# ATOMIC MASSES OF THE ELEMENTS

| Name | Symbol | Atomic Number | Atomic Mass[a] | Name | Symbol | Atomic Number | Atomic Mass[a] |
|---|---|---|---|---|---|---|---|
| Actinium | Ac | 89 | (227) | Neodymium | Nd | 60 | 144.2 |
| Aluminum | Al | 13 | 26.98 | Neon | Ne | 10 | 20.18 |
| Americium | Am | 95 | (243) | Neptunium | Np | 93 | (237) |
| Antimony | Sb | 51 | 121.8 | Nickel | Ni | 28 | 58.69 |
| Argon | Ar | 18 | 39.95 | Niobium | Nb | 41 | 92.91 |
| Arsenic | As | 33 | 74.92 | Nitrogen | N | 7 | 14.01 |
| Astatine | At | 85 | (210) | Nobelium | No | 102 | (259) |
| Barium | Ba | 56 | 137.3 | Osmium | Os | 76 | 190.2 |
| Berkelium | Bk | 97 | (247) | Oxygen | O | 8 | 16.00 |
| Beryllium | Be | 4 | 9.012 | Palladium | Pd | 46 | 106.4 |
| Bismuth | Bi | 83 | 209.0 | Phosphorus | P | 15 | 30.97 |
| Bohrium | Bh | 107 | (264) | Platinum | Pt | 78 | 195.1 |
| Boron | B | 5 | 10.81 | Plutonium | Pu | 94 | (244) |
| Bromine | Br | 35 | 79.90 | Polonium | Po | 84 | (209) |
| Cadmium | Cd | 48 | 112.4 | Potassium | K | 19 | 39.10 |
| Calcium | Ca | 20 | 40.08 | Praseodymium | Pr | 59 | 140.9 |
| Californium | Cf | 98 | (251) | Promethium | Pm | 61 | (145) |
| Carbon | C | 6 | 12.01 | Protactinium | Pa | 91 | 231.0 |
| Cerium | Ce | 58 | 140.1 | Radium | Ra | 88 | (226) |
| Cesium | Cs | 55 | 132.9 | Radon | Rn | 86 | (222) |
| Chlorine | Cl | 17 | 35.45 | Rhenium | Re | 75 | 186.2 |
| Chromium | Cr | 24 | 52.00 | Rhodium | Rh | 45 | 102.9 |
| Cobalt | Co | 27 | 58.93 | Roentgenium | Rg | 111 | (272) |
| Copper | Cu | 29 | 63.55 | Rubidium | Rb | 37 | 85.47 |
| Curium | Cm | 96 | (247) | Ruthenium | Ru | 44 | 101.1 |
| Darmstadtium | Ds | 110 | (271) | Rutherfordium | Rf | 104 | (261) |
| Dubnium | Db | 105 | (262) | Samarium | Sm | 62 | 150.4 |
| Dysprosium | Dy | 66 | 162.5 | Scandium | Sc | 21 | 44.96 |
| Einsteinium | Es | 99 | (252) | Seaborgium | Sg | 106 | (266) |
| Erbium | Er | 68 | 167.3 | Selenium | Se | 34 | 78.96 |
| Europium | Eu | 63 | 152.0 | Silicon | Si | 14 | 28.09 |
| Fermium | Fm | 100 | (257) | Silver | Ag | 47 | 107.9 |
| Fluorine | F | 9 | 19.00 | Sodium | Na | 11 | 22.99 |
| Francium | Fr | 87 | (223) | Strontium | Sr | 38 | 87.62 |
| Gadolinium | Gd | 64 | 157.3 | Sulfur | S | 16 | 32.07 |
| Gallium | Ga | 31 | 69.72 | Tantalum | Ta | 73 | 180.9 |
| Germanium | Ge | 32 | 72.64 | Technetium | Tc | 43 | (98) |
| Gold | Au | 79 | 197.0 | Tellurium | Te | 52 | 127.6 |
| Hafnium | Hf | 72 | 178.5 | Terbium | Tb | 65 | 158.9 |
| Hassium | Hs | 108 | (269) | Thallium | Tl | 81 | 204.4 |
| Helium | He | 2 | 4.003 | Thorium | Th | 90 | 232.0 |
| Holmium | Ho | 67 | 164.9 | Thulium | Tm | 69 | 168.9 |
| Hydrogen | H | 1 | 1.008 | Tin | Sn | 50 | 118.7 |
| Indium | In | 49 | 114.8 | Titanium | Ti | 22 | 47.87 |
| Iodine | I | 53 | 126.9 | Tungsten | W | 74 | 183.8 |
| Iridium | Ir | 77 | 192.2 | Uranium | U | 92 | 238.0 |
| Iron | Fe | 26 | 55.85 | Vanadium | V | 23 | 50.94 |
| Krypton | Kr | 36 | 83.80 | Xenon | Xe | 54 | 131.3 |
| Lanthanum | La | 57 | 138.9 | Ytterbium | Yb | 70 | 173.0 |
| Lawrencium | Lr | 103 | (260) | Yttrium | Y | 39 | 88.91 |
| Lead | Pb | 82 | 207.2 | Zinc | Zn | 30 | 65.41 |
| Lithium | Li | 3 | 6.941 | Zirconium | Zr | 40 | 91.22 |
| Lutetium | Lu | 71 | 175.0 | — | — | 112 | (285) |
| Magnesium | Mg | 12 | 24.31 | — | — | 113 | (284) |
| Manganese | Mn | 25 | 54.94 | — | — | 114 | (289) |
| Meitnerium | Mt | 109 | (268) | — | — | 115 | (288) |
| Mendelevium | Md | 101 | (258) | — | — | 116 | (292) |
| Mercury | Hg | 80 | 200.6 | — | — | 118 | (293) |
| Molybdenum | Mo | 42 | 95.94 | | | | |

[a]Values in parentheses are the mass number of the most stable isotope.

# GENERAL, ORGANIC, AND BIOLOGICAL CHEMISTRY

# *Structures of Life*

# GENERAL, ORGANIC, AND BIOLOGICAL CHEMISTRY

## *Structures of Life*

Third Edition

KAREN C. TIMBERLAKE

**Prentice Hall**
New York Boston San Francisco
London Toronto Sydney Tokyo Singapore Madrid
Mexico City Munich Paris Cape Town Hong Kong Montreal

Library of Congress Cataloging-in-Publication Data

Timberlake, Karen.
General, organic, and biological chemistry : structures of life / Karen C. Timberlake.—3rd ed.
p. cm.
Includes index.
ISBN 0-13-605454-4
1. Chemistry—Textbooks. I. Title.

QD33.2.T56 2010
540—dc22 2008038699

*Acquisitions Editor:* Dawn Giovanniello
*Assistant Editor:* Jessica Neumann
*Editor in Chief, Science:* Nicole Folchetti
*Marketing Manager:* Elizabeth Averbeck
*Editorial Assistant:* Lisa Tarabokjia
*Editor in Chief, Development:* Ray Mullaney
*Development Editor:* Karen Nein
*Managing Editor, Chemistry and Geosciences:* Gina M. Cheselka
*Project Manager, Science:* Beth Sweeten
*Media Editor:* Natasha Wolfe
*Art Editor:* Connie Long
*Art Studio:* Precision
*Art Director:* Maureen Eide
*Interior & Cover Design:* Suzanne Behnke
*Senior Operations Supervisor:* Alan Fischer
*Image Permissions Coordinator:* Elaine Soares
*Photo Researcher:* Eric Shrader
*Production Supervision/Composition:* Macmillan Publishing Solutions
*Cover Credit:* FoodCollection/Getty Images, Inc.


Pearson Prentice Hall
Pearson Education, Inc.
Upper Saddle River, New Jersey 07458



Printed in the United States of America
10 9 8 7 6 5 4 3

ISBN-10: 0-13-605454-4
ISBN-13: 978-0-13-605454-2

**Prentice Hall**
is an imprint of

www.pearsonhighered.com

# BRIEF CONTENTS


Prologue 1

1 Measurements 14

2 Energy and Matter 55

3 Atoms and Elements 95

4 Nuclear Chemistry 138

5 Compounds and Their Bonds 168

6 Chemical Reactions and Quantities 210

7 Gases 261

8 Solutions 295

9 Chemical Equilibrium 336

10 Acids and Bases 371

11 Introduction to Organic Chemistry: Alkanes 415

12 Alkenes, Alkynes, and Aromatic Compounds 446

13 Alcohols, Phenols, Thiols, and Ethers 479

14 Aldehydes, Ketones, and Chiral Molecules 508

15 Carbohydrates 542

16 Carboxylic Acids and Esters 575

17 Lipids 602

18 Amines and Amides 644

19 Amino Acids and Proteins 672

20 Enzymes and Vitamins 702

21 Nucleic Acids and Protein Synthesis 738

22 Metabolic Pathways for Carbohydrates 778

23 Metabolism and Energy Production 812

24 Metabolic Pathways for Lipids and Amino Acids 838

# CONTENTS


## Prologue 1

P.1 Chemistry and Chemicals 2
P.2 Scientific Method: Thinking Like a Scientist 4
HEALTH NOTE
Early Chemists: The Alchemists 6
ENVIRONMENTAL NOTE
DDT: Good Pesticide, Bad Pesticide 8
P.3 A Study Plan for Learning Chemistry 9
Concept Map 11
Chapter Review 12
Key Terms 12
Understanding the Concepts 12
Additional Questions and Problems 12
Challenge Questions 13
Answers 13

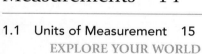

## 1 Measurements 14

1.1 Units of Measurement 15
EXPLORE YOUR WORLD
Units Listed on Labels 17
1.2 Scientific Notation 18
1.3 Measured Numbers and Significant Figures 21
1.4 Significant Figures in Calculations 24
1.5 Prefixes and Equalities 27
1.6 Writing Conversion Factors 32
CAREER FOCUS
Veterinary Technician (VT) 33
EXPLORE YOUR WORLD
SI and Metric Equalities on Product Labels 34
GREEN CHEMISTRY NOTE
Toxicology and Risk-Benefit Assessment 36
1.7 Problem Solving 37
1.8 Density 43
HEALTH NOTE
Bone Density 46
EXPLORE YOUR WORLD
Sink or Float? 46
HEALTH NOTE
Determination of Percentage of Body Fat 48
Concept Map 49
Chapter Review 49
Key Terms 50
Understanding the Concepts 50
Additional Questions and Problems 51
Challenge Questions 52
Answers 53

## 2 Energy and Matter 55

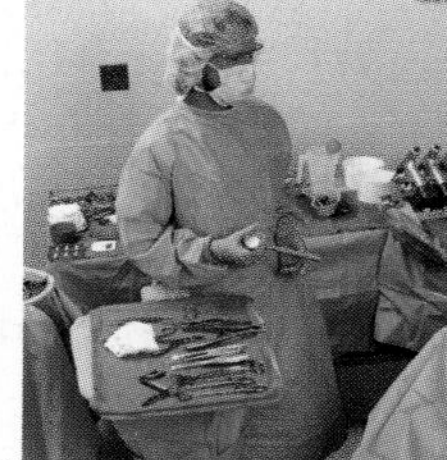

2.1 Energy 56
2.2 Temperature 59
HEALTH NOTE
Variation in Body Temperature 62
2.3 Specific Heat 63
GREEN CHEMISTRY NOTE
Carbon Dioxide and Global Warming 66
2.4 Energy and Nutrition 68
EXPLORE YOUR WORLD
Counting Calories 70
HEALTH NOTE
Losing and Gaining Weight 71
2.5 Classification of Matter 72
2.6 States and Properties of Matter 75
CAREER FOCUS
Histologist 76
2.7 Changes of State 79
HEALTH NOTE
Steam Burns 83
Concept Map 87
Chapter Review 88
Key Terms 88
Understanding the Concepts 89
Additional Questions and Problems 90
Challenge Questions 91
Answers 91

■ **Combining Ideas from Chapters 1 and 2** 93

## 3 Atoms and Elements 95

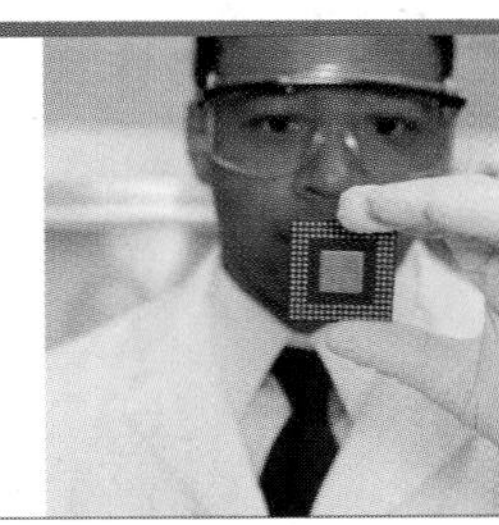

3.1 Elements and Symbols 96
HEALTH NOTE
Latin Names for Elements in Clinical Usage 97
ENVIRONMENTAL NOTE
Toxicity of Mercury 98
3.2 The Periodic Table 98
HEALTH NOTE
Elements Essential to Health 100
HEALTH NOTE
Some Important Trace Elements in the Body 104
3.3 The Atom 105
EXPLORE YOUR WORLD
Repulsion and Attraction 107
3.4 Atomic Number and Mass Number 108
CAREER FOCUS
Optician 109
3.5 Isotopes and Atomic Mass 110
3.6 Electron Energy Levels 114
GREEN CHEMISTRY NOTE
Energy-Saving Lightbulbs 116
3.7 Electron Configurations 119
3.8 Periodic Trends 126

Concept Map 131
Chapter Review 131
Key Terms 132
Understanding the Concepts 133
Additional Questions and Problems 133
Challenge Questions 134
Answers 135

## 4 Nuclear Chemistry 138

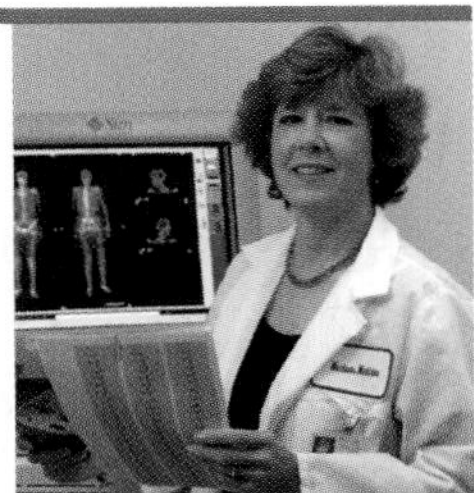

4.1 Natural Radioactivity 139
4.2 Nuclear Reactions 143
GREEN CHEMISTRY NOTE
Radon in Our Homes 146
HEALTH NOTE
Beta Emitters in Medicine 147
4.3 Radiation Measurement 150
HEALTH NOTE
Radiation and Food 151
HEALTH NOTE
Brachytherapy 152
4.4 Half-Life of a Radioisotope 153
EXPLORE YOUR WORLD
Modeling Half-Lives 155
ENVIRONMENTAL NOTE
Dating Ancient Objects 156
4.5 Medical Applications Using Radioactivity 156
HEALTH NOTE
Radiation Doses in Diagnostic and Therapeutic Procedures 158
HEALTH NOTE
Other Imaging Methods 159
4.6 Nuclear Fission and Fusion 160
GREEN CHEMISTRY NOTE
Nuclear Power Plants 162

Concept Map 163
Chapter Review 163
Key Terms 163
Understanding the Concepts 164
Additional Questions and Problems 165
Challenge Questions 166
Answers 166

## 5 Compounds and Their Bonds 168

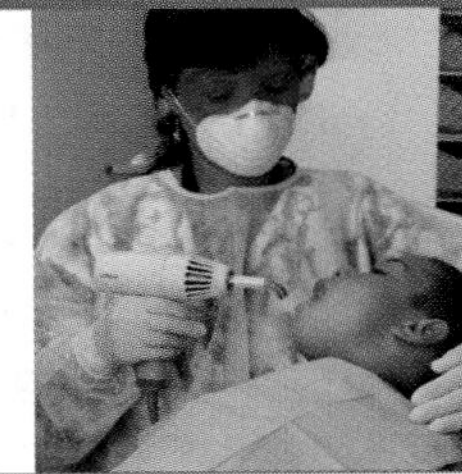

5.1 Octet Rule and Ions 169
HEALTH NOTE
Some Uses for Noble Gases 172
HEALTH NOTE
Some Important Ions in the Body 173
5.2 Ionic Compounds 174
CAREER FOCUS
Physical Therapist 175
5.3 Naming and Writing Ionic Formulas 176
5.4 Polyatomic Ions 180
5.5 Covalent Compounds 183

5.6 Naming and Writing Covalent Formulas 189
5.7 Electronegativity and Bond Polarity 192
5.8 Shapes and Polarity of Molecules 195
5.9 Attractive Forces in Compounds 200

Concept Map 202
Chapter Review 203
Key Terms 203
Understanding the Concepts 204
Additional Questions and Problems 205
Challenge Questions 206
Answers 206

# 6 Chemical Reactions and Quantities 210

6.1 Chemical Reactions 211
6.2 Types of Reactions 216
HEALTH NOTE
Smog and Health Concerns 220
6.3 Oxidation–Reduction Reactions 221
EXPLORE YOUR WORLD
Oxidation of Fruits and Vegetables 223
GREEN CHEMISTRY NOTE
Fuel Cells: Clean Energy for the Future 225
6.4 The Mole 226
6.5 Molar Mass 230
EXPLORE YOUR WORLD
Calculating Moles in the Kitchen 232
6.6 Mole Relationships in Chemical Equations 235
6.7 Mass Calculations for Reactions 237
6.8 Percent Yield and Limiting Reactants 240
6.9 Energy Changes in Chemical Reactions 246
HEALTH NOTE
Hot Packs and Cold Packs 249

Concept Map 250
Chapter Review 250
Key Terms 251
Understanding the Concepts 251
Additional Questions and Problems 253
Challenge Questions 255
Answers 255

■ **Combining Ideas from Chapters 3 to 6** 258

# 7 Gases 261

7.1 Properties of Gases 262
EXPLORE YOUR WORLD
Forming a Gas 264
7.2 Gas Pressure 264
HEALTH NOTE
Measuring Blood Pressure 266
7.3 Pressure and Volume (Boyle's Law) 267
HEALTH NOTE
Pressure–Volume Relationship in Breathing 269
7.4 Temperature and Volume (Charles's Law) 270
GREEN CHEMISTRY NOTE
Greenhouse Gases 272
7.5 Temperature and Pressure (Gay–Lussac's Law) 273
7.6 The Combined Gas Law 276
7.7 Volume and Moles (Avogadro's Law) 277
7.8 The Ideal Gas Law 281
7.9 Partial Pressures (Dalton's Law) 285
HEALTH NOTE
Blood Gases 287
HEALTH NOTE
Hyperbaric Chambers 288

Concept Map 289
Chapter Review 289
Key Terms 290
Understanding the Concepts 290
Additional Questions and Problems 291
Challenge Questions 292
Answers 293

# 8 Solutions 295

8.1 Solutions 296
HEALTH NOTE
Water in the Body 298
8.2 Electrolytes and Nonelectrolytes 300

EXPLORE YOUR WORLD
Like Dissolves Like 300
HEALTH NOTE
Electrolytes in Body Fluids 304
8.3 Solubility 305
HEALTH NOTE
Gout and Kidney Stones: A Problem of Saturation in Body Fluids 306
EXPLORE YOUR WORLD
Preparing Solutions 307
8.4 Percent Concentration 312
8.5 Molarity and Dilution 316
8.6 Physical Properties of Solutions 322
HEALTH NOTE
Colloids and Solutions in the Body 322
EXPLORE YOUR WORLD
Everyday Osmosis 325
HEALTH NOTE
Dialysis by the Kidneys and the Artificial Kidney 328
Concept Map 329
Chapter Review 330
Key Terms 330
Understanding the Concepts 331
Additional Questions and Problems 333
Challenge Questions 334
Answers 334

9
Chemical Equilibrium 336
9.1 Rates of Reactions 337
ENVIRONMENTAL NOTE
Catalytic Converters 341
9.2 Chemical Equilibrium 342
9.3 Equilibrium Constants 344
9.4 Using Equilibrium Constants 349
9.5 Changing Equilibrium Conditions: Le Châtelier's Principle 353
HEALTH NOTE
Oxygen–Hemoglobin Equilibrium and Hypoxia 357
HEALTH NOTE
Homeostasis: Regulation of Body Temperature 362
9.6 Equilibrium in Saturated Solutions 362
Concept Map 366
Chapter Review 366
Key Terms 367
Understanding the Concepts 367
Additional Questions and Problems 368
Challenge Questions 369
Answers 369

10
Acids and Bases 371
10.1 Acids and Bases 372
10.2 Strengths of Acids and Bases 377
10.3 Ionization of Water 383
10.4 The pH Scale 386
HEALTH NOTE
Stomach Acid, HCl 388
EXPLORE YOUR WORLD
Using Vegetables and Flowers as pH Indicators 393
10.5 Reactions of Acids and Bases 393
GREEN CHEMISTRY NOTE
Acid Rain 394
HEALTH NOTE
Antacids 397
10.6 Acid–Base Properties of Salt Solutions 399
10.7 Buffers 401
HEALTH NOTE
Buffers in the Blood 405
Concept Map 406
Chapter Review 406
Key Terms 407
Understanding the Concepts 407
Additional Questions and Problems 408
Challenge Questions 409
Answers 410
■ Combining Ideas from Chapters 7 to 10 412

# 11 Introduction to Organic Chemistry: Alkanes 415

11.1 Organic Compounds 416
11.2 Alkanes 419
11.3 Alkanes with Substituents 423
CAREER FOCUS
Geologist 427
HEALTH NOTE
Common Uses of Haloalkanes 428
11.4 Properties of Alkanes 429
EXPLORE YOUR WORLD
Combustion 431
HEALTH NOTE
Toxicity of Carbon Monoxide 432
GREEN CHEMISTRY NOTE
Crude Oil 433
ENVIRONMENTAL NOTE
CFCs and Ozone Depletion 434
11.5 Functional Groups 434
ENVIRONMENTAL NOTE
Functional Groups in Familiar Compounds 438

Concept Map 439
Chapter Review 440
Summary of Naming 440
Summary of Reactions 440
Key Terms 440
Understanding the Concepts 441
Additional Questions and Problems 442
Challenge Questions 443
Answers 444


# 12 Alkenes, Alkynes, and Aromatic Compounds 446

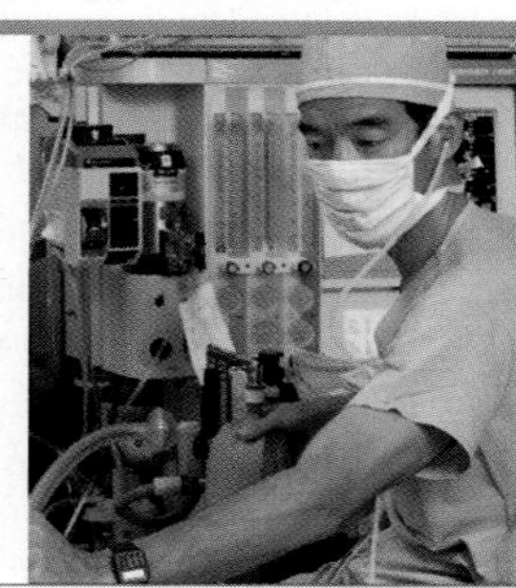


12.1 Alkenes and Alkynes 447
EXPLORE YOUR WORLD
Ripening Fruit 448
ENVIRONMENTAL NOTE
Fragrant Alkenes 450
12.2 Cis–Trans Isomers 451
EXPLORE YOUR WORLD
Modeling Cis–Trans Isomers 453
ENVIRONMENTAL NOTE
Pheromones in Insect Communication 453
HEALTH NOTE
Cis–Trans Isomers for Night Vision 454
12.3 Addition Reactions 455
EXPLORE YOUR WORLD
Unsaturation in Fats and Oils 456
HEALTH NOTE
Hydrogenation of Unsaturated Fats 458
CAREER FOCUS
Laboratory Technologist 460
12.4 Polymers of Alkenes 462
EXPLORE YOUR WORLD
Polymers and Recycling Plastics 463
12.5 Aromatic Compounds 465
HEALTH NOTE
Some Common Aromatic Compounds 466
HEALTH NOTE
Polycyclic Aromatic Hydrocarbons (PAHs) 467

Concept Map 470
Chapter Review 471
Summary of Naming 471
Summary of Reactions 472
Key Terms 472
Understanding the Concepts 473
Additional Questions and Problems 473
Challenge Questions 475
Answers 475


# 13 Alcohols, Phenols, Thiols, and Ethers 479

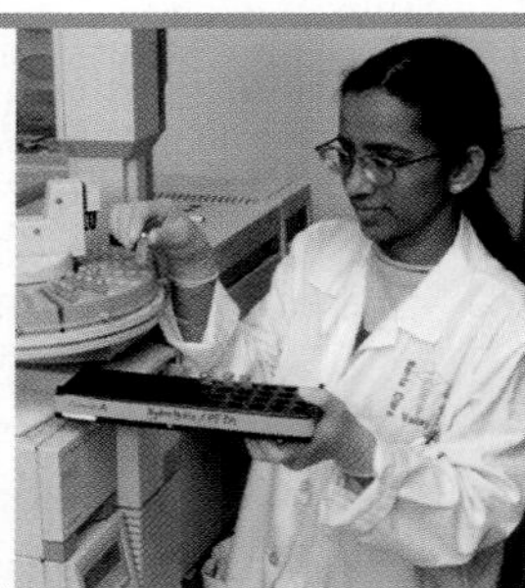


13.1 Alcohols, Phenols, and Thiols 480
EXPLORE YOUR WORLD
Alcohols in Household Products 482
HEALTH NOTE
Some Important Alcohols and Phenols 483
13.2 Ethers 486
HEALTH NOTE
Ethers as Anesthetics 489
ENVIRONMENTAL NOTE
Toxic Ethers 490

13.3 Physical Properties of Alcohols, Phenols, and Ethers 491
13.4 Reactions of Alcohols and Thiols 494
HEALTH NOTE Methanol Poisoning 496
HEALTH NOTE Oxidation of Alcohol in the Body 498
Concept Map 500
Chapter Review 501
Summary of Naming 501
Summary of Reactions 501
Key Terms 502
Understanding the Concepts 502
Additional Questions and Problems 503
Challenge Questions 504
Answers 505

14 Aldehydes, Ketones, and Chiral Molecules 508
14.1 Aldehydes and Ketones 509
ENVIRONMENTAL NOTE Vanilla 512
HEALTH NOTE Some Important Aldehydes and Ketones 513
14.2 Physical Properties of Aldehydes and Ketones 515
14.3 Oxidation and Reduction of Aldehydes and Ketones 517
14.4 Addition Reactions of Aldehydes and Ketones 521
14.5 Chiral Molecules 525
EXPLORE YOUR WORLD Using Gumdrops and Toothpicks to Model Chiral Objects 527
HEALTH NOTE Enantiomers in Biological Systems 530
Concept Map 532
Chapter Review 533
Summary of Naming 533
Summary of Reactions 533
Key Terms 534
Understanding the Concepts 534
Additional Questions and Problems 536
Challenge Questions 538
Answers 539

15 Carbohydrates 542
15.1 Carbohydrates 543
15.2 Fischer Projections of Monosaccharides 546
HEALTH NOTE Hyperglycemia and Hypoglycemia 549
15.3 Haworth Structures of Monosaccharides 551
15.4 Chemical Properties of Monosaccharides 555
HEALTH NOTE Testing for Glucose in Urine 556
15.5 Disaccharides 557
EXPLORE YOUR WORLD Sugar and Sweeteners 558
HEALTH NOTE How Sweet Is My Sweetener? 560
HEALTH NOTE Blood Types and Carbohydrates 561
CAREER FOCUS Phlebotomist 562
15.6 Polysaccharides 563
EXPLORE YOUR WORLD Polysaccharides 565
Concept Map 566
Chapter Review 566
Summary of Carbohydrates 567
Summary of Reactions 567
Key Terms 568
Understanding the Concepts 569
Additional Questions and Problems 569
Challenge Questions 570
Answers 570
■ Combining Ideas from Chapters 11 to 15 573

16 Carboxylic Acids and Esters 575
16.1 Carboxylic Acids 576
HEALTH NOTE Alpha Hydroxy Acids 579
16.2 Properties of Carboxylic Acids 580
HEALTH NOTE Carboxylic Acids in Metabolism 584

16.3 Esters 585
HEALTH NOTE
Salicylic Acid Pain Relievers 586
ENVIRONMENTAL NOTE
Plastics 587
16.4 Naming Esters 588
16.5 Properties of Esters 591
ENVIRONMENTAL NOTE
Cleaning Action of Soaps 593

Concept Map 594
Chapter Review 595
Summary of Naming 595
Summary of Reactions 595
Key Terms 596
Understanding the Concepts 596
Additional Questions and Problems 597
Challenge Questions 598
Answers 599

17
Lipids 602

17.1 Lipids 603
17.2 Fatty Acids 604
EXPLORE YOUR WORLD
Solubility of Fats and Oils 608
HEALTH NOTE
Omega-3 Fatty Acids in Fish Oils 610
17.3 Waxes, Fats, and Oils 611
17.4 Chemical Properties of Triacylglycerols 615
HEALTH NOTE
Olestra: A Fat Substitute 616
HEALTH NOTE
Trans Fatty Acids and Hydrogenation 617
GREEN CHEMISTRY NOTE
Biodiesel as an Alternative Fuel 619
EXPLORE YOUR WORLD
Types of Fats 620
17.5 Glycerophospholipids 621
17.6 Sphingolipids 624
HEALTH NOTE
Lipid Diseases 626
17.7 Steroids: Cholesterol, Bile Salts, and Steroid Hormones 627
HEALTH NOTE
Anabolic Steroids 632
17.8 Cell Membranes 633

Concept Map 636
Chapter Review 637
Summary of Reactions 637
Key Terms 637
Understanding the Concepts 638
Additional Questions and Problems 639
Challenge Questions 639
Answers 640

18
Amines and Amides 644

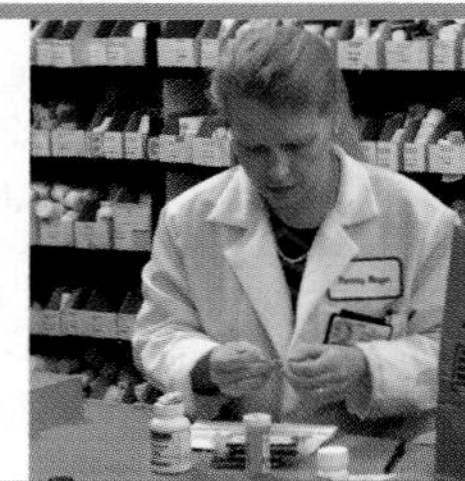

18.1 Amines 645
HEALTH NOTE
Amines in Health and Medicine 647
18.2 Properties of Amines 650
18.3 Heterocyclic Amines and Alkaloids 654
HEALTH NOTE
Synthesizing Drugs 657
18.4 Amides 658
HEALTH NOTE
Amides in Health and Medicine 662
18.5 Hydrolysis of Amides 663

Concept Map 665
Chapter Review 665
Summary of Naming 666
Summary of Reactions 666
Key Terms 667
Understanding the Concepts 667
Additional Questions and Problems 668
Challenge Questions 669
Answers 670

19
Amino Acids and Proteins 672

19.1 Proteins and Amino Acids 673
19.2 Amino Acids as Zwitterions 677
19.3 Formation of Peptides 680
CAREER FOCUS
Rehabilitation Specialist 682

19.4 Protein Structure: Primary and Secondary Levels 683
HEALTH NOTE
Polypeptides in the Body 684
HEALTH NOTE
Essential Amino Acids 687
19.5 Protein Structure: Tertiary and Quaternary Levels 687
HEALTH NOTE
Prions and Mad Cow Disease 690
HEALTH NOTE
Sickle-Cell Anemia 692
19.6 Protein Hydrolysis and Denaturation 693
EXPLORE YOUR WORLD
Denaturation of Milk Protein 694
Concept Map 696
Chapter Review 697
Key Terms 697
Understanding the Concepts 698
Additional Questions and Problems 699
Challenge Questions 699
Answers 699

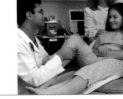

20
Enzymes and Vitamins 702

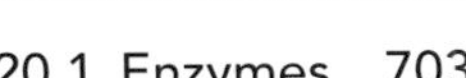

20.1 Enzymes 703
20.2 Enzyme Action 706
HEALTH NOTE
Isoenzymes as Diagnostic Tools 709
20.3 Factors Affecting Enzyme Activity 710
EXPLORE YOUR WORLD
Enzyme Activity 711
20.4 Enzyme Inhibition 713
20.5 Regulation of Enzyme Activity 717
20.6 Enzyme Cofactors and Vitamins 721
Concept Map 729
Chapter Review 730
Key Terms 730
Understanding the Concepts 731
Additional Questions and Problems 732
Challenge Questions 733
Answers 733
■ Combining Ideas from Chapters 16 to 20 735

21
Nucleic Acids and Protein Synthesis 738

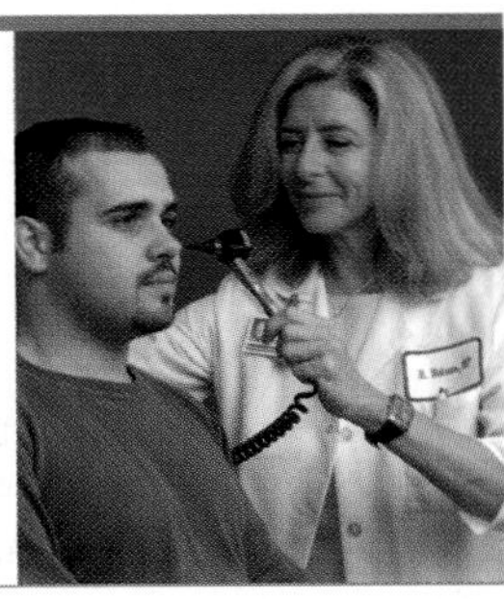

21.1 Components of Nucleic Acids 739
21.2 Primary Structure of Nucleic Acids 743
21.3 DNA Double Helix 745
21.4 DNA Replication 747
CAREER FOCUS
Occupational Therapist 749
21.5 RNA and Transcription 751
21.6 The Genetic Code 757
21.7 Protein Synthesis: Translation 758
HEALTH NOTE
Many Antibiotics Inhibit Protein Synthesis 759
21.8 Genetic Mutations 761
EXPLORE YOUR WORLD
A Model for DNA Replication and Mutation 763
21.9 Recombinant DNA 765
21.10 Viruses 768
HEALTH NOTE
Cancer 771
Concept Map 772
Chapter Review 773
Key Terms 773
Understanding the Concepts 774
Additional Questions and Problems 775
Challenge Questions 775
Answers 776

22
Metabolic Pathways for Carbohydrates 778

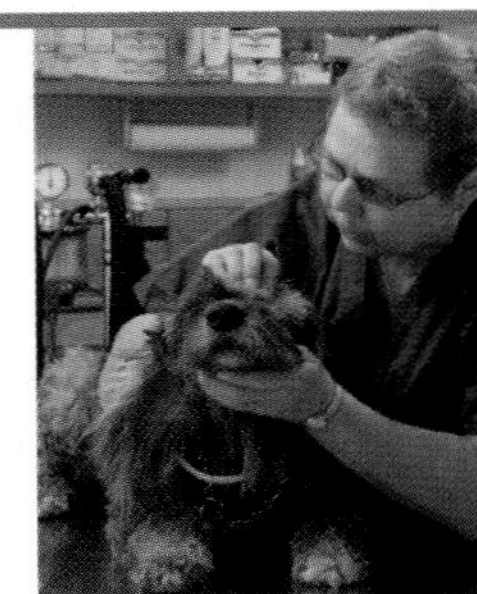

22.1 Metabolism and Cell Structure 779
22.2 ATP and Energy 782
HEALTH NOTE
ATP Energy and $Ca^{2+}$ Needed to Contract Muscles 784

22.3 Important Coenzymes in Metabolic Pathways 785
22.4 Digestion of Carbohydrates 788
EXPLORE YOUR WORLD
Carbohydrate Digestion 789
HEALTH NOTE
Lactose Intolerance 790
22.5 Glycolysis: Oxidation of Glucose 790
22.6 Pathways for Pyruvate 796
22.7 Glycogen Metabolism 799
22.8 Gluconeogenesis: Glucose Synthesis 802
Concept Map 807
Chapter Review 807
Summary of Key Reactions 808
Key Terms 808
Understanding the Concepts 809
Additional Questions and Problems 809
Challenge Questions 810
Answers 810

# 23 Metabolism and Energy Production 812

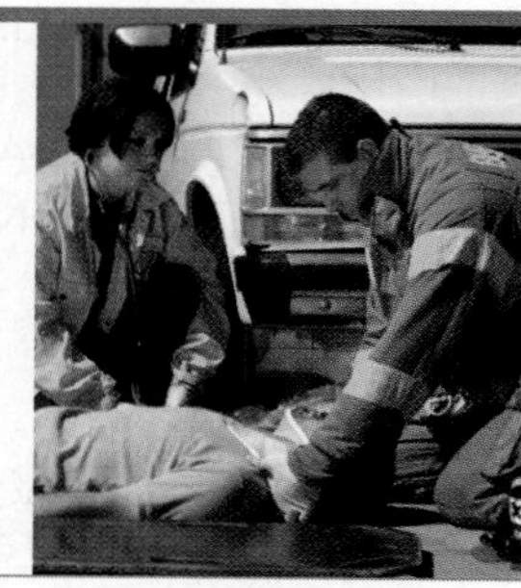

23.1 The Citric Acid Cycle 813
CAREER FOCUS
Physical Therapist 815
23.2 Electron Carriers 819
23.3 Electron Transport 822
HEALTH NOTE
Toxins: Inhibitors of Electron Transport 825
23.4 Oxidative Phosphorylation and ATP 826
23.5 ATP Energy from Glucose 828
HEALTH NOTE
ATP Synthase and Heating the Body 829
HEALTH NOTE
Efficiency of ATP Production 832
Concept Map 833
Chapter Review 833
Summary of Key Reactions 834
Key Terms 834
Understanding the Concepts 834
Additional Questions and Problems 835
Challenge Questions 836
Answers 836

# 24 Metabolic Pathways for Lipids and Amino Acids 838

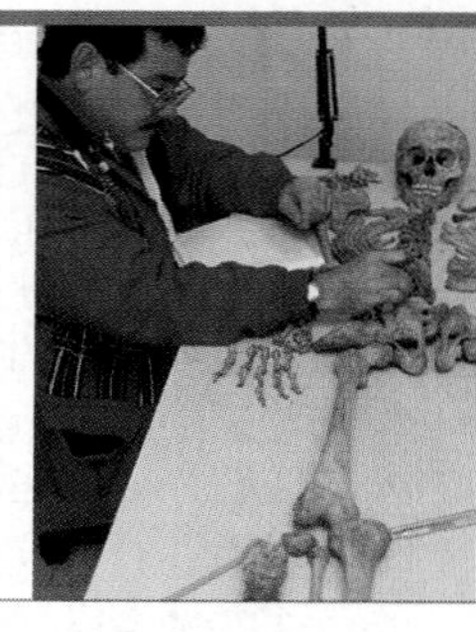

24.1 Digestion of Triacylglycerols 839
EXPLORE YOUR WORLD
Digestion of Fats 841
24.2 Oxidation of Fatty Acids 841
24.3 ATP and Fatty Acid Oxidation 846
HEALTH NOTE
Stored Fat and Obesity 847
EXPLORE YOUR WORLD
Fat Storage and Blubber 848
24.4 Ketogenesis and Ketone Bodies 849
HEALTH NOTE
Ketone Bodies and Diabetes 850
24.5 Fatty Acid Synthesis 851
24.6 Digestion of Proteins 854
24.7 Degradation of Amino Acids 856
24.8 Urea Cycle 858
24.9 Fates of the Carbon Atoms from Amino Acids 861
24.10 Synthesis of Amino Acids 863
HEALTH NOTE
Phenylketonuria (PKU) 865
HEALTH NOTE
Homocysteine and Coronary Heart Disease 866
Concept Map 868
Chapter Review 868
Summary of Key Reactions 869
Key Terms 870
Understanding the Concepts 870
Additional Questions and Problems 871
Challenge Questions 871
Answers 872

■ **Combining Ideas from Chapters 21 to 24** 874

Credits C-1

Glossary/Index I-1

# APPLICATIONS AND ACTIVITIES

## Career Focus


Veterinary Technician 33
Histologist 76
Optician 109
Physical Therapist 175
Geologist 427
Laboratory Technologist 460
Phlebotomist 562
Rehabilitation Specialist 682
Occupational Therapist 749
Physical Therapist 815


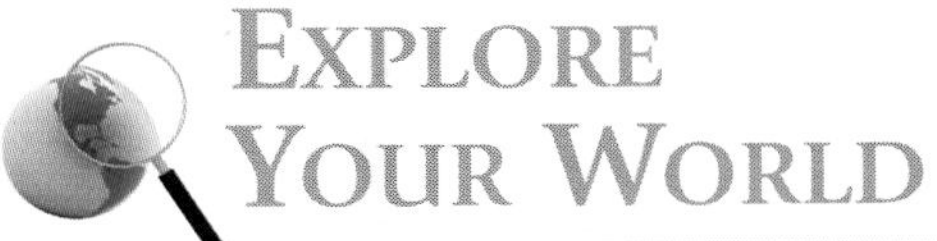

## Explore Your World


Units Listed on Labels 17
SI and Metric Equalities on Product Labels 34
Sink or Float? 46
Counting Calories 70
Repulsion and Attraction 107
Modeling Half-Lives 155
Oxidation of Fruits and Vegetables 223
Calculating Moles in the Kitchen 232
Forming a Gas 264
Like Dissolves Like 300
Preparing Solutions 307
Everyday Osmosis 325
Using Vegetables and Flowers as pH Indicators 393
Combustion 431
Ripening Fruit 448
Modeling Cis–Trans Isomers 453
Unsaturation in Fats and Oils 456
Polymers and Recycling Plastics 463
Alcohols in Household Products 482
Using Gumdrops and Toothpicks to Model Chiral Objects 527
Sugar and Sweeteners 558
Polysaccharides 565
Solubility of Fats and Oils 608
Types of Fats 620
Denaturation of Milk Protein 694
Enzyme Activity 711
A Model for DNA Replication and Mutation 763
Carbohydrate Digestion 789
Digestion of Fats 841
Fat Storage and Blubber 848

## Health Note


Early Chemists: The Alchemists 6
Bone Density 46
Determination of Percentage of Body Fat 48
Variation in Body Temperature 62
Losing and Gaining Weight 71
Steam Burns 83
Latin Names for Elements in Clinical Usage 97
Elements Essential to Health 100
Some Important Trace Elements in the Body 104
Beta Emitters in Medicine 147
Radiation and Food 151
Brachytherapy 152
Radiation Doses in Diagnostic and Therapeutic Procedures 158
Other Imaging Methods 159
Some Uses for Noble Gases 172
Some Important Ions in the Body 173
Smog and Health Concerns 220
Hot Packs and Cold Packs 249
Measuring Blood Pressure 266
Pressure–Volume Relationship in Breathing 269
Blood Gases 287
Hyperbaric Chambers 288
Water in the Body 298
Electrolytes in Body Fluids 304
Gout and Kidney Stones: A Problem of Saturation in Body Fluids 306
Colloids and Solutions in the Body 322

Dialysis by the Kidneys and the Artificial Kidney 328
Oxygen–Hemoglobin Equilibrium and Hypoxia 357
Homeostasis: Regulation of Body Temperature 362
Stomach Acid, HCl 388
Antacids 397
Buffers in the Blood 405
Common Uses of Haloalkanes 428
Toxicity of Carbon Monoxide 432
Cis–Trans Isomers for Night Vision 454
Hydrogenation of Unsaturated Fats 458
Some Common Aromatic Compounds 466
Polycyclic Aromatic Hydrocarbons (PAHs) 467
Some Important Alcohols and Phenols 483
Ethers as Anesthetics 489
Methanol Poisoning 496
Oxidation of Alcohol in the Body 498
Some Important Aldehydes and Ketones 513
Enantiomers in Biological Systems 530
Hyperglycemia and Hypoglycemia 549
Testing for Glucose in Urine 556
How Sweet Is My Sweetener? 560
Blood Types and Carbohydrates 561
Alpha Hydroxy Acids 579
Carboxylic Acids in Metabolism 584
Salicylic Acid and Pain Relievers 586
Omega-3 Fatty Acids in Fish Oils 610
Olestra: A Fat Substitute 616
Trans Fatty Acids and Hydrogenation 617
Lipid Diseases 626
Anabolic Steroids 632
Amines in Health and Medicine 647
Synthesizing Drugs 657
Amides in Health and Medicine 662
Polypeptides in the Body 684
Essential Amino Acids 687
Prions and Mad Cow Disease 690
Sickle-Cell Anemia 692
Isoenzymes as Diagnostic Tools 709
Many Antibiotics Inhibit Protein Synthesis 759
Cancer 771
ATP Energy and $Ca^{2+}$ Needed to Contract Muscles 784
Lactose Intolerance 790
Toxins: Inhibitors of Electron Transport 825
ATP Synthase and Heating the Body 829
Efficiency of ATP Production 832
Stored Fat and Obesity 847
Ketone Bodies and Diabetes 850
Phenylketonuria (PKU) 865
Homocysteine and Coronary Heart Disease 866

## ENVIRONMENTAL NOTE

DDT: Good Pesticide, Bad Pesticide 8
Toxicity of Mercury 98
Dating Ancient Objects 156
Catalytic Converters 341
CFCs and Ozone Depletion 434
Functional Groups in Familiar Compounds 438
Fragrant Alkenes 450
Pheromones in Insect Communication 453
Toxic Ethers 490
Vanilla 512
Plastics 587
Cleaning Action of Soaps 593

## GREEN CHEMISTRY NOTE

Toxicology and Risk-Benefit Assessment 36
Carbon Dioxide and Global Warming 66
Energy-Saving Lightbulbs 116
Radon in Our Homes 146
Nuclear Power Plants 162
Fuel Cells: Clean Energy for the Future 225
Greenhouse Gases 272
Acid Rain 394
Crude Oil 433
Biodiesel as an Alternative Fuel 619

## GUIDE TO PROBLEM SOLVING

Using Conversion Factors 39
Calculating Density 44
Using Density 47
Calculations Using Specific Heat 65
Calculations Using Heat of Fusion/Vaporization 80
Writing Electron Configurations with Sublevel Blocks 125
Completing a Nuclear Equation 145

Naming Ionic Compounds with Metals That Form a Single Ion 177
Naming Ionic Compounds with Variable Charge Metals 178
Writing Formulas from the Name of an Ionic Compound 179
Naming Ionic Compounds with Polyatomic Ions 183
Writing Electron-Dot Formulas 186
Naming Covalent Compounds with Two Nonmetals 190
Writing Formulas for Covalent Compounds 191
Predicting Molecular Shape (VSEPR Theory) 198
Balancing a Chemical Equation 215
Calculating the Atoms or Molecules of a Substance 228
Calculating Molar Mass 231
Calculating the Moles (or Grams) of a Substance from Grams (or Moles) 233
Using Mole–Mole Factors 236
Calculating the Masses of Reactants and Products in a Chemical Reaction 238
Calculations for Percent Yield 240
Calculating Product from a Limiting Reactant 243
Calculations Using Heat of Reaction ($\Delta H$) 248
Using the Gas Laws 267
Using Molar Volume 279
Reactions Involving Gases 280
Using the Ideal Gas Law 282
Solving for Partial Pressure 286
Writing Net Ionic Equations for an Insoluble Salt 311
Calculating Solution Concentrations 313
Using Concentration to Calculate Mass or Volume 315
Calculating Molarity 316
Calculating Dilution Quantities 319
Calculations Involving Solutions in Chemical Reactions 320
Writing the $K_c$ Expression 345
Calculating the $K_c$ Value 348
Using the $K_c$ Value 352
Calculating $K_{sp}$ 364
Calculating Solubility from $K_{sp}$ 365
Calculating $[H_3O^+]$ and $[OH^-]$ in Aqueous Solutions 385
Calculating pH of an Aqueous Solution 389
Balancing an Equation for Neutralization 396
Calculations for an Acid–Base Titration 398
Calculating pH of a Buffer 404
Naming Alkanes 425
Drawing Alkane Formulas 426
Naming Alkenes and Alkynes 449
Naming Alcohols 482
Naming Ethers 488
Naming Aldehydes 511
Naming Ketones 514
Drawing Haworth Structures 554
Naming Carboxylic Acids 578
Naming Esters 589
Naming of Amines 649
Naming Amides 660

# ABOUT THE AUTHOR

*DEDICATION*

*I dedicate this book to:*

*My husband for his patience, loving support, and preparation of late meals.*

*My son, John, daughter-in-law, Cindy, grandson, Daniel, and granddaughter, Emily, for the precious things in life.*

*The wonderful students over many years whose hard work and commitment always motivated me and put purpose in my writing.*

*FAVORITE QUOTES*

*The whole art of teaching is only the art of awakening the natural curiosity of young minds.*

*—Anatole France*

*One must learn by doing the thing; though you think you know it, you have no certainty until you try.*

*—Sophocles*

*Discovery consists of seeing what everybody has seen and thinking what nobody has thought.*

*—Albert Szent-Gyorgi*

*I never teach my pupils; I only attempt to provide the conditions in which they can learn.*

*—Albert Einstein*

**Karen Timberlake** is Professor Emerita of chemistry at Los Angeles Valley College, where she taught chemistry for allied health and preparatory chemistry for 36 years. She received her bachelor's degree in chemistry from the University of Washington and her master's degree in biochemistry from the University of California at Los Angeles.

Professor Timberlake has been writing chemistry textbooks for 33 years. During that time, her name has become associated with the strategic use of pedagogical tools that promote student success in chemistry and the application of chemistry to real-life situations. More than one million students have learned chemistry using texts, laboratory manuals, and study guides written by Karen Timberlake. In addition to *General, Organic, and Biological Chemistry: Structures of Life*, third edition, she is also the author of *Basic Chemistry*, second edition, and *Chemistry: An Introduction to General, Organic, and Biological Chemistry*, tenth edition with the accompanying *Study Guide*, *Selected Solutions Manual*, *Laboratory Manual*, and *Essential Laboratory Manual.*

Professor Timberlake belongs to numerous science and educational organizations including the American Chemical Society (ACS) and the National Science Teachers Association (NSTA). She was the Western Regional Winner of Excellence in College Chemistry Teaching Award given by Chemical Manufacturers Association. In 2004, she received the McGuffey Award in Physical Sciences from the Text and Academic Authors Association for her textbook *Chemistry: An Introduction to General, Organic, and Biological Chemistry*, eighth edition, which has demonstrated excellence over time. In 2006, she received the Textbook Excellence Award for the first edition of *Basic Chemistry.* She has participated in education grants for science teaching including the Los Angeles Collaborative for Teaching Excellence (LACTE) and a Title III grant at her college. She speaks at conferences and educational meetings on the use of student-centered teaching methods in chemistry to promote learning success of students.

Her husband, Bill, is also a chemistry professor and has contributed to writing this text. He taught preparatory and organic chemistry at Los Angeles Harbor College for 36 years. When the professors Timberlake are not writing textbooks, they relax by hiking, traveling, trying new restaurants, cooking, and playing tennis.

# PREFACE

## To the Student

Welcome to the third edition of *General, Organic, and Biological Chemistry: Structures of Life*. This chemistry text was written and designed to help you prepare for a career in a health-related profession, such as nursing, dietetics, respiratory therapy, and environmental and agricultural science. My main objective in writing this text is to make the study of chemistry an engaging and positive experience for you by relating the structure and behavior of matter to its functions in health and life. This new edition introduces rich problem-solving strategies, including new concept checks, more problem-solving guides, conceptual and challenge problems, and new sets of combined problems.

It is also my goal to help you become a critical thinker by connecting the scientific concepts with current issues concerning health and the environment. Thus, I have utilized materials that

- motivate you to learn and enjoy chemistry;
- relate chemistry to careers that interest you;
- develop problem-solving skills that lead to your success in your chemistry course; and
- promote learning and your success in your chosen career.

I hope that this textbook helps you discover exciting new ideas and gives you a rewarding experience as you develop an understanding and appreciation of the role of chemistry in your life.

## Features of this Text

You may wonder why your career path includes a class in chemistry. A common view is that chemistry is just a lot of facts to be memorized. To change this perception, I have included many features to help you learn about chemistry in your life and career choice and to give you the skills to learn chemistry successfully. These features include connections to health, the environment, and green chemistry, visual guides to problem solving, and in-chapter problem sets to work immediately that reinforce the learning of new concepts. A successful learning program in this text provides you with many learning tools, which are discussed here.

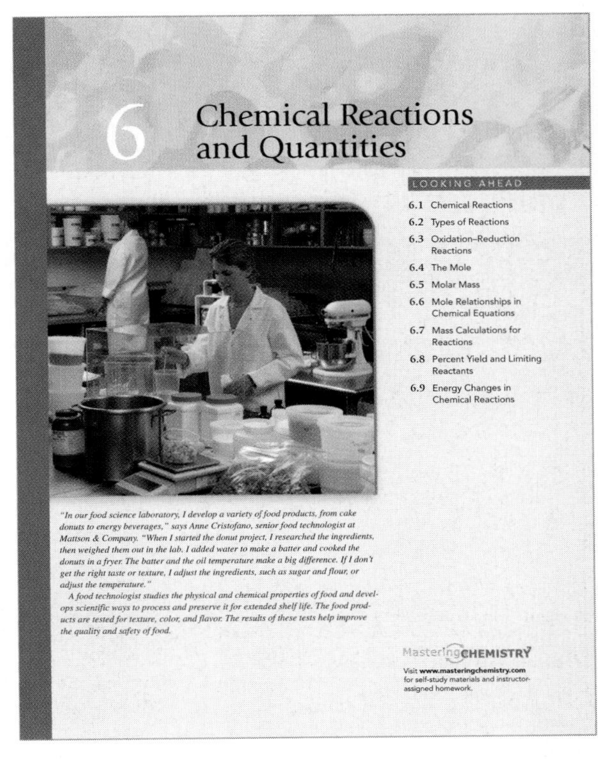

6 Chemical Reactions and Quantities

LOOKING AHEAD

6.1 Chemical Reactions
6.2 Types of Reactions
6.3 Oxidation–Reduction Reactions
6.4 The Mole
6.5 Molar Mass
6.6 Mole Relationships in Chemical Equations
6.7 Mass Calculations for Reactions
6.8 Percent Yield and Limiting Reactants
6.9 Energy Changes in Chemical Reactions

*"In our food science laboratory, I develop a variety of food products, from cake donuts to energy beverages," says Anne Cristofano, senior food technologist at Mattson & Company. "When I started the donut project, I researched the ingredients, then weighed them out in the lab. I added water to make a batter and cooked the donuts in a fryer. The batter and the oil temperature make a big difference. If I don't get the right taste or texture, I adjust the ingredients, such as sugar and flour, or adjust the temperature."*

*A food technologist studies the physical and chemical properties of food and develops scientific ways to process and preserve it for extended shelf life. The food products are tested for texture, color, and flavor. The results of these tests help improve the quality and safety of food.*

MasteringCHEMISTRY

Visit **www.masteringchemistry.com** for self-study materials and instructor-assigned homework.

## Career Focus and Real-World Applications

### This Text Was Designed to Help Students Attain Their Career Goals

**Chapter Opening Interviews with Scientists and Health Care Professionals** Each chapter begins with an interview with a professional in a career such as nursing, forensic anthropology, nuclear medicine, dentistry, and oceanography. These professionals discuss the importance of chemistry in their careers.

**CAREER FOCUS**

### Occupational Therapist

"Occupational therapists teach children and adults the skills they need for the job of living," says occupational therapist Leslie Wakasa. "When working with the pediatric population, we are crucial in educating children with disabilities, their families, caregivers, and school staff in ways to help them be as independent as they can be in all aspects of their daily lives. It's rewarding when you can show children how to feed themselves, which is a huge self-esteem issue for them. The opportunity to help people become more independent is very rewarding."

A combination of technology and occupational therapy helps children who are nonverbal to communicate and interact with their environment. By leaning on a red switch, Alex is learning to use a computer.

**Career Focus** Within the chapters are additional interviews with allied health professionals using chemistry.

**On the Web** The **MasteringChemistry Study Area** features in-depth resources for each of the health professions featured in the book and takes students through interactive case studies.

## Students Will Learn Chemistry Using Real-World Examples

**NEW Green Chemistry Notes** The new **Green Chemistry Notes** highlight the practical applications of chemistry that are beneficial to human health and the environment. The new green chemistry approach that chemists, engineers, scientists, health professionals, and researchers are taking focuses on practices and products that are "benign by design" and that provide sustainability.

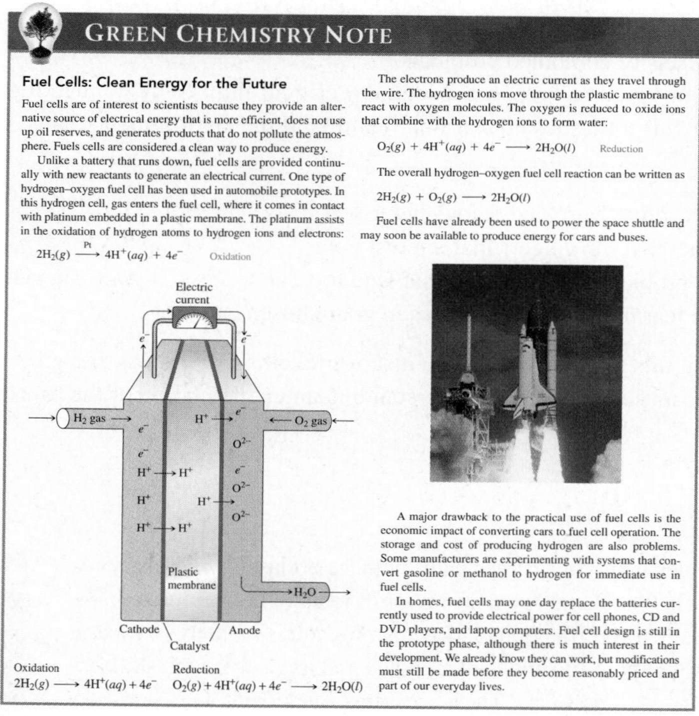

GREEN CHEMISTRY NOTE

**Fuel Cells: Clean Energy for the Future**

Fuel cells are of interest to scientists because they provide an alternative source of electrical energy that is more efficient, does not use up oil reserves, and generates products that do not pollute the atmosphere. Fuels cells are considered a clean way to produce energy.

Unlike a battery that runs down, fuel cells are provided continually with new reactants to generate an electrical current. One type of hydrogen–oxygen fuel cell has been used in automobile prototypes. In this hydrogen cell, gas enters the fuel cell, where it comes in contact with platinum embedded in a plastic membrane. The platinum assists in the oxidation of hydrogen atoms to hydrogen ions and electrons:

$$2H_2(g) \xrightarrow{Pt} 4H^+(aq) + 4e^- \quad \text{Oxidation}$$



Oxidation
$2H_2(g) \longrightarrow 4H^+(aq) + 4e^-$

Reduction
$O_2(g) + 4H^+(aq) + 4e^- \longrightarrow 2H_2O(l)$

The electrons produce an electric current as they travel through the wire. The hydrogen ions move through the plastic membrane to react with oxygen molecules. The oxygen is reduced to oxide ions that combine with the hydrogen ions to form water:

$$O_2(g) + 4H^+(aq) + 4e^- \longrightarrow 2H_2O(l) \quad \text{Reduction}$$

The overall hydrogen–oxygen fuel cell reaction can be written as

$$2H_2(g) + O_2(g) \longrightarrow 2H_2O(l)$$

Fuel cells have already been used to power the space shuttle and may soon be available to produce energy for cars and buses.

A major drawback to the practical use of fuel cells is the economic impact of converting cars to fuel cell operation. The storage and cost of producing hydrogen are also problems. Some manufacturers are experimenting with systems that convert gasoline or methanol to hydrogen for immediate use in fuel cells.

In homes, fuel cells may one day replace the batteries currently used to provide electrical power for cell phones, CD and DVD players, and laptop computers. Fuel cell design is still in the prototype phase, although there is much interest in their development. We already know they can work, but modifications must still be made before they become reasonably priced and part of our everyday lives.

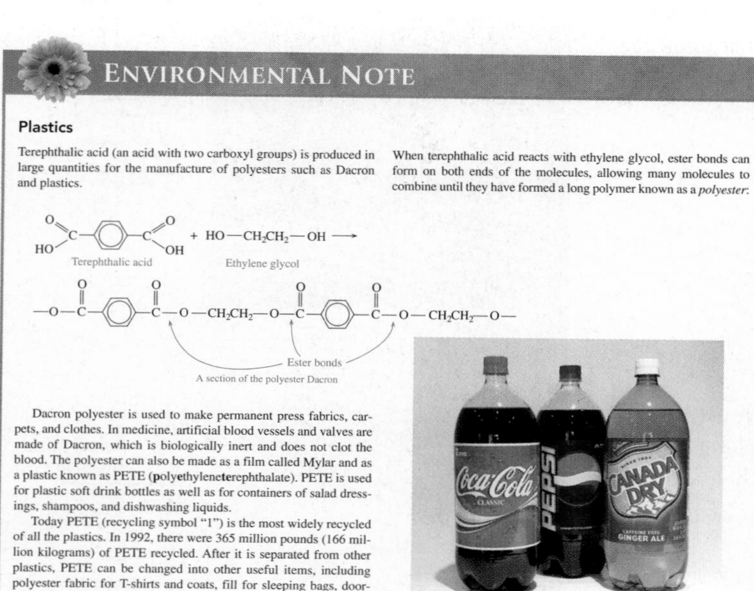

ENVIRONMENTAL NOTE

**Plastics**

Terephthalic acid (an acid with two carboxyl groups) is produced in large quantities for the manufacture of polyesters such as Dacron and plastics.

When terephthalic acid reacts with ethylene glycol, ester bonds can form on both ends of the molecules, allowing many molecules to combine until they have formed a long polymer known as a *polyester*:



Dacron polyester is used to make permanent press fabrics, carpets, and clothes. In medicine, artificial blood vessels and valves are made of Dacron, which is biologically inert and does not clot the blood. The polyester can also be made as a film called Mylar and as a plastic known as PETE (**p**oly**e**thylene**te**rephthalate). PETE is used for plastic soft drink bottles as well as for containers of salad dressings, shampoos, and dishwashing liquids.

Today PETE (recycling symbol "1") is the most widely recycled of all the plastics. In 1992, there were 365 million pounds (166 million kilograms) of PETE recycled. After it is separated from other plastics, PETE can be changed into other useful items, including polyester fabric for T-shirts and coats, fill for sleeping bags, doormats, and containers for tennis balls.

**Environmental Notes** **Environmental Notes** throughout the text relate chemistry to real-life topics in science and medicine that are interesting and motivating and support the role of chemistry in the real world. They delve into issues such as global warming, biodiesel fuels, radon, acid rain, pheromones, ozone depletion, and toxicity of mercury.

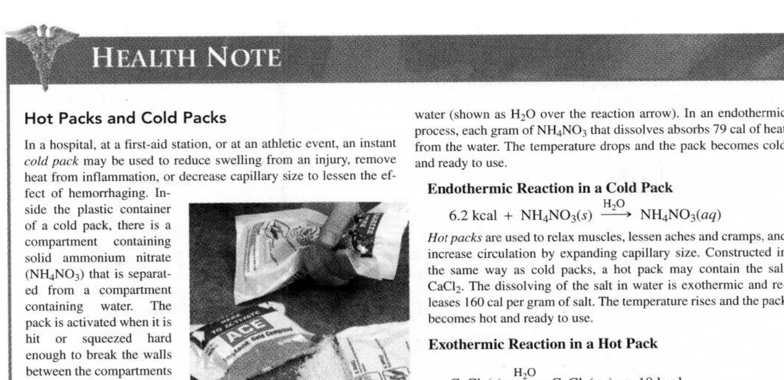

HEALTH NOTE

**Hot Packs and Cold Packs**

In a hospital, at a first-aid station, or at an athletic event, an instant *cold pack* may be used to reduce swelling from an injury, remove heat from inflammation, or decrease capillary size to lessen the effect of hemorrhaging. Inside the plastic container of a cold pack, there is a compartment containing solid ammonium nitrate ($NH_4NO_3$) that is separated from a compartment containing water. The pack is activated when it is hit or squeezed hard enough to break the walls between the compartments and cause the ammonium nitrate to mix with the water (shown as $H_2O$ over the reaction arrow). In an endothermic process, each gram of $NH_4NO_3$ that dissolves absorbs 79 cal of heat from the water. The temperature drops and the pack becomes cold and ready to use.

**Endothermic Reaction in a Cold Pack**

$$6.2\text{ kcal} + NH_4NO_3(s) \xrightarrow{H_2O} NH_4NO_3(aq)$$

*Hot packs* are used to relax muscles, lessen aches and cramps, and increase circulation by expanding capillary size. Constructed in the same way as cold packs, a hot pack may contain the salt $CaCl_2$. The dissolving of the salt in water is exothermic and releases 160 cal per gram of salt. The temperature rises and the pack becomes hot and ready to use.

**Exothermic Reaction in a Hot Pack**

$$CaCl_2(s) \xrightarrow{H_2O} CaCl_2(aq) + 18\text{ kcal}$$

**Health Notes** The many **Health Notes** in each chapter apply chemical concepts to relevant topics of health and medicine. These topics include weight loss and weight gain, artificial fats, sweeteners, anabolic steroids, alcohol, genetic diseases, viruses, and cancer.

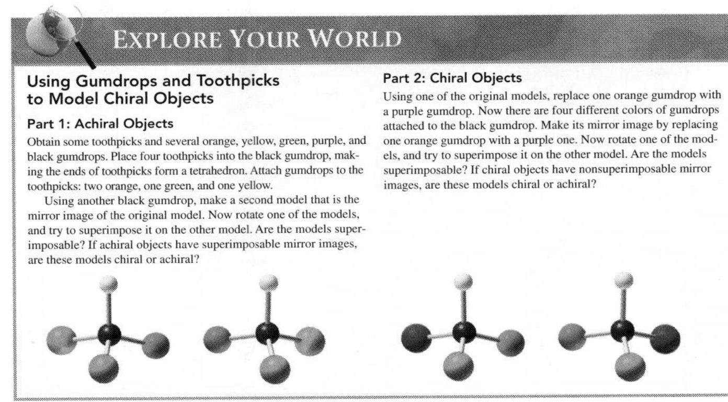

EXPLORE YOUR WORLD

**Using Gumdrops and Toothpicks to Model Chiral Objects**

**Part 1: Achiral Objects**

Obtain some toothpicks and several orange, yellow, green, purple, and black gumdrops. Place four toothpicks into the black gumdrop, making the ends of toothpicks form a tetrahedron. Attach gumdrops to the toothpicks: two orange, one green, and one yellow.

Using another black gumdrop, make a second model that is the mirror image of the original model. Now rotate one of the models, and try to superimpose it on the other model. Are the models superimposable? If achiral objects have superimposable mirror images, are these models chiral or achiral?

**Part 2: Chiral Objects**

Using one of the original models, replace one orange gumdrop with a purple gumdrop. Now there are four different colors of gumdrops attached to the black gumdrop. Make its mirror image by replacing one orange gumdrop with a purple one. Now rotate one of the models, and try to superimpose it on the other model. Are the models superimposable? If chiral objects have nonsuperimposable mirror images, are these models chiral or achiral?

**Explore Your World** **Explore Your World** contains hands-on activities that use everyday materials to encourage students to actively explore selected chemistry topics, either individually or in group-learning environments. Each activity is followed by questions to encourage critical thinking.

# Student-Friendly Approach

## Keeping Students Engaged Is the Ultimate Goal

**Student-Friendly Writing Style** To enhance student understanding, I try to use an accessible writing style, based on a carefully paced and simple development of chemical ideas, suited to the background of allied health students. All terms are precisely defined, and clear goals are set for each section of the text. Clear analogies help students visualize and understand key chemical concepts.

**Learning Goals** At the beginning of each section, a **Learning Goal** clearly identifies the key concept of the section, providing a roadmap for studying. All information contained in that section relates back to the Learning Goal. The Learning Goals for each section are also repeated in the Chapter Review so students can make sure they have mastered the key concepts.

**NEW Concept Checks** The many **Concept Checks** throughout each chapter allow students to check their understanding of new concepts. The many new Concept Checks give students an opportunity to focus on their understanding of newly introduced chemical terms and ideas.

**Concept Maps** Each chapter ends with a **Concept Map** that reviews the key concepts of each chapter and how they fit together.

**6.1 Chemical Reactions**

As we discussed in Chapter 2, a *chemical change* occurs when a substance is converted into one or more new substances. For example, when silver tarnishes, the shiny silver metal (Ag) reacts with sulfur (S) to become the dull, black substance we call *tarnish* ($Ag_2S$). (See Figure 6.1.)

LEARNING GOAL

Write a balanced chemical equation from the formulas of the reactants and products for a chemical reaction.

CONCEPT CHECK 6.4

**Moles and Particles**

Explain why 0.20 mole of aluminum is a small number, but the number of atoms in 0.20 mole is a large number: $1.2 \times 10^{23}$ atoms of aluminum.

ANSWER

The term *mole* is used as a collection term that represents $6.02 \times 10^{23}$ particles. Because atoms are submicroscopic particles, a large number of atoms are in 1 mole of aluminum.

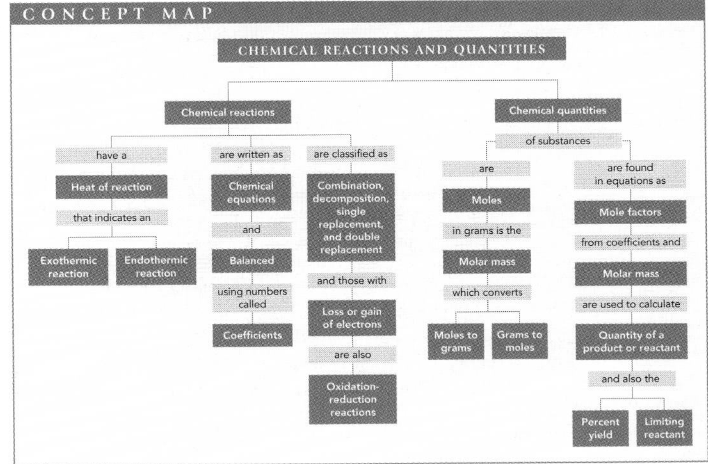

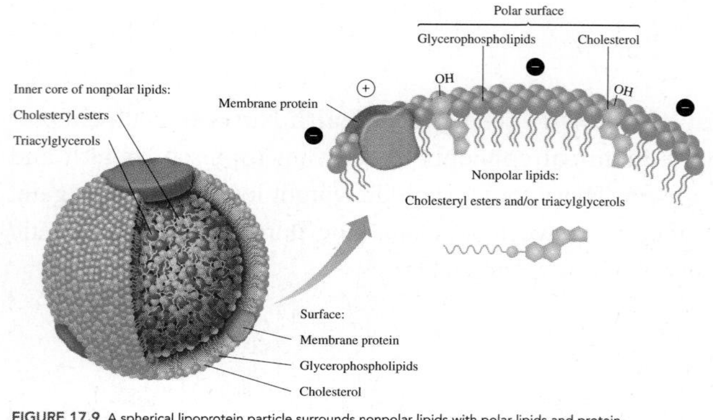


FIGURE 17.9 A spherical lipoprotein particle surrounds nonpolar lipids with polar lipids and protein for transport to body cells.

Q Why are the polar components on the surface of a lipoprotein particle and the nonpolar components at the center?

### Clear Illustrations Help Students Visualize Chemistry

The **art program** is not only beautifully rendered, but pedagogically effective as well.

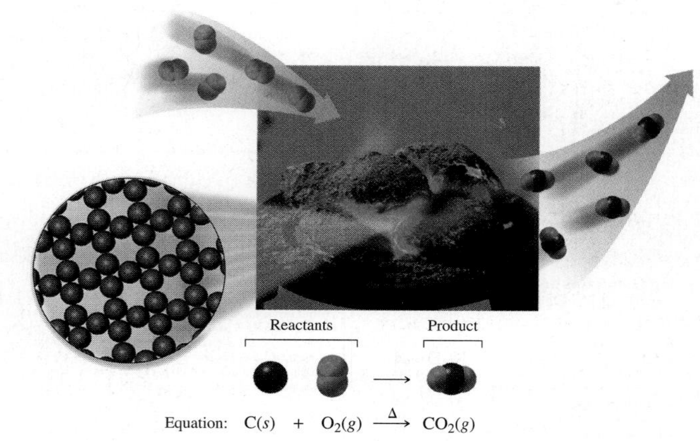


Macro-to-Micro Art

**Macro-to-Micro Art** **Macro-to-micro art** portrays the atomic structure of recognizable objects, putting chemistry in context and connecting the atomic world to the macroscopic world. A question with each figure challenges students to think critically about photos and illustrations. Many new photos expand visual connections.

# Problem Solving

## Many Tools Show Students How to Solve Problems

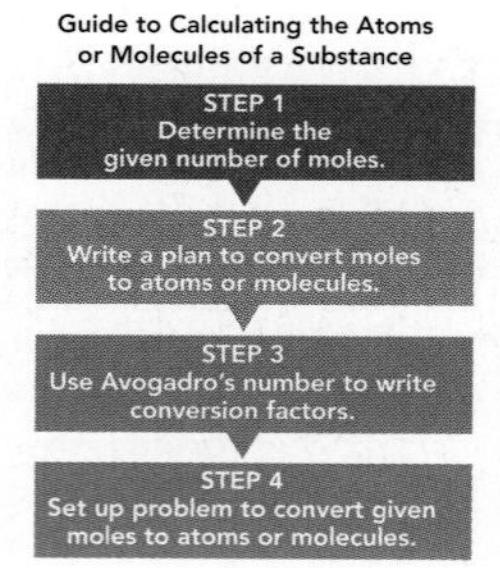


**A Visual Guide to Problem Solving** As part of a comprehensive learning program, the **Guides to Problem Solving** (GPS) illustrate the steps students need to solve problems. I clearly understand the learning challenges facing students in this course, so I walk students through the problem-solving process step by step. For each type of problem, I use a unique, color-coded flow chart that is coordinated with parallel worked examples as a visual guide for each problem-solving strategy.

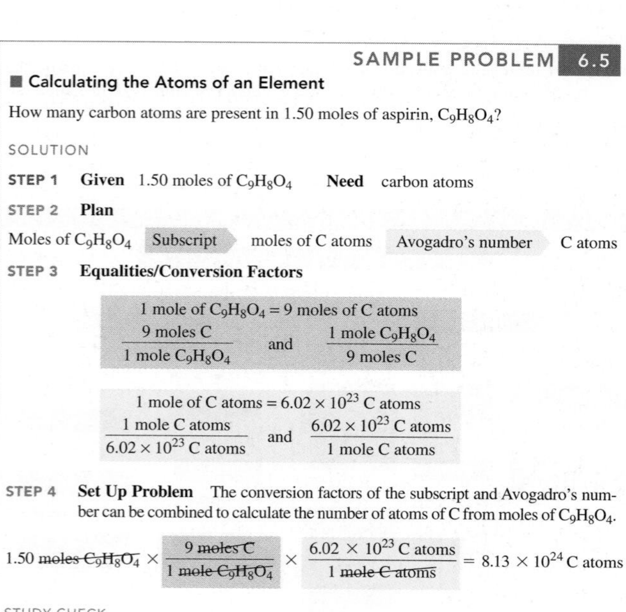

SAMPLE PROBLEM 6.5

■ Calculating the Atoms of an Element

How many carbon atoms are present in 1.50 moles of aspirin, $C_9H_8O_4$?

SOLUTION

STEP 1 **Given** 1.50 moles of $C_9H_8O_4$ **Need** carbon atoms

STEP 2 **Plan**

Moles of $C_9H_8O_4$ → Subscript → moles of C atoms → Avogadro's number → C atoms

STEP 3 **Equalities/Conversion Factors**

1 mole of $C_9H_8O_4$ = 9 moles of C atoms

$$\frac{9 \text{ moles C}}{1 \text{ mole } C_9H_8O_4} \text{ and } \frac{1 \text{ mole } C_9H_8O_4}{9 \text{ moles C}}$$

1 mole of C atoms = $6.02 \times 10^{23}$ C atoms

$$\frac{1 \text{ mole C atoms}}{6.02 \times 10^{23} \text{ C atoms}} \text{ and } \frac{6.02 \times 10^{23} \text{ C atoms}}{1 \text{ mole C atoms}}$$

STEP 4 **Set Up Problem** The conversion factors of the subscript and Avogadro's number can be combined to calculate the number of atoms of C from moles of $C_9H_8O_4$.

$$1.50 \text{ moles } C_9H_8O_4 \times \frac{9 \text{ moles C}}{1 \text{ mole } C_9H_8O_4} \times \frac{6.02 \times 10^{23} \text{ C atoms}}{1 \text{ mole C atoms}} = 8.13 \times 10^{24} \text{ C atoms}$$

STUDY CHECK

How many moles of aspirin, $C_9H_8O_4$, contain 0.480 mole of O atoms?

**Sample Problems with Study Checks** Numerous **Sample Problems** appear throughout the text to demonstrate the application of each new concept. The worked-out solutions give step-by-step explanations, provide a problem-solving model, and illustrate required calculations. Each Sample Problem is followed by a **Study Check** question that allows students to test their understanding of the problem-solving strategy.

**Integrated Questions and Problems** **Questions and Problems** at the end of each section encourage students to apply concepts and begin problem solving after each section. **Paired Problems** of each even-numbered problem with a matching odd-numbered problem guide students through solving problems. **Answers** to odd-numbered problems are given at the end of each chapter.

**End-of-Chapter Questions and Problems** **Understanding the Concepts** questions encourage students to think about the concepts they have learned. **Additional Questions and Problems** integrate the topics from the entire chapter to promote understanding and critical thinking. **Challenge Questions** are designed for group work in cooperative learning environments.

**NEW Combining Ideas Problem Sets** This **new feature** appears after every 2–4 chapters as a set of integrated problems designed to test students' cumulative understanding of the previous chapters.

COMBINING IDEAS FROM CHAPTERS 3 TO 6

CI.7 Some of the isotopes of silicon are listed in the following table:

| Isotope | % Natural Abundance | Atomic Mass | Half-Life | Radiation Emitted |
|---|---|---|---|---|
| $^{27}_{14}Si$ | | 26.99 | 4.2 s | Positron |
| $^{28}_{14}Si$ | 92.23 | 27.99 | Stable | None |
| $^{29}_{14}Si$ | 4.67 | 28.99 | Stable | None |
| $^{30}_{14}Si$ | 3.10 | 29.98 | Stable | None |
| $^{31}_{14}Si$ | | 30.99 | 2.6 h | Beta |

a. In the following table, indicate the number of protons, neutrons, and electrons for each isotope listed:

| Isotope | Number of Protons | Number of Neutrons | Number of Electrons |
|---|---|---|---|
| $^{27}_{14}Si$ | | | |
| $^{28}_{14}Si$ | | | |
| $^{29}_{14}Si$ | | | |
| $^{30}_{14}Si$ | | | |
| $^{31}_{14}Si$ | | | |

b. What is the electron configuration of silicon?
c. Calculate the atomic mass for silicon using the isotopes that have a natural abundance.
d. Write the nuclear equations for $^{27}_{14}Si$ and $^{31}_{14}Si$.
e. Write the electron-dot formula and predict the shape of $SiCl_4$.
f. How many hours are needed for a sample of $^{31}_{14}Si$ with an activity of 16 μCi to decay to 2.0 μCi?

**CI.8** $K^+$ is an electrolyte required by the human body and is found in many foods as well as salt substitutes. One of the isotopes of potassium is $^{40}_{19}K$ which has a natural abundance of 0.012% and a half-life of $1.30 \times 10^9$ years. The isotope $^{40}_{19}K$ decays to $^{40}_{20}Ca$ or to $^{40}_{18}Ar$. A typical activity for $^{40}_{19}K$ is 7.0 μCi per gram.

a. Write a nuclear equation for each type of decay.
b. Identify the particle emitted for each type of decay.
c. How many $K^+$ ions are in 3.5 oz of KCl?
d. What is the activity of 25 g of KCl, in becquerels?

CI.9 Of much concern to environmentalists is the radioactive noble gas radon-222, which can seep from the ground into basements of homes and buildings. Radon-222 is a product of the decay of radium-226 that occurs naturally in rocks and soil in much of the United States. Radon-222, which has a half-life of 3.8 days, decays by emitting an alpha particle. Radon-222, which is a gas, can be inhaled; because of that, it is strongly associated with lung cancer. Radon levels in a home can be measured with a home radon-detection kit. Environmental agencies have set the maximum level of radon-222 in a home at 4 picocuries per liter (pCi/L) of air in a home.

a. Write the equation for the decay of Ra-226.
b. Write the equation for the decay of Rn-222.
c. If a room contains 24 000 atoms of radon-222, how many atoms of radon-222 remain after 15.2 days?
d. Suppose a room in a home has a volume of 72 000 liters ($7.2 \times 10^4$ L). If the radon level is 2.5 picocuries/liter, how many alpha particles are emitted in one day? (1 Ci = $3.7 \times 10^{10}$ disintegrations per second.)

**CI.10** A gold bar has a volume of 728 $cm^3$ and a density of 19.3 $g/cm^3$.
a. What is the mass in kilograms of the gold bar?
b. How many atoms of gold are in the bar?
c. Give the number of protons and neutrons in each of the following isotopes of gold:
$^{185}_{79}Au$ $^{197}_{79}Au$ $^{198}_{79}Au$

CI.11 The following reaction occurs between a metal in Group 1A (1) or Group 2A (2) and a nonmetal:

X Y Y

a. Which spheres represent a metal? A nonmetal?
b. Which reactant has the higher electronegativity?
c. What are the ionic charges of X and Y in the product?
d. If these elements are both in period 3:
1. Write the electron configurations of the atoms.
2. Write the electron configurations of their ions.
3. Give the names of the noble gases with the same electron configurations as these ions.
4. Write the formula and name of the product.
e. Match the spheres below with atoms of Li, Na, K, and Rb.

A. B. C. D.

258

# The Most Advanced Chemistry Homework and Tutorial System

MasteringCHEMISTRY™

**www.masteringchemistry.com**

**MasteringChemistry™** is the most advanced chemistry homework and tutorial system available. This online homework and tutoring system uses the Socratic Method to coach students through problem-solving techniques, offering hints and simpler questions on request. It tutors students individually with feedback specific to their errors. MasteringChemistry helps students learn, not just practice. (See the MasteringChemistry insert at the front of the book.)

# Instructional Package

*General, Organic, and Biological Chemistry: Structures of Life*, third edition, is the nucleus of an integrated teaching and learning package of support material for both students and professors.

## For Students

**Study Guide** for *General, Organic, and Biological Chemistry*, third edition, by Karen Timberlake, is keyed to the learning goals in the text and designed to promote active learning through a variety of exercises with answers as well as practice tests. (ISBN 0321587553)

**Selected Solutions Manual** for *General, Organic, and Biological Chemistry*, third edition, by Karen Timberlake, contains the complete solutions to the odd-numbered problems. (ISBN 0321616634)

**Laboratory Manual for General, Organic, and Biological Chemistry** by Karen Timberlake. This best-selling lab manual coordinates 42 experiments with the topics in *General, Organic, and Biological Chemistry*, third edition; uses new terms during the lab; and explores chemical concepts. Laboratory investigations develop skills of manipulating equipment, reporting data, solving problems, making calculations, and drawing conclusions. (ISBN 0805349049)

**Essential Laboratory Manual** by Karen Timberlake. This manual contains 25 experiments for the standard course sequence of topics in *General, Organic, and Biological Chemistry*, third edition. (ISBN 0805330232)

## For Instructors

**Instructor Resource Center on CD/DVD** This CD/DVD includes all the art and tables from the book in JPG format for use in classroom projection or creating study materials and tests. In addition, the instructor can access the PowerPoint™ lecture outlines, featuring over 2000 slides. Also available on the discs are downloadable files of the *Instructor Manual*, a set of "clicker questions" suitable for use with classroom-response systems, and the test bank. (ISBN 0321587561)

**Transparency Pack** Contains 300 full-color transparency acetates. (ISBN 032158757X)

**Instructor Solutions Manual** Prepared by Kathy Thrush Shaginaw and Karen Timberlake, this manual highlights chapter topics and includes suggestions for the laboratory. Contains complete solution setups and answers to all problems in the text. (ISBN 0321587596)

**Printed Test Bank** Prepared by Kathy Thrush Shaginaw, Lynn Carlson, and Bill Timberlake, this test bank contains over 2000 questions in multiple-choice, matching, true-false, and short-answer format. (ISBN 0321587588)

**Online Instructor Manual for Laboratory Manual** Contains answers to report pages for the Laboratory Manual and Essential Laboratory Manual. (ISBN 0321499670)

**Course Management: Blackboard and WebCT** course management systems provide powerful course management capability. All of the content available in the Mastering-Chemistry Study Area is also available in **WebCT** and **Blackboard**. Pearson Prentice Hall offers content cartridges for these text-specific Classroom Management Systems. Visit **http://www.pearsonhighered.com** or contact your Prentice Hall sales representative for details.

Also visit the Prentice Hall catalog page for Timberlake's *General, Organic, and Biological Chemistry*, third edition, at **www.pearsonhighered.com** to download available instructor supplements.

## New to This Edition

New features have been added throughout this third edition, including the following:

- A new Prologue introduces chemistry, the scientific method, and a study plan for learning chemistry.
- New Concept Checks with Answers build conceptual understanding.
- More Guides to Problem Solving (GPS) illustrate step-by-step problem-solving strategies.
- New Green Chemistry Notes include "Biodiesel as an Alternative Fuel," "Greenhouse Gases," and "Energy-Saving Light Bulbs."
- New Health Note "Brachytherapy" has been added.
- New Career interviews include Geologist and Conservator of Photographs.
- New molecular models in problem sets improve visual understanding of chemical reactions.
- New photos and updated diagrams improve clarity and provide visual connections to real life.
- New units of measurement include parts per million (ppm) and parts per billion (ppb).
- New Sample Problems and Study Checks model problem-solving strategies.
- New Understanding the Concepts problems add more visual examples to conceptual learning.
- New inter-chapter Combining Ideas problem sets provide problems with greater depth using concepts from several chapters.

## Chapter Organization

Throughout this text, the structures of compounds and organic and biochemical molecules are related to their function. The discussion of bonding and shapes of molecules in Chapter 5 provides a foundation for understanding the structure of organic and biochemical molecules. The topic of stereochemistry and chiral organic molecules in Chapter 14 is revisited as an important concept in the understanding of structures of carbohydrates, amino acids, and chiral drugs.

The structures of molecules are related to their physical and chemical properties such as solubility in water, density, and boiling point. The structural levels of proteins are related to their function, while chemical processes that denature proteins emphasize the importance of structure to activity. Throughout the text, the atomic structure of matter is highlighted by macro-to-micro art that relates the atomic level to the macroscopic structures of real-life materials. In this way, the chemical concepts and structures of molecules are continuously related to the behavior and function of biomolecules in the body.

In each textbook I write, I consider it essential to relate every chemical concept to real-life issues of health and environment. In this text, I have added the theme of Structures of Life. All the material usually found in appendices has been integrated with the appropriate chapter material so that there are no longer any appendices at the end of the book. Because a course of chemistry for allied health may be taught in different time frames, it may be difficult to cover all the chapters in this text. However, each chapter is a complete package, which allows some chapters to be skipped or the order of presentation to be changed.

## Prologue

The **Prologue**, a new feature, introduces students to the concepts of chemicals and chemistry, discusses the scientific method, and asks students to develop a study plan for learning chemistry. A *Health Note*, "Early Chemists: The Alchemists," was added.

## Chapters 1 and 2

**Chapter 1, "Measurements,"** looks at measurement and the need to understand numerical structures of the metric system in the sciences. The section on *Scientific Notation* is now a separate section. Items added include *peta* prefix to Metric and SI Prefixes, and parts per million (ppm) and parts per billion (ppb) to percentage conversion factors.

- A new feature called *Green Chemistry Note* discusses "Toxicology and Risk-Benefit Assessment."
- *Health Note*, "Bone Density," has been rewritten to discuss changes in bone density with age.
- New *Guides to Problem Solving*, "Calculating Density" and "Using Density," use color blocks as visual guides in the step-by-step solution pathway.
- The discussion of "Temperature" has been moved to Chapter 2.

**Chapter 2, "Energy and Matter,"** now combines temperature, physical and chemical changes, energy, and matter into a single chapter that discusses energy and heat, nutritional energy values, temperature conversions, states of matter, and energy involved in changes of state. New energy problems use the SI unit of the joule (J).

- *Green Chemistry Note* updates the content of "Carbon Dioxide and Global Warming."
- New macro-to-micro art emphasizes the atomic level for changes of state.
- Many *Sample Problems* were reworked to utilize the Guide to Problem Solving strategy.
- New to this edition is an inter-chapter problem set, *Combining Ideas from Chapters 1 and 2*.

## Chapters 3 and 4

**Chapter 3, "Atoms and Elements,"** looks at elements, atoms, subatomic particles, and atomic mass. *The Periodic Table* emphasizes the numbering of groups from 1–18. Elements with atomic numbers 116 and 118 were added.

- New items include a discussion of the discovery of electrons by J. J. Thomson using the cathode ray tube. The calculation of the average atomic mass of an element uses percent abundance and isotope mass.
- Section 3.8, *Periodic Trends*, discusses periodic properties of elements including valence electrons, atomic size, and ionization energy.
- A new *Green Chemistry Note*, "Energy-Saving Lightbulbs," has been added.

**Chapter 4, "Nuclear Chemistry,"** extends the concepts of subatomic particles, atomic number, and atomic mass to a discussion of radioisotopes including the positron. Nuclear equations are written and balanced for both naturally occurring and artificially produced radioactivity. The topic of biological effects of radiation is now part of the chapter content.

- Tables of radioisotopes were expanded.
- New *Health Note*, "Brachytherapy," was added.
- Update on "Radon in Our Homes."
- The half-lives of radioisotopes are discussed, and the amount of time for a sample to decay is calculated.
- Radioisotopes that are important in the field of nuclear medicine are emphasized.

## Chapters 5 and 6

**Chapter 5, "Compounds and Their Bonds,"** describes how atoms form ionic and covalent bonds in compounds. Chemical formulas are written, and ionic compounds—including those with polyatomic ions—and covalent compounds are named. An introduction to the three-dimensional shape of molecules provides a basis for the shape of organic and biochemical compounds. The discussion of polyatomic ions, which includes more polyatomic ions, follows the formation of ionic compounds. The concept of resonance is discussed for the electron-dot formulas for compounds with multiple bonds.

- New items include a discussion on the sizes of ions compared to the sizes of their corresponding atoms.
- New questions use the electron-dot formulas or electron configurations to determine chemical formulas and names. Electronegativity leads to a discussion of the polarity of bonds and molecules.
- The section *Attractive Forces in Compounds* now appears in Chapter 5.

**Chapter 6, "Chemical Reactions and Quantities,"** includes the quantitative aspects of reactions such as the mole and molar mass (which are used in calculations of the number of particles in a quantity) and mass calculations in reactions. Equations for chemical reactions are balanced and organized into combination, decomposition, single replacement, and double replacement reactions.

- Section 6.3, *Oxidation–Reduction Reactions*, was rewritten to include oxidation–reduction in biological systems.
- A new *Green Chemistry Note*, "Fuel Cells: Clean Energy for the Future," has been added.
- Mole and mass relationships among the reactants and products are examined along with calculations of percent yield and limiting reactants.
- The material on limiting reactants has been expanded to give more examples.
- Section 6.9, *Energy Changes in Chemical Reactions*, is now included with Chapter 6.
- New to this edition is an inter-chapter problem set, *Combining Ideas from Chapters 3 to 6*.

## Chapters 7 and 8

**Chapter 7, "Gases,"** discusses the properties of a gas and calculates changes in gases using the gas laws.

- New art was added on gas pressure at different altitudes.
- The chapter includes calculations of the amount of a gas required or produced in a chemical reaction.
- New items include predicting changes in gas variables, a *Guide to Problem Solving*, "Using Molar Volume," and a *Summary* of Gas Laws.
- A new *Green Chemistry Note*, "Greenhouse Gases," on the types and sources of greenhouse gases has been added.

**Chapter 8, "Solutions,"** describes solutions, electrolytes, saturation and solubility, concentrations, osmosis, and dialysis. The volumes and molarities of solutions are used to calculate product quantities in chemical reactions.

- The topics of dilution and titration were updated and new problems on concentrations and dilution were added.
- New items include Table 8.3, *Possible Combinations of Solutes and Solvents*, and Section 8.6, *Physical Properties of Solutions*, which discusses the impact of solution particles on the lowering of freezing points and the elevation of boiling points.
- The material on electrolytes and nonelectrolytes, saturation, and osmosis has been rewritten and new questions added.

## Chapters 9 and 10

**Chapter 9, "Chemical Equilibrium,"** looks at the rates of reactions and the equilibrium condition when forward and reverse rates for a reaction become equal. Equilibrium expressions for reactions are written and equilibrium constants are calculated. Le Châtelier's principle is used to evaluate the impact on concentrations when a stress is placed on the system.

- A new Section 9.6, *Equilibrium in Saturated Solutions*, and a new Guide to Problem Solving, "Guide to Calculating $K_{sp}$," have been added.

**Chapter 10, "Acids and Bases,"** discusses acids and bases and their strengths; conjugate acid–base pairs; pH; and buffers. Section 10.1, *Acids and Bases*, now includes Brønsted–Lowry Acids and Bases.

- The acids HCN, HClO, and $HClO_4$ have been added to Table 10.1, *Naming Common Acids*.
- A *Green Chemistry Note*, "Acid Rain," updates the topic of acid rain.
- New problems related to acid rain have been added. Acid–base titration uses the neutralization reaction between an acid and a base to calculate quantities of an acid in a sample.
- The chapter includes discussions of strengths of acids and bases, their dissociation constants, acid–base properties of salt solutions, and buffers.
- New to this edition is an inter-chapter problem set, *Combining Ideas from Chapters 7 to 10*.

## Chapter 11, 12, and 13

**Chapter 11, "Introduction to Organic Chemistry: Alkanes,"** discusses the structure, nomenclature, and reactions of alkanes. Guides to Problem Solving (GPS) clarify the rules for nomenclature. An overview of functional groups and isomers describes the structure of organic chemistry and forms a basis for understanding the biomolecules of living systems.

- The subsection *Halogenation of Alkanes (Substitution)* was deleted.
- The *Health Note* "Toxicity of Carbon Monoxide" describes the products of incomplete combustion and their toxicity.
- A new *Career Focus*, "Geologist," has been added.

**Chapter 12, "Alkenes, Alkynes, and Aromatic Compounds,"** discusses alkenes and alkynes, cis–trans isomers, addition reactions, polymers of alkenes used in everyday items, and aromatic compounds.

- Section 12.2, *Cis–Trans Isomers*, has been rewritten for clarity.
- An *Explore Your World* feature, "Modeling Cis–Trans Isomers," now asks students to model cis and trans isomers using gumdrops and toothpicks.
- The discussion of addition reactions hydrogenation, halogenation, hydrohalogenation, and hydration illustrates reactions important in biological systems.
- The *Career Focus* "Laboratory Technologist" is now included in this chapter.

**Chapter 13, "Alcohols, Phenols, Ethers, and Thiols,"** discusses structures, names, properties, and reactions of alcohols, phenols, thiols, and ethers.

- The *Health Note* "Some Important Alcohols and Phenols" now includes a discussion of bisphenol A (BPA).
- Section 13.3, *Physical Properties of Alcohols, Phenols, and Ethers*, was rewritten for clarity.
- The *Health Note* "Oxidation of Methanol" is now titled "Methanol Poisoning."
- The *Health Note* "Oxidation of Alcohol in the Body" has been updated to include current methods of determining blood alcohol.

## Chapters 14 and 15

**Chapter 14, "Aldehydes, Ketones, and Chiral Molecules,"** discusses the nomenclature and structures of aldehydes and ketones.

- The subsection *Some Important Aldehydes and Ketones* is now a *Health Note*.
- Section 14.5, *Chiral Molecules*, uses simple compounds to introduce chiral molecules and chirality early in the text in preparation for the next chapter.
- An *Explore Your World* feature, "Using Gumdrops and Toothpicks to Model Chiral Objects," constructs chiral and achiral molecules by using gumdrops and toothpicks.

**Chapter 15, "Carbohydrates,"** applies the organic chemistry of alcohols, aldehydes, and ketones to biomolecules, which relates the study of chemistry to health and medicine.

- Section 15.2 is now *Fischer Projections of Monosaccharides*, and Section 15.3 is *Haworth Structures of Monosaccharides*.
- New art includes Fischer projections for all the carbohydrate structures.
- The section *Haworth Structures of Monosaccharides* is rewritten to provide clearer instructions for drawing the closed ring structures.
- The *Health Notes* "How Sweet Is My Sweetener?" and "Blood Types and Carbohydrates" have been updated with recently developed sweeteners and information on blood types.
- New to this edition is an inter-chapter problem set, *Combining Ideas from Chapters 11 to 15*.

## Chapters 16, 17, and 18

**Chapter 16, "Carboxylic Acids and Esters,"** discusses two organic families that are important in biochemical systems.

- In this new edition, there is more emphasis on the use of Le Châtelier's principle to explain direction of reactions such as esterification and acid hydrolysis of esters.

**Chapter 17, "Lipids,"** contains the functional groups of alcohols, aldehydes, and ketones in larger molecules such as triacylglycerols, glycerophospholipids, and steroids.

- Table 17.1, *Structures and Melting Points of Common Fatty Acids*, now includes arachidonic acid. The differences in the structures of prostaglandins E and F are now explained. Structures for fatty acids now include the line-bond formula. *Health Notes* of interest to students include olestra, trans fatty acids, and lipoproteins.
- A new *Green Chemistry Note*, "Biodiesel as an Alternative Fuel," has been added.
- Section 17.6, *Sphingolipids*, has been rewritten to clarify the structural differences between a sphingomyelin, ceramide, glycosphingolipid, and ganglioside. The role of lipids and cholesterol in cell membranes is discussed along with lipids that function as bile salts and steroid hormones.

**Chapter 18, "Amines and Amides,"** emphasizes the nitrogen atom in their functional groups and their names.

- New *Guides to Problem Solving* now include steps for naming amines and amides. *Health Notes* include amines and amides in health and medicine, as well as alkaloids, which are naturally occurring amines in plants.

## Chapters 19, 20, and 21

**Chapter 19, "Amino Acids and Proteins,"** connects the functional groups of amines and amides to their related biomolecules. The classification of amino acids has been rewritten to include their ionized structures.

- Table 19.2, *The 20 Amino Acids (Ionized) in Proteins*, compares the form of amino acids above, below, and at the isoelectric point (pI). The importance of the structure of proteins from primary to quaternary is related to the shapes and activity of proteins.

**Chapter 20, "Enzymes and Vitamins,"** relates the importance of the three-dimensional shape of proteins to their function as enzymes. Table 20.1, *Classification of Enzymes*, was simplified. The students learn that the shape of an enzyme is a factor in enzyme regulation and how end products might change the shape of an enzyme to increase or decrease the rate of an enzyme-catalyzed reaction. We also see that proteins change shape and lose function when subjected to pH changes and high temperatures. The important role of water-soluble vitamins as coenzymes is related to enzyme function.

- New to this edition is an inter-chapter problem set, *Combining Ideas from Chapters 16 to 20*.

**Chapter 21, "Nucleic Acids and Protein Synthesis,"** describes the nucleic acids and their importance as biomolecules that store and direct information for cellular components, growth, and reproduction. The role of complementary base pairing is highlighted in both DNA replication and the formation of mRNA during protein synthesis. Discussions include the genetic code, its relationship to the order of amino acids in a protein, and how mutations can occur when the nucleotide sequence is altered.

- The *Explore Your World* feature "A Model for DNA Replication and Mutation" is expanded to include formation of mRNA and dipeptide formation.
- The preparation and uses of recombinant DNA in forensic science and the discussion of the Human Genome Project have been updated.
- The role of DNA or RNA in viruses that utilize host cells to replicate is discussed.

## Chapters 22, 23, and 24

**Chapter 22, "Metabolic Pathways for Carbohydrates,"** describes the stages of metabolism and the digestion of carbohydrates, our most important fuel. The breakdown of glucose to pyruvate is described using the glycolytic pathway, which is followed under aerobic conditions by the decarboxylation of pyruvate to acetyl CoA. The synthesis of glycogen and the synthesis of glucose from noncarbohydrate sources are discussed.

**Chapter 23, "Metabolic Pathways and Energy Production,"** looks at the entry of acetyl CoA into the citric acid cycle and the production of reduced coenzymes for the electron transport system and oxidative phosphorylation.

- The discussion of the reactions of the citric acid cycle has been expanded and now includes the enzymes that catalyze the reactions.
- Details on the structure and function of ATP synthase are included.

**Chapter 24, "Metabolic Pathways for Lipids and Amino Acids,"** discusses the digestion of lipids and proteins and the metabolic pathways that convert fatty acids and amino acids into energy. Discussions include the conversion of excess carbohydrates to triacylglycerols in adipose tissue and how the intermediates of the citric acid cycle are converted to nonessential amino acids.

- The *Explore Your World* feature "Fat Storage and Blubber" has been updated and expanded to give clear instructions for the procedures.
- Finally, the relationships between the catabolic and anabolic pathways in metabolism are summarized.
- New to this edition is an inter-chapter problem set, *Combining Ideas from Chapters 21 to 24.*

# ACKNOWLEDGMENTS

The preparation of a new edition is a continuous effort of many people. As in my work on other textbooks, I am thankful for the support, encouragement, and dedication of many people who put in hours of tireless effort to produce a high-quality book that provides an outstanding learning package. The editorial team at Pearson Publishing has done an exceptional job. I want to thank Nicole Folchetti, editor in chief, and acquisitions editor, Dawn Giovanniello, who supported my vision of this third edition and the addition of new *Concept Checks*, *Green Chemistry Notes*, *Combining Ideas*, problem sets, and an updated art program. I much appreciate all the wonderful work of Jessica Neumann, assistant editor, who was like an angel encouraging me at each step while skillfully coordinating reviews, art, website materials, and all the things it takes to make a book come together. I am grateful to Ray Mullaney, editor in chief of science book development, and Karen Nein, developmental editor, for their watchful eyes during the writing and development of this new edition. I appreciate the work of Beth Sweeten, project manager, and Lynn Lustberg of Macmillan Publishing Solutions, who brilliantly coordinated all phases of the manuscript to the final pages of a beautiful book. Thanks to Kathy Thrush Shaginaw, manuscript reviewer, and Richard Camp, copy editor, who precisely reviewed and edited the initial and final manuscripts to make sure the words and problems were correct to help students learn chemistry.

I am especially proud of the art program in this text, which lends beauty and understanding to chemistry. I would like to thank Suzanne Behnke, art director and book designer, and Travis Amos, photo editor, whose creative ideas provided the outstanding design for the cover and pages of the book. Eric Schrader, photo researcher, was invaluable in researching and selecting vivid photos for the text so that students can see the beauty of chemistry. Thanks also to *Bio-Rad Laboratories* for their courtesy and use of *KnowItAll ChemWindows Edition* drawing software that helped me produce chemical structures for the manuscript. The macro-to-micro illustrations designed by Production Solutions and Precision Graphics give students visual impressions of the atomic and molecular organization of everyday things and are a fantastic learning tool. I want to thank Michael Rossa for the hours of proofreading all the pages. I also appreciate all the hard work in the field put in by the marketing team and Elizabeth Averbeck, marketing manager.

This text also reflects the contributions of many professors who took the time to review and edit the manuscript and provide outstanding comments, help, and suggestions. A special thanks to Kathy Thrush Shaginaw, Mark Quirie, and Timothy Kreider for their outstanding accuracy reviews of the entire manuscript. Their keen eyes and thoughtful comments were extremely helpful in the development of this text.

I am extremely grateful to an incredible group of peers for their careful assessment of all the new ideas for the text; for their suggested additions, corrections, changes, and deletions; and for providing an incredible amount of feedback about improvements for the book. In addition, I appreciate the time scientists took to let us take photos and discuss their work with them. I admire and appreciate every one of you.

If you would like to share your experience with chemistry or have questions and comments about this text, I would appreciate hearing from you.

*Karen Timberlake*
E-mail: khemist@aol.com

# REVIEWERS

**Third Edition Reviewers**

**Dana Chatellier**
*University of Delaware*

**Robin De Roo**
*Cypress College*

**Csilla Duneczky**
*Johnson County Community College*

**Fahd Z. Eissa**
*Voorhees College*

**Jeff Flowers**
*College of San Mateo*

**Margaret (Peggy) Geiger**
*Gaston College*

**Deepa Godambe**
*William Rainey Harper College*

**Karen Hammond**
*Boise State University*

**Myung W. Han**
*Columbus State Community College*

**Bruce J. Heyen**
*Tabor College*

**Ling Huang**
*Sacramento City College*

**James F. Kirby**
*Quinnipiac University*

**John R. Kiser**
*Isothermal Community College*

**Timothy Kreider**
*UMDNJ-New Jersey Medical School*

**Jeanne L. Kuhler**
*Auburn University*

**Michael Langohr**
*Tarrant County College*

**Carole LeMaster**
*Boise State University*

**Andrea D. Leonard**
*University of Louisiana, Lafayette*

**Margaret Ruth Leslie**
*Kent State University*

**Laura Lograsso**
*Macomb Community College*

**Craig P. McClure**
*University of Alabama, Birmingham*

**Emily Jellen-McCullough**
*Western Carolina University*

**Susanne McFadden**
*Tarrant County College, Northwest Campus*

**Cynthia Molitor**
*Lourdes College*

**Luis D. Montes**
*University of Central Oklahoma*

**Sun O. (Jane) Myoung**
*Sinclair Community College*

**Paula Nolibos**
*Gainesville State College*

**Marie Nguyen**
*Highline College*

**Kefa K. Onchoke**
*Stephen F. Austin State University*

**Harry Pang**
*Lee College*

**Mark Quirie**
*Algonquin College*

**Michael Sakuta**
*Georgia Perimeter College*

**Paul Sampson**
*Kent State University*

**Rhodora Snow**
*J. Sargeant Reynolds Community College*

**Kathy Thrush Shaginaw**
*Particular Solutions Inc.*

**Eric R. Taylor**
*University of Louisiana, Lafayette*

**David A. Tramontozzi**
*Macomb Community College*

**Aimee Wagner**
*Central Ohio Technical College*

**Joanne Wittbrodt**
*Wayne County Community College, Downtown Campus*

# PROLOGUE
# Chemistry in Our Lives

## LOOKING AHEAD


**P.1** Chemistry and Chemicals

**P.2** Scientific Method: Thinking like a Scientist

**P.3** A Study Plan for Learning Chemistry


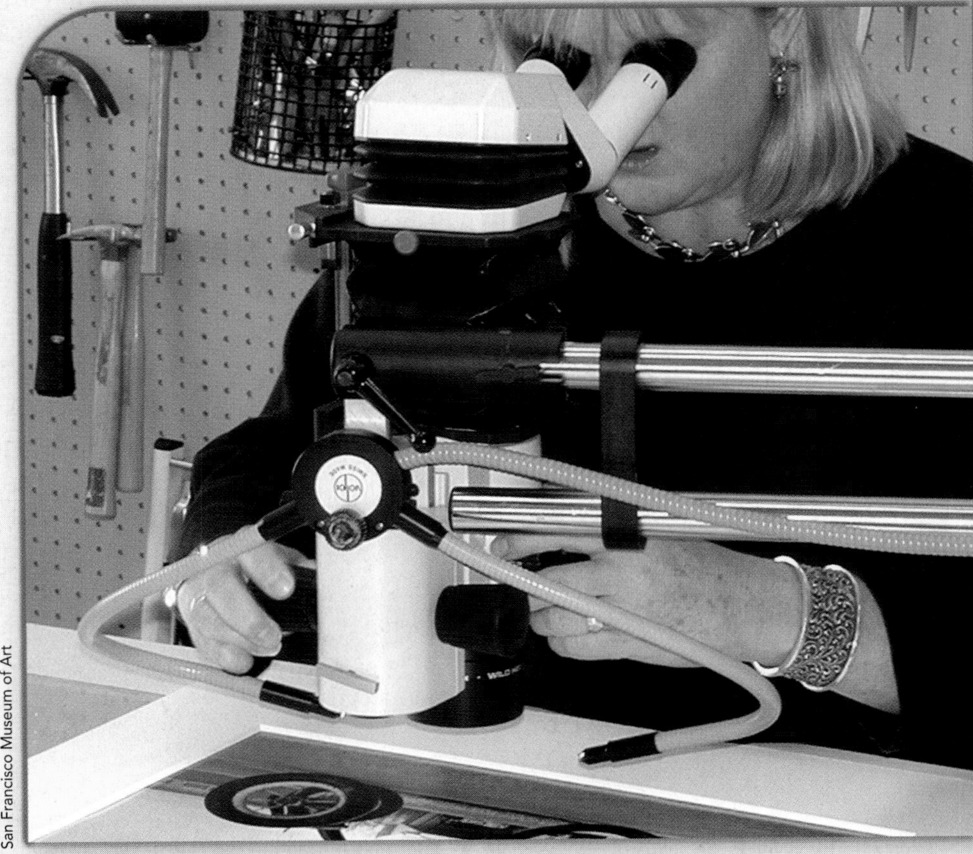

San Francisco Museum of Art

*"As a conservator of photographic materials, it is essential to have an understanding of the chemical reactions of many different photographic processes," says Theresa Andrews, Conservator of Photographs at the San Francisco Museum of Modern Art. "For example, the creation of the latent image in many photographs is based upon the light sensitivity of silver halides. Photolytic silver 'prints out' when exposed to a light source such as the sun and filamentary silver 'develops out' when an exposed photographic paper is placed in a bath with reducing agents. Photolytic silver particles are much smaller than filamentary silver particles making them more vulnerable to abrasion and image loss. This knowledge is critical when making recommendations for light levels and for the protection of photographs when they are on exhibition. Conservation treatments require informed decisions based on the reactivity of the materials within the photograph and also the compatibility of materials that might be required for repair or preservation of the photograph."*

Visit **www.masteringchemistry.com** for self-study materials and instructor-assigned homework.

What are some questions in science you have been curious about? Perhaps you are interested in how smog is formed, what causes ozone depletion, how nails form rust, or how aspirin relieves a headache. Just like you, chemists are curious about the world we live in.

- How does car exhaust produce the smog that hangs over our cities? One component of car exhaust is nitrogen oxide (NO), which forms in car engines where high temperatures convert nitrogen gas ($N_2$) and oxygen gas ($O_2$) to NO. In chemistry, these reactions are written in the form of equations such as $N_2(g) + O_2(g) \longrightarrow 2NO(g)$. The reaction of NO with oxygen in the air produces $NO_2$, which gives smog its characteristic reddish-brown color.
- Why has the ozone layer been depleted in certain parts of the atmosphere? During the 1970s, scientists discovered that substances called *chlorofluorocarbons* (CFCs) were associated with the depletion of ozone ($O_3$) over Antarctica. As CFCs are broken down by ultraviolet (UV) light, chlorine (Cl) is released and acts rapidly with ozone in the atmosphere to form chlorine oxide gas (ClO) and oxygen: $Cl(g) + O_3(g) \longrightarrow ClO(g) + O_2(g)$. This reaction causes the breakdown of ozone molecules and the destruction of the ozone layer.
- Why does an iron nail rust when exposed to air and rain? When solid iron (Fe) in a nail reacts with oxygen gas in the air, the oxidation of iron forms rust ($Fe_2O_3$): $4Fe(s) + 3O_2(g) \longrightarrow 2Fe_2O_3(s)$.

- Why does aspirin relieve a headache? When a part of the body is injured, substances called *prostaglandins* are produced that cause inflammation and pain. Aspirin acts to block the production of prostaglandins, thereby reducing inflammation, pain, and fever.

Chemists perform many different kinds of research. Some design new fuels and more efficient ways to use them. Researchers in the medical field look for evidence that will help them understand and design new treatments for diabetes, genetic defects, cancer, AIDS, and other diseases. For the chemist in the laboratory, the physician in the dialysis unit, or the agricultural scientist, chemistry plays a central role in providing understanding, assessing solutions, and making important decisions.

## P.1 Chemistry and Chemicals

**LEARNING GOAL**

Define the term *chemistry* and identify substances as chemicals.

**Chemistry** is the study of the composition, structure, properties, and reactions of matter. *Matter* is another word for all the substances that make up our world. Perhaps you imagine that chemistry is done only in a laboratory by a chemist wearing a lab coat and goggles. Actually, chemistry happens all around you every day and has a big impact on everything you use and do. You are doing chemistry when you cook food, add chlorine to a swimming pool, or start your car. A chemical reaction takes place when a nail rusts or an antacid tablet fizzes when dropped into water. Plants grow because chemical reactions convert carbon dioxide, water, and energy to carbohydrates and oxygen. Chemical reactions take place when you digest food and break it down into substances that you need for energy and health.

All the things you see around you are composed of one or more chemicals. A **chemical** is a substance that always has the same composition and properties wherever it is found. When a chemical undergoes a *chemical change*, a new substance with a new composition and properties is formed. Chemical changes take place in chemistry laboratories, manufacturing plants, and pharmaceutical labs as well as every day in nature and in our bodies. Often, the terms *chemical* and *substance* are used interchangeably to describe a specific type of matter.

TABLE P.1 Chemicals Commonly Used in Toothpaste

| Chemical | Function |
|---|---|
| Calcium carbonate | Acts as an abrasive to remove plaque |
| Sorbitol | Prevents loss of water and hardening of toothpaste |
| Carrageenan (seaweed extract) | Keeps toothpaste from hardening or separating |
| Glycerin | Makes toothpaste foam in the mouth |
| Sodium lauryl sulfate | Acts as a detergent used to loosen plaque |
| Titanium dioxide | Makes toothpaste base white and opaque |
| Triclosan | Inhibits bacteria that cause plaque and gum disease |
| Sodium fluorophosphate | Prevents formation of cavities by strengthening tooth enamel with fluoride |
| Methyl salicylate | Gives a pleasant flavor of wintergreen |

Each day you use products containing substances that were developed and prepared by chemists. Soaps and shampoos contain chemicals that combine with oils on your skin and scalp. When you shower in the morning, these oils are removed by rinsing with water. When you brush your teeth, the chemicals in toothpaste clean your teeth, prevent plaque formation, and prevent tooth decay. Some chemicals commonly contained in toothpaste are listed in Table P.1.

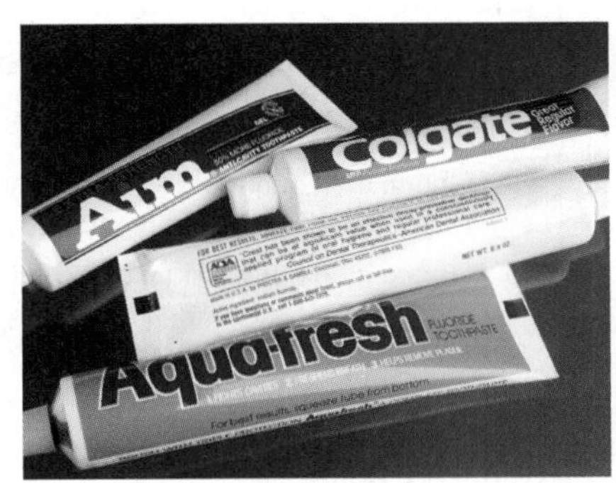


In cosmetics and lotions, chemicals are used to moisturize the skin, fight bacteria, prevent deterioration of the product, and thicken the product. Your clothes may be made of natural materials such as cotton, or synthetic substances such as nylon or polyester. Perhaps you wear a ring or watch made of gold, silver, or platinum. Your breakfast cereal is probably fortified with iron, calcium, and phosphorus, while the milk you drink is enriched with vitamins A and D. Antioxidants are chemicals added to your cereal to prevent it from spoiling. Some of the chemicals you may encounter when you cook in the kitchen are shown in Figure P.1.

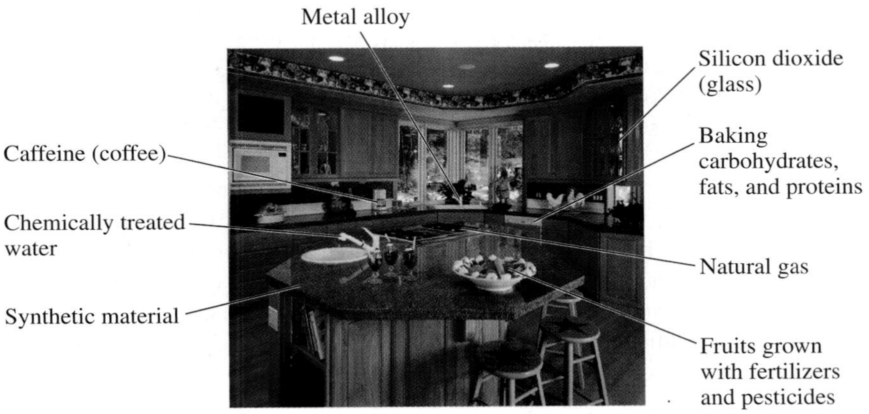


FIGURE P.1 Many of the items found in a kitchen are obtained using chemical reactions.

Q What are some other chemicals found in a kitchen?

CONCEPT CHECK P.1

## Chemicals

Why is copper wire an example of a chemical, while sunlight is not?

ANSWER

Copper wire is a substance that has the same composition and properties wherever it is found. Sunlight is not a substance and does not contain matter.

SAMPLE PROBLEM P.1

## Everyday Chemicals

Identify the chemical described by each of the following statements:

**a.** Aluminum is used to make cans.
**b.** Salt (sodium chloride) is used as a preservative.
**c.** Sugar (sucrose) is used as a sweetener.

SOLUTION

**a.** aluminum **b.** salt (sodium chloride) **c.** sugar (sucrose)

STUDY CHECK

Which of the following are chemicals?

**a.** iron **b.** tin **c.** a low temperature **d.** water

The answers for all Study Checks are included at the end of each chapter.

## QUESTIONS AND PROBLEMS

### Chemistry and Chemicals

The answers for all the magenta, odd-numbered Questions and Problems are included at the end of each chapter. Checking your answers will let you know if you understand the material.

**P.1** Obtain a vitamin bottle and observe the list of ingredients. List four. Which ones are chemicals?

**P.2** Obtain a box of breakfast cereal and observe the list of ingredients. List four. Which ones are chemicals?

**P.3** A "chemical-free" shampoo includes the following ingredients: water, cocomide, glycerin, and citric acid. Is the shampoo "chemical-free"?

**P.4** A "chemical-free" sunscreen includes the following ingredients: titanium dioxide, vitamin E, and vitamin C. Is the sunscreen "chemical-free"?

**P.5** Pesticides are chemicals. Give one advantage and one disadvantage of using pesticides.

**P.6** Sugar is a chemical. Give one advantage and one disadvantage of eating sugar.

## P.2 Scientific Method: Thinking Like a Scientist

LEARNING GOAL

Describe the activities that are part of the scientific method.

When you were very young, you explored the things around you by touching and tasting. When you grew a little older, you asked questions about the world in which you live. What is lightning? Where does a rainbow come from? Why is water blue? As an adult, you may have wondered how antibiotics work or why vitamins are important to your health. Each day you ask questions and seek answers as you organize and make sense of the world around you.

When the late Nobel Laureate Linus Pauling described his student life in Oregon, he recalled that he read many books on chemistry, mineralogy, and physics. "I mulled over the properties of materials: why are some substances colored and others not, why are some minerals or inorganic compounds hard and others soft?" He said, "I was building up this tremendous background of empirical knowledge and at the same time asking a great number of questions." Linus Pauling won two Nobel Prizes: the first, in 1954, was in chemistry for his work on the structure of proteins; the second, in 1962, was the Peace Prize.

### Scientific Method

Although the process of trying to understand nature is unique to each scientist, a set of general principles called the **scientific method** helps to describe how a scientist thinks.

1. **Observations.** The first step in the scientific method is to observe, describe, and measure an event in nature. Observations based on measurements are called *data*.
2. **Hypothesis.** After sufficient data are collected, a *hypothesis* is proposed that states a possible interpretation of the observations. The hypothesis must be stated in a way that it can be tested by experiments.
3. **Experiments.** Experiments are tests that determine the validity of the hypothesis. Often many experiments are performed, and a large amount of data is collected. If the results of the experiments are different than those predicted by the hypothesis, then a new or modified hypothesis is proposed, and new experiments are performed.
4. **Theory.** When many scientists repeat the experiments with consistent results that confirm the hypothesis, the hypothesis becomes a *theory*. Each theory, however,

continues to be tested and, based on new data, sometimes needs to be modified or even replaced. Then a new hypothesis is proposed, and the process of experimentation takes place once again.

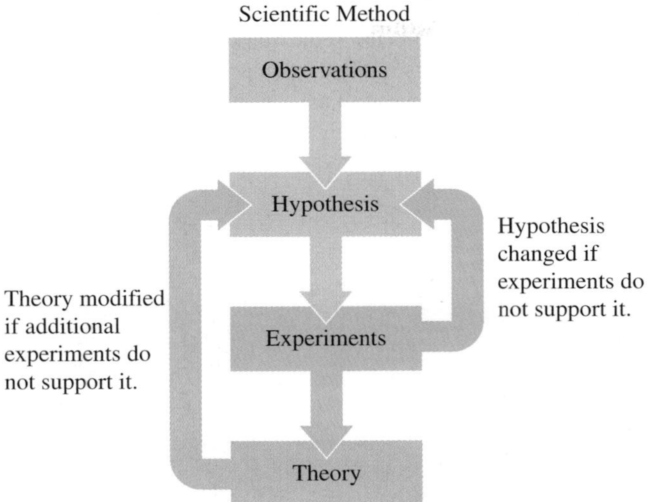

## Using the Scientific Method in Everyday Life

TUTORIAL
Scientific Method

You may be surprised to realize that you use the scientific method in your everyday life. Suppose you visit a friend in her home. Soon after you arrive, your eyes start to itch and you begin to sneeze. Then you observe that your friend has a new cat. Perhaps you ask yourself why you are sneezing and form the hypothesis that you are allergic to cats. To test your hypothesis, you leave your friend's home. If the sneezing stops, perhaps your hypothesis is correct. You test your hypothesis further by visiting another friend who also has a cat. If you start to sneeze again, then your experimental results support your hypothesis that you are allergic to cats. However, if you continue sneezing after you leave your friend's home, your hypothesis is not supported. Now you need to form a new hypothesis, which could be that you have a cold.

**CONCEPT CHECK P.2**

### Scientific Method

Label each of the following as an observation, hypothesis, or experiment:

**a.** Drinking coffee at night keeps me awake.
**b.** When I drink coffee only in the morning, I can sleep at night.
**c.** I will try drinking coffee only in the morning.

ANSWER

**a.** An observation describes what happens when I drink coffee.
**b.** An observation describes what happens if I drink coffee only in the morning.
**c.** Changing the time for drinking coffee is an experiment.

**SAMPLE PROBLEM P.2**

### Scientific Method

Identify each of the following statements as an observation or a hypothesis:

**a.** A silver tray turns a dull gray color when left uncovered.
**b.** It is warmer in summer than in winter in the northern hemisphere.
**c.** Ice cubes float in water because they are less dense.

SOLUTION

**a.** observation **b.** observation **c.** hypothesis

STUDY CHECK

The following statements are found in a student's notebook. Identify each of the following as observation (O), hypothesis (H), or experiment (E):

**a.** "Today, I planted two tomato seedlings in the garden. I put two more tomato seedlings in a closet. I will give all the plants the same amount of water and fertilizer."
**b.** "After 50 days, the tomato plants in the garden are 3 feet high with green leaves. The plants in the closet are 8 inches tall and yellow."
**c.** "Tomato plants need sunlight to grow."

# HEALTH NOTE

## Early Chemists: The Alchemists

For many centuries, chemists have studied changes in matter. From the time of the Greeks to about the sixteenth century, alchemists, early chemists who studied matter, described matter in terms of four components of nature: earth, air, fire, and water. These components had the qualities of hot, cold, damp, or dry. By the eighth century, alchemists believed that they could rearrange these qualities to change metals such as copper and lead into gold and silver. They searched for an unknown substance called a *philosopher's stone* that they thought would turn metals into gold as well as prolong youth and postpone death. Although these efforts failed, the alchemists did provide information on the processes and chemical reactions involved in the extraction of metals from ores. The alchemists also designed some of the first laboratory equipment and developed early laboratory procedures. These early efforts were some of the first observations and experiments using the scientific method.

The alchemist Paracelsus (1493–1541) thought that alchemy should be about preparing new medicines, not about producing gold. Using observation and experiments, he viewed the body as a series of chemical processes that could be unbalanced by certain chemical compounds and rebalanced by using minerals and medicines. For example, he determined that inhaled dust, not underground spirits, caused the lung diseases of miners. He also thought that goiter was a problem caused by contaminated drinking water, and he treated syphilis with compounds of mercury. His opinion of medicines was that the right dose makes the difference between a poison and a cure. Today this idea is part of the risk analysis of medicines. Paracelsus changed alchemy in ways that helped to establish modern medicine and chemistry.

## Science and Technology

When scientific information is applied to industrial and commercial uses, it is called *technology*. Such uses have made the chemical industry one of the largest industries in the United States. Every year, technology provides new materials or procedures that produce more energy, cure diseases, improve crops, and produce new kinds of synthetic materials. Table P.2 lists some of the important scientific discoveries, laws, theories, and technological innovations that have been made over the past 300 years.

**TABLE P.2** Some Important Scientific Discoveries, Laws, Theories, and Technological Innovations

| Discovery, Law, Theory, or Innovation | Date | Name | Country |
|---|---|---|---|
| Law of gravity | 1687 | Isaac Newton | England |
| Oxygen | 1774 | Joseph Priestley | England |
| Electric battery | 1800 | Alessandro Volta | Italy |
| Atomic theory | 1803 | John Dalton | England |
| Anesthesia, ether | 1842 | Crawford Long | United States |
| Nitroglycerin | 1847 | Ascanio Sobrero | Italy |
| Germ theory | 1865 | Louis Pasteur | France |
| Antiseptic surgery | 1865 | Joseph Lister | England |
| Discovery of nucleic acids | 1869 | Friedrich Miescher | Switzerland |
| Radioactivity | 1896 | Henri Becquerel | France |
| Discovery of radium | 1898 | Marie and Pierre Curie | France |
| Quantum theory | 1900 | Max Planck | Germany |
| Theory of relativity | 1905 | Albert Einstein | Germany |
| Identification of components of RNA and DNA | 1909 | Phoebus Theodore Levene | United States |
| Insulin | 1922 | Frederick Banting, Charles Best, John Macleod | Canada |
| Penicillin | 1928 | Alexander Fleming | England |
| Nylon | 1937 | Wallace Carothers | United States |
| Discovery of DNA as genetic material | 1944 | Oswald Avery | United States |
| Synthetic production of transuranium elements | 1944 | Glenn Seaborg, Arthur Wahl, Joseph Kennedy, Albert Ghiorso | United States |
| Determination of DNA structure | 1953 | Francis Crick, Rosalind Franklin, James Watson | England |
| Polio vaccine | 1954 | Jonas Salk | United States |
| | 1957 | Albert Sabin | United States |
| Laser | 1958 | Charles Townes | United States |
| | 1960 | Theodore Maiman | United States |
| Cellular phones | 1973 | Martin Cooper | United States |
| MRI (magnetic resonance imaging) | 1980 | Paul Lauterbur | United States |
| Prozac | 1988 | Ray Fuller | United States |
| HIV protease inhibitor | 1995 | Joseph Martin, Sally Redshaw | United States |

Not all scientific discoveries, however, have been positive. The production of some substances has contributed to the development of hazardous conditions in our environment. We have become concerned about the energy requirements of new products and how some materials may cause changes in our oceans and atmosphere. We want to know if the new materials can be recycled, how they are broken down, and whether there are alternate and safer processes. The ways in which we continue to utilize scientific research will strongly affect our planet and its communities in the future. These decisions can best be made if every citizen has an understanding of science.

## ENVIRONMENTAL NOTE

### DDT: Good Pesticide, Bad Pesticide

DDT (dichlorodiphenyltrichloroethane) was once one of the most commonly used pesticides. Although DDT was first made in 1874, it was not used as an insecticide until 1939. Before DDT was widely used, insect-borne diseases such as malaria and typhus were rampant in many parts of the world. Paul Müller, who discovered that DDT was an effective pesticide, was recognized for saving many lives and received the Nobel Prize for medicine and physiology in 1948. At that time, DDT was considered the ideal pesticide because it was toxic to many insects, had a low toxicity to humans and animals, and was inexpensive to prepare.

In the United States, DDT was used extensively on home gardens as well as on farm crops, particularly cotton and soybeans. Because of its stable chemical structure, DDT did not break down quickly in the environment, which meant that it did not have to be reapplied frequently. At first, everyone was pleased with DDT—crop yields increased and diseases such as malaria and typhus were under control.

However, during the early 1950s, problems attributed to DDT began to arise. Insects were becoming more resistant to the pesticide. At the same time, the public was increasingly concerned about the long-term impact of a substance that could remain in the environment for many years. The metabolic systems of humans and animals cannot break down DDT, which is soluble in fats but not in water and is stored in the fatty tissues of the body. Although the concentrations of DDT applied to crops were extremely low, the concentrations of DDT found in fish and the birds that ate the fish were as much as 10 million times greater. Although the affected birds did not die immediately, the DDT in their bodies reduced the amount of calcium in their eggshells. As a result, the incubating eggs cracked open early, causing many offspring to die. Because of this difficulty with reproduction, the populations of birds such as bald eagles and brown pelicans dropped significantly.

By 1972, DDT was banned in the United States. The Environmental Protection Agency (EPA) reported that by 1978 DDT levels were reduced by 90% in fish in Lake Michigan. Today, new types of pesticides that are more water soluble and do not persist in the environment have replaced long-lasting pesticides such as DDT. However, these new pesticides are much more toxic to humans.

## QUESTIONS AND PROBLEMS

### Scientific Method: Thinking like a Scientist

**P.7** Identify each of the following statements as an observation (O), a hypothesis (H), an experiment (E), or a theory (T): At a popular restaurant, where Chang is the head chef, the following occur:

**a.** Chang determines that sales of the chef's salad have dropped.
**b.** Chang decides that the chef's salad needs a new dressing.
**c.** In a taste test, four bowls of lettuce are prepared with four new dressings: sesame seed, oil and vinegar, blue cheese, and anchovies.
**d.** The tasters rate the dressing with sesame seeds the best.
**e.** After two weeks, Chang notes that the orders for the chef's salad with the new sesame dressing have doubled.
**f.** Chang decides that the sesame dressing improved the sales of the chef's salad because the sesame dressing improved the taste of the salad.

**P.8** Identify each of the following statements as an observation (O), a hypothesis (H), an experiment (E), or a theory (T): Lucia wants to develop a process for dyeing shirts so that the color will not fade when the shirt is washed. She proceeds with the following activities:

**a.** Lucia notices that the dye in a design on T-shirts fades when the shirt is washed.
**b.** Lucia decides that the dye needs something to help it set in the T-shirt fabric.
**c.** She places a spot of dye on each of four T-shirts and then places each one separately in water, salt water, vinegar, and baking soda and water.
**d.** After 1 hour, all the T-shirts are removed and washed with a detergent.
**e.** Lucia notices that the dye has faded on the T-shirts soaked in water, salt water, and baking soda, while the dye did not fade in the T-shirts soaked in vinegar.
**f.** Lucia thinks that the vinegar binds with the dye so it does not fade when the shirt is washed.

# P.3 A Study Plan for Learning Chemistry

**LEARNING GOAL**

Develop a study plan for learning chemistry.

Here you are taking chemistry, perhaps for the first time. Whatever your reasons are for choosing to study chemistry, you can look forward to learning many new and exciting ideas.

## Features in This Text Help You Study Chemistry

This text has been designed with a variety of study aids to complement different learning styles. On the inside of the front cover is a periodic table of the elements that provides information about the elements. On the inside of the back cover are tables that summarize useful information needed throughout the study of chemistry. Each chapter begins with *Looking Ahead*, which outlines the topics in the chapter. A *Learning Goal* at the beginning of each section previews the concepts you are to learn. A comprehensive *Glossary/Index* is included at the end of the text.

Before you begin to read a chapter, obtain an overview of the topics by reviewing the list of topics in *Looking Ahead*. As you prepare to read a section of the chapter, look at the section title and turn it into a question. For example, for Section P.1, "Chemistry and Chemicals," you could write a question that asks "What is chemistry?" or "What are chemicals?" When you are ready to read that section, review the *Learning Goal*, which tells you what you need to accomplish. As you read, try to answer the question you wrote. Throughout the chapter, you will find *Concept Checks* that will help you understand key ideas. When you come to a *Sample Problem*, take the time to work it through, and try the associated *Study Check*. Then, check your answer at the end of the chapter. If your answer does not match, you may need to study the section again. When you finish each section, immediately work through the *Questions and Problems* for practice.

Throughout the chapters, boxes titled *Health Notes*, *Green Chemistry Notes*, and *Environmental Notes* connect the chemical concepts you are studying to real-life situations. Many of the figures and diagrams throughout the text use macro-to-micro illustrations to depict the atomic level of organization of ordinary objects. These visual models illustrate the concepts described in the text and allow you to "see" the world in a microscopic way.

At the end of each chapter, you will find several study aids that complete the chapter. *Chapter Reviews* and *Concept Maps* at the end of each chapter give a summary and show the connections between important concepts. The *Key Terms* are boldfaced in the text and listed again at the end of the chapter. *Understanding the Concepts* is a set of questions that use art and structures to help you visualize concepts. *Additional Questions and Problems* and *Challenge Problems* provide more problems to test your understanding of the topics in the chapter. Answers to all the *Study Checks* and *Answers to Selected Questions and Problems* are provided at the end of the chapter.

## Using Active Learning to Learn Chemistry

A student who is an active learner continually interacts with the chemical ideas while reading the text and attending lectures. Let's see how this is done.

As you read and practice solving problems, you remain actively involved in studying, which enhances the learning process. In this way, you learn small bits of information at a time and establish the necessary foundation for understanding the next section. You may also note questions you have about the reading to discuss with your professor and laboratory instructor. Table P.3 summarizes these steps for active learning. The time you spend in lecture can also be useful as a learning time. By keeping track of the class schedule and reading the assigned material before lecture, you become aware of the new terms and concepts you need to learn. Some questions that occur during your reading may be answered during the lecture. If not, you can ask for further clarification from your professor.

**TABLE P.3** Steps in Active Learning

1. Read the set of *Looking Ahead* topics and *Learning Goals* for an overview of the material.
2. Form a question from the title of the section you are going to read.
3. Read the section looking for answers to your question.
4. Self-test by working *Concept Checks*, *Sample Problems*, and *Study Checks* within each section.
5. Complete the *Questions and Problems* that follow each section and check the magenta odd-numbered answers.
6. Proceed to the next section and repeat the above steps.

Many students think that studying with a group can be beneficial to learning. In a group, students motivate each other to study, fill in gaps, and correct misunderstandings by teaching and learning together. Studying alone does not allow the process of peer correction that takes place when you work with a group of students in your class. In a group, you can cover the ideas more thoroughly as you discuss the reading and problem solving with other students. Waiting to study until the night before an exam does not give you time to understand concepts and practice problem solving. You may ignore or avoid ideas that turn out to be important on test day.

## Thinking Scientifically About Your Study Plan

As you embark on your journey into the world of chemistry, think about your approach to studying and learning chemistry. You might consider some of the ideas in the following list. Check those ideas that will help you learn chemistry successfully. Commit to them now. Your success depends on you.

**My study of chemistry will include the following:**

_______ Reviewing the *Learning Goals*
_______ Keeping a problem notebook
_______ Reading the text as an active learner
_______ Self-testing by working the chapter problems and checking solutions in the text
_______ Reading the chapter before lecture
_______ Being an active learner in lecture
_______ Going to lecture
_______ Organizing a study group
_______ Seeing the professor during office hours
_______ Attending review sessions
_______ Organizing my own review sessions
_______ Studying a little bit as often as I can

CONCEPT CHECK P.3

### ■ A Study Plan for Chemistry

What are some advantages to studying in a group?

ANSWER

In a group, students motivate and support each other, fill in gaps, and correct misunderstandings. Ideas are discussed while reading and problem solving together.

SAMPLE PROBLEM P.3

### ■ A Study Plan for Learning Chemistry

Which of the following activities would you include in a study plan for successfully learning chemistry?

**a.** skipping a lecture
**b.** forming a study group
**c.** keeping a problem notebook
**d.** waiting to study until the night before the exam
**e.** becoming an active learner

SOLUTION

Your success in chemistry can be helped if you include the following in your study plan:

**b.** forming a study group
**c.** keeping a problem notebook
**e.** becoming an active learner

STUDY CHECK

Which of the following would help you learn chemistry?

**a.** skipping review sessions
**b.** working assigned problems
**c.** attending the professor's office hours
**d.** staying up all night before an exam
**e.** reading the assignment before a lecture

## QUESTIONS AND PROBLEMS

### A Study Plan for Studying Chemistry

**P.9** A student in your class asks you for advice on learning chemistry. Which of the following might you suggest?
**a.** Form a study group.
**b.** Skip a lecture.
**c.** Visit the professor during office hours.
**d.** Wait until the night before an exam to study.
**e.** Become an active learner.

**P.10** A student in your class asks you for advice on learning chemistry. Which of the following might you suggest?
**a.** Do the assigned problems.
**b.** Don't read the book; it's never on the test.
**c.** Attend review sessions.
**d.** Read the assignment before lecture.
**e.** Keep a problem notebook.

## CONCEPT MAP

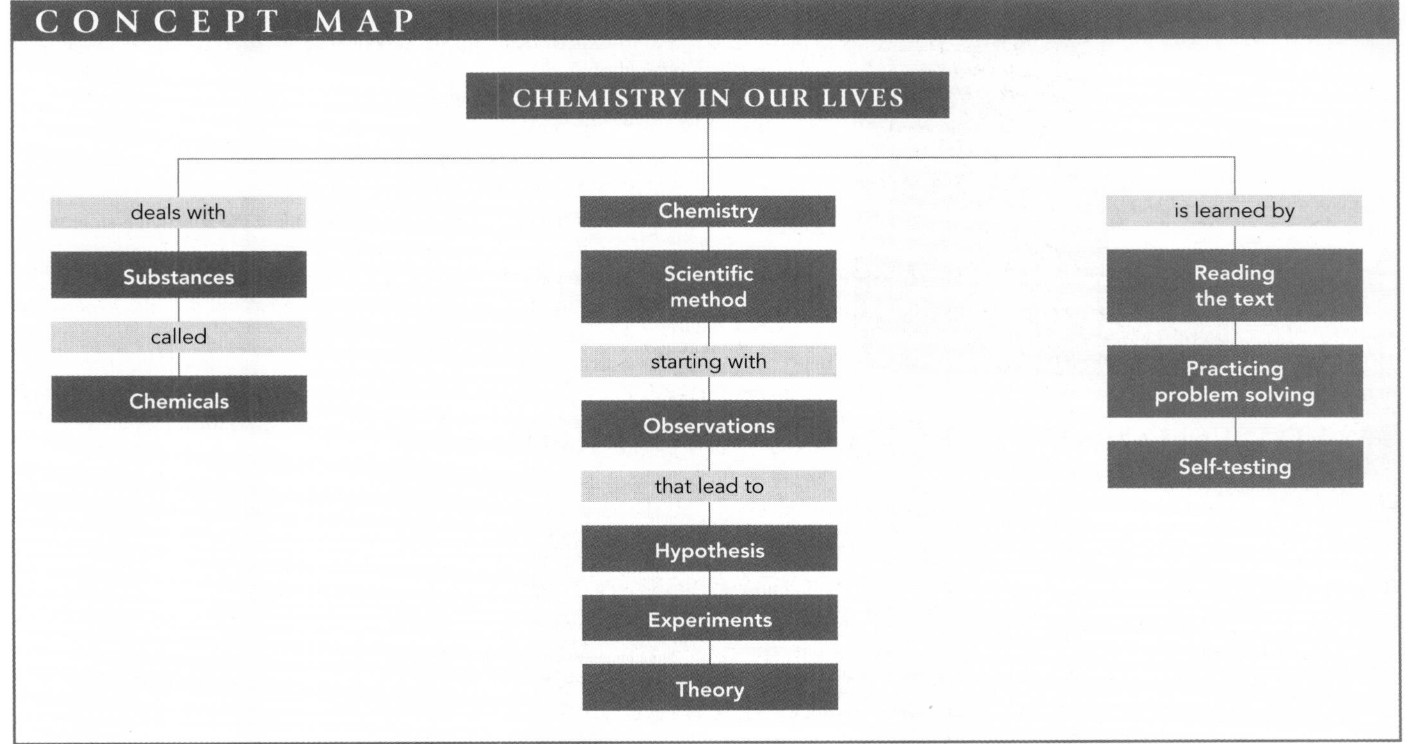

# CHAPTER REVIEW

## P.1 Chemistry and Chemicals

**LEARNING GOAL:** *Define the term* chemistry, *and identify substances as chemicals.*

Chemistry is the study of the composition of substances and the way in which they interact with other substances. A chemical is any substance used in or produced by a chemical process.

## P.2 Scientific Method: Thinking like a Scientist

**LEARNING GOAL:** *Describe the activities that are part of the scientific method.*

The scientific method is a process of explaining natural phenomena beginning with observations, a hypothesis, and experiments, which may lead to a theory when experimental results support the hypothesis. Technology involves the application of scientific information to industrial and commercial uses.

## P.3 A Study Plan for Learning Chemistry

**LEARNING GOAL:** *Develop a study plan for learning chemistry.*

A study plan for learning chemistry utilizes the visual features in the text and develops an active learning approach to study. By using the *Learning Goals* and *Concept Checks* in the chapter and working the *Sample Problems* and *Study Checks* and the problems at the end of each section, the student can successfully learn the concepts of chemistry.

# KEY TERMS

**chemical** A substance that has the same composition and properties wherever it is found.

**chemistry** A science that studies the composition of substances and the way they interact with other substances.

**experiment** A procedure that tests the validity of a hypothesis.

**hypothesis** An unverified explanation of a natural phenomenon.

**observation** Information determined by noting and recording a natural phenomenon.

**scientific method** The process of making observations, proposing a hypothesis, testing the hypothesis, and developing a theory that explains a natural event.

**theory** An explanation of an observation that has been validated by experiments that support a hypothesis.

# UNDERSTANDING THE CONCEPTS

P.11 According to Sherlock Holmes, "One must follow the rules of scientific inquiry, gathering, observing, and testing data, then formulating, modifying, and rejecting hypotheses, until only one remains." Did Sherlock use the scientific method? Why or why not?

**P.12** In "A Scandal in Bohemia," Sherlock Holmes receives a mysterious note. He states, "I have no data yet. It is a capital mistake to theorize before one has data. Insensibly one begins to twist facts to suit theories instead of theories to suit facts." What do you think Sherlock meant?

P.13 Select the correct phrase(s) to complete the following statement: If experimental results do not support your hypothesis, you should

**a.** pretend that the experimental results do support your hypothesis.
**b.** write another hypothesis.
**c.** do more experiments.

**P.14** Select the correct phrase(s) to complete the following statement: A hypothesis becomes a theory when

**a.** one experiment proves the hypothesis.
**b.** many experiments by many scientists validate the hypothesis.
**c.** you decide to call it a theory.

# ADDITIONAL QUESTIONS AND PROBLEMS

*For instructor-assigned homework, go to* ***www.masteringchemistry.com****.*

P.15 Why does the scientific method include a hypothesis?

**P.16** Why is experimentation an important part of the scientific method?

P.17 Classify each of the following statements as either an observation or a hypothesis:

**a.** Aluminum melts at 660 °C.
**b.** Dinosaurs became extinct when a large meteorite struck Earth and caused a huge dust cloud that severely decreased the amount of light reaching Earth.
**c.** The 100-yard dash was run in 9.8 seconds.

**P.18** Classify each of the following statements as either an observation or a hypothesis:

**a.** Analysis of 10 ceramic dishes showed that four dishes contained lead levels that exceeded federal safety standards.
**b.** Marble statues undergo corrosion in acid rain.
**c.** Statues corrode in acid rain because the acidity is sufficient to dissolve calcium carbonate, the major substance of marble.

## CHALLENGE QUESTIONS

**P.19** Classify each of the following statements as an observation, hypothesis, or experiment:
**a.** The bicycle tire is flat.
**b.** If I add air to the bicycle tire, it will expand to the proper size.
**c.** When I added air to the bicycle tire, it was still flat.
**d.** The bicycle tire must have a leak in it.

**P.20** Classify each of the following statements as an observation, hypothesis, or experiment:
**a.** A big log in the fire does not burn well.
**b.** If I chop the log into small pieces, it will burn better.
**c.** The smaller pieces of wood burn brighter and make a hotter fire.
**d.** The small wood pieces burn faster than burning the big log.

## ANSWERS

### ANSWERS TO STUDY CHECKS

**P.1** **a.**, **b.**, and **d.**

**P.2** **a.** E **b.** O **c.** H

**P.3** **b.**, **c.**, and **e.**

### ANSWERS TO SELECTED QUESTIONS AND PROBLEMS

**P.1** Many chemicals are listed on a vitamin bottle such as vitamin A, vitamin $B_3$, vitamin $B_{12}$, folic acid, etc.

**P.3** No. All of the ingredients listed are chemicals.

**P.5** One advantage of a pesticide is that it gets rid of insects that bite humans or animals or damage crops. One disadvantage is that a pesticide can destroy beneficial insects or be retained in a crop that is eventually eaten by animals or humans.

**P.7** **a.** O **b.** H **c.** E **d.** O **e.** O **f.** T

**P.9** **a.**, **c.**, and **e.**

**P.11** Yes. Sherlock's investigation includes making observations (gathering data), formulating a hypothesis, testing the hypothesis, and modifying it until one of the hypotheses is validated.

**P.13** **b.** and **c.**

**P.15** A hypothesis, which is a possible explanation for an observation, can be tested with experiments.

**P.17** **a.** observation **b.** hypothesis **c.** observation

**P.19** **a.** observation **b.** hypothesis **c.** experiment **d.** hypothesis

# 1 Measurements

LOOKING AHEAD


1.1 Units of Measurement

1.2 Scientific Notation

1.3 Measured Numbers and Significant Figures

1.4 Significant Figures in Calculations

1.5 Prefixes and Equalities

1.6 Writing Conversion Factors

1.7 Problem Solving

1.8 Density


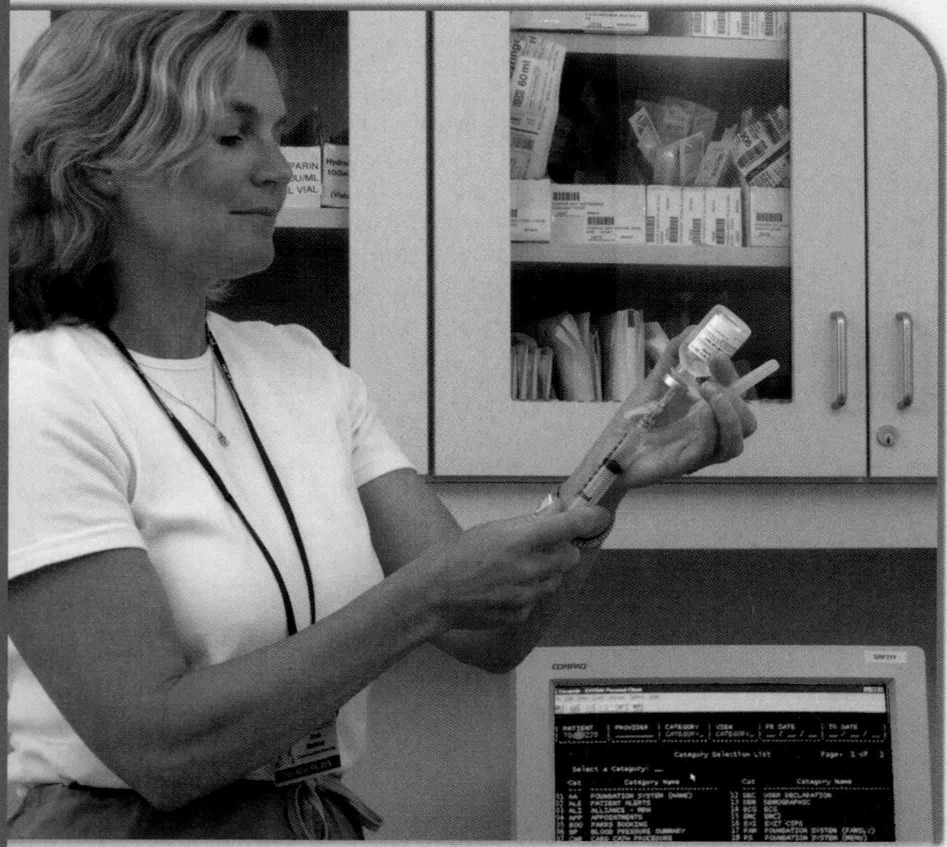


*"I use measurement in just about every part of my nursing practice," says registered nurse Vicki Miller. "When I receive a doctor's order for a medication, I have to verify that order. Then I draw a carefully measured volume from an IV or a vial to create that particular dose. Some dosage orders are specific to the size of the patient. I measure the patient's weight and calculate the dosage required for the weight of that patient."*

*Nurses use measurement each time they determine a patient's temperature, height, weight, or blood pressure. Measurement is used to obtain the correct amounts for injections and medications and to determine the volumes of fluid intake and output. For each measurement, the amounts and units are recorded in the patient's records.*

Visit **www.masteringchemistry.com** for self-study materials and instructor-assigned homework.

Chemistry and measurement are an important part of our everyday lives. Levels of toxic materials in the air, soil, and water are discussed in our newspapers. We read about radon in our homes, holes in the ozone layer, trans fatty acids, global warming, and DNA analysis. Understanding chemistry and measurement helps us make proper choices about our world.

Think about your day; you probably made some measurements. Perhaps you checked your weight by stepping on a scale. If you did not feel well, you may have taken your temperature. To make some soup, you added 2 cups of water to a package of mix. If you stopped at the gas station, you watched the gas pump measure the number of gallons of gasoline you put in the car.

Measurement is an essential part of health careers such as nursing, dental hygiene, respiratory therapy, nutrition, and veterinary technology. The temperature, height, and weight of a patient are measured in degrees Celsius, meters, and kilograms, respectively. Samples of blood and urine are collected and sent to a laboratory where glucose, pH, urea, and protein are measured by the lab technicians.

By learning about measurement, you will develop skills for solving problems and how to work with numbers in chemistry. If you intend to go into a health career, an understanding and assessment of measurements will be an important part of your evaluation of a patient's health.

## 1.1 Units of Measurement

**LEARNING GOAL**

Write the names and abbreviations for the units used in measurements of length, volume, time, and mass.

Scientists and health professionals throughout the world use the **metric system**. It is also the common measuring system in all but a few countries. In 1960, scientists adopted a modification of the metric system called the *International System of Units*, Système International (**SI**), to provide additional uniformity for units used in the sciences. In this text, we will use metric units and introduce some of the SI units.

### Length

The metric and SI unit of length is the **meter (m)**. A meter is 39.4 inches (in.), which makes it slightly longer than a yard (yd). The **centimeter (cm)** is a smaller unit of length that is commonly used in chemistry and is about as wide as your little finger. For comparison, there are 2.54 cm in 1 inch (in.). (See Figure 1.1.)

$$1\ \text{m} = 100\ \text{cm}$$

$$1\ \text{m} = 39.4\ \text{in.}$$

$$2.54\ \text{cm} = 1\ \text{in.}$$

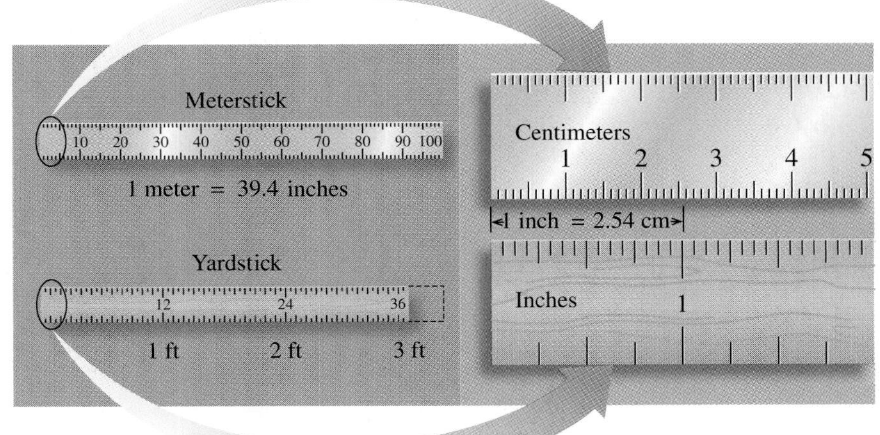


**FIGURE 1.1** Length in the metric and SI systems is based on the meter, which is slightly longer than a yard.

**Q** How many centimeters are in a length of one inch?

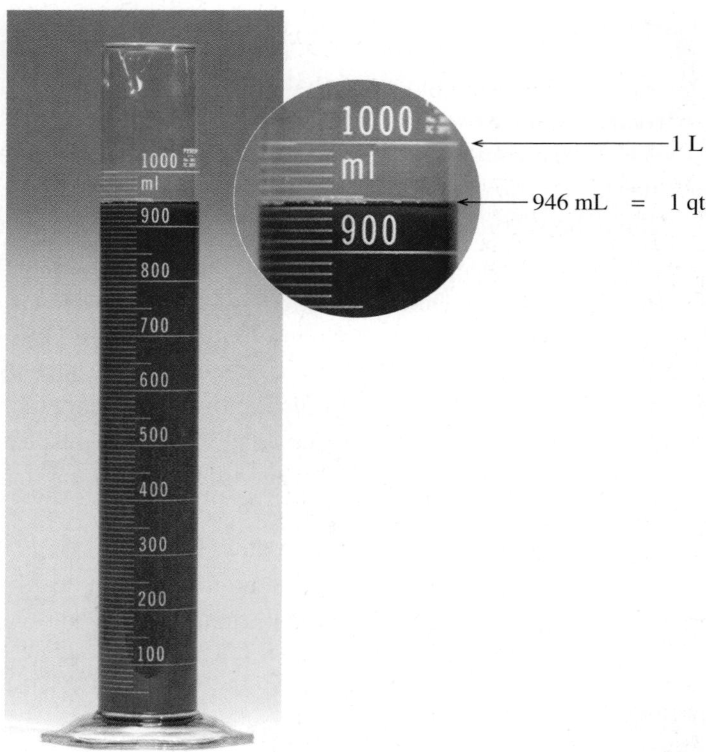


**FIGURE 1.2** Volume is the space occupied by a substance. In the metric system, volume is based on the liter, which is slightly larger than a quart.

Q How many milliliters are in 1 quart?

## Volume

**Volume** is the amount of space a substance occupies. A **liter (L)**, which is slightly larger than a quart (qt), is commonly used to measure volume. The **milliliter (mL)** is more convenient for measuring smaller volumes of fluids in hospitals and laboratories. The SI unit of volume is the cubic meter ($m^3$), a unit that is too large for practical use in the laboratory or hospital. A comparison of metric and U.S. units for volume appears in Figure 1.2.

$$1\text{ L} = 1000\text{ mL}$$
$$1\text{ L} = 1.06\text{ qt}$$
$$946\text{ mL} = 1\text{ qt}$$
$$1000\text{ L} = 1\text{ m}^3$$

## Mass

**FIGURE 1.3** On an electronic balance, mass is shown in grams as a digital readout.

Q How many grams are in 1 pound of candy?

The **mass** of an object is a measure of the quantity of material it contains. In the metric system, the unit for mass is the **gram (g)**. The SI unit of mass, the **kilogram (kg)**, is used for larger masses such as body weight. It takes 2.20 pounds (lb) to make 1 kg, and 454 g are needed to equal 1 pound.

$$1\text{ kg} = 1000\text{ g}$$
$$1\text{ kg} = 2.20\text{ lb}$$
$$454\text{ g} = 1\text{ lb}$$

You may be more familiar with the term *weight* than with mass. Weight is a measure of the gravitational pull on an object. On Earth, an astronaut with a mass of 75.0 kg has a weight of 165 lb. On the moon where the gravitational pull is one-sixth that of Earth, the astronaut has a weight of 27.5 lb. However, the mass of the astronaut is the same as on Earth, 75.0 kg. Scientists measure mass rather than weight because mass does not depend on gravity.

In a chemistry laboratory, a balance is used to measure the mass of a substance, as shown in Figure 1.3.

## Temperature

You use a thermometer to see how hot something is, how cold it is outside, or perhaps to determine if you have a fever. (See Figure 1.4.) **Temperature** tells us how hot or cold an object is. A typical laboratory thermometer consists of a glass bulb containing a liquid that expands as the temperature increases. On the **Celsius (°C) temperature scale**, water freezes at 0 °C and boils at 100 °C, while on the Fahrenheit (°F) scale, water freezes at 32 °F and boils at 212 °F. In the SI system, temperature is measured using the **Kelvin (K) temperature scale**, on which the lowest temperature possible is assigned a value of 0 K. Note that the units on the Kelvin scale are called *kelvins* (K) and are not given degree signs.

**FIGURE 1.4** A thermometer is used to determine the temperature of a substance.

**Q** What kinds of temperature readings have you made today?

## Time

We typically measure time in units of years, days, hours, minutes, or seconds. Of these, the SI and metric basic unit of time is the **second (s)**. The standard device now used to determine a second is an atomic clock. A comparison of metric and SI units for measurement is shown in Table 1.1.

**TABLE 1.1** Units of Measurement

| Measurement | Metric | SI |
|---|---|---|
| Length | Meter (m) | Meter (m) |
| Volume | Liter (L) | Cubic meter ($m^3$) |
| Mass | Gram (g) | Kilogram (kg) |
| Time | Second (s) | Second (s) |
| Temperature | Celsius degree (°C) | Kelvin (K) |

**CONCEPT CHECK 1.1**

### Units of Measurement

State the type of measurement indicated by each of the following units:

**a.** kilogram **b.** liter **c.** meter **d.** Celsius degree

ANSWER

**a.** A kilogram is a unit of mass. **b.** A liter is a unit of volume.
**c.** A meter is a unit of length. **d.** A Celsius degree is a unit of temperature.

**SAMPLE PROBLEM 1.1**

### Units of Measurement

State the type of measurement (mass, length, volume, temperature, or time) indicated by the unit in each of the following:

**a.** 45.6 kg **b.** 1.895 L **c.** 14 s **d.** 45 m **e.** 315 K

SOLUTION

**a.** mass **b.** volume **c.** time **d.** length **e.** temperature

STUDY CHECK

Write the name of the metric unit and symbol you would use to express each of the following:

**a.** length of a football field
**b.** daytime temperature
**c.** mass of salt in a shaker

### Units Listed on Labels

Read the labels on a variety of products such as sugar, salt, soft drinks, vitamins, and dental floss.

QUESTIONS

1. What metric or SI units of mea–surement are listed on the labels?
2. What type of measurement (mass, volume, etc.) do they indicate?
3. Write the metric or SI amounts in terms of a number plus a unit.

## QUESTIONS AND PROBLEMS

### Units of Measurement

In every chapter, each magenta-colored, odd-numbered exercise in Questions and Problems is paired with the next even-numbered exercise. The answers for all the magenta, odd-numbered Questions and Problems are given at the end of this chapter. The complete solutions to the odd-numbered Questions and Problems are in the *Study Guide*.

1.1 Compare the units a student in the United States and a student in Mexico would use to measure the following:
**a.** your mass
**b.** your height
**c.** amount of gasoline to fill the gas tank
**d.** temperature

**1.2** Suppose that a friend tells you the following information. Why are the statements confusing, and how would you make them clear using a metric (SI) unit?
**a.** I rode my bicycle for 15 today.
**b.** My dog weighs 25.
**c.** It is hot today. It is 30.
**d.** I started a diet and lost 1.5 last week.

1.3 State the name of the unit and the type of measurement (mass, length, volume, temperature, or time) for each of the following quantities:
**a.** 4.8 m
**b.** 325 g
**c.** 1.5 L
**d.** 480 s
**e.** 28 °C

**1.4** State the name of the unit and the type of measurement (mass, length, volume, temperature, or time) for each of the following quantities:
**a.** 0.8 mL
**b.** 3.6 m
**c.** 14 kg
**d.** 35 g
**e.** 373 K

## 1.2 Scientific Notation

**LEARNING GOAL**
Write a number in scientific notation.

In chemistry, we use numbers that are extremely small and extremely large. We might measure something as tiny as the width of a human hair, which is 0.000 008 m. Or perhaps we want to count the number of hairs on the average human scalp, which is about 100 000 hairs. (In this section, we have added spaces to help make the places easier to count in very small or very large numbers.) (See Figure 1.5.) However, it is more convenient to write these small and large numbers in scientific notation.

| Item | Value | Scientific Notation |
|---|---|---|
| Width of a human hair | 0.000 008 m | $8 \times 10^{-6}$ m |
| Hairs on a human scalp | 100 000 hairs | $1 \times 10^{5}$ hairs |

### Writing a Number in Scientific Notation

A number written in **scientific notation** has two parts: a coefficient and a power of 10. For example, the number 2400 in scientific notation is $2.4 \times 10^3$. The coefficient is 2.4, and $10^3$ shows that the power of 10 is 3. The coefficient is determined by moving the decimal point three places to the left to give a number from 1 to 9. Because we moved the decimal

**FIGURE 1.5** Humans have an average of $1 \times 10^5$ hairs on their scalps. Each hair is about $8 \times 10^{-6}$ m wide.
**Q** Why are large and small numbers written in scientific notation?

point three places to the left, the power of 10 is a positive 3, written as $10^3$. For a number greater than 1, the power of 10 is positive.

$$2400. = 2.4 \times 1000 = 2.4 \times 10 \times 10 \times 10 = 2.4 \times 10^3$$

← 3 places   Coefficient   Power of 10

When a number less than 1 is written in scientific notation, the power of 10 is negative. For example, to express the number 0.000 86 in scientific notation, the decimal point is moved to the right four places to give a coefficient of 8.6. By moving the decimal point four places to the right, the power of 10 is a negative 4, or $10^{-4}$.

$$0.000\ 86 = \frac{8.6}{10\ 000} = \frac{8.6}{10 \times 10 \times 10 \times 10} = 8.6 \times 10^{-4}$$

4 places →   Coefficient   Power of 10

Table 1.2 gives some examples of numbers written as positive and negative powers of 10. The powers of 10 are a way to keep track of the decimal point in the decimal number. Table 1.3 gives examples of writing measurements in scientific notation.

**TABLE 1.2** Some Powers of 10

| Number | Multiples of 10 | Scientific Notation | |
|---|---|---|---|
| 10 000 | $10 \times 10 \times 10 \times 10$ | $1 \times 10^4$ | |
| 1 000 | $10 \times 10 \times 10$ | $1 \times 10^3$ | |
| 100 | $10 \times 10$ | $1 \times 10^2$ | Some positive powers of 10 |
| 10 | 10 | $1 \times 10^1$ | |
| 1 | 0 | $1 \times 10^0$ | |
| 0.1 | $\frac{1}{10}$ | $1 \times 10^{-1}$ | |
| 0.01 | $\frac{1}{10} \times \frac{1}{10} = \frac{1}{100}$ | $1 \times 10^{-2}$ | |
| 0.001 | $\frac{1}{10} \times \frac{1}{10} \times \frac{1}{10} = \frac{1}{1000}$ | $1 \times 10^{-3}$ | Some negative powers of 10 |
| 0.0001 | $\frac{1}{10} \times \frac{1}{10} \times \frac{1}{10} \times \frac{1}{10} = \frac{1}{10\ 000}$ | $1 \times 10^{-4}$ | |

**TABLE 1.3** Some Measurements Written in Scientific Notation

| Measured Quantity | Measurement | Scientific Notation |
|---|---|---|
| Volume of gasoline used in United States each year | 550 000 000 000 L | $5.5 \times 10^{11}$ L |
| Diameter of Earth | 12 800 000 m | $1.28 \times 10^7$ m |
| Time for light to travel from the Sun to Earth | 500 s | $5 \times 10^2$ s |
| Mass of a typical human | 68 kg | $6.8 \times 10^1$ kg |
| Mass of a hummingbird | 0.002 kg | $2 \times 10^{-3}$ kg |
| Length of a pox virus | 0.000 000 3 m | $3 \times 10^{-7}$ m |
| Mass of a bacterium (mycoplasma) | 0.000 000 000 000 000 000 1 kg | $1 \times 10^{-19}$ kg |

## Scientific Notation and Calculators

You can enter numbers in scientific notation on many calculators using the EE or EXP key. After you enter the coefficient, push the EXP (or EE) key and enter only the power of 10; the EXP function key already includes the $\times$ 10 value. To enter a negative power of 10, push the plus/minus (+/–) key or the minus (–) key (depending on your calculator) but ***not*** the key that performs the subtraction operation "–". Some calculators require entering the sign before the power.

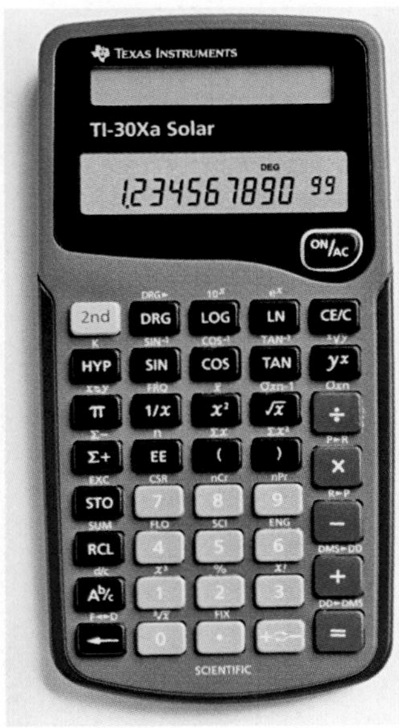


| Number to Enter | Method | Display Reads |
|---|---|---|
| $4 \times 10^6$ | 4 EXP (EE) 6 | 4 06 or $4^{06}$ or 4 E06 |
| $2.5 \times 10^{-4}$ | 2.5 EXP (EE) +/− 4 | 2.5 −04 or $2.5^{-04}$ or 2.5 E−04 |

When a calculator answer appears in scientific notation, it is usually shown in the display as a number from 1 to 9 followed by a space and the power of 10. To express this display in scientific notation, write the number, insert × 10, and use the power of 10 as an exponent.

| Calculator Display | Expressed in Scientific Notation |
|---|---|
| 7.52 04 or $7.52^{04}$ or 7.52 E04 | $7.52 \times 10^4$ |
| 5.8−02 or $5.8^{-02}$ or 5.8 E−02 | $5.8 \times 10^{-2}$ |

On many scientific calculators, a number can be converted into scientific notation using the appropriate keys. For example, the number 0.000 52 can be entered followed by hitting the 2nd or 3rd function key and the SCI key. The scientific notation appears in the calculator display as a coefficient and the power of 10.

0.000 52 [2nd or 3rd function key] [SCI] = $5.2^{-04}$ or 5.2−04 or 5.2E−4 = $5.2 \times 10^{-4}$

Key Key Display

## Converting Scientific Notation to a Standard Number

When a number in scientific notation has a positive power of 10, the standard number is written by moving the decimal point to the right for the same number of places as the power of 10. Placeholder zeros are used to give additional decimal places.

$$8.2 \times 10^2 = 8.2 \times 100 = 820$$

For a number in scientific notation with a negative power of 10, the standard number is written by moving the decimal point to the left for the same number of places. Placeholder zeros are added in front of the coefficient as needed.

$$4.3 \times 10^{-3} = 4.3 \times \frac{1}{1000} = 0.0043$$

CONCEPT CHECK 1.2

### Scientific Notation

Indicate whether the power of 10 is positive or negative when each of the following is written in scientific notation:

**a.** 45 000 m
**b.** 0.0092 g
**c.** 143 mL

ANSWER

**a.** To make a coefficient between 1 and 9, the decimal point is moved four places to the left, which gives a positive power of 10 ($4.5 \times 10^4$ m).
**b.** To make a coefficient between 1 and 9, the decimal point is moved three places to the right, which gives a negative power of 10 ($9.2 \times 10^{-3}$ g).
**c.** To make a coefficient between 1 and 9, the decimal point is moved two places to the left, which gives a positive power of 10 ($1.43 \times 10^2$ mL).

SAMPLE PROBLEM 1.2

**Scientific Notation**

1. Write the following measurements in scientific notation:
   **a.** 0.000 16 L **b.** 5 220 000 m
2. Write the following as standard numbers:
   **a.** $7.2 \times 10^{-3}$ m **b.** $2.4 \times 10^{5}$ g

SOLUTION

1. **a.** $1.6 \times 10^{-4}$ L **b.** $5.22 \times 10^{6}$ m
2. **a.** 0.0072 m **b.** 240 000 g

STUDY CHECK

Write the following measurements in scientific notation:
**a.** 425 000 m **b.** 0.000 000 8 g

## QUESTIONS AND PROBLEMS

### Scientific Notation

**1.5** Write the following measurements in scientific notation:
**a.** 55 000 m **b.** 480 g **c.** 0.000 005 cm
**d.** 0.000 14 s **e.** 0.007 85 L **f.** 670 000 kg

**1.6** Write the following measurements in scientific notation:
**a.** 180 000 000 g **b.** 0.000 06 m **c.** 750 000 kg
**d.** 0.15 m **e.** 0.024 s **f.** 1500 $m^3$

**1.7** Which number in each pair is larger?
**a.** $7.2 \times 10^{3}$ or $8.2 \times 10^{2}$ **b.** $4.5 \times 10^{-4}$ or $3.2 \times 10^{-2}$
**c.** $1 \times 10^{4}$ or $1 \times 10^{-4}$ **d.** 0.000 52 or $6.8 \times 10^{-2}$

**1.8** Which number in each pair is smaller?
**a.** $4.9 \times 10^{-3}$ or $5.5 \times 10^{-9}$
**b.** 1250 or $3.4 \times 10^{2}$
**c.** 0.000 000 4 or $5 \times 10^{-8}$
**d.** $4 \times 10^{-8}$ or $4 \times 10^{-10}$

**1.9** Write the following as standard numbers:
**a.** $1.2 \times 10^{4}$ **b.** $8.25 \times 10^{-2}$
**c.** $4 \times 10^{6}$ **d.** $5 \times 10^{-3}$

**1.10** Write the following as standard numbers:
**a.** $3.6 \times 10^{-5}$ **b.** $8.75 \times 10^{4}$
**c.** $3 \times 10^{-2}$ **d.** $2.12 \times 10^{5}$

# 1.3 Measured Numbers and Significant Figures

LEARNING GOAL

Determine the number of significant figures in measured numbers.

Whenever you make a measurement, you use some type of measuring device. For example, you may use a meterstick to measure your height, a scale to check your weight, and a thermometer to take your temperature. **Measured numbers** are the numbers you obtain when you measure a quantity such as your height, weight, or temperature.

## Measured Numbers

Suppose you are going to measure the lengths of the objects in Figure 1.6. You would select a ruler with a scale marked on it. By observing the lines on the scale, you determine the measurement for each object. Perhaps the divisions on the scale are marked as 1 cm. Another ruler might be marked in divisions of 0.1 cm. To report the length, you would first read the numerical value of the marked line. Finally, you estimate by visually dividing the space between the smallest marked lines. This estimated number is the final digit in a measured number.

For example, in Figure 1.6a, the end of the object falls between the lines marked 4 cm and 5 cm. That means that the length is 4 cm plus an estimated digit. If you estimate that the end is halfway between 4 cm and 5 cm, you would report its length as 4.5 cm. However, someone else might report the length as 4.4 cm. The last digit in a measured number can differ because people do not estimate in the same way. The ruler shown in Figure 1.6b is marked with lines at 0.1 cm. With this ruler, you can estimate the value of the hundredth's

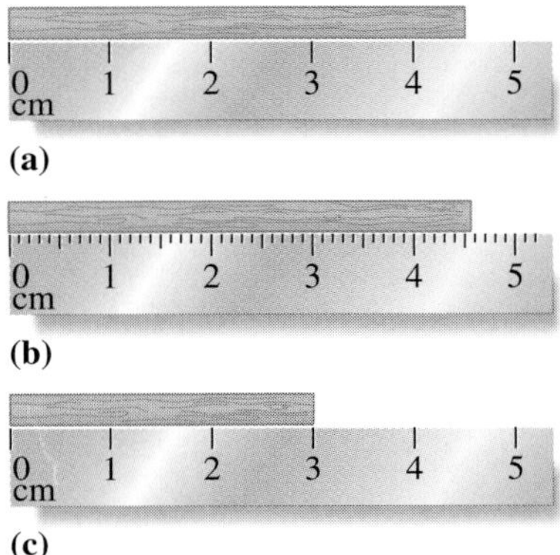


**FIGURE 1.6** The lengths of the rectangular objects are measured as **(a)** 4.5 cm and **(b)** 4.55 cm.

Q What is the length of the object in (c)?

place (0.01 cm). Perhaps you would report the length of the object as 4.55 cm, while someone else may report its length as 4.56 cm. Both results are acceptable.

Therefore, there is always uncertainty in every measurement. When a measurement ends right on a marked line, a zero is written as the estimated digit. For example, in Figure 1.6c, the measurement for length is written as 3.0 cm, not 3. This means that the uncertainty of the measurement is in the estimated digit.

## Significant Figures

SELF STUDY ACTIVITY
Significant Figures

In a measured number, the **significant figures** (**SFs**) are all the digits including the estimated digit. All nonzero numbers are counted as significant figures. Zeros may or may not be significant, depending on their position in a number. Table 1.4 gives the rules and examples of counting significant figures.

**TABLE 1.4** Significant Figures in Measured Numbers

| Rule | Measured Number | Number of Significant Figures |
|---|---|---|
| 1. **A number is a *significant figure* if it is** | | |
| **a.** not a zero | 4.5 g | 2 |
| | 122.35 m | 5 |
| **b.** a zero between nonzero digits | 205 m | 3 |
| | 5.082 kg | 4 |
| **c.** a zero at the end of a decimal number | 50. L | 2 |
| | 25.0 °C | 3 |
| | 16.00 g | 4 |
| **d.** any digit in the coefficient of a number written in scientific notation | $4.0 \times 10^5$ m | 2 |
| | $5.70 \times 10^{-3}$ g | 3 |
| 2. **A zero is *not significant* if it is** | | |
| **a.** at the beginning of a decimal number | 0.0004 lb | 1 |
| | 0.075 m | 2 |
| **b.** used as a placeholder in a large number without a decimal point | 850 000 m | 2 |
| | 1 250 000 g | 3 |

When one or more zeros in a large number are significant digits, they are shown by writing the number using scientific notation. For example, if the first zero in the measurement 500 m is significant, then it can be shown by writing the measurement as $5.0 \times 10^2$ m. In this text, we will place a decimal point after a significant zero at the end of a number. For example, a measurement written as 250. g has three significant figures, which includes the zero. The number could also be written as $2.50 \times 10^2$ g. Unless noted otherwise, we will assume that zeros at the end of large standard numbers are not significant. We would interpret 400 000 g as $4 \times 10^5$ g with one significant figure.

CONCEPT CHECK 1.3

### Significant Zeros

Underline significant zeros in each of the following measured numbers:

**a.** 0.000 250 m **b.** 70.040 g **c.** 1 020 055 mg

ANSWER

**a.** 0.000 25$\underline{0}$ m **b.** 7$\underline{0}$.$\underline{0}$4$\underline{0}$ g **c.** 1 $\underline{0}$2$\underline{0}$ $\underline{0}$55 mg

## Exact Numbers

**Exact numbers** are those obtained by counting items or from a definition that compares two units in the same measuring system. Suppose a friend asks you to tell her the number of coats in your closet or the number of classes you are taking in school. Your answer would be given by counting the items. It was not necessary for you to use any type of measuring tool. Suppose someone asks you to state the number of seconds in one minute. Without using any measuring device, you would give the definition: 60 seconds in one minute. Exact numbers are not measured, do not have a limited number of significant figures, and do not affect the number of significant figures in a calculated answer. For more examples of exact numbers, see Table 1.5.

**TABLE 1.5** Examples of Some Exact Numbers

| | Defined Equalities | |
|---|---|---|
| **Counted Numbers** | **U.S. System** | **Metric System** |
| 8 doughnuts | 1 ft = 12 in. | 1 L = 1000 mL |
| 2 baseballs | 1 qt = 4 cups | 1 m = 100 cm |
| 5 capsules | 1 lb = 16 oz | 1 kg = 1000 g |

**SAMPLE PROBLEM 1.3**

### Significant Figures

Identify each of the following numbers as measured or exact, and give the number of significant figures in each measured number:

**a.** 42.2 g **b.** three eggs **c.** $5.0 \times 10^{-4}$ cm **d.** 450 000 km **e.** $3.500 \times 10^{5}$ s

SOLUTION

**a.** measured; three
**b.** exact
**c.** measured; two
**d.** measured; two
**e.** measured; four

STUDY CHECK

State the number of significant figures in each of the following measured numbers:

**a.** 0.000 35 g **b.** 2000 m **c.** 2.0045 L

## QUESTIONS AND PROBLEMS

### Measured Numbers and Significant Figures

**1.11** Identify the numbers in each of the following statements as measured or exact:
- **a.** A person weighs 155 lb.
- **b.** The basket holds eight apples.
- **c.** In the metric system, 1 kg is equal to 1000 g.
- **d.** The distance from Denver, Colorado, to Houston, Texas, is 1720 km.

**1.12** Identify the numbers in each of the following statements as measured or exact:
- **a.** There are 31 students in the laboratory.
- **b.** The oldest known flower lived $1.2 \times 10^{8}$ years ago.
- **c.** The largest gem ever found, an aquamarine, has a mass of $10^{4}$ kg.
- **d.** A laboratory test shows a blood cholesterol level of 184 mg/100 mL.

**1.13** In each set of the following numbers, identify the measured number(s), if any:
- **a.** 3 hamburgers and 6 oz of meat
- **b.** one table and four chairs
- **c.** 0.75 lb of grapes and 350 g of butter
- **d.** 60 seconds equals 1 minute

**1.14** In each set of the following numbers, identify the exact number(s), if any:
- **a.** 5 pizzas and 50.0 g of cheese
- **b.** 6 nickels and 16 g of nickel
- **c.** 3 onions and 3 lb of potatoes
- **d.** 5 miles and 5 cars

**1.15** For each of the following measurements, indicate if the zeros are significant:
- **a.** 0.0038 m
- **b.** 5.04 cm
- **c.** 800. L
- **d.** $3.0 \times 10^{-3}$ kg
- **e.** 85 000 g

**1.16** For each of the following measurements, indicate if the zeros are significant:
- **a.** 20.05 g
- **b.** 5.00 m
- **c.** 0.000 02 L
- **d.** 120 000 years
- **e.** $8.05 \times 10^{2}$ g

**1.17** How many significant figures are in each of the following measured quantities?
**a.** 11.005 g **b.** 0.000 32 m
**c.** 36 000 000 m **d.** $1.80 \times 10^4$ g
**e.** 0.8250 L **f.** 30.0 °C

**1.18** How many significant figures are in each of the following measured quantities?
**a.** 20.60 L **b.** 1036.48 g
**c.** 4.00 m **d.** 20.8 °C
**e.** 60 800 000 g **f.** $5.0 \times 10^{-3}$ L

**1.19** In which of the following pairs do both numbers contain the same number of significant figures?
**a.** 20.5 g and 20.50 g **b.** 405 K and 405.0 K
**c.** 0.0012 s and 12 000 s **d.** 35.00 L and 0.3500 L

**1.20** In which of the following pairs do both numbers contain the same number of significant figures?
**a.** 0.005 75 g and $5.75 \times 10^{-3}$ g
**b.** 0.0250 m and 0.205 m
**c.** 150 000 s and $1.50 \times 10^4$ s
**d.** $3.8 \times 10^{-2}$ L and $3.8 \times 10^5$ L

**1.21** Write each of the following in scientific notation with two significant figures:
**a.** 5000 L **b.** 30 000 g
**c.** 100 000 m **d.** 0.000 25 cm

**1.22** Write each of the following in scientific notation with two significant figures:
**a.** 5 100 000 g **b.** 26 000 s
**c.** 40 000 m **d.** 0.000 820 kg

## 1.4 Significant Figures in Calculations

**LEARNING GOAL**

Adjust calculated answers to the correct number of significant figures.

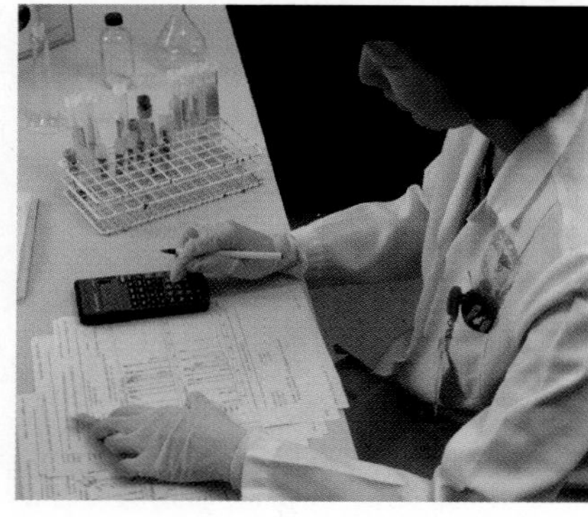

In the sciences, we measure many things: the length of a bacterium, the volume of a gas sample, the temperature of a reaction mixture, or the mass of iron in a sample. The numbers obtained from these types of measurements are often used in calculations. The number of significant figures in the measured numbers limits the number of significant figures that can be given in the calculated answer.

Using a calculator will usually help you to do calculations faster. However, calculators cannot think for you. It is up to you to enter the numbers correctly, press the right function keys, and adjust the calculator display to give an answer with the correct number of significant figures.

### Rounding Off

To calculate the area of a carpet that measures 5.5 m by 3.5 m, you multiply 5.5 times 3.5 to obtain the number 19.25 as the area in square meters. However, all four digits cannot be given in the answer because they are not all significant figures. Each measurement of length and width has only two significant figures. This means that the calculated result must be rounded off to give an answer that also has two significant figures, 19 $m^2$. When you obtain a calculator result, determine the number of significant figures for the answer and round off using the following rules.

**Rules for Rounding Off**

1. If the first digit to be dropped is *4 or less*, then it and all following digits are simply dropped from the number.
2. If the first digit to be dropped is *5 or greater*, then the last retained digit of the number is increased by 1.

| | Three Significant Figures | Two Significant Figures |
|---|---|---|
| Example 1: 8.4234 rounds off to | 8.42 | 8.4 |
| Example 2: 14.780 rounds off to | 14.8 | 15 |
| Example 3: 3256 rounds off to | 3260 ($3.26 \times 10^3$) | 3300 ($3.3 \times 10^3$) |

**CONCEPT CHECK 1.4**

**Rounding Off**

Select the correct value when 2.8456 m is rounded to each of the following:
**a.** three significant figures: 2.84 m 2.85 m 2.8 m 2.90 m
**b.** two significant figures: 2.80 m 2.8 m 2.9 m 3.0 m

ANSWER

**a.** To round 2.8456 m to three significant figures, drop the final digits 56 and increase the last retained digit to give 2.85 m.

**b.** To round 2.8456 m to two significant figures, drop the final digits 456 to give 2.8 m.

SAMPLE PROBLEM 1.4

### Rounding Off

Round off each of the following numbers to three significant figures:

**a.** 35.7823 m **b.** 0.002 627 L **c.** $3.8268 \times 10^3$ g **d.** 1.2836 kg

SOLUTION

**a.** 35.8 m **b.** 0.002 63 L **c.** $3.83 \times 10^3$ g **d.** 1.28 kg

STUDY CHECK

Round off each of the numbers in Sample Problem 1.4 to two significant figures.

## Multiplication and Division

In multiplication or division, the final answer is written so it has the same number of significant figures as the measurement with the fewest SFs.

**Example 1**

Multiply the following measured numbers: $24.65 \times 0.67$

| 24.65 | × | 0.67 | = | 16.5155 | ⟶ | 17 |
|---|---|---|---|---|---|---|
| Four SFs | | Two SFs | | Calculator display | | Final answer, rounded to two SFs |

The answer in the calculator display has more digits than the data allow. The measurement 0.67 has the least number of significant figures: two. Therefore, the calculator answer is rounded off to two significant figures.

**Example 2**

Solve the following:

$$\frac{2.85 \times 67.4}{4.39}$$

To do this problem on a calculator, enter the numbers and then press the operation keys. In this case, we might press the keys in the following order:

| 2.85 | × | 67.4 | ÷ | 4.39 | = | 43.756264 | ⟶ | 43.8 |
|---|---|---|---|---|---|---|---|---|
| Three SFs | | Three SFs | | Three SFs | | Calculator display | | Final answer, rounded to three SFs |

All of the measurements in this problem have three significant figures. Therefore, the calculator result is rounded off to give an answer, 43.8, that also has three significant figures.

## Adding Significant Zeros

Sometimes, a calculator displays a small whole number. To give an answer with the correct number of significant figures, you may need to write significant zeros after the calculator result. For example, suppose the calculator display is 4, but you used measurements that have three significant numbers. The answer 4.00 is obtained by placing two significant zeros after the 4.

| $\frac{8.00}{2.00} =$ | 4 | $\longrightarrow$ | 4.00 |
|---|---|---|---|
| 3 SFs | Calculator display | | Final answer, two zeros added to give 3 SFs |

SAMPLE PROBLEM 1.5

### Significant Figures in Multiplication and Division

Perform the following calculations of measured numbers. Give the answers with the correct number of significant figures:

**a.** $56.8 \times 0.37$ **b.** $\frac{71.4}{11}$ **c.** $\frac{(2.075)(0.585)}{(8.42)(0.004\ 50)}$ **d.** $\frac{25.0}{5.00}$

SOLUTION

**a.** 21 **b.** 6.5 **c.** 32.0 **d.** 5.00 (add significant zeros)

STUDY CHECK

Perform the following calculations of measured numbers. Give the answers with the correct number of significant figures:

**a.** $45.26 \times 0.010\ 88$ **b.** $2.6 \div 324$ **c.** $\frac{4.0 \times 8.00}{16}$

## Addition and Subtraction

In addition or subtraction, the answer is written so that it has the same number of decimal places as the measurement having the fewest decimal places.

**Example 3**

Add:

| | |
|---|---|
| 2.045 | Three decimal places |
| + 34.1 | One decimal place |
| 36.145 | Calculator display |
| 36.1 | Answer rounded to one decimal place |

**Example 4**

Subtract:

| | |
|---|---|
| 255 | Ones place |
| − 175.65 | Two decimal places |
| 79.35 | Calculator display |
| 79 | Answer rounded to ones place |

When numbers are added or subtracted to give answers ending in zero, the zero does not appear after the decimal point in the calculator display. For example, 14.5 g − 2.5 g = 12.0 g. However, if you do the subtraction on your calculator, the display shows 12. To give the correct answer, a significant zero is written after the decimal point.

**Example 5**

Add:

| | |
|---|---|
| 37.12 mL | Two decimal places |
| + 21.880 mL | Three decimal places |
| 59. | Calculator display |
| 59.00 mL | Answer; two significant zeros are written after the decimal point |

SAMPLE PROBLEM 1.6

**Significant Figures in Addition and Subtraction**

Perform the following calculations, and give the answers with the correct number of decimal places:

**a.** 27.8 cm + 0.235 cm **b.** 104.45 mL − 0.838 mL + 46 mL
**c.** 153.247 g − 14.82 g

SOLUTION

**a.** 28.0 cm **b.** 151 mL **c.** 138.43 g

STUDY CHECK

Perform the following calculations and give the answers with the correct number of decimal places:

**a.** 82.45 mg + 1.245 mg + 0.000 56 mg **b.** 4.259 L − 3.8 L

## QUESTIONS AND PROBLEMS

### Significant Figures in Calculations

1.23 Why do we usually need to round off calculations that use measured numbers?

**1.24** Why do we sometimes add a zero to a number in a calculator display?

1.25 Round off each of the following numbers to three significant figures:
**a.** 1.854 **b.** 184.2038
**c.** 0.004 738 265 **d.** 8807
**e.** $1.832 \times 10^5$

**1.26** Round off each of the numbers in problem 1.25 to two significant figures.

1.27 For the following problems, give answers with the correct number of significant figures:
**a.** $45.7 \times 0.034$ **b.** $0.002\,78 \times 5$
**c.** $\frac{34.56}{1.25}$ **d.** $\frac{(0.2465)(25)}{1.78}$

**1.28** For the following problems, give answers with the correct number of significant figures:
**a.** $400 \times 185$ **b.** $\frac{2.40}{(4)(125)}$
**c.** $0.825 \times 3.6 \times 5.1$ **d.** $\frac{3.5 \times 0.261}{8.24 \times 20.0}$

1.29 For the following problems, give answers with the correct number of decimal places:
**a.** 45.48 cm + 8.057 cm
**b.** 23.45 g + 104.1 g + 0.025 g
**c.** 145.675 mL − 24.2 mL
**d.** 1.08 L − 0.585 L

**1.30** For the following problems, give answers with the correct number of decimal places:
**a.** 5.08 g + 25.1 g
**b.** 85.66 cm + 104.10 cm + 0.025 cm
**c.** 24.568 mL − 14.25 mL
**d.** 0.2654 L − 0.2585 L

## 1.5 Prefixes and Equalities

**LEARNING GOAL**

Use the numerical values of prefixes to write a metric equality.

The special feature of the metric system of units is that a **prefix** can be attached to any unit to increase or decrease its size by some factor of 10. For example, the prefixes *milli* and *micro* are used to make the smaller units, milligram (mg) and microgram ($\mu$g). Table 1.6 lists some of the metric prefixes, their symbols, and their decimal values.

The prefix *centi* is like cents in a dollar. One cent would be a centidollar, or $\frac{1}{100}$ of a dollar. That also means that one dollar is the same as 100 cents. The prefix *deci* is like dimes in a dollar. One dime would be a decidollar, or $\frac{1}{10}$ of a dollar. That also means that one dollar is the same as 10 dimes.

SELF STUDY ACTIVITY
Metric System

The U.S. Food and Drug Administration (FDA) has determined the daily values (DVs) of nutrients for adults and children age 4 or older. Some of these recommended daily values, which use prefixes, are listed in Table 1.7.

**TABLE 1.6** Metric and SI Prefixes

| Prefix | Symbol | Numerical Value | Scientific Notation | Equality |
|---|---|---|---|---|
| **Prefixes That Increase the Size of the Unit** | | | | |
| peta | P | 1 000 000 000 000 000 | $10^{15}$ | 1 Pg = $10^{15}$ g |
| tera | T | 1 000 000 000 000 | $10^{12}$ | 1 Tg = $10^{12}$ g |
| giga | G | 1 000 000 000 | $10^{9}$ | 1 Gm = $10^{9}$ m |
| mega | M | 1 000 000 | $10^{6}$ | 1 Mg = $10^{6}$ g |
| kilo | k | 1 000 | $10^{3}$ | 1 km = $10^{3}$ m |
| **Prefixes That Decrease the Size of the Unit** | | | | |
| deci | d | 0.1 | $10^{-1}$ | 1 dL = $10^{-1}$ L<br>1 L = 10 dL |
| centi | c | 0.01 | $10^{-2}$ | 1 cm = $10^{-2}$ m<br>1 m = 100 cm |
| milli | m | 0.001 | $10^{-3}$ | 1 ms = $10^{-3}$ s<br>1 s = $10^{3}$ ms |
| micro | $\mu$ | 0.000 001 | $10^{-6}$ | 1 $\mu$g = $10^{-6}$ g<br>1 g = $10^{6}$ $\mu$g |
| nano | n | 0.000 000 001 | $10^{-9}$ | 1 nm = $10^{-9}$ m<br>1 m = $10^{9}$ nm |
| pico | p | 0.000 000 000 001 | $10^{-12}$ | 1 ps = $10^{-12}$ s<br>1 s = $10^{12}$ ps |
| femto | f | 0.000 000 000 000 001 | $10^{-15}$ | 1 fs = $10^{-15}$ s<br>1 s = $10^{15}$ fs |

**TABLE 1.7** Daily Values for Selected Nutrients

| Nutrient | Amount Recommended |
|---|---|
| Protein | 44 g |
| Vitamin C | 60 mg |
| Vitamin $B_{12}$ | 6 $\mu$g |
| Calcium | 1000 mg |
| Iron | 18 mg |
| Iodine | 150 $\mu$g |
| Magnesium | 400 mg |
| Potassium | 3500 mg |
| Sodium | 2400 mg |
| Zinc | 15 mg |

The relationship of a prefix to a unit can be expressed by replacing the prefix with its numerical value. For example, when the prefix *kilo* in kilometer is replaced with its value of 1000, we find that a kilometer is equal to 1000 meters. Other examples follow.

1 **kilo**meter (1 km) = **1000** meters (1000 m = $10^3$ m)

1 **kilo**liter (1 kL) = **1000** liters (1000 L = $10^3$ L)

1 **kilo**gram (1 kg) = **1000** grams (1000 g = $10^3$ g)

CONCEPT CHECK 1.5

### Prefixes

The storage capacity for a hard disk drive (HDD) is specified using prefixes: terabyte (TB), gigabyte (GB), or megabyte (MB). Indicate the storage capacity in bytes of each of the following hard disk drives. Suggest a reason for describing a HDD storage capacity in gigabytes or terabytes:

**a.** 5 MB **b.** 1 TB **c.** 2 GB

ANSWER

**a.** 5 MB = 5 000 000 ($5 \times 10^6$) bytes
**b.** 1 TB = 1 000 000 000 000 ($1 \times 10^{12}$) bytes
**c.** 2 GB = 2 000 000 000 ($2 \times 10^9$) bytes

Expressing HDD capacity in gigabytes or terabytes gives a more reasonable number to work with than a number with many zeros or a large power of 10.

SAMPLE PROBLEM 1.7

**Prefixes**

Fill in the blanks with the correct prefix:

**a.** 1000 grams = 1 _____ gram **b.** 0.01 meter = 1 _____ meter
**c.** $1 \times 10^6$ liters = 1 _____ liter

SOLUTION

**a.** The prefix for 1000 is *kilo*; 1000 grams = 1 kilogram.
**b.** The prefix for 0.01 is *centi*; 0.01 meter = 1 centimeter.
**c.** The prefix for $1 \times 10^6$ is *mega*; $1 \times 10^6$ liters = 1 megaliter.

STUDY CHECK

Write the correct prefix in the blanks:

**a.** 1 000 000 000 seconds = 1 _____ second
**b.** 0.01 meter = 1 _____ meter

## Measuring Length

An ophthalmologist may measure the diameter of the retina of an eye in centimeters (cm), whereas a surgeon may need to know the length of a nerve in millimeters (mm). When the prefix *centi* is used with the unit meter, it indicates the unit centimeter, a length that is one-hundredth of a meter (0.01 m). A *millimeter* measures a length of 0.001 m. There are 1000 mm in a meter.

If we compare the lengths of a millimeter and a centimeter, we find that 1 mm is 0.1 cm; there are 10 mm in 1 cm. These comparisons are examples of **equalities**, which show the relationship between two units that measure the same quantity. For example, in the equality 1 m = 100 cm, each quantity describes the same length but in a different unit. Note that each quantity in the equality expression has both a number and a unit.

| First Quantity | | | Second Quantity | |
|---|---|---|---|---|
| 1 | m | = | 100 | cm |
| ↑ | ↑ | | ↑ | ↑ |
| Number + unit | | | Number + unit | |

**Some Length Equalities**

1 m = 100 cm $= 1 \times 10^2$ cm
1 m = 1000 mm $= 1 \times 10^3$ mm
1 cm = 10 mm $= 1 \times 10^1$ mm

Some metric units for length are compared in Figure 1.7.

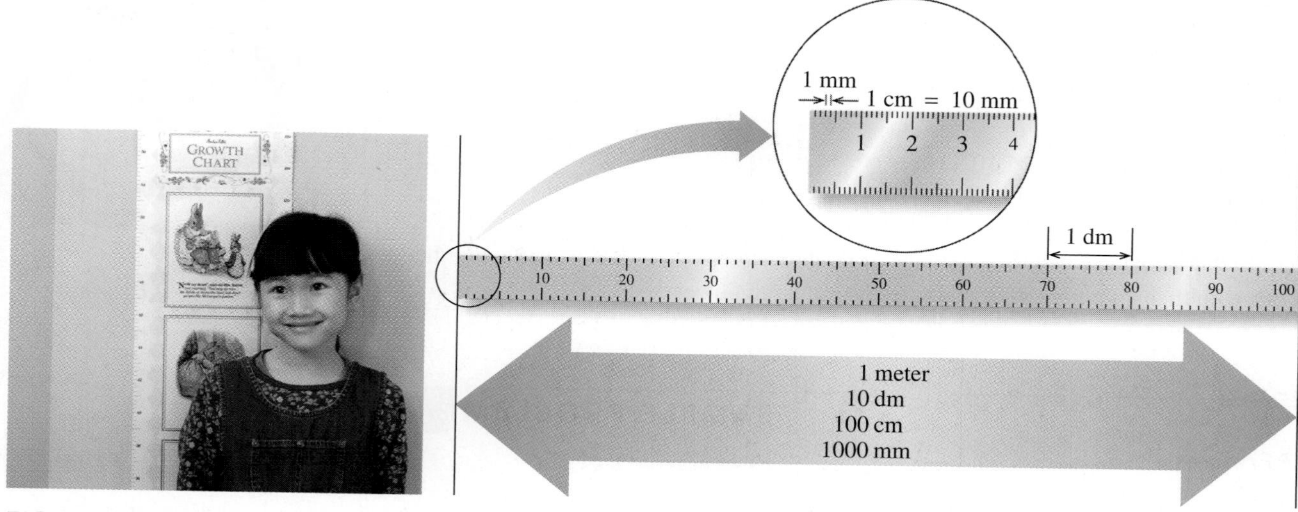


**FIGURE 1.7** The metric length of 1 meter is the same length as 10 dm, 100 cm, and 1000 mm.
**Q** How many millimeters (mm) are in 1 centimeter (cm)?

## Measuring Volume

Volumes of 1 L or smaller are common in the health sciences. When a liter is divided into 10 equal portions, each portion is a deciliter (dL). There are 10 dL in 1 L. Laboratory results for blood work are often reported in mass per deciliter. Table 1.8 lists typical laboratory tests for some substances in the blood.

When a liter is divided into a thousand parts, each smaller part is a milliliter (mL). In a 1-L container of physiological saline, there are 1000 mL of solution. (See Figure 1.8.)

**TABLE 1.8** Some Typical Laboratory Test Values

| Substance in Blood | Typical Range |
|---|---|
| Albumin | 3.5–5.0 g/dL |
| Ammonia | 20–150 μg/dL |
| Calcium | 8.5–10.5 mg/dL |
| Cholesterol | 105–250 mg/dL |
| Iron (male) | 80–160 μg/dL |
| Protein (total) | 6.0–8.0 g/dL |

**Some Volume Equalities**

$1\text{ L} = 10\text{ dL} = 1 \times 10^1\text{ dL}$

$1\text{ L} = 1000\text{ mL} = 1 \times 10^3\text{ mL}$

$1\text{ dL} = 100\text{ mL} = 1 \times 10^2\text{ mL}$

The **cubic centimeter** (**$cm^3$** or **cc**) is the volume of a cube with dimensions of 1 cm on each side. A cubic centimeter has the same volume as a milliliter, and the units are often used interchangeably.

$1\text{ cm}^3 = 1\text{ cc} = 1\text{ mL}$

When you see *1 cm*, you are reading about length; when you see *1 cc* or *1 $cm^3$* or *1 mL*, you are reading about volume. Units of volume are illustrated in Figure 1.9.

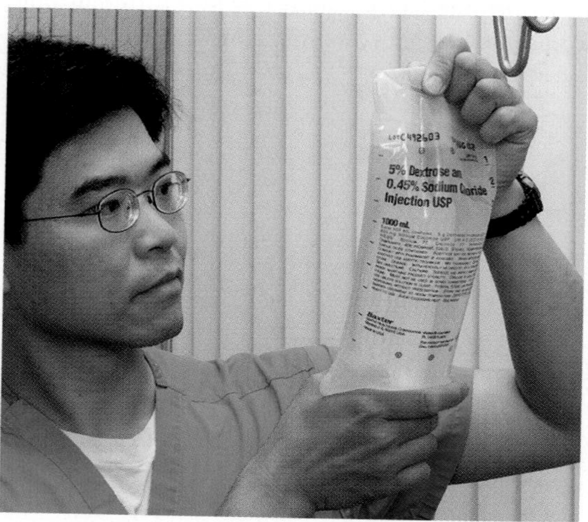


**FIGURE 1.8** A plastic intravenous fluid container contains 1000 mL.
**Q** How many liters of solution are in the intravenous fluid container?

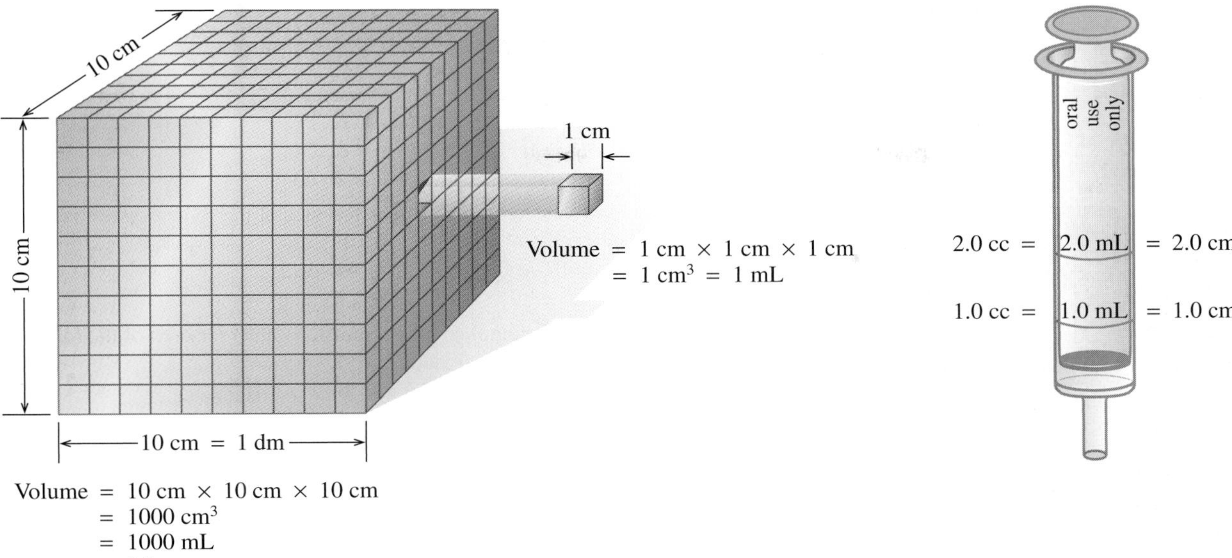


**FIGURE 1.9** A cube measuring 10 cm on each side has a volume of 1000 $cm^3$, or 1 L; a cube measuring 1 cm on each side has a volume of 1 $cm^3$ (cc) or 1 mL.

**Q** What is the relationship between a milliliter (mL) and a cubic centimeter ($cm^3$)?

## Measuring Mass

When you get a physical examination, your mass is recorded in kilograms, whereas the results of your laboratory tests are reported in grams, milligrams (mg), or micrograms ($\mu$g). A kilogram equals 1000 g. One gram represents the same mass as 1000 mg, and 1 mg equals 1000 $\mu$g.

**Some Mass Equalities**

$$1 \text{ kg} = 1000 \text{ g} = 1 \times 10^3 \text{ g}$$

$$1 \text{ g} = 1000 \text{ mg} = 1 \times 10^3 \text{ mg}$$

$$1 \text{ mg} = 1000\ \mu\text{g} = 1 \times 10^3\ \mu\text{g}$$

SAMPLE PROBLEM 1.8

### Writing Metric Relationships

Complete the following list of metric equalities:

**a.** 1 L = _____ dL

**b.** 1 km = _____ m

**c.** 1 m = _____ cm

**d.** 1 $cm^3$ = _____ mL

SOLUTION

**a.** 10 dL **b.** 1000 m **c.** 100 cm **d.** 1 mL

STUDY CHECK

Complete the following metric equalities:

**a.** 1 kg = _____ g

**b.** 1 mL = _____ L

## QUESTIONS AND PROBLEMS

### Prefixes and Equalities

**1.31** The speedometer is marked in both km/h and mph. What is the meaning of each abbreviation?

**1.32** In a French car, the odometer reads 2250. What units would this be? What units would it be if this were an odometer in a car made for the United States?

**1.33** How does the prefix *kilo* affect the gram unit in kilogram?

**1.34** How does the prefix *centi* affect the meter unit in centimeter?

**1.35** Write the abbreviation for each of the following units:
**a.** milligram **b.** deciliter
**c.** kilometer **d.** kilogram
**e.** microliter **f.** nanogram

**1.36** Write the complete name for each of the following units:
**a.** cm **b.** kg
**c.** dL **d.** Gm
**e.** $\mu$g **f.** mg

**1.37** Write the numerical values for each of the following prefixes:
**a.** centi **b.** kilo
**c.** milli **d.** deci
**e.** mega **f.** pico

**1.38** Write the complete name (prefix + unit) for each of the following numerical values:
**a.** 0.10 g **b.** $1 \times 10^{-6}$ g
**c.** 1000 g **d.** 0.01 g
**e.** 0.001 g **f.** $1 \times 10^{12}$ g

**1.39** Complete the following metric relationships:
**a.** 1 m = _____ cm **b.** 1 km = _____ m
**c.** 1 mm = _____ m **d.** 1 L = _____ mL

**1.40** Complete the following metric relationships:
**a.** 1 kg = _____ g **b.** 1 mL = _____ L
**c.** 1 g = _____ kg **d.** 1 g = _____ mg

**1.41** For each of the following pairs, which is the larger unit?
**a.** milligram or kilogram **b.** milliliter or microliter
**c.** cm or km **d.** kL or dL
**e.** nanometer or picometer

**1.42** For each of the following pairs, which is the smaller unit?
**a.** mg or g **b.** centimeter or millimeter
**c.** mm or $\mu$m **d.** mL or dL
**e.** mg or Mg

## 1.6 Writing Conversion Factors

**LEARNING GOAL**

Write a conversion factor for two units that describe the same quantity.

Many problems in chemistry and the health sciences require a change of units. You make changes in units every day. For example, suppose you spent 2.0 hours (h) on your homework, and someone asked you how many minutes that was. You must have multiplied 2.0 h × 60 min/h, because you knew an equality (1 h = 60 min) that related the two units. When you expressed 2.0 h as 120 min, you did not change the amount of time you spent studying. You changed only the unit of measurement used to express the time. You can write every equality in the form of a fraction called a **conversion factor** in which one of the quantities is the numerator, and the other is the denominator. Two conversion factors are always possible from an equality because a factor can be inverted. Be sure to include the units when you write the conversion factors.

**Two Conversion Factors for the Equality 1 h = 60 min**

$$\frac{\text{Numerator}}{\text{Denominator}} \begin{matrix}\longrightarrow\\ \longrightarrow\end{matrix} \quad \frac{60\text{ min}}{1\text{ h}} \quad \text{and} \quad \frac{1\text{ h}}{60\text{ min}}$$

These factors are read as "60 minutes per 1 hour," and "1 hour per 60 minutes." The term *per* means "divide." Some common relationships are given in Table 1.9. It is important that the equality you select to construct a conversion factor is a true relationship.

When an equality shows the relationship for two units from the same system (metric or U.S.), it is considered a definition and exact. It is not used to determine significant figures. When an equality shows the relationship of units from two different systems, the number is measured and counts toward the significant figures in a calculation. For example, in the equality 1 lb = 454 g, the measured number 454 has three significant figures. The number 1 in 1 lb is considered to be exact. An exception is the relationship of 1 in. = 2.54 cm: the value 2.54 has been defined as exact.

TABLE 1.9 Some Common Equalities

| Quantity | U.S. | Metric (SI) | Metric–U.S. |
|---|---|---|---|
| Length | 1 ft = 12 in. | 1 km = 1000 m | 2.54 cm = 1 in. |
| | 1 yard = 3 ft | 1 m = 1000 mm | 1 m = 39.4 in. |
| | 1 mile = 5280 ft | 1 cm = 10 mm | 1 km = 0.621 mi |
| Volume | 1 qt = 4 cups | 1 L = 1000 mL | 946 mL = 1 qt |
| | 1 qt = 2 pt | 1 dL = 100 mL | 1 L = 1.06 qt |
| | 1 gallon = 4 qt | 1 mL = 1 cm$^3$ | |
| Mass | 1 lb = 16 oz | 1 kg = 1000 g | 1 kg = 2.20 lb |
| | | 1 g = 1000 mg | 454 g = 1 lb |
| Time | | 1 h = 60 min | |
| | | 1 min = 60 s | |

## Metric Conversion Factors

We can write metric conversion factors for the metric relationships we have studied. For example, from the equality for meters and centimeters, we can write the following factors:

| Metric Equality | Conversion Factors |
|---|---|
| 1 m = 100 cm | $\frac{100\text{ cm}}{1\text{ m}}$ and $\frac{1\text{ m}}{100\text{ cm}}$ |

Both are proper conversion factors for the relationship; one is just the inverse of the other. The usefulness of conversion factors is enhanced by the fact that we can turn a conversion factor over and use its inverse.

## Metric–U.S. System Conversion Factors

Suppose you need to convert from pounds, a unit in the U.S. system, to kilograms in the metric (or SI) system. A relationship you could use is

1 kg = 2.20 lb

The corresponding conversion factors would be

$$\frac{2.20\text{ lb}}{1\text{ kg}} \text{ and } \frac{1\text{ kg}}{2.20\text{ lb}}$$

Figure 1.10 illustrates the contents of some packaged foods in both metric and U.S. units.

FIGURE 1.10 In the U.S., the contents of many packaged foods are listed in both U.S. and metric units.

Q What are some advantages of using the metric system?

CAREER FOCUS

### Veterinary Technician (VT)

"I am checking this dog's ears for foxtails and her eyes for signs of conjunctivitis," says Joyce Rhodes, veterinary assistant at the Sonoma Animal Hospital. "We always check a dog's teeth for tartar, because dental care is very important to the well-being of the animal. When I do need to give a medication to an animal, I use my chemistry to prepare the proper dose that the pet should take. Dosages may be in milligrams, kilograms, or milliliters."

As a member of the veterinary healthcare team, a veterinary technician (VT) assists a veterinarian in the care and handling of animals. A VT takes medical histories, collects specimens, performs laboratory procedures, prepares an animal for surgery, assists in surgical procedures, takes X-rays, talks with animal owners, and cleans teeth.

CONCEPT CHECK 1.6

### Identifying Conversion Factors

Identify the correct conversion factors for the equality for gigagrams and grams.

**a.** $\frac{1\ \text{Gg}}{1 \times 10^{9}\text{g}}$ **b.** $\frac{1 \times 10^{-9}\text{g}}{1\ \text{Gg}}$ **c.** $\frac{1 \times 10^{9}\ \text{Gg}}{1\ \text{g}}$ **d.** $\frac{1 \times 10^{9}\text{g}}{1\ \text{Gg}}$

ANSWER

Using the prefix table, we find the equality for gigagrams and grams is 1 Gg = $1 \times 10^{9}$ g. Answers **a.** and **d.** are correctly written conversion factors.

SAMPLE PROBLEM 1.9

### Writing Conversion Factors from Equalities

Write conversion factors for the relationship for the following pairs of units:

**a.** milligrams and grams **b.** quarts and milliliters

SOLUTION

| Equality | Conversion Factors | | |
|---|---|---|---|
| **a.** 1 g = 1000 mg | $\frac{1\ \text{g}}{1000\ \text{mg}}$ | and | $\frac{1000\ \text{mg}}{1\ \text{g}}$ |
| **b.** 1 qt = 946 mL | $\frac{1\ \text{qt}}{946\ \text{mL}}$ | and | $\frac{946\ \text{mL}}{1\ \text{qt}}$ |

STUDY CHECK

A zeptosecond (zs) is a very small quantity of time. As an equality, it is written

1 zs = $1 \times 10^{-21}$ s

Write the conversion factors for this equality.

EXPLORE YOUR WORLD

### SI and Metric Equalities on Product Labels

Read the labels on some food products or use the labels in Figure 1.10. List the amount of product given in different units. Write a relationship for two of the amounts for the same product and container. Look for measurements of grams and pounds or quarts and milliliters.

QUESTIONS

1. Use the stated measurement to derive a metric–U.S. conversion factor.
2. How do your results compare to the conversion factors we have described in this text?

## Conversion Factors Stated Within a Problem

Many times, a problem specifies an equality that is true only for that problem. It might be the cost of 1 kilogram of oranges or the speed of a car in kilometers per hour. Such equalities are easy to miss when you first read a problem. Let's see how conversion factors are written from statements made within a problem.

1. The motorcycle was traveling at a speed of 85 km/h.

   **Equality:** 1 h = 85 km

   **Conversion factors:** $\frac{85\ \text{km}}{1\ \text{h}}$ and $\frac{1\ \text{h}}{85\ \text{km}}$

2. One tablet contains 500 mg of vitamin C.

   **Equality:** 1 tablet = 500 mg of vitamin C

   **Conversion factors:** $\frac{500\ \text{mg vitamin C}}{1\ \text{tablet}}$ and $\frac{1\ \text{tablet}}{500\ \text{mg vitamin C}}$

## Conversion Factors for a Percentage, ppm, and ppb

Sometimes a percentage is given in a problem. The term *percent* (%) means parts per 100 parts. To write a percentage as a conversion factor, we choose a unit and express the numerical relationship of the parts of this unit to 100 parts of the whole. For example, an athlete might have 18% (18 percent) body fat by mass. (See Figure 1.11.) The percent quantity can be written as 18 mass units of body fat in every 100 mass units of body mass. Different mass units such as grams, kilograms (kg), or pounds (lb) can be used, but both units in the factor must be the same.

FIGURE 1.11 The thickness of the skin fold at the waist measured in millimeters (mm) is used to determine the amount of body fat.

Q What is the percent body fat of an athlete with a body mass of 100 kg and 16 kg of body fat?

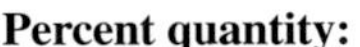

**Percent quantity:** 18% body fat by mass

**Equality:** 18 kg of body fat = 100 kg of body mass

**Conversion factors:** $\frac{100 \text{ kg body mass}}{18 \text{ kg body fat}}$ and $\frac{18 \text{ kg body fat}}{100 \text{ kg body mass}}$

or

**Equality:** 18 lb of body fat = 100 lb of body mass

**Conversion factors:** $\frac{100 \text{ lb body mass}}{18 \text{ lb body fat}}$ and $\frac{18 \text{ lb body fat}}{100 \text{ lb body mass}}$

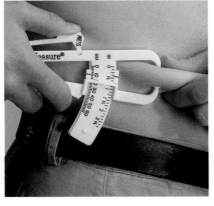

When scientists want to indicate ratios with particularly small percentage values, they use numerical relationships called *parts per million* (ppm) or *parts per billion* (ppb). The ratio of parts per million indicates milligrams of a substance per kilogram (mg/kg). The ratio of parts per billion gives the micrograms per kilogram ($\mu$g/kg). For example, the maximum amount of lead allowed by FDA in glazed pottery bowls is 5 ppm, which is 5 mg/kg.

**ppm quantity:** 5 ppm lead in glaze

**Equality:** 5 mg lead = 1 kg glaze

**Conversion factors:** $\frac{5 \text{ mg lead}}{1 \text{ kg glaze}}$ and $\frac{1 \text{ kg glaze}}{5 \text{ mg lead}}$

SAMPLE PROBLEM 1.10

### Conversion Factors Stated in a Problem

Write the conversion factors for each of the following statements:

**a.** There are 325 mg of aspirin in 1 tablet.
**b.** One kilogram of bananas costs $1.25 at the grocery store.
**c.** The EPA has set the maximum level for mercury in tuna at 0.1 ppm.

SOLUTION

**a.** $\frac{325 \text{ mg aspirin}}{1 \text{ tablet}}$ and $\frac{1 \text{ tablet}}{325 \text{ mg aspirin}}$

**b.** $\frac{\$1.25}{1 \text{ kg bananas}}$ and $\frac{1 \text{ kg bananas}}{\$1.25}$

**c.** $\frac{0.1 \text{ mg mercury}}{1 \text{ kg tuna}}$ and $\frac{1 \text{ kg tuna}}{0.1 \text{ mg mercury}}$

STUDY CHECK

What conversion factors can be written for the following statements?

**a.** A cyclist in the Tour de France bicycle race rides at the average speed of 62.2 km/h.
**b.** The permissible level of arsenic in water is 10 ppb.

# GREEN CHEMISTRY NOTE

## Toxicology and Risk-Benefit Assessment

Each day we make choices about what we do or what we eat, often without thinking about the risks associated with these choices. We are aware of the risks of cancer from smoking, and we know there is a greater risk of having an accident if we cross a street where there is no light or crosswalk.

A basic concept of toxicology is the statement of Paracelsus that the right dose is the difference between a poison and a cure. To evaluate the level of danger from various substances, natural or synthetic, a risk assessment is made by exposing laboratory animals to the substances and monitoring the health effects. Often, doses much greater than humans might encounter are given to the test animals.

Many hazardous chemicals or substances have been identified by these tests. One measure of toxicity is the $LD_{50}$, or "lethal dose," which is the concentration of the substance that causes death in 50% of the test animals. A dosage is typically measured in milligrams per kilogram (mg/kg) of body mass or micrograms per kilogram ($\mu$g/kg).

| Dosage | Units |
|---|---|
| parts per million (ppm) | milligrams per kilogram (mg/kg) |
| parts per billion (ppb) | micrograms per kilogram ($\mu$g/kg) |

Other evaluations also need to be made, but it is easy to compare $LD_{50}$ values. Parathion, a pesticide, with an $LD_{50}$ of 3 mg/kg would be highly toxic. That means that half the test animals given 3 mg of parathion per kg body mass would be expected to die. Salt (sodium chloride) with an $LD_{50}$ of 3000 mg/kg has a much lower toxicity. You would need to ingest a huge amount of salt before any toxic effect would be observed. Although the risk to animals based on dose can be evaluated in the laboratory, it is more difficult to determine the impact in the environment because there is also a difference between continued exposure and a single, large dose of the substance.

Table 1.10 lists some $LD_{50}$ values and compares pesticides and common substances in our everyday lives, in order of increasing toxicity.

**TABLE 1.10** Some $LD_{50}$ Values for Pesticides and Common Materials Tested in Rats

| Substance | $LD_{50}$ (mg/kg) |
|---|---|
| Table sugar | 29 700 |
| Baking soda | 4220 |
| Table salt | 3000 |
| Ethanol | 2080 |
| Aspirin | 1100 |
| Caffeine | 192 |
| Sodium cyanide | 6 |
| Parathion | 3 |

# QUESTIONS AND PROBLEMS

## Writing Conversion Factors

**1.43** Why can two conversion factors be written for an equality such as 1 m = 100 cm?

**1.44** How can you check that you have written the correct conversion factors for an equality?

**1.45** Write the equality and two conversion factors for the following pairs of units:
**a.** centimeters and meters
**b.** milligrams and grams
**c.** liters and milliliters
**d.** deciliters and milliliters

**1.46** Write the equality and two corresponding conversion factors for the following pairs of units:
**a.** centimeters and inches
**b.** pounds and kilograms
**c.** pounds and grams
**d.** quarts and milliliters

**1.47** Write the equality and two conversion factors for each of the following statements:
**a.** One yard is 3 feet.
**b.** One mile is 5280 feet.
**c.** One minute is 60 seconds.
**d.** A car goes 27 miles on 1 gallon of gas.
**e.** Sterling silver is 93% by mass silver.

**1.48** Write the equality and two conversion factors for each of the following statements:
**a.** One gallon is 4 quarts.
**b.** At the store, oranges are $1.29 per lb.
**c.** There are 7 days in 1 week.
**d.** One dollar has four quarters.
**e.** A ring contains 58% by mass gold.

**1.49** Write the conversion factors for each of the following statements:
**a.** A bee flies at an average speed of 3.5 m per second.
**b.** The daily requirement for potassium is 3500 mg.
**c.** An automobile traveled 46.0 km on 1.0 gal of gasoline.
**d.** The label on a bottle reads 50 mg Atenolol per tablet.
**e.** The pesticide level in plums was 29 ppb.

**1.50** Write the conversion factors for each of the following statements:
**a.** The label on a bottle reads 10 mg of furosemide per mL.
**b.** The daily requirement for iodine is 150 μg.
**c.** The nitrate level in well water was 32 ppm.
**d.** A DVD contains 17 gigabytes of information.
**e.** The price of a gallon of gas is $3.19.

## 1.7 Problem Solving

**LEARNING GOAL**

Use conversion factors to change from one unit to another.

The process of problem solving in chemistry often requires the conversion of an initial quantity given in one unit to the same quantity but in different units. By using one or more of the conversion factors we discussed in the previous section, the initial unit can be converted to the final unit:

Given quantity × One or more conversion factors = Desired quantity

Initial unit ⟶ Final unit

You may use a sequence similar to the steps in the following guide to problem solving (GPS):

**Guide to Problem Solving (GPS) Using Conversion Factors**

**STEP 1** **Given/Need** State the initial unit given in the problem and the final unit needed.

**STEP 2** **Plan** Write out a sequence of units that starts with the initial unit and progresses to the final unit for the answer. Be sure you can supply the equality for each unit conversion.

**STEP 3** **Equalities/Conversion Factors** For each change of unit in your plan, state the equality and corresponding conversion factors. Recall that equalities are derived from the metric (SI) system, the U.S. system, and statements within a problem.

**STEP 4** **Set Up Problem** Write the initial quantity and unit, and set up conversion factors that connect the units. Be sure to arrange the units in each factor so the unit in the denominator cancels the preceding unit in the numerator. Check that the units cancel properly to give the final unit. Carry out the calculations, count the significant figures in each measured number, and give a final answer with the correct number of significant figures.

Suppose a problem requires the conversion of 164 lb to kilograms. One part of this statement (164 lb) is the given quantity (initial unit), while another part (kilograms) is the final unit needed for the answer. Once you identify these units, you can determine which equalities you need to convert the initial unit to the final unit.

**STEP 1** **Given** 164 lb **Need** kg

**STEP 2** **Plan** It is helpful to decide on a plan of units. When we look at the initial units given and the final units needed, we see that one is a metric unit, and the other is a unit in the U.S. system of measurement. Therefore, the connecting conversion factor must be one that includes a metric and a U.S. unit.

lb | Metric–U.S. factor | kg

**STEP 3** **Equalities/Conversion Factors** From the discussion on U.S. and metric equalities, we can write the following equality and conversion factors:

$$1 \text{ kg} = 2.20 \text{ lb}$$

$$\frac{2.20 \text{ lb}}{1 \text{ kg}} \quad \text{and} \quad \frac{1 \text{ kg}}{2.20 \text{ lb}}$$

**STEP 4** **Set Up Problem** Now we can write the setup to solve the problem using the unit plan and a conversion factor. First, write down the initial unit, 164 lb. Then multiply by the conversion factor that has the unit lb in the denominator (bottom number) to cancel out the initial unit. The unit kg in the numerator (top number) gives the final unit for the answer.

Unit for answer goes here

$$164 \cancel{\text{lb}} \quad \times \quad \frac{1 \text{ kg}}{2.20 \cancel{\text{lb}}} \quad = \quad 74.5 \text{ kg}$$

Given (initial unit) | Conversion factor (cancels initial unit) | Answer (desired unit)

Look at how the units cancel. The unit that you want in the answer is the one that remains after all the other units have cancelled out. This is a helpful way to check that a problem is set up properly.

$$\cancel{\text{lb}} \times \frac{\text{kg}}{\cancel{\text{lb}}} = \text{kg} \quad \text{Unit needed for answer}$$

The calculation done on a calculator gives the numerical part of the answer. The calculator answer is adjusted to give a final answer with the proper number of significant figures.

$$164 \times \frac{1}{2.20} = 74.54545455 = 74.5$$

3 SFs | 3 SFs | Calculator display | 3 SFs (rounded)

The value of 74.5 combined with the final unit, kg, gives the final answer of 74.5 kg. With few exceptions, answers to numerical problems contain a number and a unit.

**CONCEPT CHECK 1.7**

### ■ Cancellation of Units

Cancel the units in the following set up and give the unit of the final answer.

$$3.5 \text{ L} \times \frac{1 \times 10^3 \text{ mL}}{1 \text{ L}} \times \frac{0.48 \text{ g}}{1 \text{ mL}} \times \frac{1 \times 10^3 \text{ mg}}{1 \text{ g}} =$$

ANSWER

All like units cancel to give mg in the numerator as the final unit for the answer.

$$3.5 \cancel{\text{L}} \times \frac{1 \times 10^3 \cancel{\text{mL}}}{1 \cancel{\text{L}}} \times \frac{0.48 \cancel{\text{g}}}{1 \cancel{\text{mL}}} \times \frac{1 \times 10^3 \text{ mg}}{1 \cancel{\text{g}}} = \text{final unit is mg}$$

SAMPLE PROBLEM 1.11

### Problem Solving Using Metric Factors

The daily recommended amount of potassium in the diet is 3500 mg. How many grams of potassium are needed each day?

SOLUTION

**STEP 1** **Given** 3500 mg **Need** g

**STEP 2** **Plan** When we look at the initial units given and the final units needed, we see that both are metric units. Therefore, the connecting conversion factor must relate two metric units.

mg → Metric factor → g

**STEP 3** **Equalities/Conversion Factors** From the discussion on prefixes and metric equalities, we can write the following equality and conversion factors:

$$1\text{ g} = 1000\text{ mg}$$

$$\frac{1\text{ g}}{1000\text{ mg}} \quad \text{and} \quad \frac{1000\text{ mg}}{1\text{ g}}$$

**STEP 4** **Set Up Problem** We write the setup using the unit plan and a conversion factor starting with the initial unit, 3500 mg. The final answer (g) is obtained by using the conversion factor that cancels the unit mg. Round off the answer to give the proper number of significant figures.

Unit for answer goes here

$$3500\ \cancel{\text{mg}} \times \frac{1\text{ g}}{1000\ \cancel{\text{mg}}} = 3.5\text{ g}$$

Given — Metric factor — Answer

STUDY CHECK

If 1890 mL of orange juice are prepared from orange juice concentrate, how many liters of orange juice is that?

**Guide to Problem Solving Using Conversion Factors**

STEP 1 State the given and needed units.

STEP 2 Write a unit plan to convert the given unit to the final unit.

STEP 3 State the equalities and conversion factors needed to cancel units.

STEP 4 Set up problem to cancel units and calculate answer.

## Using Two or More Conversion Factors

In many problems, two or more conversion factors are needed to complete the change of units. In setting up these problems, one factor follows the other. Each factor is arranged to cancel the preceding unit until the final unit is obtained. Up to this point, we have used the conversion factors one at a time and calculated an answer. You can work all problems in single steps; if you do, be sure to keep one or two extra digits in the intermediate answers and round off only the final answer to the correct number of significant figures. A more efficient way to do these problems is to use a series of two or more conversion factors set up so that the unit in the denominator of each factor cancels the unit in the preceding numerator. Both approaches are illustrated in the following sample problem.

SAMPLE PROBLEM 1.12

### Problem Solving Using Two Factors

During a volcanic eruption on Mauna Loa, Hawaii, the lava flowed at a rate of 33 meters per minute. At this rate, how far, in kilometers, can the lava travel in 45 minutes?

SOLUTION

**STEP 1** **Given** 45 min **Need** km

**STEP 2** **Plan** min → Rate factor → m → Metric factor → km

**STEP 3** **Equalities/Conversion Factors** In the problem, the information for the rate of lava flow is given as 33 m/min. We will use this rate as one of the equalities as well as the metric equality for meters and kilometers and write conversion factors for each.

$$1 \text{ min} = 33 \text{ m} \qquad \frac{1 \text{ min}}{33 \text{ m}} \text{ and } \frac{33 \text{ m}}{1 \text{ min}}$$

$$1 \text{ km} = 1000 \text{ m} \qquad \frac{1 \text{ km}}{1000 \text{ m}} \text{ and } \frac{1000 \text{ m}}{1 \text{ km}}$$

**STEP 4** **Set Up Problem** Set up the problem using the rate as a conversion factor to cancel minutes. Then use the metric factor to obtain kilometers in the final factor. Working in single steps, we can use the rate factor to convert from minutes to meters:

$$45 \cancel{\text{min}} \times \frac{33 \text{ m}}{1 \cancel{\text{min}}} = 1500 \text{ m}$$

Then we use the metric factor to cancel meters and give kilometers as the needed unit:

$$1500 \cancel{\text{m}} \times \frac{1 \text{ km}}{1000 \cancel{\text{m}}} = 1.5 \text{ km}$$

When set up as a series, the first factor cancels minutes, and the second factor cancels meters, which gives kilometers as the final unit for the answer.

$$\cancel{\text{min}} \times \frac{\cancel{\text{m}}}{\cancel{\text{min}}} \times \frac{\text{km}}{\cancel{\text{m}}} = \text{km}$$

$$45 \cancel{\text{min}} \times \frac{33 \cancel{\text{m}}}{1 \cancel{\text{min}}} \times \frac{1 \text{ km}}{1000 \cancel{\text{m}}} = 1.485 \text{ km} = 1.5 \text{ km}$$

| Given (initial unit) 2 SFs | Rate factor 2 SFs | Metric factor exact | Calculator answer | Answer (desired unit) 2 SFs |
|---|---|---|---|---|

The calculations are done in a sequence on a calculator to give the numerical part of the answer. The calculator answer is adjusted to give a final answer with the proper number of SFs.

| 45 | × | 33 | ÷ | 1000 | = | 1.485 | = | 1.5 |
|---|---|---|---|---|---|---|---|---|
| 2 SFs | | 2 SFs | | Exact | | Calculator display | | 2 SFs (rounded) |

STUDY CHECK

One medium bran muffin contains 4.2 g of fiber. How many ounces (oz) of fiber are obtained by eating three medium bran muffins if 1 lb = 16 oz? (*Hint*: number of muffins → g of fiber → lb → oz.)

Using a sequence of two or more conversion factors is an efficient way to set up and solve problems, especially if you are using a calculator. Once you have the problem set up, the calculations can be done without writing out the intermediate values. This process is worth practicing until you understand unit cancellation and the mathematical calculations.

## Clinical Calculations Using Conversion Factors

Conversion factors are also useful for calculating medications. For example, if an antibiotic is available in 5-mg tablets, the dosage can be written as a conversion factor: 5 mg/1 tablet. In many hospitals, the apothecary unit of *grain* (gr) is still in use; there are 65 mg in 1 gr. When you do a medication problem, you often start with a doctor's order that contains the quantity to give the patient. The medication dosage is used as a conversion factor.

SAMPLE PROBLEM 1.13

## Clinical Factors from a Word Problem

Synthroid is used as a replacement or supplemental therapy for diminished thyroid function. A dosage of 0.200 mg is prescribed with tablets that contain 50 $\mu$g of Synthroid. How many tablets are required to provide the prescribed medication?

SOLUTION

**STEP 1** **Given** 0.200 mg of Synthroid **Need** tablets

**STEP 2** **Plan** mg → Metric factor → $\mu$g → Clinical factor → tablets

**STEP 3** **Equalities/Conversion Factors** In the problem, the information for the dosage is given as 50 $\mu$g per tablet. We will use this as one of the equalities as well as the metric equality for milligrams and micrograms and write conversion factors for each.

$$1\text{ mg} = 1000\ \mu\text{g}$$
$$\frac{1\text{ mg}}{1000\ \mu\text{g}} \quad\text{and}\quad \frac{1000\ \mu\text{g}}{1\text{ mg}}$$

$$1\text{ tablet} = 50\ \mu\text{g}$$
$$\frac{1\text{ tablet}}{50\ \mu\text{g}} \quad\text{and}\quad \frac{50\ \mu\text{g}}{1\text{ tablet}}$$

**STEP 4** **Set Up Problem** The problem can be set up using the metric factor to cancel "milligrams," and then the clinical factor to obtain "tablets" as the final unit.

$$0.200\ \cancel{\text{mg}} \times \frac{1000\ \cancel{\mu\text{g}}}{1\ \cancel{\text{mg}}} \times \frac{1\text{ tablet}}{50\ \cancel{\mu\text{g}}} = 4\text{ tablets}$$

STUDY CHECK

An antibiotic dosage of 500 mg is ordered. If the antibiotic is supplied in liquid form as 250 mg in 5.0 mL, how many mL would be given?

SAMPLE PROBLEM 1.14

## Using a Percent as a Conversion Factor

Bronze is 80.0% by mass copper and 20.0% by mass tin. A sculptor is preparing to cast a figure that requires 1.75 lb of bronze. How many grams of copper are needed for the bronze figure?

SOLUTION

**STEP 1** **Given** 1.75 lb of bronze **Need** g of copper

**STEP 2** **Plan** lb of bronze → Metric–U.S. factor → g of bronze → Percent factor → g of copper

**STEP 3** **Equalities/Conversion Factors** Now we can write the equalities and conversion factors. One is the U.S.–metric factor for g and lb. The second is the percent factor derived from the information given in the problem.

$$1\text{ lb of bronze} = 454\text{ g of bronze}$$
$$\frac{454\text{ g bronze}}{1\text{ lb bronze}} \quad\text{and}\quad \frac{1\text{ lb bronze}}{454\text{ g bronze}}$$

$$100\text{ g of bronze} = 80.0\text{ g of copper}$$
$$\frac{80.0\text{ g copper}}{100\text{ g bronze}} \quad\text{and}\quad \frac{100\text{ g bronze}}{80.0\text{ g copper}}$$

**STEP 4** **Set Up Problem** We can set up the problem using conversion factors to cancel each unit, starting with lb bronze, until we obtain the final factor, g copper, in the numerator. After we count the significant figures in the measured quantities, we write the final answer with three significant figures.

$$\underset{\text{3 SFs}}{1.75\ \cancel{\text{lb bronze}}} \times \underset{\text{3 SFs}}{\frac{454\ \cancel{\text{g bronze}}}{1\ \cancel{\text{lb bronze}}}} \times \underset{\text{3 SFs}}{\frac{80.0\ \text{g copper}}{100\ \cancel{\text{g bronze}}}} = \underset{\text{3 SFs}}{636\ \text{g of copper}}$$

STUDY CHECK

A lean hamburger is 22% fat by weight. How many grams of fat are in 0.25 lb of the hamburger?

## QUESTIONS AND PROBLEMS

### Problem Solving

**1.51** When you convert one unit to another, how do you know which unit of the conversion factor to place in the denominator?

**1.52** When you convert one unit to another, how do you know which unit of the conversion factor to place in the numerator?

**1.53** Use metric conversion factors to solve the following problems:
- **a.** The height of a student is 175 cm. How tall is the student in meters?
- **b.** A cooler has a volume of 5500 mL. What is the capacity of the cooler in liters?
- **c.** A hummingbird has a mass of 0.0055 kg. What is the mass of the hummingbird in grams?

**1.54** Use metric conversion factors to solve the following problems:
- **a.** The daily requirement of phosphorus is 800 mg. How many grams of phosphorus are recommended?
- **b.** A glass of orange juice contains 0.85 dL of juice. How many milliliters of orange juice is that?
- **c.** A package of chocolate instant pudding contains 2840 mg of sodium. How many grams of sodium is that?

**1.55** Solve the following problems using one or more conversion factors:
- **a.** A container holds 0.750 qt of liquid. How many milliliters of lemonade will it hold?
- **b.** In England, a person is weighed in stones. If one stone has a weight of 14.0 lb, what is the mass, in kilograms, of a person who weighs 11.8 stones?
- **c.** The femur, or thighbone, is the longest bone in the body. In a 6-ft-tall person, the femur is 19.5 in. long. What is the length of that femur in millimeters?
- **d.** How many inches thick is an arterial wall that measures 0.50 $\mu$m?

**1.56** Solve the following problems using one or more conversion factors:
- **a.** You need 4.0 ounces of a steroid ointment. If there are 16 oz in 1 lb, how many grams of ointment does the pharmacist need to prepare?
- **b.** During surgery, a person receives 5.0 pints of plasma. How many milliliters of plasma were given?
- **c.** Solar flares containing hot gases can rise to 120 000 miles above the surface of the sun. What is that distance in kilometers?
- **d.** A filled gas tank contains 18.5 gallons of unleaded fuel. If a car uses 46 L, how many gallons of fuel remain in the tank?

**1.57** The singles portion of a tennis court is 27.0 ft wide and 78.0 ft long.

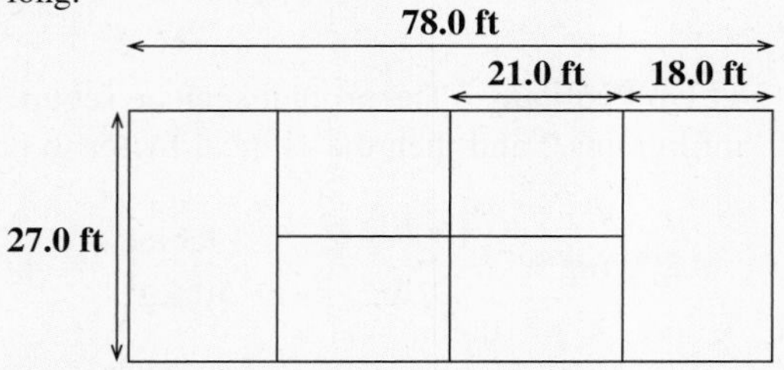


- **a.** What is the length of the court in meters?
- **b.** What is the area of the court in square meters ($m^2$)?
- **c.** If a serve is measured at 185 km per hour, how many seconds does it take for the tennis ball to travel the length of the court?

**1.58** A football field is 300 feet long between goal lines.

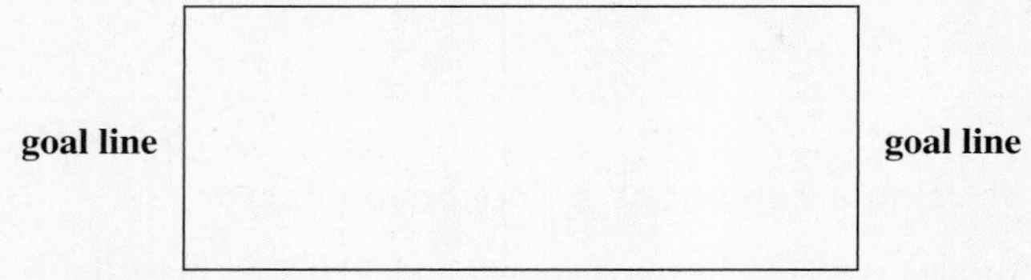


- **a.** How many meters does a player run if he catches the ball on his own goal line and scores a touchdown?
- **b.** If a player catches the football and runs 45 yards, how many meters did he gain?
- **c.** If a player runs at a speed of 36 km/h, how many seconds does it take to run from the 50-yard line to the 20-yard line?

**1.59** Using conversion factors, solve the following clinical problems:
- **a.** You have used 250 L of distilled water for a dialysis patient. How many gallons of water is that?
- **b.** A patient needs 0.024 g of a sulfa drug. There are 8-mg tablets in stock. How many tablets should be given?
- **c.** The daily dose of ampicillin for the treatment of an ear infection is 115 mg/kg of body weight. What is the daily dose, in mg, for a 34-lb child?

**1.60** Using conversion factors, solve the following clinical problems:
- **a.** The physician has ordered 1.0 g of tetracycline to be given every 6 hours to a patient. If your stock on hand is 500-mg tablets, how many will you need for 1 day's treatment?
- **b.** An intramuscular medication is given at 5.00 mg/kg of body weight. If you give 425 mg of medication to a patient, what is the patient's weight in pounds?

c. A physician has ordered 325 mg of atropine, intramuscularly. If atropine were available as 0.50 g/mL of solution, how many milliliters would you need to give?

1.61 a. Oxygen makes up 46.7% by mass of Earth's crust. How many grams of oxygen are present if a sample of Earth's crust has a mass of 325 g?
b. Magnesium makes up 2.1% by mass of Earth's crust. How many grams of magnesium are present if a sample of Earth's crust has a mass of 1.25 g?
c. A plant fertilizer contains 15% by mass nitrogen (N). In a container of soluble plant food, there are 10.0 oz of fertilizer. How many grams of nitrogen are in the container?
d. In a candy factory, the nutty chocolate bars contain 22.0% by mass pecans. If 5.0 kg of pecans were used for candy last Tuesday, how many lb of nutty chocolate bars were made?

**1.62 a.** Water is 11.2% by mass hydrogen. How many kilograms of water would contain 5.0 g of hydrogen?
**b.** Water is 88.8% by mass oxygen. How many grams of water would contain 2.25 kg of oxygen?
**c.** Blueberry fiber cakes contain 51% dietary fiber. If a package with a net weight of 12 ounces contains 6 cakes, how many grams of fiber are in each cake?
**d.** A jar of crunchy peanut butter contains 1.43 kg of peanut butter. If you use 8.0% of the peanut butter for a sandwich, how many ounces of peanut butter did you take out of the container?

## 1.8 Density

LEARNING GOAL

Calculate the density or specific gravity of a substance and use the density or specific gravity to calculate the mass or volume of a substance.

Differences in density determine whether an object will sink or float. In Figure 1.12, the density of lead is greater than the density of water, and the lead object sinks. The cork floats because cork is less dense than water.

The mass and volume of any object can be measured. However, the separate measurements do not tell us how tightly packed the substance might be. If we compare the mass of the object to its volume, we obtain a relationship called **density**:

$$\text{Density} = \frac{\text{mass of substance}}{\text{volume of substance}}$$

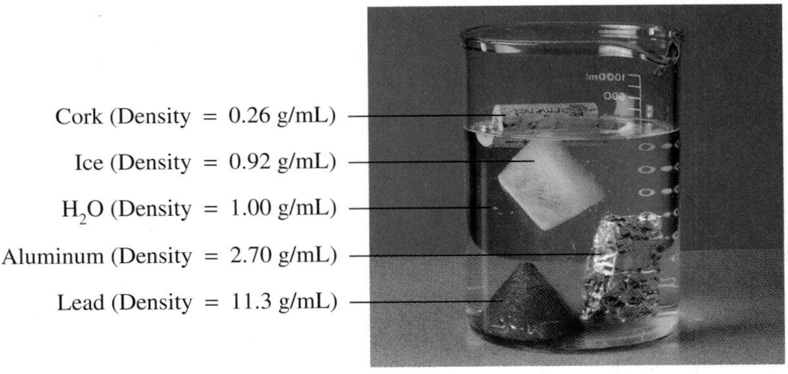


**FIGURE 1.12** Objects that sink in water are more dense than water; objects float if they are less dense.
Q Why does a cork float and a piece of lead sink?

In the metric system, the densities of solids and liquids are usually expressed as grams per cubic centimeter ($g/cm^3$) or grams per milliliter (g/mL). The density of gases is usually stated as grams per liter (g/L). Table 1.11 gives the densities of some common substances.

**TABLE 1.11** Densities of Some Common Substances

| Solids (at 25 °C) | Density (g/mL) | Liquids (at 25 °C) | Density (g/mL) | Gases (at 0 °C, 1 atm) | Density (g/L) |
|---|---|---|---|---|---|
| Cork | 0.26 | Gasoline | 0.66 | Hydrogen | 0.090 |
| Wood (maple) | 0.75 | Ethyl alcohol | 0.79 | Helium | 0.179 |
| Ice (at 0 °C) | 0.92 | Olive oil | 0.92 | Methane | 0.714 |
| Sugar | 1.59 | Water (at 4 °C) | 1.00 | Neon | 0.90 |
| Bone | 1.80 | Plasma (blood) | 1.03 | Nitrogen | 1.25 |
| Aluminum | 2.70 | Milk | 1.04 | Air (dry) | 1.29 |
| Cement | 3.00 | Mercury | 13.6 | Oxygen | 1.43 |
| Diamond | 3.52 | | | Carbon dioxide | 1.96 |
| Silver | 10.5 | | | | |
| Lead | 11.3 | | | | |
| Gold | 19.3 | | | | |

CONCEPT CHECK 1.8

## Density

(a) (b)

**a.** In drawing (a), the gray cube has a density of 4.5 g/cm$^3$. Is the density of the green cube the same, less than, or greater than the gray cube?
**b.** In drawing (b), the gray cube has a density of 4.5 g/cm$^3$. Is the density of the green cube the same, less than, or greater than the gray cube?

ANSWER

**a.** The green cube has the same volume as the gray cube, but has a greater mass. Thus, the green cube has a density that is greater than the density of the gray cube.
**b.** The green cube has the same mass as the gray cube, but the green cube has a greater volume. Thus, the green cube has a density that is less than the density of the gray cube.

SAMPLE PROBLEM 1.15

## Calculating Density

A copper sample has a mass of 44.65 g and a volume of 5.0 mL. What is the density of copper?

SOLUTION

**Guide to Calculating Density**

STEP 1 State the given and needed quantities.

STEP 2 Write the density expression.

STEP 3 Express mass in grams and volume in milliliters (mL) or cm$^3$.

STEP 4 Substitute mass and volume into density expression and solve.

STEP 1 **Given** mass = 44.65 g; volume = 5.0 mL **Need** density (g/mL)

STEP 2 **Plan** To calculate density, substitute the mass (g) and the volume (mL) of the copper sample into the expression for density.

STEP 3 **Equality/Conversion Factor**

$$\text{Density} = \frac{\text{mass of substance}}{\text{volume of substance}}$$

STEP 4 **Set Up Problem**

$$\text{Density} = \frac{\overset{4\text{ SFs}}{44.65\text{ g}}}{\underset{2\text{ SFs}}{5.0\text{ mL}}} = \frac{8.9\text{ g}}{1\text{ mL}} = \overset{2\text{ SFs}}{8.9\text{ g/mL}}$$

STUDY CHECK

What is the density (g/cm$^3$) of a silver bar that has a mass of 294 g and a volume of 28.0 cm$^3$?

## Density of Solids

The density of a solid is calculated from its mass and volume. When a solid is completely submerged, it displaces a volume of water that is equal to the volume of the solid. In Figure 1.13, the water level rises from 35.5 mL to 45.0 mL. This means that 9.5 mL of water is displaced and that the volume of the object is 9.5 mL. The density of the zinc is calculated as follows:

$$\text{Density} = \frac{68.60 \text{ g zinc}}{9.5 \text{ mL}} = 7.2 \text{ g/mL}$$

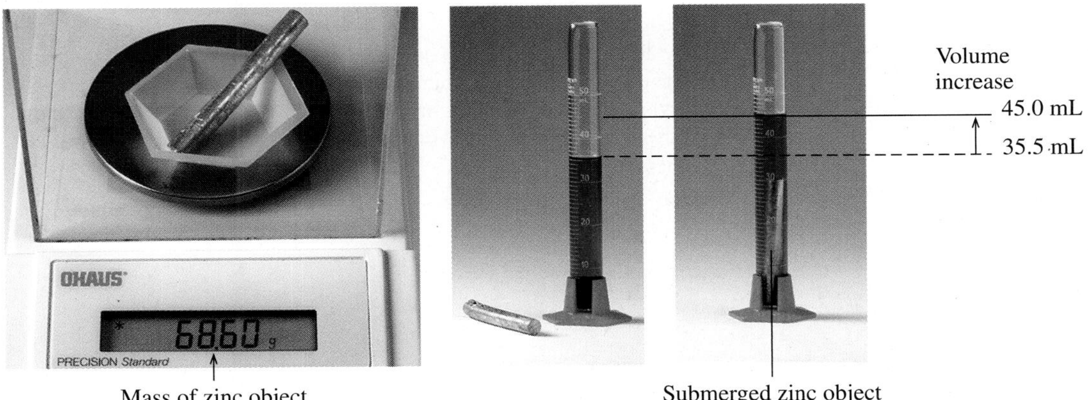


**FIGURE 1.13** The density of a solid can be determined by volume displacement because a submerged object displaces a volume of water equal to its own volume.

**Q** How is the volume of the zinc object determined?

### SAMPLE PROBLEM 1.16

#### Using Volume Displacement to Calculate Density

A lead weight used in the belt of a scuba diver has a mass of 226 g. When the weight is placed in a graduated cylinder containing 200.0 mL of water, the water level rises to 220.0 mL. What is the density of the lead weight (g/mL)?

SOLUTION

**STEP 1** **Given** mass = 226 g; water level before object submerged = 200.0 mL; water level after object submerged = 220.0 mL **Need** density (g/mL)

**STEP 2** **Plan** To calculate density, substitute the mass (g) and the volume (mL) of the lead weight into the expression for density.

**STEP 3** **Equality/Conversion Factor**

$$\text{Density} = \frac{\text{mass of substance}}{\text{volume of substance}}$$

**STEP 4** **Set Up Problem** The volume of the lead weight is equal to the volume of water displaced, which is calculated as follows:

| | | |
|---|---|---|
| | Water level after object submerged | = 220.0 mL |
| − | Water level before object submerged | = 200.0 mL |
| | Water displaced (volume of lead weight) | = 20.0 mL |

The density is calculated by dividing the mass (g) by the volume (mL). Be sure to use the volume of water the object displaced and not the original volume of water.

$$\text{Density} = \frac{226 \text{ g}}{\underset{3 \text{ SFs}}{20.0 \text{ mL}}} = \frac{11.3 \text{ g}}{1 \text{ mL}} = \underset{3 \text{ SFs}}{11.3 \text{ g/mL}}$$

STUDY CHECK

A total of 0.500 lb of glass marbles is added to 425 mL of water. The water level rises to a volume of 528 mL. What is the density (g/mL) of the glass marbles?

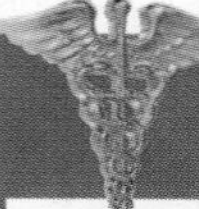

## HEALTH NOTE

### Bone Density

The density of our bones determines their health and strength. Our bones are constantly gaining and losing minerals such as calcium, magnesium, and phosphate. In childhood, bones form at a faster rate than they break down. As we age, the breakdown of bone occurs more rapidly than new bone forms. As the loss of bone minerals increases, bones begin to thin, causing a decrease in mass and density. Thinner bones lack strength, which increases the risk of fracture. Hormonal changes, disease, and certain medications can also contribute to the thinning of bone. Eventually, a condition of severe thinning of bone known as *osteoporosis* may occur. *Scanning electron micrographs* (SEMs) show (a) normal bone and (b) bone in osteoporosis caused by the loss of bone minerals.

Bone density is often determined by passing low-dose X-rays through the narrow part at the top of the femur (hip) and the spine (c). These locations are where fractures are more likely to occur, especially as we age. Bones with high density will block more of the X-rays compared to bones that are less dense. The results of a bone density test are compared to a healthy young adult as well as to other people of the same age.

Recommendations to improve bone strength include supplements of calcium and vitamin D and medications such as Fosamax, Evista, or Actonel. Weight-bearing exercise such as walking and lifting weights can also improve muscle strength, which in turn, increases bone strength.

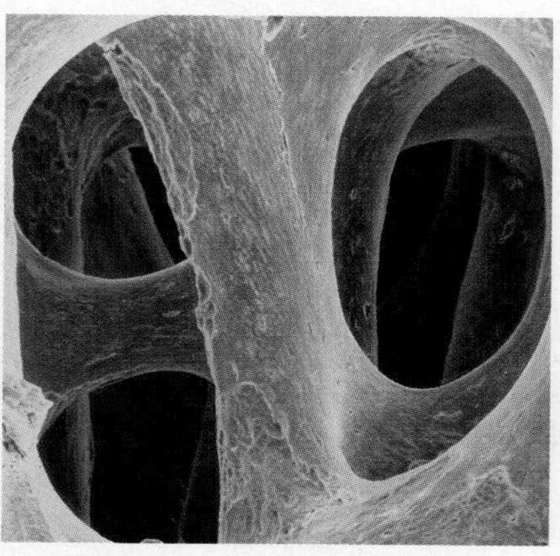

(a)

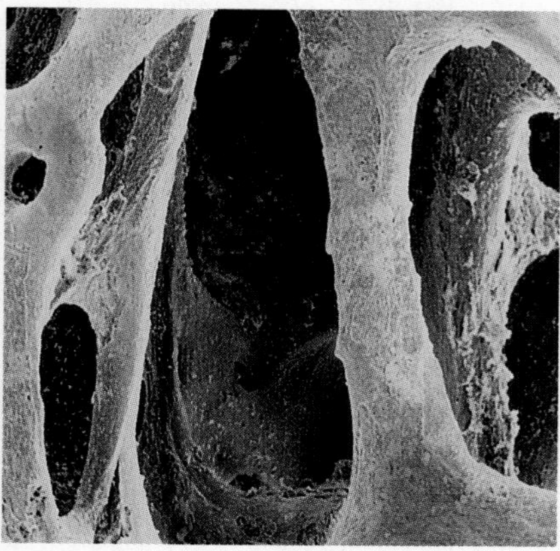

(b)

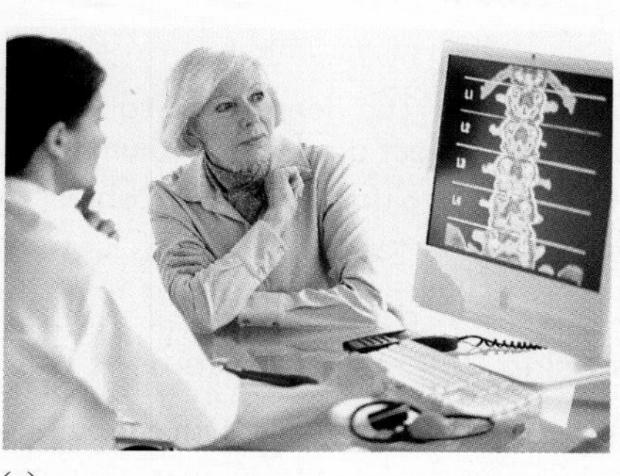

(c)

## Problem Solving Using Density

Density can be used as a conversion factor. For example, if the volume and the density of a sample are known, the mass in grams of the sample can be calculated.

## EXPLORE YOUR WORLD

### Sink or Float?

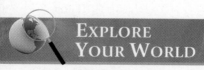

1. Fill a large container or bucket with water. Place a can of diet and a can of nondiet soft drink in the water. What happens? Using information on the label, how might you account for your observations?
2. Design an experiment to determine the substance that is the most dense in each of the following:
   **a.** water and vegetable oil
   **b.** water and ice
   **c.** rubbing alcohol and ice
   **d.** vegetable oil, water, and ice

**SAMPLE PROBLEM 1.17**

**■ Problem Solving Using Density**

If the density of milk is 1.04 g/mL, how many grams of milk are in 0.50 qt of milk?

SOLUTION

**STEP 1** **Given** 0.50 qt **Need** g

**STEP 2** **Plan**

qt → Metric–U.S. factor → L → Metric factor → mL → Density factor → g

**STEP 3** **Equalities/Conversion Factors**

$$1\text{ L} = 1.06\text{ qt} \qquad \frac{1\text{ L}}{1.06\text{ qt}} \text{ and } \frac{1.06\text{ qt}}{1\text{ L}}$$

$$1\text{ L} = 1000\text{ mL} \qquad \frac{1\text{ L}}{1000\text{ mL}} \text{ and } \frac{1000\text{ mL}}{1\text{ L}}$$

$$1\text{ mL} = 1.04\text{ g} \qquad \frac{1\text{ mL}}{1.04\text{ g}} \text{ and } \frac{1.04\text{ g}}{1\text{ mL}}$$

**STEP 4** **Set Up Problem**

$$0.50\,\cancel{\text{qt}} \times \frac{1\,\cancel{\text{L}}}{1.06\,\cancel{\text{qt}}} \times \frac{1000\,\cancel{\text{mL}}}{1\,\cancel{\text{L}}} \times \frac{1.04\text{ g}}{1\,\cancel{\text{mL}}} = 490\text{ g } (4.9 \times 10^2\text{ g})$$

2 SFs 3 SFs Exact 3 SFs 2 SFs

STUDY CHECK

How many mL of mercury are in a thermometer that contains 20.4 g of mercury? (See Table 1.11 for the density of mercury.)

Guide to Using Den.

STEP 1 State the given and needed quantities.

STEP 2 Write a plan to calculate the needed quantity.

STEP 3 Write equalities and their conversion factors including density.

STEP 4 Set up problem to solve for the needed quantity.

## Specific Gravity

**Specific gravity (sp gr)** is a ratio between the density of a substance and the density of water. Specific gravity is calculated by dividing the density of a sample by the density of water, which is 1.00 g/mL at 4 °C. A substance with a specific gravity of 1.00 has the same density as water. A substance with a specific gravity of 3.00 is three times as dense as water, whereas a substance with a specific gravity of 0.50 is just one-half as dense as water.

$$\text{Specific gravity} = \frac{\text{density of sample}}{\text{density of water}}$$

In the calculations for specific gravity, the units of density must match. Then all units cancel to leave only a number. Specific gravity is one of the few unitless values you will encounter in chemistry.

An instrument called a *hydrometer* is often used to measure the specific gravity of fluids such as battery fluid or a sample of urine. In Figure 1.14, a hydrometer is used to measure the specific gravity of a fluid.

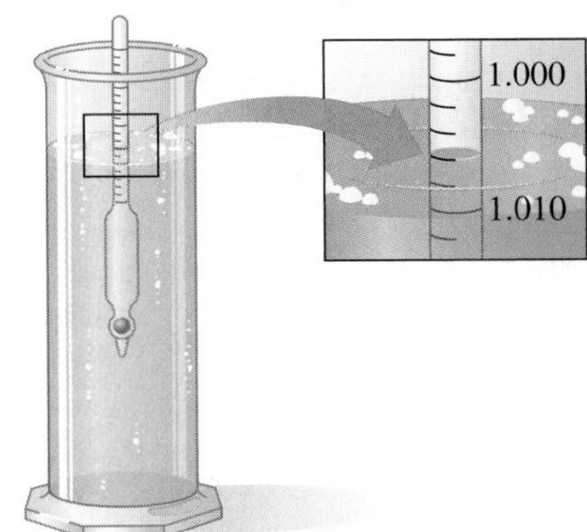


**FIGURE 1.14** When the specific gravity of beer measures 1.010 or less with a hydrometer, the fermentation process is complete.

**Q** If the hydrometer reading is 1.006, what is the density of the liquid?

SAMPLE PROBLEM 1.18

### Problem Solving with Specific Gravity

John took 2.0 teaspoons (tsp) of cough syrup (sp gr 1.20) for a persistent cough. If there is 5.0 mL in 1 tsp, what was the mass (in grams) of the cough syrup?

SOLUTION

**STEP 1** **Given** 2.0 tsp **Need** g

**STEP 2** **Plan** tsp → Metric–U.S. factor → mL → Density factor → g

**STEP 3** **Equalities/Conversion Factors** For problem solving, it is convenient to convert the specific gravity value (1.20) to density.

$$\text{Density} = (\text{sp gr}) \times 1.00\text{ g/mL} = 1.20\text{ g/mL}$$

$$1\text{ tsp} = 5.0\text{ mL} \qquad \frac{5.0\text{ mL}}{1\text{ tsp}} \text{ and } \frac{1\text{ tsp}}{5.0\text{ mL}}$$

$$1\text{ mL} = 1.20\text{ g} \qquad \frac{1\text{ mL}}{1.20\text{ g}} \text{ and } \frac{1.20\text{ g}}{1\text{ mL}}$$

**STEP 4** **Set Up Problem**

$$2.0\ \cancel{\text{tsp}} \times \frac{5.0\ \cancel{\text{mL}}}{1\ \cancel{\text{tsp}}} \times \frac{1.20\ \text{g}}{1\ \cancel{\text{mL}}} = 12\ \text{g of syrup}$$

2 SFs — 2 SFs — 3 SFs — 2 SFs

STUDY CHECK

An ebony carving has a mass of 275 g. If ebony has a specific gravity of 1.33, what is the volume of the carving?

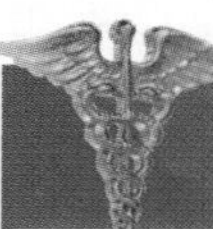

## HEALTH NOTE

### Determination of Percentage of Body Fat

Body mass is made up of protoplasm, extracellular fluid, bone, and adipose tissue. One way to determine the amount of adipose tissue is to measure the whole-body density. After the on-land mass of the body is determined, the underwater body mass is obtained by submerging the person in water. Because water helps support the body by giving it buoyancy, the underwater body mass is less. A higher percentage of body fat will make a person more buoyant, causing the underwater mass to be even lower. This occurs because fat has a lower density than the rest of the body.

The difference between the on-land mass and underwater mass, known as the *buoyant force*, is used to determine the body volume. Then the mass and volume of the person are used to calculate body density. For example, suppose a 70.0-kg person has a body volume of 66.7 L.

The body density is calculated as

$$\frac{\text{Body mass}}{\text{Body volume}} = \frac{70.0\ \text{kg}}{66.7\ \text{L}}$$
$$= 1.05\ \text{kg/L or } 1.05\ \text{g/mL}$$

When the body density is determined, it is compared with a chart that correlates the percentage of adipose tissue with body density. A person with a body density of 1.05 g/mL has 21% body fat, according to such a chart. Athletes use this procedure to determine exercise and diet programs.

## QUESTIONS AND PROBLEMS

### Density

1.63 In an old trunk, you find a piece of metal that you think may be aluminum, silver, or lead. In lab you find it has a mass of 217 g and a volume of 19.2 cm$^3$. Using Table 1.11, what is the metal you found?

**1.64** Suppose you have two 100-mL graduated cylinders. In each cylinder there is 40.0 mL of water. You also have two cubes: One is lead, and the other is aluminum. Each cube measures 2.0 cm on each side. After you carefully lower each cube into the water of its own cylinder, what will the new water level be in each of the cylinders?

1.65 Determine the density (g/mL) for each of the following:

**a.** A 20.0 mL sample of a salt solution has a mass of 24.0 g.
**b.** A cube of butter weighs 0.250 lb and has a volume of 130. mL.
**c.** A gem has a mass of 45.0 g. When the gem is placed in a graduated cylinder containing 20.0 mL of water, the water level rises to 34.5 mL.
**d.** A syrup is added to an empty container with a mass of 115.25 g. When 0.100 pint of syrup is added, the total mass of the container and syrup is 182.48 g.

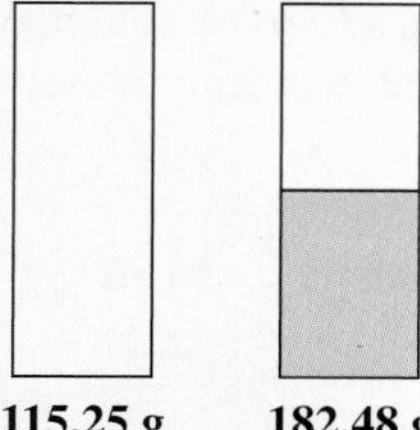


**1.66** Determine the density (g/mL) for each of the following:

**a.** A plastic material weighs 2.68 lb and has a volume of 3.5 L.
**b.** The fluid in a car battery if it has a volume of 125 mL and a mass of 155 g.
**c.** A 5.00-mL urine sample from a patient suffering from diabetes mellitus has a mass of 5.025 g.
**d.** A 10.00 L sample of oxygen gas has a mass of 0.014 kg.

**1.67** Use the density values in Table 1.11 to solve the following problems:

**a.** How many liters of ethanol contain 1.5 kg of alcohol?

**b.** How many grams of mercury are present in a barometer that holds 6.5 mL of mercury?

**c.** A sculptor has prepared a mold for casting a bronze figure. The figure has a volume of 225 mL. If bronze has a density of 7.8 g/mL, how many ounces of bronze are needed in the preparation of the bronze figure?

**d.** How many kilograms of gasoline fill a 12.0-gallon gas tank? (1 gallon = 4 qt)

**1.68** Use the density values in Table 1.11 to solve the following problems:

**a.** A graduated cylinder contains 28.0 mL of water. What is the new water level after 35.6 g of silver metal is submerged in the water?

**b.** A fish tank holds 35 gallons of water. How many pounds (lb) of water are in the fish tank?

**c.** The mass of an empty container is 88.25 g. The mass of the container and a liquid with a density of 0.758 g/mL is 150.50 g. What is the volume (mL) of the liquid in the container?

**d.** A cannon ball made of iron has a volume of 115 $cm^3$. If iron has a density of 7.86 g/$cm^3$, what is the mass, in kilograms, of the cannon ball?

**1.69** Solve the following specific gravity problems:

**a.** A urine sample has a density of 1.030 g/mL. What is the specific gravity of the sample?

**b.** A liquid has a volume of 40.0 mL and a mass of 45.0 g. What is the specific gravity of the liquid?

**c.** The specific gravity of a vegetable oil is 0.85. What is its density?

**1.70** Solve the following specific gravity problems:

**a.** A 5.0% glucose solution has a specific gravity of 1.02. What is the mass of 500. mL of glucose solution?

**b.** A bottle containing 325 g of cleaning solution is used for carpets. If the cleaning solution has a specific gravity of 0.850, what volume of solution was used?

**c.** Butter has a specific gravity of 0.86. What is the mass, in grams, of 2.15 L of butter?

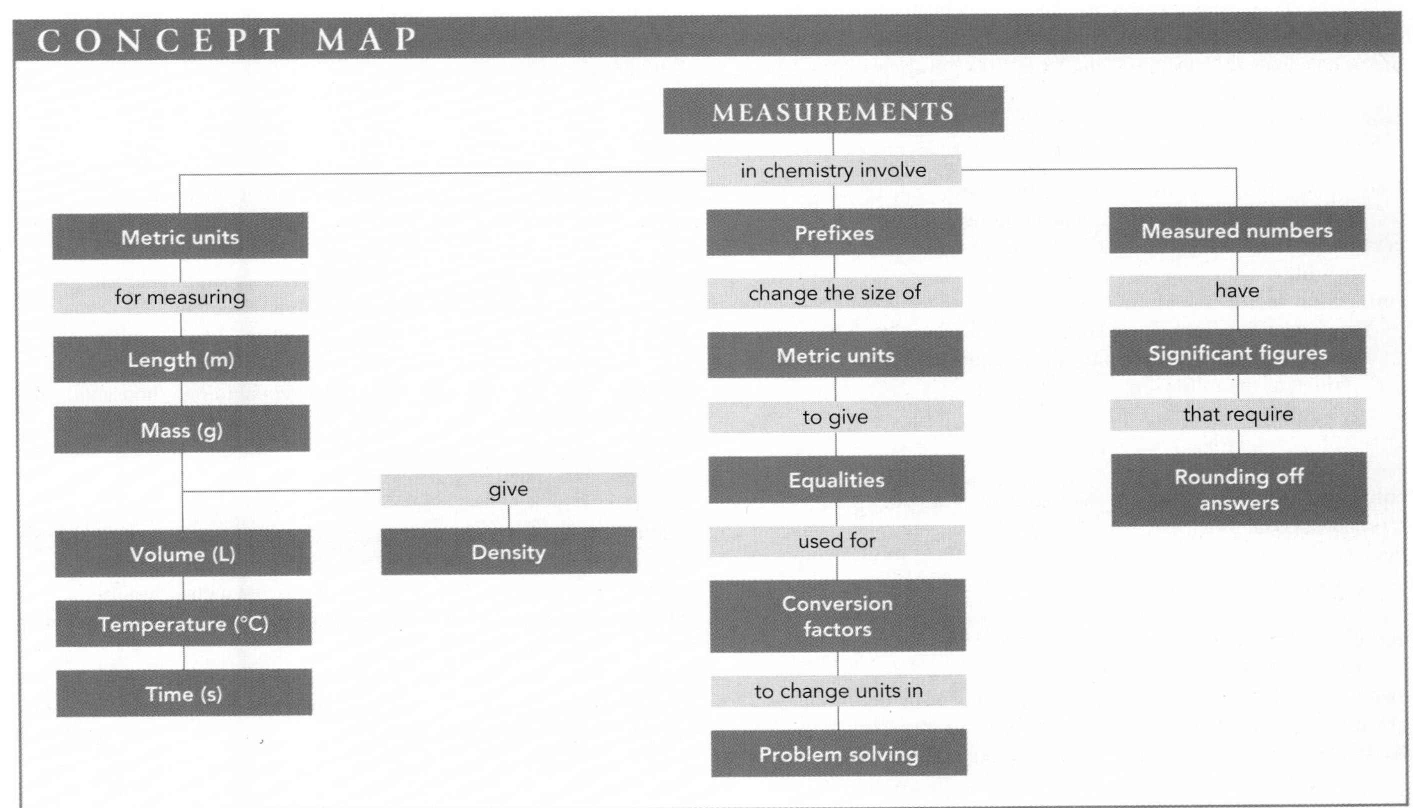


## CHAPTER REVIEW

### 1.1 Units of Measurement

**LEARNING GOAL:** *Write the names and abbreviations for the units used in measurements of length, volume, time, and mass.*

In science, physical quantities are described in units of the metric or International System (SI). Some important units are meter (m) for length, liter (L) for volume, gram (g) and kilogram (kg) for mass, degree Celsius (°C) and Kelvin (K) for temperature, and second(s) for time.

### 1.2 Scientific Notation

**LEARNING GOAL:** *Write a number in scientific notation.*

Large and small numbers can be written using scientific notation in which the decimal point is moved to give a coefficient between 1 and 9 and the number of decimal places moved shown as a power of 10. A large number will have a positive power of 10, while a small number will have a negative power of 10.

### 1.3 Measured Numbers and Significant Figures

**LEARNING GOAL:** *Determine the number of significant figures in measured numbers.*

A measured number is any number obtained by using a measuring device. An exact number is obtained by counting items or from a definition; no measuring device is used. Significant figures are the numbers reported in a measurement including the estimated digit. Zeros in front of a decimal number or at the end of a nondecimal number are not significant.

### 1.4 Significant Figures in Calculations

**LEARNING GOAL:** *Adjust calculated answers to the correct number of significant figures.*

In multiplication or division, the final answer is written so that it has the same number of significant figures as the measurement with the fewest significant figures. In addition or subtraction, the final answer is written so that it has the same number of decimal places as the measurement with the fewest decimal places.

### 1.5 Prefixes and Equalities

**LEARNING GOAL:** *Use the numerical values of prefixes to write a metric equality.*

Prefixes placed in front of a unit change the size of the unit by factors of 10. Prefixes such as *centi*, *milli*, and *micro* provide smaller units; prefixes such as *kilo* provide larger units. An equality relates two metric units that measure the same quantity of length, volume, or mass. Examples of metric equalities are 1 m = 100 cm, 1 L = 1000 mL, and 1 kg = 1000 g.

### 1.6 Writing Conversion Factors

**LEARNING GOAL:** *Write a conversion factor for two units that describe the same quantity.*

Conversion factors are used to express a relationship in the form of a fraction. Two factors can be written for any relationship in the metric or U.S. system. A percentage is written as a conversion factor by expressing matching units in the relationship as the parts to 100 parts of the whole. Extremely small percentage values are written as parts per million (ppm) or parts per billion (ppb).

### 1.7 Problem Solving

**LEARNING GOAL:** *Use conversion factors to change from one unit to another.*

Conversion factors are useful when changing a quantity expressed in one unit to a quantity expressed in another unit. In the process, a given unit is multiplied by one or more conversion factors that cancel units until the desired answer is obtained.

### 1.8 Density

**LEARNING GOAL:** *Calculate the density or specific gravity of a substance, and use the density or specific gravity to calculate the mass or volume of a substance.*

The density of a substance is a ratio of its mass to its volume, usually g/mL or g/cm$^3$. The units of density can be used as a factor to convert between the mass and volume of a substance. Specific gravity (sp gr) compares the density of a substance to the density of water, 1.00 g/mL.

## KEY TERMS

**Celsius (°C) temperature scale** A temperature scale on which water has a freezing point of 0 °C and a boiling point of 100 °C.

**centimeter (cm)** A unit of length in the metric system; there are 2.54 cm in 1 in.

**conversion factor** A ratio in which the numerator and denominator are quantities from an equality or given relationship. For example, the conversion factors for the relationship 1 kg = 2.20 lb are written as the following:

$$\frac{2.20 \text{ lb}}{1 \text{ kg}} \quad \text{and} \quad \frac{1 \text{ kg}}{2.20 \text{ lb}}$$

**cubic centimeter (cm$^3$ or cc)** The volume of a cube that has 1-cm sides; equal to 1 mL.

**density** The relationship of the mass of an object to its volume expressed as grams per cubic centimeter (g/cm$^3$), grams per milliliter (g/mL), or grams per liter (g/L).

**equality** A relationship between two units that measure the same quantity.

**exact number** A number obtained by counting or by definition.

**gram (g)** The metric unit used in measurements of mass.

**Kelvin (K) temperature scale** A temperature scale on which the lowest possible temperature is 0 K.

**kilogram (kg)** A metric mass of 1000 g and equal to 2.20 lb. The kilogram is the SI standard unit of mass.

**liter (L)** The metric unit for volume that is slightly larger than a quart.

**mass** A measure of the quantity of material in an object.

**measured number** A number obtained when a quantity is determined by using a measuring device.

**meter (m)** The metric unit for length that is slightly longer than a yard. The meter is the SI standard unit of length.

**metric system** A system of measurement used by scientists and in most countries of the world.

**milliliter (mL)** A metric unit of volume equal to one-thousandth of a L (0.001 L).

**prefix** The part of the name of a metric unit that precedes the base unit and specifies the size of the measurement. All prefixes are related on a decimal scale.

**scientific notation** A form of writing large and small numbers using a coefficient from 1 to 9, followed by a power of 10.

**second** The standard unit of time in the SI and metric system.

**SI units** The international system of units that modifies the metric system.

**significant figures** The numbers recorded in a measurement.

**specific gravity (sp gr)** A relationship between the density of a substance and the density of water:

$$\text{sp gr} = \frac{\text{density of sample}}{\text{density of water}}$$

**temperature** An indicator of the hotness or coldness of an object.

**volume** The amount of space occupied by a substance.

## UNDERSTANDING THE CONCEPTS

**1.71** In which of the following pairs do both numbers contain the same number of significant figures?

**a.** 11.0 m and 11.00 m **b.** 600.0 K and 60 K
**c.** 0.000 75 s and 75 000 s **d.** 255.0 L and $6.240 \times 10^{-2}$ L

**1.72** In which of the following pairs do both numbers contain the same number of significant figures?

**a.** $5.75 \times 10^{-3}$ g and 0.00287 g **b.** 8.05 m and 0.0805 m
**c.** 150 000 s and $1.5 \times 10^{2}$ s **d.** 0.0038 L and 75 000 mL

1.73 Indicate if each of the following is answered with an exact number or a measured number:

a. number of legs
b. height of table
c. number of chairs at the table
d. area of table top

1.74 Measure the length of each of the objects in figure (a), (b), and (c) using the metric rule in the figure. Indicate the number of significant figures for each and the estimated digit for each.

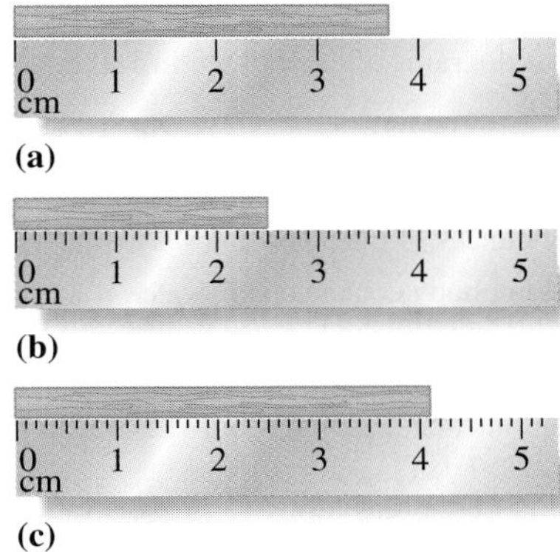


1.75 Measure the length and width of the rectangle using a metric rule:

a. What is the length and width of this rectangle measured in centimeters?
b. What is the length and width of this rectangle measured in millimeters?
c. How many significant figures are in the length measurement?
d. How many significant figures are in the width measurement?
e. What is the area of the rectangle in $cm^2$?
f. How many significant figures are in the calculated answer for area?

1.76 Each of the following diagrams represents a container of water and a cube. Some cubes float while others sink. Match diagrams A, B, C, or D with one of the following descriptions and explain your choices:

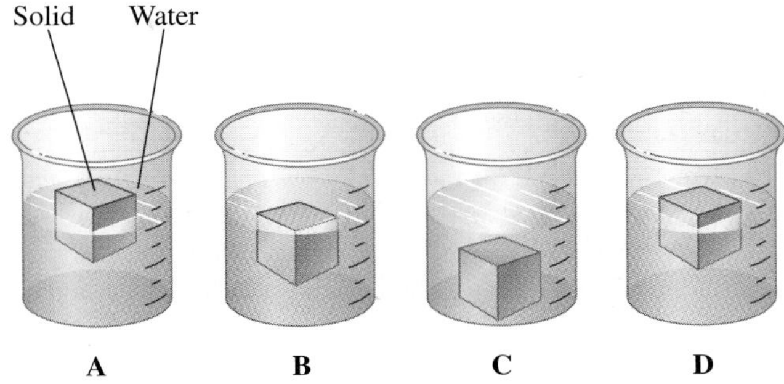


a. The cube has a greater density than water.
b. The cube has a density that is 0.60–0.80 g/mL.
c. The cube has a density that is 1/2 the density of water.
d. The cube has the same density as water.

1.77 What is the density of the solid object that is weighed and submerged in water?

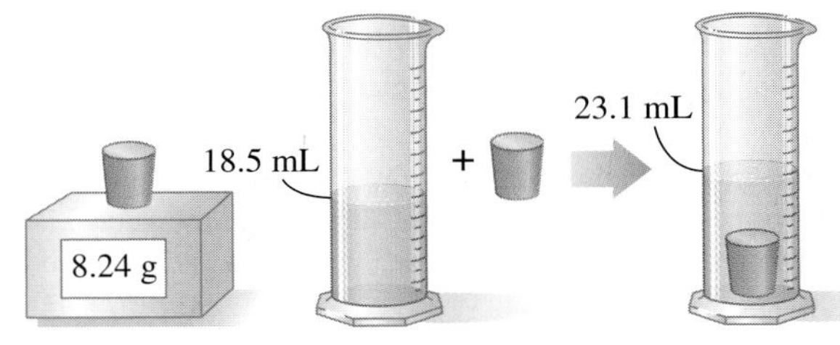


1.78 Consider the following solids. The solids A, B, and C represent gold, silver, and aluminum. If each has a mass of 10.0 g, what is the identity of each solid?

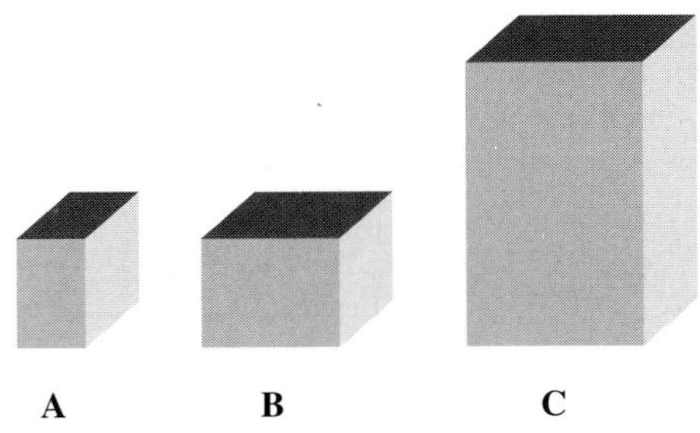


a. Density of aluminum = 2.70 g/mL
b. Density of gold = 19.3 g/mL
c. Density of silver = 10.5 g/mL

## ADDITIONAL QUESTIONS AND PROBLEMS

*For instructor-assigned homework, go to* ***www.masteringchemistry.com***.

1.79 Round off or add zeros to the following calculated answers to give a final answer with three significant figures:

a. 0.000 012 58 L
b. $3.528 \times 10^2$ kg
c. 125 111 m
d. 58.703 g
e. $3 \times 10^{-3}$ s
f. 0.010 826 g

1.80 What is the total mass, in grams, of a dessert containing 137.25 g of vanilla ice cream, 84 g of fudge sauce, and 43.7 g of nuts?

1.81 During a workout at the gym, you set the treadmill at a pace of 55.0 meters per minute. How many minutes will you walk if you cover a distance of 7500 ft?

**1.82** A fish company delivers 22 kg of salmon, 5.5 kg of crab, and 3.48 kg of oysters to your seafood restaurant.

**a.** What is the total mass, in kilograms, of the seafood?

**b.** What is the total number of pounds?

**1.83** Bill's recipe for onion soup calls for 4.0 lb of thinly sliced onions. If an onion has an average mass of 115 g, how many onions does Bill need?

**1.84** The price of 1 pound (lb) of potatoes is \$1.75. If all the potatoes sold today at the store bring in \$1420, how many kilograms (kg) of potatoes did grocery shoppers buy?

**1.85** The following nutrition information is listed on a box of crackers:

Serving size 0.50 oz (6 crackers)
Fat 4 g per serving
Sodium 140 mg per serving

**a.** If the box has a net weight (contents only) of 8.0 oz, about how many crackers are in the box?

**b.** If you ate 10 crackers, how many ounces of fat are you consuming?

**c.** How many grams of sodium are used to prepare 50 boxes of crackers?

**1.86** An aquarium store unit requires 75 000 mL of water. How many gallons of water are needed? (1 gal = 4 qt)

**1.87** In Mexico, avocados are 48 pesos per kilogram. What is the cost in cents of an avocado that weighs 0.45 lb if the exchange rate is 10.8 pesos to the dollar?

**1.88** Celeste's diet restricts her intake of protein to 24 g per day. If she eats an 8.0-oz burger that is 15.0% protein, has she exceeded her protein limit for the day? How many ounces of a burger would be allowed for Celeste?

**1.89** A sunscreen preparation contains 2.50% by mass benzyl salicylate. If a tube contains 4.0 ounces of sunscreen, how many kilograms of benzyl salicylate are needed to manufacture 325 tubes of sunscreen?

**1.90** An object has a mass of 3.15 oz. When it is submerged in a graduated cylinder initially containing 325.2 mL of water, the water level rises to 442.5 mL. What is the density (g/mL) of the object?

**1.91** What is a cholesterol level of 1.85 g/L in units of mg/dL?

**1.92** If a recycling center collects 1254 aluminum cans and there are 22 aluminum cans in 1 pound, what volume, in liters, of aluminum was collected? (See Table 1.11.)

**1.93** The water level in a graduated cylinder initially at 215 mL rises to 285 mL after a piece of lead is submerged. What is the mass in grams of the lead? (See Table 1.11.)

**1.94** A graduated cylinder contains 155 mL of water. A 15.0-g piece of iron (density = 7.86 g/cm$^3$) and a 20.0-g piece of lead are added. What is the new water level in the cylinder? (See Table 1.11.)

**1.95** How many cubic centimeters (cm$^3$) of olive oil have the same mass as 1.00 L of gasoline? (See Table 1.11.)

**1.96** What is the volume, in quarts, of 1.50 kg of ethyl alcohol? (See Table 1.11.)

**1.97** **a.** Some athletes have as little as 3.0% body fat. If such a person has a body mass of 45 kg, how many lb of body fat does that person have?

**b.** In a process called *liposuction*, a doctor removes fat deposits from a person's body. If body fat has a density of 0.94 g/mL and 3.0 liters of fat are removed, how many pounds of fat were removed from the patient?

**1.98** A mouthwash is 21.6% by mass alcohol. If each bottle contains 0.358 pint of mouthwash with a density of 0.876 g/mL, how many kilograms of alcohol are in 180 bottles of the mouthwash?

**1.99** Sterling silver is 92.5% silver by mass with a density of 10.3 g/cm$^3$. If a cube of sterling silver has a volume of 27.0 cm$^3$, how many ounces of pure silver are present?

**1.100** A typical adult body contains 55% water. If a person has a mass of 65 kg, how many pounds of water does she have in her body?

**1.101** For a 180-lb person, calculate the quantities of each of the following that must be ingested to provide the $LD_{50}$ for caffeine given in Table 1.10:

**a.** cups of coffee if one cup is 12 fluid ounces and there are 100. mg of caffeine per 6 fl oz of drip-brewed coffee

**b.** cans of cola if one can contains 50. mg of caffeine

**c.** tablets of No-Doz if one tablet contains 100. mg of caffeine

**1.102** The label on a 1-pint bottle of water lists the following components. If the density is the same as pure water and you drink three bottles of water in one day, how many milligrams of each component will you obtain?

Calcium 28 ppm
Fluoride 0.08 ppm
Magnesium 12 ppm
Potassium 3.2 ppm
Sodium 15 ppm

## CHALLENGE QUESTIONS

*The following groups of questions and problems are related to the topics in this chapter. However, they do not all follow the chapter order, and they require you to combine concepts and skills from several sections. These problems will help you increase your critical thinking skills and prepare for your next exam.*

**1.103** A balance measures mass to 0.001 g. If you determine the mass of an object that weighs about 30 g, would you record the mass as 30 g, 32 g, 32.1 g, or 32.075 g? Explain your choice by writing two to three complete sentences that describe your thinking.

**1.104** When three students use the same meterstick to measure the length of a paper clip, they obtain results of 5.8 cm, 5.75 cm, and 5.76 cm. If the meterstick has millimeter markings, what are some reasons for the different values?

**1.105** A car travels at 55 miles per hour and gets 11 kilometers per liter of gasoline. How many gallons of gasoline are needed for a 3.0-hour trip?

**1.106** A 50.0-g silver object and a 50.0-g gold object are both added to 75.5 mL of water contained in a graduated cylinder. What is the new water level in the cylinder?

**1.107** In the manufacturing of computer chips, cylinders of silicon are cut into thin wafers that are 3.00 inches in diameter and have a mass of 1.50 g of silicon. How thick (mm) is each wafer if silicon has a density of 2.33 g/cm$^3$? (The volume of a cylinder is $V = \pi r^2 h$.)

**1.108** A circular pool with a diameter of 27 ft is filled to a depth of 50. in. Assume the pool is a cylinder ($V = \pi r^2 h$).

**a.** What is the volume of water in the pool in cubic meters?

**b.** The density of water is 1.0 g/cm$^3$. What is the mass, in kilograms, of the water in the pool?

1.109 A package of aluminum foil is 66.7 yd long, 12 in. wide, and 0.000 30 in. thick. If aluminum has a density of 2.7 g/cm$^3$, what is the mass, in grams, of the foil?

**1.110** An 18-karat gold necklace is 75% gold by mass, 16% silver, and 9.0% copper.

**a.** What is the mass, in grams, of the necklace if it contains 0.24 oz silver?
**b.** How many grams of copper are in the necklace?
**c.** If 18-karat gold has a density of 15.5 g/cm$^3$, what is the volume in cubic centimeters?

# ANSWERS

## ANSWERS TO STUDY CHECKS

**1.1** **a.** meter; m **b.** degree Celsius; °C **c.** gram; g

**1.2** **a.** $4.25 \times 10^5$ m **b.** $8 \times 10^{-7}$ g

**1.3** **a.** two **b.** one **c.** five

**1.4** **a.** 36 m **b.** 0.0026 L **c.** $3.8 \times 10^3$ g **d.** 1.3 kg

**1.5** **a.** 0.4924 **b.** 0.0080 or $8.0 \times 10^{-3}$ **c.** 2.0

**1.6** **a.** 83.70 mg **b.** 0.5 L

**1.7** **a.** giga **b.** centi

**1.8** **a.** 1000 g ($1 \times 10^3$g) **b.** 0.001 mL ($1 \times 10^{-3}$mL)

**1.9** Conversion factors: $\frac{1 \text{ zs}}{1 \times 10^{-23} \text{ s}}$ and $\frac{1 \times 10^{-23} \text{ s}}{1 \text{ zs}}$

**1.10** **a.** $\frac{62.2 \text{ km}}{1 \text{ h}}$ and $\frac{1 \text{ h}}{62.2 \text{ km}}$

**b.** $\frac{10 \text{ g arsenic}}{1 \times 10^9 \text{ g water}}$ and $\frac{1 \times 10^9 \text{ g water}}{10 \text{ g arsenic}}$

**1.11** 1.89 L

**1.12** 0.44 oz

**1.13** 10 mL

**1.14** 25 g of fat

**1.15** 10.5 g/cm$^3$

**1.16** 2.20 g/mL

**1.17** 1.50 mL of mercury

**1.18** 207 mL

## ANSWERS TO SELECTED QUESTIONS AND PROBLEMS

**1.1** In the United States, **a.** weight is measured in pounds (lb), **b.** height in feet and inches, **c.** gasoline in gallons, and **d.** temperature in Fahrenheit (°F). In Mexico, **a.** mass is measured in kilograms, **b.** height in meters, **c.** gasoline in liters, and **d.** temperature in Celsius (°C).

**1.3** **a.** meter; length **b.** gram; mass **c.** liter; volume **d.** second; time **e.** degree Celsius; temperature

**1.5** **a.** $5.5 \times 10^4$ m **b.** $4.8 \times 10^2$ g **c.** $5 \times 10^{-6}$ cm **d.** $1.4 \times 10^{-4}$ s **e.** $7.85 \times 10^{-3}$ L **f.** $6.7 \times 10^5$ kg

**1.7** **a.** $7.2 \times 10^3$ **b.** $3.2 \times 10^{-2}$ **c.** $1 \times 10^4$ **d.** $6.8 \times 10^{-2}$

**1.9** **a.** 12 000 **b.** 0.0825 **c.** 4 000 000 **d.** 0.005

**1.11** **a.** measured **b.** exact **c.** exact **d.** measured

**1.13** **a.** 6 oz of meat **b.** none **c.** 0.75 lb; 350 g **d.** none (definitions are exact)

**1.15** **a.** not significant **b.** significant **c.** significant **d.** significant **e.** not significant

**1.17** **a.** 5 **b.** 2 **c.** 2 **d.** 3 **e.** 4 **f.** 3

**1.19** Both measurements in part **c** have two significant figures, and both measurements in part **d** have four significant figures.

**1.21** **a.** $5.0 \times 10^3$ L **b.** $3.0 \times 10^4$ g **c.** $1.0 \times 10^5$ m **d.** $2.5 \times 10^{-4}$ cm

**1.23** A calculator often gives more digits than the number of significant figures allowed in the answer.

**1.25** **a.** 1.85 **b.** 184 **c.** 0.004 74 **d.** 8810 **e.** $1.83 \times 10^5$

**1.27** **a.** 1.6 **b.** 0.01 **c.** 27.6 **d.** 3.5

**1.29** **a.** 53.54 cm **b.** 127.6 g **c.** 121.5 mL **d.** 0.50 L

**1.31** km/h is kilometers per hour; mi/h (mph) is miles per hour.

**1.33** The prefix *kilo* means to multiply by 1000. One kg is the same mass as 1000 g.

**1.35** **a.** mg **b.** dL **c.** km **d.** kg **e.** $\mu$L **f.** ng

**1.37** **a.** 0.01 **b.** 1000 **c.** 0.001 ($1 \times 10^{-3}$) **d.** 0.1 **e.** 1 000 000 ($1 \times 10^6$) **f.** $1 \times 10^{-12}$

**1.39** **a.** 100 cm **b.** 1000 m **c.** 0.001 m **d.** 1000 mL

**1.41** **a.** kilogram **b.** milliliter **c.** km **d.** kL **e.** nanometer

**1.43** A conversion factor can be inverted to give a second conversion factor.

**1.45** **a.** 100 cm = 1 m; $\frac{100 \text{ cm}}{1 \text{ m}}$ and $\frac{1 \text{ m}}{100 \text{ cm}}$

**b.** 1000 mg = 1 g; $\frac{1000 \text{ mg}}{1 \text{ g}}$ and $\frac{1 \text{ g}}{1000 \text{ mg}}$

**c.** 1 L = 1000 mL; $\frac{1000 \text{ mL}}{1 \text{ L}}$ and $\frac{1 \text{ L}}{1000 \text{ mL}}$

**d.** 1 dL = 100 mL; $\frac{100 \text{ mL}}{1 \text{ dL}}$ and $\frac{1 \text{ dL}}{100 \text{ mL}}$

**1.47** **a.** 3 ft = 1 yd; $\frac{3 \text{ ft}}{1 \text{ yd}}$ and $\frac{1 \text{ yd}}{3 \text{ ft}}$

**b.** 1 mile = 5280 feet; $\frac{5280 \text{ ft}}{1 \text{ mi}}$ and $\frac{1 \text{ mi}}{5280 \text{ ft}}$

**c.** 1 min = 60 sec; $\frac{60 \text{ s}}{1 \text{ min}}$ and $\frac{1 \text{ min}}{60 \text{ s}}$

**d.** 1 gal = 27 mi; $\frac{1 \text{ gal}}{27 \text{ mi}}$ and $\frac{27 \text{ mi}}{1 \text{ gal}}$

**e.** 93 g silver = 100 g sterling; $\frac{93 \text{ g silver}}{100 \text{ g sterling}}$ and $\frac{100 \text{ g sterling}}{93 \text{ g silver}}$

**1.49** **a.** $\frac{3.5 \text{ m}}{1 \text{ s}}$ and $\frac{1 \text{ s}}{3.5 \text{ m}}$

**b.** $\frac{3500 \text{ mg potassium}}{1 \text{ day}}$ and $\frac{1 \text{ day}}{3500 \text{ mg potassium}}$

**c.** $\frac{46.0\text{ km}}{1.0\text{ gal}}$ and $\frac{1.0\text{ gal}}{46.0\text{ km}}$

**d.** $\frac{50\text{ mg Atenolol}}{1\text{ tablet}}$ and $\frac{1\text{ tablet}}{50\text{ mg Atenolol}}$

**e.** $\frac{29\ \mu\text{g}}{1\text{ kg}}$ and $\frac{1\text{ kg}}{29\ \mu\text{g}}$

**1.51** The unit in the denominator must cancel with the preceding unit.

**1.53** **a.** 1.75 m **b.** 5.5 L **c.** 5.5 g

**1.55** **a.** 710. mL **b.** 75.1 kg **c.** 495 mm **d.** $2.0 \times 10^{-5}$ in.

**1.57** **a.** 23.8 m **b.** 196 $m^2$ **c.** 0.463 s

**1.59** **a.** 66 gal **b.** 3 tablets
**c.** 1800 mg ($1.8 \times 10^3$ mg)

**1.61** **a.** 152 g of oxygen **b.** 0.026 g of magnesium
**c.** 43 g of N **d.** 50. lb of chocolate bars

**1.63** lead; 11.3 g/mL

**1.65** **a.** 1.20 g/mL **b.** 0.873 g/mL
**c.** 3.10 g/mL **d.** 1.42 g/mL

**1.67** **a.** 1.9 L **b.** 88 g **c.** 62 oz **d.** 30. kg

**1.69** **a.** 1.030 **b.** 1.13 **c.** 0.85 g/mL

**1.71** **c.** 0.000 75 s and 75 000 s
**d.** 255.0 L and $6.240 \times 10^{-2}$ L

**1.73** **a.** exact **b.** measured **c.** exact **d.** measured

**1.75** **a.** length = 6.96 cm; width = 4.75 cm
**b.** length = 69.6 mm; width = 47.5 mm
**c.** 3 significant figures
**d.** 3 significant figures
**e.** 33.1 $cm^2$
**f.** 3 significant figures

**1.77** 1.8 g/mL

**1.79** **a.** 0.000 0126 L **b.** $3.53 \times 10^2$ kg
**c.** 125 000 m **d.** 58.7 g
**e.** $3.00 \times 10^{-3}$ s **f.** 0.0108 g

**1.81** 42 min

**1.83** 16 onions

**1.85** **a.** 96 crackers **b.** 0.2 oz of fat **c.** 110 g of sodium

**1.87** 91 cents

**1.89** 0.92 kg

**1.91** 185 mg/dL

**1.93** 790 g

**1.95** 720 $cm^3$

**1.97** **a.** 3.0 lb of body fat **b.** 6.2 lb

**1.99** 9.07 oz of pure silver

**1.101** **a.** 80 cups **b.** 310 cans **c.** 160 tablets

**1.103** You should record the mass as 32.075 g. Because your balance will weigh to the nearest 0.001 g, the mass values should be reported to 0.001 g.

**1.105** 6.4 gal

**1.107** 0.141 mm

**1.109** $3.8 \times 10^2$ g of aluminum foil

# Energy and Matter 2

LOOKING AHEAD

2.1 Energy
2.2 Temperature
2.3 Specific Heat
2.4 Energy and Nutrition
2.5 Classification of Matter
2.6 States and Properties of Matter
2.7 Changes of State

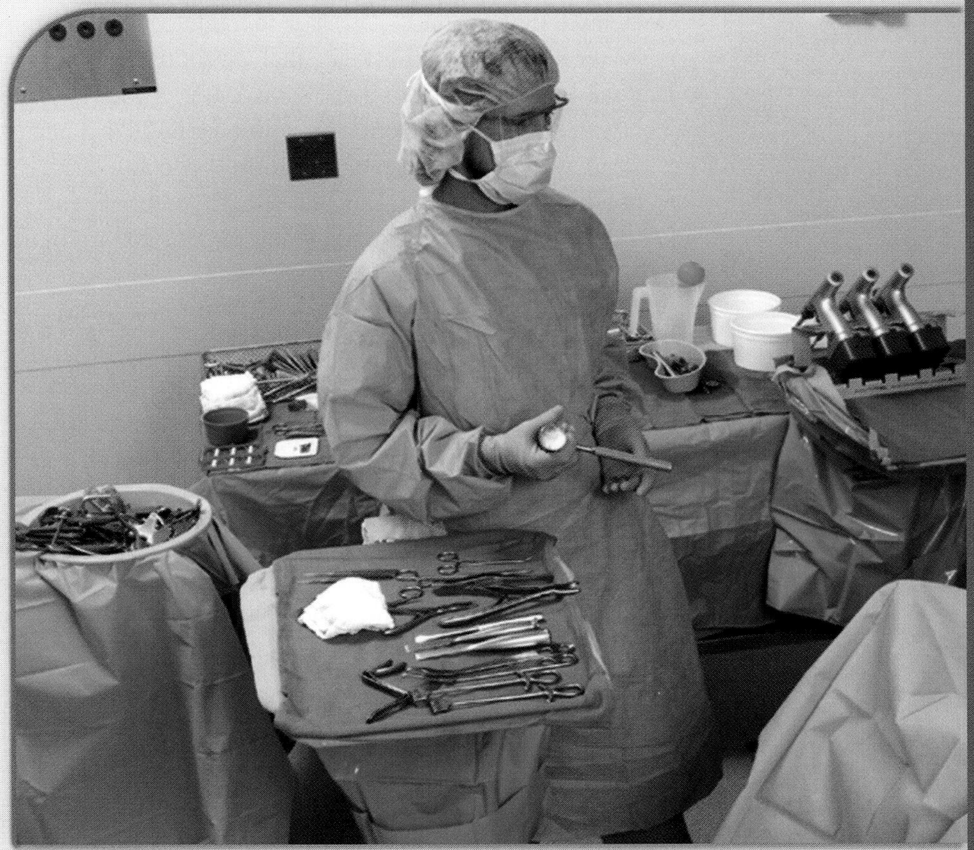

*"As a surgical technologist, I assist the doctors during surgeries," says Christopher Ayars, surgical technologist, Kaiser Hospital. "I am there to help during general or orthopedic surgery by passing instruments, holding retractors, and maintaining the sterile field. Our equipment for surgery is sterilized by steam that is heated to 270 °F, which is the same as 130 °C."*

*Surgical technologists assist with surgical procedures by preparing and maintaining surgical equipment, instruments, and supplies; providing patient care in an operating room setting; preparing and maintaining a sterile field; and ensuring that there are no breaks in aseptic technique. Instruments, which have been sterilized, are wrapped and sent to surgery where they are checked again before they are opened.*

Visit **www.masteringchemistry.com** for self-study materials and instructor-assigned homework.

Almost everything we do involves energy. We use energy when we walk, play tennis, study, and breathe. We use energy when we warm water, cook food, turn on lights, use a washing machine, and drive our cars. Of course, that energy has to come from something. In our bodies, the food we eat provides us with energy. In our homes, schools, and automobiles, burning fossil fuels such as oil, propane, or gasoline provides energy.

Every day, we see a variety of materials with many different shapes and forms. To a scientist, all of these materials are *matter*. Matter is everywhere around us. The orange juice we had for breakfast, the water we put in the coffee maker, the plastic bag we put our sandwich in, our toothbrush and toothpaste, the oxygen we inhale, and the carbon dioxide we exhale are all forms of matter.

When we look around us, we see that matter takes the physical form of a solid, a liquid, or a gas. Water is a familiar substance that we routinely observe in all three states. In the solid state, water can be an ice cube or a snowflake. It is a liquid when it comes out of a faucet or fills a pool. When water evaporates from wet clothes or boils in a pan, it forms a gas, or vapor. In all of these examples, water changes state by gaining or losing energy. For example, energy is added to melt ice cubes and to boil water in a teakettle. In contrast, energy is removed to freeze liquid water in an ice cube tray and to condense water vapor (gas) to liquid.

## 2.1 Energy

**LEARNING GOAL**

Identify energy as potential or kinetic and understand the units of energy.

When you are running, walking, dancing, or thinking, you are using energy to do **work**, any activity that requires energy. In fact, **energy** is defined as the ability to do work. Suppose you are climbing a steep hill and you become too tired to go on. At that moment, you do not have sufficient energy to do any more work. Now suppose you sit down and have lunch. In a while you will have obtained energy from the food, and you will be able to do more work and complete the climb.

FIGURE 2.1 Work is done as the rock climber moves up the cliff. At the top, the climber has more potential energy than when she started the climb.

Q What happens to the potential energy of the climber when she descends?

### Potential and Kinetic Energy

All energy can be classified as potential energy or kinetic energy. **Potential energy** is stored energy, whereas **kinetic energy** is the energy of motion. (See Figure 2.1.) Any object that is moving has kinetic energy. A boulder resting on top of a mountain has potential energy because of its location. If the boulder rolls down the mountain, the potential energy becomes kinetic energy. Water stored in a reservoir has potential energy. When it flows over the dam and falls to the stream below, its potential energy is converted to kinetic energy. Foods and fossil fuels have potential energy stored in their molecules. When you digest food or burn gasoline in your car, potential energy is converted to kinetic energy to do work.

**CONCEPT CHECK 2.1**

**Potential and Kinetic Energy**

Identify each of the following as an example of mostly potential or kinetic energy:

**a.** gasoline **b.** skating **c.** a candy bar

ANSWER

**a.** Gasoline is burned to provide energy and heat; it contains potential energy in its molecules.

**b.** A skater uses energy to move; skating is kinetic energy (energy of motion).

**c.** A candy bar has stored energy. When digested, its components provide energy for the body to do work.

## Heat and Units of Energy

**Heat** is energy that flows from a warmer object to a cooler one. A frozen pizza feels cold because heat flows from your warm hand to the pizza. Heat is associated with the motion of particles. In the frozen pizza, the particles are moving very slowly. As heat is added and the pizza becomes warmer, the motions of the particles in the pizza increase. Eventually, the particles have enough energy to make the pizza hot and ready to eat.

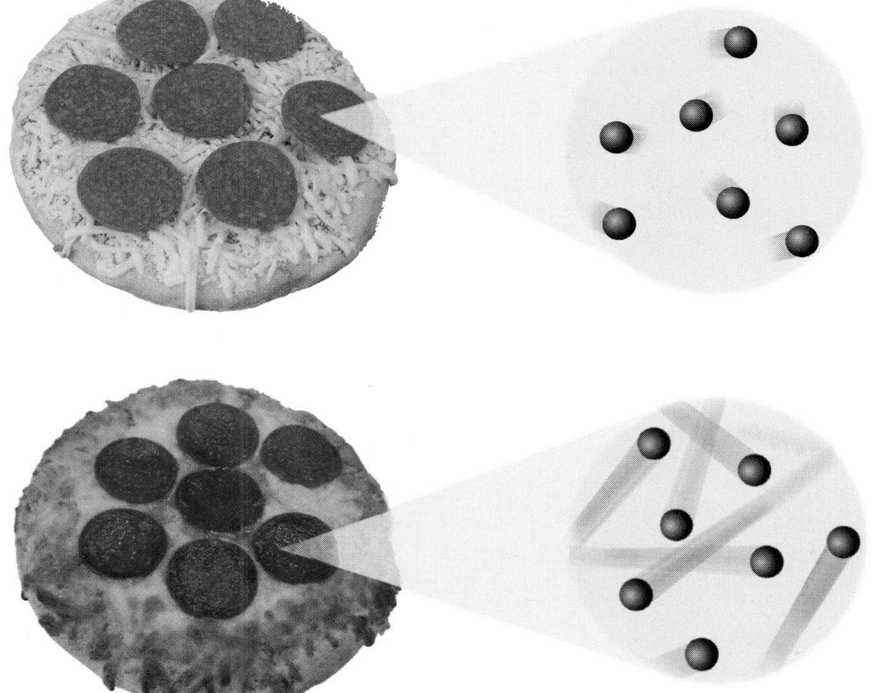

MC™ TUTORIAL
Heat

MC™ TUTORIAL
Energy Conversions

The SI unit of energy and work is the **joule** (J) (pronounced "jewel"). The joule is a small amount of energy, so scientists often use the kilojoule (kJ). When you heat water for one cup of tea, you use about 75 000 J, or 75 kJ, of heat.

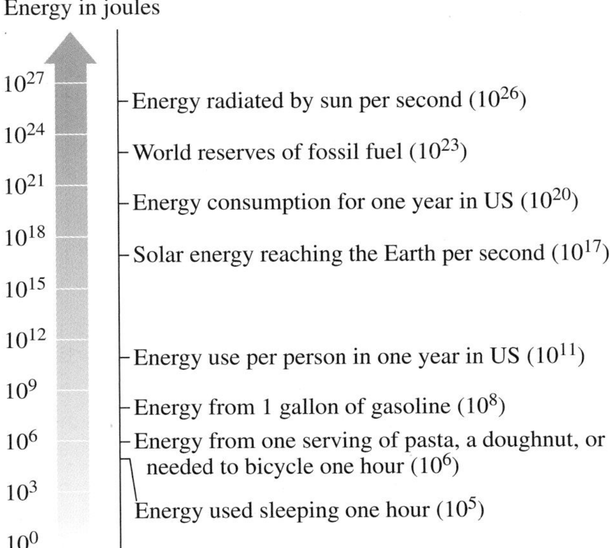

You may be more familiar with the unit **calorie (cal)**, from the Latin *caloric*, meaning "heat." The calorie was originally defined as the amount of energy (heat) needed to raise the temperature of one gram of water by 1 °C. Now one calorie is defined as exactly 4.184 J. This equality can also be written as a conversion factor:

$$1 \text{ cal} = 4.184 \text{ J (exact)}$$

$$\frac{4.184 \text{ J}}{1 \text{ cal}} \quad \text{and} \quad \frac{1 \text{ cal}}{4.184 \text{ J}}$$

One **kilocalorie (kcal)** is equal to 1000 calories, and one *kilojoule* (kJ) is 1000 joules.

$$1 \text{ kcal} = 1000 \text{ cal}$$

$$1 \text{ kJ} = 1000 \text{ J}$$

SAMPLE PROBLEM 2.1

## Energy Units

When 1.0 g of octane fuel burns in an automobile engine, 48 000 J are released. Convert this quantity of energy to the following units:

**a.** calories **b.** kilojoules

SOLUTION

**a.** calories

**STEP 1** **Given** 48 000 J **Need** calories (cal)

**STEP 2** **Plan** J → Energy factor → cal

**STEP 3** **Equalities/Conversion Factors**

$$1 \text{ cal} = 4.184 \text{ J}$$

$$\frac{1 \text{ cal}}{4.184 \text{ J}} \quad \text{and} \quad \frac{4.184 \text{ J}}{1 \text{ cal}}$$

**STEP 4** **Set Up Problem**

$$48\,000 \not{\text{J}} \times \frac{1 \text{ cal}}{4.184 \not{\text{J}}} = 11\,000 \text{ cal } (1.1 \times 10^4 \text{ cal}) \quad \text{(2 SFs)}$$

**b.** kilojoules

**STEP 1** **Given** 48 000 J **Need** kilojoules

**STEP 2** **Plan** J → Energy factor → kJ

**STEP 3** **Equalities/Conversion Factors**

$$1 \text{ kJ} = 1000 \text{ J}$$

$$\frac{1000 \text{ J}}{1 \text{ kJ}} \quad \text{and} \quad \frac{1 \text{ kJ}}{1000 \text{ J}}$$

**STEP 4** **Set Up Problem**

$$48\,000 \not{\text{J}} \times \frac{1 \text{ kJ}}{1000 \not{\text{J}}} = 48 \text{ kJ}$$

STUDY CHECK

The burning of 1.0 g of coal produces 35 000 J of energy. How many kcal are produced?

## QUESTIONS AND PROBLEMS

### Energy

2.1 Discuss the changes in the potential and kinetic energy of a roller-coaster ride as the roller coaster climbs up a ramp and goes down the other side.

**2.2** Discuss the changes in the potential and kinetic energy of a ski jumper taking the elevator to the top of the jump and skiing down the ramp.

2.3 Indicate whether each statement describes potential or kinetic energy:
**a.** water at the top of a waterfall
**b.** kicking a ball
**c.** the energy in a lump of coal
**d.** a skier at the top of a hill

**2.4** Indicate whether each statement describes potential or kinetic energy:
**a.** the energy in your food
**b.** a tightly wound spring
**c.** an earthquake
**d.** a car speeding down the freeway

2.5 A burning match releases $1.1 \times 10^3$ J. Convert the energy released by 20 matches to the following energy units:
**a.** kilojoules **b.** calories **c.** kilocalories

**2.6** A person uses 750 kcal to run a race. Convert the energy used for the race to the following energy units:
**a.** calories **b.** joules **c.** kilojoules

# 2.2 Temperature

**LEARNING GOAL**

Given a temperature, calculate a corresponding temperature on another temperature scale.

Temperature is a measure of how hot or cold a substance is compared to another substance. The temperature is an indication of the kinetic energy of the particles in a substance. Heat flows from a substance with a higher temperature to a substance with a lower temperature until the temperatures of both are the same. When you drink hot coffee or touch a hot pan, heat flows to your mouth or hand, which is at a lower temperature. When you touch an ice cube, it feels cold because heat flows from your hand to the colder ice cube.

## Celsius and Fahrenheit Temperatures

Temperatures in science, and in most of the world, are measured and reported in *Celsius* (*°C*) units. In the United States, everyday temperatures are commonly reported in *Fahrenheit* (*°F*) units. A typical room temperature of 22 °C would be the same as 72 °F. A normal human body temperature of 37.0 °C is 98.6 °F.

On the Celsius and Fahrenheit scales, the temperatures of melting ice and boiling water are used as reference points. On the Celsius scale, the freezing point of pure water is defined as exactly 0 °C and the boiling point as exactly 100 °C. On the Fahrenheit scale, pure water freezes at exactly 32 °F and boils at exactly 212 °F. On each scale, the temperature difference between freezing and boiling is divided into smaller units called *degrees*. The Celsius scale has 100 degrees between the freezing and boiling temperatures of water, compared with 180 degrees on the Fahrenheit scale. That makes a Celsius degree almost twice the size of a Fahrenheit degree: 1 °C = 1.8 °F. (See Figure 2.2.)

$$180 \text{ Fahrenheit degrees} = 100 \text{ Celsius degrees}$$

$$\frac{180 \text{ Fahrenheit degrees}}{100 \text{ Celsius degrees}} = \frac{1.8\ °\text{F}}{1\ °\text{C}}$$

In a chemistry laboratory, temperatures are measured in Celsius degrees. To convert to a Fahrenheit temperature, multiply the Celsius temperature by 1.8 and add 32 degrees. The 32 degrees adjusts the freezing point of 0 °C on the Celsius scale to 32 °F on the Fahrenheit scale. Both values, 1.8 and 32, are exact numbers. The equation for this conversion follows:

$$T_F = \underbrace{\frac{1.8\ °\text{F}(T_C)}{1\ °\text{C}}}_{\text{Changes °C to °F}} + \underbrace{32}_{\text{Adjusts freezing point}} \quad \text{or} \quad T_F = 1.8(T_C) + 32$$

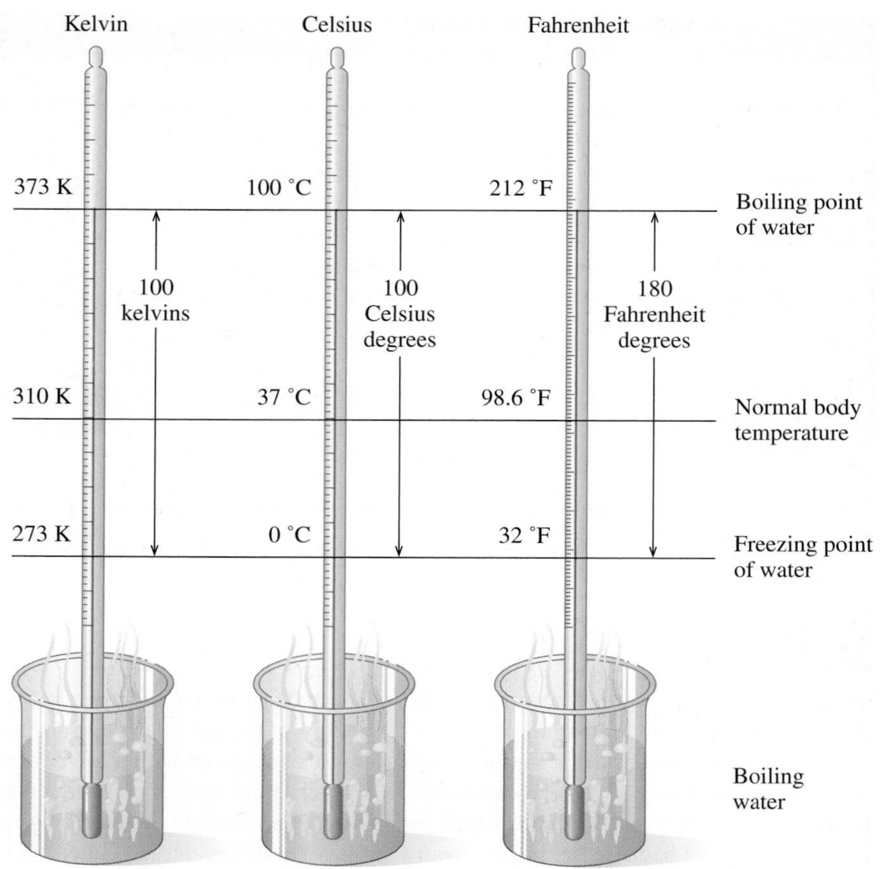


**FIGURE 2.2** A comparison of the Fahrenheit, Celsius, and Kelvin temperature scales between the freezing and boiling points of water.

**Q** What is the difference in the values for freezing on the Fahrenheit, Celsius, and Kelvin temperature scales?

**CONCEPT CHECK 2.2**

### Temperature Scales

A student in your chemistry class has designed a new temperature scale in degrees Zupa. The freezing point on this Zupa scale is 10 °Z, and the boiling point occurs at 130 °Z.

**a.** What is the relationship between degrees Zupa and degrees Celsius?
**b.** How would you adjust the freezing point?
**c.** Write an equation that relates degrees Zupa to degrees Celsius.
**d.** Convert a temperature of 35 °C to degrees Zupa.

ANSWER

**a.** On the Celsius scale, there are 100 °C between the freezing and the boiling points of water. On the Zupa scale, there are 120 °Z. Thus, 100 °C = 120 °Z and the conversion factor is 120 °Z/100 °C.
**b.** The freezing point is adjusted by adding 10 degrees.
**c.** The equation to convert °C to °Z would be written as

$$T_Z = \frac{120\ °\text{Z}\,(T_C)}{100\ °\text{C}} + 10$$

$$T_Z = 1.2\,(T_C) + 10$$

**d.** $T_Z = 1.2(35) + 10 = 42 + 10 = 52\ °\text{Z}$

**SAMPLE PROBLEM 2.2**

### Converting Celsius to Fahrenheit

The temperature of a room is set at 22 °C. If that temperature is lowered by 1 °C, it can save as much as 5% in energy costs. What temperature, in Fahrenheit degrees, should be set to lower the Celsius temperature by 1 °C?

SOLUTION

**STEP 1** **Given** 22 °C − 1 °C = 21 °C **Need** $T_F$

**STEP 2** **Plan** $T_C$ → Temperature equation → $T_F$

**STEP 3** **Equalities/Conversion Factors**

$$T_F = 1.8(T_C) + 32$$

**STEP 4** **Set Up Problem** Substitute the Celsius temperature into the equation and solve.

$$T_F = 1.8(21) + 32 \quad \text{1.8 is exact; 32 is exact}$$

$$T_F = 38 + 32$$

$$= 70.\ °F \quad \text{Answer to the ones place}$$

In the equation, *the values of 1.8 and 32 are exact numbers*. The answer is reported to the same decimal place as the initial temperature.

STUDY CHECK

In the process of making ice cream, rock salt is added to the crushed ice. If the temperature drops to –11 °C, what is it in °F?

In a chemistry laboratory, temperatures are measured in Celsius degrees. To convert from Fahrenheit to Celsius, the temperature equation is rearranged to solve for $T_C$. Start with

$$T_F = 1.8(T_C) + 32$$

Then subtract 32 from both sides.

$$T_F - 32 = 1.8(T_C) + 32 - 32$$

$$T_F - 32 = 1.8(T_C)$$

Solve the equation for $T_C$ by dividing both sides by 1.8.

$$\frac{T_F - 32}{1.8} = \frac{\cancel{1.8}(T_C)}{\cancel{1.8}}$$

$$\frac{T_F - 32}{1.8} = T_C$$

SAMPLE PROBLEM 2.3

## ■ Converting Fahrenheit to Celsius

In a type of cancer treatment called *thermotherapy*, temperatures as high as 113 °F are used to destroy cancer cells. What is that temperature in Celsius degrees?

SOLUTION

**STEP 1** **Given** 113 °F **Need** $T_C$

**STEP 2** **Plan** $T_F$ → Temperature equation → $T_C$

**STEP 3** **Equalities/Conversion Factors**

$$T_C = \frac{T_F - 32}{1.8}$$

**STEP 4** **Set Up Problem** To solve for $T_C$, substitute the Fahrenheit temperature into the equation, and solve.

$$T_C = \frac{T_F - 32}{1.8}$$

$$T_C = \frac{(113 - 32)}{1.8} \quad \text{32 is exact; 1.8 is exact}$$

$$= \frac{81}{1.8} = 45\ °C \quad \text{Answer to the ones place}$$

STUDY CHECK

A child has a temperature of 103.6 °F. What is this temperature on a Celsius thermometer?

## HEALTH NOTE

### Variation in Body Temperature

Normal human body temperature is considered to be 37.0 °C, although it varies throughout the day and from person to person. Oral temperatures of 36.1 °C are common in the morning and climb to a high of 37.2 °C between 6 P.M. and 10 P.M. Temperatures above 37.2 °C for a person at rest are usually an indication of disease. Individuals who are involved in prolonged exercise may also experience elevated temperatures. Body temperatures of marathon runners can range from 39 °C to 41 °C because heat production during exercise exceeds the body's ability to lose heat.

Changes of more than 3.5 °C from the normal body temperature begin to interfere with bodily functions. Temperatures above 41 °C, hyperthermia, can lead to convulsions, particularly in children, which may cause permanent brain damage. Heatstroke occurs above 41.1 °C. Sweat production stops, and the skin becomes hot and dry. The pulse rate is elevated, and respiration becomes weak and rapid. The person can become lethargic and lapse into a coma. Damage to internal organs is a major concern, and treatment, which must be immediate, may include immersing the person in an ice-water bath.

At the low temperature extreme of hypothermia, body temperature can drop as low as 28.5 °C. The person may appear cold and pale and have an irregular heartbeat. Unconsciousness can occur if the body temperature drops below 26.7 °C. Respiration becomes slow and shallow, and oxygenation of the tissues decreases. Treatment involves providing oxygen and increasing blood volume with glucose and saline fluids. Injecting warm fluids (37.0 °C) into the peritoneal cavity may restore the internal temperature.

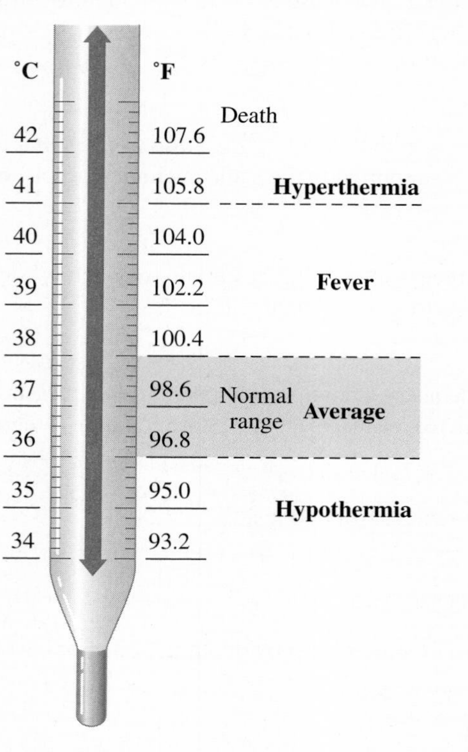


## Kelvin Temperature Scale

Scientists have learned that the coldest temperature possible is –273 °C (more precisely, –273.15 °C). On the Kelvin scale, this temperature, called absolute zero, has the value of 0 Kelvin (0 K). Units on the Kelvin scale are called kelvins (K); no degree symbol is used. Because there are no lower temperatures, the Kelvin scale has no negative numbers. Between the freezing and boiling points of water, there are 100 kelvins, which makes a kelvin equal in size to a Celsius degree.

$$1 \text{ K} = 1 \text{ °C}$$

To calculate a Kelvin temperature, add 273 to the Celsius temperature:

$$T_K = T_C + 273$$

Table 2.1 gives a comparison of some temperatures on the three scales.

**TABLE 2.1** A Comparison of Temperatures

| Example | Fahrenheit (°F) | Celsius (°C) | Kelvin (K) |
|---|---|---|---|
| Sun | 9937 | 5503 | 5776 |
| A hot oven | 450 | 232 | 505 |
| A desert | 120 | 49 | 322 |
| A high fever | 104 | 40 | 313 |
| Room temperature | 70 | 21 | 294 |
| Water freezes | 32 | 0 | 273 |
| An Alaskan winter | –66 | –54 | 219 |
| Helium boils | –452 | –269 | 4 |
| Absolute zero | –459 | –273 | 0 |

SAMPLE PROBLEM 2.4

### Converting from Celsius to Kelvin Temperature

A dermatologist may use cryogenic liquid nitrogen at –196 °C to remove skin lesions and some skin cancers. What is the temperature of the liquid nitrogen in K?

SOLUTION

To find the Kelvin temperature, we use the equation:

$$T_K = T_C + 273$$
$$T_K = -196 + 273$$
$$= 77 \text{ K}$$

STUDY CHECK

On the planet Mercury, the average night temperature is 13 K, and the average day temperature is 683 K. What are these temperatures in Celsius degrees?

## QUESTIONS AND PROBLEMS

### Temperature

2.7 Your friend who is visiting from Canada just took her temperature. When she reads 99.8, she becomes concerned that she is quite ill. How would you explain this temperature to your friend?

**2.8** You have a friend who is using a recipe for flan from a Mexican cookbook. You notice that he set your oven temperature at 175 °F. What would you advise him to do?

2.9 Solve the following temperature conversions:

**a.** 37.0 °C = ____ °F **b.** 65.3 °F = ____ °C
**c.** −27 °C = ____ K **d.** 62 °C = ____ K
**e.** 114 °F = ____ °C **f.** 72 °F = ____ K

**2.10** Solve the following temperature conversions:

**a.** 25 °C = ____ °F **b.** 155 °C = ____ °F
**c.** −25 °F = ____ °C **d.** 224 K = ____ °C
**e.** 545 K = ____ °C **f.** 875 K = ____ °F

2.11 **a.** A patient with heat stroke has a temperature of 106 °F. What does this read on a Celsius thermometer?
**b.** Because high fevers can cause convulsions in children, the doctor wants to be called if the child's temperature goes over 40. °C. Should the doctor be called if a child has a temperature of 103 °F?

**2.12 a.** Hot water is heated to 145 °F. What is the temperature of the hot water in °C?
**b.** During extreme hypothermia, a young woman's temperature dropped to 20.6 °C. What was her temperature on the Fahrenheit scale?

## 2.3 Specific Heat

LEARNING GOAL

Use specific heat to calculate heat loss or gain, temperature change, or mass of a sample.

Every substance has the ability to absorb or lose heat with temperature change. When you bake a potato, you place it in a hot oven. If you are cooking pasta, you add the pasta to boiling water. Some substances must absorb more heat than others to reach a certain temperature. These energy requirements for different substances are described in terms of a physical property called specific heat. **Specific heat** (*SH*) is the amount of heat needed to raise the temperature of exactly 1 g of a substance by exactly 1 °C. This temperature change is written as $\Delta T$ (*delta T*), where the delta symbol means "a change in."

$$\text{Specific heat}(SH) = \frac{\text{heat}}{\text{grams} \times \Delta T} = \frac{\text{cal(or J)}}{1 \text{ g} \times 1 \text{ °C}}$$

Now we can write the specific heat for water using our definition of the calorie and joule.

$$\text{Specific heat}(SH) \text{ of } H_2O(l) = \frac{1.00 \text{ cal}}{\text{g °C}} = \frac{4.184 \text{ J}}{\text{g °C}}$$

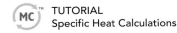

TUTORIAL
Specific Heat Calculations

If we look at Table 2.2, we see that 1 g of water requires 1.00 cal to increase its temperature by 1 °C. Water has a large specific heat that is about five times the specific heat of aluminum. Aluminum has a specific heat that is about twice that of copper. Therefore, 1 cal (4.184 J) will increase the temperature of 1 g of water by 1 °C. The same amount of heat (1 cal or 4.184 J)

**TABLE 2.2** Specific Heats of Some Substances

| Substance | Specific Heat | |
|---|---|---|
| | (cal/g °C) | (J/g °C) |
| Aluminum, Al(*s*) | 0.214 | 0.897 |
| Copper, Cu(*s*) | 0.0920 | 0.385 |
| Gold, Au(*s*) | 0.0308 | 0.129 |
| Iron, Fe(*s*) | 0.108 | 0.452 |
| Silver, Ag(*s*) | 0.0562 | 0.235 |
| Titanium, Ti(*s*) | 0.125 | 0.523 |
| Ammonia, $NH_3(g)$ | 0.488 | 2.04 |
| Ethanol, $C_2H_5OH(l)$ | 0.588 | 2.46 |
| Sodium chloride, NaCl(*s*) | 0.207 | 0.864 |
| Water, $H_2O(l)$ | 1.00 | 4.184 |

will also increase the temperature of 1 g of aluminum by about 5 °C and 1 g of copper by 10 °C. The high specific heat of water gives it the capacity to absorb or release large amounts of heat in the body, which maintains an almost constant body temperature.

CONCEPT CHECK 2.3

### Specific Heat

A 1.0-g sample of iron has a temperature of 20 °C. Referring to Table 2.2, what is the final temperature of the iron sample if 1 cal of heat is added to the iron sample?

**a.** 21 °C **b.** 25 °C **c.** 30 °C **d.** 120 °C **e.** 200 °C

Explain.

ANSWER

The specific heat of iron (0.108 cal/g °C) is about 10 times smaller than that of water (1.00 cal/g °C). Therefore, the addition of 1 cal of heat would increase the temperature of 1 g of iron about 10 times the temperature increase of 1 g of water, or by 10 °C, to 30 °C (answer **c**).

SAMPLE PROBLEM 2.5

### Calculating Specific Heat

What is the specific heat of lead if 13.6 cal are needed to raise the temperature of 35.6 g of lead by 12.5 °C?

SOLUTION

**STEP 1** **Given** heat 13.6 cal mass 35.6 g temperature change 12.5 °C

**Need** specific heat (cal/g °C)

**STEP 2** **Plan** The specific heat (*SH*) is calculated by dividing the heat by the mass (g) and by the temperature change ($\Delta T$).

$$SH = \frac{\text{heat}}{\text{mass} \quad \Delta T}$$

**STEP 3** **Substitute the given values into the specific heat relationship.**

$$\text{Specific heat } (SH) = \frac{13.6 \text{ cal}}{35.6 \text{ g} \quad 12.5 \text{ °C}} = 0.0306 \frac{\text{cal}}{\text{g °C}}$$

STUDY CHECK

What is the specific heat of sodium metal (J/g °C) if 123 J are needed to raise the temperature of 4.00 g of sodium by 25.0 °C?

TUTORIAL
Specific Heat Calculations

## Calculations Using Specific Heat

When we know the specific heat of a substance, we can rearrange the specific heat to obtain the heat equation.

$$\text{Specific heat } (SH) = \frac{\text{heat}}{\text{grams} \times \Delta T}$$

$$\text{Specific heat } (SH) \times \text{grams} \times \Delta T = \frac{\text{heat}}{\cancel{\text{grams}} \times \cancel{\Delta T}} \times \cancel{\text{grams}} \times \cancel{\Delta T}$$

$$\text{Heat} = \text{mass} \times \Delta T \times \text{specific heat } (SH)$$

The heat lost or gained is calculated by substituting the mass of the substance, the change in temperature, and the specific heat into the heat equation.

| Heat | = mass | × temperature change | × specific heat |
|---|---|---|---|
| Heat | = mass | × $\Delta T$ | × $SH$ |
| cal | = $\cancel{g}$ | × $\cancel{°C}$ | × $\frac{\text{cal}}{\cancel{g}\,\cancel{°C}}$ |
| J | = $\cancel{g}$ | × $\cancel{°C}$ | × $\frac{\text{J}}{\cancel{g}\,\cancel{°C}}$ |

### SAMPLE PROBLEM 2.6

#### ■ Calculating Heat with Temperature Increase

How many joules are absorbed by 45.2 g of aluminum (Al) if its temperature rises from 12.5 °C to 76.8 °C? (See Table 2.2.)

SOLUTION

**STEP 1** **Given** mass = 45.2 g

$SH$ for aluminum = 0.897 J/g °C

Initial temperature = 12.5 °C
Final temperature = 76.8 °C

**Need** heat in calories (cal)

**STEP 2** **Calculate the temperature change.** The temperature change $\Delta T$ is the difference between the two temperatures.

$$\Delta T = T_{\text{final}} - T_{\text{initial}} = 76.8\ °\text{C} - 12.5\ °\text{C} = 64.3\ °\text{C}$$

**STEP 3** **Write the heat equation.**

$$\text{Heat} = \text{mass} \times \Delta T \times SH$$

**STEP 4** **Substitute the given values into the equation and solve, making sure units cancel.**

$$\text{Heat} = 45.2\ \cancel{g} \times 64.3\ \cancel{°C} \times \frac{0.897\ \text{J}}{\cancel{g}\,\cancel{°C}} = 2610\ \text{J}\ (2.61 \times 10^3\ \text{J})$$

STUDY CHECK

Some cooking pans have a layer of copper on the bottom. How many kilojoules are needed to raise the temperature of 125 g of copper from 22 °C to 325 °C? (See Table 2.2.)

**Guide to Calculations Using Specific Heat**

STEP 1
List given and needed data.

STEP 2
Calculate temperature change ($\Delta T$).

STEP 3
Write the equation for heat.
Heat = mass × $\Delta T$ × $SH$
and rearrange for unknown.

STEP 4
Substitute given values and solve, making sure units cancel.

## GREEN CHEMISTRY NOTE

### Carbon Dioxide and Global Warming

Earth's climate is a product of interactions between sunlight, the atmosphere, and the oceans. The sun provides us with energy in the form of solar radiation. Some of this radiation is reflected back into space. The rest is absorbed by the clouds, atmospheric gases including carbon dioxide, and Earth's surface. For millions of years, concentrations of carbon dioxide have fluctuated. However in the past 100 years, the amount of carbon dioxide ($CO_2$) gas in our atmosphere has increased significantly. From the years 1000 to 1800, the atmospheric carbon dioxide averaged 280 ppm. But since the beginning of the Industrial Revolution in 1800, the level of atmospheric carbon dioxide has risen from about 280 ppm to about 380 ppm in 2005, or a 35% increase.

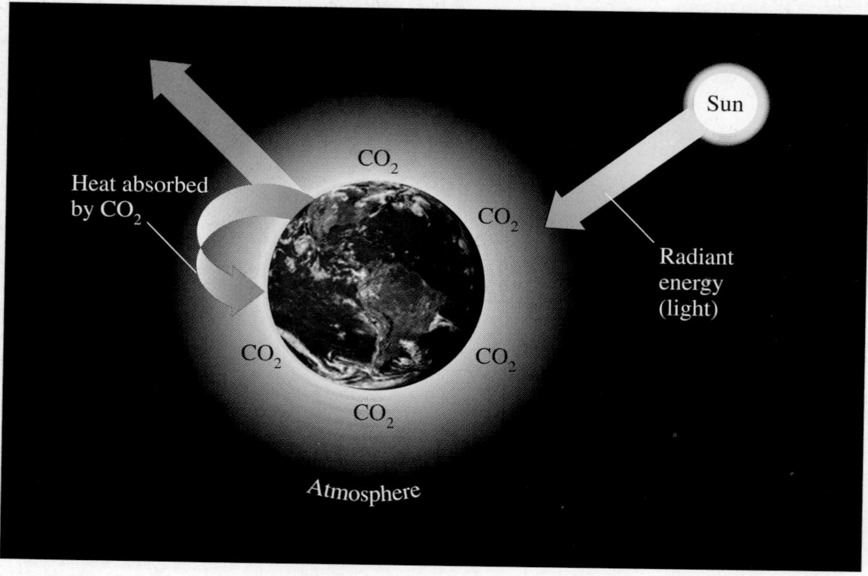


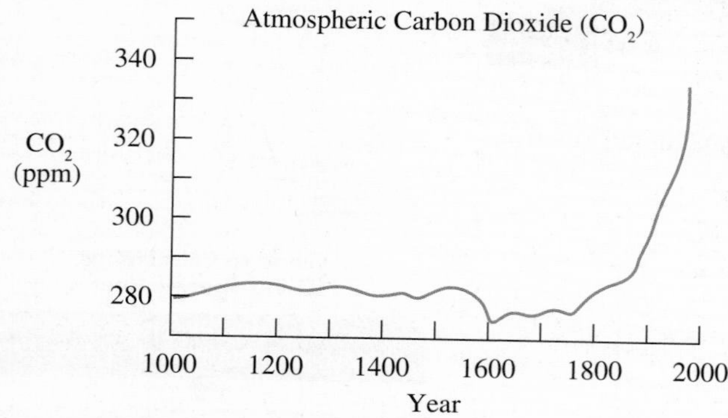


As the atmospheric $CO_2$ levels increase, more solar radiation is trapped by atmospheric gases, which raises the temperature at Earth's surface. Some scientists have estimated that if the carbon dioxide level doubles from its level before the Industrial Revolution, the average temperature globally could increase by 2.0 °C to 4.4 °C. While this may seem to be a small temperature change, it could have dramatic impact worldwide. Even now, glaciers and snow cover in much of the world have diminished. Ice sheets in Antarctica and Greenland are melting rapidly and breaking apart. Although no one knows for sure how rapidly the ice in the polar regions is melting, this accelerating change will contribute to a rise in sea level. In the twentieth century, the sea level rose 15 to 23 cm, and some scientists predict the sea level will rise 1 m in this century. Such an increase will have a major impact on coastal areas.

Until recently, the carbon dioxide level was maintained as algae in the oceans and trees in the forests utilized the carbon dioxide. However, the ability of these and other forms of plant life to absorb carbon dioxide is not keeping up with the increase in carbon dioxide levels. Most scientists agree that the primary source of the increase of carbon dioxide is the burning of fossil fuels such as gasoline, coal, and natural gas. The cutting and burning of trees in the rain forests (deforestation) also reduces the amount of carbon dioxide removed from the atmosphere.

Worldwide efforts are being made to reduce the carbon dioxide produced by burning fossil fuels that heat our homes, run our cars, and provide energy for industries. Efforts are being made to explore alternative energy sources and to reduce the effects of deforestation. Meanwhile, we can reduce energy use in our homes by using appliances that are more energy efficient and replacing incandescent light bulbs with fluorescent lights. Such an effort worldwide will reduce the possible impact of global warming and at the same time save our fuel resources.

## SAMPLE PROBLEM 2.7

### Calculating Mass Using Specific Heat

Ethanol has a specific heat of 2.46 J/g °C. When 655 J are added to a sample of ethanol, its temperature rises from 18.2 °C to 32.8 °C. What is the mass in grams of the ethanol sample?

SOLUTION

**STEP 1** **List given and needed data.**

**Given** heat = 655 J *SH* for ethanol = 2.46 J/g °C

Initial temperature = 18.2 °C

Final temperature = 32.8 °C

**Need** grams of the ethanol sample

**STEP 2** **Calculate the temperature change.** The temperature change, $\Delta T$, is the difference between the two temperatures.

$$\Delta T = 32.8\text{ °C} - 18.2\text{ °C} = 14.6\text{ °C}$$

**STEP 3** **Write the heat equation.**

$$\text{Heat} = \textit{mass} \times \Delta T \times SH$$

The heat equation must be rearranged to solve for mass, which is the heat divided by the temperature change and the specific heat.

**STEP 4** **Substitute the given values into the equation and solve, making sure units cancel.**

$$\text{Mass} = \frac{655\ \cancel{\text{J}}}{14.6\ \cancel{\text{°C}}\ \dfrac{2.46\ \cancel{\text{J}}}{\text{g}\ \cancel{\text{°C}}}}$$

$$= 18.2\text{ g}$$

STUDY CHECK

When 8.81 kJ is absorbed by a piece of iron, its temperature rises from 15 °C to 122 °C. What is the mass, in grams, if iron has a specific heat of 0.452 J/g °C?

## QUESTIONS AND PROBLEMS

### Specific Heat

**2.13** If the same amount of heat is supplied to samples of 10.0 g each of aluminum, iron, and copper, all at 15 °C, which sample would reach the highest temperature? (See Table 2.2.)

**2.14** Substances A and B are the same mass and at the same initial temperature. When the same amount of heat is added to each, the final temperature of A is 55 °C higher than the temperature of B. What does this tell you about the specific heats of A and B?

**2.15** Calculate the specific heat (J/g °C) for each of the following:

**a.** a 13.5-g sample of zinc heated from 24.2 °C to 83.6 °C that absorbs 312 J of heat

**b.** a 48.2-g sample of a metal that absorbs 345 J when temperature increases from 35.0 °C to 57.9 °C

**2.16** Calculate the specific heat (J/g °C) for each of the following:

**a.** an 18.5-g sample of tin that absorbs 183 J when its temperature increases from 35.0 °C to 78.6 °C

**b.** a 22.5-g sample of a metal that absorbs 645 J when its temperature changes from 36.2 °C to 92.0 °C

**2.17** What is the amount of heat required in each of the following?

**a.** calories to heat 25 g of water from 15 °C to 25 °C

**b.** calories to heat 150 g of water from 0 °C to 75 °C

**c.** kilocalories to heat 150 g of water in a kettle from 15 °C to 77 °C

**2.18** What is the amount of heat involved in each of the following?

**a.** calories given off when 85 g of water cools from 45 °C to 25 °C

**b.** calories given off when 25 g of water cools from 86 °C to 61 °C

**c.** kilocalories absorbed when 5.0 kg of water warms from 22 °C to 28 °C

**2.19** Calculate the energy in joules and calories

**a.** required to heat 25.0 g of water from 12.5 °C to 25.7 °C

**b.** required to heat 38.0 g of copper (Cu) from 122 °C to 246 °C

**c.** lost when 15.0 g of ethanol, $C_2H_5OH$, cools from 60.5 °C to −42.0 °C

**d.** lost when 112 g of iron, Fe, cools from 118 °C to 55 °C

**2.20** Calculate the energy in joules and calories

**a.** required to heat 5.25 g of water, $H_2O$, from 5.5 °C to 64.8 °C

**b.** lost when 75.0 g of water, $H_2O$, cools from 86.4 °C to 2.1 °C

**c.** required to heat 10.0 g of silver (Ag) from 112 °C to 275 °C

**d.** lost when 18.0 g of gold (Au) cools from 224 °C to 118 °C

**2.21** Calculate the mass in grams for each of the following:

**a.** a gold sample that absorbs 225 J to change its temperature from 15.0 °C to 47.0 °C

**b.** an iron object that loses 8.40 kJ when its temperature drops from 168.0 °C to 82.0 °C

**c.** a sample of aluminum that absorbs 8.80 kJ when heated from 12.5 °C to 26.8 °C

**d.** a sample of titanium that loses 14 200 J when it cools from 185 °C to 42 °C

**2.22** Calculate the mass in grams for each of the following:

**a.** a sample of water that absorbs 8250 J when its temperature rises from 18.4 °C to 92.6 °C

**b.** a pure silver sample that loses 3.22 kJ when its temperature drops from 145 °C to 24 °C

**c.** a sample of aluminum that absorbs 1.65 kJ when its temperature rises from 65 °C to 187 °C

**d.** an iron bar that loses 2.52 kJ when its temperature drops from 252 °C to 75 °C

## 2.4 Energy and Nutrition

**LEARNING GOAL**

Use the energy values to calculate the kilocalories (Cal) or kilojoules (kJ) in a food.

The foods we eat provide energy to do work in the body, which includes the growth and repair of cells. Vitamins and minerals are necessary for health but have little energy value. Carbohydrates are the primary fuel for the body, but if carbohydrate reserves are exhausted, fats and then proteins can be used for energy. For many years in the field of nutrition, the energy from food was measured in Calories or kilocalories. The nutritional unit **Calorie, Cal** (with an uppercase C), is the same as 1000 cal, or 1 kcal. Now the use of kilojoule (kJ) is becoming more prevalent. For example, a baked potato has an energy value of 120 Calories, which is 120 kcal or 500 kJ. A typical diet of 2000 Cal (kcal) is the same as an 8400 kJ diet.

TUTORIAL
Nutritional Energy

**Energy Values in Nutrition**

1 Cal = 1 kcal = 1000 cal

1 Cal = 4.184 kJ = 4184 J

In the laboratory, foods are burned in a calorimeter to determine their energy value. (See Figure 2.3.) Within the calorimeter, a sample of food is placed in a steel combustion chamber filled with oxygen gas. A measured quantity of water surrounds the combustion chamber. After the food sample ignites and burns, the heat released increases the temperature of the water. From the mass of the food and the temperature increase of the water, we can determine the energy content of the food.

We will assume that the energy absorbed by the calorimeter is negligible.

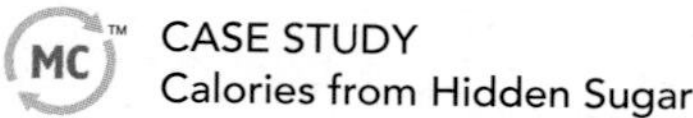
CASE STUDY
Calories from Hidden Sugar

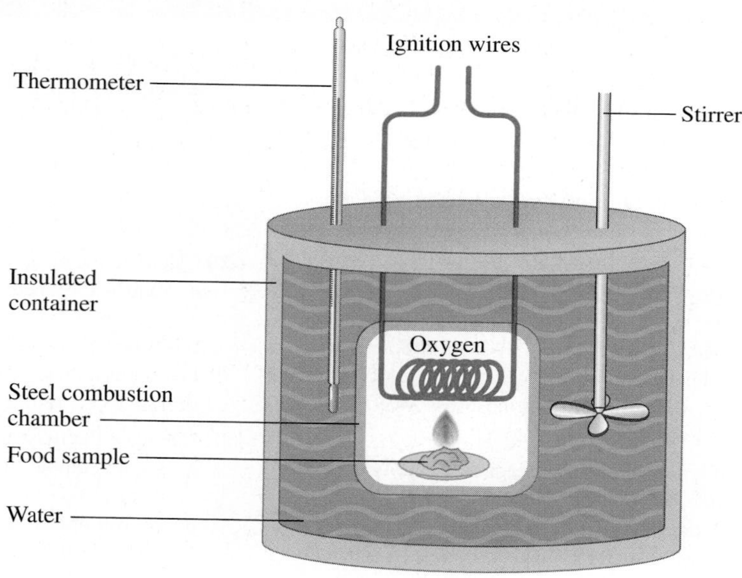


**FIGURE 2.3** The caloric value of a food sample is calculated from the heat released when the sample is burned in a calorimeter.

Q What happens to the temperature of water in a calorimeter during the combustion of a food sample?

**CONCEPT CHECK 2.4**

**Energy Values of Food**

A 2-oz serving of pasta provides 200 Cal. What is the energy value of pasta in Cal/g?

ANSWER

Using the equalities of 16 oz = 1 lb and 1 lb = 454 g, we can set up some calculations for the energy values of pasta.

$$\frac{200\ \text{Cal}}{2\ \cancel{\text{oz}}} \times \frac{16\ \cancel{\text{oz}}}{1\ \cancel{\text{lb}}} \times \frac{1\ \cancel{\text{lb}}}{454\ \text{g}} = 4\ \text{Cal/g}$$

SAMPLE PROBLEM 2.8

### Calculating Food Energy Values

A 2.3-g sample of butter, a fat, is placed in a calorimeter containing 1900 g of water at an initial temperature of 17 °C. After the complete combustion of the butter, the water has a temperature of 28 °C. Assume that the energy absorbed by the calorimeter is negligible. What is the energy value (kcal/g) and (kJ/g) of butter?

SOLUTION

With a $\Delta T = 11$ °C, the heat in kilocalories and kilojoules absorbed by the water is calculated as follows:

$$\text{Mass} \times \Delta T \times \text{specific heat of water} = \text{heat (kcal or kJ)}$$

$$1900\ \cancel{g} \times 11\ ^\circ\cancel{C} \times \frac{1.00\ \cancel{cal}}{\cancel{g}\ ^\circ\cancel{C}} \times \frac{1\ \text{kcal}}{1000\ \cancel{cal}} = 21\ \text{kcal}$$

$$1900\ \cancel{g} \times 11\ ^\circ\cancel{C} \times \frac{4.184\ \cancel{J}}{\cancel{g}\ ^\circ\cancel{C}} \times \frac{1\ \text{kJ}}{1000\ \cancel{J}} = 87\ \text{kJ}$$

Because 2.3 g of fat provided the 21 kcal (87 kJ) of heat, the energy value of butter is calculated as follows:

$$\frac{21\ \text{kcal}}{2.3\ \text{g fat}} = 9.1\ \text{kcal/g of fat} \qquad \frac{87\ \text{kJ}}{2.3\ \text{g fat}} = 38\ \text{kJ/g of fat}$$

STUDY CHECK

A 4.5-g sample of the carbohydrate sucrose, table sugar, is placed in a calorimeter. The water in the container has a mass of 1500 g and an initial temperature of 15 °C. After all the sucrose is burned, the water temperature is 27 °C. What is the energy value, in kcal/g and kJ/g, for sucrose?

## Energy Values for Foods

The **energy (caloric) values** of food are the kilocalories or kilojoules obtained from the complete combustion of 1 g of a carbohydrate, fat, or protein. (See Table 2.3.)

**TABLE 2.3** Typical Energy (Caloric) Values for the Three Food Types

| Food Type | kJ/g | kcal/g |
|---|---|---|
| Carbohydrate | 17 | 4 |
| Fat | 38 | 9 |
| Protein | 17 | 4 |

Using the energy values in Table 2.3, we can calculate the total energy of a food if the mass of each food type is known.

$$\text{Kilojoules} = \cancel{g} \times \frac{\text{kJ}}{\cancel{g}}$$

$$\text{Kilocalories} = \cancel{g} \times \frac{\text{kcal}}{\cancel{g}}$$

**Nutrition Facts**
Serving Size 14 crackers (31g)
Servings Per Container About 7

| Amount Per Serving | |
|---|---|
| Calories 120 Calories from Fat 35 | |
| Kilojoules 500 kJ from Fat 150 | |
| | % Daily Value* |
| **Total Fat** 4g | 6% |
| Saturated Fat 0.5g | 3% |
| Trans Fat 0g | |
| Polyunsaturated Fat 0.5% | |
| Monounsaturated Fat 1.5g | |
| **Cholesterol** 0mg | 0% |
| **Sodium** 310mg | 13% |
| **Total Carbohydrate** 19g | 6% |
| Dietary Fiber Less than 1g | 4% |
| Sugars 2g | |
| **Proteins** 2g | |
| Vitamin A 0% • Vitamin C 0% | |
| Calcium 4% • Iron 6% | |

*Percent Daily Values are based on a 2,000 calorie diet. Your daily values may be higher or lower depending on your calorie needs.

| | | Calories: 2,000 | 2,500 |
|---|---|---|---|
| Total Fat | Less than | 65g | 80g |
| Sat Fat | Less than | 20g | 25g |
| Cholesterol | Less than | 300mg | 300mg |
| Sodium | Less than | 2,400mg | 2,400mg |
| Total Carbohydrate | | 300g | 375g |
| Dietary Fiber | | 25g | 30g |

Calories per gram:
Fat 9 • Carbohydrate 4 • Protein 4

## Counting Calories

Obtain a food item that has a nutrition label. From the Nutrition Facts information on the label, determine the number of grams of carbohydrate, fat, and protein in one serving. Using energy values, calculate the total Calories for one serving. (Most products round off to the tens place.)

**QUESTION**

How does your total for the Calories in one serving compare to the Calories stated on the label for a single serving?

Typical values for carbohydrates, fats, and proteins are listed in Table 2.4. On packaged food, the energy content is listed in the Nutrition Facts label on the package, usually in terms of the number of Calories for one serving. The general composition and caloric content of some foods are given in Table 2.4.

**TABLE 2.4** General Composition and Energy Content of Some Foods

| Food | Carbohydrate (g) | Fat (g) | Protein (g) | Energy* |
|---|---|---|---|---|
| Banana, 1 medium | 26 | 0 | 1 | 460 kJ (110 kcal) |
| Beef, ground, 3 oz | 0 | 14 | 22 | 910 kJ (220 kcal) |
| Carrots, raw, 1 cup | 11 | 0 | 1 | 200 kJ (50 kcal) |
| Chicken, no skin, 3 oz | 0 | 3 | 20 | 460 kJ (110 kcal) |
| Egg, 1 large | 0 | 6 | 6 | 330 kJ (80 kcal) |
| Milk, 4% fat, 1 cup | 12 | 9 | 9 | 700 kJ (170 kcal) |
| Milk, nonfat, 1 cup | 12 | 0 | 9 | 360 kJ (90 kcal) |
| Potato, baked | 23 | 0 | 3 | 440 kJ (100 kcal) |
| Salmon, 3 oz | 0 | 5 | 16 | 460 kJ (110 kcal) |
| Steak, 3 oz | 0 | 27 | 19 | 1350 kJ (320 kcal) |

*Energy values are rounded to the tens place.

SAMPLE PROBLEM 2.9

## Energy Content for a Food

What is the energy content, in kJ and kcal, for a piece of chocolate cake that contains 34 g of carbohydrate, 10 g of fat, and 5 g of protein? Round the answers of kJ and kcal to the tens place.

SOLUTION

Using the energy values for carbohydrate, fat, and protein (Table 2.3), we can calculate the total number of kcal:

| Food Type | Mass | Energy Values | Energy |
|---|---|---|---|
| Carbohydrate | $34\ \cancel{g}\ \times$ | $\dfrac{17\text{ kJ (or 4 kcal)}}{1\ \cancel{g}} =$ | 580 kJ (or 140 kcal) |
| Fat | $10\ \cancel{g}\ \times$ | $\dfrac{38\text{ kJ (or 9 kcal)}}{1\ \cancel{g}} =$ | 380 kJ (or 90 kcal) |
| Protein | $5\ \cancel{g}\ \times$ | $\dfrac{17\text{ kJ (or 4 kcal)}}{1\ \cancel{g}} =$ | 90 kJ (or 20 kcal) |
| | | Total energy content = | 1050 kJ (or 250 kcal) |

STUDY CHECK

A 1-oz (28 g) serving of oat-bran hot cereal with half a cup of whole milk contains 22 g of carbohydrate, 7 g of fat, and 10 g of protein. If you eat two servings of the oat bran for breakfast, how many kilocalories will you obtain? Round the final answer to the tens place.

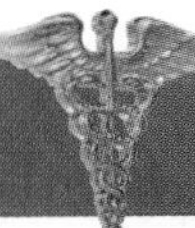

# HEALTH NOTE

## Losing and Gaining Weight

The number of kilocalories or kilojoules needed in the daily diet of an adult depends on gender, age, and level of physical activity. Some general levels of energy needs are given in Table 2.5.

**TABLE 2.5** Typical Energy Requirements for a 70.0-kg (154-lb) Adult

| Gender | Energy (kJ) | Energy (kcal) |
|---|---|---|
| Female | 10 000 | 2200 |
| Male | 12 500 | 3000 |

A person gains weight when food intake exceeds energy output. The amount of food a person eats is regulated by the hunger center in the hypothalamus, which is located in the brain. Food intake is normally proportional to the nutrient stores in the body. If these nutrient stores are low, you feel hungry; if they are high, you do not feel like eating.

A person loses weight when food intake is less than energy output. Many diet products contain cellulose, which has no nutritive value but provides bulk and makes you feel full. Some diet drugs depress the hunger center and must be used with caution, because they excite the nervous system and can elevate blood pressure. Because muscular exercise is an important way to expend energy, an increase in daily exercise aids weight loss. Table 2.6 lists some activities and the amount of energy they require.

**TABLE 2.6** Energy Expended by a 70.0-kg (154-lb) Adult

| Activity | Energy (kJ/hr) | Energy (kcal/hr) |
|---|---|---|
| Sleeping | 250 | 60 |
| Sitting | 420 | 100 |
| Walking | 840 | 200 |
| Swimming | 2100 | 500 |
| Running | 3100 | 750 |

# QUESTIONS AND PROBLEMS

## Energy and Nutrition

2.23 Using the following data, determine the kilojoules and kilocalories for each food burned in a calorimeter:

- **a.** one stalk of celery that produces energy to heat 505 g of water from 25.2 °C to 35.7 °C
- **b.** a waffle that produces energy to heat 4980 g of water from 20.6 °C to 62.4 °C

**2.24** Calculate the kilojoules and kilocalories each food provides when burned in a calorimeter:

- **a.** 1 cup of popcorn that produces energy to change the temperature of 1250 g of water from 25.5 °C to 50.8 °C
- **b.** a sample of butter that produces energy to increase the temperature of 357 g water from 22.7 °C to 38.8 °C

2.25 Using the energy values for foods, determine each of the following (round final Cal answers to the tens place):

- **a.** the total Calories for 1 cup of orange juice that contains 26 g of carbohydrate, no fat, and 2 g of protein
- **b.** the grams of carbohydrate in one apple if the apple has no fat and no protein and provides 72 kcal of energy
- **c.** the Calories in 1 tablespoon of vegetable oil, which contains 14 g of fat and no carbohydrate or protein
- **d.** the total Calories in one breakfast roll that has 30.0 g of carbohydrate, 15 g of fat, and 5 g of protein

**2.26** Using the energy values for food, determine each of the following (round final Cal answers to tens place):

- **a.** the total Calories for 2 tablespoons of crunchy peanut butter that contains 6 g of carbohydrate, 16 g of fat, and 7 g of protein
- **b.** the grams of protein in 1 cup of soup that has 110 Cal with 7 g of fat and 9 g of carbohydrate
- **c.** the grams of sugar (carbohydrate) in one can of cola if it has 140 Cal and no fat and no protein
- **d.** the grams of fat in one avocado if it has 405 Calories, 13 g of carbohydrate, and 5 g of protein

2.27 One cup of clam chowder contains 9 g of protein, 12 g of fat, and 16 g of carbohydrate. How many kilocalories are in the clam chowder? How many kilojoules are in the clam chowder? (Round the final answers to the tens place.)

**2.28** A high-protein diet contains 70.0 g of carbohydrate, 150 g of protein, and 5.0 g of fat. How many kilocalories does this diet provide? How many kilojoules does this diet provide? (Round the final answers to the tens place.)

## 2.5 Classification of Matter

**LEARNING GOAL**

Classify examples of matter as pure substances or mixtures.

*Matter* is anything that has mass and occupies space. Matter makes up all the things we use such as water, wood, plates, plastic bags, clothes, and shoes. The different types of matter are classified by their composition.

### Pure Substances

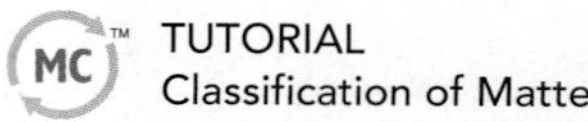


TUTORIAL
Classification of Matter

A **pure substance** is matter that has a definite composition. There are two kinds of pure substances: elements and compounds. An **element** is the simplest pure substance because it is composed of only one kind of material—for example, silver, iron, or aluminum. A full list of the elements is found on the inside front cover of this text. A **compound** is also a pure substance, but it consists of two or more elements always in the same proportion. In compounds, the elements are held together by attractions called *bonds*. For example, the compound water, $H_2O$, always has the same proportion of the elements hydrogen and oxygen. The compound, hydrogen peroxide, $H_2O_2$, is also a combination of the elements hydrogen and oxygen, but in a different ratio.

An important difference between elements and compounds is that chemical processes can break down compounds into simpler substances such as elements. You may know that ordinary table salt is the compound NaCl, which can be broken down into sodium and chlorine as seen in Figure 2.4. Compounds are not broken down through physical methods such as boiling or sifting. Chemical or physical processes cannot break down elements.

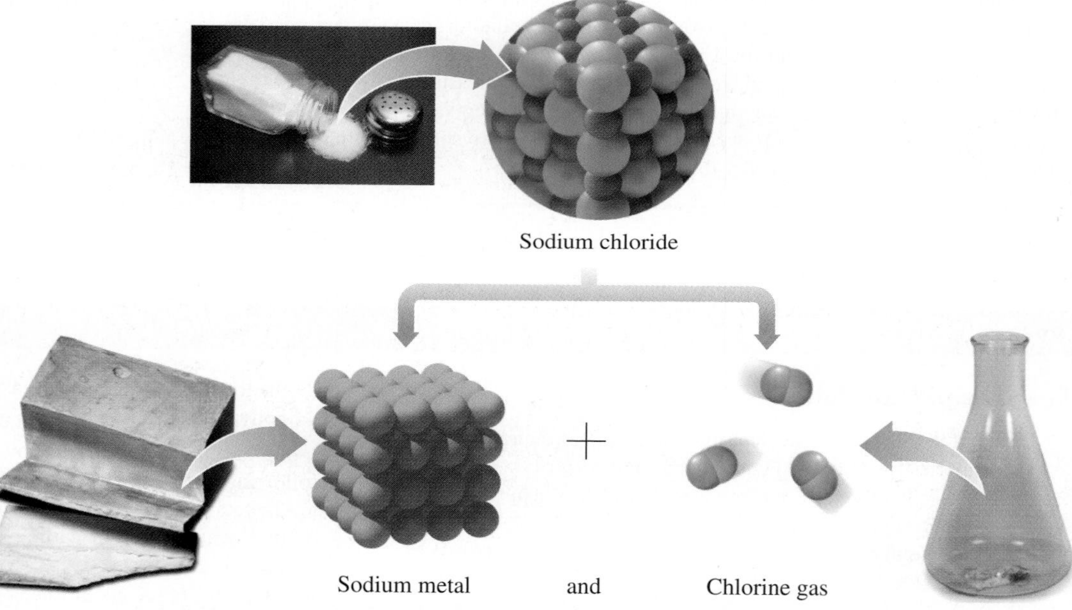


FIGURE 2.4 The decomposition of salt, NaCl, produces the elements sodium and chlorine.
Q How do elements and compounds differ?

**CONCEPT CHECK 2.5**

**Pure Substances**

Explain why each of the following pure substances is a compound, and name its elements:

**a.** a carbohydrate glucose, $C_6H_{12}O_6$, also known as blood sugar
**b.** nitrogen dioxide, $NO_2$, a reddish-brown colored gas found in smog

ANSWER

**a.** Glucose, $C_6H_{12}O_6$, has a definite composition of three elements: carbon, hydrogen, and oxygen.
**b.** Nitrogen dioxide, $NO_2$, has a definite composition of two elements: nitrogen and oxygen.

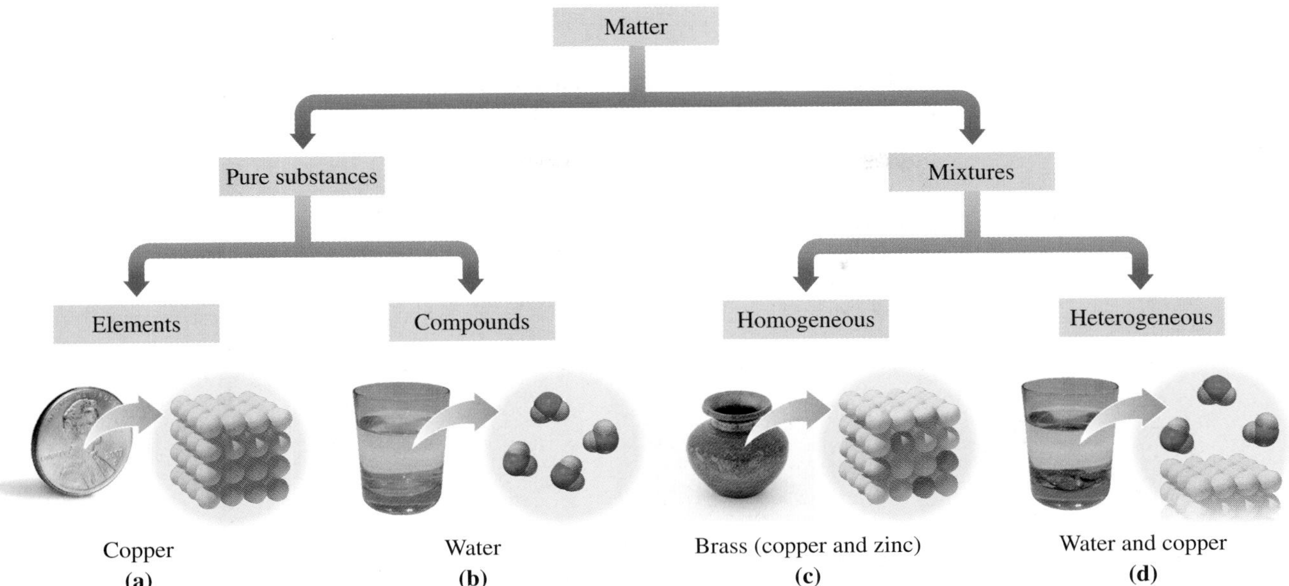


**FIGURE 2.5** Matter is organized by its components: elements, compounds, and mixtures. **(a)** The element copper consists of copper atoms. **(b)** The compound water consists of $H_2O$ molecules. **(c)** Brass is a homogeneous mixture of copper and zinc atoms. **(d)** Copper metal in water is a heterogeneous mixture of Cu atoms and $H_2O$ molecules.

**Q** Why are copper and water pure substances, but brass is a mixture?

## Mixtures

Much of the matter in our everyday lives consists of mixtures. (See Figure 2.5.) In a **mixture**, two or more substances are physically mixed, but not chemically combined. The air we breathe is a mixture of mostly oxygen and nitrogen gases. The steel in buildings and railroad tracks is a mixture of iron, nickel, carbon, and chromium. The brass in doorknobs and fixtures is a mixture of zinc and copper. Tea, coffee, and ocean water are mixtures, too. In any mixture, the composition can vary. For example, two sugar–water mixtures may look the same, but one would taste sweeter because it has a higher ratio of sugar to water. Different types of brass have different properties, depending on the ratio of copper to zinc.

Physical processes can be used to separate mixtures because there are no chemical interactions between the components. For example, a mixture of different coins such as nickels, dimes, and quarters can be separated by size; iron particles mixed with sand can be picked up with a magnet; and water is separated from cooked spaghetti by using a strainer. (See Figure 2.6.)

## Types of Mixtures

Mixtures are classified as homogeneous or heterogeneous. In a *homogeneous mixture*, also called a *solution*, the composition is uniform throughout the sample. Examples of familiar homogeneous mixtures are air, which contains oxygen and nitrogen gases; and salt water, a solution of salt and water.

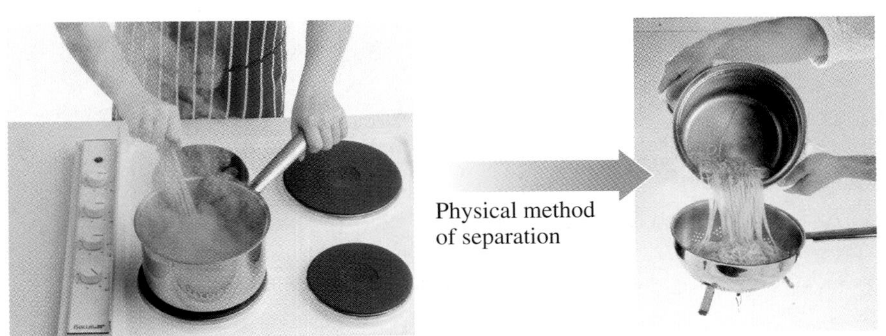


**FIGURE 2.6** A mixture of spaghetti and water is separated using a strainer, a physical method of separation.

**Q** Why can physical methods be used to separate mixtures but not compounds?

TABLE 2.7 Classification of Matter

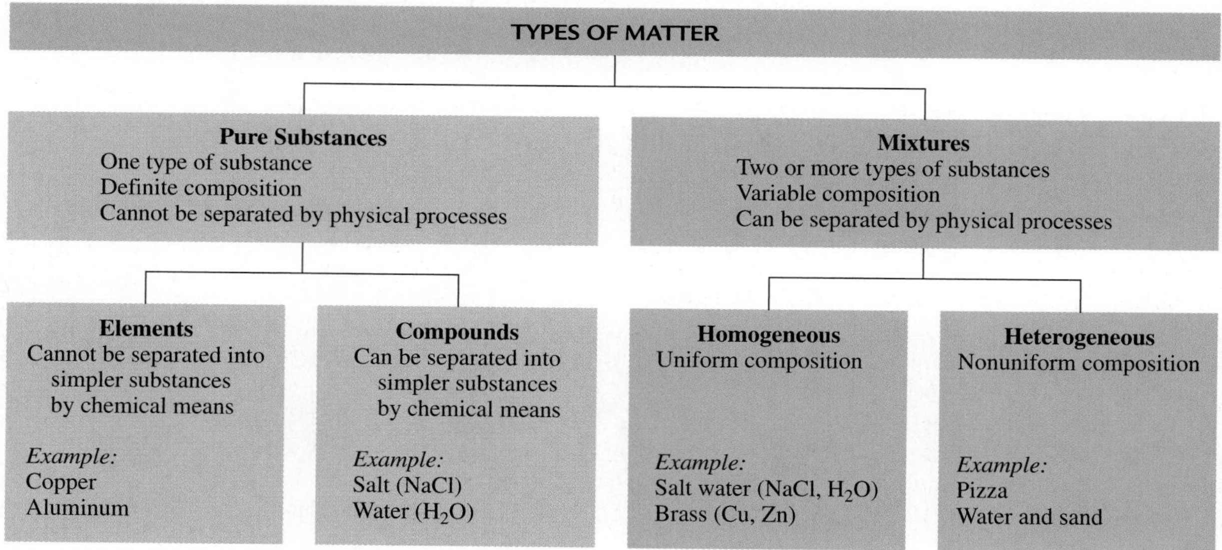


In a *heterogeneous mixture*, the components do not have a uniform composition throughout the sample. For example, a mixture of oil and water is heterogeneous because the oil floats on the surface of the water. Other examples of heterogeneous mixtures include a raisin cookie and a hot fudge sundae. Table 2.7 summarizes the classification of matter.

SAMPLE PROBLEM 2.10

## Classifying Pure Substances and Mixtures

Classify each of the following as a pure substance (element or compound) or a mixture (homogeneous or heterogeneous):

**a.** ice cream float
**b.** coffee with cream and sugar
**c.** copper wire
**d.** carbon dioxide ($CO_2$)

SOLUTION

**a.** mixture; heterogeneous with a nonuniform composition
**b.** mixture; homogeneous with uniform composition of coffee, cream, and sugar
**c.** pure substance; element
**d.** pure substance; compound with a definite ratio of two elements

STUDY CHECK

A salad dressing is prepared with oil, vinegar, and chunks of blue cheese. Is this a homogeneous or heterogeneous mixture?

# QUESTIONS AND PROBLEMS

## Classification of Matter

**2.29** Classify each of the following pure substances as an element or compound. Give a reason for your answer.
**a.** baking soda ($NaHCO_3$)
**b.** oxygen ($O_2$)
**c.** ice ($H_2O$)
**d.** aluminum foil (Al)

**2.30** Classify each of the following pure substances as an element or compound. Give a reason for your answer.
**a.** platinum (Pt) in a catalytic converter
**b.** vitamin C ($C_6H_8O_6$)
**c.** mercury in a thermometer (Hg)
**d.** carbon monoxide (CO)

**2.31** Classify each of the following mixtures as homogeneous or heterogeneous:
**a.** vegetable soup
**b.** saltwater
**c.** tea
**d.** tea with ice and a lemon slice
**e.** water and sand in an aquarium
**f.** fruit salad

**2.32** Classify each of the following mixtures as homogeneous or heterogeneous:
**a.** homogenized milk
**b.** chocolate chip ice cream
**c.** gasoline
**d.** ham and cheese sandwich
**e.** chicken noodle soup
**f.** hot tea with sweetener

## 2.6 States and Properties of Matter

On Earth, matter exists in one of three *physical states*: *solids*, *liquids*, and *gases*. All matter is made up of tiny particles. A **solid**, such as a pebble or a baseball, has a definite shape and volume. You can probably recognize several solids within your reach right now such as books, pencils, or a computer mouse. In a **solid**, strong attractive forces hold the particles close together. The particles are arranged in such a rigid pattern they can only vibrate slowly in their fixed positions. For many solids, this rigid structure produces a crystal such as that seen in amethyst. (See Figure 2.7.)

A **liquid** has a definite volume but not a definite shape. In a **liquid**, the particles move in random directions but are sufficiently attracted to each other to maintain a definite volume, although not a rigid structure. Thus, when oil, water, or vinegar is poured from one container to another, the liquid maintains its own volume but takes the shape of the new container. (See Figure 2.8.)

A **gas** does not have a definite shape or volume. When you inflate a bicycle tire, the air, which is a gas, fills the entire shape and volume of the tire. In a **gas**, the particles are far apart, have little attraction to each other, and move at high speeds, taking the shape and volume of their container. (See Figure 2.9.) Table 2.8 compares the three states of matter.

LEARNING GOAL

Identify the states and properties of matter.

FIGURE 2.7 The solid state of amethyst, a purple form of quartz.

Q Why do these crystals have a definite shape?

FIGURE 2.8 A liquid with a volume of 100 mL takes the shape of its container.

Q Why does a liquid have a definite volume but not a definite shape?

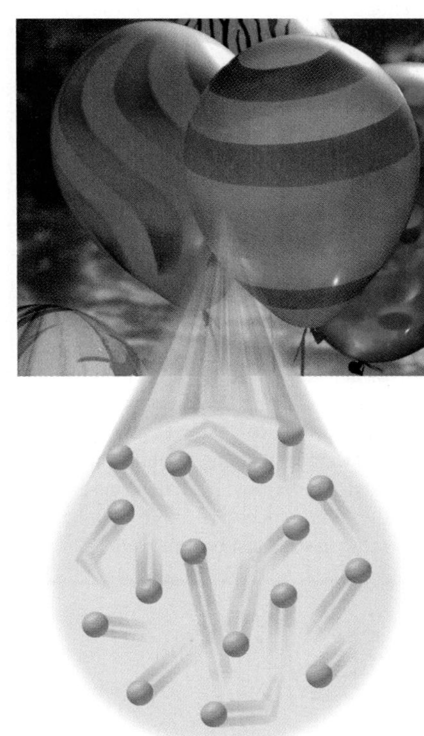

FIGURE 2.9 A gas takes the shape and volume of its container.

Q Why does a gas fill the volume of a container?

CONCEPT CHECK 2.6

### States of Matter

Identify the state(s) of matter described by the substance in each of the following:

**a.** Volume does not change in a different container.
**b.** Has an especially low density.
**c.** Shape depends on the container.
**d.** Has a definite shape and volume.

ANSWER

**a.** Both a solid and a liquid have their own volume that does not depend on the volume of their container.
**b.** In a gas, the particles are far apart, which gives a small mass per volume, or a low density.
**c.** Both a liquid and a gas take the shape of their containers.
**d.** A solid has a rigid arrangement of particles that gives it a definite shape and volume.

## Physical Properties and Physical Changes

One way to describe matter is to observe its physical properties. If you were asked to describe yourself, you might list your characteristics such as the color of your eyes and skin, or the length, color, and texture of your hair. **Physical properties** are those characteristics

## Career Focus

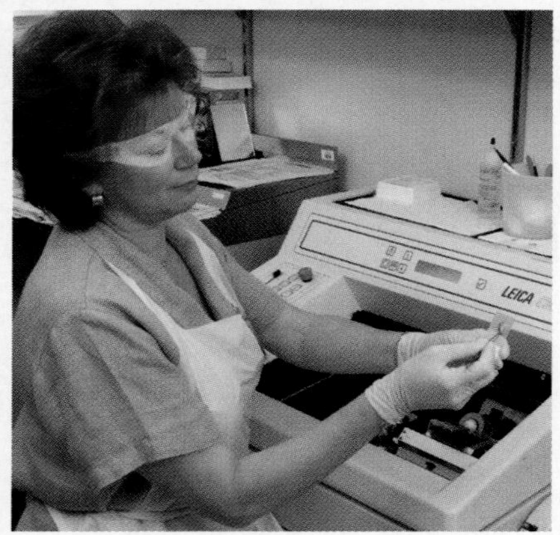

### Histologist

"While a patient is in surgery for skin cancer, some tissue around the cancer is sent to us," says Mary Ann Pipe, histology technician. "Using the Mohs surgical technique, we place the tissue block on a glass slide, chill it to −30 °C in a machine called a *cryostat*, and freeze it for longer in another machine called a *heat extractor.* From this frozen block of tissue, we cut extremely thin slices—one-thousandth of an inch—from different depths. We prepare three separate slides from skin at three different depths up to the surface of the skin. We stain the cells pink and blue by placing the slides in hemotoxin, and then in eosin. The slices are a tissue map that the doctor can easily read to determine if the margins around the skin cancer are clear or whether more tissue must be removed."

**TABLE 2.8** A Comparison of Solids, Liquids, and Gases

Ice: $H_2O$ (*s*)

Water: $H_2O$ (*l*)

Water vapor: $H_2O$ (*g*)

| Characteristic | Solid | Liquid | Gas |
|---|---|---|---|
| Shape | Has a definite shape | Takes the shape of the container | Takes the shape of the container |
| Volume | Has a definite volume | Has a definite volume | Fills the volume of the container |
| Arrangement of particles | Fixed, extremely close | Random, close | Random, far apart |
| Interaction between particles | Especially strong | Strong | Essentially none |
| Movement of particles | Extremely slow | Moderate | Exceptionally fast |
| Examples | Ice, salt, iron | Water, oil, vinegar | Water vapor, helium, air |

that can be observed or measured without affecting the identity of a substance. In chemistry, typical physical properties include the shape, state, color, melting point, and boiling point of a substance. For example, you might observe that a penny is round, orange-red, solid, and shiny. Table 2.9 gives examples of physical properties of copper found in pennies, electrical wiring, and copper pans.

**TABLE 2.9** Some Physical Properties of Copper

| Characteristic | Physical property |
|---|---|
| Color | Reddish-orange |
| Odor | Odorless |
| Melting point | 1083 °C |
| Boiling point | 2567 °C |
| State at 25 °C | Solid |
| Luster | Shiny |
| Conduction of electricity | Excellent |
| Conduction of heat | Excellent |

Water is a substance that is commonly found in all three states: solid, liquid, and gas. When matter undergoes a **physical change**, its state or its appearance will change, but its composition remains the same. The solid form of water, snow or ice, has a different appearance than its liquid or gaseous form, but all three forms are water.

The physical appearance of a substance can change in other ways, too. Suppose that you dissolve some salt in water. The appearance of the salt changes, but you could re-form the salt crystals by heating the mixture and evaporating the water. Thus in a physical change, there are no new substances produced. Table 2.10 gives more examples of physical changes.

TABLE 2.10 Examples of Some Physical Changes

| Type of Physical Change | Example |
|---|---|
| Change of state | Water boiling<br>Water freezing |
| Change of appearance | Dissolving sugar in water |
| Change of shape | Hammering a gold ingot into shiny gold leaf<br>Drawing copper into thin copper wire |
| Change of size | Cutting paper into tiny pieces for confetti<br>Grinding pepper into smaller particles |

## Chemical Properties and Chemical Changes

**Chemical properties** are those that describe the ability of a substance to change into a new substance. When **chemical changes** take place, the original substances are converted into one or more new substances, which have different chemical and physical properties. For example, wood can burn because it has the chemical property of being flammable. When wood burns, it is converted to ashes and smoke, which have different chemical and physical properties. Rusting or corrosion is a chemical property of iron. In the rain, an iron nail undergoes a chemical change when it reacts with oxygen in the air to form rust, a new substance. Table 2.11 gives examples of chemical changes, and Table 2.12 summarizes physical and chemical properties and changes.

TABLE 2.11 Examples of Some Chemical Changes

| Type of Chemical Change | Changes in Chemical Properties |
|---|---|
| Tarnishing of silver | Shiny, silver metal reacts in air to give a black, grainy coating. |
| Burning wood | A piece of pine burns with a bright flame, producing heat, ashes, carbon dioxide, and water vapor. |
| Caramelizing sugar | At high temperatures, white, granular sugar changes to a smooth, caramel-colored substance. |
| Formation of rust | Iron, which is gray and shiny, combines with oxygen to form orange-red rust. |

TABLE 2.12 Summary of Physical and Chemical Properties and Changes

| | Physical | Chemical |
|---|---|---|
| **Property** | A characteristic of the substance such as color, shape, odor, luster, size, melting point, and density. | A characteristic that indicates the ability of a substance to form another substance: paper can burn, iron can rust, and silver can tarnish. |
| **Change** | A change in a physical property that retains the identity of the substance: a change of state, a change in size, or a change in shape. | A change in which the original substance is converted to one or more new substances: paper burns, iron rusts, silver tarnishes. |

CONCEPT CHECK 2.7

### Physical and Chemical Properties

Classify each of the following as a physical or chemical property:

**a.** Water is a liquid at room temperature.
**b.** Gasoline is flammable.
**c.** Aluminum foil has a shiny appearance.

ANSWER

**a.** A liquid is a state of matter, which makes it a physical property.
**b.** The burning or flammability of gasoline changes it to different substances with new properties, which is a chemical property.
**c.** The shininess of a substance does not change the type of substance; it is a physical property.

SAMPLE PROBLEM 2.11

### Physical and Chemical Changes

Classify each of the following as a physical or chemical change:

**a.** An ice cube melts to form liquid water.
**b.** Bleach removes a stain.
**c.** An enzyme breaks down the lactose in milk.
**d.** Peppercorns are ground into flakes.

SOLUTION

**a.** Physical change; the ice cube changes state.
**b.** Chemical change; a change occurs in the composition of the stain.
**c.** Chemical change; a change occurs in the composition of lactose.
**d.** Physical change; a change of size does not change composition.

STUDY CHECK

Which of the following are chemical changes?

**a.** Water freezes on a pond.
**b.** Gas bubbles form when baking powder is placed in vinegar.
**c.** A log is chopped for firewood.
**d.** A log is burned in a fireplace.

## QUESTIONS AND PROBLEMS

### States and Properties of Matter

**2.33** Indicate whether each of the following describes a gas, a liquid, or a solid:
**a.** This substance has no definite volume or shape.
**b.** The particles in a substance do not interact strongly with each other.
**c.** The particles in a substance are held in a definite structure.

**2.34** Indicate whether each of the following describes a gas, a liquid, or a solid:
**a.** The substance has a definite volume but takes the shape of the container.
**b.** The particles in this substance are very far apart.
**c.** This substance occupies the entire volume of the container.

**2.35** Describe each of the following as a physical or chemical property:
**a.** Chromium is a steel-gray solid.
**b.** Hydrogen reacts readily with oxygen.
**c.** Nitrogen freezes at –210 °C.
**d.** Milk will sour when left in a warm room.

**2.36** Describe each of the following as a physical or chemical property:
**a.** Neon is a colorless gas at room temperature.
**b.** Apple slices turn brown when exposed to air.
**c.** Phosphorus will ignite when exposed to air.
**d.** At room temperature, mercury is a liquid.

**2.37** What type of change, physical or chemical, takes place in each of the following?
**a.** Water vapor condenses to form rain.
**b.** Cesium metal reacts explosively with water.
**c.** Gold melts at 1064 °C.
**d.** A puzzle is cut into 1000 pieces.
**e.** Sugar dissolves in water.

**2.38** What type of change, physical or chemical, takes place in each of the following?
**a.** Gold is hammered into thin sheets.
**b.** A silver pin tarnishes in the air.
**c.** A tree is cut into boards at a sawmill.
**d.** Food is digested.
**e.** A chocolate bar melts.

**2.39** Describe each property of the element fluorine as physical or chemical.
- **a.** is highly reactive
- **b.** is a gas at room temperature
- **c.** has a pale, yellow color
- **d.** will explode in the presence of hydrogen
- **e.** has a melting point of –220 °C

**2.40** Describe each property of the element zirconium as physical or chemical.
- **a.** melts at 1852 °C
- **b.** is resistant to corrosion
- **c.** has a grayish-white color
- **d.** ignites spontaneously in air when finely divided
- **e.** is a shiny metal

## 2.7 Changes of State

**LEARNING GOAL**

Describe the changes of state between solids, liquids, and gases; calculate the energy involved.

Matter undergoes a **change of state** when it is converted from one state to another state. (See Figure 2.10.)

When heat is added to a solid, the particles in the rigid structure move faster. At a temperature called the **melting point (mp)**, the particles in the solid gain sufficient energy to overcome the attractive forces that hold them together. The particles in the solid separate and move about in random patterns. The substance is **melting**, changing from a solid to a liquid.

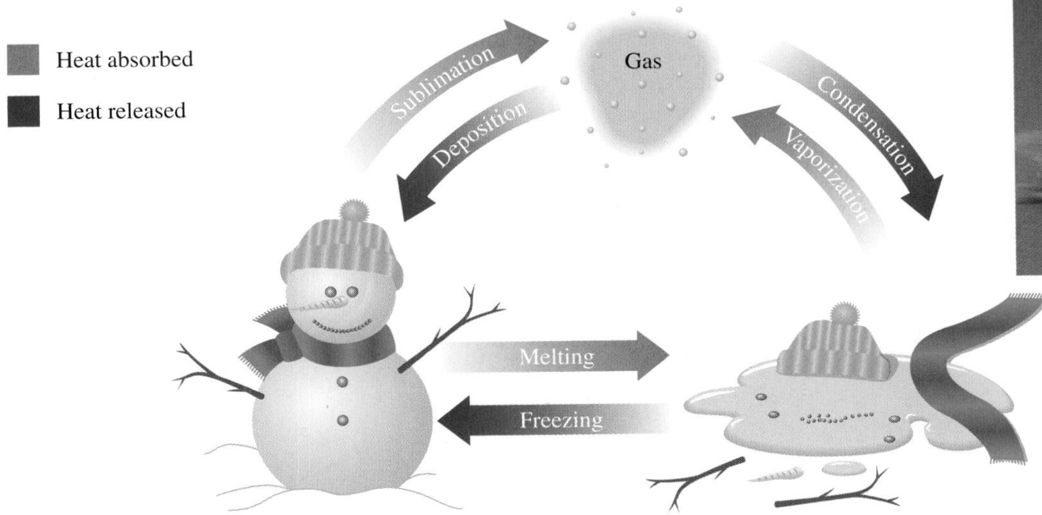


**FIGURE 2.10** A summary of the changes of state.
**Q** Is heat added or released when liquid water freezes?

If the temperature of a liquid is lowered, the reverse process takes place. Kinetic energy is lost, the particles slow down, and attractive forces pull the particles close together. The substance is **freezing**. A liquid changes to a solid at its **freezing point (fp)**, which is the same temperature as the melting point. Every substance has its own freezing (melting) point: Water freezes (melts) at 0 °C, gold freezes (melts) at 1064 °C, and nitrogen freezes (melts) at –210 °C.

During a change of state, the temperature of a substance remains constant. Suppose we have a glass containing ice and water. The ice melts when heat is added at 0 °C, forming more liquid. The liquid freezes when heat is removed at 0 °C.

### Heat of Fusion

During melting, energy called the **heat of fusion** is added to separate the particles of a solid. For example, 334 joules (80. calories) of heat are needed to melt 1 g of ice at its melting point (0 °C).

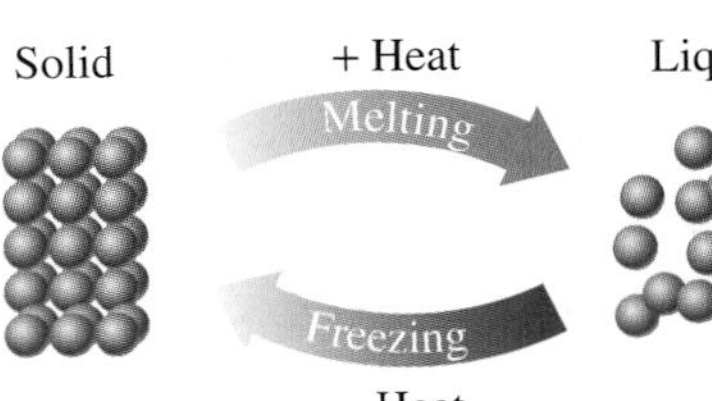


**Heat of Fusion for Water**

$$\frac{334\ \text{J}}{1\ \text{g of H}_2\text{O}} \qquad \frac{80.\ \text{cal}}{1\ \text{g of H}_2\text{O}}$$

The heat of fusion (334 J/g or 80. cal/g) is also the amount of heat that must be removed to freeze 1 g of water at its freezing point (0 °C). Water is sometimes sprayed in fruit orchards during especially cold and sometimes subfreezing weather. If the air temperature drops to 0 °C, the water begins to freeze. Heat is released as the water molecules bond together, which warms the air and protects the fruit.

To determine the amount of heat needed to melt a sample of ice, multiply the mass of the ice by its heat of fusion. There is no temperature change in the calculation because temperature remains constant as long as the ice is melting.

**Calculating Heat to Melt (or Freeze) Water**

Heat = mass × heat of fusion

$$\text{J} = \cancel{\text{g}} \times \frac{334\ \text{J}}{\cancel{\text{g}}}$$

$$\text{cal} = \cancel{\text{g}} \times \frac{80.\ \text{cal}}{\cancel{\text{g}}}$$

SAMPLE PROBLEM 2.12

### Heat of Fusion

Ice cubes at 0 °C with a mass of 26 g are added to your soft drink.

**a.** How much heat (joules) must be added to melt all the ice at 0 °C?
**b.** What happens to the temperature of your soft drink? Why?

SOLUTION

**a.** The heat in joules required to melt the ice is calculated as follows:

**STEP 1** **Given** 26 g of $H_2O(s)$ **Need** joules to melt ice

**STEP 2** g of ice → Heat of fusion → J

**STEP 3** **Equalities/Conversion Factors**

$$1\ \text{g}\ H_2O(s \longrightarrow l) = 334\ \text{J}$$

$$\frac{334\ \text{J}}{1\ \text{g}\ H_2O} \quad \text{and} \quad \frac{1\ \text{g}\ H_2O}{334\ \text{J}}$$

**STEP 4** **Set Up Problem**

$$26\ \cancel{\text{g}\ H_2O} \times \frac{334\ \text{J}}{1\ \cancel{\text{g}\ H_2O}} = 8700\ \text{J}$$

**b.** The soft drink will be colder because heat from the soft drink is providing the energy to melt the ice.

STUDY CHECK

In a freezer, 150. g water at 0 °C is placed in an ice cube tray. How much heat, in kilojoules, must be removed to form ice cubes at 0 °C?

**Guide to Calculations Using Heat of Fusion/Vaporization**

STEP 1 List grams of substance and change of state.

STEP 2 Write the plan to convert grams to heat and desired unit.

STEP 3 Write the heat conversion factor and metric factor if needed.

STEP 4 Set up the problem with factors.

## Boiling and Condensation

Water in a mud puddle disappears, unwrapped food dries out, and clothes hung on a clothesline dry. **Evaporation** is taking place as molecules of liquid water with sufficient energy escape from the liquid surface and enter the gas phase. (See Figure 2.11a.) The loss of the "hot" water molecules removes heat, which cools the remaining liquid water. As heat is added, more and more water molecules evaporate. At the **boiling point (bp)**, the molecules of a liquid acquire the energy needed to change to a gas. The **boiling** of a liquid occurs as gas bubbles form throughout the liquid and then rise to the surface and escape. (See Figure 2.11b.)

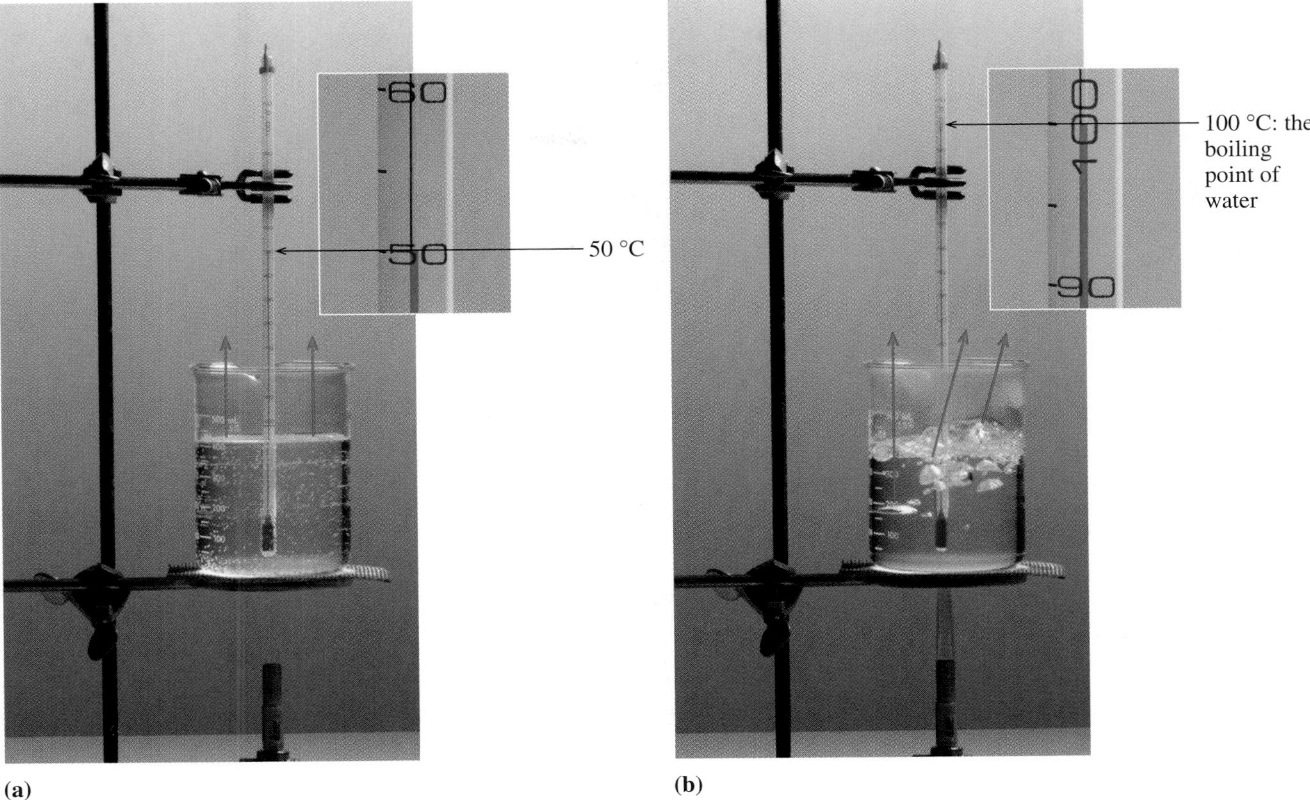


**FIGURE 2.11** **(a)** Evaporation occurs at the surface of a liquid. **(b)** Boiling occurs as bubbles of gas form throughout the liquid.

Q Why does water evaporate faster at 80 °C than at 20 °C?

When heat is removed, a reverse process takes place. In condensation, water vapor is converted back to liquid as the water molecules lose kinetic energy and slow down. Condensation occurs at the same temperature as boiling but differs because heat is removed. You may have noticed that condensation occurs when you take a hot shower and the water vapor forms water droplets on a mirror. Because a substance loses heat as it condenses, its surroundings become warmer. That is why, when a rainstorm is approaching, we notice a warming of the air as gaseous water molecules condense to rain.

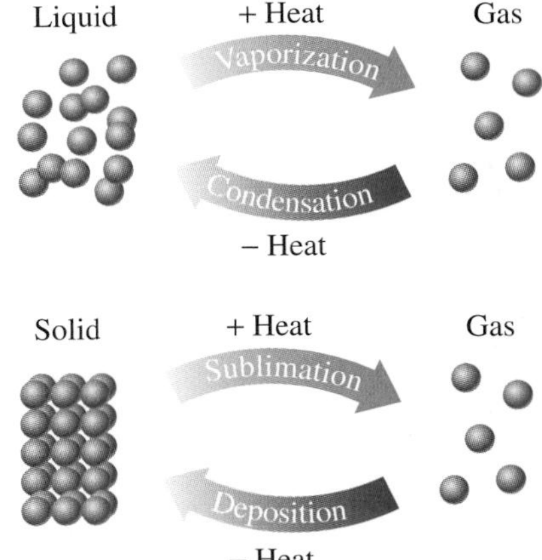


## Sublimation

In a process called **sublimation**, the particles on the surface of a solid change directly to a gas with no temperature change and without going through the liquid state. In the reverse process of sublimation called *deposition*, gas particles change directly to solid.

**Heat of Sublimation for Water**

$$\frac{2590 \text{ J}}{1 \text{ g of } H_2O} \qquad \frac{620. \text{ cal}}{1 \text{ g of } H_2O}$$

For example, dry ice, which is solid carbon dioxide ($CO_2$), undergoes sublimation at –78 °C. It is called "dry" because it does not form a liquid as it warms. In extremely cold areas, snow does not melt but sublimes directly to water vapor. In a frost-free refrigerator, the water in the ice on the walls of the freezer and in frozen foods sublimes when warm air is circulated through the compartment during the defrost cycle. When frozen foods are left in the freezer for a long time, so much water sublimes that foods, especially meat, become dry and shrunken, a condition called *freezer burn*. Deposition occurs in a freezer when water vapor forms ice crystals on the surface of freezer bags and frozen food.

Freeze-dried foods prepared by sublimation are convenient for long-term storage and for camping and hiking. A food that has been frozen is placed in a vacuum chamber where it dries as the ice sublimes. The dried food retains all of its nutritional value and needs only

water to be edible. A food that is freeze-dried does not need refrigeration because bacteria cannot grow without moisture.

## Heat of Vaporization

The energy that must be added to vaporize exactly 1 g of liquid to gas at its boiling point is called the **heat of vaporization**. For water, 540 cal or 2260 J are needed to convert 1 g of water to vapor at 100 °C. This amount of heat is released when 1 g of water vapor (gas) changes to liquid at 100 °C. Therefore, 540 cal/g or 2260 J/g is also the *heat of condensation* of water.

**Heat of Vaporization for Water**

$$\frac{2260\ \text{J}}{1\ \text{g of H}_2\text{O}} \qquad \frac{540\ \text{cal}}{1\ \text{g of H}_2\text{O}}$$

To calculate the amount of heat added to vaporize (or removed to condense) a sample of water, the mass of the sample is multiplied by the heat of vaporization. As before, no temperature change occurs during a change of state.

**Calculating Heat to Vaporize (or Condense) Water**

Heat = mass × heat of vaporization

$$\text{cal} = \cancel{\text{g}} \times \frac{540\ \text{cal}}{\cancel{\text{g}}}$$

$$\text{J} = \cancel{\text{g}} \times \frac{2260\ \text{J}}{\cancel{\text{g}}}$$

Just as substances have different melting and boiling points, they also have different heats of fusion and heats of vaporization, as shown in Table 2.13. The heat of vaporization is always greater than the heat of fusion. (See Figure 2.12.)

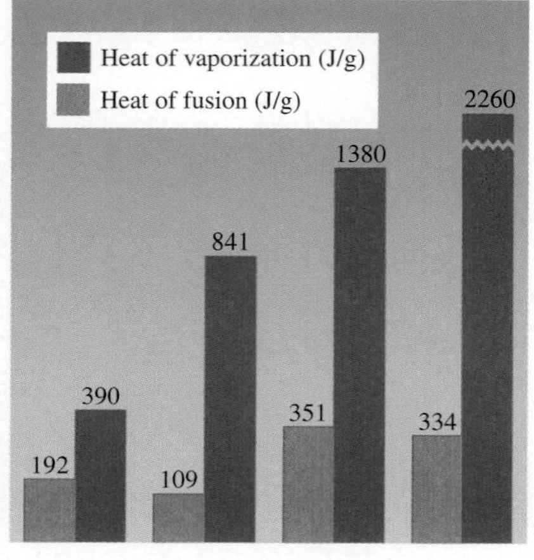


**FIGURE 2.12** For any substance, the heat of vaporization is greater than the heat of fusion.

**Q** Why does the formation of a gas require more energy than the formation of a liquid of the same substance?

**TABLE 2.13** Heats of Fusion and Heats of Vaporization for Selected Substances

| Liquid | Formula | Melting Point (°C) | Heat of Fusion (J/g) | Boiling Point (°C) | Heat of Vaporization (J/g) |
|---|---|---|---|---|---|
| Water | $H_2O$ | 0 | 334 | 100 | 2260 |
| Ethanol | $C_2H_5OH$ | –114 | 109 | 78 | 841 |
| Ammonia | $NH_3$ | –78 | 351 | –33 | 1380 |
| Acetone | $C_3H_6O$ | –95 | 98 | 56 | 335 |
| Mercury | Hg | –39 | 11 | 357 | 294 |
| Acetic acid | $C_2H_4O_2$ | 17 | 192 | 118 | 390 |

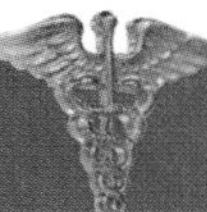

## HEALTH NOTE

### Steam Burns

Hot water at 100 °C will cause burns and damage to the skin. However, getting steam on the skin is even more dangerous. If 25 g of hot water at 100 °C falls on a person's skin, the temperature of the water will drop to body temperature, 37 °C. The heat released during cooling burns the skin. The amount of heat can be calculated from the temperature change, 63 °C.

$$25\,\cancel{g} \times 63\,\cancel{°C} \times \frac{4.184\text{ J}}{\cancel{g}\,\cancel{°C}} = 6600\text{ J released}$$

For comparison, we can calculate the amount of heat released when 25 g of steam at 100 °C hits the skin. First, the steam condenses to water (liquid) at 100 °C:

$$25\,\cancel{g} \times \frac{2260\text{ J}}{1\,\cancel{g}} = 57\,000\text{ J released}$$

The total amount of heat released from the condensation and cooling of the steam is calculated as follows:

$$\begin{aligned} \text{Condensation (100 °C)} &= 57\,000\text{ J} \\ \text{Cooling (100 °C to 37 °C)} &= 6600\text{ J} \\ \text{Heat released} &= 64\,000\text{ J (rounded)} \end{aligned}$$

The amount of heat released from steam is 10 times greater than the heat from the same amount of hot water.

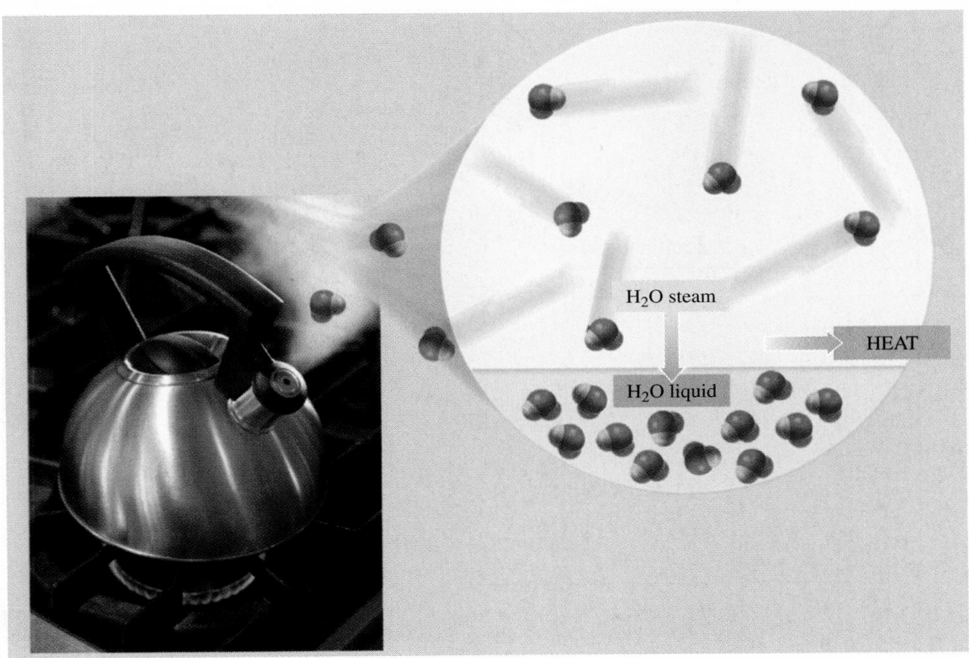


SAMPLE PROBLEM 2.13

### Using Heat of Vaporization

In a sauna, 150 g of water is converted to steam at 100 °C. How many kilocalories of heat are needed?

SOLUTION

**STEP 1** **Given** 150 g of $H_2O(l)$ to $H_2O(g)$ **Need** kilocalories of heat to change state

**STEP 2** **Plan** g of $H_2O$ → Heat of vaporization → cal → Metric factor → kcal

**STEP 3** **Equalities/Conversion Factors**

$$1\text{ g } H_2O\ (l \rightarrow g) = 540\text{ cal}$$
$$\frac{540\text{ cal}}{1\text{ g } H_2O} \text{ and } \frac{1\text{ g } H_2O}{540\text{ cal}}$$

$$1\text{ kcal} = 1000\text{ cal}$$
$$\frac{1000\text{ cal}}{1\text{ kcal}} \text{ and } \frac{1\text{ kcal}}{1000\text{ cal}}$$

STEP 4 **Set Up Problem**

$$150 \text{ g } \cancel{H_2O} \times \frac{540 \cancel{\text{cal}}}{1 \text{ g } \cancel{H_2O}} \times \frac{1 \text{ kcal}}{1000 \cancel{\text{cal}}} = 81 \text{ kcal}$$

STUDY CHECK

When steam from a pan of boiling water reaches a cool window, it condenses. How much heat, in kilocalories (kcal), is released when 25 g of steam condenses at 100 °C?

## Heating and Cooling Curves

All the changes of state during the heating of a solid can be illustrated visually. In a heating curve, the temperature is shown on the vertical axis, and the addition of heat is shown on the horizontal axis. (See Figure 2.13a.)

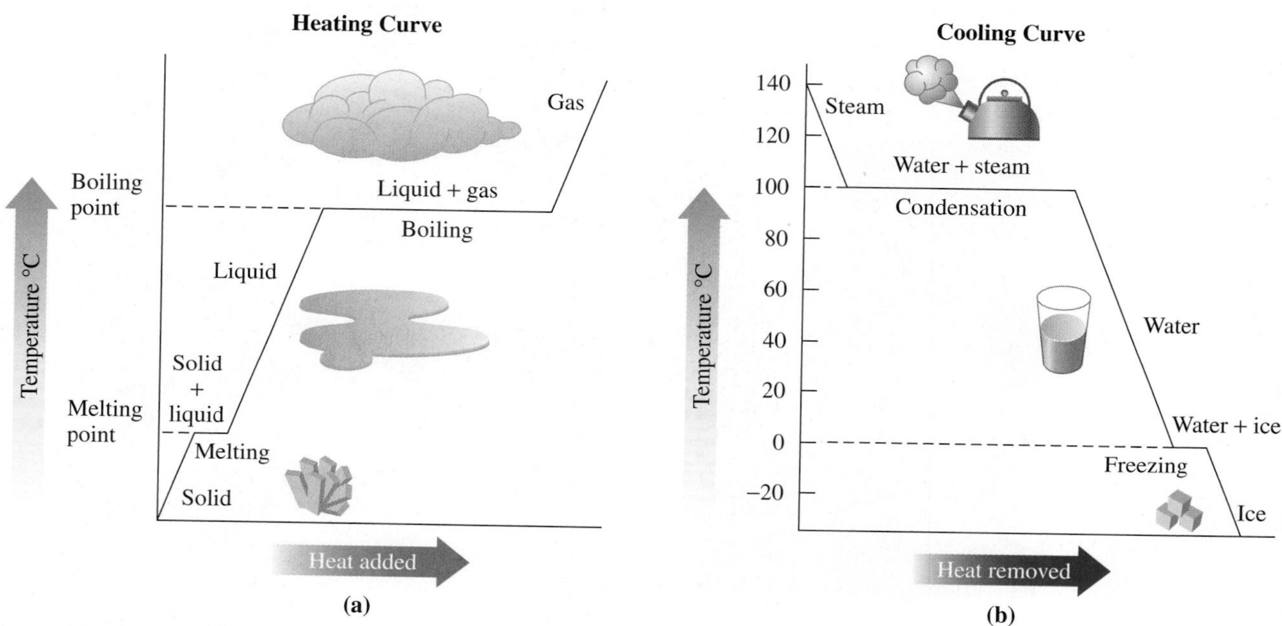


**FIGURE 2.13** **(a)** A heating curve diagrams the temperature increases and changes in state as heat is added. **(b)** A cooling curve for water.

**Q** What does the horizontal line at 100 °C represent on the heating and cooling curves for water?

## Steps on a Heating Curve

The first diagonal line indicates a warming of a solid as heat is added. When the melting temperature is reached, a horizontal line, or plateau, indicates that the solid is melting. As melting takes place, the solid is changing to a liquid without any change in temperature.

Once all of the particles are in the liquid state, heat that is added will increase the temperature of the liquid. This increase is drawn as a diagonal line from the melting point to the boiling point temperature. Once the liquid reaches its boiling point, a horizontal line indicates that the temperature remains constant as liquid changes to gas. Because the heat of vaporization is larger than the heat of fusion, the horizontal line at the boiling point is longer than the line at the melting point. Once all the liquid becomes a gas, adding more heat increases the temperature of the gas.

CONCEPT CHECK 2.8

**Heating Curve**

Using the melting and boiling points of acetone in Table 2.13, identify the state or change of state as heat is added to a sample of acetone starting at –110 °C and stopping at 70 °C. (*Hint*: Sketch the heating curve.)

**a.** –95 °C
**b.** –80 °C
**c.** 0 °C
**d.** 70 °C

ANSWER

**a.** A horizontal line at –95 °C indicates the melting of acetone.
**b.** At –80 °C, which is higher than the melting point, acetone is a liquid.
**c.** At 0 °C, which is higher than the melting point, acetone is a liquid.
**d.** At 70 °C, which is higher than the boiling point, acetone is a gas.

## Steps on a Cooling Curve

A cooling curve is a diagram of the cooling process. In the diagram, the temperature is plotted on the vertical axis, and the removal of heat is plotted on the horizontal axis. (See Figure 2.13b.) Initially, a diagonal line to the boiling (condensation) point is drawn to show that heat is removed from a substance, cooling the gas until it begins to condense. A horizontal line (plateau) is drawn at the condensation point (same as the boiling point) to indicate the change of state as the gas condenses to form a liquid. After all of the gas has changed into liquid, further cooling lowers the temperature. The decrease in temperature is shown as a diagonal line from the condensation point temperature to the freezing point temperature. At the freezing point, another horizontal line indicates that liquid is changing to solid at the freezing point temperature. Once all of the substance is frozen, a loss of heat decreases the temperature below its freezing point, which is shown as a diagonal line below the freezing point.

## Combining Energy Calculations

Up to now, we have calculated one step in a heating or cooling curve. However, many problems require a combination of steps that include a temperature change as well as a change of state. The heat is calculated for each step separately and then added together to find the total energy as seen in Sample Problem 2.14.

SELF STUDY ACTIVITY
Heat, Energy, and Changes of State

SAMPLE PROBLEM 2.14

**Combining Heat Calculations**

Using Table 2.13 and the specific heat of ethanol (2.46 J/g °C), calculate the total heat, in joules, needed to convert 15.0 g of ethanol at 25.0 °C to gas at 78.0 °C.

SOLUTION

**STEP 1** **Given** 15.0 g of ethanol at 25.0 °C
**Need** heat (J) needed to warm the ethanol and change it to gas

**STEP 2** When several changes occur, draw a diagram of heating and changes of state.

Total heat = joules needed to warm ethanol from 25.0 °C to 78.0 °C
+ joules to change liquid to gas at 78.0 °C

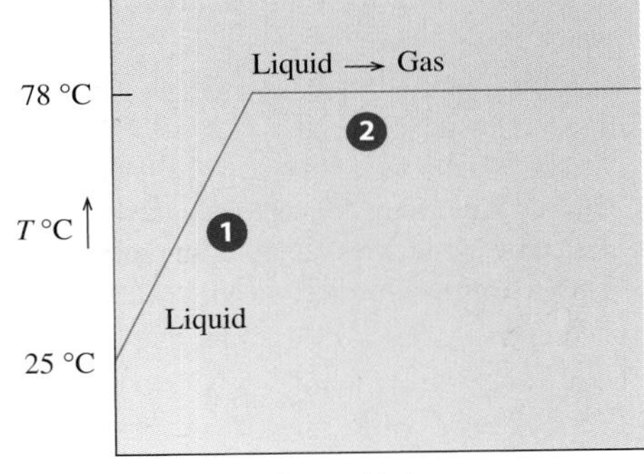

**STEP 3** **Equalities/Conversion Factors**

$$SH_{\text{ethanol}} = \frac{2.46\ \text{J}}{\text{g}\ ^\circ\text{C}}$$

$$\frac{2.46\ \text{J}}{\text{g}\ ^\circ\text{C}} \text{ and } \frac{\text{g}\ ^\circ\text{C}}{2.46\ \text{J}}$$

$$1\ \text{g of ethano}(l \rightarrow g) = 841\ \text{J}$$

$$\frac{841\ \text{J}}{1\ \text{g ethanol}} \text{ and } \frac{1\ \text{g ethanol}}{841\ \text{J}}$$

**STEP 4** **Set Up Problem** $\Delta T = 78.0\ ^\circ\text{C} - 25.0\ ^\circ\text{C} = 53.0\ ^\circ\text{C}$

Heat needed to warm ethanol (liquid) (25.0 °C) to ethanol (liquid) (78.0 °C):

$$15.0\ \cancel{\text{g}} \times 53.0\ \cancel{^\circ\text{C}} \times \frac{2.46\ \text{J}}{\cancel{\text{g}}\ \cancel{^\circ\text{C}}} = 1960\ \text{J}$$

Heat needed to change ethanol (liquid) to ethanol (gas) at 78.0 °C:

$$15.0\ \cancel{\text{g}} \times \frac{841\ \text{J}}{1\ \cancel{\text{g}}} = 12\ 600\ \text{J}$$

Calculate the total heat:

| | |
|---|---|
| Heating ethanol (25.0 °C to 78.0 °C) | 1 960 J |
| Changing liquid to gas (at 78.0 °C) | 12 600 J |
| Total heat needed | 14 600 J (rounded) |

STUDY CHECK

How many kilojoules (kJ) are released when 25.0 g of steam at 100 °C condenses, cools to 0 °C, and freezes? (*Hint*: The solution will require three energy calculations.)

## QUESTIONS AND PROBLEMS

### Changes of State

**2.41** Identify each of the following changes of state as melting, freezing, condensation, sublimation, or deposition:
- **a.** The solid structure of a substance breaks down as liquid forms.
- **b.** Coffee is freeze-dried.
- **c.** Water on the street turns to ice during a cold wintry night.
- **d.** Crystals of ice form on a package of frozen corn.

**2.42** Identify each of the following changes of state as melting, freezing, condensation, sublimation, or deposition:
- **a.** Dry ice in an ice-cream cart disappears.
- **b.** Snow on the ground turns to liquid water.
- **c.** Heat is removed from 125 g of liquid water at 0 °C.
- **d.** In a warm room, a person's glasses fog up.

**2.43** Calculate the heat needed at 0 °C to make each of the following changes of state. Indicate whether heat was absorbed or released.
- **a.** calories to melt 65 g of ice
- **b.** calories to melt 17 g of ice
- **c.** kilocalories to freeze 225 g of water

**2.44** Calculate the heat needed at 0 °C to make each of the following changes of state. Indicate whether heat was absorbed or released.
- **a.** calories to freeze 35 g of water
- **b.** calories to freeze 250 g of water
- **c.** kilocalories to melt 140 g of ice

**2.45** Identify each of the following changes of state as evaporation, boiling, or condensation:
- **a.** The water vapor in the clouds changes to rain.
- **b.** Wet clothes dry on a clothesline.
- **c.** Lava flows into the ocean, and steam forms.
- **d.** After a hot shower, your bathroom mirror is covered with water.

**2.46** Identify each of the following changes of state as evaporation, boiling, or condensation:
- **a.** At 100 °C, the water in a pan changes to steam.
- **b.** On a cool morning, the windows in your car fog up.
- **c.** A shallow pond dries up in the summer.
- **d.** Your teakettle whistles when the water is ready for tea.

**2.47** Calculate the heat change at 100 °C in each of the following problems. Indicate whether heat was absorbed or released.
**a.** calories to vaporize 10.0 g of water
**b.** kilocalories to vaporize 50.0 g of water
**c.** kilocalories to condense 8.0 kg of steam

**2.48** Calculate the heat change at 100 °C in each of the following problems. Indicate whether heat was absorbed or released.
**a.** calories to condense 10.0 g of steam
**b.** kilocalories to condense 75 g of steam
**c.** kilocalories to vaporize 44 g of water

**2.49** Draw a heating curve for a sample of ice that is heated from –20 °C to 140 °C. Indicate the segment of the graph that corresponds to each of the following:
**a.** solid **b.** melting point **c.** liquid
**d.** boiling point **e.** gas

**2.50** Draw a cooling curve for a sample of steam that cools from 110 °C to –10 °C. Indicate the segment of the graph that corresponds to each of the following:
**a.** solid **b.** freezing point **c.** liquid
**d.** condensation point (boiling point) **e.** gas

**2.51** Using the values for the heat of fusion, specific heat of water, or heat of vaporization, calculate the amount of heat energy in each of the following:
**a.** calories needed to warm 20.0 g of water at 15 °C to 72 °C (one step)
**b.** calories need to melt 50.0 g of ice at 0 °C and to warm the liquid to 65 °C (two steps)
**c.** kilojoules given off when 15 g of steam condenses at 100 °C and the liquid cools to 0 °C (two steps)
**d.** kilocalories needed to melt 24 g of ice at 0 °C, to warm the liquid to 100 °C, and to vaporize it at 100 °C (three steps)

**2.52** Using the values for the heat of fusion, specific heat of water, or heat of vaporization, calculate the amount of heat energy in each of the following:
**a.** calories removed to condense 125 g of steam at 100 °C and to cool the liquid to 15 °C (two steps)
**b.** joules needed to melt a 525-g ice cube at 0 °C and to warm the liquid to 15 °C (two steps)
**c.** kilocalories removed to condense 85 g of steam at 100 °C, cool the liquid to 0 °C, and freeze it at 0 °C (three steps)
**d.** calories to warm 55 mL of water (density = 1.0 g/mL) from 10 °C to 100 °C and vaporize it at 100 °C (two steps)

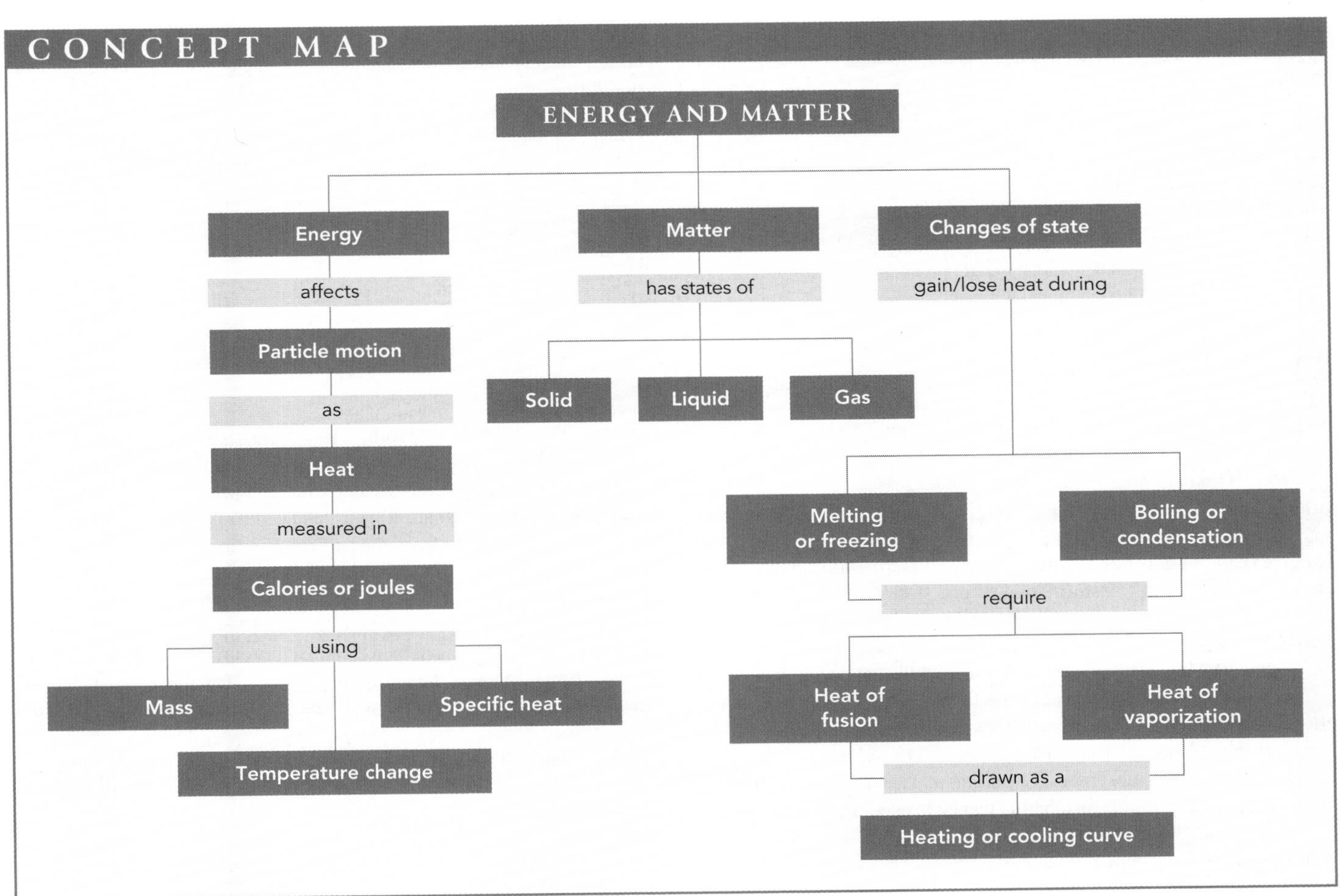

# CHAPTER REVIEW

## 2.1 Energy

**LEARNING GOAL:** *Identify energy as potential or kinetic and understand the units of energy.*

Energy is the ability to do work. Potential energy is stored energy; kinetic energy is the energy of motion. Common units of energy are the calorie (cal), kilocalorie (kcal), joule (J), and kilojoule (kJ). One cal is equal to 4.184 J.

## 2.2 Temperature

**LEARNING GOAL:** *Given a temperature, calculate a corresponding temperature on another temperature scale.*

In science, temperature is measured in Celsius degrees (°C) or kelvins (K). In the United States, the Fahrenheit scale (°F) is still in use. On the Celsius scale, there are 100 units between the freezing point (0 °C) and the boiling point of water (100 °C). On the Fahrenheit scale, there are 180 units between the freezing point (32 °F) and boiling point of water (212 °F). A Fahrenheit temperature is related to its Celsius temperature by the equation $T_F = 1.8\,T_C + 32$. The SI temperature of Kelvin is related to the Celsius temperature by the equation $T_K = T_C + 273$.

## 2.3 Specific Heat

**LEARNING GOAL:** *Use specific heat to calculate heat loss or gain, temperature change, or mass of a sample.*

Specific heat is the amount of energy required to raise the temperature of exactly 1 g of a substance by exactly 1 °C. The heat lost or gained by a substance is determined by multiplying its mass (g), the temperature change ($\Delta T$), and its specific heat (cal/g °C or J/g °C).

## 2.4 Energy and Nutrition

**LEARNING GOAL:** *Use the energy values to calculate the kilocalories (kcal) or kilojoules (kJ) in a food.*

The nutritional Calorie is the same amount of energy as 1 kcal or 1000 calories. The energy content of a food is the sum of kilocalories or kilojoules from carbohydrate, fat, and protein.

## 2.5 Classification of Matter

**LEARNING GOAL:** *Classify examples of matter as pure substances or mixtures.*

Matter is classified as pure substances or mixtures. Pure substances, which are elements or compounds, have fixed compositions, and mixtures have variable compositions. The substances in mixtures can be separated using physical methods.

## 2.6 States and Properties of Matter

**LEARNING GOAL:** *Identify the states and properties of matter.*

Matter is anything that has mass and occupies space. The three states of matter are solid, liquid, and gas. A physical property is a characteristic of a substance. A physical change occurs when physical properties change but not the identity of the substance. A chemical property indicates the ability of a substance to change into another substance. In a chemical change, at least one substance forms a new substance with new physical properties.

## 2.7 Changes of State

**LEARNING GOAL:** *Describe the changes of state between solids, liquids, and gases; calculate the energy involved.*

Melting occurs when the particles in a solid absorb enough energy to break apart and form a liquid. The amount of energy required to convert exactly 1 g of solid to liquid is its heat of fusion. For water, 80. cal or 334 J must be added to melt 1 g of ice. Boiling is the vaporization of a liquid at its boiling point. The heat of vaporization is the amount of heat needed to convert exactly 1 g of liquid to vapor. For water, 540 cal or 2260 J are needed to vaporize 1 g of liquid water. A heating or cooling curve illustrates the changes in temperature and state as heat is added to or removed from a substance. Plateaus on the graph indicate changes of state with no change in temperature.

# KEY TERMS

**boiling** The formation of bubbles of gas throughout a liquid.

**boiling point (bp)** The temperature at which a liquid changes to gas (boils) and gas changes to liquid (condenses).

**calorie (cal)** The amount of heat energy that raises the temperature of exactly 1 g of water exactly 1 °C; 1 cal = 4.184 J.

**Calorie (Cal)** A nutritional unit of energy equal to 1000 cal, or 1 kcal.

**change of state** The transformation of one state of matter to another; for example, from solid to liquid, liquid to solid, and liquid to gas.

**chemical change** A change during which the original substance is converted into a new substance with a different composition and new chemical and physical properties.

**chemical properties** The properties that indicate the ability of a substance to change to a new substance.

**compound** A pure substance consisting of two or more elements, with a definite composition, that can be broken down into simpler substance only by chemical methods.

**condensation** The change of state of a gas to a liquid.

**cooling curve** A diagram that illustrates temperature changes and changes of state for a substance as heat is removed.

**deposition** The reverse process of sublimation, with gas particles changing directly into a solid.

**element** A pure substance containing only one type of matter, which cannot be broken down by chemical methods.

**energy** The ability to do work.

**energy (caloric) value** The kilocalories obtained per gram of the three food types: carbohydrate, fat, and protein.

**evaporation** The formation of a gas (vapor) by the escape of high-energy molecules from the surface of a liquid.

**freezing** A change of state from liquid to solid.

**freezing point (fp)** The temperature at which a liquid changes to a solid (freezes) and a solid changes to a liquid (melts).

**gas** A state of matter characterized by no definite shape or volume. Particles in a gas move rapidly.

**heat** The energy associated with the motion of particles in a substance.

**heat of fusion** The energy required to melt exactly 1 g of a substance at its melting point. For water, 80. cal (334 J) are needed to melt 1 g of ice; 80. cal (334 J) are released when 1 g of water freezes.

**heat of vaporization** The energy required to vaporize exactly 1 g of a substance at its boiling point. For water, 540 calories (2260 J) are needed to vaporize exactly 1 g of liquid; 1 g of steam gives off 540 cal (2260 J) when it condenses.

**heating curve** A diagram that shows the temperature changes and changes of state of a substance as it is heated.

**joule (J)** The SI unit of heat energy; 4.184 J = 1 cal.

**kilocalorie (kcal)** An amount of heat energy equal to 1000 calories.

**kinetic energy** The energy of motion.

**liquid** A state of matter that takes the shape of its container but has a definite volume.

**melting** A change of state that involves the conversion of a solid to a liquid.

**melting point (mp)** The temperature at which a solid becomes a liquid (melts). It is the same temperature as the freezing point.

**mixture** The physical combination of two or more substances that does not change the identities of the substances.

**physical change** The change in which the physical appearance of a substance changes, but the chemical composition stays the same.

**physical properties** The properties that can be observed or measured without affecting the identity of a substance.

**potential energy** An inactive type of energy that is stored for future use.

**pure substance** Matter composed of elements or compounds that has a definite composition.

**solid** A state of matter that has its own shape and volume.

**specific heat** A quantity of heat that changes the temperature of exactly 1 g of a substance by exactly 1 °C.

**sublimation** The change of state in which a solid is transformed directly to a gas without forming a liquid first.

**work** An activity that requires energy.

## UNDERSTANDING THE CONCEPTS

2.53 Select the warmer temperature in each pair.

**a.** 10 °C or 10 °F **b.** 30 °C or 15 °F

**c.** −10 °C or 32 °F **d.** 200 °C or 200 K

**2.54** Compost can be made at home from grass clippings, some kitchen scraps, and dry leaves. As microbes break down organic matter, heat is generated and the compost can reach a temperature of 155 °F, which kills most pathogens. What is this temperature in Celsius degrees?

2.55 After a week, biochemical reactions in compost slow, and the temperature drops to 45 °C. The dark brown organic-rich mixture is ready for use in the garden. What is this temperature in Fahrenheit degrees? In kelvins?

**2.56** Determine the energy to heat three cubes (gold, aluminum, and silver), each with a volume of 10.0 $cm^3$ from 15 °C to 25 °C. Refer to Tables 1.11 and 2.2. What do you notice about the energy needed for each?

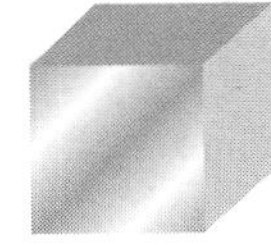

2.57 A 70.0-kg person had a quarter-pound cheeseburger, french fries, and a chocolate shake. According to Table 2.6, determine each of the following:

**a.** the number of hours of sleep needed to "burn off" the kilocalories in this meal

**b.** the number of hours of running needed to "burn off" the kilocalories in this meal

| Item | Protein (g) | Fat (g) | Carbohydrate (g) |
|---|---|---|---|
| Cheeseburger | 31 | 29 | 34 |
| French fries | 3 | 11 | 26 |
| Chocolate shake | 11 | 9 | 6 |

**2.58** Identify each of the following as an element, compound, or mixture:

**a.**

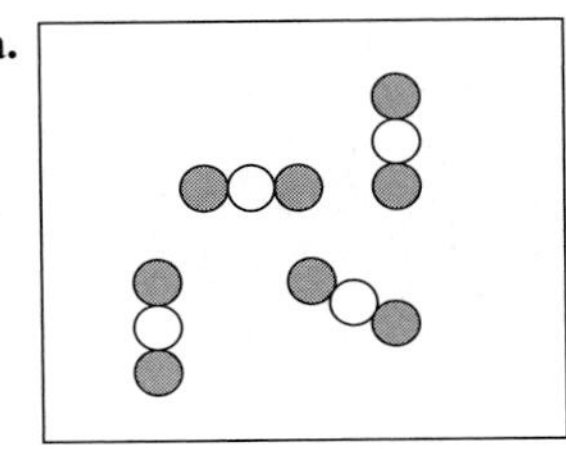

**b.**

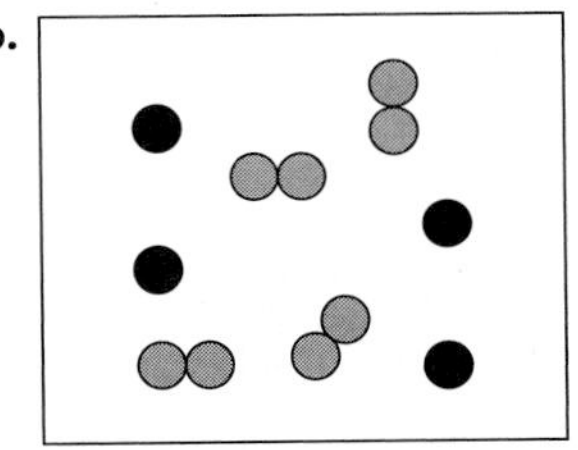

**c.**

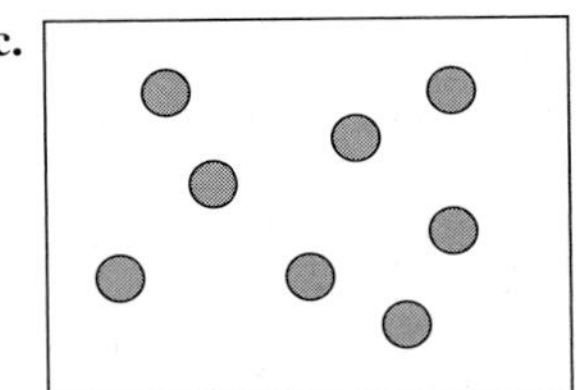

2.59 Which diagram illustrates a heterogeneous mixture? Explain your choice. Which diagrams illustrate a homogeneous mixture? Explain your choice.

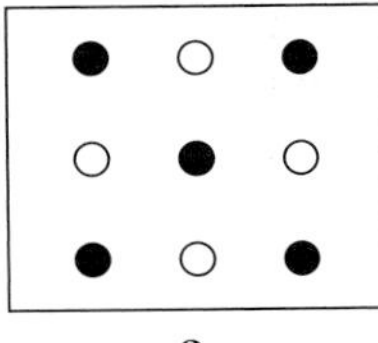
**a.**

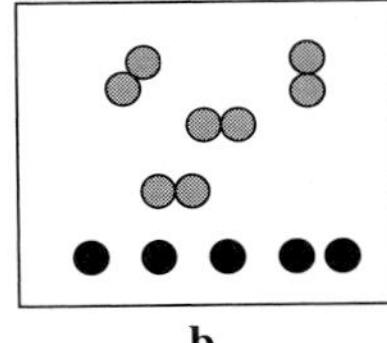
**b.**

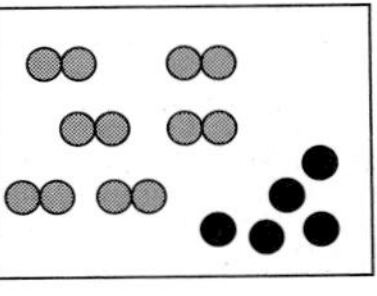
**c.**

**2.60** Classify each of the following as a homogeneous mixture or heterogeneous mixture:

**a.** lemon-flavored water
**b.** stuffed mushrooms
**c.** chicken noodle soup
**d.** ketchup
**e.** hard-boiled egg
**f.** eye drops

**2.61 a.** How does perspiration during heavy exercise cool the body?
**b.** Why do clothes dry more quickly on a hot summer day than on a cold winter day?

**2.62 a.** When a sports injury occurs during a game, a spray such as ethyl chloride may be used to numb an area of the skin. Explain how a substance such as ethyl chloride that evaporates quickly can numb the skin.
**b.** Why does water in a wide, flat, shallow dish evaporate more quickly than the same amount of water in a tall, narrow glass?

**2.63** The following is a heating curve for chloroform, a solvent for fats, oils, and waxes:

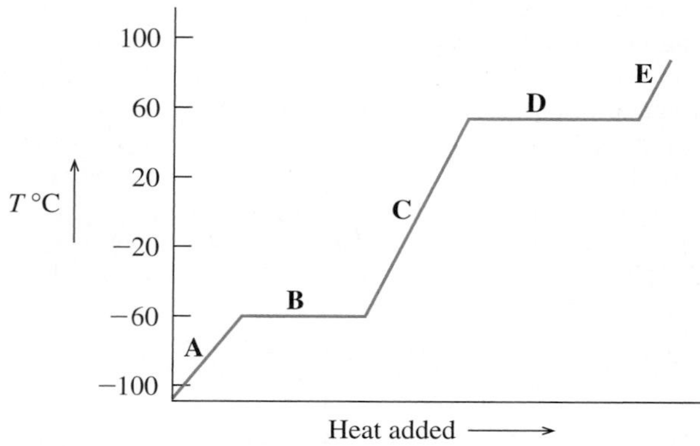


**a.** What is the melting point of chloroform?
**b.** What is the boiling point of chloroform?
**c.** On the heating curve, identify the segments A, B, C, D, and E as solid, liquid, gas, melting, or boiling.
**d.** At the following temperatures, is chloroform a solid, liquid, or gas? –80 °C; –40 °C; 25 °C; 80 °C

**2.64** Associate the following diagrams with a segment on the heating curve for water:

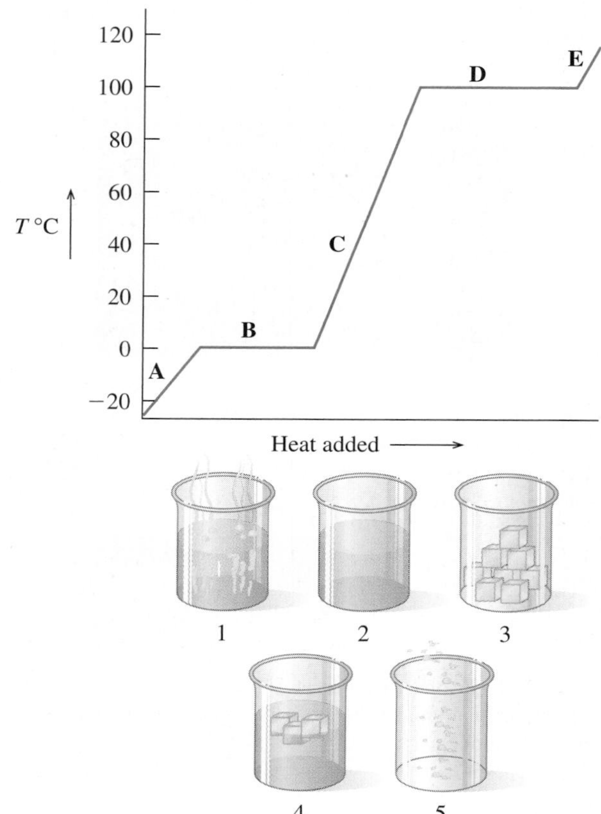


## ADDITIONAL QUESTIONS AND PROBLEMS

*For instructor-assigned homework, go to* ***www.masteringchemistry.com*****.**

**2.65** On a hot day, the beach sand gets hot, but the water stays cool. Compare the specific heat of sand to that of water.

**2.66** Why do drops of liquid water form on a glass of iced tea?

**2.67** When it rains or snows, the air temperature seems warmer. Explain.

**2.68** Water is sprayed on the ground of an orchard when temperatures are near freezing to keep the fruit from freezing. Explain.

**2.69** Calculate the following temperatures in degrees Fahrenheit:

**a.** The highest recorded temperature in the world was 58.0 °C in El Azizia, Libya, on September 13, 1922.
**b.** The lowest recorded temperature in the world was –89.2 °C in Vostok Station, Antarctica, July 21, 1983.

**2.70** Calculate the following temperatures in degrees Celsius:
**a.** The highest recorded temperature in the continental United States was 134 °F in Death Valley, California, on July 10, 1913.
**b.** The lowest recorded temperature in the continental United States was –70. °F in Rodgers Pass, Montana, on January 20, 1954.

2.71 A large bottle of water (883 g) at 4 °C is removed from the refrigerator. How many kilojoules (kJ) are absorbed to warm the water to a room temperature of 27 °C?

**2.72** If you used the 2100 kcal you expend in energy in one day to heat 50 000 g of water at 20. °C, what would be its new temperature?

2.73 A typical diet in the United States provides 15% of its calories from protein, 45% from carbohydrates, and the remainder from fats. Calculate the grams of protein, carbohydrate, and fat to be included each day in diets having the following caloric requirements:
**a.** 1200 kcal **b.** 1900 kcal **c.** 2600 kcal

**2.74** For lunch, your friend has a slice of pizza, a cola soft drink, and ice cream. What is the total number of kilocalories your friend obtained from this meal? How many hours will your friend need to swim to "burn off" the kilocalories in this meal if your friend has a mass of 70.0 kg? (See Table 2.6.)

| Item | Protein (g) | Fat (g) | Carbohydrate (g) |
|---|---|---|---|
| Pizza | 13 | 10 | 29 |
| Cola | 0 | 0 | 51 |
| Ice cream | 8 | 28 | 44 |

2.75 If you want to lose 1 pound of "fat," which is 15% water, how many kilocalories do you need to expend?

**2.76** Calculate the Cal (kcal) in 1 cup of whole milk: 12 g of carbohydrate, 9 g of fat, and 9 g of protein.

2.77 Identify each of the following as solid, liquid, or gas:
**a.** popcorn in a bag **b.** water in a garden hose
**c.** a computer mouse **d.** air in a tire
**e.** hot tea

**2.78** Identify each of the following as solid, liquid, or gas:
**a.** vitamin tablets in a bottle **b.** helium in a balloon
**c.** milk in a glass **d.** the air you breathe
**e.** charcoal briquettes on a barbecue

2.79 The melting point of chloroform is –64 °C, and its boiling point is 61 °C. Sketch a heating curve for chloroform from –100 °C to 100 °C.
**a.** What is the state of chloroform at –75 °C?
**b.** What happens on the curve at –64 °C?
**c.** What is the state of chloroform at –18 °C?
**d.** What is the state of chloroform at 80 °C?
**e.** At what temperature will both solid and liquid be present?

**2.80** A pitcher containing 0.75 L of water at 4 °C is removed from the refrigerator. How many kilojoules are needed to warm the water to a room temperature of 27 °C?

2.81 A hot-water bottle contains 725 g of water at 65 °C. If the water cools to body temperature (37 °C), how many kilocalories of heat could be transferred to sore muscles?

**2.82** An ice cube tray holds 325 g of water. If the water initially has a temperature of 25 °C, how many kilojoules of heat must be removed to cool and freeze the water at 0 °C?

2.83 How many kilocalories of heat are released when 45 g of steam at 100 °C is converted to liquid water at 15 °C?

**2.84** The melting point of benzene is 5.5 °C, and its boiling point is 80.1 °C. Sketch a heating curve for benzene from 0 °C to 100 °C.
**a.** What is the state of benzene at 15 °C?
**b.** What happens on the curve at 5.5 °C?
**c.** What is the state of benzene at 63 °C?
**d.** What is the state of benzene at 98 °C?
**e.** At what temperature will both liquid and gas be present?

## CHALLENGE QUESTIONS

2.85 A 25-g sample of an alloy at 98 °C is placed in 50. g of water at 15 °C. If the final temperature reached by the alloy sample and water is 27 °C, what is the specific heat (cal/g °C) of the alloy?

**2.86** A 0.50-g sample of vegetable oil is placed in a calorimeter. When the sample is burned, 18.9 kJ are given off. What is the caloric value, in kcal/g, of the oil?

2.87 How many kilojoules of heat are released when 35.0 g of steam at 100 °C is converted to ice at 0 °C?

**2.88** A 45-g piece of ice at 0 °C is added to a sample of water at 8 °C. All of the ice melts, and the temperature of the water decreases to 0 °C. How many grams of water were in the sample?

2.89 Rearrange the heat equation to solve for each of the following:
**a.** the mass, in grams, of water that absorbs 8250 J when its temperature rises from 18.3 °C to 92.6 °C
**b.** the mass, in grams, of a gold sample that absorbs 225 J when the temperature rises from 15.0 °C to 47.0 °C
**c.** the rise in temperature ($\Delta T$) when a 20.0-g sample of iron absorbs 1580 J
**d.** the specific heat of a metal when 8.50 g of the metal absorbs 28 cal and the temperature rises from 12 °C to 24 °C

**2.90** The combustion of 1.0 g of gasoline releases 11 kcal of heat (density of gasoline = 0.74 g/mL).
**a.** How many megajoules are released when 1.0 gal of gasoline burns?
**b.** When a color television is on for 2.0 h, 300 kJ are used. How long can a color television run on the energy from 1.0 gal of gasoline?

2.91 A 3.0-kg block of lead is taken from a furnace at 300. °C and placed on a large block of ice at 0 °C. The specific heat of lead is 0.13 J/g °C. If all the heat given up by the lead is used to melt ice, how much ice is melted if the temperature of the lead drops to 0 °C?

**2.92** In a large building, oil is used in a steam boiler heating system. The combustion of 1.0 lb of oil provides $2.4 \times 10^7$ J.
**a.** How many kg of oil are needed to heat 150 kg of water from 22 °C to 100 °C?
**b.** How many kg of oil are needed to provide steam from 150 kg of water at 100 °C?

## ANSWERS

### ANSWERS TO STUDY CHECKS

**2.1** 8.4 kcal

**2.2** 12 °F

**2.3** 39.8 °C

**2.4** night –260. °C; day 410. °C

**2.5** $SH$ = 1.23 J/g °C

**2.6** 14.6 kJ

**2.7** 182 g of iron

**2.8** 4.0 kcal/g of sucrose; 17 kJ/g of sucrose

**2.9** 380 kcal

**2.10** Salad dressing is a heterogeneous mixture with a nonuniform composition.

**2.11** b. and d. are chemical changes

**2.12** 50.1 kJ

**2.13** 14 kcal; 24 kcal

**2.14** 75.4 kJ

## ANSWERS TO SELECTED QUESTIONS AND PROBLEMS

**2.1** As the car goes up the ramp, kinetic energy changes to potential energy. As the car descends, potential energy changes to kinetic energy. At the bottom, all the energy is kinetic.

**2.3** **a.** potential **b.** kinetic **c.** potential **d.** potential

**2.5** **a.** 22 kJ **b.** 5300 cal **c.** 5.3 kcal

**2.7** In the United States, the Fahrenheit scale is in common use. On a Fahrenheit thermometer, normal body temperature is 98.6 °F. A temperature of 99.8 °F would indicate a mild fever. On the Celsius scale, her temperature is 37.7 °C.

**2.9** **a.** 98.6 °F **b.** 18.5 °C **c.** 246 K **d.** 335 K **e.** 46 °C **f.** 295 K

**2.11** **a.** 41 °C
**b.** No. The temperature is equivalent to 39 °C.

**2.13** Copper has the lowest specific heat of the samples and will reach the highest temperature.

**2.15** **a.** 0.389 J/g °C **b.** 0.313 J/g °C

**2.17** **a.** 250 cal **b.** 11 000 cal **c.** 9.3 kcal

**2.19** **a.** 1380 J; 330. cal **b.** 1810 J; 434 cal **c.** 3780 J; 904 cal **d.** 3200 J; 760 cal

**2.21** **a.** 54.5 g of gold **b.** 216 g of iron **c.** 686 g of aluminum **d.** 190. g of titanium

**2.23** **a.** 5.30 kcal; 22.2 kJ **b.** 208 kcal; 870. kJ

**2.25** **a.** 110 Cal **b.** 18 g **c.** 130 Cal **d.** 280 Cal

**2.27** 210 kcal; 870 kJ

**2.29** **a.** compound; contains four elements in definite composition
**b.** element; consists of one type of pure substance
**c.** compound; consists of two elements in a definite composition
**d.** element; consists of one type of pure substance

**2.31** **a.** heterogeneous **b.** homogeneous **c.** homogeneous **d.** heterogeneous **e.** heterogeneous **f.** heterogeneous

**2.29** **a.** gas **b.** gas **c.** solid

**2.33** **a.** gas **b.** gas **c.** solid

**2.35** **a.** physical **b.** chemical **c.** physical **d.** chemical

**2.37** **a.** physical **b.** chemical **c.** physical **d.** physical **e.** physical

**2.39** **a.** chemical **b.** physical **c.** physical **d.** chemical **e.** physical

**2.41** **a.** melting **b.** sublimation **c.** freezing **d.** deposition

**2.43** **a.** 5200 cal absorbed **b.** 1400 cal absorbed **c.** 18 kcal released

**2.45** **a.** condensation **b.** evaporation **c.** boiling **d.** condensation

**2.47** **a.** 5400 cal absorbed **b.** 27 kcal absorbed **c.** 4300 kcal released

**2.49**

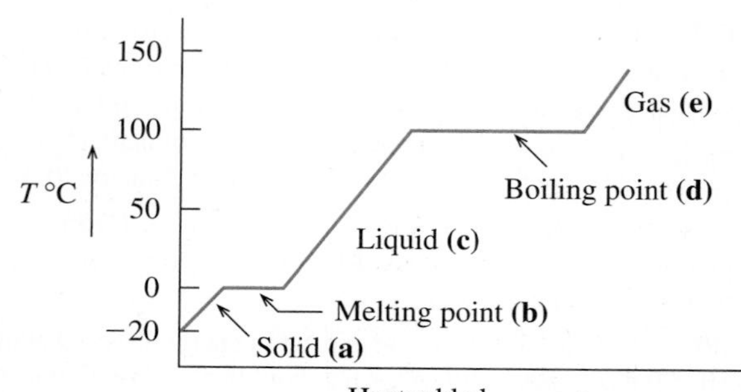


**2.51** **a.** 1100 cal **b.** 7300 cal **c.** 40. kJ **d.** 17 kcal

**2.53** **a.** 10 °C **b.** 30 °C **c.** 32 °F **d.** 200 °C

**2.55** 113 °F; 318 K

**2.57** **a.** 15 h sleeping **b.** 1.2 h running

**2.59** Mixtures b. and c. are not the same throughout and are heterogeneous. Mixture a. is the same throughout and is homogeneous.

**2.61** **a.** The heat from the skin is used to evaporate the water (perspiration). Therefore, the skin is cooled.
**b.** On a hot day, there are more molecules with sufficient energy to become water vapor.

**2.63** **a.** −60 °C **b.** 60 °C
**c.** A is solid. B is melting. C is liquid. D is boiling. E is gas.
**d.** At −80 °C, it is solid; at −40 °C, it is liquid; at 25 °C, it is liquid; at 80 °C, it is gas.

**2.65** Sand must have a lower specific heat than water. When both substances absorb the same amount of heat, the final temperature of the sand will be higher than that of water.

**2.67** When water vapor condenses or liquid water freezes, heat is released, which warms the air.

**2.69** **a.** 136 °F **b.** −129 °F

**2.71** 85 kJ

**2.73** **a.** 45 g of protein, 140 g of carbohydrate, 53 g of fat
**b.** 71 g of protein, 210 g of carbohydrate, 84 g of fat
**c.** 98 g of protein, 290 g of carbohydrate, 120 g of fat

**2.75** 3500 kcal

**2.77** **a.** solid **b.** liquid **c.** solid **d.** gas **e.** liquid

**2.79** **a.** solid **b.** solid chloroform melts **c.** liquid **d.** gas **e.** −64 °C

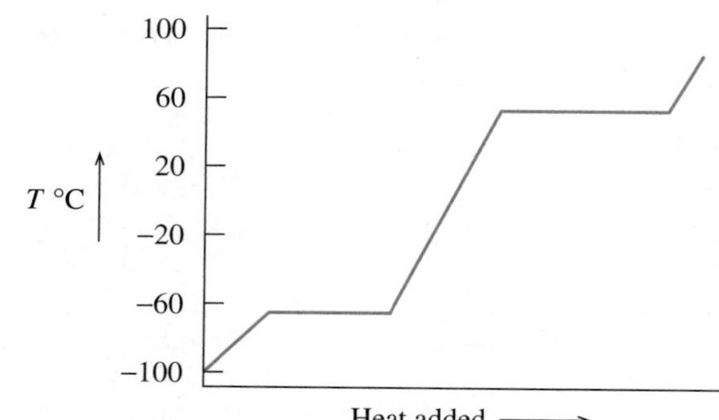


**2.81** 20. kcal

**2.83** 28 kcal

**2.85** $\frac{0.34\text{ cal}}{\text{g °C}}$

**2.87** 105.4 kJ

**2.89** **a.** 26.5 g **b.** 54.5 g of gold **c.** 175 °C **d.** $\frac{0.27\text{ cal}}{\text{g °C}}$

**2.91** 350 g of ice

# COMBINING IDEAS FROM CHAPTERS 1 AND 2

**CI.1** Gold, one of the most sought after metals in the world, has a density of 19.3 g/cm$^3$, a melting point of 1064 °C, a specific heat of 0.129 J/g °C, and a heat of fusion of 63.6 J/g. A gold nugget found in Alaska in 1998 weighs 20.17 lb.

**a.** How many significant figures are in the measurement of the nugget's weight?

**b.** What is the mass of the nugget in kilograms?

**c.** If the nugget is pure gold, what would its volume be in cm$^3$?

**d.** What is the melting point of gold in degrees Fahrenheit and kelvins?

**e.** How many kilojoules are required to heat the nugget from 500. °C to 1064 °C and convert all the gold to liquid? How many kcal is that? (*Hint*: Draw a heating curve for gold.)

**f.** Gold is sold in troy ounces (ozt). One ozt is equal to 31.1 g. If the current price of gold is \$895/ozt, what is the nugget worth?

**CI.2** The mileage for a motorcycle with a fuel-tank capacity of 22 L is 35 miles per gal. The density of gasoline is 0.74 g/mL.

**a.** How long a trip, in kilometers, can be made on a full tank of gasoline?

**b.** If 1 gallon of gasoline costs \$3.85, then what would be the price of fuel for the trip?

**c.** If the average speed during the trip is 44 mi/h, how many hours will it take to reach the destination?

**d.** What is the mass, in kilograms, of the fuel in the tank?

**e.** When 1.0 g of gasoline burns, 46 kJ of energy are released. How many kilojoules are produced when the fuel in one full tank is burned?

**CI.3** Answer the following questions for the water samples A and B shown in the diagrams:

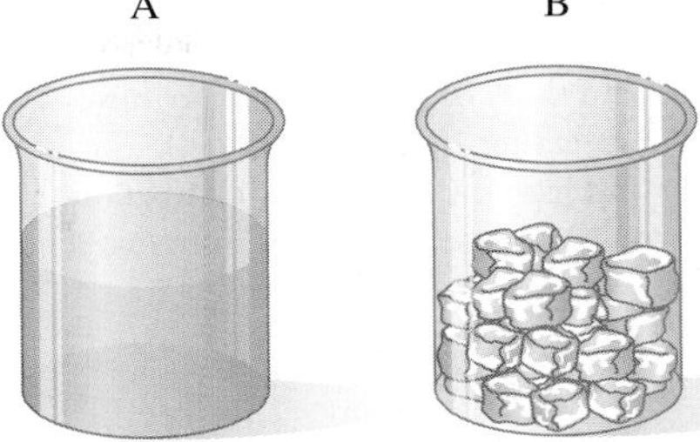


**a.** Which sample has its own shape?

**b.** When each sample is transferred to another container, what happens to its volume?

**c.** Match the diagrams (1, 2, or 3) that represent the water particles with sample A and B. Give a reason for your choice.

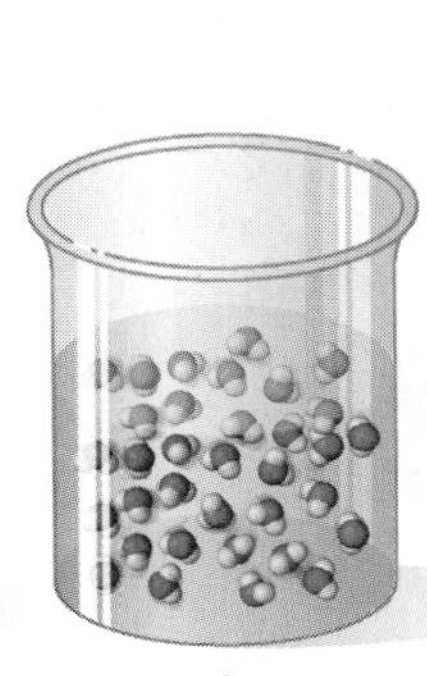

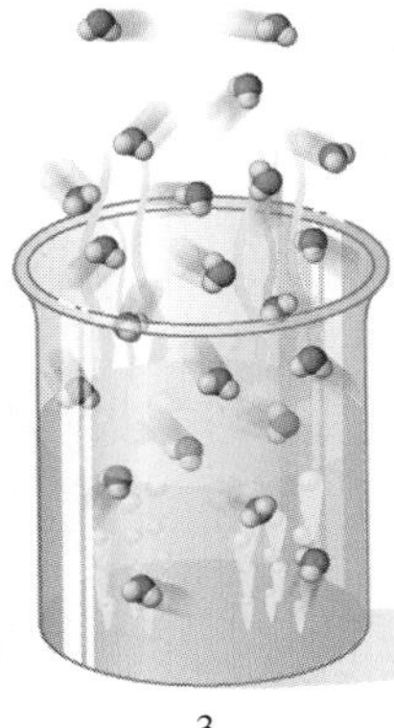


**d.** When the water in sample A changes to sample B, the process is called ___________, which occurs at a temperature called the ___________. This is an example of a ___________ change.
When the water in sample B changes to sample A, the process is called ___________, which occurs at a temperature called the ___________. This is an example of a ___________ change.

**e.** What happens to the solid water particles when melting occurs?

**f.** If the water in sample A has a mass of 19.8 g and a temperature of 45 °C, how much heat, in joules, is removed to form ice at 0 °C?

**CI.4** The label of a lemon poppyseed energy bar lists the nutrition facts as 4 g of fat, 23 g of carbohydrate, and 10 g of protein.

a. Using the energy values of carbohydrate (4 kcal/g), fat (9 kcal/g), and protein (4 kcal/g), what are the kilocalories (Calories) listed for the lemon poppyseed bar?
b. What is the energy value of the energy bar in kilojoules?
c. If the bar has a mass of 48 g, how many kilojoules are obtained from eating 10. g of the bar?
d. If you are walking (840 kJ/h), how many minutes will you need to walk to use the energy from two lemon poppyseed bars?

**CI.5** In a box of nails, there are 75 iron nails weighing 0.250 lb. The density of iron is 7.86 g/cm$^3$. The specific heat of iron is 0.450 J/g °C.

a. What is the volume, in cm$^3$, of all the iron nails in the box?
b. If 30 nails are added to a graduated cylinder containing 17.6 mL of water, what is the new level of water in the cylinder?
c. How many joules must be added to the nails in the box to raise the temperature from 16 °C to 125 °C?

**CI.6** A hot tub is filled with 450 gal of water, which has a density of 1.0 g/mL.

a. What is the volume, in liters, of the water in the tub?
b. What is the mass, in kilograms, of the water in the tub?
c. How many kilocalories are needed to heat the water from 62 °F to 105 °F?
d. If the hot tub heater provides 1400 kcal per minute, how long, in hours, will it take to heat the water in the hot tub from 62 °F to 105 °F?

## ANSWERS

**CI.1** a. Four significant figures are in the measurement of 20.17 lb.
b. 9.17 kg
c. 475 cm$^3$
d. 1947 °F; 1337 K
e. 1250 kJ; 298.8 kcal
f. $264 000
d. freezing; freezing point; 0 °C; physical; melting; melting point; 0 °C; physical
e. The solid water particles break apart from their fixed arrangement to have a more random arrangement, but they are still close together.
f. 10 300 J

**CI.3** a. B
b. The volumes of both A and B remain the same.
c. A is liquid water represented by diagram 2. In liquid water, the water particles are in a random arrangement but close together. B is solid water represented by diagram 1. In solid water, the water particles are fixed in a definite arrangement.

**CI.5** a. 14.4 cm$^3$
b. 23.4 mL
c. 5570 J or $5.57 \times 10^3$ J

# Atoms and Elements

3

## LOOKING AHEAD


3.1 Elements and Symbols
3.2 The Periodic Table
3.3 The Atom
3.4 Atomic Number and Mass Number
3.5 Isotopes and Atomic Mass
3.6 Electron Energy Levels
3.7 Electron Configurations
3.8 Periodic Trends


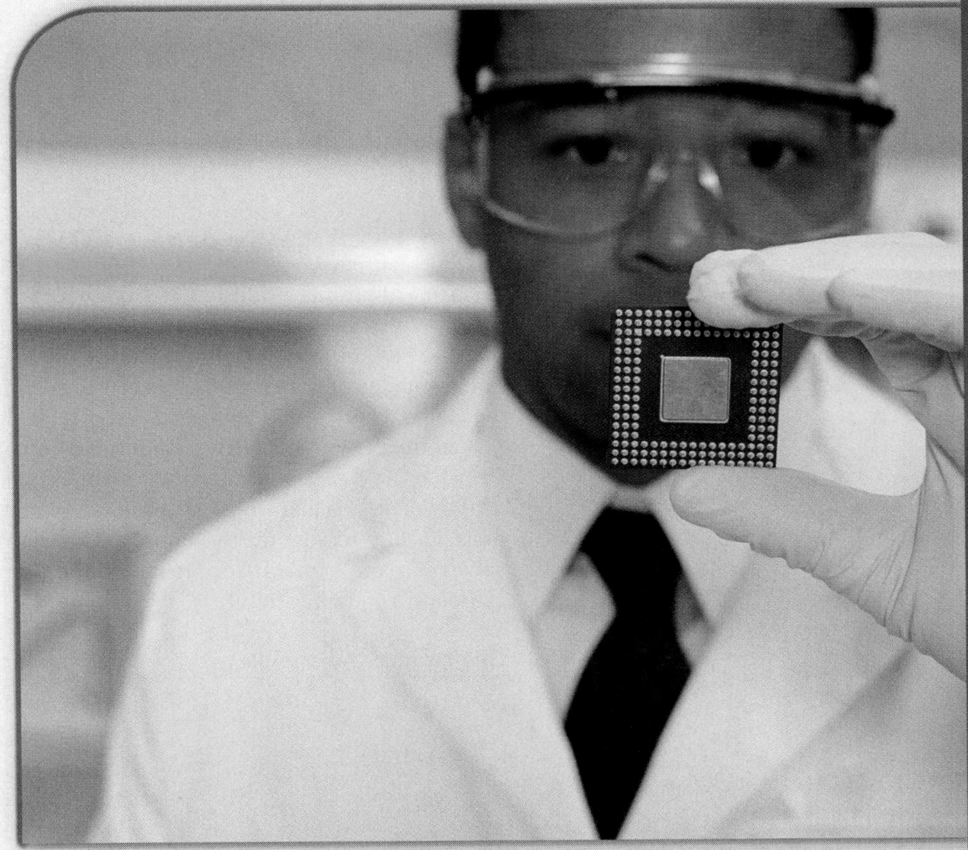

*"The unique qualities of semiconducting metals make it possible for us to create sophisticated electronic circuits," says Tysen Streib, Global Product Manager, Applied Materials. "Elements from columns 3A, 4A, and 5A of the periodic table often make good semiconductors because they readily form covalently bonded crystals. When small amounts of impurities are added, free-flowing electrons or holes can travel through the crystal with very little interference. Without these covalent bonds and loosely bound electrons, we wouldn't have any of the microchips that we use in computers, cell phones, and thousands of other devices."*

*Materials scientists study the chemical properties of materials to find new uses for them in products such as cars, bridges, and clothing. They also develop materials that can be used as superconductors or in integrated-circuit chips and fuel cells. Chemistry is important in materials science because it provides information about structure and composition.*

Visit **www.masteringchemistry.com** for self-study materials and instructor-assigned homework.

All matter is composed of *elements*, of which there are 117 different kinds. Of these, 88 elements occur naturally and make up all the substances in our world. Many elements are already familiar to you. Perhaps you use aluminum in the form of foil or drink soft drinks from aluminum cans. You may have a ring or necklace made of gold, silver, or perhaps platinum. If you play tennis or golf, then you may have noticed that your racket or clubs may be made from the elements titanium or carbon. In our bodies, compounds of calcium and phosphorus form the structure of bones and teeth, iron and copper are needed in the formation of red blood cells, and iodine is required for the proper functioning of the thyroid.

The amounts of certain elements are crucial to the proper growth and function of the body. Low levels of iron can lead to anemia, while low levels of iodine can cause hypothyroidism and goiter. Lab tests are used to confirm that elements such as iron, copper, zinc, or iodine are within normal ranges in a patient's blood serum. A dietitian may recommend beef for iron and zinc, whole grains and leafy green vegetables for magnesium, dairy products for calcium, and iodized table salt and seafood for iodine.

## 3.1 Elements and Symbols

**LEARNING GOAL**

Given the name of an element, write its correct symbol; from the symbol, write the correct name.

*Elements* are primary substances from which all other things are built. Elements cannot be broken down into simpler substances. Over the centuries, elements have been named for planets, mythological figures, minerals, colors, geographic locations, and famous people. Some sources of names of elements are listed in Table 3.1. The names and symbols of all the elements are found on the inside cover of this text.

**Chemical symbols** are one- and two-letter abbreviations for the names of the elements. Only the first letter of an element's symbol is capitalized. If the symbol has a second letter, it is lowercase so that we know when a different element is indicated. If two letters are capitalized, they represent the symbols of two different elements. For example, the element cobalt has the symbol Co. However, the two capital letters CO specify two elements, carbon (C) and oxygen (O).

| One-Letter Symbols | | Two-Letter Symbols | |
|---|---|---|---|
| C | carbon | Co | cobalt |
| S | sulfur | Si | silicon |
| N | nitrogen | Ne | neon |
| I | iodine | Ni | nickel |

**TABLE 3.1** Some Elements and Their Names

| Element | Source of Name |
|---|---|
| Uranium | The planet Uranus |
| Titanium | Titans (mythology) |
| Chlorine | *Chloros*: "greenish yellow" (Greek) |
| Iodine | *Ioeides*: "violet" (Greek) |
| Magnesium | Magnesia, a mineral |
| Californium | California |
| Curium | Marie and Pierre Curie |

Although most of the symbols use letters from the current names, some are derived from their ancient Latin or Greek names. For example, Na, the symbol for sodium, comes from the Latin word *natrium*. The symbol for iron, Fe, is derived from the Latin name *ferrum*. Table 3.2 lists the names and symbols of some common elements. Learning their names and symbols will greatly help your learning of chemistry. A complete list of all the elements and their symbols appears on the inside front cover of this text.

**CONCEPT CHECK 3.1**

**Symbols of the Elements**

The symbol for carbon is C, and the symbol for sulfur is S. However, the symbol for cesium is Cs not CS. Why?

ANSWER

When the symbol for an element has two letters, the first letter is capitalized, but the second letter is lowercase. If both letters are capitalized such as in CS, then two elements—carbon and sulfur—are indicated.

TABLE 3.2 Names and Symbols of Some Common Elements

| Name[a] | Symbol | Name[a] | Symbol | Name[a] | Symbol |
|---|---|---|---|---|---|
| Aluminum | Al | Gold (*aurum*) | Au | Phosphorus | P |
| Argon | Ar | Helium | He | Platinum | Pt |
| Arsenic | As | Hydrogen | H | Potassium (*kalium*) | K |
| Barium | Ba | Iodine | I | Radium | Ra |
| Boron | B | Iron (*ferrum*) | Fe | Silicon | Si |
| Bromine | Br | Lead (*plumbum*) | Pb | Silver (*argentum*) | Ag |
| Cadmium | Cd | Lithium | Li | Sodium (*natrium*) | Na |
| Calcium | Ca | Magnesium | Mg | Strontium | Sr |
| Carbon | C | Manganese | Mn | Sulfur | S |
| Chlorine | Cl | Mercury (*hydrargyrum*) | Hg | Tin (*stannum*) | Sn |
| Chromium | Cr | Neon | Ne | Titanium | Ti |
| Cobalt | Co | Nickel | Ni | Uranium | U |
| Copper (*cuprum*) | Cu | Nitrogen | N | Zinc | Zn |
| Fluorine | F | Oxygen | O | | |

[a]Names given in parentheses are ancient Latin or Greek words from which the symbols are derived.

Aluminum

Carbon

Gold

Silver

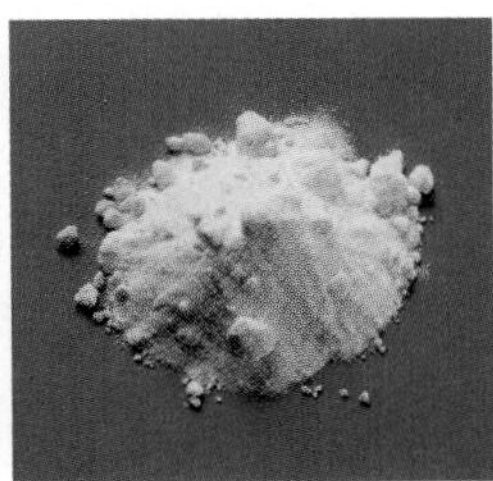
Sulfur

SAMPLE PROBLEM 3.1

### Writing Chemical Symbols

What are the chemical symbols for the following elements?

**a.** nickel **b.** niobium **c.** nitrogen **d.** neon

SOLUTION

**a.** Ni **b.** Nb **c.** N **d.** Ne

STUDY CHECK

What are the chemical symbols for silicon, strontium, and silver?

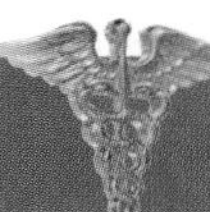

## HEALTH NOTE

### Latin Names for Elements in Clinical Usage

In medicine, the Latin name *natrium* may be used for sodium, an important electrolyte in body fluids and cells. An increase in serum sodium, a condition called *hypernatremia*, may occur when water is lost because of profuse sweating, severe diarrhea, or vomiting, or when there is inadequate water intake. A decrease in sodium, a condition called *hyponatremia*, may occur when a person takes in a large amount of water or fluid-replacement solutions. Conditions that occur in cardiac failure, liver failure, and malnutrition can also cause hyponatremia.

The Latin name *kalium* may be used for potassium, the most common electrolyte inside the cells. Potassium regulates osmotic pressure, acid–base balance, nerve and muscle excitability, and the function of cellular enzymes. Serum potassium measures potassium outside the cells, which amounts to only 2 percent of total body potassium. An increase in serum potassium (*hyperkalemia*) may occur when cells are severely injured, in renal failure when potassium is not properly excreted, and in Addison's disease. A severe loss of potassium (*hypokalemia*) may occur during excessive vomiting, diarrhea, renal tubular defects, and glucose or insulin therapy.

## QUESTIONS AND PROBLEMS

### Elements and Symbols

**3.1** Write the symbols for the following elements:

**a.** copper **b.** silicon
**c.** potassium **d.** nitrogen
**e.** iron **f.** barium
**g.** lead **h.** strontium

**3.2** Write the symbols for the following elements:

**a.** oxygen **b.** lithium
**c.** sulfur **d.** aluminum
**e.** hydrogen **f.** neon
**g.** tin **h.** gold

**3.3** Write the name of the element for each of the following symbols:

**a.** C **b.** Cl
**c.** I **d.** Hg
**e.** F **f.** Ar
**g.** Zn **h.** Ni

**3.4** Write the name of the element for each of the following symbols:

**a.** He **b.** P
**c.** Na **d.** Mg
**e.** Ca **f.** Br
**g.** Cd **h.** Si

**3.5** What elements are in the following substances?

**a.** table salt, $NaCl$
**b.** plaster casts, $CaSO_4$
**c.** Demerol, $C_{15}H_{22}ClNO_2$
**d.** antacid, $CaCO_3$

**3.6** What elements are in the following substances?

**a.** water, $H_2O$
**b.** baking soda, $NaHCO_3$
**c.** lye, $NaOH$
**d.** sugar, $C_{12}H_{22}O_{11}$

## ENVIRONMENTAL NOTE

### Toxicity of Mercury

Mercury is a silvery, shiny element that is a liquid at room temperature. Mercury can enter the body through inhalation as a vapor, contact with the skin, or foods or water that have been contaminated with mercury. In the body, mercury destroys proteins and disrupts cell function. Long-term exposure to mercury can damage the brain and kidneys, cause mental retardation, and decrease physical development. Blood, urine, and hair samples are used to test for mercury.

In both freshwater and saltwater, bacteria convert mercury into toxic methylmercury, which primarily attacks the central nervous system (CNS). Because fish absorb methylmercury, we are exposed to mercury when we eat mercury-contaminated fish. As levels of mercury ingested from fish became a concern, the Food and Drug Administration (FDA) set a maximum level of one part mercury per million parts seafood (1 ppm), which is the same as 1 $\mu$g mercury in every gram of seafood. Fish higher in the food chain such as swordfish and shark can have such high levels of mercury that the Environmental Protection Agency (EPA) recommends they be consumed no more than once a week.

One of the worst incidents of mercury poisoning occurred in Minamata and Niigata, Japan, in 1950. At that time, the ocean was polluted with high levels of mercury from industrial wastes. Because fish were a major food in the Japanese diet, more than 2000 people were affected with mercury poisoning and died or developed neural damage. In the U.S., between 1988 and 1997, industry decreased the use of mercury by 75% by banning mercury in paint and pesticides, reducing mercury in batteries, and regulating mercury in other products.

This mercury fountain, housed in glass, was designed by Calder for the 1937 World's Fair in Paris

## 3.2 The Periodic Table

**LEARNING GOAL**

Use the periodic table to identify the group and the period of an element and decide whether it is a metal, nonmetal, or metalloid.

As more elements were discovered, it became necessary to organize them with some type of classification system. By the late 1800s, scientists recognized that certain elements looked alike and behaved in much the same way. In 1872, a Russian chemist, Dmitri Mendeleev, arranged the 60 elements known at that time into groups with similar properties and placed them in order of increasing mass. Today, this arrangement of 117 elements is known as the **periodic table**. (See Figure 3.1.)

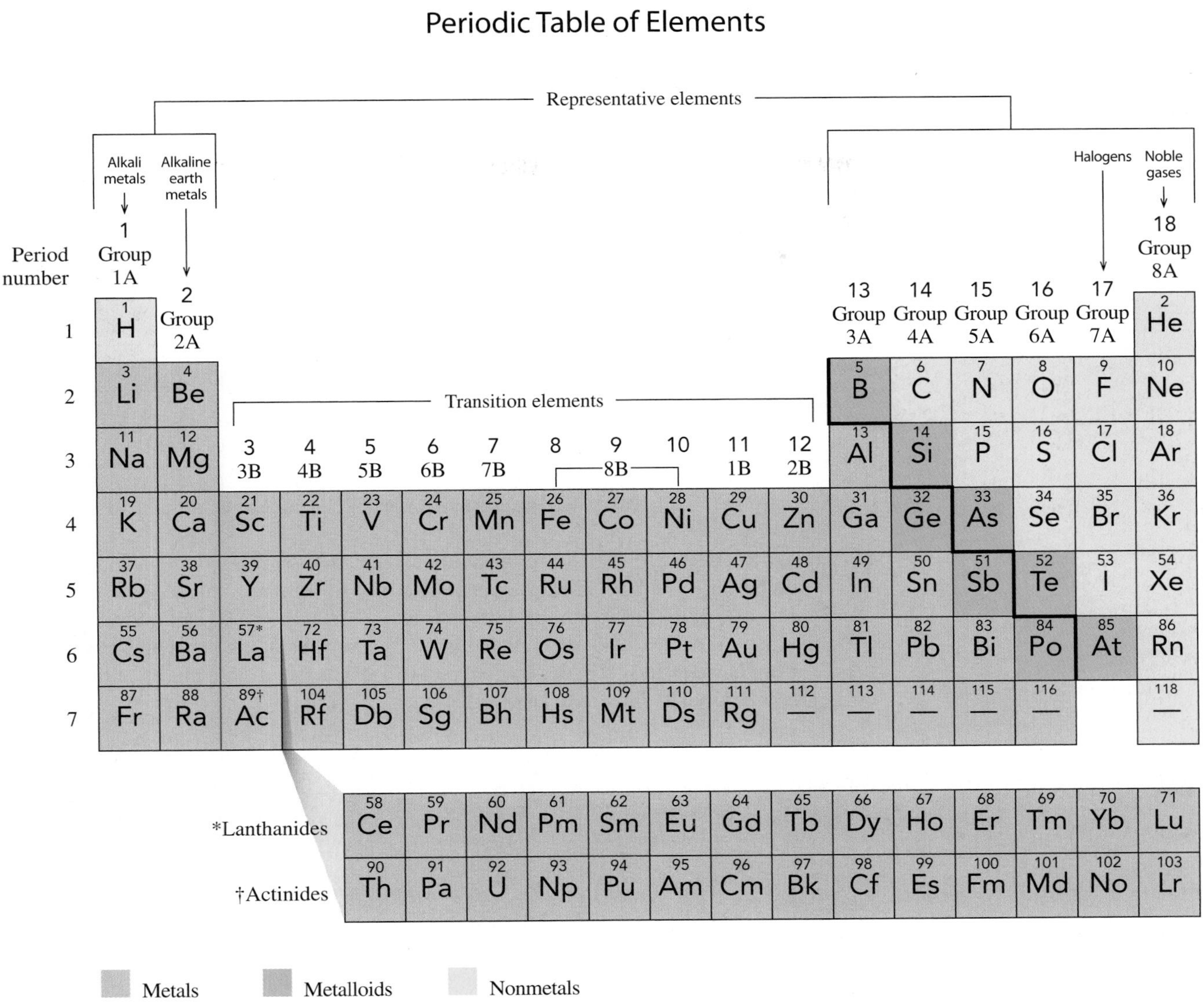

Periodic Table of Elements

Representative elements

Alkali metals · Alkaline earth metals · Transition elements · Halogens · Noble gases

| Period number | 1 Group 1A | 2 Group 2A | 3 3B | 4 4B | 5 5B | 6 6B | 7 7B | 8 8B | 9 8B | 10 8B | 11 1B | 12 2B | 13 Group 3A | 14 Group 4A | 15 Group 5A | 16 Group 6A | 17 Group 7A | 18 Group 8A |
|---|---|---|---|---|---|---|---|---|---|---|---|---|---|---|---|---|---|---|
| 1 | 1 H | | | | | | | | | | | | | | | | | 2 He |
| 2 | 3 Li | 4 Be | | | | | | | | | | | 5 B | 6 C | 7 N | 8 O | 9 F | 10 Ne |
| 3 | 11 Na | 12 Mg | | | | | | | | | | | 13 Al | 14 Si | 15 P | 16 S | 17 Cl | 18 Ar |
| 4 | 19 K | 20 Ca | 21 Sc | 22 Ti | 23 V | 24 Cr | 25 Mn | 26 Fe | 27 Co | 28 Ni | 29 Cu | 30 Zn | 31 Ga | 32 Ge | 33 As | 34 Se | 35 Br | 36 Kr |
| 5 | 37 Rb | 38 Sr | 39 Y | 40 Zr | 41 Nb | 42 Mo | 43 Tc | 44 Ru | 45 Rh | 46 Pd | 47 Ag | 48 Cd | 49 In | 50 Sn | 51 Sb | 52 Te | 53 I | 54 Xe |
| 6 | 55 Cs | 56 Ba | 57* La | 72 Hf | 73 Ta | 74 W | 75 Re | 76 Os | 77 Ir | 78 Pt | 79 Au | 80 Hg | 81 Tl | 82 Pb | 83 Bi | 84 Po | 85 At | 86 Rn |
| 7 | 87 Fr | 88 Ra | 89† Ac | 104 Rf | 105 Db | 106 Sg | 107 Bh | 108 Hs | 109 Mt | 110 Ds | 111 Rg | 112 — | 113 — | 114 — | 115 — | 116 — | | 118 — |

| | | | | | | | | | | | | | | |
|---|---|---|---|---|---|---|---|---|---|---|---|---|---|---|
| *Lanthanides | 58 Ce | 59 Pr | 60 Nd | 61 Pm | 62 Sm | 63 Eu | 64 Gd | 65 Tb | 66 Dy | 67 Ho | 68 Er | 69 Tm | 70 Yb | 71 Lu |
| †Actinides | 90 Th | 91 Pa | 92 U | 93 Np | 94 Pu | 95 Am | 96 Cm | 97 Bk | 98 Cf | 99 Es | 100 Fm | 101 Md | 102 No | 103 Lr |

Metals Metalloids Nonmetals

**FIGURE 3.1** Groups and periods in the periodic table.
**Q** What is the symbol of the alkali metal in Period 3?

## Periods and Groups

Each horizontal row in the table is called a **period**. The number of elements in the periods increases going down the periodic table. Each row is counted from the top of the table as Period 1 to Period 7. The first period contains only the elements hydrogen (H) and helium (He). The second period contains eight elements: lithium (Li), beryllium (Be), boron (B), carbon (C), nitrogen (N), oxygen (O), fluorine (F), and neon (Ne). The third period also contains eight elements, beginning with sodium (Na) and ending with argon (Ar). The fourth period, which begins with potassium (K), and the fifth period, which begins with rubidium (Rb), have 18 elements each. The sixth period, which begins with cesium (Cs), has 32 elements. The seventh period as of today contains the 31 remaining elements although it could go as high as 32. (See Figure 3.2.)

Each vertical column on the periodic table contains a **group** (or family) of elements that have similar properties. At the top of each column is a number that is assigned to each group. The elements in the first two columns on the left of the periodic table and the last six columns on the right are called the **representative elements**. For many years, they have been given group numbers 1A–8A. On some periodic tables, the group numbers may be written with Roman numerals: IA–VIIIA. In the center of the periodic table is a block

TUTORIAL
Elements and Symbols in the Periodic Table

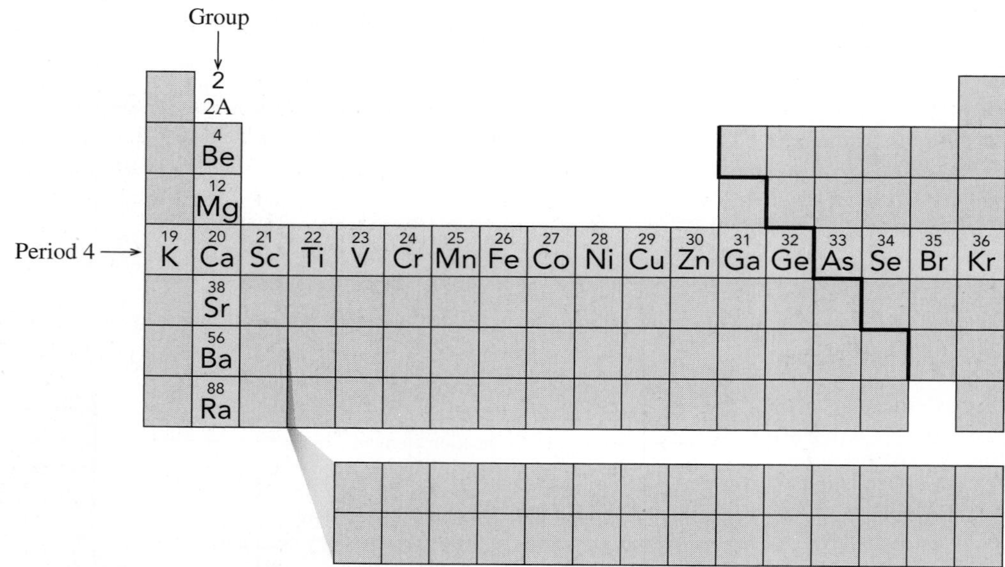


**FIGURE 3.2** On the periodic table, each vertical column represents a group of elements, and each horizontal row of elements represents a period.

**Q** Are the elements Si, P, and S part of a group or a period?

of elements known as the **transition elements**, which are designated with the letter "B." A newer numbering system assigns group numbers of 1 to 18 across the periodic table. Because both systems of group numbers are currently in use, they are both indicated on the periodic table in this text and are included in our discussions of elements and group numbers. The lanthanides and actinides that are part of Periods 6 and 7 are placed at the bottom of the periodic table to allow it to fit on a page.

## HEALTH NOTE

### Elements Essential to Health

Many elements are essential for the well-being and survival of the human body. The four elements oxygen, carbon, hydrogen, and nitrogen are the most important elements that make up carbohydrates, fats, proteins, and DNA. Most of the hydrogen and oxygen is found in water, which makes up 55% to 60% of our body mass. Some examples and the amounts present in a 60-kg person are listed in Table 3.3.

**TABLE 3.3** Elements Essential to Health

| Element | Symbol | Amount in a 60-kg Person |
|---|---|---|
| Oxygen | O | 39 kg |
| Carbon | C | 11 kg |
| Hydrogen | H | 6 kg |
| Nitrogen | N | 1.5 kg |
| Calcium | Ca | 1 kg |
| Phosphorus | P | 600 g |
| Potassium | K | 120 g |
| Sulfur | S | 120 g |
| Sodium | Na | 86 g |
| Chlorine | Cl | 81 g |
| Magnesium | Mg | 16 g |
| Iron | Fe | 3.6 g |
| Fluorine | F | 2.2 g |
| Zinc | Zn | 2.0 g |
| Copper | Cu | 60 mg |
| Iodine | I | 20 mg |

## Classification of Groups

Several groups in the periodic table have special names. (See Figure 3.3.) Group 1A (1) elements—lithium (Li), sodium (Na), potassium (K), rubidium (Rb), cesium (Cs), and francium (Fr)—make up a family of elements known as the **alkali metals**. (See Figure 3.4.) The elements within this group are soft, shiny metals that are good conductors of heat and electricity and have relatively low melting points. Alkali metals react vigorously with water and form white products when they combine with oxygen.

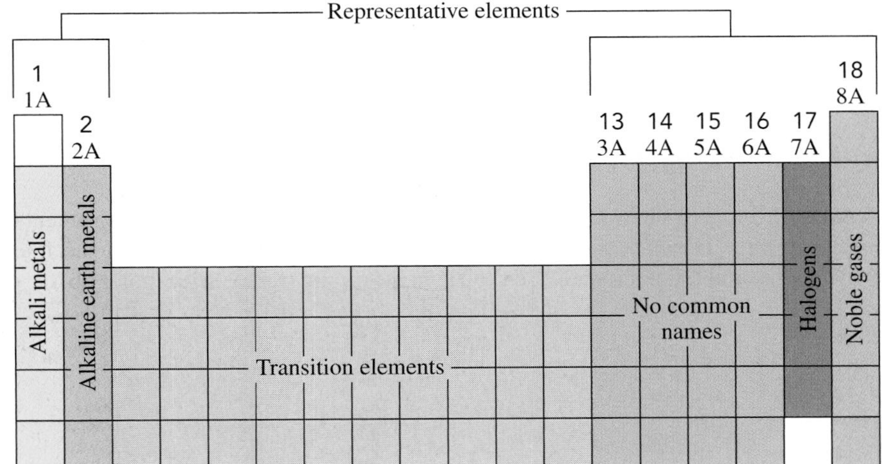


**FIGURE 3.3** Certain groups on the periodic table have common names.

**Q** What is the common name for the group of elements that includes helium and argon?

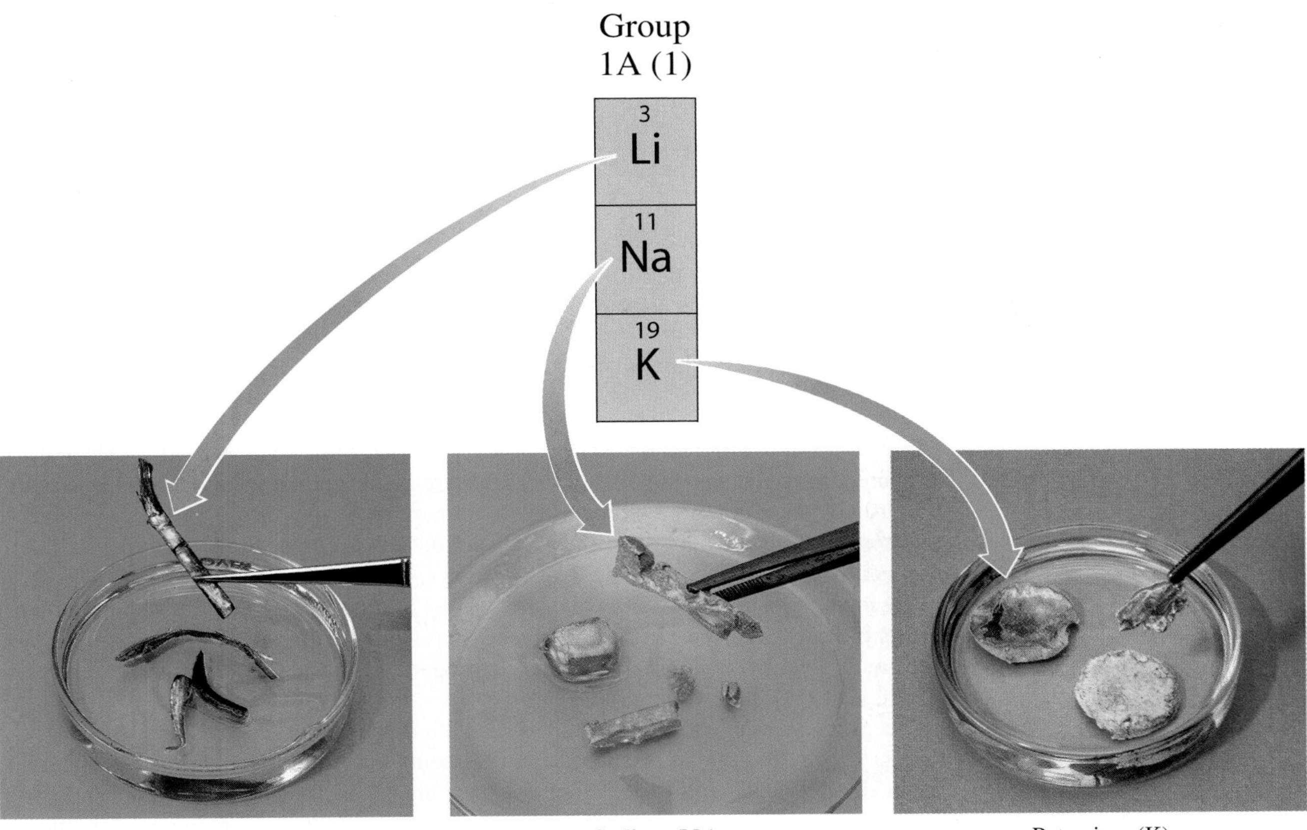


**FIGURE 3.4** Lithium (Li), sodium (Na), and potassium (K) are some alkali metals from Group 1A (1).

**Q** What physical properties do these alkali metals have in common?

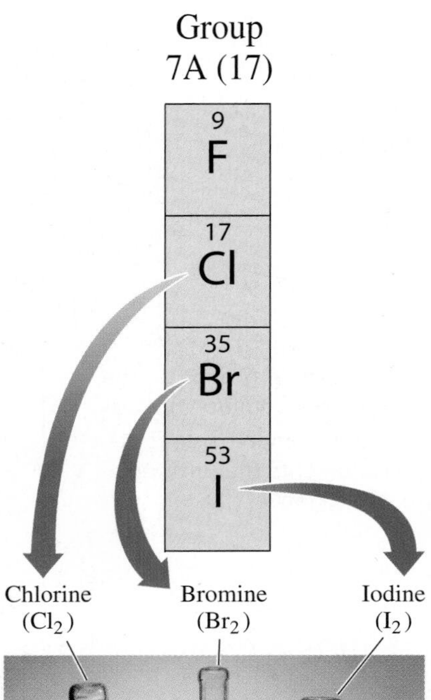


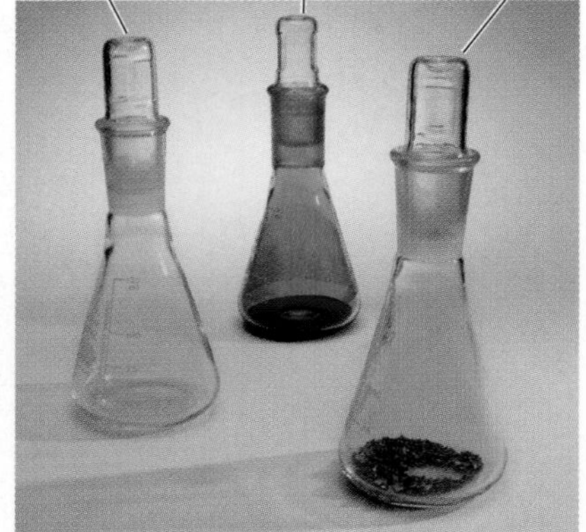

**FIGURE 3.5** Chlorine ($Cl_2$), bromine ($Br_2$), and iodine ($I_2$) are examples of halogens from Group 7A (17).

**Q** What elements are in the halogen group?

Although hydrogen (H) is at the top of Group 1A (1), it is not an alkali metal and has properties that are distinctly different than the rest of the elements in this group. Thus hydrogen is not included in the classification of alkali metals. In some periodic tables, H is placed at the top of Group 7A (17).

Group 2A (2) elements—beryllium (Be), magnesium (Mg), calcium (Ca), strontium (Sr), barium (Ba), and radium (Ra)—are called the **alkaline earth metals**. They are also shiny metals like those in Group 1A (1), but they are not as reactive.

The **halogens** are found on the right side of the periodic table in Group 7A (17). They include the elements fluorine (F), chlorine (Cl), bromine (Br), iodine (I), and astatine (At), as shown in Figure 3.5. The halogens, especially fluorine and chlorine, are highly reactive and form compounds with most of the elements.

Group 8A (18) contains the **noble gases**: helium (He), neon (Ne), argon (Ar), krypton (Kr), xenon (Xe), and radon (Rn). They are quite unreactive and are seldom found in combination with other elements.

## Metals, Nonmetals, and Metalloids

Another feature of the periodic table is the heavy zigzag line that separates the elements into the *metals* and the *nonmetals*. The metals are those elements on the left of the line *except for hydrogen*, and the nonmetals are the elements on the right. (See Figure 3.6.)

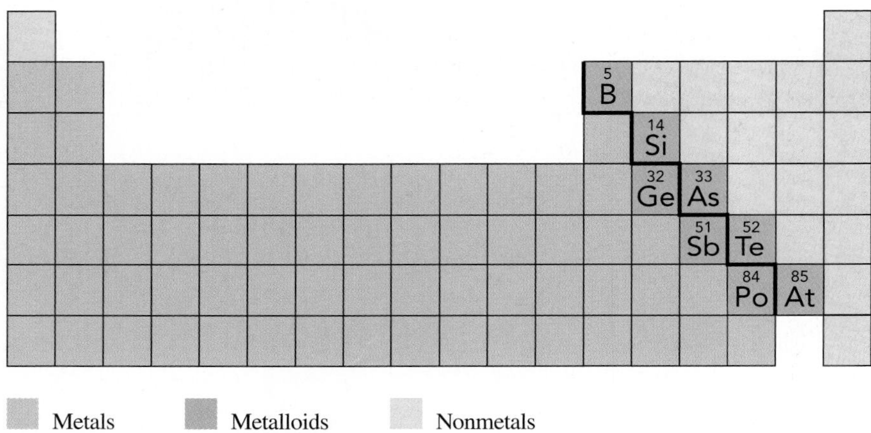


**FIGURE 3.6** Along the heavy zigzag line on the periodic table that separates the metals and nonmetals are metalloids, which exhibit characteristics of both metals and nonmetals.

**Q** On which side of the heavy zigzag line are the nonmetals located?

In general, most **metals** are shiny solids. They can be shaped into wires (ductile) or hammered into a flat sheet (malleable). Metals are good conductors of heat and electricity. They usually melt at higher temperatures than nonmetals. All of the metals are solids at room temperature, except for mercury (Hg), which is a liquid. Some typical metals are magnesium (Mg), copper (Cu), gold (Au), silver (Ag), iron (Fe), and tin (Sn).

**Nonmetals** are not especially shiny, malleable, or ductile, and they are often poor conductors of heat and electricity. They typically have low melting points and low densities. You may have heard of nonmetals such as hydrogen (H), carbon (C), nitrogen (N), oxygen (O), chlorine (Cl), and sulfur (S).

Except for aluminum, the elements located along the heavy line are **metalloids**: B, Si, Ge, As, Sb, Te, Po, and At. Metalloids are elements that exhibit some properties that are typical of the metals and other properties that are characteristic of the nonmetals. For example, they are better conductors of heat and electricity than the nonmetals, but not as good as the metals. The metalloids are semiconductors because they can be easily modified to function as conductors or insulators. Table 3.4 compares some characteristics of silver, a metal, with those of antimony, a metalloid, and sulfur, a nonmetal.

TABLE 3.4 Some Characteristics of a Metal, a Metalloid, and a Nonmetal

| Silver (Ag) | Antimony (Sb) | Sulfur (S) |
|---|---|---|
| Metal | Metalloid | Nonmetal |
| Shiny | Blue-gray, shiny | Dull, yellow |
| Extremely ductile | Brittle | Brittle |
| Can be hammered into sheets (malleable) | Shatters when hammered | Shatters when hammered |
| Good conductor of heat and electricity | Poor conductor of heat and electricity | Poor conductor, good insulator |
| Used in coins, jewelry, tableware | Used to harden lead, color glass and plastics | Used in gunpowder, rubber, fungicides |
| Density 10.5 g/mL | Density 6.7 g/mL | Density 2.1 g/mL |
| Melting point 962 °C | Melting point 630 °C | Melting point 113 °C |

CONCEPT CHECK 3.2

### Groups and Periods on the Periodic Table

Consider the elements aluminum, silicon, and phosphorus.

**a.** In what group and period are they found?
**b.** Identify each as a metal, metalloid, or nonmetal.

ANSWER

**a.** They are all found in Period 3. Aluminum is in Group 3A (13), silicon is in Group 4A (14), and phosphorus is in Group 5A (15).
**b.** Aluminum is a metal, silicon is a metalloid, and phosphorus is a nonmetal.

SAMPLE PROBLEM 3.2

### Classification of Elements

Use the periodic table to classify each of the following elements by its group and period, group name (if any), and if it is a metal, nonmetal, or metalloid:

**a.** Na **b.** Si **c.** I **d.** Sn

SOLUTION

**a.** Na (sodium), Group 1A (1), Period 3, is an alkali metal.
**b.** Si (silicon), Group 4A (14), Period 3, is a metalloid.
**c.** I (iodine), Group 7A (17), Period 5, halogen, is a nonmetal.
**d.** Sn (tin), Group 4A (14), Period 5, is a metal.

STUDY CHECK

Give the symbol of the element represented by the following:
**a.** Group 5A (15), Period 4
**b.** a noble gas in Period 6
**c.** a metalloid in Period 2

## QUESTIONS AND PROBLEMS

### The Periodic Table

3.7 Identify the group or period number described by each of the following statements:
**a.** contains the elements C, N, and O
**b.** begins with helium
**c.** the alkali metals
**d.** ends with neon

**3.8** Identify the group or period number described by each of the following statements:
**a.** contains Na, K, and Rb
**b.** the row that begins with Li
**c.** the noble gases
**d.** contains F, Cl, Br, and I

**3.9** Classify each of the following as an alkali metal, alkaline earth metal, transition element, halogen, or noble gas:
**a.** Ca **b.** Fe **c.** Xe **d.** Na **e.** Cl

**3.10** Classify each of the following as an alkali metal, alkaline earth metal, transition element, halogen, or noble gas:
**a.** Ne **b.** Mg **c.** Cu **d.** Br **e.** Ba

**3.11** Give the symbol of the element described by the following:
**a.** Group 4A, Period 2
**b.** a noble gas in Period 1
**c.** an alkali metal in Period 3
**d.** Group 2, Period 4
**e.** Group 13, Period 3

**3.12** Give the symbol of the element described by the following:
**a.** an alkaline earth metal in Period 2
**b.** Group 15, Period 3
**c.** a noble gas in Period 4
**d.** a halogen in Period 5
**e.** Group 4A, Period 4

**3.13** Identify each of the following elements as a metal, nonmetal, or metalloid:
**a.** calcium **b.** sulfur
**c.** a shiny element **d.** a poor conductor of heat
**e.** located in Group 8A **f.** phosphorus
**g.** boron **h.** silver

**3.14** Identify each of the following elements as a metal, nonmetal, or metalloid:
**a.** located in Group 2A
**b.** a good conductor of electricity
**c.** chlorine
**d.** arsenic
**e.** an element that is not shiny
**f.** oxygen
**g.** nitrogen
**h.** aluminum

## HEALTH NOTE

### Some Important Trace Elements in the Body

Some metals and nonmetals known as *trace elements* are essential to the proper functioning of the body. Although they are required in minute amounts, their absence can disrupt major biological processes and cause illness. The trace elements listed in Table 3.5 are present in the body combined with other elements. The adult daily value (DV) is the daily recommended amount for an adult.

**TABLE 3.5** Some Important Trace Elements in the Body

| Element | Adult DV[a] | Biological Function | Deficiency Symptoms | Dietary Sources |
|---|---|---|---|---|
| Iron (Fe) | 10 mg (males)<br>18 mg (females) | Formation of hemoglobin; enzymes | Dry skin, spoon nails, decreased hemoglobin count, anemia | Liver and other organ meats, oysters, red and dark meats, green leafy vegetables, fortified breads and cereals, egg yolk |
| Copper (Cu) | 2.0–5.0 mg | Necessary in many enzyme systems; growth; aids formation of red blood cells and collagen | Uncommon; anemia; decreased white cell count; bone demineralization | Nuts, organ meats, whole grains, shellfish, eggs, poultry, green leafy vegetables |
| Zinc (Zn) | 15 mg | Amino acid metabolism; enzyme systems; energy production; collagen | Retarded growth and bone formation; skin inflammation; loss of taste and smell; poor healing | Oysters, crab, lamb, beef, organ meats, whole grains |
| Manganese (Mn) | 2.5–5.0 mg | Necessary for some enzyme systems; collagen formation; central nervous system; fat and carbohydrate metabolism; blood clotting | Abnormal skeletal growth; impairment of central nervous system | Whole grains, wheat germ, legumes, pineapple, figs |
| Iodine (I) | 150 mg | Necessary for activity of thyroid gland | Hypothyroidism; goiter; cretinism | Seafood, iodized salt |
| Fluorine (F) | 1.5–4.0 mg | Necessary for solid tooth formation and retention of calcium in bones with aging | Dental cavities | Tea, fish, water in some areas, supplementary drops, toothpaste |

[a]Daily value

# 3.3 The Atom

LEARNING GOAL

Describe the electrical charge and location in an atom for a proton, a neutron, and an electron.

SELF STUDY ACTIVITY
Atoms and Isotopes

TUTORIAL
The Anatomy of Atoms

All the elements listed on the periodic table are made up of atoms. An **atom** is the smallest particle of an element that retains the characteristics of that element. You have probably seen the element aluminum. Imagine that you are tearing a piece of aluminum foil into smaller and smaller pieces. Now imagine that you have a piece so small that you cannot tear it apart further. Then you would have a single atom of aluminum.

The concept of the atom is relatively recent. Although the Greek philosophers in 500 B.C.E. reasoned that everything must contain minute particles they called *atomos*, the idea of atoms did not become a scientific theory until 1808. Then John Dalton (1766–1844) developed an atomic theory that proposed that atoms were responsible for the combinations of elements found in compounds.

**Dalton's Atomic Theory**

1. All matter is made up of tiny particles called atoms.
2. All atoms of a given element are similar to one another and different from atoms of other elements.
3. Atoms of two or more different elements combine to form compounds. A particular compound is always made up of the same kinds of atoms and always has the same number of each kind of atom.
4. A chemical reaction involves the rearrangement, separation, or combination of atoms. Atoms are never created or destroyed during a chemical reaction.

Although atoms are the building blocks of everything we see around us, we cannot see an atom or even a billion atoms with the naked eye. However, when billions and billions of atoms are packed together, the characteristics of each atom are added to those of the next until we can see the characteristics we associate with the element. For example, a small piece of the shiny, reddish-colored element we call copper consists of many, many copper atoms. A special kind of microscope called a *scanning tunneling microscope* (STM) produces images of individual atoms such as the atoms of carbon in graphite shown in Figure 3.7.

FIGURE 3.7 Graphite, a form of carbon, magnified millions of times by a scanning tunneling microscope. This instrument generates an image of the atomic structure. The round yellow objects are atoms.

Q Why is a microscope with extremely high magnification needed to see atoms?

## Electrical Charges in an Atom

By the end of the 1800s, experiments with electricity showed that atoms were not solid spheres, but were composed of even smaller bits of matter called **subatomic particles**, three of which are the proton, electron, and neutron. Some of these subatomic particles were discovered because they have electrical charges.

An electrical charge can be positive or negative. Experiments show that like charges repel, or push away from each other. When you brush your hair on a dry day, electrical charges that are alike build up on the brush and in your hair. As a result, your hair flies away from the brush. Opposite or unlike charges attract. The crackle of clothes taken from the clothes dryer indicates the presence of electrical charges. The clinginess of the clothing results from the attraction of opposite, unlike charges, as shown in Figure 3.8.

Positive charges repel

Negative charges repel

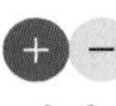

Unlike charges attract

FIGURE 3.8 Like charges repel, and unlike charges attract.

Q Why are the electrons attracted to the protons in the nucleus of an atom?

## Structure of the Atom

In 1897, J. J. Thomson, an English physicist, applied electricity to a glass tube and produced streams of small particles called *cathode rays*. Because these rays were attracted to a positively charged electrode, Thomson realized that these particles must be negatively charged. In further experiments, these particles called **electrons** were found to be much smaller than the atom and to have an extremely small mass. Because atoms are neutral, scientists soon discovered that atoms contain positively charged particles called **protons** that are much heavier than the electrons.

Thomson proposed a model for the atom in which the electrons and protons were randomly distributed through the atom. In 1911, Ernest Rutherford worked with Thomson to test this model. In Rutherford's experiment, positively charged particles were aimed at a thin sheet of gold foil. (See Figure 3.9.) If the Thomson model were correct, the particles would travel in straight paths through the gold foil. Rutherford was greatly surprised to

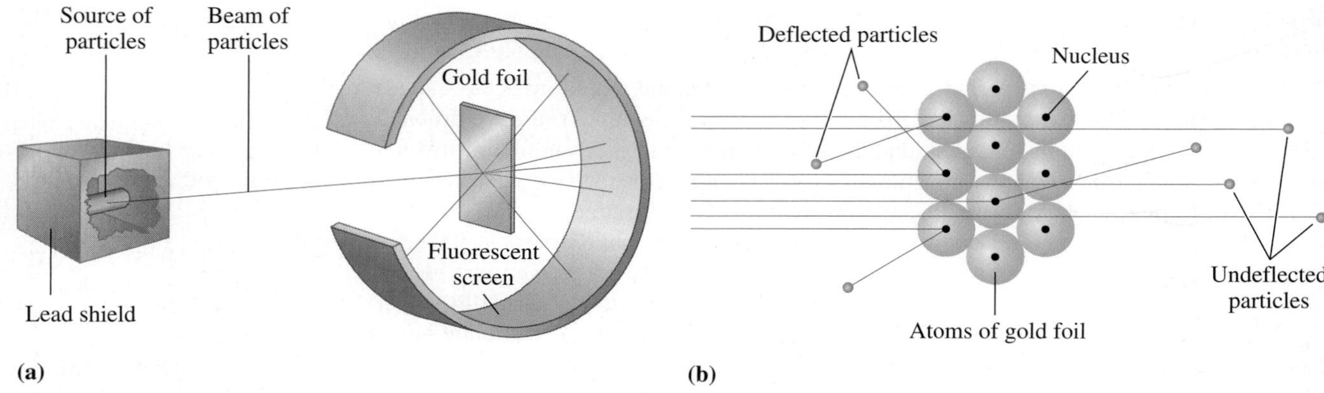


**FIGURE 3.9** **(a)** Positive particles are aimed at a piece of gold foil. **(b)** Particles that come close to the atomic nuclei are deflected from their straight path.

Q Why are some particles deflected while most pass through the gold foil undeflected?

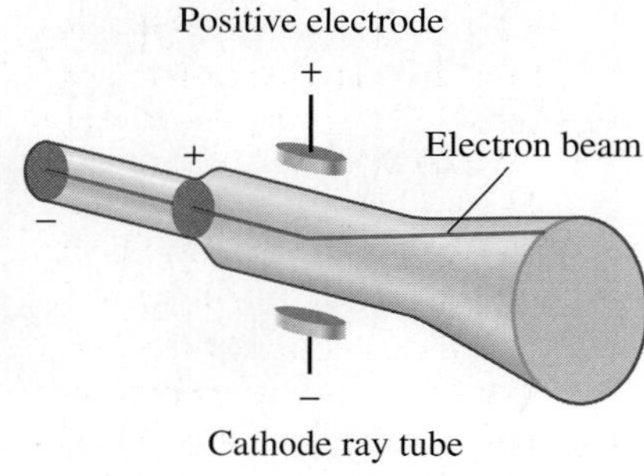


find that some of the particles were deflected slightly as they passed through the gold foil, and a few particles were deflected so much that they went back in the opposite direction. According to Rutherford, it was as though he had shot a cannonball at a piece of tissue paper, and it bounced back at him. Rutherford realized that the protons must be contained in a small, positively charged region at the center of the atom, which he called the **nucleus**. He proposed that the electrons in the atom occupy the space surrounding the nucleus through which most of the particles traveled undisturbed. Only the particles that came near this dense, positive center were deflected. If an atom were the size of a football stadium, the nucleus would be about the size of a golf ball placed in the center of the field.

Scientists knew that the nucleus was heavier than the mass of the protons and looked for another subatomic particle. Eventually, they discovered that the nucleus also contained a particle called a **neutron**, which is neutral. Thus, the masses of the protons and neutrons in the nucleus determine its mass. (See Figure 3.10.)

## Mass of the Atom

All of the subatomic particles are extremely small compared with the things you see around you. One proton has a mass of $1.7 \times 10^{-24}$ g, and the neutron is about the same. The mass of the electron is $9.1 \times 10^{-28}$ g, which is much less than a proton or neutron. Because the masses of subatomic particles are so small, chemists use a unit called an

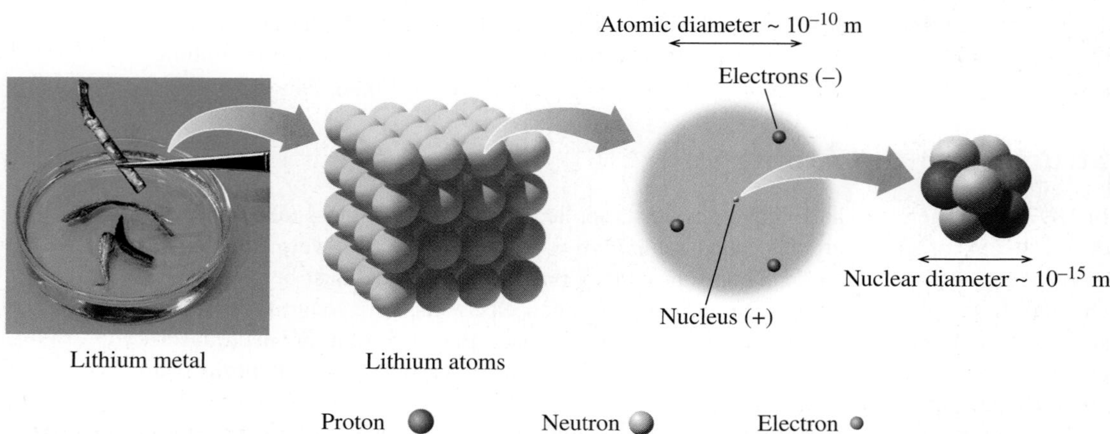


**FIGURE 3.10** In an atom, the protons and neutrons that make up most of the mass of the atom are packed into the tiny volume of the nucleus. The rapidly moving electrons surround the nucleus and account for the large volume of the atom.

Q Why can we say that an atom is mostly empty space?

**atomic mass unit (amu)**. An amu is defined as one-twelfth of the mass of the carbon atom with six protons and six neutrons, a standard with which the mass of every other atom is compared. In biology, the atomic mass unit is called a *dalton* in honor of John Dalton. On the amu scale, the proton and neutron each have a mass of about 1 amu. Because the electron mass is so small, it is usually ignored in atomic mass calculations. Table 3.6 summarizes some information about the subatomic particles in an atom.

TABLE 3.6 Particles in the Atom

| Subatomic Particle | Symbol | Electrical Charge | Approximate Mass (amu) | Location in Atom |
|---|---|---|---|---|
| Proton | $p$ or $p^+$ | 1+ | 1 | Nucleus |
| Neutron | $n$ or $n^0$ | 0 | 1 | Nucleus |
| Electron | $e^-$ | 1− | 0.0005 ($^1/_{2000}$) | Outside nucleus |

SAMPLE PROBLEM 3.3

### Identifying Subatomic Particles

Is each of the following statements *true* or *false*?

**a.** Protons are heavier than electrons.
**b.** Protons are attracted to neutrons.
**c.** Electrons are so small that they have no electrical charge.
**d.** The nucleus contains all the protons and neutrons of an atom.

SOLUTION

**a.** True
**b.** False; protons are attracted to electrons.
**c.** False; electrons have a 1− charge.
**d.** True

STUDY CHECK

*True* or *false*: The nucleus occupies a large volume in an atom.

EXPLORE YOUR WORLD

## Repulsion and Attraction

1. Obtain a tape dispenser with clear tape, a hairbrush, a comb, and a piece of paper. Tear off a piece of the tape about 20 cm long (the length of your hand). Stick the tape to the edge of a table leaving the end hanging down. Tear off a second piece of tape and slowly bring it close to the first one. What happens? Is there an attraction or repulsion?

   Slide your thumb and finger along the tape you are holding. Bring it close to the piece that is hanging from the table. What happens? Is there an attraction or repulsion? Attach the second tape to the edge of the table. Brush your hair and bring the brush close to each piece of tape hanging from the table. What do you observe?
2. Tear a small piece of paper into bits. Brush your hair several times and place the brush just above the bits of paper. Use your knowledge of electrical charges to explain your observations. Try the same experiment using a comb.

QUESTIONS

1. What happens when objects with like charges are placed close together?
2. What happens when objects with unlike charges are placed close together?

## QUESTIONS AND PROBLEMS

### The Atom

**3.15** Is a proton, neutron, or electron described by each of the following?
**a.** has the smallest mass
**b.** has a 1+ charge
**c.** is found outside the nucleus
**d.** is electrically neutral

**3.16** Is a proton, neutron, or electron described by each of the following?
**a.** has a mass about the same as a proton
**b.** is found in the nucleus
**c.** is attracted to the protons
**d.** has a 1− charge

**3.17** What did Rutherford determine about the structure of the atom from his gold-foil experiment?

**3.18** Why does the nucleus in every atom have a positive charge?

**3.19** Is each of the following statements *true* or *false*?
**a.** A proton and an electron have opposite charges.
**b.** The nucleus contains most of the mass of an atom.
**c.** Electrons repel each other.
**d.** A proton is attracted to a neutron.

**3.20** Is each of the following statements *true* or *false*?
**a.** A proton is attracted to an electron.
**b.** A neutron has twice the mass of a proton.
**c.** Neutrons repel each other.
**d.** Electrons and neutrons have opposite charges.

**3.21** On a dry day, your hair flies away when you brush it. How would you explain this?

**3.22** Sometimes clothes cling together when removed from a dryer. What kinds of charges are on the clothes?

## 3.4 Atomic Number and Mass Number

**LEARNING GOAL**

Given the atomic number and the mass number of an atom, state the number of protons, neutrons, and electrons.

All of the atoms of the same element always have the same number of protons. This feature distinguishes atoms of one element from atoms of all the other elements.

### Atomic Number

An **atomic number**, which is equal to the number of protons in the nucleus of an atom, is used to identify and define each element.

Atomic number = number of protons in an atom

TUTORIAL
Atomic Number and Mass Number

On the inside front cover of this text is a periodic table, which gives all of the elements in order of increasing atomic number. The atomic number is the whole number that appears above the symbol. For example, a hydrogen atom, with atomic number 1, has 1 proton; a lithium atom, with atomic number 3, has 3 protons; an atom of carbon, with atomic number 6, has 6 protons; gold, with atomic number 79, has 79 protons; and so forth.

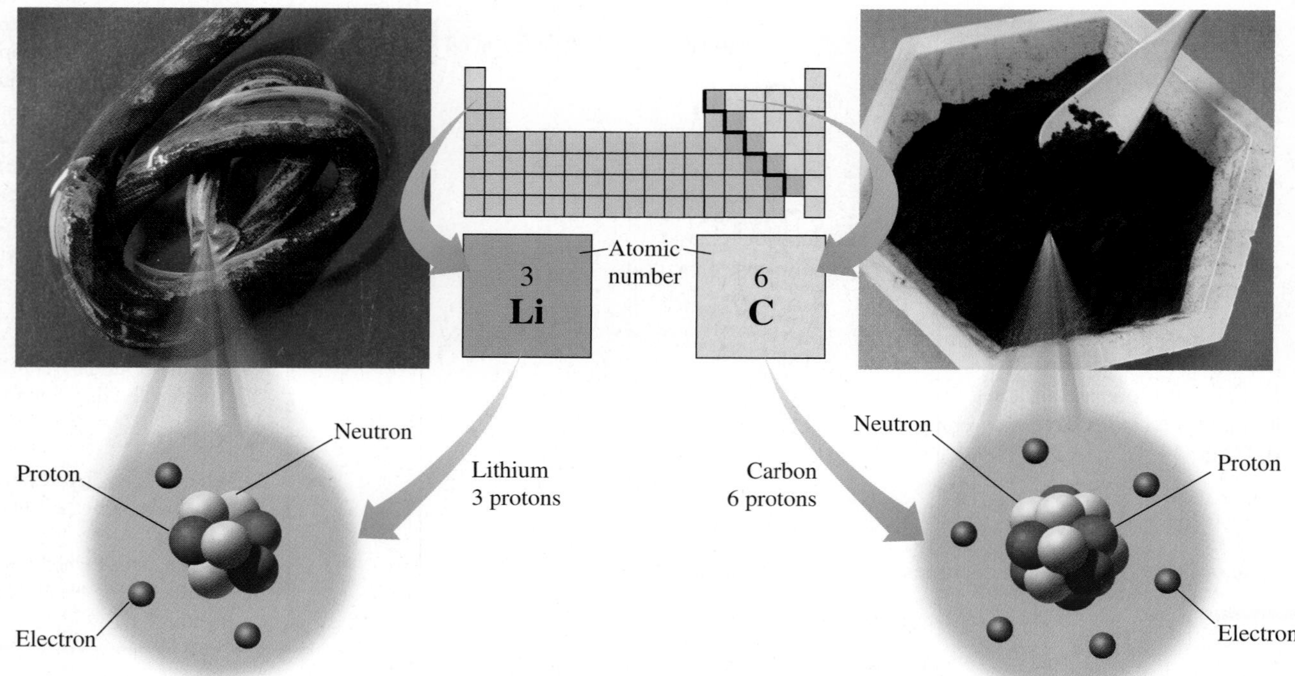


An atom is electrically neutral. That means that the number of protons in an atom is equal to the number of electrons. This electrical balance gives an atom an overall electrical charge of zero. Thus, in every atom, the atomic number also gives the number of electrons.

### Mass Number

We now know that the protons and neutrons determine the mass of the nucleus. For any atom, the **mass number** is the sum of the number of protons and neutrons in the nucleus.

Mass number = number of protons + number of neutrons

For example, an atom of oxygen that contains 8 protons and 8 neutrons has a mass number of 16.

Most elements have atoms with different numbers of neutrons. For example, some atoms of oxygen have 10 neutrons, which give a mass number of 18 (8 protons and 10 neutrons).

Table 3.7 illustrates the relationship between atomic number, mass number, and the number of protons, neutrons, and electrons in some atoms of different elements.

TABLE 3.7 Composition of Some Atoms of Different Elements

| Element | Symbol | Atomic Number | Mass Number | Number of Protons | Number of Neutrons | Number of Electrons |
|---|---|---|---|---|---|---|
| Hydrogen | H | 1 | 1 | 1 | 0 | 1 |
| Nitrogen | N | 7 | 14 | 7 | 7 | 7 |
| Chlorine | Cl | 17 | 35 | 17 | 18 | 17 |
| Chlorine | Cl | 17 | 37 | 17 | 20 | 17 |
| Iron | Fe | 26 | 57 | 26 | 31 | 26 |
| Gold | Au | 79 | 197 | 79 | 118 | 79 |

CONCEPT CHECK 3.3

### Subatomic Particles in Atoms

An atom of silver has a mass number of 109.

**a.** How many protons are in the nucleus?
**b.** How many neutrons are in the nucleus?
**c.** How many electrons are in the atom?

ANSWER

**a.** Silver (Ag) in Period 5 with atomic number 47 has 47 protons.
**b.** Neutrons are calculated by subtracting the number of protons from the mass number.

$109 - 47 = 62$ neutrons for Ag with a mass number of 109

**c.** In an atom, the number of electrons is equal to the number of protons. An atom of silver with 47 protons has 47 electrons.

SAMPLE PROBLEM 3.4

### Calculating Numbers of Protons, Neutrons, and Electrons

For an atom of iron that has a mass number of 56, determine the following:

**a.** the number of protons
**b.** the number of neutrons
**c.** the number of electrons

SOLUTION

**a.** On the periodic table, the atomic number of iron is 26. An iron atom has 26 protons.
**b.** The number of neutrons in this atom is found by subtracting the atomic number from the mass number. The number of neutrons is 30.

$$\begin{array}{ccccc} \text{Mass number} & - & \text{atomic number} & = & \text{number of neutrons} \\ 56 & - & 26 & = & 30 \end{array}$$

**c.** Because an atom is neutral, the number of electrons is equal to the number of protons. An iron atom has 26 electrons.

STUDY CHECK

How many neutrons are in the nucleus of a bromine atom that has a mass number of 80?

CAREER FOCUS

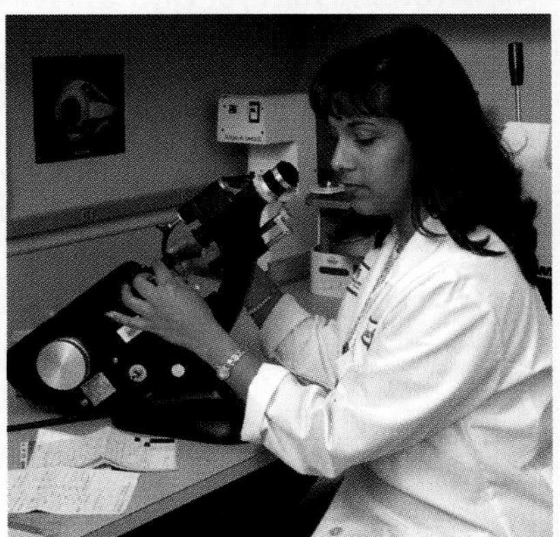

### Optician

"When a patient brings in a prescription, I help select the proper lenses, put them into a frame, and fit them properly on the patient's face," says Suranda Lara, optician, Kaiser Hospital. "If a prescription requires a thinner and lighter-weight lens, we formulate that lens. So we have to understand the different materials used to make lenses. Sometimes patients come in with their own glasses that they want to convert to sunglasses. We remove the lenses and put them into a tint bath, which turns them into sunglasses."

Opticians fit and adjust eyewear for patients who have had their eyesight tested by an ophthalmologist or optometrist. Optics and mathematics are used to select materials for frames and lenses that are compatible with patients' facial measurements and lifestyles.

## QUESTIONS AND PROBLEMS

### Atomic Number and Mass Number

**3.23** Would you use atomic number, mass number, or both to obtain the following?
- **a.** number of protons in an atom
- **b.** number of neutrons in an atom
- **c.** number of particles in the nucleus
- **d.** number of electrons in a neutral atom

**3.24** What do you know about the subatomic particles from the following?
- **a.** atomic number
- **b.** mass number
- **c.** mass number − atomic number
- **d.** mass number + atomic number

**3.25** Write the names and symbols of the elements with the following atomic numbers:

**a.** 3 **b.** 9 **c.** 20 **d.** 30
**e.** 10 **f.** 14 **g.** 53 **h.** 8

**3.26** Write the names and symbols of the elements with the following atomic numbers:

**a.** 1 **b.** 11 **c.** 19 **d.** 26
**e.** 35 **f.** 47 **g.** 15 **h.** 2

**3.27** How many protons are there in a neutral atom of the following?

**a.** magnesium **b.** zinc
**c.** iodine **d.** potassium

**3.28** How many electrons are there in a neutral atom of the following?

**a.** carbon **b.** fluorine
**c.** calcium **d.** sulfur

**3.29** Complete the following table for neutral atoms:

| Name of Element | Symbol | Atomic Number | Mass Number | Number of Protons | Number of Neutrons | Number of Electrons |
|---|---|---|---|---|---|---|
| | Al | | 27 | | | |
| | | 12 | | | 12 | |
| Potassium | | | | | 20 | |
| | | | | 16 | 15 | |
| | | | 56 | | | 26 |

**3.30** Complete the following table for neutral atoms:

| Name of Element | Symbol | Atomic Number | Mass Number | Number of Protons | Number of Neutrons | Number of Electrons |
|---|---|---|---|---|---|---|
| | N | | 15 | | | |
| Calcium | | | 42 | | | |
| | | | | 38 | 50 | |
| | | 14 | | | 16 | |
| | | 56 | 138 | | | |

# 3.5 Isotopes and Atomic Mass

**LEARNING GOAL**

Give the number of protons, electrons, and neutrons in the isotopes of an element.

We have seen that all atoms of the same element have the same number of protons and electrons. However, the atoms of any one element are not identical because they can have different numbers of neutrons.

## Isotopes

SELF STUDY ACTIVITY
Atoms and Isotopes

**Isotopes** are atoms of the same element that have different numbers of neutrons. For example, all atoms of the element magnesium (Mg) have 12 protons. However, some magnesium atoms have 12 neutrons, others have 13 neutrons, and still others have 14 neutrons. The differences in numbers of neutrons for these magnesium atoms cause their mass numbers to be different but not their chemical behavior. The three isotopes of magnesium have the same atomic number but different mass numbers.

On the periodic table, the atomic number appears above the element symbol. To distinguish between the different isotopes of an element, we write an **atomic symbol** that indicates the mass number in the upper left corner and the atomic number in the lower left corner.

Atomic Symbol for an Isotope of Magnesium

Mass number → 24
Symbol of element → Mg
Atomic number → 12

$$^{24}_{12}\text{Mg}$$

An isotope may be referred to by its name or symbol followed by the mass number such as magnesium-24 or Mg-24. Magnesium has three naturally occurring isotopes, as shown in Table 3.8.

**TABLE 3.8** Isotopes of Magnesium

| Atomic symbol | $^{24}_{12}Mg$ | $^{25}_{12}Mg$ | $^{26}_{12}Mg$ |
|---|---|---|---|
| Number of protons | 12 | 12 | 12 |
| Number of electrons | 12 | 12 | 12 |
| Mass number | **24** | **25** | **26** |
| Number of neutrons | **12** | **13** | **14** |
| Mass of isotope (amu) | 23.99 | 24.99 | 25.98 |
| % abundance | 78.70 | 10.13 | 11.17 |

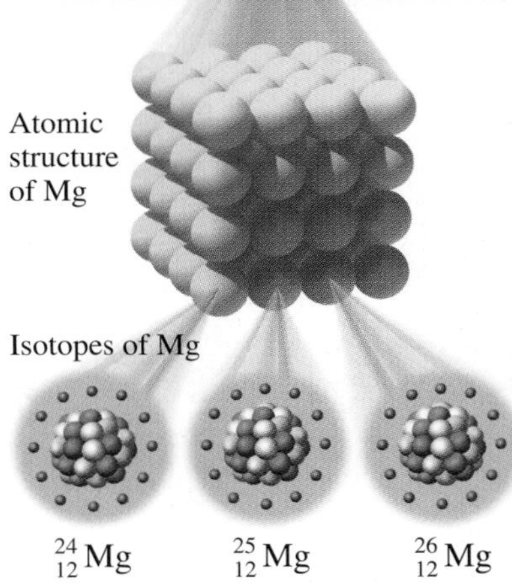


**SAMPLE PROBLEM 3.5**

### Identifying Protons and Neutrons in Isotopes

State the number of protons and neutrons in the following isotopes of neon (Ne):

**a.** $^{20}_{10}Ne$ **b.** $^{21}_{10}Ne$ **c.** $^{22}_{10}Ne$

SOLUTION

The atomic number of Ne is 10; each isotope has 10 protons. The number of neutrons in each isotope is found by subtracting the atomic number (10) from each mass number.

**a.** 10 protons; 10 neutrons (20 − 10)
**b.** 10 protons; 11 neutrons (21 − 10)
**c.** 10 protons; 12 neutrons (22 − 10)

STUDY CHECK

Write an atomic symbol for each of the following isotopes:
**a.** a nitrogen atom with 8 neutrons
**b.** an atom with 20 protons and 22 neutrons
**c.** an atom with mass number 27 and 14 neutrons

## Atomic Mass

In laboratory work, a scientist uses samples that contain many atoms of an element. Among those atoms are all of the various isotopes with their different masses. To obtain a convenient mass to work with, chemists use the mass of an "average atom" of each element. This average atom has an **atomic mass**, which is the weighted average of the mass of all of the naturally occurring isotopes of that element. On the periodic table, the atomic mass is given below the symbol of each element.

Most elements consist of several isotopes, which is one reason that the atomic masses on the periodic table are seldom whole numbers. For example, a sample of chlorine atoms consists of two isotopes, $^{35}_{17}Cl$ and $^{37}_{17}Cl$. The atomic mass of chlorine (35.45 amu) indicates that there will be a higher percentage of $^{35}_{17}Cl$ atoms. In fact, there are more than three atoms of $^{35}_{17}Cl$ for every atom of $^{37}_{17}Cl$ in a sample of chlorine atoms.

## Calculating Atomic Mass

To determine the atomic mass of an element, the percentage of each isotope and the mass of each isotope must be determined experimentally. For example, a sample of chlorine atoms consists of 75.76% of $^{35}_{17}Cl$ atoms and 24.24% of $^{37}_{17}Cl$ atoms. The atomic mass, known as a *weighted average*, is calculated using the percentage of each isotope and its mass: $^{35}_{17}Cl$ has a mass of 34.97 amu, and $^{37}_{17}Cl$ has a mass of 36.97 amu.

$$\text{Atomic mass of Cl} = \underbrace{\text{mass } ^{35}_{17}\text{Cl} \times \frac{^{35}_{17}\text{Cl}\%}{100\%}}_{\text{(mass from } ^{35}_{17}\text{Cl)}} + \underbrace{\text{mass } ^{37}_{17}\text{Cl} \times \frac{^{37}_{17}\text{Cl}\%}{100\%}}_{\text{(mass from } ^{37}_{17}\text{Cl)}}$$

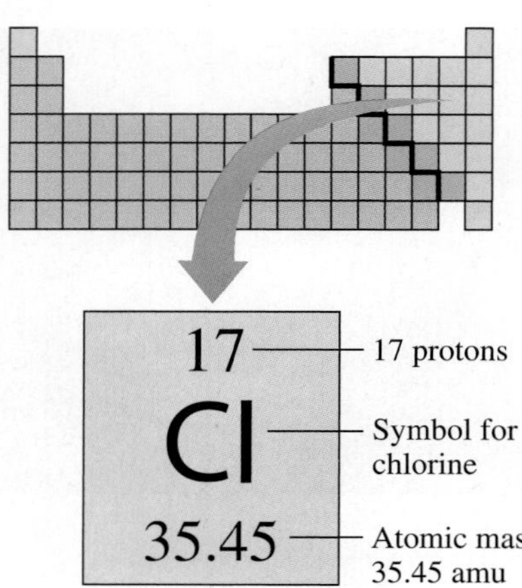

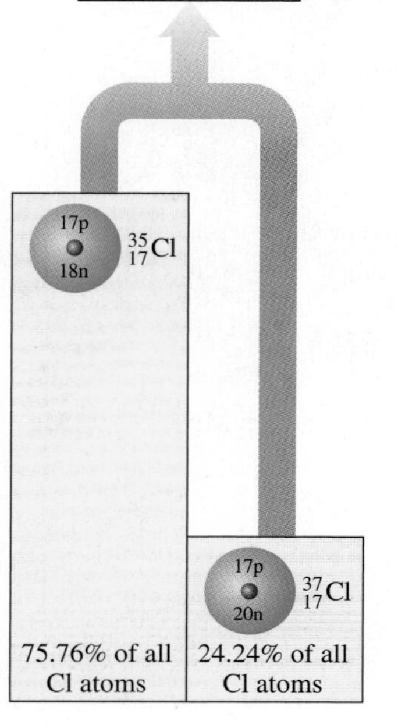


| Isotope | Mass (amu) | × | Abundance (%) | = | Contribution to Average Cl Atom |
|---|---|---|---|---|---|
| $^{35}_{17}Cl$ | 34.97 | × | $\frac{75.76}{100}$ | = | 26.49 amu |
| $^{37}_{17}Cl$ | 36.97 | × | $\frac{24.24}{100}$ | = | 8.962 amu |
| | | | Atomic mass of Cl | = | 35.45 amu |

The atomic mass of 35.45 amu is the weighted average mass of a sample of Cl atoms, although no individual Cl atom actually has this mass.

Table 3.9 lists the naturally occurring isotopes of selected elements and their atomic masses.

**TABLE 3.9 The Atomic Mass of Some Elements**

| Element | Most Common Naturally Occurring Isotopes | Atomic Mass (weighted average) |
|---|---|---|
| Lithium | $^{6}_{3}Li$, $^{7}_{3}Li$ | 6.941 amu |
| Carbon | $^{12}_{6}C$, $^{13}_{6}C$, $^{14}_{6}C$ | 12.01 amu |
| Oxygen | $^{16}_{8}O$, $^{17}_{8}O$, $^{18}_{8}O$ | 16.00 amu |
| Fluorine | $^{19}_{9}F$ | 19.00 amu |
| Sulfur | $^{32}_{16}S$, $^{33}_{16}S$, $^{34}_{16}S$, $^{36}_{16}S$ | 32.07 amu |
| Copper | $^{63}_{29}Cu$, $^{65}_{29}Cu$ | 63.55 amu |

**TUTORIAL** Atomic Mass Calculations

**CONCEPT CHECK 3.4**

### Average Atomic Mass

Magnesium consists of three naturally occurring isotopes: $^{24}_{12}Mg$, $^{25}_{12}Mg$, and $^{26}_{12}Mg$. Using the atomic mass on the periodic table, which isotope of magnesium is the most prevalent in a magnesium sample?

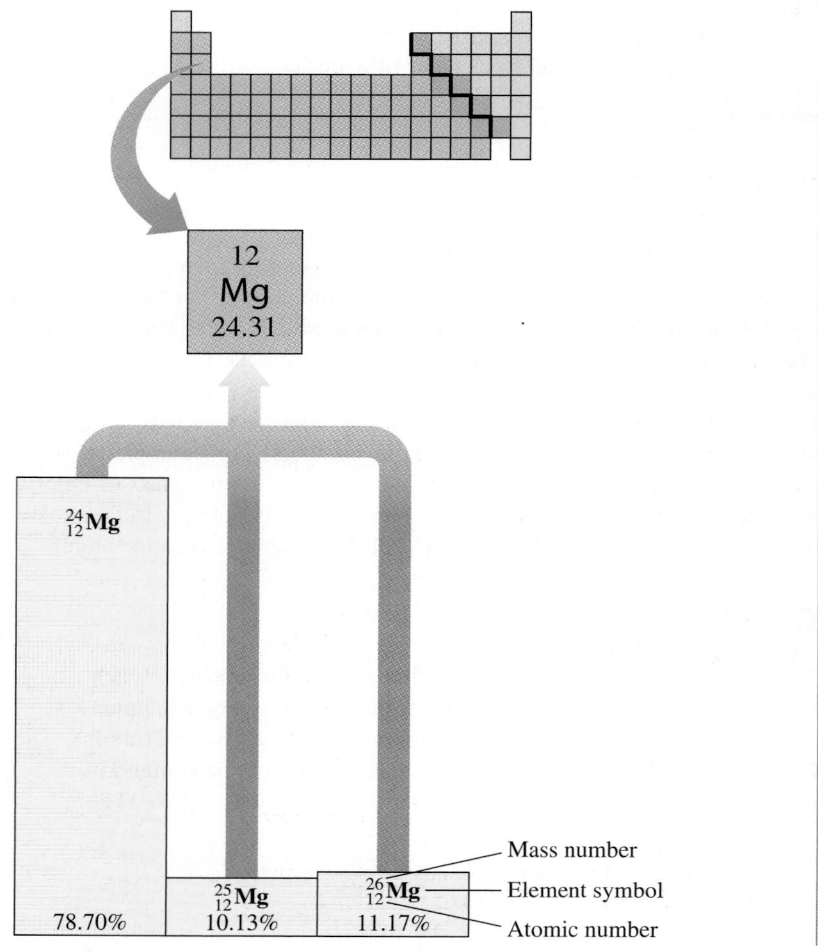

ANSWER

The atomic mass (weighted average) for all isotopes of magnesium is 24.31 amu. Thus, the isotope $^{24}_{12}Mg$ must be the most prevalent isotope in a magnesium sample.

SAMPLE PROBLEM 3.6

### Calculating Atomic Mass

Using Table 3.8, calculate the atomic mass for magnesium.

SOLUTION

| | | | | |
|---|---|---|---|---|
| $^{24}_{12}Mg$ | 23.99 | $\times$ | $\frac{78.70}{100}$ | = 18.88 amu |
| $^{25}_{12}Mg$ | 24.99 | $\times$ | $\frac{10.13}{100}$ | = 2.531 amu |
| $^{26}_{12}Mg$ | 25.98 | $\times$ | $\frac{11.17}{100}$ | = 2.902 amu |
| | Atomic mass of Mg | | | = 24.31 amu |

STUDY CHECK

There are two naturally occurring isotopes of boron. $^{10}_{5}B$ has a mass of 10.01 amu with an abundance of 19.80%, and $^{11}_{5}B$ has a mass of 11.01 amu with an abundance of 80.20%. What is the atomic mass of boron?

## QUESTIONS AND PROBLEMS

### Isotopes and Atomic Mass

**3.31** What are the number of protons, neutrons, and electrons in the following isotopes?

**a.** $^{30}_{14}Si$ **b.** $^{60}_{27}Co$

**c.** $^{80}_{34}Se$ **d.** $^{19}_{9}F$

**3.32** What are the number of protons, neutrons, and electrons in the following isotopes?

**a.** $^{2}_{1}H$ **b.** $^{14}_{7}N$

**c.** $^{26}_{14}Si$ **d.** $^{70}_{30}Zn$

**3.33** Write the atomic symbols for isotopes with the following:

**a.** 15 protons and 16 neutrons
**b.** 35 protons and 45 neutrons
**c.** 13 electrons and 14 neutrons
**d.** a chlorine atom with 18 neutrons
**e.** a mercury atom with 122 neutrons

**3.34** Write the atomic symbols for isotopes with the following:

**a.** an oxygen atom with 10 neutrons
**b.** 4 protons and 5 neutrons
**c.** 26 electrons and 30 neutrons
**d.** a mass number of 24 and 13 neutrons
**e.** a nickel atom with 32 neutrons

**3.35** There are four isotopes of sulfur with mass numbers 32, 33, 34, and 36.

**a.** Write the atomic symbol for each of these atoms.
**b.** How are these isotopes alike?
**c.** How are they different?
**d.** Why is the atomic mass of sulfur listed on the periodic table not a whole number?
**e.** Which isotope is the most abundant in a sample of sulfur?

**3.36** There are four isotopes of strontium with mass numbers 84, 86, 87, and 88.

**a.** Write the atomic symbol for each of these atoms.
**b.** How are these isotopes alike?
**c.** How are they different?
**d.** Why is the atomic mass of strontium listed on the periodic table not a whole number?
**e.** Which isotope is the most abundant in a sample of strontium?

**3.37** Copper consists of two isotopes, $^{63}_{29}Cu$ and $^{65}_{29}Cu$. If the atomic mass for copper on the periodic table is 63.55, are there more atoms of $^{63}_{29}Cu$ or $^{65}_{29}Cu$ in a sample of copper?

**3.38** There are four naturally occurring isotopes of iron: $^{54}_{26}Fe$, $^{56}_{26}Fe$, $^{57}_{26}Fe$, and $^{58}_{26}Fe$. Use the atomic mass of iron listed on the periodic table to identify the most abundant isotope.

**3.39** Two isotopes of gallium are naturally occurring, with $^{69}_{31}Ga$ at 60.11% (68.93 amu) and $^{71}_{31}Ga$ at 39.89% (70.92 amu). What is the atomic mass of gallium?

**3.40** Two isotopes of copper are naturally occurring, with $^{63}_{29}Cu$ at 69.09% (62.93 amu) and $^{65}_{29}Cu$ at 30.91% (64.93 amu). What is the atomic mass of copper?

## 3.6 Electron Energy Levels

**LEARNING GOAL**

Describe the energy levels, sublevels, and orbitals in atoms.

When we listen to a radio, use a microwave oven, turn on a light, see the colors of a rainbow, or have an X-ray, we are using various forms of *electromagnetic radiation*. Light and other electromagnetic radiation consist of energy particles called *photons* that move as a wave of energy. In a wave, the distance between the peaks is called the *wavelength*. In some types of radiation, the peaks are far apart, while in other forms of radiation they are close together. All forms of electromagnetic radiation travel at the speed of light, $3.0 \times 10^8$ meters per second, but they differ in energy and wavelength. The energy of radiation is inversely related to its wavelength. High-energy radiation such as X-rays and gamma rays has short wavelengths. X-rays and gamma rays can pass through soft substances but not metal or bone, which is why they are used to scan luggage at airports and to image bones and teeth. Low-energy forms of radiation such as microwaves and radio waves have long wavelengths. The wavelength of a typical AM radio wave or cell phone can be as long as a football field. (See Figure 3.11.)

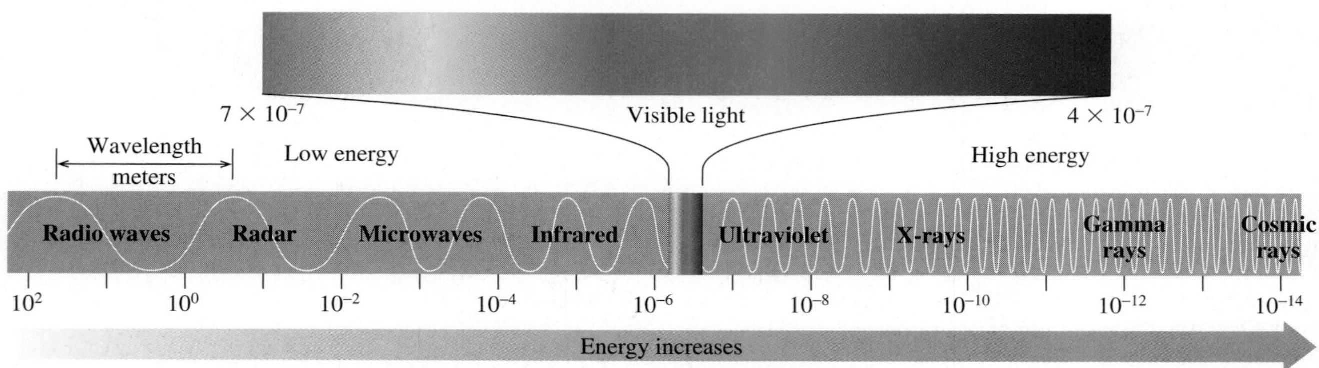


**FIGURE 3.11** The electromagnetic spectrum contains radiation with long and short wavelengths in the visible and invisible regions.

Q How does the energy of ultraviolet light compare to that of a microwave?

When sunlight passes through a prism or crystal, the light separates into a continuous color spectrum: red, orange, yellow, green, blue, indigo, and violet. These are the same colors we see in a rainbow that forms when sunlight passes through raindrops acting as prisms. In this visible spectrum, which is the only part of the electromagnetic spectrum that we can see naturally, red light has the longest wavelength and violet light has the shortest wavelength.

When the light emitted from a heated element is passed through a prism, it does not produce a continuous spectrum. Instead, an **atomic spectrum** is produced that consists of lines of different colors separated by dark areas. (See Figure 3.12.) This separation of colors indicates that only certain wavelengths of light are produced when an element is heated, which gives each element a unique atomic spectrum.

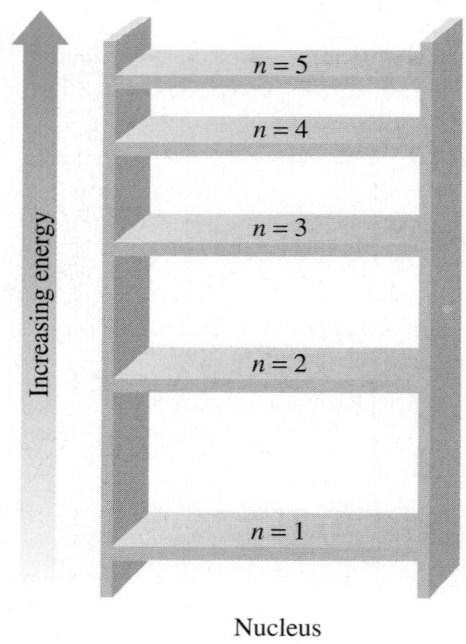


### Electron Energy Levels

Scientists associated the lines in atomic spectra with changes in the energies of the electrons. In an atom, each electron has a fixed or specific energy known as its energy level.

The energy levels are assigned values called *principal quantum numbers (n)*, which are positive integers ($n = 1, n = 2, \ldots$). Generally, electrons in the lower energy levels are closer to the nucleus, while electrons in the higher energy levels are farther away. The energy of an electron is *quantized*, which means that an electron can only have specific energy values but cannot have values between them.

As an analogy, we can think of the energy levels of an atom as similar to the shelves in a bookcase. The lowest energy level is the first shelf; the second energy level would be the second shelf. If we have a stack of books on the floor, it takes less energy to put them on the bottom shelves first, and then the second shelf, and so on. However, we could never get any book to stay in the space between the shelves. Unlike standard bookcases, however,

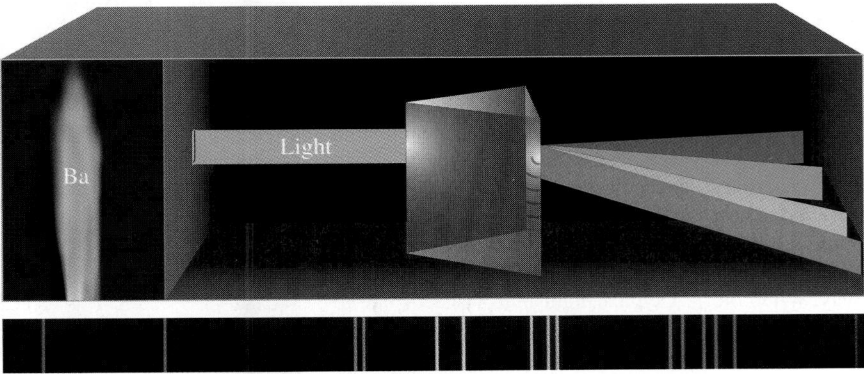


FIGURE 3.12 A spectrum unique to each element is produced as light emitted from the heated element passes through a prism, which separates the light into colored lines.

Q Why don't the elements form a continuous spectrum as seen with white light?

there is a big difference in the energy of the first and second energy levels, and thereafter the energy levels are closer.

**Principal Quantum Number (*n*)**

$1 < 2 < 3 < 4 < 5 < 6 < 7$

Energy of electrons increases →

## Changes in Energy Levels

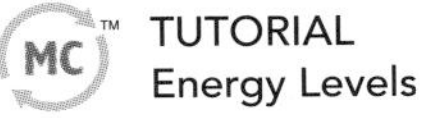


TUTORIAL
Energy Levels

When the electrons in an atom occupy the lowest energy levels, they are in their *ground state*. By absorbing energy equal to the difference in energy levels, an electron is raised to a higher energy level called the *excited state*. An electron loses energy when it falls to a lower energy level and emits electromagnetic radiation equal to the difference in energy levels. (See Figure 3.13.) If the electromagnetic radiation emitted has a wavelength in the visible range, we see a color.

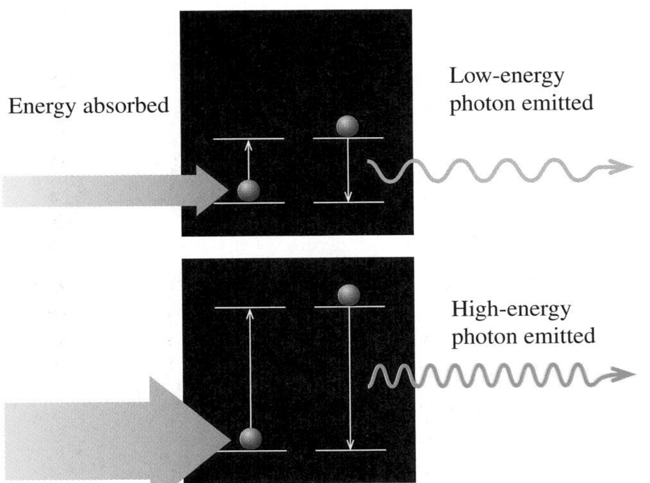


FIGURE 3.13 Electrons can absorb a specific amount of energy to move to a higher energy level. When electrons lose energy, photons with specific energies are emitted.

Q How does the energy of a photon of green light compare to the energy of a photon of red light?

There is a limit to the number of electrons allowed in each energy level. Only a few electrons can occupy the lower energy levels, while more electrons can be accommodated in higher energy levels. The maximum number of electrons allowed in any energy level is calculated using the formula $2n^2$ (two times the square of the principal quantum number).

## GREEN CHEMISTRY NOTE

### Energy-Saving Lightbulbs

A compact fluorescent light (CFL) is a type of fluorescent bulb that is replacing the standard light bulb we use in our homes and workplaces. Compared to a standard light bulb, the CFL has a longer life and uses less electricity. Within about 20 days of use, the fluorescent bulb saves enough money in electricity costs to pay for its higher initial cost.

A standard incandescent light bulb has a thin tungsten filament inside a sealed glass bulb. When the light is switched on, electricity flows through this filament, and electrical energy is converted to heat energy. When the filament reaches a temperature around 2300 °C, we see white light. We say that the light bulb is incandescent.

A fluorescent bulb produces light in a different way. When the switch is turned on, electrons move between two electrodes and collide with mercury atoms in a gas mixture of mercury and argon inside the bulb. When the electrons in the mercury atoms absorb energy from the collisions, electrons are raised to higher energy levels. As electrons fall to lower energy levels, energy in the ultraviolet range is emitted. This ultraviolet light strikes the phosphor coating inside the tube, and fluorescence occurs as visible light is emitted.

The production of light in a fluorescent bulb is more efficient than in an incandescent light bulb. A 75-watt incandescent bulb can be replaced by a 20-watt fluorescent bulb that gives the same amount of light, providing a 70% reduction in electricity costs. A typical light bulb lasts for one to two months, whereas a fluorescent light bulb lasts from one to two years.

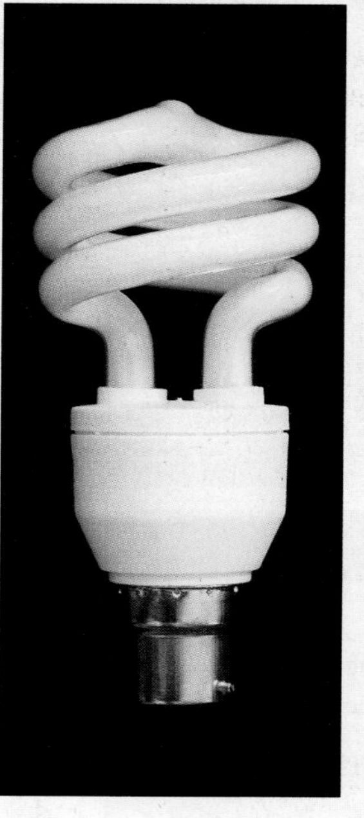

## Sublevels

Within each energy level, there are one or more **sublevels** that contain electrons with identical energy. The sublevels are identified by the letters *s*, *p*, *d*, and *f*. The number of sublevels within an energy level is equal to the principal quantum number. The first energy level ($n = 1$) has only one sublevel, 1*s*. The second energy level ($n = 2$) has two sublevels, 2*s* and 2*p*. The third energy level ($n = 3$) has three sublevels, 3*s*, 3*p*, and 3*d*. The fourth energy level ($n = 4$) has four sublevels: 4*s*, 4*p*, 4*d*, and 4*f*. (See Figure 3.14.)

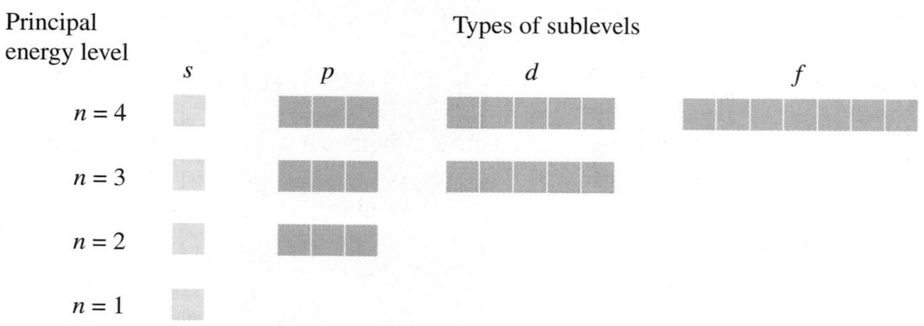


**FIGURE 3.14** The number of sublevels in an energy level is the same as the principal quantum number *n*.

**Q** How many sublevels are in energy level $n = 5$?

Within each energy level, the *s* sublevel has the lowest energy. If there are additional sublevels, the *p* sublevel has the next lowest energy, then the *d* sublevel, and finally the *f* sublevel.

**Order of Increasing Energy of Sublevels in an Energy Level**

$$s < p < d < f$$

Lowest energy ⟶ Highest energy

Energy levels $n = 5$ and higher have as many sublevels as the value of *n*, but only *s*, *p*, *d*, and *f* sublevels are needed to hold the electrons of atoms of the elements known today.

## Number of Electrons in Sublevels

A maximum number of electrons can occupy each sublevel. An *s* sublevel holds 1 or 2 electrons. A *p* sublevel takes up to 6 electrons, a *d* sublevel can hold up to 10 electrons, and an *f* sublevel holds a maximum of 14 electrons.

CONCEPT CHECK 3.5

### Energy Levels and Sublevels

Complete the following table with the notation for principal energy level and sublevels in each energy level:

| Energy Level (*n*) | Sublevels | | | |
|---|---|---|---|---|
| | *s* | *p* | *d* | *f* |
| | | | 4*d* | |
| 1 | | | | |
| | 2*s* | | | |
| | | 3*p* | | |

ANSWER

| Energy Level (*n*) | Sublevels | | | |
|---|---|---|---|---|
| | *s* | *p* | *d* | *f* |
| 4 | 4*s* | 4*p* | 4*d* | 4*f* |
| 1 | 1*s* | | | |
| 2 | 2*s* | 2*p* | | |
| 3 | 3*s* | 3*p* | 3*d* | |

## Orbitals

There is no way to know the exact location of an electron in an atom. Instead, scientists describe the location of an electron in terms of *probability*. A region in an atom where there is the highest probability of finding an electron is called an **orbital**. Suppose you could draw an imaginary circle with a 100-m radius around your chemistry classroom. There is a high probability of finding you within that area when your chemistry class is in session. Occasionally, though, you may be found outside that circle because you were sick or your car did not start.

Any orbital can have a maximum of two electrons. When an orbital contains two electrons, their spins are in opposite directions. We represent the spins of the electrons in the same orbital with one arrow pointing up and the other pointing down.

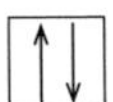

Electron spinning counterclockwise

Electron spinning clockwise

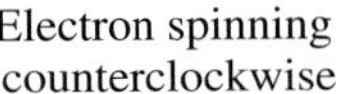

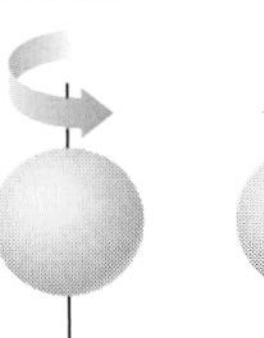

Opposite spins of electrons in an orbital

## Shapes of Orbitals

Each sublevel within an energy level is composed of the same type of orbitals. There is an *s* orbital for each *s* sublevel, *p* orbitals for each *p* sublevel, *d* orbitals for each *d* sublevel,

**FIGURE 3.15** An *s* orbital represents the region of highest probability of finding an *s* electron around the nucleus of an atom. All *s* orbitals are spherical, but the size increases at higher energy levels.

**Q** Is the probability high or low of finding an *s* electron outside an *s* orbital?

and *f* orbitals for each *f* sublevel. Each type of orbital has a unique shape. In an *s* orbital, the electrons are most likely found in a region with a spherical shape. Every *s* orbital can hold one or two electrons; there is just one *s* orbital for every *s* sublevel. Although the shape of every *s* orbital is spherical, there is an increase in the size of the *s* orbitals in higher energy levels. (See Figure 3.15.)

A *p* sublevel consists of three *p* orbitals, each of which has two lobes. The three *p* orbitals are arranged in three different directions (*x*, *y*, and *z* axes) around the nucleus. (See Figure 3.16.) Because each *p* orbital can hold up to two electrons, the three *p* orbitals can accommodate six electrons in a *p* sublevel. At higher energy levels, the shape of *p* orbitals is the same, but the volume increases.

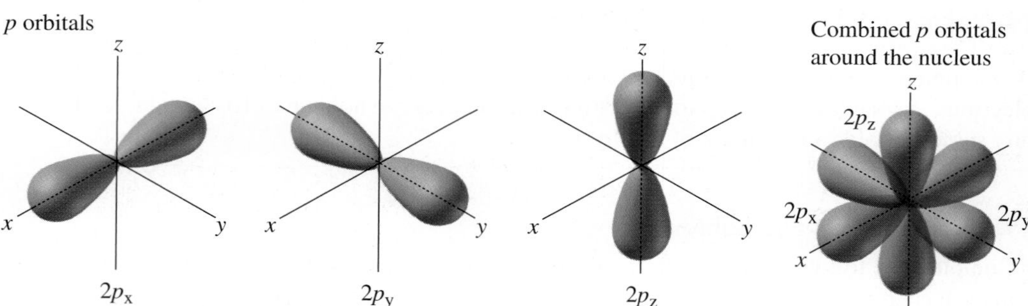


**FIGURE 3.16** Each *p* orbital has a dumbbell shape and aligns along a different axis from other *p* orbitals. Each holds a maximum of two electrons.

**Q** What is the maximum number of electrons possible in a *p* sublevel?

A *d* sublevel consists of five *d* orbitals. Each *d* orbital can hold as many as two electrons, which means that a *d* sublevel can have a maximum of 10 electrons. In the *f* sublevel, there are seven *f* orbitals. Each *f* orbital can hold up to two electrons, which means that the *f* sublevel can have as many as 14 electrons. The shapes of *d* orbitals and *f* orbitals are more complex, and we have not included them in this text.

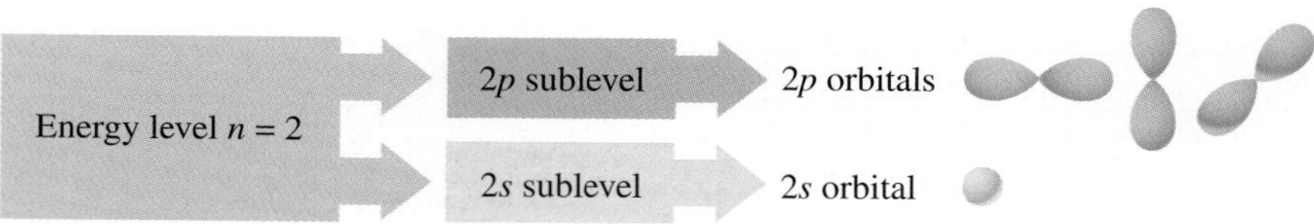


The number of electrons in the orbitals determines the number of electrons in the sublevels in each energy level. (See Table 3.10.)

**TABLE 3.10** Electron Capacity and Orbitals in Energy Levels 1–4

| Energy Level (*n*) | Electron Capacity ($2n^2$) | Orbitals | Maximum Number of Electrons in Sublevels |
|---|---|---|---|
| 1 | $2(1)^2 = 2$ | 1*s* | 2 |
| 2 | $2(2)^2 = 8$ | 2*s* | 2 |
| | | 2*p* 2*p* 2*p* | 6 |
| 3 | $2(3)^2 = 18$ | 3*s* | 2 |
| | | 3*p* 3*p* 3*p* | 6 |
| | | 3*d* 3*d* 3*d* 3*d* 3*d* | 10 |
| 4 | $2(4)^2 = 32$ | 4*s* | 2 |
| | | 4*p* 4*p* 4*p* | 6 |
| | | 4*d* 4*d* 4*d* 4*d* 4*d* | 10 |
| | | 4*f* 4*f* 4*f* 4*f* 4*f* 4*f* 4*f* | 14 |

SAMPLE PROBLEM 3.7

### Energy Levels, Sublevels, and Orbitals

Indicate the type and number of orbitals in each of the following energy levels or sublevels:

**a.** 3*p* sublevel **b.** $n = 2$ **c.** $n = 3$ **d.** 4*d* sublevel

SOLUTION

**a.** The 3*p* sublevel contains three 3*p* orbitals.
**b.** The $n = 2$ principal energy level consists of 2*s* (one) and 2*p* (three) orbitals.
**c.** The $n = 3$ principal energy level consists of 3*s* (one), 3*p* (three), and 3*d* (five) orbitals.
**d.** The 4*d* sublevel contains five 4*d* orbitals.

STUDY CHECK

What is similar and what is different for 1*s*, 2*s*, and 3*s* orbitals?

## QUESTIONS AND PROBLEMS

### Electron Energy Levels

3.41 Describe the shape of the following orbitals:
**a.** 1*s* **b.** 2*p* **c.** 5*s*

**3.42** Describe the shape of the following orbitals:
**a.** 3*p* **b.** 6*s* **c.** 4*p*

3.43 What is similar about the following?
**a.** 1*s* and 2*s* orbitals **b.** 3*s* and 3*p* sublevels
**c.** 3*p* and 4*p* sublevels **d.** three 3*p* orbitals

**3.44** What is similar about the following?
**a.** 5*s* and 6*s* orbitals **b.** 3*p* and 4*p* orbitals
**c.** 3*s* and 4*s* sublevels **d.** 2*s* and 2*p* orbitals

3.45 Indicate the number of each in the following:
**a.** orbitals in the 3*d* sublevel
**b.** sublevels in the energy level $n = 1$
**c.** orbitals in the 6*s* sublevel
**d.** orbitals in the energy level $n = 3$

**3.46** Indicate the number of each in the following:
**a.** orbitals in the energy level $n = 2$
**b.** sublevels in the energy level $n = 4$
**c.** orbitals in the 5*f* sublevel
**d.** orbitals in the 6*p* sublevel

3.47 Indicate the maximum number of electrons in the following:
**a.** 2*p* orbital
**b.** 3*p* sublevel
**c.** principal energy level $n = 4$
**d.** 5*d* sublevel

**3.48** Indicate the maximum number of electrons in the following:
**a.** 3*s* sublevel
**b.** 4*p* orbital
**c.** principal energy level $n = 3$
**d.** 4*f* sublevel

# 3.7 Electron Configurations

LEARNING GOAL

Use the periodic table to write orbital diagrams and electron configurations.

We can now look at how electrons are arranged in the orbitals within an atom. In an **orbital diagram**, boxes (or circles) represent the orbitals containing electrons. We see from an energy diagram (Figure 3.17) that the electrons in the 1*s* orbital have a lower energy level than in the 2*s* orbital.

## Period 1 Hydrogen and Helium

TUTORIAL
Electron Configurations

We can begin to draw the orbital diagrams and build the electron configurations for the elements H and He in Period 1. The 1*s* orbital (which is also the 1*s* sublevel) is used first because it has the lowest energy. Hydrogen has one electron in the 1*s* sublevel; helium has two. In the orbital diagram, the electrons for helium are shown with opposite spins.

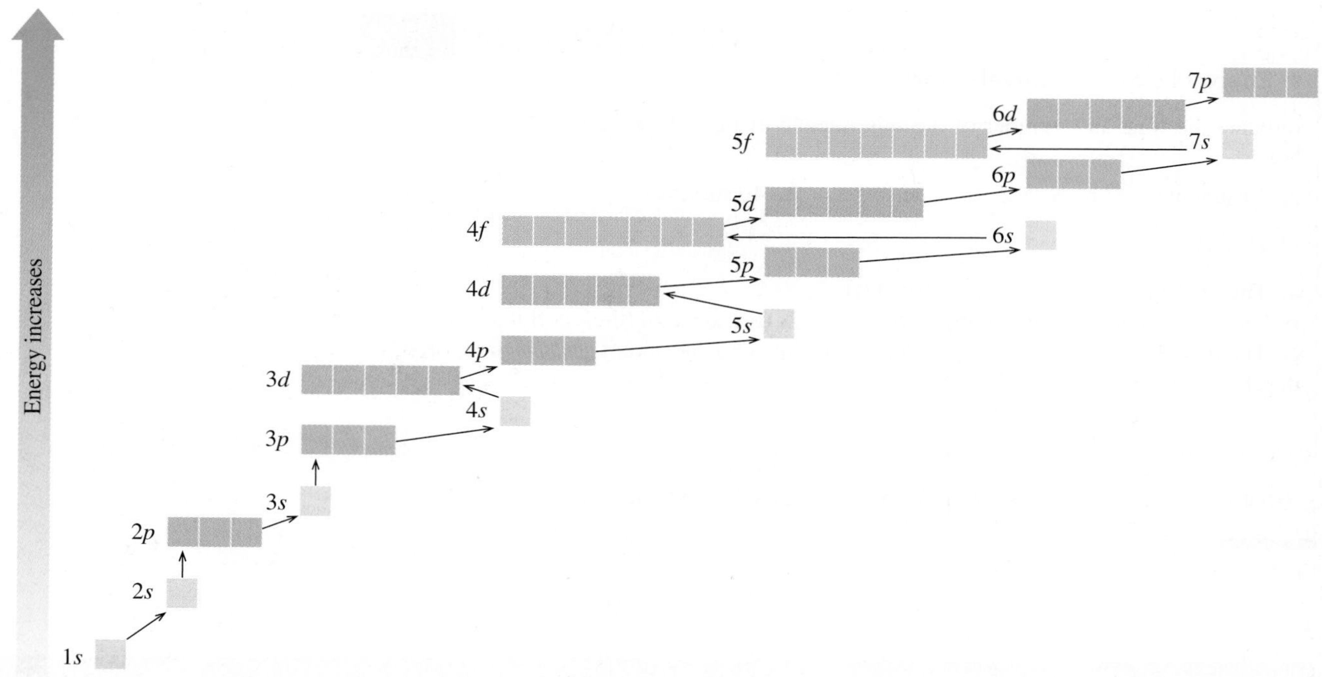


**FIGURE 3.17** The sublevels fill in order of increasing energy beginning with 1*s*. In each sublevel, each orbital will be filled with two electrons before additional electrons go to sublevels of higher energy.

**Q** Why does the 3*d* sublevel fill after the 4*s* sublevel?

The **electron configuration** of an atom is "built up" by placing the electrons of an atom in the sublevels in order of increasing energy. The electron configuration for helium is written as

Sublevel Number of electrons

$1s^2$ Read as "One *s* two"

| Atomic Number | Element | Orbital Diagram 1s | Electron Configuration |
|---|---|---|---|
| 1 | H | ↑ | $1s^1$ |
| 2 | He | ↑↓ | $1s^2$ |

## Period 2 Lithium to Neon

Period 2 begins with lithium, which has three electrons. The first two electrons fill the 1*s* orbital, while the third electron goes into the 2*s* orbital, the sublevel with the next lowest energy. In beryllium, another electron is added to complete the 2*s* orbital. Because 2*p* orbitals have equal energy, electrons from boron to nitrogen are added one at a time to give three half-filled 2*p* orbitals. In a half-filled sublevel, there is less repulsion between electrons when they are placed in separate 2*p* orbitals. From oxygen to neon, the remaining electrons must pair up using opposite spins until the 2*p* sublevel is complete. In writing the complete electron configurations for the elements in Period 2, begin with the 1*s* sublevel followed by the 2*s* and the 2*p* sublevels.

An electron configuration can also be written in an *abbreviated configuration*. The electron configuration of the preceding noble gas is replaced by writing its symbol inside square brackets. For example, the electron configuration for lithium, $1s^2 2s^1$, can be abbreviated as [He]$2s^1$, where [He] replaces $1s^2$.

| Atomic Number | Element | Orbital Diagram | | | Electron Configuration | Abbreviated Configuration |
|---|---|---|---|---|---|---|
| | | $1s$ | $2s$ | $2p$ | | |
| 3 | Li | ↑↓ | ↑ | | $1s^22s^1$ | $[He]2s^1$ |
| 4 | Be | ↑↓ | ↑↓ | | $1s^22s^2$ | $[He]2s^2$ |
| 5 | B | ↑↓ | ↑↓ | ↑ \| \| | $1s^22s^22p^1$ | $[He]2s^22p^1$ |
| 6 | C | ↑↓ | ↑↓ | ↑ \| ↑ \| | $1s^22s^22p^2$ | $[He]2s^22p^2$ |
| | | | | Unpaired electrons | | |
| 7 | N | ↑↓ | ↑↓ | ↑ \| ↑ \| ↑ | $1s^22s^22p^3$ | $[He]2s^22p^3$ |
| 8 | O | ↑↓ | ↑↓ | ↑↓ \| ↑ \| ↑ | $1s^22s^22p^4$ | $[He]2s^22p^4$ |
| 9 | F | ↑↓ | ↑↓ | ↑↓ \| ↑↓ \| ↑ | $1s^22s^22p^5$ | $[He]2s^22p^5$ |
| 10 | Ne | ↑↓ | ↑↓ | ↑↓ \| ↑↓ \| ↑↓ | $1s^22s^22p^6$ | $[He]2s^22p^6$ |

## Period 3 Sodium to Argon

In Period 3, electrons enter the orbitals of the 3*s* and 3*p* sublevels, but not the 3*d* sublevel. We notice that the elements sodium to argon, which are directly below the elements lithium to neon in Period 2, have a similar pattern of filling their *s* and *p* orbitals. We can write the complete orbital diagram for phosphorus as follows:

| $1s$ | $2s$ | $2p$ | $3s$ | $3p$ |
|---|---|---|---|---|
| ↑↓ | ↑↓ | ↑↓ \| ↑↓ \| ↑↓ | ↑↓ | ↑ \| ↑ \| ↑ |

For elements in Period 3 and above, we usually write the orbital diagrams for only the electrons in the highest energy levels. In Period 3, the symbol [Ne] replaces the electron configuration of neon, $1s^22s^22p^6$. The abbreviated configuration is convenient to use for electron configurations that contain several sublevel notations.

| Atomic Number | Element | Orbital Diagram (3*s* and 3*p* orbitals only) | | Electron Configuration | Abbreviated Configuration |
|---|---|---|---|---|---|
| | | $3s$ | $3p$ | | |
| 11 | Na | ↑ | \| \| | $1s^22s^22p^63s^1$ | $[Ne]3s^1$ |
| 12 | Mg | ↑↓ | \| \| | $1s^22s^22p^63s^2$ | $[Ne]3s^2$ |
| 13 | Al | ↑↓ | ↑ \| \| | $1s^22s^22p^63s^23p^1$ | $[Ne]3s^23p^1$ |
| 14 | Si | ↑↓ | ↑ \| ↑ \| | $1s^22s^22p^63s^23p^2$ | $[Ne]3s^23p^2$ |
| 15 | P | ↑↓ | ↑ \| ↑ \| ↑ | $1s^22s^22p^63s^23p^3$ | $[Ne]3s^23p^3$ |
| 16 | S | ↑↓ | ↑↓ \| ↑ \| ↑ | $1s^22s^22p^63s^23p^4$ | $[Ne]3s^23p^4$ |
| 17 | Cl | ↑↓ | ↑↓ \| ↑↓ \| ↑ | $1s^22s^22p^63s^23p^5$ | $[Ne]3s^23p^5$ |
| 18 | Ar | ↑↓ | ↑↓ \| ↑↓ \| ↑↓ | $1s^22s^22p^63s^23p^6$ | $[Ne]3s^23p^6$ |

SAMPLE PROBLEM 3.8

## Orbital Diagrams and Electron Configurations

For each of the following elements, write the stated type of electron notation:

**a.** orbital diagram for silicon
**b.** electron configuration for phosphorus
**c.** abbreviated electron configuration for chlorine

SOLUTION

**a.** Silicon in Period 3 has atomic number 14, which tells us that it has 14 electrons. To write the orbital diagram, we draw boxes for the orbitals up to $3p$.

| $1s$ | $2s$ | $2p$ | $3s$ | $3p$ |
|---|---|---|---|---|
| [↑↓] | [↑↓] | [↑↓][↑↓][↑↓] | [↑↓] | [↑][↑][ ] |

Add 14 electrons, starting with the $1s$ orbital. Show paired electrons in the same orbital with opposite spins, and place the last 2 electrons in different $3p$ orbitals.

| $1s$ | $2s$ | $2p$ | $3s$ | $3p$ |
|---|---|---|---|---|
| [↑↓] | [↑↓] | [↑↓][↑↓][↑↓] | [↑↓] | [↑][↑][ ] |

**b.** The electron configuration gives the electrons that fill the sublevels in order of increasing energy. Phosphorus is in Group 5A (15) in Period 3. In Periods 1 and 2, a total of 10 electrons fill sublevels: $1s^2$, $2s^2$, and $2p^6$. In Period 3, 2 electrons go into $3s^2$. The 3 remaining electrons (total of 15) are placed in the $3p$ sublevel.

P $1s^22s^22p^63s^23p^3$

**c.** In chlorine, the previous noble gas is neon. For the abbreviated configuration, write [Ne] for $1s^22s^22p^6$ followed by the electrons in the $3s$ and $3p$ sublevels.

$[Ne]3s^23p^5$

STUDY CHECK

Write the complete and abbreviated electron configurations for sulfur.

## Electron Configurations and the Periodic Table

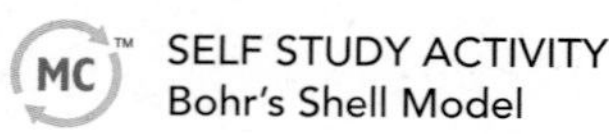


SELF STUDY ACTIVITY
Bohr's Shell Model

Until now, we have written electron configurations using the energy diagram. As configurations involve more sublevels, this becomes tedious. However, on the periodic table, the atomic numbers are arranged in order of increasing sublevel energy. The electron configurations of the elements are related to their position in the periodic table. Different sections or sublevel blocks within the table correspond to the $s$, $p$, $d$, and $f$ sublevels. (See Figure 3.18.) Therefore, we can "build up" atoms by reading the periodic table from left to right across each period.

1. The ***s* block** includes the elements hydrogen and helium as well as the elements in Group 1A (1) and Group 2A (2). This means that the final one or two electrons in the elements of the $s$ block are located in $s$ sublevels. The period number indicates the particular $s$ sublevel that is filling: $1s$, $2s$, and so on.
2. The ***p* block** consists of the elements in Group 3A (13) to Group 8A (18). There are six $p$ block elements in each period because each $p$ sublevel can hold as many as six electrons. The period number indicates the particular $p$ sublevel that is filling: $2p$, $3p$, and so on.
3. The ***d* block** first appears after calcium (atomic number 20) with the 10 columns of the transition elements. There are 10 elements in the $d$ block because each $d$ sublevel can hold as many as 10 electrons. The particular $d$ sublevel is one less ($n - 1$) than

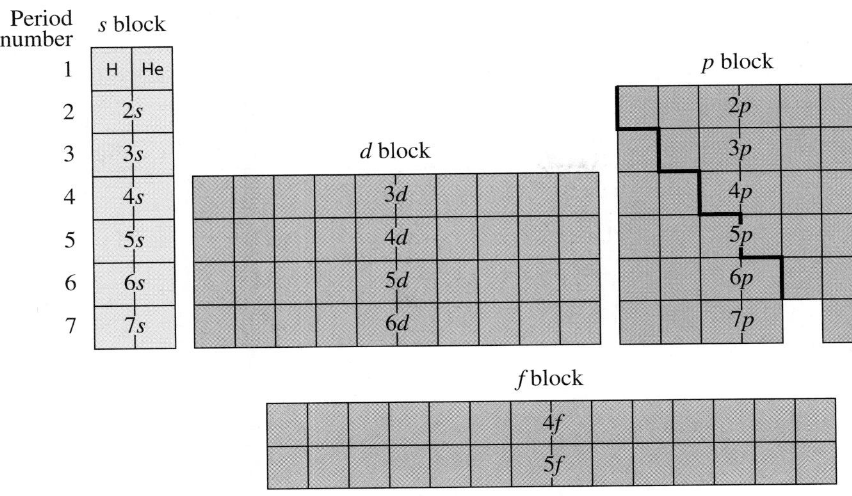


**FIGURE 3.18** An electron configuration of an atom follows the order of sublevels on the periodic table.

**Q** How many electrons are in the 1*s*, 2*s*, and 2*p* sublevels of neon?

the period number. For example, in Period 4, the first *d* block is the 3*d* sublevel. In Period 5, the second *d* block is the 4*d* sublevel.

4. The ***f* block** includes all the elements in the two rows at the bottom of the periodic table. There are 14 elements in each *f* block because an *f* sublevel can hold as many as 14 electrons. Elements that have atomic numbers higher than 57 (La) have electrons in the 4*f* block. The particular *f* sublevel is two fewer ($n - 2$) than the period number. For example, in Period 6, the first *f* block is the 4*f* sublevel. In Period 7, the second *f* block is the 5*f* sublevel.

## Writing Electron Configurations Using Sublevel Blocks

Now we can write electron configurations using the sublevel blocks on the periodic table. As before, each configuration begins at H. But now we move across the table writing down each block we come to until we reach the element for which we are writing an electron configuration.

To write the electron configuration for chlorine (atomic number 17) from the sublevel blocks on the periodic table:

| **Period** | | **Sublevel Blocks Filled** |
|---|---|---|
| 1 | 1*s* sublevel (H $\longrightarrow$ He) | $1s^2$ |
| 2 | 2*s* sublevel (Li $\longrightarrow$ Be) then 2*p* sublevel (B $\longrightarrow$ Ne) | $2s^2 \longrightarrow 2p^6$ |
| 3 | 3*s* sublevel (Na $\longrightarrow$ Mg) then 3*p* sublevel (Al $\longrightarrow$ Cl) | $3s^2 \longrightarrow 3p^?$ |

Writing the sublevel blocks in order up to chlorine gives

$1s^22s^22p^63s^23p^?$

Chlorine is the fifth element in the 3*p* block, which means that chlorine has five 3*p* electrons. The complete electron configuration for chlorine is written as

$1s^22s^22p^63s^23p^5$

## Period 4

Until now, the filling of sublevels has progressed in order. However, if we look at the sublevel blocks in Period 4, we see that the 4*s* sublevel block fills before the 3*d* orbitals. The 4*s* orbital has a slightly lower energy than the 3*d* orbitals, which means that the 4*s* sublevel has the next lowest energy following the filling of the 3*p* sublevel at the end of Period 3. This order occurs again in Period 5 when the 5*s* orbital fills before the 4*d* orbitals, and again in Period 6 when the 6*s* fills before the 5*d*.

At the beginning of Period 4, the one and two remaining electrons in potassium (19) and calcium (20) go into the 4*s* orbital. In scandium, the remaining electron goes into the 3*d* block, which continues to fill until it has 10 electrons at zinc (30). Once the 3*d* block is complete, the next six electrons go into the 4*p* block for elements gallium (31) to krypton (36).

| Atomic Number | Element | Electron Configuration | Abbreviated Configuration |
|---|---|---|---|
| **4*s* Block** | | | |
| 19 | K | $1s^22s^22p^63s^23p^64s^1$ | $[Ar]4s^1$ |
| 20 | Ca | $1s^22s^22p^63s^23p^64s^2$ | $[Ar]4s^2$ |
| **3*d* Block** | | | |
| 21 | Sc | $1s^22s^22p^63s^23p^64s^23d^1$ | $[Ar]4s^23d^1$ |
| 22 | Ti | $1s^22s^22p^63s^23p^64s^23d^2$ | $[Ar]4s^23d^2$ |
| 23 | V | $1s^22s^22p^63s^23p^64s^23d^3$ | $[Ar]4s^23d^3$ |
| 24 | Cr | $1s^22s^22p^63s^23p^64s^13d^5$ | $[Ar]4s^13d^5$ (1/2 filled *d* sublevel is stable) |
| 25 | Mn | $1s^22s^22p^63s^23p^64s^23d^5$ | $[Ar]4s^23d^5$ |
| 26 | Fe | $1s^22s^22p^63s^23p^64s^23d^6$ | $[Ar]4s^23d^6$ |
| 27 | Co | $1s^22s^22p^63s^23p^64s^23d^7$ | $[Ar]4s^23d^7$ |
| 28 | Ni | $1s^22s^22p^63s^23p^64s^23d^8$ | $[Ar]4s^23d^8$ |
| 29 | Cu | $1s^22s^22p^63s^23p^64s^13d^{10}$ | $[Ar]4s^13d^{10}$ (filled *d* sublevel is stable) |
| 30 | Zn | $1s^22s^22p^63s^23p^64s^23d^{10}$ | $[Ar]4s^23d^{10}$ |
| **4*p* Block** | | | |
| 31 | Ga | $1s^22s^22p^63s^23p^64s^23d^{10}4p^1$ | $[Ar]4s^23d^{10}4p^1$ |
| 32 | Ge | $1s^22s^22p^63s^23p^64s^23d^{10}4p^2$ | $[Ar]4s^23d^{10}4p^2$ |
| 33 | As | $1s^22s^22p^63s^23p^64s^23d^{10}4p^3$ | $[Ar]4s^23d^{10}4p^3$ |
| 34 | Se | $1s^22s^22p^63s^23p^64s^23d^{10}4p^4$ | $[Ar]4s^23d^{10}4p^4$ |
| 35 | Br | $1s^22s^22p^63s^23p^64s^23d^{10}4p^5$ | $[Ar]4s^23d^{10}4p^5$ |
| 36 | Kr | $1s^22s^22p^63s^23p^64s^23d^{10}4p^6$ | $[Ar]4s^23d^{10}4p^6$ |

## Some Exceptions in Sublevel Block Order

Within the filling of the 3*d* sublevel, exceptions occur for chromium and copper. When electrons half-fill or fill a sublevel, it is particularly stable. Thus, chromium has only one electron in the 4*s* and five electrons in the 3*d* sublevel to give the stability of a half-filled *d* sublevel. In copper, there is one electron in the 4*s* sublevel and 10 electrons in the 3*d* sublevel, which give the stability of a filled *d* sublevel.

After the 4*s* and 3*d* sublevels are completed, the 4*p* sublevel fills as expected from gallium to krypton, the noble gas that completes Period 4.

CONCEPT CHECK 3.6

### Electron Configurations

Identify the elements that have atoms with each of the following electron configurations:

**a.** $1s^22s^22p^5$

**b.** $1s^22s^22p^63s^23p^64s^23d^{10}4p^2$

**c.** $[Ar]4s^23d^6$

ANSWER

**a.** In the $p$ block, Period 2, the fifth element across is F, fluorine.
**b.** In the $p$ block, Period 4, the second element across is Ge, germanium.
**c.** In the $d$ block, Period 4, the sixth element across is Fe, iron.

SAMPLE PROBLEM 3.9

## Using Sublevel Blocks to Write Electron Configurations

Use the sublevel blocks on the periodic table to write the electron configuration for bromine.

SOLUTION

**STEP 1** Bromine is in the $p$ block and in Period 4.

**STEP 2** Beginning with $1s^2$, go across the periodic table writing each filled sublevel block as follows:

| | |
|---|---|
| Period 1 | $1s^2$ |
| Period 2 | $2s^2 \longrightarrow 2p^6$ |
| Period 3 | $3s^2 \longrightarrow 3p^6$ |
| Period 4 | $4s^2 \longrightarrow 3d^{10} \longrightarrow 4p^?$ |

**STEP 3** Five electrons in the $4p$ sublevel for Br ($4p^5$) completes the electron configuration for Br:

$1s^2 2s^2 2p^6 3s^2 3p^6 4s^2 3d^{10} 4p^5$

Guide to Writing Electron Configurations with Sublevel Blocks

STEP 1
Locate the element on the periodic table.

STEP 2
Write the filled sublevels in order going across each period.

STEP 3
Count the number of electrons in the sublevel for the given element and complete the configuration.

STUDY CHECK

Write the electron configuration for tin.

# QUESTIONS AND PROBLEMS

## Electron Configurations

**3.49** Write an orbital diagram for an atom of each of the following:
**a.** boron **b.** aluminum
**c.** phosphorus **d.** argon

**3.50** Write an orbital diagram for an atom of each of the following:
**a.** fluorine **b.** sodium
**c.** magnesium **d.** sulfur

**3.51** Write a complete electron configuration for an atom of each of the following:
**a.** nitrogen **b.** sodium
**c.** sulfur **d.** arsenic
**e.** iron

**3.52** Write a complete electron configuration for an atom of each of the following:
**a.** carbon **b.** silicon
**c.** phosphorus **d.** cobalt
**e.** gallium

**3.53** Write an abbreviated electron configuration for an atom of each of the following:
**a.** magnesium **b.** sulfur
**c.** aluminum **d.** titanium
**e.** barium

**3.54** Write an abbreviated electron configuration for an atom of each of the following:
**a.** sodium **b.** oxygen
**c.** nickel **d.** tin
**e.** silver

**3.55** Give the symbol of the element with each of the following electron configurations:
**a.** $1s^2 2s^2 2p^6 3s^2 3p^4$
**b.** $1s^2 2s^2 2p^6 3s^2 3p^6 4s^2 3d^7$
**c.** $[Ne]3s^2 3p^2$
**d.** $[Ar]4s^2 3d^{10} 4p^5$

**3.56** Give the symbol of the element with each of the following electron configurations:
**a.** $1s^2 2s^2 2p^4$
**b.** $1s^2 2s^2 2p^6 3s^2 3p^6$
**c.** $[Ne]3s^2 3p^1$
**d.** $[Ar]4s^2 3d^4$

**3.57** Give the symbol of the element that meets the following conditions:
**a.** has three electrons in energy level $n = 3$
**b.** has two $2p$ electrons
**c.** completes the $3p$ sublevel
**d.** has two electrons in the $4d$ sublevel

**3.58** Give the symbol of the element that meets the following conditions:
**a.** has five electrons in the $3p$ sublevel
**b.** has three $2p$ electrons
**c.** completes the $3s$ sublevel
**d.** has four $5p$ electrons

**3.59** Give the number of electrons in the indicated orbitals for the following:
**a.** $3d$ in zinc **b.** $2p$ in sodium
**c.** $4p$ in arsenic **d.** $5s$ in rubidium

**3.60** Give the number of electrons in the indicated orbitals for the following:
**a.** $3d$ in manganese **b.** $5p$ in antimony
**c.** $6p$ in lead **d.** $3s$ in magnesium

## 3.8 Periodic Trends

**LEARNING GOAL**

Use the electron configurations of elements to explain periodic trends.

The electron configurations of atoms are an important factor in the physical and chemical behavior of the elements. Going across a period, there is a pattern of regular change in these properties from one group to the next. Known as *periodic properties*, each property increases or decreases across a period. The trend is repeated again in each successive period. We can use the seasonal changes in temperatures as an analogy for periodic properties. In the winter, temperatures are cold and become warmer in the spring. In summer, outdoor temperatures are high, but they are lower in the fall. By winter, we expect cold temperatures again as the pattern of decreasing and increasing temperatures repeats for another year.

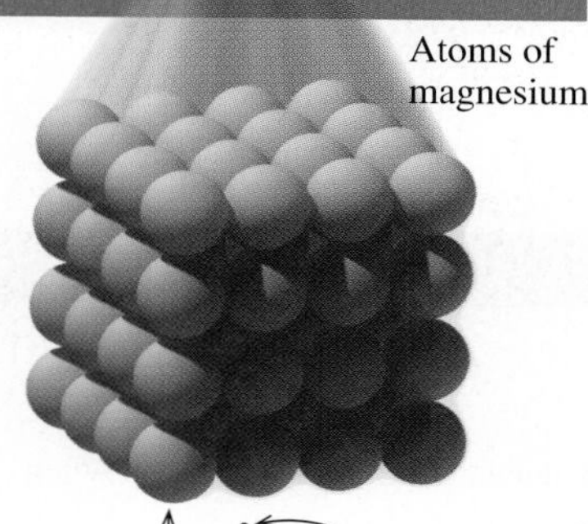

Atoms of magnesium

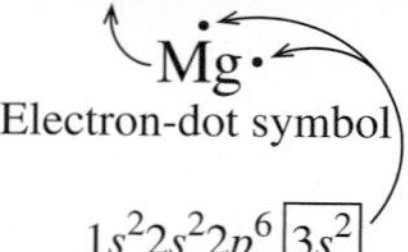


Electron-dot symbol

$1s^22s^22p^6\boxed{3s^2}$

Electron configuration of magnesium

### Group Number and Valence Electrons

If we could imagine two atoms approaching each other, the first interaction would be between those electrons in the highest filled energy levels. Chemists have determined that the chemical properties of representative elements are mostly the result of these outermost electrons, which are known as the **valence electrons**. Valence electrons occupy the $s$ and $p$ sublevels with the highest quantum number $n$. The group numbers indicate the number of valence (outer) electrons for the elements in each vertical column. For example, the elements in Group 1A (1) such as lithium, sodium, and potassium, all have one electron in the outer energy level. Looking at the sublevel block, we can represent the valence electron in the alkali metals of Group 1A (1) as $ns^1$. All the elements in Group 2A (2), the alkaline earth metals, have two (2) valence electrons, $ns^2$. The halogens in Group 7A (17) have seven (7) valence electrons, $ns^2np^5$.

We can see the repetition of the outermost $s$ and $p$ electrons for the representative elements in Periods 1 to 4 in Table 3.11. Helium is included in Group 8A (18) because it is a noble gas, but it has only two electrons in its complete energy level.

**TABLE 3.11** Valence Electrons for Representative Elements in Periods 1–4

| 1A (1) | 2A (2) | 3A (13) | 4A (14) | 5A (15) | 6A (16) | 7A (17) | 8A (18) |
|---|---|---|---|---|---|---|---|
| 1<br>H<br>$1s^1$ | | | | | | | 2<br>He<br>$1s^2$ |
| 3<br>Li<br>$2s^1$ | 4<br>Be<br>$2s^2$ | 5<br>B<br>$2s^22p^1$ | 6<br>C<br>$2s^22p^2$ | 7<br>N<br>$2s^22p^3$ | 8<br>O<br>$2s^22p^4$ | 9<br>F<br>$2s^22p^5$ | 10<br>Ne<br>$2s^22p^6$ |
| 11<br>Na<br>$3s^1$ | 12<br>Mg<br>$3s^2$ | 13<br>Al<br>$3s^23p^1$ | 14<br>Si<br>$3s^23p^2$ | 15<br>P<br>$3s^23p^3$ | 16<br>S<br>$3s^23p^4$ | 17<br>Cl<br>$3s^23p^5$ | 18<br>Ar<br>$3s^23p^6$ |
| 19<br>K<br>$4s^1$ | 20<br>Ca<br>$4s^2$ | 31<br>Ga<br>$4s^24p^1$ | 32<br>Ge<br>$4s^24p^2$ | 33<br>As<br>$4s^24p^3$ | 34<br>Se<br>$4s^24p^4$ | 35<br>Br<br>$4s^24p^5$ | 36<br>Kr<br>$4s^24p^6$ |

### Electron-Dot Symbols

An **electron-dot symbol** is a convenient way to represent the valence electrons. Valence electrons are shown as dots placed on the sides, top, or bottom of the symbol for the element—which side does not matter. However, one to four valence electrons are arranged as single dots. When there are more than four electrons, the electrons begin to pair up. Any of the following would be an acceptable electron-dot symbol for magnesium, which has two valence electrons:

**Possible Electron-Dot Symbols for the Two Valence Electrons in Magnesium**

$\dot{\text{Mg}}\cdot$ $\quad \dot{\underset{\cdot}{\text{Mg}}}$ $\quad \cdot\dot{\text{Mg}}$ $\quad \cdot\text{Mg}\cdot$ $\quad \underset{\cdot}{\text{Mg}}\cdot$ $\quad \cdot\underset{\cdot}{\text{Mg}}$

Electron-dot symbols for selected elements are given in Table 3.12.

**TABLE 3.12** Electron-Dot Symbols for Representative Elements in Periods 1–4

| | Group Number | | | | | | | |
|---|---|---|---|---|---|---|---|---|
| | 1A (1) | 2A (2) | 3A (13) | 4A (14) | 5A (15) | 6A (16) | 7A (17) | 8A (18) |
| Valence Electron Configuration | $ns^1$ | $ns^2$ | $ns^2np^1$ | $ns^2np^2$ | $ns^2np^3$ | $ns^2np^4$ | $ns^2np^5$ | $ns^2np^6$ |
| | H· | | | | | | | He: |
| | Li· | Ḃe· | ·Ḃ· | ·Ċ· (with dot below) | ·N̈· (with dot below) | ·Ö: (with dot below) | ·F̈: (with pair below) | :N̈e: (with pair below) |
| | Na· | Ṁg· | ·Ȧl· | ·Ṡi· (with dot below) | ·P̈· (with dot below) | ·S̈: (with dot below) | ·C̈l: (with pair below) | :Är: (with pair below) |
| | K· | Ċa· | ·Ġa· | ·Ġe· (with dot below) | ·Äs· (with dot below) | ·S̈e: (with dot below) | ·B̈r: (with pair below) | :K̈r: (with pair below) |

SAMPLE PROBLEM 3.10

**Writing Electron-Dot Symbols**

Write the electron-dot symbol for each of the following elements:

**a.** bromine **b.** aluminum

SOLUTION

**a.** Because the group number for bromine is 7A (17), bromine has seven valence electrons.

·B̈r: (with pair below)

**b.** Aluminum, in Group 3A (13), has three valence electrons.

·Ȧl·

STUDY CHECK

What is the electron-dot symbol for phosphorus?

## Atomic Size

Although there are no fixed boundaries to atoms, scientists have a good idea of the typical volume occupied by the electrons in atoms. The *atomic radius*, which is the distance from the nucleus to the valence (outermost) electrons, determines this volume, or atomic size. Going down a group of representative elements, the outermost electrons occupy higher energy levels, which are farther from the nucleus. Therefore, the atomic radius increases from the top to the bottom of each group. For example, in the alkali metals, Li has a valence electron in the 2*s* sublevel, Na has a valence electron in the 3*s* sublevel, K has a valence electron in the 4*s* sublevel, and Rb has a valence electron in the 5*s* sublevel. (See Figure 3.19.)

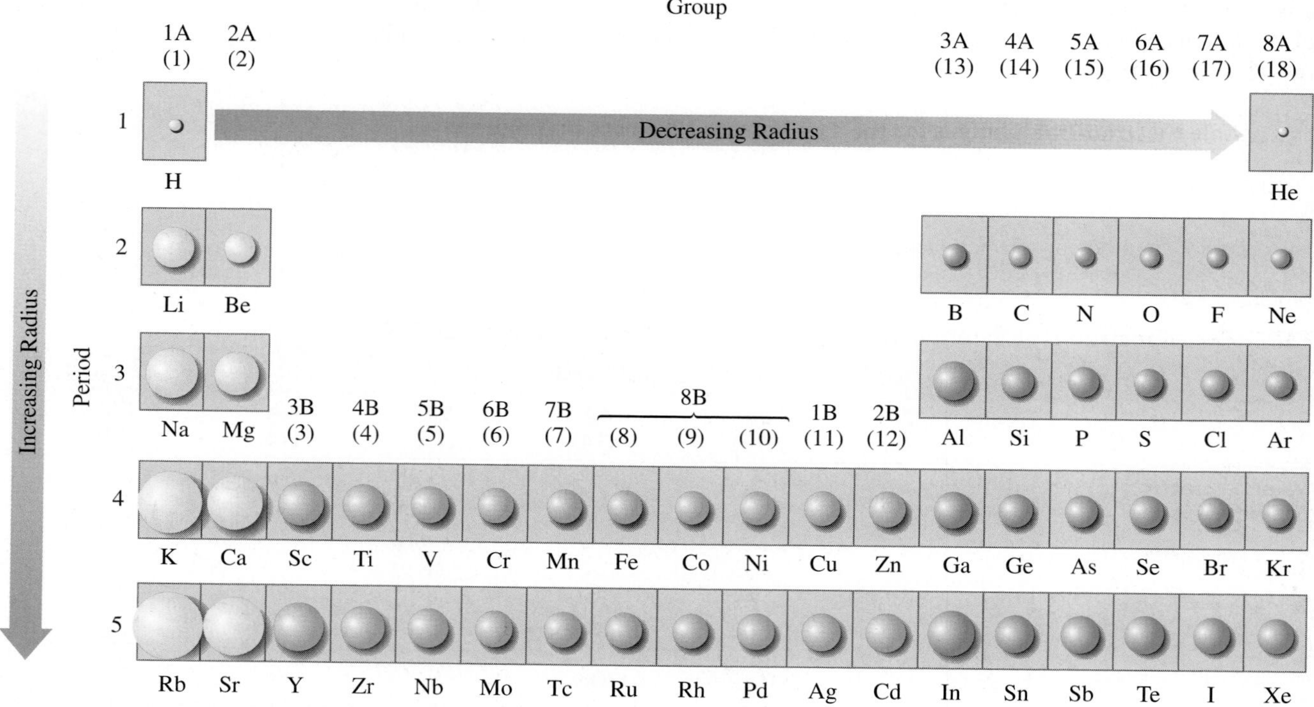


**FIGURE 3.19** The atomic radius increases going down a group but decreases going from left to right across a period.

**Q** Why does the atomic radius increase going down a group?

TUTORIAL
Ionization Energy

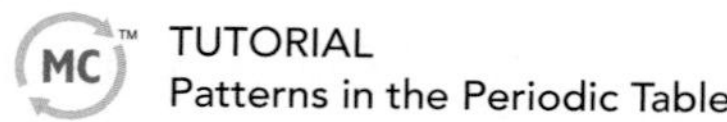


TUTORIAL
Patterns in the Periodic Table

The atomic size decreases going across a period. As the positive charge on the nucleus increases, there is an increase in attraction, which pulls all of the electrons closer. Thus, the distance to the outermost electrons decreases, and the atomic size decreases.

## Ionization Energy

Electrons are held in atoms by their attraction to the positively charged nucleus. Therefore, energy is required to remove an electron from an atom. The **ionization energy** is the energy needed to remove the least tightly bound electron from an atom in the gaseous (*g*) state. When an electron is removed from a neutral atom, a particle called a *cation*, with a 1+ charge, is formed.

$$Na(g) + \text{energy (ionization)} \longrightarrow Na^{+}(g) + e^{-}$$

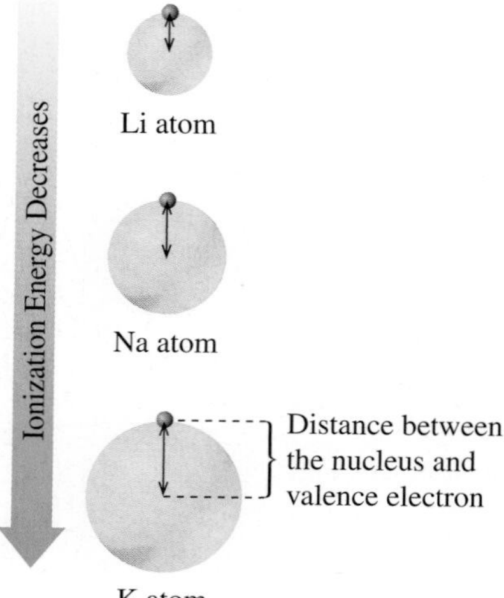


The ionization energy decreases going down a group. Less energy is needed to remove an electron because nuclear attraction decreases when electrons are farther from the nucleus. Going across a period from left to right, the ionization energy increases. As the positive charge of the nucleus increases, more energy is needed to remove an electron. (See Figure 3.20.) In Period 1, the valence electrons are close to the nucleus and strongly held. H and He have high ionization energies because a large amount of energy is required to remove an electron. The ionization energy for He is the highest of any element because He has a full, stable, energy level that is disrupted when an electron is removed. The high ionization energies of the noble gases indicate that their electron arrangements are especially stable. The slight decrease in ionization energy for Group 3A (13) occurs because the single *p* electron is farther from the nucleus and more easily removed than the electrons in the full *s* sublevel. The next decrease in ionization energy occurs for Group 6A (16) because the removal of a single *p* electron provides a half-filled, more stable *p* sublevel. In general, the ionization energy is low for metals and high for nonmetals.

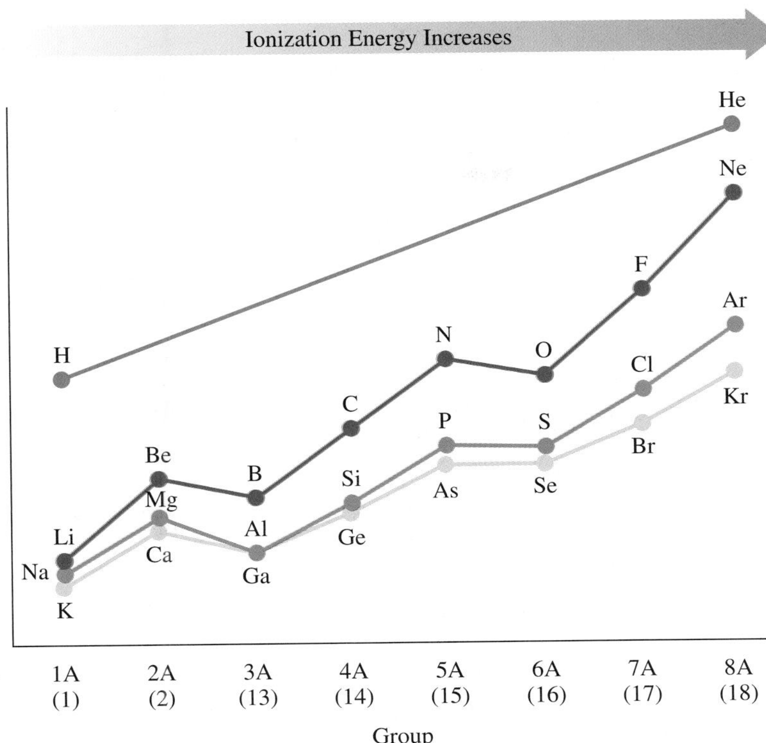


**FIGURE 3.20** Ionization energies for the representative elements tend to decrease going down a group and increase going left to right across a period.

**Q** Why is the ionization energy for Li less than for O?

CONCEPT CHECK 3.7

### Atomic Size

**a.** Match the spheres represented with atoms of Li, Na, K, and Rb.

**A.**

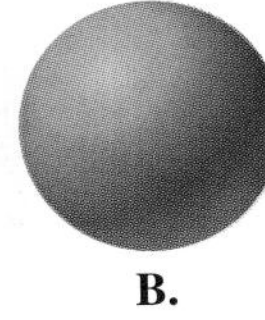
**B.**

**C.**

**D.**

**b.** Match the spheres represented with atoms of K, Ge, Ca, and Kr.

**A.**

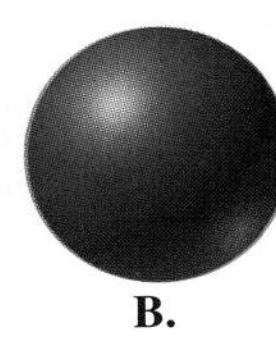
**B.**

**C.**

**D.**

ANSWER

**a.** The element at the top of a group has the smallest atomic radius. Going down the group, the atomic radius increases: Li (with the smallest radius) is C, Na is A, K is D, and Rb (with the largest radius) is B.

**b.** The element at the beginning of a period has the largest atomic radius. Going across a period, the atomic radius decreases: K (with the largest radius) is B, Ge is A, Ca is C, and Kr (with the smallest radius) is D.

SAMPLE PROBLEM 3.11

### Ionization Energy

Indicate the element in each set that has the higher ionization energy and explain your choice.

**a.** K or Na **b.** Mg or Cl **c.** F, N, or C

SOLUTION

**a.** Na. In Na, the valence electron is closer to the nucleus.
**b.** Cl. Attraction for the valence electrons increases across a period, going left to right.
**c.** F. Because fluorine has more protons than nitrogen or carbon, more energy is needed to remove a valence electron from the fluorine atom.

STUDY CHECK

Arrange Sn, Sr, and I in order of increasing ionization energy.

## QUESTIONS AND PROBLEMS

### Periodic Trends

**3.61** Write the group number using both A and B notation and 1–18 numbering of elements that have the following outer electron configurations:
**a.** $2s^2$
**b.** $3s^23p^3$
**c.** $5s^24d^{10}5p^4$

**3.62** Write the group number using both A and B notation and 1–18 numbering of elements that have the following outer electron configurations:
**a.** $4s^24p^5$
**b.** $4s^1$
**c.** $5s^24d^{10}5p^2$

**3.63** Indicate the number of valence (outermost) electrons in each of the following:
**a.** aluminum
**b.** Group 5A
**c.** F, Cl, Br, and I

**3.64** Indicate the number of valence (outermost) electrons in each of the following:
**a.** Li, Na, K, Rb, and Cs
**b.** C, Si, Ge, Sn, and Pb
**c.** Group 8A

**3.65** Write the group number and electron-dot symbol for each element:
**a.** sulfur
**b.** nitrogen
**c.** calcium
**d.** sodium
**e.** barium

**3.66** Write the group number and electron-dot symbol for each element:
**a.** carbon
**b.** oxygen
**c.** bromine
**d.** lithium
**e.** chlorine

**3.67** Using the symbol M for an atom that is a metal, draw the electron-dot symbol for an atom of a metal in the following groups:
**a.** Group 1A (1)
**b.** Group 2A (2)

**3.68** Using the symbol Nm for an atom that is a nonmetal, draw the electron-dot symbol for an atom of a nonmetal in the following groups:
**a.** Group 5A (15)
**b.** Group 7A (17)

**3.69** Place the elements in each set in order of decreasing atomic radius.
**a.** Mg, Al, Si
**b.** Cl, Br, I
**c.** I, Sb, Sr

**3.70** Place the elements in each set in order of decreasing atomic radius.
**a.** Cl, S, P
**b.** Ge, Si, C
**c.** Ba, Ca, Sr

**3.71** Select the larger atom in each pair.
**a.** Na or Cl
**b.** Na or Rb
**c.** Na or Mg

**3.72** Select the larger atom in each pair.
**a.** S or Cl
**b.** S or O
**c.** S or Se

**3.73** Arrange each set of elements in order of increasing ionization energy.
**a.** F, Cl, Br
**b.** Na, Cl, Al
**c.** Cs, Na, K

**3.74** Arrange each set of elements in order of increasing ionization energy.
**a.** O, N, C
**b.** S, P, Cl
**c.** As, P, N

**3.75** Select the element in each pair with the higher ionization energy.
**a.** Br or I
**b.** Mg or S
**c.** Si or P

**3.76** Select the element in each pair with the higher ionization energy.
**a.** O or Ne
**b.** K or Br
**c.** Ca or Ba

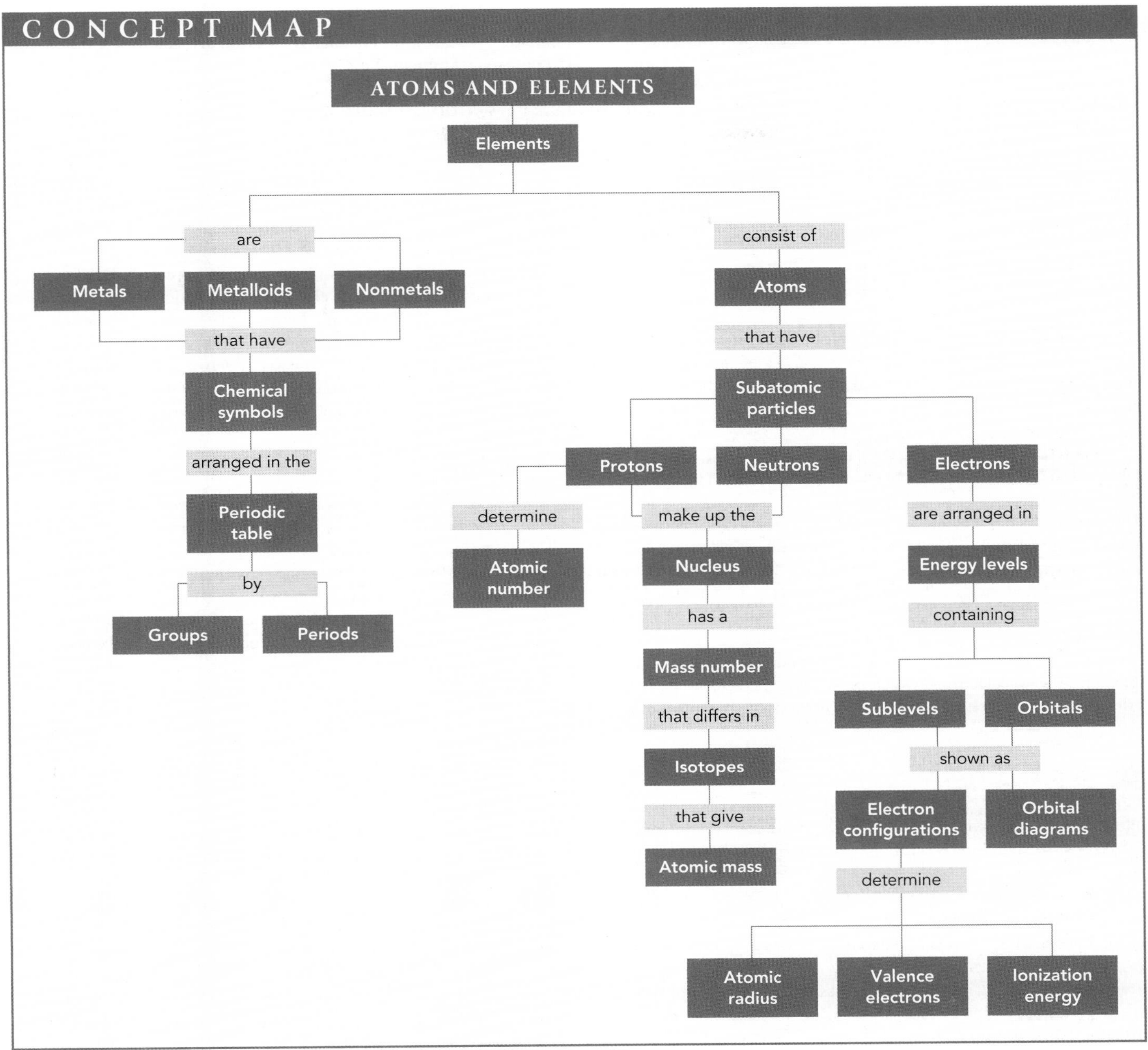


# CHAPTER REVIEW

## 3.1 Elements and Symbols

**LEARNING GOAL:** *Given the name of an element, write its correct symbol; from the symbol, write the correct name.*

Elements are the primary substances of matter. Chemical symbols are one- or two-letter abbreviations of the names of the elements.

## 3.2 The Periodic Table

**LEARNING GOAL:** *Use the periodic table to identify the group and period of an element and decide whether it is a metal, nonmetal, or metalloid.*

The periodic table is an arrangement of the elements by increasing atomic number. A vertical column on the periodic table containing elements with similar properties is called a *group*. A horizontal row is called a *period*. Elements in Group 1A (1) are called the *alkali metals*; Group 2A (2), *alkaline earth metals*; Group 7A (17), the *halogens*; and Group 8A (18), the *noble gases*. On the periodic table, metals are located on the left of the heavy zigzag line, and nonmetals are to the right of the heavy zigzag line. Except for aluminum, elements located on the heavy zigzag line are called *metalloids*.

## 3.3 The Atom

**LEARNING GOAL:** *Describe the electrical charge and location in an atom for a proton, a neutron, and an electron.*

An atom is the smallest particle that retains the characteristics of an element. Atoms are composed of three types of subatomic particles. Protons have a positive charge (+), electrons carry a negative charge (−), and neutrons are electrically neutral. The protons and neutrons are found in the tiny, dense nucleus. Electrons are located outside the nucleus.

### 3.4 Atomic Number and Mass Number

**LEARNING GOAL:** *Given the atomic number and the mass number of an atom, state the number of protons, neutrons, and electrons.*

The atomic number gives the number of protons in all the atoms of the same element. In a neutral atom, the number of protons and electrons is equal. The mass number is the total number of protons and neutrons in an atom.

### 3.5 Isotopes and Atomic Mass

**LEARNING GOAL:** *Give the number of protons, electrons, and neutrons in the isotopes of an element.*

Atoms that have the same number of protons but different numbers of neutrons are called *isotopes*. The atomic mass of an element is the average mass of all the atoms in a naturally occurring sample of that element.

### 3.6 Electron Energy Levels

**LEARNING GOAL:** *Describe the energy levels, sublevels, and orbitals in atoms.*

The atomic spectra of elements are related to the specific energy levels occupied by electrons. When energy is absorbed, an electron moves to a higher energy level; energy is lost when the electron drops to a lower energy level and emits a photon. Each element has it own unique spectrum.

An orbital is a region around the nucleus in which an electron with a specific energy is most likely to be found. Each orbital holds a maximum of two electrons, which must have opposite spins. In each principal energy level ($n$), electrons occupy orbitals within sublevels. An $s$ sublevel contains one $s$ orbital, a $p$ sublevel contains three $p$ orbitals, a $d$ sublevel contains five $d$ orbitals, and an $f$ sublevel contains seven $f$ orbitals. Each type of orbital has a unique shape.

### 3.7 Electron Configurations

**LEARNING GOAL:** *Use the periodic table to write orbital diagrams and electron configurations.*

Within a sublevel, electrons enter orbitals in the same energy level one at a time until all the orbitals are half-filled. Additional electrons enter with opposite spins until the orbitals in that sublevel are filled with two electrons each. The electrons in an atom can be written in an orbital diagram, which shows the orbitals that are occupied by paired and unpaired electrons. The electron configuration shows the number of electrons in each sublevel. An abbreviated electron configuration places the symbol of a noble gas in brackets to represent the filled sublevels. The periodic table consists of $s$, $p$, $d$, and $f$ sublevel blocks. Beginning with $1s$, an electron configuration is obtained by writing the sublevel blocks in order going across the periodic table until the element is reached.

### 3.8 Periodic Trends

**LEARNING GOAL:** *Use the electron configurations of elements to explain periodic trends.*

The properties of elements are related to the valence electrons of the atoms. With only a few minor exceptions, each group of elements has the same arrangement of valence electrons differing only in the energy level. The radius of an atom increases going down a group and decreases going across a period. The energy required to remove a valence electron is the ionization energy, which generally decreases going down a group and generally increases going across a period.

## KEY TERMS

**alkali metal** An element in Group 1A (1), except hydrogen, that is a soft, shiny metal with one electron in its outermost energy level.

**alkaline earth metal** An element in Group 2A (2) that has two electrons in its outermost energy level.

**atom** The smallest particle of an element that retains the characteristics of the element.

**atomic mass** The weighted average mass of all the naturally occurring isotopes of an element.

**atomic mass unit (amu)** A small mass unit used to describe the mass of extremely small particles such as atoms and subatomic particles; 1 amu is equal to one-twelfth the mass of a $^{12}_{6}C$ atom.

**atomic number** A number that is equal to the number of protons in an atom.

**atomic spectrum** A series of lines specific for each element produced by photons emitted by electrons dropping to lower energy levels.

**atomic symbol** An abbreviation used to indicate the mass number and atomic number of an isotope.

**chemical symbol** An abbreviation that represents the name of an element.

***d* block** The block of ten elements from Groups 3B (3) to 2B (12) in which electrons fill the five $d$ orbitals in $d$ sublevels.

**electron** A negatively charged subatomic particle having a minute mass that is usually ignored in mass calculations; its symbol is $e^-$.

**electron configuration** A list of the number of electrons in each sublevel within an atom, arranged by increasing energy.

**electron-dot symbol** The representation of an atom that shows valence electrons as dots around the symbol of the element.

***f* block** The block of 14 elements in the rows at the bottom of the periodic table in which electrons fill the seven $f$ orbitals in the $4f$ and $5f$ sublevels.

**group** A vertical column in the periodic table that contains elements having similar physical and chemical properties.

**halogen** An element in Group 7A (17)—fluorine, chlorine, bromine, iodine, and astatine—that has seven electrons in its outermost energy level.

**ionization energy** The energy needed to remove the least tightly bound electron from the outermost energy level of an atom.

**isotope** An atom that differs only in mass number from another atom of the same element. Isotopes have the same atomic number (number of protons) but different numbers of neutrons.

**mass number** The total number of neutrons and protons in the nucleus of an atom.

**metal** An element that is shiny, malleable, ductile, and a good conductor of heat and electricity. The metals are located to the left of the heavy zigzag line on the periodic table.

**metalloid** Elements with properties of both metals and nonmetals located along the heavy zigzag line on the periodic table.

**neutron** A neutral subatomic particle having a mass of about 1 amu and found in the nucleus of an atom; its symbol is $n$ or $n^0$.

**noble gas** An element in Group 8A (18) of the periodic table, generally unreactive and seldom found in combination with other elements, that has eight electrons (He has two electrons) in its outermost energy level.

**nonmetal** An element with little or no luster that is a poor conductor of heat and electricity. The nonmetals are located to the right of the heavy zigzag line on the periodic table.

**nucleus** The compact, extremely dense center of an atom, containing the protons and neutrons of the atom.
**orbital** The region around the nucleus where electrons of a certain energy are more likely to be found. The *s* orbitals are spherical; the *p* orbitals have two lobes.
**orbital diagram** A diagram that shows the distribution of electrons in the orbitals of the energy levels.
***p* block** The elements in Groups 3A (13) to 8A (18) in which electrons fill the *p* orbitals in the *p* sublevels.
**period** A horizontal row of elements in the periodic table.
**periodic table** An arrangement of elements by increasing atomic number such that elements having similar chemical behavior are grouped in vertical columns.
**proton** A positively charged subatomic particle having a mass of about 1 amu and found in the nucleus of an atom; its symbol is $p$ or $p^+$.
**representative element** An element in the first two columns on the left of the periodic table and the last six columns on the right that has a group number of 1A through 8A or 1, 2 and 13 through 18.
***s* block** The elements in Groups 1A (1) and 2A (2) in which electrons fill the *s* orbitals.
**subatomic particle** A particle within an atom; protons, neutrons, and electrons are subatomic particles.
**sublevel** A group of orbitals of equal energy within principal energy levels. The number of sublevels in each energy level is the same as the principal quantum number ($n$).
**transition element** An element in the center of the periodic table that is designated with the letter "B" or the group number of 3 through 12.
**valence electrons** Electrons in the outermost energy level of an atom.

## UNDERSTANDING THE CONCEPTS

**3.77** According to Dalton's atomic theory, which of the following are *true*?
**a.** Atoms of an element are identical to atoms of other elements.
**b.** Every element is made of atoms.
**c.** Atoms of two different elements combine to form compounds.
**d.** In a chemical reaction, some atoms disappear and new atoms appear.

**3.78** Use Rutherford's gold-foil experiment to answer each of the following:
**a.** What did Rutherford expect to happen when he aimed particles at the gold foil?
**b.** How did the results differ from what he expected?
**c.** How did he use the results to propose a model of the atom?

**3.79** Match the following with the descriptions below:
(1) protons (2) neutrons (3) electrons
**a.** atomic mass **b.** atomic number
**c.** positive charge **d.** negative charge
**e.** mass number – atomic number

**3.80** Match the following with the descriptions below:
(1) protons (2) neutrons (3) electrons
**a.** mass number **b.** surround the nucleus
**c.** nucleus **d.** charge of 0
**e.** equal to number of electrons

**3.81** Consider the following atoms in which X represents the chemical symbol of the element:

$^{16}_{8}X$ $^{16}_{9}X$ $^{18}_{10}X$ $^{17}_{8}X$ $^{18}_{8}X$

**a.** What atoms have the same number of protons?
**b.** Which atoms are isotopes? Of what element?
**c.** Which atoms have the same mass number?
**d.** What atoms have the same number of neutrons?

**3.82** For each of the following, write the symbol and name for X and the number of protons and neutrons. Which are isotopes of each other?
**a.** $^{37}_{17}X$ **b.** $^{56}_{26}X$ **c.** $^{116}_{50}X$ **d.** $^{124}_{50}X$ **e.** $^{116}_{48}X$

## ADDITIONAL QUESTIONS AND PROBLEMS

*For instructor-assigned homework, go to* ***www.masteringchemistry.com****.*

**3.83** Give the symbol and name of the element found in the following group and period on the periodic table:
**a.** Group 2A, Period 3 **b.** Group 7A, Period 4
**c.** Group 13, Period 3 **d.** Group 16, Period 2

**3.84** The following trace elements have been found to be crucial to the functions of the body. Indicate each as a metal or nonmetal.
**a.** zinc **b.** cobalt
**c.** manganese **d.** iodine
**e.** copper **f.** selenium

**3.85** Indicate if each of the following statements is *true* or *false*:
**a.** The proton is a negatively charged particle.
**b.** The neutron is 2000 times as heavy as a proton.
**c.** The atomic mass unit is based on a carbon atom with 6 protons and 6 neutrons.
**d.** The nucleus is the largest part of the atom.
**e.** The electrons are located outside the nucleus.

**3.86** Indicate if each of the following statements is *true* or *false*:
**a.** The neutron is electrically neutral.
**b.** The masses of the protons and neutrons account for most of the mass of an atom.
**c.** The charge of an electron is equal, but opposite, to the charge of a neutron.
**d.** The proton and the electron have about the same mass.
**e.** The mass number is the number of protons.

**3.87** For the following atoms, determine the number of protons, neutrons, and electrons:
**a.** $^{27}_{13}Al$ **b.** $^{52}_{24}Cr$ **c.** $^{34}_{16}S$ **d.** $^{56}_{26}Fe$ **e.** $^{136}_{54}Xe$

**3.88** For the following atoms, give the number of protons, neutrons, and electrons:
**a.** $^{22}_{10}Ne$ **b.** $^{127}_{53}I$ **c.** $^{75}_{35}Br$ **d.** $^{133}_{55}Cs$ **e.** $^{195}_{78}Pt$

**3.89** Complete the following table:

| Name | Nuclear Symbol | Number of Protons | Number of Neutrons | Number of Electrons |
|---|---|---|---|---|
| | $^{34}_{16}S$ | | | |
| | | 30 | 40 | |
| Magnesium | | | 14 | |
| | $^{220}_{86}Rn$ | | | |

**3.90** Complete the following table:

| Name | Nuclear Symbol | Number of Protons | Number of Neutrons | Number of Electrons |
|---|---|---|---|---|
| Potassium | | | 22 | |
| | $^{51}_{23}V$ | | | |
| | | 48 | 64 | |
| Barium | | | 82 | |

**3.91 a.** What electron sublevel starts to fill after completion of the 3*s* sublevel?

**b.** What electron sublevel starts to fill after completion of the 4*p* sublevel?

**c.** What electron sublevel starts to fill after completion of the 3*d* sublevel?

**d.** What electron sublevel starts to fill after completion of the 3*p* sublevel?

**3.92 a.** What electron sublevel starts to fill after completion of the 5*s* sublevel?

**b.** What electron sublevel starts to fill after completion of the 4*d* sublevel?

**c.** What electron sublevel starts to fill after completion of the 4*f* sublevel?

**d.** What electron sublevel starts to fill after completion of the 5*p* sublevel?

**3.93 a.** How many 3*d* electrons are in Fe?

**b.** How many 5*p* electrons are in Ba?

**c.** How many 4*d* electrons are in I?

**d.** How many 6*s* electrons are in Ba?

**3.94 a.** How many 3*d* electrons are in Zn?

**b.** How many 4*p* electrons are in Br?

**c.** How many 6*p* electrons are in Bi?

**d.** How many 5*s* electrons are in Cd?

**3.95** What do the elements Ca, Sr, and Ba have in common in terms of their electron configuration? Where are they located in the periodic table?

**3.96** What do the elements O, S, and Se have in common in terms of their electron configuration? Where are they located in the periodic table?

**3.97** Name the element that corresponds to each of the following:

**a.** $1s^22s^22p^63s^23p^3$

**b.** alkali metal with the smallest atomic radius

**c.** $[Kr]5s^24d^{10}$

**d.** Group 5A element with highest ionization energy

**e.** Period 3 element with largest atomic radius

**3.98** Name the element that corresponds to each of the following:

**a.** $1s^22s^22p^63s^23p^64s^13d^5$

**b.** $[Xe]6s^24f^{14}5d^{10}6p^5$

**c.** halogen with the highest ionization energy

**d.** Group 6A element with the smallest ionization energy

**e.** Period 4 element with smallest atomic radius

**3.99** Why is the ionization energy of Ca higher than K but lower than Mg?

**3.100** Why is the ionization energy of Cl lower than F but higher than S?

**3.101** Of the elements Na, P, Cl, and F, which

**a.** is a metal?

**b.** has the largest atomic radius?

**c.** has the highest ionization energy?

**d.** loses an electron most easily?

**e.** is found in Group 7A, Period 3?

**3.102** Of the elements K, Ca, Br, Kr, which

**a.** is a noble gas?

**b.** has the smallest atomic radius?

**c.** has the lowest ionization energy?

**d.** requires the most energy to remove an electron?

**e.** is found in Group 2A, Period 4?

## CHALLENGE QUESTIONS

**3.103** Of the elements K, Mg, Si, S, Cl, and Ar, which

**a.** is a metal?

**b.** is a metalloid?

**c.** is an alkali metal?

**d.** has the smallest atomic size?

**e.** has an electron arrangement $1s^22s^22p^63s^23p^4$?

**3.104** Of the elements K, Mg, Si, S, Cl, and Ar, which

**a.** has the largest atomic size?

**b.** is a halogen?

**c.** has an electron arrangement $1s^22s^22p^63s^23p^2$?

**d.** has the lowest ionization energy?

**e.** is in Group 6A (16)?

**f.** has the highest ionization energy?

**3.105** The most abundant isotope of iron is Fe-56.

**a.** How many protons, neutrons, and electrons are in this isotope?

**b.** What is the symbol of another isotope of iron with 25 neutrons?

**c.** What is the symbol of a different atom with the same mass number and 27 neutrons?

**3.106** Give the symbol of the element that has the

**a.** smallest atomic radius in Group 6A.

**b.** smallest atomic radius in Period 3.

**c.** highest ionization energy in Group 15.

**d.** lowest ionization energy in Period 3.

**3.107** If the diameter of a sodium atom is $3.14 \times 10^{-8}$ cm, how many sodium atoms would fit along a line exactly 1 inch long?

**3.108** A lead atom has a mass of $3.4 \times 10^{-22}$ g. How many lead atoms are in a cube of lead that has a volume of 2.00 $cm^3$ if the density of lead is 11.3 g/$cm^3$?

**3.109** Lead consists of four naturally occurring isotopes. Calculate the atomic mass of lead.

| Isotope | Mass | Abundance (%) |
|---|---|---|
| $^{204}_{82}Pb$ | 203.97 | 1.40 |
| $^{206}_{82}Pb$ | 205.97 | 24.10 |
| $^{207}_{82}Pb$ | 206.98 | 22.10 |
| $^{208}_{82}Pb$ | 207.98 | 52.40 |

**3.110** Indium (In) with an atomic mass of 114.8 consists of two naturally occurring isotopes: $^{113}_{49}In$ and $^{115}_{49}In$. If 4.30% of a sample of indium is $^{113}_{49}In$, which has a mass of 112.90, what is the mass of the $^{115}_{49}In$?

**3.111** Consider three elements with the following abbreviated gas notations:

$X = [Ar]4s^2 \quad Y = [Ne]3s^23p^4$
$Z = [Ar]4s^23d^{10}4p^4$

**a.** Identify each element as a metal, metalloid, or nonmetal.
**b.** Which element has the largest atomic radius?
**c.** Which elements have similar properties?
**d.** Which element has the highest ionization energy?
**e.** Which element has the smallest atomic radius?

**3.112** Indicate if the following sections of orbital diagrams are or are not possible and explain your reason:

**a.** 1*s* 2*s* 2*p* 3*s*

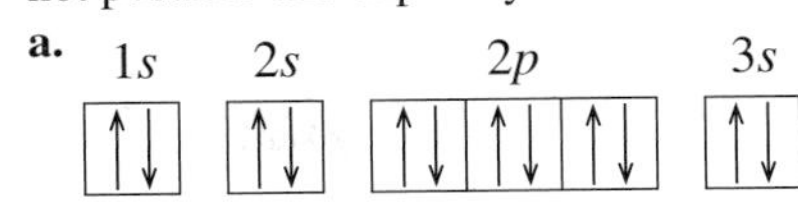

**b.** 2*s* 2*p*

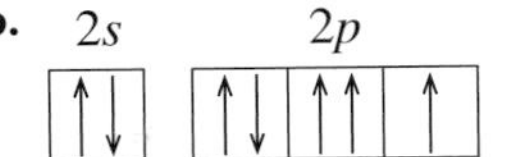

**c.** 1*s* 2*s* 2*p* 3*s*

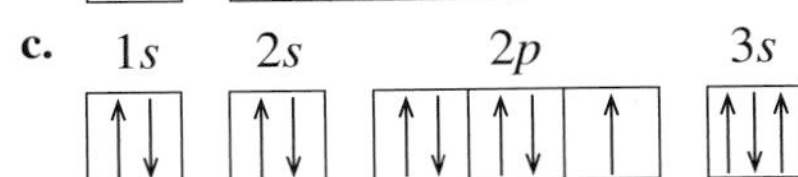

**d.** 4*s* 3*d*

[↑] [↑|↑|↑|↑|↑]

**3.113** Consider three elements with the following abbreviated electron configurations:

$X = [Ar]4s^23d^5 \quad Y = [Ar]4s^23d^{10}4p^1$

$Z = [Ar]4s^23d^{10}4p^6$

**a.** Identify each element as a metal, metalloid, or nonmetal.
**b.** Which element has the smallest atomic radius?
**c.** Which elements have similar properties?
**d.** Which element has the highest ionization energy?
**e.** Which element has a half-filled sublevel?

# ANSWERS

## ANSWERS TO STUDY CHECKS

**3.1** Si, Sr, Ag

**3.2** **a.** As **b.** Rn **c.** B

**3.3** False; most of the volume in an atom is outside the nucleus.

**3.4** 45 neutrons

**3.5** **a.** $^{15}_{7}N$ **b.** $^{42}_{20}Ca$ **c.** $^{27}_{13}Al$

**3.6** 10.81 amu

**3.7** The 1*s*, 2*s*, and 3*s* orbitals are all spherical, but they increase in volume because the electron is most likely to be found farther from the nucleus for higher energy levels.

**3.8** $1s^22s^22p^63s^23p^4$ Complete electron configuration for sulfur (S)
$[Ne]3s^23p^4$ Abbreviated electron configuration for sulfur (S)

**3.9** Tin has the electron configuration:
$1s^22s^22p^63s^23p^64s^23d^{10}4p^65s^24d^{10}5p^2$

**3.10** $\cdot\underset{\cdot}{\ddot{\mathrm{P}}}\cdot$

**3.11** Ionization energy increases going across a period: Sr is lowest, Sn is higher, and I is the highest of this set.

## ANSWERS TO SELECTED QUESTIONS AND PROBLEMS

**3.1** **a.** Cu **b.** Si **c.** K **d.** N **e.** Fe **f.** Ba **g.** Pb **h.** Sr

**3.3** **a.** carbon **b.** chlorine **c.** iodine **d.** mercury **e.** fluorine **f.** argon **g.** zinc **h.** nickel

**3.5** **a.** sodium, chlorine
**b.** calcium, sulfur, oxygen
**c.** carbon, hydrogen, chlorine, nitrogen, oxygen
**d.** calcium, carbon, oxygen

**3.7** **a.** Period 2 **b.** Group 8A (18) **c.** Group 1A (1) **d.** Period 2

**3.9** **a.** alkaline earth metal
**b.** transition element
**c.** noble gas
**d.** alkali metal
**e.** halogen

**3.11** **a.** C **b.** He **c.** Na **d.** Ca **e.** Al

**3.13** **a.** metal **b.** nonmetal **c.** metal **d.** nonmetal **e.** nonmetal **f.** nonmetal **g.** metalloid **h.** metal

**3.15** **a.** electron **b.** proton **c.** electron **d.** neutron

**3.17** Rutherford determined that an atom contains a small, compact nucleus that is positively charged.

**3.19** **a.** **b.** and **c.** are *true*, but **d.** is *false*. A proton is attracted to an electron, not a neutron.

**3.21** In the process of brushing hair, strands of hair become charged with like charges that repel each other.

**3.23** **a.** atomic number **b.** both **c.** mass number **d.** atomic number

**3.25** **a.** lithium, Li **b.** fluorine, F **c.** calcium, Ca **d.** zinc, Zn **e.** neon, Ne **f.** silicon, Si **g.** iodine, I **h.** oxygen, O

**3.27** **a.** 12 **b.** 30 **c.** 53 **d.** 19

**3.29**

| Name of Element | Symbol | Atomic Number | Mass Number | Number of Protons | Number of Neutrons | Number of Electrons |
|---|---|---|---|---|---|---|
| Aluminum | Al | 13 | 27 | 13 | 14 | 13 |
| Magnesium | Mg | 12 | 24 | 12 | 12 | 12 |
| Potassium | K | 19 | 39 | 19 | 20 | 19 |
| Sulfur | S | 16 | 31 | 16 | 15 | 16 |
| Iron | Fe | 26 | 56 | 26 | 30 | 26 |

**3.31 a.** 14 protons, 16 neutrons, 14 electrons
**b.** 27 protons, 33 neutrons, 27 electrons
**c.** 34 protons, 46 neutrons, 34 electrons
**d.** 9 protons, 10 neutrons, 9 electrons

**3.33 a.** ${}^{31}_{15}P$ **b.** ${}^{80}_{35}Br$ **c.** ${}^{27}_{13}Al$ **d.** ${}^{35}_{17}Cl$ **e.** ${}^{202}_{80}Hg$

**3.35 a.** ${}^{32}_{16}S$ ${}^{33}_{16}S$ ${}^{34}_{16}S$ ${}^{36}_{16}S$
**b.** They all have the same number of protons and electrons.
**c.** They have different numbers of neutrons, which gives them different mass numbers.
**d.** The atomic mass of S listed on the periodic table is the weighted average atomic mass of all the naturally occuring isotopes.
**e.** The isotope S-32 is most abundant because its atomic mass is closest to the weighted average atomic mass.

**3.37** Because the atomic mass of copper is closer to 63 amu, there are more atoms of ${}^{63}_{29}Cu$.

**3.39** 69.72 amu

**3.41 a.** spherical **b.** two lobes **c.** spherical

**3.43 a.** Both are spherical.
**b.** Both are part of the third energy level.
**c.** Both contain three *p* orbitals.
**d.** All have two lobes and belong in the third energy level.

**3.45 a.** There are five orbitals in the 3*d* sublevel.
**b.** There is one sublevel in the $n = 1$ energy level.
**c.** There is one orbital in the 6*s* sublevel.
**d.** There are nine orbitals in the $n = 3$ energy level.

**3.47 a.** There is a maximum of 2 electrons in a 2*p* orbital.
**b.** There is a maximum of six electrons in the 3*p* sublevel.
**c.** There is a maximum of 32 electrons in the $n = 4$ energy level.
**d.** There is a maximum of 10 electrons in the 5*d* sublevel.

**3.49 a.** 1*s* [↑↓] 2*s* [↑↓] 2*p* [↑][ ][ ]

**b.** 1*s* [↑↓] 2*s* [↑↓] 2*p* [↑↓][↑↓][↑↓] 3*s* [↑↓] 3*p* [↑][ ][ ]

**c.** 1*s* [↑↓] 2*s* [↑↓] 2*p* [↑↓][↑↓][↑↓] 3*s* [↑↓] 3*p* [↑][↑][↑]

**d.** 1*s* [↑↓] 2*s* [↑↓] 2*p* [↑↓][↑↓][↑↓] 3*s* [↑↓] 3*p* [↑↓][↑↓][↑↓]

**3.51 a.** N $1s^22s^22p^3$
**b.** Na $1s^22s^22p^63s^1$
**c.** S $1s^22s^22p^63s^23p^4$
**d.** As $1s^22s^22p^63s^23p^64s^23d^{10}4p^3$
**e.** Fe $1s^22s^22p^63s^23p^64s^23d^6$

**3.53 a.** Mg $[Ne]3s^2$
**b.** S $[Ne]3s^23p^4$
**c.** Al $[Ne]3s^23p^1$
**d.** Ti $[Ar]4s^23d^2$
**e.** Ba $[Xe]6s^2$

**3.55 a.** S **b.** Co **c.** Si **d.** Br

**3.57 a.** Al **b.** C **c.** Ar **d.** Zr

**3.59 a.** 10 **b.** 6 **c.** 3 **d.** 1

**3.61 a.** 2A (2) **b.** 5A (15) **c.** 6A (16)

**3.63 a.** 3 **b.** 5 **c.** 7

**3.65 a.** Group 6A (16) $\cdot\ddot{\underset{\cdot\cdot}{S}}:$ **b.** Group 5A (15) $\cdot\dot{\underset{\cdot}{N}}\cdot$
**c.** Group 2A (2) $\dot{C}a\cdot$ **d.** Group 1A (1) Na·
**e.** Group 2A (2) $\dot{B}a\cdot$

**3.67 a.** M· **b.** $\dot{M}\cdot$

**3.69 a.** Mg, Al, Si **b.** I, Br, Cl **c.** Sr, Sb, I

**3.71 a.** Na **b.** Rb **c.** Na

**3.73 a.** Br, Cl, F **b.** Na, Al, Cl **c.** Cs, K, Na

**3.75 a.** Br **b.** S **c.** P

**3.77 a.** false **b.** true **c.** true **d.** false

**3.79 a.** 1 and 2 **b.** 1 **c.** 1 **d.** 3 **e.** 2

**3.81 a.** ${}^{16}_{8}X$, ${}^{17}_{8}X$, and ${}^{18}_{8}X$ All have eight protons.
**b.** ${}^{16}_{8}X$, ${}^{17}_{8}X$, and ${}^{18}_{8}X$ All are isotopes of oxygen.
**c.** ${}^{16}_{8}X$ and ${}^{16}_{9}X$ have mass number 16, whereas ${}^{18}_{8}X$ and ${}^{18}_{10}X$ have mass number 18.
**d.** ${}^{16}_{8}X$ and ${}^{18}_{10}X$ both have eight neutrons.

**3.83 a.** Mg, magnesium **b.** Br, bromine
**c.** Al, aluminum **d.** O, oxygen

**3.85 a.** false **b.** false **c.** true **d.** false **e.** true

**3.87 a.** 13 protons, 14 neutrons, 13 electrons
**b.** 24 protons, 28 neutrons, 24 electrons
**c.** 16 protons, 18 neutrons, 16 electrons
**d.** 26 protons, 30 neutrons, 26 electrons
**e.** 54 protons, 82 neutrons, 54 electrons

**3.89**

| Name | Nuclear Symbol | Number of Protons | Number of Neutrons | Number of Electrons |
|---|---|---|---|---|
| Sulfur | ${}^{34}_{16}S$ | 16 | 18 | 16 |
| Zinc | ${}^{70}_{30}Zn$ | 30 | 40 | 30 |
| Magnesium | ${}^{26}_{12}Mg$ | 12 | 14 | 12 |
| Radon | ${}^{220}_{86}Rn$ | 86 | 134 | 86 |

**3.91** **a.** 3$p$ **b.** 5$s$ **c.** 4$p$ **d.** 4$s$

**3.93** **a.** 6 **b.** 6 **c.** 10 **d.** 2

**3.95** Ca, Sr, and Ba all have two valence electrons $ns^2$, which places them in Group 2A (2).

**3.97** **a.** phosphorus **b.** lithium (H is a nonmetal) **c.** cadmium **d.** nitrogen **e.** sodium

**3.99** Calcium has a greater number of protons than K. The least tightly bound electron in Ca is farther from the nucleus than in Mg and requires less energy to remove it.

**3.101** **a.** Na **b.** Na **c.** F **d.** Na **e.** Cl

**3.103** **a.** K, Mg **b.** Si **c.** K **d.** Ar **e.** S

**3.105** **a.** 26 protons, 30 neutrons, 26 electrons **b.** $^{51}_{26}Fe$ **c.** $^{51}_{24}Cr$

**3.107** $8.09 \times 10^7$ sodium atoms

**3.109** 207.2 amu

**3.111** **a.** X is a metal; Y and Z are nonmetals.
**b.** X has the largest atomic radius.
**c.** Y and Z have six valence electrons and are in Group 6A (16).
**d.** Y has the highest ionization energy.
**e.** Y has the smallest atomic radius.

**3.113** **a.** X and Y are metals and Z is a nonmetal.
**b.** Z
**c.** X and Y are both metals.
**d.** Z
**e.** X

# 4 Nuclear Chemistry

## LOOKING AHEAD


4.1 Natural Radioactivity

4.2 Nuclear Reactions

4.3 Radiation Measurement

4.4 Half-Life of a Radioisotope

4.5 Medical Applications Using Radioactivity

4.6 Nuclear Fission and Fusion


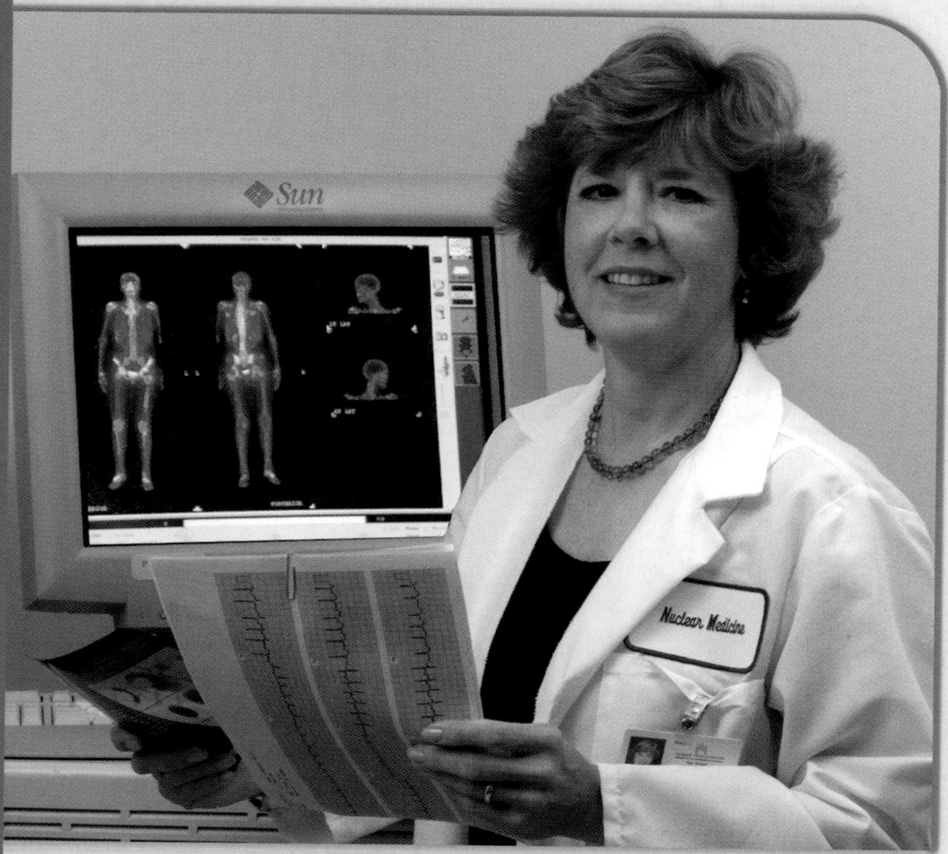


*"Everything we do in this department involves radioactive materials," says Julie Goudak, nuclear medicine technologist at Kaiser Hospital. "The radioisotopes are given in several ways. The patient may ingest an isotope, breathe it in, or receive it by an IV injection. We do many diagnostic tests, particularly of the heart function, to determine if a patient needs a cardiac CT scan."*

*A nuclear medicine technologist administers isotopes that emit radiation to determine the level of function of an organ such as the thyroid or heart, to detect the presence and size of a tumor, or to treat disease. A radioisotope locates in a specific organ, and its radiation is used by a computer to create an image of that organ. From this data, a physician can make a diagnosis and design a treatment program.*

Visit **www.masteringchemistry.com** for self-study materials and instructor-assigned homework.

A female patient, age 50, complains of nervousness, irritability, increased perspiration, brittle hair, and muscle weakness. Her hands are shaky at times, and her heart often beats rapidly. She has been experiencing weight loss. The doctor decides to test for proper thyroid activity. To get a detailed look at the thyroid, a thyroid scan is ordered. The patient is given a small amount of an iodine radioisotope, which will be taken up by the thyroid. The scan shows a higher than normal rate of uptake of the radioactive iodine, which indicates an overactive thyroid gland, a condition called *hyperthyroidism*. Treatment for hyperthyroidism includes the use of drugs to lower the level of thyroid hormone, the use of radioactive iodine to destroy thyroid cells, or surgical removal of part or the entire thyroid. In our case, the nuclear physician decides to use radioactive iodine. To begin treatment, the patient drinks a solution containing radioactive iodine. In the following few weeks, the cells that take up the radioactive iodine are destroyed by the radiation. Follow-up tests not only show that the patient's thyroid is smaller, but also that the blood level of thyroid hormone is normal once again.

The field of nuclear medicine was established in 1934 with the production of artificial radioactive substances. In 1937, the first radioactive isotope was used to treat a patient with leukemia at the University of California at Berkeley. Major strides in the use of radioactivity in medicine occurred in 1946, when a radioactive iodine isotope was successfully used to diagnose thyroid function and to treat hyperthyroidism and thyroid cancer. During the 1970s and 1980s, a variety of radioactive substances were used to produce images of organs such as the liver, spleen, thyroid gland, kidney, and brain, and to detect heart disease. Today, procedures in nuclear medicine provide information about the function and structure of every organ in the body, which allows the nuclear physician to diagnose and treat diseases early.

## 4.1 Natural Radioactivity

**LEARNING GOAL**

Describe alpha, beta, positron, and gamma radiation.

Most naturally occurring isotopes of elements up to atomic number 19 have stable nuclei. In a stable nucleus, the repulsions between the positively charged protons are balanced by other nuclear forces. Elements with atomic numbers 20 and higher usually have one or more isotopes that have unstable nuclei in which the nuclear forces cannot offset the repulsions between the protons. An unstable nucleus is radioactive, which means that it spontaneously emits small particles of energy called **radiation** to become more stable. Radiation may take the form of alpha ($\alpha$) and beta ($\beta$) particles, positrons ($\beta^+$), or pure energy such as gamma ($\gamma$) rays. An isotope that emits radiation is called a *radioisotope*. For most types of radiation, there is a change in the number of protons in the nucleus. This change means that an atom of one element is converted into an atom of a different element. This kind of nuclear change was not evident to Dalton when he made his predictions about atoms. Elements with atomic numbers of 93 and higher are produced artificially in nuclear laboratories and consist only of radioactive isotopes.

In Chapter 3, we wrote symbols for the different isotopes of an element. These symbols had the mass number written in the upper left corner and the atomic number in the lower left corner. Recall that the mass number is equal to the number of protons and neutrons in the nucleus and that atomic number is equal to the number of protons. For example, a radioactive isotope of iodine used in the diagnosis and treatment of thyroid conditions has a symbol with a mass number of 131 and an atomic number of 53:

Mass number (protons and neutrons)
Element symbol
Atomic number (protons)

$${}^{131}_{53}\text{I}$$

Radioactive isotopes are named specifically by writing the mass number after the element's name or symbol. This isotope is named iodine-131 or I-131. Table 4.1 compares some stable, nonradioactive isotopes with some radioactive isotopes.

**TABLE 4.1** Stable and Radioactive Isotopes of Some Elements

| Magnesium | Iodine | Uranium |
|---|---|---|
| **Stable Isotopes** | | |
| $^{24}_{12}Mg$<br>Magnesium-24 | $^{127}_{53}I$<br>Iodine-127 | None |
| **Radioactive Isotopes** | | |
| $^{23}_{12}Mg$<br>Magnesium-23 | $^{125}_{53}I$<br>Iodine-125 | $^{235}_{92}U$<br>Uranium-235 |
| $^{27}_{12}Mg$<br>Magnesium-27 | $^{131}_{53}I$<br>Iodine-131 | $^{238}_{92}U$<br>Uranium-238 |

MC TUTORIAL Types of Radiation

$^{4}_{2}He$
Alpha ($\alpha$) particle

$^{0}_{-1}e$
Beta ($\beta$) particle

## Types of Radiation

Different types of radiation are emitted from unstable nuclei to form more stable, lower-energy nuclei. One type of radiation consists of alpha particles. An **alpha particle** is identical to a helium (He) nucleus, which has two protons and two neutrons. An alpha particle has a mass number of 4, an atomic number of 2, and a charge of 2+. The symbol for an alpha particle is the Greek letter alpha ($\alpha$) or the symbol of a helium nucleus but with the 2+ charge omitted.

A **beta particle** is a high-energy electron that is emitted when a neutron in an unstable nucleus changes into a proton. A beta particle has a charge of 1− and a mass number of 0. It is represented by the Greek letter beta ($\beta$) or by the symbol for the electron ($e$) including the mass number and the charge:

$$^{1}_{0}n \longrightarrow {}^{1}_{1}H + {}^{0}_{-1}e \text{ (or } \beta)$$

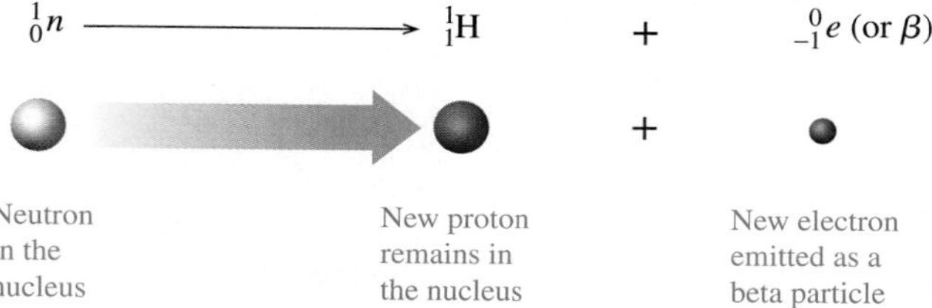


A **positron**, represented as $\beta^+$, has a positive (1+) charge with a mass number of 0, which makes it similar to a beta ($\beta$) particle, but with the opposite charge. We write the symbols of a beta particle and a positron as follows:

| | **Electron** | **Positron** |
|---|---|---|
| Mass number<br>Charge | $^{0}_{-1}e$ | $^{0}_{+1}e$ |

A positron is produced by an unstable nucleus when a proton is transformed into a neutron and a positron.

$$^{1}_{1}H \longrightarrow {}^{1}_{0}n + {}^{0}_{+1}e \text{ (or } \beta^+)$$

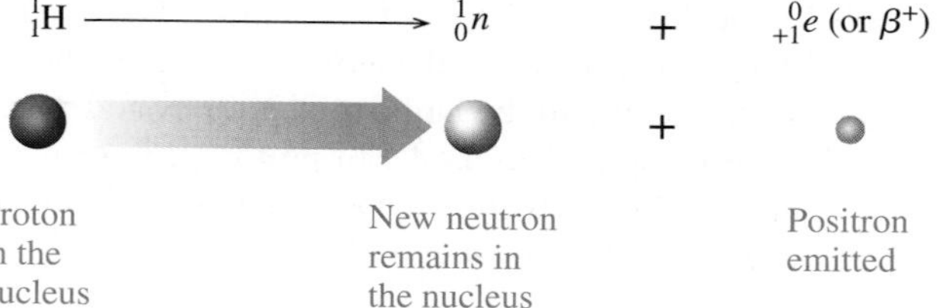


A positron is an example of *antimatter*, a term physicists use to describe a particle that is the exact opposite of another particle, in this case, an electron. When an electron and a positron collide, their minute masses are completely converted to energy in the form of gamma rays.

$$^{0}_{-1}e + {}^{0}_{+1}e \rightarrow 2\,{}^{0}_{0}\gamma$$

When the symbol $\beta$ is used with no charge, it is a beta particle rather than a positron.

**Gamma rays** are high-energy radiation, released when an unstable nucleus undergoes a rearrangement of its particles to give a more stable, lower-energy nucleus. Gamma rays are often emitted along with other types of radiation. A gamma ray is written as the Greek letter gamma ($\gamma$). Because gamma rays are energy only, zeros are used to show that a gamma ray has no mass or charge.

$^0_0\gamma$

Gamma ($\gamma$) ray

Table 4.2 summarizes the types of radiation we will use in nuclear equations.

TABLE 4.2 Some Common Forms of Radiation

| Type of Radiation | Symbol | | Mass Number | Charge |
|---|---|---|---|---|
| Alpha particle | $\alpha$ | $^4_2He$ | 4 | 2+ |
| Beta particle | $\beta$ | $^{0}_{-1}e$ | 0 | 1− |
| Positron | $\beta^+$ | $^{0}_{+1}e$ | 0 | 1+ |
| Gamma ray | $\gamma$ | $^0_0\gamma$ | 0 | 0 |
| Proton | $p$ | $^1_1H$ | 1 | 1+ |
| Neutron | $n$ | $^1_0n$ | 1 | 0 |

CONCEPT CHECK 4.1

**Radiation Particles**

Identify and write the symbol for each of the following types of radiation:

**a.** contains two protons and two neutrons
**b.** has a mass number of 0 and a 1− charge

ANSWER

**a.** An alpha ($\alpha$) particle, $^4_2He$, has two protons and two neutrons.
**b.** A beta ($\beta$) particle, $^{0}_{-1}e$, is like an electron with a mass number of 0 and a 1− charge.

## Biological Effects of Radiation

SELF STUDY ACTIVITY
Radiation and Its Biological Effects

When radiation strikes molecules in its path, electrons may be knocked away, forming unstable ions. For example, when radiation passes through the human body, it may interact with water molecules, removing electrons, and producing $H_2O^+$, which can cause undesirable chemical reactions.

The cells most sensitive to radiation are the ones undergoing rapid division—those of the bone marrow, skin, reproductive organs, and intestinal lining, as well as all cells of growing children. Damaged cells may lose their ability to produce necessary materials. For example, if radiation damages cells of the bone marrow, red blood cells may no longer be produced. If sperm cells, ova, or the cells of a fetus are damaged, birth defects may result. In contrast, cells of the nerves, muscles, liver, and adult bones are much less sensitive to radiation because they undergo little or no cellular division.

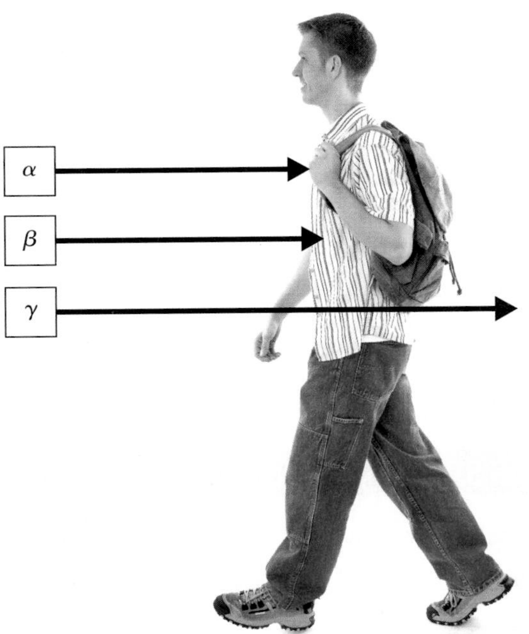


Cancer cells are another example of rapidly dividing cells. Because cancer cells are highly sensitive to radiation, large doses of radiation are used to destroy them. The normal tissue that surrounds cancer cells divides at a slower rate and suffers less damage from radiation. However, radiation itself may cause malignant tumors, leukemia, anemia, and genetic mutations.

## Radiation Protection

Radiologists, doctors, and nurses who work with radioactive isotopes must use proper radiation protection. Proper **shielding** is necessary to prevent exposure. Alpha particles, the heaviest of the radiation particles, travel only a few centimeters in the air before they collide with air molecules, acquire electrons, and become helium atoms. A piece of paper,

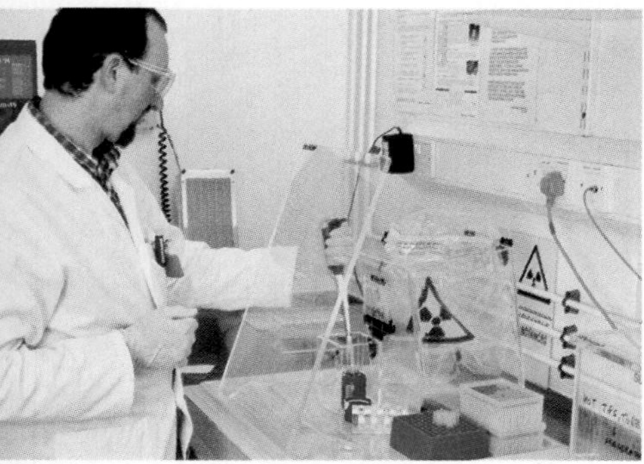

**FIGURE 4.1** A person working with radioisotopes wears protective clothing and gloves and stands behind a lead shield.

**Q** What types of radiation does the lead shield block?

**TABLE 4.3** Properties of Radiation and Shielding Required

| Property | Alpha ($\alpha$) particle | Beta ($\beta$) particle | Gamma ($\gamma$) ray |
|---|---|---|---|
| Travel distance in air | 2–4 cm | 200–300 cm | 500 m |
| Tissue depth | 0.05 mm | 4–5 mm | 50 cm or more |
| Shielding | Paper, clothing | Heavy clothing, lab coats, gloves | Lead, thick concrete |
| Typical source | Radium-226 | Carbon-14 | Technetium-99m |

clothing, and our skin are protection against alpha particles. Lab coats and gloves will also provide sufficient shielding. However, if ingested or inhaled, alpha emitters can bring about serious internal damage because of their large mass and high charge.

Beta particles move much faster and farther than alpha particles, traveling as far as several meters through air. They can pass through paper and penetrate as far as 4–5 mm into body tissue. External exposure to beta particles can burn the surface of the skin, but they are stopped before they reach the internal organs. Heavy clothing such as lab coats and gloves are needed to protect the skin from beta particles.

Gamma rays travel great distances through the air and pass through many materials, including body tissues. Only the densest shielding from substances such as lead and concrete will stop them. Because gamma rays penetrate so deeply, exposure to these rays can be extremely hazardous. When preparing radioactive materials, the radiologist wears special gloves and works behind lead-glass windows. Long tongs are used within the work area to pick up vials of radioactive material, keeping them away from the hands and body. Even the syringe used to give an injection of a gamma-emitting radioactive isotope is placed inside a special lead-glass cover. (See Figure 4.1.) Table 4.3 summarizes the shielding materials required for the various types of radiation.

If you work in an environment such as a nuclear medicine facility, try to keep the time you must spend in a radioactive area to a minimum. A certain amount of radiation is emitted every minute. Remaining in a radioactive area twice as long exposes you to twice as much radiation.

Keep your distance! The greater your distance from the radioactive source, the lower the intensity of radiation you will receive. Just by doubling your distance from the radiation source, the intensity of the radiation drops to $\left(\frac{1}{2}\right)^2$ or one-fourth of its previous value.

## SAMPLE PROBLEM 4.1

### Radiation Protection

How does the type of shielding for alpha radiation differ from that used for gamma radiation?

SOLUTION

Alpha radiation is stopped by paper and clothing. However, lead or concrete is needed for protection from gamma radiation.

STUDY CHECK

Besides shielding, what other methods help reduce exposure to radiation?

## QUESTIONS AND PROBLEMS

### Natural Radioactivity

**4.1** **a.** How are an alpha particle and a helium nucleus similar?
**b.** What symbols are used for alpha particles?
**c.** What is the source of an alpha particle?

**4.2** **a.** How are a beta particle and an electron similar?
**b.** What symbols are used for beta particles?
**c.** What is the source of a beta particle?

**4.3** Naturally occurring potassium consists of three isotopes: potassium-39, potassium-40, and radioactive potassium-41.
- **a.** Write the atomic symbol for each isotope.
- **b.** In what ways are the isotopes similar, and in what ways do they differ?

**4.4** Naturally occurring iodine is iodine-127. Medically, radioactive isotopes of iodine-125 and iodine-130 are used.
- **a.** Write the atomic symbol for each isotope.
- **b.** In what ways are the isotopes similar, and in what ways do they differ?

**4.5** Supply the missing information in the following table:

| Medical Use | Atomic Symbol | Mass Number | Number of Protons | Number of Neutrons |
|---|---|---|---|---|
| Heart imaging | ${}^{201}_{81}Tl$ | | | |
| Radiation therapy | | 60 | 27 | |
| Abdominal scan | | | 31 | 36 |
| Hyperthyroidism | ${}^{131}_{53}I$ | | | |
| Leukemia treatment | | 32 | | 17 |

**4.6** Supply the missing information in the following table:

| Medical Use | Atomic Symbol | Mass Number | Number of Protons | Number of Neutrons |
|---|---|---|---|---|
| Cancer treatment | ${}^{60}_{27}Co$ | | | |
| Brain scan | | 99 | 43 | |
| Blood flow | | 141 | 58 | |
| Bone scan | | 85 | | 47 |
| Lung function | ${}^{133}_{54}Xe$ | | | |

**4.7** Write a symbol for each of the following:
**a.** alpha particle **b.** neutron
**c.** beta particle **d.** nitrogen-15
**e.** iodine-125

**4.8** Write a symbol for each of the following:
**a.** proton **b.** gamma ray
**c.** electron **d.** positron
**e.** cobalt-60

**4.9** Identify each of the following:
**a.** ${}^{0}_{-1}X$ **b.** ${}^{4}_{2}X$
**c.** ${}^{1}_{0}X$ **d.** ${}^{24}_{11}X$
**e.** ${}^{14}_{6}X$

**4.10** Identify each of the following:
**a.** ${}^{1}_{1}X$ **b.** ${}^{32}_{15}X$
**c.** ${}^{0}_{0}X$ **d.** ${}^{59}_{26}X$
**e.** ${}^{0}_{+1}X$

**4.11**
- **a.** Why does beta radiation penetrate farther into solid material than alpha radiation?
- **b.** How does radiation cause damage to cells of the body?
- **c.** Why does the radiation technician leave the room when taking your X-ray?
- **d.** What is the purpose of wearing gloves when handling radioactive isotopes?

**4.12**
- **a.** As a nurse in an oncology unit, you may give an injection of a radioactive isotope. What are three ways you can minimize your exposure to radiation?
- **b.** Why are cancer cells more sensitive to radiation than nerve cells?
- **c.** What is the purpose of placing a lead apron on a patient who is receiving routine dental X-rays?
- **d.** Why are the walls in a radiology office built of lead or thick concrete blocks?

# 4.2 Nuclear Reactions

**LEARNING GOAL**

Write an equation showing mass numbers and atomic numbers for radioactive decay.

When a nucleus spontaneously breaks down by emitting radiation, the process is called **radioactive decay**. The process can be written using the atomic symbols of the original radioactive nucleus, the new nucleus, and the type of radiation emitted. An arrow between the atomic symbols indicates that this is a nuclear equation.

Radioactive nucleus $\longrightarrow$ new nucleus + radiation ($\alpha$, $\beta$, $\gamma$, $\beta^+$)

In a nuclear equation, the mass numbers and the atomic numbers must be equal on both sides. In most nuclear equations, there is a change in the number of protons, which gives a different element.

The changes in mass number and atomic number of an unstable nucleus that undergoes radioactive decay are shown in Table 4.4.

**TABLE 4.4** Mass Number and Atomic Number Changes due to Radiation

| Decay Process | Radiation Symbol | Change in Mass Number | Change in Atomic Number | Change in Neutron Number |
|---|---|---|---|---|
| Alpha emission | ${}^{4}_{2}He$ | −4 | −2 | −2 |
| Beta emission | ${}^{0}_{-1}e$ | 0 | +1 | −1 |
| Positron emission | ${}^{0}_{+1}e$ | 0 | −1 | +1 |
| Gamma emission | ${}^{0}_{0}\gamma$ | 0 | 0 | 0 |

We will now see how this works in the following examples and sample problems.

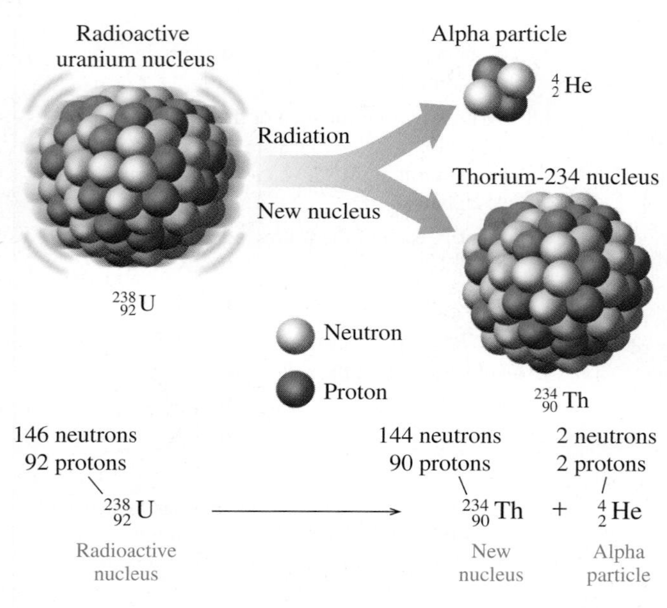


## Alpha Decay

An unstable nucleus undergoes alpha decay by emitting an alpha particle. Because an alpha particle consists of 2 protons and 2 neutrons, the mass number decreases by 4, and the atomic number decreases by 2. For example, uranium-238 emits an alpha particle to form a different nucleus with a mass number of 234. Compared to uranium with 92 protons, the new nucleus has 90 protons, which makes it thorium.

## Guide to Completing a Nuclear Equation

In another example of radioactive decay, radium-226 emits an alpha particle to form a nucleus that has a new identity with a different mass number and atomic number.

**STEP 1** **Write the incomplete nuclear equation.**

$$^{226}_{88}Ra \longrightarrow ? + ^{4}_{2}He$$

**STEP 2** **Determine the missing mass number.** In the equation, the mass number, 226, of the radium is equal to the combined mass numbers of the alpha particle and the new nucleus.

$$226 = ? + 4$$
$$226 - 4 = ?$$
$$222 = ? \text{ (mass number of new nucleus)}$$

**STEP 3** **Determine the missing atomic number.** The atomic number of radium, 88, must equal the sum of the atomic numbers of the alpha particle and the new nucleus.

$$88 = ? + 2$$
$$88 - 2 = ?$$
$$86 = ? \text{ (atomic number of new nucleus)}$$

**STEP 4** **Determine the symbol of the new nucleus.** On the periodic table, the element that has atomic number 86 is radon, Rn. The nucleus of this isotope of Rn is written as $^{222}_{86}Rn$.

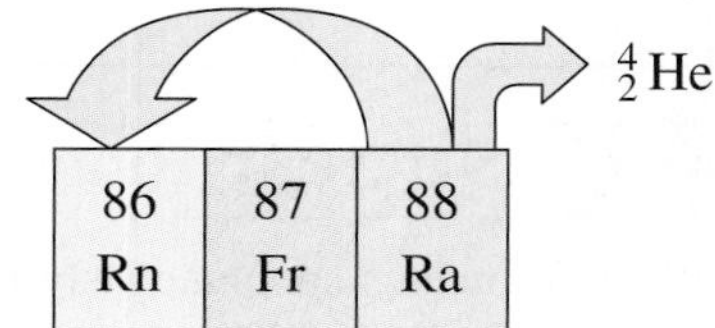


**STEP 5** **Complete the nuclear equation.**

$$^{226}_{88}Ra \longrightarrow ^{222}_{86}Rn + ^{4}_{2}He$$

In this nuclear reaction, a radium-226 nucleus decays by releasing an alpha particle and produces a radon-222 nucleus.

**CONCEPT CHECK 4.2**

### Alpha Decay

Francium-221 emits alpha particles when it decays.

**a.** Does the new nucleus have a larger or smaller mass number? By how much?

**b.** Does the new nucleus have a larger or smaller atomic number? By how much?

ANSWER

**a.** The loss of an alpha particle will give a smaller mass number to the new nucleus. Because an alpha particle is a helium nucleus, $^{4}_{2}He$, the mass number of the new nucleus will decrease by 4 from 221 to 217.

**b.** The loss of an alpha particle will give a smaller atomic number to the new nucleus. Because an alpha particle is a helium nucleus, $^{4}_{2}He$, the atomic number of the new nucleus will decrease by 2 from 87 to 85.

## SAMPLE PROBLEM 4.2

### Writing an Equation for Alpha Decay

Smoke detectors that are used in homes and apartments contain americium-241, which undergoes alpha decay. When alpha particles collide with air molecules, charged particles are produced that generate an electrical current. When smoke particles enter the detector, they interfere with the formation of charged particles in the air, and the electric current is interrupted. This causes the alarm to sound and warns the occupants of the danger of fire. Complete the following nuclear equation for the decay of americium-241:

$${}^{241}_{95}\text{Am} \longrightarrow ? + {}^{4}_{2}\text{He}$$

SOLUTION

Guide to Completing a Nuclear Equation

- STEP 1 Write the incomplete nuclear equation.
- STEP 2 Determine the missing mass number.
- STEP 3 Determine the missing atomic number.
- STEP 4 Determine the symbol of the new nucleus.
- STEP 5 Complete the nuclear equation.

**STEP 1** **Write the incomplete nuclear equation.**

$${}^{241}_{95}\text{Am} \longrightarrow ? + {}^{4}_{2}\text{He}$$

**STEP 2** **Determine the missing mass number.** In the equation, the mass number of the americium, 241, is equal to the sum of the mass numbers of the alpha particle and the new nucleus:

$$241 = ? + 4$$
$$241 - 4 = ?$$
$$237 = ? \text{ (mass number of new nucleus)}$$

**STEP 3** **Determine the missing atomic number.** The atomic number of americium, 95 must equal the sum of the atomic numbers of the alpha particle and the new nucleus:

$$95 = ? + 2$$
$$95 - 2 = ?$$
$$93 = ? \text{ (atomic number of new nucleus)}$$

**STEP 4** **Determine the symbol of the new nucleus.** On the periodic table, the element that has atomic number 93 is neptunium, Np. The symbol of this isotope of Np is written as ${}^{237}_{93}\text{Np}$.

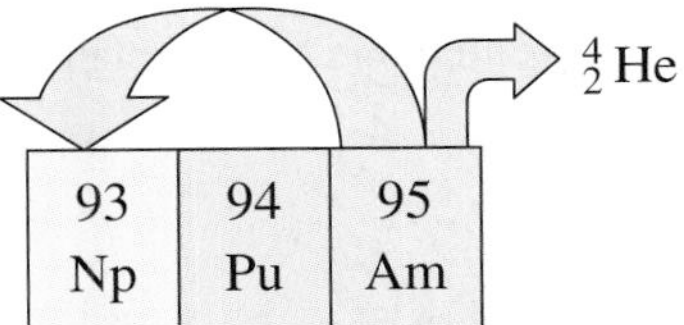


**STEP 5** **Complete the nuclear equation.**

$${}^{241}_{95}\text{Am} \longrightarrow {}^{237}_{93}\text{Np} + {}^{4}_{2}\text{He}$$

In this nuclear reaction, an Am-241 nucleus decays by releasing an alpha particle and produces a Np-237 nucleus.

STUDY CHECK

Write a balanced nuclear equation for the alpha decay of Po-214.

## Beta Decay

When an unstable nucleus emits a beta particle, the newly formed proton increases the atomic number by 1, but the mass number stays the same. For example, when carbon-14 decays by beta emission, it becomes nitrogen-14.

In the nuclear equation for beta decay, the mass number of the radioactive nucleus and the mass number of the new nucleus are the same. However, the atomic number of the new nucleus increases by 1, indicating a change of one element into another. For example, the beta decay of a carbon-14 nucleus produces a nitrogen-14 nucleus.

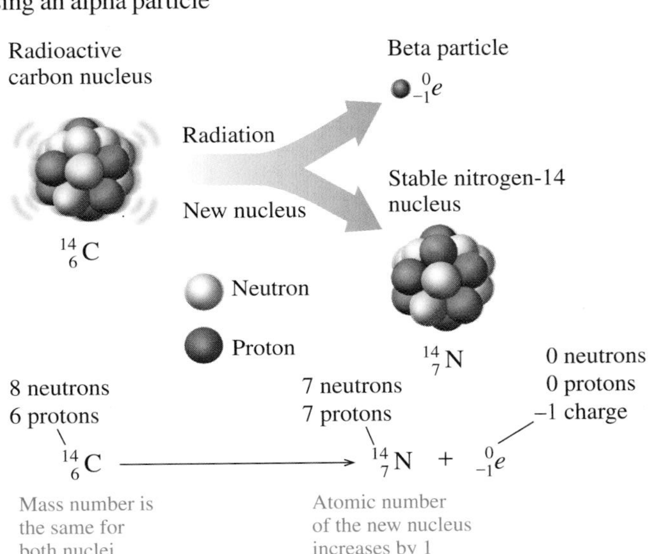

## GREEN CHEMISTRY NOTE

### Radon in Our Homes

The presence of radon has become a much publicized environmental and health issue because of the radiation danger it poses. Radioactive isotopes such as uranium-238 and radium-226 are naturally present in many types of rocks and soils. Radium-226 emits an alpha particle and is converted into radon gas, which diffuses out of the rocks and soil:

$$^{226}_{88}\text{Ra} \longrightarrow {}^{222}_{86}\text{Rn} + {}^{4}_{2}\text{He}$$

Outdoors, radon gas poses little danger because it disperses in the air. However, if the radioactive source is under a house or building, the radon gas can enter the house through cracks in the foundation or other openings. Those who live or work there may inhale the radon. Inside the lungs, radon-222 emits alpha particles to form polonium-218, which is known to cause lung cancer:

$$^{222}_{86}\text{Rn} \longrightarrow {}^{218}_{84}\text{Po} + {}^{4}_{2}\text{He}$$

Some researchers have estimated that 10% of all lung cancer deaths in the United States result from radon gas exposure. The Environmental Protection Agency (EPA) recommends that the maximum level of radon not exceed 4 picocuries (pCi) per liter of air in a home. One (1) picocurie (pCi) is equal to $10^{-12}$ curies (Ci): curies are described in section 4.3. In California, 1% of all the houses surveyed exceeded the EPA's recommended maximum radon level.

## SAMPLE PROBLEM 4.3

### Writing an Equation for Beta Decay

MC™ TUTORIAL
Writing Nuclear Equations

Write the nuclear equation for the beta decay of cobalt-60.

SOLUTION

**STEP 1 Write the incomplete nuclear equation.**

$$^{60}_{27}\text{Co} \longrightarrow ? + {}^{0}_{-1}e$$

**STEP 2 Determine the missing mass number.** In the equation, the mass number of cobalt, 60, is equal to the sum of the mass numbers of the beta particle and the new nucleus:

$$\begin{aligned} 60 &= ? + 0 \\ 60 - 0 &= ? \\ 60 &= ? \text{ (mass number of new nucleus)} \end{aligned}$$

**STEP 3 Determine the missing atomic number.** The atomic number of cobalt, 27, must equal the sum of the atomic numbers of the beta particle and the new nucleus:

$$\begin{aligned} 27 &= ? - 1 \\ 27 + 1 &= ? \\ 28 &= ? \text{ (atomic number of new nucleus)} \end{aligned}$$

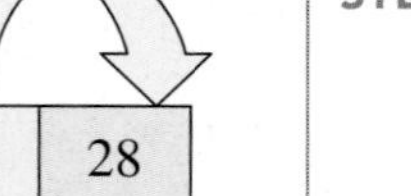


**STEP 4 Determine the symbol of the new nucleus.** On the periodic table, the element that has atomic number 28 is nickel (Ni). The symbol of this isotope is written as

$$^{60}_{28}\text{Ni}$$

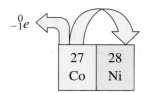

**STEP 5 Complete the nuclear equation.**

$$^{60}_{27}\text{Co} \longrightarrow {}^{60}_{28}\text{Ni} + {}^{0}_{-1}e$$

In this nuclear reaction, cobalt-60 undergoes beta decay to produce nickel-60.

STUDY CHECK

Write the nuclear equation for the beta decay of iodine-131.

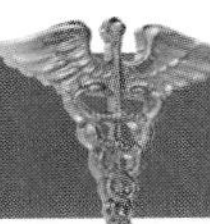

## Health Note

### Beta Emitters in Medicine

The radioactive isotopes of several biologically important elements are beta emitters. When a radiologist wants to treat a malignancy within the body, a beta emitter may be used. The short range of penetration into the tissue by beta particles is advantageous for certain conditions. For example, some malignant tumors increase the fluid within the body tissues. A compound containing phosphorus-32, a beta emitter, is injected into the body cavity where the tumor is located. The beta particles travel only a few millimeters through the tissue, so only the malignancy and any tissue within that range are affected. The growth of the tumor is slowed or stopped, and the production of fluid decreases. Phosphorus-32 is also used to treat leukemia, polycythemia vera (an excessive production of red blood cells), and lymphomas.

$$^{32}_{15}\text{P} \longrightarrow {}^{32}_{16}\text{S} + {}^{0}_{-1}e$$

Another beta emitter, iron-59, is used in blood tests to determine the level of iron in the blood and the rate of production of red blood cells by the bone marrow.

$$^{59}_{26}\text{Fe} \longrightarrow {}^{59}_{27}\text{Co} + {}^{0}_{-1}e$$

### Positron Emission

When a radioactive isotope emits a positron, the mass number does not change. However, the atomic number of the new nucleus decreases by 1. For example, manganese-49 undergoes positron emission to produce chromium-49. The atomic number of chromium (24) and the charge of the positron (+1) added together give the atomic number of manganese (25).

$$^{49}_{25}\text{Mn} \longrightarrow {}^{49}_{24}\text{Cr} + {}^{0}_{+1}e$$

TUTORIAL
Alpha, Beta, and Gamma Emitters

## Gamma Emission

Pure gamma emitters are rare, although gamma radiation accompanies most alpha and beta radiation. In radiology, one of the most commonly used gamma emitters is technetium (Tc). Because the unstable isotope of technetium decays quickly, it is written as the *metastable* (symbol m) isotope: technetium-99m, Tc-99m, or $^{99m}_{43}\text{Tc}$. By emitting energy in the form of gamma rays, the unstable nucleus becomes more stable.

$$^{99m}_{43}\text{Tc} \longrightarrow {}^{99}_{43}\text{Tc} + {}^{0}_{0}\gamma$$

Figure 4.2 summarizes the changes in the nucleus for alpha, beta, positron, and gamma radiation.

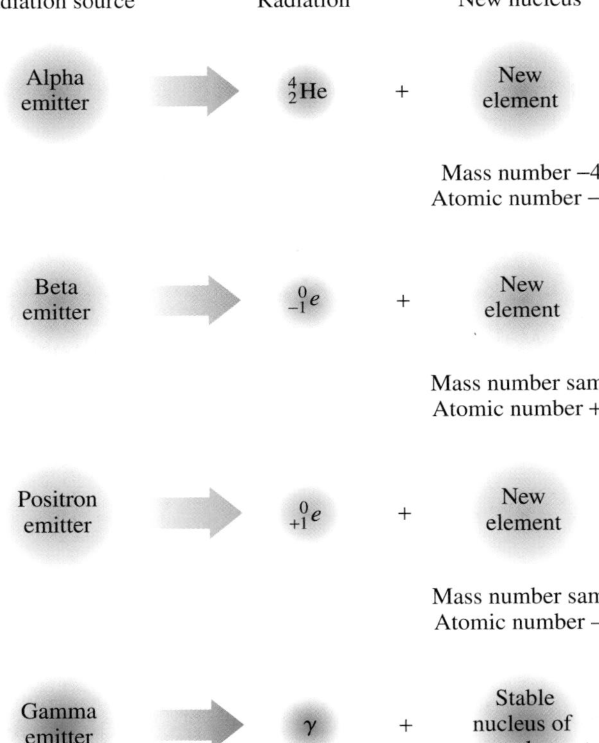


FIGURE 4.2 When the nuclei of alpha, beta, positron, and gamma emitters emit radiation, new and more stable nuclei are produced.

Q What changes occur in the number of protons and neutrons when an alpha emitter gives off radiation?

## Producing Radioactive Isotopes

Today, many radioisotopes are produced in small amounts by converting stable, nonradioactive isotopes into radioactive ones. In a process called *transmutation*, a stable nucleus is bombarded by high-speed particles such as alpha particles, protons, neutrons, and small nuclei. When one of these particles is absorbed, the nucleus becomes a radioactive isotope.

When the nonradioactive isotope boron-10 is bombarded by an alpha particle, it is converted to nitrogen-13, and a neutron is emitted.

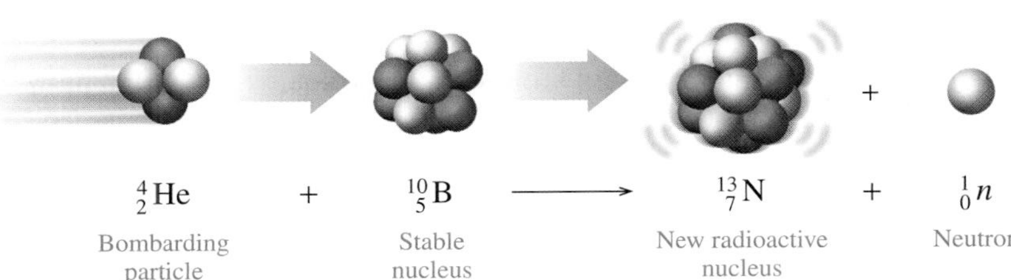

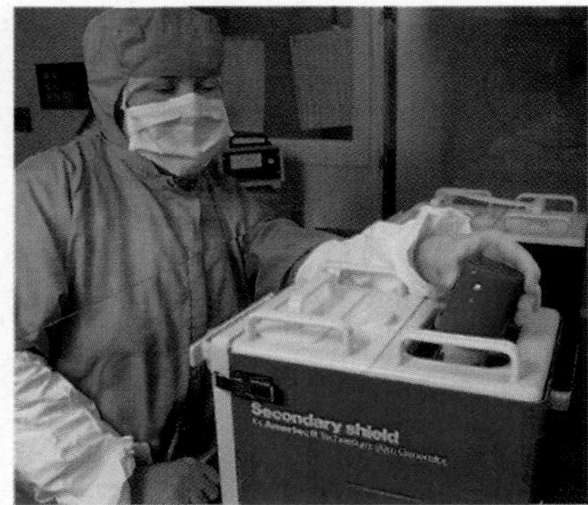


All elements that have an atomic number greater than 92 have been produced by bombardment; none of these elements occurs naturally. Most have been produced in small amounts and exist for such a short time that it is difficult to study their properties. An example is element 105, dubnium (Db), which is produced when californium-249 is bombarded with nitrogen-15:

$${}^{249}_{98}\mathrm{Cf} + {}^{15}_{7}\mathrm{N} \longrightarrow {}^{260}_{105}\mathrm{Db} + 4\,{}^{1}_{0}n$$

Technetium-99m is a radioisotope used in nuclear medicine for several diagnostic procedures, including the detection of brain tumors and examinations of the liver and spleen. The source of technetium-99m is molybdenum-99, which is produced in a nuclear reactor by neutron bombardment of molybdenum-98:

$${}^{98}_{42}\mathrm{Mo} + {}^{1}_{0}n \longrightarrow {}^{99}_{42}\mathrm{Mo}$$

Many radiology laboratories have small generators containing molybdenum-99, which decays to give technetium-99m:

$${}^{99}_{42}\mathrm{Mo} \longrightarrow {}^{99m}_{43}\mathrm{Tc} + {}^{0}_{-1}e$$

The technetium-99m radioisotope decays by emitting gamma rays. Gamma emission is desirable for diagnostic work because the gamma rays pass through the body to the detection equipment.

$${}^{99m}_{43}\mathrm{Tc} \longrightarrow {}^{99}_{43}\mathrm{Tc} + {}^{0}_{0}\gamma$$

CONCEPT CHECK 4.3

### Producing Radioactive Isotopes

Sulfur-32 is bombarded with a neutron to produce a new isotope and an alpha particle. What is the name of the new isotope?

ANSWER

To determine the name of the new isotope, we need to calculate its mass number and atomic number. Combining the mass numbers of S-32 and a neutron (32 + 1) gives a total of 33. Subtracting 4 for the alpha particle gives a mass number of 29 to the new isotope. Combining the atomic numbers of sulfur (16) and the neutron (0) and subtracting 2 for the alpha particle gives an atomic number of 14 to the new isotope. The element that has the atomic number of 14 is silicon. The new nucleus is silicon-29.

SAMPLE PROBLEM 4.4

### Writing Equations for Isotope Production

Write the equation when zinc-66 absorbs one proton (${}^{1}_{1}\mathrm{H}$) during bombardment to form a radioactive isotope.

SOLUTION

**STEP 1** **Write the incomplete nuclear equation.**

$${}^{66}_{30}\mathrm{Zn} + {}^{1}_{1}\mathrm{H} \longrightarrow ?$$

**STEP 2** **Determine the missing mass number.** In the equation, the sum of the mass numbers of zinc (66) and the proton (1) must equal the mass number of the new nucleus:

$$66 + 1 = ?$$
$$67 \quad = ? \text{ (mass number of new nucleus)}$$

**STEP 3** **Determine the missing atomic number.** The sum of the atomic numbers of zinc (30) and a proton (1) must equal the atomic number of the new nucleus:

$30 + 1 = ?$
$31 \quad = ?$ (atomic number of new nucleus)

**STEP 4** **Determine the symbol of the new nucleus.** On the periodic table, the element that has atomic number 31 is gallium, Ga. The symbol of this isotope of Ga is written as

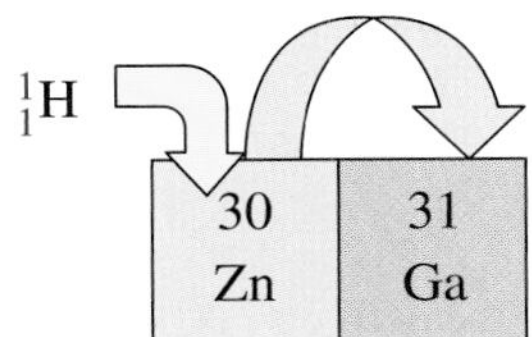


**STEP 5** **Complete the nuclear equation.**

$$^{66}_{30}\text{Zn} + ^{1}_{1}\text{H} \longrightarrow ^{67}_{31}\text{Ga}$$

Proton    New isotope

STUDY CHECK

The first radioactive isotope was produced in 1933 by the bombardment of aluminum-27 with an alpha particle to produce a radioactive isotope and one neutron. What is the balanced nuclear equation for this transmutation?

# QUESTIONS AND PROBLEMS

## Nuclear Equations

**4.13** Write a balanced nuclear equation for the alpha decay of each of the following:
**a.** $^{208}_{84}\text{Po}$ **b.** $^{232}_{90}\text{Th}$ **c.** $^{251}_{102}\text{No}$ **d.** $^{220}_{86}\text{Rn}$

**4.14** Write a balanced nuclear equation for the alpha decay of each of the following:
**a.** $^{243}_{96}\text{Cm}$ **b.** $^{252}_{99}\text{Es}$ **c.** $^{251}_{98}\text{Cf}$ **d.** $^{261}_{107}\text{Bh}$

**4.15** Write a balanced nuclear equation for the beta decay of each of the following:
**a.** $^{25}_{11}\text{Na}$ **b.** $^{20}_{8}\text{O}$
**c.** strontium-92 **d.** potassium-42

**4.16** Write a balanced nuclear equation for the beta decay of each of the following:
**a.** $^{44}_{19}\text{K}$ **b.** iron-59 **c.** iron-60 **d.** $^{141}_{56}\text{Ba}$

**4.17** Write a balanced nuclear equation for the positron decay of each of the following:
**a.** $^{26}_{14}\text{Si}$ **b.** $^{54}_{27}\text{Co}$ **c.** $^{77}_{37}\text{Rb}$ **d.** $^{93}_{45}\text{Rh}$

**4.18** Write a balanced nuclear equation for the positron decay of each of the following:
**a.** $^{8}_{5}\text{B}$ **b.** $^{13}_{7}\text{N}$ **c.** $^{40}_{19}\text{K}$ **d.** $^{118}_{54}\text{Xe}$

**4.19** Complete each of the following nuclear equations:
**a.** $^{28}_{13}\text{Al} \longrightarrow ? + ^{0}_{-1}e$
**b.** $? \longrightarrow ^{86}_{36}\text{Kr} + ^{1}_{0}n$
**c.** $^{66}_{29}\text{Cu} \longrightarrow ^{66}_{30}\text{Zn} + ?$
**d.** $? \longrightarrow ^{4}_{2}\text{He} + ^{234}_{90}\text{Th}$
**e.** $^{188}_{80}\text{Hg} \longrightarrow ? + ^{0}_{+1}e$

**4.20** Complete each of the following nuclear equations:
**a.** $^{11}_{6}\text{C} \longrightarrow ^{7}_{4}\text{Be} + ?$
**b.** $^{35}_{16}\text{S} \longrightarrow ? + ^{0}_{-1}e$
**c.** $? \longrightarrow ^{90}_{39}\text{Y} + ^{0}_{-1}e$
**d.** $^{210}_{83}\text{Bi} \longrightarrow ? + ^{4}_{2}\text{He}$
**e.** $? \longrightarrow ^{135}_{59}\text{Pr} + ^{0}_{+1}e$

**4.21** Complete each of the following bombardment reactions:
**a.** $^{9}_{4}\text{Be} + ^{1}_{0}n \longrightarrow ?$
**b.** $^{32}_{16}\text{S} + ? \longrightarrow ^{32}_{15}\text{P}$
**c.** $? + ^{1}_{0}n \longrightarrow ^{24}_{11}\text{Na} + ^{4}_{2}\text{He}$
**d.** $^{27}_{13}\text{Al} + ^{4}_{2}\text{He} \longrightarrow ? + ^{1}_{0}n$

**4.22** Complete each of the following bombardment reactions:
**a.** $^{40}_{18}\text{Ar} + ? \longrightarrow ^{43}_{19}\text{K} + ^{1}_{1}\text{H}$
**b.** $^{238}_{92}\text{U} + ^{1}_{0}n \longrightarrow ?$
**c.** $? + ^{1}_{0}n \longrightarrow ^{14}_{6}\text{C} + ^{1}_{1}\text{H}$
**d.** $? + ^{64}_{28}\text{Ni} \longrightarrow ^{272}_{111}\text{Rg} + ^{1}_{0}n$

## 4.3 Radiation Measurement

**LEARNING GOAL**

Describe the detection and measurement of radiation.

One of the most common instruments for detecting beta and gamma radiation is the Geiger counter. It consists of a metal tube filled with a gas such as argon. When radiation enters a window on the end of the tube, it produces charged particles in the gas, which produce an electrical current. Each burst of current is amplified to give a click and a reading on a meter.

$$Ar + radiation \longrightarrow Ar^{+} + e^{-}$$

Radiation is measured in several different ways. We can measure the activity of a radioactive sample or determine the impact of radiation on biological tissue.

### Measuring Radiation

When a radiology laboratory obtains a radioisotope, the activity of the sample is measured in terms of the number of nuclear disintegrations per second. The **curie (Ci)**, the original unit of activity, was defined as the number of disintegrations that occur in 1 second for 1 g of radium, which is equal to $3.7 \times 10^{10}$ disintegrations per second. The unit was named for Marie Curie, a Polish scientist, who, along with her husband, Pierre, discovered the radioactive elements radium and polonium. A newer unit of radiation activity is the **becquerel (Bq)**, which is one disintegration per second.

The **rad (radiation absorbed dose)** is a unit that measures the amount of radiation absorbed by a gram of material such as body tissue. The newer unit for absorbed dose is the **gray (Gy)**, which is equal to 100 rads.

The **rem (radiation equivalent in humans)** measures the biological effects of different kinds of radiation. Although alpha particles do not penetrate the skin, if they should enter the body by some other route, they can cause a lot of damage even though the particles travel only a short distance in tissue. High-energy radiation such as beta particles and high-energy protons and neutrons that penetrate the skin and travel into tissue cause more damage. Gamma rays are dangerous because they travel a long way through tissue and create a great deal of damage.

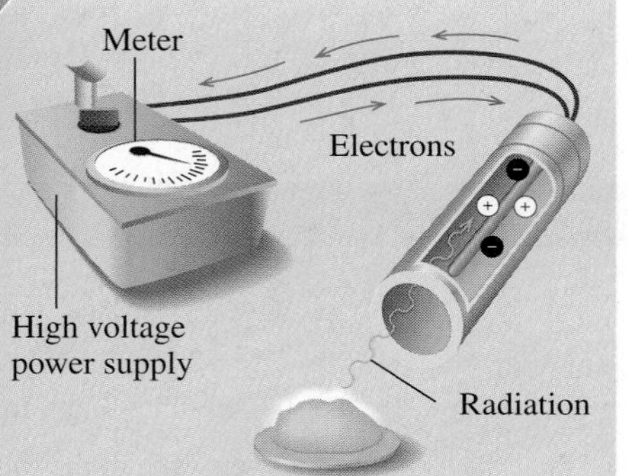


To determine the **equivalent dose** or rem dose, the absorbed dose (rads) is multiplied by a factor that adjusts for biological damage caused by a particular form of radiation. For beta and gamma radiation the factor is 1, so the biological damage in rems is the same as the absorbed radiation (rads). For high-energy protons and neutrons, the factor is about 10, and for alpha particles it is 20.

$$\text{Biological damage (rem)} = \text{absorbed dose (rad)} \times \text{factor}$$

Often the measurement for an equivalent dose will be in units of millirems (mrem). One rem is equal to 1000 mrem. The newer unit is the **sievert (Sv)**. One sievert is equal to 100 rems.

People who work in radiology laboratories wear film badges to determine their exposure to radiation. A film badge consists of a piece of photographic film in a container that is attached to clothing. Periodically, the film badges are collected and developed to determine the level of exposure to radiation.

Table 4.5 summarizes the units used to measure radiation.

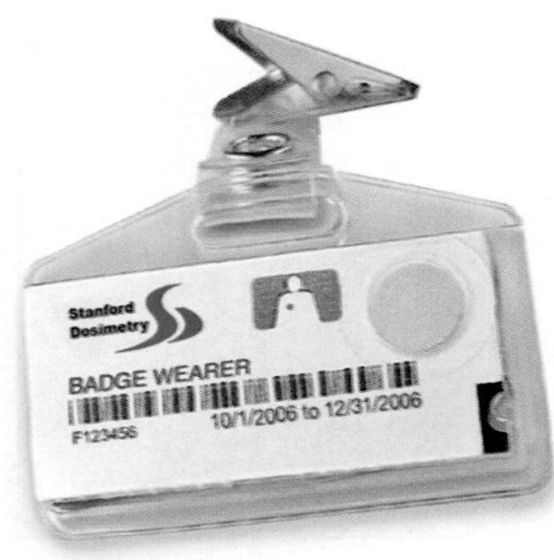


**TABLE 4.5** Some Units of Radiation Measurement

| Measurement | Common Unit | SI Unit | Relationship |
|---|---|---|---|
| Activity | curie (Ci) | becquerel (Bq) | 1 Ci $= 3.7 \times 10^{10}$ Bq |
| Absorbed dose | rad | gray (Gy) | 1 Gy = 100 rad |
| Biological damage | rem | sievert (Sv) | 1 Sv = 100 rem |

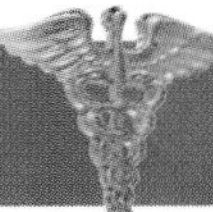

# HEALTH NOTE

## Radiation and Food

Food-borne illnesses caused by pathogenic bacteria such as *Salmonella*, *Listeria*, and *Escherichia coli* have become a major health concern in the United States. The Centers for Disease Control and Prevention (CDC) estimates that each year *E. coli* in contaminated foods infects 20 000 people in the United States, and that 500 people die. *E. coli* has been responsible for outbreaks of illness from contaminated ground beef, fruit juices, lettuce, and alfalfa sprouts.

The Food and Drug Administration (FDA) has approved the use of 0.3 kilogray (0.3 kGy) to 1 kGy of radiation produced by cobalt-60 or cesium-137 for the treatment of foods. The irradiation technology is much like that used to sterilize medical supplies. Cobalt pellets are placed in stainless steel tubes, which are arranged in racks. When food moves through the series of racks, the gamma rays pass through the food and kill the bacteria.

It is important for consumers to understand that when food is irradiated, it never comes into contact with the radioactive source. The gamma rays pass through the food to kill bacteria, but that does not make the food radioactive. The radiation kills bacteria because it stops their ability to divide and grow. We cook or heat food thoroughly for the same purpose. Radiation has little effect on the food itself because its cells are no longer dividing or growing. Thus irradiated food is not harmed although small amounts of vitamins may be lost.

Currently, tomatoes, blueberries, strawberries, and mushrooms are being irradiated to allow them to be harvested when completely ripe and extend their shelf life. (See Figure 4.3.) The FDA has also approved the irradiation of pork, poultry, and beef to decrease potential infections and to extend shelf life. Currently, irradiated vegetable and meat products are available in retail markets in South Africa. Apollo 17 astronauts ate irradiated foods on the moon, and some U.S. hospitals and nursing homes now use irradiated poultry to reduce the possibility of salmonella infections among patients. The extended shelf life of irradiated food also makes it useful for campers and military personnel. Soon consumers concerned about food safety will have a choice of irradiated meats, fruits, and vegetables at the market.

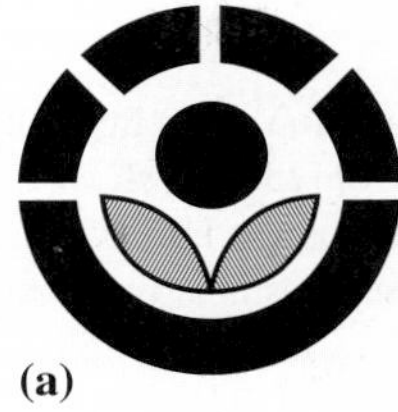

(a)

(b)

**FIGURE 4.3** **(a)** The FDA requires this symbol to appear on irradiated retail foods. **(b)** After two weeks, the irradiated strawberries on the right show no spoilage. Mold is growing on the nonirradiated ones on the left.

**Q** Why are irradiated foods used on spaceships and in nursing homes?

SAMPLE PROBLEM **4.5**

### Radiation Measurement

One treatment of bone pain involves intravenous administration of the radioisotope phosphorus-32, which is primarily incorporated into bone. A typical dose of 7 mCi can produce up to 450 rads in the bone. What is the difference between the units of mCi and rads?

SOLUTION

The millicuries (mCi) indicate the activity of the P-32 in terms of nuclei that break down in 1 second. The radiation absorbed dose (rads) is a measure of amount of radiation absorbed by the bone.

STUDY CHECK

If P-32 is a beta emitter, how do the number of rems compare to the rads?

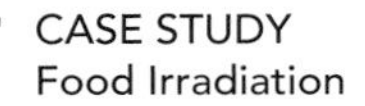

CASE STUDY
Food Irradiation

## Exposure to Radiation

Every day, we are exposed to low levels of background radiation from naturally occurring radioactive isotopes in the buildings where we live and work, in our food and water, and in the air we breathe. For example, potassium-40 is a naturally occurring isotope that is present in any potassium-containing food. Other naturally occurring radioisotopes in air

# HEALTH NOTE

## Brachytherapy

The process called *brachytherapy*, or seed implantation, is an internal form of radiation therapy. The prefix *brachy* is from the Greek word for short distance. With internal radiation, a high dose of radiation is delivered to a cancerous area, while normal tissue sustains minimal damage. Because higher doses are used, fewer treatments of shorter duration are needed. Conventional external treatment delivers a lower dose per treatment but requires six to eight weeks of treatments.

### Permanent Brachytherapy

One of the most common forms of cancer in males is prostate cancer. In addition to surgery and chemotherapy, one treatment option is to place 40 or more titanium capsules, or "seeds," in the malignant area. Each seed, which is the size of a small grain of rice, contains radioactive iodine-125, palladium-103, or cesium-131. The radiation from the seeds destroys the cancer by interfering with the reproduction of cancer cells. Because the radiation targets the cancer cells, there is minimal damage to normal tissues. Ninety percent (90%) of the radioisotopes decay within a few months because they have short half-lives.

| Isotope | I-125 | Pd-103 | Cs-131 |
|---|---|---|---|
| Half-life | 60 days | 17 days | 10 days |
| Time to deliver 90% of radiation | 7 months | 2 months | 1 month |

Almost no radiation passes out of the patient's body. The amount of radiation received by a family member is no greater than that received on a long plane flight. The titanium capsules are left in the body permanently, but the products of decay are not radioactive and cause no further damage.

### Temporary Brachytherapy

In another type of treatment for prostate cancer, long needles containing iridium-192 are placed in the tumor. However, the needles are removed after 5 to 10 minutes, depending on the activity of the iridium isotope. Compared to permanent brachytherapy, temporary brachytherapy can deliver a higher dose of radiation over a shorter time. The procedure may be repeated in a few days.

Brachytherapy is also used following breast cancer lumpectomy. An iridium-192 isotope is inserted into the catheter implanted in the space left by the removal of the tumor. The isotope is removed after 5 to 10 minutes, depending on the activity of the iridium source. Radiation is delivered primarily to the tissue surrounding the cavity that contained the tumor and where the cancer is most likely to reoccur. The procedure is repeated twice a day for five days to give an absorbed dose of 34 Gy (3400 rads). The catheter is removed, and no radioactive material remains in the body.

In conventional external beam therapy for breast cancer, a patient receives 2 Gy/treatment once a day for 35 days or about seven weeks, which gives a total absorbed dose of about 100 Gy or 10 000 rads. The external beam therapy irradiates the entire breast including the tumor cavity.

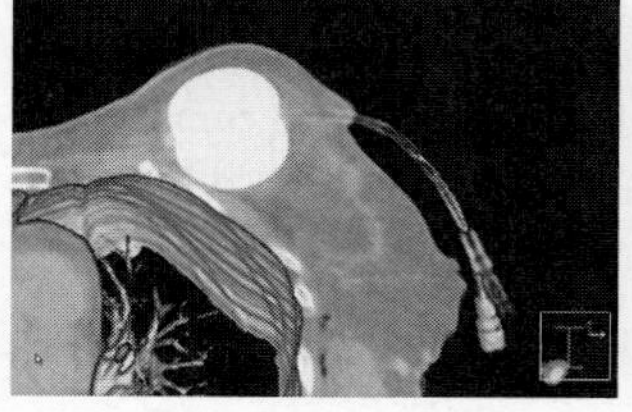

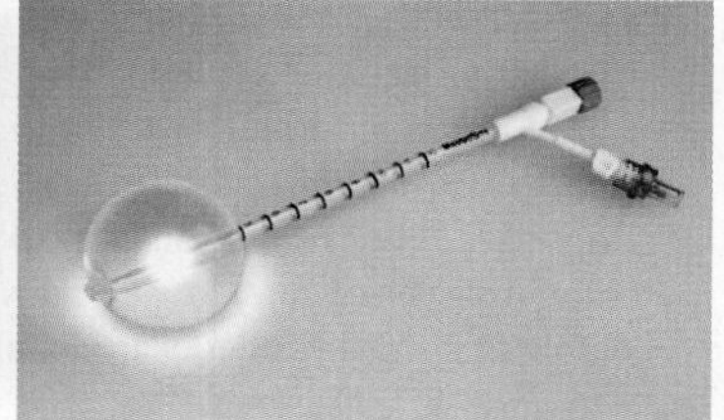

**TABLE 4.6 Average Annual Radiation Received by a Person in the United States**

| Source | Dose (mrem) |
|---|---|
| **Natural** | |
| The ground | 20 |
| Air, water, food | 30 |
| Cosmic rays | 40 |
| Wood, concrete, brick | 50 |
| **Medical** | |
| Chest X-ray | 20 |
| Dental X-ray | 20 |
| Hip X-ray | 60 |
| Lumbar spine X-ray | 70 |
| Mammogram | 40 |
| Upper gastrointestinal tract X-ray | 200 |
| **Other** | |
| Television | 20 |
| Air travel | 10 |
| Radon | 200[a] |

[a]Varies widely.

and food are carbon-14, radon-222, strontium-90, and iodine-131. The average person in the United States is exposed to about 360 mrem of radiation annually. Table 4.6 lists some common sources of radiation.

Another source of background radiation is cosmic radiation produced in space by the sun. People who live at high altitudes or travel by airplane receive a greater amount of cosmic radiation because there are fewer molecules in the atmosphere to absorb the radiation. For example, a person living in Denver receives about twice the cosmic radiation as a person living in Los Angeles. A person living close to a nuclear power plant normally does not receive much additional radiation, perhaps 0.1 millirem (mrem) in one year. (One rem equals 1000 mrem.) However, in the accident at the Chernobyl nuclear power plant in 1986 in Ukraine, people in a nearby town were estimated to have received as much as 1 rem/h.

Medical sources of radiation including dental, hip, spine, and chest X-rays and mammograms add to our radiation exposure.

## Radiation Sickness

The larger the dose of radiation received at one time, the greater the effect on the body. Exposure to radiation less than 25 rem usually cannot be detected. Whole-body exposure of 100 rem produces a temporary decrease in the number of white blood cells. When the exposure to radiation exceeds 100 rem, a person may experience one or more symptoms of radiation sickness: nausea, vomiting, fatigue, and a reduction in white-cell count. A whole-body dosage greater than 300 rem can decrease the white-cell count to zero. The victim suffers diarrhea, hair loss, and infection. Exposure to radiation of about 500 rem is expected to cause death in 50% of the people receiving that dose. This amount of radiation to the whole body is called the *lethal dose for one-half the population*, or the $LD_{50}$. The $LD_{50}$ varies for different life forms, as Table 4.7 shows. Radiation dosages of 600 rem or higher would be fatal to all humans within a few weeks.

**TABLE 4.7** Lethal Doses of Whole-Body Radiation for Some Life Forms

| Life-Form | $LD_{50}$ (rem) |
|---|---|
| Insect | 100 000 |
| Bacterium | 50 000 |
| Rat | 800 |
| Human | 500 |
| Dog | 300 |

## QUESTIONS AND PROBLEMS

### Radiation Measurement

**4.23** **a.** How does a Geiger counter detect radiation?
**b.** What SI unit and what older unit describe the activity of a radioactive sample?
**c.** What SI unit and what older unit describe the radiation dose absorbed by tissue?
**d.** What is meant by the term kilogray?

**4.24** **a.** What is background radiation?
**b.** What are the SI unit and the older unit that describe the biological effect of radiation?
**c.** What is meant by the terms mCi and mrem?
**d.** Why is a factor used to determine the equivalent dose?

**4.25** The recommended dosage of iodine-131 is 4.20 $\mu$Ci/kg of body weight. How many microcuries of iodine-131 are needed for a 70.0-kg patient with hyperthyroidism?

**4.26** **a.** The dosage of technetium-99m for a lung scan is 20 $\mu$Ci/kg of body weight. How many millicuries should be given to a 50.0-kg patient? (1 mCi = 1000 $\mu$Ci)
**b.** Suppose a person absorbed 50 mrads of alpha radiation. What would be the equivalent dose in mrems?

**4.27** Why would an airline pilot be exposed to more background radiation than the person who works at the ticket counter?

**4.28** In radiation therapy, a patient receives high doses of radiation. What symptoms of radiation sickness might the patient exhibit?

## 4.4 Half-Life of a Radioisotope

**LEARNING GOAL**

Given the half-life of a radioisotope, calculate the amount of radioisotope remaining after one or more half-lives.

The **half-life** of a radioisotope is the amount of time it takes for one-half of a sample to decay. Each radioisotope has a characteristic half-life that depends on the stability of the nucleus. For example, $^{131}_{53}I$ has a half-life of 8.0 days. As $^{131}_{53}I$ decays, it produces a beta particle and the nonradioactive isotope $^{131}_{54}Xe$:

$$^{131}_{53}I \longrightarrow ^{131}_{54}Xe + ^{0}_{-1}e$$

Suppose we have an initial sample that contains 20. g of $^{131}_{53}I$. In 8.0 days, 10. g, which is one-half of all the $^{131}_{53}I$ in the sample, will decay to give $^{131}_{54}Xe$. The decay process also produces 10. g of the product $^{131}_{54}Xe$. After another half-life or 8.0 days passes, another 5.0 g of $^{131}_{53}I$ will decay.

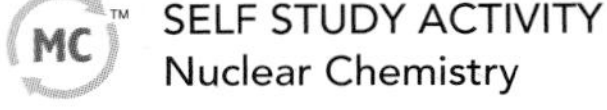

SELF STUDY ACTIVITY
Nuclear Chemistry

$$20.\text{ g of } ^{131}_{53}I \xrightarrow{\text{1 half-life}} 10.\text{ g of } ^{131}_{53}I \xrightarrow{\text{2 half-lives}} 5\text{ g of } ^{131}_{53}I \xrightarrow{\text{3 half-lives}} 2.5\text{ g of } ^{131}_{53}I$$

$^{131}_{53}I$ 20. g — 1 Half-life → $^{131}_{54}Xe$ 10. g, $^{131}_{53}I$ 10. g — 2 Half-lives → $^{131}_{54}Xe$ 15 g, $^{131}_{53}I$ 5.0 g — 3 Half-lives → $^{131}_{54}Xe$ 17.5 g, $^{131}_{53}I$ 2.5 g

A third half-life, or another 8.0 days, results in 2.5 g of the $^{131}_{53}I$ decaying to give $^{131}_{54}Xe$, which leaves 2.5 g of $^{131}_{53}I$ still capable of producing radiation. This information is summarized in Table 4.8.

**TABLE 4.8** Activity of an $^{131}_{53}I$ Sample with Time

| Time elapsed | 0 days | 8.0 days | 16 days | 24 days |
|---|---|---|---|---|
| Half-lives | 0 | 1 | 2 | 3 |
| $^{131}_{53}I$ remaining | 20. g | 10. g | 5.0 g | 2.5 g |
| $^{131}_{54}Xe$ produced | 0 g | 10. g | 15.0 g | 17.5 g |

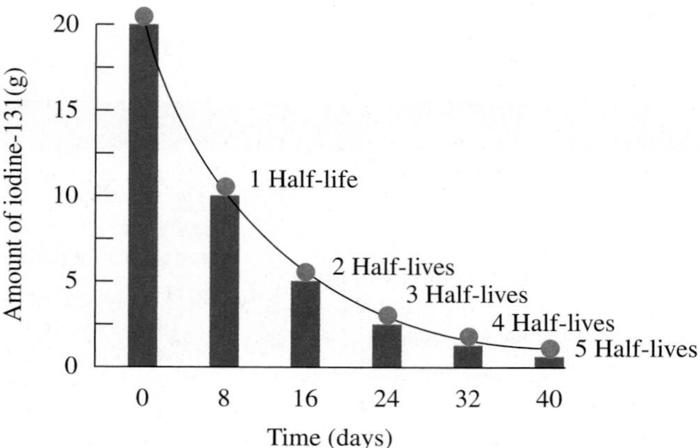


**FIGURE 4.4** The decay curve for iodine-131 shows that one-half of the radioactive sample decays and one-half remains radioactive after each half-life of 8 days.

**Q** How many grams of the 20.-g sample remain radioactive after 2 half-lives?

A **decay curve** is a diagram of the decay of a radioactive isotope. Figure 4.4 shows such a curve for the $^{131}_{53}I$ we have discussed.

CONCEPT CHECK 4.4

### Half-Lives

Iridium-192, which is used to treat cancer, has a half-life of 74 days. What happens after 74 days if the initial sample of Ir-192 has an activity of $8 \times 10^4$ Bq? Why?

ANSWER

In one half-life of iridium-192, or 74 days, half of the iridium-192 atoms will decay. Thus, after 74 days, the activity is half of the initial activity of $8 \times 10^4$ Bq, or $4 \times 10^4$ Bq.

SAMPLE PROBLEM 4.6

### Using Half-Lives of a Radioisotope

Phosphorus-32, a radioisotope used in the treatment of leukemia, has a half-life of 14 days. If a sample contains 8.0 g of phosphorus-32, how many grams of phosphorus-32 remain after 42 days?

SOLUTION

STEP 1 **Given** 8.0 g of $^{32}_{15}P$; 42 days; 14 days/half-life
**Need** g of $^{32}_{15}P$ remaining

STEP 2 **Plan**

42 days → Half-life → Number of half-lives

8.0 g of $^{32}_{15}P$ → Number of half-lives → g of $^{32}_{15}P$ remaining

STEP 3 **Equalities/Conversion Factors**

$$1 \text{ half-life} = 14 \text{ days}$$
$$\frac{14 \text{ days}}{1 \text{ half-life}} \text{ and } \frac{1 \text{ half-life}}{14 \text{ days}}$$

**STEP 4** **Set Up Problem** We can do this problem with two calculations. First, we determine the number of half-lives in the amount of time that has elapsed:

$$\text{Number of half-lives} = 42 \cancel{\text{days}} \times \frac{1 \text{ half-life}}{14 \cancel{\text{days}}} = 3 \text{ half-lives}$$

Now we determine how much of the sample decays in three half-lives and how many grams of the phosphorus remain:

$$8.0 \text{ g of } {}^{32}_{15}\text{P} \xrightarrow{\text{1 half-life}} 4.0 \text{ g of } {}^{32}_{15}\text{P} \xrightarrow{\text{1 half-life}} 2.0 \text{ g of } {}^{32}_{15}\text{P} \xrightarrow{\text{1 half-life}} 1.0 \text{ g of } {}^{32}_{15}\text{P}$$

STUDY CHECK

Iron-59 has a half-life of 44 days. If the laboratory received 8.0 g of iron-59, how many grams are still active after 176 days?

Naturally occurring isotopes of the elements are typically more stable and therefore usually have long half-lives, as shown in Table 4.9. They disintegrate slowly and produce radiation over a long period of time, even hundreds or millions of years. In contrast, many of the radioisotopes used in nuclear medicine are extremely unstable and have much shorter half-lives. They disintegrate rapidly and produce almost all their radiation in a short period of time. For example, technetium-99m emits half of its radiation in the first six hours. This means that a small amount of the radioisotope given to a patient is essentially gone within two days. The decay products of technetium-99m are totally eliminated by the body.

TUTORIAL
Radioactive Half-Lives

**TABLE 4.9** Half-Lives of Some Radioisotopes

| Element | Radioisotope | Half-Life |
|---|---|---|
| **Naturally Occurring Radioisotopes** | | |
| Carbon | ${}^{14}_{6}\text{C}$ | 5730 y |
| Potassium | ${}^{40}_{19}\text{K}$ | $1.3 \times 10^9$ y |
| Radium | ${}^{226}_{88}\text{Ra}$ | 1600 y |
| Uranium | ${}^{238}_{92}\text{U}$ | $4.5 \times 10^9$ y |
| **Some Medical Radioisotopes** | | |
| Chromium | ${}^{51}_{24}\text{Cr}$ | 28 d |
| Iodine | ${}^{131}_{53}\text{I}$ | 8 d |
| Iron | ${}^{59}_{26}\text{Fe}$ | 44 d |
| Technetium | ${}^{99m}_{43}\text{Tc}$ | 6.0 h |
| Iridium | ${}^{192}_{77}\text{Ir}$ | 74 d |

## Modeling Half-Lives

Obtain a piece of paper and a licorice stick or celery stalk. Draw a vertical and a horizontal axis on the paper. Label the vertical axis as radioactive atoms and the horizontal axis as minutes. Place the licorice stick or celery against the vertical axis and mark its height for zero minutes. In the next minute, cut the licorice stick or celery in two. (You can eat the half if you are hungry.) Place the shortened licorice stick or celery at 1 minute on the horizontal axis and mark its height. Every minute, cut the licorice stick or celery in half again and mark the shorter height at the corresponding time. Keep reducing the length by half until you cannot divide the licorice or celery in half any more. Connect the points you made for each minute. What does the curve look like? How does this curve represent the concept of a half-life for a radioisotope?

SAMPLE PROBLEM 4.7

### Dating Using Half-Lives

In Los Angeles, the remains of ancient animals have been unearthed from the La Brea Tar Pits. Suppose a bone sample from the tar pits is subjected to the carbon-14 dating method. How long ago did the animal live if the sample shows that two half-lives have passed?

SOLUTION

We can calculate the age of the bone sample by using the half-life of carbon-14 (5730 years):

$$2 \cancel{\text{half-lives}} \times \frac{5730 \text{ years}}{1 \cancel{\text{half-life}}} = 11\,500 \text{ years}$$

We would estimate that the animal lived 11 500 years ago, or about 9500 B.C.E.

STUDY CHECK

Suppose that a piece of wood found in a tomb had $\frac{1}{8}$ of its original carbon-14 activity. About how many years ago was the wood part of a living tree?

## ENVIRONMENTAL NOTE

### Dating Ancient Objects

Radiological dating is a technique used by geologists, archaeologists, and historians to determine the age of ancient objects. The age of an object derived from plants or animals (such as wood, fiber, natural pigments, bone, and cotton and woolen clothing) is determined by measuring the amount of carbon-14, a naturally occurring radioactive form of carbon. In 1960, Willard Libby received the Nobel Prize for his work developing carbon-14 dating techniques during the 1940s. Carbon-14 is produced in the upper atmosphere by the bombardment of $^{14}_{7}N$ by high-energy neutrons from cosmic rays.

$$^{1}_{0}n + {}^{14}_{7}N \longrightarrow {}^{14}_{6}C + {}^{1}_{1}H$$

Neutron from cosmic rays; Nitrogen in atmosphere; Radioactive carbon-14; Proton

The carbon-14 reacts with oxygen to form radioactive carbon dioxide, $^{14}_{6}CO_2$. Living plants continuously absorb carbon dioxide, which incorporates carbon-14 into the plant material. The uptake of carbon-14 stops when the plant dies.

$$^{14}_{6}C \longrightarrow {}^{14}_{7}N + {}^{0}_{-1}e$$

As the carbon-14 decays, the amount of radioactive carbon-14 in the plant material steadily decreases. In a process called **carbon dating**, scientists use the half-life of carbon-14 (5730 years) to calculate the length of time since the plant died. As the plant material ages, the radioactive carbon-14 decays so that the amount of radioactive carbon-14 that remains is less than in the original living plant. For example, a wooden beam found in an ancient Indian dwelling might have one-half of the carbon-14 found in living plants. Because one half-life of carbon-14 is 5730 years, the dwelling was constructed about 5730 years ago. Carbon-14 dating was used to determine that the Dead Sea Scrolls are about 2000 years old.

A radiological dating method used for determining the age of much older items is based on the radioisotope uranium-238, which decays through a series of reactions to lead-206. The uranium-238 isotope has an incredibly long half-life, about $4 \times 10^9$ (4 billion) years. Measurements of the amounts of uranium-238 and lead-206 enable geologists to determine the age of rock samples. The older rocks will have a higher percentage of lead-206 because more of the uranium-238 has decayed. The age of rocks brought back from the moon by the Apollo missions, for example, was determined using uranium-238. They were found to be about $4 \times 10^9$ years old, approximately the same age calculated for Earth.

## QUESTIONS AND PROBLEMS

### Half-Life of a Radioisotope

4.29 What is meant by the term *half-life*?

**4.30** Why are radioisotopes with short half-lives used for diagnosis in nuclear medicine?

4.31 Technetium-99m is an ideal radioisotope for scanning organs because it has a half-life of 6.0 h and is a pure gamma emitter. Suppose that 80.0 mg were prepared in the technetium generator this morning. How many milligrams would remain after the following intervals?
**a.** one half-life **b.** two half-lives
**c.** 18 h **d.** 24 h

**4.32** A sample of sodium-24 with an activity of 12 mCi is used to study the rate of blood flow in the circulatory system. If sodium-24 has a half-life of 15 h, what is the activity of the sodium after 2.5 days?

4.33 Strontium-85, used for bone scans, has a half-life of 65 days. How long will it take for the radiation level of strontium-85 to drop to one-fourth of its original level? To one-eighth?

**4.34** Fluorine-18, which has a half-life of 110 min, is used in PET scans. (See section 4.5.) If 100 mg of fluorine-18 is shipped at 8 A.M., how many milligrams of the radioisotope are still active if the sample arrives at the radiology laboratory at 1:30 P.M.?

## 4.5 Medical Applications Using Radioactivity

LEARNING GOAL

Describe the use of radioisotopes in medicine.

To determine the condition of an organ in the body, a radiologist may give a patient a radioisotope that concentrates in that organ. The cells in the body do not differentiate between a nonradioactive atom and a radioactive one. However, radioactive atoms can be detected because they emit radiation. Some radioisotopes used in nuclear medicine are listed in Table 4.10.

**TABLE 4.10 Medical Applications of Radioisotopes**

| Isotope | Half-Life | Medical Application |
|---|---|---|
| Ce-141 | 32.5 days | Gastrointestinal tract diagnosis; measuring blood flow to the heart |
| Ga-67 | 78 h | Abdominal imaging; tumor detection |
| Ga-68 | 68 min | Detection of pancreatic cancer |
| P-32 | 4.3 days | Treatment of leukemia, excess red blood cells, pancreatic cancer |
| I-125 | 60 days | Treatment of brain cancer |
| I-131 | 8 days | Imaging of thyroid; treatment of Graves' disease, goiter, and hyperthyroidism; treatment of thyroid and prostate cancer |
| Sr-85 | 65 days | Detection of bone lesions; brain scans |
| Tc-99m | 6 h | Imaging of skeleton, heart muscle, brain, liver, heart, lungs, bone, spleen, kidney, and thyroid; most widely used radioisotope in nuclear medicine |

## Scans with Radioisotopes

After a patient receives a radioisotope, the radiologist determines the level and location of radioactivity emitted by the radioisotope. An apparatus called a *scanner* is used to produce an image of the organ. The scanner moves slowly across the patient's body above the region where the organ containing the radioisotope is located. The gamma rays emitted from the radioisotope in the organ can be used to expose a photographic plate, producing a scan of the organ. On a scan, an area of decreased or increased radiation can indicate conditions such as a disease of the organ, a tumor, a blood clot, or edema.

A common method of determining thyroid function is the use of *radioactive iodine uptake* (RAIU). Taken orally, the radioisotope iodine-131 mixes with the iodine already present in the thyroid. Twenty-four hours later, the amount of iodine taken up by the thyroid is determined. A detection tube held up to the area of the thyroid gland detects the radiation coming from the iodine-131 that has located there. (See Figure 4.5.)

(a)

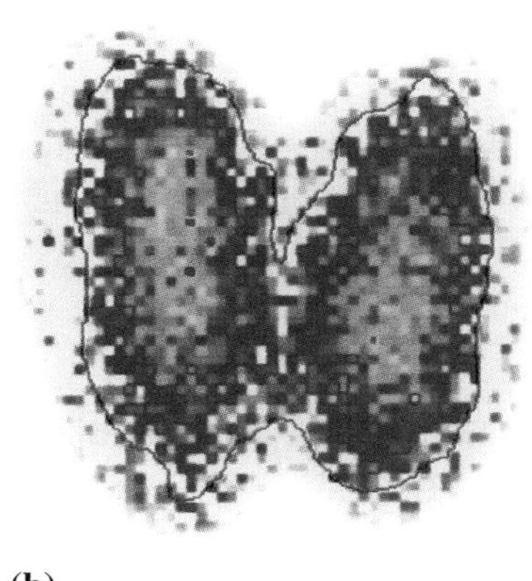

(b)

**FIGURE 4.5** **(a)** A scanner is used to detect radiation from a radioisotope that has accumulated in an organ. **(b)** A scan of the thyroid shows the accumulation of radioactive iodine-131 in the thyroid.

**Q** What type of radiation would move through body tissues to create a scan?

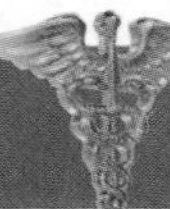

## HEALTH NOTE

### Radiation Doses in Diagnostic and Therapeutic Procedures

We can compare the levels of radiation exposure commonly used during diagnostic and therapeutic procedures in nuclear medicine. In diagnostic procedures, the radiologist uses the minimum amount of radioactive isotope needed to evaluate the condition of an organ or tissue. The doses used in radiation therapy are much greater than those used for diagnostic procedures. For example, a therapeutic dose would be used to destroy the cells in a malignant tumor. Although there will be some damage to surrounding tissue, the healthy cells are more resistant to radiation and can repair themselves. (See Table 4.11.)

**TABLE 4.11** Radiation Doses Used for Diagnostic and Therapeutic Procedures

| Organ/Condition | Dose (rem) |
|---|---|
| **Diagnostic** | |
| Liver | 0.3 |
| Thyroid | 50.0 |
| Lung | 2.0 |
| **Therapeutic** | |
| Lymphoma | 4500 |
| Skin cancer | 5000–6000 |
| Lung cancer | 6000 |
| Brain tumor | 6000–7000 |

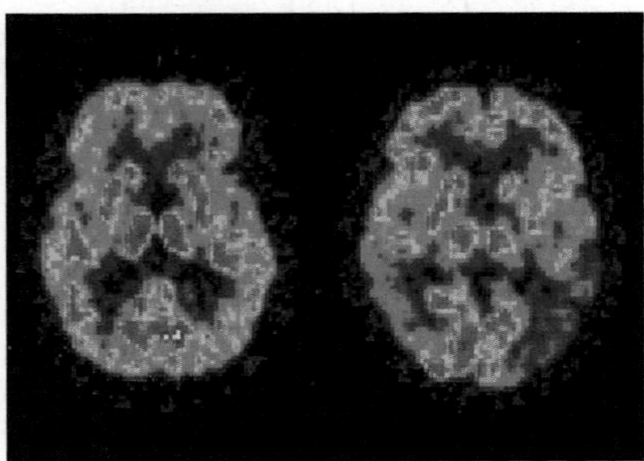

**FIGURE 4.6** These PET scans of the brain show a normal brain on the left and a brain affected by Alzheimer's disease on the right.

**Q** When positrons collide with electrons, what type of radiation is produced that gives an image of an organ?

A patient with a hyperactive thyroid will have a higher than normal level of radioactive iodine, whereas a patient with a hypoactive thyroid will record low values. If the patient has hyperthyroidism, treatment is begun to lower the activity of the thyroid. One treatment involves giving the patient a therapeutic dosage of radioactive iodine, which has a higher radiation count than the diagnostic dose. The radioactive iodine goes to the thyroid, where its radiation destroys some of the thyroid cells. The thyroid produces less thyroid hormone, bringing the hyperthyroid condition under control.

## Positron Emission Tomography (PET)

Positron emitters with short half-lives such as carbon-11, oxygen-15, nitrogen-13, and fluorine-18 are used in an imaging method called *positron emission tomography* (PET). A positron-emitting isotope such as fluorine-18 combined with substances in the body such as glucose is used to study brain function, metabolism, and blood flow.

$$^{18}_{9}\text{F} \longrightarrow {}^{18}_{8}\text{O} + {}^{0}_{+1}e$$

As positrons are emitted, they combine with electrons to produce gamma rays that are detected by computerized equipment to create a three-dimensional image of the organ. (See Figure 4.6.)

SAMPLE PROBLEM 4.8

### Medical Application of Radioactivity

In the determination of thyroid function, a patient receives an oral dose of sodium iodide (NaI) that contains 10 $\mu$Ci of iodine-131, which is a beta emitter. Write the nuclear equation for the beta decay of iodine-131.

SOLUTION

We can write the incomplete nuclear equation starting with iodine-131, which has atomic number 53:

$$^{131}_{53}\text{I} \longrightarrow ? + {}^{0}_{-1}e$$

In beta decay, the mass number (131) does not change, but the atomic number of the new nucleus increases by 1. The new atomic number is 54, which is xenon (Xe):

$$^{131}_{53}\text{I} \longrightarrow {}^{131}_{54}\text{Xe} + {}^{0}_{-1}e$$

STUDY CHECK

In an experimental treatment, a patient is given boron-10, which is taken up by malignant tumors. When bombarded with neutrons, boron-10 decays by emitting alpha particles that destroy the surrounding tumor cells. Write the equation for the nuclear reaction for this experimental procedure.

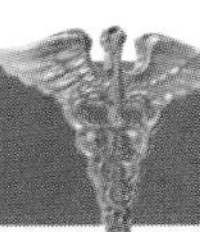

# HEALTH NOTE

## Other Imaging Methods

### Computed Tomography (CT)

Another imaging method used to detect changes within the body is *computed tomography* (CT). A computer monitors the degree of absorption of 30 000 X-ray beams directed at the brain at successive layers. Based on the densities of the tissues and fluids in the brain, the differences in absorption provide a series of images of the brain. This technique is successful in the identification of brain hemorrhages, tumors, and atrophy. (See Figure 4.7.)

### Magnetic Resonance Imaging (MRI)

*Magnetic resonance imaging* (MRI) is a powerful imaging technique that does not involve X-ray radiation. It is the least invasive imaging method available. MRI is based on the absorption of energy when the protons in hydrogen atoms are excited by a strong magnetic field. Hydrogen atoms make up 63% of all the atoms in the body. In the hydrogen nuclei, the protons act like tiny bar magnets. With no external field, the protons have random orientations. However, when placed within a large magnet, the protons align with the magnetic field. A proton aligned with the field has a lower energy than one that is aligned against the field. As the MRI scan proceeds, radiofrequency pulses of energy are applied. When a nucleus absorbs certain energy, its proton "flips" and becomes aligned against the field. Because hydrogen atoms in the body are in different chemical environments, energies of different frequencies are absorbed. The energies absorbed are calculated and converted to color images of the body. MRI is particularly useful in obtaining images of soft tissues because these tissues contain large amounts of water. (See Figure 4.8.)

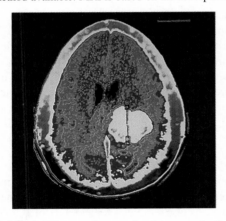

**FIGURE 4.7** A CT scan shows a brain tumor (yellow area) in the center of the right side of the brain.

Q What is the type of radiation used to give a CT scan?

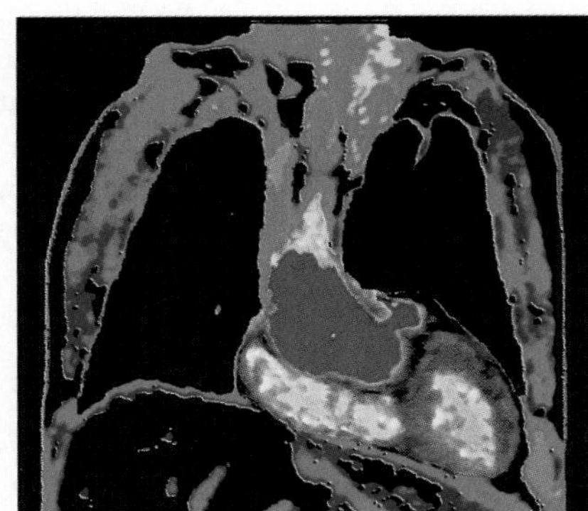

**FIGURE 4.8** An MRI scan of the heart and lungs, with the left ventricle shown in red.

Q What is the source of energy in an MRI?

# QUESTIONS AND PROBLEMS

## Medical Applications Using Radioactivity

4.35 Bone and bony structures contain calcium and phosphorus.

**a.** Why would the radioisotopes of calcium-47 and phosphorus-32 be used in the diagnosis and treatment of bone diseases?

**b.** The radioisotope strontium-89, a beta emitter, is used to treat bone cancer. Write the nuclear equation and explain why a strontium radioisotope would be used to treat bone cancer.

**4.36 a.** Technetium-99m emits only gamma radiation. Why would this type of radiation be used in diagnostic imaging rather than an isotope that also emits beta or alpha radiation?

**b.** A patient with polycythemia vera (excess production of red blood cells) receives radioactive phosphorus-32. Why would this treatment reduce the production of red blood cells in the bone marrow of the patient?

4.37 In a diagnostic test for leukemia, a patient receives 4.0 mL of a solution containing selenium-75. If the activity of the selenium-75 is 45 $\mu$Ci/mL, what is the dose received by the patient?

**4.38** A vial contains radioactive iodine-131 with an activity of 2.0 mCi per milliliter. If the thyroid test requires 3.0 mCi in an "atomic cocktail," how many milliliters are used to prepare the iodine-131 solution?

# 4.6 Nuclear Fission and Fusion

**LEARNING GOAL**

Describe the processes of nuclear fission and fusion.

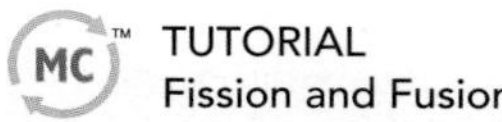

TUTORIAL
Fission and Fusion

During the 1930s, scientists bombarding uranium-235 with neutrons discovered that the U-235 nucleus splits into two medium-weight nuclei and produces a great amount of energy. This was the discovery of nuclear **fission**. The energy generated by splitting the atom was called *atomic* energy. A typical equation for nuclear fission is

$$^{1}_{0}n + ^{235}_{92}\text{U} \longrightarrow ^{91}_{36}\text{Kr} + ^{142}_{56}\text{Ba} + 3\,^{1}_{0}n + \text{energy}$$

If we could weigh these products with great accuracy, we would find that their total mass is slightly less than the mass of the starting materials. The missing mass has been converted into energy, consistent with the famous equation derived by Albert Einstein:

$$E = mc^2$$

where $E$ is the energy released, $m$ is the mass lost, and $c$ is the speed of light, $3 \times 10^8$ m/s. Even though the mass loss is very small, when it is multiplied by the speed of light squared the result is a large value for the energy released. The fission of 1 g of uranium-235 produces about as much energy as the burning of 3 tons of coal.

## Chain Reaction

Fission begins when a neutron collides with the nucleus of a uranium atom. The resulting nucleus is unstable and splits into smaller nuclei. This fission process also releases several neutrons and large amounts of gamma radiation and energy. The neutrons emitted have high energies and bombard more uranium-235 nuclei. As fission continues, there is a rapid increase in the number of high-energy neutrons capable of splitting more uranium atoms, a process called a **chain reaction**. To sustain a nuclear chain reaction, sufficient quantities of uranium-235 must be brought together to provide a critical mass in which almost all the neutrons immediately collide with more uranium-235 nuclei. So much heat and energy are released that an atomic explosion can occur. (See Figure 4.9.)

## Nuclear Fusion

In **fusion**, two small nuclei such as those in hydrogen combine to form a larger nucleus. Mass is lost, and a tremendous amount of energy is released, even more than the energy released from nuclear fission. However, a fusion reaction requires a temperature of 100 000 000 °C to overcome the repulsion of the hydrogen nuclei and cause them to undergo fusion. Fusion reactions occur continuously in the sun and other stars, providing us with heat and light. The huge amounts of energy produced by our sun come from the fusion of $6 \times 10^{11}$ kg of hydrogen every second. The following fusion reaction involves the combination of two isotopes of hydrogen.

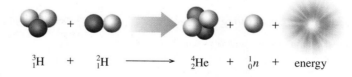

$$^{3}_{1}\text{H} + ^{2}_{1}\text{H} \longrightarrow ^{4}_{2}\text{He} + ^{1}_{0}n + \text{energy}$$

Scientists expect less radioactive waste with shorter half-lives from fusion reactors. However, fusion is still in the experimental stage because the extremely high temperatures needed have been difficult to reach and even more difficult to maintain. Research groups around the world are attempting to develop the technology needed to make the harnessing of the fusion reaction for energy a reality in our lifetime.

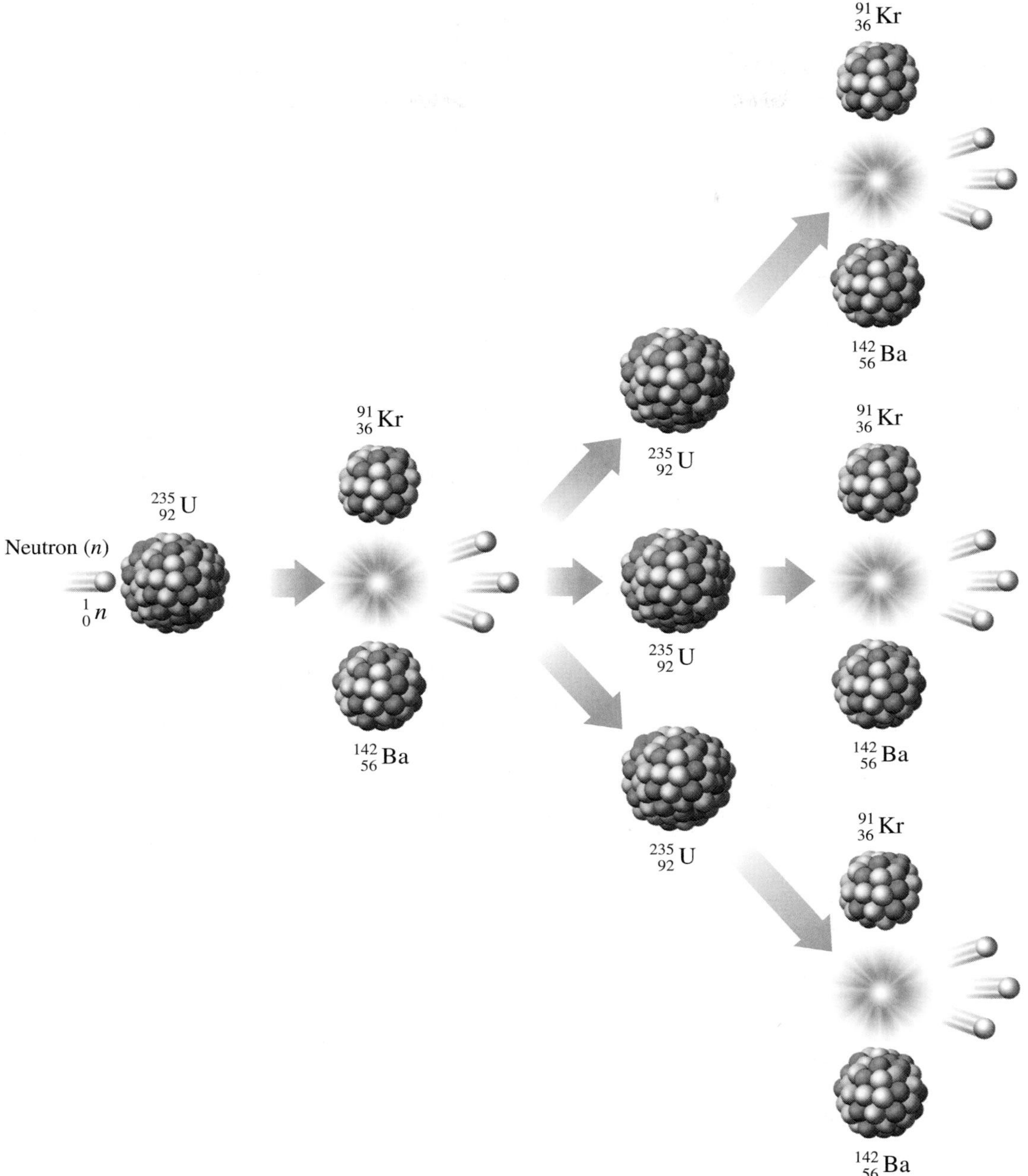


**FIGURE 4.9** In a nuclear chain reaction, the fission of each uranium-235 atom produces three neutrons that cause the nuclear fission of more and more uranium-235 atoms.

Q Why is the fission of uranium-235 called a chain reaction?

CONCEPT CHECK 4.5

### Identifying Fission and Fusion

Classify the following as pertaining to nuclear fission, nuclear fusion, or both:

**a.** Small nuclei combine to form larger nuclei.
**b.** Large amounts of energy are released.
**c.** Extraordinarily high temperatures are needed for reaction.

ANSWER

**a.** When small nuclei are combined, the process is fusion.
**b.** Large amounts of energy are generated in both the fusion and fission processes.
**c.** An extremely high temperature is required for fusion.

## GREEN CHEMISTRY NOTE

### Nuclear Power Plants

In a nuclear power plant, the quantity of uranium-235 is held below a critical mass so that it cannot sustain a chain reaction. The fission reactions are slowed by placing control rods, which absorb some of the fast-moving neutrons, among the uranium samples. In this way, less fission occurs, and there is a slower, controlled production of energy. The heat from the controlled fission is used to produce steam. The steam drives a generator, which produces electricity. Approximately 10% of the electrical energy produced in the United States is generated in nuclear power plants.

Although nuclear power plants help meet some of our energy needs, there are some problems. One of the most serious is the production of radioactive by-products that have long half-lives. It is essential that these waste products be stored safely in a place where they do not contaminate the environment. Early in 1990, the Environmental Protection Agency gave its approval for the storage of radioactive hazardous wastes in chambers 2150 ft underground. In 1998, the Waste Isolation Pilot Plant (WIPP) repository site in New Mexico was ready to receive plutonium waste from former U.S. bomb factories. Although authorities claim the caverns are safe, some people are concerned with the safe transport of the radioactive waste by trucks on the highways.

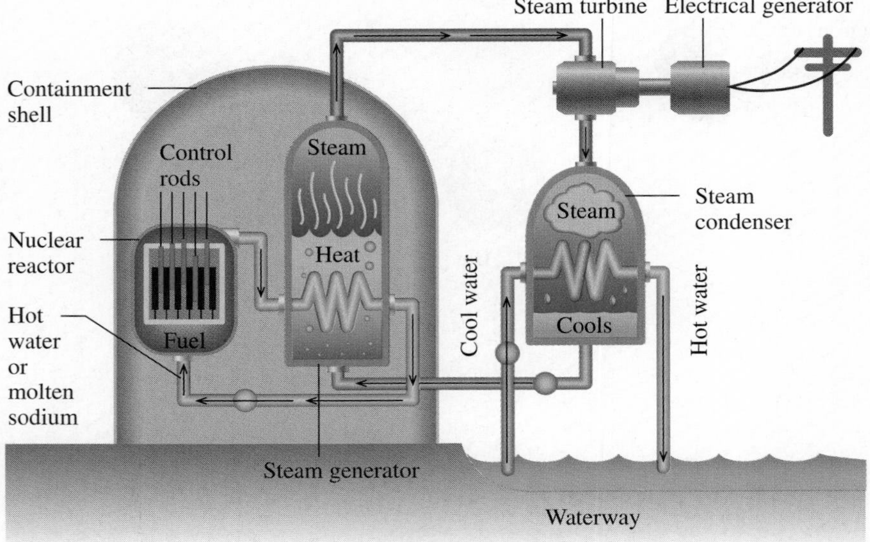


## QUESTIONS AND PROBLEMS

### Nuclear Fission and Fusion

**4.39** What is nuclear fission?

**4.40** How does a chain reaction occur in nuclear fission?

**4.41** Complete the following fission reaction:

$$^{235}_{92}\text{U} + ^{1}_{0}n \longrightarrow ^{131}_{50}\text{Sn} + ? + 2\,^{1}_{0}n + \text{energy}$$

**4.42** In another fission reaction, uranium-235 bombarded with a neutron produces strontium-94, another small nucleus, and 3 neutrons. Write the complete equation for the fission reaction.

**4.43** Indicate whether each of the following is characteristic of the fission or fusion process or both:

**a.** Neutrons bombard a nucleus.
**b.** The nuclear process occurring in the sun.
**c.** A large nucleus splits into smaller nuclei.
**d.** Small nuclei combine to form larger nuclei.

**4.44** Indicate whether each of the following is characteristic of the fission or fusion process or both:

**a.** Extremely high temperatures are required to initiate the reaction.
**b.** Less radioactive waste is produced.
**c.** Hydrogen nuclei are the reactants.
**d.** Large amounts of energy are released when the nuclear reaction occurs.

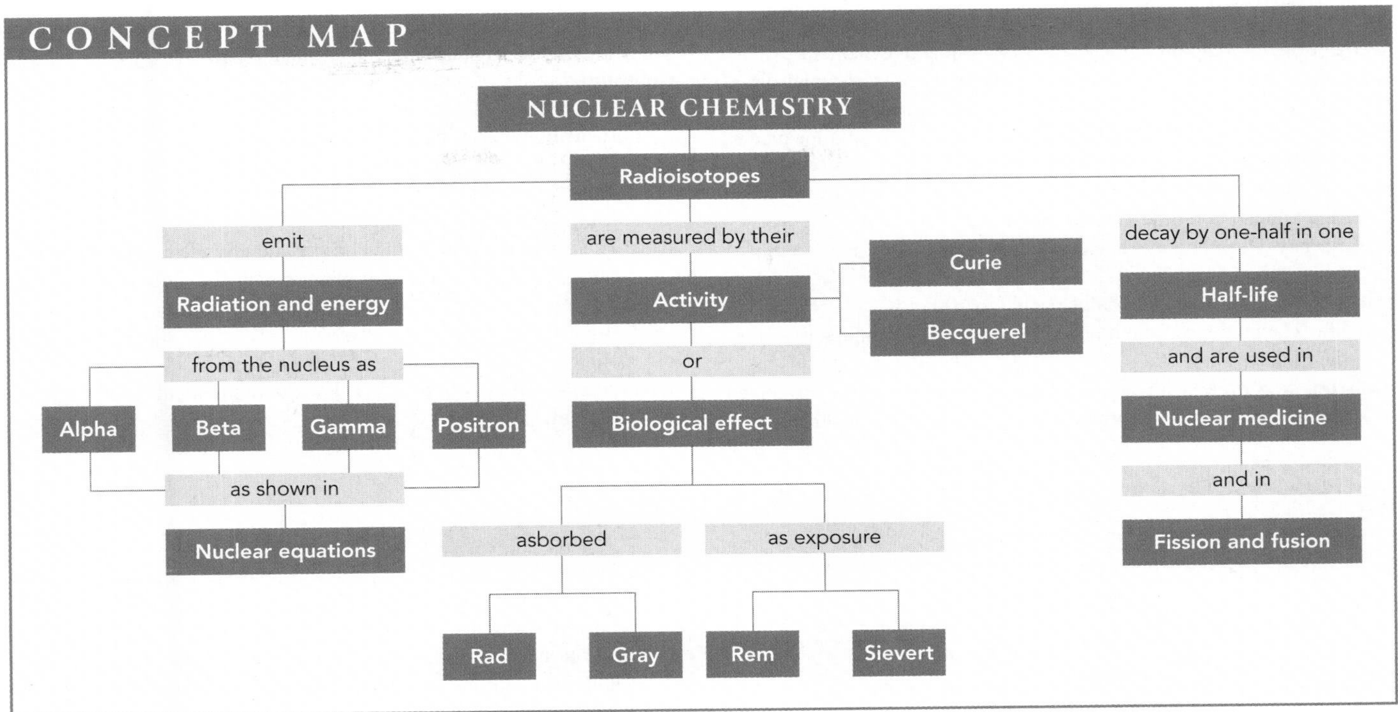


## CHAPTER REVIEW

### 4.1 Natural Radioactivity

**LEARNING GOAL:** *Describe alpha, beta, positron, and gamma radiation.*

Radioactive isotopes have unstable nuclei that break down (decay), spontaneously emitting alpha ($\alpha$), beta ($\beta$), positron ($\beta$), and gamma ($\gamma$) radiation. Because radiation can damage the cells in the body, proper protection must be used: shielding, limiting the time of exposure, and distance.

### 4.2 Nuclear Reactions

**LEARNING GOAL:** *Write an equation showing mass numbers and atomic numbers for radioactive decay.*

A balanced equation is used to represent the changes that take place in the nuclei of the reactants and products. The new isotopes and the type of radiation emitted can be determined from the symbols that show the mass numbers and atomic numbers of the isotopes in the nuclear reaction. A radioisotope is produced artificially when a nonradioactive isotope is bombarded by a small particle. Many radioactive isotopes used in nuclear medicine are produced in this way.

### 4.3 Radiation Measurement

**LEARNING GOAL:** *Describe the detection and measurement of radiation.*

In a Geiger counter, radiation produces charged particles in the gas contained in the tube, which generates an electrical current. The curie (Ci) measures the number of nuclear transformations of a radioactive sample. Activity is also measured in becquerel (Bq) units. The amount of radiation absorbed by a substance is measured in rads or the gray (Gy). The rem and the sievert (Sv) are units used to determine the biological damage from the different types of radiation.

### 4.4 Half-Life of a Radioisotope

**LEARNING GOAL:** *Given the half-life of a radioisotope, calculate the amount of radioisotope remaining after one or more half-lives.*

Every radioisotope has its own rate of emitting radiation. The time it takes for one-half of a radioactive sample to decay is called its half-life. For many medical radioisotopes, such as Tc-99m and I-131, half-lives are short. For other isotopes, usually naturally occurring ones such as C-14, Ra-226, and U-238, half-lives are extremely long.

### 4.5 Medical Applications Using Radioactivity

**LEARNING GOAL:** *Describe the use of radioisotopes in medicine.*

In nuclear medicine, radioisotopes that go to specific sites in the body are given to the patient. By detecting the radiation they emit, an evaluation can be made about the location and extent of an injury, disease, tumor, or the level of function of a particular organ. Higher levels of radiation are used to treat or destroy tumors.

### 4.6 Nuclear Fission and Fusion

**LEARNING GOAL:** *Describe the processes of nuclear fission and fusion.*

In fission, a large nucleus breaks apart into smaller pieces, releasing one or more types of radiation and a great amount of energy. In fusion, small nuclei combine to form a larger nucleus while great amounts of energy are released.

## KEY TERMS

**alpha particle** A nuclear particle identical to a helium nucleus with symbol $\alpha$ or ${}^{4}_{2}He$.

**becquerel (Bq)** A unit of activity of a radioactive sample equal to one disintegration per second.

**beta particle** A particle identical to an electron with symbol $\beta$ or ${}^{0}_{-1}e$ that forms in the nucleus when a neutron changes to a proton and an electron.

**carbon dating** A technique used to date ancient specimens that contain carbon. The age is determined by the amount of active carbon-14 that remains in the samples.

**chain reaction** A fission reaction that will continue once it has been initiated by a high-energy neutron bombarding a heavy nucleus such as uranium-235.

**curie (Ci)** A unit of radiation equal to $3.7 \times 10^{10}$ disintegrations/s.

**decay curve** A diagram of the decay of a radioactive element.

**equivalent dose** The measure of biological damage from an absorbed dose that has been adjusted for the type of radiation.

**fission** A process in which large nuclei are split into smaller pieces, releasing large amounts of energy.

**fusion** A reaction in which large amounts of energy are released when small nuclei combine to form larger nuclei.

**gamma ray** High-energy radiation (with symbol ${}^{0}_{0}\gamma$) that is emitted by an unstable nucleus.

**gray (Gy)** A unit of absorbed dose equal to 100 rads.

**half-life** The length of time it takes for one-half of a radioactive sample to decay.

**positron** A particle with no mass and a positive charge produced when a proton is transformed into a neutron and a positron.

**rad (radiation absorbed dose)** A measure of an amount of radiation absorbed by the body.

**radiation** Energy or particles released by radioactive atoms.

**radioactive decay** The process by which an unstable nucleus breaks down and releases high-energy radiation.

**rem (radiation equivalent in humans)** A measure of the biological damage caused by the various kinds of radiation (rad $\times$ radiation biological factor).

**scan** The image of a site in the body created by the detection of radiation from radioactive isotopes that have accumulated in that site.

**shielding** Materials used to provide protection from radioactive sources.

**sievert (Sv)** A unit of biological damage (equivalent dose) equal to 100 rems.

## UNDERSTANDING THE CONCEPTS

4.45 Consider the following nucleus of a radioactive isotope:

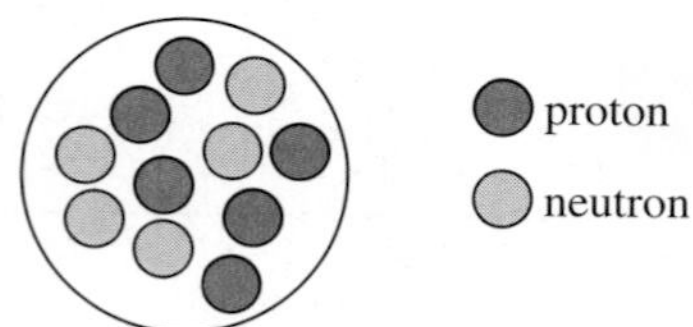


a. What is the nuclear symbol for this isotope?

b. If this isotope decays by emitting a positron, what does the resulting nucleus look like?

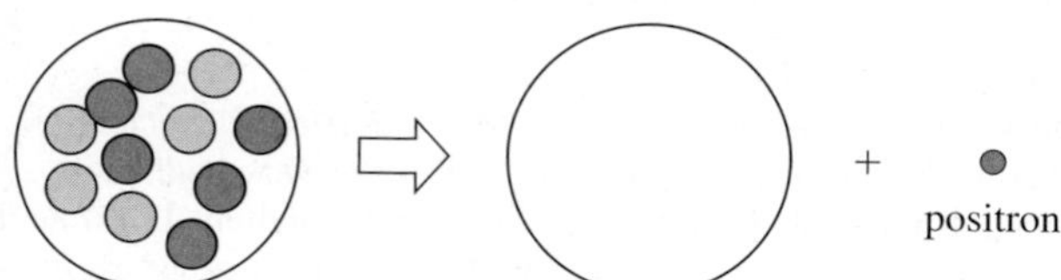


4.46 Sketch the nucleus that emits a beta particle to form the following nucleus:

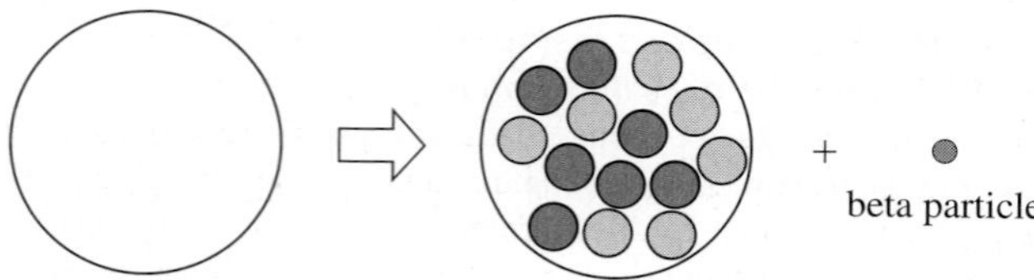


4.47 Sketch the nucleus of the atom to complete the following:

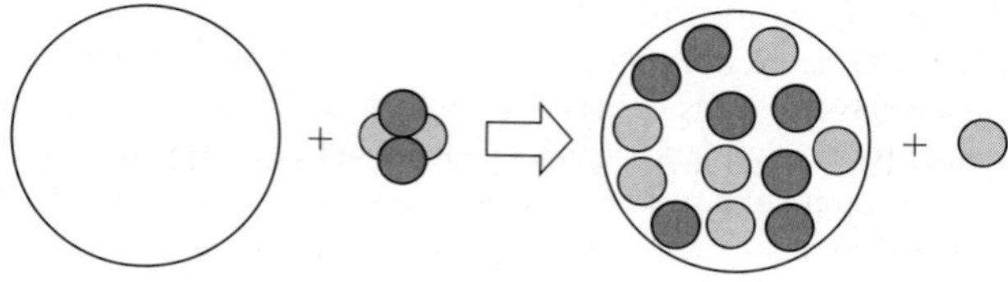


4.48 Complete the following by drawing the nucleus of the atom produced:

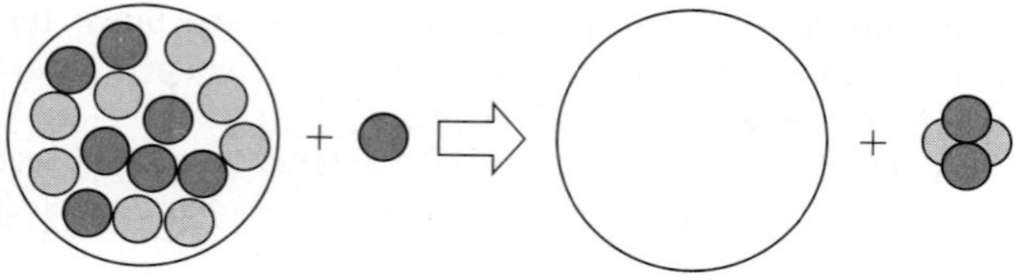


4.49 Carbon dating of small bits of charcoal used in cave paintings has determined that some of the paintings are from 10 000 to 30 000 years old. Carbon-14 has a half-life of 5730 years. In a 1 $\mu g$ sample of carbon from a live tree, the activity of ${}^{14}_{6}C$ is 6.4 $\mu Ci$. If researchers determine that 1 $\mu g$ of charcoal from a prehistoric cave painting in France has an activity of 0.80 $\mu Ci$, what is the age of the painting?

4.50 Using the decay curve for ${}^{131}_{53}I$, determine the following:

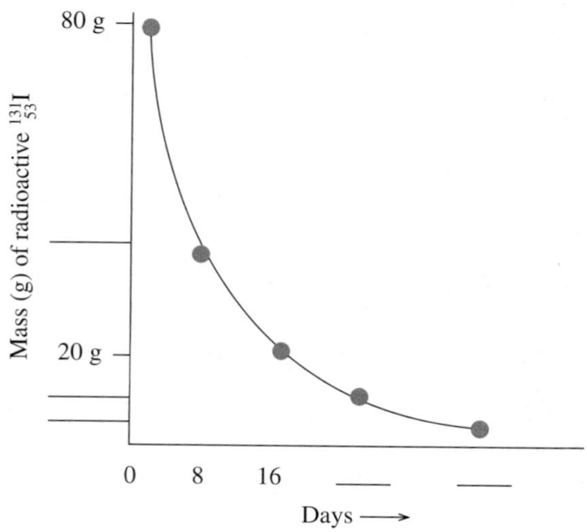


a. the values for the mass of radioactive ${}^{131}_{53}I$ on the vertical axis

b. the number of days on the horizontal axis

c. the half-life in days of ${}^{131}_{53}I$

## ADDITIONAL QUESTIONS AND PROBLEMS

*For instructor-assigned homework, go to* ***www.masteringchemistry.com.***

**4.51** Give the number of protons and number of neutrons in the nucleus of each the following:
**a.** sodium-25 **b.** nickel-61
**c.** rubidium-84 **d.** silver-110

**4.52** Give the number of protons, neutrons, and electrons in atoms of the following isotopes:
**a.** boron-10 **b.** zinc-72
**c.** iron-59 **d.** gold-198

**4.53** Describe alpha, beta, and gamma radiation in terms of the following:
**a.** type of radiation **b.** symbols

**4.54** Describe alpha, beta, and gamma radiation in terms of the following:
**a.** depth of tissue penetration
**b.** type of shielding needed for protection

**4.55** Identify each of the following as alpha decay, beta decay, positron emission, or gamma radiation:
**a.** ${}^{27m}_{13}\text{Al} \longrightarrow {}^{27}_{13}\text{Al} + {}^{0}_{0}\gamma$
**b.** ${}^{8}_{5}\text{B} \longrightarrow {}^{8}_{4}\text{Be} + {}^{0}_{+1}e$
**c.** ${}^{220}_{86}\text{Rn} \longrightarrow {}^{216}_{84}\text{Po} + {}^{4}_{2}\text{He}$

**4.56** Identify each of the following as alpha decay, beta decay, positron emission, or gamma radiation:
**a.** ${}^{127}_{55}\text{Cs} \longrightarrow {}^{127}_{54}\text{Xe} + {}^{0}_{+1}e$
**b.** ${}^{90}_{38}\text{Sr} \longrightarrow {}^{90}_{39}\text{Y} + {}^{0}_{-1}e$
**c.** ${}^{218}_{85}\text{At} \longrightarrow {}^{214}_{83}\text{Bi} + {}^{4}_{2}\text{He}$

**4.57** Write a balanced nuclear equation for each of the following:
**a.** Th-225 ($\alpha$ decay)
**b.** Bi-210 ($\alpha$ decay)
**c.** cesium-137 ($\beta$ decay)
**d.** tin-126 ($\beta$ decay)
**e.** nitrogen-13 ($\beta^+$ emission)

**4.58** Write a balanced nuclear equation for each of the following:
**a.** potassium-40 ($\beta$ decay)
**b.** sulfur-35 ($\beta$ decay)
**c.** platinum-190 ($\alpha$ decay)
**d.** Ra-210 ($\alpha$ decay)
**e.** In-113m ($\gamma$ emission)

**4.59** Complete each of the following nuclear equations:
**a.** ${}^{14}_{7}\text{N} + {}^{4}_{2}\text{He} \longrightarrow ? + {}^{1}_{1}\text{H}$
**b.** ${}^{27}_{13}\text{Al} + {}^{4}_{2}\text{He} \longrightarrow {}^{30}_{14}\text{Si} + ?$
**c.** ${}^{235}_{92}\text{U} + {}^{1}_{0}n \longrightarrow {}^{90}_{38}\text{Sr} + 3{}^{1}_{0}n + ?$

**4.60** Complete each of the following nuclear equations:
**a.** ${}^{59}_{27}\text{Co} + ? \longrightarrow {}^{56}_{25}\text{Mn} + {}^{4}_{2}\text{He}$
**b.** $? \longrightarrow {}^{14}_{7}\text{N} + {}^{0}_{-1}e$
**c.** ${}^{76}_{36}\text{Kr} + {}^{0}_{-1}e \longrightarrow ?$

**4.61** Write the symbols and a balanced nuclear equation for the following:
**a.** When two oxygen-16 atoms collide, one of the products is an alpha particle.
**b.** When californium-249 is bombarded by oxygen-18, a new isotope and four neutrons are produced.
**c.** Radon-222 undergoes alpha decay.
**d.** The particle from **c.** undergoes alpha decay.

**4.62** Write the symbols and a balanced nuclear equation for the following:
**a.** Polonium-210 decays to give lead-206.
**b.** Bismuth-211 decays by emitting an alpha particle.
**c.** The product from **b.** emits a beta particle.
**d.** When an alpha particle bombards aluminum-27, one product is silicon-30.

**4.63** If the amount of radioactive phosphorus-32 in a sample decreases from 1.2 g to 0.30 g in 28 d, what is the half-life of phosphorus-32?

**4.64** If the amount of radioactive iodine-123 in a sample decreases from 0.4 g to 0.1 g in 26.2 h, what is the half-life of iodine-123?

**4.65** Iodine-131, a beta emitter, has a half-life of 8.0 d.
**a.** Write the nuclear equation for the beta decay of iodine-131.
**b.** How many grams of a 12.0-g sample of iodine-131 would remain after 40 d?
**c.** How many days have passed if 48 g of iodine-131 decayed to 3.0 g of iodine-131?

**4.66** Cesium-137, a beta emitter, has a half-life of 30 y.
**a.** Write the nuclear equation for the beta decay of cesium-137.
**b.** How many grams of a 16-g sample of cesium-137 would remain after 90 y?
**c.** How many years will be needed for 28 g of cesium-137 to decay to 3.5 g of cesium-137?

**4.67** A nurse was accidentally exposed to potassium-42 while doing some brain scans for possible tumors. The error was not discovered until 36 h later when the activity of the potassium-42 sample was 2.0 $\mu$Ci. If potassium-42 has a half-life of 12 h, what was the activity of the sample at the time the nurse was exposed?

**4.68** A wooden object from the site of an ancient temple has a carbon-14 activity of 10 counts per minute compared with a reference piece of wood cut today that has an activity of 40 counts per minute. If the half-life for carbon-14 is 5730 y, what is the age of the ancient wood object?

**4.69** A 120-mg sample of technetium-99m is used for a diagnostic test. If technetium-99m has a half-life of 6.0 h, how much of the technetium-99m sample remains 24 h after the test?

**4.70** The half-life of oxygen-15 is 124 s. If a sample of oxygen-15 has an activity of 4000 Bq, how many minutes will elapse before it reaches an activity of 500 Bq?

**4.71** What is the purpose of irradiating meats, fruits, and vegetables?

**4.72** The irradiation of foods was approved in the United States during the 1980s.
**a.** Why have we not seen many irradiated products in our markets?
**b.** Would you buy foods that have been irradiated? Why or why not?

**4.73** What is the difference between fission and fusion?

**4.74 a.** What are the products in the fission of uranium-235 that make possible a nuclear chain reaction?
**b.** What is the purpose of placing control rods among uranium samples in a nuclear reactor?

**4.75** Where does fusion occur naturally?

**4.76** Why are scientists continuing to try to build a fusion reactor even though the high temperatures needed have been difficult to reach and maintain?

# CHALLENGE QUESTIONS

**4.77** Identify each of the following nuclear reactions as alpha decay, beta decay, positron emission, or gamma radiation:

**a.** ${}^{27}_{13}\text{Al} \longrightarrow {}^{27}_{13}\text{Al} + {}^{0}_{0}\gamma$

**b.** ${}^{8}_{5}\text{B} \longrightarrow {}^{8}_{4}\text{Be} + {}^{0}_{+1}e$

**c.** ${}^{90}_{38}\text{Sr} \longrightarrow {}^{90}_{39}\text{Y} + {}^{0}_{-1}e$

**d.** ${}^{218}_{85}\text{At} \longrightarrow {}^{214}_{83}\text{Bi} + {}^{4}_{2}\text{He}$

**4.78** Complete and balance each of the following nuclear equations:

**a.** ${}^{23m}_{12}\text{Mg} \longrightarrow \_\_\_ + {}^{0}_{0}\gamma$

**b.** ${}^{61}_{30}\text{Zn} \longrightarrow {}^{61}_{29}\text{Cu} + \_\_\_$

**c.** ${}^{241}_{95}\text{Am} + {}^{4}_{2}\text{He} \longrightarrow \_\_\_ + 2{}^{1}_{0}n$

**d.** ${}^{126}_{50}\text{Sn} \longrightarrow \_\_\_ + {}^{0}_{-1}e$

**4.79** Uranium-238 decays in a series of nuclear changes until stable ${}^{206}_{82}\text{Pb}$ is produced. Complete the following nuclear equations that are part of the ${}^{238}_{92}\text{U}$ decay series:

**a.** ${}^{238}_{92}\text{U} \longrightarrow {}^{234}_{90}\text{Th} + ?$

**b.** ${}^{234}_{90}\text{Th} \longrightarrow ? + {}^{0}_{-1}e$

**c.** $? \longrightarrow {}^{222}_{86}\text{Rn} + {}^{4}_{2}\text{He}$

**4.80** The iceman known as "Ötzi" was discovered in a high mountain pass on the Austrian-Italian border. Samples of his hair and bones had carbon-14 activity that was about 50% of that present in new hair or bone. Carbon-14 is a beta emitter.

**a.** How long ago did "Ötzi" live if the half-life for C-14 is 5730 y?

**b.** Write a nuclear equation for the decay of carbon-14.

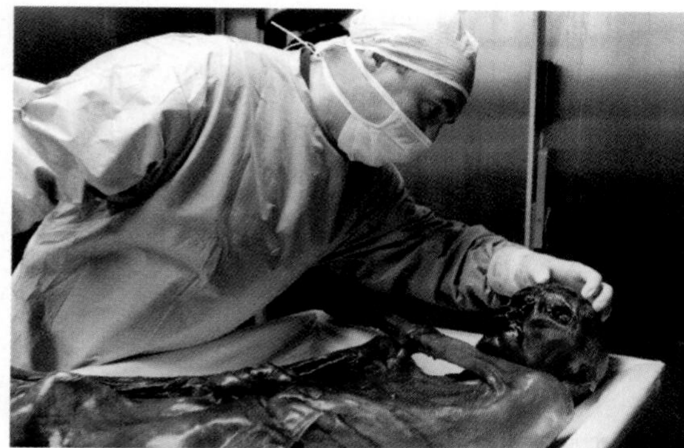

**4.81** The half-life for the radioactive decay of calcium-47 is 4.5 d. If a sample has an activity of 4.0 $\mu$Ci after 18 d, what was the initial activity of the sample?

**4.82** A 16-$\mu$g sample of sodium-24 decays to 2.0 $\mu$g in 45 h. What is the half-life of sodium-24?

**4.83** Write a balanced equation for each of the following radioactive emissions:

**a.** an alpha particle from Hg-180

**b.** a beta particle from Sn-126

**c.** a positron from Mn-49

**4.84** Write a balanced equation for each of the following radioactive emissions:

**a.** an alpha particle from Gd-148

**b.** a beta particle from Sr-90

**c.** a positron from Al-25

# ANSWERS

## ANSWERS TO STUDY CHECKS

**4.1** Distance from the radioactive source and minimizing the time of exposure

**4.2** ${}^{214}_{84}\text{Po} \longrightarrow {}^{210}_{82}\text{Pb} + {}^{4}_{2}\text{He}$

**4.3** ${}^{131}_{53}\text{I} \longrightarrow {}^{131}_{54}\text{Xe} + {}^{0}_{-1}e$

**4.4** ${}^{27}_{13}\text{Al} + {}^{4}_{2}\text{He} \longrightarrow {}^{30}_{15}\text{P} + {}^{1}_{0}n$

**4.5** For $\beta$, the factor is 1; rads and rems are equal.

**4.6** 0.50 g

**4.7** 17 200 y

**4.8** ${}^{10}_{5}\text{B} + {}^{1}_{0}n \longrightarrow {}^{4}_{2}\text{He} + {}^{7}_{3}\text{Li}$

## ANSWERS TO SELECTED QUESTIONS AND PROBLEMS

**4.1 a.** Both an alpha particle and a helium nucleus have two protons and two neutrons.

**b.** $\alpha$, ${}^{4}_{2}\text{He}$

**c.** An $\alpha$-particle is emitted from an unstable nucleus during radioactive decay.

**4.3 a.** ${}^{39}_{19}\text{K}$, ${}^{40}_{19}\text{K}$, ${}^{41}_{19}\text{K}$

**b.** They all have 19 protons and 19 electrons, but they differ in the number of neutrons.

**4.5**

| Medical Use | Atomic Symbol | Mass Number | Number of Protons | Number of Neutrons |
|---|---|---|---|---|
| Heart imaging | ${}^{201}_{81}\text{Tl}$ | 201 | 81 | 120 |
| Radiation therapy | ${}^{60}_{27}\text{Co}$ | 60 | 27 | 33 |
| Abdominal scan | ${}^{67}_{31}\text{Ga}$ | 67 | 31 | 36 |
| Hyperthyroidism | ${}^{131}_{53}\text{I}$ | 131 | 53 | 78 |
| Leukemia treatment | ${}^{32}_{15}\text{P}$ | 32 | 15 | 17 |

**4.7 a.** $\alpha$, ${}^{4}_{2}\text{He}$ **b.** ${}^{1}_{0}n$, $n$ **c.** $\beta$, ${}^{0}_{-1}e$

**d.** ${}^{15}_{7}\text{N}$ **e.** ${}^{125}_{53}\text{I}$

**4.9 a.** $\beta$ or ${}^{0}_{-1}e$ **b.** $\alpha$ or ${}^{4}_{2}\text{He}$ **c.** ${}^{1}_{0}n$

**d.** ${}^{24}_{11}\text{Na}$ **e.** ${}^{14}_{6}\text{C}$

**4.11 a.** Because $\beta$ particles are much smaller and move faster than $\alpha$ particles, they can penetrate farther into tissue.

**b.** When radiation interacts with the components of the cells, reactive species are formed that cause undesirable reactions.

**c.** Radiation technicians leave the room to increase the distance between them and the radiation. Also, a wall that contains lead shields them.

**d.** Wearing gloves shields the skin from $\alpha$ and $\beta$ radiation.

**4.13 a.** ${}^{208}_{84}\text{Po} \longrightarrow {}^{204}_{82}\text{Pb} + {}^{4}_{2}\text{He}$

**b.** ${}^{232}_{90}\text{Th} \longrightarrow {}^{228}_{88}\text{Ra} + {}^{4}_{2}\text{He}$

c. $^{251}_{102}No \longrightarrow ^{247}_{100}Fm + ^{4}_{2}He$

d. $^{220}_{86}Rn \longrightarrow ^{216}_{84}Po + ^{4}_{2}He$

**4.15** **a.** $^{25}_{11}Na \longrightarrow ^{25}_{12}Mg + ^{0}_{-1}e$
**b.** $^{20}_{8}O \longrightarrow ^{20}_{9}F + ^{0}_{-1}e$
**c.** $^{92}_{38}Sr \longrightarrow ^{92}_{39}Y + ^{0}_{-1}e$
**d.** $^{42}_{19}K \longrightarrow ^{42}_{20}Ca + ^{0}_{-1}e$

**4.17** **a.** $^{26}_{14}Si \longrightarrow ^{26}_{13}Al + ^{0}_{+1}e$
**b.** $^{54}_{27}Co \longrightarrow ^{54}_{26}Fe + ^{0}_{+1}e$
**c.** $^{77}_{37}Rb \longrightarrow ^{77}_{36}Kr + ^{0}_{+1}e$
**d.** $^{93}_{45}Rh \longrightarrow ^{93}_{44}Ru + ^{0}_{+1}e$

**4.19** **a.** $^{28}_{14}Si$ **b.** $^{87}_{36}Kr$ **c.** $^{0}_{-1}e$
**d.** $^{238}_{92}U$ **e.** $^{188}_{79}Au$

**4.21** **a.** $^{10}_{4}Be$ **b.** $^{0}_{-1}e$ **c.** $^{27}_{13}Al$ **d.** $^{30}_{15}P$

**4.23** **a.** When radiation enters the Geiger counter, charged particles are produced that create a burst of current that is detected by the instrument.
**b.** becquerel (Bq), curie (Ci)
**c.** gray (Gy), rad
**d.** 1000 Gy

**4.25** 294 $\mu$Ci

**4.27** When pilots are flying at high altitudes, there is less atmosphere to protect them from cosmic radiation.

**4.29** A half-life is the time it takes for one-half of a radioactive sample to decay.

**4.31** **a.** 40.0 mg
**b.** 20.0 mg
**c.** 10.0 mg
**d.** 5.00 mg

**4.33** 130 days, 195 days

**4.35** **a.** Because the elements Ca and P are part of bone, their radioactive isotopes will also become part of the bony structures of the body where their radiation can be used to diagnose or treat bone diseases.
**b.** $^{89}_{38}Sr \longrightarrow ^{89}_{39}Y + ^{0}_{-1}e$

Strontium (Sr) acts much like calcium (Ca) because both are Group 2A (2) elements. The body will accumulate radioactive strontium in bones in the same way that it incorporates calcium. Once the strontium isotope is absorbed by the bone, the beta radiation will destroy cancer cells.

**4.37** 180 $\mu$Ci

**4.39** Nuclear fission is the splitting of a large atom into smaller fragments with the release of large amounts of energy.

**4.41** $^{103}_{42}Mo$

**4.43** **a.** fission
**b.** fusion
**c.** fission
**d.** fusion

**4.45** **a.** $^{11}_{6}C$

**b.**

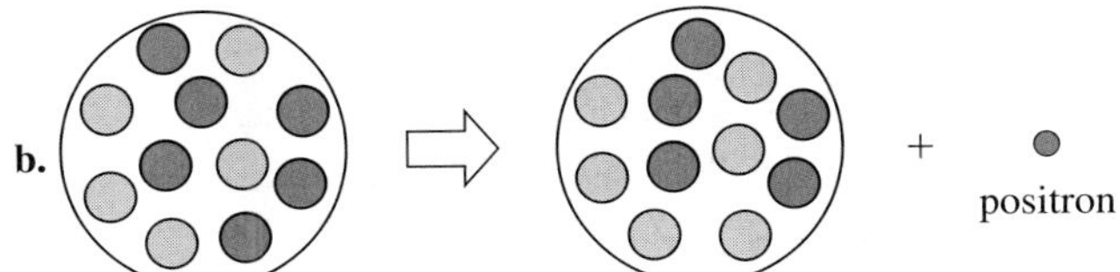


**4.47**

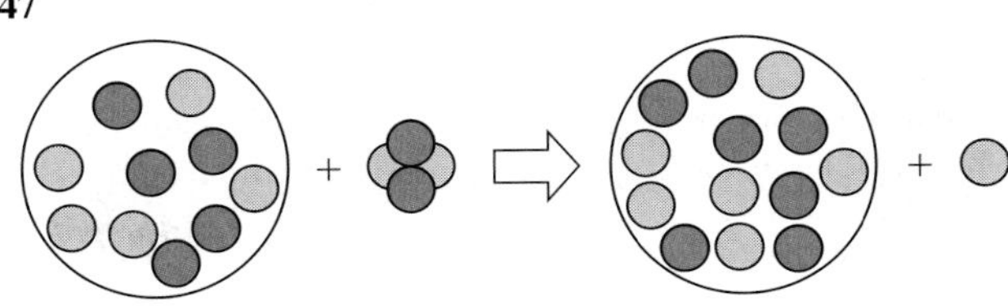

**4.49** 17 200 years old

**4.51** **a.** 11 protons and 14 neutrons
**b.** 28 protons and 33 neutrons
**c.** 37 protons and 47 neutrons
**d.** 47 protons and 63 neutrons

**4.53** **a.** In alpha decay, a helium nucleus is emitted from a radioisotope. In beta decay, a neutron in an unstable nucleus is converted to a proton and electron, which is emitted as a beta particle. In gamma emission, high-energy radiation is emitted from the nucleus of a radioisotope.
**b.** $\alpha$, $^{4}_{2}He$ $\beta$, $^{0}_{-1}e$ $\gamma$, $^{0}_{0}\gamma$

**4.55** **a.** gamma radiation
**b.** positron emission
**c.** alpha decay

**4.57** **a.** $^{225}_{90}Th \longrightarrow ^{221}_{88}Ra + ^{4}_{2}He$
**b.** $^{210}_{83}Bi \longrightarrow ^{206}_{81}Tl + ^{4}_{2}He$
**c.** $^{137}_{55}Cs \longrightarrow ^{137}_{56}Ba + ^{0}_{-1}e$
**d.** $^{126}_{50}Sn \longrightarrow ^{126}_{51}Sb + ^{0}_{-1}e$
**e.** $^{13}_{7}N \longrightarrow ^{13}_{6}C + ^{0}_{+1}e$

**4.59** **a.** $^{17}_{8}O$ **b.** $^{1}_{1}H$ **c.** $^{143}_{54}Xe$

**4.61** **a.** $^{16}_{8}O + ^{16}_{8}O \longrightarrow ^{4}_{2}He + ^{28}_{14}Si$
**b.** $^{249}_{98}Cf + ^{18}_{8}O \longrightarrow ^{263}_{106}Sg + 4^{1}_{0}n$
**c.** $^{222}_{86}Rn \longrightarrow ^{218}_{84}Po + ^{4}_{2}He$
**d.** $^{218}_{84}Po \longrightarrow ^{214}_{82}Pb + ^{4}_{2}He$

**4.63** 14 d

**4.65** **a.** $^{131}_{53}I \longrightarrow ^{0}_{-1}e + ^{131}_{54}Xe$
**b.** 0.375 g **c.** 32 d

**4.67** 16 $\mu$Ci

**4.69** 7.5 mg

**4.71** The irradiation of meats, fruits, and vegetables kills bacteria such as *E. coli* that can cause food-borne illnesses. In addition, spoilage is deterred, and shelf life is extended.

**4.73** In the fission process, an atom splits into smaller nuclei. In fusion, small nuclei combine (fuse) to form a larger nucleus.

**4.75** Fusion occurs naturally in the sun and other stars.

**4.77** **a.** gamma radiation
**b.** positron emission
**c.** beta decay **d.** alpha decay

**4.79** **a.** $^{238}_{92}U \longrightarrow ^{234}_{90}Th + ^{4}_{2}He$
**b.** $^{234}_{90}Th \longrightarrow ^{234}_{91}Pa + ^{0}_{-1}e$
**c.** $^{226}_{88}Ra \longrightarrow ^{222}_{86}Rn + ^{4}_{2}He$

**4.81** 4 half-lives; 64 $\mu$Ci

**4.83** **a.** $^{180}_{80}Hg \longrightarrow ^{176}_{78}Pt + ^{4}_{2}He$
**b.** $^{126}_{50}Sn \longrightarrow ^{126}_{51}Sb + ^{0}_{-1}e$
**c.** $^{49}_{25}Mn \longrightarrow ^{49}_{24}Cr + ^{0}_{+1}e$

# 5 Compounds and Their Bonds

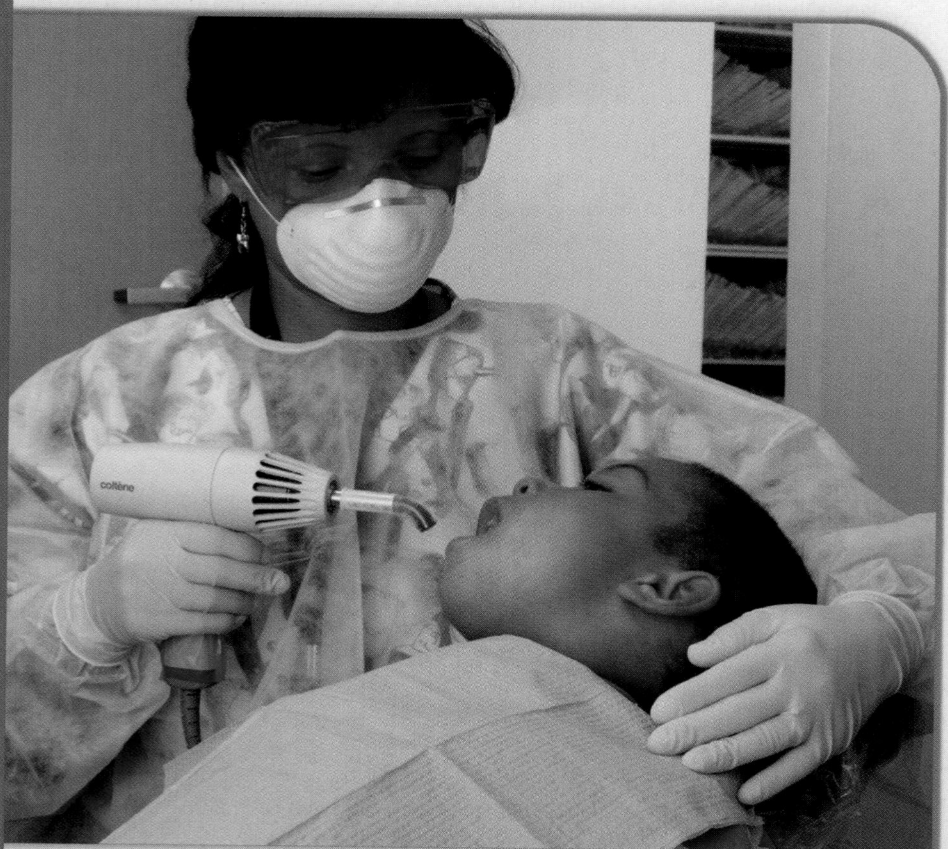


LOOKING AHEAD


5.1 Octet Rule and Ions

5.2 Ionic Compounds

5.3 Naming and Writing Ionic Formulas

5.4 Polyatomic Ions

5.5 Covalent Compounds

5.6 Naming and Writing Covalent Formulas

5.7 Electronegativity and Bond Polarity

5.8 Shapes and Polarity of Molecules

5.9 Attractive Forces in Compounds


*"One way to prevent cavities in children is to apply a thin, plastic coating called a sealant to their teeth," says Dr. Pam Alston, a dentist in private practice. "We look for teeth with deep grooves and pits that trap food. We clean the teeth and apply an etching agent, which helps the sealant bind to the teeth. Then we apply the liquid sealant, which fills in the grooves and pits, and use ultraviolet light to solidify the coating."*

*The use of fluoride compounds, such as $SnF_2$ in toothpaste and NaF in water, and mouth rinses have greatly reduced tooth decay. The fluoride ion replaces the hydroxide ion to form $Ca_{10}(PO_4)_6F_2$, which strengthens the enamel and makes it less susceptible to decay. Other compounds used in dentistry are the anesthetic known as laughing gas ($N_2O$) and Novocaine ($C_{13}H_{20}N_2O_2$).*

Visit **www.masteringchemistry.com** for self-study materials and instructor-assigned homework.

In nature, atoms of almost all the elements on the periodic table are found in combination with other atoms. Only the atoms of the noble gases—He, Ne, Ar, Kr, Xe, and Rn—do not combine in nature with other atoms. As discussed in Chapter 3, a compound is a pure substance, composed of two or more elements, with a definite composition. In a typical ionic compound, one or more electrons are transferred from the atoms of metals to atoms of nonmetals. The attraction that results is called an *ionic bond*. We use many ionic compounds every day. When we cook or bake, we use ionic compounds such as salt (NaCl) and baking soda ($NaHCO_3$). Epsom salts ($MgSO_4$) may be used to soak sore feet. Milk of magnesia ($Mg(OH)_2$) or calcium carbonate ($CaCO_3$) may be taken to settle an upset stomach. In a mineral supplement, iron is present as iron(II) sulfate ($FeSO_4$). Certain sunscreens contain zinc oxide (ZnO) and the tin(II) fluoride ($SnF_2$) in toothpaste provides fluoride to help prevent tooth decay.

The structures of ionic crystals result in the beautiful facets seen in gems. Sapphires and rubies are made of aluminum oxide ($Al_2O_3$). Impurities of chromium make rubies red, and iron and titanium make sapphires blue.

In compounds of nonmetals, covalent bonding occurs by atoms sharing one or more valence electrons. There are many more covalent compounds than there are ionic ones, and many simple covalent compounds are present in our everyday lives. For example, water ($H_2O$), oxygen ($O_2$), and carbon dioxide ($CO_2$) are all covalent compounds.

Covalent compounds consist of molecules, which are discrete groups of atoms. A molecule of water ($H_2O$) consists of two atoms of hydrogen and one atom of oxygen. When you have iced tea, perhaps you add molecules of sugar (sucrose), which is a covalent compound ($C_{12}H_{22}O_{11}$). Other covalent compounds include propane ($C_3H_8$), alcohol ($C_2H_6O$), the antibiotic amoxicillin ($C_{16}H_{19}N_3O_5S$), and the antidepressant Prozac ($C_{17}H_{18}F_3NO$).

## 5.1 Octet Rule and Ions

**LEARNING GOAL**

Using the octet rule, write the symbols of the simple ions for the representative elements.

MC™ TUTORIAL
Octet Rule and Ions

Most of the elements, except the noble gases, combine to form compounds. The noble gases are so stable that they form compounds only under extreme conditions. One explanation for the stability of noble gases is that they have an octet of 8 valence electrons. The exception is helium, which is stable with 2 electrons that fill its first energy level.

Compounds are the result of the formation of chemical bonds between two or more different elements. Ionic bonds occur when atoms of one element lose valence electrons and the atoms of another element gain valence electrons. Ionic compounds typically occur between metals and nonmetals. For example, atoms of sodium and chlorine form the ionic compound NaCl. Covalent bonds occur when atoms of nonmetals share valence electrons and form covalent compounds. For example, atoms of nitrogen and chlorine form the covalent compound $NCl_3$.

In the formation of either an ionic bond or a covalent bond, atoms lose, gain, or share valence electrons to acquire an octet. This tendency for atoms to attain a noble gas electron configuration is known as the **octet rule** and provides a key to our understanding of the ways in which atoms bond and form compounds.

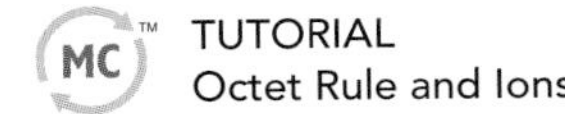


Loss and gain of electrons

Sharing electrons

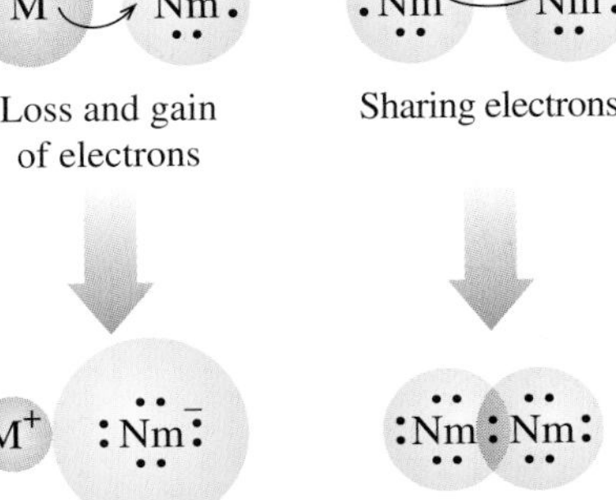


Ionic bond

Covalent bond

M is a metal
Nm is a nonmetal

### Positive Ions

In ionic bonding, **ions**, which have electrical charges, form when atoms lose or gain valence electrons to form octets. Because the ionization energies of metals of Groups 1A (1), 2A (2), and 3A (13) are low, these metal atoms readily lose their valence electrons to nonmetals. In doing so, they acquire the electron configuration of a noble gas (8 valence electrons) and form ions with positive charges. For example, when a sodium atom loses its single valence electron, the remaining electrons have the noble gas configuration of neon. By losing an electron, sodium has 10 electrons instead of 11. Because there are still 11 protons in its nucleus, the atom is no longer neutral. It has become a sodium ion and has an electrical charge, called an **ionic charge**, of 1+. In the symbol for the sodium ion, the ionic charge of 1+ is written as + in the upper right-hand corner, $Na^+$.

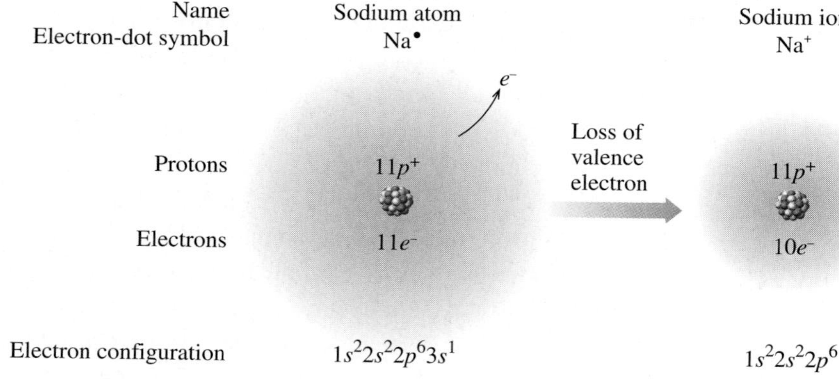


Metals in ionic compounds lose their valence electrons to form positively charged ions called **cations** (pronounced *cat'-ions*). Magnesium, a metal in Group 2A (2), attains a noble gas electron configuration like neon by losing 2 valence electrons to form a positive ion with a 2+ ionic charge. A metal ion is named by its element name. Thus, $Mg^{2+}$ is named the *magnesium* ion.

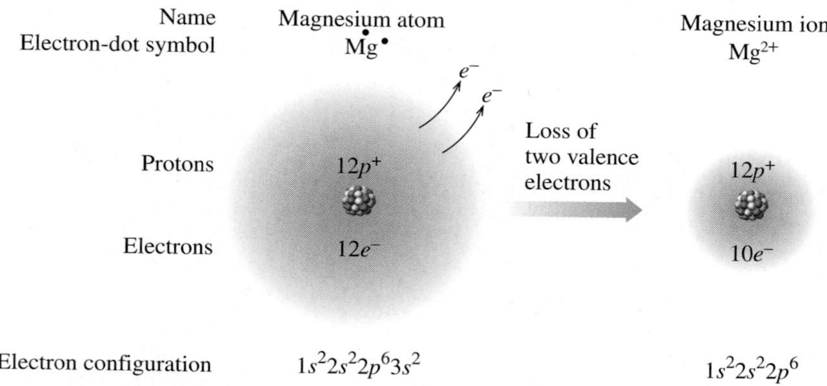


## Negative Ions

Nonmetals form negative ions when they gain valence electrons to attain an octet. For example, an atom of chlorine with 7 valence electrons obtains 1 electron to have an octet and the electron configuration of argon, a noble gas. By acquiring an electron, a chlorine atom becomes a particle called a *chloride* ion ($Cl^-$), which has a 1− charge. Ions with negative charges are called **anions** (pronounced *an'-ions*). The name of an anion uses the first syllable of the element name followed by *ide*.

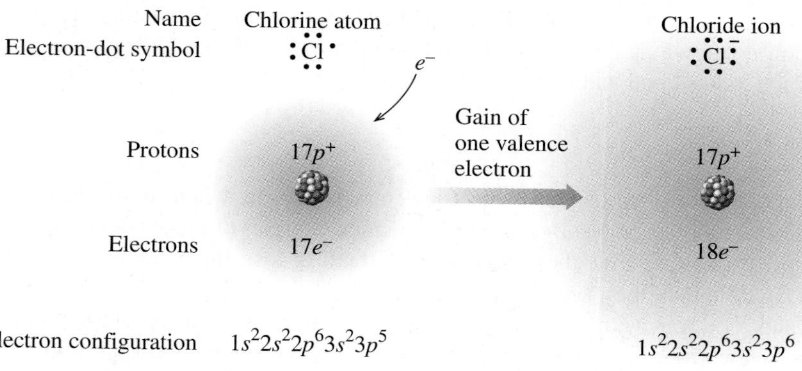


Table 5.1 lists the names of some important metal and nonmetal ions.

TABLE 5.1 Formulas and Names of Some Common Ions

| Group Number | Formula of Ion | Name of Ion | Group Number | Formula of Ion | Name of Ion |
|---|---|---|---|---|---|
| | **Metals** | | | **Nonmetals** | |
| 1A (1) | $Li^+$ | Lithium | 5A (15) | $N^{3-}$ | Nitride |
| | $Na^+$ | Sodium | | $P^{3-}$ | Phosphide |
| | $K^+$ | Potassium | 6A (16) | $O^{2-}$ | Oxide |
| 2A (2) | $Mg^{2+}$ | Magnesium | | $S^{2-}$ | Sulfide |
| | $Ca^{2+}$ | Calcium | 7A (17) | $F^-$ | Fluoride |
| | $Ba^{2+}$ | Barium | | $Cl^-$ | Chloride |
| 3A (13) | $Al^{3+}$ | Aluminum | | $Br^-$ | Bromide |
| | | | | $I^-$ | Iodide |

CONCEPT CHECK 5.1

**Ions**

**a.** Write the symbol and name of the ion that has 7 protons and 10 electrons.
**b.** State the number of protons and electrons in a calcium ion, $Ca^{2+}$.

ANSWER

**a.** The element with 7 protons is nitrogen. An ion of nitrogen with 10 electrons has an ionic charge of 3− and is called a *nitride* ion, $N^{3-}$.
**b.** In a calcium ion, $Ca^{2+}$, there are 20 protons. The ionic charge of 2+ indicates a loss of 2 electrons, which gives a total of 18 electrons in the calcium ion.

## Ionic Charges from Group Numbers

Group numbers can be used to determine the ionic charges for most ions of the representative elements. We have seen that metals lose electrons to form positive ions. The elements in Groups 1A (1), 2A (2), and 3A (13) lose 1, 2, and 3 electrons, respectively. Group 1A (1) metals form ions with 1+ charges, Group 2A (2) metals form ions with 2+ charges, and Group 3A (13) metals form ions with 3+ charges.

The nonmetals from Groups 5A (15), 6A (16), and 7A (17) form negative ions. Group 5A (15) nonmetals usually form ions with 3− charges, Group 6A (16) nonmetals form ions with 2− charges, and Group 7A (17) nonmetals form ions with 1− charges. The nonmetals of Group 4A (14) do not typically form ions. Table 5.2 lists the ionic charges for some common ions of representative elements.

TABLE 5.2 Positive and Negative Ions Have the Same Electron Configuration as the Nearest Noble Gases

| | | Metals Lose Valence Electrons | | | Nonmetals Gain Valence Electrons | | | | |
|---|---|---|---|---|---|---|---|---|---|
| Noble Gases | | 1A (1) | 2A (2) | 3A (13) | 5A (15) | 6A (16) | 7A (17) | | Noble Gases |
| **He** | ⇦ | $Li^+$ | | | | | | | |
| **Ne** | ⇦ | $Na^+$ | $Mg^{2+}$ | $Al^{3+}$ | $N^{3-}$ | $O^{2-}$ | $F^-$ | ⇨ | **Ne** |
| **Ar** | ⇦ | $K^+$ | $Ca^{2+}$ | | $P^{3-}$ | $S^{2-}$ | $Cl^-$ | ⇨ | **Ar** |
| **Kr** | ⇦ | $Rb^+$ | $Sr^{2+}$ | | | | $Br^-$ | ⇨ | **Kr** |
| **Xe** | ⇦ | $Cs^+$ | $Ba^{2+}$ | | | | $I^-$ | ⇨ | **Xe** |

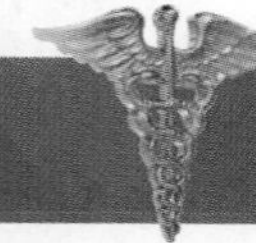

## HEALTH NOTE

### Some Uses for Noble Gases

Noble gases may be used when an unreactive substance is required. Scuba divers normally use a pressurized mixture of nitrogen and oxygen gases for breathing under water. However, when the air mixture is used at depths where pressure is high, the nitrogen gas is absorbed into the blood, where it can cause mental disorientation. To avoid this problem, a breathing mixture of oxygen and helium may be substituted. The diver still obtains the necessary oxygen, but the unreactive helium that dissolves in the blood does not cause mental disorientation. However, its lower density does change the vibrations of the vocal cords, and the diver will sound like Donald Duck.

Helium is also used to fill blimps and balloons. When dirigibles were first designed, they were filled with hydrogen, the lightest gas. However, when they encountered any type of spark or heating source, the dirigibles exploded violently because of the extreme reactivity of hydrogen gas with oxygen present in the air. Today blimps are filled with unreactive helium gas, which presents no danger of explosion.

Lighting tubes are generally filled with a noble gas such as neon or the filament would soon burn up.

## Sizes of Atoms and Their Ions

The size of ions for the representative elements compared to the size of their atoms is much smaller for metals and much larger for nonmetals.

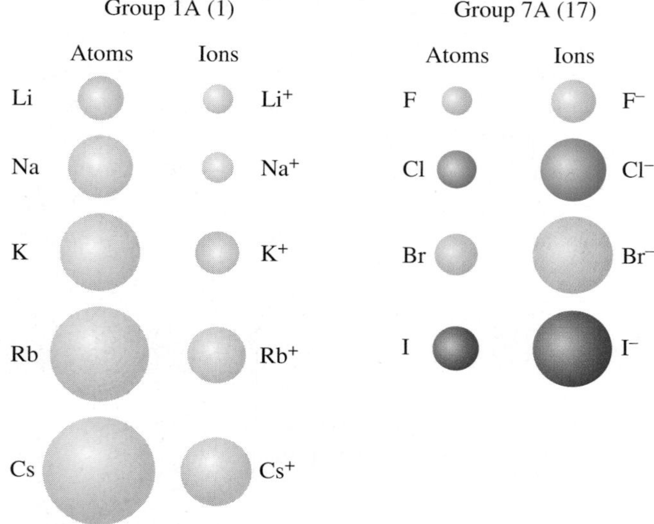


If we look at the relative sizes of the positive ions in Group 1A (1), we see that they are about half the size of their corresponding metal atoms. This size change occurs because metal atoms lose all of their valence electrons from their outermost energy levels. For example, a sodium atom has one electron in the third energy level. When that valence electron is lost and the sodium ion is formed, the outermost energy level becomes the second energy level, which has an octet.

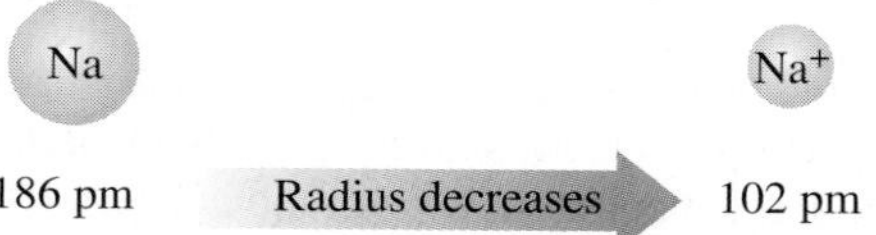


The size of nonmetal atoms increases because they gain electrons in the outermost energy level. For example, a valence electron adds to the second energy level of fluorine to complete an octet, which increases the repulsion among the electrons and increases the size of the fluoride ion.

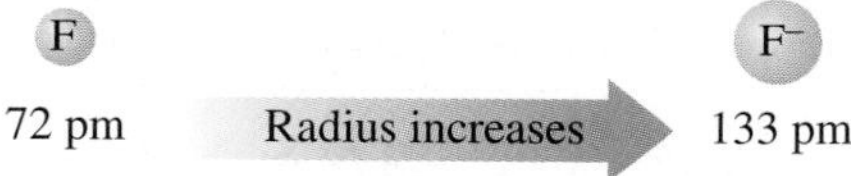


**SAMPLE PROBLEM 5.1**

### Writing Ions

Consider the elements aluminum and oxygen.

**a.** Identify each as a metal or a nonmetal.
**b.** State the number of valence electrons for each.
**c.** State the number of electrons that must be lost or gained for each to acquire an octet.
**d.** Write the symbol and name of each resulting ion, including its ionic charge.

SOLUTION

| **Aluminum** | **Oxygen** |
|---|---|
| **a.** metal | nonmetal |
| **b.** 3 valence electrons | 6 valence electrons |
| **c.** loses $3e^-$ | gains $2e^-$ |
| **d.** $Al^{3+}$, aluminum ion | $O^{2-}$, oxide ion |

STUDY CHECK

What are the symbols and names for the ions formed by potassium and sulfur?

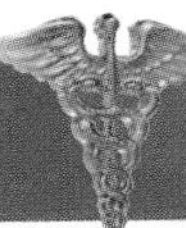

# HEALTH NOTE

## Some Important Ions in the Body

Several ions in body fluids have important physiological and metabolic functions. Some of them are listed in Table 5.3.

**TABLE 5.3** Ions in the Body

| Ion | Occurrence | Function | Source | Result of Too Little | Result of Too Much |
|---|---|---|---|---|---|
| $Na^+$ | Principal cation outside the cell | Regulation and control of body fluids | Salt, cheese, pickles, potato chips, pretzels | Hyponatremia, anxiety, diarrhea, circulatory failure, decrease in body fluid | Hypernatremia, little urine, thirst, edema |
| $K^+$ | Principal cation inside the cell | Regulation of body fluids and cellular functions | Bananas, orange juice, milk, prunes, potatoes | Hypokalemia (hypopotassemia), lethargy, muscle weakness, failure of neurological impulses | Hyperkalemia (hyperpotassemia), irritability, nausea, little urine, cardiac arrest |
| $Ca^{2+}$ | Cation outside the cell; 90% of calcium in the body in bone as $Ca_3(PO_4)_2$ or $CaCO_3$ | Major cation of bone; needed for muscle contraction | Milk, yogurt, cheese, greens, spinach | Hypocalcemia, tingling fingertips, muscle cramps, osteoporosis | Hypercalcemia, relaxed muscles, kidney stones, deep bone pain |
| $Mg^{2+}$ | Cation outside the cell; 70% of magnesium in the body in bone structure | Essential for certain enzymes, muscles, nerve control | Widely distributed (part of chlorophyll of all green plants), nuts, whole grains | Disorientation, hypertension, tremors, slow pulse | Drowsiness |
| $Cl^-$ | Principal anion outside the cell | Gastric juice, regulation of body fluids | Salt | Same as for $Na^+$ | Same as for $Na^+$ |

# QUESTIONS AND PROBLEMS

## Octet Rule and Ions

5.1 State the number of electrons that must be lost by atoms of each of the following elements to acquire a noble gas electron configuration:

**a.** Li **b.** Mg
**c.** Al **d.** Cs
**e.** Ba

**5.2** State the number of electrons that must be gained by atoms of each of the following elements to acquire a noble gas electron configuration:

**a.** Cl **b.** O
**c.** N **d.** I
**e.** P

5.3 Write the symbols of the ions with the following number of protons and electrons:

**a.** 3 protons, 2 electrons
**b.** 9 protons, 10 electrons
**c.** 12 protons, 10 electrons
**d.** 26 protons, 23 electrons

**5.4** Write the symbols of the ions with the following number of protons and electrons:
**a.** 30 protons, 28 electrons
**b.** 53 protons, 54 electrons
**c.** 82 protons, 78 electrons
**d.** 15 protons, 18 electrons

**5.5** How many protons and electrons are in the following ions?
**a.** $O^{2-}$ **b.** $K^{+}$
**c.** $Br^{-}$ **d.** $S^{2-}$

**5.6** How many protons and electrons are in the following ions?
**a.** $Sr^{2+}$ **b.** $F^{-}$
**c.** $Au^{3+}$ **d.** $Cs^{+}$

**5.7** Write the symbol for the ion of each of the following:
**a.** chlorine **b.** potassium
**c.** oxygen **d.** aluminum

**5.8** Write the symbol for the ion of each of the following:
**a.** fluorine **b.** calcium
**c.** sodium **d.** lithium

**5.9** Select the larger atom or ion in each of the following pairs:
**a.** K or $K^{+}$ **b.** $Cl^{-}$ or Cl
**c.** Ca or $Ca^{2+}$ **d.** $K^{+}$ or $Li^{+}$

**5.10** Select the smaller atom or ion in each of the following pairs:
**a.** S or $S^{2-}$ **b.** Al or $Al^{3+}$
**c.** $F^{-}$ or $Cl^{-}$ **d.** I or $I^{-}$

# 5.2 Ionic Compounds

**LEARNING GOAL**

Using charge balance, write the correct formula for an ionic compound.

MC™ TUTORIAL
Ionic Compounds

**Ionic compounds** consist of positive and negative ions. The ions are held together by strong attractions between the oppositely charged ions called **ionic bonds**.

## Properties of Ionic Compounds

The physical and chemical properties of an ionic compound such as NaCl are very different from those of the original elements. For example, the original elements of NaCl were sodium, which is a soft, shiny metal, and chlorine, which is a yellow-green poisonous gas. As positive and negative ions, however, they form table salt, NaCl, a hard, white, crystalline substance that is common in our diet. In ionic compounds, the attraction between the positive and negative ions is extremely strong, which makes the melting points of ionic compounds high, often more than 500 °C. For instance, the melting point of NaCl is 801 °C. At room temperature, ionic compounds are solids.

The structure of an ionic solid depends on the arrangement of the ions. In a crystal of NaCl, which has a cubic shape, the larger $Cl^{-}$ ions (green) are packed close together in a structure as shown in Figure 5.1. The smaller $Na^{+}$ ions (shown in gray) occupy the holes between the $Cl^{-}$ ions.

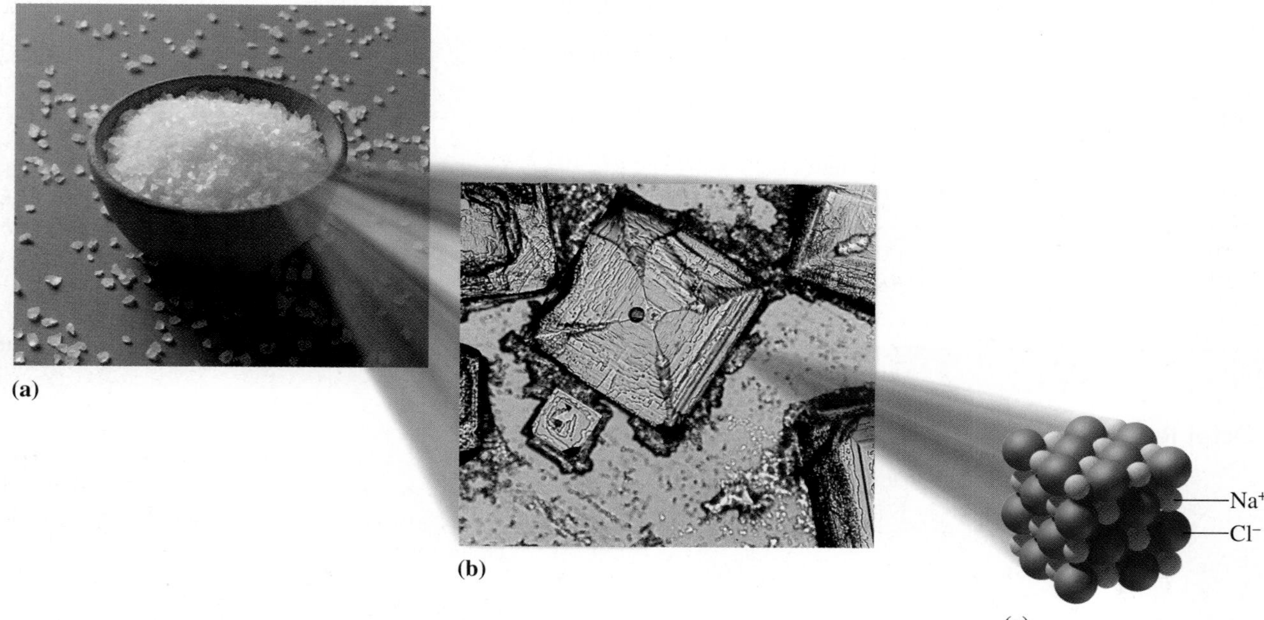


FIGURE 5.1 **(a)** The elements sodium and chlorine react to form the ionic compound sodium chloride, the compound that makes up table salt. **(b)** Crystals of NaCl under magnification. **(c)** A diagram of the arrangements of $Na^{+}$ and $Cl^{-}$ packed together in a NaCl crystal.

Q What is the type of bonding between $Na^{+}$ and $Cl^{-}$ ions in salt?

## Charge Balance in Ionic Compounds

The **formula** of an ionic compound indicates the number and kinds of ions that make up the ionic compound. The sum of the ionic charges in the formula is always zero, which means that the total amount of positive charge is equal to the total amount of negative charge. For example, the NaCl formula indicates that there is one sodium ion, $Na^+$, for every chloride ion, $Cl^-$, in the compound. Note that the ionic charges of the ions do not appear in the formula of the ionic compound.

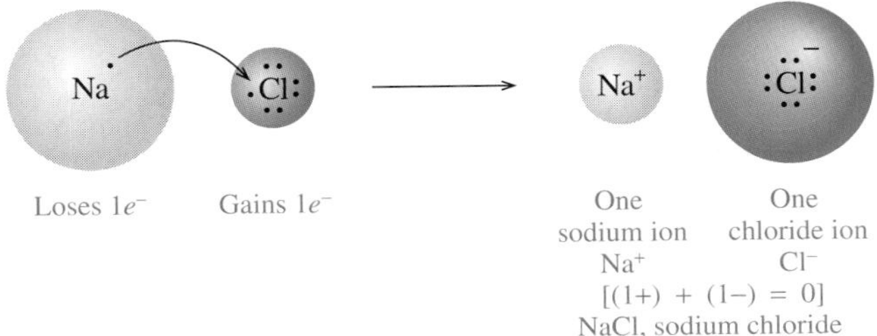


One sodium ion $Na^+$ One chloride ion $Cl^-$
$[(1+) + (1-) = 0]$
NaCl, sodium chloride

## Subscripts in Formulas

Consider a compound of magnesium and chlorine. To achieve an octet, a Mg atom loses its two valence electrons to form $Mg^{2+}$. Each Cl atom gains one electron to form $Cl^-$, which has a complete valence energy level. In this example, two $Cl^-$ ions are needed to balance the positive charge of $Mg^{2+}$. This gives the formula $MgCl_2$, magnesium chloride, in which the subscript 2 shows that two $Cl^-$ were needed for charge balance.

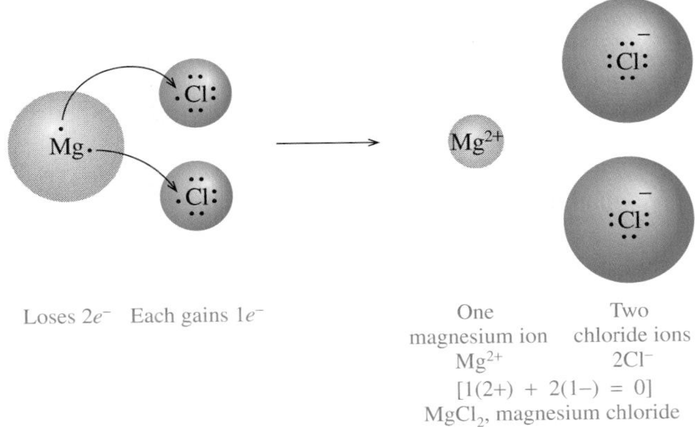


One magnesium ion $Mg^{2+}$ Two chloride ions $2Cl^-$
$[1(2+) + 2(1-) = 0]$
$MgCl_2$, magnesium chloride

## Writing Ionic Formulas from Ionic Charges

The subscripts in the formula of an ionic compound represent the number of positive and negative ions that give an overall charge of zero. Thus, we can now write a formula directly from the ionic charges of the positive and negative ions. In the formula of an ionic compound, the cation is written first and is followed by the anion. Suppose we wish to write the formula of the ionic compound containing $Na^+$ and $S^{2-}$ ions. To balance the ionic charge of the $S^{2-}$ ion, we show two $Na^+$ ions by using a subscript 2 in the formula. This gives the formula $Na_2S$, which has an overall charge of zero. When there is no subscript for a symbol such as the S in $Na_2S$, it assumed to be 1.

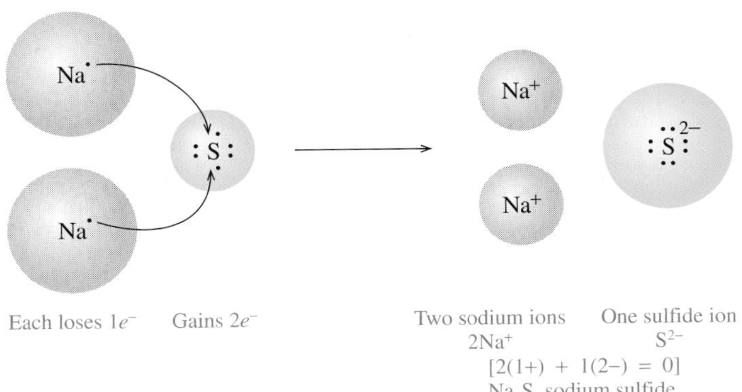


Two sodium ions $2Na^+$ One sulfide ion $S^{2-}$
$[2(1+) + 1(2-) = 0]$
$Na_2S$, sodium sulfide

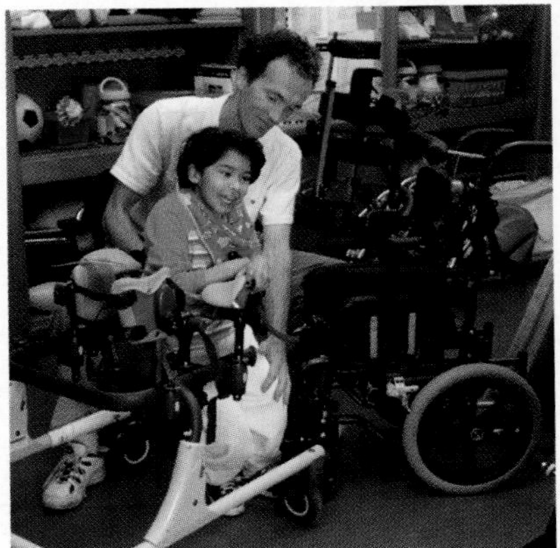

### Physical Therapist

"Physical therapists need to understand how the body, muscles, and joints function in order to recognize when something is not working and which area needs strengthening," says Vincent Leddy, a physical therapist. "Chemistry is important to understanding the body's physiology and how chemical changes in the body affect movement. I went into physical therapy because I enjoy teaching movement to children. I am guiding Maggie into her chair but allowing her to move as much as she can by herself. I help her by giving gentle pressure and reassurance so that she'll be safe in the transition. I work on getting Maggie to use her body, and the occupational therapist works on Maggie's fine motor skills and how she uses her hand on the switch or picks up objects. By using both physical and occupational therapy, we enhance the child's performance."

CONCEPT CHECK 5.2

**Writing Formulas from Ionic Charges**

Determine ionic charges and write the formula for the ionic compound formed when lithium and nitrogen react.

ANSWER

Lithium in Group 1A (1) forms $Li^+$; nitrogen in Group 5A (15) forms $N^{3-}$. The charge of 3− for $N^{3-}$ is balanced by three $Li^+$ ions. Writing the positive ion first gives the formula $Li_3N$.

## QUESTIONS AND PROBLEMS

### Ionic Compounds

**5.11** Which of the following pairs of elements are likely to form ionic compounds?
- **a.** lithium and chlorine
- **b.** oxygen and chlorine
- **c.** potassium and oxygen
- **d.** sodium and neon
- **e.** sodium and magnesium
- **f.** nitrogen and chlorine

**5.12** Which of the following pairs of elements are likely to form ionic compounds?
- **a.** helium and oxygen
- **b.** magnesium and chlorine
- **c.** chlorine and bromine
- **d.** potassium and sulfur
- **e.** sodium and potassium
- **f.** nitrogen and oxygen

**5.13** Write the correct ionic formula for compounds formed between the following ions:
- **a.** $Na^+$ and $O^{2-}$ **b.** $Al^{3+}$ and $Br^-$
- **c.** $Ba^{2+}$ and $O^{2-}$ **d.** $Mg^{2+}$ and $Cl^-$
- **e.** $Al^{3+}$ and $S^{2-}$

**5.14** Write the correct ionic formula for compounds formed between the following ions:
- **a.** $Al^{3+}$ and $Cl^-$ **b.** $Ca^{2+}$ and $S^{2-}$
- **c.** $Li^+$ and $S^{2-}$ **d.** $K^+$ and $N^{3-}$
- **e.** $K^+$ and $I^-$

**5.15** Determine the ions and write the correct formula for ionic compounds formed by the following metals and nonmetals:
- **a.** sodium and sulfur **b.** potassium and nitrogen
- **c.** aluminum and iodine **d.** lithium and oxygen

**5.16** Determine the ions and write the correct formula for ionic compounds formed by the following metals and nonmetals:
- **a.** calcium and chlorine
- **b.** barium and bromine
- **c.** sodium and phosphorus
- **d.** magnesium and oxygen

# 5.3 Naming and Writing Ionic Formulas

LEARNING GOAL

Given the formula of an ionic compound, write the correct name; given the name of an ionic compound, write the correct formula.

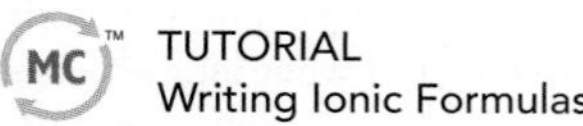

TUTORIAL
Writing Ionic Formulas

As we determined in section 5.2, the name of a metal ion is the same as its elemental name. The name of a nonmetal ion is obtained by using the first syllable of its elemental name followed by *ide*. The name of the compound includes a space between the names of the metal and nonmetal.

## Naming Ionic Compounds Containing Two Elements

In the name of an ionic compound made up of two elements, the metal ion is named followed by the name of the nonmetal ion. Subscripts are never mentioned; they are understood because of the charge balance of the ions in the compound. (See Table 5.4.)

**TABLE 5.4** Names of Some Ionic Compounds

| Compound | Metal Ion | Nonmetal Ion | Name |
|---|---|---|---|
| NaF | $Na^+$<br>Sodium | $F^-$<br>Fluoride | Sodium fluoride |
| $MgBr_2$ | $Mg^{2+}$<br>Magnesium | $Br^-$<br>Bromide | Magnesium bromide |
| $Al_2O_3$ | $Al^{3+}$<br>Aluminum | $O^{2-}$<br>Oxide | Aluminum oxide |

SAMPLE PROBLEM 5.2

## Naming Ionic Compounds

Write the name of the ionic compound $Mg_3N_2$.

SOLUTION

STEP 1 **Identify the cation and anion.** The cation from Group 2A (2) is $Mg^{2+}$, and the anion from Group 5A (15) is $N^{3-}$.

STEP 2 **Name the cation by its element name.** The cation $Mg^{2+}$ is magnesium.

STEP 3 **Name the anion by using the first syllable of its element name followed by *ide*.** The anion $N^{3-}$ is nitride.

STEP 4 **Write the name of the cation first and the name of the anion second.** $Mg_3N_2$ is named *magnesium nitride*.

STUDY CHECK

Name the compound $Ga_2S_3$.

**Guide to Naming Ionic Compounds with Metals That Form a Single Ion**

STEP 1 Identify the cation and anion.

STEP 2 Name the cation by its element name.

STEP 3 Name the anion by using the first syllable of its element name followed by *ide*.

STEP 4 Write the name of the cation first and the name of the anion second.

## Metals with Variable Charge

The transition metals typically form two or more kinds of positive ions because they lose their outer electrons as well as electrons from a lower energy level. For example, in some ionic compounds, iron is in the $Fe^{2+}$ form; in other compounds, it takes the $Fe^{3+}$ form. Copper also forms two different ions: $Cu^{+}$ is present in some compounds and $Cu^{2+}$ in others. When a metal can form two or more ions, it is not possible to predict the ionic charge from the group number. We say that it has a *variable valence* or *variable charge*.

When different ions are possible for a metal, a naming system is needed to identify the particular cation in a compound. To do this, a Roman numeral that matches the ionic charge is placed in parentheses immediately after the elemental name of the metal. For the cations of iron, $Fe^{2+}$ is named iron(II), and $Fe^{3+}$ is named iron(III). Table 5.5 lists the ions of some common metals that produce two or more ions.

Figure 5.2 shows some common ions and their location on the periodic table. Typically, the transition metals form more than one positive ion. However, zinc, cadmium, and silver

**TABLE 5.5** Some Metals That Form More Than One Positive Ion

| Element | Possible Ions | Name of Ion |
|---|---|---|
| Chromium | $Cr^{2+}$ | Chromium(II) |
| | $Cr^{3+}$ | Chromium(III) |
| Copper | $Cu^{+}$ | Copper(I) |
| | $Cu^{2+}$ | Copper(II) |
| Gold | $Au^{+}$ | Gold(I) |
| | $Au^{3+}$ | Gold(III) |
| Iron | $Fe^{2+}$ | Iron(II) |
| | $Fe^{3+}$ | Iron(III) |
| Lead | $Pb^{2+}$ | Lead(II) |
| | $Pb^{4+}$ | Lead(IV) |
| Tin | $Sn^{2+}$ | Tin(II) |
| | $Sn^{4+}$ | Tin(IV) |

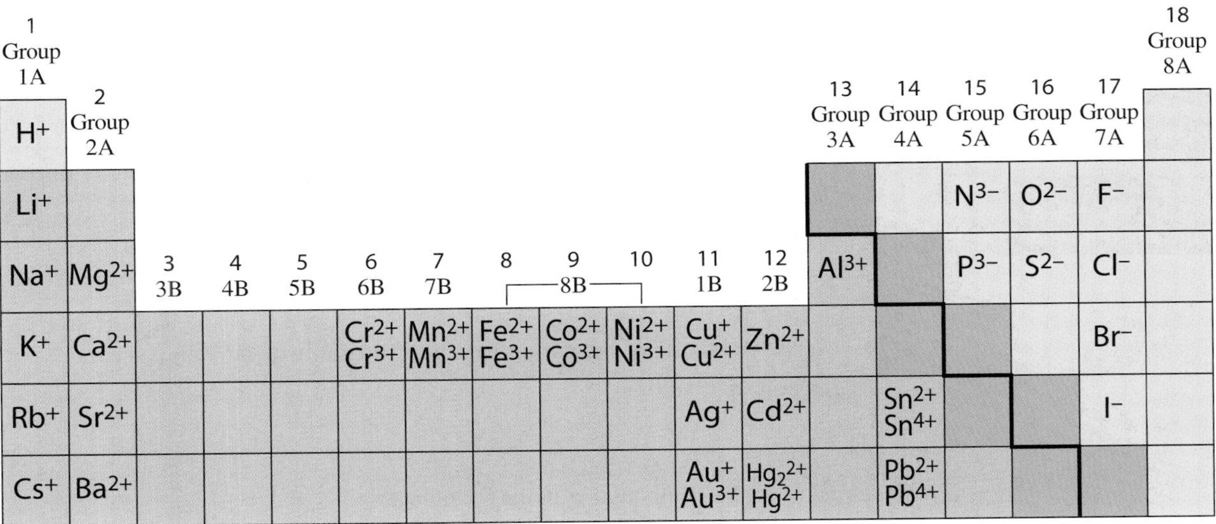


**FIGURE 5.2** On the periodic table, positive ions are produced from metals and negative ions are produced from nonmetals.

Q What are the ions produced by calcium, copper, and oxygen?

form only one ion. The ionic charges of silver, cadmium, and zinc are fixed like Group 1A (1), 2A (2), and 3A (13) metals, so their elemental names are sufficient when naming their ionic compounds. Metals in Groups 4A (14) and 5A (15) also form more than one positive ion. For example, lead and tin in Group 4A (14) form cations with charges of 2+ and 4+.

The selection of the correct Roman numeral depends on the ionic charge of the transition metal in the formula. For example, we use charge balance to calculate the charge of the copper cation in the formula $CuCl_2$. Two chloride ions each have a 1− charge, which gives a total negative charge of 2−. To balance the 2− charge, the copper ion must have a positive charge of 2+, which is a $Cu^{2+}$ ion:

**$CuCl_2$**

| | | |
|---|---|---|
| Cu charge | + $2Cl^-$ charge | = 0 |
| (?) | + 2(1−) | = 0 |
| (2+) | + (2−) | = 0 |

To indicate the copper ion $Cu^{2+}$, we place (II) after *copper* when naming the compound: copper(II) chloride.

Table 5.6 lists names of some ionic compounds in which the metals form two types of positive ions.

**TABLE 5.6 Some Ionic Compounds of Metals That Form Two Kinds of Positive Ions**

| Compound | Systematic Name |
|---|---|
| $FeCl_2$ | Iron(II) chloride |
| $Fe_2O_3$ | Iron(III) oxide |
| $Cu_3P$ | Copper(I) phosphide |
| $CuBr_2$ | Copper(II) bromide |
| $SnCl_2$ | Tin(II) chloride |
| $PbS_2$ | Lead(IV) sulfide |

**Guide to Naming Ionic Compounds with Variable Charge Metals**

STEP 1 Determine the charge of the cation from the anion.

STEP 2 Name the cation by its element name, and use a Roman numeral in parentheses for the charge.

STEP 3 Name the anion by using the first syllable of its element name followed by *ide*.

STEP 4 Write the name of the cation first and the name of the anion second.

SAMPLE PROBLEM 5.3

## Naming Ionic Compounds with Variable Charge Metal Ions

Write the name for $Cu_2S$.

SOLUTION

STEP 1 **Determine the charge of the cation from the anion.** The nonmetal S in Group 6A (16) forms the $S^{2-}$ ion. Because there are two Cu ions to balance the $S^{2-}$, the charge of each Cu ion is 1+.

| | Metal | Nonmetal |
|---|---|---|
| **Elements** | Copper | Sulfur |
| **Groups** | Transition | 6A (16) |
| **Ions** | Cu? | $S^{2-}$ |
| **Charge balance** | 2(1+) | (2−) = 0 |
| **Ions** | $Cu^+$ | $S^{2-}$ |

STEP 2 **Name the cation by its element name, and use a Roman numeral in parentheses for the charge.**

copper(I)

STEP 3 **Name the anion by using the first syllable of its element name followed by *ide*.**

sulfide

STEP 4 **Write the name of the cation first and the name of the anion second.**

copper(I) sulfide

STUDY CHECK

Write the name of the compound with the formula $Au_2O$.

SAMPLE PROBLEM 5.4

## Writing Formulas of Ionic Compounds

Write the formula for iron(III) chloride.

SOLUTION

**STEP 1** **Identify the cation and anion.** The Roman numeral (III) indicates that the charge of the iron ion is 3+, $Fe^{3+}$.

| | Metal | Nonmetal |
|---|---|---|
| **Elements** | Iron(III) | Chlorine |
| **Groups** | Transition | 7A (17) |
| **Ions** | $Fe^{3+}$ | $Cl^-$ |

**STEP 2** **Balance the charges.**

$Fe^{3+}$ $Cl^-$
$Cl^-$
$Cl^-$

$\mathbf{1}(3+) + \mathbf{3}(1-) = 0$

Becomes a subscript in the formula

**STEP 3** **Write the formula, cation first, using subscripts from the charge balance.**

$FeCl_3$

STUDY CHECK

Write the correct formula for chromium(III) oxide.

**Guide to Writing Formulas from the Name of an Ionic Compound**

STEP 1
Identify the cation and anion.

STEP 2
Balance the charges.

STEP 3
Write the formula, cation first, using subscripts from charge balance.

## QUESTIONS AND PROBLEMS

### Naming and Writing Ionic Formulas

**5.17** Write names for the following ionic compounds:
**a.** $Al_2O_3$ **b.** $CaCl_2$
**c.** $Na_2O$ **d.** $Mg_3N_2$
**e.** KI

**5.18** Write names for the following ionic compounds:
**a.** $MgCl_2$ **b.** $K_3P$
**c.** $Li_2S$ **d.** LiBr
**e.** MgO

**5.19** Why is a Roman numeral placed after the name of most transition metal ions?

**5.20** The compound $CaCl_2$ is named calcium chloride; the compound $CuCl_2$ is named copper(II) chloride. Explain why a Roman numeral is used in one name but not in the other.

**5.21** Write the names of the following Group 4A (14) and transition metal ions (include the Roman numeral when necessary):
**a.** $Fe^{2+}$ **b.** $Cu^{2+}$
**c.** $Zn^{2+}$ **d.** $Pb^{4+}$
**e.** $Cr^{3+}$

**5.22** Write the names of the following Group 4A (14) and transition metal ions (include the Roman numeral when necessary):
**a.** $Ag^+$ **b.** $Cu^+$
**c.** $Fe^{3+}$ **d.** $Sn^{2+}$
**e.** $Au^{3+}$

**5.23** Write names for the following ionic compounds:
**a.** $SnCl_2$ **b.** FeO
**c.** $Cu_2S$ **d.** CuS
**e.** $CrBr_3$ **f.** $ZnCl_2$

**5.24** Write names for the following ionic compounds:
**a.** $Ag_3P$ **b.** PbS
**c.** $Al_2O_3$ **d.** $AuCl_3$
**e.** FeS **f.** $Na_3N$

**5.25** Give the symbol of the cation in each of the following formulas:
**a.** $AuCl_3$ **b.** $Fe_2O_3$
**c.** $PbI_4$ **d.** $SnCl_2$

**5.26** Give the symbol of the cation in each of the following formulas:
**a.** $FeCl_2$ **b.** CuO
**c.** $Fe_2S_3$ **d.** $CrCl_3$

**5.27** Write formulas for the following ionic compounds:
**a.** magnesium chloride
**b.** sodium sulfide
**c.** copper(I) oxide
**d.** zinc phosphide
**e.** gold(III) nitride
**f.** chromium(II) chloride

**5.28** Write formulas for the following ionic compounds:
**a.** iron(III) oxide
**b.** barium fluoride
**c.** tin(IV) chloride
**d.** silver sulfide
**e.** copper(II) chloride
**f.** lithium nitride

## 5.4 Polyatomic Ions

**LEARNING GOAL**

Write the name and formula of a compound containing a polyatomic ion.

TUTORIAL
Polyatomic Ions

An ionic compound with three or more elements contains a **polyatomic ion**, which is a group of atoms that has an ionic charge. Most polyatomic ions consist of a nonmetal such as phosphorus, sulfur, carbon, or nitrogen that has covalent bonds to one or more oxygen atoms. However, the covalent bonds do not contain a sufficient number of electrons to complete some of the octets. Thus, 1, 2, or 3 electrons are gained by the atoms in the group to complete their octets. This electron gain gives the negatively charged polyatomic ions ionic charges of 1−, 2−, or 3−.

Fertilizer
$NaNO_3$

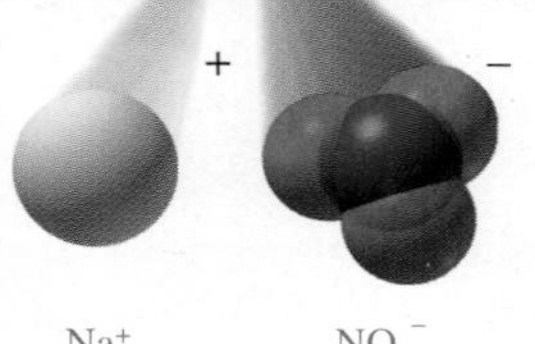


Plaster molding
$CaSO_4$

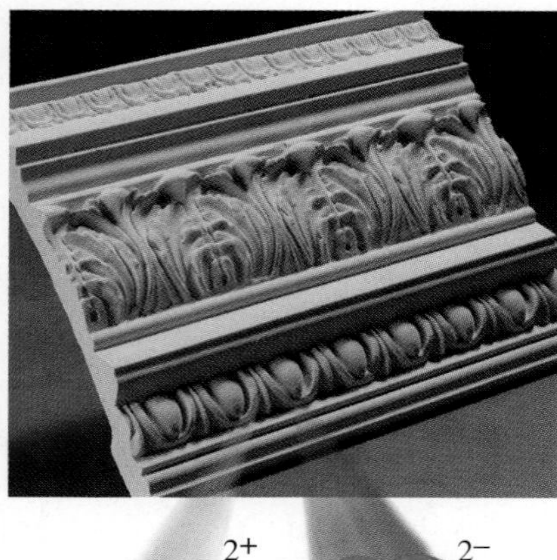

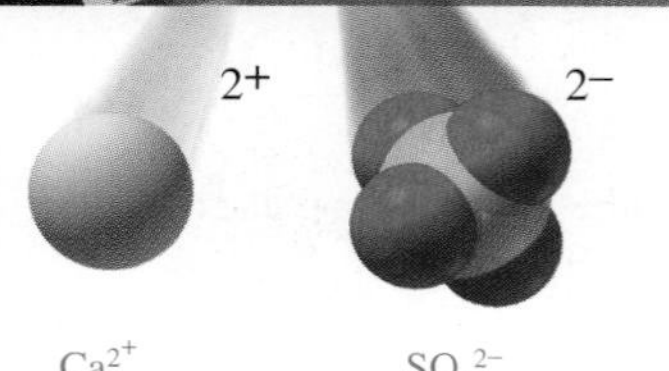


**FIGURE 5.3** Many products contain polyatomic ions, which are groups of atoms that carry an ionic charge.

**Q** Why does the sulfate ion have a 2− charge?

### Naming Polyatomic Ions

Most polyatomic ions have a negative charge. Only one common polyatomic ion, $NH_4^+$, has a 1+ ionic charge. The names of most common negatively charged polyatomic ions end in *ate*. When a related ion has one less oxygen atom, the *ite* ending is used for its name. By recognizing these endings, you can identify a polyatomic ion in the name of a compound. In the halogen family, the ions with just one oxygen atom are named by placing a prefix *hypo* in the name. The hydroxide ion ($OH^-$) and cyanide ion ($CN^-$) are exceptions to this naming pattern.

There is no easy way to learn polyatomic ions. You will need to memorize the number of oxygen atoms and the charge associated with each ion, as shown in Table 5.7. By memorizing the formulas and the names of the ions shown in the boxes, you can derive the related ions. For example, the sulfate ion is $SO_4^{2-}$. We write the formula of the sulfite ion, which has one less oxygen atom, as $SO_3^{2-}$. Note that the *ate* and *ite* ions of a particular nonmetal have the same ionic charge: sulfate and sulfite ions have 2− charges; phosphate and phosphite ions have 3− charges; nitrate and nitrite have 1− charges; chlorate and chlorite (and other halogens) have 1− charges.

The formula of hydrogen carbonate, or *bicarbonate*, can be written by placing a hydrogen cation ($H^+$) in front of the formula for carbonate, $CO_3^{2-}$, and decreasing the charge from 2− to 1− to give $HCO_3^-$. Some models of polyatomic ions are shown in Figure 5.3.

$$CO_3^{2-} + H^+ = HCO_3^-$$

**TABLE 5.7** Names and Formulas of Some Common Polyatomic Ions

| Nonmetal Element | Formula of Ion[a] | Name of Ion |
|---|---|---|
| Hydrogen | $OH^-$ | Hydroxide |
| Nitrogen | $NH_4^+$ | Ammonium |
| | $\boxed{NO_3^-}$ | Nitrate |
| | $NO_2^-$ | Nitrite |
| Chlorine | $ClO_4^-$ | Perchlorate |
| | $\boxed{ClO_3^-}$ | Chlorate |
| | $ClO_2^-$ | Chlorite |
| | $ClO^-$ | Hypochlorite |
| Carbon | $\boxed{CO_3^{2-}}$ | Carbonate |
| | $HCO_3^-$ | Hydrogen carbonate (or bicarbonate) |
| | $CN^-$ | Cyanide |
| | $C_2H_3O_2^-$ | Acetate |
| Sulfur | $\boxed{SO_4^{2-}}$ | Sulfate |
| | $HSO_4^-$ | Hydrogen sulfate (or bisulfate) |
| | $SO_3^{2-}$ | Sulfite |
| | $HSO_3^-$ | Hydrogen sulfite (or bisulfite) |
| Phosphorus | $\boxed{PO_4^{3-}}$ | Phosphate |
| | $HPO_4^{2-}$ | Hydrogen phosphate |
| | $H_2PO_4^-$ | Dihydrogen phosphate |
| | $PO_3^{3-}$ | Phosphite |

[a]Boxed formulas show the most common polyatomic ion for each element.

## Writing Formulas for Compounds Containing Polyatomic Ions

No polyatomic ion exists by itself. Like any ion, a polyatomic ion must be associated with ions of opposite charge. The bonding between polyatomic ions and other ions is one of electrical attraction. For example, the compound sodium sulfate consists of sodium ions ($Na^+$) and sulfate ions ($SO_4^{2-}$) held together by ionic bonds.

To write correct formulas for compounds containing polyatomic ions, we follow the same rules of charge balance that we used for writing the formulas of simple ionic compounds. The total negative and positive charges must equal zero. For example, consider the formula for a compound containing calcium ions and carbonate ions. The ions are written as

$Ca^{2+}$ Calcium ion    $CO_3^{2-}$ Carbonate ion

Ionic charge: $(2+) + (2-) = 0$

Because one ion of each balances the charge, the formula is written as

$CaCO_3$
Calcium carbonate

When more than one polyatomic ion is needed for charge balance, parentheses are used to enclose the formula of the ion. A subscript is written outside the closing parenthesis of the polyatomic ion to indicate the number needed for charge balance. Consider the formula for magnesium nitrate. The ions are the magnesium ion and the nitrate ion, a polyatomic ion.

$Mg^{2+}$ Magnesium ion    $NO_3^-$ Nitrate ion

To balance the 2+ ionic charge of magnesium, two polyatomic ions of nitrate are needed. In the formula, parentheses are placed around the nitrate ion, as follows:

$Mg^{2+}$ $NO_3^-$ $NO_3^-$

$(2+) + 2(1-) = 0$

Magnesium nitrate
$Mg(NO_3)_2$

Parentheses enclose the formula of the nitrate ion

Subscript outside the parentheses indicates the use of two nitrate ions

SAMPLE PROBLEM 5.5

### Writing Formulas for Ionic Compounds with Polyatomic Ions

Write the formula of aluminum bicarbonate.

SOLUTION

**STEP 1** **Identify the cation and anion.** The cation is the aluminum ion, $Al^{3+}$, and the anion is bicarbonate, $HCO_3^-$.

| | Cation | Anion |
|---|---|---|
| **Ions** | $Al^{3+}$ | $HCO_3^-$ |

**STEP 2** **Balance the charges.**

$Al^{3+}$    $HCO_3^-$ $HCO_3^-$ $HCO_3^-$

$\mathbf{1}(3+) + \mathbf{3}(1-) = 0$

Becomes a subscript in the formula

STEP 3 **Write the formula, cation first, using subscripts from the charge balance.** The formula for the compound is written by enclosing the formula of the bicarbonate ion, $HCO_3^-$, in parentheses and writing the subscript 3 outside the last parenthesis.

$$Al(HCO_3)_3$$

STUDY CHECK

Write the formula for a compound containing ammonium ion(s) and phosphate ion(s).

CONCEPT CHECK 5.3

**Polyatomic Ions in Bones and Teeth**

Bone material consists of a mineral substance called calcium hydroxyapatite, $Ca_{10}(PO_4)_6(OH)_2$, a solid formed from calcium ions and polyatomic ions. What polyatomic ions are contained in the mineral substance of bone?

ANSWER

The polyatomic ions are phosphate ions and hydroxide ions.

## Naming Compounds Containing Polyatomic Ions

When naming ionic compounds containing polyatomic ions, first we write the positive ion, usually a metal, and then the name of the polyatomic ion. It is important that you learn to recognize the polyatomic ion in the formula and name it correctly. As with other ionic compounds, no prefixes are used.

| $Na_2SO_4$ | $FePO_4$ | $Al_2(CO_3)_3$ |
|---|---|---|
| $Na_2\boxed{SO_4}$ | $Fe\boxed{PO_4}$ | $Al_2(\boxed{CO_3})_3$ |
| Sodium sulfate | Iron(III) phosphate | Aluminum carbonate |

Table 5.8 lists the formulas and names of some ionic compounds that include polyatomic ions and also gives their uses in medicine and industry.

**TABLE 5.8** Some Compounds That Contain Polyatomic Ions

| Formula | Name | Use |
|---|---|---|
| $BaSO_4$ | Barium sulfate | Radiopaque medium |
| $CaCO_3$ | Calcium carbonate | Antacid, calcium supplement |
| $Ca_3(PO_4)_2$ | Calcium phosphate | Calcium replenisher |
| $CaSO_3$ | Calcium sulfite | Preservative in cider and fruit juices |
| $CaSO_4$ | Calcium sulfate | Plaster casts |
| $AgNO_3$ | Silver nitrate | Topical anti-infective |
| $NaHCO_3$ | Sodium bicarbonate *or* Sodium hydrogen carbonate | Antacid |
| $Zn_3(PO_4)_2$ | Zinc phosphate | Dental cements |
| $FePO_4$ | Iron(III) phosphate | Food and bread enrichment |
| $K_2CO_3$ | Potassium carbonate | Alkalizer, diuretic |
| $Al_2(SO_4)_3$ | Aluminum sulfate | Antiperspirant, anti-infective |
| $AlPO_4$ | Aluminum phosphate | Antacid |
| $MgSO_4$ | Magnesium sulfate | Cathartic, Epsom salts |

SAMPLE PROBLEM 5.6

## Naming Compounds Containing Polyatomic Ions

Name the following ionic compounds:

**a.** $CaSO_4$ **b.** $Cu(NO_2)_2$

SOLUTION

| | STEP 1 | | STEP 2 | STEP 3 | STEP 4 |
|---|---|---|---|---|---|
| **Formula** | **Cation** | **Anion** | **Name of Cation** | **Name of Anion** | **Name of Compound** |
| **a.** $CaSO_4$ | $Ca^{2+}$ | $SO_4^{2-}$ | Calcium ion | Sulfate ion | Calcium sulfate |
| **b.** $Cu(NO_2)_2$ | $Cu^{2+}$ | $NO_2^-$ | Copper(II) ion | Nitrite ion | Copper(II) nitrite |

STUDY CHECK

What is the name of $Ca_3(PO_4)_2$?

**Guide to Naming Ionic Compounds with Polyatomic Ions**

STEP 1 Identify the cation and polyatomic ion (anion).

STEP 2 Name the cation using a Roman numeral, if needed.

STEP 3 Name the polyatomic ion usually ending with *ite* or *ate*.

STEP 4 Write the name of the compound, cation first and the polyatomic ion second.

## QUESTIONS AND PROBLEMS

### Polyatomic Ions

**5.29** Write the formulas including the charge for the following polyatomic ions:
**a.** hydrogen carbonate **b.** ammonium
**c.** phosphate **d.** hydrogen sulfate

**5.30** Write the formulas including the charge for the following polyatomic ions:
**a.** nitrite **b.** sulfite
**c.** hydroxide **d.** phosphite

**5.31** Name the following polyatomic ions:
**a.** $SO_4^{2-}$ **b.** $CO_3^{2-}$
**c.** $PO_4^{3-}$ **d.** $NO_3^-$

**5.32** Name the following polyatomic ions:
**a.** $OH^-$ **b.** $HSO_3^-$
**c.** $CN^-$ **d.** $NO_2^-$

**5.33** Complete the following table with the formula of the compound:

| | $OH^-$ | $NO_2^-$ | $CO_3^{2-}$ | $HSO_4^-$ | $PO_4^{3-}$ |
|---|---|---|---|---|---|
| $Li^+$ | | | | | |
| $Cu^{2+}$ | | | | | |
| $Ba^{2+}$ | | | | | |

**5.34** Complete the following table with the formula of the compound:

| | $OH^-$ | $NO_3^-$ | $HCO_3^-$ | $SO_3^{2-}$ | $PO_4^{3-}$ |
|---|---|---|---|---|---|
| $NH_4^+$ | | | | | |
| $Al^{3+}$ | | | | | |
| $Pb^{4+}$ | | | | | |

**5.35** Write the formula for the polyatomic ion in each of the following and name each compound:
**a.** $Na_2CO_3$ **b.** $NH_4Cl$
**c.** $Li_3PO_4$ **d.** $Cu(NO_2)_2$
**e.** $FeSO_3$

**5.36** Write the formula for the polyatomic ion in each of the following, and name each compound:
**a.** KOH **b.** $NaNO_3$
**c.** $CuCO_3$ **d.** $NaHCO_3$
**e.** $BaSO_4$

**5.37** Write the correct formula for the following compounds:
**a.** barium hydroxide **b.** sodium sulfate
**c.** iron(II) nitrate **d.** zinc phosphate
**e.** iron(III) carbonate

**5.38** Write the correct formula for the following compounds:
**a.** aluminum chlorate **b.** ammonium oxide
**c.** magnesium bicarbonate **d.** sodium nitrite
**e.** copper(I) sulfate

# 5.5 Covalent Compounds

LEARNING GOAL

Given the formula of a covalent compound, write its electron-dot formula.

A **covalent compound** forms when atoms of two nonmetals achieve stability by sharing electrons. Because of the nonmetals' high ionization energies, electrons are not transferred between atoms. When atoms share electrons, the bond is a **covalent bond**. Thus, in *covalent compounds*, electrons are not transferred from one atom to another, but are shared between atoms of nonmetals to achieve stability. When two or more atoms share electrons, they form **molecules**.

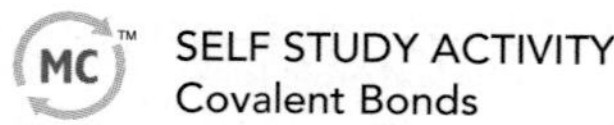

SELF STUDY ACTIVITY
Covalent Bonds

## Formation of a Hydrogen Molecule

The simplest covalent molecule is hydrogen gas, $H_2$. When two hydrogen atoms are far apart, they are not attracted to each other. As the atoms move closer, the positive charge of each nucleus attracts the electron of the other atom. This attraction pulls the atoms closer until they share a pair of valence electrons and form a *covalent bond*. In the covalent bond in $H_2$, the shared electrons give the noble gas configuration of He to each of the H atoms. Thus the atoms bonded in $H_2$ are more stable than two individual H atoms.

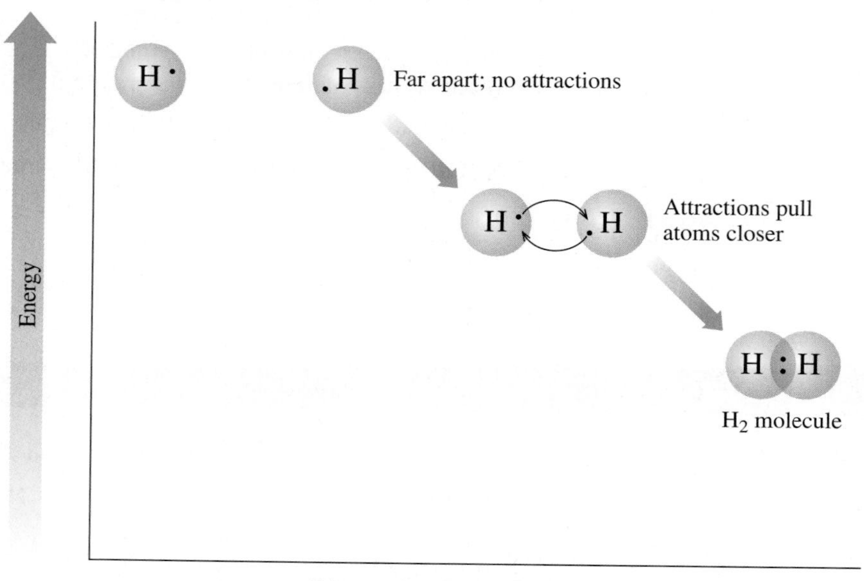


**TABLE 5.9 Elements That Exist as Diatomic, Covalent Molecules**

| Element | Diatomic Molecule | Name |
|---|---|---|
| H | $H_2$ | Hydrogen |
| N | $N_2$ | Nitrogen |
| O | $O_2$ | Oxygen |
| F | $F_2$ | Fluorine |
| Cl | $Cl_2$ | Chlorine |
| Br | $Br_2$ | Bromine |
| I | $I_2$ | Iodine |

## Electron-Dot Formulas of Covalent Molecules

The valence electrons in covalent molecules are shown using an electron-dot formula, which is also known as a Lewis structure. The shared electrons, or *bonding pairs*, are shown as two dots or a single line between atoms. The nonbonding pairs of electrons, or *lone pairs*, are placed on the outside. For example, a fluorine molecule ($F_2$) consists of two fluorine atoms, Group 7A (17), each with 7 valence electrons. Each F atom achieves an octet by sharing its unpaired valence electrons. In the $F_2$ molecule, each F atom has the noble gas configuration of neon.

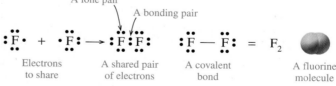

A lone pair
A bonding pair

:F· + ·F: ⟶ :F:F:    :F — F: = $F_2$

Electrons to share    A shared pair of electrons    A covalent bond    A fluorine molecule

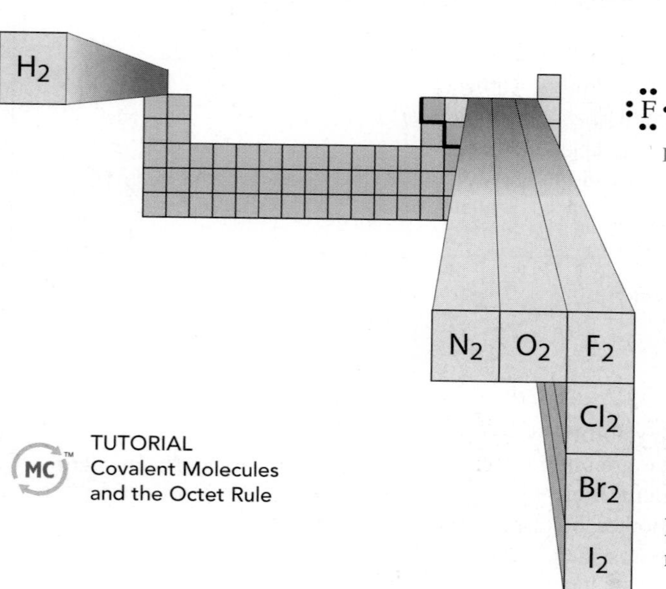


Hydrogen ($H_2$) and fluorine ($F_2$) are examples of nonmetal elements whose natural state is diatomic; that is, they contain two like atoms. The elements that exist as diatomic molecules are listed in Table 5.9.

TUTORIAL
Covalent Molecules and the Octet Rule

## Sharing Electrons Between Atoms of Different Elements

In Period 2, the number of electrons that an atom shares and the number of covalent bonds it forms are usually equal to the number of electrons needed to acquire a noble gas configuration. For example, carbon has 4 valence electrons. Because carbon needs to acquire 4 more electrons for an octet, it forms 4 covalent bonds by sharing its 4 valence electrons.

Methane, a component of natural gas, is a compound made of carbon and hydrogen. To attain an octet, each carbon atom shares 4 electrons, and each hydrogen atom shares 1 electron. In this molecule, a carbon atom forms 4 covalent bonds with 4 hydrogen atoms. The electron-dot formula for the molecule is written with the carbon atom in the center and the hydrogen atoms on the sides. Table 5.10 gives the formulas of some covalent molecules for Period 2 elements.

H<br>H : C : H<br>H

Methane, $CH_4$

**TABLE 5.10** Electron-Dot Formulas for Some Covalent Compounds

| $CH_4$ | $NH_3$ | $H_2O$ |
|---|---|---|
| **Formulas Using Electron Dots Only** | | |
| H<br>H:C̤̈:H<br>H | H:N̤̈:H<br>H | :Ö:H<br>H |
| **Formulas Using Bonds and Electron Dots** | | |
| H<br>\|<br>H—C—H<br>\|<br>H | H—N̈—H<br>\|<br>H | :Ö—H<br>\|<br>H |
| **Molecular Models** | | |
| Methane molecule | Ammonia molecule | Water molecule |

While the octet rule is useful, there are exceptions. We have already seen that a hydrogen molecule ($H_2$) requires just two electrons, or a single bond, to achieve the stability of the nearest noble gas, helium. In $BeCl_2$, Be forms only 2 covalent bonds. In $BF_3$, the nonmetal B can share only 3 valence electrons to give a total of 6 valence electrons or 3 bonds. The nonmetals typically form octets. However, atoms such as P, S, Cl, Br, and I can share more of their valence electrons and expand the octets to stable valence shells of 10, 12, or even 14 electrons. In $PCl_3$, the P atom has an octet, but in $PCl_5$ the P atom has 10 valence electrons or 5 bonds. In $H_2S$, the S atom has an octet, but in $SF_6$, there are 12 valence electrons, or 6 bonds to the sulfur atom. Table 5.11 gives the bonding patterns for some nonmetals.

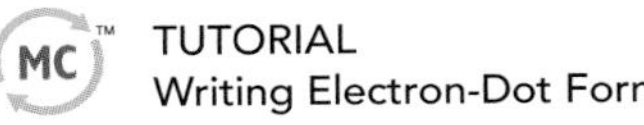

TUTORIAL
Writing Electron-Dot Formulas

**TABLE 5.11** Typical Bonding Patterns of Some Nonmetals in Covalent Compounds

| 1A (1) | 3A (13) | 4A (14) | 5A (15) | 6A (16) | 7A (17) |
|---|---|---|---|---|---|
| [a]H<br>1 bond | | | | | |
| | [a]B<br>3 bonds | C<br>4 bonds | N<br>3 bonds | O<br>2 bonds | F<br>1 bond |
| | | Si<br>4 bonds | P<br>3 bonds | S<br>2 bonds | Cl, Br, I<br>1 bond |

[a]H and B do not form eight-electron octets. H atoms share one electron pair; B atoms share three electron pairs for a set of 6 electrons.

**Guide to Writing Electron-Dot Formulas**

**STEP 1** Determine the arrangement of atoms.

**STEP 2** Determine the total number of valence electrons.

**STEP 3** Attach each bonded atom to the central atom with a pair of electrons.

**STEP 4** Place the remaining electrons as lone pairs to complete octets (two for H, six for B).

SAMPLE PROBLEM 5.7

## Writing Electron-Dot Formulas

Write the electron-dot formula for $PCl_3$, phosphorus trichloride.

SOLUTION

**STEP 1** **Determine the arrangement of atoms.** In $PCl_3$, the central atom is P because it needs the most electrons.

Cl P Cl
Cl

**STEP 2** **Determine the total number of valence electrons.** We can use the group numbers to determine the valence electrons for each of the atoms in the molecule.

| Element | Group | Atoms | Valence Electrons | = | Total |
|---|---|---|---|---|---|
| P | 5A (15) | 1 P | $\times 5e^-$ | = | $5e^-$ |
| Cl | 7A (17) | 3 Cl | $\times 7e^-$ | = | $21e^-$ |
| | Total valence electrons for $PCl_3$ | | | = | $26e^-$ |

**STEP 3** **Attach the central atom to each bonded atom by a pair of electrons.**

Cl:P:Cl (with :Cl below P) or Cl—P—Cl (with |Cl below P)

**STEP 4** **Place the remaining electrons as lone pairs to complete octets.** A total of 6 electrons ($3 \times 2e^-$) are needed to bond the central P atom to three Cl atoms. Twenty valence electrons are left:

$$26 \text{ valence } e^- - 6 \text{ bonding } e^- = 20e^- \text{ remaining}$$

The remaining electrons are placed as lone pairs around the outer Cl atoms first, which uses 18 more electrons.

:C̈l:P:C̈l: (with :C̈l: below P) or :C̈l—P—C̈l: (with :C̈l: below P)

Use the remaining two electrons to complete the octet for the P atom.

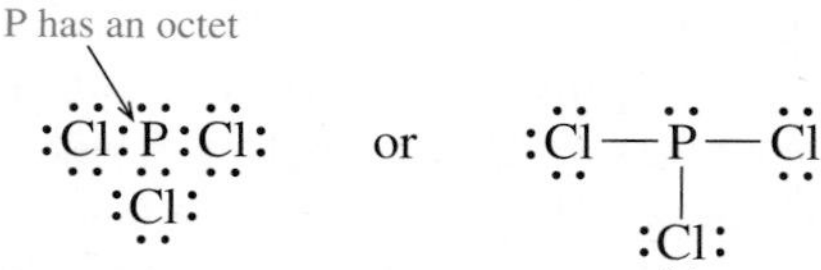

P has an octet

STUDY CHECK

Write the electron-dot formula for $Cl_2O$ (O is the central atom).

## Multiple Covalent Bonds

SELF STUDY ACTIVITY
Bonds and Bond Polarity

In many covalent compounds, two atoms share two or three pairs of electrons to complete their octets. A **double bond** occurs when two pairs of electrons are shared between two atoms; in a **triple bond**, three pairs of electrons are shared. Atoms of carbon, oxygen, nitrogen, and sulfur are most likely to form multiple bonds. Atoms of hydrogen and the halogens do not form double or triple bonds. Double and triple bonds are formed when single covalent bonds fail to complete the octets of all the atoms in the molecule. For example, in the electron-dot formula for the covalent compound $N_2$, an octet is achieved when each nitrogen atom shares 3 electrons. Thus, three covalent bonds, or a triple bond, will form.

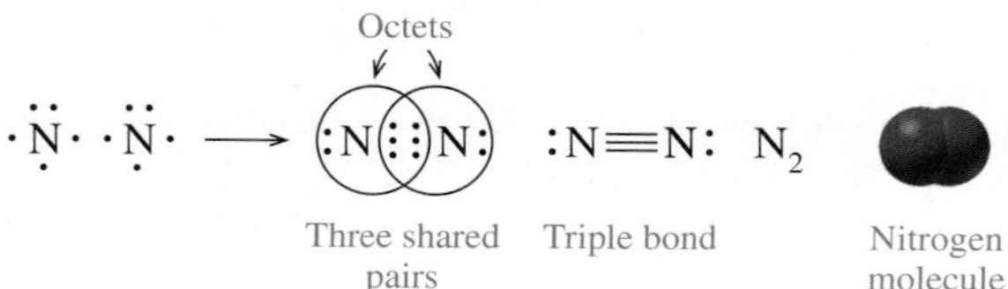

SAMPLE PROBLEM 5.8

### Writing Electron-Dot Formulas with Double Bonds

Write the electron-dot formula for $CO_2$, carbon dioxide.

SOLUTION

**STEP 1** **Determine the arrangement of atoms.** In $CO_2$, the central atom is C.

O C O

**STEP 2** **Determine the total number of valence electrons.**

| Element | Group | Atoms | Valence Electrons | = | Total |
|---|---|---|---|---|---|
| O | 6A (16) | 2 O | $\times$ 6$e^-$ | = | 12$e^-$ |
| C | 4A (14) | 1 C | $\times$ 4$e^-$ | = | 4$e^-$ |
| | Total valence electrons for $CO_2$ | | | = | 16$e^-$ |

**STEP 3** **Attach the central atom to each bonded atom by a pair of electrons.**

O:C:O or O—C—O

**STEP 4** **Arrange remaining electrons as lone pairs to complete octets.** Four (4) electrons (2 × 2 $e^-$) are used to bond the central C atom to the O atoms. The number of valence electrons remaining is

16 valence $e^-$ − 4 bonding $e^-$ = 12$e^-$ remaining

The remaining 12 electrons are placed as 6 lone pairs to complete the octets for the O atoms.

:Ö:C:Ö: or :Ö—C—Ö:

If octets are not complete, move one or more electron pairs between the central and attached atoms to form multiple bonds.

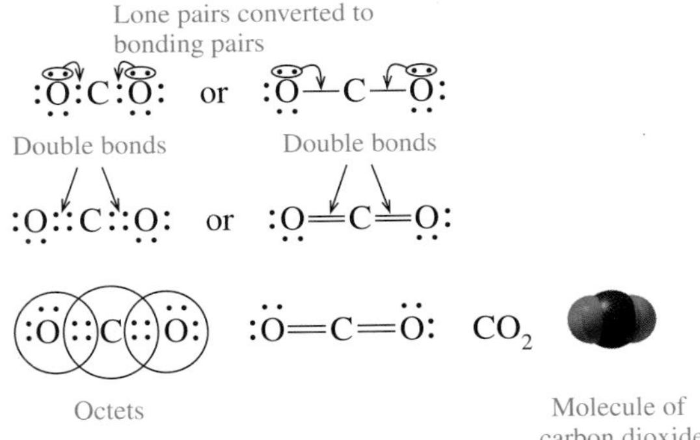


Molecule of carbon dioxide

STUDY CHECK

Write the electron-dot formula for HCN (atoms arranged as H C N).

## Resonance Structures

When a molecule or polyatomic ion contains multiple bonds, it is often possible to write more than one electron-dot formula for the same arrangement of atoms. Suppose we want to write the electron-dot formula for ozone, $O_3$, a component in the stratosphere that protects us from the ultraviolet rays of the sun. Although all 18 valence electrons are used, one of the oxygen atoms does not have an octet. One lone pair must be moved to form a double bond. But which one should be used? One possibility is to form a double bond

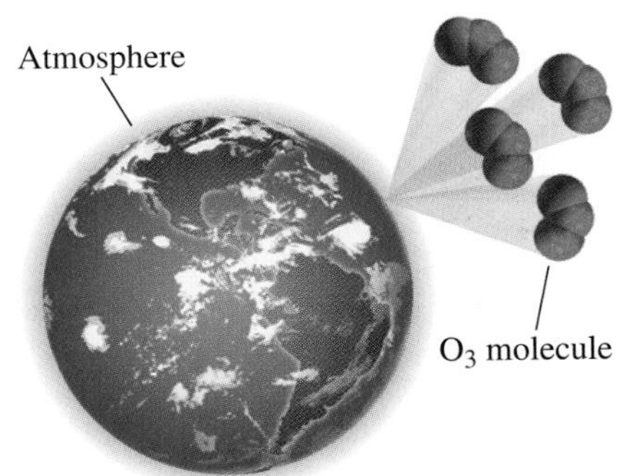

with the O atom on the left. The other possibility is to form a double bond with the O atom on the right.

:Ö—Ö—Ö:

or

:Ö—Ö—Ö: :Ö—Ö—Ö:

:Ö=Ö—Ö: ⟷ :Ö—Ö=Ö: or :Ö—Ö—Ö:

Resonance structures Hybrid

Experiments show that the actual bond is equivalent to a "one and a half" bond between the central O atom and each of the attached O atoms. In this *hybrid*, the electrons are shown spread equally over all the O atoms. When two or more electron-dot formulas can be written, they are called **resonance structures** and shown with a double-headed arrow. Although we will write resonance structures of some molecules and ions, the true structure is really a mix, or average, of the possible structures.

CONCEPT CHECK 5.4

### Resonance Structures

Explain why $SCl_2$ does not have resonance structures, but $SO_2$ does.

ANSWER

In the electron-dot formula of $SCl_2$, the single valence electrons of each chlorine atom complete the octet of the sulfur atom. However, in $SO_2$, the central sulfur atom must form a double bond with one of the oxygen atoms. Thus, two electron-dot formulas, or resonance structures, are possible.

SAMPLE PROBLEM 5.9

### Writing Resonance Structures

Write two resonance structures for sulfur dioxide, $SO_2$.

SOLUTION

**STEP 1** **Determine the arrangement of atoms.** In $SO_2$, the S atom is the central atom.

O S O

**STEP 2** **Determine the total number of valence electrons.** We can use the group numbers to determine the valence electrons for each atom in the molecule.

| Element | Group | Atoms | Valence Electrons | = | Total |
|---|---|---|---|---|---|
| S | 6A (16) | 1 S | $\times 6e^-$ | = | $6e^-$ |
| O | 6A (16) | 2 O | $\times 6e^-$ | = | $12e^-$ |
| | Total valence electrons for $SO_2$ | | | = | $18e^-$ |

**STEP 3** **Attach the central atom to each bonded atom by a pair of electrons.** We will use a single line to represent a pair of bonding electrons.

O—S—O

**STEP 4** **Arrange the remaining electrons to complete octets.** Four (4) electrons are used to write single bonds between the S atom and the O atoms. The number of valence electrons that remain is

18 valence $e^-$ − 4 bonding $e^-$ = $14e^-$ remaining

The remaining electrons are placed as lone pairs around the O atoms first. One lone pair remains, which is assigned to the S atom.

:Ö—S̈—Ö:

The octet for S is completed using one lone pair from an O atom as a bonding pair, and thus forming a double bond. Because two electron-dot formulas can be written using a lone pair from either O atom, two resonance structures are possible.

$$:\ddot{\underset{..}{O}}—\ddot{S}=\ddot{O}: \longleftrightarrow :\ddot{O}=\ddot{S}—\ddot{\underset{..}{O}}:$$

STUDY CHECK

Write three resonance structures for $SO_3$.

## QUESTIONS AND PROBLEMS

### Covalent Compounds

**5.39** What elements on the periodic table are most likely to form covalent compounds?

**5.40** How does the bond that forms between Na and Cl differ from a bond that forms between N and Cl?

**5.41** State the number of valence electrons, bonding pairs, and lone pairs in each of the following electron-dot formulas:

**a.** H:H **b.** H:Br: **c.** :Br:Br:

**5.42** State the number of valence electrons, bonding pairs, and lone pairs in each of the following electron-dot formulas:

**a.** H:O: (with H above O) **b.** H:N:H (with H below N) **c.** :Br:O: (with :Br: above Br)

**5.43** Write the electron-dot formula for each of the following molecules:

**a.** HF **b.** $SF_2$ **c.** $NBr_3$

**d.** $CH_3OH$ (methyl alcohol)

```
  H
H C O H
  H
```

**e.** $N_2H_4$ (hydrazine)

```
 H H
H N N H
```

**5.44** Write the electron-dot formula for each of the following molecules:

**a.** $H_2O$ **b.** $CCl_4$ **c.** $SiF_4$ **d.** $CF_2Cl_2$

**e.** $C_2H_6$ (ethane)

```
 H H
H C C H
 H H
```

**5.45** When is it necessary to write a multiple bond in an electron-dot formula?

**5.46** If the available valence electrons for a molecule do not complete all of the octets in an electron-dot formula, what should you do?

**5.47** What is resonance?

**5.48** When does a covalent compound have resonance?

**5.49** Write the electron-dot formula for each of the following molecules:

**a.** CO (carbon monoxide)
**b.** $H_2CCH_2$ (ethylene)
**c.** $H_2CO$ (C is the central atom)

**5.50** Write the electron-dot formula for each of the following molecules:

**a.** HCCH (acetylene)
**b.** $CS_2$ (C is the central atom)
**c.** $COCl_2$ (C is the central atom)

**5.51** Write resonance structures for $ClNO_2$ (N is the central atom).

**5.52** Write resonance structures for $N_2O$ (N N O).

## 5.6 Naming and Writing Covalent Formulas

LEARNING GOAL

Given the formula of a covalent compound, write its correct name; given the name of a covalent compound, write its formula.

When naming a covalent compound, the first nonmetal in the formula is named by its elemental name; the second nonmetal is named by its elemental name with the ending changed to *ide*. Subscripts that indicate two or more atoms of an element are expressed as prefixes placed in front of each name. Table 5.12 lists prefixes used in naming covalent compounds. The names of covalent compounds need prefixes because several different compounds can be formed from the same two nonmetals. For example, carbon and oxygen can form two different compounds: carbon monoxide (CO) and carbon dioxide ($CO_2$).

When the vowels *o* and *o* or *a* and *o* appear together, the first vowel is omitted as in carbon monoxide. In the name of a covalent compound, the prefix *mono* is usually omitted, as in NO, nitrogen oxide. Traditionally, however, CO is named carbon monoxide. Table 5.13 lists the formulas, names, and commercial uses of some covalent compounds.

**TABLE 5.12** Prefixes Used in Naming Covalent Compounds

| | | | |
|---|---|---|---|
| 1 | mono | 6 | hexa |
| 2 | di | 7 | hepta |
| 3 | tri | 8 | octa |
| 4 | tetra | 9 | nona |
| 5 | penta | 10 | deca |

**TABLE 5.13** Some Common Covalent Compounds

| Formula | Name | Commercial Uses |
|---|---|---|
| $CS_2$ | Carbon disulfide | Manufacture of rayon |
| $CO_2$ | Carbon dioxide | Carbonation of beverages; fire extinguishers; propellant in aerosols; dry ice |
| NO | Nitrogen oxide | Stabilizer |
| $N_2O$ | Dinitrogen oxide | Inhalation anesthetic: "laughing gas" |
| $SiO_2$ | Silicon dioxide | Manufacture of glass |
| $SO_2$ | Sulfur dioxide | Preserving fruits, vegetables; disinfectant in breweries; bleaching textiles |
| $SF_6$ | Sulfur hexafluoride | Electrical circuits |

CONCEPT CHECK 5.5

### Naming Covalent Compounds

Why is it that the name of the covalent compound BrCl, bromine chloride, does not include a prefix, but the name of $OCl_2$, oxygen dichloride, does?

ANSWER

When a formula has one atom of each element, no prefix (*mono*) is needed in the name bromine chloride. In $OCl_2$, two atoms of chlorine are indicated by the prefix *di*, oxygen dichloride.

SAMPLE PROBLEM 5.10

### Naming Covalent Compounds

Name the covalent compound $NCl_3$.

SOLUTION

We can use the guide for naming covalent compounds to name this covalent compound.

**STEP 1** **Name the first nonmetal by its element name.** In $NCl_3$, the first nonmetal (N) is nitrogen.

**STEP 2** **Name the second nonmetal by changing the last part of its element name to *ide*.** The second nonmetal (Cl) is named *chloride*.

**STEP 3** **Add prefixes to indicate the number of atoms of each nonmetal.** Because there is only one nitrogen atom, the prefix *mono* is understood and not used. The subscript indicating three Cl atoms is shown as the prefix *tri*.

$NCl_3$ nitrogen trichloride

STUDY CHECK

Write the name of each of the following compounds:

**a.** $SiBr_4$ **b.** $Br_2O$

**Guide to Naming Covalent Compounds with Two Nonmetals**

STEP 1
Name the first nonmetal by its element name.

STEP 2
Name the second nonmetal by using the first syllable of its element name followed by *ide*.

STEP 3
Add prefixes to indicate the number of atoms (subscripts).

## Writing Formulas from the Names of Covalent Compounds

In the name of a covalent compound, the names of two nonmetals are given along with prefixes for the number of atoms of each. To obtain a formula, we write the symbol for each element and a subscript if a prefix indicates two or more atoms.

SAMPLE PROBLEM 5.11

## Writing Formulas for Covalent Compounds

Write the formula for diboron trioxide.

SOLUTION

**STEP 1** **Write the symbols in order of the elements in the name.** The first nonmetal is boron and the second nonmetal is oxygen.

B O

**STEP 2** **Write prefixes as subscripts.** The prefix *di* in *diboron* indicates that there are two atoms of boron shown as a subscript 2 in the formula. The prefix *tri* in *trioxide* indicates that there are three atoms of oxygen shown as a subscript 3 in the formula.

$B_2O_3$

STUDY CHECK

What is the formula of iodine heptafluoride?

**Guide to Writing Formulas for Covalent Compounds**

STEP 1
Write the symbols in the order of the elements in the name.

STEP 2
Write any prefixes as subscripts.

## Summary of Naming Compounds

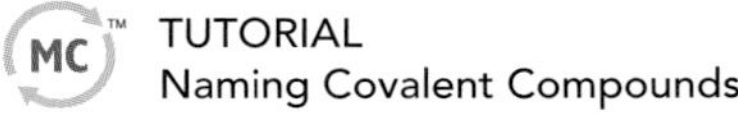


Throughout this chapter we have examined strategies for naming ionic and covalent compounds. Now we can summarize the rules, as illustrated in Figure 5.4. In general, compounds having two elements are named by stating the first element, followed by the second element with an *ide* ending. If the first element is a metal, then the compound is ionic; if the first element is a nonmetal, then the compound is covalent. For ionic compounds, it is necessary to determine whether the metal can form more than one type of positive ion; if so,

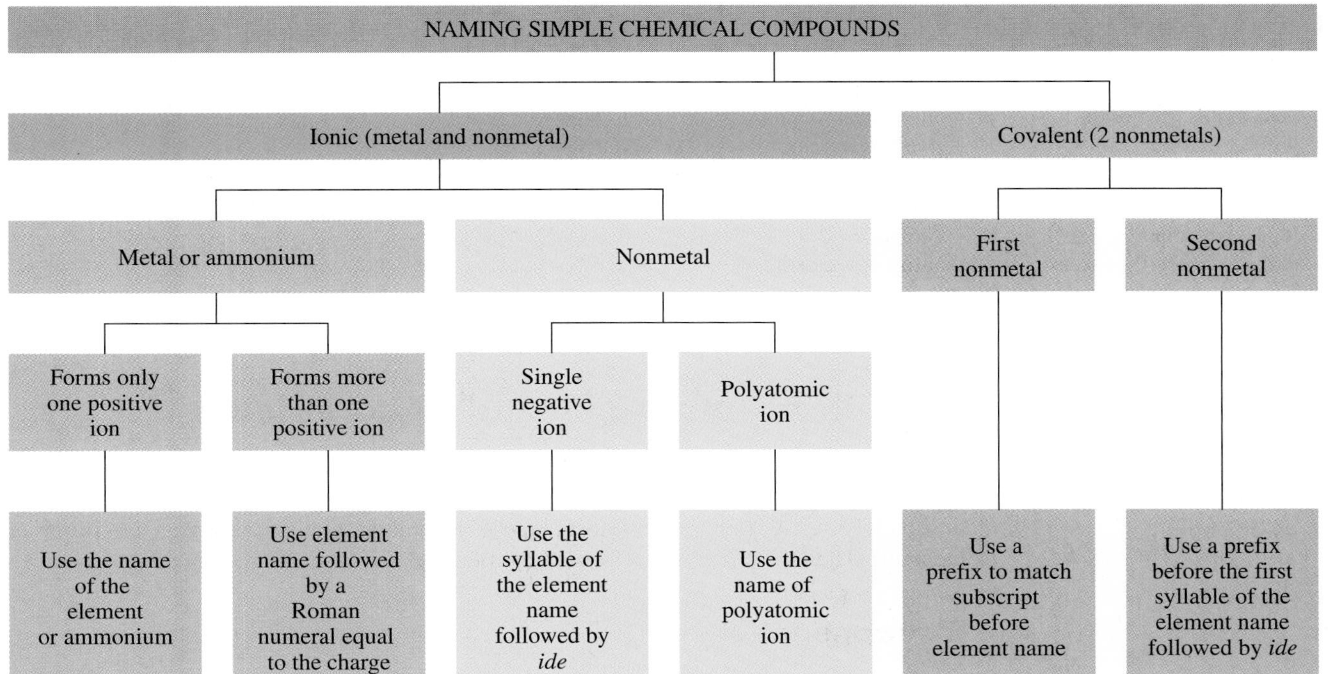


**FIGURE 5.4** A flowchart for naming ionic and covalent compounds

Q Why does the name sulfur dichloride have a prefix but magnesium chloride does not?

then a Roman numeral following the name of the metal indicates the particular ionic charge. One exception is the ammonium ion $NH_4^+$, which is also written first as a positively charged polyatomic ion. In naming covalent compounds having two elements, prefixes are necessary to indicate the number of atoms of each nonmetal as shown in that particular formula. Organic compounds of C and H such as $CH_4$ and $C_2H_6$ use a different system of naming that we will discuss in a later chapter. Ionic compounds having three or more elements include some type of polyatomic ion. They are named by ionic rules, but have an *ate* or *ite* ending when the polyatomic ion has a negative charge.

CONCEPT CHECK 5.6

**Naming Ionic and Covalent Compounds**

Identify each of the following compounds as ionic or covalent and give its name:

**a.** $Na_3P$ **b.** $SO_2$

ANSWER

**a.** $Na_3P$, consisting of a metal and nonmetal, is an ionic compound. Na is a metal that forms a single ion, $Na^+$, named *sodium*. The single negative ion, $P^{3-}$, is *phosphide*. The compound is named sodium phosphide.

**b.** $SO_2$ consists of two nonmetals; it is covalent. The first element sulfur does not need a prefix because the formula has only one atom. The second element is named *dioxide* because there are two atoms of oxygen. Thus, $SO_2$ is named sulfur dioxide.

## QUESTIONS AND PROBLEMS

### Naming and Writing Covalent Formulas

**5.53** Name the following covalent compounds:
**a.** $PBr_3$ **b.** $CBr_4$ **c.** $SiO_2$
**d.** $N_2O_3$ **e.** $SiBr_4$ **f.** $PCl_5$

**5.54** Name the following covalent compounds:
**a.** $CS_2$ **b.** $P_2O_5$ **c.** $Cl_2O$
**d.** $PCl_3$ **e.** $IBr_3$ **f.** $SO_3$

**5.55** Write the formulas of the following covalent compounds:
**a.** carbon tetrachloride **b.** carbon monoxide
**c.** phosphorus trichloride **d.** dinitrogen tetroxide
**e.** boron trifluoride **f.** sulfur hexafluoride

**5.56** Write the formulas of the following covalent compounds:
**a.** sulfur dioxide **b.** silicon tetrachloride
**c.** iodine pentafluoride **d.** dinitrogen oxide
**e.** tetraphosphorus hexoxide **f.** dinitrogen pentoxide

**5.57** Name the compounds that are found in the following:
**a.** $Al_2(SO_4)_3$ antiperspirant
**b.** $CaCO_3$ antacid
**c.** $N_2O$ "laughing gas" (inhaled anesthetic)
**d.** $Na_3PO_4$ cathartic
**e.** $(NH_4)_2SO_4$ fertilizer
**f.** $Fe_2O_3$ pigment

**5.58** Name the compounds that are found in the following:
**a.** $N_2$ Earth's atmosphere
**b.** $Mg_3(PO_4)_2$ antacid
**c.** $FeSO_4$ iron supplement in vitamins
**d.** $MgSO_4$ Epsom salts
**e.** $Cu_2O$ fungicide
**f.** $SnF_2$ prevents dental caries

# 5.7 Electronegativity and Bond Polarity

LEARNING GOAL

Use electronegativity to determine the polarity of a bond.

In this chapter, we have seen that atoms form chemical bonds by gaining, losing, or sharing valence electrons. In bonds between identical nonmetal atoms, the bonding electrons are shared equally. However, in most compounds, bonds form between atoms of different elements. Then the bonding electrons are attracted to one atom more than the other.

## Electronegativity

SELF STUDY ACTIVITY Electronegativity

**Electronegativity** is the attraction of an atom for valence electrons in a chemical bond. (See Figure 5.5.) Nonmetals have higher electronegativity values than metals. The nonmetals with the highest electronegativity values are fluorine (4.0) at the top of Group 7A (17)

Electronegativity increases →

↑ Electronegativity increases

| 1 Group 1A | 2 Group 2A | 13 Group 3A | 14 Group 4A | 15 Group 5A | 16 Group 6A | 17 Group 7A | 18 Group 8A |
|---|---|---|---|---|---|---|---|
| H 2.1 | | | | | | | |
| Li 1.0 | Be 1.5 | B 2.0 | C 2.5 | N 3.0 | O 3.5 | F 4.0 | |
| Na 0.9 | Mg 1.2 | Al 1.5 | Si 1.8 | P 2.1 | S 2.5 | Cl 3.0 | |
| K 0.8 | Ca 1.0 | Ga 1.6 | Ge 1.8 | As 2.0 | Se 2.4 | Br 2.8 | |
| Rb 0.8 | Sr 1.0 | In 1.7 | Sn 1.8 | Sb 1.9 | Te 2.1 | I 2.5 | |
| Cs 0.7 | Ba 0.9 | Tl 1.8 | Pb 1.9 | Bi 1.9 | Po 2.0 | At 2.1 | |

**FIGURE 5.5** The electronegativity of representative elements indicates the attraction of an atom for valence electrons in a chemical bond. Electronegativity values increase not only across a period but also going up a group.

**Q** What element on the periodic table has the strongest attraction for shared electrons?

and oxygen (3.5) at the top of Group 6A (16). The metal cesium at the bottom of Group 1A (1) has the lowest electronegativity value of 0.7. Smaller atoms tend to have higher electronegativity values because the valence electrons are closer to their nuclei. Electronegativity values increase from left to right across each period as well as from bottom to top of each group. The values of electronegativity for the transition metals are also low, but we will not include them in our discussion. Note that there are no electronegativity values for the noble gases because they do not typically form bonds.

## Types of Bonding

Earlier we discussed bonding as either *ionic*, in which electrons are transferred, or *covalent*, in which electrons were equally shared. The difference in the electronegativity of two atoms can be used to predict the type of bond that forms. In H—H, the electronegativity difference is zero ($2.1 - 2.1 = 0$), which means the bonding electrons are shared equally. A covalent bond between atoms with identical or very similar electronegativity values is a **nonpolar covalent bond**. However, most covalent bonds are between atoms with different electronegativity values. When electrons are shared unequally, the bond is a **polar covalent bond**. In H—Cl, an electronegativity difference of 3.0 (Cl) − 2.1 (H) = 0.9 means that the H—Cl bond is polar covalent. (See Figure 5.6.)

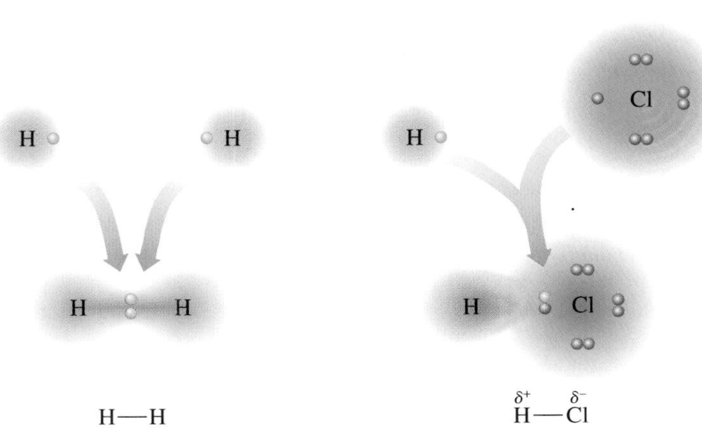


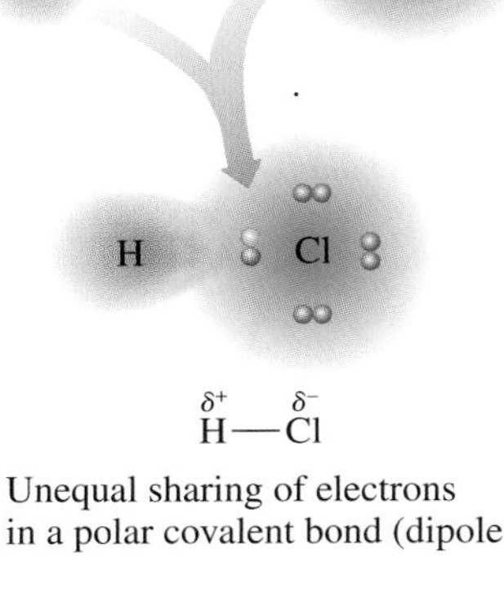


**FIGURE 5.6** In the nonpolar covalent bond of $H_2$, electrons are shared equally. In the polar covalent bond of HCl, electrons are shared unequally.

**Q** $H_2$ has a nonpolar covalent bond, but HCl has a polar covalent bond. Explain.

In a polar covalent bond, the shared electrons are attracted to the more electronegative atom, which makes it partially negative, whereas the atom with the lower electronegativity becomes partially positive. A polar covalent bond that has a separation of charges is called a **dipole**. The positive and negative ends of the dipole are indicated by the lowercase Greek letter delta with a positive or negative sign, $\delta^+$ and $\delta^-$. Sometimes an arrow pointing from the positive charge to the negative charge ($+\!\!\longrightarrow$) is used to indicate the dipole.

**Examples of Dipoles in Polar Covalent Bond**

$\overset{\delta^+}{C}—\overset{\delta^-}{O}$ $\qquad$ $\overset{\delta^+}{N}—\overset{\delta^-}{O}$ $\qquad$ $\overset{\delta^+}{Cl}—\overset{\delta^-}{F}$

$+\!\!\longrightarrow$ $\qquad$ $+\!\!\longrightarrow$ $\qquad$ $+\!\!\longrightarrow$

## Variations in Bonding

The variations in bonding are continuous; there is no definite point at which one type of bond stops and the next starts. However, we can use some general ranges for predicting the type of bond between atoms. When electronegativity differences are from 0.0 to 0.4, the electrons are shared about equally in a *nonpolar covalent bond.* As the electronegativity difference increases, the shared electrons are attracted more closely to the more electronegative atoms and the polarity of the bond increases. When the electronegativity difference is greater than 0.4 but less than 1.8, the bond is a *polar covalent bond.* (See Table 5.14.)

Eventually, the difference in electronegativity is great enough that the electrons are transferred from one atom to another, which results in an ionic bond. Differences in electronegativity of 1.8 or greater indicate that the bond is an *ionic bond.* (See Table 5.15.)

**TABLE 5.14 Electronegativity Difference and Types of Bonds**

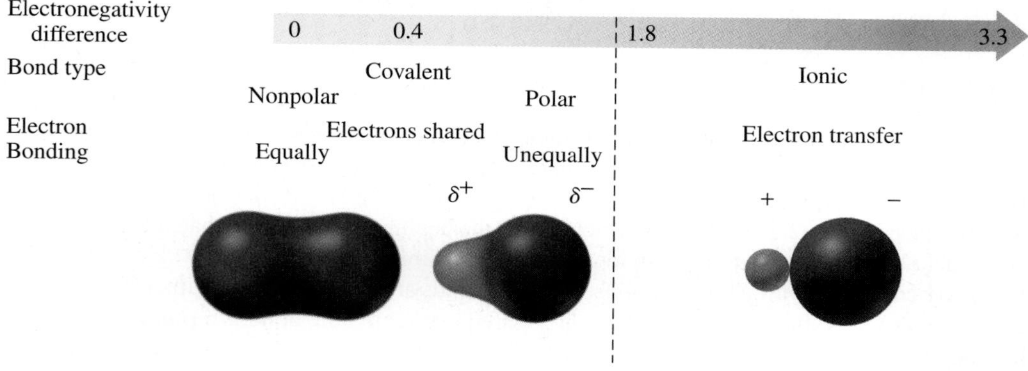


**TABLE 5.15 Predicting Bond Type from Electronegativity Differences**

| Molecule | Bond | Type of Electron Sharing | Electronegativity Difference[a] | Bond Type |
|---|---|---|---|---|
| $H_2$ | H—H | Shared equally | 2.1 − 2.1 = 0.0 | Nonpolar covalent |
| $Cl_2$ | Cl—Cl | Shared equally | 3.0 − 3.0 = 0.0 | Nonpolar covalent |
| $CH_4$ | C—H | Shared equally | 2.5 − 2.1 = 0.4 | Nonpolar covalent |
| HBr | $\overset{\delta^+}{H}—\overset{\delta^-}{Br}$ | Shared unequally | 2.8 − 2.1 = 0.7 | Polar covalent |
| HCl | $\overset{\delta^+}{H}—\overset{\delta^-}{Cl}$ | Shared unequally | 3.0 − 2.1 = 0.9 | Polar covalent |
| NaCl | $Na^+\ Cl^-$ | Electron transfer | 3.0 − 0.9 = 2.1 | Ionic |
| MgO | $Mg^{2+}\ O^{2-}$ | Electron transfer | 3.5 − 1.2 = 2.3 | Ionic |

[a]Values are taken from Figure 5.5.

SAMPLE PROBLEM 5.12

### Bond Polarity

Using electronegativity values, classify each bond as nonpolar covalent, polar covalent, or ionic:

N—N O—H Cl—As C—S O—K

SOLUTION

For each bond, we obtain the electronegativity values and calculate the difference.

| Bond | Electronegativity Difference | Type of Bond |
|---|---|---|
| N—N | 3.0 − 3.0 = 0.0 | Nonpolar covalent |
| O—H | 3.5 − 2.1 = 1.4 | Polar covalent |
| Cl—As | 3.0 − 2.0 = 1.0 | Polar covalent |
| C—S | 2.5 − 2.5 = 0.0 | Nonpolar covalent |
| O—K | 3.5 − 0.8 = 2.7 | Ionic |

STUDY CHECK

For each of the following pairs, identify the more polar bond:

**a.** Si—S or Si—N **b.** O—P or N—P

## QUESTIONS AND PROBLEMS

### Electronegativity and Bond Polarity

5.59 Describe the trend in electronegativity going from left to right across a period.

**5.60** Describe the trend in electronegativity going down a group.

5.61 Approximately what electronegativity difference would you expect for a nonpolar covalent bond?

**5.62** Approximately what electronegativity difference would you expect for a polar covalent bond?

5.63 Using the periodic table, arrange the atoms in each of the following sets in order of increasing electronegativity:
**a.** Li, Na, K **b.** Na, P, Cl **c.** O, Ca, Br

**5.64** Using the periodic table, arrange the atoms in each of the following sets in order of increasing electronegativity:
**a.** Cl, F, Br **b.** B, O, N **c.** Mg, F, S

5.65 Predict whether each of the following bonds is ionic, polar covalent, or nonpolar covalent:
**a.** Si—Br **b.** Li—F **c.** Br—F
**d.** Br—Br **e.** N—P **f.** C—O

**5.66** Predict whether each of the following bonds is ionic, polar covalent, or nonpolar covalent:
**a.** Si—O **b.** K—Cl **c.** S—F
**d.** P—Br **e.** Li—O **f.** O—P

5.67 For each of the following bonds, indicate the positive end with $\delta^+$ and the negative end with $\delta^-$. Write an arrow to show the dipole for each.
**a.** N—F **b.** Si—Br **c.** C—O
**d.** P—Br **e.** B—Cl

**5.68** For each of the following bonds, indicate the positive end with $\delta^+$ and the negative end with $\delta^-$. Write an arrow to show the dipole for each.
**a.** Si—Cl **b.** Se—F **c.** Br—F
**d.** N—H **e.** N—P

## 5.8 Shapes and Polarity of Molecules

LEARNING GOAL

Predict the three-dimensional structure of a molecule and classify it as polar or nonpolar.

With the information about valence electrons, electron-dot formulas, and polarity of bonds, we can look at the three-dimensional shapes of some molecules.

To predict molecular shape, we look at the geometry of the electron groups around a central atom. The **valence-shell electron-pair repulsion (VSEPR) theory** indicates that the electron groups will move as far apart as possible to reduce the repulsion between their negative charges. Once its electron-dot formula is written, the specific shape of a molecule can be determined.

## Two Electron Groups

In $BeCl_2$, two chlorine atoms are bonded to a central beryllium atom. Because Be has a strong attraction for its valence electrons, it forms a covalent rather than ionic compound. With only two electron groups around the central atom, the electron-dot formula of $BeCl_2$ is an exception to the octet rule. The best arrangement of two electron groups for minimal repulsion is to place them on opposite sides of the Be atom. This gives a **linear** shape and a bond angle of 180° to the $BeCl_2$ molecule.

180°

Linear

:C̤̈l—Be—C̤̈l:

Another example of a linear molecule is $CO_2$. In predicting shape, a double or triple bond is treated the same as one electron group. Thus, a multiple bond is counted as a single electron group in determining electron repulsion. In $CO_2$, the two double bonds, which are counted as one electron group each around C, are arranged on opposite sides of the C atom. With two double bonds, the shape of the $CO_2$ molecule is linear and has a bond angle of 180°.

180°

Linear

:Ö=C=Ö:

## Three Electron Groups

In $BF_3$, the central atom B is attached to fluorine atoms by three electron groups (another exception to the octet rule). The arrangement of three electron groups as far apart as possible is called **trigonal planar** and has bond angles of 120°. In $BF_3$, each electron group is bonded to an atom, which gives $BF_3$ a trigonal planar structure. Thus, the $BF_3$ molecule is flat with all the atoms in the same plane and 120° bond angles.

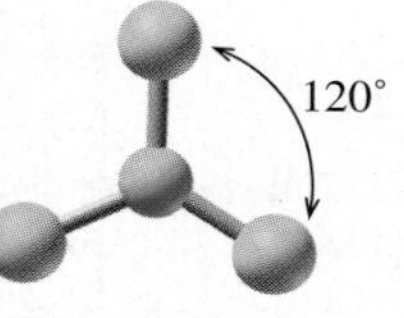


Trigonal planar

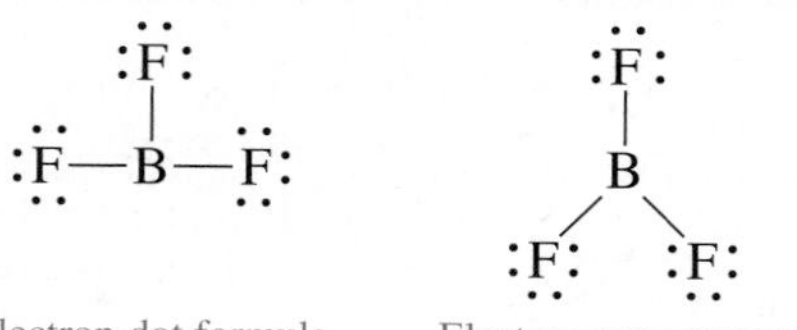

Electron-dot formula    Electron arrangement

In the electron-dot formula for $SO_2$, there is a single bond, a double bond, and a lone pair of electrons surrounding the S atom. Thus three electron groups surrounding the S atom attain a trigonal planar arrangement for minimal repulsion. But only the bonded atoms attached to the central atom determine the shape and structure of a molecule. Therefore, with two O atoms bonded to the central S atom, the structure of the $SO_2$ molecule is a **bent** shape. In the $SO_2$ molecule, the bond angle is slightly affected by the lone pair but close to 120°.

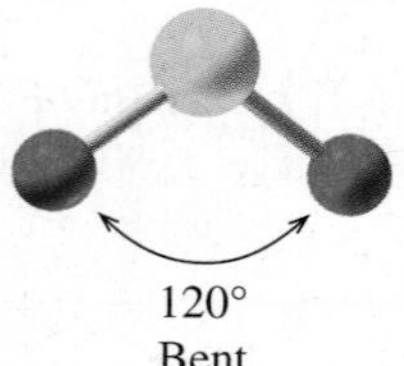

120°

Bent

:Ö—S̈=O:

Electron-dot formula    Electron arrangement

## Four Electron Groups

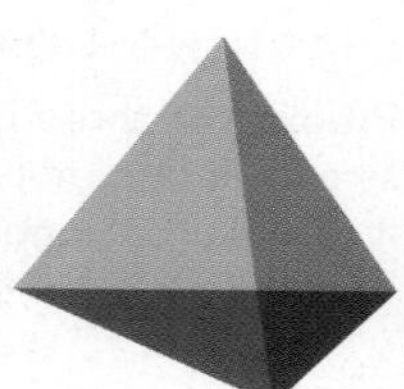

Up to now, the shapes of molecules have been in two dimensions. However, when there are four electron groups around a central atom, the minimum repulsion is obtained by placing four electron groups at the corners of a three-dimensional tetrahedron. A regular tetrahedron consists of four sides that are equilateral triangles. For molecules with four electron groups, the central atom is located in the center of a tetrahedron.

In $CH_4$, the central atom is bonded to four hydrogen atoms. From the electron-dot formula, $CH_4$ appears planar with 90° bond angles, but this is not the largest angle possible.

The best arrangement for minimal repulsion is **tetrahedral**, which places the bonded atoms at the corners of a tetrahedron to give bond angles of 109.5°.

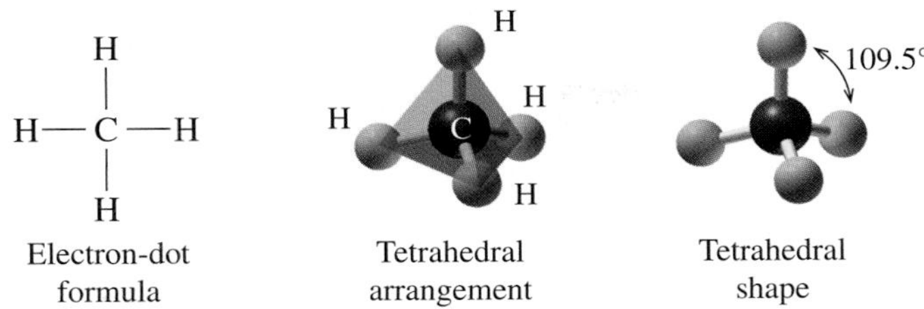


Now we will look at other molecules with four electron groups but only two or three attached atoms. For example, in ammonia, $NH_3$, the three bonded H atoms and one lone electron pair occupy the corners of a tetrahedron. Because one corner has no bonded atom, the $NH_3$ molecule has a **trigonal pyramidal** shape. In the $NH_3$ molecule, the bond angles are decreased by the strong negatively charged lone pair to about 107°.

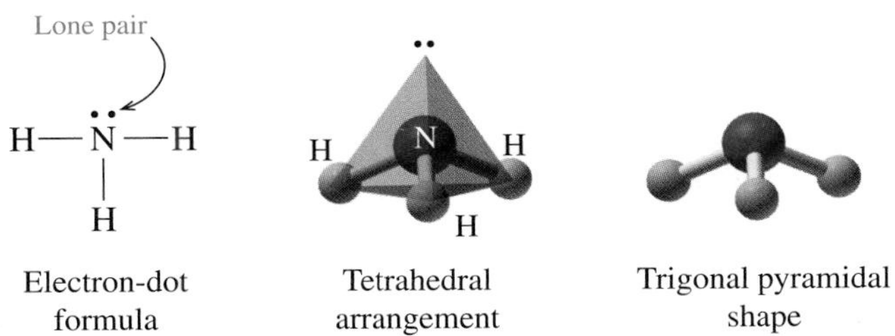


In water, $H_2O$, there are two bonded H atoms and two lone pairs of electrons. These four electron groups have a tetrahedral arrangement around the central O atom. A molecule with four electron groups but only two bonded atoms has a *bent* shape. In the $H_2O$ molecule, the bond angle is decreased because of the negatively charged lone pairs to about 105°. Table 5.16 gives the molecular shapes for molecules with two, three, and four electron groups.

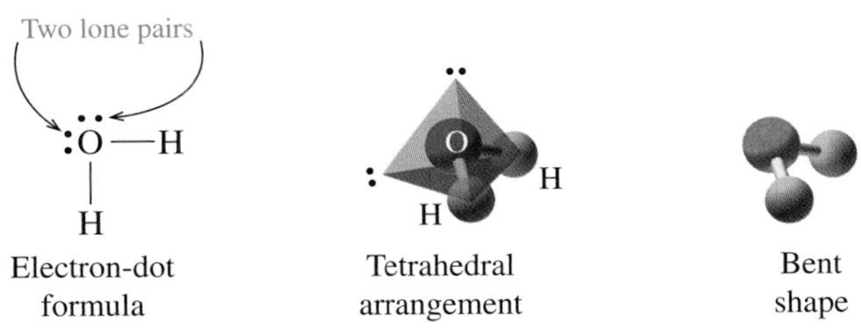


## SAMPLE PROBLEM 5.13

### Predicting Shapes

Use VSEPR theory to predict the shape of the following molecules:

**a.** $PH_3$ **b.** $H_2Se$

SOLUTION

We will use the guide to predict the shape of molecules.

**a.** $PH_3$

**STEP 1** **Write the electron-dot formula.** In the electron-dot formula for $PH_3$, there are four electron groups.

```
   ..
H—P—H
   |
   H
```

**Guide to Predicting Molecular Shape (VSEPR Theory)**

STEP 1
Write the electron-dot formula for the melecule.

STEP 2
Arrange the electron groups around the central atom to minimize repulsion.

STEP 3
Use the atoms bonded to the central atom to determine the molecular shape.

**STEP 2** **Arrange the electron groups around the central atom to minimize repulsion.** The four electron groups have a tetrahedral arrangement.

**STEP 3** **Use the atoms bonded to the central atom to determine the molecular shape.** Three bonded atoms and one lone pair give $PH_3$ a trigonal pyramidal shape.

**b.** $H_2Se$

**STEP 1** **Write the electron-dot formula.** In the electron-dot formula for $H_2Se$, there are four electron groups.

```
 ..
:Se—H
  |
  H
```

**STEP 2** **Arrange the electron groups around the central atom to minimize repulsion.** The four electron groups around Se would have a tetrahedral arrangement.

**STEP 3** **Use the atoms bonded to the central atom to determine the molecular shape.** Two bonded atoms and two lone pairs give $H_2Se$ a bent shape.

STUDY CHECK

Predict the shape of $CBr_4$.

**TABLE 5.16** Examples of Shapes of Molecules

| Molecule | Electron-Dot Formula | Bonded Atoms | Molecular Shape (angle) |
|---|---|---|---|
| **Two (2) electron groups around the central atom** | | | |
| $BeCl_2$ | :C̤̈l:Be:C̤̈l: | 2 | linear (180°) |
| $CO_2$ | :Ö::C::Ö: | 2 | linear (180°) |
| **Three (3) electron groups around the central atom** | | | |
| $BF_3$ | :F̤: above :F̤:B:F̤: | 3 | trigonal planar (120°) |
| $SO_2$ | :Ö:S̈ :: :Ö: | 2 | bent (120°) |
| **Four (4) electron groups around the central atom** | | | |
| $CH_4$ | H:C:H with H above and below | 4 | tetrahedral (109.5°) |
| $NH_3$ | H:N̈:H with H below | 3 | trigonal pyramidal (107°) |
| $H_2O$ | :Ö:H with H below | 2 | bent (105°) |

## Polarity of Molecules

We have seen that covalent bonds in molecules can be polar or nonpolar. Molecules can also be polar or nonpolar, depending on their shape. Diatomic molecules such as $H_2$ and $Cl_2$ are nonpolar because they contain one nonpolar covalent bond.

H—H Cl—Cl

Nonpolar

Molecules with two or more polar bonds can also be nonpolar if the polar bonds have a symmetrical arrangement in the molecule.

In a **polar molecule**, one end of the molecule is more negatively charged than another end. Polarity in a molecule occurs when the polar bonds do not cancel each other. This cancellation depends on the type of atoms, the electron pairs around the central atom, and the shape of the molecule. For example, the HCl molecule is polar because electrons are shared unequally in a polar covalent bond.

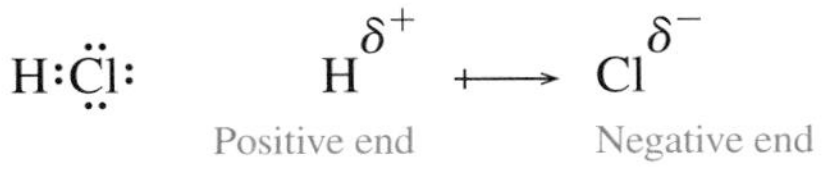

H:Cl: $\overset{\delta^+}{\text{H}}$ $\longleftrightarrow$ $\overset{\delta^-}{\text{Cl}}$

Positive end Negative end

In polar molecules with three or more atoms, the shape of the molecule determines whether the dipoles cancel or not. Often there are lone pairs around the central atom. In $H_2O$, the dipoles do not cancel, which makes the molecule positive at one end and negative at the other end. This gives the molecule a dipole.

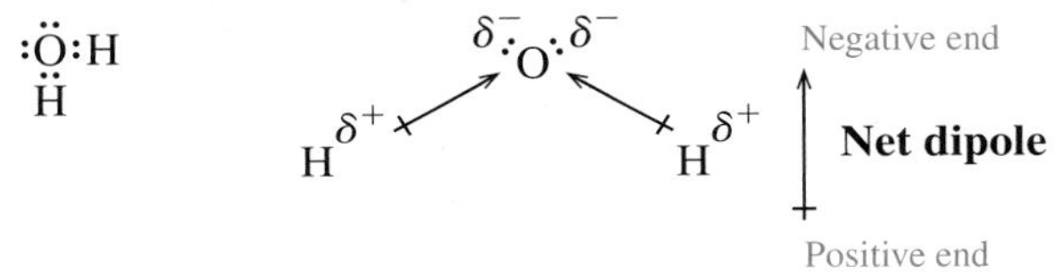

:Ö:H
H

Negative end

**Net dipole**

Positive end

In the molecule $NH_3$, there are three dipoles, but they do not cancel.

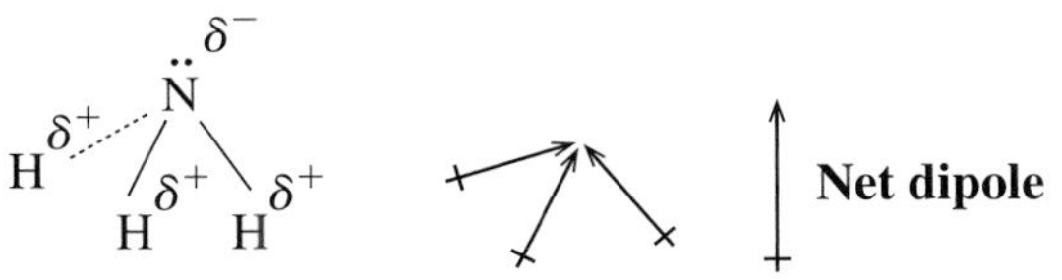

**Net dipole**

A **nonpolar molecule** occurs when the polar bonds or dipoles in a molecule cancel each other. For example, $CO_2$ and $CCl_4$ contain polar bonds. However, the symmetrical arrangement of the polar bonds cancels the dipoles, which makes $CO_2$ and $CCl_4$ molecules nonpolar.

**Examples of Nonpolar Molecules with Polar Bonds**

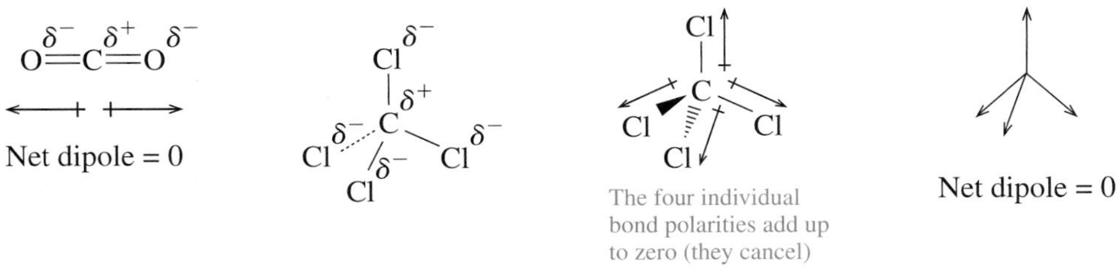

$\overset{\delta^-}{\text{O}}=\overset{\delta^+}{\text{C}}=\overset{\delta^-}{\text{O}}$

Net dipole = 0

The four individual bond polarities add up to zero (they cancel)

Net dipole = 0

SAMPLE PROBLEM 5.14

### ■ Polarity of Molecules

Determine whether each of the following molecules is polar or nonpolar:

**a.** $SiCl_4$ **b.** $OF_2$

SOLUTION

**a.** The electron-dot formula for $SiCl_4$ has four bonded atoms and no lone pairs.

$$\begin{array}{c} :\ddot{Cl}: \\ :\ddot{Cl}:\ddot{Si}:\ddot{Cl}: \\ :\ddot{Cl}: \end{array}$$

The molecule would have a tetrahedral shape. With four identical atoms bonded to the central atom and no lone pairs, the polar Si–Cl bonds cancel, and $SiCl_4$ would be nonpolar.

**b.** The electron-dot formula for $OF_2$ shows four electron groups with two bonded atoms and two lone pairs.

$$\begin{array}{l} :\ddot{O}:\ddot{F}: \\ :\ddot{F}: \end{array}$$

The molecule would have a bent shape. The two polar O–F bonds do not cancel, which makes $OF_2$ a polar molecule.

STUDY CHECK

Would $PCl_3$ be a polar or nonpolar molecule?

## QUESTIONS AND PROBLEMS

### Shapes and Polarity of Molecules

**5.69** What is the shape of a molecule if the central atom has four bonded atoms and no lone pairs?

**5.70** What is the shape of a molecule if the central atom has two bonded atoms and two lone pairs?

**5.71** In the molecule $PCl_3$, the four electron groups around the phosphorus atom are arranged in a tetrahedral geometry. However, the shape of the molecule is trigonal pyramidal. Why does the shape of the molecule have a different name from the name of the electron group geometry?

**5.72** In the molecule $H_2S$, the four electron groups around the sulfur atom are arranged in a tetrahedral geometry. However, the shape of the molecule is bent. Why does the shape of the molecule have a different name from the name of the electron group geometry?

**5.73** Compare the electron-dot formulas of $PH_3$ and $NH_3$. Why do these molecules have the same shape?

**5.74** Compare the electron-dot formulas $CH_4$ and $H_2O$. Why do these molecules have approximately the same angles but different shapes?

**5.75** Use the VSEPR theory to predict the shape of each molecule:
**a.** $OF_2$ **b.** $CCl_4$ **c.** HCN **d.** $SeO_2$

**5.76** Use the VSEPR theory to predict the shape of each molecule:
**a.** $NCl_3$ **b.** $SCl_2$ **c.** $CF_4$ **d.** $CS_2$

**5.77** The molecule $Cl_2$ is nonpolar, but HCl is polar. Explain.

**5.78** The molecules $CH_4$ and $CH_3Cl$ both contain four bonds. Why is $CH_4$ nonpolar whereas $CH_3Cl$ is polar?

**5.79** Identify the following molecules as polar or nonpolar:
**a.** HBr **b.** $NF_3$ **c.** $CBr_4$ **d.** $SO_3$

**5.80** Identify the following molecules as polar or nonpolar:
**a.** $H_2S$ **b.** $PBr_3$ **c.** $SiCl_4$ **d.** $SO_2$

## 5.9 Attractive Forces in Compounds

LEARNING GOAL

Describe the attractive forces between ions, polar molecules, and nonpolar molecules.

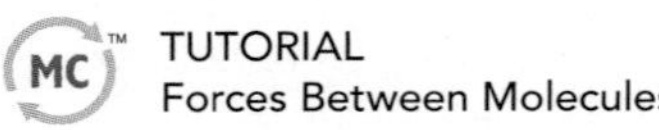


In gases, the interactions between particles are minimal, which allows gas molecules to move far apart from each other. In solids and liquids, there are sufficient interactions between the particles to hold them close together, although some solids have low melting points whereas others have extremely high melting points. Such differences in properties are explained by looking at the various kinds of attractive forces between particles.

Ionic compounds have high melting points. For example, solid NaCl melts at 801 °C. Large amounts of energy are needed to overcome the strong attractive forces between positive and negative ions. Solids that contain molecules with covalent bonds also have attractive forces, but they are weaker than those of ionic compounds.

## Dipole–Dipole Attractions and Hydrogen Bonds

For polar molecules, attractive forces called **dipole–dipole attractions** occur between the positive end of one molecule and the negative end of another. For a polar molecule with a dipole such as HCl, the partially positive H atom of one HCl molecule attracts the partially negative Cl atom in another molecule.

When a hydrogen atom is attached to highly electronegative atoms of fluorine, oxygen, or nitrogen, there are strong dipole–dipole attractions between the polar molecules. This type of attraction, called a **hydrogen bond**, occurs between the partially positive hydrogen atom of one molecule and a lone pair of electrons on a nitrogen, oxygen, or fluorine atom in another molecule. Hydrogen bonds are the strongest type of attractive forces between polar molecules. They are a major factor in the formation and structure of biological molecules such as proteins and DNA.

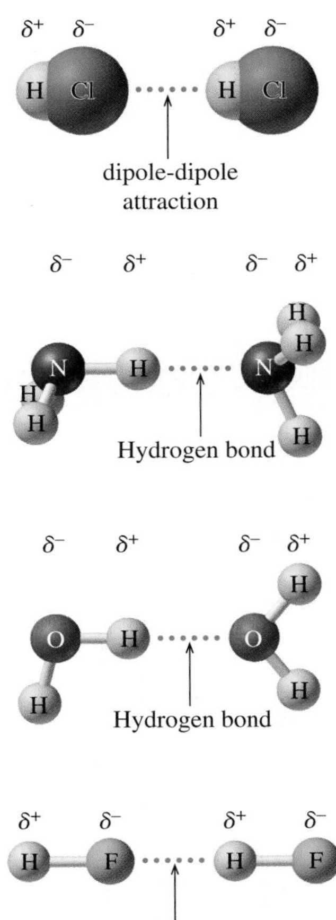


## Dispersion Forces

Nonpolar compounds can form solids but only at low temperatures. Very weak attractions called **dispersion forces** occur between nonpolar molecules. Usually, the electrons in a nonpolar molecule are distributed symmetrically. However, electrons may accumulate more in one part of the molecule than another, which forms a temporary dipole. Although dispersion forces are especially weak, they make it possible for nonpolar molecules to form liquids and solids.

The melting points of substances are related to the strength of the attractive forces within the compound. Compounds with weak attractive forces such as dispersion forces have low melting points because only a small amount of energy is needed to separate the molecules and form a liquid. Compounds with hydrogen bonds and dipole–dipole attractions require more energy to break the attractive forces between the molecules. The highest melting points are seen with ionic compounds that have extremely strong attractions between ions. Table 5.17 compares the melting points of some substances with various kinds of attractive forces. The various types of attractions between particles in solids and liquids are summarized in Table 5.18.

**TABLE 5.18** Comparison of Bonding and Attractive Forces

| Type of Force | Particle Arrangement | Example | Strength |
|---|---|---|---|
| **Ionic bonds** | + − + / − + − | $Na^+$ - - - $Cl^-$ | **Strong** |
| **Hydrogen bonds** (X = F, O, or N) | δ+ δ− δ+ δ− H X - - H X | δ+ δ− δ+ δ− H—F - - - H—F | |
| **Dipole–dipole attractions** (X and Y = different nonmetals) | δ+ δ− δ+ δ− Y X - - Y X | δ+ δ− δ+ δ− Br—Cl - - - Br—Cl | |
| **Dispersion forces** (Temporary shift of electrons in nonpolar bonds) | δ+ δ− δ+ δ− (temporary dipoles) X :X - - X :X | δ+ δ− δ+ δ− F—F - - - F—F | **Weak** |

**TABLE 5.17** Melting Points of Selected Substances

| Substance | Melting Point (°C) |
|---|---|
| **Ionic bonds** | |
| $MgF_2$ | 1248 |
| NaCl | 801 |
| **Hydrogen bonds** | |
| $H_2O$ | 0 |
| $NH_3$ | −78 |
| **Dipole–dipole attractions** | |
| HBr | −89 |
| HCl | −115 |
| **Dispersion forces** | |
| $Cl_2$ | −101 |
| $F_2$ | −220 |
| $CH_4$ | −182 |

SAMPLE PROBLEM 5.15

### Attractive Forces Between Particles

Indicate the major type of molecular interaction expected of each of the following:

**1.** dipole–dipole attractions **2.** hydrogen bonding **3.** dispersion forces

**a.** HF **b.** $I_2$ **c.** $PCl_3$

SOLUTION

**a. 2:** HF is a polar molecule that interacts with other HF molecules by hydrogen bonding.
**b. 3:** $I_2$ is nonpolar; only dispersion forces provide attractive forces.
**c. 1:** The polarity of the $PCl_3$ molecules provides dipole–dipole attractions.

STUDY CHECK

Why is the boiling point of $H_2S$ lower than that of $H_2O$?

## QUESTIONS AND PROBLEMS

### Attractive Forces in Compounds

**5.81** Identify the major type of interactive force in each of the following:
**a.** BrF **b.** KCl **c.** $CCl_4$ **d.** HF **e.** $Cl_2$

**5.82** Identify the major type of interactive force in each of the following:
**a.** HCl **b.** $MgF_2$ **c.** $PBr_3$ **d.** $Br_2$ **e.** $NH_3$

**5.83** Identify the strongest attractive forces between molecules of each of the following:
**a.** $CH_3OH$ **b.** $Cl_2$ **c.** HCl
**d.** $CCl_4$ **e.** $CH_3CH_3$

**5.84** Identify the strongest attractive forces between molecules of each of the following:
**a.** $O_2$ **b.** HF **c.** $CH_3Cl$ **d.** $H_2O$ **e.** $NH_3$

**5.85** Identify the substance in each pair that would have the higher boiling point and explain your choice:
**a.** HF or HBr **b.** HF or NaF
**c.** $MgBr_2$ or $PBr_3$ **d.** $CH_4$ or $CH_3OH$

**5.86** Identify the substance in each pair that would have the higher boiling point and explain your choice:
**a.** $MgCl_2$ or $PCl_3$ **b.** $H_2O$ or $H_2Se$
**c.** $NH_3$ or $PH_3$ **d.** $F_2$ or HF

## CONCEPT MAP

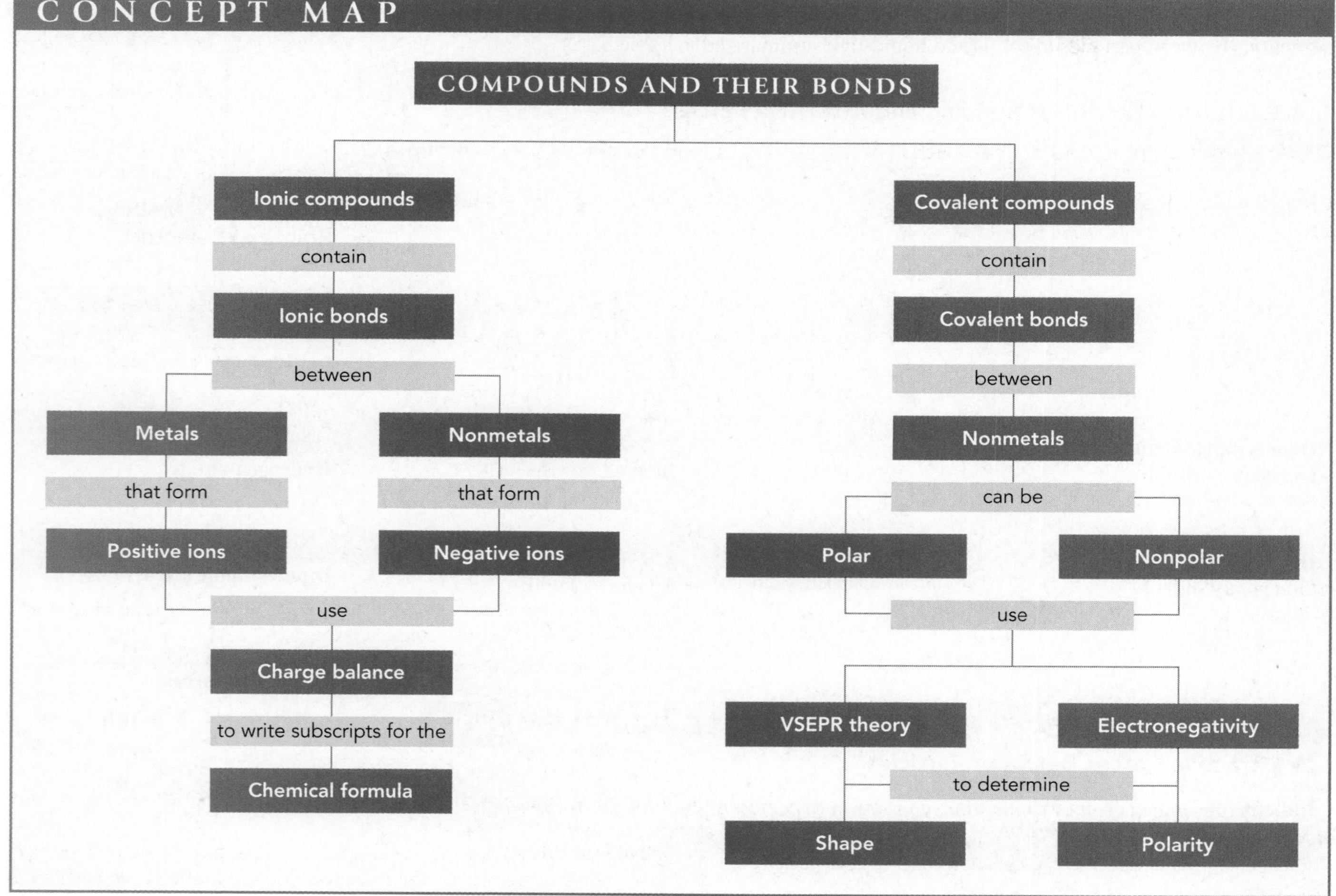

# CHAPTER REVIEW

## 5.1 Octet Rule and Ions

**LEARNING GOAL:** *Using the octet rule, write the symbols of the simple ions for the representative elements.*

The stability of the noble gases is associated with 8 electrons, an octet, in their valence shells; helium needs 2 electrons for stability. Atoms of elements in Groups 1A–7A (1, 2, 13–17) achieve stability by losing, gaining, or sharing their valence electrons in the formation of compounds. Metals of the representative elements form octets by losing valence electrons to form positively charged ions (cations): Group 1A (1), 1+, Group 2A (2), 2+, and Group 3A (13), 3+. When reacting with metals, nonmetals gain electrons to form octets and form negatively charged ions (anions): Group 5A (15), 3−, Group 6A (16), 2−, Group 7A (17), 1−.

## 5.2 Ionic Compounds

**LEARNING GOAL:** *Using charge balance, write the correct formula for an ionic compound.*

The total positive and negative ionic charge is balanced in the formula of an ionic compound. Charge balance in a formula is achieved by using subscripts after each symbol so that the overall charge is zero.

## 5.3 Naming and Writing Ionic Formulas

**LEARNING GOAL:** *Given the formula of an ionic compound, write the correct name; given the name of an ionic compound, write the correct formula.*

In naming ionic compounds, the name of the positive ion is first, followed by the name of the negative ion. Ionic compounds containing two elements end with *ide*. Except for Ag, Cd, and Zn, transition metals form cations with two or more ionic charges. The charge of the cation is determined from the total negative charge in the formula and included as a Roman numeral in the name.

## 5.4 Polyatomic Ions

**LEARNING GOAL:** *Write the name and formula of a compound containing a polyatomic ion.*

A polyatomic ion is a group of nonmetal atoms that carries an electrical charge; for example, the carbonate ion has the formula $CO_3^{2-}$. Most polyatomic ions have names that end with *ate* or *ite*.

## 5.5 Covalent Compounds

**LEARNING GOAL:** *Given the formula of a covalent compound, write its electron-dot formula (Lewis structure).*

In a covalent bond, atoms of two nonmetals share electrons such that each atom achieves an octet (or two for hydrogen). In some covalent compounds, double or triple bonds are needed to provide an octet. Resonance structures are possible when two or more electron-dot formulas can be drawn for a molecule with a multiple bond.

## 5.6 Naming and Writing Covalent Formulas

**LEARNING GOAL:** *Given the formula of a covalent compound, write its correct name; given the name of a covalent compound, write its formula.*

In the names of covalent compounds, prefixes are used to indicate the subscript in the formula. The first element is named with its name. The second element uses the first syllable of its element name followed by *ide*. Prefixes are added to indicate the number of atoms of each nonmetal.

## 5.7 Electronegativity and Bond Polarity

**LEARNING GOAL:** *Use electronegativity to determine the polarity of a bond.*

Electronegativity is the attraction of an atom for the electrons in a bond. The electronegativity values of metals are low, while those of nonmetals are high. If the bonding electrons are shared equally, then it is a nonpolar covalent bond. If the electrons are shared unequally, then it is a polar covalent bond in which the atom with the lower electronegativity is partially positive ($\delta^+$) and the atom with the higher electronegativity is partially negative ($\delta^-$). Atoms that form ionic bonds have large differences in electronegativity.

## 5.8 Shapes and Polarity of Molecules

**LEARNING GOAL:** *Predict the three-dimensional structure of a molecule and classify it as polar or nonpolar.*

The VSEPR theory indicates that the repulsion of electrons around a central atom pushes the electron groups as far apart as possible. The shape of a molecule is predicted from the arrangement of the bonded atoms and lone pairs of the central atom. The arrangement of four atoms around a central atom with no lone pairs is tetrahedral. A central atom with three atoms bonded to the central atom and one lone pair has a trigonal pyramidal shape. A central atom with two bonded atoms and two lone pairs has a bent shape.

Molecules are nonpolar if they contain nonpolar covalent bonds or have an arrangement of polar covalent bonds with dipoles that cancel out. In polar molecules, the dipoles do not cancel because there are nonidentical bonded atoms or lone pairs on the central atom.

## 5.9 Attractive Forces in Compounds

**LEARNING GOAL:** *Describe the attractive forces between ions, polar molecules, and nonpolar molecules.*

Ionic bonds consist of very strong attractive forces between oppositely charged ions. Attractive forces in polar covalent compounds are weaker than ionic bonds and include dipole–dipole attractions and hydrogen bonds. Nonpolar covalent compounds form solids using temporary dipoles called dispersion forces.

# KEY TERMS

**anion** A negatively charged ion such as $Cl^-$, $O^{2-}$, or $SO_4^{2-}$.

**bent** The shape of a molecule with two bonded atoms and two lone pairs.

**cation** A positively charged ion such as $Na^+$, $Mg^{2+}$, $Al^{3+}$, or $NH_4^+$.

**covalent bond** A bond created by the sharing of valence electrons by atoms.

**covalent compound** A combination of atoms in which noble gas configurations are attained by sharing electrons.

**dipole** The separation of positive and negative charge in a polar bond indicated by an arrow that is drawn from the more positive atom to the more negative atom.

**dipole–dipole attractions** Attractive forces between oppositely charged ends of polar molecules.

**dispersion forces** Weak dipole bonding that results from a momentary polarization of nonpolar molecules.

**double bond** A sharing of two pairs of electrons by two atoms.

**electronegativity** The relative ability of an element to attract electrons in a bond.

**formula** The group of symbols and subscripts that represent the atoms or ions in a compound.

**hydrogen bond** The attraction between a partially positive H on one molecule and a strongly electronegative atom of F, O, or N on a nearby molecule.

**ion** An atom or group of atoms having an electrical charge because of a loss or gain of electrons.

**ionic bond** The attraction between oppositely charged ions.

**ionic charge** The difference between the number of protons (positive) and the number of electrons (negative) written in the upper right corner of the symbol for the element or polyatomic ion.

**ionic compound** A compound of positive and negative ions held together by ionic bonds.

**linear** The shape of a molecule that has two bonded atoms and no lone pair.

**molecule** The smallest unit of two or more atoms held together by covalent bonds.

**nonpolar covalent bond** A covalent bond in which the electrons are shared equally between atoms.

**nonpolar molecule** A molecule that has only nonpolar bonds or in which the bond dipoles cancel.

**octet rule** Elements in Groups 1A–7A (1, 2, 13–17) react with other elements by forming ionic or covalent bonds to produce a noble gas configuration, usually eight electrons in the outer shell.

**polar covalent bond** A covalent bond in which the electrons are shared unequally between atoms.

**polar molecule** A molecule containing bond dipoles that do not cancel.

**polyatomic ion** A group of covalently bonded nonmetal atoms that has an overall electrical charge.

**resonance structures** Two or more electron-dot formulas that can be written for a molecule by placing a multiple bond between different atoms.

**tetrahedral** The shape of a molecule with four bonded atoms.

**trigonal planar** The shape of a molecule with three bonded atoms and no lone pair.

**trigonal pyramidal** The shape of a molecule that has three bonded atoms and one lone pair.

**triple bond** A sharing of three pairs of electrons by two atoms.

**valence-shell electron-pair repulsion (VSEPR) theory** A theory that predicts the shape of a molecule by placing the electron pairs on a central atom as far apart as possible to minimize the mutual repulsion of the electrons.

## UNDERSTANDING THE CONCEPTS

5.87 **a.** How does the octet rule explain the formation of a sodium ion?
**b.** What noble gas has the same electron configuration as the sodium ion?
**c.** Why are Group 1A (1) and Group 2A (2) elements found in many compounds, but not Group 8A (18) elements?

**5.88** **a.** How does the octet rule explain the formation of a chloride ion, $Cl^-$?
**b.** What noble gas has the same electron configuration as the chloride ion, $Cl^-$?
**c.** Why are Group 7A (17) elements found in many compounds, but not Group 8A (18) elements?

5.89 Identify each of the following atoms or ions:

| A | B | C | D |
|---|---|---|---|
| $15p^+$, $16n$, $18e^-$ | $8p^+$, $8n$, $8e^-$ | $30p^+$, $35n$, $28e^-$ | $26p^+$, $28n$, $23e^-$ |

| E | F |
|---|---|
| $3p^+$, $4n$, $2e^-$ | $7p^+$, $8n$, $10e^-$ |

**5.90** Identify each of the following atoms or ions:
**a.** 35 protons, 45 neutrons, and 36 electrons
**b.** 47 protons, 60 neutrons, and 46 electrons
**c.** 50 protons, 68 neutrons, and 46 electrons
**d.** 15 protons, 16 neutrons, and 15 electrons
**e.** 82 protons, 126 neutrons, and 82 electrons
**f.** 34 protons, 46 neutrons, and 36 electrons

5.91 In the following electron-dot formulas, assume X and Y are atoms of nonmetals and all bonds are polar covalent:

a. X—Y(—X)—X (X bonded above Y; one lone pair below Y)
b. X—Y—X (one lone pair above and one below Y)
c. X—Y(—X)(—X)—X (X bonded above and below Y)

Match each molecule with the correct diagram of its shape and name the shape; indicate if each molecule is polar or nonpolar.

**5.92** Consider the following bonds: Ca—O, C—O, K—O, O—O, and N—O
**a.** Which bonds are polar covalent?
**b.** Which bonds are nonpolar covalent?
**c.** Which bonds are ionic?
**d.** Arrange the covalent bonds in order of decreasing polarity.

5.93 Write the formulas and names of the ionic compounds for the elements indicated by the period and electron-dot symbols in the following table:

| Period | Electron-Dot Symbols | Formula of Compound | Name of Compound |
|---|---|---|---|
| 3 | ·X· and ·Ỵ̈· | | |
| 3 | ·Ẋ· and ·Ÿ̤· | | |
| 5 | ·X· and ·Ÿ̤: | | |

**5.94** Write the formulas and names of the ionic compounds for the elements indicated by the period and electron-dot symbols in the following table:

| Period | Electron-Dot Symbols | Formula of Compound | Name of Compound |
|---|---|---|---|
| 2 | X· and ·Ỵ̈· | | |
| 4 | ·X· and ·Ÿ̤: | | |
| 4 | ·Ẋ· and ·Ÿ̤· | | |

**5.95** Write the symbols of ions, formulas, and names of their ionic compounds using the electron configurations.

| Electron Configurations | | Symbols of Ions | | | |
|---|---|---|---|---|---|
| Metal | Nonmetal | Cation | Anion | Formula of Compound | Name of Compound |
| $1s^22s^1$ | $1s^22s^22p^63s^23p^4$ | | | | |
| $1s^22s^22p^63s^23p^64s^2$ | $1s^22s^22p^63s^23p^3$ | | | | |
| $1s^22s^22p^63s^1$ | $1s^22s^22p^63s^23p^5$ | | | | |

**5.96** Write the symbols of ions, formulas, and names of their ionic compounds using the electron configurations.

| Electron Configurations | | Symbols of Ions | | | |
|---|---|---|---|---|---|
| Metal | Nonmetal | Cation | Anion | Formula of Compound | Name of Compound |
| $1s^22s^22p^63s^2$ | $1s^22s^22p^3$ | | | | |
| $1s^22s^22p^63s^23p^64s^1$ | $1s^22s^22p^4$ | | | | |
| $1s^22s^22p^63s^23p^1$ | $1s^22s^22p^63s^23p^5$ | | | | |

# ADDITIONAL QUESTIONS AND PROBLEMS

*For instructor-assigned homework, go to* ***www.masteringchemistry.com.***

**5.97** Write the symbol for the ion of each of the following:
**a.** chloride **b.** potassium **c.** oxide **d.** aluminum

**5.98** Write the symbol for the ion of each of the following:
**a.** fluoride **b.** calcium **c.** sodium **d.** lithium

**5.99** What is the name of each of the following ions?
**a.** $K^+$ **b.** $S^{2-}$ **c.** $Ca^{2+}$ **d.** $N^{3-}$

**5.100** What is the name of each of the following ions?
**a.** $Mg^{2+}$ **b.** $Ba^{2+}$ **c.** $I^-$ **d.** $Cl^-$

**5.101** Write the formula of each of the following ionic compounds:
**a.** gold(III) chloride **b.** lead(IV) oxide
**c.** silver chloride **d.** calcium nitride
**e.** copper(I) phosphide **f.** chromium(II) chloride

**5.102** Write the formula of each of the following ionic compounds:
**a.** tin(IV) oxide **b.** iron(III) sulfide
**c.** lead(IV) sulfide **d.** chromium(III) iodide
**e.** lithium nitride **f.** gold(I) oxide

**5.103** Write the electron-dot formula for each of the following:
**a.** $Cl_2O$ **b.** $CF_4$
**c.** $H_2NOH$ (N is the central atom)
**d.** $H_2CCCl_2$

**5.104** Write the electron-dot formula for each of the following:
**a.** $H_3COCH_3$; the atoms are in the order C O C
**b.** $CS_2$; the atoms are in the order S C S
**c.** $NH_3$
**d.** $H_2CCHCN$; the atoms are in the order C C C N

**5.105** Name each of the following covalent compounds:
**a.** $NCl_3$ **b.** $SCl_2$ **c.** $N_2O$
**d.** $F_2$ **e.** $PCl_5$ **f.** $P_2O_5$

**5.106** Name each of the following covalent compounds:
**a.** $CBr_4$ **b.** $SF_6$ **c.** $Br_2$
**d.** $N_2O_4$ **e.** $SO_2$ **f.** $CS_2$

**5.107** Give the formula for each of the following:
**a.** carbon monoxide **b.** diphosphorus pentoxide
**c.** dihydrogen sulfide **d.** sulfur dichloride

**5.108** Give the formula for each of the following:
**a.** silicon dioxide **b.** carbon tetrabromide
**c.** sulfur trioxide **d.** dinitrogen oxide

**5.109** Classify each of the following compounds as ionic or covalent, and give its name:
**a.** $FeCl_3$ **b.** $Na_2SO_4$ **c.** $N_2O$
**d.** $N_2$ **e.** $PCl_5$ **f.** $CF_4$

**5.110** Classify each of the following compounds as ionic or covalent, and give its name:
**a.** $Al_2(CO_3)_3$ **b.** $SF_6$ **c.** $Br_2$
**d.** $Mg_3N_2$ **e.** $SO_2$ **f.** $CrPO_4$

**5.111** Write the formulas for the following:
**a.** tin(II) carbonate **b.** lithium phosphide
**c.** silicon tetrachloride **d.** iron(III) sulfide
**e.** carbon dioxide **f.** calcium bromide

**5.112** Write the formulas for the following:
**a.** sodium carbonate **b.** nitrogen dioxide
**c.** aluminum nitrate **d.** copper(I) nitride
**e.** potassium phosphate **f.** lead(IV) oxide

**5.113** Select the more polar bond in each of the following pairs:
**a.** C—N or C—O **b.** N—F or N—Br
**c.** Br—Cl or S—Cl **d.** Br—Cl or Br—I
**e.** N—F or N—O

**5.114** Select the more polar bond in each of the following pairs:
**a.** C—C or C—O **b.** P—Cl or P—Br
**c.** Si—S or Si—Cl **d.** F—Cl or F—Br
**e.** P—O or P—S

**5.115** Show the dipole arrow for each of the following bonds:
**a.** Si—Cl **b.** C—N **c.** F—Cl
**d.** C—F **e.** N—O

**5.116** Show the dipole arrow for each of the following bonds:
**a.** C—O **b.** N—F **c.** O—Cl
**d.** S—Cl **e.** P—F

**5.117** Classify each of the following bonds as nonpolar covalent, polar covalent, or ionic:
**a.** Si—Cl **b.** C—C **c.** Na—Cl
**d.** C—H **e.** F—F

**5.118** Classify each of the following bonds as nonpolar covalent, polar covalent, or ionic:
**a.** C—N **b.** Cl—Cl **c.** K—Br
**d.** H—H **e.** N—F

**5.119** Predict the shape and polarity of each of the following molecules: (Assume that all the bonds are polar.)
**a.** A central atom bonded with three identical bonded atoms and no lone pair.
**b.** A central atom with two bonded atoms and one lone pair.
**c.** A central atom bonded to two identical atoms and no lone pairs.

**5.120** Predict the shape and polarity of each of the following molecules: (Assume that all the bonds are polar.)
**a.** A central atom with four identical bonded atoms and no lone pairs.
**b.** A central atom with three identical bonded atoms and one lone pair.
**c.** A central atom with four bonded atoms that are not identical and no lone pair.

**5.121** Write the electron-dot formula and determine the shape for each of the following:
**a.** $NF_3$ **b.** $SiBr_4$ **c.** $BeCl_2$ **d.** $SO_2$

**5.122** Write the electron-dot formula and determine the shape for each of the following:
**a.** $SiH_4$ **b.** HCCH
**c.** $COCl_2$ (C is the central atom)
**d.** $BCl_3$

**5.123** Predict the shape and polarity of each of the following molecules:
**a.** $H_2S$ **b.** $NF_3$ **c.** $NCl_3$
**d.** $CH_3Cl$ **e.** $SiF_4$

**5.124** Predict the shape and polarity of each of the following molecules:
**a.** $H_2O$ **b.** $CF_4$ **c.** $GeH_4$
**d.** $PCl_3$ **e.** $SCl_2$

**5.125** Indicate the major type of attractive forces—(1) ionic, (2) dipole–dipole attractions, (3) hydrogen bonds, (4) dispersion forces—that occurs between particles of the following:
**a.** $NH_3$ **b.** HI **c.** $Br_2$ **d.** $Cs_2O$

**5.126** Indicate the major type of attractive force—(1) ionic, (2) dipole–dipole attraction, (3) hydrogen bond, (4) dispersion forces—that occurs between particles of the following:
**a.** $CHCl_3$ **b.** $H_2O$ **c.** LiCl **d.** $Cl_2$

## CHALLENGE QUESTIONS

**5.127** Consider the following electron-dot formulas for elements X and Y:

$X\cdot \quad \cdot\ddot{\underset{\cdot\cdot}{Y}}\cdot$

**a.** What are the group numbers of X and Y?
**b.** Will a compound of X and Y be ionic or covalent?
**c.** What ions would be formed by X and Y?
**d.** What would be the formula of a compound of X and Y?
**e.** What would be the formula of a compound of X and chlorine?
**f.** What would be the formula of a compound of Y and chlorine?

**5.128** Complete the following table for atoms or ions:

| Atom or Ion | Number of Protons | Number of Electrons | Electrons Lost/Gained |
|---|---|---|---|
| $K^+$ | | | |
| | $12p^+$ | $10e^-$ | |
| | $8p^+$ | | $2e^-$ gained |
| | | $10e^-$ | $3e^-$ lost |

**5.129** One of the ions of tin is tin(IV).
**a.** What is the symbol for this ion?
**b.** How many protons and electrons are in the ion?
**c.** What is the formula of tin(IV) oxide?
**d.** What is the formula of tin(IV) phosphate?

**5.130** Classify the following compounds as ionic or covalent and name each:
**a.** $Li_2O$ **b.** $N_2O$ **c.** $CF_4$
**d.** $Cl_2O$ **e.** $MgF_2$ **f.** CO
**g.** $CaCl_2$ **h.** $K_3PO_4$

**5.131** Name the following compounds:
**a.** $FeCl_2$ **b.** $Cl_2O_7$ **c.** $N_2$
**d.** $Ca_3(PO_4)_2$ **e.** $PCl_3$ **f.** $Al(NO_3)_3$
**g.** $PbCl_4$ **h.** $MgCO_3$ **i.** $NO_2$
**j.** $SnSO_4$ **k.** $Ba(NO_3)_2$ **l.** CuS

**5.132** Identify the most important type of attractive forces for each of following:
**a.** $C_3H_8$ **b.** $CH_3OH$ **c.** $Br_2$
**d.** HBr **e.** IBr

## ANSWERS

### ANSWERS TO STUDY CHECKS

**5.1** $K^+$ and $S^{2-}$

**5.2** gallium sulfide

**5.3** gold(I) oxide

**5.4** $Cr_2O_3$

**5.5** $(NH_4)_3PO_4$

**5.6** calcium phosphate

**5.7** $:\ddot{\underset{\cdot\cdot}{Cl}}:\ddot{\underset{\cdot\cdot}{O}}:\ddot{\underset{\cdot\cdot}{Cl}}:$ or $:\ddot{\underset{\cdot\cdot}{Cl}}—\ddot{\underset{\cdot\cdot}{O}}—\ddot{\underset{\cdot\cdot}{Cl}}:$

**5.8** $H:C:::N:$ or $H—C\equiv N:$ In HCN, there is a triple bond between C and N atoms.

**5.9** $:\ddot{\underset{\cdot\cdot}{O}}—\ddot{S}=\ddot{O}: \longleftrightarrow :\ddot{\underset{\cdot\cdot}{O}}—\ddot{S}—\ddot{\underset{\cdot\cdot}{O}}: \longleftrightarrow :\ddot{O}=\ddot{S}—\ddot{\underset{\cdot\cdot}{O}}:$ (with the third O bonded to S below: $—\,:\ddot{\underset{\cdot\cdot}{O}}:$ ; $=\,:\ddot{O}:$ ; $—\,:\ddot{\underset{\cdot\cdot}{O}}:$ respectively)

**5.10** **a.** silicon tetrabromide **b.** dibromine oxide

**5.11** $IF_7$

**5.12** **a.** Si—N **b.** O—P

**5.13** tetrahedral

**5.14** polar

**5.15** $H_2O$ forms hydrogen bonds that are stronger than the dipole–dipole attractions of $H_2S$. Thus $H_2S$ does not need as much energy to change from liquid to gas.

## ANSWERS TO SELECTED QUESTIONS AND PROBLEMS

**5.1** **a.** 1 **b.** 2 **c.** 3 **d.** 1 **e.** 2

**5.3** **a.** $Li^+$ **b.** $F^-$ **c.** $Mg^{2+}$ **d.** $Fe^{3+}$

**5.5** **a.** 8 protons, 10 electrons **b.** 19 protons, 18 electrons
**c.** 35 protons, 36 electrons **d.** 16 protons, 18 electrons

**5.7** **a.** $Cl^-$ **b.** $K^+$ **c.** $O^{2-}$ **d.** $Al^{3+}$

**5.9** **a.** K **b.** $Cl^-$ **c.** Ca **d.** $K^+$

**5.11** **a., c.,**

**5.13** **a.** $Na_2O$ **b.** $AlBr_3$ **c.** BaO **d.** $MgCl_2$ **e.** $Al_2S_3$

**5.15** **a.** $Na^+$, $S^{2-}$ $Na_2S$ **b.** $K^+$, $N^{3-}$ $K_3N$
**c.** $Al^{3+}$, $I^-$ $AlI_3$ **d.** $Li^+$, $O^{2-}$ $Li_2O$

**5.17** **a.** aluminum oxide **b.** calcium chloride
**c.** sodium oxide **d.** magnesium nitride
**e.** potassium iodide

**5.19** Most of the transition metals form more than one positive ion. The specific ion is indicated in a name by writing a Roman numeral that is the same as the ionic charge. For example, iron forms $Fe^{2+}$ and $Fe^{3+}$ ions, which are named iron(II) and iron(III).

**5.21** **a.** iron(II) **b.** copper(II)
**c.** zinc **d.** lead(IV)
**e.** chromium(III)

**5.23** **a.** tin(II) chloride **b.** iron(II) oxide
**c.** copper(I) sulfide **d.** copper(II) sulfide
**e.** chromium(III) bromide **f.** zinc chloride

**5.25** **a.** $Au^{3+}$ **b.** $Fe^{3+}$ **c.** $Pb^{4+}$ **d.** $Sn^{2+}$

**5.27** **a.** $MgCl_2$ **b.** $Na_2S$ **c.** $Cu_2O$
**d.** $Zn_3P_2$ **e.** AuN **f.** $CrCl_2$

**5.29** **a.** $HCO_3^-$ **b.** $NH_4^+$ **c.** $PO_4^{3-}$ **d.** $HSO_4^-$

**5.31** **a.** sulfate **b.** carbonate
**c.** phosphate **d.** nitrate

**5.33**

| | $OH^-$ | $NO_2^-$ | $CO_3^{2-}$ | $HSO_4^-$ | $PO_4^{3-}$ |
|---|---|---|---|---|---|
| $Li^+$ | LiOH | $LiNO_2$ | $Li_2CO_3$ | $LiHSO_4$ | $Li_3PO_4$ |
| $Cu^{2+}$ | $Cu(OH)_2$ | $Cu(NO_2)_2$ | $CuCO_3$ | $Cu(HSO_4)_2$ | $Cu_3(PO_4)_2$ |
| $Ba^{2+}$ | $Ba(OH)_2$ | $Ba(NO_2)_2$ | $BaCO_3$ | $Ba(HSO_4)_2$ | $Ba_3(PO_4)_2$ |

**5.35** **a.** $CO_3^{2-}$, sodium carbonate
**b.** $NH_4^+$, ammonium chloride
**c.** $PO_4^{3-}$, lithium phosphate
**d.** $NO_2^-$ copper(II) nitrite
**e.** $SO_3^{2-}$, iron(II) sulfite

**5.37** **a.** $Ba(OH)_2$ **b.** $Na_2SO_4$ **c.** $Fe(NO_3)_2$
**d.** $Zn_3(PO_4)_2$ **e.** $Fe_2(CO_3)_3$

**5.39** The nonmetallic elements are most likely to form covalent bonds.

**5.41** **a.** 2 valence electrons: 1 bonding pair and 0 lone pairs
**b.** 8 valence electrons: 1 bonding pair and 3 lone pairs
**c.** 14 valence electrons: 1 bonding pair and 6 lone pairs

**5.43** **a.** HF ($8\,e^-$) H:F: or H—F:
**b.** $SF_2$ ($20\,e^-$) :F:S:F: or :F—S—F:
**c.** $NBr_3$ ($26\,e^-$) :Br:N:Br: (with :Br: above N) or :Br—N—Br: (with :Br: above N)
**d.** $CH_3OH$ ($14\,e^-$) H:C:O:H (with H above and below C) or H—C—O—H (with H above and below C)
**e.** $N_2H_4$ ($14\,e^-$) H:N:N:H (with H above each N) or H—N—N—H (with H above each N)

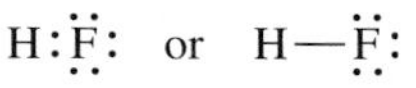

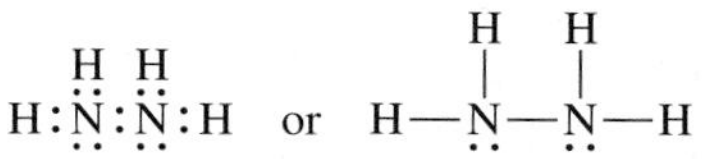

**5.45** When using all the valence electrons does not give complete octets, it is necessary to write multiple bonds.

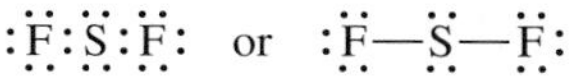

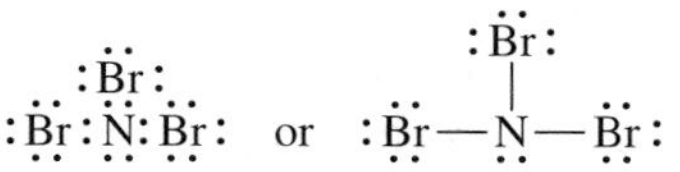

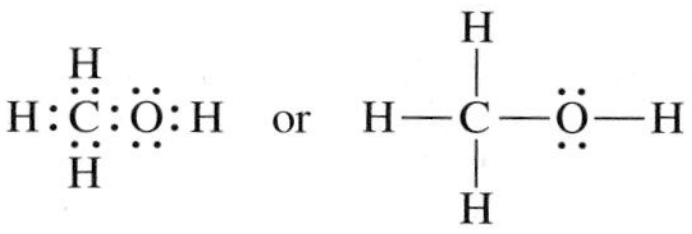

**5.47** Resonance occurs when, for the same molecule or ion, we can write two or more electron-dot formulas that have multiple bonds.

**5.49** **a.** CO ($10\,e^-$) :C:::O: or :C≡O:
**b.** $H_2CCH_2$ ($12\,e^-$) H:C::C:H (with H above each C) or H—C=C—H (with H above each C)
**c.** $H_2CO$ ($12\,e^-$) H:C:H (with :O: above C) or H—C—H (with :O: double-bonded above C)

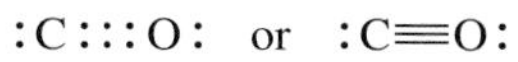

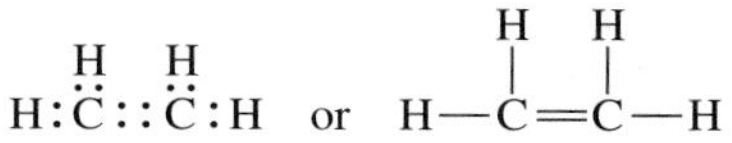

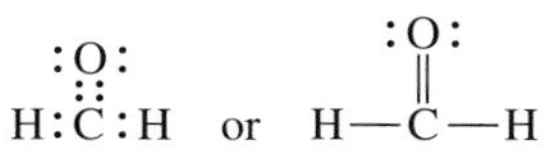

**5.51** **a.** $ClNO_2$ :Cl—N—O: (with :O: double-bonded above N) ⟷ :Cl—N=O: (with :O: single-bonded above N)

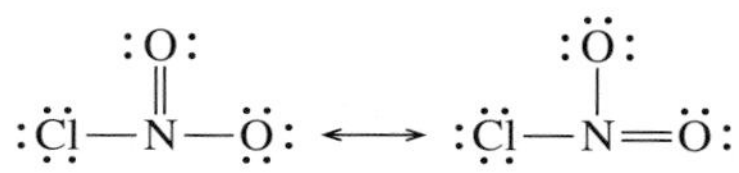

**5.53** **a.** phosphorus tribromide
**b.** carbon tetrabromide
**c.** silicon dioxide
**d.** dinitrogen trioxide
**e.** silicon tetrabromide
**f.** phosphorus pentachloride

**5.55** **a.** $CCl_4$ **b.** CO **c.** $PCl_3$
**d.** $N_2O_4$ **e.** $BF_3$ **f.** $SF_6$

**5.57** **a.** aluminum sulfate
**b.** calcium carbonate
**c.** dinitrogen oxide
**d.** sodium phosphate
**e.** ammonium sulfate
**f.** iron(III) oxide

**5.59** The electronegativity increases going from left to right across a period.

**5.61** A nonpolar covalent bond would have an electronegativity difference of 0.0 to 0.4.

**5.63** **a.** K, Na, Li **b.** Na, P, Cl **c.** Ca, Br, O

**5.65** **a.** polar covalent
**b.** ionic
**c.** polar covalent
**d.** nonpolar covalent
**e.** polar covalent
**f.** nonpolar covalent

**5.67** **a.** 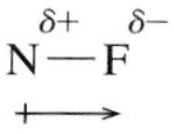 $\overset{\delta+}{N}$—$\overset{\delta-}{F}$ (⟼) **b.** 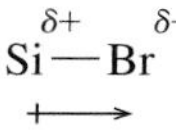 $\overset{\delta+}{Si}$—$\overset{\delta-}{Br}$ (⟼) **c.** 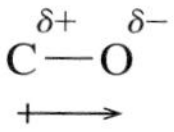 $\overset{\delta+}{C}$—$\overset{\delta-}{O}$ (⟼)
**d.** 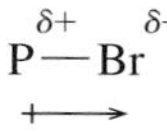 $\overset{\delta+}{P}$—$\overset{\delta-}{Br}$ (⟼) **e.** 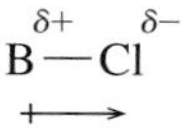 $\overset{\delta+}{B}$—$\overset{\delta-}{Cl}$ (⟼)

**5.69** tetrahedral

**5.71** The four electron groups in $PCl_3$ have a tetrahedral arrangement, but three bonded atoms and one lone pair around a central atom give a trigonal pyramidal shape.

**5.73** In both $PH_3$ and $NH_3$, there are four electron pairs; three are bonded to atoms, and one is a lone pair. The shapes of both are trigonal pyramidal.

**5.75** **a.** bent **b.** tetrahedral **c.** linear **d.** bent

**5.77** $Cl_2$ is a nonpolar molecule because there is a nonpolar covalent bond between Cl atoms, which have identical electronegativity values. In HCl, the bond is a polar bond, which makes HCl a polar molecule.

**5.79** **a.** polar **b.** polar
**c.** nonpolar **d.** nonpolar

**5.81** **a.** dipole–dipole attractions
**b.** ionic
**c.** dispersion forces
**d.** hydrogen bonds
**e.** dispersion forces

**5.83** **a.** hydrogen bonding
**b.** dispersion forces
**c.** dipole–dipole attractions
**d.** dispersion forces
**e.** dispersion forces

**5.85** **a.** HF; hydrogen bonds are stronger than dipole–dipole attractions in HBr.
**b.** NaF; ionic bonds are stronger than the hydrogen bonds in HF.
**c.** $MgBr_2$; ionic bonds are stronger than the dipole–dipole attractions in $PBr_3$.
**d.** $CH_3OH$; hydrogen bonds are stronger than the dispersion forces in $CH_4$.

**5.87** **a.** By losing one valence electron from the third energy level, sodium achieves an octet in the second energy level.
**b.** Ne
**c.** Group 1A (1) and 2A (2) elements acquire octets by losing electrons when they form compounds. Group 8A (18) elements are stable with octets (or two electrons for helium).

**5.89** **a.** $P^{3-}$ **b.** O atom **c.** $Zn^{2+}$ **d.** $Fe^{3+}$
**e.** $Li^+$ **f.** $N^{3-}$

**5.91** **a.** 2—trigonal pyramidal, polar
**b.** 1—bent, polar
**c.** 3—tetrahedral, nonpolar

**5.93**

| Period | Electron-Dot Symbols | Formula of Compound | Name of Compound |
|---|---|---|---|
| 3 | ·X· and ·Ÿ· | $Mg_3P_2$ | Magnesium phosphide |
| 3 | ·Ẋ· and ·Ÿ· | $Al_2S_3$ | Aluminum sulfide |
| 5 | ·X· and ·Ÿ: | $SrI_2$ | Strontium iodide |

**5.95**

| Electron Configurations | | Symbols of Ions | | | |
|---|---|---|---|---|---|
| Metal | Nonmetal | Cation | Anion | Formula of Compound | Name of Compound |
| $1s^22s^1$ | $1s^22s^22p^63s^23p^4$ | $Li^+$ | $S^{2-}$ | $Li_2S$ | Lithium sulfide |
| $1s^22s^22p^63s^23p^64s^2$ | $1s^22s^22p^63s^23p^3$ | $Ca^{2+}$ | $P^{3-}$ | $Ca_3P_2$ | Calcium phosphide |
| $1s^22s^22p^63s^1$ | $1s^22s^22p^63s^23p^5$ | $Na^+$ | $Cl^-$ | NaCl | Sodium chloride |

**5.97** **a.** $Cl^-$ **b.** $K^+$ **c.** $O^{2-}$ **d.** $Al^{3+}$

**5.99** **a.** potassium **b.** sulfide **c.** calcium **d.** nitride

**5.101** **a.** $AuCl_3$ **b.** $PbO_2$ **c.** AgCl
**d.** $Ca_3N_2$ **e.** $Cu_3P$ **f.** $CrCl_2$

**5.103** **a.** $Cl_2O$ (20 $e^-$) :C̤̈l:Ö̤:C̤̈l: or :C̤̈l—Ö̤—C̤̈l:

**b.** $CF_4$ (32 $e^-$)

```
 :F:
:F:C:F:
 :F:
```

**c.** $H_2NOH$ (14 $e^-$)

```
  H                  H
H:N:O:H    or    H—N—O—H
```

**d.** $H_2CCCl_2$ (24 $e^-$)

```
 H :Cl:                 H  :Cl:
H:C::C:Cl:     or    H—C=C—Cl:
```

**5.105** **a.** nitrogen trichloride
**b.** sulfur dichloride
**c.** dinitrogen oxide
**d.** fluorine
**e.** phosphorus pentachloride
**f.** diphosphorus pentoxide

**5.107** **a.** CO **b.** $P_2O_5$ **c.** $H_2S$ **d.** $SCl_2$

**5.109** **a.** ionic, iron(III) chloride
**b.** ionic, sodium sulfate
**c.** covalent, dinitrogen oxide
**d.** covalent, nitrogen
**e.** covalent, phosphorus pentachloride
**f.** covalent, carbon tetrafluoride

**5.111** **a.** $SnCO_3$ **b.** $Li_3P$ **c.** $SiCl_4$
**d.** $Fe_2S_3$ **e.** $CO_2$ **f.** $CaBr_2$

**5.113** **a.** C—O **b.** N—F **c.** S—Cl
**d.** Br—I **e.** N—F

**5.115** **a.** Si—Cl (+⟶) **b.** C—N (+⟶) **c.** F—Cl (⟵+)
**d.** C—F (+⟶) **e.** N—O (+⟶)

**5.117** **a.** polar covalent
**b.** nonpolar covalent
**c.** ionic
**d.** nonpolar covalent
**e.** nonpolar covalent

**5.119** **a.** trigonal planar, nonpolar
**b.** bent, polar
**c.** linear, nonpolar

**5.121** **a.** $NF_3$

```
:F—N—F:
   |
  :F:
```

trigonal pyramidal

**b.** $SiBr_4$

```
     :Br:
      |
:Br—Si—Br:
      |
     :Br:
```

tetrahedral

**c.** $BeCl_2$ $:\ddot{Cl}—Be—\ddot{Cl}:$ linear

**d.** $SO_2$ $[:\ddot{O}=\ddot{S}—\ddot{O}:] \longleftrightarrow [:\ddot{O}—\ddot{S}=\ddot{O}:]$ bent (120°)

**5.123** **a.** bent, polar
**b.** trigonal pyramidal, polar
**c.** trigonal pyramidal, polar
**d.** tetrahedral, polar
**e.** tetrahedral, nonpolar

**5.125** **a.** (3) hydrogen bond
**b.** (2) dipole–dipole attractions
**c.** (4) dispersion forces
**d.** (1) ionic

**5.127** **a.** X is in Group 1A (1); Y is in Group 6A (16)
**b.** ionic **c.** $X^+$, $Y^{2-}$ **d.** $X_2Y$
**e.** XCl **f.** $YCl_2$

**5.129** **a.** $Sn^{4+}$
**b.** 50 protons, 46 electrons
**c.** $SnO_2$
**d.** $Sn_3(PO_4)_4$

**5.131** **a.** iron(II) chloride
**b.** dichlorine heptoxide
**c.** nitrogen
**d.** calcium phosphate
**e.** phosphorus trichloride
**f.** aluminum nitrate
**g.** lead(IV) chloride
**h.** magnesium carbonate
**i.** nitrogen dioxide
**j.** tin(II) sulfate
**k.** barium nitrate
**l.** copper(II) sulfide

# 6 Chemical Reactions and Quantities

LOOKING AHEAD


6.1 Chemical Reactions

6.2 Types of Reactions

6.3 Oxidation–Reduction Reactions

6.4 The Mole

6.5 Molar Mass

6.6 Mole Relationships in Chemical Equations

6.7 Mass Calculations for Reactions

6.8 Percent Yield and Limiting Reactants

6.9 Energy Changes in Chemical Reactions

*"In our food science laboratory, I develop a variety of food products, from cake donuts to energy beverages," says Anne Cristofano, senior food technologist at Mattson & Company. "When I started the donut project, I researched the ingredients, then weighed them out in the lab. I added water to make a batter and cooked the donuts in a fryer. The batter and the oil temperature make a big difference. If I don't get the right taste or texture, I adjust the ingredients, such as sugar and flour, or adjust the temperature."*

*A food technologist studies the physical and chemical properties of food and develops scientific ways to process and preserve it for extended shelf life. The food products are tested for texture, color, and flavor. The results of these tests help improve the quality and safety of food.*

Visit **www.masteringchemistry.com** for self-study materials and instructor-assigned homework.

The fuel in our cars burns with oxygen to provide energy to make the car move, play the radio, and run the air conditioner. When we cook our food or bleach our hair, chemical reactions take place. In our bodies, chemical reactions convert food substances into molecules to build muscles and move them. In the leaves of trees and plants, carbon dioxide and water are converted into carbohydrates.

Some chemical reactions are simple, whereas others are quite complex. However, they can all be written with equations used to describe chemical reactions. In every chemical reaction, the atoms in the reacting substances, called *reactants*, are rearranged to give new substances called *products*.

In this chapter, we will see how equations are written and how we can determine the amount of reactant or product involved. We do the same thing at home when we use a recipe to make bread or cookies. At the automotive repair shop, a mechanic does essentially the same thing when adjusting the fuel system of an engine to allow the correct amounts of fuel and oxygen. In the hospital, a respiratory therapist evaluates the level of $CO_2$ and $O_2$ in the blood. A certain amount of $O_2$ must reach the tissues for efficient metabolic reactions. If the oxygenation of the blood is low, then the therapist will oxygenate the patient and recheck the blood oxygen levels.

## 6.1 Chemical Reactions

LEARNING GOAL

Write a balanced chemical equation from the formulas of the reactants and products for a chemical reaction.

SELF STUDY ACTIVITY
Chemical Reactions and Equations

As we discussed in Chapter 2, a *chemical change* occurs when a substance is converted into one or more new substances. For example, when silver tarnishes, the shiny silver metal (Ag) reacts with sulfur (S) to become the dull, black substance we call *tarnish* ($Ag_2S$). (See Figure 6.1.)

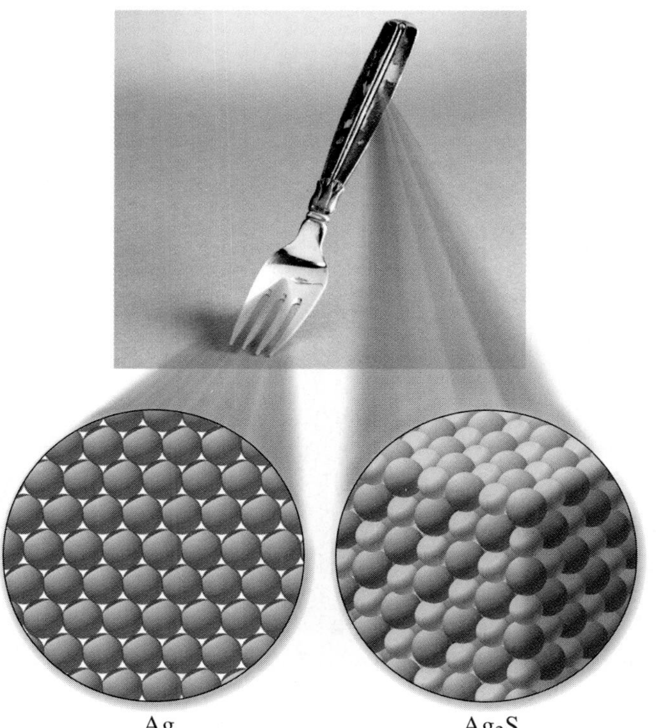


**FIGURE 6.1** A chemical change produces new substances.
**Q** Why is the formation of tarnish a chemical change?

**FIGURE 6.2** A chemical reaction forms new products with different properties. An antacid ($NaHCO_3$) tablet in water forms bubbles of carbon dioxide ($CO_2$).

**Q** What is the evidence for chemical change in this chemical reaction?

A **chemical reaction** always involves chemical change because atoms of the reacting substances form new combinations with new properties. For example, a chemical reaction takes place when an antacid tablet is dropped into a glass of water. The tablet fizzes and bubbles as $NaHCO_3$ and citric acid ($C_6H_8O_7$) in the tablet react to form carbon dioxide ($CO_2$) gas. (See Figure 6.2.) During a chemical change, new properties become visible, which are an indication that a chemical reaction has taken place. (See Table 6.1.)

**TABLE 6.1** Types of Visible Evidence of a Chemical Reaction

1. Change in the color
2. Formation of a gas (bubbles)
3. Formation of a solid (precipitate)
4. Heat (or a flame) produced or heat absorbed

CONCEPT CHECK 6.1

### Evidence of a Chemical Reaction

Indicate why each of the following is a chemical reaction:

**a.** burning propane fuel in a barbecue
**b.** using peroxide to change the color of hair

ANSWER

**a.** The production of heat during burning of propane fuel is evidence of a chemical reaction.
**b.** The change in hair color is evidence of a chemical reaction.

When you build a model airplane, prepare a new recipe, or mix a medication formulation, you follow a set of directions. These directions tell you what materials to use and the products you will obtain. In chemistry, a **chemical equation** tells us the materials we need and the products that will form in a chemical reaction.

## Writing a Chemical Equation

Suppose you work in a bicycle shop, assembling wheels and frames into bicycles. You could represent this process by a simple equation:

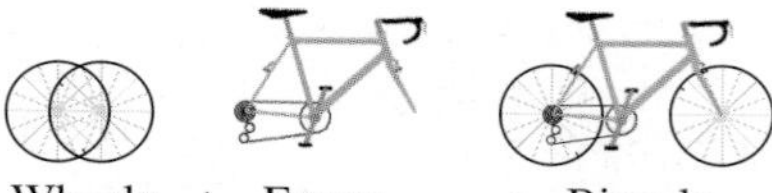

Equation: Wheels + Frame ⟶ Bicycle

MC™ SELF STUDY ACTIVITY
What Is Chemistry?

When you burn charcoal in a grill, the carbon in the charcoal combines with oxygen to form carbon dioxide. We can represent this reaction by a chemical equation that is much like the one for the bicycle:

Equation: $C(s) + O_2(g) \xrightarrow{\Delta} CO_2(g)$

In an equation, the formulas of the **reactants** are written on the left of the arrow and the formulas of the **products** on the right. When there are two or more formulas on the same side, they are separated by plus (+) signs. The delta sign (Δ) indicates that heat was used to start the reaction.

Generally, the formulas in an equation are followed by letters in parentheses that contain abbreviations for the physical state of the substances: solid (*s*), liquid (*l*), or gas or vapor (*g*). If a substance is dissolved in water, it is an aqueous (*aq*) solution. Table 6.2 summarizes some of the symbols used in equations.

**TABLE 6.2** Some Symbols Used in Writing Equations

| Symbol | Meaning |
|---|---|
| + | Separates two or more formulas |
| ⟶ | Reacts to form products |
| Δ | Reactants are heated |
| (*s*) | Solid |
| (*l*) | Liquid |
| (*g*) | Gas or vapor |
| (*aq*) | Aqueous |

## Identifying a Balanced Chemical Equation

When a chemical reaction takes place, the bonds between the atoms of the reactants are broken, and new bonds are formed to give the products. All atoms are conserved, which means that atoms cannot be gained, lost, or changed into other types of atoms during a chemical reaction. Every chemical reaction is written as a **balanced equation** that shows the same number of atoms for each element in the reactants as in the products. For example, the chemical equation we wrote above for burning carbon is *balanced* because there is one carbon atom and two oxygen atoms on each side of the arrow.

$$C(s) + O_2(g) \longrightarrow CO_2(g)$$

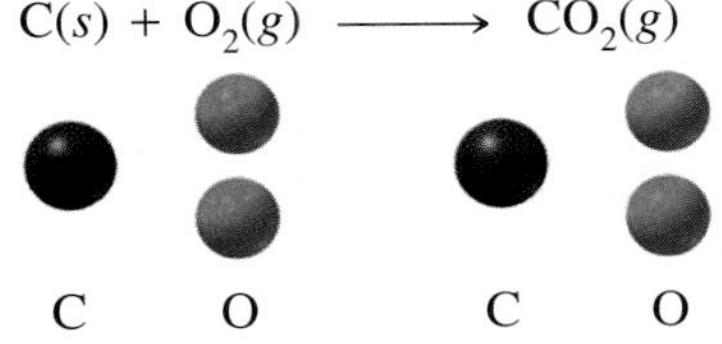


Reactant atoms = Product atoms

Now consider the reaction in which hydrogen reacts with oxygen to form water. The formulas of the reactants and products are written as follows:

$$H_2(g) + O_2(g) \longrightarrow H_2O(g)$$

When we add up the atoms of each element on each side of the arrow, we find that the equation is *not balanced*. The number of atoms on the left side does not match the number of atoms on the right side. To balance this equation, we place whole numbers called **coefficients** in front of some of the formulas. If we write a coefficient of 2 in front of $H_2O$, it represents 2 molecules of water. Now the product consists of 4 hydrogen atoms and 2 oxygen atoms. To obtain 4 H atoms on the reactant side, we must write a coefficient of 2 in front of $H_2$. Only coefficients can be used to balance a chemical equation; the formulas and their subscripts are never changed. Changing subscripts changes the chemical identities of the reactants and products. Now the numbers of hydrogen atoms and oxygen atoms are the same in the reactants as in the products. The equation is *balanced*.

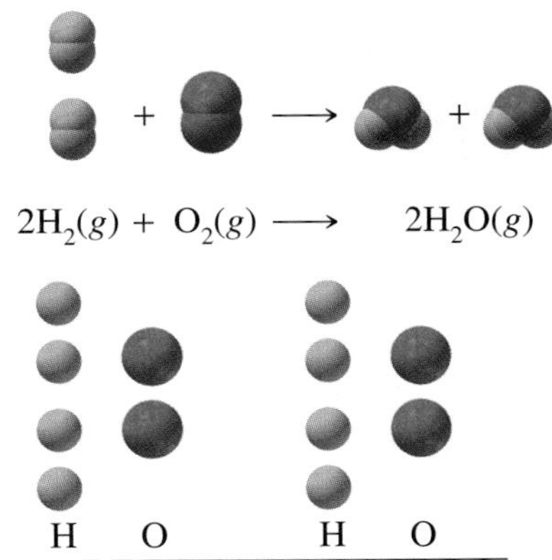


Reactant atoms = Product atoms

TUTORIAL
Balancing Chemical Equations

## Balancing a Chemical Equation

We can now show the process of balancing a chemical equation using the reaction of $CH_4$ with oxygen to produce carbon dioxide and water.

**STEP 1** **Write an equation, using the correct formulas of the reactants and products.**

$$CH_4(g) + O_2(g) \longrightarrow CO_2(g) + H_2O(g)$$

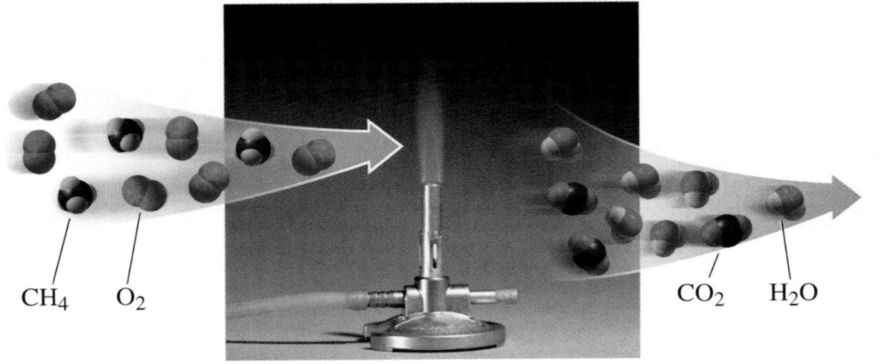

**STEP 2** **Count the atoms of each element in the reactants and products.** When we compare the atoms on the reactant side and the product side, we see that there are more hydrogen atoms on the left side and more oxygen atoms on the right.

$$CH_4(g) + O_2(g) \longrightarrow CO_2(g) + H_2O(g)$$

| Reactants | Products | |
|---|---|---|
| 1 C | 1 C | Balanced |
| 4 H | 2 H | Not balanced |
| 2 O | 3 O | Not balanced |

**STEP 3** **Use coefficients to balance each element.** Because $CH_4$ has the most atoms of an element (H), we start by balancing the 4 H atoms. This is done by placing a 2 in front of the formula for water, $2H_2O$, which gives a total of 4 H atoms on the product side. This gives a total of 4 O atoms on the product side, which we balance by placing a 2 in front of the formula $O_2$.

$$CH_4(g) + 2O_2(g) \longrightarrow CO_2(g) + 2H_2O(g)$$

**STEP 4** **Check the final equation to confirm that it is balanced.** In the final equation, the numbers of carbon, hydrogen, and oxygen atoms are the same for both reactants and products.

$$CH_4(g) + 2O_2(g) \longrightarrow CO_2(g) + 2H_2O(g) \quad \text{Balanced}$$

| Reactants | Products |
|---|---|
| 1 C atom | 1 C atom |
| 4 H atoms | 4 H atoms |
| 4 O atoms | 4 O atoms |

In a balanced equation, the coefficients must be the lowest set of whole numbers. Suppose you had added coefficients to the equation and obtained the following:

$$2CH_4(g) + 4O_2(g) \longrightarrow 2CO_2(g) + 4H_2O(g) \quad \text{Incorrect}$$

Although there are equal numbers of atoms on both sides of the equation, this is not written correctly. The correctly balanced equation is obtained by dividing all the coefficients by 2.

CONCEPT CHECK 6.2

### Balancing Chemical Equations

Indicate the number of each in the following equation:

$$Fe_2S_3(s) + 6HCl(aq) \longrightarrow 2FeCl_3(aq) + 3H_2S(g)$$

| | Reactants | Products |
|---|---|---|
| Atoms of Cl | | |
| Atoms of S | | |
| Atoms of Fe | | |
| Molecules of $H_2S$ | | |

ANSWER

The total number of atoms in each formula is obtained by multiplying through by its coefficient. The number of molecules is obtained from the coefficient.

| | Reactants | Products |
|---|---|---|
| Atoms of Cl | 6 | 6 |
| Atoms of S | 3 | 3 |
| Atoms of Fe | 2 | 2 |
| Molecules of $H_2S$ | 0 | 3 |

SAMPLE PROBLEM 6.1

## Balancing Chemical Equations

Balance the following equation:

$$Na_3PO_4(aq) + MgCl_2(aq) \longrightarrow Mg_3(PO_4)_2(s) + NaCl(aq)$$

SOLUTION

**STEP 1** **Write an equation using the correct formulas.**

$$Na_3PO_4(aq) + MgCl_2(aq) \longrightarrow Mg_3(PO_4)_2(s) + NaCl(aq)$$

**STEP 2** **Count the atoms or ions and determine if the equation is balanced.** When we compare the number of ions on the reactant and product sides, we find that the equation is not balanced. In this equation, we can balance the phosphate ion as a group because it appears on both sides of the equation.

| Reactants | Products | |
|---|---|---|
| $Na_3PO_4(aq) + MgCl_2(aq) \longrightarrow$ | $Mg_3(PO_4)_2(s) + NaCl(aq)$ | |
| $3\ Na^+$ | $1\ Na^+$ | Not balanced |
| $1\ PO_4^{3-}$ | $2\ PO_4^{3-}$ | Not balanced |
| $1\ Mg^{2+}$ | $3\ Mg^{2+}$ | Not balanced |
| $2\ Cl^-$ | $1\ Cl^-$ | Not balanced |

**STEP 3** **Use coefficients to balance each element.** We typically begin with the element in a formula that has the highest subscript values, which is $Mg_3(PO_4)_2$. A 3 in front of $MgCl_2$ balances magnesium (Mg), and a 2 in front of $Na_3PO_4$ balances the phosphate ion ($PO_4^{3-}$).

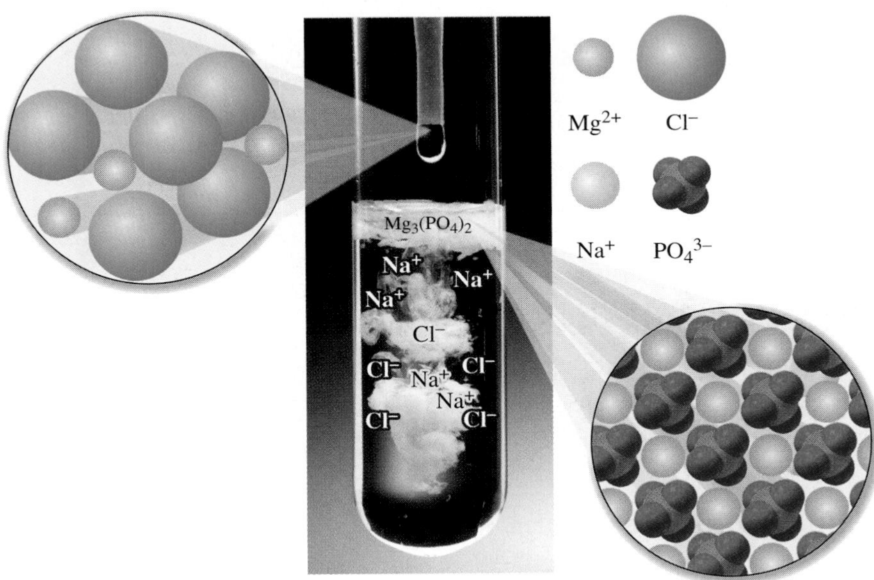


$$2Na_3PO_4(aq) + 3MgCl_2(aq) \longrightarrow 1Mg_3(PO_4)_2(s) + NaCl(aq)$$

Looking again at each of the ions in the reactants and products, we see that the sodium and chloride ions are not yet equal. A 6 in front of the NaCl balances the equation:

$$2Na_3PO_4(aq) + 3MgCl_2(aq) \longrightarrow 1Mg_3(PO_4)_2(s) + 6NaCl(aq)$$

**Guide to Balancing a Chemical Equation**

STEP 1
Write an equation using the correct formulas of the reactants and products.

STEP 2
Count the atoms or ions of each element in reactants and products.

STEP 3
Use coefficients to balance each element.

STEP 4
Check the final equation for balance.

**STEP 4** **Check to see that the final equation is balanced.** A check of the total number of atoms indicates the equation is balanced. A coefficient of 1 is understood and not usually written.

| Reactants | Products |
|---|---|
| 6 $Na^+$ | 6 $Na^+$ |
| 2 $PO_4^{3-}$ | 2 $PO_4^{3-}$ |
| 3 $Mg^{2+}$ | 3 $Mg^{2+}$ |
| 6 $Cl^-$ | 6 $Cl^-$ |

$$2Na_3PO_4(aq) + 3MgCl_2(aq) \longrightarrow Mg_3(PO_4)_2(s) + 6NaCl(aq)$$ Balanced

STUDY CHECK

Balance the following equation:

$$Fe(s) + O_2(g) \longrightarrow Fe_3O_4(s)$$

## QUESTIONS AND PROBLEMS

### Chemical Reactions

6.1 Determine whether each of the following equations is balanced or not balanced:
- a. $S(s) + O_2(g) \longrightarrow SO_3(g)$
- b. $2Al(s) + 3Cl_2(g) \longrightarrow 2AlCl_3(s)$
- c. $H_2(g) + O_2(g) \longrightarrow H_2O(g)$
- d. $C_3H_8(g) + 5O_2(g) \longrightarrow 3CO_2(g) + 4H_2O(g)$

6.2 Determine whether each of the following equations is balanced or not balanced:
- a. $PCl_3(s) + Cl_2(g) \longrightarrow PCl_5(s)$
- b. $CO(g) + 2H_2(g) \longrightarrow CH_3OH(g)$
- c. $2KClO_3(s) \longrightarrow 2KCl(s) + O_2(g)$
- d. $Mg(s) + N_2(g) \longrightarrow Mg_3N_2(s)$

6.3 Balance the following equations:
- a. $N_2(g) + O_2(g) \longrightarrow NO(g)$
- b. $HgO(s) \longrightarrow Hg(l) + O_2(g)$
- c. $Fe(s) + O_2(g) \longrightarrow Fe_2O_3(s)$
- d. $Na(s) + Cl_2(g) \longrightarrow NaCl(s)$

6.4 Balance the following equations:
- a. $Ca(s) + Br_2(l) \longrightarrow CaBr_2(s)$
- b. $P_4(s) + O_2(g) \longrightarrow P_4O_{10}(s)$
- c. $Sb_2S_3(s) + HCl(aq) \longrightarrow SbCl_3(s) + H_2S(g)$
- d. $Fe_2O_3(s) + C(s) \longrightarrow Fe(s) + CO(g)$

6.5 Balance the following equations:
- a. $Mg(s) + AgNO_3(aq) \longrightarrow Mg(NO_3)_2(aq) + Ag(s)$
- b. $Al(s) + CuSO_4(aq) \longrightarrow Cu(s) + Al_2(SO_4)_3(aq)$
- c. $Pb(NO_3)_2(aq) + NaCl(aq) \longrightarrow PbCl_2(s) + NaNO_3(aq)$
- d. $Al(s) + HCl(aq) \longrightarrow AlCl_3(aq) + H_2(g)$

6.6 Balance the following equations:
- a. $Zn(s) + H_2SO_4(aq) \longrightarrow ZnSO_4(aq) + H_2(g)$
- b. $Al(s) + H_2SO_4(aq) \longrightarrow Al_2(SO_4)_3(aq) + H_2(g)$
- c. $K_2SO_4(aq) + BaCl_2(aq) \longrightarrow BaSO_4(s) + KCl(aq)$
- d. $CaCO_3(s) \longrightarrow CaO(s) + CO_2(g)$

## 6.2 Types of Reactions

**LEARNING GOAL**

Identify a chemical reaction as a combination, decomposition, single replacement, or double replacement reaction.

A great number of reactions occur in nature, in biological systems, and in the laboratory. However, some general patterns among all reactions help us to classify them. Most fit into four general reaction types.

### Combination Reactions

Two or more reactants | combine to yield | a single product

In a **combination reaction**, two or more elements or compounds bond to form one product. For example, sulfur and oxygen combine to form the product sulfur dioxide.

**Combination**

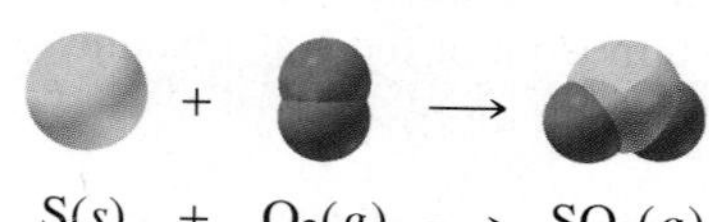

$$S(s) + O_2(g) \longrightarrow SO_2(g)$$

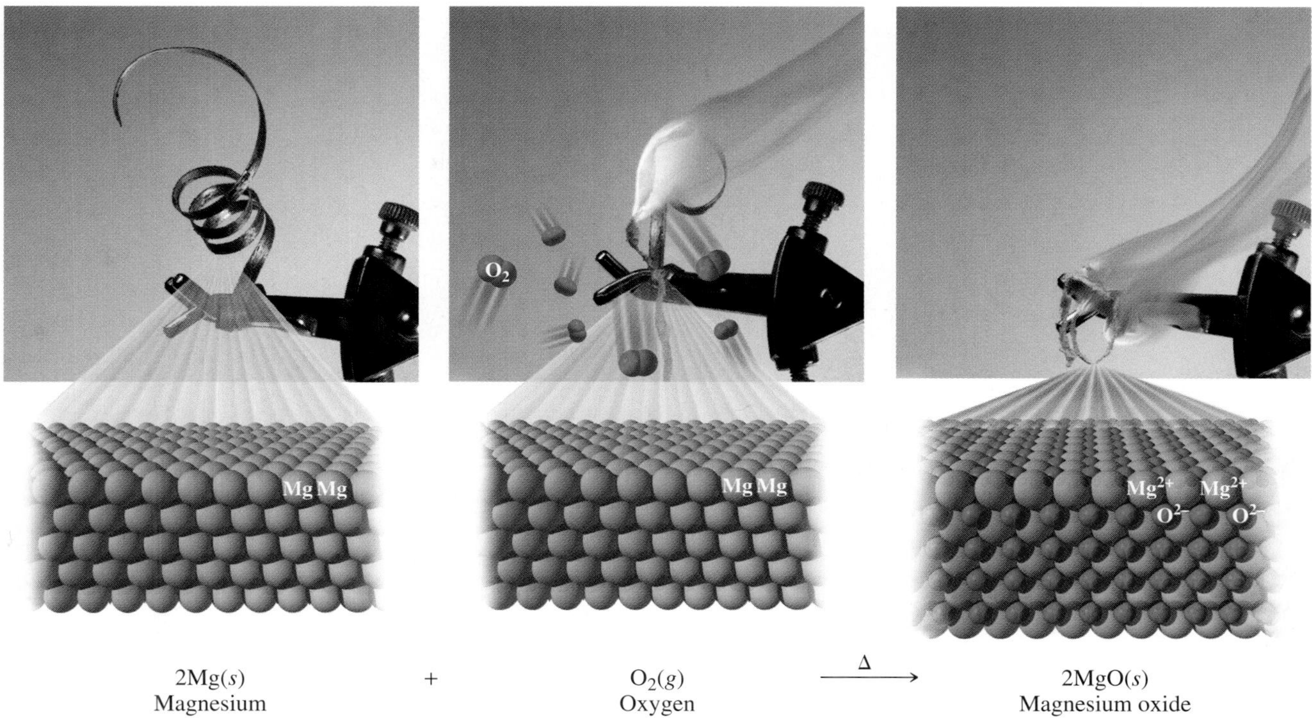


**FIGURE 6.3** In a combination reaction, two or more substances combine to form one substance as product.
**Q** What happens to the atoms of the reactants in a combination reaction?

In Figure 6.3, the elements magnesium and oxygen combine to form a single product, magnesium oxide:

$$2Mg(s) + O_2(g) \xrightarrow{\Delta} 2MgO(s)$$

## Decomposition Reactions

In a **decomposition reaction**, a reactant splits into two or more simpler products. For example, when mercury(II) oxide is heated, it breaks apart into mercury atoms and oxygen. (See Figure 6.4.)

$$2HgO(s) \xrightarrow{\Delta} 2Hg(l) + O_2(g)$$

**Decomposition**

| A reactant | splits into | two or more products |
|---|---|---|
| A B | ⟶ | A + B |

## Single Replacement Reactions

In a replacement reaction, elements in a compound are replaced by other elements. In a **single replacement reaction**, a reacting element switches place with an element in the other reacting compound.

**Single replacement**

| One element | | replaces | another element | |
|---|---|---|---|---|
| A + | B C | ⟶ | A C | + B |

In the single replacement reaction shown in Figure 6.5, zinc replaces hydrogen in hydrochloric acid, HCl(*aq*):

$$Zn(s) + 2HCl(aq) \longrightarrow ZnCl_2(aq) + H_2(g)$$

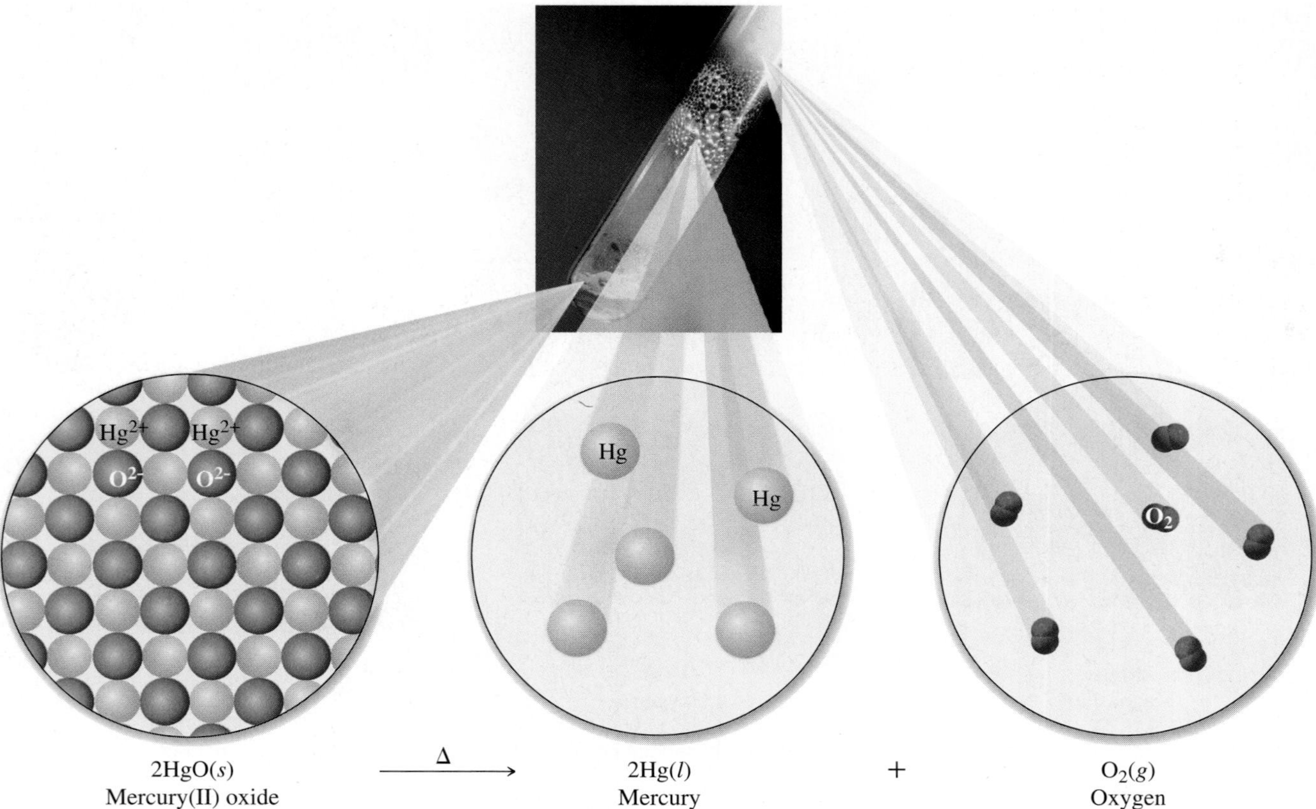


**FIGURE 6.4** In a decomposition reaction, one reactant breaks down into two or more products.
**Q** How do the differences in the reactant and products classify this as a decomposition reaction?

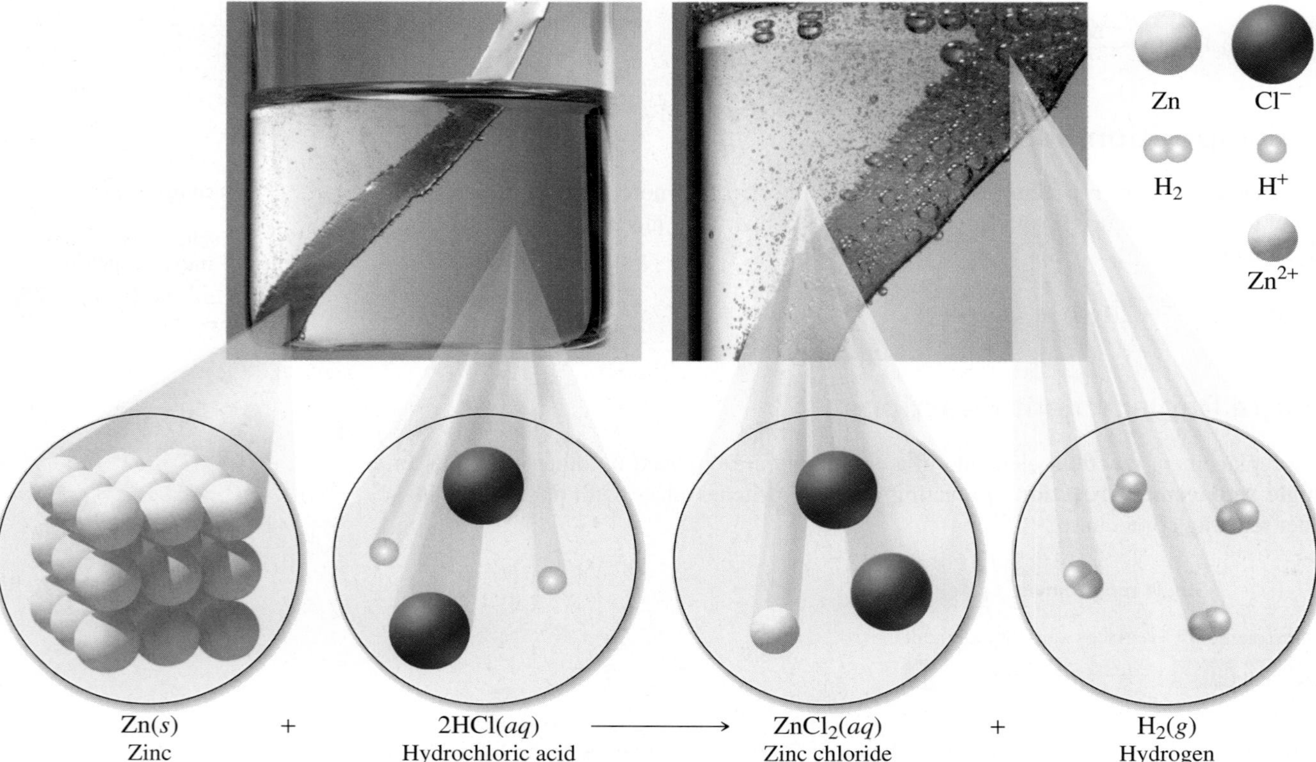


**FIGURE 6.5** In a single replacement reaction, an atom or ion replaces an atom or ion in a compound.
**Q** What changes in the formulas of the reactants identify this equation as a single replacement?

## Double Replacement Reactions

In a **double replacement reaction**, the positive ions in the reacting compounds switch places:

**Double replacement**

| Two elements | replace | each other |
|---|---|---|
| A B + C D | $\longrightarrow$ | A D + C B |

For example, in the reaction shown in Figure 6.6, barium ions change places with sodium ions in the reactants to form sodium chloride and a white solid precipitate of barium sulfate. The formulas of the products depend on the charges of the ions:

$$BaCl_2(aq) + Na_2SO_4(aq) \longrightarrow BaSO_4(s) + 2NaCl(aq)$$

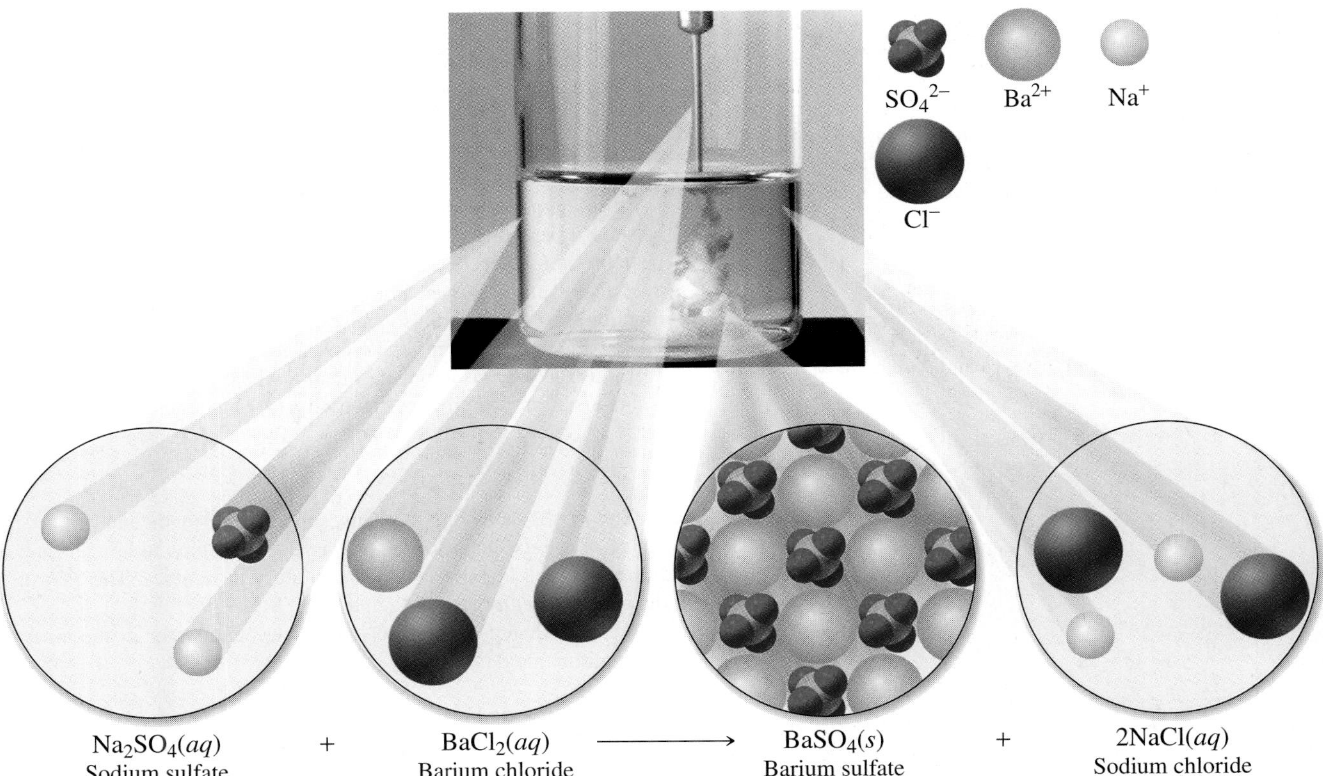


**FIGURE 6.6** In a double replacement reaction, the positive ions in the reactants replace each other.
**Q** How do the changes in the formulas of the reactants identify this equation as a double replacement reaction?

SAMPLE PROBLEM 6.2

### ■ Identifying Reactions and Predicting Products

Classify the following reactions as combination, decomposition, single replacement, or double replacement:

**a.** $2Fe_2O_3(s) + 3C(s) \longrightarrow 3CO_2(g) + 4Fe(s)$
**b.** $BaCl_2(aq) + K_2SO_4(aq) \longrightarrow BaSO_4(s) + 2KCl(aq)$

SOLUTION

**a.** In this *single replacement reaction*, a C atom replaces Fe in $Fe_2O_3$ to form the compound $CO_2$ and Fe atoms.

**b.** There are two reactants and two products, but the positive ions have exchanged places, which makes this a *double replacement reaction*.

STUDY CHECK

Nitrogen oxide gas and oxygen gas react to form nitrogen dioxide gas. Write the balanced equation and identify the reaction type.

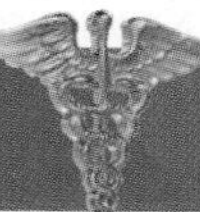

# HEALTH NOTE

## Smog and Health Concerns

There are two types of smog. One, photochemical smog, requires sunlight to initiate reactions that produce pollutants such as nitrogen oxides and ozone. The other type of smog—called *industrial* or *London smog*—occurs in areas where coal containing sulfur is burned and the unwanted product, sulfur dioxide, is emitted.

Photochemical smog is most prevalent in cities where people are dependent on cars for transportation. On a typical day in Los Angeles, for example, nitrogen oxide (NO) emissions from car exhausts increase as traffic increases on the roads. The nitrogen oxide is formed when $N_2$ and $O_2$ react at high temperatures in car and truck engines.

$$N_2(g) + O_2(g) \xrightarrow{\Delta} 2NO(g)$$

Then NO reacts with oxygen in the air to produce $NO_2$, a reddish brown gas that is irritating to the eyes and damaging to the respiratory tract.

$$2NO(g) + O_2(g) \longrightarrow 2NO_2(g)$$

When $NO_2$ is exposed to sunlight, it is converted into NO and an oxygen atom (O).

$$NO_2(g) \xrightarrow{\text{Sunlight}} NO(g) + \underset{\text{Oxygen atom}}{O(g)}$$

Oxygen atoms are so reactive that they combine with oxygen molecules in the atmosphere, forming ozone.

$$O(g) + O_2(g) \longrightarrow \underset{\text{Ozone}}{O_3(g)}$$

In the upper atmosphere (the stratosphere), ozone is beneficial because it protects us from harmful ultraviolet radiation that comes from the sun. However, in the lower atmosphere, ozone irritates the eyes and respiratory tract, where it causes coughing, decreased lung function, and fatigue. It also causes deterioration of fabrics, cracks rubber, and damages trees and crops.

Industrial smog is prevalent in areas where coal with high sulfur content is burned to produce electricity. During combustion, the sulfur is converted to sulfur dioxide.

$$S(s) + O_2(g) \longrightarrow SO_2(g)$$

The $SO_2$ is damaging to plants, suppresses growth, and it is corrosive to metals such as steel. $SO_2$ is also damaging to humans and can cause lung impairment and respiratory difficulties. The $SO_2$ in the air reacts with more oxygen to form $SO_3$.

Acid rain occurs when $SO_3$ combines with water in the air to form sulfuric acid.

$$2SO_2(g) + O_2(g) \longrightarrow 2SO_3(g)$$
$$SO_3(g) + H_2O(l) \longrightarrow \underset{\text{Sulfuric acid}}{H_2SO_4(aq)}$$

The presence of sulfuric acid in rivers and lakes causes an increase in the acidity of the water, reducing the ability of animals and plants to survive.

# QUESTIONS AND PROBLEMS

## Types of Reactions

**6.7** **a.** Why is the following called a decomposition reaction?

$$2Al_2O_3(s) \xrightarrow{\Delta} 4Al(s) + 3O_2(g)$$

**b.** Why is the following called a single replacement reaction?

$$Br_2(g) + BaI_2(s) \longrightarrow BaBr_2(s) + I_2(g)$$

**6.8** **a.** Why is the following called a combination reaction?

$$H_2(g) + Br_2(g) \longrightarrow 2HBr(g)$$

**b.** Why is the following called a double replacement reaction?

$$AgNO_3(aq) + NaCl(aq) \longrightarrow AgCl(s) + NaNO_3(aq)$$

**6.9** Classify each of the following as a combination, decomposition, single replacement, or double replacement reaction:

**a.** $4Fe(s) + 3O_2(g) \longrightarrow 2Fe_2O_3(s)$

**b.** $Mg(s) + 2AgNO_3(aq) \longrightarrow Mg(NO_3)_2(aq) + 2Ag(s)$

**c.** $CuCO_3(s) \longrightarrow CuO(s) + CO_2(g)$

**d.** $NaOH(aq) + HCl(aq) \longrightarrow NaCl(aq) + H_2O(l)$

**e.** $Al_2(SO_4)_3(aq) + 6KOH(aq) \longrightarrow 2Al(OH)_3(s) + 3K_2SO_4(aq)$

**6.10** Classify each of the following as a combination, decomposition, single replacement, or double replacement reaction:

**a.** $CuO(s) + 2HCl(aq) \longrightarrow CuCl_2(aq) + H_2O(l)$

**b.** $2Al(s) + 3Br_2(g) \longrightarrow 2AlBr_3(s)$

**c.** $Pb(NO_3)_2(aq) + 2NaCl(aq) \longrightarrow PbCl_2(s) + 2NaNO_3(aq)$

**d.** $C_6H_{12}O_6(aq) \longrightarrow 2C_2H_6O(aq) + 2CO_2(g)$

**e.** $BaCl_2(aq) + K_2CO_3(aq) \longrightarrow BaCO_3(s) + 2KCl(aq)$

**6.11** Try your hand at predicting the products that would result from the following reactions, and balance each equation:

**a.** combination: $Mg(s) + Cl_2(g) \longrightarrow$

**b.** decomposition: $HBr(g) \longrightarrow$

**c.** single replacement: $Mg(s) + Zn(NO_3)_2(aq) \longrightarrow$

**d.** double replacement: $K_2S(aq) + Pb(NO_3)_2(aq) \longrightarrow$

**6.12** Try your hand at predicting the products that would result from the following reactions, and balance each equation:

**a.** combination: $Ca(s) + O_2(g) \longrightarrow$

**b.** decomposition: $PbO_2(s) \longrightarrow$

**c.** single replacement: $KI(s) + Cl_2(g) \longrightarrow$

**d.** double replacement: $CuCl_2(aq) + Na_2S(aq) \longrightarrow$

# 6.3 Oxidation–Reduction Reactions

LEARNING GOAL

Define the terms oxidation and reduction.

Reactions known as *oxidation* and *reduction* reactions have many important applications in our everyday lives. For example, when you see a rusty nail or tarnish on a silver spoon, you are observing oxidation and reduction reactions.

$$4Fe(s) + 3O_2(g) \longrightarrow \underset{\text{Rust}}{2Fe_2O_3(s)}$$

When you turn the lights on in your car, an oxidation–reduction reaction within your car battery provides the electricity. On a cold, wintry day, you might build a wood fire. Burning wood is an oxidation–reduction reaction. When you eat foods with starches in them, you digest the starches to give glucose, which is oxidized in your cells to give you energy along with carbon dioxide and water. Every breath you take provides oxygen to carry out oxidation in your cells.

$$C_6H_{12}O_6(aq) + 6O_2(g) \longrightarrow 6CO_2(g) + 6H_2O(l) + \text{energy}$$

## Oxidation–Reduction

In an **oxidation–reduction reaction** (*redox*), electrons are transferred from one substance to another. If one substance loses electrons, another substance must gain electrons. **Oxidation** is defined as the *loss* of electrons; **reduction** is defined as the *gain* of electrons.

One way to remember these definitions is to use the following:

**OIL RIG**

**O**xidation **I**s **L**oss of electrons.

**R**eduction **I**s **G**ain of electrons.

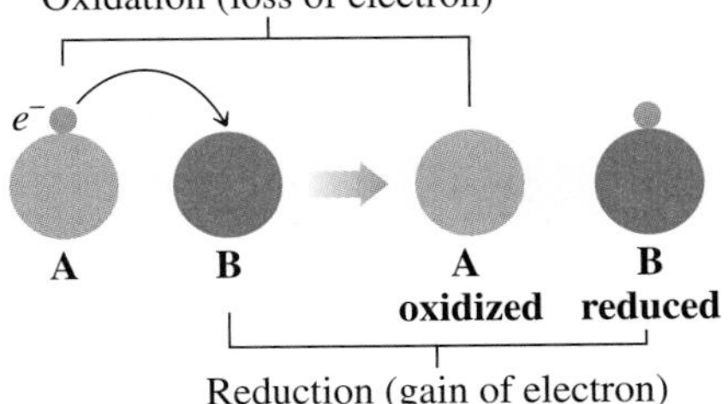


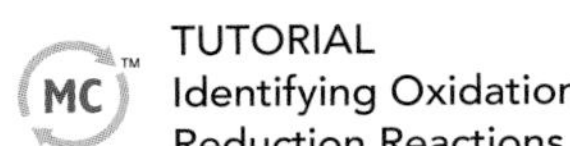


TUTORIAL
Identifying Oxidation–Reduction Reactions

## Oxidation–Reduction Involving Ions

In general, atoms of metals lose electrons to form positive ions, whereas nonmetals gain electrons to form negative ions. In terms of oxidation and reduction, atoms of a metal are oxidized, and atoms of a nonmetal are reduced. Let's look at the formation of the ionic compound CaS:

$$Ca(s) + S(s) \longrightarrow CaS(s)$$

When we looked at the formation of ionic compounds, we saw that metals lost electrons and nonmetals gained electrons. Now we can say that metals are oxidized and nonmetals are reduced.

The calcium atom loses two electrons to form calcium ion ($Ca^{2+}$); calcium is oxidized.

$$Ca \longrightarrow Ca^{2+} + 2e^- \quad \text{Oxidation; loss of electrons}$$

At the same time, the sulfur atom gains electrons to form sulfide ion ($S^{2-}$). The elemental forms of calcium and sulfur have no ionic charge; they are neutral. Many oxidation–reduction reactions include a reactant or product written in its elemental form such as $O_2(g)$ or $Zn(s)$.

$$S + 2e^- \longrightarrow S^{2-} \quad \text{Reduction; gain of electrons}$$

Therefore, the formation of CaS involves two reactions that occur simultaneously, one an oxidation and the other a reduction:

$$Ca + S \longrightarrow Ca^{2+} + S^{2-} = CaS$$

*In every oxidation–reduction reaction, the number of electrons lost is equal to the number of electrons gained.*

| Reduced | | Oxidized |
|---|---|---|
| Na | Oxidation: lose $e^-$ → | $Na^+ + e^-$ |
| Ca | | $Ca^{2+} + 2e^-$ |
| $2Br^-$ | ← Reduction: gain $e^-$ | $Br_2 + 2e^-$ |
| $Fe^{2+}$ | | $Fe^{3+} + e^-$ |

In another example, we look at a single replacement reaction between zinc and copper(II) sulfate. (See Figure 6.7.)

$$Zn(s) + CuSO_4(aq) \longrightarrow ZnSO_4(aq) + Cu(s)$$

We can rewrite the equation to show the atoms and ions:

$$Zn(s) + Cu^{2+}(aq) + SO_4^{2-}(aq) \longrightarrow Zn^{2+}(aq) + SO_4^{2-}(aq) + Cu(s)$$

In this reaction, Zn atoms lose two electrons to form $Zn^{2+}$; $Zn(s)$ is oxidized. At the same time, $Cu^{2+}$ gains two electrons to form $Cu(s)$; $Cu^{2+}$ is reduced. The $SO_4^{2-}$ ions are spectator ions and do not change.

$$Zn(s) \longrightarrow Zn^{2+}(aq) + 2e^- \quad \text{Oxidation of Zn}$$

$$Cu^{2+}(aq) + 2e^- \longrightarrow Cu(s) \quad \text{Reduction of } Cu^{2+}$$

**FIGURE 6.7** In this single replacement reaction, Zn(s) is oxidized to $Zn^{2+}$ when it provides two electrons to reduce $Cu^{2+}$ to Cu(s): $Zn(s) + Cu^{2+}(aq) \longrightarrow Cu(s) + Zn^{2+}(aq)$

**Q** In the oxidation, does Zn(s) lose or gain electrons?

CONCEPT CHECK 6.3

### Oxidation and Reduction

The following unbalanced reaction takes place in a dry-cell battery used in toys and flashlights:

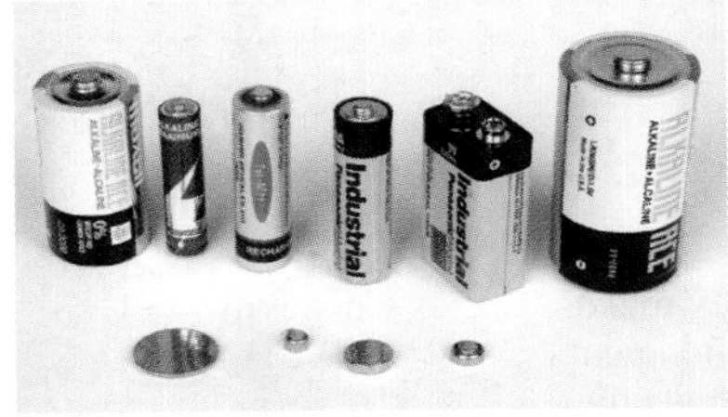


$Zn(s) \longrightarrow Zn^{2+}(aq)$

**a.** Is this reaction an oxidation or a reduction? Why?
**b.** What substance is oxidized or reduced?

ANSWER

**a.** $Zn(s)$ loses electrons to form $Zn^{2+}(aq)$, which is oxidation.

$Zn(s) \longrightarrow Zn^{2+}(aq) + 2e^-$

**b.** $Zn(s)$ is oxidized.

SAMPLE PROBLEM 6.3

### Oxidation–Reduction Reactions

In photographic film, the following decomposition reaction occurs in the presence of light. What is oxidized and what is reduced?

$2AgBr(s) \xrightarrow{\text{Light}} 2Ag(s) + Br_2(g)$

SOLUTION

To determine oxidation and reduction, we need to look at the ions and charges in the reactants and products. In AgBr, there is a silver ion ($Ag^+$) with a 1+ charge and a bromide ion ($Br^-$) with a charge of 1−. We can write the balanced reaction as follows:

$2Ag^+(s) + 2Br^-(s) \longrightarrow 2Ag(s) + Br_2(g)$

Now we can compare $Ag^+$ with the product Ag atom. In this case, each $Ag^+$ gained an electron; $Ag^+$ is reduced.

$2Ag^+(s) + 2e^- \longrightarrow 2Ag(s)$ Reduction

Then we compare $Br^-$ with the Br in the product $Br_2$. In this case, each $Br^-$ lost an electron; $Br^-$ is oxidized.

$2Br^-(s) \longrightarrow Br_2(g) + 2e^-$ Oxidation

STUDY CHECK

In the following combination reaction, which reactant is oxidized and which is reduced?

$2Li(s) + F_2(g) \longrightarrow 2LiF(s)$

### Oxidation of Fruits and Vegetables

Freshly cut surfaces of fruits and vegetables discolor when exposed to oxygen in the air. Cut three slices of a fruit or vegetable such as apple, potato, avocado, or banana. Leave one piece on the kitchen counter (uncovered). Wrap one piece in plastic wrap and leave on the kitchen counter. Dip one piece in lemon juice and leave uncovered.

QUESTIONS

1. What changes take place in each sample after 1 to 2 hours?
2. Why would wrapping fruits and vegetables slow the rate of discoloration?
3. If lemon juice contains vitamin C (an antioxidant), why would dipping a fruit or vegetable in lemon juice affect the oxidation reaction on the surface of the fruit or vegetable?
4. Other kinds of antioxidants are vitamin E, citric acid, and BHT. Look for these antioxidants on the labels of cereals, potato chips, and other foods in your kitchen. Why are antioxidants added to food products that will be stored on our kitchen shelves?

## Oxidation and Reduction in Biological Systems

Oxidation may also involve the addition of oxygen or the loss of hydrogen, and reduction may involve the loss of oxygen or the gain of hydrogen. In the cells of the body, oxidation of organic (carbon) compounds involves the transfer of hydrogen atoms (H), which are composed of electrons and protons. For example, the oxidation of a typical biochemical molecule can involve the transfer of two hydrogen atoms (or $2H^+$ and $2e^-$) to a proton acceptor such as the coenzyme FAD (flavin adenine dinucleotide). The coenzyme is reduced to $FADH_2$.

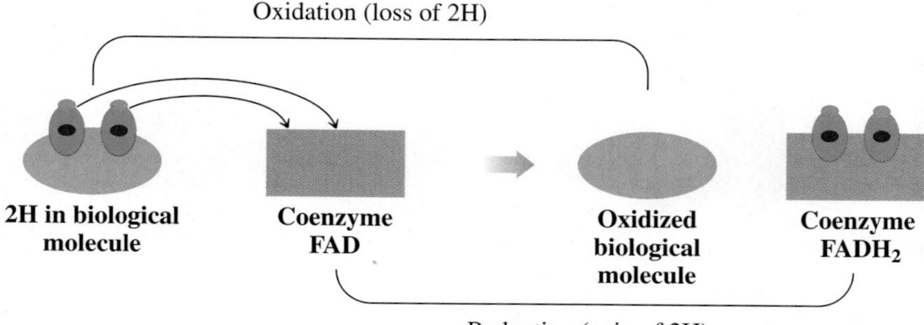


In many biochemical oxidation–reduction reactions, the transfer of hydrogen atoms is necessary for the production of energy in the cells. For example, methyl alcohol ($CH_3OH$), a poisonous substance, is metabolized in the body by the following reactions:

$$\underset{\text{Methyl alcohol}}{CH_3OH} \longrightarrow \underset{\text{Formaldehyde}}{H_2CO} + 2H \qquad \text{Oxidation: loss of H atoms}$$

The formaldehyde can be oxidized further, this time by the addition of oxygen, to produce formic acid:

$$\underset{\text{Formaldehyde}}{2H_2CO} + O_2 \longrightarrow \underset{\text{Formic acid}}{2H_2CO_2} \qquad \text{Oxidation: addition of O atoms}$$

Finally, formic acid is oxidized to carbon dioxide and water.

$$\underset{\text{Formic acid}}{2H_2CO_2} + O_2 \longrightarrow 2CO_2 + 2H_2O \qquad \text{Oxidation: addition of O atoms}$$

The intermediate products of the oxidation of methyl alcohol are quite toxic, causing blindness and possibly death as they interfere with key reactions in the cells of the body.

In summary, we find that the particular definition of oxidation and reduction we use depends on the process that occurs in the reaction. All of these definitions are summarized in Table 6.3. Oxidation always involves a loss of electrons, but it may also be seen as an addition of oxygen, or the loss of hydrogen atoms. A reduction always involves a gain of electrons, and it may also be seen as the loss of oxygen, or the gain of hydrogen.

**TABLE 6.3 Characteristics of Oxidation and Reduction**

| Oxidation | |
|---|---|
| **Always Involves** | **May Involve** |
| Loss of electrons | Addition of oxygen |
| Electrons are a product | Loss of hydrogen |
| **Reduction** | |
| **Always Involves** | **May Involve** |
| Gain of electrons | Loss of oxygen |
| Electrons are a reactant | Gain of hydrogen |

# QUESTIONS AND PROBLEMS

## Oxidation–Reduction Reactions

**6.13** Indicate whether each of the following is an oxidation or a reduction reaction:

**a.** $Na^+(aq) + e^- \longrightarrow Na(s)$
**b.** $Ni(s) \longrightarrow Ni^{2+}(aq) + 2e^-$
**c.** $Cr^{3+}(aq) + 3e^- \longrightarrow Cr(s)$
**d.** $2H^+(aq) + 2e^- \longrightarrow H_2(g)$

**6.14** Indicate whether each of the following is an oxidation or a reduction reaction:

**a.** $O_2(g) + 4e^- \longrightarrow 2O^{2-}(aq)$
**b.** $Al(s) \longrightarrow Al^{3+}(aq) + 3e^-$
**c.** $Fe^{3+}(aq) + e^- \longrightarrow Fe^{2+}(aq)$
**d.** $2Br^-(aq) \longrightarrow Br_2(g) + 2e^-$

**6.15** In the following reactions, identify which reactant is oxidized and which is reduced:

**a.** $Zn(s) + Cl_2(g) \longrightarrow ZnCl_2(s)$
**b.** $Cl_2(g) + 2NaBr(aq) \longrightarrow 2NaCl(aq) + Br_2(g)$
**c.** $2PbO(s) \longrightarrow 2Pb(s) + O_2(g)$
**d.** $2Fe^{3+}(aq) + Sn^{2+}(aq) \longrightarrow 2Fe^{2+}(aq) + Sn^{4+}(aq)$

**6.16** In the following reactions, identify which reactant is oxidized and which is reduced:

**a.** $2Li(s) + F_2(g) \longrightarrow 2LiF(s)$
**b.** $Cl_2(g) + 2KI(aq) \longrightarrow 2KCl(aq) + I_2(g)$
**c.** $Zn(s) + Cu^{2+}(aq) \longrightarrow Zn^{2+}(aq) + Cu(s)$
**d.** $Fe(s) + CuSO_4(aq) \longrightarrow FeSO_4(aq) + Cu(s)$

**6.17** In the mitochondria of human cells, energy for the production of ATP is provided by the oxidation and reduction reactions of the iron ions in the cytochromes of the electron transport chain. Identify each of the following reactions as oxidation or reduction:

**a.** $Fe^{3+} + e^- \longrightarrow Fe^{2+}$
**b.** $Fe^{2+} \longrightarrow Fe^{3+} + e^-$

**6.18** Chlorine ($Cl_2$) is a strong germicide used to disinfect drinking water and to kill microbes in swimming pools. If the product is $Cl^-$, was the $Cl_2$ oxidized or reduced?

**6.19** When linoleic acid, an unsaturated fatty acid, reacts with hydrogen, it forms a saturated fatty acid. Is linoleic acid oxidized or reduced in the hydrogenation reaction?

$$C_{18}H_{32}O_2 + 2H_2 \longrightarrow C_{18}H_{36}O_2$$

**6.20** In one of the reactions in the citric acid cycle, which provides energy for ATP synthesis, succinic acid is converted to fumaric acid:

$$\underset{\text{Succinic acid}}{C_4H_6O_4} \longrightarrow \underset{\text{Fumaric acid}}{C_4H_4O_4} + 2H$$

The reaction is accompanied by a coenzyme, flavin adenine dinucleotide (FAD):

$$FAD + 2H \longrightarrow FADH_2$$

**a.** Is succinic acid oxidized or reduced?
**b.** Is FAD oxidized or reduced?
**c.** Why would the two reactions occur together?

# GREEN CHEMISTRY NOTE

## Fuel Cells: Clean Energy for the Future

Fuel cells are of interest to scientists because they provide an alternative source of electrical energy that is more efficient, does not use up oil reserves, and generates products that do not pollute the atmosphere. Fuels cells are considered a clean way to produce energy.

Unlike a battery that runs down, fuel cells are provided continually with new reactants to generate an electrical current. One type of hydrogen–oxygen fuel cell has been used in automobile prototypes. In this hydrogen cell, gas enters the fuel cell, where it comes in contact with platinum embedded in a plastic membrane. The platinum assists in the oxidation of hydrogen atoms to hydrogen ions and electrons:

$$2H_2(g) \xrightarrow{Pt} 4H^+(aq) + 4e^- \quad \text{Oxidation}$$

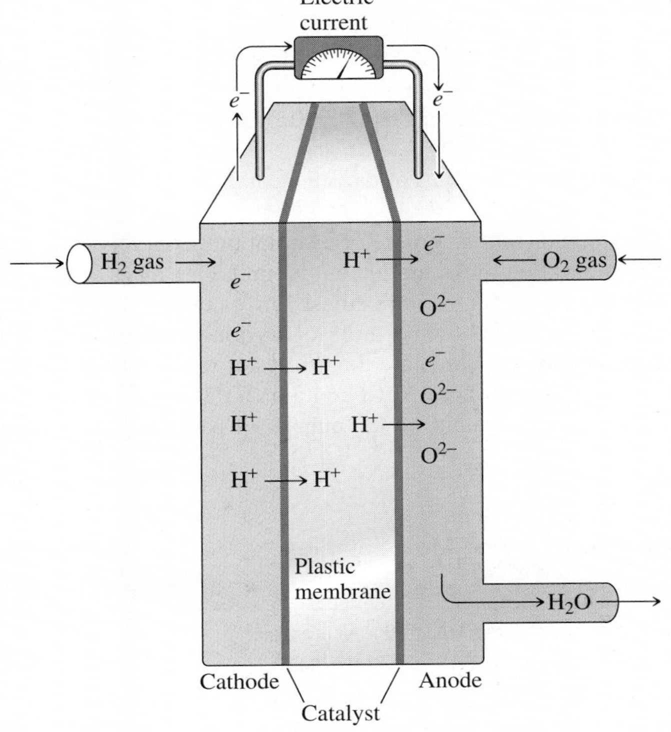


Oxidation
$2H_2(g) \longrightarrow 4H^+(aq) + 4e^-$

Reduction
$O_2(g) + 4H^+(aq) + 4e^- \longrightarrow 2H_2O(l)$

The electrons produce an electric current as they travel through the wire. The hydrogen ions move through the plastic membrane to react with oxygen molecules. The oxygen is reduced to oxide ions that combine with the hydrogen ions to form water:

$$O_2(g) + 4H^+(aq) + 4e^- \longrightarrow 2H_2O(l) \quad \text{Reduction}$$

The overall hydrogen–oxygen fuel cell reaction can be written as

$$2H_2(g) + O_2(g) \longrightarrow 2H_2O(l)$$

Fuel cells have already been used to power the space shuttle and may soon be available to produce energy for cars and buses.

A major drawback to the practical use of fuel cells is the economic impact of converting cars to fuel cell operation. The storage and cost of producing hydrogen are also problems. Some manufacturers are experimenting with systems that convert gasoline or methanol to hydrogen for immediate use in fuel cells.

In homes, fuel cells may one day replace the batteries currently used to provide electrical power for cell phones, CD and DVD players, and laptop computers. Fuel cell design is still in the prototype phase, although there is much interest in their development. We already know they can work, but modifications must still be made before they become reasonably priced and part of our everyday lives.

# 6.4 The Mole

**LEARNING GOAL**

Use Avogadro's number to determine the number of particles in a given amount of moles.

At the store, you buy eggs by the dozen. In an office, you buy pencils by the gross and paper by the ream. For a restaurant, soda is ordered by the case. In each of these examples, terms such as *dozen, gross, ream*, and *case* count the number of items present. For example, when you buy a dozen eggs, you know you will get 12 eggs in the carton.

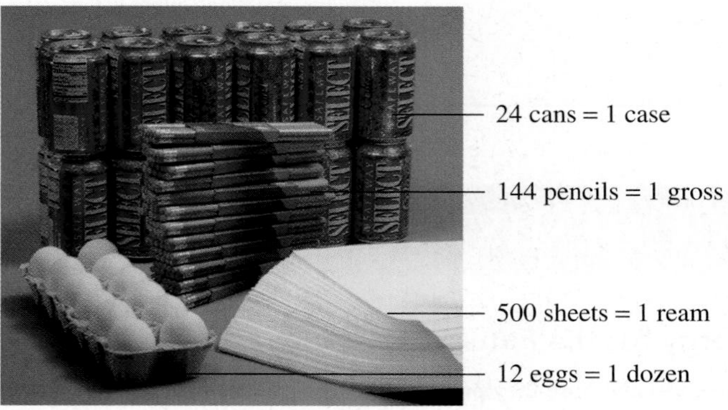


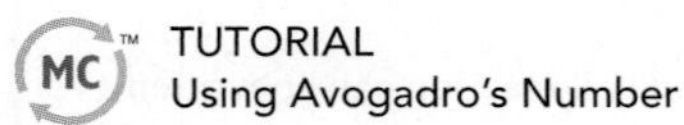

TUTORIAL
Using Avogadro's Number

## Avogadro's Number

In chemistry, tiny particles such as atoms, molecules, and ions are counted by the **mole**, a unit that contains $6.02 \times 10^{23}$ items. This immense number is called **Avogadro's number** after Amedeo Avogadro, an Italian physicist. It looks like this when written with three significant figures:

**Avogadro's Number**

$$602\ 000\ 000\ 000\ 000\ 000\ 000\ 000 = 6.02 \times 10^{23}$$

One mole of any element always contains Avogadro's number of atoms. For example, 1 mole of carbon contains $6.02 \times 10^{23}$ carbon atoms; 1 mole of aluminum contains $6.02 \times 10^{23}$ aluminum atoms; 1 mole of sulfur contains $6.02 \times 10^{23}$ sulfur atoms.

$$1 \text{ mole of an element} = 6.02 \times 10^{23} \text{ atoms of that element}$$

Avogadro's number also tells us that one mole of a compound contains $6.02 \times 10^{23}$ of the particular type of particles that make up that compound. One mole of a covalent compound contains Avogadro's number of molecules. For example, 1 mole of $CO_2$ contains $6.02 \times 10^{23}$ molecules of $CO_2$. One mole of an ionic compound contains Avogadro's number of **formula units**, which are the groups of ions represented by the formula of an ionic compound. One mole of NaCl contains $6.02 \times 10^{23}$ formula units of NaCl ($Na^+$, $Cl^-$). Table 6.4 gives examples of the number of particles in some 1-mole quantities.

**TABLE 6.4** Number of Particles in One-Mole Samples

| Substance | Number and Type of Particles |
|---|---|
| 1 mole of Al | $6.02 \times 10^{23}$ Al atoms |
| 1 mole of S | $6.02 \times 10^{23}$ S atoms |
| 1 mole of $H_2O$ | $6.02 \times 10^{23}$ $H_2O$ molecules |
| 1 mole of NaCl | $6.02 \times 10^{23}$ NaCl formula units |
| 1 mole of vitamin C ($C_6H_8O_6$) | $6.02 \times 10^{23}$ vitamin C molecules |

We can use Avogadro's number as a conversion factor to convert between the moles of a substance and number of particles it contains.

$$\frac{6.02 \times 10^{23} \text{ particles}}{1 \text{ mole}} \quad \text{and} \quad \frac{1 \text{ mole}}{6.02 \times 10^{23} \text{ particles}}$$

For example, we use Avogadro's number to convert 4.00 moles of iron to atoms of iron.

$$4.00 \cancel{\text{ moles Fe atoms}} \times \underbrace{\frac{6.02 \times 10^{23} \text{ Fe atoms}}{1 \cancel{\text{ mole Fe atoms}}}}_{\text{Avogadro's number as a conversion factor}} = 2.41 \times 10^{24} \text{ Fe atoms}$$

We can also use Avogadro's number to convert $3.01 \times 10^{24}$ molecules of $CO_2$ to moles of $CO_2$.

$$3.01 \times 10^{24} \cancel{CO_2 \text{ molecules}} \times \underbrace{\frac{1 \text{ mole } CO_2 \text{ molecules}}{6.02 \times 10^{23} \cancel{CO_2 \text{ molecules}}}}_{\text{Avogadro's number as a conversion factor}} = 5.00 \text{ moles of } CO_2 \text{ molecules}$$

Generally, in calculations that convert between moles and particles, the number of moles will be a small number compared to the number of atoms or molecules, which will be a large number.

CONCEPT CHECK 6.4

### Moles and Particles

Explain why 0.20 mole of aluminum is a small number, but the number of atoms in 0.20 mole is a large number: $1.2 \times 10^{23}$ atoms of aluminum.

ANSWER

The term *mole* is used as a collection term that represents $6.02 \times 10^{23}$ particles. Because atoms are submicroscopic particles, a large number of atoms are in 1 mole of aluminum.

SAMPLE PROBLEM 6.4

### Calculating the Number of Molecules

How many molecules are present in 1.75 moles of carbon dioxide, $CO_2$?

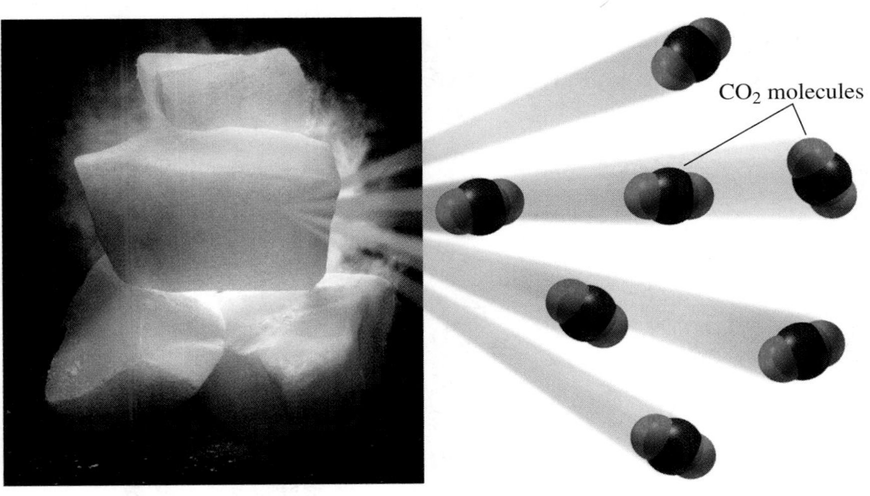


Dry ice (solid $CO_2$)

**Guide to Calculating the Atoms or Molecules of a Substance**

STEP 1
Determine the given number of moles.

STEP 2
Write a plan to convert moles to atoms or molecules.

STEP 3
Use Avogadro's number to write conversion factors.

STEP 4
Set up problem to convert given moles to atoms or molecules.

SOLUTION

**STEP 1** **Given** 1.75 moles of $CO_2$ **Need** molecules of $CO_2$

**STEP 2** **Plan** moles of $CO_2$ → Avogadro's number → molecules of $CO_2$

**STEP 3** **Equalities/Conversion Factors**

$$1 \text{ mole of } CO_2 = 6.02 \times 10^{23} \text{ molecules of } CO_2$$

$$\frac{6.02 \times 10^{23} \text{ molecules } CO_2}{1 \text{ mole } CO_2} \quad \text{and} \quad \frac{1 \text{ mole } CO_2}{6.02 \times 10^{23} \text{ molecules } CO_2}$$

**STEP 4** **Set Up Problem** Calculate the number of $CO_2$ molecules:

$$1.75 \cancel{\text{moles } CO_2} \times \frac{6.02 \times 10^{23} \text{ molecules } CO_2}{1 \cancel{\text{mole } CO_2}} = 1.05 \times 10^{24} \text{ molecules of } CO_2$$

STUDY CHECK

How many moles of water, $H_2O$, contain $2.60 \times 10^{23}$ molecules of water?

## Moles of Elements in a Formula

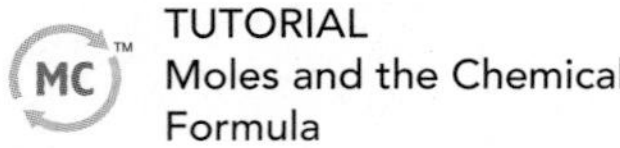

TUTORIAL
Moles and the Chemical Formula

We have seen that the subscripts in a chemical formula of a compound indicate the number of atoms of each type of element. For example, in a molecule of aspirin, chemical formula $C_9H_8O_4$, there are 9 carbon atoms, 8 hydrogen atoms, and 4 oxygen atoms. The subscripts also state the number of moles of each element in one mole of aspirin: 9 moles of carbon atoms, 8 moles of hydrogen atoms, and 4 moles of oxygen atoms.

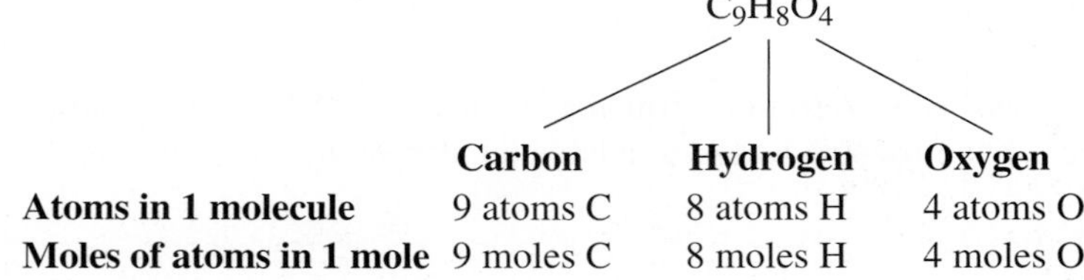

$C_9H_8O_4$

| | **Carbon** | **Hydrogen** | **Oxygen** |
|---|---|---|---|
| **Atoms in 1 molecule** | 9 atoms C | 8 atoms H | 4 atoms O |
| **Moles of atoms in 1 mole** | 9 moles C | 8 moles H | 4 moles O |

Using the subscripts from the aspirin formula, $C_9H_8O_4$, we can write the following conversion factors for each of the elements in 1 mole of aspirin:

$$\frac{9 \text{ moles C}}{1 \text{ mole } C_9H_8O_4} \quad \frac{8 \text{ moles H}}{1 \text{ mole } C_9H_8O_4} \quad \frac{4 \text{ moles O}}{1 \text{ mole } C_9H_8O_4}$$

$$\frac{1 \text{ mole } C_9H_8O_4}{9 \text{ moles C}} \quad \frac{1 \text{ mole } C_9H_8O_4}{8 \text{ moles H}} \quad \frac{1 \text{ mole } C_9H_8O_4}{4 \text{ moles O}}$$

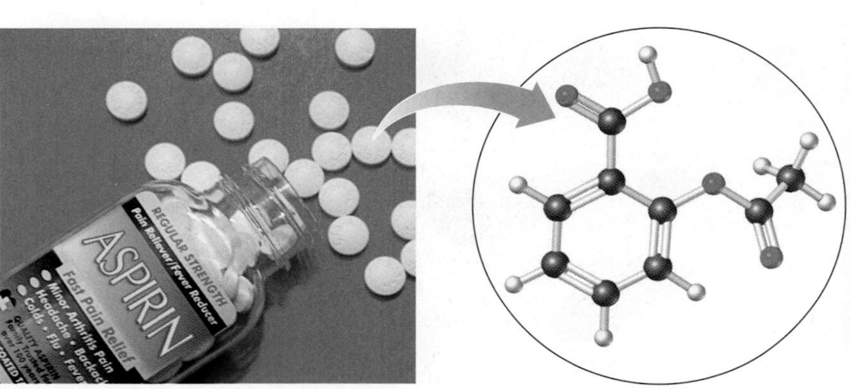


Aspirin $C_9H_8O_4$

Number of atoms in 1 molecule

Carbon (C) Hydrogen (H) Oxygen (O)

CONCEPT CHECK 6.5

### Using Subscripts of a Formula

Indicate the moles of C atoms in 1 mole of each of the following:

**a.** $C_8H_9NO_2$, acetaminophen used in Tylenol
**b.** $Zn(C_2H_3O_2)_2$, zinc dietary supplement

ANSWER

**a.** The subscript 8 indicates that there are 8 moles of C atoms in 1 mole of acetaminophen.
**b.** The subscript 2 within the parentheses indicates there are 2 moles of C in the ion $C_2H_3O_2^-$. The subscript 2 outside the parentheses indicates there are 2 moles of the ion $C_2H_3O_2^-$ in the formula. Thus there is a total of 4 (2 × 2) moles of C atoms in 1 mole of $Zn(C_2H_3O_2)_2$.

SAMPLE PROBLEM 6.5

### Calculating the Atoms of an Element

How many carbon atoms are present in 1.50 moles of aspirin, $C_9H_8O_4$?

SOLUTION

**STEP 1** **Given** 1.50 moles of $C_9H_8O_4$ **Need** carbon atoms

**STEP 2** **Plan**

Moles of $C_9H_8O_4$ → Subscript → moles of C atoms → Avogadro's number → C atoms

**STEP 3** **Equalities/Conversion Factors**

$$1 \text{ mole of } C_9H_8O_4 = 9 \text{ moles of C atoms}$$
$$\frac{9 \text{ moles C}}{1 \text{ mole } C_9H_8O_4} \quad \text{and} \quad \frac{1 \text{ mole } C_9H_8O_4}{9 \text{ moles C}}$$

$$1 \text{ mole of C atoms} = 6.02 \times 10^{23} \text{ C atoms}$$
$$\frac{1 \text{ mole C atoms}}{6.02 \times 10^{23} \text{ C atoms}} \quad \text{and} \quad \frac{6.02 \times 10^{23} \text{ C atoms}}{1 \text{ mole C atoms}}$$

**STEP 4** **Set Up Problem** The conversion factors of the subscript and Avogadro's number can be combined to calculate the number of atoms of C from moles of $C_9H_8O_4$.

$$1.50 \cancel{\text{moles } C_9H_8O_4} \times \frac{9 \cancel{\text{moles C}}}{1 \cancel{\text{mole } C_9H_8O_4}} \times \frac{6.02 \times 10^{23} \text{ C atoms}}{1 \cancel{\text{mole C atoms}}} = 8.13 \times 10^{24} \text{ C atoms}$$

STUDY CHECK

How many moles of aspirin, $C_9H_8O_4$, contain 0.480 mole of O atoms?

## QUESTIONS AND PROBLEMS

### The Mole

**6.21** What is a mole?

**6.22** What is Avogadro's number?

**6.23** Calculate each of the following:
**a.** number of Ag atoms in 0.200 mole of Ag
**b.** number of $C_3H_8O$ molecules in 0.750 mole of $C_3H_8O$
**c.** moles of Au in $2.88 \times 10^{23}$ atoms of Au

**6.24** Calculate each of the following:
**a.** number of Ni atoms in 3.4 moles of Ni
**b.** number of $Mg(OH)_2$ formula units in 1.20 moles of $Mg(OH)_2$
**c.** moles of Zn in $5.6 \times 10^{24}$ atoms of Zn

**6.25** Consider the formula for quinine, $C_{20}H_{24}N_2O_2$.
**a.** How many moles of hydrogen are in 1.0 mole of quinine?
**b.** How many moles of carbon are in 5.0 moles of quinine?
**c.** How many moles of nitrogen are in 0.020 mole of quinine?

**6.26** Consider the formula for $Al_2(SO_4)_3$, which is used in antiperspirants.
  **a.** How many moles of sulfur are present in 3.0 moles of $Al_2(SO_4)_3$?
  **b.** How many moles of aluminum ions are present in 0.40 mole of $Al_2(SO_4)_3$?
  **c.** How many moles of sulfate ions $(SO_4^{2-})$ are present in 1.5 moles of $Al_2(SO_4)_3$?

**6.27** Calculate each of the following:
  **a.** number of C atoms in 0.500 mole of C
  **b.** number of $SO_2$ molecules in 1.28 moles of $SO_2$
  **c.** moles of Fe in $5.22 \times 10^{22}$ atoms of Fe
  **d.** moles of $C_2H_5OH$ in $8.50 \times 10^{24}$ molecules of $C_2H_5OH$

**6.28** Calculate each of the following:
  **a.** number of Li atoms in 4.5 moles of Li
  **b.** number of $CO_2$ molecules in 0.0180 mole of $CO_2$
  **c.** moles of Cu in $7.8 \times 10^{21}$ atoms of Cu
  **d.** moles of $C_2H_6$ in $3.754 \times 10^{23}$ molecules of $C_2H_6$

**6.29** Calculate each of the following quantities in 2.00 moles of $H_3PO_4$:
  **a.** moles of H
  **b.** moles of O
  **c.** atoms of P
  **d.** atoms of O

**6.30** Calculate each of the following quantities in 0.185 mole of $(C_3H_5)_2O$:
  **a.** moles of C
  **b.** moles of O
  **c.** atoms of H
  **d.** atoms of C

## 6.5 Molar Mass

**LEARNING GOAL**

Determine the molar mass of a substance and use the molar mass to convert between grams and moles.

MC™ SELF STUDY ACTIVITY
Stoichiometry

A single atom or molecule is much too small to weigh, even on the most accurate balance. In fact, it takes a huge number of atoms or molecules to make a piece of a substance that you can see. An amount of water that contains Avogadro's number of water molecules is only a few sips. In the laboratory, we can use a balance to weigh out Avogadro's number of particles or 1 mole of a substance.

For any element, the quantity called its **molar mass** is the number of grams equal to the atomic mass of that element. For example, carbon has an atomic mass of 12.01 on the periodic table. This means 1 mole of carbon atoms has a mass of 12.01 g. Thus, we can use the periodic table to determine the molar mass of an element.

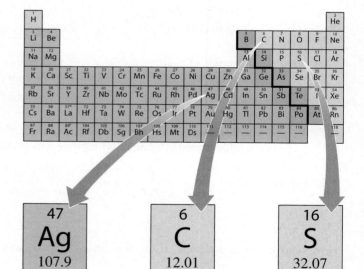

$6.02 \times 10^{23}$ atoms of C

1 mole of C atoms

12.01 g of C atoms

47 Ag 107.9 — 1 mole of silver atoms has a mass of 107.9 g

6 C 12.01 — 1 mole of carbon atoms has a mass of 12.01 g

16 S 32.07 — 1 mole of sulfur atoms has a mass of 32.07 g

### Molar Mass of a Compound

To determine the molar mass of a compound, multiply the molar mass of each element by its subscript in the formula and add the results. For example, the molar mass of sulfur trioxide, $SO_3$, is obtained by adding the molar masses of 1 mole of sulfur and 3 moles of oxygen. In our calculations, we round molar mass to the tenths (0.1 g) place.

**STEP 1** **Using the periodic table, obtain the molar masses of sulfur and oxygen.**

$$\frac{32.1\text{ g S}}{1\text{ mole S}} \qquad \frac{16.0\text{ g O}}{1\text{ mole O}}$$

**STEP 2** **Multiply each molar mass by its subscript in the formula.**
**Grams from 1 mole of S**

$$1\ \cancel{\text{mole S}} \times \frac{32.1\text{ g S}}{1\ \cancel{\text{mole S}}} = 32.1\text{ g of S}$$

**Grams from 3 moles of O**

$$3\ \cancel{\text{moles O}} \times \frac{16.0\text{ g O}}{1\ \cancel{\text{mole O}}} = 48.0\text{ g of O}$$

**STEP 3** **Obtain the molar mass of $SO_3$ by adding the masses of 1 mole of S and 3 moles of O.**

| | | |
|---|---|---|
| 1 mole of S | = | 32.1 g of S |
| 3 moles of O | = | 48.0 g of O |
| Molar mass of $SO_3$ | = | 80.1 g of $SO_3$ |

Figure 6.8 shows some 1-mole quantities of substances. Table 6.5 lists the molar mass for several 1-mole samples.

**TABLE 6.5** The Molar Mass of Selected Elements and Compounds

| Substance | Molar Mass |
|---|---|
| 1 mole of C (carbon) | 12.0 g |
| 1 mole of Na (sodium) | 23.0 g |
| 1 mole of Fe (iron) | 55.9 g |
| 1 mole of NaF (preventative for dental caries) | 42.0 g |
| 1 mole of $CaCO_3$ (antacid) | 100.1 g |
| 1 mole of $C_6H_{12}O_6$ (glucose) | 180.0 g |
| 1 mole of $C_8H_{10}N_4O_2$ (caffeine) | 194.0 g |

**One–Mole Quantities**

S

Fe

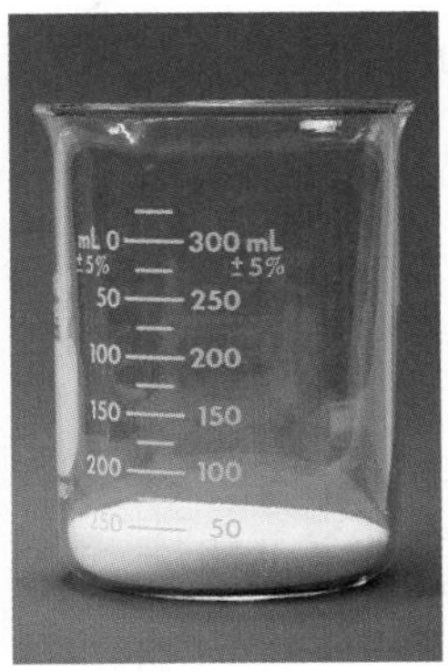


NaCl

$K_2Cr_2O_7$

$C_{12}H_{22}O_{11}$

**FIGURE 6.8** One-mole samples: sulfur, S (32.1 g); iron, Fe (55.9 g); salt, NaCl (58.5 g); potassium dichromate, $K_2Cr_2O_7$ (294.2 g); and sugar, sucrose, $C_{12}H_{22}O_{11}$ (342.0 g).

Q How is the molar mass for $K_2Cr_2O_7$ obtained?

## SAMPLE PROBLEM 6.6

### Calculating Molar Mass of Compounds

Find the molar mass of $Li_2CO_3$ used to produce the red color in fireworks.

SOLUTION

**STEP 1** **Using the periodic table, obtain the molar masses of lithium, carbon, and oxygen.**

$$\frac{6.9\text{ g Li}}{1\text{ mole Li}} \qquad \frac{12.0\text{ g C}}{1\text{ mole C}} \qquad \frac{16.0\text{ g O}}{1\text{ mole O}}$$

**STEP 2** **Multiply each molar mass by its subscript in the formula.** Grams from 2 moles of Li

$$2\ \cancel{\text{moles Li}} \times \frac{6.9\text{ g Li}}{1\ \cancel{\text{mole Li}}} = 13.8\text{ g of Li}$$

**Guide to Calculating Molar Mass**

**STEP 1** Obtain the molar mass of each element.

**STEP 2** Multiply each molar mass by the number of moles (subscript) in the formula.

**STEP 3** Calculate the molar mass by adding the masses of the elements.

Grams from 1 mole of C

$$1 \cancel{\text{mole C}} \times \frac{12.0 \text{ g C}}{1 \cancel{\text{mole C}}} = 12.0 \text{ g of C}$$

Grams from 3 moles of O

$$3 \cancel{\text{moles O}} \times \frac{16.0 \text{ g O}}{1 \cancel{\text{mole O}}} = 48.0 \text{ g of O}$$

**STEP 3** **Obtain the molar mass of $Li_2CO_3$.** Add the masses of 2 moles of Li, 1 mole of C, and 3 moles of O.

| | |
|---|---|
| 2 moles of Li | = 13.8 g of Li |
| 1 mole of C | = 12.0 g of C |
| 3 moles of O | = 48.0 g of O |
| Molar mass of $Li_2CO_3$ | = 73.8 g |

STUDY CHECK

Calculate the molar mass of salicylic acid, $C_7H_6O_3$.

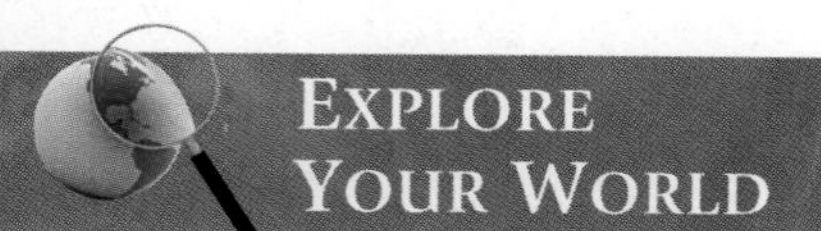

EXPLORE YOUR WORLD

### Calculating Moles in the Kitchen

The labels on food products list the components in grams and milligrams. Read the labels of some products in the kitchen and convert the amounts given in grams or milligrams to moles using molar mass.

QUESTIONS

1. How many moles of NaCl are in a box of salt containing 746 g of NaCl?
2. How many moles of sugar are contained in a 5-lb bag of sugar if sugar has the formula $C_{12}H_{22}O_{11}$?
3. A serving of cereal contains 90 mg of potassium. If there are 11 servings of cereal in the box, how many moles of $K^+$ are present in the cereal in the box?

## Calculations Using Molar Mass

The molar mass of an element or a compound is one of the most useful conversion factors in chemistry. Molar mass is used to change from moles of a substance to grams, or from grams to moles. To do these calculations, we use the molar mass as a conversion factor. For example, 1 mole of magnesium has a mass of 24.3 g. To express molar mass as an equality, we can write

$$1 \text{ mole of Mg} = 24.3 \text{ g of Mg}$$

From this equality, two conversion factors can be written.

$$\frac{24.3 \text{ g Mg}}{1 \text{ mole Mg}} \quad \text{and} \quad \frac{1 \text{ mole Mg}}{24.3 \text{ g Mg}}$$

Conversion factors are written for compounds in the same way. For example, the molar mass of the compound $H_2O$ is 2(1.0 g/mole) + 1(16.0 g/mole) = 18.0 g/mole

$$1 \text{ mole of } H_2O = 18.0 \text{ g of } H_2O$$

The conversion factors from the molar mass of $H_2O$ are written as

$$\frac{18.0 \text{ g } H_2O}{1 \text{ mole } H_2O} \quad \text{and} \quad \frac{1 \text{ mole } H_2O}{18.0 \text{ g } H_2O}$$

We can now change from moles to grams, or grams to moles, using the conversion factors derived from the molar mass. (Remember, you must determine the molar mass of the substance first.)

MC TUTORIAL Converting Between Grams and Moles

SAMPLE PROBLEM 6.7

### Converting Moles of an Element to Grams

Silver metal is used in the manufacture of tableware, mirrors, jewelry, and dental alloys. If the design for a piece of jewelry requires 0.750 mole of silver, how many grams of silver are needed?

SOLUTION

**STEP 1** **Given** 0.750 mole of Ag **Need** grams of Ag

**STEP 2** **Plan** moles of Ag → Molar mass factor → grams of Ag

**STEP 3** **Equalities/Conversion Factors**

1 mole of Ag = 107.9 g of Ag

$$\frac{107.9 \text{ g Ag}}{1 \text{ mole Ag}} \text{ and } \frac{1 \text{ mole Ag}}{107.9 \text{ g Ag}}$$

**STEP 4** **Set Up Problem** Calculate the grams of silver using the molar mass.

$$0.750 \cancel{\text{mole Ag}} \times \frac{107.9 \text{ g Ag}}{1 \cancel{\text{mole Ag}}} = 80.9 \text{ g of Ag}$$

STUDY CHECK

Calculate the number of grams of gold (Au) present in 0.124 mole of gold.

**Guide to Calculating the Moles (or Grams) of a Substance from Grams (or Moles)**

STEP 1 Determine the given number of moles (or grams).

STEP 2 Write a plan to convert moles to grams (or grams to moles).

STEP 3 Determine the molar mass and write conversion factors.

STEP 4 Set up problem to convert given moles to grams (or grams to moles).

SAMPLE PROBLEM 6.8

## Converting Mass of a Compound to Moles

A box of salt contains 737 g of NaCl. How many moles of NaCl are present in the box?

SOLUTION

**STEP 1** **Given** 737 g of NaCl **Need** moles of NaCl

**STEP 2** **Plan** grams of NaCl → Molar mass factor → moles of NaCl

**STEP 3** **Equalities/Conversion Factors** The molar mass of NaCl is the sum of the masses of one mole $Na^+$ and one mole $Cl^-$:

$$(1 \times 23.0 \text{ g/mole}) + (1 \times 35.5 \text{ g/mole}) = 58.5 \text{ g/mole}$$

1 mole of NaCl = 58.5 g of NaCl

$$\frac{58.5 \text{ g NaCl}}{1 \text{ mole NaCl}} \text{ and } \frac{1 \text{ mole NaCl}}{58.5 \text{ g NaCl}}$$

**STEP 4** **Set Up Problem** We calculate the moles of NaCl using the molar mass.

$$737 \cancel{\text{g NaCl}} \times \frac{1 \text{ mole NaCl}}{58.5 \cancel{\text{g NaCl}}} = 12.6 \text{ moles of NaCl}$$

STUDY CHECK

One gel cap of an antacid contains 311 mg of $CaCO_3$ and 232 mg of $MgCO_3$. In a recommended dosage of two gel caps, how many moles each of $CaCO_3$ and $MgCO_3$ are present?

Figure 6.9 shows the connections between the moles of a compound, mass, and number of molecules, and the moles and atoms of each element in that compound.

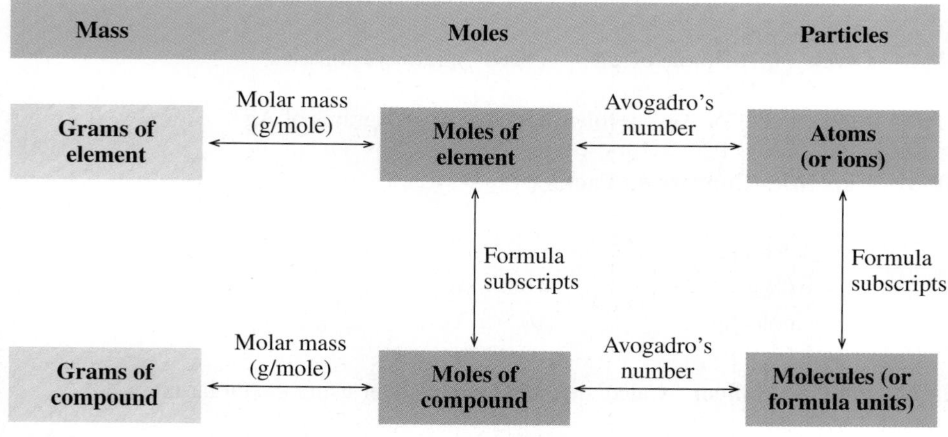


**FIGURE 6.9** The moles of a compound are related to its mass in grams by molar mass, to the number of molecules (or formula units) by Avogadro's number, and to the moles of each element by the subscripts in the formula.

**Q** What steps are needed to calculate the number of H atoms in 5.00 g of $CH_4$?

## QUESTIONS AND PROBLEMS

### Molar Mass

**6.31** Calculate the molar mass for each of the following:
- **a.** KCl (salt substitute)
- **b.** $Fe_2O_3$ (rust)
- **c.** $Li_2CO_3$ (antidepressant)
- **d.** $Al_2(SO_4)_3$ (antiperspirant)
- **e.** $Mg(OH)_2$ (antacid)
- **f.** $C_{16}H_{19}N_3O_5S$ (amoxicillin, an antibiotic)

**6.32** Calculate the molar mass for each of the following:
- **a.** $FeSO_4$ (iron supplement)
- **b.** $Al_2O_3$ (absorbent and abrasive)
- **c.** $C_7H_5NO_3S$ (saccharin)
- **d.** $C_3H_8O$ (rubbing alcohol)
- **e.** $(NH_4)_2CO_3$ (baking powder)
- **f.** $Zn(C_2H_3O_2)_2$ (dietary supplement)

**6.33** Calculate the mass in grams in each of the following:
- **a.** 2.00 moles of Na
- **b.** 2.80 moles of Ca
- **c.** 0.125 mole of Sn
- **d.** 1.76 moles of Cu

**6.34** Calculate the mass in grams in each of the following:
- **a.** 1.50 moles of K
- **b.** 2.5 moles of C
- **c.** 0.25 mole of P
- **d.** 12.5 moles of He

**6.35** Calculate the mass in grams in each of the following:
- **a.** 0.500 mole of NaCl
- **b.** 1.75 moles of $Na_2O$
- **c.** 0.225 mole of $H_2O$
- **d.** 4.42 moles of $CO_2$

**6.36** Calculate the mass in grams in each of the following:
- **a.** 2.0 moles of $MgCl_2$
- **b.** 3.5 moles of $C_3H_8$
- **c.** 5.00 moles of $C_2H_6O$
- **d.** 0.488 mole of $C_3H_6O_3$

**6.37 a.** The compound $MgSO_4$ is called Epsom salts. How many grams will you need to prepare a bath containing 5.00 moles of Epsom salts?
**b.** In a bottle of soda, there is 0.25 mole of $CO_2$. How many grams of $CO_2$ are in the bottle?

**6.38 a.** Cyclopropane, $C_3H_6$, is an anesthetic given by inhalation. How many grams are in 0.25 mole of cyclopropane?
**b.** The sedative Demerol hydrochloride has the formula $C_{15}H_{22}ClNO_2$. How many grams are in 0.025 mole of Demerol hydrochloride?

**6.39** How many moles are contained in each of the following?
- **a.** 50.0 g of Ag
- **b.** 0.200 g of C
- **c.** 15.0 g of $NH_3$
- **d.** 75.0 g of $SO_2$

**6.40** How many moles are contained in each of the following?
- **a.** 25.0 g of Ca
- **b.** 5.00 g of S
- **c.** 40.0 g of $H_2O$
- **d.** 12.2 g of $O_2$

**6.41** How many moles of S are in each of the following quantities?
- **a.** 25 g of S
- **b.** 125 g of $SO_2$
- **c.** 2.0 moles of $Al_2S_3$

**6.42** How many moles of C are in each of the following quantities?
- **a.** 75 g of C
- **b.** 0.25 mole of $C_2H_6$
- **c.** 88 g of $CO_2$

**6.43** How many atoms of N are in each of the following quantities?
- **a.** 40.0 g of N
- **b.** 1.5 moles of $N_2O_4$
- **c.** 2.0 moles of $N_2$

**6.44** How many atoms of Ag are in each of the following quantities?
- **a.** 5.0 g of Ag
- **b.** 0.40 mole of $Ag_2S$
- **c.** 0.75 g of AgCl

# 6.6 Mole Relationships in Chemical Equations

**LEARNING GOAL**

Given a quantity in moles of reactant or product, use a mole–mole factor from the balanced equation to calculate the moles of another substance in the reaction.

In an earlier section, we saw that equations are balanced in terms of the numbers of each type of atom in the reactants and products. However, when experiments are done in the laboratory or medications are prepared in the pharmacy, samples contain billions of atoms and molecules, so it is impossible to count them individually. What can be measured conveniently is mass; this is done by using a balance. Because mass is related to the number of particles through the molar mass, measuring the mass is equivalent to counting the number of particles or moles.

## Conservation of Mass

MC TUTORIAL Moles of Reactants and Products

In any chemical reaction, the total amount of matter in the reactants is equal to the total amount of matter in the products. If all of the reactants were weighed, they would have a total mass equal to the total mass of the products. This is known as the *law of conservation of mass*, which says that there is no change in the total mass of the substances reacting in a balanced chemical reaction. Thus, no material is lost or gained as original substances are changed to new substances.

For example, tarnish forms when silver reacts with sulfur to form silver sulfide.

$2Ag(s) + S(s) \longrightarrow Ag_2S(s)$

$2Ag(s)$ + $S(s)$ $\longrightarrow$ $Ag_2S(s)$

Mass of reactants = Mass of products

In this reaction, the number of silver atoms that react is two times the number of sulfur atoms. When 200 silver atoms react, 100 sulfur atoms are required. However, many more atoms would actually be present in this reaction. If we are dealing with molar amounts, then the coefficients in the equation can be interpreted in terms of moles. Thus, 2 moles of Ag react with 1 mole of sulfur to produce 1 mole of $Ag_2S$. Because the molar mass of each can be determined, the quantities of silver and sulfur can also be stated in terms of mass in grams of each. Thus, 215.8 g of Ag and 32.1 g of S react to form 247.9 g of $Ag_2S$. The total mass of the reactants (247.9 g) is equal to the 247.9 g of product. The various ways in which a chemical equation can be interpreted are seen in Table 6.6.

**TABLE 6.6 Information Available from a Balanced Equation**

| | Reactants | | | Products |
|---|---|---|---|---|
| Equation | $2Ag(s)$ | $+ S(s)$ | $\longrightarrow$ | $Ag_2S(s)$ |
| Atoms | 2 Ag atoms | + 1 S atom | $\longrightarrow$ | 1 $Ag_2S$ formula unit |
| | 200 Ag atoms | + 100 S atoms | $\longrightarrow$ | 100 $Ag_2S$ formula units |
| Avogadro's number of atoms | $2(6.02 \times 10^{23})$ Ag atoms | $+ 1(6.02 \times 10^{23})$ S atoms | $\longrightarrow$ | $1(6.02 \times 10^{23})$ $Ag_2S$ formula units |
| Moles | 2 moles of Ag | + 1 mole of S | $\longrightarrow$ | 1 mole of $Ag_2S$ |
| Mass (g) | 2(107.9 g) of Ag | + 1(32.1 g) of S | $\longrightarrow$ | 1(247.9 g) of $Ag_2S$ |
| Total mass (g) | 247.9 g | | $\longrightarrow$ | 247.9 g |

## Mole–Mole Factors from an Equation

When iron reacts with sulfur, the product is iron(III) sulfide:

$$2Fe(s) + 3S(s) \longrightarrow Fe_2S_3(s)$$

Iron (Fe) 2Fe(*s*) + Sulfur (S) 3S(*s*) ⟶ Iron(III) sulfide ($Fe_2S_3$) $Fe_2S_3(s)$

Because the equation is balanced, we know the proportions of iron and sulfur in the reaction. For this reaction, we see that 2 moles of iron reacts with 3 moles of sulfur to form 1 mole of iron(III) sulfide. From the coefficients, we can write **mole–mole factors** between reactants and between reactants and products. The coefficients used in the mole–mole factors are exact numbers; they do not limit the number of significant figures.

Fe and S: $\frac{2 \text{ moles Fe}}{3 \text{ moles S}}$ and $\frac{3 \text{ moles S}}{2 \text{ moles Fe}}$

Fe and $Fe_2S_3$: $\frac{2 \text{ moles Fe}}{1 \text{ mole } Fe_2S_3}$ and $\frac{1 \text{ mole } Fe_2S_3}{2 \text{ moles Fe}}$

S and $Fe_2S_3$: $\frac{3 \text{ moles S}}{1 \text{ mole } Fe_2S_3}$ and $\frac{1 \text{ mole } Fe_2S_3}{3 \text{ moles S}}$

## Using Mole–Mole Factors in Calculations

Whenever you prepare a recipe, adjust an engine for the proper mixture of fuel and air, or prepare medicines in a pharmaceutical laboratory, you need to know the proper amounts of reactants to use and how much of the product will form. Earlier we wrote all the possible conversion factors that can be obtained from this balanced equation: $2Fe(s) + 3S(s) \longrightarrow Fe_2S_3(s)$. Now we will show how mole–mole factors are used in chemical calculations.

**Guide to Using Mole–Mole Factors**

STEP 1 Write the given and needed moles.

STEP 2 Write a plan to convert the given to the needed moles.

STEP 3 Use coefficients to write relationships and mole–mole factors.

STEP 4 Set up problem using the mole–mole factor that cancels given moles.

SAMPLE PROBLEM 6.9

### Using Mole–Mole Factors

In the reaction of iron and sulfur, how many moles of sulfur are needed to react with 6.0 moles of iron?

$$2Fe(s) + 3S(s) \longrightarrow Fe_2S_3(s)$$

SOLUTION

**STEP 1** **Write the given and needed number of moles.** In this problem, we need to find the number of moles of S that reacts with 6.0 moles of Fe.

**Given** moles of Fe **Need** moles of S

**STEP 2** **Write the plan to convert the given to the needed moles.**

moles of Fe → Mole–mole factor → moles of S

**STEP 3** **Use coefficients to write relationships and mole–mole factors.** Use coefficients to write the mole–mole factors for the given and needed substances.

2 moles of Fe = 3 moles of S

$$\frac{2 \text{ moles Fe}}{3 \text{ moles S}} \quad \text{and} \quad \frac{3 \text{ moles S}}{2 \text{ moles Fe}}$$

**STEP 4** **Set up problem using the mole–mole factor that cancels given moles.** Use a mole–mole factor to cancel the given moles and provide needed moles.

$$6.0 \cancel{\text{moles Fe}} \times \frac{3 \text{ moles S}}{2 \cancel{\text{moles Fe}}} = 9.0 \text{ moles of S}$$

The answer is given with 2 significant figures because the given quantity 6.0 moles of Fe has 2 SFs. The values in the mole–mole factor are exact.

STUDY CHECK

Using the equation in Sample Problem 6.9, calculate the number of moles of iron(III) sulfide produced from 2.7 moles of sulfur.

## QUESTIONS AND PROBLEMS

### Mole Relationships in Chemical Equations

**6.45** Write all of the mole–mole factors for each of the following equations:

**a.** $2SO_2(g) + O_2(g) \longrightarrow 2SO_3(g)$

**b.** $4P(s) + 5O_2(s) \longrightarrow 2P_2O_5(s)$

**6.46** Write all of the mole–mole factors for each of the following equations:

**a.** $2Al(s) + 3Cl_2(g) \longrightarrow 2AlCl_3(s)$

**b.** $4HCl(g) + O_2(g) \longrightarrow 2Cl_2(g) + 2H_2O(g)$

**6.47** The reaction of hydrogen with oxygen produces water:

$$2H_2(g) + O_2(g) \longrightarrow 2H_2O(g)$$

**a.** How many moles of $O_2$ are required to react with 2.0 moles of $H_2$?

**b.** If you have 5.0 moles of $O_2$, how many moles of $H_2$ are needed for the reaction?

**c.** How many moles of $H_2O$ form when 2.5 moles of $O_2$ react?

**6.48** Ammonia is produced by the reaction of hydrogen and nitrogen:

$$N_2(g) + 3H_2(g) \longrightarrow \underset{\text{Ammonia}}{2NH_3(g)}$$

**a.** How many moles of $H_2$ are needed to react with 1.0 mole of $N_2$?

**b.** How many moles of $N_2$ reacted if 0.60 mole of $NH_3$ is produced?

**c.** How many moles of $NH_3$ are produced when 1.4 moles of $H_2$ react?

**6.49** Carbon disulfide and carbon monoxide are produced when carbon is heated with sulfur dioxide:

$$5C(s) + 2SO_2(g) \longrightarrow CS_2(l) + 4CO(g)$$

**a.** How many moles of C are needed to react with 0.500 mole of $SO_2$?

**b.** How many moles of CO are produced when 1.2 moles of C react?

**c.** How many moles of $SO_2$ are required to produce 0.50 mole of $CS_2$?

**d.** How many moles of $CS_2$ are produced when 2.5 moles of C react?

**6.50** In the acetylene torch, acetylene gas ($C_2H_2$) burns in oxygen to produce carbon dioxide and water:

$$2C_2H_2(g) + 5O_2(g) \longrightarrow 4CO_2(g) + 2H_2O(g)$$

**a.** How many moles of $O_2$ are needed to react with 2.00 moles of $C_2H_2$?

**b.** How many moles of $CO_2$ are produced when 3.5 moles of $C_2H_2$ react?

**c.** How many moles of $C_2H_2$ are required to produce 0.50 mole of $H_2O$?

**d.** How many moles of $CO_2$ are produced from 0.100 mole of $O_2$?

# 6.7 Mass Calculations for Reactions

LEARNING GOAL

Given the mass in grams of a substance in a reaction, calculate the mass in grams of another substance in the reaction.

When you perform a chemistry experiment in the laboratory, you use a laboratory balance to obtain a certain mass of reactant. From the mass in grams, you can determine the number of moles of reactant. By using mole–mole factors, you can predict the moles of product that can be produced. Then the molar mass of the product is used to convert the moles back into mass in grams. The following procedure can be used to set up and solve problems that involve calculations of quantities for substances in a chemical reaction.

**Guide to Calculating the Masses of Reactants and Products in a Chemical Reaction**

STEP 1
Use molar mass to convert grams of given to moles (if necessary).

STEP 2
Write a mole–mole factor from the coefficients in the equation.

STEP 3
Convert moles of given to moles of needed substance using mole–mole factor.

STEP 4
Convert moles of needed substance to grams using molar mass.

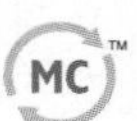

TUTORIAL
Masses of Reactants and Products

SAMPLE PROBLEM 6.10

## Mass of Products from Moles of Reactant

In the formation of smog, nitrogen reacts with oxygen to produce nitrogen oxide. Calculate the grams of NO produced when 1.50 moles of $O_2$ reacts.

$$N_2(g) + O_2(g) \longrightarrow 2NO(g)$$

SOLUTION

**STEP 1 Given** 1.50 moles of $O_2$ **Need** grams of NO

**STEP 2 Plan**

moles of $O_2$ → Mole–mole factor → moles of NO → Molar mass → grams of NO

**STEP 3 Equalities/Conversion Factors** The mole–mole factor that converts moles of $O_2$ to moles of NO is derived from the coefficients in the balanced equation:

$$1 \text{ mole of } O_2 = 2 \text{ moles of NO}$$
$$\frac{2 \text{ moles NO}}{1 \text{ mole } O_2} \text{ and } \frac{1 \text{ mole } O_2}{2 \text{ moles NO}}$$

$$1 \text{ mole of NO} = 30.0 \text{ g of NO}$$
$$\frac{30.0 \text{ g NO}}{1 \text{ mole NO}} \text{ and } \frac{1 \text{ mole NO}}{30.0 \text{ g NO}}$$

**STEP 4 Set Up Problem** First, we change the given, 1.50 moles of $O_2$, to moles of NO:

$$1.50 \cancel{\text{moles } O_2} \times \frac{2 \text{ moles NO}}{1 \cancel{\text{mole } O_2}} = 3.00 \text{ moles of NO}$$

Now, the moles of NO are converted to grams of NO using its molar mass.

$$3.00 \cancel{\text{moles NO}} \times \frac{30.0 \text{ g NO}}{1 \cancel{\text{mole NO}}} = 90.0 \text{ g of NO}$$

These two steps can also be written as a sequence of conversion factors that lead to the mass in grams of NO.

$$1.50 \cancel{\text{moles } O_2} \times \frac{2 \cancel{\text{moles NO}}}{1 \cancel{\text{mole } O_2}} \times \frac{30.0 \text{ g NO}}{1 \cancel{\text{mole NO}}} = 90.0 \text{ g of NO}$$

STUDY CHECK

Using the equation in Sample Problem 6.10, calculate the grams of NO that can be produced when 0.734 mole of $N_2$ reacts.

SAMPLE PROBLEM 6.11

## Mass of Product from Mass of Reactant

Acetylene ($C_2H_2$), used in welding, burns with oxygen.

$$2C_2H_2(g) + 5O_2(g) \longrightarrow 4CO_2(g) + 2H_2O(g)$$

How many grams of carbon dioxide are produced when 54.6 g of $C_2H_2$ are burned?

SOLUTION

**STEP 1** **Given** grams of $C_2H_2$ **Need** grams of $CO_2$

**STEP 2** **Plan** Once we convert grams of $C_2H_2$ to moles of $C_2H_2$ using its molar mass, we can use a mole–mole factor to find the moles of $CO_2$. Then the molar mass of $CO_2$ will give us the grams of $CO_2$.

grams of $C_2H_2$ → Molar mass → moles of $C_2H_2$ → Mole–mole factor → moles of $CO_2$ → Molar mass → grams of $CO_2$

**STEP 3** **Equalities/Conversion Factors** We need the molar mass of $C_2H_2$ and $CO_2$. The mole–mole factor that converts moles of $C_2H_2$ to moles of $CO_2$ is derived from the coefficients in the balanced equation.

1 mole of $C_2H_2$ = 26.0 g of $C_2H_2$

$$\frac{26.0 \text{ g } C_2H_2}{1 \text{ mole } C_2H_2} \quad \text{and} \quad \frac{1 \text{ mole } C_2H_2}{26.0 \text{ g } C_2H_2}$$

2 moles of $C_2H_2$ = 4 moles of $CO_2$

$$\frac{2 \text{ moles } C_2H_2}{4 \text{ moles } CO_2} \quad \text{and} \quad \frac{4 \text{ moles } CO_2}{2 \text{ moles } C_2H_2}$$

1 mole of $CO_2$ = 44.0 g of $CO_2$

$$\frac{44.0 \text{ g } CO_2}{1 \text{ mole } CO_2} \quad \text{and} \quad \frac{1 \text{ mole } CO_2}{44.0 \text{ g } CO_2}$$

**STEP 4** **Set Up Problem** Using our plan, we first convert grams of $C_2H_2$ to moles of $C_2H_2$.

$$54.6 \text{ g } C_2H_2 \times \frac{1 \text{ mole } C_2H_2}{26.0 \text{ g } C_2H_2} = 2.10 \text{ moles of } C_2H_2$$

Then we change moles of $C_2H_2$ to moles of $CO_2$ by using the mole–mole factor.

$$2.10 \text{ moles } C_2H_2 \times \frac{4 \text{ moles } CO_2}{2 \text{ moles } C_2H_2} = 4.20 \text{ moles of } CO_2$$

Finally, we can convert moles of $CO_2$ to grams of $CO_2$.

$$4.20 \text{ moles } CO_2 \times \frac{44.0 \text{ g } CO_2}{1 \text{ mole } CO_2} = 185 \text{ g of } CO_2$$

The solution can be obtained using the conversion factors in sequence.

$$54.6 \text{ g } C_2H_2 \times \frac{1 \text{ mole } C_2H_2}{26.0 \text{ g } C_2H_2} \times \frac{4 \text{ moles } CO_2}{2 \text{ moles } C_2H_2} \times \frac{44.0 \text{ g } CO_2}{1 \text{ mole } CO_2} = 185 \text{ g of } CO_2$$

STUDY CHECK

Using the equation in Sample Problem 6.11, calculate the grams of $CO_2$ that can be produced when 25.0 g of $O_2$ reacts.

# QUESTIONS AND PROBLEMS

## Mass Calculations for Reactions

**6.51** Sodium reacts with oxygen to produce sodium oxide.

$$4Na(s) + O_2(g) \longrightarrow 2Na_2O(s)$$

**a.** How many grams of $Na_2O$ are produced when 2.50 moles of Na react?

**b.** If you have 18.0 g of Na, how many grams of $O_2$ are required for reaction?

**c.** How many grams of $O_2$ are needed in a reaction that produces 75.0 g of $Na_2O$?

**6.52** Nitrogen gas reacts with hydrogen gas to produce ammonia by the following equation:

$$N_2(g) + 3H_2(g) \longrightarrow 2NH_3(g)$$

**a.** If you have 1.80 moles of $H_2$, how many grams of $NH_3$ can be produced?

**b.** How many grams of $H_2$ are needed to react with 2.80 g of $N_2$?

**c.** How many grams of $NH_3$ can be produced from 12.0 g of $H_2$?

**6.53** Ammonia and oxygen react to form nitrogen and water.

$$\underset{\text{Ammonia}}{4NH_3(g)} + 3O_2(g) \longrightarrow 2N_2(g) + 6H_2O(g)$$

**a.** How many grams of $O_2$ are needed to react with 8.00 moles of $NH_3$?
**b.** How many grams of $N_2$ can be produced when 6.50 g of $O_2$ reacts?
**c.** How many grams of water are formed from the reaction of 34.0 g of $NH_3$?

**6.54** Iron(III) oxide reacts with carbon to give iron and carbon monoxide.

$$Fe_2O_3(s) + 3C(s) \longrightarrow 2Fe(s) + 3CO(g)$$

**a.** How many grams of C are required to react with 2.50 moles of $Fe_2O_3$?
**b.** How many grams of CO are produced when 36.0 g of C reacts?
**c.** How many grams of Fe can be produced when 6.00 g of $Fe_2O_3$ reacts?

**6.55** Nitrogen dioxide and water react to produce nitric acid, $HNO_3$, and nitrogen oxide:

$$3NO_2(g) + H_2O(l) \longrightarrow 2HNO_3(aq) + NO(g)$$

**a.** How many grams of $H_2O$ are required to react with 28.0 g of $NO_2$?
**b.** How many grams of NO are obtained from 15.8 g of $NO_2$?
**c.** How many grams of $HNO_3$ are produced from 8.25 g of $NO_2$?

**6.56** Calcium cyanamide reacts with water to form calcium carbonate and ammonia:

$$CaCN_2(s) + 3H_2O(l) \longrightarrow CaCO_3(s) + 2NH_3(g)$$

**a.** How many grams of water are needed to react with 75.0 g of $CaCN_2$?
**b.** How many grams of $NH_3$ are produced from 5.24 g of $CaCN_2$?
**c.** How many grams of $CaCO_3$ form if 155 g of water reacts?

**6.57** When the ore lead(II) sulfide burns in oxygen, the products are lead(II) oxide and sulfur dioxide.

**a.** Write the balanced equation for the reaction.
**b.** How many grams of oxygen are required to react with 0.125 mole of lead(II) sulfide?
**c.** How many grams of sulfur dioxide can be produced when 65.0 g of lead(II) sulfide reacts?
**d.** How many grams of lead(II) sulfide are used to produce 128 g of lead(II) oxide?

**6.58** When the gases dihydrogen sulfide and oxygen react, they form the gases sulfur dioxide and water.

**a.** Write the balanced equation for the reaction.
**b.** How many grams of oxygen are required to react with 2.50 g of dihydrogen sulfide?
**c.** How many grams of sulfur dioxide can be produced when 38.5 g of oxygen reacts?
**d.** How many grams of oxygen are required to produce 55.8 g of water vapor?

## 6.8 Percent Yield and Limiting Reactants

**LEARNING GOAL**

Given the actual quantity of product, determine the percent yield for a reaction. Identify a limiting reactant when given the quantities of two or more reactants; calculate the amount of product formed from the limiting reactant.

Up to this point, we have done calculations as though the amount of product were the maximum quantity possible, or 100%. In other words, we assumed that all of the reactants were changed completely to product. Although this would be an ideal situation, it does not usually happen. As we run a reaction and transfer products from one container to another, some product is lost. There may also be side reactions that use up some of the reactants to give a different product. Thus, in a real experiment, the predicted amount of the desired product is never really obtained.

Suppose we are running a chemical reaction in the laboratory. We first measure out specific quantities of the reactants and place them in a reaction flask. Then we calculate the **theoretical yield** for the reaction, which is the amount of product we could expect if all the reactants were converted to product according to the mole ratios of the equation. The **actual yield** is the amount of product we collect when the reaction ends. Because some product is lost, the actual yield is always less than the theoretical yield. If we know the actual yield and the theoretical yield for a product, then we can express the actual yield as a **percent yield**:

$$\text{Percent yield (\%)} = \frac{\text{actual yield}}{\text{theoretical yield}} \times 100\%$$

**Guide to Calculations for Percent Yield**

**STEP 1** Write the given and needed quantities.

**STEP 2** Write a plan to calculate the theoretical yield and the percent yield.

**STEP 3** Write the molar mass for the reactant and the mole–mole factor from the balanced equation.

**STEP 4** Solve for the percent yield ratio by dividing the actual yield (given) by the theoretical yield and multiplying the result by 100%.

**SAMPLE PROBLEM 6.12**

### Calculating Percent Yield

On a spaceship, LiOH is used to absorb exhaled $CO_2$ from breathing air.

$$LiOH(s) + CO_2(g) \longrightarrow LiHCO_3(s)$$

What is the percent yield of the reaction if 50.0 g of LiOH gives 72.8 g of $LiHCO_3$?

SOLUTION

**STEP 1** **Given** 50.0 g of LiOH and 72.8 g of $LiHCO_3$ (actually produced)
**Need** % yield of $LiHCO_3$

**STEP 2** **Plan** **Calculation of theoretical yield:**

grams of LiOH → Molar mass → moles of LiOH → Mole–mole factor → moles of $LiHCO_3$ → Molar mass → grams of $LiHCO_3$

**Calculation of percent yield:**

$$\frac{\text{Actual yield}}{\text{Theoretical yield}} \times 100\%$$

**STEP 3** **Equalities/Conversion Factors**

1 mole of LiOH = 24.0 g of LiOH

$$\frac{1 \text{ mole LiOH}}{24.0 \text{ g LiOH}} \quad \text{and} \quad \frac{24.0 \text{ g LiOH}}{1 \text{ mole LiOH}}$$

1 mole of $LiHCO_3$ = 1 mole of LiOH

$$\frac{1 \text{ mole } LiHCO_3}{1 \text{ mole LiOH}} \quad \text{and} \quad \frac{1 \text{ mole LiOH}}{1 \text{ mole } LiHCO_3}$$

1 mole of $LiHCO_3$ = 68.0 g of $LiHCO_3$

$$\frac{68.0 \text{ g } LiHCO_3}{1 \text{ mole } LiHCO_3} \quad \text{and} \quad \frac{1 \text{ mole } LiHCO_3}{68.0 \text{ g } LiHCO_3}$$

**STEP 4** **Set Up Problem**
**Calculation of theoretical yield:**

$$50.0 \text{ g } \cancel{\text{LiOH}} \times \frac{1 \text{ } \cancel{\text{mole LiOH}}}{24.0 \text{ g } \cancel{\text{LiOH}}} \times \frac{1 \text{ } \cancel{\text{mole } LiHCO_3}}{1 \text{ } \cancel{\text{mole LiOH}}} \times \frac{68.0 \text{ g } LiHCO_3}{1 \text{ } \cancel{\text{mole } LiHCO_3}} = 142 \text{ g of } LiHCO_3$$

**Calculation of percent yield:**

$$\frac{\text{Actual yield (given)}}{\text{Theoretical yield (calculated)}} \times 100\% = \frac{72.8 \text{ } \cancel{\text{g } LiHCO_3}}{142 \text{ } \cancel{\text{g } LiHCO_3}} \times 100\% = 51.3\%$$

A percent yield of 51.3% means that 72.8 g of the theoretical amount of 142 g of $LiHCO_3$ was actually produced by the reaction.

STUDY CHECK

For the reaction in Sample Problem 6.12, what is the percent yield if 8.00 g of $CO_2$ produces 10.5 g of $LiHCO_3$?

## Limiting Reactants

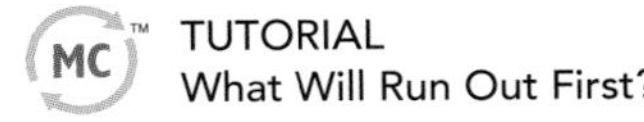


When you make peanut butter sandwiches for lunch, you need 2 slices of bread and 1 tablespoon of peanut butter for each sandwich. As an equation, we could write:

$$2 \text{ slices of bread} + 1 \text{ tablespoon of peanut butter} \longrightarrow 1 \text{ peanut butter sandwich}$$

If you have 8 slices of bread and a full jar of peanut butter, you will run out of bread after you make 4 peanut butter sandwiches. You cannot make any more sandwiches once the bread is used up, even though there is a lot of peanut butter left in the jar. The number of slices of bread has limited the number of sandwiches you can make. On a different day, you might have 8 slices of bread but only a tablespoon of peanut butter left in the peanut butter jar. You will run out of peanut butter after you make just 1 peanut butter sandwich with 6 slices of bread left over. The small amount of peanut butter available has limited the number of sandwiches you can make. This time the amount of peanut butter is limiting.

## Calculating Moles of Product from a Limiting Reactant

In a similar way, the availability of reactants in a chemical reaction can limit the amount of product that forms. In many reactions, the reactants are not combined in quantities that allow each to be used up at exactly the same time. Then one reactant is used up before the other. The reactant that is completely used up is called the **limiting reactant**. The other reactant, called the **excess reactant**, is left over. In the last analogy, the bread was the limiting reactant and the jar of peanut butter was the excess reactant.

| Bread | Peanut Butter | Sandwiches | Limiting Reactant | Excess Reactant |
|---|---|---|---|---|
| 1 loaf (20 slices) | 1 tablespoon | 1 | Peanut butter | Bread |
| 4 slices | 1 full jar | 2 | Bread | Peanut butter |
| 8 slices | 1 full jar | 4 | Bread | Peanut butter |

CONCEPT CHECK 6.6

### Limiting Reactants

You are going to plan a picnic. You have 10 spoons, 8 forks, and 6 knives. If each person requires 1 spoon, 1 fork, and 1 knife, how many people can be served lunch at your picnic?

ANSWER

The relationship of utensils required by each person can be written:

$$1 \text{ person} = 1 \text{ spoon, } 1 \text{ fork, and } 1 \text{ knife}$$

The number of people can be calculated for each utensil as:

$$10 \cancel{\text{spoons}} \times \frac{1 \text{ person}}{1 \cancel{\text{spoon}}} = 10 \text{ people}$$

$$8 \cancel{\text{forks}} \times \frac{1 \text{ person}}{1 \cancel{\text{fork}}} = 8 \text{ people}$$

$$6 \cancel{\text{knives}} \times \frac{1 \text{ person}}{1 \cancel{\text{knife}}} = 6 \text{ people} \quad \text{(smallest number of people)}$$

The limiting utensil is 6 knives, which means that 6 people (including yourself) can be at your picnic.

Consider the reaction in which hydrogen and chlorine form hydrogen chloride:

$$H_2(g) + Cl_2(g) \longrightarrow 2HCl(g)$$

Suppose the reaction mixture contains 2 moles of $H_2$ and 5 moles of $Cl_2$. From the equation, we see that 1 mole of hydrogen reacts with 1 mole of chlorine to produce 2 moles of hydrogen chloride. Now we need to calculate the amount of product that is possible from each of the reactants. We are looking for the limiting reactant, which is the one that produces the smaller amount of product.

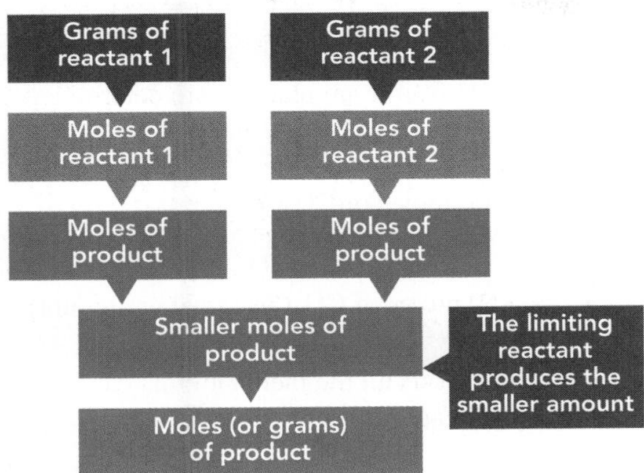


**Moles of HCl from $H_2$:**

$$2 \cancel{\text{moles } H_2} \times \frac{2 \text{ moles HCl}}{1 \cancel{\text{mole } H_2}} = 4 \text{ moles of HCl (smaller amount of product)}$$

**Moles of HCl from $Cl_2$:**

$$5 \cancel{\text{moles } Cl_2} \times \frac{2 \text{ moles HCl}}{1 \cancel{\text{mole } Cl_2}} = 10 \text{ moles of HCl (not possible)}$$

In this reaction mixture, $H_2$ is the limiting reactant. When 2 moles of $H_2$ are used up, the reaction stops. The excess reactant is the 3 moles of $Cl_2$ left over when the reaction is complete. We can show the changes in each reactant and the product as follows:

| | Reactants | | | | Product |
|---|---|---|---|---|---|
| Equation | $H_2$ | + | $Cl_2$ | $\longrightarrow$ | 2HCl |
| Initial moles | 2 moles | | 5 moles | | 0 mole |
| Moles used/formed | −2 moles | | −2 moles | | +4 moles |
| Moles left | 0 mole (2 − 2) | | 3 moles (5 − 2) | | 4 moles (0 + 4) |
| Identify as | Limiting reactant | | Excess reactant | | Product possible |

CONCEPT CHECK 6.7

### Moles of Product from Limiting Reactant

Consider the reaction for the synthesis of methanol ($CH_3OH$):

$$CO(g) + 2H_2(g) \longrightarrow CH_3OH(g)$$

In the laboratory, 3.00 moles of CO and 5.00 moles of $H_2$ are combined. Calculate the number of moles of $CH_3OH$ that can form and identify the limiting reactant.

ANSWER

**STEP 1** **Given** 3.00 moles of CO and 5.00 moles of $H_2$ **Need** moles of $CH_3OH$

**STEP 2** **Plan** We can determine the limiting reactant and the excess reactant by calculating the moles of methanol that each reactant would produce if it were all used up. The actual number of moles of $CH_3OH$ produced is from the reactant that produces the smaller number of moles.

Moles of CO → Mole–mole factor → moles of $CH_3OH$

Moles of $H_2$ → Mole–mole factor → moles of $CH_3OH$

**STEP 3** **Equalities/Conversion Factors** The mole–mole factors needed are obtained from the equation.

1 mole of CO = 1 mole of $CH_3OH$

$$\frac{1 \text{ mole } CH_3OH}{1 \text{ mole CO}} \text{ and } \frac{1 \text{ mole CO}}{1 \text{ mole } CH_3OH}$$

2 moles of $H_2$ = 1 mole of $CH_3OH$

$$\frac{1 \text{ mole } CH_3OH}{2 \text{ moles } H_2} \text{ and } \frac{2 \text{ moles } H_2}{1 \text{ mole } CH_3OH}$$

**STEP 4** **Set Up Problem** The moles of $CH_3OH$ from each reactant are determined in separate calculations.

$$3.00 \text{ moles CO} \times \frac{1 \text{ mole } CH_3OH}{1 \text{ mole CO}} = 3.00 \text{ moles of } CH_3OH$$

$$5.00 \text{ moles } H_2 \times \frac{1 \text{ mole } CH_3OH}{2 \text{ moles } H_2} = 2.50 \text{ moles of } CH_3OH \text{ (smaller amount)}$$

The smaller amount (2.5 moles of $CH_3OH$) is all the methanol that can be produced. Thus, $H_2$ is the limiting reagent and CO is in excess.

| | Reactants | | | | Product |
|---|---|---|---|---|---|
| Equation | CO | + | $2H_2$ | $\longrightarrow$ | $CH_3OH$ |
| Initial moles | 3.0 moles | | 5.0 moles | | 0 mole |
| Moles used/formed | −2.5 moles | | −5.0 moles | | +2.5 moles |
| Moles left | 0.5 mole | | 0 mole | | 2.5 moles |
| Identify as | Excess reactant | | Limiting reactant | | Product possible |

## Calculating Mass of Product from a Limiting Reactant

When the quantities of the reactants are given in grams, they must first be converted to moles. Once the limiting reactant is determined, the smaller number of moles of product is converted to grams using molar mass. This calculation is shown in Sample Problem 6.13.

SAMPLE PROBLEM 6.13

### ■ Mass of Product from a Limiting Reactant

Carbon monoxide and hydrogen gas react to form methanol, $CH_3OH$.

$$CO(g) + 2H_2(g) \longrightarrow CH_3OH(l)$$

If 48.0 g of CO and 10.0 g of $H_2$ react, how many grams of methanol can be produced?

SOLUTION

**STEP 1** **Given** 48.0 g of CO and 10.0 g of $H_2$ **Need** grams of $CH_3OH$

**STEP 2** **Plan** Convert the grams of each reactant to moles and calculate the moles of $CH_3OH$ that each reactant can produce. Then convert the number of moles of $CH_3OH$ from the limiting reactant to grams of $CH_3OH$ using molar mass.

48.0 g of CO → Molar mass → moles of CO → Mole–mole factor → moles of $CH_3OH$ (if smaller) → Molar mass → g of $CH_3OH$

or

10.0 g of $H_2$ → Molar mass → moles of $H_2$ → Mole–mole factor → moles of $CH_3OH$ (if smaller) → Molar mass → g of $CH_3OH$

**STEP 3 Equalities/Conversion Factors**

1 mole of CO = 28.0 g of CO

$$\frac{1 \text{ mole CO}}{28.0 \text{ g CO}} \quad \text{and} \quad \frac{28.0 \text{ g CO}}{1 \text{ mole CO}}$$

1 mole of CO = 1 mole of $CH_3OH$

$$\frac{1 \text{ mole CO}}{1 \text{ mole } CH_3OH} \quad \text{and} \quad \frac{1 \text{ mole } CH_3OH}{1 \text{ mole CO}}$$

1 mole of $H_2$ = 2.0 g of $H_2$

$$\frac{1 \text{ mole } H_2}{2.0 \text{ g } H_2} \quad \text{and} \quad \frac{2.0 \text{ g } H_2}{1 \text{ mole } H_2}$$

2 moles of $H_2$ = 1 mole of $CH_3OH$

$$\frac{2 \text{ moles } H_2}{1 \text{ mole } CH_3OH} \quad \text{and} \quad \frac{1 \text{ mole } CH_3OH}{2 \text{ moles } H_2}$$

1 mole of $CH_3OH$ = 32.0 g of $CH_3OH$

$$\frac{1 \text{ mole } CH_3OH}{32.0 \text{ g } CH_3OH} \quad \text{and} \quad \frac{32.0 \text{ g } CH_3OH}{1 \text{ mole } CH_3OH}$$

**STEP 4 Set Up Problem** The moles of $CH_3OH$ from each reactant can now be determined in separate calculations.

**Moles of $CH_3OH$ produced from CO:**

$$48.0 \text{ g CO} \times \frac{1 \text{ mole CO}}{28.0 \text{ g CO}} \times \frac{1 \text{ mole } CH_3OH}{1 \text{ mole CO}} = 1.71 \text{ moles of } CH_3OH$$

(smaller number of moles)

**Moles of $CH_3OH$ produced from $H_2$:**

$$10.0 \text{ g } H_2 \times \frac{1 \text{ mole } H_2}{2.0 \text{ g } H_2} \times \frac{1 \text{ mole } CH_3OH}{2 \text{ moles } H_2} = 2.5 \text{ moles of } CH_3OH$$

Because CO produces the smaller number of moles of $CH_3OH$, CO is the limiting reactant. Now the grams of product $CH_3OH$ from these reactants is calculated by converting the moles of $CH_3OH$ obtained from CO to grams using molar mass.

$$1.71 \text{ moles } CH_3OH \times \frac{32.0 \text{ g } CH_3OH}{1 \text{ mole } CH_3OH} = 54.7 \text{ g of } CH_3OH$$

STUDY CHECK

When silicon dioxide (sand) and carbon are heated, the ceramic material silicon carbide (SiC) and carbon monoxide are produced. How many grams of SiC are formed from 20.0 g of $SiO_2$ and 50.0 g of C?

$$SiO_2(s) + 3C(s) \xrightarrow{\text{Heat}} SiC(s) + 2CO(g)$$

# QUESTIONS AND PROBLEMS

## Percent Yield and Limiting Reactants

**6.59** Carbon disulfide is produced by the reaction of carbon and sulfur dioxide:

$$5C(s) + 2SO_2(g) \longrightarrow CS_2(g) + 4CO(g)$$

**a.** What is the percent yield for the reaction if 40.0 g of carbon produces 36.0 g of carbon disulfide?
**b.** What is the percent yield for the reaction if 32.0 g of sulfur dioxide produces 12.0 g of carbon disulfide?

**6.60** Iron(III) oxide reacts with carbon monoxide to produce iron and carbon dioxide:

$$Fe_2O_3(s) + 3CO(g) \longrightarrow 2Fe(s) + 3CO_2(g)$$

**a.** What is the percent yield for the reaction if 65.0 g of iron(III) oxide produces 15.0 g of iron?
**b.** What is the percent yield for the reaction if 75.0 g of carbon monoxide produces 15.0 g of carbon dioxide?

**6.61** Aluminum reacts with oxygen to produce aluminum oxide:

$4Al(s) + 3O_2(g) \longrightarrow 2Al_2O_3(s)$

The reaction of 50.0 g of aluminum and sufficient oxygen has a 75.0% yield. How many grams of aluminum oxide are produced?

**6.62** Propane ($C_3H_8$) burns in oxygen to produce carbon dioxide and water:

$C_3H_8(g) + 5O_2(g) \longrightarrow 3CO_2(g) + 4H_2O(g)$

Calculate the mass of $CO_2$ that can be produced if the reaction of 45.0 g of propane and sufficient oxygen has a 60.0% yield.

**6.63** When 30.0 g of carbon are heated with silicon dioxide, 28.2 g of carbon monoxide are produced. What is the percent yield of this reaction?

$SiO_2(s) + 3C(s) \longrightarrow SiC(s) + 2CO(g)$

**6.64** Calcium and nitrogen react to form calcium nitride:

$3Ca(s) + N_2(g) \longrightarrow Ca_3N_2(s)$

If 56.6 g of calcium are mixed with nitrogen gas and 32.4 g of calcium nitride are produced, what is the percent yield of the reaction?

**6.65** A taxi company has 10 taxis.

**a.** On a certain day, only 8 taxi drivers show up for work. How many taxis can be used to pick up passengers?

**b.** On another day, 10 taxi drivers show up for work but 3 taxis are in the repair shop. How many taxis can be driven?

**6.66** A clock maker has 15 clock faces. Each clock requires 1 face and 2 hands.

**a.** If the clock maker has 42 hands, how many clocks can be produced?

**b.** If the clock maker has only 8 hands, how many clocks can be produced?

**6.67** Nitrogen and hydrogen react to form ammonia:

$N_2(g) + 3H_2(g) \longrightarrow 2NH_3(g)$

Determine the limiting reactant in each of the following mixtures of reactants:

**a.** 3.0 moles of $N_2$ and 5.0 moles of $H_2$

**b.** 8.0 moles of $N_2$ and 4.0 moles of $H_2$

**c.** 3.0 moles of $N_2$ and 12.0 moles of $H_2$

**6.68** Iron and oxygen react to form iron(III) oxide:

$4Fe(s) + 3O_2(g) \longrightarrow 2Fe_2O_3(s)$

Determine the limiting reactant in each of the following mixtures of reactants:

**a.** 2.0 moles of Fe and 6.0 moles of $O_2$

**b.** 5.0 moles of Fe and 4.0 moles of $O_2$

**c.** 16.0 moles of Fe and 20.0 moles of $O_2$

**6.69** For each reaction, calculate the moles of product (in parentheses) when 2.00 moles of each reactant is used.

**a.** $2SO_2(g) + O_2(g) \longrightarrow 2SO_3(g)$ ($SO_3$)

**b.** $3Fe(s) + 4H_2O(l) \longrightarrow Fe_3O_4(s) + 4H_2(g)$ ($Fe_3O_4$)

**c.** $C_7H_{16}(g) + 11O_2(g) \longrightarrow 7CO_2(g) + 8H_2O(g)$ ($CO_2$)

**6.70** In each reaction, calculate the moles of product (in parentheses) when 3.00 moles of each reactant is used.

**a.** $4Li(s) + O_2(g) \longrightarrow 2Li_2O(s)$ ($Li_2O$)

**b.** $Fe_2O_3(s) + 3H_2(g) \longrightarrow 2Fe(s) + 3H_2O(l)$ (Fe)

**c.** $Al_2S_3(s) + 6H_2O(l) \longrightarrow 2Al(OH)_3(aq) + 3H_2S(g)$ ($H_2S$)

**6.71** In each reaction, calculate the moles of product (in parentheses) produced when 20.0 g of each reactant is used:

**a.** $2Al(s) + 3Cl_2(g) \longrightarrow 2AlCl_3(s)$ ($AlCl_3$)

**b.** $4NH_3(g) + 5O_2(g) \longrightarrow 4NO(g) + 6H_2O(g)$ ($H_2O$)

**c.** $CS_2(g) + 3O_2(g) \longrightarrow CO_2(g) + 2SO_2(g)$ ($SO_2$)

**6.72** For each of the following reactions, calculate the moles of product (in parentheses) when 20.0 g of each reactant is used:

**a.** $4Al(s) + 3O_2(g) \longrightarrow 2Al_2O_3(s)$ ($Al_2O_3$)

**b.** $3NO_2(g) + H_2O(l) \longrightarrow 2HNO_3(aq) + NO(g)$ ($HNO_3$)

**c.** $4NH_3(g) + 5O_2(g) \longrightarrow 4NO(g) + 6H_2O(g)$ ($H_2O$)

## 6.9 Energy Changes in Chemical Reactions

**LEARNING GOAL**

Describe the energy changes in exothermic and endothermic reactions.

Heat is energy that is lost or gained when a chemical reaction takes place. The *system* is the particular group of reactants and products we are looking at. The *surroundings* are all the things that contain and interact with the system such as the reaction flask, the laboratory room, and the air in the room. In any reaction system, there is a change in energy as reactants break apart and products form. The direction of heat flow depends on whether the products in the reaction have more or less energy than the reactants.

For a chemical reaction to take place, the molecules of the reactants must collide with each other and have the proper orientation and energy. When the molecules collide, bonds between atoms are broken and new bonds can form. The amount of energy needed to break apart those bonds is called the **activation energy**. If the energy of a collision is less than the activation energy, then the molecules bounce apart without reacting.

The concept of activation energy is analogous to climbing over a hill. To reach a destination on the other side, we must expend energy to climb to the top of the hill. Once we are at the top, we can easily run down the other side. The energy needed to get us from our starting point to the top of the hill would be the activation energy.

### Heat of Reaction

The **heat of reaction** is the amount of heat absorbed or released during a reaction that takes place at constant pressure. We determine a heat of reaction, symbol $\Delta H$, as the difference in the energy of the products and the reactants.

$$\Delta H = H_{\text{products}} - H_{\text{reactants}}$$

In the energy diagram for an **endothermic reaction** (*endo* means within), the energy of the products is greater than that of the reactants. In these reactions, heat flows out of the surroundings into the system, where it is used to convert the reactants to products. For an endothermic reaction, the heat of reaction can be written as one of the reactants. It can also be written as a $\Delta H$ value with a positive sign (+). Let us look at the equation and $\Delta H$ for the endothermic reaction in which 137 kcal of heat is needed to break down 2 moles of water into hydrogen and oxygen:

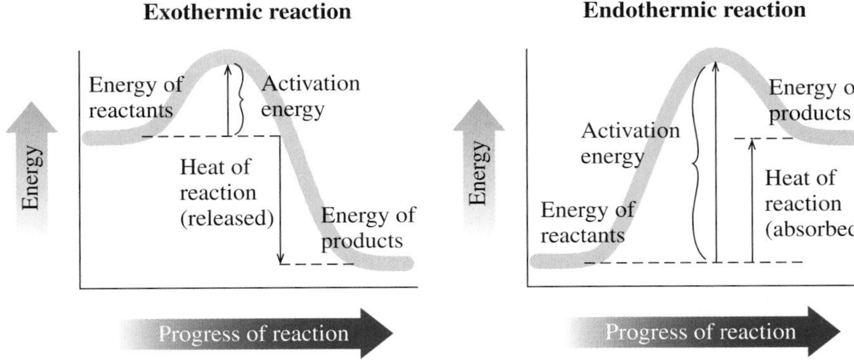


**Endothermic, Heat Required** | **Heat Is a Reactant**

$$2H_2O(l) + 137\text{ kcal} \longrightarrow 2H_2(g) + O_2(g)$$

$$2H_2O(l) \longrightarrow 2H_2(g) + O_2(g) \qquad \Delta H = +137\text{ kcal}$$

positive sign

In an **exothermic reaction** (*exo* means out), the products have less energy than the reactants. In these reactions, heat flows out of the system into the surroundings. For an exothermic reaction, the heat of reaction can be written as one of products. It can also be written as a $\Delta H$ value with a negative sign (−). The reaction for the formation of ammonia ($NH_3$) from 3 moles of hydrogen ($H_2$) and 1 mole of nitrogen ($N_2$) is exothermic.

**Exothermic, Heat Evolved** | **Heat Is a Product**

$$3H_2(g) + N_2(g) \longrightarrow 2NH_3(g) + 22.0\text{ kcal}$$

$$3H_2(g) + N_2(g) \longrightarrow 2NH_3(g) \qquad \Delta H = -22.0\text{ kcal}$$

negative sign

| Reaction | Energy Change | Heat in the Equation | Sign of $\Delta H$ |
|---|---|---|---|
| Endothermic | Heat absorbed | Reactant side | Positive sign (+) |
| Exothermic | Heat released | Product side | Negative sign (−) |

CONCEPT CHECK 6.8

## Exothermic and Endothermic Reactions

In the reaction of 1 mole of carbon with oxygen gas, the energy of the carbon dioxide produced is 93.9 kcal lower than the energy of the reactants.

**a.** Is the reaction exothermic or endothermic?
**b.** Write the equation for the reaction including the heat of the reaction.
**c.** Write the value of $\Delta H$ for this reaction.

ANSWER

**a.** When the products have a lower energy than the reactants, the reaction is exothermic.
**b.** $C(s) + O_2(g) \longrightarrow CO_2(g) + 93.9\text{ kcal}$
**c.** $\Delta H = -93.9\text{ kcal}$

## Calculations of Heat in Reactions

The value of $\Delta H$ refers to the heat change for the number of moles of each substance in the balanced equation for the reaction. Consider the following decomposition reaction:

$$2H_2O(l) \longrightarrow 2H_2(g) + O_2(g) \qquad \Delta H = 137 \text{ kcal}$$
$$2H_2O(l) + 137 \text{ kcal} \longrightarrow 2H_2(g) + O_2(g)$$

For this reaction, 137 kcal are absorbed by 2 moles of $H_2O$ to produce 2 moles of $H_2$ and 1 mole of $O_2$. We can write heat conversion factors for each substance in this reaction:

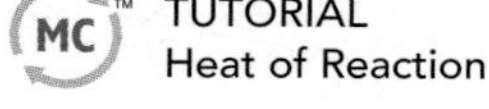

TUTORIAL
Heat of Reaction

$$\frac{137 \text{ kcal}}{2 \text{ moles } H_2O} \quad \frac{137 \text{ kcal}}{2 \text{ moles } H_2} \quad \frac{137 \text{ kcal}}{1 \text{ mole } O_2}$$

Suppose in this reaction that 12.0 g of $H_2O$ undergoes reaction. We can calculate the heat absorbed as

$$12.0 \text{ g } H_2O \times \frac{1 \text{ mole } H_2O}{18.0 \text{ g } H_2O} \times \frac{137 \text{ kcal}}{2 \text{ moles } H_2O} = 45.7 \text{ kcal}$$

**Guide to Calculations Using Heat of Reaction ($\Delta H$)**

STEP 1 List given and needed data for the equation.

STEP 2 Write a plan using heat of reaction and any molar mass needed.

STEP 3 Write the conversion factors including heat of reaction.

STEP 4 Set up the problem.

SAMPLE PROBLEM 6.14

### Calculating Heat in a Reaction

The heat of reaction for the formation of ammonia from hydrogen and nitrogen is $-92.2$ kJ:

$$N_2(g) + 3H_2(g) \longrightarrow 2NH_3(g) \qquad \Delta H = -92.2 \text{ kJ}$$

How much heat, in kilojoules, is released when 50.0 g of ammonia forms?

SOLUTION

**STEP 1** **Given** 50.0 g of $NH_3$, $\Delta H = -92.2$ kJ **Need** heat in kJ to form $NH_3$

**STEP 2** **Plan** Use conversion factors that relate the heat released to the moles of $NH_3$.

Grams of $NH_3$ → Molar mass → moles of $NH_3$ → Heat of reaction → kilojoules

**STEP 3** **Equalities/Conversion Factors**

1 mole of $NH_3$ = 17.0 g of $NH_3$

$$\frac{17.0 \text{ g } NH_3}{1 \text{ mole } NH_3} \text{ and } \frac{17.0 \text{ g of } NH_3}{1 \text{ mole } NH_3}$$

2 moles of $NH_3$ = 92.2 kJ

$$\frac{92.2 \text{ kJ}}{2 \text{ moles } NH_3} \text{ and } \frac{2 \text{ moles } NH_3}{92.2 \text{ kJ}}$$

**STEP 4** **Set Up Problem**

$$50.0 \text{ g } NH_3 \times \frac{1 \text{ mole } NH_3}{17.0 \text{ g } NH_3} \times \frac{92.2 \text{ kJ}}{2 \text{ moles } NH_3} = 136 \text{ kJ}$$

STUDY CHECK

Mercury(II) oxide decomposes to mercury and oxygen:

$$2HgO(s) \longrightarrow 2Hg(l) + O_2(g) \qquad \Delta H = 182 \text{ kJ}$$

**a.** Is the reaction exothermic or endothermic?
**b.** How many kJ are needed to react 25.0 g of mercury(II) oxide?

## QUESTIONS AND PROBLEMS

### Energy in Chemical Reactions

6.73 a. Why do chemical reactions require activation energy?
b. In an exothermic reaction, is the energy of the products higher or lower than the reactants?
c. Draw an energy diagram for an exothermic reaction.

**6.74** a. What is measured by the heat of reaction?
b. In an endothermic reaction, is the energy of the products higher or lower than the reactants?
c. Draw an energy diagram for an endothermic reaction.

6.75 Classify the following as exothermic or endothermic reactions:
a. 55 kcal is released.
b. The energy level of the products is higher than the reactants.
c. The metabolism of glucose in the body provides energy.

**6.76** Classify the following as exothermic or endothermic reactions:
a. The energy level of the products is lower than the reactants.
b. In the body, the synthesis of proteins requires energy.
c. 12 kcal is absorbed.

6.77 Classify the following as exothermic or endothermic reactions and give $\Delta H$ for each:
a. gas burning in a Bunsen burner:

$$CH_4(g) + 2O_2(g) \longrightarrow CO_2(g) + 2H_2O(g) + 210\text{ kcal}$$

b. dehydrating limestone:

$$Ca(OH)_2(s) + 65.3\text{ kJ} \longrightarrow CaO(s) + H_2O(l)$$

c. formation of aluminum oxide and iron from aluminum and iron(III) oxide:

$$2Al(s) + Fe_2O_3(s) \longrightarrow Al_2O_3(s) + 2Fe(s) + 205\text{ kcal}$$

**6.78** Classify the following as exothermic or endothermic reactions and give $\Delta H$ for each of the following:
a. combustion of propane:

$$C_3H_8(g) + 5O_2(g) \longrightarrow 3CO_2(g) + 4H_2O(g) + 530\text{ kcal}$$

b. formation of "table" salt:

$$2Na(s) + Cl_2(g) \longrightarrow 2NaCl(s) + 196\text{ kcal}$$

c. decomposition of phosphorus pentachloride:

$$PCl_5(g) + 67\text{ kJ} \longrightarrow PCl_3(g) + Cl_2(g)$$

6.79 The equation for the formation of silicon tetrachloride from silicon and chlorine is

$$Si(s) + 2Cl_2(g) \longrightarrow SiCl_4(g) \quad \Delta H = -157\text{ kcal}$$

How many kilocalories are released when 125 g of $Cl_2$ reacts with silicon?

**6.80** Methanol ($CH_3OH$), which is used as a cooking fuel, undergoes combustion to produce carbon dioxide and water:

$$2CH_3OH(l) + 3O_2(g) \longrightarrow 2CO_2(g) + 4H_2O(l) \; \Delta H = -726\text{ kJ}$$

How many kilojoules are released when 75.0 g of methanol is burned?

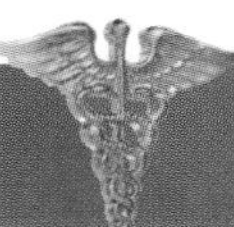

## HEALTH NOTE

### Hot Packs and Cold Packs

In a hospital, at a first-aid station, or at an athletic event, an instant *cold pack* may be used to reduce swelling from an injury, remove heat from inflammation, or decrease capillary size to lessen the effect of hemorrhaging. Inside the plastic container of a cold pack, there is a compartment containing solid ammonium nitrate ($NH_4NO_3$) that is separated from a compartment containing water. The pack is activated when it is hit or squeezed hard enough to break the walls between the compartments and cause the ammonium nitrate to mix with the water (shown as $H_2O$ over the reaction arrow). In an endothermic process, each gram of $NH_4NO_3$ that dissolves absorbs 79 cal of heat from the water. The temperature drops and the pack becomes cold and ready to use.

**Endothermic Reaction in a Cold Pack**

$$6.2\text{ kcal} + NH_4NO_3(s) \xrightarrow{H_2O} NH_4NO_3(aq)$$

*Hot packs* are used to relax muscles, lessen aches and cramps, and increase circulation by expanding capillary size. Constructed in the same way as cold packs, a hot pack may contain the salt $CaCl_2$. The dissolving of the salt in water is exothermic and releases 160 cal per gram of salt. The temperature rises and the pack becomes hot and ready to use.

**Exothermic Reaction in a Hot Pack**

$$CaCl_2(s) \xrightarrow{H_2O} CaCl_2(aq) + 18\text{ kcal}$$

## CONCEPT MAP

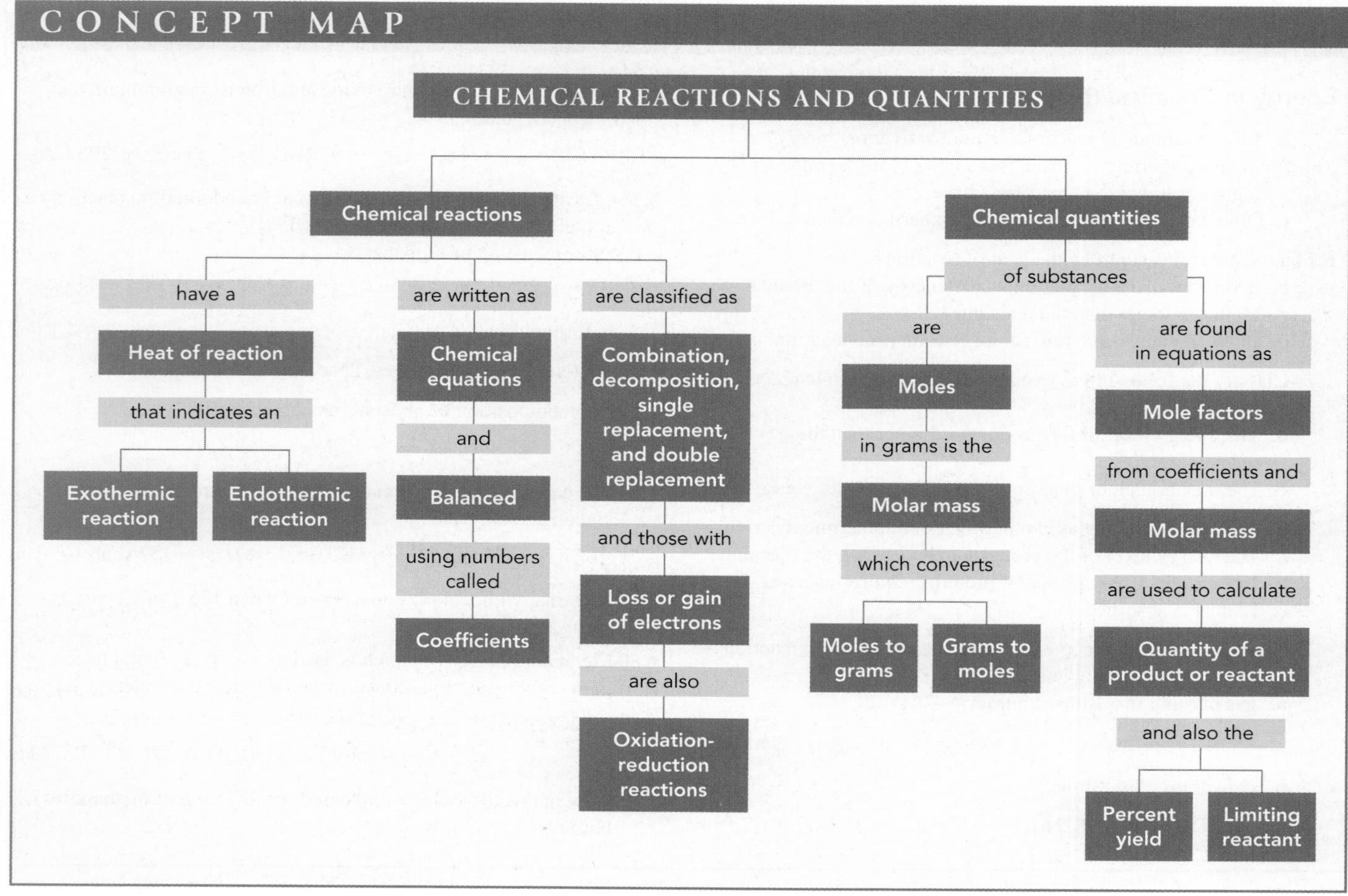


## CHAPTER REVIEW

### 6.1 Chemical Reactions

**LEARNING GOAL:** *Write a balanced chemical equation from the formulas of the reactants and products for a chemical reaction.*

A chemical reaction occurs when the atoms of the initial substances rearrange to form new substances. A chemical equation shows the formulas of the substances that react on the left side of a reaction arrow and the products that form on the right side of the reaction arrow. An equation is balanced by writing the smallest whole numbers (coefficients) in front of formulas to equalize the atoms of each element in the reactants and the products.

### 6.2 Types of Reactions

**LEARNING GOAL:** *Identify a chemical reaction as a combination, decomposition, single replacement, or double replacement reaction.*

Many chemical reactions can be organized by reaction type: combination, decomposition, single replacement, or double replacement.

### 6.3 Oxidation–Reduction Reactions

**LEARNING GOAL:** *Define the terms oxidation and reduction.*

When electrons are transferred in a reaction, it is an oxidation–reduction reaction. One reactant loses electrons, and another reactant gains electrons. Overall, the number of electrons lost and gained is equal.

### 6.4 The Mole

**LEARNING GOAL:** *Use Avogadro's number to determine the number of particles in a given amount of moles.*

One mole of an element contains $6.02 \times 10^{23}$ atoms; a mole of a compound contains $6.02 \times 10^{23}$ molecules or formula units.

### 6.5 Molar Mass

**LEARNING GOAL:** *Determine the molar mass of a substance and use the molar mass to convert between grams and moles.*

The molar mass (g/mole) of any substance is the mass in grams equal numerically to its atomic mass, or the sum of the atomic masses, which have been multiplied by their subscripts in a formula. It becomes a conversion factor when it is used to change a quantity in grams to moles, or to change a given number of moles to grams.

### 6.6 Mole Relationships in Chemical Equations

**LEARNING GOAL:** *Given a quantity in moles of reactant or product, use a mole–mole factor from the balanced equation to calculate the moles of another substance in the reaction.*

In a balanced equation, the total mass of the reactants is equal to the total mass of the products. The coefficients in an equation that describes the relationship between the moles of any two components are used to write mole–mole factors. When the number of moles for one substance is known, a mole–mole factor is used to find the moles of a different substance in the reaction.

### 6.7 Mass Calculations for Reactions

**LEARNING GOAL:** *Given the mass in grams of a substance in a reaction, calculate the mass in grams of another substance in the reaction.*

In calculations using equations, the molar masses of the substances and their mole factors are used to change the number of grams of one substance to the corresponding grams of a different substance.

### 6.8 Percent Yield and Limiting Reactants

**LEARNING GOAL:** *Given the actual quantity of product, determine the percent yield for a reaction. Identify a limiting reactant when given the quantities of two or more reactants; calculate the amount of product formed from the limiting reactant.*

The percent yield of a reaction indicates the percent of product actually produced during a reaction. The percent yield is calculated by dividing the actual yield in grams of a product by the theoretical yield in grams. A limiting reactant is the reactant that produces the smaller amount of product while some excess reactant is left over. When the mass of two or more reactants is given, the mass of a product is calculated from the product produced by the limiting reactant.

### 6.9 Energy Changes in Chemical Reactions

**LEARNING GOAL:** *Describe the energy changes in exothermic and endothermic reactions.*

In chemical reactions, the heat of reaction ($\Delta H$) is the energy difference between the reactants and the products. In an exothermic reaction, the energy of the products is lower than the reactants. Heat is released and $\Delta H$ is negative. In an endothermic reaction, the energy of the products is higher than the reactants. Heat is absorbed and the $\Delta H$ is positive.

## KEY TERMS

**activation energy** The energy needed to break the bonds of reacting molecules.

**actual yield** The actual amount of product produced by a reaction.

**Avogadro's number** The number of items in a mole; equal to $6.02 \times 10^{23}$.

**balanced equation** The final form of a chemical equation that shows the same number of atoms of each element in the reactants and products.

**chemical equation** A shorthand way to represent a chemical reaction using chemical formulas to indicate the reactants and products and coefficients to show reacting ratios.

**chemical reaction** The process by which a chemical change takes place.

**coefficients** Whole numbers placed in front of the formulas to balance the number of atoms or moles of atoms of each element on both sides of an equation.

**combination reaction** A reaction in which reactants combine to form a single product.

**decomposition reaction** A reaction in which a single reactant splits into two or more simpler substances.

**double replacement reaction** A reaction in which parts of two different reactants exchange places.

**endothermic reaction** A reaction in which the energy of the products is greater than that of the reactants.

**excess reactant** The reactant that remains when the limiting reactant is used up in a reaction.

**exothermic reaction** A reaction in which the energy of the reactants is greater than that of the products.

**formula unit** The group of ions represented by the formula of an ionic compound.

**heat of reaction** The heat (symbol $\Delta H$) absorbed or released when a reaction takes place at constant pressure.

**limiting reactant** The reactant used up during a chemical reaction; it limits the amount of product that can form.

**molar mass** The mass in grams of 1 mole of an element equal numerically to its atomic mass. The molar mass of a compound is equal to the sum of the masses of the elements in the formula.

**mole** A group of atoms, molecules, or formula units that contains $6.02 \times 10^{23}$ of these items.

**mole–mole factor** A conversion factor that relates the number of moles of two compounds derived from the coefficients in an equation.

**oxidation** The loss of electrons by a substance. Biological oxidation may involve the addition of oxygen or the loss of hydrogen.

**oxidation–reduction reaction** A reaction in which the oxidation of one reactant is always accompanied by the reduction of another reactant.

**percent yield** The ratio of the actual yield of a reaction to the theoretical yield possible for the reaction that is multiplied by 100%.

**products** The substances formed as a result of a chemical reaction.

**reactants** The initial substances that undergo change in a chemical reaction.

**reduction** The gain of electrons by a substance. Biological reduction may involve the loss of oxygen or the gain of hydrogen.

**single replacement reaction** A reaction in which an element replaces a different element in a compound.

**theoretical yield** The maximum amount of product that a reaction can produce from a given amount of reactant.

## UNDERSTANDING THE CONCEPTS

6.81 Balance each of the following by adding coefficients and identify the type of reaction for each:

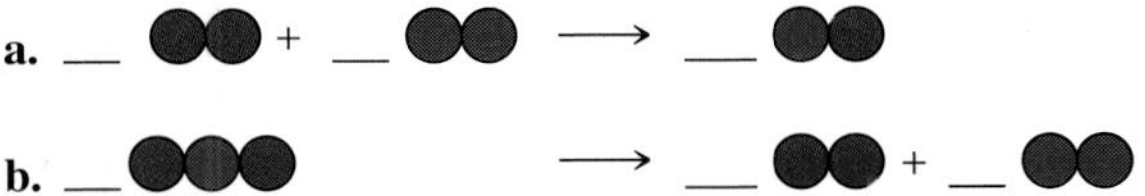

6.82 Balance each of the following by adding coefficients and identify the type of reaction for each:

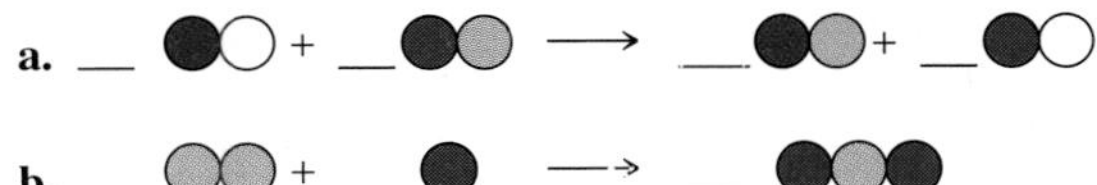

6.83 If red spheres represent oxygen atoms and blue spheres represent nitrogen atoms:

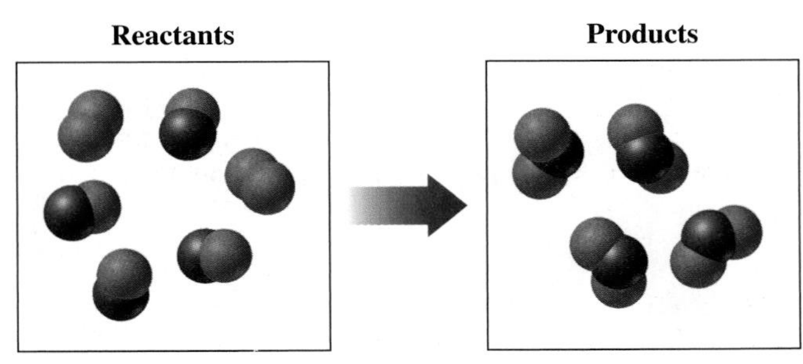

**a.** Write a balanced equation for the reaction.
**b.** Indicate the type of reaction as decomposition, combination, single replacement, or double replacement.

**6.84** If purple spheres represent iodine atoms and light blue spheres represent hydrogen atoms:

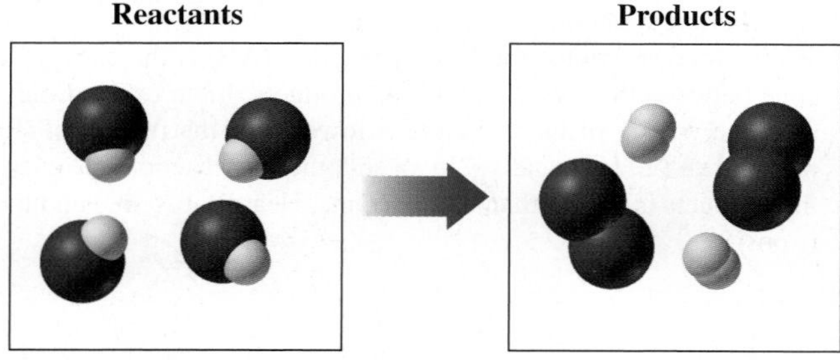


**a.** Write a balanced equation for the reaction.
**b.** Indicate the type of reaction as decomposition, combination, single replacement, or double replacement.

**6.85** If blue spheres represent nitrogen atoms and purple spheres represent iodine atoms:

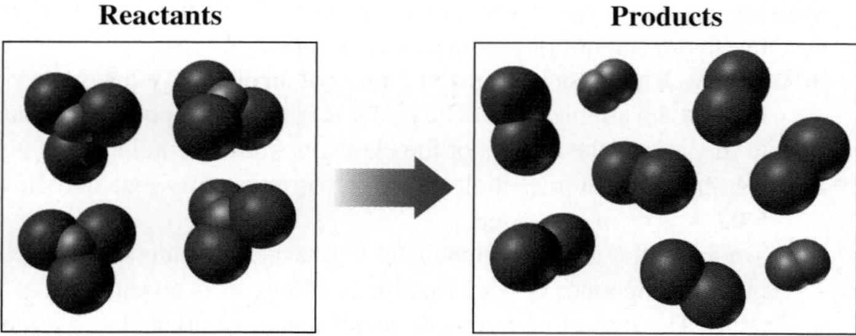


**a.** Write a balanced equation for the reaction.
**b.** Indicate the type of reaction as decomposition, combination, single replacement, or double replacement.

**6.86** If green spheres represent chlorine atoms, yellow-green spheres represent fluorine atoms, and light blue spheres represent hydrogen atoms:

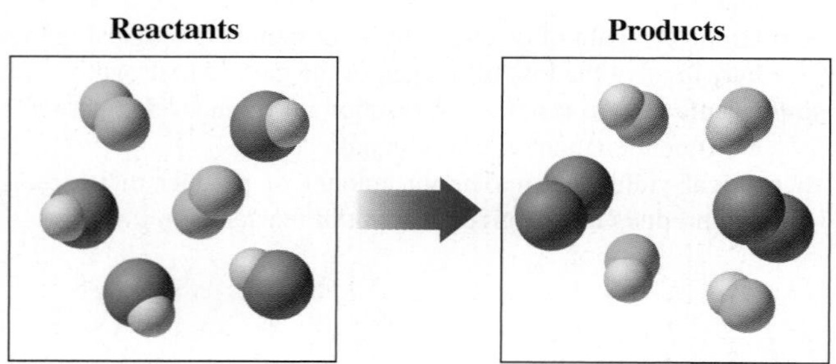


**a.** Write a balanced equation for the reaction.
**b.** Indicate the type of reaction as decomposition, combination, single replacement, or double replacement.

**6.87** If green spheres represent chlorine atoms and red spheres represent oxygen atoms:

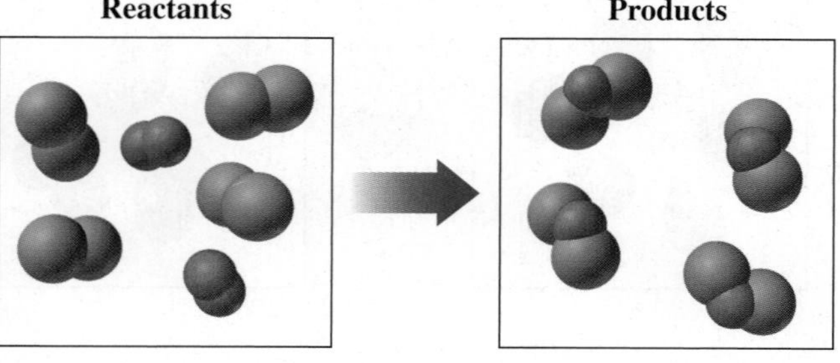


**a.** Write a balanced equation for the reaction.
**b.** Indicate the type of reaction as decomposition, combination, single replacement, or double replacement.

**6.88** If blue spheres represent nitrogen atoms and purple spheres represent iodine atoms:

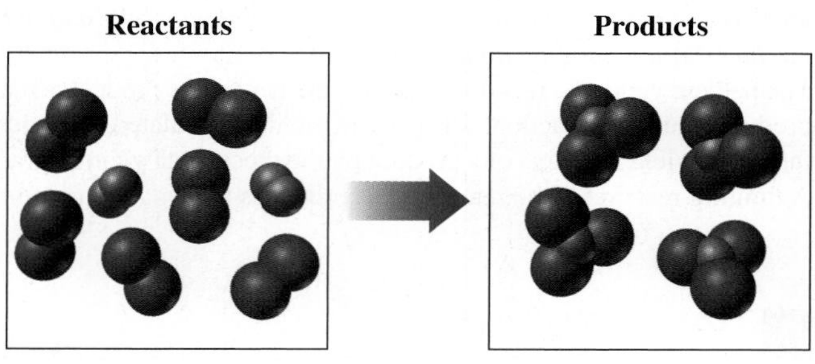


**a.** Write a balanced equation for the reaction.
**b.** Indicate the type of reaction as decomposition, combination, single replacement, or double replacement.

**6.89** Using the following models of the molecules, determine (black = C, light blue = H, yellow = S, green = Cl):

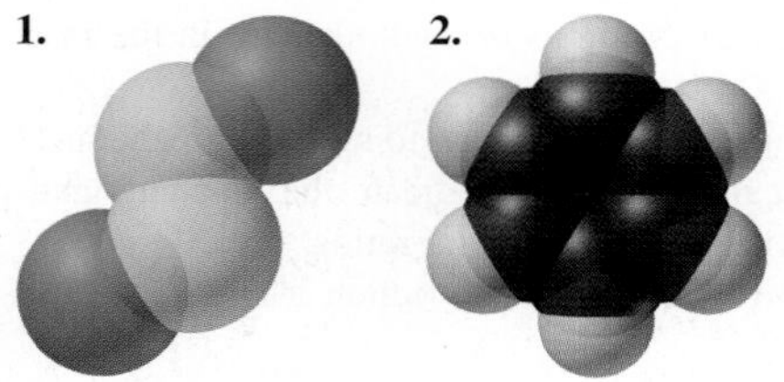


**a.** formula
**b.** molar mass
**c.** number of moles in 10.0 g

**6.90** Using the following models of the molecules, determine (black = C, light blue = H, yellow = S, red = O):

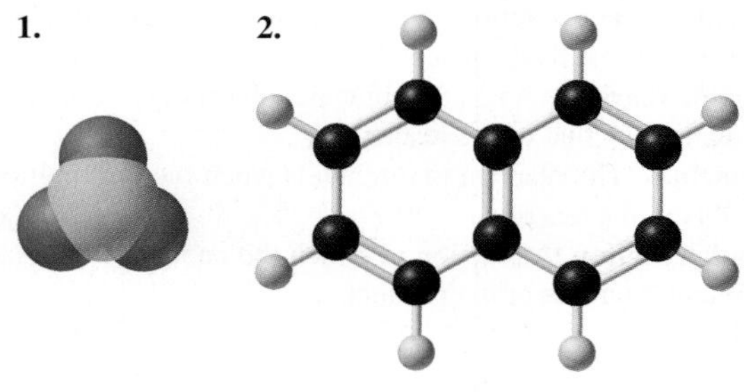


**a.** formula
**b.** molar mass
**c.** number of moles in 10.0 g

**6.91** A dandruff shampoo contains pyrithion, $C_{10}H_8N_2O_2S_2$, an antibacterial and antifungal agent.

**a.** What is the molar mass of pyrithion?
**b.** How many moles of pyrithion are in 25.0 g?
**c.** How many moles of carbon are in 25.0 g of pyrithion?

**6.92** Ammonium sulfate $(NH_4)_2SO_4$ is used in fertilizers to provide nitrogen for the soil.

**a.** How many formula units are in 0.200 mole of ammonium sulfate?

**b.** How many H atoms are in 0.100 mole of ammonium sulfate?
**c.** How many moles of ammonium sulfate contain $7.4 \times 10^{25}$ atoms of N?
**d** What is the molar mass of ammonium sulfate?

6.93 In an experiment, a piece of copper is weighed on a balance and then allowed to react with oxygen:

$$2Cu(s) + O_2(g) \longrightarrow 2CuO(s)$$

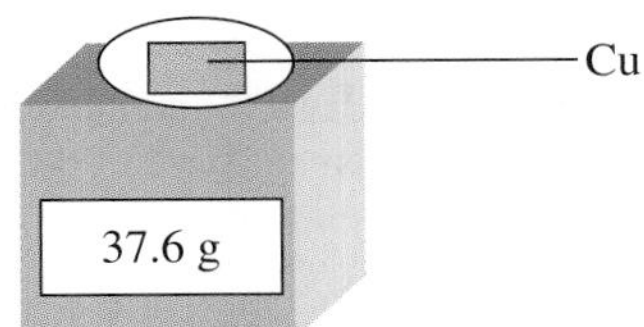


**a.** How many grams of CuO could be produced according to the equation?
**b.** How many moles of $O_2$ are required to completely react the Cu?

**6.94** Allyl sulfide $(C_3H_5)_2S$ is the substance that gives garlic its characteristic odor.

**a.** How many moles of sulfur are in 23.2 g of $(C_3H_5)_2S$?
**b.** How many hydrogen atoms are in 0.75 mole of $(C_3H_5)_2S$?
**c.** How many grams of carbon are in $4.20 \times 10^{23}$ molecules of $(C_3H_5)_2S$?
**d.** How many carbon atoms are in 15.0 g of $(C_3H_5)_2S$?

# ADDITIONAL QUESTIONS AND PROBLEMS

*For instructor-assigned homework, go to* ***www.masteringchemistry.com.***

6.95 Balance each of the following unbalanced equations and identify the type of reaction:
**a.** $NH_3(g) + HCl(g) \longrightarrow NH_4Cl(s)$
**b.** $Fe_3O_4(s) + H_2(g) \longrightarrow Fe(s) + H_2O(g)$
**c.** $Sb(s) + Cl_2(g) \longrightarrow SbCl_3(s)$
**d.** $NI_3(s) \longrightarrow N_2(g) + I_2(g)$
**e.** $KBr(aq) + Cl_2(aq) \longrightarrow KCl(aq) + Br_2(l)$
**f.** $Al_2(SO_4)_3(aq) + NaOH(aq) \longrightarrow Na_2SO_4(aq) + Al(OH)_3(s)$

**6.96** Balance each of the following unbalanced equations and identify the type of reaction:
**a.** $Li_3N(s) \longrightarrow Li(s) + N_2(g)$
**b.** $Mg(s) + N_2(g) \longrightarrow Mg_3N_2(s)$
**c.** $Mg(s) + H_3PO_4(aq) \longrightarrow Mg_3(PO_4)_2(s) + H_2(g)$
**d.** $Cr_2O_3(s) + H_2(g) \longrightarrow Cr(s) + H_2O(g)$
**e.** $Al(s) + Cl_2(g) \longrightarrow AlCl_3(s)$
**f.** $MgCl_2(aq) + AgNO_3(aq) \longrightarrow Mg(NO_3)_2(aq) + AgCl(s)$

6.97 Identify each of the following as an oxidation or a reduction reaction:
**a.** $Zn^{2+} + 2e^- \longrightarrow Zn$
**b.** $Al \longrightarrow Al^{3+} + 3e^-$
**c.** $Pb \longrightarrow Pb^{2+} + 2e^-$
**d.** $Cl_2 + 2e^- \longrightarrow 2Cl^-$

**6.98** Write a balanced chemical equation for each of the following oxidation–reduction reactions:
**a.** Sulfur reacts with molecular chlorine to form sulfur dichloride.
**b.** Molecular chlorine and sodium bromide react to form molecular bromine and sodium chloride.
**c.** Aluminum metal and iron(III) oxide react to produce aluminum oxide and elemental iron.
**d.** Copper(II) oxide reacts with elemental C to form elemental copper and carbon dioxide.

6.99 During heavy exercise and workouts, lactic acid, $C_3H_6O_3$, accumulates in the muscles, where it can cause pain and soreness.
**a.** What is the molar mass of lactic acid?
**b.** How many molecules are in 0.500 mole of lactic acid?
**c.** How many C atoms are in 1.50 moles of lactic acid?
**d.** How many grams of lactic acid contain $4.5 \times 10^{24}$ atoms of O?

**6.100** Ibuprofen, the anti-inflammatory ingredient in Advil, has the formula $C_{13}H_{18}O_2$.

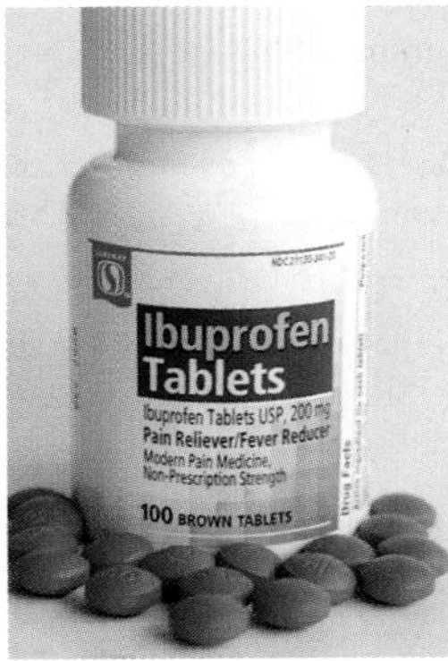


**a.** What is the molar mass of ibuprofen?
**b.** How many molecules are in 0.200 mole of ibuprofen?
**c.** How many H atoms are in 0.100 mole of ibuprofen?
**d.** How many grams of ibuprofen contain $7.4 \times 10^{25}$ atoms of C?

6.101 Calculate the molar mass of each of the following:
**a.** $FeSO_4$, iron(II) sulfate, iron supplement
**b.** $Ca(IO_3)_2$, calcium iodate, iodine source in table salt
**c.** $C_5H_8NNaO_4$, monosodium glutamate, flavor enhancer

**6.102** Calculate the molar mass of each of the following:
**a.** $Mg(HCO_3)_2$, magnesium hydrogen carbonate
**b.** $Au(OH)_3$, gold(III) hydroxide, used in gold plating
**c.** $C_{18}H_{34}O_2$, oleic acid from olive oil

6.103 How many grams are in 0.150 mole of each of the following?
**a.** K **b.** $Cl_2$ **c.** $Na_2CO_3$

**6.104** How many grams are in 2.25 moles of each of the following?
**a.** $N_2$ **b.** NaBr **c.** $C_6H_{14}$

6.105 How many moles are in 25.0 g of each of the following compounds?
**a.** $CO_2$ **b.** $Al(OH)_3$ **c.** $MgCl_2$

**6.106** How many moles are in 4.00 g of each of the following compounds?
**a.** $NH_3$ **b.** $Ca(NO_3)_2$ **c.** $SO_3$

**6.107** At a winery, glucose ($C_6H_{12}O_6$) in grapes undergoes fermentation to produce ethanol ($C_2H_6O$) and carbon dioxide:

$$\underset{\text{Glucose}}{C_6H_{12}O_6(aq)} \longrightarrow \underset{\text{Ethanol}}{2C_2H_6O(l)} + 2CO_2(g)$$

**a.** How many moles of glucose are required to form 124 g of ethanol?
**b.** How many grams of ethanol would be formed from the reaction of 0.240 kg of glucose?

**6.108** Gasohol is a fuel that contains ethanol ($C_2H_6O$), which burns in oxygen ($O_2$) to give carbon dioxide and water.
**a.** State the reactants and products for this reaction in the form of a balanced equation.
**b.** How many moles of $O_2$ are needed to completely react with 4.0 moles of $C_2H_6O$?
**c.** If a car produces 88 g of $CO_2$, how many grams of $O_2$ are used up in the reaction?
**d.** If you add 125 g of $C_2H_6O$ to your fuel, how many grams of $CO_2$ and $H_2O$ can be produced from the ethanol?

**6.109** Balance the following equation:

$$NH_3(g) + F_2(g) \longrightarrow N_2F_4(g) + HF(g)$$

**a.** How many moles of each reactant are needed to produce 4.00 moles of HF?
**b.** How many grams of $F_2$ are required to react with 1.50 moles of $NH_3$?
**c.** How many grams of $N_2F_4$ can be produced when 3.40 g of $NH_3$ reacts?

**6.110** When peroxide ($H_2O_2$) is used in rocket fuels, it produces water, oxygen, and heat:

$$2H_2O_2(l) \longrightarrow 2H_2O(l) + O_2(g)$$

**a.** If 2.00 g of $H_2O_2$ releases 5.76 kJ, what is the heat of reaction?
**b.** How many kilojoules are released when 275 g of peroxide are allowed to react?

**6.111** Ethane, $C_2H_6$, reacts with chlorine to form hexachloroethane and hydrogen chloride:

$$\underset{\text{Ethane}}{C_2H_6(g)} + 6Cl_2(g) \longrightarrow C_2Cl_6(g) + 6HCl(g)$$

**a.** How many grams of chlorine gas must react to produce 1.60 moles of hexachloroethane?
**b.** How many grams of hydrogen chloride are produced from 50.0 g of ethane and excess chlorine gas?

**6.112** Propane gas, $C_3H_8$, a fuel for many barbecues, reacts with oxygen to produce water and carbon dioxide. Propane has a density of 2.02 g/L at room temperature.

$$\underset{\text{Propane}}{C_3H_8(g)} + 5O_2(g) \longrightarrow 3CO_2(g) + 4H_2O(l)$$

**a.** How many moles of water form when 5.00 L of propane gas ($C_3H_8$) completely react?
**b.** How many grams of $CO_2$ are produced from 18.5 g of oxygen gas and excess propane?
**c.** How many grams of $H_2O$ can be produced from the reaction of $8.50 \times 10^{22}$ molecules of propane gas, $C_3H_8$?

**6.113** Acetylene gas, $C_2H_2$, burns in oxygen to produce carbon dioxide and water. If 62.0 g of $CO_2$ are produced when 22.5 g of $C_2H_2$ react with sufficient oxygen, what is the percent yield for the reaction?

**6.114** When 50.0 g of iron(III) oxide reacts with carbon monoxide, 32.8 g of iron is produced. What is the percent yield of the reaction?

$$Fe_2O_3(s) + 3CO(g) \longrightarrow 2Fe(s) + 3CO_2(g)$$

**6.115** Pentane gas, $C_5H_{12}$, reacts with oxygen to produce carbon dioxide and water:

$$\underset{\text{Pentane}}{C_5H_{12}(g)} + 8O_2(g) \longrightarrow 5CO_2(g) + 6H_2O(g)$$

**a.** How many grams of pentane must react to produce 4.0 moles of water?
**b.** How many grams of $CO_2$ are produced from 32.0 g of oxygen and excess pentane?
**c.** How many grams of $CO_2$ are formed if 44.5 g of $C_5H_{12}$ is mixed with 108 g of $O_2$?

**6.116** When nitrogen dioxide ($NO_2$) from car exhaust combines with water in the air it forms nitric acid ($HNO_3$), which causes acid rain, and nitrogen oxide.

$$3NO_2(g) + H_2O(l) \longrightarrow 2HNO_3(aq) + NO(g)$$

**a.** How many molecules of $NO_2$ are needed to react with 0.250 mole of $H_2O$?
**b.** How many grams of $HNO_3$ are produced when 60.0 g of $NO_2$ completely reacts?
**c.** How many grams of $HNO_3$ can be produced if 225 g of $NO_2$ is mixed with 55.2 g of $H_2O$?

**6.117** When a mixture of 12.8 g of Na and 10.2 g of $Cl_2$ reacts, what is the mass of NaCl that is produced?

$$2Na(s) + Cl_2(g) \longrightarrow 2NaCl(s)$$

**6.118** If a mixture of 35.8 g of $CH_4$ and 75.5 g of S reacts, how many grams of $H_2S$ are produced?

$$CH_4(g) + 4S(g) \longrightarrow CS_2(g) + 2H_2S(g)$$

**6.119** The formation of nitrogen oxide, NO, from $N_2(g)$ and $O_2(g)$, requires 21.6 kcal of heat:

$$N_2(g) + O_2(g) \longrightarrow 2NO(g) \qquad \Delta H = 21.6 \text{ kcal}$$

**a.** How many kcal are required to form 3.00 g of NO?
**b.** What is the complete equation (including heat) for the decomposition of NO?
**c.** How many kcal are released when 5.00 g of NO decomposes to $N_2$ and $O_2$?

**6.120** The formation of rust ($Fe_2O_3$) from solid iron and oxygen gas releases $1.7 \times 10^3$ kJ:

$$4Fe(s) + 3O_2(g) \longrightarrow 2Fe_2O_3(s)\ \Delta H = -1.7 \times 10^3 \text{ kJ}$$

**a.** How many kJ are released when 2.00 g of Fe of react?
**b.** How many grams of rust form when 150 kcal are released?

# CHALLENGE QUESTIONS

6.121 Write a balanced equation for each of the following reaction descriptions and identify each type of reaction:

**a.** An aqueous solution of lead(II) nitrate is mixed with aqueous sodium phosphate to produce solid lead(II) phosphate and aqueous sodium nitrate.

**b.** Gallium metal heated in oxygen gas forms solid gallium(III) oxide.

**c.** When solid sodium nitrate is heated, solid sodium nitrite and oxygen gas are produced.

**d.** Solid bismuth(III) oxide and solid carbon react to form bismuth metal and carbon monoxide gas.

**6.122** A toothpaste contains 0.24% by mass sodium fluoride (NaF) used to prevent dental caries and 0.30% by mass triclosan, $C_{12}H_7Cl_3O_2$, a preservative and antigingivitis agent. One tube contains 119 g of toothpaste.

**a.** How many moles of NaF are in the tube of toothpaste?

**b.** How many fluoride ions ($F^-$) are in the tube of toothpaste?

**c.** How many grams of sodium ion ($Na^+$) are in 1.50 g of toothpaste?

**d.** How many molecules of triclosan are in the tube of toothpaste?

6.123 A gold bar is 2.31 cm long, 1.48 cm wide, and 0.0758 cm thick.

**a.** If gold has a density of 19.3 g/mL, what is the mass of the gold bar?

**b.** How many atoms of gold are in the bar?

**c.** When the same mass of gold combines with oxygen, the oxide product has a mass of 5.61 g. How many moles of O are combined with the gold?

**d.** What is the formula of the oxide product?

**6.124** The gaseous hydrocarbon acetylene, $C_2H_2$, used in welders' torches, releases a large amount of heat when it burns according to the following equation:

$$2C_2H_2(g) + 5O_2(g) \longrightarrow 4CO_2(g) + 2H_2O(g)$$

**a.** How many moles of water are produced from the complete reaction of 64.0 g of oxygen?

**b.** How many moles of oxygen are needed to react completely with $2.25 \times 10^{24}$ molecules of acetylene?

**c.** How many grams of carbon dioxide are produced from the complete reaction of 78.0 g of acetylene?

**d.** If the reaction in part **c** produces 186 g of $CO_2$, what is the percent yield for the reaction?

6.125 Acetylene, $C_2H_2$, used in welders' torches, burns according to the following equation:

$$2C_2H_2(g) + 5O_2(g) \longrightarrow 4CO_2(g) + 2H_2O(g)$$

**a.** How many molecules of oxygen are needed to react with 22.0 g of acetylene?

**b.** How many grams of carbon dioxide could be produced from the complete reaction of the acetylene in part **a.**?

**c.** If the reaction in part **a.** produces 64.0 g of $CO_2$, what is the percent yield for the reaction?

**6.126** Consider the equation for the reaction of sodium and nitrogen to form sodium nitride:

$$Na(s) + N_2(g) \longrightarrow Na_3N(s)$$

**a.** Balance the equation.

**b.** If 80.0 g of sodium is mixed with 20.0 g of nitrogen gas, what mass of sodium nitride forms?

**c.** If the reaction in part **b.** has a percent yield of 75.0%, how much sodium nitride is actually produced?

6.127 Consider the following equation:

$$Al(s) + O_2(g) \longrightarrow Al_2O_3(s)$$

**a.** Balance the equation.

**b.** Identify the type of reaction.

**c.** How many moles of oxygen must react with 4.50 moles of Al?

**d.** How many grams of aluminum oxide are produced when 50.2 g of aluminum reacts?

**e.** When 0.500 mole of aluminum is reacted in a closed container with 8.00 g of oxygen, how many grams of aluminum oxide can form?

**f.** If 45.0 g of aluminum and 62.0 g of oxygen undergo a reaction that has a 70.0% yield, what mass of aluminum oxide forms?

# ANSWERS

## ANSWERS TO STUDY CHECKS

**6.1** $3Fe(s) + 2O_2(g) \longrightarrow Fe_3O_4(s)$

**6.2** $2NO(g) + O_2(g) \longrightarrow 2NO_2(g)$ Combination reaction

**6.3** Lithium is oxidized: $2Li(s) \longrightarrow 2Li^+(s) + 2e^-(s)$

Fluorine is reduced: $F_2(g) + 2e^- \longrightarrow 2F^-(s)$

**6.4** 0.432 mole of $H_2O$

**6.5** 0.120 mole of aspirin

**6.6** 138.0 g of salicylic acid

**6.7** 24.4 g of Au

**6.8** 0.00621 mole of $CaCO_3$, 0.00550 mole of $MgCO_3$

**6.9** 0.90 mole of $Fe_2S_3$

**6.10** 44.0 g of NO

**6.11** 27.5 g of $CO_2$

**6.12** 84.7%

**6.13** 13.4 g of SiC

**6.14** **a.** endothermic
**b.** 10.5 kJ

## ANSWERS TO SELECTED QUESTIONS AND PROBLEMS

**6.1** **a.** not balanced
**b.** balanced
**c.** not balanced
**d.** balanced

**6.3** **a.** $N_2(g) + O_2(g) \longrightarrow 2NO(g)$
**b.** $2HgO(s) \longrightarrow 2Hg(l) + O_2(g)$
**c.** $4Fe(s) + 3O_2(g) \longrightarrow 2Fe_2O_3(s)$
**d.** $2Na(s) + Cl_2(g) \longrightarrow 2NaCl(s)$

**6.5** **a.** $Mg(s) + 2AgNO_3(aq) \longrightarrow Mg(NO_3)_2(aq) + 2Ag(s)$
**b.** $2Al(s) + 3CuSO_4(aq) \longrightarrow 3Cu(s) + Al_2(SO_4)_3(aq)$
**c.** $Pb(NO_3)_2(aq) + 2NaCl(aq) \longrightarrow PbCl_2(s) + 2NaNO_3(aq)$
**d.** $2Al(s) + 6HCl(aq) \longrightarrow 2AlCl_3(aq) + 3H_2(g)$

**6.7** **a.** A single reactant breaks into two simpler substances (elements).
**b.** One element in the reacting compound is replaced by the other reactant.

**6.9** **a.** combination reaction
**b.** single replacement reaction
**c.** decomposition reaction
**d.** double replacement reaction
**e.** double replacement reaction

**6.11** **a.** $Mg(s) + Cl_2(g) \longrightarrow MgCl_2(s)$
**b.** $2HBr(g) \longrightarrow H_2(g) + Br_2(g)$
**c.** $Mg(s) + Zn(NO_3)_2(aq) \longrightarrow Zn(s) + Mg(NO_3)_2(aq)$
**d.** $K_2S(aq) + Pb(NO_3)_2(aq) \longrightarrow 2KNO_3(aq) + PbS(s)$

**6.13** **a.** reduction **b.** oxidation
**c.** reduction **d.** reduction

**6.15** **a.** Zn is oxidized; $Cl_2$ is reduced.
**b.** $Br^-$ in NaBr is oxidized; $Cl_2$ is reduced.
**c.** The $O^{2-}$ in PbO is oxidized; the $Pb^{2+}$ is reduced.
**d.** $Sn^{2+}$ is oxidized; $Fe^{3+}$ is reduced.

**6.17** **a.** reduction
**b.** oxidation

**6.19** Linoleic acid gains hydrogen atoms and is reduced.

**6.21** 1.00 mole contains $6.02 \times 10^{23}$ atoms of an element, molecules of a covalent substance, or formula units of an ionic substance.

**6.23** **a.** $1.20 \times 10^{23}$ atoms of Ag
**b.** $4.52 \times 10^{23}$ molecules of $C_3H_8O$
**c.** 0.478 mole of Au

**6.25** **a.** 24 moles of H
**b.** $1.0 \times 10^2$ moles of C
**c.** 0.040 mole of N

**6.27** **a.** $3.01 \times 10^{23}$ atoms of C
**b.** $7.71 \times 10^{23}$ molecules of $SO_2$
**c.** 0.0867 mole of Fe
**d.** 14.1 moles of $C_2H_5OH$

**6.29** **a.** 6.00 moles of H
**b.** 8.00 moles of O
**c.** $1.20 \times 10^{24}$ atoms of P
**d.** $4.82 \times 10^{24}$ atoms of O

**6.31** **a.** 74.6 g/mole **b.** 159.8 g/mole
**c.** 73.8 g/mole **d.** 342.3 g/mole
**e.** 58.3 g/mole **f.** 365.1 g/mole

**6.33** **a.** 46.0 g **b.** 112 g
**c.** 14.8 g **d.** 112 g

**6.35** **a.** 29.3 g **b.** 109 g
**c.** 4.05 g **d.** 194 g

**6.37** **a.** 602 g **b.** 11 g

**6.39** **a.** 0.463 mole **b.** 0.0167 mole
**c.** 0.882 mole **d.** 1.17 moles

**6.41** **a.** 0.78 mole of S
**b.** 1.95 moles of S
**c.** 6.0 moles of S

**6.43** **a.** $1.72 \times 10^{24}$ atoms of N
**b.** $1.8 \times 10^{24}$ atoms of N
**c.** $2.4 \times 10^{24}$ atoms of N

**6.45** **a.** $\frac{2 \text{ moles } SO_2}{1 \text{ mole } O_2}$ and $\frac{1 \text{ mole } O_2}{2 \text{ moles } SO_2}$

$\frac{2 \text{ moles } SO_2}{2 \text{ moles } SO_3}$ and $\frac{2 \text{ moles } SO_3}{2 \text{ moles } SO_2}$

$\frac{2 \text{ moles } SO_3}{1 \text{ mole } O_2}$ and $\frac{1 \text{ mole } O_2}{2 \text{ moles } SO_3}$

**b.** $\frac{4 \text{ moles P}}{5 \text{ moles } O_2}$ and $\frac{5 \text{ moles } O_2}{4 \text{ moles P}}$

$\frac{4 \text{ moles P}}{2 \text{ moles } P_2O_5}$ and $\frac{2 \text{ moles } P_2O_5}{4 \text{ moles P}}$

$\frac{5 \text{ moles } O_2}{2 \text{ moles } P_2O_5}$ and $\frac{2 \text{ moles } P_2O_5}{5 \text{ moles } O_2}$

**6.47** **a.** 1.0 mole of $O_2$ **b.** 10. moles of $H_2$
**c.** 5.0 moles of $H_2O$

**6.49** **a.** 1.25 moles of C **b.** 0.96 mole of CO
**c.** 1.0 mole of $SO_2$ **d.** 0.50 mole of $CS_2$

**6.51** **a.** 77.5 g of $Na_2O$ **b.** 6.26 g of $O_2$
**c.** 19.4 g of $O_2$

**6.53** **a.** 192 g of $O_2$ **b.** 3.79 g of $N_2$
**c.** 54.0 g of $H_2O$

**6.55** **a.** 3.65 g of $H_2O$ **b.** 3.43 g of NO
**c.** 7.53 g of $HNO_3$

**6.57** **a.** $2PbS(s) + 3O_2(g) \longrightarrow 2PbO(s) + 2SO_2(g)$
**b.** 6.00 g of $O_2$
**c.** 17.4 g of $SO_2$
**d.** 137 g of PbS

**6.59** **a.** 70.9% **b.** 63.2%

**6.61** 70.8 g of $Al_2O_3$

**6.63** 60.4%

**6.65** **a.** 8 taxis can be used to pick up passengers.
**b.** 7 taxis can be driven.

**6.67** **a.** 5.0 moles of $H_2$ **b.** 4.0 moles of $H_2$
**c.** 3.0 moles of $N_2$

**6.69** **a.** 2.00 moles of $SO_3$ **b.** 0.500 mole of $Fe_3O_4$
**c.** 1.27 moles of $CO_2$

**6.71** **a.** 0.188 mole of $AlCl_3$ **b.** 0.750 mole of $H_2O$
**c.** 0.417 mole of $SO_2$

**6.73** **a.** The activation energy is the energy required to break the bonds of the reacting molecules.
**b.** In exothermic reactions, the energy of the products is lower than the reactants.
**c.**

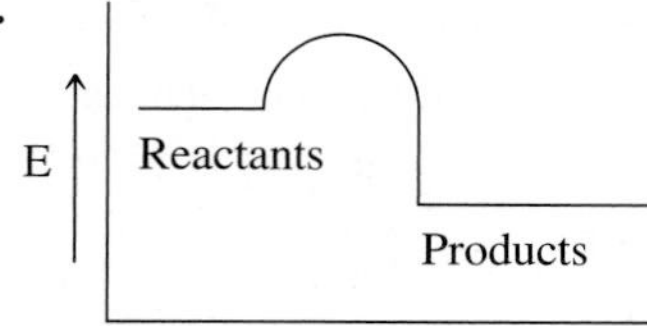


**6.75** **a.** exothermic **b.** endothermic
**c.** exothermic

**6.77** **a.** exothermic $\Delta H = -210$ kcal
**b.** endothermic $\Delta H = 65.3$ kJ
**c.** exothermic $\Delta H = -205$ kcal

**6.79** 138 kcal

**6.81** **a.** 1, 1, 2 combination reaction
**b.** 2, 2, 1 decomposition reaction

**6.83** **a.** $2NO(g) + O_2(g) \longrightarrow 2NO_2(g)$
**b.** combination reaction

**6.85** **a.** $2NI_3(s) \longrightarrow N_2(g) + 3I_2(g)$
**b.** decomposition reaction

**6.87** **a.** $2Cl_2(g) + O_2(g) \longrightarrow 2OCl_2(g)$
**b.** combination reaction

**6.89** **(1) a.** $S_2Cl_2$ **b.** 135.2 g/mole **c.** 0.0740 mole
**(2) a.** $C_6H_6$ **b.** 78.0 g/mole **c.** 0.128 mole

**6.91** **a.** 252.2 g/mole **b.** 0.0991 mole
**c.** 0.991 mole of C

**6.93** **a.** 47.1 g of CuO **b.** 0.296 mole of $O_2$

**6.95** **a.** $NH_3(g) + HCl(g) \longrightarrow NH_4Cl(s)$ Combination
**b.** $Fe_3O_4(s) + 4H_2(g) \longrightarrow 3Fe(s) + 4H_2O(g)$ Single replacement
**c.** $2Sb(s) + 3Cl_2(g)_3(s)$ Combination
**d.** $2NI_3(s) \longrightarrow N_2(g) + 3I_2(g)$ Decomposition
**e.** $2KBr(aq) + Cl_2(aq) \longrightarrow 2KCl(aq) + Br_2(l)$ Single replacement
**f.** $Al_2(SO_4)_3(aq) + 6NaOH(aq) \longrightarrow 3Na_2SO_4(aq) + 2Al(OH)_3(s)$ Double replacement

**6.97** **a.** reduction **b.** oxidation
**c.** oxidation **d.** reduction

**6.99** **a.** 90.0 g/mole
**b.** $3.01 \times 10^{23}$ molecules
**c.** $2.71 \times 10^{24}$ atoms of C
**d.** 220 g of lactic acid

**6.101** **a.** 152.0 g/mole **b.** 389.9 g/mole
**c.** 169.0 g/mole

**6.103** **a.** 5.87 g **b.** 10.7 g **c.** 15.9 g

**6.105** **a.** 0.568 mole **b.** 0.321 mole
**c.** 0.262 mole

**6.107** **a.** 1.35 moles of glucose
**b.** 123 g of ethanol

**6.109** $2NH_3(g) + 5F_2(g) \longrightarrow N_2F_4(g) + 6HF(g)$
**a.** 1.33 moles of $NH_3$ and 3.33 moles of $F_2$
**b.** 143 g of $F_2$
**c.** 10.4 g of $N_2F_4$

**6.111** **a.** 682 g of $Cl_2$
**b.** 365 g of HCl

**6.113** 81.4%

**6.115** **a.** 48 g of $C_5H_{12}$
**b.** 27.5 g of $CO_2$
**c.** 92.8 g of $CO_2$

**6.117** 16.8 g of NaCl

**6.119** **a.** 1.08 kcal
**b.** $2NO(g) \longrightarrow N_2(g) + O_2(g) + 21.6$ kcal
**c.** 1.80 kcal

**6.121** **a.** $3Pb(NO_3)_2(aq) + 2Na_3PO_4(aq) \longrightarrow Pb_3(PO_4)_2(s) + 6NaNO_3(aq)$ Double replacement
**b.** $4Ga(s) + 3O_2(g) \longrightarrow 2Ga_2O_3(s)$ Combination
**c.** $2NaNO_3(s) \longrightarrow 2NaNO_2(s) + O_2(g)$ Decomposition
**d.** $Bi_2O_3(s) + 3C(s) \longrightarrow 2Bi(s) + 3CO(g)$ Single replacement

**6.123** **a.** 5.00 g of gold
**b.** $1.53 \times 10^{22}$ Au atoms
**c.** 0.038 mole of oxygen
**d.** $Au_2O_3$

**6.125** **a.** $1.27 \times 10^{24}$ molecules of $O_2$
**b.** 74.5 g of $CO_2$
**c.** 85.9% yield

**6.127** **a.** $4Al(s) + 3O_2(g) \longrightarrow 2Al_2O_3(s)$
**b.** This is a combination reaction.
**c.** 3.38 moles of oxygen
**d.** 94.8 g of aluminum oxide
**e.** 17.0 g of aluminum oxide
**f.** 59.5 g of aluminum oxide

**CI.7** Some of the isotopes of silicon are listed in the following table:

| Isotope | % Natural Abundance | Atomic Mass | Half-Life | Radiation Emitted |
|---|---|---|---|---|
| $^{27}_{14}Si$ | | 26.99 | 4.2 s | Positron |
| $^{28}_{14}Si$ | 92.23 | 27.99 | Stable | None |
| $^{29}_{14}Si$ | 4.67 | 28.99 | Stable | None |
| $^{30}_{14}Si$ | 3.10 | 29.98 | Stable | None |
| $^{31}_{14}Si$ | | 30.99 | 2.6 h | Beta |

**a.** In the following table, indicate the number of protons, neutrons, and electrons for each isotope listed:

| Isotope | Number of Protons | Number of Neutrons | Number of Electrons |
|---|---|---|---|
| $^{27}_{14}Si$ | | | |
| $^{28}_{14}Si$ | | | |
| $^{29}_{14}Si$ | | | |
| $^{30}_{14}Si$ | | | |
| $^{31}_{14}Si$ | | | |

**b.** What is the electron configuration of silicon?
**c.** Calculate the atomic mass for silicon using the isotopes that have a natural abundance.
**d.** Write the nuclear equations for $^{27}_{14}Si$ and $^{31}_{14}Si$.
**e.** Write the electron-dot formula and predict the shape of $SiCl_4$.
**f.** How many hours are needed for a sample of $^{31}_{14}Si$ with an activity of 16 $\mu$Ci to decay to 2.0 $\mu$Ci?

**CI.8** $K^+$ is an electrolyte required by the human body and is found in many foods as well as salt substitutes. One of the isotopes of potassium is $^{40}_{19}K$ which has a natural abundance of 0.012% and a half-life of $1.30 \times 10^9$ years. The isotope $^{40}_{19}K$ decays to $^{40}_{20}Ca$ or to $^{40}_{18}Ar$. A typical activity for $^{40}_{19}K$ is 7.0 $\mu$Ci per gram.

**a.** Write a nuclear equation for each type of decay.
**b.** Identify the particle emitted for each type of decay.
**c.** How many $K^+$ ions are in 3.5 oz of KCl?
**d.** What is the activity of 25 g of KCl, in becquerels?

**CI.9** Of much concern to environmentalists is the radioactive noble gas radon-222, which can seep from the ground into basements of homes and buildings. Radon-222 is a product of the decay of radium-226 that occurs naturally in rocks and soil in much of the United States. Radon-222, which has a half-life of 3.8 days, decays by emitting an alpha particle. Radon-222, which is a gas, can be inhaled; because of that, it is strongly associated with lung cancer. Radon levels in a home can be measured with a home radon-detection kit. Environmental agencies have set the maximum level of radon-222 in a home at 4 picocuries per liter (pCi/L) of air in a home.

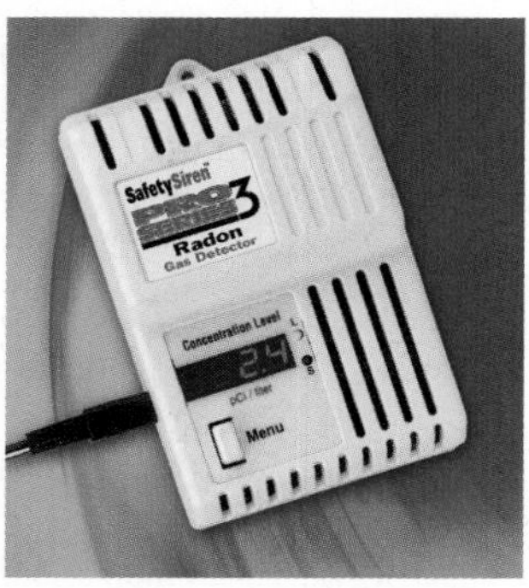


**a.** Write the equation for the decay of Ra-226.
**b.** Write the equation for the decay of Rn-222.
**c.** If a room contains 24 000 atoms of radon-222, how many atoms of radon-222 remain after 15.2 days?
**d.** Suppose a room in a home has a volume of 72 000 liters ($7.2 \times 10^4$ L). If the radon level is 2.5 picocuries/liter, how many alpha particles are emitted in one day? (1 Ci = $3.7 \times 10^{10}$ disintegrations per second.)

**CI.10** A gold bar has a volume of 728 $cm^3$ and a density of 19.3 g/$cm^3$.

**a.** What is the mass in kilograms of the gold bar?
**b.** How many atoms of gold are in the bar?
**c.** Give the number of protons and neutrons in each of the following isotopes of gold:
$^{185}_{79}Au$ $^{197}_{79}Au$ $^{198}_{79}Au$

**CI.11** The following reaction occurs between a metal in Group 1A (1) or Group 2A (2) and a nonmetal:

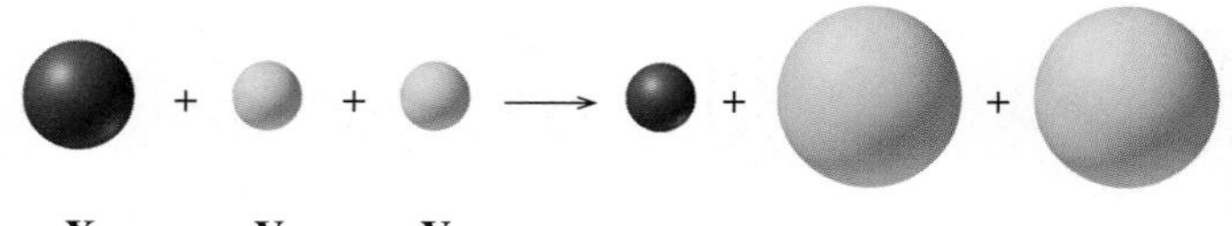


**a.** Which spheres represent a metal? A nonmetal?
**b.** Which reactant has the higher electronegativity?
**c.** What are the ionic charges of X and Y in the product?
**d.** If these elements are both in period 3:
1. Write the electron configurations of the atoms.
2. Write the electron configurations of their ions.
3. Give the names of the noble gases with the same electron configurations as these ions.
4. Write the formula and name of the product.

**e.** Match the spheres below with atoms of Li, Na, K, and Rb.

A.

B.

C.

D.

**CI.12** The active ingredient in Tums is calcium carbonate. One Tums tablet contains 500. mg of calcium carbonate.

**a.** What is the formula for calcium carbonate?
**b.** What is the molar mass of calcium carbonate?
**c.** How many moles of calcium carbonate are in one roll of Tums that contains 12 tablets?
**d.** If a person takes two Tums tablets a day, how many grams of calcium are obtained?
**e.** If the daily recommended quantity of $Ca^{2+}$ to maintain bone strength in older women is 1500 mg, how many Tums tablets are needed each day?

**CI.13** Ethanol, $C_2H_5OH$, is obtained from renewable crops such as corn, which use the sun as their source of energy. In the United States, automobiles can now use a fuel known as E10 that contains 10.0% ethanol and 90.0% unleaded gasoline by volume (%v/v). Ethanol has a melting point of −115 °C, a boiling point of 78 °C, a heat of fusion of 23.6 cal/g, and a heat of vaporization of 201 cal/g. Liquid ethanol has a density of 0.796 g/mL and a specific heat of 0.588 cal/g °C.

**a.** Draw a heating curve for ethanol from −150 °C to 100 °C.

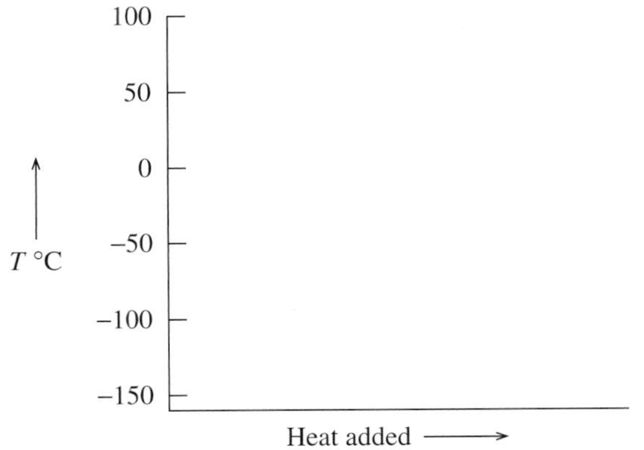


**b.** When 20.0 g of ethanol at −55 °C is heated to 37 °C, how much energy, in calories, is required?
**c.** How many kilojoules are needed to vaporize 1.00 L of ethanol at 78 °C?
**d.** If a 15-gallon gas tank is filled with E10, how many liters of ethanol are in the gas tank?
**e.** Write the balanced chemical equation for the reaction of ethanol with oxygen gas to produce carbon dioxide and water vapor.
**f.** How many kilograms of carbon dioxide, $CO_2$, are produced from the complete reaction of the ethanol in a full 15-gallon gas tank?

**CI.14** Butyric acid contributes to the characteristic odor of Parmesan cheese.

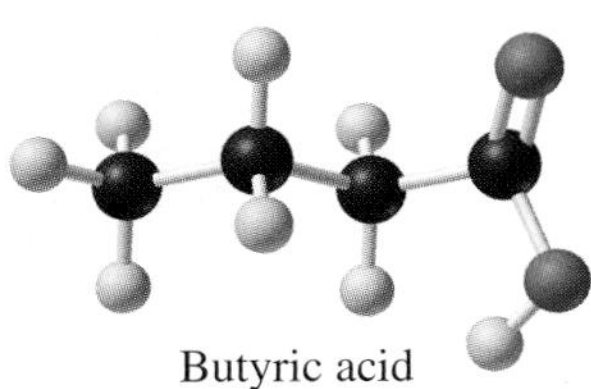

Butyric acid

**a.** If black spheres are carbon atoms, light blue spheres are hydrogen atoms, and red spheres are oxygen atoms, what is the formula of butyric acid?
**b.** What is the molar mass of butyric acid?
**c.** How many grams of butyric acid contain $3.28 \times 10^{23}$ oxygen atoms?
**d.** How many grams of carbon are in 5.28 g of butyric acid?
**e.** If butyric acid has a density of 0.959 g/mL at 20 °C, how many moles of butyric acid are in 1.56 mL of butyric acid?
**f.** Write a balanced equation for the reaction of butyric acid with oxygen gas to form carbon dioxide and water.
**g.** How many grams of oxygen are needed to completely react 1.58 g of butyric acid?
**h.** What mass of carbon dioxide is formed when 100. g of butyric acid and 100. g of oxygen react?

**CI.15** Oseltamivir, $C_{16}H_{28}N_2O_4$, is the active ingredient in Tamiflu, an antiviral drug used to treat influenza. The preparation of oseltamivir begins with the extraction of shikimic acid from the seedpods of the spice Chinese star anise. From 2.6 g of star anise, 0.13 g of shikimic acid can be obtained and used to produce one Tamiflu capsule containing 75 mg of oseltamivir. The usual adult dosage for treatment of influenza is two capsules of Tamiflu twice daily for 5 days.

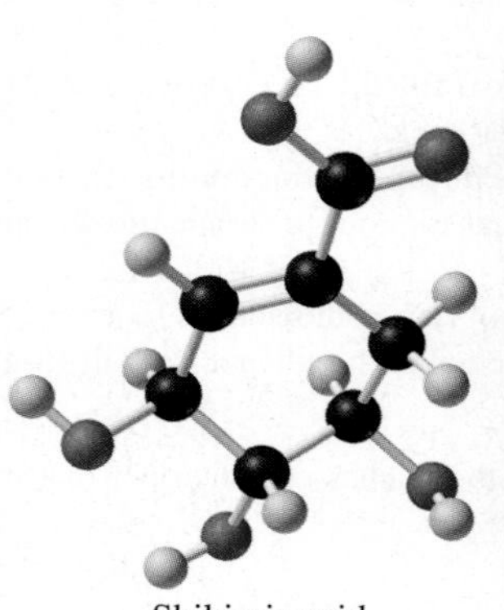

Shikimic acid

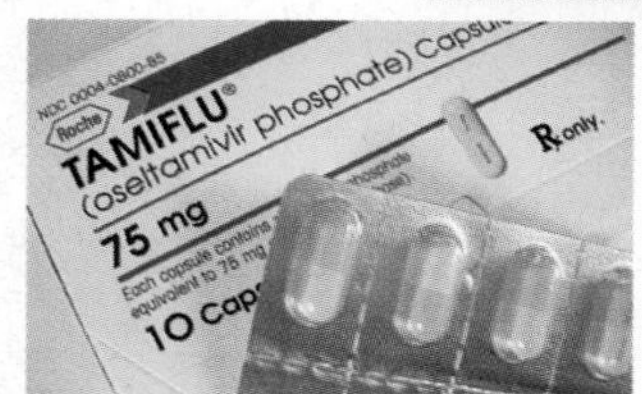


a. What is the formula of shikimic acid? (Black spheres are carbon, light blue spheres are hydrogen, and red spheres are oxygen.)

b. What is the molar mass of shikimic acid?

c. How many moles of shikimic acid are contained in 1.3 g of shikimic acid?

d. How many capsules of Tamiflu could be produced from 154 g of star anise?

e. What is the molar mass of oseltamivir?

f. How many grams of carbon are in 75 mg of oseltamivir?

g. How many kilograms of oseltamivir would be needed to treat all the people in a city with a population of 500 000 people if each person takes 2 Tamiflu capsules a day for 5 days?

**CI.16** When clothes have stains, bleach is often added to the wash to react with the soil and make the stains colorless. One brand of bleach contains 5.25% sodium hypochlorite by mass (active ingredient) with a density of 1.08 g/mL. The liquid bleach solution is prepared by bubbling chlorine gas into a solution of sodium hydroxide to produce sodium hypochlorite, sodium chloride, and water.

a. What is the formula and molar mass of sodium hypochlorite?

b. How many hypochlorite ions are present in 1 gallon of bleach solution?

c. Write the equation for the preparation of bleach.

d. How many grams of NaOH are required to produce the mass of sodium hypochlorite in 1 gallon of bleach?

e. If 165 g of $Cl_2$ is passed through a solution containing 275 g of NaOH and 162 g of sodium hypochlorite is produced, what is the percent yield for the reaction?

## ANSWERS

**CI.7 a.**

| Isotope | Number of Protons | Number of Neutrons | Number of Electrons |
|---|---|---|---|
| $^{27}_{14}Si$ | 14 | 13 | 14 |
| $^{28}_{14}Si$ | 14 | 14 | 14 |
| $^{29}_{14}Si$ | 14 | 15 | 14 |
| $^{30}_{14}Si$ | 14 | 16 | 14 |
| $^{31}_{14}Si$ | 14 | 17 | 14 |

**b.** $1s^22s^22p^63s^23p^2$

**c.** Atomic mass calculated from the three stable isotopes is 28.10 amu.

**d.** $^{27}_{14}Si \longrightarrow ^{27}_{13}Al + ^{0}_{+1}e$ and $^{31}_{14}Si \longrightarrow ^{31}_{15}P + ^{0}_{-1}e$

**e.**

```
          :C̈l:
            |
   :C̈l—Si—C̈l:
            |
          :C̤l:
```

Tetrahedral

**f.** 7.8 h

**CI.9 a.** $^{226}_{88}Ra \longrightarrow ^{222}_{86}Rn + ^{4}_{2}He$ **b.** $^{222}_{86}Rn \longrightarrow ^{218}_{84}Po + ^{4}_{2}He$

**c.** 1500 atoms of radon-222 remain

**d.** $5.8 \times 10^8$ alpha particles

**CI.11 a.** X is a metal; Y is a nonmetal.

**b.** Y has the higher electronegativity.

**c.** $X^{2+}$, $Y^-$

**d. 1.** $X = 1s^22s^22p^63s^2$ $Y = 1s^22s^22p^63s^23p^5$

**2.** $X^{2+} = 1s^22s^22p^6$ $Y^- = 1s^22s^22p^63s^23p^6$

**3.** $X^{2+}$ has the same electron configuration as Ne. $Y^-$ has the same electron configuration as Ar.

**4.** $MgCl_2$, magnesium chloride

**e.** Li is D, Na is A, K is C, and Rb is B.

**CI.13 a.**

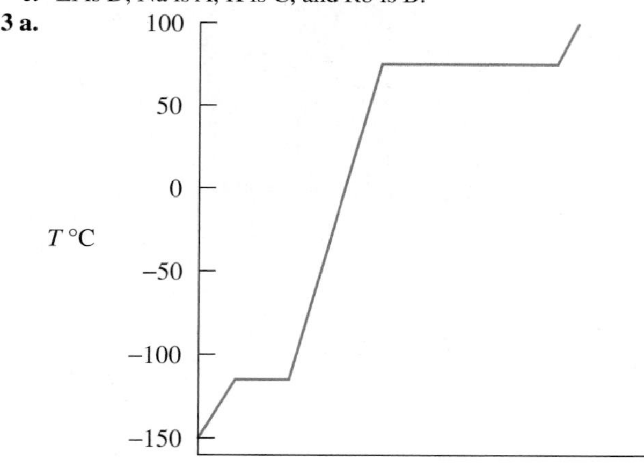


**b.** 1100 cal **c.** 669 kJ **d.** 57 L

**e.** $C_2H_5OH(l) + 3O_2(g) \longrightarrow 2CO_2(g) + 3H_2O(g)$

**f.** 86 kg of $CO_2$

**CI.15 a.** $C_7H_{10}O_5$ **b.** 174 g/mole **c.** 0.0075 mole

**d.** 59 capsules **e.** 312.0 g/mole **f.** 0.046 g of carbon

**g.** 380 kg

# 7

# Gases

LOOKING AHEAD


7.1 Properties of Gases

7.2 Gas Pressure

7.3 Pressure and Volume (Boyle's Law)

7.4 Temperature and Volume (Charles's Law)

7.5 Temperature and Pressure (Gay-Lussac's Law)

7.6 The Combined Gas Law

7.7 Volume and Moles (Avogadro's Law)

7.8 The Ideal Gas Law

7.9 Partial Pressures (Dalton's Law)

*"When oxygen levels in the blood are low, the cells in the body don't get enough oxygen," says Sunanda Tripathi, registered nurse, Santa Clara Valley Medical Center. "We use an oxygen mask to give supplemental oxygen to a patient. At a flow rate of 2 liters per minute, a patient breathes in a gaseous mixture that is about 28% oxygen, compared to 21% in ambient air."*

*When a patient has a breathing disorder, the flow and volume of oxygen into and out of the lungs are measured. A ventilator may be used if a patient has difficulty breathing. When the pressure is increased, the lungs expand. When the pressure of the incoming gas is reduced, the lung volume contracts to expel carbon dioxide. These relationships—known as gas laws—are an important part of ventilation and breathing.*

Visit **www.masteringchemistry.com** for self-study materials and instructor-assigned homework.

We all live at the bottom of a sea of gases called the atmosphere. The most important of these gases is oxygen, which constitutes about 21% of the atmosphere. Without oxygen, life on this planet would be impossible—oxygen is vital to all life processes of plants and animals. Ozone ($O_3$), formed in the upper atmosphere by the interaction of oxygen with ultraviolet light, absorbs some of the harmful radiation before it can strike Earth's surface. The other gases in the atmosphere include nitrogen (78%), argon, carbon dioxide ($CO_2$), and water vapor. Carbon dioxide gas, a product of combustion and metabolism, is used by plants in photosynthesis, a process that produces the oxygen that is essential for humans and animals.

The atmosphere has become a dumping ground for other gases, such as methane, chlorofluorocarbons (CFCs), and nitrogen oxides, as well as volatile organic compounds (VOCs), which are gases from paints, paint thinners, and cleaning supplies. The chemical reactions of these gases with sunlight and oxygen in the air are contributing to air pollution, ozone depletion, global warming, and acid rain. Such chemical changes can seriously affect our health and our lifestyle. An understanding of gases and the laws that govern gas behavior can help us understand the nature of matter and allow us to make decisions concerning important environmental and health issues.

## 7.1 Properties of Gases

LEARNING GOAL

Describe the kinetic molecular theory of gases and the properties of gases.

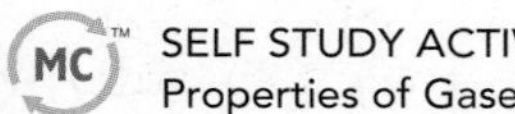


The behavior of gases is quite different from that of liquids and solids. Gas particles are far apart, whereas particles of both liquids and solids are held close together because strong attractive forces become more important at lower temperatures. This means that a gas has no definite shape or volume and will completely fill any container. Because there are great distances between its particles, a gas is less dense than a solid or liquid and can be compressed. A model for the behavior of a gas, called the **kinetic molecular theory of gases**, helps us understand gas behavior.

**Kinetic Molecular Theory of Gases**

1. **A gas consists of small particles (atoms or molecules) that move randomly with rapid velocities.** Gas molecules moving in all directions at high speeds cause a gas to fill the entire volume of a container.
2. **The attractive forces between the particles of a gas can be neglected.** Gas particles are far apart and fill a container of any size and shape.
3. **The actual volume occupied by gas molecules is extremely small compared to the volume that the gas occupies.** The volume of the container is considered equal to the volume of the gas. Most of the volume of a gas is empty space, which allows gases to be easily compressed.
4. **Gas particles are in constant motion, moving rapidly in straight paths.** When gas particles collide, they rebound and travel in new directions. Every time they hit the walls of the container, they exert pressure. An increase in the number or force of collisions against the walls of the container causes an increase in the pressure of the gas.
5. **The average kinetic energy of gas molecules is proportional to the Kelvin temperature.** Gas particles move faster as the temperature increases. At higher temperatures, gas particles hit the walls of the container with more force, producing higher pressures.

The kinetic molecular theory helps explain some of the characteristics of gases. For example, we can quickly smell perfume from a bottle that is opened on the other side of a room because its particles move rapidly in all directions. At room temperatures, the molecules of air are moving at about 1000 miles per hour. They move faster at higher temperatures and more slowly at lower temperatures. Sometimes tires and gas-filled containers explode when temperatures are too high. From the kinetic molecular theory, we know that gas particles move faster when heated, hit the walls of a container with more force, and cause a buildup of pressure inside a container.

When we talk about a gas, we describe it in terms of four properties: pressure, volume, temperature, and the amount of gas.

**Pressure (*P*)** Gas particles are extremely small and move rapidly. When they hit the walls of a container, they exert a force known as *pressure*. (See Figure 7.1.) If we heat the container, the molecules move faster and smash into the walls more often and with increased force, thus increasing the pressure. The gas particles in the air, mostly oxygen and nitrogen, exert a pressure on us called **atmospheric pressure**. (See Figure 7.2.) As altitude increases, the atmospheric pressure decreases because there are fewer particles in the air. The most common units used for gas measurement are *atmospheres* (atm) and *millimeters of mercury* (mmHg). On the TV weather report, you may hear or see the atmospheric pressure given in inches of mercury or, in countries other than the United States, kilopascals. In a chemistry lab, the unit *torr* may be used.

**Volume (*V*)** The volume of gas equals the size of the container in which the gas is placed. When you inflate a tire or a basketball, you are adding more gas particles. The increase in the number of particles hitting the walls of the tire or basketball increases the volume. Sometimes, on a cool morning, a tire looks flat. The volume of the tire has decreased because a lower temperature decreases the speed of the molecules, which in turn reduces the force of their impacts on the walls of the tire. The most common units for volume measurement are liters (L) and milliliters (mL).

**Temperature (*T*)** The temperature of a gas is related to the kinetic energy of its particles. For example, if we have a gas at 200 K in a rigid container and heat it to a temperature of 400 K, the gas particles will have twice the kinetic energy that they did at 200 K.

FIGURE 7.1 Gas particles move in straight lines within a container. The gas particles exert pressure when they collide with the walls of the container.

Q Why does heating the container increase the pressure of the gas within it?

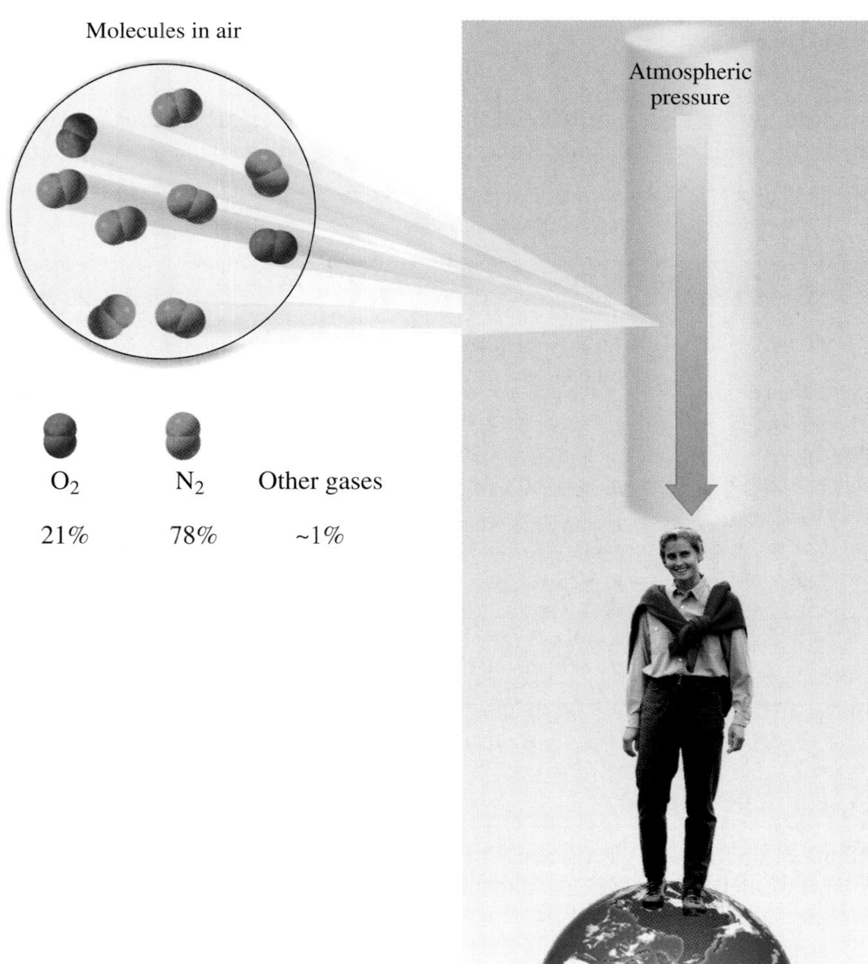


FIGURE 7.2 A column of air extending from the upper atmosphere to the surface of the Earth produces a pressure on each of us of about 1 atmosphere. While there is a lot of pressure on the body, it is balanced by the pressure inside the body.

Q Why is there less pressure at higher altitudes?

This also means that the gas at 400 K exerts twice the pressure of the gas at 200 K. Although you measure gas temperature using a Celsius thermometer, all comparisons of gas behavior and all calculations related to temperature must use the Kelvin temperature scale. No one has yet achieved the conditions for absolute zero (0 K), but we predict that the particles will have zero kinetic energy and exert zero pressure at absolute zero.

**Amount of Gas ($n$)** When you add air to a bicycle tire, you increase the amount of gas, which results in a higher pressure in the tire. Usually we measure the amount of gas by its mass (grams). In gas law calculations, we need to change the grams of gas to moles.

A summary of the four properties of a gas is given in Table 7.1.

### Forming a Gas

Obtain baking soda and a jar or a plastic bottle. You will also need an elastic glove that fits over the mouth of the jar or a balloon that fits snugly over the top of the plastic bottle. Place a cup of vinegar in the jar or bottle. Sprinkle some baking soda into the fingertips of the glove or into the balloon. Carefully fit the glove or balloon over the top of the jar or bottle. Slowly lift the fingers of the glove or the balloon so that the baking soda falls into the vinegar. Watch what happens. Squeeze the glove or balloon.

**QUESTION**

1. Describe the properties of gas that you observe as the reaction takes place between vinegar and baking soda.
2. How do you know that a gas was formed?

**TABLE 7.1** Properties That Describe a Gas

| Property | Description | Unit(s) of Measurement |
|---|---|---|
| Pressure ($P$) | The force exerted by gas against the walls of the container | atmosphere (atm); millimeters of mercury (mmHg); torr; pascal (Pa) |
| Volume ($V$) | The space occupied by the gas | liter (L); milliliter (mL); cubic meter ($m^3$) |
| Temperature ($T$) | Determines the kinetic energy and rate of motion of the gas particles | Celsius (°C); kelvin (K) *is required in calculations* |
| Amount ($n$) | The quantity of gas present in a container | grams (g); moles ($n$) *is required in calculations* |

**CONCEPT CHECK 7.1**

### Properties of Gases

Use the kinetic molecular theory to explain why a gas completely fills a container of any size and shape.

ANSWER

Gas particles move at high speeds in all directions, moving as far apart as possible until they hit the walls of a container. Thus, they completely fill a container of any size and shape.

## QUESTIONS AND PROBLEMS

### Properties of Gases

**7.1** Use the kinetic molecular theory of gases to explain each of the following:
- **a.** Gas particles move faster at higher temperatures.
- **b.** Gases can be compressed much more than liquids or solids.

**7.2** Use the kinetic molecular theory of gases to explain each of the following:
- **a.** A container of nonstick cooking spray explodes when thrown into a fire.
- **b.** The air in a hot-air balloon is heated to make the balloon rise.

**7.3** Identify the property of a gas that is measured in each of the following:
- **a.** 350 K
- **b.** space occupied by a gas
- **c.** 2.00 g of $O_2$
- **d.** force of gas particles striking the walls of the container

**7.4** Identify the property of a gas that is measured in each of the following:
- **a.** 425 K
- **b.** 1.0 atm
- **c.** 10.0 L
- **d.** 0.50 mole of He

## 7.2 Gas Pressure

**LEARNING GOAL**

Describe the units of measurement used for pressure, and change from one unit to another.

When billions and billions of gas particles hit against the walls of a container, they exert **pressure**, which is defined as a force acting on a certain area.

$$\text{Pressure } (P) = \frac{\text{force}}{\text{area}}$$

The *atmospheric pressure* can be measured using a barometer. (See Figure 7.3.) At a pressure of *exactly* 1 atmosphere (atm), the mercury column would be *exactly* 760 mm high. One **atmosphere (atm)** is defined as *exactly* 760 mmHg (millimeters of mercury). One atmosphere is also 760 *torr*, a pressure unit named to honor Evangelista Torricelli, the inventor of the barometer. Because they are equal, units of torr and mmHg are used interchangeably.

1 atm = 760 mmHg = 760 torr (exact)

1 mmHg = 1 torr (exact)

In SI units, pressure is measured in pascals (Pa); 1 atm is equal to 101 325 Pa. Because a pascal is a very small unit, pressures can be reported in kilopascals.

1 atm = 101 325 Pa = 101.325 kPa

The U.S. equivalent of 1 atm is 14.7 pounds per square inch (psi). When you use a pressure gauge to check the air pressure in the tires of a car, it may read 30–35 psi. This measurement is actually 30–35 psi above the pressure that the atmosphere exerts on the outside of the tire. Table 7.2 summarizes the various units used in the measurement of pressure.

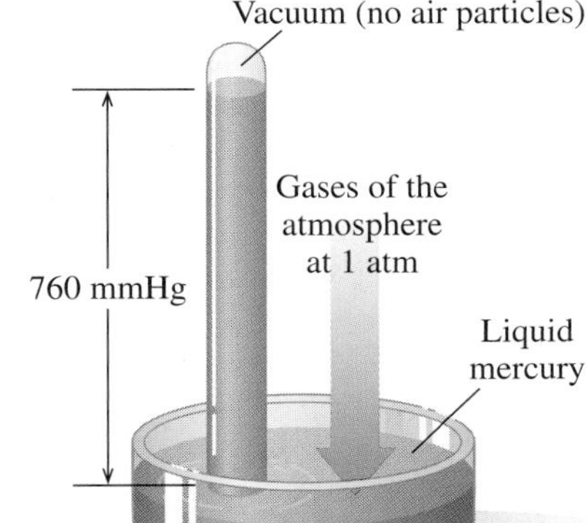


**FIGURE 7.3** A barometer: The pressure exerted by the gases in the atmosphere is equal to the downward pressure of a mercury column in a closed glass tube. The height of the mercury column measured in mmHg is called atmospheric pressure.

**Q** Why does the height of the mercury column change from day to day?

**TABLE 7.2** Units for Measuring Pressure

| Unit | Abbreviation | Unit Equivalent to 1 atm |
|---|---|---|
| Atmosphere | atm | 1 atm (exact) |
| Millimeters of Hg | mmHg | 760 mmHg (exact) |
| Torr | torr | 760 torr (exact) |
| Inches of Hg | in. Hg | 29.9 in. Hg |
| Pounds per square inch | lb/in.$^2$ (psi) | 14.7 lb/in.$^2$ |
| Pascal | Pa | 101 325 Pa |
| Kilopascal | kPa | 101.325 kPa |

TUTORIAL
Converting Between Units of Pressure

CASE STUDY
Scuba Diving and Blood Gases

If you have a barometer in your home, it probably measures pressure in inches of mercury. Atmospheric pressure changes with variations in weather and altitude. On a hot, sunny day, a column of air has more particles, which increases the pressure on the surface of the mercury. The mercury column rises, indicating a higher atmospheric pressure. On a rainy day, the atmosphere exerts less pressure, which causes the mercury column to fall. In meteorological terms, this type of weather is called a *low-pressure system*. Above sea level, the density of the gases in the air decreases, which causes lower atmospheric pressures; the atmospheric pressure is greater than 760 mmHg at the Dead Sea because it is below sea level. (See Table 7.3.)

Divers must be concerned about increasing pressures on their ears and lungs when they dive below the surface of the ocean. Because water is more dense than air, the pressure on a diver increases rapidly as the diver descends. At a depth of 33 ft below the surface of the ocean, an additional 1 atmosphere of pressure is exerted by the water on a diver, for a total of 2 atm. At 100 ft down, there is a total pressure of 4 atm on a diver. The air tanks a diver carries continuously adjust the pressure of the breathing mixture to match the increase in pressure.

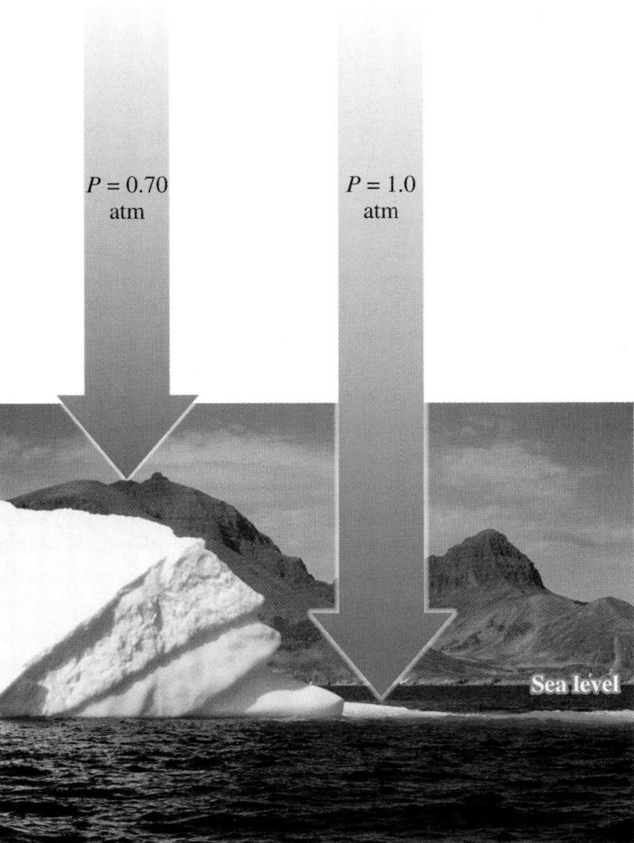


**TABLE 7.3** Altitude and Atmospheric Pressure

| Location | Altitude (km) | Atmospheric Pressure (mmHg) |
|---|---|---|
| Dead Sea | −0.40 | 800 |
| Sea level | 0 | 760 |
| Los Angeles | 0.09 | 752 |
| Las Vegas | 0.70 | 700 |
| Denver | 1.60 | 630 |
| Mount Whitney | 4.50 | 440 |
| Mount Everest | 8.90 | 253 |

SAMPLE PROBLEM 7.1

### Units of Pressure

A sample of neon gas has a pressure of 0.50 atm. Give the pressure of the neon in mmHg.

SOLUTION

The equality 1 atm = 760 mmHg can be written as conversion factors:

$$\frac{760 \text{ mmHg}}{1 \text{ atm}} \quad \text{and} \quad \frac{1 \text{ atm}}{760 \text{ mmHg}}$$

Using the appropriate conversion factor, the problem is set up as

$$0.50 \cancel{\text{atm}} \times \frac{760 \text{ mmHg}}{1 \cancel{\text{atm}}} = 380 \text{ mmHg}$$

STUDY CHECK

What is the pressure, in atmospheres, for a gas that has a pressure of 655 torr?

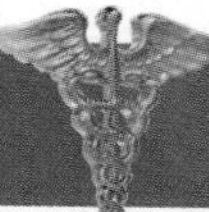

## HEALTH NOTE

### Measuring Blood Pressure

Your blood pressure is one of the vital signs a doctor or nurse checks during a physical examination. It actually consists of two separate measurements. Acting as a pump, the heart contracts to create the pressure that pushes blood through the circulatory system. During contraction, the blood pressure is at its highest; this is your *systolic* pressure. When the heart muscles relax, the blood pressure falls; this is your *diastolic* pressure. The normal range for systolic pressure is 100–120 mmHg. For diastolic pressure, it is 60–80 mmHg. These two measurements are usually expressed as a ratio such as 100/80. These values are somewhat higher in older people. When blood pressures are elevated, say, 140/90, there is a greater risk of stroke, heart attack, or kidney damage. Low blood pressure prevents the brain from receiving adequate oxygen, causing dizziness and fainting.

The blood pressures are measured by a sphygmomanometer, an instrument consisting of a stethoscope and an inflatable cuff connected to a tube of mercury called a manometer. After the cuff is wrapped around the upper arm, it is pumped up with air until it cuts off the flow of blood through the arm. With the stethoscope over the artery, the air is slowly released from the cuff. When the pressure equals the systolic pressure, blood starts to flow again, and the noise it makes is heard through the stethoscope. As air continues to be released, the cuff deflates until no sound is heard in the artery. That second pressure reading is noted as the diastolic pressure, the pressure when the heart is not contracting.

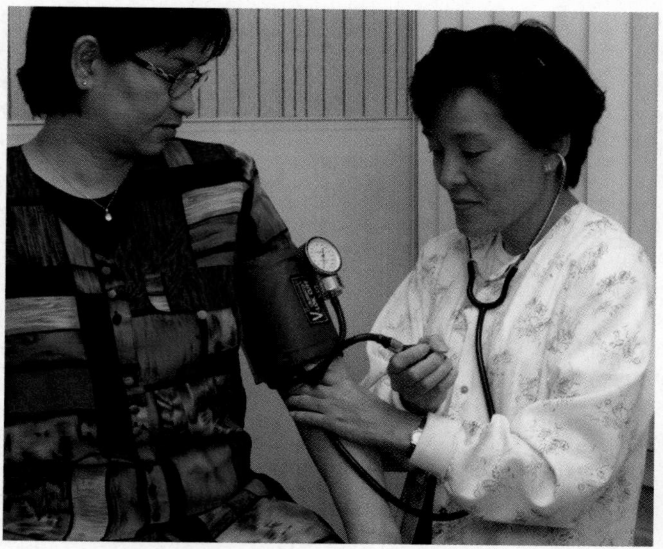

The use of digital blood pressure monitors is becoming more common. However, they have not been validated for use in all situations and can sometimes give inaccurate readings.

## QUESTIONS AND PROBLEMS

### Gas Pressure

7.5 What units are used to measure the pressure of a gas?

7.6 Which of the following statement(s) describes the pressure of a gas?
- **a.** the force of the gas particles on the walls of the container
- **b.** the number of gas particles in a container
- **c.** the volume of the container
- **d.** 3.00 atm
- **e.** 750 torr

7.7 An oxygen tank contains oxygen ($O_2$) at a pressure of 2.00 atm. What is the pressure in the tank in terms of the following units?
- **a.** torr
- **b.** mmHg

7.8 On a climb up Mt. Whitney, the atmospheric pressure is 467 mmHg. What is the pressure in terms of the following units?
- **a.** atm
- **b.** torr

## 7.3 Pressure and Volume (Boyle's Law)

**LEARNING GOAL**

Use the pressure–volume relationship (Boyle's law) to determine the new pressure or volume of a certain amount of gas at a constant temperature.

Imagine that you can see air particles hitting the walls inside a bicycle tire pump. What happens to the pressure inside the pump as you push down on the handle? As the volume decreases, there is a decrease in the surface area of the container. The air particles are crowded together, more collisions occur, and the pressure increases within the container.

When a change in one property (in this case, volume) causes a change in another property (in this case, pressure), the two properties are related. If the changes occur in opposite directions, the properties have an **inverse relationship**. The inverse relationship between the pressure and volume of a gas is known as **Boyle's law**. The law states that the volume ($V$) of a sample of gas changes inversely with the pressure ($P$) of the gas as long as there has been no change in the temperature ($T$) or amount of gas ($n$), as illustrated in Figure 7.4.

If the volume or pressure of a gas sample changes without any change in the temperature or in the amount of the gas, then the new pressure and volume will give the same $PV$ product as the initial pressure and volume. Therefore, we can set the initial and final $PV$ products equal to each other.

**Boyle's Law**

$P_1V_1 = P_2V_2$ No change in number of moles and temperature

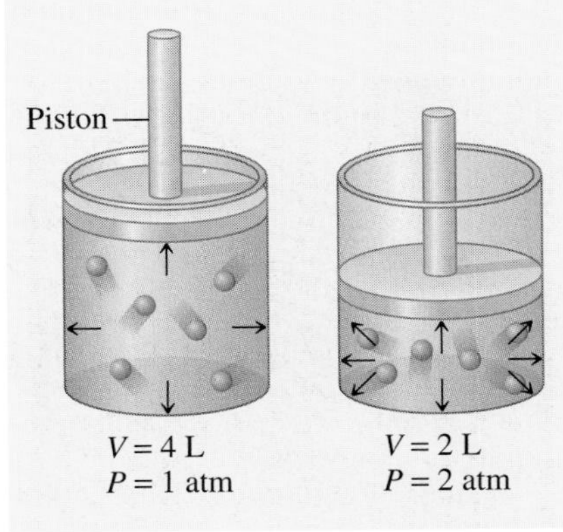


**FIGURE 7.4 Boyle's law:** As volume decreases, gas molecules become more crowded, which causes the pressure to increase. Pressure ($P$) and volume ($V$) are inversely related.

Q If the volume of a gas increases, what will happen to its pressure?

**CONCEPT CHECK 7.2**

**Boyle's Law**

State and explain the reason for the change (*increases, decreases*) in a gas that occurs for the following when $n$ and $T$ do not change:

| | Pressure | Volume |
|---|---|---|
| **a.** | | Decreases |
| **b.** | Decreases | |

ANSWER

**a.** Increases. When the volume of a gas decreases (at constant $n$ and $T$), the gas particles are closer together, which increases the number of collisions with the container walls.

**b.** Increases. When the pressure of a gas decreases (at constant $n$ and $T$), there are fewer collisions with the container walls, which indicates that the volume has increased.

TUTORIAL
Pressure and Volume

**SAMPLE PROBLEM 7.2**

**Calculating Pressure When Volume Changes**

A sample of hydrogen gas ($H_2$) has a volume of 5.0 L and a pressure of 1.0 atm. What is the new pressure if the volume is decreased to 2.0 L at constant temperature?

SOLUTION

**STEP 1** **Organize the data in a table.** In this problem, we want to know the final pressure ($P_2$) for the change in volume. In calculations with gas laws, it is helpful to organize the data in a table. Because we know that the volume decreases, we can predict that the pressure will increase.

| Conditions 1 | Conditions 2 | Know | Predict |
|---|---|---|---|
| $V_1 = 5.0$ L | $V_2 = 2.0$ L | $V$ decreases | |
| $P_1 = 1.0$ atm | $P_2 = ?$ | | $P$ increases |

**STEP 2** **Rearrange the gas law for the unknown.** For a $PV$ relationship, we use Boyle's law and solve for $P_2$ by dividing both sides by $V_2$:

$$P_1V_1 = P_2V_2$$

$$\frac{P_1V_1}{V_2} = \frac{P_2\cancel{V_2}}{\cancel{V_2}}$$

$$P_2 = P_1 \times \frac{V_1}{V_2}$$

**Guide to Using the Gas Laws**

STEP 1 Organize the data in a table of initial and final conditions.

STEP 2 Rearrange the gas law to solve for the unknown quantity.

STEP 3 Substitute values into the gas law equation to solve for the unknown.

**STEP 3** **Substitute values into the gas law to solve for the unknown.** When we substitute in the values, we see that the ratio of the volumes (volume factor) is greater than 1, which increases the pressure. The final pressure ($P_2$) has increased as we predicted in Step 1. Note that the units of volume (L) cancel to give the final pressure in atmospheres.

$$P_2 = 1.0 \text{ atm} \times \frac{5.0 \cancel{\text{L}}}{2.0 \cancel{\text{L}}} = 2.5 \text{ atm}$$

Volume factor increases pressure

STUDY CHECK

A sample of helium gas has a volume of 150 mL at 750 torr. If the volume expands to 450 mL at constant temperature, what is the new pressure in torr?

SAMPLE PROBLEM 7.3

### Calculating Volume When Pressure Changes

The gauge on a 12-L tank of compressed oxygen reads 3800 mmHg. How many liters would this same gas occupy at a pressure of 0.75 atm at constant temperature?

SOLUTION

**STEP 1** **Organize the data in a table.** To match the units for pressure, we can convert atm to mmHg, or mmHg to atm.

$$0.75 \cancel{\text{atm}} \times \frac{760 \text{ mmHg}}{1 \cancel{\text{atm}}} = 570 \text{ mmHg}$$

$$3800 \cancel{\text{mmHg}} \times \frac{1 \text{ atm}}{1 \cancel{\text{mmHg}}} = 5.0 \text{ atm}$$

Placing our information using units of mmHg for pressure in a table, we know that pressure decreases. We can predict that the volume should increase. (We could have both pressures in units of atm as well.)

| Conditions 1 | Conditions 2 | Know | Predict |
|---|---|---|---|
| $P_1 = 3800$ mmHg | $P_2 = 570$ mmHg | $P$ decreases | |
| $V_1 = 12$ L | $V_2 = ?$ | | $V$ increases |

**STEP 2** **Rearrange the gas law for the unknown.** Using Boyle's law, we solve for $V_2$. According to Boyle's law, a decrease in the pressure will cause an increase in the volume.

$$P_1V_1 = P_2V_2$$

$$\frac{P_1V_1}{P_2} = \frac{\cancel{P_2}V_2}{\cancel{P_2}}$$

$$V_2 = V_1 \times \frac{P_1}{P_2}$$

**STEP 3** **Substitute values into the gas law to solve for the unknown.** When we substitute in the values with pressures in units of mmHg or atm, the ratio of pressures (pressure factor) is greater than 1, which increases the volume.

$$V_2 = 12 \text{ L} \times \frac{3800 \cancel{\text{mmHg}}}{570 \cancel{\text{mmHg}}} = 80. \text{ L}$$

Pressure factor increases volume

Or:

$$V_2 = 12 \text{ L} \times \frac{5.0 \cancel{\text{atm}}}{0.75 \cancel{\text{atm}}} = 80. \text{ L}$$

Pressure factor increases volume

STUDY CHECK

A sample of methane gas ($CH_4$) has a volume of 125 mL at 0.600 atm pressure. How many milliliters will it occupy at a pressure of 1.50 atm at constant temperature?

## HEALTH NOTE

### Pressure–Volume Relationship in Breathing

The importance of Boyle's law becomes more apparent when you consider the mechanics of breathing. Our lungs are elastic, balloonlike structures contained within an airtight chamber called the thoracic cavity. The diaphragm, a muscle, forms the flexible floor of the cavity.

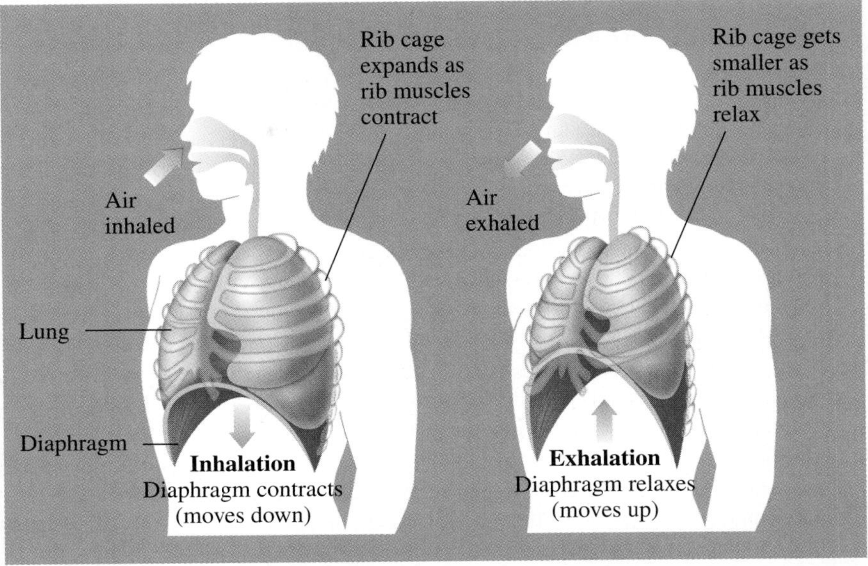


#### Inspiration

The process of taking a breath of air begins when the diaphragm contracts and the rib cage expands, causing an increase in the volume of the thoracic cavity. The elasticity of the lungs allows them to expand when the thoracic cavity expands. According to Boyle's law, the pressure inside the lungs will decrease when their volume increases, causing the pressure inside the lungs to fall below the pressure of the atmosphere. This difference in pressures produces a *pressure gradient* between the lungs and the atmosphere. In a pressure gradient, molecules flow from an area of greater pressure to an area of lower pressure. Thus, we inhale as air flows into the lungs (*inspiration*), until the pressure within the lungs becomes equal to the pressure of the atmosphere.

#### Expiration

*Expiration*, or the exhalation phase of breathing, occurs when the diaphragm relaxes and moves back up into the thoracic cavity to its resting position. This reduces the volume of the thoracic cavity, which squeezes the lungs and decreases their volume. Now the pressure in the lungs is greater than the pressure of the atmosphere, so air flows out of the lungs. Thus, breathing is a process in which pressure gradients are continuously created between the lungs and the environment because of the changes in the volume.

## QUESTIONS AND PROBLEMS

### Pressure and Volume (Boyle's Law)

**7.9** Why do scuba divers need to exhale air when they ascend to the surface of the water?

**7.10** Why does a sealed bag of chips expand when you take it to a higher altitude?

**7.11** The air in a cylinder with a piston has a volume of 220 mL and a pressure of 650 mmHg.

**a.** To obtain a higher pressure inside the cylinder at constant temperature, should the cylinder change as shown in A or B? Explain your choice.

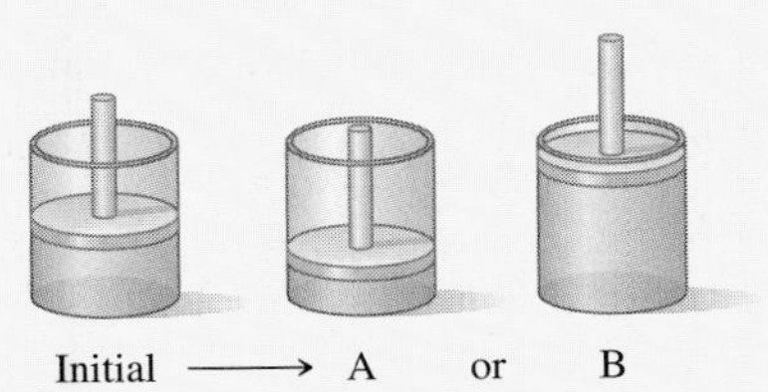


**b.** If the pressure inside the cylinder increases to 1.2 atm, what is the final volume of the cylinder? Complete the following data table:

| Property | Conditions 1 | Conditions 2 | Know | Predict |
|---|---|---|---|---|
| Pressure ($P$) | | | | |
| Volume ($V$) | | | | |

**7.12** A balloon is filled with helium gas. When the following changes are made at constant temperature, which of these diagrams (A, B, or C) shows the new volume of the balloon?

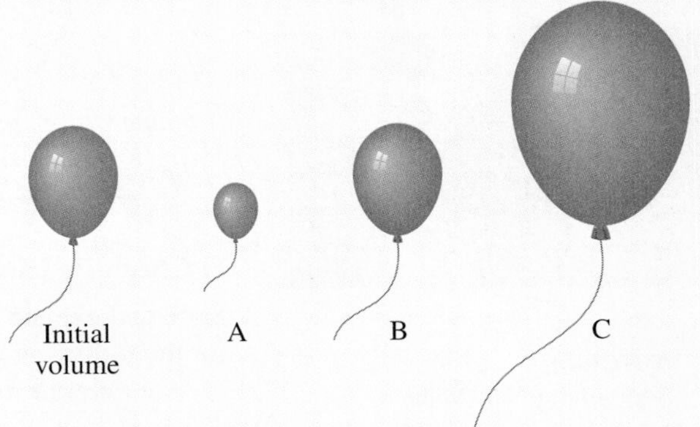


**a.** The balloon floats to a higher altitude where the outside pressure is lower.

**b.** The balloon is taken inside the house, but the atmospheric pressure remains the same.

**c.** The balloon is put in a hyperbaric chamber in which the pressure is increased.

**7.13** A gas with a volume of 4.0 L is in a closed container. Indicate what changes in pressure must have occurred if the volume undergoes the following changes at constant temperature:
**a.** The volume is compressed to 2 L.
**b.** The volume is allowed to expand to 12 L.
**c.** The volume is compressed to 0.40 L.

**7.14** A gas at a pressure of 2.0 atm is in a closed container. Indicate the changes in its volume when the pressure undergoes the following changes at constant temperature:
**a.** The pressure increases to 6.0 atm.
**b.** The pressure drops to 1.0 atm.
**c.** The pressure drops to 0.40 atm.

**7.15** A 10.0-L balloon contains helium gas at a pressure of 655 mmHg. What is the new pressure of the helium gas at each of the following volumes if there is no change in temperature?
**a.** 20.0 L **b.** 2.50 L **c.** 1500 mL

**7.16** The air in a 5.00-L tank has a pressure of 1.20 atm. What is the new pressure of the air when the air is placed in tanks that have the following volumes if there is no change in temperature?
**a.** 1.00 L **b.** 2500. mL **c.** 750. mL

**7.17** A sample of nitrogen ($N_2$) has a volume of 50.0 L at a pressure of 760 mmHg. What is the volume of the gas at each of the following pressures if there is no change in temperature?
**a.** 1500 mmHg **b.** 2.0 atm **c.** 0.500 atm

**7.18** A sample of methane ($CH_4$) has a volume of 25 mL at a pressure of 0.80 atm. What is the volume of the gas at each of the following pressures if there is no change in temperature?
**a.** 0.40 atm **b.** 2.00 atm **c.** 2500 mmHg

**7.19** Cyclopropane, $C_3H_6$, is a general anesthetic. A 5.0-L sample has a pressure of 5.0 atm. What is the volume of the anesthetic given to a patient at a pressure of 1.0 atm?

**7.20** The volume of air in a person's lungs is 615 mL at a pressure of 760 mmHg. Inhalation occurs as the pressure in the lungs drops to 752 mmHg. To what volume did the lungs expand?

**7.21** Use the words *inspiration* and *expiration* to describe the part of the breathing cycle that occurs because of each of the following:
**a.** The diaphragm contracts (flattens out).
**b.** The volume of the lungs decreases.
**c.** The pressure within the lungs is less than the atmosphere.

**7.22** Use the words *inspiration* and *expiration* to describe the part of the breathing cycle that occurs because of each of the following:
**a.** The diaphragm relaxes, moving up into the thoracic cavity.
**b.** The volume of the lungs expands.
**c.** The pressure within the lungs is greater than the atmosphere.

## 7.4 Temperature and Volume (Charles's Law)

LEARNING GOAL

Use the temperature–volume relationship (Charles's law) to determine the new temperature or volume of a certain amount of gas at a constant pressure.

MC™ TUTORIAL
Temperature and Volume

Suppose that you are going to take a ride in a hot-air balloon. The captain turns on a propane burner to heat the air inside the balloon. As the temperature rises, the air particles move faster and spread out, causing the volume of the balloon to increase. As the air is heated, it becomes less dense than the air outside, causing the balloon and its passengers to lift off. In 1787, Jacques Charles, a balloonist as well as a physicist, proposed that the volume of a gas is related to the temperature. This proposal became **Charles's law**, which states that the volume ($V$) of a gas is directly related to the temperature ($T$) when there is no change in the pressure ($P$) or amount ($n$) of gas. (See Figure 7.5.) A **direct relationship** is one in which the related properties increase or decrease together. For two conditions, we can write Charles's law as follows:

**Charles's Law**

$$\frac{V_1}{T_1} = \frac{V_2}{T_2}$$ No change in number of moles and pressure

*All temperatures used in gas law calculations must be converted to their corresponding Kelvin (K) temperatures.*

CONCEPT CHECK 7.3

### Charles's Law

State and explain the reason for the change (*increases, decreases*) in a gas that occurs for the following when $P$ and $n$ do not change:

| | Temperature | Volume |
|---|---|---|
| **a.** | Increases | |
| **b.** | Decreases | |

ANSWER

**a.** Increases. When the temperature of a gas increases (at constant $P$ and $n$), the gas particles move faster. To keep the pressure constant, the volume of the container must increase.

**b.** Decreases. When the temperature of a gas decreases (at constant $P$ and $n$), the gas particles move slower. To keep the pressure constant, the volume of the container must decrease.

SAMPLE PROBLEM 7.4

## Calculating Volume When Temperature Changes

A sample of neon gas has a volume of 5.40 L and a temperature of 15 °C. Find the new volume of the gas after the temperature has been increased to 42 °C at constant pressure.

SOLUTION

**STEP 1** **Organize the data in a table.** When the temperatures are given in degrees Celsius, they must be changed to kelvins.

$$T_1 = 15\ °\text{C} + 273 = 288\ \text{K}$$
$$T_2 = 42\ °\text{C} + 273 = 315\ \text{K}$$

| Conditions 1 | Conditions 2 | Know | Predict |
|---|---|---|---|
| $T_1 = 288$ K | $T_2 = 315$ K | $T$ increases | |
| $V_1 = 5.40$ L | $V_2 = ?$ | | $V$ increases |

**STEP 2** **Rearrange the gas law for the unknown.** In this problem, we want to know the final volume ($V_2$) when the temperature increases. Using Charles's law, we solve for $V_2$ by multiplying both sides by $T_2$:

$$\frac{V_1}{T_1} = \frac{V_2}{T_2}$$
$$\frac{V_1}{T_1} \times T_2 = \frac{V_2}{\cancel{T_2}} \times \cancel{T_2}$$
$$V_2 = V_1 \times \frac{T_2}{T_1}$$

**STEP 3** **Substitute values into the gas law to solve for the unknown.** From the table, we see that the temperature has increased. Because temperature is directly related to volume, the volume must increase. When we substitute in the values, we see that the ratio of the temperatures (temperature factor) is greater than 1, which increases the volume, as predicted:

$$V_2 = 5.40\ \text{L} \times \frac{315\ \cancel{\text{K}}}{288\ \cancel{\text{K}}} = 5.91\ \text{L}$$

Temperature factor increases volume

STUDY CHECK

A mountain climber inhales 486 mL of air at a temperature of −8 °C. What volume, in mL, will the air occupy in the lungs if the climber's body temperature is 37 °C?

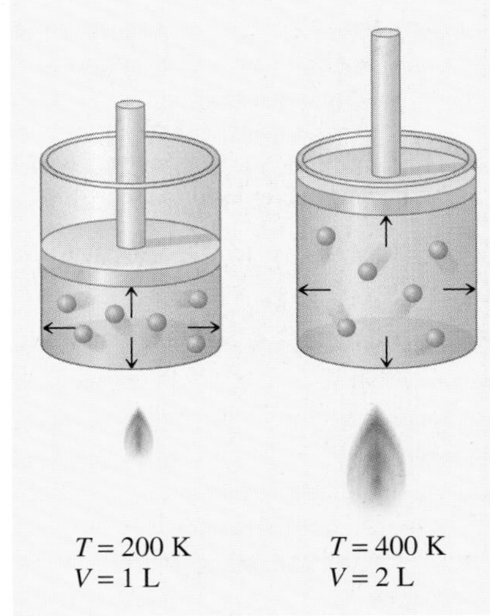


**FIGURE 7.5** **Charles's law:** The Kelvin temperature of a gas is directly related to the volume of the gas when there is no change in the pressure. When the temperature increases, making the molecules move faster, the volume must increase to maintain constant pressure.

**Q** If the temperature of a gas decreases at constant pressure, how will the volume change?

# QUESTIONS AND PROBLEMS

## Temperature and Volume (Charles's Law)

**7.23** Select the diagram that shows the new volume of a balloon when the following changes are made at constant pressure:

**a.** The temperature is changed from 100 K to 300 K.
**b.** The balloon is placed in a freezer.
**c.** The balloon is first warmed, and then returned to its starting temperature.

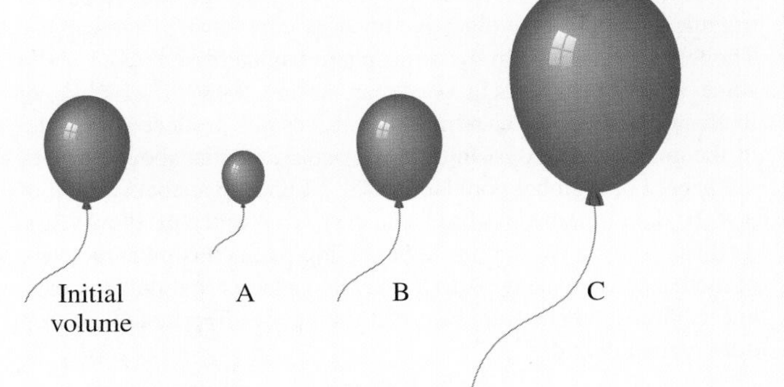

**7.24** Indicate whether the final volume of gas in each of the following is the same, larger, or smaller than the initial volume:

**a.** A volume of 500 mL of air on a cold winter day at 5 °C is breathed into the lungs, where body temperature is 37 °C.
**b.** The heater used to heat 1400 L of air in a hot-air balloon is turned off.
**c.** A balloon filled with helium at the amusement park is left in a car on a hot day.

**7.25** A sample of neon initially has a volume of 2.50 L at 15 °C. What is the new temperature, in °C, when the volume of the sample is changed at constant pressure to each of the following?

**a.** 5.00 L **b.** 1250 mL
**c.** 7.50 L **d.** 3550 mL

**7.26** A gas has a volume of 4.00 L at 0 °C. What final temperature, in degrees Celsius, is needed to cause the volume of the gas to change to the following, if $n$ and $P$ are not changed?

**a.** 100. L **b.** 1200 mL
**c.** 250 L **d.** 50.0 mL

**7.27** A balloon contains 2500 mL of helium gas at 75 °C. What is the new volume (mL) of the gas when the temperature changes to the following, if $n$ and $P$ are not changed?

**a.** 55 °C **b.** 680. K
**c.** −25 °C **d.** 240. K

**7.28** An air bubble has a volume of 0.500 L at 18 °C. If the pressure does not change, what is the volume, in liters, at each of the following temperatures?

**a.** 0 °C **b.** 425 K
**c.** −12 °C **d.** 575 K

# GREEN CHEMISTRY NOTE

## Greenhouse Gases

The term "greenhouse gases" was first used during the early 1800s for the gases in the atmosphere that trap heat. Among the greenhouse gases are carbon dioxide ($CO_2$), methane ($CH_4$), dinitrogen oxide ($N_2O$), and chlorofluorocarbons (CFCs). The molecules of greenhouse gases consist of more than two atoms that vibrate when heat is absorbed. By contrast, oxygen and nitrogen are not greenhouse gases. Because the two atoms in their molecules are so tightly bonded, they do not absorb heat.

**Percentages of Greenhouse Gases in the Atmosphere**

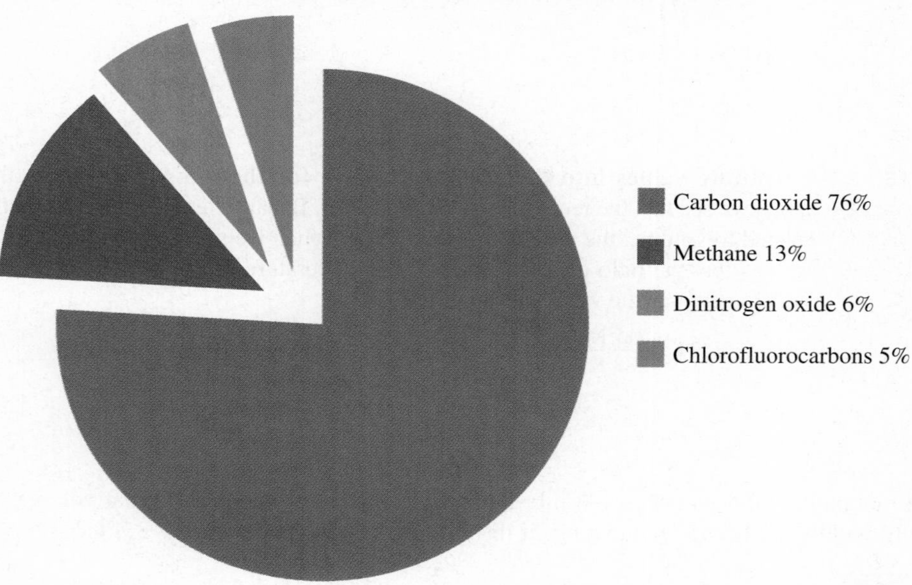


Greenhouses gases are beneficial in keeping the average surface temperature for Earth at 15 °C. Without greenhouse gases, it is estimated that the average surface temperature of Earth would be −18 °C. Most scientists say that the concentration of greenhouse gases in the atmosphere and the surface temperature of Earth are increasing because of human activities. As we discussed in Chapter 2, the increase in atmospheric carbon dioxide is mostly a result of the burning of fossil fuels and wood.

Methane ($CH_4$) is a colorless, odorless gas that is released by livestock, rice farming, the decomposition of organic plant material in landfills, and the mining, drilling, and transport of coal and oil. The contribution from livestock comes from the breakdown of organic material in the digestive tracts of cows, sheep, and camels. The level of methane in the atmosphere has increased about 150% since industrialization. In one year, as much as $5 \times 10^{11}$ kg of methane are added to the atmosphere. Livestock produce about 20% of the greenhouse gases. In one day, one cow emits about 200 g of methane. For a global population of 1.5 billion livestock, a total of $3 \times 10^8$ kg of methane is produced every day. In the past few years, methane levels have stabilized due to improvements in the recovery of methane. Methane remains in the atmosphere for about ten years, but its molecular structure causes it to trap 20 times more heat than does carbon dioxide.

Dinitrogen oxide ($N_2O$), commonly called nitrous oxide, is a colorless greenhouse gas that has a sweet odor. Most people recognize it as an anesthetic used in dentistry called "laughing gas." Although some dinitrogen oxide is released naturally from soil bacteria, its primary increases are from agricultural and industrial processes. Atmospheric dinitrogen oxide has increased by about 15% since industrialization, caused by the extensive use of fertilizers, sewage treatment plants, and car exhaust. Each year, $1 \times 10^{10}$ kg of dinitrogen oxide is added to the atmosphere. Dinitrogen oxide released today will remain in the atmosphere for about 150–180 years, where it has a greenhouse effect that is 300 times greater than that of carbon dioxide.

Chlorofluorinated gases (CFCs) are synthetic compounds containing chlorine, fluorine, and carbon. Chlorofluorocarbons were used as propellants in aerosol cans and as refrigerants in refrigerators and air conditioners. During the 1970s, scientists determined that CFCs in the atmosphere were destroying the protective ozone layer. Since then, many countries have banned the production and use of CFCs, and their levels in the atmosphere have declined slightly. Hydrofluorocarbons (HFCs), in which hydrogen atoms replace chlorine atoms, are now used as refrigerants. Although HFCs do not destroy the ozone layer, they are greenhouse gases because they trap heat in the atmosphere.

Based on current trends and climate models, scientists estimate that levels of atmospheric carbon dioxide will increase by about 2% each year up through 2025. As long as the greenhouse gases trap more heat than is reflected back into space, average surface temperatures on Earth will continue to rise. Efforts are taking place around the world to slow or decrease the emissions of greenhouse gases into the atmosphere. It is anticipated that temperatures will stabilize only when the amount of energy that reaches the surface of Earth is equal to the heat that is reflected back into space.

In 2007, former U.S. Vice President Al Gore and the United Nations Panel on Climate Change were awarded the Nobel Peace Prize for increasing global awareness of the relationship between human activities and global warming.

## 7.5 Temperature and Pressure (Gay–Lussac's Law)

**LEARNING GOAL**

Use the temperature–pressure relationship (Gay–Lussac's law) to determine the new temperature or pressure of a certain amount of gas at a constant volume.

If we could watch the molecules of a gas as the temperature rises, we would notice that they move faster and hit the sides of the container more often and with greater force. If we keep the volume of the container the same, we would observe an increase in the pressure. A temperature–pressure relationship, also known as **Gay–Lussac's law**, states that the pressure of a gas is directly related to its Kelvin temperature. This means that an increase in temperature increases the pressure of a gas, and a decrease in temperature decreases the pressure of the gas, provided the volume and number of moles of the gas remain the same. (See Figure 7.6.) The ratio of pressure ($P$) to temperature ($T$) is the same under all conditions as long as volume ($V$) and amount of gas ($n$) do not change.

**Gay–Lussac's Law**

$$\frac{P_1}{T_1} = \frac{P_2}{T_2} \quad \text{No change in number of moles and volume}$$

*All temperatures used in gas law calculations must be converted to their corresponding Kelvin (K) temperatures.*

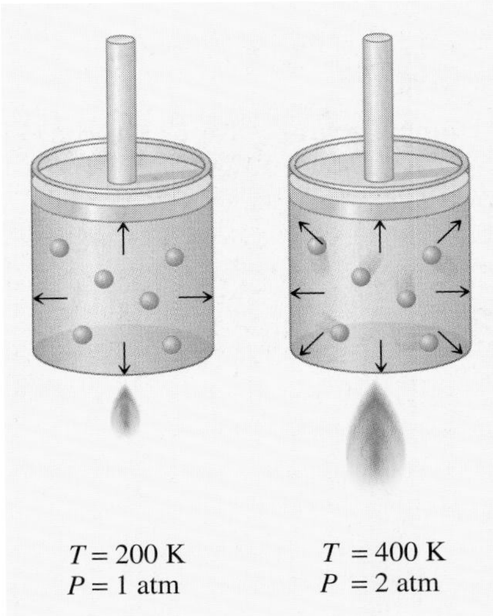


**FIGURE 7.6** Gay–Lussac's law: The pressure of a gas is directly related to the temperature of the gas. When the Kelvin temperature of a gas is doubled, the pressure is doubled at constant volume.

Q How does a decrease in the temperature of a gas affect its pressure at constant volume?

**CONCEPT CHECK 7.4**

### Gay–Lussac's Law

State and explain the reason for the change (*increases, decreases*) in a gas that occurs for the following when $V$ and $n$ do not change:

| | Temperature | Pressure |
|---|---|---|
| **a.** | Increases | |
| **b.** | Decreases | |

ANSWER

**a.** Increases. When the temperature of a gas (at constant $V$ and $n$) increases, the gas particles move faster. When the volume does not change, the gas particles collide with the walls more often and with more force, which increases the pressure.

**b.** Decreases. When the temperature of a gas (at constant $V$ and $n$) decreases, the gas particles move slower. When the volume does not change, the gas particles collide less often with the walls of the container and with less force, which decreases the pressure.

TUTORIAL
Temperature and Pressure

**SAMPLE PROBLEM 7.5**

### Calculating Pressure When Temperature Changes

Aerosol containers can be dangerous if they are heated because they can explode. Suppose a container of hair spray with a pressure of 4.0 atm at a room temperature of 25 °C is thrown into a fire. If the temperature of the gas inside the aerosol can reaches 402 °C, what will be its pressure? The aerosol container may explode if the pressure inside exceeds 8.0 atm. Would you expect it to explode?

SOLUTION

**STEP 1** **Organize the data in a table.** We must first change the temperatures to kelvins.

$$T_1 = 25\ °C + 273 = 298\ K$$

$$T_2 = 402\ °C + 273 = 675\ K$$

| Conditions 1 | Conditions 2 | Know | Predict |
|---|---|---|---|
| $P_1 = 4.0$ atm | $P_2 = ?$ | | $P$ increases |
| $T_1 = 298$ K | $T_2 = 675$ K | $T$ increases | |

**STEP 2** **Rearrange the gas law for the unknown.** Using Gay-Lussac's law, we can solve for $P_2$.

$$\frac{P_1}{T_1} = \frac{P_2}{T_2}$$

$$\frac{P_1}{T_1} \times T_2 = \frac{P_2}{\cancel{T_2}} \times \cancel{T_2}$$

$$P_2 = P_1 \times \frac{T_2}{T_1}$$

**STEP 3** **Substitute values into the gas law to solve for the unknown.** From the table, we see that the temperature has increased. Because pressure and temperature are directly related, the pressure must increase. When we substitute in the values, we see the ratio of the temperatures (temperature factor) is greater than 1, which increases pressure.

$$P_2 = 4.0\text{ atm} \times \frac{675\ \cancel{K}}{298\ \cancel{K}} = 9.1\text{ atm}$$

Temperature factor increases volume

Because the calculated pressure of 9.1 atm is greater than 8.0 atm, we expect the can to explode.

STUDY CHECK

In a storage area where the temperature has reached 55 °C, the pressure of oxygen gas in a 15.0-L steel cylinder is 965 torr. To what temperature (°C) would the gas have to be cooled to reduce the pressure to 850. torr?

**TABLE 7.4** Vapor Pressure of Water

| Temperature (°C) | Vapor Pressure (mmHg) |
|---|---|
| 0 | 5 |
| 10 | 9 |
| 20 | 18 |
| 30 | 32 |
| 37 | 47[a] |
| 40 | 55 |
| 50 | 93 |
| 60 | 149 |
| 70 | 234 |
| 80 | 355 |
| 90 | 528 |
| 100 | 760 |

[a]At body temperature.

**TABLE 7.5** Pressure and the Boiling Point of Water

| Pressure (mmHg) | Boiling Point (°C) |
|---|---|
| 270 | 70 |
| 467 | 87 |
| 630 | 95 |
| 752 | 99 |
| 760 | 100 |
| 800 | 100.4 |
| 1075 | 110 |
| 1520 (2 atm) | 120 |
| 2026 | 130 |
| 7600 (10 atm) | 180 |

## Vapor Pressure and Boiling Point

In Chapter 2, we learned that liquid molecules with sufficient kinetic energy can break away from the surface of the liquid as they become gas particles or vapor. In an open container, all the liquid will eventually evaporate. In a closed container, the vapor accumulates and creates pressure called **vapor pressure**. Each liquid exerts its own vapor pressure at a given temperature. As temperature increases, more vapor forms, and vapor pressure increases. Table 7.4 lists the vapor pressure of water at various temperatures.

A liquid reaches its boiling point when its vapor pressure becomes equal to the external pressure. As boiling occurs, bubbles of the gas form within the liquid and quickly rise to the surface. For example, at an atmospheric pressure of 760 mmHg, water will boil at 100 °C, the temperature at which its vapor pressure reaches 760 mmHg. (See Table 7.5.)

At higher altitudes, where atmospheric pressures are lower, the boiling point of water is lower than 100 °C. Earlier, we saw that the typical atmospheric pressure in Denver is 630 mmHg. This means that water in Denver needs a vapor pressure of 630 mmHg to boil. Because water has a vapor pressure of 630 mmHg at 95 °C, water boils at 95 °C in Denver.

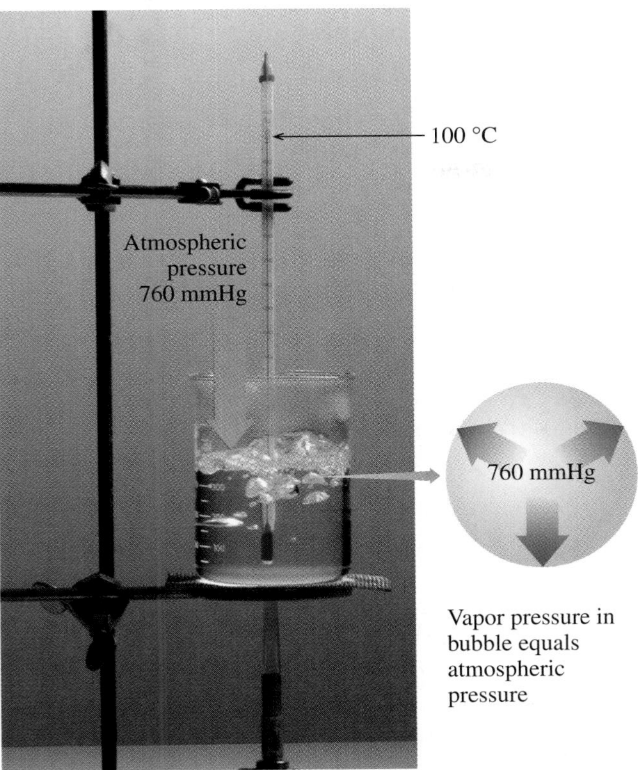

People who live at high altitudes often use pressure cookers to obtain higher temperatures when preparing food. When the external pressure is greater than 1 atm, a temperature higher than 100 °C is needed to boil water. Laboratories and hospitals use devices called *autoclaves* to sterilize laboratory and surgical equipment. An autoclave, like a pressure cooker, is a closed container that increases the total pressure above the liquid so it will boil at higher temperatures.

TUTORIAL
Vapor Pressure and Boiling Point

## QUESTIONS AND PROBLEMS

### Temperature and Pressure (Gay–Lussac's Law)

7.29 Why do aerosol cans explode if heated?

**7.30** Why is there an increased danger of the tires on a car having a blowout when the car is driven on hot pavement in the desert?

7.31 For the following, calculate the new temperature, in degrees Celsius, when pressure is changed, with $n$ and $V$ constant:
- **a.** A sample of xenon at 25 °C and 745 mmHg is cooled to give a pressure of 625 mmHg.
- **b.** A tank of argon gas with a pressure of 0.950 atm at −18 °C is heated to give a pressure of 1250 torr.

**7.32** For the following, calculate the new temperature, in degrees Celsius, when pressure is changed, with $n$ and $V$ constant:
- **a.** A tank of helium gas with a pressure of 250 torr at 0 °C is heated to give a pressure of 1500 torr.
- **b.** A sample of air at 40. °C and 745 mmHg is cooled to give a pressure of 685 mmHg.

7.33 Solve for the new pressure when each of the following temperature changes occurs, with $n$ and $V$ constant:
- **a.** A gas with an initial pressure of 1200 torr at 155 °C is cooled to 0 °C.
- **b.** A gas in an aerosol container at an initial pressure of 1.40 atm at 12 °C is heated to 35 °C.

**7.34** Solve for the new pressure in each of the following, with $n$ and $V$ constant:
- **a.** A gas with a pressure of 1.20 atm at 75 °C is cooled to −22 °C.
- **b.** A sample of $N_2$ with a pressure of 780 mmHg at −75 °C is heated to 28 °C.

7.35 Match the terms *vapor pressure, atmospheric pressure*, and *boiling point* to the following descriptions:
- **a.** the temperature at which bubbles of vapor appear within the liquid
- **b.** the pressure exerted by a gas above the surface of its liquid
- **c.** the pressure exerted on Earth by the particles in the air
- **d.** the temperature at which the vapor pressure of a liquid becomes equal to the external pressure

**7.36** In which pair(s) would boiling occur?

| | Atmospheric Pressure | Vapor Pressure |
|---|---|---|
| **a.** | 760 mmHg | 700 mmHg |
| **b.** | 480 torr | 480 mmHg |
| **c.** | 1.2 atm | 912 mmHg |
| **d.** | 1020 mmHg | 760 mmHg |
| **e.** | 740 torr | 1.0 atm |

**7.37** Explain the following observations:

**a.** Water boils at 87 °C on the top of Mt. Whitney.

**b.** Food cooks more quickly in a pressure cooker than in an open pan.

**7.38** Explain the following observations:

**a.** Boiling water at sea level is hotter than boiling water in the mountains.

**b.** Water used to sterilize surgical equipment is heated to 120 °C at 2.0 atm in an autoclave.

## 7.6 The Combined Gas Law

**LEARNING GOAL**

Use the combined gas law to find the new pressure, volume, or temperature of a gas when changes in two of these properties are given.

All the pressure–volume–temperature relationships for gases that we have studied may be combined into a single relationship called the **combined gas law**. This expression is useful for studying the effect of changes in two of these variables on the third as long as the amount of gas (number of moles) remains constant.

**Combined Gas Law**

$$\frac{P_1V_1}{T_1} = \frac{P_2V_2}{T_2} \quad \text{No change in moles of gas}$$

By using the combined gas law, we can derive any of the gas laws by omitting those properties that do not change, as seen in Table 7.6.

**TABLE 7.6** Summary of Gas Laws

| Combined Gas Law | Properties Held Constant | Relationship | Name of Gas Law |
|---|---|---|---|
| $\frac{P_1V_1}{\cancel{T_1}} = \frac{P_2V_2}{\cancel{T_2}}$ | $T, n$ | $P_1V_1 = P_2V_2$ | Boyle's |
| $\frac{\cancel{P_1}V_1}{T_1} = \frac{\cancel{P_2}V_2}{T_2}$ | $P, n$ | $\frac{V_1}{T_1} = \frac{V_2}{T_2}$ | Charles's |
| $\frac{P_1\cancel{V_1}}{T_1} = \frac{P_2\cancel{V_2}}{T_2}$ | $V, n$ | $\frac{P_1}{T_1} = \frac{P_2}{T_2}$ | Gay–Lussac's |

**CONCEPT CHECK 7.5**

### Combined Gas Law

State and explain the reason for the change (*increases, decreases, no change*) in a gas that occurs for the following when $n$ does not change:

| | Pressure | Volume | Temperature (K) |
|---|---|---|---|
| **a.** | | Twice as large | Half the Kelvin temperature |
| **b.** | Twice as large | | Twice as large |

ANSWER

**a.** Decreases. When the volume (at constant $n$) doubles, the pressure will be halved. If the temperature in Kelvin is halved, the pressure is also halved. The changes in both $V$ and $T$ decrease the pressure to one-fourth its initial value.

**b.** No change. When the Kelvin temperature of a gas (at constant $n$) is doubled, the volume is doubled. But when the pressure is twice as much, the volume must decrease to one-half. The changes offset each other, and no change occurs in the volume.

MC™ TUTORIAL
The Combined Gas Law

**SAMPLE PROBLEM 7.6**

### Using the Combined Gas Law

A 25.0-mL bubble is released from a diver's air tank at a pressure of 4.00 atm and a temperature of 11 °C. What is the volume (mL) of the bubble when it reaches the ocean surface, where the pressure is 1.00 atm and the temperature is 18 °C?

SOLUTION

**STEP 1** **Organize the data in a table.** We must first change the temperature to kelvins.

$$T_1 = 11\ °C + 273 = 284\ K$$
$$T_2 = 18\ °C + 273 = 291\ K$$

| Conditions 1 | Conditions 2 |
|---|---|
| $P_1 = 4.00$ atm | $P_2 = 1.00$ atm |
| $V_1 = 25.0$ mL | $V_2 = ?$ |
| $T_1 = 284$ K | $T_2 = 291$ K |

**STEP 2** **Rearrange the gas law for the unknown.** Because the pressure and temperature are both changing, we must use the combined gas law to solve for $V_2$.

$$\frac{P_1V_1}{T_1} = \frac{P_2V_2}{T_2}$$

$$\frac{P_1V_1}{T_1} \times \frac{T_2}{P_2} = \frac{\cancel{P_2}V_2 \times \cancel{T_2}}{\cancel{T_2} \times \cancel{P_2}}$$

$$V_2 = V_1 \times \frac{P_1}{P_2} \times \frac{T_2}{T_1}$$

**STEP 3** **Substitute the values into the gas law to solve for the unknown.** From the data table, we determine that both the pressure decrease and the temperature increase will increase the volume.

$$V_2 = 25.0\ \text{mL} \times \frac{4.00\ \cancel{\text{atm}}}{1.00\ \cancel{\text{atm}}} \times \frac{291\ \cancel{K}}{284\ \cancel{K}} = 102\ \text{mL}$$

Pressure factor increases volume; Temperature factor increases volume

STUDY CHECK

A weather balloon is filled with 15.0 L of helium at a temperature of 25 °C and a pressure of 685 mmHg. What is the pressure (mmHg) of the helium in the balloon in the upper atmosphere when the temperature is −35 °C and the volume becomes 34.0 L?

## QUESTIONS AND PROBLEMS

### The Combined Gas Law

7.39 A sample of helium gas has a volume of 6.50 L at a pressure of 845 mmHg and a temperature of 25 °C. What is the pressure of the gas, in atm, when the volume and temperature of the gas sample are changed to the following?
**a.** 1850 mL and 325 K **b.** 2.25 L and 12 °C
**c.** 12.8 L and 47 °C

**7.40** A sample of argon gas has a volume of 735 mL at a pressure of 1.20 atm and a temperature of 112 °C. What is the volume of the gas, in milliliters, when the pressure and temperature of the gas sample are changed to the following?
**a.** 658 mmHg and 281 K **b.** 0.55 atm and 75 °C
**c.** 15.4 atm and −15 °C

7.41 A 124-mL bubble of hot gases at 212 °C and 1.80 atm escapes from an active volcano. What is the temperature, in °C, of the gas in the bubble outside the volcano if the new volume of the bubble is 138 mL and the pressure is 0.800 atm?

**7.42** A scuba diver 40 ft below the ocean surface inhales 50.0 mL of compressed air in a scuba tank at a pressure of 3.00 atm and a temperature of 8 °C. What is the pressure of air in the lungs if the gas expands to 150.0 mL at a body temperature of 37 °C?

## 7.7 Volume and Moles (Avogadro's Law)

LEARNING GOAL

Use Avogadro's law to describe the relationship between the amount of a gas and its volume, and use this relationship in calculations.

In our study of the gas laws, we have looked at changes in properties for a specified amount ($n$) of gas. Now we will consider how the properties of a gas change when there is a change in the amount (number of moles or grams) of gas itself.

When you blow up a balloon, its volume increases because you are adding more air molecules. If a basketball gets a hole in it, and some of the air leaks out, its volume

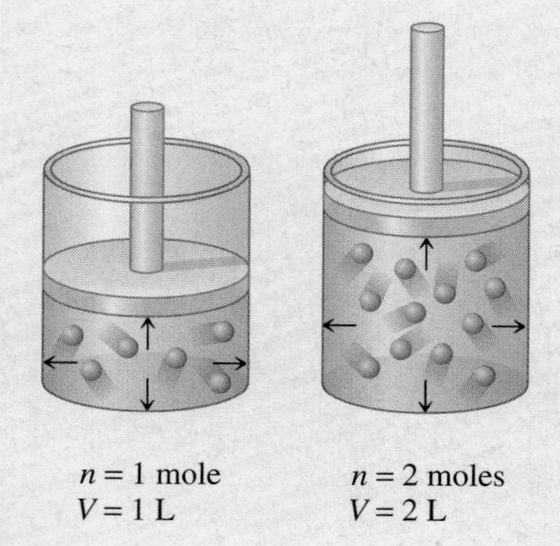


**FIGURE 7.7 Avogadro's law:** The volume of a gas is directly related to the number of moles of the gas. If the number of moles is doubled, the volume must double at constant temperature and pressure.

Q If a balloon has a leak, what happens to its volume?

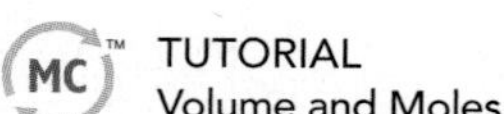
TUTORIAL
Volume and Moles

decreases. **Avogadro's law** states that the volume of a gas is directly related to the number of moles of a gas when temperature and pressure are not changed. If the number of moles of a gas is doubled, then the volume will double as long as we do not change the pressure or the temperature. (See Figure 7.7.) Under conditions of constant pressure and temperature, we can write Avogadro's law as follows:

**Avogadro's Law**

$$\frac{V_1}{n_1} = \frac{V_2}{n_2} \quad \text{No change in pressure or temperature}$$

SAMPLE PROBLEM 7.7

## Calculating Volume for a Change in Moles

A weather balloon with a volume of 44 L is filled with 2.0 moles of helium. To what volume will the balloon expand if 3.0 moles of helium are added, to give a total of 5.0 moles of helium (the pressure and temperature do not change)?

SOLUTION

**STEP 1** **Organize the data in a table.** A data table for our given information can be set up as follows:

| Conditions 1 | Conditions 2 | Know | Predict |
|---|---|---|---|
| $V_1 = 44$ L | $V_2 = ?$ | | $V$ increases |
| $n_1 = 2.0$ moles | $n_2 = 5.0$ moles | $n$ increases | |

**STEP 2** **Rearrange the gas law for the unknown.** Using Avogadro's law, we can solve for $V_2$.

$$\frac{V_1}{n_1} = \frac{V_2}{n_2}$$

$$n_2 \times \frac{V_1}{n_1} = \frac{V_2}{\cancel{n_2}} \times \cancel{n_2}$$

$$V_2 = V_1 \times \frac{n_2}{n_1}$$

**STEP 3** **Substitute the values into the gas law to solve for the unknown.** From the table, we see that the number of moles has increased. Because the number of moles and volume are directly related, the volume must increase at constant pressure and temperature. When we substitute in the values, we see the ratio of the moles (mole factor) is greater than 1, which increases volume.

$$V_2 = 44\text{ L} \times \frac{5.0\ \cancel{\text{moles}}}{2.0\ \cancel{\text{moles}}} = 110\text{ L}$$

New volume | Initial volume | Mole factor increases volume

STUDY CHECK

A sample containing 8.00 g of oxygen gas has a volume of 5.00 L. What is the volume after 4.00 g of oxygen gas is added to the balloon, if temperature and pressure do not change?

## STP and Molar Volume

Using Avogadro's law, we can say that any two gases will have equal volumes if they contain the same number of moles of gas at the same temperature and pressure. To help us make comparisons between different gases, arbitrary conditions called *standard temperature* (273 K) and *standard pressure* (1 atm), together abbreviated **STP**, were selected by scientists:

**STP Conditions**

Standard temperature is *exactly* 0 °C (273 K).

Standard pressure is *exactly* 1 atm (760 mmHg).

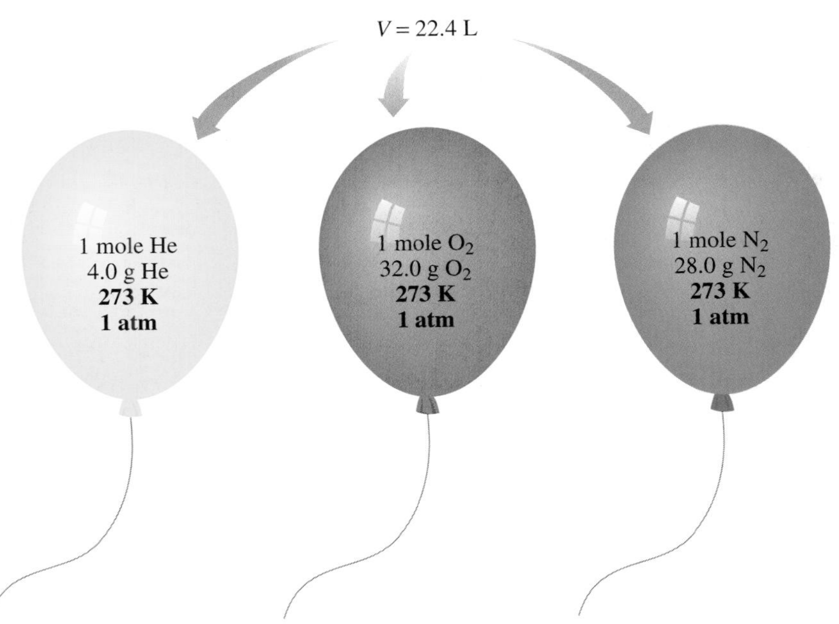


**FIGURE 7.8** Avogadro's law indicates that 1 mole of any gas at STP has a molar volume of 22.4 L.

**Q** What volume of gas is occupied by 16.0 g of methane gas, $CH_4$, at STP?

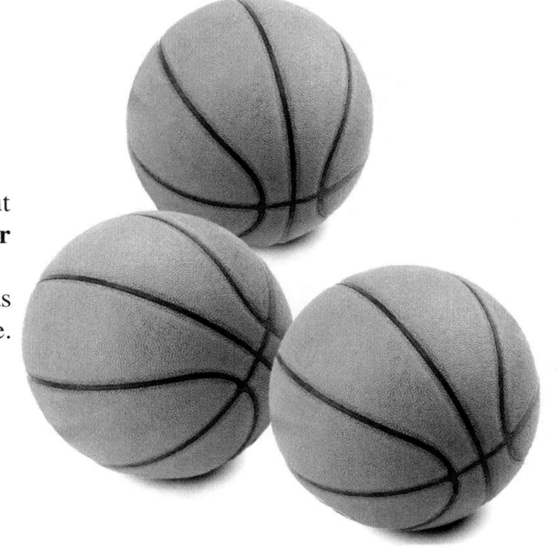

At STP, 1 mole of any gas has a volume of 22.4 L. (A volume of 22.4 L is about the same as the volume of three basketballs.) This volume is called a gas's **molar volume**. (See Figure 7.8.)

When a gas is at STP conditions (0 °C and 1 atm), its molar volume can be used as a conversion factor to convert between the number of moles of gas and its volume.

**Molar Volume Conversion Factors**

$$\frac{1 \text{ mole gas (STP)}}{22.4 \text{ L}} \quad \text{and} \quad \frac{22.4 \text{ L}}{1 \text{ mole gas (STP)}}$$

Moles of gas ⟷ Molar volume 22.4 L/mole ⟷ Volume (L) of gas

## SAMPLE PROBLEM 7.8

### Using Molar Volume to Find Volume at STP

What is the volume, in liters, of 64.0 g of $O_2$ gas at STP?

SOLUTION

Once we convert the mass of $O_2$ to moles of $O_2$, the molar volume of a gas at STP can be used to calculate the volume (L) of $O_2$.

**STEP 1** **Given** 64.0 g of $O_2(g)$ at STP **Need** volume in liters (L)

**STEP 2** **Write a plan.**

grams of $O_2$ → Molar mass → moles of $O_2$ → Molar volume → liters of $O_2$

**STEP 3** **Write conversion factors.**

1 mole of $O_2$ = 32.0 g of $O_2$

$$\frac{32.0 \text{ g } O_2}{1 \text{ mole } O_2} \quad \text{and} \quad \frac{1 \text{ mole } O_2}{32.0 \text{ g } O_2}$$

1 mole of $O_2$ (STP) = 22.4 L of $O_2$ (STP)

$$\frac{22.4 \text{ L } O_2}{1 \text{ mole } O_2} \quad \text{and} \quad \frac{1 \text{ mole } O_2}{22.4 \text{ L } O_2}$$

**STEP 4** **Set up problem with factors to cancel units.**

$$64.0 \cancel{\text{g } O_2} \times \frac{1 \cancel{\text{mole } O_2}}{32.0 \cancel{\text{g } O_2}} \times \frac{22.4 \text{ L } O_2}{1 \cancel{\text{mole } O_2}} = 44.8 \text{ L of } O_2 \text{ (STP)}$$

STUDY CHECK

How many grams of $N_2(g)$ are in 5.6 L of $N_2(g)$ at STP?

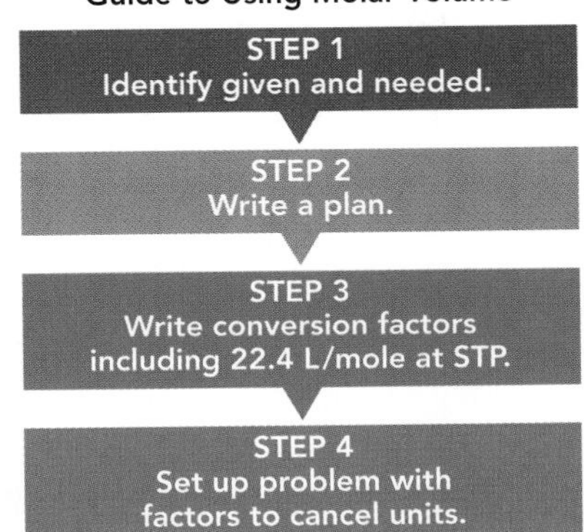

Guide to Using Molar Volume
STEP 1
Identify given and needed.
STEP 2
Write a plan.
STEP 3
Write conversion factors including 22.4 L/mole at STP.
STEP 4
Set up problem with factors to cancel units.

## Gases in Reactions at STP

We can use the molar volume at STP to determine the moles of a gas in a reaction. Once we know the moles of gas in a reaction, we can use a mole factor to determine the moles of any other substance as we have done before.

**SAMPLE PROBLEM 7.9**

### Gases in Chemical Reactions at STP

When potassium metal reacts with chlorine gas, the product is solid potassium chloride.

$$2K(s) + Cl_2(g) \longrightarrow 2KCl(s)$$

How many grams of potassium chloride are produced when 7.25 L of chlorine gas at STP reacts with excess potassium?

**Guide to Problem Solving Reactions Involving Gases**

STEP 1 Find moles of gas A using molar volume or ideal gas law.

STEP 2 Determine moles of substance B using mole–mole factor.

STEP 3 Convert moles of substance B to grams or volume.

SOLUTION

**STEP 1** **Find moles of $Cl_2$ using molar volume.** At STP, we can use molar volume (22.4 L/mole) to determine moles of $Cl_2$ gas.

$$7.25 \cancel{\text{L } Cl_2} \times \frac{1 \text{ mole } Cl_2}{22.4 \cancel{\text{L } Cl_2}} = 0.324 \text{ mole of } Cl_2$$

**STEP 2** **Determine moles of KCl using the mole–mole factor from the balanced equation.**

$$1 \text{ mole of } Cl_2 = 2 \text{ moles of KCl}$$

$$\frac{2 \text{ moles KCl}}{1 \text{ mole } Cl_2} \quad \text{and} \quad \frac{1 \text{ mole } Cl_2}{2 \text{ moles KCl}}$$

$$0.324 \cancel{\text{mole } Cl_2} \times \frac{2 \text{ moles KCl}}{1 \cancel{\text{mole } Cl_2}} = 0.648 \text{ mole of KCl}$$

**STEP 3** **Convert moles of KCl to grams.** Using the molar mass of KCl, we can determine the grams of KCl.

$$1 \text{ mole of KCl} = 74.6 \text{ g of KCl}$$

$$\frac{1 \text{ mole KCl}}{74.6 \text{ g KCl}} \quad \text{and} \quad \frac{74.6 \text{ g KCl}}{1 \text{ mole KCl}}$$

$$0.648 \cancel{\text{mole KCl}} \times \frac{74.6 \text{ g KCl}}{1 \cancel{\text{mole KCl}}} = 48.3 \text{ g of KCl}$$

These steps can also be set up as a continuous solution.

$$7.25 \cancel{\text{L } Cl_2} \times \frac{1 \cancel{\text{mole } Cl_2}}{22.4 \cancel{\text{L } Cl_2}} \times \frac{2 \cancel{\text{moles KCl}}}{1 \cancel{\text{mole } Cl_2}} \times \frac{74.6 \text{ g KCl}}{1 \cancel{\text{mole KCl}}} = 48.3 \text{ g of KCl}$$

STUDY CHECK

$H_2$ gas forms when zinc metal reacts with aqueous HCl according to the following equation:

$$Zn(s) + 2HCl(aq) \longrightarrow ZnCl_2(aq) + H_2(g)$$

How many liters of $H_2$ gas at STP are produced when 15.8 g of zinc reacts?

## QUESTIONS AND PROBLEMS

### Volume and Moles (Avogadro's Law)

**7.43** What happens to the volume of a bicycle tire or a basketball when you use an air pump to add air?

**7.44** Sometimes when you blow up a balloon and release it, it flies around the room. What is happening to the air that was in the balloon and its volume?

**7.45** A sample containing 1.50 moles of neon gas has a volume of 8.00 L. What is the new volume of gas, in liters, when the following changes occur in the quantity of the gas at constant pressure and temperature?

**a.** A leak allows one-half of the neon atoms to escape.

**b.** A sample of 25.0 g of neon is added to the 1.50 moles of neon gas in the container.

c. A sample of 3.50 moles of $O_2$ is added to the 1.50 moles of neon gas in the container.

**7.46** A sample containing 4.80 g of $O_2$ gas has a volume of 15.0 L. Pressure and temperature remain constant.
a. What is the new volume if 0.500 mole of $O_2$ gas is added?
b. Oxygen is released until the volume is 10.0 L. How many moles of $O_2$ are removed?
c. What is the volume after 4.00 g of He is added to the 4.80 g of $O_2$ gas in the container?

7.47 Use the molar volume of a gas to solve the following at STP:
a. the number of moles of $O_2$ in 44.8 L of $O_2$ gas
b. the number of moles of $CO_2$ in 4.00 L of $CO_2$ gas
c. the volume (L) of 6.40 g of $O_2$
d. the volume (mL) occupied by 50.0 g of neon

**7.48** Use molar volume to solve the following problems at STP:
a. the volume (L) occupied by 2.50 moles of $N_2$
b. the volume (mL) occupied by 0.420 mole of He
c. the number of grams of neon contained in 11.2 L of Ne gas
d. the number of moles of $H_2$ in 1620 mL of $H_2$ gas

7.49 Mg metal reacts with HCl to produce hydrogen gas:

$$Mg(s) + 2HCl(aq) \longrightarrow MgCl_2(aq) + H_2(g)$$

What volume of $H_2$ at STP is released when 8.25 g of Mg reacts?

**7.50** Aluminum oxide is formed from its elements:

$$4Al(s) + 3O_2(g) \longrightarrow 2Al_2O_3(s)$$

How many grams of Al will react with 12.0 L of $O_2$ at STP?

## 7.8 The Ideal Gas Law

**LEARNING GOAL**

Use the ideal gas law to solve for *P*, *V*, *T*, or *n* of a gas when given three of the four values in the ideal gas law.

The four properties used in the measurement of a gas—pressure ($P$), volume ($V$), temperature ($T$), and amount ($n$)—can be combined to give a single expression called the **ideal gas law**, which is written as follows:

**Ideal Gas Law**

$$PV = nRT$$

TUTORIAL Introduction to the Ideal Gas Law

Rearranging the ideal gas law shows that the four gas properties equal a constant, $R$:

$$\frac{PV}{nT} = R$$

To calculate the value of $R$, we substitute the STP conditions for molar volume into the expression: 1 mole of any gas occupies 22.4 L at STP (273 K and 1 atm).

$$R = \frac{(1.00\ \text{atm})(22.4\ \text{L})}{(1.00\ \text{mole})(273\ \text{K})} = \frac{0.0821\ \text{L} \cdot \text{atm}}{\text{mole} \cdot \text{K}}$$

The value for $R$, the **ideal gas constant**, is 0.0821 L • atm per mole • K. If we use 760 mmHg for the pressure, we obtain another useful value for $R$: 62.4 L • mmHg per mole • K.

$$R = \frac{(760\ \text{mmHg})(22.4\ \text{L})}{(1.00\ \text{mole})(273\ \text{K})} = \frac{62.4\ \text{L} \cdot \text{mmHg}}{\text{mole} \cdot \text{K}}$$

MC SELF STUDY ACTIVITY The Ideal Gas Law

The ideal gas law is a useful expression when you are given the values for any three of the four properties of a gas. In working problems using the ideal gas law, the units of each variable must match the units in the $R$ you select:

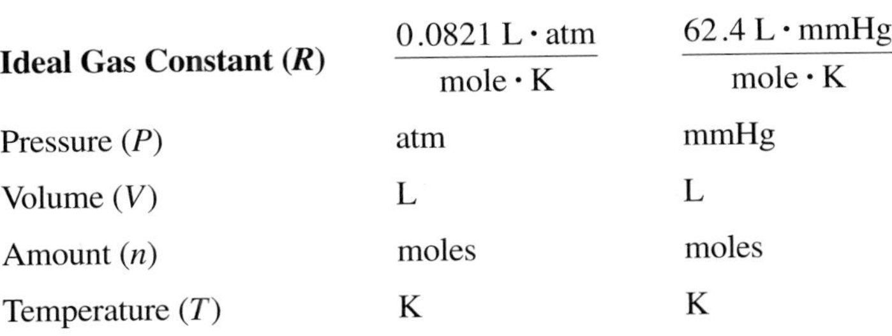

| **Ideal Gas Constant ($R$)** | $\frac{0.0821\ \text{L} \cdot \text{atm}}{\text{mole} \cdot \text{K}}$ | $\frac{62.4\ \text{L} \cdot \text{mmHg}}{\text{mole} \cdot \text{K}}$ |
|---|---|---|
| Pressure ($P$) | atm | mmHg |
| Volume ($V$) | L | L |
| Amount ($n$) | moles | moles |
| Temperature ($T$) | K | K |

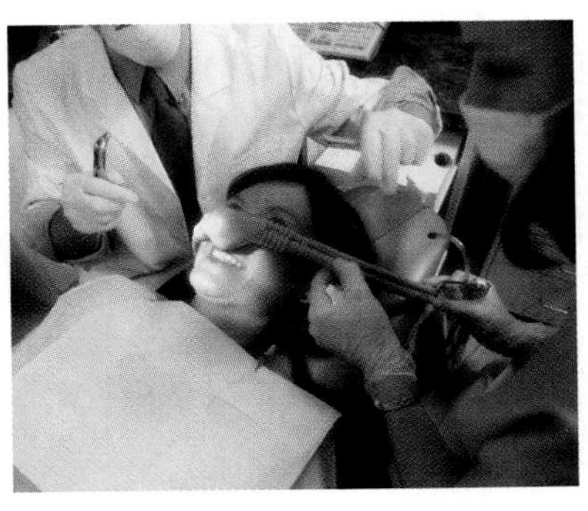

SAMPLE PROBLEM 7.10

### Using the Ideal Gas Law

Dinitrogen oxide, $N_2O$, which is used in dentistry, is an anesthetic also called "laughing gas." What is the pressure, in atmospheres, of 0.350 mole of $N_2O$ at 22 °C in a 5.00 L container?

**Guide to Using the Ideal Gas Law**

STEP 1
Organize data given for the gas.

STEP 2
Solve the ideal gas law for the unknown.

STEP 3
Substitute gas data and calculate unknown value.

SOLUTION

**STEP 1** **Organize the data, including *R*.** When three of the four quantities (*P*, *V*, *n*, and *T*) are known, we use the ideal gas law to solve for the unknown quantity. The temperature is converted from degrees Celsius to kelvins so that the units of *V*, *n*, and *T* match the units of the gas constant *R*:

$$P = ? \quad V = 5.00\text{ L} \quad n = 0.350\text{ mole} \quad R = 0.0821\frac{\text{L}\cdot\text{atm}}{\text{mole}\cdot\text{K}} \quad T = 22\text{ °C} + 273 = 295\text{ K}$$

**STEP 2** **Rearrange the ideal gas law to solve for the unknown.** By dividing both sides of the ideal gas law by *V*, we solve for pressure, *P*:

$$PV = nRT \quad \text{Ideal gas law}$$

$$P\frac{\cancel{V}}{\cancel{V}} = \frac{nRT}{V}$$

$$P = \frac{nRT}{V}$$

**STEP 3** **Substitute values to calculate unknown.**

$$P = \frac{0.350\,\cancel{\text{mole}} \times 0.0821\,\dfrac{\cancel{\text{L}}\cdot\text{atm}}{\cancel{\text{mole}}\cdot\cancel{\text{K}}} \times 295\,\cancel{\text{K}}}{5.00\,\cancel{\text{L}}} = 1.70\text{ atm}$$

STUDY CHECK

Chlorine gas, $Cl_2$, is used to purify water. How many moles of chlorine gas are in a 7.00 L tank if the gas has a pressure of 865 mmHg and a temperature of 24 °C?

SAMPLE PROBLEM 7.11

## Calculating Mass Using the Ideal Gas Law

Butane, $C_4H_{10}$, is used as a fuel for barbecues and as an aerosol propellant. If you have 108 mL of butane at 715 mmHg and 25 °C, what is the mass (g) of the butane?

SOLUTION

**STEP 1** **Organize the data, including *R*.** When three of the four quantities (*P*, *V*, *n*, and *T*) are known, we use the ideal gas law to solve for the unknown quantity. Because the pressure is given in mmHg, we will use the *R* in mmHg. The volume given in milliliters (mL) is converted to a volume in liters (L). The temperature is converted from degrees Celsius to kelvins.

| Initial values | Adjusted for units in ideal gas constant *R* |
|---|---|
| $P = 715$ mmHg | 715 mmHg |
| $V = 108$ mL | $108\,\cancel{\text{mL}} \times \dfrac{1\text{ L}}{1000\,\cancel{\text{mL}}} = 0.108\text{ L}$ |
| $n = ?$ moles of $C_4H_{10}$ | ? moles of $C_4H_{10}$ |
| $R = \dfrac{62.4\text{ L}\cdot\text{mmHg}}{\text{mole}\cdot\text{K}}$ | $\dfrac{62.4\text{ L}\cdot\text{mmHg}}{\text{mole}\cdot\text{K}}$ |
| $T = 25$ °C | 25 °C + 273 = 298 K |

**STEP 2** **Rearrange the ideal gas law to solve for the unknown.** By dividing both sides of the ideal gas law by *RT*, we solve for moles, *n*:

$$PV = nRT \quad \text{Ideal gas law}$$

$$\frac{PV}{RT} = n\frac{\cancel{RT}}{\cancel{RT}}$$

$$n = \frac{PV}{RT}$$

**STEP 3** **Substitute the known values to calculate the unknown.**

$$n = \frac{715\ \cancel{\text{mmHg}} \times 0.108\ \cancel{\text{L}}}{\dfrac{62.4\ \cancel{\text{L}} \cdot \cancel{\text{mmHg}}}{\text{mole} \cdot \cancel{\text{K}}} \times 298\ \cancel{\text{K}}} = 0.00415 \text{ mole } (4.15 \times 10^{-3} \text{ mole})$$

Now we convert the moles of butane to grams using its molar mass (58.0 g/mole).

$$0.00415\ \cancel{\text{mole } C_4H_{10}} \times \frac{58.0 \text{ g } C_4H_{10}}{1\ \cancel{\text{mole } C_4H_{10}}} = 0.241 \text{ g of } C_4H_{10}$$

STUDY CHECK

What is the volume of 1.20 g of carbon monoxide at 8 °C if it has a pressure of 724 mmHg?

SAMPLE PROBLEM 7.12

### Molar Mass of a Gas Using the Ideal Gas Law

What is the molar mass of a gas if a 3.16-g sample at 0.750 atm at 45 °C occupies a volume of 2.05 L?

SOLUTION

**STEP 1** **Given** 3.16 g of a gas, $P = 0.750$ atm, $V = 2.05$ L, $T = 45\ °\text{C} + 273 = 318$ K **Need** molar mass (g/mole)

**STEP 2** **Write a plan.** The molar mass is the grams of the gas divided by the moles. In this problem, we need to use the ideal gas law to determine the moles of the gas.

$P, V, T$ [Ideal gas law] → moles ($n$) of gas

$$\frac{3.16 \text{ g}}{\text{moles } (n) \text{ gas}} = \text{molar mass (g/mole)}$$

**STEP 3** **Write conversion factors.**

$$PV = nRT \qquad \text{Ideal gas law}$$

$$\frac{PV}{RT} = \frac{n\cancel{RT}}{\cancel{RT}}$$

$$n = \frac{PV}{RT}$$

The moles of the gas are calculated as

$$n = \frac{0.750\ \cancel{\text{atm}} \times 2.05\ \cancel{\text{L}}}{0.0821\ \dfrac{\cancel{\text{L}} \cdot \cancel{\text{atm}}}{\text{mole} \cdot \cancel{\text{K}}} \times 318\ \cancel{\text{K}}} = 0.0589 \text{ mole}$$

**Set up calculation for molar mass (g/mole).** The molar mass of the gas is obtained by dividing the mass by the moles of gas.

$$\text{Molar mass} = \frac{\text{mass}}{\text{moles}} = \frac{3.16 \text{ g}}{0.0589 \text{ mole}} = 53.7 \text{ g/mole}$$

STUDY CHECK

What is the molar mass of an unknown gas in a 1.50-L container if 0.488 g of the gas has a pressure of 0.0750 atm at 19.0 °C?

## Ideal Gas Law and Chemical Reactions

If a gas is not at STP, we use its pressure ($P$), volume ($V$), and temperature ($T$) to determine the moles of that gas involved in a reaction. Then we can determine the moles of any other substance by using the mole factors as we did in Chapter 6.

SAMPLE PROBLEM 7.13

## Ideal Gas Law and Chemical Equations

Limestone ($CaCO_3$) reacts with HCl to produce aqueous calcium chloride and carbon dioxide gas:

$$CaCO_3(s) + 2HCl(aq) \longrightarrow CaCl_2(aq) + CO_2(g) + H_2O(l)$$

How many liters of $CO_2$ are produced at 752 mmHg and 24 °C from a 25.0-g sample of limestone?

SOLUTION

**STEP 1** **Find the moles of $CaCO_3$ using molar mass.** The moles of limestone require the molar mass of limestone.

$$1 \text{ mole of } CaCO_3 = 100.1 \text{ g of } CaCO_3$$

$$\frac{100.1 \text{ g } CaCO_3}{1 \text{ mole } CaCO_3} \text{ and } \frac{1 \text{ mole } CaCO_3}{100.1 \text{ g } CaCO_3}$$

$$25.0 \cancel{\text{g } CaCO_3} \times \frac{1 \text{ mole } CaCO_3}{100.1 \cancel{\text{g } CaCO_3}} = 0.250 \text{ mole of } CaCO_3$$

**STEP 2** **Determine moles of $CO_2$ using the mole–mole factor from the balanced equation.**

$$1 \text{ mole of } CaCO_3 = 1 \text{ mole of } CO_2$$

$$\frac{1 \text{ mole } CaCO_3}{1 \text{ mole } CO_2} \text{ and } \frac{1 \text{ mole } CO_2}{1 \text{ mole } CaCO_3}$$

$$0.250 \cancel{\text{mole } CaCO_3} \times \frac{1 \text{ mole } CO_2}{1 \cancel{\text{mole } CaCO_3}} = 0.250 \text{ mole of } CO_2$$

**STEP 3** **Convert moles of $CO_2$ to volume.** Now the moles of $CO_2$ can be placed in the ideal gas law to solve for the volume (L) of gas. The ideal gas law solved for volume is

$$V = \frac{nRT}{P}$$

$$V = \frac{0.250 \cancel{\text{mole}} \times \frac{62.4 \text{ L} \cdot \cancel{\text{mmHg}}}{\cancel{\text{K}} \cdot \cancel{\text{mole}}} \times 297 \cancel{\text{K}}}{752 \cancel{\text{mmHg}}} = 6.16 \text{ L of } CO_2$$

STUDY CHECK

If 12.8 g of aluminum reacts with HCl, how many liters of $H_2$ would be formed at 715 mmHg and 19 °C?

$$2Al(s) + 6HCl(aq) \longrightarrow 2AlCl_3(aq) + 3H_2(g)$$

# QUESTIONS AND PROBLEMS

## The Ideal Gas Law

7.51 Calculate the pressure, in atmospheres, of 2.00 moles of helium gas in a 10.0-L container at 27 °C.

**7.52** What is the volume, in liters, of 4.0 moles of methane gas, $CH_4$, at 18 °C and 1.40 atm?

7.53 An oxygen gas container has a volume of 20.0 L. How many grams of oxygen are in the container if the gas has a pressure of 845 mmHg at 22 °C?

**7.54** A 10.0-g sample of krypton has a temperature of 25 °C at 575 mmHg. What is the volume, in milliliters, of the krypton gas?

7.55 A 25.0-g sample of nitrogen, $N_2$, has a volume of 50.0 L and a pressure of 630. mmHg. What is the temperature of the gas?

**7.56** A 0.226-g sample of carbon dioxide, $CO_2$, has a volume of 525 mL and a pressure of 455 mmHg. What is the temperature of the gas?

**7.57** Determine the molar mass of each of the following gases:
**a.** 0.84 g of a gas that occupies 450 mL at STP
**b.** 1.48 g of a gas that occupies 1.00 L at 685 mmHg and 22 °C
**c.** 2.96 g of a gas that occupies 2.30 L at 0.95 atm and 24 °C

**7.58** Determine the molar mass of each of the following gases:
**a.** 11.6 g of a gas that occupies 2.00 L at STP
**b.** 0.726 g of a gas that occupies 855 mL at 1.20 atm and 18 °C
**c.** 2.32 g of a gas that occupies 1.23 L at 685 mmHg and 25 °C

**7.59** Butane is used to fill gas tanks for heating. The following equation describes its combustion:

$$2C_4H_{10}(g) + 13O_2(g) \longrightarrow 8CO_2(g) + 10H_2O(g)$$

If a tank contains 55.2 g of butane, what volume, in liters, of oxygen is needed to burn all the butane at 0.850 atm and 25 °C?

**7.60** When heated to 350. °C at 0.950 atm, ammonium nitrate decomposes to produce nitrogen, water, and oxygen gases:

$$2NH_4NO_3(s) \longrightarrow 2N_2(g) + 4H_2O(g) + O_2(g)$$

**a.** How many liters of water vapor are produced when 25.8 g of $NH_4NO_3$ decomposes?
**b.** How many grams of $NH_4NO_3$ are needed to produce 10.0 L of oxygen?

**7.61** What volume, in liters, of $O_2$ at 35 °C and 1.19 atm can be produced from the decomposition of 50.0 g of $KNO_3$?

$$2KNO_3(s) \longrightarrow 2KNO_2(s) + O_2(g)$$

**7.62** Nitrogen dioxide reacts with water to produce oxygen and ammonia:

$$4NO_2(g) + 6H_2O(g) \longrightarrow 7O_2(g) + 4NH_3(g)$$

At a temperature of 415 °C and a pressure of 725 mmHg, how many grams of $NH_3$ can be produced when 4.00 L of $NO_2$ react?

## 7.9 Partial Pressures (Dalton's Law)

**LEARNING GOAL**

Use Dalton's law of partial pressures to calculate the total pressure of a mixture of gases.

TUTORIAL
Mixture of Gases

Many gas samples are a mixture of gases. For example, the air you breathe is a mixture of mostly oxygen and nitrogen gases. Scientists have observed that all gas particles in ideal gas mixtures behave in the same way. Therefore, the total pressure of the gases in a mixture is a result of the collisions of the gas particles regardless of what type of gas they are.

In a gas mixture, each gas exerts its **partial pressure**, which is the pressure it would exert if it were the only gas in the container. **Dalton's law** states that the total pressure of a gas mixture is the sum of the partial pressures of the gases in the mixture.

**Dalton's Law**

$$P_{total} = P_1 + P_2 + P_3 + \cdots$$

Total pressure of a gas mixture = sum of the partial pressures of the gases in the mixture

Suppose we have two separate tanks, one filled with helium at 2.0 atm and the other filled with argon at 4.0 atm. When the gases are combined in a single tank with the same volume and temperature, the number of gas molecules, not the type of gas, determines the pressure in a container. The pressure of the combined gas mixture in the single tank would be 6.0 atm, which is the sum of their individual or partial pressures.

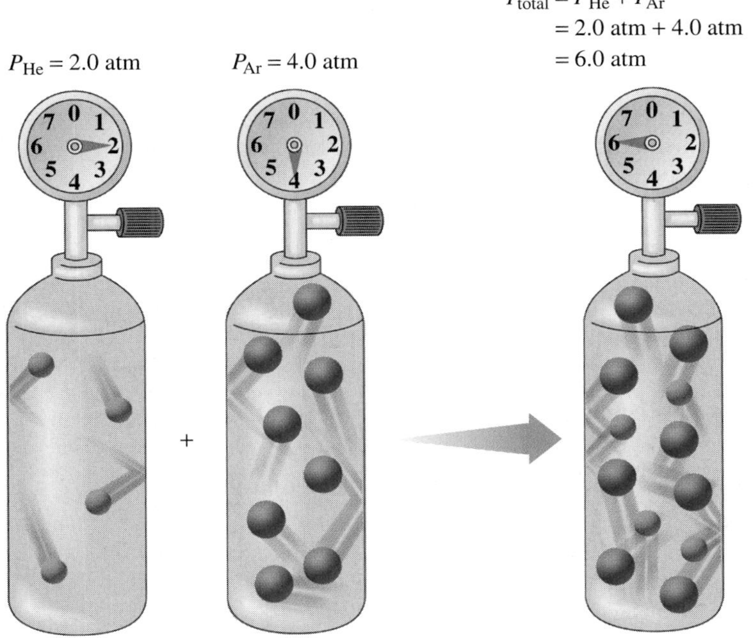

CONCEPT CHECK 7.6

**Pressure of a Gas Mixture**

One 10-L gas tank contains propane ($C_3H_8$) gas at 300. torr, and a second 10-L gas tank contains methane ($CH_4$) gas at 500. torr. After the gases from both tanks are combined in a 10-L container with no change in temperature, what is the pressure of the gas mixture?

ANSWER

Using Dalton's law of partial pressures, we find that the total pressure of the gas mixture is the sum of the partial pressures of the gases in the mixture.

$$\begin{aligned} P_{\text{total}} &= P_{\text{propane}} + P_{\text{methane}} \\ &= 300.\text{ torr} + 500.\text{ torr} \\ &= 800.\text{ torr} \end{aligned}$$

Therefore, when both propane and methane are placed in the same container, the total pressure of the mixture is 800. torr.

**TABLE 7.7** Typical Composition of Air

| Gas | Partial Pressure (mmHg) | Percentage (%) |
|---|---|---|
| Nitrogen, $N_2$ | 594 | 78 |
| Oxygen, $O_2$ | 160 | 21 |
| Carbon dioxide, $CO_2$; Argon, Ar; Water vapor, $H_2O$ (variable) | 6 | 1 |
| Total air | 760 | 100 |

## Air Is a Gas Mixture

The air you breathe is a mixture of gases. What we call the *atmospheric pressure* is actually the sum of the partial pressures of all the gases in the air. Table 7.7 lists partial pressures for the gases in air on a typical day.

SAMPLE PROBLEM 7.14

**Partial Pressure of a Gas in a Mixture**

A mixture of oxygen and helium is prepared for a scuba diver who is going to descend 200 ft below the ocean surface. At that depth, the diver breathes a gas mixture that has a total pressure of 7.00 atm. If the partial pressure of the oxygen in the tank at that depth is 1140 mmHg, what is the partial pressure of the helium?

Guide to Solving for Partial Pressure

STEP 1 Write the equation for sum of partial pressures.

STEP 2 Solve for the unknown pressure.

STEP 3 Substitute known pressures and calculate unknown.

SOLUTION

**STEP 1** **Write the equation for the sum of the partial pressures.** From Dalton's law of partial pressures, we know that the total pressure is equal to the sum of the partial pressures:

$$P_{\text{total}} = P_{O_2} + P_{\text{He}}$$

**STEP 2** **Solve for the unknown pressure.** To solve for the partial pressure of helium ($P_{\text{He}}$), we rearrange the expression to give the following:

$$\begin{aligned} P_{\text{total}} &= P_{\text{He}} + P_{O_2} \\ P_{\text{He}} &= P_{\text{total}} - P_{O_2} \end{aligned}$$

Convert units to match.

$$P_{O_2} = 1140\ \cancel{\text{mmHg}} \times \frac{1\text{ atm}}{760\ \cancel{\text{mmHg}}} = 1.50\text{ atm}$$

**STEP 3** **Substitute known pressures and calculate the unknown.**

$$\begin{aligned} P_{\text{He}} &= P_{\text{total}} - P_{O_2} \\ P_{\text{He}} &= 7.00\text{ atm} - 1.50\text{ atm} \\ &= 5.50\text{ atm} \end{aligned}$$

STUDY CHECK

An anesthetic consists of a mixture of cyclopropane gas, $C_3H_6$, and oxygen gas, $O_2$. If the mixture has a total pressure of 1.09 atm, and the partial pressure of the cyclopropane is 73 torr, what is the partial pressure (torr) of the oxygen in the anesthetic?

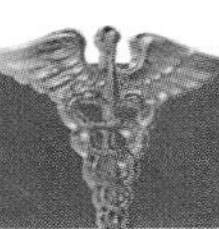

## HEALTH NOTE

### Blood Gases

Our cells continuously use oxygen and produce carbon dioxide. Both gases move in and out of the lungs through the membranes of the alveoli, the tiny air sacs at the ends of the airways in the lungs. An exchange of gases occurs in which oxygen from the air diffuses into the lungs and into the blood, while carbon dioxide produced in the cells is carried to the lungs to be exhaled. In Table 7.8, partial pressures are given for the gases in the air that we inhale (inspired air), the air in the alveoli, and the air that we exhale (expired air).

At sea level, oxygen normally has a partial pressure of 100 mmHg in the alveoli of the lungs. Because the partial pressure of oxygen in venous blood is 40 mmHg, oxygen diffuses from the alveoli into the bloodstream. The oxygen combines with hemoglobin, which carries it to the tissues of the body, where the partial pressure of oxygen can be very low, less than 30 mmHg. Oxygen diffuses from the blood where the partial pressure of $O_2$ is high into the tissues where $O_2$ pressure is low.

As oxygen is used in the cells of the body during metabolic processes, carbon dioxide is produced, so the partial pressure of $CO_2$ may be as high as 50 mmHg or more. Carbon dioxide diffuses from the tissues into the bloodstream and is carried to the lungs. There it diffuses out of the blood, where $CO_2$ has a partial pressure of 46 mmHg, into the alveoli, where the $CO_2$ is at 40 mmHg, and is exhaled. Table 7.9 gives the partial pressures of blood gases in the tissues and in oxygenated and deoxygenated blood.

**TABLE 7.8** Partial Pressures of Gases During Breathing

| | Partial Pressure (mmHg) | | |
|---|---|---|---|
| **Gas** | **Inspired Air** | **Alveolar Air** | **Expired Air** |
| Nitrogen, $N_2$ | 594 | 573 | 569 |
| Oxygen, $O_2$ | 160 | 100 | 116 |
| Carbon dioxide, $CO_2$ | 0.3 | 40 | 28 |
| Water vapor, $H_2O$ | 5.7 | 47 | 47 |
| Total | 760 | 760 | 760 |

**TABLE 7.9** Partial Pressures of Oxygen and Carbon Dioxide in Blood and Tissues

| | Partial Pressure (mmHg) | | |
|---|---|---|---|
| **Gas** | **Oxygenated Blood** | **Deoxygenated Blood** | **Tissues** |
| $O_2$ | 100 | 40 | 30 or less |
| $CO_2$ | 40 | 46 | 50 or greater |

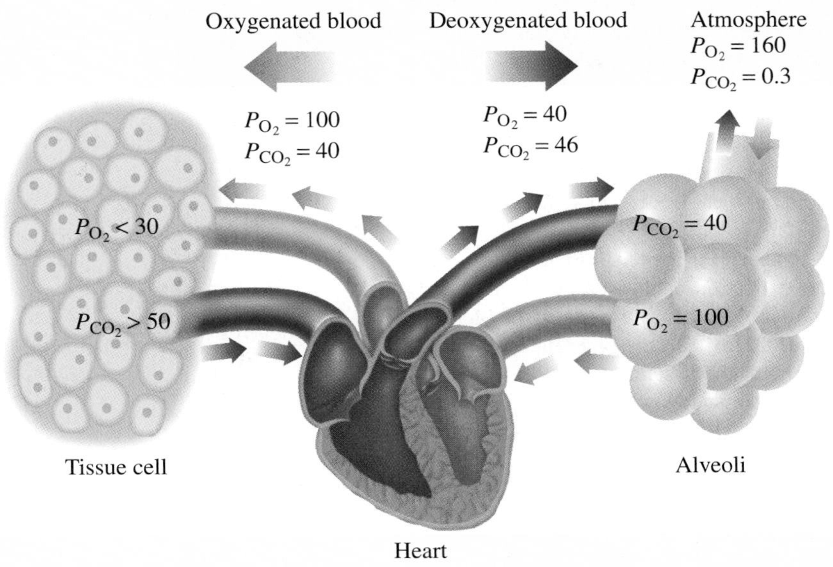

## QUESTIONS AND PROBLEMS

### Partial Pressures (Dalton's Law)

**7.63** A typical air sample in the lungs contains oxygen at 100 mmHg, nitrogen at 573 mmHg, carbon dioxide at 40 mmHg, and water vapor at 47 mmHg. Why are these pressures called partial pressures?

**7.64** Suppose a mixture contains helium and oxygen gases. If the partial pressure of helium is the same as the partial pressure of oxygen, what do you know about the number of helium atoms compared to the number of oxygen molecules? Explain.

**7.65** In a gas mixture, the partial pressures are nitrogen 425 torr, oxygen 115 torr, and helium 225 torr. What is the total pressure (torr) exerted by the gas mixture?

**7.66** In a gas mixture, the partial pressures are argon 415 mmHg, neon 75 mmHg, and nitrogen 125 mmHg. What is the total pressure (atm) exerted by the gas mixture?

**7.67** A gas mixture containing oxygen, nitrogen, and helium exerts a total pressure of 925 torr. If the partial pressures are oxygen 425 torr and helium 75 torr, what is the partial pressure (torr) of the nitrogen in the mixture?

**7.68** A gas mixture containing oxygen, nitrogen, and neon exerts a total pressure of 1.20 atm. If helium added to the mixture increases the pressure to 1.50 atm, what is the partial pressure (atm) of the helium?

**7.69** In certain lung ailments such as emphysema, there is a decrease in the ability of oxygen to diffuse into the blood.

**a.** How would the partial pressure of oxygen in the blood change?

**b.** Why does a person with severe emphysema sometimes use a portable oxygen tank?

**7.70** An injury to the head can affect the ability of a person to ventilate (breathe in and out), and so can certain drugs.

**a.** What would happen to the partial pressures of oxygen and carbon dioxide in the blood if a person cannot properly ventilate?

**b.** When a person with hypoventilation is placed on a ventilator, an air mixture is delivered at pressures that are alternately above and below the air pressure in the person's lung. How will this move oxygen gas into the lungs, and carbon dioxide out?

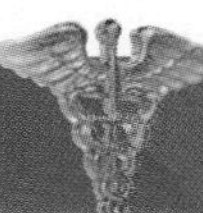

## HEALTH NOTE

### Hyperbaric Chambers

A burn patient may undergo treatment for burns and infections in a hyperbaric chamber, a device in which pressures can be obtained that are two to three times greater than atmospheric pressure. A greater oxygen pressure increases the level of dissolved oxygen in the blood and tissues. Because high levels of oxygen are toxic to many strains of bacteria, this helps fight bacterial infections. The hyperbaric chamber may also be used to counteract carbon monoxide (CO) poisoning and to treat some cancers.

The blood is normally capable of dissolving up to 95% of the oxygen available to it. Thus, if the partial pressure of the oxygen is 2280 mmHg (3 atm), 95% of that—2160 mmHg—can dissolve in the blood, saturating the tissues. In the case of carbon monoxide poisoning, this oxygen can replace the carbon monoxide that has attached to the hemoglobin.

A patient undergoing treatment in a hyperbaric chamber must also undergo decompression (reduction of pressure) at a rate that slowly reduces the concentration of dissolved oxygen in the blood. If decompression is too rapid, the oxygen dissolved in the blood may form gas bubbles in the circulatory system.

If scuba divers do not decompress slowly, they suffer a similar condition called *the bends*. While below the surface of the ocean, divers breathe air at higher pressures. At such high pressures, nitrogen gas will dissolve in their blood. If they ascend to the surface too quickly, the dissolved nitrogen forms bubbles in the blood that can produce life-threatening blood clots. The gas bubbles can also appear in the joints and tissues of the body and be quite painful. A diver suffering from the bends is placed immediately into a hyperbaric chamber, where pressure is first increased and then slowly decreased. The dissolved nitrogen can then diffuse through the lungs until atmospheric pressure is reached.

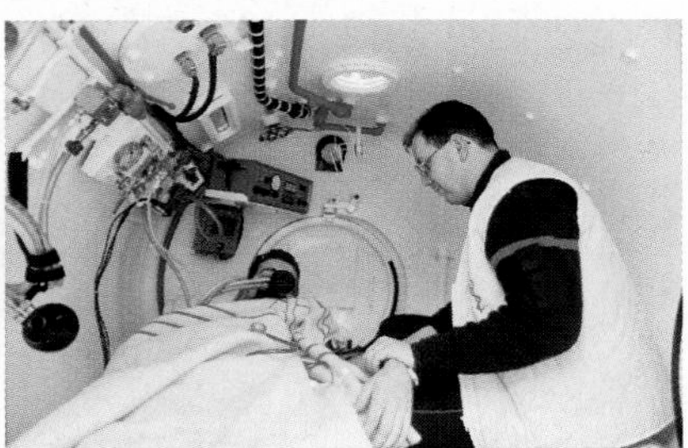

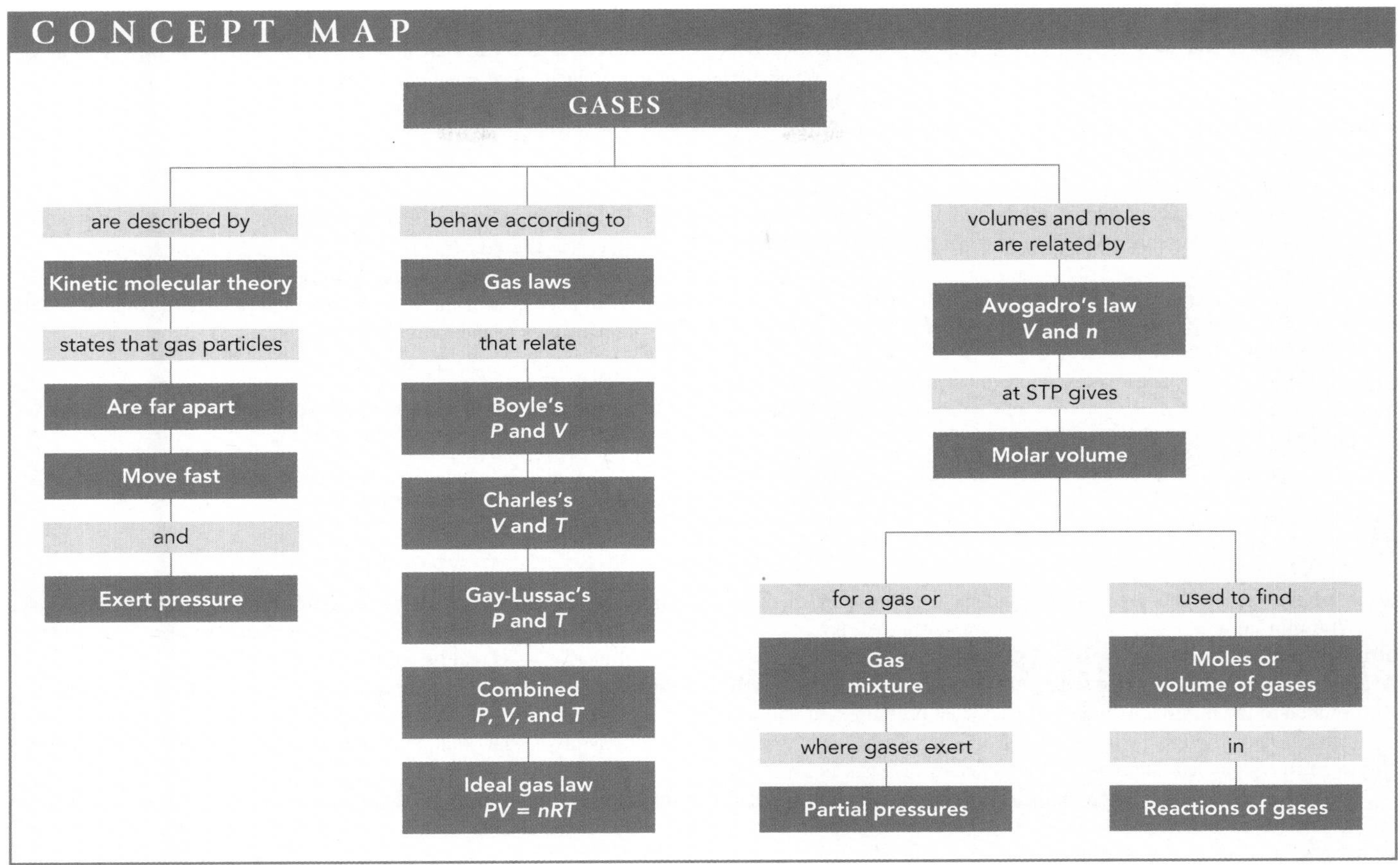


# CHAPTER REVIEW

### 7.1 Properties of Gases

**LEARNING GOAL:** *Describe the kinetic molecular theory of gases and the properties of gases.*

In a gas, particles are so far apart and moving so fast that their attractions are unimportant. A gas is described by the physical properties of pressure ($P$), volume ($V$), temperature ($T$), and amount in moles ($n$).

### 7.2 Gas Pressure

**LEARNING GOAL:** *Describe the units of measurement used for pressure, and change from one unit to another.*

A gas exerts pressure, the force of the gas particles striking the surface of a container. Gas pressure is measured in units of torr, mmHg, and atm.

### 7.3 Pressure and Volume (Boyle's Law)

**LEARNING GOAL:** *Use the pressure–volume relationship (Boyle's law) to determine the new pressure or volume of a certain amount of gas at a constant temperature.*

The volume ($V$) of a gas changes inversely with the pressure ($P$) of the gas if there is no change in the amount and temperature: $P_1V_1 = P_2V_2$. This means that the pressure increases if volume decreases; pressure decreases if volume increases.

### 7.4 Temperature and Volume (Charles's Law)

**LEARNING GOAL:** *Use the temperature–volume relationship (Charles's law) to determine the new temperature or volume of a certain amount of gas at a constant pressure.*

The volume ($V$) of a gas is directly related to its Kelvin temperature ($T$) when there is no change in the amount and pressure of the gas:

$$\frac{V_1}{T_1} = \frac{V_2}{T_2}$$

Therefore, if temperature increases, the volume of the gas increases; if temperature decreases, volume decreases.

### 7.5 Temperature and Pressure (Gay–Lussac's Law)

**LEARNING GOAL:** *Use the temperature–pressure relationship (Gay–Lussac's law) to determine the new temperature or pressure of a certain amount of gas at a constant volume.*

The pressure ($P$) of a gas is directly related to its Kelvin temperature ($T$):

$$\frac{P_1}{T_1} = \frac{P_2}{T_2}$$

This relationship means that an increase in temperature increases the pressure of a gas, and a decrease in temperature decreases the pressure, as long as the amount and volume stay constant.

### 7.6 The Combined Gas Law

**LEARNING GOAL:** *Use the combined gas law to find the new pressure, volume, or temperature of a gas when changes in two of these properties are given.*

Gas laws combine into a relationship of pressure ($P$), volume ($V$), and temperature ($T$):

$$\frac{P_1V_1}{T_1} = \frac{P_2V_2}{T_2}$$

This expression is used to determine the effect of changes in two of the variables on the third.

### 7.7 Volume and Moles (Avogadro's Law)

***LEARNING GOAL:*** *Use Avogadro's law to describe the relationship between the amount of a gas and its volume, and use this relationship in calculations.*

The volume ($V$) of a gas is directly related to the number of moles ($n$) of the gas when the pressure and temperature of the gas do not change:

$$\frac{V_1}{n_1} = \frac{V_2}{n_2}$$

If the moles of gas are increased, the volume must increase; if the moles of gas are decreased, the volume must decrease. At standard temperature (273 K) and pressure (1 atm), abbreviated STP, 1 mole of any gas has a volume of 22.4 L.

### 7.8 The Ideal Gas Law

***LEARNING GOAL:*** *Use the ideal gas law to solve for P, V, T, or n of a gas when given three of the four values in the ideal gas law.*

The ideal gas law gives the relationship of all the quantities $P$, $V$, $n$, and $T$ that describe and measure a gas: $PV = nRT$. Any of the four variables can be calculated if the other three are known.

### 7.9 Partial Pressures (Dalton's Law)

***LEARNING GOAL:*** *Use Dalton's law of partial pressures to calculate the total pressure of a mixture of gases.*

In a mixture of two or more gases, the total pressure is the sum of the partial pressures of the individual gases:

$$P_{\text{total}} = P_1 + P_2 + P_3 + \cdots$$

The partial pressure of a gas in a mixture is the pressure it would exert if it were the only gas in the container.

## KEY TERMS

**atmosphere (atm)** The pressure exerted by a column of mercury 760 mm high.

**atmospheric pressure** The pressure exerted by the atmosphere.

**Avogadro's law** A gas law that states that the volume of gas is directly related to the number of moles of gas when pressure and temperature do not change.

**Boyle's law** A gas law stating that the pressure of a gas is inversely related to the volume when temperature (K) and amount (moles) of the gas do not change.

**Charles's law** A gas law stating that the volume of a gas changes directly with a change in Kelvin temperature when pressure and amount (moles) of the gas do not change.

**combined gas law** A relationship that combines several gas laws relating pressure, volume, and temperature:

$$\frac{P_1V_1}{T_1} = \frac{P_2V_2}{T_2}$$

**Dalton's law** A gas law stating that the total pressure exerted by a mixture of gases in a container is the sum of the partial pressures that each gas would exert alone.

**direct relationship** A relationship in which two properties increase or decrease together.

**Gay–Lussac's law** A gas law stating that the pressure of a gas changes directly with a change in Kelvin temperature when the number of moles of a gas and its volume do not change.

**ideal gas constant, *R*** A numerical value that relates the quantities $P$, $V$, $n$, and $T$ in the ideal gas law, $PV = nRT$.

**ideal gas law** A law that combines the four measured properties of a gas in the equation $PV = nRT$.

**inverse relationship** A relationship in which two properties change in opposite directions.

**kinetic molecular theory of gases** A model used to explain the behavior of gases.

**molar volume** A volume of 22.4 L occupied by 1 mole of a gas at STP conditions of 0 °C (273 K) and 1 atm.

**partial pressure** The pressure exerted by a single gas in a gas mixture.

**pressure** The force exerted by gas particles that hit the walls of a container.

**STP** Standard conditions of exactly 0 °C (273 K) temperature and 1 atm pressure used for the comparison of gases.

**vapor pressure** The pressure exerted by the particles of vapor above a liquid.

## UNDERSTANDING THE CONCEPTS

7.71 At 100 °C, which of the following gases exerts

**a.** the lowest pressure?

**b.** the highest pressure?

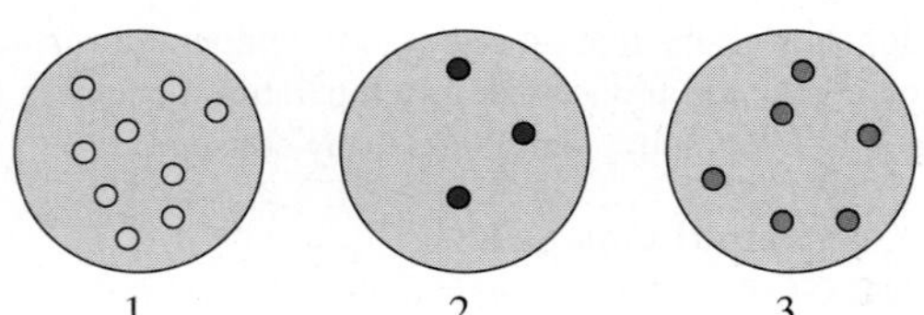


7.72 Indicate which diagram represents the volume of the gas sample in a flexible container when each of the following changes takes place:

**a.** The temperature increases at constant pressure.

**b.** The temperature decreases at constant pressure.

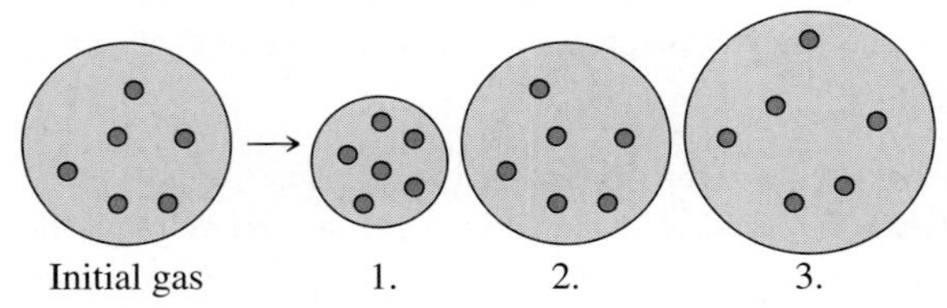


**c.** The pressure increases at constant temperature.

**d.** The pressure decreases at constant temperature.

**e.** Both the pressure and the Kelvin temperature are doubled.

7.73 A balloon is filled with helium gas with a pressure of 1.00 atm and neon gas with a pressure of 0.50 atm. For each of the following changes of the initial balloon, select the diagram (A, B, or C) that shows the final (new) volume of the balloon:

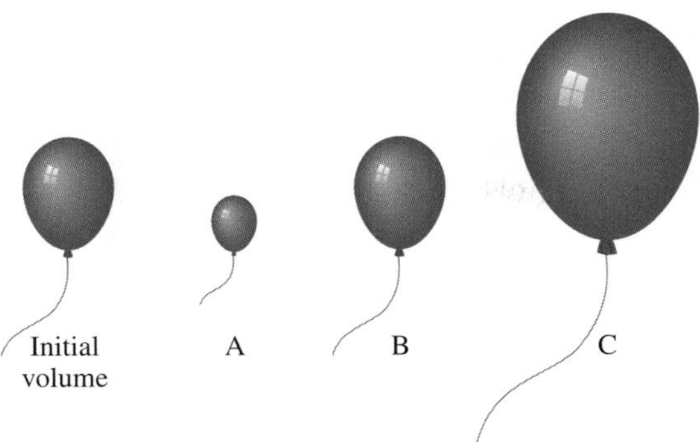


a. The balloon is put in a cold storage unit ($P$ and $n$ constant).
b. The balloon floats to a higher altitude where the pressure is less ($n$ and $T$ constant).
c. All of the neon gas is removed ($T$ and $P$ constant).
d. The Kelvin temperature doubles and one-half of the gas atoms leak out ($P$ constant).
e. 2.0 moles of $O_2$ gas are added at constant $T$ and $P$.

**7.74** Indicate if pressure increases, decreases, or stays the same in each of the following:

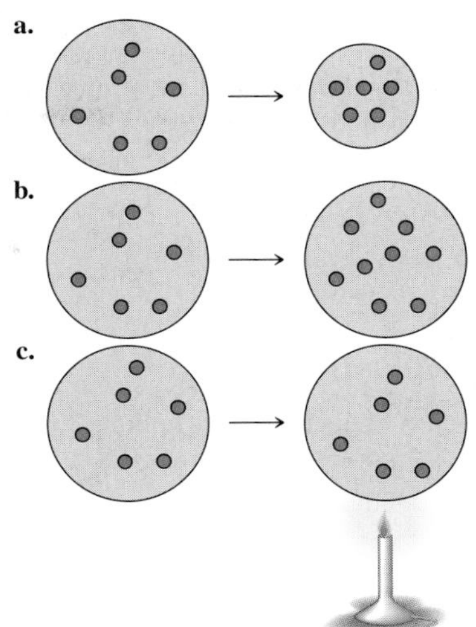


# ADDITIONAL QUESTIONS AND PROBLEMS

*For instructor-assigned homework, go to* ***www.masteringchemistry.com***.

7.75 At a restaurant, a customer chokes on a piece of food. You put your arms around the person's waist and use your fists to push up on the person's abdomen, an action called the *Heimlich maneuver*.
  **a.** How would this action change the volume of the chest and lungs?
  **b.** Why does it cause the person to expel the food item from the airway?

**7.76** An airplane is pressurized to 650. mmHg, which is the atmospheric pressure at a ski resort at an altitude of 13 000 ft.
  **a.** If air is 21% oxygen, what is the partial pressure of oxygen on the plane?
  **b.** If the partial pressure of oxygen drops below 100. mmHg, passengers become drowsy. If this happens, oxygen masks are released. What is the total cabin pressure at which oxygen masks are dropped?

7.77 In 1783, Jacques Charles launched his first balloon filled with hydrogen gas, which he chose because it was lighter than air. If the balloon has a volume of 31 000 L, how many grams of hydrogen would be needed to fill the balloon at STP?

The AEROSTATIC GLOBE
Exhibited at Paris by Mess.rs Charles & Robert
Dec.r 1 1783.


**7.78** In problem 7.77, the balloon reached an altitude of 1000 m, where the pressure was 658 mmHg and the temperature was −8 °C. What was the volume, in liters, of the balloon at these conditions?

7.79 A fire extinguisher has a pressure of 10. atm at 25 °C. What is the pressure, in atmospheres, if the fire extinguisher is used at a temperature of 75 °C?

**7.80** A weather balloon has a volume of 750 L when filled with helium at 8 °C at a pressure of 380 torr. What is the new volume of the balloon when the pressure is 0.20 atm and the temperature is −45 °C?

7.81 A sample of hydrogen ($H_2$) gas at 127 °C has a pressure of 2.00 atm. At what temperature (°C) will the pressure of the $H_2$ decrease to 0.25 atm?

**7.82** A sample of nitrogen ($N_2$) gas has a volume of 250. mL at 30. °C and a pressure of 745 mmHg. What is the volume of the nitrogen at STP?

7.83 A 2.00-L container is filled with methane gas ($CH_4$) at a pressure of 2500 mmHg and a temperature of 18 °C. How many grams of methane are in the container?

**7.84** A steel cylinder with a volume of 15.0 L is filled with 50.0 g of nitrogen gas at 25 °C. What is the pressure of the $N_2$ gas in the cylinder?

7.85 How many molecules of $CO_2$ are in 35.0 L of $CO_2(g)$ at 1.2 atm and 5 °C?

**7.86** A container is filled with $4.0 \times 10^{22}$ $O_2$ molecules at 5 °C and 845 mmHg. What is the volume, in mL, of the container?

7.87 When heated, calcium carbonate decomposes to give calcium oxide and carbon dioxide gas:

$$CaCO_3(s) \longrightarrow CaO(s) + CO_2(g)$$

If 2.00 moles of $CaCO_3$ react, how many liters of $CO_2$ gas are produced at STP?

**7.88** Magnesium reacts with oxygen to form magnesium oxide:

$$2Mg(s) + O_2(g) \longrightarrow 2MgO(s)$$

How many liters of oxygen gas at STP are needed to react completely with 8.0 g of magnesium?

**7.89** Your space ship has docked at a space station above Mars. The temperature inside the space station is a carefully controlled 24 °C at a pressure of 745 mmHg. A balloon with a volume of 425 mL drifts into the airlock, where the temperature is −95 °C and the pressure is 0.115 atm. What is the new volume of the balloon? Assume that the balloon is very elastic.

**7.90** How many liters of $H_2$ gas can be produced at STP from 25.0 g of Zn?

$$Zn(s) + 2HCl(aq) \longrightarrow ZnCl_2(aq) + H_2(g)$$

**7.91** Aluminum oxide can be formed from its elements:

$$4Al(s) + 3O_2(g) \longrightarrow 2Al_2O_3(s)$$

What volume of oxygen is needed at STP to completely react 5.4 g of aluminum?

**7.92** Glucose, $C_6H_{12}O_6$, is metabolized in living systems according to the reaction

$$C_6H_{12}O_6(s) + 6O_2(g) \longrightarrow 6CO_2(g) + 6H_2O(l)$$

How many grams of water can be produced when 12.5 L of $O_2$ reacts at STP?

**7.93** A sample of gas with a mass of 1.62 g occupies a volume of 941 mL at a pressure of 748 torr and a temperature of 20 °C. What is the molar mass of the gas?

**7.94** What is the molar mass of a gas if 1.15 g of the gas has a volume of 225 mL at STP?

**7.95** Nitrogen dioxide reacts with water to produce oxygen and ammonia:

$$4NO_2(g) + 6H_2O(g) \longrightarrow 7O_2(g) + 4NH_3(g)$$

**a.** How many liters of $O_2$ at STP are produced when $2.5 \times 10^{23}$ molecules of $NO_2$ react?

**b.** A 5.00-L sample of $H_2O(g)$ reacts at a temperature of 375 °C and a pressure of 725 mmHg. How many grams of $NH_3$ can be produced?

**7.96** Hydrogen gas can be produced in the laboratory through the reaction of aluminum metal with hydrochloric acid:

$$2Al(s) + 6HCl(aq) \longrightarrow 2AlCl_3(aq) + 3H_2(g)$$

What is the volume, in liters, of $H_2$ gas produced at STP from the reaction of 25.0 g of Al?

**7.97** A weather balloon is partially filled with helium to allow for expansion at high altitudes. At STP, a weather balloon is filled with enough helium to give a volume of 25.0 L. At an altitude of 30.0 km, where the temperature is −35 °C, it has expanded to 2460 L. The increase in volume causes it to burst, and a small parachute returns the instruments to Earth.

**a.** How many grams of helium were added to the balloon?

**b.** What was the pressure, in mmHg, of the helium inside the balloon when it burst?

**7.98** What is the total pressure, in mmHg, of a gas mixture containing argon gas at 0.25 atm, helium gas at 350 mmHg, and nitrogen gas at 360 torr?

**7.99** A gas mixture contains oxygen and argon at partial pressures of 0.60 atm and 425 mmHg. If nitrogen gas added to the sample increases the total pressure to 1250 torr, what is the partial pressure, in torr, of the nitrogen added?

**7.100** A gas mixture contains helium and oxygen at partial pressures of 255 torr and 0.450 atm. What is the total pressure, in mmHg, of the mixture after it is placed in a container one-half the volume of the original container?

## CHALLENGE QUESTIONS

**7.101** A gas sample has a volume of 4250 mL at 15 °C and 745 mmHg. What is the new temperature (°C) after the sample is transferred to a new container with a volume of 2.50 L and a pressure of 1.20 atm?

**7.102** In the fermentation of glucose (wine making), a volume of 780 mL of $CO_2$ gas was produced at 37 °C and 1.00 atm. What is the volume (L) of the gas when measured at 22 °C and 675 mmHg?

**7.103** When sensors in a car detect a collision, they cause the reaction of sodium azide, $NaN_3$:

$$2NaN_3(s) \longrightarrow 2Na(s) + 3N_2(g)$$

This generates nitrogen gas, which fills the air bags within 0.03 second.

How many liters of $N_2$ are produced at STP if the air bag contains 132 g of $NaN_3$?

**7.104** Nitrogen dioxide reacts with water to produce oxygen and ammonia:

$$4NO_2(g) + 6H_2O(g) \longrightarrow 7O_2(g) + 4NH_3(g)$$

How many liters of $O_2$ at STP are produced when $2.5 \times 10^{23}$ molecules of $NO_2$ react?

**7.105** A 1.00-g sample of dry ice ($CO_2$) is placed in a container that has a volume of 4.60 L and a temperature of 24.0 °C. Calculate the pressure of $CO_2$, in mmHg, inside the container after all the dry ice changes to a gas.

$$CO_2(s) \longrightarrow CO_2(g)$$

**7.106** A 250-mL sample of nitrogen ($N_2$) has a pressure of 745 mmHg at 30 °C. What is the mass of nitrogen?

**7.107** Hydrogen gas can be produced in the laboratory through the reaction of magnesium metal with hydrochloric acid:

$$Mg(s) + 2HCl(aq) \longrightarrow MgCl_2(aq) + H_2(g)$$

What is the volume, in liters, of $H_2$ gas produced at 24 °C and 835 mmHg, from the reaction of 12.0 g of Mg?

**7.108** In the formation of smog, nitrogen and oxygen gas react to form nitrogen dioxide. How many grams of $NO_2$ will be produced when 2.0 L of nitrogen at 840 mmHg and 24 °C are completely reacted?

$$N_2(g) + 2O_2(g) \longrightarrow 2NO_2(g)$$

**7.109** Solid aluminum reacts with aqueous $H_2SO_4$ to form $H_2$ gas and aluminum sulfate. When a sample of Al reacts, 415 mL of $H_2$ gas is produced at 23 °C at a pressure of 734 mmHg. How many grams of Al reacted?

$$2Al(s) + 3H_2SO_4(aq) \longrightarrow 3H_2(g) + Al_2(SO_4)_3(aq)$$

**7.110** When heated, solid $KClO_3$ forms solid KCl and $O_2$ gas. When a sample of $KClO_3$ is heated, 226 mL of $O_2$ gas is produced with a pressure of 719 mmHg and a temperature of 26 °C. How many grams of $KClO_3$ reacted?

$$2KClO_3(s) \longrightarrow 2KCl(s) + 3O_2(g)$$

**7.111** We saw in Chapter 1 that 1 teragram (Tg) is equal to $10^{12}$ g. In 2000, $CO_2$ emissions from the generation of electricity for use in homes in the United States were 780 Tg. In 2020, it is estimated that $CO_2$ emissions from the generation of electricity for use in homes will be 990 Tg.

**a.** Calculate the number of kilograms of $CO_2$ emitted for the years 2000 and 2020.

**b.** Calculate the number of moles of $CO_2$ emitted for the years 2000 and 2020.

**c.** What is the increase, in megagrams, for the $CO_2$ emissions between the years 2000 and 2020?

**7.112** We saw in Chapter 1 that 1 teragram (Tg) is equal to $10^{12}$ g. In 2000, $CO_2$ emissions from fuels used for transportation in the United States was 1990 Tg. In 2020, it is estimated that $CO_2$ emissions from the fuels used for transportation in the United States will be 2760 Tg.

**a.** Calculate the number of kilograms of $CO_2$ emitted for the years 2000 and 2020.

**b.** Calculate the number of moles of $CO_2$ emitted for the years 2000 and 2020.

**c.** What is the increase, in megagrams, for the $CO_2$ emitted between the years 2000 and 2020?

# ANSWERS

## ANSWERS TO STUDY CHECKS

**7.1** 0.862 atm

**7.2** 250 torr

**7.3** 50.0 mL

**7.4** 569 mL

**7.5** 16 °C

**7.6** 241 mmHg

**7.7** 7.50 L

**7.8** 7.0 g of $N_2$

**7.9** 5.41 L of $H_2$

**7.10** 0.327 mole of $Cl_2$

**7.11** 1.04 L of CO

**7.12** 104 g/mole

**7.13** 18.1 L of $H_2$

**7.14** 755 torr

## ANSWERS TO SELECTED QUESTIONS AND PROBLEMS

**7.1** **a.** At a higher temperature, gas particles have greater kinetic energy, which makes them move faster.
**b.** Because there are great distances between the particles of a gas, they can be pushed closer together and still remain a gas.

**7.3** **a.** temperature **b.** volume **c.** amount **d.** pressure

**7.5** atmospheres (atm), mmHg, torr, lb/in.$^2$, kPa

**7.7** **a.** 1520 torr **b.** 1520 mmHg

**7.9** As a diver ascends to the surface, external pressure decreases. If the air in the lungs were not exhaled, its volume would expand and severely damage the lungs. The pressure in the lungs must adjust to changes in the external pressure.

**7.11** **a.** The pressure is greater in cylinder A. According to Boyle's law, a decrease in volume pushes the gas particles closer together, which will cause an increase in the pressure.

**b.**

| Property | Conditions 1 | Conditions 2 | Know | Predict |
|---|---|---|---|---|
| Pressure ($P$) | 650 mmHg | 1.2 atm (910 mmHg) | $P$ increases | |
| Volume ($V$) | 220 mL | 160 mL | | $V$ decreases |

**7.13** **a.** The pressure doubles.
**b.** The pressure falls to one-third the initial pressure.
**c.** The pressure increases to ten times the original pressure.

**7.15** **a.** 328 mmHg **b.** 2620 mmHg **c.** 4400 mmHg

**7.17** **a.** 25 L **b.** 25 L **c.** 100. L

**7.19** 25 L

**7.21** **a.** inspiration **b.** expiration **c.** inspiration

**7.23** **a.** C **b.** A **c.** B

**7.25** **a.** 303 °C **b.** −129 °C **c.** 591 °C **d.** 136 °C

**7.27** **a.** 2400 mL **b.** 4900 mL **c.** 1800 mL **d.** 1700 mL

**7.29** An increase in temperature increases the pressure inside the can. When the pressure exceeds the pressure limit of the can, it explodes.

**7.31** **a.** −23 °C **b.** 168 °C

**7.33** **a.** 770 torr **b.** 1.51 atm

**7.35** **a.** boiling point **b.** vapor pressure **c.** atmospheric pressure **d.** boiling point

**7.37** **a.** On top of a mountain, water boils below 100 °C because the atmospheric (external) pressure is less than 1 atm.
**b.** Because the pressure inside a pressure cooker is greater than 1 atm, water boils above 100 °C. At a higher temperature, food cooks faster.

**7.39** **a.** 4.26 atm **b.** 3.07 atm **c.** 0.605 atm

**7.41** −33 °C

**7.43** The volume increases because the number of gas particles is increased.

**7.45** **a.** 4.00 L **b.** 14.6 L **c.** 26.7 L

**7.47** **a.** 2.00 moles of $O_2$ **b.** 0.179 mole of $CO_2$ **c.** 4.48 L **d.** 55 400 mL

**7.49** 7.60 L of $H_2$

**7.51** 4.93 atm

**7.53** 29.4 g of $O_2$

**7.55** 565 K (292 °C)

**7.57** **a.** 42 g/mole **b.** 39.8 g/mole **c.** 33 g/mole

**7.59** 178 L of $O_2$

**7.61** 5.25 L of $O_2$

**7.63** In a gas mixture, the pressure that each gas exerts as part of the total pressure is called the *partial pressure* of that gas. Because the air sample is a mixture of gases, the total pressure is the sum of the partial pressures of each gas in the sample.

**7.65** 765 torr

**7.67** 425 torr

**7.69** **a.** The partial pressure of oxygen will be lower than normal.
**b.** Breathing a higher concentration of oxygen will help to increase the supply of oxygen in the lungs and blood and raise the partial pressure of oxygen in the blood.

**7.71** **a.** 2 **b.** 1

**7.73** **a.** A **b.** C **c.** A **d.** B **e.** C

**7.75** **a.** The volume of the chest and lungs is decreased.
**b.** The decrease in volume increases the pressure, which can dislodge the food in the trachea.

**7.77** $2.8 \times 10^3$ g of $H_2$

**7.79** 12 atm

**7.81** −223 °C

**7.83** 4.5 g

**7.85** $1.1 \times 10^{24}$ molecules of $CO_2$

**7.87** 44.8 L of $CO_2$

**7.89** 2170 mL

**7.91** 3.4 L of $O_2$

**7.93** 42.1 g/mole

**7.95** **a.** 16 L of $O_2$ **b.** 1.02 g of $NH_3$

**7.97** **a.** 4.46 g of helium **b.** 6.73 mmHg

**7.99** 370 torr

**7.101** −66 °C

**7.103** 68.2 L of $N_2$

**7.105** 91.5 mmHg

**7.107** 11.0 L of $H_2$

**7.109** 0.297 g of Al

**7.111** **a.** $7.8 \times 10^{11}$ kg of $CO_2$ (2000), $9.9 \times 10^{11}$ kg of $CO_2$ (2020)
**b.** $1.8 \times 10^{13}$ moles of $CO_2$ (2000), $2.3 \times 10^{13}$ moles of $CO_2$ (2020)
**c.** $2.1 \times 10^8$ Mg of $CO_2$ increase

# Solutions

# 8

## LOOKING AHEAD


**8.1** Solutions

**8.2** Electrolytes and Nonelectrolytes

**8.3** Solubility

**8.4** Percent Concentration

**8.5** Molarity and Dilution

**8.6** Physical Properties of Solutions


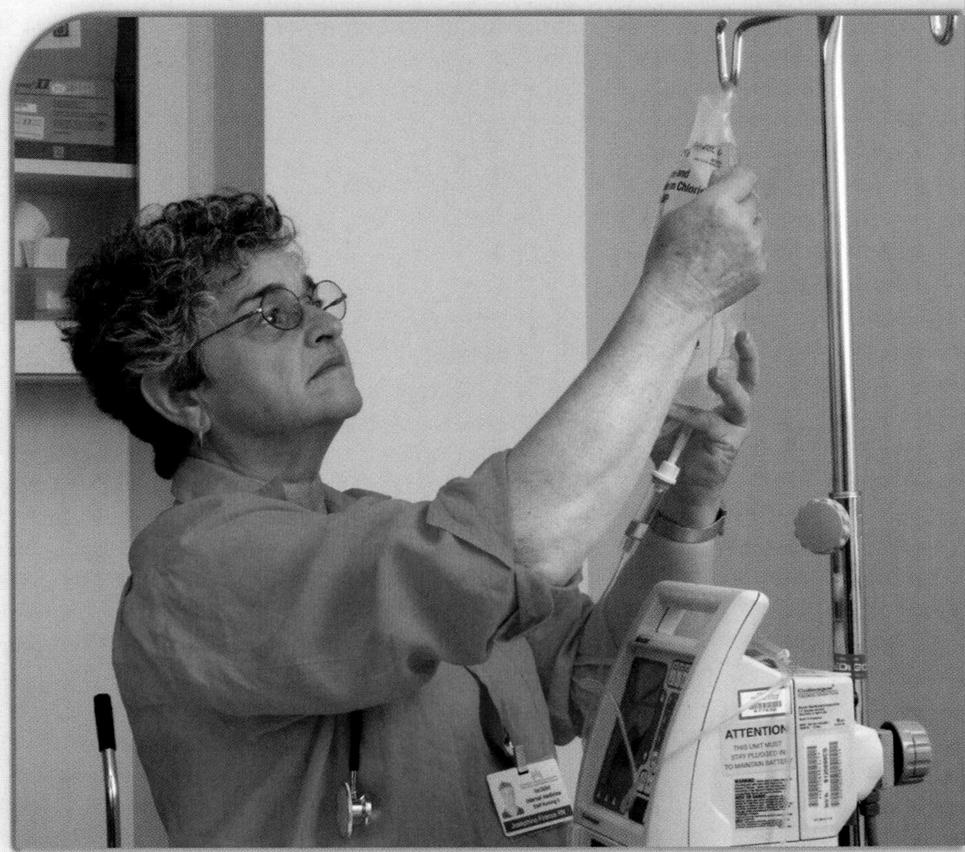


*"There is a lot of chemistry going on in the body, including drug interactions," says Josephine Firenze, registered nurse, Kaiser Hospital.*

*Normally, the body maintains a homeostasis of fluids and electrolytes. Conditions that alter the composition of body fluids can lead to convulsions, coma, or death. To halt the disease process and to establish homeostasis, a patient may be given intravenous fluid therapy. Solutions that are compatible with body fluids, such as a 5% glucose or a 0.9% saline solution, are used. An infusion pump delivers the desired number of milliliters per hour to the patient. During IV therapy, a patient is checked for fluid overload as indicated by edema (swelling) or a greater fluid input than output.*

Solutions are everywhere around us. Most consist of one substance dissolved in another. The air we breathe is a solution of primarily oxygen and nitrogen gases. Carbon dioxide gas dissolved in water makes carbonated drinks. When we make solutions of coffee or tea, we use hot water to dissolve substances from coffee beans or tea leaves. The ocean is also a solution, consisting of many salts, such as sodium chloride, dissolved in water. In a hospital, the antiseptic tincture of iodine is a solution of iodine dissolved in ethanol.

Our body fluids contain water and dissolved substances, such as glucose and urea, and ions called electrolytes, such as $K^+$, $Na^+$, $Cl^-$, $Mg^{2+}$, $HCO_3^-$, and $HPO_4^{2-}$. Proper amounts of each of these dissolved substances and water must be maintained in the body fluids. Small changes in electrolyte levels can seriously disrupt cellular processes, endangering our health. Therefore, the measurement of their concentrations is a valuable diagnostic tool.

Through the processes of osmosis and dialysis, water, essential nutrients, and waste products enter and leave the cells of the body. In osmosis, water flows in and out of the cells of the body. In dialysis, small particles in solution as well as water diffuse through semipermeable membranes. The kidneys utilize osmosis and dialysis to regulate the amount of water and electrolytes that are excreted.

## 8.1 Solutions

**LEARNING GOAL**

Identify the solute and solvent in a solution. Describe the formation of a solution.

A **solution** is a homogeneous mixture in which one substance called the **solute** is uniformly dispersed in another substance called the **solvent**. Because the solute and the solvent do not react with each other, they can be mixed in varying proportions. A little salt dissolved in water tastes slightly salty. When more salt dissolves, the water tastes very salty. Usually, the solute (in this case, salt) is the substance present in the smaller amount, whereas the solvent (in this case, water) is present in the larger amount. In a solution, the particles of the solute are evenly dispersed within the solvent. (See Figure 8.1.)

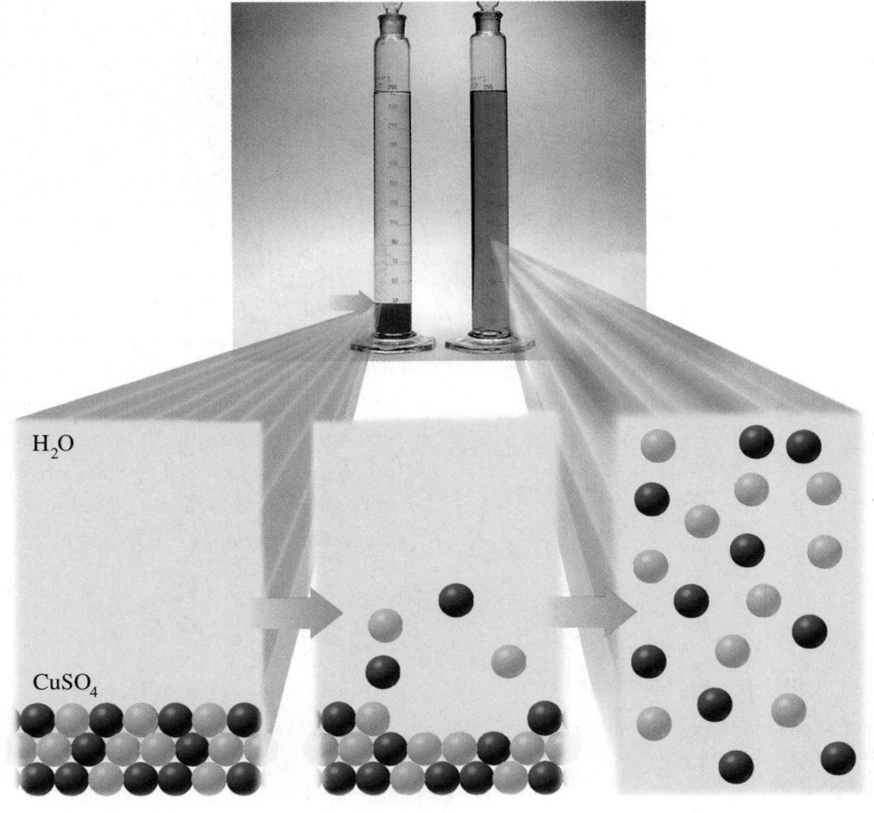


**FIGURE 8.1** A solution of copper(II) sulfate ($CuSO_4$) forms as particles of solute dissolve, move away from the crystals, and become evenly dispersed among the solvent (water) molecules.

**Q** What does the uniform blue color indicate about the $CuSO_4$ solution?

TABLE 8.1 Some Examples of Solutions

| Type | Example | Primary Solute | Solvent |
|---|---|---|---|
| **Gas Solutions** | | | |
| Gas in a gas | Air | Oxygen (gas) | Nitrogen (gas) |
| **Liquid Solutions** | | | |
| Gas in a liquid | Soda water | Carbon dioxide (gas) | Water (liquid) |
| | Household ammonia | Ammonia (gas) | Water (liquid) |
| Liquid in a liquid | Vinegar | Acetic acid (liquid) | Water (liquid) |
| Solid in a liquid | Seawater | Sodium chloride (solid) | Water (liquid) |
| | Tincture of iodine | Iodine (solid) | Ethanol (liquid) |
| **Solid Solutions** | | | |
| Liquid in a solid | Dental amalgam | Mercury (liquid) | Silver (solid) |
| Solid in a solid | Brass | Zinc (solid) | Copper (solid) |
| | Steel | Carbon (solid) | Iron (solid) |

## Types of Solutes and Solvents

Solutes and solvents may be solids, liquids, or gases. The solution that forms has the same physical state as the solvent. When sugar crystals are dissolved in water, the resulting sugar solution is liquid. Sugar is the solute, and water is the solvent. Soda water and soft drinks are prepared by dissolving carbon dioxide gas in water. The carbon dioxide gas is the solute, and water is the solvent. Table 8.1 lists some solutes and solvents and their solutions.

## Water as a Solvent

Water is one of the most common solvents in nature. In the $H_2O$ molecule, an oxygen atom shares electrons with two hydrogen atoms. Because the oxygen atom is much more electronegative, the O—H bonds are polar. In each of the polar bonds, the oxygen atom has a partial negative ($\delta^-$) charge, and the hydrogen atom has a partial positive ($\delta^+$) charge. Because of the arrangement of the polar bonds, water is a *polar solvent.*

SELF STUDY ACTIVITY
Hydrogen Bonding

*Hydrogen bonds* occur between molecules where a partially positive hydrogen is attracted to the strongly electronegative atoms of O, N, or F in other molecules. In water, hydrogen bonds are formed by the attraction between the oxygen atom of one water molecule and a hydrogen atom in another water molecule. In the diagram, hydrogen bonds are shown as dots between the water molecules. Although hydrogen bonds are much weaker than covalent or ionic bonds, there are many of them linking molecules together. As a result, hydrogen bonding plays an important role in the properties of water and biological compounds such as proteins, carbohydrates, and DNA.

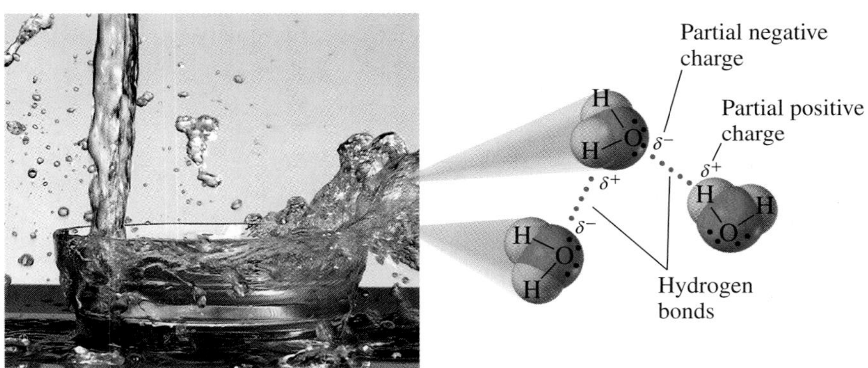

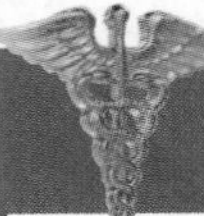

# HEALTH NOTE

## Water in the Body

The average adult body contains about 60% water by mass, and the average infant about 75%. About 60% of the body's water is contained within the cells as intracellular fluids; the other 40% makes up extracellular fluids, which include the interstitial fluid in tissue and the plasma in the blood. These external fluids carry nutrients and waste materials between the cells and the circulatory system.

**24 Hours**

| Water gain | |
|---|---|
| Liquid | 1000 mL |
| Food | 1200 mL |
| Metabolism | 300 mL |
| Total | 2500 mL |

| Water loss | |
|---|---|
| Urine | 1500 mL |
| Perspiration | 300 mL |
| Breath | 600 mL |
| Feces | 100 mL |
| Total | 2500 mL |

Every day you lose between 1500 and 3000 mL of water from the kidneys as urine, from the skin as perspiration, from the lungs as you exhale, and from the gastrointestinal tract. Serious dehydration can occur in an adult if there is a 10% loss in total body fluid. A 20% loss of fluid can be fatal. An infant suffers severe dehydration with a 5–10% loss in body fluid.

Water loss is continually replaced by the liquids and foods in the diet and from metabolic processes that produce water in the cells of the body. Table 8.2 lists the percentage by mass of water contained in some foods.

**TABLE 8.2** Percentage of Water in Some Foods

| Food | Water (% by mass) | Food | Water (% by mass) |
|---|---|---|---|
| **Vegetables** | | **Meats/Fish** | |
| Carrot | 88 | Chicken, cooked | 71 |
| Celery | 94 | Hamburger, broiled | 60 |
| Cucumber | 96 | Salmon | 71 |
| Tomato | 94 | **Grains** | |
| **Fruits** | | Cake | 34 |
| Apple | 85 | French bread | 31 |
| Banana | 76 | Noodles, cooked | 70 |
| Cantaloupe | 91 | **Milk Products** | |
| Orange | 86 | Cottage cheese | 78 |
| Strawberry | 90 | Milk, whole | 87 |
| Watermelon | 93 | Yogurt | 88 |

## Formation of Solutions

The interactions between solute and solvent will determine whether a solution will form. Initially, energy is needed to separate the particles in the solute and to move the solvent particles apart. Then energy is released as solute particles move between the solvent particles to form a solution. However, attractive forces between the solute and the solvent particles must be strong enough to provide the energy for the initial separation. These attractive forces only occur when the solute and the solvent have similar polarities. If there is no attraction between a solute and a solvent, there is not sufficient energy to form a solution. (See Table 8.3.)

**TABLE 8.3** Possible Combinations of Solutes and Solvents

| Solutions Will Form | | Solutions Will Not Form | |
|---|---|---|---|
| **Solute** | **Solvent** | **Solute** | **Solvent** |
| Polar | Polar | Polar | Nonpolar |
| Nonpolar | Nonpolar | Nonpolar | Polar |

## Solutions with Ionic and Polar Solutes

In ionic solutes such as sodium chloride, NaCl, there are strong solute-solute attractions between positively charged $Na^+$ ions and negatively charged $Cl^-$ ions. In water, a polar solvent, the hydrogen bonds provide strong solvent-solvent attractions. When a NaCl crystal is placed in water, negatively charged oxygen atoms of water molecules attract positive $Na^+$ ions, and the positively charged hydrogen atoms of other water molecules attract negative $Cl^-$ ions. (See Figure 8.2.) As soon as the $Na^+$ and $Cl^-$ ions form a solution, they undergo **hydration** as water molecules surround each ion. The strong solute-solvent attractions between the $Na^+$ and $Cl^-$ ions and the polar water molecules release the energy needed to form the solution. In the equation for the formation of the NaCl solution, the solid and aqueous NaCl are shown with the formula $H_2O$ over the arrow, which indicates that water is needed for the dissociation process but is not a reactant.

$$NaCl(s) \xrightarrow{H_2O} Na^+(aq) + Cl^-(aq)$$

In another example, we find that a polar covalent compound such as methanol, $CH_3OH$, dissolves in water because methanol has a polar —OH group that forms hydrogen bonds with water.

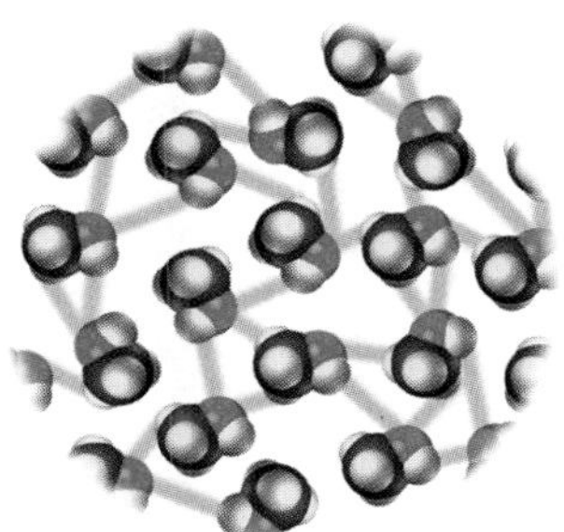

Methanol ($CH_3OH$) solute

Water solvent

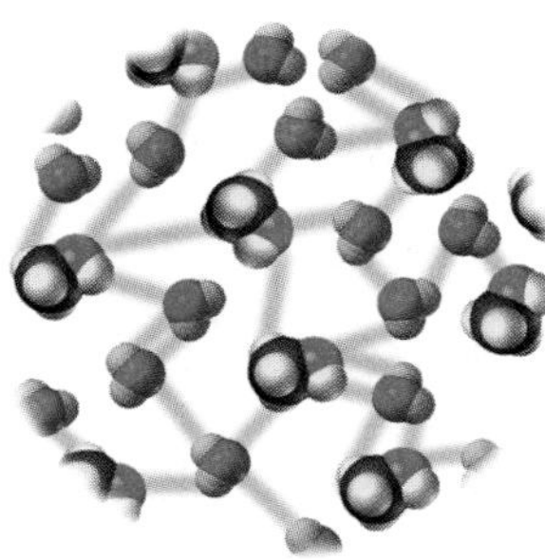

Methanol-water solution with hydrogen bonding

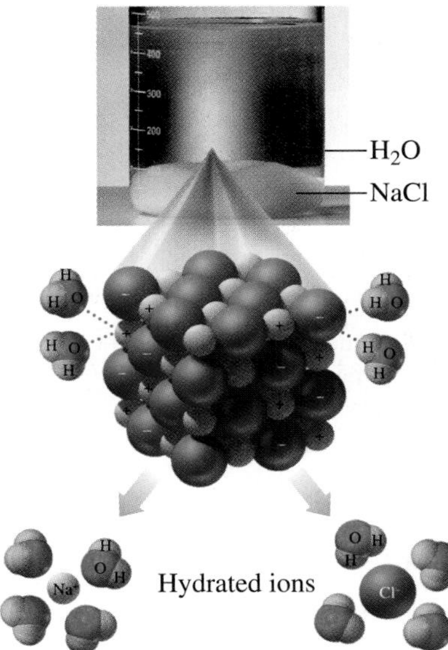


**FIGURE 8.2** Ions on the surface of a crystal of NaCl dissolve in water as they are attracted to the polar water molecules that pull the ions into solution and surround them.

Q What helps keep the $Na^+$ and $Cl^-$ ions in solution?

## Solutions with Nonpolar Solutes

Compounds containing nonpolar molecules such as iodine ($I_2$), oil, or grease do not dissolve in water, because there is little or no interaction between the particles of a nonpolar solute and the polar solvent. Nonpolar solutes require nonpolar solvents for a solution to form. The expression *"like dissolves like"* is a way of saying that the polarities of a solute and a solvent must be similar to form a solution. Figure 8.3 illustrates the formation of some polar and nonpolar solutions.

**FIGURE 8.3** Like dissolves like. **(a)** The test tubes contain an upper layer of water (polar) and a lower layer of $CH_2Cl_2$ (nonpolar). **(b)** The nonpolar solute $I_2$ dissolves in the nonpolar layer. **(c)** The ionic solute $Ni(NO_3)_2$ dissolves in the water.

Q Which layer would dissolve polar molecules of sugar?

**CONCEPT CHECK 8.1**

### Polar and Nonpolar Solutes

Indicate whether each of the following substances will form solutions with water. Explain.

**a.** KCl
**b.** octane, $C_8H_{18}$, in gasoline
**c.** ethanol, $C_2H_5OH$, in mouthwash

ANSWER

**a.** KCl is an ionic compound. The solute-solvent attractions between $K^+$ and $Cl^-$ and polar water will release the energy needed to break solute-solute and solvent-solvent bonds. Thus, a KCl solution will form.
**b.** $C_8H_{18}$ is a nonpolar substance that will not form a solution with water. The nonpolar solute-polar solvent attractions will not occur and no energy is released to form a solution.
**c.** $C_2H_5OH$ is a polar solute. Because attractions between a polar solute and polar water release energy to break solute-solute and solvent-solvent bonds, a $C_2H_5OH$ solution will form.

## QUESTIONS AND PROBLEMS

### Solutions

**8.1** Identify the solute and the solvent in each solution composed of the following:
**a.** 10.0 g of NaCl and 100.0 g of $H_2O$
**b.** 50.0 mL of ethanol, $C_2H_5OH$, and 10.0 mL of $H_2O$
**c.** 0.20 L of $O_2$ and 0.80 L of $N_2$ at STP

**8.2** Identify the solute and the solvent in each solution composed of the following:
**a.** 50.0 g of silver and 4.0 g of mercury
**b.** 100.0 mL of water and 5.0 g of sugar
**c.** 1.0 g of $I_2$ and 50.0 mL of alcohol

**8.3** Describe the formation of an aqueous KI solution.

**8.4** Describe the formation of an aqueous LiBr solution.

**8.5** Water is a polar solvent; $CCl_4$ is a nonpolar solvent. In which solvent is each of the following more likely to be soluble?
**a.** KCl, ionic
**b.** $I_2$, nonpolar
**c.** sucrose (table sugar), polar
**d.** gasoline, nonpolar

**8.6** Water is a polar solvent; hexane is a nonpolar solvent. In which solvent is each of the following more likely to be soluble?
**a.** vegetable oil, nonpolar
**b.** benzene, nonpolar
**c.** $LiNO_3$, ionic
**d.** $Na_2SO_4$, ionic

# 8.2 Electrolytes and Nonelectrolytes

LEARNING GOAL

Identify solutes as electrolytes or nonelectrolytes.

Solutes can be classified by their ability to conduct an electrical current. When **electrolytes** dissolve in water, they separate into ions that conduct electricity. When **nonelectrolytes** dissolve in water, they do not separate into ions, and their solutions do not conduct electricity.

To test solutions for ions, we can use an apparatus that consists of a battery and a pair of electrodes connected by wires to a light bulb. The light bulb glows when electricity flows, which happens only when the solution contains ions that move to each of the electrodes to complete the circuit.

### EXPLORE YOUR WORLD

#### Like Dissolves Like

Mix together small amounts of the following substances:
**a.** oil and water
**b.** water and vinegar
**c.** salt and water
**d.** sugar and water
**e.** salt and oil

QUESTIONS

1. Which of the mixtures formed a solution? Which did not?
2. Why do some mixtures form solutions, but others do not?

## Electrolytes

Electrolytes can be further classified as *strong electrolytes* and *weak electrolytes.* For all electrolytes, some or all of the solute that dissolves produces ions, a process called *dissociation.* For a **strong electrolyte**, such as sodium chloride (NaCl), 100% of the solute dissociates into ions. When the electrodes from the light bulb apparatus are placed in the NaCl solution, the light bulb is very bright.

In an equation for dissociation, the electrical charges must balance. For example, the strong electrolyte magnesium nitrate dissociates to give one magnesium ion for every two nitrate ions. However, only the ionic bonds between $Mg^{2+}$ and $NO_3^-$ are broken, not the covalent bonds within the polyatomic ion. The equation for the dissociation for $Mg(NO_3)_2$ is written as follows:

$$Mg(NO_3)_2(s) \xrightarrow{H_2O} Mg^{2+}(aq) + 2NO_3^-(aq)$$

For a **weak electrolyte** such as HF, only a small percentage of the dissolved solute dissociates into ions. Most of a weak electrolyte is present in a solution as undissociated molecules. When the electrodes are placed in a solution of a weak electrolyte, the glow of the light bulb is very dim. Thus, an aqueous solution of the weak electrolyte HF consists of mostly HF molecules and only a few $H^+$ and $F^-$ ions. As HF molecules dissociate into ions, some of $H^+$ and $F^-$ ions recombine to form HF molecules. These forward and reverse reactions of molecules to ions and back again are indicated by two arrows that point in opposite directions, as shown in the following equation:

$$HF(aq) \underset{\text{Recombination}}{\overset{\text{Dissociation}}{\rightleftharpoons}} H^+(aq) + F^-(aq)$$

## Nonelectrolytes

A nonelectrolyte such as sucrose (sugar) dissolves in water as molecules, which do not dissociate into ions. When electrodes are placed in a solution of a nonelectrolyte, the light bulb does not glow, because the solution does not conduct electricity.

$$C_{12}H_{22}O_{11}(s) \xrightarrow{H_2O} C_{12}H_{22}O_{11}(aq)$$

Sucrose — Solution of sucrose molecules

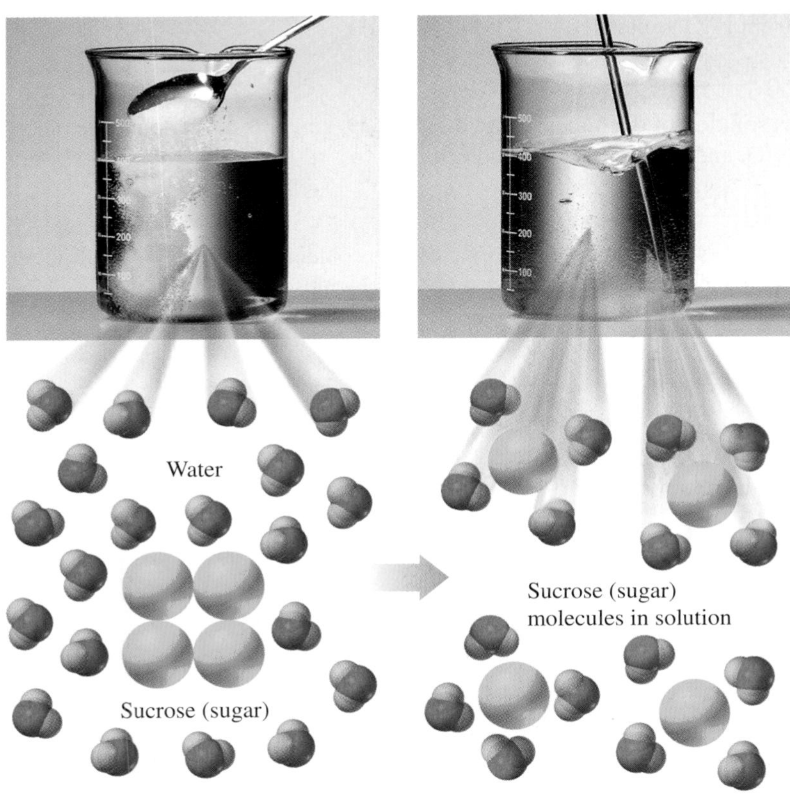


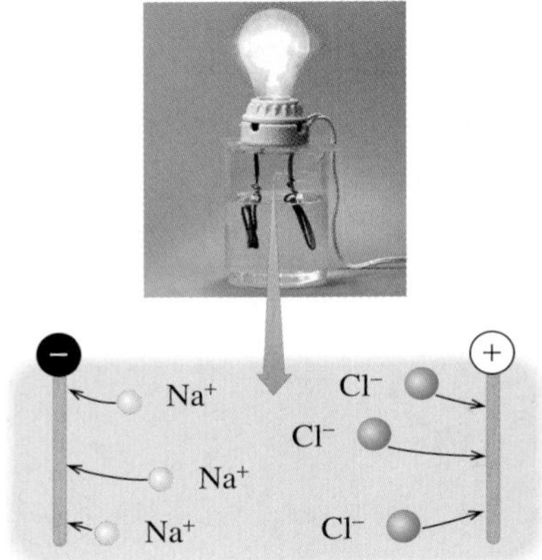


Strong electrolyte

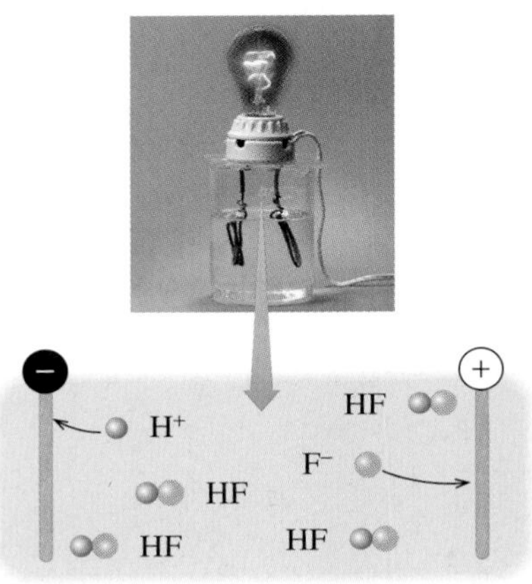


Weak electrolyte

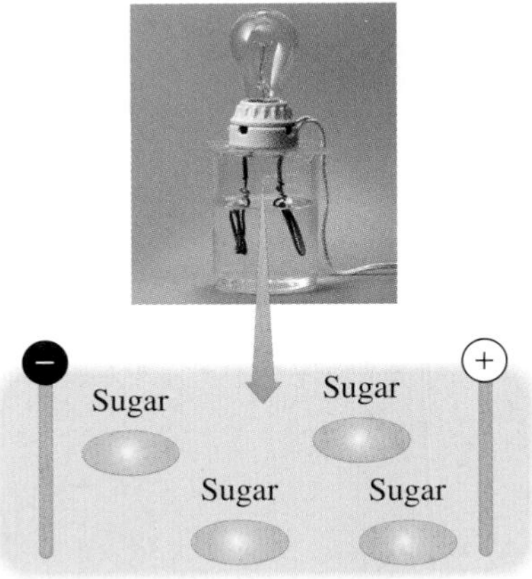


Nonelectrolyte

Table 8.4 summarizes the classification of solutes in aqueous solutions.

**TABLE 8.4** Classification of Solutes in Aqueous Solutions

| Type of Solute | Dissociation | Particles in Solution | Conducts Electricity? | Examples |
|---|---|---|---|---|
| Strong electrolyte | Complete | Ions only | Yes | Ionic compounds such as NaCl, KBr, $MgCl_2$, $NaNO_3$; NaOH, KOH; HCl, HBr, HI, $HNO_3$, $HClO_4$, $H_2SO_4$ |
| Weak electrolyte | Partial | Mostly molecules and a few ions | Yes, but poorly | HF, $H_2O$, $NH_3$, $HC_2H_3O_2$ (acetic acid) |
| Nonelectrolyte | None | Molecules only | No | Carbon compounds such as $CH_3OH$ (methanol), $C_2H_5OH$ (ethanol), $C_{12}H_{22}O_{11}$ (sucrose), $CH_4N_2O$ (urea) |

CONCEPT CHECK 8.2

### Electrolytes and Nonelectrolytes

Identify the components in each of the following aqueous solutions, and write the equation for the formation of a solution:

**a.** ammonium bromide, a strong electrolyte
**b.** urea, $CH_4N_2O$, a nonelectrolyte
**c.** hypochlorous acid, HClO, a weak electrolyte

ANSWER

**a.** An aqueous solution of the strong electrolyte, $NH_4Br$, contains $NH_4^+$ and $Br^-$ ions and the solvent $H_2O$ molecules:

$$NH_4Br(s) \xrightarrow{H_2O} NH_4^+(aq) + Br^-(aq)$$

**b.** An aqueous solution of the nonelectrolyte, $CH_4N_2O$, contains only molecules of urea, $CH_4N_2O$, and the solvent $H_2O$ molecules:

$$CH_4N_2O(s) \xrightarrow{H_2O} CH_4N_2O(aq)$$

**c.** An aqueous solution of the weak electrolyte, HClO, contains mostly HClO molecules, a few $H^+$ and $ClO^-$ ions, and the solvent $H_2O$ molecules:

$$HClO(aq) \overset{H_2O}{\rightleftharpoons} H^+(aq) + ClO^-(aq)$$

SAMPLE PROBLEM 8.1

### Solutions of Electrolytes and Nonelectrolytes

Indicate whether solutions of each of the following contain only ions, only molecules, or mostly molecules and a few ions:

**a.** $Na_2SO_4$, a strong electrolyte **b.** $CH_3OH$, a nonelectrolyte

SOLUTION

**a.** A solution of $Na_2SO_4$ contains only the ions $Na^+$ and $SO_4^{2-}$.
**b.** A nonelectrolyte such as $CH_3OH$ dissolves only as molecules.

STUDY CHECK

Boric acid, $H_3BO_3$, is a weak electrolyte. Would you expect a boric acid solution to contain only ions, only molecules, or mostly molecules and a few ions?

## Equivalents

Body fluids typically contain a mixture of several electrolytes, such as $Na^+$, $Cl^-$, $K^+$, and $Ca^{2+}$. We measure each individual ion in terms of an **equivalent (Eq)**, which is the amount of that ion equal to 1 mole of positive or negative electrical charge. For example, 1 mole of $Na^+$ ions and 1 mole of $Cl^-$ ions are each 1 equivalent or 1000 milliequivalents (mEq) because they each contain 1 mole of charge. For an ion with a charge of 2+ or 2−, there are 2 equivalents for each mole. Some examples of ions and equivalents are shown in Table 8.5.

**TABLE 8.5** Equivalents of Electrolytes

| Ion | Electrical Charge | Number of Equivalents in 1 Mole |
|---|---|---|
| $Na^+$ | 1+ | 1 Eq |
| $Ca^{2+}$ | 2+ | 2 Eq |
| $Fe^{3+}$ | 3+ | 3 Eq |
| $Cl^-$ | 1− | 1 Eq |
| $SO_4^{2-}$ | 2− | 2 Eq |

In a solution, the charge of the positive ions is always balanced by the charge of the negative ions. For example, a solution containing 25 mEq/L of $Na^+$ and 4 mEq/L of $K^+$ has a total positive charge of 29 mEq/L. If $Cl^-$ is the only anion, its concentration must be 29 mEq/L.

SAMPLE PROBLEM 8.2

## Electrolyte Concentration

In body fluids, concentrations of electrolytes are often expressed as milliequivalents (mEq) per liter. A typical concentration for $Ca^{2+}$ in the blood is 8.8 mEq/L.

**a.** How many moles of calcium ion are in 0.50 L of blood?
**b.** If chloride ion is the only other ion present, what is its concentration in mEq/L?

SOLUTION

**a.** Using the volume and the electrolyte concentration (in mEq/L), we can find the number of equivalents in 0.50 L of blood:

$$0.50\ \cancel{L} \times \frac{8.8\ \cancel{mEq\ Ca^{2+}}}{1\ \cancel{L}} \times \frac{1\ Eq\ Ca^{2+}}{1000\ \cancel{mEq\ Ca^{2+}}} = 0044\ Eq\ of\ Ca^{2+}$$

We can then convert equivalents to moles (for $Ca^{2+}$ there are 2 Eq per mole):

$$0.0044\ \cancel{Eq\ Ca^{2+}} \times \frac{1\ mole\ Ca^{2+}}{2\ \cancel{Eq\ Ca^{2+}}} = 0.0022\ mole\ of\ Ca^{2+}$$

**b.** If the concentration of $Ca^{2+}$ is 8.8 mEq/L, then the concentration of $Cl^-$ must be 8.8 mEq/L to balance the charge.

STUDY CHECK

A Ringer's solution for intravenous fluid replacement contains 155 mEq $Cl^-$ per liter of solution. If a patient receives 1250 mL of Ringer's solution, how many moles of chloride were given?

# QUESTIONS AND PROBLEMS

## Electrolytes and Nonelectrolytes

**8.7** KF is a strong electrolyte, and HF is a weak electrolyte. How are they different?

**8.8** NaOH is a strong electrolyte, and $CH_3OH$ is a nonelectrolyte. How are they different?

**8.9** The following soluble salts are strong electrolytes. For each, write a balanced equation for their dissociation in water.
**a.** KCl **b.** $CaCl_2$ **c.** $K_3PO_4$ **d.** $Fe(NO_3)_3$

**8.10** The following soluble salts are strong electrolytes. For each, write a balanced equation for their dissociation in water.
**a.** LiBr **b.** $NaNO_3$ **c.** $FeCl_3$ **d.** $Mg(NO_3)_2$

**8.11** Indicate whether aqueous solutions of the following will contain only ions, only molecules, or mostly molecules and a few ions:
**a.** acetic acid ($HC_2H_3O_2$), found in vinegar, a weak electrolyte
**b.** NaBr, a strong electrolyte
**c.** fructose ($C_6H_{12}O_6$), a nonelectrolyte

**8.12** Indicate whether aqueous solutions of the following will contain only ions, only molecules, or mostly molecules and a few ions:
**a.** $Na_2SO_4$, a strong electrolyte
**b.** ethanol, $C_2H_5OH$, a nonelectrolyte
**c.** HCN, hydrocyanic acid, a weak electrolyte

**8.13** Indicate the type of electrolyte represented in the following equations:

**a.** $K_2SO_4(s) \xrightarrow{H_2O} 2K^+(aq) + SO_4^{2-}(aq)$

**b.** $NH_4OH(aq) \overset{H_2O}{\rightleftharpoons} NH_4^+(aq) + OH^-(aq)$

**c.** $C_6H_{12}O_6(s) \xrightarrow{H_2O} C_6H_{12}O_6(aq)$

**8.14** Indicate the type of electrolyte represented in the following equations:

**a.** $CH_3OH(l) \xrightarrow{H_2O} CH_3OH(aq)$

**b.** $MgCl_2(s) \xrightarrow{H_2O} Mg^{2+}(aq) + 2Cl^-(aq)$

**c.** $HClO(aq) \overset{H_2O}{\rightleftharpoons} H^+(aq) + ClO^-(aq)$

8.15 Indicate the number of equivalents in each of the following:

**a.** 1 mole of $K^+$ **b.** 2 moles of $OH^-$
**c.** 1 mole of $Ca^{2+}$ **d.** 3 moles of $CO_3^{\ 2-}$

**8.16** Indicate the number of equivalents in each of the following:

**a.** 1 mole of $Mg^{2+}$ **b.** 0.5 mole of $H^+$
**c.** 4 moles of $Cl^-$ **d.** 2 moles of $Fe^{3+}$

8.17 A physiological saline solution contains 154 mEq/L each of $Na^+$ and $Cl^-$. How many moles each of $Na^+$ and $Cl^-$ are in 1.00 L of the saline solution?

**8.18** A solution to replace potassium loss contains 40. mEq/L each of $K^+$ and $Cl^-$. How many moles each of $K^+$ and $Cl^-$ are in 1.5 L of the solution?

8.19 A solution contains 40. mEq/L of $Cl^-$ and 15 mEq/L of $HPO_4^{\ 2-}$. If $Na^+$ is the only cation in the solution, what is the $Na^+$ concentration in milliequivalents per liter?

**8.20** A sample of Ringer's solution contains the following concentrations (mEq/L) of cations: $Na^+$ 147, $K^+$ 4, and $Ca^{2+}$ 4. If $Cl^-$ is the only anion in the solution, what is the $Cl^-$ concentration in milliequivalents per liter?

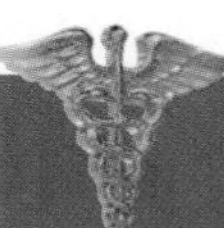

# HEALTH NOTE

## Electrolytes in Body Fluids

The concentrations of electrolytes present in body fluids and in intravenous fluids given to a patient are often expressed in milliequivalents per liter (mEq/L) of solution:

$$1 \text{ Eq} = 1000 \text{ mEq}$$

Table 8.6 gives the concentrations of some typical electrolytes in blood plasma. There is a charge balance because the total number of positive charges is equal to the total number of negative charges. The use of a specific intravenous solution depends on the nutritional, electrolyte, and fluid needs of the individual patient. Examples of various types of solutions are given in Table 8.7.

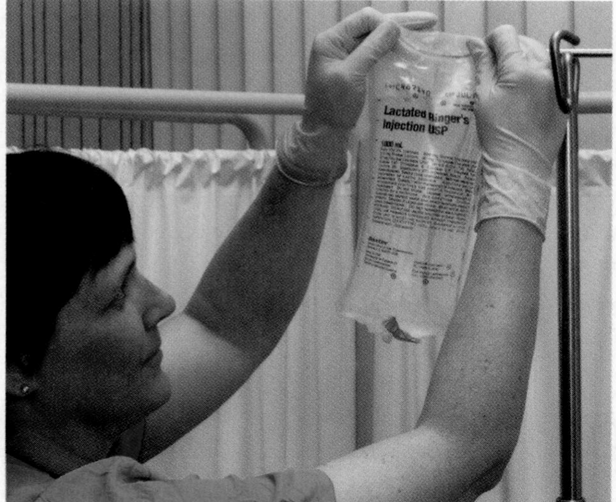


**TABLE 8.6** Some Typical Concentrations of Electrolytes in Blood Plasma

| Electrolyte | Concentration (mEq/L) |
|---|---|
| **Cations** | |
| $Na^+$ | 138 |
| $K^+$ | 5 |
| $Mg^{2+}$ | 3 |
| $Ca^{2+}$ | 4 |
| Total | 150 |
| **Anions** | |
| $Cl^-$ | 110 |
| $HCO_3^-$ | 30 |
| $HPO_4^{\ 2-}$ | 4 |
| Proteins | 6 |
| Total | 150 |

**TABLE 8.7** Electrolyte Concentrations in Intravenous Replacement Solutions

| Solution | Electrolytes (mEq/L) | Use |
|---|---|---|
| Sodium chloride (0.9%) | $Na^+$ 154, $Cl^-$ 154 | Replacement of fluid loss |
| Potassium chloride with 5% dextrose | $K^+$ 40, $Cl^-$ 40 | Treatment of malnutrition (low potassium levels) |
| Ringer's solution | $Na^+$ 147, $K^+$ 4, $Ca^{2+}$ 4, $Cl^-$ 155 | Replacement of fluids and electrolytes lost through dehydration |
| Maintenance solution with 5% dextrose | $Na^+$ 40, $K^+$ 35, $Cl^-$ 40, lactate$^-$ 20, $HPO_4^{\ 2-}$ 15 | Maintenance of fluid and electrolyte levels |
| Replacement solution (extracellular) | $Na^+$ 140, $K^+$ 10, $Ca^{2+}$ 5, $Mg^{2+}$ 3, $Cl^-$ 103, acetate$^-$ 47, citrate$^{3-}$ 8 | Replacement of electrolytes in extracellular fluids |

# 8.3 Solubility

**LEARNING GOAL**

Define solubility; distinguish between an unsaturated and a saturated solution.

SELF STUDY ACTIVITY
Solubility

The term **solubility** describes the amount of a solute that can dissolve in a given amount of solvent. Many factors, such as the type of solute, the type of solvent, and the temperature, affect solubility. Solubility is usually expressed in grams of solute in 100 grams of solvent and is the maximum amount of solute that can be dissolved at a certain temperature. If a solute readily dissolves when added to the solvent, the solution does not contain the maximum amount of solute. We call the solution an **unsaturated solution**.

A solution that contains all the solute that can dissolve is a **saturated solution**.

When a solution is saturated, the rate of the reaction that dissolves the solute becomes equal to the rate of recrystallization. Then there is no further change in the amount of dissolved solute in solution.

$$\text{Solid solute} \underset{\text{Crystallizes}}{\overset{\text{Dissolves}}{\rightleftarrows}} \text{saturated solution}$$

We can prepare a saturated solution by adding solute greater than needed for solubility. Stirring the solution will dissolve the maximum amount of solute and leave the excess on the bottom of the container. Once we have a saturated solution, the addition of more solute will increase only the amount of undissolved solute.

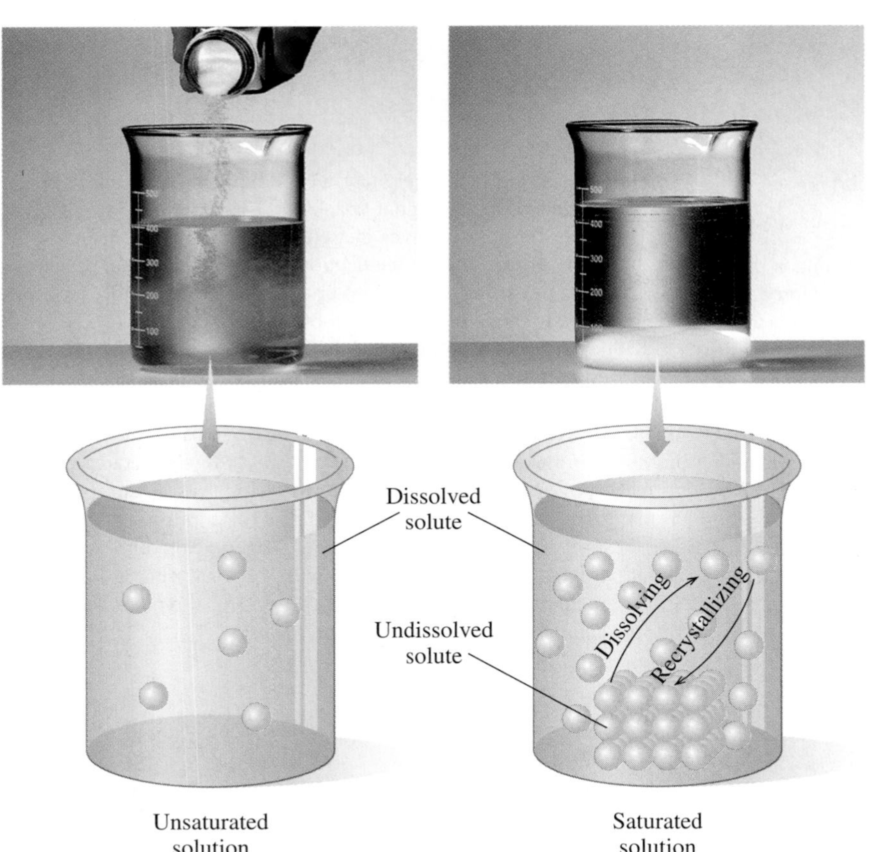


SAMPLE PROBLEM 8.3

■ **Saturated Solutions**

At 20 °C, the solubility of KCl is 34 g/100 g of water. In the laboratory, a student mixes 75 g of KCl with 200. g of water at a temperature of 20 °C.

**a.** How much of the KCl can dissolve?
**b.** Is the solution saturated or unsaturated?
**c.** What is the mass of any solid KCl in the bottom of the container?

SOLUTION

**a.** KCl has a solubility of 34 g of KCl in 100 g of water. Using solubility as a conversion factor, the maximum amount of KCl that can dissolve in 200. g of water is calculated as follows:

$$200.\ \cancel{g\ H_2O} \times \frac{34\ g\ KCl}{100\ \cancel{g\ H_2O}} = 68\ g\ of\ KCl$$

**b.** Because 75 g of KCl exceeds the amount that can dissolve in 200. g of water, the KCl solution is saturated.

**c.** If we add 75 g of KCl to 200. g of water and only 68 g of KCl can dissolve, there is 7 g of solid (undissolved) KCl on the bottom of the container.

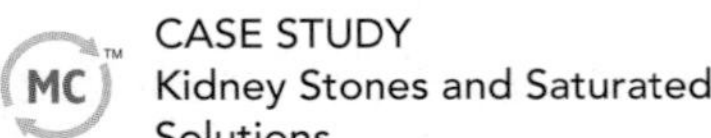

CASE STUDY
Kidney Stones and Saturated Solutions

STUDY CHECK

At 50 °C, the solubility of $NaNO_3$ is 110 g/100 g of water. How many grams of $NaNO_3$ are needed to make a saturated $NaNO_3$ solution with 50. g of water at 50 °C?

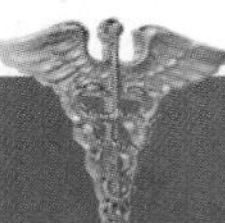

# HEALTH NOTE

## Gout and Kidney Stones: A Problem of Saturation in Body Fluids

The conditions of gout and kidney stones involve compounds in the body that exceed their solubility levels and form solid products. Gout affects adults, primarily men, over the age of 40. Attacks of gout may occur when the concentration of uric acid in blood plasma exceeds its solubility, which is 7 mg/100 mL of plasma at 37 °C. Insoluble deposits of needle-like crystals of uric acid can form in the cartilage, tendons, and soft tissues, where they cause painful gout attacks. They may also form in the tissues of the kidneys, where they can cause renal damage. High levels of uric acid in the body can be caused by an increase in uric acid production, failure of the kidneys to remove uric acid, or by a diet with an overabundance of foods containing purines, which are metabolized to uric acid in the body. Foods in the diet that contribute to high levels of uric acid include certain meats, sardines, mushrooms, asparagus, and beans. Drinking alcoholic beverages may also significantly increase uric acid levels and bring about gout attacks.

Treatment for gout involves diet changes and drugs. Depending on the levels of uric acid, a medication such as probenecid can be used to help the kidneys eliminate uric acid, or allopurinol can be administered to block the production of uric acid by the body.

Kidney stones are solid materials that form in the urinary tract. Most kidney stones are composed of calcium phosphate and calcium oxalate, although they can be solid uric acid. The excessive ingestion of minerals and insufficient water intake can cause the concentration of mineral salts to exceed their solubility and lead to the formation of kidney stones. When a kidney stone passes through the urinary tract, it causes considerable pain and discomfort, necessitating the use of painkillers and possibly surgery. Sometimes ultrasound is used to break up kidney stones. Persons prone to kidney stones are advised to drink six to eight glasses of water every day to prevent saturation levels of minerals in the urine.

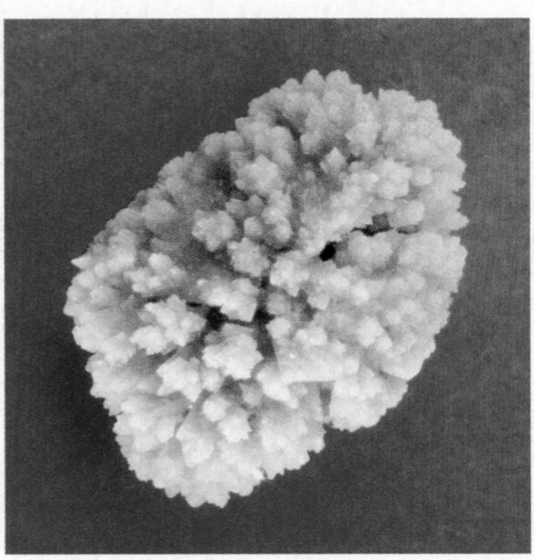

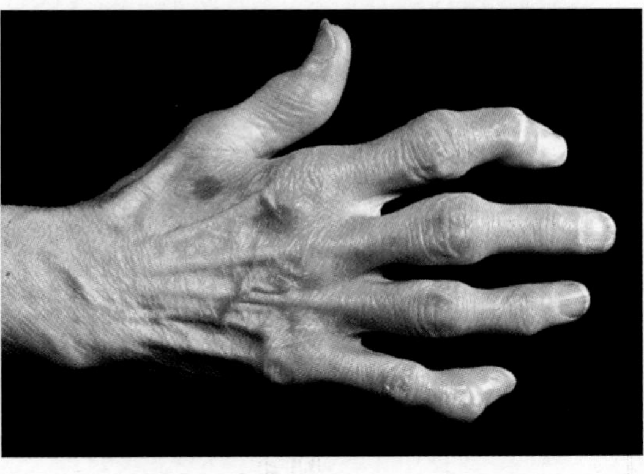

## EXPLORE YOUR WORLD

### Preparing Solutions

Place $\frac{1}{2}$ cup of cold water in a glass. Begin adding 1 tablespoon of sugar at a time and stir thoroughly. Count the number of tablespoons of sugar you add. As the sugar solution becomes more concentrated, you may need to stir for a few minutes until all the sugar dissolves. Each time observe the solution after several minutes to determine when it is saturated.

Repeat the above activity with $\frac{1}{2}$ cup of warm water. Count the number of tablespoons of sugar you need to form a saturated solution.

**QUESTIONS**

1. How did you know when you obtained a saturated solution?
2. How much sugar dissolved in the warm water compared to the cold water?

## Effect of Temperature on Solubility

The solubility of most solids becomes greater as temperature increases, which means that solutions usually can contain more dissolved solute at higher temperatures. A few substances show little change in solubility at higher temperatures, and a few are less soluble. (See Figure 8.4.) For example, when you add sugar to iced tea, some undissolved sugar may quickly form on the bottom of the glass. But if you add sugar to hot tea, many teaspoons of sugar are needed before solid sugar appears. Hot tea dissolves more sugar than does cold tea because the solubility of sugar is much greater at a higher temperature. When a saturated solution is carefully cooled, it becomes a *supersaturated solution* because it contains more solute than the solubility allows. Such a solution is unstable, and if the solution is agitated or if a solute crystal is added, the excess solute will crystallize once again to give a saturated solution.

The solubility of a gas in water decreases as the temperature increases. At higher temperatures, more gas molecules have the energy to escape from the solution. Perhaps you have observed the bubbles escaping from a cold carbonated soft drink as it warms. At high temperatures, bottles containing carbonated solutions may burst as more gas molecules leave the solution and increase the gas pressure inside the bottle. Biologists have found that increased temperatures in rivers and lakes cause the amount of dissolved oxygen to decrease until the warm water can no longer support a biological community. Electricity-generating plants are required to have their own ponds to use with their cooling towers to lessen the threat of thermal pollution to surrounding waterways.

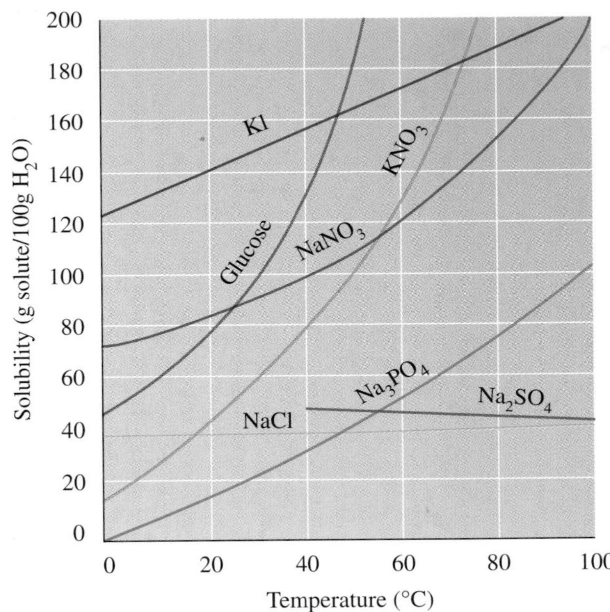


**FIGURE 8.4** In water, most common solids are more soluble as the temperature increases.

**Q** Compare the solubility of $NaNO_3$ at 20 °C and 60 °C.

## Henry's Law

**Henry's law** states that the solubility of gas in a liquid is directly related to the pressure of that gas above the liquid. At higher pressures, there are more gas molecules available to enter and dissolve in the liquid. A can of soda is carbonated by using $CO_2$ gas at high pressure to increase the solubility of the $CO_2$ in the beverage. When you open the can at atmospheric pressure, the pressure on the $CO_2$ drops, which decreases the solubility of $CO_2$. As a result, bubbles of $CO_2$ rapidly escape from the solution. The burst of bubbles is even more noticeable when you open a warm can of soda.

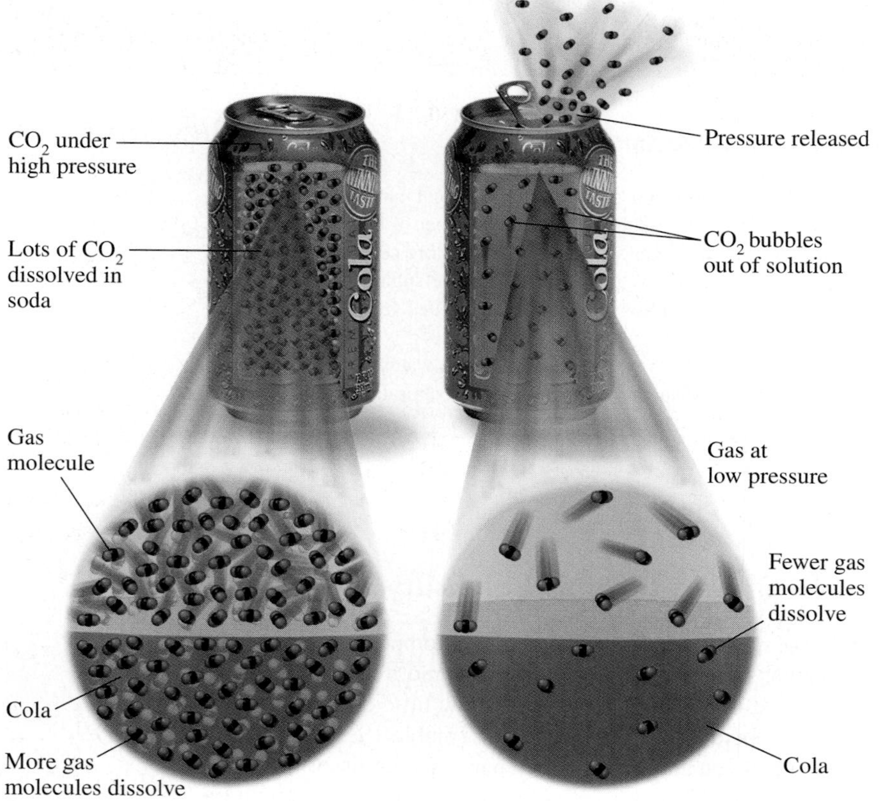


SAMPLE PROBLEM 8.4

### Factors Affecting Solubility

Indicate whether the solubility of the solute will increase or decrease in each of the following situations:

**a.** dissolving sugar using 80 °C water instead of 25 °C water
**b.** effect on the dissolved $O_2$ in a lake as it warms

SOLUTION

**a.** An increase in the temperature increases the solubility of the sugar.
**b.** An increase in the temperature decreases the solubility of $O_2$ gas.

STUDY CHECK

At 10 °C, the solubility of $KNO_3$ is 30 g/100 g $H_2O$. Would you expect the solubility of $KNO_3$ to be higher or lower at 40 °C? Explain.

## Soluble and Insoluble Salts

TUTORIAL Solubility

Up to now, we have considered ionic compounds called **soluble salts** that dissolve in water. However, some ionic compounds do not separate into ions in water. They are **insoluble salts** that remain as solids even in contact with water.

Salts that are soluble in water typically contain at least one of the following ions: $Li^+$, $Na^+$, $K^+$, $NH_4^+$, $NO_3^-$, or $C_2H_3O_2^-$. Most salts containing $Cl^-$ are soluble, but AgCl, $PbCl_2$, or $Hg_2Cl_2$ are not; they are insoluble chloride salts. Similarly, most salts containing $SO_4^{2-}$ are soluble, but a few are insoluble (See Table 8.8). Most other salts are insoluble

**TABLE 8.8** Solubility Rules for Ionic Solids in Water

| Soluble if Salt Contains | | Insoluble if Salt Contains |
|---|---|---|
| $NH_4^+$, $Li^+$, $Na^+$, $K^+$ $NO_3^-$, $C_2H_3O_2^-$ (acetate) | ← but are soluble with | $CO_3^{2-}$, $S^{2-}$ $PO_4^{3-}$, $OH^-$ |
| $Cl^-$, $Br^-$, $I^-$ | but are not soluble with → | $Ag^+$, $Pb^{2+}$, or $Hg_2^{2+}$ |
| $SO_4^{2-}$ | but are not soluble with → | $Ba^{2+}$, $Pb^{2+}$, $Ca^{2+}$, $Sr^{2+}$ |

and do not dissolve in water. (See Figure 8.5.) In an insoluble salt, attractions between its positive and negative ions are too strong for the polar water molecules to break. We can use the solubility rules to predict whether a salt (a solid ionic compound) would be expected to dissolve in water. Table 8.9 illustrates the use of these rules.

In medicine, the insoluble salt $BaSO_4$ is used as an opaque substance to enhance X-rays of the gastrointestinal tract. $BaSO_4$ is so insoluble that it does not dissolve in gastric fluids.

CdS

FeS

$PbCrO_4$

$Ni(OH)_2$

**FIGURE 8.5** Mixing certain aqueous solutions produces insoluble salts.

**Q** What makes each of these salts insoluble in water?

**TABLE 8.9** Using Solubility Rules

| Ionic Compound | Solubility in Water | Reasoning |
|---|---|---|
| $K_2S$ | Soluble | Contains $K^+$ |
| $Ca(NO_3)_2$ | Soluble | Contains $NO_3^-$ |
| $PbCl_2$ | Insoluble | Is an insoluble chloride |
| NaOH | Soluble | Contains $Na^+$ |
| $AlPO_4$ | Insoluble | Contains no soluble ions |

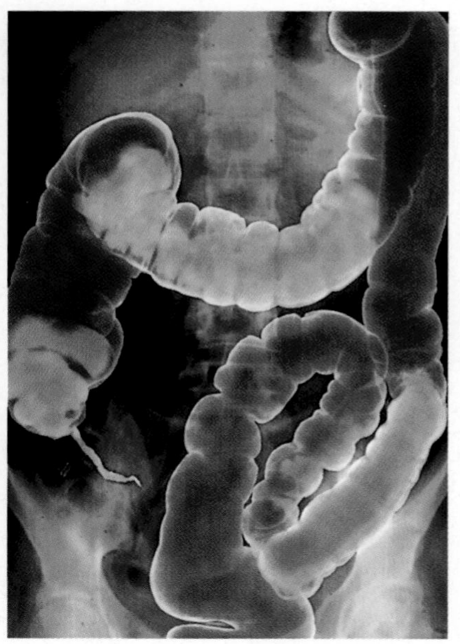

**FIGURE 8.6** A barium sulfate enhanced X-ray of the abdomen shows the large intestine.

**Q** Is $BaSO_4$ a soluble or an insoluble substance?

(See Figure 8.6.) Other barium salts cannot be used; they would dissolve in water, releasing $Ba^{2+}$, which is poisonous.

CONCEPT CHECK 8.3

### Soluble and Insoluble Salts

Predict whether each of the following salts is soluble in water and explain why:

**a.** $Na_3PO_4$ **b.** $CaCO_3$

ANSWER

**a.** The salt $Na_3PO_4$ is soluble in water because a compound that contains $Na^+$ is soluble.

**b.** The salt $CaCO_3$ is not soluble. The compound does not contain a soluble positive ion, which means that a calcium salt containing $CO_3^{2-}$ is not soluble.

## Formation of a Solid

We can use solubility rules to predict whether a solid, called a *precipitate*, forms when two solutions of ionic compounds are mixed. A solid forms when two ions of an insoluble salt come in contact with one another. For example, when a solution of $AgNO_3$ ($Ag^+$ and $NO_3^-$) is mixed with a solution of NaCl ($Na^+$ and $Cl^-$), the white insoluble salt AgCl is produced. We can write the equation for a double replacement reaction. However, the chemical equation does not show the individual ions to help us decide which, if any, insoluble salt would form. To help us determine any insoluble salt, we can first write the reactants to show all the ions present when the two solutions are mixed:

$$Ag^+(aq) + NO_3^-(aq) + Na^+(aq) + Cl^-(aq) \longrightarrow$$

Then we look at the cations and anions to see if any of the combinations would be an insoluble salt. The new combination AgCl forms an insoluble salt.

**STEP 1** **Write the reactant ions.**

**Reactants (initial combinations)**

$Ag^+(aq) + NO_3^-(aq)$

$Na^+(aq) + Cl^-(aq)$

**STEP 2** **Write the product combinations.**

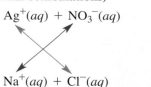

| Mixture (new combinations) | | Product |
|---|---|---|
| $Ag^+(aq) + Cl^-(aq)$ | $\longrightarrow$ | $AgCl(s)$ |
| $Na^+(aq) + NO_3^-(aq)$ | | |

**STEP 3** **Write the ionic equation including the solid.** Show that a precipitate forms, while the ions $Na^+$ and $NO_3^-$ are in solution:

$$Ag^+(aq) + NO_3^-(aq) + Na^+(aq) + Cl^-(aq) \longrightarrow AgCl(s) + Na^+(aq) + NO_3^-(aq)$$

**STEP 4** **Write the net ionic equation.** Now we can remove the $Na^+$ and $NO_3^-$ ions known as *spectator ions* because they are unchanged during the reaction:

$$Ag^+(aq) + \underbrace{\cancel{NO_3^-(aq)} + \cancel{Na^+(aq)}}_{\text{Spectator ions}} + Cl^-(aq) \longrightarrow AgCl(s) + \underbrace{\cancel{Na^+(aq)} + \cancel{NO_3^-(aq)}}_{\text{Spectator ions}}$$

Finally, a **net ionic equation** can be written that gives the chemical reaction that occurred. The $Na^+$ and $NO_3^-$ ions, the spectator ions, are removed from the ionic equation we wrote above:

$$Ag^+(aq) + Cl^-(aq) \longrightarrow AgCl(s)$$

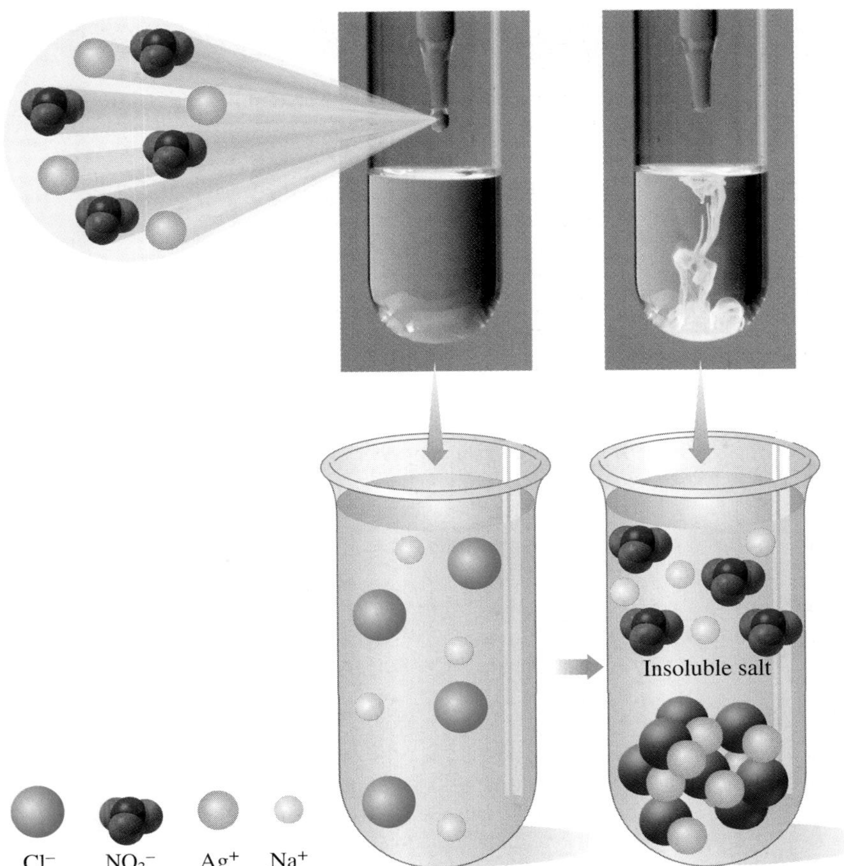


| Type of Equation | | | |
|---|---|---|---|
| **Chemical** | $AgNO_3(aq)$ | $+ NaCl(aq) \longrightarrow$ | $AgCl(s) + NaNO_3(aq)$ |
| **Ionic** | $Ag^+(aq)$ | $+ Na^+(aq) + Cl^-(aq) \longrightarrow$ | $AgCl(s) + Na^+(aq)$ |
| **Net ionic** | $Ag^+(aq)$ | $+ Cl^-(aq) \longrightarrow$ | $AgCl(s)$ |

## SAMPLE PROBLEM 8.5

### Formation of an Insoluble Salt

Solutions of $BaCl_2$ and $K_2SO_4$ are mixed and a white solid forms.

**a.** Write the net ionic equation.
**b.** What is the white solid that forms?

SOLUTION

**a. STEP 1** $Ba^{2+}(aq) + Cl^-(aq) + K^+(aq) + SO_4^{2-}(aq)$

**STEP 2** $BaSO_4(s)$ is insoluble.

**STEP 3** $Ba^{2+}(aq) + 2Cl^-(aq) + 2K^+(aq) + SO_4^{2-}(aq) \longrightarrow BaSO_4(s) + 2Cl^-(aq) + 2K^+(aq)$

**STEP 4** $Ba^{2+}(aq) + SO_4^{2-}(aq) \longrightarrow BaSO_4(s)$

**b.** $BaSO_4$ is the white solid.

STUDY CHECK

Predict whether a solid might form in each of the following mixtures of solutions. If so, write the net ionic equation for the reaction.

**a.** $NH_4Cl(aq) + Ca(NO_3)_2(aq)$ **b.** $Pb(NO_3)_2(aq) + KCl(aq)$

**Guide to Writing Net Ionic Equations for an Insoluble Salt**

**STEP 1** Write the ions of the reactants.

**STEP 2** Write the new combinations of ions and determine if any are insoluble.

**STEP 3** Write the ionic equation including the solid.

**STEP 4** Write the net ionic equation by removing spectator ions.

## QUESTIONS AND PROBLEMS

### Solubility

**8.21** State whether each of the following refers to a saturated or unsaturated solution:
**a.** A crystal added to a solution does not change in size.
**b.** A sugar cube completely dissolves when added to a cup of coffee.

**8.22** State whether each of the following refers to a saturated or unsaturated solution:
**a.** A spoonful of salt added to boiling water dissolves.
**b.** A layer of sugar forms on the bottom of a glass of tea as ice is added.

Use this table for problems 8.23–8.26.

**Solubility (g/100 g $H_2O$)**

| Substance | 20 °C | 50 °C |
|---|---|---|
| KCl | 34 | 43 |
| $NaNO_3$ | 88 | 110 |
| $C_{12}H_{22}O_{11}$ (sugar) | 204 | 260 |

**8.23** Using the above table, determine whether each of the following solutions will be saturated or unsaturated at 20 °C:
**a.** adding 25 g of KCl to 100. g of $H_2O$
**b.** adding 11 g of $NaNO_3$ to 25 g of $H_2O$
**c.** adding 400. g of sugar to 125 g of $H_2O$

**8.24** Using the above table, determine whether each of the following solutions will be saturated or unsaturated at 50 °C:
**a.** adding 25 g of KCl to 50. g of $H_2O$
**b.** adding 150. g of $NaNO_3$ to 75 g of $H_2O$
**c.** adding 80. g of sugar to 25 g of $H_2O$

**8.25** A solution containing 80. g of KCl in 200. g of $H_2O$ at 50 °C is cooled to 20 °C.
**a.** How many grams of KCl remain in solution at 20 °C?
**b.** How many grams of solid KCl crystallized after cooling?

**8.26** A solution containing 80. g of $NaNO_3$ in 75 g of $H_2O$ at 50 °C is cooled to 20 °C.
**a.** How many grams of $NaNO_3$ remain in solution at 20 °C?
**b.** How many grams of solid $NaNO_3$ crystallized after cooling?

**8.27** Explain the following observations:
**a.** More sugar dissolves in hot tea than in iced tea.
**b.** Champagne in a warm room goes flat.
**c.** A warm can of soda has more spray when opened than a cold one.

**8.28** Explain the following observations:
**a.** An open can of soda loses its "fizz" quicker at room temperature than in the refrigerator.
**b.** Chlorine gas in tap water escapes as the water warms to room temperature.
**c.** Less sugar dissolves in iced coffee than in hot coffee.

**8.29** Predict whether each of the following ionic compounds is soluble in water:
**a.** LiCl **b.** AgCl **c.** $BaCO_3$
**d.** $K_2O$ **e.** $Fe(NO_3)_3$

**8.30** Predict whether each of the following ionic compounds is soluble in water:
**a.** PbS **b.** NaI **c.** $Na_2S$
**d.** $Ag_2O$ **e.** $CaSO_4$

**8.31** Determine whether a solid forms when solutions containing the following salts are mixed. If so, write the ionic equation and the net ionic equation.
**a.** KCl and $Na_2S$ **b.** $AgNO_3$ and $K_2S$
**c.** $CaCl_2$ and $Na_2SO_4$ **d.** $CuCl_2$ and $Li_3PO_4$

**8.32** Determine whether a solid forms when solutions containing the following salts are mixed. If so, write the ionic equation and the net ionic equation.
**a.** $Na_3PO_4$ and $AgNO_3$ **b.** $K_2SO_4$ and $Na_2CO_3$
**c.** $Pb(NO_3)_2$ and $Na_2CO_3$ **d.** $BaCl_2$ and KOH

## 8.4 Percent Concentration

**LEARNING GOAL**

Calculate the percent concentration of a solute in a solution; use percent concentration to calculate the amount of solute or solution.

The amount of solute dissolved in a certain amount of solution is called the **concentration** of the solution. We will look at the concentrations that are a ratio of a certain amount of solute in a given amount of solution:

$$\text{Concentration of a solution} = \frac{\text{amount of solute}}{\text{amount of solution}}$$

### Mass Percent

In the mass percent (% m/m) of a solution, the units of mass of the solute and solution must be the same. Typically, a mass percent (% m/m) describes the mass of the solute in grams for exactly 100 g of solution. If the mass of the solute is given as kilograms, then the mass of the solution must also be kilograms. The mass of the solution is the sum of the mass of the solute and the mass of the solvent:

$$\text{Mass percent (m/m)} = \frac{\text{mass of solute(g)}}{\text{mass of solute(g)} + \text{mass of solvent(g)}} \times 100\%$$

$$= \frac{\text{mass of solute(g)}}{\text{mass of solution(g)}} \times 100\%$$

Suppose we prepared a solution by mixing 8.00 g of KCl (solute) with 42.00 g of water (solvent). Together the mass of the solute and mass of solvent give the mass of the solution (8.00 g + 42.00 g = 50.00 g). The mass percent is calculated by substituting in the values into the mass percent expression:

$$\underbrace{\frac{8.00 \text{ g KCl}}{50.00 \text{ g solution}}}_{\substack{8.00 \text{ g KCl} + 42.00 \text{ g } H_2O \\ (\text{Solute} + \text{Solvent})}} \times 100\% = 16.0\% \text{ (m/m)}$$

Add 8.00 g of KCl.

Add water until the mass of the solution is 50.00 g.

**CONCEPT CHECK 8.4**

### Mass Percent Concentration

A NaBr solution is prepared by adding 10.0 g of NaBr to 100. g of $H_2O$. Is the final concentration of the NaBr solution equal to 9.09% (m/m), 10.0% (m/m), or 90.0% (m/m)? Explain your reasoning.

ANSWER

The final concentration of the NaBr is equal to 9.09% (m/m). The mass of the solute is 10.0 g of NaBr, and the mass of the solution is 110.0 g (10.0 g of NaBr + 100.0 g of $H_2O$):

$$\frac{10.0 \text{ g NaBr}}{110.0 \text{ g of solution}} \times 100\% = 9.09\% \text{ (m/m) NaBr}$$

**SAMPLE PROBLEM 8.6**

### Calculating Mass Percent

What is the mass percent of a solution prepared by dissolving 30.0 g of NaOH in 120.0 g of $H_2O$?

SOLUTION

**STEP 1** **Given** 30.0 g of NaOH and 120.0 g of $H_2O$
**Need** mass percent (m/m) of NaOH

**STEP 2** **Plan** The mass percent is calculated by using the mass in grams of the solute and solution in the definition of mass percent.

**STEP 3** **Equalities/Conversion Factors**

$$\text{Mass percent (m/m)} = \frac{\text{mass of solute}}{\text{mass of solute} + \text{mass of solvent}} \times 100\%$$

$$\text{Mass percent (m/m)} = \frac{\text{grams of solute}}{\text{grams of solution}} \times 100\%$$

**STEP 4** **Set Up Problem** The mass of the solute and the solution are obtained from the data:

$$\begin{aligned} \text{Mass of solute} &= \phantom{+}30.0 \text{ g NaOH} \\ \text{Mass of solvent} &= +120.0 \text{ g } H_2O \\ \hline \text{Mass of solution} &= \phantom{+}150.0 \text{ g solution} \end{aligned}$$

$$\text{Mass percent (m/m)} = \frac{30.0 \text{ g NaOH}}{150.0 \text{ g solution}} \times 100\%$$

$$= 20.0\% \text{ (m/m) NaOH}$$

STUDY CHECK

What is the mass percent (m/m) of NaCl in a solution made by dissolving 2.0 g of NaCl in 56.0 g of $H_2O$?

**Guide to Calculating Solution Concentrations**

**STEP 1** State the given and needed concentration.

**STEP 2** Write a plan to calculate needed concentration.

**STEP 3** Write equalities and conversion factors.

**STEP 4** Set up problem to calculate answer.

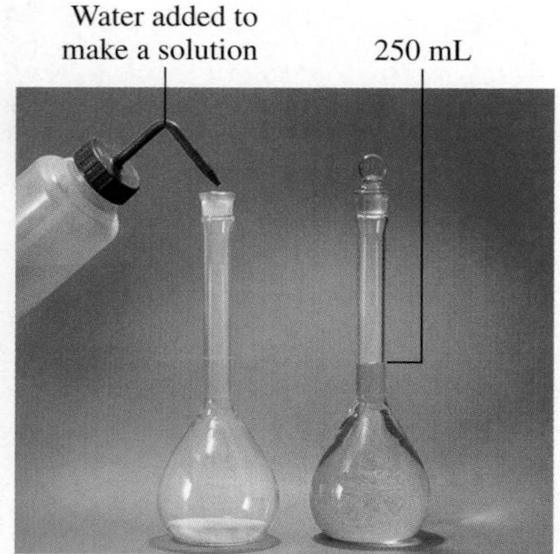


5.0 g of KI 2.0% (m/v) KI solution

## Volume Percent

Because the volumes of liquids or gases are easily measured, the concentrations of their solutions are often expressed as **volume percent** (v/v). The units of volume used in the ratio must be the same, for example, both in milliliters or both in liters.

$$\text{Volume percent (v/v)} = \frac{\text{volume of solute}}{\text{volume of solution}} \times 100\%$$

We interpret a volume/volume percent as the volume of solute in 100 mL of solution. In the wine industry, a label that reads 12% (v/v) means 12 mL of alcohol in 100 mL of wine.

## Mass/Volume Percent

A **mass/volume percent** (m/v), or weight/volume percent (w/v), is calculated by dividing the grams of the solute by the volume (mL) of solution and multiplying by 100%. The mass/volume percent is widely used in hospitals and pharmacies for the preparation of intravenous solutions and medicines.

$$\text{Mass/volume percent (m/v)} = \frac{\text{grams of solute}}{\text{milliliters of solution}} \times 100\%$$

MC™ TUTORIAL Calculating Percent Concentration

SAMPLE PROBLEM 8.7

### Calculating Percent Concentration

A student prepared a solution by dissolving 5.0 g of KI in enough water to give a final volume of 250 mL. What is the mass/volume percent (m/v) of the KI solution?

SOLUTION

**STEP 1** **Given** 5.0 g of KI and 250 mL of solution

**Need** mass/volume percent (m/v) of KI

**STEP 2** **Plan** The mass/volume percent is calculated by using the mass in grams of the solute and the volume in mL of the solution in the definition of mass/volume percent.

**STEP 3** **Equalities/Conversion Factors** Write the mass/volume percent expression.

$$\text{Mass/volume percent (m/v)} = \frac{\text{grams of solute}}{\text{milliliters of solution}} \times 100\%$$

**STEP 4** **Set Up Problem** Substitute solute and solution quantities into the mass/volume percent expression.

$$\text{Mass/volume percent (\% m/v)} = \frac{\overset{\text{Mass of solute}}{5.0 \text{ g KI}}}{\underset{\text{Volume of solution}}{250 \text{ mL solution}}} \times 100\% = 2.0\% \text{ (m/v) KI}$$

STUDY CHECK

What is the mass/volume percent (m/v) of $Br_2$ in a solution prepared by dissolving 12 g of bromine ($Br_2$) in enough carbon tetrachloride to make 250 mL of solution?

MC™ TUTORIAL Percent Concentration as a Conversion Factor

## Percent Concentrations as Conversion Factors

In the preparation of solutions, we often need to calculate the amount of solute or solution. Then the percent concentration is useful as a conversion factor. The value of 100 in the denominator of a percent expression is an *exact* number. Some examples of percent concentrations, their meanings, and possible conversion factors are given in Table 8.10.

**TABLE 8.10** Conversion Factors from Percent Concentrations

| Percent Concentration | Meaning | Conversion Factors | | |
|---|---|---|---|---|
| 15% (m/m) KCl | There are 15 g of KCl in 100 g of solution. | $\frac{15 \text{ g KCl}}{100 \text{ g solution}}$ | and | $\frac{100 \text{ g solution}}{15 \text{ g KCl}}$ |
| 5% (m/v) glucose | There are 5 g of glucose in 100 mL of solution. | $\frac{5 \text{ g glucose}}{100 \text{ mL solution}}$ | and | $\frac{100 \text{ mL solution}}{5 \text{ g glucose}}$ |
| 12% (v/v) ethanol | There are 12 mL of ethanol in 100 mL of solution. | $\frac{12 \text{ mL ethanol}}{100 \text{ mL solution}}$ | and | $\frac{100 \text{ mL solution}}{12 \text{ mL ethanol}}$ |

## SAMPLE PROBLEM 8.8

### Using Mass/Volume Percent to Find Mass of Solute

A topical antibiotic is 1.0% (m/v) Clindamycin. How many grams of Clindamycin are in 60. mL of the 1.0% (m/v) solution?

SOLUTION

**STEP 1** **Given** 1.0% (m/v) Clindamycin
**Need** grams of Clindamycin

**STEP 2** **Plan** milliliters of solution → % (m/v) factor → grams of Clindamycin

**STEP 3** **Equalities/Conversion Factors** The percent (m/v) indicates the grams of a solute in every 100 mL of a solution. The 1.0% (m/v) can be written as two conversion factors:

$$100 \text{ mL of solution} = 1.0 \text{ g of Clindamycin}$$

$$\frac{1.0 \text{ g Clindamycin}}{100 \text{ mL solution}} \quad \text{and} \quad \frac{100 \text{ mL solution}}{1.0 \text{ g Clindamycin}}$$

**STEP 4** **Set Up Problem** The volume of the solution is converted to mass of solute using the conversion factor:

$$60. \cancel{\text{mL solution}} \times \frac{1.0 \text{ g Clindamycin}}{100 \cancel{\text{mL solution}}} = 0.60 \text{ g of Clindamycin}$$

STUDY CHECK

Calculate the grams of KCl in 225 g of an 8.00% (m/m) KCl solution.

**Guide to Using Concentration to Calculate Mass or Volume**

STEP 1 State the given and needed quantities.

STEP 2 Write a plan to calculate mass or volume.

STEP 3 Write equalities and conversion factors including concentration.

STEP 4 Set up problem to calculate mass or volume.

## QUESTIONS AND PROBLEMS

### Percent Concentration

8.33 What is the difference between a 5% (m/m) glucose solution and a 5% (m/v) glucose solution?

**8.34** What is the difference between a 10.% (v/v) methyl alcohol ($CH_3OH$) solution and a 10.% (m/m) methyl alcohol solution?

8.35 Calculate the mass percent (m/m) for the solute in each of the following solutions:
**a.** 25 g of KCl and 125 g of $H_2O$
**b.** 12 g of sugar in 225 g of tea solution with sugar

**8.36** Calculate the mass percent (m/m) for the solute in each of the following solutions:
**a.** 75 g of NaOH in 325 g of NaOH solution
**b.** 2.0 g of KOH in 20.0 g of $H_2O$

8.37 Calculate the mass/volume percent (m/v) for the solute in each of the following solutions:
**a.** 75 g of $Na_2SO_4$ in 250 mL of a $Na_2SO_4$ solution
**b.** 39 g of sucrose in 355 mL of a carbonated drink

**8.38** Calculate the mass/volume percent (m/v) for the solute in each of the following solutions:
**a.** 2.50 g of KCl in 50.0 mL of solution
**b.** 7.5 g of casein in 120 mL of low-fat milk

**8.39** Calculate the amount of solute needed to prepare the following solutions:
- **a.** 50.0 mL of a 5.0% (m/v) KCl solution
- **b.** 1250 mL of a 4.0% (m/v) $NH_4Cl$ solution

**8.40** Calculate the amount of solute needed to prepare the following solutions:
- **a.** 150 mL of a 40.0% (m/v) $LiNO_3$ solution
- **b.** 450 mL of a 2.0% (m/v) KCl solution

**8.41** A mouthwash contains 22.5% alcohol by volume. If the bottle of mouthwash contains 355 mL, what is the volume, in milliliters, of the alcohol?

**8.42** A bottle of champagne is 11% alcohol by volume. If there are 750 mL of champagne in the bottle, how many milliliters of alcohol are present?

**8.43** A patient receives 100. mL of 20.% (m/v) mannitol solution every hour.
- **a.** How many grams of mannitol are given in 1 hour?
- **b.** How many grams of mannitol does the patient receive in 15 hours?

**8.44** A patient receives 250 mL of a 4.0% (m/v) amino acid solution twice a day.
- **a.** How many grams of amino acids are in 250 mL of solution?
- **b.** How many grams of amino acids does the patient receive in 1 day?

**8.45** A patient needs 100. g of glucose in the next 12 hours. How many liters of a 5% (m/v) glucose solution must be given?

**8.46** A patient received 2.0 g of NaCl in 8 hours. How many milliliters of a 0.90% (m/v) NaCl (saline) solution were delivered?

## 8.5 Molarity and Dilution

**LEARNING GOAL**

Calculate the molarity of a solution; use molarity to calculate the moles of solute or the volume of a solution. Describe the dilution of a solution.

When the solutes of solutions take part in reactions, chemists are often interested in the number of reacting particles. For this purpose, chemists use **molarity (M)**, a concentration that states the number of moles of solute in exactly 1 liter of solution. The molarity of a solution can be calculated knowing the moles of solute and the volume of solution in liters.

$$\text{Molarity (M)} = \frac{\text{moles of solute}}{\text{liters of solution}}$$

For example, if 1.0 mole of NaCl were dissolved in enough water to prepare 1.0 L of solution, the resulting NaCl solution has a molarity of 1.0 M. The abbreviation M indicates the units of moles per liter (moles/L):

$$\text{M} = \frac{\text{moles of solute}}{\text{liters of solution}} = \frac{1.0 \text{ mole NaCl}}{1.0 \text{ L}} = 1.0 \text{ M NaCl}$$

**SAMPLE PROBLEM 8.9**

### Calculating Molarity

What is the molarity (M) of 60.0 g of NaOH in 0.250 L of solution?

**Guide to Calculating Molarity**
- STEP 1 State the given quantities.
- STEP 2 Write a plan to calculate molarity.
- STEP 3 Write equalities and conversion factors needed.
- STEP 4 Set up problem to calculate molarity.

SOLUTION

**STEP 1** **Given** 60.0 g of NaOH in 0.250 L of solution
**Need** molarity (moles/L)

**STEP 2** **Plan** The calculation of molarity requires the moles of NaOH and the volume of the solution in liters.

$$\text{Molarity (M)} = \frac{\text{moles of solute}}{\text{liters of solution}}$$

grams of NaOH → Molar mass → $\frac{\text{moles NaOH}}{\text{volume (L)}}$ = M NaOH solution

**STEP 3** **Equalities/Conversion Factors**

1 mole of NaOH = 40.0 g of NaOH

$$\frac{1 \text{ mole NaOH}}{40.0 \text{ g NaOH}} \text{ and } \frac{40.0 \text{ g NaOH}}{1 \text{ mole NaOH}}$$

**STEP 4** **Set Up Problem**

$$\text{Moles of NaOH} = 60.0\ \cancel{\text{g NaOH}} \times \frac{1\ \text{mole NaOH}}{40.0\ \cancel{\text{g NaOH}}} = 1.50\ \text{moles of NaOH}$$

The molarity is calculated by dividing the moles of NaOH by the volume in liters.

$$\frac{1.50\ \text{moles NaOH}}{0.250\ \text{L}} = \frac{6.00\ \text{moles NaOH}}{1\ \text{L}} = 6.00\ \text{M NaOH}$$

STUDY CHECK

What is the molarity of a solution that contains 75.0 g of $KNO_3$ dissolved in 0.350 L of solution?

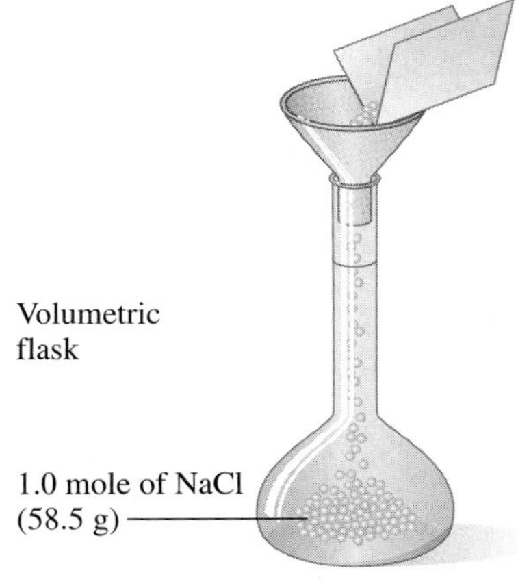


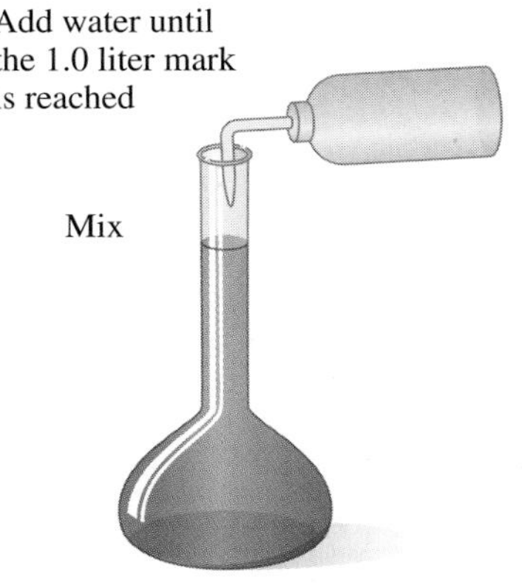


A 1.0 molar NaCl solution

## Molarity as a Conversion Factor

When we need to calculate the moles of solute or the volume of solution, the molarity is used as a conversion factor. The volume (1 L) is an exact number. Examples of conversion factors from molarity are given in Table 8.11.

Using the molarity of the solution with the molar mass of the solute, we can calculate the volume of solution needed as illustrated in Sample Problem 8.10.

**TABLE 8.11** Some Examples of Molar Solutions

| Molarity | Meaning | Conversion Factors | | |
|---|---|---|---|---|
| 6.0 M HCl | 6.0 moles of HCl in 1 liter of solution | $\frac{6.0\ \text{moles HCl}}{1\ \text{L}}$ | and | $\frac{1\ \text{L}}{6.0\ \text{moles HCl}}$ |
| 0.20 M NaOH | 0.20 mole of NaOH in 1 liter of solution | $\frac{0.20\ \text{mole NaOH}}{1\ \text{L}}$ | and | $\frac{1\ \text{L}}{0.20\ \text{mole NaOH}}$ |

SAMPLE PROBLEM 8.10

### ■ Using Molarity to Find Volume

How many liters of a 2.00 M NaCl solution are needed to provide 67.3 g of NaCl?

SOLUTION

**STEP 1** **Given** 67.3 g of NaCl from a 2.00 M NaCl solution
**Need** liters of NaCl solution

**STEP 2** **Plan** The volume of the NaCl solution is calculated using the moles of NaCl and molarity of the NaCl solution:

Grams of NaCl → Molar mass → moles of NaCl → Molarity → liters of NaCl solution

**STEP 3** **Equalities/Conversion Factors**

$$1\ \text{mole of NaCl} = 58.5\ \text{g of NaCl}$$

$$\frac{1\ \text{mole NaCl}}{58.5\ \text{g NaCl}} \quad \text{and} \quad \frac{58.5\ \text{g NaCl}}{1\ \text{mole NaCl}}$$

The molarity of any solution can be written as two conversion factors:

$$1\ \text{L of NaCl} = 2.00\ \text{moles of NaCl}$$

$$\frac{1\ \text{L NaCl}}{2.00\ \text{moles NaCl}} \quad \text{and} \quad \frac{2.00\ \text{moles NaCl}}{1\ \text{L NaCl}}$$

**STEP 4 Set Up Problem**

$$\text{Liters of NaCl} = 67.3 \cancel{\text{g NaCl}} \times \frac{1 \cancel{\text{mole NaCl}}}{58.5 \cancel{\text{g NaCl}}} \times \frac{1 \text{ L NaCl}}{2.00 \cancel{\text{moles NaCl}}}$$

$$= 0.575 \text{ L of NaCl solution}$$

STUDY CHECK

How many moles of HCl are present in 750 mL of a 6.0 M HCl solution?

## Dilution

TUTORIAL
Dilution

In chemistry and biology, we often prepare dilute solutions from more concentrated (stock) solutions. In a process called **dilution**, a solvent, usually water, is added to a solution, which increases the volume. In an everyday example, you are making a dilution when you add three cans of water to a can of concentrated orange juice.

When a solution is diluted, the amount of solute before dilution is equal to the amount of solute in the diluted solution. (See Figure 8.7.)

$$\underset{\text{Concentrated solution}}{\text{Grams or moles of solute}} = \underset{\text{Diluted solution}}{\text{grams or moles of solute}}$$

We can write this equality in terms of the concentration, $C$, and the volume, $V$.

$$\underset{\text{Concentrated solution}}{C_1V_1} = \underset{\text{Diluted solution}}{C_2V_2}$$

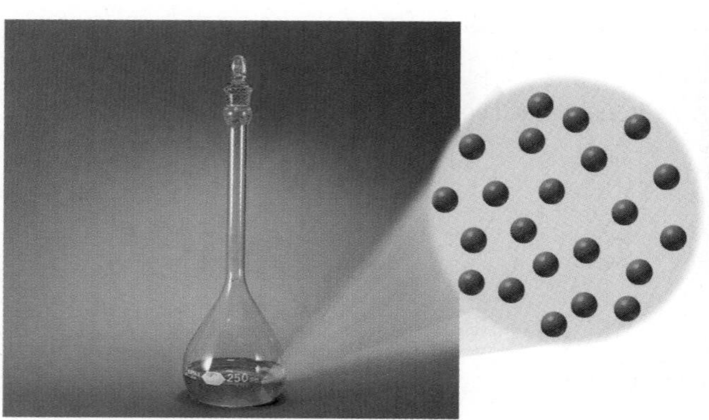

**FIGURE 8.7** When water is added to a concentrated solution, there is no change in the number of particles, but the solute particles spread out as the volume of the diluted solution increases.

Q What is the concentration of the diluted solution after an equal volume of water is added to a sample of 6 M HCl solution?

We know from the discussion of percent concentration that the grams of solute are obtained from the volume and the percent concentration.

Grams of solute = percent (grams/100 mL) × volume (mL)

We can express the number of grams for the concentrated solution as $\%_1V_1$ and the number of grams in the diluted solution as $\%_2V_2$.

Grams of solute = grams of solute
Concentrated solution = Diluted solution

$$\%_1V_1 = \%_2V_2$$

When the concentration is given as molarity (M), the moles of solute are obtained from the volume (liters) and the molarity.

Moles of solute = molarity (moles/L) × volume (L)

Expressing the number of moles in the concentrated solution as $M_1V_1$ and the number of moles in the diluted solution as $M_2V_2$, the equality is written as follows:

Moles of solute = moles of solute
Concentrated solution = Diluted solution

$$M_1V_1 = M_2V_2$$

If we are given any 3 of the 4 variables, we can rearrange the dilution expression to solve for the unknown quantity as seen in Sample Problem 8.11.

SAMPLE PROBLEM 8.11

### Molarity of a Diluted Solution

What is the molarity of a solution prepared when 75.0 mL of a 4.00 M KCl solution is diluted to a volume of 0.500 L?

SOLUTION

**STEP 1** **Give Data in a Table** We make a table of the molar concentrations and volumes of the initial and diluted solutions. For the calculation, units must be the same.

| | | |
|---|---|---|
| **Initial:** | $M_1 = 4.00$ M KCl solution | $V_1 = 75.0$ mL $= 0.0750$ L |
| **Diluted:** | $M_2 = ?$ M KCl solution | $V_2 = 0.500$ L |

**STEP 2** **Plan** The unknown molarity can be calculated by solving the dilution expression for $M_2$:

$$M_1V_1 = M_2V_2$$

Divide both sides by $V_2$

$$\frac{M_1V_1}{V_2} = M_2\frac{\cancel{V_2}}{\cancel{V_2}}$$

$$M_2 = M_1 \times \frac{V_1}{V_2}$$

**STEP 3** **Set Up Problem** The values from the table are placed into the dilution expression:

$$M_2 = 4.00\ \text{M} \times \frac{0.075\ \cancel{\text{L}}}{0.500\ \cancel{\text{L}}} = 0.600\ \text{M KCl solution (diluted)}$$

STUDY CHECK

You need to prepare 600. mL of 2.00 M NaOH solution from a 10.0 M NaOH solution. What volume of the 10.0 M NaOH solution do you use?

**Guide to Calculating Dilution Quantities**

STEP 1
Prepare a table of the initial and diluted volumes and concentrations.

STEP 2
Write a plan that solves the dilution expression for the unknown quantity.

STEP 3
Set up problem by placing known quantities in dilution expression.

## Solutions and Chemical Reactions

When chemical reactions involve aqueous solutions, we use molarity and volume to determine the moles of the substances required or produced. Using the balanced chemical equation, we can determine the volume of a solution from the molarity and moles of a solute as seen in Sample Problem 8.12.

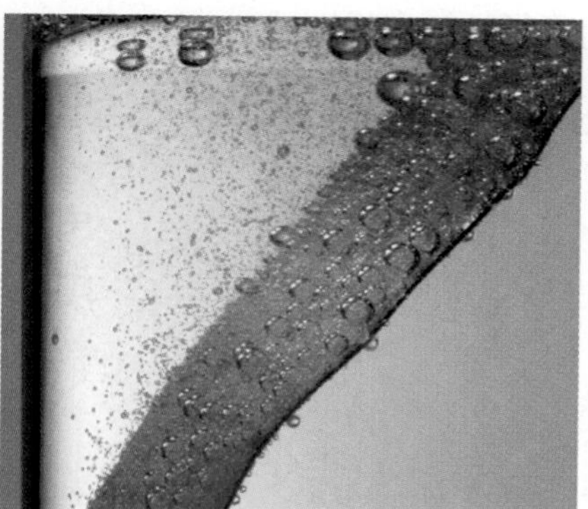

SAMPLE PROBLEM 8.12

## Volume of a Solution in a Reaction

Zinc reacts with HCl to produce $ZnCl_2$ and hydrogen gas $H_2$:

$$Zn(s) + 2HCl(aq) \longrightarrow ZnCl_2(aq) + H_2(g)$$

How many liters of a 1.50 M HCl solution completely react with 5.32 g of zinc?

SOLUTION

**STEP 1** **Given** 5.32 g of Zn and a 1.50 M HCl solution
**Need** liters of HCl solution

**STEP 2** **Plan** We start the problem with the grams of Zn given and use its molar mass to calculate moles. Then we can use the mole–mole factor from the equation and the molarity of the HCl as conversion factors:

Grams of Zn → Molar mass → moles of Zn → Mole–mole factor → moles of HCl → Molarity → L of HCl solution

**Guide to Calculations Involving Solutions in Chemical Reactions**

STEP 1
State the given and needed quantities.

STEP 2
Write a plan to calculate needed quantity or concentration.

STEP 3
Write equalities and conversion factors including mole–mole and concentration factors.

STEP 4
Set up problem to calculate needed quantity or concentration.

**STEP 3** **Equalities/Conversion Factors**

Molar mass of Zn
1 mole of Zn = 65.4 g of Zn

$$\frac{1 \text{ mole Zn}}{65.4 \text{ g Zn}} \text{ and } \frac{65.4 \text{ g Zn}}{1 \text{ mole Zn}}$$

Mole-mole factor
1 mole of Zn = 2 moles of HCl

$$\frac{1 \text{ mole Zn}}{2 \text{ moles HCl}} \text{ and } \frac{2 \text{ moles HCl}}{1 \text{ mole Zn}}$$

Molarity of HCl solution
1 L of HCl solution = 1.50 moles of HCl

$$\frac{1 \text{ L HCl}}{1.50 \text{ moles HCl}} \text{ and } \frac{1.50 \text{ moles HCl}}{1 \text{ L HCl}}$$

**STEP 4** **Set Up Problem** We can write the problem setup as seen in our plan:

$$5.32 \cancel{\text{g Zn}} \times \frac{1 \cancel{\text{mole Zn}}}{65.4 \cancel{\text{g Zn}}} \times \frac{2 \cancel{\text{moles HCl}}}{1 \cancel{\text{mole Zn}}} \times \frac{1 \text{ L HCl}}{1.50 \cancel{\text{moles HCl}}} = 0.108 \text{ L of HCl solution}$$

STUDY CHECK

Using the reaction in Sample Problem 8.12, how many grams of zinc can react with 225 mL of 0.200 M HCl solution?

Figure 8.8 gives a summary of the pathways and conversion factors needed for substances, including solutions, involved in chemical reactions.

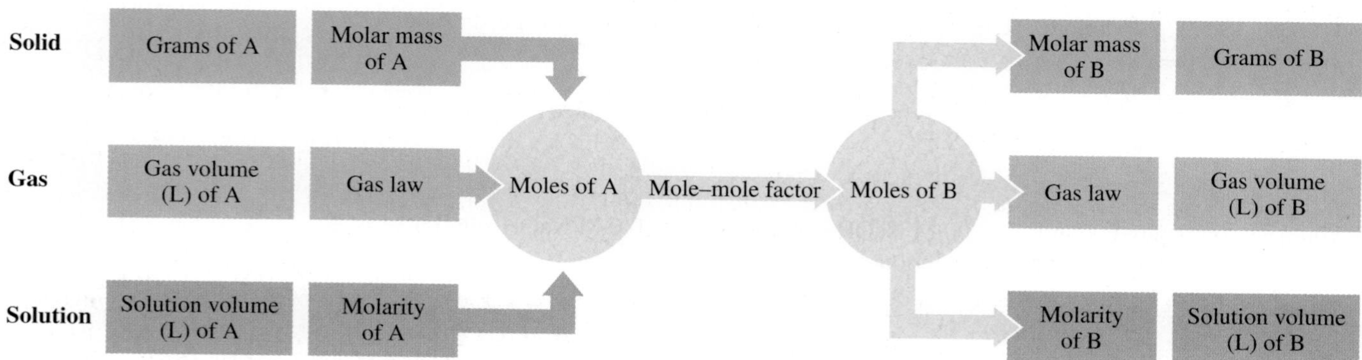


**FIGURE 8.8** In calculations involving chemical reactions, substance A is converted to moles of A using molar mass (if solid), gas laws (if gas), or molarity (if solution). Then moles of A are converted to moles of substance B, which are converted to grams of solid, liters of gas, or liters of solution, as needed.

**Q** What sequence of conversion factors would you use to calculate the number of grams of $CaCO_3$ needed to react with 1.50 L of a 2.00 M HCl solution in the reaction: $2HCl(aq) + CaCO_3(s) \longrightarrow CaCl_2(aq) + CO_2(g) + H_2O(l)$?

## QUESTIONS AND PROBLEMS

### Molarity and Dilution

**8.47** Calculate the molarity (M) of the following solutions:
- **a.** 2.0 moles of glucose in 4.0 L of glucose solution
- **b.** 4.0 g of KOH in 2.0 L of KOH solution
- **c.** 5.85 g of NaCl in 400. mL of NaCl solution

**8.48** Calculate the molarity (M) of the following solutions:
- **a.** 0.50 mole of glucose in 0.200 L of glucose solution
- **b.** 36.5 g of HCl in 1.0 L of HCl solution
- **c.** 30.0 g of NaOH in 350. mL of NaOH solution

**8.49** Calculate the moles of solute needed to prepare each of the following:
- **a.** 1.0 L of a 3.0 M NaCl solution
- **b.** 0.40 L of a 1.0 M KBr solution
- **c.** 125 mL of a 2.0 M $MgCl_2$ solution

**8.50** Calculate the moles of solute needed to prepare each of the following:
- **a.** 5.0 L of a 2.0 M $CaCl_2$ solution
- **b.** 4.0 L of a 0.10 M NaOH solution
- **c.** 215 mL of a 4.0 M $HNO_3$ solution

**8.51** Calculate the grams of solute needed to prepare each of the following:
- **a.** 2.0 L of a 1.5 M NaOH solution
- **b.** 4.0 L of a 0.20 M KCl solution
- **c.** 25.0 mL of 6.0 M HCl solution

**8.52** Calculate the grams of solute needed to prepare each of the following:
- **a.** 2.0 L of a 6.0 M NaOH solution
- **b.** 5.0 L of a 0.10 M $CaCl_2$ solution
- **c.** 175 mL of a 3.00 M $NaNO_3$ solution

**8.53** What volume is needed for each of the following:
- **a.** liters of a 2.0 M NaOH solution to obtain 3.0 moles of NaOH
- **b.** liters of a 1.5 M NaCl solution to obtain 15 moles of NaCl
- **c.** milliliters of a 0.800 M $Ca(NO_3)_2$ solution to obtain 0.0500 moles of $Ca(NO_3)_2$

**8.54** What volume is needed for each of the following:
- **a.** liters of 4.0 M KCl solution to obtain 0.100 mole of KCl
- **b.** liters of a 6.0 M HCl solution to obtain 5.0 moles of HCl
- **c.** milliliters of a 2.5 M $K_2SO_4$ solution to obtain 1.2 moles of $K_2SO_4$

**8.55** Calculate the final concentration of each of the following diluted solutions:
- **a.** 2.0 L of a 6.0 M HCl solution is added to water so that the final volume is 6.0 L.
- **b.** Water is added to 0.50 L of a 12 M NaOH solution to make 3.0 L of a diluted NaOH solution.
- **c.** A 10.0-mL sample of 25% (m/v) KOH solution is diluted with water so that the final volume is 100.0 mL.
- **d.** A 50.0-mL sample of 15% (m/v) $H_2SO_4$ solution is added to water to give a final volume of 250 mL.

**8.56** Calculate the final concentration of each of the following diluted solutions:
- **a.** 1.0 L of a 4.0 M $HNO_3$ solution is added to water so that the final volume is 8.0 L.
- **b.** Water is added to 0.25 L of a 6.0 M KOH solution to make 2.0 L of a diluted KOH solution.
- **c.** A 50.0-mL sample of 8.0% (m/v) NaOH is diluted with water so that the final volume is 200.0 mL.
- **d.** A 5.0-mL sample of 50.0% (m/v) acetic acid ($HC_2H_3O_2$) solution is added to water to give a final volume of 25 mL.

**8.57** What is the final volume of each of the following diluted solutions?
- **a.** liters of a 0.20 M HCl solution prepared from 20.0 mL of a 6.0 M HCl solution
- **b.** milliliters of a 2.0% (m/v) NaOH solution prepared from 50.0 mL of a 10.0% (m/v) NaOH solution
- **c.** liters of a 0.50 M $H_3PO_4$ solution prepared from 0.500 L of a 6.0 M $H_3PO_4$ solution
- **d.** milliliters of a 5.0% (m/v) glucose solution prepared from 75 mL of a 12% (m/v) glucose solution

**8.58** What is the final volume (mL) of each of the following diluted solutions?
- **a.** a 1.0% (m/v) KOH solution prepared from 10.0 mL of a 20.0% KOH solution
- **b.** a 0.10 M HCl solution prepared from 25 mL of a 6.0 M HCl solution
- **c.** a 1.0 M NaOH solution prepared from 50.0 mL of a 12 M NaOH solution
- **d.** a 1.0% (m/v) NaCl solution prepared from 18 mL of a 4.0% (m/v) NaCl solution

**8.59** Answer the following for the reaction

$$Pb(NO_3)_2(aq) + 2KCl(aq) \longrightarrow PbCl_2(s) + 2KNO_3(aq)$$

- **a.** How many grams of $PbCl_2$ will be formed from 50.0 mL of 1.50 M KCl solution?
- **b.** How many milliliters of 2.00 M $Pb(NO_3)_2$ solution will react with 50.0 mL of 1.50 M KCl solution?

**8.60** Answer the following for the reaction

$$NiCl_2(aq) + 2NaOH(aq) \longrightarrow Ni(OH)_2(s) + 2NaCl(aq)$$

- **a.** How many milliliters of 0.200 M NaOH solution are needed to react with 18.0 mL of 0.500 M $NiCl_2$ solution?
- **b.** How many grams of $Ni(OH)_2$ are produced from the reaction of 35.0 mL of 1.75 M NaOH solution?

**8.61** Answer the following for the reaction

$$Mg(s) + 2HCl(aq) \longrightarrow MgCl_2(aq) + H_2(g)$$

- **a.** How many milliliters of a 6.00 M HCl solution are required to react with 15.0 g of magnesium?
- **b.** How many moles of hydrogen gas form when 0.500 L of 2.00 M HCl solution reacts?

**8.62** The calcium carbonate in limestone reacts with HCl to produce a calcium chloride solution and carbon dioxide gas:

$$CaCO_3(s) + 2HCl(aq) \longrightarrow CaCl_2(aq) + H_2O(l) + CO_2(g)$$

- **a.** How many milliliters of 0.200 M HCl solution can react with 8.25 g of $CaCO_3$?
- **b.** How many moles of $CO_2$ form when 15.5 mL of 3.00 M HCl solution react?

## 8.6 Physical Properties of Solutions

**LEARNING GOAL**

Identify a mixture as a solution, a colloid, or a suspension. Describe how the particles of a solution affect the physical properties of a solution.

The solute particles in a solution play an important role in determining the properties of that solution. In most of the solutions discussed so far, the solute is dissolved as small particles that are uniformly dispersed throughout the solvent to give a homogeneous solution. When you observe a solution, such as salt water, you cannot visually distinguish the solute from the solvent. The solution appears transparent, although it may have a color. The particles are so small that they go through filters and through semipermeable membranes. A **semipermeable membrane** allows solvent molecules such as water and very small solute particles to pass through but does not allow the passage of large solute molecules.

### Colloids

The particles in a colloidal dispersion, or **colloid**, are much larger than solute particles in a solution. Colloidal particles are large molecules, such as proteins, or groups of molecules or ions. Colloids are homogeneous mixtures that do not separate or settle out. Colloidal particles are small enough to pass through filters but too large to pass through semipermeable membranes. Table 8.12 lists several examples of colloids.

HEALTH NOTE

**Colloids and Solutions in the Body**

In the body, colloids are retained by semipermeable membranes. For example, the intestinal lining allows solution particles to pass into the blood and lymph circulatory systems. However, the colloids from foods are too large to pass through the membrane, and they remain in the intestinal tract. Digestion breaks down large colloidal particles, such as starch and protein, into smaller particles, such as glucose and amino acids, that can pass through the intestinal membrane and enter the circulatory system. Human digestive processes cannot break down certain foods, such as bran, a fiber, and they move through the intestine intact.

Because large proteins, such as enzymes, are colloids, they remain inside cells. However, many of the substances that must be obtained by cells, such as oxygen, amino acids, electrolytes, glucose, and minerals, can pass through cellular membranes. Waste products, such as urea and carbon dioxide, pass out of the cell to be excreted.

**TABLE 8.12** Examples of Colloids

| | Substance Dispersed | Dispersing Medium |
|---|---|---|
| Fog, clouds, sprays | Liquid | Gas |
| Dust, smoke | Solid | Gas |
| Shaving cream, whipped cream, soapsuds | Gas | Liquid |
| Styrofoam, marshmallows | Gas | Solid |
| Mayonnaise, butter, homogenized milk, hand lotions | Liquid | Liquid |
| Cheese, butter | Liquid | Solid |
| Blood plasma, paints (latex), gelatin | Solid | Liquid |

### Suspensions

**Suspensions** are heterogeneous, nonuniform mixtures that are very different from solutions or colloids. The particles of a suspension are so large that they can often be seen with the naked eye. These particles are trapped by filters and semipermeable membranes.

The weight of the suspended solute particles causes them to settle out soon after mixing. If you stir muddy water, it mixes but then quickly separates as the suspended particles settle to the bottom and leave clear liquid at the top. You can find suspensions among the medications in a hospital or in your medicine cabinet. These include Kaopectate, calamine lotion, antacid mixtures, and liquid penicillin. It is important to "shake well before using" to suspend all the particles before giving a medication that is a suspension.

Water-treatment plants make use of the properties of suspensions to purify water. When flocculants such as aluminum sulfate or iron(III) sulfate are added to untreated water, they react with small particles of impurities to form large suspended particles called *floc*. In the water-treatment plant, a system of filters traps the suspended particles but allows clean water to pass through.

Table 8.13 compares the different types of mixtures, and Figure 8.9 illustrates some properties of solutions, colloids, and suspensions.

**TABLE 8.13** Comparison of Solutions, Colloids, and Suspensions

| Type of Mixture | Type of Particle | Settling | Separation |
|---|---|---|---|
| Solution | Small particles such as atoms, ions, or small molecules | Particles do not settle | Particles cannot be separated by filters or semipermeable membranes |
| Colloid | Larger molecules or groups of molecules or ions | Particles do not settle | Particles can be separated by semipermeable membranes but not by filters |
| Suspension | Very large particles that may be visible | Particles settle rapidly | Particles can be separated by filters |

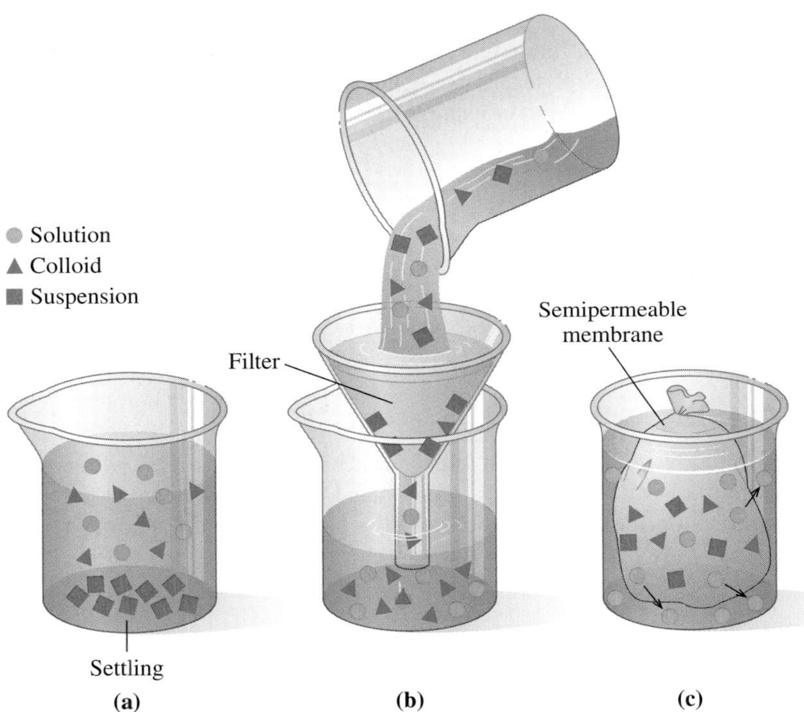


**FIGURE 8.9** Properties of different types of mixtures: **(a)** suspensions settle out; **(b)** suspensions are separated by a filter; **(c)** solution particles go through a semipermeable membrane, but colloids and suspensions do not.

**Q** A filter paper can be used to separate suspension particles from a solution, but a semipermeable membrane is needed to separate colloids from a solution. Explain.

**CONCEPT CHECK 8.5**

## Classifying Types of Mixtures

Classify each of the following as a solution, colloid, or suspension:

**a.** a mixture that has particles that settle upon standing
**b.** a mixture whose solute particles pass through both filters and membranes
**c.** an enzyme, which is a large protein molecule, that cannot pass through cellular membranes, but does pass through a filter

ANSWER

**a.** A suspension has very large particles that settle upon standing.
**b.** A solution contains particles small enough to pass through both filters and membranes.
**c.** A colloid is a particle that is small enough to pass through a filter but too large to pass through a membrane.

## Freezing Point Lowering and Boiling Point Elevation

When a solute is added to water, the physical properties such as freezing point and boiling point change. The freezing point is lowered and boiling point is raised. These types of changes in physical properties known as *colligative properties* depend on the number of solute particles in the solution.

In many cold wintry areas, salt is spread on sidewalks and roads. The salt lowers the freezing point, which causes the ice to melt. In both cold and hot regions, antifreeze is added to the radiator of a car to lower the temperature at which water freezes and to increase the temperature at which water boils. Antifreeze prevents the water in the radiator from forming ice in the cold and from boiling over on a hot desert highway.

The solute particles disrupt the formation of the solid ice structure. Thus, a lower temperature is required to freeze the water in the solution. The greater the solute concentration, the lower the freezing point will be. One mole of particles in 1000 g of water lowers the freezing point from 0 °C to −1.86 °C. If there are 2 moles of particles in 1000 g of water, the freezing point drops to −3.72 °C. A similar change occurs with the boiling point of water. One mole of particles in 1000 g of water raises the boiling point by 0.52 °C, from 100. °C to 100.52 °C.

As we discussed in section 8.2, a solute that is a nonelectrolyte dissolves as molecules, whereas a solute that is a strong electrolyte dissolves entirely as ions. The solute in antifreeze, which is ethylene glycol, $C_2H_6O_2$, dissolves as molecules.

Nonelectrolyte:

$$1 \text{ mole of } C_2H_6O_2(l) = 1 \text{ mole of } C_2H_6O_2(aq)$$

Strong electrolytes:

$$1 \text{ mole of NaCl}(s) = \underbrace{1 \text{ mole of Na}^+(aq) + 1 \text{ mole of Cl}^-(aq)}_{2 \text{ moles of particles } (aq)}$$

$$1 \text{ mole of CaCl}_2(s) = \underbrace{1 \text{ mole of Ca}^{2+}(aq) + 2 \text{ moles of Cl}^-(aq)}_{3 \text{ moles of particles } (aq)}$$

The effect of $CaCl_2$ used to salt icy roads is to produce 3 moles of particles, which will lower the freezing point of water three times more than 1 mole of ethylene glycol. The effect of solute particles on the freezing point and the boiling point is summarized in Table 8.14.

**TABLE 8.14** Effect of Solute Concentration on Freezing and Boiling Points of 1000 g of Water

| | Type of Solute | Moles of Solute Particles | Freezing Point | Boiling Point |
|---|---|---|---|---|
| Pure Water | None | 0 | 0 °C | 100 °C |
| Temperature change | | 1 mole | $\Delta T_f = 1.86$ °C | $\Delta T_b = 0.52$ °C |
| 1 mole of ethylene glycol | Nonelectrolyte | 1 mole | −1.86 °C | 100.52 °C |
| 1 mole of NaCl | Strong electrolyte | 2 moles | −3.72 °C | 101.04 °C |
| 1 mole of $CaCl_2$ | Strong electrolyte | 3 moles | −5.58 °C | 101.56 °C |

## Osmotic Pressure

The movement of water into and out of the cells of almost all living things is an important biological process that depends on the solute concentration. In a process called **osmosis**, water molecules move through a semipermeable membrane from the solution with the lower concentration of solute into a solution with the higher solute concentration. In an osmosis apparatus, water is placed on one side of a semipermeable membrane and sucrose (sugar) solution on the other side. The semipermeable membrane allows water molecules to flow back and forth but blocks the sucrose molecules because they are too large to pass through the membrane. Because the sucrose solution has a higher solute concentration, there are more water molecules flowing into the sucrose solution and the volume of the sucrose solution increases, while the volume on the other side decreases. The movement of the water dilutes the sucrose solution to equalize (or attempt to equalize) the concentrations on both sides of the membrane.

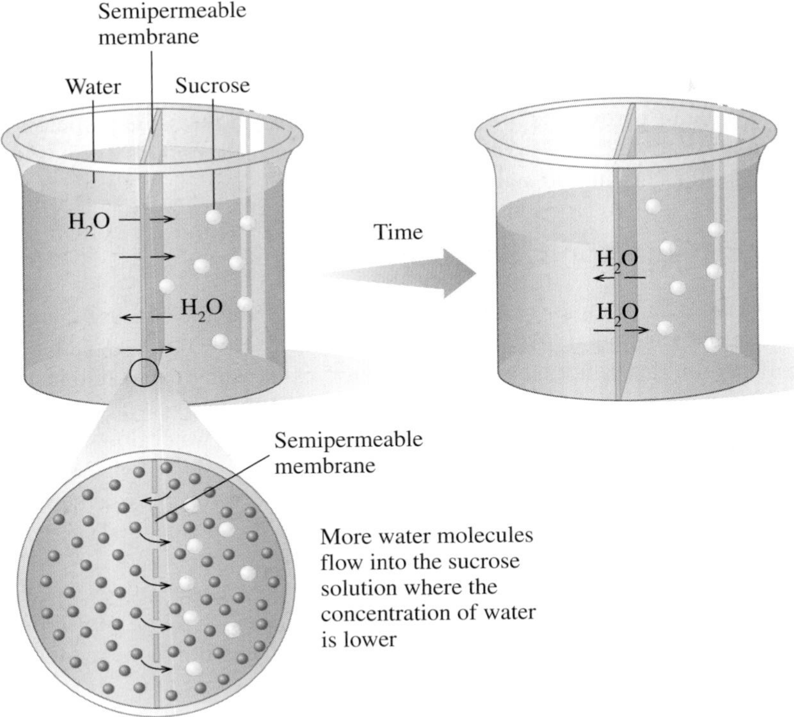


Eventually, the height of the sucrose solution creates sufficient pressure to equalize the flow of water between the two compartments. This pressure, called **osmotic pressure**, prevents the flow of additional water into the more concentrated solution. Then there is no further change in the volumes of the two solutions. The osmotic pressure depends on the concentration of solute particles in the solution. The greater the number of particles dissolved, the higher its osmotic pressure. In this example, the sucrose solution has a higher osmotic pressure than pure water, which has an osmotic pressure of zero.

In a process called *reverse osmosis*, a pressure greater than the **osmotic pressure** is applied to a solution. The flow of water is reversed so that water flows out of the solution with the higher solute concentration. This process of reverse osmosis is used in desalination plants to obtain pure water from sea (salt) water.

## Everyday Osmosis

1. Place a few pieces of dried fruit such as raisins, prunes, or banana chips in water. Observe them after 1 hour or more. Look at them again the next day.
2. Place some grapes in a concentrated salt-water solution. Observe them after 1 hour or more. Look at them again the next day.
3. Place one potato slice in water and another slice in a concentrated saltwater solution. After 1 or 2 hours observe the shapes and sizes of the slices. Look at them again the next day.

### QUESTIONS

1. How did the shape of the dried fruit change after being in water? Explain.
2. How did the appearance of the grapes change after being in a concentrated salt solution? Explain.
3. How does the appearance of the potato slice that was placed in water compare to the appearance of the potato slice placed in salt water? Explain.
4. At the grocery store, why are sprinklers used to spray water on fresh produce such as lettuce, carrots, and cucumbers?

SELF STUDY ACTIVITY
Diffusion

TUTORIAL
Osmosis

CONCEPT CHECK 8.6

### Osmotic Pressure

A 2% (m/v) sucrose solution and an 8% (m/v) sucrose solution are separated by a semipermeable membrane.

**a.** Which sucrose solution exerts the greater osmotic pressure?
**b.** In what direction does water flow initially?
**c.** Which solution will have the higher level of liquid at equilibrium?

ANSWER

**a.** The 8% (m/v) sucrose solution has the higher solute concentration, more solute particles, and the greater osmotic pressure.
**b.** Initially, water will flow out of the 2% (m/v) solution into the more concentrated 8% (m/v) solution.
**c.** The level of the 8% (m/v) solution will be higher.

## Isotonic Solutions

Because the cell membranes in biological systems are semipermeable, osmosis is an ongoing process. The solutes in body solutions such as blood, tissue fluids, lymph, and plasma all exert osmotic pressure. Most intravenous solutions are **isotonic solutions**, which exert the same osmotic pressure as body fluids. *Iso* means "equal to," and *tonic* refers to the osmotic pressure of the solution in the cell. In the hospital, isotonic solutions, or **physiological solutions**, include 0.9% (m/v) NaCl solution and 5% (m/v) glucose solution. These physiological solutions exert the same osmotic pressure as the particles in the body fluids, which is 0.3 mole of particles in 1 L. Although they are not the same particles, a 0.9% (m/v) NaCl solution as well as a 5% (m/v) glucose solution each contains 0.3 mole of particles ($Na^+$ and $Cl^-$ ions or glucose molecules) in 1 L.

## Hypotonic and Hypertonic Solutions

A red blood cell placed in an isotonic solution retains its normal volume because there is an equal flow of water into and out of the cell. (See Figure 8.10a.) However, if a red blood cell is placed in a solution that is not isotonic, the differences in osmotic pressure inside and outside the cell can drastically alter the volume of the cell. When a red blood cell is placed in pure water, a **hypotonic solution** (*hypo* means "lower than"), water flows into the cell by osmosis. (See Figure 8.10b.) The increase in fluid causes the cell to swell, and possibly burst—a process called **hemolysis**. A similar process occurs when you place dehydrated food, such as raisins or dried fruit, in water. The water enters the cells, and the food becomes plump and smooth.

If a red blood cell is placed in a **hypertonic solution**, which has a higher solute concentration (*hyper* means "greater than"), water leaves the cell by osmosis. Suppose a red blood cell is placed in a 10% (m/v) NaCl solution. Because the osmotic pressure in the red blood

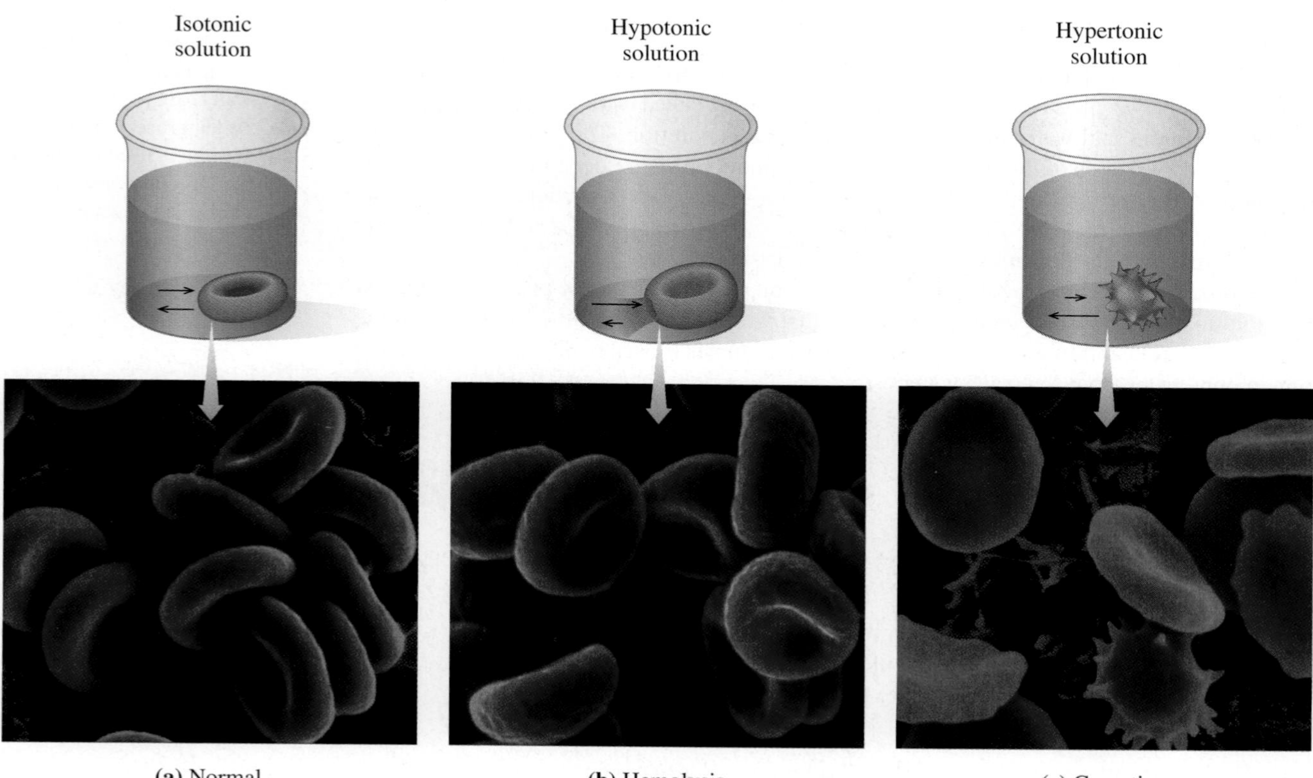


**FIGURE 8.10** **(a)** In an isotonic solution, a red blood cell retains its normal volume. **(b)** Hemolysis: In a hypotonic solution, water flows into a red blood cell, causing it to swell and burst. **(c)** Crenation: In a hypertonic solution, water leaves the red blood cell, causing it to shrink.

**Q** What happens to a red blood cell placed in a 4% NaCl solution?

cell is equal to that of a 0.90% (m/v) NaCl solution, the 10% (m/v) NaCl solution has a much greater osmotic pressure. As water is lost, the cell shrinks—a process called **crenation**. (See Figure 8.10c.) A similar process occurs when making pickles, which uses a hypertonic salt solution that causes the cucumbers to shrivel as they lose water.

## SAMPLE PROBLEM 8.13

### Isotonic, Hypotonic, and Hypertonic Solutions

Describe each of the following solutions as isotonic, hypotonic, or hypertonic. Indicate whether a red blood cell placed in each solution will undergo hemolysis, crenation, or no change.

**a.** a 5.0% (m/v) glucose solution
**b.** a 0.2% (m/v) NaCl solution

SOLUTION

**a.** A 5.0% (m/v) glucose solution is isotonic. A red blood cell will not undergo any change.
**b.** A 0.2% (m/v) NaCl solution is hypotonic. A red blood cell will undergo hemolysis.

STUDY CHECK

What is the effect of a 10% (m/v) glucose solution on a red blood cell?

## Dialysis

**Dialysis** is a process that is similar to osmosis. In dialysis, a semipermeable membrane, called a *dialyzing membrane*, permits small solute molecules and ions as well as solvent water molecules to pass through, but it retains large particles, such as colloids. Dialysis is a way to separate solution particles from colloids.

Suppose we fill a cellophane bag with a solution containing NaCl, glucose, starch, and protein and place it in pure water. Cellophane is a dialyzing membrane, and the sodium ions, chloride ions, and glucose molecules will pass through it into the surrounding water. However, starch and protein remain inside because they are colloids. Water molecules will flow by osmosis into the cellophane bag. Eventually the concentrations of sodium ions, chloride ions, and glucose molecules inside and outside the dialysis bag become equal. To remove more NaCl or glucose, the cellophane bag must be placed in a fresh sample of pure water.

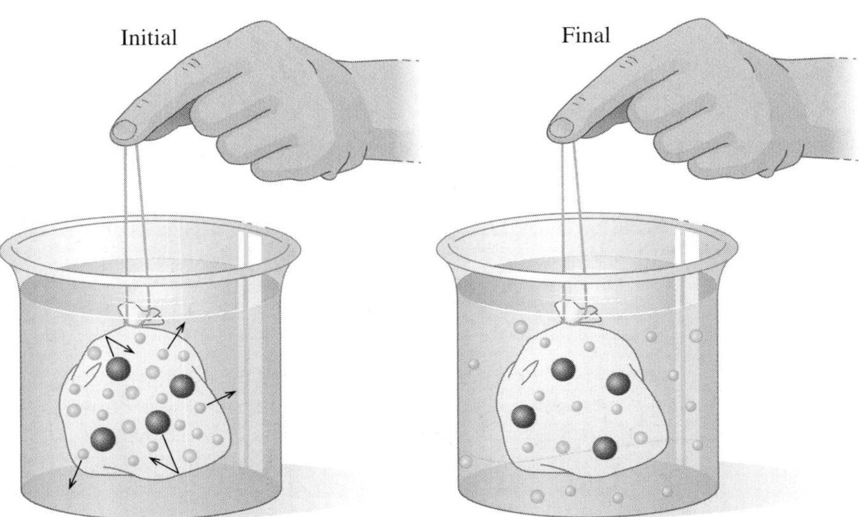

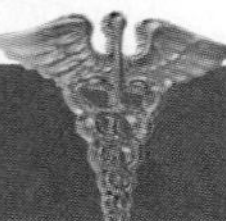

# HEALTH NOTE

## Dialysis by the Kidneys and the Artificial Kidney

The fluids of the body undergo dialysis by the membranes of the kidneys, which remove waste materials, excess salts, and water. In an adult, each kidney contains about 2 million nephrons. At the top of each nephron, there is a network of arterial capillaries called the *glomerulus*.

As blood flows into the glomerulus, small particles, such as amino acids, glucose, urea, water, and certain ions, will move through the capillary membranes into the nephron. As this solution moves through the nephron, substances still of value to the body (such as amino acids, glucose, certain ions, and 99% of the water) are reabsorbed. The major waste product, urea, is excreted in the urine.

### Hemodialysis

If the kidneys fail to dialyze waste products, increased levels of urea can become life threatening in a relatively short time. A person with kidney failure must use an artificial kidney, which cleanses the blood by **hemodialysis**.

A typical artificial kidney machine contains a large tank filled with about 100 L of water containing selected electrolytes. In the center of this dialyzing bath (dialysate), there is a dialyzing coil or membrane made of cellulose tubing. As the patient's blood flows through the dialyzing coil, the highly concentrated waste products dialyze out of the blood. No blood is lost, because the membrane is not permeable to large particles such as red blood cells.

Dialysis patients do not produce much urine. As a result, they retain large amounts of water between dialysis treatments, which produces a strain on the heart. The intake of fluids for a dialysis patient may be restricted to as little as a few teaspoons of water a day. In the dialysis procedure, the pressure of the blood is increased as it circulates through the dialyzing coil so water can be squeezed out of the blood. For some dialysis patients, 2–10 L of water may be removed during one treatment. Dialysis patients typically have from two to three treatments a week, each treatment requiring about 5–7 hr. Some of the newer treatments require less time. For many patients, dialysis is done at home with a home dialysis unit.

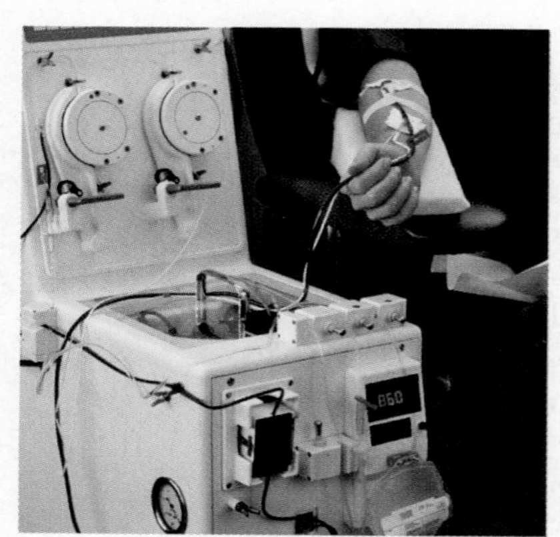

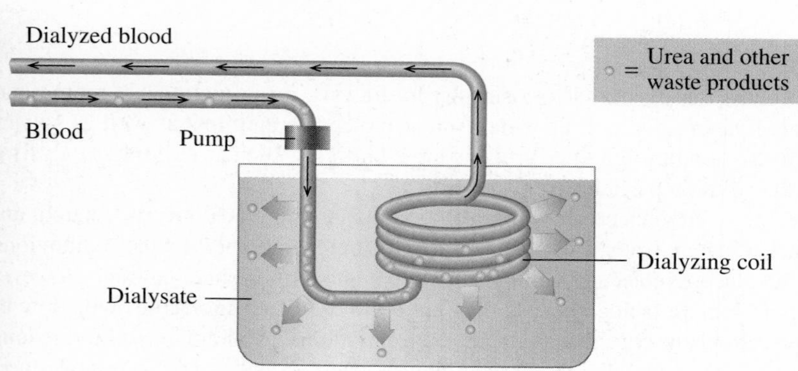


# QUESTIONS AND PROBLEMS

## Physical Properties of Solutions

8.63 Identify the following as characteristic of a solution, colloid, or suspension:
**a.** a mixture that cannot be separated by a semipermeable membrane
**b.** a mixture that settles out upon standing

**8.64** Identify the following as characteristic of a solution, colloid, or suspension:
**a.** Particles of this mixture remain inside a semipermeable membrane but pass through filters.
**b.** The particles of solute in this mixture are very large and visible.

8.65 How many moles of each of the following strong electrolytes are needed to give the same freezing point lowering as 0.12 mole of the nonelectrolyte ethylene glycol in 1000 g of water?
**a.** NaCl
**b.** $K_3PO_4$

**8.66** Two solutions, A and B, are separated by a semipermeable membrane. Indicate the solution that has the greater osmotic pressure and the direction in which water will move.
**a.** A is 0.1 M NaCl and B is 0.2 M $K_2SO_4$
**b.** A is 0.3 M LiBr and B is 0.2 M $K_3PO_4$

8.67 A 10% (m/v) starch solution is separated from pure water by an osmotic membrane.
**a.** Which liquid has the higher osmotic pressure?
**b.** In which direction will water flow initially?
**c.** In which compartment will the volume level rise?

**8.68** Two solutions, a 0.1% (m/v) albumin solution and a 2% (m/v) albumin solution, are separated by a semipermeable membrane. (Albumins are colloidal proteins.)
**a.** Which compartment has the higher osmotic pressure?
**b.** In which direction will water flow initially?
**c.** In which compartment will the volume level rise?

8.69 Indicate the compartment (A or B) that will increase in volume for each of the following pairs of solutions separated by semipermeable membranes:

| | A | B |
|---|---|---|
| **a.** | 5.0% (m/v) starch | 10% (m/v) starch |
| **b.** | 4% (m/v) albumin | 8% (m/v) albumin |
| **c.** | 0.1% (m/v) sucrose | 10% (m/v) sucrose |

**8.70** Indicate the compartment (A or B) that will increase in volume for each of the following pairs of solutions separated by semipermeable membranes:

| | A | B |
|---|---|---|
| **a.** | 20% (m/v) starch | 10% (m/v) starch |
| **b.** | 10% (m/v) albumin | 2% (m/v) albumin |
| **c.** | 0.5% (m/v) sucrose | 5% (m/v) sucrose |

8.71 Are the following solutions isotonic, hypotonic, or hypertonic compared with a red blood cell?
**a.** distilled $H_2O$
**b.** 1% (m/v) glucose
**c.** 0.90% (m/v) NaCl
**d.** 5.0% (m/v) glucose

**8.72** Will a red blood cell undergo crenation, hemolysis, or no change in each of the following solutions?
**a.** 1% (m/v) glucose
**b.** 2% (m/v) NaCl
**c.** 5% (m/v) NaCl
**d.** 0.1% (m/v) NaCl

8.73 Each of the following mixtures is placed in a dialyzing bag and immersed in distilled water. Which substances will be found outside the bag in the distilled water?
**a.** NaCl solution
**b.** starch (colloid) and alanine (amino acid) solution
**c.** NaCl solution and starch (colloid)
**d.** urea solution

**8.74** Each of the following mixtures is placed in a dialyzing bag and immersed in distilled water. Which substances will be found outside the bag in the distilled water?
**a.** KCl solution and glucose solution
**b.** an albumin solution (colloid)
**c.** an albumin solution (colloid), KCl solution, and glucose solution
**d.** urea solution and NaCl solution

## CONCEPT MAP

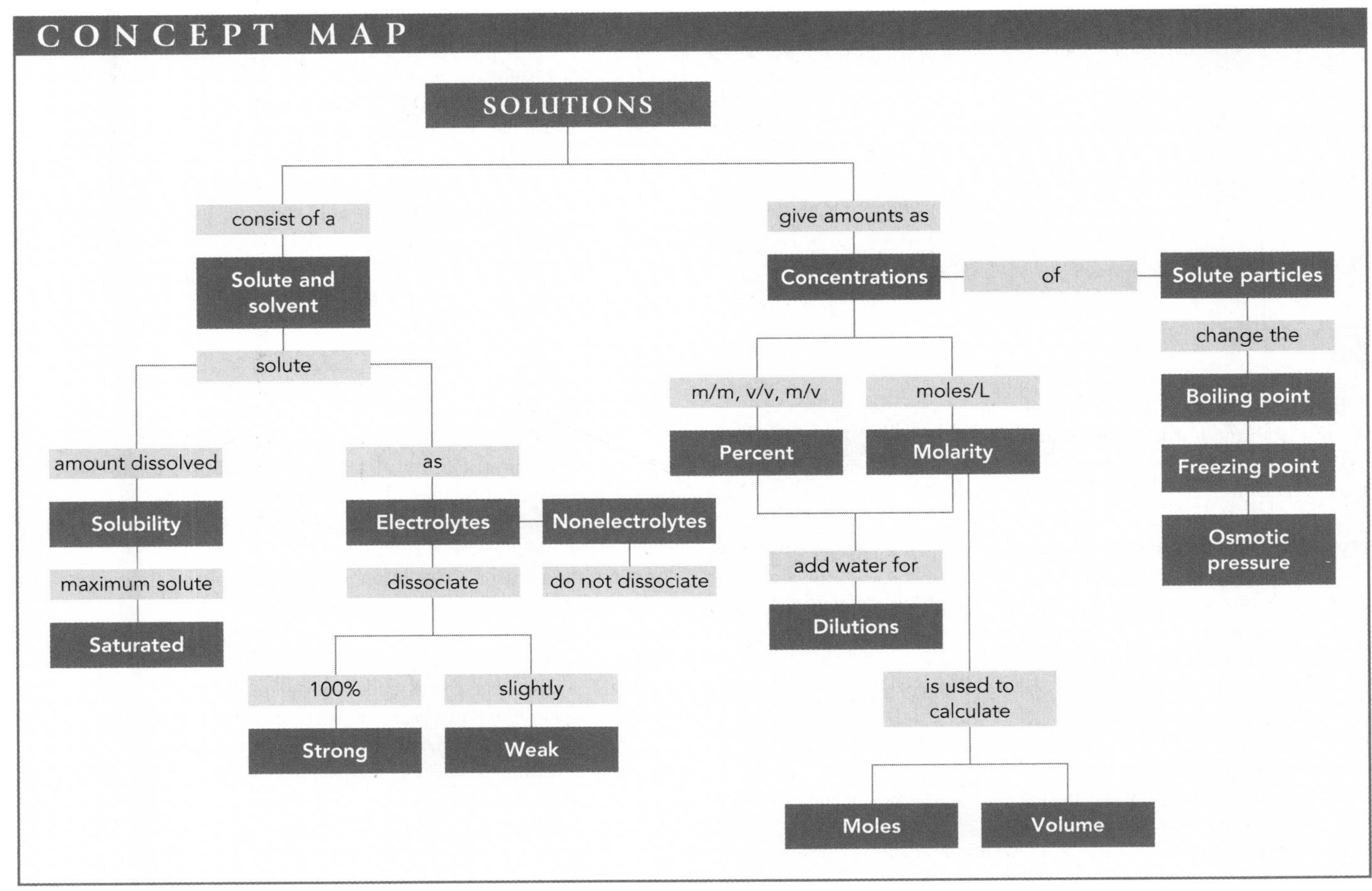

# CHAPTER REVIEW

## 8.1 Solutions

**LEARNING GOAL:** *Identify the solute and solvent in a solution. Describe the formation of a solution.*

A solution forms when a solute dissolves in a solvent. In a solution, the particles of solute are evenly distributed in the solvent. The solute and solvent may be solid, liquid, or gas. The polar O—H bond leads to hydrogen bonding in water molecules. An ionic solute dissolves in water—a polar solvent—because the polar water molecules attract and pull the ions into solution, where they become hydrated. The expression "like dissolves like" means that a polar or ionic solute dissolves in a polar solvent while a nonpolar solute requires a nonpolar solvent.

## 8.2 Electrolytes and Nonelectrolytes

**LEARNING GOAL:** *Identify solutes as electrolytes or nonelectrolytes.*

Substances that release ions in water are called electrolytes because the solution will conduct an electrical current. Strong electrolytes are completely ionized, whereas weak electrolytes are only partially ionized. Nonelectrolytes are substances that dissolve in water to produce molecules and cannot conduct electrical currents. An equivalent is the amount of an electrolyte that carries 1 mole of positive or negative charge. One mole of $Na^+$ is 1 equivalent. One mole of $Ca^{2+}$ is 2 equivalents. In fluid replacement solutions, the concentrations of electrolytes are expressed as mEq/L of solution.

## 8.3 Solubility

**LEARNING GOAL:** *Define solubility; distinguish between an unsaturated and a saturated solution.*

A solution that contains the maximum amount of dissolved solute is a saturated solution. The solubility of a solute is the maximum amount of a solute that can dissolve in 100 g of solvent. A solution containing less than the maximum amount of dissolved solute is unsaturated. An increase in temperature increases the solubility of most solids in water but decreases the solubility of gases in water. Salts that are soluble in water usually contain $Li^+$, $Na^+$, $K^+$, $NH_4^+$, $NO_3^-$, or acetate $C_2H_3O_2^-$. An ionic equation consists of writing all the dissolved substances in an equation for the formation of an insoluble salt as individual ions. A net ionic equation is written by removing all the ions not involved in the chemical change (spectator ions) from the ionic equation.

## 8.4 Percent Concentration

**LEARNING GOAL:** *Calculate the percent concentration of a solute in a solution; use percent concentration to calculate the amount of solute or solution.*

The concentration of a solution is the amount of solute dissolved in a certain amount of solution. Mass percent expresses the ratio of the mass of solute to the mass of solution multiplied by 100. Percent concentration is also expressed as volume/volume (v/v) and mass/volume (m/v) ratios. In calculations of grams or milliliters of solute or solution, the percent concentration is used as a conversion factor.

## 8.5 Molarity and Dilution

**LEARNING GOAL:** *Calculate the molarity of a solution; use molarity to calculate the moles of solute or the volume of a solution. Describe the dilution of a solution.*

Molarity is the moles of solute per liter of solution. Units of molarity, moles/liter, are used in conversion factors to solve for moles of solute or volume of solution. In dilution, the volume of solvent increases and the solute concentration decreases. If the mass or solution volume and molarity of substances in a reaction are given, the balanced equation can be used to determine the quantities or concentrations of any of the other substances in the reaction.

## 8.6 Physical Properties of Solutions

**LEARNING GOAL:** *Identify a mixture as a solution, a colloid, or suspension. Describe how the particles of a solution affect the physical properties of a solution.*

Colloids contain particles that do not settle out and which pass through most filters but not semipermeable membranes. Suspensions have very large particles that settle out of solution. Colligative properties are the physical properties that change when solute dissolves in water.

In osmosis, solvent (water) passes through a semipermeable membrane from a solution with a lower osmotic pressure (lower solute concentration) to a solution with a higher osmotic pressure (higher solute concentration). Isotonic solutions have osmotic pressures equal to that of body fluids. A red blood cell maintains its volume in an isotonic solution but swells and may burst (hemolyze) in a hypotonic solution and shrinks (crenates) in a hypertonic solution. In dialysis, water and small solute particles pass through a dialyzing membrane, while larger particles are retained.

# KEY TERMS

**colloids** Mixtures having particles that are moderately large. Colloids pass through filters but cannot pass through semipermeable membranes.

**concentration** A measure of the amount of solute that is dissolved in a specified amount of solution.

**crenation** The shriveling of a cell due to water leaving the cell when the cell is placed in a hypertonic solution.

**dialysis** A process in which water and small solute particles pass through a semipermeable membrane.

**dilution** A process by which water (solvent) is added to a solution to increase the volume and decrease (dilute) the concentration of the solute.

**electrolyte** A substance that produces ions when dissolved in water; its solution conducts electricity.

**equivalent (Eq)** The amount of a positive or negative ion that supplies 1 mole of electrical charge.

**hemodialysis** A cleansing of the blood by an artificial kidney using the principle of dialysis.

**hemolysis** A swelling and bursting of red blood cells in a hypotonic solution due to an increase in fluid volume.

**Henry's law** The solubility of a gas in a liquid is directly related to the pressure of that gas above the liquid.

**hydration** The process of surrounding dissolved ions by water molecules.

**hypertonic solution** A solution that has a higher osmotic pressure than the red blood cells of the body.

**hypotonic solution** A solution that has a lower osmotic pressure than the red blood cells of the body.

**insoluble salts** Ionic compounds that do not dissolve in water.

**ionic equation** An equation for a reaction in solution that gives all the individual ions, both reacting ions and spectator ions.

**isotonic solution** A solution that has the same osmotic pressure as that of the red blood cells of the body.

**mass percent (m/m)** The grams of solute in exactly 100 grams of solution.

**mass/volume percent (m/v)** The grams of solute in exactly 100 mL of solution.

**molarity (M)** The number of moles of solute in exactly 1 L of solution.

**net ionic equation** An equation for a reaction that gives only the reactants and products involved in a chemical change.

**nonelectrolyte** A substance that dissolves in water as molecules; its solution will not conduct an electrical current.

**osmosis** The flow of a solvent, usually water, through a semipermeable membrane into a solution of higher solute concentration.

**osmotic pressure** The pressure that prevents the flow of water into the more concentrated solution.

**physiological solution** A solution that exerts the same osmotic pressure as normal body fluids.

**saturated solution** A solution containing the maximum amount of solute that can dissolve at a given temperature. Any additional solute will remain undissolved in the container.

**semipermeable membrane** A membrane that permits the passage of certain substances while blocking or retaining others.

**solubility** The maximum amount of solute that can dissolve in exactly 100 g of solvent, usually water, at a given temperature.

**soluble salts** Ionic compounds that dissolve in water.

**solute** The component in a solution that changes state upon dissolving; if no change in state occurs, it is the component present in the smaller quantity.

**solution** A homogeneous mixture in which the solute is made up of small particles (ions or molecules) that can pass through filters and semipermeable membranes.

**solvent** The substance in which the solute dissolves; usually the component present in greatest amount.

**strong electrolyte** A polar or ionic compound that ionizes completely when it dissolves in water. Its solution is a good conductor of electricity.

**suspension** A mixture in which the solute particles are large enough and heavy enough to settle out and be retained by both filters and semipermeable membranes.

**unsaturated solution** A solution that contains less solute than can be dissolved.

**volume percent (v/v)** A percent concentration that relates the volume of the solute to the volume of the solution.

**weak electrolyte** A substance that produces only a few ions along with many molecules when it dissolves in water. Its solution is a weak conductor of electricity.

## UNDERSTANDING THE CONCEPTS

**8.75** Select the diagram that represents the solution formed by a solute ⚭ that is a

**a.** nonelectrolyte

**b.** weak electrolyte

**c.** strong electrolyte

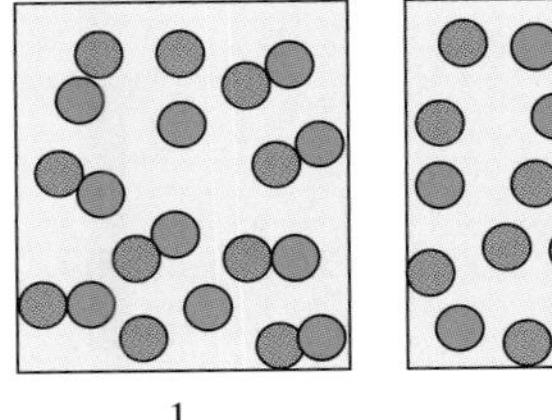

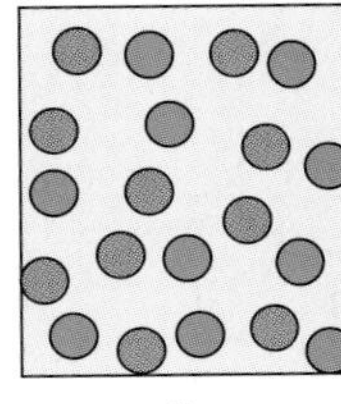

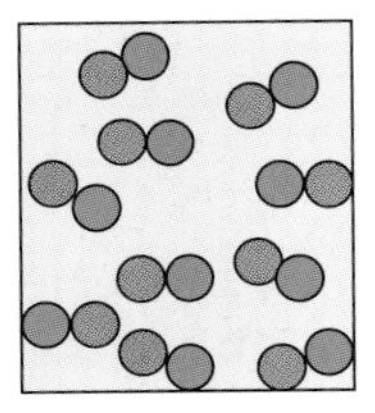

1. 2. 3.

**8.76** Match the diagrams with the following:

**a.** a polar solute and a polar solvent

**b.** a nonpolar solute and a polar solvent

**c.** a nonpolar solute and a nonpolar solvent

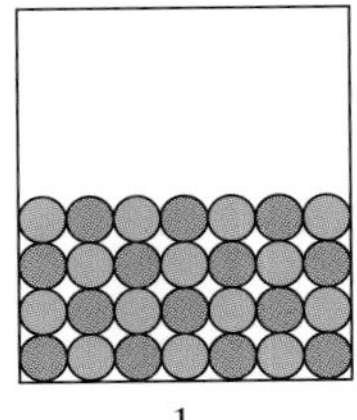

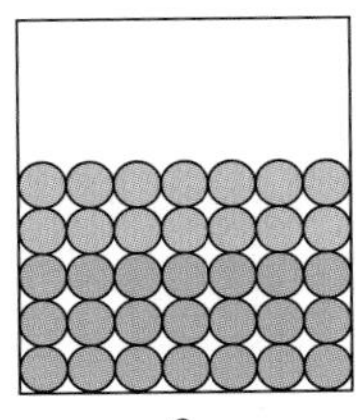

1. 2.

**8.77** A pickle is made by soaking a cucumber in brine, a saltwater solution. What makes the smooth cucumber become wrinkled like a prune?

**8.78** Do you think solution (1) has undergone heating or cooling to give the solid shown in (2) and (3)?

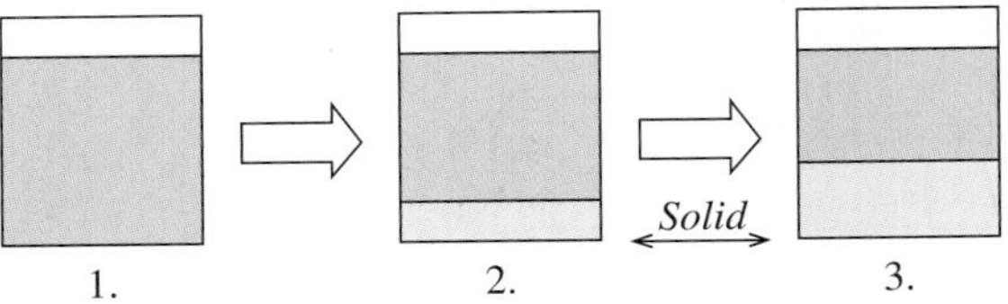


**8.79** Select the container that represents the dilution of a 4% (m/v) NaCl solution to each of the following:

**a.** 2% (m/v) NaCl

**b.** 1% (m/v) NaCl

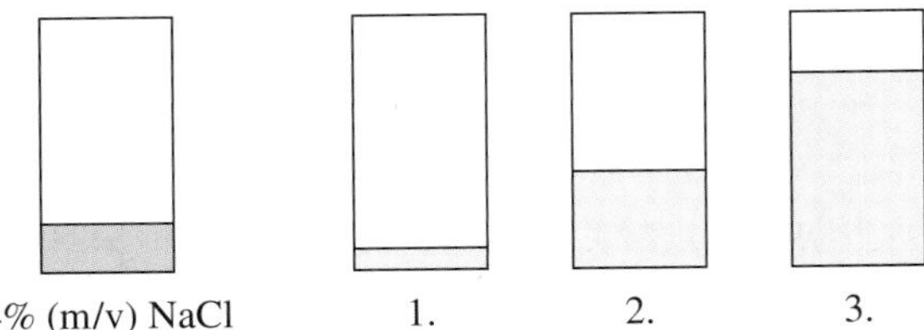


**8.80** Why do the lettuce leaves in a salad wilt after a vinaigrette dressing containing salt is added?

Use the following beakers and solutions for questions 8.81 and 8.82:

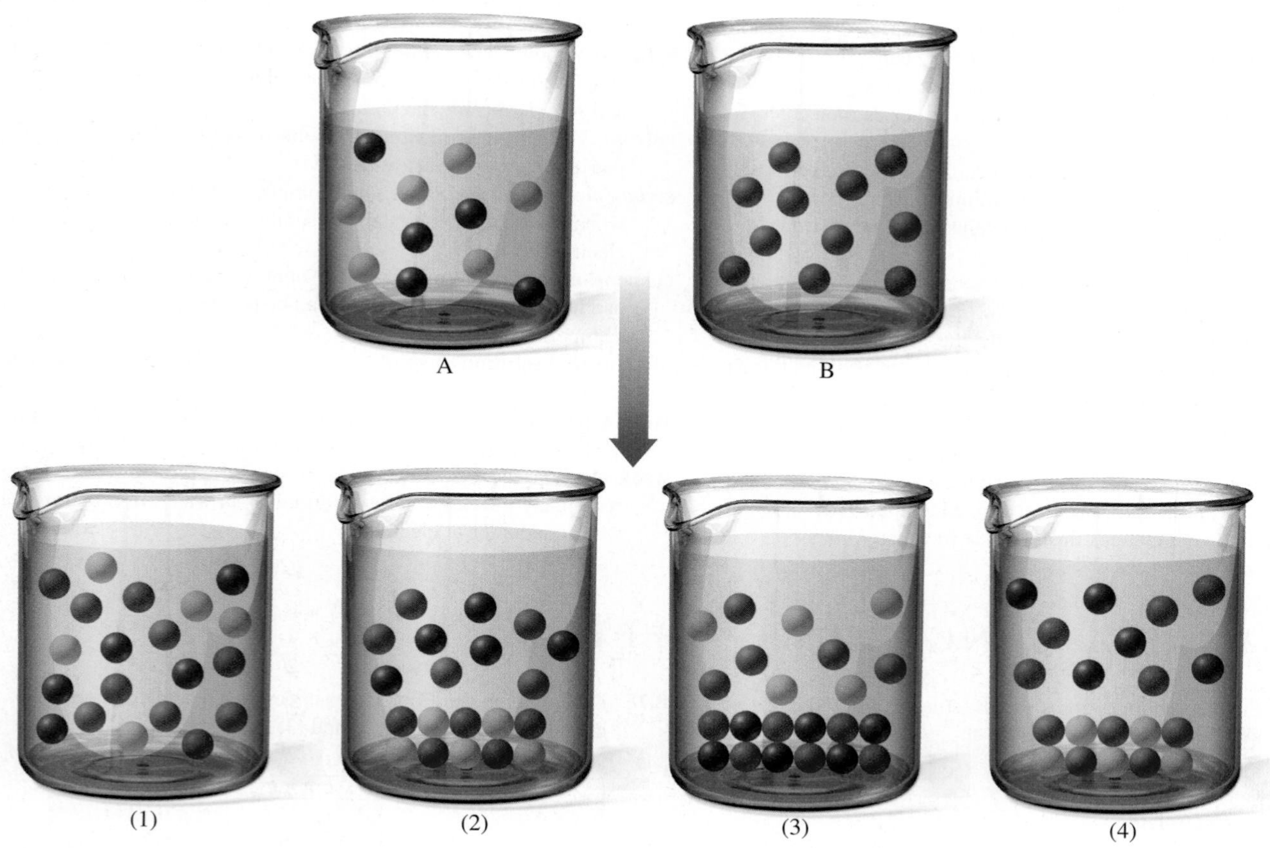


**8.81** Use the following:

$Na^+$  $Cl^-$   $Ag^+$  $NO_3^-$  

**a.** Select the beaker (1, 2, 3, or 4) that contains the products after the solutions in beakers A and B are mixed.
**b.** If an insoluble salt forms, write the ionic equation.
**c.** If a reaction occurs, write the net ionic equation.

**8.82** Use the following:

$K^+$  $NO_3^-$   $NH_4^+$  $Br^-$  

**a.** Select the beaker (1, 2, 3, or 4) that contains the products after the solutions in beakers A and B are mixed.
**b.** If an insoluble salt forms, write the ionic equation.
**c.** If a reaction occurs, write the net ionic equation.

**8.83** A semipermeable membrane separates two compartments, A and B. If the levels of solutions in A and B are equal initially, select the diagram that illustrates the final levels for each of the following:

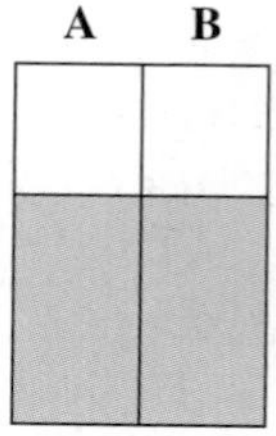


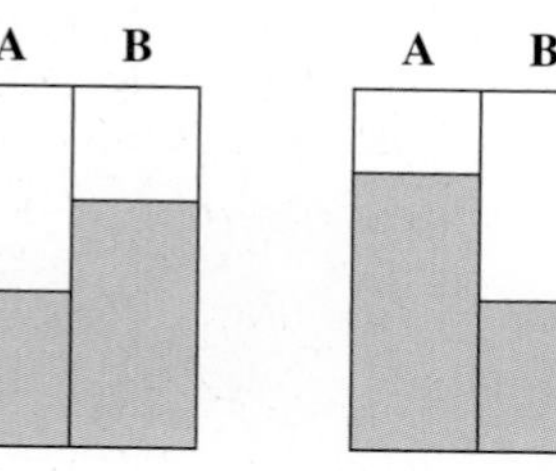


| | A | B |
|---|---|---|
| **a.** | 2% (m/v) starch | 8% (m/v) starch |
| **b.** | 1% (m/v) starch | 1% (m/v) starch |
| **c.** | 5% (m/v) sucrose | 1% (m/v) sucrose |
| **d.** | 0.1% (m/v) sucrose | 1% (m/v) sucrose |

**8.84** Select the diagram that represents the shape of a red blood cell when placed in each of the following solutions:

1. Normal red blood cell

2.

3.

**a.** 0.90% (m/v) NaCl
**b.** 10% (m/v) glucose
**c.** 0.01% (m/v) NaCl
**d.** 5.0% (m/v) glucose
**e.** 1% (m/v) glucose

# ADDITIONAL QUESTIONS AND PROBLEMS

**8.85** Why does iodine dissolve in hexane but not in water?

**8.86** How do temperature and pressure affect the solubility of solids and gases in water?

**8.87** If NaCl has a solubility of 36.0 g in 100 g of $H_2O$ at 20 °C, how many grams of water are needed to prepare a saturated solution containing 80.0 g of NaCl?

**8.88** If the solid NaCl in a saturated solution of NaCl continues to dissolve, why is there no change in the concentration of the NaCl solution?

**8.89** Potassium nitrate has a solubility of 34 g of $KNO_3$ in 100 g of $H_2O$ at 20 °C. State if each of the following forms an unsaturated or saturated solution at 20 °C:
**a.** 34 g of $KNO_3$ and 200. g of $H_2O$
**b.** 17 g of $KNO_3$ and 50. g of $H_2O$
**c.** 68 g of $KNO_3$ and 150. g of $H_2O$

**8.90** Potassium fluoride has a solubility of 92 g of KF in 100 g of $H_2O$ at 18 °C. State if each of the following forms an unsaturated or saturated solution at 18 °C:
**a.** 46 g of KF and 100 g of $H_2O$
**b.** 46 g of KF and 50 g of $H_2O$
**c.** 184 g of KF and 150 g of $H_2O$

**8.91** Calculate the mass percent (m/m) of a solution containing 15.5 g of $Na_2SO_4$ and 75.5 g of $H_2O$.

**8.92** How many grams of $K_2CO_3$ are in 750 mL of a 3.5% (m/v) $K_2CO_3$ solution?

**8.93** A patient receives all her nutrition from fluids given through the vena cava. Every 12 hours, 750 mL of a solution that is 4% (m/v) amino acids (protein) and 25% (m/v) glucose (carbohydrate) is given along with 500 mL of a 10% (m/v) lipid (fat).
**a.** In 1 day, how many grams of amino acids, glucose, and lipid are given to the patient?
**b.** How many kilocalories does she obtain in 1 day?

**8.94** An 80-proof brandy is 40.0% (v/v) ethyl alcohol. The "proof" is twice the percent concentration of alcohol in the beverage. How many milliliters of alcohol are present in 750 mL of brandy?

**8.95** How many milliliters of a 12% (v/v) propyl alcohol solution would you need to obtain 4.5 mL of propyl alcohol?

**8.96** How many liters of a 5.0% (m/v) glucose solution would you need to obtain 75 g of glucose?

**8.97** If you were in the laboratory, how would you prepare 0.250 L of a 2.00 M KCl solution?

**8.98** What is the molarity of a solution containing 15.6 g of KCl in 274 mL of solution?

**8.99** A solution is prepared with 70.0 g of $HNO_3$ and 130.0 g of $H_2O$. It has a density of 1.21 g/mL.
**a.** What is the mass percent (m/m) of the $HNO_3$ solution?
**b.** What is the total volume of the solution?
**c.** What is the mass/volume percent (m/v)?
**d.** What is its molarity (M)?

**8.100** What is the molarity of a 15% (m/v) NaOH solution?

**8.101** How many grams of solute are in each of the following solutions?
**a.** 2.5 L of 3.0 M $Al(NO_3)_3$ solution
**b.** 75 mL of 0.50 M $C_6H_{12}O_6$ solution

**8.102** How many grams of solute are in each of the following solutions?
**a.** 428 mL of a 0.450 M $Na_2SO_4$ solution
**b.** 10.5 mL of a 2.50 M $AgNO_3$ solution
**c.** 28.4 mL of a 6.00 M $H_3PO_4$ solution

**8.103** Why would a solution made by mixing solutions of $NaNO_3$ and KCl be clear, while a combination of KCl and $Pb(NO_3)_2$ solution produces a solid?

**8.104** Indicate whether each of the following is soluble in water:
**a.** KCl **b.** $MgSO_4$ **c.** PbS
**d.** $AgNO_3$ **e.** $Ca(OH)_2$

**8.105** Write the net ionic equation to show the formation of a precipitate (insoluble salt) when the following solutions are mixed. Write *none* if there is no precipitate.
**a.** $AgNO_3(aq)$ and $NaCl(aq)$
**b.** $NaCl(aq)$ and $KNO_3(aq)$
**c.** $Na_2SO_4(aq)$ and $BaCl_2(aq)$

**8.106** Write the net ionic equation to show the formation of a precipitate (insoluble salt) when the following solutions are mixed. Write *none* if there is no precipitate.
**a.** $Ca(NO_3)_2(aq)$ and $Na_2S(aq)$
**b.** $Na_3PO_4(aq)$ and $Pb(NO_3)_2(aq)$
**c.** $FeCl_3(aq)$ and $NH_4NO_3(aq)$

**8.107** Calculate the molarity of the solution when water is added to prepare each of the following solutions:
**a.** 25.0 mL of 0.200 M NaBr solution diluted to 50.0 mL
**b.** 15.0 mL of 1.20 M $K_2SO_4$ solution diluted to 40.0 mL
**c.** 75.0 mL of 6.00 M NaOH solution diluted to 255 mL

**8.108** Calculate the molarity of the solution when water is added to prepare each of the following solutions:
**a.** 25.0 mL of 18.0 M HCl solution diluted to 500. mL
**b.** 50.0 mL of 1.50 M NaCl solution diluted to 125 mL
**c.** 4.50 mL of 8.50 M KOH solution diluted to 75.0 mL

**8.109** What is the final volume, in mL, when 25.0 mL of 5.00 M HCl solution is diluted to each of the following concentrations?
**a.** 2.50 M HCl
**b.** 1.00 M HCl
**c.** 0.500 M HCl

**8.110** What is the final volume, in mL, when 5.00 mL of 12.0 M NaOH solution is diluted to each of the following concentrations?
**a.** 0.600 M **b.** 1.00 M **c.** 2.50 M

**8.111** The antacid Amphogel contains aluminum hydroxide $Al(OH)_3$. How many milliliters of 6.00 M HCl solution are required to react with 60.0 mL of 1.00 M $Al(OH)_3$ solution?

$$Al(OH)_3(s) + 3HCl(aq) \longrightarrow AlCl_3(aq) + 3H_2O(l)$$

**8.112** Calcium carbonate, $CaCO_3$, reacts with stomach acid (HCl, hydrochloric acid) according to the following equation:

$$CaCO_3(s) + 2HCl(aq) \longrightarrow CaCl_2(aq) + H_2O(l) + CO_2(g)$$

Tums, an antacid, contains $CaCO_3$. If Tums is added to 20.0 mL of 0.400 M HCl solution, how many grams of $CO_2$ gas are produced?

**8.113** Why would solutions with high salt content be used to prepare dried flowers?

**8.114** Why would a dialysis unit (artificial kidney) use isotonic concentrations of NaCl, KCl, $NaHCO_3$, and glucose in the dialysate?

**8.115** Why can't you drink seawater even if you are stranded on a desert island?

**8.116** A patient on dialysis has a high level of urea, a high level of sodium, and a low level of potassium in the blood. Why is the dialyzing solution prepared with a high level of potassium but no sodium or urea?

# CHALLENGE QUESTIONS

8.117 How many grams of NO gas can be produced from 80.0 mL of a 4.00 M $HNO_3$ solution and excess Cu?

$$3Cu(s) + 8HNO_3(aq) \longrightarrow 3Cu(NO_3)_2(aq) + 4H_2O(l) + 2NO(g)$$

8.118 Osmolarity (Osm) is the molar concentration of the particles—molecules and/or ions—in a solution. In physiological solutions, 5% (m/v) glucose ($C_6H_{12}O_6$) and 0.9% (m/v) NaCl, the osmolarity must be the same as for the blood, which is 0.3 Osm. Calculate the osmolarity of each solute compound in these two physiological solutions.

8.119 Indicate whether each of the following ionic compounds is soluble (S) or insoluble (I) in water:

**a.** $Na_3PO_4$ **b.** $PbBr_2$ **c.** KCl
**d.** $(NH_4)_2S$ **e.** $MgCO_3$ **f.** $FePO_4$

8.120 Write the net ionic equation to show the formation of a precipitate (insoluble salt) when the following solutions are mixed. Write *none* if no insoluble salt forms.

**a.** $AgNO_3 + Na_2SO_4$ **b.** $KCl + Pb(NO_3)_2$
**c.** $CaCl_2 + Mg_3(PO_4)_2$ **d.** $Na_2SO_4 + BaCl_2$

8.121 In a laboratory experiment, a 10.0-mL sample of NaCl solution is poured into an evaporating dish with a mass of 24.10 g. The combined mass of the evaporating dish and NaCl solution is 36.15 g. After heating, the evaporating dish and dry NaCl have a combined mass of 25.50 g.

**a.** What is the % (m/m) of the NaCl solution?
**b.** What is the molarity (M) of the NaCl solution?
**c.** If water is added to 10.0 mL of the initial NaCl solution to give a final volume of 60.0 mL, what is the molarity of the dilute NaCl solution?

8.122 A solution contains 4.56 g of KCl in 175 mL of solution. If the density of the KCl solution is 1.12 g/mL, what are the % (m/m) and molarity, M, for the potassium chloride solution?

8.123 A solution is prepared by dissolving 22.0 g of NaOH in 118.0 g water. The NaOH solution has a density of 1.15 g/mL.

**a.** What is the % (m/m) concentration of the NaOH solution?
**b.** What is the total volume (mL) of the solution?
**c.** What is the molarity (M) of the solution?

8.124 How many milliliters of a 1.75 M LiCl solution contain 15.2 g of LiCl?

8.125 How many grams of NaBr are contained in 75.0 mL of a 1.50 M NaBr solution?

8.126 Magnesium reacts with HCl to produce magnesium chloride and hydrogen gas:

$$Mg(s) + 2HCl(aq) \longrightarrow MgCl_2(aq) + H_2(g)$$

What is the molarity of the HCl solution if 250. mL of the HCl solution reacts with magnesium to produce 4.20 L of $H_2$ gas measured at STP?

# ANSWERS

## ANSWERS TO STUDY CHECKS

**8.1** A solution of a weak electrolyte will contain both molecules and ions.

**8.2** 0.194 mole of $Cl^-$

**8.3** 57 g of $NaNO_3$

**8.4** A higher solubility is more likely because the solubility of most solids increases when the temperature increases.

**8.5** **a.** No solid forms.
**b.** $Pb^{2+}(aq) + 2Cl^-(aq) \longrightarrow PbCl_2(s)$

**8.6** 3.4% (m/m) NaCl solution

**8.7** 4.8% (m/v) $Br_2$ in $CCl_4$

**8.8** 18 g of KCl

**8.9** 2.12 M $KNO_3$ solution

**8.10** 4.5 moles of HCl

**8.11** 120. mL

**8.12** 1.47 g of Zn

**8.13** The red blood cell will shrink (crenate).

## ANSWERS TO SELECTED QUESTIONS AND PROBLEMS

**8.1** **a.** NaCl, solute; water, solvent
**b.** water, solute; ethanol, solvent
**c.** oxygen, solute; nitrogen, solvent

**8.3** The polar water molecules pull the $K^+$ and $I^-$ ions away from the solid and into solution, where they are hydrated.

**8.5** **a.** water **b.** $CCl_4$ **c.** water **d.** $CCl_4$

**8.7** In a solution of KF, only the ions of $K^+$ and $F^-$ are present in the solvent. In an HF solution, there are a few ions of $H^+$ and $F^-$ present, but mostly dissolved HF molecules.

**8.9** **a.** $KCl(s) \xrightarrow{H_2O} K^+(aq) + Cl^-(aq)$
**b.** $CaCl_2(s) \xrightarrow{H_2O} Ca^{2+}(aq) + 2Cl^-(aq)$
**c.** $K_3PO_4(s) \xrightarrow{H_2O} 3K^+(aq) + PO_4^{3-}(aq)$
**d.** $Fe(NO_3)_3(s) \xrightarrow{H_2O} Fe^{3+}(aq) + 3NO_3^-(aq)$

**8.11** **a.** mostly molecules and a few ions
**b.** ions only
**c.** molecules only

**8.13** **a.** strong electrolyte
**b.** weak electrolyte
**c.** nonelectrolyte

**8.15** **a.** 1 Eq **b.** 2 Eq **c.** 2 Eq **d.** 6 Eq

**8.17** 0.154 mole of $Na^+$, 0.154 mole of $Cl^-$

**8.19** 55 mEq/L

**8.21** **a.** saturated **b.** unsaturated

**8.23** **a.** unsaturated **b.** unsaturated **c.** saturated

**8.25** **a.** 68 g of KCl **b.** 12 g of KCl

**8.27** **a.** The solubility of solid solutes typically increases as temperature increases.
**b.** The solubility of a gas is less at a higher temperature.
**c.** Gas solubility is less at a higher temperature and the $CO_2$ pressure in the can is increased.

**8.29** **a.** soluble **b.** insoluble **c.** insoluble
**d.** soluble **e.** soluble

**8.31** **a.** No solid forms.

**b.** $2Ag^+(aq) + \cancel{2NO_3^-}(aq) + \cancel{2K^+}(aq) + S^{2-}(aq) \longrightarrow Ag_2S(s) + \cancel{2NO_3^-}(aq) + \cancel{2K^+}(aq)$

$2Ag^+(aq) + S^{2-}(aq) \longrightarrow Ag_2S(s)$

**c.** $Ca^{2+}(aq) + \cancel{2Cl^-}(aq) + \cancel{2Na^+}(aq) + SO_4^{2-}(aq) \longrightarrow CaSO_4(s) + \cancel{2Cl^-}(aq) + \cancel{2Na^+}(aq)$

$Ca^{2+}(aq) + SO_4^{2-}(aq) \longrightarrow CaSO_4(s)$

**d.** $3Cu^{2+}(aq) + \cancel{6Cl^-}(aq) + \cancel{6Li^+}(aq) + 2PO_4^{3-}(aq) \longrightarrow Cu_3(PO_4)_2(s) + \cancel{6Cl^-}(aq) + \cancel{6Li^+}(aq)$

$3Cu^{2+}(aq) + 2PO_4^{3-}(aq) \longrightarrow Cu_3(PO_4)_2(s)$

**8.33** 5% (m/m) is 5 g of glucose in 100 g of solution, whereas 5% (m/v) is 5 g of glucose in 100 mL of solution.

**8.35** **a.** 17% (m/m) **b.** 5.3% (m/m)

**8.37** **a.** 30.% (m/v) **b.** 11% (m/v)

**8.39** **a.** 2.5 g of KCl **b.** 50. g of $NH_4Cl$

**8.41** 79.9 mL of alcohol

**8.43** **a.** 20. g of mannitol
**b.** 300 g of mannitol

**8.45** 2 L

**8.47** **a.** 0.50 M glucose solution
**b.** 0.036 M KOH solution
**c.** 0.250 M NaCl solution

**8.49** **a.** 3.0 moles of NaCl
**b.** 0.40 mole of KBr
**c.** 0.25 mole of $MgCl_2$

**8.51** **a.** 120 g of NaOH
**b.** 60. g of KCl
**c.** 5.5 g of HCl

**8.53** **a.** 1.5 L **b.** 10. L **c.** 62.5 mL

**8.55** **a.** 2.0 M HCl solution
**b.** 2.0 M NaOH solution
**c.** 2.5% (m/v) KOH solution
**d.** 3.0% (m/v) $H_2SO_4$ solution

**8.57** **a.** 0.60 L **b.** 250 mL **c.** 6.0 L **d.** 180 mL

**8.59** **a.** 10.4 g of $PbCl_2$
**b.** 18.8 mL of $Pb(NO_3)_2$ solution

**8.61** **a.** 206 mL of HCl solution
**b.** 0.500 mole of $H_2$ gas

**8.63** **a.** solution **b.** suspension

**8.65** **a.** 0.060 mole of NaCl (0.12 mole of particles)
**b.** 0.030 mole of $K_3PO_4$ (0.12 mole of particles)

**8.67** **a.** starch
**b.** from pure water into the starch
**c.** starch

**8.69** **a.** B 10% (m/v) starch
**b.** B 8% (m/v) albumin
**c.** B 10% (m/v) sucrose

**8.71** **a.** hypotonic **b.** hypotonic
**c.** isotonic **d.** isotonic

**8.73** **a.** NaCl **b.** alanine **c.** NaCl **d.** urea

**8.75** **a.** 3 **b.** 1 **c.** 2

**8.77** The skin of the cucumber acts like a semipermeable membrane and the more dilute solution inside flows into the brine solution.

**8.79** **a.** 2 **b.** 3

**8.81** **a.** beaker 3

**b.** $Na^+(aq) + Cl^-(aq) + Ag^+(aq) + NO_3^-(aq) \longrightarrow AgCl(s) + Na^+(aq) + NO_3^-(aq)$

**c.** $Ag^+(aq) + Cl^-(aq) \longrightarrow AgCl(s)$

**8.83** **a.** 2 **b.** 1 **c.** 3 **d.** 2

**8.85** Because iodine is a nonpolar molecule, it will dissolve in hexane, a nonpolar solvent. Iodine does not dissolve in water, because water is a polar solvent.

**8.87** 222 g of water

**8.89** **a.** unsaturated solution
**b.** saturated solution
**c.** saturated solution

**8.91** 17.0% (m/m)

**8.93** **a.** 60 g of amino acids, 380 g of glucose, and 100 g of lipids
**b.** 2700 kcal

**8.95** 38 mL of solution

**8.97** To make a 2.00 M KCl solution, weigh out 37.3 g of KCl (0.500 mole) and place in a volumetric flask. Add water to dissolve the KCl and give a final volume of 0.250 liter.

**8.99** **a.** 35.0% (m/m) $HNO_3$
**b.** 165 mL
**c.** 42.4% (m/v) $HNO_3$
**d.** 6.73 M

**8.101** **a.** 1600 g of $Al(NO_3)_3$
**b.** 6.8 g of $C_6H_{12}O_6$

**8.103** When solutions of $NaNO_3$ and KCl are mixed, no insoluble products are formed. All the combinations of salts are soluble. When KCl and $Pb(NO_3)_2$ solutions are mixed, the insoluble salt $PbCl_2$ forms.

**8.105** **a.** $Ag^+(aq) + Cl^-(aq) \longrightarrow AgCl(s)$
**b.** none
**c.** $Ba^{2+}(aq) + SO_4^{2-}(aq) \longrightarrow BaSO_4(s)$

**8.107** **a.** 0.100 M NaBr solution
**b.** 0.450 M $K_2SO_4$ solution
**c.** 1.76 M NaOH solution

**8.109** **a.** 50.0 mL of HCl solution
**b.** 125 mL of HCl solution
**c.** 250. mL of HCl solution

**8.111** 30.0 mL of HCl solution

**8.113** The solution will dehydrate the flowers because water will flow out of the cells of the flowers into the more concentrated salt solution.

**8.115** Drinking seawater will cause water to flow out of the body cells and further dehydrate a person.

**8.117** 2.40 g of NO

**8.119** **a.** $Na^+$ salts are soluble.
**b.** The halide salts containing $Pb^{2+}$ are insoluble.
**c.** $K^+$ salts are soluble.
**d.** Salts containing $NH_4^+$ ions are soluble.
**e.** Salts containing $CO_3^{2-}$ are usually insoluble.
**f.** Salts containing $PO_4^{3-}$ and $Fe^{3+}$ are insoluble.

**8.121** **a.** 11.6% (m/m) **b.** 2.39 M **c.** 0.383 M

**8.123** **a.** 15.7% (m/m) NaOH
**b.** 122 mL
**c.** 4.51 M

**8.125** 11.6 g of NaBr

# 9 Chemical Equilibrium

LOOKING AHEAD


9.1 Rates of Reactions

9.2 Chemical Equilibrium

9.3 Equilibrium Constants

9.4 Using Equilibrium Constants

9.5 Changing Equilibrium Conditions: Le Châtelier's Principle

9.6 Equilibrium in Saturated Solutions

*"I use radioactive isotopes to understand the cycling of elements like carbon and phosphorus in the ocean," explains Claudia Benitez-Nelson, a chemical oceanographer and Associate Professor of Geological Sciences at the University of South Carolina. "For example, I use thorium-234 to trace how and when particles are formed and transported to the bottom of the ocean. I also examine the biological consumption of the nutrient phosphorus by measuring fluctuations over time in the levels of the naturally occurring radioactive isotopes of phosphorus. My knowledge of chemistry is essential for understanding nutrient biogeochemistry and carbon sequestration in the oceans."*

*Oceanographers study the oceans and the plants and animals that live there. They study marine life, the chemical compounds in the ocean, the shape and composition of the ocean floor, and the effects of waves and tides.*

Visit **www.masteringchemistry.com** for self-study materials and instructor-assigned homework.

Earlier we looked at chemical reactions and determined the amounts of substances that react and the products that form. Now we are interested in how fast a reaction goes. If we know how fast a medication acts on the body, we can adjust the time over which the medication is taken. In construction, substances are added to cement to make it dry faster so work can continue. Some reactions such as explosions or the formation of precipitates in a solution are very fast. We know that when we roast a turkey or bake a cake that the reaction is slower. Some reactions such as the tarnishing of silver and the aging of the body are even slower. (See Figure 9.1.) We will see that some reactions need energy to keep running, whereas other reactions produce energy. We burn gasoline in our automobile engines to produce energy to make our cars move. We will also look at the effect of changing the concentrations of reactants or products on the rate of reaction.

Up to now, we have considered a reaction as proceeding in a forward direction from reactants to products. However, in many reactions a reverse reaction also takes place as products collide to reform reactants. When the forward and reverse reactions take place at the same rates the amounts of reactants and products stay the same. When this balance in forward and reverse rate is reached, we say that the reaction has reached *equilibrium*. At equilibrium, both reactants and products are present, though some reaction mixtures contain mostly reactants and form only a few products, while others contain mostly products and few reactants.

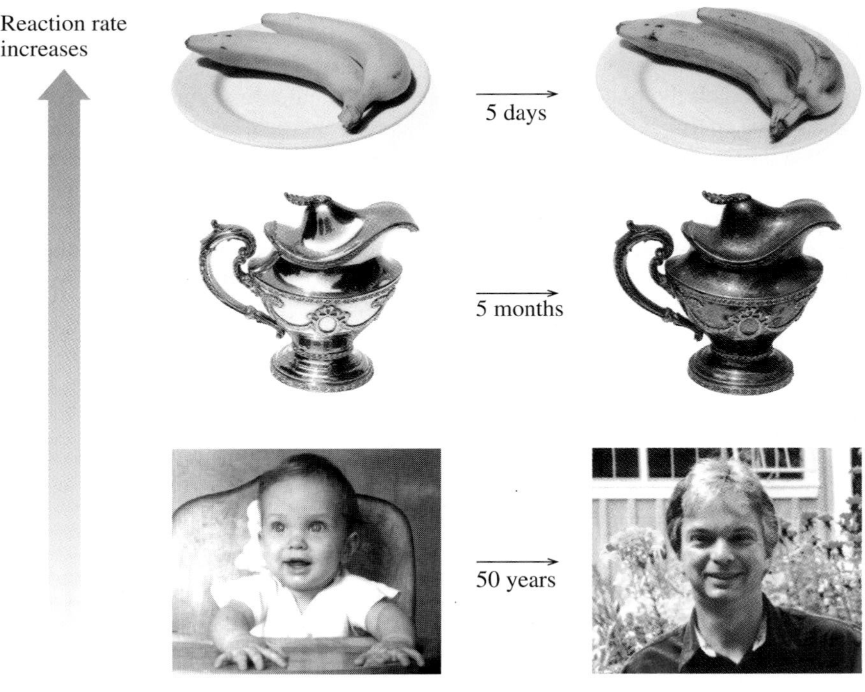


**FIGURE 9.1** Reaction rates vary greatly for everyday processes. A banana ripens in a few days, silver tarnishes in a few months, while the aging process of humans takes many years.

**Q** How would you compare the rates of the reaction that forms sugars in plants by photosynthesis with the reactions that digest sugars in the body?

## 9.1 Rates of Reactions

**LEARNING GOAL**

Describe how temperature, concentration, and catalysts affect the rate of a reaction.

For a chemical reaction to take place, the molecules of the reactants must come in contact with each other. The **collision theory** indicates that a reaction takes place only when molecules collide with the proper orientation and with sufficient energy. Many collisions can occur, but only a few actually lead to the formation of product. For example, consider the reaction of nitrogen ($N_2$) and oxygen ($O_2$) molecules. (See Figure 9.2.) To form the nitrogen oxide (NO) product, the collisions between the $N_2$ and the $O_2$ molecules must place the atoms in the proper alignment. If the molecules are not aligned properly, no reaction takes place.

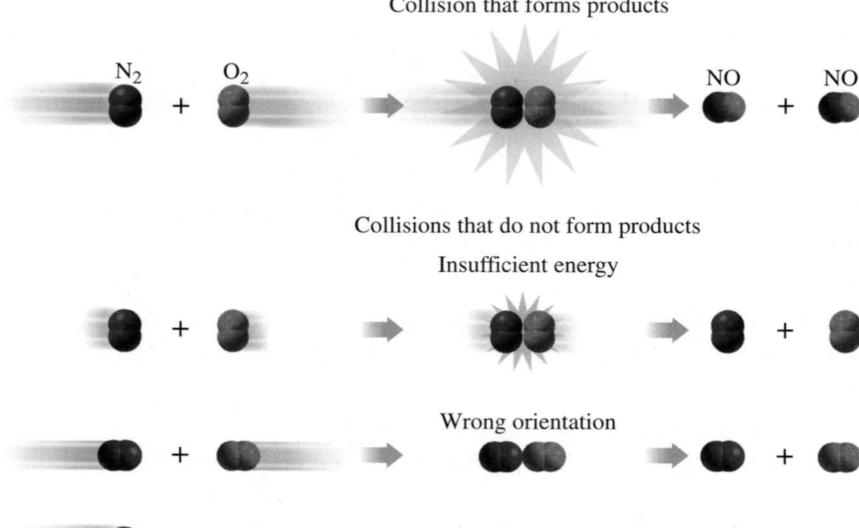


**FIGURE 9.2** Reacting molecules must collide, have a minimum amount of energy, and the proper orientation to form products.

**Q** What happens when reacting molecules collide with the minimum energy but do not have the proper orientation?

## Activation Energy

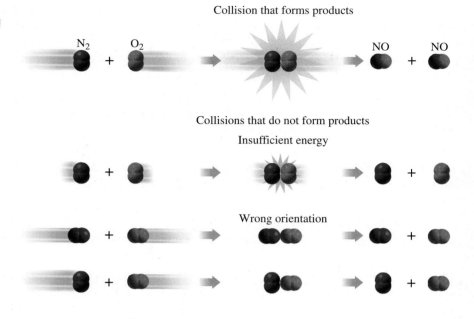

Even when a collision has the proper orientation, there still must be sufficient energy to break the bonds between the atoms of the reactants. The **activation energy** is the amount of energy required to break the bonds between atoms of reactants. In Figure 9.3, activation energy appears as an energy hill. The concept of activation energy is analogous to climbing a hill. To reach a destination on the other side, we must have the energy needed to climb to the top of the hill. Once we are at the top, we can run down the other side. The energy needed to get us from our starting point to the top of the hill would be our activation energy.

In the same way, a collision must provide enough energy to push the reactants to the top of the energy hill. Then the reactants may be converted to products. If the energy provided

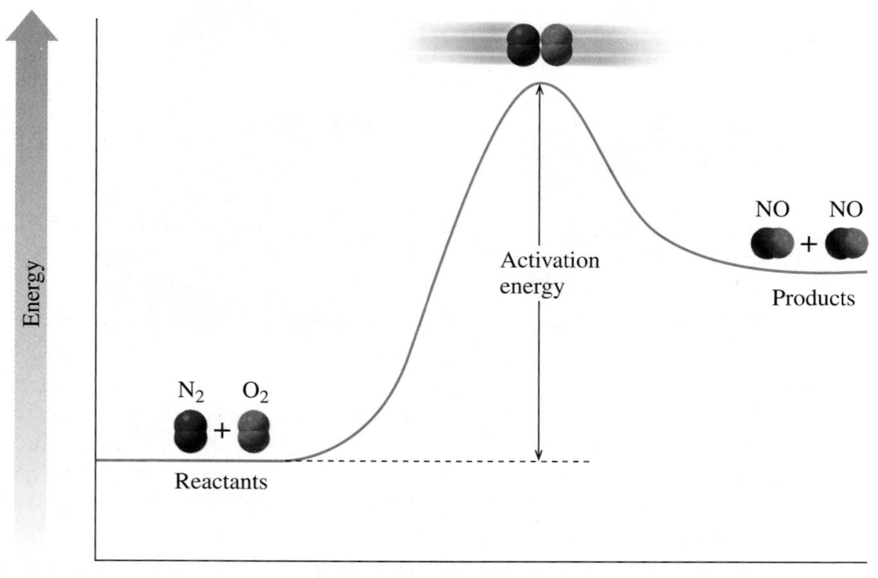


**FIGURE 9.3** The activation energy is the energy needed to convert the colliding molecules into product.

**Q** What happens in a collision of reacting molecules that have the proper orientation but not the energy of activation?

by the collision is less than the activation energy, the molecules simply bounce apart, and no reaction occurs. The features that lead to a successful reaction are summarized as follows:

**Three Conditions Required for a Reaction to Occur**

| | |
|---|---|
| **1. Collision** | The reactants must collide. |
| **2. Orientation** | The reactants must align properly to break and form bonds. |
| **3. Energy** | The collision must provide the energy of activation. |

## Reaction Rates

The **rate** (or speed) **of reaction** is determined by measuring the amount of a reactant used up, or the amount of a product formed, in a certain period of time:

$$\text{Rate of reaction} = \frac{\text{change in concentration}}{\text{change in time}}$$

Perhaps we can describe the rate of reaction by the analogy of eating a pizza. When we start to eat, we have a whole pizza. As time goes by, there are fewer slices of pizza left. If we know how long it took to eat the pizza, we could determine the rate at which the pizza was consumed. Let's assume 4 slices are eaten every 8 minutes. That gives a rate of $\frac{1}{2}$ slice per minute. After 16 minutes, all 8 slices are gone.

 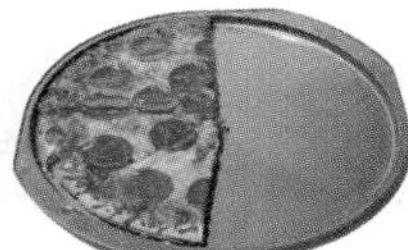 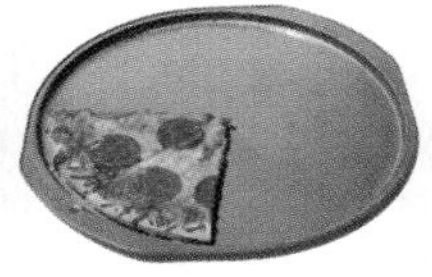 

**Rate at which pizza slices are eaten**

| **Slices eaten** | 0 | 4 slices | 6 slices | 8 slices |
|---|---|---|---|---|
| **Time (min)** | 0 | 8 min | 12 min | 16 min |

$$\text{Rate} = \frac{4 \text{ slices}}{8 \text{ min}} = \frac{1 \text{ slice}}{2 \text{ min}} = \frac{\frac{1}{2} \text{ slice}}{1 \text{ min}}$$

TUTORIAL
Factors That Affect Rate

## Factors That Affect the Rate of a Reaction

Some reactions go very fast, while others are very slow. For any reaction, the rate is affected by changes in temperature, changes in the concentration of the reactants, and the addition of catalysts.

**Temperature** At higher temperatures, the increase in kinetic energy makes the reacting molecules move faster. As a result, more collisions occur, and more colliding molecules have sufficient energy to react and form products. If we want food to cook faster, we use more heat to raise the temperature. When body temperature rises, there is an increase in the pulse rate, rate of breathing, and metabolic rate. On the other hand, we slow down reactions by lowering the temperature. We refrigerate perishable foods to retard spoilage and make them last longer. For some injuries, we apply ice to lessen the bruising process.

**Concentrations of Reactants** For virtually all reactions, the rate of a reaction increases when the concentrations of the reactants increases. When there are more reacting molecules, more collisions can occur, and the reaction goes faster. (See Figure 9.4.) For example, a person having difficulty breathing may be given oxygen. The increase in the number of oxygen molecules in the lungs increases the rate at which oxygen combines with hemoglobin and helps the patient breathe more easily.

| Reactants in reaction flask | Possible collisions |
|---|---|
| 1 red, 1 green | 1 |
| 2 red, 1 green | 2 |
| 2 red, 2 green | 4 |

**FIGURE 9.4** Increasing the concentration of a reactant increases the number of collisions that are possible.

**Q** How many collisions are possible if one more red reactant is added?

**Catalysts** Another way to speed up a reaction is to lower the activation energy. We saw that the activation energy is the energy needed to break apart the bonds of the reacting molecules. If a collision provides less energy than the activation energy, the bonds do not break apart and the molecules bounce apart. A **catalyst** speeds up a reaction by providing a different way for the reaction to proceed that has a lower activation energy. When activation energy is lowered, more collisions provide sufficient energy for reactants to form product. During a reaction, a catalyst is not changed or consumed.

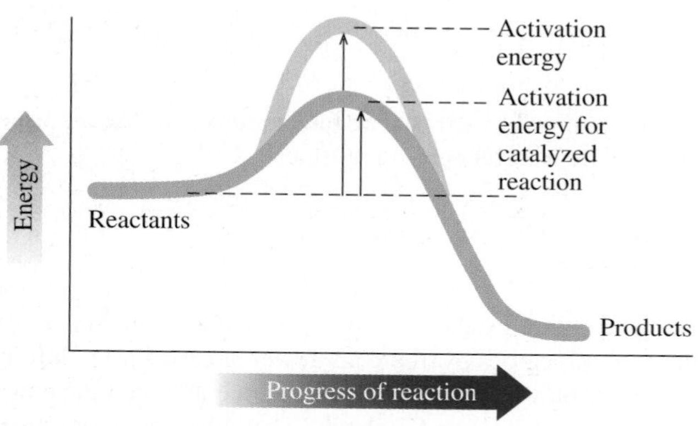


**TABLE 9.1 Factors That Increase Reaction Rate**

| Factor | Reason |
|---|---|
| More reactants | More collisions |
| Higher temperature | More collisions, more collisions with energy of activation |
| Adding a catalyst | Lowers energy of activation |

Catalysts have many uses in industry. In the manufacturing of margarine, hydrogen ($H_2$) is added to vegetable oils. Normally, the reaction is very slow because it has a high activation energy. However, when platinum (Pt) is used as a catalyst, the reaction occurs rapidly. In the body, biocatalysts called enzymes make most metabolic reactions proceed at rates necessary for proper cellular activity. A summary of the factors affecting reaction rates is given in Table 9.1.

CONCEPT CHECK 9.1

**Rate of Reactions**

Describe how decreasing the concentration of a reactant would change the rate of a reaction.

ANSWER

If the concentration of a reactant is decreased, there will be fewer collisions of the reactant molecules, which would slow the rate of reaction.

SAMPLE PROBLEM 9.1

**Factors That Affect the Rate of Reaction**

Indicate whether the following changes will increase, decrease, or have no effect upon the rate of reaction:

**a.** increase in temperature
**b.** increase in the number of reactant molecules
**c.** adding a catalyst

SOLUTION

**a.** increase **b.** increase **c.** increase

STUDY CHECK

How does the lowering of temperature affect the rate of reaction?

# ENVIRONMENTAL NOTE

## Catalytic Converters

For over 20 years, manufacturers have been required to include catalytic converters on gasoline automobile engines. When gasoline burns, the products found in the exhaust of a car contain high levels of pollutants. These include carbon monoxide (CO) from incomplete combustion, hydrocarbons such as $C_8H_{18}$ (octane) from unburned fuel, and nitrogen oxide (NO) from the reaction of $N_2$ and $O_2$ at the high temperatures reached within the engine. Carbon monoxide is toxic, and nitrogen oxide is involved in the formation of smog and acid rain.

The purpose of a catalytic converter is to lower the activation energy for reactions that convert each of these pollutants into substances such as $CO_2$, $N_2$, $O_2$, and $H_2O$, which are already present in the atmosphere.

$$2CO(g) + O_2(g) \longrightarrow 2CO_2(g)$$
$$2C_8H_{18}(g) + 25O_2(g) \longrightarrow 16CO_2(g) + 18H_2O(g)$$
$$2NO(g) \longrightarrow N_2(g) + O_2(g)$$

A catalytic converter consists of solid-particle catalysts, such as platinum (Pt) and palladium (Pd), on a ceramic honeycomb that provides a large surface area and facilitates contact with pollutants. As the pollutants pass through the converter, they react with the catalysts. Today, we all use unleaded gasoline because lead interferes with the ability of the Pt and Pd catalysts in the converter to react with the pollutants.

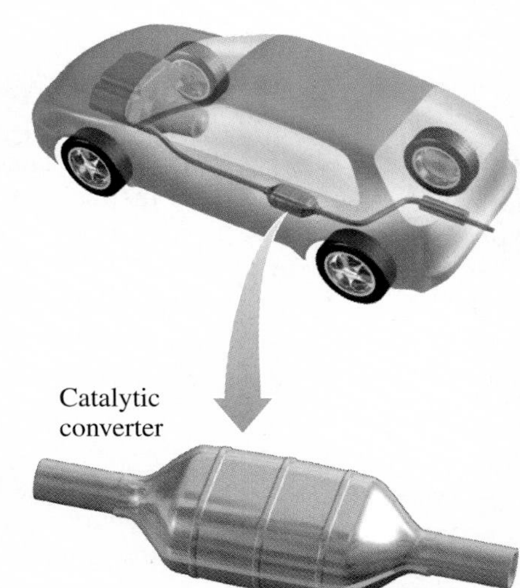


$2NO(g) \longrightarrow N_2(g) + O_2(g)$

NO absorbed on catalyst

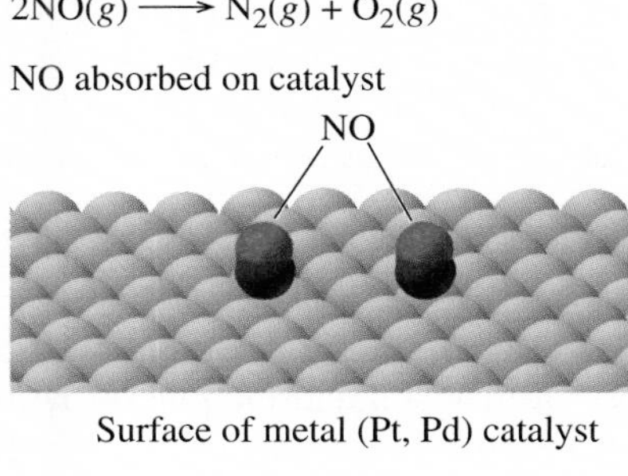


NO dissociates

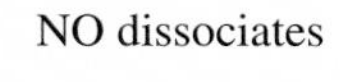

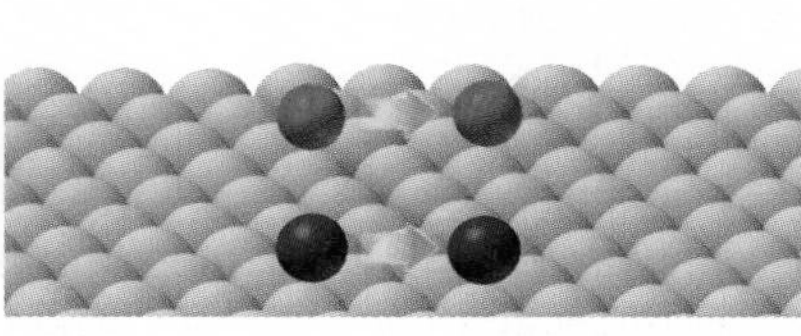

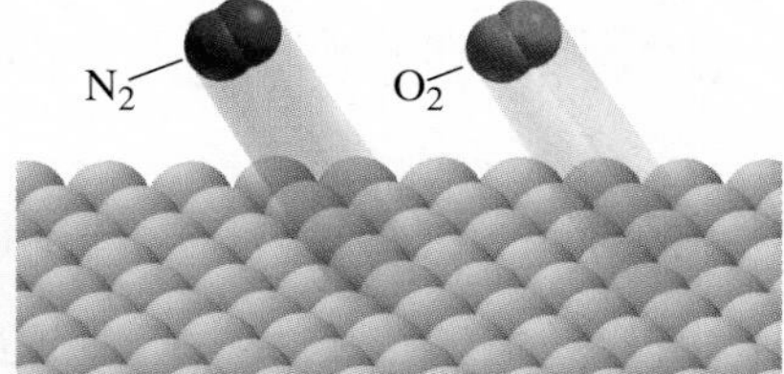


Surface of metal (Pt, Pd) catalyst

$2CO(g) + O_2(g) \longrightarrow 2CO_2(g)$

CO and $O_2$ absorbed on catalyst

$O_2$ dissociates

Surface of metal (Pt, Pd) catalyst

# QUESTIONS AND PROBLEMS

## Rates of Reactions

9.1 **a.** What is meant by the rate of a reaction?
**b.** Why does bread grow mold more quickly at room temperature than in the refrigerator?

**9.2** **a.** How does a catalyst affect the activation energy?
**b.** Why is pure oxygen used in cases of respiratory distress?

9.3 In the following reaction, what happens to the number of collisions when more $Br_2$ molecules are added?

$$H_2(g) + Br_2(g) \longrightarrow 2HBr(g)$$

**9.4** In the following reaction, what happens to the number of collisions when the temperature of the reaction is decreased?

$$H_2(g) + Br_2(g) \longrightarrow 2HBr(g)$$

**9.5** How would each of the following change the rate of the reaction shown here?

$$2SO_2(g) + O_2(g) \longrightarrow 2SO_3(g)$$

**a.** adding $SO_2$
**b.** raising the temperature
**c.** adding a catalyst
**d.** removing some $SO_2$

**9.6** How would each of the following change the rate of the reaction shown here?

$$2NO(g) + 2H_2(g) \longrightarrow N_2(g) + 2H_2O(g)$$

**a.** adding more NO
**b.** lowering the temperature
**c.** removing some $H_2$
**d.** adding a catalyst

## 9.2 Chemical Equilibrium

LEARNING GOAL

Use the concept of reversible reactions to explain chemical equilibrium.

In earlier chapters, we considered the *forward reaction* in an equation and assumed that all of the reactants were converted to products. However, most of the time reactants are not completely converted to products, because a *reverse reaction* takes place in which products come together and form the reactants. When a reaction proceeds in both a forward and reverse direction, it is said to be reversible. We have looked at other reversible processes. For example, the melting of solids to form liquids and the freezing of liquids into solids is a reversible physical change. Even in our daily life we have reversible events. We go from home to school, and we return from school to home. We go up an escalator and come back down. We put money in our bank account and take money out.

TUTORIAL
Chemical Equilibrium

An analogy for a forward and reverse reaction can be found in the phrase "We are going to the grocery store." Although we mention our trip in one direction, we know that we will also return home from the grocery store. Because our trip has both a forward and reverse direction, we can say the trip is reversible. It is not very likely that we would stay at the grocery store forever.

A trip to the grocery store can be used to illustrate another aspect of reversible reactions. Perhaps the grocery store is nearby and we usually walk. However, we can change our rate. Suppose that one day we drive to the store, which increases our rate and gets us to the store faster. Correspondingly, a car also increases the rate at which we return home.

### Reversible Reactions

MC SELF STUDY ACTIVITY
Equilibrium

A **reversible reaction** proceeds in both the forward and reverse directions. That means there are two reaction rates: the rate of the forward reaction and the rate of the reverse reaction. When molecules begin to react, the rate of the forward reaction is faster than the rate of the reverse reaction. As reactants are consumed and products accumulate, the rate of the forward reaction decreases and the rate of the reverse reaction increases.

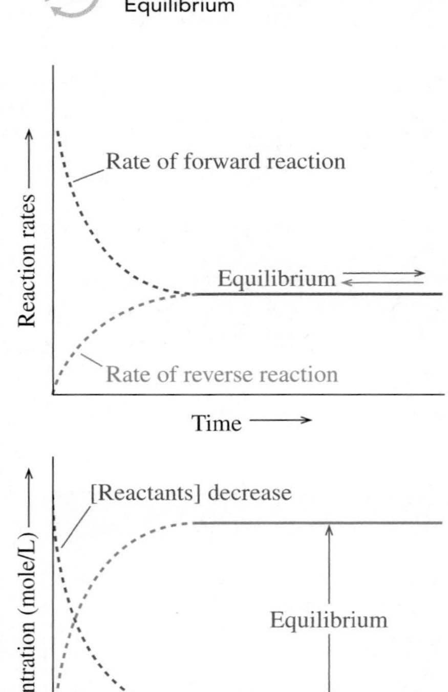


### Equilibrium

Eventually, the rates of the forward and reverse reactions are equal; the reactants form products as often as products form reactants. A reaction reaches **chemical equilibrium** when there is no further change in the concentrations of the reactants and products.

**At equilibrium:**

The rate of the forward reaction is equal to the rate of the reverse reaction.

No further changes occur in the concentrations of reactants and products, even though the two reactions continue at equal but opposite rates.

Let us look at the process as the reaction of $H_2$ and $I_2$ proceeds to equilibrium. (See Figure 9.5.) Initially, only $H_2$ and $I_2$ are present. Soon, a few molecules of HI are produced by the forward reaction. With more time, additional HI molecules are produced. As the concentration of HI increases, more HI molecules collide and react in the reverse direction.

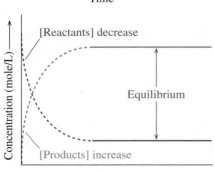

Forward reaction: $H_2(g) + I_2(g) \longrightarrow 2HI(g)$

Reverse reaction: $2HI(g) \longrightarrow H_2(g) + I_2(g)$

As HI product builds up, the rate of the reverse reaction increases, while the rate of the forward reaction decreases. Eventually the rates become equal, which means the reaction

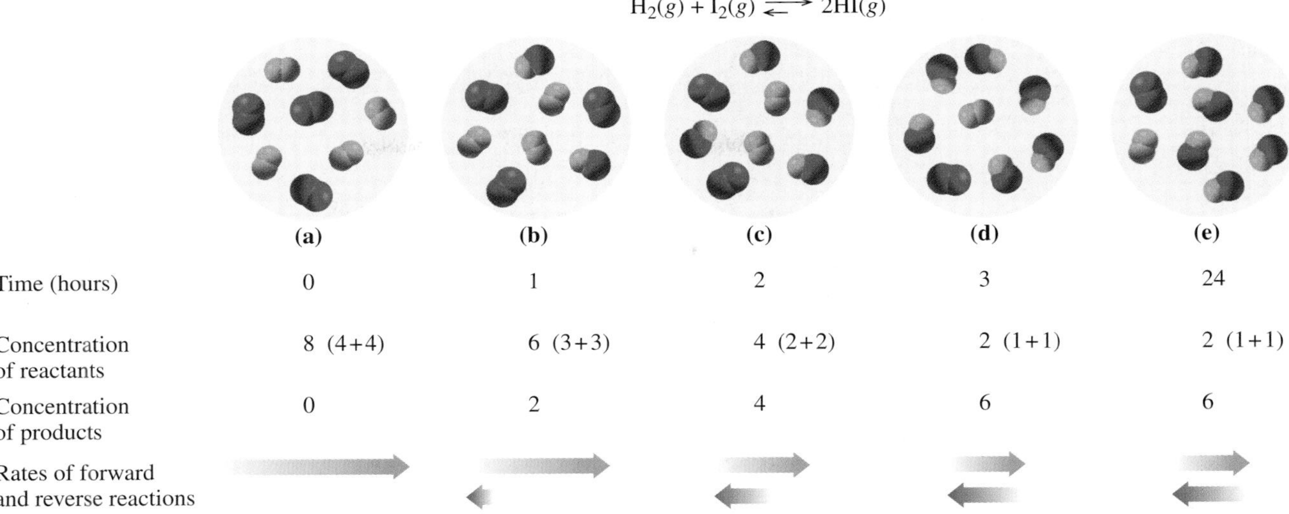


**FIGURE 9.5** **(a)** Initially, the reaction flask contains only the reactants $H_2$ and $I_2$. **(b)** The forward reaction between $H_2$ and $I_2$ begins to produce 2HI. **(c)** As the reaction proceeds, there are fewer molecules of $H_2$ and $I_2$ and more molecules of HI, which increases the rate of the reverse reaction. **(d)** At equilibrium, the concentrations of reactants $H_2$ and $I_2$ and product HI are constant. **(e)** The reaction continues with the rate of the forward reaction equal to the rate of the reverse reaction.

**Q** How do the rates of the forward and reverse reactions compare once a chemical reaction reaches equilibrium?

has reached equilibrium. Even though the concentrations remain constant at equilibrium, the forward and reverse reactions continue to occur. The forward and reverse reactions are usually shown together in a single equation by using a double arrow. A reversible reaction is two opposing reactions that occur at the same time.

$$H_2(g) + I_2(g) \underset{\text{Reverse reaction}}{\overset{\text{Forward reaction}}{\rightleftarrows}} 2HI(g)$$

## SAMPLE PROBLEM 9.2

### Reversible Reactions

Write the forward and reverse reactions for each of the following:

**a.** $N_2(g) + 3H_2(g) \rightleftarrows 2NH_3(g)$ **b.** $2CO(g) + O_2 \rightleftarrows 2CO_2(g)$

SOLUTION

The equations are separated into forward and reverse reactions.

**a.** Forward reaction: $N_2(g) + 3H_2(g) \longrightarrow 2NH_3(g)$
Reverse reaction: $2NH_3(g) \longrightarrow N_2(g) + 3H_2(g)$

**b.** Forward reaction: $2CO(g) + O_2(g) \longrightarrow 2CO_2(g)$
Reverse reaction: $2CO_2(g) \longrightarrow 2CO(g) + O_2(g)$

STUDY CHECK

Write the equation for the equilibrium reaction that contains the following reverse reaction:

$2HBr(g) \longrightarrow H_2(g) + Br_2(g)$

## CONCEPT CHECK 9.2

### Reaction Rates and Equilibrium

Complete each of the following with equal or not equal, faster or slower, change or do not change:

**a.** Before equilibrium is reached, the concentrations of the reactants and products ________.

**b.** Initially, reactants placed in a container have a ________ rate of reaction than the rate of reaction of the products.
**c.** At equilibrium, the rate of the forward reaction is ________ to the rate of the reverse reaction.
**d.** At equilibrium, the concentrations of the reactants and products ________.

ANSWER

**a.** Until the rates of the forward and reverse reactions become equal, the concentrations of the reactants and products will *change*.
**b.** When there are only reactants in the container, the rate of the forward reaction will be *faster* than the rate of the reverse reaction.
**c.** Equilibrium is reached when the rates of the forward and reverse reactions become *equal*.
**d.** At equilibrium, when the rates of the forward and reverse reactions become equal, the concentrations of the reactants and products *do not change*.

## QUESTIONS AND PROBLEMS

### Chemical Equilibrium

9.7 What is meant by the term "reversible reaction"?

**9.8** When does a reversible reaction reach equilibrium?

9.9 Which of the following processes are reversible?
**a.** breaking a glass **b.** melting snow **c.** heating a pan

**9.10** Which of the following processes are at equilibrium?
**a.** Opposing rates of reaction are equal.
**b.** Concentrations of reactants and products are equal.
**c.** Concentrations of reactants and products do not change.

# 9.3 Equilibrium Constants

LEARNING GOAL

Calculate the equilibrium constant for a reversible reaction given the concentrations of reactants and products at equilibrium.

At equilibrium, reactions occur in opposite directions at the same rate, which means the concentrations of the reactants and products remain constant. We can use a ski lift as an analogy. Early in the morning, skiers at the bottom of the mountain begin to ride the ski lift up to the slopes. As skiers reach the top of the mountain, they ski down. Eventually, the number of people riding up the ski lift becomes equal to the number of people skiing down the mountain. There is no further change in the number of skiers on the slopes; the system is at equilibrium.

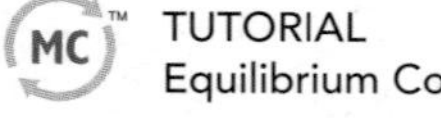
TUTORIAL
Equilibrium Constant

## Equilibrium Constant Expression

Because the concentrations in a reaction at equilibrium no longer change, they can be used to set up a relationship between the products and the reactants. Suppose we write a general equation for reactants A and B that form products C and D. The small italic letters are the coefficients in the balanced equation.

$$aA + bB \rightleftharpoons cC + dD$$

An **equilibrium constant expression** for the reaction multiplies the concentrations of the products together and divides by the concentrations of the reactants. Each concentration is raised to a power that is its coefficient in the balanced chemical reaction. The square bracket around each substance indicates the concentration is expressed in moles per liter (M). The **equilibrium constant,** $K_c$, is the numerical value obtained by substituting molar concentrations at equilibrium into the expression. For our general reaction, the equilibrium constant expression is

Equilibrium constant — Equilibrium constant expression

$$K_c = \frac{\text{Products}}{\text{Reactants}} = \frac{[C]^c\,[D]^d}{[A]^a\,[B]^b}$$

(exponents $c$, $d$, $a$, $b$: Coefficients)

For the reaction of $H_2$ and $I_2$ to form HI, we use the following steps to write the equilibrium constant expression:

**STEP 1** **Write the balanced equilibrium equation:**

$$H_2(g) + I_2(g) \rightleftharpoons 2HI(g)$$

**STEP 2** **Write the concentrations of the products as the numerator and reactants as the denominator:**

$$\frac{\text{Products}}{\text{Reactants}} \longrightarrow \frac{[HI]}{[H_2][I_2]}$$

**STEP 3** **Write the coefficient of each substance as an exponent:**

$$K_c = \frac{[HI]^2}{[H_2][I_2]}$$

CONCEPT CHECK 9.3

### Equilibrium Constant Expression

Select the correctly written equilibrium constant expression for the following reaction, and explain your choice:

$$CH_4(g) + H_2O(g) \rightleftharpoons CO(g) + 3H_2(g)$$

**a.** $K_c = \frac{[CO]]3H_2]}{[CH_4]]H_2O]}$ **b.** $K_c = \frac{[CO][H_2]^3}{[CH_4][H_2O]}$

**c.** $K_c = \frac{[CH_4][H_2O]}{[CO][H_2]^3}$ **d.** $K_c = \frac{[CO][H_2]}{[CH_4][H_2O]}$

ANSWER

The correct equilibrium constant expression is **b.** The products are written in the numerator and the reactants are in the denominator. Because $H_2$ has a coefficient of 3 in the balanced equation, an exponent of 3 is used with the concentration of $H_2$.

SAMPLE PROBLEM 9.3

### Writing Equilibrium Constant Expressions

Write the equilibrium constant expression for the following:

$$2SO_2(g) + O_2(g) \rightleftharpoons 2SO_3(g)$$

SOLUTION

**STEP 1** **Write the balanced equilibrium equation:**

$$2SO_2(g) + O_2(g) \rightleftharpoons 2SO_3(g)$$

**STEP 2** **Write the concentrations of the products as the numerator and reactants as the denominator:**

$$\frac{\text{Products}}{\text{Reactants}} \longrightarrow \frac{[SO_3]}{[SO_2][O_2]}$$

**STEP 3** **Write the coefficient of each substance as an exponent:**

$$K_c = \frac{[SO_3]^2}{[SO_2]^2[O_2]}$$

**Guide to Writing the $K_c$ Expression**

STEP 1
Write the balanced equilibrium equation.

STEP 2
Write the concentrations of the products as the numerator and reactants as the denominator.

STEP 3
Write the coefficient of each substance in the equation as an exponent.

$CaCO_3(s) \rightleftharpoons CaO(s) + CO_2(g)$

$T = 800\ °C$

$T = 800\ °C$

**FIGURE 9.6** At equilibrium at constant temperature, the concentration of $CO_2$ is the same regardless of the amounts of $CaCO_3(s)$ and $CaO(s)$ in the container.

**Q** Why are the concentrations of $CaO(s)$ and $CaCO_3(s)$ not included in $K_c$ for the decomposition of $CaCO_3$?

STUDY CHECK

Write the balanced chemical equation that would give the following equilibrium constant expression:

$$K_c = \frac{[NO_2]^2}{[NO]^2[O_2]}$$

## Heterogeneous Equilibrium

Up to now, our examples have been reactions that involve only gases. A reaction in which all the reactants and products are in the same physical state is a **homogenous equilibrium**. When the reactants and products are in two or more physical states, the equilibrium is termed a **heterogeneous equilibrium**. In the following example, solid calcium carbonate reaches equilibrium with solid calcium oxide and carbon dioxide gas; this is a heterogeneous equilibrium. (See Figure 9.6.)

$$CaCO_3(s) \rightleftharpoons CaO(s) + CO_2(g)$$

In contrast to gases, the concentrations of pure solids and pure liquids in a heterogeneous equilibrium are constant; they do not change. Therefore, pure solids and liquids are not included in the equilibrium constant expression. For this heterogeneous equilibrium, the $K_c$ expression does not include the concentration of $CaCO_3(s)$ or $CaO(s)$. It is written as $K_c = [CO_2]$.

SAMPLE PROBLEM 9.4

### Heterogeneous Equilibrium Constant Expression

Write the equilibrium constant expression for the following reaction at equilibrium:

$$4HCl(g) + O_2(g) \rightleftharpoons 2H_2O(l) + 2Cl_2(g)$$

SOLUTION

**STEP 1** **Write the balanced equilibrium equation:**

$$4HCl(g) + O_2(g) \rightleftharpoons 2H_2O(l) + 2Cl_2(g)$$

**STEP 2** **Write the concentrations of the products as the numerator and reactants as the denominator:**

$$\frac{\text{Products}}{\text{Reactants}} \longrightarrow \frac{[Cl_2]}{[HCl][O_2]}$$

In the equilibrium constant expression for a heterogeneous reaction, the concentration of the liquid $H_2O$ is not included.

**STEP 3** **Write the coefficient of each substance as an exponent:**

$$K_c = \frac{[Cl_2]^2}{[HCl]^4[O_2]}$$

STUDY CHECK

Solid iron(II) oxide and carbon monoxide gas are in equilibrium with solid iron and carbon dioxide gas. Write the equation and the equilibrium constant expression for this reaction.

## Calculating Equilibrium Constants

The numerical value of the equilibrium constant is calculated from the equilibrium constant expression by substituting experimentally measured concentrations of the reactants and products at equilibrium into the expression. For example, the equilibrium constant expression for the reaction of $H_2$ and $I_2$ is written

$$H_2(g) + I_2(g) \rightleftharpoons 2HI(g) \qquad K_c = \frac{[HI]^2}{[H_2][I_2]}$$

In the first experiment, the molar concentrations for the reactants and products at equilibrium are found to be $[H_2] = 0.10$ M, $[I_2] = 0.20$ M, and $[HI] = 1.04$ M. When we substitute these values into the equilibrium constant expression, we obtain the numerical value of the equilibrium constant:

| **Reactants** | **Products** |
|---|---|
| $[H_2] = 0.10$ M | $[HI] = 1.04$ M |
| $[I_2] = 0.20$ M | |

$$K_c = \frac{[HI]^2}{[H_2][I_2]} = \frac{[1.04]^2}{[0.10][0.20]} = 54$$

In experiments 2 and 3, we look at different equilibrium concentrations of reactants and products for the $H_2$, $I_2$, and HI system at the same temperature. When the concentrations of reactants and products are measured in each equilibrium sample and used to calculate the $K_c$ for the reaction, the same value of $K_c$ is obtained for each. (See Table 9.2.) Thus, a reaction at a specific temperature can have only one value for the equilibrium constant.

**TABLE 9.2** Equilibrium Constant for $H_2(g) + I_2(g) \rightleftharpoons 2HI(g)$ at 427 °C

| Experiment | $[H_2]$ | $[I_2]$ | $[HI]$ | $K_c = \frac{[HI]^2}{[H_2][I_2]}$ |
|---|---|---|---|---|
| 1 | 0.10 M | 0.20 M | 1.04 M | 54 |
| 2 | 0.20 M | 0.20 M | 1.47 M | 54 |
| 3 | 0.30 M | 0.17 M | 1.66 M | 54 |

The units of $K_c$ depend on the specific equation. In the example of $[H_2]$, $[I_2]$, and $[HI]$, $K_c$ has the units of $[M]^2/[M]^2$, which results in a value with no units. However, in the following example, the [M] units would not cancel, because $[M]^2/[M]^4 = 1/[M]^2 = [M]^{-2}$. Usually $K_c$ is given without units. At 500 K, the value of $K_c$ for the following reaction is $1.7 \times 10^2$. (In this text, we will give $K_c$ without units.)

$$N_2(g) + 3H_2(g) \rightleftharpoons 2NH_3(g)$$

$$K_c = \frac{[NH_3]^2}{[N_2][H_2]^3} = 1.7 \times 10^2$$

SAMPLE PROBLEM 9.5

### Calculating an Equilibrium Constant

The decomposition of dinitrogen tetroxide forms nitrogen dioxide:

$$N_2O_4(g) \rightleftharpoons 2NO_2(g)$$

What is the value of $K_c$ at 100 °C if a reaction mixture at equilibrium contains $[N_2O_4] = 0.45$ M and $[NO_2] = 0.31$ M?

**Guide to Calculating the $K_c$ Value**

STEP 1
Write the $K_c$ expression for the equilibrium.

STEP 2
Substitute equilibrium (molar) concentrations and calculate $K_c$.

SOLUTION

**Given** reactant: $[N_2O_2] = 0.45$ M product: $[NO_2] = 0.31$ M

**Need** $K_c$ value

STEP 1 **The equilibrium expression is written using the coefficients in the balanced equation as exponents of the molar concentrations:**

$$K_c = \frac{[NO_2]^2}{[N_2O_4]}$$

STEP 2 **Substitute the molar concentrations given for the equilibrium mixture into the equilibrium constant expression and calculate the $K_c$ value:**

$$K_c = \frac{[0.31]^2}{[0.45]} = 0.21$$

STUDY CHECK

Ammonia decomposes when heated to give nitrogen and hydrogen:

$$2NH_3(g) \rightleftharpoons 3H_2(g) + N_2(g)$$

Calculate the equilibrium constant if an equilibrium mixture contains $[NH_3] = 0.040$ M, $[N_2] = 0.20$ M, and $[H_2] = 0.60$ M.

## QUESTIONS AND PROBLEMS

### Equilibrium Constants

**9.11** Write the equilibrium constant expression, $K_c$, for each of the following reactions:

**a.** $CH_4(g) + 2H_2S(g) \rightleftharpoons CS_2(g) + 4H_2(g)$

**b.** $2NO(g) \rightleftharpoons N_2(g) + O_2(g)$

**c.** $2SO_3(g) + CO_2(g) \rightleftharpoons CS_2(g) + 4O_2(g)$

**9.12** Write the equilibrium constant expression, $K_c$, for each of the following reactions:

**a.** $2HBr(g) \rightleftharpoons H_2(g) + Br_2(g)$

**b.** $CO(g) + 2H_2(g) \rightleftharpoons CH_3OH(g)$

**c.** $CH_4(g) + Cl_2(g) \rightleftharpoons CH_3Cl(g) + HCl(g)$

**9.13** Identify each of the following as a homogeneous or heterogeneous equilibrium:

**a.** $2O_3(g) \rightleftharpoons 3O_2(g)$

**b.** $2NaHCO_3(s) \rightleftharpoons Na_2CO_3(s) + CO_2(g) + H_2O(g)$

**c.** $CH_4(g) + H_2O(g) \rightleftharpoons 3H_2(g) + CO(g)$

**d.** $4HCl(g) + O_2(g) \rightleftharpoons 2H_2O(l) + 2Cl_2(g)$

**9.14** Identify each of the following as a homogeneous or heterogeneous equilibrium:

**a.** $CO(g) + H_2(g) \rightleftharpoons C(s) + H_2O(g)$

**b.** $CO(g) + 2H_2(g) \rightleftharpoons CH_3OH(l)$

**c.** $CS_2(g) + 4H_2(g) \rightleftharpoons CH_4(g) + 2H_2S(g)$

**d.** $Br_2(g) + Cl_2(g) \rightleftharpoons 2BrCl(g)$

**9.15** Write the equilibrium constant expression for each of the reactions in problem 9.13.

**9.16** Write the equilibrium constant expression for each of the reactions in problem 9.14.

**9.17** What is the $K_c$ for the following reaction at equilibrium if $[NO_2] = 0.21$ M and $[N_2O_4] = 0.030$ M?

$$N_2O_4(g) \rightleftharpoons 2NO_2(g)$$

**9.18** What is the $K_c$ for the following reaction at equilibrium if $[CO] = 0.20$ M, $[H_2O] = 0.30$ M, $[CO_2] = 0.30$ M, and $[H_2] = 0.033$ M?

$$CO_2(g) + H_2(g) \rightleftharpoons CO(g) + H_2O(g)$$

**9.19** What is the $K_c$ for the following reaction at equilibrium at 1000 °C if $[H_2] = 0.30$ M, $[CO] = 0.50$ M, $[CH_4] = 1.8$ M, and $[H_2O] = 2.0$ M?

$$CO(g) + 3H_2(g) \rightleftharpoons CH_4(g) + H_2O(g)$$

**9.20** What is the $K_c$ for the following reaction at equilibrium at 500 °C if $[H_2] = 0.40$ M, $[N_2] = 0.44$ M, and $[NH_3] = 2.2$ M?

$$N_2(g) + 3H_2(g) \rightleftharpoons 2NH_3(g)$$

# 9.4 Using Equilibrium Constants

**LEARNING GOAL**

Use an equilibrium constant to predict the extent of reaction and to calculate equilibrium concentrations.

We have seen that the values of $K_c$ can be large or small. We can now look at the $K_c$ values to predict how far the reaction proceeds to products at equilibrium. When a $K_c$ is large, the numerator (products) is greater than the concentrations of the reactants in the denominator:

$$\frac{\textbf{[Products]}}{\text{[Reactants]}} = \textbf{Large } K_c$$

When a $K_c$ is small, the numerator is smaller than the denominator, which means that the reaction favors the reactants:

$$\frac{\text{[Products]}}{\textbf{[Reactants]}} = \text{Small } K_c$$

Using a general reaction and its equilibrium constant expression, we can look at the relative concentrations of reactant A and product B:

$$A(g) \rightleftharpoons B(g) \quad K_c = \frac{[B]}{[A]}$$

For a large $K_c$, [B] is greater than [A]. For example, if the $K_c$ is $1 \times 10^3$, or 1000, [B] would be 1000 times greater than [A] at equilibrium:

$$K_c = \frac{[B]}{[A]} = 1000 \quad \text{or rearranged} \quad [B] = 1000[A]$$

For a small $K_c$, [A] is greater than [B]. For example, if the $K_c$ is $1 \times 10^{-2}$, [A] is 100 times greater than [B] at equilibrium:

$$K_c = \frac{[B]}{[A]} = \frac{1}{100} \quad \text{or rearranged} \quad [A] = 100[B]$$

Equilibrium mixtures with different values of $K_c$ are illustrated in Figure 9.7.

## Equilibrium with a Large $K_c$

A reaction with a large $K_c$ forms a substantial amount of product by the time equilibrium is established. The greater the value of $K_c$, the more the equilibrium favors the products. A reaction with a very large $K_c$ essentially goes to completion to give mostly products. Consider the reaction of $SO_2$ and $O_2$, which has a large $K_c$. At equilibrium, the reaction mixture contains mostly products and very little reactants:

$$2SO_2(g) + O_2(g) \rightleftharpoons 2SO_3(g)$$

$$K_c = \frac{[SO_3]^2}{[SO_2]^2\,[O_2]} \quad \frac{\text{Mostly products}}{\text{Few reactants}} = 3.4 \times 10^2 \quad \text{Reaction favors products}$$

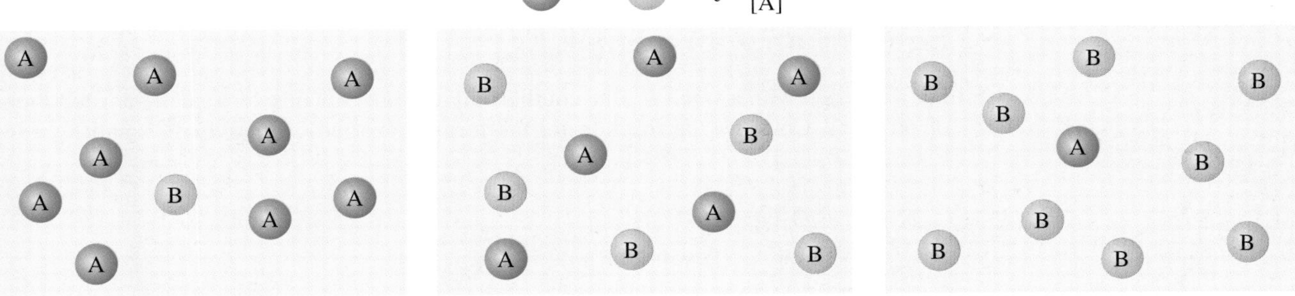


**FIGURE 9.7** A reaction with $K_c < 1$ contains a higher concentration of reactant [A] than product [B]. A reaction with $K_c$ of about 1.0 has about the same concentrations of product [B] as reactant [A]. A reaction with $K_c > 1$ has a higher concentration of product [B] than reactant [A].

**Q** Does a reaction in which [A] = 100[B] at equilibrium have a $K_c$ greater than, about equal to, or less than 1?

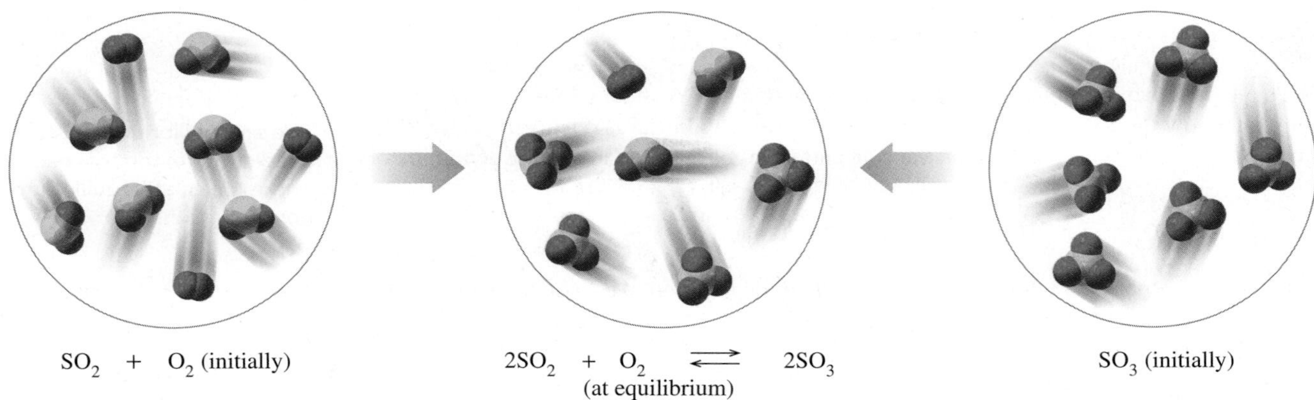


**FIGURE 9.8** One sample initially contains $SO_2$ and $O_2$, while another sample contains only $SO_3$. At equilibrium, mostly $SO_3$ and only small amounts of $SO_2$ and $O_2$ are present in the equilibrium mixture.

**Q** Why is the same equilibrium mixture obtained from reactants as from products?

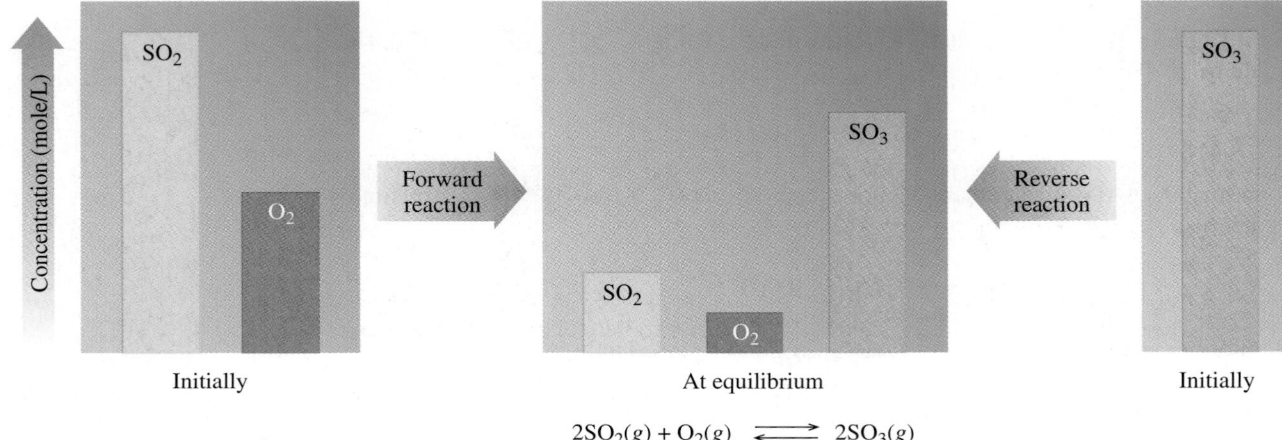


**FIGURE 9.9** In the reaction of $SO_2$ and $O_2$, the equilibrium favors the formation of product $SO_3$, which results in a large $K_c$.

**Q** Why is an equilibrium mixture obtained after starting with pure $SO_3$?

We can start the reaction with only the reactants $SO_2$ and $O_2$, or we can start the reaction with just the product $SO_3$. (See Figure 9.8.) In one reaction, $SO_2$ and $O_2$ form $SO_3$; in the other, $SO_3$ reacts to form $SO_2$ and $O_2$. However, in both equilibrium mixtures, the concentration of $SO_3$ is much higher than the concentrations of $SO_2$ and $O_2$. (See Figure 9.9.) Because there is more product than reactant at equilibrium, the energy of activation for the forward reaction must be lower than the energy of activation for the reverse reaction.

## Equilibrium with a Small $K_c$

For a reaction with a small $K_c$, the equilibrium mixture contains very small concentrations of products. Consider the reaction for the formation of NO, which has a small $K_c$. (See Figure 9.10.)

$$N_2(g) + O_2(g) \rightleftarrows 2NO(g)$$

$$K_c = \frac{[NO]^2}{[N_2][O_2]} \quad \frac{\text{Few products}}{\text{Mostly reactants}} = 2 \times 10^{-9}$$

Reaction favors reactants

Whether the reaction begins with only the reactants, $N_2$ and $O_2$, or with the product, NO, the equilibrium mixture contains mostly reactants and very little product. The energy of activation for the forward reaction is much greater than the energy of activation for the reverse reaction. Reactions with very small $K_c$ produce essentially no products.

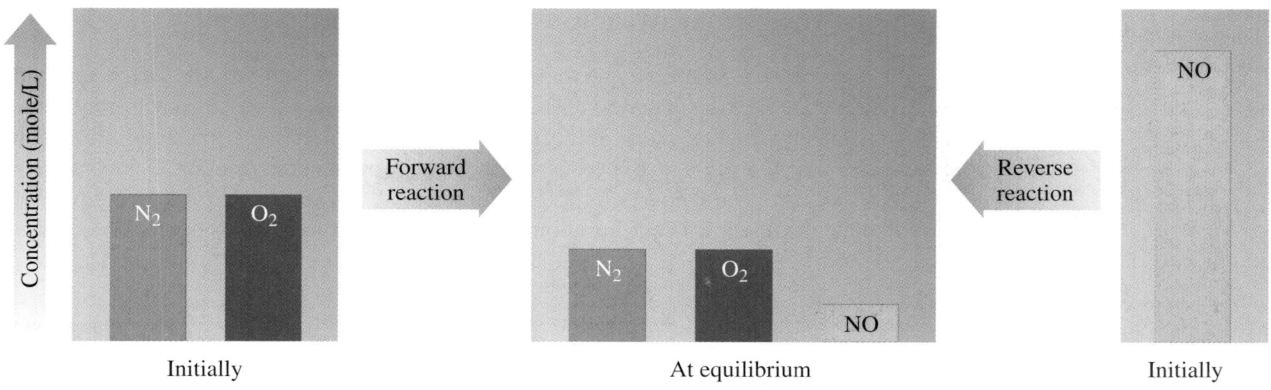


$$N_2(g) + O_2(g) \rightleftharpoons 2NO(g)$$

**FIGURE 9.10** At equilibrium, the reaction $N_2 + O_2 \rightleftharpoons 2NO$ favors the reactants and the reaction mixture at equilibrium contains mostly $N_2$ and $O_2$, which results in a small $K_c$.

**Q** Starting with only NO in a closed container, how do the forward and reverse reactions change as equilibrium is reached?

| Small $K_c$ | $K_c \approx 1$ | Large $K_c$ |
|---|---|---|
| Favors reactants | | Favors products |
| Products << Reactants<br>Little reaction takes place | Products ≈ Reactants<br>Moderate reaction | Products >> Reactants<br>Reaction complete |

**FIGURE 9.11** The equilibrium constant, $K_c$, indicates how far a reaction goes to products. A reaction with a large $K_c$ contains mostly products; a reaction with a small $K_c$ contains mostly reactants.

**Q** Does a reaction with a $K_c = 1.2 \times 10^{15}$ contain mostly reactants or products at equilibrium?

Reactions with equilibrium constants close to 1 have about the same concentrations of reactants and products. (See Figure 9.11.) Table 9.3 lists some equilibrium constants and the extent of their reaction.

**TABLE 9.3** Examples of Reactions with Large and Small $K_c$ Values

| Reactants | | Products | $K_c$ | Equilibrium Favors |
|---|---|---|---|---|
| $2CO(g) + O_2(g)$ | $\rightleftharpoons$ | $2CO_2(g)$ | $2 \times 10^{11}$ | Products |
| $2H_2(g) + S_2(g)$ | $\rightleftharpoons$ | $2H_2S(g)$ | $1.1 \times 10^{7}$ | Products |
| $N_2(g) + 3H_2(g)$ | $\rightleftharpoons$ | $2NH_3(g)$ | $1.6 \times 10^{2}$ | Products |
| $PCl_5(g)$ | $\rightleftharpoons$ | $PCl_3(g) + Cl_2(g)$ | $1.2 \times 10^{-2}$ | Reactants |
| $N_2(g) + O_2(g)$ | $\rightleftharpoons$ | $2NO(g)$ | $2 \times 10^{-9}$ | Reactants |

**CONCEPT CHECK 9.4**

### Extent of Reaction

Predict whether the equilibrium favors the reactants or products for each of the following reactions:

**a.** $2H_2(g) + O_2(g) \rightleftharpoons 2H_2O(g)$ $\quad K_c = 2.9 \times 10^{82}$ at 25 °C

**b.** $PCl_5(g) \rightleftharpoons PCl_3(g) + Cl_2(g)$ $\quad K_c = 1.2 \times 10^{-2}$ at 225 °C

ANSWER

**a.** When a $K_c$ has a large value, it indicates that there are high concentrations of products in the numerator and low concentrations of reactants in the denominator. Thus, this equilibrium favors the products.

**b.** When a $K_c$ has a small value, it indicates that there are low concentrations of products in the numerator and high concentrations of reactants in the denominator. Thus, this equilibrium favors the reactants.

TUTORIAL
Calculations Using the Equililbrium Constant

## Calculating Concentrations at Equilibrium

When a reaction goes essentially all to products, we can use the mole-mole factors we studied earlier to calculate the quantity of a product. However, many reactions reach equilibrium without using up all the reactants. If this is the case, then we need to use the equilibrium constant to calculate the amounts of products that can be formed in the reaction. For example, if we know the equilibrium constant for a reaction and all the concentrations except one, we can calculate the unknown concentration using the equilibrium constant expression.

**Guide to Using the $K_c$ Value**

STEP 1
Write the $K_c$ expression for the equilibrium equation.

STEP 2
Solve the $K_c$ expression for the unknown concentration.

STEP 3
Substitute the known values into the rearranged $K_c$ expression.

STEP 4
Check answer by using calculated concentration in the $K_c$ expression.

SAMPLE PROBLEM 9.6

### Calculating Concentration Using an Equilibrium Constant

Phosgene ($COCl_2$) is a toxic substance that is produced by the reaction of carbon monoxide and chlorine; the $K_c$ for the reaction is 5.0.

$$CO(g) + Cl_2(g) \rightleftharpoons COCl_2(g)$$

If the equilibrium concentrations for the reaction are $[Cl_2] = 0.25$ M and $[COCl_2] = 0.80$ M, what is the equilibrium concentration of $CO(g)$?

SOLUTION

**Given** $[Cl_2] = 0.25$ M, $[COCl_2] = 0.80$ M, $K_c = 5.0$
**Need** [CO]

**STEP 1** **Write the $K_c$ expression for the equilibrium.** Using the balanced chemical equation, the equilibrium constant expression is written as

$$K_c = \frac{[COCl_2]}{[CO][Cl_2]}$$

**STEP 2** **Solve the $K_c$ expression for the unknown concentration.** To rearrange the expression for [CO], we multiply both sides by [CO], which cancels the [CO] on the right side:

$$K_c[CO] = \frac{[COCl_2] \times \cancel{[CO]}}{\cancel{[CO]}[Cl_2]}$$

$$K_c[CO] = \frac{[COCl_2]}{[Cl_2]}$$

To solve for [CO], we divide both sides by $K_c$ and cancel:

$$\frac{\cancel{K_c}[CO]}{\cancel{K_c}} = \frac{[COCl_2]}{K_c[Cl_2]}$$

$$[CO] = \frac{[COCl_2]}{K_c[Cl_2]}$$

**STEP 3** **Substitute the known values into the rearranged $K_c$ expression.** Substituting the concentrations for the equilibrium mixture and the $K_c$ value into the equilibrium constant expression gives the CO concentration:

$$[CO] = \frac{[COCl_2]}{K_c[Cl_2]}$$

$$[CO] = \frac{[0.80]}{5.0 \times [0.25]} = 0.64 \text{ M}$$

STEP 4 **Check the answer.** We check the answer by substituting the calculated concentration into the $K_c$ expression:

$$K_c = \frac{[COCl_2]}{[CO][Cl_2]}$$

$$K_c = \frac{[0.80]}{[0.64][0.25]} = 5.0$$

↗ Calculated

STUDY CHECK

Ethanol can be produced by reacting ethylene ($C_2H_4$) with water vapor. At 327 °C, the $K_c$ is $9 \times 10^3$:

$$C_2H_4(g) + H_2O(g) \rightleftharpoons C_2H_5OH(g)$$

If an equilibrium mixture has concentrations of $[C_2H_4] = 0.020$ M and $[H_2O] = 0.015$ M, what is the equilibrium concentration of $C_2H_5OH$?

## QUESTIONS AND PROBLEMS

### Using Equilibrium Constants

9.21 Indicate whether each of the following equilibrium mixtures contain mostly products, mostly reactants, or both reactants and products:

**a.** $Cl_2(g) + 2NO(g) \rightleftharpoons 2NOCl(g)$ $K_c = 3.7 \times 10^8$

**b.** $H_2O(g) + CH_4(g) \rightleftharpoons CO(g) + 3H_2(g)$ $K_c = 4.7$

**c.** $3O_2(g) \rightleftharpoons 2O_3(g)$ $K_c = 1.7 \times 10^{-56}$

**9.22** Indicate whether each of the following equilibrium mixtures contain mostly products, mostly reactants, or both reactants and products:

**a.** $CO(g) + Cl_2(g) \rightleftharpoons COCl_2(g)$ $K_c = 5.0$

**b.** $2HF(g) \rightleftharpoons H_2(g) + F_2(g)$ $K_c = 1.0 \times 10^{-95}$

**c.** $2NO(g) + O_2(g) \rightleftharpoons 2NO_2(g)$ $K_c = 6.0 \times 10^{13}$

9.23 The equilibrium constant, $K_c$, for the equilibrium

$$H_2(g) + I_2(g) \rightleftharpoons 2HI(g)$$

is 54 at 425 °C. If the equilibrium mixture contains 0.030 M HI and 0.015 M $I_2$, what is the equilibrium concentration of $H_2$?

**9.24** The equilibrium constant, $K_c$, for the equilibrium

$$N_2O_4(g) \rightleftharpoons 2NO_2(g)$$

is $4.6 \times 10^{-3}$. If the equilibrium mixture contains 0.050 M $NO_2$, what is the concentration of $N_2O_4$?

9.25 The $K_c$ at 100 °C is 2.0 for the reaction

$$2NOBr(g) \rightleftharpoons 2NO(g) + Br_2(g)$$

If the system at equilibrium contains [NO] = 2.0 M and $[Br_2] =$ 1.0 M, what is the [NOBr]?

**9.26** An equilibrium mixture at 225 °C contains 0.14 M $NH_3$ and 0.18 M $H_2$ for the reaction

$$3H_2(g) + N_2(g) \rightleftharpoons 2NH_3(g)$$

If the $K_c$ at this temperature is $1.7 \times 10^2$, what is the equilibrium concentration of $N_2$?

# 9.5 Changing Equilibrium Conditions: Le Châtelier's Principle

We have seen that when a reaction reaches equilibrium, the rates of the forward and reverse reactions are equal, and the concentrations remain constant. Now we will look at what happens to a system at equilibrium when changes occur in reaction conditions such as changes in temperature, concentration, and pressure.

LEARNING GOAL

Use Le Châtelier's principle to describe the changes made in equilibrium concentrations when reaction conditions change.

## Le Châtelier's Principle

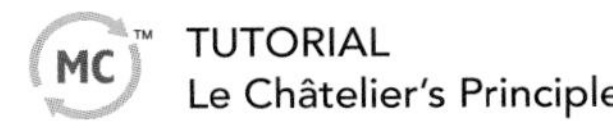


In the previous section, we saw that in a system at equilibrium, the forward and reverse reactions occur at equal rates. Thus, at equilibrium, the concentrations of the substances do not change. However, any changes in the reaction conditions will disturb the equilibrium. Removing one of the substances or adding more of one of the substances can change the concentration. The volume (pressure) can change or there may be a change in temperature. When we alter any of the conditions of a system at equilibrium, the rates of the forward and reverse reactions will no longer be equal. We say that a *stress* is placed on the equilibrium. We use **Le Châtelier's principle** to determine the direction that the equilibrium must shift to relieve that stress and reestablish equilibrium.

> **Le Châtelier's Principle**
>
> When a stress (change in conditions) is placed on a reaction at equilibrium, the equilibrium shifts in the direction that relieves the stress.

## Effect of Concentration Changes

We will use the equilibrium for the reaction of $PCl_5$ to illustrate the stress caused by a change in concentration and to show how the system reacts to the stress. Consider the following reaction, which has a $K_c$ of 0.042 at 250 °C:

$$PCl_5(g) \rightleftarrows PCl_3(g) + Cl_2(g)$$

For a reaction at a given temperature, there is only one equilibrium constant. Even if there are changes in the concentrations of the components, the $K_c$ value does not change. What will change are the concentrations of the other components in the reaction to relieve the stress. For example, we can see that an equilibrium mixture that contains 1.20 M $PCl_5$, 0.20 M $PCl_3$, and 0.25 M $Cl_2$ has a $K_c$ of 0.042:

$$K_c = \frac{[PCl_3][Cl_2]}{[PCl_5]} = \frac{[0.20][0.25]}{[1.20]} = 0.042$$

Suppose that now we add $PCl_5$ to the equilibrium mixture to increase $[PCl_5]$ to 2.00 M. If we substitute the concentrations into the equilibrium expression at this point, the ratio of products to reactants is 0.025, which is smaller than the $K_c$ of 0.042.

$$\frac{\text{Products}}{\text{Reactants (added)}} \quad \frac{[PCl_3][Cl_2]}{[PCl_5]} = \frac{[0.20][0.25]}{[2.00]} = 0.025 < K_c$$

Because a $K_c$ cannot change for a reaction at a given temperature, adding more $PCl_5$ places a stress on the system. (See Figure 9.12.) Forming more of the products can relieve this stress. According to Le Châtelier's principle, adding reactants causes the equilibrium to *shift* toward the products.

Add $PCl_5$

$$PCl_5(g) \rightleftarrows PCl_3(g) + Cl_2(g)$$

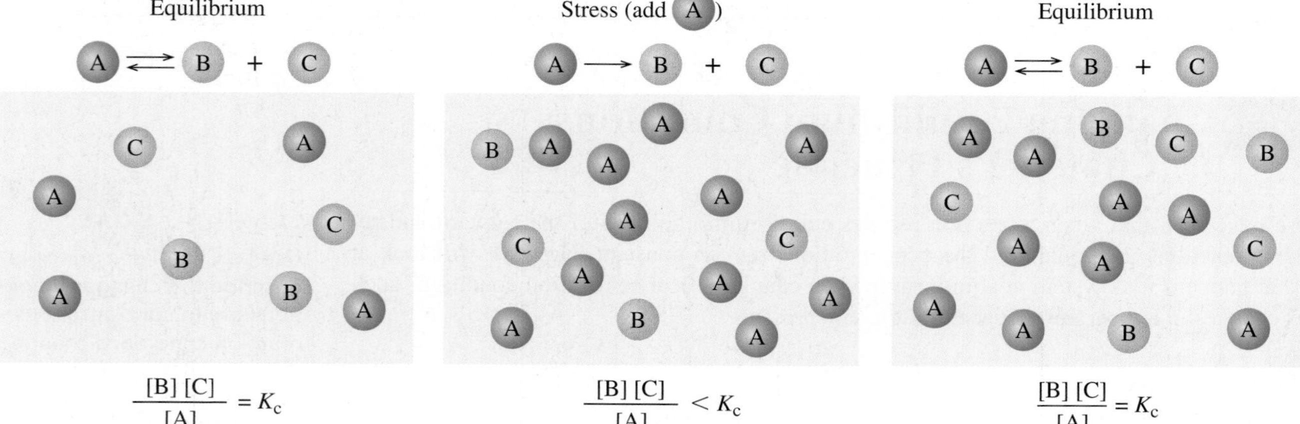


**FIGURE 9.12** The addition of A places stress on the equilibrium of A $\rightleftarrows$ B + C. To relieve the stress, the forward reaction converts some A to B + C and the equilibrium is reestablished.

**Q** When C is added, does the equilibrium shift to products or reactants? Why?

In our experiment, equilibrium is reestablished with new concentrations of $[PCl_5] = 1.94$ M, $[PCl_3] = 0.26$, and $[Cl_2] = 0.31$ M. The resulting equilibrium mixture now contains more reactants and products, but their new concentrations in the equilibrium expression are once again equal to the $K_c$.

$$K_c = \frac{[PCl_3][Cl_2]}{[PCl_5]} = \frac{[0.26][0.31]}{[1.94]} = 0.042 = K_c \quad \text{New higher concentrations}$$

Suppose that in another experiment some $PCl_5$ is removed from the original equilibrium mixture, which lowers the $[PCl_5]$ to 0.76 M. Now the ratio of the products to the reactants is greater than the $K_c$ value of 0.042. The removal of some of the reactant has placed a stress on the equilibrium:

$$\frac{\text{Products}}{\text{Reactants (removed)}} = \frac{[PCl_3][Cl_2]}{[PCl_5]} = \frac{[0.20][0.25]}{[0.76]} = 0.066 > K_c$$

In this case, the stress is relieved as the reverse reaction converts some products to reactants. Using Le Châtelier's principle, we see that removing some reactant *shifts* the equilibrium toward the reactants.

Remove $PCl_5$

$$PCl_5(g) \rightleftharpoons PCl_3(g) + Cl_2(g)$$

In this experiment, equilibrium is reestablished with new concentrations of $[PCl_5] = 0.80$ M, $[PCl_3] = 0.16$ M, and $[Cl_2] = 0.21$ M. The resulting equilibrium mixture now contains lower concentrations of reactants and products, but their new concentrations in the equilibrium expression once again are equal to the $K_c$.

$$K_c = \frac{[PCl_3][Cl_2]}{[PCl_5]} = \frac{[0.16][0.21]}{[0.80]} = 0.042 = K_c \quad \text{New lower concentrations}$$

There can also be changes in the concentrations of other components in this reaction. We could increase or decrease the amount of one of the products in this reaction. Suppose the $[Cl_2]$ is doubled, which makes the product/reactant ratio greater than $K_c$:

$$\frac{[PCl_3][Cl_2]}{[PCl_5]} = \frac{[0.20][0.50]}{[1.20]} = 0.083 > K_c$$

With an increase in the concentration of $Cl_2$, the rate of the reverse reaction increases and converts some of the products to reactants. Using Le Châtelier's principle, we see that the addition of a product causes a *shift* toward the reactants.

Add $Cl_2$

$$PCl_5(g) \rightleftharpoons PCl_3(g) + Cl_2(g)$$

On the other hand, we could remove some $Cl_2$, which would decrease $[Cl_2]$ and *shift* the equilibrium toward the products.

Remove $Cl_2$

$$PCl_5(g) \rightleftharpoons PCl_3(g) + Cl_2(g)$$

In summary, Le Châtelier's principle indicates that a stress caused by adding a substance at equilibrium is relieved by shifting the reaction away from that substance. When some of a substance is removed, the equilibrium shifts toward that substance. These features of Le Châtelier's principle are summarized in Table 9.4.

## Catalysts

Sometimes a catalyst is added to a reaction. Earlier we showed that a catalyst speeds up a reaction by lowering the activation energy. As a result, the rates of the forward and reverse reactions both increase. The time required to reach equilibrium is shorter, but the same ratios of products and reactants are attained. Therefore, a catalyst speeds up the forward and reverse reactions, but it has no effect on the equilibrium constant.

**TABLE 9.4** Effect of Concentration Changes on Equilibrium
$PCl_5(g) \rightleftarrows PCl_3(g) + Cl_2(g)$

| Stress | Shift | Equilibrium Changes | | |
|---|---|---|---|---|
| | | $PCl_5(g)$ | $PCl_3(g)$ | $Cl_2(g)$ |
| Increase $PCl_5$ | Toward products | Added | More | More |
| Decrease $PCl_5$ | Toward reactants | Removed | Less | Less |
| Increase $PCl_3$ | Toward reactants | More | Added | Less |
| Decrease $PCl_3$ | Toward products | Less | Removed | More |
| Increase $Cl_2$ | Toward reactants | More | Less | Added |
| Decrease $Cl_2$ | Toward products | Less | More | Removed |

CONCEPT CHECK 9.5

**Effect of Changes in Concentrations**

Describe the effect of each of the following changes on the following reaction at equilibrium:

$$CO(g) + H_2O(g) \rightleftarrows CO_2(g) + H_2(g)$$

**a.** increasing [CO] **b.** increasing $[H_2]$ **c.** decreasing $[H_2O]$
**d.** decreasing $[CO_2]$ **e.** adding a catalyst

ANSWER

According to Le Châtelier's principle, when stress is applied to a reaction at equilibrium, the equilibrium will shift to relieve the stress.

**a.** When the reactant [CO] is increased, the rate of the forward reaction increases to shift the equilibrium to the products.
**b.** When the product $[H_2]$ is increased, the rate of the reverse reaction increases to shift the equilibrium to the reactants.
**c.** When the reactant $[H_2O]$ is decreased, the rate of the forward reaction decreases to shift the equilibrium to the reactants.
**d.** When the product $[CO_2]$ is decreased, the rate of the reverse reaction decreases to shift the equilibrium to the products.
**e.** When a catalyst is added, it changes the rates of the forward and reverse reactions equally, which does not cause a shift in the equilibrium.

## Effect of Volume (Pressure) Changes on Equilibrium

Reactions that involve gases exert pressure. Although the volume and therefore pressure can change, the value of the equilibrium constant does not change at a given temperature. Using the gas laws, we know that increasing the volume of the container decreases the pressure, while decreasing the volume increases the pressure.

According to Le Châtelier's principle, decreasing the number of moles of gas relieves the stress of increased pressure. This means that the reaction shifts toward the fewer number of moles. Let's look at the effect of decreasing the volume of the equilibrium mixture that originally contained 1.20 M $PCl_5$, 0.20 M $PCl_3$, and 0.25 M $Cl_2$ with a $K_c$ of 0.042:

$$PCl_5(g) \rightleftarrows PCl_3(g) + Cl_2(g)$$

$$K_c = \frac{[PCl_3][Cl_2]}{[PCl_5]} = \frac{[0.20][0.25]}{[1.20]} = 0.042$$

If we decrease the volume by half, all the molar concentrations are doubled. In the equation there are more moles of products than reactants, so there is an increase in the product/reactant ratio.

$$\frac{[PCl_3][Cl_2]}{[PCl_5]} = \frac{[0.40][0.50]}{[2.40]} = 0.083 > K_c$$

To relieve the stress, the equilibrium shifts toward the reactants, which reduces the concentrations of the products and increases the concentrations of the reactant. (See Figure 9.13.)

Decrease $V$

$PCl_5(g) \rightleftharpoons PCl_3(g) + Cl_2(g)$
1 mole 2 moles

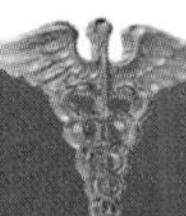

# HEALTH NOTE

## Oxygen-Hemoglobin Equilibrium and Hypoxia

The transport of oxygen involves an equilibrium between hemoglobin (Hb), oxygen, and oxyhemoglobin ($HbO_2$):

$$Hb + O_2 \rightleftharpoons HbO_2$$

When the $O_2$ level is high in the alveoli of the lung, the reaction favors the product $HbO_2$. In the tissues where $O_2$ concentration is low, the reverse reaction releases the oxygen from the hemoglobin. The equilibrium expression is written

$$K_c = \frac{[HbO_2]}{[Hb][O_2]}$$

At normal atmospheric pressure, oxygen diffuses into the blood because the partial pressure of oxygen in the alveoli is higher than that in the blood. At altitudes above 8000 ft, the decrease in the amount of oxygen in the air results in a significant reduction of oxygen to the blood and body tissues. At an altitude of 18 000 feet, a person will obtain 29% less oxygen. When oxygen levels are lowered, a person may experience hypoxia, which has symptoms that include increased respiratory rate, headache, decreased mental acuteness, fatigue, decreased physical coordination, nausea, vomiting, and cyanosis. A similar problem occurs in persons with a history of lung disease that impairs gas diffusion in the alveoli or in persons who have a reduced number of red blood cells, which occurs in smokers.

From the equilibrium expression, we see that a decrease in oxygen will shift the equilibrium to the reactants. Such a shift depletes the concentration of $HbO_2$ and causes the hypoxia condition:

$$Hb + O_2 \longleftarrow HbO_2$$

Immediate treatment of altitude sickness includes hydration, rest, and if necessary, descending to a lower altitude. The adaptation to lowered oxygen levels requires about 10 days. During this time, the bone marrow increases red blood cell production providing hemoglobin. A person living at a high altitude can have 50% more red blood cells than someone at sea level. This increase in hemoglobin causes a shift in the equilibrium back toward $HbO_2$ product. Eventually, the higher concentration of $HbO_2$ will provide more oxygen to the tissues and the symptoms of hypoxia will lessen:

$$Hb + O_2 \longrightarrow HbO_2$$

For some who climb high mountains, it is important to stop and acclimatize for several days at increasing altitudes. At very high altitudes, it may be necessary to use an oxygen tank.

$A(g) \rightleftharpoons B(g) + C(g)$

| Increase $V$: A → B + C | Equilibrium: A ⇌ B + C | Decrease $V$: A ← B + C |
|---|---|---|
| 5 moles A | 6 moles A | 7 moles A |
| 3 moles B | 2 moles B | 1 mole B |
| 3 moles C | 2 moles C | 1 mole C |
| 11 moles | 10 moles | 9 moles |

**FIGURE 9.13** The decrease in the volume of the container places stress on the equilibrium: $A(g) \rightleftharpoons B(g) + C(g)$. To relieve the stress, the reverse reaction converts some products to reactants, which gives a smaller number of moles of gas, reduces pressure, and reestablishes the equilibrium. When the volume increases, the forward reaction converts reactants to products to increase the moles of gas and relieve the stress.

**Q** If you want to increase the products, would you increase or decrease the volume of the reaction container?

When equilibrium is reestablished, the new concentrations are $[PCl_5] = 2.52$ M, $[PCl_3] =$ 0.28 M, and $[Cl_2] = 0.38$ M. The resulting equilibrium mixture contains new concentrations of reactants and products that are now equal to the $K_c$ value, as the following shows:

| At volume (1) | At volume (2) |
|---|---|
| $[PCl_3] = 0.20$ M | 0.28 M |
| $[Cl_2] = 0.25$ M | 0.38 M |
| $[PCl_5] = 1.20$ M | 2.52 M |

$$K_c = \frac{[PCl_3][Cl_2]}{[PCl_5]} = \frac{[0.20][0.25]}{[1.20]} = \frac{[0.28][0.38]}{[2.52]} = 0.042$$

On the other hand, when volume increases and pressure decreases, the reaction shifts toward the greater number of moles. Suppose that the volume is doubled. Then the molar concentrations of all the gases decrease by half. Because there are more moles of products than reactants, there is a decrease in the product/reactant ratio as follows:

$$\frac{[PCl_3][Cl_2]}{[PCl_5]} = \frac{[0.10][0.13]}{[0.60]} = 0.022 < K_c$$

Now the equilibrium has to shift toward the products to relieve the stress, increasing the molar concentrations of the products.

Increase $V$

$$PCl_5(g) \rightleftarrows PCl_3(g) + Cl_2(g)$$

1 mole → 2 moles

When equilibrium is reestablished, the new concentrations are $[PCl_5] = 0.56$ M, $[PCl_3] =$ 0.14 M, and $[Cl_2] = 0.17$ M. The resulting equilibrium mixture contains new concentrations of reactants and products that are now equal to the $K_c$ value:

| At volume (1) | At volume (2) |
|---|---|
| $[PCl_3] = 0.20$ M | 0.14 M |
| $[Cl_2] = 0.25$ M | 0.17 M |
| $[PCl_5] = 1.20$ M | 0.56 M |

$$K_c = \frac{[PCl_3][Cl_2]}{[PCl_5]} = \frac{[0.20][0.25]}{[1.20]} = \frac{[0.14][0.17]}{[0.56]} = 0.042$$

When a reaction has the same number of moles of reactants as products, a volume change does not affect the equilibrium. There is no effect on equilibrium because the molar concentrations of the reactants and products change in the same way. Consider the reaction of $H_2$ and $I_2$ to form HI, which has a $K_c$ of 54:

$$H_2(g) + I_2(g) \rightleftarrows 2HI(g)$$

2 moles of gas — 2 moles of gas

Suppose we start with $[H_2] = 0.060$ M, $[I_2] = 0.015$ M, $[HI] = 0.22$ M, giving us

$$\frac{[HI]^2}{[H_2][I_2]} = \frac{[0.22]^2}{[0.060][0.015]} = 54$$

If the volume is decreased by half, the pressure will double, and all the molar concentrations double. However, the equation has the same number of moles of products as reactants, so there is no effect on the equilibrium. The product/reactant ratio stays the same. We can see this by substituting the increased concentrations into the equilibrium constant expression, as follows:

| **At volume (1)** | **At volume (2)** |
|---|---|
| $[HI] = 0.22\ M$ | $0.44\ M$ |
| $[H_2] = 0.060\ M$ | $0.120\ M$ |
| $[I_2] = 0.015\ M$ | $0.030\ M$ |

$$K_c = \frac{[HI]^2}{[H_2][I_2]} = \frac{[0.22]^2}{[0.060][0.015]} = \frac{[0.44]^2}{[0.120][0.030]} = 54$$

SAMPLE PROBLEM 9.7

### Effect of Changes in Volume

Indicate whether the effect of decreasing the volume for each of the following equilibria causes the number of moles of product to increase or decrease:

**a.** $C_2H_2(g) + 2H_2(g) \rightleftharpoons C_2H_6(g)$
**b.** $2NO_2(g) \rightleftharpoons 2NO(g) + O_2(g)$
**c.** $CO(g) + H_2O(g) \rightleftharpoons CO_2(g) + H_2(g)$

SOLUTION

To relieve the stress of decreasing the volume, the equilibrium shifts toward the side with the fewer moles of gaseous components.

**a.** The equilibrium shifts to $C_2H_6$ (product) to reduce the number of moles of gas. The number of moles of product is increased.

$$\underset{\text{3 moles of gas}}{C_2H_2(g) + 2H_2(g)} \longrightarrow \underset{\text{1 mole of gas}}{C_2H_6(g)}$$

**b.** The equilibrium shifts to $NO_2$ (reactant) to reduce the number of moles of gas. The number of moles of product is decreased.

$$\underset{\text{2 moles of gas}}{2NO_2(g)} \longleftarrow \underset{\text{3 moles of gas}}{2NO(g) + O_2(g)}$$

**c.** There is no shift in equilibrium because there is no change in the number of moles; the moles of reactant are equal to the moles of product. The number of moles of product does not change.

$$\underset{\text{2 moles of gas}}{CO(g) + H_2O(g)} \rightleftharpoons \underset{\text{2 moles of gas}}{CO_2(g) + H_2(g)}$$

STUDY CHECK

Suppose you want to increase the yield of product in the following reaction. Would you increase or decrease the volume of the reaction container?

$$CO(g) + 2H_2(g) \rightleftharpoons CH_3OH(g)$$

## Effect of a Change in Temperature on Equilibrium

In the effects of changes on equilibrium, we have seen that shifts in equilibrium occur to reestablish the same value of the equilibrium constant. However, if we change the temperature of a system at equilibrium, we change the value of $K_c$. When the temperature of an equilibrium system increases, the favored reaction is the one that removes the heat. When heat is added to an endothermic reaction, the equilibrium shifts to the products to use up

**TABLE 9.5** Equilibrium Shifts for Temperature Changes in an Endothermic Reaction

| $K_c$ | Temperature Change | Equilibrium Shift | Change in $K_c$ Value |
|---|---|---|---|
| $\frac{[NO]^2}{[N_2][O_2]}$ | ⇧ Increase | More product $\frac{[NO]^2}{[N_2][O_2]}$ Less reactant | ⇧ Increases |
| $\frac{[NO]^2}{[N_2][O_2]}$ | ⇩ Decrease | Less product $\frac{[NO]^2}{[N_2][O_2]}$ More reactant | ⇩ Decreases |

heat. The value of $K_c$ increases because the shift increases the product concentration and decreases the reactant concentration.

Increase $T$; increase $K_c$

$$N_2(g) + O_2(g) + \text{heat} \rightleftharpoons 2NO(g)$$

If the temperature is lowered, the equilibrium shifts to increase the concentrations of the reactants, and the value of $K_c$ decreases. (See Table 9.5.)

Decrease $T$; decrease $K_c$

$$N_2(g) + O_2(g) + \text{heat} \rightleftharpoons 2NO(g)$$

For an exothermic reaction, the addition of heat favors the reverse reaction, which uses up heat. The value of $K_c$ for an exothermic reaction decreases when the temperature increases.

Increase $T$; decrease $K_c$

$$2SO_2(g) + O_2(g) \rightleftharpoons 2SO_3(g) + \text{heat}$$

If heat is removed, the equilibrium of an exothermic reaction favors the products, which provides heat. (See Table 9.6.)

Decrease $T$; increase $K_c$

$$2SO_2(g) + O_2(g) \rightleftharpoons 2SO_3(g) + \text{heat}$$

**TABLE 9.6** Equilibrium Shifts for Temperature Changes in an Exothermic Reaction

| $K_c$ | Temperature Change | Equilibrium Shift | Change in $K_c$ Value |
|---|---|---|---|
| $\frac{[SO_3]^2}{[SO_2]^2[O_2]}$ | ⇧ Increase | Less product $\frac{[SO_3]^2}{[SO_2]^2[O_2]}$ More reactant | ⇩ Decreases |
| $\frac{[SO_3]^2}{[SO_2]^2[O_2]}$ | ⇩ Decrease | More product $\frac{[SO_3]^2}{[SO_2]^2[O_2]}$ Less reactant | ⇧ Increases |

SAMPLE PROBLEM 9.8

### Effect of Temperature Change on Equilibrium

Indicate the change in the concentration of products and the change in $K_c$ when the temperature of each of the following reactions at equilibrium is increased:

**a.** $N_2(g) + 3H_2(g) \rightleftharpoons 2NH_3(g) + 92\text{ kJ}$

**b.** $N_2(g) + O_2(g) + 180\text{ kJ} \rightleftharpoons 2NO(g)$

SOLUTION

**a.** The addition of heat shifts an exothermic reaction to reactants, which decreases the concentration of the products. The $K_c$ will decrease.

**b.** The addition of heat shifts an endothermic reaction to products, which increases the concentration of the products. The $K_c$ will increase.

STUDY CHECK

Indicate the change in the concentration of reactants and the $K_c$ when there is a decrease in the temperature of each of the reactions at equilibrium in Sample Problem 9.8.

Table 9.7 summarizes the ways we can use Le Châtelier's principle to determine the shift in equilibrium that relieves a stress caused by change in a condition.

**TABLE 9.7** Effects of Condition Changes on Equilibrium

| Condition | Change (Stress) | Reaction to Remove Stress |
|---|---|---|
| **Concentration** | Add reactant | Forward |
| | Remove reactant | Reverse |
| | Add product | Reverse |
| | Remove product | Forward |
| **Volume (container)** | Decrease | Toward fewer moles in the gas phase |
| | Increase | Toward more moles in the gas phase |
| **Temperature** | **Endothermic reaction** | |
| | Raise $T$ | Forward, new value for $K_c$ |
| | Lower $T$ | Reverse, new value for $K_c$ |
| | **Exothermic reaction** | |
| | Raise $T$ | Reverse, new value for $K_c$ |
| | Lower $T$ | Forward, new value for $K_c$ |
| **Catalyst** | Increases rates equally | No effect |

## QUESTIONS AND PROBLEMS

### Changing Equilibrium Conditions: Le Châtelier's Principle

**9.27 a.** Does the addition of reactant to an equilibrium mixture cause the product/reactant ratio to be higher or lower than the $K_c$?

**b.** According to Le Châtelier's principle, how is equilibrium in part **a** established?

**9.28 a.** What is the effect on the $K_c$ when the temperature of an exothermic reaction is lowered?

**b.** According to Le Châtelier's principle, how is equilibrium in part **a** established?

**9.29** In the lower atmosphere, oxygen is converted to ozone ($O_3$) by the energy provided from lightning:

$$3O_2(g) + \text{heat} \rightleftharpoons 2O_3(g)$$

For each of the following changes at equilibrium, indicate whether the equilibrium shifts to products, reactants, or does not shift:

**a.** adding $O_2(g)$

**b.** adding $O_3(g)$

**c.** raising the temperature

**d.** decreasing the volume of the container

**e.** adding a catalyst

**9.30** Ammonia is produced by reacting nitrogen gas and hydrogen gas:

$$N_2(g) + 3H_2(g) \rightleftharpoons 2NH_3(g) + 92 \text{ kJ}$$

For each of the following changes at equilibrium, indicate whether the equilibrium shifts to products, reactants, or does not shift:

**a.** removing $N_2(g)$
**b.** lowering the temperature
**c.** adding $NH_3(g)$
**d.** adding $H_2(g)$
**e.** increasing the volume of the container

**9.31** Hydrogen chloride can be made by reacting hydrogen gas and chlorine gas:

$$H_2(g) + Cl_2(g) + \text{heat} \rightleftharpoons 2HCl(g)$$

For each of the following changes at equilibrium, indicate whether the equilibrium shifts to products, reactants, or does not shift:

**a.** adding $H_2(g)$
**b.** increasing the temperature
**c.** removing $HCl(g)$
**d.** adding a catalyst
**e.** removing $Cl_2(g)$

**9.32** When heated, carbon reacts with water to produce carbon monoxide and hydrogen:

$$C(s) + H_2O(g) + \text{heat} \rightleftharpoons CO(g) + H_2(g)$$

For each of the following changes at equilibrium, indicate whether the equilibrium shifts to products, reactants, or does not shift:

**a.** increasing the temperature
**b.** adding $C(s)$
**c.** removing $CO(g)$ as it forms
**d.** adding $H_2O(g)$
**e.** decreasing the volume of the container

## HEALTH NOTE

### Homeostasis: Regulation of Body Temperature

In a physiological system of equilibrium called *homeostasis*, changes in our environment are balanced by changes in our bodies. It is crucial to our survival that we balance heat gain with heat loss. If we do not lose enough heat, our body temperature rises. At high temperatures, the body can no longer regulate our metabolic reactions. If we lose too much heat, body temperature drops. At low temperatures, essential functions proceed too slowly.

The skin plays an important role in the maintenance of body temperature. When the outside temperature rises, receptors in the skin send signals to the brain. The temperature-regulating part of the brain stimulates the sweat glands to produce perspiration. As perspiration evaporates from the skin, heat is removed, and the body temperature is lowered.

In cold temperatures, epinephrine is released, causing an increase in metabolic rate, which increases the production of heat. Receptors on the skin signal the brain to contract the blood vessels. Less blood flows through the skin, and heat is conserved. The production of perspiration stops to lessen the heat lost by evaporation.

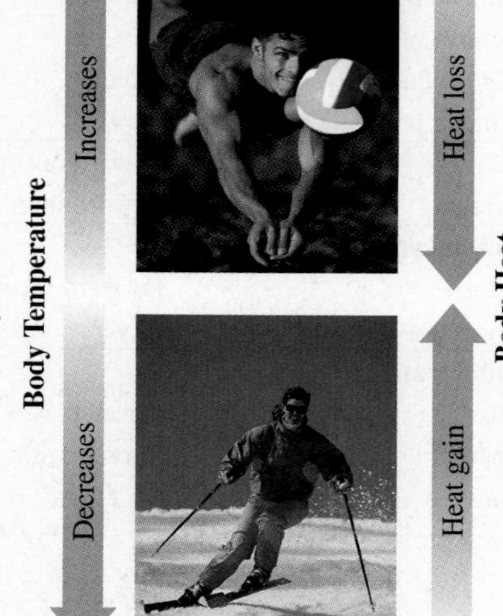


## 9.6 Equilibrium in Saturated Solutions

**LEARNING GOAL**

Write the solubility product expression for a slightly soluble salt and calculate its $K_{sp}$. Use the $K_{sp}$ to determine the solubility of a slightly soluble salt.

Until now, we have looked primarily at equilibrium in the context of gases. However, there are also equilibrium systems that involve aqueous solutions, some of which are saturated solutions or contain insoluble salts. Everyday examples of solubility equilibrium in solution are found in tooth decay and kidney stones. When bacteria in the mouth react with sugars in food, acids are produced that dissolve the enamel of a tooth, which is made of a mineral called hydroxyapatite, $Ca_5(PO_4)_3OH$. Kidney stones are composed of calcium salts such as calcium oxalate, $CaC_2O_4$, and calcium phosphate, $Ca_3(PO_4)_2$, which are rather insoluble. When $Ca^{2+}$ ions and oxalate $C_2O_4^{2-}$ ions exceed their solubility in the kidneys, they will precipitate, forming solid $CaC_2O_4$:

$$Ca^{2+}(aq) + C_2O_4^{2-}(aq) \rightleftharpoons CaC_2O_4(s)$$

$$3Ca^{2+}(aq) + 2PO_4^{3-}(aq) \rightleftharpoons Ca_3(PO_4)_2(s)$$

To understand the role of solubility in biology and the environment, we can look at the equilibrium that occurs in saturated solutions.

## Solubility Product Constant

In Chapter 8, we learned that a saturated solution contains some undissolved solute in contact with the maximum amount of dissolved solute. A saturated solution is a dynamic system in which the rate of dissolution for a solute has become equal to the rate of solute recrystallization out of solution. As long as the temperature remains constant, the concentration of the ions in the saturated solution is constant. Let us look at the equilibrium equation for the dissolution of $CaC_2O_4$, which is written with the solid solute on the left and the ions in solution on the right:

$$CaC_2O_4(s) \rightleftharpoons Ca^{2+}(aq) + C_2O_4^{2-}(aq)$$

At equilibrium, the concentrations of the $Ca^{2+}$ and $C_2O_4^{2-}$ are constant. We can represent the solubility of $CaC_2O_4$ by an equilibrium expression called the **solubility product constant, $K_{sp}$**. As in other heterogeneous equilibria (section 9.3), the concentration of the solid is constant and not included in the $K_{sp}$:

$$K_{sp} = [Ca^{2+}][C_2O_4^{2-}]$$

In another example, we consider the equilibrium of solid calcium fluoride and its ions $Ca^{2+}$ and $F^-$:

$$CaF_2(s) \rightleftharpoons Ca^{2+}(aq) + 2F^-(aq)$$

At equilibrium, the rate of dissolving for $CaF_2$ is equal to the rate of its recrystallization, which means the concentrations of the ions remain constant. The solubility product for this solubility is written as the product of the ion concentrations. As with other equilibrium expressions, the $[F^-]$ is raised to the power of 2 because there is a coefficient of 2 in the equilibrium equation:

$$K_{sp} = [Ca^{2+}][F^-]^2$$

CONCEPT CHECK 9.6

### Writing the Solubility Product Expression

For each of the following slightly soluble salts, write the equilibrium equation and the solubility product expression:

**a.** AgBr **b.** $Li_2CO_3$

ANSWER

**a.** In the equation, the solid salt is written on the left in equilibrium with the ions $Ag^+$ and $Br^-$ in aqueous solution; the solubility product expression, $K_{sp}$, gives the product of the molar concentrations of the ions:

$$AgBr(s) \rightleftharpoons Ag^+(aq) + Br^-(aq) \qquad K_{sp} = [Ag^+][Br^-]$$

**b.** In the equation, the solid salt is written on the left in equilibrium with the ions $2Li^+$ and $CO_3^{2-}$ in aqueous solution; the solubility product expression, $K_{sp}$, gives the molar concentrations of the ions with $[Li^+]$ with an exponent of 2, which is its coefficient in the balanced equation:

$$Li_2CO_3(s) \rightleftharpoons 2Li^+(aq) + CO_3^{2-}(aq) \qquad K_{sp} = [Li^+]^2[CO_3^{2-}]$$

**TABLE 9.8 Solubility Product Constants ($K_{sp}$) for Selected Ionic Compounds (25 °C)**

| Formula | $K_{sp}$ |
|---|---|
| $AgCl$ | $1.8 \times 10^{-10}$ |
| $Ag_2SO_4$ | $1.2 \times 10^{-5}$ |
| $BaCO_3$ | $2.0 \times 10^{-9}$ |
| $BaSO_4$ | $1.1 \times 10^{-10}$ |
| $CaF_2$ | $3.2 \times 10^{-11}$ |
| $Ca(OH)_2$ | $6.5 \times 10^{-6}$ |
| $CaSO_4$ | $2.4 \times 10^{-5}$ |
| $PbCl_2$ | $1.5 \times 10^{-6}$ |
| $PbCO_3$ | $7.4 \times 10^{-14}$ |

## Calculating the Solubility Product Constant

Experiments in the lab can measure the concentrations of ions in a saturated solution. For example, we can make a saturated solution of $CaCO_3$ by adding solid $CaCO_3$ to water and stirring until equilibrium is reached. Then we would measure the concentrations of $Ca^{2+}$ and $CO_3^{2-}$ in solution. Suppose that a saturated solution of $CaCO_3$ has $[Ca^{2+}] = 7.1 \times 10^{-5}$ M and $[CO_3^{2-}] = 7.1 \times 10^{-5}$ M.

**STEP 1** **Write the equilibrium equation for solubility:**

$$CaCO_3(s) \rightleftharpoons Ca^{2+}(aq) + CO_3^{2-}(aq)$$

**STEP 2** **Write the solubility product expression ($K_{sp}$):**

$$K_{sp} = [Ca^{2+}][CO_3^{2-}]$$

**STEP 3** **Substitute the molar concentrations of the ions into the $K_{sp}$ expression:**

$$K_{sp} = [7.1 \times 10^{-5}][7.1 \times 10^{-5}] = 5.0 \times 10^{-9}$$

Table 9.8 gives values of $K_{sp}$ for a selected group of ionic compounds at 25 °C.

**Guide to Calculating $K_{sp}$**

STEP 1
Write the equilibrium equation for the dissociation of the ionic compound.

STEP 2
Write the $K_{sp}$ expression with the molarity of each ion raised to a power equal to its coefficient.

STEP 3
Substitute the molarity of each ion into the $K_{sp}$ and calculate.

SAMPLE PROBLEM 9.9

### Calculating a Solubility Product Constant

A saturated solution of strontium fluoride, $SrF_2$, has $[Sr^{2+}] = 8.7 \times 10^{-4}$ M and $[F^-] = 1.7 \times 10^{-3}$ M. What is the value of $K_{sp}$ for $SrF_2$?

SOLUTION

**STEP 1** **Write the equilibrium equation for solubility:**

$$SrF_2(s) \rightleftharpoons Sr^{2+}(aq) + 2F^-(aq)$$

**STEP 2** **Write the solubility product expression, $K_{sp}$:**

$$K_{sp} = [Sr^{2+}][F^-]^2$$

**STEP 3** **Substitute the molar concentrations of the ions into the $K_{sp}$ expression:**

$$K_{sp} = [8.7 \times 10^{-4}][1.7 \times 10^{-3}]^2 = 2.5 \times 10^{-9}$$

STUDY CHECK

What is the $K_{sp}$ of silver iodide, AgI, if a saturated solution has $[Ag^+] = 9.2 \times 10^{-9}$ M and $[I^-] = 9.2 \times 10^{-9}$ M?

## Solubility ($S$) and $K_{sp}$

The *solubility* ($S$) of a slightly soluble salt is the number of moles of solute that dissolve in 1 liter of solution. For example, the solubility of CdS is found experimentally to be $1 \times 10^{-12}$ M. This means that $1 \times 10^{-12}$ mole of CdS in 1 liter dissociates into $Cd^{2+}$ and $S^{2-}$ ions: $[Cd^{2+}] = 1 \times 10^{-12}$ M and $[S^{2-}] = 1 \times 10^{-12}$ M.

$$CdS(s) \rightleftharpoons Cd^{2+}(aq) + S^{2-}(aq)$$

$$S = 1 \times 10^{-12} \text{ mole/L}$$

If we know the $K_{sp}$ of a salt, we can calculate the molarity of each ion and determine the solubility of a slightly soluble salt as shown in Sample Problem 9.10.

SAMPLE PROBLEM 9.10

## Calculating the Solubility of a Slightly Soluble Salt

Calculate the solubility ($S$) of $PbSO_4$ if the $K_{sp}$ is $1.6 \times 10^{-8}$.

SOLUTION

**STEP 1** **Write the equilibrium equation for solubility:**

$$PbSO_4(s) \rightleftarrows Pb^{2+}(aq) + SO_4^{2-}(aq)$$

**STEP 2** **Write the solubility product expression, $K_{sp}$:**

$$K_{sp} = [Pb^{2+}][SO_4^{2-}]$$

**STEP 3** **Show the molarity of the ions as $S$ in the equation with the known value of $K_{sp}$:**

$$K_{sp} = [S][S] = 1.6 \times 10^{-8}$$

**STEP 4** **Solve for the solubility $S$:**

$$S \times S = S^2 = 1.6 \times 10^{-8}$$
$$S = \sqrt{1.6 \times 10^{-8}} = 1.3 \times 10^{-4} \text{ mole/L}$$

STUDY CHECK

Calculate the solubility ($S$) of NiS if NiS has a $K_{sp}$ of $4 \times 10^{-20}$.

**Guide to Calculating Solubility from $K_{sp}$**

STEP 1
Write the equilibrium equation for the dissociation of the ionic compound.

STEP 2
Write the $K_{sp}$ expression.

STEP 3
Substitute $S$ for the molarity of each ion into the $K_{sp}$.

STEP 4
Calculate the solubility ($S$).

Earlier we described kidney stones as crystals composed of calcium salts, such as calcium oxalate, $CaC_2O_4$. Kidney stones form when the ion product $[Ca^{2+}][C_2O_4^{2-}]$ is equal to or greater than the solubility product $K_{sp}$. Normally, the urine contains substances such as magnesium and citrate ions that prevent the formation of kidney stones. Some of the factors that contribute to the formation of kidney stones are drinking too little water, limited activity, consuming foods with high levels of oxalate, and some metabolic diseases. Prevention includes drinking large quantities of water and decreasing consumption of foods high in oxalate, such as spinach, rhubarb, and soybean products.

# QUESTIONS AND PROBLEMS

## Equilibrium in Saturated Solutions

9.33 For each of the following slightly soluble salts, write the equilibrium equation and the solubility product expression:
  **a.** $MgCO_3$
  **b.** $PbI_2$
  **c.** $Ag_3PO_4$

**9.34** For each of the following slightly soluble salts, write the equilibrium equation and the solubility product expression:
  **a.** $PbSO_4$
  **b.** $Al(OH)_3$
  **c.** $BaF_2$

9.35 A saturated solution of barium sulfate, $BaSO_4$, has $[Ba^{2+}] = 1 \times 10^{-5}$ M and $[SO_4^{2-}] = 1 \times 10^{-5}$ M. What is the value of $K_{sp}$ for $BaSO_4$?

**9.36** A saturated solution of silver bromide, AgBr, has $[Ag^+] = 7.1 \times 10^{-7}$ M and $[Br^-] = 7.1 \times 10^{-7}$ M. What is the value of $K_{sp}$ for AgBr?

9.37 A saturated solution of silver carbonate, $Ag_2CO_3$, has $[Ag^+] = 2.6 \times 10^{-4}$ M and $[CO_3^{2-}] = 1.3 \times 10^{-4}$ M. What is the value of $K_{sp}$ for $Ag_2CO_3$?

**9.38** A saturated solution of barium fluoride, $BaF_2$, has $[Ba^{2+}] = 3.6 \times 10^{-3}$ M and $[F^-] = 7.2 \times 10^{-3}$ M. What is the value of $K_{sp}$ for $BaF_2$?

9.39 What are $[Cu^+]$ and $[I^-]$ in a saturated CuI solution if the $K_{sp}$ of CuI is $1 \times 10^{-12}$?

**9.40** What are $[Sn^{2+}]$ and $[S^{2-}]$ in a saturated SnS solution if the $K_{sp}$ of SnS is $1 \times 10^{-26}$?

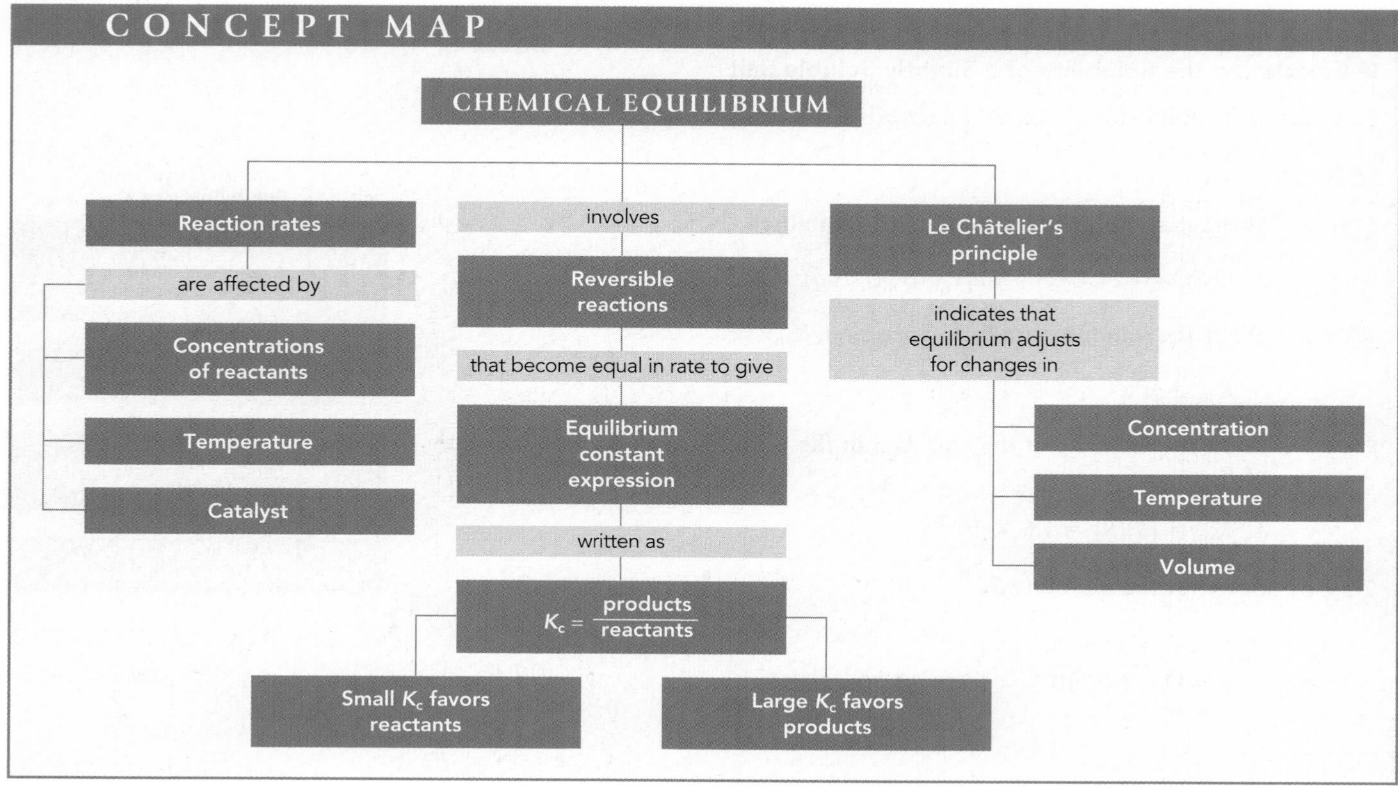


# CHAPTER REVIEW

## 9.1 Rates of Reactions

**LEARNING GOAL:** *Describe how temperature, concentration, and catalysts affect the rate of a reaction.*

The rate of a reaction is the speed at which the reactants are converted to products. Increasing the concentrations of reactants, raising the temperature, or adding a catalyst can increase the rate of a reaction.

## 9.2 Chemical Equilibrium

**LEARNING GOAL:** *Use the concept of reversible reactions to explain chemical equilibrium.*

Chemical equilibrium occurs in a reversible reaction when the rate of the forward reaction becomes equal to the rate of the reverse reaction. At equilibrium, no further change occurs in the concentrations of the reactants and products as the forward and reverse reactions continue.

## 9.3 Equilibrium Constants

**LEARNING GOAL:** *Calculate the equilibrium constant for a reversible reaction given the concentrations of reactants and products at equilibrium.*

An equilibrium constant, $K_c$, is the ratio of the concentrations of the products to the concentrations of the reactants with each concentration raised to a power equal to its coefficient in the chemical equation. For heterogeneous reactions, only gases are placed in the equilibrium expression.

## 9.4 Using Equilibrium Constants

**LEARNING GOAL:** *Use an equilibrium constant to predict the extent of reaction and to calculate equilibrium concentrations.*

A large value of $K_c$ indicates the equilibrium favors the products and could go nearly to completion, whereas a small value of $K_c$ shows that the equilibrium favors the reactants. Equilibrium constants can be used to calculate the concentration of a component in the equilibrium mixture.

## 9.5 Changing Equilibrium Conditions: Le Châtelier's Principle

**LEARNING GOAL:** *Use Le Châtelier's principle to describe the changes made in equilibrium concentrations when reaction conditions change.*

The addition of reactants or removal of products favors the forward reaction. Removal of reactants or addition of products favors the reverse reaction. A decrease in the volume of a reaction container changes the pressure of gases at equilibrium causing a shift to the side with the fewer number of moles. Raising or lowering the temperature for exothermic and endothermic reactions changes the value of $K_c$ and shifts the equilibrium for a reaction.

## 9.6 Equilibrium in Saturated Solutions

**LEARNING GOAL:** *Write the solubility product expression for a slightly soluble salt and calculate its $K_{sp}$. Use the $K_{sp}$ to determine the solubility of a slightly soluble salt.*

In a saturated solution of a slightly soluble salt, the rate of dissolving the solute is equal to the rate of recrystallization. In a saturated solution, the concentrations of the ions from the solute are constant and can be used to calculate the solubility product constant ($K_{sp}$) for the salt. If the $K_{sp}$ is known, the solubility of the salt can be calculated.

## KEY TERMS

**activation energy** The energy required to break apart the bonds of the reacting molecules.

**catalyst** A substance that increases the rate of reaction by lowering the activation energy.

**chemical equilibrium** The point at which the forward and reverse reactions take place at the same rate so that there is no further change in concentrations of reactants and products.

**collision theory** A model for a chemical reaction that states that molecules must collide with sufficient energy in order to form products.

**equilibrium constant expression** The ratio of the concentrations of products to the concentrations of reactants with each component raised to an exponent equal to the coefficient of that compound in the chemical equation.

**equilibrium constant, $K_c$** The numerical value obtained by substituting the equilibrium concentrations of the components into the equilibrium constant expression.

**heterogeneous equilibrium** An equilibrium system in which the components are in different states.

**homogenous equilibrium** An equilibrium system in which all components are in the same state.

**Le Châtelier's principle** When a stress is placed on a system at equilibrium, the equilibrium shifts to relieve that stress.

**rate of reaction** The speed at which reactants are used to form product(s).

**reversible reaction** A reaction in which a forward reaction occurs from reactants to products, and a reverse reaction occurs from products back to reactants.

**solubility product constant, $K_{sp}$** The product of the concentrations of the ions in a saturated solution of a slightly soluble salt with each concentration raised to a power equal to its coefficient in the equilibrium equation.

## UNDERSTANDING THE CONCEPTS

9.41 Would the reaction shown in the diagrams have a large or small equilibrium constant?

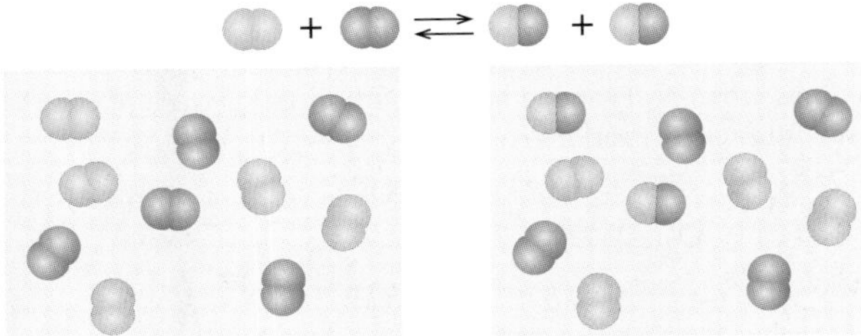


**9.42** Would the reaction shown in the diagrams have a large or small equilibrium constant?

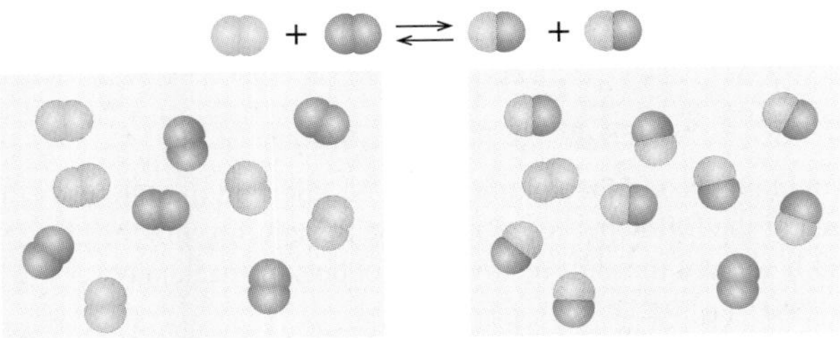


9.43 **a.** Would $T_2$ be higher or lower than $T_1$ for the reaction shown in the diagrams?
**b.** Would $K_c$ for $T_2$ be larger or smaller than the $K_c$ for $T_1$?

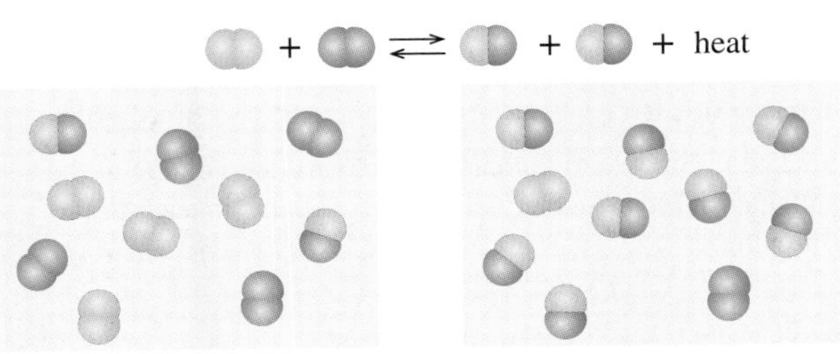


**9.44** **a.** Would the reaction shown in the diagrams be exothermic or endothermic?
**b.** To increase $K_c$ for this reaction, would you raise or lower the temperature?

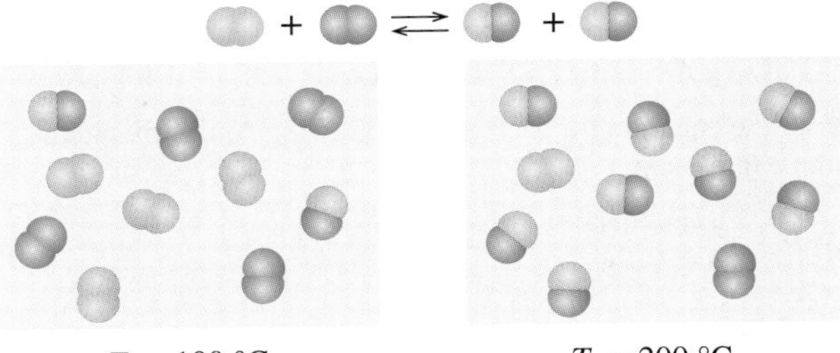


9.45 Consider the following reaction at equilibrium:

$$C_2H_4(g) + Cl_2(g) \rightleftarrows C_2H_4Cl_2(g) + \text{heat}$$

Indicate how each of the following will shift the equilibrium:
**a.** raising the temperature of the reaction
**b.** decreasing the volume of the reaction container
**c.** adding a catalyst
**d.** adding $Cl_2$

**9.46** Consider the following reaction at equilibrium:

$$N_2(g) + O_2(g) + \text{heat} \rightleftarrows 2NO(g)$$

Indicate how each of the following will shift the equilibrium:
**a.** raising the temperature of the reaction
**b.** decreasing the volume of the reaction container
**c.** adding a catalyst
**d.** adding $N_2$

9.47 If a salt has the solubility product expression $K_{sp} = [Fe^{3+}][OH^-]^3$, what is the equilibrium equation for the solubility?

**9.48** If a salt has the solubility product expression $K_{sp} = [Bi^{3+}]^2[S^{2-}]^3$, what is the equilibrium equation for the solubility?

# ADDITIONAL QUESTIONS AND PROBLEMS

*For instructor-assigned homework, go to* ***www.masteringchemistry.com***.

**9.49** Write the equilibrium constant expression for each of the following reactions:

**a.** $CH_4(g) + 2O_2(g) \rightleftharpoons CO_2(g) + 2H_2O(g)$

**b.** $4NH_3(g) + 3O_2(g) \rightleftharpoons 2N_2(g) + 6H_2O(g)$

**c.** $C(s) + 2H_2(g) \rightleftharpoons CH_4(g)$

**9.50** Write the equilibrium constant expression for each of the following reactions:

**a.** $2C_2H_6(g) + 7O_2(g) \rightleftharpoons 4CO_2(g) + 6H_2O(g)$

**b.** $2NaHCO_3(s) \rightleftharpoons Na_2CO_3(s) + CO_2(g) + H_2O(g)$

**c.** $4NH_3(g) + 5O_2(g) \rightleftharpoons 4NO(g) + 6H_2O(g)$

**9.51** For each of the following reactions at equilibrium, indicate if the equilibrium mixture contains mostly products, mostly reactants, or both products and reactants:

**a.** $H_2(g) + Cl_2(g) \rightleftharpoons 2HCl(g)$ $K_c = 1.3 \times 10^{34}$

**b.** $2NOBr(g) \rightleftharpoons 2NO(g) + Br_2(g)$ $K_c = 2.0$

**c.** $2NOCl(g) \rightleftharpoons Cl_2(g) + 2NO(g)$ $K_c = 2.7 \times 10^{-9}$

**9.52** For each of the following reactions at equilibrium, indicate if the equilibrium mixture contains mostly products, mostly reactants, or both products and reactants:

**a.** $2H_2O(g) \rightleftharpoons 2H_2(g) + O_2(g)$ $K_c = 4 \times 10^{-48}$

**b.** $N_2(g) + 3H_2(g) \rightleftharpoons 2NH_3(g)$ $K_c = 0.30$

**c.** $2SO_2(g) + O_2(g) \rightleftharpoons 2SO_3(g)$ $K_c = 1.2 \times 10^{9}$

**9.53** Write the equation for each of the following equilibrium constant expressions:

**a.** $K_c = \dfrac{[SO_2][Cl_2]}{[SO_2Cl_2]}$

**b.** $K_c = \dfrac{[BrCl]^2}{[Br_2][Cl_2]}$

**c.** $K_c = \dfrac{[CH_4][H_2O]}{[CO][H_2]^3}$

**d.** $K_c = \dfrac{[N_2O][H_2O]^3}{[O_2]^2[NH_3]^2}$

**9.54** Write the equation for each of the following equilibrium constant expressions:

**a.** $K_c = \dfrac{[CO_2][H_2]}{[CO][H_2O]}$

**b.** $K_c = \dfrac{[H_2][F_2]}{[HF]^2}$

**c.** $K_c = \dfrac{[O_2][HCl]^4}{[Cl_2]^2[H_2O]^2}$

**d.** $K_c = \dfrac{[CS_2][H_2]^4}{[CH_4][H_2S]^2}$

**9.55** Consider the reaction

$$2NH_3(g) \rightleftharpoons N_2(g) + 3H_2(g)$$

**a.** Write the equilibrium constant expression for $K_c$.

**b.** What is the $K_c$ for the reaction if at equilibrium the concentrations are $[NH_3] = 0.20$ M, $[H_2] = 0.50$ M, and $[N_2] = 3.0$ M?

**9.56** Consider the reaction

$$2SO_2(g) + O_2(g) \rightleftharpoons 2SO_3(g)$$

**a.** Write the equilibrium constant expression for $K_c$.

**b.** What is the $K_c$ for the reaction if at equilibrium the concentrations are $[SO_2] = 0.10$ M, $[O_2] = 0.12$ M, and $[SO_3] = 0.60$ M?

**9.57** The equilibrium constant for the following reaction is 5.0 at 100 °C. If an equilibrium mixture contains $[NO_2] = 0.50$ M, what is the $[N_2O_4]$?

$$2NO_2(g) \rightleftharpoons N_2O_4(g)$$

**9.58** The equilibrium constant for the following reaction is 0.20 at 1000 °C. If an equilibrium mixture contains solid carbon, $[H_2O] = 0.40$ M, and $[CO] = 0.40$ M, what is the $[H_2]$?

$$C(s) + H_2O(g) \rightleftharpoons CO(g) + H_2(g)$$

**9.59** According to Le Châtelier's principle, does the equilibrium shift to products or reactants when $O_2$ is added to the equilibrium mixture of each of the following reactions?

**a.** $3O_2(g) \rightleftharpoons 2O_3(g)$

**b.** $2CO_2(g) \rightleftharpoons 2CO(g) + O_2(g)$

**c.** $P_4(g) + 5O_2(g) \rightleftharpoons P_4O_{10}(s)$

**d.** $2SO_2(g) + 2H_2O(g) \rightleftharpoons 2H_2S(g) + 3O_2(g)$

**9.60** According to Le Châtelier's principle, what is the effect on the products when $N_2$ is added to the equilibrium mixture of each of the following reactions?

**a.** $2NH_3(g) \rightleftharpoons 3H_2(g) + N_2(g)$

**b.** $N_2(g) + O_2(g) \rightleftharpoons 2NO(g)$

**c.** $2NO_2(g) \rightleftharpoons N_2(g) + 2O_2(g)$

**d.** $4NH_3(g) + 3O_2(g) \rightleftharpoons 2N_2(g) + 6H_2O(g)$

**9.61** Would decreasing the volume of the equilibrium mixture of each of the following reactions cause the equilibrium to shift, and if so, will the shift be toward products or reactants?

**a.** $3O_2(g) \rightleftharpoons 2O_3(g)$

**b.** $2CO_2(g) \rightleftharpoons 2CO(g) + O_2(g)$

**c.** $P_4(g) + 5O_2(g) \rightleftharpoons P_4O_{10}(s)$

**d.** $2SO_2(g) + 2H_2O(g) \rightleftharpoons 2H_2S(g) + 3O_2(g)$

**9.62** Would increasing the volume of the equilibrium mixture of each of the following reactions cause the equilibrium to shift, and if so, will the shift be toward products or reactants?

**a.** $2NH_3(g) \rightleftharpoons 3H_2(g) + N_2(g)$

**b.** $N_2(g) + O_2(g) \rightleftharpoons 2NO(g)$

**c.** $2NO_2(g) \rightleftharpoons N_2(g) + 2O_2(g)$

**d.** $4NH_3(g) + 3O_2(g) \rightleftharpoons 2N_2(g) + 6H_2O(g)$

**9.63** For each of the following $K_c$ values, indicate whether the equilibrium mixture contains mostly reactants, mostly products, or similar amounts of reactants and products:

**a.** $N_2(g) + O_2(g) \rightleftharpoons 2NO(g)$ $K_c = 1 \times 10^{-30}$

**b.** $H_2(g) + Br(g) \rightleftharpoons 2HBr(g)$ $K_c = 2.0 \times 10^{19}$

**9.64** Indicate if you would increase or decrease the volume of the container to *increase* the yield of the products in each of the following:

**a.** $2C(s) + O_2(g) \rightleftharpoons 2CO(g)$

**b.** $2CH_4(g) \rightleftharpoons C_2H_2(g) + 3H_2(g)$

**c.** $2H_2(g) + O_2(g) \rightleftharpoons 2H_2O(g)$

9.65 For each of the following slightly soluble salts, write the equilibrium equation and the solubility product expression:
**a.** $CuCO_3$ **b.** $PbF_2$ **c.** $Fe(OH)_3$

**9.66** For each of the following slightly soluble salts, write the equilibrium equation and the solubility product expression:
**a.** CuS **b.** $Ag_2SO_4$ **c.** $Zn(OH)_2$

9.67 A saturated solution of iron(II) sulfide, FeS, has $[Fe^{2+}] = 7.7 \times 10^{-10}$ M and $[S^{2-}] = 7.7 \times 10^{-10}$ M. What is the value of $K_{sp}$ for FeS?

**9.68** A saturated solution of copper(I) chloride, CuCl, has $[Cu^{+}] = 1.1 \times 10^{-3}$ M and $[Cl^{-}] = 1.1 \times 10^{-3}$ M. What is the value of $K_{sp}$ for CuCl?

9.69 A saturated solution of manganese(II) hydroxide, $Mn(OH)_2$, has $[Mn^{2+}] = 3.7 \times 10^{-5}$ M and $[OH^{-}] = 7.4 \times 10^{-5}$ M. What is the value of $K_{sp}$ for $Mn(OH)_2$?

**9.70** A saturated solution of silver chromate, $Ag_2CrO_4$, has $[Ag^{+}] = 1.3 \times 10^{-4}$ M and $[CrO_4^{2-}] = 6.5 \times 10^{-5}$ M. What is the value of $K_{sp}$ for $Ag_2CrO_4$?

9.71 What are $[Cd^{2+}]$ and $[S^{2-}]$ in a saturated CdS solution if the $K_{sp}$ of CdS is $1.0 \times 10^{-24}$?

**9.72** What are $[Cu^{2+}]$ and $[CO_3^{2-}]$ in a saturated $CuCO_3$ solution if the $K_{sp}$ of $CuCO_3$ is $1 \times 10^{-26}$?

## CHALLENGE QUESTIONS

9.73 You mix 0.10 mole of $PCl_5$ with 0.050 mole of $PCl_3$ and 0.050 mole of $Cl_2$ in a 1.0 L flask.

$$PCl_5(g) \rightleftharpoons PCl_3(g) + Cl_2(g) \quad K_c = 4.2 \times 10^{-2}$$

**a.** Is the reaction at equilibrium?
**b.** If not, will the reaction proceed in the forward or reverse direction?

**9.74** You mix 0.10 mole of NO, 0.10 mole of NOBr, and 0.10 mole of $Br_2$ in a 1.0 L container.

$$2NOBr(g) \rightleftharpoons 2NO(g) + Br_2(g) \quad K_c = 2.0 \text{ at } 100\ °C$$

**a.** Is the reaction at equilibrium?
**b.** If not, will the reaction proceed in the forward or reverse direction?

9.75 Consider the following reaction:

$$PCl_5(g) \rightleftharpoons PCl_3(g) + Cl_2(g)$$

**a.** Write the equilibrium constant expression.
**b.** Initially 0.60 mole of $PCl_5$ is placed in 1.00 L flask. At equilibrium, there is 0.16 mole of $PCl_3$ in the flask. What are the equilibrium concentrations of the $PCl_5$ and $Cl_2$?
**c.** What is the equilibrium constant for the reaction?
**d.** If 0.20 mole of $Cl_2$ is added to the equilibrium mixture, will $[PCl_5]$ increase or decrease?

**9.76** The $K_c$ at 100 °C is 2.0 for the reaction

$$2NOBr(g) \rightleftharpoons 2NO(g) + Br_2(g)$$

In an experiment, 1.0 mole of NO, 1.0 mole of NOBr, and 1.0 mole of $Br_2$ was placed in a 1.0 L container.
**a.** What is the equilibrium constant expression for the reaction?
**b.** Is the system at equilibrium?
**c.** If not, will the rate of the forward or reverse reaction initially speed up?
**d.** Which concentration(s) will be greater than 1.0 mole/L at equilibrium, and which will be less than 1.0 mole/L?

9.77 For the reaction

$$C(s) + CO_2(g) \rightleftharpoons 2CO(g)$$

the equilibrium mixture contains solid carbon, [CO] = 0.030 M, and $[CO_2]$ = 0.060 M.
**a.** What is the value of $K_c$ for the reaction at this temperature?
**b.** What is the effect of adding more $CO_2$ to the equilibrium mixture?
**c.** What is the effect of decreasing the volume of the container?

**9.78** Indicate how each of the following will affect the equilibrium concentration of CO in the following reaction:

$$C(s) + H_2O(g) + 31\text{ kcal} \rightleftharpoons CO(g) + H_2(g)$$

**a.** add $H_2$
**b.** increase the temperature of the reaction
**c.** increase the volume of the container
**d.** add C(*s*)
**e.** decrease the volume of the container
**f.** add a catalyst
**g.** decrease the temperature of the reaction
**h.** remove $H_2O$

9.79 The antacid milk of magnesia, which contains $Mg(OH)_2$, is used to neutralize excess stomach acid. If the solubility of $Mg(OH)_2$ in water is $9.7 \times 10^{-3}$ g/L, what is the $K_{sp}$?

**9.80** In a saturated solution of $CaF_2$, the $[F^{-}] = 2.2 \times 10^{-3}$ M. What is $[Ca^{2+}]$?

## ANSWERS

### ANSWERS TO STUDY CHECKS

**9.1** Lowering the temperature will decrease the rate of reaction.

**9.2** $H_2(g) + Br_2(g) \rightleftharpoons 2HBr(g)$

**9.3** $2NO(g) + O_2(g) \rightleftharpoons 2NO_2(g)$

**9.4** $FeO(s) + CO(g) \rightleftharpoons Fe(s) + CO_2(g)$

$$K_c = \frac{[CO_2]}{[CO]}$$

**9.5** $K_c = 27$

**9.6** $[C_2H_5OH] = 2.7$ M

**9.7** Decreasing the volume will increase the yield of product.

**9.8** **a.** A decrease in temperature will decrease the concentration of reactants and increase the $K_c$ value.
**b.** A decrease in temperature will increase the concentration of reactants and decrease the $K_c$ value.

**9.9** $K_{sp} = 8.5 \times 10^{-17}$

**9.10** The solubility of NiS is $2 \times 10^{-10}$ M.

### ANSWER TO SELECTED QUESTIONS AND PROBLEMS

**9.1** **a.** The rate of the reaction indicates how fast the products form.
**b.** Reactions go faster at higher temperatures.

**9.3** The number of collisions will increase when the number of $Br_2$ molecules is increased.

**9.5** **a.** increase **b.** increase
**c.** increase **d.** decrease

**9.7** A reversible reaction is one in which a forward reaction converts reactants to products, while a reverse reaction converts products to reactants.

**9.9** **a.** not reversible **b.** reversible **c.** reversible

**9.11** **a.** $K_c = \frac{[CS_2][H_2]^4}{[CH_4][H_2S]^2}$ **b.** $K_c = \frac{[N_2][O_2]}{[NO]^2}$

**c.** $K_c = \frac{[CS_2][O_2]^4}{[SO_3]^2[CO_2]}$

**9.13** **a.** homogeneous equilibrium
**b.** heterogeneous equilibrium
**c.** homogeneous equilibrium
**d.** heterogeneous equilibrium

**9.15** **a.** $K_c = \frac{[O_2]^3}{[O_3]^2}$ **b.** $K_c = [CO_2][H_2O]$

**c.** $K_c = \frac{[H_2]^3[CO]}{[CH_4][H_2O]}$ **d.** $K_c = \frac{[Cl_2]^2}{[HCl]^4[O_2]}$

**9.17** $K_c = 1.5$

**9.19** $K_c = 260$

**9.21** **a.** mostly products
**b.** both reactants and products
**c.** mostly reactants

**9.23** $[H_2] = 1.1 \times 10^{-3}$ M

**9.25** $[NOBr] = 1.4$ M

**9.27** **a.** When more reactant is added to an equilibrium mixture, the product/reactant ratio is initially less than $K_c$.
**b.** According to Le Châtelier's principle, equilibrium is reestablished when the forward reaction forms more products to make the product/reactant ratio equal the $K_c$ again.

**9.29** **a.** Equilibrium shifts to products.
**b.** Equilibrium shifts to reactants.
**c.** Equilibrium shifts to products.
**d.** Equilibrium shifts to products.
**e.** No shift in equilibrium occurs.

**9.31** **a.** Equilibrium shifts to products.
**b.** Equilibrium shifts to products.
**c.** Equilibrium shifts to products.
**d.** No shift in equilibrium occurs.
**e.** Equilibrium shifts to reactants.

**9.33** **a.** $MgCO_3(s) \rightleftharpoons Mg^{2+}(aq) + CO_3^{2-}(aq)$;
$K_{sp} = [Mg^{2+}][CO_3^{2-}]$
**b.** $PbI_2(s) \rightleftharpoons Pb^{2+}(aq) + 2I^-(aq)$; $K_{sp} = [Pb^{2+}][I^-]^2$
**c.** $Ag_3PO_4(s) \rightleftharpoons 3Ag^+(aq) + PO_4^{3-}(aq)$;
$K_{sp} = [Ag^+]^3[PO_4^{3-}]$

**9.35** $K_{sp} = 1 \times 10^{-10}$

**9.37** $K_{sp} = 8.8 \times 10^{-12}$

**9.39** $[Cu^+] = 1 \times 10^{-6}$ M; $[I^-] = 1 \times 10^{-6}$ M

**9.41** The reaction would have a small equilibrium constant.

**9.43** **a.** $T_2$ is lower than $T_1$.
**b.** $K_c$ for $T_2$ is larger than $K_c$ for $T_1$.

**9.45** **a.** shift toward reactants
**b.** shift toward products
**c.** no change
**d.** shift toward products

**9.47** $Fe(OH)_3(s) \rightleftharpoons Fe^{3+}(aq) + 3OH^-(aq)$

**9.49** **a.** $K_c = \frac{[CO_2][H_2O]^2}{[CH_4][O_2]^2}$ **b.** $K_c = \frac{[N_2]^2[H_2O]^6}{[NH_3]^4[O_2]^3}$

**c.** $K_c = \frac{[CH_4]}{[H_2]^2}$

**9.51** **a.** mostly products
**b.** both products and reactants
**c.** mostly reactants

**9.53** **a.** $SO_2Cl_2(g) \rightleftharpoons SO_2(g) + Cl_2(g)$
**b.** $Br_2(g) + Cl_2(g) \rightleftharpoons 2BrCl(g)$
**c.** $CO(g) + 3H_2(g) \rightleftharpoons CH_4(g) + H_2O(g)$
**d.** $2O_2(g) + 2NH_3(g) \rightleftharpoons N_2O(g) + 3H_2O(g)$

**9.55** **a.** $K_c = \frac{[N_2][H_2]^3}{[NH_3]^2}$ **b.** $K_c = 9.4$

**9.57** $[N_2O_4] = 1.3$ M

**9.59** **a.** Equilibrium shifts to products.
**b.** Equilibrium shifts to reactants.
**c.** Equilibrium shifts to products.
**d.** Equilibrium shifts to reactants.

**9.61** **a.** Equilibrium shifts to products.
**b.** Equilibrium shifts to reactants.
**c.** Equilibrium shifts to products.
**d.** Equilibrium shifts to reactants.

**9.63** **a.** A small $K_c$ indicates that the equilibrium mixture contains mostly reactants.
**b.** A large $K_c$ indicates that the equilibrium mixture contains mostly products.

**9.65** **a.** $CuCO_3(s) \rightleftharpoons Cu^{2+}(aq) + CO_3^{2-}(aq)$;
$K_{sp} = [Cu^{2+}][CO_3^{2-}]$
**b.** $PbF_2(s) \rightleftharpoons Pb^{2+}(aq) + 2F^-(aq)$; $K_{sp} = [Pb^{2+}][F^-]^2$
**c.** $Fe(OH)_3(s) \rightleftharpoons Fe^{3+}(aq) + 3OH^-(aq)$;
$K_{sp} = [Fe^{3+}][OH^-]^3$

**9.67** $K_{sp} = 5.9 \times 10^{-19}$

**9.69** $K_{sp} = 2.0 \times 10^{-13}$

**9.71** $[Cd^{2+}] = 1.0 \times 10^{-12}$ M; $[S^{2-}] = 1.0 \times 10^{-12}$ M

**9.73** **a.** The reaction is not at equilibrium.
**b.** The reaction will proceed in the forward direction.

**9.75** **a.** $K_c = \frac{[PCl_3][Cl_2]}{[PCl_5]}$
**b.** At equilibrium, the concentrations are $[Cl_2] = 0.16$ M, $[PCl_5] = 0.84$ M.
**c.** $K_c = 0.058$
**d.** $[PCl_5]$ will increase.

**9.77** **a.** $K_c = 0.015$
**b.** If more $CO_2$ is added, the equilibrium will shift to the products.
**c.** If the container volume is decreased, the equilibrium will shift to the reactants.

**9.79** $K_{sp} = 2.0 \times 10^{-11}$

# Acids and Bases

10

LOOKING AHEAD


10.1 Acids and Bases

10.2 Strengths of Acids and Bases

10.3 Ionization of Water

10.4 The pH Scale

10.5 Reactions of Acids and Bases

10.6 Acid–Base Properties of Salt Solutions

10.7 Buffers

*"In a stat lab, we are sent blood samples of patients in emergency situations," says Audrey Trautwein, clinical laboratory technician, Stat Lab, Santa Clara Valley Medical Center. "We may need to assess the status of a trauma patient in ER or a patient who is in surgery. For example, an acidic blood pH diminishes cardiac function and affects the actions of certain drugs. In a stat situation, it is critical that we obtain our results fast. This is done using a blood gas analyzer. As I put a blood sample into the analyzer, a small probe draws out a measured volume, which is tested simultaneously for pH,* $P_{O_2}$*, and* $P_{CO_2}$*, as well as for electrolytes, glucose, and hemoglobin. In about one minute we have our test results, which are sent to the doctor's computer."*

Lemons, grapefruit, and vinegar taste sour because they contain acids. We have acid in our stomach that helps us digest food. We produce lactic acid in our muscles when we exercise. Acid from bacteria turns milk sour to make cottage cheese or yogurt. Bases are solutions that neutralize acids. Sometimes we take antacids such as milk of magnesia to offset the effects of too much stomach acid.

The pH of a solution describes its acidity. The lungs and the kidneys are the primary organs that regulate the pH of body fluids, including blood and urine. Major changes in the pH of the body fluids can severely affect biological activities within the cells. Buffers are present to prevent large fluctuations in pH.

In the environment, the pH of rain, water, and soil can have significant effects. When rain becomes too acidic, it can dissolve marble statues and accelerate the corrosion of metals. In lakes and ponds, the acidity of water can affect the ability of fish to survive. The acidity of the soil around plants affects their growth. If the soil pH is too acidic or too basic, the roots of the plant cannot take up some nutrients. Most plants thrive in soil with a nearly neutral pH, although certain plants such as orchids, camellias, and blueberries require a more acidic soil.

## 10.1 Acids and Bases

**LEARNING GOAL**

Describe and name Arrhenius and Brønsted–Lowry acids and bases; identify conjugate acid–base pairs.

The term *acid* comes from the Latin word *acidus*, which means "sour." We are familiar with the sour tastes of vinegar, lemons, and other common acidic foods.

In 1887, the Swedish chemist Svante Arrhenius was the first to describe **acids** as substances that produce hydrogen ions ($H^+$) when they dissolve in water. For example, hydrogen chloride ionizes in water to give hydrogen ions, $H^+$, and chloride ions, $Cl^-$. The hydrogen ions, $H^+$, give acids a sour taste, change blue litmus indicator to red, and corrode some metals.

$$HCl(g) \xrightarrow{H_2O} H^+(aq) + Cl^-(aq)$$

Polar covalent compound — Ionization in water — Hydrogen ion

### Naming Acids

Acids dissolve in water to produce hydrogen ions along with a negative ion that may be a simple nonmetal anion or a polyatomic ion.

When an acid dissolves in water to produce a hydrogen ion and a simple nonmetal anion, the prefix *hydro* is used before the name of the nonmetal, and its *ide* ending is changed to *ic acid*. For example, hydrogen chloride (HCl) dissolves in water to form HCl(*aq*), which is named hydrochloric acid. An exception is hydrogen cyanide (HCN), which as an acid is named hydrocyanic acid, HCN(*aq*). When an acid contains an oxygen-containing polyatomic ion, the name of the acid comes from the name of the polyatomic ion. The *ate* in the name is replaced with *ic acid*. If the acid contains a polyatomic ion with an *ite* ending, its name ends with *ous acid*. The names of some common acids and their anions are listed in Table 10.1.

**CONCEPT CHECK 10.1**

**Naming Acids**

**a.** If $H_2SO_4$ is named sulfuric acid, what is the name of $H_2SO_3$? Why?
**b.** In part **a**, why is the prefix *hydro* not used at the beginning of either name?

ANSWER

**a.** $H_2SO_3$ is named sulfurous acid. The acid of a polyatomic anion that ends in *ate* replaces the *ate* ending with *ic acid*. The acid of the polyatomic anion that ends in *ite* replaces the *ite* ending with *ous acid*.
**b.** The prefix *hydro* is used only when the anion is a simple nonmetal anion or $CN^-$, and not with an acid that includes a polyatomic anion.

**TABLE 10.1** Naming Common Acids

| Acid | Name of Acid | Anion | Name of Anion |
|---|---|---|---|
| $HCl$ | **Hydro**chlor**ic acid** | $Cl^-$ | Chlor**ide** |
| $HBr$ | **Hydro**brom**ic acid** | $Br^-$ | Brom**ide** |
| $HCN$ | **Hydro**cyan**ic acid** | $CN^-$ | Cyan**ide** |
| $HNO_3$ | Nitr**ic acid** | $NO_3^-$ | Nitr**ate** |
| $HNO_2$ | Nitr**ous acid** | $NO_2^-$ | Nitr**ite** |
| $H_2SO_4$ | Sulfur**ic acid** | $SO_4^{2-}$ | Sulf**ate** |
| $H_2SO_3$ | Sulfur**ous acid** | $SO_3^{2-}$ | Sulf**ite** |
| $H_2CO_3$ | Carbon**ic acid** | $CO_3^{2-}$ | Carbon**ate** |
| $H_3PO_4$ | Phosphor**ic acid** | $PO_4^{3-}$ | Phosph**ate** |
| $HClO_4$ | **Per**chlor**ic acid** | $ClO_4^-$ | **Per**chlor**ate** |
| $HClO_3$ | Chlor**ic acid** | $ClO_3^-$ | Chlor**ate** |
| $HClO_2$ | Chlor**ous acid** | $ClO_2^-$ | Chlor**ite** |
| $HClO$ | Hypochlor**ous acid** | $ClO^-$ | Hypochlor**ite** |
| $HC_2H_3O_2$ | Acet**ic acid** | $C_2H_3O_2^-$ | Acet**ate** |

## Bases

You may be familiar with some bases such as antacids, ammonia, drain openers, and oven cleaners. According to the Arrhenius theory, **bases** are ionic compounds that dissociate into cations and hydroxide ions ($OH^-$) when they dissolve in water. For example, sodium hydroxide is an Arrhenius base that dissociates in water to give sodium ions, $Na^+$, and hydroxide ions, $OH^-$.

Most Arrhenius bases are formed from Groups 1A (1) and 2A (2) metals, such as $NaOH$, $KOH$, $LiOH$, and $Ca(OH)_2$. Bases such as $Al(OH)_3$ and $Fe(OH)_3$ are strong, but they are fairly insoluble. The hydroxide ions ($OH^-$) give Arrhenius bases common characteristics such as a bitter taste and a slippery feel. A base turns litmus indicator blue and phenolphthalein indicator pink.

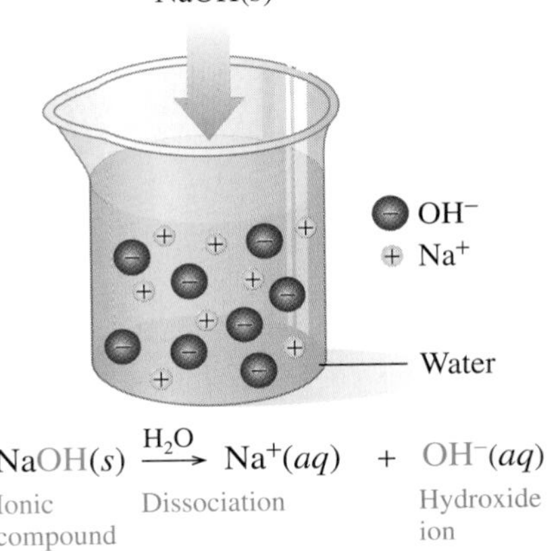


$$NaOH(s) \xrightarrow{H_2O} Na^+(aq) + OH^-(aq)$$

Ionic compound — Dissociation — Hydroxide ion

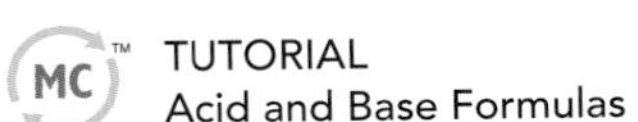
TUTORIAL
Acid and Base Formulas

TUTORIAL
Naming Acids and Bases

## Naming Bases

Typical Arrhenius bases are named as *hydroxides*.

| Bases | Name |
|---|---|
| $NaOH$ | Sodium **hydroxide** |
| $KOH$ | Potassium **hydroxide** |
| $Ca(OH)_2$ | Calcium **hydroxide** |
| $Al(OH)_3$ | Aluminum **hydroxide** |

**CONCEPT CHECK 10.2**

### Dissociation of an Arrhenius Base

Write an equation for the dissociation of calcium hydroxide in water.

ANSWER

When calcium hydroxide, $Ca(OH)_2$, dissolves in water, the solution contains calcium ions ($Ca^{2+}$) and twice as many hydroxide ions ($OH^-$). The equation is written as

$$Ca(OH)_2(s) \xrightarrow{H_2O} Ca^{2+}(aq) + 2OH^-(aq)$$

SAMPLE PROBLEM 10.1

**Names and Formulas of Acids and Bases**

**a.** Name each of the following as an acid or base:
**1.** $H_3PO_4$ **2.** NaOH

**b.** Write the formula of each of the following acids:
**1.** nitrous acid **2.** hydrobromic acid

SOLUTION

**a. 1.** phosphoric acid **2.** sodium hydroxide

**b. 1.** $HNO_2$ **2.** HBr

STUDY CHECK

**a.** Give the name for $HClO_3$.

**b.** Write the formula of iron(III) hydroxide.

## Brønsted–Lowry Acids and Bases

In 1923, J. N. Brønsted in Denmark and T. M. Lowry in Great Britain expanded the definition of acids and bases. A **Brønsted–Lowry acid** donates a proton (hydrogen ion, $H^+$) to another substance, and a **Brønsted–Lowry base** accepts a proton.

A Brønsted–Lowry acid is a proton ($H^+$) donor.
A Brønsted–Lowry base is a proton ($H^+$) acceptor.

A free, dissociated proton ($H^+$) does not actually exist in water. Its attraction to polar water molecules is so strong that the proton bonds to the water molecule and forms a **hydronium ion, $H_3O^+$**.

$$\mathrm{H{-}\ddot{O}{:}(H)} + \mathrm{H^+} \longrightarrow \left[\mathrm{H{-}\ddot{O}(H){-}H}\right]^+$$

Water Proton Hydronium ion

We can write the formation of a hydrochloric acid solution as a transfer of a proton from hydrogen chloride to water. By accepting a proton in the reaction, water is acting as a base according to the Brønsted–Lowry concept.

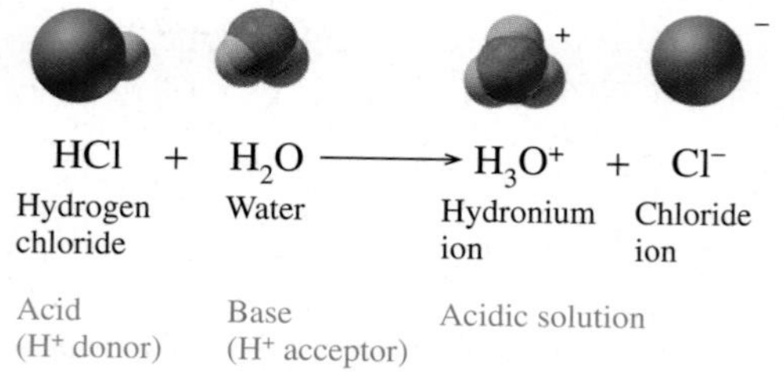


$$HCl + H_2O \longrightarrow H_3O^+ + Cl^-$$

Hydrogen chloride; Water; Hydronium ion; Chloride ion

Acid ($H^+$ donor); Base ($H^+$ acceptor); Acidic solution

In another reaction, ammonia ($NH_3$) reacts with water. Because the nitrogen atom of $NH_3$ has a stronger attraction for a proton, water acts as an acid by donating a proton.

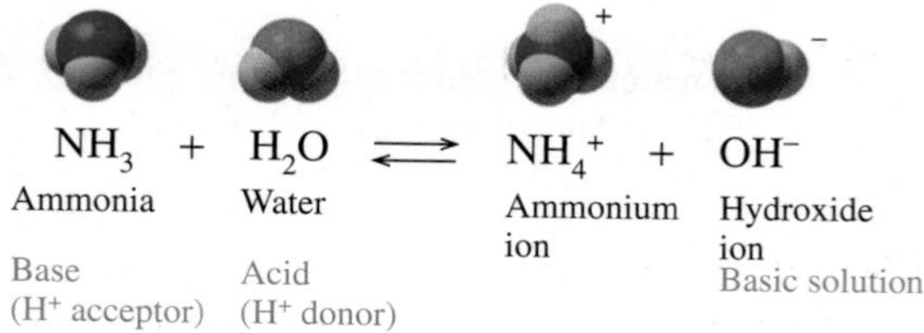


$$NH_3 + H_2O \rightleftarrows NH_4^+ + OH^-$$

Ammonia; Water; Ammonium ion; Hydroxide ion

Base ($H^+$ acceptor); Acid ($H^+$ donor); Basic solution

Table 10.2 compares some characteristics of acids and bases.

**TABLE 10.2 Some Characteristics of Acids and Bases**

| Characteristic | Acids | Bases |
|---|---|---|
| Reaction: Arrhenius | Produce $H^+$ | Produce $OH^-$ |
| Reaction: Brønsted–Lowry | Donate $H^+$ | Accept $H^+$ |
| Electrolytes | Yes | Yes |
| Taste | Sour | Bitter, chalky |
| Feel | May sting | Slippery |
| Litmus | Red | Blue |
| Phenolphthalein | Colorless | Pink |
| Neutralization | Neutralize bases | Neutralize acids |

SAMPLE PROBLEM 10.2

### Acids and Bases

In each of the following equations, identify the reactant that is a Brønsted–Lowry acid and the reactant that is a Brønsted–Lowry base:

**a.** $HBr(aq) + H_2O(l) \longrightarrow H_3O^+(aq) + Br^-(aq)$

**b.** $H_2O(l) + CN^-(aq) \rightleftarrows HCN(aq) + OH^-(aq)$

SOLUTION

**a.** HBr, Brønsted–Lowry acid; $H_2O$, Brønsted–Lowry base

**b.** $H_2O$, Brønsted–Lowry acid; $CN^-$, Brønsted–Lowry base

STUDY CHECK

When $HNO_3$ reacts with water, water acts as a Brønsted–Lowry base. Write the equation for the reaction.

## Conjugate Acid–Base Pairs

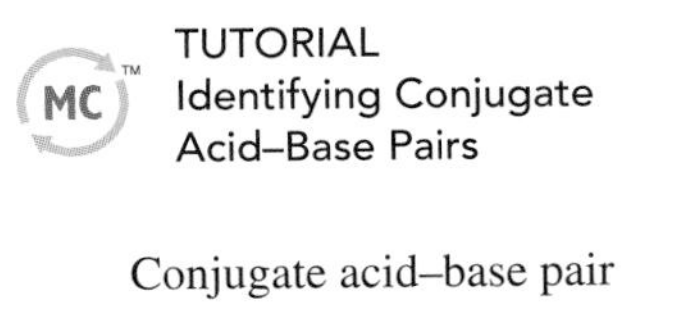


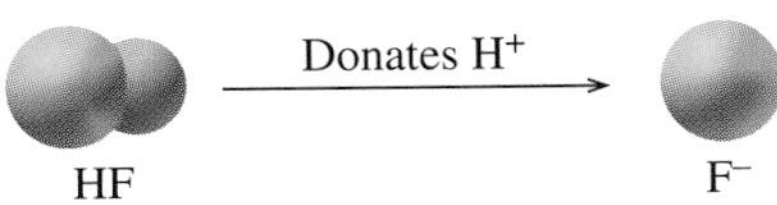


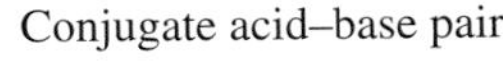


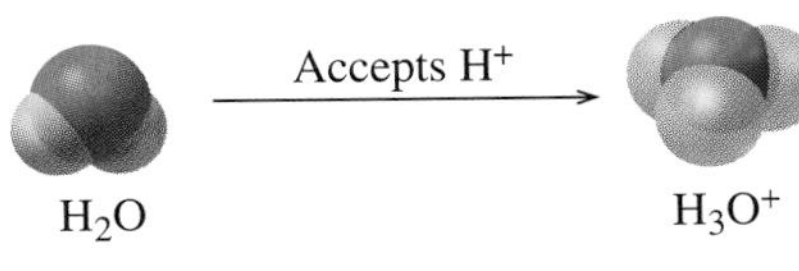


According to the Brønsted–Lowry theory, a **conjugate acid–base pair** consists of molecules or ions related by the loss or gain of one $H^+$. Every acid–base reaction contains two conjugate acid–base pairs because protons are transferred in both the forward and reverse reactions. When the acid HA donates $H^+$, the conjugate base $A^-$ forms. When the base B accepts the $H^+$, it forms the conjugate acid $BH^+$. We can write a general equation for a Brønsted–Lowry acid–base reaction as follows:

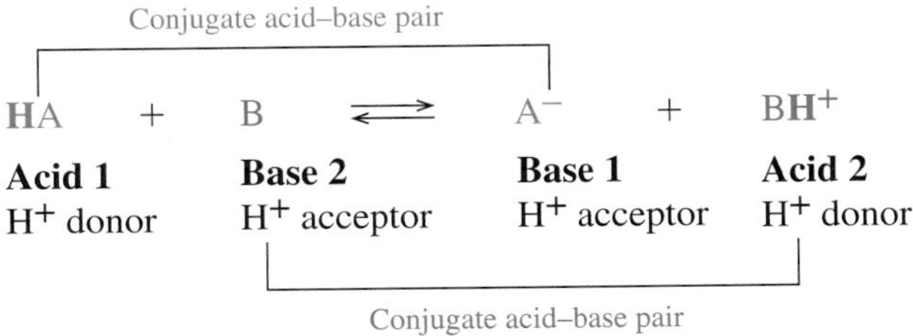


Now we can identify the conjugate acid–base pairs in a reaction such as hydrofluoric acid and water. Because the reaction is reversible, the conjugate acid $H_3O^+$ can transfer a proton to the conjugate base $F^-$ and re-form the acid HF. Using the relationship of loss and

gain of one $H^+$, we identify the conjugate acid–base pairs as HF and $F^-$ along with $H_3O^+$ and $H_2O$.

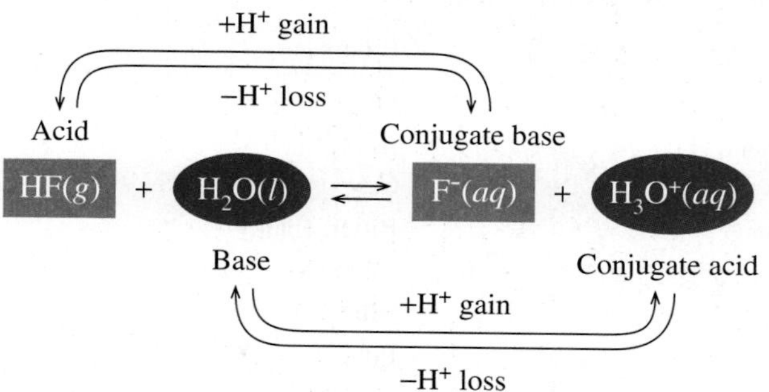


In another proton-transfer reaction, ammonia, $NH_3$, accepts $H^+$ from $H_2O$ to form the conjugate acid $NH_4^+$ and conjugate base $OH^-$. Each of these conjugate acid–base pairs, $NH_3$ and $NH_4^+$ as well as $H_2O$ and $OH^-$, are related by the loss and gain of one $H^+$.

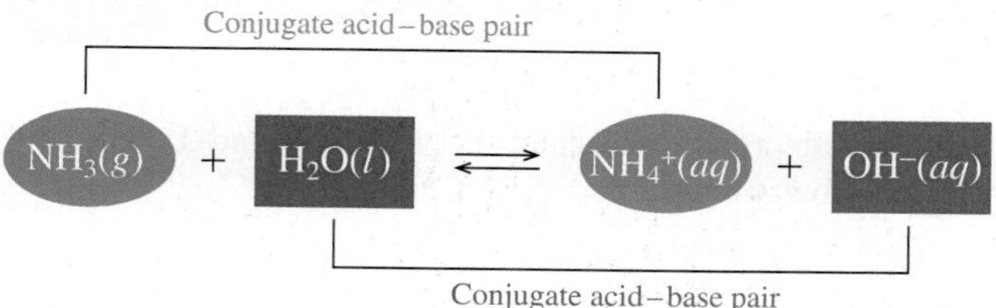


In these two examples, we see that water can act as an acid when it donates $H^+$ or a base when it accepts $H^+$. Substances that can act as both acids and bases are **amphoteric**. For water, the most common amphoteric substance, the acidic or basic behavior depends on the other reactant. Water donates $H^+$ when it reacts with a stronger base and accepts $H^+$ when it reacts with a stronger acid. Another example of an amphoteric substance is bicarbonate, $HCO_3^-$. With a stronger base, $HCO_3^-$ donates $H^+$ to give $CO_3^{2-}$. But when $HCO_3^-$ reacts with a stronger acid, it accepts a proton to form $H_2CO_3$.

SAMPLE PROBLEM 10.3

### Conjugate Acid–Base Pairs

Write the formula of the conjugate base of each of the following Brønsted–Lowry acids:

**a.** $HClO_3$ **b.** $H_2CO_3$

SOLUTION

The conjugate base forms when the acid donates a proton.

**a.** $ClO_3^-$ is the conjugate base that forms when $HClO_3$ donates $H^+$.
**b.** $HCO_3^-$ is the conjugate base that forms when $H_2CO_3$ donates $H^+$.

STUDY CHECK

Write the conjugate acid of each of the following Brønsted–Lowry bases:

**a.** $HS^-$ **b.** $NO_2^-$

SAMPLE PROBLEM 10.4

### Identifying Conjugate Acid–Base Pairs

Identify the conjugate acid–base pairs in the following equation:

$$HBr(aq) + NH_3(aq) \longrightarrow Br^-(aq) + NH_4^+(aq)$$

SOLUTION

Acting as a Brønsted–Lowry acid, HBr donates $H^+$ to form $Br^-$ as its conjugate base. The $NH_3$, acting as a Brønsted–Lowry base, accepts $H^+$ to form its conjugate acid $NH_4^+$. One conjugate acid–base pair is HBr and $Br^-$, and the other is $NH_4^+$ and $NH_3$.

STUDY CHECK

In the following reaction, identify the conjugate acid–base pairs:

$$HCN(aq) + SO_4^{2-}(aq) \rightleftharpoons CN^-(aq) + HSO_4^-(aq)$$

## QUESTIONS AND PROBLEMS

### Acids and Bases

**10.1** Indicate whether each of the following statements is characteristic of an acid or a base:
**a.** has a sour taste
**b.** neutralizes bases
**c.** produces $H^+$ ions in water
**d.** is named potassium hydroxide

**10.2** Indicate whether each of the following statements is characteristic of an acid or a base:
**a.** neutralizes acids **b.** produces $OH^-$ in water
**c.** has a slippery feel **d.** turns litmus red

**10.3** Name each of the following acids and bases:
**a.** HCl **b.** $Ca(OH)_2$ **c.** $H_2CO_3$
**d.** $HNO_3$ **e.** $H_2SO_3$ **f.** $Fe(OH)_2$

**10.4** Name each of the following acids and bases:
**a.** $Al(OH)_3$ **b.** HBr **c.** $H_2SO_4$
**d.** KOH **e.** $HNO_2$ **f.** $HClO_3$

**10.5** Write formulas for the following acids and bases:
**a.** magnesium hydroxide **b.** hydrofluoric acid
**c.** phosphoric acid **d.** lithium hydroxide
**e.** copper(II) hydroxide

**10.6** Write formulas for the following acids and bases:
**a.** barium hydroxide **b.** hydroiodic acid
**c.** nitric acid **d.** iron(III) hydroxide
**e.** sodium hydroxide

**10.7** In each of the following, identify the Brønsted–Lowry acid and Brønsted–Lowry base:
**a.** $HI(aq) + H_2O(l) \longrightarrow H_3O^+(aq) + I^-(aq)$
**b.** $F^-(aq) + H_2O(l) \rightleftharpoons HF(aq) + OH^-(aq)$

**10.8** In each of the following, identify the Brønsted–Lowry acid and the Brønsted–Lowry base:
**a.** $CO_3^{2-}(aq) + H_2O(l) \rightleftharpoons HCO_3^-(aq) + OH^-(aq)$
**b.** $H_2SO_4(aq) + H_2O(l) \longrightarrow H_3O^+(aq) + HSO_4^-(aq)$

**10.9** Write the formula and name of the conjugate base for each of the following acids:
**a.** HF **b.** $H_2O$ **c.** $H_2CO_3$ **d.** $HSO_4^-$

**10.10** Write the formula and name of the conjugate base for each of the following acids:
**a.** $HCO_3^-$ **b.** $H_3O^+$ **c.** $HPO_4^{2-}$ **d.** $HNO_2$

**10.11** Write the formula and name of the conjugate acid for each of the following bases:
**a.** $CO_3^{2-}$ **b.** $H_2O$ **c.** $H_2PO_4^-$ **d.** $Br^-$

**10.12** Write the formula and name of the conjugate acid for each of the following bases:
**a.** $SO_4^{2-}$ **b.** $CN^-$
**c.** $OH^-$ **d.** $ClO_2^-$, chlorite ion

**10.13** Identify the Brønsted–Lowry acid–base pairs in the following equations:
**a.** $H_2CO_3(aq) + H_2O(l) \rightleftharpoons H_3O^+(aq) + HCO_3^-(aq)$
**b.** $NH_4^+(aq) + H_2O(l) \rightleftharpoons H_3O^+(aq) + NH_3(aq)$
**c.** $HCN(aq) + NO_2^-(aq) \rightleftharpoons CN^-(aq) + HNO_2(aq)$

**10.14** Identify the Brønsted–Lowry acid–base pairs in the following equations:
**a.** $H_3PO_4(aq) + H_2O(l) \rightleftharpoons H_3O^+(aq) + H_2PO_4^-(aq)$
**b.** $CO_3^{2-}(aq) + H_2O(l) \rightleftharpoons OH^-(aq) + HCO_3^-(aq)$
**c.** $H_3PO_4(aq) + NH_3(aq) \rightleftharpoons NH_4^+(aq) + H_2PO_4^-(aq)$

# 10.2 Strengths of Acids and Bases

LEARNING GOAL

Write equations for the dissociation of strong and weak acids; write the equilibrium expression for a weak acid.

The *strength* of acids is determined by the moles of $H_3O^+$ that are produced for each mole of acid that dissolves. The *strength* of bases is determined by the moles of $OH^-$ that are produced for each mole of base that dissolves. In the process called **dissociation**, an acid or base separates into ions in water. Acids and bases vary greatly in their ability to produce $H_3O^+$ or $OH^-$. Strong acids and strong bases dissociate completely. In water, weak acids and weak bases dissociate only slightly, leaving most of the initial acid or base undissociated.

**TABLE 10.3 Some Conjugate Acid–Base Pairs**

Increasing acid strength ↑ | Increasing base strength ↓

| Acid | | Conjugate Base | |
|---|---|---|---|
| **Strong acids** | | | |
| Perchloric acid | $HClO_4$ | $ClO_4^-$ | Perchlorate ion |
| Sulfuric acid | $H_2SO_4$ | $HSO_4^-$ | Hydrogen sulfate ion |
| Hydroiodic acid | $HI$ | $I^-$ | Iodide ion |
| Hydrobromic acid | $HBr$ | $Br^-$ | Bromide ion |
| Hydrochloric acid | $HCl$ | $Cl^-$ | Chloride ion |
| Nitric acid | $HNO_3$ | $NO_3^-$ | Nitrate ion |
| **Weak acids** | | | |
| Hydronium ion | $H_3O^+$ | $H_2O$ | Water |
| Hydrogen sulfate ion | $HSO_4^-$ | $SO_4^{2-}$ | Sulfate ion |
| Phosphoric acid | $H_3PO_4$ | $H_2PO_4^-$ | Dihydrogen phosphate ion |
| Nitrous acid | $HNO_2$ | $NO_2^-$ | Nitrite ion |
| Hydrofluoric acid | $HF$ | $F^-$ | Fluoride ion |
| Acetic acid | $HC_2H_3O_2$ | $C_2H_3O_2^-$ | Acetate ion |
| Carbonic acid | $H_2CO_3$ | $HCO_3^-$ | Bicarbonate ion |
| Hydrosulfuric acid | $H_2S$ | $HS^-$ | Hydrogen sulfide ion |
| Ammonium ion | $NH_4^+$ | $NH_3$ | Ammonia |
| Hydrocyanic acid | $HCN$ | $CN^-$ | Cyanide ion |
| Bicarbonate ion | $HCO_3^-$ | $CO_3^{2-}$ | Carbonate ion |
| Hydrogen sulfide ion | $HS^-$ | $S^{2-}$ | Sulfide ion |
| Water | $H_2O$ | $OH^-$ | Hydroxide ion |

## Strong and Weak Acids

**Strong acids** are examples of strong electrolytes because they donate protons so easily that their dissociation in water is virtually complete. For example, when the strong acid HCl dissociates in water, $H^+$ is transferred to $H_2O$, and the resulting solution contains essentially only the ions $H_3O^+$ and $Cl^-$. We consider the reaction of HCl in $H_2O$ as going nearly 100% to products. Therefore, the equation for a strong acid such as HCl is written with a single arrow to the products:

$$HCl(g) + H_2O(l) \longrightarrow H_3O^+(aq) + Cl^-(aq)$$

There are only a handful of strong acids. All other acids are weak acids. Table 10.3 lists the strong acids along with some common weak acids, from strongest to weakest acid.

Weak acids are weak electrolytes. **Weak acids** dissociate slightly in water, which means that only a small percentage of the weak acid donates $H^+$ to $H_2O$. Thus, a weak acid reacts with water to form only a small amount of $H_3O^+$ ions. Even at high concentrations, weak acids produce low concentrations of $H_3O^+$ ions. (See Figure 10.1.) Many of the products you drink or use at home contain weak acids. In carbonated soft drinks, for example, $CO_2$ dissolves in water to form carbonic acid, $H_2CO_3$. A weak acid such as $H_2CO_3$ reaches equilibrium between the mostly undissociated $H_2CO_3$ molecules and the ions $H_3O^+$ and $HCO_3^-$. Such a reaction is written with a double arrow. A longer reverse arrow may be used to indicate that the equilibrium favors the undissociated reactants:

$$\underset{\text{Carbonic acid}}{H_2CO_3(aq)} + H_2O(l) \rightleftharpoons H_3O^+(aq) + \underset{\text{Bicarbonate ion}}{HCO_3^-(aq)}$$

Citric acid is a weak acid found in fruits and fruit juices such as lemons, oranges, and grapefruit. Vinegar contains another weak acid known as acetic acid, $HC_2H_3O_2$. In the vinegar used in salad dressings, acetic acid is present typically as a 5% (m/v) acetic acid solution:

$$\underset{\text{Acetic acid}}{HC_2H_3O_2(l)} + H_2O(l) \rightleftharpoons H_3O^+(aq) + \underset{\text{Acetate ion}}{C_2H_3O_2^-(aq)}$$

FIGURE 10.1 A strong acid such as HCl is completely dissociated (≈100%) in solution, whereas a solution of a weak acid such as $HC_2H_3O_2$ contains mostly molecules and a few ions.

Q What is the difference between a strong acid and a weak acid?

In summary, if HA is a strong acid in water, the solution consists of the ions $H_3O^+$ and $A^-$. However, if HA is a weak acid, the aqueous solution consists mostly of undissociated HA and only a few $H_3O^+$ and $A^-$ ions. (See Figure 10.2.)

Strong acid: $HA(aq) + H_2O(l) \longrightarrow H_3O^+(aq) + A^-(aq)$ (100% dissociated)

Weak acid: $HA(aq) + H_2O(l) \rightleftarrows H_3O^+(aq) + A^-(aq)$ (small % dissociated)

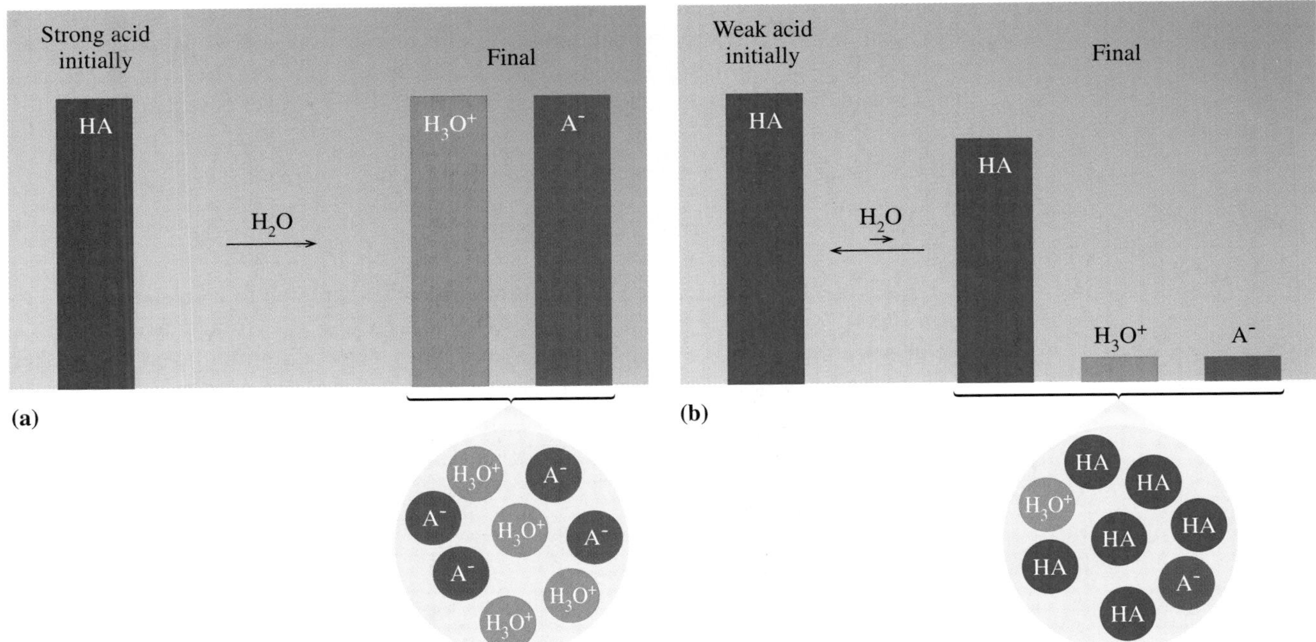


FIGURE 10.2 **(a)** A strong acid dissociates in water to give $H_3O^+$ and $A^-$ ions. **(b)** A weak acid in water dissociates only slightly to form a solution containing only a few $H_3O^+$ and $A^-$ ions and mostly undissociated HA molecules.

Q How does the height of the $H_3O^+$ and $A^-$ in the bar diagram change for a strong acid compared to a weak acid?

## Strong and Weak Bases

As strong electrolytes, **strong bases** dissociate completely in water. Because these strong bases are ionic compounds, they dissociate in water to give an aqueous solution of a metal ion and hydroxide ion. The Group 1A (1) hydroxides are very soluble in water, which can give high concentrations of $OH^-$ ions. The other strong bases are much less soluble in water, but they dissolve completely as ions. For example, when KOH, a strong base, dissociates in water, the solution consists only of the ions $K^+$ and $OH^-$:

$$KOH(s) \xrightarrow{H_2O} K^+(aq) + OH^-(aq)$$

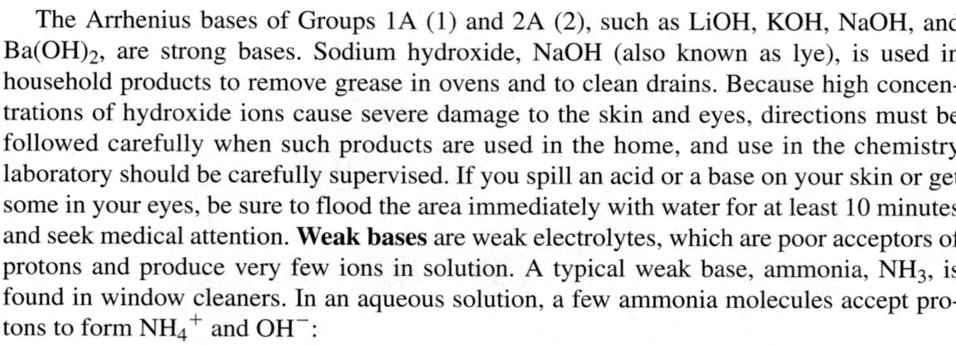

The Arrhenius bases of Groups 1A (1) and 2A (2), such as LiOH, KOH, NaOH, and $Ba(OH)_2$, are strong bases. Sodium hydroxide, NaOH (also known as lye), is used in household products to remove grease in ovens and to clean drains. Because high concentrations of hydroxide ions cause severe damage to the skin and eyes, directions must be followed carefully when such products are used in the home, and use in the chemistry laboratory should be carefully supervised. If you spill an acid or a base on your skin or get some in your eyes, be sure to flood the area immediately with water for at least 10 minutes and seek medical attention. **Weak bases** are weak electrolytes, which are poor acceptors of protons and produce very few ions in solution. A typical weak base, ammonia, $NH_3$, is found in window cleaners. In an aqueous solution, a few ammonia molecules accept protons to form $NH_4^+$ and $OH^-$:

$$\underset{\text{Ammonia}}{NH_3(g)} + H_2O(l) \rightleftharpoons \underset{\text{Ammonium hydroxide}}{NH_4^+(aq) + OH^-(aq)}$$

## Direction of Reaction

There is a relationship between the components in each conjugate acid–base pair. The strong acids that donate protons easily have weak conjugate bases that do not readily accept protons. This conjugate base is a very weak base. As the strength of the acid decreases, the strength of its conjugate base increases.

In any acid–base reaction, there are two acids and two bases. However, one acid is stronger than the other acid, and one base is stronger than the other base. By comparing their relative strengths, we can determine the direction of the reaction. For example, the strong acid $H_2SO_4$ gives up protons to water. The hydronium ion $H_3O^+$ produced is a weaker acid than $H_2SO_4$, and the conjugate base $HSO_4^-$ is a weaker base than water:

$$\underset{\text{Stronger acid}}{H_2SO_4(aq)} + \underset{\text{Stronger base}}{H_2O(l)} \longrightarrow \underset{\text{Weaker acid}}{H_3O^+(aq)} + \underset{\text{Weaker base}}{HSO_4^-(aq)} \quad \text{Strongly favors products}$$

Let's look at another reaction in which water donates a proton to carbonate $CO_3^{2-}$ to form $HCO_3^-$ and $OH^-$. From Table 10.3, we see that $HCO_3^-$ is a stronger acid than $H_2O$. We also see that $OH^-$ is a stronger base than $CO_3^{2-}$. The equilibrium favors the weaker acid and base reactants, as shown by the long arrow for the reverse reaction:

$$\underset{\text{Weaker base}}{CO_3^{2-}(aq)} + \underset{\text{Weaker acid}}{H_2O(l)} \rightleftharpoons \underset{\text{Stronger acid}}{HCO_3^-(aq)} + \underset{\text{Stronger base}}{OH^-(aq)} \quad \text{Strongly favors reactants}$$

**SAMPLE PROBLEM 10.5**

### ■ Direction of Reaction

Does equilibrium favor the reactants or products in the following reaction?

$$HF(aq) + H_2O(l) \rightleftharpoons H_3O^+(aq) + F^-(aq)$$

SOLUTION

From Table 10.3, we see that HF is a weaker acid than $H_3O^+$ and that $H_2O$ is a weaker base than $F^-$. Equilibrium favors the reverse direction and therefore the reactants:

$$\underset{\text{Weaker acid}}{HF(aq)} + \underset{\text{Weaker base}}{H_2O(l)} \rightleftarrows \underset{\text{Stronger acid}}{H_3O^+(aq)} + \underset{\text{Stronger base}}{F^-(aq)}$$

STUDY CHECK

Does the reaction of nitric acid and water favor the reactants or the products?

## Dissociation Constants for Weak Acids

TUTORIAL
Using Dissociation Constants

We have seen that reactions of weak acids in water reach equilibrium. If HA is a weak acid, the concentrations of $H_3O^+$ and $A^-$ are small, which means that the equilibrium favors the reactants:

$$HA(aq) + H_2O(l) \rightleftarrows H_3O^+(aq) + A^-(aq)$$

As we have seen, acids have different strengths depending on how much they dissociate in water. Because the dissociation of strong acids in water is essentially complete, the reaction is not considered to be an equilibrium situation. However, because weak acids in water dissociate only slightly, the ion products reach equilibrium with the undissociated weak acid molecules. Thus, an equilibrium expression can be written for weak acids that gives the ratio of the concentrations of products to the weak acid reactants. As with other equilibrium constants, the molar concentration of the products is divided by the molar concentration of the reactants:

$$\frac{[H_3O^+][A^-]}{[HA][H_2O]}$$

Because water is a pure liquid, its concentration, which is constant, is omitted from the equilibrium constant, called the **acid dissociation constant**, $\boldsymbol{K_a}$ (or acid ionization constant). Thus for a weak acid HA, the $K_a$ is written

$$K_a = \frac{[H_3O^+][A^-]}{[HA]} \quad \text{Acid dissociation constant}$$

Let's consider the equilibrium of carbonic acid, which dissociates in water to form bicarbonate and hydronium ions:

$$H_2CO_3(aq) + H_2O(l) \rightleftarrows HCO_3^-(aq) + H_3O^+(aq)$$

The $K_a$ expression for carbonic acid at 25 °C is

$$K_a = \frac{[H_3O^+][HCO_3^-]}{[H_2CO_3]} = 4.3 \times 10^{-7}$$

The $K_a$ measured for carbonic acid is small, which confirms that the equilibrium of carbonic acid in water favors the reactants. (Recall that the concentration units are omitted in the values given for equilibrium constants.)

We can conclude that weak acids will have small $K_a$ values because their equilibria favor the reactants. The smaller the $K_a$ value, the weaker the acid. On the other hand, strong acids, which are essentially 100% dissociated, have large $K_a$ values, although these values are not usually measured. Table 10.4 gives some $K_a$ values for selected weak acids.

**TABLE 10.4** $K_a$ **Values for Selected Weak Acids**

| Name | Formula | $K_a$ |
|---|---|---|
| Phosphoric acid | $H_3PO_4$ | $7.5 \times 10^{-3}$ |
| Hydrofluoric acid | $HF$ | $7.2 \times 10^{-4}$ |
| Nitrous acid | $HNO_2$ | $4.5 \times 10^{-4}$ |
| Formic acid | $HCHO_2$ | $1.8 \times 10^{-4}$ |
| Acetic acid | $HC_2H_3O_2$ | $1.8 \times 10^{-5}$ |
| Carbonic acid | $H_2CO_3$ | $4.3 \times 10^{-7}$ |
| Dihydrogen phosphate | $H_2PO_4^-$ | $6.2 \times 10^{-8}$ |
| Hydrocyanic acid | $HCN$ | $4.9 \times 10^{-10}$ |
| Bicarbonate | $HCO_3^-$ | $5.6 \times 10^{-11}$ |
| Hydrogen phosphate | $HPO_4^{2-}$ | $2.2 \times 10^{-13}$ |

We have described strong and weak acids in several ways. Table 10.5 summarizes the characteristics of acids in terms of strength and equilibrium position.

**TABLE 10.5** **Characteristics of Acids**

| Characteristic | Strong Acids | Weak Acids |
|---|---|---|
| Equilibrium position | Toward ionized products | Toward unionized reactants |
| $K_a$ | Large | Small |
| $[H_3O^+]$ and $[A^-]$ | 100% of initial [HA] | Small percent of initial [HA] |
| Conjugate bases | Weak | Strong |

CONCEPT CHECK 10.3

### Acid Dissociation Constants

Acid HX has a $K_a$ of $4.0 \times 10^{-4}$, and acid HY has $K_a$ of $8.0 \times 10^{-6}$. If each acid has a 0.10 M concentration, which solution has the higher concentration of $H_3O^+$?

ANSWER

Acid HX has a larger $K_a$ value than acid HY. When acid HX dissolves in water, there is more dissociation of HX, which gives a higher concentration of $H_3O^+$ and $X^-$ ions in solution.

SAMPLE PROBLEM 10.6

### Writing Acid Dissociation Constants

Write the expression for the acid dissociation constant for nitrous acid.

SOLUTION

The equation for the dissociation of nitrous acid is written

$$HNO_2(aq) + H_2O(l) \rightleftarrows H_3O^+(aq) + NO_2^-(aq)$$

The acid dissociation constant is written as the concentrations of the products divided by the concentration of the undissociated weak acid:

$$K_a = \frac{[H_3O^+][NO_2^-]}{[HNO_2]}$$

STUDY CHECK

Which is the stronger acid, nitrous acid or carbonic acid? Why?

## QUESTIONS AND PROBLEMS

### Strengths of Acids and Bases

10.15 What is meant by the phrase, "A strong acid has a weak conjugate base"?

**10.16** What is meant by the phrase, "A weak acid has a strong conjugate base"?

10.17 Identify the stronger acid in each pair:
**a.** HBr or $HNO_2$
**b.** $H_3PO_4$ or $HSO_4^-$
**c.** HCN or $H_2CO_3$

**10.18** Identify the stronger acid in each pair:
**a.** $NH_4^+$ or $H_3O^+$
**b.** $H_2SO_4$ or HCN
**c.** $H_2O$ or $H_2CO_3$

10.19 Identify the weaker acid in each pair:
**a.** HCl or $HSO_4^-$
**b.** $HNO_2$ or HF
**c.** $HCO_3^-$ or $NH_4^+$

**10.20** Identify the weaker acid in each pair:
**a.** $HNO_3$ or $HCO_3^-$
**b.** $HSO_4^-$ or $H_2O$
**c.** $H_2SO_4$ or $H_2CO_3$

10.21 Predict whether the equilibrium for each of the following reactions favors the reactants or the products:
**a.** $H_2CO_3(aq) + H_2O(l) \rightleftharpoons H_3O^+(aq) + HCO_3^-(aq)$
**b.** $NH_4^+(aq) + H_2O(l) \rightleftharpoons H_3O^+(aq) + NH_3(aq)$
**c.** $HCl(aq) + NH_3(aq) \rightleftharpoons Cl^-(aq) + NH_4^+(aq)$

**10.22** Predict whether the equilibrium for each of the following reactions favors the reactants or the products:
**a.** $H_3PO_4(aq) + H_2O(l) \rightleftharpoons H_3O^+(aq) + H_2PO_4^-(aq)$
**b.** $CO_3^{2-}(aq) + H_2O(l) \rightleftharpoons OH^-(aq) + HCO_3^-(aq)$
**c.** $HS^-(aq) + H_2O(l) \rightleftharpoons H_3O^+(aq) + S^{2-}(aq)$

10.23 Write an equation for the acid–base reaction between ammonium ion and sulfate ion. Why does the equilibrium favor the reactants?

**10.24** Write an equation for the acid–base reaction between nitrous acid and sulfate ion. Why does the equilibrium favor the reactants?

10.25 Consider the following acids and their dissociation constants:

$$H_2SO_3(aq) + H_2O(l) \rightleftharpoons H_3O^+(aq) + HSO_3^-(aq) \quad K_a = 1.2 \times 10^{-2}$$

$$HS^-(aq) + H_2O(l) \rightleftharpoons H_3O^+(aq) + S^{2-}(aq) \quad K_a = 1.3 \times 10^{-19}$$

**a.** Which is the stronger acid, $H_2SO_3$ or $HS^-$?
**b.** What is the conjugate base of $H_2SO_3$?
**c.** Which acid has the weaker conjugate base?
**d.** Which acid has the stronger conjugate base?
**e.** Which acid produces more ions?

**10.26** Consider the following acids and their dissociation constants:

$$HPO_4^{2-}(aq) + H_2O(l) \rightleftharpoons H_3O^+(aq) + PO_4^{3-}(aq) \quad K_a = 2.2 \times 10^{-13}$$

$$HCHO_2(aq) + H_2O(l) \rightleftharpoons H_3O^+(aq) + CHO_2^-(aq) \quad K_a = 1.8 \times 10^{-4}$$

**a.** Which is the weaker acid, $HPO_4^{2-}$ or $HCHO_2$?
**b.** What is the conjugate base of $HPO_4^{2-}$?
**c.** Which acid has the weaker conjugate base?
**d.** Which acid has the stronger conjugate base?
**e.** Which acid produces more ions?

10.27 Phosphoric acid reacts with water to form dihydrogen phosphate and hydronium ion. Write the equation and equilibrium expression for the dissociation of the acid.

**10.28** Carbonic acid, a weak acid, reacts with water to form bicarbonate and hydronium ion. Write the equation and equilibrium expression for the dissociation of the acid.

# 10.3 Ionization of Water

We have seen that in acid–base reactions water is amphoteric; it can act either as an acid or as a base. Does this observation mean that water can be both an acid and a base? Yes, this is exactly what happens with water molecules in pure water. Let's see how this happens. One water molecule acts as an acid by donating a $H^+$ to another water molecule, which acts as a base. The products are the conjugate acid $H_3O^+$ and the conjugate base $OH^-$. Let's take a look at the conjugate acid–base pairs of water:

**LEARNING GOAL**

Use the ion-product constant of water to calculate the $[H_3O^+]$ and $[OH^-]$ in an aqueous solution.

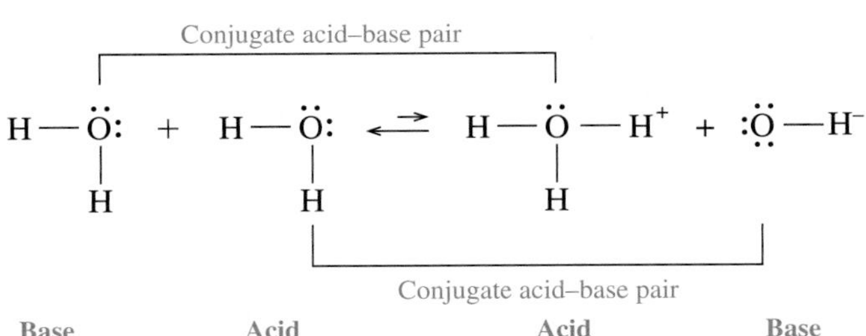

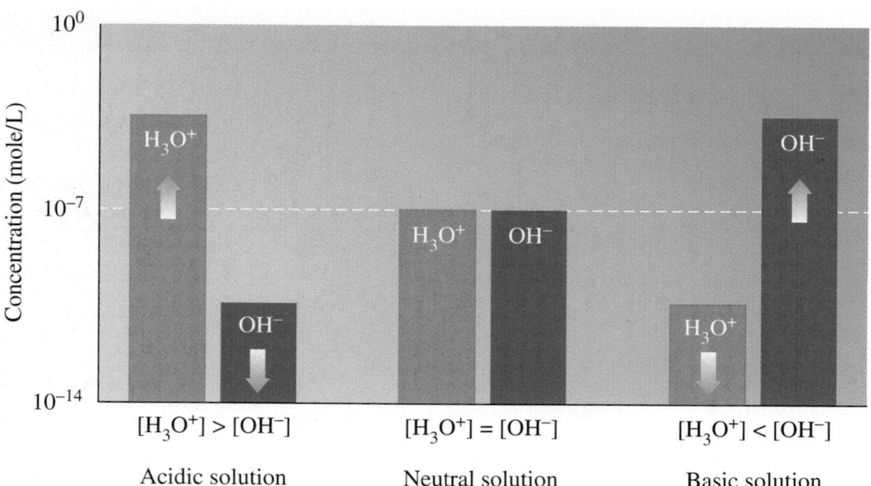


**FIGURE 10.3** In a neutral solution, $[H_3O^+]$ and $[OH^-]$ are equal. In acidic solutions, the $[H_3O^+]$ is greater than the $[OH^-]$. In basic solutions, the $[OH^-]$ is greater than the $[H_3O^+]$.

**Q** Is a solution that has $[H_3O^+] = 1.0 \times 10^{-3}$ M acidic, basic, or neutral?

In the ionization of water, there is both a forward and a reverse reaction:

$$H_2O(l) + H_2O(l) \rightleftharpoons H_3O^+(aq) + OH^-(aq)$$

Every time a $H^+$ is transferred between two water molecules, the products are one $H_3O^+$ and one $OH^-$. Experiments have determined that in pure water the concentrations of $H_3O^+$ and $OH^-$ at 25 °C are each $1.0 \times 10^{-7}$ M. Square brackets around the symbols indicate their concentrations in moles per liter (M):

Pure water $\quad [H_3O^+] = [OH^-] = 1.0 \times 10^{-7}\text{ M}$

When we multiply these concentrations, it forms the **ion-product constant of water, $K_w$,** which is $1.0 \times 10^{-14}$ at 25 °C. The concentration units are omitted in the $K_w$ value.

$$K_w = [H_3O^+] \times [OH^-]$$
$$= (1.0 \times 10^{-7}\text{ M})(1.0 \times 10^{-7}\text{ M}) = 1.0 \times 10^{-14}$$

The $K_w$ value of $1.0 \times 10^{-14}$ is important because it applies to any aqueous solution at 25 °C: all aqueous solutions have $H_3O^+$ and $OH^-$.

When the $[H_3O^+]$ and $[OH^-]$ in a solution are equal, the solution is **neutral**. However, most solutions are not neutral and have different concentrations of $[H_3O^+]$ and $[OH^-]$. If acid is added to water, there is an increase in $[H_3O^+]$ and a decrease in $[OH^-]$, which makes an acidic solution. If base is added, $[OH^-]$ increases and $[H_3O^+]$ decreases, which makes a basic solution. (See Figure 10.3.) However, for any aqueous solution, whether it is neutral, acidic, or basic, the product $[H_3O^+] \times [OH^-]$ is equal to $K_w$ ($1.0 \times 10^{-14}$) at 25 °C. Therefore, if the $[H_3O^+]$ is given, $K_w$ can be used to calculate the $[OH^-]$. Or if the $[OH^-]$ is given, $K_w$ can be used to calculate the $[H_3O^+]$. (See Table 10.6.)

$$K_w = [H_3O^+] \times [OH^-]$$

$$[OH^-] = \frac{K_w}{[H_3O^+]} \qquad [H_3O^+] = \frac{K_w}{[OH^-]}$$

**TABLE 10.6** Examples of $[H_3O^+]$ and $[OH^-]$ in Neutral, Acidic, and Basic Solutions

| Type of Solution | $[H_3O^+]$ | $[OH^-]$ | $K_w$ (25 °C) |
|---|---|---|---|
| Neutral | $1.0 \times 10^{-7}$ M | $1.0 \times 10^{-7}$ M | $1.0 \times 10^{-14}$ |
| Acidic | $1.0 \times 10^{-2}$ M | $1.0 \times 10^{-12}$ M | $1.0 \times 10^{-14}$ |
| Acidic | $2.5 \times 10^{-5}$ M | $4.0 \times 10^{-10}$ M | $1.0 \times 10^{-14}$ |
| Basic | $1.0 \times 10^{-8}$ M | $1.0 \times 10^{-6}$ M | $1.0 \times 10^{-14}$ |
| Basic | $5.0 \times 10^{-11}$ M | $2.0 \times 10^{-4}$ M | $1.0 \times 10^{-14}$ |

To illustrate these calculations, let's determine the $[H_3O^+]$ for a solution that has an $[OH^-] = 1.0 \times 10^{-6}$ M.

**STEP 1** **Write the $K_w$ for water:**

$$K_w = [H_3O^+][OH^-] = 1.0 \times 10^{-14}$$

**STEP 2** **Rearrange the $K_w$ to solve for the unknown.** Dividing through by the $[OH^-]$ gives

$$\frac{K_w}{[OH^-]} = \frac{[H_3O^+] \times \cancel{[OH^-]}}{\cancel{[OH^-]}}$$

$$[H_3O^+] = \frac{1.0 \times 10^{-14}}{[OH^-]}$$

**STEP 3** **Substitute the $[OH^-]$ and calculate the $[H_3O^+]$:**

$$[H_3O^+] = \frac{1.0 \times 10^{-14}}{[1.0 \times 10^{-6}]} = 1.0 \times 10^{-8}\text{ M}$$

Because the $[OH^-]$ of $1.0 \times 10^{-6}$ M is larger than the $[H_3O^+]$ of $1.0 \times 10^{-8}$ M, the solution is basic.

SAMPLE PROBLEM 10.7

## Calculating $[H_3O^+]$ and $[OH^-]$ in Solution

A vinegar solution has a $[H_3O^+] = 2.0 \times 10^{-3}$ M at 25 °C. What is the $[OH^-]$ of the vinegar solution? Is the solution acidic, basic, or neutral?

SOLUTION

**STEP 1** **Write the $K_w$ for water:**

$$K_w = [H_3O^+] \times [OH^-] = 1.0 \times 10^{-14}$$

**STEP 2** **Arrange the $K_w$ to solve for the unknown.** Rearranging the $K_w$ for $OH^-$ gives

$$\frac{K_w}{[H_3O^+]} = \frac{\cancel{[H_3O^+]} \times [OH^-]}{\cancel{[H_3O^+]}}$$

$$[OH^-] = \frac{1.0 \times 10^{-14}}{[H_3O^+]}$$

**STEP 3** **Substitute the known $[H_3O^+]$ and calculate:**

$$[OH^-] = \frac{1.0 \times 10^{-14}}{[2.0 \times 10^{-3}]} = 5.0 \times 10^{-12}\text{ M}$$

Because the $[H_3O^+]$ of $2.0 \times 10^{-3}$ M is much larger than the $[OH^-]$ of $5.0 \times 10^{-12}$ M, the solution is acidic.

STUDY CHECK

What is the $[H_3O^+]$ of an ammonia cleaning solution with an $[OH^-] = 4.0 \times 10^{-4}$ M? Is the solution acidic, basic, or neutral?

**Guide to Calculating $[H_3O^+]$ and $[OH^-]$ in Aqueous Solutions**

STEP 1
Write the $K_w$ for water.

STEP 2
Solve the $K_w$ for the unknown $[H_3O^+]$ or $[OH^-]$.

STEP 3
Substitute the known $[H_3O^+]$ or $[OH^-]$ and calculate.

## QUESTIONS AND PROBLEMS

### Ionization of Water

**10.29** Why are the concentrations of $H_3O^+$ and $OH^-$ equal in pure water?

**10.30** What is the meaning and value of $K_w$?

**10.31** In an acidic solution, how does the concentration of $H_3O^+$ compare to the concentration of $OH^-$?

**10.32** If a base is added to pure water, why does the $[H_3O^+]$ decrease?

**10.33** Indicate whether the following are acidic, basic, or neutral solutions at 25 °C:
- **a.** $[H_3O^+] = 2.0 \times 10^{-5}$ M
- **b.** $[H_3O^+] = 1.4 \times 10^{-9}$ M
- **c.** $[OH^-] = 8.0 \times 10^{-3}$ M
- **d.** $[OH^-] = 3.5 \times 10^{-10}$ M

**10.34** Indicate whether the following are acidic, basic, or neutral solutions at 25 °C:
- **a.** $[H_3O^+] = 6.0 \times 10^{-12}$ M
- **b.** $[H_3O^+] = 1.4 \times 10^{-4}$ M
- **c.** $[OH^-] = 5.0 \times 10^{-12}$ M
- **d.** $[OH^-] = 4.5 \times 10^{-2}$ M

**10.35** Calculate the $[H_3O^+]$ of each aqueous solution with the following $[OH^-]$ at 25 °C:
- **a.** coffee, $1.0 \times 10^{-9}$ M
- **b.** soap, $1.0 \times 10^{-6}$ M
- **c.** cleanser, $2.0 \times 10^{-5}$ M
- **d.** lemon juice, $4.0 \times 10^{-13}$ M

**10.36** Calculate the $[H_3O^+]$ of each aqueous solution with the following $[OH^-]$ at 25 °C:
- **a.** NaOH, $1.0 \times 10^{-2}$ M
- **b.** aspirin, $1.8 \times 10^{-11}$ M
- **c.** milk of magnesia, $1.0 \times 10^{-5}$ M
- **d.** sea water, $2.5 \times 10^{-6}$ M

**10.37** Calculate the $[OH^-]$ of each aqueous solution with the following $[H_3O^+]$ at 25 °C:
- **a.** vinegar, $1.0 \times 10^{-3}$ M
- **b.** urine, $5.0 \times 10^{-6}$ M
- **c.** ammonia, $1.8 \times 10^{-12}$ M
- **d.** NaOH, $4.0 \times 10^{-13}$ M

**10.38** Calculate the $[OH^-]$ of each aqueous solution with the following $[H_3O^+]$ at 25 °C:
- **a.** baking soda, $1.0 \times 10^{-8}$ M
- **b.** orange juice, $2.0 \times 10^{-4}$ M
- **c.** milk, $5.0 \times 10^{-7}$ M
- **d.** bleach, $4.8 \times 10^{-12}$ M

## 10.4 The pH Scale

**LEARNING GOAL**

Calculate pH from $[H_3O^+]$; given the pH, calculate the $[H_3O^+]$ and $[OH^-]$ of a solution.

CASE STUDY
Hyperventilation and Blood pH

SELF STUDY ACTIVITY
The pH Scale

Many kinds of careers such as respiratory therapy, food processing, medicine, agriculture, spa and pool maintenance, and soap manufacturing require personnel to measure the $[H_3O^+]$ and $[OH^-]$ of solutions. The proper levels of acidity are necessary for soil to support plant growth, and to prevent algae in swimming pool water. Measuring the acidity levels of blood and urine checks the function of the kidneys.

On the pH scale, a number between 0 and 14 represents the $H_3O^+$ concentration for most solutions. A neutral solution has a pH of 7.0 at 25 °C. An acidic solution has a pH value less than 7. A basic solution has a pH value greater than 7. (See Figure 10.4.)

| | | |
|---|---|---|
| Acidic solution | $pH < 7$ | $[H_3O^+] > 1.0 \times 10^{-7}$ M |
| Neutral solution | $pH = 7$ | $[H_3O^+] = 1.0 \times 10^{-7}$ M |
| Basic solution | $pH > 7$ | $[H_3O^+] < 1.0 \times 10^{-7}$ M |

In the laboratory, a pH meter is commonly used to determine the pH of a solution. There are also various indicators and pH papers that turn specific colors when placed in solutions of different pH values. The pH is found by comparing the colors to a color chart. (See Figure 10.5.)

**CONCEPT CHECK 10.4**

### pH of Solutions

Consider the pH of the following items:

| Item | pH |
|---|---|
| Rootbeer | 5.8 |
| Kitchen cleaner | 10.9 |
| Pickles | 3.5 |
| Glass cleaner | 7.6 |
| Cranberry juice | 2.9 |

**a.** Place the pH values of the preceding items in order of most acidic to most basic.
**b.** Which item has the highest $[H_3O^+]$?
**c.** Which item has the highest $[OH^-]$?

ANSWER

**a.** The most acidic item is the one with the lowest pH, and the most basic is the item with the highest pH: cranberry juice (2.9), pickles (3.5), rootbeer (5.8), glass cleaner (7.6), kitchen cleaner (10.9).
**b.** The item with the highest $[H_3O^+]$ would have the lowest pH value, which is cranberry juice.
**c.** The item with the highest $[OH^-]$ would have the highest pH value, which is kitchen cleaner.

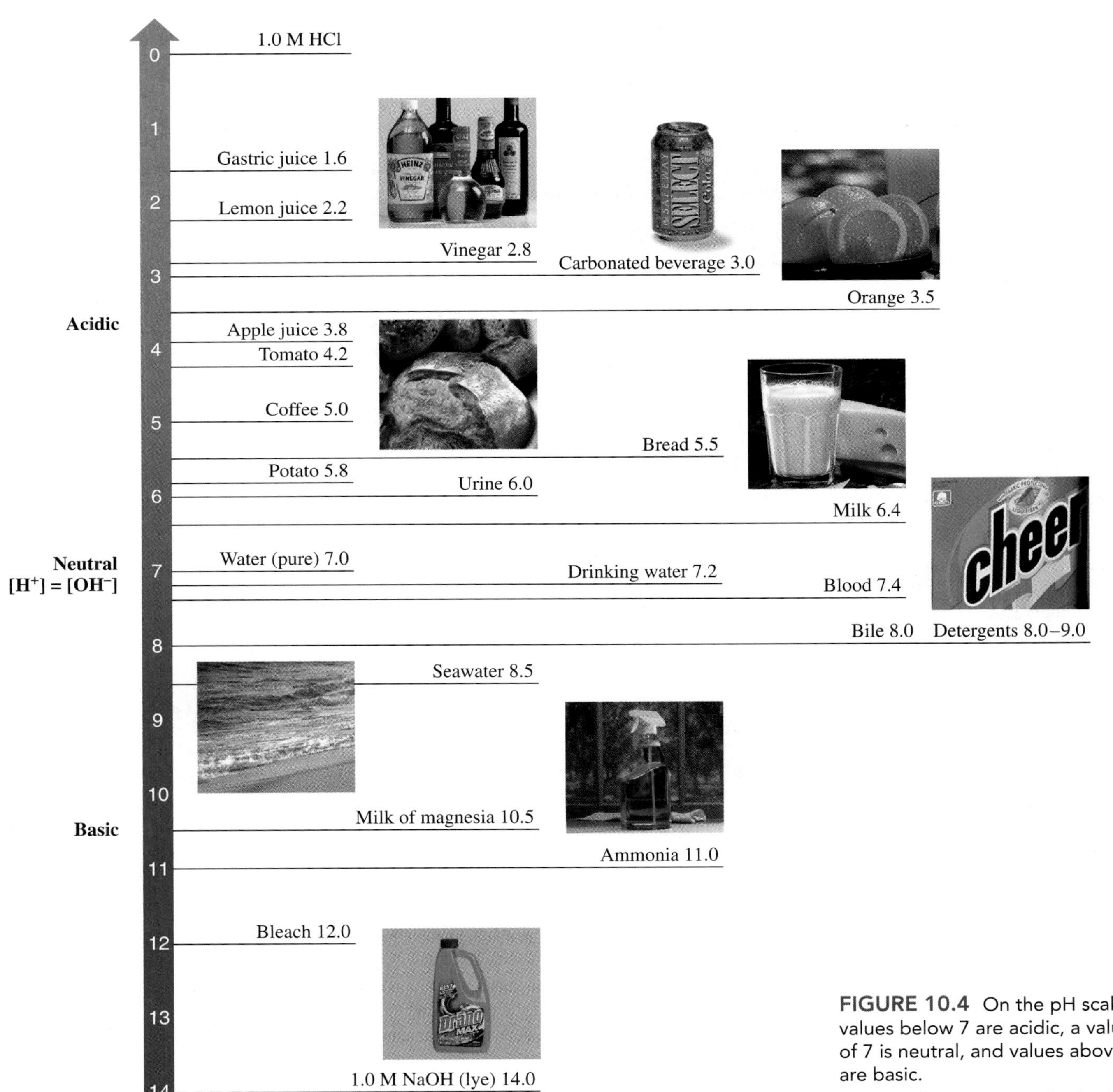


**FIGURE 10.4** On the pH scale, values below 7 are acidic, a value of 7 is neutral, and values above 7 are basic.

**Q** Is apple juice an acidic, basic, or neutral solution?

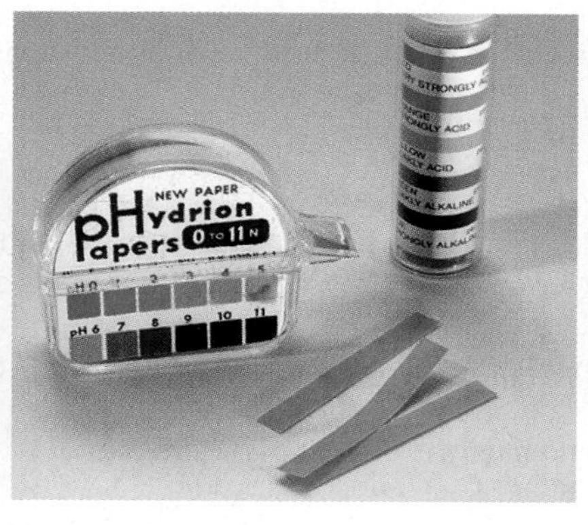

(a) (b) (c)

**FIGURE 10.5** The pH of a solution can be determined using **(a)** a pH meter, **(b)** pH paper, and **(c)** indicators that turn different colors corresponding to different pH values.

Q If a pH meter reads 4.00, is the solution acidic, basic, or neutral?

## Calculating the pH of Solutions

MC™ TUTORIAL Logarithms

The pH scale is a log scale that corresponds to the hydrogen-ion concentrations of aqueous solutions. Mathematically, **pH** is the negative logarithm (base 10) of the $H_3O^+$ concentration:

$$pH = -\log[H_3O^+]$$

MC™ TUTORIAL The pH Scale

Essentially, the negative powers of 10 in the molar concentrations are converted to positive numbers. For example, a lemon juice solution with $[H_3O^+] = 1.0 \times 10^{-2}$ M has a pH of 2.00. This can be calculated using the pH equation:

$$pH = -\log[1.0 \times 10^{-2}]$$

$$pH = -(-2.00)$$

$$= 2.00$$

The number of *decimal places* in the pH value is the same as the number of significant figures in the $[H_3O^+]$.

$$[H_3O^+] = 1.0 \times 10^{-2} \qquad pH = 2.00$$

Two significant figures — Two decimal places

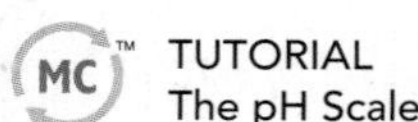

### HEALTH NOTE

#### Stomach Acid, HCl

When a person sees, smells, thinks about, or tastes food, the gastric glands in the stomach begin to secrete a strongly acidic solution of HCl. In a single day, a person may secrete as much as 2000 mL of gastric juice.

The HCl in the gastric juice activates a digestive enzyme called *pepsin* that breaks down proteins in food entering the stomach. The secretion of HCl continues until the stomach has a pH of about 2, which is the optimum pH for activating the digestive enzymes without ulcerating the stomach lining. Normally, large quantities of viscous mucus are secreted within the stomach to protect its lining from acid and enzyme damage.

### CONCEPT CHECK 10.5

#### Calculating pH

Indicate if the pH values given for the following are correct or incorrect, and state why:

**a.** $[H_3O^+] = 1 \times 10^{-6}$ pH = –6.0
**b.** $[OH^-] = 1.0 \times 10^{-10}$ pH = 10.00
**c.** $[H_3O^+] = 1.0 \times 10^{-6}$ pH = 6.00
**d.** $[OH^-] = 1 \times 10^{-2}$ pH = 12.0

ANSWER

**a.** Incorrect. The pH of this solution is 6.0, which has a positive value, not negative.
**b.** Incorrect. The pH is calculated from the $[H_3O^+]$, not $[OH^-]$. This solution has a $[H_3O^+]$ of $1.0 \times 10^{-4}$, for a pH of 4.00. There are two zeros after the decimal point to match the two significant figures in the coefficient of 1.0.
**c.** Correct. The pH has two zeros after the decimal point to match the two significant figures in the coefficient of 1.0.
**d.** Correct. The pH is calculated from the $[H_3O^+] = 1 \times 10^{-12}$ with one zero after the decimal point to match the one significant figure in the coefficient.

## Steps for a pH Calculation

The pH of a solution is determined using the *log* key and *changing the sign*. For example, to calculate the pH of a vinegar solution with $[H_3O^+] = 2.4 \times 10^{-3}$ M, you can use the following steps:

**Guide to Calculating pH of an Aqueous Solution**

STEP 1 Enter the $[H_3O^+]$ value.

STEP 2 Press the *log* key and *change the sign.*

STEP 3 Adjust the number of digits to the *right* of the decimal point to equal SFs in the coefficient.

**Display Shows**

**STEP 1** **Enter the $[H_3O^+]$ value.** Enter 2.4 and press [EE or EXP]. 2.4 00 or 2.4 00 or 2.4 E00

Enter 3 and press [+/-] to change the power to −3. (For calculators without a change sign key, consult the instructions for the calculator.) 2.4 −03 or 2.4−03 or 2.4 E−03

**STEP 2** **Press the [log] key.** −2.619789

**Change the sign.** 2.619789

The steps can be combined to give the calculator sequence as follows:

$$pH = -\log[2.4 \times 10^{-3}] = 2.4 \text{ [EE or EXP] } 3 \text{ [+/-] [log] [+/-]}$$
$$= 2.619789$$

Be sure to check the instructions for your calculator. On some calculators, the numbers are entered as they appear in the pH expression as follows:

−2.4 [log] [EE] −03

**STEP 3** **Adjust significant figures.** In a pH value, the number to the *left* of the decimal point is an *exact* number derived from the power of ten. The number of digits to the *right* of the decimal point is equal to the number of significant figures in the coefficient:

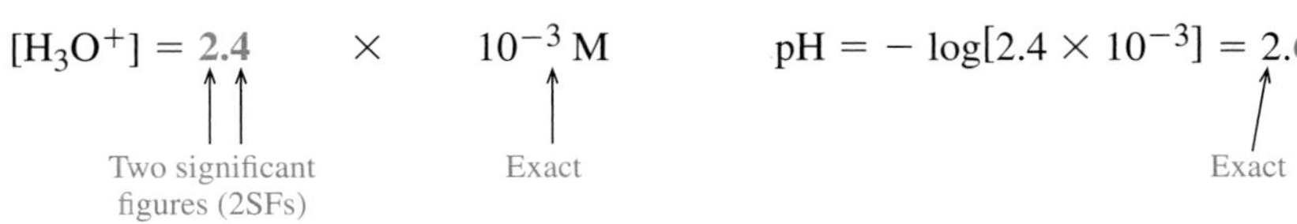


Because pH is a log scale, a change of one pH unit corresponds to a ten-fold change in $[H_3O^+]$. It is important to note that the pH decreases as the $[H_3O^+]$ increases. For example, a solution with a pH of 2.00 has a $[H_3O^+]$ 10 times higher than a solution with a pH of 3.00, and 100 times higher than a solution with a pH of 4.00.

**SAMPLE PROBLEM 10.8**

### Calculating pH

Determine the pH for the following solutions:

**a.** $[H_3O^+] = 1.0 \times 10^{-5}$ M **b.** $[H_3O^+] = 5 \times 10^{-8}$ M

SOLUTION

**a. STEP 1** **Enter the $[H_3O^+]$:**

**Display**

1.0 [EE or EXP] 5 [+/-] 1.0 −05 or 1.0 − 05 or 1.0 E − 05

**STEP 2** **Press the *log* key and the *change sign* key:**

[log] [+/-] 5

**STEP 3** **Adjust the number of digits to the *right* of the decimal point to equal the number of significant figures in the coefficient:**

$1.0 \times 10^{-5}$ M pH = 5.00

2 SFs → 2 digits to the *right* of the decimal point

**b. STEP 1 Enter the $[H_3O^+]$:**

**Display**

5 [EE or EXP] 8 [+/−] $5^{-08}$ or 5 − 08 or 5 E − 08

**STEP 2 Press the *log* key and the *change sign* key:**

[log] [+/−] 7.301029

**STEP 3 Adjust the number of digits to the *right* of the decimal point to equal the significant figures in the coefficient:**

$5 \times 10^{-8}$ M pH = 7.3

1 SF → 1 digit to the *right* of the decimal point

STUDY CHECK

What is the pH of bleach with $[H_3O^+] = 4.2 \times 10^{-12}$ M?

SAMPLE PROBLEM 10.9

## Calculating pH from $[OH^-]$

What is the pH of an ammonia solution at 25 °C with $[OH^-] = 3.7 \times 10^{-3}$ M?

SOLUTION

**STEP 1 Enter the $[H_3O^+]$.** Because $[OH^-]$ is given for the ammonia solution, we have to calculate $[H_3O^+]$ using the ion-product constant of water, $K_w$. Dividing through by $[OH^-]$ gives $[H_3O^+]$.

$$\frac{K_w}{[OH^-]} = \frac{[H_3O^+]\,[\cancel{OH^-}]}{[\cancel{OH^-}]}$$

$$[H_3O^+] = \frac{1.0 \times 10^{-14}}{[3.7 \times 10^{-3}]} = 2.7 \times 10^{-12}\text{ M}$$

**Display**

2.7 [EE or EXP] 12 [+/−] = $2.7^{-12}$ or 2.7 − 12 or 2.7 E−12

**STEP 2 Press the *log* key, and then the *change sign* key:**

[log] [+/−] 11.56863

**STEP 3 Adjust the number of digits to the *right* of the decimal point to equal the SFs in the coefficient:**

$2.7 \times 10^{-12}$ M pH = 11.57

2 SFs → 2 digits *after* the decimal point

STUDY CHECK

Calculate the pH of a sample of acid rain that has $[OH^-] = 2 \times 10^{-10}$ M.

## Calculating $[H_3O^+]$ from pH

In another calculation, we are given the pH of a solution and asked to determine the $[H_3O^+]$. This is a reverse of the pH calculation:

$$[H_3O^+] = 10^{-pH}$$

For pH values that are not whole numbers, the calculation requires the use of the *$10^x$* key, which is usually a 2nd function key. On some calculators, this operation is done using the *inverse* key and the *log* key.

SAMPLE PROBLEM 10.10

## Calculating $[H_3O^+]$ from pH

Calculate $[H_3O^+]$ for each of the following solutions:

**a.** coffee, pH of 5.0
**b.** baking soda, pH of 8.25

SOLUTION

**a.** coffee, pH of 5.0

**STEP 1** **Enter the pH value and press the *change sign* key:**

**Display**

5.0 [+/−] — $-5.0$

**STEP 2** **Convert −pH to concentration.** Press the *2nd function* key and then the *10*$^x$ key:

[2nd] [$10^x$] — 0.00001 or $1.^{-05}$ or $1-05$

Or press the *inverse* key and then the *log* key:

[inv] [log] — 0.00001 or $1.^{-05}$ or $1-05$

On some calculators, the numbers are entered as they appear:

$10^x - 5.0$

Write the display in scientific notation with units of concentration: $1 \times 10^{-5}$ M.

**STEP 3** **Adjust the significant figures in the coefficient.** The pH value of 5.0 has only one digit to the *right* of the decimal point, which means the $[H_3O^+]$ is written with only one significant figure:

$$[H_3O^+] = 1 \times 10^{-5}\ M$$

**b.** baking soda, pH of 8.25

**STEP 1** **Enter the pH value and press the *change sign* key:**

**Display**

8.25 [+/−] — $-8.25$

**STEP 2** **Convert –pH to concentration.** Press the *2nd function* key and then the *10*$^x$ key.

[2nd] [$10^x$] — $5.62341^{-09}$ or $5.62341-09$ or 5.62341 E-09

Or press the *inverse* key and then the *log* key.

[inv] [log] — $5.62341^{-09}$ or $5.62341-09$ or 5.62341 E-09

Write the display in scientific notation with units of concentration: $5.62341 \times 10^{-9}$ M.

**STEP 3** **Adjust the significant figures in the coefficient.** Because the pH value of 8.25 has two digits to the *right* of the decimal point, the $[H_3O^+]$ is written with two significant figures:

$$[H_3O^+] = 5.6 \times 10^{-9}\ M$$

STUDY CHECK

What is the $[H_3O^+]$ and $[OH^-]$ of a beer that has a pH of 4.50?

A comparison of $[H_3O^+]$, $[OH^-]$, and their corresponding pH values is given in Table 10.7.

**TABLE 10.7 A Comparison of $[H_3O^+]$, $[OH^-]$, and Corresponding pH Values at 25 °C**

| $[H_3O^+]$ | pH | $[OH^-]$ | |
|---|---|---|---|
| $10^0$ | 0 | $10^{-14}$ | |
| $10^{-1}$ | 1 | $10^{-13}$ | |
| $10^{-2}$ | 2 | $10^{-12}$ | |
| $10^{-3}$ | 3 | $10^{-11}$ | Acidic |
| $10^{-4}$ | 4 | $10^{-10}$ | |
| $10^{-5}$ | 5 | $10^{-9}$ | |
| $10^{-6}$ | 6 | $10^{-8}$ | |
| $10^{-7}$ | 7 | $10^{-7}$ | Neutral |
| $10^{-8}$ | 8 | $10^{-6}$ | |
| $10^{-9}$ | 9 | $10^{-5}$ | |
| $10^{-10}$ | 10 | $10^{-4}$ | |
| $10^{-11}$ | 11 | $10^{-3}$ | Basic |
| $10^{-12}$ | 12 | $10^{-2}$ | |
| $10^{-13}$ | 13 | $10^{-1}$ | |
| $10^{-14}$ | 14 | $10^0$ | |

## QUESTIONS AND PROBLEMS

### The pH Scale

**10.39** Why does a neutral solution have a pH of 7.00 at 25 °C?

**10.40** If you know the $[OH^-]$, how can you determine the pH of a solution?

**10.41** State whether each of the following solutions is acidic, basic, or neutral:

**a.** blood, pH 7.38 **b.** vinegar, pH 2.8
**c.** drain cleaner, pH 11.2 **d.** coffee, pH 5.5
**e.** tomatoes, pH 4.2 **f.** chocolate cake, pH 7.6

**10.42** State whether each of the following solutions is acidic, basic, or neutral:

**a.** soda, pH 3.2
**b.** shampoo, pH 5.7
**c.** laundry detergent, pH 9.4
**d.** rain, pH 5.8
**e.** honey, pH 3.9
**f.** cheese, pH 7.4

**10.43** Calculate the pH of each solution given the following $[H_3O^+]$ or $[OH^-]$ values:

**a.** $[H_3O^+] = 1.0 \times 10^{-4}$ M
**b.** $[H_3O^+] = 3.0 \times 10^{-9}$ M
**c.** $[OH^-] = 1.0 \times 10^{-5}$ M
**d.** $[OH^-] = 2.5 \times 10^{-11}$ M
**e.** $[H_3O^+] = 6.7 \times 10^{-8}$ M
**f.** $[OH^-] = 8.2 \times 10^{-4}$ M

**10.44** Calculate the pH of each solution given the following $[H_3O^+]$ or $[OH^-]$ values:

**a.** $[H_3O^+] = 1.0 \times 10^{-8}$ M
**b.** $[H_3O^+] = 5.0 \times 10^{-6}$ M
**c.** $[OH^-] = 4.0 \times 10^{-2}$ M
**d.** $[OH^-] = 8.0 \times 10^{-3}$ M
**e.** $[H_3O^+] = 4.7 \times 10^{-2}$ M
**f.** $[OH^-] = 3.9 \times 10^{-6}$ M

**10.45** Complete the following table:

| $[H_3O^+]$ | $[OH^-]$ | pH | Acidic, Basic, or Neutral? |
|---|---|---|---|
| | $1.0 \times 10^{-6}$ M | | |
| | | 3.00 | |
| $2.8 \times 10^{-5}$ M | | | |
| | | 4.62 | |

**10.46** Complete the following table:

| $[H_3O^+]$ | $[OH^-]$ | pH | Acidic, Basic, or Neutral? |
|---|---|---|---|
| | | 10.00 | |
| | | | Neutral |
| $6.4 \times 10^{-12}$ M | | | |
| | | 11.3 | |

# EXPLORE YOUR WORLD

## Using Vegetables and Flowers as pH Indicators

Many flowers and vegetables with strong color, especially reds and purples, contain compounds that change color with changes in pH. Some examples are red cabbage, cranberry juice, and cranberry drinks.

### Materials Needed

Red cabbage, water, and a saucepan; or cranberry juice or drinks

Several glasses or small glass containers, and some tape and a pen or pencil to mark the containers

Several colorless household solutions such as vinegar, lemon juice, other fruit juices; baking soda; antacids; aspirin; window cleaners; soaps; shampoos; and detergents

### Procedure

1. Obtain a bottle of cranberry juice or cranberry drink, or use red cabbage to prepare the red cabbage pH indicator as follows: Tear up several red cabbage leaves and place them in a saucepan and cover with water. Boil for about 5 minutes. Cool and collect the purple solution.
2. Place small amounts of each household solution into separate clear glass containers, and mark what each one is. If the sample is a solid or a thick liquid, add a small amount of water. Add some cranberry juice or some red cabbage indicator until you obtain a color.
3. Observe the colors of the various samples. The colors that indicate acidic solutions are the red and pink colors (pH 1–4) and the pink to lavender colors (pH 5–6). A neutral solution has about the same purple color as the indicator. Bases will give blue to green color (pH 8–11) or a yellow color (pH 12–13).
4. Arrange your samples by color and pH. Classify each of the solutions as acidic (pH 1–6), neutral (pH 7), or basic (pH 8–13).
5. Try to make an indicator using other colorful fruits or flowers.

### QUESTIONS

1. Which products that tested acidic listed an acid on their labels?
2. Which products that tested basic listed a base on their labels?
3. How many products were neutral?
4. Which flowers or vegetables behaved as indicators?

# 10.5 Reactions of Acids and Bases

**LEARNING GOAL**

Write balanced equations for reactions of acids with metals, carbonates, and bases.

Typical reactions of acids and bases include the reactions of acids with metals, bases, and carbonate or bicarbonate ions. For example, when you drop an antacid tablet in water, the bicarbonate ion and citric acid in the tablet react to produce carbon dioxide bubbles, a salt, and water.

## Acids and Metals

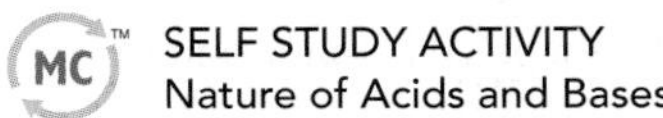

SELF STUDY ACTIVITY
Nature of Acids and Bases

Acids react with certain metals to produce hydrogen gas ($H_2$) and a salt, which is an ionic compound that does not contain $H^+$ or $OH^-$. Metals that react with acids include potassium, sodium, calcium, magnesium, aluminum, zinc, iron, and tin. In these single replacement reactions, the metal ion replaces the hydrogen in the acid:

$$\underset{\text{Metal}}{Mg(s)} + \underset{\text{Acid}}{2HCl(aq)} \longrightarrow \underset{\text{Salt}}{MgCl_2(aq)} + \underset{\text{Hydrogen}}{H_2(g)}$$

$$\underset{\text{Metal}}{Zn(s)} + \underset{\text{Acid}}{2HCl(aq)} \longrightarrow \underset{\text{Salt}}{ZnCl_2(aq)} + \underset{\text{Hydrogen}}{H_2(g)}$$

## Acids and Carbonates

When an acid is added to a carbonate or bicarbonate (hydrogen carbonate), the products are carbon dioxide gas, water, and an ionic compound (salt). The acid reacts with $CO_3^{2-}$ or $HCO_3^-$ to produce carbonic acid, $H_2CO_3$, which breaks down rapidly to $CO_2$ and $H_2O$. The net ionic equation is written by omitting the metal ions and chloride ions that are not reacting:

$$\underset{\text{Acid}}{2HCl(aq)} + \underset{\text{Carbonate}}{Na_2CO_3(aq)} \longrightarrow \underset{\text{Carbon dioxide}}{CO_2(g)} + \underset{\text{Water}}{H_2O(l)} + \underset{\text{Salt}}{2NaCl(aq)}$$

$$\underset{\text{Acid}}{HCl(aq)} + \underset{\text{Bicarbonate}}{NaHCO_3(aq)} \longrightarrow \underset{\text{Carbon dioxide}}{CO_2(g)} + \underset{\text{Water}}{H_2O(l)} + \underset{\text{Salt}}{NaCl(aq)}$$

## Green Chemistry Note

### Acid Rain

Natural rain is slightly acidic, with a pH of 5.6. In the atmosphere, carbon dioxide combines with water to form carbonic acid, a weak acid, which dissociates to give hydronium ions and bicarbonate:

$$CO_2(g) + H_2O(l) \rightleftharpoons H_2CO_3(aq)$$
$$H_2CO_3(aq) + H_2O(l) \rightleftharpoons H_3O^+(aq) + HCO_3^-(aq)$$

However, in many parts of the world, rain has become considerably more acidic. *Acid rain* is a term given to precipitation such as rain, snow, hail, or fog in which the water has a pH that is less than 5.6. In the United States, pH values of rain have decreased to about 4–4.5. In some parts of the world, pH values have been reported as low as 2.6, which is about as acidic as lemon juice or vinegar. Because the calculation of pH involves powers of 10, a pH value of 2.6 would be 1000 times more acidic than natural rain.

Although natural sources such as volcanoes and forest fires release $SO_2$, the primary sources of acid rain today are from the burning of fossil fuels in automobiles and coal in industrial plants. When coal and oil are burned, the sulfur impurities combine with oxygen in the air to produce $SO_2$ and $SO_3$. The reaction of $SO_3$ with water forms sulfuric acid, $H_2SO_4$, a strong acid:

$$S(g) + O_2(g) \longrightarrow SO_2(g)$$
$$2SO_2(g) + O_2(g) \longrightarrow 2SO_3(g)$$
$$SO_3(g) + H_2O(l) \longrightarrow H_2SO_4(aq)$$

In an effort to decrease the formation of acid rain, legislation has required a reduction in $SO_2$ emissions. Coal-burning plants have installed equipment called "scrubbers" that absorb $SO_2$ before it is emitted. In a smokestack, "scrubbing" removes 95% of the $SO_2$ as the flue gases containing $SO_2$ pass through limestone ($CaCO_3$) and water. The end product, $CaSO_4$, also called "gypsum," is used in agriculture and to prepare cement products.

Nitrogen oxide forms at high temperatures in the engines of automobiles as air containing nitrogen and oxygen gases is burned. As nitrogen oxide is emitted into the air, it combines with more oxygen to form nitrogen dioxide, which is responsible for the brown color of smog. When nitrogen dioxide dissolves in water in the atmosphere, nitric acid, a strong acid, forms:

$$N_2(g) + O_2(g) \longrightarrow 2NO(g)$$
$$2NO(g) + O_2(g) \longrightarrow 2NO_2(g)$$
$$3NO_2(g) + H_2O(g) \longrightarrow 2HNO_3(aq) + NO(g)$$

Air currents in the atmosphere carry the sulfuric acid and nitric acid many thousands of kilometers before they precipitate in areas far away from the site of the initial contamination. The acids in acid rain have detrimental effects on marble and limestone structures, lakes, and forests. Throughout the world, monuments made of marble (a form of $CaCO_3$) are deteriorating as acid rain dissolves the marble:

1994

Marble statue in Washington Square Park

$$CaCO_3(s) + H_2SO_4(aq) \longrightarrow CaSO_4(aq) + H_2O(l) + CO_2(g)$$

Acid rain is also changing the pH of many lakes and streams in parts of the United States and Europe. When the pH of a lake falls below 4.5–5, most fish and plant life cannot survive. As the soil near a lake becomes more acidic, aluminum becomes more soluble. Increased levels of aluminum ion in lakes are toxic to fish and other water animals.

Trees and forests are susceptible to acid rain, too. Acid rain breaks down the protective waxy coating on leaves and interferes with photosynthesis. Tree growth is impaired as nutrients and minerals in the soil dissolve and wash away. In Eastern Europe, acid rain is causing an environmental disaster. Nearly 70% of the forests in the Czech Republic have been severely damaged, and some parts of the land are so acidic that crops will not grow.

## Acids and Bases

In a reaction called **neutralization**, acids react with bases to produce a salt and water. The $H^+$ of an acid and the $OH^-$ of a strong base combine to form water as one product. The salt is the cation from the base and the anion from the acid. We can write the following equation for the neutralization reaction between HCl and NaOH:

$$\underset{\text{Acid}}{HCl(aq)} + \underset{\text{Base}}{NaOH(aq)} \longrightarrow \underset{\text{Salt}}{NaCl(aq)} + \underset{\text{Water}}{H_2O(l)}$$

If we write the strong acid HCl and the strong base NaOH as ions, we see that $H^+$ combines with $OH^-$ to form water, leaving the ions $Na^+$ and $Cl^-$ in solution:

$$H^+(aq) + Cl^-(aq) + Na^+(aq) + OH^-(aq) \longrightarrow Na^+(aq) + Cl^-(aq) + H_2O(l) \quad \text{Ionic equation}$$

Now we omit the ions that do not change during the reaction (spectator ions):

$$H^+(aq) + \cancel{Cl^-(aq)} + \cancel{Na^+(aq)} + OH^-(aq) \longrightarrow \cancel{Na^+(aq)} + \cancel{Cl^-(aq)} + H_2O(l)$$

The *net ionic equation* for the neutralization is the reaction of $H^+$ and $OH^-$ to form $H_2O$:

$$H^+(aq) + OH^-(aq) \longrightarrow H_2O(l) \quad \text{Net ionic equation}$$

## Balancing Neutralization Equations

In a neutralization reaction, one $H^+$ always combines with one $OH^-$. Therefore, coefficients are needed to balance $H^+$ in the acid with the $OH^-$ in the base. We balance the neutralization of HCl and $Ba(OH)_2$ as follows:

**STEP 1** **Write the reactants and products:**

$$HCl(aq) + Ba(OH)_2(s) \longrightarrow H_2O(l) + \text{salt}$$

**STEP 2** **Balance the $H^+$ in the acid with the $OH^-$ in the base.** Placing a 2 in front of the HCl provides $2H^+$ for the $2OH^-$ in $Ba(OH)_2$:

$$2HCl(aq) + Ba(OH)_2(s) \longrightarrow H_2O(l) + \text{salt}$$

**STEP 3** **Balance the $H_2O$ with the $H^+$ and $OH^-$.** Use a coefficient of 2 in front of $H_2O$ to balance $2H^+$ and $2OH^-$.

$$2HCl(aq) + Ba(OH)_2(s) \longrightarrow \mathbf{2}H_2O(l) + \text{salt}$$

**STEP 4** **Write the salt from the remaining ions in the acid and base.** The ions $Ba^{2+}$ and $2Cl^-$ are used to write the formula of the salt as $BaCl_2$:

$$\mathbf{2HCl}(aq) + \mathbf{Ba}(OH)_2(s) \longrightarrow 2H_2O(l) + \mathbf{BaCl_2}(aq)$$

SAMPLE PROBLEM **10.11**

### Reactions of Acids

Write a balanced equation for the reaction of HCl(*aq*) with each of the following:

**a.** Al(*s*) **b.** $K_2CO_3(s)$ **c.** $Mg(OH)_2(s)$

SOLUTION

**a.** Al

**STEP 1** **Write the reactants and products.** When a metal reacts with an acid, the products are $H_2$ gas and a salt:

$$Al(s) + HCl(aq) \longrightarrow H_2(g) + \text{salt}$$

**STEP 2** **Determine the formula of the salt.** When Al(*s*) dissolves, it forms $Al^{3+}$, which is balanced by $3Cl^-$ from HCl:

$$\mathbf{Al}(s) + \mathbf{HCl}(aq) \longrightarrow H_2(g) + \mathbf{AlCl_3}(aq)$$

**STEP 3** **Balance the equation:**

$$\mathbf{2}Al(s) + \mathbf{6}HCl(aq) \longrightarrow \mathbf{3}H_2(g) + \mathbf{2}AlCl_3(aq)$$

**b.** $K_2CO_3$

**STEP 1** **Write the reactants and products.** When a carbonate reacts with an acid, the products are $CO_2(g)$, $H_2O(l)$, and a salt:

$$K_2CO_3(s) + HCl(aq) \longrightarrow CO_2(g) + H_2O(l) + \text{salt}$$

**STEP 2** **Determine the formula of the salt.** When $K_2CO_3(s)$ dissolves, it forms $K^+$, which is balanced by $1Cl^-$ from HCl:

$$K_2CO_3(s) + \mathbf{HCl}(aq) \longrightarrow CO_2(g) + H_2O(l) + \mathbf{KCl}(aq)$$

**STEP 3** **Balance the equation.** A coefficient of 2 in front of KCl balances the 2K in $K_2CO_3$, and a coefficient of 2 in front of HCl balances the 2 Cl in 2KCl:

$$K_2CO_3(s) + \mathbf{2}HCl(aq) \longrightarrow CO_2(g) + H_2O(l) + \mathbf{2}KCl(aq)$$

**c.** $Mg(OH)_2$

Guide to Balancing an Equation for Neutralization

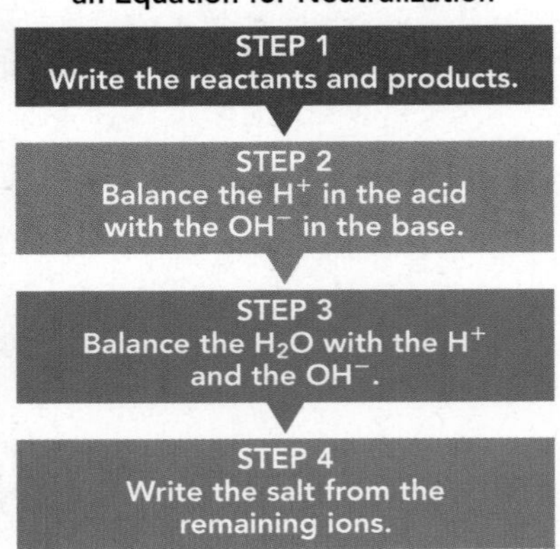
STEP 1
Write the reactants and products.
STEP 2
Balance the H+ in the acid with the OH− in the base.
STEP 3
Balance the H2O with the H+ and the OH−.
STEP 4
Write the salt from the remaining ions.

**STEP 1** **Write the reactants and products.** When a base reacts with an acid, the products are $H_2O(l)$ and a salt:

$$Mg(OH)_2(s) + HCl(aq) \longrightarrow H_2O(l) + \text{salt}$$

**STEP 2** **Balance the $H^+$ in the acid with the $OH^-$ in the base.** Placing a 2 in front of the HCl provides $2H^+$ for $2OH^-$ in $Mg(OH)_2$:

$$Mg(OH)_2(s) + \mathbf{2HCl}(aq) \longrightarrow H_2O(l) + \text{salt}$$

**STEP 3** **Balance the $H_2O$ with the $H^+$ and $OH^-$:**

$$Mg(OH)_2(s) + 2HCl(aq) \longrightarrow \mathbf{2H_2O}(l) + \text{salt}$$

**STEP 4** **Write the salt from the remaining ions in the acid and base:**

$$\mathbf{Mg}(OH)_2(s) + \mathbf{2HCl}(aq) \longrightarrow 2H_2O(l) + \mathbf{MgCl_2}(aq)$$

STUDY CHECK

Write the balanced equation for the reaction between $H_2SO_4$ and $NaHCO_3$.

## Acid–Base Titration

Suppose we need to find the molarity of an HCl solution of unknown concentration. We can do this by a laboratory procedure called **titration** in which we neutralize an acid sample with a known amount of base. In our titration, we first place a measured volume of the acid in a flask and add a few drops of an *indicator* such as phenolphthalein. An indicator is a compound that dramatically changes color when the pH of the solution changes. In an acidic solution, phenolphthalein is colorless. Then we fill a buret with a NaOH solution of known molarity and carefully add NaOH to the acid in the flask, as shown in Figure 10.6.

In the titration, we neutralize the acid by adding a volume of base that contains a matching number of moles of $OH^-$. We know that neutralization has taken place when the

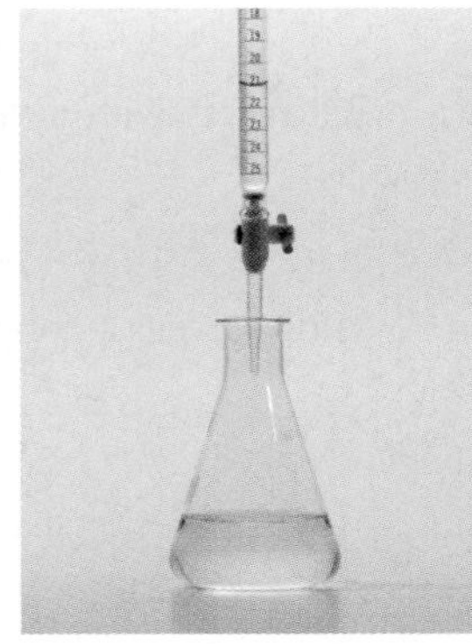

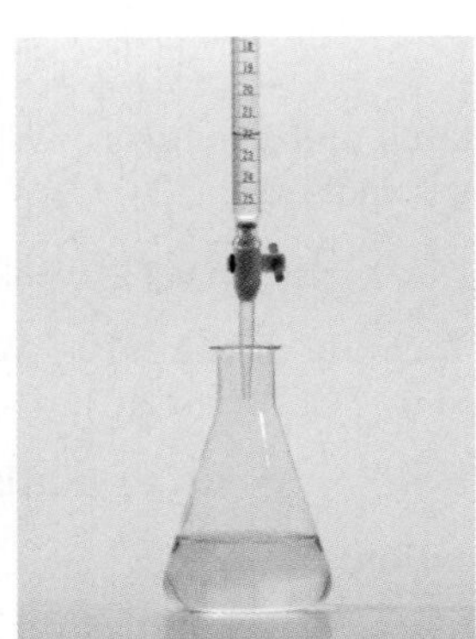

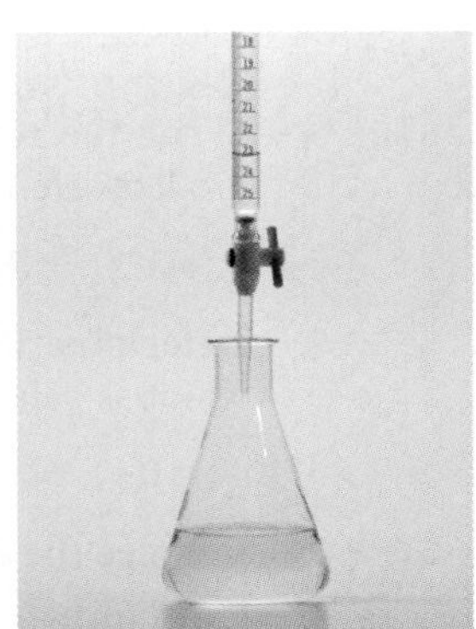

FIGURE 10.6 The titration of an acid. A known volume of an acid is placed in a flask with an indicator and titrated with a measured volume of NaOH to the neutralization point.

Q What data is needed to determine the molarity of the acid in the flask?

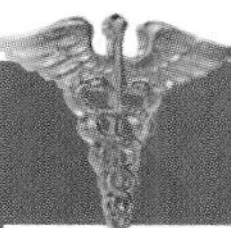

## HEALTH NOTE

### Antacids

Antacids are substances used to neutralize excess stomach acid (HCl). Some antacids are mixtures of aluminum hydroxide and magnesium hydroxide. These hydroxides are not very soluble in water, so the levels of available $OH^-$ are not damaging to the intestinal tract. However, aluminum hydroxide has the side effects of producing constipation and binding phosphate in the intestinal tract, which may cause weakness and loss of appetite. Magnesium hydroxide has a laxative effect. These side effects are less likely when a combination of the antacids is used.

$$Al(OH)_3(aq) + 3HCl(aq) \longrightarrow AlCl_3(aq) + 3H_2O(l)$$

$$Mg(OH)_2(s) + 2HCl(aq) \longrightarrow MgCl_2(aq) + 2H_2O(l)$$

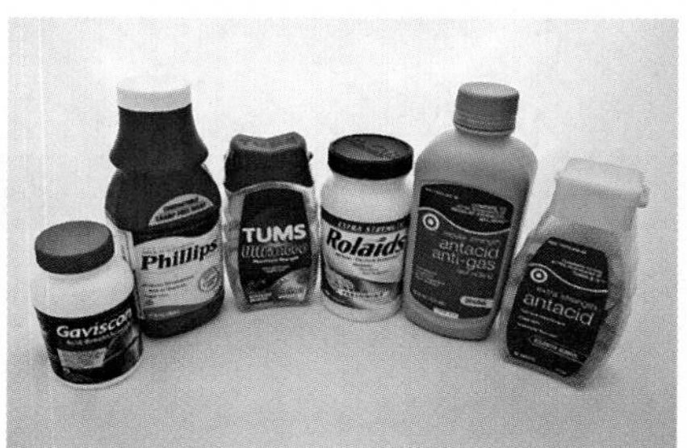


Some antacids use calcium carbonate to neutralize excess stomach acid. About 10% of the calcium is absorbed into the bloodstream, where it elevates the levels of serum calcium. Calcium carbonate is not recommended for patients who have peptic ulcers or a tendency to form kidney stones.

$$CaCO_3(s) + 2HCl(aq) \longrightarrow H_2O(l) + CO_2(g) + CaCl_2(aq)$$

Still other antacids contain sodium bicarbonate. This type of antacid has a tendency to increase blood pH and elevate sodium levels in the body fluids. It also is not recommended in the treatment of peptic ulcers.

$$NaHCO_3(s) + HCl(aq) \longrightarrow NaCl(aq) + CO_2(g) + H_2O(l)$$

The neutralizing substances in some antacid preparations are given in Table 10.8.

**TABLE 10.8** Basic Compounds in Some Antacids

| Antacid | Base(s) |
|---|---|
| Amphojel | $Al(OH)_3$ |
| Milk of magnesia | $Mg(OH)_2$ |
| Mylanta, Maalox, Di-Gel, Gelusil, Riopan | $Mg(OH)_2$, $Al(OH)_3$ |
| Bisodol, Rolaids | $CaCO_3$, $Mg(OH)_2$ |
| Titralac, Tums, Pepto-Bismol | $CaCO_3$ |
| Alka-Seltzer | $NaHCO_3$, $KHCO_3$ |

phenolphthalein in the solution changes from colorless to pink. This is called the neutralization *endpoint*. From the volume added and molarity of the NaOH, we can calculate the number of moles of NaOH and then the concentration of the acid.

**SAMPLE PROBLEM 10.12**

### Titration of an Acid

A 25.0-mL sample of an HCl solution is placed in a flask with a few drops of phenolphthalein (indicator). If 32.6 mL of a 0.185 M NaOH solution is needed to reach the endpoint, what is the concentration (M) of the HCl solution?

$$NaOH(aq) + HCl(aq) \longrightarrow NaCl(aq) + H_2O(l)$$

SOLUTION

**STEP 1** **Given** 32.6 mL of 0.185 M NaOH; 25.0 mL of HCl = 0.0250 L of HCl
**Need** molarity of HCl

**STEP 2** **Plan**

mL of NaOH solution → [Metric factor] → L → [Molarity factor] → moles of NaOH → [Mole-mole factor] → moles of HCl → [Divide by liters] → M HCl solution

**STEP 3** **Equalities/Conversion Factors**

1 L of NaOH = 1000 mL of NaOH

$$\frac{1\ L}{1000\ mL} \text{ and } \frac{1000\ mL}{1\ L}$$

1 L of NaOH = 0.185 mole of NaOH

$$\frac{1\ L}{0.185\ mole\ NaOH} \text{ and } \frac{0.185\ mole\ NaOH}{1\ L}$$

1 mole of HCl = 1 mole of NaOH

$$\frac{1\ mole\ HCl}{1\ mole\ NaOH} \text{ and } \frac{1\ mole\ NaOH}{1\ mole\ HCl}$$

**STEP 4** **Set Up Problem**

$$32.6\ \cancel{\text{mL NaOH}}\ \text{solution} \times \frac{1\ \cancel{\text{L NaOH}}}{1000\ \cancel{\text{mL NaOH}}} \times \frac{0.185\ \cancel{\text{mole NaOH}}}{1\ \cancel{\text{L NaOH}}} \times \frac{1\ \text{mole HCl}}{1\ \cancel{\text{mole NaOH}}}$$

$$= 0.00603\ \text{mole of HCl solution}$$

$$\text{Molarity HCl} = \frac{0.00603\ \text{mole HCl}}{0.0250\ \text{L HCl}} = 0.241\ \text{M HCl solution}$$

**Guide to Calculations for an Acid–Base Titration**

STEP 1 State the given and needed quantities and concentrations.

STEP 2 Write a plan to calculate molarity or volume.

STEP 3 State equalities and conversion factors, including concentration.

STEP 4 Set up problem to calculate needed quantity.

STUDY CHECK

What is the molarity of an HCl solution if 28.6 mL of a 0.175 M NaOH solution is needed to neutralize a 25.0-mL sample of the HCl solution?

## QUESTIONS AND PROBLEMS

### Reactions of Acids and Bases

**10.47** Complete and balance the equation for each of the following reactions:

**a.** $ZnCO_3(s) + HBr(aq) \longrightarrow$

**b.** $Zn(s) + HCl(aq) \longrightarrow$

**c.** $HCl(aq) + NaHCO_3(s) \longrightarrow$

**d.** $H_2SO_4(aq) + Mg(OH)_2(s) \longrightarrow$

**10.48** Complete and balance the equations for each of the following reactions:

**a.** $KHCO_3(s) + HCl(aq) \longrightarrow$

**b.** $Ca(s) + H_2SO_4(aq) \longrightarrow$

**c.** $HNO_3(aq) + Al(OH)_3(s) \longrightarrow$

**d.** $Na_2CO_3(s) + H_2SO_4(aq)$

**10.49** Balance each of the following neutralization reactions:

**a.** $HCl(aq) + Mg(OH)_2(s) \longrightarrow MgCl_2(aq) + H_2O(l)$

**b.** $H_3PO_4(aq) + LiOH(aq) \longrightarrow Li_3PO_4(aq) + H_2O(l)$

**10.50** Balance each of the following neutralization reactions:

**a.** $HNO_3(aq) + Ba(OH)_2(s) \longrightarrow Ba(NO_3)_2(aq) + H_2O(l)$

**b.** $H_2SO_4(aq) + Al(OH)_3(s) \longrightarrow Al_2(SO_4)_3(aq) + H_2O(l)$

**10.51** Write a balanced equation for the neutralization of each of the following:

**a.** $H_2SO_4(aq)$ and $NaOH(aq)$

**b.** $HCl(aq)$ and $Fe(OH)_3(s)$

**c.** $H_2CO_3(aq)$ and $Mg(OH)_2(s)$

**10.52** Write a balanced equation for the neutralization of each of the following:

**a.** $H_3PO_4(aq)$ and $NaOH(aq)$

**b.** $HI(aq)$ and $LiOH(aq)$

**c.** $HNO_3(aq)$ and $Ca(OH)_2(s)$

**10.53** What is the molarity of an HCl solution if 5.00 mL of a HCl solution is titrated with 28.6 mL of a 0.145 M NaOH solution?

$$HCl(aq) + NaOH(aq) \longrightarrow NaCl(aq) + H_2O(l)$$

**10.54** If 29.7 mL of 0.205 M KOH is required to completely neutralize 25.0 mL of a $HC_2H_3O_2$ solution, what is the molarity of the acetic acid solution?

$$HC_2H_3O_2(aq) + KOH(aq) \longrightarrow KC_2H_3O_2(aq) + H_2O(l)$$

**10.55** If 38.2 mL of 0.163 M KOH is required to neutralize completely 25.0 mL of a $H_2SO_4$ solution, what is the molarity of the acid solution?

$$H_2SO_4(aq) + 2KOH(aq) \longrightarrow K_2SO_4(aq) + 2H_2O(l)$$

**10.56** A solution of 0.162 M NaOH is used to neutralize 25.0 mL of a $H_2SO_4$ solution. If 32.8 mL of a NaOH solution is required to reach the endpoint, what is the molarity of the $H_2SO_4$ solution?

$$H_2SO_4(aq) + 2NaOH(aq) \longrightarrow Na_2SO_4(aq) + 2H_2O(l)$$

**10.57** A solution of 0.204 M NaOH is used to neutralize 50.0 mL of a $H_3PO_4$ solution. If 16.4 mL of a NaOH solution is required to reach the endpoint, what is the molarity of the $H_3PO_4$ solution?

$$H_3PO_4(aq) + 3NaOH(aq) \longrightarrow Na_3PO_4(aq) + 3H_2O(l)$$

**10.58** A solution of 0.312 M KOH is used to neutralize 15.0 mL of a $H_3PO_4$ solution. If 28.3 mL of a KOH solution is required to reach the endpoint, what is the molarity of the $H_3PO_4$ solution?

$$H_3PO_4(aq) + 3KOH(aq) \longrightarrow K_3PO_4(aq) + 3H_2O(l)$$

## 10.6 Acid–Base Properties of Salt Solutions

**LEARNING GOAL**

Predict whether a salt will form an acidic, basic, or neutral solution.

When a salt dissolves in water, it dissociates into cations and anions. Solutions of salts can be acidic, basic, or neutral. Anions and cations from strong acids and bases do not affect pH; however, anions from weak acids and cations from weak bases change the pH of an aqueous solution.

### Salts That Form Neutral Solutions

*A solution of a salt containing a cation from a strong base and an anion from a strong acid will be neutral.* For example, a salt such as $NaNO_3$ forms a neutral solution:

$$NaNO_3(s) \xrightarrow{H_2O} \underset{\text{Does not change H}^+}{Na^+(aq)} + \underset{\text{Does not attract H}^+\text{ from water}}{NO_3^-(aq)}$$

Neutral solution (pH = 7.0)

The cation, $Na^+$, from the strong base NaOH does not change the $H^+$ concentration and the anion, $NO_3^-$, from the strong acid $HNO_3$ does not attract $H^+$ from water. Thus, there is no effect on the pH of water; the solution is neutral, with a pH of 7.0. Salts such as NaCl, KCl, $KNO_3$, and KBr contain cations from strong bases and anions from strong acids and form neutral solutions.

**Some Components of Neutral Salt Solutions**

Cations of strong bases: Group 1A (1): $Li^+$, $Na^+$, $K^+$
Group 2A (2): $Ca^{2+}$, $Mg^{2+}$, $Sr^{2+}$, $Ba^{2+}$

Anions of strong acids: $Cl^-$, $Br^-$, $I^-$, $NO_3^-$, $ClO_4^-$

### Salts That Form Basic Solutions

*A salt solution containing the cation from a strong base and the anion from a weak acid produces a basic solution.* Suppose we have a solution of the salt NaF, which contains $Na^+$ and $F^-$ ions:

$$NaF(s) \xrightarrow{H_2O} \underset{\text{Does not change H}^+}{Na^+(aq)} + \underset{\text{Attracts H}^+\text{ from water}}{F^-(aq)}$$

The metal ion $Na^+$ has no effect on the pH of the solution. However, $F^-$ is the conjugate base of the weak acid HF. Thus, $F^-$ will attract a proton from water and form $OH^-$ in solution, which makes it basic:

$$F^-(aq) + H_2O(l) \rightleftarrows HF(aq) + OH^-(aq) \quad \text{Basic solution (pH > 7.0)}$$

Other salts with anions from weak acids such as NaCN, $KNO_2$, and $Na_2SO_4$ also produce basic solutions.

**Some Components of Basic Salt Solutions**

Cations of strong bases: Group 1A (1): $Li^+$, $Na^+$, $K^+$
Group 2A (2): $Ca^{2+}$, $Mg^{2+}$, $Sr^{2+}$, $Ba^{2+}$

Anions of weak acids: $F^-$, $NO_2^-$, $CN^-$, $CO_3^{2-}$, $SO_4^{2-}$, $C_2H_3O_2^-$, $S^{2-}$, $PO_4^{3-}$

### Salts That Form Acidic Solutions

MC™ TUTORIAL Salts of Weak Acids and Bases

*A salt solution containing a cation from a weak base and an anion from a strong acid produces an acidic solution.* Suppose we have a solution of the salt $NH_4Cl$, which contains $NH_4^+$ and $Cl^-$ ions:

$$NH_4Cl(s) \xrightarrow{H_2O} \underset{\text{Donates H}^+\text{ to water}}{NH_4^+(aq)} + \underset{\text{Does not attract H}^+\text{ from water}}{Cl^-(aq)}$$

**TABLE 10.9** Cations and Anions of Salts in Neutral, Basic, and Acidic Salt Solutions

| Type of Solution | Cations | Anions | pH |
|---|---|---|---|
| **Neutral** | From strong bases: Group 1A (1): $Li^+$, $Na^+$, $K^+$ Group 2A (2): $Ca^{2+}$, $Mg^{2+}$, $Sr^{2+}$, $Ba^{2+}$ (but not $Be^{2+}$) | From strong acids: $Cl^-$, $Br^-$, $I^-$, $NO_3^-$, $ClO_4^-$ | 7.0 |
| **Basic** | From strong bases: Group 1A (1): $Li^+$, $Na^+$, $K^+$ Group 2A (2): $Ca^{2+}$, $Mg^{2+}$, $Sr^{2+}$, $Ba^{2+}$ (but not $Be^{2+}$) | From weak acids: $F^-$, $NO_2^-$, $CN^-$, $CO_3^{2-}$, $SO_4^{2-}$, $C_2H_3O_2^-$, $S^{2-}$, $PO_4^{3-}$ | $> 7.0$ |
| **Acidic** | From weak bases: $NH_4^+$ and $Be^{2+}$, $Al^{3+}$, $Zn^{2+}$, $Cr^{3+}$, $Fe^{3+}$ (small, highly charged metal ions) | From strong acids: $Cl^-$, $Br^-$, $I^-$, $NO_3^-$, $ClO_4^-$ | $< 7.0$ |

The anion $Cl^-$ has no effect on the pH of the solution. However, as a weak acid, the cation $NH_4^+$ donates a proton to water, which produces $H_3O^+$:

$$NH_4^+(aq) + H_2O(l) \rightleftharpoons NH_3(aq) + H_3O^+(aq) \quad \text{Acidic solution (pH} < 7.0)$$

**Some Components of Acidic Salt Solutions**

Cations of weak bases: $NH_4^+$ and $Be^{2+}$, $Al^{3+}$, $Zn^{2+}$, $Cr^{3+}$, $Fe^{3+}$ (small, highly charged metal ions)

Anions of strong acids: $Cl^-$, $Br^-$, $I^-$, $NO_3^-$, $ClO_4^-$

Table 10.9 summarizes the cations and anions of salts that form neutral, basic, and acidic solutions. Table 10.10 summarizes the acid–base properties of some typical salts in water.

Sometimes a salt contains the cation of a weak base and the anion of a weak acid. For example, when $NH_4F$ dissociates in water, it produces $NH_4^+$ and $F^-$. We have seen that $NH_4^+$ forms an acidic solution and $F^-$ forms a basic solution. The ion that reacts to a greater extent with water determines whether the solution is acidic or basic. The salt solution will be neutral only if the ions react with water to the same extent. The determination of these reactions is complex and will not be considered in this text.

**TABLE 10.10** Acid–Base Properties of Some Salt Solutions

| Typical Salts | Types of Ions | pH | Solution |
|---|---|---|---|
| $NaCl$, $MgBr_2$, $KNO_3$ | Cation from a strong base Anion from a strong acid | 7.0 | Neutral |
| $NaF$, $MgCO_3$, $KNO_2$ | Cation from a strong base Anion from a weak acid | $>7.0$ | Basic |
| $NH_4Cl$, $FeBr_3$, $Al(NO_3)_3$ | Cation from a weak base Anion from a strong acid | $<7.0$ | Acidic |

SAMPLE PROBLEM 10.13

## Predicting the Acid–Base Properties of Salt Solutions

Predict whether solutions of each of the following salts would be acidic, basic, or neutral:

**a.** KCN **b.** $NH_4Br$ **c.** $NaNO_3$

SOLUTION

**a.** KCN

There are only six strong acids; all other acids are weak. Bases with cations from Groups 1A (1) and 2A (2) are strong; all other bases are weak. For the salt

KCN, the cation is from a strong base (KOH), but the anion is from a weak acid (HCN):

$$KCN(s) \xrightarrow{H_2O} K^+(aq) + CN^-(aq)$$

The cation $K^+$ has no effect on pH. However, the anion $CN^-$ will attract protons from water to produce a basic solution:

$$CN^-(aq) + H_2O(l) \rightleftarrows HCN(aq) + OH^-(aq)$$

**b.** $NH_4Br$
In the salt $NH_4Br$, the cation is from a weak base, $NH_3$, but the anion is from a strong acid, HBr:

$$NH_4Br(s) \xrightarrow{H_2O} NH_4^+(aq) + Br^-(aq)$$

The anion $Br^-$ has no effect on pH because it is from HBr, a strong acid. However, the cation $NH_4^+$ will donate protons to water to produce an acidic solution:

$$NH_4^+(aq) + H_2O(l) \rightleftarrows NH_3(aq) + H_3O^+(aq)$$

**c.** $NaNO_3$
The salt $NaNO_3$ contains a cation from a strong base (NaOH) and an anion from a strong acid ($HNO_3$). Thus, there is no change of pH; the salt solution is neutral:

$$NaNO_3(s) \xrightarrow{H_2O} Na^+(aq) + NO_3^-(aq)$$

STUDY CHECK

Would a solution of $Na_3PO_4$ be acidic, basic, or neutral?

## QUESTIONS AND PROBLEMS

### Acid–Base Properties of Salt Solutions

**10.59** Why does a salt containing a cation from a strong base and an anion from a weak acid form a basic solution?

**10.60** Why does a salt containing a cation from a weak base and an anion from a strong acid form an acidic solution?

**10.61** Predict whether each of the following salts will form an acidic, basic, or neutral solution. For acidic and basic solutions, write an equation for the reaction that takes place.
**a.** $MgCl_2$ **b.** $NH_4NO_3$ **c.** $Na_2CO_3$ **d.** $K_2S$

**10.62** Predict whether each of the following salts will form an acidic, basic, or neutral solution. For acidic and basic solutions, write an equation for the reaction that takes place.
**a.** $Na_2SO_4$ **b.** KBr **c.** $BaCl_2$ **d.** $NH_4I$

# 10.7 Buffers

LEARNING GOAL

Describe the role of buffers in maintaining the pH of a solution.

The pH of water and most solutions changes drastically when a small amount of acid or base is added. However, if a solution is buffered, there is little change in pH. A **buffer solution** is a solution that maintains pH by neutralizing added acid or base. For example, blood contains buffers that maintain a consistent pH of about 7.4. If the pH of the blood goes slightly above or below 7.4, changes in our oxygen levels and our metabolic processess can be drastic enough to cause death. Even though we obtain acids and bases from foods and cellular reactions, the buffers in the body absorb those compounds so effectively that the pH of the blood remains essentially unchanged. (See Figure 10.7.)

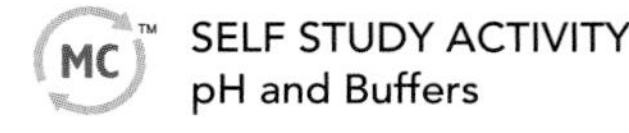


In a buffer, an acid must be present to react with any $OH^-$ that is added, and a base must be available to react with any added $H_3O^+$. However, that acid and base must not neutralize each other. Therefore, a combination of an acid–base conjugate pair is used in buffers.

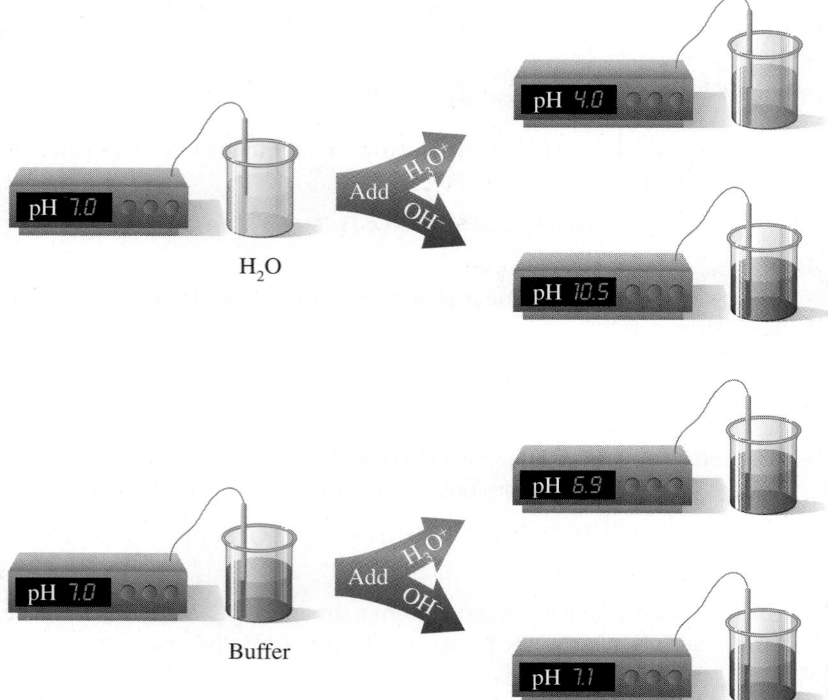


**FIGURE 10.7** Adding an acid or a base to water changes the pH drastically, but a buffer resists pH change when small amounts of acid or base are added.

**Q** Why does the pH change several pH units when acid is added to water but not when acid is added to a buffer?

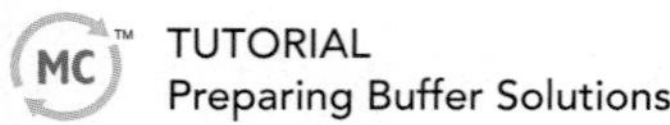


TUTORIAL
Preparing Buffer Solutions

Most buffer solutions consist of nearly equal concentrations of a weak acid and a salt containing its conjugate base. (See Figure 10.8.) Buffers may also contain a weak base and the salt of the weak base, which contains its conjugate acid.

For example, a buffer can be made from the weak acid acetic acid ($HC_2H_3O_2$), and its salt, sodium acetate ($NaC_2H_3O_2$). As a weak acid, acetic acid dissociates slightly in water to form $H_3O^+$ and a very small amount of $C_2H_3O_2^-$. The presence of sodium acetate provides a much larger concentration of acetate ion ($C_2H_3O_2^-$), which is necessary for its buffering capability:

$$\underset{\text{Large amount}}{HC_2H_3O_2(aq)} + H_2O(l) \rightleftharpoons H_3O^+(aq) + \underset{\text{Large amount}}{C_2H_3O_2^-(aq)}$$

Let's see how this buffer solution maintains the $H_3O^+$ concentration. When a small amount of acid is added, it will combine with the acetate ion (anion) as the equilibrium shifts to the reactant acetic acid. There will be a small decrease in the $[C_2H_3O_2^-]$ and a small increase in $[HC_2H_3O_2]$, but the $[H_3O^+]$ will not change very much:

$$HC_2H_3O_2(aq) + H_2O(l) \longleftarrow H_3O^+(aq) + C_2H_3O_2^-(aq)$$

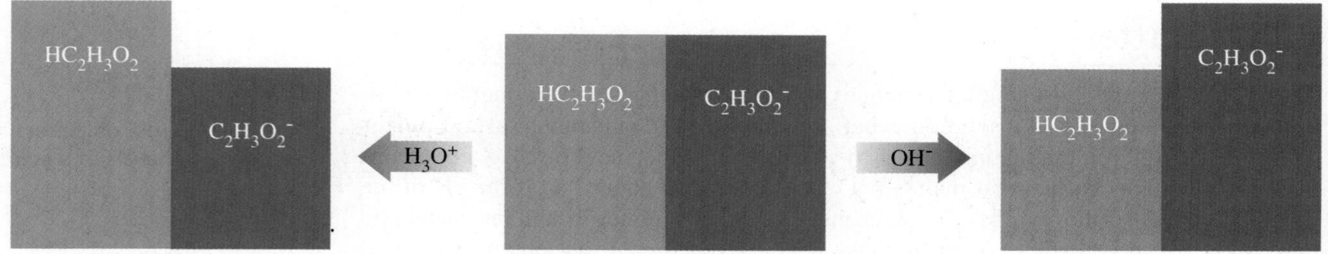


**FIGURE 10.8** The buffer described here consists of about equal concentrations of acetic acid ($HC_2H_3O_2$) and its conjugate base acetate ion ($C_2H_3O_2^-$). Adding $H_3O^+$ to the buffer uses up some $C_2H_3O_2^-$, whereas adding $OH^-$ neutralizes some $HC_2H_3O_2$. The pH of the solution is maintained as long as the added amounts of acid or base are small compared to the concentrations of the buffer components.

**Q** How does this acetic acid/acetate ion buffer maintain pH?

If a small amount of base is added to this buffer solution, it is neutralized by the acetic acid, and acetate and water are produced. The $[HC_2H_3O_2]$ decreases slightly, and the $[C_2H_3O_2^-]$ increases slightly, but again the $[H_3O^+]$ does not change very much:

$$HC_2H_3O_2(aq) + OH^-(aq) \longrightarrow H_2O(l) + C_2H_3O_2^-(aq)$$

**CONCEPT CHECK 10.6**

### Identifying Buffer Solutions

Indicate whether each of the following would make a buffer solution:

**a.** HCl (a strong acid) and NaCl
**b.** $H_3PO_4$ (a weak acid)
**c.** HF (a weak acid) and NaF

ANSWER

**a.** No. A buffer requires a weak acid, not a strong acid, and a salt containing its conjugate base.
**b.** No. A weak acid is part of a buffer, but the salt containing the conjugate base of the weak acid is also needed.
**c.** Yes. This mixture would be a buffer because it contains a weak acid and a salt containing its conjugate base $F^-$.

## Calculating the pH of a Buffer

By rearranging the $K_a$ expression to give $[H_3O^+]$, we can obtain the ratio of the acetic acid/acetate buffer:

MC TUTORIAL Calculating the pH of a Buffer

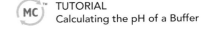

$$K_a = \frac{[H_3O^+][C_2H_3O_2^-]}{[HC_2H_3O_2]}$$

Solving for $[H_3O^+]$ gives

$$[H_3O^+] = K_a \times \frac{[HC_2H_3O_2]}{[C_2H_3O_2^-]}$$

Because $K_a$ is a constant, the $[H_3O^+]$ is determined by the $[HC_2H_3O_2]/[C_2H_3O_2^-]$ ratio. As long as the addition of small amounts of either acid or base changes the ratio of $[HC_2H_3O_2]/[C_2H_3O_2^-]$ only slightly, the changes in $[H_3O^+]$ will be small and the pH will be maintained. It is important to note that the amount of acid or base that is added must be small compared to the supply of the buffer components $HC_2H_3O_2$ and $C_2H_3O_2^-$. If a large amount of acid or base is added, the buffering capacity of the system may be exceeded.

Other buffers can be prepared from conjugate acid–base pairs such as $H_2PO_4^-/HPO_4^{2-}$, $HPO_4^{2-}/PO_4^{3-}$, $HCO_3^-/CO_3^{2-}$, or $NH_4^+/NH_3$. The pH of the buffer solution will depend on the acid–base pair chosen.

**SAMPLE PROBLEM 10.14**

### pH of a Buffer

The $K_a$ for acetic acid, $HC_2H_3O_2$, is $1.8 \times 10^{-5}$. What is the pH of a buffer prepared with 1.0 M $HC_2H_3O_2$ and 1.0 M $C_2H_3O_2^-$?

SOLUTION

$$HC_2H_3O_2(aq) + H_2O(l) \rightleftharpoons H_3O^+(aq) + C_2H_3O_2^-(aq)$$

**Guide to Calculating pH of a Buffer**

- STEP 1 Write the $K_a$ expression.
- STEP 2 Rearrange the $K_a$ for $[H_3O^+]$.
- STEP 3 Substitute in the [HA] and $[A^-]$.
- STEP 4 Use $[H_3O^+]$ to calculate pH.

STEP 1 **Write the $K_a$ expression:**

$$K_a = \frac{[H_3O^+][C_2H_3O_2^-]}{[HC_2H_3O_2]}$$

STEP 2 **Rearrange $K_a$ for $[H_3O^+]$:**

$$[H_3O^+] = K_a \times \frac{[HC_2H_3O_2]}{[C_2H_3O_2^-]}$$

STEP 3 **Substitute [HA] and $[A^-]$.** Substituting these values in the expression for $[H_3O^+]$ gives

$$[H_3O^+] = 1.8 \times 10^{-5} \times \frac{[1.0]}{[1.0]}$$

$$[H_3O^+] = 1.8 \times 10^{-5}\ M$$

STEP 4 **Use $[H_3O^+]$ to calculate pH.** Using the concentration of $[H_3O^+]$ in the pH expression gives the pH of the buffer:

$$pH = -\log[1.8 \times 10^{-5}] = 4.74$$

STUDY CHECK

The acid-base pair in a buffer is $H_2PO_4^-/HPO_4^{2-}$, which has a $K_a$ of $6.2 \times 10^{-8}$. What is the pH of a buffer that is 0.10 M $H_2PO_4^-$ and 0.50 M $HPO_4^{2-}$?

## QUESTIONS AND PROBLEMS

### Buffers

**10.63** Consider the following: (a) NaOH and NaCl, (b) $H_2CO_3$ and $NaHCO_3$, (c) HF and KF, (d) KCl and NaCl. Which of these represent a buffer system? Explain.

**10.64** Consider the following: (a) $H_3PO_4$, (b) $NaNO_3$, (c) $HC_2H_3O_2$ and $NaC_2H_3O_2$, and (d) HCl and NaOH. Which of these represent a buffer system? Explain.

**10.65** Consider the buffer system of hydrofluoric acid, HF, and its salt, NaF:

$$HF(aq) + H_2O(l) \rightleftharpoons H_3O^+(aq) + F^-(aq)$$

**a.** What is the purpose of the buffer system?
**b.** Why does a buffer require a salt that contains the same conjugate base as the acid?
**c.** How does the buffer react when some $H_3O^+$ is added?
**d.** How does the buffer react when some $OH^-$ is added?

**10.66** Consider the buffer system of nitrous acid, $HNO_2$, and its salt, $NaNO_2$:

$$HNO_2(aq) + H_2O(l) \rightleftharpoons H_3O^+(aq) + NO_2^-(aq)$$

**a.** What is the purpose of a buffer system?
**b.** What is the purpose of $NaNO_2$ in the buffer?
**c.** How does the buffer react when some $H_3O^+$ is added?
**d.** How does the buffer react when some $OH^-$ is added?

**10.67** Nitrous acid has a $K_a$ of $4.5 \times 10^{-4}$. What is the pH of a buffer solution containing 0.10 M $HNO_2$ and 0.10 M $NO_2^-$?

**10.68** Acetic acid has a $K_a$ of $1.8 \times 10^{-5}$. What is the pH of a buffer solution containing 0.15 M $HC_2H_3O_2$ (acetic acid) and 0.15 M $C_2H_3O_2^-$?

**10.69** Compare the pH of a HF buffer that contains 0.10 M HF and 0.10 M NaF with another HF buffer that contains 0.060 M HF and 0.120 M NaF. (See Table 10.4.)

**10.70** Compare the pH of a $H_2CO_3$ buffer that contains 0.10 M $H_2CO_3$ and 0.10 M $NaHCO_3$ with another $H_2CO_3$ buffer that contains 0.15 M $H_2CO_3$ and 0.050 M $NaHCO_3$. (See Table 10.4.)

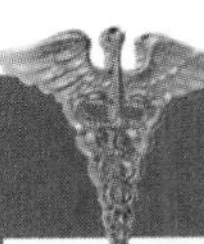

# HEALTH NOTE

## Buffers in the Blood

The arterial blood has a normal pH of 7.35–7.45. If changes in $H_3O^+$ lower the pH below 6.8 or raise it above 8.0, cells cannot function properly and death may result. In our cells, $CO_2$ is continually produced as an end product of cellular metabolism. Some $CO_2$ is carried to the lungs for elimination, and the rest dissolves in body fluids such as plasma and saliva, forming carbonic acid. As a weak acid, carbonic acid dissociates to give bicarbonate and $H_3O^+$. More of the anion $HCO_3^-$ is supplied by the kidneys to give an important buffer system in the body fluid, the $H_2CO_3/HCO_3^-$ buffer:

$$CO_2 + H_2O \rightleftharpoons H_2CO_3 \rightleftharpoons H_3O^+ + HCO_3^-$$

Excess $H_3O^+$ entering the body fluids reacts with $HCO_3^-$, and excess $OH^-$ reacts with the carbonic acid:

$$H_2CO_3(aq) + H_2O(l) \longleftarrow H_3O^+(aq) + HCO_3^-(aq)$$

Equilibrium shifts left

$$H_2CO_3(aq) + OH^-(aq) \longrightarrow H_2O(l) + HCO_3^-(aq)$$

Equilibrium shifts right

For the carbonic acid, we can write the equilibrium expression as

$$K_a = \frac{[H_3O^+][HCO_3^-]}{[H_2CO_3]}$$

To maintain the normal blood pH (7.35–7.45), the ratio of $H_2CO_3/HCO_3^-$ needs to be about 1 to 10, which is obtained by typical concentrations in the blood of 0.0024 M $H_2CO_3$ and 0.024 M $HCO_3^-$:

$$[H_3O^+] = K_a \times \frac{[H_2CO_3]}{[HCO_3^-]}$$

$$= 4.3 \times 10^{-7} \times \frac{[0.0024]}{[0.024]} = 4.3 \times 10^{-7} \times 0.10 = 4.3 \times 10^{-8}\,M$$

$$pH = -\log(4.3 \times 10^{-8}) = 7.37$$

In the body, the concentration of carbonic acid is closely associated with the partial pressure of $CO_2$. Table 10.11 lists the normal values for arterial blood. If the $CO_2$ level rises, producing more $H_2CO_3$, the equilibrium produces more $H_3O^+$, which lowers the pH. This condition is called acidosis. Difficulty with ventilation or gas diffusion can lead to respiratory acidosis, which can happen in emphysema or when an accident or depressive drugs affect the medulla of the brain.

A lowering of the $CO_2$ level leads to a high blood pH, a condition called alkalosis. Excitement, trauma, or a high temperature may cause a person to hyperventilate, which expels large amounts of $CO_2$. As the partial pressure of $CO_2$ in the blood falls below normal, the equilibrium shifts from $H_2CO_3$ to $CO_2$ and $H_2O$. This shift decreases the $[H_3O^+]$ and raises the pH. Table 10.12 lists some of the conditions that lead to changes in the blood pH and some possible treatments. The kidneys also regulate $H_3O^+$ and $HCO_3^-$ components, but they do so more slowly than the adjustment made by the lungs through ventilation.

**TABLE 10.11** Normal Values for Blood Buffer in Arterial Blood

| | |
|---|---|
| $P_{CO_2}$ | 40 mm Hg |
| $H_2CO_3$ | 2.4 mmoles/L of plasma |
| $HCO_3^-$ | 24 mmoles/L of plasma |
| pH | 7.35–7.45 |

**TABLE 10.12** Acidosis and Alkalosis: Symptoms, Causes, and Treatments

| Respiratory Acidosis: $CO_2$ ↑ pH ↓ | |
|---|---|
| Symptoms: | Failure to ventilate, suppression of breathing, disorientation, weakness, coma |
| Causes: | Lung disease blocking gas diffusion (e.g., emphysema, pneumonia, bronchitis, and asthma); depression of respiratory center by drugs, cardiopulmonary arrest, stroke, poliomyelitis, or nervous system disorders |
| Treatment: | Correction of disorder, infusion of bicarbonate |

| Metabolic Acidosis: $H^+$ ↑ pH ↓ | |
|---|---|
| Symptoms: | Increased ventilation, fatigue, confusion |
| Causes: | Renal disease, including hepatitis and cirrhosis; increased acid production in diabetes mellitus, hyperthyroidism, alcoholism, and starvation; loss of alkali in diarrhea; acid retention in renal failure |
| Treatment: | Sodium bicarbonate given orally, dialysis for renal failure, insulin treatment for diabetic ketosis |

| Respiratory Alkalosis: $CO_2$ ↓ pH ↑ | |
|---|---|
| Symptoms: | Increased rate and depth of breathing, numbness, light-headedness, tetany |
| Causes: | Hyperventilation due to anxiety, hysteria, fever, exercise; reaction to drugs such as salicylate, quinine, and antihistamines; conditions causing hypoxia (e.g., pneumonia, pulmonary edema, and heart disease) |
| Treatment: | Elimination of anxiety-producing state, rebreathing into a paper bag |

| Metabolic Alkalosis: $H^+$ ↓ pH ↑ | |
|---|---|
| Symptoms: | Depressed breathing, apathy, confusion |
| Causes: | Vomiting, diseases of the adrenal glands, ingestion of excess alkali |
| Treatment: | Infusion of saline solution, treatment of underlying diseases |

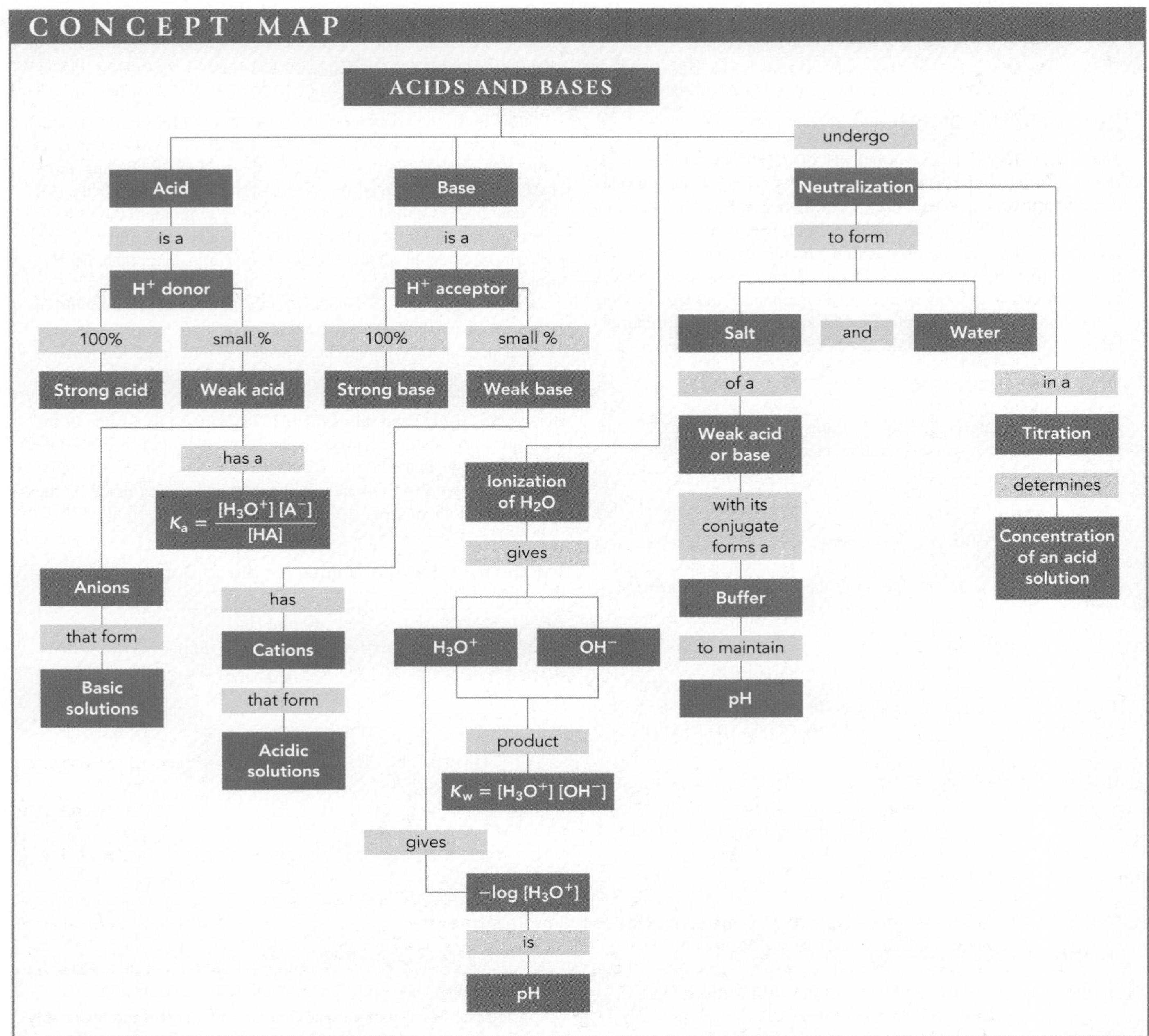


## CHAPTER REVIEW

### 10.1 Acids and Bases

**LEARNING GOAL:** *Describe and name Arrhenius and Brønsted–Lowry acids and bases; identify conjugate acid–base pairs.*

An Arrhenius acid produces $H^+$ and an Arrhenius base produces $OH^-$ in aqueous solutions. Acids taste sour, may sting, and neutralize bases. Bases taste bitter, feel slippery, and neutralize acids.

According to the Brønsted–Lowry theory, acids are proton ($H^+$) donors and bases are proton acceptors. Two conjugate acid–base pairs are present in an acid–base reaction. Each acid–base pair is related by the loss or gain of one $H^+$. For example, when the aqueous acid HF donates $H^+$, the $F^-$ it forms is its conjugate base because $F^-$ is capable of accepting $H^+$. The other acid–base pair would be $H_2O$ and $H_3O^+$:

$$HF(aq) + H_2O(l) \rightleftharpoons H_3O^+(aq) + F^-(aq)$$

### 10.2 Strengths of Acids and Bases

**LEARNING GOAL:** *Write equations for the dissociation of strong and weak acids; write the equilibrium expression for a weak acid.*

In strong acids, all the $H^+$ in the acid is donated to $H_2O$; in a weak acid, only a small percentage of acid molecules produce $H_3O^+$. Strong bases are hydroxides of Groups 1A (1) and 2A (2) that dissociate completely in water. An important weak base is ammonia, $NH_3$. In water, weak acids and weak bases produce only a few ions when equilibrium is reached. The reaction for a weak acid can be written as $HA + H_2O \rightleftharpoons H_3O^+ + A^-$. The acid dissociation expression is written as $K_a = \dfrac{[H_3O^+][A^-]}{[HA]}$.

### 10.3 Ionization of Water

**LEARNING GOAL:** *Use the ion-product constant of water to calculate the $[H_3O^+]$ and $[OH^-]$ in an aqueous solution.*

In pure water, a few molecules transfer protons to other water molecules, producing small but equal amounts of $[H_3O^+]$ and $[OH^-]$, such that each has a concentration of $1 \times 10^{-7}$ mole/L. The ion-product constant, $K_w$, $= [H_3O^+] \times [OH^-] = 1 \times 10^{-14}$ at 25 °C, applies to all aqueous solutions. In acidic solutions, the $[H_3O^+]$ is greater than the $[OH^-]$. In basic solutions, the $[OH^-]$ is greater than the $[H_3O^+]$.

### 10.4 The pH Scale

**LEARNING GOAL:** *Calculate pH from $[H_3O^+]$; given the pH, calculate the $[H_3O^+]$ and $[OH^-]$ of a solution.*

The pH scale is a range of numbers, typically from 0 to 14, which relates to the $[H_3O^+]$ of the solution. A neutral solution has a pH of 7. In acidic solutions, the pH is below 7; in basic solutions, the pH is above 7. Mathematically, pH is the negative logarithm of the hydronium ion concentration ($-\log[H_3O^+]$).

### 10.5 Reactions of Acids and Bases

**LEARNING GOAL:** *Write balanced equations for reactions of acids with metals, carbonates, and bases.*

When an acid reacts with a metal, hydrogen gas and a salt are produced. The reaction of an acid with a carbonate or bicarbonate produces carbon dioxide, a salt, and water. In neutralization, an acid reacts with a base to produce a salt and water. In titration, an acid sample is neutralized with a known amount of a base. From the volume and molarity of the base, the concentration of the acid is calculated.

### 10.6 Acid–Base Properties of Salt Solutions

**LEARNING GOAL:** *Predict whether a salt will form an acidic, basic, or neutral solution.*

A salt of a weak acid contains an anion that removes protons from water and makes the solution basic. A salt of a weak base contains an ion that donates a proton to water, producing an acidic solution. Salts of strong acids and bases give neutral solutions because they contain ions that do not affect the pH.

### 10.7 Buffers

**LEARNING GOAL:** *Describe the role of buffers in maintaining the pH of a solution.*

A buffer solution resists changes in pH when small amounts of acid or base are added. A buffer contains either a weak acid and its salt or a weak base and its salt. The weak acid reacts with added $OH^-$, and the anion of the salt reacts with added $H^+$. Buffers are important in maintaining the pH of the blood.

## KEY TERMS

**acid** A substance that dissolves in water and produces hydrogen ions ($H^+$), according to the Arrhenius theory. All acids are proton donors, according to the Brønsted–Lowry theory.

**acid dissociation constant ($K_a$)** The product of the concentrations of the ions from the dissociation of a weak acid divided by the concentration of the weak acid.

**amphoteric** Substances that can act as either an acid or a base in water.

**base** A substance that dissolves in water and produces hydroxide ions ($OH^-$), according to the Arrhenius theory. All bases are proton acceptors, according to the Brønsted–Lowry theory.

**Brønsted–Lowry acids and bases** An acid is a proton donor; a base is a proton acceptor.

**buffer solution** A solution of a weak acid and its conjugate base or a weak base and its conjugate acid that maintains the pH by neutralizing added acid or base.

**conjugate acid–base pair** An acid and base that differ by one $H^+$. When an acid donates a proton, the product is its conjugate base, which is capable of accepting a proton in the reverse reaction.

**dissociation** The separation of an acid or base into ions in water.

**hydronium ion, $H_3O^+$** The ion formed by the attraction of a proton ($H^+$) to a $H_2O$ molecule.

**ion-product constant of water, $K_w$** The product of $[H_3O^+]$ and $[OH^-]$ in solution; $K_w = [H_3O^+][OH^-]$.

**neutral** The term that describes a solution with equal concentrations of $H_3O^+$ and $OH^-$.

**neutralization** A reaction between an acid and a base to form a salt and water.

**pH** A measure of the $[H_3O^+]$ in a solution; $pH = -\log[H_3O^+]$.

**strong acid** An acid that completely ionizes in water.

**strong base** A base that completely ionizes in water.

**titration** The addition of base to an acid sample to determine the concentration of the acid.

**weak acid** An acid that is a poor donor of $H^+$ and dissociates only slightly in water.

**weak base** A base that is a poor acceptor of $H^+$ and produces only a small number of ions in water.

## UNDERSTANDING THE CONCEPTS

**10.71** In each of the following diagrams of acid solutions, determine if each diagram represents a strong acid or a weak acid. The acid has the formula HX.

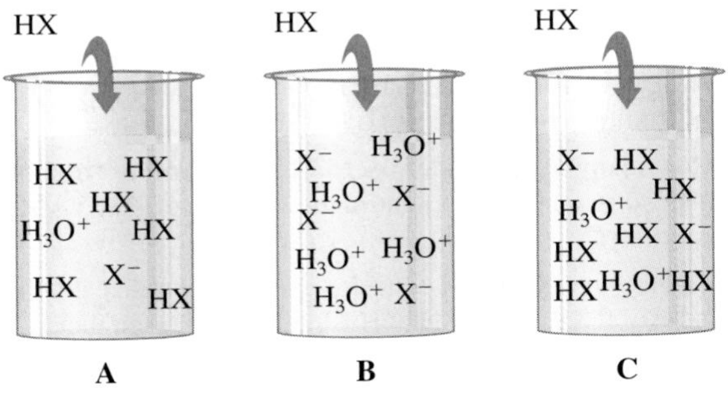


**10.72** Adding a few drops of a strong acid to water will lower the pH appreciably. However, adding the same number of drops to a buffer does not appreciably alter the pH. Why?

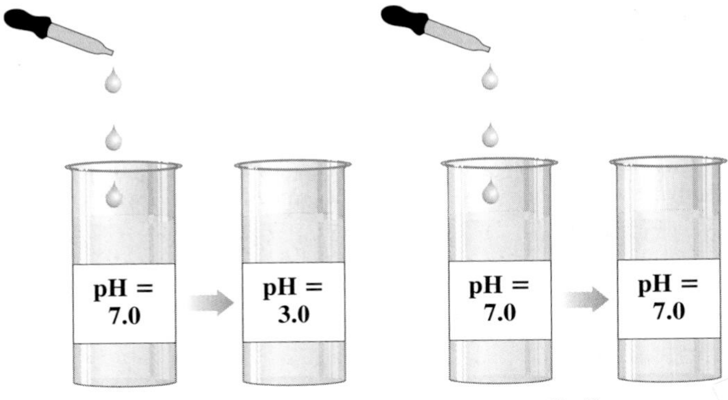

10.73 Sometimes, during stress or trauma, a person can start to hyperventilate. Then the person might breathe into a paper bag to avoid fainting.

a. What changes occur in the blood pH during hyperventilation?
b. How does breathing into a paper bag help return blood pH to normal?

**10.74** In the blood plasma, pH is maintained by the carbonic acid–bicarbonate buffer system.
a. How is pH maintained when acid is added to the buffer system?
b. How is pH maintained when base is added to the buffer system?

# ADDITIONAL QUESTIONS AND PROBLEMS

*For instructor-assigned homework, go to* ***www.masteringchemistry.com****.*

10.75 Identify each of the following as an acid, base, or salt, and give its name:
a. LiOH b. $Ca(NO_3)_2$ c. HBr
d. $Ba(OH)_2$ e. $H_2CO_3$ f. $HClO_2$

**10.76** Identify each of the following as an acid, base, or salt, and give its name:
a. $H_3PO_4$ b. $MgBr_2$ c. $NH_3$
d. $H_2SO_4$ e. NaCl f. KOH

10.77 Are each of the following examples acidic, basic, or neutral?
a. rain, pH 5.2 b. tears, pH 7.5 c. tea, pH 3.8
d. cola, pH 2.5 e. photo developer, pH 12.0

**10.78** Are each of the following examples acidic, basic, or neutral?
a. saliva, pH 6.8 b. urine, pH 5.9
c. pancreatic juice, pH 8.0
d. bile, pH 8.4 e. blood, pH 7.45

10.79 One ingredient in some antacids is $Mg(OH)_2$.
a. If the base is not very soluble in water, why is it considered a strong base?
b. What is the neutralization reaction of $Mg(OH)_2$ with stomach acid, HCl?

**10.80** Acetic acid, $HC_2H_3O_2$, found in vinegar, is a weak acid. Why?

10.81 Using Table 10.3, identify the stronger acid in each of the following pairs:
a. HF or HCN b. $H_3O^+$ or $NH_4^+$
c. $HNO_2$ or $HC_2H_3O_2$ d. $H_2O$ or $HCO_3^-$

**10.82** Using Table 10.3, identify the stronger base in each of the following pairs:
a. $H_2O$ or $Cl^-$ b. $OH^-$ or $NH_3$
c. $SO_4^{2-}$ or $NO_2^-$ d. $CO_3^{2-}$ or $H_2O$

10.83 Determine the pH for the following solutions:
a. $[H_3O^+] = 2.0 \times 10^{-8}$ M b. $[H_3O^+] = 5.0 \times 10^{-2}$ M
c. $[OH^-] = 3.5 \times 10^{-4}$ M d. $[OH^-] = 0.0054$ M

**10.84** Determine the pH for the following solutions:
a. $[OH^-] = 1.0 \times 10^{-7}$ M
b. $[H_3O^+] = 4.2 \times 10^{-3}$ M
c. $[H_3O^+] = 0.0001$ M
d. $[OH^-] = 8.5 \times 10^{-9}$ M

10.85 Are the solutions in Problem 10.83 acidic, basic, or neutral?

**10.86** Are the solutions in Problem 10.84 acidic, basic, or neutral?

10.87 What are the $[H_3O^+]$ and $[OH^-]$ for a solution with the following pH values?
a. 3.00 b. 6.48 c. 8.85
d. 11.00 e. 9.20

**10.88** What are the $[H_3O^+]$ and $[OH^-]$ for a solution with the following pH values?
a. 10.0 b. 5.0 c. 7.00
d. 6.5 e. 1.82

10.89 Solution A has a pH of 4.5, and solution B has a pH of 6.7.
a. Which solution is more acidic?
b. What is the $[H_3O^+]$ in each?
c. What is the $[OH^-]$ in each?

**10.90** Solution X has a pH of 9.5, and solution Y has a pH of 7.5.
a. Which solution is more acidic?
b. What is the $[H_3O^+]$ in each?
c. What is the $[OH^-]$ in each?

10.91 What is the $[OH^-]$ in a solution that contains 0.225 g of NaOH in 0.250 L of solution?

**10.92** What is the $[H_3O^+]$ in a solution that contains 1.54 g of $HNO_3$ in 0.500 L of solution?

10.93 What is the pH of a solution prepared by dissolving 2.5 g of HCl in water to make 425 mL of solution?

**10.94** What is the pH of a solution prepared by dissolving 1.00 g of $Ca(OH)_2$ in water to make 875 mL of solution?

10.95 Calculate the volume (mL) of a 0.150 M NaOH solution that will completely neutralize the following:
a. 25.0 mL of a 0.288 M HCl solution
b. 10.0 mL of a 0.560 M $H_2SO_4$ solution

**10.96** How many milliliters of 0.215 M NaOH solution are needed to completely neutralize 2.50 mL of 0.825 M $H_2SO_4$ solution?

10.97 A solution of 0.205 M NaOH is used to neutralize 20.0 mL of $H_2SO_4$. If 45.6 mL of NaOH is required to reach the endpoint, what is the molarity of the $H_2SO_4$ solution?

$$H_2SO_4(aq) + 2NaOH(aq) \longrightarrow Na_2SO_4(aq) + 2H_2O(l)$$

**10.98** A 10.0-mL sample of vinegar, which is an aqueous solution of acetic acid, $HC_2H_3O_2$, requires 16.5 mL of 0.500 M NaOH to reach the endpoint in a titration. What is the molarity of the acetic acid solution?

$$HC_2H_3O_2(aq) + NaOH(aq) \longrightarrow NaC_2H_3O_2(aq) + H_2O(l)$$

**10.99** Will solutions of the following salts be acidic, basic, or neutral?
**a.** KF **b.** NaCN **c.** $NH_4NO_3$ **d.** NaBr

**10.100** Will solutions of the following salts be acidic, basic, or neutral?
**a.** $K_2SO_4$ **b.** $KNO_2$ **c.** $MgCl_2$ **d.** $NH_4Cl$

**10.101** A buffer is made by dissolving $H_3PO_4$ and $NaH_2PO_4$ in water.
**a.** Write an equation that shows how this buffer neutralizes added acid.
**b.** Write an equation that shows how this buffer neutralizes added base.
**c.** Calculate the pH of this buffer if it is 0.10 M $H_3PO_4$ and 0.10 M $H_2PO_4^-$; the $K_a$ for $H_3PO_4$ is $7.5 \times 10^{-3}$.
**d.** Calculate the pH of this buffer if it is 0.50 M $H_3PO_4$ and 0.20 M $H_2PO_4^-$; the $K_a$ for $H_3PO_4$ is $7.5 \times 10^{-3}$.

**10.102** A buffer is made by dissolving $HC_2H_3O_2$ and $NaC_2H_3O_2$ in water.
**a.** Write an equation that shows how this buffer neutralizes added acid.
**b.** Write an equation that shows how this buffer neutralizes added base.
**c.** Calculate the pH of this buffer if it is 0.10 M $HC_2H_3O_2$ and 0.10 M $C_2H_3O_2^-$; the $K_a$ for $HC_2H_3O_2$ is $1.8 \times 10^{-5}$.
**d.** Calculate the pH of this buffer if it is 0.20 M $HC_2H_3O_2$ and 0.40 M $C_2H_3O_2^-$; the $K_a$ for $HC_2H_3O_2$ is $1.8 \times 10^{-5}$.

## CHALLENGE QUESTIONS

**10.103** Complete the following table:

| Acid | Conjugate base |
|---|---|
| $H_2O$ | |
| | $CN^-$ |
| $HNO_2$ | |
| | $H_2PO_4^-$ |

**10.104** Complete the following table:

| Base | Conjugate acid |
|---|---|
| | $HS^-$ |
| | $H_3O^+$ |
| $NH_3$ | |
| $HCO_3^-$ | |

**10.105** Consider the following:
1. $H_2S$ 2. $H_3PO_4$ 3. $HCO_3^-$
**a.** For each, write the formula of the conjugate base.
**b.** For each, write the $K_a$ expression.
**c.** Write the formula of the weakest acid.
**d.** Write the formula of the strongest acid.

**10.106** Identify the conjugate acid–base pairs in each of the following equations and state whether the equilibrium mixture contains mostly products or mostly reactants:
**a.** $NH_3(aq) + HNO_3(aq) \rightleftharpoons NH_4^+(aq) + NO_3^-(aq)$
**b.** $H_2O(l) + HBr(aq) \rightleftharpoons H_3O^+(aq) + Br^-(aq)$
**c.** $HNO_2(aq) + HS^-(aq) \rightleftharpoons H_2S(g) + NO_2^-(aq)$
**d.** $Cl^-(aq) + H_2O(l) \rightleftharpoons OH^-(aq) + HCl(aq)$

**10.107** Complete and balance each of the following:
**a.** $ZnCO_3(s) + H_2SO_4(aq) \longrightarrow$
**b.** $Al(s) + HNO_3(aq) \longrightarrow$
**c.** $H_3PO_4(aq) + Ca(OH)_2(aq) \longrightarrow$
**d.** $KHCO_3(s) + HNO_3(aq) \longrightarrow$

**10.108** Predict whether a solution of each of the following salts is acidic, basic, or neutral. For salts that form acidic or basic solutions, write a balanced equation for the reaction.
**a.** $NH_4Br$ **b.** $KNO_2$ **c.** $Mg(NO_3)_2$
**d.** $BaF_2$ **e.** $K_2S$

**10.109** Determine each of the following for a 0.050 M KOH solution:
**a.** $[H_3O^+]$ **b.** pH
**c.** products when reacted with $H_3PO_4$
**d.** milliliters required to neutralize 40.0 mL of 0.035 M $H_2SO_4$

**10.110** Consider the reaction of KOH and $HNO_2$.
**a.** Write the balanced chemical equation.
**b.** Calculate the milliliters of 0.122 M KOH required to neutralize 36.0 mL of 0.250 M $HNO_2$.
**c.** Determine whether the final solution would be acidic, basic, or neutral.

**10.111** One of the most acidic lakes in the United States is Little Echo Pond in the Adirondacks in New York. Recently, this lake had a pH of 4.2, well below the recommended pH of 6.5.

**a.** What is the $[H_3O^+]$ and $[OH^-]$ of Little Echo Pond?
**b.** What is the $[H_3O^+]$ and $[OH^-]$ of a lake that has a pH of 6.5?
**c.** One way to raise the pH of an acidic lake (and restore aquatic life) is to add limestone ($CaCO_3$). How many grams of $CaCO_3$ are needed to neutralize 1.0 kL of the acidic water from Little Echo Pond if the acid is written as HA?

$$2HA + CaCO_3(s) \longrightarrow CaA_2 + CO_2(g) + H_2O(l)$$

**10.112** The daily output of stomach acid (gastric juice) is 1000 mL to 2000 mL. Prior to a meal, stomach acid (HCl) typically has a pH of 1.42.
**a.** What is the $[H_3O^+]$ of stomach acid?
**b.** The antacid Maalox contains 200. mg of $Al(OH)_3$ per tablet. Write the neutralization equation and calculate the milliliters of stomach acid neutralized by two tablets of Maalox.
**c.** The antacid milk of magnesia contains 400. mg of $Mg(OH)_2$ per teaspoon. Write the neutralization equation and calculate the milliliters of stomach acid that are neutralized by 1 tablespoon of milk of magnesia (1 tablespoon = 3 teaspoons).

# ANSWERS

## ANSWERS TO STUDY CHECKS

**10.1** **a.** chloric acid **b.** $Fe(OH)_3$

**10.2** $HNO_3(aq) + H_2O(l) \longrightarrow H_3O^+(aq) + NO_3^-(aq)$

**10.3** A base accepts a proton to form its conjugate acid.
**a.** $H_2S$ **b.** $HNO_2$

**10.4** The conjugate acid–base pairs are $HCN/CN^-$ and $SO_4^{2-}/HSO_4^-$.

**10.5** $HNO_3 + H_2O \rightleftharpoons H_3O^+ + NO_3^-$
The products are favored because $HNO_3$ is a stronger acid than $H_3O^+$.

**10.6** Nitrous acid has a larger $K_a$ than carbonic acid; it dissociates more in $H_2O$, forms more $[H_3O^+]$, and is a stronger acid.

**10.7** $[H_3O^+] = 2.5 \times 10^{-11}$ M, basic

**10.8** 11.38

**10.9** 4.3

**10.10** $[H_3O^+] = 3.2 \times 10^{-5}$ M, $[OH^-] = 3.1 \times 10^{-10}$ M

**10.11** $H_2SO_4(aq) + 2NaHCO_3(s) \longrightarrow Na_2SO_4(aq) + 2CO_2(g) + 2H_2O(l)$

**10.12** 0.200 M HCl

**10.13** The anion $PO_4^{3-}$ reacts with $H_2O$ forming the weak acid $HPO_4^{2-}$ and $OH^-$, which makes the solution basic.

**10.14** pH = 7.91

## ANSWERS TO SELECTED QUESTIONS AND PROBLEMS

**10.1** **a.** acid **b.** acid **c.** acid **d.** base

**10.3** **a.** hydrochloric acid **b.** calcium hydroxide
**c.** carbonic acid **d.** nitric acid
**e.** sulfurous acid **f.** iron(II) hydroxide

**10.5** **a.** $Mg(OH)_2$ **b.** HF **c.** $H_3PO_4$
**d.** LiOH **e.** $Cu(OH)_2$

**10.7** **a.** HI is the acid (proton donor) and $H_2O$ is the base (proton acceptor).
**b.** $H_2O$ is the acid (proton donor) and $F^-$ is the base (proton acceptor)

**10.9** **a.** $F^-$, fluoride ion
**b.** $OH^-$, hydroxide ion
**c.** $HCO_3^-$, bicarbonate ion *or* hydrogen carbonate ion
**d.** $SO_4^{2-}$, sulfate ion

**10.11** **a.** $HCO_3^-$, bicarbonate ion *or* hydrogen carbonate ion
**b.** $H_3O^+$, hydronium ion
**c.** $H_3PO_4$, phosphoric acid
**d.** HBr, hydrobromic acid

**10.13** **a.** acid $H_2CO_3$, conjugate base $HCO_3^-$
base $H_2O$, conjugate acid $H_3O^+$
**b.** acid $NH_4^+$, conjugate base $NH_3$
base $H_2O$, conjugate acid $H_3O^+$
**c.** acid HCN, conjugate base $CN^-$
base $NO_2^-$, conjugate acid $HNO_2$

**10.15** A strong acid is a good proton donor, whereas its conjugate base is a poor proton acceptor.

**10.17** **a.** HBr **b.** $HSO_4^-$ **c.** $H_2CO_3$

**10.19** **a.** $HSO_4^-$ **b.** $HNO_2$ **c.** $HSO_3^-$

**10.21** **a.** reactants **b.** reactants **c.** products

**10.23** The reactants are favored because $NH_4^+$ is a weaker acid than $HSO_4^-$:

$$NH_4^+(aq) + SO_4^{2-}(aq) \rightleftharpoons NH_3(aq) + HSO_4^-(aq)$$

**10.25** **a.** $H_2SO_3$ **b.** $HSO_3^-$ **c.** $H_2SO_3$
**d.** $HS^-$ **e.** $H_2SO_3$

**10.27** $H_3PO_4(aq) + H_2O(l) \rightleftharpoons H_3O^+(aq) + H_2PO_4^-(aq)$

$$K_a = \frac{[H_3O^+][H_2PO_4^-]}{[H_3PO_4]}$$

**10.29** In pure water, $[H_3O^+] = [OH^-]$ because one of each is produced every time a proton transfers from one water molecule to another.

**10.31** In an acidic solution, the $[H_3O^+]$ is greater than the $[OH^-]$.

**10.33** **a.** acidic **b.** basic **c.** basic **d.** acidic

**10.35** **a.** $1.0 \times 10^{-5}$ M **b.** $1.0 \times 10^{-8}$ M
**c.** $5.0 \times 10^{-10}$ M **d.** $2.5 \times 10^{-2}$ M

**10.37** **a.** $1.0 \times 10^{-11}$ M **b.** $2.0 \times 10^{-9}$ M
**c.** $5.6 \times 10^{-3}$ M **d.** $2.5 \times 10^{-2}$ M

**10.39** In a neutral solution, the $[H_3O^+]$ is $1.0 \times 10^{-7}$ M and the pH is 7.00, which is the negative value of the power of 10.

**10.41** **a.** basic **b.** acidic **c.** basic
**d.** acidic **e.** acidic **f.** basic

**10.43** **a.** 4.00 **b.** 8.52 **c.** 9.00
**d.** 3.40 **e.** 7.17 **f.** 10.92

**10.45**

| $[H_3O^+]$ | $[OH^-]$ | pH | Acidic, Basic, or Neutral? |
|---|---|---|---|
| $1.0 \times 10^{-8}$ M | $1.0 \times 10^{-6}$ M | 8.00 | Basic |
| $1.0 \times 10^{-3}$ M | $1.0 \times 10^{-11}$ M | 3.00 | Acidic |
| $2.8 \times 10^{-5}$ M | $3.6 \times 10^{-10}$ M | 4.55 | Acidic |
| $2.4 \times 10^{-5}$ M | $4.2 \times 10^{-10}$ M | 4.62 | Acidic |

**10.47** **a.** $ZnCO_3(s) + 2HBr(aq) \longrightarrow ZnBr_2(aq) + CO_2(g) + H_2O(l)$
**b.** $Zn(s) + 2HCl(aq) \longrightarrow ZnCl_2(aq) + H_2(g)$
**c.** $HCl(aq) + NaHCO_3(s) \longrightarrow NaCl(aq) + H_2O(l) + CO_2(g)$
**d.** $H_2SO_4(aq) + Mg(OH)_2(s) \longrightarrow MgSO_4(aq) + 2H_2O(l)$

**10.49** **a.** $2HCl(aq) + Mg(OH)_2(s) \longrightarrow MgCl_2(aq) + 2H_2O(l)$
**b.** $H_3PO_4(aq) + 3LiOH(aq) \longrightarrow Li_3PO_4(aq) + 3H_2O(l)$

**10.51** **a.** $H_2SO_4(aq) + 2NaOH(aq) \longrightarrow Na_2SO_4(aq) + 2H_2O(l)$
**b.** $3HCl(aq) + Fe(OH)_3(s) \longrightarrow FeCl_3(aq) + 3H_2O(l)$
**c.** $H_2CO_3(aq) + Mg(OH)_2(s) \longrightarrow MgCO_3(s) + 2H_2O(l)$

**10.53** 0.829 M HCl

**10.55** 0.125 M $H_2SO_4$

**10.57** 0.0223 M $H_3PO_4$

**10.59** The anion from the weak acid removes a proton from $H_2O$ to make a basic solution.

**10.61** **a.** neutral
**b.** acidic, $NH_4^+(aq) + H_2O(l) \rightleftharpoons NH_3(aq) + H_3O^+(aq)$
**c.** basic, $CO_3^{2-}(aq) + H_2O(l) \rightleftharpoons HCO_3^-(aq) + OH^-(aq)$
**d.** basic, $S^{2-}(aq) + H_2O(l) \rightleftharpoons HS^-(aq) + OH^-(aq)$

**10.63** (b) and (c) are buffer systems. (b) contains the weak acid $H_2CO_3$ and its salt $NaHCO_3$. (c) contains HF, a weak acid, and its salt KF.

**10.65** **a.** A buffer system keeps the pH constant.
**b.** The conjugate base neutralizes any $H_3O^+$ added.
**c.** The added $H_3O^+$ reacts with $F^-$ from NaF.
**d.** The added $OH^-$ is neutralized by the HF.

**10.67** pH = 3.35

**10.69** The pH of the 0.10 M HF/0.10 M NaF buffer is 3.14. The pH of the 0.060 M HF/0.120 M NaF buffer is 3.44.

**10.71** **A.** weak acid **B.** strong acid **C.** weak acid

**10.73** **a.** Hyperventilation will lower the $CO_2$ level in the blood, which lowers the $H_2CO_3$ concentration, which decreases the $H_3O^+$ and increases the blood pH.
**b.** Breathing into a bag will increase the $CO_2$ level, increase the $H_2CO_3$, increase $H_3O^+$, and lower the blood pH.

**10.75** **a.** base, lithium hydroxide **b.** salt, calcium nitrate
**c.** acid, hydrobromic acid **d.** base, barium hydroxide
**e.** acid, carbonic acid **f.** acid, chlorous acid

**10.77** **a.** acidic **b.** basic **c.** acidic **d.** acidic **e.** basic

**10.79** **a.** The $Mg(OH)_2$ that dissolves is completely dissociated, making it a strong base.
**b.** $Mg(OH)_2(aq) + 2HCl(aq) \longrightarrow MgCl_2(aq) + 2H_2O(l)$

**10.81** **a.** HF **b.** $H_3O^+$ **c.** $HNO_2$ **d.** $HCO_3^-$

**10.83** **a.** pH 7.70 **b.** pH 1.30 **c.** pH 10.54 **d.** pH 11.73

**10.85** **a.** basic **b.** acidic **c.** basic **d.** basic

**10.87** **a.** $[H_3O^+] = 1.0 \times 10^{-3}$ M; $[OH^-] = 1.0 \times 10^{-11}$ M
**b.** $[H_3O^+] = 3.3 \times 10^{-7}$ M; $[OH^-] = 3.0 \times 10^{-8}$ M
**c.** $[H_3O^+] = 1.4 \times 10^{-9}$ M; $[OH^-] = 7.1 \times 10^{-6}$ M
**d.** $[H_3O^+] = 1.0 \times 10^{-11}$ M; $[OH^-] = 1.0 \times 10^{-3}$ M
**e.** $[H_3O^+] = 6.3 \times 10^{-10}$ M; $[OH^-] = 1.6 \times 10^{-5}$ M

**10.89** **a.** A
**b.** A, $[H_3O^+] = 3 \times 10^{-5}$ M B, $[H_3O^+] = 2 \times 10^{-7}$ M
**c.** A, $[OH^-] = 3 \times 10^{-10}$ M B, $[OH^-] = 5 \times 10^{-8}$ M

**10.91** $[OH^-] = 0.0225$ M

**10.93** pH = 0.80

**10.95** **a.** 48.0 mL of NaOH solution
**b.** 74.7 mL of NaOH solution

**10.97** 0.234 M $H_2SO_4$

**10.99** **a.** basic **b.** basic **c.** acidic **d.** neutral

**10.101** **a.** $H_2PO_4^-(aq) + H_3O^+(aq) \longrightarrow H_3PO_4(aq) + H_2O(l)$
**b.** $H_3PO_4(aq) + OH^-(aq) \longrightarrow H_2PO_4^-(aq) + H_2O(l)$
**c.** pH = 2.12 **d.** pH = 1.72

**10.103**

| Acid | Conjugate base |
|---|---|
| $H_2O$ | $OH^-$ |
| HCN | $CN^-$ |
| $HNO_2$ | $NO_2^-$ |
| $H_3PO_4$ | $H_2PO_4^-$ |

**10.105** **a.** 1. $HS^-$ 2. $H_2PO_4^-$ 3. $CO_3^{2-}$
**b.** 1. $\dfrac{[H_3O^+][HS^-]}{[H_2S]}$ 2. $\dfrac{[H_3O^+][H_2PO_4^-]}{[H_3PO_4]}$
3. $\dfrac{[CO_3^{2-}][H_3O^+]}{[HCO_3^-]}$
**c.** $HCO_3^-$ **d.** $H_3PO_4$

**10.107** **a.** $ZnCO_3(s) + H_2SO_4(aq) \longrightarrow ZnSO_4(aq) + CO_2(g) + H_2O(l)$
**b.** $2Al(s) + 6HNO_3(aq) \longrightarrow 2Al(NO_3)_3(aq) + 3H_2(g)$
**c.** $2H_3PO_4(aq) + 3Ca(OH)_2(aq) \longrightarrow Ca_3(PO_4)_2(s) + 6H_2O(l)$
**d.** $KHCO_3(s) + HNO_3(aq) \longrightarrow KNO_3(aq) + CO_2(g) + H_2O(l)$

**10.109** **a.** $[H_3O^+] = 2.0 \times 10^{-13}$ M
**b.** pH = 12.70
**c.** $3KOH(aq) + H_3PO_4(aq) \longrightarrow K_3PO_4(aq) + 3H_2O(l)$
**d.** 56 mL of KOH solution

**10.111** **a.** $[H_3O^+] = 6 \times 10^{-5}$ M; $[OH^-] = 2 \times 10^{-10}$ M
**b.** $[H_3O^+] = 3 \times 10^{-7}$ M; $[OH^-] = 3 \times 10^{-8}$ M
**c.** 3 g of $CaCO_3$

**CI.17** Methane is a major component of purified natural gas used for heating and cooking. When 1 mole of methane gas burns with oxygen to produce carbon dioxide and water vapor, 883 kJ of heat is produced. Methane gas has a density of 0.715 g/L at STP. For transport, the volume of natural gas is decreased by cooling it to −163 °C, which gives liquefied natural gas (LNG) with a density of 0.45 g/mL. A tank on a ship can hold 7.0 million gallons of LNG.

**a.** Write the electron-dot formula and the molecular formula of methane if it consists of one carbon atom bonded to four hydrogen atoms.
**b.** What is the mass, in kilograms, of LNG (assume that LNG is all methane) transported in one tank on a ship?
**c.** What is the volume, in liters, of methane gas when the LNG in one tank is converted to gas at STP?
**d.** Write the balanced equation for the reaction of methane and oxygen in a gas burner.

**e.** How many kilograms of oxygen are needed to react with all of the methane provided by one tank of LNG?
**f.** How much heat, in kilojoules, is released from burning all of the methane in one tank of LNG?

**CI.18** Automobile exhaust is a major cause of air pollution. The pollutants formed from gasoline include nitrogen oxide, which is produced at high temperatures in an automobile engine from nitrogen and oxygen gases in the air. Once emitted into the air, nitrogen oxide reacts with oxygen to produce nitrogen dioxide, a reddish-brown gas with a sharp, pungent odor that makes up smog. A component of gasoline is octane, $C_8H_{18}$, which has a density of 0.803 g/cm$^3$. In 1 year, a typical automobile uses 550 gal of gasoline and produces 41 lb of nitrogen oxide.

**a.** Write balanced equations for the production of nitrogen oxide and nitrogen dioxide.
**b.** If all the nitrogen oxide emitted by one automobile is converted to nitrogen dioxide in the atmosphere, how many kilograms of nitrogen dioxide are produced in 1 year by a single automobile?
**c.** Write a balanced equation for the reaction of octane with oxygen gas to give carbon dioxide and water vapor.
**d.** How many moles of $C_8H_{18}$ are present in 15.2 gal of octane?
**e.** How many liters of carbon dioxide (at STP) would this car produce in 1 year? (Assume complete reaction of octane.)

**CI.19** A piece of magnesium with a mass of 0.121 g is added to 50.0 mL of 1.00 M HCl at a temperature of 22.0 °C. When the magnesium dissolves, the solution reaches a temperature of 33.0 °C:

$$Mg(s) + 2HCl(aq) \longrightarrow MgCl_2(aq) + H_2(g)$$

**a.** What is the limiting reactant?
**b.** What volume of hydrogen gas would be produced if the pressure is 750. mm Hg and the temperature 33 °C?

c. How many joules were released by the reaction of the magnesium? Assume the density of HCl solution is 1.00 g/mL and the specific heat of HCl solution is the same as for water.
d. What is the heat of reaction for Mg in J/g? In kJ/mole?

**CI.20** In wine making, sugar ($C_6H_{12}O_6$) from grapes undergoes fermentation in the absence of oxygen to produce ethanol and carbon dioxide. A bottle of vintage port wine has a volume of 750 mL and contains 135 mL of ethanol ($C_2H_6O$). Ethanol has a density of 0.789 g/mL. In 1.5 lb of grapes, there are 26 g of grape sugar.

a. Calculate the percent concentration of ethanol by volume (v/v).
b. What is the molarity (M) of ethanol in the port wine?
c. Write the balanced equation for the fermentation reaction of grape sugar.
d. How many grams of sugar from grapes are required to produce one bottle of port wine?
e. How many bottles of port wine can be produced from 1.0 ton of grapes? (1 ton = 2000 lb)

**CI.21** Consider the following reaction at equilibrium:

$$2H_2(g) + S_2(g) \rightleftharpoons 2H_2S(g) + \text{heat}$$

In a 10.0-L container, an equilibrium mixture contains 2.0 g of $H_2$, 10. g of $S_2$, and 68 g of $H_2S$.
a. What is the $K_c$ value for this equilibrium mixture?
b. If $H_2$ is added to the mixture, how will the equilibrium shift?
c. How will the equilibrium shift if the mixture is placed in a 5.00-L container with no change in temperature?
d. If a 5.00-L container has an equilibrium mixture of 0.30 mole of $H_2$ and 2.5 moles of $H_2S$, what is the equilibrium concentration of $S_2$ if temperature is the same?
e. Will an increase in temperature increase or decrease the $K_c$ value?

**CI.22** A mixture of 25.0 g of $CS_2$ gas and 30.0 g of $O_2$ gas is placed in 10.0-L closed container and heated to 125 °C. The products of complete reaction are carbon dioxide gas and sulfur dioxide gas.
a. Write a balanced equation for the reaction.
b. How many grams of $CO_2$ are produced?
c. What is the partial pressure of the remaining reactant?
d. What is the final pressure in the container?

**CI.23** A metal completely reacts with 34.8 mL of 0.520 M HCl.

a. Write a balanced equation for the reaction of the metal M and $HCl(aq)$ to form $MCl_3(aq)$ and $H_2$ gas.
b. What volume, in milliliters, of $H_2$ at STP is produced?
c. How many moles of metal M reacted?
d. If the metal has a mass of 0.420 g, use your results from part **c** to determine the molar mass of the metal M.
e. What is the name and symbol of metal M in part **d**?
f. Write the balanced equation for the reaction using the symbol of the metal from part **e**.

**CI.24** In a teaspoon (5.0 mL) of a common liquid antacid, there are 200. mg of $Ca(OH)_2$ and 200. mg of $Al(OH)_3$. A 0.080 M HCl solution, which is similar to stomach acid, is used to neutralize 5.0 mL of the liquid antacid.

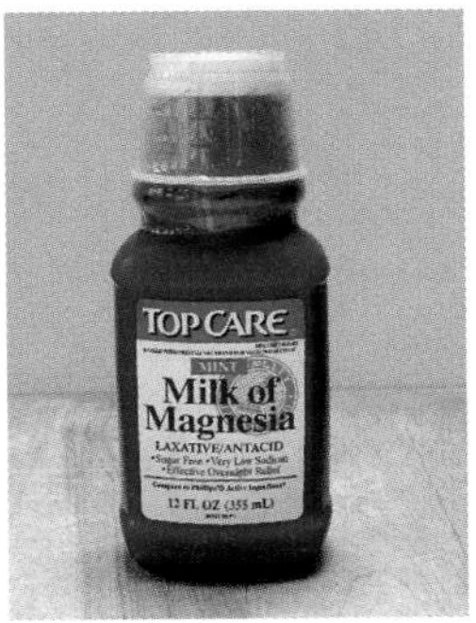

a. Write the equation for the neutralization of HCl and $Ca(OH)_2$.
b. Write the equation for the neutralization of HCl and $Al(OH)_3$.
c. What is the pH of the HCl solution?
d. How many milliliters of the HCl solution is needed to neutralize the $Ca(OH)_2$?
e. How many milliliters of the HCl solution is needed to neutralize the $Al(OH)_3$?

## ■ ANSWERS

**CI.17** a.

```
      H
      |
  H—C—H   CH4
      |
      H
```

b. $1.2 \times 10^7$ kg of LNG (methane)
c. $1.7 \times 10^{10}$ L of methane at STP
d. $CH_4(g) + 2O_2(g) \longrightarrow CO_2(g) + 2H_2O(g)$
e. $4.8 \times 10^7$ kg of $O_2$
f. $6.6 \times 10^{11}$ kJ

**CI.19** a. Mg is the limiting reactant.
b. 0.127 L of $H_2$
c. $2.30 \times 10^3$ J
d. $1.90 \times 10^4$ J/g, 462 kJ/mole

**CI.21** a. $K_c = 250$
b. If $H_2$ is added, the equilibrium will shift toward the products.
c. If the volume decreases, the equilibrium shifts toward the products.
d. $[S_2] = 0.28$ mole/L
e. An increase in temperature will decrease the value of $K_c$.

**CI.23** a. $2M(s) + 6HCl(aq) \longrightarrow 2MCl_3(aq) + 3H_2(g)$
b. 203 mL of $H_2$
c. $6.03 \times 10^{-3}$ mole of M
d. 69.7 g/mole
e. Gallium, Ga
f. $2Ga(s) + 6HCl(aq) \longrightarrow 2GaCl_3(aq) + 3H_2(g)$

# Introduction to Organic Chemistry: Alkanes

# 11

## LOOKING AHEAD


**11.1** Organic Compounds

**11.2** Alkanes

**11.3** Alkanes with Substituents

**11.4** Properties of Alkanes

**11.5** Functional Groups


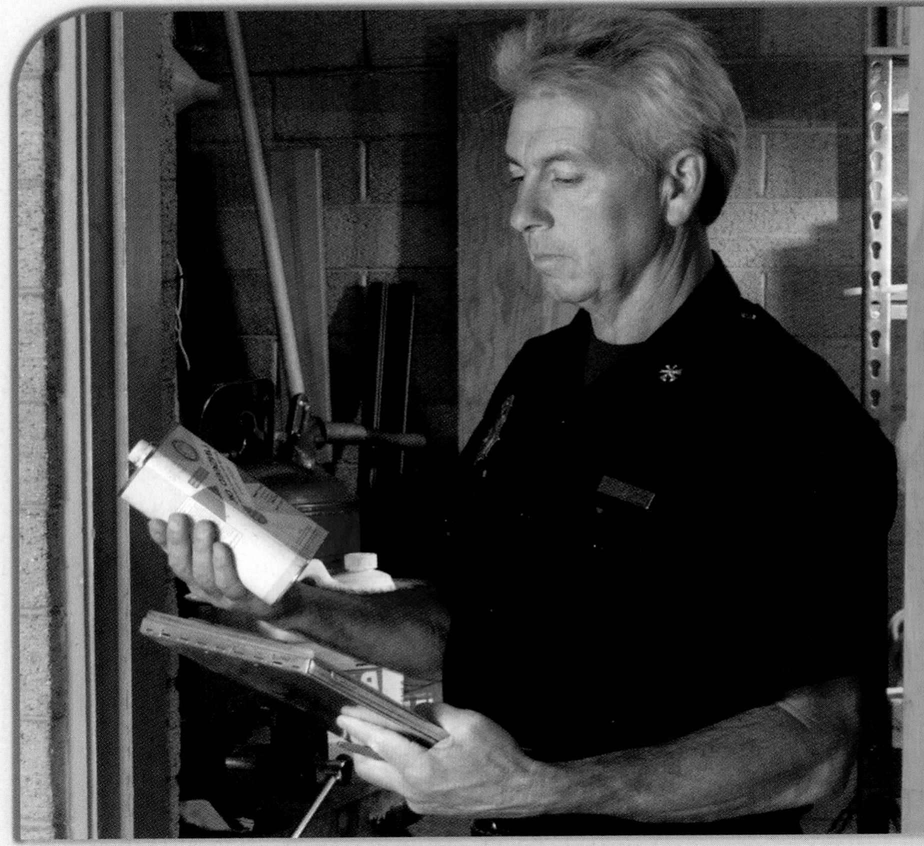

*"When we have a hazardous materials spill, the first thing we do is isolate it," says Don Dornell, assistant fire chief, Burlingame Fire Station. "Then our technicians and a county chemist identify the product from its flammability and solubility in water so we can use the proper materials to clean up the spill. We use different methods for alcohol, which mixes with water, than for gasoline, which floats. Because hydrocarbons are volatile, we use foam to cover them and trap the vapors. At oil refineries, we will use foams, but many times we squirt water on the tanks to cool the contents below their boiling points, too. By knowing the boiling point of the product and its density and vapor density, we know if it floats or sinks in water and where its vapors will go."*

*Organic chemistry* is the chemistry of compounds that contain carbon and hydrogen. The element carbon has a special role in chemistry because it bonds with other carbon atoms to give a vast array of molecules. The variety of molecules is so great that we find organic compounds in many common products we use, such as gasoline, medicine, shampoos, plastic bottles, and perfumes. The food we eat is composed of different organic compounds that supply us with fuel for energy and the carbon atoms needed to build and repair the cells of our bodies.

Although many organic compounds occur in nature, chemists have synthesized even more. The cotton, wool, or silk in your clothes contains naturally occurring organic compounds, whereas materials such as polyester, nylon, or plastic have been synthesized through organic reactions. Sometimes it is convenient to synthesize a molecule in the lab even though that molecule is also found in nature. For example, vitamin C synthesized in a laboratory has the same structure as the vitamin C in oranges or lemons. In these chapters on organic chemistry, you will learn about the structures and reactions of organic molecules, which will provide a foundation for understanding the more complex molecules of biochemistry.

## 11.1 Organic Compounds

**LEARNING GOAL**

Identify characteristic properties of organic or inorganic compounds.

At the beginning of the nineteenth century, scientists classified chemical compounds as inorganic and organic. An inorganic compound was a substance that was composed of minerals, and an organic compound was a substance that came from an organism, thus the origin of the word "organic." Early scientists thought that some type of "vital force," which could be found only in living cells, was required to synthesize an organic compound. This perception was shown to be incorrect in 1828 when the German chemist Friedrick Wöhler synthesized urea, a product of protein metabolism, by heating an inorganic compound, ammonium cyanate.

$$\underset{\text{Ammonium cyanate (inorganic)}}{NH_4CNO} \xrightarrow{\text{Heat}} \underset{\text{Urea (organic)}}{H_2N-\overset{\overset{\displaystyle O}{\|}}{C}-NH_2}$$

We now define organic chemistry as the study of carbon compounds. **Organic compounds** always contain carbon (C), usually hydrogen (H), and sometimes other nonmetallic elements such as oxygen (O), sulfur (S), nitrogen (N), phosphorus (P), or a halogen such as chlorine (Cl). In any organic compound, there are always four bonds to every carbon. Organic compounds are usually nonpolar, with weak attractions between molecules, which accounts for their low melting and boiling points. Typically, organic compounds are not soluble in water. For example, vegetable oil, which is a mixture of organic compounds, does not dissolve in water, but floats on top. Many organic compounds undergo combustion and burn vigorously in air.

In contrast, many of the inorganic compounds are ionic, which leads to high melting and boiling points. Inorganic compounds that have ionic or polar covalent bonds are usually soluble in water. Most inorganic substances do not burn in air. Table 11.1 contrasts some of the properties associated with organic compounds, such as propane ($C_3H_8$) and inorganic compounds, such as sodium chloride (NaCl). (See Figure 11.1.)

TABLE 11.1 Some Typical Properties of Organic and Inorganic Compounds

| Property | Organic | Example: $C_3H_8$ | Inorganic | Example: NaCl |
|---|---|---|---|---|
| Elements | C and H, sometimes O, S, N, P, or (F, Br, I) Cl | C and H | Most metals and nonmetals | Na and Cl |
| Bonding | Mostly covalent | Covalent (4 bonds to each C) | Many are ionic, some covalent | Ionic |
| Polarity of bonds | Nonpolar, unless a very electronegative atom is present | Nonpolar | Most are ionic or polar covalent, a few are nonpolar covalent | Ionic |
| Melting point | Usually low | −188 °C | Usually high | 801 °C |
| Boiling point | Usually low | −42 °C | Usually high | 1413 °C |
| Flammability | High | Burns in air | Low | Does not burn |
| Solubility in water | Not soluble, unless a polar group is present | No | Most are soluble, unless nonpolar | Yes |

CONCEPT CHECK 11.1

### Properties of Organic Compounds

Indicate whether the following properties are most typical of organic or inorganic compounds:

**a.** not soluble in water **b.** high melting point **c.** burns in air

ANSWER

**a.** Many organic compounds are not soluble in water.
**b.** Inorganic compounds are most likely to have high melting points.
**c.** Organic compounds are most likely to be flammable.

**FIGURE 11.1** Propane, $C_3H_8$, is an organic compound, whereas sodium chloride, NaCl, is an inorganic compound.

Q Why is propane used as a fuel?

## Bonding in Organic Compounds

**Hydrocarbons**, as the name suggests, are organic compounds that consist of only carbon and hydrogen. In the simplest hydrocarbon, methane ($CH_4$), the carbon atom forms an octet by sharing four valence electrons with four hydrogen atoms. In the electron-dot formula, each shared pair of electrons represents a single bond. In organic molecules, every carbon atom has four bonds. A hydrocarbon is referred to as a *saturated hydrocarbon* when all of the bonds in the molecule are single bonds. An **expanded structural formula** is written when we show the bonds between all of the atoms.

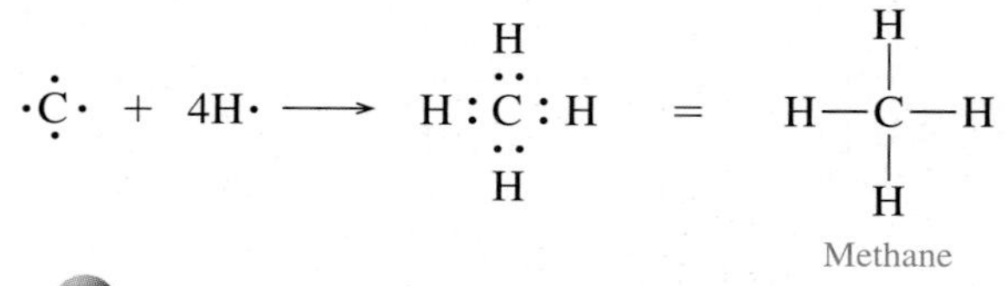

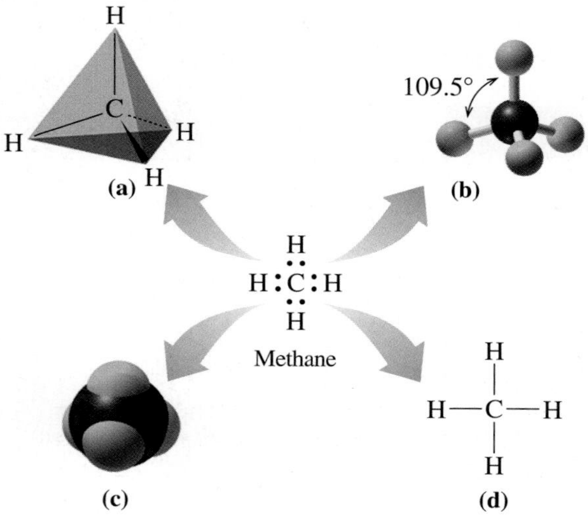

$$\cdot\dot{\underset{\cdot}{C}}\cdot + 4H\cdot \longrightarrow H:\overset{H}{\underset{H}{\ddot{\underset{..}{C}}}}:H \;=\; H-\overset{H}{\underset{H}{\overset{|}{\underset{|}{C}}}}-H$$

Methane

(a) (b) 109.5° Methane (c) (d)

FIGURE 11.2 Representations of methane, $CH_4$: **(a)** tetrahedron, **(b)** ball-and-stick model, **(c)** space-filling model, **(d)** expanded structural formula.

Q Why does methane have a tetrahedral shape and not a flat shape?

## The Tetrahedral Structure of Carbon

The VSEPR theory (Chapter 5) predicts that a molecule with four atoms bonded to a central atom has a tetrahedral shape. In $CH_4$, the bonds from the carbon atom to the four hydrogen atoms are directed to the corners of a tetrahedron with bond angles of 109.5°. The structure of methane is illustrated as both a ball-and-stick model and a space-filling model in Figure 11.2.

In ethane, $C_2H_6$, each carbon atom is bonded to another carbon and three hydrogen atoms. As in methane, each carbon retains the tetrahedral shape with bond angles close to 109.5°. In the ball-and-stick model of ethane, $C_2H_6$, two tetrahedra are attached to each other. (See Figure 11.3.)

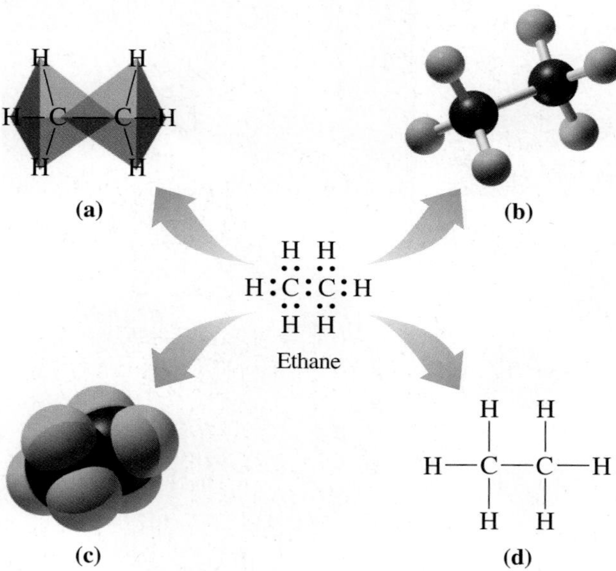


FIGURE 11.3 Representations of ethane, $C_2H_6$: **(a)** tetrahedral shape of each carbon, **(b)** ball-and-stick model, **(c)** space-filling model, **(d)** expanded structural formula.

Q How is the tetrahedral shape maintained by each carbon in a molecule with two carbon atoms?

## QUESTIONS AND PROBLEMS

### Organic Compounds

11.1 Identify the following as formulas of organic or inorganic compounds:
**a.** KCl **b.** $C_4H_{10}$ **c.** $C_3H_6O$
**d.** $H_2SO_4$ **e.** $CaCl_2$ **f.** $C_2H_5Cl$

**11.2** Identify the following as formulas of organic or inorganic compounds:
**a.** $C_6H_{12}O_6$ **b.** $Na_2SO_4$ **c.** $I_2$
**d.** $C_4H_9Cl$ **e.** $C_{10}H_{22}$ **f.** $CH_4$

11.3 Identify the following properties as most typical of organic or inorganic compounds:
**a.** soluble in water **b.** low boiling point
**c.** burns in air **d.** high melting point

**11.4** Identify the following properties as most typical of organic or inorganic compounds:
**a.** contains Na **b.** boils at −50 °C
**c.** covalent bonds **d.** produces ions in water

11.5 Match the following physical and chemical properties with the compounds ethane, $C_2H_6$, or sodium bromide, NaBr:
**a.** boils at −89 °C **b.** burns vigorously
**c.** solid at 250 °C **d.** dissolves in water

**11.6** Match the following physical and chemical properties with the compounds cyclohexane, $C_6H_{12}$, or calcium nitrate, $Ca(NO_3)_2$:
**a.** melts at 500 °C **b.** insoluble in water
**c.** produces ions in water **d.** is a liquid at room temperature

11.7 Why is the shape of the $CH_4$ molecule three-dimensional rather than two-dimensional?

**11.8** In a propane molecule with three carbon atoms, what is the geometry around each carbon atom?

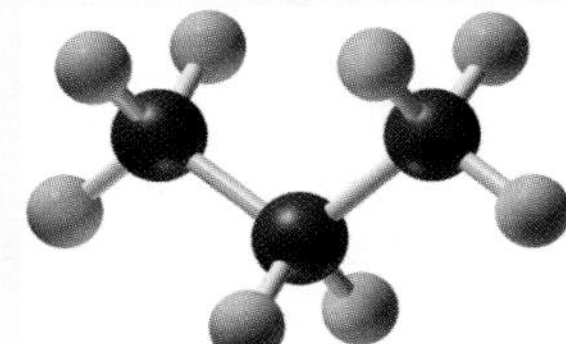
Propane

# 11.2 Alkanes

**LEARNING GOAL**
Write the IUPAC names and condensed structural formulas for alkanes.

More than 90% of the compounds in the world are organic compounds. This large number of carbon compounds is possible because the covalent bond between carbon atoms (C—C) is very strong, allowing carbon atoms to form long, stable chains. To help us study this large group of compounds, we organize them into classes that have similar structures and chemical properties.

The **alkanes** are a class of hydrocarbons in which the atoms are connected by single bonds. One of the most common uses of alkanes is as fuels. Methane, used in gas heaters and gas cooktops, is an alkane with one carbon atom. The alkanes ethane, propane, and butane contain two, three, and four carbon atoms, respectively, connected in a row or a *continuous chain*. These names are part of the **IUPAC** (International Union of Pure and Applied Chemistry) **system**, which chemists use to name organic compounds. Alkanes with five or more carbon atoms in a chain are named using Greek prefixes: *pent*(5), *hex*(6), *hept*(7), *oct*(8), *non*(9), and *dec*(10). (See Table 11.2.)

MC™ TUTORIAL
IUPAC Naming of Alkanes

**TABLE 11.2** IUPAC Names for the First Ten Alkanes

| Number of Carbon Atoms | Prefix | Name | Molecular Formula | Condensed Structural Formula |
|---|---|---|---|---|
| 1 | Meth | Methane | $CH_4$ | $CH_4$ |
| 2 | Eth | Ethane | $C_2H_6$ | $CH_3—CH_3$ |
| 3 | Prop | Propane | $C_3H_8$ | $CH_3—CH_2—CH_3$ |
| 4 | But | Butane | $C_4H_{10}$ | $CH_3—CH_2—CH_2—CH_3$ |
| 5 | Pent | Pentane | $C_5H_{12}$ | $CH_3—CH_2—CH_2—CH_2—CH_3$ |
| 6 | Hex | Hexane | $C_6H_{14}$ | $CH_3—CH_2—CH_2—CH_2—CH_2—CH_3$ |
| 7 | Hept | Heptane | $C_7H_{16}$ | $CH_3—CH_2—CH_2—CH_2—CH_2—CH_2—CH_3$ |
| 8 | Oct | Octane | $C_8H_{18}$ | $CH_3—CH_2—CH_2—CH_2—CH_2—CH_2—CH_2—CH_3$ |
| 9 | Non | Nonane | $C_9H_{20}$ | $CH_3—CH_2—CH_2—CH_2—CH_2—CH_2—CH_2—CH_2—CH_3$ |
| 10 | Dec | Decane | $C_{10}H_{22}$ | $CH_3—CH_2—CH_2—CH_2—CH_2—CH_2—CH_2—CH_2—CH_2—CH_3$ |

## Condensed Structural Formulas

In a **condensed structural formula**, each carbon atom and its attached hydrogen atoms are written as a group. A subscript indicates the number of hydrogen atoms bonded to each carbon atom.

$$\begin{array}{c}\text{H}\\ |\\ \text{H}-\text{C}-\\ |\\ \text{H}\end{array} = CH_3- \qquad \begin{array}{c}\text{H}\\ |\\ -\text{C}-\\ |\\ \text{H}\end{array} = -CH_2-$$

Expanded Condensed Expanded Condensed

By contrast, the molecular formula gives the total number of each kind of atom but does not indicate their arrangement in the molecule. When a molecule consists of a chain of three or more carbon atoms, the carbon atoms do not lie in a straight line. The tetrahedral shape of carbon arranges the carbon bonds in a zigzag pattern, which is seen in the ball-and-stick model of hexane. An abbreviated structure called the **line-bond formula** shows only the bonds from carbon to carbon. The ends of the lines and the corners where the lines meet are understood to be carbon atoms attached to the proper number of hydrogen atoms to give four bonds. (See Figure 11.4.)

Alkane name: Hexane

Molecular formula: $C_6H_{14}$

Ball-and-stick model

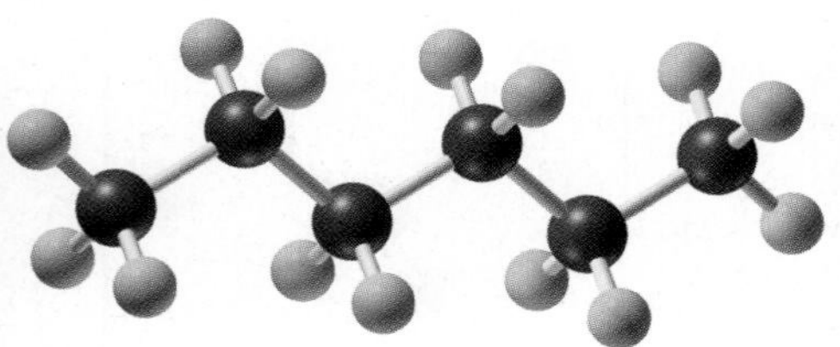

Expanded structural formula

$$\begin{array}{c}\text{H}\ \ \text{H}\ \ \text{H}\ \ \text{H}\ \ \text{H}\ \ \text{H}\\ \text{H}-\text{C}-\text{C}-\text{C}-\text{C}-\text{C}-\text{C}-\text{H}\\ \text{H}\ \ \text{H}\ \ \text{H}\ \ \text{H}\ \ \text{H}\ \ \text{H}\end{array}$$

Condensed structural formulas

$$CH_3\diagup CH_2 \diagdown CH_2 \diagup CH_2 \diagdown CH_2 \diagup CH_3$$

$$CH_3-CH_2-CH_2-CH_2-CH_2-CH_3$$

Line-bond formula

/\/\/

**FIGURE 11.4** A ball-and-stick model and structural formulas of hexane.

**Q** Why do the carbon atoms in hexane appear to be arranged in a zigzag chain?

Because an alkane has only single C—C bonds, the groups attached to each C are not in fixed positions. They can rotate freely about the bond connecting the carbon atoms. This motion is analogous to the independent rotation of the wheels of a toy car. Thus different arrangements, known as *conformations*, occur during the rotation about a single bond.

Suppose we could look at butane, $C_4H_{10}$, as it rotates. Sometimes the $-CH_3$ groups line up in front of each other, and at other times they are opposite each other. As the $-CH_3$ groups turn around the single bond, many arrangements are possible. Butane can be depicted by a variety of two-dimensional condensed structural formulas, as shown in Table 11.3. All of these condensed structural formulas represent the same compound with four carbon atoms.

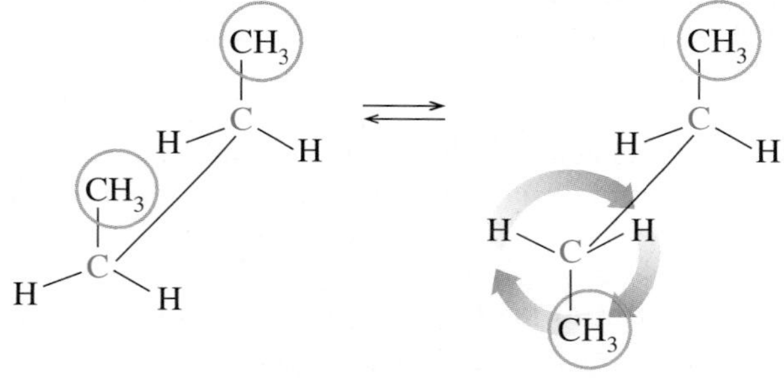


**TABLE 11.3** Structural Representations for Butane, $C_4H_{10}$

**Expanded structural formula**

$$\begin{array}{c}\text{H}\ \ \text{H}\ \ \text{H}\ \ \text{H}\\ \text{H}-\text{C}-\text{C}-\text{C}-\text{C}-\text{H}\\ \text{H}\ \ \text{H}\ \ \text{H}\ \ \text{H}\end{array}$$

**Condensed structural formulas**

$CH_3-CH_2-CH_2-CH_3$

$$\begin{array}{ll}CH_2 & -CH_2\\ | & \ \ |\\ CH_3 & \ \ CH_3\end{array} \qquad \begin{array}{l}CH_3\\ |\\ CH_2-CH_2\\ \qquad\ \ |\\ \qquad\ \ CH_3\end{array} \qquad \begin{array}{c}CH_3\\ |\\ CH_2\\ |\\ CH_2\\ |\\ CH_3\end{array}$$

$$\begin{array}{l}CH_3-CH_2\\ \qquad\ \ |\\ \qquad\ \ CH_2-CH_3\end{array} \qquad \begin{array}{l}CH_3\\ |\\ CH_2-CH_2-CH_3\end{array} \qquad CH_3\diagdown CH_2 \diagup CH_2 \diagdown CH_3$$

**Line-bond formulas**

/\/ \/\

SAMPLE PROBLEM 11.1

### Drawing Structural Formulas for Alkanes

A molecule of butane, $C_4H_{10}$, has four carbon atoms in a row. What are its expanded, condensed, and line-bond structural formulas?

SOLUTION

In the expanded structural formula, the four carbon atoms are connected to each other and to hydrogen atoms with single bonds to give each carbon atom a total of four bonds. In the condensed structural formula, each carbon atom and its attached hydrogen atoms are written as $CH_3$— or —$CH_2$—. The line-bond formula shows only the carbon-to-carbon bonds.

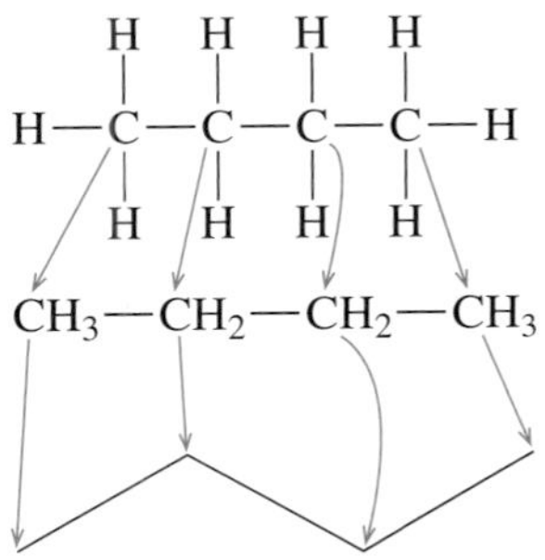

H H H H
H—C—C—C—C—H Expanded structural formula
H H H H

$CH_3—CH_2—CH_2—CH_3$ Condensed structural formula

Line-bond formula

STUDY CHECK

Write the expanded, condensed, and line-bond structural formulas of pentane, $C_5H_{12}$.

## Cycloalkanes

Hydrocarbons can also form cyclic structures called **cycloalkanes**, which have two fewer hydrogen atoms than the corresponding alkanes. Thus, the simplest cycloalkane, cyclopropane, $C_3H_6$, has a ring of three carbon atoms bonded to six hydrogen atoms. A simplified formula, which omits the hydrogen atoms and looks like a geometric figure, is a convenient way to show cyclic structures. Each corner of the triangle represents a carbon atom with four bonds to other carbon and hydrogen atoms.

The ball-and-stick models, their condensed structural formulas, and geometric formulas for several cycloalkanes are shown in Table 11.4. A cycloalkane is named by adding the prefix *cyclo* to the name of the alkane with the same number of carbon atoms.

SAMPLE PROBLEM 11.2

### Naming Alkanes

Give the IUPAC name for each of the following:

**a.** $CH_3—CH_2—CH_2—CH_2—CH_3$ **b.** 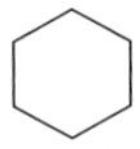 (hexagon) **c.** $CH_3—CH_2—CH_3$

SOLUTION

**a.** A chain with five carbon atoms is pentane.
**b.** The ring of six carbon atoms is named cyclohexane.
**c.** This alkane is named propane because it has three carbon atoms.

STUDY CHECK

What is the IUPAC name of the following compound?

(square)

**TABLE 11.4** Formulas of Some Common Cycloalkanes

| | | | |
|---|---|---|---|
| **Ball-and-Stick Models** | | | |
|  | 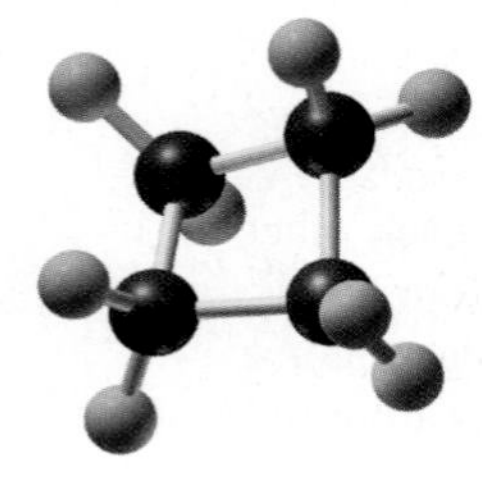 | 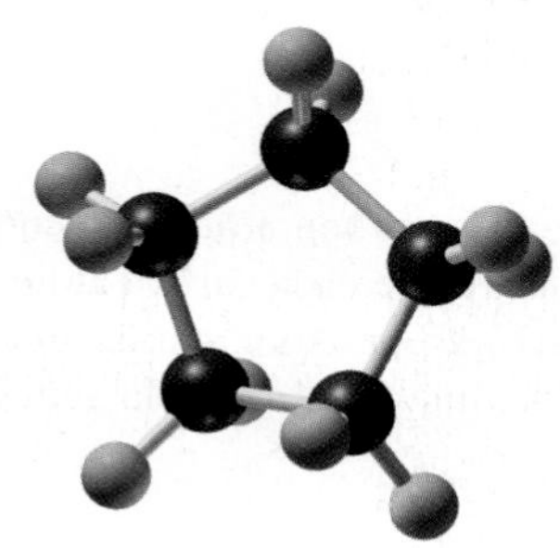 | 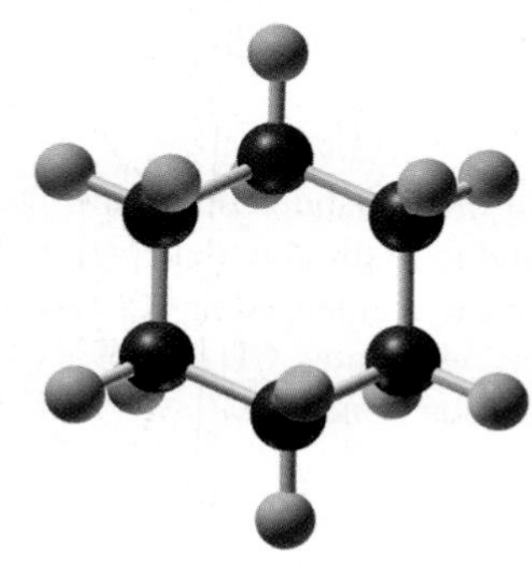 |
| **Condensed Structural Formulas** | | | |
| $CH_2$ / $H_2C—CH_2$ (three-membered ring) | $H_2C—CH_2$ / $H_2C—CH_2$ (four-membered ring) | $CH_2$ / $H_2C$ $CH_2$ / $H_2C—CH_2$ (five-membered ring) | $CH_2$ / $H_2C$ $CH_2$ / $H_2C$ $CH_2$ / $CH_2$ (six-membered ring) |
| **Geometric Formulas** | | | |
|  |  |  |  |
| **Name** | | | |
| Cyclopropane | Cyclobutane | Cyclopentane | Cyclohexane |

## QUESTIONS AND PROBLEMS

### Alkanes

**11.9** Write the stated type of structural formula for each of the following:
- **a.** an expanded structural formula for propane
- **b.** the condensed structural formula for hexane
- **c.** a line-bond formula for hexane

**11.10** Write the stated type of structural formula for each of the following:
- **a.** an expanded structural formula for butane
- **b.** the condensed structural formula for octane
- **c.** a line-bond formula for decane

**11.11** Give the IUPAC name for each of the following:

**a.** $CH_3$ | $CH_2—CH_2—CH_2$ | $CH_3$

**b.** (zigzag line-bond formula)

**c.** $CH_2—CH_3$ | $CH_2$ | $CH_3—CH_2—CH_2$

**d.** 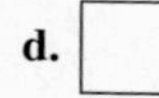

**11.12** Give the IUPAC name for each of the following alkanes:

**a.** $CH_4$

**b.** (zigzag line-bond formula)

**c.** $CH_3$ | $CH_2$ | $CH_3$

**d.** (hexagon)

**11.13** Write the condensed structural formula or geometric formula for each of the following:
- **a.** methane
- **b.** ethane
- **c.** pentane
- **d.** cyclopropane

**11.14** Write the condensed structural formula or geometric formula for each of the following:
- **a.** propane
- **b.** hexane
- **c.** heptane
- **d.** cyclopentane

## 11.3 Alkanes with Substituents

**LEARNING GOAL**

Write the IUPAC names for alkanes with substituents.

When an alkane has four or more carbon atoms, the atoms can be arranged so that a side group called a **branch** or **substituent** is attached to a carbon chain. For example, there are two different ball-and-stick models for the molecular formula $C_4H_{10}$. One model is shown as a chain of four carbon atoms. In the other model, a carbon atom is attached as a branch or substituent to a carbon in a chain of three atoms. (See Figure 11.5.) An alkane with at least one branch is called a **branched alkane**. When two compounds have the same molecular formula but different arrangements of atoms, they are called **isomers**.

In another example, we can write three different structural isomers that have the molecular formula $C_5H_{12}$ as follows:

**Isomers of $C_5H_{12}$**

| Alkane | Branched Alkanes | |
|---|---|---|
| $CH_3—CH_2—CH_2—CH_2—CH_3$ | $\begin{array}{c}\quad CH_3 \\ \quad \vert \\ CH_3—CH—CH_2—CH_3\end{array}$ | $\begin{array}{c}CH_3 \\ \vert \\ CH_3—C—CH_3 \\ \vert \\ CH_3\end{array}$ |

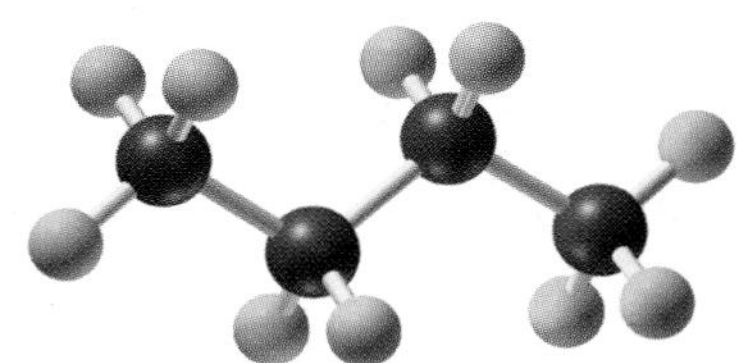

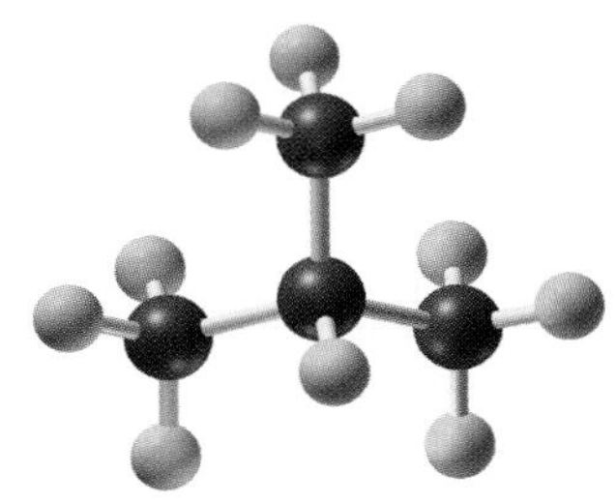

**FIGURE 11.5** The isomers of $C_4H_{10}$ have the same number and type of atoms, which are bonded in a different order.

**Q** What makes these molecules isomers?

The number of structural isomers for alkanes increases rapidly as the number of carbon atoms increases.

**Possible Isomers for Alkanes with 1–10 Carbon Atoms**

| Number of Carbon Atoms | Numbers of Isomers |
|---|---|
| 1 | 1 |
| 2 | 1 |
| 3 | 1 |
| 4 | 2 |
| 5 | 3 |
| 6 | 5 |
| 7 | 9 |
| 8 | 18 |
| 9 | 35 |
| 10 | 75 |

### SAMPLE PROBLEM 11.3

#### Isomers

Identify each pair of condensed structural formulas as isomers or the same molecule:

**a.** $\begin{array}{l}CH_3 \quad CH_3 \\ \vert \qquad\quad \vert \\ CH_2—CH_2\end{array}$ and $\begin{array}{l}CH_2—CH_2—CH_3 \\ \vert \\ CH_3\end{array}$

**b.** $\begin{array}{l}\qquad\quad CH_3 \\ \qquad\quad \vert \\ CH_3—CH—CH_2—CH_2—CH_3\end{array}$ and $\begin{array}{l}\qquad\quad CH_3 \quad CH_3 \\ \qquad\quad \vert \qquad\quad \vert \\ CH_3—CH—CH—CH_3\end{array}$

SOLUTION

**a.** The condensed structural formulas represent the same molecule because they both have four C atoms in a chain with no substituents.

**b.** These are isomers because the molecular formula $C_6H_{14}$ is identical, but the C atoms are bonded in a different order. One has a $—CH_3$ group attached to a five-carbon chain, and the other has two $—CH_3$ groups attached to a four-carbon chain.

STUDY CHECK

Is the following condensed structural formula an isomer or identical to the molecules in Sample Problem 11.3b?

$$\begin{array}{c}CH_3 \\ \vert \\ CH_3—CH_2—CH—CH_2—CH_3\end{array}$$

### Substituents in Alkanes

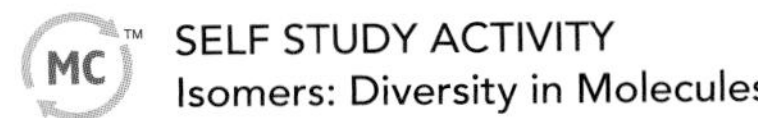

SELF STUDY ACTIVITY
Isomers: Diversity in Molecules

In the IUPAC names for alkanes, a carbon branch is named as an **alkyl group**, which is an alkane that is missing one hydrogen atom. The alkyl group is named by replacing the *ane* ending of the corresponding alkane name with *yl*. Alkyl groups cannot exist on their own;

**TABLE 11.5 Names and Formulas of Some Common Substituents**

| Substituent | Name |
|---|---|
| $CH_3—$ | Methyl |
| $CH_3—CH_2—$ | Ethyl |
| $CH_3—CH_2—CH_2—$ | Propyl |
| $CH_3—\underset{\vert}{CH}—CH_3$ | Isopropyl |
| F—, Cl—, Br—, I— | Fluoro, chloro, bromo, iodo |

TUTORIAL Naming Alkanes with Substituents

they must be attached to a carbon chain. When a halogen atom is attached to a carbon chain, it is named as a *halo* group: fluoro (F), chloro (Cl), bromo (Br), or iodo (I). Some of the common groups attached to carbon chains are illustrated in Table 11.5.

## Rules for Naming Alkanes with Substituents

In the IUPAC system, a carbon chain with a substituent is numbered to give the location of that substituent. Let's take a look at how we use the IUPAC system to name the following alkane:

$$CH_3—\overset{\overset{CH_3}{\vert}}{CH}—CH_2—CH_2—CH_3$$

**STEP 1** **Write the alkane name of the longest chain of carbon atoms.** In this alkane, the longest chain has five carbon atoms, which is *pentane*:

$$CH_3—\overset{\overset{CH_3}{\vert}}{CH}—CH_2—CH_2—CH_3 \qquad \text{pentane}$$

**STEP 2** **Number the carbon atoms starting from the end nearest a substituent.** Once you start numbering, continue in that same direction:

$$\underset{1}{CH_3}—\underset{2}{\overset{\overset{CH_3}{\vert}}{CH}}—\underset{3}{CH_2}—\underset{4}{CH_2}—\underset{5}{CH_3} \qquad \text{pentane}$$

**STEP 3** **Give the location and name of each substituent as a prefix to the alkane name.** Place a hyphen between the number and the substituent name:

$$\underset{1}{CH_3}—\underset{2}{\overset{\overset{CH_3}{\vert}}{CH}}—\underset{3}{CH_2}—\underset{4}{CH_2}—\underset{5}{CH_3} \qquad \text{2-methylpentane}$$

Below are more examples giving the locations of the substituents. Place the names of different substituents in alphabetical order.

$$\underset{1}{CH_3}—\underset{2}{\overset{\overset{CH_3}{\vert}}{CH}}—\underset{3}{\overset{\overset{Cl}{\vert}}{CH}}—\underset{4}{CH_2}—\underset{5}{CH_3} \qquad \text{3-chloro-2-methylpentane}$$

Use a prefix (*di*, *tri*, *tetra*) to indicate a group that appears more than once. Use commas to separate two or more numbers. However, prefixes are not used to determine the alphabetical order:

$$\underset{1}{CH_3}—\underset{2}{\overset{\overset{CH_3}{\vert}}{CH}}—\underset{3}{\overset{\overset{CH_3}{\vert}}{CH}}—\underset{4}{CH_2}—\underset{5}{CH_3} \qquad \text{2,3-dimethylpentane}$$

When there are two or more substituents, the main chain is numbered in the direction that gives the lowest set of numbers:

$$\underset{5}{CH_3}—\underset{4}{\overset{\overset{Br}{\vert}}{CH}}—\underset{3}{CH_2}—\underset{2}{\overset{\overset{CH_3}{\vert}}{\underset{\underset{Br}{\vert}}{C}}}—\underset{1}{CH_3} \qquad \text{2,4-dibromo-2-methylpentane}$$

No number is necessary for a compound with one or two carbon atoms and one substituent:

| | |
|---|---|
| $CH_3—Br$ | bromomethane |
| $CH_3—CH_2—Cl$ | chloroethane |

## Naming Cycloalkanes

TUTORIAL
Naming Cycloalkanes

When one substituent is attached to a carbon atom in a ring, the name of the substituent is placed in front of the cycloalkane name. No number is needed for a single alkyl group or halogen atom because the carbon atoms in the cycloalkane are equivalent. However, if two or more groups are attached, the ring is numbered to show the location of each group. The numbering starts by assigning carbon 1 to the substituent that gives the lowest numbers to the other substituents. When there are two substituents, the one that comes first alphabetically is attached to carbon 1. We may count clockwise or counterclockwise around a cycloalkane to give the lowest combination of numbers to the substituents.

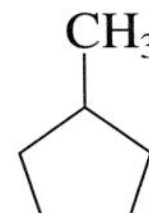

Methylcyclopentane

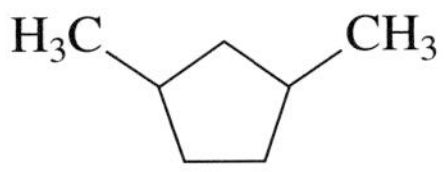

$H_3C$ $CH_3$

1,3-Dimethylcyclopentane

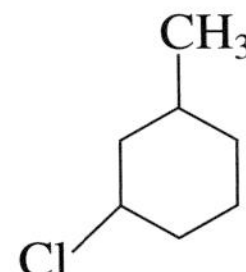

1-Chloro-3-methylcyclohexane

CONCEPT CHECK 11.2

### Naming Compounds with Substituents

A six-carbon chain has a $CH_3—$ group attached to carbon 2 and a $Cl—$ atom attached to carbon 3. What is the name of this compound?

ANSWER

The $CH_3—$ group is named as a methyl and the $Cl—$ atom is named as a chloro. In alphabetical order, these substituents are named 3-chloro-2-methyl. The six-carbon chain is named hexane, and the compound is named 3-chloro-2-methylhexane.

SAMPLE PROBLEM 11.4

### Writing IUPAC Names

Give the IUPAC name for the following alkane:

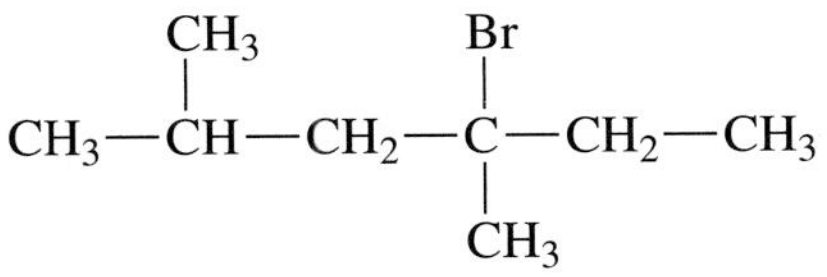

```
       CH3        Br
       |          |
CH3—CH—CH2—C—CH2—CH3
                  |
                  CH3
```

SOLUTION

**STEP 1** **Write the alkane name of the longest chain of carbon atoms.** In this alkane, the longest chain has six carbon atoms, which is *hexane*:

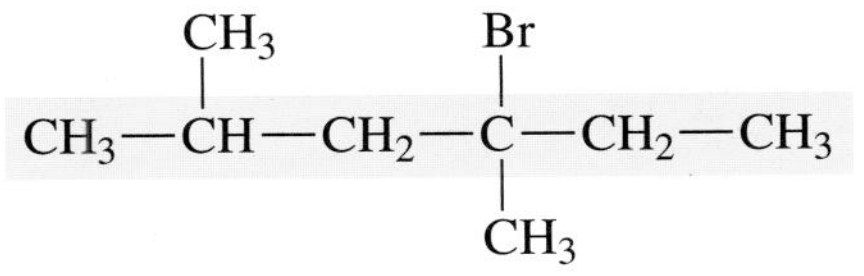

```
       CH3        Br
       |          |
CH3—CH—CH2—C—CH2—CH3        hexane
                  |
                  CH3
```

**Guide to Naming Alkanes**

STEP 1
Write the alkane name of the longest chain of carbon atoms.

STEP 2
Number the carbon atoms starting from the end nearest a substituent.

STEP 3
Give the location and name of each substituent (alphabetical order) as a prefix to the name of the main chain.

**STEP 2** **Number the carbon atoms starting from the end nearest a substituent:**

$$\begin{array}{cccccc} & CH_3 & & Br & & \\ & | & & | & & \\ CH_3- & CH- & CH_2- & C- & CH_2- & CH_3 \\ & & & | & & \\ & & & CH_3 & & \\ 1 & 2 & 3 & 4 & 5 & 6 \end{array}$$

hexane

**STEP 3** **Give the location and name of each substituent in front of the name of the longest chain. List the names of different substituents in alphabetical order.** Place hyphens between the numbers and the substituent names and add commas to separate two or more numbers. A prefix (*di*, *tri*, *tetra*) indicates a group that appears more than once.

$$\begin{array}{cccccc} & CH_3 & & Br & & \\ & | & & | & & \\ CH_3- & CH- & CH_2- & C- & CH_2- & CH_3 \\ & & & | & & \\ & & & CH_3 & & \\ 1 & 2 & 3 & 4 & 5 & 6 \end{array}$$

4-bromo-2,4-dimethylhexane

STUDY CHECK

Give the IUPAC name for the following compound:

$$\begin{array}{ccccccc} & & CH_3 & & CH_3 & & \\ & & | & & | & & \\ CH_3- & CH_2- & CH- & CH_2- & CH- & CH_2- & Cl \end{array}$$

## Drawing Structural Formulas for Alkanes

The IUPAC name gives all the information needed to draw the condensed structural formula of an alkane. Suppose you are asked to draw the condensed structural formula of 2,3-dimethylbutane. The alkane name gives the number of carbon atoms in the longest chain. The names in the beginning indicate the substituents and where they are attached. We can break down the name in the following way.

**2,3-Dimethylbutane**

| 2,3- | di | methyl | but | ane |
|---|---|---|---|---|
| Substituents on carbons 2 and 3 | Two identical groups | $CH_3-$ alkyl groups | 4 carbon atoms in the main chain | Single C—C bonds |

SAMPLE PROBLEM 11.5

### Drawing Condensed Structural Formulas from IUPAC Names

Write the condensed structural formula for 2,3-dimethylbutane.

SOLUTION

We can use the following guide to draw the condensed structural formula:

**Guide to Drawing Alkane Formulas**

STEP 1
Draw the main chain of carbon atoms.

STEP 2
Number the chain and place the substituents on the carbons indicated by the numbers.

STEP 3
Add the correct number of hydrogen atoms to give four bonds to each C atom.

**STEP 1** **Draw the main chain of carbon atoms.** For butane, we draw a chain of four carbon atoms:

C—C—C—C

**STEP 2** **Number the chain and place the substituents on the carbons indicated by the numbers.** The first part of the name indicates two methyl groups ($CH_3-$), one on carbon 2 and one on carbon 3:

$$\begin{array}{cccc} & \text{Methyl} & \text{Methyl} & \\ & CH_3 & CH_3 & \\ & | & | & \\ C- & C- & C- & C \\ 1 & 2 & 3 & 4 \end{array}$$

**STEP 3** **Add the correct number of hydrogen atoms to give four bonds to each C atom:**

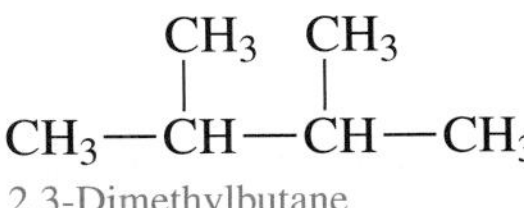

2,3-Dimethylbutane

STUDY CHECK

Draw the condensed structural formula for 2,4-dimethylpentane.

## Haloalkanes

In a **haloalkane**, halogen atoms replace hydrogen atoms in an alkane. The halogen substituents are numbered and arranged alphabetically, just as we did with the alkyl groups. Many times chemists use the common, traditional name for these compounds rather than the systematic IUPAC name. Simple haloalkanes are commonly named as alkyl halides; the carbon group is named as an alkyl group followed by the halide name:

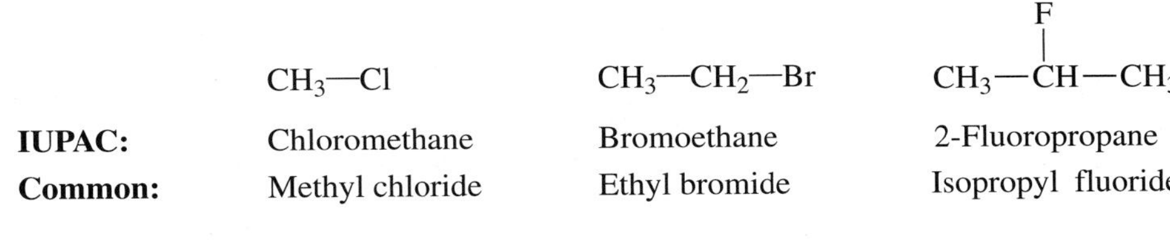

| | $CH_3—Cl$ | $CH_3—CH_2—Br$ | $CH_3—CH(F)—CH_3$ |
|---|---|---|---|
| **IUPAC:** | Chloromethane | Bromoethane | 2-Fluoropropane |
| **Common:** | Methyl chloride | Ethyl bromide | Isopropyl fluoride |

SAMPLE PROBLEM 11.6

### Naming Haloalkanes

Freon 11 and Freon 12 are compounds, known as *chlorofluorocarbons* (CFCs), that were used as refrigerants and aerosol propellants. What are their IUPAC names?

$CCl_3F$ (Cl—C—F with Cl above and Cl below)

Freon 11

$CCl_2F_2$ (F—C—F with Cl above and Cl below)

Freon 12

SOLUTION

Freon 11, trichlorofluoromethane; Freon 12, dichlorodifluoromethane.

STUDY CHECK

Ethylene dibromide is the common name of a haloalkane used as a fumigant. What is its IUPAC name?

H—C(Br)(H)—C(Br)(H)—H

Ethylene dibromide

CAREER FOCUS

### Geologist

"Chemistry underpins geology," says Vic Abadie, consulting geologist. "I am a self-employed geologist consulting in exploration for petroleum and natural gas. Predicting the occurrence of an oil reservoir depends in part on understanding chemical reactions of minerals. This is because over geologic time such reactions create or destroy pore spaces that host crude oil or gas in a reservoir rock formation. Chemical analysis can match oil in known reservoir formations with distant formations that generated oil and from which oil migrated into the reservoirs in the geologic past. This can help identify target areas to explore for new reservoirs."

"I evaluate proposals to drill for undiscovered oil and gas. I recommend that my clients invest in proposed wells that my analysis suggests have strong geologic and economic merit. This is a commercial application of the scientific method: the proposal to drill is the hypothesis, and the drill bit tests it. A successful well validates the hypothesis and generates oil or gas production and revenue for my clients and me. I do this and other consulting for private and corporate clients. The risk is high, the work is exciting, and my time is flexible."

TUTORIAL
Drawing Haloalkanes and Branched Alkanes

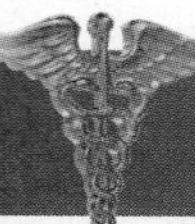

# HEALTH NOTE

## Common Uses of Haloalkanes

Some common uses of haloalkanes include solvents and anesthetics. For many years, carbon tetrachloride was widely used in dry cleaners and in home spot removers to take oils and grease out of clothes. However, this use was discontinued when carbon tetrachloride was found to be toxic to the liver, where it can cause cancer. Today, dry cleaners use other halogenated compounds such as dichloromethane; 1,1,1-trichloroethane; and 1,1,2-trichloro-1,2,2-trifluoroethane.

| $CH_2Cl_2$ | $Cl_3C—CH_3$ | $FCl_2C—CClF_2$ |
|---|---|---|
| Dichloromethane | 1,1,1-Trichloroethane | 1,1,2-Trichloro-1,2,2-trifluoroethane |

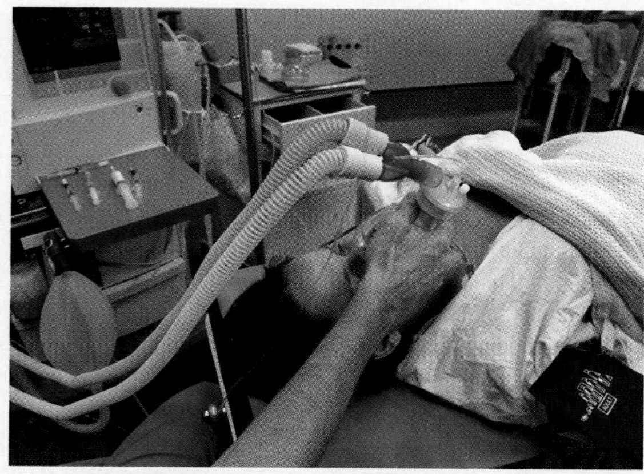

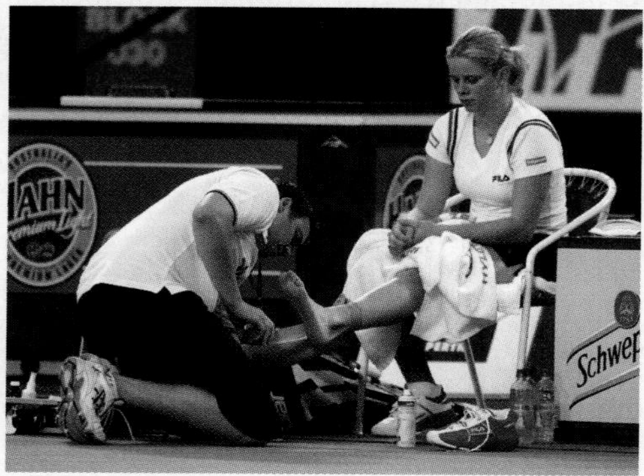

General anesthetics are compounds that are inhaled or injected to cause a loss of sensation so that surgery or other procedures can be done without causing pain to the patient. As nonpolar compounds, anesthetics are soluble in the nonpolar nerve membranes, where they decrease the ability of the nerve cells to conduct the sensation of pain. Trichloromethane, commonly called chloroform, $CHCl_3$, was once used as an anesthetic, but it is toxic and may be carcinogenic. One of the most widely used general anesthetics is halothane (2-bromo-2-chloro-1,1,1-trifluoroethane), also called Fluothane. It has a pleasant odor, is nonexplosive, has few side effects, undergoes few reactions, and is eliminated quickly from the body.

```
    F   Cl
    |   |
F — C — C — Br     Halothane (Fluothane)
    |   |
    F   H
```

For minor surgeries, a local anesthetic such as chloroethane (ethyl chloride), $CH_3—CH_2—Cl$, is applied to an area of the skin. Chloroethane evaporates quickly, which cools the skin and causes a loss of sensation.

# QUESTIONS AND PROBLEMS

## Alkanes with Substituents

**11.15** Indicate whether each of the following pairs of condensed structural formulas represent isomers or the same molecule:

```
a.        CH3                   CH3
          |                     |
    CH3 — CH — CH3      and     CH — CH3
                                |
                                CH3

b.        CH3                   CH3           CH3
          |                     |             |
    CH3 — CH — CH2 — CH3  and   CH2 — CH2 — CH2

c.  CH3   CH3                    CH3  CH3
    |     |                      |    |
    CH2 — CH — CH2 — CH3  and    CH3 — CH — CH — CH3
```

**11.16** Indicate whether each of the following pairs of condensed structural formulas represent isomers or the same molecule:

```
a.        CH3                  CH3
          |                    |
    CH3 — C — CH3      and     CH — CH2 — CH3
          |                    |
          CH3                  CH3

b.        CH3  CH3  CH3
          |    |    |
    CH3 — CH — CH — CH2    and

          CH3       CH3
          |         |
    CH3 — CH — CH2 — CH — CH3

c.        CH3                                  CH3
          |                                    |
    CH3 — CH — CH2 — CH3   and   CH3 — CH2 — CH — CH3
```

**11.17** Give the IUPAC name for each of the following alkanes:

a. $\quad CH_3$
$CH_3-CH-CH_2-CH_3$

b. $\quad CH_3$
$CH_3-C-CH_3$
$\quad CH_3$

c. $\quad\quad CH_3 \quad CH_3$
$CH_3-CH_2-CH-CH-CH_3$

d. $CH_3 \quad\quad CH_2-CH_3$
$CH_3-C-CH_2-CH-CH_2-CH_3$
$\quad CH_3$

**11.18** Give the IUPAC name for each of the following alkanes:

a. $\quad CH_3$
$CH_3-CH-CH_2-CH_2-CH_3$

b. $\quad CH_3 \quad CH_3$
$CH_3-CH-CH-CH_3$

c. $\quad\quad CH_3 \quad\quad CH_3$
$CH_3-CH_2-CH-CH_2-CH-CH_3$

d. $\quad\quad CH_2-CH_3$
$CH_3-CH_2-CH-CH-CH_2-CH_3$
$\quad\quad CH_2-CH_3$

**11.19** Give the IUPAC name for each of the following:

a. Cl (on cyclopentane)

b. $CH_3$ (on cyclohexane)

c. $CH_3$, Br (on cyclobutane)

d. Cl, Br (on cyclopentane)

**11.20** Give the IUPAC name for each of the following:

a. Cl (on cyclobutane)

b. $CH_3$, Br (on cyclopentane)

c. $CH_3$, $CH_2-CH_3$ (on cyclohexane)

d. Cl, Cl (on cyclohexane)

**11.21** Draw a condensed structural formula for each of the following alkanes:

a. 2-methylbutane
b. 3,3-dimethylpentane
c. 2,3,5-trimethylhexane
d. 3-ethyl-2,5-dimethyloctane

**11.22** Draw a condensed structural formula for each of the following alkanes:

a. 3-ethylpentane
b. 3-ethyl-2-methylpentane
c. 2,2,3,5-tetramethylhexane
d. 4-ethyl-2,2-dimethyloctane

**11.23** Draw the structural formula for each of the following cycloalkanes using their geometric formulas:

a. methylcyclopentane
b. chlorocyclohexane
c. 1,3-dimethylcyclobutane
d. 1-bromo-2,3-dimethylcyclopentane

**11.24** Draw the structural formula for each of the following cycloalkanes using their geometric formulas:

a. bromocyclopropane
b. ethylcyclohexane
c. 1,2-dichlorocyclobutane
d. 1,3-dibromocyclopentane

**11.25** Give the IUPAC name for each of the following compounds:

a. $CH_3-CH_2-Br$
b. $CH_3-CH_2-CH_2-F$
c. $\quad CH_3$
$CH_3-CH-Cl$
d. $CHCl_3$

**11.26** Give the IUPAC name for each of the following compounds:

a. $\quad\quad Cl$
$CH_3-CH_2-CH-CH_3$
b. $CCl_4$
c. $\quad CH_3$
$CH_3-C-I$
$\quad CH_3$
d. $CH_3F$

**11.27** Write the condensed structural formula for each of the following compounds:

a. 2-chloropropane
b. 2-bromo-3-chlorobutane
c. methyl bromide
d. tetrabromomethane

**11.28** Write the condensed structural formula for each of the following compounds:

a. 1,1,2,2-tetrabromopropane
b. 2-bromopropane
c. 2,3-dichloro-2-methylbutane
d. dibromodichloromethane

## 11.4 Properties of Alkanes

**LEARNING GOAL**

Identify the properties of alkanes, and write chemical equations for combustion.

Many types of alkanes are the components of fuels that power our cars and oil that heats our homes. You may have used a mixture of hydrocarbons such as mineral oil as a laxative or petrolatum (Vaseline) to soften your skin. The differences in uses of many of the alkanes result from their physical properties, including solubility, density, and boiling point.

## Solubility and Density

CASE STUDY
Hazardous Materials

Alkanes are nonpolar, which makes them insoluble in water. However, they are soluble in nonpolar solvents such as other alkanes. Alkanes have densities from 0.6 g/mL to about 0.8 g/mL, which is less dense than water (1.0 g/mL). If there is an oil spill in the ocean, the alkanes in the crude oil remain on the surface and spread over a large area. In the *Exxon Valdez* oil spill in 1989, 40 million liters of oil covered over 25 000 square kilometers of water in Prince William Sound, Alaska. (See Figure 11.6.) If the crude oil reaches the beaches and inlets, there can be considerable damage to beaches, shellfish, fish, birds, and wildlife habitats. Cleanup includes both mechanical and chemical methods. In one method, a nonpolar compound that is "oil-attracting" is used to pick up oil, which is then scraped off into recovery tanks. Most of the cleanup started in 1989 and ended by 1991. Surveys in 2002 indicated that some oil still remains on the shoreline and that of the 30 species injured, most are recovering. However, the recovery of about 10 species, including some seals, birds, and fish, is not known.

**FIGURE 11.6** In oil spills, large quantities of oil spread over the water.

**Q** What physical properties cause oil to remain on the surface of water?

## Some Uses of Alkanes

The first four alkanes—methane, ethane, propane, and butane—are gases at room temperature and are widely used as heating fuels.

Alkanes having 5–8 carbon atoms (pentane, hexane, heptane, and octane) are liquids at room temperature. They are highly volatile, which makes them useful in fuels such as gasoline. Liquid alkanes with 9–17 carbon atoms have higher boiling points and are found in kerosene, diesel, and jet fuels. Motor oil is a mixture of high-molecular-weight liquid hydrocarbons and is used to lubricate the internal components of engines. Mineral oil is a mixture of liquid hydrocarbons and is used as a laxative and a lubricant. Alkanes with 18 or more carbon atoms are waxy solids at room temperature. The high-molecular-weight alkanes, known as paraffins, are used in waxy coatings on fruits and vegetables to retain moisture, inhibit mold growth, and enhance appearance. (See Figure 11.7.) Petrolatum, or Vaseline, is a mixture of low-boiling liquid hydrocarbons that are encapsulated in solid hydrocarbons. It is used in ointments and cosmetics and as a lubricant.

## Melting and Boiling Points

**FIGURE 11.7** The solid alkanes that make up waxy coatings on fruits and vegetables help retain moisture, inhibit mold, and enhance appearance.

**Q** Why does the waxy coating help the fruits and vegetables retain moisture?

Alkanes have the lowest melting and boiling points of all the organic compounds. The only attractions between nonpolar alkanes in the solid and liquid states result from dispersion forces. In longer carbon chains, the greater number of electrons produces more attractions between molecules, which results in higher melting and boiling points:

| $CH_4$ | $CH_3—CH_3$ | $CH_3—CH_2—CH_3$ |
|---|---|---|
| Methane, bp −164 °C | Ethane, bp −89 °C | Propane, bp −42 °C |

The boiling points of branched alkanes are generally lower than straight-chain alkanes with the same number of carbon atoms. The branched chain alkanes tend to be more compact, which reduces the amount of contact between the molecules. Cycloalkanes have higher boiling points than the straight-chain alkanes. Because rotation of carbon bonds is restricted, cycloalkanes maintain a rigid structure. Those rigid structures are like a set of dishes that can be stacked closely together with many points of contact and therefore many attractions to each other. We can compare the boiling points of alkanes and cycloalkanes with five carbon atoms as shown in Table 11.6.

## Combustion of Alkanes

An alkane undergoes **combustion** when it reacts completely with oxygen to produce carbon dioxide, water, and energy. Carbon–carbon single bonds are difficult to break, which makes alkanes the least reactive family of organic compounds. However, alkanes burn readily in oxygen:

$$\text{Alkane} + O_2 \longrightarrow CO_2 + H_2O + \text{energy}$$

Methane is the gas we use to cook our foods and heat our homes. Propane is the gas used in portable heaters and gas barbecues. (See Figure 11.8.)

**TABLE 11.6** Comparison of Boiling Points of Alkanes and Cycloalkanes with Five Carbons

| Formula | Name | Boiling Point (°C) |
|---|---|---|
| **Cycloalkanes** | | |
| (cyclopentane ring) | Cyclopentane | 49 |
| (cyclobutane ring with $CH_3$) | Methylcyclobutane | 36.3 |
| **Alkane** | | |
| $CH_3—CH_2—CH_2—CH_2—CH_3$ | Pentane | 36 |
| **Branched alkanes** | | |
| $CH_3—CH(CH_3)—CH_2—CH_3$ | 2-Methylbutane | 28 |
| $CH_3—C(CH_3)_2—CH_3$ | Dimethylpropane | 10 |

Gasoline, a mixture of liquid hydrocarbons, is the fuel that powers our cars, lawn mowers, and snow blowers. As alkanes, they all undergo combustion. The equations for the combustion of methane ($CH_4$) and propane ($C_3H_8$) follow:

$$\underset{\text{Methane}}{CH_4} + 2O_2 \longrightarrow CO_2 + 2H_2O + \text{energy}$$

$$\underset{\text{Propane}}{C_3H_8} + 5O_2 \longrightarrow 3CO_2 + 4H_2O + \text{energy}$$

In the cells of our bodies, energy is produced by the combustion of glucose. Although a series of reactions is involved, we can write the overall combustion of glucose in our cells as follows:

$$C_6H_{12}O_6 + 6O_2 \xrightarrow{\text{Enzymes}} 6CO_2 + 6H_2O + \text{energy}$$

**FIGURE 11.8** The propane fuel in the tank undergoes combustion, which provides energy.

Q What is the balanced equation for the combustion of propane?

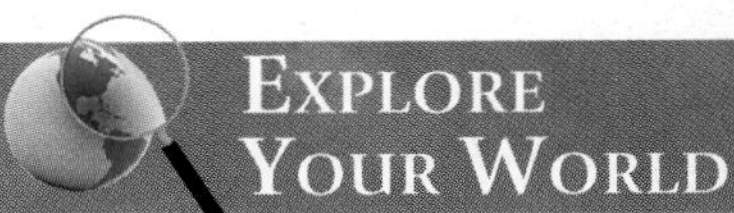


## Combustion

In this exploration, we will look at the behavior of the products of combustion. You will need one or two candles, a Pyrex glass such as a measuring cup, and some matches or wooden splints.

Hold a Pyrex cup upside down, and place a burning match inside it. The match will continue to burn as long as oxygen is available. Light a candle and hold the inverted Pyrex cup above it for 15–20 seconds. Remove the cup from the candle and immediately place a burning match into it. The $CO_2$ accumulated from the combustion of the candle should extinguish the match.

Add some water and a lot of ice to the same Pyrex cup. It should become cold to the touch. Wipe the bottom of the cup and carefully hold the bottom of the Pyrex cup over a burning candle. Look for condensation as water is formed from the combustion reaction.

### QUESTIONS

1. What are the products of combustion?
2. What was the evidence for the production of $CO_2$?
3. What observations gave evidence for the production of $H_2O$ during combustion?

TUTORIAL
Writing Balanced Equations for Combustion of Alkanes

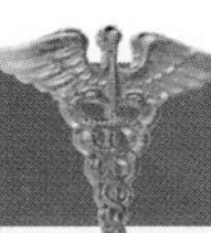

CASE STUDY
Poison in the Home: Carbon Monoxide

SAMPLE PROBLEM 11.7

## Combustion

Write a balanced equation for the complete combustion of butane.

SOLUTION

The balanced equation for the complete combustion of butane can be written

$$2C_4H_{10} + 13O_2 \longrightarrow 8CO_2 + 10H_2O$$

STUDY CHECK

Write a balanced equation for the complete combustion of the following:

$$\begin{array}{c} \quad CH_3 \\ \quad | \\ CH_3-CH-CH_2-CH_3 \end{array}$$

# HEALTH NOTE

## Toxicity of Carbon Monoxide

When a propane heater, fireplace, or wood stove is used in a closed room, there must be adequate ventilation. If the supply of oxygen is limited, *incomplete combustion* from burning gas, oil, or wood produces carbon monoxide. The incomplete combustion of methane in natural gas is written as follows:

$$\underset{\text{Limited oxygen supply}}{2CH_4(g) + 3O_2(g)} \longrightarrow \underset{\text{Carbon monoxide}}{2CO(g)} + 4H_2O(g) + \text{heat}$$

Carbon monoxide (CO) is a colorless, odorless, poisonous gas. When inhaled, CO passes into the bloodstream, where it attaches to hemoglobin. When CO binds to the hemoglobin, it reduces the amount of oxygen ($O_2$) reaching the organs and cells. As a result, a healthy person can experience a reduction in exercise capability, visual perception, and manual dexterity.

When the amount of hemoglobin bound to CO (COHb) is about 10%, a person may experience shortness of breath, mild headache, and drowsiness. Heavy smokers can have levels of COHb in their blood as high as 9%. When as much as 30% of the hemoglobin is bound to CO, a person may experience more severe symptoms, including dizziness, mental confusion, severe headache, and nausea. If 50% or more of the hemoglobin is bound to CO, a person could become unconscious and die if not treated immediately with oxygen.

# QUESTIONS AND PROBLEMS

## Properties of Alkanes

**11.29** Heptane has a density of 0.68 g/mL and boils at 98 °C.
- **a.** Draw the condensed structural formula of heptane.
- **b.** Is it a solid, liquid, or gas at room temperature?
- **c.** Is it soluble in water?
- **d.** Will it float or sink in water?

**11.30** Nonane has a density of 0.72 g/mL and boils at 151 °C.
- **a.** Draw the condensed structural formula of nonane.
- **b.** Is it a solid, liquid, or gas at room temperature?
- **c.** Is it soluble in water?
- **d.** Will it float or sink in water?

**11.31** In each of the following pairs of hydrocarbons, which one would you expect to have the higher boiling point?
- **a.** pentane or heptane
- **b.** propane or cyclopropane
- **c.** hexane or 2-methylpentane

**11.32** In each of the following pairs of hydrocarbons, which one would you expect to have the higher boiling point?
- **a.** propane or butane
- **b.** hexane or cyclohexane
- **c.** 2,2-dimethylpentane or heptane

**11.33** Write a balanced equation for the complete combustion of each of the following compounds:
- **a.** ethane
- **b.** cyclopropane, $C_3H_6$
- **c.** octane
- **d.** cyclohexane, $C_6H_{12}$

**11.34** Write a balanced equation for the complete combustion of each of the following compounds:
- **a.** hexane
- **b.** cyclopentane, $C_5H_{10}$
- **c.** nonane
- **d.** 2-methylbutane

# GREEN CHEMISTRY NOTE

## Crude Oil

Crude oil, or petroleum, contains a wide variety of hydrocarbons. At an oil refinery, the components in crude oil are separated by fractional distillation, a process that removes groups or fractions of hydrocarbons by continually heating the mixture to higher temperatures. (See Table 11.7.) Fractions containing alkanes with longer carbon chains require higher temperatures before they reach their boiling temperature and form gases. The gases are removed and passed through a distillation column where they cool and condense back to liquids. The major use of crude oil is to obtain gasoline. To increase the production of gasoline, heating oils are broken down using specialized catalysts to give the lower-weight alkanes.

**TABLE 11.7** Typical Alkane Mixtures Obtained by Distillation of Crude Oil

| Distillation Temperatures (°C) | Number of Carbon Atoms | Product |
|---|---|---|
| Below 30 | 1–4 | Natural gas |
| 30–200 | 5–12 | Gasoline |
| 200–250 | 12–16 | Kerosene, jet fuel |
| 250–350 | 16–18 | Diesel fuel, heating oil |
| 350–450 | 18–25 | Lubricating oil |
| Nonvolatile residue | Over 25 | Asphalt, tar |

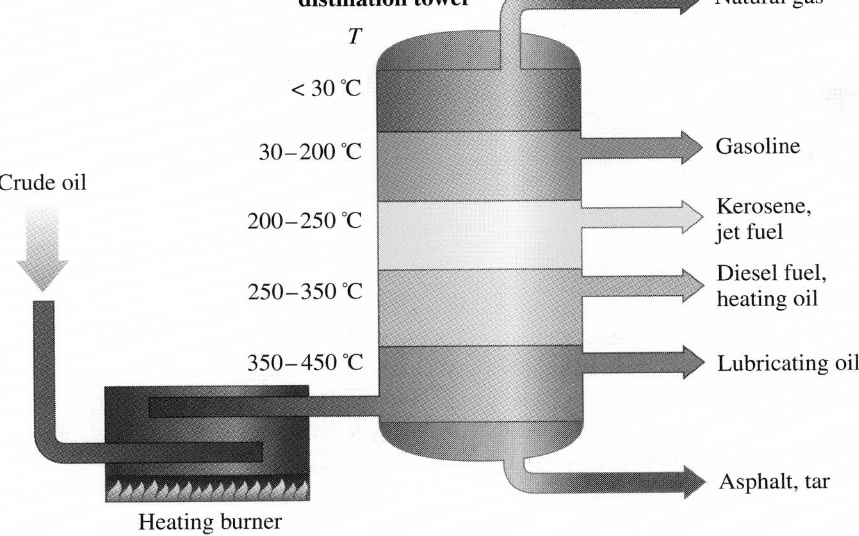

## ENVIRONMENTAL NOTE

### CFCs and Ozone Depletion

The compounds called *chlorofluorocarbons* (CFCs) were used as propellants for hair sprays and paints, and as refrigerants in home and car air conditioners. Two widely used CFCs, Freon 11 ($CCl_3F$) and Freon 12 ($CCl_2F_2$), were developed during the 1920s as nontoxic refrigerants, which were safer than the sulfur dioxide and ammonia used at the time:

```
     Cl                Cl
     |                 |
 Cl—C—F            F—C—F
     |                 |
     Cl                Cl
  Freon 11          Freon 12
```

In the stratosphere, a layer of ozone ($O_3$) absorbs the ultraviolet (UV) radiation of the Sun and acts as a protective shield for plants and animals on Earth. Ozone is produced in the stratosphere when oxygen reacts with ultraviolet light and breaks into oxygen atoms that quickly combine with oxygen molecules to form ozone. In the color image, the pink areas have the lowest levels of ozone.

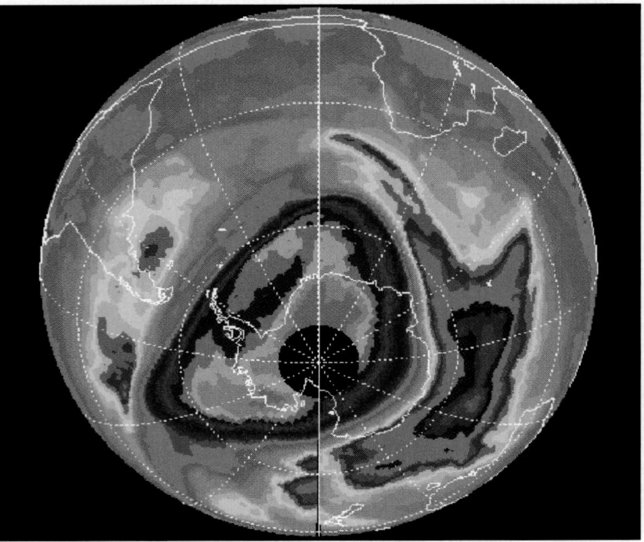

In the color image, the pink areas have the lowest levels of ozone.

$$O_2 \xrightarrow{\text{UV light}} O + O$$
$$O_2 + O \longrightarrow O_3$$

During the 1970s, scientists became concerned that CFCs entering the atmosphere were accelerating the depletion of ozone and threatening the stability of the ozone layer. CFCs decompose in the upper atmosphere in the presence of UV light to produce highly reactive chlorine atoms:

$$CCl_3F \xrightarrow{\text{UV light}} CCl_2F + Cl$$

The reactive chlorine atoms catalyze the breakdown of ozone molecules:

$$Cl + O_3 \longrightarrow ClO + O_2$$
$$ClO + O_3 \longrightarrow Cl + 2O_2$$

It has been estimated that one chlorine atom, also called a *radical*, can destroy as many as 100 000 ozone molecules. Normally, there is a balance between the ozone and oxygen in the atmosphere, but the rapid destruction of ozone has upset that equilibrium.

Reports of polar ozone depletion over Antarctica in March 1985 prompted scientists to call for a freeze on the production of CFCs. In some areas, as much as 50% of the ozone had been depleted, causing an ozone hole to appear at certain times of the year.

There is evidence of thinning in the ozone layer over the Arctic as well, but to a somewhat lesser degree due to warmer temperatures. It is interesting that in the lower atmosphere ozone is an automobile and industrial pollutant, but in the stratosphere ozone is a life-protecting compound.

Today, the use of CFCs is being phased out. However, it is expected that ozone levels will remain low for several decades due to the stability of CFCs. Chemical companies are developing substitutes for CFCs that are not as damaging to the ozone. Replacement compounds such as hydrochlorofluorocarbons (HCFCs) contain chlorine atoms, but these compounds break down in the lower atmosphere, reducing the amount of chlorine that reaches the stratosphere. Hydrofluorocarbons (HFCs), which contain no chlorine, are being considered as another replacement for CFCs. However, the potential effects of fluorine compounds on ozone destruction must still be determined.

## 11.5 Functional Groups

**LEARNING GOAL**

Classify organic molecules according to their functional groups.

SELF STUDY ACTIVITY
Functional Groups

TUTORIAL
Identifying Functional Groups

In organic compounds, carbon atoms are most likely to bond with nonmetals such as hydrogen, oxygen, nitrogen, sulfur, phosphorus, and halogens. Table 11.8 lists the number of covalent bonds most often formed by these elements in order to achieve a complete set of valence electrons. Hydrogen and the halogens form one covalent bond, and carbon forms four covalent bonds. Nitrogen forms three covalent bonds, whereas oxygen and sulfur each form two covalent bonds.

Organic compounds number in the millions, and more are synthesized every day. Within this vast number of compounds, there are specific groups of atoms called **functional groups** that give compounds similar properties. The identification of functional groups allows us to classify organic compounds according to their structure, to name compounds within each family, and to predict their chemical reactions. We will focus on recognizing the patterns of atoms that make up each of the functional groups, which we will discuss in more detail in the following chapters.

**TABLE 11.8** Covalent Bonds for Elements in Organic Compounds

| Element | Group | Covalent Bonds | Structure of Atoms |
|---|---|---|---|
| H | 1A (1) | 1 | H— |
| C | 4A (4) | 4 | —C— (with bonds above and below) |
| N, P | 5A (15) | 3 | —N̈— —P̈— (with bond above) |
| O, S | 6A (16) | 2 | —Ö— —S̈— (with two unshared pairs) |
| F, Cl, Br, I | 7A (17) | 1 | —X: (X = F, Cl, Br, I) (with three unshared pairs) |

Alkene

Alkyne

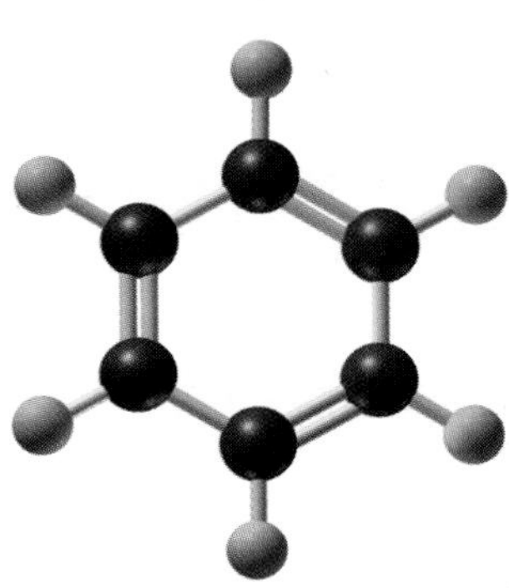
Aromatic

## Alkenes, Alkynes, and Aromatic Compounds

In the hydrocarbon family, there are also alkenes, alkynes, and aromatics. An **alkene** contains one or more double bonds between carbon atoms; an **alkyne** contains a triple bond. An **aromatic** compound contains benzene, a molecule that has a ring of six carbon atoms with one hydrogen atom attached to each carbon. The benzene structure is represented as a hexagon with a circle in the center:

| | Alkene | Alkyne | Aromatic |
|---|---|---|---|
| Structure | $H_2C{=}CH_2$ (H's on each C) | H—C≡C—H | benzene ring with one H on each carbon |
| Functional group | >C=C< | —C≡C— | benzene ring (hexagon with circle) |
| Condensed structural formula | $H_2C{=}CH_2$ | HC≡CH | |

Alcohol

## Alcohols, Thiols, and Ethers

The characteristic functional group in an **alcohol** is the *hydroxyl* (—OH) *group* bonded to a carbon atom. In an **ether**, the characteristic structural feature is an oxygen atom bonded to two carbon atoms. The oxygen atom also has two unshared pairs of electrons, but they are not shown in the condensed structural formulas. In a **thiol**, the functional group —SH is bonded to a carbon atom.

Thiol

| | Alcohol | Thiol | Ether |
|---|---|---|---|
| | $CH_3$—$CH_2$—**OH** | $CH_3$—$CH_2$—**SH** | $CH_3$—**O**—$CH_3$ |
| Functional group | **—O—H** | **—S—H** | **—O—** |

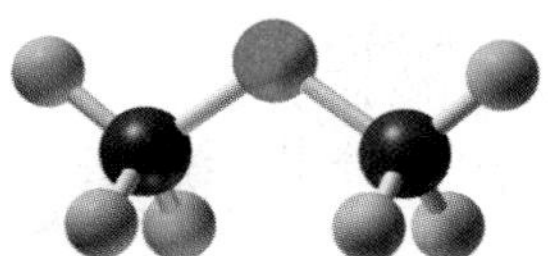
Ether

## Aldehydes and Ketones

The aldehydes and ketones contain a **carbonyl group** (C=O), which is a carbon with a double bond to oxygen. In an **aldehyde**, the first carbon of a carbon chain is a carbonyl group that is bonded to a hydrogen atom. Only the simplest aldehyde, $CH_2O$, has a carbonyl group attached to two hydrogen atoms. In a **ketone**, the carbonyl group is bonded to two other carbon atoms.

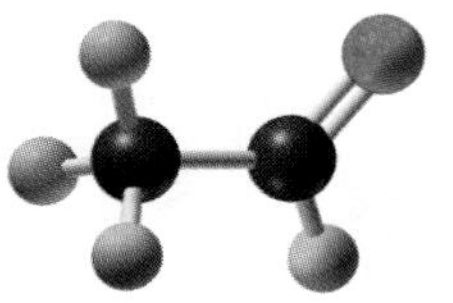
Aldehyde

| | Aldehyde | Ketone |
|---|---|---|
| | $CH_3$—**C**(=**O**)—**H** | $CH_3$—**C**(=**O**)—$CH_3$ |
| Functional group | —**C**(=**O**)—H | —C(=O)— |

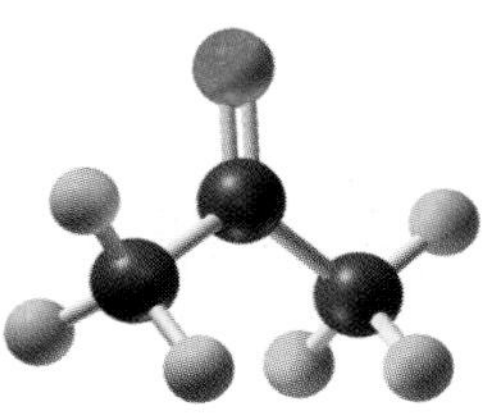
Ketone

CONCEPT CHECK 11.3

### Identifying Functional Groups

Describe the differences among the functional groups found in alcohols, ethers, and thiols.

ANSWER

In alcohols, the functional group is a hydroxyl group (—OH) attached to a carbon atom. The functional group in ethers is an oxygen atom bonded to two carbon atoms (—O—). In thiols, the functional group —SH is attached to a carbon atom.

SAMPLE PROBLEM 11.8

### Classifying Organic Compounds

Classify the following organic compounds according to their functional groups:

**a.** $CH_3—CH_2—CH_2—OH$

**b.** $CH_3—CH{=}CH—CH_3$

**c.** $CH_3—CH_2—\overset{\overset{\displaystyle O}{\|}}{C}—CH_2—CH_3$

**d.** $CH_3—\overset{\overset{\displaystyle SH}{|}}{C}H—CH_3$

SOLUTION

**a.** When the functional group —OH is bonded to a carbon atom, the compound is an alcohol.
**b.** An alkene contains one or more double bonds between carbon atoms.
**c.** A ketone contains a carbonyl group bonded to two other carbon atoms.
**d.** When the functional group —SH is bonded to a carbon atom, the compound is a thiol.

STUDY CHECK

Why is $CH_3—CH_2—O—CH_3$ an ether?

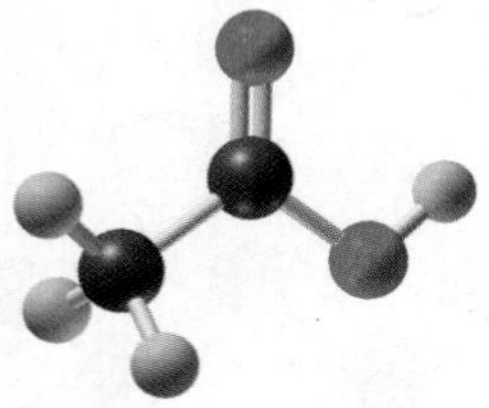

## Carboxylic Acids and Esters

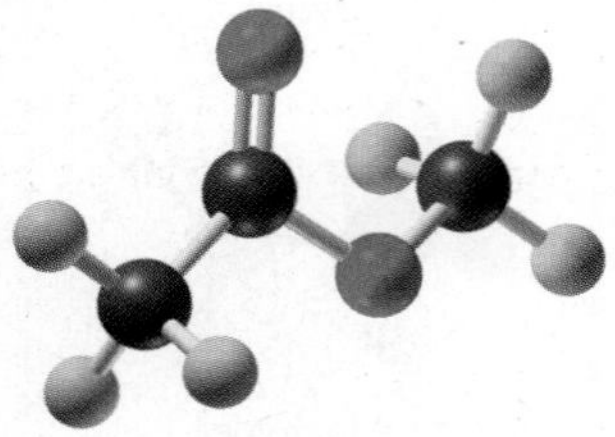

Carboxylic acid

Ester

In a **carboxylic acid**, the functional group is the *carboxyl group*, which is a combination of the *carbo*nyl and hydro*xyl* groups. In a carboxylic acid, the first carbon atom is part of a carboxyl group:

$$CH_3—\overset{\overset{\displaystyle \mathbf{O}}{\|}}{\mathbf{C}}—\mathbf{O}—\mathbf{H} \quad \text{or} \quad CH_3\mathbf{COOH}$$

Carboxylic acid

$$\text{Functional group} \quad —\overset{\overset{\displaystyle \mathbf{O}}{\|}}{\mathbf{C}}—\mathbf{O}—\mathbf{H} \quad \text{or} \quad —\mathbf{COOH}$$

An **ester** is similar to a carboxylic acid, except that the oxygen of the carboxyl group is attached to a carbon and not to hydrogen:

$$CH_3—\overset{\overset{\displaystyle \mathbf{O}}{\|}}{\mathbf{C}}—\mathbf{O}—CH_3 \quad \text{or} \quad CH_3\mathbf{COO}CH_3$$

Ester

$$\text{Functional group} \quad —\overset{\overset{\displaystyle \mathbf{O}}{\|}}{\mathbf{C}}—\mathbf{O}— \quad \text{or} \quad —\mathbf{COO}—$$

## Amines and Amides

In an **amine**, the central atom is a nitrogen atom. Amines are derivatives of ammonia, $NH_3$, in which carbon atoms replace one, two, or three of the hydrogen atoms:

$$\mathbf{NH_3} \qquad CH_3{-}\mathbf{NH_2} \qquad CH_3{-}\underset{\displaystyle CH_3}{\underset{|}{\mathbf{N}}}\mathbf{H} \qquad CH_3{-}\underset{\displaystyle CH_3}{\underset{|}{\mathbf{N}}}{-}CH_3$$

Ammonia     Examples of amines

In an **amide**, the hydroxyl group of a carboxylic acid is replaced by a nitrogen group:

$$CH_3{-}\overset{\displaystyle O}{\overset{\|}{\mathbf{C}}}{-}\mathbf{NH_2}$$

Amide

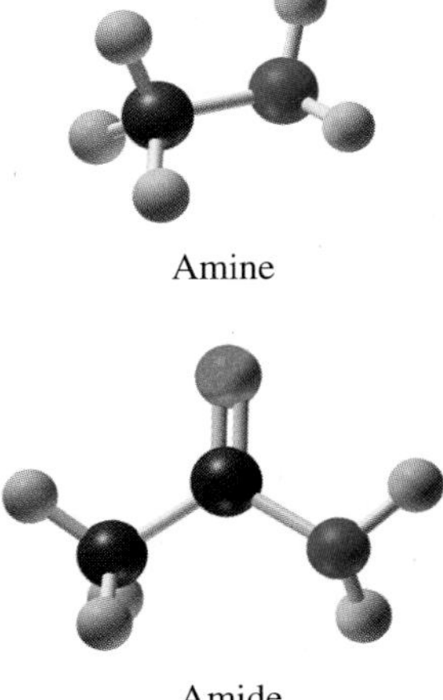

Amine

Amide

> **CONCEPT CHECK 11.4**
>
> **The Amine Functional Group**
>
> Describe the functional group found in amines.
>
> ANSWER
>
> The amine functional group has a central nitrogen atom bonded to one, two, or three carbon atoms.

A list of the common functional groups in organic compounds is shown in Table 11.9.

**TABLE 11.9** Classification of Organic Compounds

| Class | Example | Functional Group | Characteristic |
|---|---|---|---|
| Alkene | $H_2\mathbf{C}{=}\mathbf{C}H_2$ | $>C{=}C<$ | Carbon–carbon double bond |
| Alkyne | $H\mathbf{C}{\equiv}\mathbf{C}H$ | $-C{\equiv}C-$ | Carbon–carbon triple bond |
| Aromatic | $C_6H_6$ (benzene ring with H on each carbon) | benzene ring | Benzene ring (six carbon atoms and six hydrogen atoms) |
| Haloalkane | $CH_3{-}\mathbf{Cl}$ | $-F$, $-Cl$, $-Br$, $-I$ | One or more halogen atoms |
| Alcohol | $CH_3{-}CH_2{-}\mathbf{OH}$ | $-OH$ | Hydroxyl group ($-OH$) |
| Ether | $CH_3{-}\mathbf{O}{-}CH_3$ | $-O-$ | Oxygen atom bonded to two carbons |
| Thiol | $CH_3{-}\mathbf{SH}$ | $-SH$ | Thiol group ($-SH$) |
| Aldehyde | $CH_3{-}\overset{\mathbf{O}}{\overset{\|}{\mathbf{C}}}{-}\mathbf{H}$ | $-\overset{O}{\overset{\|}{C}}{-}H$ | Carbonyl group (carbon–oxygen double bond) with $-H$ |
| Ketone | $CH_3{-}\overset{\mathbf{O}}{\overset{\|}{\mathbf{C}}}{-}CH_3$ | $-\overset{O}{\overset{\|}{C}}-$ | Carbonyl group (carbon–oxygen double bond) between carbon atoms |
| Carboxylic acid | $CH_3{-}\overset{\mathbf{O}}{\overset{\|}{\mathbf{C}}}{-}\mathbf{O}{-}\mathbf{H}$ | $-\overset{O}{\overset{\|}{C}}{-}O{-}H$ | Carboxyl group (carbon–oxygen double bond and $-OH$) |
| Ester | $CH_3{-}\overset{\mathbf{O}}{\overset{\|}{\mathbf{C}}}{-}\mathbf{O}{-}CH_3$ | $-\overset{O}{\overset{\|}{C}}{-}O-$ | Carboxyl group with $-H$ replaced by a carbon |
| Amine | $CH_3{-}\mathbf{NH_2}$ | $-\overset{|}{N}-$ | Nitrogen atom with one or more carbon groups |
| Amide | $CH_3{-}\overset{\mathbf{O}}{\overset{\|}{\mathbf{C}}}{-}\mathbf{NH_2}$ | $-\overset{O}{\overset{\|}{C}}{-}\overset{|}{N}-$ | Carbonyl group bonded to nitrogen |

SAMPLE PROBLEM 11.9

## Identifying Functional Groups

Classify the following organic compounds according to their functional groups:

a. $CH_3—CH_2—NH—CH_3$

b. $CH_3—\overset{\overset{\displaystyle O}{\|}}{C}—O—CH_2—CH_3$

c. $CH_3—CH_2—\overset{\overset{\displaystyle O}{\|}}{C}—OH$

SOLUTION

a. amine b. ester c. carboxylic acid

STUDY CHECK

How does a carboxylic acid differ from an ester?

MC TUTORIAL Drawing Organic Compounds with Functional Groups

# ENVIRONMENTAL NOTE

## Functional Groups in Familiar Compounds

The flavors and odors of foods and many household products can be attributed to the functional groups of organic compounds. As we discuss these familiar products, look for the functional groups we have described.

$CH_3—CH_2—OH$
Ethyl alcohol

$CH_3—\underset{}{\overset{\overset{\displaystyle OH}{|}}{C}H}—CH_3$
Isopropyl alcohol

Ethyl alcohol is the alcohol found in alcoholic beverages. Isopropyl alcohol is another alcohol commonly used to disinfect skin before giving injections and to treat cuts.

Ketones and aldehydes are in many items we use or eat each day. Acetone, or dimethyl ketone, is produced in great amounts commercially. Acetone is used as an organic solvent because it dissolves a wide variety of organic substances. You may be familiar with acetone as fingernail polish remover. Ketones and aldehydes used in the food industry are found in flavorings such as vanilla, cinnamon, and spearmint. When we buy a small bottle of liquid flavoring, the aldehyde or ketone is dissolved in alcohol because the compounds are not very soluble in water. The aldehyde butyraldehyde adds a "buttery" taste to foods and margarine.

$CH_3—CH_2—CH_2—\overset{\overset{\displaystyle O}{\|}}{C}—H$
Butyraldehyde "butter" flavoring

The sour tastes of vinegar and fruit juices and the pain from ant stings are all due to carboxylic acids. Acetic acid is the carboxylic acid that makes up vinegar. Aspirin also contains a carboxylic acid group. Esters found in fruits produce the pleasant aromas and tastes of bananas, oranges, pears, and pineapples. Esters are also used as solvents in many household cleaners, polishes, and glues.

One of the characteristics of fish is their odor, which is due to the amines produced when proteins decay; they have a particularly pungent and offensive odor.

$CH_3—\overset{\overset{\displaystyle O}{\|}}{C}—OH$
Acetic acid (in vinegar)

$CH_3—\overset{\overset{\displaystyle O}{\|}}{C}—O—CH_2—CH_2—CH_3$
Propyl acetate (pears)

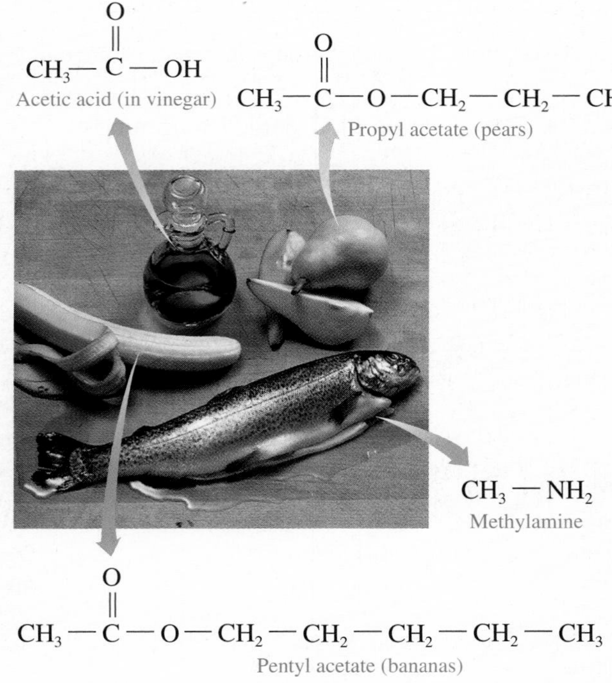

$CH_3—NH_2$
Methylamine

$CH_3—\overset{\overset{\displaystyle O}{\|}}{C}—O—CH_2—CH_2—CH_2—CH_2—CH_3$
Pentyl acetate (bananas)

$H_2N—CH_2—CH_2—CH_2—CH_2—NH_2$
Putrescine

$H_2N—CH_2—CH_2—CH_2—CH_2—CH_2—NH_2$
Cadaverine

Alkaloids are biologically active amines synthesized by plants to ward off insects and animals. Some typical alkaloids include caffeine, nicotine, histamine, and the decongestant epinephrine. Many are painkillers and hallucinogens, such as morphine, LSD, marijuana, and cocaine. Certain parts of our neurons have receptor sites that respond to the various alkaloids. By modifying the structures of certain alkaloids to eliminate side effects, chemists have synthesized painkillers such as Novocain and codeine, and other drugs, such as Valium.

## QUESTIONS AND PROBLEMS

### Functional Groups

**11.35** Identify the class of compounds that contains each of the following functional groups:

**a.** hydroxyl group attached to a carbon chain
**b.** carbon–carbon double bond
**c.** carbonyl group attached to a hydrogen atom
**d.** carboxyl group attached to two carbon atoms

**11.36** Identify the class of compounds that contains each of the following functional groups:

**a.** a nitrogen atom attached to one or more carbon atoms
**b.** carboxyl group
**c.** oxygen atom bonded to two carbon atoms
**d.** a carbonyl group between two carbon atoms

**11.37** Classify the following molecules according to their functional groups. The possibilities are alcohol, ether, ketone, carboxylic acid, or amine.

**a.** $CH_3-CH_2-O-CH_2-CH_3$
**b.** $CH_3-CH(OH)-CH_3$
**c.** $CH_3-C(=O)-CH_2-CH_3$
**d.** $CH_3-CH_2-CH_2-COOH$
**e.** $CH_3-CH_2-NH_2$

**11.38** Classify the following molecules according to their functional groups. The possibilities are alkene, aldehyde, carboxylic acid, ester, or amide.

**a.** $CH_3-CH_2-C(=O)-O-CH_2-CH_3$
**b.** $CH_3-C(=O)-NH_2$
**c.** $CH_3-CH_2-CH_2-C(=O)-H$
**d.** $CH_3-CH_2-CH_2-COOH$
**e.** $CH_3-CH{=}CH-CH_3$

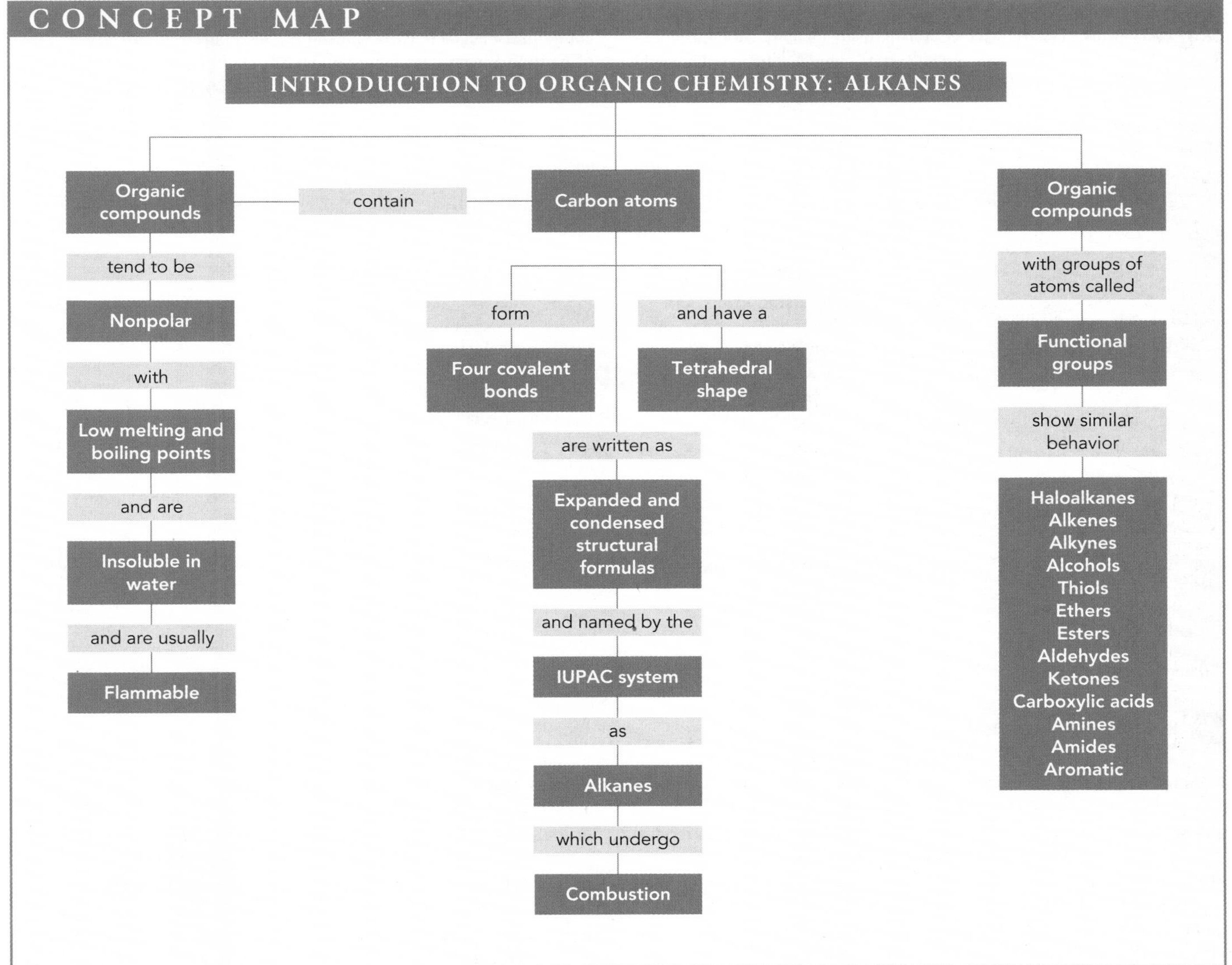

# CHAPTER REVIEW

## 11.1 Organic Compounds

**LEARNING GOAL:** *Identify characteristic properties of organic or inorganic compounds.*

Organic compounds have covalent bonds, and most form nonpolar molecules. Often, they have low melting points and low boiling points, are not very soluble in water, produce molecules in solutions, and burn vigorously in air. In contrast, many inorganic compounds are ionic or contain polar covalent bonds and form polar molecules. Many have high melting and boiling points, are usually soluble in water, produce ions in water, and do not burn in air. Carbon atoms share four valence electrons to form four covalent bonds. In the simplest organic molecule, methane, $CH_4$, the four bonds that bond hydrogen to the carbon atom are directed to the corners of a tetrahedron with bond angles of 109.5°.

## 11.2 Alkanes

**LEARNING GOAL:** *Write the IUPAC names and condensed structural formulas for alkanes.*

Alkanes are hydrocarbons that have only C—C single bonds. In the expanded structural formula, a separate line is drawn for every bonded atom. A condensed structural formula depicts groups composed of each carbon atom and its attached hydrogen atoms. In a line-bond formula, only the carbon–carbon bonds are drawn. In cycloalkanes, the carbon atoms form a ring or cyclic structure. The name is written by placing the prefix *cyclo* before the alkane name with the same number of carbon atoms. The IUPAC system is used to name organic compounds in a systematic manner. The IUPAC name indicates the number of carbon atoms.

## 11.3 Alkanes with Substituents

**LEARNING GOAL:** *Write the IUPAC names for alkanes with substituents.*

In an alkane, the carbon atoms are connected in a chain and bonded to hydrogen atoms. Substituents such as alkyl groups can replace hydrogen atoms on an alkane. A haloalkane contains one or more F, Cl, Br, or I atoms. In the IUPAC system, halogen atoms are named as *fluoro*, *chloro*, *bromo*, or *iodo* substituents attached to the main chain. In the common name, the name of the alkyl group precedes the halide, for example methyl chloride.

## 11.4 Properties of Alkanes

**LEARNING GOAL:** *Identify the properties of alkanes, and write chemical equations for combustion.*

As nonpolar molecules, alkanes are not soluble in water. They are less dense than water. With only weak attractions, they have low melting and boiling points. For alkanes of similar mass, cycloalkanes have higher boiling points and branched alkanes have lower boiling points than the nonbranched chain alkanes. Although the C—C bonds in alkanes resist most reactions, alkanes undergo combustion. In combustion, or burning, alkanes react with oxygen to produce carbon dioxide and water.

## 11.5 Functional Groups

**LEARNING GOAL:** *Classify organic molecules according to their functional groups.*

An organic molecule contains a characteristic group of atoms called a *functional group* that determines the molecule's family name and chemical reactivity. Functional groups are used to classify organic compounds, act as reactive sites in the molecule, and provide a system of naming for organic compounds. Some common functional groups include the hydroxyl group (—OH) in alcohols, the carbonyl group (C═O) in aldehydes and ketones, a nitrogen (N) atom —N— (with a bond above N) in amines, and a nitrogen and carbonyl group in amides.

# SUMMARY OF NAMING

| Type | Example | Characteristic | Structure |
|---|---|---|---|
| Alkane | Propane | Single C—C bonds | $CH_3—CH_2—CH_3$ |
| | Methylpropane | | $CH_3—CH(CH_3)—CH_3$ |
| Haloalkane | 1-Chloropropane | Halogen atom | $CH_3—CH_2—CH_2—Cl$ |
| Cycloalkane | Cyclobutane | Carbon ring | □ |

# SUMMARY OF REACTIONS

COMBUSTION

Alkane + $O_2$ ⟶ $CO_2$ + $H_2O$ + energy

# KEY TERMS

**alcohol** A class of organic compounds that contains the hydroxyl (—OH) group bonded to a carbon atom.

**aldehyde** A class of organic compounds that contains a carbonyl group (C═O) bonded to at least one hydrogen atom.

**alkanes** Hydrocarbons containing only single bonds between carbon atoms.

**alkenes** Hydrocarbons that contain carbon–carbon double bonds (C═C).

**alkyl group** An alkane minus one hydrogen atom. Alkyl groups are named like the alkanes except a *yl* ending replaces *ane*.

**alkynes** Hydrocarbons that contain carbon–carbon triple bonds (C≡C).

**amide** A class of organic compounds in which the hydroxyl group of a carboxylic acid is replaced by a nitrogen group.

**amine** A class of organic compounds that contains a nitrogen atom bonded to one or more carbon atoms.

**aromatic** A compound that contains benzene. Benzene has a six-carbon ring with only one hydrogen atom attached to each carbon.

**branch** A carbon group bonded to the main carbon chain.

**branched alkane** A single-bonded hydrocarbon containing a substituent bonded to the main chain.

**carbonyl group** A functional group that contains a double bond between a carbon atom and an oxygen atom (C═O).

**carboxylic acid** A class of organic compounds that contains the carboxyl functional group.

**combustion** A chemical reaction in which an alkane reacts with oxygen to produce $CO_2$, $H_2O$, and energy.

**condensed structural formula** A structural formula that shows the arrangement of the carbon atoms in a molecule but groups each carbon atom with its bonded hydrogen atoms.

**cycloalkane** An alkane that is a ring or cyclic structure.

**ester** A class of organic compounds that contains a —COO— group with an oxygen atom bonded to carbon.

**ether** A class of organic compounds that contains an oxygen atom bonded to two carbon atoms (—O—).

**expanded structural formula** A type of structural formula that shows the arrangement of the atoms by showing each bond in the hydrocarbon as C—H, C—C, C═C, or C≡C.

**functional group** A group of atoms that determines the physical and chemical properties and naming of a class of organic compounds.

**haloalkane** A type of alkane that contains one or more halogen atoms.

**hydrocarbons** Organic compounds consisting of only carbon and hydrogen.

**isomers** Organic compounds in which identical molecular formulas have different arrangements of atoms.

**IUPAC system** The system for naming organic compounds devised by the International Union of Pure and Applied Chemistry.

**ketone** A class of organic compounds in which a carbonyl group is bonded to two carbon atoms.

**line-bond formula** A type of structural formula that shows only the bonds from carbon to carbon.

**organic compounds** Compounds made of carbon that typically have covalent bonds, are nonpolar molecules, have low melting and boiling points, are insoluble in water, and are flammable.

**substituent** Groups of atoms such as an alkyl group or a halogen bonded to the main chain or ring of carbon atoms.

**thiol** A class of organic molecules that contains the —SH functional group bonded to a carbon atom.

## UNDERSTANDING THE CONCEPTS

11.39 Sunscreens contain compounds that absorb UV light such as oxybenzone and 2-ethylhexyl-*p*-methoxycinnamate:

Identify the functional groups in each of the following UV-absorbing compounds used in suncreens:

**a.** oxybenzone

$CH_3O$—(benzene ring, with OH)—C(═O)—(benzene ring)

**b.** 2-ethylhexyl-*p*-methoxycinnamate

$CH_3$—O—(benzene ring)—CH═CH—C(═O)—O—$CH_2$—CH($CH_2$—$CH_3$)—$(CH_2)_3$—$CH_3$

**11.40** Oxymetazoline is a vasoconstrictor used in nasal decongestant sprays such as Afrin:

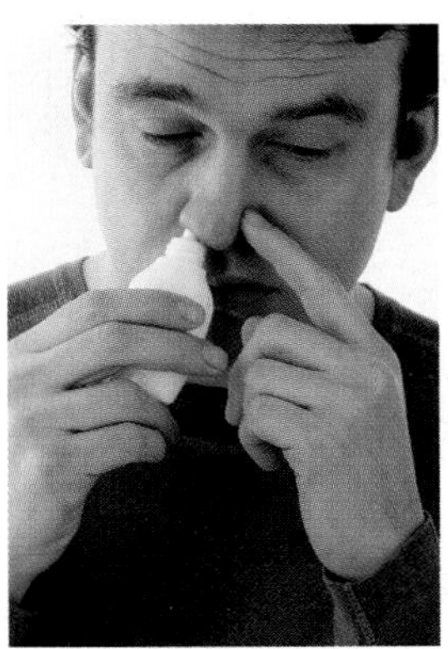

What functional groups are in oxymetazoline?

Benzene ring with OH, $(CH_3)_3C$, $CH_3$, $CH_3$, and $CH_2$ bonded to an imidazoline ring (N, NH)

11.41 Decimemide is used as an anticonvulsant:

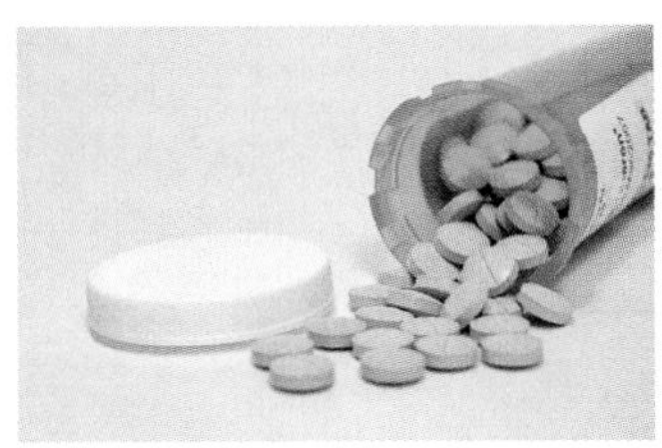

What functional groups are in decimemide?

$CH_3(CH_2)_9O$—(benzene ring with two $CH_3O$ groups)—C(═O)—$NH_2$

**11.42** The odor and taste of pineapples is from ethyl butyrate:

What functional group is in ethyl butyrate?

$$CH_3-CH_2-CH_2-\overset{\overset{\displaystyle O}{\|}}{C}-O-CH_2-CH_3$$

## ADDITIONAL QUESTIONS AND PROBLEMS

*For instructor-assigned homework, go to* ***www.masteringchemistry.com.***

**11.43** Compare organic and inorganic compounds in terms of each of the following:

**a.** types of bonds **b.** solubility in water
**c.** melting points **d.** flammability

**11.44** Identify each of the following compounds as organic or inorganic:

**a.** $Na_2SO_4$ **b.** $CH_2{=}CH_2$
**c.** $Cr_2O_3$ **d.** $C_{12}H_{22}O_{11}$

**11.45** Match the following physical and chemical properties with the compound butane, $C_4H_{10}$, or potassium chloride, KCl:

**a.** melts at −138 °C **b.** burns vigorously in air
**c.** melts at 770 °C **d.** produces ions in water
**e.** is a gas at room temperature

**11.46** Match the following physical and chemical properties with the compound cyclohexane, $C_6H_{12}$, or calcium nitrate, $Ca(NO_3)_2$:

**a.** contains only covalent bonds
**b.** melts above 500 °C
**c.** is insoluble in water
**d.** is a liquid at room temperature
**e.** produces ions in water

**11.47** Identify the functional group in each of the following:

**a.** $CH_3-NH_2$

**b.** $CH_3-\overset{\overset{\displaystyle O}{\|}}{C}-CH_3$

**c.** $CH_3-\overset{\overset{\displaystyle O}{\|}}{C}-O-CH_2-CH_3$

**d.** $CH_3-CH_2-CH_2-OH$

**11.48** Identify the functional group in each of the following:

**a.** $CH_3-C{\equiv}CH$
**b.** $CH_3-CH_2-CH_2-SH$
**c.** $CH_3-O-CH_2-CH_3$
**d.** 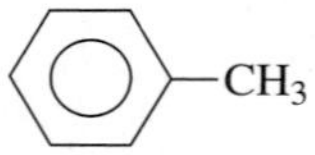 (benzene ring)$-CH_3$

**11.49** Write the name of each of the following substituents:

**a.** $CH_3-$ **b.** $CH_3-CH_2-CH_2-$ **c.** $Cl-$

**11.50** Write the name of each of the following substituents:

**a.** $Br-$

**b.** $CH_3-\underset{}{\overset{\overset{\displaystyle CH_3}{|}}{CH}}-$

**c.** $CH_3-CH_2-$

**11.51** Give the IUPAC name for each of the following:

**a.** 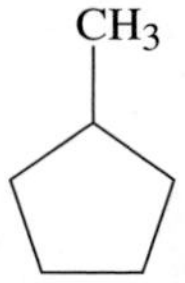 (cyclopentane ring with $CH_3$ substituent)

**b.** $Cl-CH_2-\overset{\overset{\displaystyle Br}{|}}{CH}-CH_2-Br$

**c.** $CH_3-\overset{\overset{\displaystyle CH_3}{|}}{CH}-\underset{\underset{\displaystyle CH_2-CH_2-CH_3}{|}}{CH}-CH_3$

**d.** $CH_3-CH_2-\overset{\overset{\displaystyle Cl}{|}}{\underset{\underset{\displaystyle CH_2-CH_3}{|}}{C}}-CH_2-CH_3$

**11.52** Give the IUPAC name for each of the following:

**a.** $CH_3-CH_2-\overset{\overset{\displaystyle CH_3}{|}}{\underset{\underset{\displaystyle CH_3}{|}}{C}}-CH_3$

**b.** $CH_3-CH_2-Cl$

**c.** $CH_3-CH_2-\overset{\overset{\displaystyle CH_3-CH_2}{|}}{CH}-CH_2-\overset{\overset{\displaystyle Br}{|}}{CH}-CH_3$

**d.**  (cyclohexane ring)

11.53 Draw the condensed structural formula for each of the following molecules:
**a.** 3-ethylhexane **b.** 1,3-dimethylcyclopentane
**c.** 1,3-dichloro-3-methylheptane **d.** bromocyclobutane

**11.54** Draw the condensed structural formula for each of the following molecules:
**a.** ethylcyclopropane **b.** 2-methylhexane
**c.** isopropylcyclopentane **d.** 1,1-dichloropentane

11.55 Draw the line-bond formula for each of the following molecules:
**a.** pentane **b.** 2,3-dimethylhexane
**c.** 2-bromo-4-methylheptane

**11.56** Draw the line-bond formula for each of the following molecules:
**a.** butane **b.** 2,3,3-trimethylpentane
**c.** 3,4,5-trimethyloctane

11.57 Identify the compound in each of the following pairs that has the higher boiling point:
**a.** pentane or heptane **b.** pentane or cyclopentane
**c.** hexane or 2-methylpentane

**11.58** Identify the compound in each of the following pairs that has the higher boiling point:
**a.** butane or octane **b.** cyclohexane or hexane
**c.** propane or pentane

11.59 Write a balanced equation for the complete combustion of each of the following:
**a.** propane **b.** $C_5H_{12}$ **c.** cyclobutane **d.** octane

**11.60** Write a balanced equation for the complete combustion of each of the following:
**a.** hexane **b.** methylcyclohexane
**c.** cyclopentane **d.** 2-methylpropane

11.61 Match each of the descriptions (**a–f**) with a corresponding term in the following list: alkane, alkene, alkyne, alcohol, ether, aldehyde, ketone, carboxylic acid, ester, amine, functional group, isomers.
**a.** an organic compound that contains a hydroxyl group bonded to a carbon
**b.** a hydrocarbon that contains one or more carbon–carbon double bonds
**c.** an organic compound in which the carbon of a carbonyl group is bonded to a hydrogen
**d.** a hydrocarbon that contains only carbon–carbon single bonds
**e.** an organic compound in which the carbon of a carbonyl group is bonded to a hydroxyl group
**f.** an organic compound that contains a nitrogen atom bonded to one or more carbon atoms

**11.62** Match each of the descriptions (**a–f**) with a corresponding term in the following list: alkane, alkene, alkyne, alcohol, ether, aldehyde, ketone, carboxylic acid, ester, amine, functional group, isomers.
**a.** organic compounds with identical molecular formulas that differ only in the arrangement of atoms
**b.** an organic compound in which the hydrogen atom of a carboxyl group is replaced by a carbon atom
**c.** an organic compound that contains an oxygen atom bonded to two carbon atoms
**d.** a hydrocarbon that contains a carbon–carbon triple bond
**e.** a characteristic group of atoms that make compounds behave and react in a particular way
**f.** an organic compound in which the carbonyl group is bonded to two carbon atoms

## CHALLENGE QUESTIONS

11.63 In an automobile engine, "knocking" occurs when the combustion of gasoline occurs too rapidly. The octane number of gasoline represents the ability of a gasoline mixture to reduce knocking. A sample of gasoline is compared with heptane, rated 0, because it reacts with severe knocking, and 2,2,4-trimethylpentane, which has a rating of 100 because of its low knocking. Draw the condensed structural formula, give the molecular formula, and write the balanced equation for the complete combustion of 2,2,4-trimethylpentane.

**11.64** Draw the structures of the following halogenated compounds, which are used as refrigerants:
**a.** Freon 14, tetrafluoromethane
**b.** Freon 114, 1,2-dichloro-1,1,2,2-tetrafluoroethane
**c.** Freon C318, octafluorocyclobutane

11.65 The density of pentane, a component of gasoline, is 0.63 g/mL. The heat of combustion for pentane is 845 kcal per mole.
**a.** Write the balanced equation for the complete combustion of pentane.
**b.** What is the molar mass?
**c.** How much heat is produced when 1 gallon of pentane is burned (1 gallon = 3.78 liters)?
**d.** How many liters of $CO_2$ at STP are produced from the complete combustion of 1 gallon of pentane?

**11.66** Draw the condensed structural formulas of two esters and a carboxylic acid that each have the molecular formula $C_3H_6O_2$.

11.67 Draw all the possible structures of an organic compound with 6 carbon atoms that has a 4-carbon chain.

**11.68** Draw all the possible structures of an organic compound with 4 carbon atoms that has a 3-carbon ring and a hydroxyl group.

11.69 Consider the compound propane.
**a.** Draw the condensed structural formula.
**b.** Write the balanced equation for the complete combustion of propane.
**c.** How many grams of $O_2$ are needed to react with 12.0 L of propane gas at STP?
**d.** How many grams of $CO_2$ would be produced from the reaction in part **c**?

**11.70** Consider the compound ethylcyclopentane.
**a.** Draw the geometric formula.
**b.** Write the balanced equation for the complete combustion of ethylcyclopentane.
**c.** Calculate the grams of $O_2$ required for the reaction of 25.0 g of ethylcyclopentane.
**d.** How many liters of $CO_2$ would be produced at STP from the reaction in part **c**?

11.71 A tank on an outdoor heater contains 5.0 lb of propane.
**a.** Write the balanced equation for the complete combustion of propane.
**b.** How many kilograms of $CO_2$ are produced by the complete combustion of all 5.0 lb of propane?

**11.72** A butane fireplace lighter contains 56.0 g of butane.
**a.** Write the balanced equation for the complete combustion of butane.
**b.** How many grams of oxygen are needed for the complete combustion of the butane in the lighter?

# ANSWERS

## ANSWERS TO STUDY CHECKS

**11.1**

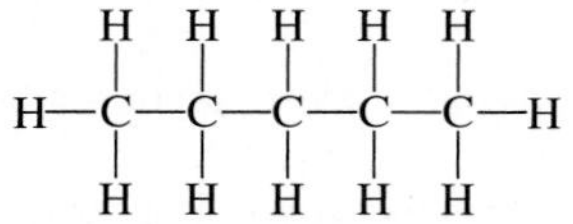

```
   H  H  H  H  H
   |  |  |  |  |
H—C—C—C—C—C—H
   |  |  |  |  |
   H  H  H  H  H
```

$CH_3—CH_2—CH_2—CH_2—CH_3$

**11.2** cyclobutane

**11.3** This is another isomer of $C_6H_{14}$. There is a five-carbon chain with a carbon group bonded to the middle (third) carbon.

**11.4** 1-chloro-2,4-dimethylhexane

**11.5**

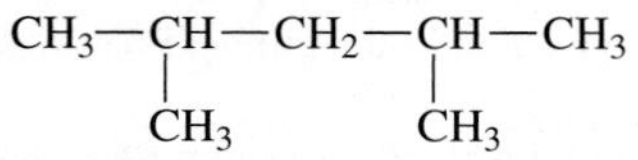

```
CH3—CH—CH2—CH—CH3
    |       |
    CH3     CH3
```

**11.6** 1,2-dibromoethane

**11.7**

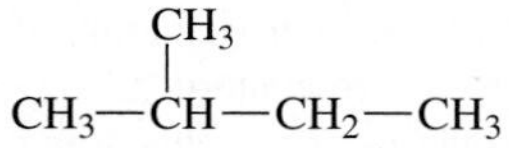

```
    CH3
    |
CH3—CH—CH2—CH3 = C5H12
```

$C_5H_{12} + 8O_2 \longrightarrow 5CO_2 + 6H_2O$

**11.8** $CH_3—CH_2—O—CH_3$ contains the functional group C—O—C; it is an ether.

**11.9** A carboxylic acid has a carboxyl group —COOH. In an ester, the oxygen atom of the carboxyl group is attached to another carbon atom, instead of hydrogen.

## ANSWERS TO SELECTED QUESTIONS AND PROBLEMS

**11.1** **a.** inorganic **b.** organic **c.** organic **d.** inorganic **e.** inorganic **f.** organic

**11.3** **a.** inorganic **b.** organic **c.** organic **d.** inorganic

**11.5** **a.** ethane **b.** ethane **c.** NaBr **d.** NaBr

**11.7** VSEPR theory predicts that the four bonds in $CH_4$ will be as far apart as possible, which means that the hydrogen atoms are at the corners of a tetrahedron.

**11.9** **a.**

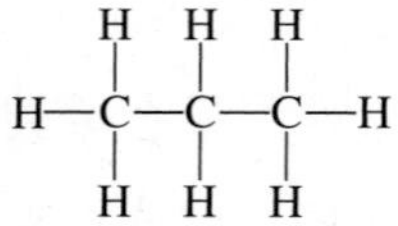

```
   H  H  H
   |  |  |
H—C—C—C—H
   |  |  |
   H  H  H
```

**b.** $CH_3—CH_2—CH_2—CH_2—CH_2—CH_3$

**c.**

**11.11** **a.** pentane **b.** heptane **c.** hexane **d.** cyclobutane

**11.13** **a.** $CH_4$ **b.** $CH_3—CH_3$ **c.** $CH_3—CH_2—CH_2—CH_2—CH_3$ **d.**

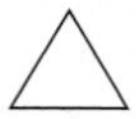

**11.15** **a.** same molecule
**b.** isomers of $C_5H_{12}$
**c.** isomers of $C_6H_{14}$

**11.17** **a.** 2-methylbutane
**b.** 2,2-dimethylpropane
**c.** 2,3-dimethylpentane
**d.** 4-ethyl-2,2-dimethylhexane

**11.19** **a.** chlorocyclopentane
**b.** methylcyclohexane
**c.** 1-bromo-3-methylcyclobutane
**d.** 1-bromo-2-chlorocyclopentane

**11.21** **a.**

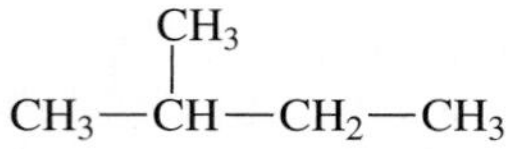

```
    CH3
    |
CH3—CH—CH2—CH3
```

**b.**

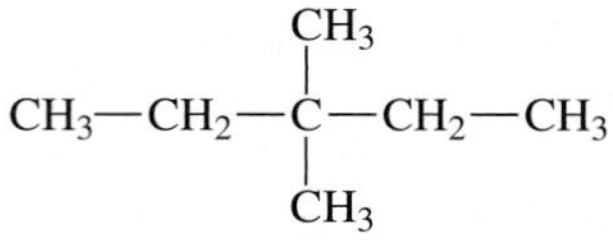

```
        CH3
        |
CH3—CH2—C—CH2—CH3
        |
        CH3
```

**c.**

```
    CH3 CH3     CH3
    |   |       |
CH3—CH—CH—CH2—CH—CH3
```

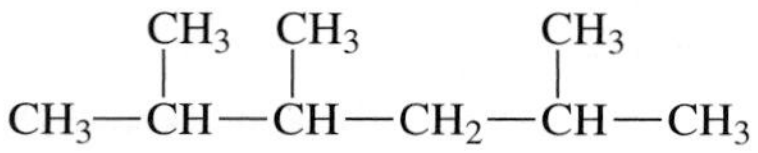

**d.**

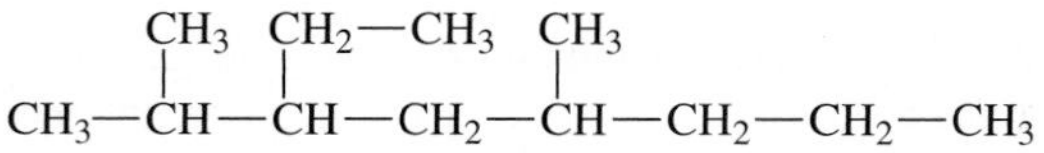

```
    CH3 CH2—CH3 CH3
    |   |       |
CH3—CH—CH—CH2—CH—CH2—CH2—CH3
```

**11.23** **a.** $CH_3$ **b.** Cl

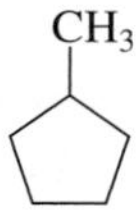

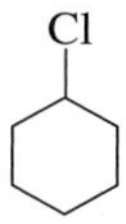

**c.** $CH_3$ $H_3C$ **d.** Br $CH_3$ $CH_3$

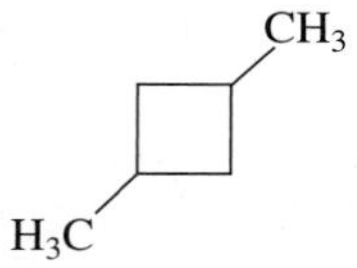

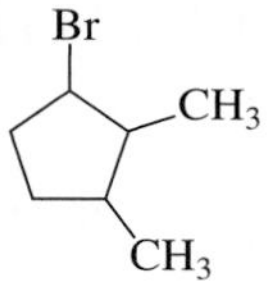

**11.25** **a.** bromoethane
**b.** 1-fluoropropane
**c.** 2-chloropropane
**d.** trichloromethane

**11.27** **a.**

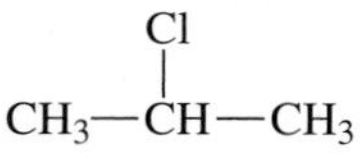

```
    Cl
    |
CH3—CH—CH3
```

**b.**

```
    Br  Cl
    |   |
CH3—CH—CH—CH3
```

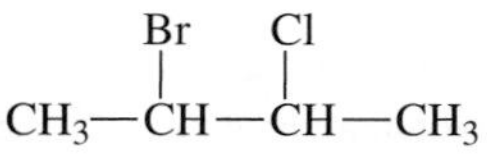

**c.** $CH_3Br$ **d.** $CBr_4$

**11.29** **a.** $CH_3—CH_2—CH_2—CH_2—CH_2—CH_2—CH_3$
**b.** liquid
**c.** insoluble in water
**d.** float

**11.31** **a.** heptane
**b.** cyclopropane
**c.** hexane

**11.33** **a.** $2C_2H_6 + 7O_2 \longrightarrow 4CO_2 + 6H_2O$
**b.** $2C_3H_6 + 9O_2 \longrightarrow 6CO_2 + 6H_2O$
**c.** $2C_8H_{18} + 25O_2 \longrightarrow 16CO_2 + 18H_2O$
**d.** $C_6H_{12} + 9O_2 \longrightarrow 6CO_2 + 6H_2O$

**11.35 a.** alcohol **b.** alkene **c.** aldehyde **d.** ester

**11.37 a.** ether **b.** alcohol **c.** ketone **d.** carboxylic acid **e.** amine

**11.39 a.** aromatic, ether, alcohol, ketone
**b.** aromatic, ether, alkene, ester

**11.41** aromatic, ether, amide

**11.43 a.** Organic compounds have covalent bonds; inorganic compounds have ionic as well as polar covalent bonds and a few have nonpolar covalent bonds.
**b.** Most organic compounds are insoluble in water; many inorganic compounds are soluble in water.
**c.** Most organic compounds have low melting points; inorganic compounds have high melting points.
**d.** Most organic compounds are flammable; inorganic compounds are not usually flammable.

**11.45 a.** butane
**b.** butane
**c.** potassium chloride
**d.** potassium chloride
**e.** butane

**11.47 a.** amine **b.** ketone **c.** ester **d.** alcohol

**11.49 a.** methyl **b.** propyl **c.** chloro

**11.51 a.** methylcyclopentane
**b.** 1,2-dibromo-3-chloropropane
**c.** 2,3-dimethylhexane
**d.** 3-chloro-3-ethylpentane

**11.53 a.**
$$\begin{array}{c}\qquad\qquad CH_2-CH_3\\ \qquad\qquad | \\ CH_3-CH_2-CH-CH_2-CH_2-CH_3\end{array}$$

**b.** 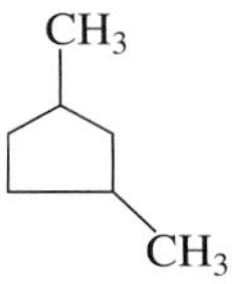 $CH_3$ $CH_3$

**c.**
$$\begin{array}{c}Cl\\ | \\ Cl-CH_2-CH_2-C-CH_2-CH_2-CH_2-CH_3\\ | \\ CH_3\end{array}$$

**d.** 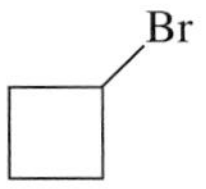 Br

**11.55 a.**

**b.**

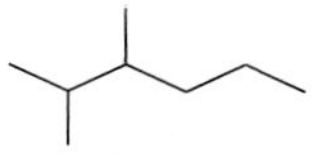

**c.** 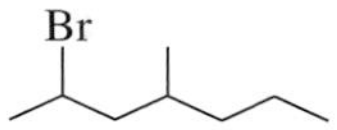 Br

**11.57 a.** heptane
**b.** cyclopentane
**c.** hexane

**11.59 a.** $C_3H_8 + 5O_2 \longrightarrow 3CO_2 + 4H_2O$
**b.** $C_5H_{12} + 8O_2 \longrightarrow 5CO_2 + 6H_2O$
**c.** $C_4H_8 + 6O_2 \longrightarrow 4CO_2 + 4H_2O$
**d.** $2C_8H_{18} + 25O_2 \longrightarrow 16CO_2 + 18H_2O$

**11.61 a.** alcohol **b.** alkene **c.** aldehyde **d.** alkane **e.** carboxylic acid **f.** amine

**11.63** Condensed structural formula:
$$\begin{array}{c}CH_3 \qquad\qquad CH_3\\ | \qquad\qquad\quad | \\ CH_3-C-CH_2-CH-CH_3\\ | \\ CH_3\end{array}$$
Molecular formula: $C_8H_{18}$
Combustion reaction:
$2C_8H_{18} + 25O_2 \longrightarrow 16CO_2 + 18H_2O$

**11.65 a.** $C_5H_{12} + 8O_2 \longrightarrow 5CO_2 + 6H_2O$
**b.** 72.0 g/mole
**c.** $2.8 \times 10^4$ kcal
**d.** 3700 L of $CO_2$

**11.67**
$$\begin{array}{c}CH_3\;\; CH_3\\ |\qquad | \\ CH_3-CH-CH-CH_3\end{array} \qquad \begin{array}{c}CH_3\\ | \\ CH_3-C-CH_2-CH_3\\ | \\ CH_3\end{array}$$

**11.69 a.** $CH_3-CH_2-CH_3$
**b.** $C_3H_8 + 5O_2 \longrightarrow 3CO_2 + 4H_2O$
**c.** 85.7 g of $O_2$
**d.** 70.7 g of $CO_2$

**11.71 a.** $C_3H_8 + 5O_2 \longrightarrow 3CO_2 + 4H_2O$
**b.** 6.8 kg of $CO_2$

# 12 Alkenes, Alkynes, and Aromatic Compounds

LOOKING AHEAD


12.1 Alkenes and Alkynes

12.2 Cis–Trans Isomers

12.3 Addition Reactions

12.4 Polymers of Alkenes

12.5 Aromatic Compounds


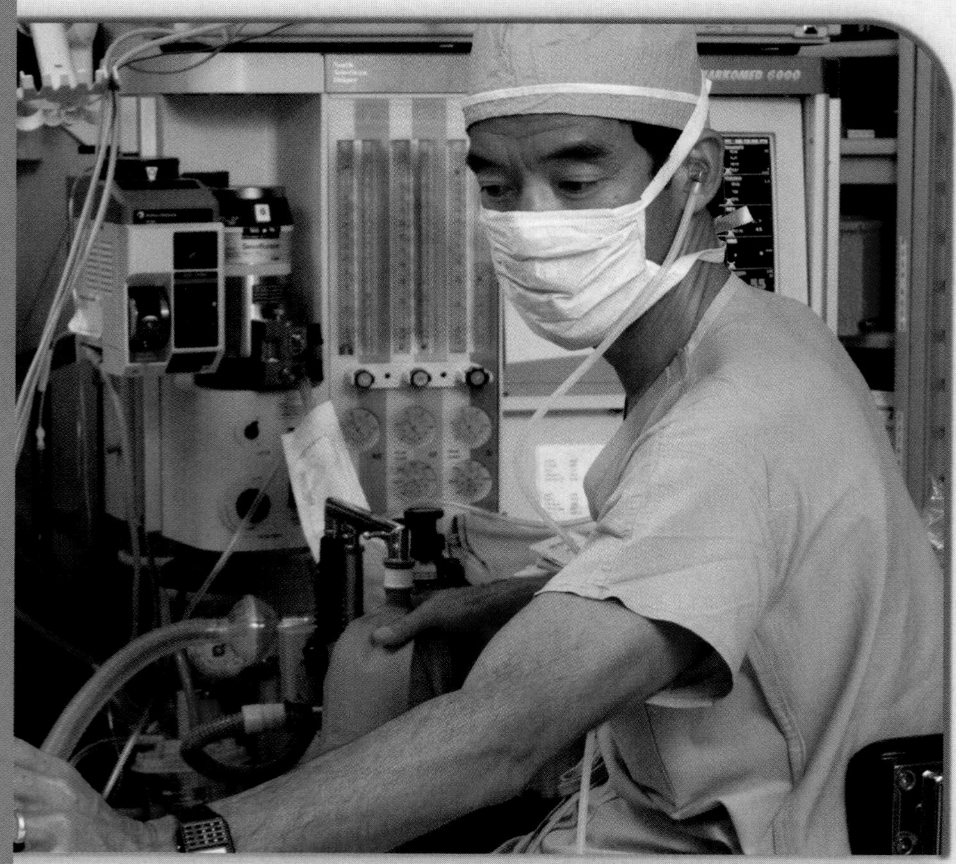

*"During surgery, I work with the surgeon to provide a safe level of anesthetics that renders the patient free from pain," says Mark Noguchi, nurse anesthetist (CRNA), Kaiser Hospital. "We do spinal and epidural blocks as well as general anesthetics, which means the patient is totally asleep. We use a variety of pharmaceutical agents, including halothane ($C_2HBrClF_3$) and bupivacain ($C_{18}H_{28}N_2O$), as well as muscle relaxants such as midazolam ($C_{18}H_{13}ClFN_3$), to achieve the results we want for the surgical situation. We also assess the patient's overall hemodynamic status. If blood is lost, we replace components such as plasma, platelets, and coagulation factors. We also monitor the heart rate and run EKGs to determine cardiac function."*

Visit **www.masteringchemistry.com** for self-study materials and instructor-assigned homework.

In Chapter 11, we looked primarily at alkanes that contain only single bonds. Now we will investigate hydrocarbons that contain one or more double bonds or triple bonds between carbon atoms. When we cook with vegetable oils such as corn oil, safflower oil, or olive oil, we are using organic compounds called *lipids* that have one or more double bonds in their long carbon chains. Animal fats also contain long chains of carbon atoms but with fewer double bonds. If we compare the two types of fats, we find considerable differences in their physical and chemical properties. Vegetable oils are liquid at room temperature, whereas animal fats are solid. Because double bonds are more reactive than single bonds, oils are oxidized by oxygen in the air, especially at warm temperatures, forming products that have rancid, unpleasant odors.

## 12.1 Alkenes and Alkynes

**LEARNING GOAL**

Write the IUPAC names for alkenes and alkynes; give common names for simple structures.

Alkenes and alkynes are families of hydrocarbons that contain double and triple bonds, respectively. They are called *unsaturated hydrocarbons* because they do not contain the maximum number of hydrogen atoms that could be attached to each carbon atom, as do alkanes. These unsaturated hydrocarbons react with hydrogen gas to increase the number of hydrogen atoms to become alkanes, which are *saturated hydrocarbons* because they do have the maximum number of hydrogen atoms possible.

### Identifying Alkenes and Alkynes

An **alkene** contains one or more carbon-carbon double bond that forms when adjacent carbon atoms share two pairs of valence electrons. Recall that a carbon atom always forms four covalent bonds. In the simplest alkene, ethene, $C_2H_4$, two carbon atoms are connected by a double bond, and each is also attached to two H atoms. (See Figure 12.1.)

Ethene, commonly called ethylene, is an important plant hormone involved in promoting the ripening of fruit. Commercially grown fruit, such as avocados, bananas, and tomatoes, are often picked before they are ripe. Before the fruit is brought to market, it is exposed to ethylene to accelerate the ripening process. Ethylene also accelerates the breakdown of cellulose in plants, which causes flowers to wilt and leaves to fall from trees.

In an **alkyne**, a triple bond forms when two carbon atoms share three pairs of valence electrons. In a triple bond, each carbon atom is attached to two other atoms. The simplest alkyne, ethyne ($C_2H_2$)—commonly called acetylene—is used in welding, where it reacts with oxygen to produce flames with temperatures above 3300 °C.

Ethene

H₂C=CH₂ structure:

H\ /H
C=C
H/ \H

Ethyne

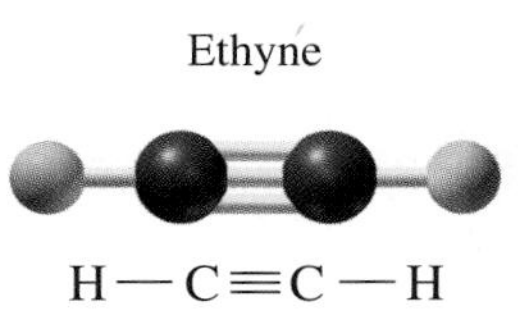

H—C≡C—H

FIGURE 12.1 Ball-and-stick models of ethene and ethyne show the functional groups of double or triple bonds.

Q Why are these compounds called unsaturated hydrocarbons?

### Structures of Alkenes and Alkynes

In ethene, two $CH_2$ groups are connected by a double bond, which represents two pairs of electrons. We already know that carbon has four electrons and needs four bonds to achieve a stable octet. In a double bond, each carbon atom is attached to three other atoms (one carbon and two hydrogens). According to VSEPR theory (Chapter 5), the three groups bonded to each carbon in the double bond are planar and arranged at angles of 120°.

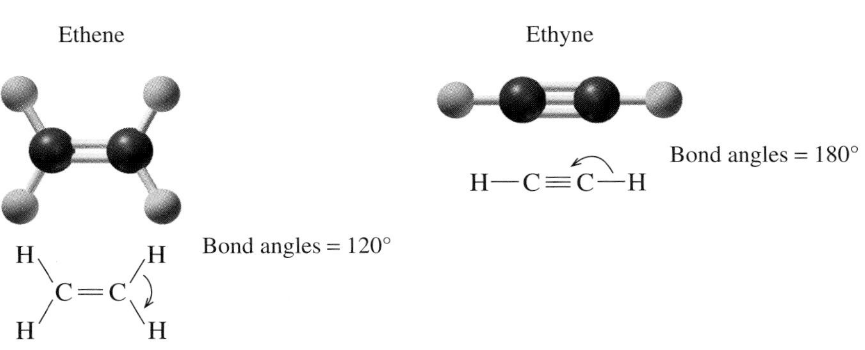

In the simplest alkyne, ethyne, two CH groups are connected by a triple bond. According to VSEPR theory, the two groups bonded to each carbon in the triple bond are linear and arranged at angles of 180°.

**CONCEPT CHECK 12.1**

**Identifying Alkanes, Alkenes, and Alkynes**

Classify each of the following condensed structural formulas as an alkane, alkene, or alkyne:

**a.** $CH_3{-}C{\equiv}C{-}CH_3$
**b.** $CH_3{-}CH_2{-}CH_3$
**c.** $CH_3{-}CH_2{-}CH_2{-}CH{=}CH_2$

ANSWER

**a.** A condensed structural formula with a triple bond is an alkyne.
**b.** A condensed structural formula with only single bonds between carbon atoms is an alkane.
**c.** A condensed structural formula with a double bond is an alkene.

MC™ TUTORIAL Naming Alkenes and Alkynes

## Naming Alkenes and Alkynes

The IUPAC names for alkenes and alkynes are similar to those of alkanes. For alkenes or alkynes, the name is based on the longest carbon chain that contains the double or triple bond.

See Table 12.1 for a comparison of the naming for alkanes, alkenes, and alkynes.

**TABLE 12.1 Comparison of Names for Alkanes, Alkenes, and Alkynes**

| Alkane | Alkene | Alkyne |
|---|---|---|
| $H_3C{-}CH_3$<br>Ethane | $H_2C{=}CH_2$<br>Ethene (ethylene) | $HC{\equiv}CH$<br>Ethyne (acetylene) |
| $CH_3{-}CH_2{-}CH_3$<br>Propane | $CH_3{-}CH{=}CH_2$<br>Propene | $CH_3{-}CH{\equiv}CH$<br>Propyne |

**STEP 1** **Name the longest carbon chain that contains the double or triple bond.** Replace the corresponding alkane ending with *ene* for an alkene and *yne* for an alkyne. Cyclic alkenes are named as *cycloalkenes.*

**STEP 2** **Number the longest chain from the end nearer the double or triple bond.** Indicate the position of the double or triple bond using the lowest number:

$$\underset{4}{CH_3}{-}\underset{3}{CH_2}{-}\underset{2}{CH}{=}\underset{1}{CH_2}$$
1-Butene

$$\underset{1}{CH_3}{-}\underset{2}{CH}{=}\underset{3}{CH}{-}\underset{4}{CH_3}$$
2-Butene

$$\underset{1}{CH_3}{-}\underset{2}{C}{\equiv}\underset{3}{C}{-}\underset{4}{CH_3}$$
2-Butyne

Alkenes or alkynes with two or three carbon atoms do not need numbers. For example, the double bond in propene must be between carbon 1 and carbon 2, which can be written $CH_2{=}CH{-}CH_3$ or $CH_3{-}CH{=}CH_2$.

**STEP 3** **Give the location and name of each substituent (alphabetical order) as a prefix to the alkene or alkyne name:**

$$\underset{1}{CH_2}{=}\underset{2}{CH}{-}\underset{3}{CH_2}{-}\underset{4}{\overset{\overset{\large CH_3}{|}}{CH}}{-}\underset{5}{CH_3}$$
4-Methyl-1-pentene

$$\underset{1}{CH_3}{-}\underset{2}{\overset{\overset{\large CH_3}{|}}{C}}{=}\underset{3}{\overset{\overset{\large CH_3}{|}}{C}}{-}\underset{4}{CH_3}$$
2,3-Dimethyl-2-butene

$$\underset{4}{CH_3}{-}\underset{3}{\overset{\overset{\large Cl}{|}}{CH}}{-}\underset{2}{C}{\equiv}\underset{1}{CH}$$
3-Chloro-1-butyne

**EXPLORE YOUR WORLD**

### Ripening Fruit

Obtain two unripe (green) bananas. Place one in a plastic bag and seal the bag. Leave both bananas on the counter. Check the bananas twice a day for 2 or 3 days and observe any difference in the ripening process.

**QUESTIONS**

1. What compound helps ripen the bananas?
2. What are some possible reasons for any difference in the ripening rate?
3. If you wish to ripen an avocado, what procedure might you use?

In a **cycloalkene** with a substituent, the double bond is understood to be between carbons 1 and 2, and the ring is numbered to give the lowest number to the substituent:

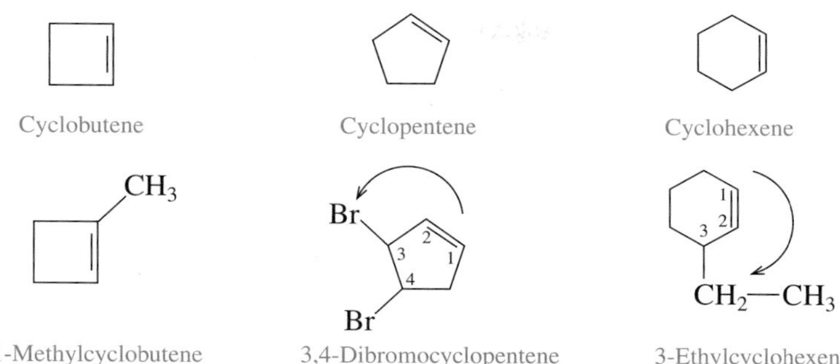


CONCEPT CHECK 12.2

### Comparing Alkenes and Alkynes

Compare the condensed structural formulas of propane, propene, and propyne.

ANSWER

Propane, propene, and propyne each contain three carbon atoms. Propane contains only single bonds, propene contains a double bond, and propyne contains a triple bond. Propane has eight hydrogen atoms, propene has six hydrogen atoms, and propyne has four hydrogen atoms.

SAMPLE PROBLEM 12.1

### Naming Alkenes and Alkynes

Write the IUPAC name for each of the following:

**a.** $CH_3—\underset{\displaystyle |}{\overset{CH_3}{CH}}—CH{=}CH—CH_3$ **b.** $CH_3—CH_2—C{\equiv}C—CH_2—CH_3$

SOLUTION

**a. STEP 1 Name the longest carbon chain that contains the double or triple bond.** There are five carbon atoms in the longest carbon chain containing the double bond. Replacing the corresponding alkane ending with *ene* gives pentene.

**STEP 2 Number the longest chain from the end nearer the double or triple bond.** The number of the first carbon in the double bond is used to give the location of the double bond:

$$\underset{5}{CH_3}—\underset{4}{\overset{CH_3}{CH}}—\underset{3}{CH}{=}\underset{2}{CH}—\underset{1}{CH_3} \qquad \text{2-pentene}$$

**STEP 3 Give the location and name of each substituent (alphabetical order) as a prefix to the alkene or alkyne name.** The methyl group is located on carbon 4:

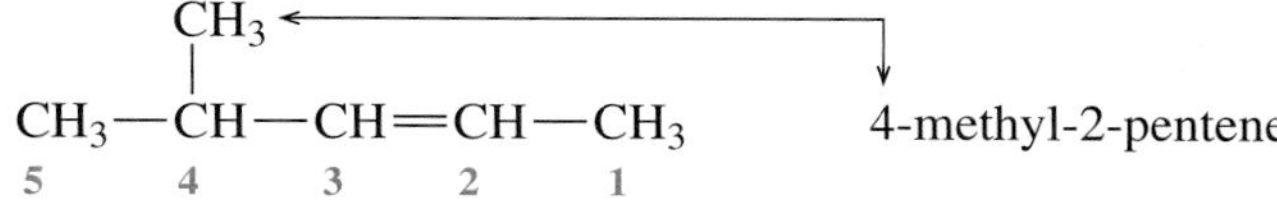


**Guide to Naming Alkenes and Alkynes**

STEP 1 Name the longest carbon chain with a double or triple bond.

STEP 2 Number the carbon chain starting from the end nearer a double or triple bond.

STEP 3 Give the location and name of each substituent (alphabetical order) as a prefix to the name, if needed.

**b.** STEP 1 **Name the longest carbon chain that contains the double or triple bond.** There are six carbon atoms in the longest chain containing the triple bond. Replacing the corresponding alkane ending with *yne* gives hexyne.

STEP 2 **Number the main chain from the end nearer the double or triple bond.** The number of the first carbon in the triple bond is used to give the location of the triple bond:

$$\underset{1}{CH_3}-\underset{2}{CH_2}-\underset{3}{C}\equiv\underset{4}{C}-\underset{5}{CH_2}-\underset{6}{CH_3} \qquad \text{3-hexyne}$$

STEP 3 **Give the location and name of each substituent (alphabetical order) as a prefix to the alkene or alkyne name.** There are no substituents in this formula.

STUDY CHECK

Draw the condensed structural formula for each of the following:

**a.** 2-pentyne

**b.** 3-methylcyclopentene

## ENVIRONMENTAL NOTE

### Fragrant Alkenes

The odors you associate with lemons, oranges, roses, and lavender are due to volatile compounds that are synthesized by the plants. The pleasant flavors and fragrances of many fruits and flowers are often due to unsaturated compounds. They were some of the first kinds of compounds to be extracted from natural plant material. In ancient times, they were highly valued in their pure forms. Limonene and myrcene give the characteristic odors and flavors to lemons and bay leaves, respectively. Geraniol and citronellal give roses and lemon grass their distinct aromas. In the food and perfume industries, these compounds are extracted or synthesized and used as perfumes and flavorings.

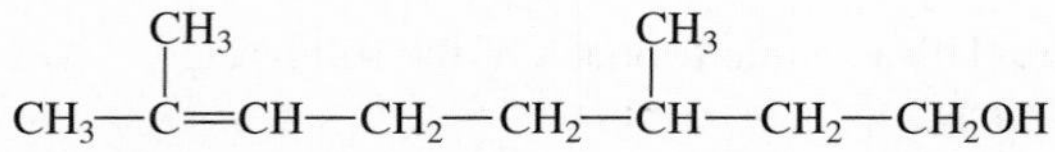
CH3
CH3
CH3—C=CH—CH2—CH2—CH—CH2—CH2OH

Geraniol, roses

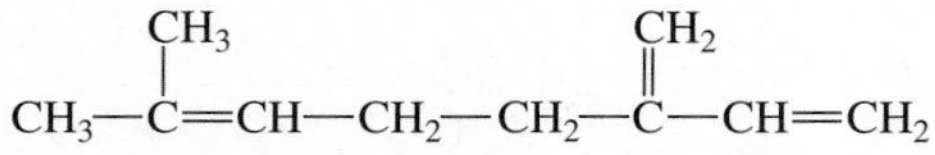
CH3
CH2
CH3—C=CH—CH2—CH2—C—CH=CH2

Myrcene, bay leaves

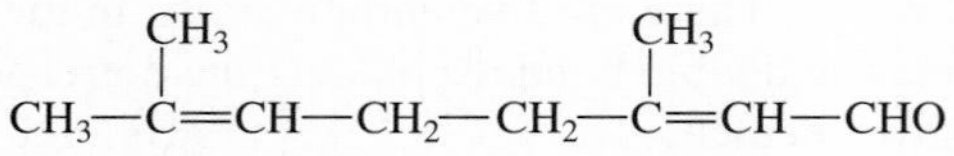
CH3
CH3
CH3—C=CH—CH2—CH2—C=CH—CHO

Citronellal, lemongrass

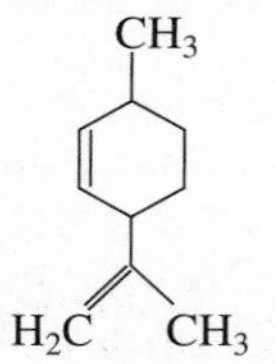
CH3
H2C
CH3

Limonene, lemons and oranges

## QUESTIONS AND PROBLEMS

### Alkenes and Alkynes

**12.1** Identify the following as alkenes, cycloalkenes, or alkynes:

a. 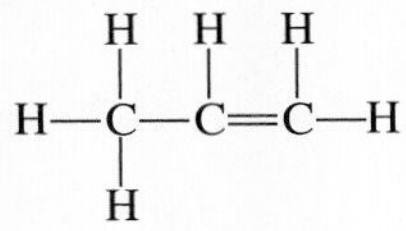 $H-\overset{H}{\underset{H}{C}}-\overset{H}{C}=\overset{H}{C}-H$

b. $CH_3-CH_2-C\equiv C-H$

c.

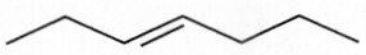

d. 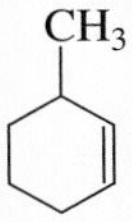 $CH_3$

**12.2** Identify the following as alkenes, cycloalkenes, or alkynes:

a. 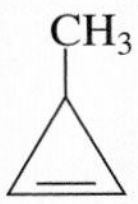 $CH_3$

b.

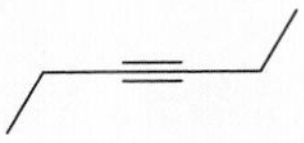

c. 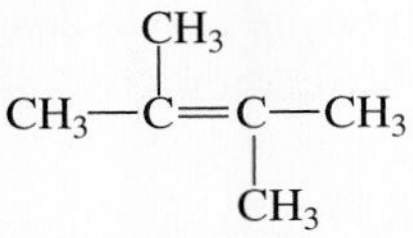 $CH_3-\overset{CH_3}{C}=\underset{CH_3}{C}-CH_3$

d. 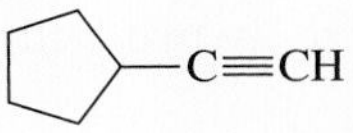 $-C\equiv CH$

**12.3** Give the IUPAC name for each of the following:

a. $CH_2=CH_2$

b. 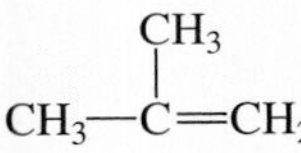 $CH_3-\overset{CH_3}{C}=CH_2$

c. $CH_3-\overset{Br}{CH}-C\equiv C-CH_3$

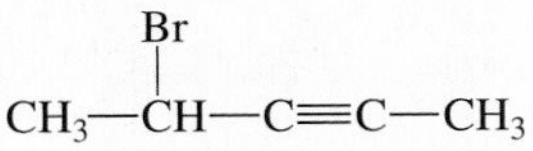

d.

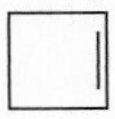

e. 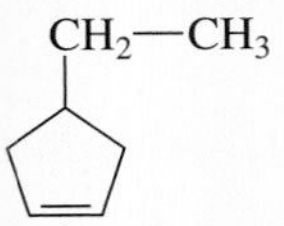 $CH_2-CH_3$

f.

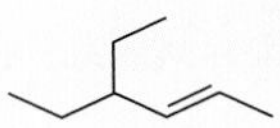

**12.4** Give the IUPAC name for each of the following:

a. $CH_2=CH-CH_2-CH_2-CH_2-CH_3$

b. 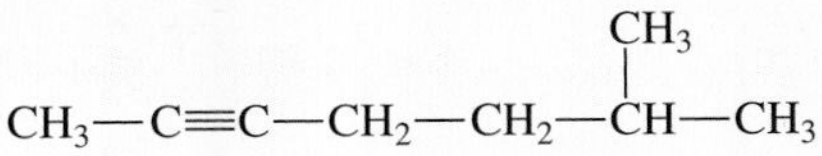 $CH_3-C\equiv C-CH_2-CH_2-\overset{CH_3}{CH}-CH_3$

c. $CH_3$, $CH_3$

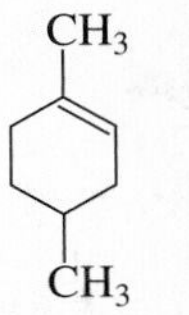

d. 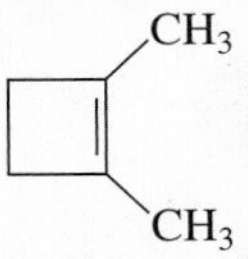 $CH_3$, $CH_3$

e. 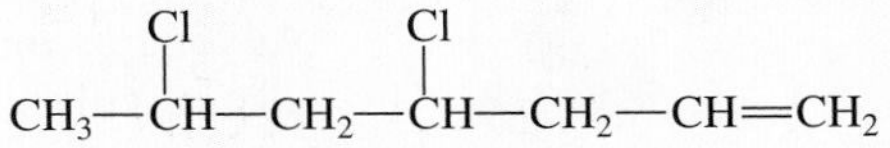 $CH_3-\overset{Cl}{CH}-CH_2-\overset{Cl}{CH}-CH_2-CH=CH_2$

f. 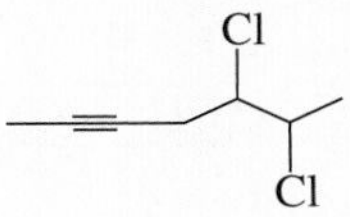 Cl, Cl

**12.5** Draw the condensed structural formula for each of the following compounds:

a. propene
b. 1-pentene
c. 2-methyl-1-butene
d. 3-methylcyclohexene
e. 2-chloro-3-hexyne
f. 1-butyne
g. 5-bromo-1-pentene

**12.6** Draw the condensed structural formula for each of the following compounds:

a. 1-methylcyclopentene
b. 3-methyl-1-butyne
c. 3,4-dimethyl-1-pentene
d. 4-ethyl-1-methylcyclohexene
e. 1,2-dichlorocyclopentene
f. propyne
g. 2-methyl-2-hexene

## 12.2 Cis–Trans Isomers

**LEARNING GOAL**

Write the condensed structural formulas and names for the cis–trans isomers of alkenes.

In alkenes, the double bond is rigid, which means that the groups attached to the double bond do not rotate. (See *Explore Your World* "Modeling Cis–Trans Isomers.") Therefore, alkenes may have two different structures or isomers indicated by the prefix *cis* or *trans*. In a **cis isomer**, two large groups, usually alkyl groups or halogen atoms, are on the same side of the double bond. In the **trans isomer**, the large groups are on opposite sides of the double bond. For example, cis–trans isomers can be written for 2-butene. (See Figure 12.2.) In general, trans isomers are more stable than their cis counterparts because the large groups attached to the double bond are farther apart. As with any pair of isomers, the cis–trans isomers of 2-butene are different compounds with different

SELF STUDY ACTIVITY
Geometric Isomers

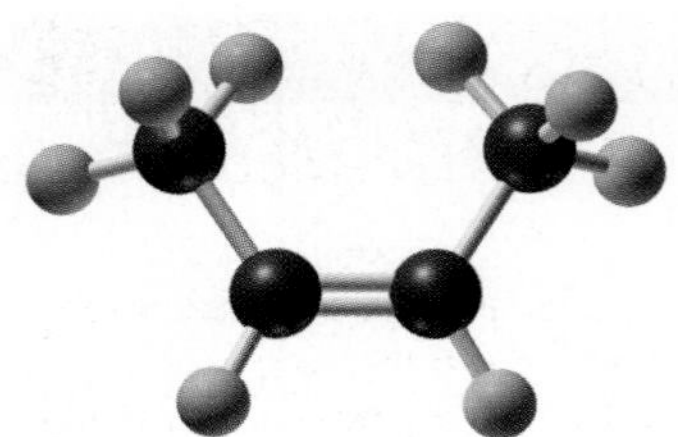

*cis*-2-Butene

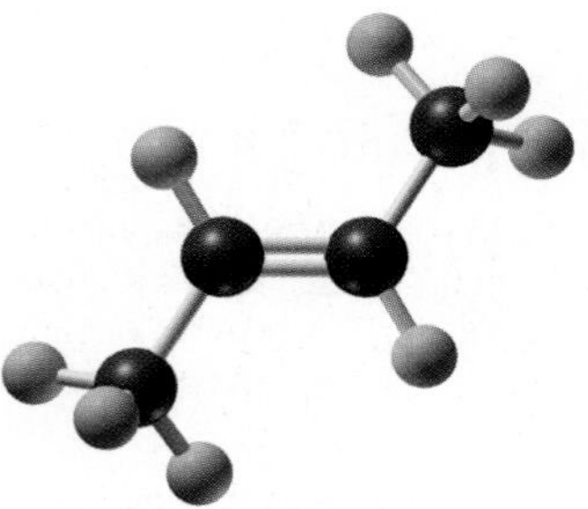

*trans*-2-Butene

**FIGURE 12.2** Ball-and-stick models of the cis and trans isomers of 2-butene.

**Q** What feature in 2-butene accounts for the cis and trans isomers?

physical properties, such as melting and boiling points, as well as different chemical properties:

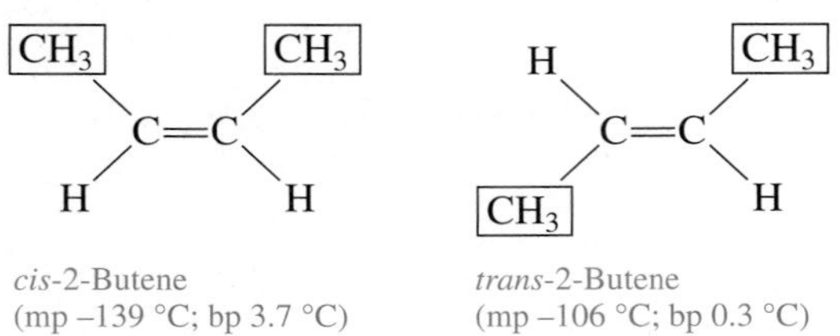


As long as the two groups attached to each carbon in the double bond are different, an alkene will show cis–trans isomers. Another example of cis–trans isomers is the following:

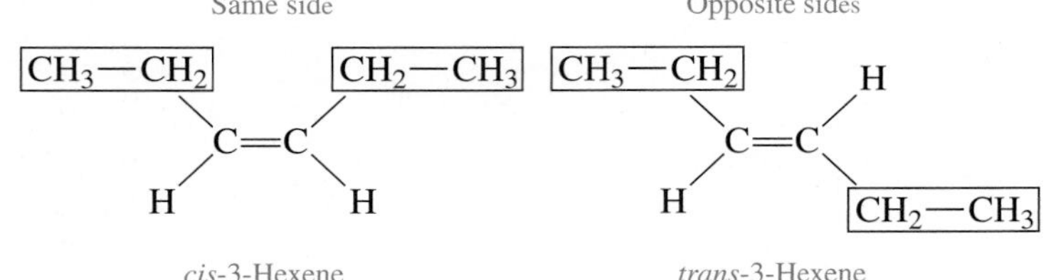


An alkene does not have cis–trans isomers if identical groups are attached to one of the carbon atoms in the double bond. For example, in 1-butene there are two hydrogen atoms on carbon 1. In 2-methylpropene there are two methyl groups on carbon 2:

H CH$_2$—CH$_3$ H CH$_3$

Identical atoms C=C C=C Identical groups

H H H CH$_3$

1-Butene 2-Methylpropene

Alkynes do not have cis–trans isomers, because the carbons in the triple bond are each attached to only one group:

$$H—C\equiv C—CH_3 \qquad CH_3—C\equiv C—CH_2—CH_3$$

TUTORIAL
Cis–Trans Isomers

## CONCEPT CHECK 12.3

### Cis-Trans Isomers

Consider the compound 2-hexene.

**a.** What alkyl groups are attached to the carbon atoms in the double bond?
**b.** In *cis*-2-hexene, are the alkyl groups attached on the same side or opposite sides of the double bond?
**c.** In *trans*-2-hexene, are the hydrogen atoms attached on the same side or opposite sides of the double bond?
**d.** Why does 1-hexene not have cis-trans isomers?

ANSWER

**a.** In 2-hexene, carbon 2 is attached to a methyl ($CH_3$—) group and carbon 3 is attached to a propyl ($CH_3$—$CH_2$—$CH_2$—) group.
**b.** In *cis*-2-hexene, the methyl and propyl groups are attached on the same side of the double bond.
**c.** In *trans*-2-hexene, the hydrogen atoms are attached on opposite sides of the double bond.
**d.** In the condensed structural formula of 1-hexene, carbon 1 is attached to two hydrogen atoms. Because the two H atoms are identical, 1-hexene cannot have cis–trans isomers.

# Explore Your World

## Modeling Cis–Trans Isomers

Because cis–trans isomerism is not easy to visualize, here are some things you can do to understand the difference in rotation around a single bond compared to a double bond and how it affects groups that are attached to the carbon atoms in the double bond.

Put the fingertips of your index fingers together. This is a model of a single bond. Consider the index fingers as a pair of carbon atoms, and think of your thumbs and other fingers as other parts of a carbon chain. While your index fingers are touching, twist your hands and change the position of the thumbs relative to each other. Notice how the relationship of your other fingers changes.

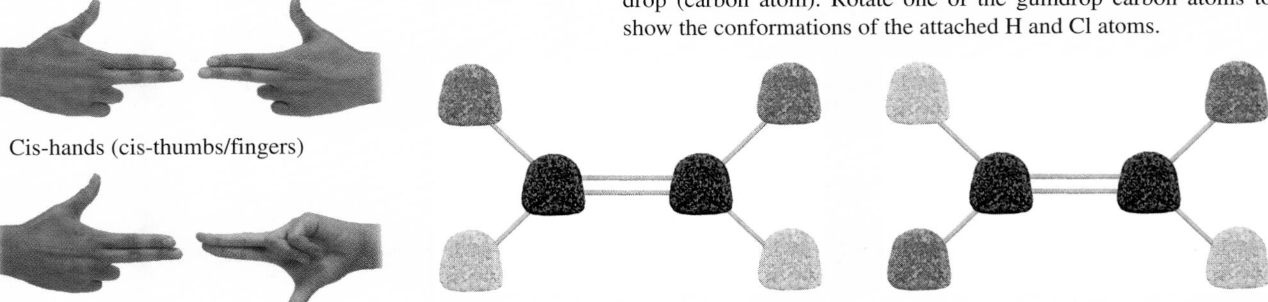

Cis-hands (cis-thumbs/fingers)

Trans-hands (trans-thumbs/fingers)

Now place the tips of your index fingers and middle fingers together in a model of a double bond. As you did before, twist your hands to try to move the thumbs apart. What happens? Can you change the location of your thumbs relative to each other without breaking the double bond? The difficulty of moving your hands with two fingers touching represents the lack of rotation about a double bond. You have made a model of a cis isomer when both thumbs are on the same side. If you turn one hand over so one thumb points down and the other thumb points up, you have made a model of a trans isomer.

## Using Gumdrops and Toothpicks to Model Cis–Trans Isomers

Obtain some toothpicks and yellow, green, and black gumdrops. The black gumdrops represent C atoms, the yellow gumdrops represent H atoms, and the green gumdrops represent Cl atoms. Place a toothpick between two black gumdrops. Use three more toothpicks to attach two yellow gumdrops, and one green gumdrop to each black gumdrop (carbon atom). Rotate one of the gumdrop carbon atoms to show the conformations of the attached H and Cl atoms.

Remove a toothpick and yellow gumdrop from each black gumdrop. Place a second toothpick between the black gumdrops which makes a double bond. Try to twist the double bond of toothpicks. Can you do it? When you observe the location of the green gumdrops, does the model you made represent a cis or trans isomer? Why? If your model is a cis isomer, how would you change it to a trans isomer? If your model is a trans isomer, how would you change it to a cis isomer?

# Environmental Note

## Pheromones in Insect Communication

Many insects emit minute quantities of chemicals called *pheromones* to send messages to other individuals of the same species. Some pheromones warn of danger, while others call for defense, mark a trail, or attract the opposite sex. During the past 40 years, the structures of many pheromones have been chemically determined. One of the most studied is bombykol, the sex pheromone produced by the female silkworm moth. Even a few nanograms of bombykol will attract male silkworm moths from distances of over 1 kilometer. The bombykol molecule is a 16-carbon chain with one cis double bond, one trans double bond, and an alcohol group. The effectiveness of many of these pheromones depends on the cis or trans configuration of the double bonds in the molecules. A certain species will respond to one isomer but not the other.

Scientists are interested in synthesizing pheromones to use as nontoxic alternatives to pesticides. When placed in a trap, bombykol can be used to isolate male silkworm moths. When a synthetic pheromone is released in a field, the males cannot locate the females, which disrupts the reproductive cycle. This technique has been successful in controlling the oriental fruit moth, the grapevine moth, and the pink bollworm.

H, H, H, H
$HOCH_2(CH_2)_7CH_2$–CH=CH–CH=CH–$CH_2CH_2CH_3$

Bombykol, sex attractant for the silkworm moth

# HEALTH NOTE

## Cis–Trans Isomers for Night Vision

The retinas of the eyes consist of two types of cells: rods and cones. The rods on the edge of the retina allow us to see in dim light, and the cones, in the center, produce our vision in bright light. The rods contain a substance called *rhodopsin* that absorbs light. Rhodopsin is composed of *cis*-11-retinal, an unsaturated compound, attached to a protein. When rhodopsin absorbs light, the *cis*-11-retinal isomer is converted to its trans isomer, which changes its shape. The trans form no longer fits, and it separates from the protein. The change from the cis to trans isomer and the separation from the protein generate an electrical signal that the brain converts into an image.

An enzyme (isomerase) converts the trans isomer back to the *cis*-11-retinal isomer and the rhodopsin re-forms. If there is a deficiency of rhodopsin in the rods of the retina, night blindness may occur. One common cause of night blindness is a lack of vitamin A in the diet. We obtain vitamin A from $\beta$-carotene, which is found in foods such as carrots, squash, and spinach. In the small intestine, $\beta$-carotene is converted to vitamin A, which can be converted to *cis*-11-retinal or stored in the liver for future use. Without a sufficient quantity of retinal, not enough rhodopsin is produced to enable us to see adequately in dim light.

### Cis–Trans Isomers of Retinal

Cis double bond — Light → — Trans double bond

*cis*-11-Retinal → *trans*-11-Retinal

## CONCEPT CHECK 12.4

### Identifying Cis and Trans Isomers

Identify each of the following statements as describing a cis or trans isomer. Give the name of each.

**a.** In an isomer of 3-hexene, the ethyl groups are attached on opposite sides of the double bond.

**b.** In an isomer of 2,3-dibromo-2-butene, the bromine atoms are attached on the same side of the double bond.

ANSWER

**a.** When the alkyl groups are attached on the opposite sides of the carbon atoms of the double bond, the isomer is a trans isomer; *trans*-3-hexene.

**b.** When the bromine atoms are attached on the same side of the double bond, the isomer is a cis isomer; *cis*-2,3-dibromo-2-butene.

## SAMPLE PROBLEM 12.2

### Naming Cis–Trans Isomers

Name each of the following as a cis or trans isomer:

**a.** Br(H)C=C(Cl)(H) — Br and Cl on the upper side, H and H on the lower side

**b.** $CH_3$(H)C=C(Br)($CH_2—CH_3$) — $CH_3$ and Br on the upper side, H and $CH_2—CH_3$ on the lower side

SOLUTION

**a.** This isomer is a cis isomer because the Br and Cl atoms are on the same side of the double bond; *cis*-1-bromo-2-chloroethene.

**b.** This isomer is a trans isomer because the $CH_3—$ group and $—CH_2—CH_3$ group are on opposite sides of the double bond; *trans*-3-bromo-2-pentene.

STUDY CHECK

Is the following compound *cis*- or *trans*-3-heptene?

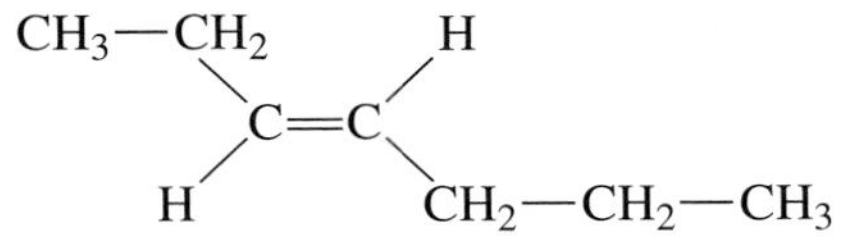

$$\begin{array}{ccc} CH_3{-}CH_2 & & H \\ & C{=}C & \\ H & & CH_2{-}CH_2{-}CH_3 \end{array}$$

## QUESTIONS AND PROBLEMS

### Cis–Trans Isomers

12.7 Which of the following can be written as cis–trans isomers?

a. $CH_2{=}CH{-}CH_3$

b. $CH_3{-}CH_2{-}CH{=}CH{-}CH_3$

c. 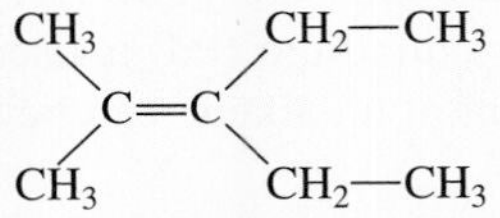 $\begin{array}{ccc} CH_3 & & CH_2{-}CH_3 \\ & C{=}C & \\ CH_3 & & CH_2{-}CH_3 \end{array}$

**12.8** Which of the following do not have cis–trans isomers?

a. 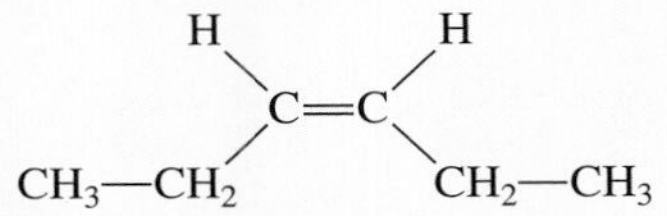 $\begin{array}{ccc} H & & H \\ & C{=}C & \\ CH_3{-}CH_2 & & CH_2{-}CH_3 \end{array}$

b. $CH_3{-}CH_2{-}CH_2{-}CH{=}CH_2$

c. 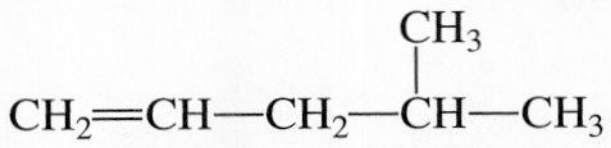 $CH_2{=}CH{-}CH_2{-}\underset{}{\overset{CH_3}{\overset{|}{C}}}H{-}CH_3$

12.9 Write the IUPAC name of each of the following using *cis* or *trans* prefixes:

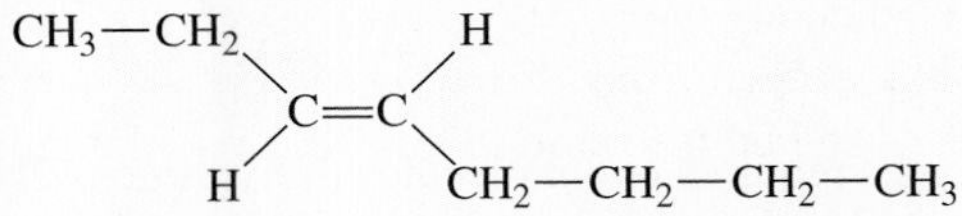

a. 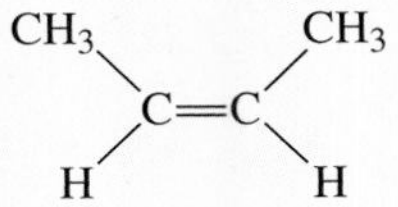 $\begin{array}{ccc} CH_3 & & CH_3 \\ & C{=}C & \\ H & & H \end{array}$

b. $\begin{array}{ccc} CH_3{-}CH_2 & & H \\ & C{=}C & \\ H & & CH_2{-}CH_2{-}CH_2{-}CH_3 \end{array}$

c. $\begin{array}{ccc} CH_3{-}CH_2{-}CH_2 & & CH_2{-}CH_3 \\ & C{=}C & \\ H & & H \end{array}$

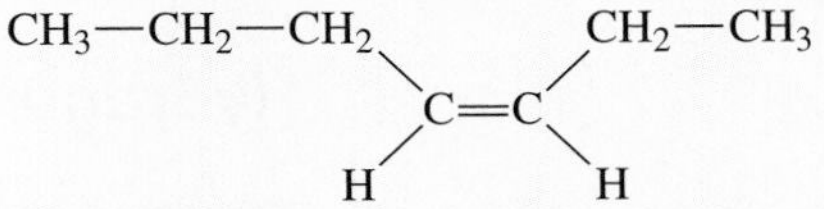

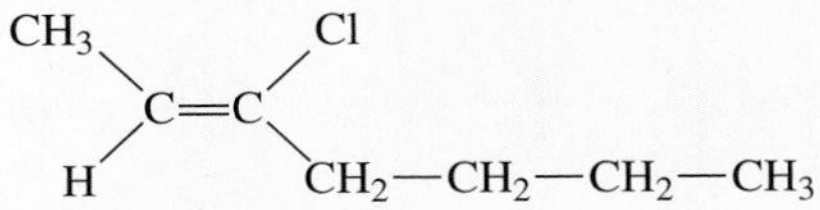

**12.10** Write the IUPAC name of each of the following using *cis* or *trans* prefixes:

a. 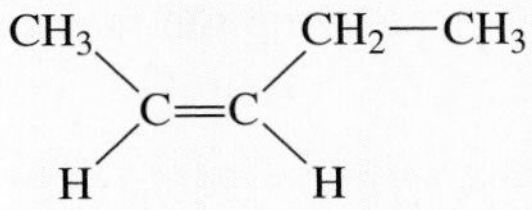 $\begin{array}{ccc} CH_3 & & CH_2{-}CH_3 \\ & C{=}C & \\ H & & H \end{array}$

b. $\begin{array}{ccc} CH_3 & & Cl \\ & C{=}C & \\ H & & CH_2{-}CH_2{-}CH_2{-}CH_3 \end{array}$

c. $\begin{array}{ccc} CH_3{-}CH_2{-}CH_2 & & H \\ & C{=}C & \\ H & & CH_3 \end{array}$

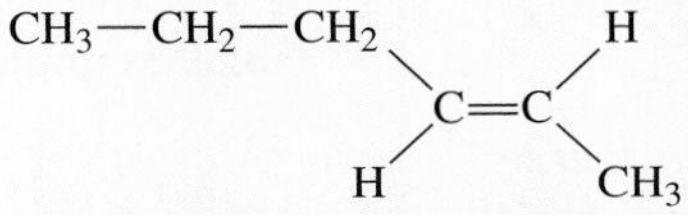

12.11 Draw the condensed structural formula for each of the following:

a. *trans*-1-chloro-2-butene

b. *cis*-2-pentene

c. *trans*-3-heptene

**12.12** Draw the condensed structural formula for each of the following:

a. *cis*-3-hexene

b. *trans*-2-pentene

c. *cis*-4-octene

## 12.3 Addition Reactions

LEARNING GOAL

Write the condensed structural formulas and names for the organic products of addition reactions of alkenes and alkynes.

The most characteristic reaction of alkenes and alkynes is the **addition** of atoms or groups of atoms to the carbons of the double or triple bond. Addition occurs because double and triple bonds are easily broken, which provides electrons to form new single bonds. The general equation for the addition of a reactant A—B to an alkene can be written as follows:

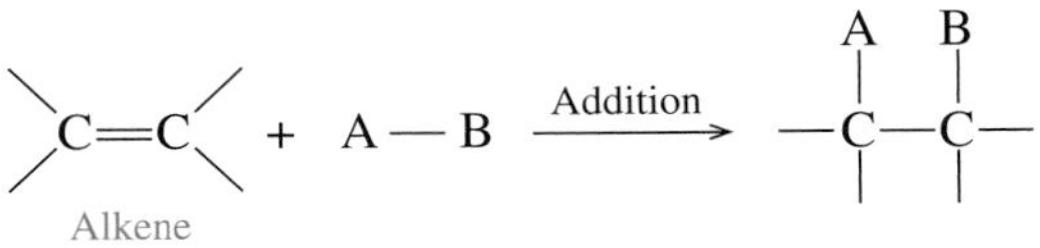

$$\underset{\text{Alkene}}{>C{=}C<} + A{-}B \xrightarrow{\text{Addition}} -\overset{A}{\overset{|}{\underset{|}{C}}}-\overset{B}{\overset{|}{\underset{|}{C}}}-$$

The addition reactions have different names that depend on the type of reactant we add to the alkene, as shown in Table 12.2.

**TABLE 12.2 Summary of Addition Reactions**

| Name of Addition Reaction | Reactants | Catalysts | Products |
|---|---|---|---|
| Hydrogenation | Alkene + $H_2$ | Pt, Ni, or Pd | Alkane |
| | Alkyne + $2H_2$ | Pt, Ni, or Pd | Alkane |
| Halogenation | Alkene + $Cl_2$ ($Br_2$) | | Haloalkane |
| | Alkyne + $2Cl_2$ ($2Br_2$) | | Haloalkane |
| Hydrohalogenation | Alkene + HCl (HBr) | | Haloalkane |
| Hydration | Alkene + $H_2O$ | $H^+$ (strong acid) | Alcohol |

## Hydrogenation

MC TUTORIAL Addition Reactions

In a reaction called **hydrogenation**, H atoms add to a double bond or triple bond to form alkanes. During hydrogenation, double or triple bonds are converted to single bonds. A catalyst such as platinum (Pt), nickel (Ni), or palladium (Pd) is used to speed up the reaction. The general equation for hydrogenation of an alkene can be written as follows:

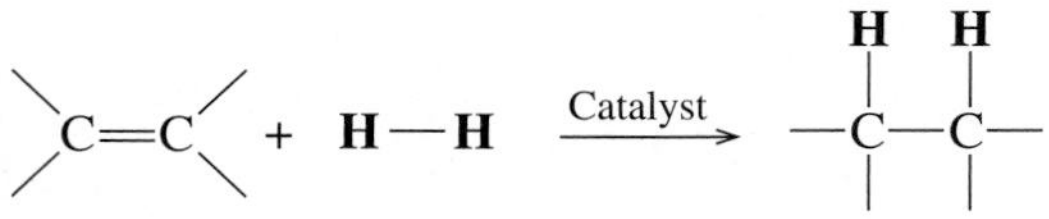

$$\text{>C=C<} + \text{H—H} \xrightarrow{\text{Catalyst}} \text{—CH—CH—}$$

Alkene → Alkane

Some examples of the hydrogenation of alkenes follow:

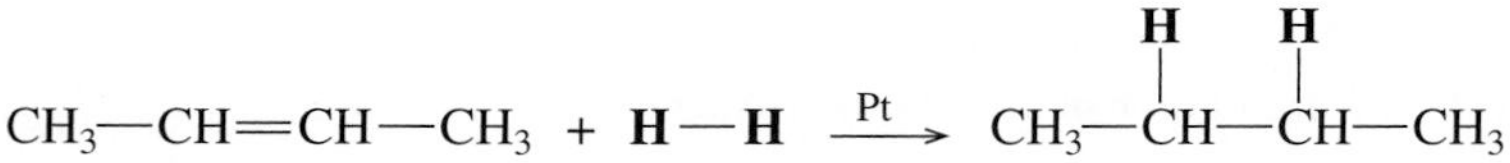

$$CH_3—CH=CH—CH_3 + H—H \xrightarrow{Pt} CH_3—CH—CH—CH_3 \text{ (with H on each middle C)}$$

2-Butene → Butane

$$\text{Cyclohexene} + H—H \xrightarrow{Ni} \text{Cyclohexane}$$

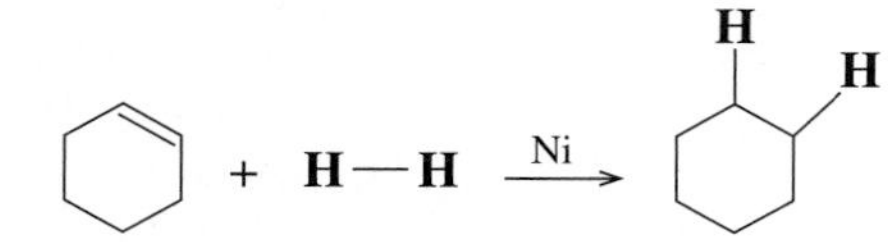

Cyclohexene → Cyclohexane

The complete hydrogenation of alkynes requires two molecules of hydrogen ($2H_2$) to form the alkane product:

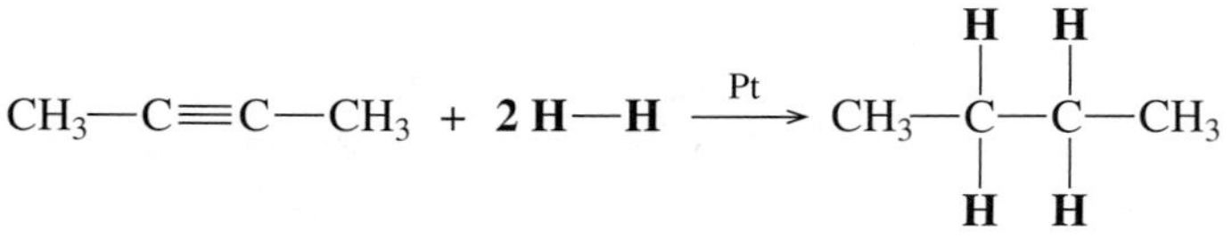

$$CH_3—C\equiv C—CH_3 + 2\,H—H \xrightarrow{Pt} CH_3—CH_2—CH_2—CH_3$$

2-Butyne → Butane

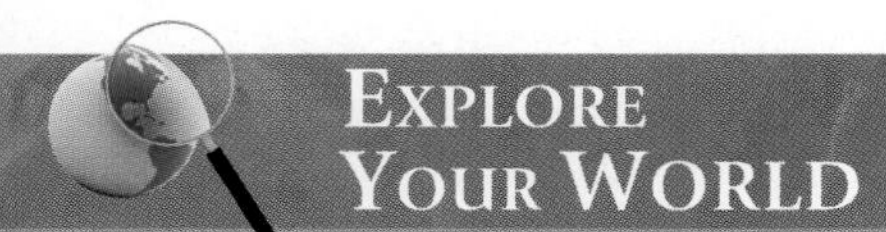

### Unsaturation in Fats and Oils

Read the labels on some containers of vegetable oils, margarine, peanut butter, and shortenings.

**QUESTIONS**

1. What terms on the label tell you that the compounds contain double bonds?
2. A label on a bottle of canola oil lists saturated, polyunsaturated, and monounsaturated fats. What do these terms tell you about the type of bonding in the fats?
3. A peanut butter label states that it contains partially hydrogenated vegetable oils or completely hydrogenated vegetable oils. What does this tell you about the type of reaction that took place in preparing the peanut butter?

**SAMPLE PROBLEM 12.3**

■ **Writing Equations for Hydrogenation**

Write the condensed structural formula for the product of the following hydrogenation reactions:

**a.** $CH_3—CH=CH_2 + H_2 \xrightarrow{Pt} ?$ **b.**  Cyclopentene $+ H_2 \xrightarrow{Pt} ?$ **c.** $HC\equiv CH + 2H_2 \xrightarrow{Ni} ?$

SOLUTION

In an addition reaction, hydrogen adds to the double or triple bond to give an alkane.

**a.** $CH_3—CH_2—CH_3$ **b.** (cyclopentane) **c.** $CH_3—CH_3$

STUDY CHECK

Draw the condensed structural formula of the product of the hydrogenation of 2-methyl-1-butene using a platinum catalyst.

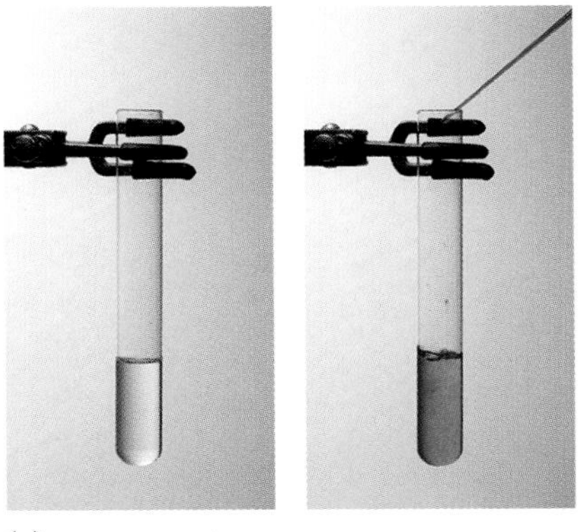

(a)

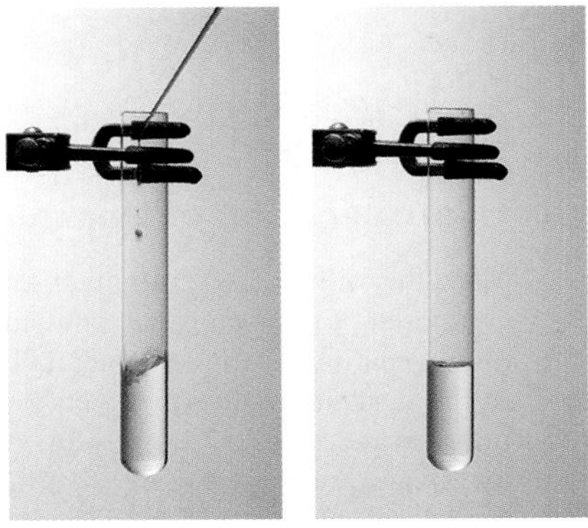

(b)

FIGURE 12.3 **(a)** When bromine is added to an alkane in the first test tube, the red color of bromine remains because the alkane does not react or reacts slowly. **(b)** When bromine is added to an alkene in the second test tube, the red color immediately disappears as bromine atoms add to the double bond.

Q Will the red color disappear when bromine is added to cyclohexane or cyclohexene?

## Halogenation

In the **halogenation** reactions of alkenes or alkynes, halogen atoms such as chlorine or bromine are added to the double or triple bonds. The reaction occurs readily, without the use of any catalyst, and adds halogen atoms to yield a di- or tetrahaloalkane product. In the general equation for halogenation, the symbol X—X or $X_2$ is used for $Cl_2$ or $Br_2$:

$$>C=C< + X—X \longrightarrow —\overset{X}{\underset{|}{\overset{|}{C}}}—\overset{X}{\underset{|}{\overset{|}{C}}}—$$

Here are some examples of adding $Cl_2$ or $Br_2$ to alkenes:

$$\underset{\text{Ethene}}{CH_2=CH_2} + Cl—Cl \longrightarrow \underset{\text{1,2-Dichloroethane}}{\overset{Cl}{\overset{|}{C}}H_2—\overset{Cl}{\overset{|}{C}}H_2}$$

Cyclohexene + Br—Br ⟶ 1,2-Dibromocyclohexane

$$\underset{\text{Propyne}}{CH_3—C\equiv C—H} + 2Cl—Cl \longrightarrow \underset{\text{1,1,2,2-Tetrachloropropane}}{CH_3—\overset{Cl}{\underset{Cl}{\overset{|}{\underset{|}{C}}}}—\overset{Cl}{\underset{Cl}{\overset{|}{\underset{|}{C}}}}—H}$$

The addition reaction of bromine is sometimes used to test for the presence of double and triple bonds, as shown in Figure 12.3.

SAMPLE PROBLEM 12.4

### Writing Products of Halogenation

Write the condensed structural formula of the product of the following reaction:

$$CH_3—\overset{CH_3}{\overset{|}{C}}=CH_2 + Br_2 \longrightarrow$$

SOLUTION

The addition of bromine to an alkene places a bromine atom on each of the carbon atoms of the double bond.

$$CH_3-\underset{\underset{Br}{|}}{\overset{\overset{CH_3}{|}}{C}}-\underset{\underset{Br}{|}}{CH_2}$$

STUDY CHECK

What is the name of the product formed when chlorine is added to 1-butene?

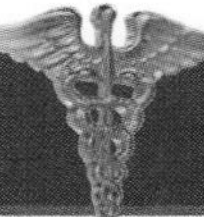

## HEALTH NOTE

### Hydrogenation of Unsaturated Fats

Vegetable oils such as corn oil or safflower oil are unsaturated fats composed of fatty acids that contain double bonds. The process of hydrogenation is used commercially to convert the double bonds in the unsaturated fats in vegetable oils to saturated fats such as margarine, which are more solid. Adjusting the amount of added hydrogen produces partially hydrogenated fats such as soft margarine, solid margarine in sticks, and shortenings, which are used in cooking. For example, oleic acid is a typical unsaturated fatty acid in olive oil and has a cis double bond at carbon 9. When oleic acid is hydrogenated, it is converted to stearic acid, a saturated fatty acid:

$$\underset{\text{Oleic acid (the cis isomer is found in olive oil and other unsaturated fats)}}{\overset{CH_3(CH_2)_7 \qquad (CH_2)_7\overset{\overset{O}{\|}}{C}OH}{\underset{H \qquad\qquad H}{C=C}}} + H_2 \xrightarrow{Pt} \underset{\text{Stearic acid (found in saturated fats)}}{CH_3(CH_2)_7-CH_2-CH_2-(CH_2)_7\overset{\overset{O}{\|}}{C}OH}$$

Oleic acid (the cis isomer is found in olive oil and other unsaturated fats)

Stearic acid (found in saturated fats)

## Hydrohalogenation

In the reaction called **hydrohalogenation**, a hydrogen halide (HCl, HBr, or HI) adds to an alkene to yield a haloalkane. The hydrogen atom bonds to one carbon of the double bond, and the halogen atom adds to the other carbon. The general reaction, in which HX represents HCl, HBr, or HI, can be written as follows:

$$\underset{\text{Alkene}}{>C=C<} + H-X \longrightarrow \underset{\text{Haloalkane (alkyl halide)}}{-\underset{|}{\overset{\overset{H}{|}}{C}}-\underset{|}{\overset{\overset{X}{|}}{C}}-}$$

Two examples of hydrohalogenation follow:

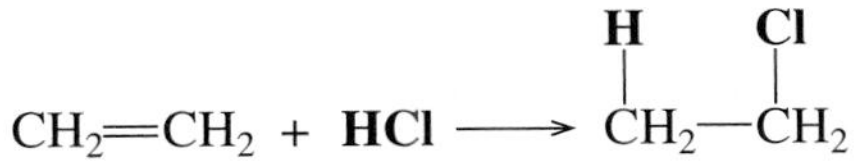

$$CH_2{=}CH_2 + \mathbf{HCl} \longrightarrow \overset{\mathbf{H}}{\underset{|}{C}}H_2{-}\overset{\mathbf{Cl}}{\underset{|}{C}}H_2$$

Ethene (ethylene) Chloroethane (ethyl chloride)

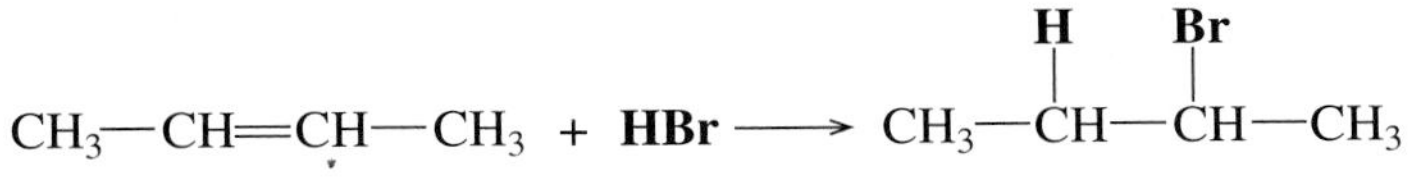

$$CH_3{-}CH{=}CH{-}CH_3 + \mathbf{HBr} \longrightarrow CH_3{-}\overset{\mathbf{H}}{\underset{|}{C}}H{-}\overset{\mathbf{Br}}{\underset{|}{C}}H{-}CH_3$$

2-Butene 2-Bromobutane

## Steps in Addition Reactions of H—X to Alkenes

We have seen that in the addition reaction of an alkene, two groups add to the carbons in the double bond to give a saturated compound. To understand how the addition of H—X or H—OH takes place, we can consider the two steps involved when HBr adds to ethene. First, a pair of electrons in the double bond reacts with a proton ($H^+$) from the HBr, which is shown by a curved arrow. This reaction produces a **carbocation** (a carbon cation) with a positive charge. In the second step, a pair of electrons from the bromide ion $Br^-$ reacts rapidly with the carbocation.

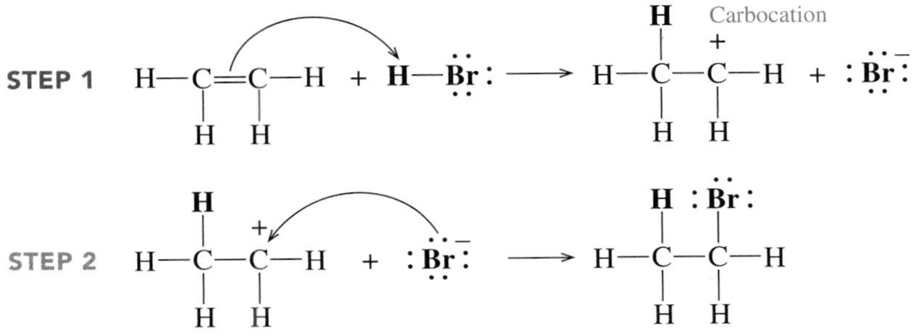

**STEP 1** H—C(H)=C(H)—H + H—:Br: ⟶ H—C(H)(**H**)—C⁺(H)—H + :Br:⁻ (Carbocation)

**STEP 2** H—C(H)(**H**)—C⁺(H)—H + :Br:⁻ ⟶ H—C(H)(**H**)—C(H)(**:Br:**)—H

Bromoethane

## Markovnikov's Rule

When HBr adds to a symmetrical alkene, a single product is formed. However, when HBr adds to a double bond in an unsymmetrical alkene, two products are possible. In 1870, Vladimir Markovnikov, a Russian chemist, observed that when HX adds to a double bond, the H attaches to the carbon that has more hydrogen atoms, and the X attaches to the carbon that has fewer hydrogen atoms. This observation is now called **Markovnikov's rule**.

When an unsymmetrical alkene forms a carbocation, the more stable form is the one where the $C^+$ is attached to the most alkyl groups. Therefore, in the initial step, the $H^+$ adds to the carbon that has fewer alkyl groups, which is the carbon in the double bond that has the greater number of hydrogen atoms.

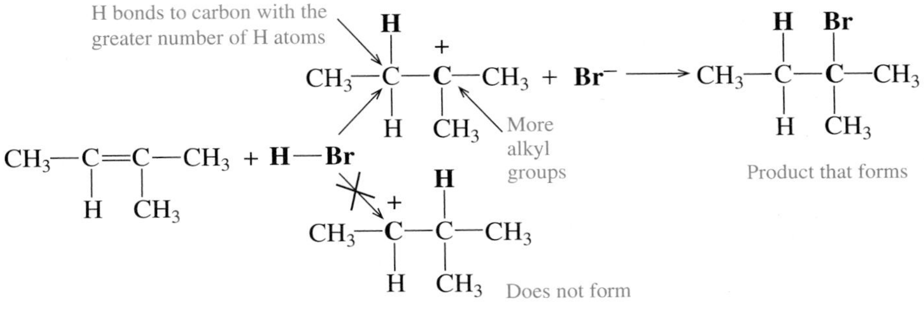

$CH_3{-}C(H){=}C(CH_3){-}CH_3$ + **H—Br**

→ $CH_3{-}C(\mathbf{H})(H){-}C^+(CH_3){-}CH_3$ + **Br⁻** ⟶ $CH_3{-}C(\mathbf{H})(H){-}C(\mathbf{Br})(CH_3){-}CH_3$

H bonds to carbon with the greater number of H atoms

More alkyl groups

Product that forms

→ (crossed out) $CH_3{-}C^+(H){-}C(\mathbf{H})(CH_3){-}CH_3$ Does not form

CONCEPT CHECK 12.5

### Markovnikov's Rule

**a.** Why would you use Markovnikov's rule to determine the product for the addition of HBr to 1-hexene but not to 3-hexene?
**b.** What is the name of the product for the addition of HBr to 1-hexene?
**c.** What is the name of the product for the addition of HBr to 3-hexene?

ANSWER

**a.** Markovnikov's rule is used to determine the product when HBr is added to 1-hexene because 1-hexene is unsymmetrical with a different number of alkyl groups attached to the carbon atoms in the double bond. Thus, the product is formed from the carbocation that has more alkyl groups attached. Markovnikov's rule is not needed when HBr is added to 3-hexene, because 3-hexene is symmetrical.
**b.** The H of HBr adds to carbon 1, which has more hydrogen atoms, and the Br adds to carbon 2 to form 2-bromohexane.
**c.** Since 3-hexene is symmetrical, addition of HBr gives 3-bromohexane.

CAREER FOCUS

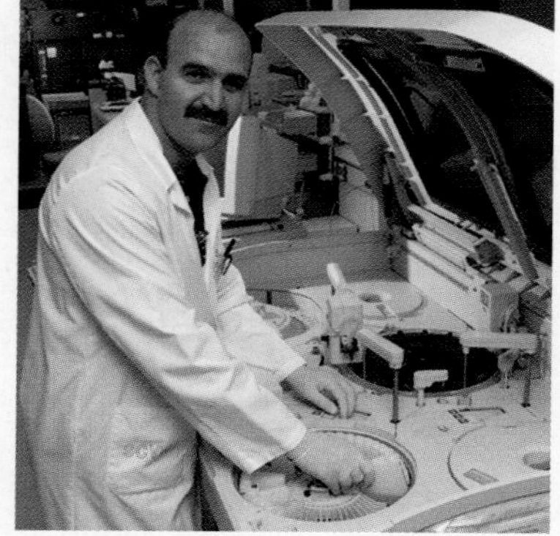

### Laboratory Technologist

"We use serum or plasma specimens, which are collected in tubes, spun down, and separated," says Fariborz Azarchehr, laboratory technologist. "I place the specimens in an analyzer, which adds reagents that react chemically with various components in the blood. Their products are then measured using spectrophotometry. We use the test results to determine normal, elevated, or decreased values of compounds that circulate in the blood including electrolytes such as sodium, or potassium. I also test for high cholesterol and triglycerides. Doctors want to know about any abnormal results."

Laboratory technologists analyze the components of body fluids for abnormal levels using automated machines that perform several tests simultaneously. The results are analyzed and passed on to doctors.

SAMPLE PROBLEM 12.5

### Addition to Alkenes

Predict the organic product for each of the following reactions:

**a.** $CH_3—CH=CH—CH_3 + HBr \longrightarrow$

**b.** $CH_3—\underset{}{\overset{CH_3}{\overset{|}{C}}}=CH—CH_3 + HCl \longrightarrow$

SOLUTION

**a.** This is a symmetrical alkene. Only one product forms when the $H^+$ and $Br^-$ add to the carbons of the double bond:

$$CH_3—CH_2—\overset{Br}{\overset{|}{C}}H—CH_3$$

**b.** In the double bond of this unsymmetrical alkene, carbon 3 has the greater number of hydrogen atoms. Using Markovnikov's rule, the H from HCl adds to carbon 3 and the Cl adds to carbon 2. The product is the most substituted alkyl halide.

$$CH_3—\underset{\underset{Cl}{|}}{\overset{\overset{CH_3}{|}}{C}}—CH_2—CH_3$$

STUDY CHECK

Draw the condensed structural formula and give the name of the organic product obtained when HBr adds to 1-methylcyclopentene.

## Hydration

In a reaction called **hydration**, alkenes react with water (HOH) when catalyzed by a strong acid such as $H_2SO_4$. In this reaction, H— attaches to one of the carbon atoms in the double bond, and —OH attaches to the other carbon. Hydration is used to prepare alcohols, which have the functional group —OH. In the general equation, water is written H—OH, and the acid is represented by $H^+$:

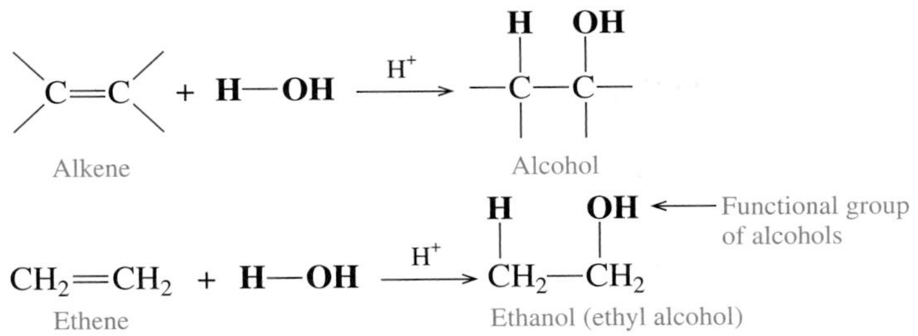

$$\text{C=C (Alkene)} + \text{H—OH} \xrightarrow{H^+} \text{—C(H)—C(OH)— (Alcohol)}$$

$$\underset{\text{Ethene}}{CH_2{=}CH_2} + H{-}OH \xrightarrow{H^+} \underset{\text{Ethanol (ethyl alcohol)}}{\overset{H\quad OH}{CH_2{-}CH_2}}$$

OH ← Functional group of alcohols

The addition of water to a double bond in an unsymmetrical alkene follows Markovnikov's rule: the H— from HOH attaches to the carbon that already has more H atoms:

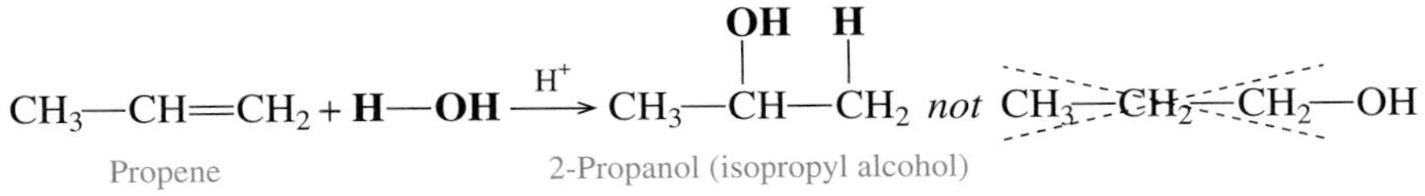

$$\underset{\text{Propene}}{CH_3{-}CH{=}CH_2} + H{-}OH \xrightarrow{H^+} \underset{\text{2-Propanol (isopropyl alcohol)}}{CH_3{-}\overset{OH}{CH}{-}\overset{H}{CH_2}} \text{ not } CH_3{-}CH_2{-}CH_2{-}OH$$

SAMPLE PROBLEM 12.6

## Writing Products of Hydration

Write the condensed structural formulas for the products that form in the following hydration reactions:

**a.** $CH_3{-}CH_2{-}CH_2{-}CH{=}CH_2 + HOH \xrightarrow{H^+}$

**b.** 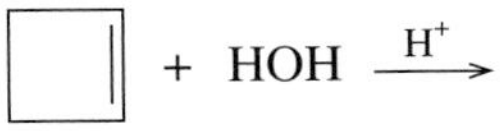 (cyclobutene) + HOH $\xrightarrow{H^+}$

SOLUTION

**a.** The H— and —OH from water (HOH) add to the carbon atoms in the double bond. Using Markovnikov's rule, the H— adds to the $CH_2$, which has more H atoms, and the —OH groups attaches to the CH:

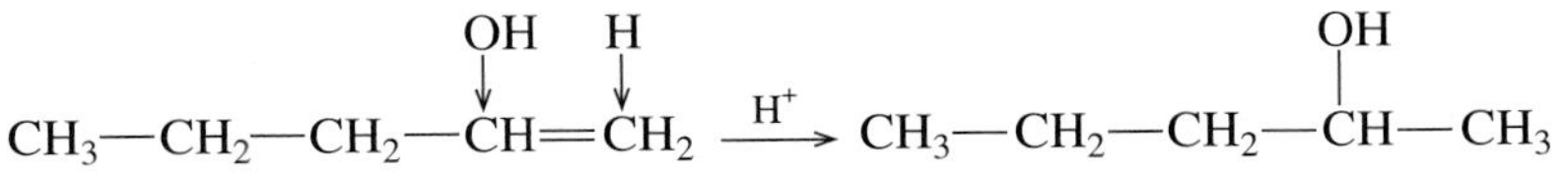

$$CH_3{-}CH_2{-}CH_2{-}\overset{OH\downarrow}{CH}{=}\overset{H\downarrow}{CH_2} \xrightarrow{H^+} CH_3{-}CH_2{-}CH_2{-}\overset{OH}{CH}{-}CH_3$$

**b.** In cyclobutene, each carbon atom in the double bond has one H. The H— from water adds to one carbon in the double bond, and the —OH group adds to the other carbon. It is not necessary to use Markovnikov's rule, because cyclobutene is symmetrical:

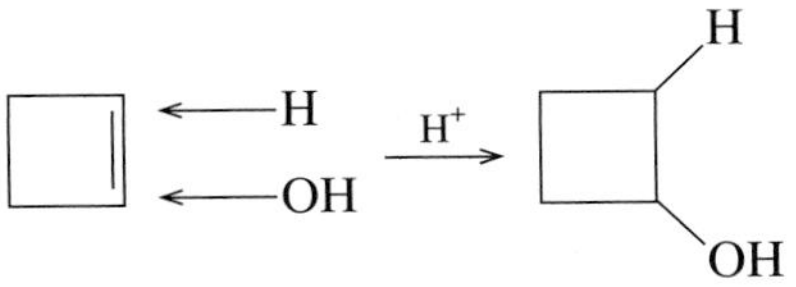

(cyclobutene) ← H, ← OH $\xrightarrow{H^+}$ (cyclobutane with H and OH)

STUDY CHECK

Draw the condensed structural formula for the alcohol obtained by the hydration of 2-methyl-2-butene.

## QUESTIONS AND PROBLEMS

### Addition Reactions

**12.13** Give the condensed structural formula and name of the products in each of the following reactions:

**a.** $CH_3—CH_2—CH_2—CH{=}CH_2 + H_2 \xrightarrow{Pt}$

**b.** $CH_2{=}C(CH_3)—CH_2—CH_3 + Cl_2 \longrightarrow$

**c.**  cyclobutene $+ Br_2 \longrightarrow$

**d.** cyclopentene $+ H_2 \xrightarrow{Pt}$

**e.** 2-methyl-2-butene $+ Cl_2 \longrightarrow$

**f.** 2-pentyne $+ 2H_2 \xrightarrow{Pd}$

**12.14** Give the condensed structural formula and name of the products in each of the following reactions:

**a.** $CH_3—CH_2—CH{=}CH_2 + Br_2 \longrightarrow$

**b.** cyclohexene $+ H_2 \xrightarrow{Pt}$

**c.** *cis*-2-butene $+ H_2 \xrightarrow{Pt}$

**d.** $CH_3—C(CH_3){=}CH—CH_2—CH_3 + Cl_2 \longrightarrow$

**e.** 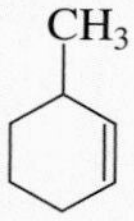 1-methylcyclohexene (ring with $CH_3$) $+ Br_2 \longrightarrow$

**f.** $CH_3—CH(CH_3)—C{\equiv}CH + 2Cl_2 \longrightarrow$

**12.15** Give the condensed structural formulas of the products in each of the following reactions, using Markovnikov's rule when necessary:

**a.** $CH_3—CH{=}CH—CH_3 + HBr \longrightarrow$

**b.** cyclopentene $+ HOH \xrightarrow{H^+}$

**c.** $CH_2{=}CH—CH_2—CH_3 + HCl \longrightarrow$

**d.** $CH_3—C(CH_3){=}C(CH_3)—CH_3 + HI \longrightarrow$

**e.** $CH_3—CH_2—C(CH_3){=}CH—CH_3 + HBr \longrightarrow$

**f.** 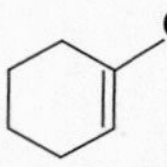 1-methylcyclohexene (ring with $CH_3$) $+ HOH \xrightarrow{H^+}$

**12.16** Give the condensed structural formulas of the products in each of the following reactions, using Markovnikov's rule when necessary:

**a.** $CH_3—C(CH_3){=}CH—CH_3 + HCl \longrightarrow$

**b.** $CH_3—CH_2—CH{=}CH—CH_2—CH_3 + HOH \xrightarrow{H^+}$

**c.** $CH_3—C(CH_3){=}CH_2 + HBr \longrightarrow$

**d.** 4-methylcyclopentene + HOH $\xrightarrow{H^+}$

**e.**  cyclohexene $+ HBr \longrightarrow$

**f.** $CH_3—C{\equiv}C—CH_3 + 2HCl \longrightarrow$

**12.17** Write an equation, including any catalysts, for each of the following reactions:

**a.** hydrogenation of methylpropene

**b.** addition of hydrogen chloride to cyclopentene

**c.** addition of bromine to 2-pentene

**d.** hydration of propene

**e.** addition of chlorine to 2-butyne

**12.18** Write an equation, including any catalysts, for each of the following reactions:

**a.** hydration of 1-methylcyclobutene

**b.** hydrogenation of 3-hexene

**c.** addition of hydrogen bromide to 2-methyl-2-butene

**d.** addition of chlorine to 2,3-dimethyl-2-pentene

**e.** addition of HCl to 1-methylcyclopentene

## 12.4 Polymers of Alkenes

**LEARNING GOAL**

Draw condensed structural formulas of monomers that form a polymer or a three-monomer section of a polymer.

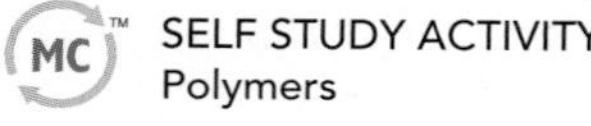


A **polymer** is a large molecule that consists of small repeating units called **monomers**. In the past hundred years, the plastics industry has made synthetic polymers that are in many of the materials we use every day, such as carpeting, plastic wrap, nonstick pans, plastic cups, and rain gear. In medicine, synthetic polymers are used to replace diseased or damaged body parts such as hip joints, teeth, heart valves, and blood vessels. (See Figure 12.4.) There are about 100 billion kg of plastics now produced every year, which is over 15 kg for every person on Earth.

Many of the synthetic polymers are made by addition reactions of monomers that are small alkenes. Many polymerization reactions require high temperature and high pressure.

In polymerization, addition reactions join one monomer to the next to form a long carbon chain that contains as many as 1000 monomers. Polyethylene, a polymer made from ethylene monomers, is used in plastic bottles, film, and plastic dinnerware. More polyethylene is produced worldwide than any other polymer.

$$CH_2{=}CH_2 + CH_2{=}CH_2 + CH_2{=}CH_2 \longrightarrow -CH_2-CH_2-[CH_2-CH_2]_{many}-CH_2-CH_2-$$

Monomer unit repeats

Ethene (ethylene) monomers — Polyethylene section

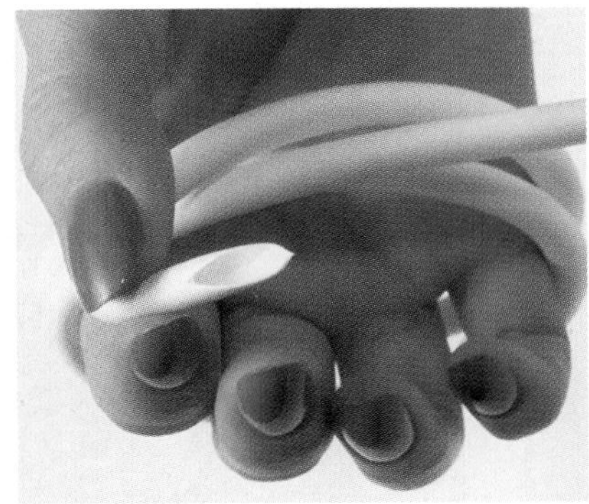

**FIGURE 12.4** Synthetic polymers are used to replace diseased veins and arteries.

Q Why are the substances in these plastic devices called polymers?

Table 12.3 lists several alkene monomers that are used to produce common synthetic polymers, and Figure 12.5 shows examples of each. The alkane-like nature of these plastic synthetic polymers makes them unreactive. Thus, they do not decompose easily (they are nonbiodegradable). As a result, they have become significant contributors to pollution. Efforts are being made to make them more degradable.

**TABLE 12.3** Some Alkenes and Their Polymers

| Monomer | Polymer Section | Common Uses |
|---|---|---|
| $CH_2{=}CH_2$ Ethene (ethylene) | $-CH_2-CH_2-CH_2-CH_2-CH_2-CH_2-$ Polyethylene | Plastic bottles, film, insulation materials |
| $CH_2{=}CHCl$ Chloroethene (vinyl chloride) | $-CH_2-CHCl-CH_2-CHCl-CH_2-CHCl-$ Polyvinyl chloride (PVC) | Plastic pipes and tubing, garden hoses, garbage bags |
| $CH_2{=}CHCH_3$ Propene (propylene) | $-CH_2-CH(CH_3)-CH_2-CH(CH_3)-CH_2-CH(CH_3)-$ Polypropylene | Ski and hiking clothing, carpets, artificial joints |
| $F_2C{=}CF_2$ Tetrafluoroethene | $-CF_2-CF_2-CF_2-CF_2-CF_2-CF_2-$ Polytetrafluoroethylene (Teflon®) | Nonstick coatings |
| $CH_2{=}CCl_2$ 1,1-Dichloroethene | $-CH_2-CCl_2-CH_2-CCl_2-CH_2-CCl_2-$ Polydichloroethylene (Saran™) | Plastic film and wrap |
| $H_2C{=}CH-C_6H_5$ Phenylethene (styrene) | $-CH_2-CH(C_6H_5)-CH_2-CH(C_6H_5)-CH_2-CH(C_6H_5)-$ Polystyrene | Plastic coffee cups and cartons, insulation |

## EXPLORE YOUR WORLD

### Polymers and Recycling Plastics

1. Make a list of the items you use or have in your room or home that are made of polymers.
2. Recycling information on the bottom or side of a plastic bottle includes a triangle with a code number that identifies the type of polymer used to make the plastic. Make a collection of several different kinds of plastic bottles. Try to find plastic items with each type of polymer.

**QUESTIONS**

1. What are the most common types of plastics among the plastic containers in your collection?
2. What are the monomer units of some of the plastics you looked at?

Polyethylene

Polyvinyl chloride

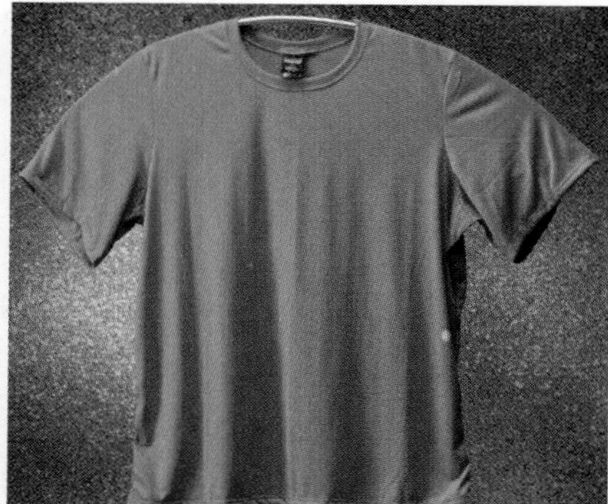
Polypropylene

Polytetrafluoroethylene (Teflon®)

Polydichloroethylene (Saran™)

Polystyrene

**FIGURE 12.5** Synthetic polymers provide a wide variety of items that we use every day.
**Q** What are some alkenes used to make the polymers in these plastic items?

You can identify the type of polymer used to manufacture a plastic item by looking for the recycle symbol (arrows in a triangle) found on the label or on the bottom of the plastic container. The number 5 or the letters PP inside the triangle is the code for a polypropylene plastic. It is important to recycle plastic material rather than add to our growing landfills.

| 1 | 2 | 3 | 4 | 5 | 6 | 7 |
|---|---|---|---|---|---|---|
| PETE | HDPE | PVC | LDPE | PP | PS | O |
| Polyethylene terephthalate | High-density polyethylene | Polyvinyl chloride | Low-density polyethylene | Polypropylene | Polystyrene | Other |

Today, many products such as lumber, tables and benches, trash receptacles, and pipes used for irrigation systems are made from recycled plastics.

SAMPLE PROBLEM 12.7

## Polymers

What are the names and condensed structural formulas of the starting monomers for the following polymers?

**a.** polypropylene

**b.** Saran™

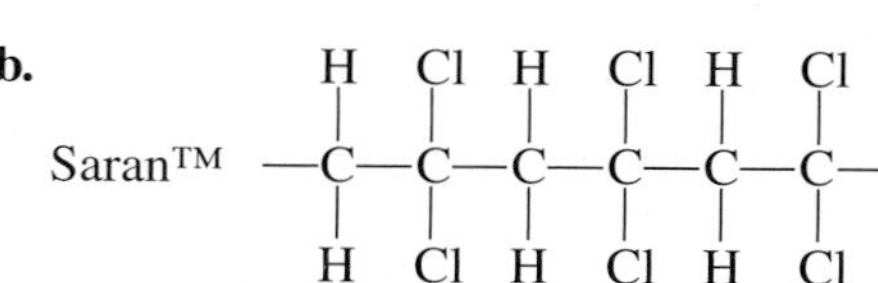

SOLUTION

**a.** propene (propylene), $CH_2{=}CH{-}CH_3$ (the $CH_3$ is attached to the second carbon)  **b.** 1,1-dichloroethene, $CH_2{=}CCl_2$

STUDY CHECK

What is the name and condensed structural formula of the monomer for PVC?

## QUESTIONS AND PROBLEMS

### Polymers of Alkenes

12.19 What is a polymer?

**12.20** What is a monomer?

12.21 Write an equation that represents the formation of a part of the Teflon polymer from three of the monomer units.

**12.22** Write an equation that represents the formation of a part of the polystyrene polymer from three of the monomer units.

12.23 The plastic polyvinylidene difluoride, PVDF, is made from monomers of 1,1-difluoroethene. Write the structure of the polymer formed from the addition of three monomers of 1,1-difluoroethene.

**12.24** An alkene called acrylonitrile is the monomer used to form the polymer used in the fabric material called Orlon. Write an equation that represents the formation of a part of the polyacrylonitrile polymer from three of the monomer units.

Acrylonitrile $CH_2{=}CH{-}CN$ (the CN is attached to the second carbon)

## 12.5 Aromatic Compounds

LEARNING GOAL

Describe the bonding in benzene. Name aromatic compounds and draw their structural formulas and the products formed by substitution reactions.

In 1825, Michael Faraday isolated a hydrocarbon called *benzene*, which had the molecular formula $C_6H_6$. Because many compounds containing benzene had fragrant odors, the family of benzene compounds became known as **aromatic compounds**. A **benzene** molecule consists of a ring of six carbon atoms with one hydrogen atom attached to each carbon. Each carbon atom uses three valence electrons to bond to the hydrogen atom and two adjacent carbons. That leaves one valence electron to share in a double bond with an adjacent carbon. When first discovered, scientists expected benzene to be very reactive, like alkenes, but it was found to be much less reactive. It behaved more like an alkane. In 1865, August Kekulé proposed that the carbon atoms in benzene were arranged in a flat ring with alternating single and double bonds between the carbon atoms. This idea led to two ways of writing the benzene structure:

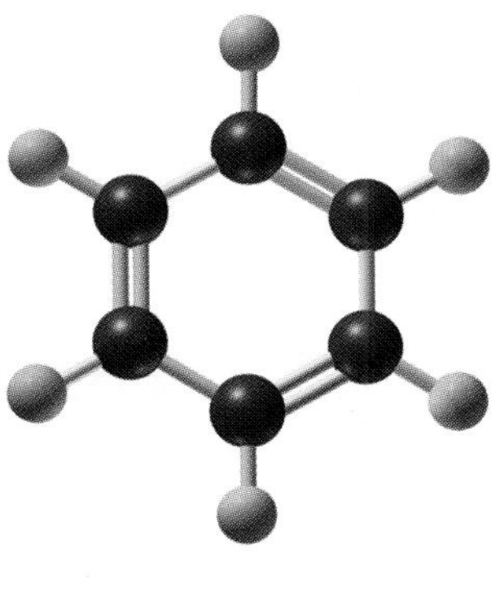

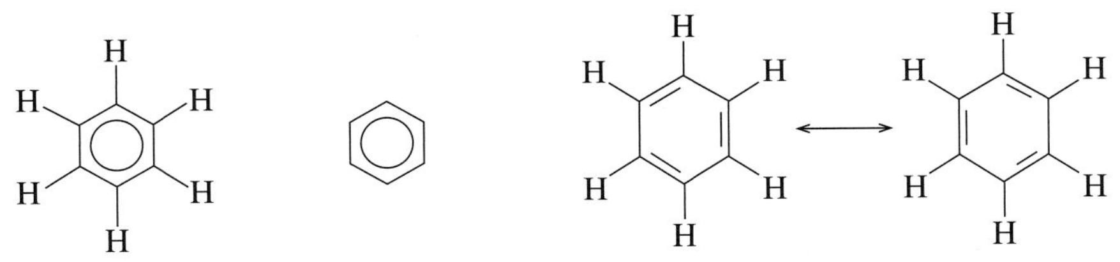

Structures for benzene

However, there is only one structure of benzene. Today we know that all the bonds in benzene are identical and that the electrons are shared equally. This unique feature makes aromatic compounds especially stable. Today, the benzene structure is represented as a hexagon with a circle in the center.

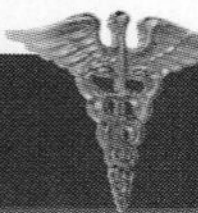

## HEALTH NOTE

### Some Common Aromatic Compounds

Aromatic compounds are common in nature and in medicine. Toluene is used as a reactant to make drugs, dyes, and explosives such as TNT (trinitrotoluene). The benzene ring is found in some amino acids (the building blocks of proteins); in pain relievers such as aspirin, acetaminophen, and ibuprofen; and in flavorings such as vanillin.

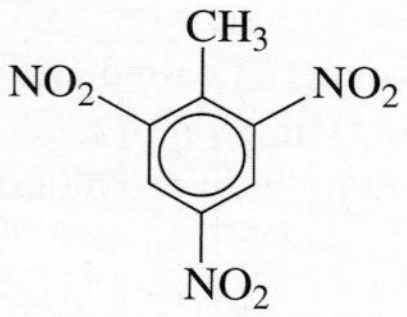

TNT (2,4,6-trinitrotoluene)

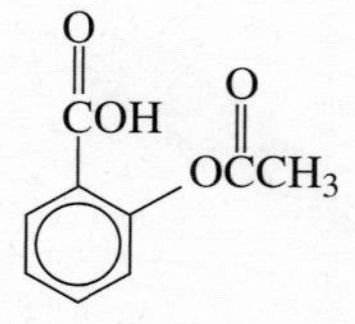

Aspirin

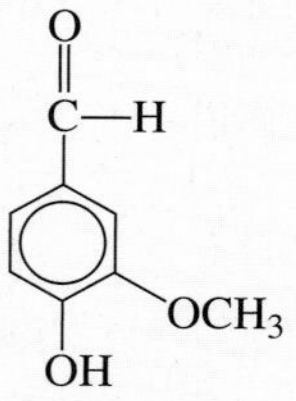

Vanillin

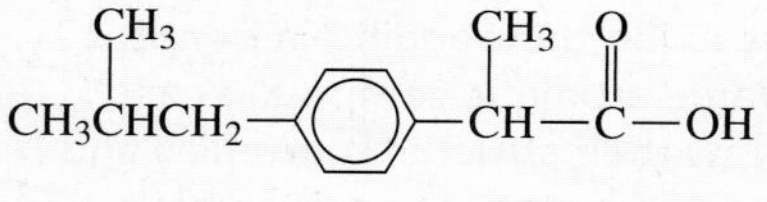

Ibuprofen

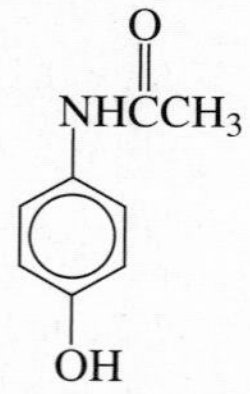

Acetaminophen

MC TUTORIAL Naming Aromatic Compounds

## Naming Aromatic Compounds

Aromatic compounds that contain a benzene ring with a single substituent are usually named as benzene derivatives. However, many of these compounds have been important for many years and still use their common names. Names such as toluene, ethylbenzene, aniline, and phenol are allowed by IUPAC rules:

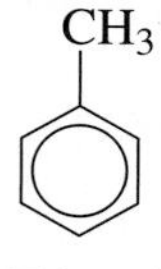

Toluene (methylbenzene) 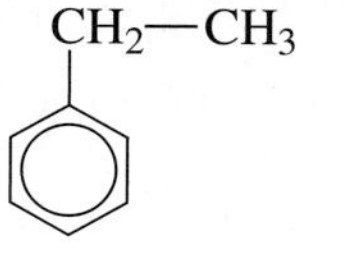 Ethylbenzene 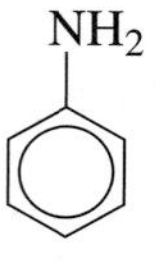 Aniline (benzenamine) 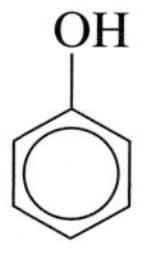 Phenol (hydroxybenzene)

When a benzene ring is a substituent, $C_6H_5$—, it is named as a phenyl group:

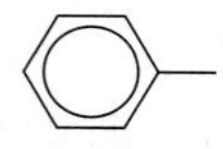

Phenyl group 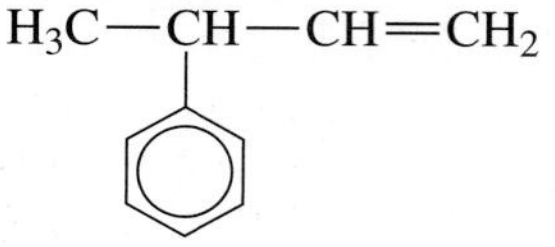 3-Phenyl-1-butene

When there are two substituents, the benzene ring is numbered to give the lowest numbers to the substituents. When a common name, such as toluene, phenol, or aniline, can be used, the carbon atom attached to the methyl, hydroxyl, or amine group is numbered as carbon 1. The position of two substituents is often shown by prefixes. The prefix **ortho** (*o*) indicates a 1,2 arrangement, **meta** (*m*) is a 1,3 arrangement, and **para** (*p*) is used for 1,4 arrangements.

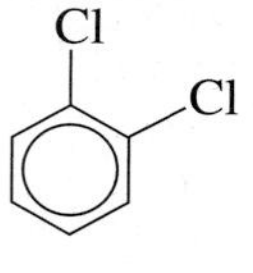

1,2-Dichlorobenzene *o*-dichlorobenzene 1,3-Dichlorobenzene *m*-dichlorobenzene 1,4-Dichlorobenzene *p*-dichlorobenzene

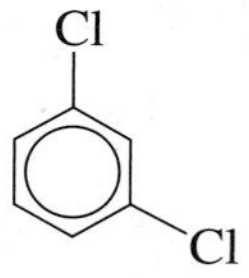

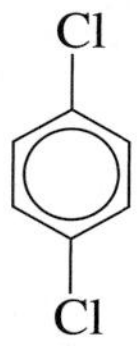

The common name xylene is used for the isomers of dimethylbenzene:

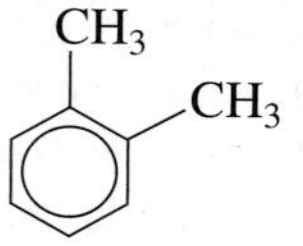

1,2-Dimethylbenzene *o*-xylene 1,3-Dimethylbenzene *m*-xylene 1,4-Dimethylbenzene *p*-xylene

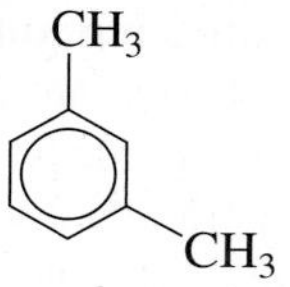

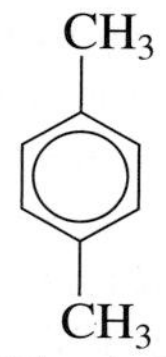

When there are three or more substituents on the benzene ring, numbers are used to show their arrangement. The substituents are numbered to give the lowest numbers and named alphabetically:

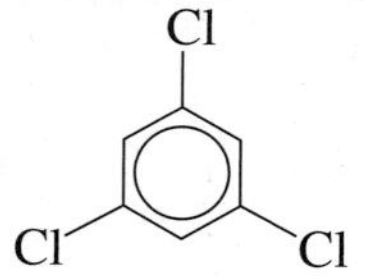

1,3,5-Trichlorobenzene 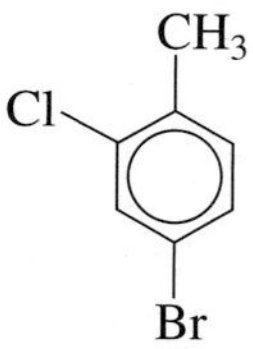 4-Bromo-2-chlorotoluene 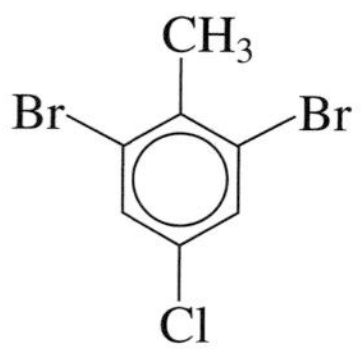 2,6-Dibromo-4-chlorotoluene

SAMPLE PROBLEM 12.8

### Naming Aromatic Compounds

Give IUPAC and any common name for each of the following aromatic compounds:

**a.** 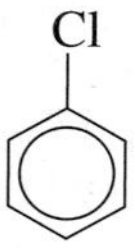 **b.** 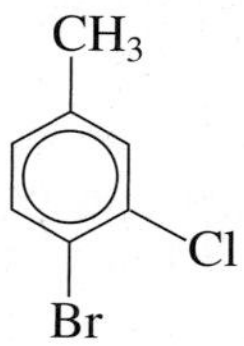 **c.**

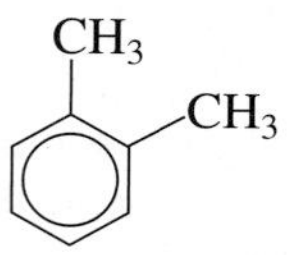

SOLUTION

**a.** chlorobenzene
**b.** 4-bromo-3-chlorotoluene
**c.** 1,2-dimethylbenzene; *o*-xylene

STUDY CHECK

Name the following compound:

$CH_2—CH_3$

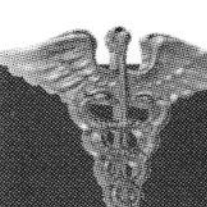

$CH_2—CH_3$

# HEALTH NOTE

## Polycyclic Aromatic Hydrocarbons (PAHs)

Large aromatic compounds known as polycyclic aromatic hydrocarbons are formed by fusing together two or more benzene rings edge to edge. In a fused-ring compound, neighboring benzene rings share two or more carbon atoms. Naphthalene, with two benzene rings, is known for its use in mothballs. Anthracene, with three rings, is used in the manufacture of dyes.

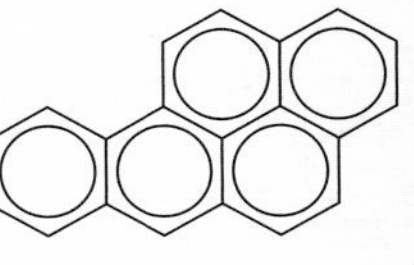

Benz[a]pyrene

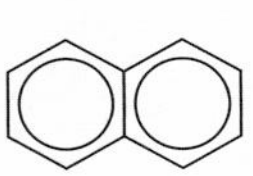

Naphthalene

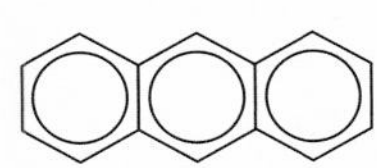

Anthracene

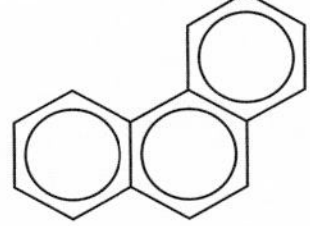

Phenanthrene

When a polycyclic compound contains the three fused rings of phenanthrene, it may act as a carcinogen, a substance known to cause cancer. For example, some aromatic compounds in cigarette smoke cause cancer, as shown in the lung tissue of a heavy smoker. Benz[a]pyrene, a product of combustion, has been identified in coal tar, tobacco smoke, barbecued meats, and automobile exhaust.

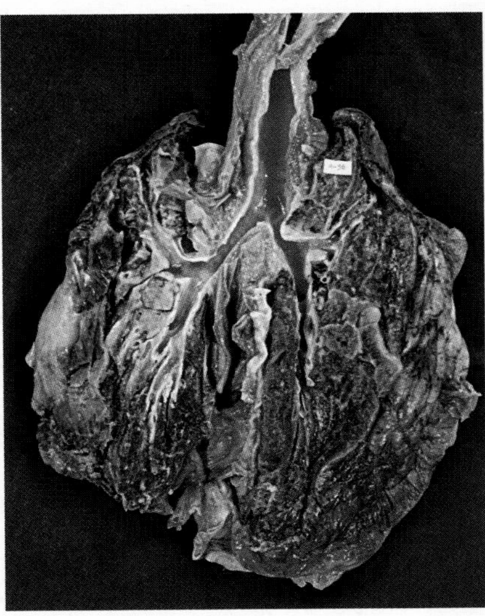

Compounds containing five or more fused benzene rings such as benz[a]pyrene are potent carcinogens. The molecules interact with the DNA in the cells, causing abnormal cell growth and cancer. Increased exposure to carcinogens increases the chance of DNA alterations in the cells.

## Properties of Aromatic Compounds

The symmetrical structure of benzene allows the cyclic structures to stack close together, which contributes to the higher melting points and boiling points of benzene and its derivatives. For example, hexane melts at −95 °C, while benzene melts at 6 °C. Among the disubstituted benzene compounds, the para isomers are more symmetric and have higher melting points than the ortho and meta isomers: *o*-xylene melts at −26 °C and *m*-xylene melts at −48 °C, while *p*-xylene melts at 13 °C.

Aromatic compounds are less dense than water, although they are somewhat denser than other hydrocarbons. Halogenated benzene compounds are denser than water. Aromatic hydrocarbons are insoluble in water and are used as solvents for other organic compounds. Only those containing strongly polar functional groups such as —OH or —COOH will be more soluble. Benzene and other aromatic compounds are resistant to reactions that break up the aromatic system, although they are flammable, as are other hydrocarbon compounds.

MC TUTORIAL Substitution Reactions of Aromatic Compounds

## Chemical Properties

The most important type of reaction for benzene and aromatic compounds is **substitution**, in which an atom or group of atoms replaces a hydrogen atom on a benzene ring. A substitution reaction, rather than addition, retains the stability of the aromatic bonding system. Substitution reactions of benzene include halogenation, nitration, and sulfonation.

### Halogenation

In the chlorination or bromination of benzene, a chlorine or bromine atom replaces a hydrogen atom on the benzene ring. A catalyst such as $FeCl_3$ is required for chlorination; $FeBr_3$ is a catalyst in bromination:

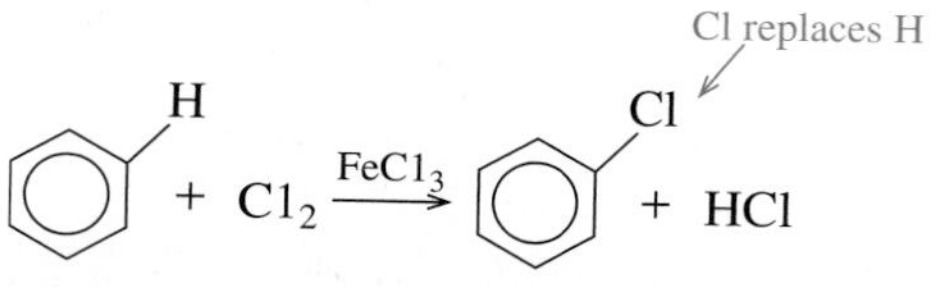

Cl replaces H

$$C_6H_5{-}H + Cl_2 \xrightarrow{FeCl_3} C_6H_5{-}Cl + HCl$$

Chlorobenzene

When toluene (methylbenzene) undergoes halogenation, a mixture of isomers is obtained as products. However, the presence of a methyl group in toluene has the effect of producing mostly ortho and para isomers. In most substitution reactions of toluene, the meta isomer is produced in very small amounts:

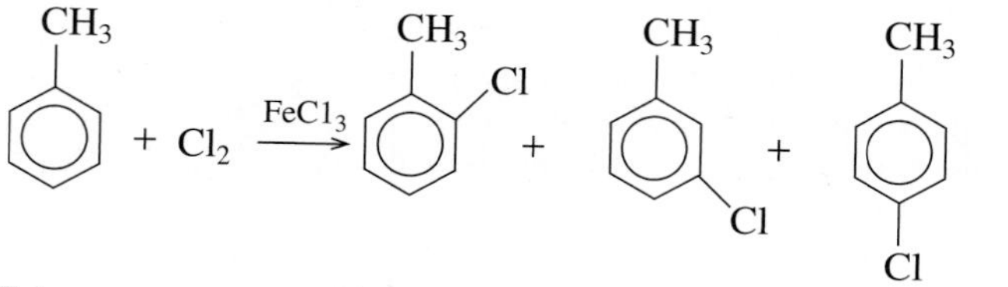

$$\text{Toluene} + Cl_2 \xrightarrow{FeCl_3} \text{o-Chlorotoluene} + \text{m-Chlorotoluene (very little)} + \text{p-Chlorotoluene}$$

Toluene; *o*-Chlorotoluene; *m*-Chlorotoluene (very little); *p*-Chlorotoluene

### Nitration

When benzene is heated with nitric acid, nitrobenzene is produced. Sulfuric acid ($H_2SO_4$) is required as a catalyst for the nitration:

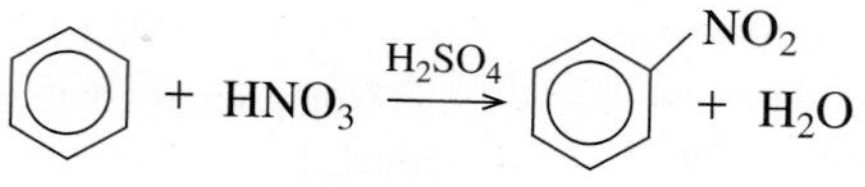

$$C_6H_6 + HNO_3 \xrightarrow{H_2SO_4} C_6H_5{-}NO_2 + H_2O$$

Nitrobenzene

### Sulfonation

When benzene reacts with a mixture of $SO_3 + H_2SO_4$, known as "fuming sulfuric acid," the product is benzenesulfonic acid:

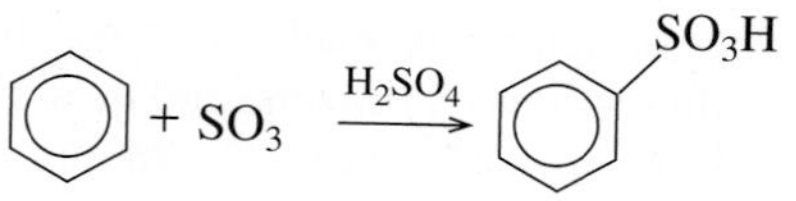

$$C_6H_6 + SO_3 \xrightarrow{H_2SO_4} C_6H_5{-}SO_3H$$

Benzenesulfonic acid

The sulfonation of aromatic compounds is one way to produce sulfa drugs:

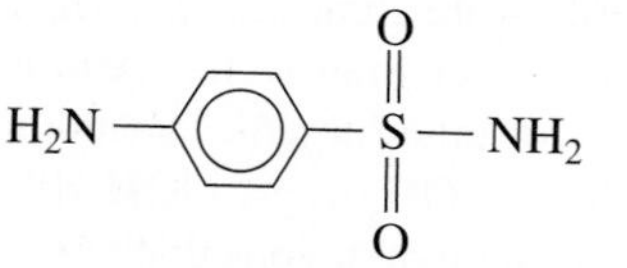

$$H_2N{-}C_6H_4{-}S(=O)_2{-}NH_2$$

Sulfanilamide, a sulfa drug

## CONCEPT CHECK 12.6

### Reactions of Aromatic Compounds

Consider the reactions of cyclohexene and benzene with chlorine ($Cl_2$).

**a.** What is required (if anything) by each compound to react with $Cl_2$?
**b.** Identify the reaction for each compound as addition or substitution.
**c.** What is the name of the product of each reaction?

ANSWER

**a.** Cyclohexene reacts readily with $Cl_2$; no catalyst is needed. The reaction of benzene and $Cl_2$ requires a catalyst such as $FeCl_3$.
**b.** The reaction of $Cl_2$ with cyclohexene is an addition reaction, whereas the reaction of $Cl_2$ with benzene is a substitution.
**c.** The reaction of $Cl_2$ with cyclohexene forms 1,2-dichlorocyclohexane. The reaction of $Cl_2$ with benzene produces chlorobenzene.

## SAMPLE PROBLEM 12.9

### Reactions of Benzene

Write the structure of the organic product when benzene reacts with the following:

**a.** $Br_2$ and $FeBr_3$ **b.** $HNO_3$ and $H_2SO_4$

SOLUTION

**a.** 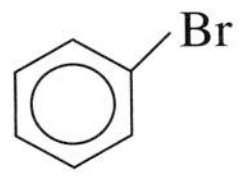 Br **b.** 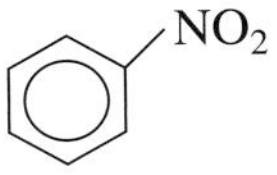 $NO_2$

STUDY CHECK

A chemist needs to synthesize chlorobenzene. If benzene is available in the lab, how could she prepare this compound?

## QUESTIONS AND PROBLEMS

### Aromatic Compounds

**12.25** Cyclohexane and benzene each have six carbon atoms. How are they different?

**12.26** In the Health Note "Some Common Aromatic Compounds," what part of each molecule is the aromatic portion?

**12.27** Give the IUPAC and any common name for each of the following:

**a.** 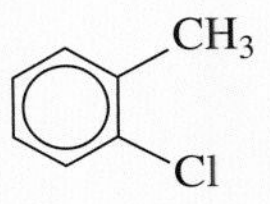 $CH_3$, Cl **b.** 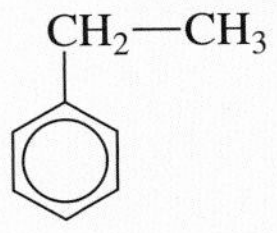 $CH_2—CH_3$ **c.** 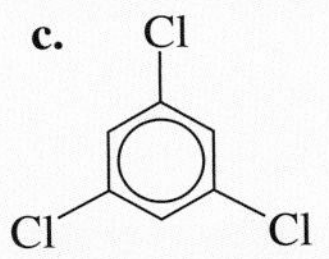 Cl, Cl, Cl

**d.** 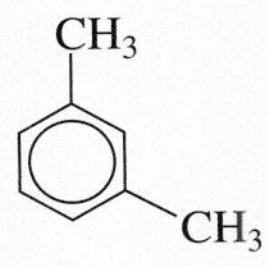 $CH_3$, $CH_3$ **e.** 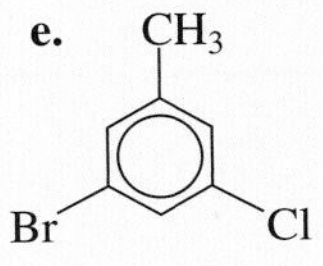 $CH_3$, Br, Cl **f.** 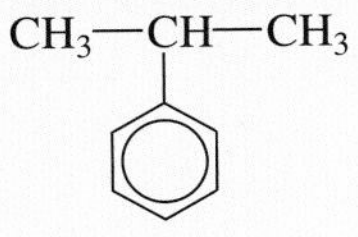 $CH_3—CH—CH_3$

**12.28** Give the IUPAC and any common name for each of the following:

**a.**

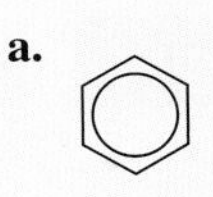

**b.**

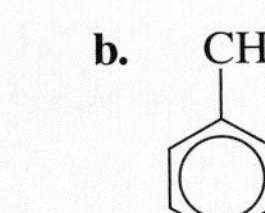


**c.**

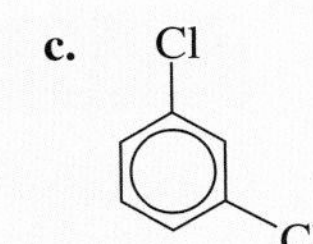


**d.** 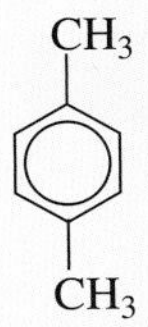 $CH_3$, $CH_3$

**e.**

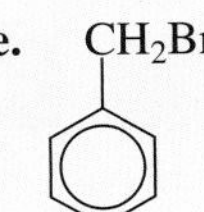


**f.**

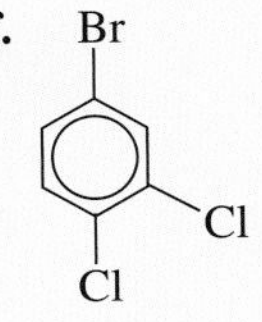


**12.29** Draw the condensed structural formula for each of the following compounds:
**a.** methylbenzene
**b.** 1-bromo-3-chlorobenzene
**c.** 1-ethyl-4-methylbenzene
**d.** *p*-chlorotoluene

**12.30** Draw the condensed structural formula for each of the following compounds:
**a.** benzene
**b.** *o*-chloromethylbenzene
**c.** propylbenzene
**d.** 1,2,4-trichlorobenzene

**12.31** Alkenes undergo addition reactions, but benzene does not. How does benzene react and why?

**12.32** What is the product of the reaction of styrene with HCl? Explain.

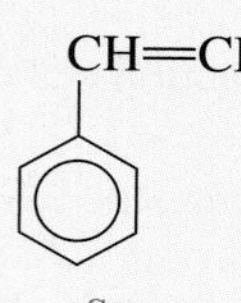

Styrene

**12.33** Draw the structures of the organic product(s), if any, for the following reactants:

**a.** benzene + $Cl_2$ $\xrightarrow{FeCl_3}$

**b.** benzene + $HNO_3$ $\xrightarrow{H_2SO_4}$

**12.34** Draw the structures of the organic product(s), if any, for the following reactants:

**a.** toluene + $Br_2$ $\xrightarrow{FeBr_3}$

**b.** benzene + $SO_3$ $\xrightarrow{H_2SO_4}$

## CONCEPT MAP

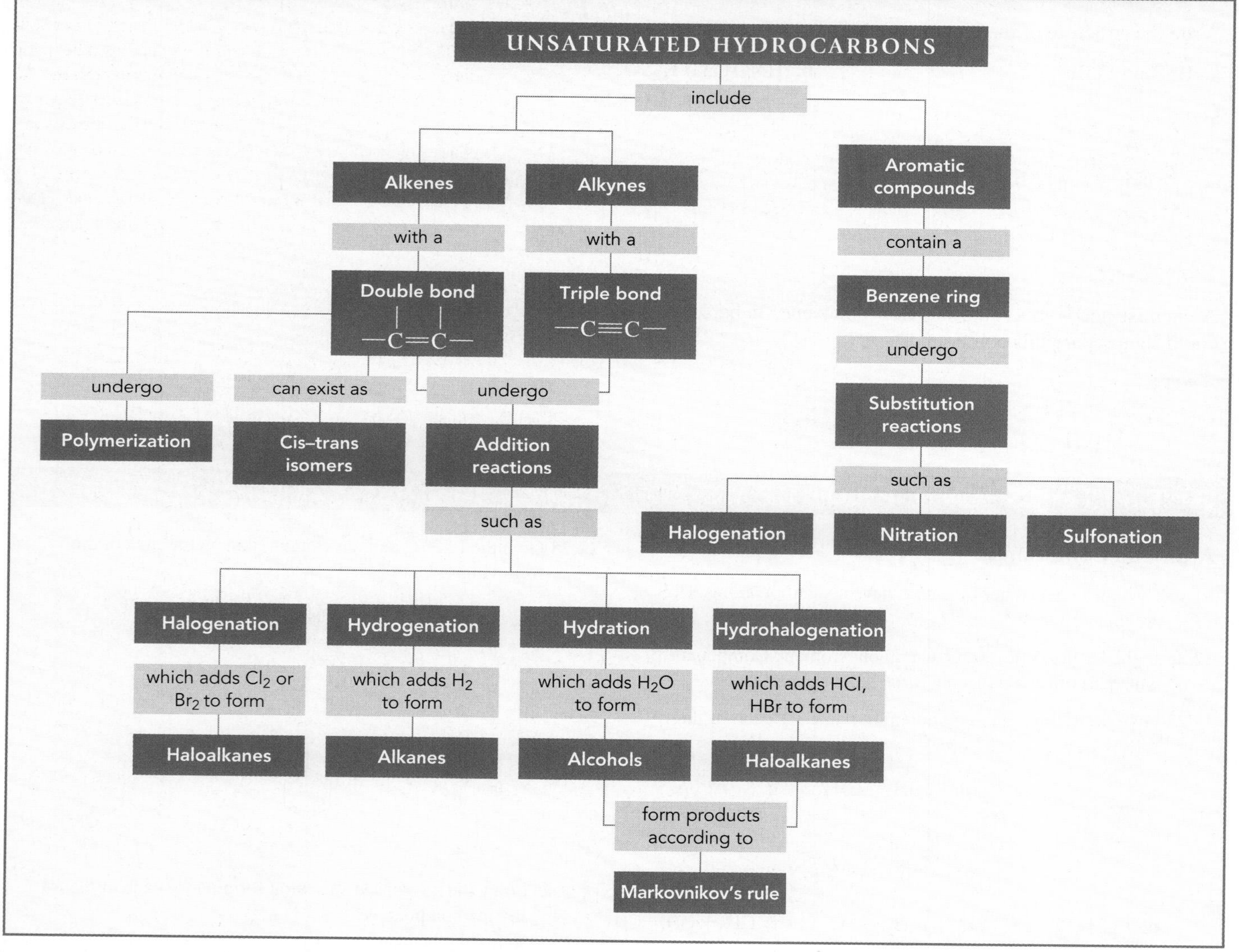

UNSATURATED HYDROCARBONS

include

Alkenes — with a — Double bond ($-C{=}C-$)

Alkynes — with a — Triple bond ($-C{\equiv}C-$)

Aromatic compounds — contain a — Benzene ring — undergo — Substitution reactions — such as — Halogenation, Nitration, Sulfonation

Double bond — undergo — Polymerization

Double bond — can exist as — Cis–trans isomers

Double bond and Triple bond — undergo — Addition reactions — such as:

Halogenation — which adds $Cl_2$ or $Br_2$ to form — Haloalkanes

Hydrogenation — which adds $H_2$ to form — Alkanes

Hydration — which adds $H_2O$ to form — Alcohols

Hydrohalogenation — which adds HCl, HBr to form — Haloalkanes

Alcohols and Haloalkanes — form products according to — Markovnikov's rule

# CHAPTER REVIEW

## 12.1 Alkenes and Alkynes

**LEARNING GOAL:** *Write the IUPAC names for alkenes and alkynes; give common names for simple structures.*

Alkenes are unsaturated hydrocarbons that contain carbon–carbon double bonds (C=C). Alkynes contain a triple bond (C≡C). The IUPAC names of alkenes end with *ene*, while alkyne names end with *yne*. The main chain is numbered from the end nearer the double or triple bond. In a cycloalkene, the double bond is carbon 1 and 2, and the ring is numbered to give the lower numbers to any substituents, which are named alphabetically.

## 12.2 Cis–Trans Isomers

**LEARNING GOAL:** *Write the condensed structural formulas and names for the cis-trans isomers of alkenes.*

Isomers of alkenes occur when the carbon atoms in the double bond are connected to different atoms or groups. In the cis isomer, alkyl groups or halogen atoms are on the same side of the double bond, whereas in the trans isomer, they are connected on opposite sides of the double bond.

## 12.3 Addition Reactions

**LEARNING GOAL:** *Write the condensed structural formulas and names for the organic products of addition reactions of alkenes and alkynes.*

The addition of small molecules to the double bond is a characteristic reaction of alkenes. Hydrogenation adds hydrogen atoms to the double bond of an alkene to yield an alkane. Halogenation adds bromine or chlorine atoms to produce dihaloalkanes. Hydrogen halides and water can also add to a double bond. When there are a different number of hydrogen atoms attached to the carbons in the double bond, Markovnikov's rule states that the H from the reactant (H—X or H—OH) adds to the carbon with the greater number of hydrogen atoms.

## 12.4 Polymers of Alkenes

**LEARNING GOAL:** *Draw condensed structural formulas of monomers that form a polymer or a three-monomer section of a polymer.*

Polymers are long-chain molecules that consist of many repeating units of smaller carbon molecules called monomers. In nature, cellulose and starch are polymers of glucose, and proteins are polymers of amino acids. Many materials that we use every day are synthetic polymers, including carpeting, plastic wrap, nonstick pans, and nylon. These synthetic materials are often made by addition reactions in which a catalyst links the carbon atoms from various kinds of alkene molecules.

## 12.5 Aromatic Compounds

**LEARNING GOAL:** *Describe the bonding in benzene. Name aromatic compounds and draw their structural formulas and the products formed by substitution reactions.*

Most aromatic compounds contain benzene, a cyclic structure containing six CH units. The structure of benzene is represented as a hexagon with a circle in the center. Aromatic compounds containing benzene are named using the parent name benzene, although common names such as toluene are retained. The benzene ring is numbered, and the substituents are listed in alphabetical order. For two substituents, the positions are often shown by the prefixes *ortho* (1,2-), *meta* (1,3-), and *para* (1,4-). Aromatic compounds undergo substitution reactions such as halogenation, nitration, and sulfonation. They do not undergo addition reactions, which would disrupt their stable aromatic bonding system.

# SUMMARY OF NAMING

| Type | Example | Characteristic | Structure |
|---|---|---|---|
| Alkene | Propene (propylene) | Double bond | $CH_3—CH=CH_2$ |
| | *cis*-1,2-dibromoethene | Large groups on same side | Br Br<br>C=C<br>H H |
| | *trans*-1,2-dibromoethene | Large groups on opposite sides | Br H<br>C=C<br>H Br |
| Cycloalkene | Cyclopropene | Double bond in a carbon ring | |
| Alkyne | Propyne | Triple bond | $CH_3—C≡CH$ |
| Aromatic | Benzene | Aromatic ring of six carbons | |
| | Methylbenzene or toluene | | $CH_3$ |
| | 1,4-dichlorobenzene or *para*-dichlorobenzene | | Cl<br>Cl |

## SUMMARY OF REACTIONS

### HYDROGENATION

$$CH_2{=}CH{-}CH_3 + H_2 \xrightarrow{Pt} CH_3{-}CH_2{-}CH_3$$

Propene → Propane

$$CH_3{-}C{\equiv}CH + 2H_2 \xrightarrow{Pt} CH_3{-}CH_2{-}CH_3$$

Propyne → Propane

### HALOGENATION

$$CH_2{=}CH{-}CH_3 + Cl_2 \longrightarrow CH_2(Cl){-}CH(Cl){-}CH_3$$

Propene → 1,2-Dichloropropane

### SUBSTITUTION REACTIONS OF BENZENE

Benzene $\xrightarrow[FeCl_3]{Cl_2}$ chlorobenzene (Cl) — Halogenation

Benzene $\xrightarrow[H_2SO_4]{HNO_3}$ nitrobenzene ($NO_2$) — Nitration

Benzene $\xrightarrow[H_2SO_4]{SO_3}$ benzenesulfonic acid ($SO_3H$) — Sulfonation

### HYDROHALOGENATION

Markovnikov's rule

$$CH_2{=}CH{-}CH_3 + HCl \longrightarrow CH_3{-}CH(Cl){-}CH_3$$

Propene → 2-Chloropropane

### HYDRATION OF ALKENES

Markovnikov's rule

$$CH_2{=}CH{-}CH_3 + H{-}OH \xrightarrow{H^+} CH_3{-}CH(OH){-}CH_3$$

Propene → 2-Propanol

## KEY TERMS

**addition** A reaction in which atoms or groups of atoms bond to a double bond. Addition reactions include the addition of hydrogen (hydrogenation), halogens (halogenation), hydrogen halides (hydrohalogenation), and water (hydration).

**alkene** A hydrocarbon containing a carbon–carbon double bond.

**alkyne** A hydrocarbon containing a carbon–carbon triple bond.

**aromatic compounds** Compounds that usually have fragrant odors and often contain the ring structure of benzene.

**benzene** A ring of six carbon atoms each of which is attached to a hydrogen atom, $C_6H_6$.

**carbocation** A carbon cation that has only three bonds and a positive charge and is formed during the addition reactions of hydration and hydrohalogenation.

**cis isomer** An isomer of an alkene in which large groups are attached to the same side of the double bond.

**cycloalkene** A cyclic hydrocarbon that contains a double bond in the ring.

**halogenation** The addition of $Cl_2$ or $Br_2$ to an alkene or benzene to form halogen-containing compounds.

**hydration** An addition reaction in which the components of water, H— and —OH, bond to the carbon–carbon double bond to form an alcohol.

**hydrogenation** The addition of hydrogen ($H_2$) to the double bond of alkenes to yield alkanes.

**hydrohalogenation** The addition of a hydrogen halide such as HCl or HBr to a double bond.

**Markovnikov's rule** When adding HX or HOH to alkenes with different numbers of groups attached to the double bonds, the H— adds to the carbon that has the greater number of hydrogen atoms.

**meta** A method of naming that indicates substituents at carbons 1 and 3 of a benzene ring.

**monomer** The small organic molecule that is repeated many times in a polymer.

**ortho** A method of naming that indicates substituents at carbons 1 and 2 of a benzene ring.

**para** A method of naming that indicates substituents at carbons 1 and 4 of a benzene ring.

**polymer** A very large molecule that is composed of many small, repeating structural units that are identical.

**substitution** The reactions of benzene and other aromatic compounds in which an atom or group of atoms replaces a hydrogen on a benzene ring.

**trans isomer** An isomer of an alkene in which large groups are attached on opposite sides of the double bond.

## UNDERSTANDING THE CONCEPTS

12.35 Draw a part of the polymer of Teflon using four monomers of 1,1,2,2-tetrafluoroethene.

12.36 A garden hose is made of polyvinylchloride (PVC) from chloroethene (vinyl chloride). Draw a part of the polymer (use four monomers) for PVC.

12.37 Explosives used in mining contain TNT or 2,4,6-trinitrotoluene.

**a.** If the functional group *nitro* is —$NO_2$, what is the structural formula of TNT?

**b.** TNT is actually a mixture of isomers of trinitrotoluene. Draw two possible isomers.

12.38 Margarine is produced from the hydrogenation of vegetable oils, which contain unsaturated fatty acids. How many grams of hydrogen are required to completely saturate 75.0 g oleic acid, $C_{18}H_{34}O_2$, which has one double bond?

## ADDITIONAL QUESTIONS AND PROBLEMS

*For instructor-assigned homework, go to* ***www.masteringchemistry.com.***

12.39 Compare the formulas and bonding in propane, cyclopropane, propene, and propyne.

12.40 Compare the formulas and bonding in butane, cyclobutane, cyclobutene, and 2-butyne.

12.41 Give the IUPAC name for each of the following compounds:

**a.** Cl (on a cyclopentane ring)

**b.**
```
       Cl          CH3
       |           |
CH3—CH—CH2—CH—CH3
```

**c.**
```
        CH3
        |
CH2=C—CH2—CH2—CH3
```

**d.** $CH_3—CH_2—C≡C—CH_3$

12.42 Give the IUPAC name for each of the following compounds:

**a.** Cl (on a cyclopentene ring, at a carbon of the double bond)

**b.**
```
CH3        H
    \     /
     C=C
    /     \
  H        CH2—CH3
```

**c.** Cl, Cl (on a cyclohexene ring)

**d.**
```
                CH3
                |
CH2=CH—CH—CH3
```

**12.43** Write the condensed structural formula of each of the following compounds:
**a.** 1,2-dibromocyclopentene
**b.** 2-pentyne
**c.** *cis*-2-heptene
**d.** 3-chloro-2-methyl-1-pentene

**12.44** Write the condensed structural formula of each of the following compounds:
**a.** *trans*-3-hexene
**b.** 2-bromo-3-chlorocyclohexene
**c.** 2,3-dichloro-1-butene
**d.** 3-iodo-1-propyne

**12.45** Indicate if the following pairs represent structural isomers, cis–trans isomers, or identical compounds:

**a.** 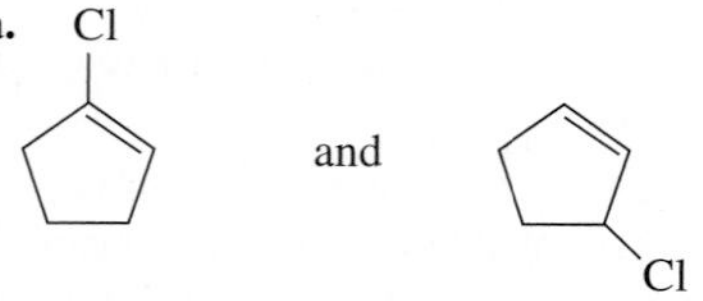 Cl on cyclopentene (Cl on double-bond carbon) and cyclopentene with Cl (on carbon adjacent to double bond)

**b.** 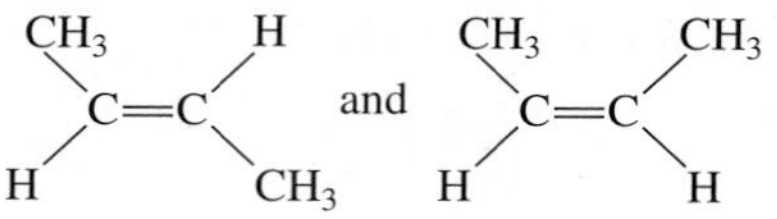 $CH_3(H)C{=}C(H)(CH_3)$ (trans) and $CH_3(H)C{=}C(CH_3)(H)$ (cis)

**12.46** Indicate if the following pairs represent structural isomers, cis–trans isomers, or identical compounds:

**a.** 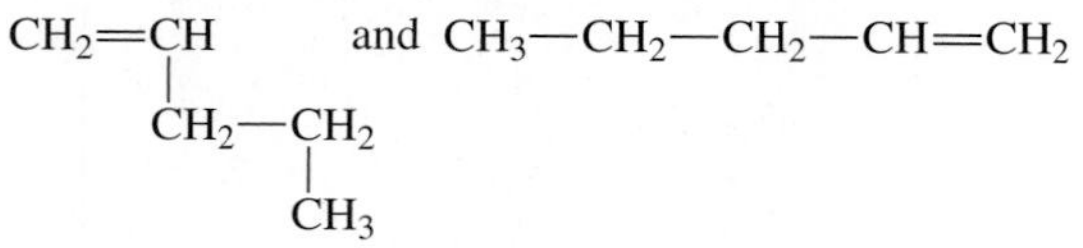 $CH_2{=}CH{-}CH_2{-}CH_2{-}CH_3$ (drawn as $CH_2{=}CH$ with $CH_2{-}CH_2$ below and $CH_3$) and $CH_3{-}CH_2{-}CH_2{-}CH{=}CH_2$

**b.** 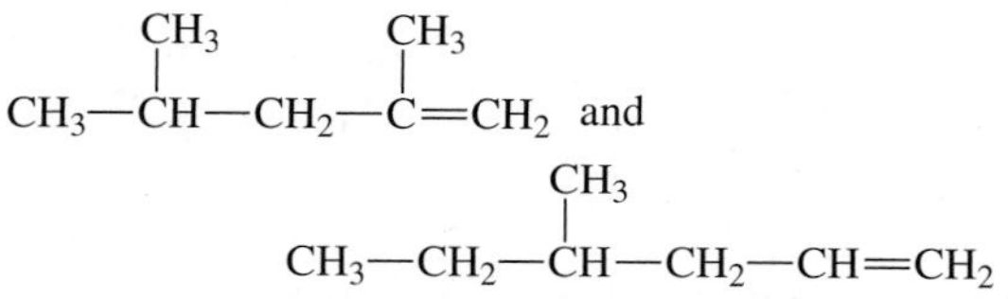 $CH_3{-}CH(CH_3){-}CH_2{-}C(CH_3){=}CH_2$ and $CH_3{-}CH_2{-}CH(CH_3){-}CH_2{-}CH{=}CH_2$

**12.47** Methylcyclopentane is formed by four different cycloalkenes that react with hydrogen ($H_2$) in the presence of a Ni catalyst. Draw the condensed structural formulas of each of these alkenes.

**12.48** Draw the condensed structural formulas and give the names for all the isomers of $C_4H_8$ including cyclic and cis–trans isomers.

**12.49** Write the condensed structural formulas for the cis and trans isomers for each of the following:
**a.** 2-pentene **b.** 2-chloro-3-hexene

**12.50** Write the condensed structural formulas for the cis and trans isomers for each of the following:
**a.** 2-butene **b.** 2-hexene

**12.51** Give the name of the product from complete hydrogenation of each of the following:
**a.** 3-methyl-2-pentene
**b.** cyclohexene
**c.** 2-pentyne

**12.52** Give the name of the product from complete hydrogenation of each of the following:
**a.** 3-hexene
**b.** 2-methyl-2-butene
**c.** propyne

**12.53** Write the condensed structural formulas of the products, if any, for the following:

**a.** $CH_3{-}CH{=}CH{-}CH_3 + HBr \longrightarrow$

**b.** 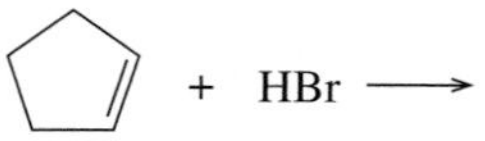 cyclopentene $+ HBr \longrightarrow$

**c.** $CH_3{-}CH{=}CH{-}CH_3 + Cl_2 \longrightarrow$

**12.54** Write the condensed structural formulas of the products, if any, for the following:

**a.** $CH_3{-}CH{=}CH{-}CH_3 + HOH \xrightarrow{H^+}$

**b.** 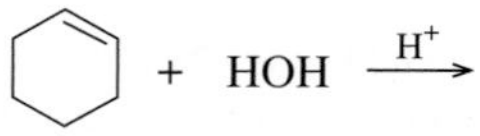 cyclohexene $+ HOH \xrightarrow{H^+}$

**c.** 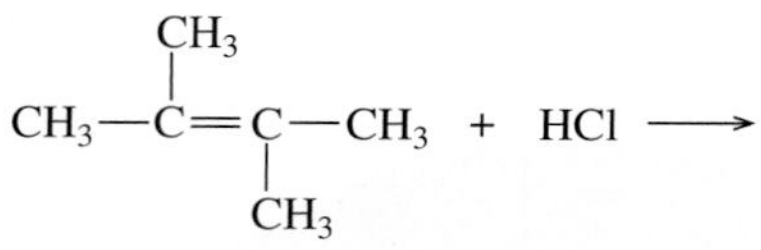 $CH_3{-}C(CH_3){=}C(CH_3){-}CH_3 + HCl \longrightarrow$

**12.55** What is the condensed structural formula of the organic compound needed to prepare each of the following products?

**a.** 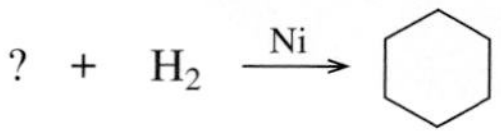 $? + H_2 \xrightarrow{Ni}$ cyclohexane

**b.** 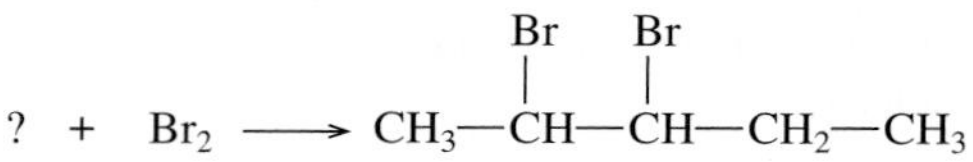 $? + Br_2 \longrightarrow CH_3{-}CH(Br){-}CH(Br){-}CH_2{-}CH_3$

**12.56** What is the condensed structural formula of the organic compound needed to prepare each of the following products?

**a.** 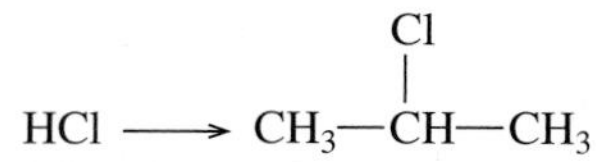 $? + HCl \longrightarrow CH_3{-}CH(Cl){-}CH_3$

**b.** 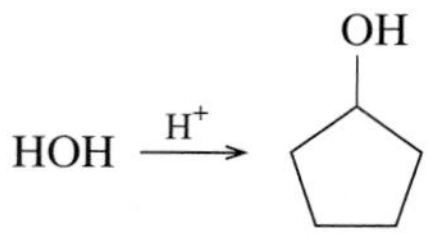 $? + HOH \xrightarrow{H^+}$ cyclopentanol (OH on cyclopentane)

**12.57** Copolymers contain more than one type of monomer. One copolymer used in medicine is made of alternating units of styrene and acrylonitrile. Write a section of the copolymer that would have three each of these alternating units. (For structure of styrene, see Table 12.3.)

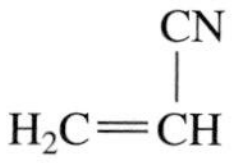

$H_2C{=}CH{-}CN$

Acrylonitrile

**12.58** Lucite, or Plexiglas, is a polymer of methylmethacrylate. Write the part of the polymer that is made from the addition of three of these monomers.

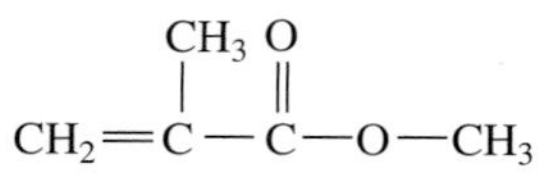

$CH_2{=}C(CH_3){-}C({=}O){-}O{-}CH_3$

Methylmethacrylate

12.59 Name the organic product(s) produced, if any, in each of the following reactions:

**a.** benzene and $Cl_2 \xrightarrow{FeCl_3}$

**b.** toluene and $Br_2 \xrightarrow{FeBr_3}$

**c.** benzene and $SO_3 \xrightarrow{H_2SO_4}$

**d.** benzene and $Br_2 \xrightarrow{light}$

**12.60** Write the condensed structural formula for each of the following:
**a.** ethylbenzene
**b.** *m*-dichlorobenzene
**c.** 1,2,4-trimethylbenzene
**d.** 1,4-dimethylbenzene

12.61 Name each of the following aromatic compounds:

**a.** 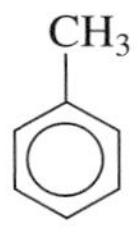 benzene ring with $CH_3$

**b.** 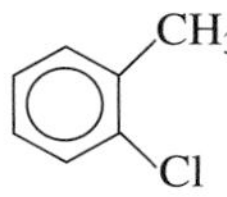 benzene ring with $CH_3$ and adjacent Cl

**c.** 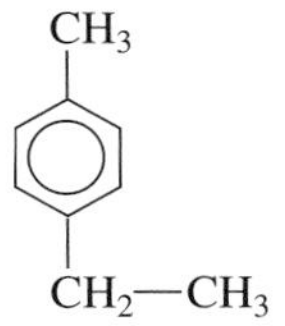 benzene ring with $CH_3$ at top and $CH_2—CH_3$ at bottom (para)

**d.** 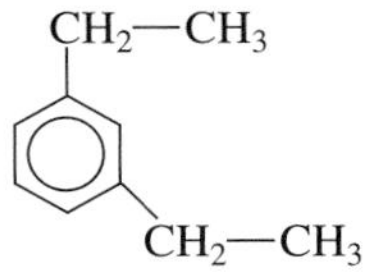 benzene ring with $CH_2—CH_3$ and $CH_2—CH_3$ at meta position

**12.62** What reactants and catalysts are needed to synthesize the following products?
**a.** nitrobenzene
**b.** benzenesulfonic acid
**c.** bromobenzene

## CHALLENGE QUESTIONS

12.63 If a female silkworm moth secretes 50 ng of bombykol, a sex attractant, how many molecules did she secrete? (See Environmental Note "Pheromones in Insect Communication.")

**12.64** How many grams of hydrogen are needed to hydrogenate 30.0 g of 2-butene?

12.65 Using each of the following carbon chains for $C_5H_{10}$, write and name all the possible alkenes, including those with cis and trans isomers:

C—C—C—C—C

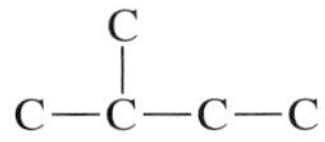

C—C(—C)—C—C

**12.66** Acetylene gas reacts with oxygen and burns at high temperature in an acetylene torch:
**a.** Write the balanced equation for the complete combustion of acetylene.
**b.** How many grams of oxygen are needed to react with 8.5 L of acetylene at STP?
**c.** How many liters of $CO_2$ (at STP) are produced when 30.0 g of acetylene undergoes combustion?

## ANSWERS

### ANSWERS TO STUDY CHECKS

**12.1** **a.** $CH_3—C≡C—CH_2—CH_3$ **b.** 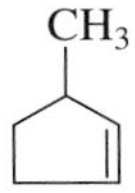 cyclopentene with $CH_3$

**12.2** *trans*-3-heptene

**12.3** $CH_3—CH(CH_3)—CH_2—CH_3$

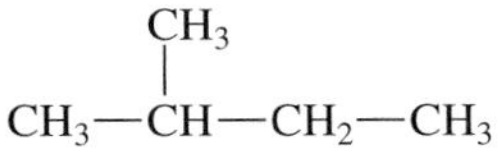

**12.4** 1,2-dichlorobutane

**12.5** cyclopentane with $CH_3$ and Br on same carbon; 1-bromo-1-methylcyclopentane

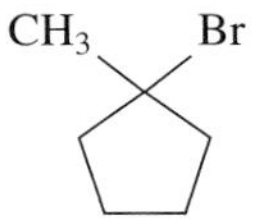

**12.6** $CH_3—C(CH_3)(OH)—CH_2—CH_3$

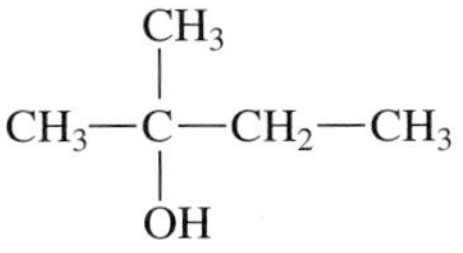

**12.7** The monomer of PVC, polyvinyl chloride, is chloroethene:

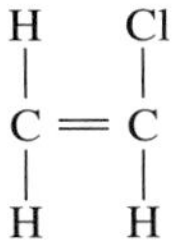

H(H)C=C(Cl)H

**12.8** 1,3-diethylbenzene; *m*-diethylbenzene

**12.9** Chlorobenzene can be prepared from benzene and chlorine, using $FeCl_3$ as a catalyst.

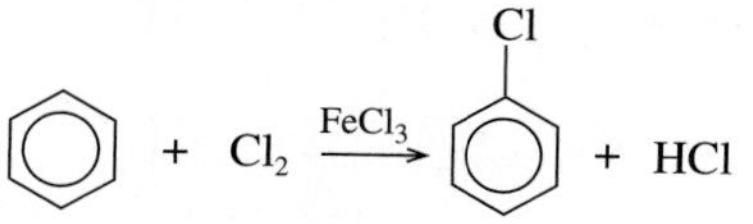

$$C_6H_6 + Cl_2 \xrightarrow{FeCl_3} C_6H_5Cl + HCl$$

## ANSWERS TO SELECTED QUESTIONS AND PROBLEMS

**12.1** **a.** An alkene has a double bond.
**b.** An alkyne has a triple bond.
**c.** An alkene has a double bond.
**d.** A cycloalkene has a double bond in a ring.

**12.3** **a.** ethene
**b.** 2-methylpropene
**c.** 4-bromo-2-pentyne
**d.** cyclobutene
**e.** 4-ethylcyclopentene
**f.** 4-ethyl-2-hexene

**12.5** **a.** $CH_3-CH=CH_2$
**b.** $CH_2=CH-CH_2-CH_2-CH_3$
**c.** 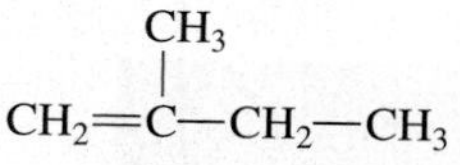 $CH_2=C(CH_3)-CH_2-CH_3$
**d.** 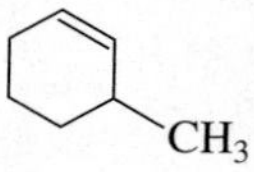 (cyclohexene ring with $CH_3$ substituent)
**e.** 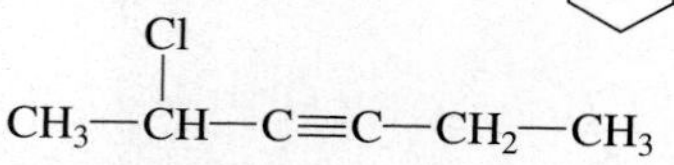 $CH_3-CH(Cl)-C\equiv C-CH_2-CH_3$
**f.** $H-C\equiv C-CH_2-CH_3$
**g.** $Br-CH_2-CH_2-CH_2-CH=CH_2$

**12.7** **a.** There are no cis–trans isomers.
**b.** This alkene has cis–trans isomers.
**c.** There are no cis–trans isomers.

**12.9** **a.** *cis*-2-butene **b.** *trans*-3-octene **c.** *cis*-3-heptene

**12.11** **a.** 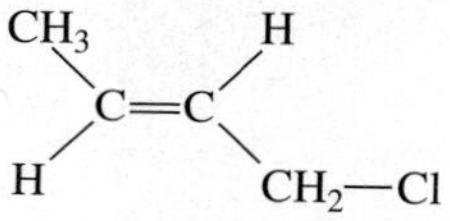 $CH_3(H)C=C(H)(CH_2-Cl)$ ($CH_3$ and H on top; H and $CH_2-Cl$ on bottom)
**b.** $CH_3(H)C=C(CH_2-CH_3)(H)$ ($CH_3$ and $CH_2-CH_3$ on top; H and H on bottom)
**c.** $CH_3-CH_2(H)C=C(H)(CH_2-CH_2-CH_3)$ ($CH_3-CH_2$ and H on top; H and $CH_2-CH_2-CH_3$ on bottom)

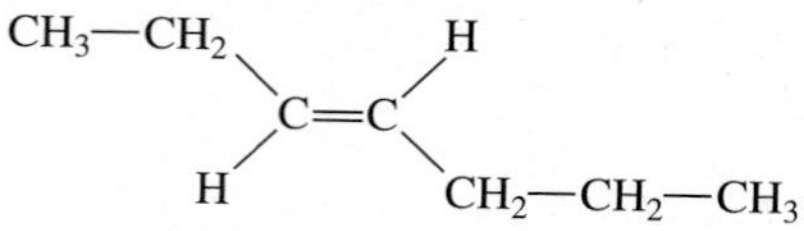

**12.13** **a.** $CH_3-CH_2-CH_2-CH_2-CH_3$ Pentane
**b.** 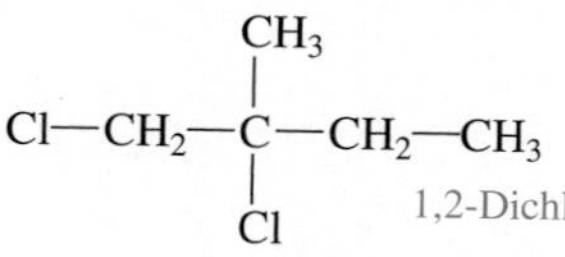 $Cl-CH_2-C(CH_3)(Cl)-CH_2-CH_3$ 1,2-Dichloro-2-methylbutane
**c.** 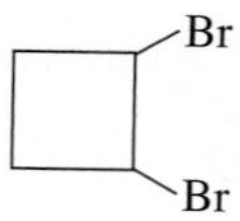 (cyclobutane with two Br) 1,2-Dibromocyclobutane
**d.** 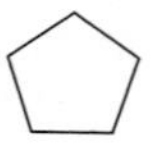 (cyclopentane ring) Cyclopentane
**e.** 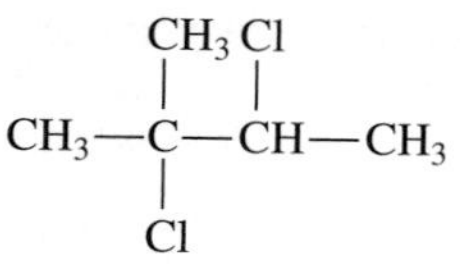 $CH_3-C(CH_3)(Cl)-CH(Cl)-CH_3$ 2,3-Dichloro-2-methylbutane
**f.** $CH_3-CH_2-CH_2-CH_2-CH_3$ Pentane

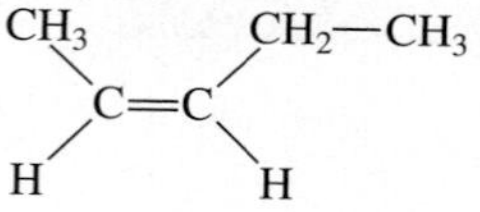

**12.15** **a.** 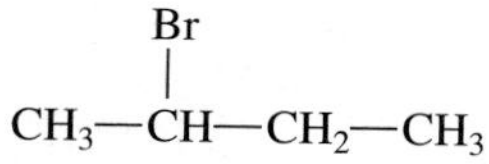 $CH_3-CH(Br)-CH_2-CH_3$ **b.** 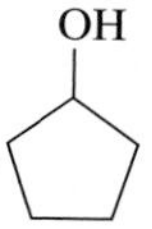 (cyclopentane ring with OH)
**c.** 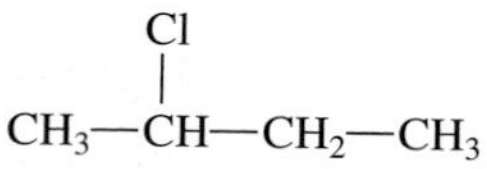 $CH_3-CH(Cl)-CH_2-CH_3$ **d.** 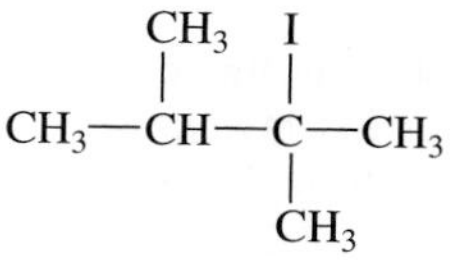 $CH_3-CH(CH_3)-C(I)(CH_3)-CH_3$
**e.** 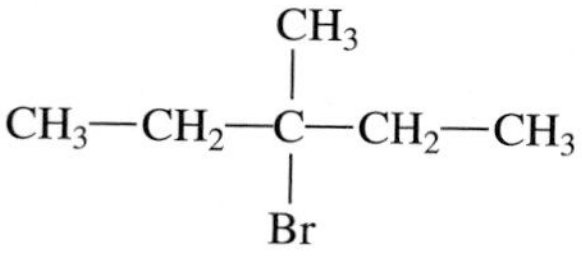 $CH_3-CH_2-C(CH_3)(Br)-CH_2-CH_3$
**f.** 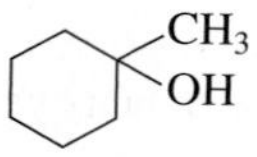 (cyclohexane ring with $CH_3$ and OH on the same carbon)

**12.17**
**a.** 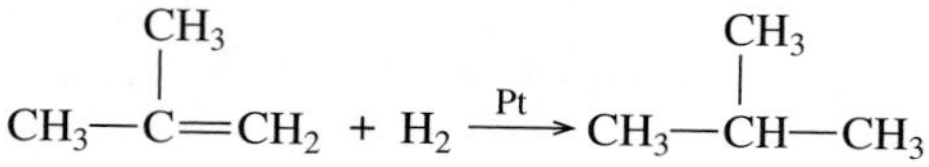 $CH_3-C(CH_3)=CH_2 + H_2 \xrightarrow{Pt} CH_3-CH(CH_3)-CH_3$
**b.** (cyclopentene) + HCl ⟶ (chlorocyclopentane)
**c.** $CH_3-CH=CH-CH_2-CH_3 + Br_2 \longrightarrow CH_3-CH(Br)-CH(Br)-CH_2-CH_3$
**d.** 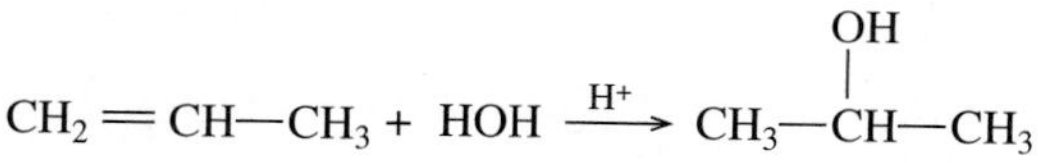 $CH_2=CH-CH_3 + HOH \xrightarrow{H^+} CH_3-CH(OH)-CH_3$
**e.** 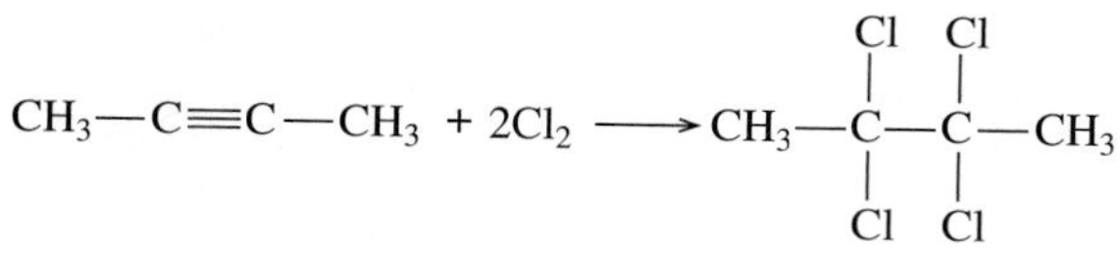 $CH_3-C\equiv C-CH_3 + 2Cl_2 \longrightarrow CH_3-CCl_2-CCl_2-CH_3$

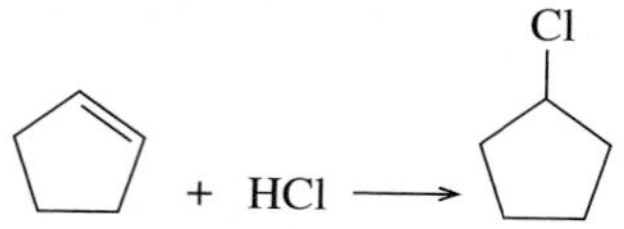

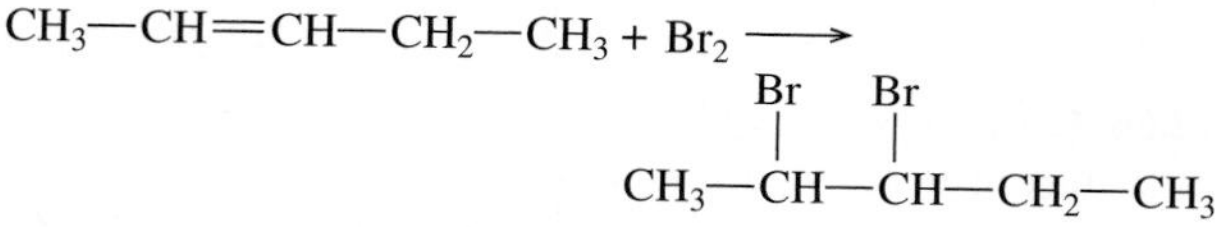

**12.19** A polymer is a very large molecule composed of small units that are repeated many times.

**12.21** $3F-C(F)=C(F)-F \longrightarrow -CF_2-CF_2-CF_2-CF_2-CF_2-CF_2-$

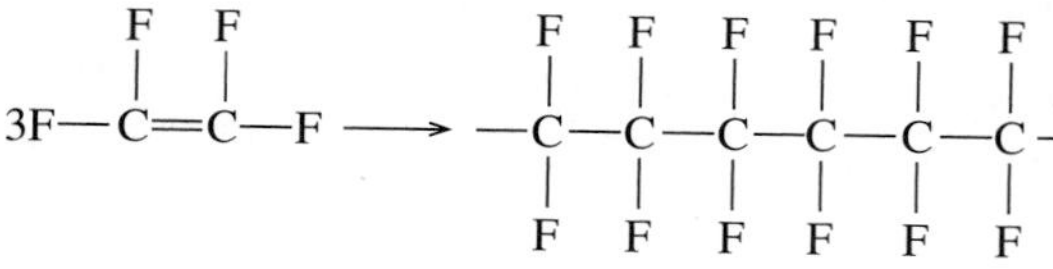

**12.23** $-CF_2-CH_2-CF_2-CH_2-CF_2-CH_2-$

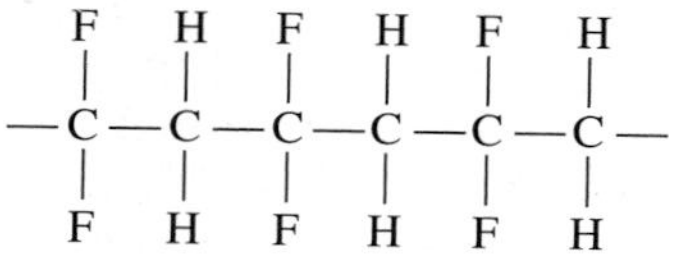

**12.25** Cyclohexane, $C_6H_{12}$, is a cycloalkane in which six carbon atoms in a ring are linked by single bonds. In benzene, $C_6H_6$, electrons are shared equally by the six carbon atoms.

**12.27** **a.** 1-chloro-2-methylbenzene, 2-chlorotoluene, *o*-chlorotoluene
**b.** ethylbenzene
**c.** 1,3,5-trichlorobenzene
**d.** 3-methyltoluene, *m*-xylene, 1,3-dimethylbenzene, *m*-dimethylbenzene, *m*-methyltoluene
**e.** 3-bromo-5-chlorotoluene, 1-bromo-3-chloro-5-methylbenzene
**f.** isopropylbenzene

**12.29** **a.** $CH_3$ **b.** Br, Cl **c.** $CH_2—CH_3$, $CH_3$ **d.** $CH_3$, Cl

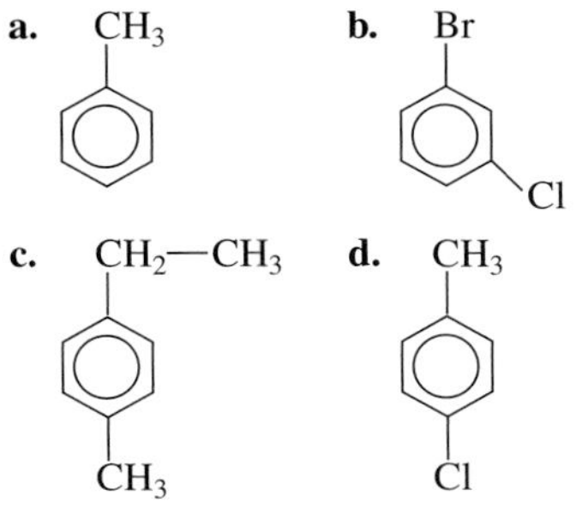

**12.31** Benzene undergoes substitution reactions because a substitution reaction allows benzene to retain the stability of the aromatic system.

**12.33** **a.** Cl **b.** $NO_2$

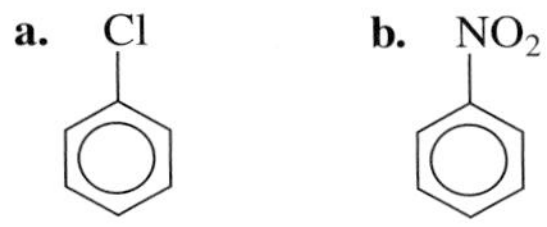

**12.35**

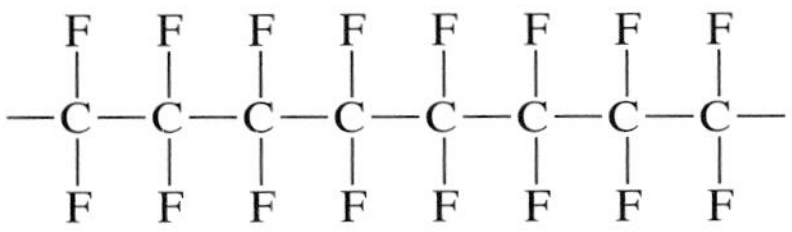

F F F F F F F F
—C—C—C—C—C—C—C—C—
F F F F F F F F

**12.37** **a.** $CH_3$, $NO_2$, $NO_2$, $NO_2$

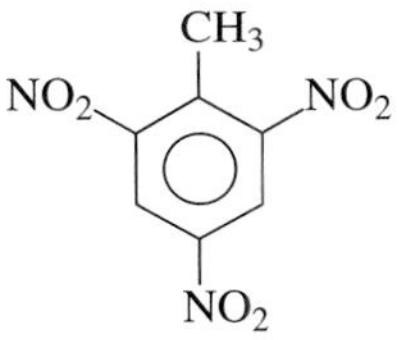

**b.** $CH_3$, $O_2N$, $NO_2$, $NO_2$ $CH_3$, $O_2N$, $NO_2$, $NO_2$ $CH_3$, $NO_2$, $O_2N$, $NO_2$

$CH_3$, $NO_2$, $NO_2$, $NO_2$ $CH_3$, $NO_2$, $O_2N$, $NO_2$

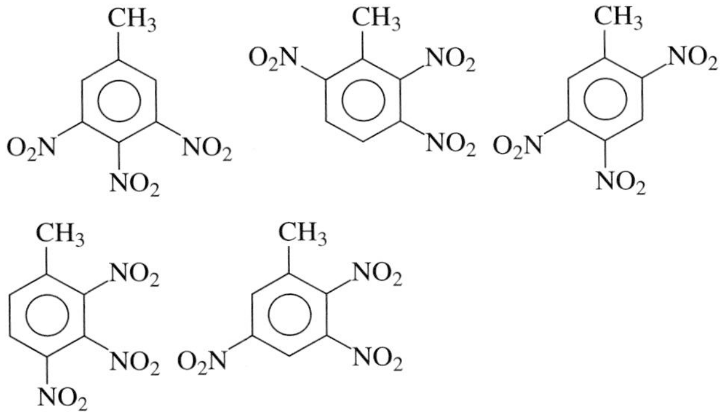

**12.39** All the compounds have three carbon atoms. The formula of propane is $C_3H_8$; the formulas of propene and cyclopropane are both $C_3H_6$ and the formula of propyne is $C_3H_4$. Propane is a saturated alkane, and cyclopropane is a saturated cyclic hydrocarbon. Both propene and propyne are unsaturated hydrocarbons, but propene has a double bond and propyne has a triple bond.

**12.41** **a.** chlorocyclopentane
**b.** 2-chloro-4-methylpentane
**c.** 2-methyl-1-pentene
**d.** 2-pentyne

**12.43** **a.** Br, Br

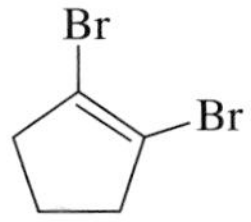

**b.** $CH_3—C{\equiv}C—CH_2—CH_3$

**c.** $CH_3$, $CH_2—CH_2—CH_2—CH_3$
C=C
H, H

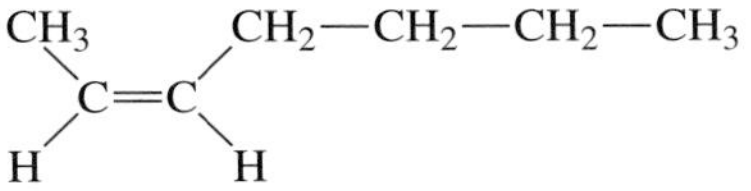

**d.** $CH_2{=}C(CH_3)—CH(Cl)—CH_2—CH_3$

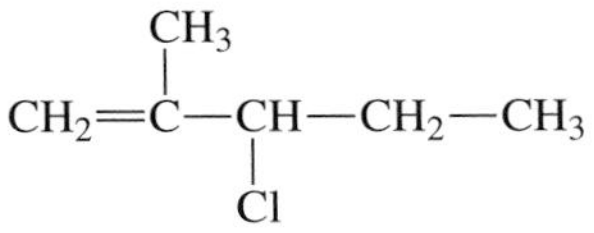

**12.45** **a.** structural isomers
**b.** cis–trans isomers

**12.47** $CH_3$ $CH_3$ $CH_3$ $CH_2$

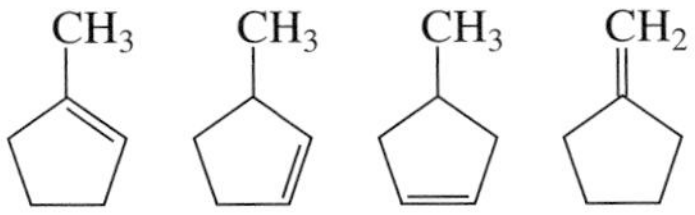

**12.49** **a.** $CH_3$, H
C=C *trans*-2-Pentene
H, $CH_2—CH_3$

$CH_3$, $CH_2—CH_3$
C=C *cis*-2-Pentene
H, H

**b.** $CH_3—CH_2$, H
C=C *trans*-3-Hexene
H, $CH_2—CH_3$

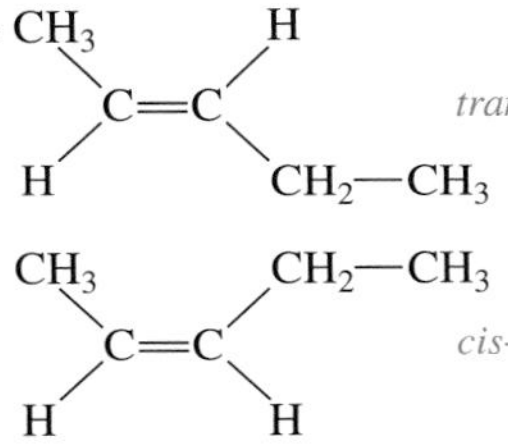

$CH_3—CH_2$, $CH_2—CH_3$
C=C *cis*-3-Hexene
H, H

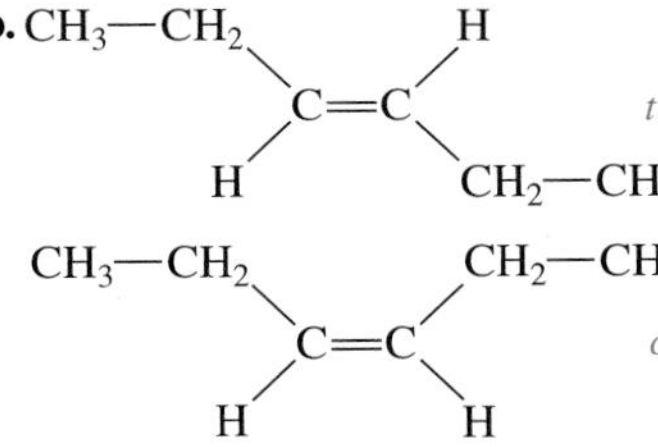

**12.51** **a.** 3-methylpentane
**b.** cyclohexane
**c.** pentane

**12.53** **a.** $CH_3—CH_2—CH(Br)—CH_3$

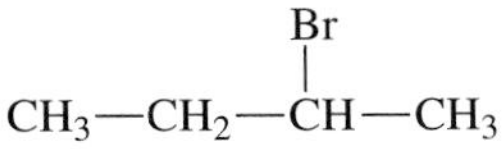

**b.** Br

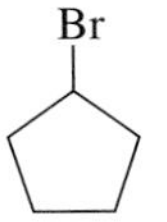

**c.** $CH_3—CH(Cl)—CH(Cl)—CH_3$

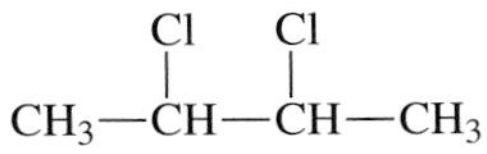

**12.55**

**a.**  (cyclohexene structure)

**b.** $CH_3—CH=CH—CH_2—CH_3$

**12.57**

$$—\overset{H}{\underset{H}{C}}—\overset{C_6H_5}{\underset{H}{C}}—\overset{H}{\underset{H}{C}}—\overset{CN}{\underset{H}{C}}—\overset{H}{\underset{H}{C}}—\overset{C_6H_5}{\underset{H}{C}}—\overset{H}{\underset{H}{C}}—\overset{CN}{\underset{H}{C}}—\overset{H}{\underset{H}{C}}—\overset{C_6H_5}{\underset{H}{C}}—\overset{H}{\underset{H}{C}}—\overset{CN}{\underset{H}{C}}—$$

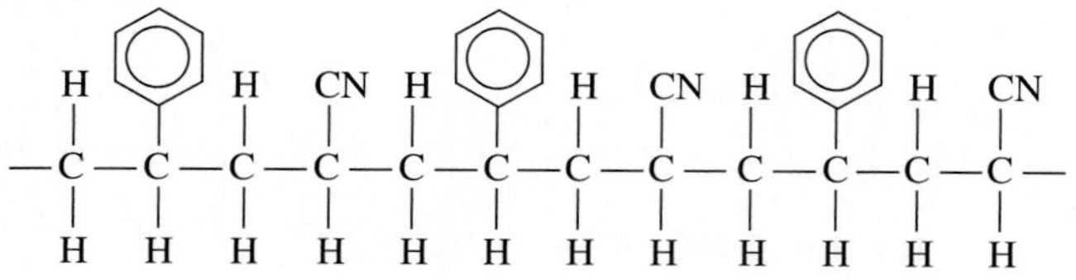

**12.59** **a.** chlorobenzene
**b.** *o*-bromotoluene, *m*-bromotoluene, *p*-bromotoluene
**c.** benzenesulfonic acid
**d.** no products

**12.61** **a.** methylbenzene, toluene
**b.** 1-chloro-2-methylbenzene, *o*-chlorotoluene, 2-chlorotoluene
**c.** 1-ethyl-4-methylbenzene, *p*-ethylmethylbenzene, *p*-ethyltoluene
**d.** 1,3-diethylbenzene, *m*-diethylbenzene

**12.63** $1 \times 10^{14}$ molecules of bombykol

**12.65**

| | |
|---|---|
| $CH_3—CH=CH—CH_2—CH_3$ | *cis*-2-pentene or *trans*-2-pentene |
| $H_2C=CH—CH_2—CH_2—CH_3$ | 1-pentene |
| $CH_2=\overset{CH_3}{C}—CH_2—CH_3$ | 2-methyl-1-butene |
| $CH_3—\overset{CH_3}{C}=CH—CH_3$ | 2-methyl-2-butene |
| $CH_3—\overset{CH_3}{CH}—CH=CH_2$ | 3-methyl-1-butene |

# Alcohols, Phenols, Thiols, and Ethers

13

LOOKING AHEAD

**13.1** Alcohols, Phenols, and Thiols
**13.2** Ethers
**13.3** Physical Properties of Alcohols, Phenols, and Ethers
**13.4** Reactions of Alcohols and Thiols

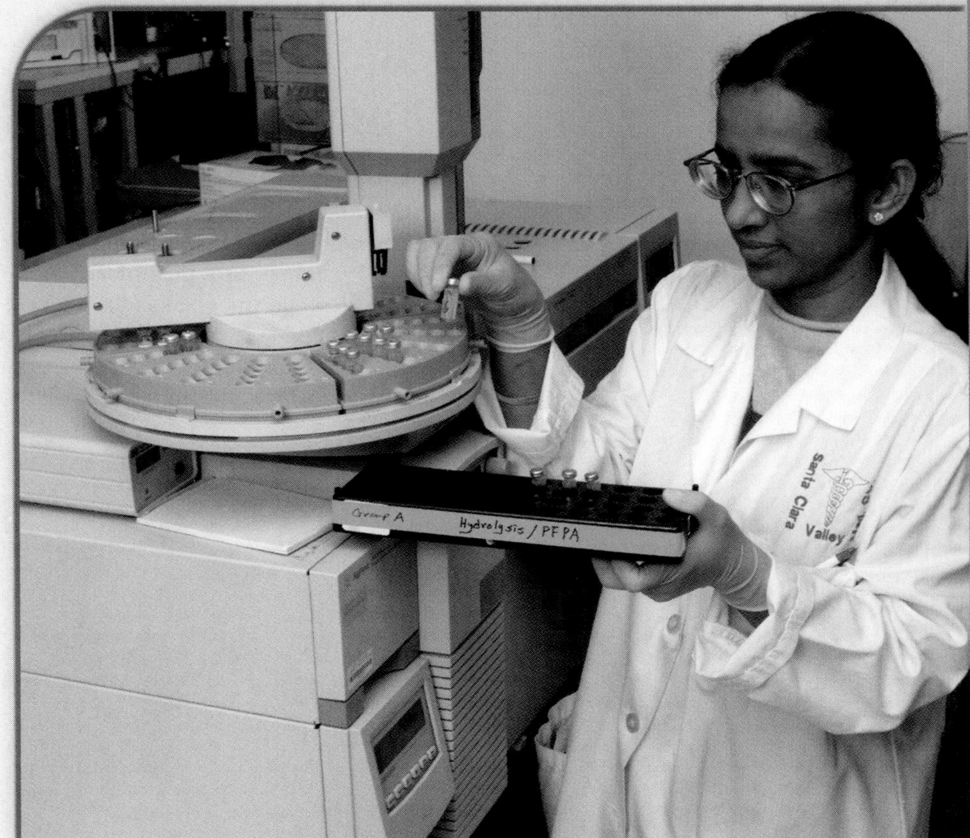


*"We use mass spectrometry to analyze and confirm the presence of drugs," says Valli Vairavan, clinical lab technologist—mass spectrometry, Santa Clara Valley Medical Center. "A mass spectrometer separates and identifies compounds including drugs by mass. When we screen a urine sample, we look for metabolites, which are the products of drugs that have metabolized in the body. If the presence of one or more drugs such as heroin and cocaine is indicated, we confirm it by using mass spectrometry."*

*Drugs or their metabolites are detected in urine 24–48 hours after use. Cocaine metabolizes to benzoylecgonine and hydroxycocaine, morphine to morphine-3-glucuronide, and heroin to acetylmorphine. Amphetamines and methamphetamines are detected unchanged.*

In this chapter, we will look at organic compounds that contain single bonds to Group 6A (16) atoms of oxygen and sulfur. Alcohols, which contain the hydroxyl group (—OH), are commonly found in nature and used in industry and at home. For centuries, grains, vegetables, and fruits have been fermented to produce the ethanol present in alcoholic beverages. The hydroxyl group is important in biomolecules, such as sugars and starches, as well as in steroids, such as cholesterol and estradiol. Menthol is a cyclic alcohol with a minty odor and flavor that is used in cough drops, shaving creams, and ointments. Ethers are compounds that contain an oxygen atom connected to two carbon atoms (—O—). They are important solvents in chemistry and medical laboratories. Beginning in 1842, diethyl ether was used for about 100 years as a general anesthetic. Today less flammable and more easily tolerated anesthetics are used. Thiols, which contain the —SH group, give the strong odors we associate with garlic and onions.

## 13.1 Alcohols, Phenols, and Thiols

**LEARNING GOAL**

Give IUPAC and common names for alcohols, phenols, and thiols; draw their condensed structural formulas. Classify alcohols as primary, secondary, or tertiary.

As we learned in Chapter 11, alcohols are a class of organic compounds that contain an oxygen (O) atom, shown in red in the ball-and-stick models. Thiols contain a sulfur (S) atom, shown in yellow. In an **alcohol**, a **hydroxyl group** (—OH) replaces a hydrogen atom in a hydrocarbon. In a **phenol**, the hydroxyl group is attached to an aromatic ring. Molecules of alcohols and phenols have a bent shape around the oxygen atom, similar to that of water. An alkyl or aromatic group replaces one hydrogen atom.

**Thiols** are a family of sulfur-containing organic compounds that have a *thiol* (—SH) *group*. They have structures similar to alcohols except that —SH takes the place of —OH.

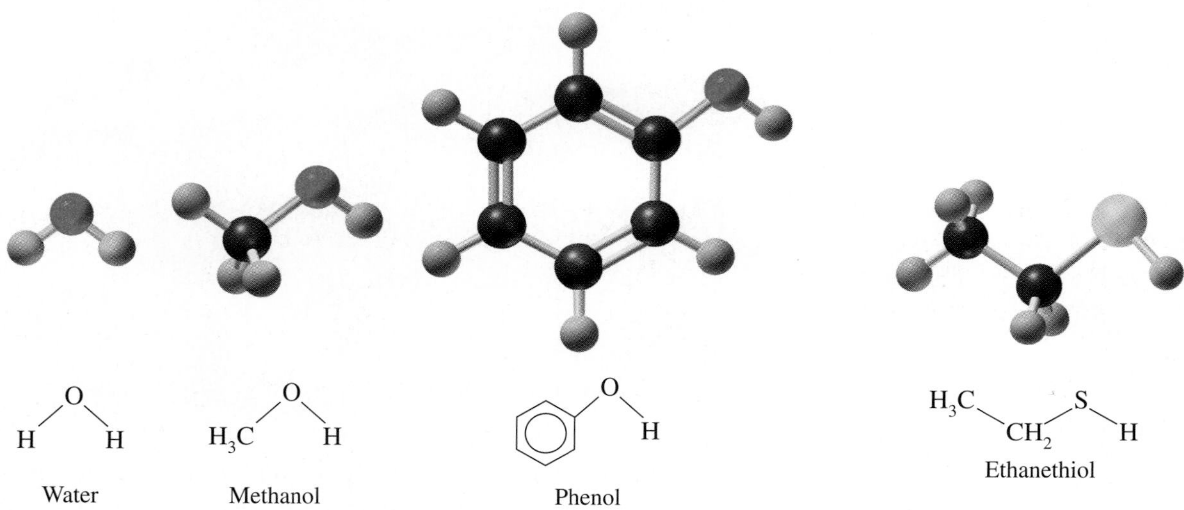


### Classification of Alcohols

SELF STUDY ACTIVITY
Alcohols and Thiols

Alcohols are classified by the number of carbon groups attached to the carbon atom bonded to the hydroxyl (—OH) group. **A primary (1°) alcohol** has one alkyl group attached to the carbon atom bonded to the —OH. The simplest alcohol, methanol, which has a carbon attached to three H atoms but no alkyl group, is considered a primary alcohol. A **secondary (2°) alcohol** has two alkyl groups, and a **tertiary (3°) alcohol** has three alkyl groups.

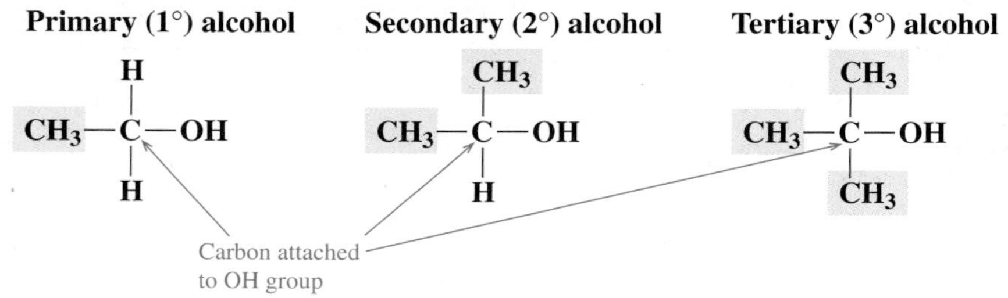

CONCEPT CHECK 13.1

**Classifying Alcohols**

Classify each of the following alcohols as primary (1°), secondary (2°), or tertiary (3°):

**a.** $CH_3—CH_2—CH_2—OH$ **b.** 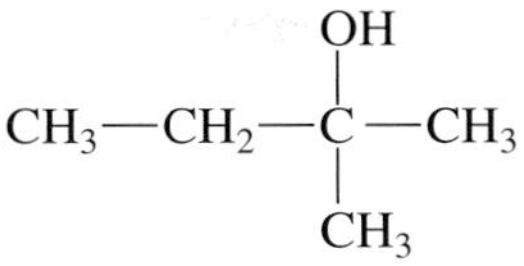 $CH_3—CH_2—C(OH)(CH_3)—CH_3$ **c.** cyclopentane ring bearing OH

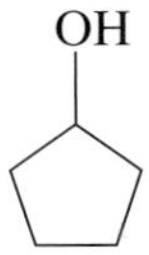

ANSWER

**a.** One alkyl group attached to the carbon atom bonded to the —OH makes this a primary (1°) alcohol.

**b.** Three alkyl groups attached to the carbon atom bonded to the —OH makes this a tertiary (3°) alcohol.

**c.** In a cyclic alcohol, there are two carbon atoms attached to the carbon atom bonded to the —OH, which makes this a secondary (2°) alcohol.

## Naming Alcohols, Phenols, and Thiols

The IUPAC rules for the naming of alcohols, phenols, and thiols are similar to those we used to name other families of organic compounds. The alcohol family is indicated by an *ol* ending, which is numbered to show the location of the hydroxyl group on the main chain.

## Naming Alcohols

In the IUPAC system, the alcohol family is indicated by the *ol* ending.

**STEP 1** **Name the longest carbon chain containing the —OH group.** Replace the *e* in the alkane name with *ol*:

$CH_3—CH_2—CH_2—OH$ propanol

**STEP 2** **Number the longest chain starting at the end closer to the —OH group.** For simple alcohols, the common name (shown in parentheses) gives the name of the carbon chain as an alkyl group followed by *alcohol.*

$\underset{3}{CH_3}—\underset{2}{CH_2}—\underset{1}{CH_2}—OH$ 1-propanol (propyl alcohol)

Alcohols with one or two carbon atoms do not require a number for the hydroxyl group.

$CH_3—OH$ Methanol (methyl alcohol)

$CH_3—CH_2—OH$ Ethanol (ethyl alcohol)

$Cl—CH_2—CH_2—OH$ 2-Chloroethanol

**STEP 3** **Name and number other substituents relative to the —OH group:**

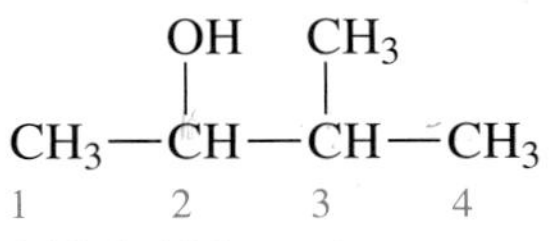

$\underset{1}{CH_3}—\underset{2}{CH(OH)}—\underset{3}{CH(CH_3)}—\underset{4}{CH_3}$ 3-Methyl-2-butanol

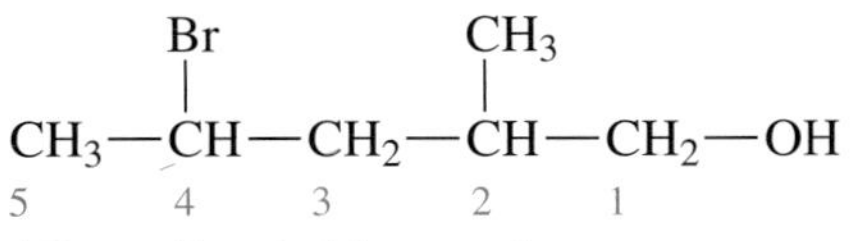

$\underset{5}{CH_3}—\underset{4}{CH(Br)}—\underset{3}{CH_2}—\underset{2}{CH(CH_3)}—\underset{1}{CH_2}—OH$ 4-Bromo-2-methyl-1-pentanol

**STEP 4** **Name a cyclic alcohol as a *cycloalkanol.*** For other substituents, the ring is numbered with the —OH group on carbon 1. Compounds with no other substituents on the ring do not require a number for the hydroxyl group:

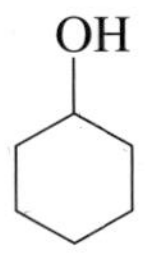

Cyclohexanol (cyclohexane ring bearing OH) 2-Methylcyclopentanol (cyclopentane ring bearing OH and $CH_3$)

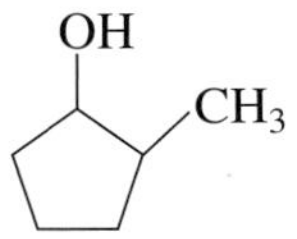

TUTORIAL
Naming Alcohols, Phenols, and Thiols

TUTORIAL
Drawing Alcohols, Phenols, and Thiols

**Guide to Naming Alcohols**

STEP 1 Name the longest carbon chain with the —OH group.

STEP 2 Number the longest chain starting at the end closer to the —OH.

STEP 3 Name substituents counting from the —OH.

STEP 4 Name a cyclic alcohol as a *cycloalkanol*.

SAMPLE PROBLEM 13.1

### Naming Alcohols

Give the IUPAC name for the following:

$$\text{a. } CH_3—\underset{}{\overset{\displaystyle CH_3}{\overset{|}{C}H}}—CH_2—\overset{\displaystyle OH}{\overset{|}{C}H}—CH_3$$

SOLUTION

**STEP 1** **Name the longest carbon chain containing the —OH group.** The parent chain is pentane; the alcohol is named pentanol.

**STEP 2** **Number the longest chain starting at the end closer to the —OH group.** The carbon chain is numbered to give the position of the —OH group as carbon 2 to give 2-pentanol.

**STEP 3** **Name and number other substituents relative to the —OH group.** With a methyl group on carbon 4, the compound is named 4-methyl-2-pentanol.

STUDY CHECK

Give the IUPAC name for the following:

$$CH_3—\overset{\displaystyle Cl}{\overset{|}{C}H}—CH_2—CH_2—OH$$

EXPLORE YOUR WORLD

### Alcohols in Household Products

Read the labels on household products such as mouthwashes, cold remedies, rubbing alcohol, and flavoring extracts. Look for names of alcohols, such as ethyl alcohol, isopropyl alcohol, thymol, and menthol.

QUESTIONS

1. What part of the name tells you that it is an alcohol?
2. What alcohol is usually meant by the term "alcohol"?
3. What is the percentage of alcohol in the products?
4. Write out the structures of the alcohols you find listed on the labels. You may need to use the Internet or a reference book for some structures.

## Naming Phenols

The term *phenol* is the IUPAC name for a benzene ring bonded to a hydroxyl group (—OH) and is used in the name of the family of organic compounds derived from phenol. When there is a second substituent, the benzene ring is numbered starting from the carbon 1, which is bonded to the —OH group. The terms *ortho*, *meta*, and *para* are used for the common names of simple phenols:

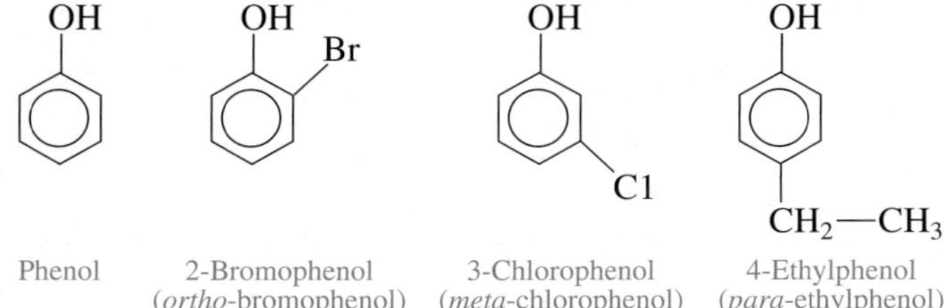


Phenol | 2-Bromophenol (*ortho*-bromophenol) | 3-Chlorophenol (*meta*-chlorophenol) | 4-Ethylphenol (*para*-ethylphenol)

Certain disubstituted phenols have common names based on historical uses. The methylphenols are commonly named as *cresols*, while benzenediols, which are benzene rings with two —OH groups, have a variety of common names:

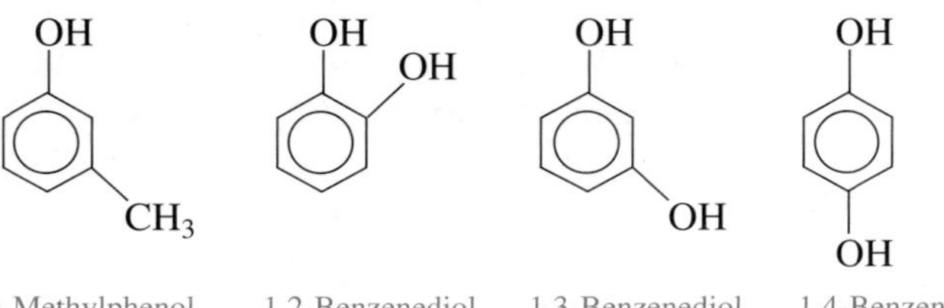


3-Methylphenol (*meta*-cresol) | 1,2-Benzenediol (catechol) | 1,3-Benzenediol (resorcinol) | 1,4-Benzenediol (hydroquinone)

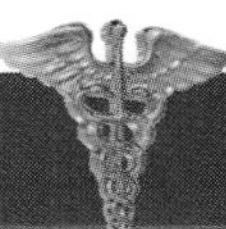

# HEALTH NOTE

## Some Important Alcohols and Phenols

*Methanol* (*methyl alcohol*), the simplest alcohol, is found in many solvents and paint removers. If ingested, methanol is oxidized to formaldehyde, which can cause headaches, blindness, and death. Methanol is used to make plastics, medicines, and fuels. In car racing, it is used as a fuel because it is less flammable and has a higher octane rating than does gasoline.

*Ethanol* (*ethyl alcohol*) has been known since prehistoric times as an intoxicating product formed by the fermentation of grains, sugars, and starches:

$$C_6H_{12}O_6 \xrightarrow{\text{Fermentation}} 2CH_3{-}CH_2{-}OH + 2CO_2$$

Ethanol for commercial uses is produced by allowing ethene and water to react at high temperatures and pressures. Ethanol is used as a solvent for perfumes, varnishes, and some medicines, such as tincture of iodine. Recent interest in alternative fuels has led to increased production of ethanol by the fermentation of sugars from grains such as corn, wheat, and rice. "Gasohol" is a mixture of ethanol and gasoline used as a fuel:

$$H_2C{=}CH_2 + H_2O \xrightarrow{300\ ^\circ C,\ 200\ \text{atm, catalyst}} CH_3{-}CH_2{-}OH$$

*1,2,3-Propanetriol* (*glycerol or glycerin*), a trihydroxy alcohol, is a viscous liquid obtained from oils and fats during the production of soaps. The presence of several polar —OH groups makes it strongly attracted to water, a feature that makes glycerin useful as a skin softener in products such as skin lotions, cosmetics, shaving creams, and liquid soaps:

$$HO{-}CH_2{-}\underset{}{\overset{\displaystyle OH}{\overset{|}{C}}H}{-}CH_2{-}OH$$

1,2,3-Propanetriol (glycerol)

*1,2-Ethanediol* (*ethylene glycol*) is used as antifreeze in heating and cooling systems. It is also a solvent for paints, inks, and plastics, and it is used in the production of synthetic fibers such as Dacron. If ingested, it is extremely toxic. In the body, it is oxidized to oxalic acid, which forms insoluble salts in the kidneys that cause renal damage, convulsions, and death. Because its sweet taste is attractive to pets and children, ethylene glycol solutions must be carefully stored:

$$HO{-}CH_2{-}CH_2{-}OH \xrightarrow{[O]} HO{-}\overset{\displaystyle O}{\overset{\|}{C}}{-}\overset{\displaystyle O}{\overset{\|}{C}}{-}OH$$

1,2-Ethanediol (ethylene glycol) → Oxalic acid

*Phenols* are found in several of the essential oils of plants, which produce the odor or flavor of the plant. Eugenol is found in cloves, vanillin in vanilla bean, isoeugenol in nutmeg, and thymol in thyme and mint. Thymol has a pleasant, minty taste and is used in mouthwashes and by dentists to disinfect a cavity before adding a filling compound.

*Bisphenol A* (BPA) is used to make polycarbonate, a clear plastic that is used to manufacture beverage bottles, including baby bottles. Washing polycarbonate bottles with certain detergents or at high temperatures disrupts the polymer, causing small amounts of BPA to leach from the bottles. Because BPA is an estrogen mimic, there are concerns about the harmful effects from low levels of BPA. In April 2008, Canada banned the use of polycarbonate baby bottles. Plastic bottles and containers made of polycarbonate have the recycling symbol "7".

$$HO{-}C_6H_4{-}\underset{\displaystyle CH_3}{\underset{|}{\overset{\displaystyle CH_3}{\overset{|}{C}}}}{-}C_6H_4{-}OH$$

Bisphenol A (BPA)

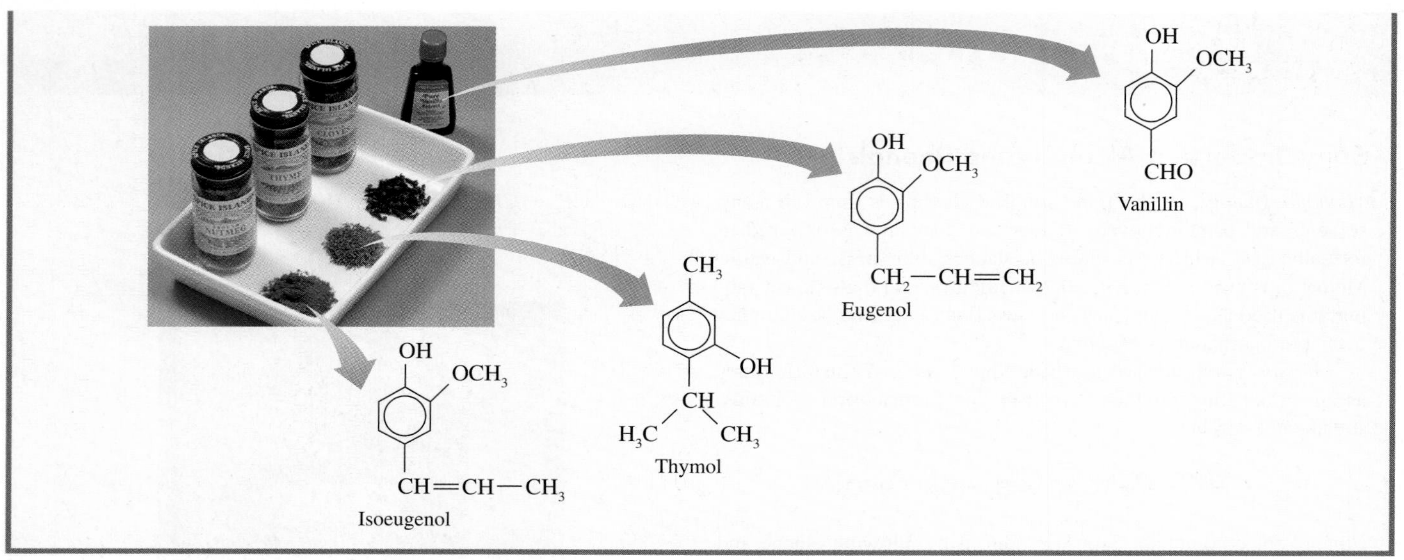


CONCEPT CHECK 13.2

### Naming Phenols

Give the IUPAC and common name for the following:

Br OH

ANSWER

The compound is a *phenol* because the —OH group is attached to a benzene ring. The ring is numbered starting with carbon attached to the —OH group in the direction that gives the bromine the lower number. The IUPAC name for the compound is 2-bromophenol; its common name is *ortho*-bromophenol or *o*-bromophenol.

## Naming Thiols

In the IUPAC system, thiols are named by adding *thiol* to the alkane name of the longest carbon chain bonded to the —SH group. The location of the —SH group is indicated by numbering the carbon chain from the end nearer the —SH group:

| $CH_3—OH$ | $CH_3—SH$ | $CH_3—CH(SH)—CH_2—CH_3$ |
|---|---|---|
| Methanol | Methanethiol | 2-Butanethiol |

An important property of thiols is a strong, sometimes disagreeable, odor. Methanethiol is the characteristic odor of oysters and cheddar cheese. (See Figure 13.1.) To help us detect natural gas (methane) leaks, a small amount of ethanethiol is added to the gas supply. There are thiols in the spray emitted when a skunk senses danger. The odor of onions is due to 1-propanethiol, which is also a lachrymator, a substance that makes eyes tear. Garlic contains thiols such as 2-propene-1-thiol. We can break this name down as follows:

| 2- | Prop | ene | -1- | thiol |
|---|---|---|---|---|
| Carbon 2 has C=C | 3 carbons in chain | alkene | on carbon 1 | —SH group |

| $H_3C(H)C=C(H)CH_2—SH$ | $CH_3—CH_2—CH_2—SH$ | $CH_2=CH—CH_2—SH$ |
|---|---|---|
| *trans*-2-Butene-1-thiol (in skunk spray) | 1-Propanethiol (in onions) | 2-Propene-1-thiol (in garlic) |

**FIGURE 13.1** Thiols are sulfur-containing compounds with a —SH group.
**Q** Why do thiols have structures similar to alcohols?

**SAMPLE PROBLEM 13.2**

### Thiols

Draw the condensed structural formula of the following:

**a.** 1-butanethiol **b.** cyclohexanethiol

SOLUTION

**a.** This compound has a —SH group on the first carbon of a butane chain:

$$CH_3—CH_2—CH_2—CH_2—SH$$

**b.** This compound has a —SH group on cyclohexane:

[cyclohexane ring with SH substituent]

STUDY CHECK

What is the condensed structural formula of ethanethiol?

## QUESTIONS AND PROBLEMS

### Alcohols, Phenols, and Thiols

**13.1** Classify each of the following as a primary (1°), secondary (2°), or tertiary (3°) alcohol:

**a.** $CH_3—CH(CH_3)—CH_2—CH_2—OH$

**b.** $CH_3—CH_2—CH_2—CH_2—OH$

**c.** $CH_3—C(OH)(CH_3)—CH_2—CH_3$

**d.** [skeletal structure with OH]

**13.2** Classify each of the following as a primary (1°), secondary (2°), or tertiary (3°) alcohol:

**a.** 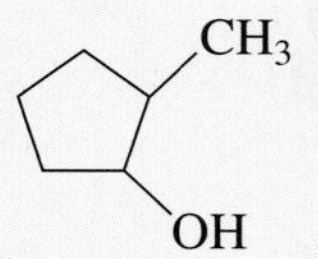 $CH_3$ / $OH$ (on cyclopentane ring)

**b.** $CH_3-\underset{}{\overset{CH_3}{\overset{|}{C}H}}-CH_2-OH$

**c.** 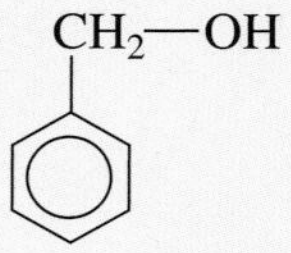 $CH_2-OH$ (on benzene ring)

**d.** $CH_3-CH_2-CH_2-\overset{CH_3}{\underset{CH_3}{C}}-OH$

**13.3** Give the IUPAC name for each of the following alcohols:

**a.** $CH_3-CH_2-OH$ **b.** $CH_3-CH_2-\overset{OH}{CH}-CH_3$

**c.** $CH_3-\overset{OH}{CH}-CH_2-CH_2-CH_3$ **d.** 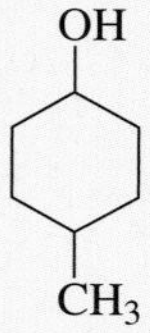 OH / $CH_3$ (on cyclohexane ring)

**13.4** Give the IUPAC name for each of the following alcohols:

**a.** 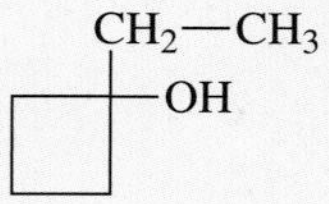 $CH_2-CH_3$ / $OH$ (on cyclobutane ring) **b.** $CH_3-CH_2-\overset{CH_3}{CH}-CH_2-OH$

**c.** $CH_3-CH_2-\overset{CH_3}{CH}-\overset{CH_3}{CH}-CH_2-OH$

**d.** $CH_3-CH_2-\overset{OH}{CH}-CH_2-CH_3$

**13.5** Draw the condensed structural formula of each of the following alcohols:

**a.** 1-propanol **b.** methyl alcohol
**c.** 3-pentanol **d.** 2-methyl-2-butanol
**e.** cyclohexanol

**13.6** Draw the condensed structural formula of each of the following alcohols:

**a.** ethyl alcohol
**b.** 3-methyl-1-butanol
**c.** 2,4-dichlorocyclohexanol
**d.** propyl alcohol
**e.** 1,3-cyclopentanediol

**13.7** Name each of the following phenols:

**a.** 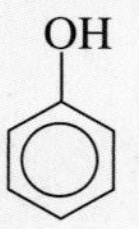 OH (on benzene ring) **b.** 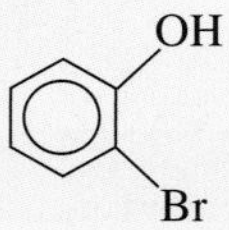 OH / Br (on benzene ring)

**c.** 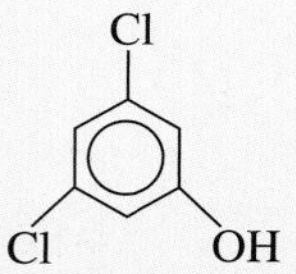 Cl / Cl / OH (on benzene ring) **d.** 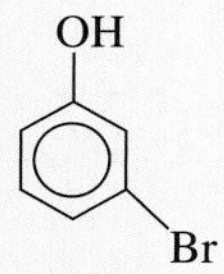 OH / Br (on benzene ring)

**13.8** Name each of the following phenols:

**a.** 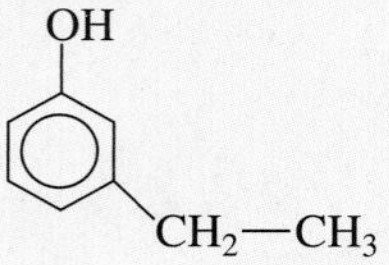 OH / $CH_2-CH_3$ (on benzene ring) **b.** 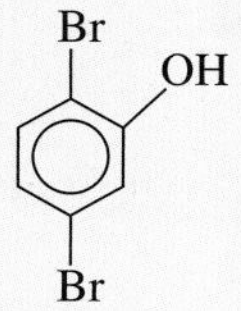 Br / OH / Br (on benzene ring)

**c.** 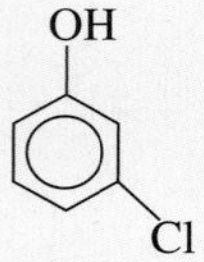 OH / Cl (on benzene ring) **d.** 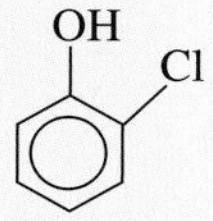 OH / Cl (on benzene ring)

**13.9** Draw the condensed structural formula of each of the following phenols:

**a.** *m*-bromophenol **b.** *p*-chlorophenol
**c.** 2,5-dichlorophenol **d.** *o*-phenylphenol

**13.10** Draw the condensed structural formula of each of the following phenols:

**a.** *o*-ethylphenol
**b.** 2,4-dichlorophenol
**c.** 2,4-dimethylphenol
**d.** 2-ethyl-5-methylphenol

**13.11** Give the IUPAC name for each of the following thiols:

**a.** $CH_3-SH$ **b.** $CH_3-\overset{SH}{CH}-CH_3$

**c.** $CH_3-\overset{CH_3}{CH}-\overset{CH_3}{CH}-CH_2-SH$

**d.** 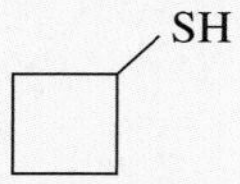 SH (on cyclobutane ring)

**13.12** Give the IUPAC name for each of the following thiols:

**a.** $CH_3-CH_2-CH_2-SH$

**b.** $CH_3-CH_2-CH_2-\overset{SH}{CH}-CH_3$

**c.** $CH_3-\overset{CH_3}{\underset{CH_3}{C}}-CH_2-SH$ **d.** 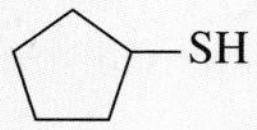 SH (on cyclopentane ring)

## 13.2 Ethers

**LEARNING GOAL**

Give the IUPAC and common names of ethers; draw the condensed structural formula.

An **ether** contains an oxygen atom that is attached by single bonds to two carbon groups that are alkyls or aromatic rings. Ethers have a bent structure like that of water and alcohols, except both hydrogen atoms are replaced by alkyl groups.

## Naming Ethers

TUTORIAL
Naming Ethers

TUTORIAL
Drawing Ethers

Simple ethers use their common names. Write the name of each alkyl or aromatic group attached to the oxygen atom in alphabetical order followed by the word *ether*.

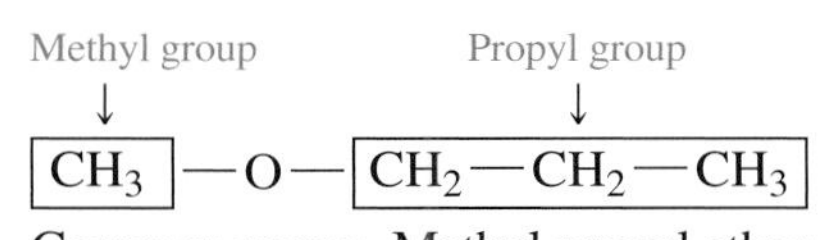


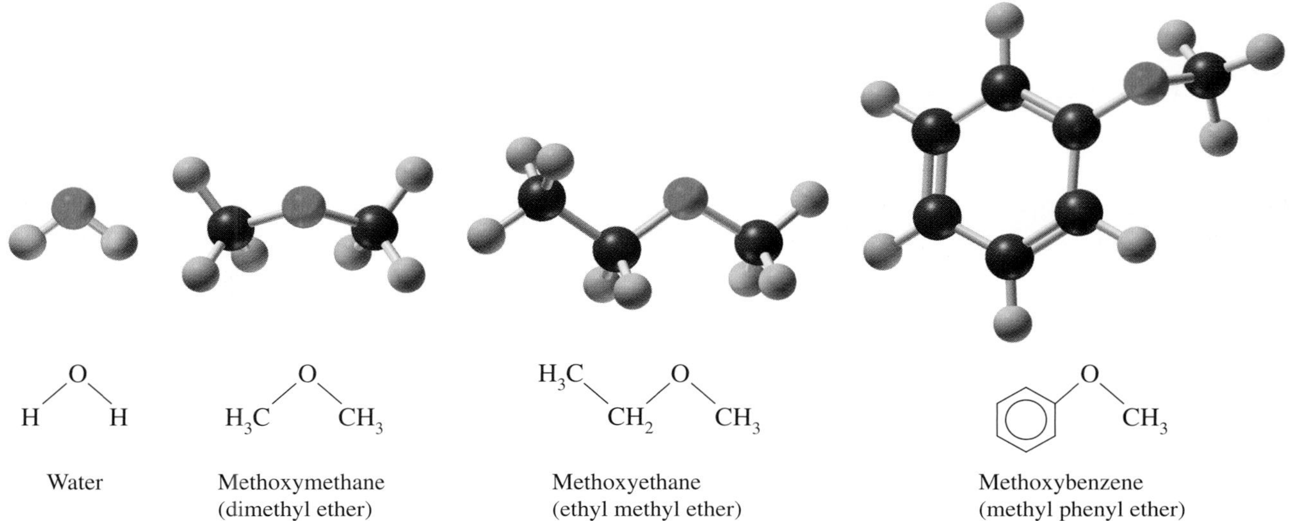


This ether can also be named using the IUPAC system using the following steps:

**STEP 1** **Write the alkane name of the longer carbon chain:**

$$CH_3—O—\underbrace{CH_2—CH_2—CH_3}_{\text{Longer carbon chain}} \qquad \text{propane}$$

**STEP 2** **Name the oxygen and smaller alkyl group as a substituent called an *alkoxy group*:**

$$\boxed{CH_3—O}—CH_2—CH_2—CH_3 \qquad \text{methoxypropane}$$

↑ Methoxy group

**STEP 3** **Number the longer carbon chain from the end nearer the alkoxy group to give the location of the alkoxy group:**

$$CH_3—O—\underset{1}{CH_2}—\underset{2}{CH_2}—\underset{3}{CH_3} \qquad \text{1-methoxypropane}$$

More examples of naming ethers with both IUPAC and common names follow:

$CH_3—O—CH_3$
Methoxymethane (dimethyl ether)

$CH_3—CH_2—O—CH_2—CH_3$
Ethoxyethane (diethyl ether)

$CH_3—\underset{}{CH}(O—CH_3)—CH_2—CH_3$
2-Methoxybutane

$CH_3—CH_2—O—C_6H_5$
Ethoxybenzene (ethyl phenyl ether)

$C_6H_5—O—C_6H_5$
Phenoxybenzene (diphenyl ether)

SAMPLE PROBLEM 13.3

## Ethers

Give the IUPAC name for the following:

$CH_3—CH_2—O—CH_2—CH_2—CH_2—CH_3$

SOLUTION

**Guide to Naming Ethers**

STEP 1 Write the alkane name of the longer carbon chain.

STEP 2 Name the oxygen and smaller alkyl group as an *alkoxy group.*

STEP 3 Number the longer chain from the end nearer the alkoxy group and give its location.

**STEP 1** **Write the alkane name of the longer carbon chain:**

$CH_3—CH_2—O—\underbrace{CH_2—CH_2—CH_2—CH_3}_{\text{Longer carbon chain}}$ butane

**STEP 2** **Name the oxygen and smaller alkyl group as a substituent called an alkoxy group:**

$\boxed{CH_3—CH_2—O}—CH_2—CH_2—CH_2—CH_3$ ethoxybutane

Ethoxy group

**STEP 3** **Number the longer carbon chain from the end nearer the alkoxy group and give its location.**

$CH_3—CH_2—O—\overset{}{\underset{1}{CH_2}}—\underset{2}{CH_2}—\underset{3}{CH_2}—\underset{4}{CH_3}$ 1-ethoxybutane

STUDY CHECK

What is the common name of ethoxybenzene?

## Isomers of Alcohols and Ethers

Alcohols and ethers can have the same molecular formula. For example, we can write condensed structural formulas for the isomers with the molecular formula $C_2H_6O$ as follows:

| $CH_3—CH_2—OH$ | $CH_3—O—CH_3$ |
|---|---|
| Ethanol (ethyl alcohol) | Methoxymethane (dimethyl ether) |

CONCEPT CHECK 13.3

## Isomers of Alcohols and Ethers

Determine the molecular formulas of the following alcohols and ethers. Identify the compounds that are structural isomers. Explain.

1-butanol, 2-butanol, methyl ethyl ether, diethyl ether, 3-pentanol, methyl propyl ether

ANSWER

The molecular formulas are as follows:

| | | | |
|---|---|---|---|
| 1-Butanol | $C_4H_{10}O$ | 2-Butanol | $C_4H_{10}O$ |
| Methyl ethyl ether | $C_3H_8O$ | Diethyl ether | $C_4H_{10}O$ |
| 3-Pentanol | $C_5H_{12}O$ | Methyl propyl ether | $C_4H_{10}O$ |

Structural isomers have the same number of carbon atoms, hydrogen atoms, and oxygen atoms but in different arrangements.

Four of these compounds are structural isomers: 1-butanol, 2-butanol, diethyl ether, and methyl propyl ether.

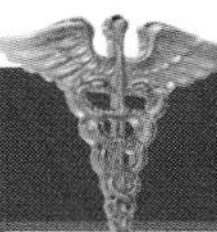

## HEALTH NOTE

### Ethers as Anesthetics

*Anesthesia* is the loss of all sensation and consciousness. A general anesthetic is a substance that blocks signals to the awareness centers in the brain, so the person has a loss of memory, a loss of feeling pain, and an artificial sleep. The term *ether* has been associated with anesthesia because diethyl ether was the most widely used anesthetic for more than a hundred years. Although it is easy to administer, ether is very volatile and highly flammable. A small spark in the operating room could cause an explosion. Since the 1950s, anesthetics such as Forane (isoflurane), Ethrane (enflurane), and Penthrane (methoxyflurane) have been developed that are not as flammable and do not cause nausea. Most of these anesthetics retain the ether group, but the addition of many halogen atoms reduces the volatility and flammability of the ethers. More recently, they have been replaced by halothane (2-bromo-2-chloro-1,1,1-trifluoroethane), discussed in Chapter 11, because of the side effects of the ether-type inhalation anesthetics.

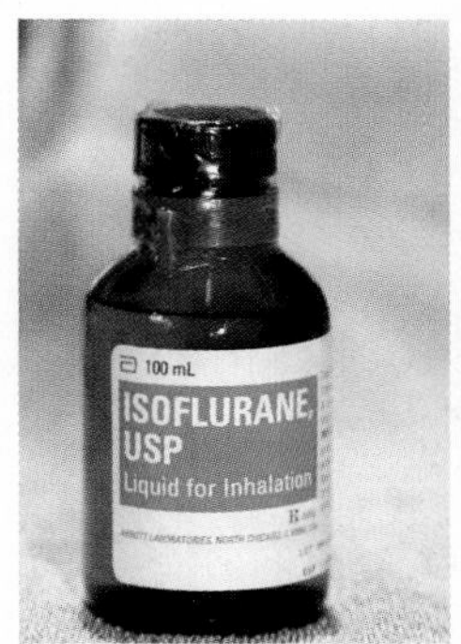


```
   F  Cl     F          F       F  F          Cl  F      H
   |  |      |          |       |  |          |   |      |
F—C—C—O—C—F      F—C—O—C—C—Cl      Cl—C—C—O—C—H
   |  |      |          |       |  |          |   |      |
   F  H      H          H       F  H          H   F      H
```

Forane® (isoflurane) | Ethrane® (enflurane) | Penthrane® (methoxyflurane)

## SAMPLE PROBLEM 13.4

### Isomers

Draw the condensed structural formulas and give the IUPAC and common names of two alcohols and one ether with a molecular formula of $C_3H_8O$.

SOLUTION

To draw the condensed structural formulas for alcohols, the hydroxyl group is bonded to two different atoms in a chain of three carbon atoms. For the ether, two alkyl groups are bonded to an oxygen atom:

$CH_3—CH_2—CH_2—OH$
1-Propanol (propyl alcohol)

$CH_3—CH(OH)—CH_3$
2-Propanol (isopropyl alcohol)

$CH_3—CH_2—O—CH_3$
Methoxyethane (ethyl methyl ether)

STUDY CHECK

Write the IUPAC names of the unbranched isomers of $C_4H_{10}O$.

## Cyclic Ethers

A **cyclic ether** contains an oxygen atom in a carbon ring. They are *heterocyclic compounds* because there is a ring with one or more atoms that are not carbon. The cyclic ethers are usually given common names. The five-atom rings with an oxygen atom use common names derived from the aromatic ring *furan*. The four-atom cyclic ethers are not common. The rings are numbered from the oxygen atom as 1:

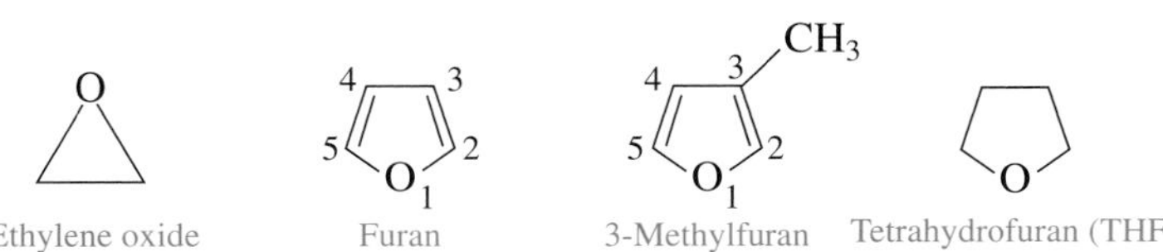


Ethylene oxide | Furan | 3-Methylfuran | Tetrahydrofuran (THF)

An unsaturated ether ring of six atoms is named *pyran*:

Pyran Tetrahydropyran (THP) 4-Methylpyran

Cyclic ethers containing two oxygen atoms in a ring of six atoms are called *dioxanes*. The oxygen atoms are numbered because they can take different positions in the ring:

1,4-Dioxane 1,3-Dioxane

## ENVIRONMENTAL NOTE

### Toxic Ethers

*Dioxin* is a term used for a group of highly toxic compounds composed of dioxanes bonded to aromatic rings. One of the most toxic is 2,3,7,8-tetrachlorodibenzo-*p*-dioxin (TCDD), now considered carcinogenic (cancer causing) because its structure interferes with DNA. Dioxin is formed during forest fires and as a by-product of many industrial processes involving chlorine, such as chemical and pesticide manufacturing and pulp and paper bleaching. The herbicide Agent Orange used in Vietnam was contaminated by highly toxic dioxin, which formed during the synthesis of Agent Orange.

2,4,5-Trichlorophenoxyacetic acid
(2,4,5-T; Agent Orange)

2,3,7,8-Tetrachlorodibenzo-*p*-dioxin
(TCDD, "dioxin")

**SAMPLE PROBLEM 13.5**

### Cyclic Ethers

Identify the following as a cyclic alcohol, ether, or cyclic ether:

**a.** **b.** **c.**

SOLUTION

**a.** A cyclic ether has an oxygen atom in the ring.
**b.** A cyclic alcohol has a hydroxyl group bonded to a cycloalkane.
**c.** An ether has an oxygen atom with single bonds to two carbon groups.

STUDY CHECK

What is the difference between furan and pyran?

## QUESTIONS AND PROBLEMS

### Ethers

**13.13** Give the IUPAC name and a common name for each of the following ethers:

**a.** $CH_3—O—CH_2—CH_3$ **b.** (cyclohexyl)—O—$CH_3$

**c.** (cyclobutyl)—O—$CH_2—CH_3$

**d.** $CH_3—O—CH_2—CH_2—CH_3$

**13.14** Give the IUPAC name and a common name for each of the following ethers:

**a.** $CH_3—CH_2—O—CH_2—CH_2—CH_3$

**b.** (phenyl)—O—$CH_3$ **c.** (cyclopentyl)—O—$CH_2—CH_3$

**d.** $CH_3—O—CH_3$

**13.15** Draw the condensed structural formula for each of the following ethers:

**a.** ethyl propyl ether **b.** cyclopropyl ethyl ether
**c.** methoxycyclopentane **d.** 1-ethoxy-2-methylbutane
**e.** 2,3-dimethoxypentane

**13.16** Draw the condensed structural formula for each of the following ethers:

**a.** diethyl ether **b.** diphenyl ether
**c.** ethoxycyclohexane
**d.** 2-methoxy-2,3-dimethylbutane
**e.** 1,2-dimethoxybenzene

**13.17** Indicate whether each of the following pairs represent isomers, the same compound, or different compounds:

**a.** 2-pentanol and 2-methoxybutane
**b.** 2-butanol and cyclobutanol
**c.** ethyl propyl ether and 2-methyl-1-butanol

**13.18** Indicate whether each of the following pairs represent isomers, the same compound, or different compounds:

**a.** 2-methoxybutane and 3-methyl-2-butanol
**b.** 1-hexanol and dipropyl ether
**c.** 2-methyl-2-propanol and diethyl ether

**13.19** Give the name for each of the following cyclic ethers:

**a.** (O in five-membered ring) **b.** 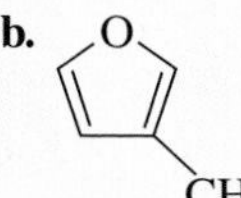

**c.** 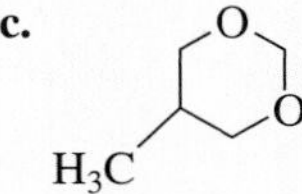


**13.20** Give the name for each of the following cyclic ethers:

**a.** (O in five-membered ring) **b.** (O, O, $H_3C$) **c.** 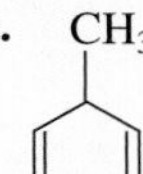


# 13.3 Physical Properties of Alcohols, Phenols, and Ethers

**LEARNING GOAL**

Describe some physical properties of alcohols, phenols, and ethers.

In Chapters 11 and 12, we learned that hydrocarbons, which are composed of only carbon and hydrogen, are nonpolar. In this chapter, we have looked at compounds containing the element oxygen. The high electronegativity of oxygen determines the boiling points and solubility in water of alcohols and ethers.

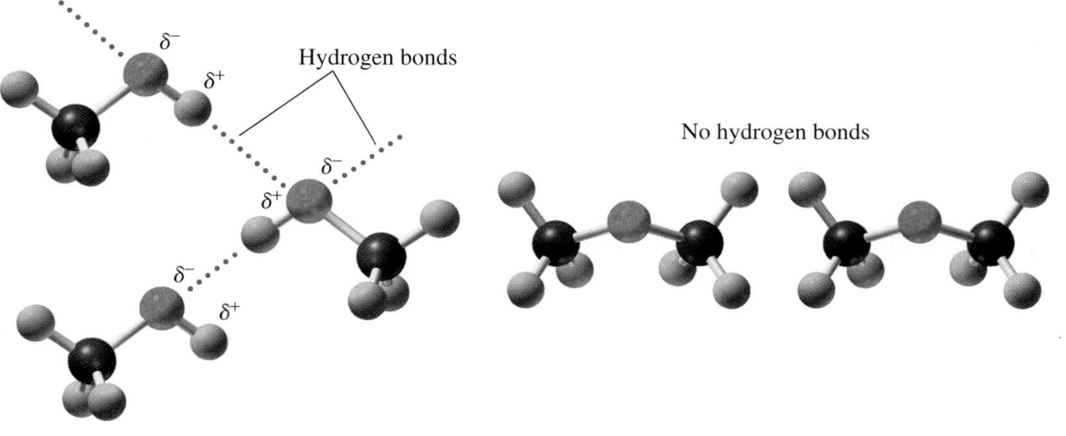


## Boiling Points

In an alcohol, the electronegativity of the oxygen makes the O—H bond very polar, which gives the hydrogen in O—H a partially positive charge. Hydrogen bonds form between the oxygen of one alcohol and hydrogen in the O—H of another alcohol.

TUTORIAL
Physical Properties of Alcohols and Ethers

Ethers do not form hydrogen bonds with other ether molecules, because they do not have a polar O—H bond.

Because of hydrogen bonding, alcohols have much higher boiling points than ethers of similar mass. In alcohols, higher temperatures are required to provide the energy needed to break the many hydrogen bonds between alcohol molecules. The boiling points of ethers are similar to those of alkanes because ether and alkanes do not form hydrogen bonds.

## Solubility in Water

The electronegativity of the oxygen atom influences the solubility of both alcohol and ethers in water. In alcohols, the atoms in the O—H group form hydrogen bonds with the H and O atoms of water. As the number of carbon atoms increases, the solubility effect of the —OH group is diminished. Only an alcohol with one to four carbon atoms is soluble in water. Alcohols with five or more carbon atoms are not soluble.

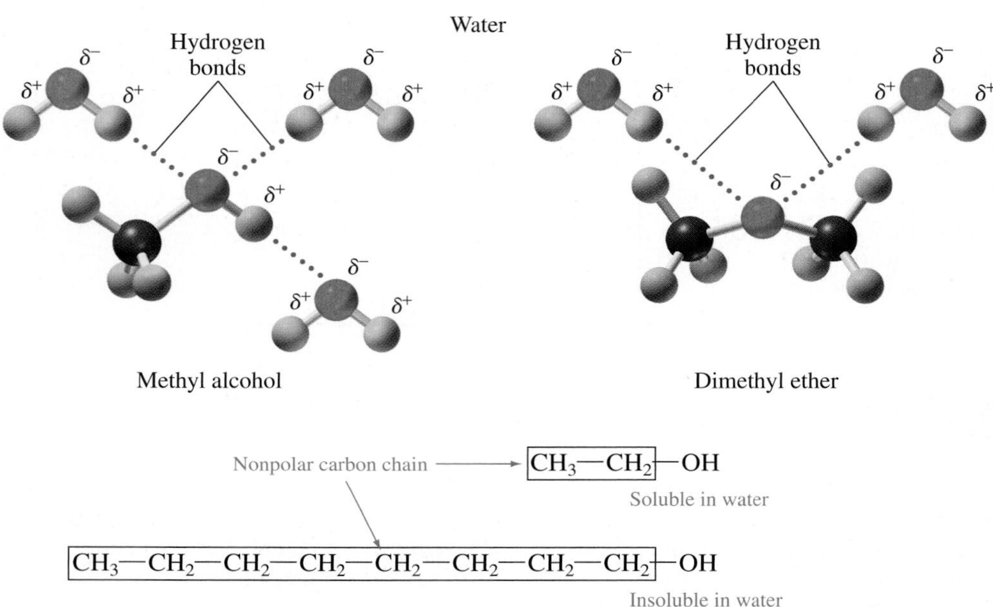


An ether with 2 or 3 carbon atoms is soluble in water because the electronegative oxygen atom forms hydrogen bonds with the hydrogen atoms in water. However, ethers cannot form as many hydrogen bonds with water as alcohols. Thus, ethers are less soluble in water than alcohols, but they are more soluble than alkanes. Table 13.1 compares the boiling points and solubility of some alkanes, alcohols, and ethers of similar mass.

**TABLE 13.1 Solubility and Boiling Points of Some Typical Alkanes, Alcohols, and Ethers of Similar Molar Mass**

| Compound | Condensed Structural Formula | Molar Mass (g/mole) | Boiling Point (°C) | Soluble in Water? |
|---|---|---|---|---|
| Propane | $CH_3—CH_2—CH_3$ | 44 | −42 | No |
| Dimethyl ether | $CH_3—O—CH_3$ | 46 | −23 | Yes |
| Ethanol | $CH_3—CH_2—OH$ | 46 | 78 | Yes |
| Butane | $CH_3—CH_2—CH_2—CH_3$ | 58 | 0 | No |
| Ethyl methyl ether | $CH_3—O—CH_2—CH_3$ | 60 | 8 | Yes |
| 1-Propanol | $CH_3—CH_2—CH_2—OH$ | 60 | 97 | Yes |

Ethers such as diethyl ether are very useful as solvents for hydrocarbons. However, ether vapors are highly flammable and react with oxygen to form explosive compounds. The utmost care must be taken when working with ethers.

CONCEPT CHECK 13.4

**Properties of Alcohols and Ethers**

Consider 1-butanol and diethyl ether, which are isomers of $C_4H_{10}O$.

**a.** Which has a higher boiling point? Explain.
**b.** Which is more soluble in water? Explain

ANSWER

**a.** The —OH group in 1-butanol forms hydrogen bonds, requiring more energy and a higher temperature to boil. Diethyl ether does not form hydrogen bonds with other molecules of diethyl ether.
**b.** The —OH in 1-butanol can form more hydrogen bonds with water than diethyl ether. Thus, 1-butanol is more soluble in water than diethyl ether.

## Phenols

Phenol has a high boiling point (182 °C) because the O—H group allows phenol molecules to hydrogen bond with other phenol molecules. Phenol is slightly soluble in water because phenol molecules can form hydrogen bonds with water molecules. In water, the O—H group of phenol ionizes slightly, which makes it a weak acid ($K_a = 1 \times 10^{-10}$). In fact, an early name for phenol was *carbolic acid*. Phenol is very corrosive and highly irritating to the skin; it can cause severe burns and ingestion can be fatal. Dilute solutions of phenol were previously used in hospitals as antiseptics, but they have generally been replaced.

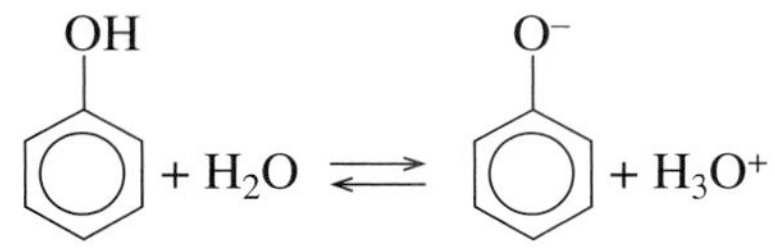

OH
Phenol $+ H_2O \rightleftharpoons$ Phenoxide ion $+ H_3O^+$
O⁻

SAMPLE PROBLEM 13.6

**Physical Properties of Alcohols, Ethers, and Phenols**

Predict which compound in each of the following pairs will be more soluble in water:

**a.** butane or 1-propanol **b.** 1-propanol or 1-heptanol

SOLUTION

**a.** 1-Propanol is more soluble because it can form hydrogen bonds with water.
**b.** The 1-propanol is more soluble because it has a shorter carbon chain.

STUDY CHECK

Dimethyl ether and ethanol both have molar masses of 46 g/mole. However, ethanol has a much higher boiling point than dimethyl ether. How would you explain this difference in boiling points?

## QUESTIONS AND PROBLEMS

### Physical Properties of Alcohols, Phenols, and Ethers

13.21 Predict the compound with the higher boiling point in the following pairs:
**a.** ethane or methanol **b.** diethyl ether or 1-butanol
**c.** 1-butanol or pentane

**13.22** Glycerol (1,2,3-propanetriol) has a boiling point of 290 °C. 1-Pentanol, which has about the same molar mass as glycerol, boils at 138 °C. Why is the boiling point of glycerol so much higher?

**13.23** Are each of the following soluble in water? Explain.

a. $CH_3—CH_2—OH$  b. $CH_3—O—CH_3$

c. $CH_3—CH_2—CH_2—CH_2—CH_2—CH_2—OH$

d. OH (attached to a benzene ring)

**13.24** Give an explanation for the following observations:

**a.** Ethanol is soluble in water, but propane is not.

**b.** Dimethyl ether is soluble in water, but pentane is not.

**c.** 1-Propanol is soluble in water, but 1-hexanol is not.

# 13.4 Reactions of Alcohols and Thiols

LEARNING GOAL

Write equations for the combustion, dehydration, and oxidation of alcohols and thiols.

In Chapter 11, we learned that hydrocarbons undergo combustion in the presence of oxygen. Alcohols burn with oxygen, too. For example, in a restaurant, a dessert may be prepared by pouring a liquor on fruit or ice cream and lighting it. (See Figure 13.2.) The combustion of the ethanol in the liquor proceeds as follows:

$$CH_3—CH_2—OH + 3O_2 \longrightarrow 2CO_2 + 3H_2O + \text{energy}$$

FIGURE 13.2 A flaming dessert is prepared using a liquor that undergoes combustion.

Q What is the equation for the combustion of the ethanol in the liquor?

## Dehydration of Alcohols to Form Alkenes

Earlier we saw that water can be added to alkenes to yield alcohols. In the reverse reaction, alcohols lose a water molecule when they are heated (180 °C) with an acid catalyst such as $H_2SO_4$. During the **dehydration** of an alcohol, H— and —OH are removed from *adjacent carbon atoms of the same alcohol* to produce a water molecule. A double bond forms between the same two carbon atoms to produce an alkene product:

$$\text{—C(H)—C(OH)—} \xrightarrow[\text{Heat}]{H^+} \text{>C=C<} + \mathbf{H_2O}$$

Alcohol Alkene Water

**Examples**

$$H—C(H)(H)—C(OH)(H)—H \xrightarrow[\text{Heat}]{H^+} H_2C=CH_2 + \mathbf{H_2O}$$

Ethanol Ethene

$$\text{Cyclopentanol} \xrightarrow[\text{Heat}]{H^+} \text{Cyclopentene} + \mathbf{H_2O}$$

Cyclopentanol Cyclopentene

TUTORIAL
Dehydration and Oxidation of Alcohols

The dehydration of a secondary alcohol can result in the formation of two products. **Saytzeff's rule** states that the major product is the one that forms by removing the hydrogen from the carbon atom that has the smaller number of hydrogen atoms. A hydrogen atom is easier to remove from the carbon atom adjacent to the carbon atom attached to the —OH group that has the fewer hydrogen atoms and thus the most alkyl groups:

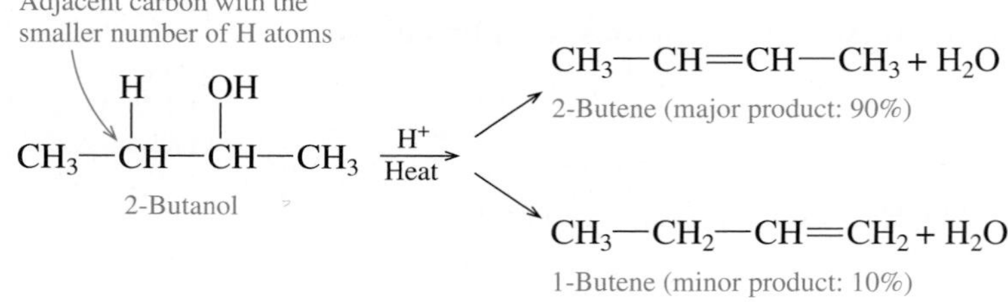

CONCEPT CHECK 13.5

### Dehydration of Alcohols

Consider the dehydration of 1-pentanol and 2-pentanol.

**a.** Is Saytzeff's rule needed to determine the dehydration product from each alcohol?
**b.** What is the name of the major dehydration product from each alcohol?

ANSWER

**a.** Saytzeff's rule is used to determine the major product from the dehydration of 2-pentanol but not from the dehydration of 1-pentanol. Carbon 2 in 2-pentanol is attached to adjacent carbon atoms with different numbers of hydrogen atoms.
**b.** The 1-pentanol loses the —OH from carbon 1 and a —H from carbon 2 to form 1-pentene. This is the only possible product. Using Saytzeff's rule, dehydration of 2-pentanol removes the —OH from carbon 2 and a —H from carbon 3, which has the smaller number of H atoms. The major product is 2-pentene.

SAMPLE PROBLEM 13.7

### Dehydration of Alcohols

Draw the condensed structural formula for the alkenes produced by the dehydration of the following alcohols:

**a.** $CH_3-CH_2-\underset{|}{\overset{OH}{CH}}-CH_2-CH_3 \xrightarrow[\text{Heat}]{H^+}$ **b.** 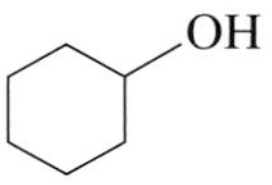 (cyclohexane ring)—OH $\xrightarrow[\text{Heat}]{H^+}$

SOLUTION

**a.** Because the molecule is a symmetrical alcohol, the —H may be removed from the either carbon adjacent to the carbon attached to the —OH group, which forms the following product:

$$CH_3-CH_2-CH=CH-CH_3$$

**b.** The —OH of this alcohol is removed along with a —H from an adjacent carbon. Remember that the hydrogen atoms are not drawn in this type of geometric formula:

STUDY CHECK

What is the name of the alkene produced by the dehydration of cyclopentanol?

SAMPLE PROBLEM 13.8

### Predicting Reactants

Draw the condensed structural formula of the alcohol that is needed to produce each of the following products:

**a.**  (cyclopentene) **b.** $CH_3-\underset{\underset{CH_3}{|}}{C}=CH-CH_3$

SOLUTION

**a.** 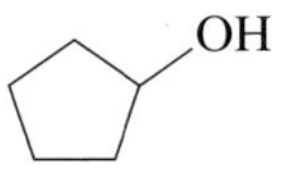 (cyclopentane ring)—OH **b.** $CH_3-\overset{\overset{OH}{|}}{\underset{\underset{CH_3}{|}}{C}}-CH_2-CH_3$ or $CH_3-\underset{\underset{CH_3}{|}}{CH}-\overset{\overset{OH}{|}}{CH}-CH_3$

STUDY CHECK

What is the name of an alcohol that forms 2-methylpropene?

## Formation of Ethers

Ethers form when the dehydration of alcohols occurs at lower temperatures (130° C) in the presence of an acid catalyst. Then the components of water are removed from two molecules: an H— from one alcohol, and the —OH from another. When the remaining portions of the two alcohols join, an ether is produced:

$$\underset{\text{Methanol}}{CH_3-OH} + \underset{\text{Methanol}}{HO-CH_3} \xrightarrow[\text{Heat}]{H^+} \underset{\text{Dimethyl ether}}{CH_3-O-CH_3} + H_2O$$

## Oxidation of Alcohols

As we know from Chapter 6, **oxidation** is a loss of hydrogen atoms or the addition of oxygen. In organic chemistry, we find that an oxidation reaction also occurs when there is an increase in the number of carbon–oxygen bonds. In a reduction reaction, the product has fewer bonds between carbon and oxygen:

$$\underset{\text{Alkane}}{CH_3-CH_3} \underset{\text{Reduction}}{\overset{\text{Oxidation}}{\rightleftharpoons}} \underset{\text{Alcohol (1°)}}{\overset{\text{1 bond to O}}{CH_3-CH_2-OH}} \underset{\text{Reduction}}{\overset{\text{Oxidation}}{\rightleftharpoons}} \underset{\text{Aldehyde}}{\overset{\text{2 bonds to O}}{CH_3-C(=O)-H}} \underset{\text{Reduction}}{\overset{\text{Oxidation}}{\rightleftharpoons}} \underset{\text{Carboxylic acid}}{\overset{\text{3 bonds to O}}{CH_3-C(=O)-OH}}$$

## Oxidation of Primary and Secondary Alcohols

The oxidation of a primary alcohol produces an aldehyde, which contains a double bond between carbon and oxygen. The oxidation occurs by removing two hydrogen atoms, one from the —OH group and another from the carbon that is bonded to the —OH. To indicate the presence of an oxidizing agent, such as $KMnO_4$ or $K_2Cr_2O_7$, reactions are often written with the symbol [O]:

$$\underset{\substack{\text{Methanol}\\ \text{(methyl alcohol)}}}{H-CH(OH)-H} \xrightarrow{[O]} \underset{\substack{\text{Methanal}\\ \text{(formaldehyde)}}}{H-C(=O)-H} + H_2O$$

$$\underset{\substack{\text{Ethanol}\\ \text{(ethyl alcohol)}}}{CH_3-CH_2-OH} \xrightarrow{[O]} \underset{\substack{\text{Ethanal}\\ \text{(acetaldehyde)}}}{CH_3-C(=O)-H} + H_2O$$

Aldehydes oxidize further by the addition of oxygen to form a carboxylic acid. This step occurs so readily that it is often difficult to isolate the aldehyde product during oxidation:

$$\underset{\substack{\text{Ethanal}\\ \text{(acetaldehyde)}}}{CH_3-C(=O)-H} \xrightarrow{[O]} \underset{\substack{\text{Ethanoic acid}\\ \text{(acetic acid)}}}{CH_3-C(=O)-OH}$$

We will learn more about carboxylic acids in Chapter 16.

In the oxidation of secondary alcohols, the products are ketones. One hydrogen is removed from the —OH and another from the carbon bonded to the —OH group. The result

**HEALTH NOTE**

### Methanol Poisoning

*Methanol*, or "wood alcohol," is a highly toxic alcohol present in products such as windshield-washer fluid, Sterno, and paint strippers. Methanol is rapidly absorbed in the gastrointestinal tract. In the liver, it is metabolized to formaldehyde and then formic acid, a substance that causes nausea, severe abdominal pain, and blurred vision. Blindness can occur because the intermediate products destroy the retina of the eye. As little as 4 mL of methanol can produce blindness. The formic acid, which is not readily eliminated from the body, lowers blood pH so severely that just 30 mL of methanol can lead to coma and death.

The treatment for methanol poisoning involves giving sodium bicarbonate to neutralize the formic acid in the blood. In some cases, ethanol is given intravenously to the patient. The enzymes in the liver pick up ethanol molecules to oxidize instead of methanol molecules. This process gives time for the methanol to be eliminated via the lungs without the formation of its dangerous oxidation products.

is a ketone that has the carbon-oxygen double bond attached to alkyl groups on both sides. There is no further oxidation of a ketone because there are no hydrogen atoms attached to the carbon of the ketone group:

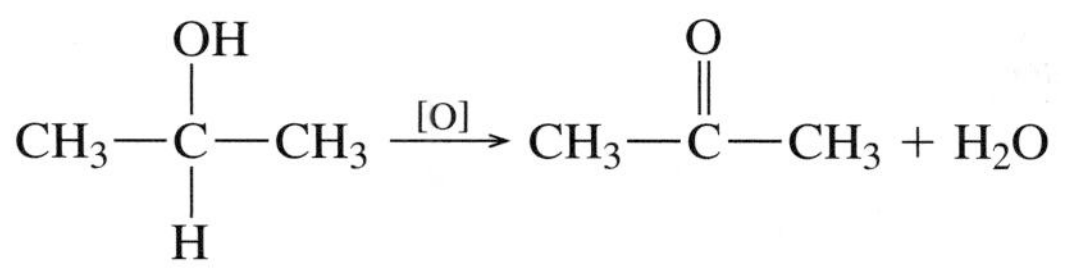

$$\underset{\substack{\text{2-Propanol}\\\text{(isopropyl alcohol)}}}{CH_3-\overset{\overset{\displaystyle OH}{|}}{\underset{\underset{\displaystyle H}{|}}{C}}-CH_3} \xrightarrow{[O]} \underset{\substack{\text{Propanone}\\\text{(dimethyl ketone; acetone)}}}{CH_3-\overset{\overset{\displaystyle O}{\|}}{C}-CH_3} + H_2O$$

Tertiary alcohols do not oxidize readily, because there are no hydrogen atoms on the carbon bonded to the —OH group. Because C—C bonds are usually too strong to oxidize, tertiary alcohols resist oxidation:

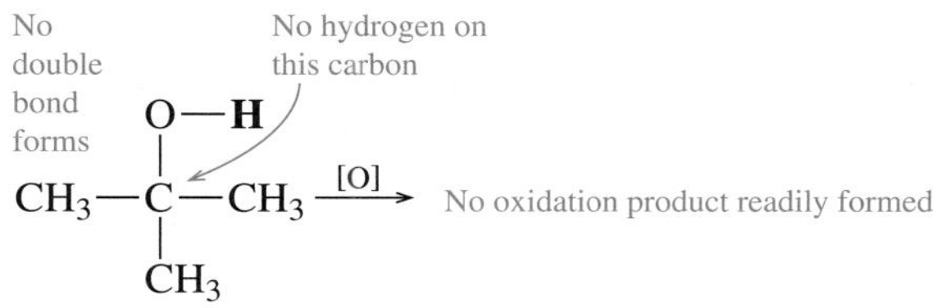

No double bond forms

No hydrogen on this carbon

$$\underset{\text{3° Alcohol}}{CH_3-\overset{\overset{\displaystyle O-H}{|}}{\underset{\underset{\displaystyle CH_3}{|}}{C}}-CH_3} \xrightarrow{[O]} \text{No oxidation product readily formed}$$

SAMPLE PROBLEM 13.9

## Oxidation of Alcohols

Draw the condensed structural formula of the aldehyde or ketone formed by the oxidation of each of the following:

**a.** 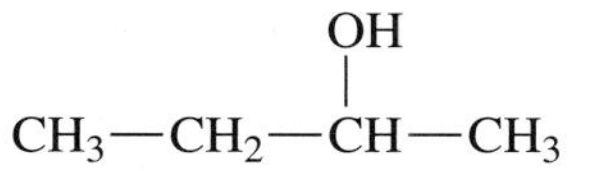 $CH_3-CH_2-\overset{\overset{\displaystyle OH}{|}}{CH}-CH_3$

**b.** $CH_3-CH_2-CH_2-OH$

SOLUTION

**a.** A secondary (2°) alcohol oxidizes to a ketone:

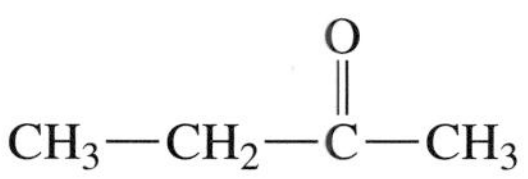

$$CH_3-CH_2-\overset{\overset{\displaystyle O}{\|}}{C}-CH_3$$

**b.** A primary (1°) alcohol oxidizes to an aldehyde:

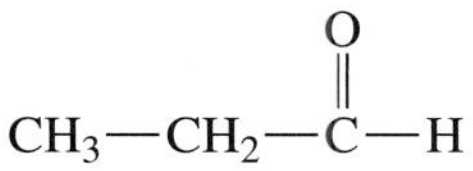

$$CH_3-CH_2-\overset{\overset{\displaystyle O}{\|}}{C}-H$$

STUDY CHECK

Draw the condensed structural formula of the product formed by the oxidation of 2-propanol.

MC™ CASE STUDY
Alcohol Toxicity

During vigorous exercise, lactic acid accumulates in the muscles and causes fatigue. When the activity level is decreased, oxygen enters the muscles. The secondary —OH group in lactic acid is oxidized to a ketone group in pyruvic acid, which eventually is oxidized to

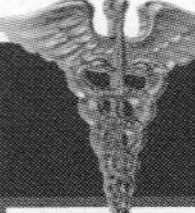

## HEALTH NOTE

### Oxidation of Alcohol in the Body

Ethanol is the most commonly abused drug in the United States. When ingested in small amounts, ethanol may produce a feeling of euphoria despite the fact that it is a depressant. In the liver, enzymes such as alcohol dehydrogenase oxidize ethanol to acetaldehyde, a substance that impairs mental and physical coordination. If the blood alcohol concentration exceeds 0.4%, coma or death may occur. Table 13.2 gives some of the typical behaviors exhibited at various levels of blood alcohol.

$$\underset{\text{Ethanol (ethyl alcohol)}}{CH_3{-}CH_2{-}OH} \xrightarrow{[O]} \underset{\text{Ethanal (acetaldehyde)}}{CH_3{-}\overset{\overset{\displaystyle O}{\|}}{C}{-}H} \xrightarrow{[O]} 2CO_2 + H_2O$$

The acetaldehyde produced from ethanol in the liver is further oxidized to acetic acid, which is eventually converted to carbon dioxide and water. However, the intermediate products of acetaldehyde and acetic acid can cause considerable damage while they are present within the cells of the liver.

**TABLE 13.2** Typical Behaviors Exhibited by a 150-lb Person Consuming Alcohol

| Number of Beers (12 oz) or Glasses of Wine (5 oz) in 1 hour | Blood Alcohol Level (% m/v) | Typical Behavior |
|---|---|---|
| 1 | 0.025 | Slightly dizzy, talkative |
| 2 | 0.05 | Euphoria, loud talking and laughing |
| 4 | 0.10 | Loss of inhibition, loss of coordination, drowsiness, legally drunk in most states |
| 8 | 0.20 | Intoxicated, quick to anger, exaggerated emotions |
| 12 | 0.30 | Unconscious |
| 16–20 | 0.40–0.50 | Coma and death |

A person weighing 150 lb requires about one hour to metabolize 10 ounces of beer. However, the rate of metabolism of ethanol varies between nondrinkers and drinkers. Typically, nondrinkers and social drinkers can metabolize 12–15 mg of ethanol/dL of blood in one hour, but an alcoholic can metabolize as much as 30 mg of ethanol/dL in one hour. Some effects of alcohol metabolism include an increase in liver lipids (fatty liver), an increase in serum triglycerides, gastritis, pancreatitis, ketoacidosis, alcoholic hepatitis, and psychological disturbances.

When alcohol is present in the blood, it evaporates through the lungs. Thus, the percentage of alcohol in the lungs can be used to calculate the blood alcohol concentration (BAC). Several devices are used to measure the BAC. When a Breathalyzer is used, a suspected drunk driver exhales through a mouthpiece into a solution containing the orange $Cr^{6+}$ ion. Any alcohol present in the exhaled air is oxidized, which reduces the orange $Cr^{6+}$ to a green $Cr^{3+}$:

$$\underset{\text{Ethanol}}{CH_3{-}CH_2{-}OH} + \underset{\text{Orange}}{Cr^{6+}} \xrightarrow{[O]} \underset{\text{Acetic acid}}{CH_3{-}\overset{\overset{\displaystyle O}{\|}}{C}{-}OH} + \underset{\text{Green}}{Cr^{3+}}$$

The Alcosensor uses an oxidation of alcohol in a fuel cell to generate an electric current that is measured. The Intoxilyzer measures the amount of light absorbed by the alcohol molecules.

Sometimes alcoholics are treated with a drug called Antabuse (disulfiram), which prevents the oxidation of acetaldehyde to acetic acid. As a result, acetaldehyde accumulates in the blood, which causes nausea, profuse sweating, headache, dizziness, vomiting, and respiratory difficulties. Because of these unpleasant side effects, the patient is less likely to use alcohol.

$CO_2$ and $H_2O$. The muscles in highly trained athletes are capable of taking up greater quantities of oxygen so that vigorous exercise can be maintained for longer periods of time.

Secondary alcohol → OH; Keto group → C=O

$$\underset{\text{Lactic acid}}{CH_3{-}\overset{\overset{\displaystyle OH}{|}}{CH}{-}\overset{\overset{\displaystyle O}{\|}}{C}{-}OH} \xrightarrow{\text{Lactic acid dehydrogenase}} \underset{\text{Pyruvic acid}}{CH_3{-}\overset{\overset{\displaystyle O}{\|}}{C}{-}\overset{\overset{\displaystyle O}{\|}}{C}{-}OH}$$

## Oxidation of Thiols

Thiols also undergo oxidation by a loss of hydrogen atoms from the —SH groups. The oxidized product is called a **disulfide**:

$$\underset{\text{Methanethiol}}{CH_3{-}S{-}H + H{-}S{-}CH_3} \xrightarrow{[O]} \underset{\text{Dimethyl disulfide}}{CH_3{-}S{-}S{-}CH_3} + H_2O$$

Much of the protein in the hair is cross-linked by disulfide bonds, which occur mostly between the thiol groups of the amino acid cysteine:

$$\text{Protein Chain}-CH_2-SH + HS-CH_2-\text{Protein Chain} \xrightarrow{[O]}$$

Cysteine side groups

$$\text{Protein Chain}-CH_2-S-S-CH_2-\text{Protein Chain} + H_2O$$

Disulfide bond

When a person is given a "perm," a reducing substance is used to break the disulfide bonds. While the hair is still wrapped around the curlers, an oxidizing substance is then applied that causes new disulfide bonds to form between different parts of the protein hair strands, which gives the hair a new shape.

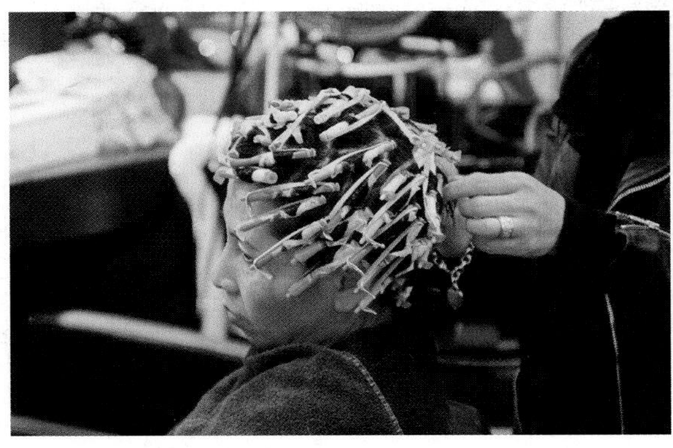

TUTORIAL
Oxidation of Thiols

## QUESTIONS AND PROBLEMS

### Reactions of Alcohols and Thiols

13.25 Draw the condensed structural formula of the alkene that is the major product from each of the following dehydration reactions:

a. $CH_3-CH_2-CH_2-CH_2-OH \xrightarrow[\text{Heat}]{H^+}$

b. 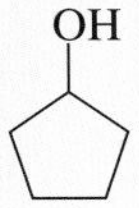 cyclopentane ring with OH $\xrightarrow[\text{Heat}]{H^+}$

c. 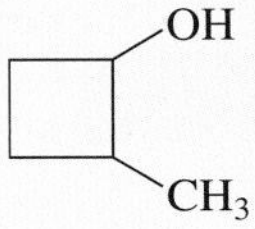 cyclobutane ring with OH and $CH_3$ on adjacent carbons $\xrightarrow[\text{Heat}]{H^+}$

d. $CH_3-CH_2-CH_2-\overset{OH}{\overset{|}{CH}}-CH_3 \xrightarrow[\text{Heat}]{H^+}$

13.26 Draw the condensed structural formula of the alkene that is the major product from each of the following dehydration reactions:

a. $CH_3-\overset{CH_3}{\overset{|}{CH}}-CH_2-OH \xrightarrow[\text{Heat}]{H^+}$

b. $CH_3-\overset{OH}{\overset{|}{CH}}-\overset{CH_3}{\overset{|}{CH}}-CH_2-CH_3 \xrightarrow[\text{Heat}]{H^+}$

c. 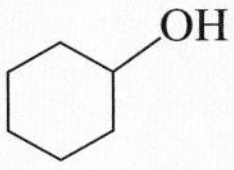 cyclohexane ring with OH $\xrightarrow[\text{Heat}]{H^+}$

d. 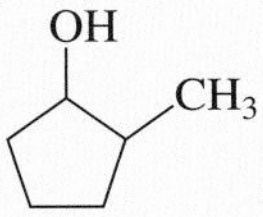 cyclopentane ring with OH and $CH_3$ on adjacent carbons $\xrightarrow[\text{Heat}]{H^+}$

13.27 Draw the condensed structural formula of the ether produced by each of the following reactions:

a. $2CH_3-OH \xrightarrow[\text{Heat}]{H^+}$

b. $2CH_3-CH_2-CH_2-OH \xrightarrow[\text{Heat}]{H^+}$

13.28 Draw the condensed structural formula of the ether produced by each of the following reactions:

a. $2CH_3-CH_2-OH \xrightarrow[\text{Heat}]{H^+}$

b. $2CH_3-\overset{CH_3}{\overset{|}{CH}}-CH_2-OH \xrightarrow[\text{Heat}]{H^+}$

13.29 What alcohol(s) could be used to produce each of the following compounds?

a. $CH_2{=}CH_2$

b. $CH_3-O-CH_2-CH_3$

c. 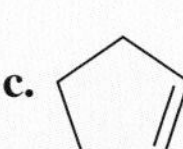

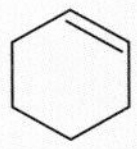

13.30 What alcohol(s) could be used to produce each of the following compounds?

a. $CH_3-CH_2-O-CH_2-CH_3$

b. $CH_3-\overset{CH_3}{\overset{|}{C}}{=}CH-CH_3$

c. 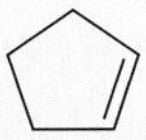 cyclopentene ring

13.31 Draw the condensed structural formula of the aldehyde or ketone produced when each of the following alcohols is oxidized [O] (if no reaction, write *none*):

a. $CH_3-CH_2-CH_2-CH_2-CH_2-OH$

b. $CH_3-CH_2-\overset{OH}{\overset{|}{CH}}-CH_3$

c. 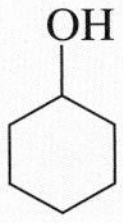 cyclohexane ring with OH

d. $CH_3-\overset{OH}{\overset{|}{CH}}-CH_2-\overset{CH_3}{\overset{|}{CH}}-CH_3$

e. $CH_3-\overset{CH_3}{\overset{|}{CH}}-CH_2-CH_2-OH$

13.32 Draw the condensed structural formula of the aldehyde or ketone produced when each of the following alcohols is oxidized [O] (if no reaction, write *none*):

a. 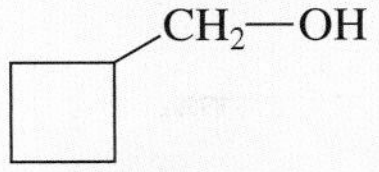 cyclobutane ring with $CH_2-OH$

b. $CH_3-\overset{CH_3}{\overset{|}{CH}}-CH_2-\underset{CH_3}{\underset{|}{CH}}-OH$

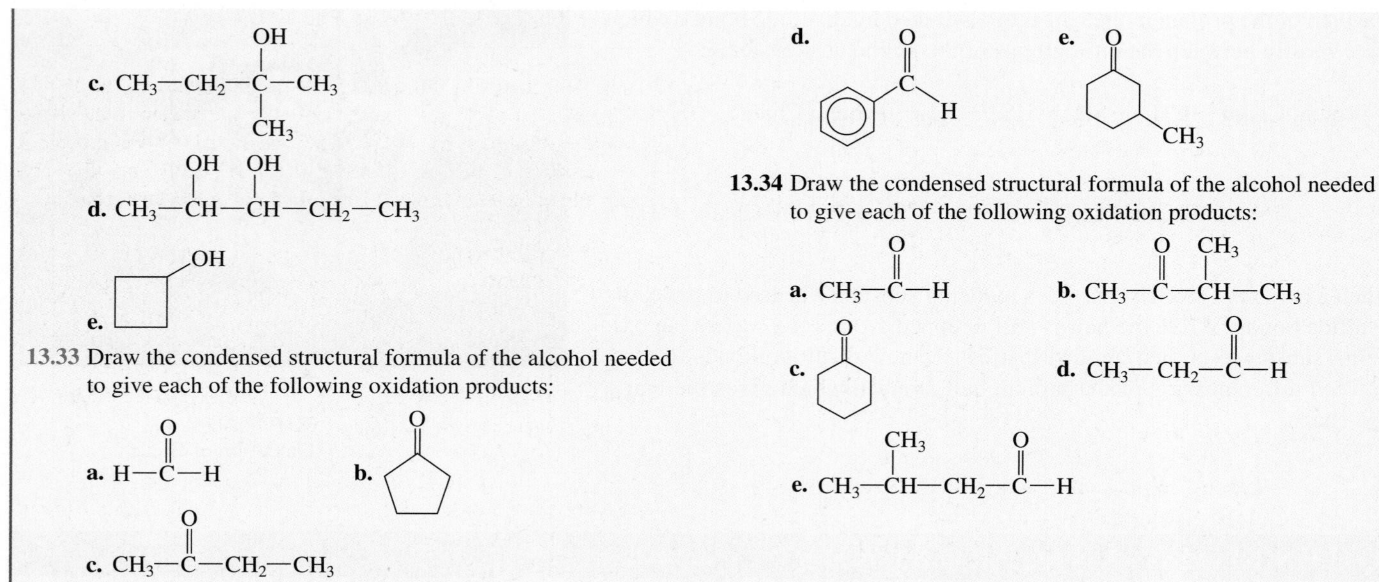

**13.33** Draw the condensed structural formula of the alcohol needed to give each of the following oxidation products:

**13.34** Draw the condensed structural formula of the alcohol needed to give each of the following oxidation products:

## CONCEPT MAP

**ALCOHOLS, PHENOLS, THIOLS, AND ETHERS**

with

- **Carbon–sulfur single bonds**
  - are
  - **Thiols**
    - that form
    - **Disulfides**
- **Carbon–oxygen single bonds**
  - are the
  - **Alcohols**
    - undergo
    - **Reactions**
      - such as
      - **Dehydration**
        - to form
        - **Alkenes**
        - **Ethers**
      - **Oxidation of**
        - 1° forms
        - **Aldehydes**
          - oxidize to
          - **Carboxylic acids**
        - 2° forms
        - **Ketones**
  - **Phenols**
  - **Ethers**

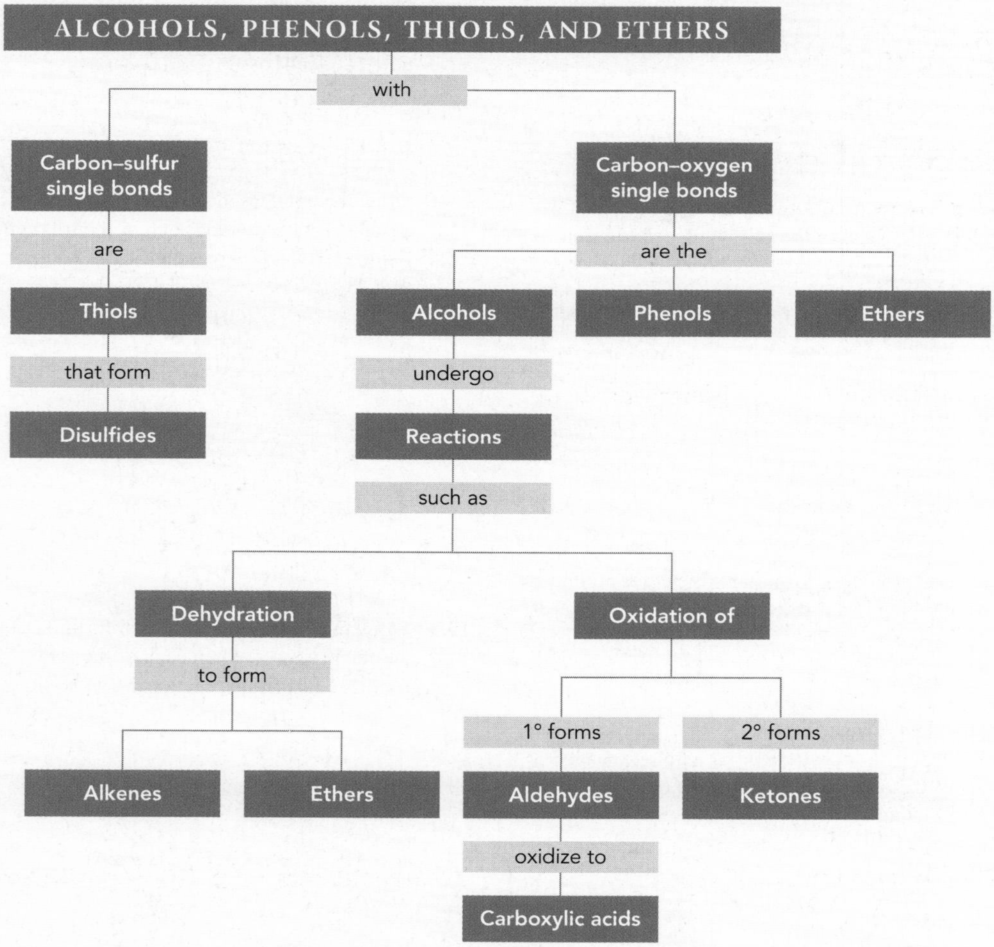

# CHAPTER REVIEW

## 13.1 Alcohols, Phenols, and Thiols

**LEARNING GOAL:** *Give IUPAC and common names for alcohols, phenols, and thiols; draw their condensed structural formulas. Classify alcohols as primary, secondary, or tertiary.*

The functional group of an alcohol is the hydroxyl group —OH bonded to a carbon chain. In a phenol, the hydroxyl group is bonded to an aromatic ring. In thiols, the functional group is —SH, which is analogous to the —OH group of alcohols. Alcohols are classified according to the number of alkyl or aromatic groups bonded to the carbon that holds the —OH. In a primary (1°) alcohol, one group is attached to the hydroxyl carbon. In a secondary (2°) alcohol, two groups are attached. In a tertiary (3°) alcohol, there are three groups bonded to the hydroxyl carbon. In the IUPAC system, the names of alcohols have *ol* endings, and the location of the —OH group is given by numbering the carbon chain. Simple alcohols are generally named by their common names with the alkyl name preceding the term *alcohol*. A cyclic alcohol is named as a cycloalkanol. An aromatic alcohol is named as a phenol.

## 13.2 Ethers

**LEARNING GOAL:** *Give the IUPAC and common names of ethers; draw the condensed structural formula.*

In an ether, an oxygen atom is connected by single bonds to two alkyl or aromatic groups. In the common names of ethers, the alkyl groups are listed alphabetically followed by the name *ether*. In the IUPAC name, the smaller alkyl group with the oxygen is named as an alkoxy group and is attached to the longer alkane chain, which is numbered to give the location of the alkoxy group. Some alcohols and ethers are isomers, which means that they have the same molecular formulas.

## 13.3 Physical Properties of Alcohols, Phenols, and Ethers

**LEARNING GOAL:** *Describe some physical properties of alcohols, phenols, and ethers.*

The —OH group allows alcohols to hydrogen bond, which causes alcohols to have higher boiling points than alkanes and ethers of similar mass. Short-chain alcohols and ethers can hydrogen bond with water, which makes them soluble.

## 13.4 Reactions of Alcohols and Thiols

**LEARNING GOAL:** *Write equations for the combustion, dehydration, and oxidation of alcohols and thiols.*

At high temperatures, alcohols dehydrate in the presence of an acid to yield alkenes. At lower temperatures, two molecules of alcohol lose —H and —OH to produce an ether. Primary alcohols are oxidized to aldehydes, which can oxidize further to carboxylic acids. Secondary alcohols are oxidized to ketones. Tertiary alcohols do not oxidize. Thiols undergo oxidation to form disulfides.

# SUMMARY OF NAMING

| Structure | Family | IUPAC Name | Common Name |
|---|---|---|---|
| $CH_3—\mathbf{OH}$ | Alcohol | Methanol | Methyl alcohol |
| $C_6H_5—\mathbf{OH}$ (benzene ring—OH) | Phenol | Phenol | Phenol |
| $CH_3—\mathbf{SH}$ | Thiol | Methanethiol | |
| $CH_3—\mathbf{O}—CH_3$ | Ether | Methoxymethane | Dimethyl ether |
| (five-membered ring with O) | Cyclic ether | Furan | |
| $CH_3—\mathbf{S}—\mathbf{S}—CH_3$ | Disulfide | Dimethyldisulfide | |

# SUMMARY OF REACTIONS

## COMBUSTION OF ALCOHOLS

$$CH_3—CH_2—OH + 3O_2 \longrightarrow 2CO_2 + 3H_2O$$

Ethanol, Oxygen, Carbon dioxide, Water

## DEHYDRATION OF ALCOHOLS TO FORM ALKENES

$$CH_3—CH_2—CH_2—OH \xrightarrow[\text{Heat}]{H^+} CH_3—CH{=}CH_2 + H_2O$$

1-Propanol → Propene

## FORMATION OF ETHERS

$$CH_3—OH + HO—CH_3 \xrightarrow[\text{Heat}]{H^+} CH_3—O—CH_3 + H_2O$$

Methanol → Dimethyl ether

## OXIDATION OF PRIMARY ALCOHOLS TO FORM ALDEHYDES

$$CH_3—CH_2(OH) \xrightarrow{[O]} CH_3—C(=O)—H + H_2O$$

Ethanol → Acetaldehyde

## OXIDATION OF SECONDARY ALCOHOLS TO FORM KETONES

$$CH_3—CH(OH)—CH_3 \xrightarrow{[O]} CH_3—C(=O)—CH_3 + H_2O$$

2-Propanol → Propanone

### OXIDATION OF THIOLS TO FORM DISULFIDES

$$CH_3—S—H + H—S—CH_3 \xrightarrow{[O]} CH_3—S—S—CH_3 + H_2O$$

Methanethiol Dimethyl disulfide

### OXIDATION OF ALDEHYDES TO CARBOXYLIC ACIDS

$$CH_3—\overset{O}{\overset{\|}{C}}—H \xrightarrow{[O]} CH_3—\overset{O}{\overset{\|}{C}}—OH$$

Acetaldehyde Acetic acid

## KEY TERMS

**alcohol** An organic compound that contains the hydroxyl (—OH) functional group attached to a carbon chain.

**cyclic ether** A compound that contains an oxygen atom in a carbon ring.

**dehydration** A reaction that removes water from an alcohol in the presence of an acid to form alkenes at high temperature, or ethers at lower temperatures.

**disulfide** A compound formed from thiols; disulfides contain the —S—S— functional group.

**ether** An organic compound in which an oxygen atom is bonded to two alkyl or two aromatic groups, or a mix of the two.

**hydroxyl group** The —OH functional group.

**oxidation** The loss of two hydrogen atoms from a reactant to give a more oxidized compound, e.g., primary alcohols oxidize to aldehydes, secondary alcohols oxidize to ketones. An oxidation can also be the addition of an oxygen atom as in the oxidation of aldehydes to carboxylic acids.

**phenol** An organic compound that has an —OH group attached to a benzene ring.

**primary (1°) alcohol** An alcohol that has one alkyl group bonded to the alcohol carbon atom.

**Saytzeff's rule** In the dehydration of an alcohol, hydrogen is removed from the carbon that already has the smaller number of hydrogen atoms to form an alkene.

**secondary (2°) alcohol** An alcohol that has two alkyl groups bonded to the carbon atom with the —OH group.

**tertiary (3°) alcohol** An alcohol that has three alkyl groups bonded to the carbon atom with the —OH.

**thiol** An organic compound that contains a thiol group (—SH).

## UNDERSTANDING THE CONCEPTS

**13.35** Urushiol is a substance in poison ivy and poison oak that causes itching and blistering of the skin. Identify the functional groups in urushiol:

(Structure: benzene ring with OH, OH, and $CH_2(CH_2)_4CH_3$ substituents)

**13.36** BHA is an antioxidant used as a preservative in foods, such as baked goods, butter, meats, and snack foods. Identify the functional groups in BHA:

(Structure: benzene ring with OH, $C(CH_3)_3$, and O—$CH_3$ substituents)

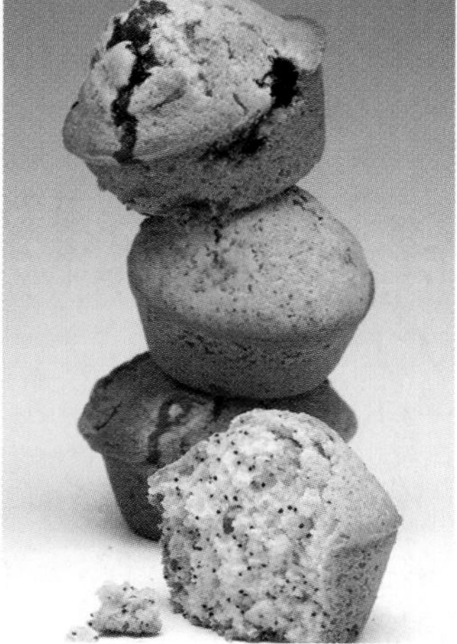

**13.37** Menthol gives a peppermint taste and odor used in candy and throat lozenges. Identify the functional groups in menthol:

(Structure: cyclohexane ring with $CH_3$, OH, and $CH(CH_3)_2$ substituents)

**13.38** Vanillin is a flavoring obtained from the seeds of the vanilla bean. Identify the functional groups in vanillin:

(Structure: benzene ring with C(=O)—H, O—$CH_3$, and OH substituents)

# ADDITIONAL QUESTIONS AND PROBLEMS

*For instructor-assigned homework, go to* ***www.masteringchemistry.com.***

**13.39** Classify each of the following as a primary (1°), secondary (2°), or tertiary alcohol (3°):

**a.** 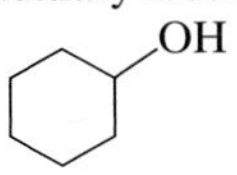 cyclohexane ring with OH
**b.** 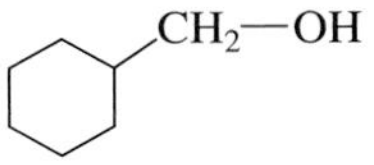 cyclohexane ring with $CH_2—OH$

**c.** 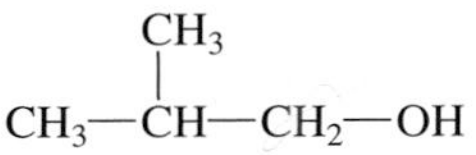 $CH_3—CH(CH_3)—CH_2—OH$
**d.** 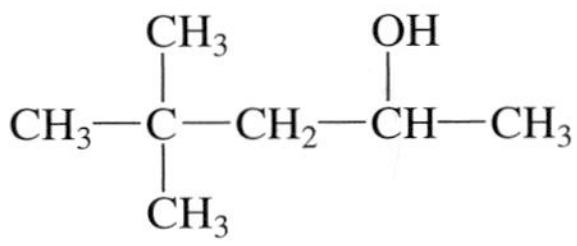 $CH_3—C(CH_3)_2—CH_2—CH(OH)—CH_3$

**e.** $HO—CH_2—CH_2—CH_3$

**f.** 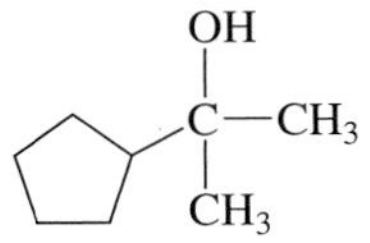 cyclopentane ring with $C(OH)(CH_3)—CH_3$

**13.40** Classify each of the following as a primary (1°), secondary (2°), or tertiary alcohol (3°):

**a.** 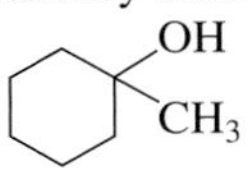 cyclohexane ring with OH and $CH_3$ on the same carbon
**b.** 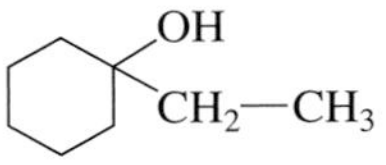 cyclohexane ring with OH and $CH_2—CH_3$ on the same carbon

**c.** 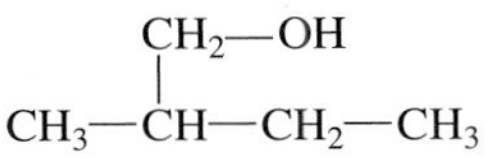 $CH_3—CH(CH_2—OH)—CH_2—CH_3$
**d.** 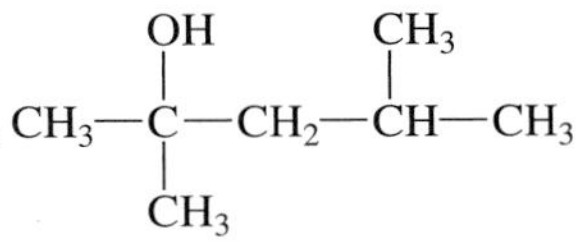 $CH_3—C(OH)(CH_3)—CH_2—CH(CH_3)—CH_3$

**e.** $CH_3—CH_2—CH_2—CH_2—OH$

**f.** 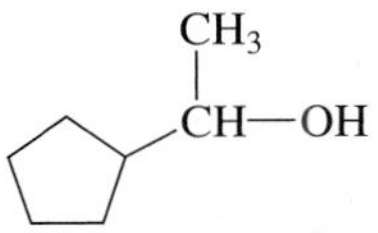 cyclopentane ring with $CH(CH_3)—OH$

**13.41** Identify each of the following as an alcohol, a phenol, an ether, a cyclic ether, or a thiol:

**a.** 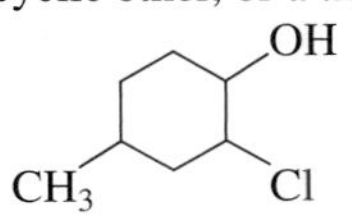 cyclohexane ring with OH, $CH_3$, and Cl
**b.** 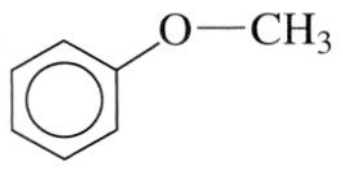 benzene ring with $O—CH_3$

**c.** 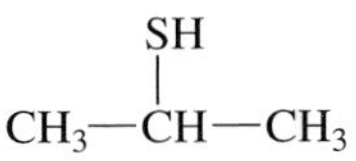 $CH_3—CH(SH)—CH_3$
**d.** 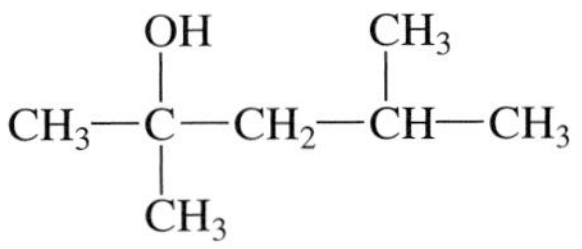 $CH_3—C(OH)(CH_3)—CH_2—CH(CH_3)—CH_3$

**e.** $CH_3—CH_2—CH_2—O—CH_3$
**f.** 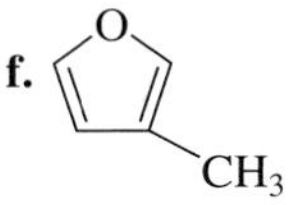 furan ring with $CH_3$

**g.** 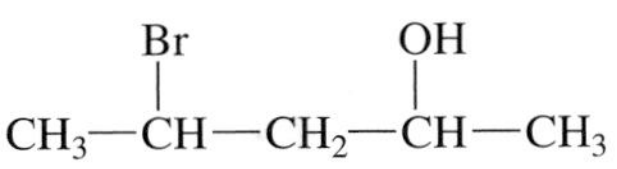 $CH_3—CH(Br)—CH_2—CH(OH)—CH_3$
**h.** 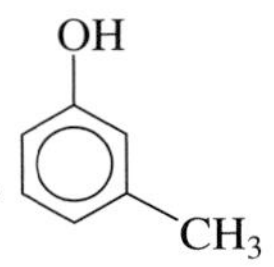 benzene ring with OH and $CH_3$ (meta)

**13.42** Identify each of the following as an alcohol, a phenol, an ether, a cyclic ether, or a thiol:

**a.**  benzene ring with OH and Cl (para)
**b.** $CH_3—CH_2—CH_2—SH$

**c.** 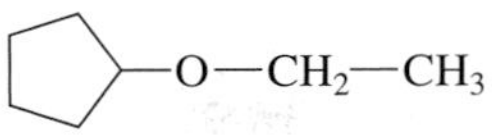 cyclopentane ring with $O—CH_2—CH_3$
**d.** 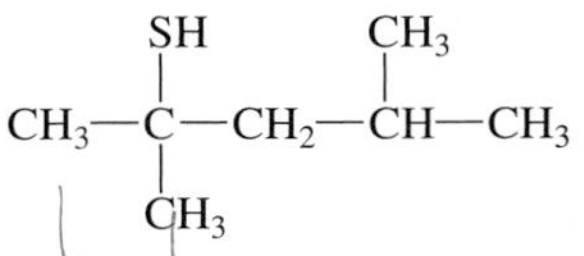 $CH_3—C(SH)(CH_3)—CH_2—CH(CH_3)—CH_3$

**e.** 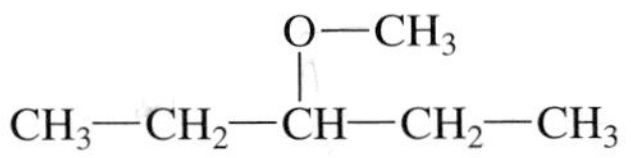 $CH_3—CH_2—CH(O—CH_3)—CH_2—CH_3$
**f.** 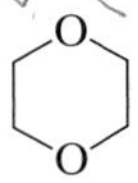 six-membered ring with two O atoms (1,4-dioxane)

**g.** 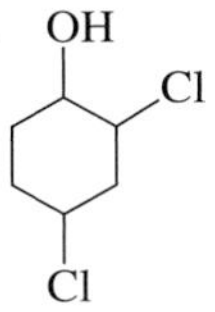 cyclohexane ring with OH, Cl, and Cl
**h.** 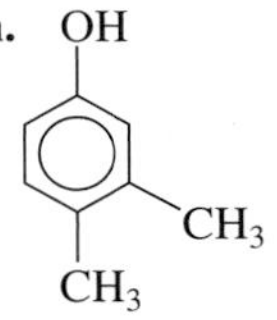 benzene ring with OH, $CH_3$, and $CH_3$

**13.43** Give the IUPAC and common names (if any) for each of the compounds in problem 13.41.

**13.44** Give the IUPAC and common names (if any) for each of the compounds in problem 13.42.

**13.45** Draw the condensed structural formula of each of the following compounds:

**a.** 3-methylcyclopentanol
**b.** *p*-chlorophenol
**c.** 2-methyl-3-pentanol
**d.** phenyl ethyl ether
**e.** 3-pentanethiol
**f.** *ortho*-cresol
**g.** 2,4-dibromophenol

**13.46** Draw the condensed structural formula of each of the following compounds:

**a.** 3-methoxypentane
**b.** *meta*-chlorophenol
**c.** 2,3-pentanediol
**d.** methyl propyl ether
**e.** methanethiol
**f.** 3-methyl-2-butanol
**g.** 3,4-dichlorocyclohexanol

**13.47** Draw the condensed structural formulas of all the alcohols with a molecular formula $C_4H_{10}O$.

**13.48** Draw the condensed structural formulas of all the ethers with a molecular formula $C_5H_{12}O$.

**13.49** Which compound in each of the following pairs would you expect to have the higher boiling point? Explain.

**a.** butane or 1-propanol
**b.** 1-propanol or ethyl methyl ether
**c.** ethanol or 1-butanol

**13.50** Which compound in each of the following pairs would you expect to have the higher boiling point? Explain.

**a.** propane or ethyl alcohol
**b.** 2-propanol or 2-pentanol
**c.** diethyl ether or 1-butanol

**13.51** Explain why each of the following compounds would be soluble or insoluble in water:

**a.** 2-propanol **b.** dimethyl ether **c.** 1-hexanol

**13.52** Explain why each of the following compounds would be soluble or insoluble in water:

**a.** glycerol **b.** butane **c.** 1,3-hexanediol

**13.53** Draw the condensed structural formula for the alkene (major product), aldehyde, ether, ketone, or *none* produced in each of the following:

**a.** $CH_3—CH_2—CH_2—OH \xrightarrow[\text{Heat}]{H^+}$

**b.** $CH_3—CH_2—CH_2—OH \xrightarrow{[O]}$

c. $CH_3-CH_2-CH(OH)-CH_3 \xrightarrow[\text{Heat}]{H^+}$

d. $CH_3-CH_2-CH(OH)-CH_3 \xrightarrow{[O]}$

e. $2CH_3-CH_2-CH_2-OH \xrightarrow{H^+}$

f. 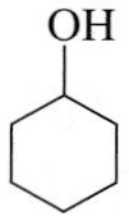 Cyclohexanol (OH on cyclohexane ring) $\xrightarrow[\text{Heat}]{H^+}$

g. 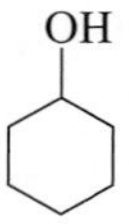 Cyclohexanol (OH on cyclohexane ring) $\xrightarrow{[O]}$

**13.54** Draw the condensed structural formula for the alkene (major product), aldehyde, ether, ketone, or *none* produced in each of the following:

a. $CH_3-CH(CH_3)-CH_2-OH \xrightarrow[\text{Heat}]{H^+}$

b. $CH_3-CH(CH_3)-CH(OH)-CH_3 \xrightarrow[\text{Heat}]{H^+}$

c. $CH_3-CH(CH_3)-CH(OH)-CH_3 \xrightarrow{[O]}$

d. 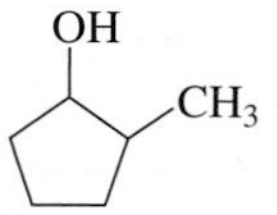 2-Methylcyclopentanol (OH and $CH_3$ on adjacent ring carbons) $\xrightarrow[\text{Heat}]{H^+}$

e. 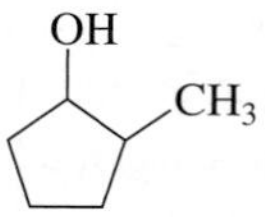 2-Methylcyclopentanol (OH and $CH_3$ on adjacent ring carbons) $\xrightarrow{[O]}$

f. $2CH_3-CH_2-OH \xrightarrow[\text{Heat}]{H^+}$

g. $CH_3-CH_2-CH_2-CH(OH)-CH_3 \xrightarrow[\text{Heat}]{H^+}$

**13.55** Sometimes several steps are needed to prepare a compound. Using a combination of the reactions we have studied, indicate how you might prepare the following from the starting substance given. For example, 2-propanol could be prepared from 1-propanol by first dehydrating the alcohol to give propene and then hydrating it again to give 2-propanol according to Markovnikov's rule, as follows:

$$CH_3-CH_2-CH_2-OH \xrightarrow[\text{Heat}]{H^+} CH_3-CH=CH_2 + H_2O$$

$$\xrightarrow{H^+} CH_3-CH(OH)-CH_3$$

2-Propanol

a. Prepare 2-chloropropane from 1-propanol.

b. Prepare 2-methylpropane from 2-methyl-2-propanol.

c. Prepare $CH_3-C(=O)-CH_3$ from 1-propanol.

**13.56** As in problem 13.55, indicate how you might prepare the following from the starting substance given:

a. Prepare 1-pentene from 1-pentanol.

b. Prepare chlorocyclohexane from cyclohexanol.

c. Prepare 1,2-dibromobutane from 1-butanol.

**13.57** Identify the functional groups in the following molecule:

[Structure: steroid skeleton with $CH_3$ groups, OH, and C=O; labels: $CH_3$, $CH_3$, OH, O]

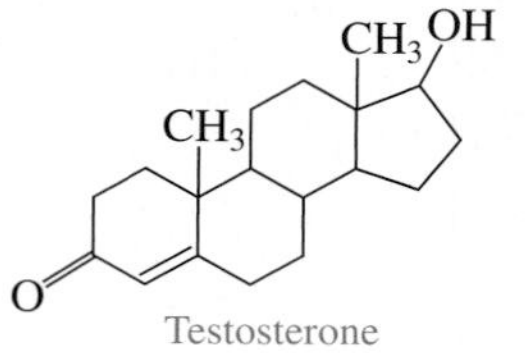

Testosterone

**13.58** Identify the functional groups in the following molecule:

[Structure: labels: $CH_3$, OH, $CH_3$, O, $CH_3$, $CH_2CH_2CH_2CH_2CH_3$]

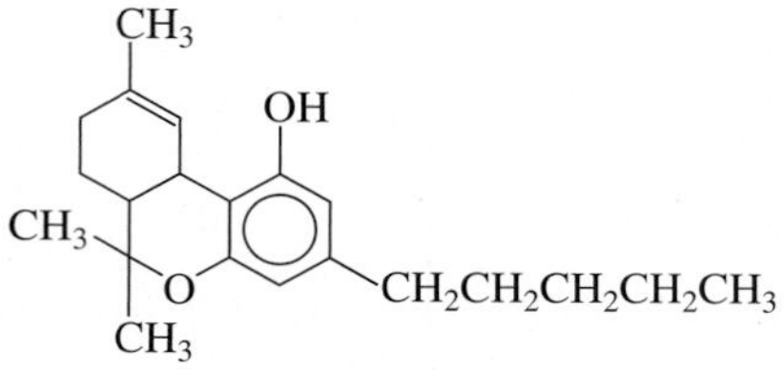

Tetrahydrocannabinol (THC)

**13.59** Hexylresorcinol, an antiseptic ingredient used in mouthwashes and throat lozenges, has the IUPAC name of 4-hexyl-1,3-benzenediol. Draw its condensed structural formula.

**13.60** Menthol, which has a minty flavor, is used in throat sprays and lozenges. Thymol is used as a topical antiseptic to destroy mold. For each, give their IUPAC names. What is similar and what is different about their structures?

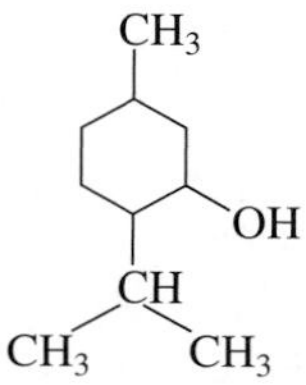

[Structures: cyclohexane ring (Menthol) and benzene ring (Thymol), each with $CH_3$, OH, and $CH(CH_3)_2$ substituents]

Menthol 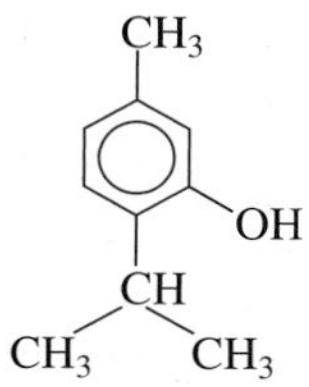 Thymol

## CHALLENGE QUESTIONS

**13.61** Draw the condensed structural formula for each of the following naturally occurring compounds:

a. 2,5-dichlorophenol, a defense pheromone of a grasshopper.

b. Skunk scent, a mixture of 3-methyl-1-butanethiol and *trans*-2-butene-1-thiol.

c. Pentachlorophenol, a wood preservative.

**13.62** Dimethyl ether and ethyl alcohol both have the molecular formula $C_2H_6O$. One has a boiling point of −24 °C, and the other, 79 °C. Draw the condensed structural formula of each compound. Decide which boiling point goes with which compound and explain.

**13.63** A compound with the formula $C_4H_8O$ is synthesized from 2-methyl-1-propanol and oxidizes easily to give a carboxylic acid. Draw the condensed structural formula of the compound.

**13.64** Methyl *tert*-butyl ether (MTBE), or 2-methoxy-2-methylpropane, has been used as a fuel additive for gasoline to boost the octane rating and to reduce CO emissions.

**a.** If fuel mixtures are required to contain 2.7% oxygen by mass, how many grams of MTBE must be present in each 100. g of gasoline?
**b.** How many liters of MTBE would be in 1.0 L of fuel if the density of both gasoline and MTBE is 0.740 g/mL?
**c.** Write the equation for the complete combustion of MTBE.
**d.** How many liters of air containing 21% (v/v) $O_2$ are required at STP to completely react (combust) 1.00 L of liquid MTBE?

**13.65** Draw the condensed structural formulas and give the IUPAC names of all the alcohols that have the formula $C_5H_{12}O$.

# ANSWERS

## ANSWERS TO STUDY CHECKS

**13.1** 3-chloro-1-butanol

**13.2** $CH_3—CH_2—SH$

**13.3** ethyl phenyl ether

**13.4** 1-butanol, 2-butanol, 1-methoxypropane, ethoxyethane

**13.5** Both are unsaturated cyclic ethers, but furan has five atoms in the ring and pyran has six atoms.

**13.6** Ethanol molecules can hydrogen bond with each other, but ether molecules cannot. Thus, a higher temperature is required to break the hydrogen bonds between ethanol molecules.

**13.7** cyclopentene

**13.8** 2-methyl-1-propanol, 2-methyl-2-propanol

**13.9** $CH_3—\overset{\overset{\large O}{\|}}{C}—CH_3$

## ANSWERS TO SELECTED QUESTIONS AND PROBLEMS

**13.1** **a.** 1° **b.** 1° **c.** 3° **d.** 2°

**13.3** **a.** ethanol **b.** 2-butanol
**c.** 2-pentanol **d.** 4-methylcyclohexanol

**13.5** **a.** $CH_3—CH_2—CH_2—OH$
**b.** $CH_3—OH$
**c.** $CH_3—CH_2—\overset{\overset{\large OH}{|}}{CH}—CH_2—CH_3$
**d.** $CH_3—\underset{\underset{\large CH_3}{|}}{\overset{\overset{\large OH}{|}}{C}}—CH_2—CH_3$
**e.** cyclohexane ring with OH

**13.7** **a.** phenol
**b.** 2-bromophenol, *o*-bromophenol
**c.** 3,5-dichlorophenol
**d.** 3-bromophenol, *m*-bromophenol

**13.9** **a.** benzene ring with OH and Br (meta)
**b.** benzene ring with OH and Cl (para)
**c.** benzene ring with OH, Cl, Cl
**d.** benzene ring with OH and a phenyl group

**13.11** **a.** methanethiol **b.** 2-propanethiol
**c.** 2,3-dimethyl-1-butanethiol **d.** cyclobutanethiol

**13.13** **a.** methoxyethane, ethyl methyl ether
**b.** methoxycyclohexane, cyclohexyl methyl ether
**c.** ethoxycyclobutane, cyclobutyl ethyl ether
**d.** 1-methoxypropane, methyl propyl ether

**13.15** **a.** $CH_3—CH_2—O—CH_2—CH_2—CH_3$
**b.** $CH_3—CH_2—O—$ cyclopropane ring
**c.** cyclopentane ring with $O—CH_3$
**d.** $CH_3—CH_2—O—CH_2—\overset{\overset{\large CH_3}{|}}{CH}—CH_2—CH_3$
**e.** $CH_3—\overset{\overset{\large O—CH_3}{|}}{CH}—\underset{\underset{\large O—CH_3}{|}}{CH}—CH_2—CH_3$

**13.17 a.** isomers ($C_5H_{12}O$) **b.** different compounds
**c.** isomers ($C_5H_{12}O$)

**13.19 a.** tetrahydrofuran **b.** 3-methylfuran
**c.** 5-methyl-1,3-dioxane

**13.21 a.** methanol **b.** 1-butanol **c.** 1-butanol

**13.23 a.** yes, hydrogen bonding
**b.** yes, hydrogen bonding
**c.** no, long carbon chain diminishes effect of —OH group
**d.** yes (slightly), hydrogen bonding

**13.25 a.** $CH_3—CH_2—CH=CH_2$ **b.** (cyclopentene)
**c.** (1-methylcyclobutene, $CH_3$) **d.** $CH_3—CH_2—CH=CH—CH_3$

**13.27 a.** $CH_3—O—CH_3$
**b.** $CH_3—CH_2—CH_2—O—CH_2—CH_2—CH_3$

**13.29 a.** $CH_3—CH_2—OH$ **b.** $CH_3—OH + CH_3—CH_2—OH$
**c.** (cyclohexanol, OH)

**13.31 a.** $CH_3—CH_2—CH_2—CH_2—C(=O)—H$
**b.** $CH_3—CH_2—C(=O)—CH_3$ **c.** (cyclohexanone, O)
**d.** $CH_3—C(=O)—CH_2—CH(CH_3)—CH_3$
**e.** $CH_3—CH(CH_3)—CH_2—C(=O)—H$

**13.33 a.** $CH_3—OH$ **b.** (cyclopentanol, OH)
**c.** $CH_3—CH_2—CH(OH)—CH_3$ **d.** (benzene ring with $CH_2—OH$)
**e.** (cyclohexane ring with OH and $CH_3$)

**13.35** phenol, alcohol

**13.37** cycloalkane, alcohol

**13.39 a.** 2° **b.** 1° **c.** 1°
**d.** 2° **e.** 1° **f.** 3°

**13.41 a.** alcohol **b.** ether **c.** thiol
**d.** alcohol **e.** ether **f.** cyclic ether
**g.** alcohol **h.** phenol

**13.43 a.** 2-chloro-4-methylcyclohexanol
**b.** methoxybenzene, methyl phenyl ether
**c.** 2-propanethiol
**d.** 2,4-dimethyl-2-pentanol
**e.** 1-methoxypropane, methyl propyl ether
**f.** 3-methylfuran
**g.** 4-bromo-2-pentanol
**h.** *meta*-cresol, 3-methylphenol

**13.45 a.** (cyclopentane ring with OH and $CH_3$) **b.** (benzene ring with OH and Cl, para)
**c.** $CH_3—CH(CH_3)—CH(OH)—CH_2—CH_3$ **d.** (benzene ring)$—O—CH_2—CH_3$
**e.** $CH_3—CH_2—CH(SH)—CH_2—CH_3$ **f.** (benzene ring with $CH_3$ and OH, ortho)
**g.** (benzene ring with OH, Br, Br)

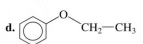

**13.47** $CH_3—CH_2—CH_2—CH_2—OH$
$CH_3—CH(CH_3)—CH_2—OH$
$CH_3—CH(OH)—CH_2—CH_3$
$CH_3—C(OH)(CH_3)—CH_3$

**13.49 a.** 1-propanol, hydrogen bonding
**b.** 1-propanol, hydrogen bonding
**c.** 1-butanol, higher molar mass

**13.51 a.** soluble, hydrogen bonding
**b.** soluble, hydrogen bonding
**c.** insoluble, long carbon chain diminishes effect of polar —OH on hydrogen bonding

**13.53 a.** $CH_3—CH=CH_2$ **b.** $CH_3—CH_2—C(=O)—H$
**c.** $CH_3—CH=CH—CH_3$ **d.** $CH_3—CH_2—C(=O)—CH_3$
**e.** $CH_3—CH_2—CH_2—O—CH_2—CH_2—CH_3$
**f.** (cyclohexene) **g.** (cyclohexanone, O)

**13.55 a.** $CH_3—CH_2—CH_2—OH \xrightarrow[\text{Heat}]{H^+}$
$CH_3—CH=CH_2 + HCl \longrightarrow CH_3—CH(Cl)—CH_3$

**b.** 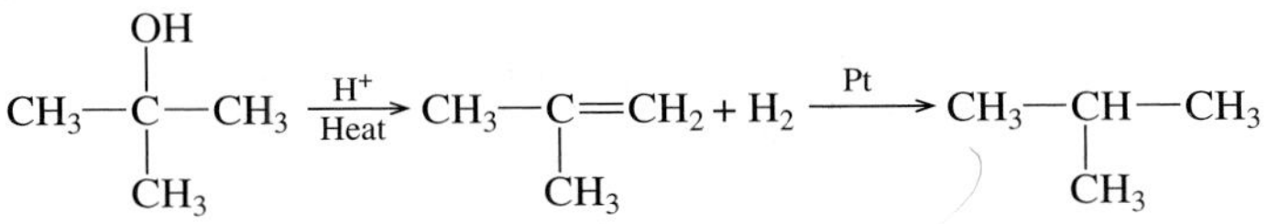 $CH_3-\underset{CH_3}{\overset{OH}{C}}-CH_3 \xrightarrow[Heat]{H^+} CH_3-\underset{CH_3}{C}=CH_2 + H_2 \xrightarrow{Pt} CH_3-\underset{CH_3}{CH}-CH_3$

**c.** $CH_3-CH_2-CH_2-OH \xrightarrow[Heat]{H^+} CH_3-CH=CH_2 + H_2O \xrightarrow[Heat]{H^+} CH_3-\overset{OH}{CH}-CH_3 \xrightarrow{[O]} CH_3-\overset{O}{\overset{\|}{C}}-CH_3$

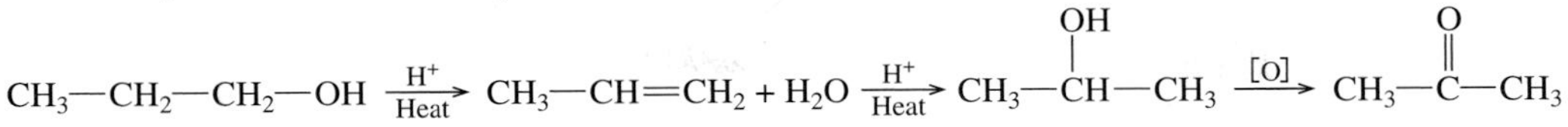

**13.57** cycloalkane, cycloalkene, ketone, and alcohol functional groups

**13.59** Benzene ring with OH; OH on adjacent (ortho) position; $CH_2-CH_2-CH_2-CH_2-CH_2-CH_3$ para to the first OH (4-hexylresorcinol)

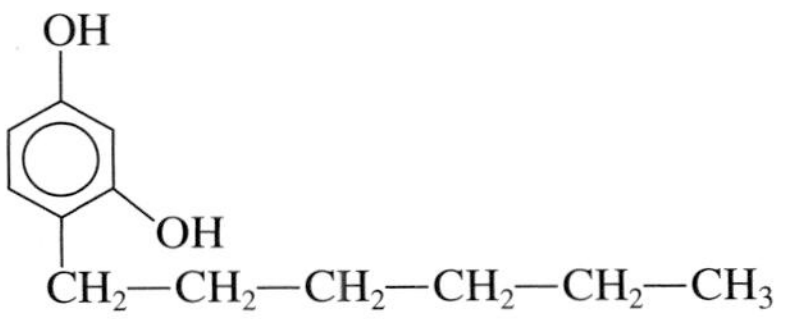

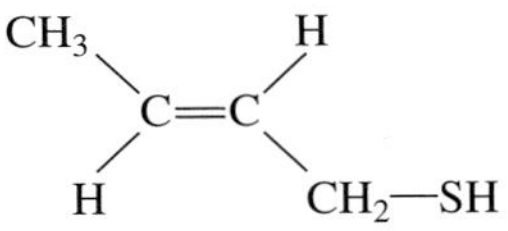

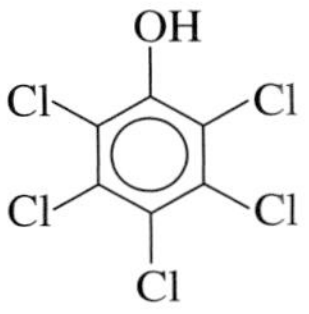

**13.61 a.** 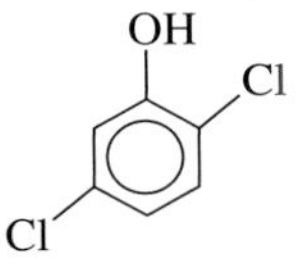 Benzene ring with OH, Cl ortho to OH, and Cl at the 5-position (2,5-dichlorophenol)

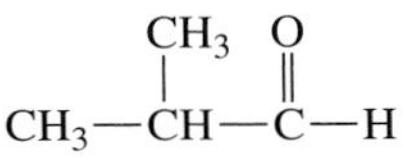

**b.** 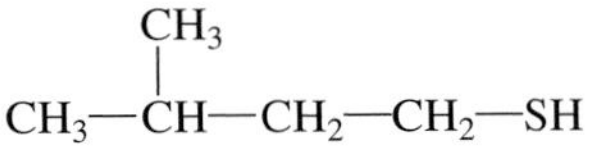 $CH_3-\overset{CH_3}{CH}-CH_2-CH_2-SH$

$\overset{CH_3}{\underset{H}{}}C=C\overset{H}{\underset{CH_2-SH}{}}$ (CH₃ and H on one carbon; H and $CH_2-SH$ on the other, CH₃ and $CH_2-SH$ trans)

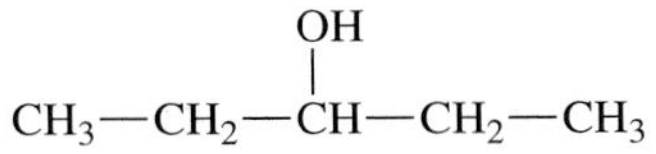

**c.** Benzene ring with OH and five Cl (pentachlorophenol)

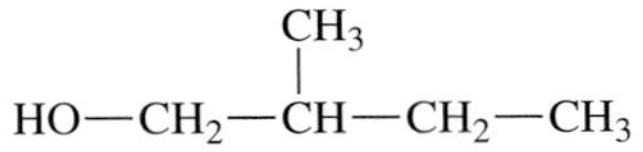

**13.63** $CH_3-\overset{CH_3}{CH}-\overset{O}{\overset{\|}{C}}-H$

**13.65**

| | |
|---|---|
| $CH_3-CH_2-CH_2-CH_2-CH_2-OH$ | 1-pentanol |
| $CH_3-\overset{OH}{CH}-CH_2-CH_2-CH_3$ | 2-pentanol |
| $CH_3-CH_2-\overset{OH}{CH}-CH_2-CH_3$ | 3-pentanol |
| $HO-CH_2-\overset{CH_3}{CH}-CH_2-CH_3$ | 2-methyl-1-butanol |
| $HO-CH_2-CH_2-\overset{CH_3}{CH}-CH_3$ | 3-methyl-1-butanol |
| $CH_3-\underset{OH}{\overset{CH_3}{C}}-CH_2-CH_3$ | 2-methyl-2-butanol |
| $CH_3-\overset{OH}{CH}-\overset{CH_3}{CH}-CH_3$ | 3-methyl-2-butanol |
| $CH_3-\underset{CH_3}{\overset{CH_3}{C}}-CH_2-OH$ | 2,2-dimethyl-1-propanol |

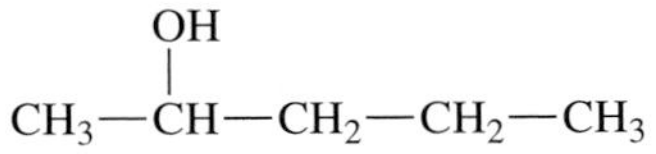

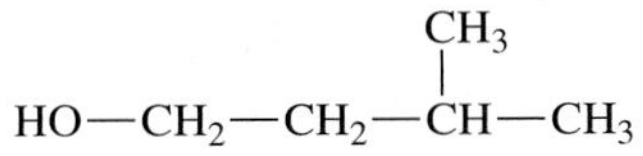

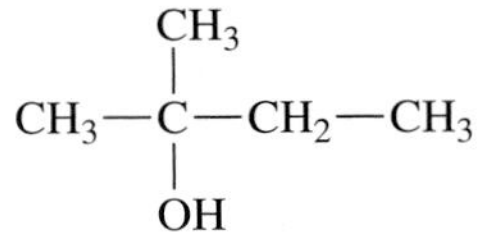

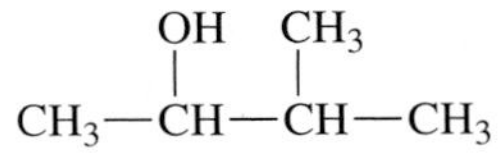

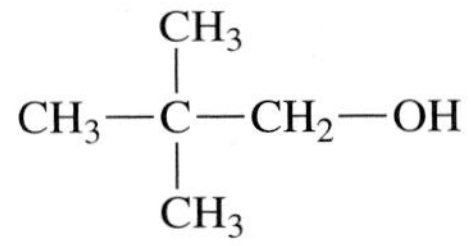

# 14 Aldehydes, Ketones, and Chiral Molecules

LOOKING AHEAD


14.1 Aldehydes and Ketones

14.2 Physical Properties of Aldehydes and Ketones

14.3 Oxidation and Reduction of Aldehydes and Ketones

14.4 Addition Reactions of Aldehydes and Ketones

14.5 Chiral Molecules

*"Dentures replace natural teeth that are extracted due to cavities, bad gums, or trauma," says Dr. Irene Hilton, dentist, La Clinica De La Raza. "I make an impression of teeth using alginate, which is a polysaccharide extracted from seaweed. I mix the compound with water and place the gel-like material in the patient's mouth, where it becomes a hard, cementlike substance. I fill this mold with gypsum ($CaSO_4$) and water, which form a solid to which I add teeth made of plastic or porcelain. When I get a good match to the patient's own teeth, I prepare a preliminary wax denture. This is placed in the patient's mouth to check the bite and adjust the position of the replacement teeth. Then a permanent denture is made using a hard plastic polymer (methyl methacrylate)."*

Visit **www.masteringchemistry.com** for self-study materials and instructor-assigned homework.

In this chapter, we will study two families of organic compounds: aldehydes and ketones. Many of the odors that you associate with flavorings and perfumes are due a carbon–oxygen double bond called a *carbonyl group* (C=O). Aldehydes in foods and perfumes provide the odors and flavors of vanilla, almond, and cinnamon. In biology, you may have seen specimens preserved in a solution of formaldehyde. You probably notice the odor of a ketone if you use paint or nail polish remover.

In later chapters, we will see how the carbonyl group influences the structures of carbohydrates, proteins, and nucleic acids. Aldehydes and ketones are also important compounds in industry, providing the solvents and reactants that make up many common materials we use in our lives.

## 14.1 Aldehydes and Ketones

LEARNING GOAL

Identify compounds with the carbonyl group as aldehydes and ketones. Give the IUPAC and common names for aldehydes and ketones; draw their condensed structural formulas.

In an **aldehyde**, the carbon of the carbonyl group is bonded to at least one hydrogen atom. That carbon may also be bonded to another hydrogen atom, a carbon of an alkyl group, or an aromatic ring. (See Figure 14.1.) In a **ketone**, the carbonyl group is bonded to two alkyl groups or aromatic rings.

### Structure of the Carbonyl Group

SELF STUDY ACTIVITY Aldehydes and Ketones

TUTORIAL Naming Aldehydes and Ketones

The carbonyl group consists of a carbon–oxygen double bond with bonds at angles of 120° to two other atoms. The double bond in the carbonyl group is similar to that of alkenes, except the carbonyl group has a dipole. The oxygen atom with two lone pairs of electrons is much more electronegative than the carbon atom. Therefore, the carbonyl group has a strong dipole with a partial negative charge ($\delta^-$) on the oxygen and a partial positive charge ($\delta^+$) on the carbon. The polarity of the carbonyl group strongly influences the physical and chemical properties of aldehydes and ketones.

There are several ways to draw the structural formulas of aldehydes and ketones. In the condensed structural formula, the aldehyde group may be drawn as separate atoms, or it may be written as —CHO at the beginning of a carbon chain. An aldehyde would not be written as —COH, which looks like a hydroxyl group. The keto group (C=O) located in the middle of the carbon chain is sometimes written as CO. For convenience, the line-bond formulas are also used, with the functional group atoms written separately. Isomers, which have the same molecular formula, can be written for aldehydes and ketones as follows:

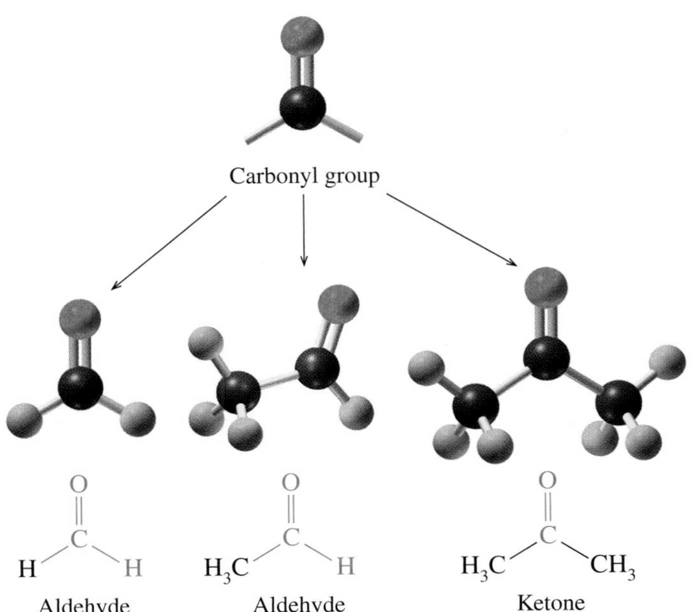


**FIGURE 14.1** The carbonyl group in aldehydes and ketones.

Q If aldehydes and ketones both contain a carbonyl group, how can you differentiate between compounds from each family?

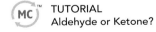

MC TUTORIAL Aldehyde or Ketone?

**Formulas for Isomers of $C_3H_6O$**

**Aldehyde**

$$CH_3-CH_2-\overset{\overset{\displaystyle O}{\|}}{C}-H \;=\; CH_3-CH_2-CHO \;=$$

**Ketone**

$$CH_3-\overset{\overset{\displaystyle O}{\|}}{C}-CH_3 \;=\; CH_3-CO-CH_3 \;=$$

CONCEPT CHECK 14.1

**Identifying Aldehydes and Ketones**

Identify each of the following compounds as an aldehyde or ketone:

a. $CH_3-\underset{\underset{\displaystyle CH_3}{|}}{\overset{\overset{\displaystyle CH_3}{|}}{C}}-CH_2-\overset{\overset{\displaystyle O}{\|}}{C}-H$

b. (cyclopentyl)$-\overset{\overset{\displaystyle O}{\|}}{C}-CH_3$

c. (benzene ring)$-CHO$

d. 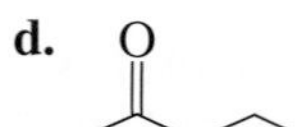

ANSWER

**a.** When the carbon atom of the carbonyl group (C=O) is attached to a hydrogen atom, the compound is an aldehyde.

**b.** When the carbon atom of the carbonyl group (C=O) is attached to two carbon atoms, the compound is a ketone.

**c.** When the carbon atom of the carbonyl group (C=O) is attached to a hydrogen atom, the compound is an aldehyde.

**d.** When the carbon atom of the carbonyl group (C=O) is attached to two carbon atoms, the compound is a ketone.

## Naming Aldehydes

In the IUPAC names of aldehydes, the *e* of the alkane name is replaced with *al*.

**STEP 1** **Name the longest carbon chain containing the carbonyl group by replacing the *e* in the corresponding alkane name with *al*.** No number is needed for the aldehyde group because it always appears at the beginning of the chain.

$$CH_3-CH_2-\overset{\overset{\displaystyle O}{\|}}{C}-H$$

Propanal

The IUPAC system names the aldehyde of benzene as benzaldehyde:

(benzene ring)$-\overset{\overset{\displaystyle O}{\|}}{C}-H$

Benzaldehyde

The first four unbranched aldehydes are often referred to by their common names, which end in *aldehyde*. (See Figure 14.2.) The roots (*form-*, *acet-*, *propion-*, and *butyr-*) of these common names are derived from Latin or Greek words.

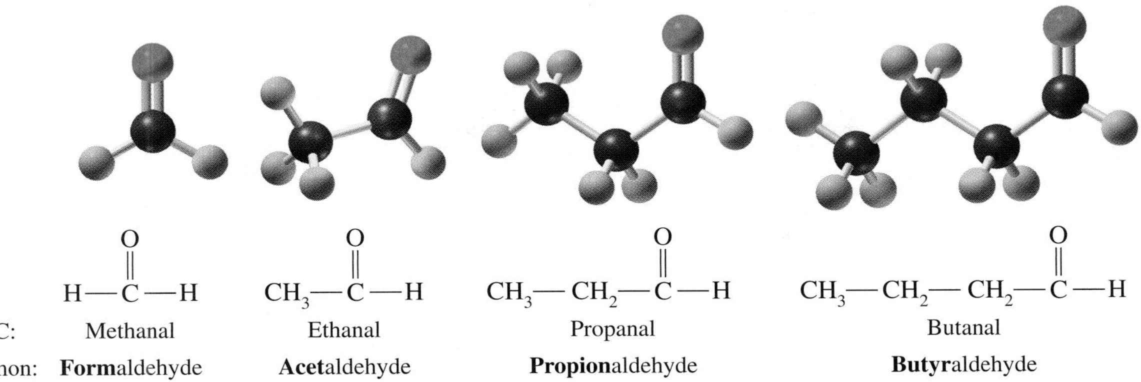

| | $H{-}\overset{\overset{\large O}{\|}}{C}{-}H$ | $CH_3{-}\overset{\overset{\large O}{\|}}{C}{-}H$ | $CH_3{-}CH_2{-}\overset{\overset{\large O}{\|}}{C}{-}H$ | $CH_3{-}CH_2{-}CH_2{-}\overset{\overset{\large O}{\|}}{C}{-}H$ |
|---|---|---|---|---|
| IUPAC: | Methanal | Ethanal | Propanal | Butanal |
| Common: | **Form**aldehyde | **Acet**aldehyde | **Propion**aldehyde | **Butyr**aldehyde |

FIGURE 14.2 In the structures of aldehydes, the carbonyl group is always the end carbon.
Q Why is the carbon in the carbonyl group in aldehydes always at the end of the chain?

STEP 2 **Name and number any substituents on the carbon chain by counting the carbonyl carbon as carbon 1.** In an aldehyde, the —OH group is counted as a substituent and named *hydroxy*:

$$\underset{\text{2-Methylpropanal}}{CH_3{-}\overset{\overset{\large CH_3}{|}}{CH}{-}\overset{\overset{\large O}{\|}}{C}{-}H} \qquad \underset{\text{4-Methylpentanal}}{CH_3{-}\overset{\overset{\large CH_3}{|}}{CH}{-}CH_2{-}CH_2{-}\overset{\overset{\large O}{\|}}{C}{-}H}$$

SAMPLE PROBLEM 14.1

## Naming Aldehydes

Give the IUPAC names for the following aldehydes:

**a.** $CH_3{-}CH_2{-}\overset{\overset{\large OH}{|}}{CH}{-}CH_2{-}\overset{\overset{\large O}{\|}}{C}{-}H$ **b.** Cl—(benzene ring)—$\overset{\overset{\large O}{\|}}{C}{-}H$

SOLUTION

**a.** STEP 1 **Name the longest carbon chain by replacing the *e* with *al*.** The longest carbon chain containing the carbonyl group has five carbon atoms. It is named by replacing the *e* in the alkane name with *al* to give pentanal.

STEP 2 **Name and number substituents by counting from the carbonyl group.** The —OH group on carbon 3 is named hydroxy, which gives an IUPAC name of 3-hydroxypentanal.

**b.** STEP 1 **Name the longest carbon chain by replacing the *e* with *al*.** The longest carbon chain consists of a benzene ring attached to a carbonyl group, which is named benzaldehyde.

STEP 2 **Name and number substituents by counting from the carbonyl group.** Counting from carbon 1 attached to the carbonyl group, the chloro group is attached to carbon 4. The name is 4-chlorobenzaldehyde.

STUDY CHECK

What are the IUPAC and common names of the aldehyde with three carbon atoms?

**Guide to Naming Aldehydes**

STEP 1
Name the longest carbon chain by replacing the e in the alkane name with *al*.

STEP 2
Name and number substituents by counting the carbonyl group as carbon 1.

## ENVIRONMENTAL NOTE

### Vanilla

Vanilla has been used as a flavoring for over a thousand years. After drinking a beverage made from powdered vanilla and cocoa beans with Emperor Montezuma in Mexico, the Spanish conquistador Hernán Cortés took vanilla back to Europe, where it became popular for flavoring and for scenting perfumes and tobacco. Thomas Jefferson introduced vanilla to the United States during the late 1700s. Today, much of the vanilla we use in the world is grown in Mexico, Madagascar, Réunion, Seychelles, Tahiti, Sri Lanka, Java, the Philippines, and Africa.

The vanilla plant is a member of the orchid family. There are many species of *Vanilla*, but *Vanilla planifolia* (or *V. fragrans*) is considered to produce the best flavor. The vanilla plant grows like a vine and can grow to 100 feet in length. Its flowers are hand-pollinated to produce a green fruit that is picked in 8 or 9 months. The fruit is sun-dried to form a long, dark brown pod, which is called "vanilla bean" because it looks like a string bean. The flavor and fragrance of the vanilla bean comes from the tiny black seeds found inside the dried bean.

The seeds and pod are used to flavor desserts such as custards and ice cream. The extract of vanilla is made by chopping up vanilla beans and mixing them with a 35% ethanol–water mixture. The liquid, which contains the aldehyde *vanillin*, is drained from the bean residue and used for flavoring.

$$\text{HO}-\text{C}_6\text{H}_3(\text{O}-\text{CH}_3)-\overset{\overset{\displaystyle O}{\|}}{\text{C}}-\text{H}$$

Vanillin

## Naming Ketones

Aldehydes and ketones are some of the most important classes of organic compounds. Because they have played a major role in organic chemistry for more than a century, the common names for unbranched ketones are still in use. In the common names, the alkyl groups bonded to the carbonyl group are named as substituents and listed alphabetically followed by *ketone*. Acetone, which is another name for propanone, has been retained by the IUPAC system.

In the IUPAC system, the name of a ketone is obtained by replacing the *e* in the corresponding alkane name with *one*.

**STEP 1** **Name the longest carbon chain containing the carbonyl group by replacing the *e* in the corresponding alkane name with *one*.**

**STEP 2** **Number the main chain starting from the end nearer the carbonyl group.** Place the number of the carbonyl carbon in front of the ketone name. (Propanone and butanone do not require numbers.)

$$CH_3-\overset{\overset{\displaystyle O}{\|}}{C}-CH_3 \qquad CH_3-CH_2-\overset{\overset{\displaystyle O}{\|}}{C}-CH_3 \qquad CH_3-CH_2-\overset{\overset{\displaystyle O}{\|}}{C}-CH_2-CH_3$$

Propanone (dimethyl ketone; acetone) — Butanone (ethyl methyl ketone) — 3-Pentanone (diethyl ketone)

**STEP 3** **Name and number any substituents on the carbon chain.** In a ketone, an —OH group is a substituent and named *hydroxy*:

$$CH_3-\overset{\overset{\displaystyle O}{\|}}{C}-\overset{\overset{\displaystyle CH_3}{|}}{CH}-CH_3 \qquad CH_3-\overset{\overset{\displaystyle OH}{|}}{CH}-\overset{\overset{\displaystyle O}{\|}}{C}-CH_2-CH_3$$

3-Methylbutanone — 2-Hydroxy-3-pentanone

STEP 4 **For cyclic ketones, the prefix *cyclo* is used in front of the ketone name.** Any substituents are located by numbering the ring starting with the carbonyl carbon as carbon 1. The ring is numbered so that the substituents have the lowest possible number:

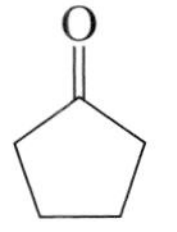

Cyclopentanone

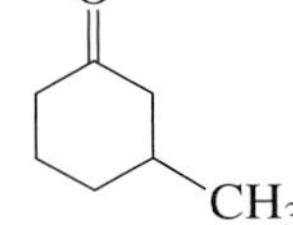

3-Methylcyclohexanone

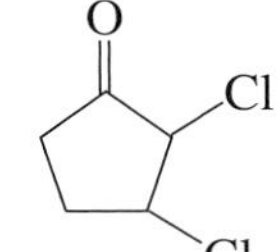

2,3-Dichlorocyclopentanone

# HEALTH NOTE

## Some Important Aldehydes and Ketones

*Formaldehyde*, the simplest aldehyde, is a colorless gas with a pungent odor. Commercially, formaldehyde is used to make fabrics, insulation materials, carpeting, pressed wood products such as plywood, and plastics for kitchen counters. An aqueous solution called formalin, which contains 40% formaldehyde, is used as a germicide and to preserve biological specimens. Exposure to formaldehyde fumes can irritate the eyes, nose, and upper respiratory tract and cause skin rashes, headaches, dizziness, and general fatigue. Formaldehyde is classified as a carcinogen.

*Acetone*, or propanone (dimethyl ketone), which is the simplest ketone, is a colorless liquid with a mild odor that has wide use as a solvent in cleaning fluids, paint and nail polish removers, and rubber cement. It is extremely flammable, and care must be taken when using acetone. In the body, acetone may be produced in uncontrolled diabetes, fasting, and high-protein diets when large amounts of fats are metabolized for energy.

$CH_3-\overset{O}{\overset{\|}{C}}-\overset{O}{\overset{\|}{C}}-CH_3$

Butanedione

Several naturally occurring aromatic aldehydes are used to flavor food and as fragrances in perfumes. Benzaldehyde is found in almonds, vanillin in vanilla beans, and cinnamaldehyde in cinnamon:

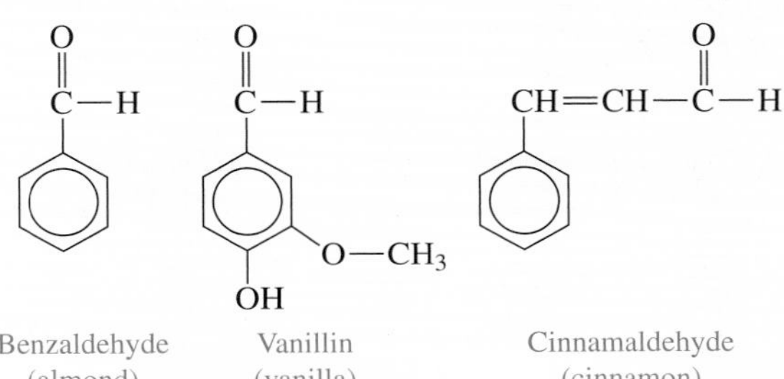

Benzaldehyde (almond) Vanillin (vanilla) Cinnamaldehyde (cinnamon)

The flavor of butter or margarine is from butanedione, muscone is used to make musk perfumes, and oil of spearmint contains carvone:

$CH_2-CH_2-CH_2-CH_2-CH_2-CH(CH_3)-CH_2$ / $CH_2-CH_2-CH_2-CH_2-CH_2-CH_2-CH_2$ \ $C=O$ (ring)

Muscone (musk)

Carvone (spearmint oil)

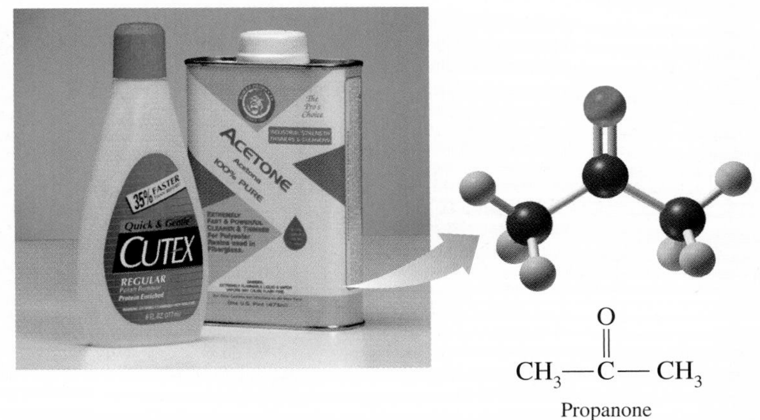


$CH_3-\overset{O}{\overset{\|}{C}}-CH_3$

Propanone

**Guide to Naming Ketones**

**STEP 1** Name the longest carbon chain by replacing the e in the alkane name by *one*.

**STEP 2** Number the carbon chain starting from the end nearer the carbonyl group and indicate its location.

**STEP 3** Name and number any substituents on other carbons in the chain.

**STEP 4** For cyclic ketones, add the prefix *cyclo* and number substituents from the carbonyl carbon as carbon 1.

SAMPLE PROBLEM 14.2

## Names of Ketones

Give the IUPAC name for the following ketone:

$$CH_3-\underset{}{\overset{CH_3}{\overset{|}{C}H}}-CH_2-\overset{O}{\overset{\|}{C}}-CH_3$$

SOLUTION

**STEP 1** **Name the longest carbon chain by replacing the *e* with *one*.** The longest chain containing the carbonyl has five carbon atoms, which is named by replacing the *e* of the alkane name: pentanone.

**STEP 2** **Number the carbon chain from the end nearer the ketone group.** The carbonyl group on carbon 2 gives 2-pentanone.

**STEP 3** **Name and number any substituents on the chain.** Counting from the end nearer the carbonyl group places the methyl group on carbon 4. The IUPAC name is 4-methyl-2-pentanone.

STUDY CHECK

What is the common name of 3-hexanone?

# QUESTIONS AND PROBLEMS

## Aldehydes and Ketones

**14.1** Identify the following compounds as aldehydes or ketones:

a. $CH_3-CH_2-\overset{O}{\overset{\|}{C}}-CH_3$

b. (skeletal structure with O and H)

c. (cyclopentanone ring with $CH_3$)

d. (cyclohexane with $\overset{O}{\overset{\|}{C}}-H$)

**14.2** Identify the following compounds as aldehydes or ketones:

a. 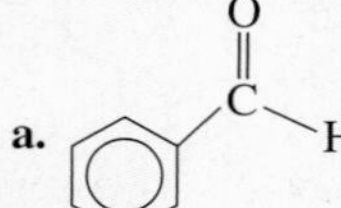

b. $CH_3-\overset{CH_3}{\overset{|}{C}H}-\overset{O}{\overset{\|}{C}}-H$

c. 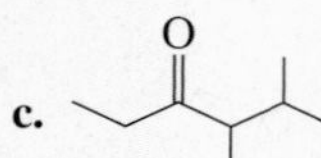

d. (cyclohexane with $\overset{O}{\overset{\|}{C}}-CH_2-CH_3$)

**14.3** Indicate if each of the following pairs of formulas represents (1) isomers, (2) the same compound, or (3) different compounds:

a. $CH_3-\overset{O}{\overset{\|}{C}}-CH_3$ and $CH_3-CH_2-\overset{O}{\overset{\|}{C}}-H$

b. (skeletal structure) and (skeletal structure)

c. $CH_3-\overset{O}{\overset{\|}{C}}-CH_2-CH_3$ and $CH_3-CH_2-\overset{O}{\overset{\|}{C}}-CH_3$

**14.4** Indicate if each of the following pairs of formulas represents (1) isomers, (2) the same compound, or (3) different compounds:

a. 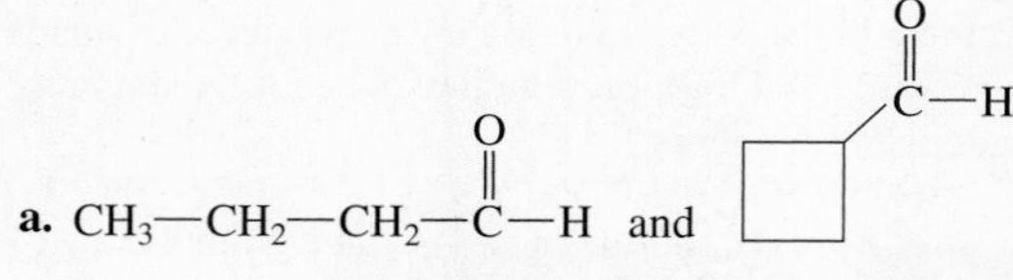

$CH_3-CH_2-CH_2-\overset{O}{\overset{\|}{C}}-H$ and (cyclobutane with $\overset{O}{\overset{\|}{C}}-H$)

b. (skeletal structure with O) and (skeletal structure with O)

c. (cyclohexanone) and (cyclohexenol with OH)

**14.5** Give the IUPAC name for each of the following compounds:

a. $CH_3-CH_2-\overset{O}{\overset{\|}{C}}-H$

b. $CH_3-CH_2-\overset{O}{\overset{\|}{C}}-\overset{CH_3}{\overset{|}{C}H}-CH_3$

c. $CH_3-\overset{Br}{\overset{|}{C}H}-CH_2-\overset{O}{\overset{\|}{C}}-H$

d. (skeletal structure with O)

e. (cyclohexanone with $CH_3$)

f. (benzene ring with $\overset{O}{\overset{\|}{C}}-H$ and Cl)

**14.6** Give the IUPAC name for each of the following compounds:

**a.** $CH_3-CH_2-CH_2-\overset{\text{O}}{\overset{\|}{C}}-H$

**b.** $CH_3-\overset{CH_3}{\overset{|}{CH}}-CH_2-\overset{\text{O}}{\overset{\|}{C}}-CH_3$ **c.** 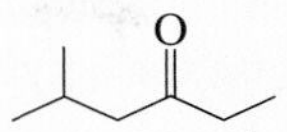 (skeletal structure)

**d.** 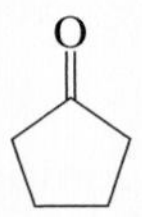 (cyclopentanone ring, =O) **e.** 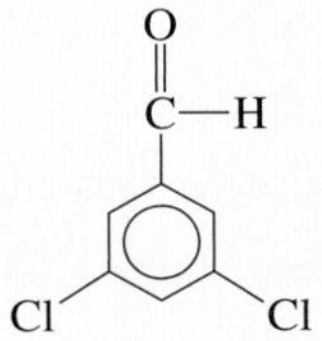 (benzene ring with $\overset{\text{O}}{\overset{\|}{C}}-H$; Cl, Cl)

**f.** $CH_3-CH_2-CH_2-\overset{CH_3}{\overset{|}{CH}}-\overset{\text{O}}{\overset{\|}{C}}-H$

**14.7** Give a common name for each of the following compounds:

**a.** $CH_3-\overset{\text{O}}{\overset{\|}{C}}-H$ **b.** $CH_3-\overset{\text{O}}{\overset{\|}{C}}-CH_2-CH_2-CH_3$

**c.** $H-\overset{\text{O}}{\overset{\|}{C}}-H$

**14.8** Give the common name for each of the following compounds:

**a.** $CH_3-\overset{\text{O}}{\overset{\|}{C}}-CH_2-CH_3$

**b.** $CH_3-CH_2-\overset{\text{O}}{\overset{\|}{C}}-CH_2-CH_3$

**c.** $CH_3-CH_2-\overset{\text{O}}{\overset{\|}{C}}-H$

**14.9** Draw the condensed structural formula for each of the following compounds:
**a.** acetaldehyde
**b.** 4-methyl-2-pentanone
**c.** 2,3-dibromobutanal
**d.** methyl butyl ketone
**e.** 3-methylpentanal

**14.10** Draw the condensed structural formula for each of the following compounds:
**a.** propionaldehyde
**b.** butanal
**c.** 3,4-dichlorohexanal
**d.** 4-bromobutanone
**e.** acetone

**14.11** Anisaldehyde, from Korean mint or blue licorice, is one of the medicinal herbs used in Chinese medicine. If its IUPAC name is 4-methoxybenzaldehyde, what is its condensed structural formula?

**14.12** The IUPAC name of vanillin, a naturally occurring compound in vanilla beans, is 4-hydroxy-3-methoxybenzaldehyde. What is the structural formula of vanillin?

## 14.2 Physical Properties of Aldehydes and Ketones

At room temperature, formaldehyde and acetaldehyde are gases. Aldehydes containing from 3 to 10 carbon atoms are liquids. The polar carbonyl group with a partially negative oxygen atom and a partially positive carbon atom has an influence on the boiling points and the solubility of aldehydes and ketones in water.

**LEARNING GOAL**

Compare the boiling points and solubility of aldehydes and ketones to those of alkanes and alcohols.

### Boiling Points

The polar carbonyl group gives aldehydes and ketones higher boiling points than alkanes and ethers of similar mass. The increase in boiling points is due to dipole–dipole attractions:

MC™ TUTORIAL Properties of Aldehydes and Ketones

Dipole–dipole attractions

$$>C^{\delta+}=O^{\delta-}\cdots\cdots>C^{\delta+}=O^{\delta-}\cdots\cdots>C^{\delta+}=O^{\delta-}$$

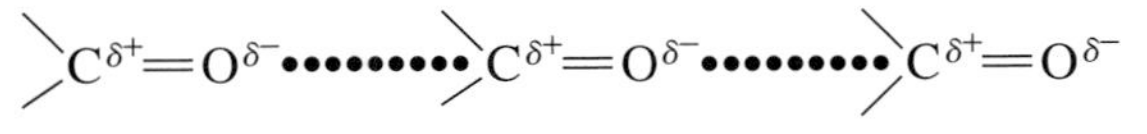

However, because there is no hydrogen on the oxygen atom, aldehydes and ketones cannot form hydrogen bonds with each other. Thus, they have boiling points that are lower than alcohols of similar molar mass:

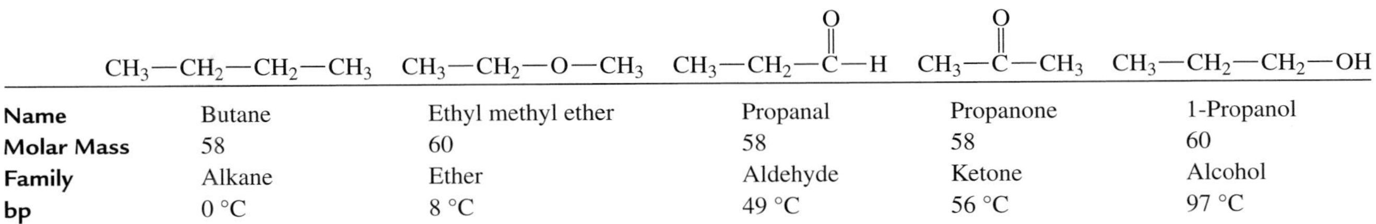

| | $CH_3-CH_2-CH_2-CH_3$ | $CH_3-CH_2-O-CH_3$ | $CH_3-CH_2-\overset{\text{O}}{\overset{\|}{C}}-H$ | $CH_3-\overset{\text{O}}{\overset{\|}{C}}-CH_3$ | $CH_3-CH_2-CH_2-OH$ |
|---|---|---|---|---|---|
| **Name** | Butane | Ethyl methyl ether | Propanal | Propanone | 1-Propanol |
| **Molar Mass** | 58 | 60 | 58 | 58 | 60 |
| **Family** | Alkane | Ether | Aldehyde | Ketone | Alcohol |
| **bp** | 0 °C | 8 °C | 49 °C | 56 °C | 97 °C |

**Increasing boiling point** →

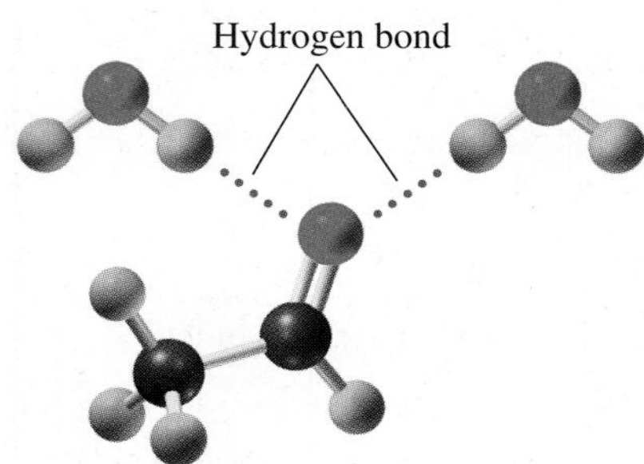


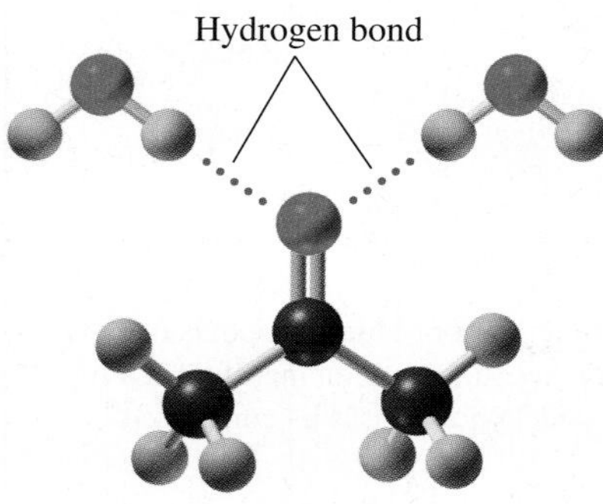


**FIGURE 14.3** Hydrogen bonding of acetaldehyde and acetone with water.

**Q** Would you expect propanal to be soluble in water?

## Solubility of Aldehydes and Ketones in Water

Although aldehydes and ketones do not hydrogen bond with each other, the electronegative oxygen atom does hydrogen bond with water molecules. Carbonyl compounds with one to four carbons are very soluble in water. However, those with five carbon atoms or more are not very soluble, because the alkyl portions diminish the effect of the polar carbonyl group. (See Figure 14.3.)

Table 14.1 compares the boiling points of some carbonyl compounds, as well as their solubilities in water.

**TABLE 14.1** Comparison of Physical Properties of Some Selected Compounds

| Compound | Boiling Point (°C) | Solubility in Water |
|---|---|---|
| Methanal (formaldehyde) | −21 | Very soluble |
| Ethanal (acetaldehyde) | 21 | Very soluble |
| Propanal (propionaldehyde) | 49 | Soluble |
| Propanone (acetone) | 56 | Soluble |
| Butanal (butyraldehyde) | 75 | Soluble |
| Butanone | 80 | Soluble |
| Pentanal | 103 | Slightly soluble |
| 2-Pentanone | 102 | Slightly soluble |
| 3-Pentanone | 102 | Slightly soluble |
| Hexanal | 129 | Not soluble |
| 2-Hexanone | 127 | Not soluble |
| 3-Hexanone | 124 | Not soluble |
| Acetophenone | 202 | Not soluble |

**CONCEPT CHECK 14.2**

### Boiling Points

Arrange the compounds pentane, 2-butanol, and butanone in order of increasing boiling points. Explain.

ANSWER

The only attractions between molecules of alkanes such as pentane are weak dispersion forces. With no dipole–dipole attractions or hydrogen bonds, pentane has the lowest boiling point of the three compounds. With a polar carbonyl group, butanone has dipole–dipole attractions but no hydrogen bonds. Butanone has a higher boiling point than pentane. Molecules of 2-butanol can form hydrogen bonds with other butanol molecules. The 2-butanol would have the highest boiling point of the three compounds. The actual boiling points are pentane (36 °C), butanone (80 °C), and 2-butanol (100 °C).

**SAMPLE PROBLEM 14.3**

### Boiling Point and Solubility

Would you expect ethanol ($CH_3—CH_2—OH$) to have a higher or lower boiling point than ethanal ($CH_3—CHO$)? Explain.

SOLUTION

Ethanol would have a higher boiling point because its molecules can hydrogen bond with each other, whereas molecules of ethanal cannot.

STUDY CHECK

If acetone molecules cannot hydrogen bond with each other, why is acetone soluble in water?

## QUESTIONS AND PROBLEMS

### Physical Properties of Aldehydes and Ketones

**14.13** Which compound in each of the following pairs would have the higher boiling point? Explain.

**a.** $CH_3{-}CH_2{-}CH_3$ or $CH_3{-}\overset{\displaystyle O}{\overset{\|}{C}}{-}H$

**b.** propanal or pentanal

**c.** butanal or 1-butanol

**14.14** Which compound in each of the following pairs would have the higher boiling point? Explain.

**a.** 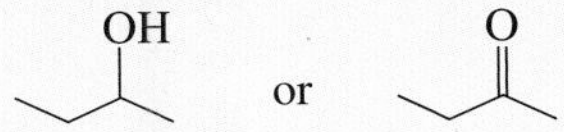 (skeletal structure of 2-butanol, with OH) or (skeletal structure of 2-butanone, with O)

**b.** pentane or butanone

**c.** propanone or pentanone

**14.15** Which compound in each of the following pairs would be more soluble in water? Explain.

**a.** $CH_3{-}\overset{\displaystyle O}{\overset{\|}{C}}{-}CH_2{-}CH_3$ or $CH_3{-}\overset{\displaystyle O}{\overset{\|}{C}}{-}\overset{\displaystyle O}{\overset{\|}{C}}{-}CH_3$

**b.** propane or acetaldehyde

**c.** acetone or 2-pentanone

**14.16** Which compound in each of the following pairs would be more soluble in water? Explain.

**a.** $CH_3{-}CH_2{-}CH_3$ or $CH_3{-}CH_2{-}CHO$

**b.** propanone or 3-hexanone

**c.** propane or propanone

**14.17** Would you expect an aldehyde with a formula of $C_8H_{16}O$ to be soluble in water? Explain.

**14.18** Would you expect an aldehyde with a formula of $C_3H_6O$ to be soluble in water? Explain.

# 14.3 Oxidation and Reduction of Aldehydes and Ketones

**LEARNING GOAL**

Draw the condensed structural formulas of reactants and products for the oxidation or reduction of aldehydes and ketones.

In Chapter 13, we saw that aldehydes produced by the oxidation of primary alcohols oxidize readily to carboxylic acids. In fact, they oxidize so easily that aldehydes exposed to the air in the laboratory quickly form carboxylic acids. In contrast, ketones produced by the oxidation of secondary alcohols do not undergo further oxidation. Let's review examples of the oxidation reactions of primary and secondary alcohols that form aldehydes and ketones.

$$\underset{\text{Ethanol (1°)}}{CH_3{-}CH_2{-}OH} \xrightarrow{\text{Oxidation}} \underset{\text{Ethanal}}{CH_3{-}\overset{\displaystyle O}{\overset{\|}{C}}{-}H} \xrightarrow{\text{Further oxidation}} \underset{\text{Ethanoic acid}}{CH_3{-}\overset{\displaystyle O}{\overset{\|}{C}}{-}OH}$$

$$\underset{\text{2-Propanol (2°)}}{CH_3{-}\overset{\displaystyle OH}{\overset{|}{CH}}{-}CH_3} \xrightarrow{\text{Oxidation}} \underset{\text{Propanone}}{CH_3{-}\overset{\displaystyle O}{\overset{\|}{C}}{-}CH_3} \xrightarrow{\text{Further oxidation}} \text{no reaction}$$

TUTORIAL
Oxidation–Reduction Reactions of Aldehydes and Ketones

## Tollens' Test

The ease of oxidation of aldehydes allows certain mild oxidizing agents to oxidize the aldehyde functional group without oxidizing other functional groups such as alcohols or ethers. In the laboratory, **Tollens' test** may be used to distinguish between aldehydes and ketones. Tollens' reagent, a solution of $Ag^+$ ($AgNO_3$) and ammonia, oxidizes aldehydes, but not ketones. The silver ion is reduced to metallic silver, which forms a layer called a "silver mirror" on the inside of the container:

$$\underset{\text{Acetaldehyde}}{CH_3{-}\overset{\displaystyle O}{\overset{\|}{C}}{-}H} + \underset{\text{Tollens' reagent}}{2Ag^+} \xrightarrow{[O]} \underset{\text{Silver mirror}}{2Ag(s)} + \underset{\text{Acetic acid}}{CH_3{-}\overset{\displaystyle O}{\overset{\|}{C}}{-}OH}$$

Commercially, a similar process is used to make mirrors by applying a solution of $AgNO_3$ and ammonia on glass with a spray gun. (See Figure 14.4.)

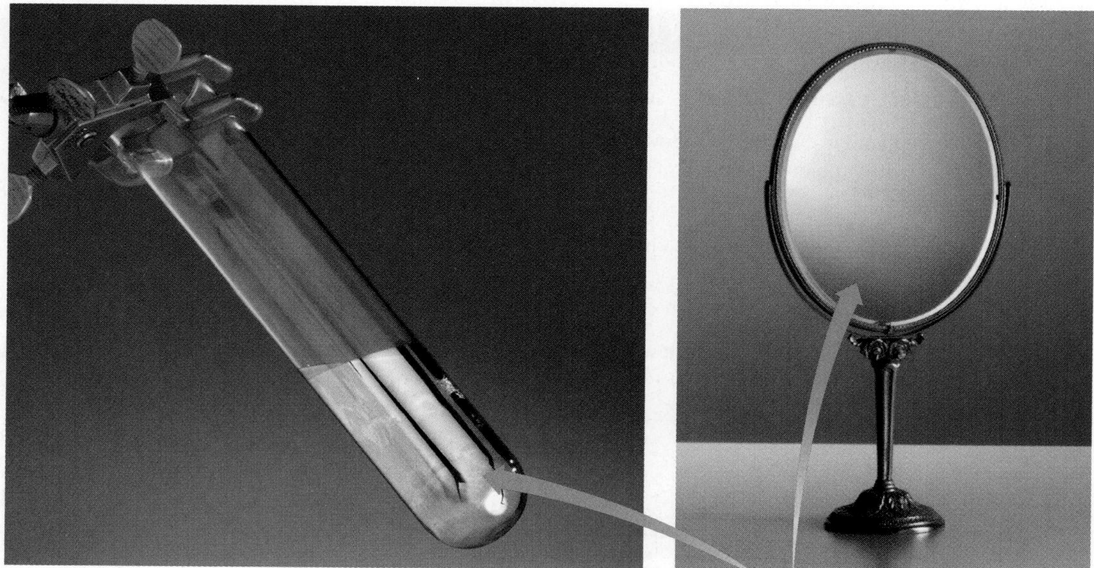

$$Ag^+ + 1e^- \longrightarrow Ag(s)$$

**FIGURE 14.4** In Tollens' test, a "silver mirror" forms when the oxidation of an aldehyde reduces silver ions to metallic silver. The silvery surface of a mirror is formed in a similar way.

Q What is the product of the oxidation of an aldehyde?

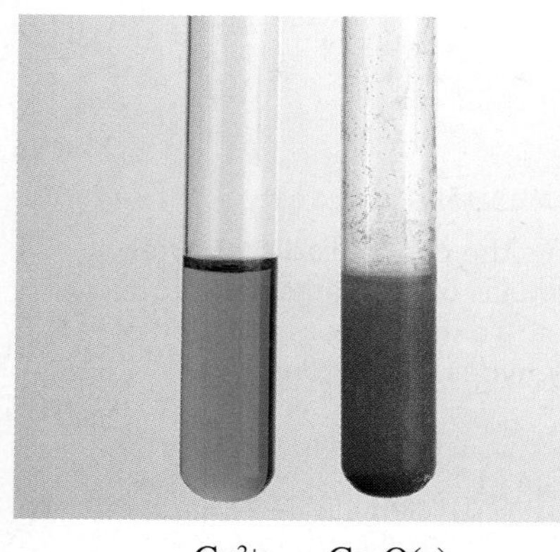


**FIGURE 14.5** The blue $Cu^{2+}$ in Benedict's solution forms a brick-red solid of $Cu_2O$ in a positive test for many sugars and aldehydes with adjacent hydroxyl groups.

Q Which test tube indicates that glucose is present?

Another test, called **Benedict's test**, gives a positive test with compounds that have an aldehyde functional group and an adjacent hydroxyl group. When Benedict's solution containing $Cu^{2+}$ ($CuSO_4$) ions is added to this type of aldehyde and heated, a brick-red solid of $Cu_2O$ forms. (See Figure 14.5.) The test is negative with simple aldehydes and ketones:

$$\underset{\text{2-Hydroxypropanal}}{CH_3-\overset{OH}{\overset{|}{CH}}-\overset{O}{\overset{\|}{C}}-H} + \underset{\text{Benedict's reagent}}{2Cu^{2+}} \longrightarrow \underset{\text{Brick-red solid}}{Cu_2O(s)} + \underset{\text{2-Hydroxypropanoic acid}}{CH_3-\overset{OH}{\overset{|}{CH}}-\overset{O}{\overset{\|}{C}}-OH}$$

Because many sugars such as glucose contain this type of aldehyde grouping, Benedict's reagent can be used to determine the presence of glucose in blood or urine:

$$\underset{\text{D-Glucose}}{\begin{array}{c} O \\ \| \\ C-H \\ | \\ H-C-OH \\ | \\ HO-C-H \\ | \\ H-C-OH \\ | \\ H-C-OH \\ | \\ CH_2OH \end{array}} + \underset{\text{(blue)}}{\underset{\text{Benedict's}}{2Cu^{2+}}} \longrightarrow \underset{\text{D-Gluconic acid}}{\begin{array}{c} O \quad OH \\ \diagdown\ \diagup \\ C \\ | \\ H-C-OH \\ | \\ HO-C-H \\ | \\ H-C-OH \\ | \\ H-C-OH \\ | \\ CH_2OH \end{array}} + \underset{\text{(brick red)}}{Cu_2O(s)}$$

SAMPLE PROBLEM 14.4

## Alcohol Oxidation

Draw the condensed structural formula of the alcohol needed to give each of the following oxidation products:

**a.** $CH_3-\overset{O}{\overset{\|}{C}}-CH_2-CH_3$ **b.** $CH_3-\overset{CH_3}{\overset{|}{CH}}-\overset{O}{\overset{\|}{C}}-H$ **c.** $CH_3-\overset{O}{\overset{\|}{C}}-OH$

SOLUTION

**a.** A secondary alcohol oxidizes to a ketone:

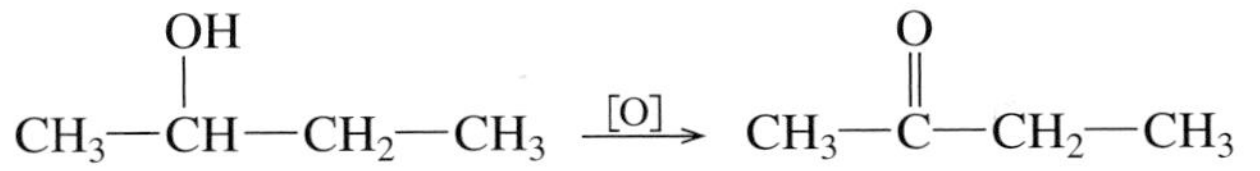

$$CH_3-\underset{}{\overset{OH}{\overset{|}{C}H}}-CH_2-CH_3 \xrightarrow{[O]} CH_3-\overset{O}{\overset{\|}{C}}-CH_2-CH_3$$

**b.** A primary alcohol oxidizes to an aldehyde with a mild oxidizing agent:

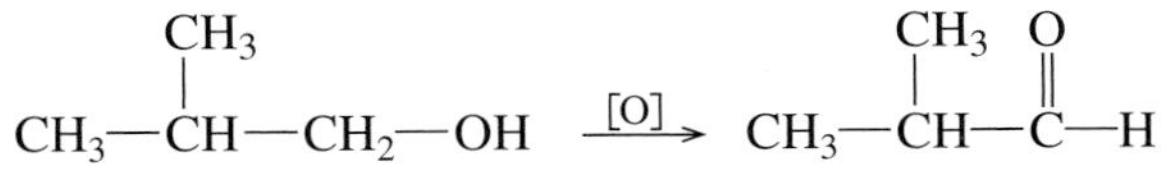

$$CH_3-\overset{CH_3}{\overset{|}{C}H}-CH_2-OH \xrightarrow{[O]} CH_3-\overset{CH_3}{\overset{|}{C}H}-\overset{O}{\overset{\|}{C}}-H$$

**c.** A primary alcohol oxidizes to an aldehyde, which oxidizes further to a carboxylic acid:

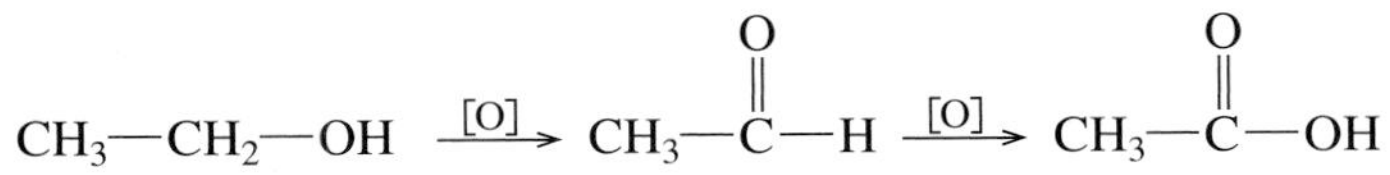

$$CH_3-CH_2-OH \xrightarrow{[O]} CH_3-\overset{O}{\overset{\|}{C}}-H \xrightarrow{[O]} CH_3-\overset{O}{\overset{\|}{C}}-OH$$

STUDY CHECK

What is the IUPAC name of the alcohol that oxidized to cyclohexanone?

SAMPLE PROBLEM 14.5

**Tollens' Test**

Draw the condensed structural formula of the product of oxidation, if any, when Tollens' reagent is added to each of the following compounds:

**a.** propanal **b.** propanone **c.** 2-methylbutanal

SOLUTION

Tollens' reagent will oxidize aldehydes but not ketones.

**a.** 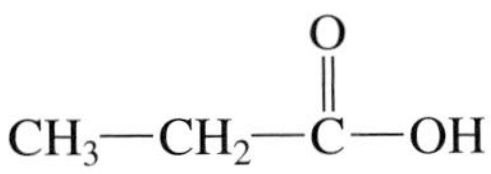 $CH_3-CH_2-\overset{O}{\overset{\|}{C}}-OH$ **b.** no reaction **c.** 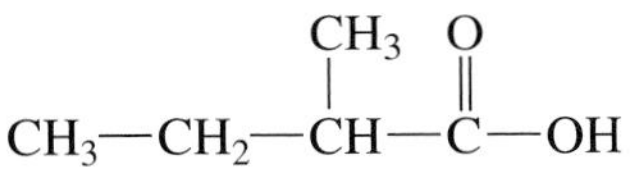 $CH_3-CH_2-\overset{CH_3}{\overset{|}{C}H}-\overset{O}{\overset{\|}{C}}-OH$

STUDY CHECK

Why does a silver mirror form when Tollens' reagent is added to a test tube containing benzaldehyde?

## Reduction of Aldehydes and Ketones

Aldehydes and ketones are reduced by sodium borohydride ($NaBH_4$) or hydrogen ($H_2$). **Reduction** decreases the number of carbon–oxygen bonds by the addition of hydrogen or the loss of oxygen. Aldehydes are reduced to primary alcohols, and ketones are reduced to secondary alcohols. A catalyst such as nickel, platinum, or palladium is needed for hydrogenation.

**Aldehydes Reduce to Primary Alcohols**

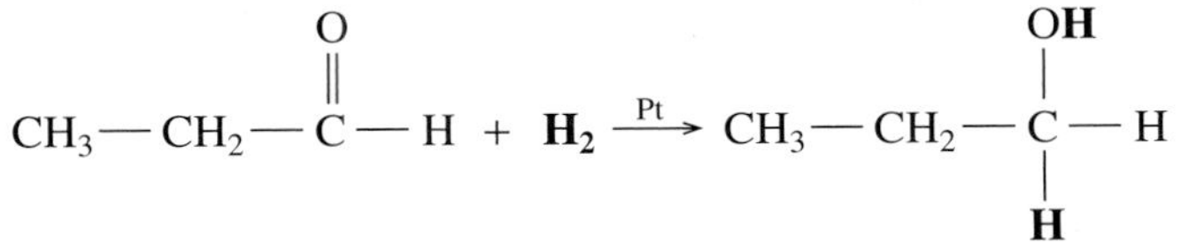

$$CH_3-CH_2-\overset{O}{\overset{\|}{C}}-H + \mathbf{H_2} \xrightarrow{Pt} CH_3-CH_2-\underset{\mathbf{H}}{\underset{|}{\overset{\mathbf{OH}}{\overset{|}{C}}}}-H$$

Propionaldehyde 1-Propanol (1° alcohol)

**Ketones Reduce to Secondary Alcohols**

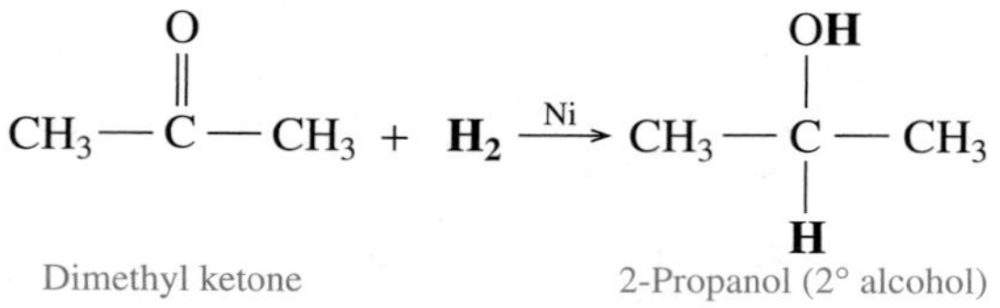

$$CH_3-\overset{\overset{\displaystyle O}{\|}}{C}-CH_3 + \mathbf{H_2} \xrightarrow{Ni} CH_3-\underset{\underset{\displaystyle \mathbf{H}}{|}}{\overset{\overset{\displaystyle \mathbf{OH}}{|}}{C}}-CH_3$$

Dimethyl ketone 2-Propanol (2° alcohol)

CONCEPT CHECK 14.3

### Reduction of Aldehydes and Ketones

Two isomers have the molecular formula $C_4H_8O$. One can be reduced to give 1-butanol, and the other can be reduced to give 2-butanol. What are the IUPAC names of the two isomers?

ANSWER

When an aldehyde is reduced, the product is a primary (1°) alcohol. The aldehyde that would be reduced to 1-butanol would have four carbons with an aldehyde group on the beginning carbon, which is named butanal.

When a ketone is reduced, the product is a secondary (2°) alcohol. The ketone that would be reduced to 2-butanol would have four carbons with a keto group on carbon 2, which is named butanone. Thus, the two isomers with molecular formula $C_4H_8O$ are butanal and butanone.

SAMPLE PROBLEM 14.6

### Reduction of Carbonyl Groups

Write an equation for the reduction of cyclopentanone in the presence of a nickel catalyst.

SOLUTION

The reacting molecule is a cyclic ketone that has five carbon atoms. Hydrogen atoms will add to the carbon and oxygen in the carbonyl group to form the corresponding secondary alcohol:

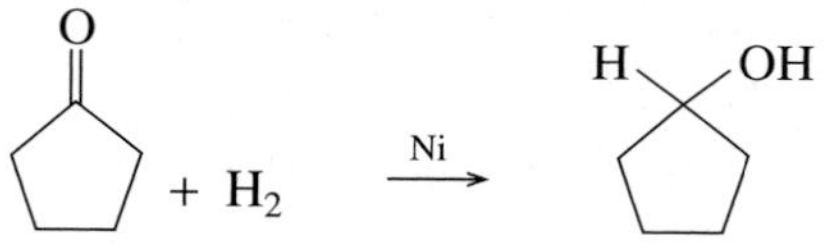

Cyclopentanone + $H_2$ $\xrightarrow{Ni}$ Cyclopentanol (H, OH)

STUDY CHECK

What is the name of the product obtained from the hydrogenation of propionaldehyde?

## QUESTIONS AND PROBLEMS

### Oxidation and Reduction of Aldehydes and Ketones

**14.19** Draw the condensed structural formula of the alcohol needed to give each of the following oxidation products:

**a.** formaldehyde **b.** cyclopentanone
**c.** 2-butanone **d.** benzaldehyde
**e.** 3-methylcyclohexanone

**14.20** Draw the condensed structural formula of the alcohol needed to give each of the following oxidation products:

**a.** acetaldehyde **b.** 3-methylbutanone
**c.** cyclohexanone **d.** propionaldehyde
**e.** 3-methylbutanal

**14.21** Draw the condensed structural formula of the aldehyde or ketone product when each of the following alcohols is oxidized [O] (if no reaction, write *none*):

**a.** $CH_3-CH_2-CH_2-CH_2-CH_2-OH$

**b.** $\begin{array}{c} \phantom{CH_3-CH_2-}OH\phantom{-CH_3} \\ | \\ CH_3-CH_2-CH-CH_3 \end{array}$

**c.** cyclohexane ring with OH

**d.** $\begin{array}{c} \phantom{CH_3-}OH\phantom{-CH_2-}CH_3\phantom{-CH_3} \\ \phantom{CH_3-}|\phantom{-CH_2-}|\phantom{-CH_3} \\ CH_3-CH-CH_2-CH-CH_3 \end{array}$

**e.** $\begin{array}{c} \phantom{CH_3-}CH_3\phantom{-CH_2-CH_2-OH} \\ | \\ CH_3-CH-CH_2-CH_2-OH \end{array}$

**14.22** Draw the condensed structural formula of the aldehyde or ketone product when each of the following alcohols is oxidized [O] (if no reaction, write *none*):

**a.** cyclobutane ring with $-CH_2-OH$

**b.** $\begin{array}{c} \phantom{CH_3-}CH_3\phantom{-CH_2-CH-OH} \\ | \\ CH_3-CH-CH_2-CH-OH \\ \phantom{CH_3-CH-CH_2-}|\phantom{-OH} \\ \phantom{CH_3-CH-CH_2-}CH_3\phantom{-OH} \end{array}$

**c.** $\begin{array}{c} \phantom{CH_3-CH_2-}OH\phantom{-CH_3} \\ | \\ CH_3-CH_2-C-CH_3 \\ | \\ \phantom{CH_3-CH_2-}CH_3\phantom{-CH_3} \end{array}$

**d.** $\begin{array}{c} \phantom{CH_3-CH-}OH\phantom{-CH_2-CH_3} \\ | \\ CH_3-CH-CH-CH_2-CH_3 \\ | \\ \phantom{CH_3-}OH\phantom{-CH-CH_2-CH_3} \end{array}$

**e.** cyclobutane ring with OH

**14.23** Give the condensed structural formula of the organic product formed when each of the following is reduced by hydrogen in the presence of a nickel catalyst:

**a.** butyraldehyde **b.** acetone

**c.** 3-bromohexanal **d.** 2-methyl-3-pentanone

**14.24** Give the condensed structural formula of the organic product formed when each of the following is reduced by hydrogen in the presence of a nickel catalyst:

**a.** ethyl propyl ketone

**b.** formaldehyde

**c.** 3-chlorocyclopentanone

**d.** 2-pentanone

# 14.4 Addition Reactions of Aldehydes and Ketones

**LEARNING GOAL**

Write the products of the addition of alcohols to aldehydes and ketones.

One of the most common reactions of aldehydes and ketones is the addition of polar molecules to the carbonyl group. The carbonyl group is reactive because of the polarity of the C═O double bond. In addition reactions, the partially negative part of the adding molecule bonds with the partially positively charged carbonyl carbon. The partially positive part, usually a proton, combines with the partially negatively charged carbonyl oxygen. This type of addition to the carbonyl group can be illustrated as follows:

$$\overset{\delta^+}{C}=\overset{\delta^-}{O} + \overset{\delta^+}{X}-\overset{\delta^-}{Y} \longrightarrow \begin{array}{c} O-X \\ | \\ -C- \\ | \\ Y \end{array}$$

Carbonyl group of aldehyde or ketone — Adding molecule

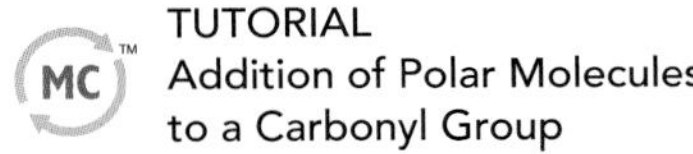

MC
TUTORIAL
Addition of Polar Molecules to a Carbonyl Group


In general, aldehydes are more reactive than ketones because the carbonyl carbon is more positive in aldehydes. Also, the presence of two alkyl groups in ketones makes it more difficult for a molecule to form bonds with the carbon in the carbonyl group.

## Addition of Water

The components of water add to aldehydes and ketones to give carbonyl hydrates in the presence of acid or base. The partially negative —OH group bonds with the carbonyl carbon, while the —H bonds to the partially negative oxygen. In water, the simplest aldehyde, formaldehyde, forms its hydrate called *formalin*, which is used to preserve tissues. Other aldehydes form hydrates in water as well, but not with as high a percentage as formaldehyde. The carbonyl group in ketones also reacts with water, but their hydrates are not very stable:

$$\underset{\text{Formaldehyde}}{H_2C{=}O} + H_2O \underset{}{\overset{H^+}{\rightleftharpoons}} \underset{\text{Formalin}}{H_2C(OH)_2}$$

$$\underset{\text{Acetaldehyde}}{(H_3C)(H)C{=}O} + H_2O \overset{H^+}{\rightleftharpoons} \underset{\text{Hydrate}}{(H_3C)(H)C(OH)_2}$$

Chloral, which is an aldehyde with chlorine atoms, forms a hydrate known as *chloral hydrate*, the substance in "knock out" drops:

$$\underset{\text{Chloral}}{(Cl_3C)(H)C{=}O} + H_2O \rightleftharpoons \underset{\text{Chloral hydrate}}{(Cl_3C)(H)C(OH)_2}$$

## Acetal Formation

TUTORIAL
Formation of Acetals

Similar to the addition of water to form hydrates, aldehydes and ketones react with alcohols in the presence of an acid catalyst to form **acetals**. (Ketal is an older term previously used for acetals from ketones.) In the acetal product, the two alkoxy groups are added to the carbonyl carbon and a molecule of water is eliminated:

$$\underset{\text{Acetaldehyde}}{CH_3{-}C({=}O){-}H} + \underset{\text{Methyl alcohol}}{2CH_3{-}OH} \overset{H^+}{\rightleftharpoons} \underset{\text{Acetaldehyde dimethyl acetal}}{CH_3{-}C(O{-}CH_3)_2{-}H} + H_2O$$

$$\underset{\text{Propanone}}{CH_3{-}C({=}O){-}CH_3} + \underset{\text{Ethyl alcohol}}{2CH_3{-}CH_2{-}OH} \overset{H^+}{\rightleftharpoons} \underset{\text{Propanone diethyl acetal}}{CH_3{-}C(O{-}CH_2{-}CH_3)_2{-}CH_3} + H_2O$$

$$\underset{\text{Cyclohexanone}}{C_6H_{10}{=}O} + \underset{\text{Methyl alcohol}}{2CH_3{-}OH} \overset{H^+}{\rightleftharpoons} \underset{\text{Cyclohexanone dimethyl acetal}}{C_6H_{10}(O{-}CH_3)_2} + H_2O$$

## Hemiacetal Intermediate

In the process of forming acetals, an intermediate called a **hemiacetal** forms when one of the two alcohol molecules adds to the carbonyl carbon. The hemiacetal has an —OH and an alkoxy group bonded to the same carbon atom. The term *hemi* indicates that the hemiacetal is halfway to an acetal. Most of the hemiacetal intermediates are unstable and difficult to isolate from the reaction mixture, which is indicated by the brackets around the hemiacetal structure. In the next step, the second alcohol is added to produce the more stable acetal. Acetals are stable and can be isolated from the reaction mixture:

$$\underset{\text{Acetaldehyde}}{CH_3-\overset{\overset{\displaystyle O}{\|}}{C}-H} + \underset{\text{Methyl alcohol}}{CH_3-OH} \overset{H^+}{\rightleftharpoons} \left\{ \underset{\text{Hemiacetal intermediate}}{CH_3-\overset{\overset{\displaystyle O-CH_3}{|}}{\underset{\underset{\displaystyle OH}{|}}{C}}-H} \right\} + CH_3-OH \overset{H^+}{\rightleftharpoons} \underset{\text{Acetaldehyde dimethyl acetal}}{CH_3-\overset{\overset{\displaystyle O-CH_3}{|}}{\underset{\underset{\displaystyle O-CH_3}{|}}{C}}-H} + H_2O$$

Cyclohexanone + $CH_3-OH$ $\overset{H^+}{\rightleftharpoons}$ {Hemiacetal intermediate (cyclohexane carbon bearing HO and $O-CH_3$)} + $CH_3-OH$ $\overset{H^+}{\rightleftharpoons}$ Cyclohexanone dimethyl acetal (cyclohexane carbon bearing $CH_3-O$ and $O-CH_3$) + $H_2O$

Both the step to the hemiacetal and the step to the acetal are reversible. As predicted by Le Châtelier's principle, the forward reaction to form the acetal is favored by removing water from the reaction mixture. The reverse reaction, which is the hydrolysis of an acetal, is favored by adding water to drive the equilibrium back to the ketone or aldehyde.

CONCEPT CHECK 14.4

### Hemiacetals and Acetals

From the following descriptions, identify the compound as a hemiacetal or an acetal:

**a.** a molecule that contains a carbon atom attached to a hydroxyl group and an ethoxy group
**b.** a molecule that contains a carbon atom attached to two ethoxy groups
**c.** intermediate that forms when one molecule of an alcohol adds to a ketone
**d.** product that forms when two molecules of an alcohol add to an aldehyde

ANSWER

**a.** A hemiacetal contains a carbon atom attached to a hydroxyl group and an ethoxy group.
**b.** An acetal contains a carbon atom attached to two ethoxy groups.
**c.** A hemiacetal involves the addition of one molecule of an alcohol to a ketone.
**d.** An acetal involves the addition of two molecules of an alcohol to an aldehyde.

SAMPLE PROBLEM 14.7

### Acetals

Draw the condensed structural formulas of the hemiacetal and acetal products when methanol adds to propionaldehyde.

SOLUTION

To form the hemiacetal, the hydrogen from the alcohol adds to the oxygen of the carbonyl group to form a new hydroxyl group. The remaining part of the alcohol adds to the carbon atom in the carbonyl group. The acetal forms when a second molecule of methanol is added to the carbonyl carbon atom:

$$\underset{\text{Aldehyde}}{CH_3-CH_2-\overset{\overset{\displaystyle O}{\|}}{C}-H} + \underset{\text{Methyl alcohol}}{HO-CH_3} \overset{H^+}{\rightleftharpoons} \underset{\text{Hemiacetal}}{CH_3-CH_2-\overset{\overset{\displaystyle OH}{|}}{\underset{\underset{\displaystyle O-CH_3}{|}}{C}}-H} + \underset{\text{Methyl alcohol}}{HO-CH_3} \overset{H^+}{\rightleftharpoons} \underset{\text{Acetal}}{CH_3-CH_2-\overset{\overset{\displaystyle O-CH_3}{|}}{\underset{\underset{\displaystyle O-CH_3}{|}}{C}}-H} + H_2O$$

STUDY CHECK

What is the condensed structural formula of the acetal produced when methanol adds to propanone?

## Cyclic Hemiacetals

MC TUTORIAL Cyclic Hemiacetals

One very important type of hemiacetal that can be isolated is a cyclic hemiacetal that forms when the carbonyl group and the —OH group are in the *same* molecule:

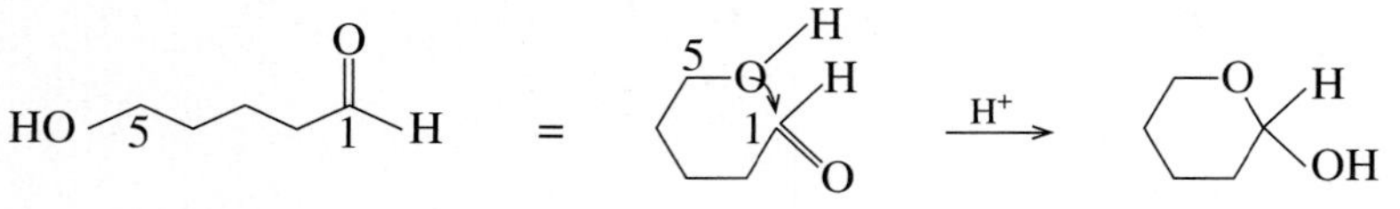

Open chain

Cyclic hemiacetal

The five- and six-atom cyclic hemiacetals and acetals are more stable than their open-chain structures. For example, glucose, a simple sugar, forms a hemiacetal when the hydroxyl group on carbon 5 bonds with the carbonyl group. The hemiacetal of glucose is so stable that almost all the glucose (99%) exists as the hemiacetal in aqueous solution:

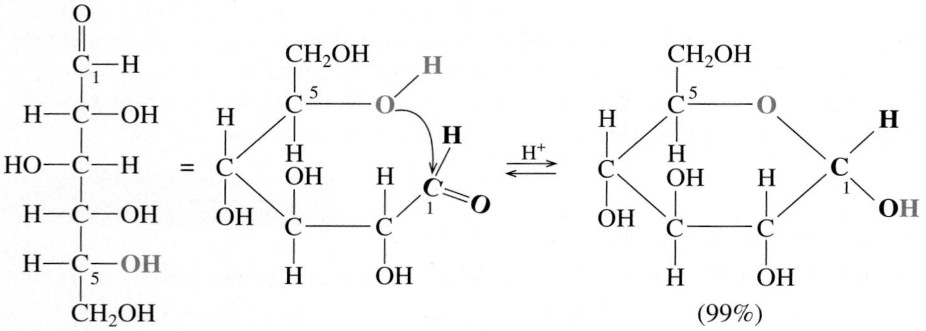

Glucose

Formation of cyclic hemiacetal

(99%)

We will discuss carbohydrates and their structures in Chapter 15.

An alcohol can add to the cyclic hemiacetal to form a cyclic acetal. This reaction is also very important in carbohydrate chemistry. It is the linkage used by glucose molecules to bond to other glucose molecules to form long chains:

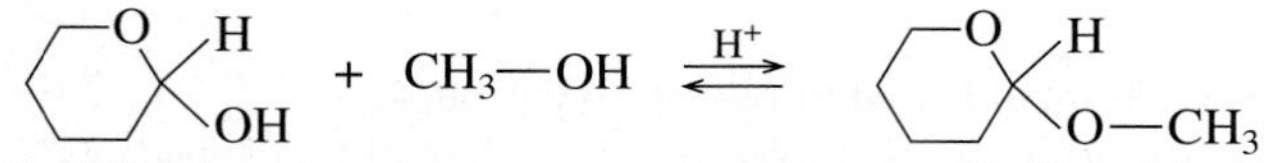

Cyclic hemiacetal + $CH_3—OH$ $\overset{H^+}{\rightleftharpoons}$ Cyclic acetal

## QUESTIONS AND PROBLEMS

### Addition Reactions of Aldehydes and Ketones

**14.25** Draw the condensed structural formula of the organic product formed by the addition of water to each of the following:

**a.** acetaldehyde **b.** formaldehyde

**14.26** Draw the condensed structural formula of the organic product formed by the addition of water to each of the following:

**a.** propanal **b.** propanone

**14.27** Indicate whether each of the following structural formulas is a hemiacetal, acetal, or neither:

**a.** $CH_3—CH_2—O—CH_2—OH$

**b.** $CH_3—CH_2—CH_2—C(O—CH_3)(OH)—H$

**c.** $CH_3—C(O—CH_2—CH_3)(O—CH_2—CH_3)—CH_2—CH_3$

**d.** cyclohexane ring with OH and $O—CH_2—CH_3$ on the same carbon

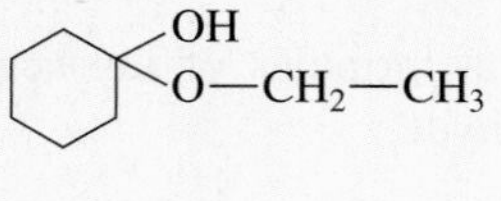

**e.** 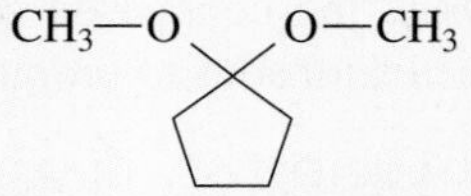 $CH_3—O$ and $O—CH_3$ on the same carbon of a cyclopentane ring

**14.28** Indicate whether each of the following structural formulas is a hemiacetal, acetal, or neither:

**a.** $CH_3—CH_2—O—CH_2—CH_3$

**b.** $HO—CH_2—CH_2—O—CH_2—CH_2—O—CH_3$

**c.** $CH_3—C(O—CH_2—CH_3)(OH)—CH_3$

**d.** 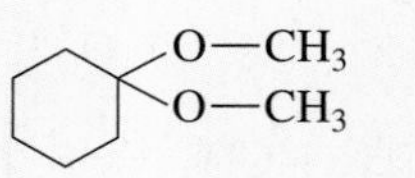 cyclohexane ring with two $O—CH_3$ groups on the same carbon

**e.** 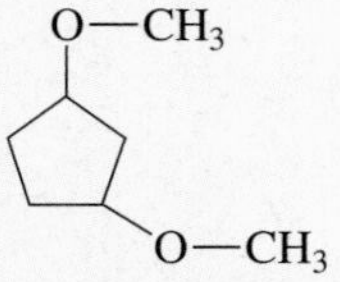 cyclopentane ring with $O—CH_3$ groups on different carbons

14.29 Draw the condensed structural formula of the hemiacetal formed by adding one methanol molecule to each of the following compounds:
**a.** ethanal **b.** propanone
**c.** cyclopentanone **d.** butanal

**14.30** Draw the condensed structural formula of the hemiacetal formed by adding one ethanol molecule to each of the following compounds:
**a.** propanal **b.** 2-butanone
**c.** cyclohexanone **d.** formaldehyde

14.31 Draw the condensed structural formula of the acetal formed by adding a second methanol to the compounds in problem 14.29.

**14.32** Draw the condensed structural formula of the acetal formed by adding a second ethanol to the compounds in problem 14.30.

## 14.5 Chiral Molecules

LEARNING GOAL
Identify chiral and achiral carbon atoms in an organic molecule.

In the preceding chapters, we have looked at isomers. Let's review those now. Molecules are structural isomers when they have the same molecular formula but different bonding arrangements:

**Isomers**

| | | |
|---|---|---|
| $C_2H_6O$ | $CH_3—CH_2—OH$ <br> Ethanol | $CH_3—O—CH_3$ <br> Dimethyl ether |
| $C_3H_6O$ | $CH_3—CH_2—C(=O)—H$ <br> Propanal | $CH_3—C(=O)—CH_3$ <br> Propanone |

Another group of isomers called **stereoisomers** have identical molecular formulas, too, but they are not structural isomers. In stereoisomers, the atoms are bonded in the same sequence but differ in the way they are arranged in space.

### Chirality

When stereoisomers have mirror images that are different, they are said to have "handedness." If you hold your right hand up to a mirror, you see its mirror image, which matches your left hand. (See Figure 14.6.)

If you turn your palms toward each other, you also have mirror images. If you look at the palms of your hands, your thumbs are on opposite sides. If you place your right hand over your left hand, you cannot match up all the parts of the hands: palms, backs, thumbs, and little fingers. The thumbs and little fingers can be matched, but then the palms and backs of your hands are facing each other. Your hands are mirror images that cannot be

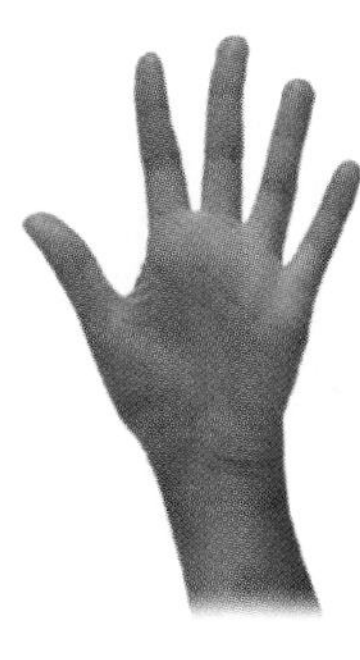
Left hand

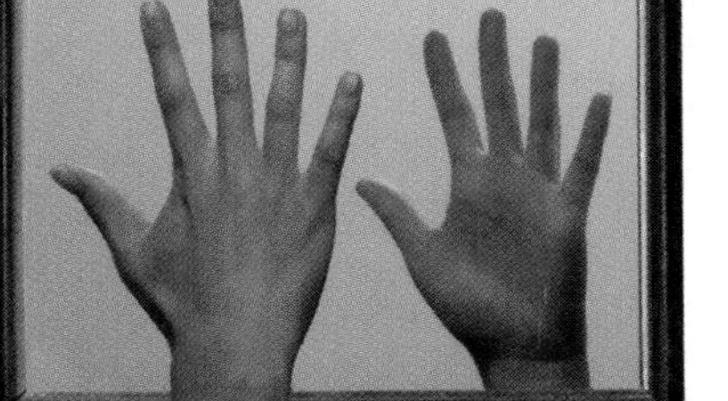
Mirror image of right hand

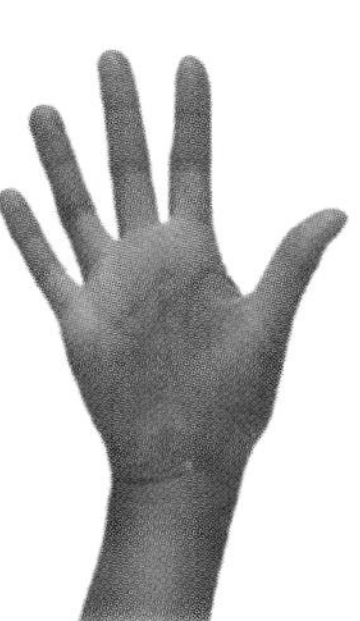
Right hand

FIGURE 14.6 The left and right hands are chiral because they have mirror images that cannot be superimposed on each other.
Q Why are your shoes chiral objects?

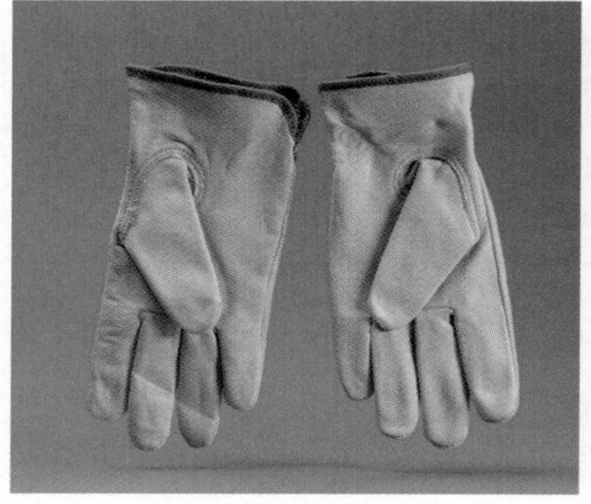
Chiral

Golf club, chiral

Achiral

Achiral

Chiral

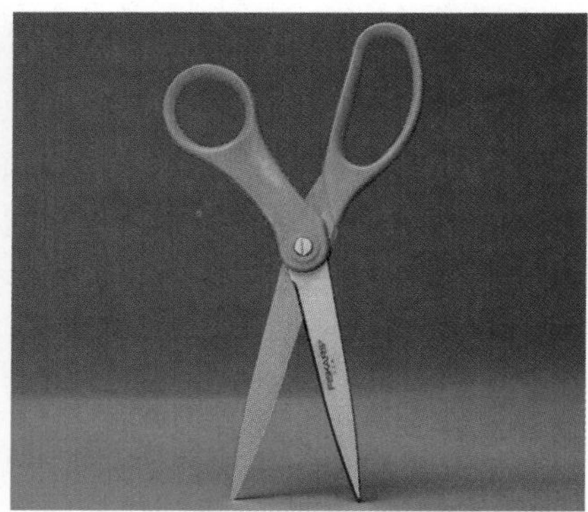
Right-handed scissors, chiral

**FIGURE 14.7** Everyday objects can be chiral or achiral.
**Q** Why are some of the above objects chiral and others achiral?

superimposed on each other. When organic molecules have mirror images but cannot be completely matched, we say that they are *nonsuperimposable*.

Objects such as hands that have nonsuperimposable mirror images are **chiral**. Left and right shoes are chiral; left- and right-handed golf clubs are chiral. When we think of how difficult it is to put a left-hand glove on our right hand, put a right shoe on our left foot, or use left-handed scissors if we are right handed, we begin to realize that certain properties of mirror images are very different.

Sometimes a mirror image can be superimposed on the original. For example, all parts of the mirror image of a plain drinking glass can be matched to the glass. When one mirror image can be superimposed on the other, the object is **achiral**. (See Figure 14.7.)

CONCEPT CHECK 14.5

### Everyday Chiral Objects

Classify each of the following objects as chiral or achiral:

**a.** left ear
**b.** flip-flop beach sandal
**c.** plain golf ball

ANSWER

**a.** A left ear is chiral because it cannot be superimposed on the right ear.
**b.** The mirror image of a left flip-flop is the right flip-flop. They are chiral because they are not superimposable.
**c.** A golf ball is achiral because the mirror images are superimposable.

## EXPLORE YOUR WORLD

### Using Gumdrops and Toothpicks to Model Chiral Objects

#### Part 1: Achiral Objects

Obtain some toothpicks and several orange, yellow, green, purple, and black gumdrops. Place four toothpicks into the black gumdrop, making the ends of toothpicks form a tetrahedron. Attach gumdrops to the toothpicks: two orange, one green, and one yellow.

Using another black gumdrop, make a second model that is the mirror image of the original model. Now rotate one of the models, and try to superimpose it on the other model. Are the models superimposable? If achiral objects have superimposable mirror images, are these models chiral or achiral?

#### Part 2: Chiral Objects

Using one of the original models, replace one orange gumdrop with a purple gumdrop. Now there are four different colors of gumdrops attached to the black gumdrop. Make its mirror image by replacing one orange gumdrop with a purple one. Now rotate one of the models, and try to superimpose it on the other model. Are the models superimposable? If chiral objects have nonsuperimposable mirror images, are these models chiral or achiral?

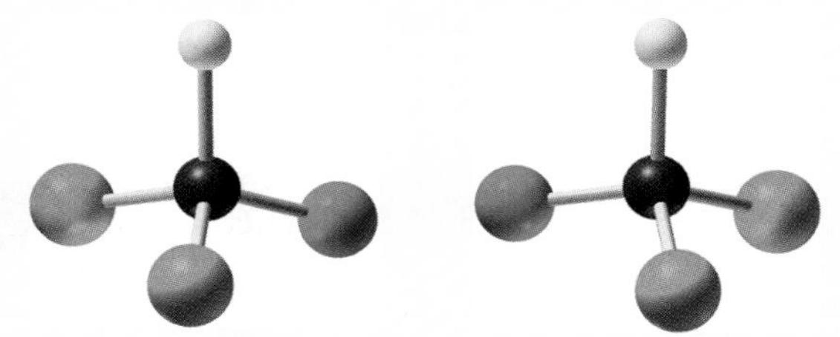

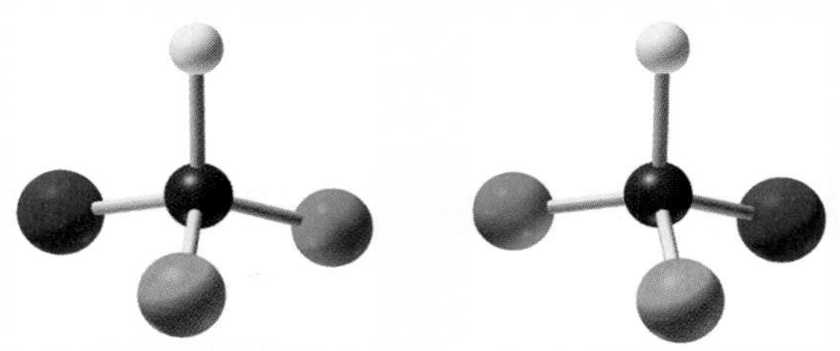

## Chiral Carbon Atoms

A carbon compound is chiral if it has at least one carbon atom bonded to four different atoms or groups. This type of carbon atom is called a **chiral carbon** because there are two different ways that it can bond to four atoms or groups of atoms. The resulting structures are mirror images of each other. Let's look at the mirror images of a carbon bonded to four different atoms. (See Figure 14.8.) If we line up the hydrogen and iodine atoms in the mirror images, the bromine and chlorine atoms appear on opposite sides. No matter how we turn the models, we cannot align all four atoms at the same time. When stereoisomers cannot be superimposed, they are called **enantiomers**.

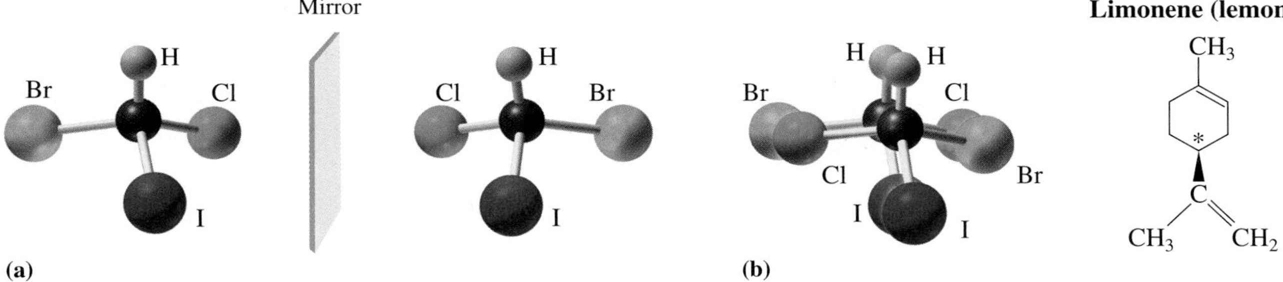


**FIGURE 14.8** **(a)** The enantiomers of a chiral molecule are mirror images. **(b)** The enantiomers of a chiral molecule cannot be superimposed on each other.

Q Why is the carbon atom in this compound a chiral carbon?

**Limonene (lemons)**

$CH_3$ … $CH_3$ $CH_2$

**Limonene (oranges)**

$CH_3$ … $H_2C$ $CH_3$

Molecules in nature also have mirror images, and often one stereoisomer has a different biological effect than the other one. For some compounds, one enantiomer has a certain odor, and the other enantiomer has a completely different odor. For example, the compound limonene has one chiral carbon in the carbon ring indicated by an asterisk; limonene has two enantiomers. One enantiomer of limonene smells like lemons, while its mirror image has the odor of oranges. If two or more atoms bonded to a particular carbon are the same, the atoms can be aligned (superimposed), and the mirror images represent the same structure. (See Figure 14.9.)

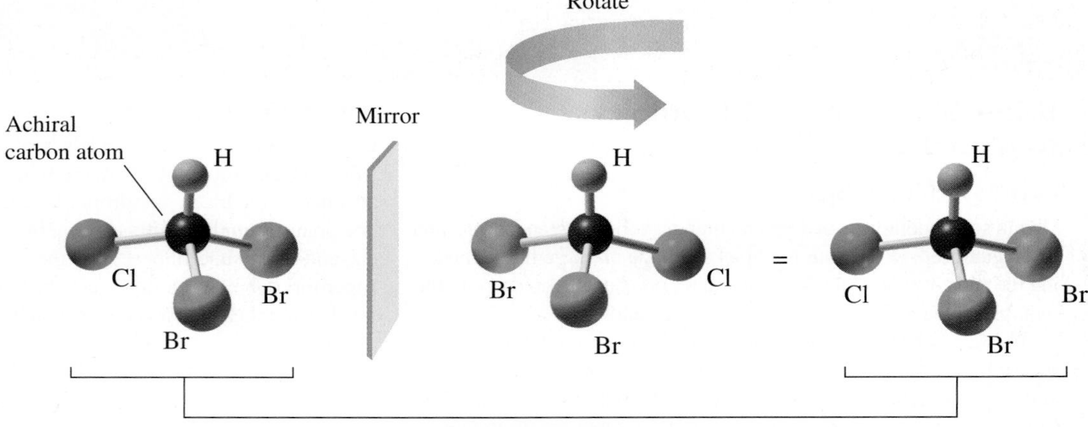


**FIGURE 14.9** The mirror images of an achiral compound can be superimposed on each other.
**Q** Why can the mirror images of the compound be superimposed?

**SAMPLE PROBLEM 14.8**

### Chiral Carbons

For each of the following, indicate whether the carbon in red is chiral or achiral:

**a.** $Cl—C(Cl)(H)—CH_3$

**b.** $CH_3—C(OH)(H)—CH_2—CH_3$

**c.** $CH_3—C(=O)—CH_2—CH_3$

**d.** $CH_3—CH_2—C(CH_3)(H)—C(=O)—H$

SOLUTION

**a.** Achiral. Two of the substituents on the carbon are the same (—Cl). A chiral carbon must be bonded to four different groups or atoms.
**b.** Chiral. Carbon 2 is bonded to four different groups: one —OH, one $—CH_3$, one $—CH_2—CH_3$, and one —H.
**c.** Achiral. Carbon 2 is bonded to only three groups, not four.
**d.** Chiral. Carbon 2 is bonded to four different groups: one —H, one $—CH_3$, one $—CH_2—CH_3$, and one —CHO.

STUDY CHECK

Circle the two chiral carbons in the structural formula of the carbohydrate erythrose:

$HO—CH_2—CH(OH)—CH(OH)—C(=O)—H$

Erythrose

## Drawing Fischer Projections

Emil Fischer devised a simplified system for drawing stereoisomers that shows the arrangements of the atoms. Fischer received the Nobel Prize in Chemistry in 1902 for his contributions to carbohydrate and protein chemistry. Using his method, called a **Fischer**

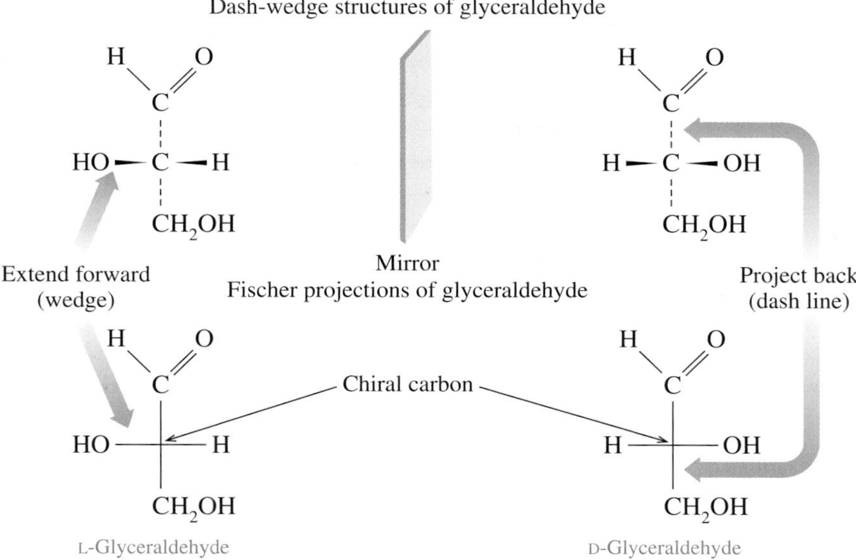


**FIGURE 14.10** In a Fischer projection, the chiral carbon atom is at the center with horizontal lines for bonds that extend toward the viewer and vertical lines for bonds that point away.

**Q** Why does glyceraldehyde have only one chiral carbon atom?

**projection**, the carbon chain is written vertically with the most highly oxidized carbon at the top. Horizontal lines represent bonds that project forward in the three-dimensional structure. Vertical lines represent bonds that project backward. Each intersection of lines represents a carbon atom that is usually chiral.

For glyceraldehyde, the carbonyl group, which is the most highly oxidized group in the molecule, is written at the top. The letter L is assigned to the left-handed stereoisomer, which has the —OH group on the left of the chiral carbon. The letter D is assigned to the right-handed structure, where the —OH is on the right of the chiral carbon. Today, the "D- and L-" system is used primarily to identify the enantiomers of carbohydrates and amino acids. Let's look at how glyceraldehyde, the simplest sugar, is converted from a three-dimensional view to a Fischer projection. (See Figure 14.10.)

Fischer projections can also be written for compounds that have two or more chiral carbons. For example, in the following mirror images, the chiral carbon atom at each intersection is bonded to four different groups. To draw the mirror image, the positions of the substituents on the horizontal lines are reversed:

```
     CH2OH                          CH2OH
  H ──┼── Br    reverse H     Br ──┼── H
 Br ──┼── H     and Br   ⇒     H ──┼── Br
     CH3                            CH3
```

We can also draw the mirror image of the carbohydrate erythrose by changing the sides of the —OH groups on the two chiral carbons:

```
   H   O           H   O
    \ //            \ //
     C               C
 HO ─┼─ H         H ─┼─ OH
 HO ─┼─ H         H ─┼─ OH
    CH2OH           CH2OH
 L-Erythrose     D-Erythrose
```

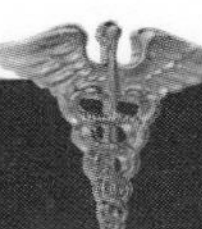

# HEALTH NOTE

## Enantiomers in Biological Systems

Most compounds that are active in biological systems consist of only one enantiomer. Rarely are both enantiomers of biological molecules active. This happens because the enzymes and cell surface receptors on which metabolic reactions take place are themselves chiral. Thus, only one enantiomer interacts with its enzymes or receptors; the other is inactive. The chiral receptor fits the arrangement of the substituents in only one enantiomer; its mirror image does not fit properly. (See Figure 14.11.)

A substance called *carvone* has two enantiomers. One enantiomer gives the odor of spearmint oil, while the other enantiomer produces the odor of caraway seeds. The chiral receptor sites in the olfactory cells in the nasal cavity and the gustatory cells in the taste buds on the tongue fit the shape of only one enantiomer. Thus, our senses of smell and taste are responsive to the chirality of molecules.

### Enantiomers of Carvone

From spearmint oil — From caraway seeds

In the brain, one enantiomer of LSD affects the production of serotonin, affecting sensory perception and possibly leading to hallucinations. However, its enantiomer produces little effect in the brain. The behavior of nicotine and epinephrine (adrenaline) also depends upon only one of their enantiomers. For example, one enantiomer of nicotine is more toxic than the other. Only one enantiomer of epinephrine is responsible for the constriction of blood vessels.

Chiral carbon

Nicotine — Adrenalin (epinephrine)

A substance used to treat Parkinson's disease is L-dopa, which is converted to dopamine in the brain, where it raises the serotonin level. However, the D-dopa enantiomer is not effective for the treatment of Parkinson's disease.

L-Dopa, anti-Parkinsonian drug — D-Dopa has no biological effect

For many drugs, only one of the enantiomers is biologically active. However, for many years, drugs have been produced that were mixtures of their enantiomers. Today, drug researchers are using *chiral technology* to produce the active enantiomers of chiral drugs. Chiral catalysts are being designed that direct the formation of just one enantiomer rather than both. The benefits of producing only the active enantiomer include using a lower dose, enhancing activity, reducing interactions with other drugs, and eliminating possible harmful side effects from the inactive enantiomer. Several active enantiomers are now being produced such as L-dopa and the active enantiomer of the popular analgesic ibuprofen used in Advil, Motrin, and Nuprin.

Ibuprofen

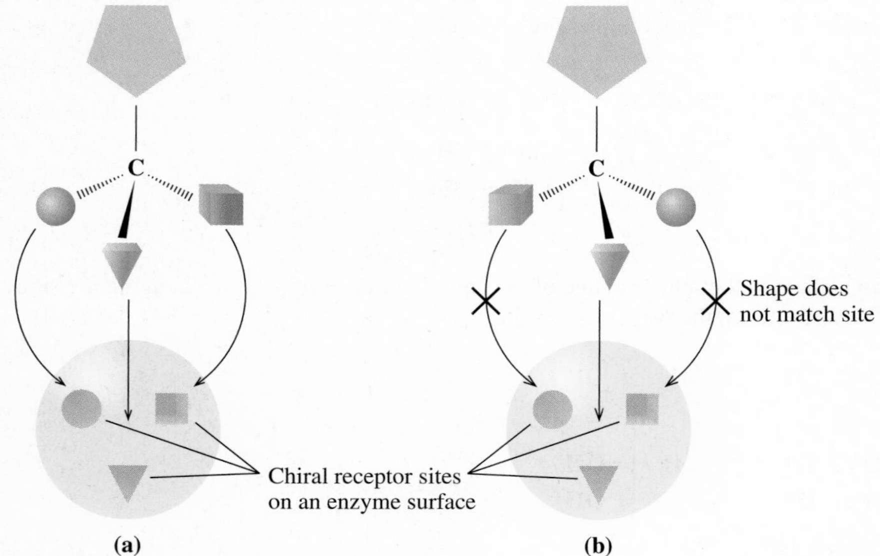


**FIGURE 14.11** **(a)** The substituents on the biologically active enantiomer bind to all the sites on a chiral receptor; **(b)** its enantiomer does not bind properly and is not active biologically.

**Q** Why doesn't the mirror image of the active enantiomer fit into a chiral receptor site?

SAMPLE PROBLEM 14.9

## Fischer Projections

Determine if each Fischer projection is chiral or achiral. If chiral, identify it as the D or L isomer and draw the mirror image.

```
     CH2OH               CH3              CHO
a. HO—+—H        b. HO—+—H       c. H—+—OH
     CH3                 CH3              CH3
```

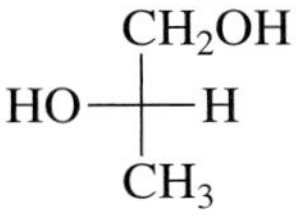

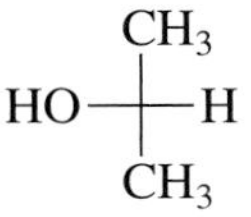

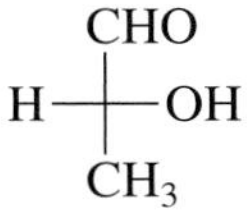

SOLUTION

**a.** Chiral. The carbon at the intersection that is attached to four different substituents is the L isomer because the —OH is on the left. Its mirror image is written by reversing the —H and —OH:

```
  CH2OH
H—+—OH
  CH3
```

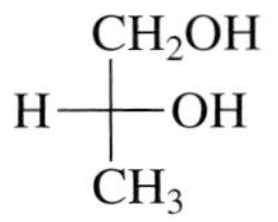

**b.** Achiral. The carbon atom at the intersection is attached to two identical groups (—$CH_3$).

**c.** Chiral. The carbon atom at the intersection is attached to four different substituents. It is the D isomer because the —OH is on the right. The mirror image is written by reversing the —H and —OH:

```
   CHO
HO—+—H
   CH3
```

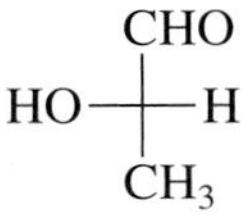

STUDY CHECK

Draw the Fischer projections for the D and L stereoisomers of 2-hydroxypropanal.

# QUESTIONS AND PROBLEMS

## Chiral Molecules

**14.33** Identify each of the following structures as chiral or achiral. If chiral, indicate the chiral carbon.

```
         OH                       Br
         |                        |
a. CH3—CH—CH3          b. CH3—CH—CH2—CH3

        CH3  O                          O
         |   ||                         ||
c. CH3—CH—C—H          d. CH3—CH2—C—CH3
```

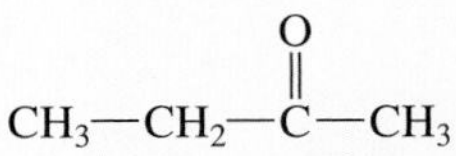

**14.34** Identify each of the following structures as chiral or achiral. If chiral, indicate the chiral carbon.

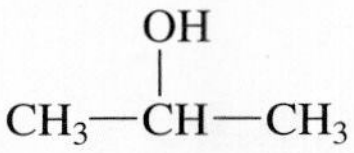

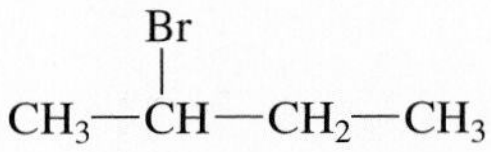

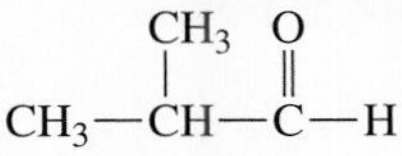

```
        Cl        Cl
        |         |
a. CH3—C—CH2—CH—CH3
        |
        CH3

        Br                     OH OH
        |                       |  |
b. CH3—C=CH—CH3         c. CH3—C—CH—CH3
                                |
                                OH
             Cl
             |
d. Br—CH2—CH—CH3
```

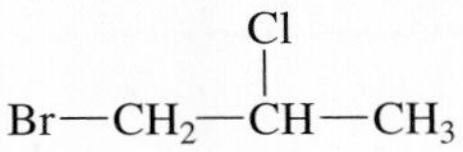

**14.35** Identify the chiral carbon in each of the following naturally occurring compounds:

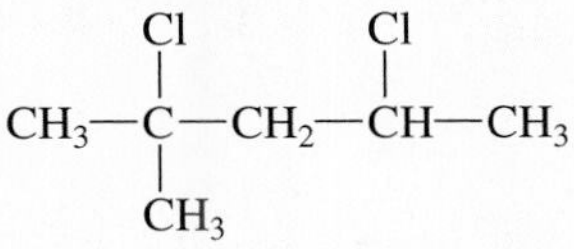

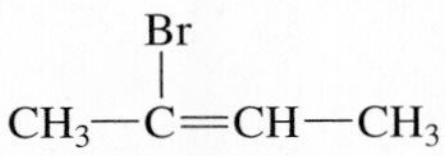

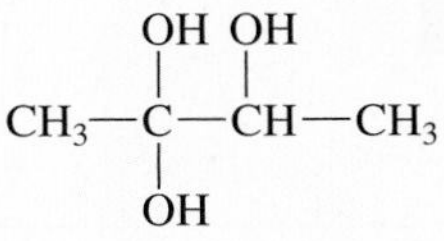

a. citronellol, one enantiomer has the geranium odor

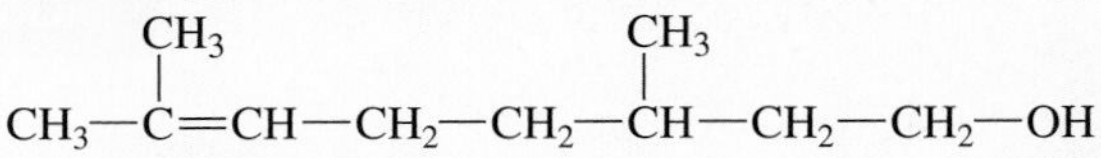

```
      CH3                 CH3
      |                   |
CH3—C=CH—CH2—CH2—CH—CH2—CH2—OH
```

b. alanine, amino acid

```
      CH3 O
       |  ||
H2N—CH—C—OH
```

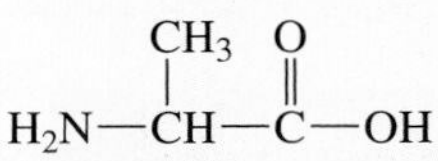

**14.36** Identify the chiral carbon in each of the following naturally occurring compounds:

a. amphetamine (Benzedrine), stimulant, treatment of hyperactivity

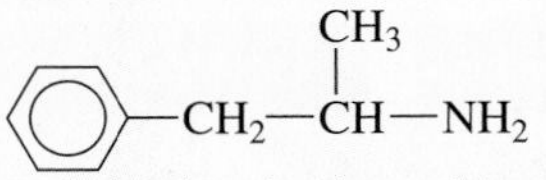

```
                 CH3
                 |
(C6H5)—CH2—CH—NH2
```

b. Norepinephrine, increases blood pressure and nerve transmission

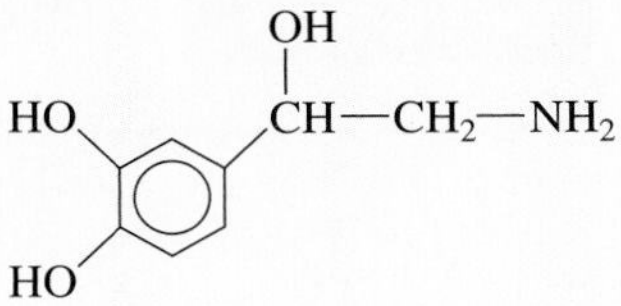

```
                        OH
                        |
HO—(benzene ring)—CH—CH2—NH2
HO—
```

**14.37** Draw the Fischer projection for each of the following dash-wedge structures:

**a.** H; C; HO, Br, $CH_3$ **b.** $CH_3$; C; Cl, Br, OH **c.** CHO; C; HO, H, $CH_2CH_3$

**14.38** Draw the Fischer projection for each of the following dash-wedge structures:

**a.** CHO; C; HO, Br, $CH_2OH$ **b.** CHO; C; H, OH, $CH_2OH$ **c.** CHO; C; HO, H, $CH_2OH$

**14.39** Indicate whether each pair of Fischer projections represent enantiomers or identical structures:

**a.** $CH_3$; Br–C–Cl; $CH_3$ and $CH_3$; Cl–C–Br; $CH_3$

**b.** CHO; HO–C–H; $CH_3$ and CHO; H–C–OH; $CH_3$

**c.** $CH_3$; Cl–C–Br; H and $CH_3$; Br–C–Cl; H

**d.** COOH; H–C–OH; $CH_3$ and COOH; HO–C–H; $CH_3$

**14.40** Indicate whether each pair of Fischer projections represent enantiomers or identical structures:

**a.** $CH_2OH$; Br–C–Cl; $CH_3$ and $CH_2OH$; Cl–C–Br; $CH_3$

**b.** CHO; H–C–H; $CH_3$ and CHO; H–C–H; $CH_3$

**c.** $CH_3$; H–C–OH; $CH_2CH_3$ and $CH_3$; HO–C–H; $CH_2CH_3$

**d.** COOH; H–C–$NH_2$; $CH_3$ and COOH; $H_2N$–C–H; $CH_3$

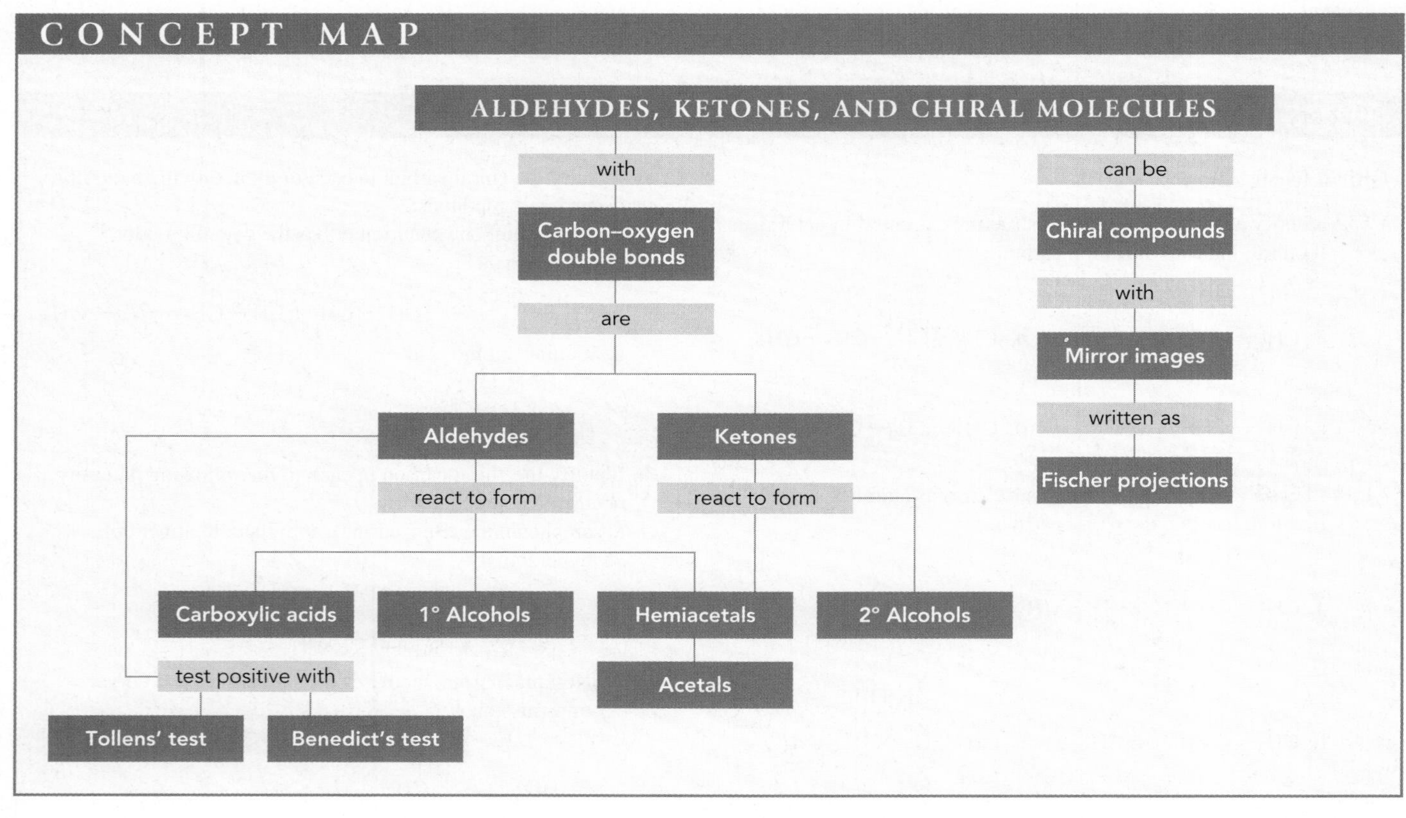

# CHAPTER REVIEW

## 14.1 Aldehydes and Ketones

**LEARNING GOAL:** *Identify compounds with the carbonyl group as aldehydes and ketones. Give the IUPAC and common names for aldehydes and ketones; draw their condensed structural formulas.*

Aldehydes and ketones contain a carbonyl group (C=O), which consists of a double bond between a carbon and an oxygen atom. However, in contrast to the C=C double bond, the C=O is strongly polar. In aldehydes, the carbonyl group appears at the end of carbon chains attached to at least one hydrogen atom. In ketones, the carbonyl group occurs between two alkyl or aromatic groups. In the IUPAC system, the *e* in the corresponding alkane is replaced with *al* for aldehydes and *one* for ketones. For ketones with more than four carbon atoms in the main chain, the carbonyl group is numbered to show its location. Many of the simple aldehydes and ketones use common names. Many aldehydes and ketones are found in biological systems, flavorings, and drugs.

## 14.2 Physical Properties of Aldehydes and Ketones

**LEARNING GOAL:** *Compare the boiling points and solubility of aldehydes and ketones to those of alkanes and alcohols.*

Because they contain a polar carbonyl group, aldehydes and ketones have higher boiling points than alkanes and ethers of similar molar mass. Their boiling points are lower than alcohols because aldehydes and ketones cannot hydrogen bond with each other. However, aldehydes and ketones can hydrogen bond with water molecules, which makes carbonyl compounds with one to four carbon atoms soluble in water.

## 14.3 Oxidation and Reduction of Aldehydes and Ketones

**LEARNING GOAL:** *Draw the condensed structural formulas of reactants and products for the oxidation or reduction of aldehydes and ketones.*

Primary alcohols can be oxidized to aldehydes, whereas secondary alcohols can oxidize to ketones. Aldehydes are easily oxidized to carboxylic acids, but ketones do not oxidize further. Aldehydes, but not ketones, react with Tollens' reagent to give "silver mirrors." In Benedict's test, aldehydes with adjacent hydroxyl groups reduce blue $Cu^{2+}$ to give a brick-red $Cu_2O$ solid. The reduction of aldehydes with hydrogen produces primary alcohols, while ketones are reduced to secondary alcohols.

## 14.4 Addition Reactions of Aldehydes and Ketones

**LEARNING GOAL:** *Write the products of the addition of alcohols to aldehydes and ketones.*

Water and alcohols can add to the carbonyl group of aldehydes and ketones. The addition of one alcohol forms a hemiacetal, while the addition of two alcohols forms an acetal. Hemiacetals are not usually stable, except for cyclic hemiacetals, which are the most common form of simple sugars such as glucose.

## 14.5 Chiral Molecules

**LEARNING GOAL:** *Identify chiral and achiral carbon atoms in an organic molecule.*

Chiral molecules are molecules with mirror images that cannot be superimposed on each other. These types of stereoisomers are called enantiomers. A chiral molecule must have at least one chiral carbon, which is a carbon bonded to four different atoms or groups of atoms. The Fischer projection is a simplified way to draw the arrangements of atoms by placing the carbon atoms at the intersection of vertical and horizontal lines. The names of the mirror images are labeled D or L to differentiate between enantiomers of carbohydrates and amino acids.

# SUMMARY OF NAMING

| Structure | Family | IUPAC Name | Common Name |
|---|---|---|---|
| $H-\overset{O}{\overset{\|}{C}}-H$ | Aldehyde | Methanal | Formaldehyde |
| $CH_3-\overset{O}{\overset{\|}{C}}-CH_3$ | Ketone | Propanone | Acetone; Dimethyl ketone |

# SUMMARY OF REACTIONS

## OXIDATION OF ALDEHYDES TO CARBOXYLIC ACIDS

$$\underset{\text{Acetaldehyde}}{CH_3-\overset{O}{\overset{\|}{C}}-H} \xrightarrow{[O]} \underset{\text{Acetic acid}}{CH_3-\overset{O}{\overset{\|}{C}}-OH}$$

## REDUCTION OF ALDEHYDES TO PRIMARY ALCOHOLS

$$\underset{\text{Acetaldehyde}}{CH_3-\overset{O}{\overset{\|}{C}}-H} + H_2 \xrightarrow{Ni} \underset{\text{Ethanol}}{CH_3-\overset{OH}{\overset{|}{CH_2}}}$$

## REDUCTION OF KETONES TO SECONDARY ALCOHOLS

$$\underset{\text{Acetone}}{CH_3-\overset{O}{\overset{\|}{C}}-CH_3} + H_2 \xrightarrow{Ni} \underset{\text{2-Propanol}}{CH_3-\overset{OH}{\overset{|}{CH}}-CH_3}$$

## ADDITION OF WATER TO ALDEHYDES

$$\underset{\text{Formaldehyde}}{H_2C{=}O} + H_2O \underset{}{\overset{H^+}{\rightleftharpoons}} \underset{\text{Formalin}}{H_2C(OH)_2}$$

$$\underset{\text{Acetaldehyde}}{H_3C(H)C{=}O} + H_2O \overset{H^+}{\rightleftharpoons} \underset{\text{Hydrate}}{H_3C(H)C(OH)_2}$$

## ADDITION OF ALCOHOLS TO FORM HEMIACETALS AND ACETALS FROM ALDEHYDES

$$\underset{\text{Formaldehyde}}{H{-}\overset{O}{\overset{\|}{C}}{-}H} + \underset{\text{Methanol}}{CH_3{-}OH} \overset{H^+}{\rightleftharpoons} \left\{\underset{\text{Hemiacetal}}{H{-}C(O{-}CH_3)(OH){-}H}\right\} + CH_3{-}OH \overset{H^+}{\rightleftharpoons} \underset{\text{Acetal}}{H{-}C(O{-}CH_3)_2{-}H} + H_2O$$

## FROM KETONES

$$\underset{\text{Acetone}}{CH_3{-}\overset{O}{\overset{\|}{C}}{-}CH_3} + \underset{\text{Methanol}}{CH_3{-}OH} \overset{H^+}{\rightleftharpoons} \left\{\underset{\text{Hemiacetal}}{CH_3{-}C(O{-}CH_3)(OH){-}CH_3}\right\} + CH_3{-}OH \overset{H^+}{\rightleftharpoons} \underset{\text{Acetal}}{CH_3{-}C(O{-}CH_3)_2{-}CH_3} + H_2O$$

# KEY TERMS

**acetal** The product of the addition of two alcohols to an aldehyde or ketone.

**achiral** Molecules with mirror images that are superimposable.

**aldehyde** An organic compound with a carbonyl functional group and at least one hydrogen attached to the carbon in the carbonyl group.

**Benedict's test** A test for aldehydes with adjacent hydroxyl groups in which $Cu^{2+}$ ($CuSO_4$) ions in Benedict's reagent are reduced to a brick-red solid of $Cu_2O$.

**chiral** Objects or molecules that have nonsuperimposable mirror images.

**chiral carbon** A carbon atom that is bonded to four different atoms or groups.

**enantiomers** Stereoisomers that are mirror images that cannot be superimposed.

**Fischer projection** A system for drawing stereoisomers; carbon atoms are shown at intersections of horizontal lines for bonds projecting forward and vertical lines for bonds projecting backward. The most highly oxidized carbon is at the top.

**hemiacetal** The product of the addition of one alcohol to the double bond of the carbonyl group in aldehydes and ketones.

**ketone** An organic compound in which the carbonyl functional group is bonded to two alkyl or aromatic groups.

**reduction** A decrease in the number of carbon–oxygen bonds by the addition of hydrogen to a carbonyl bond. Aldehydes are reduced to primary alcohols; ketones to secondary alcohols.

**stereoisomers** Isomers that have atoms bonded in the same order but with different arrangements in space.

**Tollens' test** A test for aldehydes in which $Ag^+$ in Tollens' reagent is reduced to metallic silver, which forms a "silver mirror" on the walls of the container.

# UNDERSTANDING THE CONCEPTS

**14.41** Which of the following will give a positive Tollens' test?

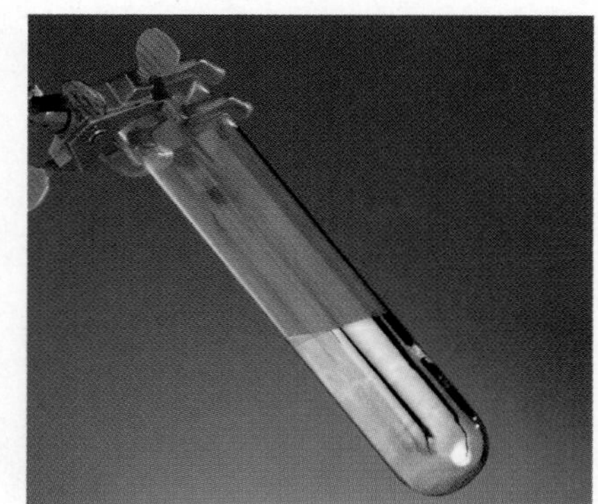

**a.** $CH_3{-}CH_2{-}\overset{O}{\overset{\|}{C}}{-}H$ **b.** $CH_3{-}\overset{O}{\overset{\|}{C}}{-}H$

**c.** $CH_3{-}O{-}CH_2{-}CH_3$ **d.** $CH_3{-}CH_2{-}CH_2{-}OH$

**e.** $CH_3{-}\overset{OH}{\overset{|}{C}H}{-}CH_3$ **f.** cyclopropyl$-\overset{O}{\overset{\|}{C}}{-}H$

**14.42** Citronellal, a constituent of oil of citronella as well as lemon and lemon grass, is used in perfumes and as an insect repellent:

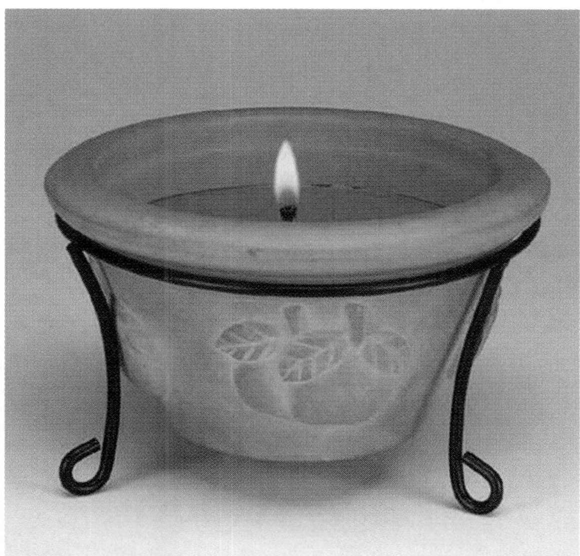

$$CH_3-\overset{\overset{\displaystyle CH_3}{|}}{C}=CH-CH_2-CH_2-\overset{\overset{\displaystyle CH_3}{|}}{C}H-CH_2-\overset{\overset{\displaystyle O}{\|}}{C}-H$$

**a.** Complete the IUPAC name
______, ______-di________ - ______-octenal.

**b.** What does the *en* in octenal signify?

**c.** What does the *al* in octenal signify?

**d.** Write the balanced equation for the combustion of citronellal when burned in a candle to repel insects.

**14.43** Identify the functional groups in each of the following:

**a.** **almonds**

$$\overset{\overset{\displaystyle O}{\|}}{C}-H \text{ attached to a benzene ring}$$

**b.** **vanilla extract or vanilla beans**

$$\overset{\overset{\displaystyle O}{\|}}{C}-H \text{ on a benzene ring bearing } O-CH_3 \text{ and } OH$$

**c.** **cinnamon sticks**

$$C_6H_5-CH=CH-\overset{\overset{\displaystyle O}{\|}}{C}-H$$

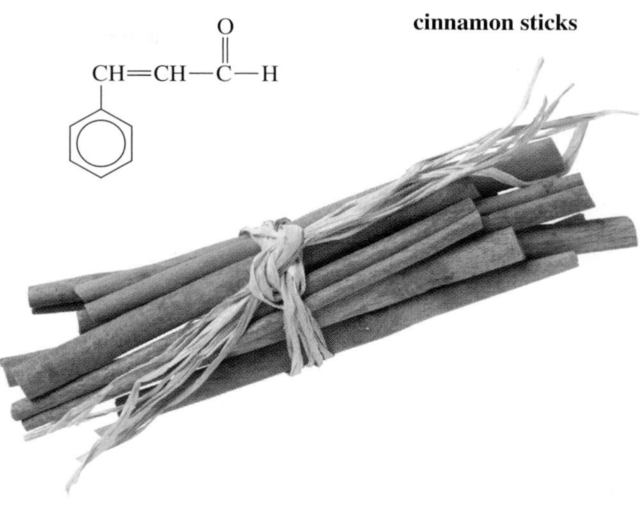

**d.** **mint leaves**

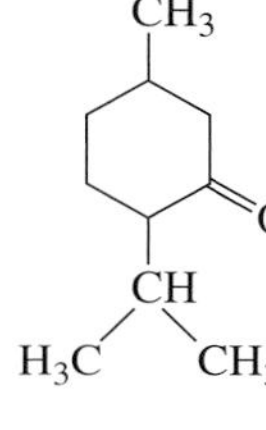

**e.**

$$CH_3-\overset{\overset{\displaystyle O}{\|}}{C}-\overset{\overset{\displaystyle O}{\|}}{C}-CH_3$$

**butter**

Match each of the preceding formulas with the following names:

1. 2,3-butanedione
2. benzaldehyde
3. 2-isopropyl-5-methylcyclohexanone
4. cinnamaldehyde
5. 4-hydroxy-3-methoxybenzaldehyde

**14.44** Draw the condensed structural formula and line-bond formula for each of the following:
**a.** 2-heptanone, an alarm pheromone of bees
**b.** 2,6-dimethyl-3-heptanone, communication pheromone of bees
**c.** *trans*-2-hexenal, an alarm pheromone of ants
**d.** 2,6-dimethyl-5-heptenal, communication pheromone of ants

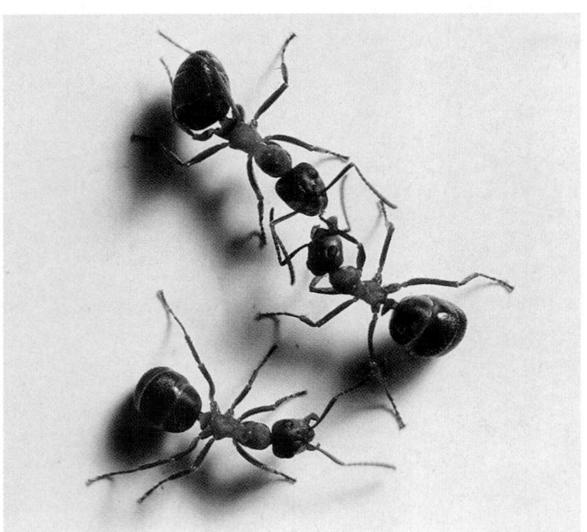

## ADDITIONAL QUESTIONS AND PROBLEMS

*For instructor-assigned homework, go to* ***www.masteringchemistry.com****.*

**14.45** Write the isomers for the carbonyl compounds of $C_4H_8O$.

**14.46** Why does the C=O double bond have a dipole, whereas the C=C does not?

**14.47** Give the IUPAC and common names (if any) for each of the following compounds:

**a.** [cyclopentanone ring with Br on C2 and Cl on C4]

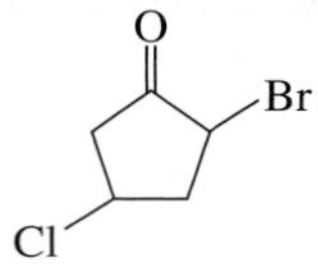

**b.** [benzene ring with CHO, OH, and Cl substituents]

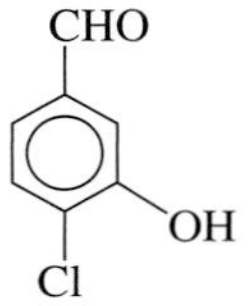

**c.** $Cl—CH_2—CH_2—\overset{O}{\overset{\|}{C}}—H$

**d.** $CH_3—CH_2—\overset{O}{\overset{\|}{C}}—CH_2—\overset{Cl}{\overset{|}{C}H}—CH_3$

**e.** $CH_3—\overset{Cl}{\overset{|}{C}H}—\overset{O}{\overset{\|}{C}}—CH_2—CH_3$

**14.48** Give the IUPAC and common names (if any) for each of the following compounds:

**a.** $CH_3—CH_2—\overset{O}{\overset{\|}{C}}—CH_3$

**b.** [benzene ring with CHO (C(=O)H) and two Cl substituents at meta positions]

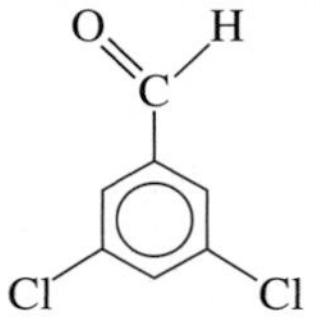

**c.** [cyclopentanone ring with Cl on adjacent carbon]

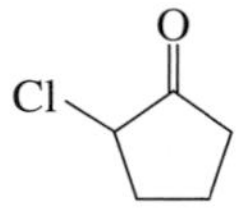

**d.** $CH_3—\overset{CH_3}{\overset{|}{C}H}—\overset{CH_3}{\overset{|}{C}H}—CH_2—\overset{O}{\overset{\|}{C}}—H$

**e.** [benzene ring attached to C(=O)—$CH_3$]

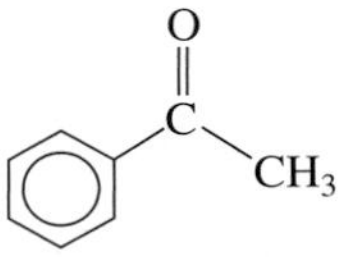

**14.49** Draw the condensed structural formula of each of the following:
**a.** 3-methylcyclopentanone
**b.** 4-chlorobenzaldehyde
**c.** 3-chloropropionaldehyde
**d.** ethyl methyl ketone
**e.** 3-methylhexanal

**14.50** Draw the condensed structural formula of each of the following:
**a.** propionaldehyde
**b.** 2-chlorobutanal
**c.** 2-methylcyclohexanone
**d.** 3,5-dimethylhexanal
**e.** 3-bromocyclopentanone

**14.51** Which of the following compounds are soluble in water?

**a.** $CH_3—CH_2—CH_2—CH_3$

**b.** $CH_3—CH_2—\overset{O}{\overset{\|}{C}}—H$

**c.** $CH_3—\overset{O}{\overset{\|}{C}}—CH_3$

**d.** $CH_3—CH_2—CH_2—OH$

**e.** $CH_3—CH_2—\overset{O}{\overset{\|}{C}}—CH_2—CH_2—CH_3$

**14.52** Which of the following compounds are soluble in water?

**a.** $CH_3—CH_2—\overset{O}{\overset{\|}{C}}—CH_3$

**b.** $H—\overset{O}{\overset{\|}{C}}—H$

**c.** $CH_3—\overset{O}{\overset{\|}{C}}—H$

**d.** $CH_3—CH_2—CH_3$

**e.** $CH_3—CH_2—\overset{CH_3}{\overset{|}{C}H}—CH_2—CH_2—\overset{O}{\overset{\|}{C}}—H$

**14.53** In each of the following pairs of compounds, select the compound with the higher boiling point:

a. $CH_3—CH_2—OH$ or $CH_3—C(=O)—H$

b. $CH_3—CH_2—CH_2—CH_3$ or $CH_3—CH_2—C(=O)—H$

c. $CH_3—CH_2—CH_2—OH$ or $CH_3—C(=O)—CH_3$

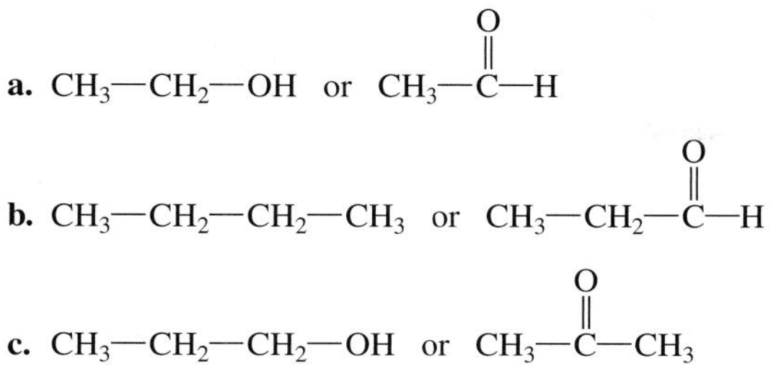

**14.54** In each of the following pairs of compounds, select the compound with the higher boiling point:

a. $CH_3—C(=O)—H$ or $CH_3—CH_2—CH_2—CH_2—C(=O)—H$

b. $CH_3—CH_2—CH_2—CH_3$ or $CH_3—C(=O)—CH_3$

c. $CH_3—CH_2—C(=O)—H$ or $CH_3—CH(OH)—CH_3$

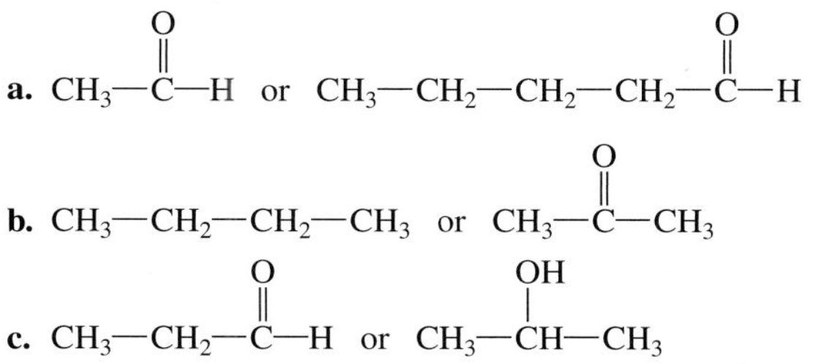

**14.55** Identify the chiral carbons, if any, in each of the following compounds:

a. $H—CCl_2—CH(Cl)—O—H$ (H—C(Cl)(Cl)—C(Cl)(H)—O—H)

b. $CH_3—C(H)=C(CH_3)—CH_3$

c. $HO—CH_2—CH(OH)—CH_2—OH$

d. $CH_3—CH(NH_2)—C(=O)—H$

e. $CH_3—CH_2—CH(Br)—CH_2—CH_2—CH_3$

f. cyclohexane ring with OH

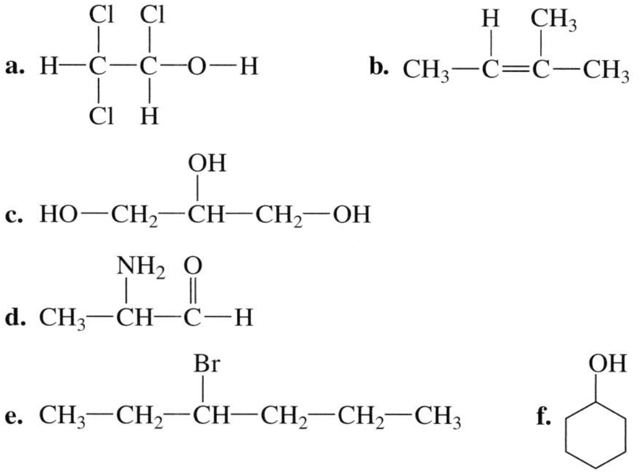

**14.56** Identify the chiral carbons, if any, in each of the following compounds:

a. $CH_3—CH(O—CH_3)—CH_3$

b. $CH_3—CH(OH)—C(=O)—CH_3$

c. $CH_3—C(OH)(OH)—CH_3$

d. $CH_3—CH(CH_3)—C(=O)—CH_3$

e. $CH_3—C(Br)(OH)—CH_2—CH_3$

f. cyclohexane ring with Cl on opposite carbons (1,4-dichlorocyclohexane)

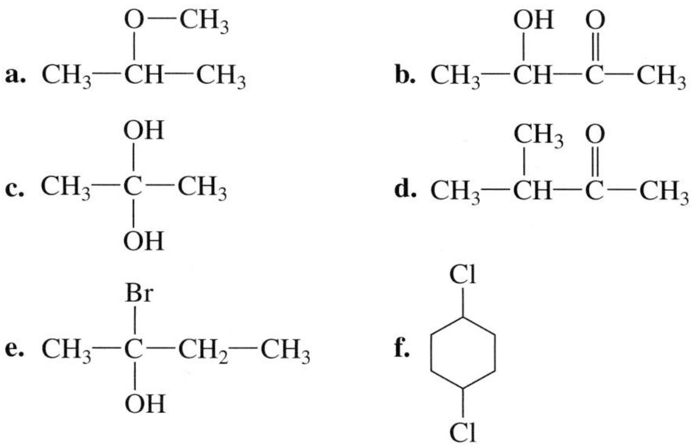

**14.57** Identify each of the following pairs of Fischer projections as enantiomers or identical compounds:

a. Fischer projection: top CHO; H—|—OH; bottom $CH_2OH$ and top CHO; HO—|—H; bottom $CH_2OH$

b. top $CH_2OH$; H—|—OH; bottom $CH_2OH$ and top $CH_2OH$; HO—|—H; bottom $CH_2OH$

c. top $CH_2OH$; H—|—Cl; bottom $CH_3$ and top $CH_2OH$; H—|—Cl; bottom $CH_3$

d. top OH; H—|—OH; bottom $CH_3$ and top OH; HO—|—H; bottom $CH_3$

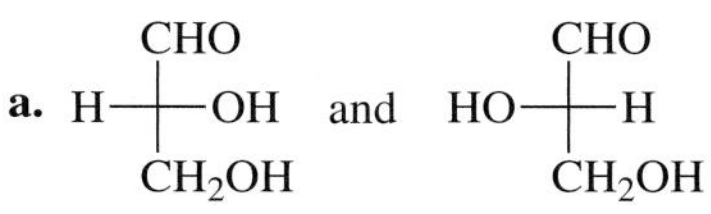

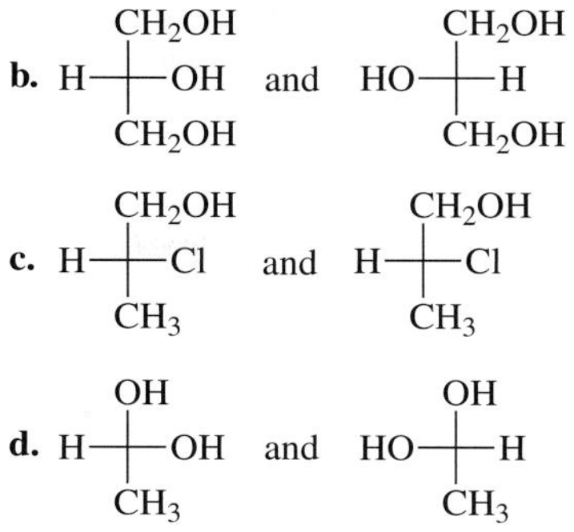

**14.58** Identify each of the following pairs of Fischer projections as enantiomers or identical compounds:

a. top $CH_2—OH$; H—|—Cl; bottom $CH_2—CH_3$ and top $CH_2—OH$; Cl—|—H; bottom $CH_2—CH_3$

b. top $CH_2—OH$; H—|—OH; bottom $CH_2—OH$ and top $CH_2—OH$; HO—|—H; bottom $CH_2—OH$

c. top $CH_2—OH$; H—|—Cl; bottom $CH_3$ and top $CH_2—OH$; H—|—Cl; bottom $CH_3$

d. top CHO; H—|—OH; bottom $CH_2—OH$ and top CHO; HO—|—H; bottom $CH_2—OH$

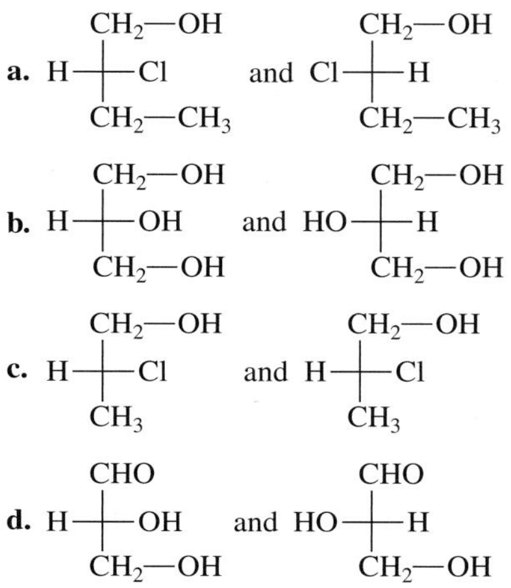

**14.59** Draw the condensed structural formula of the organic product when each of the following is oxidized:

a. $CH_3—CH_2—CH_2—OH$

b. $CH_3—CH(OH)—CH_2—CH_2—CH_3$

c. $CH_3—CH_2—CH_2—C(=O)—H$

d. cyclohexane ring with OH

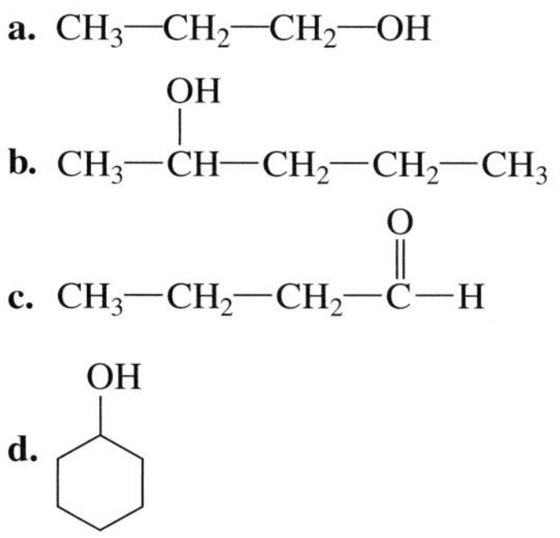

**14.60** Draw the condensed structural formula of the organic product when each of the following is oxidized:

a. $CH_3—CH_2—CH(OH)—CH_2—OH$

b. $CH_3—CH_2—CH(OH)—CH_3$

c. $CH_3—CH(CH_3)—CH_2—C(=O)—H$

d. cyclohexane ring attached to $CH(OH)—CH_3$

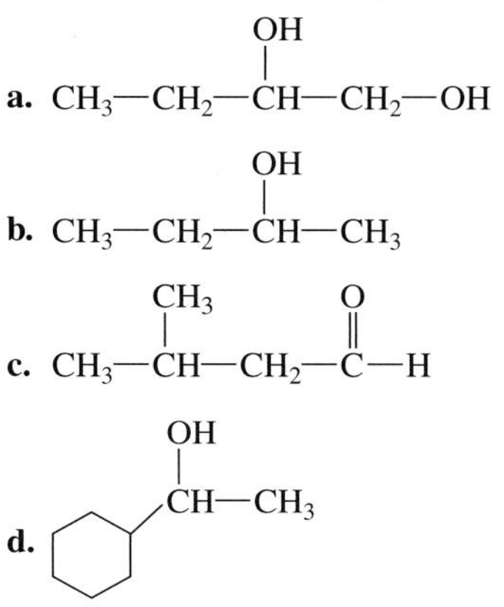

**14.61** Draw the condensed structural formula of the organic product when hydrogen and a nickel catalyst reduce each of the following:

**a.** $CH_3-\overset{\overset{\large O}{\|}}{C}-CH_3$ **b.** (benzene ring)$-CH_2-\overset{\overset{\large O}{\|}}{C}-H$

**c.** $CH_3-\underset{}{\overset{\overset{\large CH_3}{|}}{C}H}-CH_2-\overset{\overset{\large O}{\|}}{C}-CH_3$

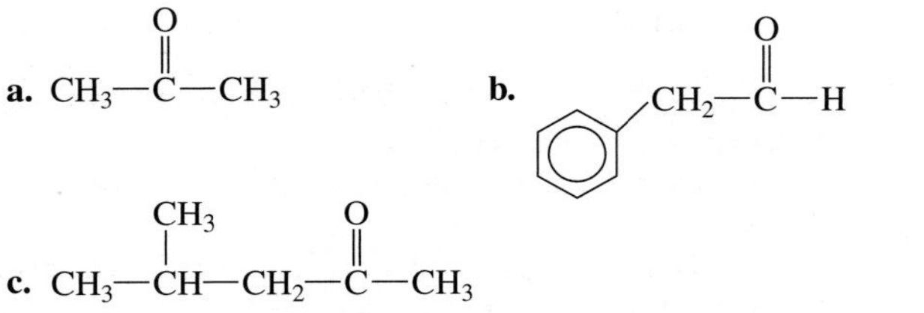

**14.62** Draw the condensed structural formula of the organic product when hydrogen and a nickel catalyst reduce each of the following:

**a.** $CH_3-\overset{\overset{\large O}{\|}}{C}-H$ **b.** (cyclopentanone with $CH_3$) **c.** $H-\overset{\overset{\large O}{\|}}{C}-H$

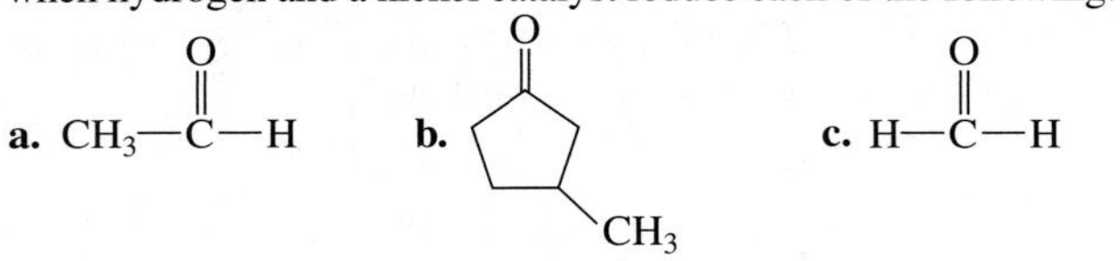

**14.63** Using reactions such as dehydration, hydrogenation, oxidation, reduction, and hydration, indicate how you might prepare the following from the starting substance given:
**a.** propene to propanone
**b.** butanal to 1,2-dibromobutane
**c.** butanal to butanone

**14.64** Using reactions such as dehydration, hydrogenation, oxidation, reduction, and hydration, indicate how you might prepare the following from the starting substance given:
**a.** pentanal to 1-pentene **b.** 1-butanol to butanone
**c.** cyclohexene to cyclohexanone

**14.65** Give the name of the alcohol, aldehyde, or ketone product for each of the following:
**a.** oxidation of 1-propanol **b.** oxidation of 2-pentanol
**c.** reduction of 2-butanone **d.** oxidation of cyclohexanol

**14.66** Give the name of the alcohol, aldehyde, or ketone product for each of the following:
**a.** reduction of butyraldehyde
**b.** oxidation of 3-methyl-2-pentanol
**c.** reduction of 4-methyl-2-hexanone
**d.** oxidation of 3-methylcyclopentanol

**14.67** Identify the following as hemiacetals or acetals. Give the names of the carbonyl compounds and alcohols used in their synthesis.

**a.** $CH_3-CH_2-\overset{\overset{\large O-CH_3}{|}}{\underset{\underset{\large O-CH_3}{|}}{C}}-H$

**b.** $CH_3-CH_2-\overset{\overset{\large O-CH_2-CH_3}{|}}{\underset{\underset{\large OH}{|}}{C}}-CH_3$

**c.** $CH_3-CH_2-O$ $O-CH_2-CH_3$ (on cyclohexane carbon)

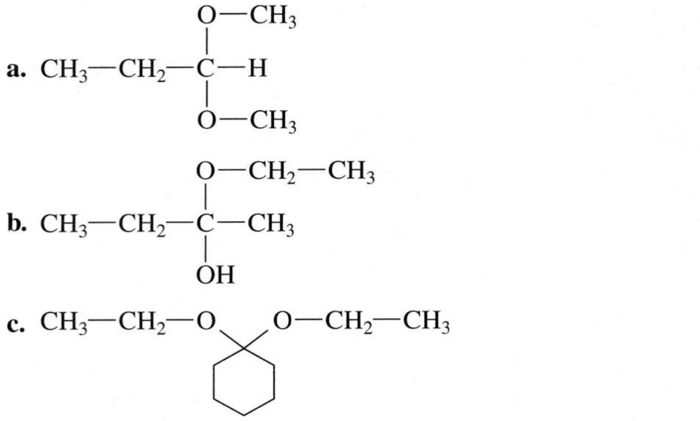

**14.68** Identify the following as hemiacetals or acetals. Give the names of the carbonyl compounds and alcohols used in their synthesis.

**a.** $CH_3-CH_2-\overset{\overset{\large O-CH_3}{|}}{\underset{\underset{\large OH}{|}}{C}}-H$ **b.** $HO$ $O-\overset{\overset{\large CH_3}{|}}{C}H-CH_3$ (on cyclohexane carbon)

**c.** $CH_3-\overset{\overset{\large O-CH_2-CH_2-CH_3}{|}}{\underset{\underset{\large O-CH_2-CH_2-CH_3}{|}}{C}}-H$

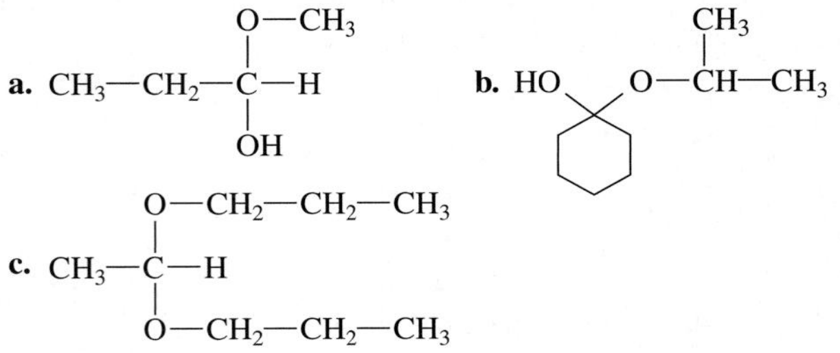

## CHALLENGE QUESTIONS

**14.69** A compound with the formula $C_4H_8O$ is synthesized from 2-butanol and cannot be oxidized further. What is the structure and name of the compound?

**14.70 a.** Write the balanced equation for the reduction of butanone using a Pt catalyst.
**b.** How many milliliters of $H_2$ gas at STP are needed to reduce 1.56 g of butanone?

**14.71** Use the following structures to answer the true/false questions below:

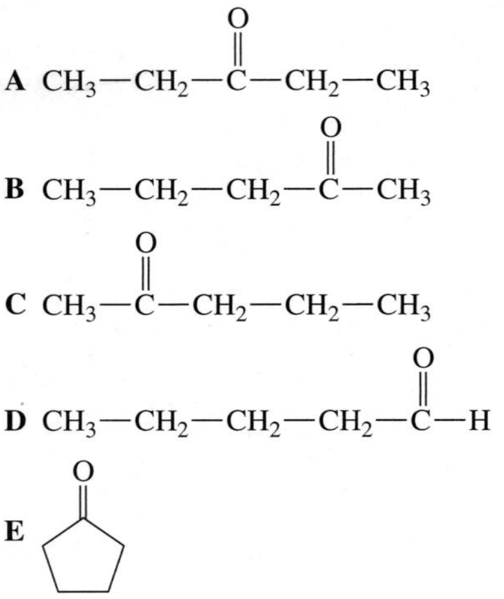

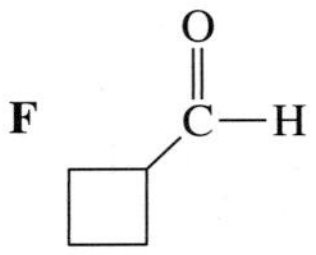

**A** $CH_3-CH_2-\overset{\overset{\large O}{\|}}{C}-CH_2-CH_3$

**B** $CH_3-CH_2-CH_2-\overset{\overset{\large O}{\|}}{C}-CH_3$

**C** $CH_3-\overset{\overset{\large O}{\|}}{C}-CH_2-CH_2-CH_3$

**D** $CH_3-CH_2-CH_2-CH_2-\overset{\overset{\large O}{\|}}{C}-H$

**E** (cyclopentanone)

**F** (cyclobutane)$-\overset{\overset{\large O}{\|}}{C}-H$

True or False?
**a.** **A** and **B** are isomers.
**b.** **A** and **C** are the same compound.
**c.** **B** and **C** are the same compound.
**d.** **E** and **F** are isomers.
**e.** **A** is chiral.
**f.** **D** and **F** are aldehydes.
**g.** **B** and **E** are ketones.

**14.72** Draw the structures and give the IUPAC names of all the aldehydes and ketones that have the formula $C_5H_{10}O$.

**14.73** Compound A is 1-propanol. When compound A is heated with strong acid, it dehydrates to form compound B ($C_3H_6$). When compound A is oxidized, compound C ($C_3H_6O$) forms. What are the structures and names of compounds A, B, and C?

**14.74** Compound X is 2-propanol. When compound X is heated with strong acid, it dehydrates to form compound Y ($C_3H_6$). When compound X is oxidized, compound Z ($C_3H_6O$) forms, which cannot be oxidized further. What are the structures and names of compounds X, Y, and Z?

# ANSWERS

## ANSWERS TO STUDY CHECKS

**14.1** propanal (IUPAC), propionaldehyde (common)

**14.2** ethyl propyl ketone

**14.3** The oxygen atom in the carbonyl group of acetone hydrogen bonds with water molecules.

**14.4** cyclohexanol

**14.5** The oxidation of benzaldehyde reduces $Ag^+$ to metallic silver, which forms a silvery coating on the walls of the test tube.

**14.6** 1-propanol

**14.7** $CH_3—C(O—CH_3)_2—CH_3$ (O—$CH_3$ above and below C)

**14.8** $HO—CH_2—\overset{*}{C}H(OH)—\overset{*}{C}H(OH)—\overset{O}{\overset{\|}{C}}—H$

**14.9**

| CHO | CHO |
|---|---|
| H—+—OH | HO—+—H |
| $CH_3$ | $CH_3$ |
| D-2-Hydroxypropanal | L-2-Hydroxypropanal |

## ANSWERS TO SELECTED QUESTIONS AND PROBLEMS

**14.1** **a.** ketone **b.** aldehyde
**c.** ketone **d.** aldehyde

**14.3** **a.** (1) isomers **b.** (1) isomers
**c.** (2) the same compound

**14.5** **a.** propanal
**b.** 2-methyl-3-pentanone
**c.** 3-bromobutanal
**d.** 2-pentanone
**e.** 3-methylcyclohexanone
**f.** 4-chlorobenzaldehyde

**14.7** **a.** acetaldehyde
**b.** methyl propyl ketone
**c.** formaldehyde

**14.9** **a.** $CH_3—\overset{O}{\overset{\|}{C}}—H$ **b.** $CH_3—\overset{O}{\overset{\|}{C}}—CH_2—\overset{CH_3}{\overset{|}{C}H}—CH_3$

**c.** $CH_3—\overset{Br}{\overset{|}{C}H}—\overset{Br}{\overset{|}{C}H}—\overset{O}{\overset{\|}{C}}—H$

**d.** $CH_3—\overset{O}{\overset{\|}{C}}—CH_2—CH_2—CH_2—CH_3$

**e.** $CH_3—CH_2—\overset{CH_3}{\overset{|}{C}H}—CH_2—\overset{O}{\overset{\|}{C}}—H$

**14.11** CHO (on benzene ring, para) $OCH_3$

**14.13** **a.** $CH_3—\overset{O}{\overset{\|}{C}}—H$ has a higher boiling point because it has a polar carbonyl group.
**b.** Pentanal has a higher molar mass and thus a higher boiling point.
**c.** 1-Butanol has a higher boiling point because it can hydrogen bond with other 1-butanol molecules.

**14.15** **a.** $CH_3—\overset{O}{\overset{\|}{C}}—\overset{O}{\overset{\|}{C}}—CH_3$, more hydrogen bonding
**b.** acetaldehyde, hydrogen bonding
**c.** acetone, lower number of carbon atoms

**14.17** No. The long carbon chain diminishes the effect of the carbonyl group.

**14.19** **a.** $CH_3—OH$ **b.** OH (on cyclopentane ring)

**c.** $CH_3—CH_2—\overset{OH}{\overset{|}{C}H}—CH_3$

**d.** 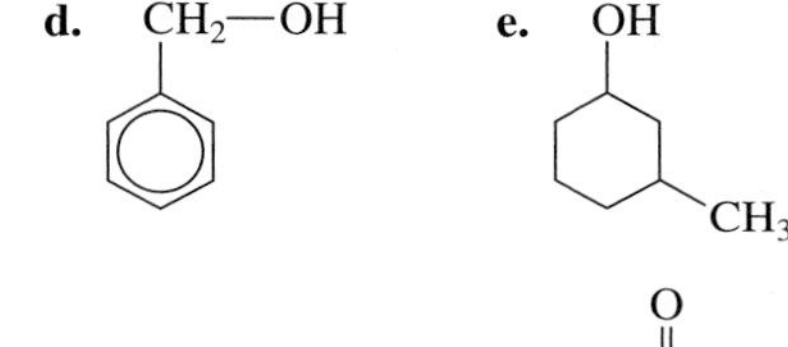


**14.21** **a.** $CH_3—CH_2—CH_2—CH_2—\overset{O}{\overset{\|}{C}}—H$

**b.** $CH_3—CH_2—\overset{O}{\overset{\|}{C}}—CH_3$ **c.** O (on cyclohexane ring)

**d.** $CH_3—\overset{O}{\overset{\|}{C}}—CH_2—\overset{CH_3}{\overset{|}{C}H}—CH_3$

**e.** $CH_3—\overset{CH_3}{\overset{|}{C}H}—CH_2—\overset{O}{\overset{\|}{C}}—H$

**14.23** **a.** $CH_3—CH_2—CH_2—CH_2—OH$

**b.** $CH_3—\overset{OH}{\overset{|}{C}H}—CH_3$

**c.** $CH_3—CH_2—CH_2—\overset{Br}{\overset{|}{C}H}—CH_2—CH_2—OH$

**d.** $CH_3—\overset{CH_3}{\overset{|}{C}H}—\underset{OH}{\underset{|}{C}H}—CH_2—CH_3$

**14.25** **a.** $CH_3—\underset{OH}{\underset{|}{\overset{OH}{\overset{|}{C}}}}—H$ **b.** $H—\underset{OH}{\underset{|}{\overset{OH}{\overset{|}{C}}}}—H$

**14.27 a.** hemiacetal **b.** hemiacetal **c.** acetal
**d.** hemiacetal **e.** acetal

**14.29 a.** $CH_3-C(O-CH_3)(OH)-H$ **b.** $CH_3-C(O-CH_3)(OH)-CH_3$

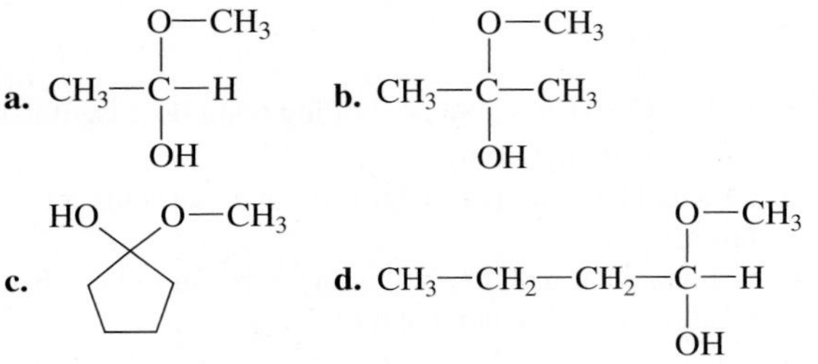

**c.** cyclopentane with HO and $O-CH_3$ on the same carbon **d.** $CH_3-CH_2-CH_2-C(O-CH_3)(OH)-H$

**14.31 a.** $CH_3-C(O-CH_3)(O-CH_3)-H$ **b.** $CH_3-C(O-CH_3)(O-CH_3)-CH_3$

**c.** cyclopentane with $CH_3-O$ and $O-CH_3$ on the same carbon

**d.** $CH_3-CH_2-CH_2-C(O-CH_3)(O-CH_3)-H$

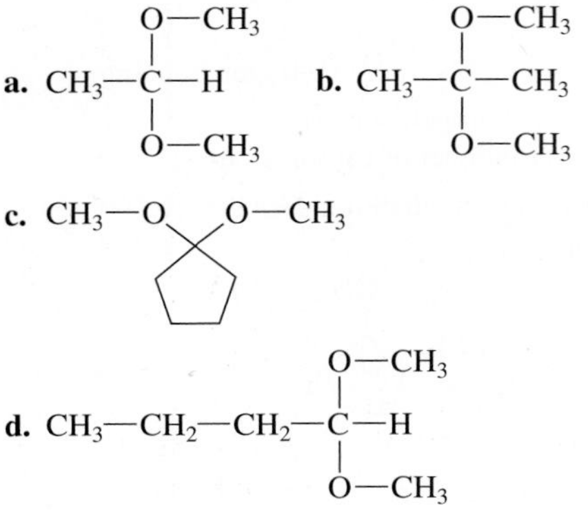

**14.33 a.** achiral
**b.** chiral $CH_3-CH(Br)-CH_2-CH_3$ (Chiral carbon: the CH bearing Br)
**c.** achiral
**d.** achiral

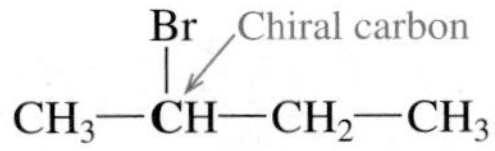

**14.35 a.** $CH_3-C(CH_3)=CH-CH_2-CH_2-CH(CH_3)-CH_2-CH_2-OH$ (Chiral carbon: the CH bearing $CH_3$)

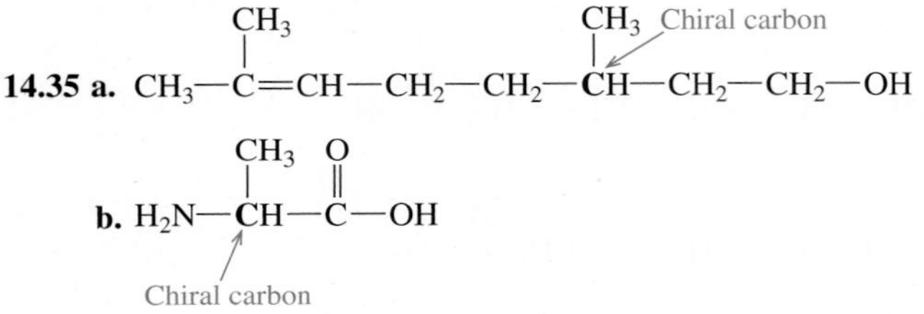

**b.** $H_2N-CH(CH_3)-C(=O)-OH$ (Chiral carbon: the CH)

**14.37 a.** Fischer projection: top H; left HO; right Br; bottom $CH_3$ **b.** top $CH_3$; left Cl; right Br; bottom OH **c.** top CHO; left HO; right H; bottom $CH_2CH_3$

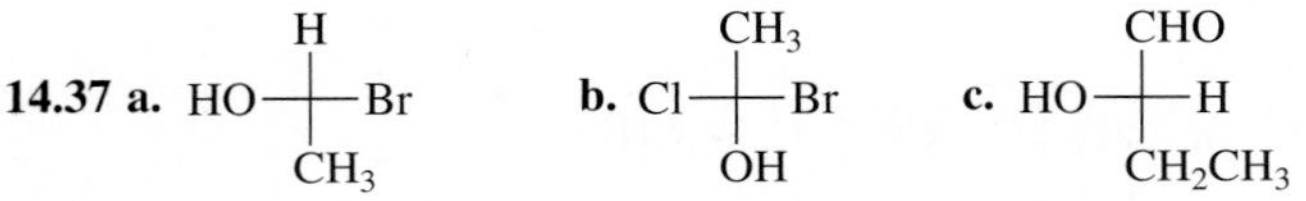

**14.39 a.** identical **b.** enantiomers
**c.** enantiomers **d.** enantiomers

**14.41** a, b, and f

**14.43 a.** aldehyde, aromatic
**b.** aldehyde, ether, phenol, aromatic
**c.** aldehyde, alkene, aromatic
**d.** ketone, cycloalkane
**e.** ketone
**a.** 2 **b.** 5 **c.** 4 **d.** 3 **e.** 1

**14.45**

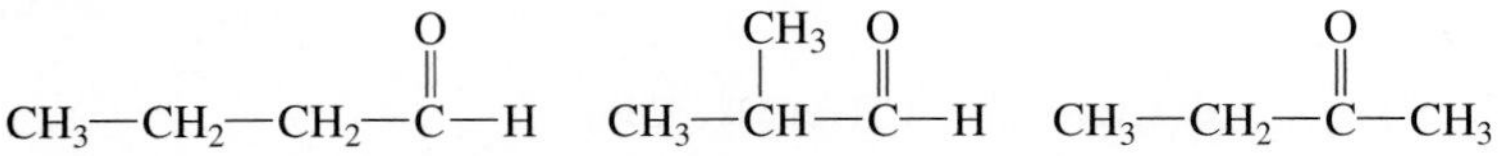

$CH_3-CH_2-CH_2-C(=O)-H$ $CH_3-CH(CH_3)-C(=O)-H$ $CH_3-CH_2-C(=O)-CH_3$

**14.47 a.** 2-bromo-4-chlorocyclopentanone
**b.** 4-chloro-3-hydroxybenzaldehyde
**c.** 3-chloropropanal; 3-chloropropionaldehyde
**d.** 5-chloro-3-hexanone
**e.** 2-chloro-3-pentanone

**14.49 a.** cyclopentanone (C=O) with $CH_3$ on ring carbon 3 **b.** benzene ring with CHO and Cl para

**c.** $Cl-CH_2-CH_2-C(=O)-H$

**d.** $CH_3-CH_2-C(=O)-CH_3$

**e.** $CH_3-CH_2-CH_2-CH(CH_3)-CH_2-C(=O)-H$

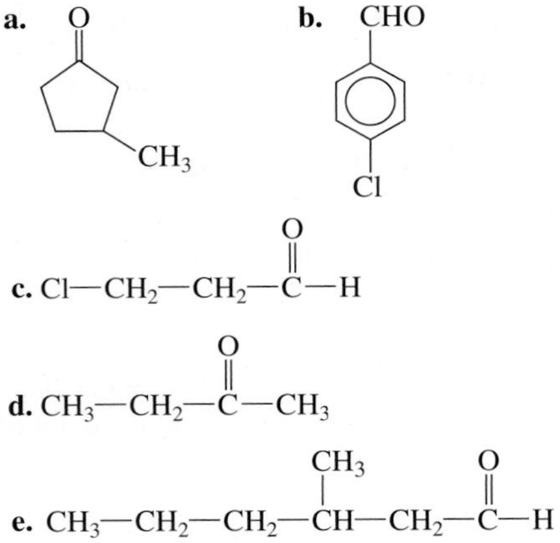

**14.51** b, c, and **d**

**14.53 a.** $CH_3-CH_2-OH$

**b.** $CH_3-CH_2-C(=O)-H$

**c.** $CH_3-CH_2-CH_2-OH$

**14.55 a.** $H-C(Cl)(Cl)-C(Cl)(H)-O-H$ (second C circled) **b.** none **c.** none

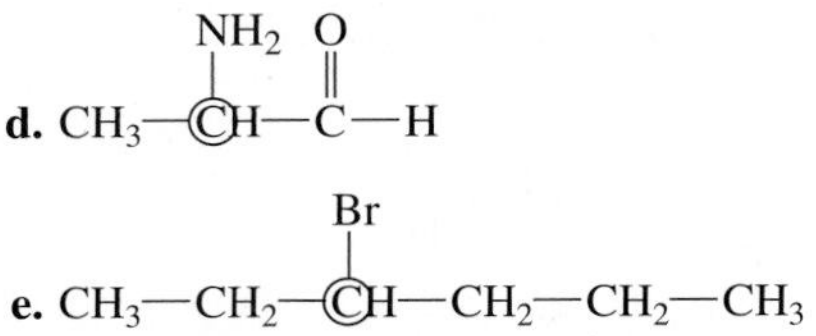

**d.** $CH_3-CH(NH_2)-C(=O)-H$ (CH circled)

**e.** $CH_3-CH_2-CH(Br)-CH_2-CH_2-CH_3$ (CH circled) **f.** none

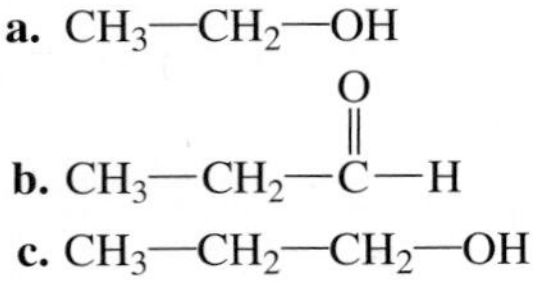

**14.57 a.** enantiomers **b.** identical
**c.** identical **d.** identical

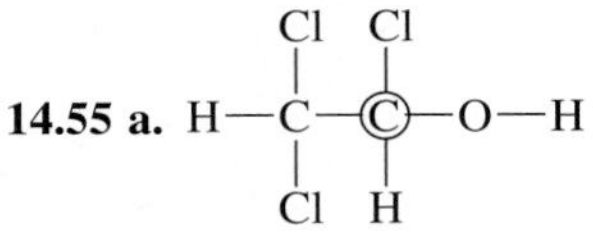

**14.59 a.** $CH_3-CH_2-C(=O)-H \xrightarrow{\text{Further oxidation}} CH_3-CH_2-C(=O)-OH$

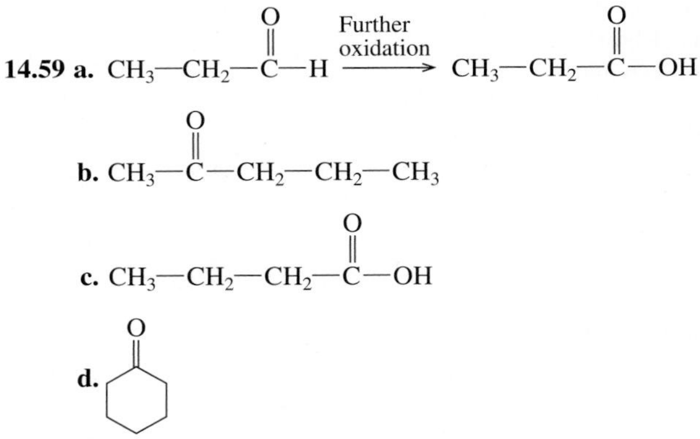

**b.** $CH_3-C(=O)-CH_2-CH_2-CH_3$

**c.** $CH_3-CH_2-CH_2-C(=O)-OH$

**d.** cyclohexanone

**14.61 a.** $CH_3-CH(OH)-CH_3$

**b.** benzene ring $-CH_2-CH_2-OH$

**c.** $CH_3-CH(CH_3)-CH_2-CH(OH)-CH_3$

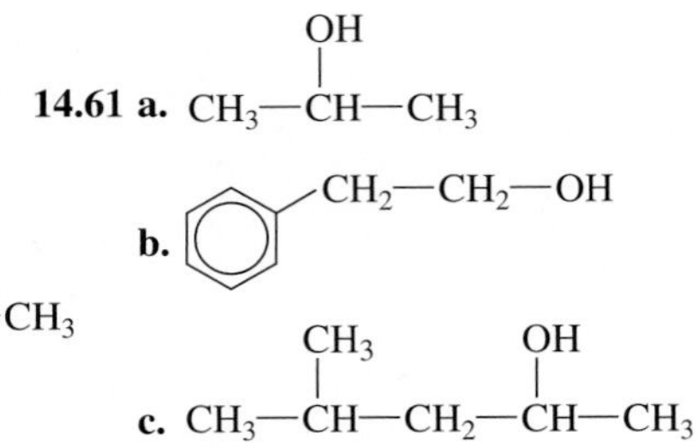

**14.63 a.** 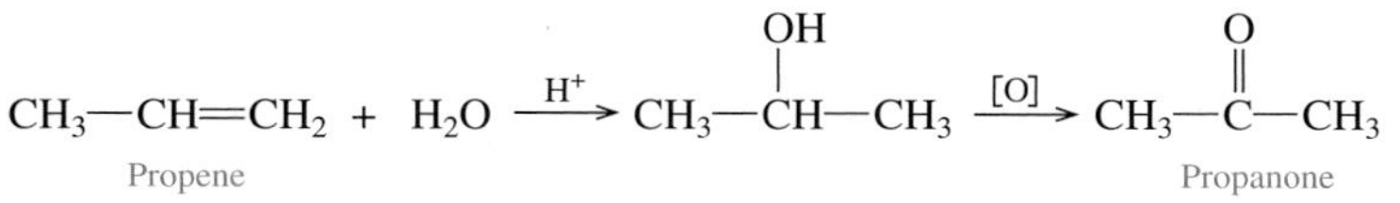 $CH_3{-}CH{=}CH_2 + H_2O \xrightarrow{H^+} CH_3{-}\underset{}{\overset{OH}{\overset{|}{C}H}}{-}CH_3 \xrightarrow{[O]} CH_3{-}\overset{O}{\overset{\|}{C}}{-}CH_3$

Propene ... Propanone

**b.** 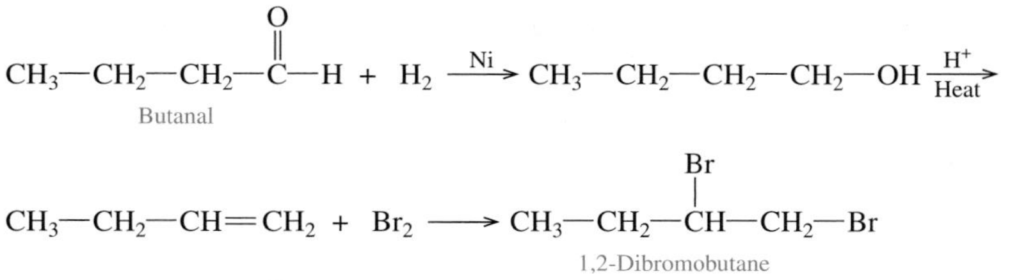 $CH_3{-}CH_2{-}CH_2{-}\overset{O}{\overset{\|}{C}}{-}H + H_2 \xrightarrow{Ni} CH_3{-}CH_2{-}CH_2{-}CH_2{-}OH \xrightarrow[Heat]{H^+}$

Butanal

$CH_3{-}CH_2{-}CH{=}CH_2 + Br_2 \longrightarrow CH_3{-}CH_2{-}\overset{Br}{\overset{|}{C}H}{-}CH_2{-}Br$

1,2-Dibromobutane

**c.** $CH_3{-}CH_2{-}CH_2{-}\overset{O}{\overset{\|}{C}}{-}H + H_2 \xrightarrow{Ni} CH_3{-}CH_2{-}CH_2{-}CH_2{-}OH \xrightarrow[Heat]{H^+}$

Butanal

$CH_3{-}CH_2{-}CH{=}CH_2 + H_2O \xrightarrow{H^+} CH_3{-}CH_2{-}\overset{OH}{\overset{|}{C}H}{-}CH_3 \xrightarrow{[O]} CH_3{-}CH_2{-}\overset{O}{\overset{\|}{C}}{-}CH_3$

Butanone

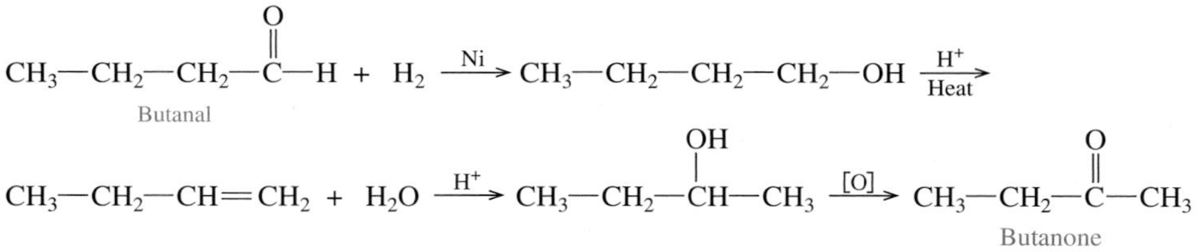

**14.65 a.** propanal **b.** 2-pentanone
**c.** 2-butanol **d.** cyclohexanone

**14.67 a.** acetal; propanal and methanol
**b.** hemiacetal; butanone and ethanol
**c.** acetal; cyclohexanone and ethanol

**14.69** $CH_3{-}\overset{CH_3}{\overset{|}{C}H}{-}\overset{O}{\overset{\|}{C}}{-}H$ 2-methylpropanal

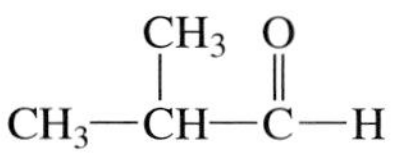

**14.71 a.** true **b.** false **c.** true **d.** true
**e.** false **f.** true **g.** true

**14.73** $CH_3{-}CH_2{-}CH_2{-}OH$ A. 1-propanol
$CH_3{-}CH{=}CH_2$ B. propene
$CH_3{-}CH_2{-}\overset{O}{\overset{\|}{C}}{-}H$ C. propanal

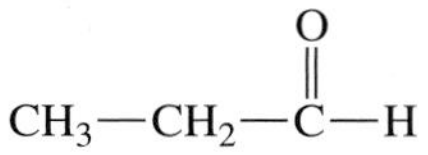

# 15 Carbohydrates

LOOKING AHEAD


**15.1** Carbohydrates

**15.2** Fischer Projections of Monosaccharides

**15.3** Haworth Structures of Monosaccharides

**15.4** Chemical Properties of Monosaccharides

**15.5** Disaccharides

**15.6** Polysaccharides

*"We use a refractometer to measure sugar content in a small sample of juices from the grapes in different areas of the vineyard," says Leslie Bucher, laboratory director at Bouchaine Winery. "We also measure the alcohol content during fermentation and run tests for sulfur, pH, and total acid."*

*As grapes ripen, there is an increase in the sugars, which are the monosaccharides fructose and glucose. The sugar content is affected by soil conditions and the amount of sun and water. When the grapes are ripe and sugar content is at a desirable level, they are harvested. During fermentation, enzymes from yeast convert about half the sugar to ethanol, and half to carbon dioxide. Grapes harvested with 22.5% sugar will ferment to produce a wine with 12.5–13.5% alcohol content.*

Visit **www.masteringchemistry.com** for self-study materials and instructor-assigned homework.

Carbohydrates are the most abundant of all the organic compounds in nature. In plants, energy from the Sun converts carbon dioxide and water into the carbohydrate glucose. Many of the glucose molecules are made into long-chain polymers of starch that store energy or into cellulose to build the structural framework of the plant. About 65% of the foods in our diet consist of carbohydrates. Each day we utilize carbohydrates known as *starches* in foods such as bread, pasta, potatoes, and rice. Other carbohydrates called *disaccharides* include sucrose (table sugar) and lactose in milk. During digestion and cellular metabolism, carbohydrates are converted into glucose, which is oxidized further in our cells to provide our bodies with energy and to provide the cells with carbon atoms for building molecules of proteins, lipids, and nucleic acids. Cellulose has other important uses, too. The wood in our furniture, the pages in this book, and the cotton in our clothing are made of cellulose.

## 15.1 Carbohydrates

**LEARNING GOAL**

Classify a monosaccharide as an aldose or ketose, and indicate the number of carbon atoms.

**Carbohydrates** such as table sugar, lactose in milk, and cellulose are all made of carbon, hydrogen, and oxygen. Simple sugars, which have formulas of $C_n(H_2O)_n$, were once thought to be hydrates of carbon, thus the name *carbohydrate*. In a series of reactions called *photosynthesis*, energy from the Sun is used to combine the carbon atoms from carbon dioxide ($CO_2$) and the hydrogen and oxygen atoms of water into the carbohydrate glucose:

$$6CO_2 + 6H_2O + \text{energy} \underset{\text{Respiration}}{\overset{\text{Photosynthesis}}{\rightleftharpoons}} \underset{\text{Glucose}}{C_6H_{12}O_6} + 6O_2$$

In the body, glucose is oxidized in a series of metabolic reactions known as *respiration*, which releases chemical energy to do work in the cells. Carbon dioxide and water are produced and returned to the atmosphere. The combination of photosynthesis and respiration is called the *carbon cycle*, in which energy from the Sun is stored in plants by photosynthesis and made available to us when the carbohydrates in our diets are metabolized. (See Figure 15.1.)

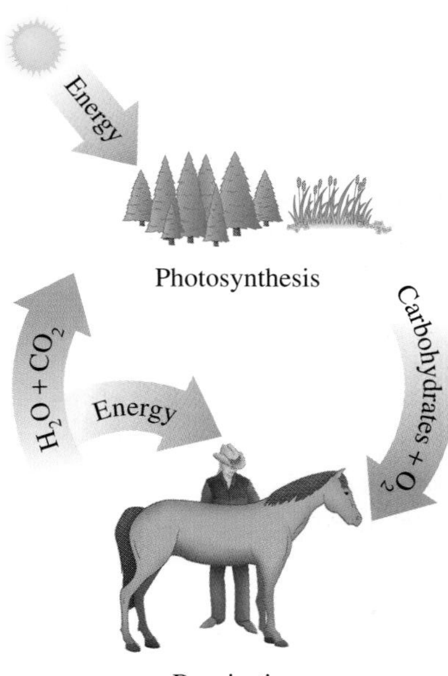


**FIGURE 15.1** During photosynthesis, energy from the Sun combines $CO_2$ and $H_2O$ to form glucose ($C_6H_{12}O_6$) and $O_2$. During respiration in the body, carbohydrates are oxidized to $CO_2$ and $H_2O$, while energy is produced.

**Q** What are the reactants and products of respiration?

### Types of Carbohydrates

The simplest carbohydrates are the **monosaccharides**. A monosaccharide cannot be split or hydrolyzed into smaller carbohydrates. One of the most common carbohydrates, glucose, $C_6H_{12}O_6$, is a monosaccharide. A **disaccharide** consists of two monosaccharide units joined together. Likewise, a disaccharide can be split into two monosaccharide units. For example, ordinary table sugar, sucrose, $C_{12}H_{22}O_{11}$, is a disaccharide that can be split by water (hydrolysis) in the presence of an acid or an enzyme to give one molecule of glucose and one molecule of another monosaccharide, fructose:

$$\underset{\text{Sucrose}}{C_{12}H_{22}O_{11}} + H_2O \xrightarrow{H^+ \text{ or enzyme}} \underset{\text{Glucose}}{C_6H_{12}O_6} + \underset{\text{Fructose}}{C_6H_{12}O_6}$$

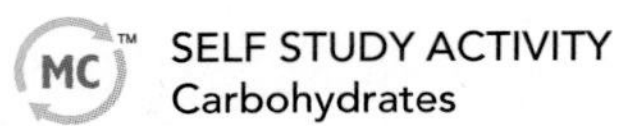


**Polysaccharides** are carbohydrates that are naturally occurring polymers containing many monosaccharide units. In the presence of an acid or an enzyme, a polysaccharide can be completely hydrolyzed to yield many molecules of monosaccharide:

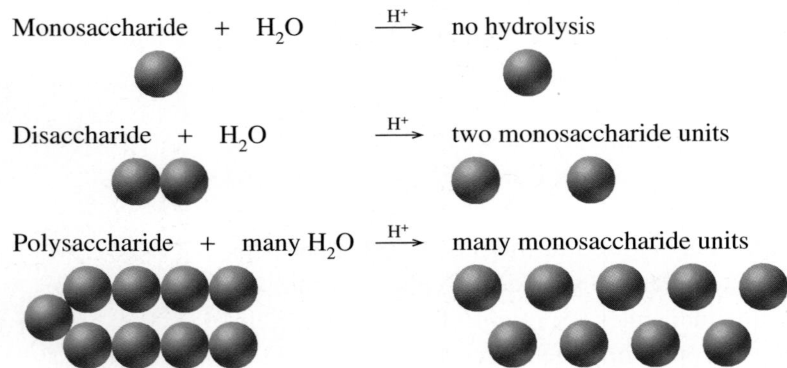


## Monosaccharides

MC TUTORIAL Types of Carbohydrates

Monosaccharides are simple sugars that have a chain of three to eight carbon atoms, one in a carbonyl group and the rest attached to hydroxyl groups. There are two types of monosaccharide structures. In an **aldose**, the carbonyl group is on the first carbon (—CHO); a **ketose** contains the carbonyl group on the second carbon atom as a ketone (C=O):

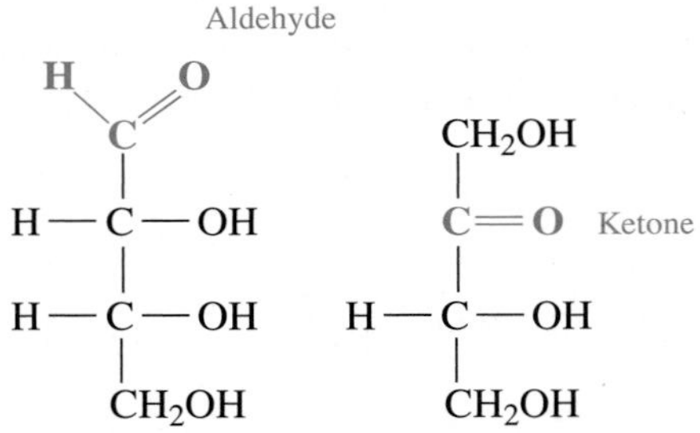

MC TUTORIAL Carbonyls in Carbohydrates

Aldehyde

H—C=O (CHO) / H—C—OH / H—C—OH / $CH_2OH$

Erythrose, an aldose

$CH_2OH$ / C=O Ketone / H—C—OH / $CH_2OH$

Erythrulose, a ketose

A monosaccharide with three carbon atoms is a *triose*, one with four carbon atoms is a *tetrose*, a *pentose* has five carbons, and a *hexose* contains six carbons. We can use both classification systems to indicate the type of carbonyl group and the number of carbon atoms. An aldopentose is a five-carbon monosaccharide that is an aldehyde; a ketohexose would be a six-carbon monosaccharide that is a ketone:

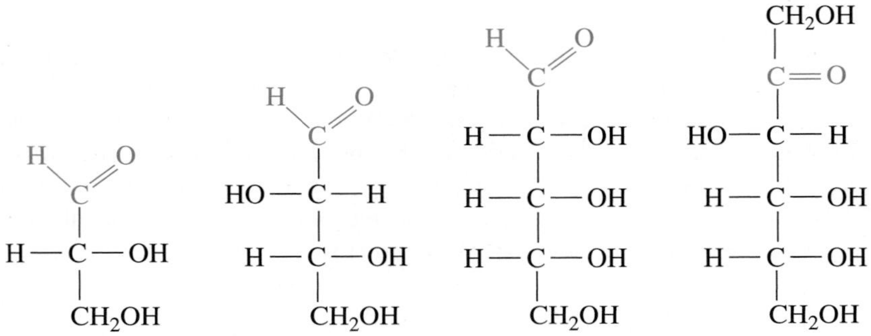

CHO / H—C—OH / $CH_2OH$

Glyceraldehyde (aldotriose)

CHO / HO—C—H / H—C—OH / $CH_2OH$

Threose (aldotetrose)

CHO / H—C—OH / H—C—OH / H—C—OH / $CH_2OH$

Ribose (aldopentose)

$CH_2OH$ / C=O / HO—C—H / H—C—OH / H—C—OH / $CH_2OH$

Fructose (ketohexose)

CONCEPT CHECK 15.1

### Monosaccharides

Classify each of the following monosaccharides to indicate their carbonyl group and number of carbon atoms:

**a.**

$CH_2OH$
|
C=O
|
H—C—OH
|
H—C—OH
|
$CH_2OH$

Ribulose

**b.**

H O
\ //
C
|
H—C—OH
|
HO—C—H
|
H—C—OH
|
H—C—OH
|
$CH_2OH$

Glucose

ANSWER

**a.** Ribulose has five carbon atoms, which makes it a pentose. The ketone (keto) group makes it a ketopentose.

**b.** Glucose has six carbon atoms, which makes it a hexose. The aldehyde (aldo) group makes it an aldohexose.

## QUESTIONS AND PROBLEMS

### Carbohydrates

**15.1** What reactants are needed for photosynthesis and respiration?

**15.2** What is the relationship between photosynthesis and respiration?

**15.3** What is a monosaccharide? A disaccharide?

**15.4** What is a polysaccharide?

**15.5** What functional groups are found in all monosaccharides?

**15.6** What is the difference between an aldose and a ketose?

**15.7** What are the functional groups and number of carbons in a ketopentose?

**15.8** What are the functional groups and number of carbons in an aldohexose?

**15.9** Classify each of the following monosaccharides as an aldose or ketose:

**a.**

$CH_2OH$
|
C=O
|
HO—C—H
|
H—C—OH
|
H—C—OH
|
$CH_2OH$

Fructose

**b.**

CHO
|
H—C—OH
|
H—C—OH
|
H—C—OH
|
$CH_2OH$

Ribose

**c.**

$CH_2OH$
|
C=O
|
$CH_2OH$

Dihydroxyacetone

**d.**

CHO
|
H—C—OH
|
HO—C—H
|
H—C—OH
|
$CH_2OH$

Xylose

**e.**

CHO
|
H—C—OH
|
HO—C—H
|
HO—C—H
|
H—C—OH
|
$CH_2OH$

Galactose

**15.10** Classify each of the monosaccharides in problem 15.9 according to the number of carbon atoms in the chain.

## 15.2 Fischer Projections of Monosaccharides

**LEARNING GOAL**

Use Fischer projections to draw the D or L isomers of glucose, galactose, and fructose.

SELF STUDY ACTIVITY
Forms of Carbohydrates

In Chapter 14, we learned that chiral compounds exist as mirror images that cannot be superimposed. Many monosaccharides exist as mirror images.

### Fischer Projections

Let's take a look again at the Fischer projection for the simplest aldose, glyceraldehyde. By convention, the carbon chain is written vertically with the aldehyde group (most oxidized carbon) at the top. The letter L is assigned to the stereoisomer if the —OH group is on the left of the chiral carbon. In D-glyceraldehyde, the —OH is on the right. The carbon atom in the —$CH_2OH$ group at the bottom of the Fischer projection is not chiral, because it does not have four different groups bonded to it:

L-Glyceraldehyde D-Glyceraldehyde

TUTORIAL
Identifying Chiral Carbons in Monosaccharides

Most of the carbohydrates we will study have carbon chains with five or six carbon atoms. Because there are several chiral carbons, the chiral carbon *farthest* from the carbonyl group is used to determine the D or L isomer. The following are the Fischer projections for the D and L isomers of ribose, a five-carbon monosaccharide, and glucose, a six-carbon monosaccharide. In each of the mirror images, it is important to understand that the —OH groups on all the chiral carbon atoms are reversed from one side to the other. For example, in L-ribose, the —OH groups are all written on the left side of the horizontal lines. In the mirror image, D-ribose, the —OH groups are all written on the right side of the horizontal lines.

TUTORIAL
Drawing Fischer Projections of Monosaccharides

TUTORIAL
Identifying D and L Sugars

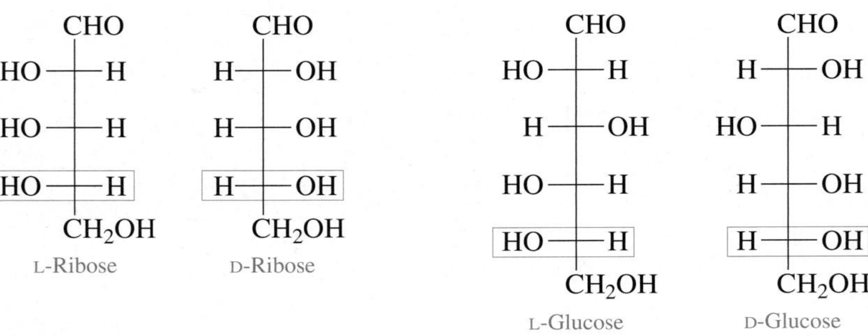


**CONCEPT CHECK 15.2**

**Fischer Projections**

How does the Fischer projection of D-galactose differ from that of D-glucose?

ANSWER

In the Fischer projections, the direction of the —OH group on the chiral carbon atoms differs only at carbon 4, extending to the left in D-galactose and to the right in D-glucose.

SAMPLE PROBLEM 15.1

### Identifying D and L Isomers of Sugars

Identify the following Fischer projection as D- or L-ribose:

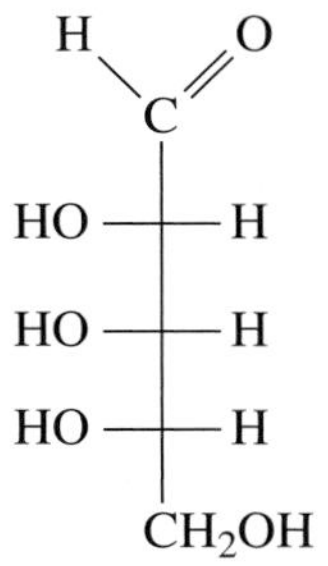

```
H     O
 \   //
   C
   |
HO—+—H
   |
HO—+—H
   |
HO—+—H
   |
  CH2OH
```

SOLUTION

In ribose, carbon 4 is the chiral atom farthest from the carbonyl group. Because the hydroxyl group on carbon 4 is on the left, this is L-ribose:

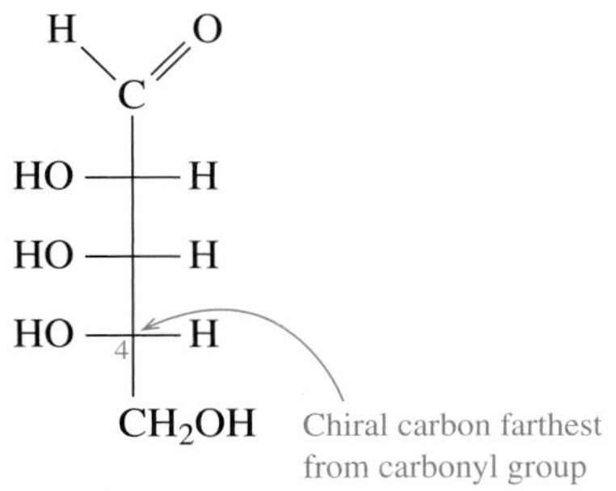

```
H     O
 \   //
   C
   |
HO—+—H
   |
HO—+—H
   |
HO—+—H   (4)
   |
  CH2OH
```

Chiral carbon farthest from carbonyl group

STUDY CHECK

Draw the Fischer projection for D-ribose.

## Some Important Monosaccharides

The hexoses glucose, galactose, and fructose are important monosaccharides. Although we can draw Fischer projections for D and L isomers, the D isomers are commonly found in nature and used in the cells of the body. The Fischer projections for the D isomers are written as follows:

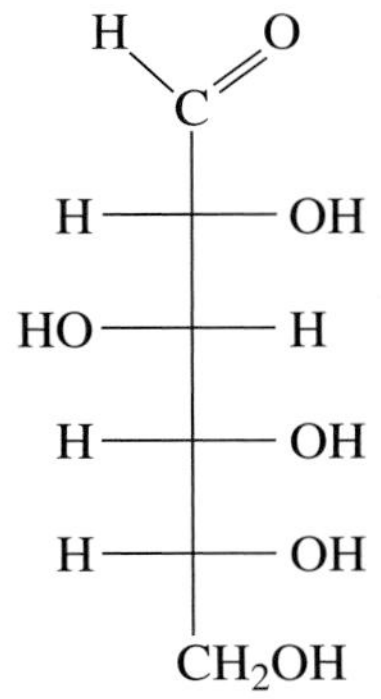

```
  H     O          H     O
   \   //           \   //            CH2OH
     C                C                 |
     |                |                C=O
 H ——+—— OH       H ——+—— OH            |
     |                |            HO ——+—— H
HO ——+—— H       HO ——+—— H             |
     |                |             H ——+—— OH
 H ——+—— OH      HO ——+—— H             |
     |                |             H ——+—— OH
 H ——+—— OH       H ——+—— OH            |
     |                |               CH2OH
   CH2OH            CH2OH
```

D-Glucose 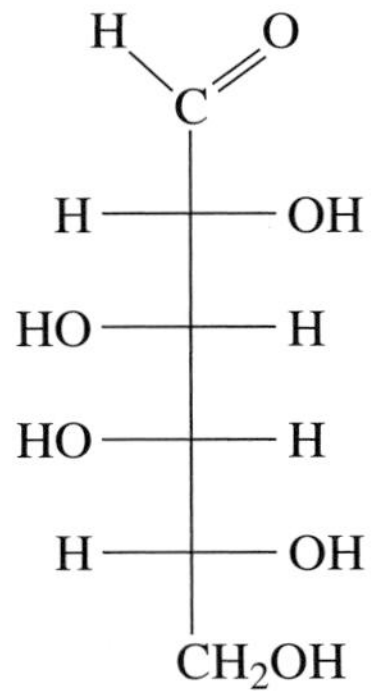 D-Galactose 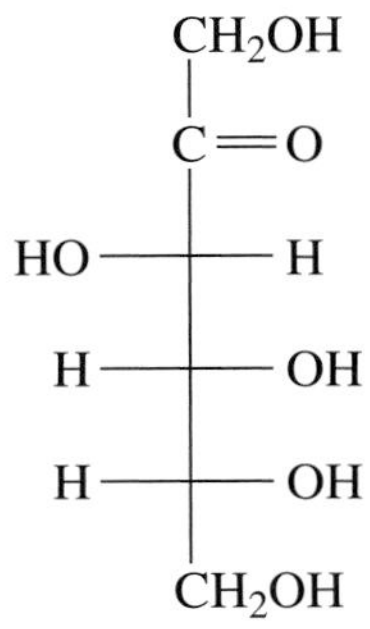 D-Fructose

The most common hexose, D-**glucose**, $C_6H_{12}O_6$, also known as dextrose and blood sugar, is found in fruits, vegetables, corn syrup, and honey. It is a building block of the disaccharides sucrose, lactose, and maltose, and polysaccharides such as starch, cellulose, and glycogen.

In the body, glucose normally occurs at a concentration of 70–90 mg/dL (1 dL = 100 mL) of blood. Excess glucose is converted to glycogen and stored in the liver and muscle. When the amount of glucose exceeds what is needed for energy or glycogen, the excess glucose is converted to fat, which can be stored in unlimited amounts:

Glycogen (liver and muscle)

$\uparrow\downarrow$

Fat $\xleftarrow{\text{Excess}}$ Glucose $\xrightarrow{\text{Metabolism}}$ $CO_2$ + $H_2O$ + energy

Glucose → Urine

**Galactose** is an aldohexose that is obtained as a hydrolysis product of the disaccharide lactose, a sugar found in milk and milk products. Galactose is important in the cellular membranes of the brain and nervous system. The only difference in the Fischer projections of D-glucose and D-galactose is the arrangement of the —OH group on carbon 4:

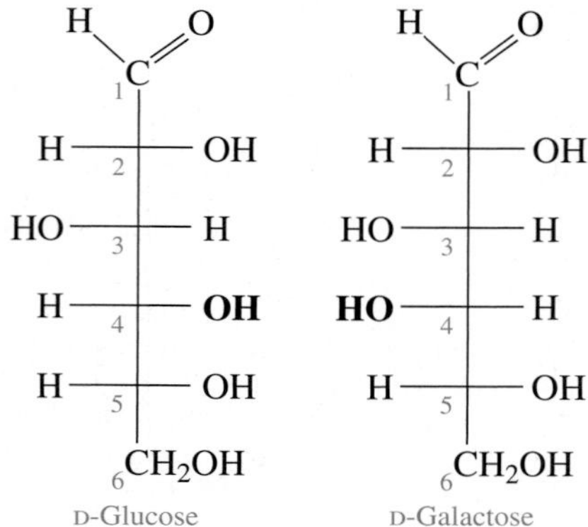


In a condition called *galactosemia*, an enzyme needed to convert galactose to glucose is missing. The accumulation of galactose in the blood and tissues can lead to cataracts, mental retardation, and cirrhosis. The treatment for galactosemia is the removal of all galactose-containing foods, mainly milk and milk products, from the diet. If this is done for an infant immediately after birth, the damaging effects of galactose accumulation can be avoided.

In contrast to glucose and galactose, **fructose** is a ketohexose. The structure of fructose differs from glucose at carbons 1 and 2 by the location of the carbonyl group:

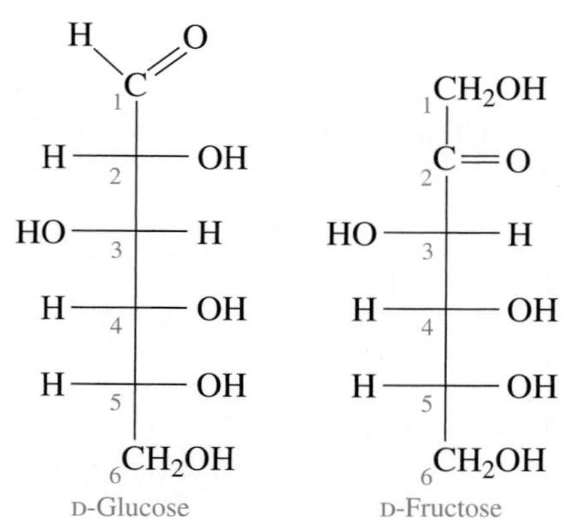


Fructose is the sweetest of the carbohydrates, twice as sweet as sucrose (table sugar). This characteristic makes fructose popular with dieters because less fructose, and therefore fewer calories, is needed to provide a pleasant taste. After fructose enters the bloodstream, it is converted to its isomer, glucose. (See Figure 15.2.) Fructose, also

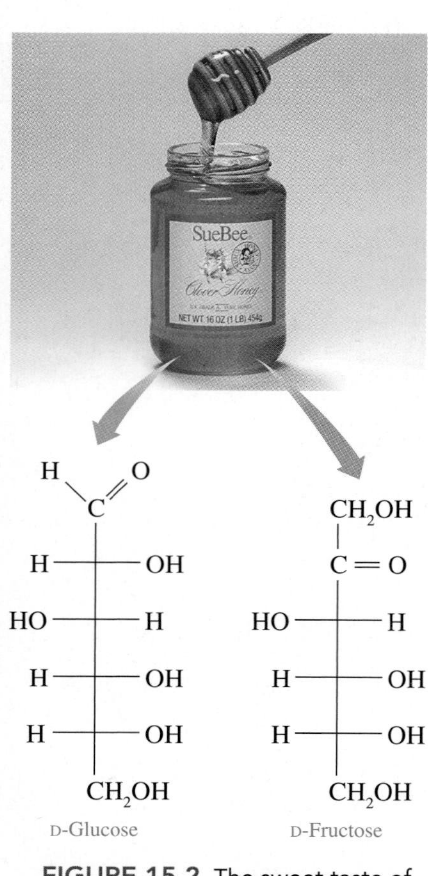


**FIGURE 15.2** The sweet taste of honey is due to the monosaccharides D-glucose and D-fructose.

**Q** What are some differences in the Fischer projections of D-glucose and D-fructose?

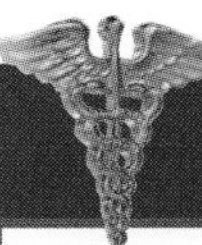

## HEALTH NOTE

### Hyperglycemia and Hypoglycemia

In the body, glucose normally occurs at a concentration of 70–90 mg/dL (1 dL = 100 mL) of blood. However, the amount of glucose in the blood depends on the time that has passed since eating. In the first hour after a meal, the level of glucose rises to about 130 mg/dL of blood and then decreases over the next 2–3 hours as it is used in the tissues.

A doctor may order a glucose tolerance test to evaluate the body's ability to return to normal glucose concentration in response to the ingestion of a specified amount of glucose. The patient fasts for 12 hours and then drinks a solution containing glucose. A blood sample is taken immediately, followed by more blood samples each half-hour for 2 hours, and then every hour for a total of 5 hours. If the blood glucose exceeds 140 mg/dL in plasma and remains high, hyperglycemia may be indicated. The term *glyc* or *gluco* refers to "sugar." The prefix *hyper* means above or over, *hypo* means below or under, and the suffix *emia* means "in the blood." Thus, the blood sugar level in *hyperglycemia* is above normal and below normal in *hypoglycemia*.

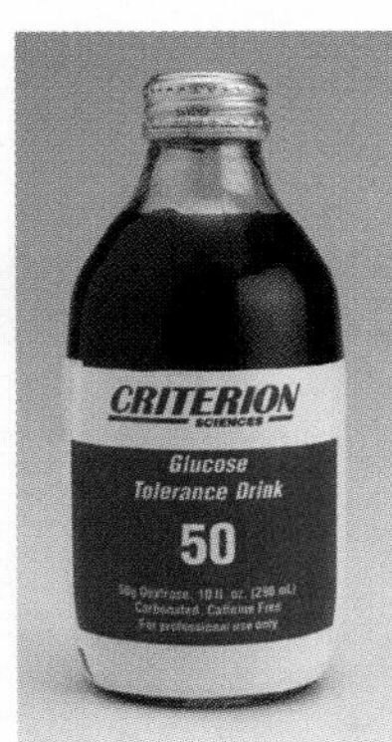


An example of a disease that can cause hyperglycemia is diabetes mellitus, which occurs when the pancreas is unable to produce sufficient quantities of insulin. As a result, glucose levels in the body fluids can rise as high as 350 mg/dL in plasma. Symptoms of diabetes in people under the age of 40 include thirst, excessive urination, increased appetite, and weight loss. In older adults, diabetes is sometimes a consequence of excessive weight gain.

When a person is hypoglycemic, the blood glucose level rises and then decreases rapidly to levels as low as 40 mg/dL plasma. In some cases, hypoglycemia is caused by overproduction of insulin by the pancreas. Low blood glucose can cause dizziness, general weakness, and muscle tremors. A diet may be prescribed that consists of several small meals high in protein and low in carbohydrate. Some hypoglycemic patients are finding success with diets that include more complex carbohydrates rather than simple sugars.

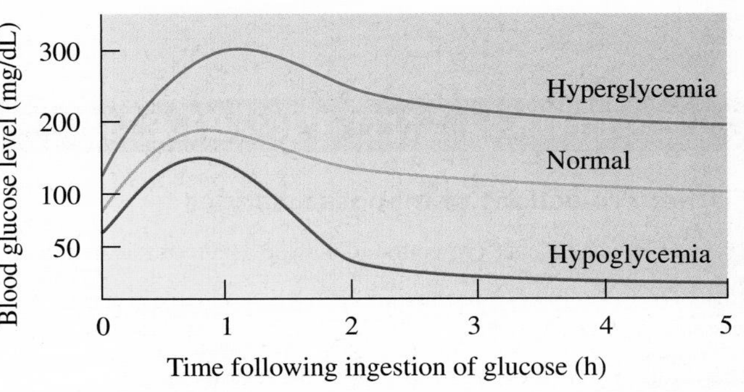


called levulose and fruit sugar, is found in fruit juices and honey. Fructose is also obtained as one of the hydrolysis products of sucrose, the disaccharide known as table sugar.

## SAMPLE PROBLEM 15.2

### Monosaccharides

Ribulose has the following Fischer projection:

```
      CH2OH
       |
       C=O
       |
  H ───┼─── OH
       |
  H ───┼─── OH
       |
      CH2OH
```

**a.** Identify the compound as D- or L-ribulose.
**b.** Draw the Fischer projection of its mirror image.

SOLUTION

**a.** The compound is D-ribulose because the —OH is on the right side of the chiral carbon farthest from the carbonyl group.

**b.** To draw the mirror image, all the —OH groups on the chiral carbon atoms are written on the opposite side. L-Ribulose has the following Fischer projection:

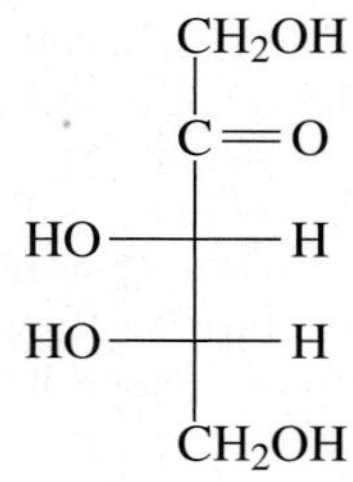

$CH_2OH$
C=O
HO—H
HO—H
$CH_2OH$

STUDY CHECK

What type of carbohydrate is ribulose?

## QUESTIONS AND PROBLEMS

### Fischer Projections of Monosaccharides

**15.11** How is a Fischer projection identified as a D or L isomer?

**15.12** Draw the Fischer projection for D-glyceraldehyde and L-glyceraldehyde.

**15.13** Identify each of the following as the D or L isomer:

**a.** 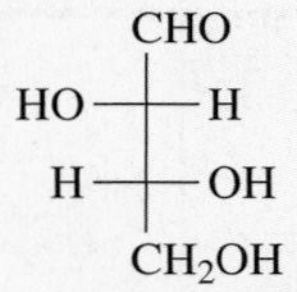
CHO
HO—H
H—OH
$CH_2OH$
Threose

**b.** 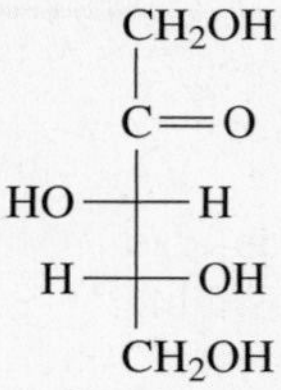
$CH_2OH$
C=O
HO—H
H—OH
$CH_2OH$
Xylulose

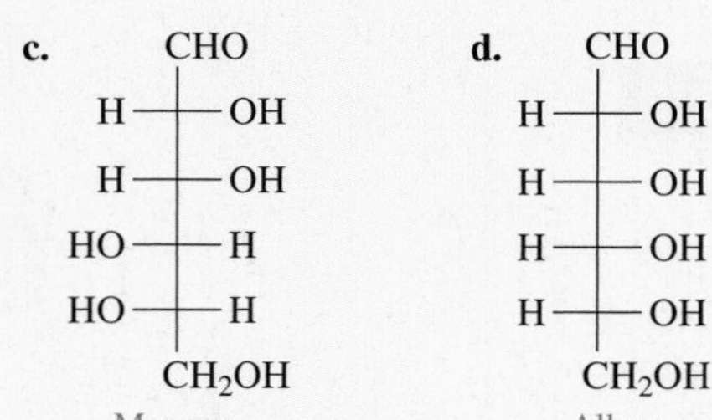
**c.** Mannose **d.** Allose

**15.14** Identify each of the following as the D or L isomer:

**a.** 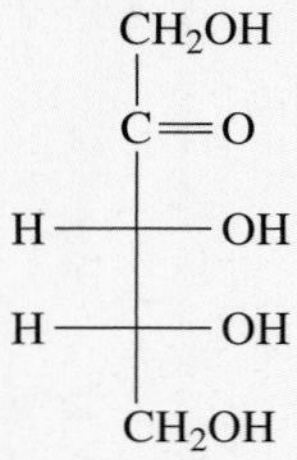
$CH_2OH$
C=O
H—OH
H—OH
$CH_2OH$
Ribulose

**b.** 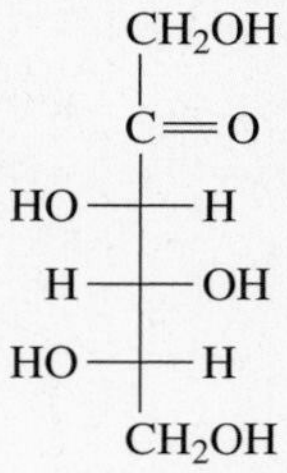
$CH_2OH$
C=O
HO—H
H—OH
HO—H
$CH_2OH$
Sorbose

**c.** 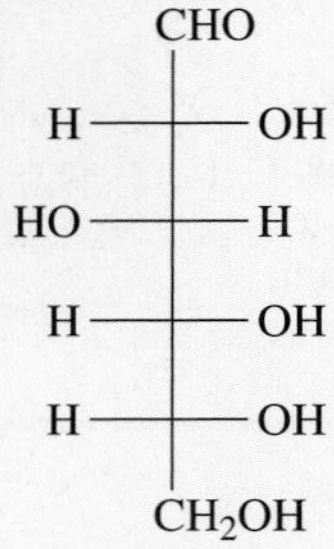
CHO
H—OH
HO—H
H—OH
H—OH
$CH_2OH$
Glucose

**d.** 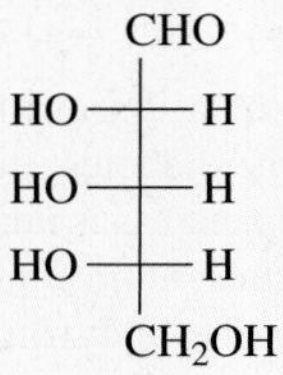
CHO
HO—H
HO—H
HO—H
$CH_2OH$
Ribose

**15.15** Draw the Fischer projections for the mirror images for **a–d** in problem 15.13.

**15.16** Draw the Fischer projections for the mirror images for **a–d** in problem 15.14.

**15.17** Draw the Fischer projections for D-glucose and L-glucose.

**15.18** Draw the Fischer projections for D-fructose and L-fructose.

**15.19** How does the Fischer projection for D-galactose differ from D-glucose?

**15.20** How does the Fischer projection for D-fructose differ from D-glucose?

**15.21** Identify the monosaccharide that fits each of the following descriptions:
**a.** also called blood sugar
**b.** not metabolized in galactosemia
**c.** also called fruit sugar

**15.22** Identify the monosaccharide that fits each of the following descriptions:
**a.** high blood levels in diabetes
**b.** obtained as a hydrolysis product of lactose
**c.** the sweetest of the monosaccharides

# 15.3 Haworth Structures of Monosaccharides

**LEARNING GOAL**

Draw and identify the Haworth structures of monosaccharides.

In Chapter 14, we saw that an aldehyde group reacts with one alcohol molecule to form a hemiacetal. This same reaction occurs when a carbonyl group and an —OH group are in the *same* molecule, which forms a *cyclic hemiacetal*. While the carbonyl group in the open chain could react with several of the —OH groups, the most stable form of pentoses and hexoses are their hemiacetals with five- or six-atom rings. For the aldohexose in the following diagram, the oxygen atom in the hydroxyl group on carbon 5 forms a bond with the carbonyl carbon 1 to produce a heterocyclic six-atom ring containing an oxygen atom and an —OH group on carbon 1:

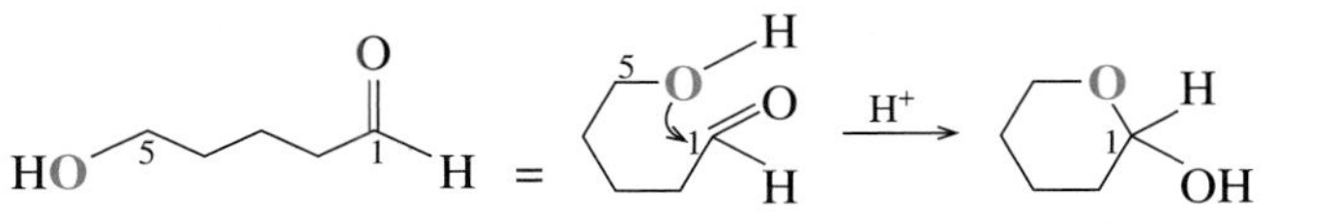

MC™ TUTORIAL
Drawing Cyclic Sugars

Open chain $\xrightarrow{H^+}$ Heterocyclic hemiacetal

## Drawing Haworth Structures for Cyclic Forms

Let's look at how we draw the **Haworth structure**, a representation of the cyclic hemiacetals of the monosaccharides for some D isomers, starting with the open-chain structure of D-glucose. Traditionally, Fischer projections represent the chiral carbon intersections of vertical and horizontal lines. In this text, we will show the carbon chain when it helps understanding.

**STEP 1** **Turn the open-chain structure of D-glucose clockwise.** This places the —OH groups on the right of the vertical open chain below the carbon atoms and the —OH group on the left of the open chain above its carbon atom:

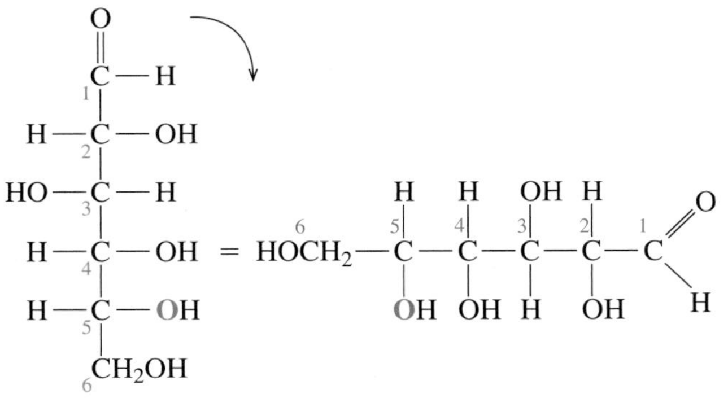

D-Glucose (open chain)

**STEP 2** **Fold the carbon chain into a hexagon by moving carbon 5 above carbon 3.** In all D-monosaccharides including D-glucose, the $—CH_2OH$ group (carbon 6) is placed above carbon 5, and the —OH group on carbon 5 is written next to the carbonyl carbon. To complete the Haworth structure, draw a bond from the oxygen of the —OH group to the carbonyl carbon:

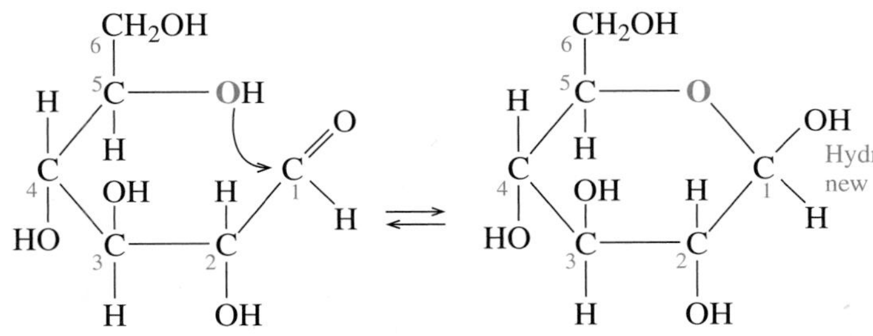

Carbon-5 oxygen bonds to carbonyl

Cyclic hemiacetal structure

Hydroxyl group on new chiral carbon

**STEP 3** **In the Haworth structure for the hemiacetal, the —OH group forms on carbon 1.** In the Haworth structure, the corners of the ring represent carbon atoms. There are two ways to draw the —OH on carbon 1, either up or down, which gives two isomers called **anomers**. The —OH group is drawn down in the $\alpha$ (alpha) anomer and up in the $\beta$ (beta) anomer:

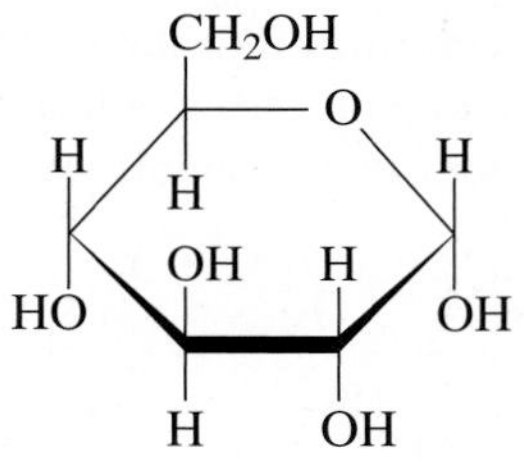

$\alpha$-D-Glucose

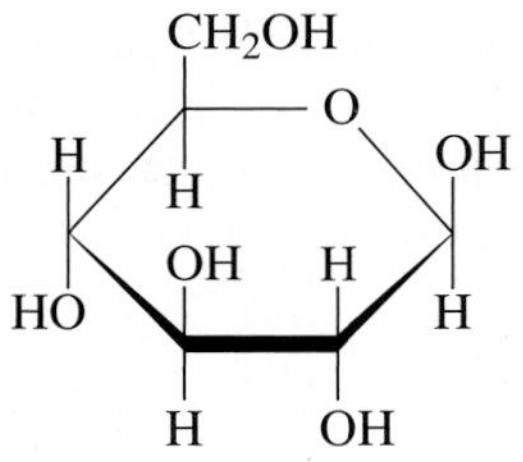

$\beta$-D-Glucose

## Mutarotation of $\alpha$- and $\beta$-D-glucose

In aqueous solution, the Haworth structure of $\alpha$-D-glucose opens and closes to form $\beta$-D-glucose. In this process called **mutarotation**, each anomer converts to the open chain and back again. As the ring opens and closes, the hydroxyl (—OH) group on carbon 1 forms either the $\alpha$ or the $\beta$ anomer. At equilibrium, a glucose solution contains a mixture of 36% of the $\alpha$ anomer and 64% of the $\beta$ anomer. Although the open chain is an essential part of mutarotation, only a trace amount of the open chain is present at any given time:

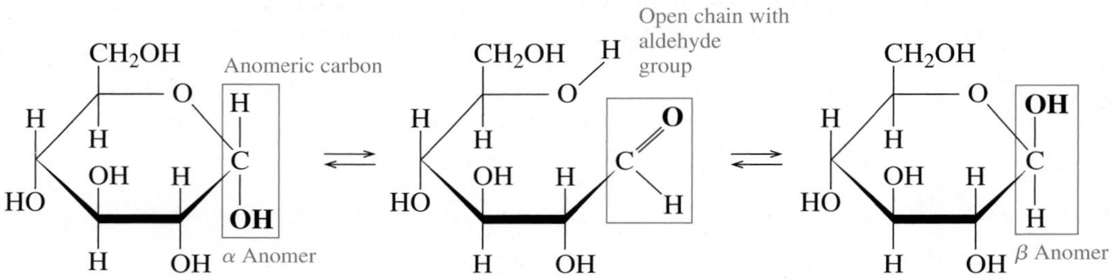

Anomeric carbon

$\alpha$ Anomer

Open chain with aldehyde group

$\beta$ Anomer

$\alpha$-D-Glucose
(36% in equilibrium mixture)

D-Glucose
open chain (trace)

$\beta$-D-Glucose
(64% in equilibrium mixture)

## Haworth Structures of Galactose

Galactose is an aldohexose that differs from glucose only in the arrangement of the —OH group on carbon 4. Thus, its Haworth structure is similar to glucose, except that in galactose the —OH on carbon 4 is up. Galactose also exists as $\alpha$ and $\beta$ anomers and undergoes mutarotation via the open-chain form in aqueous solution:

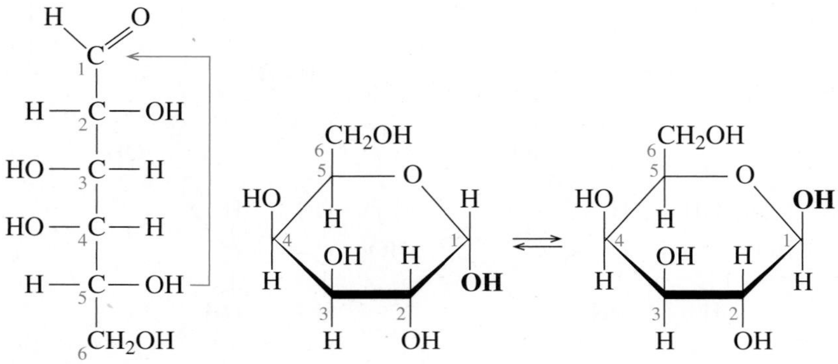

D-Galactose

$\alpha$-D-Galactose

$\beta$-D-Galactose

## Haworth Structures of Fructose

In contrast to glucose and galactose, fructose is a ketohexose. The Haworth structure for fructose is a stable five-atom ring. The hemiacetal forms when the hydroxyl group on carbon 5 reacts with the ketone group on carbon 2. In fructose, the anomeric carbon, which is carbon 2, is bonded to —$CH_2OH$ and a hydroxyl group (—OH). Mutarotation of the anomeric carbon 2 gives $\alpha$ and $\beta$ anomers:

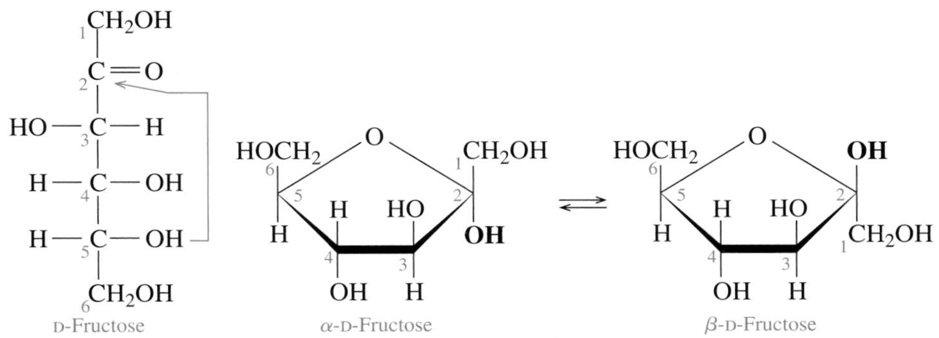


CONCEPT CHECK 15.3

### Anomers

**a.** Why is the Haworth structure of D-galactose a hemiacetal?
**b.** What is the difference between $\alpha$ and $\beta$ anomers of D-galactose?

ANSWER

**a.** D-galactose consists of both a carbonyl group as the aldehyde and several hydroxyl groups. A stable six-atom cyclic structure forms when the hydroxyl group on carbon 5 reacts with the carbonyl group at carbon 1. The resulting structure is a cyclic hemiacetal.
**b.** When the hemiacetal forms, an —OH appears on carbon 1. Two isomers called *anomers* are possible because the —OH can form above or below the ring. In the $\alpha$ anomer, the —OH is drawn down, and for the $\beta$ anomer, the —OH is drawn up.

SAMPLE PROBLEM 15.3

### Drawing Haworth Structures for Sugars

D-Mannose, a carbohydrate found in immunoglobulins, has the following open-chain structure. Draw the Haworth structure for $\beta$-D-mannose anomer:

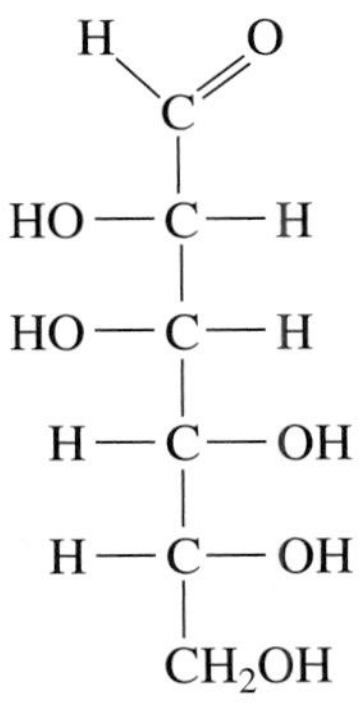

D-Mannose

**Guide to Drawing Haworth Structures**

**STEP 1**
Turn the open-chain structure clockwise 90°.

**STEP 2**
Fold the chain into a hexagon and bond the O on carbon 5 to the carbon of the carbonyl group.

**STEP 3**
Draw the new —OH group on carbon 1 down to give the $\alpha$ anomer or up to give the $\beta$ anomer.

SOLUTION

**STEP 1** **Turn the open-chain structure to the right.**

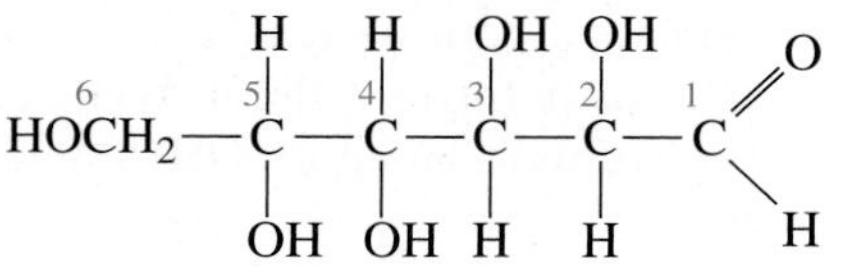

$HOCH_2$—C—C—C—C—CHO (carbons 6 to 1; upper substituents H, H, OH, OH; lower substituents OH, OH, H, H)

**STEP 2** **Fold the carbon chain into a hexagon (move carbons 4, 5, and 6 clockwise).** Draw the —$CH_2OH$ group above carbon 5 and the —OH group next to the carbonyl. Complete the Haworth structure by bonding the O of the —OH group with the C of the carbonyl group:

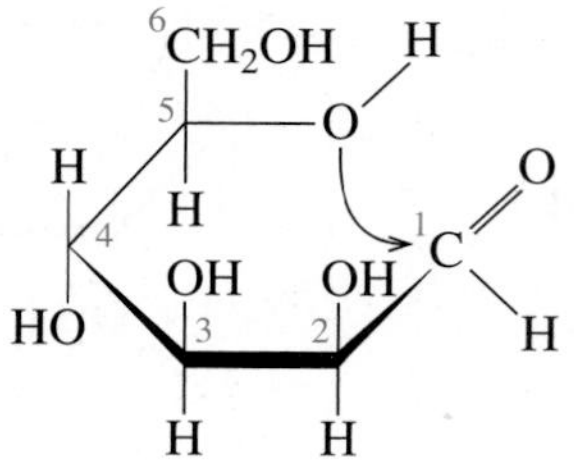

**STEP 3** **In the Haworth structure, draw the hydroxyl group on carbon 1 up to make the $\beta$-D-mannose anomer:**

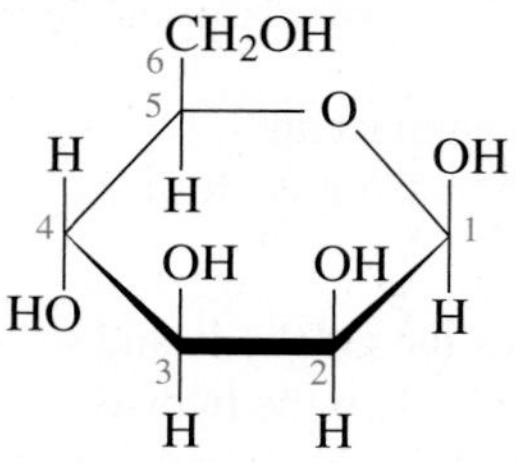

$\beta$-D-Mannose

STUDY CHECK

Draw the Haworth structure for $\alpha$-D-glucose.

# QUESTIONS AND PROBLEMS

## Haworth Structures of Monosaccharides

**15.23** Name the kind and number of atoms in the ring portion of the Haworth structure of glucose.

**15.24** Name the kind and number of atoms in the ring portion of the Haworth structure of fructose.

**15.25** Draw the Haworth structures for the $\alpha$ and $\beta$ anomers of D-glucose.

**15.26** Draw the Haworth structures for the $\alpha$ and $\beta$ anomers of D-fructose.

**15.27** Identify each of the following Haworth structures as the $\alpha$ or $\beta$ anomer:

**a.** **b.**

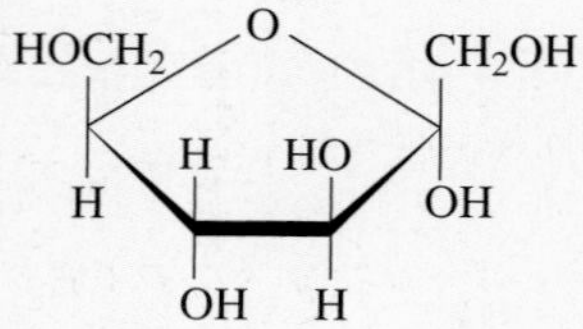

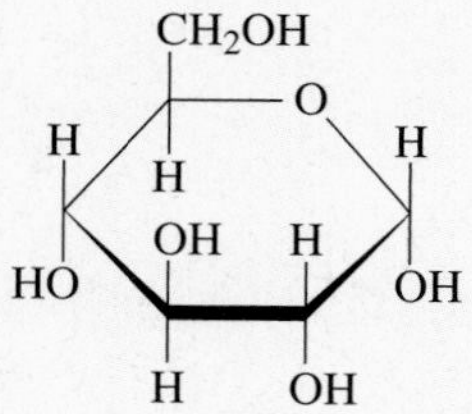

**15.28** Identify each of the following Haworth structures as the $\alpha$ or $\beta$ anomer:

**a.**

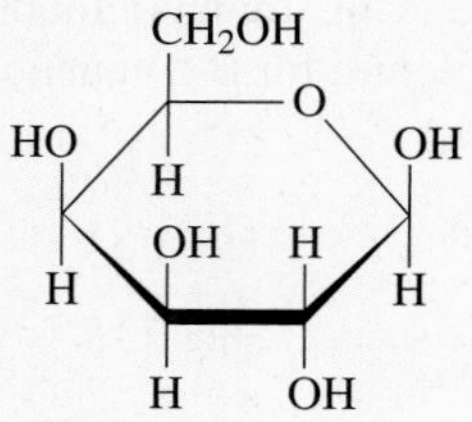

**b.**

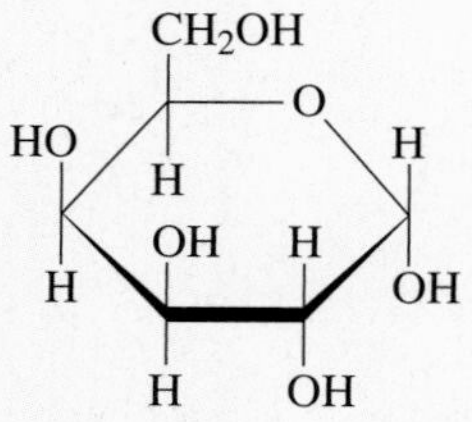

## 15.4 Chemical Properties of Monosaccharides

**LEARNING GOAL**

Identify the products of oxidation or reduction of monosaccharides; determine whether a carbohydrate is a reducing sugar.

Monosaccharides contain functional groups that can undergo chemical reactions. In an aldose, the aldehyde group can be oxidized to a carboxylic acid. The carbonyl group in both an aldose and a ketose can be reduced to give a hydroxyl group. The hydroxyl groups can react with other compounds to form a variety of derivatives that are important in biological structures.

### Oxidation of Monosaccharides

Although monosaccharides exist mostly in cyclic form, a small amount of the open-chain structure is always present, which provides an aldehyde group. When Benedict's reagent is added, the aldehyde group is oxidized and $Cu^{2+}$ is reduced to $Cu^{+}$, which forms a brick-red precipitate of $Cu_2O$. Monosaccharides, including all the aldohexoses, that reduce another substance are called **reducing sugars**.

$$\begin{array}{c} O \\ \| \\ C-H \\ | \\ H-C-OH \\ | \\ HO-C-H \\ | \\ H-C-OH \\ | \\ H-C-OH \\ | \\ CH_2OH \end{array} \quad + \underset{\text{Blue}}{2Cu^{2+}} \xrightarrow{[O]} \quad \overset{\text{Oxidized}}{\begin{array}{c} O \\ \| \\ C-OH \\ | \\ H-C-OH \\ | \\ HO-C-H \\ | \\ H-C-OH \\ | \\ H-C-OH \\ | \\ CH_2OH \end{array}} \quad + \overset{\text{Reduced}}{\underset{\text{Brick-red}}{Cu_2O(s)}}$$

Open chain of D-Glucose, a reducing sugar — D-Gluconic acid

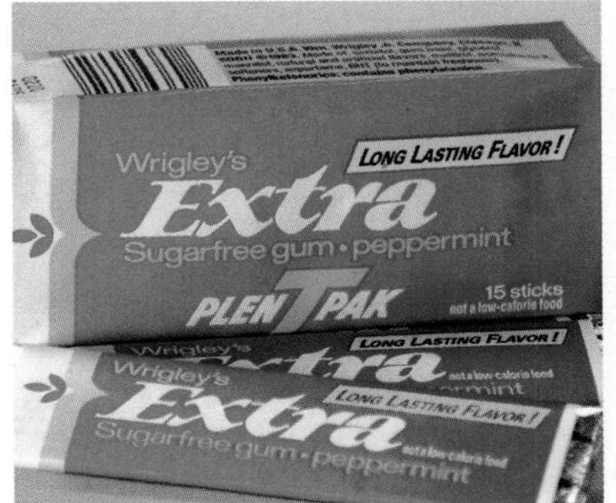


Fructose, a ketohexose, is also a reducing sugar. Usually a ketone cannot be oxidized. However, in a basic Benedict's solution, a rearrangement moves the carbonyl group from carbon 2 to carbon 1. As a result, this rearrangement converts fructose to glucose, which provides an aldehyde group that can be oxidized:

$$\begin{array}{c} {}_1CH_2OH \\ | \\ {}_2C=O \\ | \\ HO-C-H \\ | \\ H-C-OH \\ | \\ H-C-OH \\ | \\ CH_2OH \end{array} \quad \xrightleftharpoons{\text{Rearrangement}} \quad \begin{array}{c} H\diagdown\ \diagup O \\ {}_1C \\ | \\ H-{}_2C-OH \\ | \\ HO-C-H \\ | \\ H-C-OH \\ | \\ H-C-OH \\ | \\ CH_2OH \end{array}$$

D-Fructose (ketose) — D-Glucose (aldose)

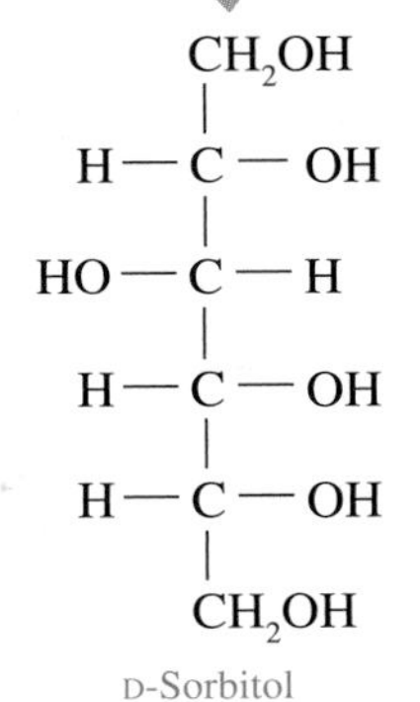

D-Sorbitol

### Reduction of Monosaccharides

The reduction of the carbonyl group in monosaccharides produces sugar alcohols, which are also called *alditols*. D-Glucose is reduced to D-glucitol, better known as *sorbitol*. D-Mannose is reduced to give D-mannitol. The sugar alcohols are named by changing the *ose* ending of the monosaccharide to *itol.*

$$
\begin{array}{c}
\text{O} \\
\| \\
\text{C}-\text{H} \\
| \\
\text{H}-\text{C}-\text{OH} \\
| \\
\text{HO}-\text{C}-\text{H} \\
| \\
\text{H}-\text{C}-\text{OH} \\
| \\
\text{H}-\text{C}-\text{OH} \\
| \\
\text{CH}_2\text{OH}
\end{array}
\xrightarrow{H_2}
\begin{array}{c}
\text{CH}_2\text{OH} \\
| \\
\text{H}-\text{C}-\text{OH} \\
| \\
\text{HO}-\text{C}-\text{H} \\
| \\
\text{H}-\text{C}-\text{OH} \\
| \\
\text{H}-\text{C}-\text{OH} \\
| \\
\text{CH}_2\text{OH}
\end{array}
$$

D-Glucose D-Glucitol or D-Sorbitol

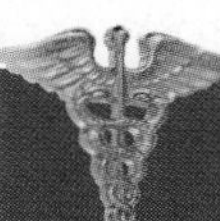

CASE STUDY
Diabetes and Blood Glucose

Sugar alcohols such as sorbitol, xylitol from xylose, and mannitol from mannose are used as sweeteners in many sugar-free products such as diet drinks and sugarless gum, as well as products for people with diabetes. However, there are some side effects of these sugar substitutes. Some people experience some discomfort, such as gas and diarrhea, from the ingestion of sugar alcohols. The development of cataracts in diabetics is attributed to the accumulation of sorbitol in the lens of the eye.

## HEALTH NOTE

### Testing for Glucose in Urine

Normally, blood glucose flows through the kidneys and is reabsorbed into the bloodstream. However, if the blood level exceeds about 160 mg of glucose/dL of blood, the kidneys cannot reabsorb it all, and glucose spills over into the urine, a condition known as glucosuria. A symptom of diabetes mellitus is a high level of glucose in the urine.

Benedict's test can be used to determine the presence of glucose in urine. The amount of copper(I) oxide ($Cu_2O$) formed is proportional to the concentration of reducing sugar present in the urine. Low to moderate levels of reducing sugar turn the solution green; solutions with high glucose levels turn Benedict's yellow or brick-red. Table 15.1 lists some colors associated with the concentration of glucose in the urine.

In another clinical test that is more specific for glucose, the enzyme glucose oxidase is used. The oxidase enzyme converts glucose to gluconic acid and hydrogen peroxide ($H_2O_2$). The peroxide produced reacts with a dye in the test strip to produce different colors. The level of glucose present in the urine is found by matching the color produced to a color chart on the container.

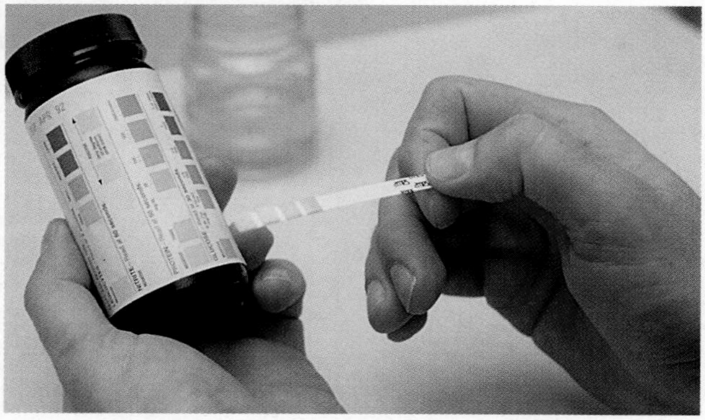

**TABLE 15.1** Glucose Test Results

| Color (of Benedict's test) | Glucose Present in Urine | |
|---|---|---|
| | % (m/v) | mg/dL |
| Blue | 0 | 0 |
| Blue-green | 0.25 | 250 |
| Green | 0.50 | 500 |
| Yellow | 1.00 | 1000 |
| Brick-red | 2.00 | 2000 |

CONCEPT CHECK 15.4

### Reducing Sugars

**a.** Why is D-glucose a *reducing sugar*?

**b.** In a laboratory test using Benedict's reagent, a sample of urine turns brick-red. According to Table 15.1, what might this test result indicate?

ANSWER

**a.** The aldehyde in D-glucose is easily oxidized by Benedict's reagent. A carbohydrate that reduces $Cu^{2+}$ to $Cu^{+}$ is called a reducing sugar.

**b.** This result indicates a high level of reducing sugar (probably glucose) in the urine. One common cause of this condition is diabetes mellitus.

## QUESTIONS AND PROBLEMS

### Chemical Properties of Monosaccharides

**15.29** Draw the product xylitol produced from the reduction of D-xylose:

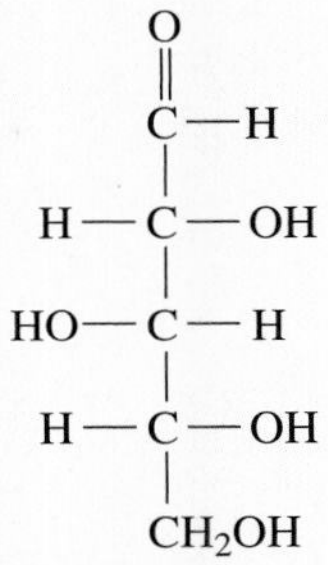

O
‖
C—H
|
H—C—OH
|
HO—C—H
|
H—C—OH
|
$CH_2OH$

D-Xylose

**15.30** Draw the product mannitol produced from the reduction of D-mannose:

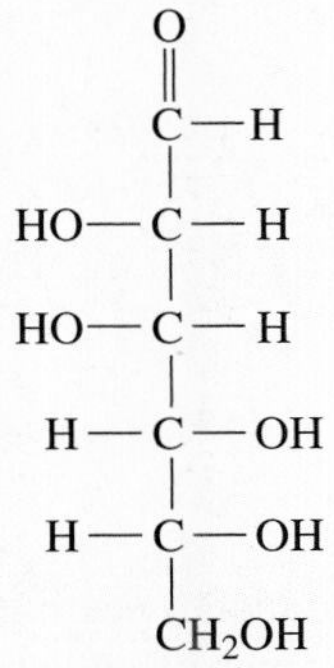

O
‖
C—H
|
HO—C—H
|
HO—C—H
|
H—C—OH
|
H—C—OH
|
$CH_2OH$

D-Mannose

**15.31** Write the oxidation and reduction products of D-arabinose. What is the name of the sugar alcohol produced by reduction?

O
‖
C—H
|
HO—C—H
|
H—C—OH
|
H—C—OH
|
$CH_2OH$

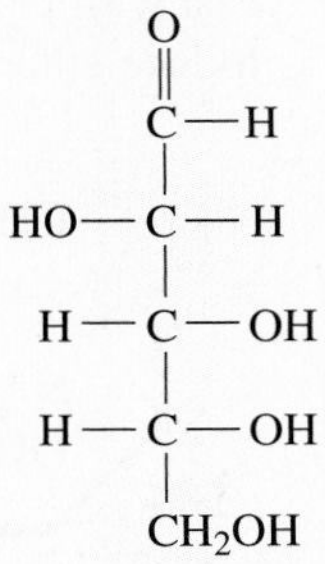

D-Arabinose

**15.32** Write the oxidation and reduction products of D-ribose. What is the name of the sugar alcohol produced by reduction?

O
‖
C—H
|
H—C—OH
|
H—C—OH
|
H—C—OH
|
$CH_2OH$

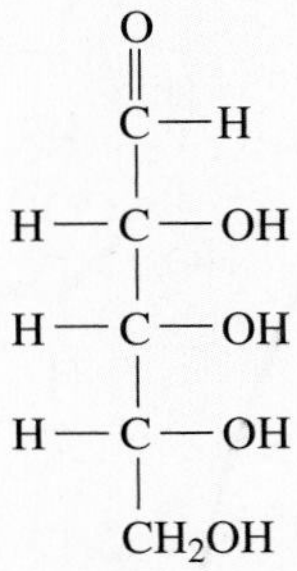

D-Ribose

## 15.5 Disaccharides

LEARNING GOAL

Describe the monosaccharide units and glycosidic bonds in disaccharides.

A disaccharide is composed of two monosaccharides linked together. When monosaccharides combine, they form an acetal. The reaction occurs between the anomeric hydroxyl group as a hemiacetal and one of the hydroxyl groups as the alcohol on a second monosaccharide. The most common disaccharides are maltose, lactose, and sucrose. Their

## Sugar and Sweeteners

Add a tablespoon of sugar to a glass of water and stir. Taste. Add more tablespoons of sugar, stir, and taste. If you have other carbohydrates such as fructose, honey, cornstarch, arrowroot, or flour, add some of each to separate glasses of water and stir. If you have some artificial sweeteners, add a few drops of the sweetener or a package, if solid, to a glass of water. Taste each.

### QUESTIONS

1. Which substance is the most soluble in water?
2. Place the substances in order from the one that tastes least sweet to the sweetest.
3. How does your list compare to Table 15.2?
4. How does the sweetness of sucrose compare with the artificial sweeteners?
5. Check the labels of food products in your kitchen. Look for sugars such as sucrose and fructose or artificial sweeteners such as aspartame or sucralose on the label. How many grams of sugar are in a serving of the food?

hydrolysis, by an acid or an enzyme (maltase, lactase, and sucrase), gives the following monosaccharides:

$$\text{Maltose} + H_2O \xrightarrow{H^+ \text{ or maltase}} \text{glucose} + \text{glucose}$$

$$\text{Lactose} + H_2O \xrightarrow{H^+ \text{ or lactase}} \text{glucose} + \text{galactose}$$

$$\text{Sucrose} + H_2O \xrightarrow{H^+ \text{ or sucrase}} \text{glucose} + \text{fructose}$$

**Maltose**, or malt sugar, is a disaccharide. A **glycosidic bond** between two glucose molecules forms when one glucose acting as a hemiacetal reacts with a hydroxyl group in another glucose. In maltose, the glycosidic bond that joins the two glucose molecules is an $\alpha$-1,4 linkage, which shows that the —OH on carbon 1 of $\alpha$-D-glucose is bonded to carbon 4 of the second glucose. In maltose, the —OH group on carbon 1 gives $\alpha$ and $\beta$ anomers. Maltose is a reducing sugar because the hemiacetal —OH on carbon 1 opens and closes, which provides an aldehyde group. Maltose is used in cereals, candies, and the brewing of beverages. When maltose from the starches in barley and other grains is hydrolyzed by yeast with maltase enzyme, glucose is obtained. This glucose can undergo fermentation to produce ethanol:

α-D-Glucose + α-D-Glucose

↓

α-1,4-Glycosidic bond

+ $H_2O$

α Anomer

α-Maltose, a disaccharide

**Lactose**, milk sugar, is a disaccharide found in milk and milk products. (See Figure 15.3.) The bond in lactose is a $\beta$-1,4-glycosidic bond because the $\beta$ anomer of galactose forms a bond with the hydroxyl group on carbon 4 of glucose. In lactose, the —OH group on the hemiacetal carbon 1 gives $\alpha$ and $\beta$ anomers. Lactose is a reducing sugar because the hemiacetal on carbon 1 provides an open chain with an aldehyde group that can be oxidized.

Lactose makes up 6–8% of human milk and about 4–5% of cow's milk, and it is used in products that attempt to duplicate mother's milk. Some people do not produce sufficient quantities of the enzyme needed to hydrolyze lactose, and the sugar remains undigested, causing abdominal cramps and diarrhea. In some commercial milk products, an enzyme called lactase is added to break down lactose.

**Sucrose** consists of an $\alpha$-D-glucose and $\beta$-D-fructose molecule joined by an $\alpha,\beta$-1,2-glycosidic bond. (See Figure 15.4.) Unlike maltose and lactose, the glycosidic bond

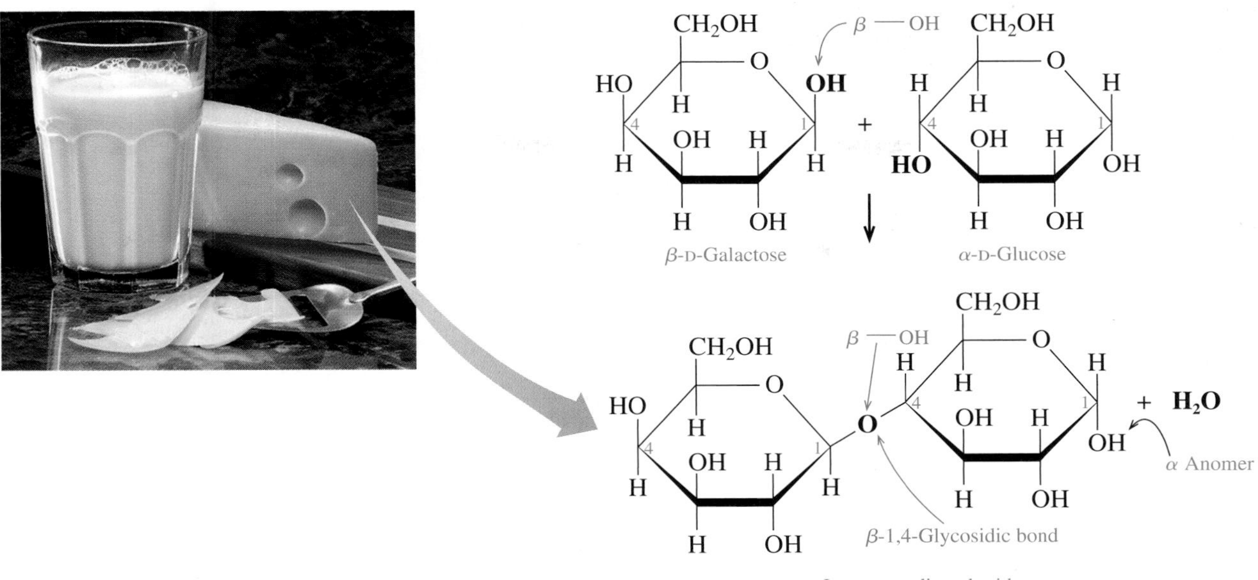


**FIGURE 15.3** α-Lactose, a disaccharide found in milk and milk products, contains β-D-galactose and α-D-glucose.

**Q** What type of glycosidic bond links β-D-galactose and α-D-glucose in α-lactose?

in sucrose is between carbon 1 of glucose and carbon 2 of fructose. Thus, sucrose does not have a hemiacetal on carbon 1 and cannot form an open chain. Sucrose cannot react with Benedict's reagent and is not a reducing sugar.

The sugar we use to sweeten our cereal, coffee, and tea is sucrose. Most of the sucrose for table sugar comes from sugar cane (20% by mass) or sugar beets (15% by mass). Both the raw and refined forms of sugar are sucrose. Some estimates indicate that each person in the United States consumes an average of 68 kg (150 lb) of sucrose every year either by itself or in a variety of food products. In the body, the enzyme sucrase hydrolyzes sucrose to glucose and fructose.

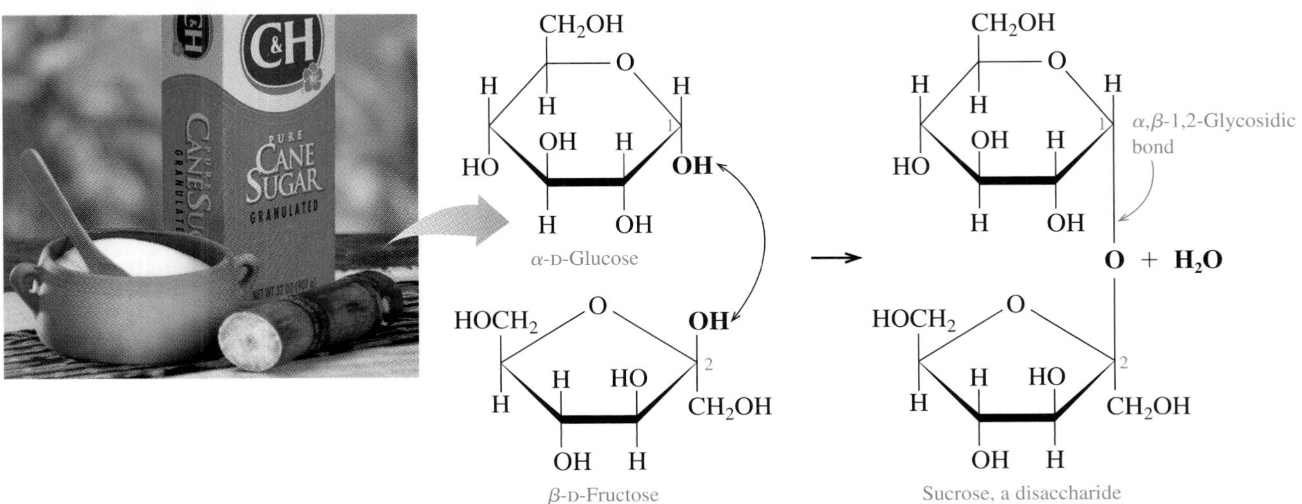


**FIGURE 15.4** Sucrose, a disaccharide obtained from sugar beets and sugar cane, contains α-D-glucose and β-D-fructose.

**Q** Why is sucrose a nonreducing sugar?

# HEALTH NOTE

## How Sweet Is My Sweetener?

Although many of the monosaccharides and disaccharides taste sweet, they differ considerably in their degree of sweetness. Dietetic foods contain sweeteners that are noncarbohydrate or carbohydrates that are sweeter than sucrose. Some examples of sweeteners compared with sucrose are shown in Table 15.2.

Sucralose is made from sucrose by replacing some of the hydroxyl groups with chlorine atoms:

Sucralose

Aspartame, which is marketed as NutraSweet, is used in a large number of sugar-free products. It is a noncarbohydrate sweetener made of aspartic acid and a methyl ester of phenylalanine. It does have some caloric value, but it is so sweet that only a very small quantity is needed. However, phenylalanine, one of the breakdown products, poses a danger to anyone who cannot metabolize it properly, a condition called phenylketonuria (PKU):

$$H_2N{-}CH(CH_2COOH){-}C(=O){-}NH{-}CH(CH_2C_6H_5){-}C(=O){-}O{-}CH_3$$

From aspartic acid From phenylalanine Methyl ester

Aspartame (NutraSweet)

Another artificial sweetener, Neotame, is a modification of the aspartame structure. The addition of a large alkyl group to the amine group prevents enzymes from breaking the amide bond between aspartic acid and phenylalanine. Thus, phenylalanine is not produced when Neotame is used as a sweetener. Very small amounts of Neotame are needed because it is about 10 000 times sweeter than sucrose:

$$H_3C{-}C(CH_3)_2{-}CH_2{-}CH_2{-}NH{-}CH(CH_2COOH){-}C(=O){-}NH{-}CH(CH_2C_6H_5){-}C(=O){-}O{-}CH_3$$

Large alkyl group to modify Aspartame

Neotame

**TABLE 15.2 Relative Sweetness of Sugars and Artificial Sweeteners**

| | Sweetness Relative to Sucrose (= 100) |
|---|---|
| **Monosaccharides** | |
| Galactose | 30 |
| Glucose | 75 |
| Fructose | 175 |
| **Disaccharides** | |
| Lactose | 16 |
| Maltose | 33 |
| Sucrose | 100 = reference standard |
| **Sugar Alcohols (Polyols)** | |
| Sorbitol | 60 |
| Maltitol | 80 |
| Xylitol | 100 |
| **Artificial Sweeteners (Noncarbohydrate)** | |
| Aspartame | 18 000 |
| Saccharin | 45 000 |
| Sucralose | 60 000 |
| Neotame | 1 000 000 |

Saccharin has been used as a noncarbohydrate artificial sweetener for the past 25 years. The use of saccharin has been banned in Canada because studies indicate that it may cause bladder tumors. However, it is still approved for use by the FDA in the United States.

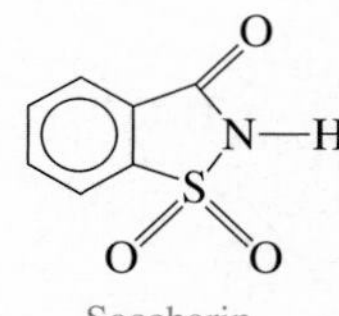


Saccharin

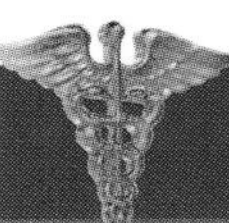

# HEALTH NOTE

## Blood Types and Carbohydrates

Every individual's blood can be typed as one of four blood groups: A, B, AB, and O. Although there is some variation among ethnic groups in the United States, the incidence of blood types in the general population is about 43% O, 40% A, 12% B, and 5% AB.

The blood types A, B, and O are determined by saccharides attached to the surface of red blood cells. In type O, the end saccharides are *N*-acetylglucosamine, galactose, and fucose. These same three end saccharides also occur in type A and type B blood. In type A, the galactose is bonded to *N*-acetylgalactosamine. In type B, the galactose is bonded to another galactose. Thus, blood types A and B are determined by an end *N*-acetylgalactosamine (type A) or an end galactose (type B). In type AB, both sequences are at the ends of the saccharide chains. The structures of these monosaccharides are as follows:

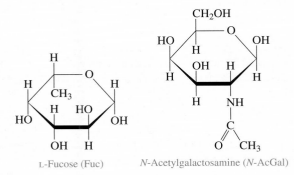

*N*-Acetylglucosamine (*N*-AcGlu)

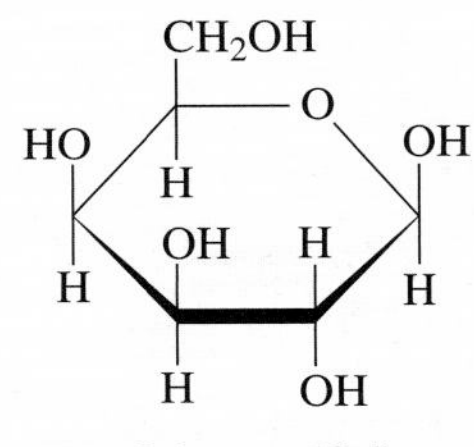

D-Galactose (Gal)

L-Fucose (Fuc)

*N*-Acetylgalactosamine (*N*-AcGal)

A person with type A blood produces antibodies against type B, whereas a person with type B blood produces antibodies against type A. Type AB blood produces no antibodies, whereas type O produces antibodies against both types A and B. Thus, if a person with type A blood receives a transfusion of type B blood, factors in the recipient's blood will cause the donor's red blood cells to clump together, or agglutinate.

People with type O can donate to individuals with all blood types; they are universal donors. However, a type O person can receive only type O blood. People with type AB blood can receive all blood types because they do not have antibodies for types A and B; they are universal recipients.

Terminal saccharide that determines blood type

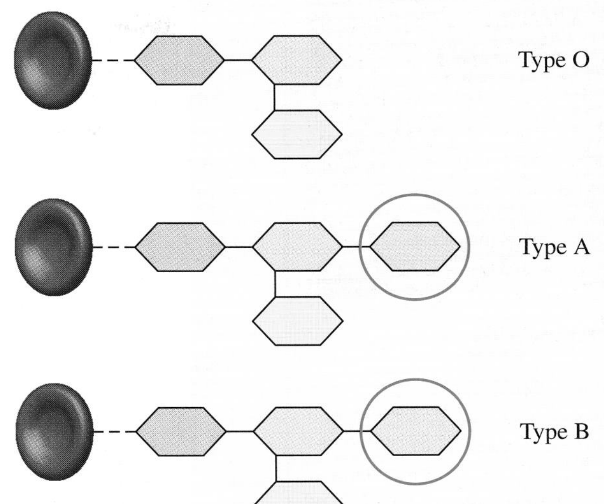


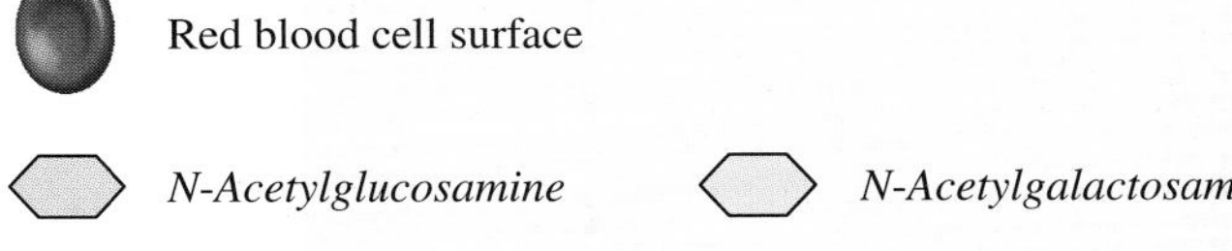


Table 15.3 summarizes the compatibility of blood groups for transfusion.

**TABLE 15.3 Compatibility of Blood Groups**

| Blood Type | Antibodies Against | Can Receive |
|---|---|---|
| A | B | A, O |
| B | A | B, O |
| AB[a] | None | A, B, AB, O |
| O[b] | A, B | O |

[a]AB universal recipient
[b]O universal donor

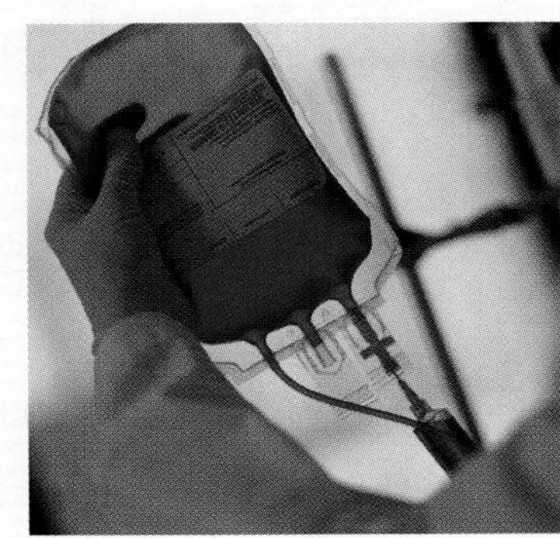

## CAREER FOCUS

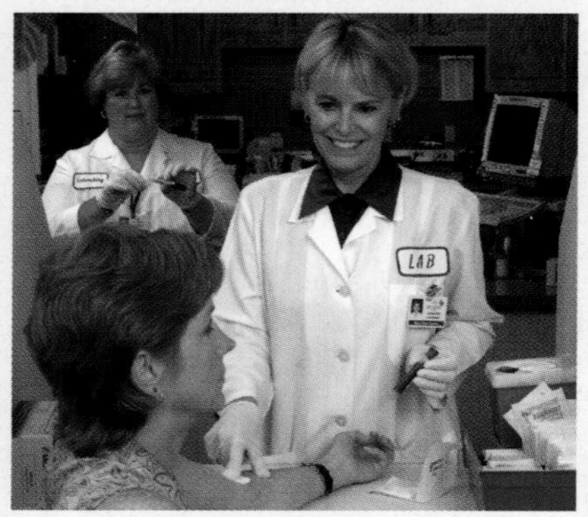


### Phlebotomist

As part of the medical team, phlebotomists collect and process blood for laboratory tests. They work directly with patients, calming them if necessary before the collection of blood. Phlebotomists are trained to collect blood in a safe manner and provide patient care if fainting occurs. Blood is drawn through venipuncture methods such as syringe, vacutainer, and fingerstick. They also prepare patients for procedures such as glucose tolerance tests. In the preparation of specimens for analysis, a phlebotomist determines media, inoculation method, and reagents for culture setup.

## CONCEPT CHECK 15.5

### Glycosidic Bonds

Why is the glycosidic bond in maltose called an $\alpha$-1,4-glycosidic bond whereas in lactose it is called a $\beta$-1,4-glycosidic bond?

ANSWER

In maltose, the hydroxyl group on the hemiacetal (carbon 1) is down, which makes it the $\alpha$ anomer. When the hydroxyl group from the $\alpha$ anomer of one glucose forms an acetal with the hydroxyl group on carbon 4 of another glucose, the glycosidic bond is an $\alpha$-1,4-glycosidic bond. In lactose, a hydroxyl group from the $\beta$ anomer of galactose forms an acetal with the hydroxyl group on carbon 4 of glucose. Then the glycosidic bond is a $\beta$-1,4-glycosidic bond.

## SAMPLE PROBLEM 15.4

### Glycosidic Bonds in Disaccharides

Melebiose is a disaccharide that is 30 times sweeter than sucrose:

Melebiose

a. What are the monosaccharide units in melebiose?
b. What type of glycosidic bond links the monosaccharides?
c. Identify the structure as $\alpha$- or $\beta$-melebiose.

SOLUTION

a. The monosaccharide on the left side is $\alpha$-D-galactose; on the right is $\alpha$-D-glucose.
b. The monosaccharide units are linked by an $\alpha$-1,6-glycosidic bond.
c. The downward position of the hydroxyl group on the carbon 1 hemiacetal of the D-glucose makes it $\alpha$-melebiose.

STUDY CHECK

Cellobiose is a disaccharide composed of two $\beta$-D-glucose molecules linked by a $\beta$-1,4-glycosidic linkage. Draw a structural formula for $\beta$-cellobiose.

## QUESTIONS AND PROBLEMS

### Disaccharides

15.33 Give the monosaccharide units produced by hydrolysis, the type of glycosidic bond, and the identity of the disaccharide including the $\alpha$ or $\beta$ anomer for each of the following:

a.

b.

**15.34** Give the monosaccharide units produced by hydrolysis, the type of glycosidic bond, and the identity of the disaccharide including the $\alpha$ or $\beta$ anomer for each of the following:

**a.**

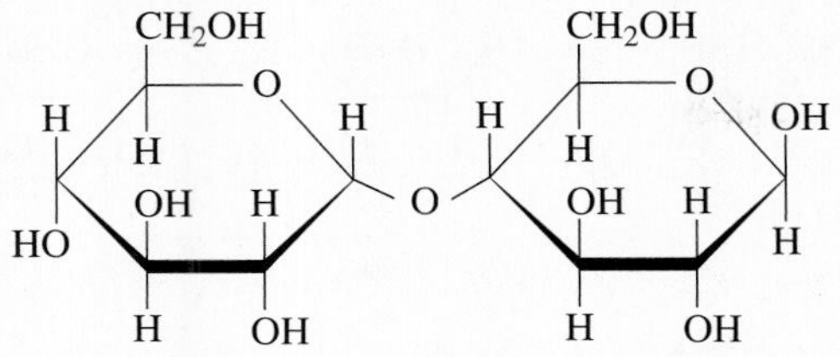

**b.**

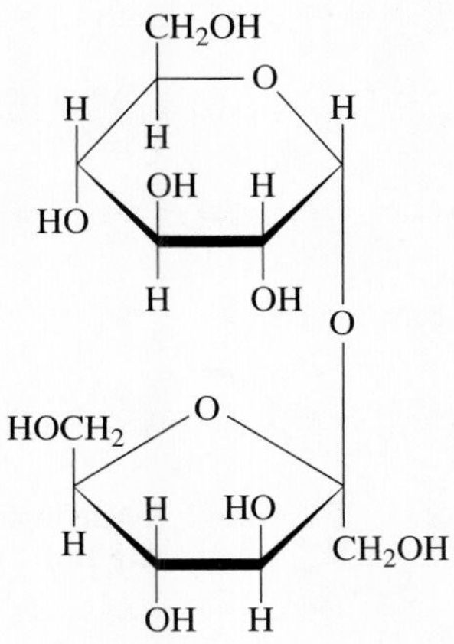

15.35 Indicate whether each disaccharide in problem 15.33 is a reducing sugar or not.

**15.36** Indicate whether each disaccharide in problem 15.34 is a reducing sugar or not.

15.37 Identify the disaccharide that fits each of the following descriptions:

**a.** ordinary table sugar
**b.** found in milk and milk products
**c.** also called malt sugar
**d.** hydrolysis gives galactose and glucose

**15.38** Identify the disaccharide that fits each of the following descriptions:

**a.** not a reducing sugar
**b.** composed of two glucose units
**c.** also called milk sugar
**d.** hydrolysis gives glucose and fructose

## 15.6 Polysaccharides

**LEARNING GOAL**

Describe the structural features of amylose, amylopectin, glycogen, and cellulose.

A **polysaccharide** is a polymer of many monosaccharides joined together. Four biologically important polysaccharides—amylose, amylopectin, cellulose, and glycogen—are all polymers of D-glucose that differ only in the type of glycosidic bonds and the amount of branching in the molecule.

Starch, a storage form of glucose in plants, is found as insoluble granules in rice, wheat, potatoes, beans, and cereals. Starch is composed of two kinds of polysaccharides, amylose and amylopectin. **Amylose**, which makes up about 20% of starch, consists of 250 to 4000 $\alpha$-D-glucose molecules connected by $\alpha$-1,4-glycosidic bonds in a continuous chain. Sometimes called a straight-chain polymer, polymers of amylose are actually coiled in helical fashion.

**Amylopectin**, which makes up as much as 80% of plant starch, is a branched-chain polysaccharide. Like amylose, $\alpha$-1,4-glycosidic bonds connect the glucose molecules. However, at about every 25 glucose units, there is a branch of glucose molecules attached by an $\alpha$-1,6-glycosidic bond between carbon 1 of the branch and carbon 6 in the main chain. (See Figure 15.5.)

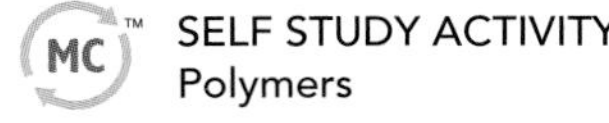

SELF STUDY ACTIVITY
Polymers

Starches hydrolyze easily in water and acid to give shorter glucose chains called *dextrins*, which then hydrolyze to maltose and finally glucose. In our bodies, these complex carbohydrates are digested by the enzymes amylase (in saliva) and maltase. The glucose obtained usually provides about 50% of our nutritional calories.

$$\text{Amylose, amylopectin} \xrightarrow{H^+ \text{ or amylase}} \text{dextrins} \xrightarrow{H^+ \text{ or amylase}} \text{maltose} \xrightarrow{H^+ \text{ or maltase}} \text{many D-glucose units}$$

**Glycogen**, or animal starch, is a polymer of glucose that is stored in the liver and muscle of animals. It is hydrolyzed in our cells at a rate that maintains the blood level of glucose and provides energy between meals. The structure of glycogen is very similar to that of amylopectin, found in plants, except that glycogen is more highly branched. In glycogen, $\alpha$-1,4-glycosidic bonds join the glucose units, and branches occurring about every 10 to 15 glucose units are attached by $\alpha$-1,6-glycosidic bonds.

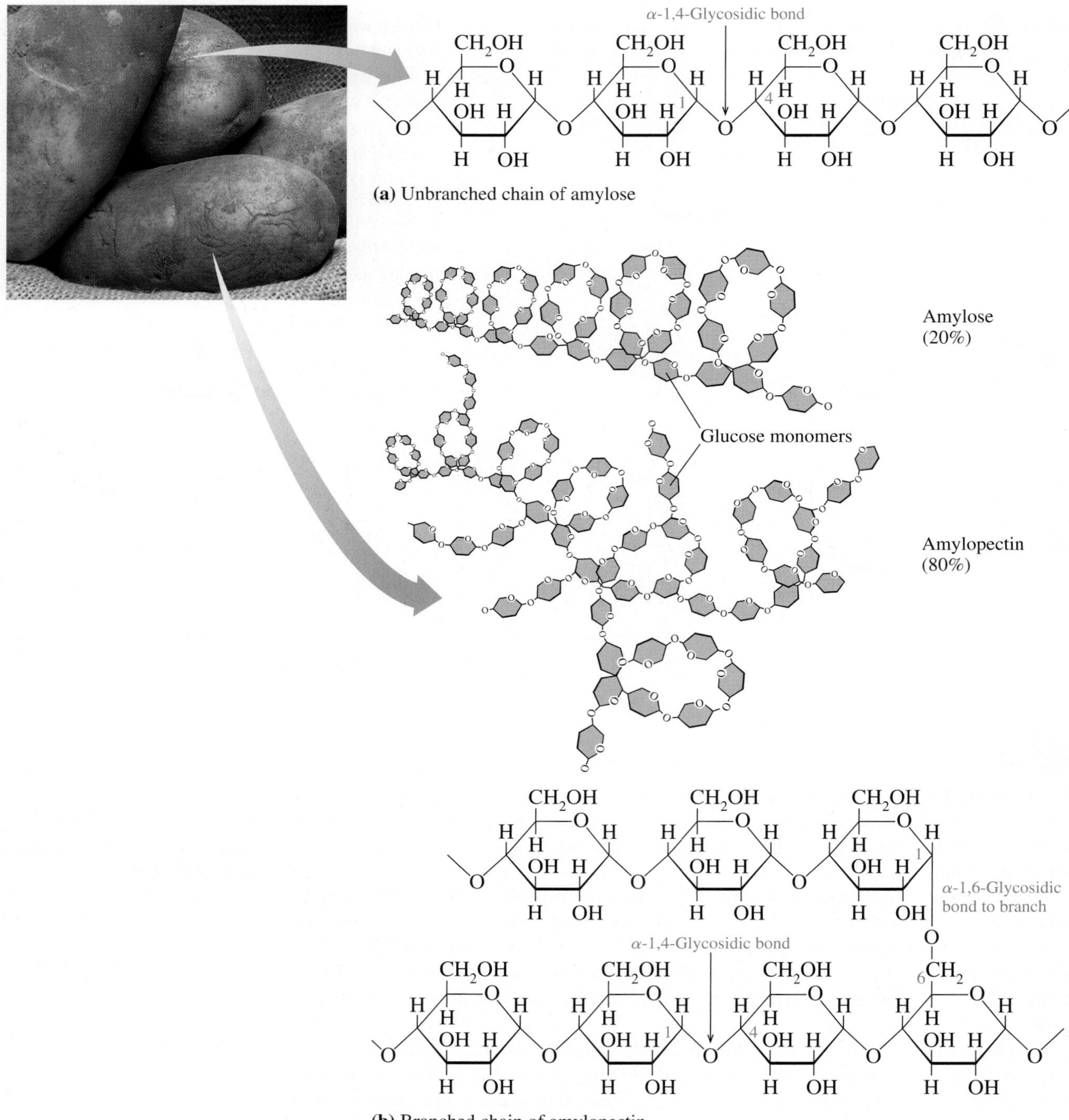


**FIGURE 15.5** The structure of amylose **(a)** is a straight-chain polysaccharide of glucose units, and amylopectin **(b)** is a branched chain of glucose.

**Q** What are the two types of glycosidic bonds that link glucose molecules in amylopectin?

**Cellulose** is the major structural material of wood and plants. Cotton is almost pure cellulose. In cellulose, glucose molecules form a long unbranched chain similar to that of amylose. However, $\beta$-1,4-glycosidic bonds link the glucose units in cellulose. The $\beta$ isomers do not form coils like the $\alpha$ isomers but are aligned in parallel rows that are held in place by hydrogen bonds between hydroxyl groups in adjacent chains. This arrangement makes cellulose insoluble in water and gives a rigid structure to the cell walls in wood and fiber that is more resistant to hydrolysis than the starches. (See Figure 15.6.)

Humans have an enzyme called $\alpha$-amylase in saliva and pancreatic juices that hydrolyzes the $\alpha$-1,4-glycosidic bonds of the starches but not the $\beta$-1,4-glycosidic bonds

Cellulose

β-1,4-Glycosidic bond

**FIGURE 15.6** The polysaccharide cellulose is composed of β-1,4-glycosidic bonds.
**Q** Why are humans unable to digest cellulose?

of cellulose. Thus, humans cannot digest cellulose. Animals such as horses, cows, and goats can obtain glucose from cellulose because their digestive systems contain bacteria that provide enzymes such as cellulase to hydrolyze β-1,4-glycosidic bonds.

## Iodine Test

In the **iodine test**, iodine ($I_2$) is used to test for the presence of starch. The unbranched helical shape of the polysaccharide amylose in starch interacts with iodine to form a deep blue-black complex. Amylopectin, cellulose, and glycogen produce reddish-purple and brown colors. Such colors do not develop when iodine is added to samples of mono- or disaccharides.

### SAMPLE PROBLEM 15.5

#### Structures of Polysaccharides

Identify the polysaccharide described by each of the following:

**a.** a polysaccharide that is stored in the liver and muscle tissues
**b.** an unbranched polysaccharide containing β-1,4-glycosidic bonds
**c.** a starch containing α-1,4- and α-1,6-glycosidic bonds

SOLUTION

**a.** glycogen **b.** cellulose **c.** amylopectin, glycogen

STUDY CHECK

Amylose and amylopectin are both glucose polymers. How do they differ?

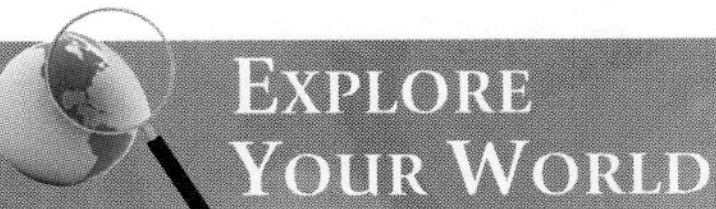


### Polysaccharides

Read the nutrition label on a box of crackers, cereal, bread, chips, or pasta. The major ingredient in crackers is flour, a starch. Chew on a single cracker for 4 or 5 minutes. An enzyme (amylase) in your saliva breaks apart the bonds in starch.

QUESTIONS

1. How are carbohydrates listed?
2. What other carbohydrates are listed?
3. How did the taste of the cracker change during the time that you chewed it?
4. What happened to the starches in the cracker as the amylase enzyme in your saliva reacted with the amylose and amylopectin?

## QUESTIONS AND PROBLEMS

### Polysaccharides

**15.39** Describe the similarities and differences in the following:
- **a.** amylose and amylopectin
- **b.** amylopectin and glycogen

**15.40** Describe the similarities and differences in the following:
- **a.** amylose and cellulose
- **b.** cellulose and glycogen

**15.41** Give the name of one or more polysaccharides that matches each of the following descriptions:
- **a.** not digestible by humans
- **b.** the storage form of carbohydrates in plants
- **c.** contains only $\alpha$-1,4-glycosidic bonds
- **d.** the most highly branched polysaccharide

**15.42** Give the name of one or more polysaccharides that matches each of the following descriptions:
- **a.** the storage form of carbohydrates in animals
- **b.** contains only $\beta$-1,4-glycosidic bonds
- **c.** contains both $\alpha$-1,4- and $\alpha$-1,6-glycosidic bonds
- **d.** produces maltose during digestion

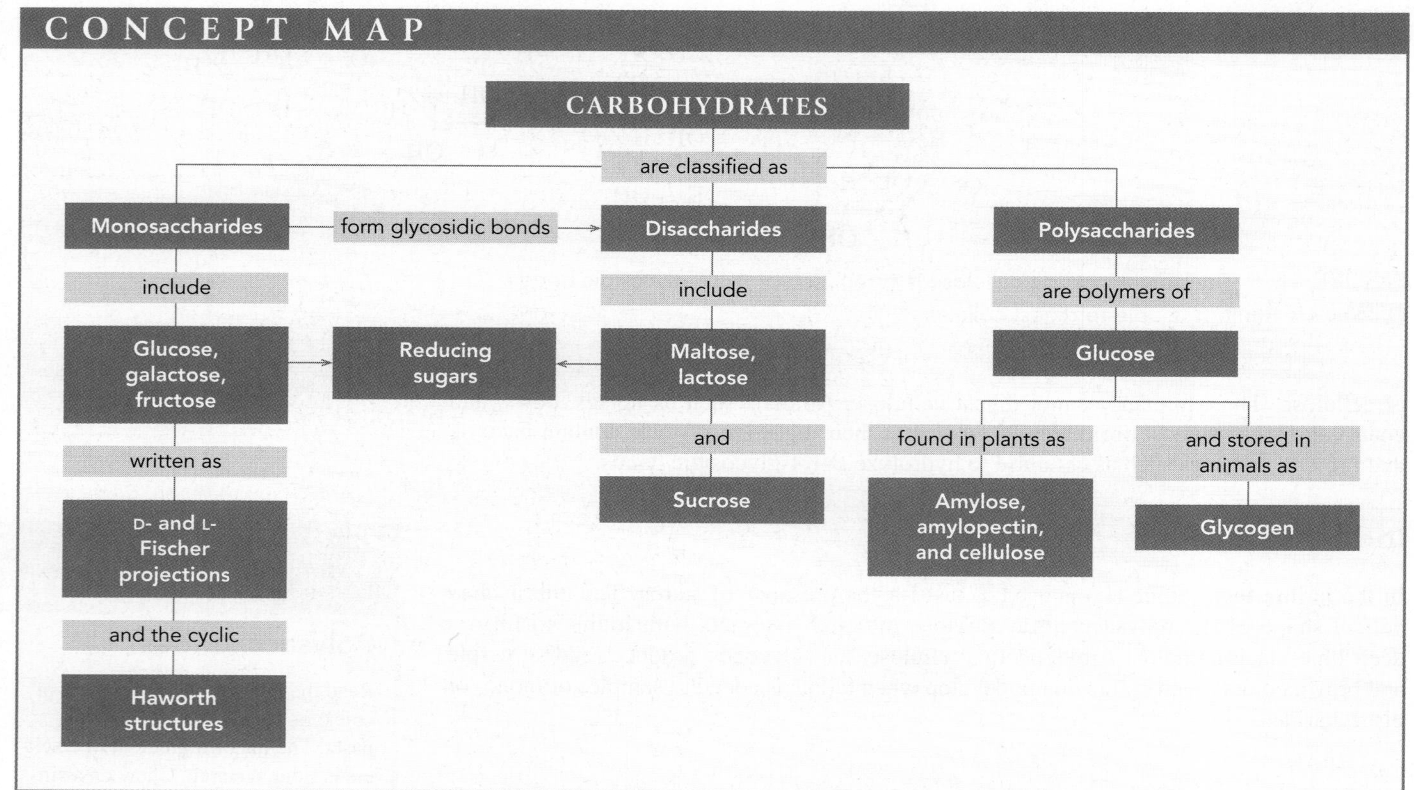


## CHAPTER REVIEW

### 15.1 Carbohydrates

**LEARNING GOAL:** *Classify a monosaccharide as an aldose or ketose, and indicate the number of carbon atoms.*

Carbohydrates are classified as monosaccharides (simple sugars), disaccharides (two monosaccharide units), and polysaccharides (many monosaccharide units). Monosaccharides are polyhydroxy aldehydes (aldoses) or ketones (ketoses). Monosaccharides are also classified by their number of carbon atoms: *triose, tetrose, pentose*, or *hexose*.

### 15.2 Fischer Projections of Monosaccharides

**LEARNING GOAL:** *Use Fischer projections to draw the D or L isomers of glucose, galactose, and fructose.*

Chiral molecules can exist in two different forms, which are mirror images of each other. In a Fischer projection (straight chain), the prefixes D- and L- are used to distinguish between the mirror images. In D isomers, the —OH is on the right of the chiral carbon farthest from the carbonyl carbon; it is on the left in L isomers. Important monosaccharides are the aldohexoses glucose and galactose and the ketohexose fructose.

### 15.3 Haworth Structures of Monosaccharides

**LEARNING GOAL:** *Draw and identify the Haworth structures of monosaccharides.*

The predominant form of monosaccharides is the cyclic arrangement of five or six atoms. The cyclic structure forms by a reaction between an —OH (usually the one on carbon 5 in hexoses) with the carbonyl group of the same molecule. The mutarotation of the hydroxyl group on carbon 1 (or 2 in fructose) gives $\alpha$ and $\beta$ anomers of the cyclic monosaccharide.

### 15.4 Chemical Properties of Monosaccharides

**LEARNING GOAL:** *Identify the products of oxidation or reduction of monosaccharides; determine whether a carbohydrate is a reducing sugar.*

The aldehyde group in an aldose can be oxidized to a carboxylic acid, while the carbonyl group in an aldose or a ketose can be reduced to give a hydroxyl group. Monosaccharides that are reducing sugars have an aldehyde group in the open chain that is oxidized.

### 15.5 Disaccharides

**LEARNING GOAL:** *Describe the monosaccharide units and glycosidic bonds in disaccharides.*

Disaccharides are two monosaccharide units joined together by a glycosidic bond. In the most common disaccharides maltose, lactose, and sucrose, there is at least one glucose unit.

### 15.6 Polysaccharides

**LEARNING GOAL:** *Describe the structural features of amylose, amylopectin, glycogen, and cellulose.*

Polysaccharides are polymers of monosaccharide units. Amylose is an unbranched chain of glucose with $\alpha$-1,4-glycosidic bonds, and amylopectin is a branched polymer of glucose with $\alpha$-1,4- and $\alpha$-1,6-glycosidic bonds. Glycogen, the storage form of glucose in animals, is similar to amylopectin with more branching. Cellulose is also a polymer of glucose, but in cellulose the glycosidic bonds are $\beta$-1,4-bonds rather than $\alpha$-1,4-bonds in amylose.

## SUMMARY OF CARBOHYDRATES

| Carbohydrate | Food Sources | |
|---|---|---|
| **Monosaccharides** | | |
| Glucose | Fruit juices, honey, corn syrup | |
| Galactose | Lactose hydrolysis | |
| Fructose | Fruit juices, honey, sucrose hydrolysis | |
| **Disaccharides** | | **Monosaccharides** |
| Maltose | Germinating grains, starch hydrolysis | Glucose + glucose |
| Lactose | Milk, yogurt, ice cream | Glucose + galactose |
| Sucrose | Sugar cane, sugar beets | Glucose + fructose |
| **Polysaccharides** | | |
| Amylose | Rice, wheat, grains, cereals | Unbranched polymer of glucose joined by $\alpha$-1,4-glycosidic bonds |
| Amylopectin | Rice, wheat, grains, cereals | Branched polymer of glucose joined by $\alpha$-1,4- and $\alpha$-1,6-glycosidic bonds |
| Glycogen | Liver, muscles | Highly branched polymer of glucose joined by $\alpha$-1,4- and $\alpha$-1,6-glycosidic bonds |
| Cellulose | Plant fiber, bran, beans, celery | Unbranched polymer of glucose joined by $\beta$-1,4-glycosidic bonds |

## SUMMARY OF REACTIONS

### FORMATION OF DISACCHARIDES

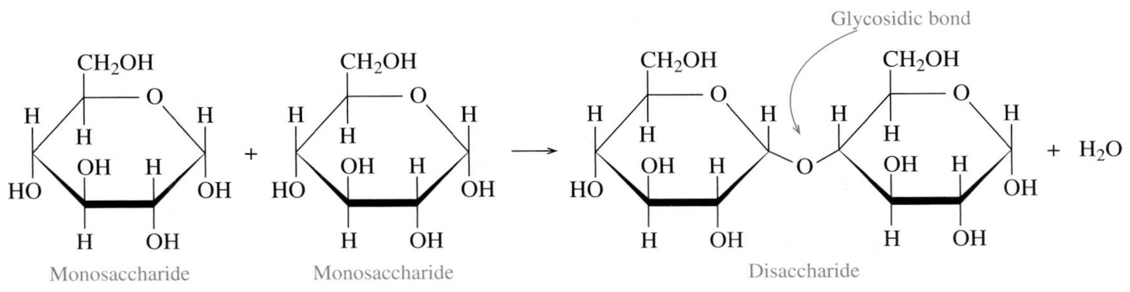

Monosaccharide + Monosaccharide $\longrightarrow$ Disaccharide (Glycosidic bond) + $H_2O$

## OXIDATION AND REDUCTION OF MONOSACCHARIDES

$$
\begin{array}{c}
CH_2OH \\
|\\
H-C-OH \\
|\\
HO-C-H \\
|\\
H-C-OH \\
|\\
H-C-OH \\
|\\
CH_2OH \\
\text{D-Glucitol}
\end{array}
\xleftarrow{\text{Reduction}}
\begin{array}{c}
CHO \\
|\\
H-C-OH \\
|\\
HO-C-H \\
|\\
H-C-OH \\
|\\
H-C-OH \\
|\\
CH_2OH \\
\text{D-Glucose}
\end{array}
\xrightarrow{\text{Oxidation}}
\begin{array}{c}
COOH \\
|\\
H-C-OH \\
|\\
HO-C-H \\
|\\
H-C-OH \\
|\\
H-C-OH \\
|\\
CH_2OH \\
\text{D-Gluconic acid}
\end{array}
$$

## HYDROLYSIS OF DISACCHARIDES

$$\text{Sucrose} + H_2O \xrightarrow{H^+ \text{ or sucrase}} \text{glucose} + \text{fructose}$$

$$\text{Lactose} + H_2O \xrightarrow{H^+ \text{ or lactase}} \text{glucose} + \text{galactose}$$

$$\text{Maltose} + H_2O \xrightarrow{H^+ \text{ or maltase}} \text{glucose} + \text{glucose}$$

## HYDROLYSIS OF POLYSACCHARIDES

$$\text{Amylose, amylopectin} \xrightarrow{H^+ \text{ or enzymes}} \text{many D-glucose units}$$

# KEY TERMS

**aldose** A monosaccharide that contains an aldehyde group.

**amylopectin** A branched-chain polymer of starch composed of glucose units joined by $\alpha$-1,4- and $\alpha$-1,6-glycosidic bonds.

**amylose** An unbranched polymer of starch composed of glucose units joined by $\alpha$-1,4-glycosidic bonds.

**anomers** The isomers of cyclic hemiacetals of monosaccharides that have a hydroxyl group on carbon 1 (or carbon 2). In the $\alpha$ anomer, the —OH is drawn downward; in the $\beta$ anomer, the —OH is up.

**carbohydrate** A simple or complex sugar composed of carbon, hydrogen, and oxygen.

**cellulose** An unbranched polysaccharide composed of glucose units linked by $\beta$-1,4-glycosidic bonds that cannot be hydrolyzed by the human digestive system.

**disaccharide** A carbohydrate composed of two monosaccharides joined by a glycosidic bond.

**fructose** A monosaccharide, also called levulose and fruit sugar, that is found in honey and fruit juices; it is combined with glucose in sucrose.

**galactose** A monosaccharide that occurs combined with glucose in lactose.

**glucose** The most prevalent monosaccharide in the diet. An aldohexose found in fruits, vegetables, corn syrup, and honey that is also known as blood sugar and dextrose. Most polysaccharides are polymers of glucose.

**glycogen** A polysaccharide formed in the liver and muscles for the storage of glucose as an energy reserve. It is composed of glucose in a highly branched polymer joined by $\alpha$-1,4- and $\alpha$-1,6-glycosidic bonds.

**glycosidic bond** The bond that forms when the hydroxyl group of one monosaccharide reacts with the hydroxyl group of another monosaccharide; it is the type of bond that links monosaccharide units in di- or polysaccharides.

**Haworth structure** The cyclic structure that represents the closed chain of a monosaccharide.

**iodine test** A test for amylose that forms a blue-black color after iodine is added to the sample.

**ketose** A monosaccharide that contains a ketone group.

**lactose** A disaccharide consisting of glucose and galactose found in milk and milk products.

**maltose** A disaccharide consisting of two glucose units; it is obtained from the hydrolysis of starch and germinating grains.

**monosaccharide** A polyhydroxy compound that contains an aldehyde or ketone group.

**mutarotation** The conversion between $\alpha$ and $\beta$ anomers via an open chain.

**polysaccharide** A polymer of many monosaccharide units, usually glucose. Polysaccharides differ in the types of glycosidic bonds and the amount of branching in the polymer.

**reducing sugar** A carbohydrate with an aldehyde group capable of reducing the $Cu^{2+}$ in Benedict's reagent.

**sucrose** A disaccharide composed of glucose and fructose; a nonreducing sugar, commonly called table sugar or "sugar."

## UNDERSTANDING THE CONCEPTS

15.43 Isomaltose, obtained from the breakdown of starch, has the following Haworth structure:

a. Is isomaltose a mono-, di-, or polysaccharide?
b. What are the monosaccharides in isomaltose?
c. What is the glycosidic link in isomaltose?
d. Is this the $\alpha$ or $\beta$ form of isomaltose?
e. Would isomaltose be a reducing sugar?

**15.44** Sophorose, a carbohydrate found in certain types of beans, has the following Haworth structure:

a. Is sophorose a mono-, di-, or polysaccharide?
b. What are the monosaccharides in sophorose?
c. What is the glycosidic link in sophorose?
d. Is this the $\alpha$ or $\beta$ anomer of sophorose?
e. Is sophorose a reducing sugar?

15.45 Melezitose, a carbohydrate found in tree sap, has the following Haworth structure:

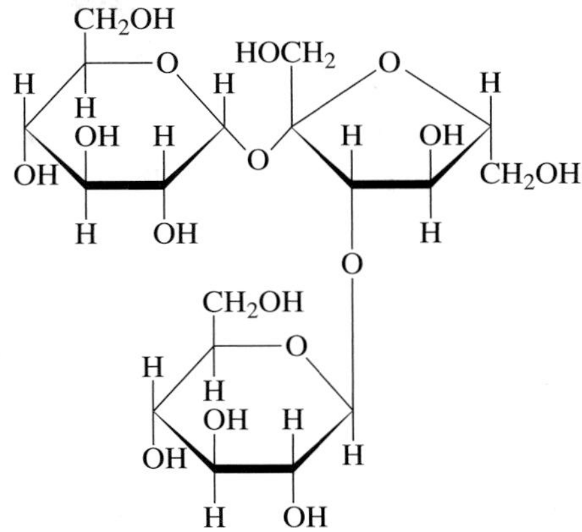


a. Is melezitose a mono-, di-, tri-, or polysaccharide?
b. What are the monosaccharides in melezitose?

**15.46** What are the disaccharides and polysaccharides present in each of the following?

(a) (b) (c) (d)

## ADDITIONAL QUESTIONS AND PROBLEMS

*For instructor-assigned homework, go to* ***www.masteringchemistry.com.***

15.47 What are the differences in the Fischer projections of D-fructose and D-galactose?

**15.48** What are the differences in the Fischer projections of D-glucose and D-fructose?

15.49 What are the differences in the Fischer projections of D-galactose and L-galactose?

**15.50** What are the differences in the Haworth structures of $\alpha$-D-glucose and $\beta$-D-glucose?

15.51 Consider the sugar D-gulose:

```
        O
        ‖
        C—H
        |
    H—C—OH
        |
    H—C—OH
        |
   HO—C—H
        |
    H—C—OH
        |
      CH2OH
```

D-Gulose

a. Draw the Fischer projection for L-gulose.
b. Draw the Haworth structures for $\alpha$- and $\beta$-D-gulose.

**15.52** Consider the open-chain structure for D-gulose in question 15.51.
  **a.** Draw the structure and give the name of the product formed by the reduction of D-gulose.
  **b.** Draw the structure and give the name of the product formed by the oxidation of D-gulose.

**15.53** D-Sorbitol, a sweetener found in seaweed and berries, contains only hydroxyl functional groups. When D-sorbitol is oxidized, it forms D-glucose. Draw the Fischer projection of D-sorbitol.

**15.54** Raffinose is a trisaccharide found in Australian manna and in cottonseed meal. It is composed of three different monosaccharides. Identify the monosaccharides in raffinose.

$CH_2OH$ — O; HO, H, OH, H, H, H, OH, HO — O — $CH_2$ — O; H, H, OH, H, H, OH — O — $CH_2OH$ — O; H, H, HO, $CH_2OH$, OH, H

**15.55** If $\alpha$-galactose is dissolved in water, $\beta$-galactose is eventually present. Explain how this occurs.

**15.56** Why are lactose and maltose considered reducing sugars, but sucrose is not?

**15.57** $\beta$-Cellobiose is a disaccharide obtained from the hydrolysis of cellulose. It is quite similar to maltose except it has a $\beta$-1,4-glycosidic bond. Draw the Haworth structure of $\beta$-cellobiose.

**15.58** The disaccharide trehalose found in mushrooms is composed of two $\alpha$-D-glucose molecules joined by an $\alpha$-1,1-glycosidic bond. Draw the Haworth structure of trehalose.

# CHALLENGE QUESTIONS

**15.59** Gentiobiose is found in saffron.
  **a.** Gentiobiose contains two glucose molecules linked by a $\beta$-1,6-glycosidic bond. Draw the Haworth structure of $\alpha$-gentiobiose.
  **b.** Would gentiobiose be a reducing sugar? Explain.

**15.60** Identify the open-chain formula that matches each of the following:
  **a.** L-mannose  **b.** a ketopentose
  **c.** an aldopentose  **d.** a ketohexose

| A | B | C | D |
|---|---|---|---|
| CHO | CHO | $CH_2OH$ | $CH_2OH$ |
| H—C—OH | H—C—OH | C=O | C=O |
| HO—C—H | H—C—OH | HO—C—H | H—C—OH |
| H—C—OH | HO—C—H | H—C—OH | HO—C—H |
| $CH_2OH$ | HO—C—H | $CH_2OH$ | HO—C—H |
| | $CH_2OH$ | | $CH_2OH$ |

# ANSWERS

## ANSWERS TO STUDY CHECKS

**15.1**
H—C=O
H—C—OH
H—C—OH
H—C—OH
$CH_2OH$

**15.2** Ribulose is a ketopentose.

**15.3**
$CH_2OH$ — O; H, H, H, OH, H, HO, OH, H, OH

**15.4**
$CH_2OH$ — O; H, H, OH, H, HO, H, H, OH — O — $CH_2OH$ — O; H, OH, H, OH, H, H, H, OH

**15.5** Both amylose and amylopectin contain glucose units connected by $\alpha$-1,4-glycosidic bonds. However, in amylopectin, branches of glucose units are connected by $\alpha$-1,6-glycosidic bonds about every 25 glucose units on the chain.

## ANSWERS TO SELECTED QUESTIONS AND PROBLEMS

**15.1** Photosynthesis requires $CO_2$, $H_2O$, and the energy from the Sun. Respiration requires $O_2$ from the air and glucose from our foods.

**15.3** Monosaccharides can be a chain of three to eight carbon atoms, one in a carbonyl group as an aldehyde or ketone, and the rest attached to hydroxyl groups. A monosaccharide cannot be split or hydrolyzed into smaller carbohydrates. A disaccharide consists of two monosaccharide units joined together that can be split.

**15.5** Hydroxyl groups are found in all monosaccharides along with a carbonyl on the first or second carbon.

**15.7** A ketopentose contains hydroxyl and ketone functional groups and has five carbon atoms.

**15.9** **a.** ketose **b.** aldose **c.** ketose **d.** aldose **e.** aldose

**15.11** In the D isomer, the —OH on the chiral carbon atom at the bottom of the chain is on the right side, whereas in the L isomer, the —OH appears on the left side.

**15.13** **a.** D **b.** D **c.** L **d.** D

**15.15** **a.**

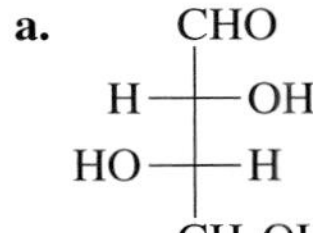

**b.**

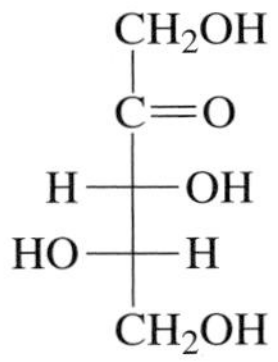

$CH_2OH$
C=O
H—C—OH
HO—C—H
$CH_2OH$

**c.**

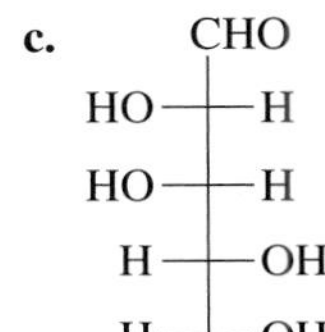

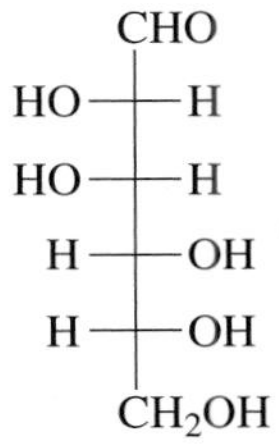

**d.**

CHO
HO—C—H
HO—C—H
HO—C—H
HO—C—H
$CH_2OH$

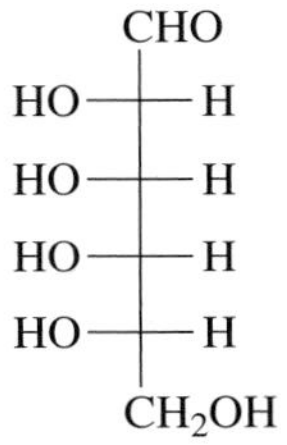

**15.17**

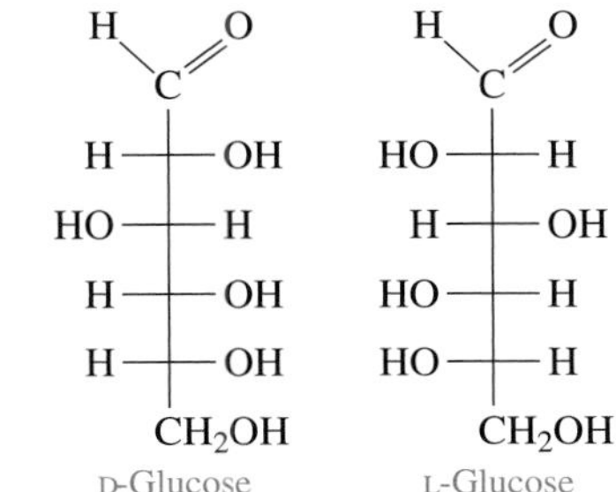

D-Glucose L-Glucose

**15.19** In D-galactose, the hydroxyl on carbon four extends to the left. In D-glucose, this hydroxyl goes to the right.

**15.21** **a.** glucose **b.** galactose **c.** fructose

**15.23** In the cyclic structure of glucose, there are five carbon atoms and an oxygen atom.

**15.25**

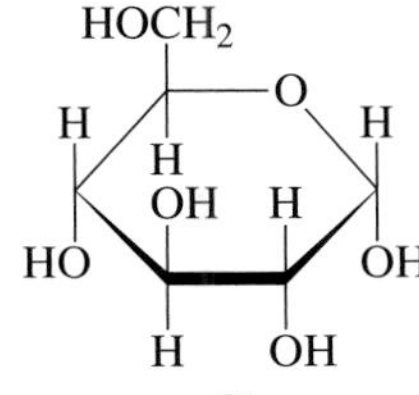

α-D-Glucose

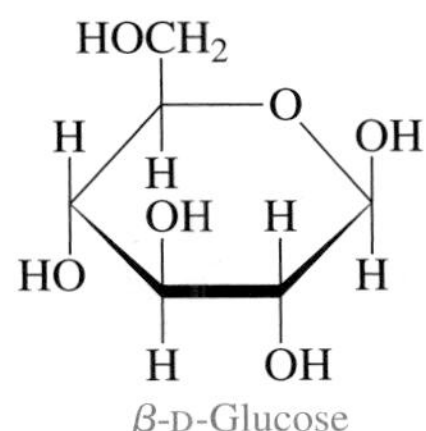

β-D-Glucose

**15.27** **a.** α anomer **b.** α anomer

**15.29**

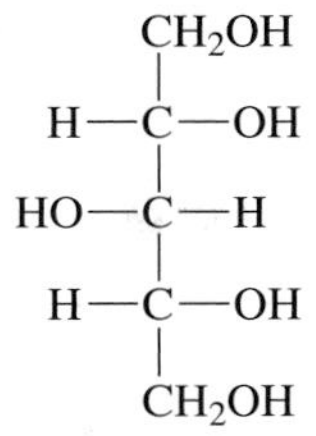

$CH_2OH$
H—C—OH
HO—C—H
H—C—OH
$CH_2OH$

Xylitol

**15.31** Oxidation product:

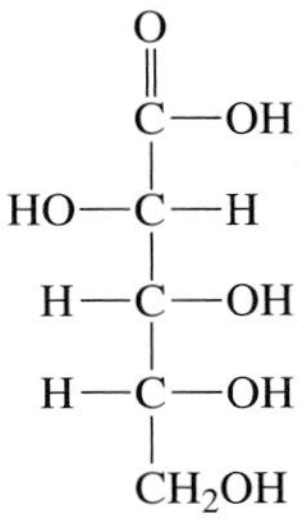

O
‖
C—OH
HO—C—H
H—C—OH
H—C—OH
$CH_2OH$

Reduction product (sugar alcohol):

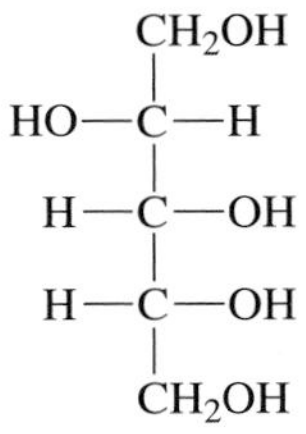

$CH_2OH$
HO—C—H
H—C—OH
H—C—OH
$CH_2OH$

D-Arabitol

**15.33** **a.** galactose and glucose, β-1,4-glycosidic bond, β-lactose
**b.** glucose and glucose, α-1,4-glycosidic bond, α-maltose

**15.35** **a.** reducing sugar
**b.** reducing sugar

**15.37** **a.** sucrose **b.** lactose
**c.** maltose **d.** lactose

**15.39** **a.** Amylose is an unbranched polymer of glucose units joined by α-1,4-glycosidic bonds; amylopectin is a branched polymer of glucose joined by α-1,4- and α-1,6-glycosidic bonds.
**b.** Amylopectin, which is produced in plants, is a branched polymer of glucose, joined by α-1,4- and α-1,6-glycosidic bonds. Glycogen, which is produced in animals, is a highly branched polymer of glucose, joined by α-1,4- and α-1,6-glycosidic bonds.

**15.41** **a.** cellulose **b.** amylose, amylopectin
**c.** amylose **d.** glycogen

**15.43** **a.** disaccharide **b.** α-D-glucose
**c.** α-1,6-glycosidic bond
**d.** α **e.** yes

**15.45** **a.** trisaccharide
**b.** 2 glucose and 1 fructose

**15.47** D-Fructose is a ketohexose, whereas D-galactose is an aldohexose. In galactose, the —OH on carbon 4 is on the left; in fructose, the —OH is on the right.

**15.49** D-Galactose is the mirror image of L-galactose. In D-galactose, the —OH groups on carbon 2 and 5 are on the right side, but they are on the left for carbon 3 and 4. In L-galactose, the —OH groups are reversed; carbons 2 and 5 have —OH on the left, and carbons 3 and 4 have —OH on the right.

**15.51 a.**

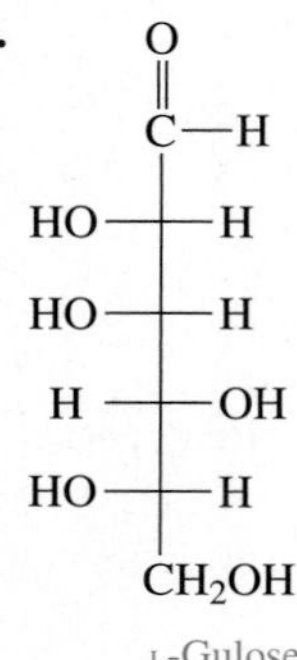


L-Gulose

**b.**

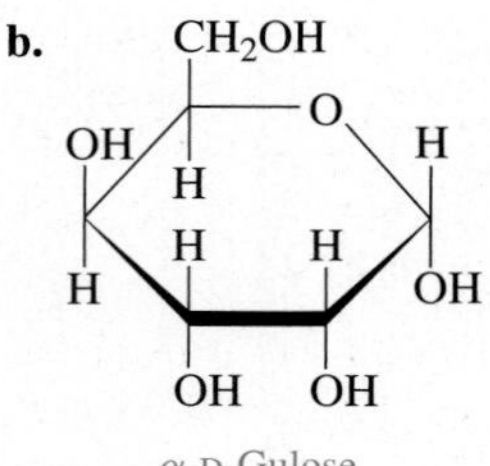


α-D-Gulose

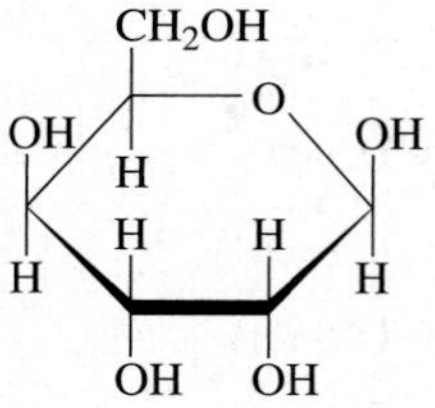

β-D-Gulose

**15.53**

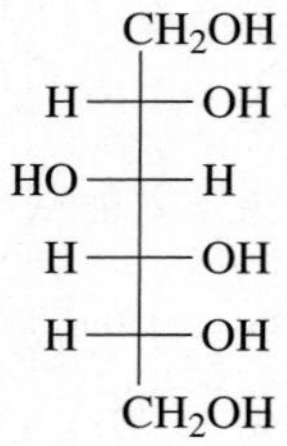

$CH_2OH$
H—OH
HO—H
H—OH
H—OH
$CH_2OH$

**15.55** When the $\alpha$-galactose forms an open-chain structure, it can close to form either $\alpha$- or $\beta$-galactose.

**15.57**

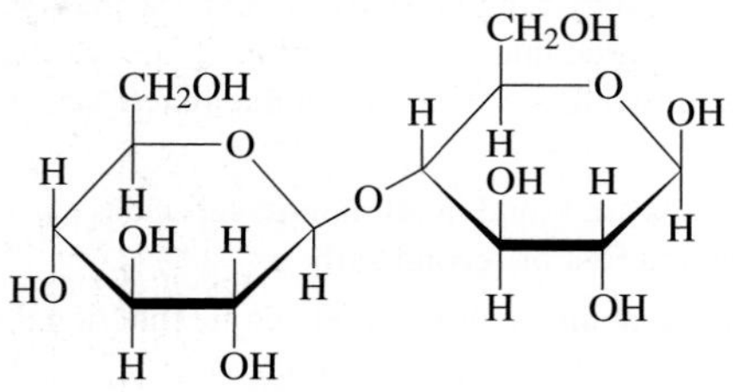

**15.59 a.**

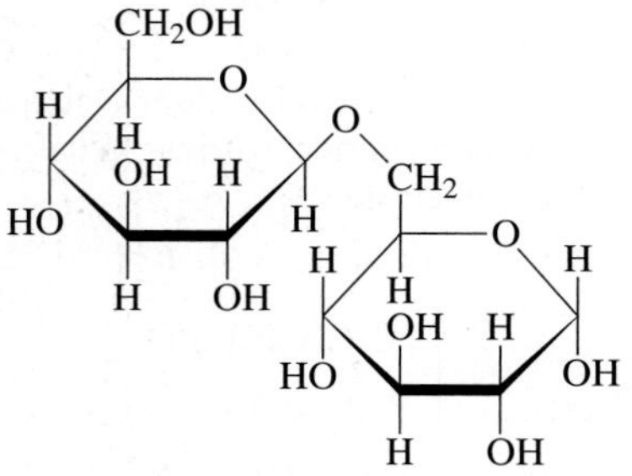

**b.** Yes. Gentiobiose is a reducing sugar. The ring with the hemiacetal with the —OH group can open up to form an aldehyde that can be oxidized.

**CI.25** A compound called butylated hydroxytoluene, or BHT, has been added to cereal and other foods since 1947 as an antioxidant. Its IUPAC name is 1-hydroxy-2,6-dimethylethyl-4-methylbenzene. The formula of the alkyl group dimethylethyl is

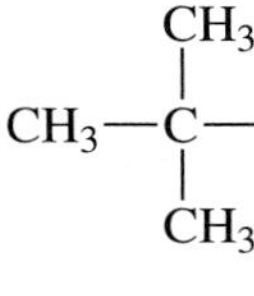

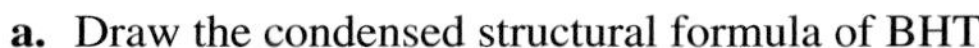

a. Draw the condensed structural formula of BHT.
b. BHT is produced from 4-methylphenol and 2-methylpropene. Draw the condensed structural formulas of these reactants.
c. What are the molecular formula and molar mass of BHT?
d. The FDA (Food and Drug Administration) allows a maximum of 50. ppm of BHT added to cereal. How many mg of BHT could be added to a box of cereal that contains 15 oz of dry cereal?

**CI.26** Used in "sunless" tanning lotions, the compound 1,3-dihydroxy-2-propanone, or dihydroxyacetone (DHA), darkens the skin without sun. DHA reacts with amino acids in the dead cells in the outer surface of the skin. A typical drugstore lotion contains 4.0 % (mass/volume) DHA.

a. Draw the condensed structural formula of DHA.
b. What are the functional groups in DHA?
c. What are the molecular formula and molar mass of DHA?
d. Why is DHA a ketotriose?
e. A bottle of sunless tanning lotion contains 177 mL of lotion. How many milligrams of DHA are in a bottle?

**CI.27** Acetone (propanone), a clear liquid solvent with an acrid odor, is used to remove nail polish, paints, and resins. It has a low boiling point and is highly flammable.

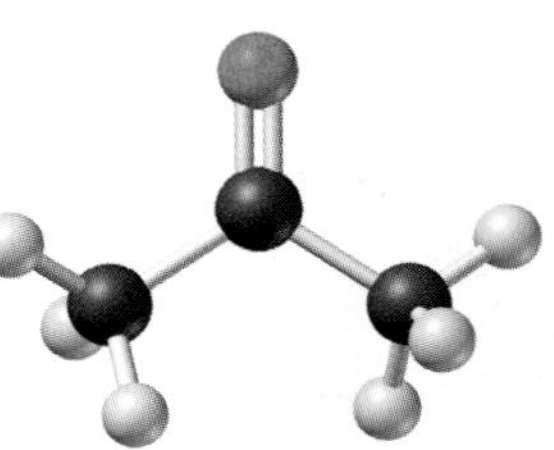

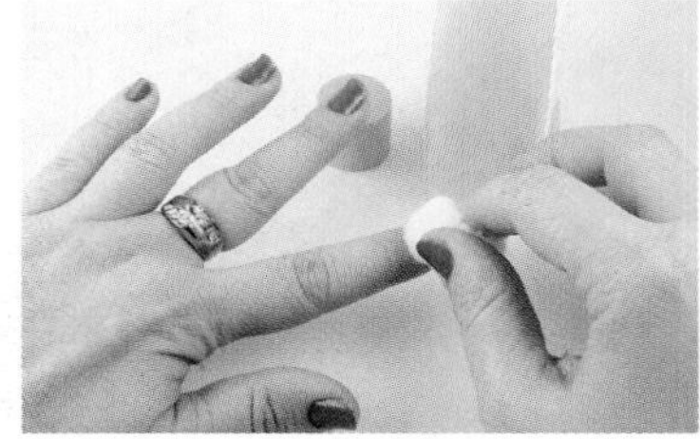

a. Draw the condensed structural formula of propanone.
b. What are the molecular formula and molar mass of propanone?
c. Draw the condensed structural formula of the alcohol that can be oxidized to produce propanone.

**CI.28** Acetone (propanone) has a density of 0.786 g/mL and a heat of combustion of 428 kcal/mole. Use your answers to problem CI.27 to solve the following:
a. Write the equation for the complete combustion reaction of propanone.
b. How much heat, in kilojoules, is released if 2.58 g of propanone reacts with oxygen?
c. How many grams of oxygen gas are needed to react with 15.0 mL of propanone?
d. How many liters of carbon dioxide gas are produced at STP in part **c**?

**CI.29** Panose is a trisaccharide that is being considered as a possible sweetener by the food industry.

a. What are the monosaccharides, A, B, and C, in panose?
b. What type of bond connects the monosaccharides A and B?
c. What type of bond connects the monosaccharides B and C?
d. Is the structure drawn as $\alpha$ or $\beta$ panose?
e. Why would panose be a reducing sugar?

**CI.30** Ionone is a compound that gives violets their aroma. The small edible purple flowers of violets are used on salads and to make teas. An antioxidant called anthocyanin produces the blue and purple colors of violets. Liquid ionone has a density of 0.935 g/mL.

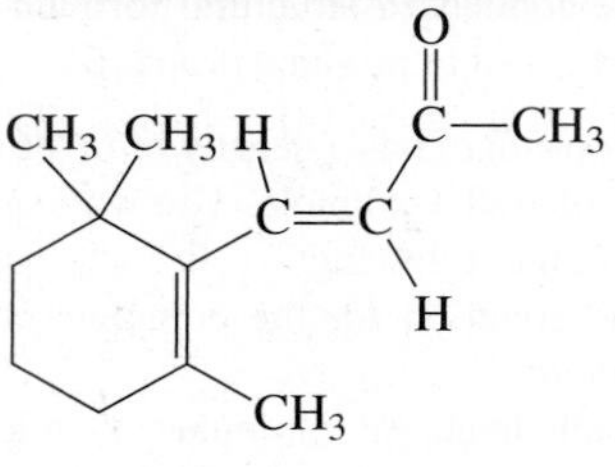

```
                          O
                          ‖
CH3  CH3  H               C—CH3
  \   /    \             /
   \ /      C═══C
  ⌐ \      /     \
 |   ‖            H
  \_/ \
       CH3
```

Ionone

**a.** What functional groups are present in ionone?
**b.** Is the double bond on the side chain cis or trans?
**c.** What are the molecular formula and molar mass of ionone?
**d.** How many moles are in 2.00 mL of ionone?
**e.** When ionone reacts with hydrogen in the presence of a platinum catalyst, hydrogen adds to the double bonds and converts the ketone group to an alcohol. What is the condensed structural formula and molecular formula of the product?
**f.** How many mL of hydrogen gas are needed at STP to completely react 5.0 mL of ionone?

## ■ ANSWERS

**CI.25 a.**

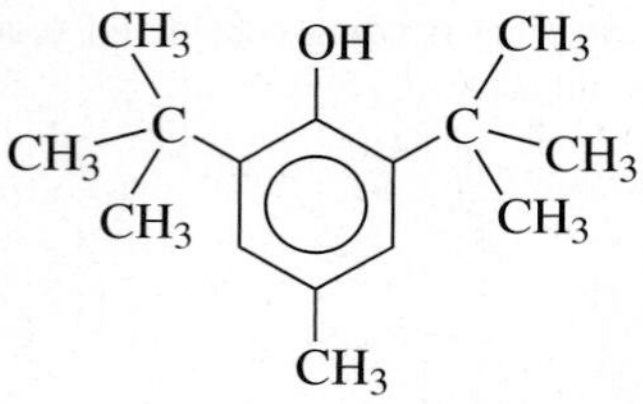

```
       CH3       OH       CH3
         \       |        /
  CH3 —— C —— ⟨benzene⟩ —— C —— CH3
         /       |        \
       CH3      CH3        CH3
```

**b.**

```
     OH
     |
 ⟨benzene⟩                     CH3
     |                          |
    CH3                 CH2═C—CH3
```

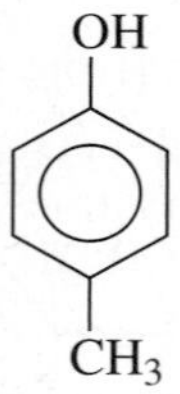

4-Methylphenol 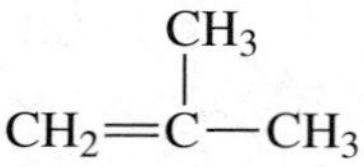        2-Methylpropene

**c.** $C_{15}H_{24}O$; 220. g/mole
**d.** 21 mg

**CI.27 a.**

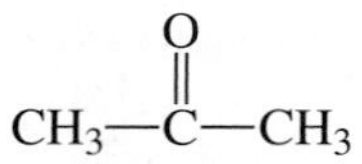

```
         O
         ‖
CH3—C—CH3
```

**b.** $C_3H_6O$; 58.0 g/mole

**c.**

```
         OH
         |
CH3—CH—CH3
```

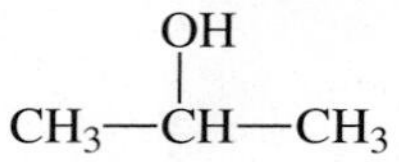

**CI.29 a.** A, B, and C are all glucose.
**b.** An $\alpha$-1,6-glycosidic bond links A and B.
**c.** An $\alpha$-1,4-glycosidic bond links B and C.
**d.** $\beta$ panose
**e.** Panose is a reducing sugar because the hydroxyl group on the anomeric carbon 1 of structure C allows glucose (structure C) to form the aldehyde.

# Carboxylic Acids and Esters

# 16

LOOKING AHEAD


16.1 Carboxylic Acids

16.2 Properties of Carboxylic Acids

16.3 Esters

16.4 Naming Esters

16.5 Properties of Esters

*"There are many carboxylic acids, including the alpha hydroxy acids, that are found today in skin products," says Dr. Ken Peterson, pharmacist and cosmetic chemist, Oakland, California. "When you take a carboxylic acid called a fatty acid and react it with a strong base, you get a salt called soap. Soap has a high pH because the weak fatty acid and the strong base won't have a neutral pH of 7. If you take soap and drop its pH down to 7, you will convert the soap to the fatty acid. When I create fragrances, I use my nose and my chemistry background to identify and break down the reactions that produce good scents. Many fragrances are esters, which form when an alcohol reacts with a carboxylic acid. For example, the ester that smells like pineapple is made from ethanol and butyric acid."*

Carboxylic acids are similar to the weak acids we studied in Chapter 10. They have a sour or tart taste, produce hydronium ions in water, and neutralize bases. You encounter carboxylic acids when you taste the vinegar in a salad dressing, which is a solution of acetic acid and water, or experience the sour taste of citric acid in a grapefruit or lemon. When a carboxylic acid combines with an alcohol, an ester and water are produced. Fats and oils are esters of glycerol and fatty acids, which are long-chain carboxylic acids. Esters produce the pleasant aromas and flavors of many fruits, such as bananas, strawberries, and oranges.

## 16.1 Carboxylic Acids

**LEARNING GOAL**

Give the common names, IUPAC names, and condensed structural formulas of carboxylic acids.

In Chapter 14, we described the carbonyl group (C═O) as the functional group in aldehydes and ketones. In a **carboxylic acid**, a hydroxyl group is attached to the carbonyl group, forming a **carboxyl group**. The carboxyl functional group may be attached to an alkyl group or an aromatic group.

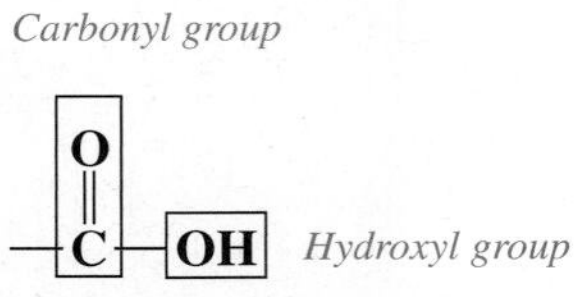

*Carbonyl group*

$$-\overset{\overset{\displaystyle O}{\|}}{C}-OH$$

*Hydroxyl group*

Carboxyl group

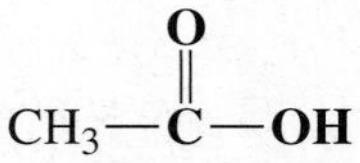

$$CH_3-\overset{\overset{\displaystyle O}{\|}}{C}-OH$$

Acetic acid

$$CH_3-(CH_2)_{16}-\overset{\overset{\displaystyle O}{\|}}{C}-OH$$

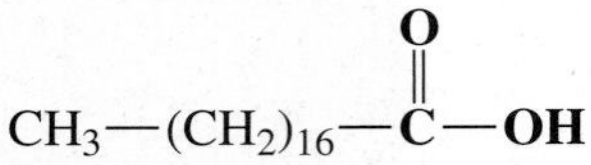

Stearic acid (a fatty acid in fats and oils)

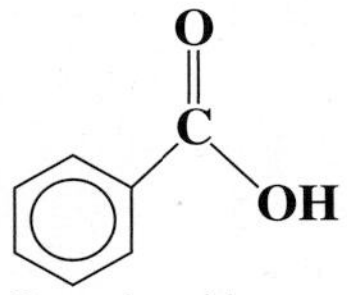

$$C_6H_5-\overset{\overset{\displaystyle O}{\|}}{C}-OH$$

Benzoic acid (aromatic acid)

The carboxyl group can be written in several different ways. For example, the condensed structural formula and line-bond formula for propanoic acid can be written as follows:

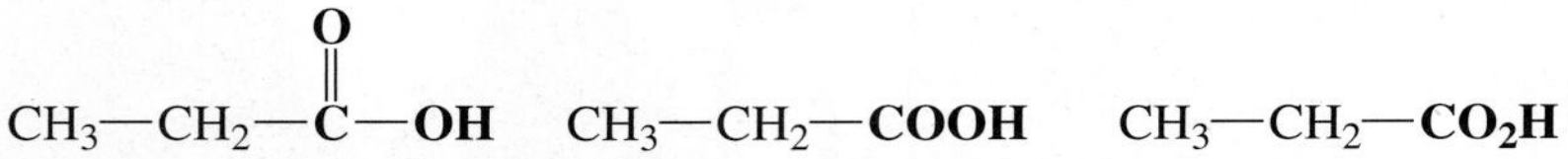

$$CH_3-CH_2-\overset{\overset{\displaystyle O}{\|}}{C}-OH \quad CH_3-CH_2-COOH \quad CH_3-CH_2-CO_2H$$

Some condensed structural formulas for propanoic acid

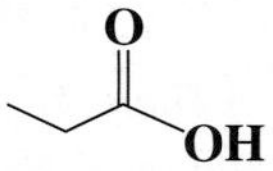

Line-bond formula

### Naming Carboxylic Acids

MC™ SELF STUDY ACTIVITY Carboxylic Acids

The IUPAC names of carboxylic acids use the alkane names of the corresponding carbon chains.

**STEP 1** **Identify the carbon chain containing the carboxyl group and replace the *e* of the alkane name with *oic acid*.** The carboxylic acid of benzene is named benzoic acid.

**STEP 2** **Give the location and names of substituents on the main chain.** Number the carbon chain beginning with the carboxyl carbon as 1:

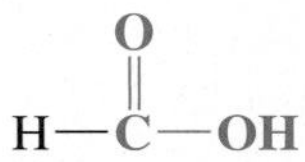

$$H-\overset{\overset{\displaystyle O}{\|}}{C}-OH$$

Methanoic acid

$$CH_3-\overset{\overset{\displaystyle CH_3}{|}}{CH}-\overset{\overset{\displaystyle O}{\|}}{C}-OH$$

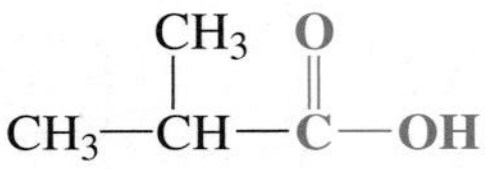

2-Methylpropanoic acid

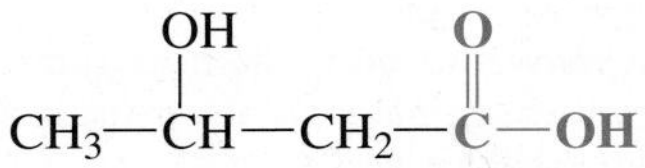

$$CH_3-\overset{\overset{\displaystyle OH}{|}}{CH}-CH_2-\overset{\overset{\displaystyle O}{\|}}{C}-OH$$

3-Hydroxybutanoic acid

For benzoic acid, where the carboxyl group is bonded to carbon 1, the ring is numbered to give the lowest possible numbers. As with other aromatic compounds, the prefixes *ortho*, *meta*, and *para* may be used to show the position of one other substituent:

| Benzoic acid | 4-Aminobenzoic acid (*p*-aminobenzoic acid) | 3,4-Dichlorobenzoic acid |
|---|---|---|
| $C_6H_5-\overset{O}{\overset{\|}{C}}-OH$ | $C-OH$ at carbon 1, $NH_2$ at carbon 4 | $C-OH$ at carbon 1, Cl at carbons 3 and 4 |

Many carboxylic acids are still named by their common names, which are derived from their natural sources. In Chapter 14, we named aldehydes using the prefixes that represent the typical sources of carboxylic acids.

When using the common names, the Greek letters alpha ($\alpha$), beta ($\beta$), and gamma ($\gamma$) are assigned to the carbons adjacent to the carboxyl carbon:

$$CH_3-\underset{}{\overset{CH_3}{\overset{|}{CH}}}-CH_2-\overset{O}{\overset{\|}{C}}-OH$$

| | | | | |
|---|---|---|---|---|
| IUPAC | 4 | 3 | 2 | 1 |
| Common | $\gamma$ | $\beta$ | $\alpha$ | |

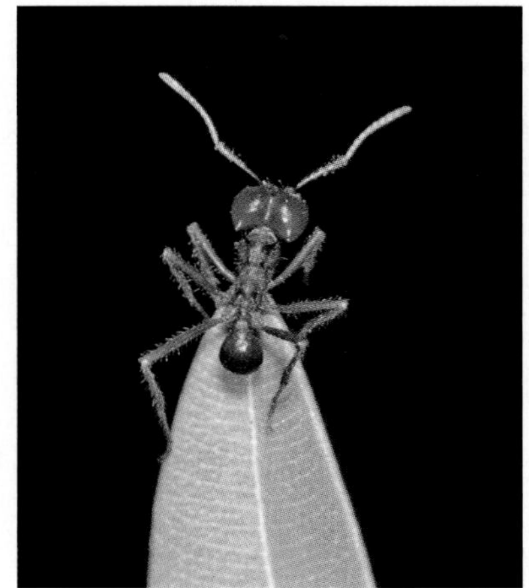

Formic acid is injected under the skin during bee or red ant stings and other insect bites. Acetic acid is the oxidation product of the ethanol in wines and apple cider. The resulting solution of acetic acid and water is known as vinegar. Propionic acid is obtained from the fats of dairy products. Butyric acid gives the foul odor to rancid butter. (See Table 16.1.)

**TABLE 16.1 Names and Natural Sources of Some Carboxylic Acids**

| Condensed Structural Formula | IUPAC Name | Common Name |
|---|---|---|
| $H-\overset{O}{\overset{\|}{C}}-OH$ | Methanoic acid | Formic acid |
| $CH_3-\overset{O}{\overset{\|}{C}}-H$ | Ethanoic acid | Acetic acid |
| $CH_3-CH_2-\overset{O}{\overset{\|}{C}}-OH$ | Propanoic acid | Propionic acid |
| $CH_3-CH_2-CH_2-\overset{O}{\overset{\|}{C}}-OH$ | Butanoic acid | Butyric acid |

**CONCEPT CHECK 16.1**

### Naming Carboxylic Acids

Why can the following condensed structural formula be named as propanoic acid or propionic acid?

$$CH_3-CH_2-\overset{O}{\overset{\|}{C}}-OH$$

TUTORIAL
Naming and Drawing Carboxylic Acids

ANSWER

The longest carbon chain containing the carboxyl group has three carbon atoms. In the IUPAC system, the *e* in propane is replaced by *oic acid*, to give the name propanoic acid. It has the common name propionic acid.

SAMPLE PROBLEM 16.1

■ **Naming Carboxylic Acids**

Give the IUPAC and common name, if any, for each of the following carboxylic acids:

**a.** (skeletal structure: four-carbon chain with C=O and OH at the end, $CH_3$ on the second carbon)

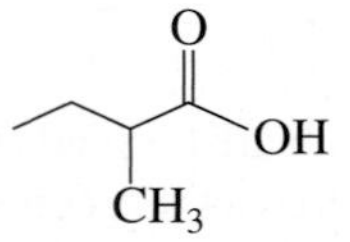

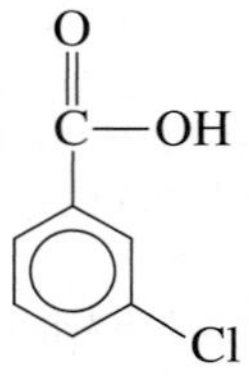

**b.** (benzene ring with $C(=O)—OH$ and Cl in the meta position)

**Guide to Naming Carboxylic Acids**

STEP 1: For nonaromatics, identify the carbon chain containing carboxyl group and replace the *e* in the alkane name by *oic acid.*

STEP 2: Give the location and names of substituents on the main chain.

SOLUTION

**a.** STEP 1 **In the IUPAC system, name the longest carbon chain containing the carboxyl group by replacing the *e* in the alkane name with *oic acid.*** A carboxylic acid with four carbon atoms is named butanoic acid; the common name is butyric acid.

STEP 2 **Give the location and names of the substituents on the carbon chain by counting the carboxyl carbon as carbon 1.** With a methyl group on the second carbon, the IUPAC name is 2-methylbutanoic acid. For the common name, the Greek letter $\alpha$ specifies the carbon atom next to the carboxyl carbon, $\alpha$-methylbutyric acid.

**b.** STEP 1 **In the IUPAC system, name the longest carbon chain containing the carboxyl group by replacing the *e* in the alkane name with *oic acid.*** An aromatic carboxylic acid is named as benzoic acid.

STEP 2 **The carbon attached to the carboxyl group is carbon 1.** With the —Cl on carbon 3, the IUPAC name is 3-chlorobenzoic acid. For the common name, the —Cl is on the *meta* (*m*) carbon, which gives *meta*-chlorobenzoic acid or *m*-chlorobenzoic acid.

STUDY CHECK

Draw the condensed structural formula of 3-phenylpropanoic acid.

**FIGURE 16.1** Vinegar is a 5% solution of acetic acid and water.

**Q** What is the IUPAC name for acetic acid?

## Preparation of Carboxylic Acids

Carboxylic acids can be prepared from primary alcohols or aldehydes. As we saw in Chapter 13, there is an increase in carbon–oxygen bonds as a primary alcohol is oxidized to an aldehyde. Oxidation continues easily as oxygen is added to yield a carboxylic acid. For example, when ethyl alcohol in wine is exposed to oxygen in the air, vinegar is produced. The oxidation process converts the ethyl alcohol (primary alcohol) to acetaldehyde, and then to acetic acid, the carboxylic acid in vinegar. (See Figure 16.1.)

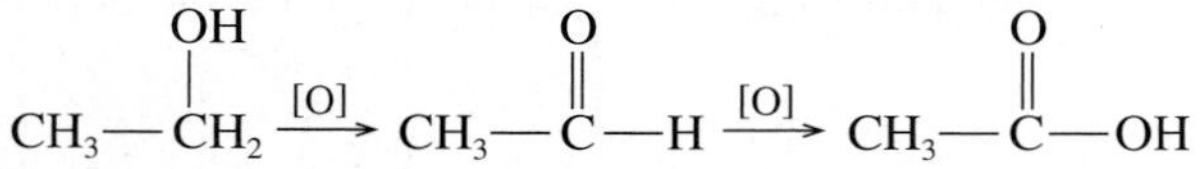

$$CH_3—CH_2—OH \xrightarrow{[O]} CH_3—\overset{O}{\overset{\|}{C}}—H \xrightarrow{[O]} CH_3—\overset{O}{\overset{\|}{C}}—OH$$

Ethanol (ethyl alcohol) → Ethanal (acetaldehyde) → Ethanoic acid (acetic acid)

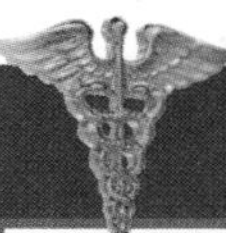

## HEALTH NOTE

### Alpha Hydroxy Acids

Alpha hydroxy acids (AHAs) are naturally occurring carboxylic acids found in fruits, milk, and sugar cane. Cleopatra reportedly bathed in sour milk to smooth her skin. Dermatologists use products with high concentrations (20–70%) of AHAs to remove acne scars and in skin peels to reduce irregular pigmentation and age spots. Lower concentrations (8–10%) of AHAs are added to skin care products for the purpose of smoothing fine lines, improving skin texture, and cleansing pores. Several different alpha hydroxy acids may be found in skin care products singly or in combination. Glycolic acid and lactic acid are most frequently used.

Recent studies indicate that products with AHAs increase sensitivity of the skin to sun and UV radiation. It is recommended that a sunscreen with a sun protection factor (SPF) of at least 15 be used when treating the skin with products that include AHAs. Products containing AHAs at concentrations under 10% and pH values greater than 3.5 are generally considered safe. However, the Food and Drug Administration (FDA) has reports of AHAs causing skin irritation including blisters, rashes, and discoloration of the skin. The FDA does not require product safety reports from cosmetic manufacturers, although they are responsible for marketing safe products. The FDA advises that you test any product containing AHAs on a small area of skin before you use it on a large area.

| Alpha Hydroxy Acid (Source) | Structure |
|---|---|
| Glycolic acid (sugar cane, sugar beet) | $HO{-}CH_2{-}\overset{\overset{\displaystyle O}{\|}}{C}{-}OH$ |
| Lactic acid (sour milk) | $CH_3{-}\overset{\overset{\displaystyle OH}{\|}}{CH}{-}\overset{\overset{\displaystyle O}{\|}}{C}{-}OH$ |
| Tartaric acid (grapes) | $HO{-}\overset{\overset{\displaystyle O}{\|}}{C}{-}\overset{\overset{\displaystyle OH}{\|}}{CH}{-}\overset{\overset{\displaystyle OH}{\|}}{CH}{-}\overset{\overset{\displaystyle O}{\|}}{C}{-}OH$ |
| Malic acid (apples, grapes) | $HO{-}\overset{\overset{\displaystyle O}{\|}}{C}{-}CH_2{-}\overset{\overset{\displaystyle OH}{\|}}{CH}{-}\overset{\overset{\displaystyle O}{\|}}{C}{-}OH$ |
| Citric acid (citrus fruits: lemons, oranges, grapefruit) | $HO{-}\underset{\underset{\displaystyle CH_2{-}COOH}{\|}}{\overset{\overset{\displaystyle CH_2{-}COOH}{\|}}{C}}{-}COOH$ |

SAMPLE PROBLEM 16.2

### Preparation of Carboxylic Acids

Write an equation for the oxidation of 1-propanol and name each product.

SOLUTION

A primary alcohol oxidizes to an aldehyde, which can oxidize further to a carboxylic acid:

$$\underset{\text{1-Propanol (propyl alcohol)}}{CH_3{-}CH_2{-}CH_2{-}OH} \xrightarrow{[O]} \underset{\text{Propanal (propionaldehyde)}}{CH_3{-}CH_2{-}\overset{\overset{\displaystyle O}{\|}}{C}{-}H} \xrightarrow{[O]} \underset{\text{Propanoic acid (propionic acid)}}{CH_3{-}CH_2{-}\overset{\overset{\displaystyle O}{\|}}{C}{-}OH}$$

STUDY CHECK

Draw the condensed structural formula of the carboxylic acid produced by the oxidation of 1-butanol.

## QUESTIONS AND PROBLEMS

### Carboxylic Acids

16.1 What carboxylic acid is responsible for the pain of an ant sting?

**16.2** What carboxylic acid is found in vinegar?

16.3 Explain the differences in the condensed structural formulas of propanal and propanoic acid.

**16.4** Explain the differences in the condensed structural formulas of benzaldehyde and benzoic acid.

**16.5** Give the IUPAC and common name (if any) for each of the following carboxylic acids:

a. $CH_3-\overset{O}{\overset{\|}{C}}-OH$

b. 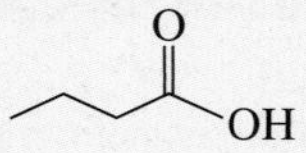 (skeletal structure: four-carbon chain ending in C(=O)OH)

c. $CH_3-\overset{Cl}{\overset{|}{CH}}-\overset{O}{\overset{\|}{C}}-OH$

d. 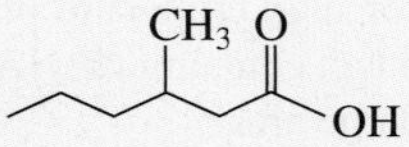 (skeletal structure with $CH_3$ branch, ending in C(=O)OH)

e. 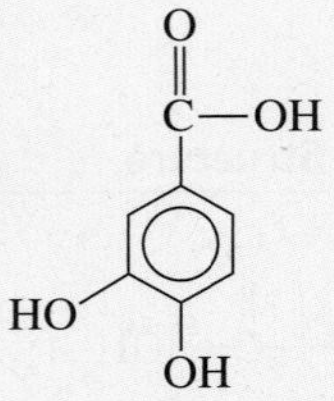 (benzene ring with $\overset{O}{\overset{\|}{C}}-OH$, HO, and OH substituents)

f. $CH_3-\overset{Br}{\overset{|}{CH}}-CH_2-CH_2-\overset{O}{\overset{\|}{C}}-OH$

**16.6** Give the IUPAC and common name (if any) for each of the following carboxylic acids:

a. $H-\overset{O}{\overset{\|}{C}}-OH$

b. 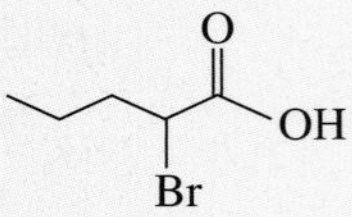 (skeletal structure with Br substituent, ending in C(=O)OH)

c. (benzene ring with $\overset{O}{\overset{\|}{C}}-OH$)

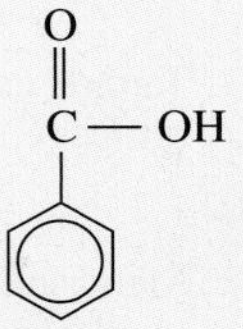

d. 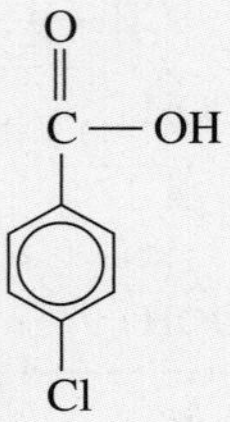 (benzene ring with $\overset{O}{\overset{\|}{C}}-OH$ and Cl)

e. $CH_3-\overset{CH_3}{\overset{|}{CH}}-CH_2-\overset{O}{\overset{\|}{C}}-OH$

f. $Cl-CH_2-\overset{O}{\overset{\|}{C}}-OH$

**16.7** Draw the condensed structural formula of each of the following carboxylic acids:

**a.** propionic acid **b.** benzoic acid
**c.** 2-chloroethanoic acid **d.** 3-hydroxypropanoic acid
**e.** $\alpha$-methylbutyric acid **f.** 3,5-dibromoheptanoic acid

**16.8** Draw the condensed structural formula of each of the following carboxylic acids:

**a.** butyric acid **b.** 3-ethylbenzoic acid
**c.** $\alpha$-hydroxyacetic acid **d.** 2,4-dibromobutanoic acid
**e.** *m*-methylbenzoic acid **f.** 4,4-dibromohexanoic acid

**16.9** Draw the condensed structural formula of the carboxylic acid formed by the oxidation of each of the following:

**a.** $CH_3-OH$ **b.** $CH_3-\overset{O}{\overset{\|}{C}}-H$

**c.** $CH_3-\overset{CH_3}{\overset{|}{CH}}-CH_2-CH_2-OH$

**d.** 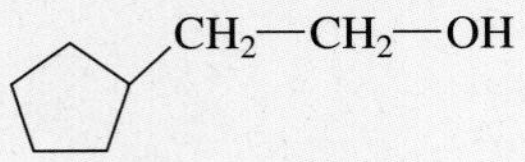 (cyclopentane ring with $CH_2-CH_2-OH$)

**16.10** Draw the condensed structural formula of the carboxylic acid formed by the oxidation of each of the following:

**a.** $CH_3-CH_2-CH_2-CH_2-CH_2-CH_2-OH$

**b.** $CH_3-CH_2-CH_2-CH_2-\overset{O}{\overset{\|}{C}}-H$

**c.** $CH_3-\overset{CH_3}{\overset{|}{CH}}-CH_2-\overset{O}{\overset{\|}{C}}-H$

**d.** 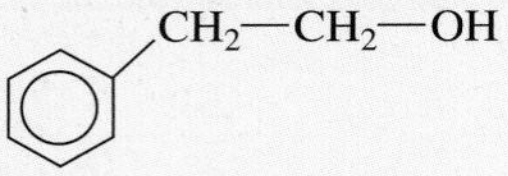 (benzene ring with $CH_2-CH_2-OH$)

## 16.2 Properties of Carboxylic Acids

**LEARNING GOAL**

Describe the boiling points, solubility, and ionization of carboxylic acids in water.

Carboxylic acids are among the most polar organic compounds because the functional group consists of two polar groups: a hydroxyl (—OH) group and a carbonyl (C=O) group:

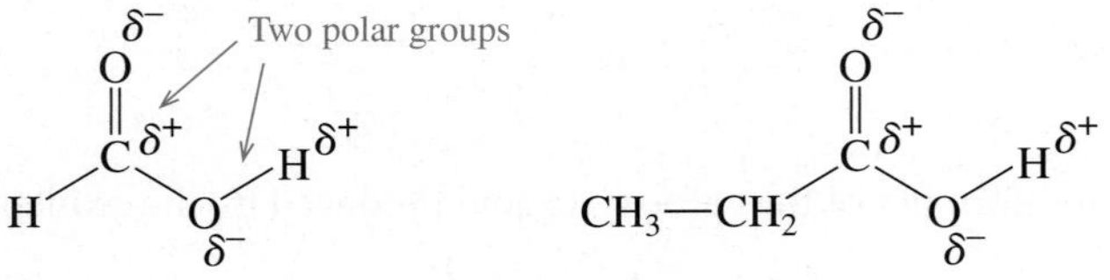

Two polar groups

$H-\overset{O^{\delta-}}{\overset{\|}{C}^{\delta+}}-O^{\delta-}-H^{\delta+}$ $CH_3-CH_2-\overset{O^{\delta-}}{\overset{\|}{C}^{\delta+}}-O^{\delta-}-H^{\delta+}$

The —OH group is similar to the functional group in alcohols, and the C=O double bond is similar to that of aldehydes and ketones.

### Boiling Points

The polar —OH group allows carboxylic acids to form several hydrogen bonds with other carboxylic acid molecules as well as with water. This effect of hydrogen bonds

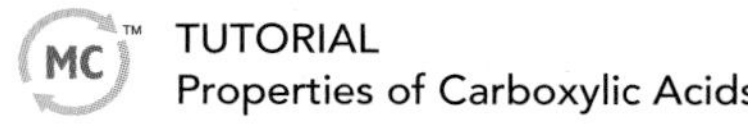


gives carboxylic acids higher boiling points than alcohols, ketones, and aldehydes of similar mass:

| | $CH_3-CH_2-\overset{O}{\overset{\|\|}{C}}-H$ | $CH_3-CH_2-CH_2-OH$ | $CH_3-\overset{O}{\overset{\|\|}{C}}-OH$ |
|---|---|---|---|
| **Compound** | Propanal | 1-Propanol | Ethanoic acid |
| **Molar mass** | 58 | 60 | 60 |
| **Bp** | 49 °C | 97 °C | 118 °C |

An important reason for the higher boiling points of carboxylic acids is that two carboxylic acids form hydrogen bonds between their carboxyl groups, resulting in a *dimer*. As a dimer, the mass of the carboxylic acid is effectively doubled, which means that a higher temperature is required to reach the boiling point:

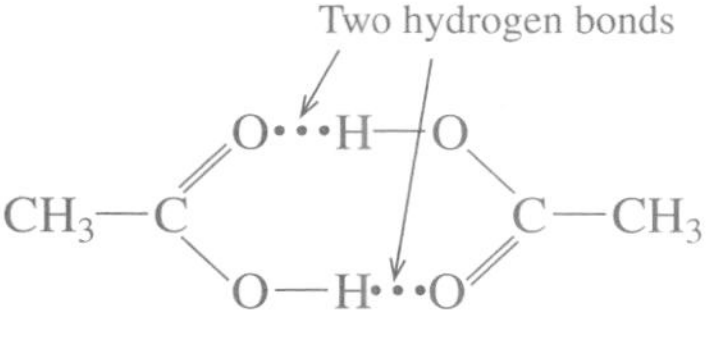

A dimer of two ethanoic acid molecules

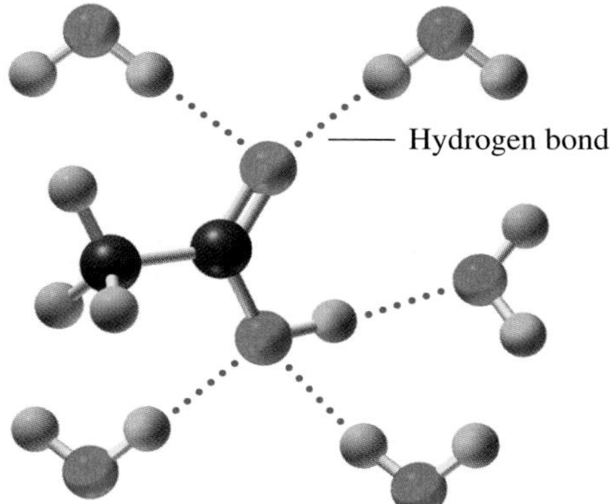


**FIGURE 16.2** Acetic acid forms hydrogen bonds with water molecules.

**Q** Why do the atoms in the carboxyl group hydrogen bond with water molecules?

## Solubility in Water

Carboxylic acids with one to four carbons are very soluble in water because the carboxyl group forms hydrogen bonds with several water molecules. (See Figure 16.2.) However, as the length of the carbon chain increases, the nonpolar portion reduces solubility. Carboxylic acids having five or more carbons are not very soluble in water. Table 16.2 lists boiling point, solubility, and acid dissociation constant for some selected carboxylic acids.

**TABLE 16.2** Properties of Selected Carboxylic Acids

| IUPAC name | Bp (°C) | Soluble in water? | Acid Dissociation Constants (25 °C) |
|---|---|---|---|
| Methanoic acid | 101 | Yes | $1.8 \times 10^{-4}$ |
| Ethanoic acid | 118 | Yes | $1.8 \times 10^{-5}$ |
| Propanoic acid | 141 | Yes | $1.3 \times 10^{-5}$ |
| Butanoic acid | 164 | Yes | $1.5 \times 10^{-5}$ |
| Pentanoic acid | 187 | Slightly | $1.5 \times 10^{-5}$ |
| Hexanoic acid | 205 | Slightly | $1.4 \times 10^{-5}$ |
| Benzoic acid | 250 | Slightly | $6.5 \times 10^{-5}$ |

**CONCEPT CHECK 16.2**

### Boiling Points

Propanal (bp 49 °C) and ethanoic acid (bp 118 °C) have similar molar masses. Explain why ethanoic acid has a higher boiling point than propanal.

ANSWER

In the liquid state, hydrogen bonds between the carboxyl groups of two ethanoic acid molecules form a dimer. As a dimer, the molar mass of ethanoic acid is essentially doubled, which requires higher temperatures to form a gas. Ethanal does not form hydrogen bonds in the liquid state.

SAMPLE PROBLEM 16.3

### Properties of Carboxylic Acids

Put the following organic compounds in order of increasing boiling points: butanoic acid, pentane, and 2-butanol.

SOLUTION

The boiling point increases when the molecules of a compound can form hydrogen bonds or have dipole–dipole attractions. The alkane has the lowest boiling point because alkanes cannot hydrogen bond. Alcohols and carboxylic acids have higher boiling points than alkanes because they form hydrogen bonds. However, carboxylic acids can form stable dimers to increase their effective molar mass and therefore their boiling points.

Pentane $<$ 2-butanol $<$ butanoic acid

STUDY CHECK

Why would methanoic acid (molar mass 46, bp 101 °C) have a higher boiling point than ethanol (molar mass 46, bp 78 °C)?

## Acidity of Carboxylic Acids

One of the most important properties of carboxylic acids is their ionization in water, which makes them weak acids (Chapter 10). In the ionization, a carboxylic acid donates a proton to a water molecule to produce an anion called a **carboxylate ion** and a hydronium ion:

$$\underset{\substack{\text{Carboxylic acid}\\\text{(acetic acid)}}}{CH_3-\overset{\overset{\displaystyle O}{\|}}{C}-OH} + H_2O \rightleftharpoons \underset{\substack{\text{Carboxylate ion}\\\text{(acetate ion)}}}{CH_3-\overset{\overset{\displaystyle O}{\|}}{C}-O^-} + \underset{\substack{\text{Hydronium}\\\text{ion}}}{H_3O^+}$$

Carboxylic acids are more acidic than other organic compounds, including phenols. Only a small percentage (~1%) of the carboxylic acid molecules in a dilute solution are ionized, which means that most of the acid is not ionized. The acid dissociation constants of most carboxylic acids are between $10^{-4}$ to $10^{-5}$, as seen in Table 16.2.

SAMPLE PROBLEM 16.4

### Ionization of Carboxylic Acids in Water

Write the equation for the ionization of propionic acid in water.

SOLUTION

The ionization of propionic acid produces a carboxylate ion and a hydronium ion:

$$CH_3-CH_2-\overset{\overset{\displaystyle O}{\|}}{C}-OH + H_2O \rightleftharpoons CH_3-CH_2-\overset{\overset{\displaystyle O}{\|}}{C}-O^- + H_3O^+$$

STUDY CHECK

Write an equation for the ionization of formic acid in water.

## Neutralization of Carboxylic Acids

Because carboxylic acids are weak acids, they are completely neutralized by strong bases such as NaOH and KOH. The products are water and a **carboxylic acid salt**, which is a carboxylate ion and the metal ion from the base. The carboxylate ion is named by replacing the *ic acid* ending of the acid name with *ate*.

$$\mathrm{H{-}\overset{\overset{\displaystyle O}{\|}}{C}{-}OH} + \mathrm{NaOH} \longrightarrow \mathrm{H{-}\overset{\overset{\displaystyle O}{\|}}{C}{-}O^-Na^+} + H_2O$$

Methanoic acid (formic acid) → Sodium methanoate (sodium formate)

$$\mathrm{C_6H_5{-}\overset{\overset{\displaystyle O}{\|}}{C}{-}OH} + \mathrm{KOH} \longrightarrow \mathrm{C_6H_5{-}\overset{\overset{\displaystyle O}{\|}}{C}{-}O^-K^+} + H_2O$$

Benzoic acid → Potassium benzoate

FIGURE 16.3 Preservatives and flavor enhancers in soups and seasonings are often carboxylic acids or their salts.

Q What is the carboxylic acid salt produced by the neutralization of butanoic acid and lithium hydroxide?

Sodium propionate, a preservative, is added to bread, cheeses, and bakery items to inhibit the spoilage of the food by microorganisms. Sodium benzoate, an inhibitor of mold and bacteria, is added to juices, margarine, relishes, salads, and jams. Monosodium glutamate (MSG) is added to meats, fish, vegetables, and bakery items to enhance flavor, although it causes headaches in some people. (See Figure 16.3.)

$$\mathrm{CH_3{-}CH_2{-}\overset{\overset{\displaystyle O}{\|}}{C}{-}O^-Na^+}$$

Sodium propionate

$$\mathrm{C_6H_5{-}\overset{\overset{\displaystyle O}{\|}}{C}{-}O^-Na^+}$$

Sodium benzoate

$$\mathrm{HO{-}\overset{\overset{\displaystyle O}{\|}}{C}{-}\overset{\overset{\displaystyle NH_2}{|}}{C}H{-}CH_2{-}CH_2{-}\overset{\overset{\displaystyle O}{\|}}{C}{-}O^-Na^+}$$

Monosodium glutamate

Carboxylic acid salts are ionic compounds with strong attractions between ions of metals such as $Li^+$, $Na^+$, and $K^+$ and the negatively charged carboxylate ion. Like most salts, the carboxylic acid salts are solids at room temperature, have high melting points, and are usually soluble in water.

SAMPLE PROBLEM 16.5

## Neutralization of a Carboxylic Acid

Write the equation for the neutralization of propanoic acid (propionic acid) with sodium hydroxide.

SOLUTION

The neutralization of an acid with a base produces the salt of the acid and water:

$$\mathrm{CH_3{-}CH_2{-}\overset{\overset{\displaystyle O}{\|}}{C}{-}OH} + \mathrm{NaOH} \longrightarrow \mathrm{CH_3{-}CH_2{-}\overset{\overset{\displaystyle O}{\|}}{C}{-}O^-Na^+} + H_2O$$

Propanoic acid (propionic acid) → Sodium propanoate (sodium propionate)

STUDY CHECK

What carboxylic acid will give potassium butanoate (potassium butyrate) when it is neutralized by KOH?

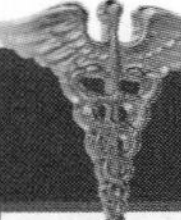

# HEALTH NOTE

## Carboxylic Acids in Metabolism

Several carboxylic acids are part of the metabolic processes within our cells. For example, during glycolysis, a molecule of glucose is broken down into two molecules of pyruvic acid, or actually its carboxylate ion pyruvate. During strenuous exercise when oxygen levels are low (anaerobic), pyruvic acid is reduced to give lactic acid or the lactate ion. The buildup of lactate ion in muscle leads to fatigue and pain.

$$\underset{\text{Pyruvic acid}}{CH_3-\overset{\overset{O}{\|}}{C}-\overset{\overset{O}{\|}}{C}-OH} + 2H \xrightarrow{\text{Reduction}} \underset{\text{Lactic acid}}{CH_3-\overset{\overset{OH}{|}}{CH}-\overset{\overset{O}{\|}}{C}-OH}$$

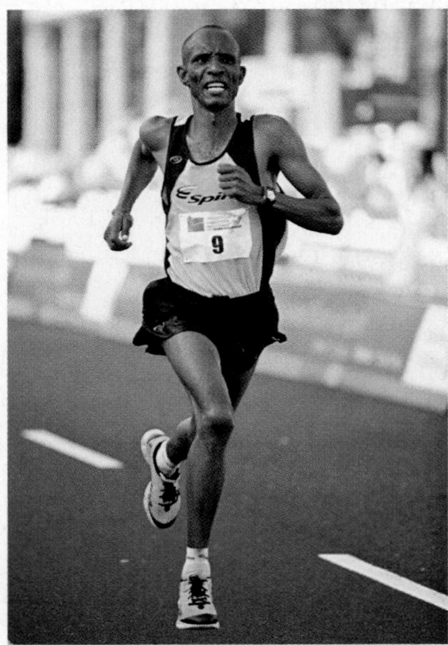

In the citric acid cycle, also called the Krebs cycle, di- and tricarboxylic acids are oxidized and decarboxylated (loss of $CO_2$) to produce energy for the cell. These carboxylic acids are normally referred to by their common names. At the start of the citric acid cycle, citric acid with six carbons is converted to five-carbon $\alpha$-ketoglutaric acid. Citric acid is also the acid that gives the sour tastes to citrus fruits such as lemons and grapefruits.

Citric acid: COOH–$CH_2$–C(OH)(COOH)–$CH_2$–COOH $\xrightarrow{[O]}$ $\alpha$-Ketoglutaric acid: COOH–$CH_2$–$CH_2$–C(=O)–COOH + $CO_2$

The citric acid cycle continues as $\alpha$-ketoglutaric acid loses $CO_2$ to give a four-carbon succinic acid. Then a series of reactions converts succinic acid to oxaloacetic acid. We see that some of the functional groups we have studied along with reactions such as hydration and oxidation are part of the metabolic processes that take place in our cells.

Succinic acid: COOH–$CH_2$–$CH_2$–COOH $\xrightarrow{[O]}$ Fumaric acid: COOH–C(H)=C(H)–COOH $\xrightarrow{H_2O}$

Malic acid: COOH–C(OH)(H)–$CH_2$–COOH $\xrightarrow{[O]}$ Oxaloacetic acid: COOH–C(=O)–$CH_2$–COOH

At the pH of the aqueous environment in the cells, the carboxylic acids are ionized, which means it is actually the carboxylate ions that take part in the reactions of citric acid cycle. For example, in water, succinic acid is in equilibrium with its carboxylate ion succinate.

Succinic acid: COOH–$CH_2$–$CH_2$–COOH + $2H_2O$ $\rightleftharpoons$ Succinate ion: $COO^-$–$CH_2$–$CH_2$–$COO^-$ + $2H_3O^+$

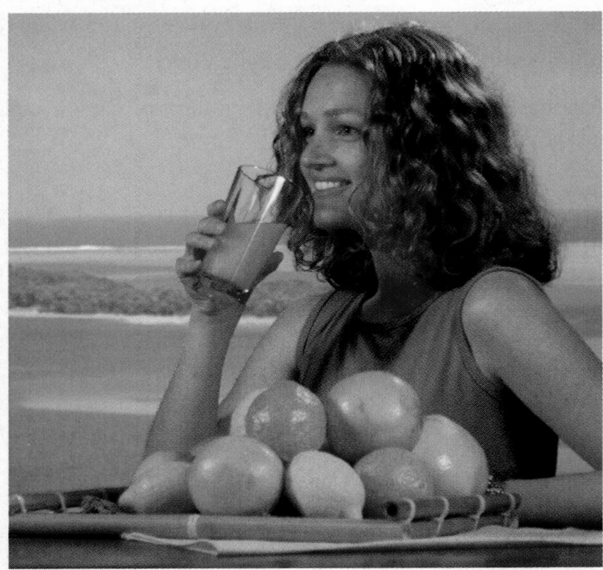

## QUESTIONS AND PROBLEMS

### Properties of Carboxylic Acids

**16.11** Identify the compound in each of the following pairs that has the higher boiling point. Explain.
**a.** ethanoic acid (acetic acid) or butanoic acid
**b.** 1-propanol or propanoic acid
**c.** butanone or butanoic acid

**16.12** Identify the compound in each of the following pairs that has the higher boiling point. Explain.
**a.** propanone (acetone) or propanoic acid
**b.** propanoic acid or hexanoic acid
**c.** ethanol or ethanoic acid (acetic acid)

**16.13** Identify the compound in each of the following groups that is the most soluble in water. Explain.
**a.** propanoic acid, hexanoic acid, benzoic acid
**b.** pentane, 1-butanol, propanoic acid

**16.14** Identify the compound in each of the following groups that is the most soluble in water. Explain.
**a.** butanone, butanoic acid, butane
**b.** acetic acid, pentanoic acid, octanoic acid

**16.15** Write an equation for the ionization of each of the following carboxylic acids in water:
**a.** $H-\overset{\overset{O}{\|}}{C}-OH$ **b.** $CH_3-CH_2-\overset{\overset{O}{\|}}{C}-OH$
**c.** acetic acid

**16.16** Write an equation for the ionization of each of the following carboxylic acids in water:
**a.** $CH_3-\overset{\overset{CH_3}{|}}{CH}-\overset{\overset{O}{\|}}{C}-OH$
**b.** $\alpha$-hydroxyacetic acid
**c.** butanoic acid

**16.17** Write an equation for the reaction of each of the following carboxylic acids with NaOH:
**a.** formic acid
**b.** propanoic acid
**c.** benzoic acid

**16.18** Write an equation for the reaction of each of the following carboxylic acids with KOH:
**a.** acetic acid
**b.** 2-methylbutanoic acid
**c.** *p*-chlorobenzoic acid

**16.19** Give the IUPAC and common names, if any, of the carboxylic acid salts in problem 16.17.

**16.20** Give the IUPAC and common names, if any, of the carboxylic acid salts in problem 16.18.

# 16.3 Esters

A carboxylic acid reacts with an alcohol to form an **ester** and water. In an ester, the —H of the carboxylic acid is replaced by an alkyl group. Fats and oils in our diets contain esters of long-chain carboxylic acids. The aromas and flavors of many fruits including bananas, oranges, and strawberries are because of esters.

LEARNING GOAL

Name an ester; write equations for the formation and hydrolysis of an ester.

MC TUTORIAL Writing Esterification Equations

| **Carboxylic acid** | **Ester** |
|---|---|
| $CH_3-\overset{\overset{O}{\|}}{C}-O-H$ | $CH_3-\overset{\overset{O}{\|}}{C}-O-CH_3$ |
| Ethanoic acid (acetic acid) | Methyl ethanoate (methyl acetate) |

## Esterification

In a reaction called **esterification**, an ester is produced when a carboxylic acid and an alcohol react in the presence of an acid catalyst (usually $H_2SO_4$). An excess of the alcohol reactant is used to favor the formation of the ester product. In this reaction, the —OH removed from the carboxylic acid and the —H removed from the alcohol combine to form water:

$$\underset{\text{Ethanoic acid (acetic acid)}}{CH_3-\overset{\overset{O}{\|}}{C}-O-H} + \underset{\text{Methanol (methyl alcohol)}}{H-O-CH_3} \xrightleftharpoons{H^+,\ heat} \underset{\text{Methyl ethanoate (methyl acetate)}}{CH_3-\overset{\overset{O}{\|}}{C}-O-CH_3} + H-O-H$$

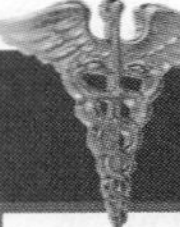

# HEALTH NOTE

## Salicylic Acid and Pain Relievers

Chewing on a piece of willow bark was used as a way to relieve pain for many centuries. By the 1800s, chemists discovered that salicylic acid was the agent in the bark responsible for the relief of pain. However, salicylic acid, which has both a carboxylic group and a hydroxyl group, irritates the stomach lining. A less irritating ester of salicylic acid and acetic acid, called acetylsalicylic acid or "aspirin," was prepared in 1899 by the Bayer chemical company in Germany. In some aspirin preparations, a buffer is added to neutralize the carboxylic acid group and lessen its irritation of the stomach. Aspirin is used as an analgesic (pain reliever), antipyretic (fever reducer), and anti-inflammatory agent. Many people take a daily low-dose aspirin, which has been found to lower the risk of heart attack and stroke.

$$\text{Salicylic acid } (C_6H_4(OH){-}COOH) + HO{-}\overset{\displaystyle O}{\overset{\|}{C}}{-}CH_3 \xrightarrow{H^+} \text{Acetylsalicylic acid, aspirin } (C_6H_4(O{-}\overset{\displaystyle O}{\overset{\|}{C}}{-}CH_3){-}COOH) + H_2O$$

Salicylic acid — Acetic acid — Acetylsalicylic acid, aspirin

Oil of wintergreen, or methyl salicylate, has a spearmint odor and flavor. Because it can pass through the skin, methyl salicylate is used in skin ointments, where it acts as a counterirritant, producing heat to soothe sore muscles.

$$\text{Salicylic acid } (C_6H_4(OH){-}COOH) + HO{-}CH_3 \xrightarrow{H^+} \text{Methyl salicylate } (C_6H_4(OH){-}\overset{\displaystyle O}{\overset{\|}{C}}{-}O{-}CH_3) + H_2O$$

Salicylic acid — Methyl alcohol — Methyl salicylate (oil of wintergreen)

For example, the ester responsible for the flavor and odor of pears can be prepared using acetic acid and 1-propanol. The equation for this esterification is written as follows:

$$CH_3{-}\overset{\displaystyle O}{\overset{\|}{C}}{-}\mathbf{OH} + \mathbf{H}{-}O{-}CH_2{-}CH_2{-}CH_3 \underset{}{\overset{H^+,\text{ heat}}{\rightleftharpoons}} CH_3{-}\overset{\displaystyle O}{\overset{\|}{C}}{-}O{-}CH_2{-}CH_2{-}CH_3 + \mathbf{H_2O}$$

Ethanoic acid (acetic acid) — 1-Propanol (propyl alcohol) — Propyl ethanoate (propyl acetate)

SAMPLE PROBLEM 16.6

### Writing Esterification Equations

The ester that is present in apples and pineapples can be synthesized from butyric acid and methyl alcohol. What is the equation for the formation of the ester in apples?

SOLUTION

$$CH_3{-}CH_2{-}CH_2{-}\overset{\displaystyle O}{\overset{\|}{C}}{-}\mathbf{OH} + \mathbf{H}{-}O{-}CH_3 \overset{H^+,\text{ heat}}{\rightleftharpoons} CH_3{-}CH_2{-}CH_2{-}\overset{\displaystyle O}{\overset{\|}{C}}{-}O{-}CH_3 + \mathbf{H_2O}$$

Butanoic acid (butyric acid) — Methanol (methyl alcohol) — Methyl butanoate (methyl butyrate)

STUDY CHECK

What carboxylic acid and alcohol are needed to form the following ester, which gives flavor and odor to apricots? (*Hint*: Separate the O and C=O of the ester group and add —H and —OH to give the original alcohol and carboxylic acid.)

$$CH_3—CH_2—\overset{\overset{\displaystyle O}{\|}}{C}—O—CH_2—CH_2—CH_2—CH_2—CH_3$$

## ENVIRONMENTAL NOTE

### Plastics

Terephthalic acid (an acid with two carboxyl groups) is produced in large quantities for the manufacture of polyesters such as Dacron and plastics.

When terephthalic acid reacts with ethylene glycol, ester bonds can form on both ends of the molecules, allowing many molecules to combine until they have formed a long polymer known as a *polyester*:

$$HOOC—C_6H_4—COOH + HO—CH_2CH_2—OH \longrightarrow$$

Terephthalic acid        Ethylene glycol

$$—O—\overset{\overset{\displaystyle O}{\|}}{C}—C_6H_4—\overset{\overset{\displaystyle O}{\|}}{C}—O—CH_2CH_2—O—\overset{\overset{\displaystyle O}{\|}}{C}—C_6H_4—\overset{\overset{\displaystyle O}{\|}}{C}—O—CH_2CH_2—O—$$

Ester bonds

A section of the polyester Dacron

Dacron polyester is used to make permanent press fabrics, carpets, and clothes. In medicine, artificial blood vessels and valves are made of Dacron, which is biologically inert and does not clot the blood. The polyester can also be made as a film called Mylar and as a plastic known as PETE (**p**oly**e**thylene**te**rephthalate). PETE is used for plastic soft drink bottles as well as for containers of salad dressings, shampoos, and dishwashing liquids.

Today PETE (recycling symbol "1") is the most widely recycled of all the plastics. In 1992, there were 365 million pounds (166 million kilograms) of PETE recycled. After it is separated from other plastics, PETE can be changed into other useful items, including polyester fabric for T-shirts and coats, fill for sleeping bags, doormats, and containers for tennis balls.

## QUESTIONS AND PROBLEMS

### Esters

16.21 Identify each of the following as an aldehyde, a ketone, a carboxylic acid, or an ester:

**a.** $CH_3—\overset{\overset{\displaystyle O}{\|}}{C}—H$

**b.** $CH_3—\overset{\overset{\displaystyle O}{\|}}{C}—O—CH_3$

**c.** $CH_3—CH_2—\overset{\overset{\displaystyle O}{\|}}{C}—CH_3$

**d.** $CH_3—CH_2—\overset{\overset{\displaystyle O}{\|}}{C}—O—H$

**16.22** Identify each of the following as an aldehyde, a ketone, a carboxylic acid, or an ester:

**a.** $CH_3-\overset{\overset{\displaystyle O}{\|}}{C}-OH$ **b.** $CH_3-\overset{\overset{\displaystyle O}{\|}}{C}-O-CH_2-CH_3$

**c.** $CH_3-CH_2-\overset{\overset{\displaystyle O}{\|}}{C}-H$

**d.** $CH_3-\overset{\overset{\displaystyle CH_3}{|}}{CH}-\overset{\overset{\displaystyle O}{\|}}{C}-O-CH_2-CH_3$

**16.23** Draw the condensed structural formula of the ester formed when each of the following reacts with methyl alcohol:
**a.** acetic acid **b.** butyric acid **c.** benzoic acid

**16.24** Draw the condensed structural formula of the ester formed when each of the following reacts with methyl alcohol:
**a.** formic acid
**b.** propionic acid
**c.** 2-methylpentanoic acid

**16.25** Draw the condensed structural formula of the ester formed when each of the following react:

**a.** $CH_3-CH_2-\overset{\overset{\displaystyle O}{\|}}{C}-OH + HO-CH_2-CH_2-CH_3 \overset{H^+}{\rightleftarrows}$

**b.**

$CH_3-CH_2-CH_2-CH_2-\overset{\overset{\displaystyle O}{\|}}{C}-OH + HO-\overset{\overset{\displaystyle CH_3}{|}}{CH}-CH_3 \overset{H^+}{\rightleftarrows}$

**16.26** Draw the condensed structural formula of the ester formed when each of the following react:

**a.** $CH_3-CH_2-\overset{\overset{\displaystyle O}{\|}}{C}-OH + HO-CH_3 \overset{H^+}{\rightleftarrows}$

**b.** $C_6H_5-\overset{\overset{\displaystyle O}{\|}}{C}-OH + HO-CH_2-CH_2-CH_2-CH_3 \overset{H^+}{\rightleftarrows}$ (benzene ring attached to C)

## 16.4 Naming Esters

**LEARNING GOAL**

Write the IUPAC and common names for esters; draw condensed structural formulas.

The name of an ester consists of two words taken from the names of the alcohol and the acid. The first word indicates the *alkyl* part of the alcohol. The second word is the *carboxylate* name of the carboxylic acid. The IUPAC names of esters use the IUPAC names for the carbon chain of the acid, while the common names of esters use the common names of the acids. Let's take a look at the following ester, which has the odor and flavor of peppermint. We can separate the structure into two parts, one from the alcohol and one from the carbon chain of the acid. By writing and naming the alcohol and carboxylic acid that produced the ester, we can determine the name of the ester.

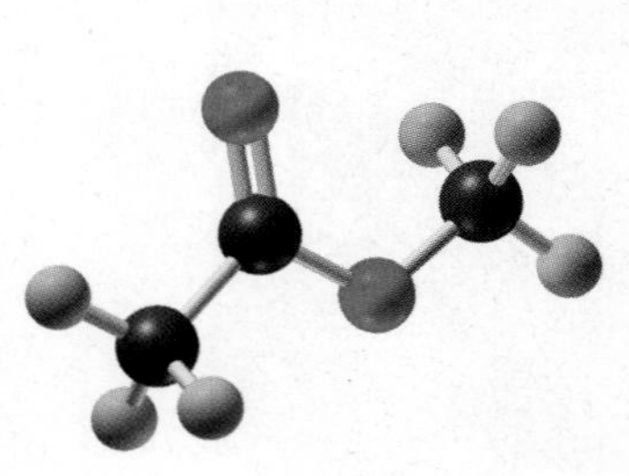

Methyl ethanoate
(methyl acetate)

$$CH_3-O-\overset{\overset{\displaystyle O}{\|}}{C}-CH_3$$

From alcohol (alkyl) From carboxylic acid (carboxylate)

$$CH_3-O-H + H-O-\overset{\overset{\displaystyle O}{\|}}{C}-CH_3$$

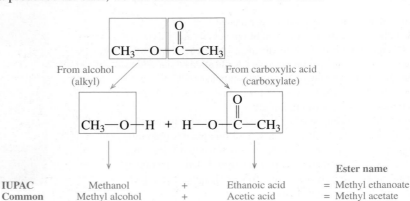

| | | | | Ester name |
|---|---|---|---|---|
| IUPAC | Methanol | + | Ethanoic acid | = Methyl ethanoate |
| Common | Methyl alcohol | + | Acetic acid | = Methyl acetate |

The following examples of some typical esters show the IUPAC as well as the common names of esters:

$CH_3-CH_2-O-\overset{\overset{\displaystyle O}{\|}}{C}-CH_3$
Ethyl ethanoate
(ethyl acetate)

$CH_3-O-\overset{\overset{\displaystyle O}{\|}}{C}-CH_2-CH_3$
Methyl propanoate
(methyl propionate)

$CH_3-CH_2-O-\overset{\overset{\displaystyle O}{\|}}{C}-C_6H_5$
Ethyl benzoate

Many of the fragrances of perfumes and flowers and the flavors of fruits are due to esters. Small esters are volatile so we can smell them and soluble in water so we can taste them. Several of these are listed in Table 16.3.

TABLE 16.3 Some Esters in Fruits and Flavorings

| Condensed Structural Formula and Name | Flavor/Odor |
|---|---|
| $CH_3-\overset{\overset{\displaystyle O}{\|}}{C}-O-CH_2-CH_2-CH_3$<br>Propyl ethanoate<br>(propyl acetate) | Pears |
| $CH_3-\overset{\overset{\displaystyle O}{\|}}{C}-O-CH_2-CH_2-CH_2-CH_2-CH_3$<br>Pentyl ethanoate<br>(pentyl acetate) | Bananas |
| $CH_3-\overset{\overset{\displaystyle O}{\|}}{C}-O-CH_2-CH_2-CH_2-CH_2-CH_2-CH_2-CH_2-CH_3$<br>Octyl ethanoate<br>(octyl acetate) | Oranges |
| $CH_3-CH_2-CH_2-\overset{\overset{\displaystyle O}{\|}}{C}-O-CH_2-CH_3$<br>Ethyl butanoate<br>(ethyl butyrate) | Pineapples |
| $CH_3-CH_2-CH_2-\overset{\overset{\displaystyle O}{\|}}{C}-O-CH_2-CH_2-CH_2-CH_2-CH_3$<br>Pentyl butanoate<br>(pentyl butyrate) | Apricots |

CONCEPT CHECK 16.3

### Esterification

The odor and flavor of apples is the ester from ethanol and pentanoic acid. What is the IUPAC name of the ester?

ANSWER

The first part of an ester name comes from the alkyl part of ethanol, which would be ethyl. The second part is obtained from the name of the carboxylic acid by replacing *ic acid* with *ate*. The name of the ester for apple flavor is ethyl pentanoate.

SAMPLE PROBLEM 16.7

### Naming Esters

TUTORIAL
Naming Esters

Write the IUPAC and common names of the following ester:

$$CH_3-CH_2-\overset{\overset{\displaystyle O}{\|}}{C}-O-CH_2-CH_2-CH_3$$

SOLUTION

**STEP 1** **Write the name of the carbon chain from the alcohol as an *alkyl* group.** The alcohol that is part of the ester is propanol, which is named as the alkyl group propyl.

**STEP 2** **For the IUPAC name, replace the *ic acid* in the carboxylic acid name with *ate*.** The carboxylic acid with three carbon atoms is propanoic acid. Replacing the *ic acid* with *ate* gives the IUPAC name of propyl propanoate.

**Guide to Naming Esters**

STEP 1
Write the name of the carbon chain from the alcohol as an *alkyl* group

STEP 2
Change the *ic acid* of the acid name to *ate*.

The common name of propionic acid gives the common name for the ester of propyl propionate:

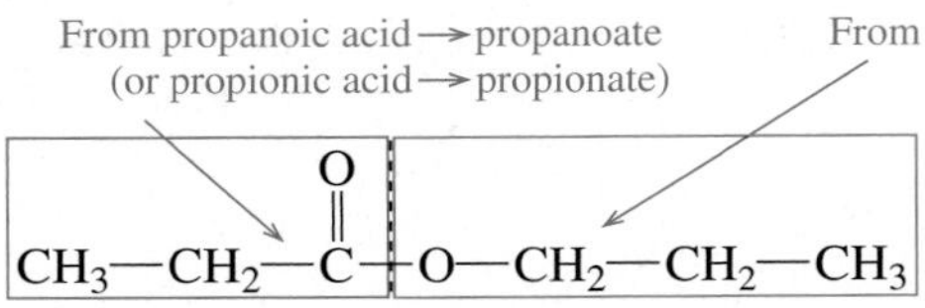

From propanoic acid ⟶ propanoate (or propionic acid ⟶ propionate)    From propyl alcohol ⟶ propyl

$$CH_3-CH_2-\overset{O}{\overset{\|}{C}}-O-CH_2-CH_2-CH_3$$

IUPAC name: propyl propanoate
Common name: propyl propionate

STUDY CHECK

Draw the condensed structural formula of ethyl heptanoate that gives odor and flavor to grapes.

## QUESTIONS AND PROBLEMS

### Naming Esters

**16.27** Give the names of the carboxylic acid and alcohol needed to produce each of the following esters:

**a.** $H-\overset{O}{\overset{\|}{C}}-O-CH_3$    **b.** $CH_3-\overset{O}{\overset{\|}{C}}-O-CH_3$

**c.** $CH_3-CH_2-CH_2-\overset{O}{\overset{\|}{C}}-O-CH_3$

**d.** $CH_3-\overset{CH_3}{\overset{|}{CH}}-CH_2-\overset{O}{\overset{\|}{C}}-O-CH_2-CH_3$

**16.28** Give the names of the carboxylic acid and alcohol needed to produce each of the following esters:

**a.** $CH_3-CH_2-\overset{O}{\overset{\|}{C}}-O-CH_2-CH_3$

**b.** $CH_3-CH_2-CH_2-CH_2-CH_2-\overset{O}{\overset{\|}{C}}-O-CH_3$

**c.** $CH_3-CH_2-\underset{CH_3}{\underset{|}{CH}}-\overset{O}{\overset{\|}{C}}-O-CH_3$

**d.** $CH_3-CH_2-\overset{O}{\overset{\|}{C}}-O-CH_2-CH_2-CH_2-CH_3$

**16.29** Name each of the following esters:

**a.** $CH_3-O-\overset{O}{\overset{\|}{C}}-H$

**b.** $CH_3-O-\overset{O}{\overset{\|}{C}}-CH_3$

**c.** $CH_3-O-\overset{O}{\overset{\|}{C}}-CH_2-CH_2-CH_3$

**d.** $CH_3-\overset{CH_3}{\overset{|}{CH}}-CH_2-\overset{O}{\overset{\|}{C}}-O-CH_2-CH_3$

**16.30** Name each of the following esters:

**a.** $CH_3-CH_2-O-\overset{O}{\overset{\|}{C}}-CH_2-CH_2-CH_3$

**b.** $CH_3-O-\overset{O}{\overset{\|}{C}}-CH_2-CH_2-CH_2-CH_2-CH_3$

**c.** $CH_3-O-\overset{O}{\overset{\|}{C}}-CH_2-\overset{CH_3}{\overset{|}{CH}}-CH_3$

**d.** $CH_3-CH_2-\overset{O}{\overset{\|}{C}}-O-CH_2-CH_2-CH_2-CH_3$

**16.31** Draw the condensed structural formula of each of the following esters:
**a.** methyl acetate
**b.** butyl formate
**c.** ethyl pentanoate
**d.** 2-bromopropyl propanoate

**16.32** Draw the condensed structural formula of each of the following esters:
**a.** hexyl acetate
**b.** propyl propionate
**c.** ethyl 2-hydroxybutanoate
**d.** methyl benzoate

**16.33** What is the ester responsible for the flavor and odor of each of the following fruits?
**a.** banana  **b.** orange  **c.** apricot

**16.34** What flavor would you notice if you smelled or tasted each of the following?
**a.** ethyl butanoate  **b.** propyl acetate  **c.** octyl acetate

# 16.5 Properties of Esters

Esters have boiling points higher than those of alkanes but lower than those of alcohols and carboxylic acids of similar mass. Because ester molecules do not have hydroxyl groups, they cannot hydrogen bond to each other:

**LEARNING GOAL**

Describe the boiling points and solubility of esters; draw the condensed structural formulas of the hydrolysis products.

| | $CH_3—CH_2—CH_2—CH_3$ | $CH_3—O—CH_2—CH_3$ | $CH_3—O—\overset{\overset{O}{\|}}{C}—H$ | $CH_3—CH_2—CH_2—OH$ | $CH_3—\overset{\overset{O}{\|}}{C}—OH$ |
|---|---|---|---|---|---|
| | Butane | Methoxyethane | Methyl methanoate | 1-Propanol | Ethanoic acid |
| Type | Alkane | Ether | Ester | Alcohol | Carboxylic acid |
| Bp | 0 °C | 11 °C | 32 °C | 97 °C | 118 °C |
| Mass | 58 | 60 | 60 | 60 | 60 |

Increasing boiling points →

## Solubility in Water

Esters with only a few carbon atoms are soluble in water. The partially negative oxygen of the carbonyl group forms hydrogen bonds with the partially positive hydrogen atoms of water molecules. The solubility of esters decreases as the number of carbon atoms increases.

## Acid Hydrolysis of Esters

In **hydrolysis**, water splits apart esters when heated in the presence of a strong acid, usually $H_2SO_4$ or HCl. The products of acid hydrolysis are the carboxylic acid and alcohol. Therefore, hydrolysis is the reverse of the esterification reaction. However, in an application of Le Châtelier's principle, using a large quantity of water favors the formation of the carboxylic acid and alcohol products. When hydrolysis of biological compounds occurs in the cells, an enzyme replaces the acid as the catalyst. During hydrolysis, —OH from a water molecule bonds to the carbon atom in the carbonyl group of the ester to form the carboxylic acid:

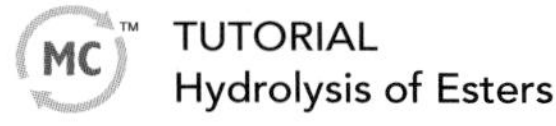

MC™ TUTORIAL Hydrolysis of Esters

$$CH_3—\overset{\overset{O}{\|}}{C}—O—CH_3 + H—OH \underset{}{\overset{H^+}{\rightleftharpoons}} CH_3—\overset{\overset{O}{\|}}{C}—O—H + CH_3—OH$$

Methyl ethanoate (methyl acetate) + Water ⇌ Ethanoic acid (acetic acid) + Methanol (methyl alcohol)

**SAMPLE PROBLEM 16.8**

### ■ Acid Hydrolysis of Esters

Aspirin that has been stored for a long time may undergo hydrolysis in the presence of water and heat. What are the hydrolysis products of aspirin? Why does a bottle of old aspirin smell like vinegar?

[Structure: benzene ring with —C(=O)—OH and —O—C(=O)—CH₃ substituents]

Aspirin (acetylsalicylic acid)

SOLUTION

To write the hydrolysis products, separate the compound at the ester bond. Complete the formula of the carboxylic acid by adding —OH (from water) to the carbonyl group and an —H to complete the alcohol. The acetic acid in the products gives the vinegar odor to a sample of aspirin that has hydrolyzed:

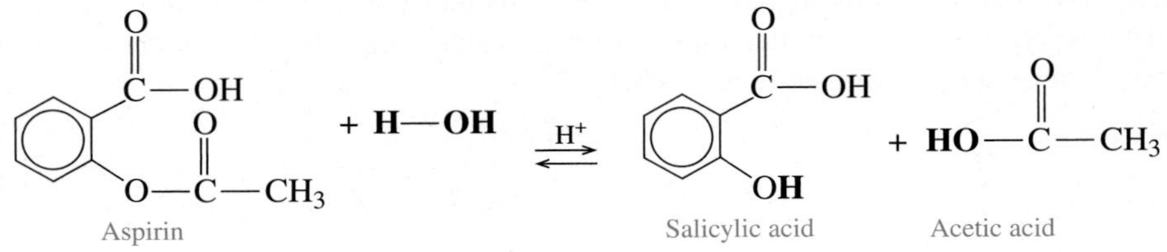

$$\text{Aspirin} + \mathbf{H{-}OH} \underset{}{\overset{H^+}{\rightleftharpoons}} \text{Salicylic acid} + \mathbf{HO}{-}\overset{\overset{\large O}{\|}}{C}{-}CH_3 \text{ (Acetic acid)}$$

Aspirin

Salicylic acid

Acetic acid

STUDY CHECK

What are the names of the products from the acid hydrolysis of ethyl propanoate (ethyl propionate)?

## Base Hydrolysis of Esters (Saponification)

When an ester undergoes hydrolysis with a strong base such as NaOH or KOH, the products are the carboxylic acid salt and the corresponding alcohol. The base hydrolysis reaction is also called **saponification**, which refers to the reaction of a long-chain fatty acid with NaOH to make soap. The carboxylic acid, which is produced in acid hydrolysis, is converted to its carboxylate ion by a strong base:

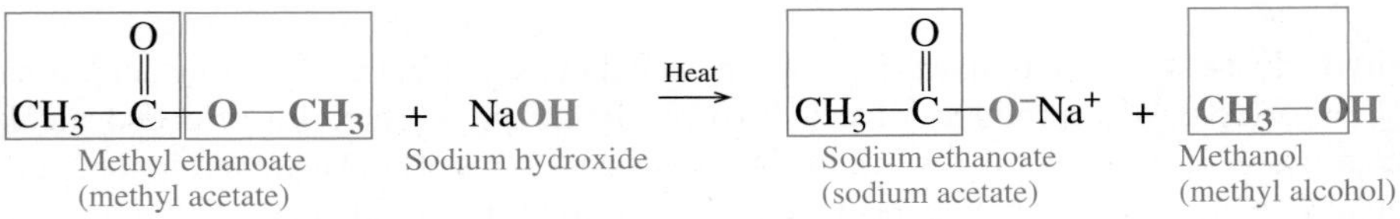

$$CH_3{-}\overset{\overset{O}{\|}}{C}{-}O{-}CH_3 + NaOH \xrightarrow{\text{Heat}} CH_3{-}\overset{\overset{O}{\|}}{C}{-}O^-Na^+ + CH_3{-}OH$$

Methyl ethanoate (methyl acetate) | Sodium hydroxide | Sodium ethanoate (sodium acetate) | Methanol (methyl alcohol)

CONCEPT CHECK 16.4

### Hydrolysis of Esters

Ethyl methanoate has a fruity, lemon fragrance. Name the products of the following reactions of ethyl methanoate:

**a.** acid hydrolysis with HCl

**b.** saponification with KOH

ANSWER

**a.** The products of the acid hydrolysis of ethyl methanoate are the alcohol ethanol and a carboxylic acid methanoic acid.

**b.** The products of the base hydrolysis of ethyl methanoate with KOH are the alcohol ethanol and the carboxylic acid salt potassium methanoate.

SAMPLE PROBLEM 16.9

### Base Hydrolysis of Esters

Ethyl acetate is a solvent widely used for fingernail polish, plastics, and lacquers. Write the equation of the hydrolysis of ethyl acetate by NaOH.

SOLUTION

The hydrolysis of ethyl acetate by NaOH gives the salt of acetic acid and ethyl alcohol:

$$CH_3{-}\overset{\overset{\displaystyle O}{\|}}{C}{-}O{-}CH_2{-}CH_3 + NaOH \xrightarrow{\text{Heat}} CH_3{-}\overset{\overset{\displaystyle O}{\|}}{C}{-}O^-Na^+ + HO{-}CH_2{-}CH_3$$

Ethyl ethanoate (ethyl acetate) — Sodium ethanoate (sodium acetate) — Ethanol (ethyl alcohol)

STUDY CHECK

Draw the condensed structural formulas of the products from the hydrolysis of methyl benzoate by KOH.

## ENVIRONMENTAL NOTE

### Cleaning Action of Soaps

For many centuries, soaps were made by heating a mixture of animal fats (tallow) with lye, a basic solution obtained from wood ashes. In the soap-making process, fats, which are esters of long-chain carboxylic acids, undergo saponification with the strong base in lye.

Fatty acid

$$CH_3CH_2CH_2CH_2CH_2CH_2CH_2CH_2CH_2CH_2CH_2CH_2CH_2CH_2CH_2CH_2CH_2{-}\overset{\overset{\displaystyle O}{\|}}{C}{-}OH + NaOH \longrightarrow$$

Carboxylic acid salt ("soap")

$$CH_3CH_2CH_2CH_2CH_2CH_2CH_2CH_2CH_2CH_2CH_2CH_2CH_2CH_2CH_2CH_2CH_2{-}\overset{\overset{\displaystyle O}{\|}}{C}{-}O^-Na^+$$

Nonpolar tail (hydrophobic) — Polar head (hydrophilic)

Today soaps are also prepared from fats such as coconut oil. Perfumes are added to give a pleasant-smelling soap. Because a soap is the salt of a long-chain fatty acid, the two ends of a soap molecule have different polarities. The long carbon chain end is nonpolar and *hydrophobic* (water-fearing). It is soluble in nonpolar substances such as oil or grease, but it is not soluble in water. The carboxylate salt end is ionic and *hydrophilic* (water-loving). It is very soluble in water but not in oils or grease.

When soap is used to clean grease or oil, the nonpolar ends of the soap molecules dissolve in the nonpolar fats and oils that accompany dirt. The water-loving salt ends of the soap molecules extend outside where they can dissolve in water. The soap molecules coat the oil or grease, forming clusters called *micelles*. The ionic ends of the soap molecules provide polarity to the micelles, which makes them soluble in water. As a result, small globules of oil and fat coated with soap molecules are pulled into the water and rinsed away.

One of the problems of using soaps is that the carboxylate end reacts with ions in water such as $Ca^{2+}$ and $Mg^{2+}$ and forms insoluble substances.

$$2CH_3(CH_2)_{16}COO^- + Mg^{2+} \longrightarrow [CH_3(CH_2)_{16}COO^-]_2Mg^{2+}$$

Stearate ion — Magnesium ion — Magnesium stearate (insoluble)

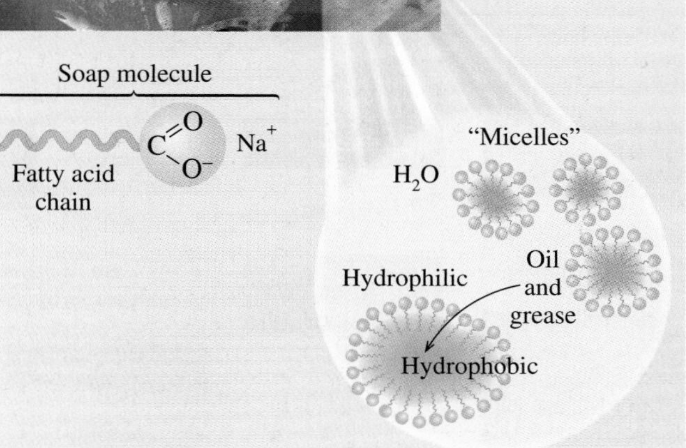

## QUESTIONS AND PROBLEMS

### Properties of Esters

**16.35** For each of the following pairs of compounds, select the compound that has the higher boiling point:

a. $\mathrm{CH_3-\overset{O}{\overset{\|}{C}}-O-CH_3}$ or $\mathrm{CH_3-\overset{O}{\overset{\|}{C}}-OH}$

b. $\mathrm{CH_3-\overset{O}{\overset{\|}{C}}-O-CH_3}$ or $\mathrm{CH_3-CH_2-CH_2-CH_2-OH}$

c. $\mathrm{CH_3-CH_2-CH_2-CH_3}$ or $\mathrm{CH_3-O-\overset{O}{\overset{\|}{C}}-CH_3}$

**16.36** For each of the following pairs of compounds, select the compound that has the higher boiling point:

a. $\mathrm{H-\overset{O}{\overset{\|}{C}}-O-CH_3}$ or $\mathrm{CH_3-CH_2-CH_2-OH}$

b. $\mathrm{CH_3-\overset{O}{\overset{\|}{C}}-O-CH_3}$ or $\mathrm{CH_3-CH_2-\overset{O}{\overset{\|}{C}}-OH}$

c. $\mathrm{CH_3-O-CH_2-CH_3}$ or $\mathrm{CH_3-O-\overset{O}{\overset{\|}{C}}-H}$

**16.37** What are the products of the acid hydrolysis of an ester?

**16.38** What are the products of the base hydrolysis of an ester?

**16.39** Draw the condensed structural formulas of the products from the acid- or base-catalyzed hydrolysis of each of the following compounds:

a. $\mathrm{CH_3-CH_2-\overset{O}{\overset{\|}{C}}-O-CH_3 + NaOH \longrightarrow}$

b. $\mathrm{CH_3-\overset{O}{\overset{\|}{C}}-O-CH_2-CH_2-CH_3 + H_2O \overset{H^+}{\rightleftharpoons}}$

c. $\mathrm{CH_3-CH_2-CH_2-\overset{O}{\overset{\|}{C}}-O-CH_2-CH_3 + H_2O \overset{H^+}{\rightleftharpoons}}$

d. $\mathrm{C_6H_5-\overset{O}{\overset{\|}{C}}-O-CH_2-CH_3 + H_2O \overset{H^+}{\rightleftharpoons}}$

e. $\mathrm{C_6H_5-\overset{O}{\overset{\|}{C}}-O-CH_2-CH_3 + NaOH \longrightarrow}$

**16.40** Draw the condensed structural formulas of the products from the acid- or base-catalyzed hydrolysis of each of the following compounds:

a. $\mathrm{CH_3-CH_2-\overset{O}{\overset{\|}{C}}-O-CH_2-CH_2-CH_2-CH_3 + H_2O \overset{H^+}{\rightleftharpoons}}$

b. $\mathrm{H-\overset{O}{\overset{\|}{C}}-O-CH_2-CH_3 + NaOH \longrightarrow}$

c. $\mathrm{CH_3-CH_2-\overset{O}{\overset{\|}{C}}-O-CH_3 + H_2O \overset{H^+}{\rightleftharpoons}}$

d. $\mathrm{CH_3-CH_2-\overset{O}{\overset{\|}{C}}-O-C_6H_5 + H_2O \overset{H^+}{\rightleftharpoons}}$

e. $\mathrm{C_6H_5-CH_2-\overset{O}{\overset{\|}{C}}-O-CH_2-CH_3 + NaOH \longrightarrow}$

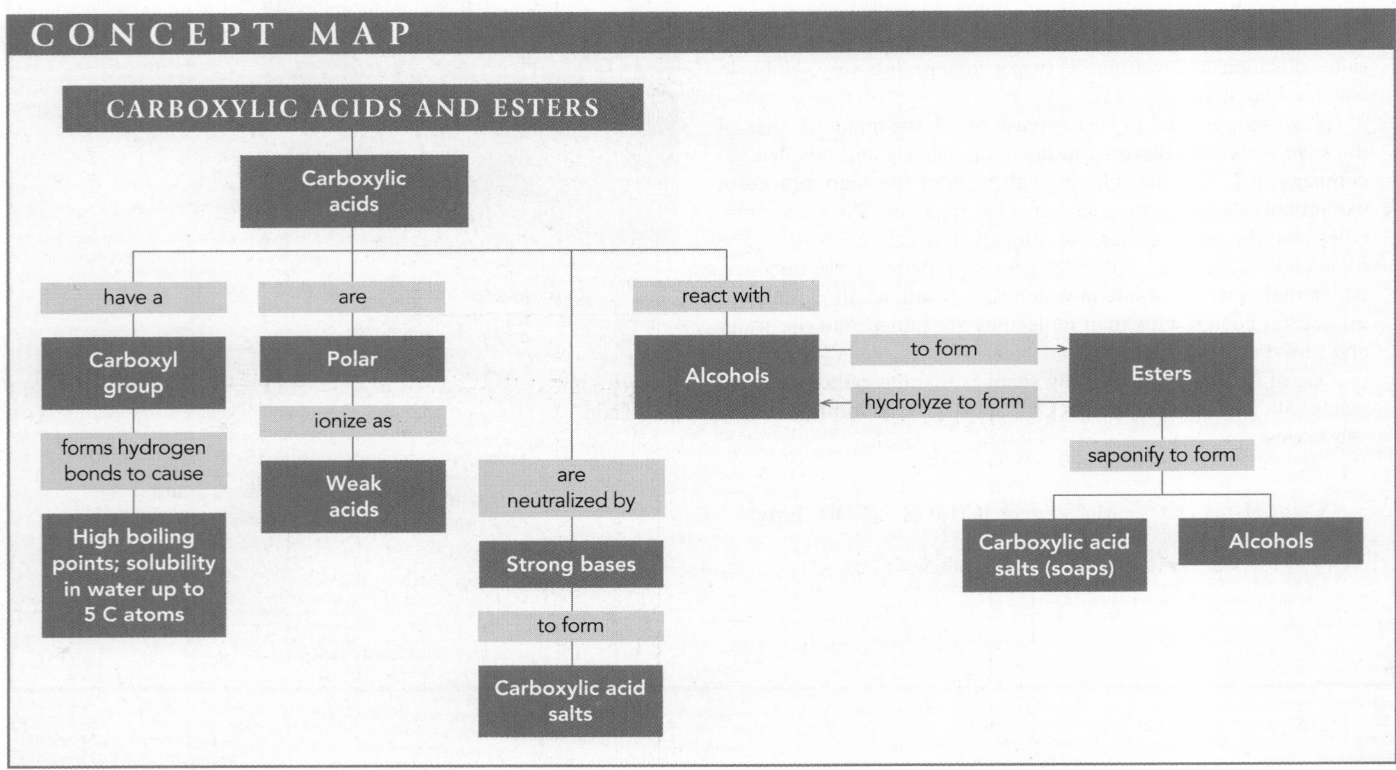

## CHAPTER REVIEW

### 16.1 Carboxylic Acids

**LEARNING GOAL:** *Give the common names, IUPAC names, and condensed structural formulas of carboxylic acids.*
A carboxylic acid contains the carboxyl functional group, which is a hydroxyl group connected to the carbonyl group.

### 16.2 Properties of Carboxylic Acids

**LEARNING GOAL:** *Describe the boiling points, solubility, and ionization of carboxylic acids in water.*
The carboxyl group contains polar bonds of O—H and C=O, which makes a carboxylic acid with one to four carbon atoms very soluble in water. As weak acids, carboxylic acids ionize slightly by donating a proton to water to form carboxylate and hydronium ions. Carboxylic acids are neutralized by base, producing the carboxylate salt and water.

### 16.3 Esters

**LEARNING GOAL:** *Name an ester; write equations for the formation and hydrolysis of an ester.*
In an ester, an alkyl or aromatic group has replaced the H of the hydroxyl group of a carboxylic acid. In the presence of a strong acid, a carboxylic acid reacts with an alcohol to produce an ester. A molecule of water is removed: —OH from the carboxylic acid, and —H from the alcohol molecule.

### 16.4 Naming Esters

**LEARNING GOAL:** *Write the IUPAC and common names for esters; draw condensed structural formulas.*
The names of esters consist of two words, one from the alcohol and the other from the carboxylic acid with the *ic acid* ending replaced by *ate*.

### 16.5 Properties of Esters

**LEARNING GOAL:** *Describe the boiling points and solubility of esters; draw the condensed structural formulas of the hydrolysis products.*
Esters undergo acid hydrolysis by adding water to yield the carboxylic acid and alcohol (or phenol). Base hydrolysis, or saponification, of an ester produces the carboxylate salt and an alcohol.

## SUMMARY OF NAMING

| Family | Condensed Structural Formula | IUPAC Name | Common Name |
|---|---|---|---|
| Carboxylic acid | $CH_3—\overset{O}{\overset{\|\|}{C}}—OH$ | Ethanoic acid | Acetic acid |
| Carboxylic acid salt | $CH_3—\overset{O}{\overset{\|\|}{C}}—O^-Na^+$ | Sodium ethanoate | Sodium acetate |
| Ester | $CH_3—\overset{O}{\overset{\|\|}{C}}—O—CH_3$ | Methyl ethanoate | Methyl acetate |

## SUMMARY OF REACTIONS

### IONIZATION OF A CARBOXYLIC ACID IN WATER

$$CH_3—\overset{O}{\overset{||}{C}}—OH + H_2O \rightleftarrows CH_3—\overset{O}{\overset{||}{C}}—O^- + H_3O^+$$

Ethanoic acid (acetic acid); Ethanoate ion (acetate ion); Hydronium ion

### NEUTRALIZATION OF A CARBOXYLIC ACID

$$CH_3—CH_2—\overset{O}{\overset{||}{C}}—OH + NaOH \longrightarrow CH_3—CH_2—\overset{O}{\overset{||}{C}}—O^-Na^+ + H_2O$$

Propanoic acid (propionic acid); Sodium hydroxide; Sodium propanoate (sodium propionate)

### ESTERIFICATION: CARBOXYLIC ACID AND AN ALCOHOL

$$CH_3—\overset{O}{\overset{||}{C}}—OH + HO—CH_3 \overset{H^+}{\rightleftarrows} CH_3—\overset{O}{\overset{||}{C}}—O—CH_3 + H_2O$$

Ethanoic acid (acetic acid); Methanol (methyl alcohol); Methyl ethanoate (methyl acetate)

ACID HYDROLYSIS OF AN ESTER

$$CH_3-\overset{\displaystyle O}{\overset{\|}{C}}-O-CH_3 + H-OH \overset{H^+}{\rightleftharpoons} CH_3-\overset{\displaystyle O}{\overset{\|}{C}}-OH + H-O-CH_3$$

Methyl ethanoate (methyl acetate) — Ethanoic acid (acetic acid) — Methanol (methyl alcohol)

BASE HYDROLYSIS OF AN ESTER (SAPONIFICATION)

$$CH_3-CH_2-\overset{\displaystyle O}{\overset{\|}{C}}-O-CH_3 + NaOH \xrightarrow{Heat} CH_3-CH_2-\overset{\displaystyle O}{\overset{\|}{C}}-O^-Na^+ + H-O-CH_3$$

Methyl propanoate (methyl propionate) — Sodium hydroxide — Sodium propanoate (sodium propionate) — Methanol (methyl alcohol)

## KEY TERMS

**carboxyl group** A functional group found in carboxylic acids composed of carbonyl and hydroxyl groups.

$$-\overset{\displaystyle O}{\overset{\|}{C}}-OH \quad \text{Carboxyl group}$$

**carboxylate ion** The anion produced when a carboxylic acid donates a proton to water.

**carboxylic acid** An organic compound containing the carboxyl group.

**carboxylic acid salt** The product of neutralization of a carboxylic acid; a carboxylate ion and the metal ion from the base.

**ester** An organic compound in which an alkyl group replaces the hydrogen atom in a carboxylic acid.

**esterification** The formation of an ester from a carboxylic acid and an alcohol with the elimination of a molecule of water in the presence of an acid catalyst.

**hydrolysis** The splitting of a molecule by the addition of water. Esters hydrolyze to produce a carboxylic acid and an alcohol.

**saponification** The hydrolysis of an ester with a strong base to produce a salt of the carboxylic acid and an alcohol.

## UNDERSTANDING THE CONCEPTS

**16.41** Propyl acetate is the ester that gives the odor and flavor of pears.

**a.** What is the condensed structural formula of propyl acetate?
**b.** Write an equation for the formation of propyl acetate.
**c.** Write an equation for the acid hydrolysis of propyl acetate.
**d.** Write an equation for the base hydrolysis of propyl acetate with NaOH.
**e.** How many mL of 0.208 M NaOH are needed to completely hydrolyze (saponify) 1.58 g of propyl acetate?

**16.42** Ethyl octanoate is a flavor component of mangos.

**a.** What is the condensed structural formula of ethyl octanoate?
**b.** Write an equation for the formation of ethyl octanoate.
**c.** Write an equation for the acid hydrolysis of ethyl octanoate.
**d.** Write an equation for the base hydrolysis of ethyl octanoate with NaOH.
**e.** How many mL of 0.315 M NaOH are needed to completely hydrolyze (saponify) 2.84 g of ethyl octanoate?

# ADDITIONAL QUESTIONS AND PROBLEMS

*For instructor-assigned homework, go to* ***www.masteringchemistry.com****.*

16.43 Give the IUPAC and common names (if any) for each of the following compounds:

**a.** 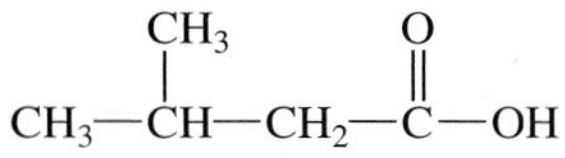 $CH_3-\overset{CH_3}{\overset{|}{C}H}-CH_2-\overset{O}{\overset{\|}{C}}-OH$

**b.** $\overset{O}{\overset{\|}{C}}-O-CH_2-CH_3$

**c.** $CH_3-CH_2-O-\overset{O}{\overset{\|}{C}}-CH_2-CH_3$

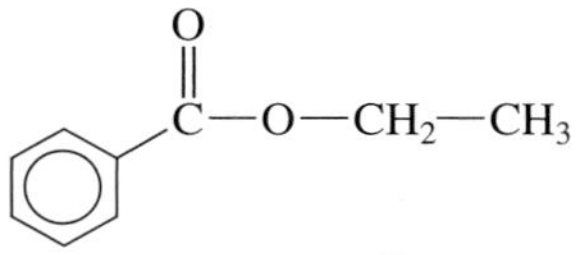

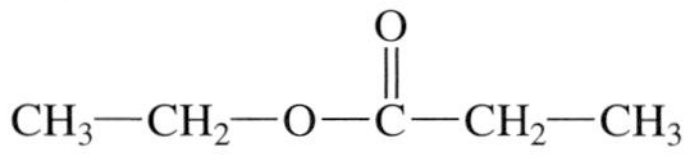

**d.** 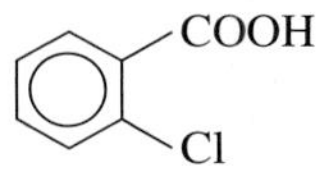 COOH, Cl

**e.** 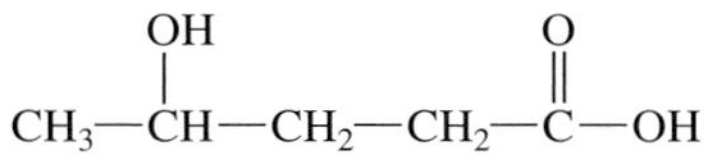 $CH_3-\overset{OH}{\overset{|}{C}H}-CH_2-CH_2-\overset{O}{\overset{\|}{C}}-OH$

**f.** 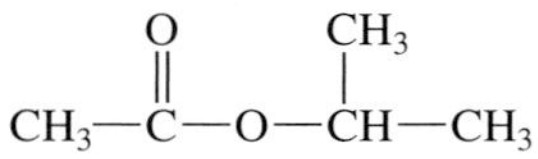 $CH_3-\overset{O}{\overset{\|}{C}}-O-\overset{CH_3}{\overset{|}{C}H}-CH_3$

**16.44** Give the IUPAC and common names (if any) for each of the following compounds:

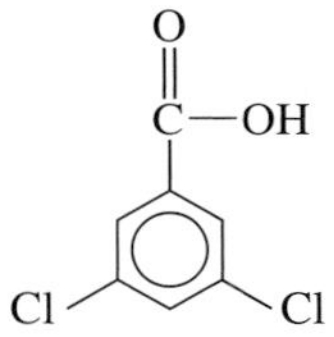

**a.** 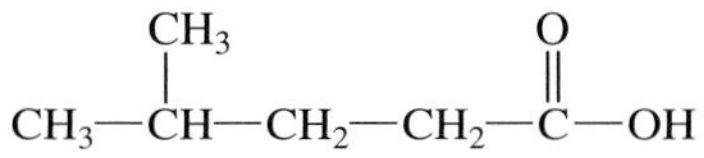 $CH_3-\overset{CH_3}{\overset{|}{C}H}-CH_2-CH_2-\overset{O}{\overset{\|}{C}}-OH$

**b.** $\overset{O}{\overset{\|}{C}}-OH$, Cl, Cl

**c.** $\overset{O}{\overset{\|}{C}}-O-CH_3$

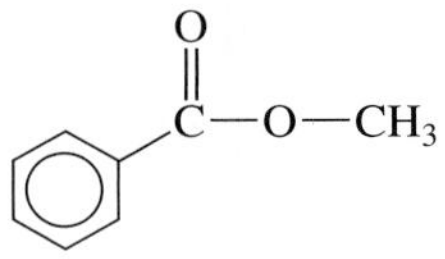

**d.** 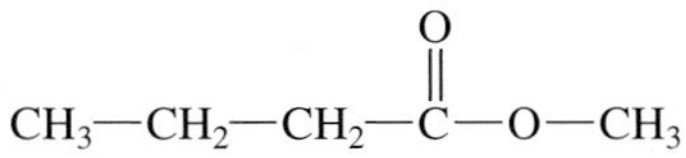 $CH_3-CH_2-CH_2-\overset{O}{\overset{\|}{C}}-O-CH_3$

**e.** 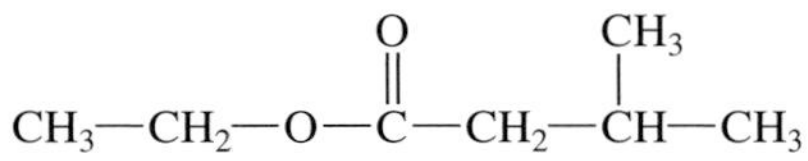 $CH_3-CH_2-O-\overset{O}{\overset{\|}{C}}-CH_2-\overset{CH_3}{\overset{|}{C}H}-CH_3$

**f.** 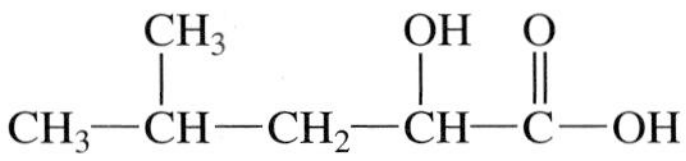 $CH_3-\overset{CH_3}{\overset{|}{C}H}-CH_2-\overset{OH}{\overset{|}{C}H}-\overset{O}{\overset{\|}{C}}-OH$

16.45 Draw the condensed structural formulas of at least three carboxylic acids with the molecular formula $C_5H_{10}O_2$.

**16.46** Draw the condensed structural formulas of at least three esters with the formula $C_4H_8O_2$.

16.47 Draw the condensed structural formula of each of the following:
**a.** methyl acetate
**b.** *p*-chlorobenzoic acid
**c.** $\beta$-chloropropionic acid
**d.** ethyl butanoate
**e.** 3-methylpentanoic acid
**f.** ethyl benzoate

**16.48** Draw the condensed structural formula of each of the following:
**a.** $\alpha$-bromobutyric acid
**b.** ethyl butyrate
**c.** 2-methyloctanoic acid
**d.** 3,5-dimethylhexanoic acid
**e.** propyl acetate
**f.** 3,4-dibromobenzoic acid

16.49 For each of the following pairs, identify the compound that would have the higher boiling point. Explain.

**a.** 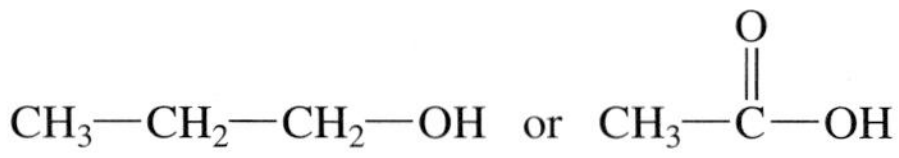 $CH_3-CH_2-CH_2-OH$ or $CH_3-\overset{O}{\overset{\|}{C}}-OH$

**b.** $CH_3-CH_2-CH_2-CH_3$ or $CH_3-CH_2-\overset{O}{\overset{\|}{C}}-OH$

**c.** $CH_3-\overset{O}{\overset{\|}{C}}-OH$ or $CH_3-CH_2-CH_2-\overset{O}{\overset{\|}{C}}-OH$

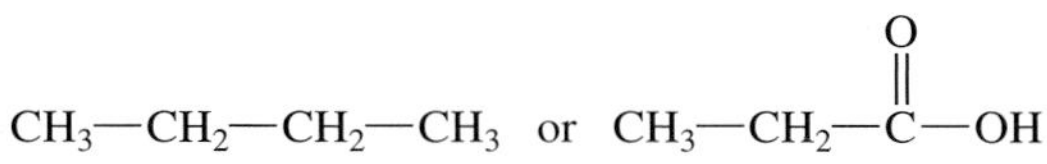

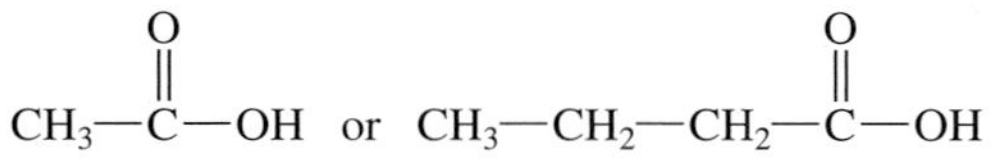

**16.50** For each of the following pairs, identify the compound that would have the higher boiling point. Explain.

**a.** 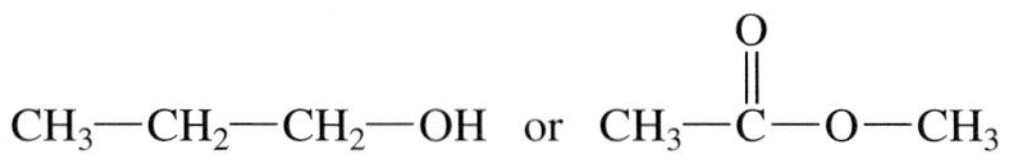 $CH_3-CH_2-CH_2-OH$ or $CH_3-\overset{O}{\overset{\|}{C}}-O-CH_3$

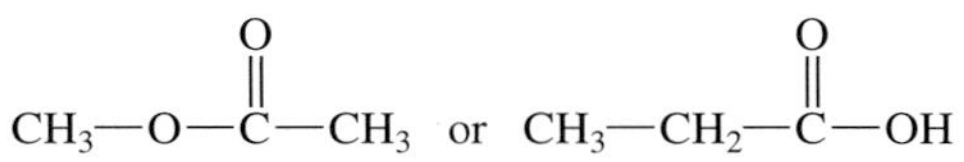

**b.** $CH_3-O-\overset{O}{\overset{\|}{C}}-CH_3$ or $CH_3-CH_2-\overset{O}{\overset{\|}{C}}-OH$

**c.** $CH_3-\overset{O}{\overset{\|}{C}}-O-CH_3$ or $CH_3-CH_2-CH_2-CH_3$

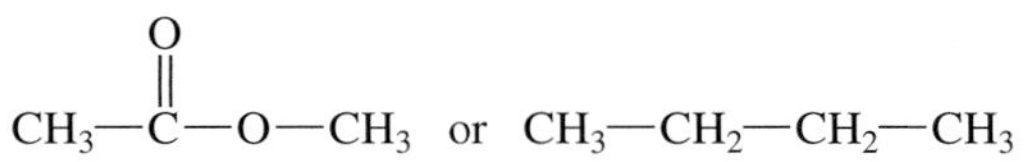

16.51 Why does acetic acid have a higher boiling point than either 1-propanol or methyl formate when they all have the same molar mass?

**16.52** Propionic acid, 1-butanol, and butanal all have the same molar mass. The possible boiling points are 76 °C, 118 °C, and 141 °C. Match the compounds with the boiling points and explain your choice.

16.53 Which of the following compounds are soluble in water?

**a.** $CH_3-CH_2-CH_2-CH_2-CH_3$

**b.** 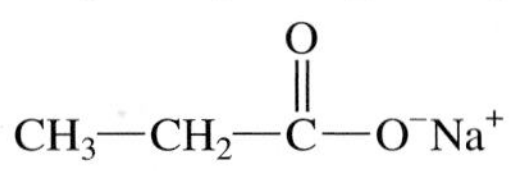 $CH_3-CH_2-\overset{O}{\overset{\|}{C}}-O^-Na^+$

**c.** $CH_3-\overset{O}{\overset{\|}{C}}-O-CH_3$

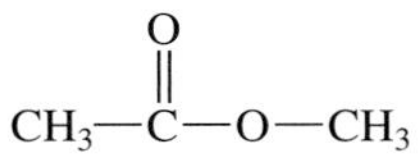

**d.** $CH_3-CH_2-CH_2-OH$

**e.** 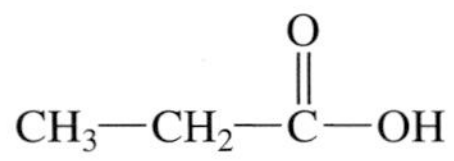 $CH_3-CH_2-\overset{O}{\overset{\|}{C}}-OH$

**16.54** Which of the following compounds are soluble in water?

**a.** $CH_3-CH_2-CH_2-\overset{O}{\overset{\|}{C}}-OH$

**b.** $CH_3-CH_2-\overset{O}{\overset{\|}{C}}-O-CH_2-CH_2-CH_3$

**c.** $CH_3-CH_2-CH_2-CH_3$

**d.** $CH_3-(CH_2)_8-CH_2-OH$

**e.** $CH_3-CH_2-CH_2-O-CH_2-CH_2-CH_3$

**16.55** Draw the products of the following reactions:

**a.** $CH_3-CH_2-\overset{O}{\overset{\|}{C}}-OH + H_2O \rightleftarrows$

**b.** $CH_3-CH_2-\overset{O}{\overset{\|}{C}}-OH + KOH \longrightarrow$

**c.** $CH_3-CH_2-\overset{O}{\overset{\|}{C}}-OH + CH_3-OH \overset{H^+}{\rightleftarrows}$

**d.** 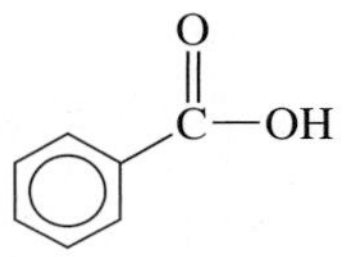 $C_6H_5-\overset{O}{\overset{\|}{C}}-OH + CH_3-CH_2-OH \overset{H^+}{\rightleftarrows}$

**16.56** Draw the products of the following reactions:

**a.** $CH_3-\overset{O}{\overset{\|}{C}}-OH + NaOH \longrightarrow$

**b.** $CH_3-\overset{O}{\overset{\|}{C}}-OH + H_2O \rightleftarrows$

**c.** $CH_3-\overset{CH_3}{\overset{|}{CH}}-\overset{O}{\overset{\|}{C}}-OH + KOH \longrightarrow$

**d.** $CH_3-\overset{CH_3}{\overset{|}{CH}}-\overset{O}{\overset{\|}{C}}-OH + CH_3-OH \overset{H^+}{\rightleftarrows}$

**16.57** Give the IUPAC names of the carboxylic acid and alcohol needed to prepare each of the following esters:

**a.** $CH_3-\overset{CH_3}{\overset{|}{CH}}-CH_2-\overset{O}{\overset{\|}{C}}-O-CH_3$

**b.** 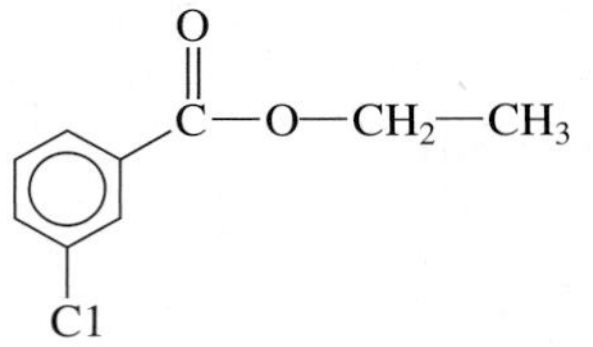 $ClC_6H_4-\overset{O}{\overset{\|}{C}}-O-CH_2-CH_3$ (Cl in the 3-position of the ring)

**c.** $CH_3-(CH_2)_4-\overset{O}{\overset{\|}{C}}-O-CH_3$

**16.58** Give the IUPAC names of the carboxylic acid and alcohol needed to prepare each of the following esters:

**a.** $CH_3-CH_2-CH_2-\overset{O}{\overset{\|}{C}}-O-CH_2-CH_3$

**b.** 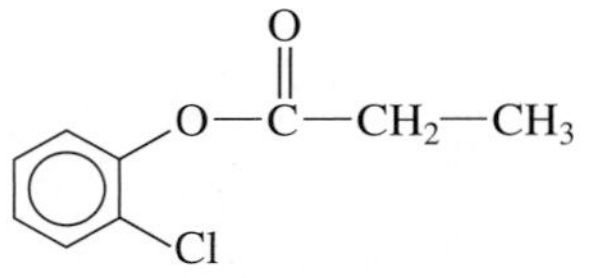 $ClC_6H_4-O-\overset{O}{\overset{\|}{C}}-CH_2-CH_3$ (Cl in the 2-position of the ring)

**c.** $CH_3-\overset{CH_3}{\overset{|}{CH}}-\overset{CH_3}{\overset{|}{CH}}-\overset{O}{\overset{\|}{C}}-O-CH_3$

**16.59** Draw the products of the following reactions:

**a.** $CH_3-CH_2-\overset{O}{\overset{\|}{C}}-O-\overset{CH_3}{\overset{|}{CH}}-CH_3 + H_2O \overset{H^+}{\rightleftarrows}$

**b.** $CH_3-\overset{CH_3}{\overset{|}{CH}}-\overset{O}{\overset{\|}{C}}-O-CH_2-CH_2-CH_3 + NaOH \longrightarrow$

**16.60** Draw the products of the following reactions:

**a.** $CH_3-CH_2-\overset{O}{\overset{\|}{C}}-O-\overset{CH_3}{\overset{|}{CH}}-CH_3 + NaOH \longrightarrow$

**b.** $CH_3-\overset{CH_3}{\overset{|}{CH}}-\overset{O}{\overset{\|}{C}}-O-CH_2-CH_2-CH_3 + H_2O \overset{H^+}{\rightleftarrows}$

## CHALLENGE QUESTIONS

**16.61** Using the reactions we have studied, indicate how you might prepare the following from the starting substance given:
**a.** acetic acid from ethene
**b.** butyric acid from 1-butanol

**16.62** Using the reactions we have studied, indicate how you might prepare the following from the starting substance given:
**a.** pentanoic acid from 1-pentanol
**b.** ethyl acetate from two molecules of ethanol

**16.63** Methyl benzoate is not soluble in water; however, when it is heated with KOH, the ester forms soluble products. Write an equation for the reaction and explain what happens. When HCl is added to the product in solution, a white solid forms. What is the solid?

**16.64** Hexanoic acid is not soluble in water. However, when hexanoic acid is added to a NaOH solution, a soluble product forms. Explain.

16.65 Salicylic acid could be named *o*-hydroxybenzoic acid.
  **a.** What two reactive functional groups are present?
  **b.** Draw the condensed structural formula of the ester product that forms when the hydroxyl group of salicylic acid reacts with acetic acid.
  **c.** Draw the condensed structural formula of methyl salicylate, oil of wintergreen, formed when salicylic acid forms an ester with methyl alcohol.

**16.66** What volume (mL) of 0.100 M NaOH is needed to neutralize 3.00 g of benzoic acid?

# ANSWERS

## ANSWERS TO STUDY CHECKS

**16.1** $C_6H_5-CH_2-CH_2-\overset{\overset{O}{\|}}{C}-OH$

**16.2** $CH_3-CH_2-CH_2-\overset{\overset{O}{\|}}{C}-OH$

**16.3** Two methanoic acid molecules form a dimer, which gives an effective molar mass that is double that of the single acid molecule. Thus, a higher boiling point is required than for ethanol.

**16.4** $H-\overset{\overset{O}{\|}}{C}-OH + H_2O \rightleftharpoons H-\overset{\overset{O}{\|}}{C}-O^- + H_3O^+$

**16.5** butanoic acid, butyric acid

**16.6** propanoic (propionic) acid and 1-pentanol

**16.7** $CH_3-CH_2-CH_2-CH_2-CH_2-CH_2-\overset{\overset{O}{\|}}{C}-O-CH_2-CH_3$

**16.8** propanoic (propionic) acid and ethanol

**16.9** $C_6H_5-\overset{\overset{O}{\|}}{C}-O^-K^+ + CH_3-OH$

## ANSWERS TO SELECTED QUESTIONS AND PROBLEMS

**16.1** methanoic acid (formic acid)

**16.3** Each compound contains three carbon atoms. They differ because propanal, an aldehyde, contains a carbonyl group bonded to a hydrogen. In propanoic acid, the carbonyl group connects to a hydroxyl group forming a carboxyl group.

**16.5** **a.** ethanoic acid (acetic acid)
  **b.** butanoic acid (butyric acid)
  **c.** 2-chloropropanoic acid ($\alpha$-chloropropionic acid)
  **d.** 3-methylhexanoic acid
  **e.** 3,4-dihydroxybenzoic acid
  **f.** 4-bromopentanoic acid

**16.7**
  **a.** $CH_3-CH_2-\overset{\overset{O}{\|}}{C}-OH$
  **b.** $C_6H_5-\overset{\overset{O}{\|}}{C}-OH$
  **c.** $Cl-CH_2-\overset{\overset{O}{\|}}{C}-OH$
  **d.** $HO-CH_2-CH_2-\overset{\overset{O}{\|}}{C}-OH$
  **e.** $CH_3-CH_2-\underset{\underset{CH_3}{|}}{CH}-\overset{\overset{O}{\|}}{C}-OH$
  **f.** $CH_3-CH_2-\underset{\underset{Br}{|}}{CH}-CH_2-\underset{\underset{Br}{|}}{CH}-CH_2-\overset{\overset{O}{\|}}{C}-OH$

**16.9** **a.** $H-\overset{\overset{O}{\|}}{C}-OH$  **b.** $CH_3-\overset{\overset{O}{\|}}{C}-OH$
  **c.** $CH_3-\underset{}{\overset{\overset{CH_3}{|}}{CH}}-CH_2-\overset{\overset{O}{\|}}{C}-OH$
  **d.** $C_5H_9-CH_2-\overset{\overset{O}{\|}}{C}-OH$ (cyclopentyl)

**16.11** **a.** Butanoic acid has a higher molar mass and would have a higher boiling point.
  **b.** Propanoic acid can form more hydrogen bonds and would have a higher boiling point.
  **c.** Butanoic acid can form hydrogen bonds and would have a higher boiling point.

**16.13** **a.** Propanoic acid has the smaller alkyl group, which makes it more soluble.
  **b.** Propanoic acid forms more hydrogen bonds.

**16.15** **a.** $H-\overset{\overset{O}{\|}}{C}-OH + H_2O \rightleftharpoons H-\overset{\overset{O}{\|}}{C}-O^- + H_3O^+$
  **b.** $CH_3-CH_2-\overset{\overset{O}{\|}}{C}-OH + H_2O \rightleftharpoons CH_3-CH_2-\overset{\overset{O}{\|}}{C}-O^- + H_3O^+$
  **c.** $CH_3-\overset{\overset{O}{\|}}{C}-OH + H_2O \rightleftharpoons CH_3-\overset{\overset{O}{\|}}{C}-O^- + H_3O^+$

**16.17** **a.** $H-\overset{\overset{O}{\|}}{C}-OH + NaOH \longrightarrow H-\overset{\overset{O}{\|}}{C}-O^-Na^+ + H_2O$

**b.** $CH_3-CH_2-\overset{O}{\overset{\|}{C}}-OH + NaOH \longrightarrow$

$$CH_3-CH_2-\overset{O}{\overset{\|}{C}}-O^-Na^+ + H_2O$$

**c.** $C_6H_5-\overset{O}{\overset{\|}{C}}-OH + NaOH \longrightarrow C_6H_5-\overset{O}{\overset{\|}{C}}-O^-Na^+ + H_2O$

**16.19 a.** sodium methanoate, sodium formate
**b.** sodium propanoate, sodium propionate
**c.** sodium benzoate

**16.21 a.** aldehyde
**b.** ester
**c.** ketone
**d.** carboxylic acid

**16.23 a.** $CH_3-\overset{O}{\overset{\|}{C}}-O-CH_3$

**b.** $CH_3-CH_2-CH_2-\overset{O}{\overset{\|}{C}}-O-CH_3$

**c.** $C_6H_5-\overset{O}{\overset{\|}{C}}-O-CH_3$

**16.25 a.** $CH_3-CH_2-\overset{O}{\overset{\|}{C}}-O-CH_2-CH_2-CH_3$

**b.** $CH_3-CH_2-CH_2-CH_2-\overset{O}{\overset{\|}{C}}-O-\underset{}{\overset{CH_3}{\overset{|}{C}H}}-CH_3$

**16.27 a.** methanoic acid (formic acid) and methanol (methyl alcohol)
**b.** ethanoic acid (acetic acid) and methanol (methyl alcohol)
**c.** butanoic acid (butyric acid) and methanol (methyl alcohol)
**d.** 3-methylbutanoic acid ($\beta$-methylbutyric acid) and ethanol (ethyl alcohol)

**16.29 a.** methyl methanoate (methyl formate)
**b.** methyl ethanoate (methyl acetate)
**c.** methyl butanoate (methyl butyrate)
**d.** ethyl 3-methylbutanoate (ethyl $\beta$-methyl butyrate)

**16.31**

**a.** $CH_3-\overset{O}{\overset{\|}{C}}-O-CH_3$

**b.** $H-\overset{O}{\overset{\|}{C}}-O-CH_2-CH_2-CH_2-CH_3$

**c.** $CH_3-CH_2-CH_2-CH_2-\overset{O}{\overset{\|}{C}}-O-CH_2-CH_3$

**d.** $CH_3-CH_2-\overset{O}{\overset{\|}{C}}-O-CH_2-\overset{Br}{\overset{|}{C}H}-CH_3$

**16.33 a.** pentyl ethanoate (pentyl acetate)
**b.** octyl ethanoate (octyl acetate)
**c.** pentyl butanoate (pentyl butyrate)

**16.35**

**a.** $CH_3-\overset{O}{\overset{\|}{C}}-OH$

**b.** $CH_3-CH_2-CH_2-CH_2-OH$

**c.** $CH_3-O-\overset{O}{\overset{\|}{C}}-CH_3$

**16.37** The products of the acid hydrolysis of an ester are an alcohol and a carboxylic acid.

**16.39 a.** $CH_3-CH_2-\overset{O}{\overset{\|}{C}}-O^-Na^+$ and $CH_3-OH$

**b.** $CH_3-\overset{O}{\overset{\|}{C}}-OH$ and $CH_3-CH_2-CH_2-OH$

**c.** $CH_3-CH_2-CH_2-\overset{O}{\overset{\|}{C}}-OH$ and $CH_3-CH_2-OH$

**d.** $C_6H_5-\overset{O}{\overset{\|}{C}}-OH$ and $CH_3-CH_2-OH$

**e.** $C_6H_5-\overset{O}{\overset{\|}{C}}-O^-Na^+$ and $CH_3-CH_2-OH$

**16.41 a.** $CH_3-CH_2-CH_2-O-\overset{O}{\overset{\|}{C}}-CH_3$

**b.** $CH_3-CH_2-CH_2-OH + HO-\overset{O}{\overset{\|}{C}}-CH_3 \xrightleftharpoons{H^+,\ heat}$

$$CH_3-CH_2-CH_2-O-\overset{O}{\overset{\|}{C}}-CH_3 + H_2O$$

**c.** $CH_3-CH_2-CH_2-O-\overset{O}{\overset{\|}{C}}-CH_3 + H_2O \xrightleftharpoons{H^+}$

$$CH_3-CH_2-CH_2-OH + HO-\overset{O}{\overset{\|}{C}}-CH_3$$

**d.**

$$CH_3-CH_2-CH_2-O-\overset{O}{\overset{\|}{C}}-CH_3 + NaOH \xrightarrow{Heat}$$

$$CH_3-CH_2-CH_2-OH + Na^+\ {}^-O-\overset{O}{\overset{\|}{C}}-CH_3$$

**e.** 74.5 mL of 0.208 M NaOH

**16.43 a.** 3-methylbutanoic acid, $\beta$-methylbutyric acid
**b.** ethyl benzoate
**c.** ethyl propanoate, ethyl propionate
**d.** 2-chlorobenzoic acid, *ortho*-chlorobenzoic acid
**e.** 4-hydroxypentanoic acid
**f.** 2-propyl ethanoate, isopropyl acetate

**16.45**

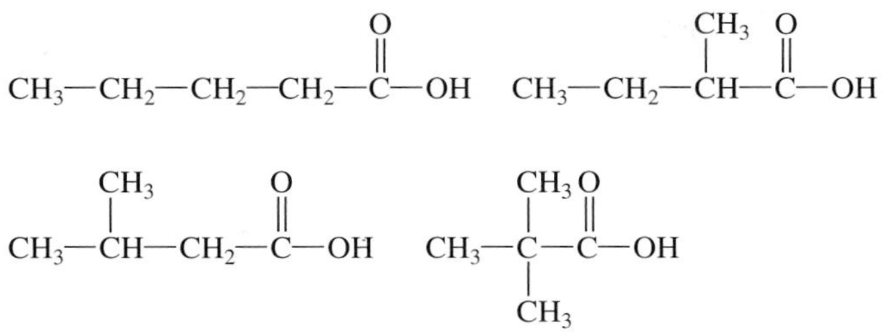

$CH_3-CH_2-CH_2-CH_2-\overset{O}{\overset{\|}{C}}-OH$ $\quad CH_3-CH_2-\underset{}{\overset{CH_3}{\overset{|}{CH}}}-\overset{O}{\overset{\|}{C}}-OH$

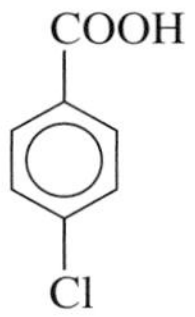

$CH_3-\overset{CH_3}{\overset{|}{CH}}-CH_2-\overset{O}{\overset{\|}{C}}-OH$ $\quad CH_3-\underset{CH_3}{\underset{|}{\overset{CH_3}{\overset{|}{C}}}}-\overset{O}{\overset{\|}{C}}-OH$

**16.47 a.** 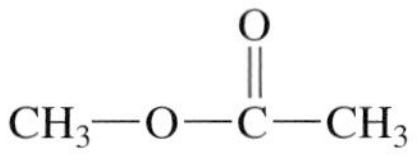 $CH_3-O-\overset{O}{\overset{\|}{C}}-CH_3$ $\quad$ **b.** $Cl-C_6H_4-COOH$ (para)

**c.** $Cl-CH_2-CH_2-\overset{O}{\overset{\|}{C}}-OH$

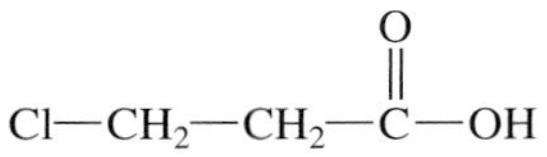

**d.** 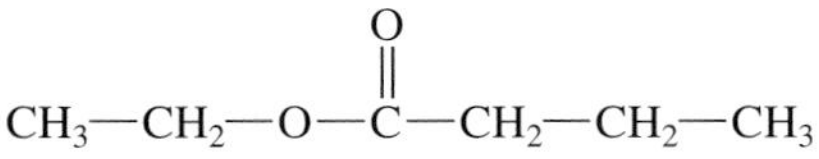 $CH_3-CH_2-O-\overset{O}{\overset{\|}{C}}-CH_2-CH_2-CH_3$

**e.** 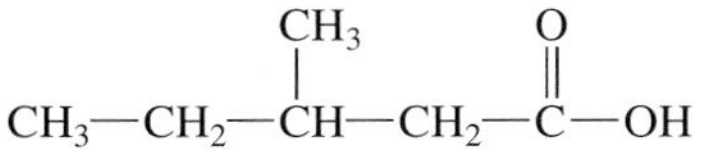 $CH_3-CH_2-\overset{CH_3}{\overset{|}{CH}}-CH_2-\overset{O}{\overset{\|}{C}}-OH$

**f.** 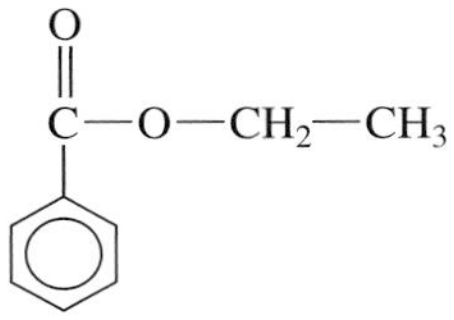 $C_6H_5-\overset{O}{\overset{\|}{C}}-O-CH_2-CH_3$

**16.49 a.** Ethanoic acid has a higher boiling point than 1-propanol because two molecules of ethanoic acid hydrogen bond to form a dimer, which effectively doubles the molar mass and requires a higher temperature to reach the boiling point.
**b.** Propanoic acid forms hydrogen bonds, but butane does not.
**c.** Butanoic acid has a higher molar mass than ethanoic acid and requires a higher temperature to reach the boiling point.

**16.51** The presence of two polar groups in the carboxyl group allows hydrogen bonding and the formation of a dimer that doubles the effective molar mass.

**16.53** **b**, **c**, **d**, and **e** are all soluble in water

**16.55 a.** 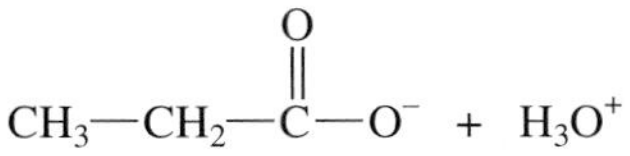 $CH_3-CH_2-\overset{O}{\overset{\|}{C}}-O^- + H_3O^+$

**b.** $CH_3-CH_2-\overset{O}{\overset{\|}{C}}-O^-K^+ + H_2O$

**c.** $CH_3-CH_2-\overset{O}{\overset{\|}{C}}-O-CH_3 + H_2O$

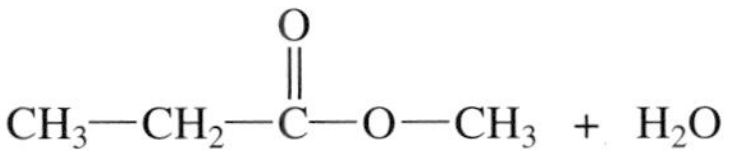

**d.** 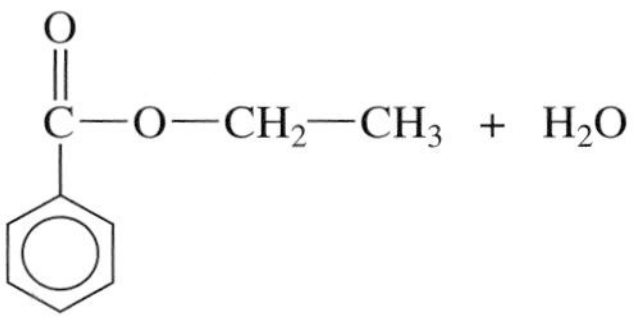 $C_6H_5-\overset{O}{\overset{\|}{C}}-O-CH_2-CH_3 + H_2O$

**16.57 a.** 3-methylbutanoic acid and methanol
**b.** 3-chlorobenzoic acid and ethanol
**c.** hexanoic acid and methanol

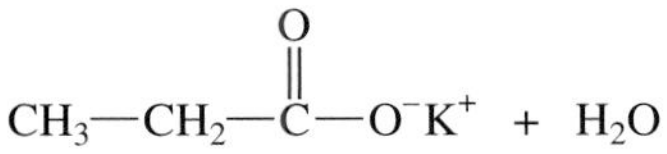

**16.59 a.** 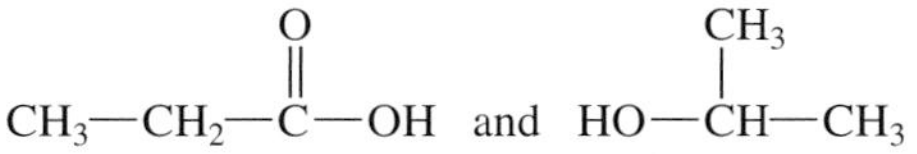 $CH_3-CH_2-\overset{O}{\overset{\|}{C}}-OH$ and $HO-\overset{CH_3}{\overset{|}{CH}}-CH_3$

**b.** 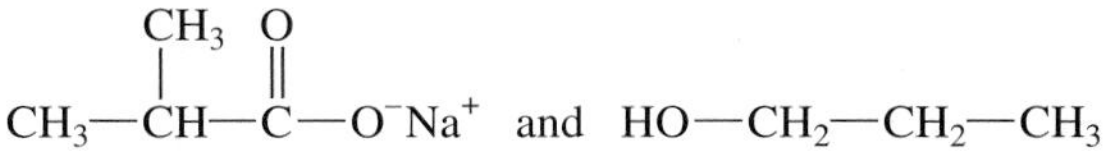 $CH_3-\overset{CH_3}{\overset{|}{CH}}-\overset{O}{\overset{\|}{C}}-O^-Na^+$ and $HO-CH_2-CH_2-CH_3$

**16.61**

**a.** 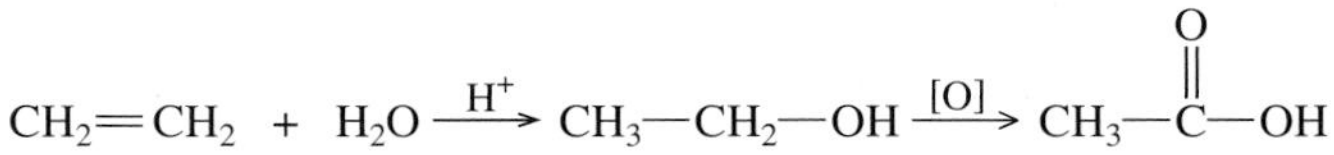 $CH_2{=}CH_2 + H_2O \xrightarrow{H^+} CH_3-CH_2-OH \xrightarrow{[O]} CH_3-\overset{O}{\overset{\|}{C}}-OH$

**b.** 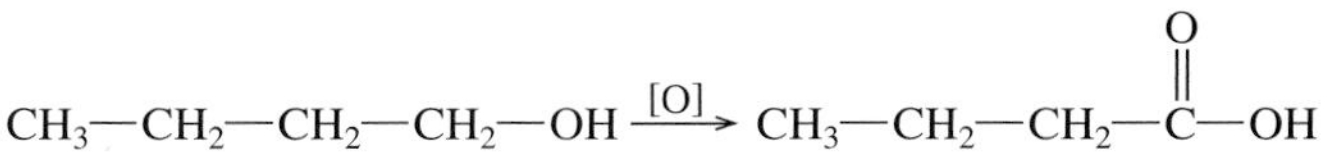 $CH_3-CH_2-CH_2-CH_2-OH \xrightarrow{[O]} CH_3-CH_2-CH_2-\overset{O}{\overset{\|}{C}}-OH$

**16.63** $C_6H_5-\overset{O}{\overset{\|}{C}}-O-CH_3 + KOH \longrightarrow$

$C_6H_5-\overset{O}{\overset{\|}{C}}-O^-K^+ + CH_3-OH$

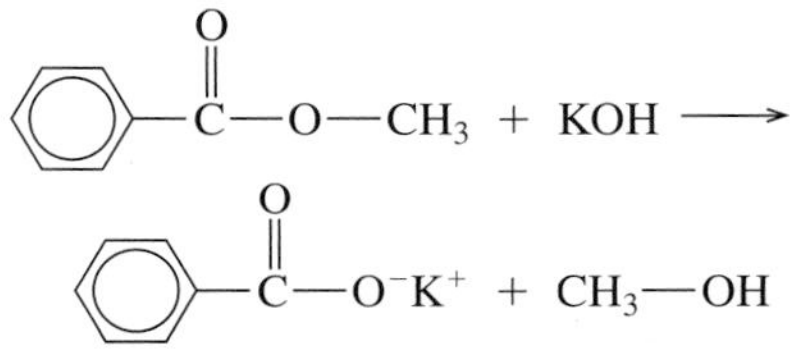

In KOH solution, the ester undergoes saponification to form soluble salt of potassium benzoate. When acid is added to the soluble salt potassium benzoate, it is converted to insoluble benzoic acid.

**16.65 a.** phenol and carboxylic acid

**b.** 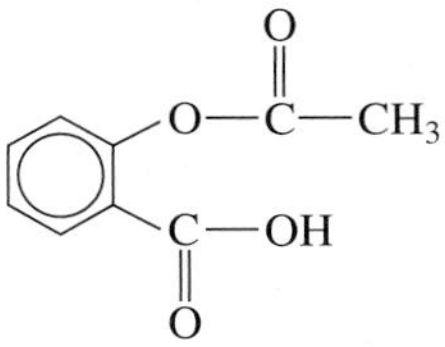 $C_6H_4(-O-\overset{O}{\overset{\|}{C}}-CH_3)(-\overset{O}{\overset{\|}{C}}-OH)$ (ortho)

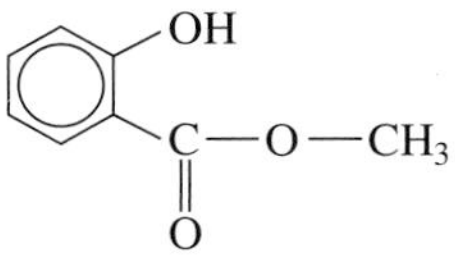

**c.** $C_6H_4(-OH)(-\overset{O}{\overset{\|}{C}}-O-CH_3)$ (ortho)

# 17 Lipids

LOOKING AHEAD


17.1 Lipids

17.2 Fatty Acids

17.3 Waxes, Fats, and Oils

17.4 Chemical Properties of Triacylglycerols

17.5 Glycerophospholipids

17.6 Sphingolipids

17.7 Steroids: Cholesterol, Bile Salts, and Steroid Hormones

17.8 Cell Membranes


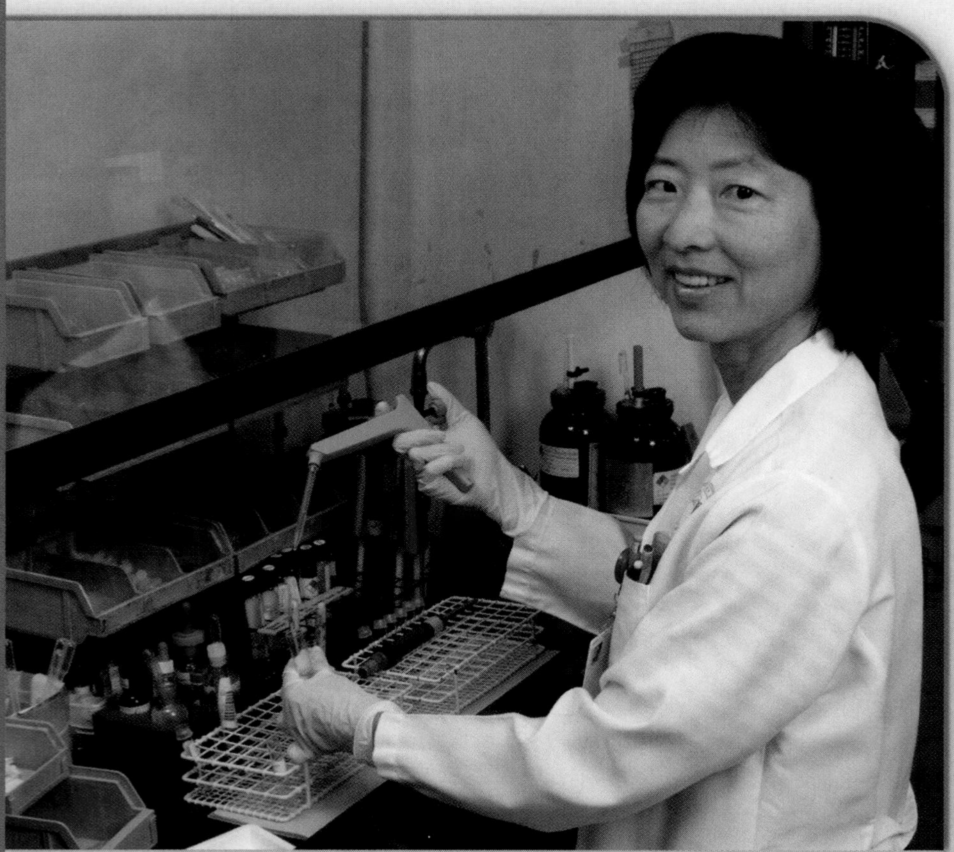

*"In our toxicology lab, we measure the drugs in samples of urine or blood," says Penny Peng, assistant supervisor of chemistry, toxicology lab, Santa Clara Valley Medical Center. "But first we extract the drugs from the fluid and concentrate them so they can be detected in the machine we use. We extract the drugs by using different organic solvents such as methanol, ethyl acetate, or methylene chloride, and by changing the pH. We evaporate most of the organic solvent to concentrate any drugs it may contain. A small sample of the concentrate is placed into a machine called a gas chromatograph. As the gas moves over a column, the drugs in it are separated. From the results, we can identify as many as 10 to 15 different drugs from one urine sample."*

Visit **www.masteringchemistry.com** for self-study materials and instructor-assigned homework.

When we talk of fats and oils, waxes, steroids, cholesterol, and fat-soluble vitamins, we are discussing lipids. Lipids are naturally occurring compounds that vary considerably in structure but share a common feature of being soluble in nonpolar solvents but not in water. Fats, which are one family of lipids, have many functions in the body, such as storing energy and protecting and insulating internal organs. Other types of lipids are found in nerve fibers and in hormones, which act as chemical messengers. Lipids are components of cell membranes. Because they are not soluble in water, they function to separate the internal contents of cells from the external environment.

Many people are concerned about the amounts of saturated fats and cholesterol in our diets. Researchers suggest that saturated fats and cholesterol are associated with diseases such as diabetes; cancers of the breast, pancreas, and colon; and atherosclerosis, a condition in which deposits of lipid materials (plaques) accumulate in the coronary blood vessels. In atherosclerosis, plaques restrict the flow of blood to the tissue, causing necrosis (death) of the tissue. In the heart, plaque accumulation could result in a *myocardial infarction* (heart attack).

The American Institute for Cancer Research (AICR) has recommended that our diet contain more fiber and starch by adding more vegetables, fruits, and whole grains and moderate amounts of foods with low levels of fat and cholesterol such as fish, poultry, lean meats, and low-fat dairy products. AICR also suggests that we limit our intake of foods high in fat and cholesterol such as eggs, nuts, french fries, fatty or organ meats, cheeses, butter, and coconut and palm oil.

## 17.1 Lipids

**LEARNING GOAL**
Describe the classes of lipids.

**Lipids** are a family of biomolecules that have the common property of being soluble in organic solvents but not in water. The word "lipid" comes from the Greek word *lipos*, meaning "fat" or "lard." Typically, the lipid content of a cell can be extracted using a nonpolar solvent such as ether or chloroform. Lipids are an important feature in cell membranes, fat-soluble vitamins, and steroid hormones.

### Types of Lipids

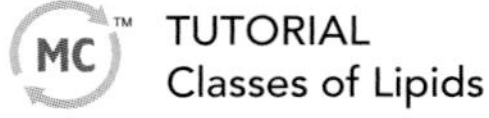

TUTORIAL
Classes of Lipids

Within the lipid family, there are specific structures that distinguish the different types of lipids. Lipids such as waxes, fats, oils, and glycerophospholipids are esters that can be hydrolyzed to give fatty acids along with other products, including an alcohol. Sphingolipids contain an alcohol called sphingosine, and glycosphingolipids contain a carbohydrate as well. Steroids do not contain fatty acids but are characterized by the steroid nucleus of four fused carbon rings. Steroids cannot be hydrolyzed. Figure 17.1 illustrates the types and general structures of lipids we will discuss in this chapter.

**SAMPLE PROBLEM 17.1**

**Classes of Lipids**

What type of lipid does not contain fatty acids?

SOLUTION

The steroids are a group of lipids with no fatty acids.

STUDY CHECK

What type of lipid contains a carbohydrate?

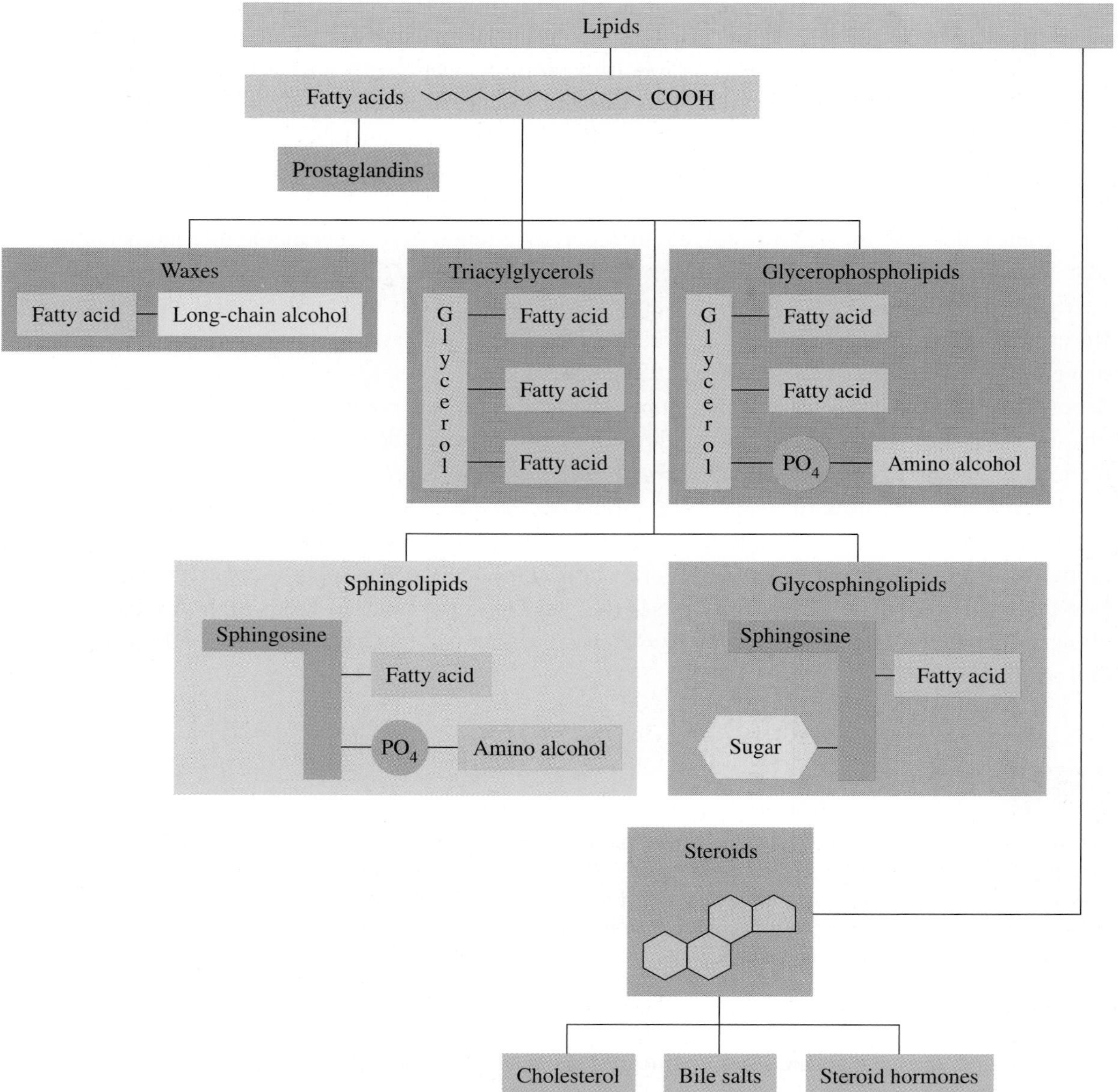


**FIGURE 17.1** Structures for some classes of lipids that are naturally occurring compounds in cells and tissues.
**Q** What property do waxes, triacylglycerols, and steroids have in common?

## QUESTIONS AND PROBLEMS

### Lipids

**17.1** What are some functions of lipids in the body?

**17.2** What are some of the different kinds of lipids?

**17.3** Lipids are not soluble in water. Are lipids polar or nonpolar molecules?

**17.4** Which of the following solvents might be used to dissolve an oil stain?

**a.** water  **b.** $CCl_4$
**c.** diethyl ether  **d.** benzene
**e.** NaCl solution

# 17.2 Fatty Acids

**LEARNING GOAL**

Draw the condensed structural formula of a fatty acid and identify it as saturated or unsaturated.

The fatty acids are the simplest type of lipids and are found as components in more complex lipids. A **fatty acid** contains a long unbranched carbon chain attached to a carboxylic acid group at one end. Although the carboxylic acid part is hydrophilic, the long hydrophobic carbon chain makes long-chain fatty acids insoluble in water. Most naturally occurring fatty acids have an even number of carbon atoms, usually between 10 and 20. An example of a fatty acid is lauric acid, a 12-carbon acid found in coconut oil. In a simplified structure of a fatty acid called a line-bond formula, the carbon chain is written as a zigzag line that indicates the bonds between carbon atoms. In a zigzag line representation of a fatty acid, the ends and bends of the zigzag line are the carbon atoms. The structural formula of lauric acid can be written in several forms as follows:

SELF STUDY ACTIVITY
Fats

**Writing Formulas for Lauric Acid**

$$CH_3-(CH_2)_{10}-\overset{\overset{\displaystyle O}{\|}}{C}-OH \qquad CH_3-(CH_2)_{10}-COOH$$

$$CH_3-CH_2-CH_2-CH_2-CH_2-CH_2-CH_2-CH_2-CH_2-CH_2-CH_2-C(=O)OH$$

Condensed structural formula

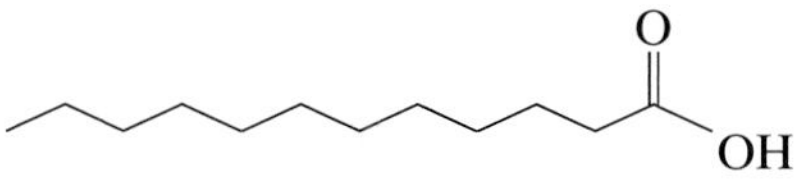

Line-bond structural formula

A **saturated fatty acid** contains only single carbon–carbon bonds, which makes the properties of a long-chain fatty acid similar to those of an alkane. In a **monounsaturated fatty acid**, the long carbon chain has one double bond, which makes its properties similar to those of an alkene. A **polyunsaturated fatty acid** has at least two carbon–carbon double bonds. Table 17.1 lists some of the typical fatty acids in lipids.

## Cis and Trans Isomers of Unsaturated Fatty Acids

Unsaturated fatty acids can be written as cis and trans isomers in the same way as the cis and trans alkene structures we looked at in Chapter 12. For example, oleic acid, a monounsaturated fatty acid found in olives and corn, has one double bond at carbon 9. We can show its cis and trans structural formulas using the line-bond notation. The cis structure is the most prevalent isomer found in naturally occurring unsaturated fatty acids. In the cis isomer, the carbon chain has a "kink" at the double bond site. As we will see, the cis bond has a major impact on the properties of unsaturated fatty acids.

*cis*-Oleic acid
cis double bond

*trans*-Oleic acid
trans double bond

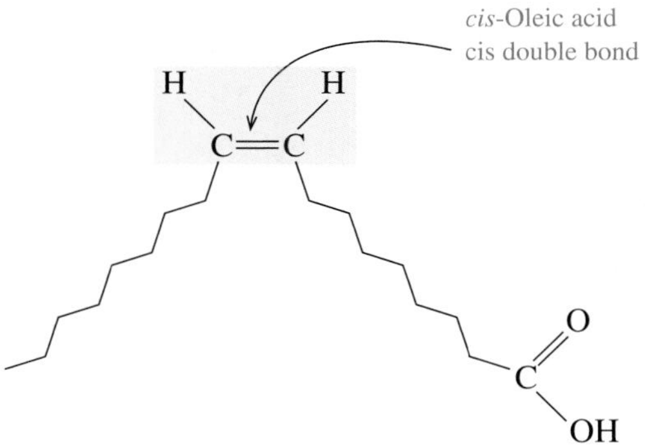

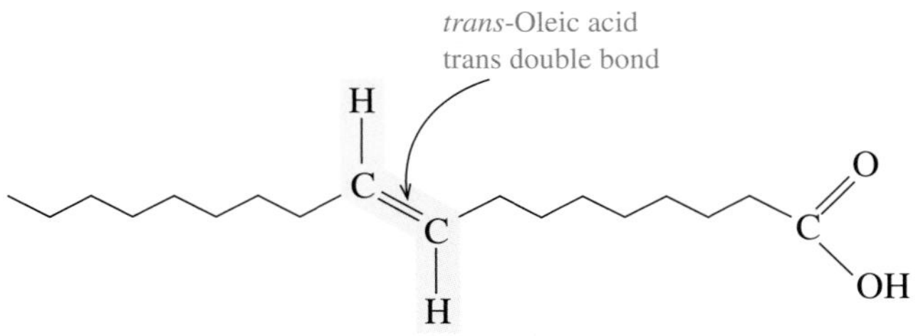

The human body is capable of synthesizing most fatty acids from carbohydrates or other fatty acids. However, humans do not synthesize sufficient amounts of polyunsaturated fatty acids, such as linoleic acid, linolenic acid, and arachidonic acid. Because these fatty acids must be obtained from the diet, they are known as *essential fatty acids*. In infants, a deficiency of essential fatty acids can cause skin dermatitis. However, the role of fatty acids in adult nutrition is not well understood. Adults do not usually have a deficiency of essential fatty acids.

TABLE 17.1 Structures and Melting Points of Common Fatty Acids

| Name | Carbon Atoms | Source | Melting Point (°C) | Structures |
|---|---|---|---|---|
| **Saturated Fatty Acids** | | | | |
| Lauric acid | 12 | Coconut | 43 | $CH_3-(CH_2)_{10}-COOH$ 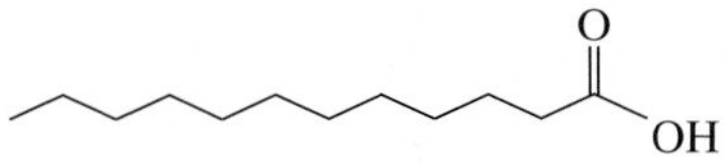 |
| Myristic acid | 14 | Nutmeg | 54 | $CH_3-(CH_2)_{12}-COOH$ 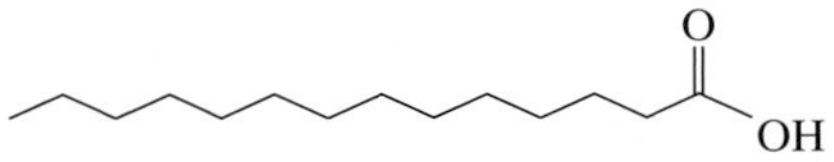 |
| Palmitic acid | 16 | Palm | 62 | $CH_3-(CH_2)_{14}-COOH$ 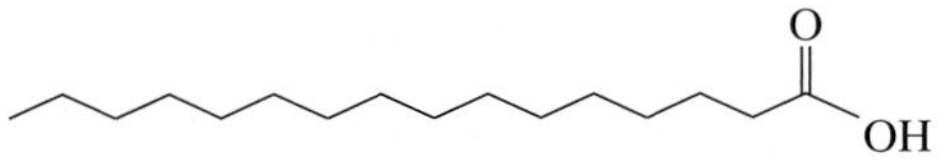 |
| Stearic acid | 18 | Animal fat | 69 | $CH_3-(CH_2)_{16}-COOH$ 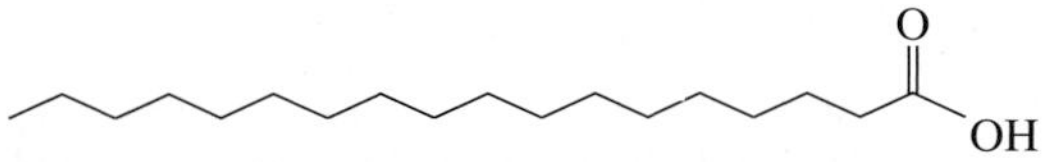 |
| **Monounsaturated Fatty Acids** | | | | |
| Palmitoleic acid | 16 | Butter | 0 | $CH_3-(CH_2)_5-CH{=}CH-(CH_2)_7-COOH$ 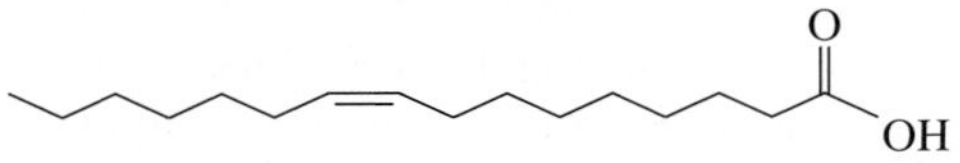 |
| Oleic acid | 18 | Olives, corn | 13 | $CH_3-(CH_2)_7-CH{=}CH-(CH_2)_7-COOH$ 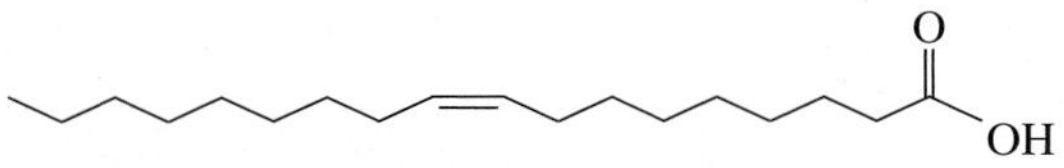 |
| **Polyunsaturated Fatty Acids** | | | | |
| Linoleic acid | 18 | Soybeans, sunflowers | −9 | $CH_3-(CH_2)_4-CH{=}CH-CH_2-CH{=}CH-(CH_2)_7-COOH$ 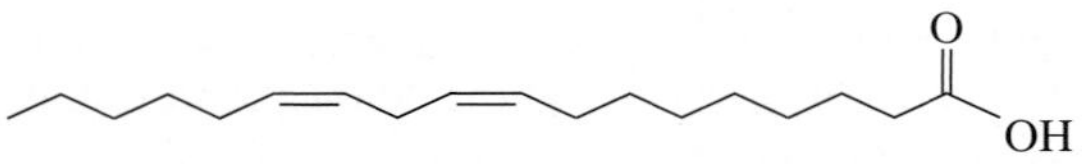 |
| Linolenic acid | 18 | Corn | −17 | $CH_3-(CH_2-CH{=}CH)_3-(CH_2)_7-COOH$ 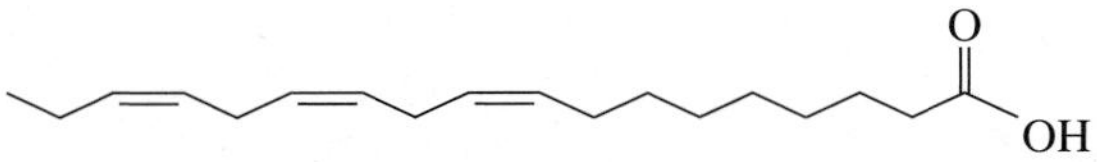 |
| Arachidonic acid | 20 | Meat, eggs, fish | −50 | $CH_3-(CH_2)_3-(CH_2-CH{=}CH)_4-(CH_2)_3-COOH$ 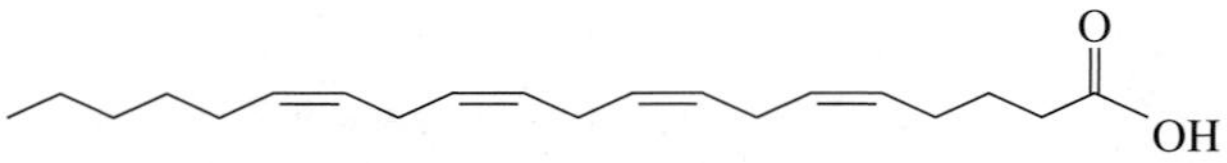 |

## Properties of Fatty Acids

Saturated fatty acids fit close together in a regular pattern, which allows strong attractions to occur between the carbon chains. As a result, a significant amount of energy and high temperatures are required to separate the fatty acids and melt the fat. As the length of the carbon chain increases, more interactions occur between the carbon chains, which results in higher melting points. Saturated fatty acids are usually solids at room temperature.

In unsaturated fatty acids, the cis double bonds cause the carbon chain to bend or "kink," which gives the molecules an irregular shape. As a result, fewer interactions occur

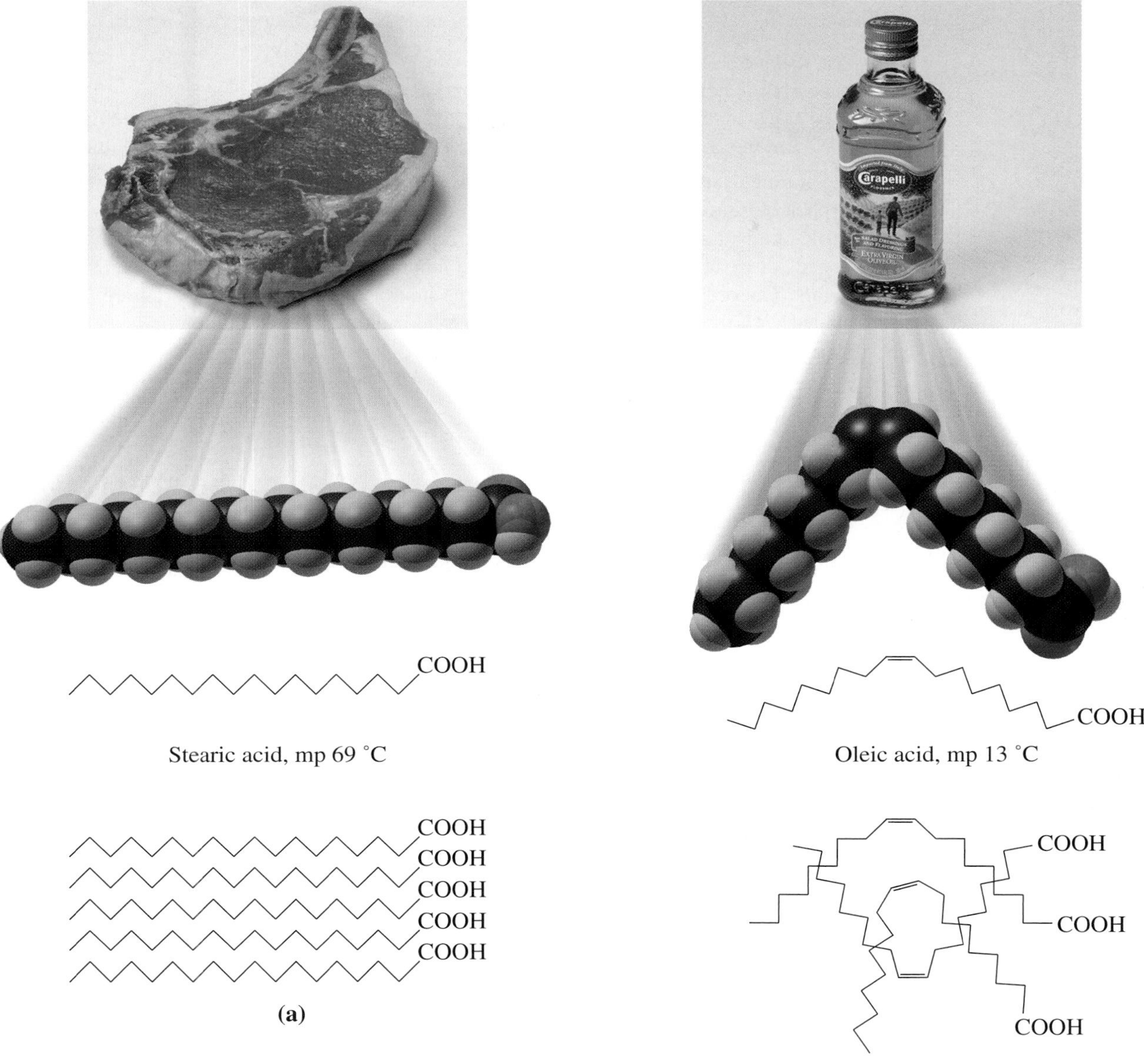


**FIGURE 17.2** **(a)** In saturated fatty acids, the molecules fit closely together to give high melting points. **(b)** In unsaturated fatty acids, molecules cannot pack closely together, resulting in lower melting points.

Q Why does the cis double bond affect the melting points of unsaturated fatty acids?

between carbon chains. Consequently, less energy is required to separate the molecules, which makes the melting points of unsaturated fats lower than those of saturated fats. (See Figure 17.2.) Most unsaturated fats are liquid oils at room temperature.

We might think of saturated fatty acids as potato chips with matching shapes that stack close together in a container. Similarly, irregularly shaped chips would be like unsaturated fatty acids that do not pack close together.

**CONCEPT CHECK 17.1**

### Fatty Acids

**1.** Using Table 17.1, identify the following:

**a.** an 18-carbon fatty acid that is saturated
**b.** a monounsaturated fatty acid found in olives
**c.** an 18-carbon fatty acid with three double bonds

## Solubility of Fats and Oils

Place some water in a small bowl. Add a drop of a vegetable oil. Then add a few more drops of the oil. Record your observations. Now add a few drops of liquid soap and mix. Record your observations.

Place a small amount of fat such as margarine, butter, shortening, or vegetable oil on a dish or plate. Run water over it. Record your observations. Mix some soap with the fat substance and run water over it again. Record your observations.

### QUESTIONS

1. Do the drops of oil in the water separate or do they come together? Explain.
2. How does the soap affect the oil layer?
3. Why don't the fats on the dish or plate wash off with water?
4. In general, what is the solubility of lipids in water?
5. Why does soap help to wash the fats off the plate?

TUTORIAL
Structures and Properties of Fatty Acids

**2.** List the fatty acids in part 1 in order of increasing melting points. Explain.

ANSWER

**1. a.** Stearic acid is a saturated 18-carbon fatty acid.
**b.** Oleic acid is a monounsaturated fatty acid with one double bond found in olives.
**c.** Linolenic acid is a polyunsaturated 18-carbon fatty acid with three double bonds.

**2.** Saturated fatty acids have carbon chains with only single bonds that allow them to pack close together and form molecular attractions. Unsaturated fats contain cis double bonds that place a "kink" in the carbon chain that does not allow the fatty acids to pack close together. Thus, unsaturated fats have lower melting points than saturated fats. The order of increasing melting points for the fatty acids in part 1 are linolenic acid with three double bonds (−9 °C), oleic acid with one double bond (13 °C), and stearic acid with single bonds (69 °C).

SAMPLE PROBLEM 17.2

### Structures and Properties of Fatty Acids

Consider the condensed structural formula of oleic acid:

$$CH_3-(CH_2)_7-CH{=}CH-(CH_2)_7-\overset{\overset{\displaystyle O}{\|}}{C}-OH$$

**a.** Why is this substance an acid?
**b.** How many carbon atoms are in oleic acid?
**c.** Is it a saturated or unsaturated fatty acid?
**d.** Is it most likely to be solid or liquid at room temperature?
**e.** Would it be soluble in water?

SOLUTION

**a.** Oleic acid contains a carboxylic acid group.
**b.** It contains 18 carbon atoms.
**c.** It is an unsaturated fatty acid.
**d.** It is liquid at room temperature.
**e.** No, its long hydrocarbon chain makes it insoluble in water.

STUDY CHECK

Palmitoleic acid is a fatty acid with the following formula:

$$CH_3-(CH_2)_5-CH{=}CH-(CH_2)_7-\overset{\overset{\displaystyle O}{\|}}{C}-OH$$

**a.** How many carbon atoms are in palmitoleic acid?
**b.** Is it a saturated or unsaturated fatty acid?
**c.** Is it most likely to be solid or liquid at room temperature?

## Prostaglandins

**Prostaglandins (PGs)** are hormone-like substances produced in low amounts in most cells of the body. The prostaglandins, also known as *eicosanoids*, are formed from arachidonic acid, the polyunsaturated fatty acid with 20 carbon atoms (*eicos* is the Greek word for 20). Swedish chemists first discovered prostaglandins and named them "prostaglandin E" (soluble in ether) and "prostaglandin F" (soluble in phosphate buffer, or *fosfat* in Swedish). The various kinds of prostaglandins differ by the substituents attached to the five-carbon ring. Prostaglandin E (PGE) has a ketone group on carbon 9, whereas prostaglandin F (PGF) has a hydroxyl group. The number of double bonds is shown as a subscript 1 or 2:

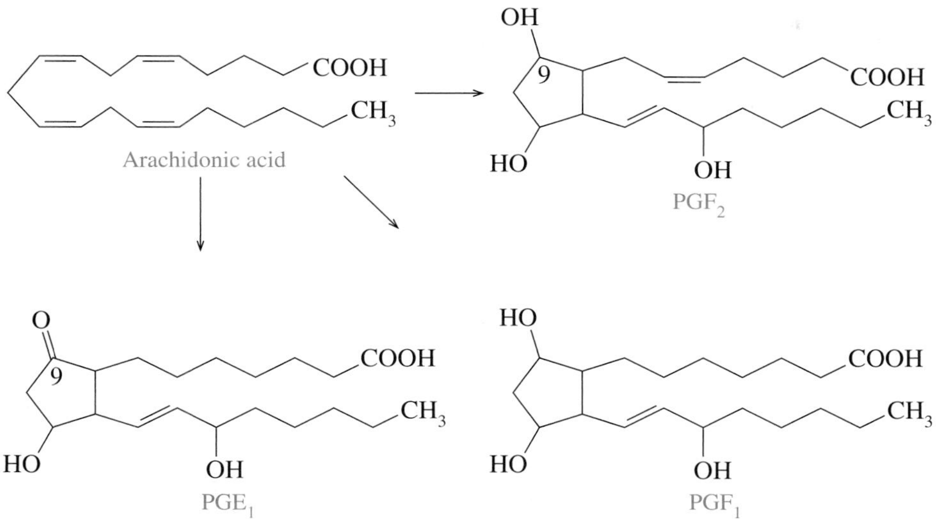

COOH
$CH_3$
Arachidonic acid

OH
9
COOH
$CH_3$
HO
OH
$PGF_2$

O
9
COOH
$CH_3$
HO
OH
$PGE_1$

HO
COOH
$CH_3$
HO
OH
$PGF_1$

Although prostaglandins are broken down quickly, they have potent physiological effects. Some prostaglandins increase blood pressure, and others lower blood pressure. Other prostaglandins stimulate contraction and relaxation in the smooth muscle of the uterus during the birth process. When tissues are injured, arachidonic acid present in the blood is converted to prostaglandins such as PGE and PGF that produce inflammation and pain in the area:

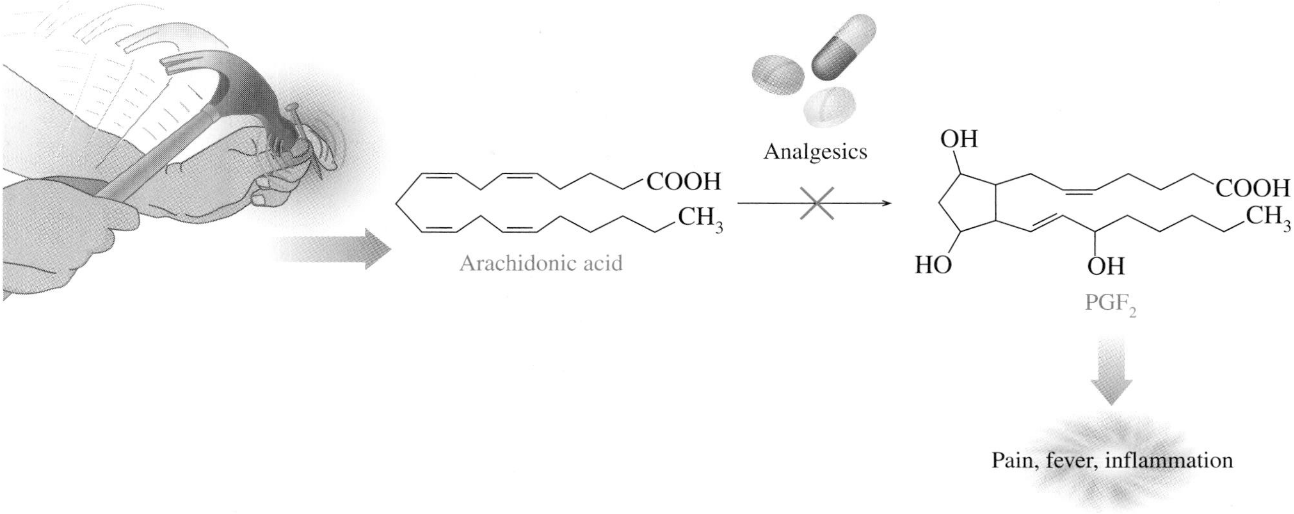

COOH
$CH_3$
Arachidonic acid
Analgesics
OH
COOH
$CH_3$
HO
OH
$PGF_2$
Pain, fever, inflammation

The treatment of pain, fever, and inflammation is based on inhibiting the enzymes that convert arachidonic acid to prostaglandins. Several nonsteroidal anti-inflammatory drugs (NSAIDs), such as aspirin, block the production of prostaglandins and in doing so decrease pain and inflammation and reduce fever (antipyretics). Ibuprofen has similar anti-inflammatory and analgesic effects. Other NSAIDs include naproxen (Aleve and Naprosyn), ketoprofen (Actron), and nabumetone (Relafen). Long-term use of such products can result in liver, kidney, and gastrointestinal damage. Some prostaglandins are being tested as inhibitors of gastric secretion for use in the treatment of stomach ulcers.

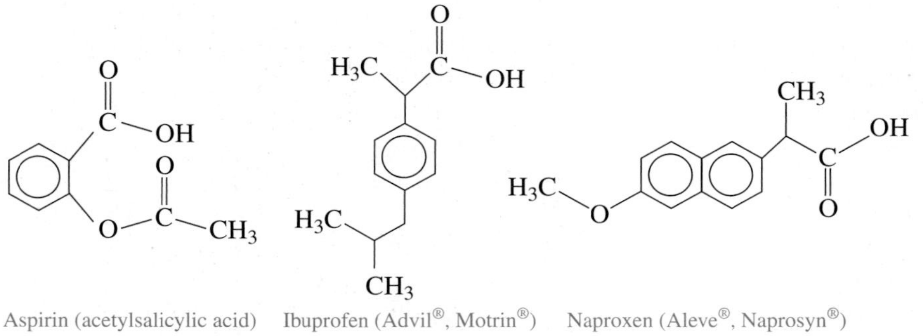

Aspirin (acetylsalicylic acid) Ibuprofen (Advil®, Motrin®) Naproxen (Aleve®, Naprosyn®)

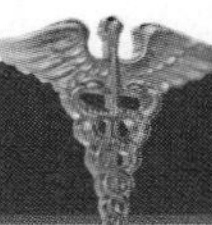

## Health Note

### Omega-3 Fatty Acids in Fish Oils

Over the past several decades, Americans have been changing their diets to include more polyunsaturated fats and fewer saturated fats. This change is a response to research that indicates that atherosclerosis and heart disease are associated with high levels of fats in the diet. However, the Inuit people of Alaska have a diet with high levels of polyunsaturated fats as well as high levels of blood cholesterol, but a very low occurrence of atherosclerosis and heart attacks. The fats in the Inuit diet are primarily polyunsaturated fats from fish rather than from land animals.

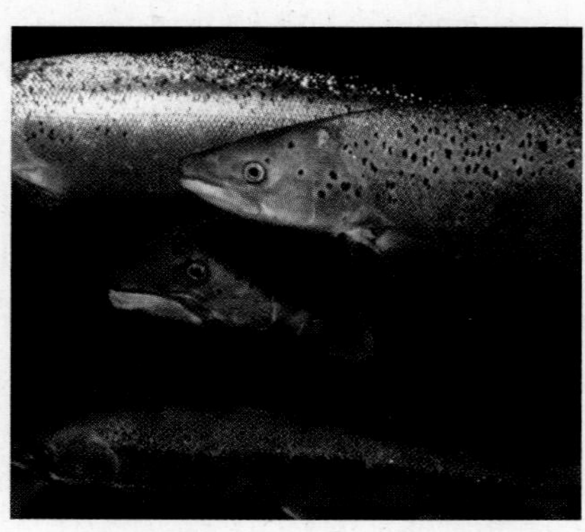

Both fish and vegetable oils have high levels of polyunsaturated fats. The fatty acids in vegetable oils are omega-6 acids, in which the first double bond occurs at carbon 6 counting from the end of the carbon chain. Two common omega-6 acids are linoleic acid and arachidonic acid. However, the fatty acids in the fish oils are mostly the omega-3 type, in which the first double bond occurs at the third carbon counting from the methyl group. Three common omega-3 fatty acids in fish are linolenic acid, eicosapentaenoic acid (EPA), and docosahexaenoic acid (DHA).

In atherosclerosis and heart disease, cholesterol forms plaques that adhere to the walls of the blood vessels. Blood pressure rises as blood has to squeeze through a smaller opening in the blood vessel. As more plaque forms, there is also a possibility of blood clots blocking the blood vessels and causing a heart attack. Omega-3 fatty acids lower the tendency of blood platelets to stick together, thereby reducing the possibility of blood clots. However, high levels of omega-3 fatty acids can increase bleeding if the ability of the platelets to form blood clots is reduced too much. It does seem that a diet that includes fish such as salmon, tuna, and herring can provide higher amounts of the omega-3 fatty acids, which help lessen the possibility of developing heart disease.

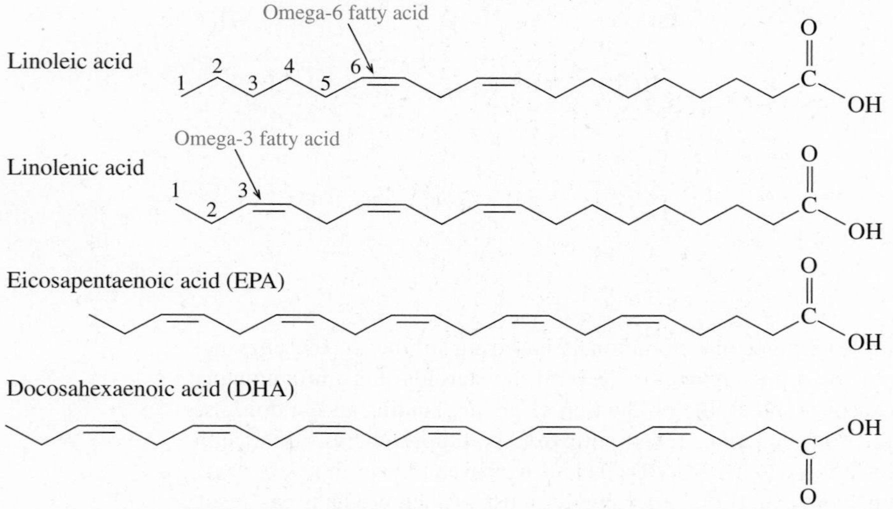

Linoleic acid — Omega-6 fatty acid

Linolenic acid — Omega-3 fatty acid

Eicosapentaenoic acid (EPA)

Docosahexaenoic acid (DHA)

## QUESTIONS AND PROBLEMS

### Fatty Acids

17.5 Describe some similarities and differences in the structures of a saturated fatty acid and an unsaturated fatty acid.

**17.6** Stearic acid and linoleic acid both have 18 carbon atoms. Why does stearic acid melt at 69 °C, but linoleic acid melts at −9 °C?

17.7 Draw the line-bond formula of the following fatty acids:
**a.** palmitic acid **b.** oleic acid

**17.8** Draw the line-bond formula of the following fatty acids:
**a.** stearic acid **b.** linoleic acid

17.9 Which of the following fatty acids are saturated and which are unsaturated?
**a.** lauric acid **b.** linolenic acid
**c.** palmitoleic acid **d.** stearic acid

**17.10** Which of the following fatty acids are saturated and which are unsaturated?
**a.** linoleic acid **b.** palmitic acid
**c.** myristic acid **d.** oleic acid

17.11 How does the structure of a fatty acid with a cis double bond differ from the structure of a fatty acid with a trans double bond?

**17.12** In each pair, identify the fatty acid with the lower melting point. Explain.
**a.** myristic acid and stearic acid
**b.** stearic acid and linoleic acid
**c.** oleic acid and linolenic acid

17.13 What is the difference in the location of the first double bond in an omega-3 and an omega-6 fatty acid? (See Health Note "Omega-3 Fatty Acids in Fish Oils.")

**17.14 a.** What are some sources of omega-3 and omega-6 fatty acids? (See Health Note "Omega-3 Fatty Acids in Fish Oils.")
**b.** How may omega-3 fatty acids help in lowering the risk of heart disease?

17.15 Compare the structures and functional groups of arachidonic acid and $PGE_1$.

**17.16** Compare the structures and functional groups of PGE and PGF.

17.17 What are some effects of prostaglandins in the body?

**17.18** How do nonsteroidal anti-inflammatory drugs reduce inflammation?

# 17.3 Waxes, Fats, and Oils

**LEARNING GOAL**

Draw the condensed structural formula of a wax, fat, or oil produced by the reaction of a fatty acid and an alcohol or glycerol.

Waxes are found in many plants and animals. Coatings of carnauba wax on fruits and the leaves and stems of plants help to prevent loss of water and damage from pests. Waxes on the skin, fur, and feathers of animals and birds provide a waterproof coating. A **wax** is an ester of a saturated fatty acid and a long-chain alcohol, each containing from 14 to 30 carbon atoms.

The formulas of some common waxes are given in Table 17.2. Beeswax obtained from honeycombs and carnauba wax from palm trees are used to give a protective coating to furniture, cars, and floors. Jojoba wax is used in making candles and cosmetics such as lipstick. Lanolin, a mixture of waxes obtained from wool, is used in hand and facial lotions to aid retention of water, which softens the skin.

Ester bond

$$\text{Fatty acid}-\overset{\displaystyle O}{\overset{\|}{C}}-O-\text{Long-chain alcohol}$$

Wax

**TABLE 17.2** Some Typical Waxes

| Type | Condensed Structural Formula | Source | Uses |
|---|---|---|---|
| Beeswax | $CH_3-(CH_2)_{14}-\overset{O}{\overset{\|}{C}}-O-(CH_2)_{29}-CH_3$ | Honeycomb | Candles, shoe polish, wax paper |
| Carnauba wax | $CH_3-(CH_2)_{24}-\overset{O}{\overset{\|}{C}}-O-(CH_2)_{29}-CH_3$ | Brazilian palm tree | Waxes for furniture, cars, floors, shoes |
| Jojoba wax | $CH_3-(CH_2)_{18}-\overset{O}{\overset{\|}{C}}-O-(CH_2)_{19}-CH_3$ | Jojoba | Candles, soaps, cosmetics |

## Fats and Oils: Triacylglycerols

In the body, fatty acids are stored as fats and oils known as **triacylglycerols**. These substances, also called *triglycerides*, are triesters of glycerol (a trihydroxy alcohol) and fatty acids. The general formula of a triacylglycerol follows:

$$\begin{array}{l} CH_2-O-\overset{\displaystyle O}{\overset{\|}{C}}\sim\sim\sim\sim\sim \\ | \\ CH-O-\overset{\displaystyle O}{\overset{\|}{C}}\sim\sim\sim\sim\sim \\ | \\ CH_2-O-\overset{\displaystyle O}{\overset{\|}{C}}\sim\sim\sim\sim\sim \end{array}$$

Triacylglycerol

| Glycerol | |
|---|---|
| G | — Fatty acid |
| l y c e | — Fatty acid |
| r o l | — Fatty acid |

SELF STUDY ACTIVITY Triacylglycerols

In Chapter 16, we saw that esters are produced from the esterification reaction between a carboxylic acid and an alcohol. In a triacylglycerol, three hydroxyl groups on glycerol form ester bonds with the carboxyl groups of three fatty acids. For example, glycerol and three molecules of stearic acid form glyceryl tristearate, which is commonly named tristearin. In these complex molecules, bonds between carbon atoms may be omitted to give a condensed structure:

$$\begin{array}{l} CH_2-O-H + HO-\overset{\displaystyle O}{\overset{\|}{C}}-(CH_2)_{16}CH_3 \\ | \\ CH-O-H + HO-\overset{\displaystyle O}{\overset{\|}{C}}-(CH_2)_{16}CH_3 \\ | \\ CH_2-O-H + HO-\overset{\displaystyle O}{\overset{\|}{C}}-(CH_2)_{16}CH_3 \end{array} \longrightarrow \begin{array}{l} CH_2-\mathbf{O}-\overset{\displaystyle \mathbf{O}}{\overset{\|}{\mathbf{C}}}-(CH_2)_{16}CH_3 \\ | \\ CH-\mathbf{O}-\overset{\displaystyle \mathbf{O}}{\overset{\|}{\mathbf{C}}}-(CH_2)_{16}CH_3 + 3H_2O \\ | \\ CH_2-\mathbf{O}-\overset{\displaystyle \mathbf{O}}{\overset{\|}{\mathbf{C}}}-(CH_2)_{16}CH_3 \end{array}$$

Glycerol; 3 Stearic acid molecules; Glyceryl tristearate (tristearin, a fat); Ester bond

Most fats and oils are mixed triacylglycerols that contain two or three different fatty acids. For example, a mixed triacylglycerol might be made from lauric acid, myristic acid, and palmitic acid. One possible structure for the mixed triacylglycerol follows:

$$\begin{array}{ll} CH_2-O-\overset{\displaystyle O}{\overset{\|}{C}}-(CH_2)_{10}CH_3 & \text{Lauric acid} \\ | & \\ CH-O-\overset{\displaystyle O}{\overset{\|}{C}}-(CH_2)_{12}CH_3 & \text{Myristic acid} \\ | & \\ CH_2-O-\overset{\displaystyle O}{\overset{\|}{C}}-(CH_2)_{14}CH_3 & \text{Palmitic acid} \end{array}$$

A mixed triacylglycerol

Triacylglycerols are the major form of energy storage for animals. Animals that hibernate eat large quantities of plants, seeds, and nuts that contain high levels of fats and oils. Prior to hibernation, these animals, such as polar bears, gain as much as 14 kilograms a week. As the external temperature drops, the animal goes into hibernation. The body temperature drops to nearly freezing, and cellular activity, respiration, and heart rate are dramatically reduced. Animals that live in extremely cold climates will hibernate for 4–7 months. During this time, stored fat is their only source of energy.

CONCEPT CHECK 17.2

### Triacylglycerols

Name the triacylglycerol that is formed by the esterification of glycerol with each of the following fatty acids:

**a.** $CH_3-(CH_2)_{12}-COOH$
**b.** $CH_3-(CH_2)_5-CH=CH-(CH_2)_7-COOH$

ANSWER

**a.** The saturated fatty acid with 14 carbon atoms is myristic acid. The triacylglycerol of glycerol and myristic acid is named glyceryl trimyristate or trimyristin (common).
**b.** The monounsaturated fatty acid with 16 carbon atoms is palmitoleic acid. The triacylglycerol of glycerol and palmitoleic acid is named glyceryl tripalmitoleate or tripalmitolein (common).

SAMPLE PROBLEM 17.3

### Writing Structures for a Triacylglycerol

Draw the condensed structural formula of glyceryl tripalmitoleate (tripalmitolein).

SOLUTION

Glyceryl tripalmitoleate (tripalmitolein) is the triacylglycerol that contains ester bonds between glycerol and three palmitoleic acid molecules:

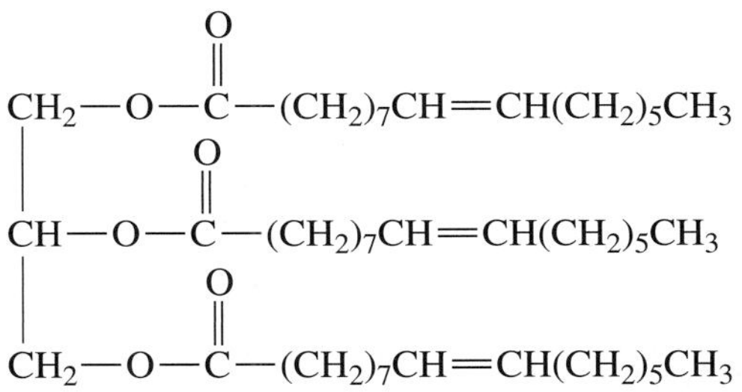

$$\begin{array}{l} CH_2-O-\overset{\overset{\Large O}{\|}}{C}-(CH_2)_7CH=CH(CH_2)_5CH_3 \\ | \\ CH-O-\overset{\overset{\Large O}{\|}}{C}-(CH_2)_7CH=CH(CH_2)_5CH_3 \\ | \\ CH_2-O-\overset{\overset{\Large O}{\|}}{C}-(CH_2)_7CH=CH(CH_2)_5CH_3 \end{array}$$

Glyceryl tripalmitoleate (tripalmitolein)

STUDY CHECK

Draw the condensed structural formula of the triacylglycerol containing three molecules of myristic acid.

## Melting Points of Fats and Oils

A **fat** is a triacylglycerol that is solid at room temperature and usually comes from animal sources such as meat, whole milk, butter, and cheese.

An **oil** is a triacylglycerol that is usually a liquid at room temperature and is obtained from a plant source. Olive oil and peanut oil are monounsaturated because they contain large amounts of oleic acid. Oils from corn, cottonseed, safflowers, and sunflowers are polyunsaturated because they contain large amounts of fatty acids with two or more double bonds. (See Figure 17.3.) Palm oil and coconut oil are solids at room temperature because they consist mostly of saturated fatty acids.

The amounts of saturated, monounsaturated, and polyunsaturated fatty acids in some typical fats and oils are shown in Figure 17.4.

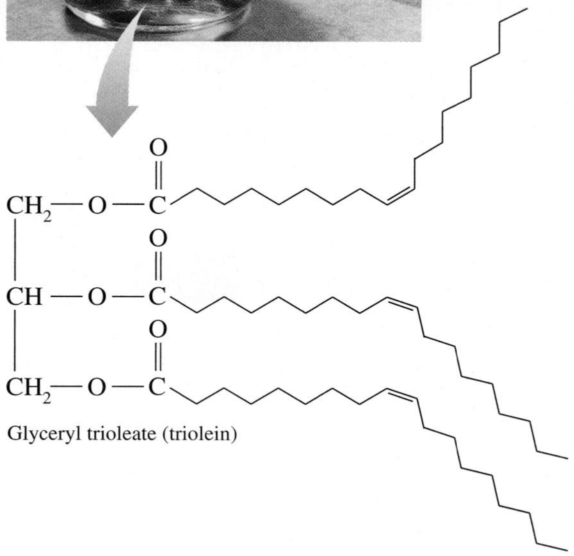

O
‖
$CH_2$—O—C
O
‖
CH—O—C
O
‖
$CH_2$—O—C

Glyceryl trioleate (triolein)

**FIGURE 17.3** Vegetable oils such as olive oil, corn oil, and safflower oil contain unsaturated fats.

**Q** Why is olive oil a liquid at room temperature?

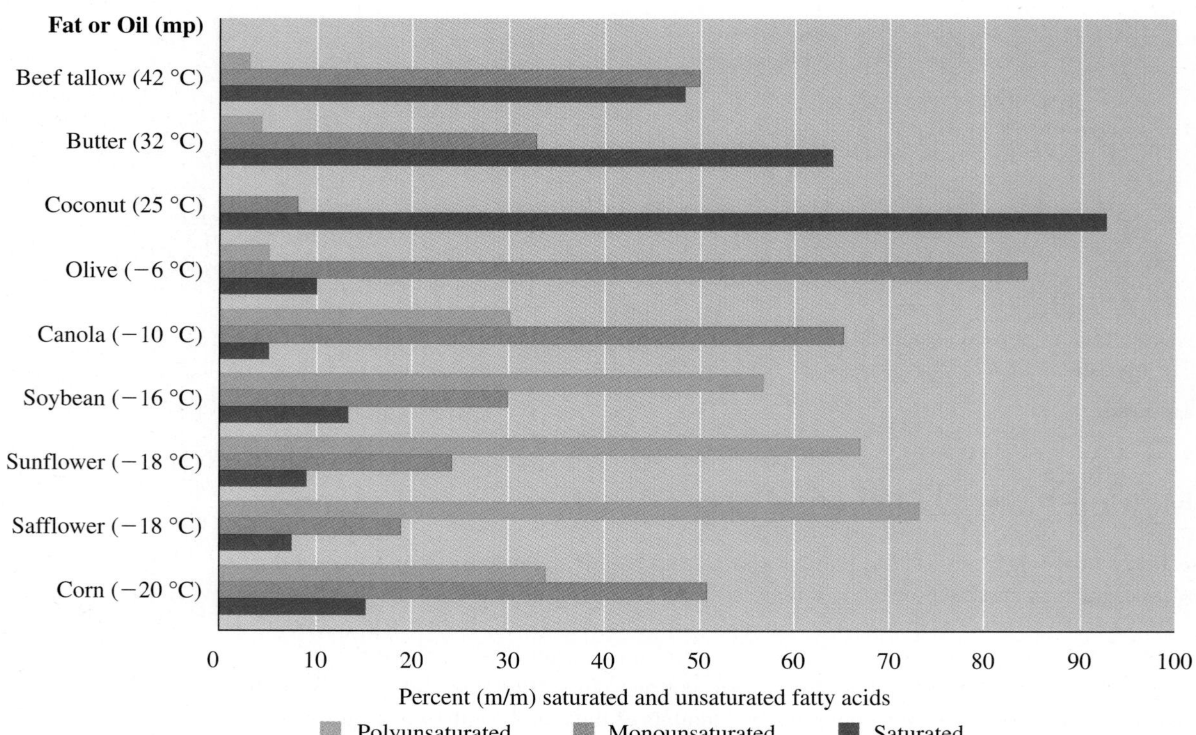


**FIGURE 17.4** Vegetable oils have low melting points because they have a higher percentage of unsaturated fatty acids than do animal fats.

**Q** Why is the melting point of butter higher than olive or canola oil?

Saturated fatty acids have higher melting points than unsaturated fatty acids because they pack together more tightly. Animal fats usually contain more saturated fatty acids than do vegetable oils. Therefore the melting points of animal fats are higher than those of vegetable oils.

## QUESTIONS AND PROBLEMS

### Waxes, Fats, and Oils

17.19 Draw the condensed structural formula of an ester in beeswax formed from myricyl alcohol, $CH_3(CH_2)_{29}OH$, and palmitic acid.

**17.20** Draw the condensed structural formula of an ester in jojoba wax formed from arachidic acid, a 20-carbon saturated fatty acid, and 1-docosanol, $CH_3(CH_2)_{21}OH$.

17.21 Draw the condensed structural formula of a triacylglycerol that contains stearic acid and glycerol.

**17.22** A mixed triacylglycerol contains two palmitic acid molecules and one oleic acid molecule. Draw two possible condensed structural formulas (isomers) for the compound.

17.23 Draw the condensed structural formula of glyceryl tripalmitate (tripalmitin).

**17.24** Draw the condensed structural formula of glyceryl trioleate (triolein).

17.25 Safflower oil is polyunsaturated, whereas olive oil is monounsaturated. Explain.

**17.26** Why does olive oil have a lower melting point than butter fat?

17.27 Why does coconut oil, a vegetable oil, have a melting point similar to fats from animal sources?

**17.28** A label on a bottle of 100% sunflower seed oil states that it is lower in saturated fats than all the leading oils.

**a.** How does the percentage of saturated fats in sunflower seed oil compare to that of safflower, corn, and canola oil? (See Figure 17.4.)

**b.** Is the claim valid?

# 17.4 Chemical Properties of Triacylglycerols

LEARNING GOAL

Draw the structure of the product when a triacylglycerol is hydrogenated, hydrolyzed, or oxidized.

The chemical reactions of the triacylglycerols (fats and oils) are the same as those we discussed for alkenes (Chapter 12) and esters (Chapter 16). Next, we will look at the hydrogenation and the hydrolysis and saponification of fats and oils.

## Hydrogenation

TUTORIAL
Hydrogenation and Hydrolysis of Triacylglycerols

In the **hydrogenation** of an unsaturated fat, hydrogen is added to carbon–carbon double bonds to form carbon–carbon single bonds. The hydrogen gas is bubbled through the heated oil, typically in the presence of a nickel catalyst:

$$-CH{=}CH- + \mathbf{H_2} \xrightarrow{Ni} -\overset{\mathbf{H}}{\underset{H}{\overset{|}{\underset{|}{C}}}}-\overset{\mathbf{H}}{\underset{H}{\overset{|}{\underset{|}{C}}}}-$$

For example, when hydrogen adds to all of the double bonds of glyceryl trioleate (triolein), the product is the saturated fat glyceryl tristearate (tristearin):

$$\begin{array}{l} CH_2-O-\overset{O}{\overset{\|}{C}}-(CH_2)_7CH{=}CH(CH_2)_7CH_3 \\ | \\ CH-O-\overset{O}{\overset{\|}{C}}-(CH_2)_7CH{=}CH(CH_2)_7CH_3 \\ | \\ CH_2-O-\overset{O}{\overset{\|}{C}}-(CH_2)_7CH{=}CH(CH_2)_7CH_3 \end{array} + 3H_2 \xrightarrow{Ni} \begin{array}{l} CH_2-O-\overset{O}{\overset{\|}{C}}-(CH_2)_{16}CH_3 \\ | \\ CH-O-\overset{O}{\overset{\|}{C}}-(CH_2)_{16}CH_3 \\ | \\ CH_2-O-\overset{O}{\overset{\|}{C}}-(CH_2)_{16}CH_3 \end{array}$$

Glyceryl trioleate (triolein) Glyceryl tristearate (tristearin)

In commercial hydrogenation, the addition of hydrogen is stopped before all the double bonds in a liquid vegetable oil become completely saturated. Complete hydrogenation gives a very brittle product, whereas the partial hydrogenation of a liquid vegetable oil

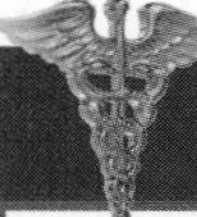

# HEALTH NOTE

## Olestra: A Fat Substitute

In 1968, food scientists designed an artificial fat called *olestra* as a source of nutrition for premature babies. However, olestra could not be digested and was never used for that purpose. Later, scientists realized that olestra had the flavor and texture of a fat without the calories.

Olestra is manufactured by obtaining the fatty acids from the fats in cottonseed or soybean oils and bonding the fatty acids with the hydroxyl groups on sucrose. Chemically, olestra is composed of six to eight long-chain fatty acids attached by ester links to a sugar (sucrose) rather than to a glycerol molecule found in fats. This structure makes olestra a very large molecule that cannot be absorbed through the intestinal walls. The enzymes and bacteria in the intestinal tract are unable to break down the olestra molecule, and it travels through the intestinal tract undigested.

The large molecule of olestra also combines with fat-soluble vitamins (A, D, E, and K) as well as the carotenoids from the foods we eat before they can be absorbed through the intestinal wall. Carotenoids are plant pigments in fruits and vegetables that protect against cancer, heart disease, and macular degeneration, a form of blindness in the elderly. The FDA now requires manufacturers to add the four vitamins, but not the carotenoids, to olestra products. There have been reports of some adverse reactions, including diarrhea, abdominal cramps, and anal leakage, indicating that olestra may act as a laxative in some people. However, the manufacturers contend there is no direct proof that olestra is the cause of those effects.

Snack foods made with olestra are now in supermarkets nationwide. Since there are already low-fat snacks on the market, it remains to be seen whether olestra will have any significant effect on reducing the problem of obesity.

**Fatty acids**

$CH_3(CH_2)_6COOH$

$CH_3(CH_2)_8COOH$

Olestra

changes it to a soft, semisolid fat. As the semisolid fat becomes more saturated, the melting point increases, and the substance becomes more solid at room temperature. By controlling the amount of hydrogen, manufacturers can produce the various types of products on the market today, such as soft margarines, solid stick margarines, and solid shortenings. (See Figure 17.5.) Although these products now contain more saturated fatty acids than the original oils, they contain no cholesterol, unlike similar products from animal sources, such as butter and lard.

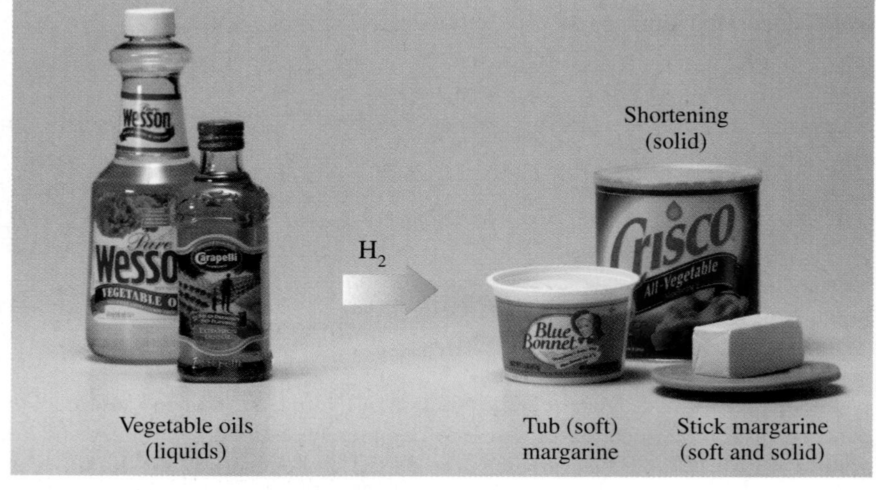


**FIGURE 17.5** Many soft margarines, stick margarines, and solid shortenings are produced by the partial hydrogenation of vegetable oils.

Q How does hydrogenation change the structure of the fatty acids in the vegetable oils?

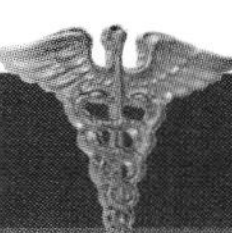

# HEALTH NOTE

## Trans Fatty Acids and Hydrogenation

During the early 1900s, margarine became a popular replacement for highly saturated fats such as butter and lard. Margarine is produced by partially hydrogenating the unsaturated fats in vegetable oils such as safflower oil, corn oil, canola oil, cottonseed oil, and sunflower oil. Fats that are more saturated are more resistant to oxidation.

In vegetable oils, the unsaturated fats usually contain cis double bonds. As hydrogenation occurs, double bonds are converted to single bonds. However, a small amount of the cis double bonds are converted to trans double bonds, which causes a change in the overall structure of the fatty acids. If the label on a product states that the oils have been "partially hydrogenated," that product will also contain trans fatty acids. In the United States, it is estimated that 2–4% of our total calories comes from trans fatty acids.

The concern about trans fatty acids is that their altered structure may make them behave like saturated fatty acids in the body. During the 1980s, research indicated that trans fatty acids have an effect on blood cholesterol similar to that of saturated fats, although study results vary. Several studies reported that trans fatty acids raise the levels of LDL-cholesterol, low-density lipoproteins containing cholesterol that can accumulate in the arteries. (LDLs and HDLs are described in the section on lipoproteins later in the chapter.) Some studies also report that trans fatty acids lower HDL-cholesterol, high-density lipoproteins that carry cholesterol to the liver to be excreted. However, other studies did not report any decrease in HDL-cholesterol. In some American and European studies, an increased risk of breast cancer was associated with increased intake of trans fatty acids. However, these studies are not conclusive, and not all studies have supported such findings. Current evidence does not yet indicate that the intake of trans fatty acids is a significant risk factor for heart disease. The trans fatty acids controversy will continue to be debated as more research is done.

Foods containing trans fatty acids include milk, bread, fried foods, ground beef, baked goods, stick margarine, butter, soft margarine, cookies, crackers, and vegetable shortening. The American Heart Association recommends that margarine should have no more than 2 grams of saturated fat per tablespoon, and a liquid vegetable oil should be the first ingredient. They also recommend the use of soft margarine, which is only slightly hydrogenated and therefore has fewer trans fatty acids.

Many health organizations agree that fat should account for less than 30% of daily calories (the current average for Americans is 34%) and saturated fat should be less than 10% of total calories. Lowering the overall fat intake would also decrease the amount of trans fatty acids. The Food and Drug Administration and the U.S. Department of Agriculture are encouraging the use of new food labels to inform consumers of the fat content of food. Since the beginning of 2006, the amount of trans fats has been included on the Nutritional Facts panel on food products. The best advice may be to reduce total fat in the diet by using fats and oils sparingly, cooking with little or no fat, substituting olive oil or canola oil for other oils, and limiting the use of coconut oil and palm oil, which are high in saturated fatty acids.

There are several products on the market, including peanut butter and butterlike spreads, that have 0% trans fatty acids. On the labels, they state that their products are nonhydrogenated, which avoids the production of the undesirable trans fatty acid. However, in the list of natural vegetable oils, such as soy and canola oil, there is also palm oil. Because palm oil has a melting point of 30 °C, palm oil increases the overall melting point of the spread and gives a product that is solid at room temperature. However, palm oil contains high amounts of saturated fatty acids and has a similar effect in the body as do stearic acid (18 carbons) and fats derived from animal sources. Health experts recommend that we limit the amount of saturated fats, including palm oil, in our diets.

*cis*-Oleic acid

$H_2$/Ni

Ni catalyst

Isomerization

Addition of $H_2$

Undesired side product (*trans*-oleic acid)

Desired saturated product (stearic acid)

## Oxidation of Unsaturated Fats

A fat or oil becomes rancid when its double bonds are oxidized in the presence of oxygen and microorganisms. The products are short-chain fatty acids and aldehydes that have disagreeable odors:

$$-CH{=}CH- \xrightarrow{[O]} -\overset{\overset{O}{\|}}{C}-H + H-\overset{\overset{O}{\|}}{C}- \xrightarrow{[O]} -\overset{\overset{O}{\|}}{C}-OH + HO-\overset{\overset{O}{\|}}{C}-$$

Unsaturated fatty acids — Short-chain aldehydes — Short-chain carboxylic acids

If a vegetable oil does not contain an antioxidant, it will oxidize rather easily. You can detect oil that has become rancid by its unpleasant odor. If oil is covered tightly and stored in a refrigerator, the process of oxidation can be slowed and the oil will last longer.

Oxidation also occurs in the oils that accumulate on the surface of the skin during heavy exercise.

At body temperature, microorganisms on the skin promote rapid oxidation of the oils as they are exposed to oxygen and water. The resulting short-chain aldehydes and fatty acids account for the body odor associated with working out and heavy perspiration.

## Hydrolysis

Triacylglycerols are hydrolyzed (split by water) in the presence of strong acids such HCl or $H_2SO_4$ or digestive enzymes called *lipases*. The products of hydrolysis of the ester bonds are glycerol and three fatty acids. The polar glycerol is soluble in water, but the fatty acids with their long hydrocarbon chains are not.

Water adds to ester bonds

$$\begin{array}{l} CH_2-O-\overset{\overset{O}{\|}}{C}-(CH_2)_{14}CH_3 \\ | \\ CH-O-\overset{\overset{O}{\|}}{C}-(CH_2)_{14}CH_3 \\ | \\ CH_2-O-\overset{\overset{O}{\|}}{C}-(CH_2)_{14}CH_3 \end{array} + \mathbf{3H_2O} \xrightarrow{H^+ \text{ or lipase}} \begin{array}{l} CH_2-\mathbf{OH} \\ | \\ CH-\mathbf{OH} \\ | \\ CH_2-\mathbf{OH} \end{array} + \mathbf{3HO}-\overset{\overset{O}{\|}}{C}-(CH_2)_{14}CH_3$$

Glyceryl tripalmitate (tripalmitin) — Glycerol — 3 Palmitic acid molecules

## Saponification

When a fat is heated with a strong base such as sodium hydroxide, saponification (base hydrolysis) of the fat gives glycerol and the sodium salts of the fatty acids, which are soaps. When NaOH is used, a solid soap is produced that can be molded into a desired shape; KOH produces a softer, liquid soap. Polyunsaturated oils produce softer soaps. Names like "coconut" or "avocado shampoo" tell you the sources of the oil used in the reaction:

$$\text{Fat or oil} + \text{strong base} \longrightarrow \text{glycerol} + \text{salts of fatty acids (soaps)}$$

$$\begin{array}{l} CH_2-O-\overset{\overset{O}{\|}}{C}-(CH_2)_{14}CH_3 \\ | \\ CH-O-\overset{\overset{O}{\|}}{C}-(CH_2)_{14}CH_3 \\ | \\ CH_2-O-\overset{\overset{O}{\|}}{C}-(CH_2)_{14}CH_3 \end{array} + \mathbf{3NaOH} \longrightarrow \begin{array}{l} CH_2-\mathbf{OH} \\ | \\ CH-\mathbf{OH} \\ | \\ CH_2-\mathbf{OH} \end{array} + \mathbf{3Na^{+}\,{}^{-}O}-\overset{\overset{O}{\|}}{C}-(CH_2)_{14}CH_3$$

Glyceryl tripalmitate (tripalmitin) — Glycerol — 3 Sodium palmitate (soap)

## GREEN CHEMISTRY NOTE

### Biodiesel as an Alternative Fuel

**Biodiesel** is a name of a nonpetroleum fuel that can be used in place of diesel fuel. Biodiesel is produced from renewable biological resources such as vegetable oils (primarily soybean), waste vegetable oils from restaurants, and some animal fats. Biodiesel is nontoxic and biodegradable.

Biodiesel is prepared from triacylglycerols and alcohols (usually ethanol) to form ethyl esters and glycerol. The glycerol that separates from the fat is used in soaps and other products. The reaction of triacylglycerols is catalyzed by a base such as NaOH or KOH at low temperatures to give a very high percentage of the fatty acid esters, which make up the biodiesel product.

$$\text{Triacylglycerol} + 3\ \text{ethanol} \longrightarrow 3\ \text{ethyl ester (biodiesel)} + \text{glycerol}$$

In many cases, diesel engines need only slight modification to use biodiesel. Manufacturers of diesel cars, trucks, boats, and tractors have different suggestions for the percentage of biodiesel to use, ranging from 2% (B2) blended with standard diesel fuel to using 100% pure biodiesel (B100). For example, B20 is 20 percent by volume of biodiesel blended with 80 percent by volume petroleum diesel. In 2006, $9.8 \times 10^{14}$ liters of biodiesel were used in the United States. Fuel stations in Europe and the United States are now stocking biodiesel fuel.

Compared to diesel fuel from petroleum, biodiesel burns in an engine to produce much lower levels of carbon dioxide emissions, particulates, unburned hydrocarbons, and polycyclic aromatic hydrocarbons that cause lung cancer. Because biodiesel has extremely low sulfur content, it does not contribute to the formation of the sulfur oxides that produce acid rain. The energy output from the combustion of biodiesel is almost the same as energy produced by petroleum diesel.

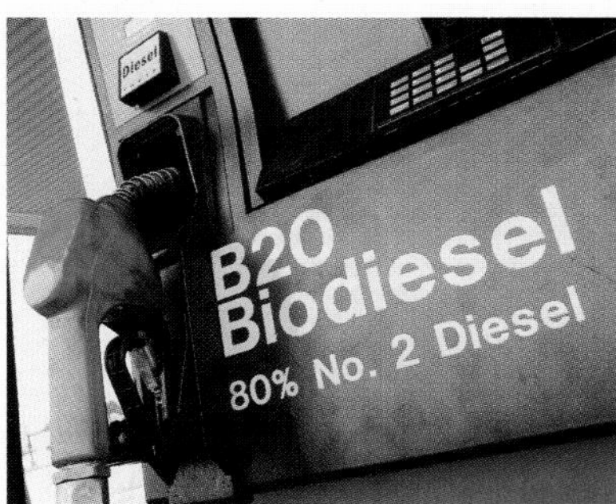


$$\begin{array}{l} H_2C{-}O{-}\overset{O}{\overset{\|}{C}}{-}(CH_2)_{12}{-}CH_3 \\ \quad| \\ H{-}C{-}O{-}\overset{O}{\overset{\|}{C}}{-}(CH_2)_7{-}CH{=}CH{-}(CH_2)_7{-}CH_3 \\ \quad| \\ H_2C{-}O{-}\overset{O}{\overset{\|}{C}}{-}(CH_2)_{16}{-}CH_3 \end{array} + 3CH_3{-}CH_2{-}OH$$

Triacylglycerol from vegetable oil — Ethanol

$$\xrightarrow{\text{NaOH catalyst}} \begin{array}{l} H_2C{-}OH \\ \quad| \\ H{-}C{-}OH \\ \quad| \\ H_2C{-}OH \end{array} + \begin{array}{l} CH_3{-}CH_2{-}O{-}\overset{O}{\overset{\|}{C}}{-}(CH_2)_{12}{-}CH_3 \\ CH_3{-}CH_2{-}O{-}\overset{O}{\overset{\|}{C}}{-}(CH_2)_7{-}CH{=}CH{-}(CH_2)_7{-}CH_3 \\ CH_3{-}CH_2{-}O{-}\overset{O}{\overset{\|}{C}}{-}(CH_2)_{16}{-}CH_3 \end{array}$$

Glycerol — Ethyl esters used for biodiesel

CONCEPT CHECK 17.3

### Hydrogenation, Hydrolysis, and Saponification

Identify each of the following as hydrogenation, hydrolysis, or saponification and identify the products:

**a.** the reaction of palm oil with KOH
**b.** the reaction of glyceryl trilinoleate from safflower oil with water and HCl
**c.** the reaction of corn oil and hydrogen ($H_2$) using a nickel catalyst

EXPLORE YOUR WORLD

## Types of Fats

Read the labels on food products that contain fats, such as butter, margarine, vegetable oils, peanut butter, and potato chips. Look for terms such as saturated, monounsaturated, polyunsaturated, and partially or fully hydrogenated.

### QUESTIONS

1. How many grams of saturated, monounsaturated, and polyunsaturated fat are in one serving of the product?
2. What type(s) of fats or oils are in the product?
3. What percent of the total fat is saturated fat? Unsaturated fat?
4. If the product is a vegetable oil, what information is given about how to store it? Why?
5. The label on a container of peanut butter states that the cottonseed and canola oils used to make the peanut butter have been fully hydrogenated. What are the typical products that would form when hydrogen is added?
6. For each packaged food, determine the following:
   **a.** How many grams of fat are in one serving of the food?
   **b.** Using the caloric value for fat (9 kcal/gram of fat), how many Calories (kilocalories) come from the fat in one serving?
   **c.** What is the percentage of fat in one serving?

ANSWER

**a.** The reaction of palm oil with KOH is saponification, and the products are glycerol and the potassium salts of the fatty acids, which are soaps.
**b.** In acid hydrolysis, glyceryl trilinoleate reacts with water, which splits the ester bonds to produce glycerol and three molecules of linoleic acid.
**c.** In hydrogenation, $H_2$ adds to double bonds in corn oil, which produces a more saturated and thus more solid fat.

SAMPLE PROBLEM 17.4

### Reactions of Lipids

Write the equation for the reaction catalyzed by the enzyme lipase that hydrolyzes trilaurin (glyceryl trilaurate) during the digestion process.

SOLUTION

$$\begin{array}{l} CH_2-O-\overset{O}{\overset{\|}{C}}-(CH_2)_{10}CH_3 \\ | \\ CH-O-\overset{O}{\overset{\|}{C}}-(CH_2)_{10}CH_3 + 3H_2O \xrightarrow{\text{Lipase}} \\ | \\ CH_2-O-\overset{O}{\overset{\|}{C}}-(CH_2)_{10}CH_3 \end{array}$$

Glyceryl trilaurate (trilaurin)

$$\begin{array}{l} CH_2-OH \\ | \\ CH-OH + 3HO-\overset{O}{\overset{\|}{C}}-(CH_2)_{10}CH_3 \\ | \\ CH_2-OH \end{array}$$

Glycerol     3 Lauric acid molecules

STUDY CHECK

What is the name of the product formed when a triacylglycerol containing oleic acid and linoleic acid is completely hydrogenated?

## QUESTIONS AND PROBLEMS

### Chemical Properties of Triacylglycerols

**17.29** Write an equation for the hydrogenation of glyceryl trioleate, a fat formed from glycerol and three oleic acid units.

**17.30** Write an equation for the hydrogenation of glyceryl trilinolenate, a fat formed from glycerol and three linolenic acid units.

**17.31** A label on a container of margarine states that it contains partially hydrogenated corn oil.
**a.** How has the liquid corn oil been changed?
**b.** Why is the margarine product solid?

**17.32** Why should a bottle of vegetable oil that has no preservatives be tightly covered and refrigerated?

**17.33 a.** Write an equation for the acid hydrolysis of glyceryl trimyristate (trimyristin).
**b.** Write an equation for the NaOH saponification of glyceryl trimyristate (trimyristin).

**17.34 a.** Write an equation for the acid hydrolysis of glyceryl trioleate (triolein).
**b.** Write an equation for the NaOH saponification of glyceryl trioleate (triolein).

**17.35** Compare the structure of a triacylglycerol to the structure of olestra.

**17.36** A vegetable oil is partially hydrogenated.

**a.** Are all or just some of the double bonds converted to single bonds?

**b.** What happens to some of the cis double bonds during hydrogenation?

**c.** How can you reduce the amount of trans fatty acids in your diet?

**17.37** Draw the product of the hydrogenation of the following triacylglycerol:

$$\begin{array}{l} \quad\quad\quad\quad\quad\;\; O \\ \quad\quad\quad\quad\quad\;\; \| \\ CH_2—O—C—(CH_2)_{16}CH_3 \\ |\quad\quad\quad\quad\;\; O \\ |\quad\quad\quad\quad\;\; \| \\ CH—O—C—(CH_2)_7CH{=}CH(CH_2)_7CH_3 \\ |\quad\quad\quad\quad\;\; O \\ |\quad\quad\quad\quad\;\; \| \\ CH_2—O—C—(CH_2)_{16}CH_3 \end{array}$$

**17.38** Draw all the products that would be obtained when the triacylglycerol in problem 17.37 undergoes complete hydrolysis.

# 17.5 Glycerophospholipids

**LEARNING GOAL**

Describe the characteristics of glycerophospholipids.

The **glycerophospholipids** are a family of lipids similar to triacylglycerols except that one hydroxyl group of glycerol is replaced by the ester of phosphoric acid and an amino alcohol, bonded through a phosphodiester bond. We can compare the general structures of a triacylglycerol and a glycerophospholipid as follows:

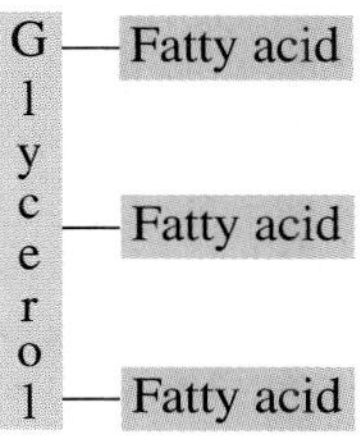


Triacylglycerol (triglyceride)

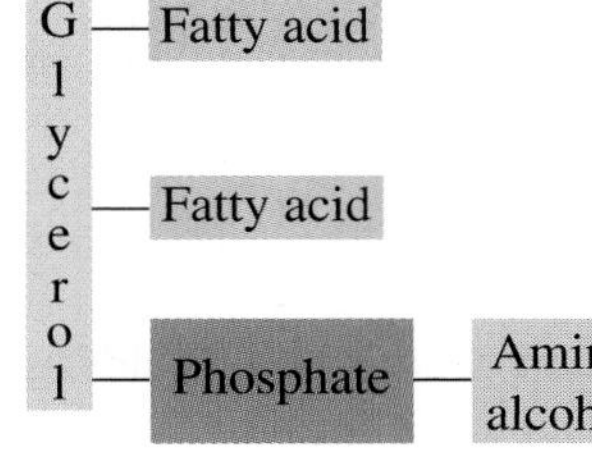


Glycerophospholipid

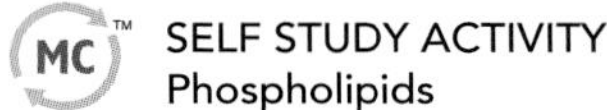


## Phosphate Esters

In this group of compounds, ester bonds form between a hydroxyl group of an alcohol and phosphoric acid to give ester products similar to those formed with carboxylic acids:

$$\mathrm{HO—\overset{\overset{\displaystyle O}{\|}}{\underset{\underset{\displaystyle OH}{|}}{P}}—OH + HO—CH_3 \longrightarrow HO—\overset{\overset{\displaystyle O}{\|}}{\underset{\underset{\displaystyle OH}{|}}{P}}—O—CH_3 + H_2O}$$

Phosphoric acid + Alcohol ⟶ Phosphate ester + Water

The phosphate ester forms a diester by reaction with a second alcohol:

$$\mathrm{HO—\overset{\overset{\displaystyle O}{\|}}{\underset{\underset{\displaystyle OH}{|}}{P}}—O—CH_3 + HO—CH_3 \longrightarrow CH_3—O—\overset{\overset{\displaystyle O}{\|}}{\underset{\underset{\displaystyle OH}{|}}{P}}—O—CH_3 + H_2O}$$

Phosphate ester + Alcohol ⟶ Phosphate diester + Water

MC TUTORIAL The Split Personality of Glycerophospholipids

Three amino alcohols found in glycerophospholipids are choline, serine, and ethanolamine. In the body, at a physiological pH of 7.4, these amino alcohols are ionized:

$$\mathrm{HO—CH_2—CH_2—\overset{\overset{\displaystyle CH_3}{|}}{\underset{\underset{\displaystyle CH_3}{|}}{N^+}}—CH_3}$$

Choline

$$\mathrm{HO—CH_2—\overset{\overset{\displaystyle \overset{+}{N}H_3}{|}}{CH}—COO^-}$$

Serine

$$\mathrm{HO—CH_2—CH_2—\overset{+}{N}H_3}$$

Ethanolamine

**Lecithins** and **cephalins** are two types of glycerophospholipids that are particularly abundant in brain and nerve tissues as well as in egg yolks, wheat germ, and yeast. Lecithins contain choline, and cephalins usually contain ethanolamine and sometimes serine. In the following structural formulas, palmitic acid is used as an example of a fatty acid:

$$\begin{array}{l} CH_2-O-\overset{\displaystyle O}{\overset{\|}{C}}-(CH_2)_{14}CH_3 \\ | \\ CH-O-\overset{\displaystyle O}{\overset{\|}{C}}-(CH_2)_{14}CH_3 \\ | \\ CH_2-O-\overset{\displaystyle O}{\overset{\|}{P}}-O-\underbrace{CH_2CH_2\overset{+}{N}(CH_3)_3}_{\text{Choline}} \\ \qquad\quad\;\; | \\ \qquad\quad\;\; O^- \end{array} \quad \begin{array}{l} \left.\right\} \text{Nonpolar fatty acids} \\ \\ \text{Polar} \end{array}$$

A lecithin

$$\begin{array}{l} CH_2-O-\overset{\displaystyle O}{\overset{\|}{C}}-(CH_2)_{14}CH_3 \\ | \\ CH-O-\overset{\displaystyle O}{\overset{\|}{C}}-(CH_2)_{14}CH_3 \\ | \\ CH_2-O-\overset{\displaystyle O}{\overset{\|}{P}}-O-\underbrace{CH_2CH_2\overset{+}{N}H_3}_{\text{Ethanolamine}} \\ \qquad\quad\;\; | \\ \qquad\quad\;\; O^- \end{array}$$

A cephalin

Glycerophospholipids contain both polar and nonpolar regions, which allow them to interact with both polar and nonpolar substances. The ionized amine and phosphate portion, called "the head," is polar and strongly attracted to water. (See Figure 17.6.) The two fatty acids connected to the glycerol molecule represent the nonpolar "tails" of the glycerophospholipid. The hydrocarbon chains that make up the "tails" are only soluble in other nonpolar substances, mostly lipids.

*Glycerophospholipids* are the most abundant lipids in cell membranes, where they play an important role in cellular permeability. They make up much of the myelin sheath that protects nerve cells. In the body fluids, glycerophospholipids combine with the less polar triglycerides and cholesterol to make them more soluble as they are transported in the body.

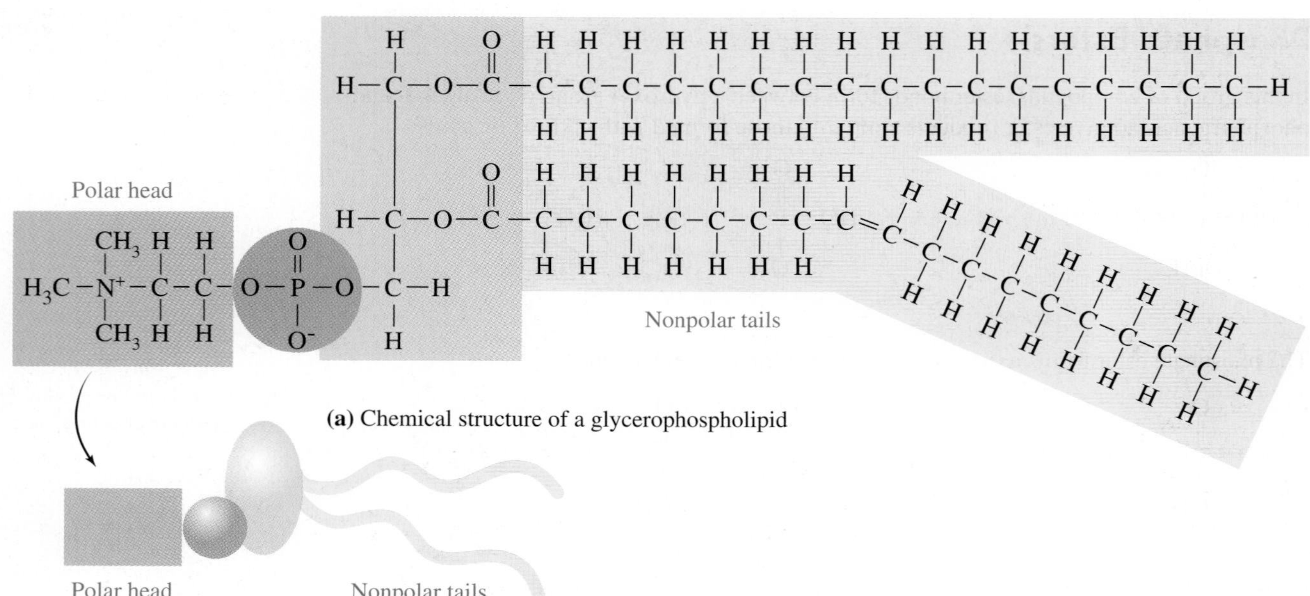


FIGURE 17.6 (a) In a glycerophospholipid, a polar "head" contains the ionized amino alcohol and phosphoric acid groups, while the two fatty acids make up the nonpolar "tails." (b) A simplified drawing indicates the polar region and the nonpolar region.

Q Why are glycerophospholipids polar?

## SAMPLE PROBLEM 17.5

### Drawing Glycerophospholipid Structures

Draw the condensed structural formula of the cephalin that contains stearic acid and serine. Describe each component in the glycerophospholipid.

SOLUTION

In general, glycerophospholipids are composed of a glycerol molecule in which two carbon atoms are attached to fatty acids such as stearic acid. The third carbon atom is attached via an ester bond to phosphate linked to an amino alcohol. In this example, the amino alcohol is serine:

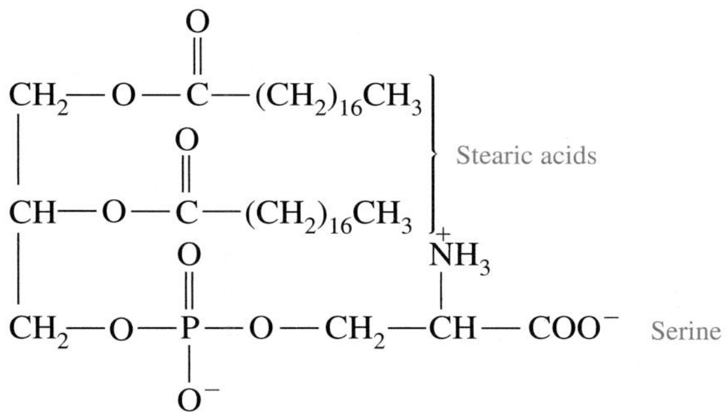

```
              O
              ‖
CH2—O—C—(CH2)16CH3  ⎫
 |            O         ⎬ Stearic acids
 |            ‖         ⎪
CH—O—C—(CH2)16CH3   ⎭
 |            O              +
 |            ‖             NH3
 |            ‖              |
CH2—O—P—O—CH2—CH—COO−   Serine
              |
              O−
```

STUDY CHECK

What are the four components of glycerophospholipids?

## QUESTIONS AND PROBLEMS

### Glycerophospholipids

**17.39** Describe the differences between triacylglycerols and glycerophospholipids.

**17.40** Describe the differences between lecithins and cephalins.

**17.41** Draw the structure of a glycerophospholipid containing two molecules of palmitic acid and ethanolamine. What is another name for this type of glycerophospholipid?

**17.42** Draw the structure of a glycerophospholipid that contains choline and palmitic acids.

**17.43** Identify the following glycerophospholipid and list its components:

```
              O
              ‖
CH2—O—C—(CH2)7CH=CH(CH2)7CH3
 |            O
 |            ‖
CH—O—C—(CH2)16CH3
 |            O
 |            ‖                +
CH2—O—P—O—CH2—CH2—NH3
              |
              O−
```

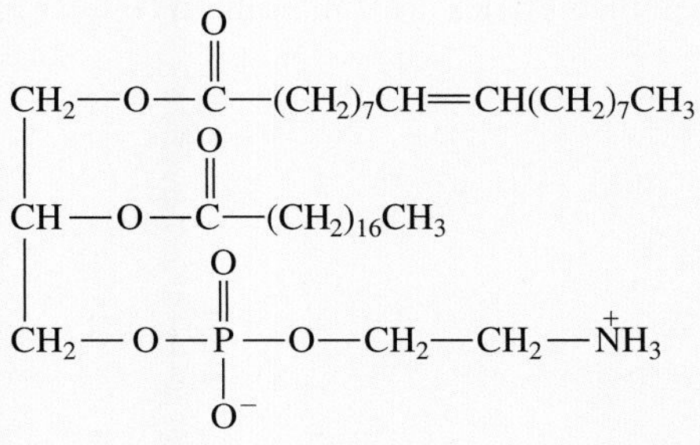

**17.44** Identify the following glycerophospholipid and list its components:

```
              O
              ‖
CH2—O—C—(CH2)14CH3
 |            O
 |            ‖
CH—O—C—(CH2)16CH3
 |            O                      CH3
 |            ‖                      | +
CH2—O—P—O—CH2—CH2—N—CH3
              |                      |
              O−                     CH3
```

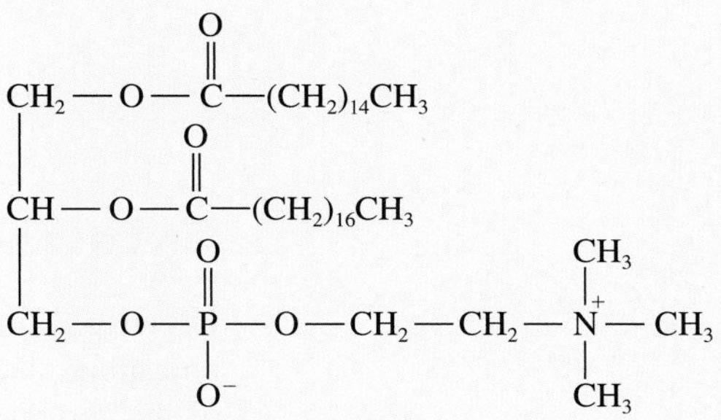

## 17.6 Sphingolipids

**LEARNING GOAL**

Describe the types of lipids that contain sphingosine.

**Sphingolipids** are lipids that contain a long-chain amino alcohol called *sphingosine*, rather than glycerol.

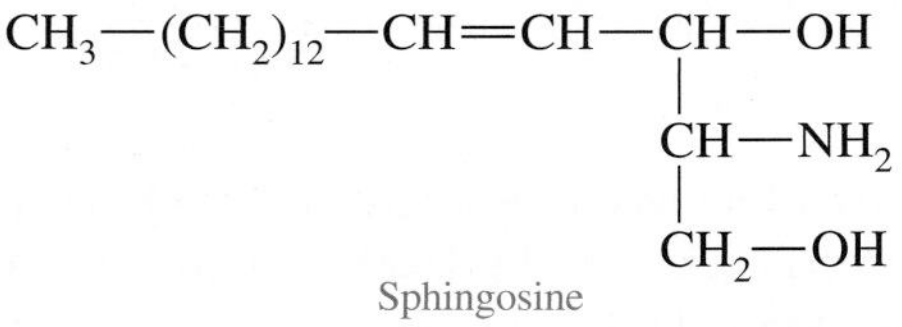

$$
\begin{array}{l}
CH_3-(CH_2)_{12}-CH{=}CH-CH-OH \\
\qquad\qquad\qquad\qquad\qquad\quad\; | \\
\qquad\qquad\qquad\qquad\qquad\; CH-NH_2 \\
\qquad\qquad\qquad\qquad\qquad\quad\; | \\
\qquad\qquad\qquad\qquad\qquad\; CH_2-OH
\end{array}
$$

Sphingosine

In **ceramides**, the $-NH_2$ group of sphingosine is attached by an *amide* link to a fatty acid:

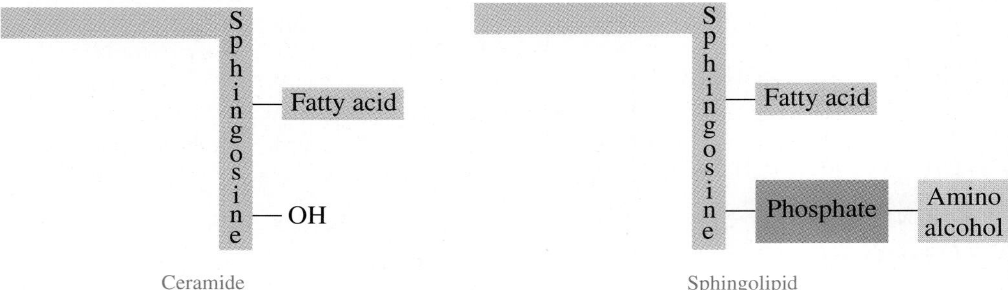


Ceramide

Sphingolipid

One of the most abundant groups of sphingolipids is the **sphingomyelins**, in which the $-OH$ of a ceramide forms a phosphate ester of choline, an amino alcohol. The sphingomyelins are abundant in the white matter of the myelin sheath, a coating surrounding the nerve cells that increases the speed of nerve impulses and insulates and protects the nerve cells:

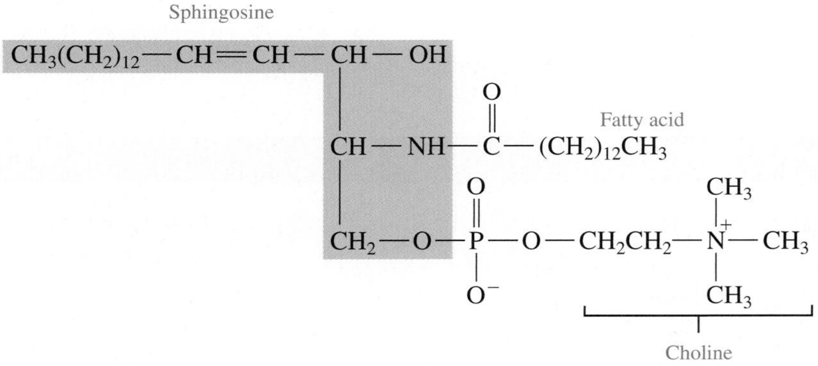

$$
\begin{array}{l}
\text{Sphingosine} \\
CH_3(CH_2)_{12}-CH{=}CH-CH-OH \\
\qquad\qquad\qquad\qquad\quad | \qquad\quad\; O \qquad\quad \text{Fatty acid} \\
\qquad\qquad\qquad\qquad\quad | \qquad\quad\; \| \\
\qquad\qquad\qquad\qquad CH-NH-C-(CH_2)_{12}CH_3 \\
\qquad\qquad\qquad\qquad\quad | \qquad\quad O \qquad\qquad\qquad\quad CH_3 \\
\qquad\qquad\qquad\qquad\quad | \qquad\quad \| \qquad\qquad\qquad\qquad | \\
\qquad\qquad\qquad\qquad CH_2-O-P-O-CH_2CH_2-\overset{+}{N}-CH_3 \\
\qquad\qquad\qquad\qquad\qquad\qquad\; | \qquad\qquad\qquad\qquad\; | \\
\qquad\qquad\qquad\qquad\qquad\qquad O^- \qquad\qquad\qquad\quad CH_3 \\
\qquad\qquad\qquad\qquad\qquad\qquad\qquad\qquad\quad \underbrace{\qquad\qquad\qquad\qquad}_{\text{Choline}}
\end{array}
$$

Sphingomyelin (a sphingolipid)

### Glycosphingolipids

**Glycosphingolipids** are sphingolipids that contain carbohydrates. In a **cerebroside**, one monosaccharide (galactose or glucose) forms a $\beta$-glycosidic bond with the $-OH$ of the ceramide. Cerebrosides are present primarily in the brain and the myelin shealth. Glycosphingolipids on the surface of cell membranes are important to cellular recognition and tissue immunity.

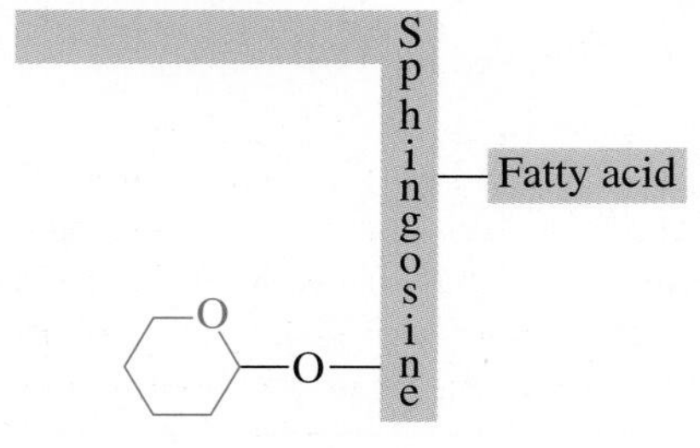


Cerebroside

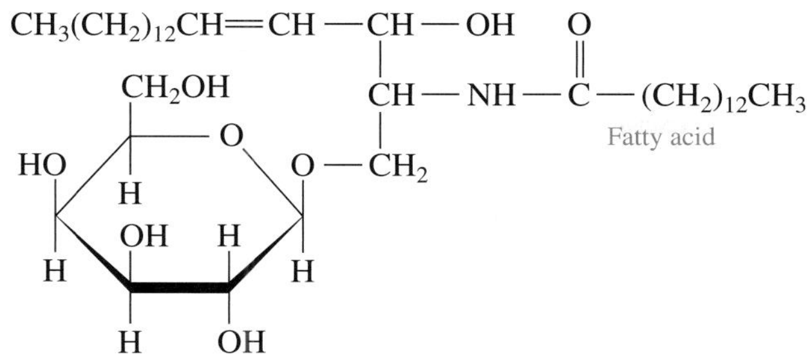

Sphingosine

$CH_3(CH_2)_{12}CH{=}CH{-}CH{-}OH$

$CH{-}NH{-}C(=O){-}(CH_2)_{12}CH_3$

Fatty acid

$CH_2OH$ HO O O $-CH_2$ H OH H H H H OH

Galactose

Galactocerebroside (a glycosphingolipid)

A **ganglioside** is similar to a cerebroside but contains chains of two to seven monosaccharides bonded to a ceramide. Gangliosides are found in the neurons of the brain and on the surface of cell membranes where they act as receptors for hormones, viruses, and certain drugs. In Tay–Sachs disease, the ganglioside known as $GM_2$ accumulates because of a genetic defect in hexosaminidase A, an enzyme needed for the removal of the *N*-acetyl-D-galactosamine.

$CH_3{-}(CH_2)_{12}{-}CH{=}CH{-}CH{-}OH$

$CH_2{-}NH{-}C(=O){-}(CH_2)_{12}{-}CH_3$

*N*-Acetyl-D-galactosamine

D-Galactose

D-Glucose

$CH_2OH$ $CH_2OH$ $CH_2OH$ OH O O O O O O O OH OH OH OH NH $O{=}C$ $CH_3$ $CH_2$

$CH_3{-}C(=O){-}NH$ O CHOH CHOH $CH_2OH$ $COO^-$ OH

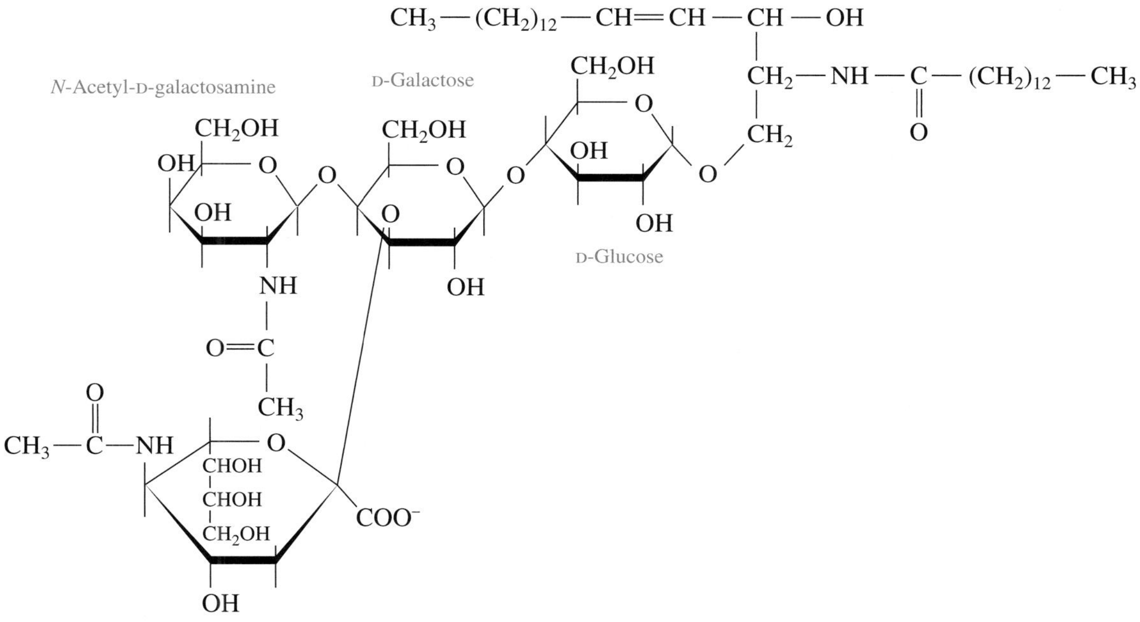

Glycosphingolipid $GM_2$ or Tay–Sachs ganglioside

CONCEPT CHECK 17.4

**Sphingolipids**

Describe the similarities and differences between the structures of sphingomyelin, cerebrosides, and gangliosides.

ANSWER

Sphingomyelin, cerebrosides, and gangliosides are all sphingolipids that contain the ceramide structure in which sphingosine is bonded to a fatty acid by an amide bond. In sphingomyelin, the —OH of a ceramide forms a phosphate ester with the amino alcohol choline. In cerebrosides, the —OH of a ceramide is bonded to one monosaccharide, galactose, or glucose. In gangliosides, the —OH of a ceramide is bonded to a chain of two to seven monosaccharides.

## SAMPLE PROBLEM 17.6

### Glycosphingolipid

In Fabry's disease, the ganglioside shown here accumulates due to a deficiency of $\alpha$-galactosidase. Identify the components A–E in this glycosphingolipid:

A

$CH_3(CH_2)_{12}CH{=}CH{-}CH{-}OH$

$CH{-}NH{-}C({=}O){-}(CH_2)_{16}CH_3$ (B)

$CH_2{-}O{-}$ [glucose E]$\ {-}O{-}$ [galactose D]$\ {-}O{-}$ [galactose C]

C D E

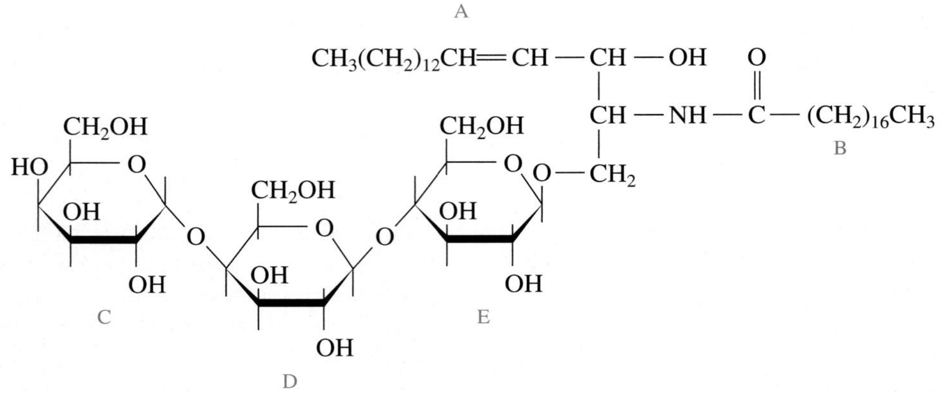

SOLUTION

In this glycosphingolipid, the components are sphingosine (A); stearic acid (B); two galactose units (C, D); and one glucose (E).

STUDY CHECK

How do we know that this glycosphingolipid is a ganglioside rather than a cerebroside?

## HEALTH NOTE

### Lipid Diseases

Many lipid diseases (*lipidoses*) involve the excessive accumulation of a sphingolipid because an enzyme needed for its breakdown is deficient or absent. The accumulation of these sphingolipids may enlarge the spleen, liver, and bone marrow cells (Gaucher's disease) and cause mental retardation, seizures, blindness, or death in early infancy. Some lipid storage diseases are listed in Table 17.3.

In multiple sclerosis, sphingomyelins are lost from the myelin sheath, which protects the neurons in the brain and spinal cord. As the disease progresses, the myelin sheath deteriorates. Scars form on the neurons and impair the transmission of nerve signals. The symptoms of multiple sclerosis include various levels of muscle weakness and loss of coordination and vision depending on the amount of damage. The cause of multiple sclerosis is not yet known, although some researchers suggest that a virus is involved.

**TABLE 17.3** Lipid Diseases

| Name of Disease | Lipid Stored | Type | Enzyme Absent |
|---|---|---|---|
| Fabry's | Gal-gal-glucosylceramide | Ganglioside | $\alpha$-Galactosidase |
| Gaucher's | Glucosylceramide | Cerebroside | $\beta$-Glucosidase |
| Niemann–Pick | Sphingomyelin | Sphingolipid | Sphingomyelinase |
| Tay–Sachs | $GM_2$ ganglioside | Ganglioside | Hexosaminidase A |

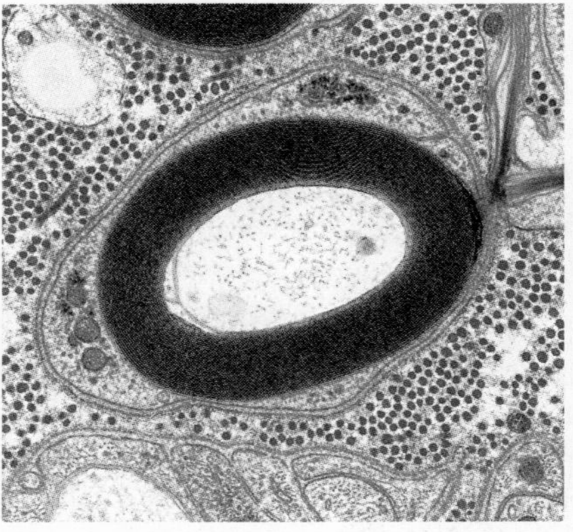

## QUESTIONS AND PROBLEMS

### Sphingolipids

**17.45** Describe the differences between glycerophospholipids and ceramides.

**17.46** Describe the differences between a cerebroside and a ganglioside.

**17.47** Draw the structure of a cerebroside containing palmitic acid and galactose.

**17.48** What amino alcohol is found in sphingomyelin? Draw the structure of a sphingomyelin containing palmitic acid.

# 17.7 Steroids: Cholesterol, Bile Salts, and Steroid Hormones

**LEARNING GOAL**

Describe the structures of steroids.

**Steroids** are compounds containing the steroid nucleus, which consists of three cyclohexane rings and one cyclopentane ring fused together. Although they are large molecules, steroids do not hydrolyze to give fatty acids and alcohols. The four rings in the steroid nucleus are designated A, B, C, and D. The carbon atoms are numbered beginning with the carbons in ring A and ending with the two methyl groups:

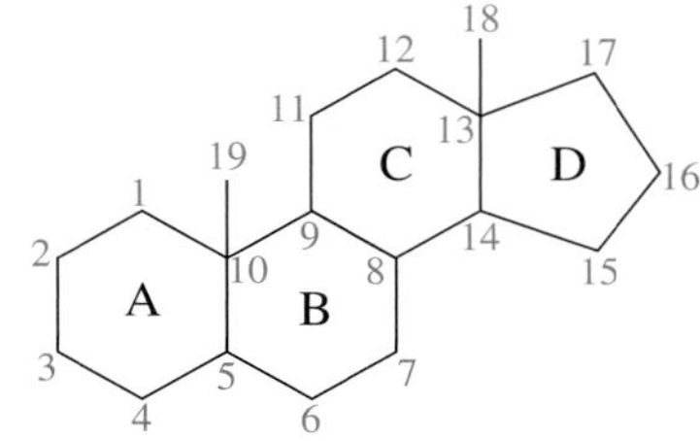


Steroid

MC TUTORIAL Cholesterol

## Cholesterol

Attaching other atoms and groups of atoms to the steroid nucleus forms a wide variety of steroid compounds. **Cholesterol**, which is one of the most important and abundant steroids in the body, is a *sterol* because it contains an oxygen atom as a hydroxyl (—OH) group on carbon 3. Like many steroids, cholesterol has a double bond between carbon 5 and carbon 6, methyl groups at carbon 10 and carbon 13, and a carbon chain at carbon 17. In other steroids, the oxygen atom typically at carbon 3 forms a carbonyl (C=O) group:

Cholesterol

## Cholesterol in the Body

Cholesterol is a component of cellular membranes, myelin sheaths, and brain and nerve tissues. It is also found in the liver, bile salts, and skin, where it forms vitamin D. In the adrenal gland, cholesterol is used to synthesize steroid hormones. Cholesterol in the body is obtained from eating meats, milk, and eggs. The liver synthesizes cholesterol from fats, carbohydrates, and proteins. There is no cholesterol in vegetable and plant products.

**TABLE 17.4 Cholesterol Content of Some Foods**

| Food | Serving Size | Cholesterol (mg) |
|---|---|---|
| Liver (beef) | 3 oz | 370 |
| Large egg | 1 | 200 |
| Lobster | 3 oz | 175 |
| Fried chicken | $3\frac{1}{2}$ oz | 130 |
| Hamburger | 3 oz | 85 |
| Chicken (no skin) | 3 oz | 75 |
| Fish (salmon) | 3 oz | 40 |
| Butter | 1 tablespoon | 30 |
| Whole milk | 1 cup | 35 |
| Skim milk | 1 cup | 5 |
| Margarine | 1 tablespoon | 0 |

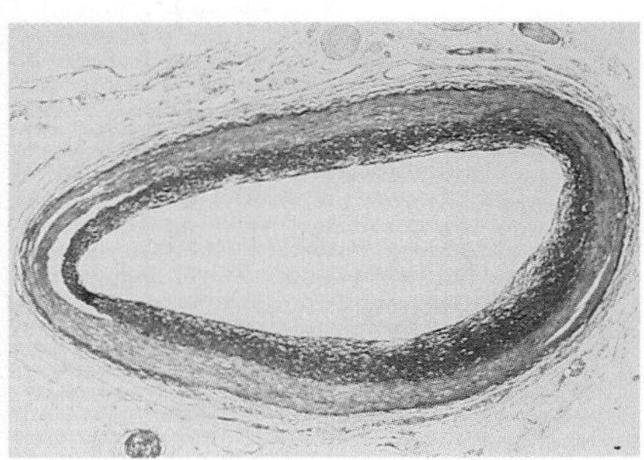

(a)

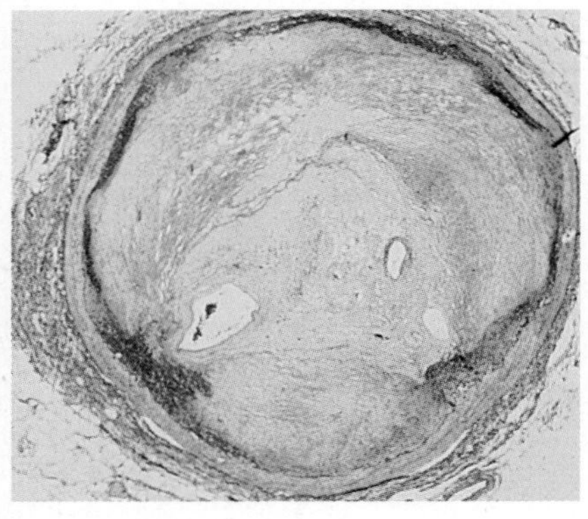

(b)

**FIGURE 17.7** Excess cholesterol forms plaque that can block an artery, resulting in a heart attack. **(a)** A normal, open artery shows no buildup of plaque. **(b)** An artery that is almost completely clogged by atherosclerotic plaque.

Q What property of cholesterol would cause it to form deposits along the coronary arteries?

If a diet is high in cholesterol, the liver produces less. A typical daily American diet includes 400–500 mg of cholesterol, one of the highest in the world. The American Heart Association has recommended that we consume no more than 300 mg of cholesterol a day. The cholesterol contents of some typical foods are listed in Table 17.4.

High levels of cholesterol are associated with the accumulation of lipid deposits (plaque) that line and narrow the coronary arteries. (See Figure 17.7.) Clinically, cholesterol levels are considered elevated if the total plasma cholesterol level exceeds 200 mg/dL.

Saturated fats in the diet may stimulate the production of cholesterol by the liver. A diet that is low in foods containing cholesterol and saturated fats appears to be helpful in reducing the serum cholesterol level. Other factors that may also increase the risk of heart disease are family history, lack of exercise, smoking, obesity, diabetes, gender, and age.

**SAMPLE PROBLEM 17.7**

### Cholesterol

Refer to the structure of cholesterol for the following questions:

**a.** What part of cholesterol is the steroid nucleus?
**b.** What features have been added to the steroid nucleus in cholesterol?
**c.** What classifies cholesterol as a sterol?

SOLUTION

**a.** The four fused rings form the steroid nucleus.
**b.** The cholesterol molecule contains an alcohol (—OH) group on the first ring, methyl groups on carbons 10 and 13, one double bond in the second ring, and a branched carbon chain on the fourth ring.
**c.** The alcohol group determines the sterol classification.

STUDY CHECK

Why is cholesterol in the lipid family?

## Bile Salts

Bile salts are synthesized in the liver from cholesterol and stored in the gallbladder. When bile is secreted into the small intestine, the bile salts mix with the water-insoluble fats and oils in our diets. The bile salts with their nonpolar and polar regions act much like soaps, breaking apart and emulsifying large globules of fat. The emulsions that form have a larger surface area for the lipases, enzymes that digest fat. Bile salts also help in the absorption of cholesterol into the intestinal mucosa.

From cholic acid (a bile acid) — From glycine (an amino acid)

[Structure: steroid nucleus with HO, OH, $CH_3$ groups, side chain —C(=O)—N(H)—$CH_2$—C(=O)$O^-Na^+$]

Sodium glycocholate (a bile salt)

When large amounts of cholesterol accumulate in the gallbladder, cholesterol can precipitate out and form gallstones. (See Figure 17.8.) Gallstones are composed of almost

100% cholesterol, with some calcium salts, fatty acids, and glycerophospholipids. If a gallstone passes into the bile duct, the pain can be severe. If the gallstone obstructs the duct, bile cannot be excreted. Then bile pigments known as bilirubin enter the blood where they cause jaundice, which gives a yellow color to the skin and eyes.

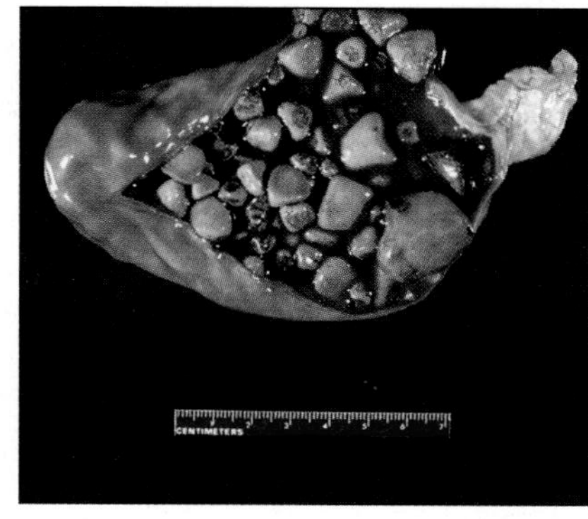

FIGURE 17.8 Gallstones form in the gallbladder when cholesterol levels are high.

Q What type of steroid is stored in the gallbladder?

## Lipoproteins: Transporting Lipids

In the body, lipids must be transported through the bloodstream to tissues where they are stored, used for energy, or used to make hormones. However, most lipids are nonpolar and insoluble in the aqueous environment of blood. They are made more soluble by combining them with glycerophospholipids and proteins to form water-soluble complexes called **lipoproteins**. In general, lipoproteins are spherical particles with an outer surface of polar proteins and glycerophospholipids that surround hundreds of nonpolar molecules of triacylglycerols and cholesteryl esters. (See Figure 17.9.) Cholesteryl esters are the prevalent form of cholesterol in the blood. They are formed by the esterification of the hydroxyl group in cholesterol with a fatty acid:

Ester bond

$CH_3-(CH_2)_{14}-C(=O)-O-$ (cholesterol ring system with $CH_3$ groups)

Cholesteryl ester

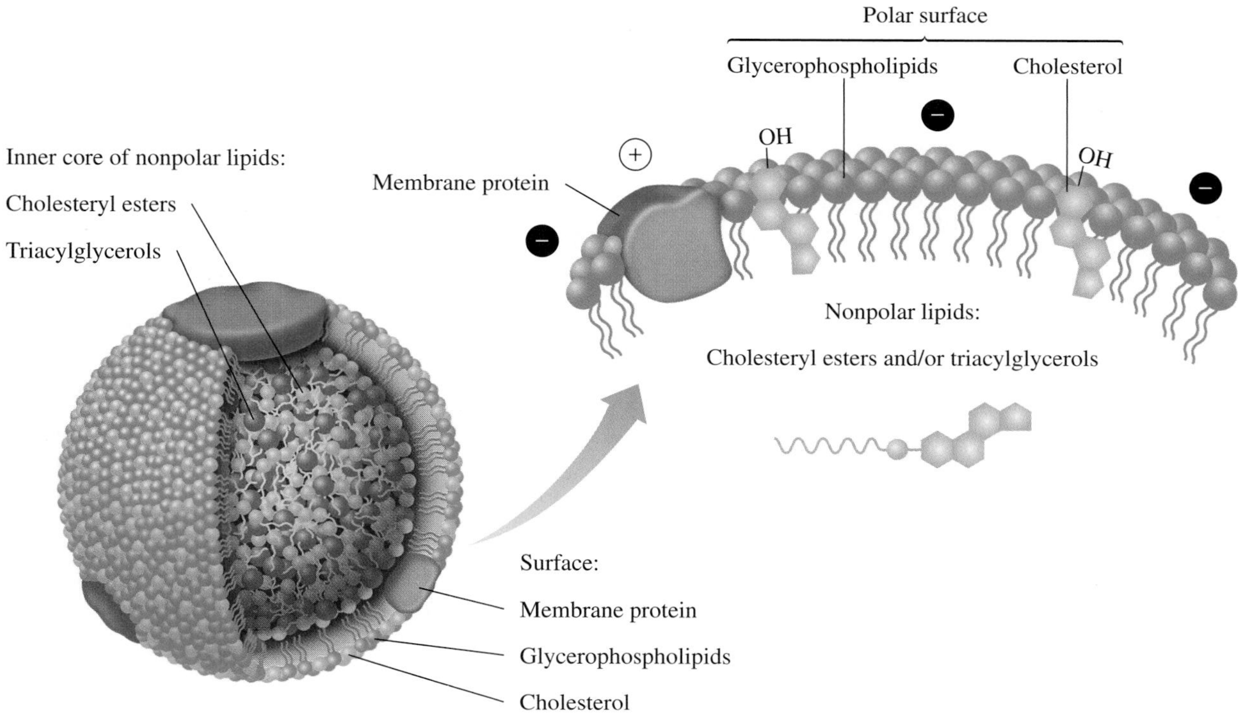


FIGURE 17.9 A spherical lipoprotein particle surrounds nonpolar lipids with polar lipids and protein for transport to body cells.

Q Why are the polar components on the surface of a lipoprotein particle and the nonpolar components at the center?

**TABLE 17.5** Composition and Properties of Plasma Lipoproteins

| | Chylomicron | VLDL | LDL | HDL |
|---|---|---|---|---|
| **Density (g/mL)** | 0.940 | 0.950–1.006 | 1.006–1.063 | 1.063–1.210 |
| | | **Composition (% by mass)** | | |
| **Type of Lipid** | | | | |
| Triacylglycerol | 86 | 55 | 6 | 4 |
| Phospholipids | 7 | 18 | 22 | 24 |
| Cholesterol | 2 | 7 | 8 | 2 |
| Cholesteryl esters | 3 | 12 | 42 | 15 |
| Protein | 2 | 8 | 22 | 55 |

Types of lipoproteins differ in density, lipid composition, and function. They include chylomicrons, very-low-density lipoprotein (VLDL), low-density lipoprotein (LDL), and high-density lipoprotein (HDL). The LDLs form when the triacylglycerol portion is removed from VLDLs. The density of the lipoproteins increases as the percentage of protein increases. (See Table 17.5.) The chylomicrons and the VLDLs transport triacylglycerols, glycerophospholipids, and cholesterol to the tissues for storage or to the muscles for energy. (See Figure 17.10.) The LDLs transport cholesterol to tissues to be used for the synthesis of cell membranes, steroid hormones, and bile salts. When the level of LDL exceeds the amount of cholesterol needed by the tissues, the LDLs deposit cholesterol in the arteries, which can restrict blood flow and increase the risk of developing heart disease and/or myocardial infarctions (heart attacks). This is why LDL cholesterol is called "bad" cholesterol.

The HDLs remove excess cholesterol from the tissues and carry it to the liver, where it is converted to bile salts and eliminated. When HDL levels are high, cholesterol that is not needed by the tissues is carried to the liver for elimination rather than deposited in the arteries, which gives the HDLs the name of "good" cholesterol. Most of the cholesterol in the body is synthesized in the liver, although some comes from the diet. However, a person on a high-fat diet reabsorbs cholesterol from the bile salts, causing less cholesterol to be eliminated. In addition, higher levels of saturated fats stimulate the synthesis of cholesterol by the liver.

Because high cholesterol levels are associated with the onset of atherosclerosis and heart disease, the serum levels of LDL and HDL are generally determined as part of a medical

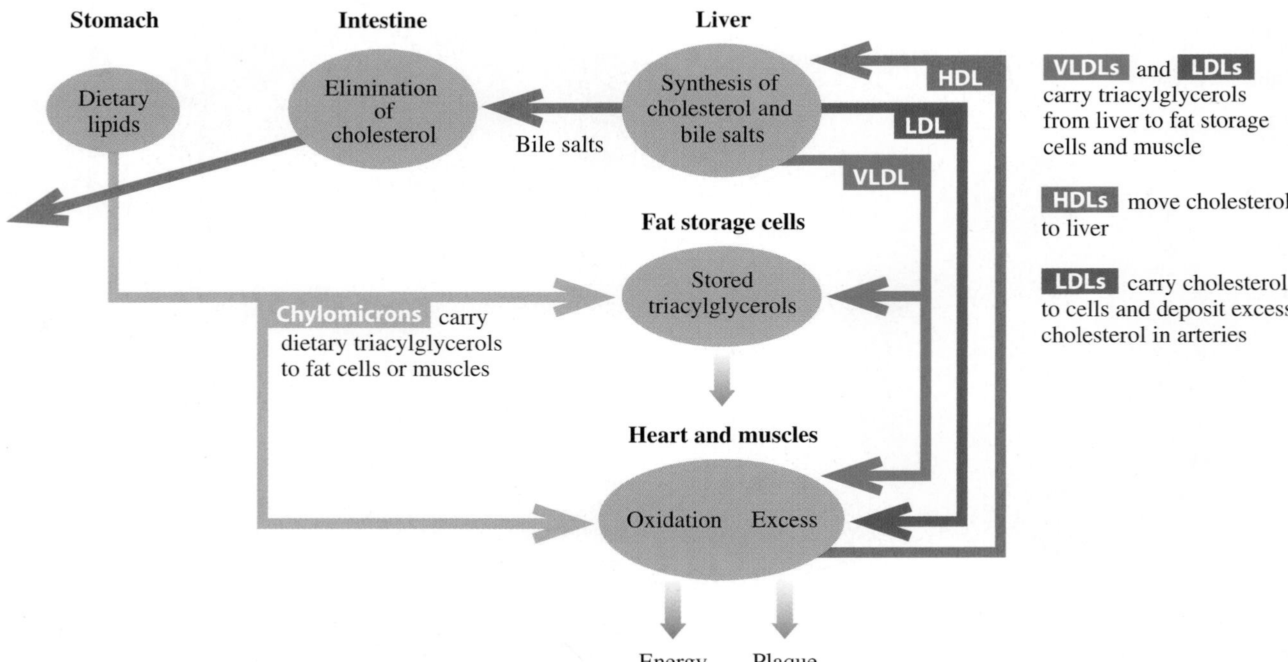


**FIGURE 17.10** Lipoproteins such as HDLs and LDLs transport nonpolar lipids and cholesterol to cells and the liver.
**Q** What type of lipoprotein transports cholesterol to the liver?

examination. For adults, recommended levels for total cholesterol are less than 200 mg/dL with LDL less than 130 mg/dL and HDL higher than 40 mg/dL. A lower level of serum cholesterol decreases the risk of heart disease. Increased HDL levels are found in people who exercise regularly and eat less saturated fat.

## Steroid Hormones

The word *hormone* comes from the Greek "to arouse" or "to excite." Hormones are chemical messengers that serve as a communication system from one part of the body to another. The *steroid* hormones, which include the sex hormones and the adrenocortical hormones, are closely related in structure to cholesterol and depend on cholesterol for their synthesis.

Two of the male sex hormones, *testosterone* and *androsterone*, promote the growth of muscle and of facial hair and the maturation of the male sex organs and of sperm.

The *estrogens*, a group of female sex hormones, direct the development of female sexual characteristics: the uterus increases in size, fat is deposited in the breasts, and the pelvis broadens. *Progesterone* prepares the uterus for the implantation of a fertilized egg. If an egg is not fertilized, the levels of progesterone and estrogen drop sharply, and menstruation follows. Synthetic forms of the female sex hormones are used in birth-control pills. As with other kinds of steroids, side effects include weight gain and a greater risk of forming blood clots. The structures of some steroid hormones follow:

| Hormone | Biological Effects |
|---|---|
| 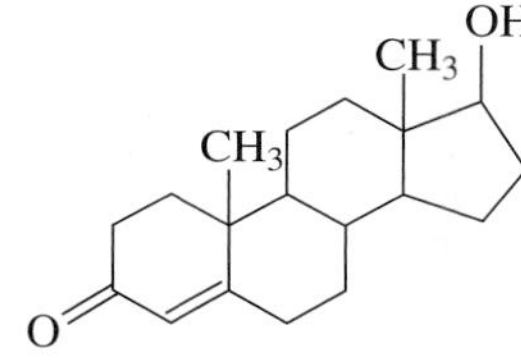 Testosterone (androgen) (produced in testes) | Development of male organs; male sexual characteristics including muscles and facial hair; sperm formation |
| Estradiol (estrogen) (produced in ovaries) | Development of female sexual characteristics; ovulation |
| Progesterone (produced in ovaries) | Prepares uterus for fertilized egg |
| Norethindrone (synthetic progestin) | Contraceptive (birth-control) pill |

## Adrenal Corticosteroids

The adrenal glands, located on the top of each kidney, produce the corticosteroids. *Aldosterone*, a mineralocorticoid, is responsible for electrolyte and water balance by the kidneys. *Cortisone*, a glucocorticoid, increases the blood glucose level and stimulates the synthesis of glycogen in the liver from amino acids. Synthetic corticoids such as *prednisone* are derived from cortisone and used medically for reducing inflammation and treating asthma and rheumatoid arthritis, although health problems can result from long-term use.

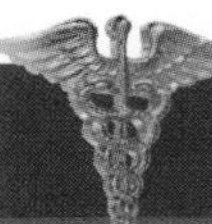

## HEALTH NOTE

### Anabolic Steroids

Some of the physiological effects of testosterone are to increase muscle mass and decrease body fat. Derivatives of testosterone called *anabolic steroids* that enhance these effects have been synthesized. Although they have some medical uses, anabolic steroids have been used in rather high dosages by some athletes in an effort to increase muscle mass. Such use is banned by most sports organizations.

Use of anabolic steroids in attempting to improve athletic strength can cause side effects including hypertension, fluid retention, increased hair growth, sleep disturbances, and acne. Over a long period, their use may cause irreversible liver damage and decreased sperm production.

### Some Anabolic Steroids

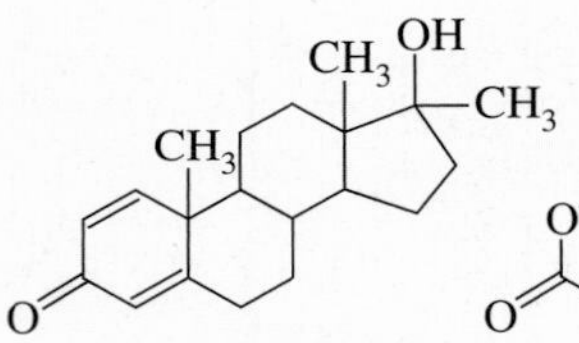

Methandienone

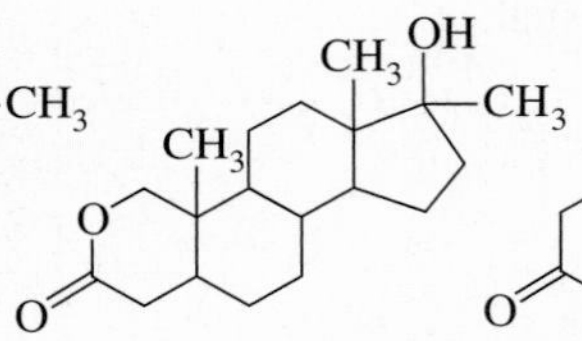

Oxandrolone

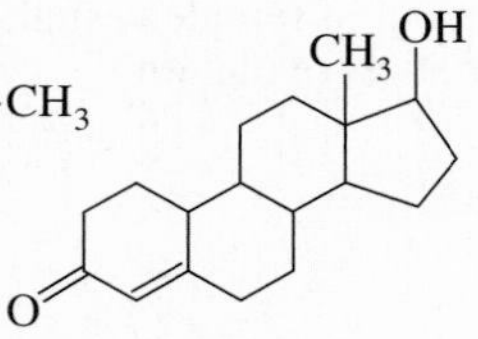

Nandrolone

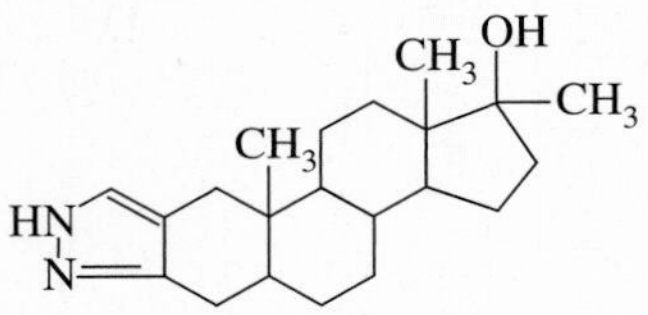

Stanozolol

### Corticosteroids

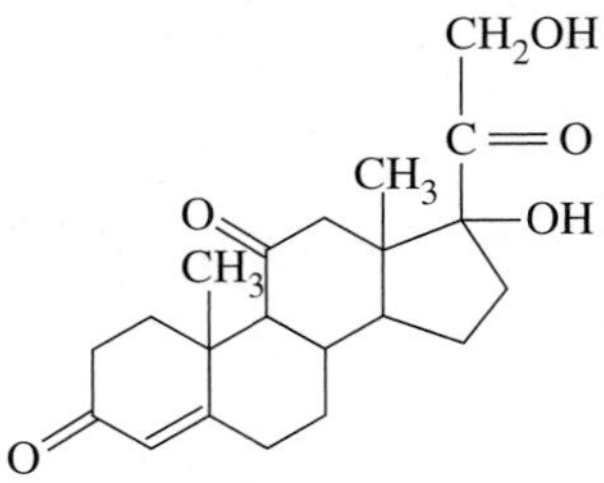

Cortisone (produced in adrenal gland)

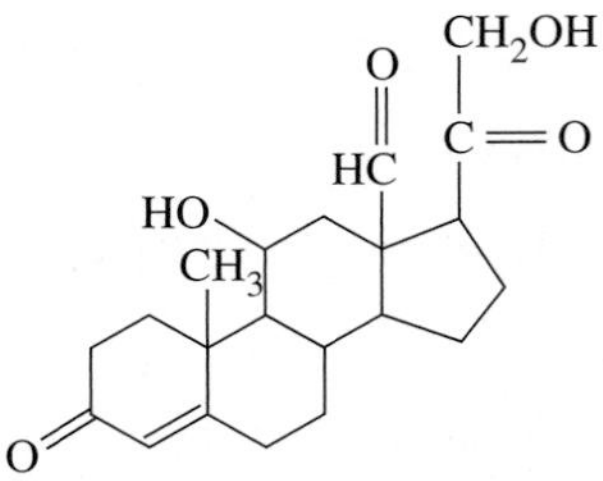

Aldosterone (mineralocorticoid) (produced in adrenal gland)

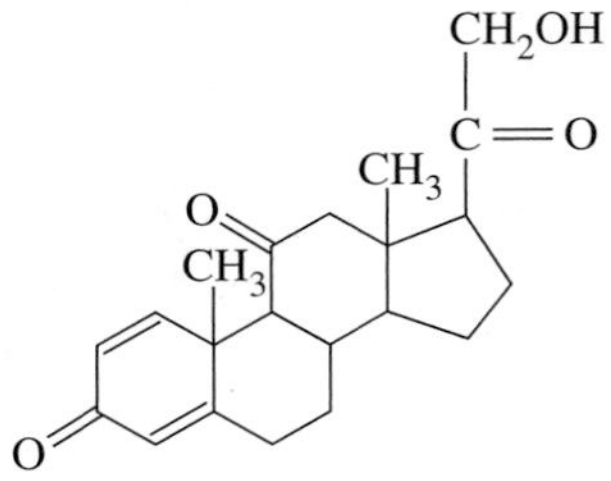

Prednisone (synthetic corticoid)

### Biological Effects

| Cortisone | Aldosterone | Prednisone |
|---|---|---|
| Increases the blood glucose and glycogen levels from fatty acids and amino acids | Increases the reabsorption of $Na^+$ in kidneys; retention of water | Reduces inflammation; treatment of asthma and rheumatoid arthritis |

SAMPLE PROBLEM 17.8

### Steroid Hormones

What are the groups on the steroid nucleus in the sex hormones estradiol and testosterone?

SOLUTION

Estradiol contains an aromatic ring, one methyl group, a hydroxyl group, and a phenol. Testosterone contains a ketone group, two methyl groups, an alkene, and a hydroxyl group.

STUDY CHECK

What are the similarities and differences in the structures of testosterone and the anabolic steroid nandrolone?

## QUESTIONS AND PROBLEMS

### Steroids: Cholesterol, Bile Salts, and Steroid Hormones

17.49 Draw the structure for the steroid nucleus.

**17.50** Which of the following compounds are derived from cholesterol?
**a.** glyceryl tristearate **b.** cortisone
**c.** bile salts **d.** testosterone
**e.** estradiol

17.51 What is the function of bile salts in digestion?

**17.52** Why are gallstones composed of cholesterol?

17.53 What is the general structure of lipoproteins?

**17.54** Why are lipoproteins needed to transport lipids in the bloodstream?

17.55 How do chylomicrons differ from very-low-density lipoproteins?

**17.56** How do LDLs differ from HDLs?

17.57 Why are LDLs called "bad" cholesterol?

**17.58** Why are HDLs called "good" cholesterol?

17.59 What are the similarities and differences between the sex hormones estradiol and testosterone?

**17.60** What are the similarities and differences between the adrenal hormone cortisone and the synthetic corticoid prednisone?

17.61 Which of the following are male sex hormones?
**a.** cholesterol **b.** aldosterone
**c.** estrogen **d.** testosterone
**e.** choline

**17.62** Which of the following are adrenal corticosteroids?
**a.** cholesterol **b.** aldosterone
**c.** estrogen **d.** testosterone
**e.** choline

## 17.8 Cell Membranes

LEARNING GOAL

Describe the composition and function of the lipid bilayer in cell membranes.

The membrane of a cell separates the contents of the cell from the external fluids. It is semipermeable so that nutrients can enter the cell and waste products can leave. The main components of a cell membrane are glycerophospholipids and sphingolipids. Earlier in this chapter, we saw that glycerophospholipids consist of a nonpolar region or "tail" with long-chain fatty acids and a polar region or "head" from phosphoric acid and amino alcohols that ionize at physiological pH. The lipid composition of the membranes of human red blood cells and bacterial cells is given in Table 17.6.

MC™ SELF STUDY ACTIVITIES
Membrane Structure
Diffusion
Osmosis
Active Transport

**TABLE 17.6** Lipid Composition of Cell Membranes

| Type of Lipid | Human Red Blood Cells (% m/m) | Bacterial Cells (% m/m) |
|---|---|---|
| **Glycerophospholipids** | | |
| Choline | 19 | 0 |
| Ethanolamine | 18 | 65 |
| Serine | 8 | 0 |
| **Triacylglycerol** | 0 | 18 |
| **Sphingomyelin** | 18 | 0 |
| **Glycosphingolipids** | 10 | 0 |
| **Cholesterol** | 25 | 0 |
| **Others** | 2 | 17 |

Data adapted from Mathews, C. K., Van Holde, K. K., and Ahem, K. G. *Biochemistry*; Addison Wesley/Longman/Benjamin Cummings: New York, 2000, p. 322.

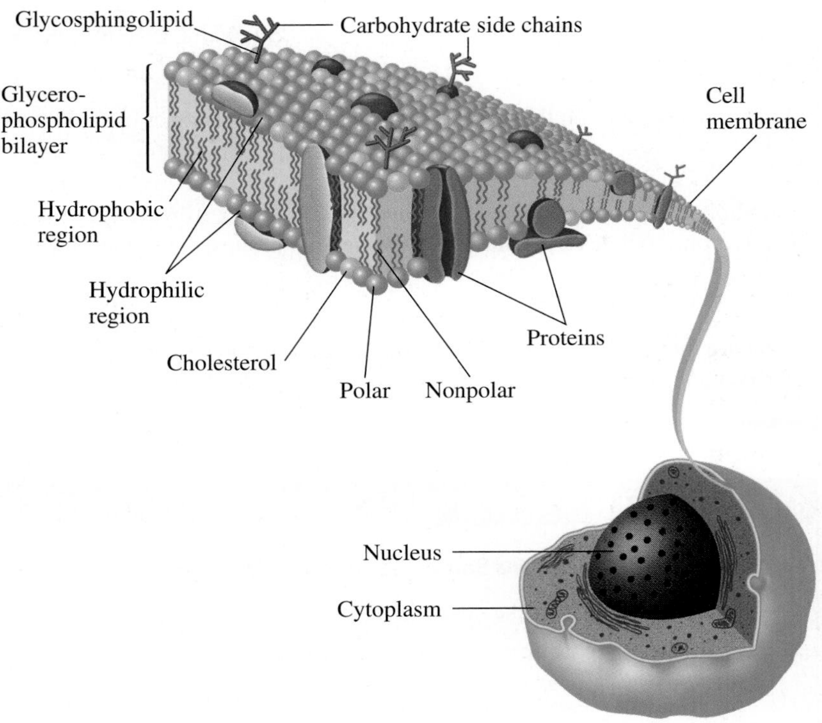


**FIGURE 17.11** In the fluid mosaic model of a cell membrane, proteins and cholesterol are embedded in a lipid bilayer of glycerophospholipids. The bilayer forms a membrane-type barrier with polar heads at the membrane surfaces and the nonpolar tails in the center away from the water.

**Q** What types of fatty acids are found in the glycerophospholipids of the lipid bilayer?

In a cell membrane, two rows of glycerophospholipids are arranged like a sandwich. Their nonpolar tails, which are hydrophobic ("water-fearing"), move to the center, while their polar heads, which are hydrophilic ("water-loving"), align on the outer edges of the membrane. This double row arrangement of glycerophospholipids is called a **lipid bilayer**. (See Figure 17.11.) One row of glycerophospholipids forms the outside surface of the membrane, which is in contact with the external fluids, and the other row forms the inside surface of the membrane, which is in contact with the internal contents of the cell.

Most of the glycerophospholipids in the lipid bilayer contain unsaturated fatty acids. Because of the kinks in the carbon chains at the cis double bonds, the glycerophospholipids do not fit closely together. As a result, the lipid bilayer is not a rigid, fixed structure, but one that is dynamic and fluid-like. This liquid-like bilayer also contains proteins, carbohydrates, and cholesterol molecules. For this reason, the model of biological membranes is referred to as the **fluid mosaic model** of membranes.

In the fluid mosaic model, peripheral proteins emerge on just one of the surfaces, outer or inner. The integral proteins extend through the entire lipid bilayer and appear on both surfaces of the membrane. Some proteins and lipids on the outer surface of the cell membrane are attached to carbohydrates to form glycoproteins and glycosphingolipids. These carbohydrate chains project into the surrounding fluid environment, where they are responsible for cell recognition and communication with chemical messengers such as hormones and neurotransmitters. In animals, cholesterol molecules embedded among the glycerophospholipids make up 20–25% of the lipid bilayer. Because cholesterol molecules are large and rigid, they reduce the flexibility of the lipid bilayer and add strength to the cell membrane.

## Transport through Cell Membranes

Ions and molecules flow in and out of the cell in several ways. In the simplest transport mechanism called *diffusion* or *passive transport*, ions and small molecules migrate from a higher concentration to a lower concentration. For example, some ions as well as small molecules such as $O_2$, urea, and water diffuse through cell membranes. If their concentration

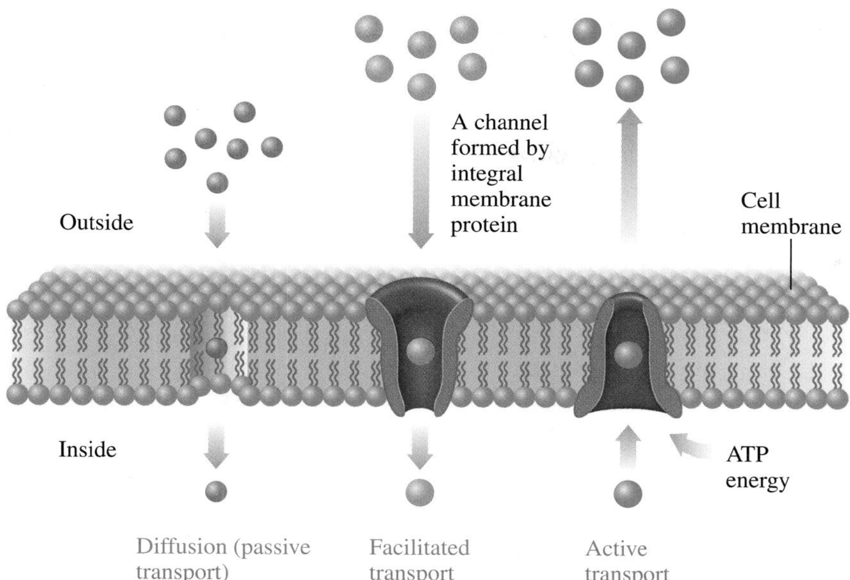


**FIGURE 17.12** Substances are transported across a cell membrane by either diffusion, facilitated transport, or by active transport.

**Q** What is the difference between diffusion and facilitated transport?

is greater outside the cell than inside, they diffuse into the cell. If water has a higher concentration in the cell, it diffuses out of the cell.

Another type of transport, called *facilitated transport*, increases the rate of diffusion for substances that diffuse too slowly by passive diffusion to meet cell needs. This process utilizes the integral proteins that extend from one edge of the cell membrane to the other. These protein channels allow transport of chloride ion ($Cl^-$), bicarbonate ion ($HCO_3^-$), and glucose molecules in and out of the cell.

Certain ions, such as $K^+$, $Na^+$, and $Ca^{2+}$, move across a cell membrane against a concentration gradient. For example, the $K^+$ concentration is greater inside a cell, and the $Na^+$ concentration is greater outside. However, in the conduction of nerve impulses and contraction of muscles, $K^+$ moves into the cell, and $Na^+$ moves out. To move an ion from a lower to a higher concentration requires energy, which is accomplished by a process known as *active transport*. In active transport, a protein complex called a $Na^+/K^+$ pump breaks down adenosine triphosphate (ATP) to adenosine diphosphate (ADP), which releases energy to move $Na^+$ and $K^+$ against their concentration gradients. (See Figure 17.12.)

SAMPLE PROBLEM 17.9

## ■ Lipid Bilayer in the Cell Membranes

Describe the role of glycerophospholipids in the lipid bilayer.

SOLUTION

Glycerophospholipids consist of polar and nonpolar parts. In a cell membrane, an alignment of the nonpolar sections toward the center with the polar sections on the outside produces a barrier that prevents the contents of a cell from mixing with the fluids on the outside of the cell.

STUDY CHECK

Why are protein channels needed in the lipid bilayer?

## QUESTIONS AND PROBLEMS

### Cell Membranes

**17.63** What types of lipids are found in cell membranes?

**17.64** Describe the structure of a lipid bilayer.

**17.65** What is the function of the lipid bilayer in a cell membrane?

**17.66** How do the unsaturated fatty acids in the glycerophospholipids affect the structure of cell membranes?

**17.67** What is the difference between peripheral and integral proteins?

**17.68** What components are attached to carbohydrates on the outer surface of a cell membrane?

**17.69** What is the function of the carbohydrates on a cell membrane surface?

**17.70** Describe how a cell membrane is semipermeable.

**17.71** What are some ways that substances move in and out of cells?

**17.72** Identify the type of transport described by each of the following:

**a.** A molecule moves through a protein channel.

**b.** $O_2$ moves into the cell from a higher concentration outside the cell.

**c.** An ion moves from low to high concentration in the cell.

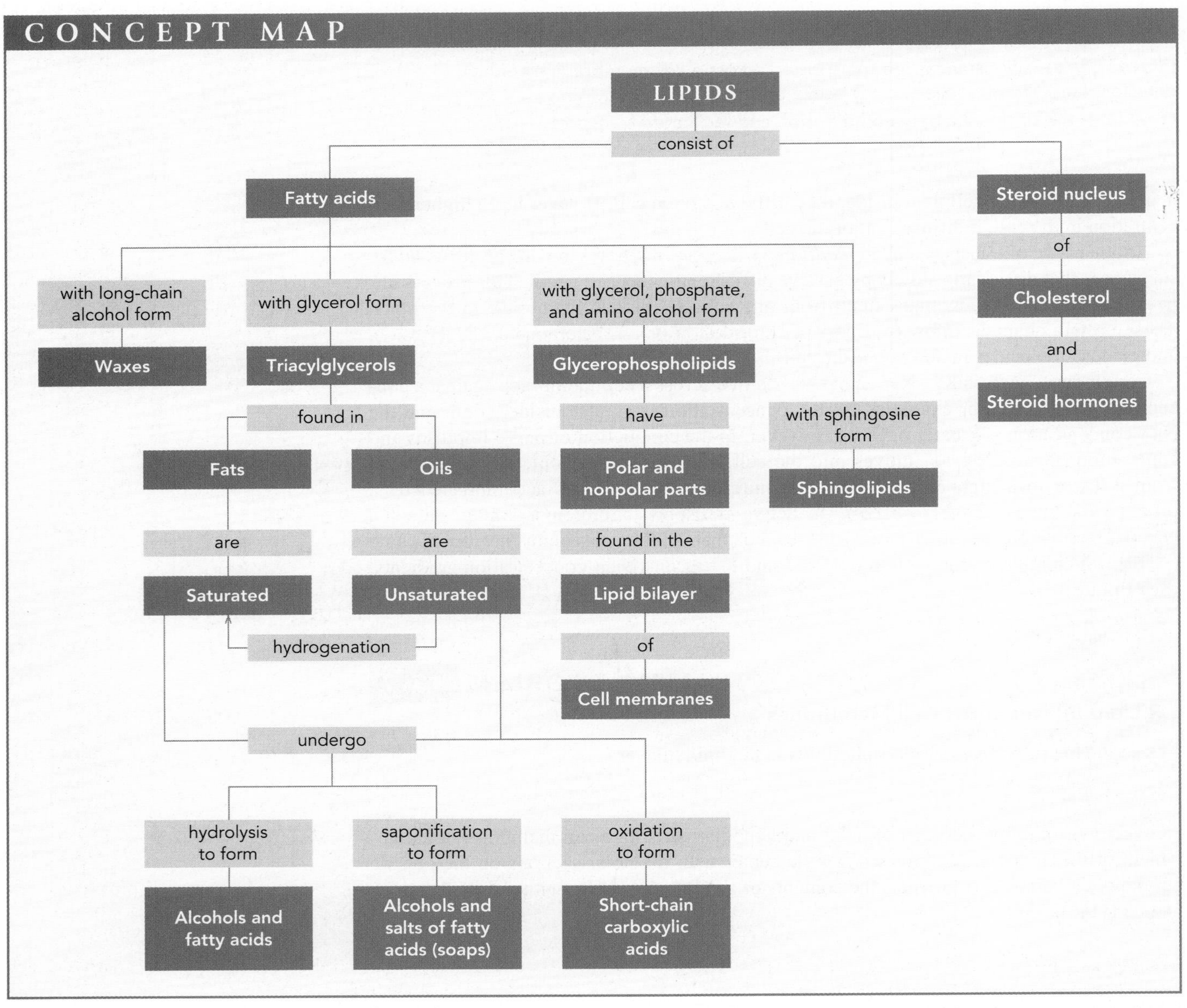

# CHAPTER REVIEW

## 17.1 Lipids

**LEARNING GOAL:** *Describe the classes of lipids.*

Lipids are nonpolar compounds that are not soluble in water. Classes of lipids include waxes, fats and oils, glycerophospholipids, and steroids.

## 17.2 Fatty Acids

**LEARNING GOAL:** *Draw the condensed structural formula of a fatty acid and identify it as saturated or unsaturated.*

Fatty acids are unbranched carboxylic acids that typically contain an even number (12–18) of carbon atoms. Fatty acids may be saturated, monounsaturated with one double bond, or polyunsaturated with two or more double bonds. The double bonds in unsaturated fatty acids are almost always cis.

## 17.3 Waxes, Fats, and Oils

**LEARNING GOAL:** *Draw the condensed structural formula of a wax, fat, or oil produced by the reaction of a fatty acid and an alcohol or glycerol.*

A wax is an ester of a long-chain fatty acid and a long-chain alcohol. The triacylglycerols of fats and oils are esters of glycerol with three long-chain fatty acids. Fats contain more saturated fatty acids and have higher melting points than most vegetable oils.

## 17.4 Chemical Properties of Triacylglycerols

**LEARNING GOAL:** *Draw the structure of the product when a triacylglycerol is hydrogenated, hydrolyzed, or oxidized.*

The hydrogenation of unsaturated fatty acids converts double bonds to single bonds. The oxidation of unsaturated fatty acids produces short-chain fatty acids with disagreeable odors. The hydrolysis of the ester bonds in fats or oils produces glycerol and fatty acids. In saponification, a fat heated with a strong base produces glycerol and the salts of the fatty acids (soaps).

## 17.5 Glycerophospholipids

**LEARNING GOAL:** *Describe the characteristics of glycerophospholipids.*

Glycerophospholipids are esters of glycerol with two fatty acids and a phosphate group attached to an amino alcohol.

## 17.6 Sphingolipids

**LEARNING GOAL:** *Describe the types of lipids that contain sphingosine.*

In sphingolipids, the alcohol sphingosine forms a bond with a fatty acid and a phosphate–amino alcohol group. In glycosphingolipids, sphingosine is bonded to a fatty acid and one or more monosaccharides.

## 17.7 Steroids: Cholesterol, Bile Salts, and Steroid Hormones

**LEARNING GOAL:** *Describe the structures of steroids.*

Steroids are lipids containing the steroid nucleus, which is a fused structure of four rings. Steroids include cholesterol, bile salts, and vitamin D. Lipids, which are nonpolar, are transported through the aqueous environment of the blood by forming lipoproteins. Lipoproteins, such as chylomicrons and LDL, transport triacylglycerols from the intestines and the liver to fat cells for storage and muscles for energy. HDLs transport cholesterol from the tissues to the liver for elimination. The steroid hormones are closely related in structure to cholesterol and depend on cholesterol for their synthesis. The sex hormones, such as estrogen and testosterone, are responsible for sexual characteristics and reproduction. The adrenal corticosteroids, such as aldosterone and cortisone, regulate water balance and glucose levels in the cells.

## 17.8 Cell Membranes

**LEARNING GOAL:** *Describe the composition and function of the lipid bilayer in cell membranes.*

All animal cells are surrounded by a semipermeable membrane that separates the cellular contents from the external fluids. The membrane is composed of two rows of glycerophospholipids in a lipid bilayer. Nutrients and waste products move through the cell membrane using passive transport (diffusion), facilitated transport, or active transport.

# SUMMARY OF REACTIONS

### ESTERIFICATION

$$\text{Glycerol} + 3\text{fatty acid molecules} \longrightarrow \text{triacylglycerol} + 3H_2O$$

### HYDROGENATION OF TRIACYLGLYCEROLS

$$\text{Triacylglycerol (unsaturated)} + H_2 \xrightarrow{\text{Ni}} \text{triacylglycerol (saturated)}$$

### OXIDATION OF UNSATURATED FATTY ACIDS

$$\text{Fatty acids (unsaturated)} \longrightarrow \text{(short-chain aldehydes)} \longrightarrow \text{(short-chain carboxylic acids)}$$

### HYDROLYSIS OF TRIACYLGLYCEROLS

$$\text{Triacylglycerol} + 3H_2O \xrightarrow{\text{HCl}} \text{glycerol} + 3 \text{ fatty acid molecules}$$

### SAPONIFICATION OF TRIACYLGLYCEROLS

$$\text{Triacylglycerol} + 3\text{NaOH} \longrightarrow \text{glycerol} + 3 \text{ sodium salts of fatty acids}$$

# KEY TERMS

**biodiesel** A nonpetroleum fuel that can be used in place of diesel fuel; produced from renewable biological resources.

**cephalin** A glycerophospholipid found in brain and nerve tissues that incorporates the amino alcohol serine or ethanolamine.

**ceramide** A lipid in which sphingosine is attached to a fatty acid by an *amide* link.

**cerebroside** A glycolipid consisting of sphingosine, a fatty acid, and a monosaccharide (usually galactose).

**cholesterol** The most prevalent of the steroid compounds; needed for cellular membranes and the synthesis of vitamin D, hormones, and bile salts.

**fat** A triacylglycerol that is solid at room temperature and usually comes from animal sources.

**fatty acid** A long-chain carboxylic acid found in many lipids.

**fluid mosaic model** The concept that cell membranes are lipid bilayer structures that contain an assortment of polar lipids and proteins in a dynamic, fluid arrangement.

**ganglioside** A glycolipid consisting of sphingosine, a fatty acid, and two or more monosaccharides.

**glycerophospholipid** A polar lipid of glycerol attached to two fatty acids and a phosphate group connected to an amino alcohol such as choline, serine, or ethanolamine.

**glycosphingolipid** The phospholipid that combines sphingosine with a fatty acid bonded to the nitrogen group and one or more monosaccharides bonded by a glycosidic link, which replaces the —OH group of sphingosine.

**hydrogenation** The addition of hydrogen to unsaturated fats.

**lecithins** Glycerophospholipids containing choline as the amino alcohol.

**lipid bilayer** A model of a cell membrane in which glycerophospholipids are arranged in two rows.

**lipids** A family of compounds that is nonpolar in nature and not soluble in water; includes fats, waxes, glycerophospholipids, and steroids.

**lipoprotein** A combination of nonpolar lipids with glycerophospholipids and proteins to form a polar complex that can be transported through body fluids.

**monounsaturated fatty acid** A fatty acid with one double bond.

**oil** A triacylglycerol that is usually a liquid at room temperature and is obtained from a plant source.

**polyunsaturated fatty acid** A fatty acid that contains two or more double bonds.

**prostaglandins (PGs)** A number of compounds derived from arachidonic acid that regulate several physiological processes.

**saturated fatty acids** Fatty acids that have no double bonds; they have higher melting points than unsaturated fatty acids and are usually solid at room temperatures.

**sphingolipids** Types of lipids in which glycerol is replaced by sphingosine.

**sphingomyelins** Sphingolipids that consist of ceramide attached to a phosphate ester of choline, an amino alcohol.

**steroids** Types of lipid composed of a multicyclic ring system.

**triacylglycerols** A family of lipids composed of three fatty acids bonded through ester bonds to glycerol, a trihydroxy alcohol.

**wax** The ester of a long-chain alcohol and a long-chain saturated fatty acid.

## UNDERSTANDING THE CONCEPTS

17.73 Palmitic acid is obtained from palm oil as glyceryl tripalmitate. Draw the condensed structural formula of glyceryl tripalmitate.

**17.74** Jojoba wax in candles consists of stearic acid and a 22-carbon saturated alcohol. Draw the condensed structural formula of jojoba wax.

17.75 Sunflower oil can be used to make margarine. A triacylglycerol in sunflower oil consists of two linoleic acids and one oleic acid.

**a.** Draw the condensed structural formulas for two isomers of the triacylglycerol in sunflower oil.

**b.** Using one of the isomers, write the reaction that would be used when sunflower oil is used to make solid margarine.

**17.76** Identify each of the following as saturated, monounsaturated, polyunsaturated, omega-3, or omega-6 fatty acid:

**a.** $CH_3—(CH_2)_4—CH=CH—CH_2—CH=CH—(CH_2)_7—COOH$

**b.** linolenic acid

**c.** $CH_3—(CH_2)_{14}—COOH$

**d.** $CH_3—(CH_2)_7—CH=CH—(CH_2)_7—COOH$

## ADDITIONAL QUESTIONS AND PROBLEMS

*For instructor-assigned homework, go to* ***www.masteringchemistry.com****.*

17.77 Among the ingredients in lipstick are beeswax, carnauba wax, hydrogenated vegetable oils, and glyceryl tricaprate (tricaprin). What types of lipids have been used? Draw the condensed structural formula of glyceryl tricaprate (tricaprin). Capric acid is the saturated 10-carbon fatty acid.

**17.78** Because peanut oil floats on the top of peanut butter, many brands of peanut butter are hydrogenated. A solid product then forms that is mixed into the peanut butter and does not separate. If a triacylglycerol in peanut oil that contains one palmitic acid, one oleic acid, and one linoleic acid is completely hydrogenated, what is the product?

17.79 Trans fats are produced during the hydrogenation of polyunsaturated oils.

**a.** What is the typical configuration of the double bond in a monounsaturated fatty acid?
**b.** How does a trans fatty acid differ from a cis fatty acid?
**c.** Draw the condensed structural formula of *trans*-oleic acid.

**17.80** One mole of glyceryl trioleate (triolein) is completely hydrogenated. Draw the condensed structural formula of the product. How many moles of hydrogen are required? How many grams of hydrogen? How many liters of hydrogen are needed if the reaction is run at STP?

17.81 On the list of ingredients in a cosmetic product are glyceryl tristearate (tristearin) and a lecithin. Draw the condensed structural formula of glyceryl tristearate and a lecithin with palmitic acids and choline.

**17.82** Some typical meals at fast-food restaurants are listed here. Calculate the number of kilocalories from fat and the percentage of total kilocalories due to fat (1 gram of fat = 9 kcal). Would you expect the fats to be mostly saturated or unsaturated? Why?

**a.** a chicken dinner, 830 kcal, 46 g of fat
**b.** a quarter-pound cheeseburger, 518 kcal, 29 g of fat
**c.** pepperoni pizza (three slices), 560 kcal, 18 g of fat
**d.** beef burrito, 470 kcal, 21 g of fat
**e.** deep-fried fish (three pieces), 480 kcal, 28 g of fat

17.83 Identify each of the following as a fatty acid, soap, triacylglycerol, wax, glycerophospholipid, sphingolipid, or steroid:

**a.** beeswax **b.** cholesterol
**c.** lecithin **d.** glyceryl tripalmitate (tripalmitin)
**e.** sodium stearate **f.** safflower oil
**g.** sphingomyelin **h.** whale blubber
**i.** adipose tissue **j.** progesterone
**k.** cortisone **l.** stearic acid

**17.84** Why would an animal that lives in a cold climate have more unsaturated triacylglycerols in its body fat than an animal that lives in a warm climate?

17.85 Identify the components (**1–6**) contained in each of the following lipids (**a–f**):

**1.** glycerol **2.** fatty acid
**3.** phosphate **4.** amino alcohol
**5.** steroid nucleus **6.** sphingosine

**a.** estrogen **b.** cephalin
**c.** wax **d.** triacylglycerol
**e.** glycerophospholipid **f.** sphingomyelin

**17.86** Which of the following are found in cell membranes?

**a.** cholesterol **b.** triacylglycerols
**c.** carbohydrates **d.** proteins
**e.** waxes **f.** glycerophospholipids
**g.** sphingolipids **h.** prostaglandins

## CHALLENGE QUESTIONS

17.87 Match each type of lipoprotein (**1–4**) with its description (**a–h**).

**1.** chylomicron **2.** VLDL **3.** LDL **4.** HDL

**a.** "good" cholesterol
**b.** transports most of the cholesterol to the cells
**c.** carries triacylglycerols from the intestine to the fat cells
**d.** transports cholesterol to the liver
**e.** has the greatest abundance of protein
**f.** "bad" cholesterol
**g.** carries triacylglycerols synthesized in the liver to the muscles
**h.** has the lowest density

**17.88 a.** Which of the following fatty acids has the lowest melting point? Explain.
**b.** Which of the following fatty acids has the highest melting point? Explain.

**1.** $CH_3—(CH_2)_{16}—COOH$ Stearic acid
**2.** $CH_3—(CH_2)_4—CH{=}CH—CH_2—CH{=}CH—(CH_2)_7—COOH$ Linoleic acid
**3.** $CH_3—(CH_2)_7—CH{=}CH—(CH_2)_7—COOH$ Oleic acid

17.89 Draw the condensed structural formula of a glycerophospholipid that is made from stearic acid, palmitic acid, and a phosphate bonded to ethanolamine.

**17.90** Olive oil consists of a high percentage of glyceryl trioleate (triolein).

**a.** Draw the condensed structural formula for glyceryl trioleate (triolein).
**b.** How many liters of $H_2$ gas at STP are needed to completely saturate 100. g of glyceryl trioleate (triolein)?
**c.** How many mL of 0.250 M NaOH are needed to completely saponify 100. g of glyceryl trioleate (triolein)?

**17.91** A sink drain can become clogged with solid fat such as glyceryl tristearate (tristearin).

**a.** How would adding lye (NaOH) to the sink drain remove the blockage?

**b.** Write an equation for the reaction that occurs.

# ANSWERS

## ANSWERS TO STUDY CHECKS

**17.1** a glycosphingolipid

**17.2** **a.** 16
**b.** unsaturated
**c.** liquid

**17.3**

$$\begin{array}{l} CH_2-O-\overset{\overset{\displaystyle O}{\|}}{C}-(CH_2)_{12}-CH_3 \\ | \\ CH-O-\overset{\overset{\displaystyle O}{\|}}{C}-(CH_2)_{12}-CH_3 \\ | \\ CH_2-O-\overset{\overset{\displaystyle O}{\|}}{C}-(CH_2)_{12}-CH_3 \end{array}$$

**17.4** glyceryl tristearate (tristearin)

**17.5** Glycerophospholipids contain glycerol, fatty acids, a phosphate, and an amino alcohol.

**17.6** Cerebrosides contain only one monosaccharide, and gangliosides contain two or more monosaccharide units.

**17.7** Cholesterol is not soluble in water; it is classified with the lipid family.

**17.8** Testosterone and nandrolone both contain a steroid nucleus with one double bond and a ketone group in the first ring, and a methyl and alcohol group on the five-carbon ring. Nandrolone does not have the second methyl group at the first and second ring fusion that is seen in the structure of testosterone.

**17.9** Protein channels allow ions and polar molecules to flow in and out of the cell through the lipid bilayer.

## ANSWERS TO SELECTED QUESTIONS AND PROBLEMS

**17.1** Lipids provide energy, protection, and insulation for the organs in the body. Lipids are also an important part of cell membranes.

**17.3** Because lipids are not soluble in water, a polar solvent, they are nonpolar molecules.

**17.5** All fatty acids contain a long chain of carbon atoms with a carboxylic acid group. Saturated fatty acids contain only carbon–carbon single bonds; unsaturated fatty acids contain one or more double bonds.

**17.7** **a.** palmitic acid

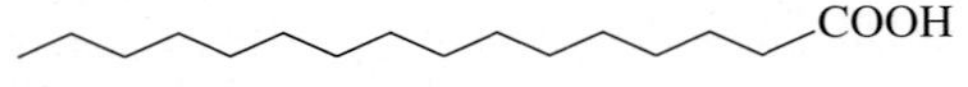


**b.** oleic acid

COOH

**17.9** **a.** saturated
**b.** unsaturated
**c.** unsaturated
**d.** saturated

**17.11** In a cis fatty acid, the hydrogen atoms are on the same side of the double bond, which produces a bend in the carbon chain. In a trans fatty acid, the hydrogen atoms are on opposite sides of the double bond, which gives a carbon chain without any bend.

**17.13** In an omega-3 fatty acid, there is a double bond on carbon 3 counting from the methyl group, whereas in an omega-6 fatty acid, there is a double bond beginning at carbon 6 counting from the methyl group.

**17.15** Arachidonic acid contains four double bonds and no side groups. In $PGE_1$, a part of the chain forms cyclopentane and there are hydroxyl and ketone functional groups.

**17.17** Prostaglandins raise or lower blood pressure, stimulate contraction and relaxation of smooth muscle, and may cause inflammation and pain.

**17.19** $CH_3-(CH_2)_{14}-\overset{\overset{\displaystyle O}{\|}}{C}-O-(CH_2)_{29}-CH_3$

**17.21**

$$\begin{array}{l} CH_2-O-\overset{\overset{\displaystyle O}{\|}}{C}-(CH_2)_{16}-CH_3 \\ | \\ CH-O-\overset{\overset{\displaystyle O}{\|}}{C}-(CH_2)_{16}-CH_3 \\ | \\ CH_2-O-\overset{\overset{\displaystyle O}{\|}}{C}-(CH_2)_{16}-CH_3 \end{array}$$

**17.23**

$$\begin{array}{l} CH_2-O-\overset{\overset{\displaystyle O}{\|}}{C}-(CH_2)_{14}-CH_3 \\ | \\ CH-O-\overset{\overset{\displaystyle O}{\|}}{C}-(CH_2)_{14}-CH_3 \\ | \\ CH_2-O-\overset{\overset{\displaystyle O}{\|}}{C}-(CH_2)_{14}-CH_3 \end{array}$$

**17.25** Safflower oil contains fatty acids with two or more double bonds; olive oil contains a large amount of oleic acid, which has only one (monounsaturated) double bond.

**17.27** Although coconut oil comes from a plant source, it has large amounts of saturated fatty acids and small amounts of unsaturated fatty acids.

**17.29**

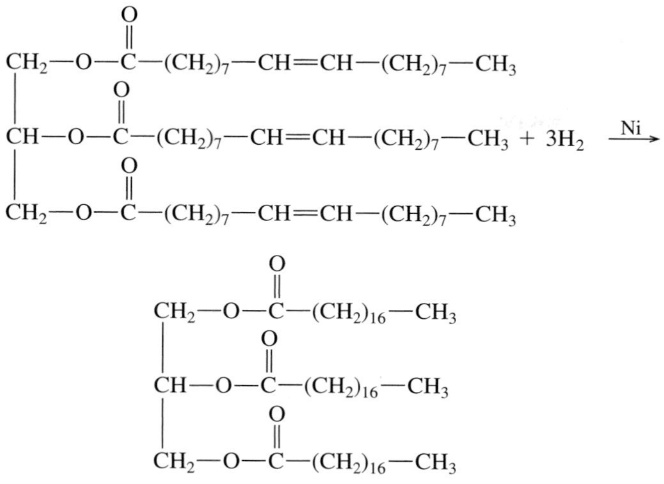

**17.31** **a.** Some of the double bonds in the unsaturated fatty acids have been converted to single bonds.
**b.** It now contains mostly saturated fatty acids.

**17.33** **a.**

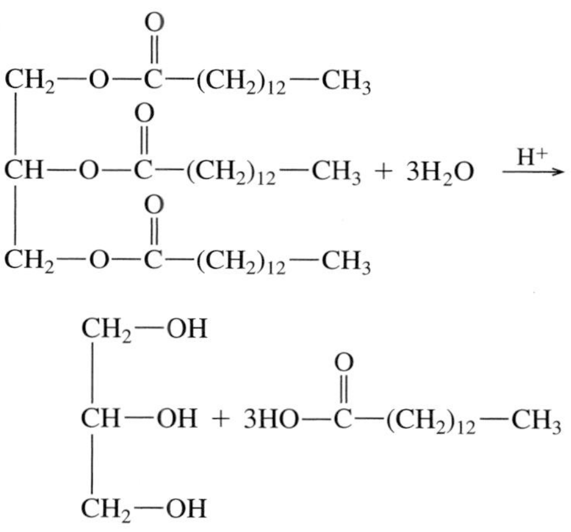

**b.**

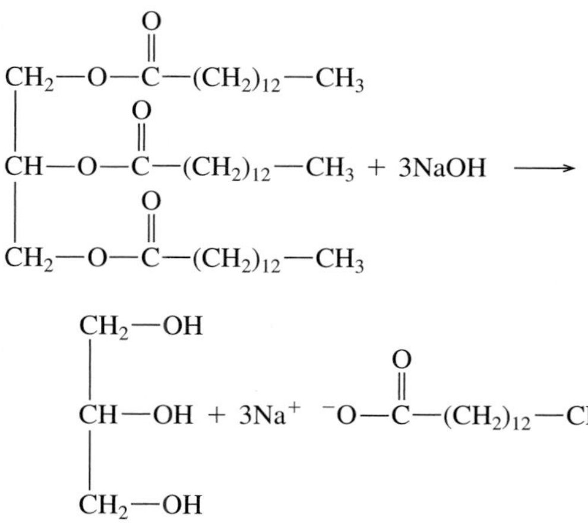

**17.35** A triacylglycerol is composed of glycerol with three hydroxyl groups that form ester links with three long-chain fatty acids. In olestra, six to eight long-chain fatty acids form ester links with the hydroxyl groups on sucrose, a sugar. The olestra cannot be digested because our enzymes cannot break down the large olestra molecule.

**17.37**

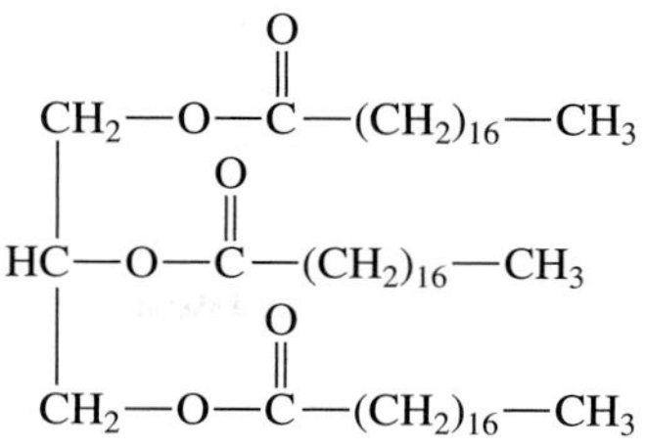

**17.39** A triacylglycerol consists of glycerol and three fatty acids. A glycerophospholipid consists of glycerol, two fatty acids, a phosphate group, and an amino alcohol.

**17.41**

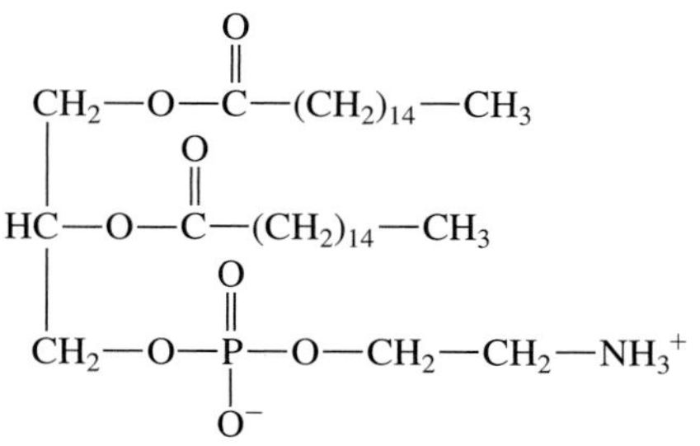

This is a cephalin

**17.43** This glycerophospholipid is a cephalin. It contains glycerol, oleic acid, stearic acid, a phosphate, and ethanolamine.

**17.45** A ceramide contains the amino alcohol sphingosine (instead of glycerol) and one fatty acid. A glycerophospholipid consists of glycerol, two fatty acids, a phosphate group, and an amino alcohol.

**17.47**

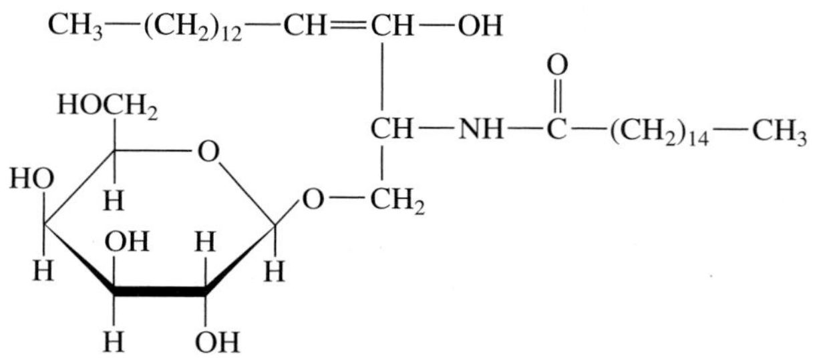

**17.49**

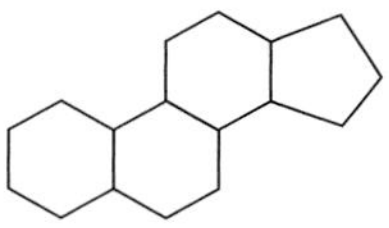

**17.51** Bile salts act to emulsify fat globules, allowing the fat to be more easily digested.

**17.53** Lipoproteins are large, spherically shaped structures that transport lipids in the bloodstream. They consist of an outside layer of glycerophospholipids and proteins surrounding an inner core of hundreds of nonpolar lipids and cholesteryl esters.

**17.55** Chylomicrons have a lower density than VLDLs. They pick up triacylglycerols from the intestine, whereas VLDLs transport triacylglycerols synthesized in the liver.

**17.57** "Bad" cholesterol is the cholesterol carried by LDLs that can form deposits called plaque in the arteries, which narrow the arteries.

**17.59** Both estradiol and testosterone contain the steroid nucleus and a hydroxyl group. Testosterone has a ketone group, a double bond, and two methyl groups. Estradiol has a benzene ring, a hydroxyl group in place of the ketone, and a methyl group.

**17.61** **d.** Testosterone is a male sex hormone.

**17.63** The lipids in a cell membrane are glycerophospholipids with smaller amounts of glycolipids and cholesterol.

**17.65** The lipid bilayer in a cell membrane surrounds the cell and separates the contents of the cell from the external fluids.

**17.67** The peripheral proteins in the membrane emerge on the inner or outer surface only, whereas the integral proteins extend through the membrane to both surfaces.

**17.69** The carbohydrates (glycoproteins and glycosphingolipids) on the surface of cells act as receptors for cell recognition and chemical messengers such as neurotransmitters.

**17.71** Substances move through cell membranes by passive transport, facilitated transport, and active transport.

**17.73**

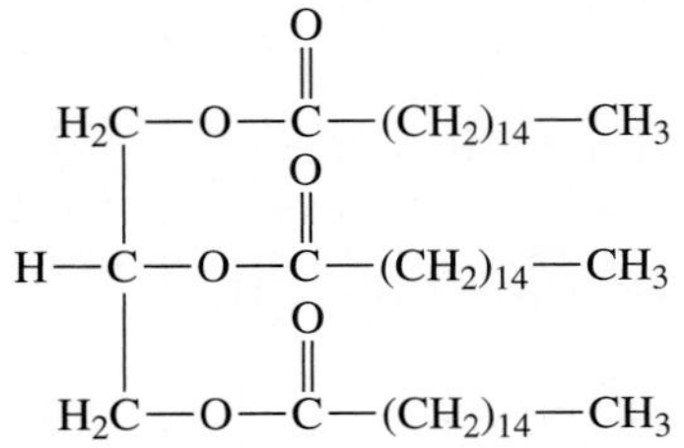

$$\begin{array}{l} H_2C{-}O{-}\overset{O}{\overset{\|}{C}}{-}(CH_2)_{14}{-}CH_3 \\ \;| \\ H{-}C{-}O{-}\overset{O}{\overset{\|}{C}}{-}(CH_2)_{14}{-}CH_3 \\ \;| \\ H_2C{-}O{-}\overset{O}{\overset{\|}{C}}{-}(CH_2)_{14}{-}CH_3 \end{array}$$

**17.75** **a.**

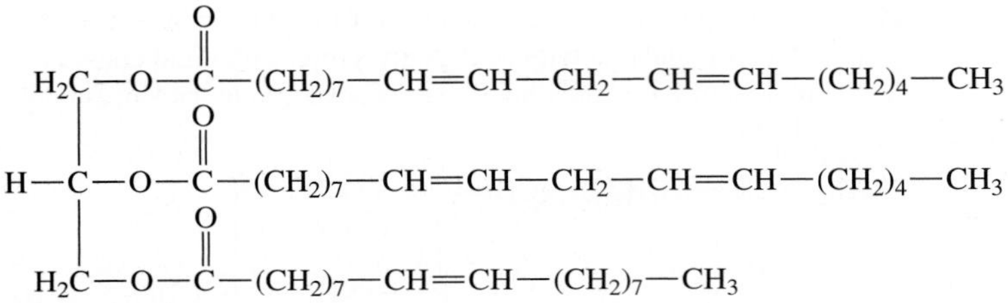

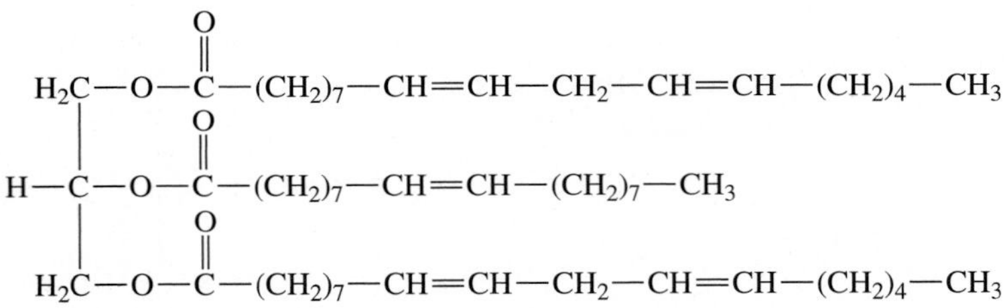

$$\begin{array}{l} H_2C{-}O{-}\overset{O}{\overset{\|}{C}}{-}(CH_2)_7{-}CH{=}CH{-}CH_2{-}CH{=}CH{-}(CH_2)_4{-}CH_3 \\ \;| \\ H{-}C{-}O{-}\overset{O}{\overset{\|}{C}}{-}(CH_2)_7{-}CH{=}CH{-}CH_2{-}CH{=}CH{-}(CH_2)_4{-}CH_3 \\ \;| \\ H_2C{-}O{-}\overset{O}{\overset{\|}{C}}{-}(CH_2)_7{-}CH{=}CH{-}(CH_2)_7{-}CH_3 \end{array}$$

$$\begin{array}{l} H_2C{-}O{-}\overset{O}{\overset{\|}{C}}{-}(CH_2)_7{-}CH{=}CH{-}CH_2{-}CH{=}CH{-}(CH_2)_4{-}CH_3 \\ \;| \\ H{-}C{-}O{-}\overset{O}{\overset{\|}{C}}{-}(CH_2)_7{-}CH{=}CH{-}(CH_2)_7{-}CH_3 \\ \;| \\ H_2C{-}O{-}\overset{O}{\overset{\|}{C}}{-}(CH_2)_7{-}CH{=}CH{-}CH_2{-}CH{=}CH{-}(CH_2)_4{-}CH_3 \end{array}$$

**b.**

$$\begin{array}{l} H_2C{-}O{-}\overset{O}{\overset{\|}{C}}{-}(CH_2)_7{-}CH{=}CH{-}CH_2{-}CH{=}CH{-}(CH_2)_4{-}CH_3 \\ \;| \\ H{-}C{-}O{-}\overset{O}{\overset{\|}{C}}{-}(CH_2)_7{-}CH{=}CH{-}(CH_2)_7{-}CH_3 + 5H_2 \xrightarrow{Ni} \\ \;| \\ H_2C{-}O{-}\overset{O}{\overset{\|}{C}}{-}(CH_2)_7{-}CH{=}CH{-}CH_2{-}CH{=}CH{-}(CH_2)_4{-}CH_3 \end{array}$$

$$\begin{array}{l} H_2C{-}O{-}\overset{O}{\overset{\|}{C}}{-}(CH_2)_{16}{-}CH_3 \\ \;| \\ H{-}C{-}O{-}\overset{O}{\overset{\|}{C}}{-}(CH_2)_{16}{-}CH_3 \\ \;| \\ H_2C{-}O{-}\overset{O}{\overset{\|}{C}}{-}(CH_2)_{16}{-}CH_3 \end{array}$$

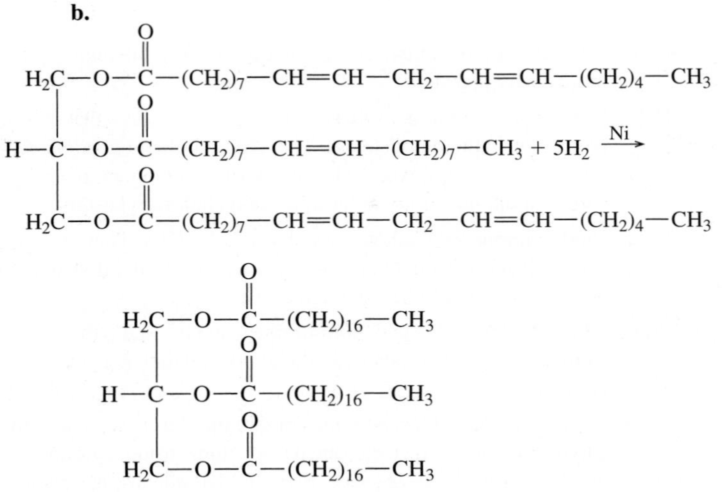

**17.77** Beeswax and carnauba are waxes. Vegetable oil and glyceryl tricaprate (tricaprin) are triacylglycerols.

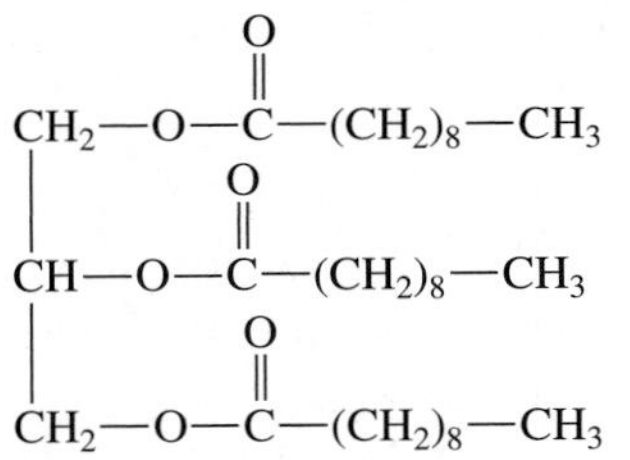

$$\begin{array}{l} CH_2{-}O{-}\overset{O}{\overset{\|}{C}}{-}(CH_2)_8{-}CH_3 \\ \;| \\ CH{-}O{-}\overset{O}{\overset{\|}{C}}{-}(CH_2)_8{-}CH_3 \\ \;| \\ CH_2{-}O{-}\overset{O}{\overset{\|}{C}}{-}(CH_2)_8{-}CH_3 \end{array}$$

Glyceryl tricaprate (tricaprin)

**17.79** **a.** A typical unsaturated fatty acid has a cis double bond.

**b.** A cis unsaturated fatty acid contains hydrogen atoms on the same side of each double bond. A trans unsaturated fatty acid has hydrogen atoms on opposite sides of the double bond that forms during hydrogenation:

**c.**

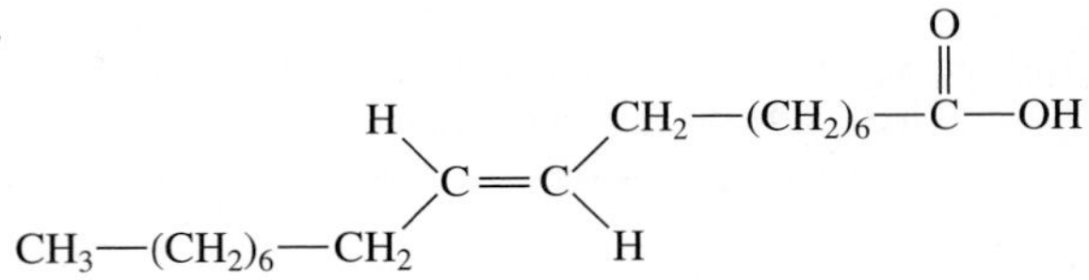

$$\begin{array}{l} \quad\quad\quad\quad\quad H \quad\quad\quad CH_2{-}(CH_2)_6{-}\overset{O}{\overset{\|}{C}}{-}OH \\ \quad\quad\quad\quad\quad\quad C{=}C \\ CH_3{-}(CH_2)_6{-}CH_2 \quad\quad\quad H \end{array}$$

**17.81**

$$\begin{array}{l} CH_2{-}O{-}\overset{O}{\overset{\|}{C}}{-}(CH_2)_{16}{-}CH_3 \\ \;| \\ HC{-}O{-}\overset{O}{\overset{\|}{C}}{-}(CH_2)_{16}{-}CH_3 \\ \;| \\ CH_2{-}O{-}\overset{O}{\overset{\|}{C}}{-}(CH_2)_{16}{-}CH_3 \end{array}$$

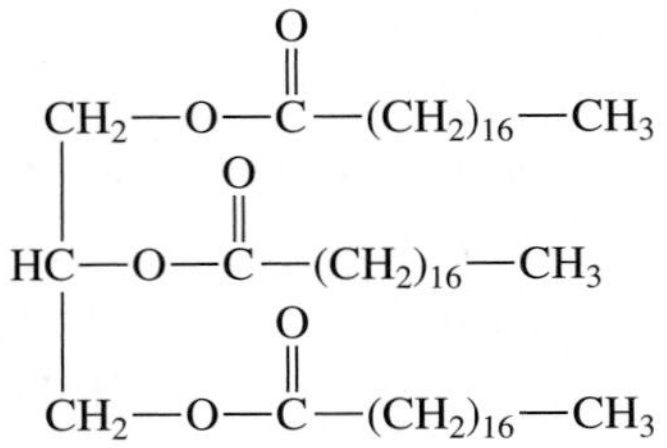

Glyceryl tristearate (tristearin)

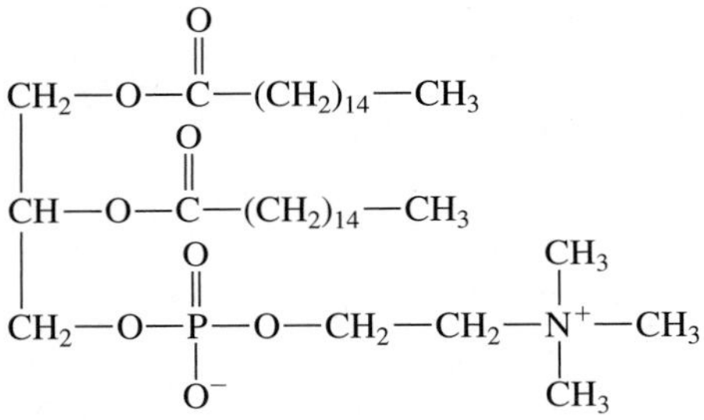

$$\begin{array}{l} CH_2{-}O{-}\overset{O}{\overset{\|}{C}}{-}(CH_2)_{14}{-}CH_3 \\ \;| \\ CH{-}O{-}\overset{O}{\overset{\|}{C}}{-}(CH_2)_{14}{-}CH_3 \\ \;| \\ CH_2{-}O{-}\overset{O}{\overset{\|}{P}}{-}O{-}CH_2{-}CH_2{-}\overset{CH_3}{\overset{|}{\underset{\underset{CH_3}{|}}{N^+}}}{-}CH_3 \\ \quad\quad\quad\quad\;\; O^- \end{array}$$

Lecithin

**17.83** Stearic acid **(l)** is a fatty acid. Sodium stearate **(e)** is a soap. Glyceryl tripalmitate **(d)**, safflower oil **(f)**, whale blubber **(h)**, and adipose tissue **(i)** are triacylglycerols. Beeswax **(a)** is a wax. Lecithin **(c)** is a glycerophospholipid. Sphingomyelin **(g)** is a sphingolipid. Cholesterol **(b)**, progesterone **(j)**, and cortisone **(k)** are steroids.

**17.85** **a.** 5
**b.** 1, 2, 3, 4
**c.** 2
**d.** 1, 2
**e.** 1, 2, 3, 4
**f.** 2, 3, 4, 6

**17.87** **a.** 4
**b.** 3
**c.** 1
**d.** 4
**e.** 4
**f.** 3
**g.** 2
**h.** 1

**17.89**

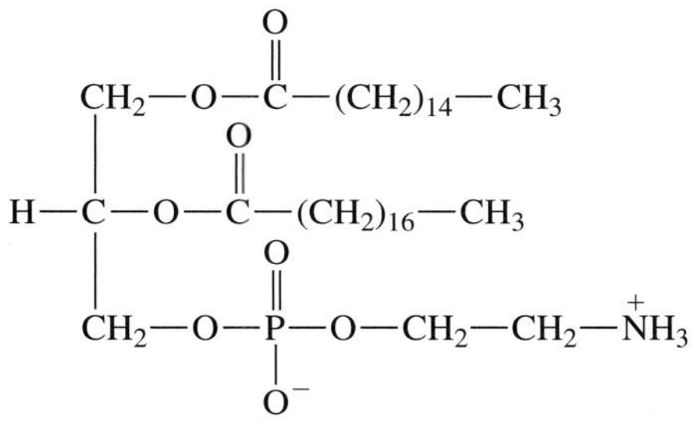

$$\begin{array}{l} CH_2-O-\overset{\overset{\displaystyle O}{\|}}{C}-(CH_2)_{14}-CH_3 \\ | \\ H-C-O-\overset{\overset{\displaystyle O}{\|}}{C}-(CH_2)_{16}-CH_3 \\ | \\ CH_2-O-\overset{\overset{\displaystyle O}{\|}}{\underset{\underset{\displaystyle O^-}{|}}{P}}-O-CH_2-CH_2-\overset{+}{N}H_3 \end{array}$$

**17.91** **a.** Adding NaOH would hydrolyze lipids such as glyceryl tristearate (tristearin), forming glycerol and salts of the fatty acids that are soluble in water and wash down the drain.

**b.**

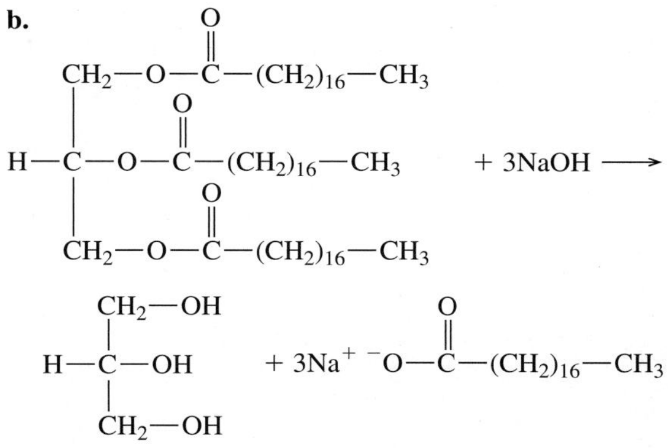

$$\begin{array}{l} CH_2-O-\overset{\overset{\displaystyle O}{\|}}{C}-(CH_2)_{16}-CH_3 \\ | \\ H-C-O-\overset{\overset{\displaystyle O}{\|}}{C}-(CH_2)_{16}-CH_3 \quad + 3NaOH \longrightarrow \\ | \\ CH_2-O-\overset{\overset{\displaystyle O}{\|}}{C}-(CH_2)_{16}-CH_3 \end{array}$$

$$\begin{array}{l} CH_2-OH \\ | \\ H-C-OH \\ | \\ CH_2-OH \end{array} \quad + 3Na^+ \; {}^-O-\overset{\overset{\displaystyle O}{\|}}{C}-(CH_2)_{16}-CH_3$$

Glycerol  Salts of stearic acid

# 18 Amines and Amides

LOOKING AHEAD


18.1 Amines

18.2 Properties of Amines

18.3 Heterocyclic Amines and Alkaloids

18.4 Amides

18.5 Hydrolysis of Amides


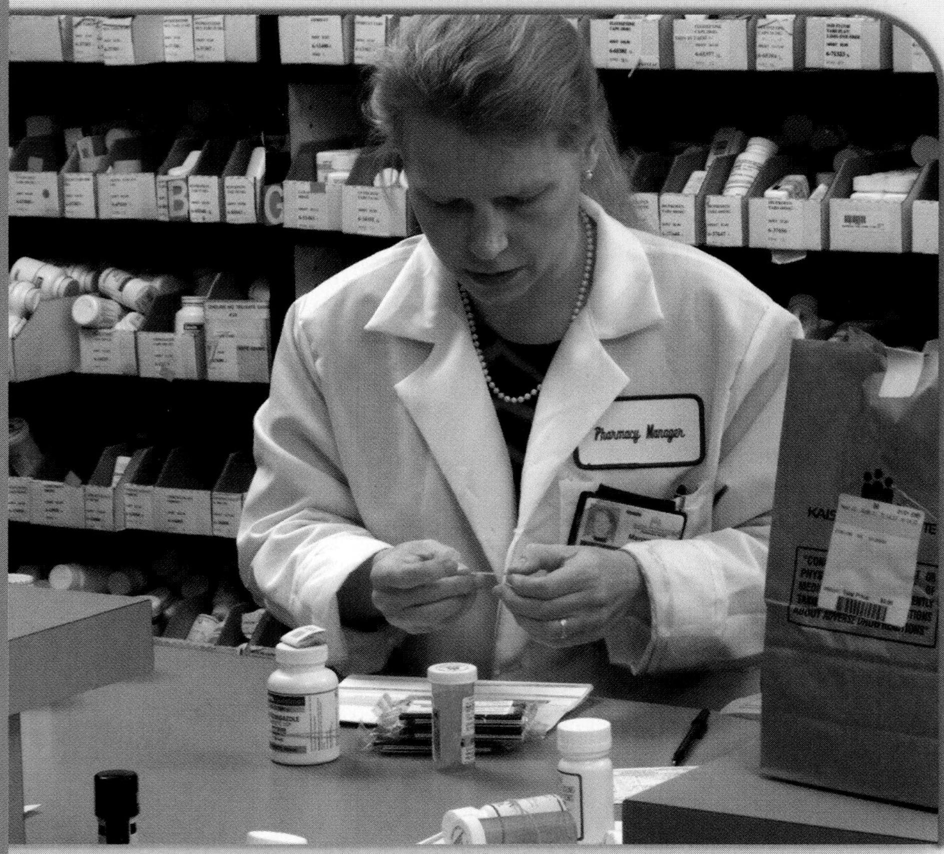


*"The pharmacy is one of the many factors in the final integration of chemistry and medicine in patient care," says Dorothea Lorimer, pharmacist, Kaiser Hospital. "If someone is allergic to a medication, I have to find out if a new medication has similar structural features. For instance, some people are allergic to sulfur. If there is sulfur in the new medication, there is a chance it will cause a reaction."*

*A prescription indicates a specific amount of a medication. At the pharmacy, the chemical name, formula, and quantity in milligrams or micrograms are checked. Then the prescribed number of capsules is prepared and placed in a container. If it is a liquid medication, a specific volume is measured and poured into a bottle.*

Visit **www.masteringchemistry.com** for self-study materials and instructor-assigned homework.

Amines and amides are organic compounds that contain nitrogen. Many nitrogen-containing compounds are important to life as components of amino acids, proteins, and nucleic acids (DNA and RNA). Many amines that exhibit strong physiological activity are used in medicine as decongestants, anesthetics, and sedatives. Examples include dopamine, histamine, epinephrine, and amphetamine.

Alkaloids such as caffeine, nicotine, cocaine, and digitalis, which demonstrate powerful physiological activity, are naturally occurring amines obtained from plants. In amides, the functional group consists of a carboxyl group attached to an amine. In biochemistry, the amide bond that links amino acids in a protein is called a peptide bond. Some medically important amides include acetaminophen (Tylenol) used to reduce fever; phenobarbital, a sedative and anticonvulsant medication; and penicillin, an antibiotic.

## 18.1 Amines

**LEARNING GOAL**

Classify amines as primary (1°), secondary (2°), or tertiary (3°). Name amines using common and IUPAC names; draw the condensed structural formulas given the names.

**Amines** are derivatives of ammonia ($NH_3$) in which one or more hydrogen atoms is replaced with alkyl or aromatic groups. From Table 11.8, we know that a nitrogen atom has one lone pair along with three bonds. In methylamine, a methyl group replaces one hydrogen atom in ammonia. The bonding of two methyl groups to the nitrogen atom gives dimethylamine. In trimethylamine, methyl groups replace all three hydrogen atoms attached to the nitrogen atom.

### Classification of Amines

SELF STUDY ACTIVITY
Amine and Amide Functional Groups

Amines are classified by counting the number of carbon atoms directly bonded to a nitrogen atom. In a *primary (1°) amine*, a nitrogen atom is bonded to one carbon. In a *secondary (2°) amine*, a nitrogen atom is bonded to two carbons. In a *tertiary (3°) amine*, a nitrogen atom is bonded to three carbons.

In each of the following models of ammonia and amines, the atoms are arranged around the nitrogen atom in a trigonal pyramidal shape:

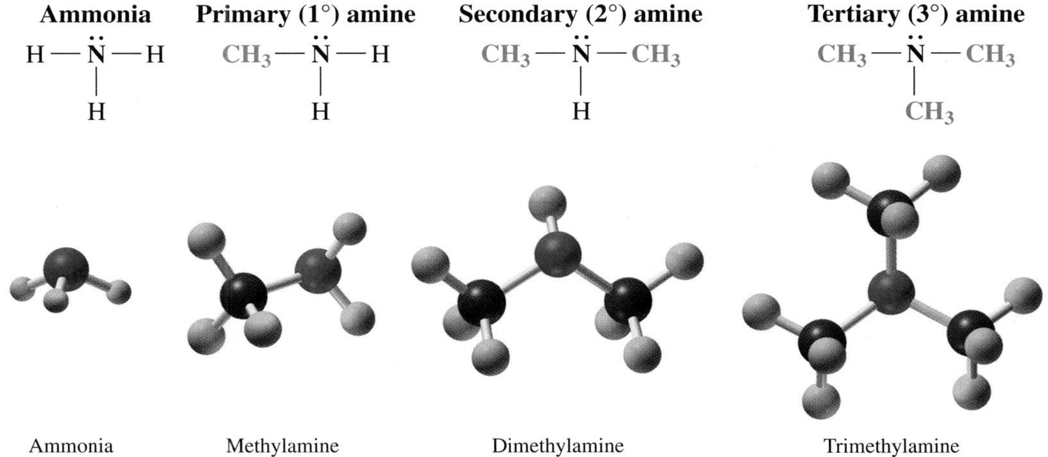


Ammonia Methylamine Dimethylamine Trimethylamine

### Line-Bond Formulas for Amines

MC TUTORIAL
Know What Amine?

We can draw line-bond formulas for amines just as we did for other organic compounds. For example, we can draw the following line-bond formulas and classify each of the amines:

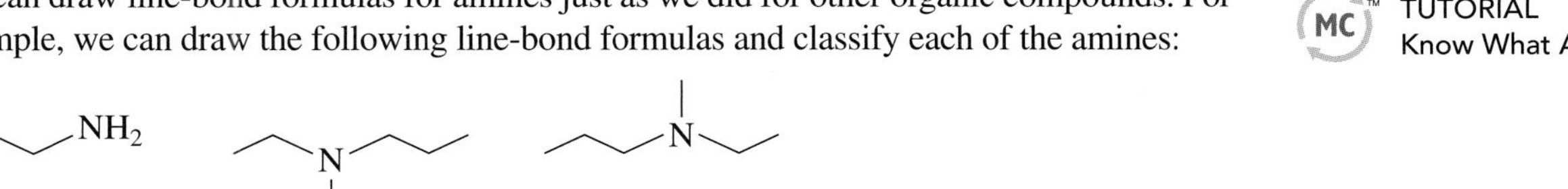


Primary amine (1°) Secondary amine (2°) Tertiary amine (3°)

MC™ TUTORIAL
Drawing Amines

SAMPLE PROBLEM 18.1

## Classifying Amines

Classify the following amines as primary (1°), secondary (2°), or tertiary (3°):

**a.** 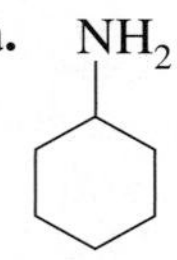 Cyclohexane ring bearing $NH_2$

**b.** 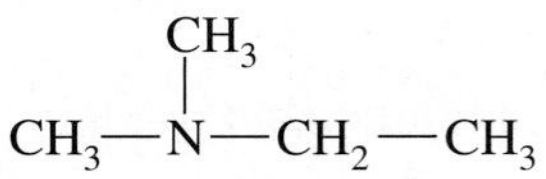 $CH_3—N(CH_3)—CH_2—CH_3$

**c.** 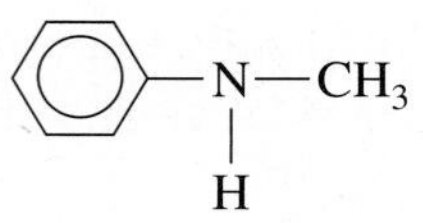 Benzene ring—$N(H)—CH_3$

**d.** 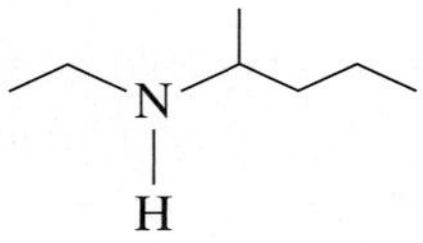 Line-bond structure with N bonded to H

SOLUTION

**a.** This is a primary (1°) amine because there is one alkyl group (cyclohexyl) attached to a nitrogen atom.

**b.** This is a tertiary (3°) amine. There are three alkyl groups (two methyls and one ethyl) attached to the nitrogen atom.

**c.** This is a secondary (2°) amine with two carbon groups, methyl and phenyl, bonded to the nitrogen atom.

**d.** The nitrogen atom in this line-bond formula is bonded to two carbon atoms, which makes it a secondary (2°) amine.

STUDY CHECK

Classify the following amine as primary (1°), secondary (2°), or tertiary (3°):

$$CH_3—CH_2—N(CH_3)—CH_2—CH_3$$

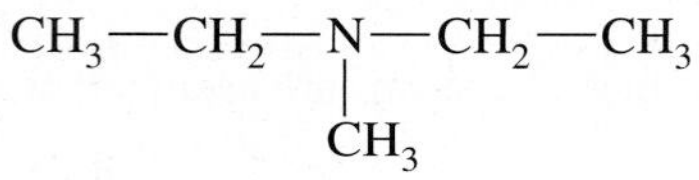

## Naming Amines

Several systems are used for naming amines. For simple amines, the common names are often used. In the common name, the alkyl groups bonded to the nitrogen atom are listed in alphabetical order. The prefixes *di* and *tri* are used to indicate two and three identical substituents.

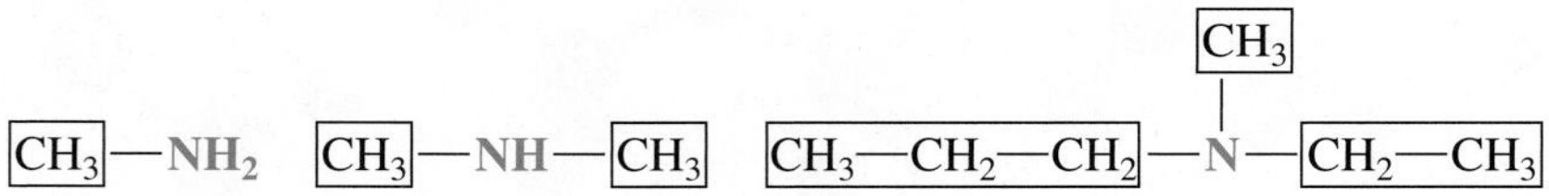

$CH_3—NH_2$ Methylamine

$CH_3—NH—CH_3$ Dimethylamine

$CH_3—CH_2—CH_2—N(CH_3)—CH_2—CH_3$ Ethylmethylpropylamine

CONCEPT CHECK 18.1

## Common Names of Amines

Give a common name for each of the following amines:

**a.** $CH_3—CH_2—NH_2$ **b.** 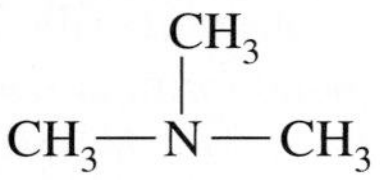 $CH_3—N(CH_3)—CH_3$

ANSWER

**a.** This amine has one ethyl group attached to the nitrogen atom; its name is ethylamine.

**b.** The common name for an amine with three methyl groups attached to the nitrogen atom is trimethylamine.

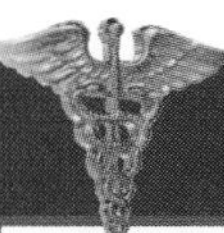

## HEALTH NOTE

### Amines in Health and Medicine

In the body, the production of histamine increases the response to allergic reactions or injury. Histamine dilates blood vessels, increases the permeability of the cells, and causes redness and swelling. Using an antihistamine such as diphenylhydramine helps reduce the effects of histamine.

Histamine

Diphenylhydramine

In the body, hormones called *biogenic amines* carry messages between the central nervous system and nerve cells. Epinephrine (adrenaline) and norepinephrine (noradrenaline) are released by the adrenal medulla in "fight or flight" situations to raise the blood glucose level and move blood to the muscles. The prefix *nor* in a drug name means there is one less $-CH_3$ group on the nitrogen atom. Norepinephrine is used in remedies for colds, hay fever, and asthma because it contracts the capillaries in the mucous membranes of the respiratory passages. Parkinson's disease is a result of a deficiency in another biogenic amine called dopamine.

Epinephrine (adrenaline)

Norepinephrine (noradrenaline)

Dopamine

Produced synthetically, amphetamines (known as "uppers") are stimulants of the central nervous system much like epinephrine, but they also increase cardiovascular activity and depress the appetite. They are sometimes used to bring about weight loss, but they can cause chemical dependency. Benzedrine and Neo-Synephrine (phenylephrine) are used in medications to reduce respiratory congestion from colds, hay fever, and asthma. Sometimes, Benzedrine is used to combat the desire to sleep. Methedrine may be used to treat depression and in the illegal form is known as "speed" or "crank." The prefix *meth* means that there is one more methyl group on the nitrogen atom.

Benzedrine (amphetamine)

Neo-Synephrine (phenylephrine)

Methamphetamine (methedrine)

The IUPAC names for amines are similar to the names we used for alcohols, except that the *e* in the parent alkane name is replaced with *amine*:

| $CH_4$ | $CH_3-\mathbf{OH}$ | $CH_3-\mathbf{NH_2}$ |
|---|---|---|
| Methane | Methan**ol** | Methan**amine** |

**STEP 1 Name the longest carbon chain bonded to the N atom by replacing the *e* with *amine*:**

| $CH_3-NH_2$ | $CH_3-CH_2-NH_2$ |
|---|---|
| Methanamine | Ethanamine |

**STEP 2 Number the carbon chain to show the position of the amine group and other substituents:**

$CH_3-CH_2-CH_2-NH_2$ 1-Propan**amine**

$CH_3-CH(NH_2)-CH_3$ 2-Propan**amine**

$CH_3-CH(NH_2)-CH_2-CH_3$ 2-Butan**amine**

$CH_3-CH(CH_3)-CH_2-CH_2-NH_2$ 3-Methyl-1-butan**amine**

**STEP 3** **In secondary and tertiary amines, use the prefix *N*- to name alkyl groups attached to the N atom.** Alkyl groups attached to the N atom are listed alphabetically:

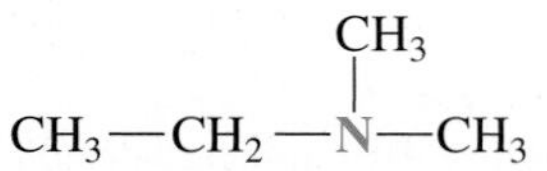

$$CH_3-CH_2-\overset{\displaystyle CH_3}{\overset{|}{N}}-CH_3$$
*N,N*-Dimethylethanamine

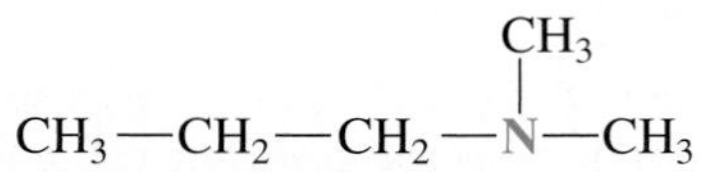

$$CH_3-CH_2-CH_2-\overset{\displaystyle CH_3}{\overset{|}{N}}-CH_3$$
*N,N*-Dimethyl-1-propanamine

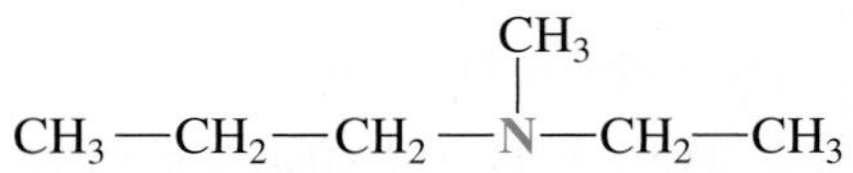

$$CH_3-CH_2-CH_2-\overset{\displaystyle CH_3}{\overset{|}{N}}-CH_2-CH_3$$
*N*-Ethyl-*N*-methyl-1-propanamine

An amine with two amine functional groups is named as a *diamine*. For example, the amines 1,4-butanediamine and 1,5-pentanediamine contribute to the odors of decaying flesh:

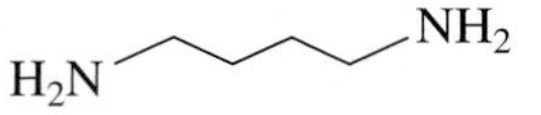

$H_2N$ ⁄⁄⁄ $NH_2$
1,4-Butanediamine
(putrescine)

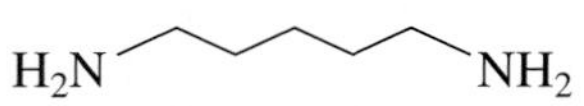

$H_2N$ ⁄⁄⁄ $NH_2$
1,5-Pentanediamine
(cadaverine)

In amines where another functional group takes priority, the $-NH_2$ group is named as a substituent *amino* group and numbered to show its location. For the major functional groups we have studied, the increasing priority follows the increase in oxidation:

$$\text{Low priority} \quad -NH_2 < -OH < -\overset{\displaystyle O}{\overset{||}{C}}- < -\overset{\displaystyle O}{\overset{||}{C}}-H < -\overset{\displaystyle O}{\overset{||}{C}}-OH \quad \text{High priority}$$

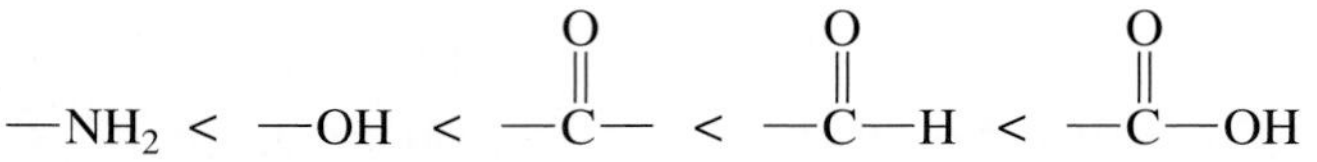

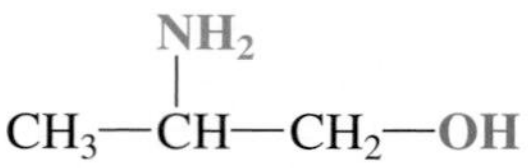

$$CH_3-\overset{\displaystyle NH_2}{\overset{|}{CH}}-CH_2-OH$$
2-Amino-1-propanol

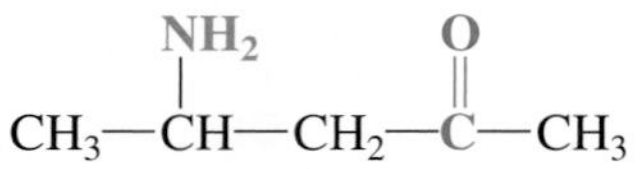

$$CH_3-\overset{\displaystyle NH_2}{\overset{|}{CH}}-CH_2-\overset{\displaystyle O}{\overset{||}{C}}-CH_3$$
4-Amino-2-pentanone

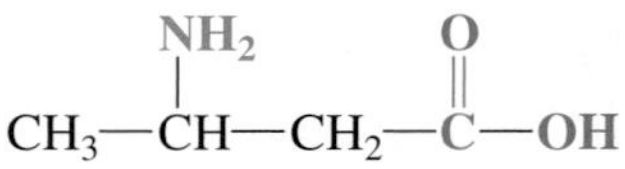

$$CH_3-\overset{\displaystyle NH_2}{\overset{|}{CH}}-CH_2-\overset{\displaystyle O}{\overset{||}{C}}-OH$$
3-Aminobutanoic acid

CONCEPT CHECK 18.2

### IUPAC Names of Amines with Substituents

An amine has the name *N*-methyl-1-hexanamine.

**a.** How many carbon atoms are in the carbon chain attached to the N atom?
**b.** What is indicated by the "1" in the 1-hexanamine part of the name?
**c.** What is indicated by the "*N*-methyl" part of the name?
**d.** What is the condensed structural formula of the amine?
**e.** If the N atom were attached to the second carbon of the chain, how would the compound be named?

ANSWER

**a.** In a hexanamine, the carbon chain attached to the N atom has 6 carbon atoms.
**b.** The "1" in 1-hexanamine indicates that the N atom is attached to carbon 1 of the chain.
**c.** The "*N*-methyl" part of the name indicates that a methyl group ($-CH_3$) is attached to the N atom.
**d.** The condensed structural formula of *N*-methyl-1-hexanamine is as follows:

$$CH_3-CH_2-CH_2-CH_2-CH_2-CH_2-NH-CH_3$$

**e.** If the N atom were attached to the second carbon of the chain, the compound would be named *N*-methyl-2-hexanamine.

SAMPLE PROBLEM 18.2

### IUPAC Names for Amines

Give the IUPAC name of the following amine:

$$CH_3-CH_2-CH_2-CH_2-NH-CH_2-CH_3$$

SOLUTION

**STEP 1** **Name the longest carbon chain bonded to the *N* atom by replacing the *e* with *amine*.** The four-carbon chain attached to a nitrogen atom is named by replacing the *e* in butane with *amine*: butanamine.

**STEP 2** **Number the carbon chain to show the position of the amine group and other substituents.** The N atom in the amine group is attached to carbon 1 of butanamine: 1-butanamine.

**STEP 3** **In secondary and tertiary amines, use the prefix *N*- to name alkyl groups attached to the N atom.** An ethyl group attached to the N atom is indicated as *N*-ethyl. The name of the amine is *N*-ethyl-1-butanamine.

STUDY CHECK

Draw the condensed structural formula of *N*-ethyl-1-propanamine.

**Guide to IUPAC Naming of Amines**

**STEP 1** Name the longest carbon chain bonded to the N atom by replacing the e with *amine*.

**STEP 2** Number the carbon chain to show the position of the amine group and other substituents.

**STEP 3** In secondary and tertiary amines, use the prefix *N*- to name groups attached to the N atom.

## Aromatic Amines

The aromatic amines use the name *aniline*, which is approved by IUPAC:

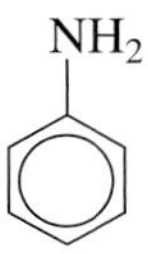

$NH_2$ | $NH_2$, Br | H, N—$CH_3$ | $CH_3$, N—$CH_3$

Aniline 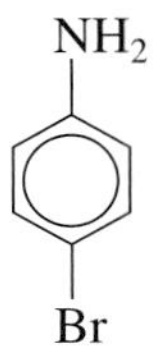 | 4-Bromoaniline (*p*-bromoaniline) 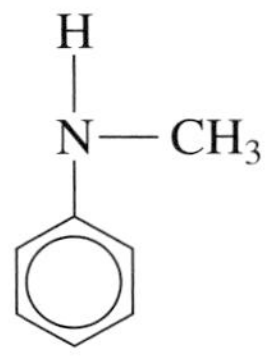 | *N*-Methylaniline 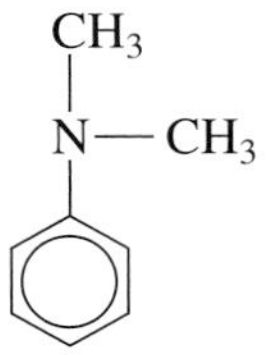 | *N*,*N*-Dimethylaniline

## QUESTIONS AND PROBLEMS

### Amines

**18.1** What is a primary amine?

**18.2** What is a tertiary amine?

**18.3** Classify each of the following amines as primary (1°), secondary (2°), or tertiary (3°):

**a.** $CH_3—CH_2—CH_2—NH_2$

**b.** $CH_3—N(H)—CH_2—CH_3$

**c.** 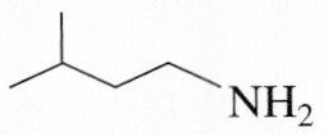 $NH_2$ (skeletal structure)

**d.** 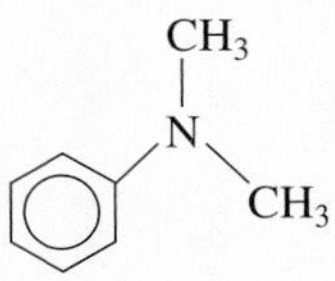 $CH_3$, N, $CH_3$ (attached to benzene ring)

**e.** $CH_3—CH(CH_3)—N(CH_3)—CH_2—CH_3$

**18.4** Classify each of the following amines as primary (1°), secondary (2°), or tertiary (3°):

**a.** $CH_3—CH_2—CH(NH_2)—CH_3$

**b.** $CH_3—CH_2—N(CH_3)—CH_2—CH_3$

**c.** 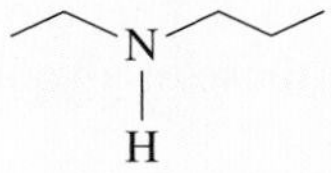 N, H (skeletal structure)

**d.** $CH_3$, CH—$NH_2$ (attached to benzene ring)

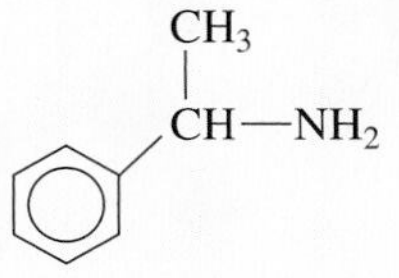

**e.** $CH_3—N(H)—C(CH_3)_2—CH_3$

**18.5** Write the common and IUPAC names for each of the following:

**a.** $CH_3—CH_2—NH_2$

**b.** $CH_3—NH—CH_2—CH_2—CH_3$

**c.** $CH_3—CH_2—N(CH_3)—CH_2—CH_3$

**d.** $CH_3—CH(NH_2)—CH_3$

**18.6** Write the common and IUPAC names for each of the following:

**a.** $CH_3—CH_2—CH_2—NH_2$

**b.** $CH_3—NH—CH_2—CH_3$

**c.** $CH_3—CH_2—CH_2—CH_2—NH_2$

**d.** $CH_3—CH_2—N(CH_2—CH_3)—CH_2—CH_3$

**18.7** Write the IUPAC names for each of the following:

**a.** $CH_3—CH(NH_2)—CH_2—CH_3$

**b.** benzene ring with $NH_2$ and Cl on adjacent carbons

**c.** $H_2N—CH_2—CH_2—C(=O)—H$

**d.** benzene ring—$NH—CH_2—CH_3$

**18.8** Write the IUPAC names for each of the following:

**a.** $CH_3—C(=O)—CH(NH_2)—CH_3$

**b.** $CH_3—CH(NH_2)—CH_2—CH_2—CH_2—NH_2$

**c.** benzene ring with $NH—CH_3$ and Br para to each other

**d.** benzene ring—$N(CH_3)—CH_2—CH_3$

**18.9** Draw the condensed structural formula for each of the following amines:

**a.** ethylamine **b.** *N*-methylaniline

**c.** butylpropylamine **d.** 2-pentanamine

**18.10** Draw the condensed structural formula for each of the following amines:

**a.** dimethylamine **b.** *p*-chloroaniline

**c.** *N,N*-diethylaniline **d.** 1-amino-3-pentanone

# 18.2 Properties of Amines

**LEARNING GOAL**

Describe the boiling points and solubility of amines; write equations for the ionization and neutralization of amines.

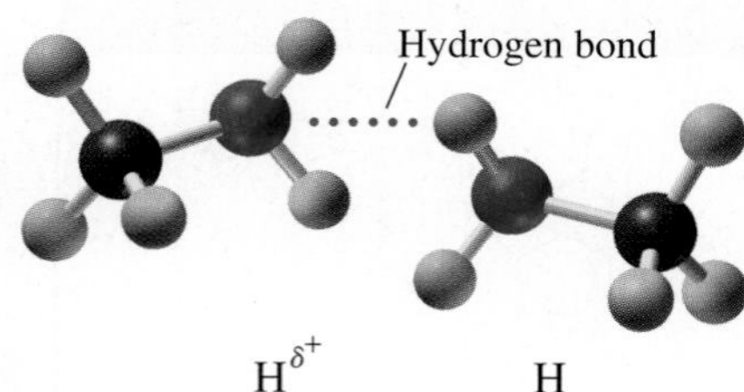


$CH_3—\overset{H^{\delta+}}{N^{\delta-}}(H):\cdots\cdots H^{\delta+}—N^{\delta-}(H)—CH_3$

Amines have boiling points higher than alkanes of similar mass but lower than the alcohols:

| $CH_3—CH_3$ | $CH_3—NH_2$ | $CH_3—OH$ |
|---|---|---|
| Ethane | Methanamine | Methanol |
| bp −84 °C | bp −7 °C | bp 65 °C |

Because amines contain a polar N—H bond, they form hydrogen bonds. However, nitrogen is not as electronegative as oxygen, which makes the hydrogen bonds in amines weaker. The $—NH_2$ in primary (1°) amines, which have two N—H bonds, can form more hydrogen bonds, which gives them higher boiling points than the secondary (2°) amines of the same mass. It is not possible for tertiary (3°) amines to hydrogen bond with each other (no N—H bonds), which makes their boiling points much lower and similar to those of alkanes:

| $CH_3—CH_2—CH_2—NH_2$ | $CH_3—CH_2—NH—CH_3$ | $CH_3—N(CH_3)—CH_3$ |
|---|---|---|
| Propylamine (1°) | Ethylmethylamine (2°) | Trimethylamine (3°) |
| bp 48 °C | bp 36 °C | bp 3 °C |

## Solubility in Water

Like alcohols, the smaller amines, including tertiary ones, are soluble because they form hydrogen bonds with water. (See Figure 18.1.) However, in amines with more than six carbon atoms, the effect of hydrogen bonding is diminished. As with alcohols, the nonpolar alkyl part of the molecules decreases the solubility of an amine in water.

**CONCEPT CHECK 18.3**

### Boiling Points and Solubility of Amines

**a.** If the compounds trimethylamine and ethylmethylamine have the same molar mass, why is the boiling point of trimethylamine (3 °C) lower than that of ethylmethylamine (37 °C)?

**b.** Why is $CH_3—CH_2—NH—CH_2—CH_3$ more soluble in water than

$$CH_3—CH_2—CH_2—CH_2—\underset{}{\overset{H}{\overset{|}{N}}}—CH_2—CH_2—CH_3?$$

ANSWER

**a.** With polar N—H bonds, ethylmethylamine molecules form hydrogen bonds. Thus, a higher temperature is required to break the hydrogen bonds and form a gas. However, trimethylamine, which is a tertiary amine, does not have N—H bonds and cannot hydrogen bond with other trimethylamine molecules.

**b.** Hydrogen bonding is sufficient to make amines with six or fewer carbon atoms soluble in water. Amines with seven or more carbon atoms are not soluble because the effect of hydrogen bonding is not sufficient to overcome the effect of the large hydrocarbon groups that are nonpolar and not soluble in water.

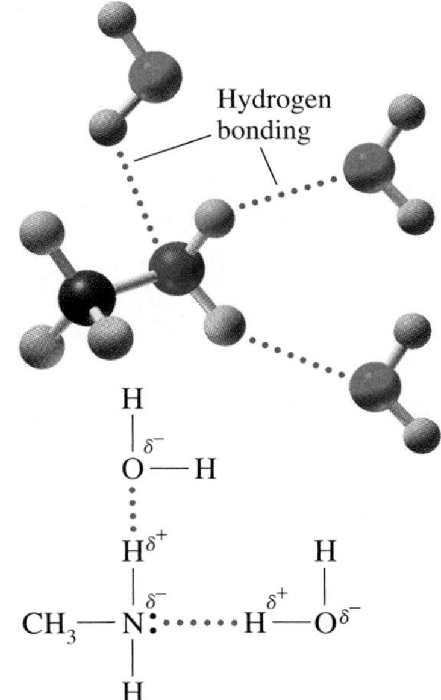


**FIGURE 18.1** Hydrogen bonding occurs between amines and water molecules.

**Q** Why are tertiary (3°) amines soluble in water?

TUTORIAL
Reactions of Amines

## Ionization of an Amine in Water

In Chapter 10, we saw that ammonia ($NH_3$) acts as a Brønsted–Lowry base because it accepts a proton ($H^+$) from water to produce an ammonium ion ($NH_4^+$) and a hydroxide ion ($OH^-$):

$$\ddot{N}H_3 + H_2O \rightleftharpoons NH_4^+ + OH^-$$

Ammonia — Ammonium ion — Hydroxide ion

In water, amines also act as Brønsted–Lowry bases because the lone electron pair on the nitrogen atom accepts a proton from water. The products are an alkyl ammonium ion and hydroxide ion. The name of the alkyl ammonium ion is similar to the common amine name, but *amine* is replaced by *ammonium ion*:

$$CH_3—\ddot{N}H_2 + H_2O \rightleftharpoons CH_3—\overset{+}{N}H_3 + OH^-$$

Methylamine — Methylammonium ion — Hydroxide ion

Secondary and tertiary amines also accept a proton to form ammonium ions:

$$CH_3—\underset{\underset{CH_3}{|}}{\ddot{N}H} + H_2O \rightleftharpoons CH_3—\underset{\underset{CH_3}{|}}{\overset{+}{N}H_2} + OH^-$$

Dimethylamine — Dimethylammonium ion — Hydroxide ion

## Basicity of Amines

Because amines act as weak bases by accepting protons from water and producing hydroxide ions, their aqueous solutions are basic. We can write the equilibrium constant $K$ for methylamine as follows:

MC SELF STUDY ACTIVITY
Amines as Bases

$$K = \frac{[CH_3—NH_3^+][OH^-]}{[CH_3—NH_2]} = 4.4 \times 10^{-4}$$

Most of the $K$ values for amines are less than $10^{-3}$ at 25 °C, which means that the equilibrium favors the amine molecules. Aqueous solutions of amines have basic pH values and turn red litmus paper blue. We can compare the strengths of some amines by looking at their $K$ values:

| | Ammonia | 1° Amine | | 2° Amine | 3° Amine |
|---|---|---|---|---|---|
| | $NH_3$ | $CH_3—NH_2$ | $CH_3—CH_2—NH_2$ | $CH_3—NH—CH_3$ | $CH_3—\underset{}{\overset{CH_3}{\overset{|}{N}}}—CH_3$ |
| $K$ | $1.8 \times 10^{-5}$ | $4.4 \times 10^{-4}$ | $5.6 \times 10^{-4}$ | $5.1 \times 10^{-4}$ | $5.3 \times 10^{-5}$ |

## Amine Salts

When you squeeze lemon juice on fish, the "fishy odor" of the amines is removed by converting them to amine salts. In a *neutralization reaction*, an amine acts as a base and reacts with an acid to form an **amine salt**. The lone pair of electrons on the nitrogen atom accepts a proton $H^+$ from an acid to give an amine salt; no water is formed. An amine salt is named by replacing the *amine* part of the name with *ammonium* followed by the name of the negative ion.

## Neutralization of an Amine

| Amine | Acid | | Amine salt |
|---|---|---|---|
| $CH_3—\ddot{N}H_2$ | $+ HCl$ | $\longrightarrow$ | $CH_3—\overset{+}{N}H_3\ Cl^-$ |
| Methyl**amine** | | | Methyl**ammonium chloride** |

$$CH_3—\ddot{N}H(CH_3) + HCl \longrightarrow CH_3—\overset{+}{N}H_2(CH_3)\ Cl^-$$

Dimethyl**amine** → Dimethyl**ammonium chloride**

The ammonium ions are classified as primary (1°), secondary (2°), and tertiary (3°) depending on the number of alkyl groups bonded to the N atom:

$$CH_3—\overset{+}{N}H_3 \qquad CH_3—\overset{+}{N}H_2(CH_3) \qquad CH_3—\overset{+}{N}H(CH_3)_2$$

Primary (1°) Secondary (2°) Tertiary (3°)

In a **quaternary ammonium ion**, a nitrogen atom bonds to four carbon groups. In the quaternary ion, the nitrogen atom has a positive charge just as it does in other amine salts. Choline, an amino alcohol present in glycerophospholipids, is a quaternary ammonium ion:

$$CH_3—\overset{+}{N}(CH_3)_2—CH_3\ Cl^- \qquad HO—CH_2—CH_2—\overset{+}{N}(CH_3)_2—CH_3$$

Tetramethylammonium chloride Choline

The quaternary salts differ from other amine salts because the nitrogen atom is not bonded to an H atom. Thus, quaternary salts do not react with bases.

## Properties of Amine Salts

Amine salts are ionic compounds with strong attractions between the positively charged ammonium ion and an anion, usually chloride. Like most salts, amine salts are solid at room temperature, odorless, and soluble in water and body fluids. For this reason, amines used as drugs are converted to their amine salts. The amine salt of ephedrine is used as a bronchodilator and in decongestant products such as Sudafed. The amine salt of diphenhydramine is used in products such as Benadryl for relief of itching and pain from skin irritations and rashes. (See Figure 18.2.) In pharmaceuticals, the naming of the amine salt follows an older method of giving the amine name followed by the name of the acid:

$$HO—CH(C_6H_5)—CH(CH_3)—\overset{+}{N}H_2—CH_3\ Cl^- \qquad (C_6H_5)_2CH—O—CH_2—CH_2—\overset{+}{N}H(CH_3)_2\ Cl^-$$

Ephedrine hydrochloride
ephedrine HCl
Sudafed®

Diphenhydramine hydrochloride
diphenylhydramine HCl
Benadryl®

**FIGURE 18.2** Decongestants and products that relieve itch and skin irritations can contain ammonium salts.

**Q** Why are ammonium salts used in drugs rather than the biologically active amines?

When an amine salt reacts with a strong base such as NaOH, it is converted back to the amine, which is also called the free amine or free base:

$$CH_3{-}NH_3^+\,Cl^- + NaOH \longrightarrow CH_3{-}NH_2 + NaCl + H_2O$$

The narcotic cocaine is typically extracted from coca leaves using an acidic solution to give a white, solid amine salt, which is cocaine hydrochloride. It is the salt of cocaine (cocaine hydrochloride) that is smuggled and used illegally on the street. "Crack cocaine" is the free amine or free base of the amine obtained by treating the cocaine hydrochloride with NaOH and ether, a process known as "free-basing." The solid product is known as "crack cocaine" because it makes a cracking noise when heated. The free amine is rapidly absorbed when smoked and gives stronger highs than the cocaine hydrochloride, which makes crack cocaine more addictive:

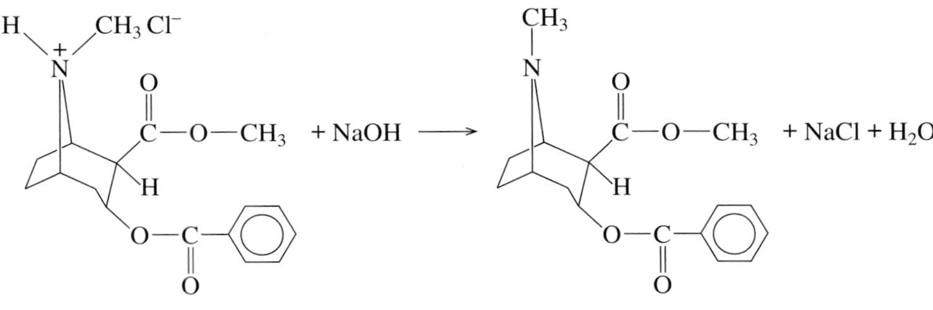


MC™ CASE STUDY
Death by Chocolate?

## CONCEPT CHECK 18.4

### Reacting an Amine with HCl

Consider the reaction of dimethylamine with HCl.

**a.** What type of reaction takes place?
**b.** What type of product forms?
**c.** What is the name of the product that forms?

ANSWER

**a.** The reaction of an amine acting as a base and an acid is neutralization.
**b.** The product that forms is an amine salt.
**c.** The product is dimethylammonium chloride.

## SAMPLE PROBLEM 18.3

### Reactions of Amines

Write an equation that shows ethylamine

**a.** ionizing as a weak base in water.
**b.** neutralized by HCl.

SOLUTION

**a.** In water, ethylamine acts as a weak base by accepting a proton from water to produce ethylammonium hydroxide:

$$CH_3{-}CH_2{-}NH_2 + H{-}OH \rightleftharpoons CH_3{-}CH_2{-}NH_3^+ + OH^-$$

**b.** $CH_3{-}CH_2{-}NH_2 + HCl \longrightarrow CH_3{-}CH_2{-}NH_3^+Cl^-$

STUDY CHECK

What is the condensed structural formula of the salt formed by the reaction of trimethylamine and HCl?

## QUESTIONS AND PROBLEMS

### Properties of Amines

**18.11** Identify the compound in each pair that has the higher boiling point. Explain.

**a.** $CH_3-CH_2-NH_2$ or $CH_3-CH_2-OH$

**b.** $CH_3-NH_2$ or $CH_3-CH_2-CH_2-NH_2$

**c.** $CH_3-\overset{CH_3}{\overset{|}{N}}-CH_3$ or $CH_3-CH_2-CH_2-NH_2$

**18.12** Identify the compound in each pair that has the higher boiling point. Explain.

**a.** $CH_3-CH_2-CH_2-CH_3$ or $CH_3-CH_2-CH_2-NH_2$

**b.** $CH_3-NH_2$ or $CH_3-CH_2-NH_2$

**c.** $CH_3-CH_2-CH_2-OH$ or $CH_3-\overset{NH_2}{\overset{|}{CH}}-CH_3$

**18.13** Propylamine (59 g/mole) has a boiling point of 48 °C, and ethylmethylamine (59 g/mole) has a boiling point of 37 °C. Butane (58 g/mole) has a much lower boiling point of –1 °C. Explain.

**18.14** Assign the boiling point of 3 °C, 48 °C, or 97 °C to the appropriate compound: 1-propanol, propylamine, and trimethylamine.

**18.15** Indicate if each of the following is soluble in water. Explain.

**a.** $CH_3-CH_2-NH_2$ **b.** $CH_3-NH-CH_3$

**c.** $CH_3-CH_2-CH_2-\overset{CH_2-CH_2-CH_3}{\overset{|}{N}}-CH_2-CH_2-CH_3$

**d.** $CH_3-\overset{NH_2}{\overset{|}{CH}}-CH_2-CH_3$

**18.16** Indicate if each of the following is soluble in water. Explain.

**a.** $CH_3-CH_2-CH_2-NH_2$

**b.** $CH_3-CH_2-CH_2-NH-CH_2-CH_3$

**c.** $CH_3-\overset{CH_3}{\overset{|}{N}}-CH_3$ **d.** $C_6H_5-\overset{H}{\overset{|}{N}}-C_6H_5$

**18.17** Write an equation for the ionization of each of the following amines in water:

**a.** methylamine

**b.** dimethylamine

**c.** aniline

**18.18** Write an equation for the ionization of each of the following amines in water:

**a.** ethylamine

**b.** propylamine

**c.** *N*-methylaniline

**18.19** Write the condensed structural formula of the amine salt obtained when each of the amines in problem 18.17 reacts with HCl.

**18.20** Write the condensed structural formula of the amine salt obtained when each of the amines in problem 18.18 reacts with HCl.

**18.21** Novocain, a local anesthetic, is the amine salt of procaine:

$$H_2N-C_6H_4-\overset{O}{\overset{\|}{C}}-O-CH_2-CH_2-\underset{CH_2-CH_3}{\underset{|}{\overset{CH_2-CH_3}{\overset{|}{N}}}}$$

Procaine

**a.** What is the condensed structural formula of the amine salt (procaine hydrochloride) formed when procaine reacts with HCl? (Hint: The tertiary amine reacts with HCl.)

**b.** Why is procaine hydrochloride used rather than procaine?

**18.22** Lidocaine (Xylocaine) is used as a local anesthetic and cardiac depressant:

$$(CH_3)_2C_6H_3-NH-\overset{O}{\overset{\|}{C}}-CH_2-\underset{CH_2-CH_3}{\underset{|}{\overset{CH_2-CH_3}{\overset{|}{N}}}}$$

Lidocaine (Xylocaine®)

**a.** What is the condensed structural formula of the amine salt formed when lidocaine reacts with HCl?

**b.** Why is the amine salt of lidocaine used rather than the amine?

## 18.3 Heterocyclic Amines and Alkaloids

**LEARNING GOAL**

Identify heterocyclic amines; distinguish between the types of heterocyclic amines.

A **heterocyclic amine** is a cyclic organic compound that contains one or more nitrogen atoms in the ring. The heterocyclic amine rings typically consist of five or six atoms and one or more nitrogen atoms. Of the five-atom rings, the simplest one is pyrrolidine, which is a ring of four carbon atoms and a nitrogen atom, all with single bonds. Pyrrole is a five-atom ring with one nitrogen atom and two double bonds. Imidazole is a five-atom ring that contains two nitrogen atoms.

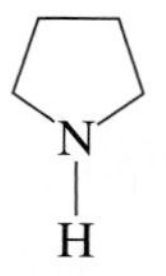

Pyrrolidine

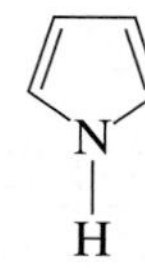

Pyrrole

Imidazole

Some of the pungent aroma and taste we associate with black pepper is due to a compound called *piperidine*, which is a six-atom heterocyclic ring with a nitrogen atom. The fruit from the black pepper plant is dried and ground to give the black pepper we use to season our foods.

Many of the other six-atom heterocyclic amines are aromatic. Pyridine is similar to benzene, except it has a nitrogen atom in place of a carbon atom. Pyrimidine, which is found in nucleic acids, is also similar to benzene, except it has two nitrogen atoms. In purine, another component of nucleic acids, a pyrimidine ring is fused with imidazole.

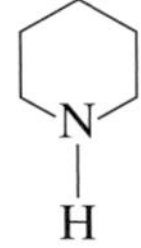

Piperidine 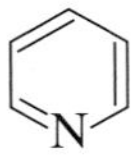  Pyridine  Pyrimidine 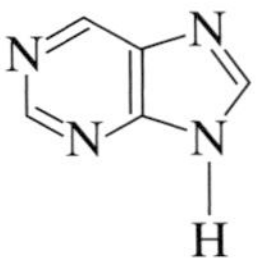  Purine

**CONCEPT CHECK 18.5**

**Heterocyclic Amines**

Identify each of the following heterocyclic amines:

**a.** 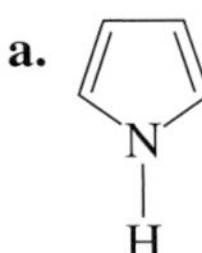 **b.** 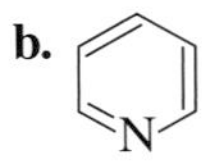 **c.**

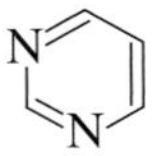

ANSWER

**a.** Pyrrole has a five-atom ring with one nitrogen atom.
**b.** Pyridine has a six-atom ring similar to benzene with one nitrogen atom.
**c.** Pyrimidine has a six-atom ring similar to benzene with two nitrogen atoms.

MC TUTORIAL Identifying Types of Heterocyclic Amines

## Alkaloids: Amines in Plants

**Alkaloids** are physiologically active nitrogen-containing compounds produced by plants. The term *alkaloid* refers to the "alkali-like" or basic characteristics we have seen for amines. Certain alkaloids are used in anesthetics, in antidepressants, and as stimulants, although many are habit forming.

As a stimulant, nicotine increases the level of adrenaline in the blood, which increases the heart rate and blood pressure. Nicotine is responsible for the addiction of smoking. Nicotine has a simple alkaloid structure that includes a pyrrolidine ring. Coniine, which is obtained from hemlock, is an extremely toxic alkaloid that contains a piperidine ring.

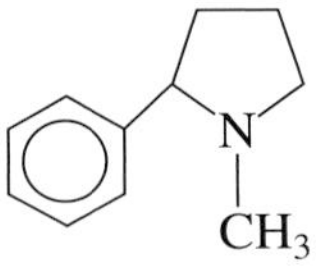

Nicotine 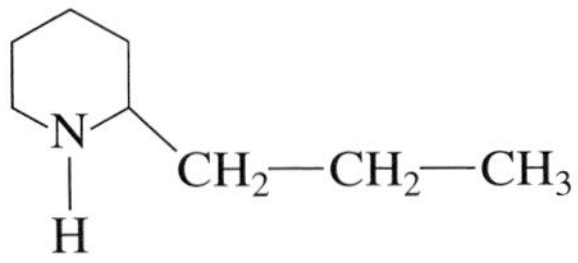  Coniine

Caffeine contains an imidazole ring and is a central nervous system stimulant. Present in coffee, tea, soft drinks, chocolate, and cocoa, caffeine increases alertness, but it may cause nervousness and insomnia. Caffeine is also used in certain pain relievers to counteract the drowsiness caused by an antihistamine. (See Figure 18.3.)

**FIGURE 18.3** Coffee beans contain caffeine, which is an alkaloid that is a stimulant of the central nervous system.

**Q** Why is caffeine considered an alkaloid?

Several alkaloids are used in medicine. Quinine, obtained from the bark of the cinchona tree, has been used in the treatment of malaria since the 1600s. Atropine from belladonna is used in low concentrations to accelerate slow heart rates and as an anesthetic for eye examinations.

Quinine

Atropine

For many centuries, morphine and codeine, alkaloids found in the opium poppy plant, have been used as effective painkillers. (See Figure 18.4.) Codeine, which is structurally similar to morphine, is used in some prescription painkillers and cough syrups. Heroin, obtained by a chemical modification of morphine, is strongly addictive and is not used medically.

Heroin

**FIGURE 18.4** The green, unripe poppy seed capsule contains a milky sap (opium) that is the source of the alkaloids morphine and codeine.

**Q** Where is the piperidine ring in the structures of morphine and codeine?

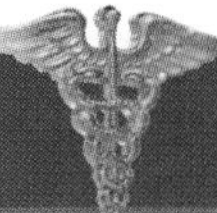

# HEALTH NOTE

## Synthesizing Drugs

One area of research in pharmacology is the synthesis of compounds that retain the anesthetic characteristic of naturally occurring alkaloids such as cocaine and morphine without the addictive side effects. For example, cocaine is an effective anesthetic, but it is addictive. Research chemists modified the structure of cocaine but kept the benzene group and nitrogen atom. The synthetic products procaine and lidocaine retain the anesthetic qualities of the natural alkaloid without the addictive side effects:

The structure of morphine was also modified to make a synthetic alkaloid, meperidine, or Demerol, which acts as an effective painkiller:

Meperidine (Demerol®)

Cocaine

Procaine (Novocaine®)

Lidocaine (Xylocaine®)

SAMPLE PROBLEM 18.4

### Heterocyclic Amines

Identify the heterocyclic amines in the alkaloids nicotine and caffeine.

SOLUTION

In nicotine, the heterocyclic amine is the five-atom ring of pyrrolidine. Caffeine contains a purine, which is pyrimidine and imidazole fused together.

STUDY CHECK

What is the heterocyclic amine in meperidine (Demerol)?

## QUESTIONS AND PROBLEMS

### Heterocyclic Amines and Alkaloids

**18.23** Identify the following as amines or heterocyclic amines:

a. 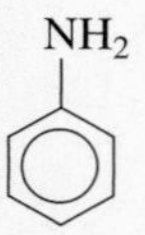 $NH_2$ on a benzene ring

b. 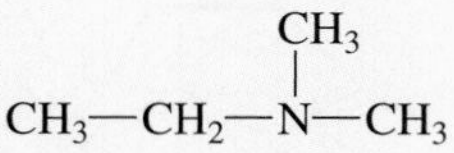 $CH_3—CH_2—N(CH_3)—CH_3$

c. 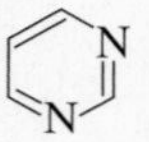 (pyrimidine ring)

d. 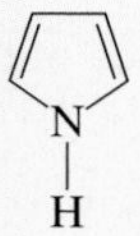 (pyrrole ring, N—H)

**18.24** Identify the following as amines or heterocyclic amines:

a. 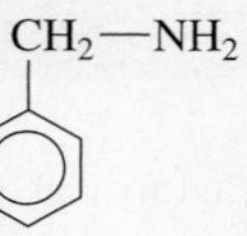 $CH_2—NH_2$ on a benzene ring

b. 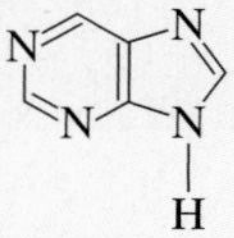 (purine ring, N—H)

c. 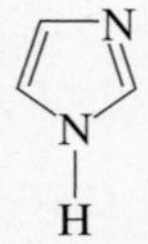 (imidazole ring, N—H)

d. 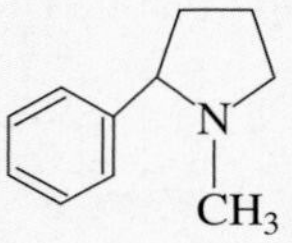 (benzene ring attached to a pyrrolidine ring, N—$CH_3$)

**18.25** Identify the types of heterocyclic amines in problem 18.23.

**18.26** Identify the types of heterocyclic amines in problem 18.24.

**18.27** Low levels of serotonin in the brain appear to be associated with depressed states. What type of heterocyclic amine is serotonin?

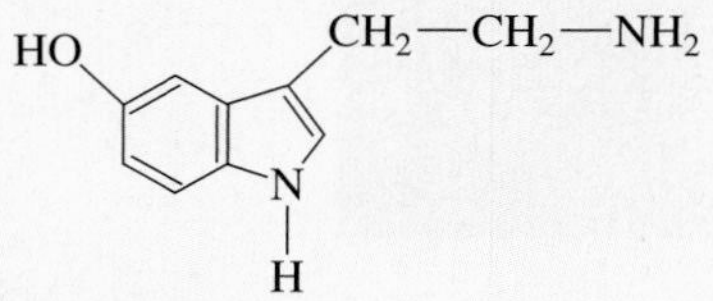

HO, $CH_2—CH_2—NH_2$, N—H

Serotonin

**18.28** LSD is made from lysergic acid, which is produced by a fungus that grows on rye. What types of heterocyclic amines are in lysergic acid?

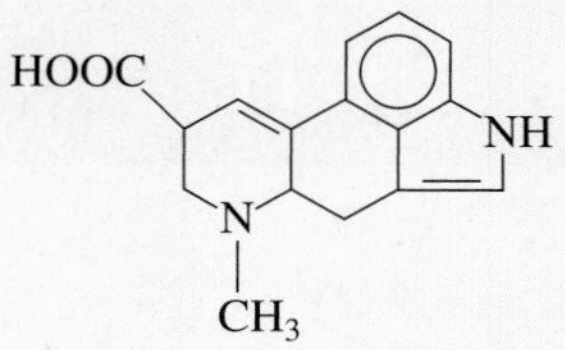

HOOC, NH, N—$CH_3$

Lysergic acid

## 18.4 Amides

**LEARNING GOAL**

Write the amide products of amidation, and give their common and IUPAC names.

The **amides** are derivatives of carboxylic acids in which an amino group replaces the hydroxyl group:

| **Carboxylic acid** | **Amide** |
|---|---|
| Ethanoic acid (acetic acid) | Ethanamide (acetamide) |

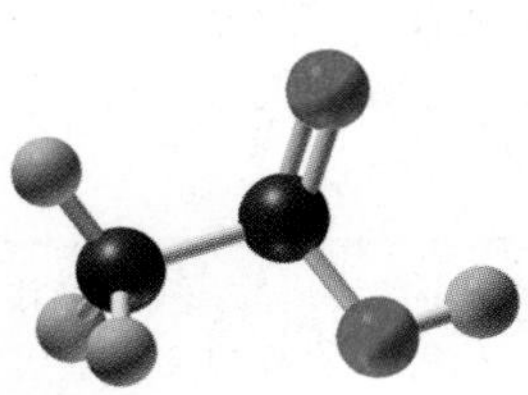

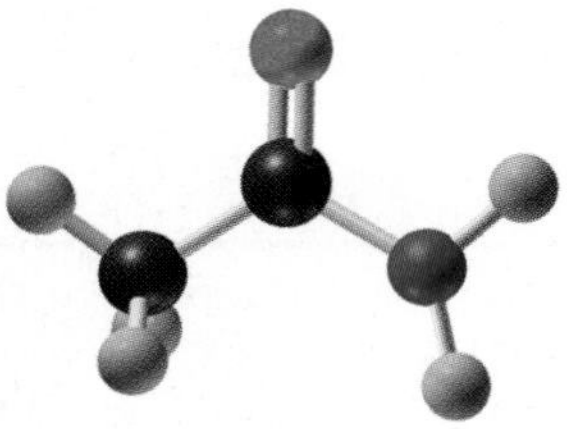

### Preparation of Amides

TUTORIAL
Amidation Reactions

An amide is produced in a reaction called **amidation**, in which a carboxylic acid reacts with ammonia or a primary or secondary amine. A molecule of water is eliminated, and the fragments of the carboxylic acid and amine molecules join to form the amide, much like the formation of an ester. Because a hydrogen atom must be lost from the amines, only primary and secondary amines undergo amidation:

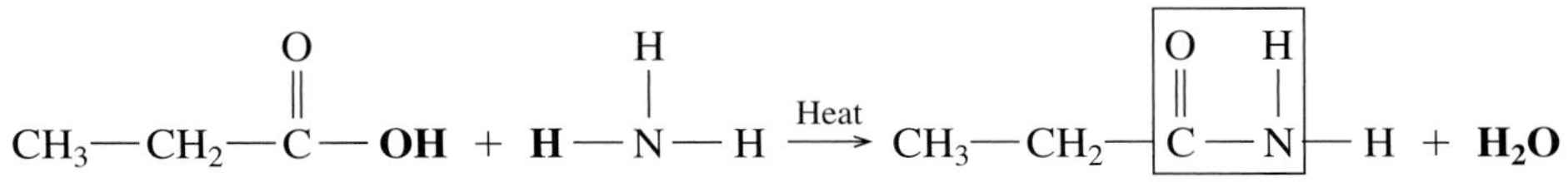

$$CH_3{-}CH_2{-}\overset{\overset{\large O}{\|}}{C}{-}\mathbf{OH} + \mathbf{H}{-}\overset{\overset{\large H}{|}}{N}{-}H \xrightarrow{\text{Heat}} CH_3{-}CH_2{-}\boxed{\overset{\overset{\large O}{\|}}{C}{-}\overset{\overset{\large H}{|}}{N}}{-}H + \mathbf{H_2O}$$

Propanoic acid (propionic acid) — Ammonia — Propanamide (propionamide)

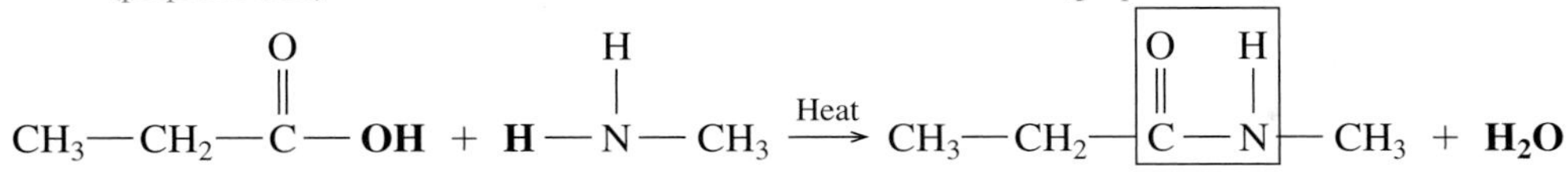

$$CH_3{-}CH_2{-}\overset{\overset{\large O}{\|}}{C}{-}\mathbf{OH} + \mathbf{H}{-}\overset{\overset{\large H}{|}}{N}{-}CH_3 \xrightarrow{\text{Heat}} CH_3{-}CH_2{-}\boxed{\overset{\overset{\large O}{\|}}{C}{-}\overset{\overset{\large H}{|}}{N}}{-}CH_3 + \mathbf{H_2O}$$

Propanoic acid (propionic acid) — Methylamine — *N*-Methylpropanamide (*N*-methylpropionamide)

SAMPLE PROBLEM 18.5

## Amidation

Give the condensed structural formula of the amide product in each of the following reactions:

**a.**

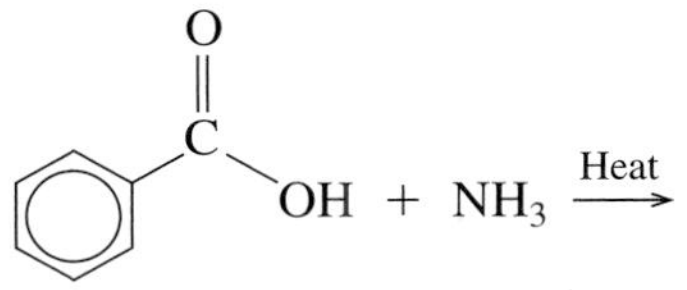

$$C_6H_5{-}\overset{\overset{\large O}{\|}}{C}{-}OH + NH_3 \xrightarrow{\text{Heat}}$$

**b.**

$$CH_3{-}\overset{\overset{\large O}{\|}}{C}{-}OH + NH_2{-}CH_2{-}CH_3 \xrightarrow{\text{Heat}}$$

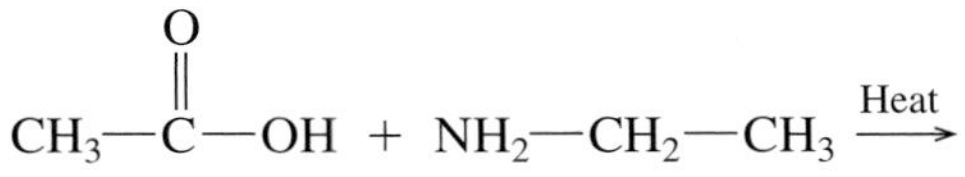

SOLUTION

**a.** The condensed structural formula of the amide product can be written by attaching the carbonyl group from the acid to the nitrogen atom of the amine. —OH is removed from the acid and —H from the amine to form water:

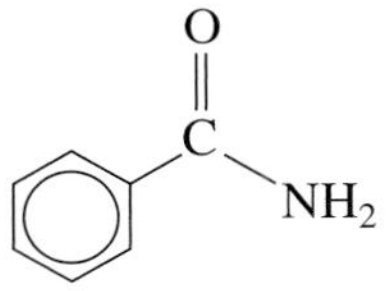

$$C_6H_5{-}\overset{\overset{\large O}{\|}}{C}{-}NH_2$$

**b.**

$$CH_3{-}\overset{\overset{\large O}{\|}}{C}{-}\overset{\overset{\large H}{|}}{N}{-}CH_2{-}CH_3$$

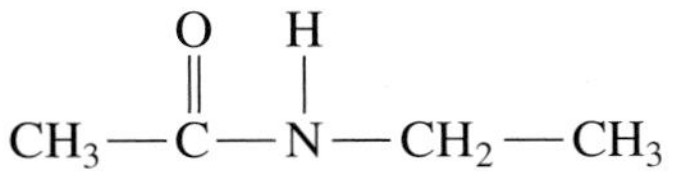

STUDY CHECK

What are the condensed structural formulas of the carboxylic acid and amine needed to prepare the following amide? (Hint: Separate the N and C=O of the amide group, and add —H and —OH to give the original amine and carboxylic acid.)

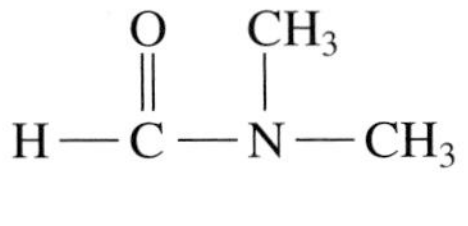

$$H{-}\overset{\overset{\large O}{\|}}{C}{-}\overset{\overset{\large CH_3}{|}}{N}{-}CH_3$$

## Naming Amides

In both the common and IUPAC names, amides are named by dropping the *ic acid* or *oic acid* from the carboxylic acid names (IUPAC or common) and adding the suffix *amide*. In the common names, the position of a substituent is shown with $\alpha$ or $\beta$ just as we used for the common names of carboxylic acids (Chapter 16):

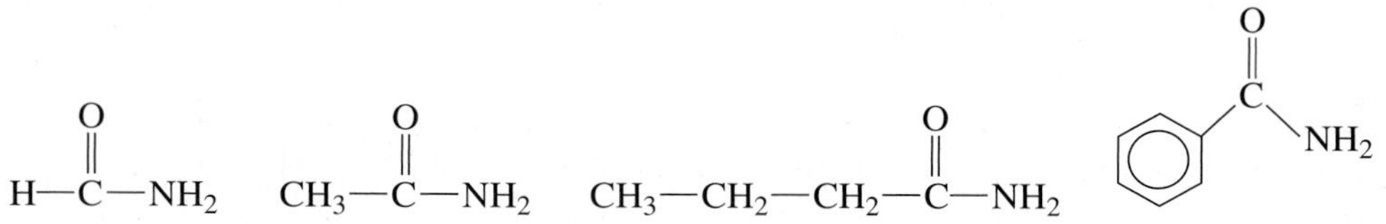

$H-C(=O)-NH_2$ — Methanamide (formamide)

$CH_3-C(=O)-NH_2$ — Ethanamide (acetamide)

$CH_3-CH_2-CH_2-C(=O)-NH_2$ — Butanamide (butyramide)

$C_6H_5-C(=O)-NH_2$ — Benzamide

When alkyl groups are attached to the nitrogen atom, *N*- or *N,N*- precedes the name of the amide depending on whether there are one or two groups:

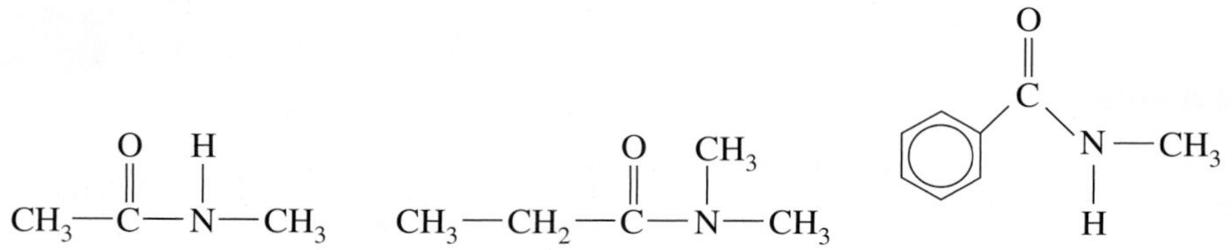

$CH_3-C(=O)-NH-CH_3$ — *N*-Methylethanamide (*N*-methylacetamide)

$CH_3-CH_2-C(=O)-N(CH_3)-CH_3$ — *N,N*-Dimethylpropanamide (*N,N*-dimethylpropionamide)

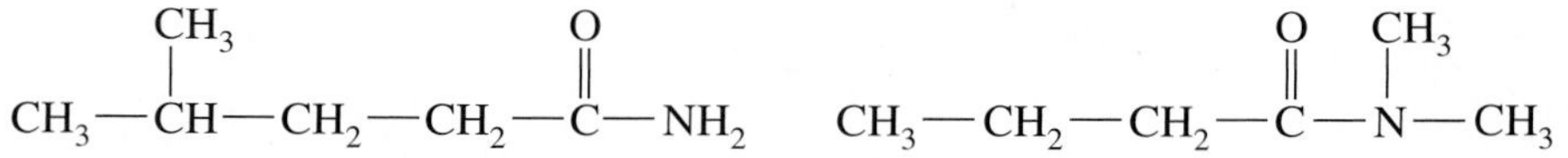

$C_6H_5-C(=O)-NH-CH_3$ — *N*-Methylbenzamide

$CH_3-CH(CH_3)-CH_2-CH_2-C(=O)-NH_2$ — 4-Methylpentanamide

$CH_3-CH_2-CH_2-C(=O)-N(CH_3)-CH_3$ — *N,N*-Dimethylbutanamide (*N,N*-dimethylbutyramide)

**CONCEPT CHECK 18.6**

### IUPAC Names of Amides

An amide has the name *N*-ethylpentanamide.

**a.** What is the IUPAC name of the carboxylic acid used in the amidation reaction to form this amide?

**b.** What is indicated by the "*N*-ethyl" part of the name?

**c.** If a methyl group were also attached to the N atom, how would the amide be named?

ANSWER

**a.** Pentanamide indicates that there are 5 carbon atoms. The corresponding carboxylic acid used in the amidation reaction would be pentanoic acid.

**b.** The "*N*-ethyl" part of the name indicates that an ethyl group ($CH_3-CH_2-$) is attached to the N atom.

**c.** If the N atom were attached to an ethyl group and a methyl group, the amide would be named *N*-ethyl-*N*-methylpentanamide.

**Guide to Naming Amides**

STEP 1
Identify the corresponding carboxylic acid of the amide.

STEP 2
Name the amide by replacing the *oic* or *ic* acid in the name of the corresponding carboxylic acid by *amide*.

STEP 3
Name a substituent on the N atom using the prefix *N*– and the alkyl name.

**SAMPLE PROBLEM 18.6**

### Naming Amides

Give the IUPAC and common names for each of the following amides:

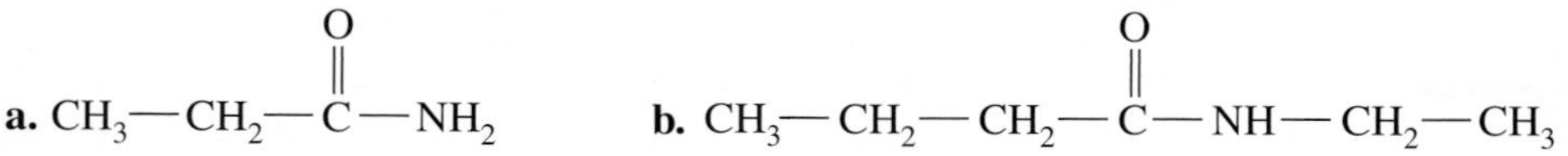

**a.** $CH_3-CH_2-C(=O)-NH_2$ **b.** $CH_3-CH_2-CH_2-C(=O)-NH-CH_2-CH_3$

SOLUTION

**a. STEP 1** **Identify the corresponding carboxylic acid of the amide.** The IUPAC name of the corresponding carboxylic acid is propanoic acid. The common name of the corresponding carboxylic acid is propionic acid.

STEP 2 **Name the amide by replacing the *oic* or *ic acid* in the name of the corresponding carboxylic acid by *amide*.** The *oic acid* ending of propanoic acid is replaced with *amide* to give the IUPAC name of propanamide. Replacing the *ic acid* ending of propionic acid with *amide* gives the common name of propionamide.

STEP 3 **Name a substituent on the N atom using the prefix *N*- and the alkyl name.** This compound has no substituent on the N atom.

**b.** STEP 1 **Identify the corresponding carboxylic acid of the amide.** The IUPAC name of the corresponding carboxylic acid is butanoic acid. The common name of the corresponding carboxylic acid is butyric acid.

STEP 2 **Name the amide by replacing the *oic* or *ic acid* in the name of the corresponding carboxylic acid by *amide*.** The *oic acid* ending of butanoic acid is replaced by *amide* to give the IUPAC name butanamide. Replacing the *ic acid* ending of butryic acid with *amide* gives the common name butyramide.

STEP 3 **Name a substituent on the N atom using the prefix *N*- and the alkyl name.** The ethyl group attached to the nitrogen atom is named *N-ethyl*. The IUPAC name is *N*-ethylbutanamide, and the common name is *N*-ethylbutyramide.

STUDY CHECK

Draw the condensed structural formula of *N*,*N*-dimethylbenzamide.

## Physical Properties of Amides

The amides do not have the properties of bases that we saw for the amines. Only formamide is a liquid at room temperature, while the other amides are solids. For primary amides, the $-NH_2$ group can form hydrogen bonds, which gives primary amides high melting points. The melting points of the secondary amides are lower because there is only one N—H bond, and the number of hydrogen bonds decreases. Tertiary amides have even lower melting points because they have no N—H bonds and thus cannot form hydrogen bonds with other tertiary amides.

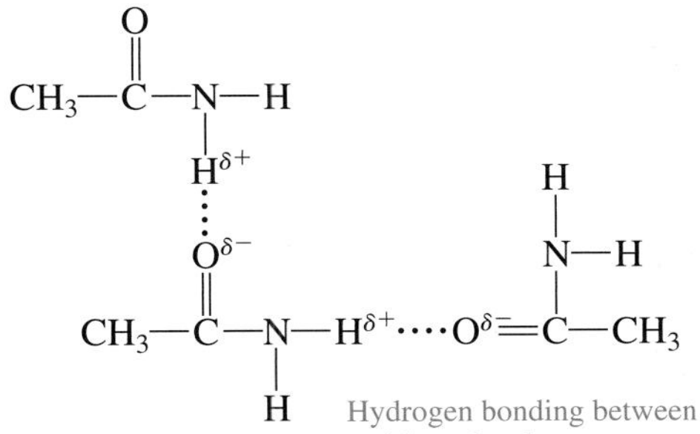

```
            O
            ‖
   CH3—C—N—H
              |
             Hδ+                        H
              :                          |
             Oδ−                        N—H
              ‖                          |
      CH3—C—N—Hδ+····Oδ−=C—CH3
                 |
                 H
```

Hydrogen bonding between amide molecules

The amides with one to five carbon atoms are soluble in water because they can hydrogen bond with water molecules:

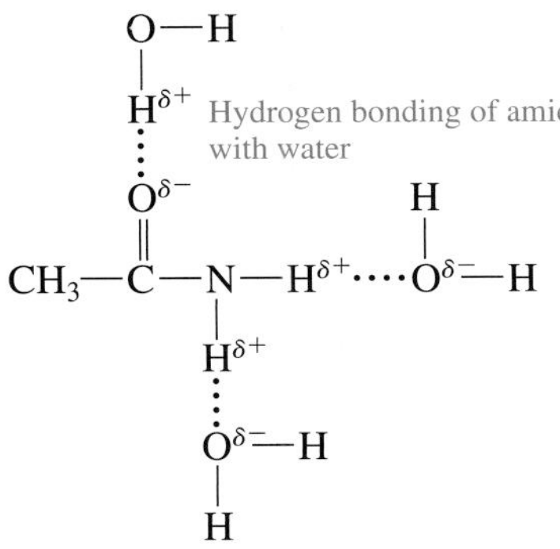

```
          O—H
          |
          Hδ+
          :
          Oδ−              H
          ‖                |
   CH3—C—N—Hδ+····Oδ−—H
             |
            Hδ+
             :
            Oδ−—H
             |
             H
```

Hydrogen bonding of amides with water

# HEALTH NOTE

## Amides in Health and Medicine

The simplest natural amide is urea, an end product of protein metabolism in the body. The kidneys remove urea from the blood and provide for its excretion in urine. If the kidneys malfunction, urea is not removed and builds to a toxic level, a condition called uremia. Urea is also used as a component of fertilizer to increase nitrogen in the soil.

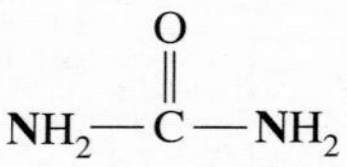

$$NH_2-\overset{\overset{O}{\|}}{C}-NH_2$$

Urea

Synthetic amides are used as substitutes for sugar and aspirin. Saccharin is a very powerful sweetener and is used as a sugar substitute. The sweetener aspartame is made from two amino acids: aspartic acid and phenylalanine.

Aspirin substitutes contain phenacetin or acetaminophen, which is used in Tylenol. Like aspirin, acetaminophen reduces fever and pain, but it has little anti-inflammatory effect.

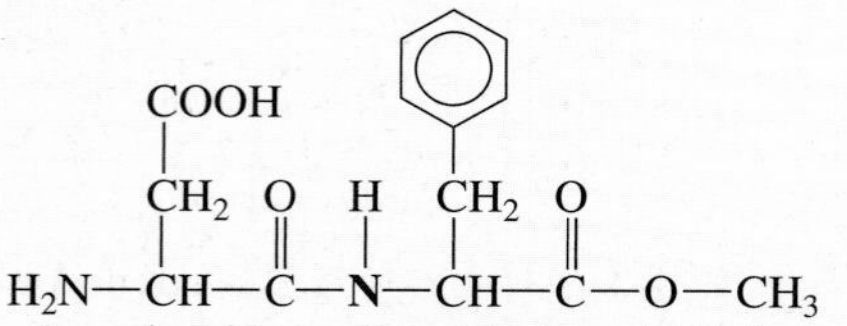

$$H_2N-\underset{\underset{COOH}{|}}{\overset{}{CH}}(CH_2)-\overset{O}{\overset{\|}{C}}-\overset{H}{\overset{|}{N}}-\overset{C_6H_5-CH_2}{CH}-\overset{O}{\overset{\|}{C}}-O-CH_3$$

Aspartic acid — Phenylalanine — Methyl ester

Aspartame

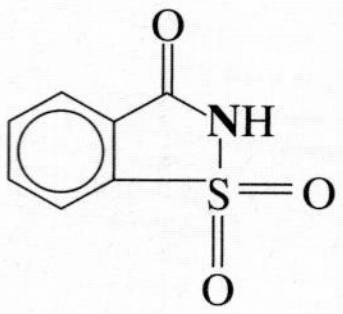

(Saccharin: benzene ring fused to C=O, NH, $S(=O)_2$)

Saccharin

$$CH_3-CH_2-O-[C_6H_4]-\overset{H}{\overset{|}{N}}-\overset{O}{\overset{\|}{C}}-CH_3$$

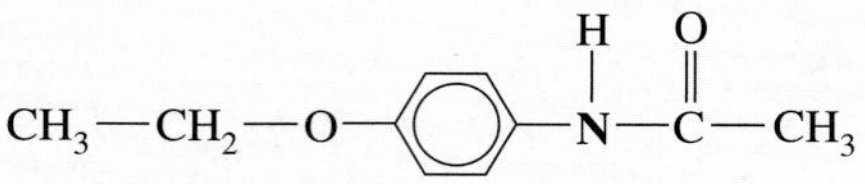

Phenacetin

$$HO-[C_6H_4]-\overset{H}{\overset{|}{N}}-\overset{O}{\overset{\|}{C}}-CH_3$$

Acetaminophen

Many barbiturates are cyclic amides of barbituric acid that act as sedatives in small dosages or sleep inducers in larger dosages. They are often habit forming. Barbiturate drugs include phenobarbital (Luminal), pentobarbital (Nembutal), and secobarbital (Seconal).

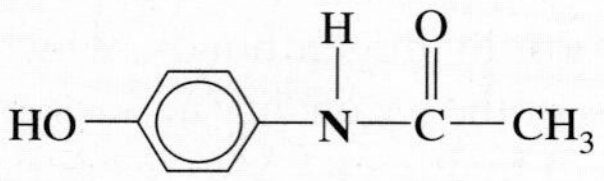

($CH_3-CH_2$ and $C_6H_5$ on barbiturate ring)

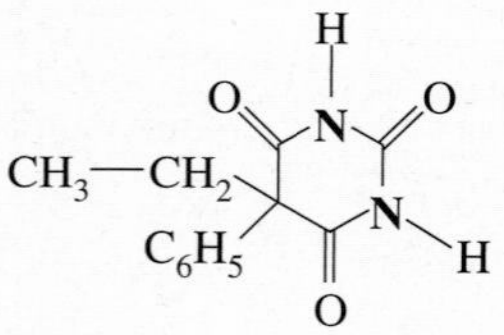

Luminal® (phenobarbital)

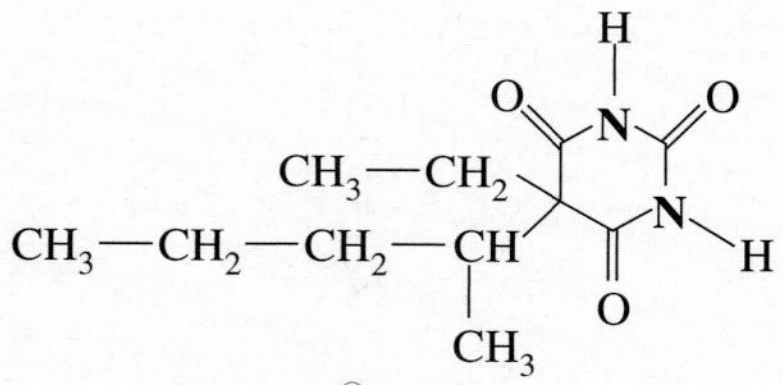

($CH_3-CH_2$ and $CH_3-CH_2-CH_2-CH(CH_3)$ on barbiturate ring)

Nembutal® (pentobarbital)

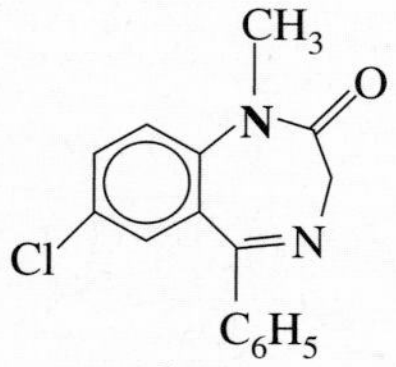

(benzodiazepine ring with $CH_3$ on N, C=O, Cl, =N, $C_6H_5$)

Valium® (diazepam)

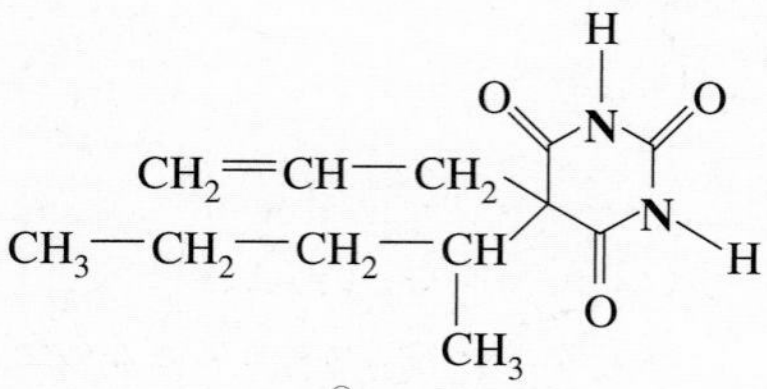

($CH_2=CH-CH_2$ and $CH_3-CH_2-CH_2-CH(CH_3)$ on barbiturate ring)

Seconal® (secobarbital)

$$H_2N-\overset{O}{\overset{\|}{C}}-O-CH_2-\underset{CH_2-CH_2-CH_3}{\overset{CH_3}{C}}-CH_2-O-\overset{O}{\overset{\|}{C}}-NH_2$$

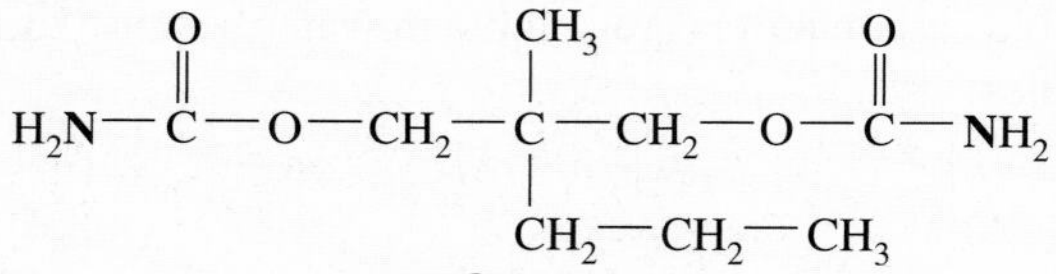

Equanil® (meprobamate)

## QUESTIONS AND PROBLEMS

### Amides

18.29 Draw the condensed structural formula of the amide formed in each of the following reactions:

a. $CH_3-\overset{O}{\overset{\|}{C}}-OH + NH_3 \xrightarrow{\text{Heat}}$

b. $CH_3-\overset{O}{\overset{\|}{C}}-OH + NH_2-CH_2-CH_3 \xrightarrow{\text{Heat}}$

c. 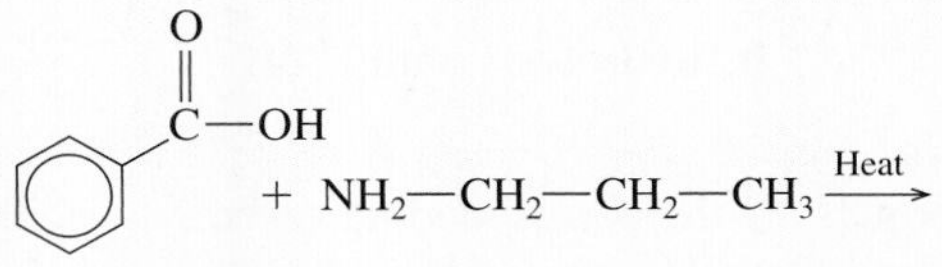 $C_6H_5-\overset{O}{\overset{\|}{C}}-OH + NH_2-CH_2-CH_2-CH_3 \xrightarrow{\text{Heat}}$

18.30 Draw the condensed structural formula of the amide formed in each of the following reactions:

a. $CH_3-CH_2-CH_2-CH_2-\overset{O}{\overset{\|}{C}}-OH + NH_3 \xrightarrow{\text{Heat}}$

b. $CH_3-\overset{CH_3}{\overset{|}{CH}}-CH_2-\overset{O}{\overset{\|}{C}}-OH + NH_2-CH_2-CH_2-CH_3 \xrightarrow{\text{Heat}}$

c. 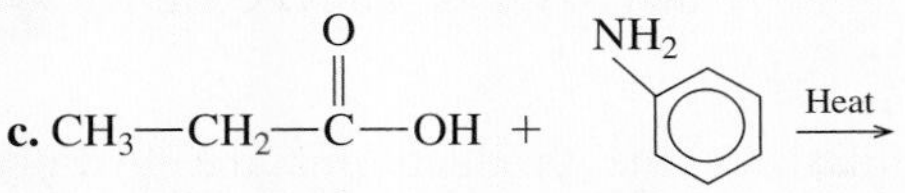 $CH_3-CH_2-\overset{O}{\overset{\|}{C}}-OH + C_6H_5NH_2 \xrightarrow{\text{Heat}}$

18.31 Give the IUPAC and common name (if any) for each of the following amides:

a. $CH_3-\overset{O}{\overset{\|}{C}}-NH-CH_3$

b. $CH_3-CH_2-CH_2-\overset{O}{\overset{\|}{C}}-NH_2$

c. $H-\overset{O}{\overset{\|}{C}}-NH_2$

d. 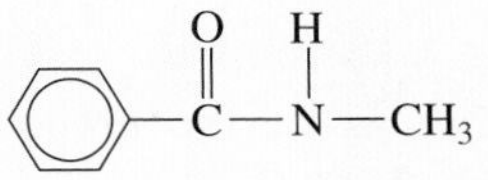 $C_6H_5-\overset{O}{\overset{\|}{C}}-\overset{H}{\overset{|}{N}}-CH_3$

18.32 Give the IUPAC and common name (if any) for each of the following amides:

a. $CH_3-CH_2-\overset{O}{\overset{\|}{C}}-\overset{H}{\overset{|}{N}}-CH_2-CH_3$

b. $CH_3-CH_2-CH_2-CH_2-CH_2-\overset{O}{\overset{\|}{C}}-NH_2$

c. $CH_3-\overset{O}{\overset{\|}{C}}-\overset{CH_3}{\overset{|}{N}}-CH_2-CH_2-CH_3$

d. 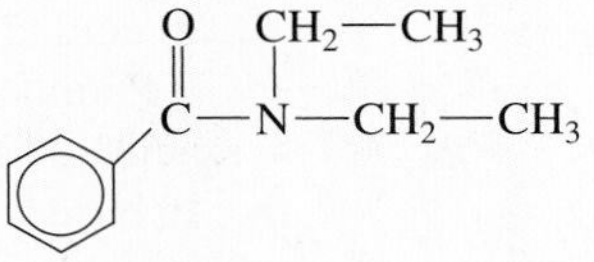 $C_6H_5-\overset{O}{\overset{\|}{C}}-\overset{CH_2-CH_3}{\overset{|}{N}}-CH_2-CH_3$

18.33 Draw the condensed structural formula for each of the following amides:

a. propionamide
b. pentanamide
c. methanamide
d. *N*-ethylbenzamide
e. *N*-ethylbutyramide

18.34 Draw the condensed structural formula for each of the following amides:

a. formamide
b. *N,N*-dimethylbenzamide
c. 3-methylbutyramide
d. hexanamide
e. *N*-propylpentanamide

18.35 For each of the following pairs, identify the compound that has the higher melting point. Explain.

a. acetamide or *N*-methylacetamide
b. butane or propionamide
c. *N,N*-dimethylpropanamide or *N*-methylpropanamide

18.36 For each of the following pairs, identify the compound that has the higher melting point. Explain.

a. propane or acetamide
b. *N*-methylacetamide or propanamide
c. *N,N*-dimethylpropanamide or *N*-methylpropanamide

## 18.5 Hydrolysis of Amides

As we have seen, amide bonds are formed by the elimination of water. The reverse reaction, called **hydrolysis**, occurs when water is added back to the amide bond to split the molecule. When an acid is used, the hydrolysis products of an amide are the carboxylic acid and the ammonium salt. In base hydrolysis, the amide produces the salt of the carboxylic acid and ammonia or the amine.

**LEARNING GOAL**

Write equations for the hydrolysis of amides.

### Acid Hydrolysis of Amides

$$CH_3-\overset{O}{\overset{\|}{C}}-NH_2 + HOH + HCl \longrightarrow CH_3-\overset{O}{\overset{\|}{C}}-OH + NH_4^+Cl^-$$

Ethanamide (acetamide) → Ethanoic acid (acetic acid) + Ammonium chloride

**Base Hydrolysis of Amides**

$$\underset{\substack{N\text{-Methylpropanamide} \\ (N\text{-methylpropionamide})}}{CH_3-CH_2-\overset{\overset{\displaystyle O}{\|}}{C}-NH-CH_3} + NaOH \longrightarrow \underset{\substack{\text{Sodium propanoate, a salt} \\ \text{(sodium propionate)}}}{CH_3-CH_2-\overset{\overset{\displaystyle O}{\|}}{C}-O^- Na^+} + \underset{\substack{\text{Methanamine} \\ \text{(methylamine)}}}{NH_2-CH_3}$$

CONCEPT CHECK 18.7

## Acid and Base Hydrolysis of Amides

Give the names of the products when *N*-ethylpropanamide undergoes each of the following:

**a.** hydrolysis with HCl

**b.** hydrolysis with KOH

ANSWER

**a.** In acid (HCl) hydrolysis, the products are the corresponding carboxylic acid and the amine salt. The acid hydrolysis of *N*-ethylpropanamide with HCl forms propanoic acid and ethylammonium chloride.

**b.** In base (KOH) hydrolysis, the products are the corresponding carboxylic acid salt and the amine. The base hydrolysis of *N*-ethylpropanamide with KOH forms potassium propanoate and ethylamine.

SAMPLE PROBLEM 18.7

## Hydrolysis of Amides

Write the condensed structural formulas for the products for the hydrolysis of *N*-methylpentanamide with NaOH.

SOLUTION

Hydrolysis of the amide with a base produces a carboxylate salt (sodium pentanoate) and the corresponding amine (methylamine):

$$CH_3-CH_2-CH_2-CH_2-\overset{\overset{\displaystyle O}{\|}}{C}-O^- Na^+ + NH_2-CH_3$$

STUDY CHECK

Draw the condensed structural formulas of the products from the hydrolysis of *N*-methylbutyramide with HBr.

# QUESTIONS AND PROBLEMS

## Hydrolysis of Amides

**18.37** Draw the condensed structural formulas for the products of the acid hydrolysis of each of the following amides with HCl:

**a.** $CH_3-\overset{\overset{\displaystyle O}{\|}}{C}-NH_2$

**b.** $CH_3-CH_2-\overset{\overset{\displaystyle O}{\|}}{C}-NH_2$

**c.** $CH_3-CH_2-CH_2-\overset{\overset{\displaystyle O}{\|}}{C}-NH-CH_3$

**d.** $C_6H_5-\overset{\overset{\displaystyle O}{\|}}{C}-NH_2$ (benzene ring attached to the carbonyl carbon)

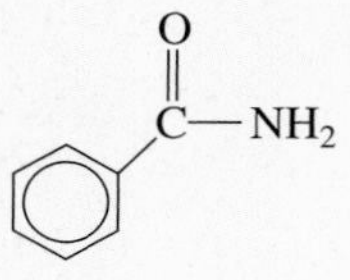

**e.** *N*-ethylpentanamide

**18.38** Draw the condensed structural formulas for the products of the base hydrolysis of each of the following amides with NaOH:

**a.** $CH_3-CH_2-CH(CH_3)-C(=O)-NH_2$

**b.** $CH_3-CH_2-CH_2-C(=O)-N(CH_2-CH_3)-CH_2-CH_3$

**c.** $C_6H_5-C(=O)-N(CH_3)-CH_2-CH_2-CH_2-CH_3$

**d.** $CH_3-CH(Cl)-C(=O)-N(CH_3)-CH_2-CH_3$

**e.** *N*-propylbenzamide

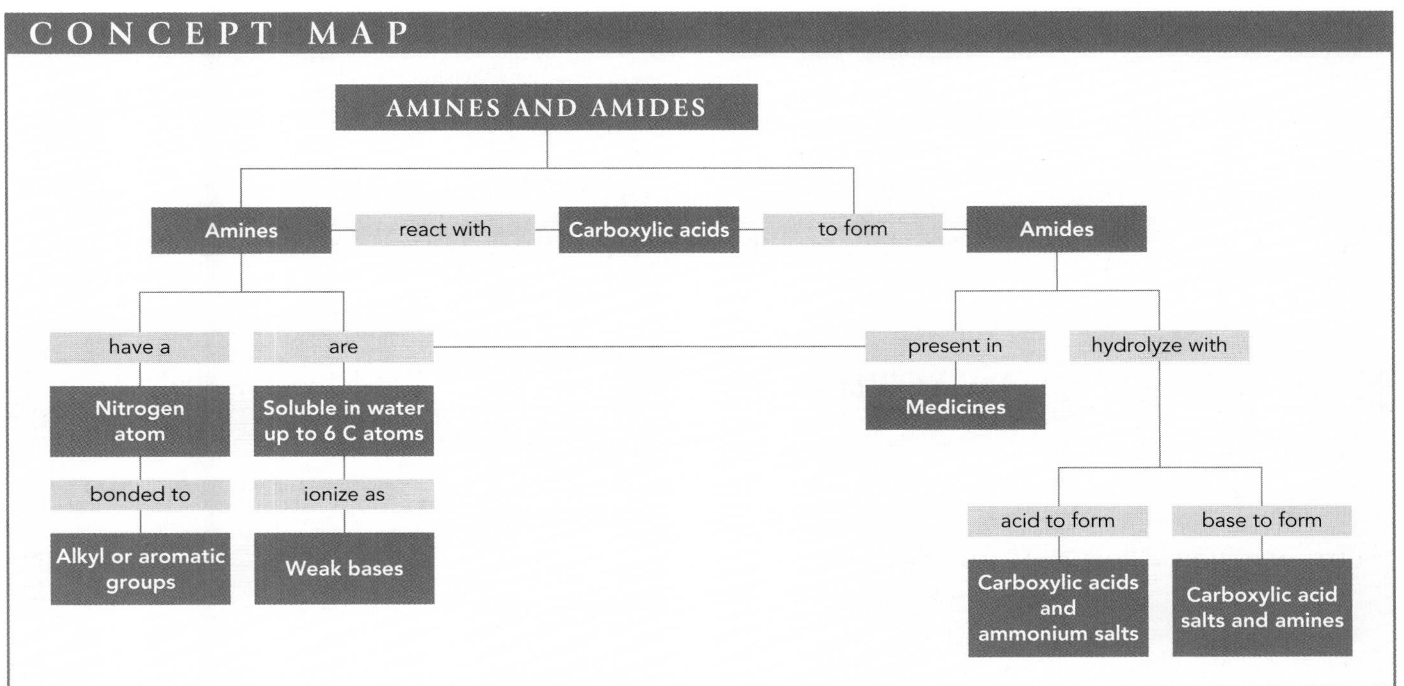


# CHAPTER REVIEW

## 18.1 Amines

**LEARNING GOAL:** *Classify amines as primary (1°), secondary (2°), or tertiary (3°). Name amines using common and IUPAC names; draw the condensed structural formulas given the names.*

A nitrogen atom attached to one, two, or three alkyl or aromatic groups forms a primary (1°), secondary (2°), or tertiary (3°) amine. In the IUPAC system, the *amine* suffix is added to the alkane name (after dropping the *e*) of the longer carbon chain. Groups attached to the nitrogen atom use a *N*- prefix. When other functional groups are present, the $-NH_2$ is named as an amino group. In the common names of simple amines, the alkyl groups are listed alphabetically followed by the suffix *amine*.

## 18.2 Properties of Amines

**LEARNING GOAL:** *Describe the boiling points and solubility of amines; write equations for the ionization and neutralization of amines.*

Primary and secondary amines form hydrogen bonds, which make their boiling points higher than alkanes of similar mass but lower than those of alcohols. Amines with up to six carbon atoms are soluble in water. In water, amines act as weak bases because the nitrogen atom accepts a proton from water to produce ammonium and hydroxide ions. When amines react with acids, they form amine salts, which are named as ammonium salts. As ionic compounds, amine salts are solids, soluble in water, and odorless compared to the amines. Quaternary ammonium salts contain four carbon groups bonded to the nitrogen atom.

## 18.3 Heterocyclic Amines and Alkaloids

**LEARNING GOAL:** *Identify heterocyclic amines; distinguish between the types of heterocyclic amines.*

Heterocyclic amines are cyclic organic compounds that contain one or more nitrogen atoms in the ring. The amine rings typically consist of five or six atoms and one or more nitrogen atoms. Alkaloids such as caffeine and nicotine are naturally occurring amines derived from plants. Many are known for their physiological activity.

### 18.4 Amides

**LEARNING GOAL:** *Write the amide products of amidation, and give their common and IUPAC names.*

Amides are derivatives of carboxylic acids in which the hydroxyl group is replaced by $-NH_2$ or a primary or secondary amine group. Amides are formed when carboxylic acids react with ammonia or primary or secondary amines in the presence of heat. Amides are named by replacing the *ic acid* or *oic acid* with *amide*. Any carbon group attached to the nitrogen atom is named using the *N*- prefix.

### 18.5 Hydrolysis of Amides

**LEARNING GOAL:** *Write equations for the hydrolysis of amides.*

Hydrolysis of an amide by an acid produces a carboxylic acid and an amine salt. Hydrolysis by a base produces the salt of the carboxylic acid and an amine.

## SUMMARY OF NAMING

| Family | Condensed Structural Formula | IUPAC Name | Common Name |
|---|---|---|---|
| Amine | $CH_3-CH_2-NH_2$ | Ethanamine | Ethylamine |
| | $CH_3-CH_2-NH-CH_3$ | *N*-Methylethanamine | Ethylmethylamine |
| Amine salt | $CH_3-CH_2-NH_3^+Cl^-$ | Ethylammonium chloride | Ethylammonium chloride |
| Amide | $CH_3-\overset{\overset{\large O}{\parallel}}{C}-NH_2$ | Ethanamide | Acetamide |

## SUMMARY OF REACTIONS

### IONIZATION OF AMINES IN WATER

$$\underset{\text{Methylamine}}{CH_3-\overset{\overset{\large H}{|}}{\underset{\underset{\large H}{|}}{N}}} + HOH \rightleftarrows \underset{\text{Methylammonium ion}}{CH_3-\overset{\overset{\large H}{|}}{\underset{\underset{\large H}{|}}{N^+}}-H} + \underset{\text{Hydroxide ion}}{OH^-}$$

### FORMATION OF AMINE SALTS

$$\underset{\text{Methylamine}}{CH_3-\overset{\overset{\large H}{|}}{\underset{\underset{\large H}{|}}{N}}} + HCl \longrightarrow \underset{\text{Methylammonium chloride}}{CH_3-\overset{\overset{\large H}{|}}{\underset{\underset{\large H}{|}}{N^+}}-H\ Cl^-}$$

### FORMATION OF AMIDES

$$\underset{\substack{\text{Propanoic acid}\\\text{(propionic acid)}}}{CH_3-CH_2-\overset{\overset{\large O}{\parallel}}{C}-OH} + \underset{\text{Ammonia}}{H-\overset{\overset{\large H}{|}}{N}-H} \xrightarrow{\text{Heat}} \underset{\substack{\text{Propanamide}\\\text{(propionamide)}}}{CH_3-CH_2-\overset{\overset{\large O}{\parallel}}{C}-\overset{\overset{\large H}{|}}{N}-H} + H_2O$$

$$\underset{\substack{\text{Propanoic acid}\\\text{(propionic acid)}}}{CH_3-CH_2-\overset{\overset{\large O}{\parallel}}{C}-OH} + \underset{\substack{\text{Methanamine}\\\text{(methylamine)}}}{H-\overset{\overset{\large H}{|}}{N}-CH_3} \xrightarrow{\text{Heat}} \underset{\substack{N\text{-Methylpropanamide}\\(N\text{-methylpropionamide})}}{CH_3-CH_2-\overset{\overset{\large O}{\parallel}}{C}-\overset{\overset{\large H}{|}}{N}-CH_3} + H_2O$$

## ACID HYDROLYSIS OF AMIDES

$$CH_3-\overset{\overset{\displaystyle O}{\|}}{C}-NH_2 + HOH + HCl \longrightarrow CH_3-\overset{\overset{\displaystyle O}{\|}}{C}-OH + NH_4^+Cl^-$$

Ethanamide (acetamide) — Ethanoic acid (acetic acid) — Ammonium chloride

## BASE HYDROLYSIS OF AMIDES

$$CH_3-CH_2-\overset{\overset{\displaystyle O}{\|}}{C}-NH-CH_3 + NaOH \longrightarrow CH_3-CH_2-\overset{\overset{\displaystyle O}{\|}}{C}-O^-Na^+ + NH_2-CH_3$$

*N*-Methylpropanamide (*N*-methylpropionamide) — Sodium propanoate (sodium propionate) — Methanamine (methylamine)

# KEY TERMS

**alkaloids** Amines having physiological activity that are produced in plants.

**amidation** The formation of an amide from a carboxylic acid and ammonia or an amine.

**amides** Organic compounds containing the carbonyl group attached to an amino group or a substituted nitrogen atom.

**amines** Organic compounds containing a nitrogen atom attached to one, two, or three hydrocarbon groups.

**amine salt** An ionic compound produced from an amine and an acid.

**heterocyclic amine** A cyclic organic compound that contains one or more nitrogen atoms in the ring.

**hydrolysis** The splitting of a molecule by the addition of water. Amides yield the corresponding carboxylic acid and amine or their salts.

**quaternary ammonium ion** An amine ion in which the nitrogen atom is bonded to four carbon groups.

# UNDERSTANDING THE CONCEPTS

18.39 The sweetener aspartame is made from two amino acids: aspartic acid and phenylalanine. Identify the functional groups in aspartame.

$$H_2N-\underset{\underset{\displaystyle \overset{\displaystyle O}{\overset{\|}{C}}-OH}{|}}{\overset{}{CH}}\text{(}CH_2\text{)}-\overset{\overset{\displaystyle O}{\|}}{C}-\overset{\overset{\displaystyle H}{|}}{N}-\overset{\overset{\displaystyle CH_2-C_6H_5}{|}}{CH}-\overset{\overset{\displaystyle O}{\|}}{C}-O-CH_3$$

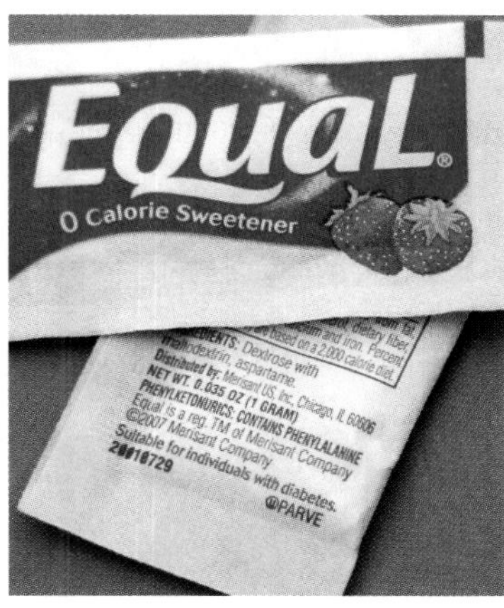


**18.40** Some aspirin substitutes contain phenacetin to reduce fever. Identify the functional groups in phenacetin.

$$CH_3-CH_2-O-C_6H_4-NH-\overset{\overset{\displaystyle O}{\|}}{C}-CH_3$$

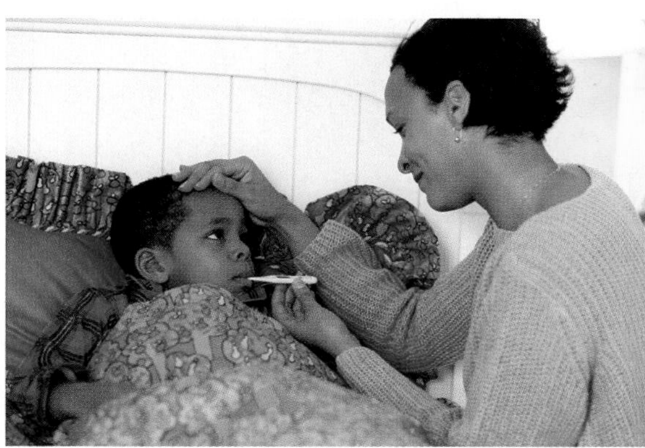

# ADDITIONAL QUESTIONS AND PROBLEMS

*For instructor-assigned homework, go to* ***www.masteringchemistry.com***.

**18.41** The insect repellent DEET can be made from 3-methylbenzoic acid and *N,N*-diethylamine. What is the condensed structural formula of DEET?

**18.42** Nylon 66 is a polymer used to make shirts and jackets. The condensed structural formula of one unit of Nylon 66 is shown below. Draw the condensed structural formulas of the carboxylic acid and amine that are polymerized to make Nylon 66.

$$-\underbrace{\overset{\overset{\displaystyle O}{\|}}{C}-CH_2-CH_2-CH_2-CH_2-\overset{\overset{\displaystyle O}{\|}}{C}}_{\text{6 carbon atoms}}-NH-\underbrace{CH_2-CH_2-CH_2-CH_2-CH_2-CH_2}_{\text{6 carbon atoms}}-NH-$$

Nylon 66

**18.43** There are four amine isomers with the molecular formula $C_3H_9N$. Draw their condensed structural formulas. Give the common name and classify each as a primary (1°), secondary (2°), or tertiary (3°) amine.

**18.44** There are four amide isomers with the molecular formula $C_3H_7NO$. Draw their condensed structural formulas.

**18.45** Name and classify each of the following compounds as a primary (1°), secondary (2°), or tertiary (3°) amine or as a quaternary ammonium salt:

**a.** $$\begin{array}{l} \quad\quad\;\; CH_2-CH_3 \\ \quad\quad\;\; | \\ CH_3-N-CH_2-CH_3 \end{array}$$

**b.** $CH_3-CH_2-CH_2-CH_2-NH_2$

**c.** $CH_3-CH_2-CH_2-NH-CH_2-CH_3$

**18.46** Name and classify each of the following compounds as a primary (1°), secondary (2°), or tertiary (3°) amine or as a quaternary ammonium salt:

**a.** $$\begin{array}{l} NH-CH_3 \\ | \\ C_6H_5 \end{array}$$

**b.** $$\begin{array}{l} \quad\quad\;\; CH_3 \quad\quad\quad\quad\; CH_3 \\ \quad\quad\;\; | \quad\quad\quad\quad\quad\quad | \\ CH_3-CH-CH_2-N-CH_2-CH_3 \end{array}$$

**c.** $$\begin{array}{l} \quad\quad\;\; CH_2-CH_3 \\ \quad\quad\;\; |_{+} \\ CH_3-N-CH_2-CH_3 \quad Cl^- \\ \quad\quad\;\; | \\ \quad\quad\;\; CH_3 \end{array}$$

**18.47** Draw the condensed structural formula of each of the following compounds:
**a.** 3-pentanamine **b.** cyclohexylamine
**c.** dimethylammonium chloride **d.** triethylamine

**18.48** Draw the condensed structural formula of each of the following compounds:
**a.** 3-amino-2-hexanol
**b.** tetramethylammonium bromide
**c.** *N,N*-dimethylaniline
**d.** butylethylmethylamine

**18.49** In each of the following pairs, indicate the compound that has the higher boiling point. Explain.
**a.** 1-butanol or butanamine
**b.** trimethylamine or propylamine

**18.50** In each of the following pairs, indicate the compound that has the higher boiling point. Explain.
**a.** butylamine or diethylamine
**b.** butane or propylamine

**18.51** In each of the following pairs, indicate the compound that is more soluble in water. Explain.
**a.** ethylamine or dibutylamine
**b.** trimethylamine or *N*-ethylcyclohexylamine

**18.52** In each of the following pairs, indicate the compound that is more soluble in water. Explain.
**a.** butylamine or pentane
**b.** butyramide or hexane

**18.53** Give the IUPAC name for each of the following amides:

**a.** $H-\overset{\overset{O}{\|}}{C}-NH_2$ **b.** $CH_3-CH_2-\overset{\overset{O}{\|}}{C}-NH_2$

**c.** $CH_3-\overset{\overset{O}{\|}}{C}-\overset{\overset{H}{|}}{N}-CH_3$

**18.54** Give the IUPAC name for each of the following amides:

**a.** $CH_3-CH_2-CH_2-\overset{\overset{O}{\|}}{C}-NH-CH_2-CH_3$

**b.** $CH_3-\overset{\overset{O}{\|}}{C}-\overset{\overset{CH_3}{|}}{N}-CH_2-CH_2-CH_2-CH_3$

**c.** $CH_3-\overset{\overset{O}{\|}}{C}-\overset{\overset{CH_3}{|}}{N}-CH_3$

**18.55** Give the name of the alkaloid described in each of the following:
**a.** from the bark of the cinchona tree used in malaria treatment
**b.** found in tobacco
**c.** found in coffee and tea
**d.** a painkiller found in the opium poppy plant

**18.56** Identify the heterocyclic amine in each of the following:
**a.** caffeine **b.** Demerol
**c.** nicotine **d.** quinine

**18.57** Write the condensed structural formulas of the products of the following reactions:
**a.** $CH_3-CH_2-NH_2 + H_2O \rightleftarrows$
**b.** $CH_3-CH_2-NH_2 + HCl \longrightarrow$
**c.** $CH_3-CH_2-NH-CH_3 + H_2O \rightleftarrows$

**18.58** Write the condensed structural formulas of the products of the following reactions:
**a.** $CH_3-CH_2-NH-CH_3 + HCl \longrightarrow$
**b.** $CH_3-CH_2-CH_2-NH_3^+Cl^- + NaOH \longrightarrow$
**c.** $CH_3-CH_2-\overset{\overset{CH_3}{|}}{N}H_2^+Cl^- + NaOH \longrightarrow$

**18.59** Voltaren is indicated for acute and chronic treatment of the symptoms of rheumatoid arthritis. Name the functional groups in this molecule.

$CH_2-\overset{\overset{O}{\|}}{C}-O^-Na^+$
NH
Cl Cl

**18.60** Toradol is used in dentistry to relieve pain. Name the functional groups in this molecule.

$\overset{\overset{O}{\|}}{C}OH$
C
O
N

## CHALLENGE QUESTIONS

**18.61** Use the Internet or a reference book such as the *Merck Index* or *Physicians' Desk Reference* to look up the structural formula of the following medicinal drugs. List the functional groups in each compound.
**a.** Keflex, an antibiotic
**b.** Inderal, a $\beta$-channel blocker used to treat heart irregularities
**c.** ibuprofen, an anti-inflammatory agent
**d.** Aldomet (methyldopa)
**e.** Percodan, a narcotic pain reliever
**f.** triamterene, a diuretic

**18.62** Many amine-containing drugs are given to patients in their salt form, such as hydrochloride or sulfate. What might be the reason?

**18.63** Use the $K$ of methylamine to calculate the pH of a 1.0 M solution of methylamine.

**18.64** Kevlar is a lightweight polymer used in tires and bulletproof vests. Part of the strength of Kevlar is due to hydrogen bonds between polymer chains. The polymer chain is shown below:

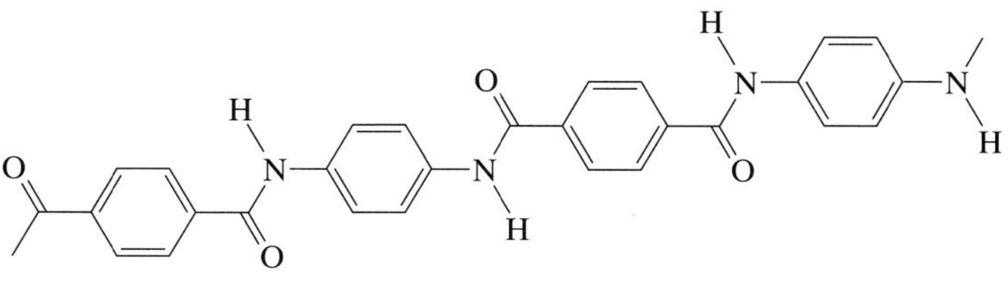

**a.** Draw the condensed structural formulas of the carboxylic acid and amine that are polymerized to make Kevlar.
**b.** What feature of Kevlar will give the hydrogen bonds between the polymer chains?

# ANSWERS

## ANSWERS TO STUDY CHECKS

**18.1** tertiary (3°)

**18.2** $CH_3{-}CH_2{-}\underset{|}{\overset{H}{N}}{-}CH_2{-}CH_2{-}CH_3$ (H on N)

**18.3** $CH_3{-}\overset{+}{N}(CH_3)_2{-}H\ Cl^-$ (N bonded to two $CH_3$ groups above and below)

**18.4** piperidine

**18.5** $H{-}\overset{O}{\overset{\|}{C}}{-}OH$ and $H{-}N(CH_3){-}CH_3$

**18.6** $C_6H_5{-}\overset{O}{\overset{\|}{C}}{-}N(CH_3){-}CH_3$

**18.7** $CH_3{-}CH_2{-}CH_2{-}\overset{O}{\overset{\|}{C}}{-}OH$ and $CH_3{-}\overset{+}{N}H_3\ Br^-$

## ANSWERS TO SELECTED QUESTIONS AND PROBLEMS

**18.1** In a primary amine, there is one alkyl group (and two hydrogens) attached to a nitrogen atom.

**18.3** **a.** primary (1°) **b.** secondary (2°) **c.** primary (1°) **d.** tertiary (3°) **e.** tertiary (3°)

**18.5** **a.** ethylamine, ethanamine
**b.** methylpropylamine, *N*-methyl-1-propanamine
**c.** diethylmethylamine, *N*-ethyl-*N*-methylethanamine
**d.** isopropylamine, 2-propanamine

**18.7** **a.** 2-butanamine **b.** 2-chloroaniline
**c.** 3-aminopropanal **d.** *N*-ethylaniline

**18.9** **a.** $CH_3{-}CH_2{-}NH_2$ **b.** $C_6H_5{-}NH{-}CH_3$

**c.** $CH_3{-}CH_2{-}CH_2{-}CH_2{-}N(H){-}CH_2{-}CH_2{-}CH_3$

**d.** $CH_3{-}CH(NH_2){-}CH_2{-}CH_2{-}CH_3$

**18.11** **a.** $CH_3{-}CH_2{-}OH$ has a higher boiling point because the $-OH$ forms stronger hydrogen bonds than the $-NH_2$.
**b.** $CH_3{-}CH_2{-}CH_2{-}NH_2$ has the higher boiling point because it has a greater molar mass.
**c.** $CH_3{-}CH_2{-}CH_2{-}NH_2$ has the higher boiling point because it is a primary amine that forms hydrogen bonds. A tertiary amine cannot form hydrogen bonds with other tertiary amines.

**18.13** As a primary amine, propylamine can form two hydrogen bonds, which gives it the highest boiling point. Ethylmethylamine, a secondary amine, can form one hydrogen bond, and butane cannot form hydrogen bonds. Thus, butane has the lowest boiling point of the three compounds.

**18.15** **a.** Yes, amines with fewer than six carbon atoms are soluble in water.
**b.** Yes, amines with fewer than six carbon atoms are soluble in water.
**c.** No, an amine with nine carbon atoms is not soluble in water.
**d.** Yes, amines with fewer than six carbon atoms are soluble in water.

**18.17** **a.** $CH_3{-}NH_2 + H_2O \rightleftarrows CH_3{-}NH_3^+ + OH^-$

**b.** $CH_3{-}NH{-}CH_3 + H_2O \rightleftarrows CH_3{-}\overset{+}{N}H_2{-}CH_3 + OH^-$

**c.** $C_6H_5{-}NH_2 + H_2O \rightleftarrows C_6H_5{-}NH_3^+ + OH^-$

**18.19** **a.** $CH_3{-}\overset{+}{N}H_3\ Cl^-$

**b.** $CH_3{-}\overset{+}{N}H_2{-}CH_3\ Cl^-$ **c.** $C_6H_5{-}\overset{+}{N}H_3\ Cl^-$

**18.21** **a.** $H_2N{-}C_6H_4{-}\overset{O}{\overset{\|}{C}}{-}O{-}CH_2{-}CH_2{-}\overset{+}{N}(CH_2{-}CH_3)_2{-}H\ Cl^-$

**b.** The amine salt (Novocain) is more soluble in aqueous body fluids than procaine.

**18.23** **a.** amine **b.** amine
**c.** heterocyclic amine **d.** heterocyclic amine

**18.25** **c.** pyrimidine **d.** pyrrole

**18.27** pyrrole

**18.29** **a.** $CH_3{-}\overset{O}{\overset{\|}{C}}{-}NH_2$

**b.** $CH_3{-}\overset{O}{\overset{\|}{C}}{-}N(H){-}CH_2{-}CH_3$

**c.** $C_6H_5{-}\overset{O}{\overset{\|}{C}}{-}N(H){-}CH_2{-}CH_2{-}CH_3$

**18.31** **a.** *N*-methylethanamide (*N*-methylacetamide)
**b.** butanamide (butyramide)
**c.** methanamide (formamide)
**d.** *N*-methylbenzamide

**18.33** **a.** $CH_3{-}CH_2{-}\overset{O}{\overset{\|}{C}}{-}NH_2$

**b.** $CH_3{-}CH_2{-}CH_2{-}CH_2{-}\overset{O}{\overset{\|}{C}}{-}NH_2$

**c.** $H{-}\overset{O}{\overset{\|}{C}}{-}NH_2$ **d.** $C_6H_5{-}\overset{O}{\overset{\|}{C}}{-}N(H){-}CH_2{-}CH_3$

**e.** $CH_3{-}CH_2{-}CH_2{-}\overset{O}{\overset{\|}{C}}{-}N(H){-}CH_2{-}CH_3$

**18.35 a.** Acetamide has the higher melting point because it forms more hydrogen bonds as a primary amide than *N*-methylpropanamide, which is a secondary amide.

**b.** Propionamide has the higher melting point because it forms hydrogen bonds, but butane does not.

**c.** *N*-methylpropanamide has the higher melting point because it forms hydrogen bonds as a secondary amide, but *N,N*-dimethylpropanamide cannot form hydrogen bonds as a tertiary amide.

**18.37 a.** $CH_3-\overset{\overset{O}{\|}}{C}-OH + NH_4^+Cl^-$

**b.** $CH_3-CH_2-\overset{\overset{O}{\|}}{C}-OH + NH_4^+Cl^-$

**c.** $CH_3-CH_2-CH_2-\overset{\overset{O}{\|}}{C}-OH + CH_3-NH_3^+Cl^-$

**d.** 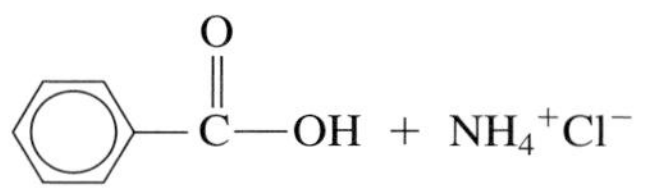 $C_6H_5-\overset{\overset{O}{\|}}{C}-OH + NH_4^+Cl^-$

**e.** $CH_3-CH_2-CH_2-CH_2-\overset{\overset{O}{\|}}{C}-OH +$

$CH_3-CH_2-NH_3^+Cl^-$

**18.39** amine, carboxylic acid, amide, aromatic, ester

**18.41** $C_6H_4(CH_3)-\overset{\overset{O}{\|}}{C}-N(CH_2-CH_3)_2$

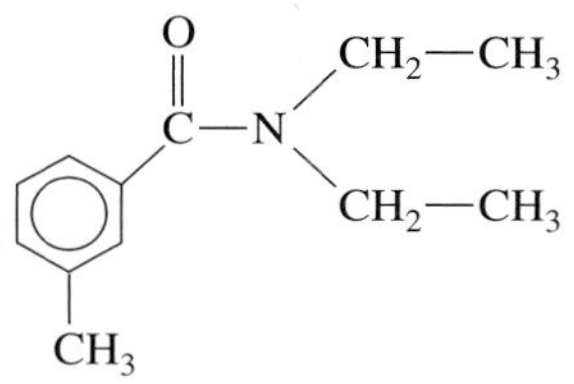

**18.43** $CH_3-CH_2-CH_2-NH_2$

Propylamine (1°)

$CH_3-CH_2-NH-CH_3$

Ethylmethylamine (2°)

$CH_3-\underset{}{\overset{\overset{CH_3}{|}}{N}}-CH_3$

Trimethylamine (3°)

$CH_3-\overset{\overset{CH_3}{|}}{CH}-NH_2$

Isopropylamine (1°)

**18.45 a.** diethylmethylamine (common), *N*-ethyl-*N*-methylethanamine; tertiary (3°)

**b.** butylamine (common), 1-butanamine; primary (1°)

**c.** ethylpropylamine (common), *N*-ethyl-1-propanamine; secondary (2°)

**18.47 a.** $CH_3-CH_2-\overset{\overset{NH_2}{|}}{CH}-CH_2-CH_3$ **b.** 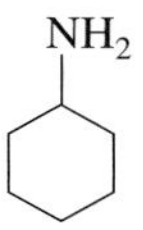 cyclohexylamine ($C_6H_{11}-NH_2$)

**c.** $CH_3-\overset{\overset{CH_3}{|}}{NH_2^+}\ Cl^-$

**d.** $CH_3-CH_2-\overset{\overset{CH_2-CH_3}{|}}{N}-CH_2-CH_3$

**18.49 a.** An alcohol with an —OH group such as 1-butanol forms stronger hydrogen bonds than an amine and has a higher boiling point than an amine.

**b.** Propylamine, a primary amine, forms hydrogen bonds and has a higher boiling point than trimethylamine, a tertiary amine that does not form hydrogen bonds.

**18.51 a.** Ethylamine is a small amine that is soluble because it forms hydrogen bonds with water. Dibutylamine has two large nonpolar alkyl groups that decrease the solubility in water.

**b.** Trimethylamine is a small tertiary amine that is soluble because it hydrogen bonds with water.

**18.53 a.** methanamide

**b.** propanamide

**c.** *N*-methylethanamide

**18.55 a.** quinine

**b.** nicotine

**c.** caffeine

**d.** morphine, codeine

**18.57 a.** $CH_3-CH_2-NH_3^+ + OH^-$

**b.** $CH_3-CH_2-NH_3^+\ Cl^-$

**c.** $CH_3-CH_2-\overset{+}{N}H_2-CH_3 + OH^-$

**18.59** carboxylate salt, aromatic, amine, haloaromatic

**18.61 a.** aromatic, amine, amide, carboxylic acid, cycloalkene

**b.** aromatic, ether, alcohol, amine

**c.** aromatic, carboxylic acid

**d.** phenol, amine, carboxylic acid

**e.** aromatic, ether, alcohol, amine, ketone

**f.** aromatic, amine

**18.63** The pH is 12.32.

# 19 Amino Acids and Proteins

LOOKING AHEAD


**19.1** Proteins and Amino Acids

**19.2** Amino Acids as Zwitterions

**19.3** Formation of Peptides

**19.4** Protein Structure: Primary and Secondary Levels

**19.5** Protein Structure: Tertiary and Quaternary Levels

**19.6** Protein Hydrolysis and Denaturation

*"This lamb is fed with Lamb Lac, which is a chemically formulated replacement for ewe's milk," says part-time farmer Dennis Samuelson. "Its mother had triplets and didn't have enough milk to feed them all, so they weren't thriving the way the other lambs were. The Lamb Lac includes dried skim milk, dried whey, milk proteins, egg albumin, the amino acids methionine and lysine, vitamins, and minerals."*

*A veterinary technician diagnoses and treats diseases of animals, takes blood and tissue samples, and administers drugs and vaccines. Agricultural technologists assist in the study of farm crops to increase productivity and ensure a safe food supply. They look for ways to improve crop yields, develop safer methods of weed and pest control, and design methods to conserve soil and water.*

Visit **www.masteringchemistry.com** for self-study materials and instructor-assigned homework.

The word "protein" is derived from the Greek word *proteios*, meaning "first." Made of amino acids, proteins provide structure in membranes, build cartilage and connective tissue, transport oxygen in blood and muscle, direct biological reactions as enzymes, defend the body against infection, and control metabolic processes as hormones. Proteins can even be a source of energy.

Protein molecules, compared with many of the compounds we have studied, can be gigantic. Insulin has a molar mass of 5800 g/mole, and hemoglobin has a molar mass of about 67 000 g/mole. Some virus proteins are even larger, having molar masses of more than 40 million g/mole. Yet all proteins in humans are polymers made up of only 20 different amino acids. Each kind of protein is composed of amino acids arranged in a specific sequence that determines the characteristics of the protein and its biological action.

Proteins perform many functions in the body: making up skin and hair, moving muscles, carrying oxygen, and regulating metabolism. All of these different functions depend on the structures and chemical behavior of amino acids, the building blocks. We will see how peptide bonds link amino acids and how the sequence of the amino acids in these protein polymers directs the formation of unique three-dimensional structures.

## 19.1 Proteins and Amino Acids

**LEARNING GOAL**

Classify proteins by their functions in the body. Give the name and abbreviation of an amino acid and draw its ionized structure.

The many kinds of proteins perform different functions in the body. Some proteins form structural components such as cartilage, muscles, hair, and nails. Wool, silk, feathers, and horns in animals are made of proteins. Proteins that function as enzymes regulate biological reactions such as digestion and cellular metabolism. Other proteins, such as hemoglobin and myoglobin, transport oxygen in the blood and muscle. (See Figure 19.1.) Table 19.1 gives examples of proteins that are classified by their functions in biological systems.

**TABLE 19.1** Classification of Some Proteins and Their Functions

| Class of Protein | Function in the Body | Examples |
|---|---|---|
| Structural | Provide structural components | *Collagen* is in tendons and cartilage. *Keratin* is in hair, skin, wool, and nails. |
| Contractile | Move muscles | *Myosin* and *actin* contract muscle fibers. |
| Transport | Carry essential substances throughout the body | *Hemoglobin* transports oxygen. *Lipoproteins* transport lipids. |
| Storage | Store nutrients | *Casein* stores protein in milk. *Ferritin* stores iron in the spleen and liver. |
| Hormone | Regulate body metabolism and nervous system | *Insulin* regulates blood glucose level. *Growth hormone* regulates body growth. |
| Enzyme | Catalyze biochemical reactions in the cells | *Sucrase* catalyzes the hydrolysis of sucrose. *Trypsin* catalyzes the hydrolysis of proteins. |
| Protection | Recognize and destroy foreign substances | *Immunoglobulins* stimulate immune responses. |

**FIGURE 19.1** The horns, feathers, and wool of animals are made of proteins.

**Q** What class of protein would be in horns?

### Amino Acids

TUTORIAL
Protein Building Blocks

TUTORIAL
Proteins "R" Us

SELF STUDY ACTIVITY
Functions of Proteins

Proteins are composed of building blocks called amino acids. Every **amino acid** has a central carbon atom ($\alpha$ carbon) bonded to an ammonium group ($-NH_3^+$), a carboxylate group ($-COO^-$), a hydrogen atom ($-H$), and a side chain called an *R group*. The differences in the 20 $\alpha$-amino acids present in human proteins are due to the unique characteristics of the R groups.

At the pH of most body fluids, amino acids are ionized. Under physiological conditions, the carboxylic acid groups ($-COOH$) lose $H^+$ to give carboxylate groups ($-COO^-$), and the amino groups ($-NH_2$) accept $H^+$ to give ammonium groups ($-NH_3^+$).

**General Structure of an α-Amino Acid**

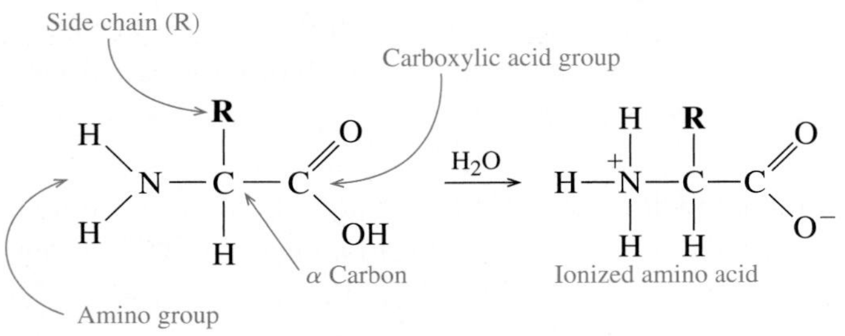

Side chain (R)

Carboxylic acid group

$$\mathrm{H_2N{-}\underset{H}{\overset{R}{C}}{-}COOH} \xrightarrow{H_2O} \mathrm{H{-}\overset{+}{N}H_2{-}\underset{H}{\overset{R}{C}}{-}COO^-}$$

Amino group

α Carbon

Ionized amino acid

## Classification of Amino Acids

**Nonpolar amino acids** contain alkyl or aromatic R groups, which make them *hydrophobic* ("water fearing"). **Polar amino acids (neutral)** contain polar R groups such as hydroxyl ($-OH$), thiol ($-SH$), and amide ($-CONH_2$) that interact with water; they are *hydrophilic* ("water attracting"). **Acidic amino acids** contain R groups that have carboxylate ($-COO^-$), and **basic amino acids** contain R groups that have ammonium ($-NH_3^+$). The R groups of acidic and basic amino acids interact with water, which makes them hydrophilic.

The ionized structures of the 20 α-amino acids found in proteins at physiological pH with their R groups highlighted in yellow, common names, and three-letter abbreviations are listed in Table 19.2. The isoelectric points, known as pI values, are discussed in Section 19.2.

SAMPLE PROBLEM 19.1

### Structural Formulas of Amino Acids

Draw the condensed structural formula of the given ionized amino acid, and write the abbreviation for each of the following:

**a.** serine
**b.** aspartic acid

SOLUTION

**a.** The ionized form of serine is written by attaching $-NH_3^+$, $-COO^-$, $-H$, and the R group ($-CH_2-OH$) to the α carbon atom:

Serine (Ser)

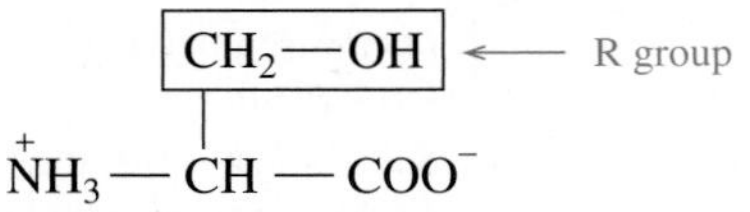

$$\overset{+}{N}H_3-\underset{}{\overset{\boxed{CH_2-OH}}{CH}}-COO^-$$

← R group

**b.** The ionized form of aspartic acid is written by attaching $-NH_3^+$, $-COO^-$, $-H$, and the R group ($-CH_2-COO^-$) to the alpha carbon atom.

Aspartic acid (Asp)

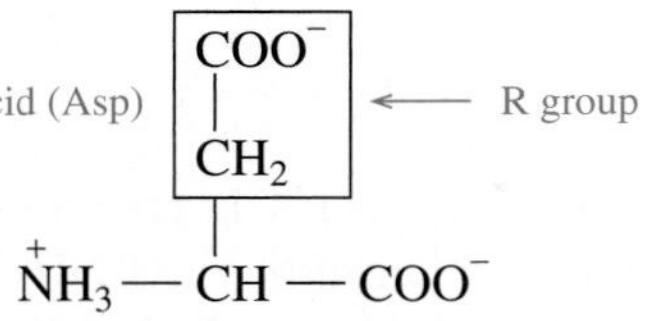

$$\overset{+}{N}H_3-\overset{\boxed{\begin{array}{c}COO^-\\|\\CH_2\end{array}}}{CH}-COO^-$$

← R group

STUDY CHECK

Classify the amino acids in the sample problem as polar or nonpolar.

TABLE 19.2 The 20 Amino Acids (Ionized) in Proteins

**Nonpolar Amino Acids**

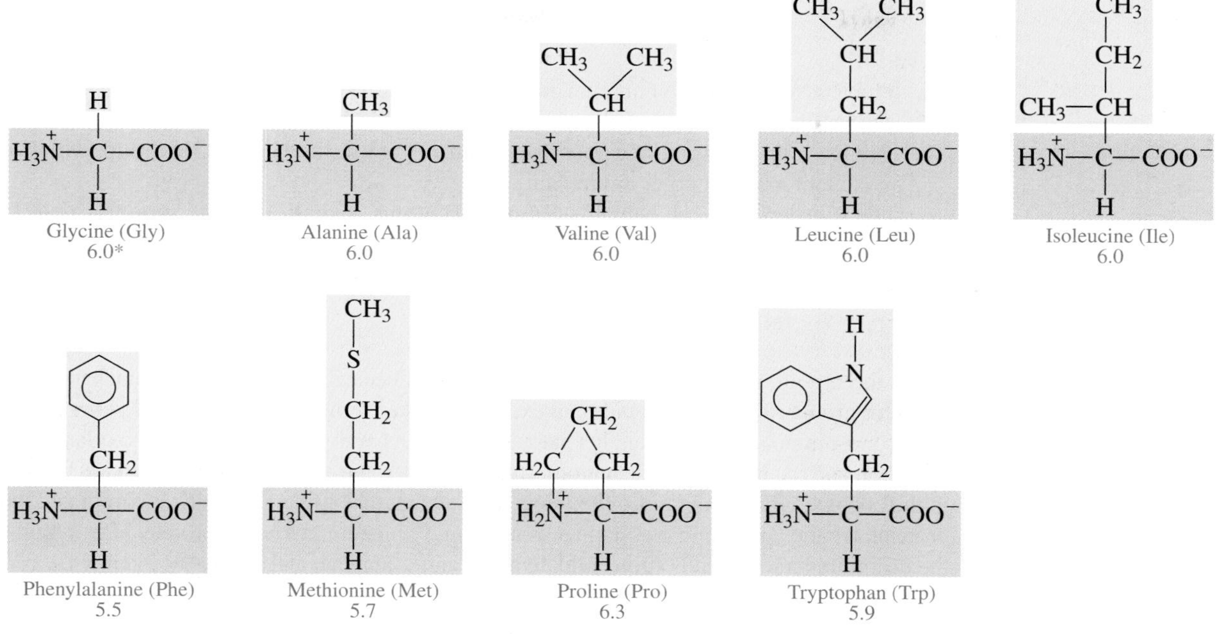


**Polar Amino Acids (Neutral)**

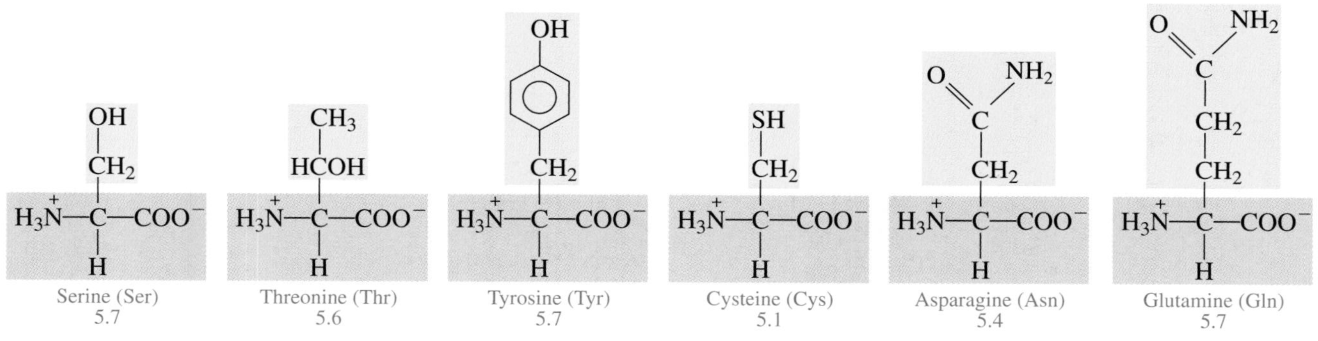


**Polar Amino Acids (Acidic)**

**Polar Amino Acids (Basic)**

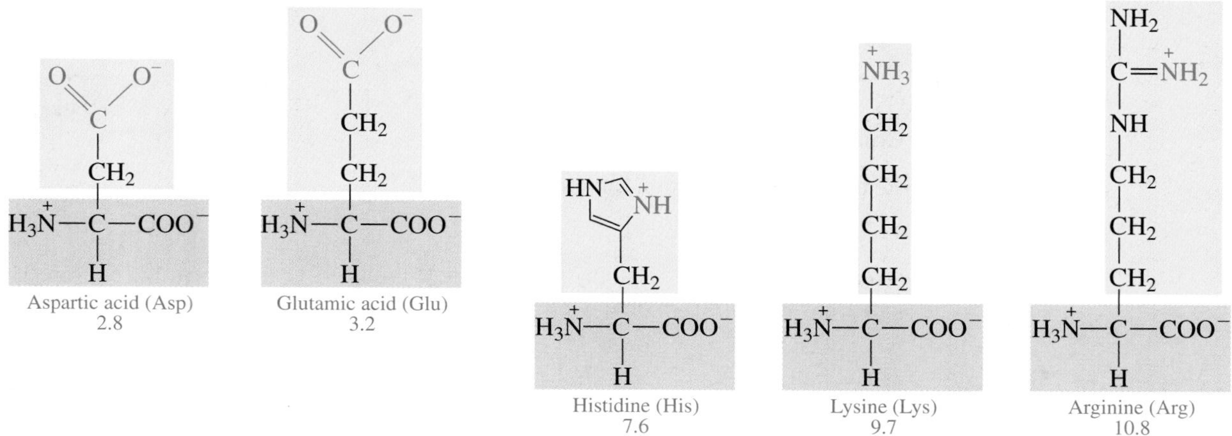


*Isoelectric points (pI)

CONCEPT CHECK 19.1

**R Groups and Polarity of Amino Acids**

Compare the types of atoms in the R groups and the polarity of each of the following:

**a.** valine **b.** threonine **c.** lysine

ANSWER

**a.** The R group in valine contains only C atoms and H atoms, which makes valine a nonpolar amino acid.

**b.** The R group in threonine contains C atoms, H atoms, and an —OH group, which makes threonine a polar amino acid.

**c.** The R group in lysine contains C atoms, H atoms, and an $—NH_3^+$ group, which makes lysine a polar (basic) amino acid.

## Amino Acid Stereoisomers

All of the $\alpha$-amino acids except for glycine are chiral because the $\alpha$ carbon is attached to four different groups. Thus amino acids can exist as D and L isomers. We can write Fischer projections for $\alpha$-amino acids as we did in Chapter 14 for aldehydes by placing the carboxylate group at the top and the R group at the bottom. In the L isomer, the $—NH_3^+$ group is on the left, and in the D isomer, it is on the right. In biological systems, the only amino acids incorporated into proteins are the L isomers; D amino acids are found in nature but not in proteins. Let's look at the enantiomers for L- and D-glyceraldehyde, L- and D-alanine, and L- and D-cysteine:

| CHO<br>HO—┼—H<br>$CH_2OH$ | CHO<br>H—┼—OH<br>$CH_2OH$ |
|---|---|
| L-Glyceraldehyde | D-Glyceraldehyde |
| ⇩ | ⇩ |
| $COO^-$<br>$H_3\overset{+}{N}$—┼—H<br>$CH_3$ | $COO^-$<br>H—┼—$\overset{+}{N}H_3$<br>$CH_3$ |
| L-Alanine | D-Alanine |
| $COO^-$<br>$H_3\overset{+}{N}$—┼—H<br>$CH_2SH$ | $COO^-$<br>H—┼—$\overset{+}{N}H_3$<br>$CH_2SH$ |
| L-Cysteine | D-Cysteine |

SAMPLE PROBLEM 19.2

**Chiral Amino Acids**

Write the Fischer projection for L-serine.

SOLUTION

In L-serine, the $—COO^-$ is at the top, and the R group $—CH_2OH$ is at the bottom. The L isomer has the $—NH_3^+$ on the left:

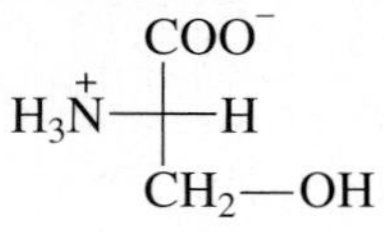

$COO^-$<br>$H_3\overset{+}{N}$—┼—H<br>$CH_2$—OH

L-Serine

STUDY CHECK

How does the Fischer projection for D-serine differ from L-serine?

## QUESTIONS AND PROBLEMS

### Proteins and Amino Acids

**19.1** Classify each of the following proteins according to its function:
**a.** hemoglobin, carries oxygen in the blood
**b.** collagen, a major component of tendons and cartilage
**c.** keratin, a protein found in hair
**d.** amylases, catalyze hydrolysis of starch

**19.2** Classify each of the following proteins according to its function:
**a.** insulin, a hormone needed for glucose utilization
**b.** antibodies, disable foreign proteins
**c.** casein, milk protein
**d.** lipases, catalyze the hydrolysis of lipids

**19.3** Describe the functional groups found in all $\alpha$-amino acids.

**19.4** How does the polarity of the R group in leucine compare to the R group in serine?

**19.5** Draw the ionized form of each of the following amino acids:
**a.** alanine **b.** threonine
**c.** glutamic acid **d.** phenylalanine

**19.6** Draw the ionized form of each of the following amino acids:
**a.** lysine **b.** aspartic acid
**c.** leucine **d.** tyrosine

**19.7** Classify the amino acids in problem 19.5 as hydrophobic (nonpolar) or hydrophilic (polar neutral, acidic, or basic).

**19.8** Classify the amino acids in problem 19.6 as hydrophobic (nonpolar) or hydrophilic (polar neutral, acidic, or basic).

**19.9** Give the name of the amino acid represented by each of the following three-letter abbreviations:
**a.** Ala **b.** Val **c.** Lys **d.** Cys

**19.10** Give the name of the amino acid represented by each of the following three-letter abbreviations:
**a.** Trp **b.** Met **c.** Pro **d.** Gly

**19.11** Draw the Fischer projection for each of the following amino acids:
**a.** L-valine **b.** D-cysteine

**19.12** Draw the Fischer projection for each of the following amino acids:
**a.** L-threonine **b.** D-valine

# 19.2 Amino Acids as Zwitterions

LEARNING GOAL

Draw the zwitterion of an amino acid at its isoelectric point and its ionized structure at pH values above or below its isoelectric point.

TUTORIAL
pH, pI, and Amino Acid Ionization

At a specific pH known as the **isoelectric point (pI)**, the positive and negative charges of an ionized amino acid are equal. This ionized structure is called a **zwitterion**, which has an overall charge of zero:

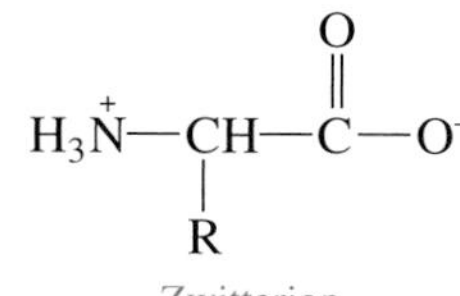

Zwitterion

The pI values for the zwitterions are included in the list of the amino acids in Table 19.2.

As zwitterions, amino acids have very high melting points because they are salts. The ionic charges of the zwitterions make amino acids soluble in water, but not in organic solvents.

## Zwitterions of Nonpolar and Polar Amino Acids (Neutral)

The zwitterions of the nonpolar and polar (neutral) amino acids exist at pH values from 5.1 to 6.3. Let's look at the how the zwitterion of glycine reacts in acid and base. In a solution that is more acidic (lower pH) than its pI of 6.0, the $—COO^-$ group of glycine accepts an $H^+$ to form —COOH. Because of the remaining $—NH_3^+$, glycine has an overall positive charge (1+):

$$H_3\overset{+}{N}-\underset{H}{CH}-\overset{O}{\overset{\|}{C}}-O^- + H_3O^+ \rightleftarrows H_3\overset{+}{N}-\underset{H}{CH}-\overset{O}{\overset{\|}{C}}-OH + H_2O$$

Zwitterion ion accepts $H^+$ — Positively charged ion

When glycine is placed in a solution that is more basic (higher pH) than its pI of 6.0, the $—NH_3^+$ group donates $H^+$ to form $—NH_2$. Because of the remaining carboxylate group $—COO^-$, glycine has an overall negative charge (1−):

| Condition | pH < pI | pH = pI | pH > pI |
|---|---|---|---|
| **Change in $H^+$** | $[H^+]$ ⇑ | None | $[H^+]$ ⇓ |
| **Change in ionized groups** | $-COOH$<br>$-NH_3^+$ | $-COO^-$<br>$-NH_3^+$ | $-COO^-$<br>$-NH_2$ |
| **Overall charge** | 1+ | 0 | 1− |

$$\boxed{H_3\overset{+}{N}}-\underset{H}{CH}-\overset{O}{\overset{\|}{C}}-O^- + OH^- \longrightarrow \boxed{H_2N}-\underset{H}{CH}-\overset{O}{\overset{\|}{C}}-O^- + H_2O$$

Zwitterion donates H⁺ — Negatively charged ion

In another example, we look at the changes in the zwitterion of alanine with a pI of 6.0 when it is placed in a more acidic solution and in a more basic solution:

← pH decreases — pH increases →

$$\overset{+}{N}H_3-\underset{CH_3}{CH}-\overset{O}{\overset{\|}{C}}-OH \underset{H_3O^+}{\overset{OH^-}{\rightleftharpoons}} \overset{+}{N}H_3-\underset{CH_3}{CH}-\overset{O}{\overset{\|}{C}}-O^- \underset{H_3O^+}{\overset{OH^-}{\rightleftharpoons}} NH_2-\underset{CH_3}{CH}-\overset{O}{\overset{\|}{C}}-O^-$$

Alanine at pH < 6 (charge = 1+) — Zwitterion of alanine pH = 6.0 (charge = 0) — Alanine at pH > 6 (charge = 1−)

CONCEPT CHECK 19.2

### Zwitterions of Amino Acids

Consider the amino acid cysteine.

**a.** What is the pI of cysteine, and what does it mean?
**b.** At a pH of 2.0, how does the zwitterion change?
**c.** At a pH of 8.0, how does the zwitterion change?

ANSWER

**a.** From Table 5.2, the pI of cysteine is 5.1. This means that at pH of 5.1 cysteine exists as a zwitterion with a net charge of zero.
**b.** From Table 5.2, a pH of 2.0 is more acidic and below the pI of cysteine. Then the $-COO^-$ accepts $H^+$ to give $-COOH$. The remaining $-NH_3^+$ group gives cysteine a positive charge (1+).
**c.** From Table 5.2, a pH of 8.0 is more basic and above the pI of cysteine. Then the $-NH_3^+$ donates $H^+$ to give $-NH_2$. The remaining $-COO^-$ gives cysteine a negative charge (1−).

## Zwitterions of Acidic and Basic Amino Acids

In physiological solutions, all of the R groups of the acidic and basic amino acids are ionized. The zwitterions of acidic amino acids exist only at lower pH values from 2.8 to 3.2, when a carboxylate group accepts $H^+$ to give an overall charge of zero. The zwitterions of basic amino acids exist only at higher pH values from 7.6 to 10.8, when an amino group donates $H^+$ to give an overall charge of zero.

← pH decreases — pH increases →

$$H_3\overset{+}{N}-\underset{\underset{\underset{O}{\overset{\|}{C}}-OH}{|}}{\underset{CH_2}{CH}}-\overset{O}{\overset{\|}{C}}-OH \underset{H_3O^+}{\overset{OH^-}{\rightleftharpoons}} H_3\overset{+}{N}-\underset{\underset{\underset{O}{\overset{\|}{C}}-OH}{|}}{\underset{CH_2}{CH}}-\overset{O}{\overset{\|}{C}}-O^- \underset{H_3O^+}{\overset{OH^-}{\rightleftharpoons}} H_3\overset{+}{N}-\underset{\underset{\underset{O}{\overset{\|}{C}}-O^-}{|}}{\underset{CH_2}{CH}}-\overset{O}{\overset{\|}{C}}-O^- \underset{H_3O^+}{\overset{OH^-}{\rightleftharpoons}} H_2N-\underset{\underset{\underset{O}{\overset{\|}{C}}-O^-}{|}}{\underset{CH_2}{CH}}-\overset{O}{\overset{\|}{C}}-O^-$$

Aspartic acid pH < 2 (charge = 1+) — Zwitterion pH = 2.8 (charge = 0) — Aspartic acid at pH 7 (charge = 1−) — Aspartic acid pH > 10 (charge = 2−)

SAMPLE PROBLEM 19.3

**Amino Acids as Zwitterions**

Draw the zwitterion of serine at pH 5.7, which is the pI of serine.

SOLUTION

At the pI of 5.7, serine exists as a zwitterion with both a carboxylate and an ammonium group:

$$\overset{+}{N}H_3-\underset{}{\overset{\overset{\displaystyle OH}{|}}{\overset{CH_2}{|}}}\!\!\!\!\!CH-\overset{\overset{\displaystyle O}{\|}}{C}-O^-$$

Zwitterion of serine

STUDY CHECK

Draw the ionized structure of serine at a pH of 3.

## Electrophoresis

It is possible to separate a mixture of amino acids using a laboratory method called **electrophoresis**. A buffered amino acid mixture is applied to a gel on a thin plate or piece of filter paper that is connected to two electrodes. A voltage applied to the electrodes causes the positively charged amino acids to move toward the negative electrode, and the negatively charged amino acids to move toward the positive electrode. Any amino acid at its isoelectric point with a zero net charge would not move. After several hours, the sample is removed. It can be sprayed with a dye such as ninhydrin to make the amino acids visible, which are identified by their direction and rate of migration toward the electrodes. The amino acids are recovered separately by cutting the filter paper or removing the amino acids from the gel. Electrophoresis is a method used in medicine to screen for the sickle-cell trait in newborn infants.

Suppose we have a mixture of valine (pI 6.0), aspartic acid (pI 2.8), and lysine (pI 9.7) in a buffer of pH 6.0. When the mixture is placed between two electrodes at a high voltage, the aspartic acid, which has a negative charge at pH 6.0, moves to the positive electrode (anode). (See Figure 19.2.) The lysine, which has a positive charge at a pH of 6.0, moves toward the negative electrode (cathode). Valine, which is neutral at pH 6.0, does not move in the presence of an electric field.

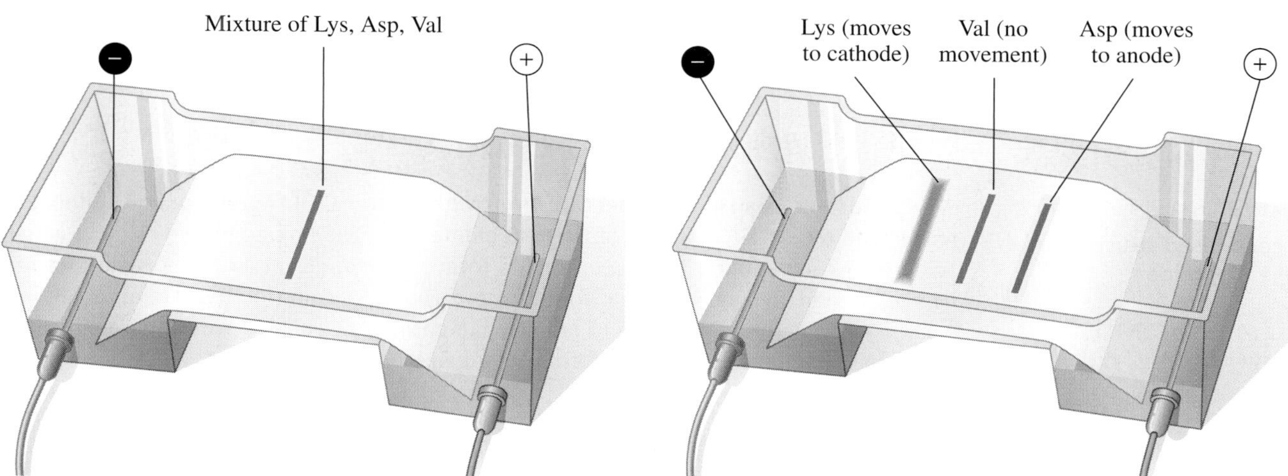


**FIGURE 19.2** A positively charged amino acid (pH < pI) moves toward the negative electrode; a negatively charged amino acid (pH > pI) moves toward the positive electrode; an amino acid with no net charge (pH = pI) does not migrate.

**Q** How would the three amino acids migrate if the mixture were buffered to pH 9.7, the pI of lysine?

CONCEPT CHECK 19.3

### Ionized Forms of Amino Acids

Explain each of the following:

**a.** Glutamic acid moves toward the positive electrode during electrophoresis at a pH of 7.0.

**b.** The pI of lysine is much higher than the pI of phenylalanine.

ANSWER

**a.** A pH of 7.0 is higher (more basic) than the pI of 3.2 for glutamic acid. At a pH of 7.0, glutamic acid would have two negatively charged $-COO^-$ groups and one $-NH_3^+$, which gives an overall negative charge of 1−.

**b.** At a pH of 5.5, the nonpolar phenylalanine forms a zwitterion with a zero net charge. However, lysine is a basic amino acid with two $-NH_3^+$ groups and one $-COO^-$. To form the zwitterion of lysine, a more basic environment is needed so that an $-NH_3^+$ group donates $H^+$ to give $-NH_2$ and a zwitterion with a net charge of zero. Thus, lysine has a higher pI because it requires a higher pH to form the zwitterion.

## QUESTIONS AND PROBLEMS

### Amino Acids as Zwitterions

**19.13** Draw the zwitterion of each of the following amino acids:
**a.** glycine **b.** cysteine **c.** threonine **d.** alanine

**19.14** Draw the zwitterion of each of the following amino acids:
**a.** phenylalanine **b.** methionine
**c.** leucine **d.** valine

**19.15** Draw the positive ion (acidic ion) of each of the amino acids in problem 19.13 at a pH below 1.0.

**19.16** Draw the negative ion (basic ion) of each of the amino acids in problem 19.13 at a pH above 12.0.

**19.17** Would each of the following ions of valine exist at a pH above, below, or at pI?

**a.** $H_2N-CH(CH(CH_3)_2)-COO^-$

**b.** $H_3\overset{+}{N}-CH(CH(CH_3)_2)-COOH$

**c.** $H_3\overset{+}{N}-CH(CH(CH_3)_2)-COO^-$

**19.18** Would each of the following ions of serine exist at a pH above, below, or at pI?

**a.** $H_3\overset{+}{N}-CH(CH_2OH)-COO^-$

**b.** $H_3\overset{+}{N}-CH(CH_2OH)-COOH$

**c.** $H_2N-CH(CH_2OH)-COO^-$

# 19.3 Formation of Peptides

LEARNING GOAL

Draw the condensed structural formula of a dipeptide.

SELF STUDY ACTIVITY
Structure of Proteins

A **peptide bond** is an amide bond that forms when the $-COO^-$ group of one amino acid reacts with the $-NH_3^+$ group of the next amino acid. The linking of two or more amino acids forms a **peptide**. Two amino acids form a *dipeptide*, three amino acids form a *tripeptide*, and four amino acids form a *tetrapeptide*. A chain of five amino acids is a *pentapeptide*, and longer chains of amino acids form *polypeptides*. We can write the amidation reaction for the zwitterion forms of two amino acids as follows:

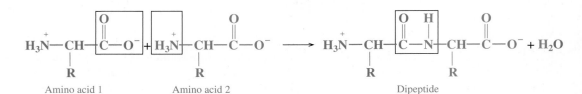

$$H_3\overset{+}{N}-\underset{R}{CH}-\overset{O}{\overset{\|}{C}}-O^- + H_3\overset{+}{N}-\underset{R}{CH}-\overset{O}{\overset{\|}{C}}-O^- \longrightarrow H_3\overset{+}{N}-\underset{R}{CH}-\overset{O}{\overset{\|}{C}}-\overset{H}{\overset{|}{N}}-\underset{R}{CH}-\overset{O}{\overset{\|}{C}}-O^- + H_2O$$

Amino acid 1 Amino acid 2 Dipeptide

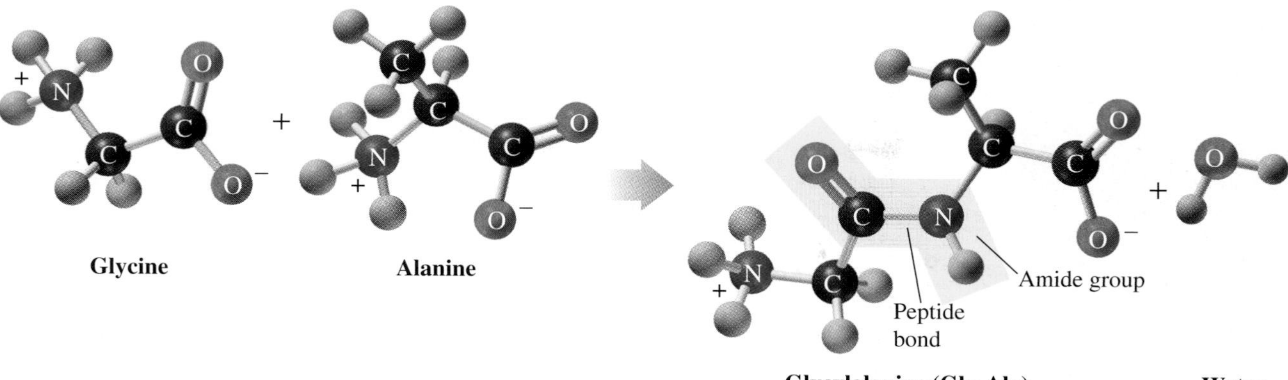


FIGURE 19.3 A peptide bond between glycine and alanine as zwitterions forms the dipeptide glycylalanine.
Q What functional groups in glycine and alanine form the peptide bond?

We can write the formation of the dipeptide glycylalanine (Gly-Ala) between glycine and alanine as follows. (See Figure 19.3.) In this peptide, glycine is written on the left. Because the glycine has a free $-NH_3^+$, it is the **N terminal** amino acid. The amino acid alanine written on the right has a free $-COO^-$ and is called the **C terminal** amino acid.

$$\underset{\text{Glycine}}{H_3\overset{+}{N}-CH_2-\overset{\overset{\displaystyle O}{\|}}{C}-O^-} + \underset{\text{Alanine}}{H_3\overset{+}{N}-\underset{\underset{\displaystyle CH_3}{|}}{CH}-\overset{\overset{\displaystyle O}{\|}}{C}-O^-} \longrightarrow \underset{\text{Glycylalanine (Gly-Ala)}}{\overset{\text{N terminal}}{H_3\overset{+}{N}-CH_2}-\boxed{\overset{\overset{\displaystyle O}{\|}}{C}-\overset{\overset{\displaystyle H}{|}}{N}}-\overset{\text{C terminal}}{\underset{\underset{\displaystyle CH_3}{|}}{CH}-\overset{\overset{\displaystyle O}{\|}}{C}-O^-}} + H_2O$$

## Naming Peptides

In the name of a peptide, each amino acid beginning from the N terminal end has the *ine* (or *ic acid*) replaced by *yl.* The last amino acid at the C terminal end of the peptide has its full name. For example, a tripeptide consisting of alanine, glycine, and serine is named as alan**yl**glyc**yl**serine. For convenience, the order of amino acids in the peptide is often written as the sequence of three-letter abbreviations:

$$\underset{\substack{\text{From alanine}\\ \text{alanyl}}}{\boxed{H_3\overset{+}{N}-\underset{\underset{\displaystyle CH_3}{|}}{CH}-\overset{\overset{\displaystyle O}{\|}}{C}}}\boxed{\underset{\substack{\text{From glycine}\\ \text{glycyl}}}{-NH-CH_2-\overset{\overset{\displaystyle O}{\|}}{C}}}\boxed{\underset{\substack{\text{From serine}\\ \text{serine}}}{-NH-\underset{\underset{\displaystyle CH_2OH}{|}}{CH}-\overset{\overset{\displaystyle O}{\|}}{C}-O^-}}$$

Alanylglycylserine
(Ala-Gly-Ser)

CONCEPT CHECK 19.4

### Structure and Names of Peptides

Consider the dipeptide Val-Thr:

**a.** What amino acid is the N terminal amino acid?
**b.** What amino acid is the C terminal amino acid?
**c.** How are the amino acids connected?
**d.** Draw the condensed structural formula of Val-Thr.
**e.** Give the name of the dipeptide.

## CAREER FOCUS

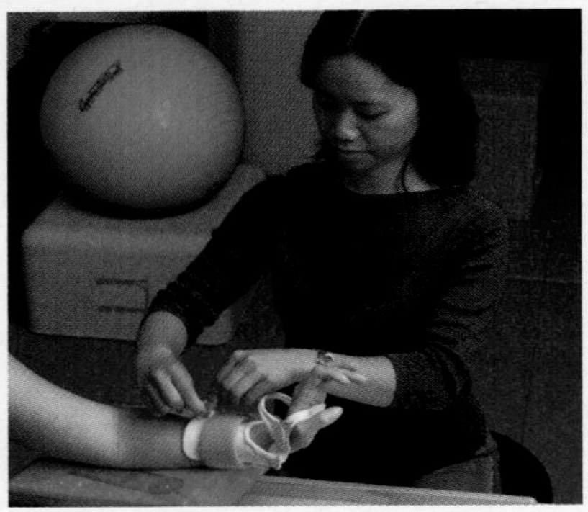

### Rehabilitation Specialist

"I am interested in the biomechanical part of rehabilitation, which involves strengthening activities that help people return to the activities of daily living," says Minna Robles, rehabilitation specialist. "Here I am fitting a patient with a wrist extension splint that allows her to lift her hand. This exercise will also help the muscles and soft tissues in that wrist area to heal. An understanding of the chemicals of the body, how they interact, and how we can affect the body on a chemical level is important in understanding our work. One technique we use is called myofacial release. We apply pressure to a part of the body, which helps to increase circulation. By increasing circulation, we can move the soft tissues better, which improves movement and range of motion."

ANSWER

**a.** Valine, the first amino acid in the peptide, has a free $—NH_3^+$, which makes it the N terminal amino acid.

**b.** Threonine, the last amino acid in the peptide, has a free $—COO^-$, which makes it the C terminal amino acid.

**c.** The amino acids valine and threonine are connected by a peptide bond, which is an amide bond between the C=O of valine and the N—H of threonine.

**d.**

```
        CH3             CH3
        |               |
    H3C—CH              CH—OH
        |    O  H       |    O
        |    ‖  |       |    ‖
   H3N⁺—CH—C—N—CH—C—O⁻
```

**e.** In the name of a peptide, the ending *ine* (or *ic acid*) of each amino acid preceding the C terminal amino acid is changed to *yl*. The C terminal amino acid does not change its name. The dipeptide is named valylthreonine.

SAMPLE PROBLEM 19.4

### Identifying a Tripeptide

Consider the following tripeptide:

```
             O               O               O
             ‖               ‖               ‖
  H3N⁺—CH—C—NH—CH—C—NH—CH—C—O⁻
        |            |            |
      HC—OH         CH2          CH2
        |            |            |
       CH3         HC—CH3       C6H5 (phenyl)
                     |
                    CH3
```

**a.** What amino acid is the N terminal? What amino acid is the C terminal?

**b.** What is the three-letter abbreviation for the tripeptide?

**c.** What is the name of the tripeptide?

SOLUTION

**a.** Threonine is the N terminal; phenylalanine is the C terminal.

**b.** Thr-Leu-Phe

**c.** Beginning at the N terminal, the amino acids in the tripeptide are threonine, leucine, and phenylalanine. Changing the *ine* endings of the amino acids preceding the C terminal amino acid (name does not change) gives the name threonylleucylphenylalanine.

STUDY CHECK

What is the name of the pentapeptide called *enkephalin*, a natural painkiller produced in the body, if it has the abbreviation Tyr-Gly-Gly-Phe-Met?

## QUESTIONS AND PROBLEMS

### Formation of Peptides

**19.19** Draw the condensed structural formula of each of the following peptides, and give the abbreviation for their names:

**a.** alanylcysteine **b.** serylphenylalanine
**c.** glycylalanylvaline **d.** valylisoleucyltryptophan

**19.20** Draw the condensed structural formula of each of the following peptides, and give the abbreviation for their names:

**a.** methionylaspartic acid
**b.** alanyltryptophan
**c.** methionylglutaminyllysine
**d.** histidylglycylglutamylalanine

# 19.4 Protein Structure: Primary and Secondary Levels

When there are more than 50 amino acids in a chain, the polypeptide is usually called a **protein**. Each protein in our cells has a unique sequence of amino acids that determines its biological function.

LEARNING GOAL

Describe the primary and secondary structures of a protein.

TUTORIAL
Peptides Are Chains of Amino Acids

## Primary Structure

The **primary structure** of a protein is the particular sequence of amino acids held together by peptide bonds. For example, a hormone that stimulates the thyroid to release thyroxine is a tripeptide with the amino acid sequence Glu-His-Pro:

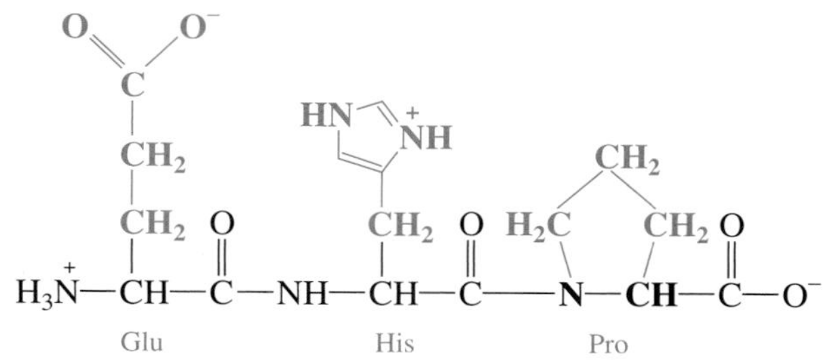

$$H_3\overset{+}{N}-CH-C(=O)-NH-CH-C(=O)-N-CH-C(=O)-O^-$$

Glu His Pro

Although other amino acid sequences are possible, such as His-Pro-Glu or Pro-His-Glu, they do not produce hormonal activity. Only the tripeptide with the Glu-His-Pro sequence of amino acids has hormonal activity. Thus, the biological function of peptides and proteins depends on the specific sequence of the amino acids.

The first protein to have its primary structure determined was insulin, which is a hormone that regulates the glucose level in the blood. The primary structure of human insulin has two polypeptide chains. Chain A has 21 amino acids, and chain B has 30 amino acids. The polypeptide chains are held together by disulfide bonds formed by the R groups of the cysteine amino acids in each of the chains. (See Figure 19.4.)

The primary structure of insulin in humans is very similar to the primary structure of insulin in cows (bovine). Only the three amino acids at positions 8, 9, and 10 in chain A and position 30 in chain B vary from one species to another. For many years, bovine insulin obtained from the pancreas of cows was used to treat diabetics who lacked insulin. Today, human insulin produced through genetic engineering is used in the treatment of diabetes.

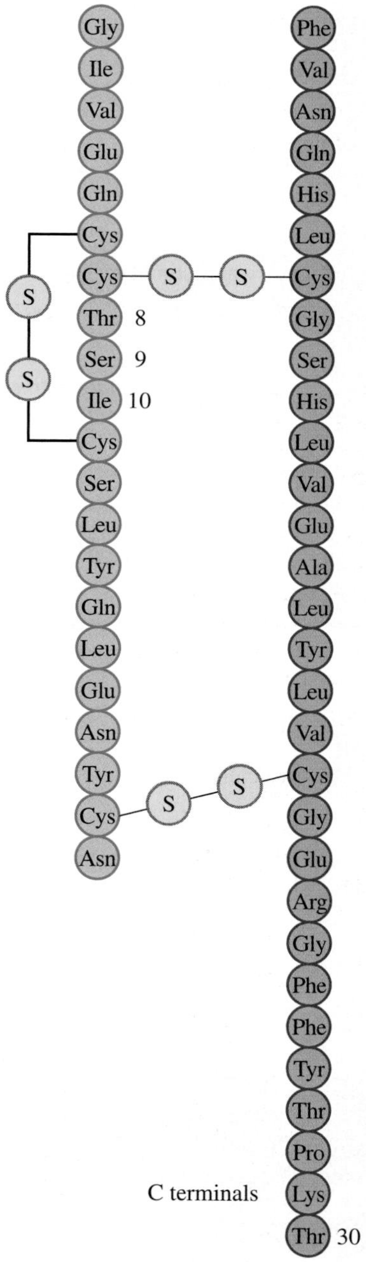

A chain — N terminals — B chain

A chain: Gly, Ile, Val, Glu, Gln, Cys, Cys, Thr 8, Ser 9, Ile 10, Cys, Ser, Leu, Tyr, Gln, Leu, Glu, Asn, Tyr, Cys, Asn

B chain: Phe, Val, Asn, Gln, His, Leu, Cys, Gly, Ser, His, Leu, Val, Glu, Ala, Leu, Tyr, Leu, Val, Cys, Gly, Glu, Arg, Gly, Phe, Phe, Tyr, Thr, Pro, Lys, Thr 30

C terminals

S S S S S S

FIGURE 19.4 The sequence of amino acids in human insulin is its primary structure.

Q What kinds of bonds occur in the primary structure of a protein?

CONCEPT CHECK 19.5

**Primary Structure**

What are the abbreviations of the possible tetrapeptides containing two valines, one proline, and one histidine if the C terminal is proline?

ANSWER

The C terminal of proline in the possible tetrapeptides would be preceded by three different sequences of two valines and one histidine: Val-Val-His-Pro, Val-His-Val-Pro, and His-Val-Val-Pro.

## Secondary Structure

The **secondary structure** of a protein describes the type of structure that forms when amino acids form hydrogen bonds within a polypeptide or between polypeptides. The three most common types of secondary structure are the *alpha helix*, the *beta-pleated sheet*, and the *triple helix*.

## HEALTH NOTE

### Polypeptides in the Body

Enkephalins and endorphins are natural painkillers produced in the body. They are polypeptides that bind to receptors in the brain to give relief from pain. This effect appears to be responsible for the runner's high and the temporary loss of pain when severe injury occurs.

The *enkephalins*, which are found in the thalamus and the spinal cord, are pentapeptides, the smallest molecules with opiate activity. The amino acid sequence of an enkephalin is found in the longer amino acid sequence of the endorphins.

Four groups of *endorphins* have been identified: $\alpha$-endorphin contains 16 amino acids, $\beta$-endorphin contains 31 amino acids, $\gamma$-endorphin has 17 amino acids, and $\delta$-endorphin has 27 amino acids. Endorphins may produce their sedating effects by preventing the release of substance P, a polypeptide with 11 amino acids, which has been found to transmit pain impulses to the brain.

$\alpha$-Endorphin

Tyr—Gly—Gly—Phe—Met—Thr—Ser—Glu—Lys—Ser—Glu—Thr—Pro—Leu—Val—Thr—Leu—Phe—Lys—Asn—Ala—Ile—Ile—Lys—Asn—Ala—Tyr—Lys—Lys—Gly—Glu

Enkephalin (Tyr—Gly—Gly—Phe—Met)

$\beta$-Endorphin

When cells are damaged, a polypeptide called bradykinin is released, which stimulates the release of prostaglandins:

Arg—Pro—Pro—Gly—Phe—Ser—Pro—Phe—Arg

Bradykinin

Two hormones produced by the pituitary gland are the nonapeptides (nine-amino-acid peptides) oxytocin and vasopressin. Oxytocin stimulates uterine contractions in labor, and vasopressin is an antidiuretic hormone that regulates blood pressure by adjusting the amount of water reabsorbed by the kidneys. The structures of these nonapeptides are very similar. Only the amino acids in positions 3 and 8 are different. However, the difference of two amino acids greatly affects how the two hormones function in the body.

1 Cys—S—S—6 Cys—7 Pro—8 Leu/Arg—9 Gly—C(=O)—$NH_2$

1 Cys—2 Tyr—3 Ile/Phe—4 Gln—5 Asn—6 Cys

**Oxytocin**

**Vasopressin**

In an **alpha helix ($\alpha$ helix)**, hydrogen bonds form between each N—H group and the oxygen of a C=O group of an amino acid in the next turn of the $\alpha$ helix. (See Figure 19.5.) Because there are many hydrogen bonds along the polypeptide, it has the helical shape of a coiled telephone cord. All the R groups of the different amino acids in the polypeptide extend to the outside of the helix.

SELF STUDY ACTIVITY
Primary and Secondary Structure

TUTORIAL
The Shapes of Protein Chains: Helices and Sheets

Another type of secondary structure is known as the **beta-pleated sheet ($\beta$-pleated sheet)**. In a $\beta$-pleated sheet, polypeptide chains are held together side by side by hydrogen bonds between the peptide chains. In a $\beta$-pleated sheet of silk fibroin, the small R groups of the prevalent amino acids, glycine, alanine, and serine, extend above and below the sheet. This arrangement of amino acids results in a series of $\beta$-pleated sheets that are stacked close together. The hydrogen bonds holding the $\beta$-pleated sheets tightly in place account for the strength and durability of fibrous proteins such as silk. (See Figure 19.6.)

In some proteins, the polypeptide chain consists of mostly the $\alpha$ helix secondary structure, whereas other proteins consist of mostly the $\beta$-pleated sheet structure. Another group of proteins have a mixture with some sections of the polypeptide chain in $\alpha$ helices and other sections in the $\beta$-pleated sheet structure. The tendency to form a certain type of secondary structure depends on the amino acids in a particular segment of the polypeptide chain. Amino acids such as valine, proline, serine, and aspartic acid are found in $\beta$-pleated sheet regions. The $\alpha$ helix region has large amounts of amino acids such as alanine, histidine, leucine, and methionine.

The secondary structure in silk is a beta-pleated sheet.

**Collagen**, which is the most abundant protein in the body, makes up 25–35% of all protein in vertebrates. It is found in connective tissue, blood vessels, skin, tendons, ligaments,

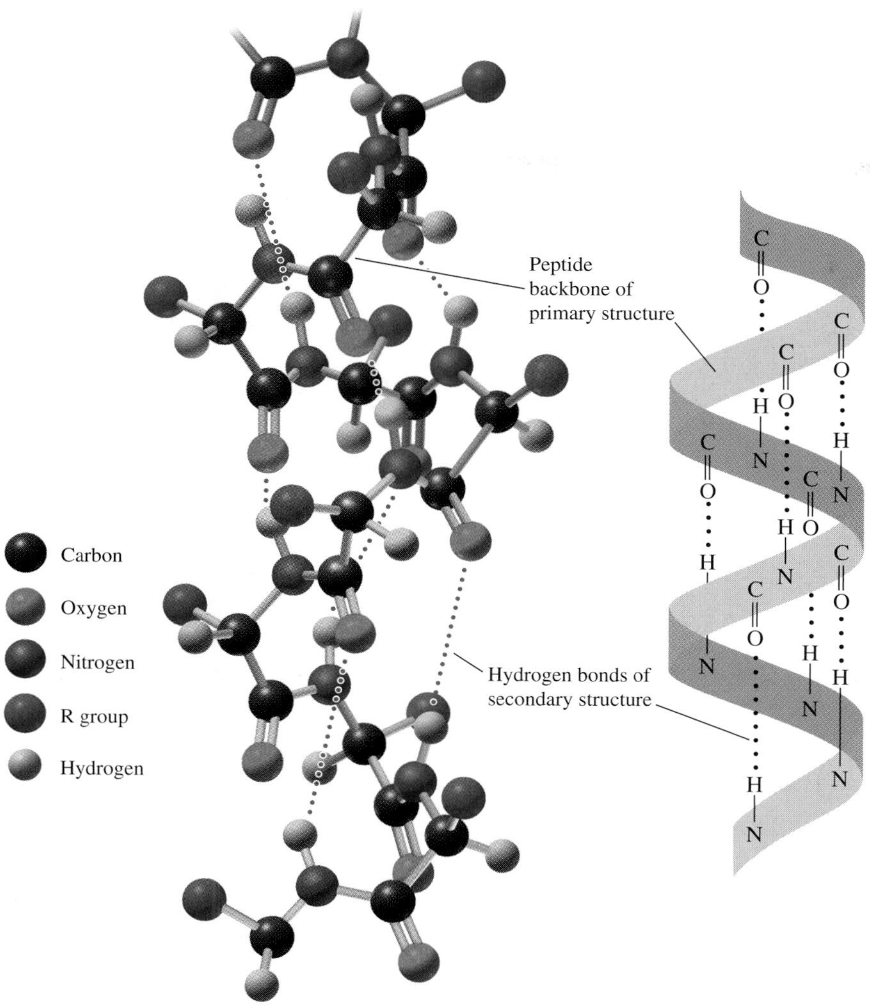

**FIGURE 19.5** The $\alpha$ (alpha) helix acquires a coiled shape from hydrogen bonds between the N—H of the peptide bond in one loop and the C═O of the peptide bond in the next loop.

Q What are the partial charges of the H in N—H and the O in C═O that permits hydrogen bonds to form?

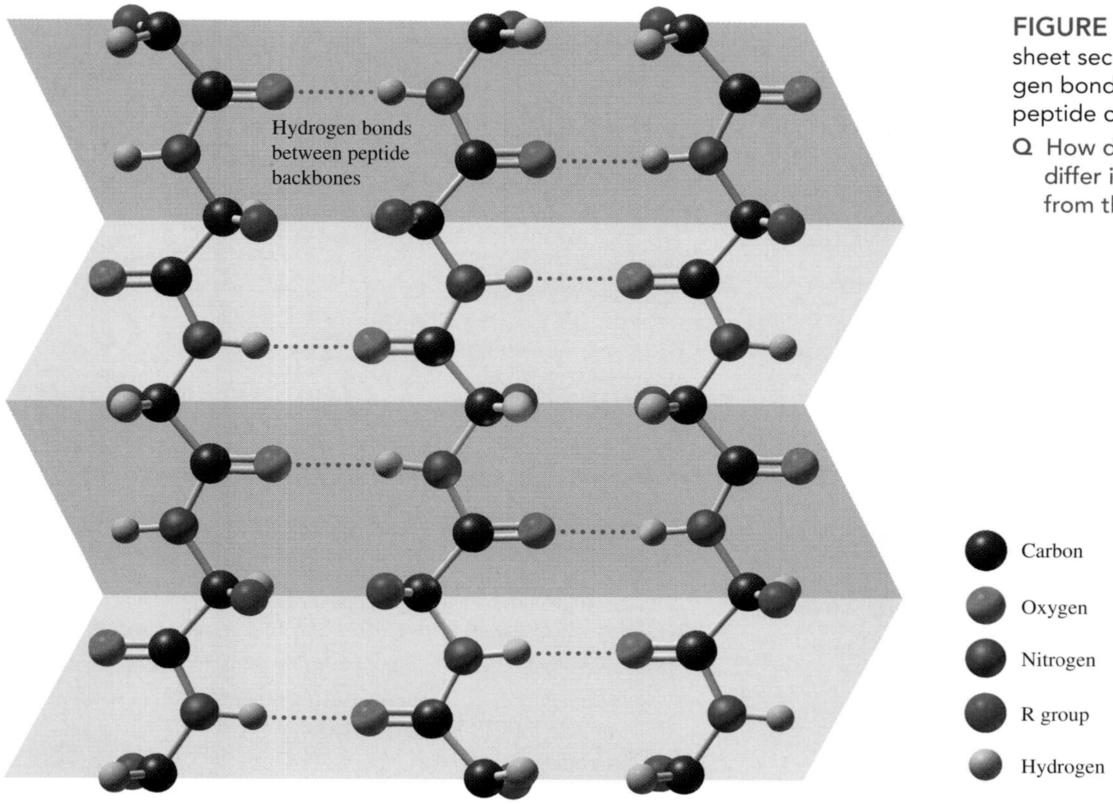

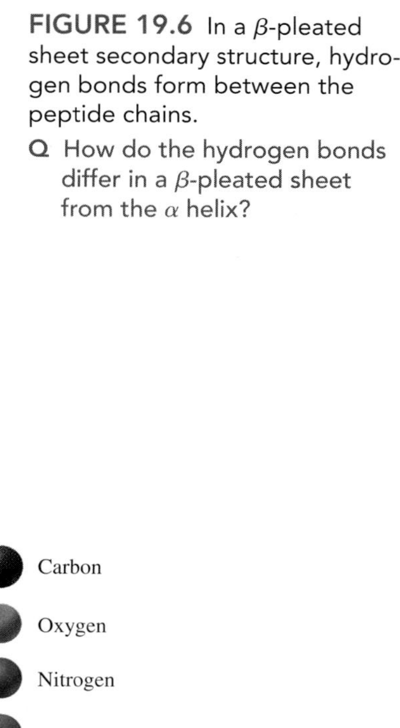


**FIGURE 19.6** In a $\beta$-pleated sheet secondary structure, hydrogen bonds form between the peptide chains.

Q How do the hydrogen bonds differ in a $\beta$-pleated sheet from the $\alpha$ helix?

Triple helix 3 $\alpha$-helix peptide chains

**FIGURE 19.7** Hydrogen bonds between polar R groups in three polypeptide chains form the triple helices that combine to make fibers of collagen.

**Q** What are some of the amino acids in collagen that form hydrogen bonds between the polypeptide chains?

the cornea of the eye, and cartilage. The strong structure of collagen is a result of three polypeptides woven together like a braid to form a **triple helix**, as seen in Figure 19.7.

Collagen has a high content of glycine (33%), proline (22%), and alanine (12%), and smaller amounts of hydroxyproline and hydroxylysine, which are modified forms of proline and lysine. These —OH groups provide additional hydrogen bonds between the peptide chains to give strength to the collagen triple helix. When several triple helices wrap together as a braid, they form the fibrils that make up connective tissues and tendons. When a diet is deficient in vitamin C, collagen is weakened because the enzymes needed to form hydroxyproline and hydroxylysine require vitamin C. Collagen becomes less elastic as a person ages because additional cross-links form between the fibrils. Bones, cartilage, and tendons become more brittle, and wrinkles are seen as the skin loses elasticity.

$$\begin{array}{c} OH \\ | \\ CH \\ \diagup \quad \diagdown \\ CH_2 \quad CH_2 \\ | \qquad | \\ H_2N^+ - CH - COO^- \end{array}$$

Hydroxyproline

$$\begin{array}{c} \overset{+}{N}H_3 \\ | \\ CH_2 \\ | \\ H - C - OH \\ | \\ CH_2 \\ | \\ CH_2 \\ | \\ H_3N^+ - CH - COO^- \end{array}$$

Hydroxylysine

SAMPLE PROBLEM 19.5

### Identifying Secondary Structures

Indicate the secondary structure ($\alpha$ helix, $\beta$-pleated sheet, or triple helix) described in each of the following statements:

**a.** a coiled peptide chain held in place by hydrogen bonding between peptide bonds in the same chain

**b.** a structure that has hydrogen bonds between polypeptide chains arranged side by side

SOLUTION

**a.** $\alpha$ helix **b.** $\beta$-pleated sheet

STUDY CHECK

What is the secondary structure in collagen?

## QUESTIONS AND PROBLEMS

### Protein Structure: Primary and Secondary Levels

19.21 What type of bonding occurs in the primary structure of a protein?

**19.22** How can two proteins with exactly the same number and type of amino acids have different primary structures?

19.23 Two peptides each contain one molecule of valine and two molecules of serine. What are their possible primary structures?

**19.24** What are three different types of secondary protein structure?

19.25 What happens to the primary structure of a protein when a protein forms a secondary structure?

**19.26** In an $\alpha$ helix, how does bonding occur between the amino acids in the polypeptide chain?

19.27 What is the difference in bonding between an $\alpha$ helix and a $\beta$-pleated sheet?

**19.28** How is the secondary structure of a $\beta$-pleated sheet different from that of a triple helix?

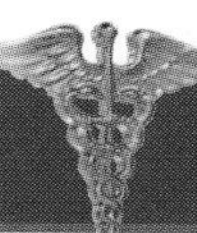

## HEALTH NOTE

### Essential Amino Acids

Of the 20 amino acids used to build the proteins in the body, only 10 can be synthesized in the body. The other 10 amino acids, listed in Table 19.3, are **essential amino acids** that cannot be synthesized and must be obtained from the proteins in the diet.

TABLE 19.3 Essential Amino Acids

| | |
|---|---|
| Arginine (Arg)* | Methionine (Met) |
| Histidine (His)* | Phenylalanine (Phe) |
| Isoleucine (Ile) | Threonine (Thr) |
| Leucine (Leu) | Tryptophan (Trp) |
| Lysine (Lys) | Valine (Val) |

*Required in diets of children, not adults

*Complete proteins*, which contain all of the essential amino acids, are found in most animal products, such as eggs, milk, meat, fish, and poultry. However, gelatin and plant proteins such as grains, beans, and nuts are *incomplete proteins* because they are deficient in one or more of the essential amino acids. Diets that rely on plant foods for protein must contain a variety of protein sources to obtain all the essential amino acids. For example, a diet of rice and beans contains all the essential amino acids because rice and beans have complementary proteins. Rice contains the methionine and tryptophan deficient in beans, while beans contain the lysine that is lacking in rice. (See Table 19.4.)

TABLE 19.4 Amino Acid Deficiency in Selected Vegetables and Grains

| Food Source | Amino Acids Missing |
|---|---|
| Eggs, milk, meat, fish, poultry | None |
| Wheat, rice, oats | Lysine |
| Corn | Lysine, tryptophan |
| Beans | Methionine, tryptophan |
| Peas | Methionine |
| Almonds, walnuts | Lysine, tryptophan |
| Soy | Low in methionine |

# 19.5 Protein Structure: Tertiary and Quaternary Levels

LEARNING GOAL

Describe the tertiary and quaternary structures of a protein.

The **tertiary structure** of a protein involves attractions and repulsions between the R groups of the amino acids in the polypeptide chain. As interactions occur between different parts of the peptide chain, segments of the chain twist and bend until the protein acquires a specific three-dimensional shape.

## Cross-Links in Tertiary Structures

SELF STUDY ACTIVITY
Tertiary and Quaternary Structure

Many proteins are **globular proteins** because they acquire compact, spherical shapes when the secondary structures of their polypeptide chains fold over on top of each other. Globular proteins carry out cell functions such as synthesis, transport, and metabolism. The tertiary structure of a globular protein is stabilized by interactions between the R groups of the amino acids in one region of the polypeptide chain with the R groups of amino acids in other regions of the protein. (See Figure 19.8.) Table 19.5 lists the stabilizing interactions of tertiary structures, which are detailed as follows:

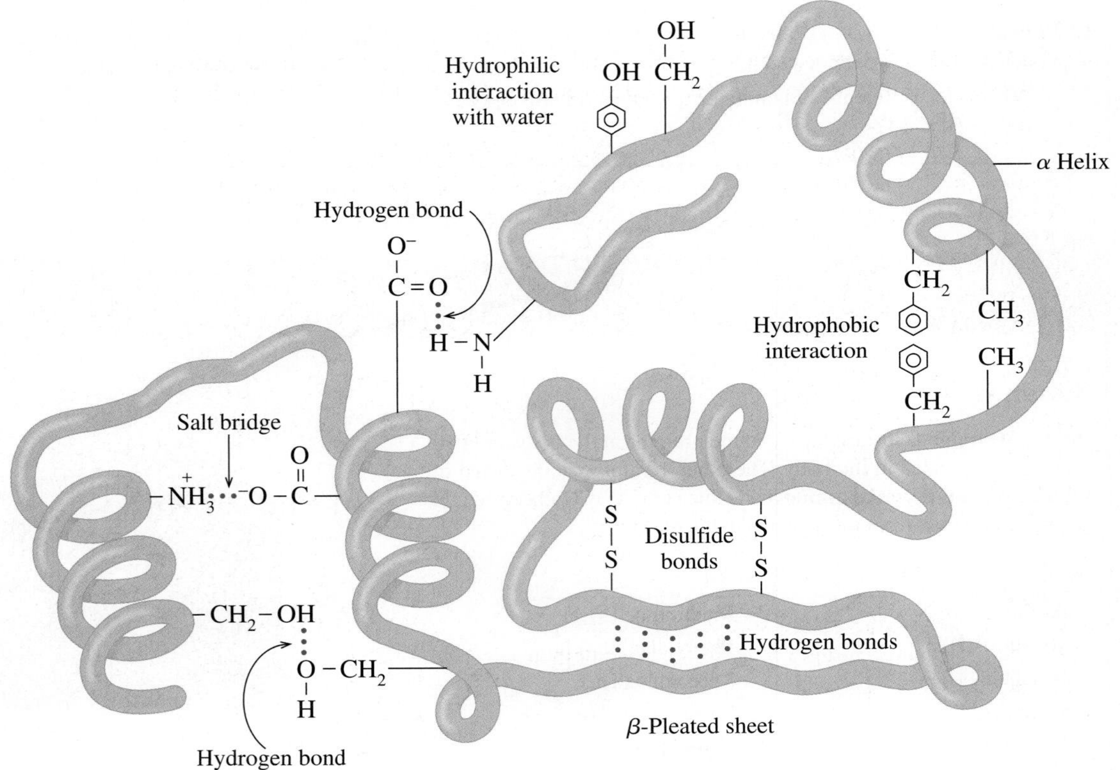


**FIGURE 19.8** Interactions between amino acid R groups fold a protein into a specific three-dimensional shape called its tertiary structure.

**Q** Why would one section of the protein chain move to the center while another section remains on the surface of the tertiary structure?

**TABLE 19.5 Some Cross-Links in Tertiary Structures**

| | Nature of Bonding |
|---|---|
| **Hydrophobic interactions** | Interactions between nonpolar groups |
| **Hydrophilic interactions** | Attractions between polar or ionized groups and water on the surface of the tertiary structure |
| **Salt bridges** | Ionic interactions between ionized acidic and basic amino acids |
| **Hydrogen bonds** | Occur between H and O or N |
| **Disulfide bonds** | Strong covalent links between sulfur atoms of two cysteine amino acids |

MC TUTORIAL
Levels of Structure in Proteins

1. **Hydrophobic interactions** are interactions between two nonpolar R groups. Within a protein, the amino acids with nonpolar R groups push as far away from the aqueous environment as possible, which forms a hydrophobic center at the interior of the protein molecule.
2. **Hydrophilic interactions** are attractions between the external aqueous environment and amino acids that have polar or ionized R groups. The polar R groups move to the outer surface where they hydrogen bond with water.
3. **Salt bridges** are ionic bonds between the ionized R groups of basic and acidic amino acids. For example, at physiological pH, the R group of lysine ($-NH_3^+$) attracts the R group of glutamic acid ($-COO^-$) to form an ionic bond called a salt bridge. If the pH changes, the basic and acidic R groups lose their ionic charges and cannot form salt bridges, which causes a change in the shape of the protein.
4. **Hydrogen bonds** form between the H of one R group and the O or N of another polar amino acid. For example, a hydrogen bond can occur between the $-OH$ groups of two serines or between the $-OH$ of serine and the $-NH_2$ in the R group of glutamine.
5. **Disulfide bonds** ($-S-S-$) are covalent bonds that form between the $-SH$ groups of cysteines in the polypeptide chain. In some proteins, there are several disulfide bonds between the R groups of cysteines in the polypeptide chain.

**CONCEPT CHECK 19.6**

**Structural Levels in Proteins**

In a tertiary structure of a globular protein, the R groups of lysine and aspartic acid interact.

**a.** What type of interaction occurs?

**b.** What happens to this interaction when acid is added to the protein?

ANSWER

**a.** The R group of lysine contains $-NH_3^+$, and the R group of aspartic acid contains $-COO^-$. The interaction between positively and negatively charged R groups is an ionic attraction called a salt bridge.

**b.** If acid is added to the protein until the pH equals the pI of the aspartic acid, the zwitterion forms. The $-COO^-$ accepts $H^+$ to form $-COOH$, which causes a loss of ionic attraction, and breaks down the salt bridge.

SAMPLE PROBLEM 19.6

**Cross-Links in Tertiary Structures**

What type of interaction would you expect between the R groups of the following amino acids in a tertiary structure?

**a.** cysteine and cysteine
**b.** glutamic acid and lysine

SOLUTION

**a.** Because cysteine has an R group containing $-SH$, a disulfide bond will form.
**b.** An ionic bond (salt bridge) can form by the interaction of the $-COO^-$ of glutamic acid and the $-NH_3^+$ of lysine.

STUDY CHECK

Would you expect to find valine and leucine in a globular protein on the outside or the inside of the tertiary structure? Why?

## Examples of Globular and Fibrous Proteins

Myoglobin is a globular protein that stores oxygen in skeletal muscle. High concentrations of myoglobin have been found in the muscles of sea mammals, such as seals and whales, that stay under the water for long periods. Myoglobin contains 153 amino acids in a single polypeptide chain with about three-fourths of the chain in the $\alpha$ helix secondary structure. The polypeptide chain, including its helical regions, forms a compact tertiary structure by folding upon itself. (See Figure 19.9.) Within the tertiary structure, a pocket of amino acids and a heme group binds and stores oxygen ($O_2$).

The **fibrous proteins** are proteins that consist of long, thin, fiber-like shapes. They are typically involved in the structure of cells and tissues. Two types of fibrous protein are the $\alpha$- and $\beta$-keratins. The ***α*-keratins** are the proteins that make up hair, wool, skin, and nails. In hair, three $\alpha$ helices coil together like a braid to form a fibril. Within the fibril, the $\alpha$ helices are held together by disulfide ($-S-S-$) linkages between the R groups of the many cysteine amino acids in hair. Several fibrils bind together to form a strand of hair. (See Figure 19.10.)

The $\beta$-keratins are the type of proteins found in the feathers of birds and scales of reptiles. In $\beta$-keratins, the proteins consist of large amounts of twisted $\beta$-pleated sheet structure.

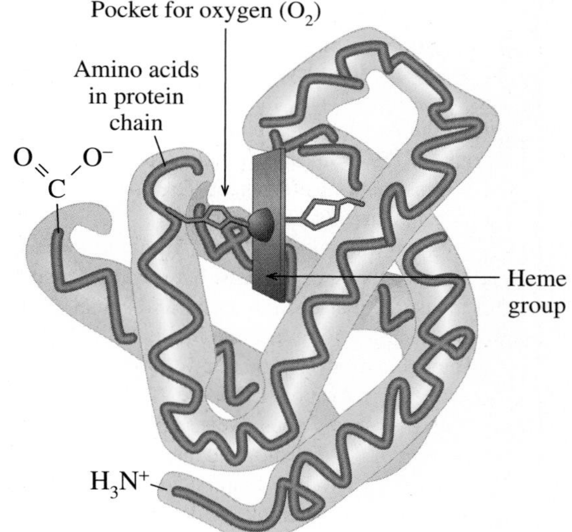


**FIGURE 19.9** Myoglobin is a globular protein with a heme pocket in its tertiary structure that binds oxygen to be carried to the tissues.

**Q** Would hydrophilic amino acids be found on the outside or inside of the myoglobin structure?

## Quaternary Structure: Hemoglobin

When a biologically active protein consists of two or more polypeptide chains or subunits, the structural level is referred to as a **quaternary structure**. Hemoglobin, a globular protein that transports oxygen in blood, consists of four polypeptide chains, two $\alpha$ chains and two $\beta$ chains.

**FIGURE 19.10** The fibrous proteins of α-keratin wrap together to form fibrils that make up hair and wool. The proteins called β-keratins are found in the feathers of birds and scales of reptiles.

Q Why does hair have a large amount of cysteine amino acids?

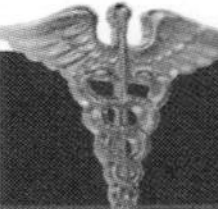

## HEALTH NOTE

### Prions and Mad Cow Disease

Until recently, researchers thought that only viruses or bacteria were responsible for transmitting diseases. Now a group of diseases has been found in which the infectious agents are proteins called *prions*. Bovine spongiform encephalopathy (BSE), or "mad cow disease," is a fatal brain disease of cattle in which the brain fills with cavities, resembling a sponge. In the noninfectious form of the prion $PrP^c$, the N-terminal portion is a random coil. (See structure at right.) Although the noninfectious form may be ingested from meat products, its structure can change to what is known as $PrP^s$, or *prion-related protein scrapie*. In this infectious form, which has disastrous effects on the brain and spinal cord, the end of the peptide chain folds into a beta-pleated sheet. The conditions that cause this structural change are not yet known.

BSE was diagnosed in Great Britain in 1986. The protein is present in nerve tissue of animals, but it is not found in their meat. Control measures that exclude brain and spinal cord from animal feed are now in place to reduce the incidence of BSE.

The human variant of this disease is called Creutzfeldt-Jakob disease (CJD). Around 1955, Dr. Carleton Gajdusek was studying the Fore people of Papua, New Guinea, where many tribe members were dying of the neurological disease known as "kuru." Among the Fore, it was a custom to cannibalize members of the tribe upon their death. Gajdusek eventually determined that this practice was responsible for transmitting the infectious agent from one tribe member to another.

After Gajdusek identified the infectious agent in kuru as similar to the prions that cause BSE, he received the Nobel Prize in Physiology or Medicine in 1976.

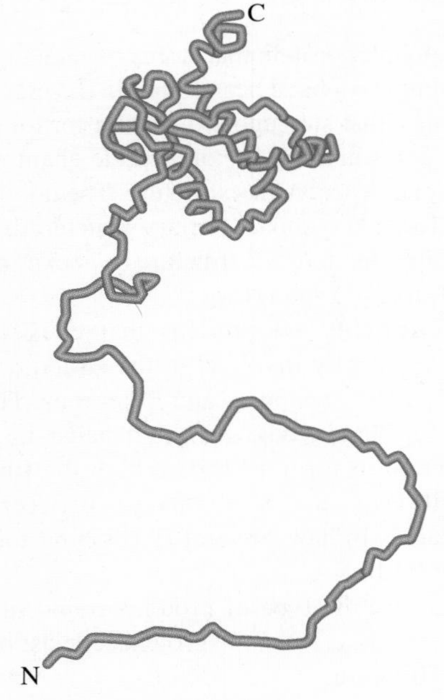


In the quaternary structure, the subunits are held together by the same interactions that stabilize their tertiary structures, such as hydrogen bonds and salt bridges between R groups, disulfide bonds, and hydrophobic interactions. (See Figure 19.11.) Each subunit of the hemoglobin contains a heme group that binds oxygen. In the adult hemoglobin molecule, all four subunits ($\alpha_2\beta_2$) must be combined for the hemoglobin to properly function as an oxygen carrier. Therefore, the complete quaternary structure of hemoglobin can bind and transport four molecules of oxygen.

Hemoglobin and myoglobin have similar biological functions. Hemoglobin carries oxygen in the blood, whereas myoglobin carries oxygen in muscle. Myoglobin, a single polypeptide chain with a molar mass of 17 000 g/mole, has about one-fourth the molar mass of hemoglobin (67 000 g/mole). The tertiary structure of the single polypeptide myoglobin is almost identical to the tertiary structure of each of the subunits of hemoglobin. Myoglobin stores just one molecule of oxygen, just as each subunit of hemoglobin carries one oxygen molecule. The similarity in tertiary structures allows each protein to bind and release oxygen in a similar manner. Table 19.6 and Figure 19.12 summarize the structural levels of proteins.

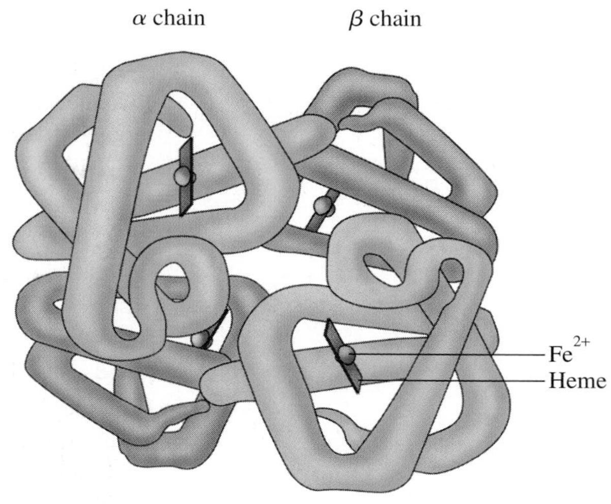


**FIGURE 19.11** The quaternary structure of hemoglobin consists of four polypeptide subunits, each containing a heme group that binds an oxygen molecule.

**Q** What is the difference between a tertiary structure and a quaternary structure?

**TABLE 19.6** Summary of Structural Levels in Proteins

| Structural Level | Characteristics |
|---|---|
| Primary | The sequence of amino acids |
| Secondary | The α helix, β-pleated sheet, or a triple helix forms by hydrogen bonding between peptide bonds along the chain |
| Tertiary | A protein folds into a compact, three-dimensional shape stabilized by interactions between R groups of amino acids |
| Quaternary | Two or more protein subunits combine to form a biologically active protein |

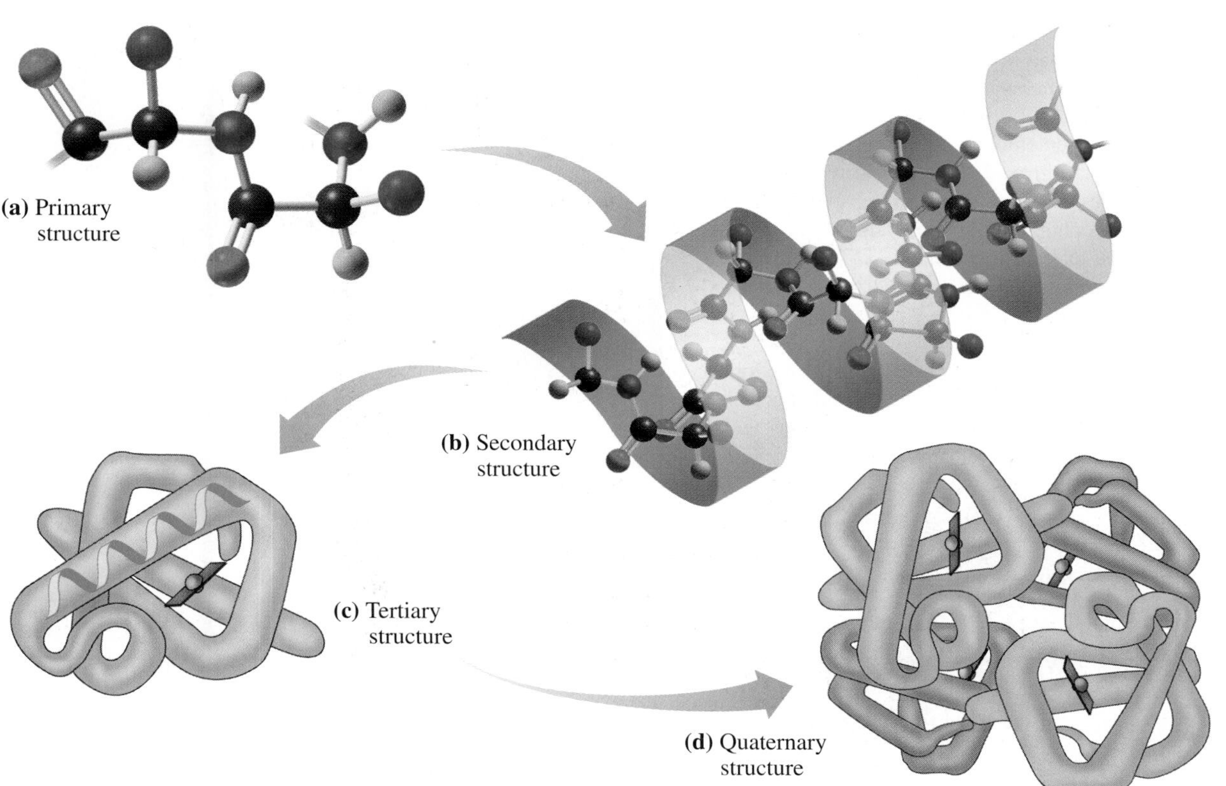


**FIGURE 19.12** Proteins consist of **(a)** primary, **(b)** secondary, **(c)** tertiary, and sometimes **(d)** quaternary structural levels.

**Q** What is the difference between a primary structure and a tertiary structure?

CONCEPT CHECK 19.7

**Structures of Proteins**

Indicate which of the following are present in the primary, secondary, tertiary, and quaternary structures of proteins:

**a.** peptide bonds
**b.** hydrogen bonds between adjacent peptides
**c.** hydrogen bonds within a single peptide
**d.** hydrophobic interactions
**e.** association of four polypeptide chains

ANSWER

**a.** Peptide bonds are present at all levels of protein structures.
**b.** Hydrogen bonds between adjacent peptides occur in the secondary structures such as $\beta$-pleated sheets and triple helices.
**c.** Hydrogen bonds within a single peptide is a characteristic of the secondary structure of an $\alpha$ helix.
**d.** Hydrophobic interactions between two nonpolar R groups occur in the tertiary and quaternary structures of proteins.
**e.** The association of four polypeptide chains occurs in the quaternary structures of proteins.

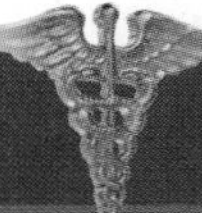

## HEALTH NOTE

### Sickle-Cell Anemia

Sickle-cell anemia is a disease caused by an abnormality in the shape of one of the subunits of the hemoglobin protein. In the $\beta$ chain, the sixth amino acid, glutamic acid, which is polar acidic, is replaced by valine, a nonpolar amino acid.

Because valine has a nonpolar R group, it is attracted to the nonpolar regions of other beta hemoglobin chains. The affected red blood cells (RBC) change from a rounded shape to a crescent shape, like a sickle, which interferes with their ability to transport adequate quantities of oxygen. Hydrophobic interactions also cause sickle-cell hemoglobin molecules to stick together. They form insoluble fibers of sickle-cell hemoglobin that clog capillaries, where they cause inflammation, pain, and organ damage. Critically low oxygen levels may occur in the affected tissues.

In sickle-cell anemia, both genes for the altered hemoglobin must be inherited. However, a few sickled cells are found in persons who carry one gene for sickle-cell hemoglobin, a condition that is also known to provide protection from malaria.

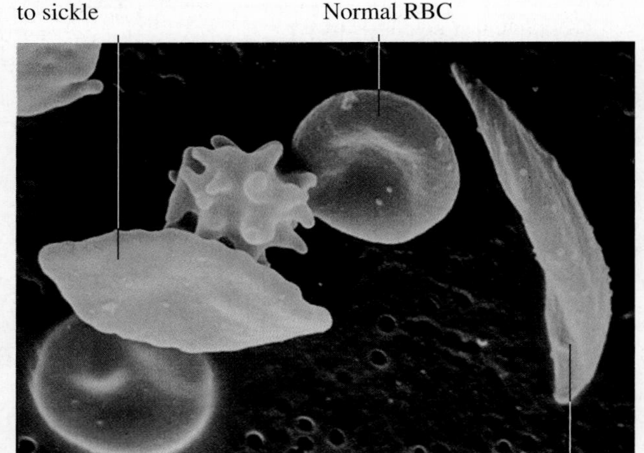


Polar amino acid

Normal $\beta$ chain: Val—His—Leu—Thr—Pro—[Glu]—Glu—Lys—

Sickled $\beta$ chain: Val—His—Leu—Thr—Pro—[Val]—Glu—Lys—

Nonpolar amino acid

SAMPLE PROBLEM 19.7

**Identifying Protein Structure**

Indicate whether the following conditions are responsible for primary, secondary, tertiary, or quaternary protein structures:

**a.** Disulfide bonds form between portions of a protein chain.
**b.** Peptide bonds form a chain of amino acids.

SOLUTION

**a.** Disulfide bonds help to stabilize the tertiary structure of a protein.
**b.** The sequence of amino acids in a polypeptide is a primary structure.

STUDY CHECK

What structural level is represented by the interaction of the two subunits in insulin?

## QUESTIONS AND PROBLEMS

### Protein Structure: Tertiary and Quaternary Levels

19.29 What type of interaction would you expect between the following groups in a tertiary structure?
**a.** two cysteines **b.** glutamic acid and lysine
**c.** serine and aspartic acid **d.** two leucines

**19.30** What type of interaction would you expect between the following groups in a tertiary structure?
**a.** phenylalanine and leucine
**b.** aspartic acid and histidine
**c.** asparagine and tyrosine
**d.** alanine and proline

19.31 A portion of a polypeptide chain contains the following sequence of amino acids:

-Leu-Val-Cys-Asp-

**a.** Which amino acid can form a disulfide cross-link?
**b.** Which amino acids are likely to be found on the inside of the protein structure? Why?
**c.** Which amino acids would be found on the outside of the protein? Why?
**d.** How does the primary structure of a protein affect its tertiary structure?

**19.32** In myoglobin, about one-half of the 153 amino acids have nonpolar R groups.
**a.** Where would you expect those amino acids to be located in the tertiary structure?
**b.** Where would you expect the polar R groups to be?
**c.** Why is myoglobin more soluble in water than silk or wool?

19.33 State whether the following statements describe the primary, secondary, tertiary, or quaternary protein structure:
**a.** R groups interact to form disulfide bonds or ionic bonds.
**b.** Peptide bonds join amino acids in a polypeptide chain.
**c.** Several polypeptides in a $\beta$-pleated sheet are held together by hydrogen bonds between adjacent chains.
**d.** Hydrogen bonding between amino acids in the same polypeptide gives a coiled shape to the protein.

**19.34** State whether the following statements describe the primary, secondary, tertiary, or quaternary protein structure:
**a.** Hydrophobic R groups seeking a nonpolar environment move toward the inside of the folded protein.
**b.** Protein chains of collagen form a triple helix.
**c.** An active protein contains four tertiary subunits.
**d.** In sickle-cell anemia, valine replaces glutamic acid in the $\beta$ chain.

# 19.6 Protein Hydrolysis and Denaturation

LEARNING GOAL

Describe the hydrolysis and denaturation of proteins.

TUTORIAL
Protein Demolition

Peptide bonds can be hydrolyzed to give individual amino acids. This process occurs in the stomach when enzymes such as pepsin or trypsin catalyze the hydrolysis of proteins to give amino acids. This hydrolysis disrupts the primary structure by breaking the covalent amide bonds that link the amino acids. In the digestion of proteins, the amino acids are absorbed through the intestinal walls and carried to the cells where they can be used to synthesize new proteins:

$$\overset{+}{H_3N}-\underset{\underset{CH_3}{|}}{CH}-\overset{\overset{O}{\|}}{C}-NH-CH_2-\overset{\overset{O}{\|}}{C}-NH-\underset{\underset{CH_2OH}{|}}{CH}-\overset{\overset{O}{\|}}{C}-O^-$$

Alanylglycylserine (Ala-Gly-Ser)

$$\Big\downarrow \; H_2O \;\; \text{Enzyme}$$

$$\overset{+}{H_3N}-\underset{\underset{CH_3}{|}}{CH}-\overset{\overset{O}{\|}}{C}-O^- + \overset{+}{H_3N}-CH_2-\overset{\overset{O}{\|}}{C}-O^- + \overset{+}{H_3N}-\underset{\underset{CH_2OH}{|}}{CH}-\overset{\overset{O}{\|}}{C}-O^-$$

Alanine (Ala) Glycine (Gly) Serine (Ser)

EXPLORE YOUR WORLD

### Denaturation of Milk Protein

Place some milk in each of five glasses. Add the following to the milk samples in glasses 1–4. The fifth glass of milk is a reference sample.

1. Vinegar, drop by drop. Stir.
2. One-half teaspoon of meat tenderizer. Stir.
3. One teaspoon of fresh pineapple juice. (Canned juice has been heated and cannot be used.)
4. One teaspoon of fresh pineapple juice after the juice is heated to boiling.

#### QUESTIONS

1. How did the appearance of the milk change in each of the samples?
2. What enzyme is listed on the package label of the tenderizer?
3. How does the effect of the heated pineapple juice compare with that of the fresh juice? Explain.
4. Why is cooked pineapple used when making gelatin (a protein) desserts?

## Denaturation of Proteins

**Denaturation** of a protein occurs when there is a disruption of any of the bonds that stabilize the secondary, tertiary, or quaternary structure. However, the covalent amide bonds of the primary structure are not affected.

The loss of secondary and tertiary structures occurs when conditions change, such as increasing the temperature or making the pH very acidic or basic. If the pH changes, the basic and acidic R groups lose their ionic charges and cannot form salt bridges, which causes a change in the shape of the protein. Denaturation can also occur with the addition of certain organic compounds or heavy metal ions, or through mechanical agitation.

When there is a disruption of the interactions between the R groups, a globular protein unfolds like a loose piece of cooked spaghetti. With the loss of its overall shape (tertiary structure), the protein is no longer biologically active. (See Figure 19.13.)

### Heat

Heat denatures proteins by breaking apart hydrogen bonds and the hydrophobic interactions between nonpolar R groups. Few proteins can remain biologically active above 50 °C. Whenever you cook food, you are using heat to denature protein. The nutritional value of the proteins in food is not changed, but they are made more digestible. High temperatures are also used to disinfect surgical instruments and gowns by denaturing the proteins of any bacteria present.

### Acids and Bases

When an acid or a base is added to a protein, the change in pH breaks down hydrogen bonds and disrupts the ionic bonds (salt bridges). In the preparation of yogurt and cheese, bacteria that produce lactic acid are added to denature the milk protein and produce solid casein. Tannic acid, a weak acid used in burn ointments, is used to coagulate proteins at the site of the burn, forming a protective cover and preventing further loss of fluid from the burn.

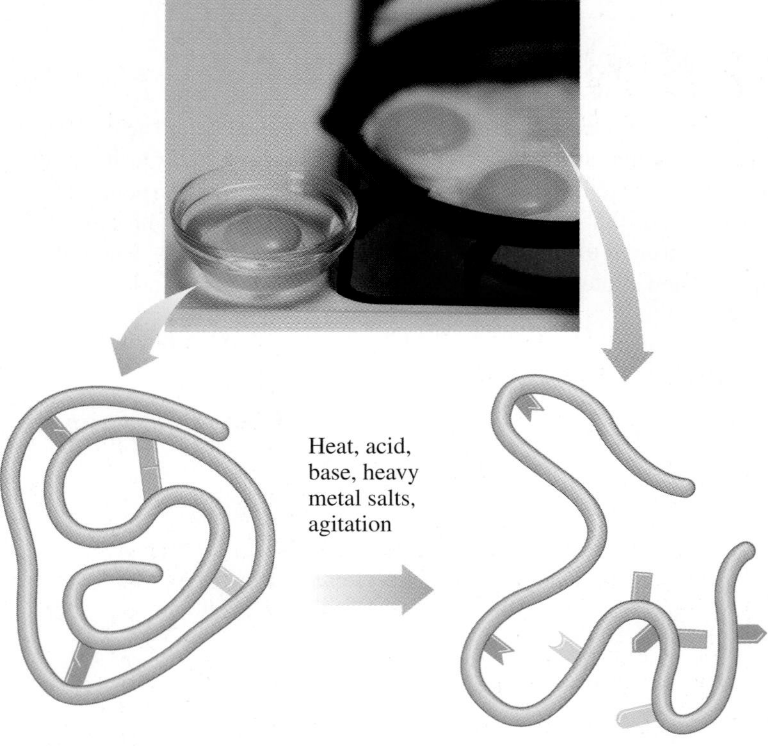


**FIGURE 19.13** Denaturation of a protein occurs when the bonds of the tertiary structure are disrupted, which destroys the shape and renders the protein biologically inactive.

Q What are some ways in which proteins are denatured?

## Organic Compounds

Ethanol and isopropyl alcohol act as disinfectants by forming their own hydrogen bonds with a protein and disrupting the hydrophobic interactions. An alcohol swab is used to clean wounds or to prepare the skin for an injection because the alcohol passes through the cell walls and coagulates the proteins inside the bacteria.

## Heavy Metal Ions

Heavy metal ions such as $Ag^{+}$, $Pb^{2+}$, and $Hg^{2+}$ denature protein by forming bonds with ionic R groups or reacting with disulfide (—S—S—) bonds. In hospitals, a dilute (1%) solution of $AgNO_3$ is placed in the eyes of newborn babies to destroy the bacteria that cause gonorrhea. If heavy metals are ingested, they act as poisons by severely denaturing body proteins and disrupting metabolic reactions. An antidote is a high-protein food such as milk, eggs, or cheese that combines with the heavy metal ions until the stomach can be pumped.

## Agitation

The whipping of cream and the beating of egg whites are examples of using mechanical agitation to denature protein. The whipping action stretches the polypeptide chains until the stabilizing interactions are disrupted.

CONCEPT CHECK 19.8

### Denaturation of Proteins

Describe the denaturation process in each of the following:

**a.** An appetizer known as ceviche is prepared without heat by placing slices of raw fish in a solution of lemon or lime juice. After 3 or 4 hours, the fish appears to be "cooked."

**b.** In baking sliced potatoes and milk to prepare scalloped potatoes, the milk curdles (forms solids).

ANSWER

**a.** The acids in lemon or lime juice break down the hydrogen bonds between polar R groups and disrupt salt bridges, which denature the proteins of the fish.

**b.** The heat during baking breaks apart hydrogen bonds and hydrophobic interactions between nonpolar R groups. When the milk denatures, the proteins become insoluble and form solids called curds.

SAMPLE PROBLEM 19.8

### Effects of Denaturation

What happens to the tertiary structure of a globular protein when it is placed in an acidic solution?

SOLUTION

An acid causes denaturation by disrupting the hydrogen bonds and the ionic bonds between the R groups. A loss in interactions causes the tertiary structure to lose stability. As the protein unfolds, both the shape and biological function are lost.

STUDY CHECK

Why is a dilute solution of $AgNO_3$ used to disinfect the eyes of newborn infants?

## QUESTIONS AND PROBLEMS

### Protein Hydrolysis and Denaturation

19.35 What products would result from the complete hydrolysis of Gly-Ala-Ser?

**19.36** Would the hydrolysis products of the tripeptide Ala-Ser-Gly be the same or different from the products in problem 19.35? Explain.

19.37 What dipeptides could be produced from the partial hydrolysis of His-Met-Gly-Val?

**19.38** What tripeptides could be produced from the partial hydrolysis of Ser-Leu-Gly-Gly-Ala?

19.39 What structural level of a protein is affected by hydrolysis?

**19.40** What structural level of a protein is affected by denaturation?

19.41 Indicate the changes in the secondary and tertiary structural levels of proteins for each of the following:

**a.** An egg placed in water at 100 °C is soft boiled in about 3 minutes.
**b.** Prior to giving an injection, the skin is wiped with an alcohol swab.
**c.** Surgical instruments are placed in a 120 °C autoclave.
**d.** During surgery, a wound is closed by cauterization (heat).

**19.42** Indicate the changes in the secondary and tertiary structural levels of proteins for each of the following:

**a.** Tannic acid is placed on a burn.
**b.** Milk is heated to 60 °C to make yogurt.
**c.** To avoid spoilage, seeds are treated with a solution of $HgCl_2$.
**d.** Hamburger is cooked at high temperatures to destroy *E. coli* bacteria that may cause intestinal illness.

## CONCEPT MAP

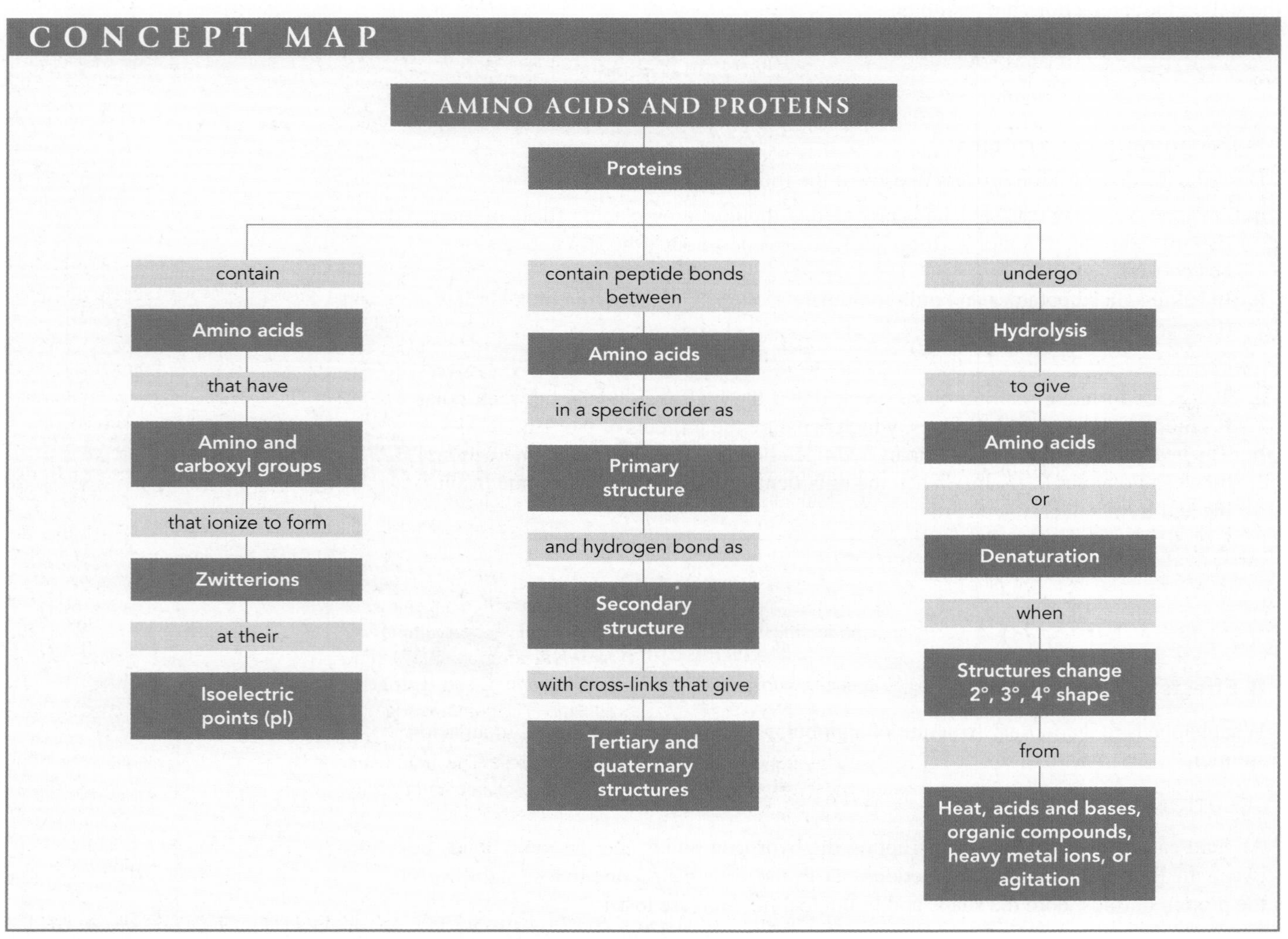

# CHAPTER REVIEW

## 19.1 Proteins and Amino Acids

**LEARNING GOAL:** *Classify proteins by their functions in the body. Give the name and abbreviation of an amino acid and draw its ionized structure.*

Some proteins are enzymes or hormones, whereas others are important in structure, transport, protection, storage, and muscle contraction. A group of 20 amino acids provides the molecular building blocks of proteins. Attached to the central $\alpha$ (alpha) carbon of each amino acid are an ammonium group, a carboxylate group, and a unique R group. The R group gives an amino acid the property of being nonpolar, polar, acidic, or basic.

## 19.2 Amino Acids as Zwitterions

**LEARNING GOAL:** *Draw the zwitterion of an amino acid at its isoelectric point and its ionized structure at pH values above or below its isoelectric point.*

Amino acids exist as dipolar ions called zwitterions, as positive ions at low pH, and as negative ions at high pH levels. At the isoelectric point, zwitterions have a net charge of zero.

## 19.3 Formation of Peptides

**LEARNING GOAL:** *Draw the condensed structural formula of a dipeptide.*

Peptides form when an amide bond links the carboxylate group of one amino acid and the ammonium group of a second amino acid. Long chains of amino acids are called proteins.

## 19.4 Protein Structure: Primary and Secondary Levels

**LEARNING GOAL:** *Describe the primary and secondary structures of a protein.*

The primary structure of a protein is its sequence of amino acids. In the secondary structure, hydrogen bonds between peptide groups produce a characteristic shape such as an $\alpha$ helix, $\beta$-pleated sheet, or a triple helix.

## 19.5 Protein Structure: Tertiary and Quaternary Levels

**LEARNING GOAL:** *Describe the tertiary and quaternary structures of a protein.*

In globular proteins, the polypeptide chain, including $\alpha$-helical and $\beta$-pleated sheet regions, folds upon itself to form a tertiary structure. A tertiary structure is stabilized by interactions that move hydrophobic R groups to the inside and hydrophilic R groups to the outside surface, and by attractions between R groups that form hydrogen bonds, disulfide bonds, and salt bridges. In a quaternary structure, two or more tertiary subunits must combine for biological activity. They are held together by the same interactions found in tertiary structures.

## 19.6 Protein Hydrolysis and Denaturation

**LEARNING GOAL:** *Describe the hydrolysis and denaturation of proteins.*

Denaturation of a protein occurs when heat or other denaturing agents destroy the structure of the protein (but not the primary structure) until biological activity is lost.

# KEY TERMS

**acidic amino acid** An amino acid that has an R group with a carboxylate ($—COO^-$) ion.

**$\alpha$ (alpha) helix** A secondary level of protein structure, in which hydrogen bonds connect the N—H of one peptide bond with the C=O of a peptide bond farther down the chain to form a coiled or corkscrew structure.

**$\alpha$-keratins** Fibrous proteins containing mostly $\alpha$ helices found in hair, nails, and skin.

**amino acid** The building block of proteins, consisting of an ammonium group, a carboxylate group, and a unique R group attached to the $\alpha$ carbon.

**basic amino acid** An amino acid that contains an R group with an ammonium ($—NH_3^+$) ion.

**$\beta$ (beta)-pleated sheet** A secondary level of protein structure that consists of hydrogen bonds between peptide links in parallel polypeptide chains.

**C terminal** The end amino acid in a peptide chain with a free carboxylate ($—COO^-$) group.

**collagen** The most abundant form of protein in the body, which is composed of fibrils of triple helices with hydrogen bonding between —OH groups of hydroxyproline and hydroxylysine.

**denaturation** The loss of secondary and tertiary protein structure caused by heat, acids, bases, organic compounds, heavy metals, and/or agitation.

**disulfide bonds** Covalent —S—S— bonds that form between the —SH groups of two cysteines in a protein to stabilize the tertiary structure.

**electrophoresis** The use of electrical current to separate proteins or other charged molecules with different isoelectric points.

**essential amino acids** Amino acids that must be supplied by the diet because they are not synthesized by the body.

**fibrous proteins** Proteins that are insoluble in water; consisting of polypeptide chains with $\alpha$ helices or $\beta$-pleated sheets, and comprising the fibers of hair, wool, skin, nails, and silk.

**globular proteins** Proteins that acquire a compact shape from attractions between the R groups of the amino acids in the protein.

**hydrogen bonds** The interactions between water and the polar R groups such as —OH, $—NH_2$, and —COOH on the outside surface of a polypeptide chain.

**hydrophilic interactions** The attractions between polar R groups on the protein surface and water.

**hydrophobic interactions** The attractions between nonpolar R groups on the inside of a globular protein.

**isoelectric point (pI)** The pH at which an amino acid exists as a zwitterion with a net charge of zero.

**N terminal** The end amino acid in a peptide with a free $—NH_3^+$ group.

**nonpolar amino acids** Amino acids with nonpolar R groups containing only C and H atoms.

**peptide** The combination of two or more amino acids joined by peptide bonds; dipeptide, tripeptide, and so on.

**peptide bond** The amide bond in peptides that joins the carboxylate group of one amino acid with the ammonium group in the next amino acid.

**polar amino acids (neutral)** Amino acids with polar R groups.

**primary structure** The specific sequence of the amino acids in a protein.

**protein** Polypeptides containing many amino acids linked together by peptide bonds that are biologically active.

**quaternary structure** A protein structure in which two or more protein subunits form an active protein.

**salt bridge** The attraction between the ionized R groups of basic and acidic amino acids in the tertiary structure of a protein.

**secondary structure** The formation of an $\alpha$ helix, $\beta$-pleated sheet, or triple helix.

**tertiary structure** The folding of the secondary structure of a protein into a compact structure that is stabilized by the interactions of R groups such as ionic and disulfide bonds.

**triple helix** The protein structure found in collagen consisting of three polypeptide chains woven together like a braid.

**zwitterion** The dipolar form of an amino acid consisting of two oppositely charged ionic regions, $-NH_3^+$ and $-COO^-$.

## UNDERSTANDING THE CONCEPTS

**19.43** Seeds and vegetables are often deficient in one or more essential amino acids. Using the following table, state whether the given combinations would provide the essential amino acids lysine, tryptophan, and methionine.

| Source | Lysine | Tryptophan | Methionine |
|---|---|---|---|
| Oatmeal | No | Yes | Yes |
| Rice | No | Yes | Yes |
| Garbanzo beans | Yes | No | Yes |
| Lima beans | Yes | No | No |
| Cornmeal | No | No | Yes |

**a.** rice and garbanzo beans
**b.** lima beans and cornmeal
**c.** a salad of garbanzo beans and lima beans

**19.44** Seeds and vegetables are often deficient in one or more essential amino acids. Using the table in question 19.43, state whether the following combinations would provide the essential amino acids lysine, tryptophan, and methionine:
**a.** rice and lima beans
**b.** rice and oatmeal
**c.** oatmeal and lima beans

Consider the following structures of cysteine to answer questions 19.45 and 19.46:

(1) $H_2N-CH(CH_2-SH)-COO^-$

(2) $H_3\overset{+}{N}-CH(CH_2-SH)-COOH$

(3) $H_3\overset{+}{N}-CH(CH_2-SH)-COO^-$

(4) $H_2N-CH(CH_2-SH)-COOH$

**19.45** If cysteine, an amino acid prevalent in hair, has a pI of 5.1, which structure would it have in solutions with the following pH values?
**a.** pH = 10.5 **b.** pH = 5.1 **c.** pH = 1.8

**19.46** If cysteine, an amino acid prevalent in hair, has a pI of 5.1, which structure would it have in solutions with the following pH values?
**a.** pH = 2.0 **b.** pH = 3.5 **c.** pH = 9.1

**19.47** For each of the following pairs of R groups, identify the amino acids and the type of cross-link that forms between them:

**a.** $-CH_2-\overset{O}{\overset{\|}{C}}-NH_2$ and $HO-CH_2-$

**b.** $-CH_2-\overset{O}{\overset{\|}{C}}-O^-$ and $H_3\overset{+}{N}-(CH_2)_4-$

**c.** $-CH_2-SH$ and $HS-CH_2-$

**d.** $-CH_2-\underset{}{\overset{CH_3}{\overset{|}{CH}}}-CH_3$ and $CH_3-$

**19.48** Consider a mixture of the amino acids lysine, valine, and aspartic acid at pH 6.0 that is subjected to an electric voltage.
**a.** Indicate which amino acid would migrate toward the positive electrode (+), the negative electrode (−), or remain stationary.

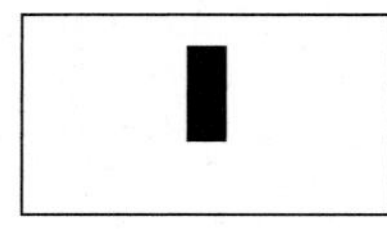

Mixture of amino acids

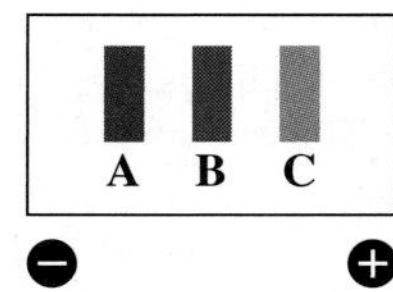


**b.** If the mixture is the result of hydrolyzing a tripeptide, what are the possible sequences if one unit of each amino acid is present?
**c.** If present in an enzyme, which of these amino acids would
1. be found in hydrophobic regions?
2. be found in hydrophilic regions?
3. form hydrogen bonds?
4. form salt bridges?
5. form disulfide bonds?

# ADDITIONAL QUESTIONS AND PROBLEMS

*For instructor-assigned homework, go to* ***www.masteringchemistry.com.***

19.49 **a.** What are some functions of $\alpha$-keratins?
**b.** What amino acids give strength to the $\alpha$-keratins?

**19.50 a.** Where is collagen found?
**b.** What type of secondary structure is used to form collagen?

19.51 **a.** Draw the condensed structural formula of Ser-Lys-Asp.
**b.** Would you expect to find this segment at the center or at the surface of a globular protein? Why?

**19.52 a.** Draw the condensed structural formula of Val-Ala-Leu.
**b.** Would you expect to find this segment at the center or at the surface of a globular protein? Why?

19.53 Would you expect the following segments in a polypeptide to have an $\alpha$ helix or $\beta$-pleated sheet secondary structure?
**a.** a segment with a high content of Val, Pro, and Ser
**b.** a segment with a high content of His, Met, and Leu

**19.54** What type of interaction would you expect between the following R groups in a tertiary structure?
**a.** threonine and asparagine
**b.** valine and alanine
**c.** arginine and aspartic acid

19.55 If serine were replaced by valine in a protein, how would the tertiary structure be affected?

**19.56** If you eat rice, what other vegetable protein source(s) could you eat to ingest all essential amino acids?

19.57 Draw the condensed structural formula of each of the following amino acids at pH 4:
**a.** serine **b.** alanine **c.** lysine

**19.58** Draw the condensed structural formula of each of the following amino acids at pH 11:
**a.** cysteine **b.** aspartic acid **c.** valine

# CHALLENGE QUESTIONS

19.59 Indicate the overall net charge (1−, 0, or 1+) for each of the following amino acids at the following pH values:
**a.** serine at pH 5.7
**b.** lysine at pH 7.7
**c.** methionine at pH 7.6
**d.** isoleucine at pH 3.0
**e.** leucine at pH 9.0

**19.60** Indicate the overall net charge (1−, 0, or 1+) for each of the following amino acids at the given pH values:
**a.** serine at pH 3.0
**b.** lysine at pH 9.7
**c.** methionine at pH 10.0
**d.** isoleucine at pH 8.5
**e.** leucine at pH 3.5

19.61 A mixture of cysteine, aspartic acid, and histidine are placed on a gel for electrophoresis. A buffer of pH 5.1 is placed on the gel.
**a.** Which amino acid will migrate toward the positive electrode?
**b.** Which amino acid will migrate toward the negative electrode?
**c.** Which amino acid will remain at the same place it was originally placed?

**19.62** The proteins placed on a gel for electrophoresis have the following isoelectric points: albumin, 4.9; hemoglobin, 6.8; and lysozyme, 11.0. A buffer of pH 6.8 is placed on the gel.
**a.** Which protein will migrate toward the positive electrode?
**b.** Which protein will migrate toward the negative electrode?
**c.** Which protein will remain at the same place it was originally placed?

19.63 What are some differences between each of the following?
**a.** secondary and tertiary protein structures
**b.** essential and nonessential amino acids
**c.** polar and nonpolar amino acids
**d.** dipeptides and tripeptides

**19.64** What are some differences between each of the following?
**a.** an ionic bond (salt bridge) and a disulfide bond
**b.** fibrous and globular proteins
**c.** $\alpha$ helix and $\beta$-pleated sheet
**d.** tertiary and quaternary structures of proteins

19.65 In the preparation of meringue for a pie, tartaric acid is added and the egg whites are whipped. What causes the meringue to form?

**19.66** How does denaturation of a protein differ from its hydrolysis?

# ANSWERS

## ANSWERS TO STUDY CHECKS

**19.1** **a.** polar **b.** polar

**19.2** In the Fischer projection of D-serine, the $-NH_3^+$ group is on the right side.

**19.3**

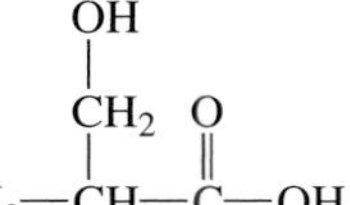


**19.4** tyrosylglycylglycylphenylalanylmethionine

**19.5** a triple helix

**19.6** Both are nonpolar and would be found on the inside of the tertiary structure.

**19.7** quaternary

**19.8** The heavy metal $Ag^+$ denatures the proteins in bacteria that cause gonorrhea.

## ANSWERS TO SELECTED QUESTIONS AND PROBLEMS

**19.1** **a.** transport **b.** structural
**c.** structural **d.** enzyme

**19.3** All amino acids contain a carboxylate group and an ammonium group on the $\alpha$ carbon.

**19.5**

**a.** $H_3\overset{+}{N}-CH(CH_3)-C(=O)-O^-$

**b.** $H_3\overset{+}{N}-CH(CH(OH)CH_3)-C(=O)-O^-$

**c.** $H_3\overset{+}{N}-CH(CH_2CH_2COO^-)-C(=O)-O^-$

**d.** $H_3\overset{+}{N}-CH(CH_2C_6H_5)-C(=O)-O^-$

**19.7** **a.** hydrophobic (nonpolar)
**b.** hydrophilic (polar, neutral)
**c.** hydrophilic (acidic)
**d.** hydrophobic (nonpolar)

**19.9** **a.** alanine **b.** valine
**c.** lysine **d.** cysteine

**19.11**

**a.** Fischer projection: $COO^-$ (top); $H_3\overset{+}{N}$ (left), H (right); $CH(CH_3)_2$ (bottom: CH with $H_3C$ and $CH_3$)

**b.** Fischer projection: $COO^-$ (top); H (left), $\overset{+}{N}H_3$ (right); $CH_2SH$ (bottom)

**19.13**

**a.** $H_3\overset{+}{N}-CH(H)-C(=O)-O^-$

**b.** $H_3\overset{+}{N}-CH(CH_2SH)-C(=O)-O^-$

**c.** $H_3\overset{+}{N}-CH(CH(OH)CH_3)-C(=O)-O^-$

**d.** $H_3\overset{+}{N}-CH(CH_3)-C(=O)-O^-$

**19.15**

**a.** $H_3\overset{+}{N}-CH(H)-C(=O)-OH$

**b.** $H_3\overset{+}{N}-CH(CH_2SH)-C(=O)-OH$

**c.** $H_3\overset{+}{N}-CH(CH(OH)CH_3)-C(=O)-OH$

**d.** $H_3\overset{+}{N}-CH(CH_3)-C(=O)-OH$

**19.17** **a.** above pI **b.** below pI **c.** at pI

**19.19**

**a.** $H_3\overset{+}{N}-CH(CH_3)-C(=O)-NH-CH(CH_2SH)-C(=O)-O^-$

Ala-Cys

**b.** $H_3\overset{+}{N}-CH(CH_2OH)-C(=O)-NH-CH(CH_2C_6H_5)-C(=O)-O^-$

Ser-Phe

**c.** $H_3\overset{+}{N}-CH(H)-C(=O)-NH-CH(CH_3)-C(=O)-NH-CH(CH(CH_3)_2)-C(=O)-O^-$

Gly-Ala-Val

**d.** $H_3\overset{+}{N}-CH(CH(CH_3)_2)-C(=O)-NH-CH(CH(CH_3)CH_2CH_3)-C(=O)-NH-CH(CH_2\text{-indolyl})-C(=O)-O^-$

Val-Ile-Trp

**19.21** Amide bonds form to connect the amino acids that make up the protein.

**19.23** Val-Ser-Ser, Ser-Val-Ser, or Ser-Ser-Val

**19.25** The primary structure remains unchanged and intact as hydrogen bonds form between carbonyl oxygen atoms and amino hydrogen atoms in the secondary structure.

**19.27** In the $\alpha$ helix, hydrogen bonds form between the carbonyl oxygen atom and the amino hydrogen atom in the next turn of the helix. In the $\beta$-pleated sheet, hydrogen bonds occur between parallel peptides or across sections of a long polypeptide chain.

**19.29** **a.** disulfide bond **b.** salt bridge
**c.** hydrogen bond **d.** hydrophobic interaction

**19.31** **a.** cysteine
**b.** Leucine and valine will be found on the inside of the protein because they are hydrophobic.
**c.** The cysteine and aspartic acid would be on the outside of the protein because they are polar.
**d.** The order of the amino acids (the primary structure) provides the R groups whose interactions determine the tertiary structure of the protein.

**19.33** **a.** tertiary and quaternary
**b.** primary **c.** secondary **d.** secondary

**19.35** The products would be the amino acids glycine, alanine, and serine.

**19.37** His-Met, Met-Gly, Gly-Val

**19.39** Hydrolysis splits the amide linkages in the primary structure.

**19.41** **a.** Placing an egg in boiling water coagulates the proteins of the egg by disrupting hydrogen bonds and hydrophobic interactions.
**b.** Using an alcohol swab coagulates the proteins of any bacteria present by forming hydrogen bonds and disrupting hydrophobic interactions.
**c.** The heat from an autoclave will coagulate the proteins of any bacteria on the surgical instruments by disrupting hydrogen bonds and hydrophobic interactions.
**d.** Heat will coagulate the surrounding proteins to close the wound by disrupting hydrogen bonds and hydrophobic interactions.

**19.43** **a.** yes **b.** no **c.** no

**19.45** **a.** (1) **b.** (3) **c.** (2)

**19.47** **a.** asparagine and serine, hydrogen bond
**b.** aspartic acid and lysine, salt bridge
**c.** cysteine and cysteine, disulfide bond
**d.** leucine and alanine, hydrophobic interaction

**19.49** **a.** α-Keratins are fibrous proteins that provide structure to hair, wool, skin, and nails.
**b.** α-Keratins have a high content of cysteine.

**19.51** **a.**

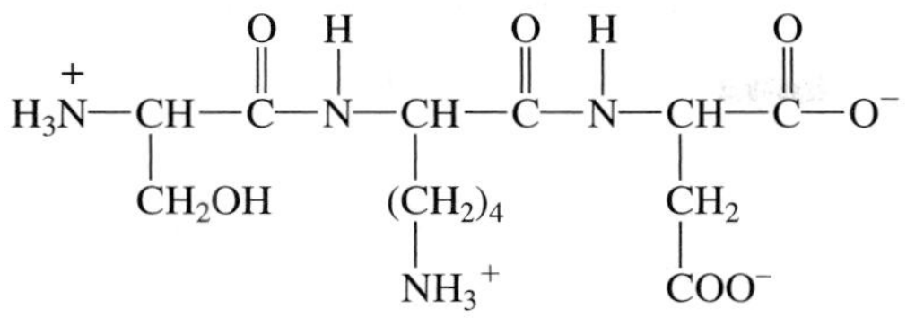

$$\overset{+}{H_3N}-\underset{\displaystyle CH_2OH}{\underset{|}{CH}}-\overset{\displaystyle O}{\overset{\|}{C}}-\overset{\displaystyle H}{\overset{|}{N}}-\underset{\displaystyle \underset{\displaystyle NH_3^+}{\underset{|}{(CH_2)_4}}}{\underset{|}{CH}}-\overset{\displaystyle O}{\overset{\|}{C}}-\overset{\displaystyle H}{\overset{|}{N}}-\underset{\displaystyle \underset{\displaystyle COO^-}{\underset{|}{CH_2}}}{\underset{|}{CH}}-\overset{\displaystyle O}{\overset{\|}{C}}-O^-$$

**b.** This segment contains polar R groups, which would be found on the surface of a globular protein where they hydrogen bond with water.

**19.53** **a.** β-pleated sheet **b.** α helix

**19.55** Serine is a polar amino acid, whereas valine is nonpolar. Serine would form hydrogen bonds with water on the outside surface of the protein. However, valine would pull that part of the peptide chain to the center of the tertiary structure where it forms hydrophobic interactions.

**19.57** **a.** $$H_3\overset{+}{N}-\underset{\displaystyle CH_2OH}{\underset{|}{CH}}-\overset{\displaystyle O}{\overset{\|}{C}}-OH$$

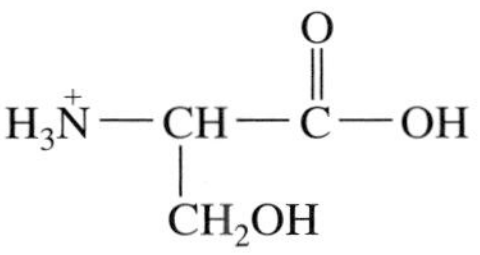

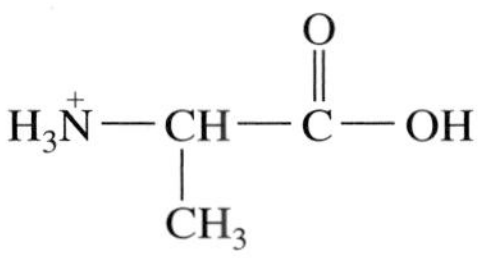

**b.** $$H_3\overset{+}{N}-\underset{\displaystyle CH_3}{\underset{|}{CH}}-\overset{\displaystyle O}{\overset{\|}{C}}-OH$$

**c.** $$H_3\overset{+}{N}-\underset{\displaystyle \underset{\displaystyle \overset{+}{N}H_3}{\underset{|}{(CH_2)_4}}}{\underset{|}{CH}}-\overset{\displaystyle O}{\overset{\|}{C}}-OH$$

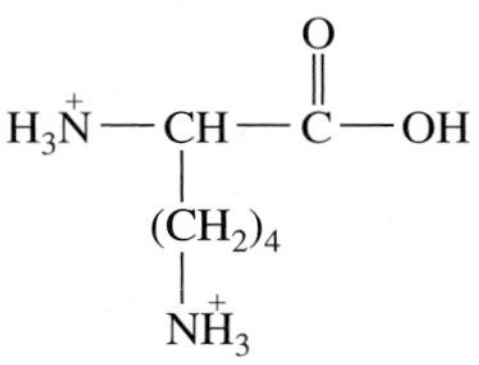

**19.59** **a.** 0 **b.** 1+ **c.** 1− **d.** 1+ **e.** 1−

**19.61** **a.** Aspartic acid (1−) will migrate to the positive electrode.
**b.** Histidine (1+) will migrate to the negative electrode.
**c.** Cysteine (0) will not move from where it is placed.

**19.63** **a.** In the secondary structure of proteins, hydrogen bonds form a helix or a pleated sheet; the tertiary structure is determined by hydrogen bonds as well as by disulfide bonds and salt bridges.
**b.** Nonessential amino acids can be synthesized by the body; essential amino acids must be supplied by the diet.
**c.** Polar amino acids have hydrophilic R groups, whereas nonpolar amino acids have hydrophobic R groups.
**d.** A dipeptide contains two amino acids, but a tripeptide contains three amino acids.

**19.65** The tartaric acid and the mechanical whipping (agitation) of the egg white denatures the proteins, which turn into solids as meringue.

# 20 Enzymes and Vitamins

## LOOKING AHEAD

**20.1** Enzymes

**20.2** Enzyme Action

**20.3** Factors Affecting Enzyme Activity

**20.4** Enzyme Inhibition

**20.5** Regulation of Enzyme Activity

**20.6** Enzyme Cofactors and Vitamins

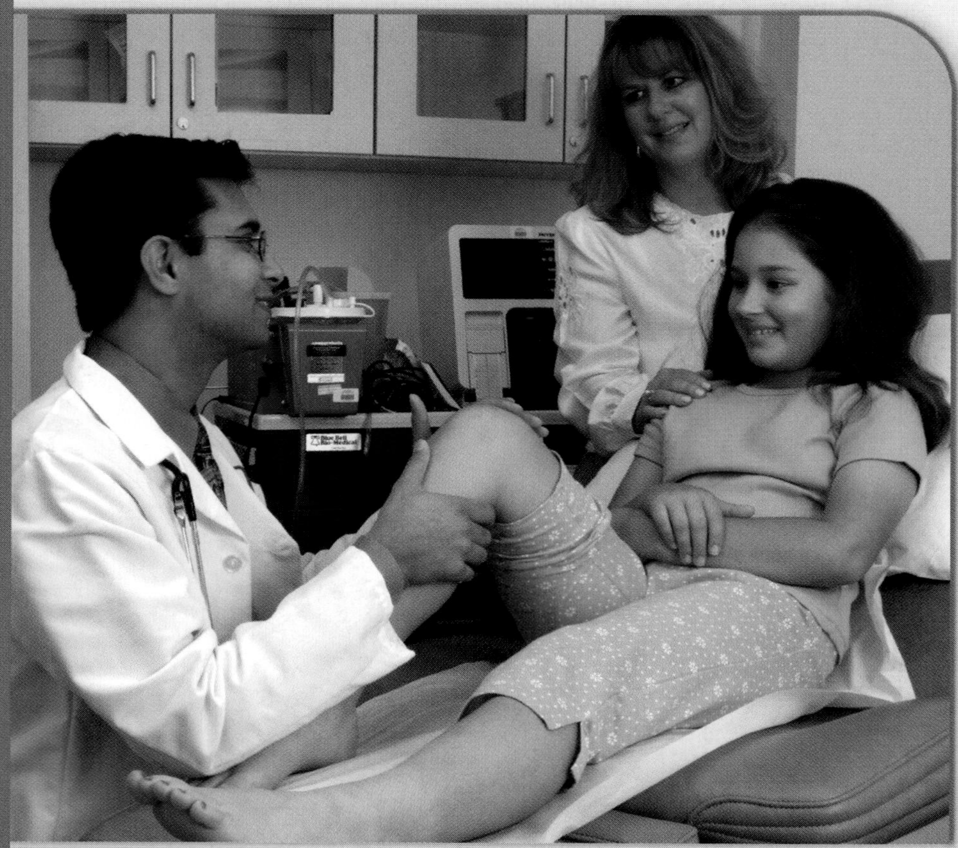

*"At a time when we have a shortage of health care professionals, I think of myself as a physician extender," says Pushpinder Beasley, orthopedic physician assistant, Kaiser Hospital. "We can put a significant amount of time into our patient care. Just today, I examined a child's knee. One of the most common injuries to children is disruption of either knee ligaments or the soft tissue around the knees. In this child's case, we were checking her anterior ligaments, also known as ACL. I think an important role of the health care professional is to earn the trust of young people."*

*As part of a health care team, physician assistants examine patients, order laboratory tests, make diagnoses, report patient progress, order therapeutic procedures, and, in most states, prescribe medications.*

Visit **www.masteringchemistry.com** for self-study materials and instructor-assigned homework.

Every second, thousands of chemical reactions occur in the cells of the human body. For example, many reactions occur to digest the food we eat, convert the products to chemical energy, and synthesize proteins and other macromolecules in our cells. In the laboratory, we can carry out reactions that hydrolyze polysaccharides, fats, or proteins, but we must use a strong acid or base, high temperatures, and long reaction times. In the cells of our body, these reactions must take place at rates that meet our physiological and metabolic needs. To make this happen, enzymes catalyze the chemical reactions in our cells, with a different enzyme for every reaction. Digestive enzymes in the mouth, stomach, and small intestine catalyze the hydrolysis of carbohydrate, fats, and proteins. Enzymes in the mitochondria extract energy from biomolecules to give us energy.

Every enzyme responds to what comes into the cells and to what the cells need. Enzymes keep reactions going when our cells need certain products and turn off reactions when they don't need those products.

Many enzymes require cofactors to function properly. Cofactors are inorganic metal ions (minerals) or organic compounds such as vitamins. We obtain minerals such as zinc ($Zn^{2+}$) and iron ($Fe^{3+}$) and vitamins from our diets. A lack of minerals and vitamins can lead to certain nutritional diseases. For example, rickets is a deficiency of vitamin D, and scurvy occurs when a diet is low in vitamin C.

## 20.1 Enzymes

LEARNING GOAL

Describe how enzymes function as catalysts; name and classify them.

Biological catalysts known as **enzymes** catalyze nearly all the chemical reactions that take place in the body. As we discussed in Chapter 9, a *catalyst* increases the rate of a reaction by changing the way a reaction takes place; the enzyme itself is not changed. An uncatalyzed reaction in a cell may take place eventually, but not at a rate fast enough for survival. For example, the hydrolysis of proteins in our diet would eventually occur without a catalyst, but the reactions would not occur fast enough to meet the body's requirements for amino acids. The chemical reactions in our cells must occur at incredibly fast rates under mild conditions of pH 7.4 and a body temperature of 37 °C. Enzymes permit cells to use energy and materials efficiently while responding to cellular needs.

As catalysts, enzymes lower the activation energy for a chemical reaction. (See Figure 20.1.) Less energy is required to convert reactant molecules to products, which increases the rate of a biochemical reaction compared to the rate of the uncatalyzed reaction. The rates of enzyme-catalyzed reactions are much faster than the rates of the uncatalyzed reactions. Some enzymes can increase the rate of a biological reaction by a factor of a billion, a trillion, or even a hundred million trillion compared to the rate of the uncatalyzed reaction. For example, an enzyme in the blood called carbonic anhydrase converts carbon dioxide and water to carbonic acid. In 1 minute, 1 molecule of carbonic anhydrase can catalyze the reaction of about 1 million molecules of carbon dioxide. An enzyme does not affect the equilibrium position, because the rates of both the forward and reverse directions increase.

$$CO_2 + H_2O \xrightleftharpoons{\text{Carbonic anhydrase}} H_2CO_3$$

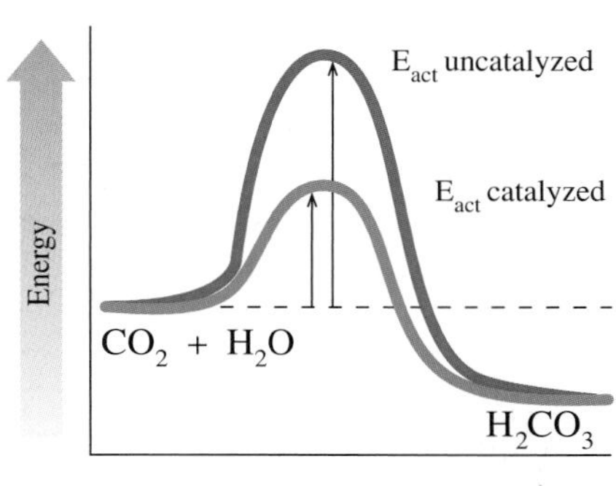


**FIGURE 20.1** The enzyme carbonic anhydrase lowers the activation energy needed for the reaction of $CO_2$ and $H_2O$.

Q Why are enzymes needed in biological reactions?

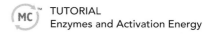

TUTORIAL
Enzymes and Activation Energy

### Names and Classification of Enzymes

The name of an enzyme describes the compound or the reaction that is catalyzed. The actual names of enzymes are derived by replacing the end of the name of the reaction or reacting compound with the suffix *ase*. For example, an *oxidase* is an enzyme that catalyzes an oxidation reaction, and a *dehydrogenase* is an enzyme that removes hydrogen atoms.

The enzyme named *sucrase* hydrolyzes the compound sucrose, and an enzyme named *lipase* hydrolyzes a lipid. Some enzymes use names that end in the suffix *in*, such as *papain* found in papaya; *rennin* found in milk; and *pepsin* and *trypsin*, enzymes that catalyze the hydrolysis of proteins.

The International Commission on Enzymes has classified enzymes according to the six general types of reactions they catalyze. (See Table 20.1.)

**TABLE 20.1 Classification of Enzymes**

| Class | Typical Subclass/Function |
|---|---|
| **1. Oxidoreductases**<br>Catalyze oxidation–reduction reactions | *Oxidases* oxidize a substance.<br>*Reductases* reduce a substance.<br>*Dehydrogenases* remove two H atoms to form a double bond. |
| $CH_3-CH_2-OH + NAD^+ \xrightarrow{\text{Alcohol dehydrogenase}} CH_3-C(=O)-H + NADH + H^+$<br>Ethanol, Coenzyme → Acetaldehyde, Coenzyme | |
| **2. Transferases**<br>Transfer groups between two compounds | *Transaminases* move amino groups between molecules.<br>*Kinases* move phosphate groups. |
| $CH_3-CH(NH_3^+)-COO^- + {}^-OOC-C(=O)-CH_2CH_2-COO^- \xrightleftharpoons{\text{Alanine transaminase}} CH_3-C(=O)-COO^- + {}^-OOC-CH(NH_3^+)-CH_2CH_2-COO^-$<br>Alanine, α-Ketoglutarate ⇌ Pyruvate, Glutamate | |
| **3. Hydrolases**<br>Add water to break bonds | *Peptidases* hydrolyze peptide bonds.<br>*Lipases* hydrolyze ester bonds in lipids.<br>*Amylases* hydrolyze 1,4-glycosidic bonds in amylose. |
| $-NH-CH(R)-C(=O)-NH-CH(R)-COO^- + H_2O \xrightarrow{\text{Peptidase}} -NH-CH(R)-C(=O)-O^- + H_3\overset{+}{N}-CH(R)-COO^-$<br>Polypeptide C terminal → Shorter polypeptide, Amino acid from C terminal | |
| **4. Lyases**<br>Add or remove groups without hydrolysis or oxidation that may result in a double bond | *Decarboxylases* remove $CO_2$.<br>*Hydrases* add $H_2O$.<br>*Dehydrases* remove $H_2O$.<br>*Deaminases* remove $NH_3$. |
| $CH_3-C(=O)-COO^- + H^+ \xrightarrow{\text{Pyruvate decarboxylase}} CH_3-C(=O)-H + CO_2$<br>Pyruvate → Acetaldehyde, Carbon dioxide | |
| **5. Isomerases**<br>Rearrange atoms to form isomers | *Isomerases* convert cis and trans bonds.<br>*Epimerases* convert D and L isomers. |
| Maleate (cis ${}^-OOC-CH=CH-COO^-$) $\xrightleftharpoons{\text{Maleate isomerase}}$ Fumarate (trans ${}^-OOC-CH=CH-COO^-$) | |
| **6. Ligases**<br>Join molecules using ATP energy<br>(See Section 22.2) | *Synthetases* combine molecules.<br>*Carboxylases* add $CO_2$. |
| ${}^-OOC-C(=O)-CH_3 + CO_2 + ATP \xrightarrow{\text{Pyruvate carboxylase}} {}^-OOC-C(=O)-CH_2-COO^- + ADP + P_i + H^+$<br>Pyruvate → Oxaloacetate | $P_i$ (inorganic phosphate $HPO_4^{2-}$) |

CONCEPT CHECK 20.1

## Classes of Enzymes

Identify the general class of enzyme that catalyzes each of the following reactions:

**a.** a kinase that moves a phosphate group from one reactant to another
**b.** a peptidase that hydrolyzes a peptide bond in a protein
**c.** a decarboxylase that removes a carbon as $CO_2$ from a reactant

ANSWER

**a.** A kinase that moves a phosphate group from one reactant to another is part of the *transferase* class of enzymes.
**b.** A peptidase that hydrolyzes a peptide bond in a protein is part of the *hydrolase* class of enzymes.
**c.** A decarboxylase that removes a carbon as $CO_2$ from a reactant is part of the *lyase* class of enzymes.

SAMPLE PROBLEM 20.1

## Naming Enzymes

What class of enzymes catalyzes each of the following?

**a.** the transfer of an amino group
**b.** the removal of hydrogen from lactate

SOLUTION

**a.** The class of enzymes called *transferases* includes enzymes that move functional groups, such as an amino group from one reactant to another.
**b.** The class of enzymes called *oxidoreductases* includes enzymes, such as lactate dehydrogenase, that remove two H atoms from lactate.

STUDY CHECK

What is the class of the enzyme lipase that catalyzes the hydrolysis of ester bonds in triglycerides?

# QUESTIONS AND PROBLEMS

## Enzymes

**20.1** Why do chemical reactions in the body require enzymes?

**20.2** How do enzymes make chemical reactions in the body proceed at faster rates?

**20.3** What type of reaction is catalyzed by each of the following classes of enzymes?
**a.** oxidoreductases **b.** transferases **c.** hydrolases

**20.4** What type of reaction is catalyzed by each of the following classes of enzymes?
**a.** lyases **b.** isomerases **c.** ligases

**20.5** What is the name of the class of enzymes that catalyzes each of the following reactions?
**a.** hydrolysis of sucrose
**b.** addition of oxygen
**c.** converting glucose ($C_6H_{12}O_6$) to fructose ($C_6H_{12}O_6$)
**d.** moving an amino group from one molecule to another

**20.6** What is the name of the class of enzymes that catalyzes each of the following reactions?
**a.** addition of water to a double bond
**b.** removing hydrogen atoms
**c.** splitting peptide bonds in proteins
**d.** removing $CO_2$ from pyruvate

**20.7** Identify the class of enzyme that catalyzes each of the following reactions:

**a.** 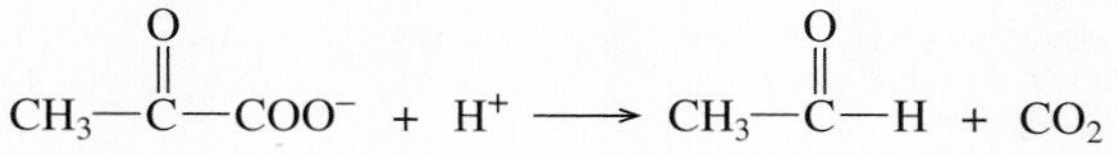 $CH_3-\overset{\overset{O}{\|}}{C}-COO^- + H^+ \longrightarrow CH_3-\overset{\overset{O}{\|}}{C}-H + CO_2$

**b.** 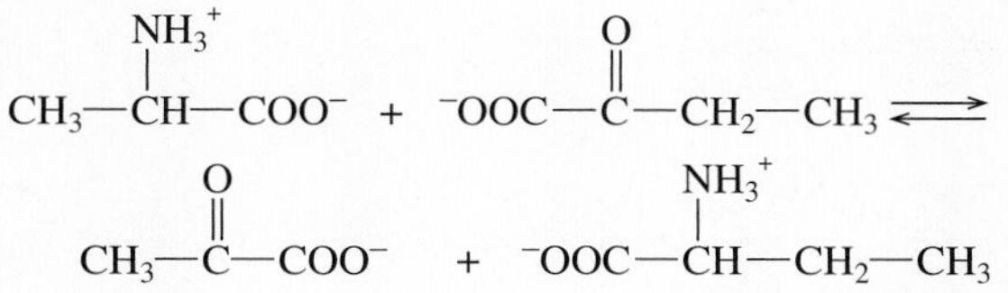 $CH_3-\overset{\overset{NH_3^+}{|}}{CH}-COO^- + {}^-OOC-\overset{\overset{O}{\|}}{C}-CH_2-CH_3 \rightleftharpoons CH_3-\overset{\overset{O}{\|}}{C}-COO^- + {}^-OOC-\overset{\overset{NH_3^+}{|}}{CH}-CH_2-CH_3$

**20.8** Identify the class of enzyme that catalyzes each of the following reactions:

**a.** $CH_3-\overset{\overset{O}{\|}}{C}-COO^- + CO_2 + ATP \longrightarrow$

$$^-OOC-CH_2-\overset{\overset{O}{\|}}{C}-COO^- + ADP + P_i$$

**b.** $CH_3-CH_2-OH + NAD^+ \longrightarrow$

$$CH_3-\overset{\overset{O}{\|}}{C}-H + NADH + H^+$$

**20.9** Name the enzyme that catalyzes each of the following reactions:
**a.** oxidizes succinate
**b.** adds water to fumarate
**c.** removes 2H from an alcohol

**20.10** Name the enzyme that catalyzes each of the following reactions:
**a.** hydrolyzes sucrose
**b.** transfers an amino group from aspartate
**c.** removes a carboxylate group from pyruvate

## 20.2 Enzyme Action

**LEARNING GOAL**

Describe the role of an enzyme in an enzyme-catalyzed reaction.

Nearly all enzymes are globular proteins. Each has a unique three-dimensional shape that recognizes and binds a small group of reacting molecules, which are called **substrates**. The tertiary structure of an enzyme plays an important role in how that enzyme catalyzes reactions.

MC™ SELF STUDY ACTIVITY
How Enzymes Work

### Active Site

In a catalyzed reaction, an enzyme must first bind to a substrate in a way that favors catalysis. A typical enzyme is much larger than its substrate. However, within the enzyme's large tertiary structure is a region called the **active site**, where the enzyme binds a substrate or substrates and catalyzes the reaction. (See Figure 20.2.) This active site is often a small pocket that closely fits the structure of the substrate. Within the active site, R groups from specific amino acids interact with the R groups on the substrate to form hydrogen bonds, salt bridges, and hydrophobic interactions. The active site of a particular enzyme fits the shape of only a few types of substrates, which makes the enzyme very specific about the type of substrate it binds.

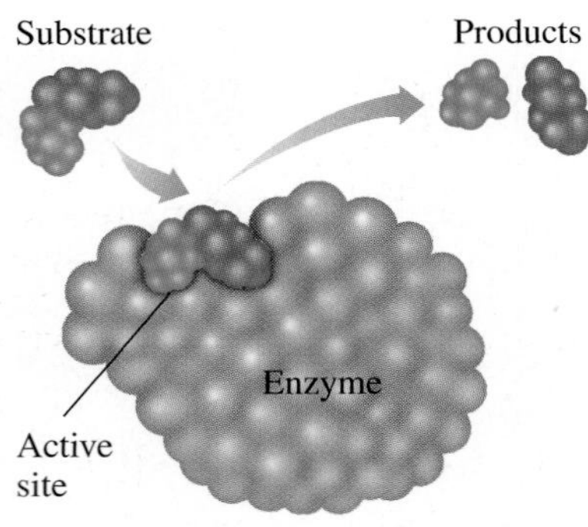


**FIGURE 20.2** On the surface of an enzyme, a small region called an active site binds a substrate and catalyzes a reaction of that substrate.

Q Why does an enzyme catalyze a reaction of only certain substrates?

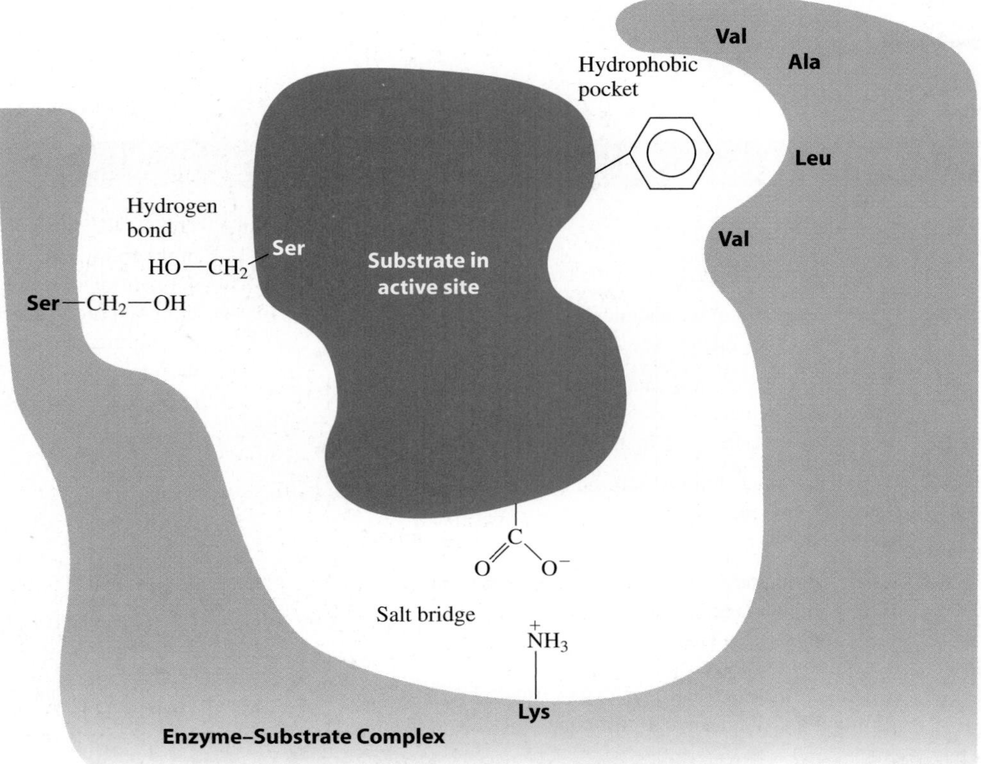

TABLE 20.2 Types of Enzyme Specificity

| Type | Reaction Type | Example |
|---|---|---|
| Absolute | Catalyze one type of reaction for a single substrate | Urease catalyzes only the hydrolysis of urea. |
| Group | Catalyze one type of reaction for similar substrates | Hexokinase adds a phosphate group to hexoses. |
| Linkage | Catalyze one type of reaction for a specific type of bond | Chymotrypsin catalyzes the hydrolysis of peptide bonds. |

Some enzymes show absolute specificity by catalyzing only one reaction of one specific substrate. Other enzymes catalyze a reaction for a group of substrates. Still other enzymes catalyze a reaction for a specific type of bond in a substrate. Types of enzyme specificity are listed in Table 20.2.

## Enzyme-Catalyzed Reaction

The proper alignment of a substrate within the active site forms an **enzyme–substrate (ES) complex**. This combination of an enzyme and a substrate provides an alternative pathway for the reaction with a lower activation energy. Within the active site, amino acid side chains take part in catalyzing the chemical reaction. For example, acidic and basic side chains remove protons from or provide protons for the substrate. As soon as the catalyzed reaction is complete, the products are released from the enzyme so it can bind to a new substrate molecule.

We can write the catalyzed reaction of an enzyme (E) with a substrate (S) to form product (P) as follows:

**Step 1** $E + S \rightleftharpoons ES$

**Step 2** $ES \longrightarrow E + P$

$$\underset{\text{Enzyme + substrate}}{E + S} \rightleftharpoons \underset{\text{ES complex}}{ES} \longrightarrow \underset{\text{Enzyme + product}}{E + P}$$

Let's consider the hydrolysis of sucrose by sucrase. When a molecule of sucrose binds to the active site of sucrase, its glycosidic bond is in a position favorable for reaction. The amino acid side chains catalyze the hydrolysis of sucrose with water to give the products glucose and fructose.

$$\underset{\text{Sucrase + sucrose}}{E + S} \rightleftharpoons \underset{\text{sucrase–sucrose complex}}{\text{ES complex}} \longrightarrow \underset{\text{sucrase + glucose + fructose}}{E + P_1 + P_2}$$

Because the structures of the products are no longer attracted to the active site, they are released, and the sucrase binds another sucrose substrate. (See Figure 20.3.)

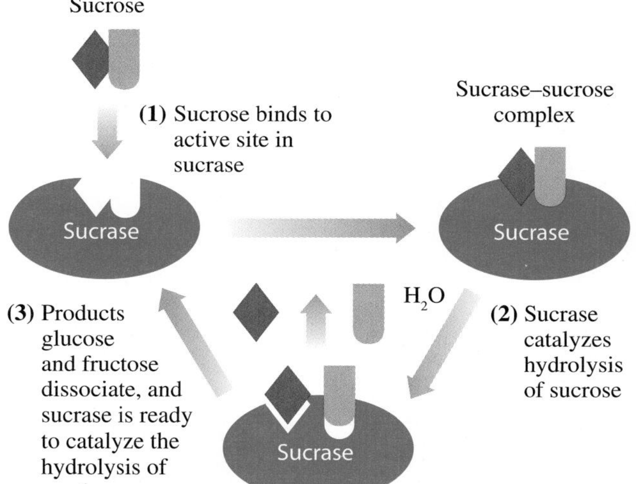
Sucrose
(1) Sucrose binds to active site in sucrase
Sucrase
Sucrase–sucrose complex
Sucrase
$H_2O$
(2) Sucrase catalyzes hydrolysis of sucrose
(3) Products glucose and fructose dissociate, and sucrase is ready to catalyze the hydrolysis of another sucrose
Sucrase

FIGURE 20.3 At the active site, sucrose is aligned for the hydrolysis reaction. The monosaccharides produced dissociate from the active site, and the enzyme is ready to bind to another sucrose molecule.

Q Why does the enzyme-catalyzed hydrolysis of sucrose go faster than the hydrolysis of sucrose in the chemistry laboratory?

## Lock-and-Key and Induced-Fit Models

An early theory of enzyme action, called the **lock-and-key model**, described the active site as having a rigid, nonflexible shape. Thus, only those substrates with shapes that fit exactly into the active site are able to bind with that enzyme. The shape of the active site is analogous to a lock, and the proper substrate is the key that fits into the lock. (See Figure 20.4a.)

While the lock-and-key model explains the binding of substrates for many enzymes, certain enzymes have a broader range of specificity than the lock-and-key model allows. In the **induced-fit model**, there is an interaction between both the enzyme and substrate. (See Figure 20.4b.) The active site adjusts to fit the shape of the substrate more closely. At the same time, the substrate adjusts its shape to better adapt to the geometry of the active site. As a result, the reacting section of the substrate becomes aligned exactly with the groups in the active site that catalyze the reaction.

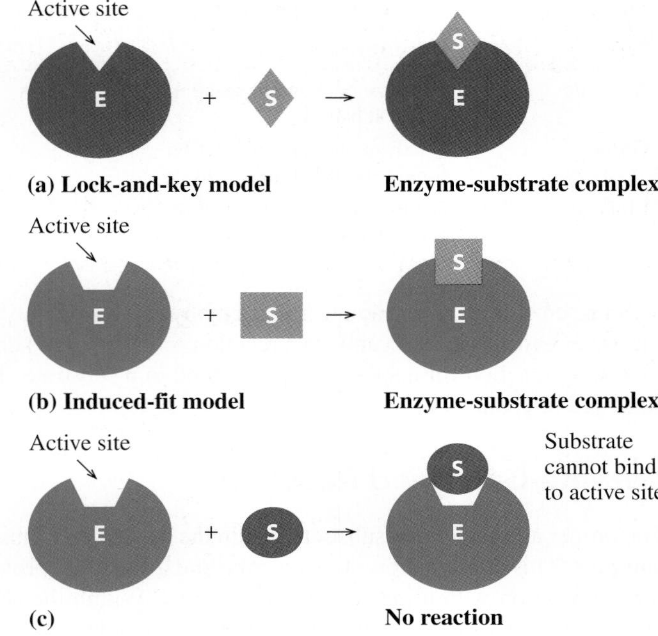


**FIGURE 20.4** **(a)** In the lock-and-key model, a substrate fits the shape of the active site and forms an enzyme–substrate complex. **(b)** In the induced-fit model, a flexible active site and substrate adjust shape to provide the best fit for the reaction. **(c)** A substrate that does not fit or induce a fit in the active site cannot undergo catalysis by the enzyme.

Q How does the induced-fit model differ from the lock-and-key model?

In the induced-fit model, substrate and enzyme work together to acquire a geometrical arrangement that lowers the activation energy. A different substrate would not induce these structural changes, and no catalysis would occur. (See Figure 20.4c.)

CONCEPT CHECK 20.2

### Specificity of Enzymes

Why would the lock-and-key model of enzyme action explain why certain enzymes have absolute specificity, but the induced-fit model would explain why other enzymes have group specificity?

ANSWER

In the lock-and-key model of enzyme action, the shape of the substrate must fit the active site precisely. Therefore, an enzyme that has absolute specificity reacts with only a single substrate. In the induced-fit model, the shapes of an active site and substrate adjust to give the best fit to catalyze a reaction. An enzyme with group specificity can catalyze substrates that have similar shapes.

SAMPLE PROBLEM 20.2

### The Enzyme Active Site

What is the function of the active site in an enzyme?

SOLUTION

The R groups of the active site bind the substrate by forming hydrogen bonds, salt bridges, and hydrophobic interactions with the substrate and catalyze the reaction.

STUDY CHECK

How do the lock-and-key and the induced-fit models differ in their description of the active site in an enzyme?

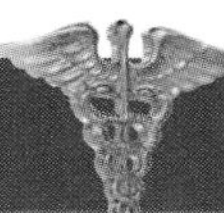

# HEALTH NOTE

## Isoenzymes as Diagnostic Tools

*Isoenzymes* are different forms of an enzyme that catalyze the same reaction in different cells or tissues of the body. Isoenzymes consist of quaternary structures with slight variations in the amino acids in the polypeptide subunits. For example, five isoenzymes of *lactate dehydrogenase (LDH)* catalyze the conversion between lactate and pyruvate.

$$\underset{\text{Lactate}}{CH_3-\overset{\displaystyle OH}{\overset{|}{C}H}-COO^-} \xrightleftharpoons{\text{Lactate dehydrogenase}} \underset{\text{Pyruvate}}{CH_3-\overset{\displaystyle O}{\overset{\|}{C}}-COO^-} + 2H$$

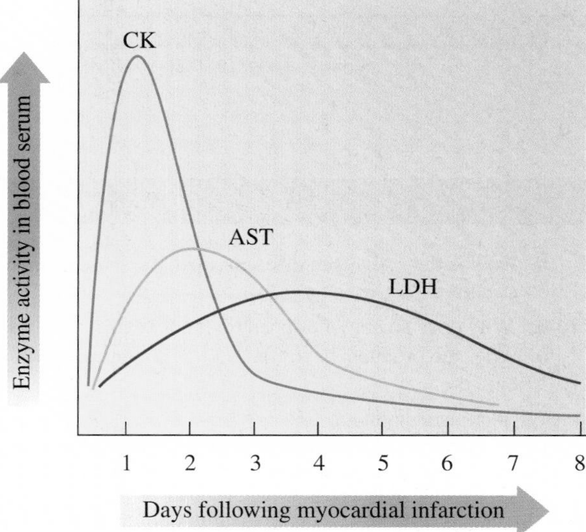


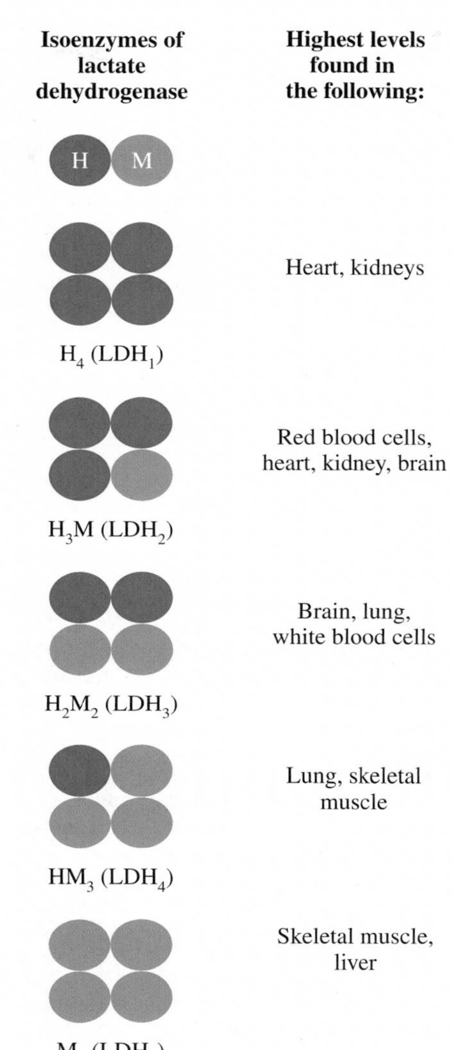


Each LDH isoenzyme contains a mix of polypeptide subunits, M and H. In the liver and muscle, lactate is converted to pyruvate by the $LDH_5$ isoenzyme with four M subunits, designated $M_4$. In the heart, the same reaction is catalyzed by the $LDH_1$ isoenzyme ($H_4$) containing four H subunits. Different combinations of the M and H subunits are found in the LDH isoenzymes of the brain, red blood cells, kidney, and white blood cells.

The different forms of an enzyme allow a medical diagnosis of damage or disease to a particular organ or tissue. In healthy tissues, isoenzymes function within the cells. However, when a disease damages a particular organ, cells die, which releases cell contents including the isoenzymes into the blood. Measurements of the elevated levels of specific isoenzymes in the blood serum help to identify the disease and its location in the body. For example, an elevation in the serum $LDH_5$, which is the $M_4$ isoenzyme of lactate dehydrogenase, indicates liver damage or disease. When a myocardial infarction (MI), or heart attack, damages the cells in heart muscle, an increase in the level of $LDH_1$ ($H_4$) isoenzyme is detected in the blood serum. (See Table 20.3.)

**TABLE 20.3 Isoenzymes of Lactate Dehydrogenase and Creatine Kinase**

| Isoenzyme | Abundant in | Subunits |
|---|---|---|
| **Lactate Dehydrogenase (LDH)** | | |
| $LDH_1$ | Heart, kidneys | $H_4$ |
| $LDH_2$ | Red blood cells, heart, kidney, brain | $H_3M$ |
| $LDH_3$ | Brain, lung, white blood cells | $H_2M_2$ |
| $LDH_4$ | Lung, skeletal muscle | $HM_3$ |
| $LDH_5$ | Skeletal muscle, liver | $M_4$ |
| **Creatine Kinase (CK)** | | |
| $CK_1$ | Brain, lung | BB |
| $CK_2$ | Heart | MB |
| $CK_3$ | Skeletal muscle, red blood cells | MM |

## HEALTH NOTE (CONTINUED)

### Isoenzymes as Diagnostic Tools *(Continued)*

Another isoenzyme used diagnostically is creatine kinase (CK), which consists of two types of polypeptide subunits. Subunit B is prevalent in the brain, and subunit M predominates in muscle. Normally only $CK_3$ (subunits MM) is present in low amounts in the blood serum. However, in a patient who has suffered a myocardial infarction (MI), the level of $CK_2$ (subunits MB) is elevated within 4–6 hours and reaches a peak in about 24 hours. Table 20.4 lists some enzymes used to diagnose tissue damage and diseases of certain organs.

**TABLE 20.4** Serum Enzymes Used in Diagnosis of Tissue Damage

| Condition | Diagnostic Enzymes Elevated |
|---|---|
| Heart attack or liver disease (cirrhosis, hepatitis) | Lactate dehydrogenase (LDH)<br>Aspartate transaminase (AST) |
| Heart attack | Creatine kinase (CK) |
| Hepatitis | Alanine transaminase (ALT) |
| Liver (carcinoma) or bone disease (rickets) | Alkaline phosphatase (ALP) |
| Pancreatic disease | Amylase, cholinesterase, lipase (LPS) |
| Prostate carcinoma | Acid phosphatase (ACP)<br>Prostate specific antigen (PSA) |

## QUESTIONS AND PROBLEMS

### Enzyme Action

20.11 Match the terms, (1) enzyme–substrate complex, (2) enzyme, and (3) substrate, with each of the following:
- **a.** has a tertiary structure that recognizes the substrate
- **b.** the combination of an enzyme with the substrate
- **c.** has a structure that fits the active site of an enzyme

**20.12** Match the terms, (1) active site, (2) lock-and-key model, and (3) induced-fit model, with each of the following:
- **a.** the portion of an enzyme where catalytic activity occurs
- **b.** an active site that adapts to the shape of a substrate
- **c.** an active site that has a rigid shape

20.13 **a.** Write an equation that represents an enzyme-catalyzed reaction.
**b.** How is the active site different from the whole enzyme structure?

**20.14 a.** Why does an enzyme speed up the reaction of a substrate?
**b.** After the products have formed, what happens to the enzyme?

20.15 What are isoenzymes?

**20.16** How is the LDH isoenzyme in the heart different from the LDH isoenzyme in the liver?

20.17 A patient arrives in emergency complaining of chest pains. What enzymes would you test for in the blood serum?

**20.18** A patient who is an alcoholic has elevated levels of LDH and AST. What condition might be indicated?

# 20.3 Factors Affecting Enzyme Activity

LEARNING GOAL

**Describe the effect of temperature, pH, concentration of enzyme, and concentration of substrate on enzyme activity.**

The **activity** of an enzyme describes how fast an enzyme catalyzes the reaction that converts a substrate to product. This activity is strongly affected by reaction conditions, which include the temperature, pH, concentration of the substrate, and concentration of the enzyme. (See Section 19.6 to review the conditions that denature proteins.)

## Temperature

TUTORIAL
Denaturation and Enzyme Activity

Enzymes are very sensitive to temperature. At low temperatures, most enzymes show little activity because there is not a sufficient amount of energy for the catalyzed reaction to take place. At higher temperatures, enzyme activity increases as reacting molecules move faster to cause more collisions with enzymes. Enzymes are most active at **optimum temperature**, which is 37 °C, or body temperature, for most enzymes. (See Figure 20.5.) At temperatures above 50 °C, the tertiary structure, and thus the shape of most proteins, is

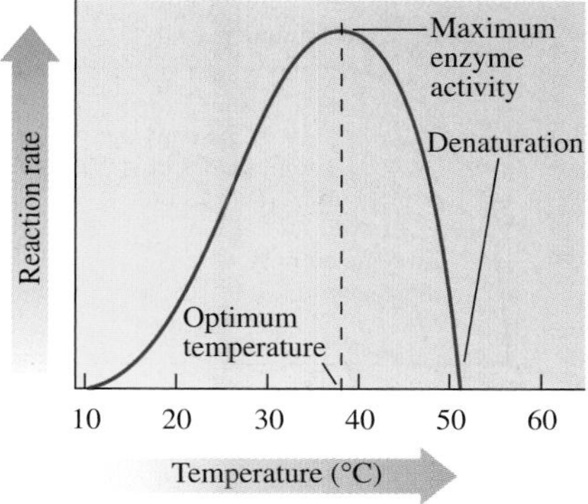


**FIGURE 20.5** An enzyme attains maximum activity at its optimum temperature, usually 37 °C. Lower temperatures slow the rate of reaction, and temperatures above 50 °C denature an enzyme, resulting in a loss of catalytic activity.

Q Why is 37 °C the optimum temperature for many enzymes?

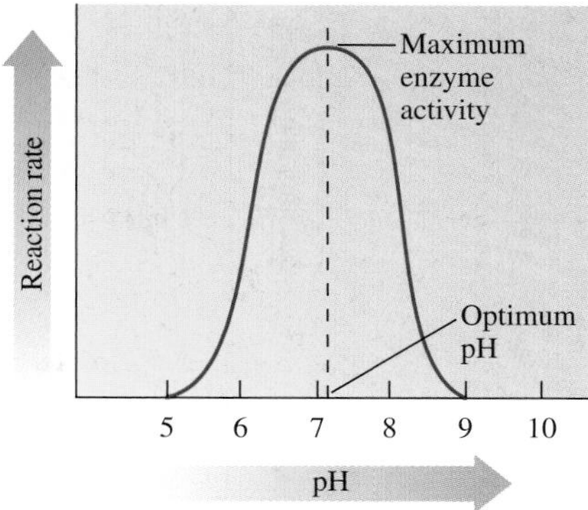


**FIGURE 20.6** Enzymes are most active at their optimum pH. At a higher or lower pH, denaturation of the enzyme causes a loss of catalytic activity.

Q Why does the digestive enzyme pepsin have an optimum pH of 2?

destroyed, which causes a loss in enzyme activity. For this reason, equipment in hospitals and laboratories is sterilized in autoclaves where the high temperatures denature the enzymes in harmful bacteria. A high fever in the body may be helpful in denaturing enzymes in bacteria that cause infection.

## pH

Enzymes are most active at their **optimum pH**, the pH that maintains the proper tertiary structure of the protein. (See Figure 20.6.) If a pH value is above or below the optimum pH, the R group interactions are disrupted, which destroys the tertiary structure and the active site. As a result, the enzyme no longer binds substrate properly, and no reaction occurs. Small changes in pH can be reversed that permit an enzyme to regain its structure and activity. However, large variations from optimum pH permanently destroy the structure of the enzyme.

Enzymes in most cells have optimum pH values at physiological pH around 7.4. However, enzymes in the stomach have a low optimum pH because they hydrolyze proteins at the acidic pH in the stomach. For example, pepsin, a digestive enzyme in the stomach, has an optimum pH of 1.5–2. Between meals, the pH in the stomach is 4 or 5, and pepsin shows little or no digestive activity. When food enters the stomach, the secretion of HCl lowers the pH to about 2, which activates pepsin. Table 20.5 lists the optimum pH values for selected enzymes.

**TABLE 20.5** Optimum pH for Selected Enzymes

| Enzyme | Location | Substrate | Optimum pH |
|---|---|---|---|
| Pepsin | Stomach | Peptide bonds | 1.5–2.0 |
| Sucrase | Small intestine | Sucrose | 6.2 |
| Amylase | Pancreas | Amylose | 6.7–7.0 |
| Urease | Liver | Urea | 7.0 |
| Trypsin | Small intestine | Peptide bonds | 7.7–8.0 |
| Lipase | Pancreas | Lipid (ester bonds) | 8.0 |
| Arginase | Liver | Arginine | 9.7 |

### Enzyme Activity

The enzymes on the surface of a freshly cut apple, avocado, or banana react with oxygen in the air to turn the surface brown. An antioxidant, such as vitamin C in lemon juice, prevents the oxidation reaction. Cut an apple, an avocado, or a banana into several slices. Place one slice in a plastic zipper bag, squeeze out all the air, and close the zipper lock. Dip another slice in lemon juice and place it on a plate. Sprinkle another slice with a crushed vitamin C tablet. Leave another slice alone as a control. Observe the surface of each of your samples. Record your observations immediately, then every hour for 6 hours or longer.

**QUESTIONS**

1. Which slice(s) shows the most oxidation (turns brown)?
2. Which slice(s) shows little or no oxidation?
3. How was the oxidation reaction on each slice affected by treatment with an antioxidant?

## Enzyme and Substrate Concentration

In any catalyzed reaction, the substrate must first bind with the enzyme to form the enzyme–substrate complex. For a particular substrate concentration, an increase in enzyme concentration increases the rate of the catalyzed reaction. At higher enzyme concentrations,

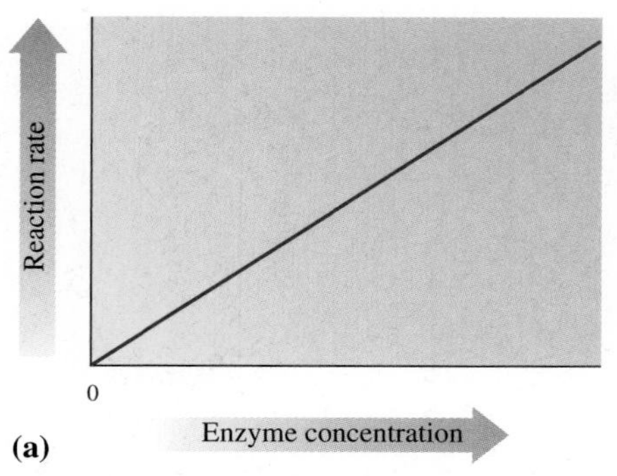


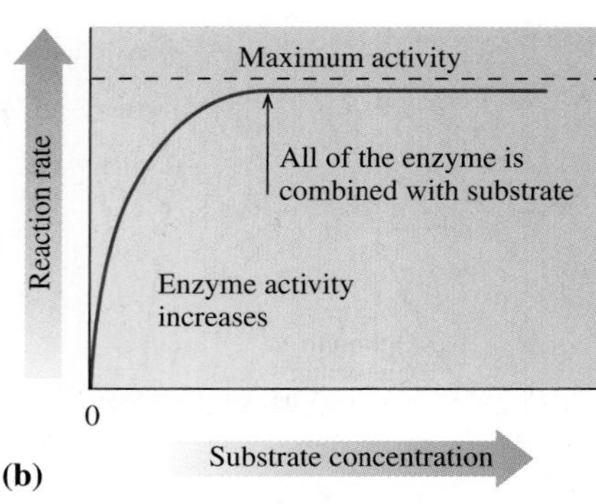


**FIGURE 20.7** **(a)** The rate of reaction increases when the enzyme concentration increases with substrate. **(b)** Increasing the substrate concentration increases the rate of reaction until the enzyme molecules are saturated with substrate.

**Q** What happens to the rate of reaction when substrate saturates the enzyme?

MC TUTORIAL
Enzyme and Substrate Concentrations

more molecules are available to bind and catalyze the reaction. As long as the substrate concentration is greater than the enzyme concentration, there is a direct relationship between the enzyme concentration and enzyme activity. (See Figure 20.7a.)

For a particular enzyme concentration, an increase in substrate increases the rate of the reaction until all the enzymes molecules are involved in catalyzing the reaction continuously. When the substrate concentration is high enough to bind with all the enzyme molecules, the rate of the catalyzed reaction reaches a maximum. After that, the addition of more substrate does not increase the rate. (See Figure 20.7b.)

CONCEPT CHECK 20.3

### Enzyme Activity

Describe how each of the following affects the activity of an enzyme:

**a.** decreasing the pH from the optimum pH
**b.** increasing the temperature from the optimum temperature
**c.** increasing the substrate concentration at constant temperature and pH

ANSWER

**a.** A more acidic environment disrupts the hydrogen bonds and salt bridges of the tertiary structure, which causes a loss of enzyme activity.
**b.** When the temperature is increased above the optimum temperature, the tertiary structure breaks down (denaturation), the shape of the active site deteriorates, and enzyme activity is lost.
**c.** An increase in a substrate concentration increases the rate of reaction until all the enzyme is combining with substrate continuously. Then the reaction rate is constant.

SAMPLE PROBLEM 20.3

### Factors Affecting Enzymatic Activity

Describe what effect the following changes would have on the rate of the reaction catalyzed by urease:

$$H_2N{-}\overset{\overset{\displaystyle O}{\|}}{C}{-}NH_2 + H_2O \xrightarrow{\text{Urease}} 2NH_3 + CO_2$$

Urea

**a.** increasing the urea concentration
**b.** lowering the temperature to 10 °C

SOLUTION

**a.** An increase in urea concentration will increase the rate of reaction until all the enzyme molecules bind to urea. Then no further increase in rate occurs.

**b.** Because 10 °C is lower than the optimum temperature of 37 °C, there is a decrease in the rate of the reaction.

STUDY CHECK

If urease has an optimum pH of 7.0, what is the effect of lowering the pH to 3.0?

## QUESTIONS AND PROBLEMS

### Factors Affecting Enzyme Action

**20.19** Trypsin, a peptidase that hydrolyzes polypeptides, functions in the small intestine at an optimum pH of 7.7–8.0. How is the rate of a trypsin-catalyzed reaction affected by each of the following conditions?

**a.** lowering the concentration of polypeptides
**b.** changing the pH to 3.0
**c.** running the reaction at 75 °C
**d.** adding more trypsin

**20.20** Pepsin, a peptidase that hydrolyzes proteins, functions in the stomach at an optimum pH of 1.5–2.0. How is the rate of a pepsin-catalyzed reaction affected by each of the following conditions?

**a.** increasing the concentration of proteins
**b.** changing the pH to 5.0
**c.** running the reaction at 0 °C
**d.** using less pepsin

**20.21** The following graph shows the curves for pepsin, sucrase, and trypsin. Estimate the optimum pH for each.

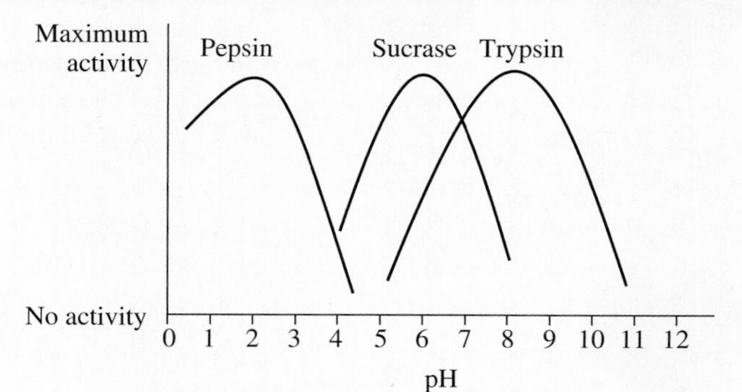


**20.22** Refer to the graph in problem 20.21 to determine if the reaction rate in each condition will be at the optimum rate or not.

**a.** trypsin, pH 5.0
**b.** sucrase, pH 5.0
**c.** pepsin, pH 4.0
**d.** trypsin, pH 8.0
**e.** pepsin, pH 2.0

# 20.4 Enzyme Inhibition

LEARNING GOAL

Describe competitive and noncompetitive inhibition and reversible and irreversible inhibition.

TUTORIAL
Enzyme Inhibition

Many kinds of molecules called **inhibitors** cause enzymes to lose catalytic activity. Although inhibitors act differently, they all prevent the active site from binding with a substrate. An enzyme with a reversible inhibitor can regain enzymatic activity, but an enzyme attached to an irreversible inhibitor loses enzymatic activity permanently.

## Reversible Inhibition

In **reversible inhibition**, an inhibitor causes a loss of enzymatic activity that can be reversed. A reversible inhibitor can act in different ways but does not form covalent bonds with the enzyme. Reversible inhibition can be competitive or noncompetitive. In competitive inhibition, an inhibitor competes for the active site, whereas in noncompetitive inhibition, the inhibitor acts on a site that is not the active site.

A **competitive inhibitor** has a structure that is so similar to the substrate it can bond to the enzyme just like the substrate. Thus, the competitive inhibitor competes with the substrate for the active site on the enzyme. As long as the inhibitor occupies the active site, the substrate cannot bind to the enzyme, and no reaction takes place. (See Figure 20.8.)

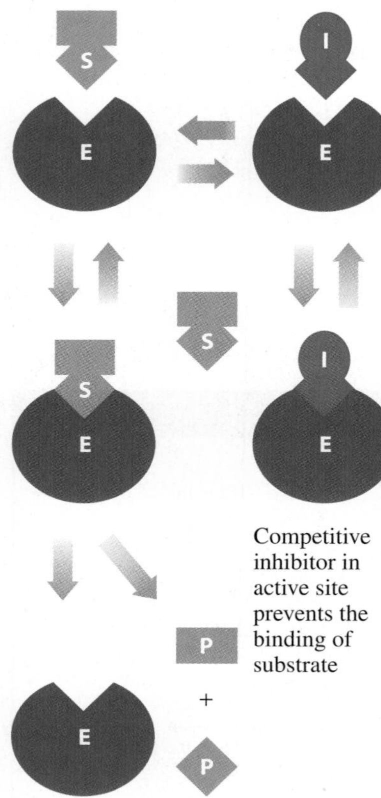


FIGURE 20.8 With a structure similar to the substrate for an enzyme, a competitive inhibitor also fits the active site and competes with the substrate when both are present.

Q Does an increase in substrate concentration reverse the inhibition by a competitive inhibitor?

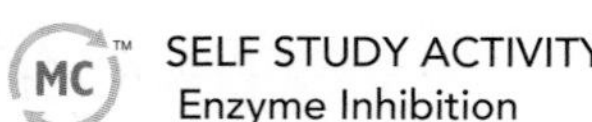


SELF STUDY ACTIVITY
Enzyme Inhibition

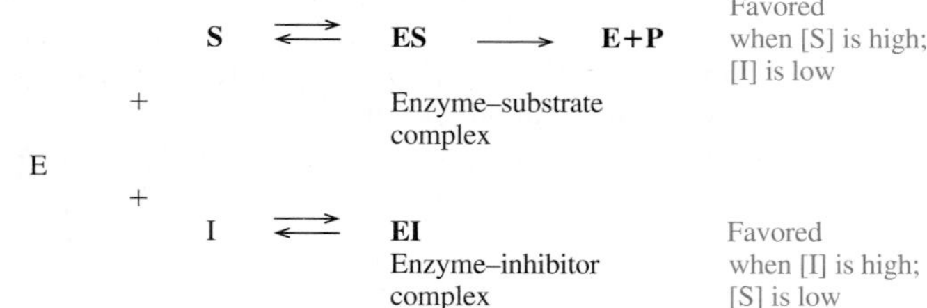


As long as the concentration of the inhibitor is substantial, there is a loss of enzymatic activity. However, adding more substrate displaces the competitive inhibitor, which increases the rate of the reaction. As more enzyme molecules bind to substrate (ES), enzymatic activity is regained.

Malonate is a competitive inhibitor of the enzyme succinate dehydrogenase. Because malonate has a structure similar to succinate, the two substances compete for the active site on the dehydrogenase. As long as malonate (inhibitor) occupies the active site, no reaction occurs. When more succinate is added, more active sites will fill with substrate, and there will be less inhibition.

Succinate: $^{-}OOC{-}CH_2{-}CH_2{-}COO^{-}$    Malonate: $^{-}OOC{-}CH_2{-}COO^{-}$

Succinate    Malonate

Some bacterial infections are treated with competitive inhibitors called antimetabolites. Sulfanilamide, one of the first sulfa drugs, competes with PABA (*p*-aminobenzoic acid), which is an essential substance (metabolite) in the growth cycle of bacteria:

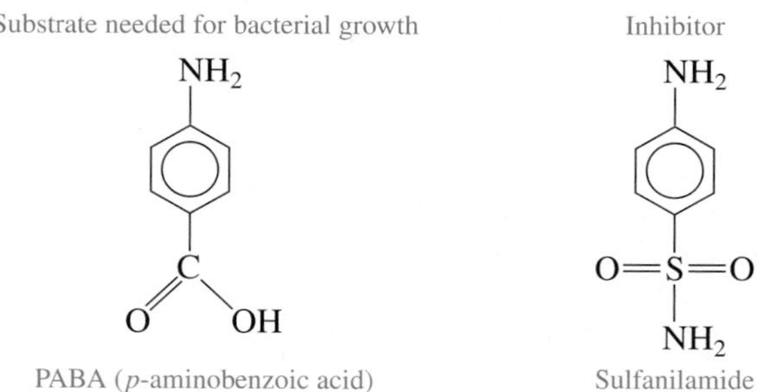


PABA (*p*-aminobenzoic acid)    Sulfanilamide

The structure of a **noncompetitive inhibitor** does not resemble the substrate and does not compete for the active site. Instead, a noncompetitive inhibitor binds to a site on the enzyme that is not the active site. When the noncompetitive inhibitor is bonded to the enzyme, the shape of the enzyme is distorted. Inhibition occurs because the substrate cannot fit in the active site or because it does not fit properly. Without the proper alignment of substrate with the amino acid side groups, no catalysis can take place. (See Figure 20.9.)

Because a noncompetitive inhibitor is not competing for the active site, the addition of more substrate does not reverse this type of inhibition. However, enzyme activity can be regained by lowering the concentration of the noncompetitive inhibitor and thus making more enzyme molecules available. Examples of noncompetitive inhibitors are the heavy metal ions $Pb^{2+}$, $Ag^{+}$, and $Hg^{2+}$ that bond with amino acid side groups such as $-COO^{-}$ or with $-OH$. Catalytic activity is restored when chemical reagents remove the inhibitors.

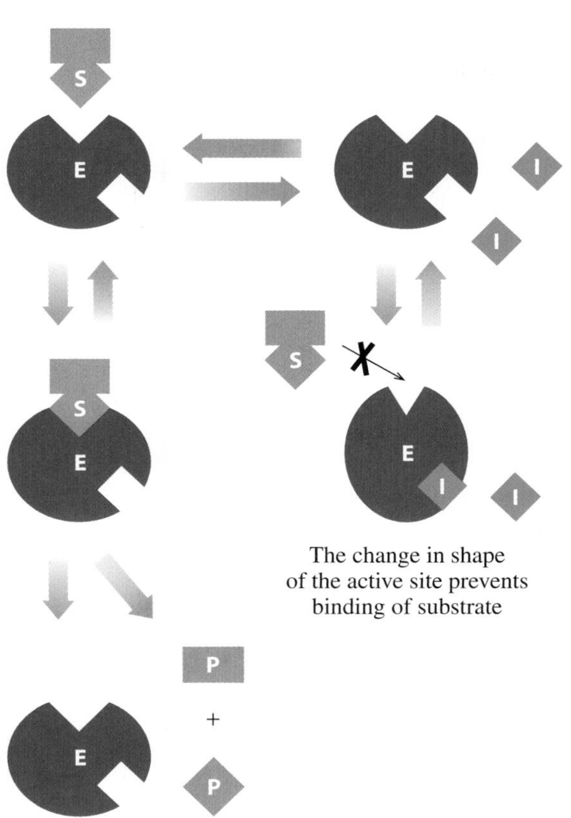


**FIGURE 20.9** A noncompetitive inhibitor (I) binds to an enzyme at a site other than the active site, which distorts the enzyme and prevents the proper binding and catalysis of the substrate at the active site.

**Q** Does an increase in the substrate concentration reverse the inhibition by a noncompetitive inhibitor?

## Irreversible Inhibition

In **irreversible inhibition**, a toxic substance causes an enzyme to permanently lose enzymatic activity. These inhibitors form a covalent bond with an amino acid side group within the active site, which prevents the substrate from entering the active site or prevents catalytic activity.

Insecticides and nerve gases act as irreversible inhibitors of acetylcholinesterase, an enzyme needed for nerve conduction. The compound DFP (diisopropyl fluorophosphate) forms a covalent bond with the side chain $-CH_2-OH$ of serine in the active site. When acetylcholinesterase is inhibited, the transmission of nerve impulses is blocked, and paralysis occurs.

$$\underset{\text{Enzyme—Serine}}{\text{(E)}-\mathbf{CH_2-OH}} + \underset{\text{DFP (diisopropyl fluorophosphate)}}{F-P(=O)(O-CH(CH_3)_2)_2} \longrightarrow \underset{\text{Serine covalently bonded to DFP}}{\text{(E)}-\mathbf{CH_2-O}-P(=O)(O-CH(CH_3)_2)_2} + \mathbf{H}F$$

**Antibiotics** produced by bacteria, mold, or yeast are irreversible inhibitors used to inhibit bacterial growth. For example, penicillin inhibits a transpeptidase enzyme needed to catalyze a step in the formation of cell walls in bacteria but not human cell membranes. Penicillin, an irreversible inhibitor, forms a covalent bond with the R group ($-CH_2-OH$) of a serine in the polypeptide of transpeptidase that is stable and cannot be hydrolyzed. The resulting enzyme is inactive.

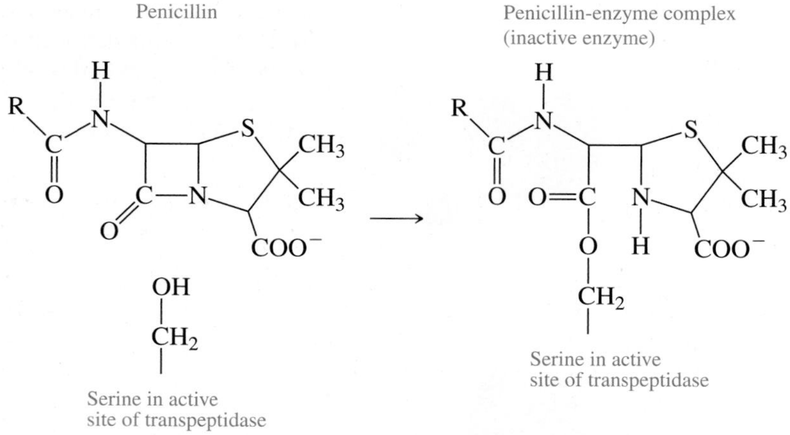

Penicillin

Penicillin-enzyme complex (inactive enzyme)

Serine in active site of transpeptidase

Serine in active site of transpeptidase

Without a complete cell wall, bacteria cannot survive, and the infection is stopped. However, some bacteria are resistant to penicillin because they produce penicillinase, an enzyme that breaks down penicillin. The penicillinase hydrolyzes the four-atom ring converting penicillin to penicillinoic acid, which is inactive:

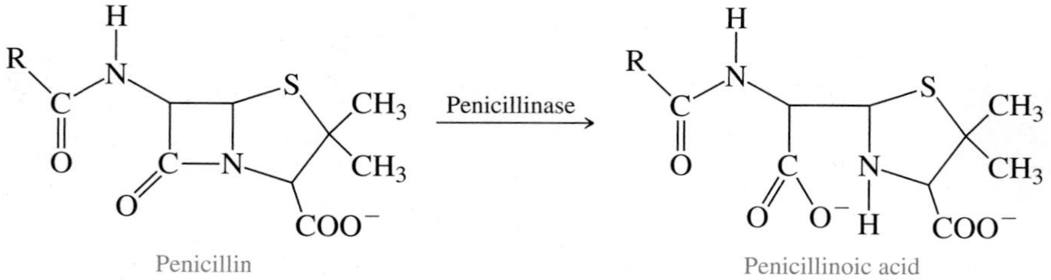

Penicillinase

Penicillin

Penicillinoic acid

Over the years, derivatives of penicillin to which bacteria have not yet become resistant have been produced. Examples of some irreversible enzyme inhibitors are listed in Table 20.6.

**TABLE 20.6** Examples of Irreversible Enzyme Inhibitors

| Name | Structure | Source | Inhibitory Action |
|---|---|---|---|
| Cyanide | $CN^-$ | Bitter almonds | Bonds to metal ions in enzymes in electron transport |
| Sarin | 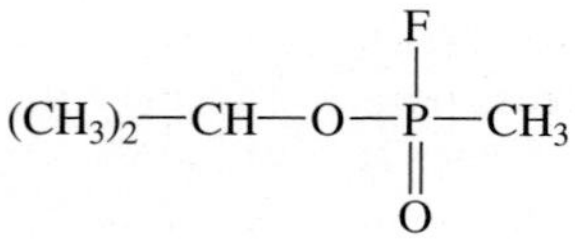 $(CH_3)_2-CH-O-P(=O)(F)-CH_3$ | Nerve gas | Similar to DFP |
| Parathion | 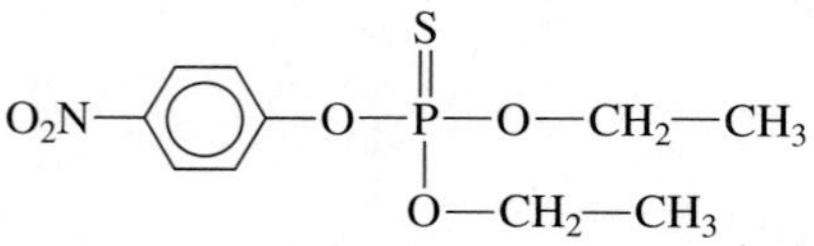 $O_2N-C_6H_4-O-P(=S)(-O-CH_2-CH_3)-O-CH_2-CH_3$ | Insecticide | Similar to DFP |
| Penicillin | 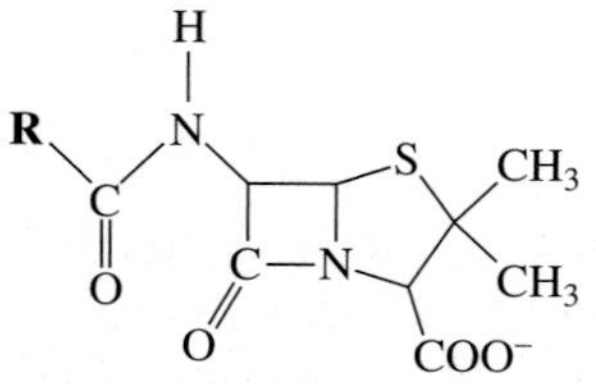 | *Penicillium* fungus | Inhibits enzymes that build cell walls in bacteria |

**R Groups for Penicillin Derivatives**

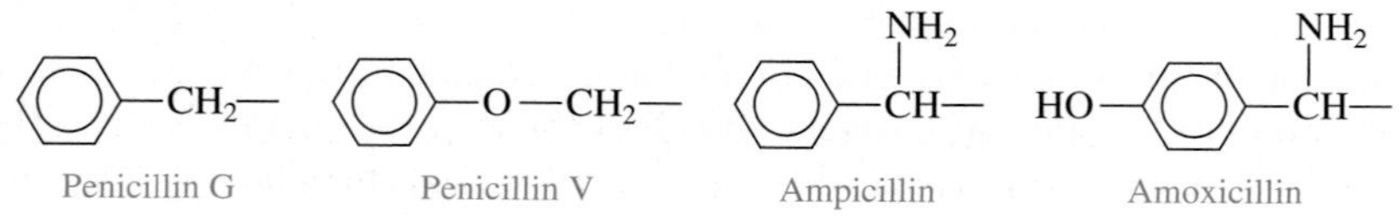

| Penicillin G | Penicillin V | Ampicillin | Amoxicillin |
|---|---|---|---|
| $C_6H_5-CH_2-$ | $C_6H_5-O-CH_2-$ | $C_6H_5-CH(NH_2)-$ | $HO-C_6H_4-CH(NH_2)-$ |

CONCEPT CHECK 20.4

**Enzyme Inhibition**

Describe the type of inhibition for each of the following:

**a.** an inhibitor that has a structure similar to that of the substrate
**b.** an inhibitor that binds to the surface of the enzyme and changes its shape
**c.** the inhibitor Sarin, a nerve gas that forms covalent bonds with the R group of serine in the active site of acetylcholinesterase, an enzyme involved in nerve impulses

ANSWER

**a.** When an inhibitor has a structure similar to that of the substrate, it competes with the substrate for the active site. This type of inhibition is competitive inhibition, which is reversed by increasing the concentration of the substrate.
**b.** When an inhibitor binds to the surface of the enzyme, it changes the shape of the enzyme and the active site. This type of inhibition is noncompetitive inhibition because the inhibitor does not have a similar shape to the substrate and does not compete with the substrate for the active site.
**c.** Sarin is a noncompetitive inhibitor. Because it forms a stable, covalent bond with an R group in the active site of the enzyme, the inhibition of Sarin is irreversible.

## QUESTIONS AND PROBLEMS

### Enzyme Inhibition

20.23 Indicate whether the following describe (1) a competitive or a noncompetitive enzyme inhibitor and if they are (2) reversible or irreversible:
**a.** The inhibitor has a structure similar to the substrate.
**b.** The effect of the inhibitor cannot be reversed by adding more substrate.
**c.** The inhibitor competes with the substrate for the active site.
**d.** The structure of the inhibitor is not similar to the substrate.
**e.** The addition of more substrate reverses the inhibition.

**20.24** Oxaloacetate is an inhibitor of succinate dehydrogenase:

$$\begin{array}{c} COO^- \\ | \\ CH_2 \\ | \\ CH_2 \\ | \\ COO^- \end{array} \qquad \begin{array}{c} COO^- \\ | \\ CH_2 \\ | \\ C{=}O \\ | \\ COO^- \end{array}$$

Succinate  Oxaloacetate

**a.** Would you expect oxaloacetate to be a competitive or a noncompetitive inhibitor? Why?
**b.** Would oxaloacetate bind to the active site or elsewhere on the enzyme?
**c.** How would you reverse the effect of the inhibitor?

20.25 Methanol and ethanol are oxidized by alcohol dehydrogenase. In methanol poisoning, ethanol is given intravenously to prevent the formation of formaldehyde that has toxic effects.
**a.** Draw the structures of methanol and ethanol.
**b.** Would ethanol compete for the active site or bind to a different site?
**c.** Would ethanol be a competitive or noncompetitive inhibitor of methanol oxidation?

**20.26** In humans, the antibiotic amoxicillin (a type of penicillin) is used to treat certain bacterial infections.
**a.** Does the antibiotic inhibit enzymes in humans?
**b.** Why does the antibiotic kill bacteria but not humans?
**c.** Is amoxicillin a reversible or irreversible inhibitor?

# 20.5 Regulation of Enzyme Activity

LEARNING GOAL

Describe the role of zymogens, feedback control, and allosteric enzymes in regulating enzyme activity.

In an enzyme-catalyzed reaction, compounds are produced in the amounts and at the times they are needed. This means that the rate of a catalyzed reaction must be controlled so it can speed up when more molecules of a compound are needed and slow down when that compound is no longer needed.

## Zymogens

TUTORIAL
Regulating Enzyme Action

Many enzymes are active as soon as they are synthesized and acquire their tertiary structure. However, **zymogens**, or *proenzymes*, are produced as an inactive form and stored in an organ such as the pancreas. Many zymogens are inactive forms of enzymes that hydrolyze protein such as the digestive enzymes. Zymogens are transported to the parts of the body where their active form is needed. A zymogen is converted to the active form by the removal of a polypeptide section with up to 40 amino acids, which uncovers the active site of the enzyme. If zymogen activation occurs in the storage organ such as pancreas, the tissue within the pancreas is digested, which can result in a painful condition called *pancreatitis.*

Most protein hormones, such as insulin, as well as digestive enzymes and the enzymes needed for blood clotting, are initially synthesized as zymogens. (See Table 20.7.) For example, the hormone *insulin* is synthesized in an inactive form called *proinsulin*. To form insulin (Chapter 19), a polypeptide containing 33 amino acids is removed.

**TABLE 20.7** Example of Zymogens and Their Active Forms

| Zymogen (Inactive Enzyme) | Produced in | Activated in | Enzyme (Active) |
|---|---|---|---|
| Proinsulin | Pancreas | Pancreas | Insulin |
| Chymotrypsinogen | Pancreas | Small intestine | Chymotrypsin |
| Pepsinogen | Gastric mucosa | Stomach | Pepsin |
| Trypsinogen | Pancreas | Small intestine | Trypsin |
| Fibrinogen | Blood | Damaged tissues | Fibrin |
| Prothrombin | Blood | Damaged tissues | Thrombin |

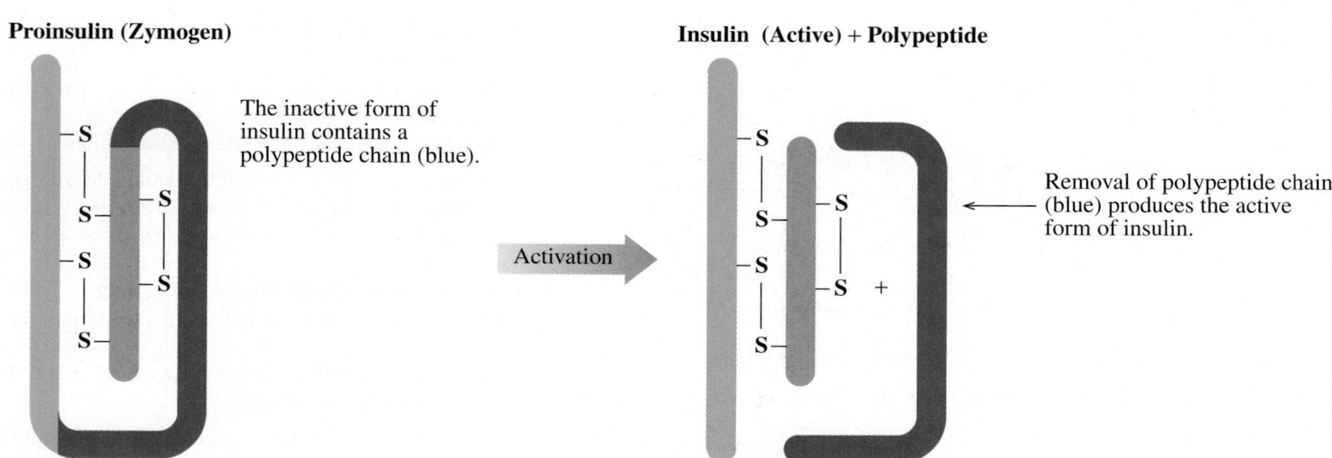


The zymogen of a digestive enzyme called pepsinogen is produced in the gastric mucosal cells that line the stomach. As food enters the stomach, HCl is secreted. Under these acidic conditions (about pH 2), a polypeptide of 42 amino acids is hydrolyzed from pepsinogen to form pepsin, which is the active enzyme that digests proteins in our foods:

$$\text{Pepsinogen} \xrightarrow{H^+} \text{pepsin} + \text{peptides} + \text{amino acids}$$

Several digestive enzymes, such as *trypsinogen*, *chymotrypsinogen*, and *procarboxypeptidase*, are produced as inactive enzymes and stored in the pancreas. After food is ingested and reaches the small intestine, hormones trigger the release of the zymogens of the digestive enzymes from the pancreas. When the zymogens enter the small intestine, they are converted into active enzymes by proteases that remove peptide sections from their protein chains. The result is the active form of the enzyme. For example, an enzyme called enteropeptidase removes a hexapeptide from trypsinogen to give active trypsin. Trypsin in turn removes peptide sections from the zymogens chymotrypsinogen and procarboxypeptidase to give the active forms chymotrypsin and carboxypeptidase.

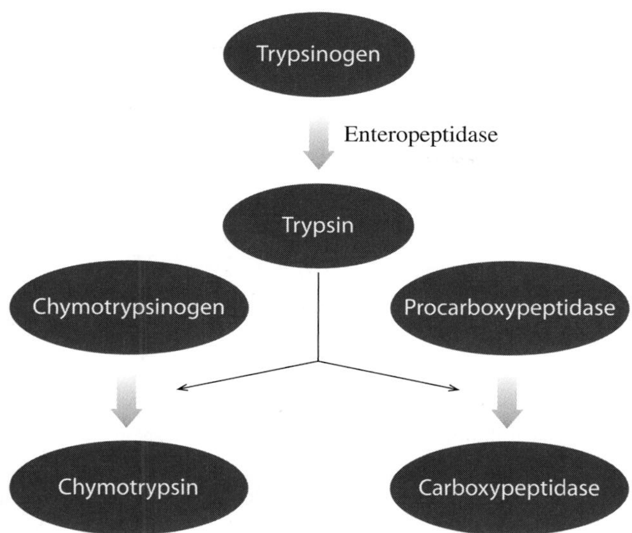


## Feedback Control

Certain enzymes known as **allosteric enzymes** are capable of binding a regulator molecule that is different from the substrate. The binding of a regulator causes a change in the shape of the enzyme and therefore a change in the active site. There are both positive and negative regulators. A *positive regulator* speeds up a reaction by causing a change in the shape of the active site that permits the substrate to bind more effectively. A *negative regulator* slows down the rate of catalysis by preventing the proper binding of the substrate. In **feedback control**, the end product acts as a negative regulator. (See Figure 20.10.) When the end product is present in sufficient amounts for the cell, some end product molecules bind to the first enzyme in the reaction pathway ($E_1$), which is an allosteric enzyme. The inhibition of the reaction of the initial substrate stops the production of any intermediate compounds in the reaction pathway. The entire enzyme-catalyzed reaction sequence shuts down.

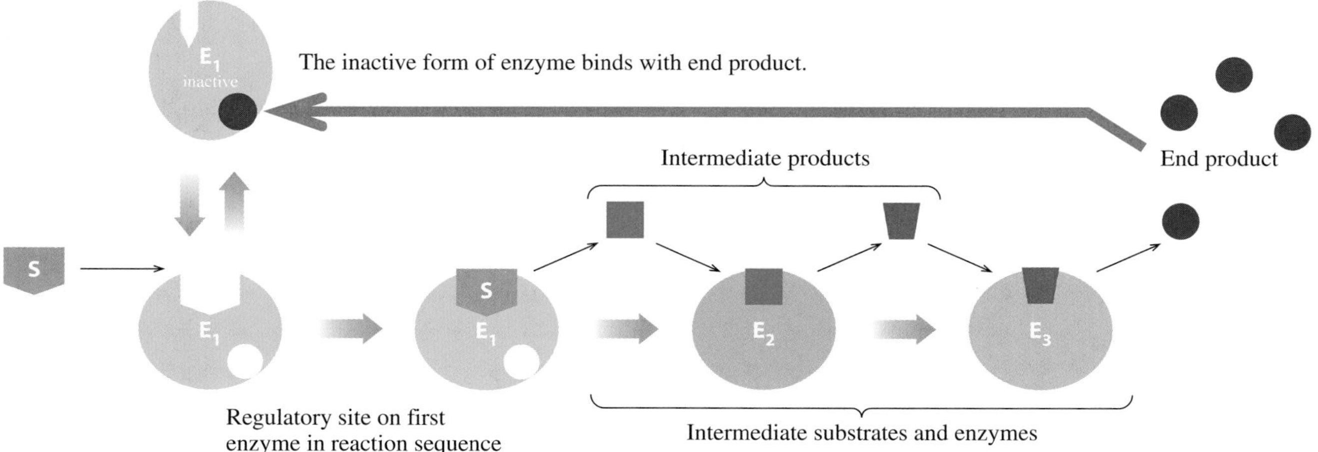


**FIGURE 20.10** In feedback control, the end product binds to a regulatory site on the first enzyme in the reaction pathway, which prevents the formation of all intermediate compounds needed in the synthesis of the end product.
**Q** Do the intermediate enzymes in a reaction sequence have regulatory sites?

When the level of end product is too low, the regulator dissociates from the allosteric enzyme ($E_1$), which unblocks the active site. The enzyme becomes active and binds to the initial substrate once again. Thus, feedback control allows the reaction only when the end product is needed by the cell. This control prevents the accumulation of unneeded end product, thereby conserving the materials in the cell.

Let's look at feedback control in a reaction pathway with five enzymes that converts the amino acid threonine to isoleucine, another amino acid. When isoleucine accumulates in the cell, it binds to the first enzyme in the pathway, threonine deaminase, $E_1$:

$$\underset{\text{Threonine}}{H_3\overset{+}{N}-\underset{\underset{CH_3}{|}}{\overset{CH-OH}{|}}CH-COO^-} \xrightarrow[\text{Threonine deaminase}]{E_1} \xrightarrow{E_2} \xrightarrow{E_3} \xrightarrow{E_4} \xrightarrow{E_5} \underset{\text{Isoleucine}}{H_3\overset{+}{N}-CH(CH(CH_3)CH_2CH_3)-COO^-}$$

Feedback control (isoleucine inhibits $E_1$, Threonine deaminase)

The binding of isoleucine changes the shape of the deaminase, which prevents threonine from binding with the active site. The entire reaction pathway is turned off. None of the intermediate products from the other enzymes in the pathway can inhibit the first enzyme. As isoleucine is utilized in the cell, its concentration decreases, which causes the threonine deaminase to release the end-product inhibitor. The tertiary shape of the deaminase returns to its active form and the reaction sequence once again converts threonine to isoleucine.

CONCEPT CHECK 20.5

### Regulation of Enzyme Activity

Why are the enzymes trypsin and chymotrypsin produced as zymogens in the pancreas rather than as active enzymes?

ANSWER

Trypsin and chymotrypsin are digestive enzymes that break down proteins. If they were produced as active enzymes in the pancreas, they would digest the proteins of the pancreas. They are produced as zymogens that are activated when digestive activity is needed.

SAMPLE PROBLEM 20.4

### Enzyme Regulation

How is the rate of a reaction sequence regulated in feedback control?

SOLUTION

When the end product of a reaction sequence is produced at sufficient levels for the cell, some product molecules bind to the first enzyme in the sequence, which shuts down all the reactions that follow and stops the production of end product.

STUDY CHECK

Why is pepsin, a digestive enzyme, produced as a zymogen?

## QUESTIONS AND PROBLEMS

### Regulation of Enzyme Activity

**20.27** Why are many of the enzymes that act on proteins synthesized as zymogens?

**20.28** The zymogen trypsinogen produced in the pancreas is activated in the small intestine, where it catalyzes the digestion and hydrolysis of proteins. Explain how the activation of the zymogen while still in the pancreas can lead to an inflammation of the pancreas called pancreatitis.

**20.29** In feedback control, how does the end product of a reaction sequence regulate enzyme activity?

**20.30** Why are the second or third enzymes in a reaction sequence function not used as regulatory enzymes?

**20.31** How does an allosteric enzyme function as a regulatory enzyme?

**20.32** What is the difference between a negative regulator and a positive regulator?

**20.33** Indicate if the following statements describe (1) a zymogen, (2) a positive regulator, (3) a negative regulator, or (4) an allosteric enzyme:

**a.** It slows down a reaction, but its shape is different from that of the substrate.

**b.** An enzyme that binds a regulator molecules that differs from the substrate.

**c.** It is produced as an inactive enzyme.

**20.34** Indicate if the following statements describe (1) a zymogen, (2) a positive regulator, (3) a negative regulator, or (4) an allosteric enzyme:

**a.** It is activated when a peptide section is removed from its protein chain.

**b.** It speeds up a reaction, but it is not the substrate.

**c.** When it binds to end product, it stops the formation of more end product.

# 20.6 Enzyme Cofactors and Vitamins

LEARNING GOAL

Describe the types of cofactors found in enzymes.

Enzymes known as **simple enzymes** consist only of proteins. However, many enzymes require small molecules such as vitamins or metal ions called **cofactors** to catalyze reactions properly. When the cofactor is a small organic molecule, it is known as a **coenzyme**. If an enzyme requires a cofactor, neither the protein structure nor the cofactor alone has catalytic activity.

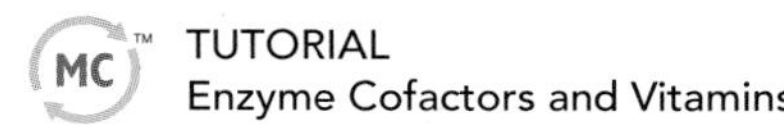


**Forms of Active Enzymes**

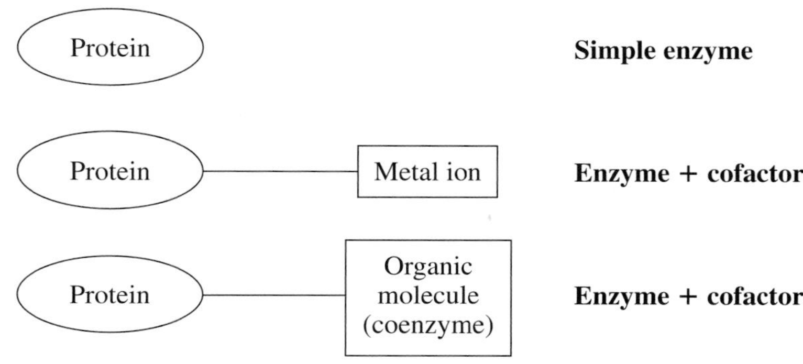


## Metal Ions

Many enzymes must contain a metal ion to carry out their catalytic activity. The metal ions are bonded to one or more of the amino acid side chains. The metal ions from the minerals that we obtain from foods in our diet have various functions in catalysis. Ions such as $Fe^{2+}$ and $Cu^{2+}$ are used by oxidases, losing or gaining electrons in oxidation and reduction reactions. Other metal ions such as $Zn^{2+}$ stabilize the amino acid side chains during hydrolysis reactions. Some metal cofactors required by enzymes are listed in Table 20.8.

TABLE 20.8 Enzymes and the Metal Ions Required as Cofactors

| Enzyme | Metal Ion Cofactor | Function |
|---|---|---|
| Cytochrome oxidase | $Cu^{2+}$ | Oxidation–reduction |
| Catalase<br>Cytochrome oxidase | $Fe^{2+}/Fe^{3+}$ | Oxidation–reduction |
| Alcohol dehydrogenase | $Zn^{2+}$ | Used with $NAD^+$ |
| Carbonic anhydrase | | |
| Carboxypeptidase A | | |
| Glucose-6-phosphatase | $Mg^{2+}$ | Hydrolyzes phosphate esters |
| Arginase | $Mn^{2+}$ | Removes electrons |
| Urease | $Ni^{2+}$ | Hydrolyzes amides |

Let's look at an example of a metal ion in an enzyme-catalyzed reaction. The enzyme carboxypeptidase A cleaves the C terminal amino acid of a protein when that amino acid has a bulky hydrophobic or aromatic side chain. (See Figure 20.11.) With the substrate in the active site, the $Zn^{2+}$ helps to stabilize the negative charge on the oxygen atom of the carbonyl group and promotes the hydrolysis of the peptide bond.

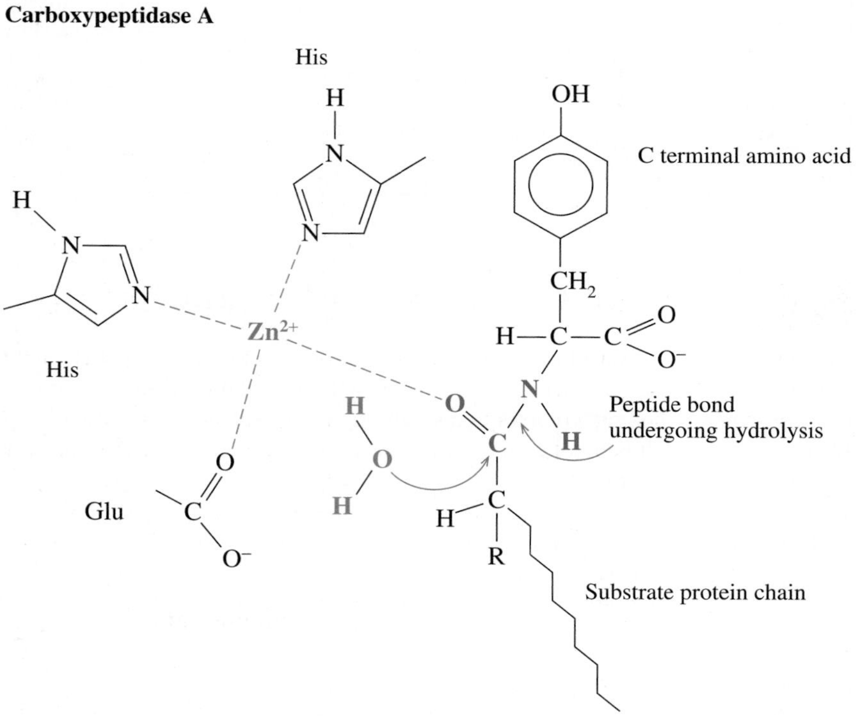

**FIGURE 20.11** A $Zn^{2+}$ cofactor aids in the hydrolysis of the peptide bond of a bulky C terminal amino acid by helping to stabilize the carbonyl oxygen.

**Q** When would the $Zn^{2+}$ be utilized as a cofactor by other enzymes?

**Carboxypeptidase A**

His, His, Glu, $Zn^{2+}$, C terminal amino acid, Peptide bond undergoing hydrolysis, Substrate protein chain

> **SAMPLE PROBLEM 20.5**
>
> **Enzyme Cofactors**
>
> Indicate whether each of the following is active as a simple enzyme or requires a cofactor:
>
> **a.** a polypeptide that needs $Mg^{2+}$ for catalytic activity
> **b.** an active enzyme composed only of a polypeptide chain
> **c.** an enzyme that consists of a quaternary structure attached to vitamin $B_6$
>
> SOLUTION
>
> **a.** The enzyme requires a cofactor.
> **b.** An active enzyme that consists of only a polypeptide chain is a simple enzyme.
> **c.** The enzyme requires a cofactor.
>
> STUDY CHECK
>
> Which of the nonprotein portions of the enzymes in Sample Problem 20.5 is a coenzyme?

## Vitamins and Coenzymes

**Vitamins** are organic molecules that are essential for normal health and growth. They are required in trace amounts and are obtained from the diet because sufficient amounts are not synthesized in the body. Before vitamins were discovered, it was known that lime juice prevented the disease scurvy in sailors and that cod liver oil could prevent rickets. In 1912, scientists found that in addition to carbohydrates, fats, and proteins, certain other factors called vitamins must be obtained from the diet.

Vitamins are classified into two groups by solubility: water-soluble and fat-soluble. **Water-soluble vitamins** have polar groups such as —OH and —COOH, which make them soluble in the aqueous environment of the cells. The **fat-soluble vitamins** are nonpolar compounds, which are soluble in the fat (lipid) components of the body such as fat deposits and cell membranes.

## Water-Soluble Vitamins

Most water-soluble vitamins are not stored in the body, because excess amounts are eliminated in the urine each day. Therefore, the water-soluble vitamins must be in the foods of our daily diets. Because many water-soluble vitamins are easily destroyed by heat, oxygen, and ultraviolet light, care must be taken in food preparation, processing, and storage. Because refining grains such as wheat causes a loss of vitamins, during the 1940s the Committee on Food and Nutrition of the National Research Council began to recommend dietary enrichment of cereal grains. Thiamine ($B_1$), riboflavin ($B_2$), niacin, and iron were in the first group of added nutrients recommended. We now see the Recommended Daily Allowance (RDA) for many vitamins and minerals on food product labels such as cereals and bread.

The water-soluble vitamins are required by many enzymes as cofactors to carry out certain aspects of catalytic action. (See Table 20.9.) The coenzymes do not remain bonded to a particular enzyme, but are used repeatedly by different enzymes to facilitate an enzyme-catalyzed reaction. (See Figure 20.12.) Thus, only small amounts of coenzymes are required in the cells.

*Thiamine* (vitamin $B_1$) was the first B vitamin to be identified, thus the abbreviation $B_1$. The coenzyme thiamine pyrophosphate (TPP) is obtained when a synthetase adds two

TABLE 20.9 Function, RDA, Sources, and Deficiency Symptoms of Water-Soluble Vitamins

| Vitamin | Function | RDA (Adults) | Sources | Deficiency Symptoms |
|---|---|---|---|---|
| Thiamine (vitamin $B_1$) | Decarboxylation | 1.2 mg | Liver, yeast, whole grain bread, cereals, milk | Beriberi: fatigue, poor appetite, weight loss, nerve degeneration, heart failure |
| Riboflavin (vitamin $B_2$) | Electron transfer | 1.2–1.8 mg | Beef liver, chicken, eggs, green leafy vegetables, dairy foods, peanuts, whole grains | Dermatitis, dry skin, tongue inflammation, cataracts |
| Niacin (vitamin $B_3$) | Oxidation–reduction | 14–18 mg | Brewer's yeast, chicken, beef, fish, liver, brown rice, whole grains | Pellagra: dermatitis, muscle fatigue, loss of appetite, diarrhea, mouth sores, mental disorders |
| Pantothenic acid (vitamin $B_5$) | Acetyl group transfer | 5 mg | Salmon, beef, liver, eggs, brewer's yeast, whole grains, fresh vegetables | Fatigue, retarded growth, muscle cramps, anemia |
| Pyridoxine (vitamin $B_6$) | Transamination | 1.3–2.0 mg | Meat, liver, fish, nuts, whole grains, spinach | Dermatitis, fatigue, anemia, retarded growth |
| Cobalamin (vitamin $B_{12}$) | Methyl group transfer | 2.0–2.6 $\mu$g | Liver, beef, kidney, chicken, fish, milk products | Pernicious anemia, malformed red blood cells, nerve damage |
| Ascorbic acid (vitamin C) | Collagen synthesis, healing of wounds | 60–95 mg | Blueberries, oranges, strawberries, cantaloupe, tomatoes, peppers, broccoli, cabbage, spinach | Scurvy: bleeding gums, weakened connective tissues, slow-healing wounds, anemia |
| Biotin | Carboxylation | 30 $\mu$g | Liver, yeast, nuts, eggs | Dermatitis, loss of hair, fatigue, anemia, nausea, depression |
| Folic acid (folate) | Methyl group transfer | 400 $\mu$g | Green leafy vegetables, beans, meat, seafood, yeast, asparagus, whole grains enriched with folic acid | Abnormal red blood cells, anemia, intestinal-tract disturbances, loss of hair, growth impairment, depression, spina bifida |

**FIGURE 20.12** The active forms of many enzymes require the combination of the protein with a coenzyme.

**Q** What is the function of water-soluble vitamins in enzymes?

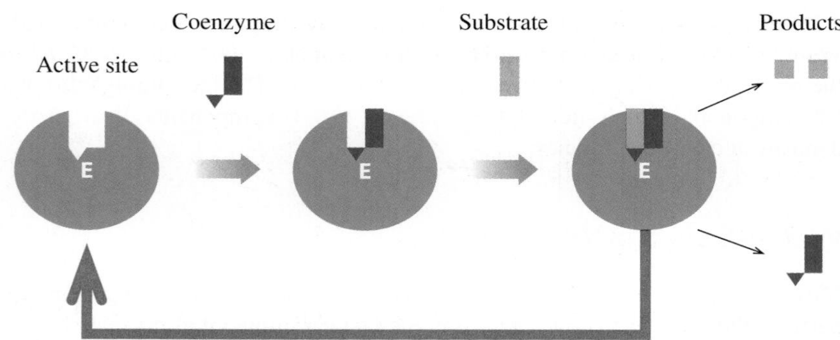


phosphate groups from ATP to the alcohol group of thiamine. (ATP and AMP are discussed in Section 22.2.)

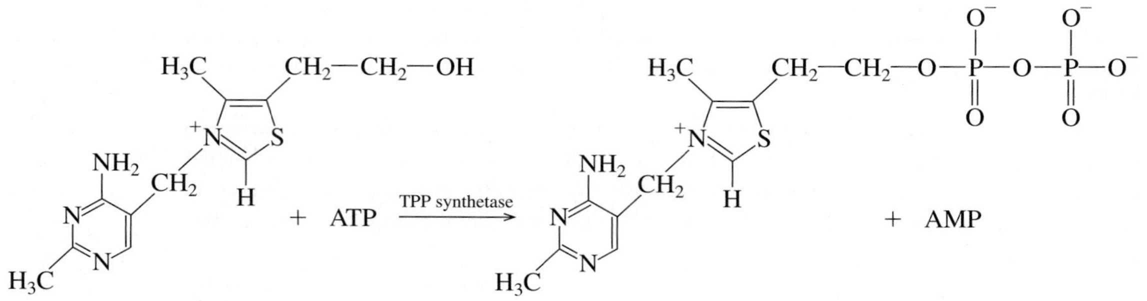

Thiamine (vitamin $B_1$) + ATP $\xrightarrow{\text{TPP synthetase}}$ Thiamine pyrophosphate (TPP) + AMP

The TPP coenzyme is involved in the decarboxylation reactions of $\alpha$-keto carboxylic acids and reactions that cleave bonds to carbonyl carbons of $\alpha$-hydroxy ketones.

*Riboflavin* (vitamin $B_2$) is used to make the coenzymes flavin adenine dinucleotide (FAD) and flavin mononucleotide (FMN). The *ribo* part of the name comes from the sugar alcohol ribitol in the *riboflavin* molecule. Enzymes called *flavoenzymes* use the coenzymes FAD and FMN to catalyze oxidation–reduction reactions of carbohydrates, fats, and proteins.

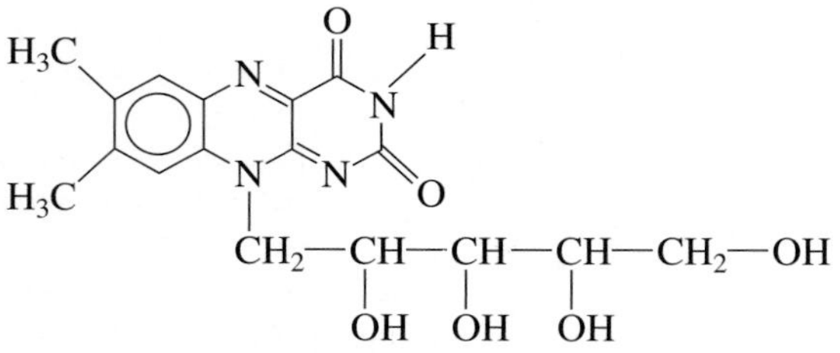

Riboflavin (vitamin $B_2$)

*Niacin* (vitamin $B_3$) is a component of coenzymes nicotinamide adenine dinucleotide ($NAD^+$) and $NADP^+$, the phosphate form of $NAD^+$. The name *niacin* was assigned to the vitamin because its actual name, *nicotinic acid*, might be confused with nicotine. These coenzymes participate in oxidation–reduction, energy-production reactions in carbohydrate, fat, and protein metabolism.

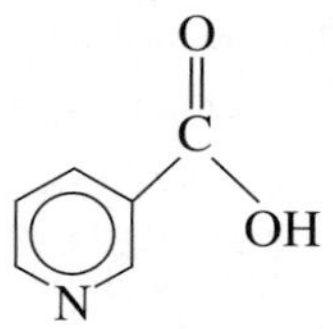

Niacin (vitamin $B_3$)

*Pantothenic acid* (vitamin $B_5$) is part of a complex coenzyme known as coenzyme A. Coenzyme A transfers a two-carbon acetyl group from pyruvate to the citric acid cycle for the production of energy. Coenzyme A is also involved in the conversion of amino acids and lipids to glucose as well as in the synthesis of cholesterol and steroid hormones.

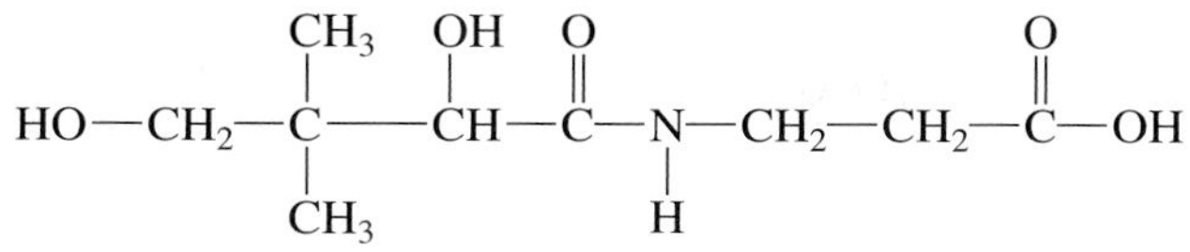

Pantothenic acid (vitamin $B_5$)

*Pyridoxine* (vitamin $B_6$) and *pyridoxal* (an aldehyde) are converted to the coenzyme pyridoxal phosphate (PLP). The PLP coenzyme participates in enzyme-catalyzed reactions such as transamination of amino acids and decarboxylation.

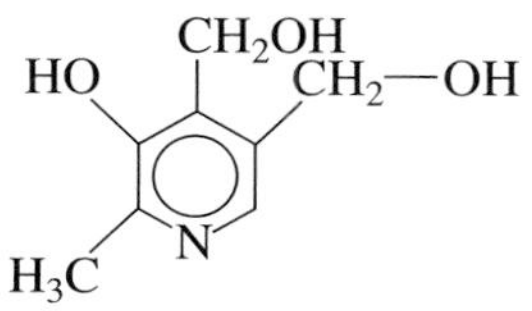

Pyridoxine (vitamin $B_6$)

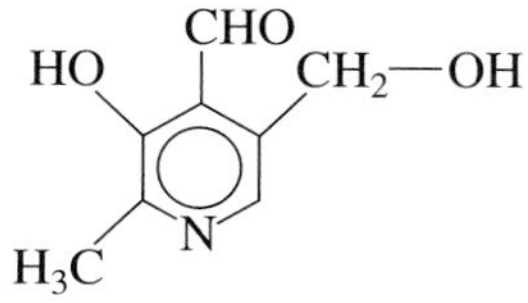

Pyridoxal (vitamin $B_6$)

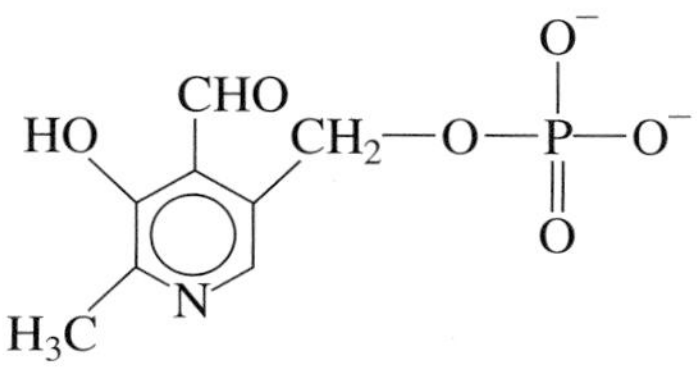

Pyridoxal phosphate (PLP)

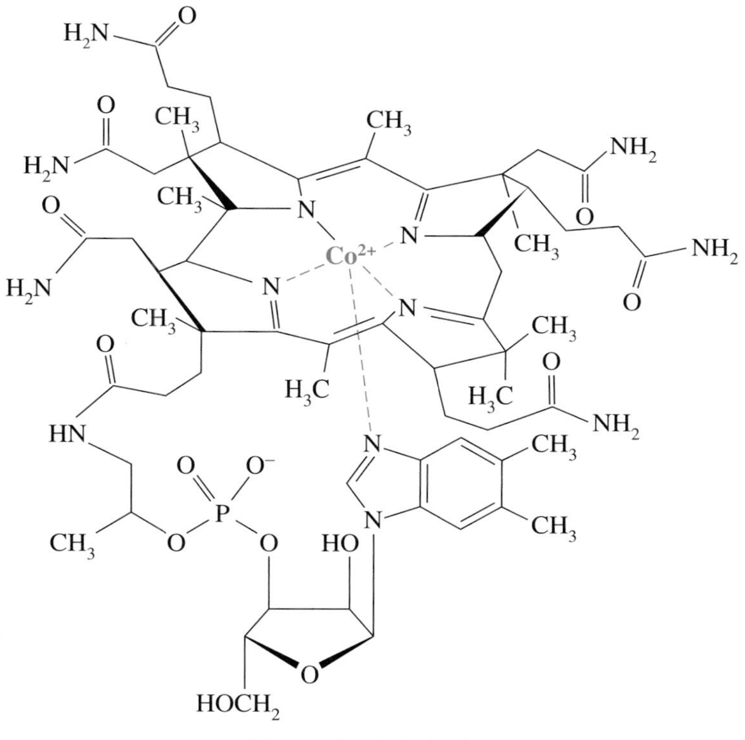

Vitamin $B_{12}$ (cobalamin)

*Cobalamin* (vitamin $B_{12}$) is a coenzyme consisting of four pyrrole rings with a cobalt ion ($Co^{2+}$) in the center. In its coenzyme form, cobalamin participates in the transfer of methyl groups, molecular rearrangements, the formation of red blood cells, and the synthesis of acetylcholine for nerve cells. Because vitamin $B_{12}$ is not present in plants, strict vegetarians can experience symptoms of pernicious anemia.

*Ascorbic acid* (vitamin C) has a simple chemical structure compared to most of the other vitamins. Its major function in the cells is its role in the synthesis of hydroxyproline and hydroxylysine, which are needed to form collagen. Collagen is the protein found in tendons, connective tissue, bone structure, and skin. (See Figure 20.13.)

**FIGURE 20.13** Oranges, lemons, peppers, and tomatoes contain vitamin C, or ascorbic acid.

**Q** What happens to any excess vitamin C that is consumed over the course of a day?

CH$_2$OH
CHOH
O O
HO OH

Ascorbic acid (vitamin C)

*Biotin* is a coenzyme for enzymes that transfer a carboxyl group in the reaction of pyruvate to oxaloacetate or acetyl CoA to malonyl CoA, which occurs in the synthesis of fatty acids.

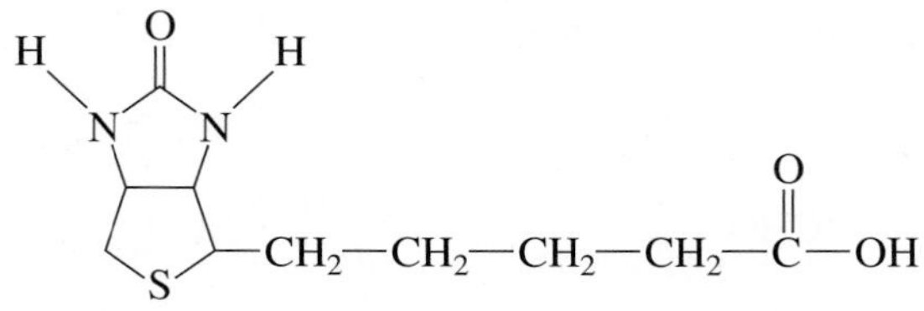

H O H
N N
O
S —CH$_2$—CH$_2$—CH$_2$—CH$_2$—C—OH

Biotin

*Folic acid* (folate) is composed of a pyrimidine ring, *p*-aminobenzoic acid (PABA), and glutamate. The vitamin was discovered during the 1930s when people with a form of anemia were cured with extracts from liver or yeast. Folic acid is also found in spinach leaves, hence the name *folium*, Latin for *leaf*. In the cells, an enzyme called dihydrofolate reductase adds hydrogen atoms to the atoms in the heterocyclic ring of folate to yield the coenzyme tetrahydrofolate (THF). This coenzyme is used in reactions that transfer single-carbon groups and synthesize purines and pyrimidines to make DNA and RNA. It also plays a role with cobalamin in the production of red blood cells.

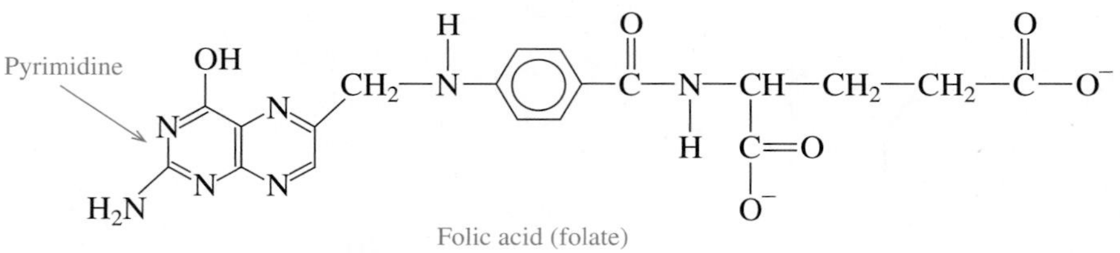

Heterocyclic ring | *p*-Aminobenzoic acid | Glutamate

Pyrimidine
OH
CH$_2$—N(H)—C$_6$H$_4$—C(=O)—N(H)—CH(C(=O)O$^-$)—CH$_2$—CH$_2$—C(=O)—O$^-$
H$_2$N

Folic acid (folate)

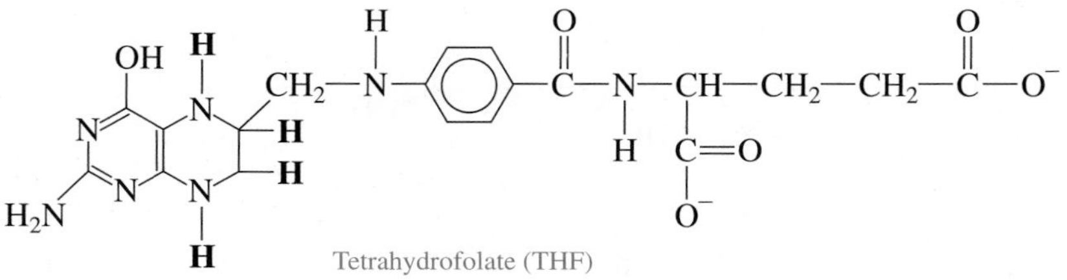

OH **H**
CH$_2$—N(H)—C$_6$H$_4$—C(=O)—N(H)—CH(C(=O)O$^-$)—CH$_2$—CH$_2$—C(=O)—O$^-$
**H**
**H**
H$_2$N
**H**

Tetrahydrofolate (THF)

Some compounds related to folate bring about remissions in people with leukemia. For example, 4-aminofolate, referred to medically as *methotrexate*, acts as a competitive inhibitor of the dihydrofolate reductase that forms THF. The growth of cells, including tumor cells, depends on THF to build purines and thymine. By inhibiting the reductase enzyme with methotrexate, THF cannot be produced, and the rapid growth of tumor cells is blocked.

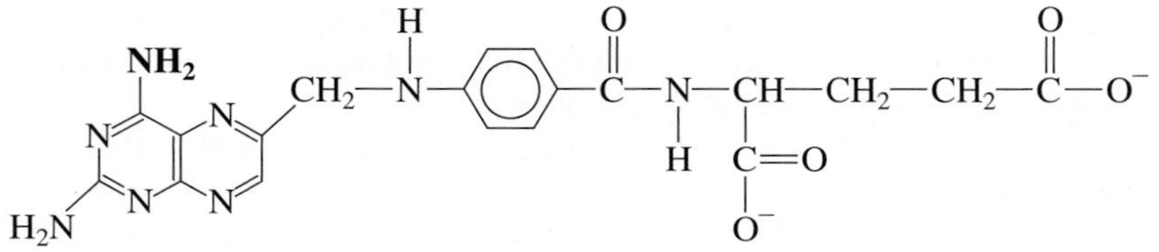

**NH$_2$**
CH$_2$—N(H)—C$_6$H$_4$—C(=O)—N(H)—CH(C(=O)O$^-$)—CH$_2$—CH$_2$—C(=O)—O$^-$
H$_2$N

4- Aminofolate (methotrexate)

## Fat-Soluble Vitamins

The fat-soluble vitamins—A, D, E, and K—are not involved as coenzymes, but they are important in processes such as vision, formation of bone, protection from oxidation, and proper blood clotting. (See Table 20.10.) Because the fat-soluble vitamins are stored in the body and not eliminated, it is possible to take too much, which could be toxic.

**TABLE 20.10** Function, RDA, Sources, and Deficiency Symptoms of Fat-Soluble Vitamins

| Vitamin | Function | RDA (Adults) | Sources | Deficiency Symptoms |
|---|---|---|---|---|
| Retinol (vitamin A) | Vision, synthesis of RNA | 800 $\mu$g | Yellow and green fruits and vegetables | Night blindness, immune system repression, slowed growth rickets |
| Cholecalciferol (vitamin $D_3$) | Regulation of absorption of P and Ca | 5–10 $\mu$g | Sunlight, cod liver oil, enriched milk, eggs | Rickets, weak bone structure, osteomalacia |
| Tocopherol (vitamin E) | Antioxidant, cell protection | 15 mg | Meats, whole grains, vegetables | Hemolysis, anemia |
| Menaquinone (vitamin $K_2$) | Blood clotting | 90–120 $\mu$g | Liver, spinach, cauliflower | Prolonged bleeding time, bruising |

Vitamin A consists of three different forms depending on the oxidation of the functional group: *retinol* (alcohol), *retinal* (aldehyde), and *retinoic acid* (carboxylic acid). Vitamin A is obtained from animal sources in the diet or the $\beta$-carotenes of plants, which are converted to vitamin A in the liver. The retinol in the retinas of the eyes accumulates in the rod and cone cells, where it plays a role in vision. Vitamin A is also involved in the synthesis of RNA and glycoproteins. (See Figure 20.14.)

**FIGURE 20.14** Yellow and green fruits and vegetables contain vitamin A.

**Q** Why is vitamin A called a fat-soluble vitamin?

$\beta$-Carotene

Liver enzymes

Retinol (vitamin A)

The most prevalent form of vitamin D is vitamin $D_3$, or *cholecalciferol*. Technically, this is not a vitamin, because it is not required in the diet. In skin, vitamin $D_3$ is synthesized from 7-dehydrocholesterol by the ultraviolet rays from sunlight. In regions of limited sunlight, vitamin $D_3$ is added to milk products to avoid a vitamin $D_3$ deficiency. Its function in the body is to regulate the absorption of phosphorus and calcium during bone growth.

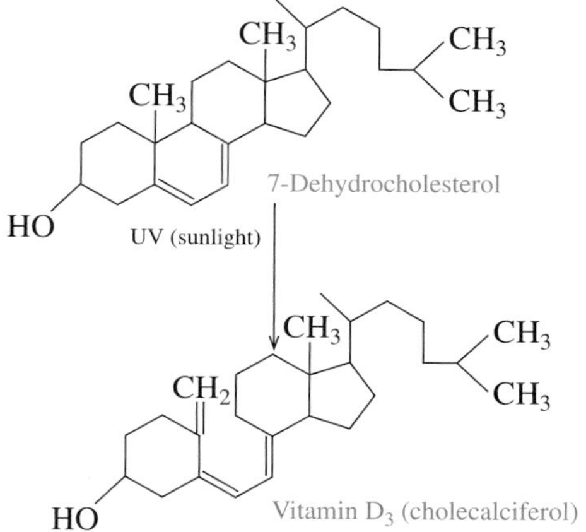

Vitamin E, or *tocopherol*, has a major role in cells as an antioxidant, but not much is known about the mechanism of its activity. It appears to protect the cells in the body by removing damaging chemicals and by preventing the oxidation of unsaturated fatty acids. Vitamin E has been used to reduce the damage to the retinas that can be caused by the high oxygen levels needed for respiration by premature infants.

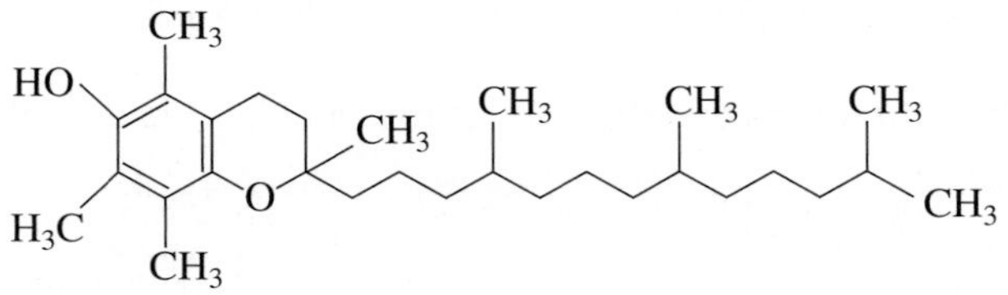

Vitamin E (tocopherol)

Vitamin $K_1$, or *phylloquinone*, a substance found in plants, has a large saturated side chain. Vitamin $K_2$, or *menaquinone*, found in animals, has a very long unsaturated side chain. Vitamin $K_2$ takes part in the synthesis of zymogens needed for blood clotting.

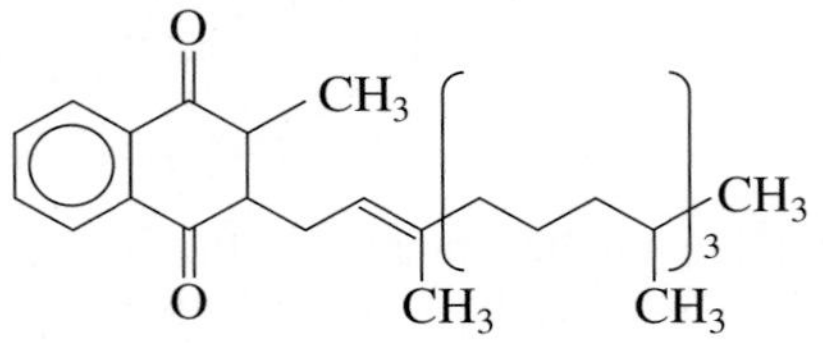

Vitamin $K_1$ (phylloquinone)

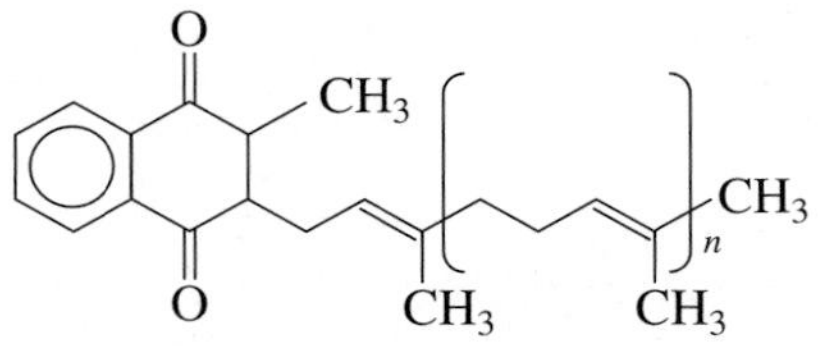

Vitamin $K_2$ (menaquinone)

CONCEPT CHECK 20.6

**Vitamins**

Identify the vitamin(s) described by each of the following:

**a.** is synthesized in the skin by sunlight
**b.** contains a $Co^{2+}$ ion
**c.** is fat soluble
**d.** can lead to scurvy and slow-healing wounds if deficient in the diet

ANSWER

**a.** Vitamin $D_3$ (cholecalciferol) is synthesized in the skin by sunlight.
**b.** Vitamin $B_{12}$ (cobalamin) contains a $Co^{2+}$ ion.
**c.** Vitamins A (retinol), D, E (tocopherol), and K (menaquinone) are fat soluble.
**d.** Vitamin C (ascorbic acid) deficiency can lead to scurvy and slow-healing wounds.

SAMPLE PROBLEM 20.6

**Vitamins**

Why do you need a certain amount of thiamine and riboflavin in your diet every day but not vitamin A or D?

SOLUTION

Water-soluble vitamins like thiamine and riboflavin are not stored in the body, whereas fat-soluble vitamins such as A and D are stored in the liver. Any excess of thiamine or riboflavin are eliminated in the urine and must be replenished each day from the diet.

STUDY CHECK

Why are fresh fruits rather than cooked fruits recommended as a source of vitamin C?

## QUESTIONS AND PROBLEMS

### Enzyme Cofactors and Vitamins

**20.35** Is the enzyme described in each of the following statements a simple enzyme or one that requires a cofactor?
**a.** requires vitamin $B_1$ (thiamine)
**b.** needs $Zn^{2+}$ for catalytic activity
**c.** its active form consists of two polypeptide chains

**20.36** Is the enzyme described in each of the following statements a simple enzyme or one that requires a cofactor?
**a.** requires vitamin $B_2$ (riboflavin)
**b.** its active form composed of 155 amino acids
**c.** uses $Cu^{2+}$ during catalysis

**20.37** Give the abbreviation for each of the following coenzymes:
**a.** tetrahydrofolate
**b.** nicotinamide adenine dinucleotide

**20.38** Give the abbreviation for each of the following coenzymes:
**a.** flavin adenine dinucleotide
**b.** thiamine pyrophosphate

**20.39** Identify a vitamin that is a component of each of the following coenzymes:
**a.** coenzyme A **b.** tetrahydrofolate (THF)
**c.** $NAD^+$

**20.40** Identify a vitamin that is a component of each of the following coenzymes:
**a.** thiamine pyrophosphate
**b.** FAD
**c.** pyridoxal phosphate

**20.41** What vitamin may be deficient in the following conditions?
**a.** rickets **b.** scurvy **c.** pellagra

**20.42** What vitamin may be deficient in the following conditions?
**a.** poor night vision
**b.** pernicious anemia
**c.** beriberi

**20.43** The RDA for pyridoxine (vitamin $B_6$) is 2 mg daily. Why will it not improve your nutrition to take 100 mg of pyridoxine daily?

**20.44** The RDA for vitamin A is 3 mg daily. What would happen if you took 25 mg of vitamin A every day?

**20.45** What is the change in the structure of pyridoxine ($B_6$) that yields the coenzyme PLP?

**20.46** What is the change in the structure of folate that yields the coenzyme THF?

## CONCEPT MAP

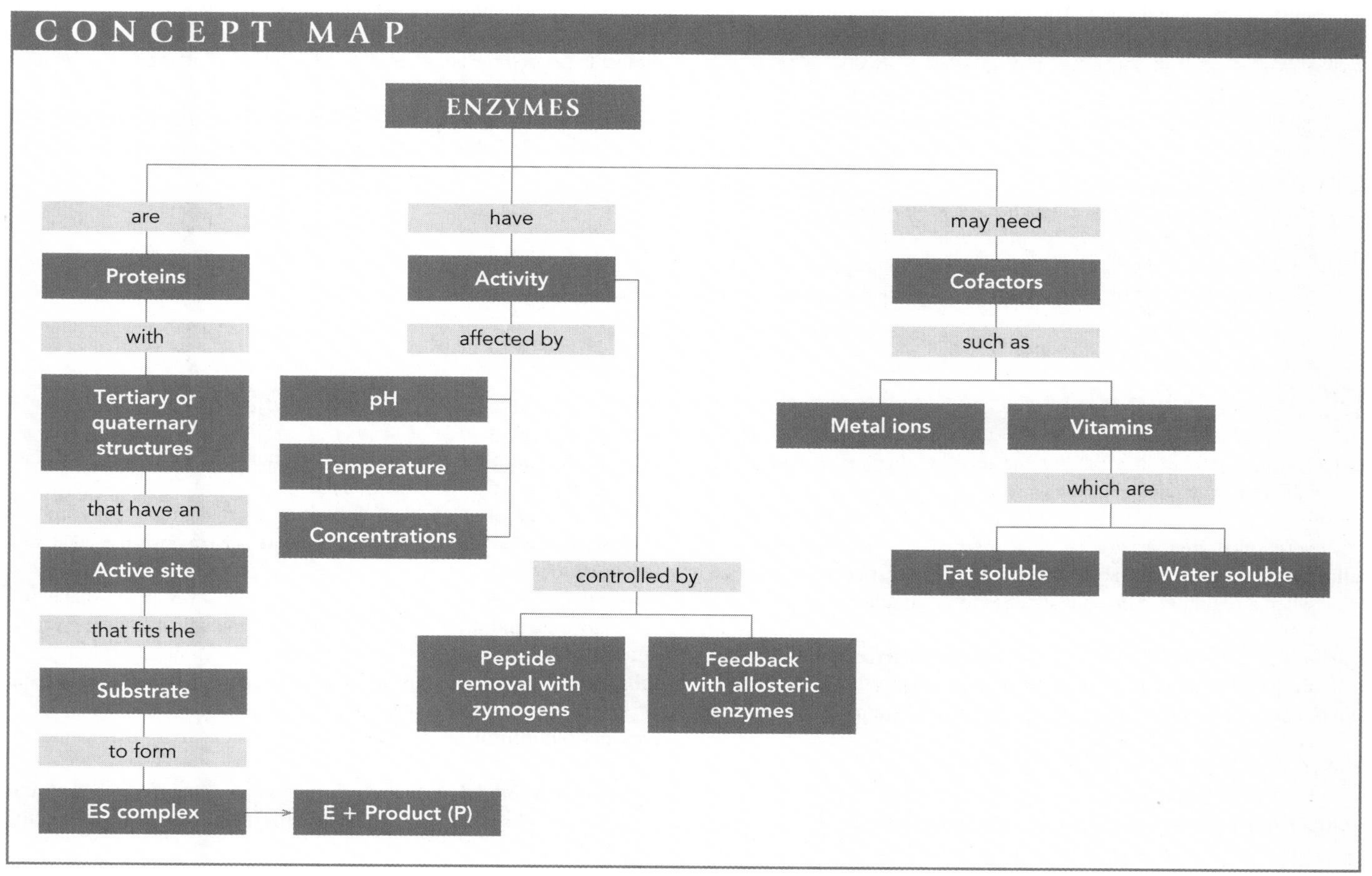

# CHAPTER REVIEW

## 20.1 Enzymes

**LEARNING GOAL:** *Describe how enzymes function as catalysts; name and classify them.*

Enzymes are globular proteins that act as biological catalysts by lowering activation energy and accelerating the rate of cellular reactions. The names of most enzymes ending in *ase* describe the compound or reaction catalyzed by the enzyme. Enzymes are classified by the main type of reaction they catalyze, such as oxidoreductase, transferase, or isomerase.

## 20.2 Enzyme Action

**LEARNING GOAL:** *Describe the role of an enzyme in an enzyme-catalyzed reaction.*

Within the tertiary structure of an enzyme, a small pocket called the active site binds the substrates. In the lock-and-key model, a substrate precisely fits the shape of the active site. In the induced-fit model, substrates induce the active site to change structure to give an optimal fit by the substrate. In the enzyme–substrate complex, catalysis takes place when amino acid side chains react with a substrate. The products are released, and the enzyme is available to bind another substrate molecule.

## 20.3 Factors Affecting Enzyme Action

**LEARNING GOAL:** *Describe the effect of temperature, pH, concentration of enzyme, and concentration of substrate on enzyme activity.*

Enzymes are most effective at optimum temperature, usually 37 °C, and optimum pH, usually 7.4. The rate of an enzyme-catalyzed reaction decreases as temperature and pH go above or below the optimum values. An increase in substrate concentration increases the reaction rate of an enzyme-catalyzed reaction. If an enzyme is saturated, adding more substrate will not increase the reaction rate.

## 20.4 Enzyme Inhibition

**LEARNING GOAL:** *Describe competitive and noncompetitive inhibition and reversible and irreversible inhibition.*

An inhibitor reduces the activity of an enzyme or makes it inactive. A competitive inhibitor has a structure similar to the substrate and competes for the active site. When the active site is occupied, the enzyme cannot catalyze the reaction of the substrate. A noncompetitive inhibitor attaches elsewhere on the enzyme, changing the shape of both the enzyme and its active site. As long as the noncompetitive inhibitor is attached, the altered active site cannot bind with substrate.

## 20.5 Regulation of Enzyme Activity

**LEARNING GOAL:** *Describe the role of zymogens, feedback control, and allosteric enzymes in regulating enzyme activity.*

Insulin and digestive enzymes are produced as inactive forms called zymogens. They are converted to active forms by the removal of a peptide portion from their protein chains. The rate of an enzyme-catalyzed reaction can be increased or decreased by regulator molecules that bind to a regulator site on an allosteric enzyme. The regulator molecule changes the shape of the enzyme and therefore the shape of the active site. A positive regulator increases the rate, whereas a negative regulator decreases the rate. In feedback control, the end product of a reaction sequence binds to a regulator site on the first enzyme, which is an allosteric enzyme, to decrease product formation.

## 20.6 Enzyme Cofactors and Vitamins

**LEARNING GOAL:** *Describe the types of cofactors found in enzymes.*

Simple enzymes are biologically active as a protein only, whereas other enzymes require small organic molecules or metal ions called cofactors. A cofactor may be a metal ion, such as $Cu^{2+}$ or $Fe^{2+}$, or an organic molecule called a coenzyme. A vitamin is a small organic molecule needed for health and normal growth. Vitamins are obtained in small amounts through the foods in the diet. The water-soluble vitamins B and C function as coenzymes. The fat-soluble vitamins are A, D, E, and K. Vitamin A is important in vision, vitamin D for proper bone growth, vitamin E is an antioxidant, and vitamin K is required for proper blood clotting.

# KEY TERMS

**active site** A pocket in a part of the tertiary enzyme structure that binds substrate and catalyzes a reaction.

**activity** The rate at which an enzyme catalyzes the reaction that converts substrate to product.

**allosteric enzyme** An enzyme that regulates the rate of a reaction when a regulator molecule attaches to a site other than the active site.

**antibiotics** Substances usually produced by bacteria, mold, or yeast that inhibit the growth of bacteria.

**coenzyme** An organic molecule, usually a vitamin, required as a cofactor in enzyme action.

**cofactor** A metal ion or an organic molecule that is necessary for a biologically functional enzyme.

**competitive inhibitor** A molecule with a structure similar to the substrate that inhibits enzyme action by competing for the active site.

**enzymes** Globular proteins, sometimes with cofactors, that catalyze biological reactions.

**enzyme–substrate (ES) complex** An intermediate consisting of an enzyme that binds to a substrate in an enzyme-catalyzed reaction.

**fat-soluble vitamins** Vitamins that are not soluble in water and can be stored in the liver and body fat.

**feedback control** A type of inhibition in which an end product inhibits the first enzyme in a sequence of enzyme-catalyzed reactions.

**induced-fit model** A model of enzyme action in which the shape of a substrate and the active site of the enzyme adjust to give an optimal fit.

**inhibitors** Substances that make an enzyme inactive by interfering with its ability to react with a substrate.

**irreversible inhibition** The loss of enzymatic activity that cannot be reversed.

**lock-and-key model** A model of enzyme action in which the substrate is like a key that fits the specific shape of the active site (the lock).

**noncompetitive inhibitor** A type of inhibitor that alters the shape of an enzyme as well as the active site so that the substrate cannot bind properly.

**optimum pH** The pH at which an enzyme is most active.

**optimum temperature** The temperature at which an enzyme is most active.

**reversible inhibition** The loss of enzymatic activity by an inhibitor whose effect can be reversed.

**simple enzyme** An enzyme that is active as a polypeptide only.

**substrate** The molecule that reacts in the active site in an enzyme-catalyzed reaction.

**vitamins** Organic molecules that are essential for normal health and growth and are obtained in small amounts from the diet.

**water-soluble vitamins** Vitamins that are soluble in water; they cannot be stored in the body, are easily destroyed by heat, ultraviolet light, and oxygen, and function as coenzymes.

**zymogen** An inactive form of an enzyme that is activated by the removal of a peptide portion from one end of the protein.

## UNDERSTANDING THE CONCEPTS

20.47 Ethylene glycol ($HO—CH_2—CH_2—OH$) is a major component of antifreeze. In the body, it is first converted to HOOC—CHO (oxoethanoic acid) and then to HOOC—COOH (oxalic acid), which is toxic.

**a.** What class of enzyme catalyzes both of the reactions of ethylene glycol?

**b.** The treatment for the ingestion of ethylene glycol is an intravenous solution of ethanol. How might this help prevent toxic levels of oxalic acid in the body?

**20.48** Adults who are lactose intolerant cannot break down the disaccharide in milk products. To help digest dairy food, a product known as Lactaid can be added to milk. The milk is then refrigerated for 24 hours.

**a.** What enzyme is present in Lactaid, and what is the major class of this enzyme?

**b.** What might happen to the enzyme if the digestion product were stored in a warm area?

20.49 Fresh pineapple contains the enzyme bromelain that degrades proteins.

**a.** The directions on a gelatin package say not to add fresh pineapple. However, canned pineapple, where pineapple is heated to high temperatures, can be added. Why?

**b.** Fresh pineapple can be used as a marinade to tenderize tough meat. Why?

**20.50** Beano contains an enzyme that breaks down polysaccharides into smaller, more digestible sugars, which diminishes the gas formation that can occur after eating foods such as vegetables and beans.

**a.** The label says "contains alpha-galactosidase." What class of enzyme is present in beano?

**b.** What is the substrate for the enzyme?

**c.** The directions indicate you should not cook with or heat beano. Why?

## ADDITIONAL QUESTIONS AND PROBLEMS

*For instructor-assigned homework, go to* ***www.masteringchemistry.com.***

20.51 Why do the cells in the body have so many enzymes?

**20.52** Are all the possible enzymes present at the same time in a cell?

20.53 How are enzymes different from the catalysts used in chemistry laboratories?

**20.54** Why do enzymes function only under mild conditions?

20.55 Indicate whether each of the following would be a substrate (S) or an enzyme (E):
**a.** lactose **b.** lactase **c.** urease
**d.** trypsin **e.** pyruvate **f.** transaminase

**20.56** Indicate whether each of the following would be a substrate (S) or an enzyme (E):
**a.** glucose **b.** hydrolase **c.** maleate isomerase
**d.** alanine **e.** amylose **f.** amylase

20.57 Give the substrate of each of the following enzymes:
**a.** urease
**b.** lactase
**c.** aspartate transaminase
**d.** phenylalanine hydroxylase

**20.58** Give the substrate of each of the following enzymes:
**a.** maltase **b.** fructose oxidase
**c.** phenolase **d.** sucrase

20.59 Predict the major class of each of the following enzymes:
**a.** acyltransferase **b.** oxidase
**c.** lipase **d.** decarboxylase

**20.60** Predict the major class for each of the following enzymes:
**a.** cis–trans isomerase **b.** reductase
**c.** carboxylase **d.** peptidase

20.61 How would the lock-and-key theory explain that sucrase hydrolyses sucrose but not lactose?

**20.62** How does the induced-fit model of enzyme action allow an enzyme to catalyze a reaction of a group of substrates?

20.63 If a blood test indicates a high level of LDH and CK, what could be the cause?

**20.64** If a blood test indicates a high level of ALT, what could be the cause?

20.65 Indicate whether an enzyme is saturated or unsaturated in each of the following conditions:
**a.** adding more substrate does not increase the rate of reaction
**b.** doubling the substrate concentration doubles the rate of reaction

**20.66** Indicate whether each of the following enzymes would be functional:
**a.** pepsin, a digestive enzyme, at pH 2
**b.** an enzyme at 37 °C, if the enzyme is from a type of thermophilic bacteria that have an optimum temperature of 100 °C

20.67 How does reversible inhibition differ from irreversible inhibition?

**20.68** How does competitive reversible inhibition differ from noncompetitive reversible inhibition?

20.69 **a.** What type of an inhibitor is the antibiotic amoxicillin?
**b.** Why can amoxicillin be used to treat bacterial infections?

**20.70** **a.** A gardener using Parathion develops a headache, dizziness, nausea, blurred vision, excessive salivation, and muscle twitching. What might be happening to the gardener?
**b.** Why must humans be careful when using insecticides?

20.71 The zymogen pepsinogen is produced in the gastric mucosa.
**a.** How and where does pepsinogen become the active form pepsin?
**b.** Why are proteases such as pepsin produced in inactive forms?

**20.72** Thrombin is an enzyme that helps produce blood clotting when an injury and bleeding occur.
**a.** What would be the name of the zymogen of thrombin?
**b.** Why would the active form of thrombin be produced only when an injury to tissue occurs?

20.73 What is an allosteric enzyme?

**20.74** Why can some regulator molecules speed up a reaction, while others slow it down?

20.75 In feedback control, what type of regulator modifies the catalytic activity of the reaction pathway?

**20.76** Why aren't the intermediate products in a reaction sequence used in feedback control?

20.77 Does each of the following statements describe a simple enzyme or an enzyme that requires a cofactor?
**a.** contains $Mg^{2+}$ in the active site
**b.** has catalytic activity as a tertiary protein structure
**c.** requires folic acid for catalytic activity

**20.78** Does each of the following statements describe a simple enzyme or an enzyme that requires a cofactor?
**a.** contains riboflavin or vitamin $B_2$
**b.** has four subunits of polypeptide chains
**c.** requires $Fe^{3+}$ in the active site for catalytic activity

20.79 Match the following vitamins with their coenzymes:
**(1)** $NAD^+$ **(2)** TPP **(3)** coenzyme A
**a.** pantothenic acid ($B_5$)
**b.** niacin ($B_3$)
**c.** thiamine ($B_1$)

**20.80** Match the following vitamins with their coenzymes:
**(1)** pyridoxal phosphate **(2)** THF **(3)** FAD
**a.** folate
**b.** riboflavin ($B_2$)
**c.** pyridoxine

20.81 Why are only small amounts of vitamins needed in the cells when there are several enzymes that require coenzymes?

**20.82** Why is there a daily requirement for vitamins?

20.83 Match each of the following vitamins with their deficiency symptoms or conditions:
**(1)** night blindness
**(2)** weak bone structure
**(3)** pellagra
**a.** niacin **b.** vitamin A **c.** vitamin D

**20.84** Match each of the following vitamins with their deficiency symptoms or conditions:
**(1)** bleeding **(2)** anemia **(3)** scurvy
**a.** cobalamin
**b.** vitamin C
**c.** vitamin K

## CHALLENGE QUESTIONS

20.85 Lactase is an enzyme that hydrolyzes lactose to glucose and galactose.

**a.** What are the reactants and products of the reaction?
**b.** Draw an energy diagram for the reaction with and without lactase.
**c.** How does lactase make the reaction go faster?

20.86 Maltase is an enzyme that hydrolyzes maltose into two glucose molecules.

**a.** What are the reactants and products of the reaction?
**b.** Draw an energy diagram for the reaction with and without maltase.
**c.** How does maltase make the reaction go faster?

20.87 What is the class of the enzyme that would catalyze each of the following reactions?

**a.** 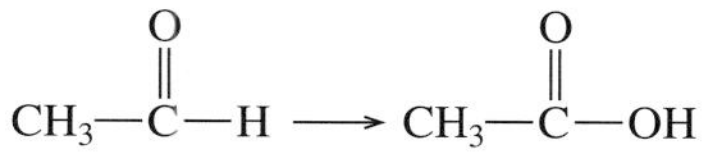 $CH_3{-}\overset{O}{\overset{\|}{C}}{-}H \longrightarrow CH_3{-}\overset{O}{\overset{\|}{C}}{-}OH$

**b.** $\overset{+}{N}H_3{-}CH_2{-}\overset{O}{\overset{\|}{C}}{-}NH{-}\overset{CH_3}{\overset{|}{C}H}{-}\overset{O}{\overset{\|}{C}}{-}O^- + H_2O \longrightarrow$

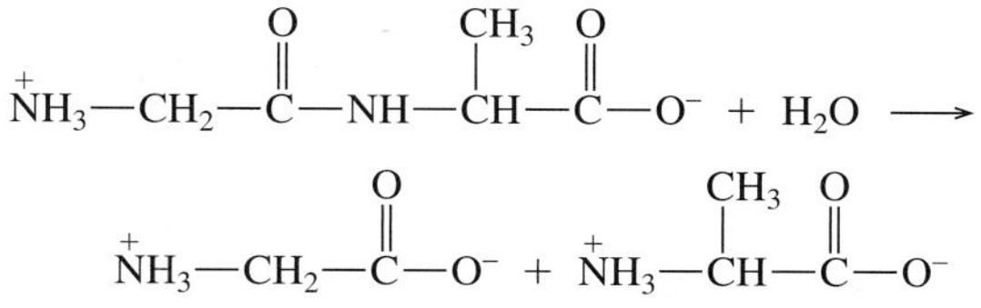

$\overset{+}{N}H_3{-}CH_2{-}\overset{O}{\overset{\|}{C}}{-}O^- + \overset{+}{N}H_3{-}\overset{CH_3}{\overset{|}{C}H}{-}\overset{O}{\overset{\|}{C}}{-}O^-$

**c.** $CH_3{-}CH{=}CH{-}CH_3 + H_2O \longrightarrow$

$CH_3{-}CH_2{-}\overset{OH}{\overset{|}{C}H}{-}CH_3$

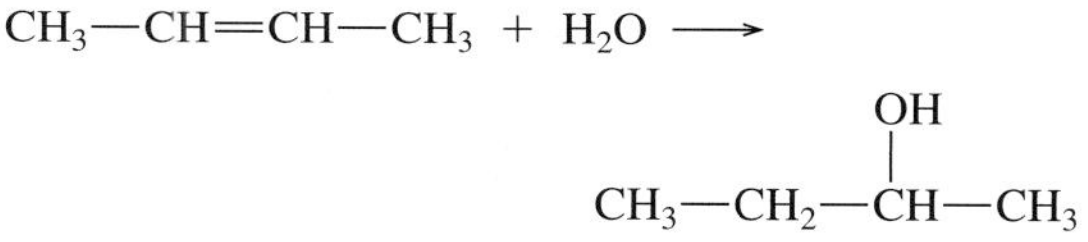

20.88 What is the class of the enzyme that would catalyze each of the following reactions?

**a.** 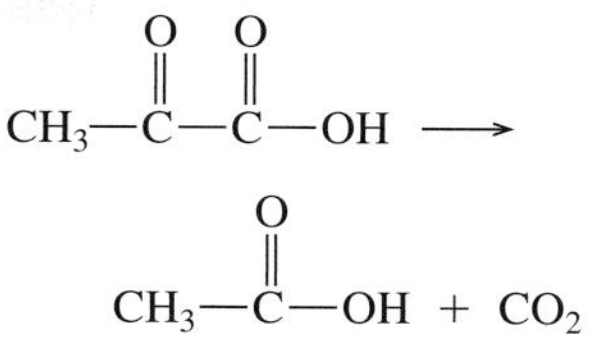 $CH_3{-}\overset{O}{\overset{\|}{C}}{-}\overset{O}{\overset{\|}{C}}{-}OH \longrightarrow$

$CH_3{-}\overset{O}{\overset{\|}{C}}{-}OH + CO_2$

**b.** 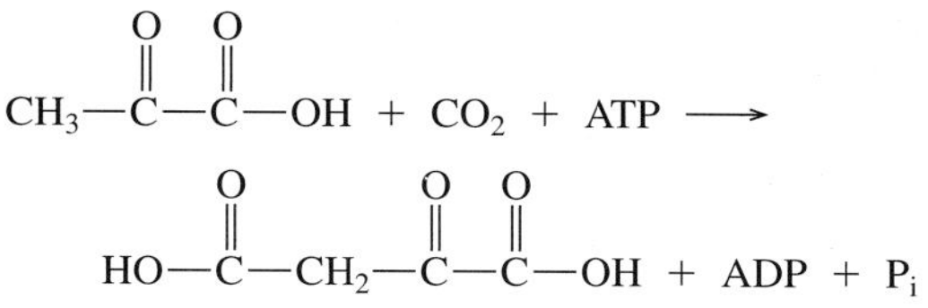 $CH_3{-}\overset{O}{\overset{\|}{C}}{-}\overset{O}{\overset{\|}{C}}{-}OH + CO_2 + ATP \longrightarrow$

$HO{-}\overset{O}{\overset{\|}{C}}{-}CH_2{-}\overset{O}{\overset{\|}{C}}{-}\overset{O}{\overset{\|}{C}}{-}OH + ADP + P_i$

**c.** glucose-6-phosphate $\longrightarrow$ fructose-6-phosphate

## ANSWERS

### ANSWERS TO STUDY CHECKS

**20.1** hydrolase

**20.2** In the lock-and-key model, the shape of a substrate fits the shape of the active site exactly. In the induced-fit model, the substrate and the active site adjust shape to provide the best fit.

**20.3** At a pH lower than the optimum pH, denaturation will decrease the activity of urease.

**20.4** Pepsin hydrolyzes proteins in the foods we ingest. It is synthesized as a zymogen, pepsinogen, to prevent its digestion of the proteins that make up the organs in the body.

**20.5** vitamin $B_6$

**20.6** Water-soluble vitamins are easily destroyed by heat.

### ANSWERS TO SELECTED QUESTIONS AND PROBLEMS

**20.1** Chemical reactions can occur without enzymes, but the rates are too slow. Catalyzed reactions, which are many times faster, provide the amounts of products needed by the cell at a particular time.

**20.3** **a.** oxidation–reduction
**b.** transfer of a group from one substance to another
**c.** hydrolysis (splitting) of molecules with the addition of water

**20.5** **a.** hydrolase **b.** oxidoreductase
**c.** isomerase **d.** transferase

**20.7** **a.** lyase **b.** transferase

**20.9** **a.** succinate oxidase
**b.** fumarate hydrase
**c.** alcohol dehydrogenase

**20.11** **a.** enzyme (2)
**b.** enzyme–substrate complex (1)
**c.** substrate (3)

**20.13** **a.** $E + S \rightleftarrows ES \longrightarrow E + P$
**b.** The active site is a region or pocket within the tertiary structure of an enzyme that accepts the substrate, aligns the substrate for reaction, and catalyzes the reaction.

**20.15** Isoenzymes are slightly different forms of an enzyme that catalyze the same reaction in different organs and tissues of the body.

**20.17** A doctor might run tests for the enzymes CK, LDH, and AST to determine if the patient had a heart attack.

**20.19** **a.** The rate would decrease.
**b.** The rate would decrease.
**c.** The rate would decrease.
**d.** The rate increases as long as there is free substrate to react.

**20.21** pepsin, pH 2; sucrase, pH 6; trypsin, pH 8

**20.23** **a.** (1) competitive, (2) reversible
**b.** (1) noncompetitive, (2) may be either
**c.** (1) competitive, (2) reversible
**d.** (1) noncompetitive, (2) may be either
**e.** (1) competitive, (2) reversible

**20.25 a.** methanol, $CH_3—OH$; ethanol, $CH_3—CH_2—OH$
**b.** Ethanol has a similar structure to methanol and could compete for the active site.
**c.** Ethanol is a competitive inhibitor of methanol oxidation.

**20.27** Enzymes that act on proteins are proteases and would digest the proteins of the organ where they are produced if they were active immediately upon synthesis.

**20.29** In feedback control, the product binds to the first enzyme in a series and changes the shape of the active site. If the active site can no longer bind the substrate effectively, the reaction will stop.

**20.31** When a regulator molecule binds to an allosteric site, the shape of the enzyme is altered, which makes the active site more reactive or less reactive and thereby increases or decreases the rate of the reaction.

**20.33 a.** (3) negative regulator
**b.** (4) allosteric enzyme
**c.** (1) zymogen

**20.35 a.** an enzyme that requires a cofactor
**b.** an enzyme that requires a cofactor
**c.** a simple enzyme

**20.37 a.** THF
**b.** $NAD^+$

**20.39 a.** pantothenic acid (vitamin $B_5$)
**b.** folic acid
**c.** niacin (vitamin $B_3$)

**20.41 a.** vitamin D or cholecalciferol
**b.** ascorbic acid or vitamin C
**c.** niacin or vitamin $B_3$

**20.43** Vitamin $B_6$ is a water-soluble vitamin, which means that each day any excess of vitamin $B_6$ is eliminated from the body.

**20.45** The side chain $—CH_2OH$ on the ring is oxidized to $—CHO$, and the other $—CH_2OH$ forms a phosphate ester.

**20.47 a.** oxidoreductase
**b.** Ethanol would act as a competitive inhibitor of ethylene glycol, saturate the alcohol dehydrogenase enzyme, and allow ethylene glycol to be removed from the body without producing oxalic acid.

**20.49 a.** Fresh pineapple contains an enzyme that breaks down protein, which means that the gelatin dessert would not turn solid. The high temperatures used to prepare canned pineapple denature the enzyme so it no longer can break down protein.
**b.** The enzyme in fresh pineapple juice can be used to tenderize tough meat because the enzyme breaks down proteins.

**20.51** The many different reactions that take place in cells require different enzymes because enzymes react with only a certain type of substrate.

**20.53** Enzymes are catalysts that are proteins and function only at mild temperature and pH. Catalysts used in chemistry laboratories are usually inorganic materials that can function at high temperatures and in strongly acidic or basic conditions.

**20.55 a.** S **b.** E **c.** E **d.** E **e.** S **f.** E

**20.57 a.** urea **b.** lactose
**c.** aspartate **d.** phenylalanine

**20.59 a.** transferase **b.** oxidoreductase
**c.** hydrolase **d.** lyase

**20.61** Sucrose fits the shape of the active site in sucrase, but lactose does not.

**20.63** A heart attack may be the cause.

**20.65 a.** saturated **b.** unsaturated

**20.67** In reversible inhibition, the inhibitor can dissociate from the enzyme, whereas in irreversible inhibition, the inhibitor forms a strong covalent bond with the enzyme and does not dissociate. Irreversible inhibitors act as poisons to enzymes.

**20.69 a.** Antibiotics such as amoxicillin are irreversible inhibitors.
**b.** Antibiotics inhibit enzymes needed to form cell walls in bacteria, not humans.

**20.71 a.** When pepsinogen enters the stomach, the low pH cleaves a peptide from its protein chain to form pepsin.
**b.** An active protease would digest the proteins of the stomach rather than the proteins in foods.

**20.73** An allosteric enzyme contains sites for regulators that alter the enzyme and speed up or slow down the rate of the catalyzed reaction.

**20.75** This would be feedback control because the end product of the reaction pathway binds to the enzyme to decrease or stop the first reaction in the reaction pathway.

**20.77 a.** requires a cofactor
**b.** simple enzyme
**c.** requires a cofactor (coenzyme)

**20.79 a.** (3) coenzyme A
**b.** (1) $NAD^+$
**c.** (2) TPP

**20.81** A vitamin combines with an enzyme only when the enzyme and coenzyme are needed to catalyze a reaction. When the enzyme is not needed, the vitamin dissociates for use by other enzymes in the cell.

**20.83 a.** niacin, (3) pellagra
**b.** vitamin A, (1) night blindness
**c.** vitamin D, (2) weak bone structure

**20.85 a.** The reactant is lactose and the products are glucose and galactose.
**b.**

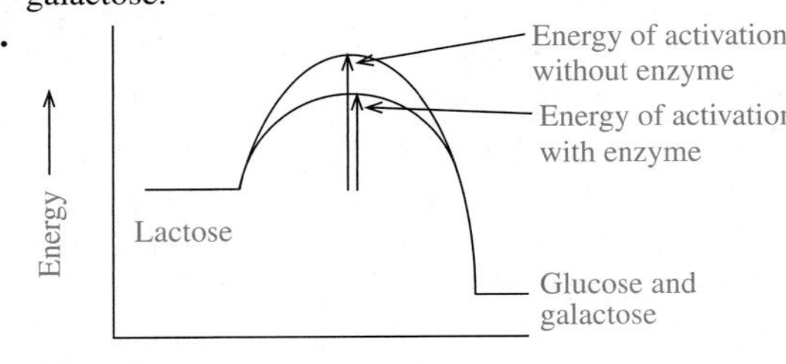


**c.** By lowering the energy of activation, the enzyme furnishes a lower energy pathway by which the reaction can take place.

**20.87 a.** oxidoreductase
**b.** hydrolase
**c.** lyase

**CI.31** The plastic known as PETE (**p**oly**e**thylene**te**rephthalate) is used to make plastic soft drink bottles and containers for salad dressings, shampoos, and dishwashing liquids. Today, PETE is the most widely recycled of all the plastics. PETE is a polymer of terephthalic acid and ethylene glycol. In a single year, 1.7 billion ($10^9$) pounds of PETE are recycled. After PETE is separated from other plastics, it can be used in polyester fabric, fill for sleeping bags, doormats, and tennis ball containers. The density of PETE is 1.38 g/mL.

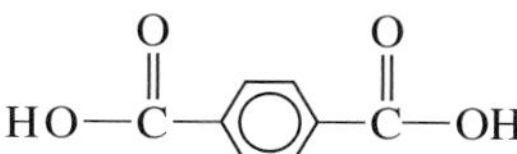

Terephthalic acid

$HO—CH_2—CH_2—OH$

Ethylene glycol

**a.** Draw the condensed structural formula of the ester formed from one molecule of terephthalic acid and one molecule of ethylene glycol.
**b.** Draw the condensed structural formula of the product formed when a second molecule of ethylene glycol reacts with the ester you drew for the answer in part **a**.
**c.** How many kilograms of PETE are recycled in 1 year?
**d.** What volume, in liters, of PETE is recycled in 1 year?
**e.** Suppose a landfill with an area of a football field and a depth of 5.0 m holds $2.7 \times 10^7$ L of recycled PETE. If all of the PETE that is recycled in a year were placed instead in landfills, how many would it fill?

**CI.32** Using the Internet or a reference book such as the *Merck Index* or *Physicians' Desk Reference*, look up the structural formulas of the following medicinal drugs and list the functional groups in the compounds. You may need to refer to the cross-index of names at the back of the reference book.
**a.** baclofen, a muscle relaxant
**b.** anethole, a licorice flavoring agent in anise and fennel
**c.** alibendol, an antispasmodic drug
**d.** pargyline, an antihypertensive drug
**e.** naproxen, nonsteroid anti-inflammatory drug

**CI.33** The insect repellent DEET is an amide that can be made from 3-methylbenzoic acid and diethylamine. A 6.0-fl-oz can of DEET repellent contains 25% DEET by mass (1 qt = 32 fluid ounces). Assume that the density of DEET solution in a can is 1.0 g/mL.
**a.** Draw the condensed structural formulas for the reaction that forms DEET.
**b.** What are the molecular formulas of 3-methylbenzoic acid, diethylamine, and DEET?

**c.** What are the molar masses of 3-methylbenzoic acid, diethylamine, and DEET?
**d.** How many grams of DEET are in one spray can?
**e.** How many molecules of DEET are in one spray can?
**f.** If 10.0 g of 3-methylbenzoic acid and 10.0 g of diethylamine react and 12.5 g of DEET are produced, what is the percent yield for the reaction?

**CI.34** Glyceryl trimyristate (trimyristin) is found in the seeds of the nutmeg (*Myristica fragrans*). The oil known as nutmeg butter contains 75% trimyristin. Ground nutmeg, which is sweet, is used to flavor many foods. It is used as a lubricant and fragrance in soaps and shaving creams. Isopropyl myristate is used to increase absorption of skin creams. Draw the condensed structural formula for each of the following:

**a.** myristic acid
**b.** glyceryl trimyristate (trimyristin)
**c.** isopropyl myristate
**d.** products of the hydrolysis of glyceryl trimyristate with an acid catalyst
**e.** products of the saponification of glyceryl trimyristate with KOH
**f.** reactant and product for oxidation of myristyl alcohol to myristic acid

**CI.35** Hyaluronic acid (HA), a polymer of about 25 000 disaccharide units, is a natural component of eye and joint fluid as well as of skin and cartilage. Due to the ability of HA to absorb water, it is used in skin care products and injections to smooth wrinkles and for treatment of arthritis. The repeating disaccharide units in HA consist of D-gluconic acid and D-acetylglucosamine.

[Structure of hyaluronic acid: repeating units of D-acetylglucosamine ($CH_2OH$, OH, $NH-C(=O)-CH_3$) and D-gluconic acid (COOH, OH, OH) joined by O linkages]

D-Acetylglucosamine is an amide derived from acetic acid and D-glucosamine, in which an amino group ($-NH_2$) replaces the hydroxyl on carbon 2 of D-glucose. Another natural polymer called chitin is found in the shells of lobsters and crabs. Chitin is made of repeating units of D-acetylglucosamine connected by $\beta$-1,4-glycosidic bonds.

a. Draw the Haworth structures for the oxidation reaction of the hydroxyl group on carbon 6 in $\beta$-D-glucose to form $\beta$-gluconic acid.
b. Draw the Haworth structure of $\beta$-D-glucosamine.
c. Draw the Haworth structure for the amide product of D-glucosamine and acetic acid.
d. What are the two types of glycosidic bonds that link the monosaccharides?
e. Draw the structure of a section of chitin with three $\beta$-D-acetylglucosamine units linked by $\beta$-1,4–glycosidic bonds.

**CI.36** In response to signals from the nervous system, the hypothalamus secretes a polypeptide hormone known as gonadotropin-releasing factor (GnRF), which stimulates the pituitary gland to release other hormones into the bloodstream. Two of the hormones are known as gonadotropins, which are luteinizing hormone (LH), and follicle-stimulating hormone (FSH). GnRF is a decapeptide with the following primary structure: Glu—His—Tyr—Ser—Tyr—Gly—Leu—Arg—Pro—Gly.

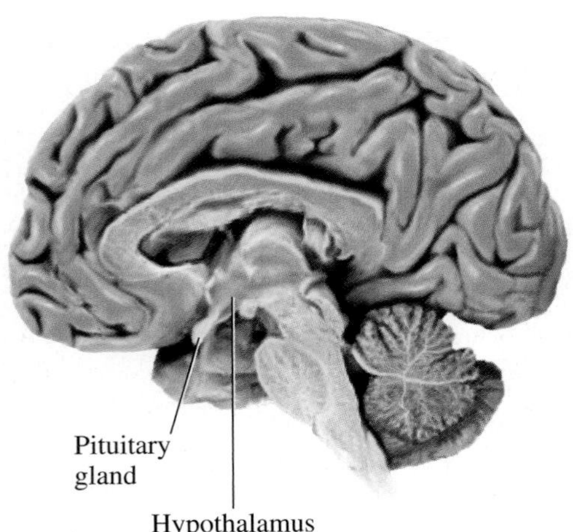


a. What is the N terminal amino acid?
b. What is the C terminal amino acid?
c. Which amino acids are nonpolar or polar neutral?
d. Write the condensed structural formulas of the acidic or basic amino acids at physiological pH.
e. Write the primary structure of the first three amino acids starting from the N terminal amino acid at physiological pH.
f. When the level of LH or FSH is high in the bloodstream, the hypothalamus stops secreting GnRF. What type of regulation of proteins does this represent?

## ■ ANSWERS

**CI.31** a. $HO-C(=O)-C_6H_4-C(=O)-O-CH_2-CH_2-OH$

b. $HO-CH_2-CH_2-O-C(=O)-C_6H_4-C(=O)-O-CH_2-CH_2-OH$

c. $7.7 \times 10^8$ kg of PETE
d. $5.6 \times 10^8$ L of PETE
e. 21 landfills

**CI.33** a. $H_3C-C_6H_4-C(=O)-OH + H-N(CH_2-CH_3)-CH_2-CH_3 \longrightarrow$

$H_3C-C_6H_4-C(=O)-N(CH_2-CH_3)-CH_2-CH_3 + H_2O$

b. $C_8H_8O_2$ (3-methylbenzoic acid), $C_4H_{11}N$ (diethylamine), $C_{12}H_{17}NO$ (DEET)

**c.** 136 g/mole (3-methylbenzoic acid), 73.0 g/mole (diethylamine), 191 g/mole (DEET)

**d.** 44 g of DEET

**e.** $1.4 \times 10^{23}$ molecules

**f.** 89.3% yield of DEET

**CI.35** **a.**

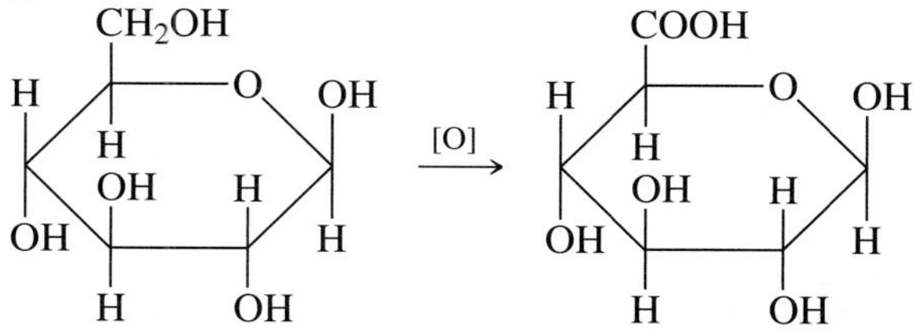

$CH_2OH$ (ring structure) $\xrightarrow{[O]}$ $COOH$ (ring structure)

**b.** (ring structure with $CH_2OH$, $NH_2$)

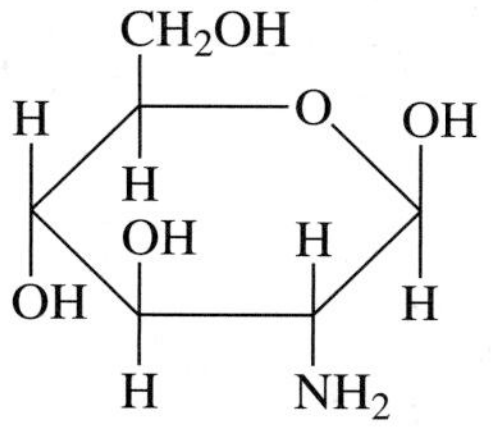

**c.** (ring structure with $CH_2OH$, NH—C=O—$CH_3$)

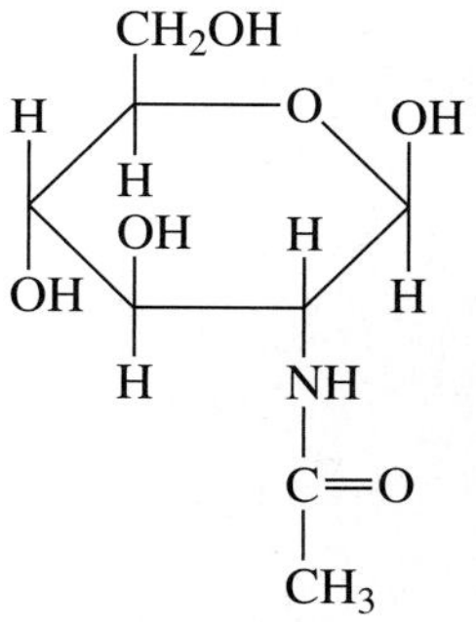

**d.** They are $\beta$-1,4- and $\beta$-1,3-glycosidic bonds.

**e.** (polymer chain of three rings with $CH_2OH$, N—H, C=O, $CH_3$)

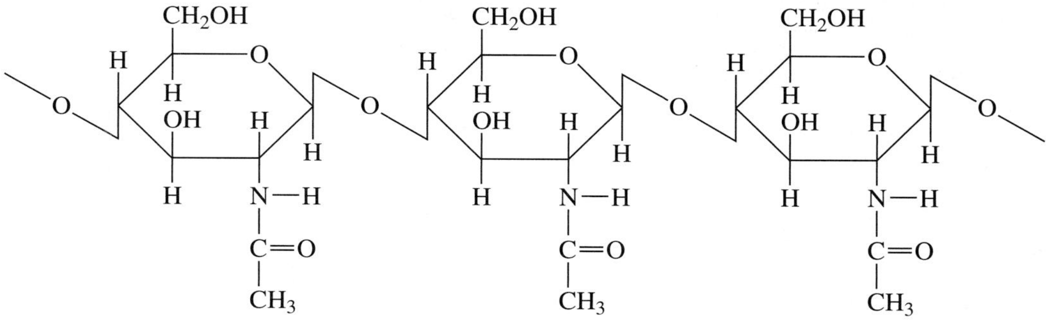

# 21 Nucleic Acids and Protein Synthesis

LOOKING AHEAD


21.1 Components of Nucleic Acids
21.2 Primary Structure of Nucleic Acids
21.3 DNA Double Helix
21.4 DNA Replication
21.5 RNA and Transcription
21.6 The Genetic Code
21.7 Protein Synthesis: Translation
21.8 Genetic Mutations
21.9 Recombinant DNA
21.10 Viruses


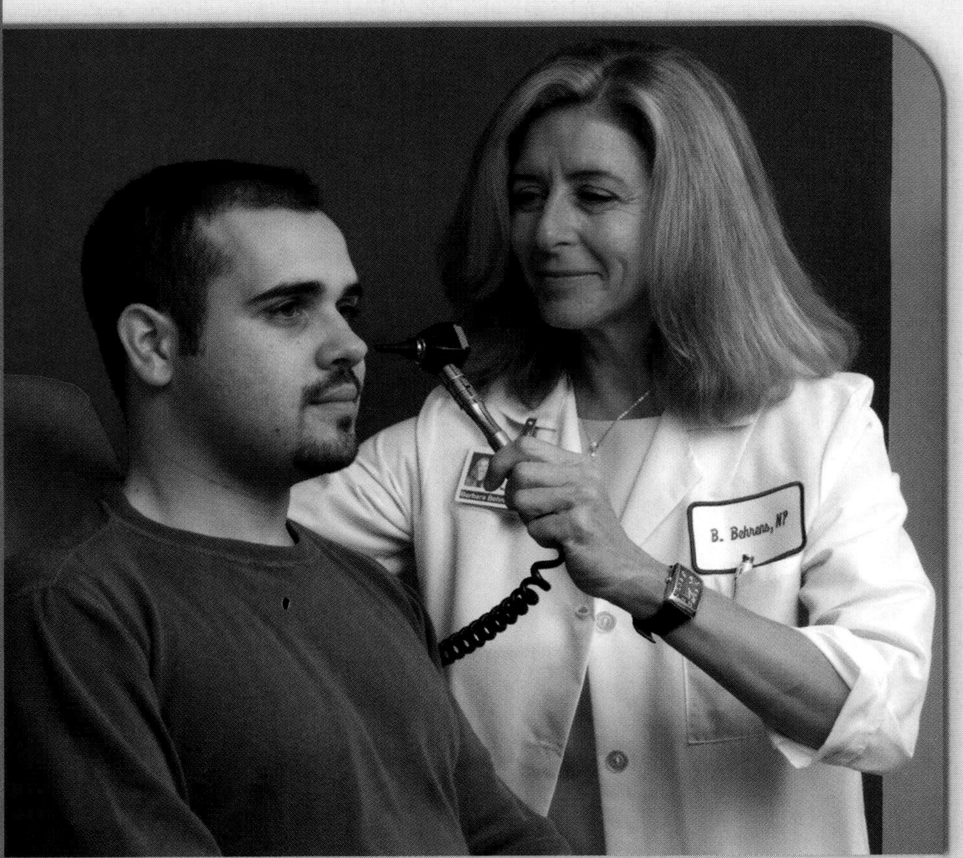


*"I run the Hepatitis C Clinic, where patients are often anxious when diagnosed," says Barbara Behrens, nurse practitioner, Hepatitis C Clinic, Kaiser Hospital. "The treatment for hepatitis C can produce significant reactions such as a radical drop in blood count. When this happens, I get help to them within 24 hours. I monitor our patients very closely, and many call me whenever they need to."*

*Hepatitis C is an RNA virus, or retrovirus, that causes liver inflammation, often resulting in chronic liver disease. Unlike many viruses to which we eventually develop immunity, the hepatitis C virus undergoes mutations so rapidly that scientists have not been able to produce vaccines. People who carry the virus are contagious throughout their lives and are able to pass the virus to other people.*

Nucleic acids are large molecules found in the nuclei of cells that store information and direct activities for cellular growth and reproduction. Deoxyribonucleic acid (DNA), the genetic material in the nucleus of a cell, contains all the information needed for the development of a complete living organism. The way you grow, your hair, your eyes, your physical appearance, and all the activities of all the cells in your body are determined by a set of directions contained within the DNA of your cells.

All of the genetic information in the cell is called the *genome*. Every time a cell divides, the information in the genome is copied and passed on to the new cells. This replication process must duplicate the genetic instructions exactly. Some sections of DNA called *genes* contain the information to make a particular protein.

As a cell requires protein, another type of nucleic acid, ribonucleic acid (RNA), translates the genetic information in DNA and carries that information to the ribosomes, where the synthesis of protein takes place. However, mistakes may occur that lead to mutations that affect the synthesis of a certain protein.

## 21.1 Components of Nucleic Acids

**LEARNING GOAL**

Describe the bases and ribose sugars that make up the nucleic acids DNA and RNA.

There are two closely related types of nucleic acids: *deoxyribonucleic acid* (**DNA**) and *ribonucleic acid* (**RNA**). Both are unbranched polymers of repeating monomer units known as *nucleotides*. A DNA molecule may contain several million nucleotides; smaller RNA molecules may contain up to several thousand. Each nucleotide has three components: a base, a five-carbon sugar, and a phosphate group. When $—PO_3^{2-}$ is part of a larger molecule, it is called a *phosphoryl group*. (See Figure 21.1.)

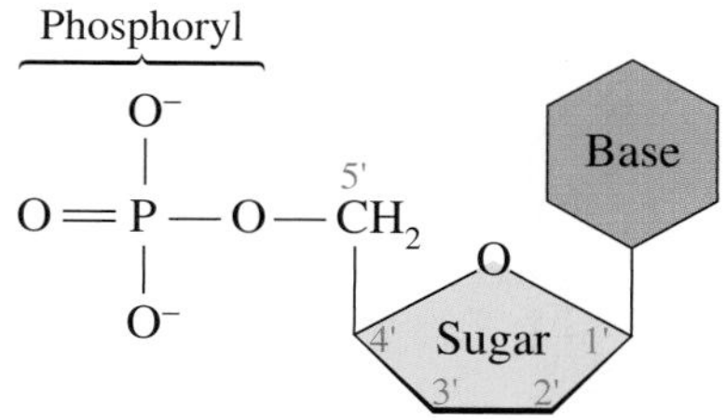


FIGURE 21.1 A diagram of the general structure of a nucleotide found in nucleic acids.

Q In a nucleotide, what types of groups are bonded to a five-carbon sugar?

### Bases

The **bases** in nucleic acids are derivatives of *pyrimidine* or *purine*:

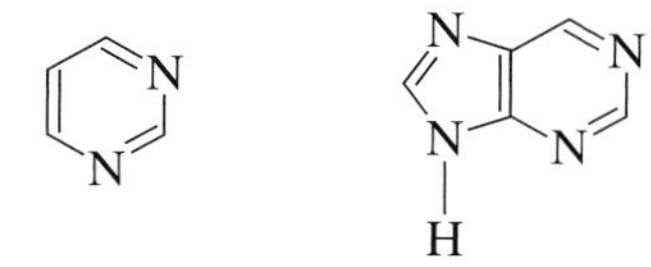

Pyrimidine

Purine

In DNA, the purine bases with double rings are adenine (A) and guanine (G), and the pyrimidine bases with single rings are cytosine (C) and thymine (T). In RNA, thymine (5-methyluracil) is replaced by uracil (U); adenine (A), guanine (G), and cytosine (C) are the same as in DNA. (See Figure 21.2.)

**FIGURE 21.2** DNA contains the bases A, G, C, and T; RNA contains A, G, C, and U.

**Q** Which bases are found in DNA?

Pyrimidines

Cytosine (C)
(DNA and RNA)

Thymine (T)
(DNA only)

Uracil (U)
(RNA only)

Purines

Adenine (A)
(DNA and RNA)

Guanine (G)
(DNA and RNA)

MC™ TUTORIAL
Nucleic Acid Building Blocks

## Ribose and Deoxyribose Sugars

Ribose in RNA

In RNA, the five-carbon sugar is *ribose*, which gives the letter R in the abbreviation RNA. The atoms in the pentose sugars are numbered with primes (1′, 2′, 3′, 4′, and 5′) to differentiate them from the atoms in the bases. In DNA, the five-carbon sugar is *deoxyribose*, which is similar to ribose except that there is no hydroxyl group (—OH) on C2′. The *deoxy* prefix means "without oxygen" and provides the D in DNA.

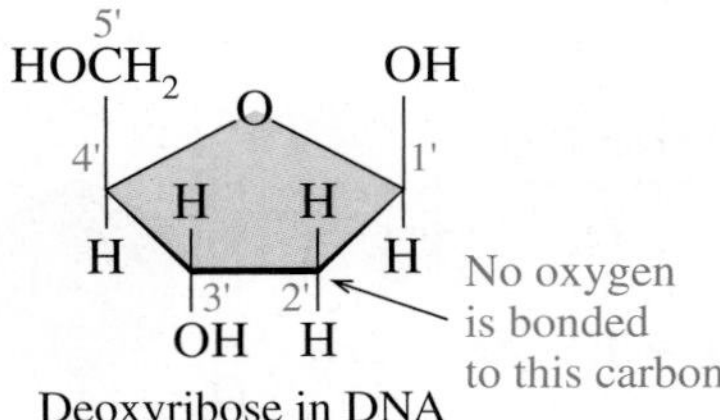

Deoxyribose in DNA

CONCEPT CHECK 21.1

**Components of Nucleic Acids**

Identify each of the following bases as a purine or pyrimidine. Indicate if each base is found in RNA, DNA, or both.

**a.**

**b.**

ANSWER

**a.** Guanine is a purine found in both RNA and DNA.

**b.** Uracil is a pyrimidine found only in RNA.

## Nucleosides and Nucleotides

A **nucleoside** is produced when a pyrimidine or a purine forms a glycosidic bond to C1′ of a sugar, either ribose or deoxyribose. For example, adenine, a purine, and ribose form a nucleoside called aden**osine**:

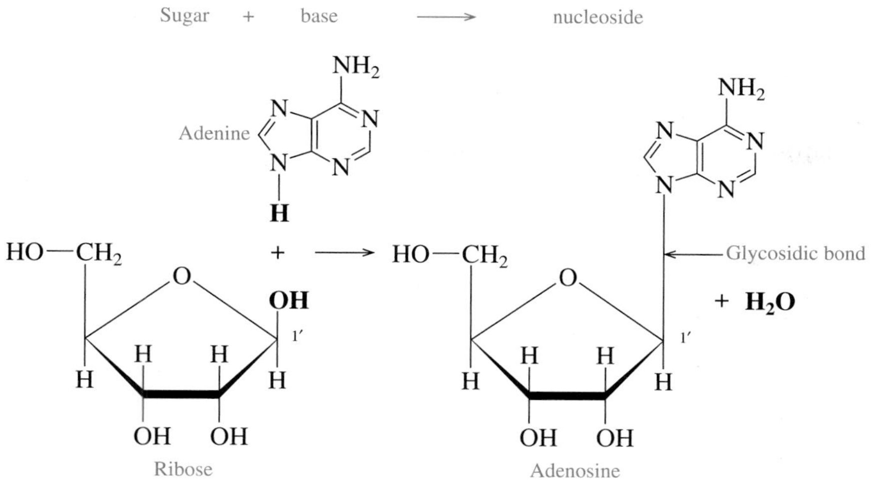

Sugar + base ⟶ nucleoside



**Nucleotides** are formed when the C5′—OH group of ribose or deoxyribose in a nucleoside forms a phosphate ester. Other hydroxyl groups on ribose can also form phosphate esters, but only the 5′-monophosphate nucleotides are found in RNA and DNA. All the nucleotides in RNA and DNA are shown in Figure 21.3.

## Naming Nucleosides and Nucleotides

The name of a nucleoside that contains a purine ends with *osine*, whereas a nucleoside that contains a pyrimidine ends with *idine*. The names of nucleosides of DNA add *deoxy* to the beginning of their names. The corresponding nucleotides in RNA and DNA are named by adding *5′-monophosphate*. Although the letters A, G, C, U, and T represent the bases, they are often used in the abbreviations of the respective nucleosides and nucleotides. The

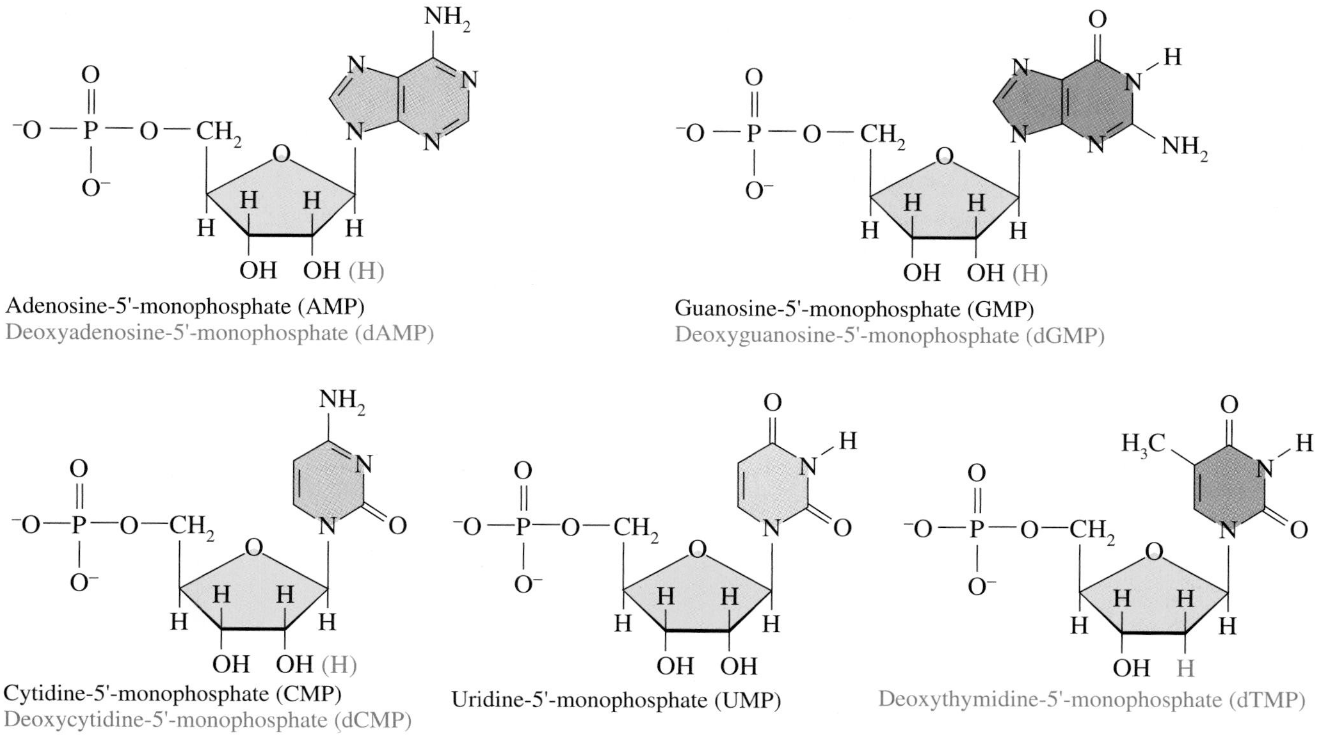

**FIGURE 21.3** The nucleotides of RNA are similar to those of DNA, except in DNA (shown in magenta) the sugar is deoxyribose and deoxythymidine replaces uridine.

**Q** What are two differences in the nucleotides of RNA and DNA?

**TABLE 21.1** Names of Nucleosides and Nucleotides in DNA and RNA

| Base | Nucleosides | Nucleotides |
|---|---|---|
| **RNA** | | |
| Adenine (A) | Adenosine (A) | Adenosine-5′-monophosphate (AMP) |
| Guanine (G) | Guanosine (G) | Guanosine-5′-monophosphate (GMP) |
| Cytosine (C) | Cytidine (C) | Cytidine-5′-monophosphate (CMP) |
| Uracil (U) | Uridine (U) | Uridine-5′-monophosphate (UMP) |
| **DNA** | | |
| Adenine (A) | Deoxyadenosine (A) | Deoxyadenosine-5′-monophosphate (dAMP) |
| Guanine (G) | Deoxyguanosine (G) | Deoxyguanosine-5′-monophosphate (dGMP) |
| Cytosine (C) | Deoxycytidine (C) | Deoxycytidine-5′-monophosphate (dCMP) |
| Thymine (T) | Deoxythymidine (T) | Deoxythymidine-5′-monophosphate (dTMP) |

names of the bases, nucleosides, and nucleotides in DNA and RNA and their abbreviations are listed in Table 21.1.

## Formation of Nucleoside Di- and Triphosphates

The phosphoryl in any nucleoside 5′-monophosphate can bond to one or two additional phosphate groups to form di- and triphosphates. For example, adding one phosphate to AMP gives ADP (*adenosine-5′-diphosphate*). Adding another phosphate to ADP gives ATP (*adenosine-5′-triphosphate*). (See Figure 21.4.) Of the triphosphates, ATP is of particular

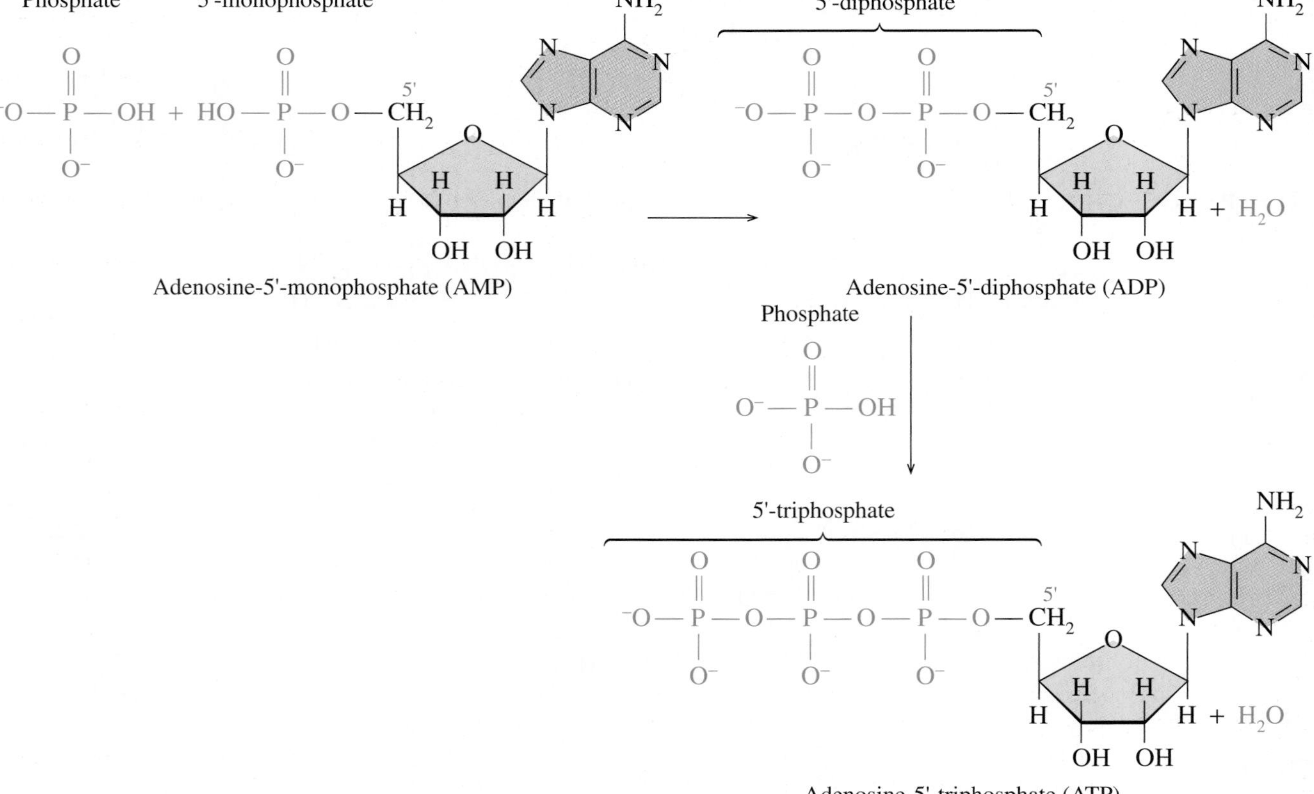


**FIGURE 21.4** The addition of one or two phosphate groups to AMP forms adenosine-5′-diphosphate (ADP) and adenosine-5′-triphosphate (ATP).

**Q** How does the structure of deoxyguanosine triphosphate (dGTP) differ from ATP?

interest because it is the major source of energy for most energy-requiring activities in the cell. In other examples, phosphate is added to GMP to yield GDP and GTP, and to dCMP to form dCDP and dCTP. GTP is an energy source for protein synthesis, and CTP is an intermediate in phospholipid synthesis.

### SAMPLE PROBLEM 21.1

#### Nucleotides

For each of the following nucleotides, identify the components and whether the nucleotide is found in DNA, RNA, or both:

**a.** deoxyguanosine-5′-monophosphate (dGMP)
**b.** adenosine-5′-monophosphate (AMP)

SOLUTION

**a.** This nucleotide of deoxyribose, guanine, and a phosphoryl group is found in DNA.
**b.** This nucleotide of ribose, adenine, and a phosphoryl group is found in RNA.

STUDY CHECK

What is the name and abbreviation of the DNA nucleotide of cytosine?

## QUESTIONS AND PROBLEMS

### Components of Nucleic Acids

21.1 Identify each of the following bases as a purine or pyrimidine:
**a.** thymine **b.**

21.2 Identify each of the following bases as a purine or pyrimidine:
**a.** guanine **b.**

21.3 Identify the bases in problem 21.1 as components of RNA, DNA, or both.

21.4 Identify the bases in problem 21.2 as components of RNA, DNA, or both.

21.5 What are the names and abbreviations of the four nucleotides in DNA?

21.6 What are the names and abbreviations of the four nucleotides in RNA?

21.7 Identify each of the following as a nucleoside or nucleotide:
**a.** adenosine **b.** deoxycytidine
**c.** uridine **d.** cytidine-5′-monophosphate

21.8 Identify each of the following as a nucleoside or nucleotide:
**a.** deoxythymidine **b.** guanosine
**c.** adenosine **d.** uridine-5′-monophosphate

21.9 Draw the structure of deoxyadenosine-5′-monophosphate (dAMP).

21.10 Draw the structure of uridine-5′-monophosphate (UMP).

## 21.2 Primary Structure of Nucleic Acids

LEARNING GOAL

Describe the primary structures of RNA and DNA.

The **nucleic acids** are polymers of many nucleotides in which the 3′-hydroxyl group of the sugar in one nucleotide bonds to the phosphoryl group on the 5′-carbon atom in the sugar of the next nucleotide. This link between the sugars in adjacent nucleotides is referred to as a **phosphodiester bond**. As more nucleotides are added using phosphodiester bonds, a backbone forms that consists of alternating sugar and phosphate groups. The bases, which are attached to each sugar, extend out from the sugar-phosphate backbone. Each nucleic acid has its own unique sequence of bases, which is known as its **primary structure**.

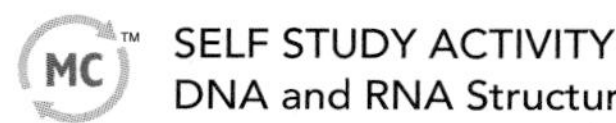

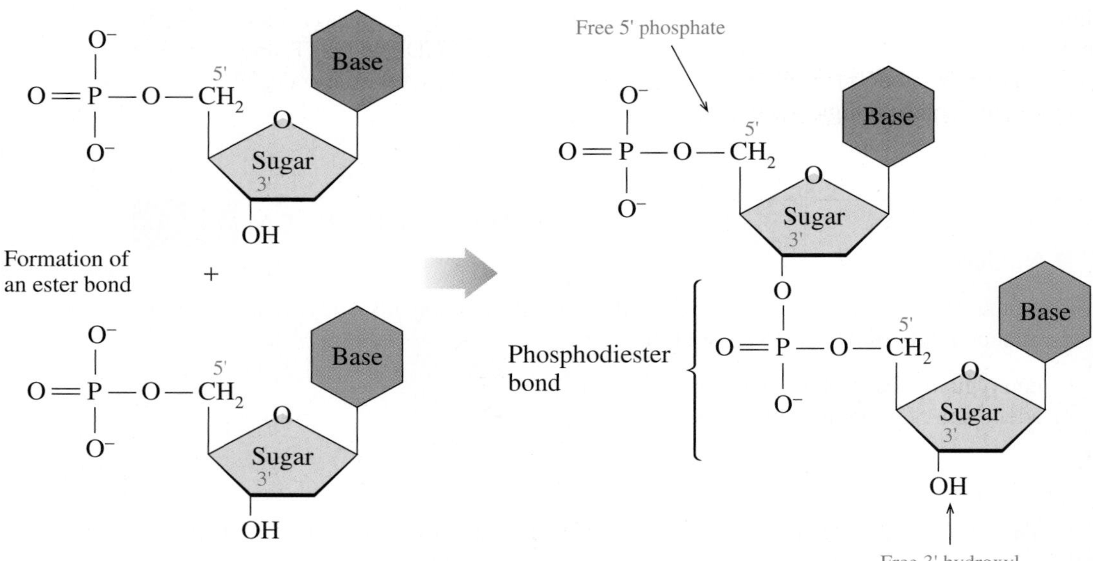


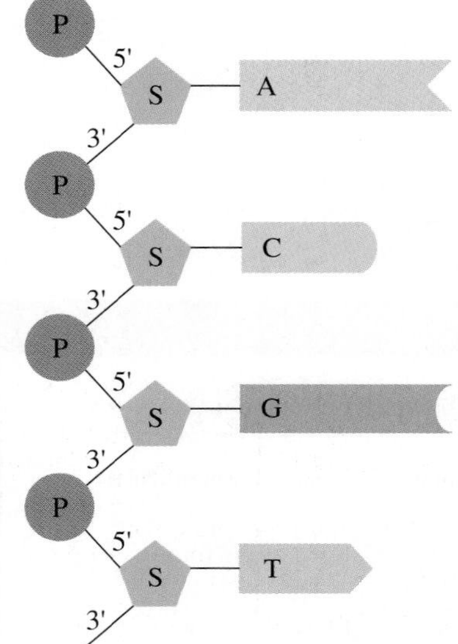


In any nucleic acid, the sugar at one end has an unreacted, or free, 5′-phosphate terminal end, and the sugar at the other end has a free 3′-hydroxyl group. A nucleic acid sequence is read from the sugar with the free 5′-phosphate to the sugar with the free 3′-hydroxyl group. The order of nucleotides is often written using only the letters of the bases. For example, the nucleotide sequence starting with adenine (free 5′-phosphate end) in the section of RNA shown in Figure 21.5 is 5′—A—C—G—U—3′.

**RNA (ribonucleic acid)**

Free 5' end

Adenine (A)

Cytosine (C)

3'–5' Phosphodiester bond

Guanine (G)

Uracil (U)

Free 3' end

**FIGURE 21.5** In the primary structure of an RNA, A, C, G, and U are linked by 3′–5′ phosphodiester bonds.

**Q** Where are the free 5′-phosphate and 3′-hydroxyl groups of ribose?

SAMPLE PROBLEM 21.2

### Bonding of Nucleotides

Draw the structure of an RNA dinucleotide formed by two CMP.

SOLUTION

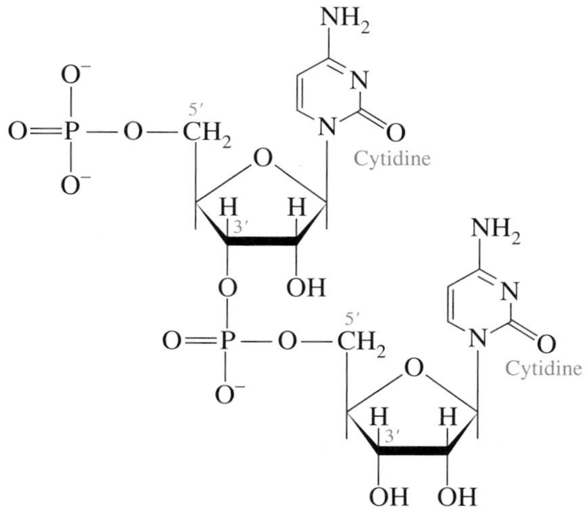

STUDY CHECK

In the dinucleotide of cytidine shown in the solution to Sample Problem 21.2, identify the free 5′-phosphate group and the free 3′-hydroxyl (—OH) group.

## QUESTIONS AND PROBLEMS

### Primary Structure of Nucleic Acids

21.11 How are the nucleotides held together in a nucleic acid chain?

**21.12** How do the ends of a nucleic acid polymer differ?

21.13 Write the structure of the dinucleotide GC that would be in RNA.

**21.14** Write the structure of the dinucleotide AT that would be in DNA.

# 21.3 DNA Double Helix

LEARNING GOAL

Describe the double helix of DNA.

During the 1940s, biologists determined that DNA in a variety of organisms had a specific relationship between bases: the amount of adenine (A) was equal to the amount of thymine (T), and the amount of guanine (G) was equal to the amount of cytosine (C). Eventually, biologists determined that adenine is always paired (1:1) with thymine, and guanine is always paired (1:1) with cytosine. (See Table 21.2.) This relationship, known as *Chargaff's rules*, can be summarized as follows:

Number of purine molecules = Number of pyrimidine molecules

A = T

G = C

In 1953, James Watson and Francis Crick proposed that DNA was a **double helix** that consists of two polynucleotide strands winding about each other like a spiral staircase. (See Figure 21.6.) The sugar-phosphate backbones are analogous to the outside railings with the bases arranged like steps along the inside. One strand goes in the 5′–3′ direction, and the other strand goes in the 3′–5′ direction.

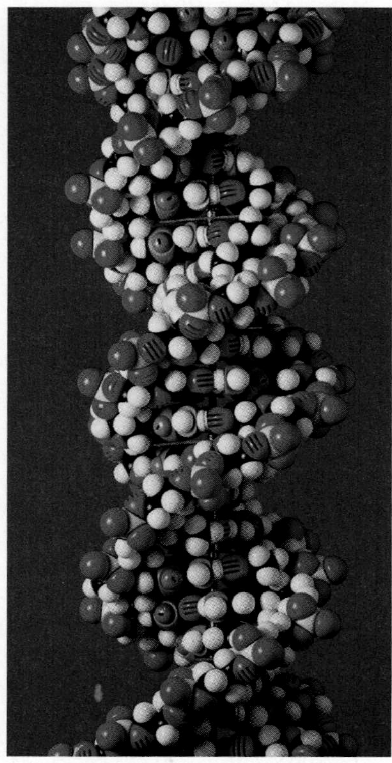

FIGURE 21.6 This space-filling model shows the double helix that is the characteristic shape of DNA molecules.

Q What is meant by the term *double helix*?

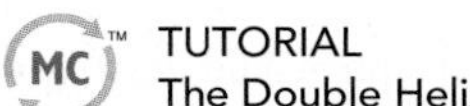

TUTORIAL
The Double Helix

**TABLE 21.2** Percentages of Bases in the DNAs of Selected Organisms

| Organism | %A | %T | %G | %C |
|---|---|---|---|---|
| Human | 30 | 30 | 20 | 20 |
| Chicken | 28 | 28 | 22 | 22 |
| Salmon | 28 | 28 | 22 | 22 |
| Corn (maize) | 27 | 27 | 23 | 23 |
| *Neurospora* | 23 | 23 | 27 | 27 |

## Complementary Base Pairs

Each of the bases along a polynucleotide strand forms hydrogen bonds to a specific base on the opposite DNA strand. Adenine bonds only to thymine and guanine bonds only to cytosine. (See Figure 21.7.) The pairs A—T and G—C are called **complementary base pairs**. The specific pairing of the bases occurs because adenine and thymine form only two hydrogen bonds, while cytosine and guanine form three hydrogen bonds. This specific pairing of the bases explains why DNA has equal amounts of A and T bases and equal amounts of G and C.

Since each base pair contains a purine and a pyrimidine, the total width of the two pairs of bases A—T and G—C is the same. Thus, the two polynucleotide strands of a DNA molecule are the same distance apart all along the DNA polymer. There are no C—T, C—A, G—T, or G—A pairs in DNA because such base-pair combinations cannot form as many hydrogen bonds or maintain a constant distance between the two DNA backbones. (See Figure 21.8.)

SAMPLE PROBLEM 21.3

### Complementary Base Pairs

Write the complementary base sequence for the following segment of a strand of DNA:

5′—A—C—G—A—T—C—T—3′

SOLUTION

In the complementary segment of DNA, A pairs with T, and G pairs with C:

Given segment of DNA: 5′—A—C—G—A—T—C—T—3′
: : : : : : :
Complementary segment: 3′—T—G—C—T—A—G—A—5′

STUDY CHECK

What sequence of bases is complementary to a DNA segment with the base sequence of 5′—G—G—T—T—A—A—C—C—3′?

## QUESTIONS AND PROBLEMS

### DNA Double Helix

**21.15** How are the two strands of nucleic acid in DNA held together?

**21.16** What is meant by complementary base pairing?

**21.17** Write the base sequence in a new DNA segment if the original segment has the following base sequence:
**a.** 5′—A—A—A—A—A—A—3′
**b.** 5′—G—G—G—G—G—G—3′
**c.** 5′—A—G—T—C—C—A—G—G—T—3′
**d.** 5′—C—T—G—T—A—T—A—C—G—T—T—A—3′

**21.18** Write the base sequence in a new DNA segment if the original segment has the following base sequence:
**a.** 5′—T—T—T—T—T—T—3′
**b.** 5′—C—C—C—C—C—C—C—C—C—3′
**c.** 5′—A—T—G—G—C—A—3′
**d.** 5′—A—T—A—T—G—C—G—C—T—A—A—A—3′

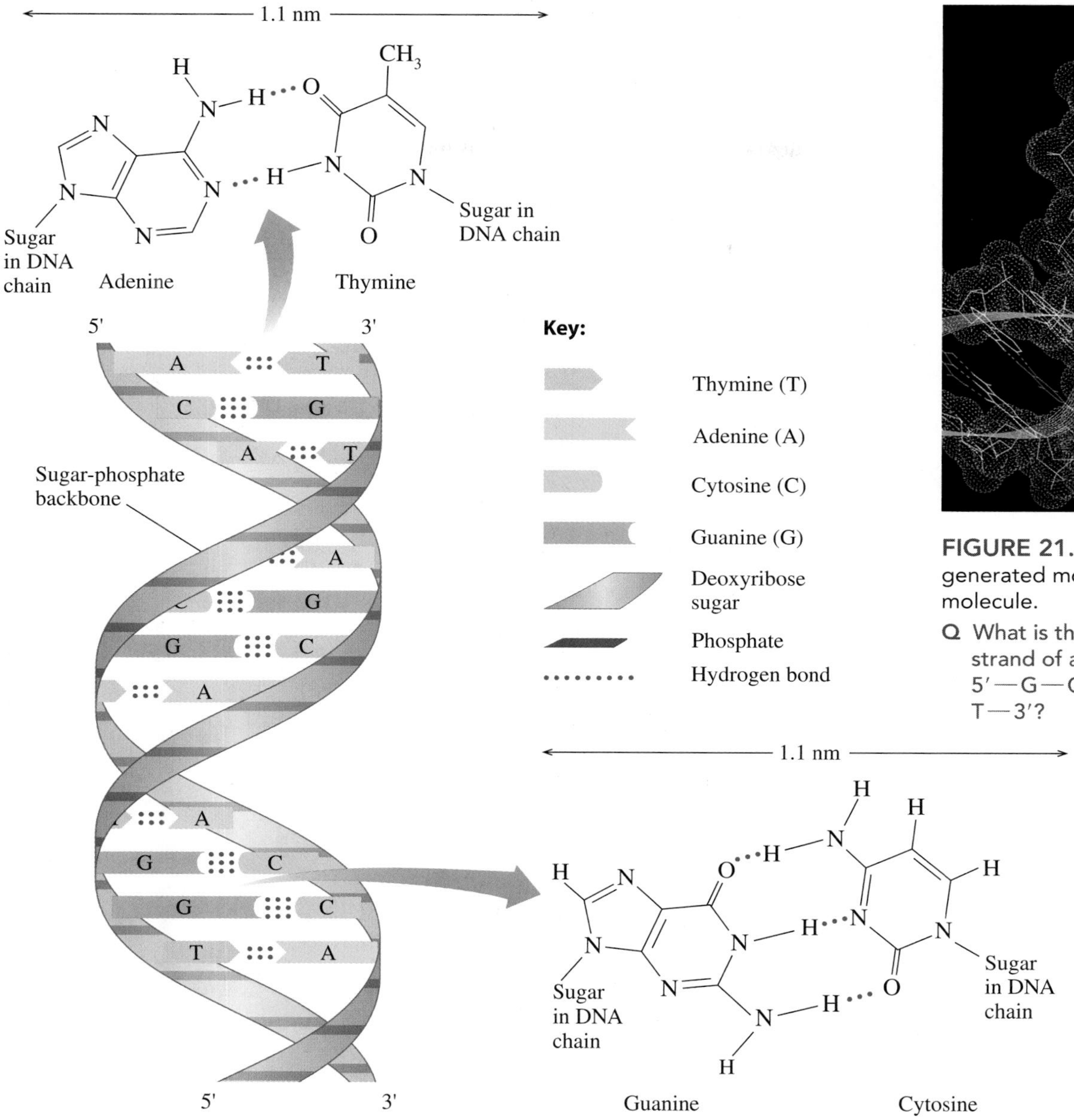

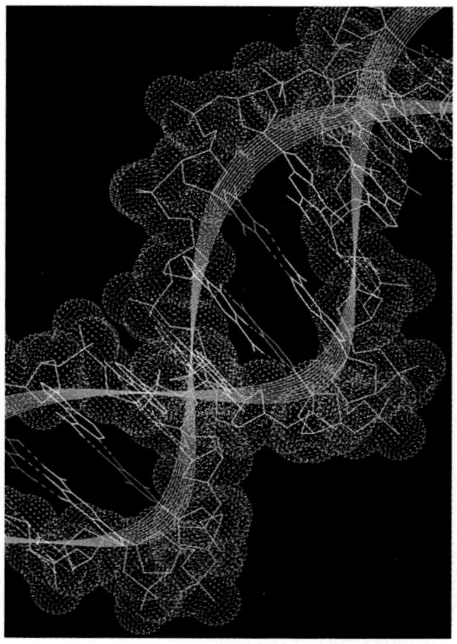

FIGURE 21.7 Hydrogen bonds between complementary base pairs hold the polynucleotide strands together in the double helix of DNA.

Q Why are G—C base pairs more stable than A—T base pairs?

FIGURE 21.8 A computer-generated model of a DNA molecule.

Q What is the complementary strand of a DNA section of 5′—G—G—C—C—T—T—3′?

## 21.4 DNA Replication

DNA found in the cells of animals, plants, and bacteria is chemically similar and has the same function, which is to preserve genetic information. As cells divide, copies of DNA are produced that transfer genetic information to the new cells.

LEARNING GOAL

Describe the process of DNA replication.

### Replication and Energy

TUTORIAL
DNA Replication

In DNA **replication**, the strands in the parent DNA molecule separate, which allows the synthesis of complementary strands of DNA. The replication process begins when an enzyme called *helicase* catalyzes the unwinding of a portion of the double helix by breaking the hydrogen bonds between the complementary bases. These single strands now act as

SELF STUDY ACTIVITY
DNA Replication

templates for the synthesis of new complementary strands of DNA. (See Figure 21.9.) Within the nucleus, nucleoside triphosphates for each base are available so that each exposed base on the template strand can form hydrogen bonds with its complementary base in the nucleoside triphosphate.

Each nucleoside triphosphate bonds to a sugar at the end of a growing strand with the hydrolysis of a phosphate bond. For example, T in the template bonds with A in ATP, and G

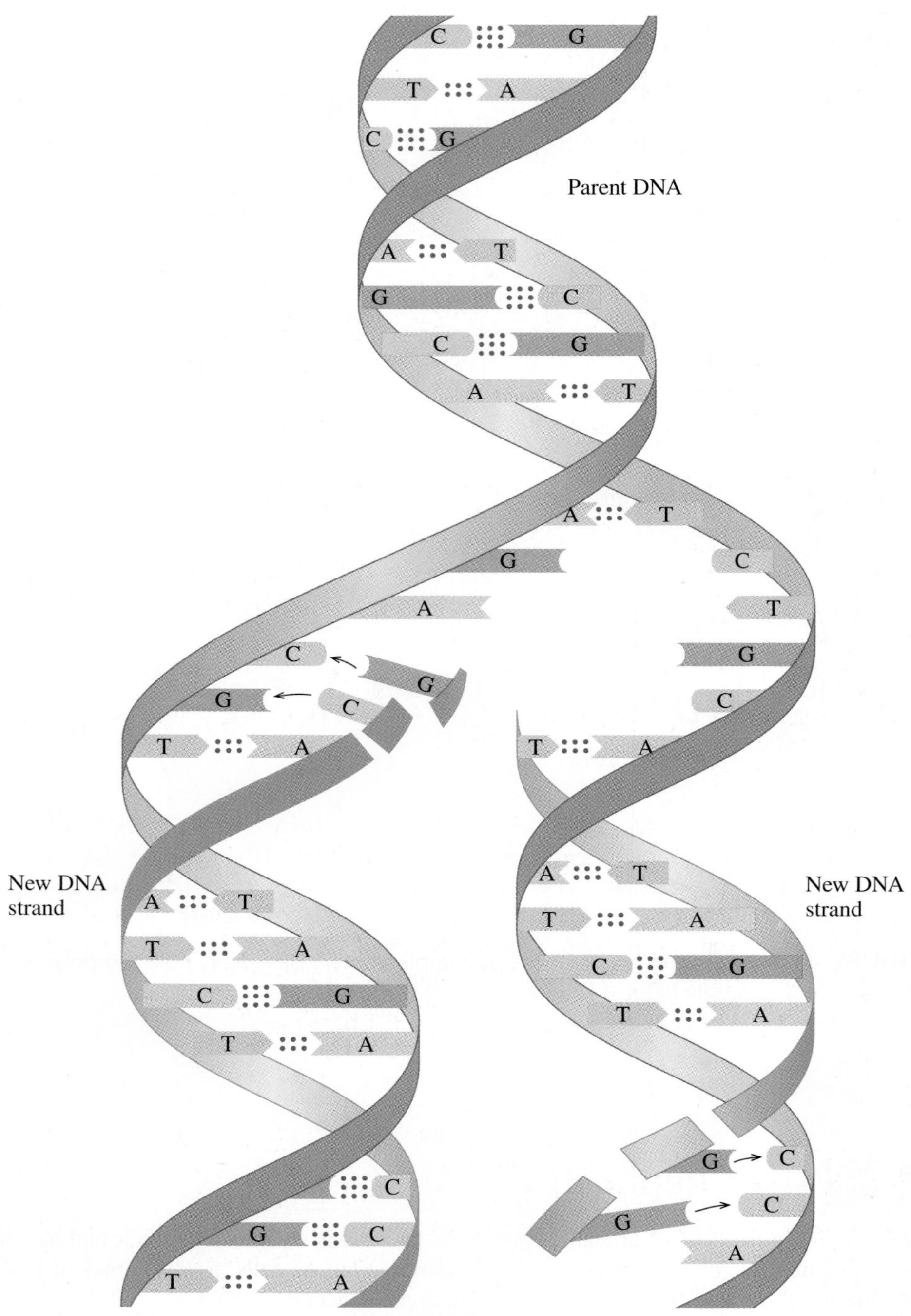


**FIGURE 21.9** In DNA replication, the separate strands of the parent DNA are the templates for the synthesis of complementary strands, which produce two exact copies of DNA.

**Q** How many strands of the parent DNA are contained in each of the daughter DNAs?

on the template strand bonds with CTP. As the base pairs form, *DNA polymerase* catalyzes the formation of phosphodiester bonds between the nucleotides. The hydrolysis of pyrophosphate releases energy for the new bonds. In this way, energy is provided to join each new nucleotide to the backbone of a growing DNA strand. (See Figure 21.10.)

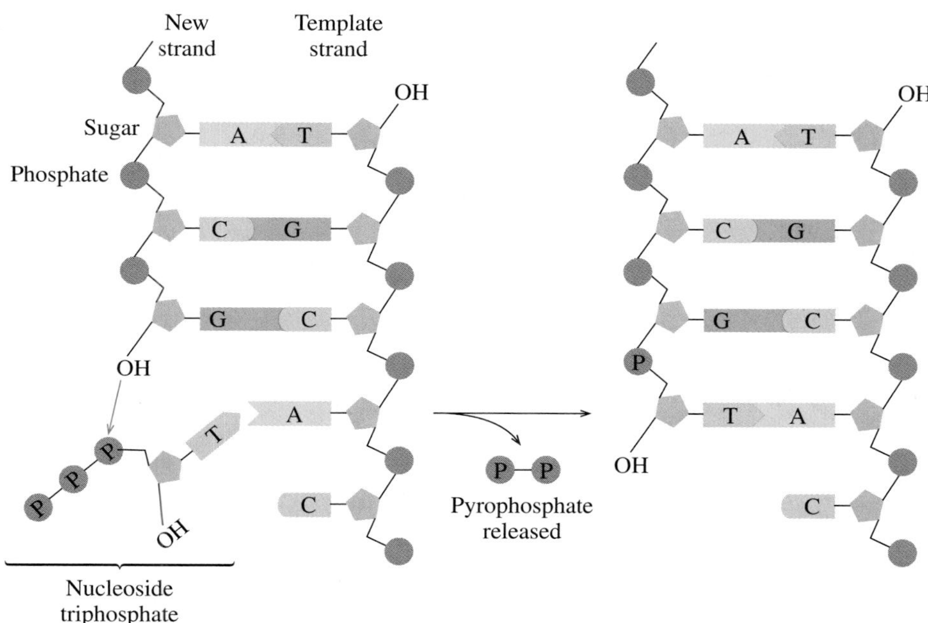


**FIGURE 21.10** Energy for the formation of a bond between thymidine triphosphate and the 3′—OH of the preceding sugar is provided by the removal of two phosphates (as pyrophosphate).

**Q** Why are nucleoside triphosphates used to provide the complementary bases instead of nucleoside monophosphates?

Eventually the entire double helix of the parent DNA is copied. In each new DNA molecule, one strand of the double helix is from the original DNA, and one is a newly synthesized strand. This process, called *semi-conservative replication*, produces two new DNAs called *daughter DNAs* that are identical to each other and exact copies of the original parent DNA. In the process of DNA replication, complementary base pairing ensures the correct placements of bases in the new DNA strands.

## Direction of Replication

Now that we have seen the overall process, we can take a look at some of the details that are important in understanding DNA replication. The unwinding of DNA by *helicase* occurs simultaneously in several sections along the parent DNA molecule. As a result, *DNA polymerase* can catalyze the replication process at each of these open DNA sections called **replication forks**. However, DNA polymerase catalyzes only phosphodiester bonds between the 5′-phosphate of one nucleotide and the 3′-hydroxyl of the next, which means that DNA polymerases have to move in opposite directions along the separated strands of DNA. The new DNA strand that grows in the 5′–3′ direction, the *leading strand*, is synthesized continuously. The other new DNA, the *lagging strand*, is synthesized in the opposite direction, which is in the reverse 3′–5′ direction. In this lagging strand, short sections called **Okazaki fragments** are synthesized at the same time by several *DNA polymerases* and connected to form a continuous strand by *DNA ligases* to give a single 3′–5′ DNA strand. (See Figure 21.11.)

### CAREER FOCUS

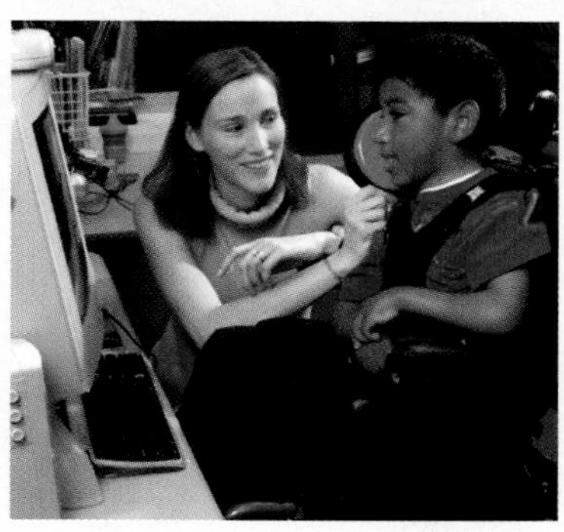

### Occupational Therapist

"Occupational therapists teach children and adults the skills they need for the job of living," says occupational therapist Leslie Wakasa. "When working with the pediatric population, we are crucial in educating children with disabilities, their families, caregivers, and school staff in ways to help them be as independent as they can be in all aspects of their daily lives. It's rewarding when you can show children how to feed themselves, which is a huge self-esteem issue for them. The opportunity to help people become more independent is very rewarding."

A combination of technology and occupational therapy helps children who are nonverbal to communicate and interact with their environment. By leaning on a red switch, Alex is learning to use a computer.

SELF STUDY ACTIVITY
DNA Replication

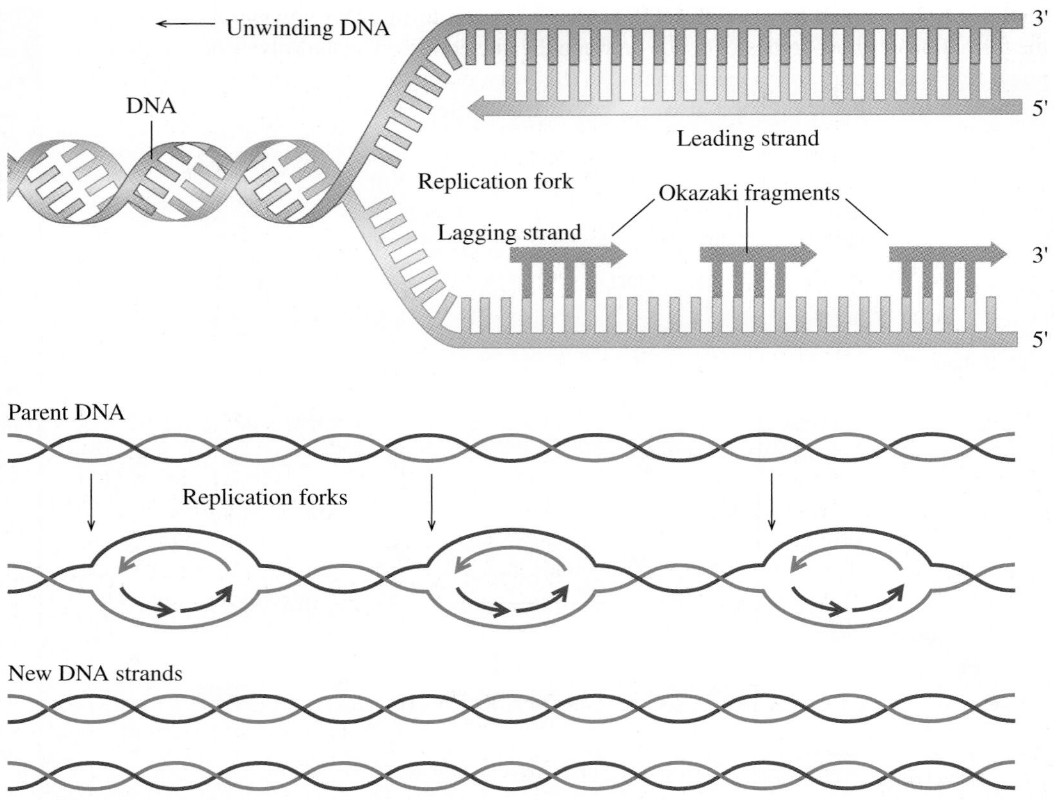


**FIGURE 21.11** At each replication fork, DNA polymerase synthesizes a continuous DNA strand in the 5′ to 3′ direction. In the new 3′ to 5′ DNA strand, small Okazaki fragments are produced that are joined by DNA ligase.

Q Why is only one of the new DNA strands synthesized in a continuous direction?

## CONCEPT CHECK 21.2

### DNA Replication

In an original DNA strand, a segment has the base sequence 5′—A—G—T—3′.

**a.** What is the sequence of nucleotides in the daughter DNA strand that is complementary to this segment?

**b.** Why would the complementary sequence in the daughter DNA strand be synthesized as Okazaki fragments that require a DNA ligase?

ANSWER

**a.** Only one possible nucleotide can pair with each base in the original segment. Thymine will pair only with adenine, cytosine only with guanine, and adenine only with thymine to give the complementary base sequence: 3′—T—C—A—5′.

**b.** The DNA produced in the 3′–5′ direction, called the lagging strand, is synthesized as short sections, which are joined by DNA ligase.

## QUESTIONS AND PROBLEMS

### DNA Replication

**21.19** What is the function of the enzyme helicase in DNA replication?

**21.20** What is the function of the enzyme DNA polymerase in DNA replication?

**21.21** What process ensures that the replication of DNA produces identical copies?

**21.22** Why are Okazaki fragments needed in the synthesis of the lagging strand?

# 21.5 RNA and Transcription

LEARNING GOAL

Identify the different types of RNA; describe the synthesis of mRNA.

Ribonucleic acid, RNA, which makes up most of the nucleic acid found in the cell, is involved with transmitting the genetic information needed to operate the cell. Similar to DNA, RNA molecules are unbranched polymers of nucleotides. However, RNA differs from DNA in several important ways:

1. The sugar in RNA is ribose rather than the deoxyribose found in DNA.
2. In RNA, the base uracil replaces thymine.
3. RNA molecules are single-stranded nucleic acids.
4. RNA molecules are much smaller than DNA molecules.

## Types of RNA

There are three major types of RNA in the cells: *messenger RNA*, *ribosomal RNA*, and *transfer RNA*. (See Table 21.3.) Ribosomal RNA (**rRNA**), the most abundant type of RNA, is combined with proteins in the ribosomes. Ribosomes, which are the sites within the cells where protein synthesis occurs, consist of two subunits: a large subunit and a small subunit. (See Figure 21.12.) Cells that synthesize large numbers of proteins have thousands of ribosomes.

TABLE 21.3 Types of RNA Molecules in Humans

| Type | Abbreviation | Percentage of Total RNA | Function in the Cell |
|---|---|---|---|
| Ribosomal RNA | rRNA | 80 | Major component of the ribosomes |
| Messenger RNA | mRNA | 5 | Carries information for protein synthesis from the DNA in the nucleus to the ribosomes |
| Transfer RNA | tRNA | 15 | Brings amino acids to the ribosomes for protein synthesis |

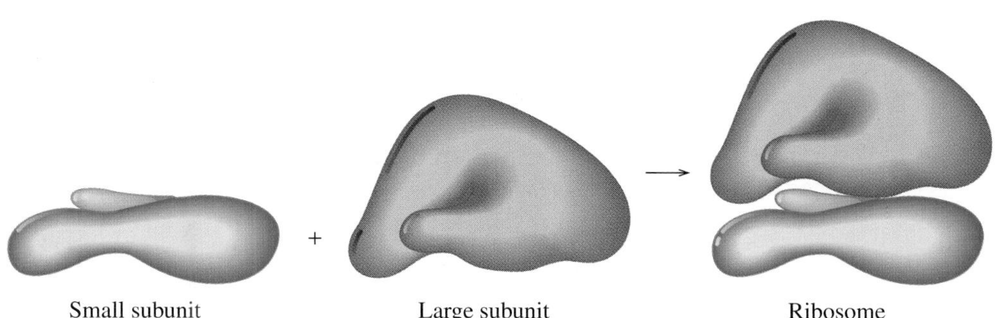


FIGURE 21.12 A typical prokaryotic ribosome consists of a small subunit and a large subunit.

Q Why would there be many thousands of ribosomes in a cell?

Messenger RNA (**mRNA**) carries genetic information from the DNA, located in the nucleus of the cell, to the ribosomes, located in the cytoplasm of the cell. Each gene segment of DNA produces a specific mRNA for a particular protein that is needed in the cell. The size of an mRNA depends on the number of nucleotides in that gene.

Transfer RNA (**tRNA**), the smallest of the RNA molecules, interprets the genetic information in mRNA and brings specific amino acids to the ribosome for protein synthesis. Only the tRNA molecules can translate the genetic information into amino acids for proteins. Each of the 20 amino acids has one or more different tRNA molecules. The structures of the tRNAs are similar, consisting of 70–90 nucleotides. Hydrogen bonds between some of the complementary bases in the chain produce loops that give some double-stranded regions.

Although the structure of tRNA is complex, we draw tRNA as a cloverleaf to illustrate its features. All tRNA molecules have a 3′ end with the nucleotide sequence ACC—, which is known as the *acceptor stem*. An enzyme attaches an amino acid by forming an ester bond with the free —OH of the acceptor stem. Each tRNA contains an **anticodon**, which is a series of three bases that complements three bases on an mRNA. (See Figure 21.13.)

(a.)

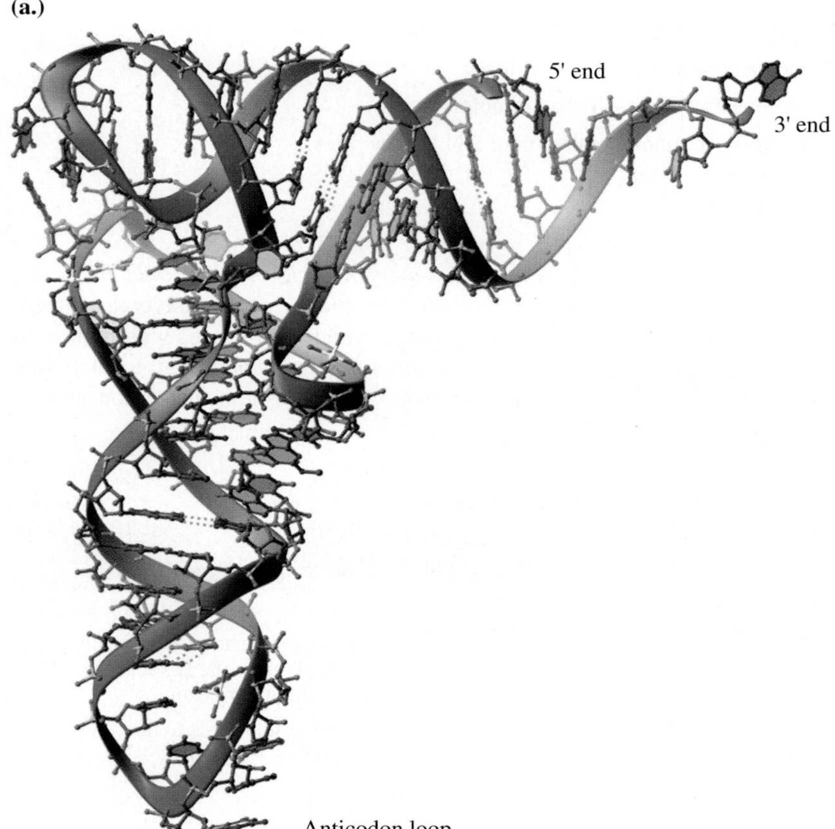


(b.)

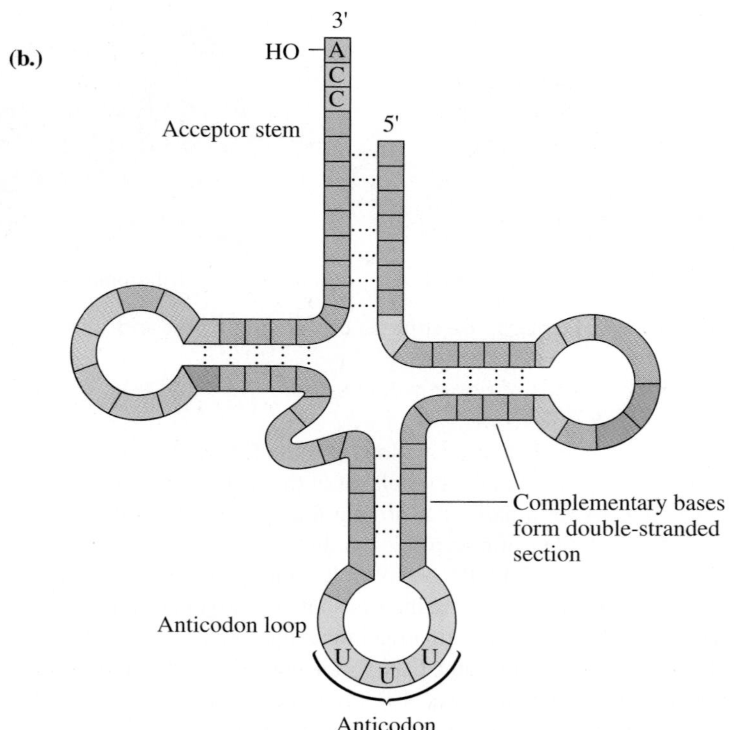


**FIGURE 21.13** **(a)** In the L shape of a transfer RNA, some sections of the ribose–phosphate backbone form regions of complementary base bonding. **(b)** A typical tRNA molecule has an acceptor stem that attaches to an amino acid and an anticodon loop that complements a codon on mRNA.

**Q** Why will different tRNAs have different bases in the anticodon loop?

SAMPLE PROBLEM 21.4

**Types of RNA**

What is the function of mRNA in a cell?

SOLUTION

The mRNA molecules carry instructions for the synthesis of a protein from the DNA in the nucleus to the ribosomes in the cytoplasm.

STUDY CHECK

What is the function of tRNA in a cell?

## RNA and Protein Synthesis

We now look at the overall processes involved in transferring genetic information encoded in the DNA to the production of proteins. In the nucleus, the genetic information for the synthesis of a protein is copied from a gene in DNA to make a messenger RNA (mRNA), a process called **transcription**. The mRNA molecules move out of the nucleus into the cytoplasm, where they combine with the ribosomes. Then in a process called **translation**, tRNA molecules convert the mRNA information into amino acids, which are placed in the proper sequence to synthesize a protein. (See Figure 21.14.)

$$\text{DNA} \xrightarrow{\text{Transcription}} \text{mRNA} \xrightarrow{\text{Translation}} \text{protein}$$

## Transcription: Synthesis of mRNA

Transcription begins when the section of a DNA molecule that contains the gene to be copied unwinds. Within this unwound portion of DNA called a *transcription bubble*, RNA polymerase moves along the template strand in a 3′ to 5′ direction. The mRNA forms with bases that are complementary to the DNA template. In mRNA synthesis, C and G form pairs, T (in DNA) pairs with A (in mRNA), and A (in DNA) pairs with U (in mRNA). When RNA polymerase reaches the termination site, transcription ends, and the new mRNA is released. The unwound portion of the DNA returns to its double helix structure. (See Figure 21.15.)

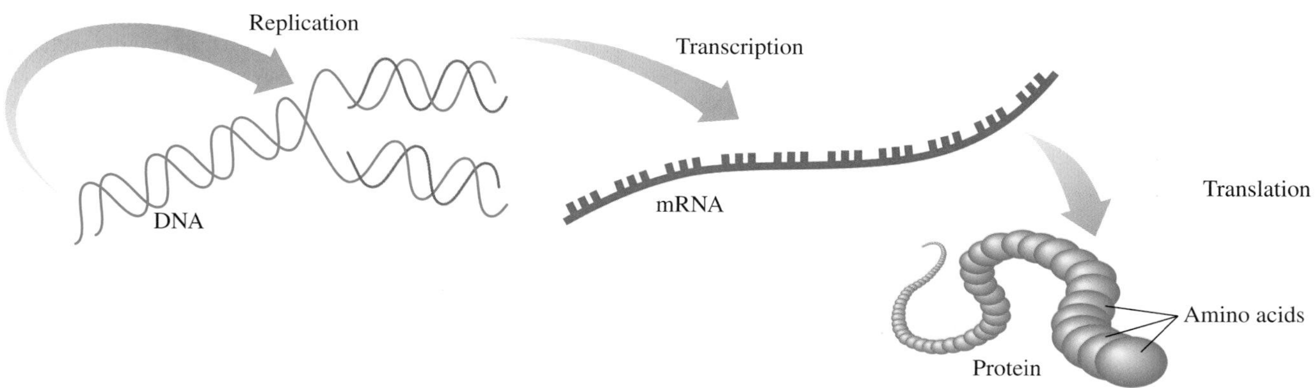


**FIGURE 21.14** The genetic information in DNA is replicated in cell division and is used to produce messenger RNAs that code for amino acids needed for protein synthesis.

Q What is the difference between transcription and translation?

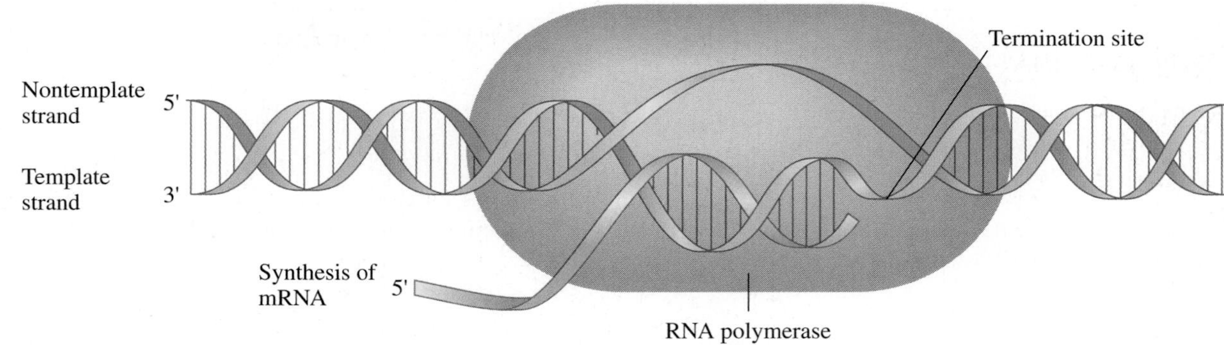


**FIGURE 21.15** DNA undergoes transcription when RNA polymerase makes a complementary copy of a gene using the 3′ to 5′ strand as the template.

**Q** Why is the mRNA connected in a 5′ to 3′ direction?

RNA polymerase →

| | |
|---|---|
| Section of bases on DNA template: | 3′—G—A—A—C—T—5′ |
| | ↓ ↓ ↓ ↓ ↓ |
| Complementary base sequence in mRNA: | 5′—C—U—U—G—A—3′ |

**SAMPLE PROBLEM 21.5**

**■ RNA Synthesis**

The sequence of bases in a part of the DNA template for mRNA is 3′—C—G—A—T—C—A—5′. What is the corresponding mRNA produced?

SOLUTION

To form the mRNA, the bases in the DNA template are paired with their complementary bases: G with C, C with G, T with A, and A with U.

| | |
|---|---|
| Portion of DNA template: | 3′—C—G—A—T—C—A—5′ |
| Complementary bases in mRNA: | 5′—G—C—U—A—G—U—3′ |

STUDY CHECK

What is the DNA template that codes for the mRNA segment with the nucleotide sequence 5′—G—G—G—U—U—U—A—A—A—3′?

## Processing of mRNA

The DNA in eukaryotes—organisms including plants and animals—contains sections known as *exons* and *introns*. **Exons**, which code for proteins, are mixed in with sections called **introns** that do not code for protein. A newly formed mRNA called a *pre-mRNA* is a copy of the entire DNA template, including the noncoding introns. Before the pre-mRNA leaves the nucleus, the introns must be removed. This processing of pre-RNA produces a functional mRNA that leaves the nucleus to deliver the genetic information to the ribosomes for the synthesis of protein. (See Figure 21.16.)

SELF STUDY ACTIVITY
The Lactose Operon in *E. coli*

## Regulation of Transcription

The synthesis of mRNA occurs when cells require a particular protein; it does not occur randomly. The regulation of mRNA synthesis takes place at the transcription level, where the absence or presence of end products determines which mRNAs are needed for specific proteins. For example, *E. coli* bacteria that grow on lactose need $\beta$-galactosidase to hydrolyze lactose to glucose and galactose. When the lactose level is low, $\beta$-galactosidase is not needed; the transcription of its mRNA is turned off. When lactose enters the cell and

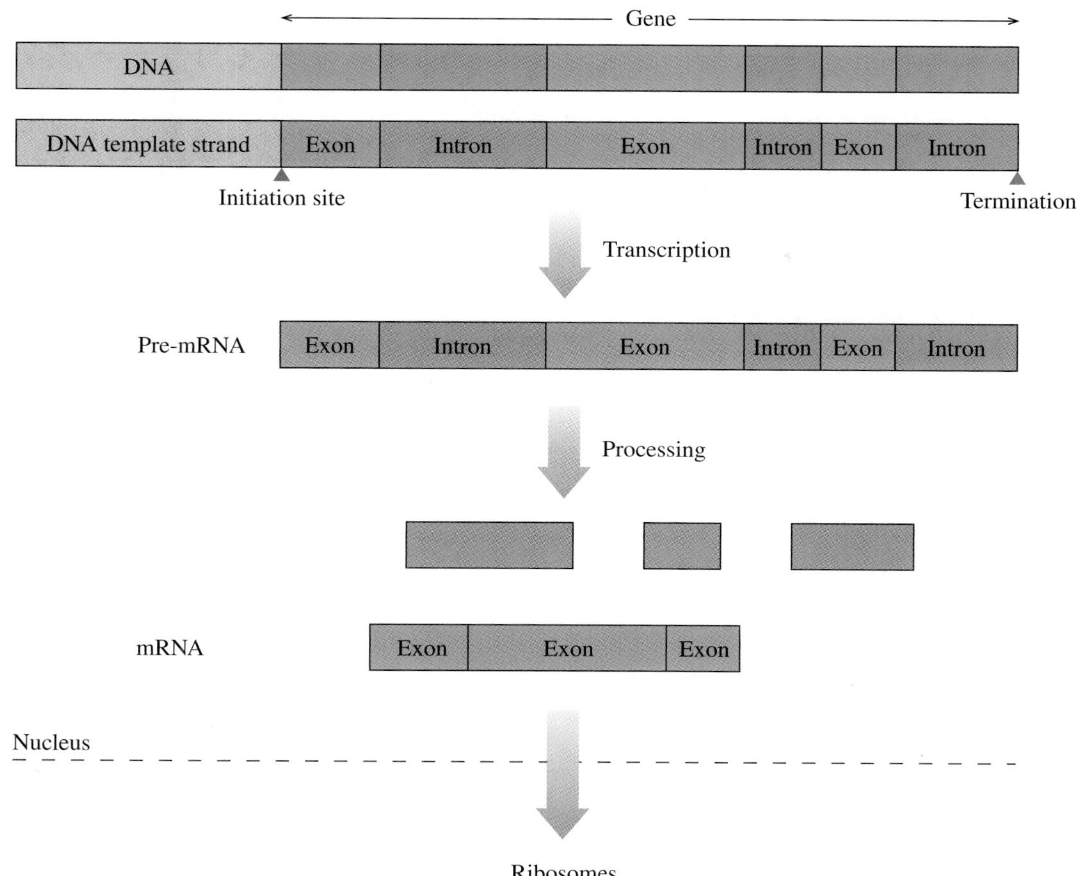


**FIGURE 21.16** A pre-RNA, containing copies of the exons and introns from the gene, is processed to remove the introns and form mRNA that codes for a protein.

**Q** What is the difference between exons and introns?

$\beta$-galactosidase is required, lactose initiates the synthesis of mRNA for the enzyme. This process, known as **enzyme induction**, occurs when high levels of a substrate turn on the transcription of the genes that produce the mRNAs that code for specific enzymes.

Within a gene, sections of DNA called **operons** regulate the synthesis of related proteins. Each operon has a **control site** followed by the **structural genes** that produce the mRNAs for specific proteins. (See Figure 21.17.)

In front of the lactose operon, there is a **regulatory gene** that produces an mRNA for the synthesis of a **repressor** protein that blocks the synthesis of $\beta$-galactosidase by RNA polymerase. When lactose enters the cell, it combines with the repressor and removes it from the control site. Without a repressor, RNA polymerase proceeds to the structural genes, which now produces the mRNAs needed for the synthesis of the lactose enzymes.

MC™ TUTORIAL
Activating and Inhibiting Genes

**CONCEPT CHECK 21.3**

### Transcription

Describe why transcription will or will not take place in each of the following conditions:

**a.** A repressor binds to the control site.
**b.** An inducer binds to the repressor protein.

ANSWER

**a.** Transcription will not take place as long as a repressor is attached to the control site, which blocks the synthesis of mRNA by RNA polymerase.
**b.** Transcription will take place when an inducer attaches to the repressor, which removes it from the control site.

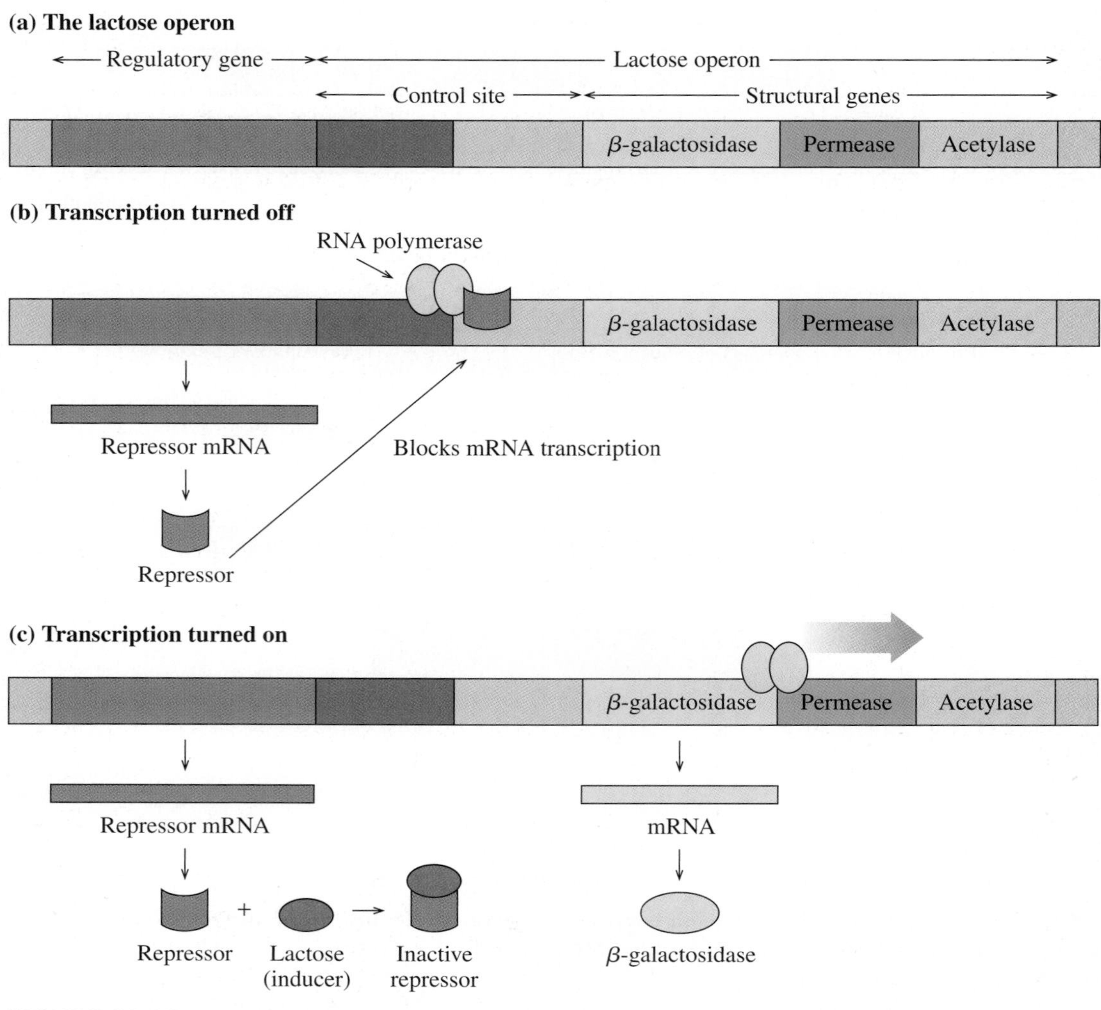


**FIGURE 21.17** **(a)** The lactose operon consists of a control site and structural genes. **(b)** Without lactose, a repressor protein blocks the transcription of enzymes for lactose. **(c)** Lactose, an inducer, removes the repressor to allow the transcription of enzymes for lactose hydrolysis.

**Q** Why is transcription blocked when no lactose is present in the cell?

## QUESTIONS AND PROBLEMS

### RNA and Transcription

**21.23** What are the three different types of RNA?

**21.24** What is the function of each type of RNA?

**21.25** What is the composition of a ribosome?

**21.26** What is the smallest RNA?

**21.27** What is meant by the term "transcription"?

**21.28** What bases in mRNA are used to complement the bases A, T, G, and C in DNA?

**21.29** Write the corresponding section of mRNA produced from the following section of DNA template:

3′—C—C—G—A—A—G—G—T—T—C—A—C—5′

**21.30** Write the corresponding section of mRNA produced from the following section of DNA template:

3′—T—A—C—G—G—C—A—A—G—C—T—A—5′

**21.31** What are introns and exons?

**21.32** What kind of processing do mRNA molecules undergo before they leave the nucleus?

**21.33** What is an operon?

**21.34** Why does the operon model control protein synthesis at the transcription level?

**21.35** How is the lactose operon turned off in *E. coli* that grow on lactose?

**21.36** How is the lactose operon activated in *E. coli* that grow on lactose?

## 21.6 The Genetic Code

The overall function of the different types of RNA in the cell is to facilitate the task of synthesizing proteins. After the genetic information encoded in DNA is transcribed into mRNA molecules, the mRNAs move out of the nucleus to the ribosomes in the cytoplasm. At the ribosomes, the genetic information in the mRNAs is converted into a sequence of amino acids in protein:

**LEARNING GOAL**

Describe the function of the codons in the genetic code.

$$\text{mRNA} \xrightarrow[\text{}]{\text{Translation at the ribosomes in the cytoplasm}} \text{protein}$$

### Codons

The **genetic code** consists of a series of three nucleotides (triplet) in mRNA called a **codon**. Each codon specifies an amino acid and its sequence in a protein. Early work on protein synthesis showed that repeating triplets of uracil, UUU, produced a polypeptide that contained only phenylalanine. Therefore, a sequence of 5′—UUU—UUU—UUU—3′ codes for three phenylalanines:

MC™ TUTORIAL Genetic Code

| | |
|---|---|
| Codons in mRNA | 5′—UUU—UUU—UUU—3′ |
| Translation | ↓ ↓ ↓ |
| Amino acid sequence | —Phe — Phe — Phe— |

Codons have been determined for all 20 amino acids. A total of 64 codons are possible from the triplet combinations of A, G, C, and U. (See Table 21.4.) Three of these, UGA, UAA, and UAG, are stop signals that code for the termination of protein synthesis. All the other three-base codons specify amino acids; one amino acid can have several codons. For example, glycine has four codons: GGU, GGC, GGA, and GGG. The triplet AUG has two roles in protein synthesis. At the beginning of an mRNA, the codon AUG signals the start of protein synthesis. In the middle of a series of codons, the AUG codon specifies the amino acid methionine.

**TABLE 21.4** mRNA Codons: The Genetic Code for Amino Acids

| First Letter | Second Letter U | Second Letter C | Second Letter A | Second Letter G | Third Letter |
|---|---|---|---|---|---|
| U | UUU Phe | UCU Ser | UAU Tyr | UGU Cys | U |
| | UUC Phe | UCC Ser | UAC Tyr | UGC Cys | C |
| | UUA Leu | UCA Ser | UAA STOP | UGA STOP | A |
| | UUG Leu | UCG Ser | UAG STOP | UGG Trp | G |
| C | CUU Leu | CCU Pro | CAU His | CGU Arg | U |
| | CUC Leu | CCC Pro | CAC His | CGC Arg | C |
| | CUA Leu | CCA Pro | CAA Gln | CGA Arg | A |
| | CUG Leu | CCG Pro | CAG Gln | CGG Arg | G |
| A | AUU Ile | ACU Thr | AAU Asn | AGU Ser | U |
| | AUC Ile | ACC Thr | AAC Asn | AGC Ser | C |
| | AUA Ile | ACA Thr | AAA Lys | AGA Arg | A |
| | [a]AUG START/Met | ACG Thr | AAG Lys | AGG Arg | G |
| G | GUU Val | GCU Ala | GAU Asp | GGU Gly | U |
| | GUC Val | GCC Ala | GAC Asp | GGC Gly | C |
| | GUA Val | GCA Ala | GAA Glu | GGA Gly | A |
| | GUG Val | GCG Ala | GAG Glu | GGG Gly | G |

[a]START codon signals the initiation of a peptide chain.
STOP codons signal the end of a peptide chain.

CONCEPT CHECK 21.4

**The Genetic Code**

Indicate the nucleotides in mRNA that code for the following:

**a.** the amino acid phenylalanine
**b.** the amino acid proline
**c.** the start of a polypeptide

ANSWER

**a.** In mRNA, the codons UUU and UUC would place the amino acid phenylalanine (Phe) in a polypeptide.
**b.** In mRNA, the codons CCU, CCC, CCA, and CCG would place the amino acid proline (Pro) in a polypeptide.
**c.** The codon AUG in mRNA signals the start of the synthesis of a polypeptide.

SAMPLE PROBLEM 21.6

**Codons**

What is the sequence of amino acids coded by the following codons in mRNA?

5′—GUC—AGC—CCA—3′

SOLUTION

According to Table 21.4, GUC codes for valine, AGC for serine, and CCA for proline. The sequence of amino acids is Val-Ser-Pro.

STUDY CHECK

What tripeptide is coded for by the following codons in mRNA?

5′—AAU—GCU—UGU—3′

## QUESTIONS AND PROBLEMS

### The Genetic Code

21.37 What is a codon?

**21.38** What is the genetic code?

21.39 What amino acid is coded for by each of the following codons?
**a.** CUU **b.** UCA
**c.** GGU **d.** AGG

**21.40** What amino acid is coded for by each of the following codons?
**a.** AAA **b.** GUC
**c.** CGG **d.** GCA

21.41 When does the codon AUG signal the start of a protein? When does it code for the amino acid methionine?

**21.42** The codons UAA and UAG do not code for amino acids. What is their role as codons in mRNA?

## 21.7 Protein Synthesis: Translation

LEARNING GOAL

Describe the process of protein synthesis from mRNA.

SELF STUDY ACTIVITY
Translation

Once a molecule of mRNA is synthesized, it migrates out of the nucleus into the cytoplasm to the ribosomes. In the *translation* process, tRNA molecules, amino acids, and enzymes convert the codons on mRNA into amino acids to build a protein.

### Activation of tRNA

Molecules of tRNA read the codons of mRNA and pick up the corresponding amino acids. Each tRNA molecule contains a loop called the *anticodon*, which is a triplet of bases that

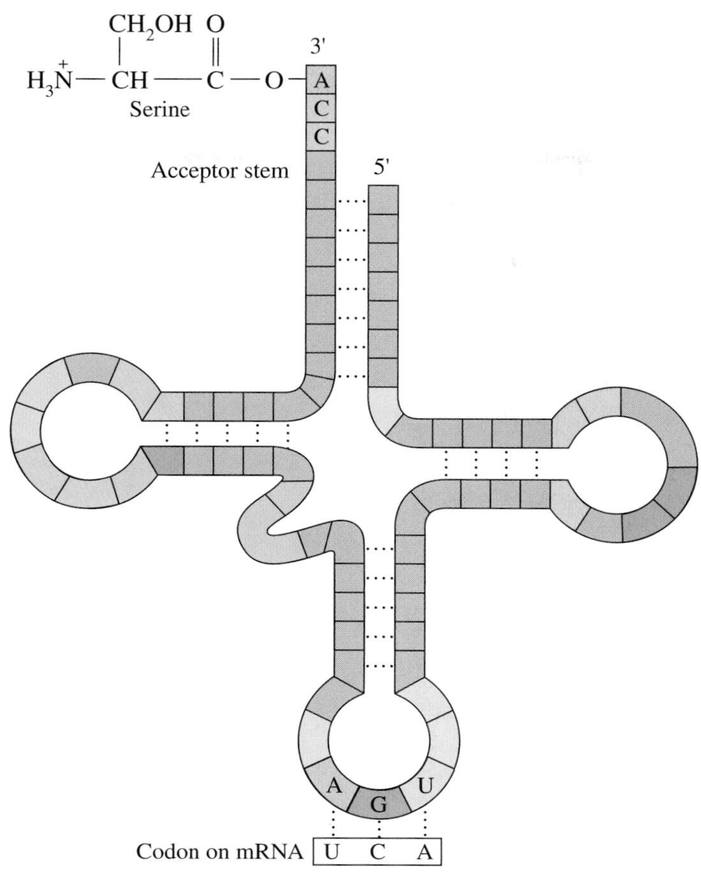


**FIGURE 21.18** An activated tRNA with anticodon AGU bonds to serine at the acceptor stem.

**Q** What is the codon for serine for this tRNA?

complements a codon in an mRNA. An amino acid is attached to the acceptor stem of each tRNA by an enzyme called *aminoacyl–tRNA synthetase*. Each amino acid has a different synthetase. (See Figure 21.18.) Activation takes place when a *tRNA synthetase* uses the anticodon of a tRNA to form an ester bond between the carboxylate group of its amino acid and the hydroxyl group on the acceptor stem. Each synthetase then checks the tRNA–amino acid combination and hydrolyzes any incorrect combinations.

## Initiation and Chain Elongation

Protein synthesis begins when an mRNA combines with the ribosome. The first codon in an mRNA is a *start* codon, AUG. Therefore, a tRNA with an anticodon of UAC and the amino acid methionine forms hydrogen bonds with the AUG codon. (See Figure 21.19.) In *chain elongation*, another tRNA carries a second amino acid to the adjacent codon on the mRNA. With two amino acids close together, a peptide bond forms. Then the first tRNA detaches from the ribosome, and the ribosome shifts to the next codon on the mRNA, a process called *translocation*. As the next tRNA attaches to the open binding site, its amino acid attaches to the growing peptide chain. As another tRNA detaches, the ribosome moves along the mRNA to read the next codon. Sometimes several ribosomes, called a *polysome*, translate a single strand of mRNA simultaneously to produce several copies of the peptide chain at the same time.

## Chain Termination

Eventually, a ribosome encounters a stop codon—UAA, UGA, or UAG—that signals the termination of polypeptide synthesis. The stop codons have no corresponding tRNAs but are recognized by proteins called *release factors*, which release the completed polypeptide chain from the ribosome. The initial amino acid methionine is usually removed from the beginning of the polypeptide chain. The R groups of the amino acids along the polypeptide chain interact to give the tertiary structure of a biologically active protein.

## HEALTH NOTE

### Many Antibiotics Inhibit Protein Synthesis

Several antibiotics stop bacterial infections by interfering with the synthesis of proteins needed by the bacteria. Some antibiotics act only on bacterial cells, binding to the ribosomes in bacteria but not those in human cells. A description of some of these antibiotics is given in Table 21.5.

**TABLE 21.5** Antibiotics That Inhibit Protein Synthesis in Bacterial Cells

| Antibiotic | Effect on Ribosomes to Inhibit Protein Synthesis |
|---|---|
| Chloramphenicol | Inhibits peptide bond formation and prevents the binding of tRNA |
| Erythromycin | Inhibits peptide chain growth by preventing the translocation of the ribosome along the mRNA |
| Puromycin | Causes release of an incomplete protein by ending the growth of the polypeptide early |
| Streptomycin | Prevents the proper attachment of the initial tRNA |
| Tetracycline | Prevents the binding of tRNAs |

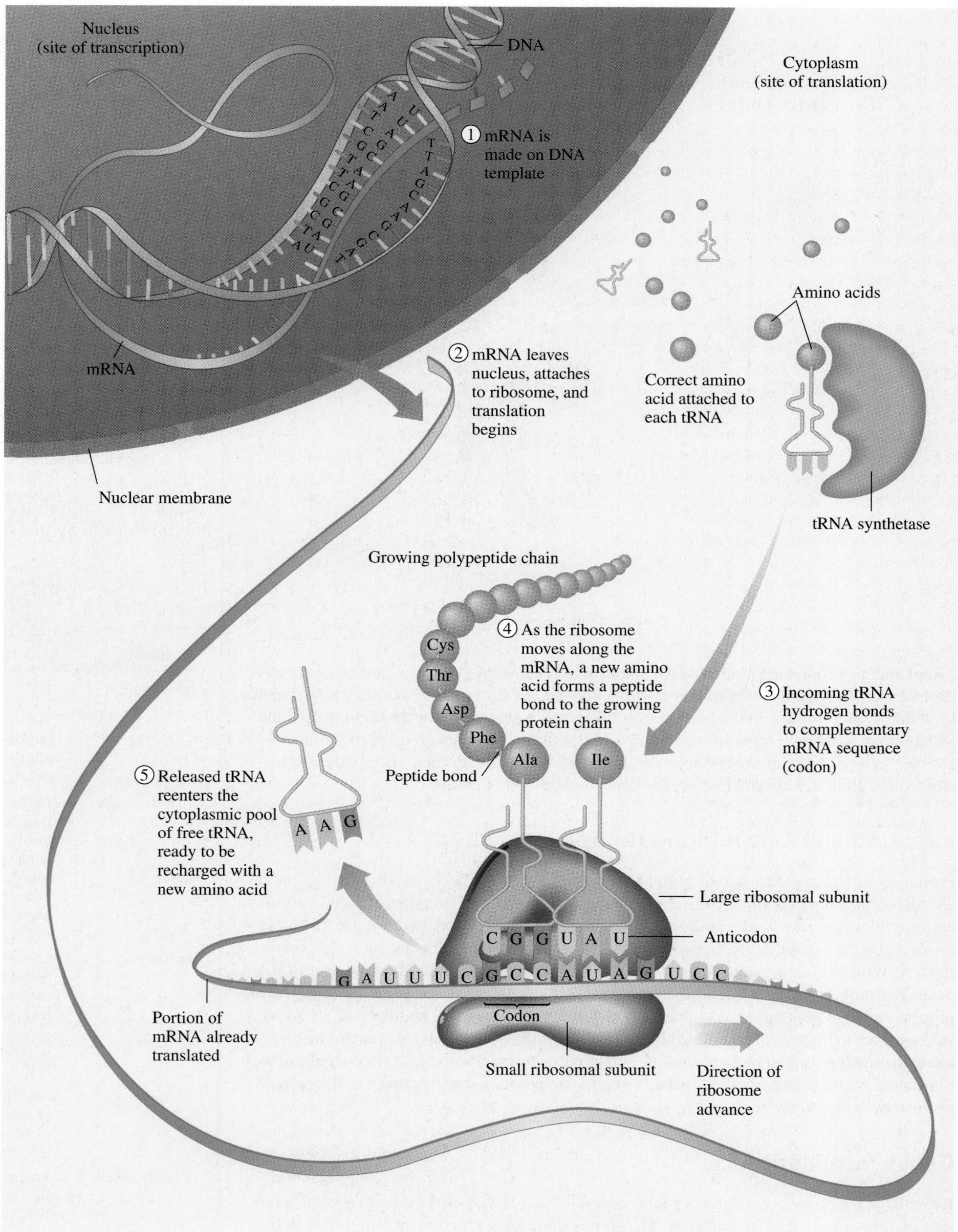


**FIGURE 21.19** In the translation process, the mRNA synthesized by transcription attaches to a ribosome, and tRNAs pick up their amino acids and place them in a growing peptide chain.

**Q** How is the correct amino acid placed in the peptide chain?

SAMPLE PROBLEM 21.7

## Protein Synthesis: Translation

What order of amino acids would you expect in a peptide for the mRNA sequence of 5′—UCA—AAA—GCC—CUU—3′?

SOLUTION

Each of the codons specifies a particular amino acid. Using Table 21.4, we write a peptide with the following amino acid sequence:

mRNA codons: 5′—UCA—AAA—GCC—CUU—3′

Amino acid sequence: — Ser — Lys — Ala — Leu —

STUDY CHECK

Where would protein synthesis stop in the following series of bases in an mRNA?

5′—GGG—AGC—AGU—UAG—GUU—3′

MC™ TUTORIAL Following the Instructions in DNA

MC™ SELF STUDY ACTIVITY Overview of Protein Synthesis

# QUESTIONS AND PROBLEMS

### Protein Synthesis: Translation

21.43 What is the difference between a *codon* and an *anticodon*?

**21.44** Why are there at least 20 different tRNAs?

21.45 What are the three steps of translation?

**21.46** Where does protein synthesis take place?

21.47 What amino acid sequence would you expect from each of the following mRNA segments?
- **a.** 5′—AAA—AAA—AAA—3′
- **b.** 5′—UUU—CCC—UUU—CCC—3′
- **c.** 5′—UAC—GGG—AGA—UGU—3′

**21.48** What amino acid sequence would you expect from each of the following mRNA segments?
- **a.** 5′—AAA—CCC—UUG—GCC—3′
- **b.** 5′—CCU—CGA—AGC—CCA—UGA—3′
- **c.** 5′—AUG—CAC—AAA—GAA—GUA—CUU—3′

21.49 How is a peptide chain extended?

**21.50** What is meant by "translocation"?

21.51 The following is a portion of DNA is in the template DNA strand:

3′—GCT—TTT—CAA—AAA—5′

- **a.** What is the corresponding mRNA section?
- **b.** What are the anticodons of the tRNAs?
- **c.** What amino acids will be placed in the peptide chain?

**21.52** The following is a portion of DNA is in the template DNA strand:

3′—TGT—GGG—GTT—ATT—5′

- **a.** What is the corresponding mRNA section?
- **b.** What are the anticodons of the tRNAs?
- **c.** What amino acids will be placed in the peptide chain?

# 21.8 Genetic Mutations

LEARNING GOAL

Describe some ways in which DNA is altered to cause mutations.

A **mutation** is a change in the nucleotide sequence of DNA. Such a change may alter the sequence of amino acids, affecting the structure and function of a protein in a cell. Mutations result from X-rays, overexposure to sun (ultraviolet or UV light), chemicals called *mutagens*, and possibly some viruses. If a mutation occurs in a somatic cell (a cell other than a reproductive cell), the altered DNA is limited to that cell and its daughter cells. If there is uncontrolled growth, the mutation could lead to cancer. If a mutation occurs in a germ cell (egg or sperm), then all DNA produced will contain the same genetic change. When a mutation severely alters the function of structural proteins or enzymes, the new cells may not survive or the person may exhibit a disease or condition that is a result of a genetic defect.

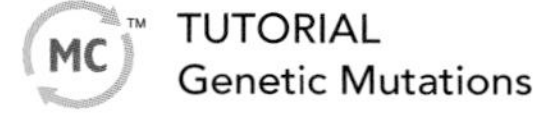

MC™ TUTORIAL Genetic Mutations

## Types of Mutations

Consider a triplet of bases CCG in the coding strand of DNA, which produces the codon GGC in mRNA. At the ribosome, tRNA would place the amino acid glycine in the peptide

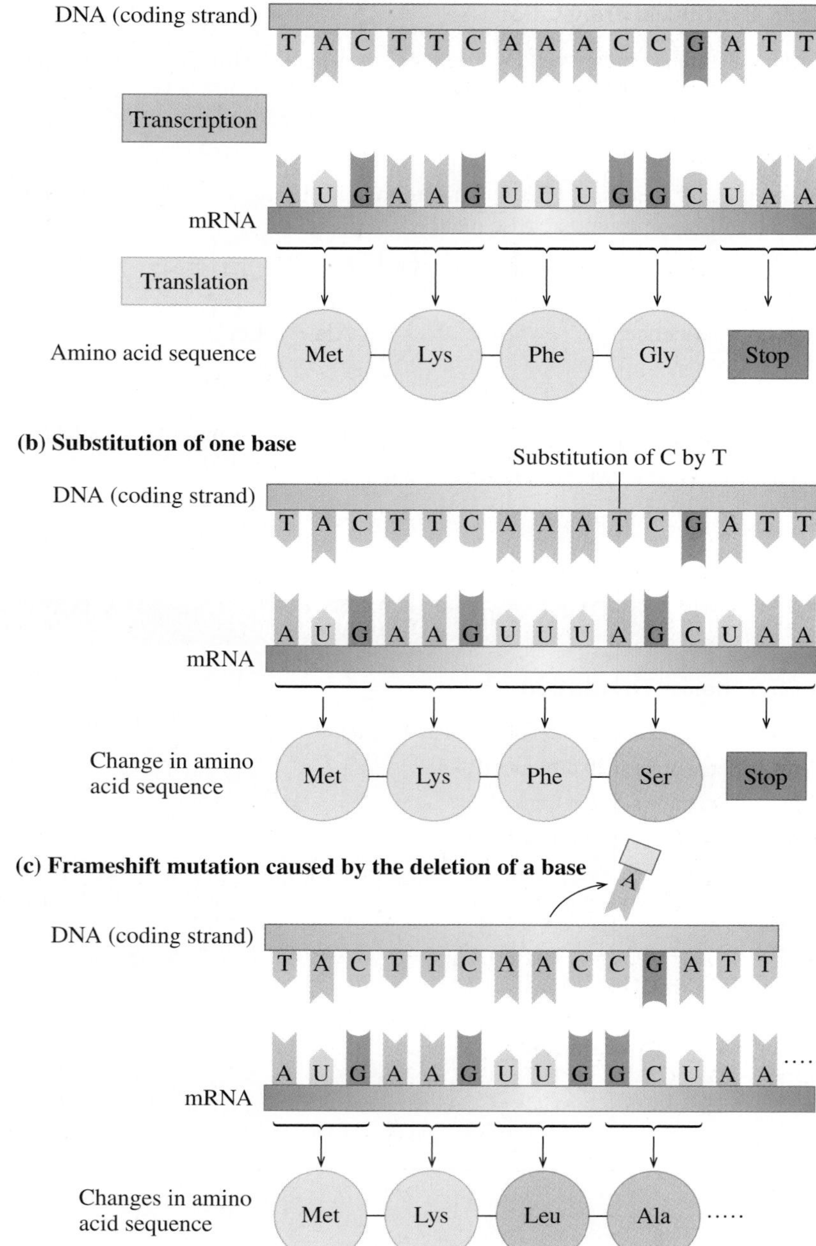


**FIGURE 21.20** An alteration in the DNA coding strand (template) produces a change in the sequence of amino acids in the protein, which may lead to a mutation. **(a)** A normal DNA leads to the correct amino acid order in a protein. **(b)** The substitution of a base in DNA leads to a change in the mRNA codon and a change in the amino acid. **(c)** The deletion of a base causes a frameshift mutation, which changes the amino acid order that follows the mutation.

Q When would a substitution mutation cause protein synthesis to stop?

chain. (See Figure 21.20a.) Now, suppose that T replaces the first C in the DNA triplet, which gives TCG as the triplet. Then the codon produced in the mRNA is AGC, which brings the tRNA with the amino acid serine to add to the peptide chain. The replacement of one base in the coding strand of DNA with another is called a **substitution mutation**. With a change of nucleotides in the codon, a different amino acid may be inserted into the polypeptide. Substitution is the most common way in which mutations occur. (See Figure 21.20b.)

In a **frameshift mutation**, a base is added to or deleted from the normal order of bases in the coding strand of DNA. Suppose now an A is deleted from the triplet AAA, which gives a new triplet of AAC. The next triplet becomes CGA rather than CCG, and so on. All the triplets shift over by one base, which changes all the codons that follow and leads to a different sequence of amino acids from that point. Figure 21.20c illustrates a frameshift mutation by deletion.

## Effect of Mutations

When a mutation causes a change in the amino acid sequence, the structure of the resulting protein can be altered severely and may lose biological activity. If the protein is an enzyme, it may no longer bind to its substrate or react with the substrate at the active site. When an altered enzyme cannot catalyze a reaction, certain substances may accumulate until they act as poisons in the cell, or substances vital to survival may not be synthesized. If a defective enzyme occurs in a major metabolic pathway or in the building of a cell membrane, the mutation can be lethal. When a protein deficiency is hereditary, the condition is called a **genetic disease**.

DNA $\xrightarrow{\text{X-rays, UV sunlight, mutagens, viruses}}$ alteration of DNA $\longrightarrow$ defective protein $\longrightarrow$ genetic disease (germ cells) or cancer (somatic cells)

SAMPLE PROBLEM 21.8

### Mutations

An mRNA has the sequence of codons 5′—CCC—AGA—GCC—3′. If a base substitution in the DNA changes the mRNA codon of AGA to GGA, how is the amino acid sequence affected in the resulting protein?

SOLUTION

The mRNA sequence —CCC—AGA—GCC— codes for the following amino acids: proline, arginine, and alanine. When the mutation occurs, the new sequence of the mRNA codons is —CCC—GGA—GCC—, which codes for proline, glycine, and alanine. The basic amino acid arginine is replaced by nonpolar glycine.

| | *Normal* | *After Mutation* |
|---|---|---|
| mRNA codons | —CCC—[AGA]—GCC— | —CCC—[GGA]—GCC— |
| Amino acids | — Pro —[Arg]— Ala — | — Pro —[Gly]— Ala — |

STUDY CHECK

How might the protein made from this mRNA be affected by this mutation?

### A Model for DNA Replication and Mutation

1. Cut out 16 rectangular pieces of paper. Using 8 rectangular pieces for DNA strand 1, write two each of the following nucleotide symbols: A═, T═, G≡, and C≡.
2. Using the other 8 rectangular pieces for DNA strand 2, write two of each of the following nucleotide symbols: ═A, ═T, ≡G, and ≡C.
3. Place the pieces for strand 1 in random order.
4. Using the DNA segment strand 1 you made in part 3, select the correct bases to build the complementary segment of DNA strand 2.
5. Using the rectangular pieces for nucleotides, put together a DNA segment using a template strand of —A—T—T—G—C—C—. What is the mRNA from this segment of DNA? What is the dipeptide that would form from this mRNA?
6. In the DNA segment of part 5, change the G to an A. What is the mRNA from this segment of DNA? What is the dipeptide that forms? How could this change in codons lead to a mutation?

## Genetic Diseases

A genetic disease is the result of a defective enzyme caused by a mutation in its genetic code. For example, phenylketonuria (PKU) results when DNA cannot direct the synthesis of the enzyme phenylalanine hydroxylase, required for the conversion of phenylalanine to tyrosine. In an attempt to break down the phenylalanine, other enzymes in the cells convert it to phenylpyruvate. The accumulation of phenylalanine and phenylpyruvate in the blood can lead to severe brain damage and mental retardation. If PKU is detected in a newborn baby, a diet is prescribed that eliminates all the foods that contain phenylalanine. Preventing the buildup of the phenylpyruvate ensures normal growth and development.

The amino acid tyrosine is needed in the formation of melanin, the pigment that gives the color to our skin and hair. If the enzyme that converts tyrosine to melanin is defective, no melanin is produced, a genetic disease known as albinism. Persons and animals with no melanin have no skin or hair pigment. (See Figure 21.21.) Table 21.6 lists some other common genetic diseases and the type of metabolism or area affected.

FIGURE 21.21 A peacock with albinism does not produce the melanin needed to the make bright colors of its feathers.

Q Why are traits such as albinism related to the gene?

$$C_6H_5—CH_2—CH(NH_3^+)—COO^- \longrightarrow C_6H_5—CH_2—C(=O)—COO^-$$

Phenylalanine → Phenylpyruvate → Phenylketonuria (PKU)

Phenylalanine ↓ (blocked) Phenylalanine hydroxylase

$$HO—C_6H_4—CH_2—CH(NH_3^+)—COO^- \not\longrightarrow \text{Melanin (pigments)}$$

Tyrosine → Albinism

TABLE 21.6 Some Genetic Diseases

| Genetic Disease | Result |
|---|---|
| Galactosemia | The transferase enzyme required for the metabolism of galactose-1-phosphate is absent. Accumulation of Gal-1-P leads to cataracts and mental retardation. It occurs in about 1 in every 50 000 births. |
| Cystic fibrosis | One of the most common inherited diseases in children. Thick mucus secretions make breathing difficult and block pancreatic function. |
| Down syndrome | The leading cause of mental retardation, occurring in about 1 of every 800 live births although mother's age strongly influences its occurence. Mental and physical problems including heart and eye defects are the result of the formation of three chromosomes, usually chromosome 21, instead of a pair. |
| Familial hypercholesterolemia | A mutation of a gene on chromosome 19 results in high cholesterol levels that lead to early coronary heart disease in people 30–40 years old. |
| Muscular dystrophy (MD) (Duchenne) | One of 10 forms of MD. A mutation in the X chromosome results in the low or abnormal production of *dystrophin*. This muscle-destroying disease appears at about age 5 with death by age 20 and occurs in about 1 of 10,000 males. |
| Huntington's disease (HD) | Appearing in middle age, HD affects the nervous system, leading to total physical impairment. It is the result of a mutation in a gene on chromosome 4, which can now be mapped to test people in families with HD. There are about 30 000 people with Huntington's disease in the United States. |
| Sickle-cell anemia | A defective hemoglobin from a mutation in a gene on chromosome 11 decreases the oxygen-carrying ability of red blood cells, which take on a sickled shape, causing anemia and plugged capillaries from red blood cell aggregation. In the United States, about 72 000 people are affected by sickle cell anemia. |
| Hemophilia | One or more defective blood-clotting factors lead to poor coagulation, excessive bleeding, and internal hemorrhages. There are about 20 000 hemophilia patients in the United States. |
| Tay-Sachs disease | Hexosaminidase A is defective, causing an accumulation of gangliosides resulting in mental retardation, loss of motor control, and early death. |

## QUESTIONS AND PROBLEMS

### Genetic Mutations

21.53 What is a substitution mutation?

**21.54** How does a substitution mutation in the genetic code for an enzyme affect the order of amino acids in that protein?

21.55 What is the effect of a frameshift mutation on the amino acid sequence in the polypeptide?

**21.56** How can a mutation decrease the activity of a protein?

21.57 How is protein synthesis affected if the normal base sequence TTT in the DNA template is changed to TTC?

**21.58** How is protein synthesis affected if the normal base sequence CCC is changed to ACC?

21.59 Consider the following portion of mRNA produced by the normal order of DNA nucleotides:

5′—ACA—UCA—CGG—GUA—3′

**a.** What is the amino acid order produced for normal DNA?
**b.** What is the amino acid order if a mutation changes UCA to ACA?
**c.** What is the amino acid order if a mutation changes CGG to GGG?
**d.** What happens to protein synthesis if a mutation changes UCA to UAA?
**e.** What happens if a G is added to the beginning of the mRNA segment?
**f.** What happens if the A is removed from the beginning of the mRNA segment?

**21.60** Consider the following portion of mRNA produced by the normal order of DNA nucleotides:

5′—CUU—AAA—CGA—GUU—3′

**a.** What is the amino acid order produced for normal DNA?
**b.** What is the amino acid order if a mutation changes CUU to CCU?
**c.** What is the amino acid order if a mutation changes CGA to AGA?
**d.** What happens to protein synthesis if a mutation changes AAA to UAA?
**e.** What happens if a G is added to the beginning of the mRNA segment?
**f.** What happens if the C is removed from the beginning of the mRNA segment?

21.61 **a.** A base substitution changes a codon for an enzyme from GCC to GCA. Why is there no change in the amino acid order in the protein?
**b.** In sickle-cell anemia, a base substitution in hemoglobin replaces glutamic acid (a polar acidic amino acid) with valine. Why does the replacement of one amino acid cause such a drastic change in biological function?

**21.62 a.** A base substitution for an enzyme replaces leucine (a nonpolar amino acid) with alanine. Why does this change in amino acids have little effect on the biological activity of the enzyme?
**b.** A base substitution replaces cytosine in the codon UCA with adenine. How would this substitution affect the amino acids in the protein?

# 21.9 Recombinant DNA

Techniques in the field of genetic engineering permit scientists to cut and recombine DNA fragments to form **recombinant DNA**. The technology of recombinant DNA is used to produce human insulin for diabetics, the antiviral substance interferon, blood clotting factor VIII, and human growth hormone.

**LEARNING GOAL**

Describe the preparation and uses of recombinant DNA.

SELF STUDY ACTIVITIES
Applications of DNA Technology
Restriction Enzymes

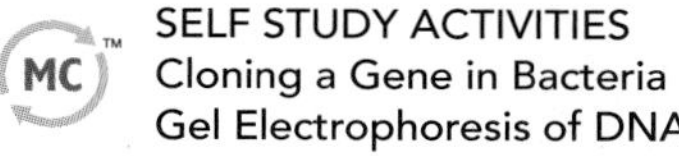

SELF STUDY ACTIVITIES
Cloning a Gene in Bacteria
Gel Electrophoresis of DNA

## Preparing Recombinant DNA

Most of the work in recombinant DNA is done with *Escherichia coli (E. coli)* bacteria. The DNA in bacterial cells exists as small circular molecules called *plasmids*, which are easy to isolate and capable of replication. Initially, *E. coli* cells are soaked in a detergent solution to dissolve the plasma membrane. The contents of the cells, including the plasmids, are released and collected. A *restriction enzyme*, which breaks phosphodiester bonds in DNA between specific nucleotides, is used to cut open the circular DNA strands in the plasmids. (See Figure 21.22.)

The same enzymes are also used to cut out a piece of DNA from a different organism, such as the gene that produces insulin or growth hormone. The cut-out genes are then mixed with the plasmids that were cut open. The ends of the foreign DNA piece and the ends of the opened plasmids are joined by a DNA ligase. Then the altered plasmids containing the recombined DNA are placed in a fresh culture of *E. coli* bacteria, where they can be reabsorbed into the bacterial cells.

The new gene that was inserted in the plasmids is copied as the genetically engineered *E. coli* cells start to replicate. In a single day, one *E. coli* bacterium is capable of producing a million copies of itself including the foreign DNA, a process known as gene cloning. If

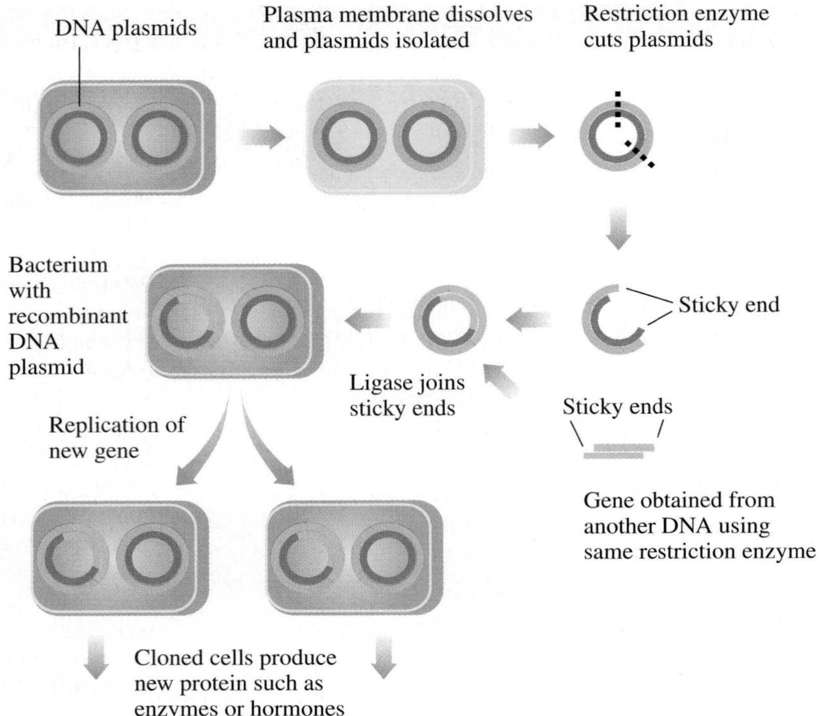


**FIGURE 21.22** Recombinant DNA is formed by placing a gene from another organism in a plasmid DNA of the bacterium, which causes the bacterium to produce a non-bacterial protein such as insulin or growth hormone.

**Q** How can recombinant DNA help a person with a genetic disease?

**TABLE 21.7** Therapeutic Products of Recombinant DNA

| Product | Therapeutic Use |
|---|---|
| Human insulin | Treat diabetes |
| Erythropoietin (EPO) | Treat anemia; stimulate production of erythrocytes |
| Human growth hormone (HGH) | Stimulate growth |
| Interferon | Treat cancer and viral disease |
| Tumor necrosis factor (TNF) | Destroy tumor cells |
| Monoclonal antibodies | Transport drugs needed to treat cancer and transplant rejection |
| Epidermal growth factor (EGF) | Stimulate healing of wounds and burns |
| Human blood clotting factor VIII | Treat hemophilia; allows blood to clot normally |
| Interleukins | Stimulate immune system; treat cancer |
| Prourokinase | Destroy blood clots; treat myocardial infarctions |

the inserted DNA codes for the human insulin protein, the altered plasmids begin to synthesize human insulin. Eventually, a large number of cells with the new DNA produce the insulin protein. Table 21.7 lists some of the products developed through recombinant DNA technology that are now used therapeutically.

## DNA Fingerprinting

SELF STUDY ACTIVITY
DNA Fingerprinting

SELF STUDY ACTIVITY
Analyzing DNA Fragments Using Gel Electrophoresis

In a process called DNA fingerprinting, restriction enzymes are used to cut DNA into smaller fragments called RFLPs (restriction fragment length polymorphisms). The RFLPs are separated by size by placing them on a gel. The gel is treated with a radioactive isotope that adheres to specific base sequences in the RFLPs. A piece of X-ray film placed over the gel is exposed by the radiation from the RFLPs. The pattern of dark and light bands on the film is known as a DNA fingerprint, which represents the order of nucleotides. (See Figure 21.23.) Scientists estimate that the odds of two people who are not identical twins producing the same DNA fingerprint are less than one in a billion.

One application of DNA fingerprinting is in forensic science, where DNA from samples of blood, hair, or semen is used to connect a suspect with a crime. Recently, DNA fingerprinting has been used to gain the release of individuals who were wrongly convicted. Other applications of DNA fingerprinting are determining the biological parents of a child, establishing the identity of a deceased person, and matching recipients with organ donors.

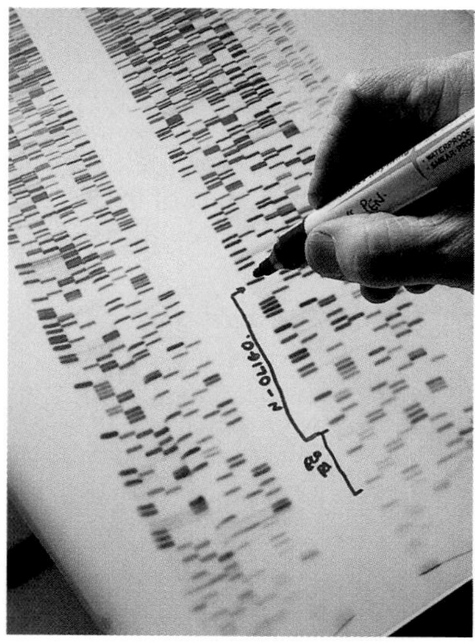

FIGURE 21.23 A scientist analyzes a nucleotide sequence in DNA from a human gene. Dark and light bands on the film represent the order of nucleotides. The marked sequences are involved in the growth of melanoma cancer cells.

Q What causes DNA fragments to appear on X-ray film?

## Human Genome Project

During the 1970s, scientists began to use restriction enzymes to map the location of genes within the DNA of the genome, which contains the hereditary information of an organism. By 1987, the genome of *E. coli* was determined. More recently, these techniques combined with new computer programs have compiled the map of the human genome, which contains about 30 000 genes.

Scientists think that most of the genome is not functional and has perhaps been carried from generation to generation for millions of years. Large blocks of genes are copied from one human chromosome to another even though they no longer code for needed proteins. Thus, the coding portions of the genes seem to make up only about 1% of the total genome. The results of the genome project will help us identify defective genes that lead to genetic disease. Today, DNA fingerprinting is used to screen for genes responsible for genetic diseases such as sickle-cell anemia, cystic fibrosis, breast cancer, colon cancer, Huntington's disease, and Lou Gehrig's disease.

## Polymerase Chain Reaction

The process of gene cloning using recombinant DNA requires living cells such as *E. coli*. In 1987, a process called **polymerase chain reaction (PCR)** made it possible to produce multiple copies of (amplify) the DNA in a short time. In the PCR technique, a sequence of a DNA molecule is selected to copy, and the DNA is heated to separate the strands. Primers that are complementary to a small group of nucleotides on each side of the sequence to be copied are added to the ends of the templates. The DNA strands with their primers are mixed with DNA polymerase and a mixture of deoxyribonucleotides to produce complementary strands for the DNA section. Then the process is repeated with the new batch of DNA. After several cycles of the PCR process, millions of copies of the initial DNA section are produced. (See Figure 21.24.)

SELF STUDY ACTIVITY
The Human Genome Project: Human Chromosome 17

CONCEPT CHECK 21.5

**Recombinant DNA**

What is the function of restriction enzymes in recombinant DNA?

ANSWER

Restriction enzymes are used to cut out a particular piece of DNA from a gene and to cut open the circular plasmids in a bacterium where the foreign DNA attaches.

## QUESTIONS AND PROBLEMS

### Recombinant DNA

21.63 Why are *E. coli* bacteria used in recombinant DNA procedures?

**21.64** What is a plasmid?

21.65 How are plasmids obtained from *E. coli*?

**21.66** Why are restriction enzymes mixed with the plasmids?

21.67 How is a gene for a particular protein inserted into a plasmid?

**21.68** Why is DNA polymerase useful in criminal investigations?

21.69 What is a DNA fingerprint?

**20.70** What beneficial proteins are produced from recombinant DNA technology?

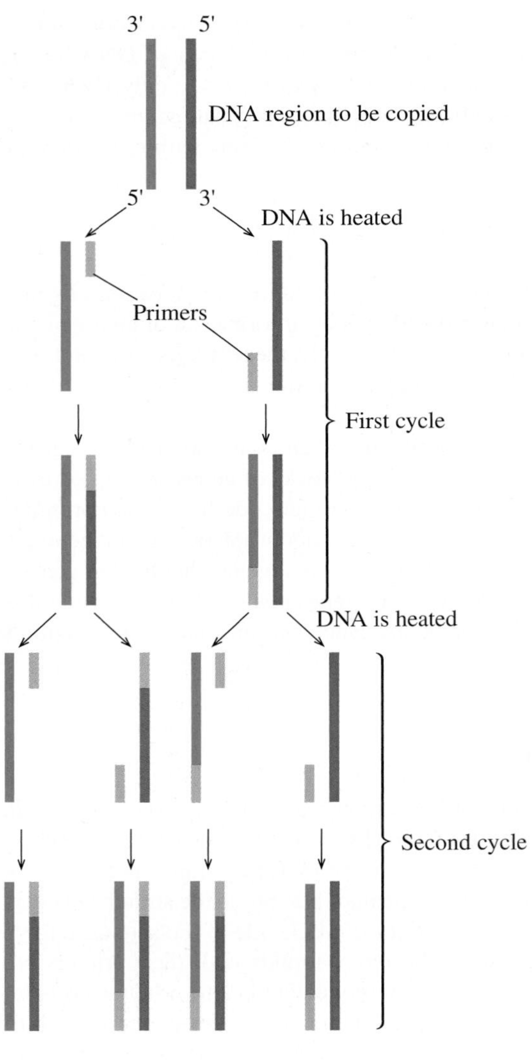


**FIGURE 21.24** Each cycle of the polymerase chain reaction doubles the number of copies of the DNA section.

**Q** Why are the DNA strands heated at the start of each cycle?

**TABLE 21.8** Some Diseases Caused by Viral Infection

| Disease | Virus |
|---|---|
| Common cold | Coronavirus (over 100 types) |
| Influenza | Orthomyxovirus |
| Warts | Papovavirus |
| Herpes | Herpesvirus |
| HPV | Human papillomavirus |
| Leukemia, cancers, AIDS | Retrovirus |
| Hepatitis | Hepatitis A virus (HAV), hepatitis B virus (HBV), hepatitis C virus (HCV) |
| Mumps | Paramyxovirus |
| Mononucleosis | Epstein–Barr virus (EBV) |
| Chicken pox (shingles) | Varicella zoster virus (VZV) |

## 21.10 Viruses

**LEARNING GOAL**

Describe the methods by which a virus infects a cell.

**Viruses** are small particles of 3 to 200 genes that cannot replicate without a host cell. A typical virus contains a nucleic acid, DNA or RNA, but not both, inside a protein coat. A virus does not have the necessary materials such as nucleotides and enzymes to synthesize proteins and to grow. The only way a virus can replicate (make additional copies of itself) is to invade a host cell and take over the materials necessary for protein synthesis and growth. Some infections caused by viruses invading human cells are listed in Table 21.8. There are also viruses that attack bacteria, plants, and animals.

A viral infection begins when an enzyme in the protein coat of the virus makes a hole in the host cell, allowing the viral nucleic acid to enter and mix with the materials in the host cell. (See Figure 21.25.) If the virus contains DNA, the host cell begins to replicate the viral DNA in the same way it would replicate normal DNA. Viral DNA produces viral RNA, and a protease produces a protein coat to form a viral particle that leaves the cell. (See Figure 21.26.) The cell synthesizes so many virus particles, the cell eventually bursts and releases new viruses to infect more cells.

Vaccines are inactive forms of viruses that boost the immune response by causing the body to produce antibodies to the virus. Several childhood diseases, such as polio, mumps, chicken pox, and measles, can be prevented through the use of vaccines.

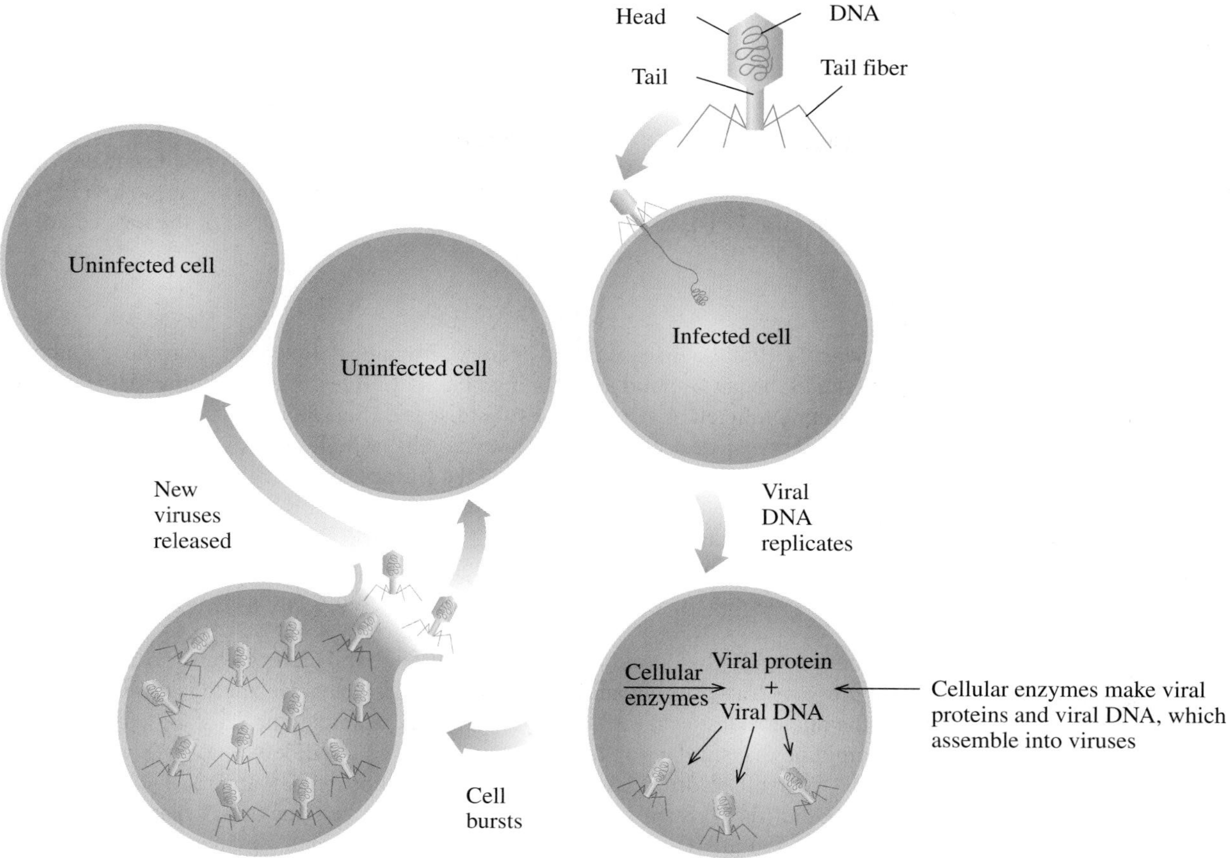


**FIGURE 21.25** After a virus attaches to the host cell, it injects its viral DNA and uses the host cell's amino acids to synthesize viral protein, nucleic acids, enzymes, and ribosomes to make viral RNA. When the cell bursts, the new viruses are released to infect other cells.

**Q** Why does a virus need a host cell for replication?

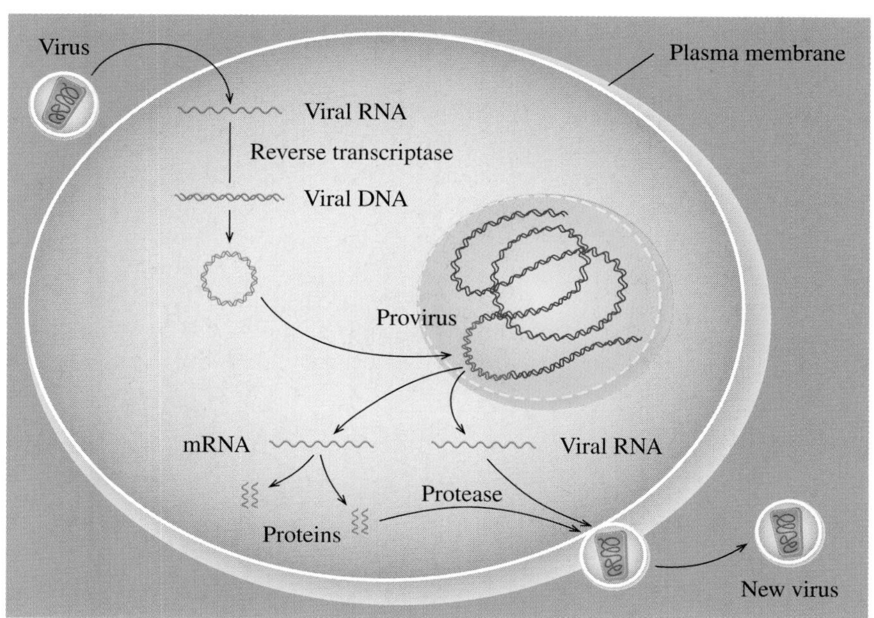


**FIGURE 21.26** After a retrovirus injects its viral RNA into a cell, it forms a DNA strand by reverse transcription. The DNA forms a double-stranded DNA called a provirus, which joins the host cell DNA. When the cell replicates, the provirus produces the viral RNA needed to produce more virus particles.

**Q** What is reverse transcription?

## Reverse Transcription

SELF STUDY ACTIVITY
HIV Reproductive Cycle

A virus that contains RNA as its genetic material is a **retrovirus**. Once inside the host cell, the retrovirus must first make viral DNA using a process known as *reverse transcription*. A retrovirus contains a polymerase enzyme called *reverse transcriptase* that uses the viral RNA template to synthesize complementary strands of DNA. Once produced, the DNA strands form double-stranded DNA using the nucleotides present in the host cell. This newly formed viral DNA, called a *provirus*, integrates with the DNA of the host cell.

## AIDS

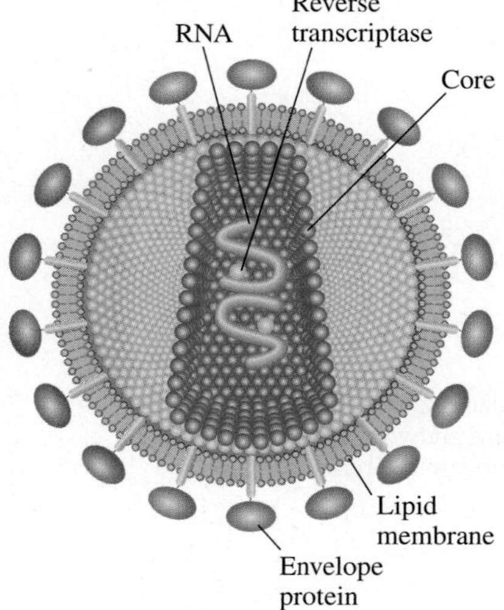


**FIGURE 21.27** HIV virus causes AIDS, which destroys the immune system in the body.

**Q** Is HIV a DNA virus or an RNA retrovirus?

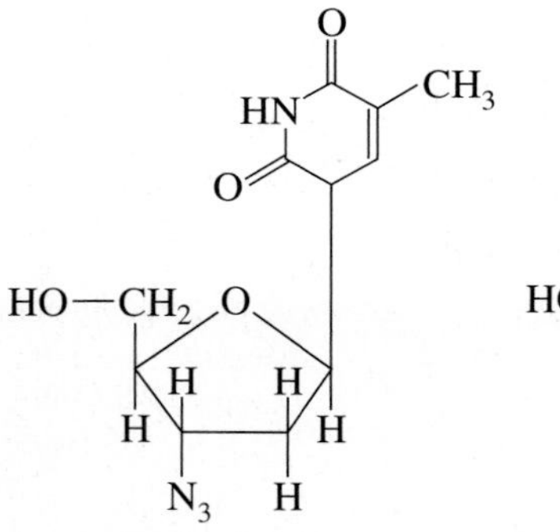

During the early 1980s, a disease called acquired immune deficiency syndrome, commonly known as AIDS, began to claim an alarming number of lives. We now know that HIV virus (human immunodeficiency virus) causes the disease. (See Figure 21.27.) HIV is a retrovirus that infects and destroys T4 lymphocyte cells, which are involved in the immune response. After the HIV binds to receptors on the surface of a T4 cell, the virus injects viral RNA into the host cell. As a retrovirus, the genes of the viral RNA direct the formation of viral DNA. The gradual depletion of T4 cells reduces the ability of the immune system to destroy harmful organisms. The AIDS syndrome is characterized by opportunistic infections such as *Pneumocystis carinii*, which causes pneumonia, and *Kaposi's sarcoma*, a skin cancer.

Treatment for AIDS is based on attacking the HIV at different points in its life cycle, including reverse transcription and protein synthesis. Nucleoside analogs mimic the structures of the nucleosides used for DNA synthesis. For example, the drug AZT (3′-azido-3′-deoxythymidine) is similar to thymidine, and ddI (2′,3′-dideoxyinosine) is similar to guanosine. Two other drugs are 2′,3′-dideoxycytidine (ddC) and 2′,3′-didehydro-3′-deoxythymidine (d4T). Such compounds are found in the "cocktails" that are providing extended remission of HIV infections. When a nucleoside analog is incorporated into viral DNA, the lack of a hydroxyl group on the 3′-carbon in the sugar prevents the formation of the sugar–phosphate bonds and stops the replication of the virus.

3'-azido-3'-deoxythymidine (AZT)

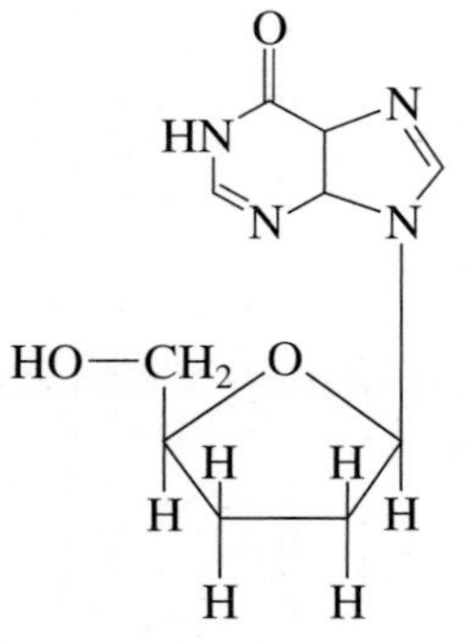

2',3'-Dideoxyinosine (ddI)

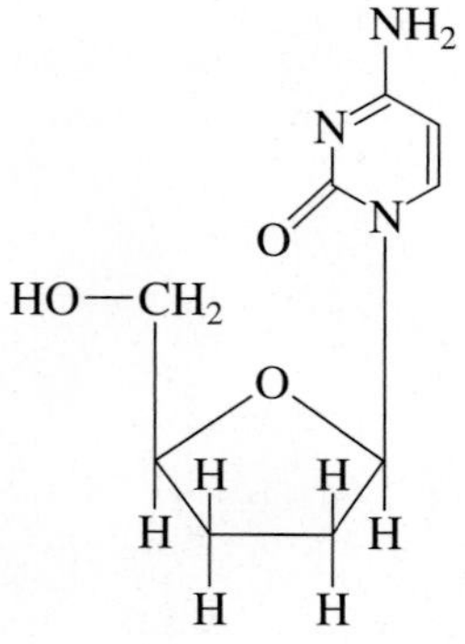

2',3'-Dideoxycytidine (ddC)

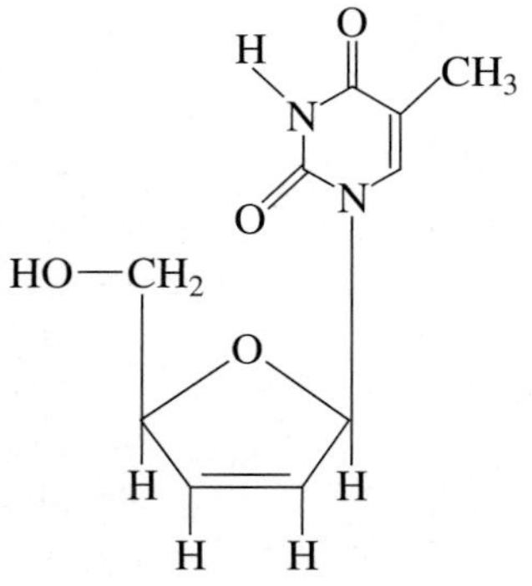

2',3'-Didehydro-3'-deoxythymidine (d4T)

The newest and most powerful anti-HIV drugs are the protease inhibitors such as saquinavir (Invirase), indinavir, and ritonavir. The inhibition of protease prevents the synthesis of proteins needed to make more copies of the virus. Researchers are not yet certain how long protease inhibitors will be beneficial for a person with AIDS.

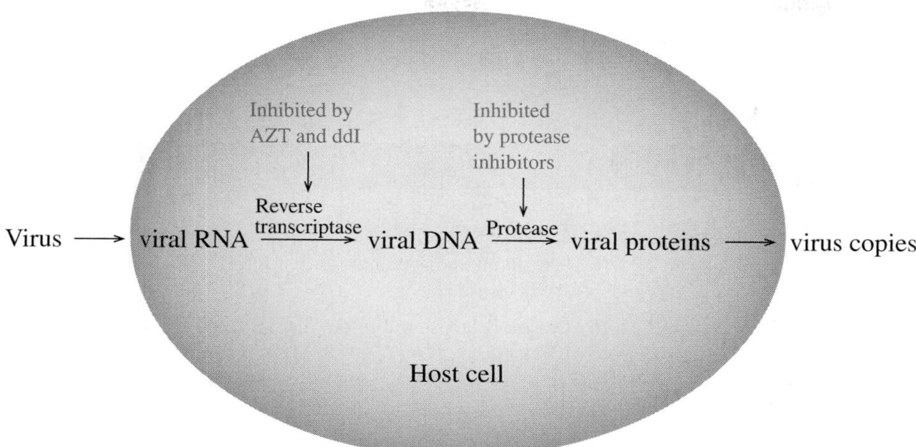


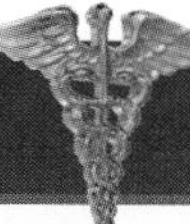

## HEALTH NOTE

### Cancer

In an adult body, many cells do not continue to reproduce. When cells in the body begin to grow and multiply inappropriately, they are called a tumor. If the effect of these tumors is limited, they are benign. When they invade other tissues and interfere with normal functions of the body, the tumors are cancerous. Cancer can be caused by chemical and environmental substances, by radiation, or by oncogenic viruses, which are viruses associated with human cancers. (See Table 21.9.)

Some reports estimate that chemical and environmental substances initiate 70–80% of all human cancers. A carcinogen is any substance that increases the chance of inducing a tumor. Known carcinogens include dyes, cigarette smoke, and asbestos. More than 90% of all persons with lung cancer are smokers. A carcinogen causes cancer by reacting with the DNA molecules in a cell, which alters the growth of that cell. Some known carcinogens are listed in Table 21.10.

Radiant energy from sunlight or medical radiation is another type of environmental factor. Skin cancer has become one of the most prevalent forms of cancer. The DNA damage in the exposed areas of the skin may eventually cause mutations. The cells lose their ability to control protein synthesis. This type of uncontrolled cell division becomes skin cancer. The incidence of malignant melanoma, one of the most serious skin cancers, has been rapidly increasing. Some possible factors for this increase may be the popularity of sun tanning as well as the reduction of the ozone layer, which absorbs much of the harmful radiation from sunlight.

Some cancers such as retinoblastoma and breast cancer appear to occur more frequently in families. Research indicates that a missing or defective gene is responsible.

**TABLE 21.9** Human Cancers Caused by Oncogenic Viruses

| Virus | Disease |
|---|---|
| **RNA viruses** | |
| Human T-cell lymphotropic virus-type I (HTLV-I) | Leukemia |
| **DNA viruses** | |
| Epstein–Barr virus (EBV) | Burkitt's lymphoma (cancer of white blood B cells) |
| | Nasopharyngeal carcinoma |
| | Hodgkin's disease |
| Hepatitis B virus (HBV) | Liver cancer |
| Herpes simplex virus (type 2) | Cervical and uterine cancer |
| Papilloma virus | Cervical and colon cancer, genital warts |

**TABLE 21.10** Some Chemical and Environmental Carcinogens

| Carcinogen | Tumor Site |
|---|---|
| Asbestos | Lung, respiratory tract |
| Arsenic | Skin, lung |
| Cadmium | Prostate, kidneys |
| Chromium | Lung |
| Nickel | Lung, sinuses |
| Aflatoxin | Liver |
| Nitrites | Stomach |
| Aniline dyes | Bladder |
| Vinyl chloride | Liver |

**CONCEPT CHECK 21.6**

**Viruses**

Why are viruses unable to replicate on their own?

ANSWER

Viruses contain only packets of DNA or RNA but not the necessary replication machinery that includes enzymes and nucleosides.

## QUESTIONS AND PROBLEMS

### Viruses

21.71 What type of genetic information is found in a virus?

**21.72** Why do viruses need to invade a host cell?

21.73 A virus contains viral RNA.

**a.** Why would reverse transcription be used in the life cycle of this type of virus?

**b.** What is the name of this type of virus?

**21.74** What is the purpose of a vaccine?

21.75 How do nucleoside analogs disrupt the life cycle of the HIV-1 virus?

**21.76** How do protease inhibitors disrupt the life cycle of the HIV-1 virus?

## CONCEPT MAP

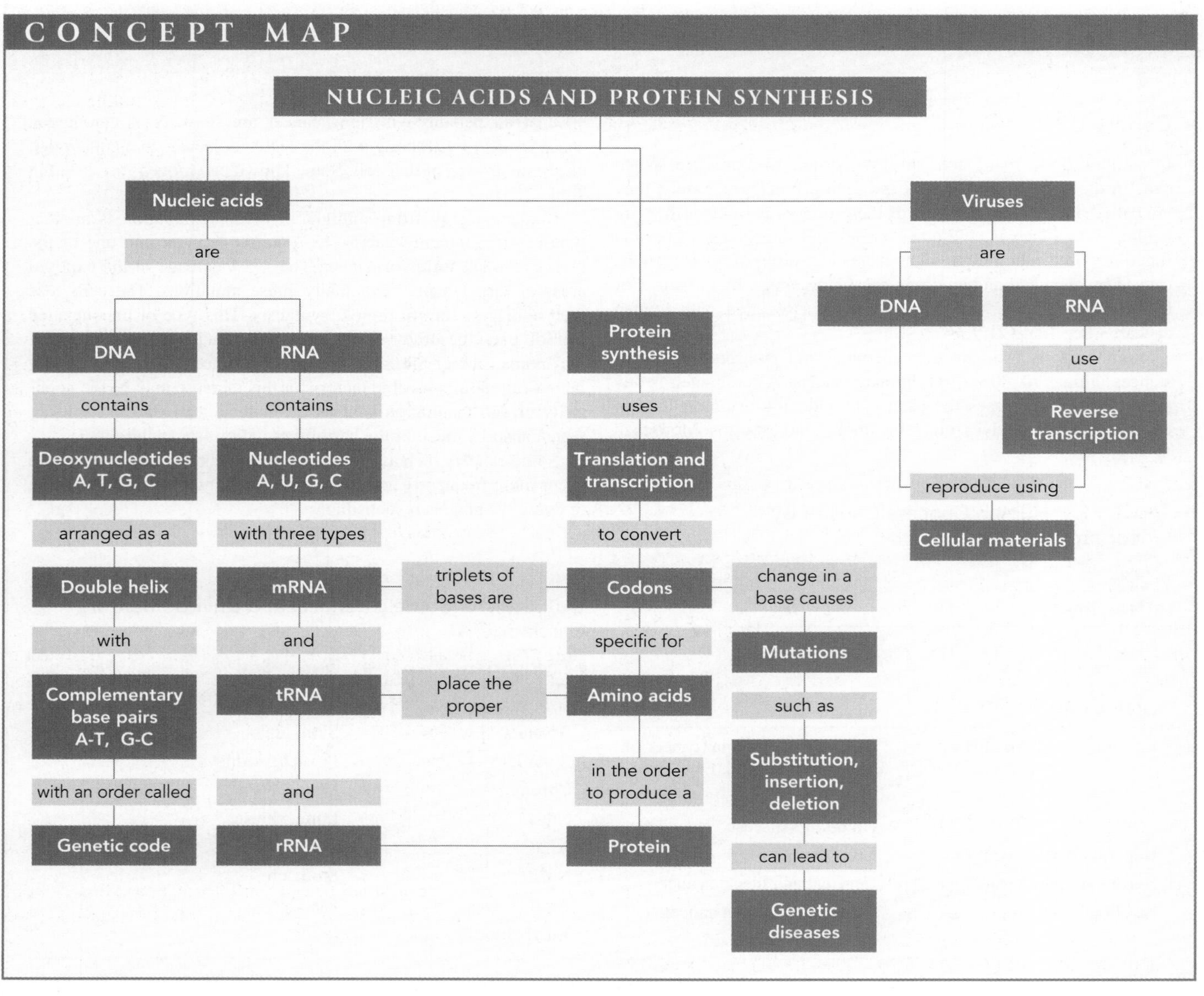

# CHAPTER REVIEW

## 21.1 Components of Nucleic Acids

**LEARNING GOAL:** *Describe the bases and ribose sugars that make up the nucleic acids DNA and RNA.*

Nucleic acids, such as deoxyribonucleic acid (DNA) and ribonucleic acid (RNA), are polymers of nucleotides. A nucleoside is a combination of a pentose sugar and a base. A nucleotide is composed of three parts: a pentose sugar, a base, and a phosphoryl group. In DNA, the sugar is deoxyribose and the base can be adenine, thymine, guanine, or cytosine. In RNA, the sugar is ribose, and uracil replaces thymine.

## 21.2 Primary Structure of Nucleic Acids

**LEARNING GOAL:** *Describe the primary structures of RNA and DNA.*

Each nucleic acid has its own unique sequence of bases known as its primary structure. In a nucleic acid polymer, the 3′—OH of each ribose sugar in RNA or deoxyribose sugar in DNA forms a phosphodiester bond to the phosphate group of the 5′-carbon atom group of the sugar in the next nucleotide to give a backbone of alternating sugar and phosphate groups. There is a free 5′-phosphate at one end of the polymer and a free 3′—OH group at the other end.

## 21.3 DNA Double Helix

**LEARNING GOAL:** *Describe the double helix of DNA.*

A DNA molecule consists of two strands of nucleotides that are wound around each other like a spiral staircase. The two strands are held together by hydrogen bonds between complementary base pairs, A with T, and G with C.

## 21.4 DNA Replication

**LEARNING GOAL:** *Describe the process of DNA replication.*

During DNA replication, DNA polymerase makes new DNA strands along each of the original DNA strands that serve as templates. Complementary base pairing ensures the correct pairing of bases to give identical copies of the original DNA.

## 21.5 RNA and Transcription

**LEARNING GOAL:** *Identify the different types of RNA; describe the synthesis of mRNA.*

The three types of RNA differ by function in the cell: ribosomal RNA makes up most of the structure of the ribosomes, messenger RNA carries genetic information from the DNA to the ribosomes, and transfer RNA places the correct amino acids in a growing peptide chain. Transcription is the process by which RNA polymerase produces mRNA from one strand of DNA. The bases in the mRNA are complementary to the DNA, except U is paired with A in RNA. The production of mRNA occurs when certain proteins are needed in the cell. In enzyme induction, the appearance of a substrate in a cell removes a repressor from the control site, which allows RNA polymerase to produce mRNA at the structural genes.

## 21.6 The Genetic Code

**LEARNING GOAL:** *Describe the function of the codons in the genetic code.*

The genetic code consists of a series of codons, which are sequences of three bases that specify the order for the amino acids in a protein. There are 64 codons for the 20 amino acids, which means there are multiple codons for most amino acids. The codon AUG signals the start of transcription, and codons UAG, UGA, and UAA signal it to stop.

## 21.7 Protein Synthesis: Translation

**LEARNING GOAL:** *Describe the process of protein synthesis from mRNA.*

Proteins are synthesized at the ribosomes in a translation process that includes three steps: initiation, translocation, and termination. During translation, tRNAs bring the appropriate amino acids to the ribosome, and peptide bonds form. When the polypeptide is released, it takes on its secondary and tertiary structures and becomes a functional protein in the cell.

## 21.8 Genetic Mutations

**LEARNING GOAL:** *Describe some ways in which DNA is altered to cause mutations.*

A genetic mutation is a change of one or more bases in the DNA sequence that alters the structure and ability of the resulting protein to function properly. In a substitution, one codon is altered, and a frameshift mutation inserts or deletes a base, which changes all the codons after the base change.

## 21.9 Recombinant DNA

**LEARNING GOAL:** *Describe the preparation and uses of recombinant DNA.*

A recombinant DNA is prepared by inserting a DNA segment—a gene—into the DNA present in plasmids of *E. coli* bacteria. As the altered bacterial cells replicate, the protein expressed by the foreign DNA segment is produced. In criminal investigation, large quantities of DNA are obtained from smaller amounts by DNA polymerase chain reactions.

## 21.10 Viruses

**LEARNING GOAL:** *Describe the methods by which a virus infects a cell.*

Viruses containing DNA or RNA must invade host cells to use the machinery within the cell for the synthesis of more viruses. For a retrovirus containing RNA, a viral DNA is synthesized by reverse transcription using the nucleotides and enzymes in the host cell. In the treatment of AIDS, nucleoside analogs inhibit the reverse transcriptase of the HIV-1 virus, and protease inhibitors disrupt the catalytic activity of protease needed to produce proteins for the synthesis of more viruses.

# KEY TERMS

**anticodon** The triplet of bases in the center loop of tRNA that is complementary to a codon on mRNA.

**bases** Nitrogen-containing compounds found in DNA and RNA: adenine (A), thymine (T), cytosine (C), guanine (G), and uracil (U).

**codon** A sequence of three bases in mRNA that specifies a certain amino acid to be placed in a protein. A few codons signal the start or stop of protein synthesis.

**complementary base pairs** In DNA, adenine is always paired with thymine (A—T or T—A), and guanine is always paired with cytosine (G—C or C—G). In forming RNA, adenine is paired with uracil (A—U).

**control site** A section of DNA that regulates protein synthesis.

**DNA** Deoxyribonucleic acid; the genetic material of all cells containing nucleotides with deoxyribose sugar, phosphate, and the four bases adenine, thymine, guanine, and cytosine.

**double helix** The helical shape of the double chain of DNA that is like a spiral staircase with a sugar–phosphate backbone on the outside and base pairs like stair steps on the inside.

**enzyme induction** A model of cellular regulation in which protein synthesis is induced by a substrate.

**exons** The sections in a DNA template that code for proteins.

**frameshift mutation** A mutation that inserts or deletes a base in a DNA sequence.

**genetic code** The sequence of codons in mRNA that specifies the amino acid order for the synthesis of protein.

**genetic disease** A physical malformation or metabolic dysfunction caused by a mutation in the base sequence of DNA.

**introns** The sections in DNA that do not code for proteins.

**mRNA** Messenger RNA; produced in the nucleus from DNA to carry the genetic information to the ribosomes for the construction of a protein.

**mutation** A change in the DNA base sequence that alters the formation of a protein in the cell.

**nucleic acids** Large molecules composed of nucleotides; found as a double helix in DNA and as the single strands of RNA.

**nucleoside** The combination of a pentose sugar and a base.

**nucleotides** Building blocks of a nucleic acid consisting of a base, a pentose sugar (ribose or deoxyribose), and a phosphoryl group.

**Okazaki fragments** The short segments formed by DNA polymerase in the daughter DNA strand that runs in the 3′ to 5′ direction.

**operon** A group of genes, including a control site and structural genes, whose transcription is controlled by the same regulatory gene.

**phosphodiester bond** The phosphate link that joins the 3′-hydroxyl group in one nucleotide to the phosphate group on the 5′-carbon atom in the next nucleotide.

**polymerase chain reaction (PCR)** A procedure in which a strand of DNA is copied many times by mixing it with DNA polymerase and a mixture of deoxyribonucleotides.

**primary structure** The sequences of nucleotides in nucleic acids.

**recombinant DNA** DNA combined from different organisms to form new, synthetic DNA.

**regulatory gene** A gene in front of the control site that produces a repressor.

**replication** The process of duplicating DNA by pairing the bases on each parent strand with their complementary base.

**replication forks** The open sections in unwound DNA strands where DNA polymerase begins the replication process.

**repressor** A protein that interacts with the control site in an operon to prevent the transcription of mRNA.

**retrovirus** A virus that contains RNA as its genetic material and that synthesizes a complementary DNA strand inside a cell.

**RNA** Ribonucleic acid; a type of nucleic acid that is a single strand of nucleotides containing adenine, cytosine, guanine, and uracil.

**rRNA** Ribosomal RNA; the most prevalent type of RNA and a major component of the ribosomes.

**structural genes** The sections of DNA that code for the synthesis of proteins.

**substitution mutation** A mutation that replaces one base in a DNA with a different base.

**transcription** The transfer of genetic information from DNA by the formation of mRNA.

**translation** The interpretation of the codons in mRNA as amino acids in a peptide.

**tRNA** Transfer RNA; an RNA that places a specific amino acid into a peptide chain at the ribosome. There is one or more tRNA for each of the 20 different amino acids.

**virus** Small particles containing DNA or RNA in a protein coat that require a host cell for replication.

## UNDERSTANDING THE CONCEPTS

**21.77** Answer the following questions for the given section of DNA:

**a.** Complete the bases in the parent and template strands.

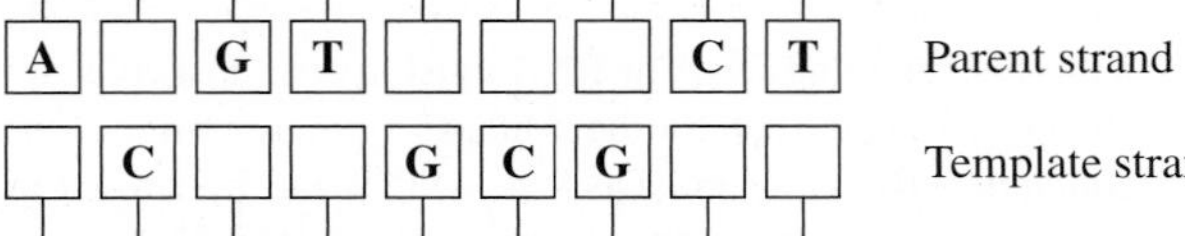


**b.** Using the template strand, write the mRNA sequence.

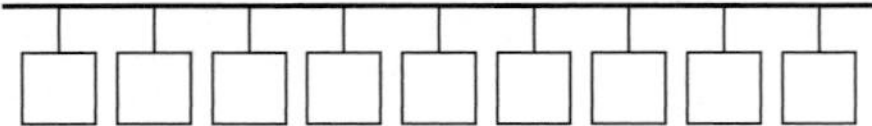

**c.** Write the 3-letter symbols of the amino acids that would go into the peptide from the mRNA you wrote in part **b**.

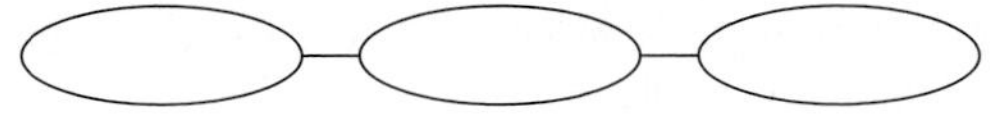

**21.78** Suppose a mutation occurs in the DNA section in problem 21.77, and the first base in the parent chain, adenine, is replaced by guanine.

**a.** What type of mutation has occurred?

**b.** Using the template strand that results from this mutation, write the order of bases in the altered mRNA.

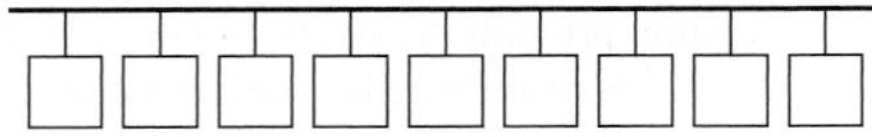

**c.** Write the 3-letter symbols of the amino acids that would go into the peptide from the mRNA you wrote in part **b**.

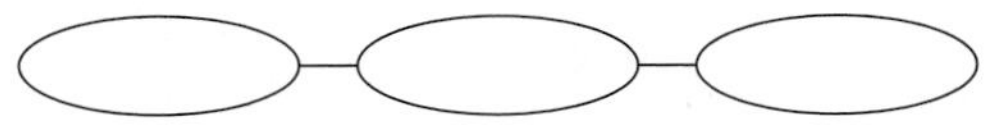

**d.** What effect, if any, might this mutation have on the structure and/or function of the resulting protein?

# ADDITIONAL QUESTIONS AND PROBLEMS

*For instructor-assigned homework, go to* ***www.masteringchemistry.com.***

21.79 Identify each of the following bases as a pyrimidine or a purine:
**a.** cytosine **b.** adenine **c.** uracil
**d.** thymine **e.** guanine

**21.80** Indicate if each of the bases in problem 21.79 are found in DNA only, RNA only, or both DNA and RNA.

21.81 Identify the base and sugar in each of the following nucleosides:
**a.** deoxythymidine **b.** adenosine
**c.** cytidine **d.** deoxyguanosine

**21.82** Identify the base and sugar in each of the following nucleotides:
**a.** CMP **b.** dAMP
**c.** dGMP **d.** UMP

21.83 How do the bases thymine and uracil differ?

**21.84** How do the bases cytosine and uracil differ?

21.85 Draw the structure of CMP.

**21.86** Draw the structure of dGMP.

21.87 What is similar about the primary structure of RNA and DNA?

**21.88** What is different about the primary structure of RNA and DNA?

21.89 If the DNA double helix in salmon contains 28% adenine, what is the percentage of thymine, guanine, and cytosine?

**21.90** If the DNA double helix in humans contains 20% cytosine, what is the percentage of guanine, adenine, and thymine?

21.91 In DNA, how many hydrogen bonds form between each of the following:
**a.** adenine and thymine **b.** guanine and cytosine

**21.92** How does polymerase chain reaction (PCR) produce many copies of a DNA section?

21.93 Write the complementary base sequence for each of the following DNA segments:
**a.** 5′—G—A—C—T—T—A—G—G—C—3′
**b.** 3′—T—G—C—A—A—A—C—T—A—G—C—T—5′
**c.** 5′—A—T—C—G—A—T—C—G—A—T—C—G—3′

**21.94** Write the complementary base sequence for each of the following DNA segments:
**a.** 5′—T—T—A—C—G—G—A—C—C—G—C—3′
**b.** 5′—A—T—A—G—C—C—C—T—T—A—C—T—G—G—3′
**c.** 3′—G—G—C—C—T—A—C—C—T—T—A—A—C—G—A—C—G—5′

21.95 In DNA replication, what is the difference in the synthesis of the leading strand and the lagging strand?

**21.96** How are the Okazaki fragments joined to the growing DNA strand?

21.97 Where are the DNA strands of the original DNA found in the double helix of each of the daughter DNA molecules?

**21.98** How can replication occur at several places along a DNA double helix?

21.99 Match the following statements with rRNA, mRNA, or tRNA:
**a.** is the smallest type of RNA
**b.** makes up the highest percentage of RNA in the cell
**c.** carries genetic information from the nucleus to the ribosomes

**21.100** Match the following statements with rRNA, mRNA, or tRNA:
**a.** combines with proteins to form ribosomes
**b.** brings amino acids to the ribosomes for protein synthesis
**c.** acts as a template for protein synthesis

21.101 What are the possible codons for each of the following amino acids?
**a.** threonine **b.** serine **c.** cysteine

**21.102** What are the possible codons for each of the following amino acids?
**a.** valine **b.** proline **c.** histidine

21.103 What is the amino acid for each of the following codons?
**a.** AAG **b.** AUU **c.** CGU

**21.104** What is the amino acid for each of the following codons?
**a.** CAA **b.** GGC **c.** AAC

21.105 Endorphins are polypeptides that reduce pain. What is the amino acid order for the following mRNA that codes for a pentapeptide that is an endorphin called leucine enkephalin?

5′—AUG—UAC—GGU—GGA—UUU—CUA—UAA—3′

**21.106** Endorphins are polypeptides that reduce pain. What is the amino acid order for the following mRNA that codes for a pentapeptide that is an endorphin called methionine enkephalin?

5′—AUG—UAC—GGU—GGA—UUU—AUG—UAA—3′

21.107 What is the anticodon on tRNA for each of the following codons in an mRNA?
**a.** AGC **b.** UAU **c.** CCA

**21.108** What is the anticodon on tRNA for each of the following codons in an mRNA?
**a.** GUG **b.** CCC **c.** GAA

# CHALLENGE QUESTIONS

21.109 Oxytocin is a nonapeptide with nine amino acids. How many nucleotides would be found in the mRNA for this protein?

**21.110** Why are there no base pairs in DNA between adenine and guanine or thymine and cytosine?

21.111 What is the difference between a DNA virus and a retrovirus?

**21.112** A protein contains 35 amino acids. How many nucleotides would be found in the mRNA for this protein?

# ANSWERS

## ANSWERS TO STUDY CHECKS

**21.1** deoxycytidine-5′-monophosphate (dCMP)

**21.2**

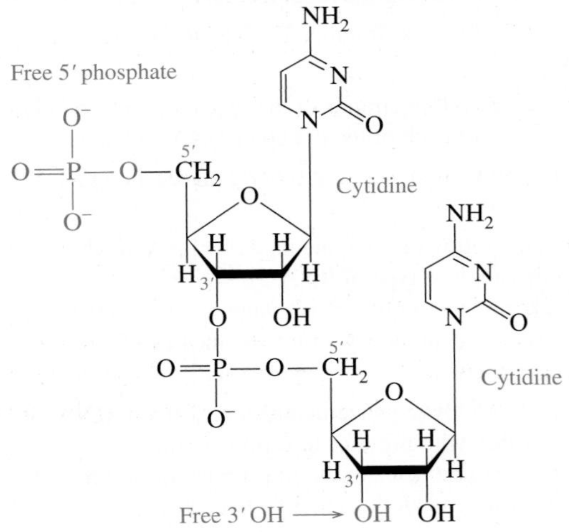

Free 5′ phosphate

Cytidine

Cytidine

Free 3′ OH

**21.3** 3′—C—C—A—A—T—T—G—G—5′

**21.4** Each type of tRNA matches a specific codon to a specific amino acid and brings the amino acids to the ribosomes for protein synthesis.

**21.5** 3′—C—C—C—A—A—A—T—T—T—5′

**21.6** Asn—Ala—Cys

**21.7** at UAG

**21.8** If the substitution of an amino acid in the polypeptide affects an interaction essential to functional structure on the binding of a substrate, the resulting protein could be less effective or nonfunctional.

## ANSWERS TO SELECTED QUESTIONS AND PROBLEMS

**21.1** **a.** pyrimidine **b.** pyrimidine

**21.3** **a.** DNA **b.** both DNA and RNA

**21.5** deoxyadenosine-5′-monophosphate (dAMP), deoxythymidine-5′-monophosphate (dTMP), deoxycytidine-5′-monophosphate (dCMP), and deoxyguanosine-5′-monophosphate (dGMP)

**21.7** **a.** nucleoside **b.** nucleoside
**c.** nucleoside **d.** nucleotide

**21.9**

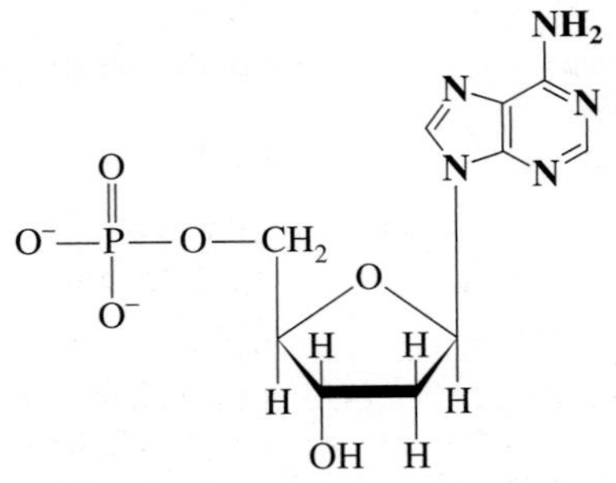

**21.11** The nucleotides in nucleic acids are held together by phosphodiester bonds between the 3′—OH of a sugar (ribose or deoxyribose) and a phosphate group on the 5′-carbon of another sugar.

**21.13**

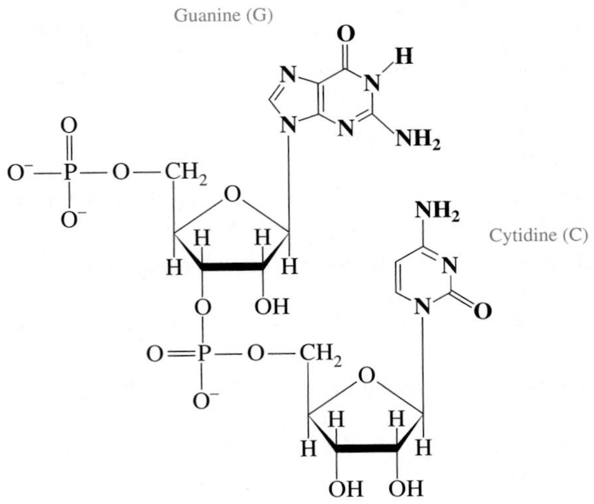

Guanine (G)

Cytidine (C)

**21.15** The two DNA strands are held together by hydrogen bonds between the bases in each strand.

**21.17** **a.** 3′—T—T—T—T—T—T—5′
**b.** 3′—C—C—C—C—C—C—5′
**c.** 3′—T—C—A—G—G—T—C—C—A—5′
**d.** 3′—G—A—C—A—T—A—T—G—C—A—A—T—5′

**21.19** The enzyme helicase unwinds the DNA helix to prepare the parent DNA strands for the synthesis of daughter DNA strands.

**21.21** Once the DNA strands separate, the DNA polymerase pairs each of the bases with its complementary base and produces two exact copies of the original DNA.

**21.23** ribosomal RNA, messenger RNA, and transfer RNA

**21.25** A ribosome consists of a small subunit and a large subunit.

**21.27** In transcription, the sequence of nucleotides on a DNA template (one strand) is used to produce the base sequences of a messenger RNA.

**21.29** 5′—G—G—C—U—U—C—C—A—A—G—U—G—3′

**21.31** In eukaryotic cells, genes contain sections called exons that code for proteins and sections called introns that do not code for protein.

**21.33** An operon is a section of DNA that regulates the synthesis of one or more proteins.

**21.35** When the lactose level is low in *E. coli*, a repressor produced by the mRNA from the regulatory gene binds to the control site, which blocks the synthesis of mRNA from the genes preventing the synthesis of protein.

**21.37** A codon is a three-base sequence in mRNA that codes for a specific amino acid in a protein.

**21.39** **a.** leucine (Leu) **b.** serine (Ser)
**c.** glycine (Gly) **d.** arginine (Arg)

**21.41** When AUG is the first codon, it signals the start of protein synthesis. Thereafter, AUG codes for methionine.

**21.43** A codon is a base triplet in the mRNA. An anticodon is the complementary triplet on a tRNA for a specific amino acid.

**21.45** initiation, chain elongation, and termination

**21.47** **a.** —Lys—Lys—Lys—
**b.** —Phe—Pro—Phe—Pro—
**c.** —Tyr—Gly—Arg—Cys—

**21.49** The new amino acid is joined by a peptide bond to the peptide chain. The ribosome moves to the next codon, which attaches to a tRNA carrying the next amino acid.

**21.51** **a.** 5′—CGA—AAA—GUU—UUU—3′
**b.** GCU, UUU, CAA, AAA
**c.** using codons in mRNA: —Arg—Lys—Val—Phe—

**21.53** A base in DNA is replaced by a different base.

**21.55** In a frameshift mutation caused by a deletion or an addition, all the codons from the mutation onward are changed, which changes the order of amino acids in the rest of the polypeptide chain.

**21.57** The normal triplet TTT forms a codon AAA, which codes for lysine. The mutation TTC forms a codon AAG, which also codes for lysine. There is no effect on the amino acid sequence.

**21.59** **a.** —Thr—Ser—Arg—Val—
**b.** —Thr—Thr—Arg—Val—
**c.** —Thr—Ser—Gly—Val—
**d.** —Thr—STOP. Protein synthesis would terminate early. If this occurs early in the formation of the polypeptide, the resulting protein will probably be nonfunctional.
**e.** The new protein will contain the sequence —Asp—Ile—Thr—Gly—.
**f.** The new protein will contain the sequence —His—His—Gly—.

**21.61** **a.** GCC and GCA both code for alanine.
**b.** A vital ionic cross-link in the tertiary structure of hemoglobin cannot be formed when the polar glutamic acid is replaced by valine, which is nonpolar. The resulting hemoglobin is malformed and less capable of carrying oxygen.

**21.63** *E. coli* bacterial cells contain several small circular plasmids of DNA that can be isolated easily. After the recombinant DNA is formed, *E. coli* multiply rapidly, producing many copies of the recombinant DNA in a relatively short time.

**21.65** *E. coli* are soaked in a detergent solution that dissolves the plasma membrane and releases the cell contents including the plasmids, which are collected.

**21.67** When a gene has been obtained using restriction enzymes, it is mixed with the plasmids that have been opened by the same enzymes. When mixed together in a fresh *E. coli* culture, the sticky ends of the DNA fragments bond with the sticky ends of the plasmid DNA to form a recombinant DNA.

**21.69** In DNA fingerprinting, restriction enzymes cut a sample DNA into fragments, which are sorted by size by gel electrophoresis. After tagging the DNA fragments with a radioactive isotope, a piece of X-ray film placed over the gel is exposed by the radioactivity to give a pattern of dark and light bands known as a DNA fingerprint.

**21.71** DNA or RNA, but not both

**21.73** **a.** A viral RNA is used to synthesize a viral DNA to produce the proteins for the protein coat, which allows the virus to replicate and leave the cell.
**b.** retrovirus

**21.75** Nucleoside analogs such as AZT and ddI are similar to the nucleosides required to make viral DNA in reverse transcription. However, they interfere with the ability of the DNA to form and thereby disrupt the life cycle of the HIV-1 virus.

**21.77**

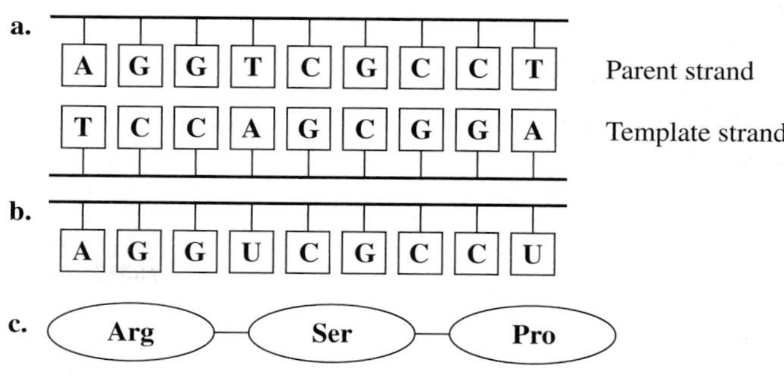


**21.79** **a.** pyrimidine **b.** purine **c.** pyrimidine
**d.** pyrimidine **e.** purine

**21.81** **a.** thymine and deoxyribose **b.** adenine and ribose
**c.** cytosine and ribose **d.** guanine and deoxyribose

**21.83** They are both pyrimidines, but thymine has a methyl group.

**21.85**

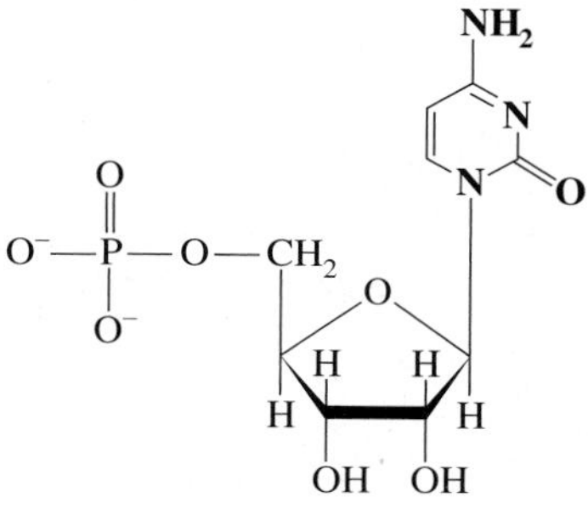


**21.87** They are both polymers of nucleotides connected through phosphodiester bonds between alternating sugar and phosphate groups with bases extending out from each sugar.

**21.89** 28% T, 22% G, and 22% C

**21.91** **a.** two **b.** three

**21.93** **a.** 3′—C—T—G—A—A—T—C—C—G—5′
**b.** 5′—A—C—G—T—T—T—G—A—T—C—G—A—3′
**c.** 3′—T—A—G—C—T—A—G—C—T—A—G—C—5′

**21.95** DNA polymerase synthesizes the leading strand continuously in the 5′ to 3′ direction. The lagging strand is synthesized in small segments called Okazaki fragments because it must grow in the 3′ to 5′ direction.

**21.97** One strand of the parent DNA is found in each of the two copies of the daughter DNA molecule.

**21.99** **a.** tRNA **b.** rRNA **c.** mRNA

**21.101** **a.** ACU, ACC, ACA, and ACG
**b.** UCU, UCC, UCA, UCG, AGU, and AGC
**c.** UGU and UGC

**21.103** **a.** lysine **b.** isoleucine **c.** arginine

**21.105** START—Tyr—Gly—Gly—Phe—Leu—STOP

**21.107** **a.** UCG **b.** AUA **c.** GGU

**21.109** Three nucleotides are needed to code for each amino acid plus the start and stop codons of three nucleotides each, which makes a minimum total of 33 nucleotides.

**21.111** A DNA virus attaches to a cell and injects viral DNA that uses the host cell to produce copies of the DNA to make viral RNA. A retrovirus injects viral RNA from which complementary DNA is produced by reverse transcription.

# 22 Metabolic Pathways for Carbohydrates

## LOOKING AHEAD


**22.1** Metabolism and Cell Structure

**22.2** ATP and Energy

**22.3** Important Coenzymes in Metabolic Pathways

**22.4** Digestion of Carbohydrates

**22.5** Glycolysis: Oxidation of Glucose

**22.6** Pathways for Pyruvate

**22.7** Glycogen Metabolism

**22.8** Gluconeogenesis: Glucose Synthesis


*"I was checking this dog's ears for foxtails and her eyes for signs of conjunctivitis," says Joyce Rhodes, veterinary assistant at the Sonoma Animal Hospital. "We always check a dog's teeth for tartar, because dental care is very important to the well-being of the animal. When I do need to give a medication to an animal, I use my chemistry to prepare the proper dose that the pet should take. Dosages may be in milligrams, kilograms, or milliliters."*

*As a member of the veterinary health care team, a veterinary technician (VT) assists a veterinarian in the care and handling of animals. A VT takes medical histories, collects specimens, performs laboratory procedures, prepares an animal for surgery, assists in surgical procedures, takes X-rays, talks with animal owners, and cleans teeth.*

Visit **www.masteringchemistry.com** for self-study materials and instructor-assigned homework.

When we eat food such as a tuna fish sandwich, the polysaccharides, lipids, and proteins are digested to smaller molecules that are absorbed into the cells of our bodies. As glucose, fatty acids, and amino acids are broken down further, energy is released. This energy is used in the cells to synthesize high-energy compounds such as adenosine triphosphate (ATP). Our cells utilize ATP energy when they do work such as contracting muscles, synthesizing large molecules, sending nerve impulses, and moving substances across cell membranes.

All the chemical reactions that take place in living cells to break down or build molecules are known as *metabolism*. In a metabolic pathway, reactions are linked together in a series, each catalyzed by a specific enzyme to produce an end product. In this and the following chapters, we will look at these pathways and the ways they produce energy and cellular compounds.

## 22.1 Metabolism and Cell Structure

**LEARNING GOAL**

Describe three stages of metabolism.

The term **metabolism** refers to all the chemical reactions that provide energy and the substances required for continued cell growth. There are two types of metabolic reactions: catabolic and anabolic. In **catabolic reactions**, complex molecules are broken down to simpler ones with an accompanying release of energy. **Anabolic reactions** utilize energy available in the cell to build large molecules from simple ones.

We can think of the catabolic processes in metabolism as consisting of three stages. (See Figure 22.1.) Let's use that tuna fish sandwich for our example. In stage 1 of metabolism, the processes of digestion break down the large macromolecules into small monomer units. The polysaccharides in the bread break down to monosaccharides, the lipids in the mayonnaise break down to glycerol and fatty acids, and the proteins from the tuna yield amino acids. These digestion products diffuse into the bloodstream for transport to cells. In stage 2, carbohydrates are broken down further to give a three-carbon compound called *pyruvate*. Other degradation pathways for lipids and proteins can also provide pyruvate. Under aerobic conditions, pyruvate is degraded to a two-carbon acetyl group that is activated when combined with coenzyme A to give acetyl CoA. In stage 3, the two carbon atoms from acetyl CoA enter the citric acid cycle (discussed in Chapter 23) for further oxidation to produce $CO_2$ and reduced coenzymes. As long as the cells have oxygen, the reduced coenzymes transfer hydrogen ions and electrons to electron transport where most of the ATP energy in the cell is produced.

### Cell Structure for Metabolism

To understand the relationships among metabolic reactions, we need to look at where metabolic reactions take place in the cells of plants and animals. The cells in plants and animals are *eukaryotic* cells, which have a nucleus and other structures surrounded by membranes. (See Figure 22.2.) Single-celled organisms such as bacteria are *prokaryotic* cells, which have no nucleus.

In a eukaryotic cell, a *cell membrane* is a lipid bilayer that separates the materials inside the cell from the aqueous environment surrounding the cell. In addition, the outer surface of the cell membrane contains structures that allow cells to communicate with each other. The *nucleus* contains the genes that control DNA replication and protein synthesis within the cell. The **cytoplasm** consists of all the materials between the nucleus and the cell membrane. The **cytosol**, which is the fluid part of the cytoplasm, is an aqueous solution of electrolytes and enzymes that catalyze many of the cell's chemical reactions.

Within the cytoplasm, specialized structures carry out specific functions in the cell. We have already seen (Chapter 21) that the *ribosomes* are the sites of protein synthesis using mRNA templates. The *endoplasmic reticulum* consists of two forms: a rough endoplasmic reticulum where proteins are processed for secretion and phospholipids are synthesized, and a smooth endoplasmic reticulum where fats and steroids are synthesized. The *Golgi*

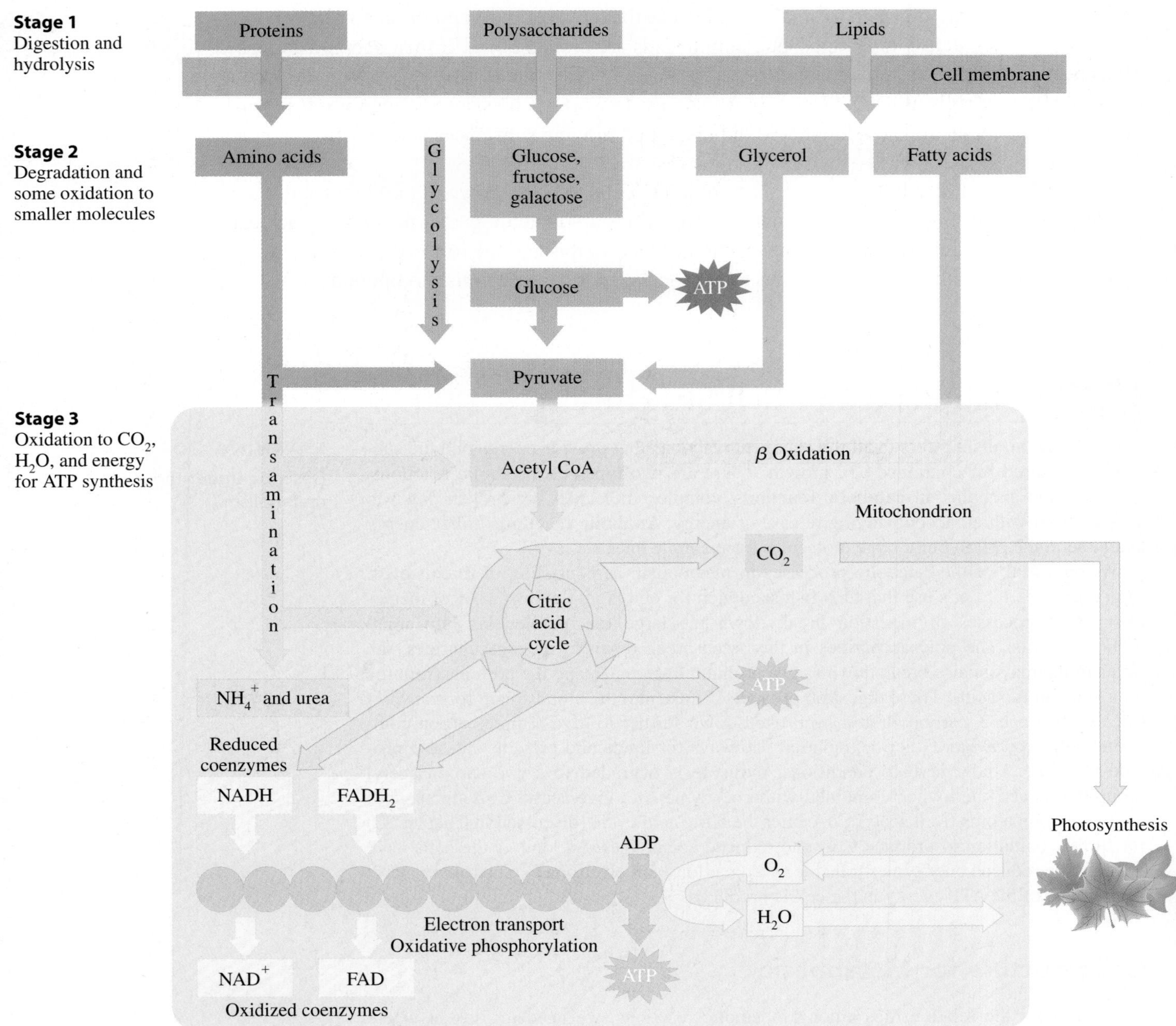


**FIGURE 22.1** In the three stages of catabolic metabolism, foods are digested and degraded into smaller molecules, which are oxidized to produce energy.

**Q** Where is most of the ATP energy produced in the cells?

*complex* modifies proteins it receives from the rough endoplasmic reticulum, secretes these modified proteins into fluid surrounding the cell, and forms glycoproteins and cell membranes. *Lysosomes* contain enzymes that break down recyclable cellular structures that are no longer needed by the cell. The **mitochondria** are the energy-producing factories of the cells. A mitochondrion consists of an outer membrane and an inner membrane, with an intermembrane space between them. The fluid section surrounded by the inner membrane is called the *matrix*. Enzymes located in the matrix and along the inner membrane catalyze the oxidation of carbohydrates, fats, and amino acids. All of these oxidation pathways lead to $CO_2$, $H_2O$, and energy, which are used to form energy-rich compounds. Table 22.1 summarizes some of the functions of the cellular components in animal cells.

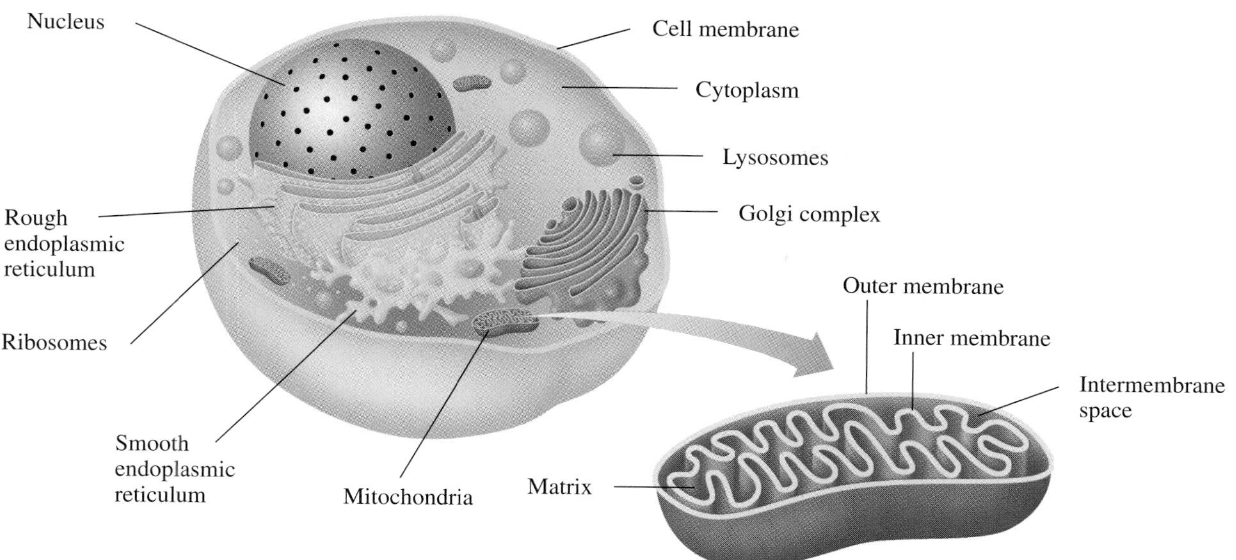


**FIGURE 22.2** The diagram illustrates the major components of a typical animal cell.
**Q** What is the cytoplasm in a cell?

**TABLE 22.1** Locations and Functions of Components in Animal Cells

| Component | Description and Function |
|---|---|
| Cell membrane | Separates the contents of a cell from the external environment and contains structures that communicate with other cells |
| Cytoplasm | Consists of all of the cellular contents between the cell membrane and nucleus |
| Cytosol | Fluid part of the cytoplasm that contains enzymes for many of the cell's chemical reactions including glycolysis and glucose and fatty acid synthesis |
| Endoplasmic reticulum | Rough type processes proteins for secretion and synthesizes phospholipids; smooth type synthesizes fats and steroids |
| Golgi complex | Modifies and secretes proteins from the endoplasmic reticulum and synthesizes cell membranes |
| Lysosomes | Contain hydrolytic enzymes that digest and recycle old cell structures |
| Mitochondria | Contain the structures for the synthesis of ATP from energy-producing reactions |
| Nucleus | Contains genetic information for the replication of DNA and the synthesis of protein |
| Ribosomes | Sites of protein synthesis using mRNA templates |

CONCEPT CHECK 22.1

### Metabolism and Cell Structure

Identify the following as catabolic or anabolic reactions:

**a.** digestion of polysaccharides
**b.** synthesis of proteins
**c.** oxidation of glucose to $CO_2$ and $H_2O$

ANSWER

**a.** The breakdown of large molecules involves catabolic reactions.
**b.** The synthesis of large molecules requires energy and involves anabolic reactions.
**c.** The breakdown of monomers such as glucose involves catabolic reactions.

## QUESTIONS AND PROBLEMS

### Metabolism and Cell Structure

22.1 What stage of metabolism involves the digestion of polysaccharides?

**22.2** What stage of metabolism involves the conversion of small molecules to $CO_2$, $H_2O$, and energy for the synthesis of ATP?

22.3 What is meant by a *catabolic reaction* in metabolism?

**22.4** What is meant by an *anabolic reaction* in metabolism?

22.5 Match each of the following with its function in the cell: (1) lysosome, (2) Golgi complex, (3) smooth endoplasmic reticulum.

**a.** synthesis of fats and steroids
**b.** contains hydrolytic enzymes
**c.** modifies products from rough endoplasmic reticulum

**22.6** Match each of the following with its function in the cell: (1) mitochondria, (2) rough endoplasmic reticulum, (3) cell membrane.

**a.** separates cell contents from external surroundings
**b.** sites of energy production
**c.** synthesizes proteins for secretion

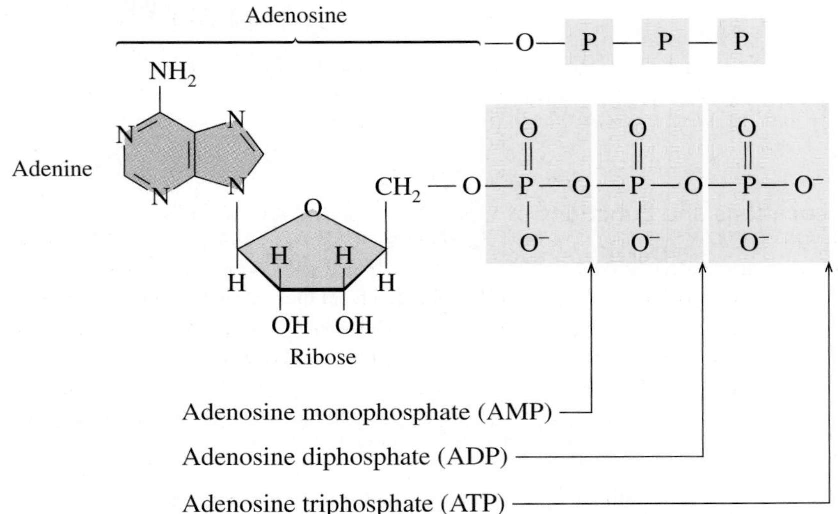


**FIGURE 22.3** Adenosine triphosphate (ATP) hydrolyzes to form ADP and AMP, along with a release of energy.

**Q** How much energy is released when a phosphoryl group is cleaved from one mole of ATP?

## 22.2 ATP and Energy

**LEARNING GOAL**

Describe the role of ATP in catabolic and anabolic reactions.

In our cells, the energy released from the oxidation of the food we eat is used to form a compound called *adenosine triphosphate* (abbreviated as **ATP**). As we saw in Chapter 21, the ATP molecule is composed of the base adenine, a ribose sugar, and three phosphoryl groups ($-PO_3^{2-}$). (See Figure 22.3.)

### Hydrolysis of ATP Yields Energy

In the cells, there are a variety of "high-energy" compounds. The most important of these is adenosine triphosphate, or ATP, which undergoes hydrolysis to give energy, adenosine diphosphate (abbreviated as **ADP**), and $HPO_4^{2-}$, called inorganic phosphate (abbreviated as $P_i$). The cleavage of inorganic phosphate ($P_i$) releases energy of 7.3 kcal per mole of ATP, or 31 kJ per mole of ATP. This equation can be written as follows:

$$ATP^{4-} + H_2O \longrightarrow ADP^{3-} + HPO_4^{2-} + H^+ + 7.3\,\text{kcal/mole (31 kJ/mole)}$$

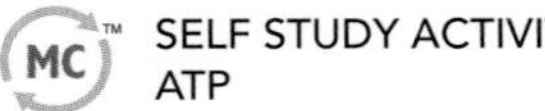


However, in this text, we often write equations such as this in an abbreviated form as follows:

$$ATP \longrightarrow ADP + P_i + 7.3\,\text{kcal/mole (31 kJ/mole)}$$

Adenosine—O— P — P — P

Adenosine triphosphate (ATP)

↓ $H_2O$

Adenosine—O— P — P + $P_i$ + 7.3 kcal/mole (31 kJ/mole)

Adenosine diphosphate (ADP)

↓ $H_2O$

Adenosine—O— P + $P_i$ + 7.3 kcal/mole (31 kJ/mole)

Adenosine monophosphate (AMP)

P = $-PO_3^{2-}$, phosphoryl

$P_i$ = $HPO_4^{2-}$, inorganic phosphate

The ADP can also hydrolyze to form adenosine monophosphate (AMP) and an inorganic phosphate ($P_i$). The abbreviated equation is written as follows:

$$\text{ADP} \longrightarrow \text{AMP} + P_i + 7.3 \text{ kcal/mole (31 kJ/mole)}$$

Every time we contract muscles, move substances across cellular membranes, send nerve signals, or synthesize an enzyme, we use energy from ATP hydrolysis. In a cell that is doing work (anabolic processes), 1–2 million ATP molecules may be hydrolyzed in one second. The amount of ATP hydrolyzed in one day can be as much as our body mass, even though only about 1 gram of ATP is present in all our cells at any given time.

When we take in food, the resulting catabolic reactions provide energy to regenerate ATP in our cells. Then 7.3 kcal/mole (31 kJ/mole) is used to make ATP from ADP and $P_i$. (See Figure 22.4.)

$$\text{ADP} + P_i + 7.3 \text{ kcal/mole (31 kJ/mole)} \longrightarrow \text{ATP}$$

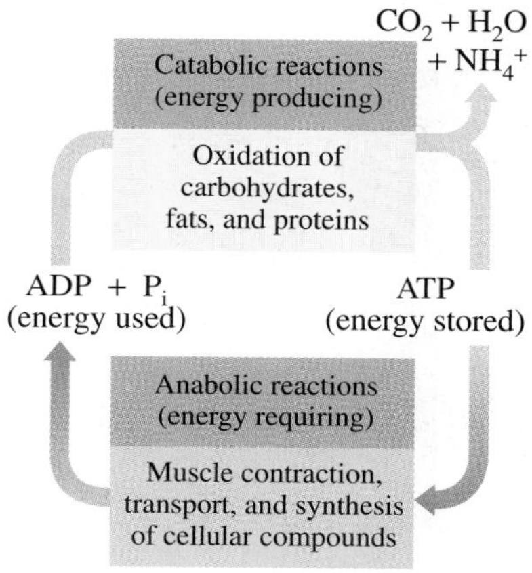

$CO_2 + H_2O + NH_4^+$

Catabolic reactions (energy producing)

Oxidation of carbohydrates, fats, and proteins

ADP + $P_i$ (energy used)

ATP (energy stored)

Anabolic reactions (energy requiring)

Muscle contraction, transport, and synthesis of cellular compounds

**FIGURE 22.4** ATP, the energy-storage molecule, connects the energy-producing reactions with the energy-requiring reactions that do work in the cells.

**Q** What type of reaction provides energy for ATP synthesis?

## ATP Drives Reactions

ATP and other energy-rich compounds are combined with metabolic reactions and processes that require energy. ATP is very useful in the body because it can be used to drive reactions that require energy and do not occur on their own. For example, the glucose obtained from carbohydrates must add a phosphoryl group to start its breakdown in the cell. However, the cost of adding a phosphoryl group to glucose is 3.3 kcal/mole (14 kJ/mole), which means that the reaction does not occur spontaneously in the cell. By combining the reaction with the hydrolysis of an energy-rich compound such as ATP, the reaction takes place because the energy from hydrolysis pushes, or "drives," the energy-requiring reaction:

MC™ TUTORIAL ATP: Energy Rich

| | | | |
|---|---|---|---|
| ATP | ⟶ | ADP + $P_i$ + 7.3 kcal/mole (31 kJ/mole) | Provides energy |
| Glucose + $P_i$ + 3.3 kcal/mole (14 kJ/mole) | ⟶ | glucose-6-phosphate | Requires energy |
| ATP + Glucose | ⟶ | ADP + glucose-6-phosphate + 4.0 kcal/mole (17 kJ/mole) | |

The coupling of a reaction that requires energy with a reaction that supplies energy is a very important concept in biochemical pathways. Many of the reactions essential to a cell for survival cannot proceed by themselves, but they can be made to proceed by coupling them with a reaction that releases energy. Similar kinds of combined reactions are also used to transmit nerve impulses, transport substances across membranes to higher concentrations, and to contract muscles.

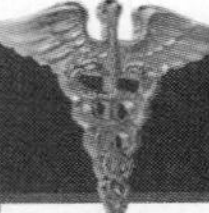

# HEALTH NOTE

## ATP Energy and $Ca^{2+}$ Needed to Contract Muscles

Our muscles consist of thousands of parallel fibers. Within these muscle fibers are fibrils composed of two kinds of proteins called filaments. Arranged in alternating rows, the thick filaments of myosin overlap the thin filaments containing actin. During a muscle contraction, the thin filaments slide inward over the thick filaments causing a shortening of the muscle fibers.

Calcium ion ($Ca^{2+}$) and ATP play an important role in muscle contraction. An increase in the $Ca^{2+}$ concentration in the muscle fibers causes the filaments to slide, while a decrease stops the process. In a relaxed muscle, the $Ca^{2+}$ concentration is low. However, when a nerve impulse reaches the muscle, calcium channels in the membrane open, and $Ca^{2+}$ flows into the fluid surrounding the filaments. The muscle contracts as myosin binds to actin and pulls the filaments inward. The energy for the contraction is provided by the hydrolysis of ATP to ADP + $P_i$.

Muscle contraction continues as long as both ATP and $Ca^{2+}$ levels are high around the filaments. When the nerve impulse ends, the calcium channels close. The $Ca^{2+}$ concentration decreases as energy from ATP pumps the remaining $Ca^{2+}$ out of the filaments, which causes the muscle to relax. In rigor mortis, $Ca^{2+}$ concentration remains high within the muscle fibers, causing a continued state of rigidity. After approximately 24 hours, $Ca^{2+}$ decreases due to cellular deterioration, and the muscles relax.

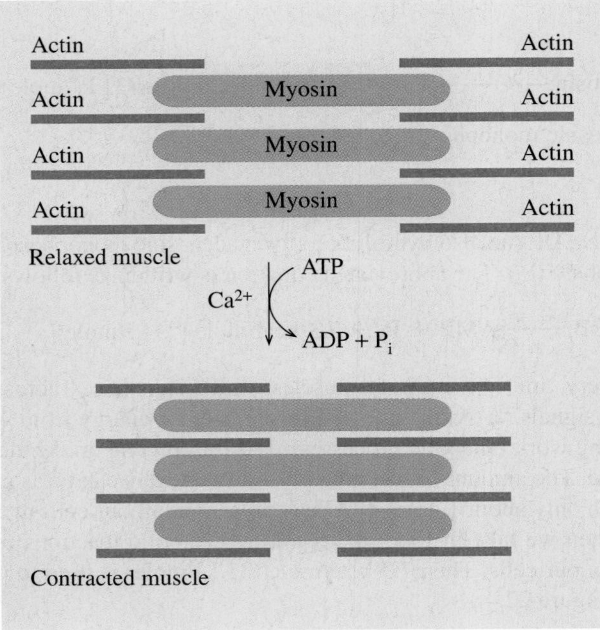


CONCEPT CHECK 22.2

### High-Energy Compounds

Describe the components of ATP, ADP, and AMP.

ANSWER

ATP, ADP, and AMP all contain the nucleoside adenosine, which is the base adenine and ribose sugar. In ATP, adenosine is attached to three phosphoryl groups; in ADP, adenosine is attached to two phosphoryl groups; and in AMP, adenosine is attached to one.

SAMPLE PROBLEM 22.1

### Hydrolysis of ATP

Write an abbreviated form of the equation for the hydrolysis of ATP.

SOLUTION

The abbreviated form of the equation for the hydrolysis of ATP produces ADP, $P_i$, and energy:

$$\text{ATP} \longrightarrow \text{ADP} + \text{P}_i + \text{energy}$$

STUDY CHECK

How much energy is released from the hydrolysis of ATP to ADP and $P_i$?

## QUESTIONS AND PROBLEMS

### ATP and Energy

22.7 Why is ATP considered an energy-rich compound?

**22.8** What is meant when we say that the hydrolysis of ATP is used to "drive" a reaction?

22.9 Phosphoenolpyruvate (PEP) is a high-energy compound that releases 14.8 kcal/mole of energy when it hydrolyzes to pyruvate and $P_i$. This reaction can be combined with the synthesis of ATP from ADP and $P_i$.

**a.** Write an equation for the energy-releasing reaction of PEP.

**b.** Write an equation for the energy-requiring reaction that forms ATP.

**c.** Write the overall equation for the combined reaction including the net energy change.

**22.10** The phosphorylation of glycerol to glycerol-3-phosphate requires 2.2 kcal/mole and is driven by the hydrolysis of ATP.

**a.** Write an equation for the energy-releasing reaction of ATP.

**b.** Write an equation for the energy-requiring reaction that forms glycerol-3-phosphate.

**c.** Write the overall equation for the combined reaction including the net energy change.

# 22.3 Important Coenzymes in Metabolic Pathways

**LEARNING GOAL**

Describe the components and functions of the coenzymes FAD, $NAD^+$, and coenzyme A.

Before we look at the metabolic reactions that extract energy from our food, we need to review some ideas about oxidation and reduction reactions. (See Chapter 6.) An *oxidation* reaction involves the loss of hydrogen ions and electrons by a substance or an increase in oxygen. When an enzyme catalyzes an oxidation reaction, hydrogen atoms are removed from a substrate as hydrogen ions, $2H^+$, and electrons, $2e^-$:

$$2\text{H atoms (removed in oxidation)} \longrightarrow 2H^+ + 2e^-$$

*Reduction* is the gain of hydrogen ions and electrons or a decrease in oxygen. When hydrogen ions and electrons are picked up by a coenzyme, it is reduced.

**Oxidation: Loss of H, loss of $e^-$, or increase of O** →

$$\underset{\text{Alkane}}{CH_3{-}CH_3} \underset{}{\overset{[O]}{\rightleftharpoons}} \underset{\text{Alcohol (1°)}}{CH_3{-}\overset{\overset{\large OH}{|}}{C}H_2} \overset{[O]}{\rightleftharpoons} \underset{\text{Aldehyde}}{CH_3{-}\overset{\overset{\large O}{\|}}{C}{-}H} \overset{[O]}{\rightleftharpoons} \underset{\text{Carboxylic acid}}{CH_3{-}\overset{\overset{\large O}{\|}}{C}{-}OH}$$

$$\underset{\text{Alcohol (2°)}}{CH_3{-}\overset{\overset{\large OH}{|}}{C}H{-}CH_3} \overset{[O]}{\rightleftharpoons} \underset{\text{Ketone}}{CH_3{-}\overset{\overset{\large O}{\|}}{C}{-}CH_3}$$

← **Reduction: Gain of H, gain of $e^-$, or decrease of O**

As we saw in Chapter 20, the structures of many coenzymes include the water-soluble B vitamins we obtain from the foods in our diets. Now we will look at the structures of several important coenzymes in their oxidized and reduced forms.

## $NAD^+$

**$NAD^+$** (nicotinamide adenine dinucleotide) is an important coenzyme in which the vitamin *niacin* provides the *nicotinamide* group, which is bonded to ribose and adenosine diphosphate (ADP). (See Figure 22.5.) The $NAD^+$ coenzyme participates in reactions that produce

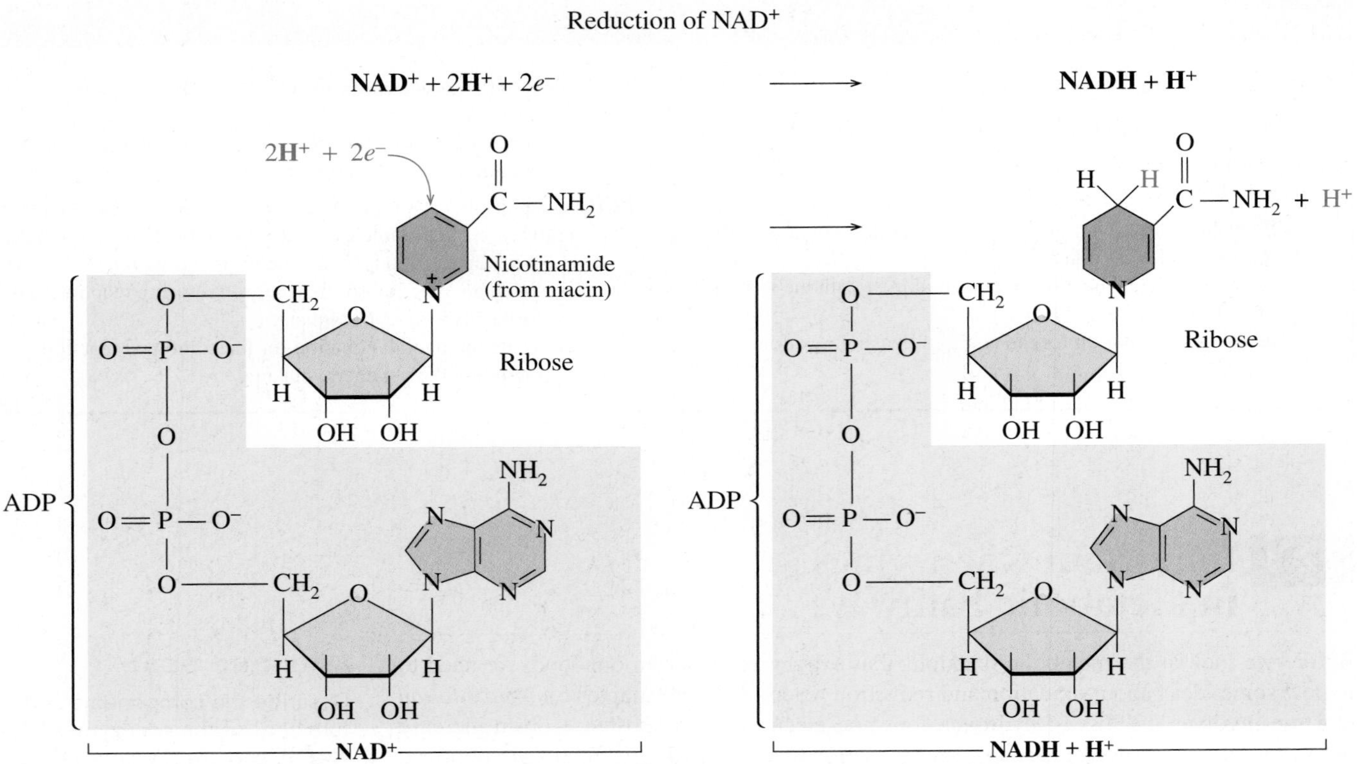

Reduction of $NAD^+$

$NAD^+ + 2H^+ + 2e^- \longrightarrow NADH + H^+$

$2H^+ + 2e^-$ Nicotinamide (from niacin) Ribose ADP $NAD^+$ $NADH + H^+$

FIGURE 22.5 The coenzyme $NAD^+$ (nicotinamide adenine dinucleotide), which consists of adenosine diphosphate, nicotinamide from the vitamin niacin, and ribose, is reduced to $NADH + H^+$.

Q Why is the conversion of $NAD^+$ to NADH and $H^+$ called a reduction?

a carbon–oxygen (C=O) double bond such as the oxidation of alcohols to aldehydes and ketones. The $NAD^+$ is reduced when the carbon in the pyridine ring of nicotinamide accepts a hydrogen ion and two electrons, leaving one $H^+$. Let's look at the reactions that take place when ethanol is oxidized in the liver to acetaldehyde using $NAD^+$:

**Oxidation**

$$\underset{\text{Ethanol}}{CH_3{-}CH_2{-}OH} \xrightleftharpoons{\text{Alcohol dehydrogenase}} \underset{\text{Acetaldehyde}}{CH_3{-}\overset{O}{\overset{\|}{C}}{-}H} + 2H^+ + 2e^-$$

**Reduction**

$$NAD^+ + 2H^+ + 2e^- \rightleftharpoons NADH + H^+$$

**Overall oxidation–reduction reaction**

$$\underset{\text{Ethanol}}{CH_3{-}CH_2{-}OH} + NAD^+ \xrightleftharpoons{\text{Alcohol dehydrogenase}} \underset{\text{Acetaldehyde}}{CH_3{-}\overset{O}{\overset{\|}{C}}{-}H} + NADH + H^+$$

## FAD

**FAD** (flavin adenine dinucleotide) is a coenzyme that contains adenosine diphosphate (ADP) and riboflavin. Riboflavin (vitamin $B_2$) consists of ribitol (a sugar alcohol) and flavin. As a coenzyme, two nitrogen atoms in the flavin part of the FAD coenzyme accept two hydrogens, which reduces the FAD to $FADH_2$. (See Figure 22.6.)

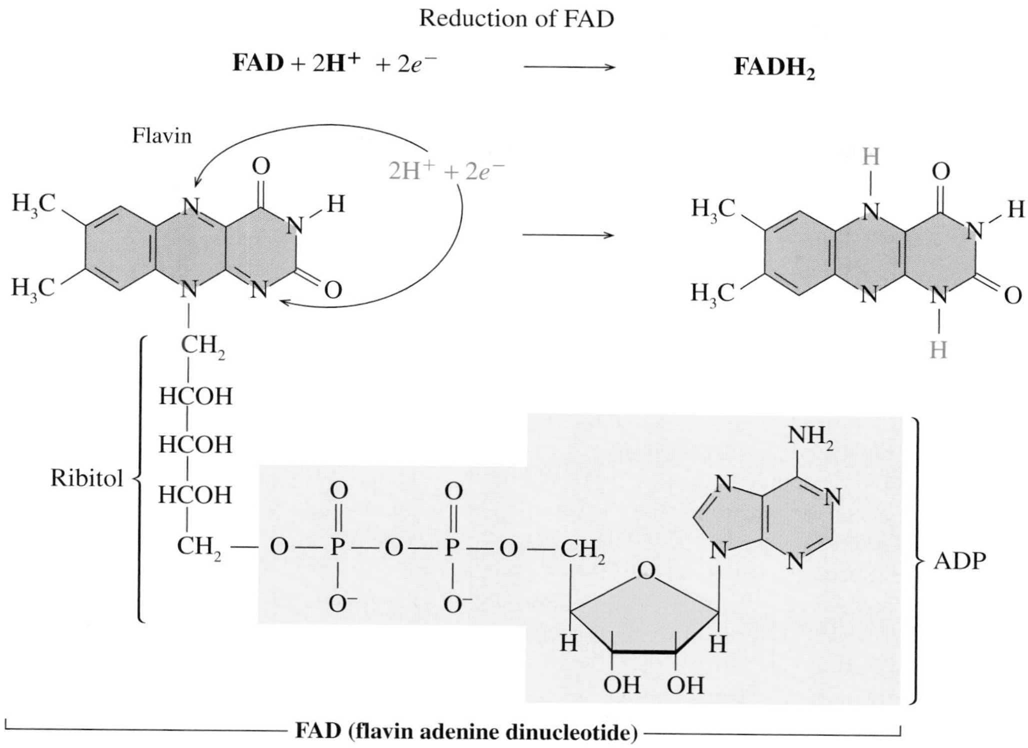

Reduction of FAD

$$FAD + 2H^+ + 2e^- \longrightarrow FADH_2$$

Flavin

Ribitol

ADP

FAD (flavin adenine dinucleotide)

FIGURE 22.6 The coenzyme FAD (flavin adenine dinucleotide) made from riboflavin (vitamin $B_2$) and adenosine diphosphate is reduced to $FADH_2$.

Q What is the type of reaction in which FAD accepts hydrogen?

FAD typically participates in oxidation reactions that produce a carbon–carbon (C=C) double bond:

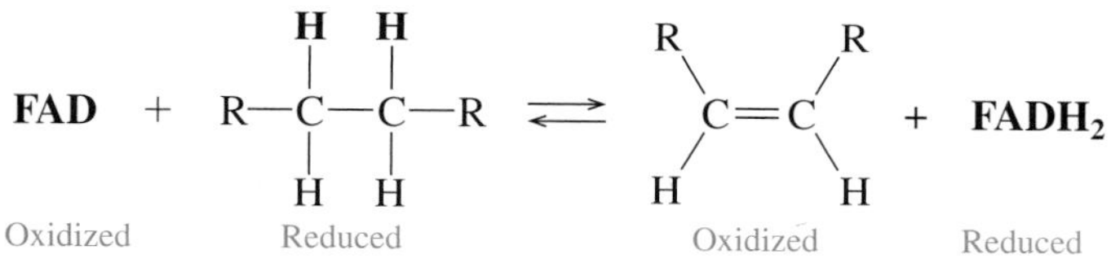

$$\text{FAD} + \text{R—CH—CH—R} \rightleftharpoons \text{RHC=CHR} + \text{FADH}_2$$

Oxidized | Reduced | Oxidized | Reduced

## Coenzyme A

**Coenzyme A (CoA)** is made up of several components. An aminoethanethiol is attached to pantothenic acid (vitamin $B_5$), which is bonded to adenosine-3′-phosphate (phosphorylated ADP). (See Figure 22.7.)

One of the main functions of coenzyme A is to prepare small acyl groups (represented by the letter A) such as acetyl for reactions with enzymes. The important reactive feature of coenzyme A is the thiol (—SH). When the —SH group of coenzyme A bonds to a two-carbon acetyl group, it produces an energy-rich thioester **acetyl CoA**.

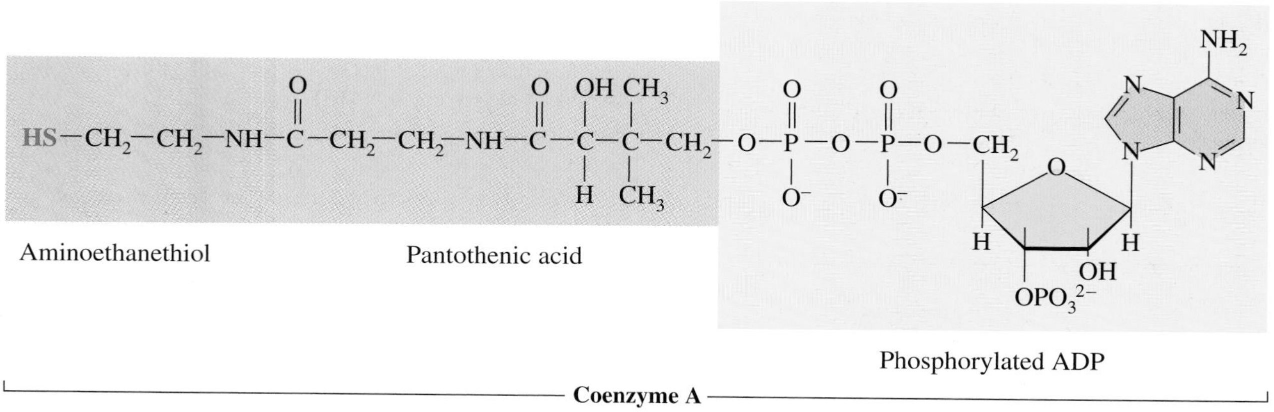

HS—CH₂—CH₂—NH—C(=O)—CH₂—CH₂—NH—C(=O)—CH(OH)—C(CH₃)₂—CH₂—O—P(=O)(O⁻)—O—P(=O)(O⁻)—O—CH₂—(ribose-3′-OPO₃²⁻)—adenine

Aminoethanethiol | Pantothenic acid | Phosphorylated ADP

Coenzyme A

FIGURE 22.7 Coenzyme A consists of aminoethanethiol bonded to pantothenic acid (vitamin $B_5$), which is attached to the diphosphate of adenosine-3′-phosphate (phosphorylated adenosine diphosphate).

Q What part of coenzyme A reacts with a two-carbon acetyl group?

Thioester

$$CH_3{-}\overset{\displaystyle O}{\overset{\|}{C}}{-}S{-}CoA$$

Acetyl CoA

In biochemistry, several abbreviations are used for coenzyme A and the ester acetyl coenzyme A. For discussions in this text, we will use CoA for coenzyme A and acetyl CoA when the acetyl group is attached to the sulfur atom (—S—) in coenzyme A. In equations, we will show the (—SH) group in coenzyme A as HS—CoA and the —S— in the structure of the acetyl CoA product to emphasize the reaction of the thiol (—SH) group.

CONCEPT CHECK 22.3

### Coenzymes

Describe the reactive part of each of the following coenzymes and the way each participates in metabolic pathways:

**a.** FAD **b.** $NAD^+$ **c.** coenzyme A

ANSWER

**a.** When two nitrogen atoms in the flavin accept $2H^+$ and $2e^-$, FAD is reduced to $FADH_2$. FAD is the coenzyme in oxidation reactions that produce a carbon–carbon (C═C) double bond.

**b.** When a carbon atom in the pyridine ring of nicotinamide accepts $H^+$ and $2e^-$, $NAD^+$ is reduced to NADH. The $NAD^+$ coenzyme participates in reactions that produce a carbon–oxygen (C═O) double bond.

**c.** The thiol (HS—) group of aminoethanethiol in coenzyme A combines with an acetyl group to form acetyl coenzyme A. The CoA participates in the transfer of acyl groups, usually acetyl groups.

SAMPLE PROBLEM 22.2

### Coenzymes in Metabolic Pathways

What vitamin is part of each of the following coenzymes?

**a.** FAD **b.** $NAD^+$ **c.** CoA

SOLUTION

**a.** FAD contains riboflavin (vitamin $B_2$).
**b.** $NAD^+$ contains nicotinamide from niacin (vitamin $B_3$).
**c.** CoA contains pantothenic acid (vitamin $B_5$).

STUDY CHECK

What is the abbreviation of the reduced form of FAD?

## QUESTIONS AND PROBLEMS

### Important Coenzymes in Metabolic Pathways

22.11 Identify one or more coenzymes with each of the following components:
**a.** pantothenic acid **b.** niacin **c.** ribitol

**22.12** Identify one or more coenzymes with each of the following components:
**a.** riboflavin **b.** adenine **c.** aminoethanethiol

22.13 Give the abbreviation for each of the following:
**a.** the reduced form of $NAD^+$
**b.** the oxidized form of $FADH_2$

**22.14** Give the abbreviation for each of the following:
**a.** the reduced form of FAD
**b.** the oxidized form of NADH

22.15 What coenzyme picks up hydrogen when a carbon–carbon double bond is formed?

**22.16** What coenzyme picks up hydrogen when a carbon–oxygen double bond is formed?

## 22.4 Digestion of Carbohydrates

LEARNING GOAL

Give the sites and products of the digestion of carbohydrates.

In stage 1 of metabolism, foods undergo **digestion**, a process that converts large molecules to smaller ones that can be absorbed by the body. We begin the digestion of carbohydrates as soon as we chew food. (See Figure 22.8.) *Amylase*, an enzyme produced in the salivary glands, hydrolyzes some of the α-glycosidic bonds in amylose and amylopectin, producing maltose, glucose, and smaller polysaccharides called dextrins, which contain three to eight

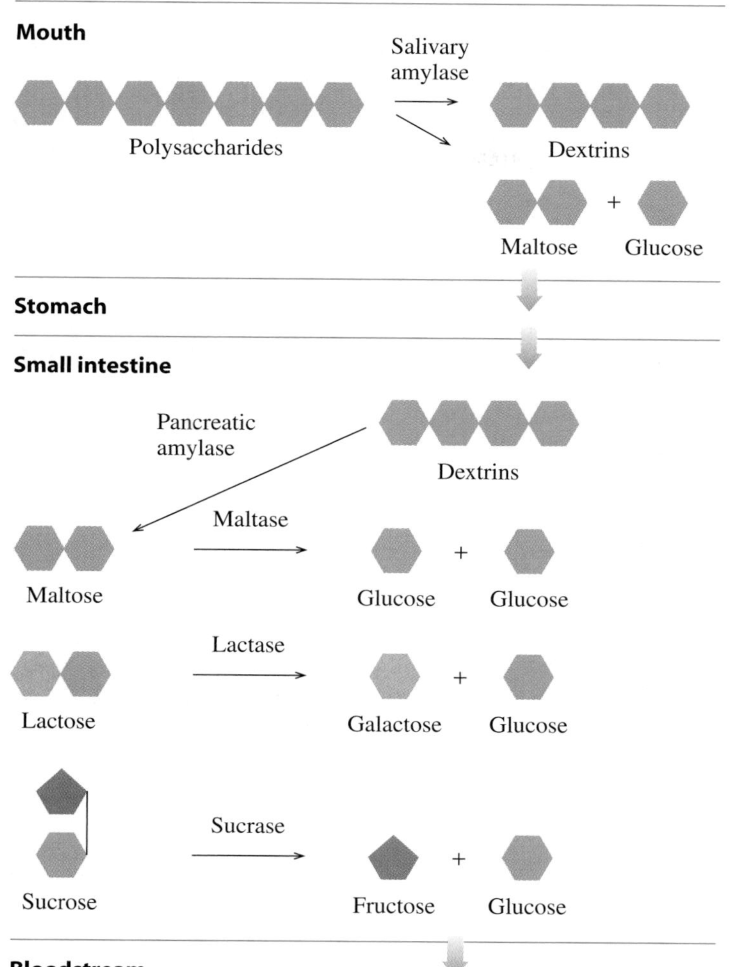


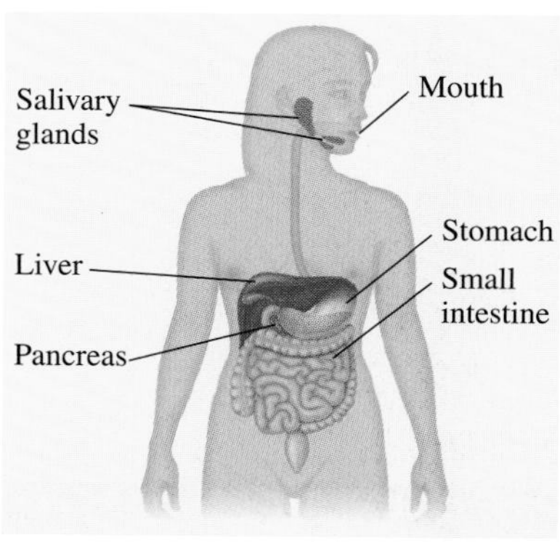

**FIGURE 22.8** In stage 1 of catabolic metabolism, the digestion of carbohydrates begins in the mouth and is completed in the small intestine.

**Q** Why is there little or no digestion of carbohydrates in the stomach?

glucose units. After swallowing, the partially digested starches enter the acidic environment of the stomach, where the low pH soon stops further carbohydrate digestion.

## Digestion of Disaccharides

In the small intestine, which has a pH of about 8, an $\alpha$-amylase produced in the pancreas hydrolyzes the remaining polysaccharides to maltose and glucose. (See Chapter 15 to review carbohydrates.) A branching enzyme hydrolyzes the glycosidic bonds in amylopectin. Then, enzymes produced in the mucosal cells that line the small intestine hydrolyze maltose as well as lactose and sucrose. The hydrolysis reactions for the three common dietary disaccharides are written as follows:

$$\text{Lactose} + H_2O \xrightarrow{\text{Lactase}} \text{galactose} + \text{glucose}$$

$$\text{Sucrose} + H_2O \xrightarrow{\text{Sucrase}} \text{fructose} + \text{glucose}$$

$$\text{Maltose} + H_2O \xrightarrow{\text{Maltase}} \text{glucose} + \text{glucose}$$

The monosaccharides are absorbed through the intestinal wall into the bloodstream, which carries them to the liver where fructose and galactose are converted to glucose.

### EXPLORE YOUR WORLD

### Carbohydrate Digestion

1. Obtain a cracker or small piece of bread and chew it for 2–3 minutes. During that time observe any change in the taste.
2. Some milk products contain Lactaid, which is the lactase that digests lactose. Look for the brands of milk and ice cream that contain Lactaid or lactase enzyme.

**QUESTIONS**

1. **a.** How does the taste of the cracker or bread change after you have chewed it for 2–3 minutes? What could be an explanation?
   **b.** What part of carbohydrate digestion occurs in the mouth?
2. **a.** Write an equation for the digestion of lactose.
   **b.** Where does lactose undergo digestion?

**SAMPLE PROBLEM 22.3**

### Digestion of Carbohydrates

Indicate the carbohydrate that undergoes digestion in each of the following sites:

**a.** mouth **b.** stomach **c.** small intestine

SOLUTION

**a.** starches amylose and amylopectin ($\alpha$-1,4-glycosidic bonds only)
**b.** essentially no digestion of carbohydrates
**c.** dextrins, maltose, sucrose, and lactose

STUDY CHECK

Describe the digestion of amylose, a polymer of glucose molecules joined by $\alpha$-glycosidic bonds.

## QUESTIONS AND PROBLEMS

### Digestion of Carbohydrates

22.17 What is the general type of reaction that occurs during the digestion of carbohydrates?

**22.18** Why is $\alpha$-amylase produced in the salivary glands and in the pancreas?

22.19 Complete the following equations by filling in the missing words:

**a.** ____________ + $H_2O$ $\longrightarrow$ galactose + glucose

**b.** Sucrose + $H_2O$ $\longrightarrow$ ____________ + ____________

**c.** Maltose + $H_2O$ $\longrightarrow$ glucose + ____________

**22.20** Give the site and the enzyme for each of the reactions in problem 22.19.

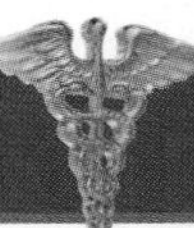

## HEALTH NOTE

### Lactose Intolerance

The disaccharide in milk is lactose, which is broken down by *lactase* in the intestinal tract to monosaccharides that are a source of energy. Infants and small children produce lactase to break down the lactose in milk. It is rare for an infant to lack the ability to produce lactase. However, the production of lactase decreases as many people age, which causes lactose intolerance. This condition affects approximately 25% of the people in the United States. A deficiency of lactase occurs in adults in many parts of the world, but in the United States it is prevalent among the African-American, Hispanic, and Asian populations.

When lactose is not broken down into glucose and galactose, it cannot be absorbed through the intestinal wall and remains in the intestinal tract. In the intestines, the lactose undergoes fermentation to products that include lactic acid and gases such as methane ($CH_4$) and $CO_2$. Symptoms of lactose intolerance, which appear approximately $\frac{1}{2}$ to 1 hour after ingesting milk or milk products, include nausea, abdominal cramps, and diarrhea. The severity of the symptoms depends on how much lactose is present in the food and how much lactase a person produces.

### Treatment of Lactose Intolerance

One way to reduce the reaction to lactose is to avoid products that contain lactose, including milk and milk products such as cheese, butter, and ice cream. However, it is important to consume foods that provide the body with calcium. Many people with lactose intolerance seem to tolerate yogurt, which is a good source of calcium. Although there is lactose in yogurt, the bacteria in yogurt may produce some lactase, which helps to digest the lactose. A person who is lactose intolerant should also know that some foods that may not seem to be dairy products contain lactose. For example, baked goods, cereals, breakfast drinks, salad dressings, and even lunchmeat can contain lactose in their ingredients. You must read food labels carefully to see if the ingredients include "milk" or "lactose."

The enzyme lactase is now available in many forms, such as tablets that are taken with meals, drops that are added to milk, or as additives in many dairy products such as milk. When lactase is added to milk that is left in the refrigerator for 24 hours, the lactose level is reduced by 70–90%. Lactase pills or chewable tablets are taken when a person begins to eat a meal that contains dairy foods. If taken too far ahead of the meal, the lactase will be degraded by stomach acid. If taken following a meal, the lactose will have already entered the lower intestine.

## 22.5 Glycolysis: Oxidation of Glucose

LEARNING GOAL

Describe the conversion of glucose to pyruvate in glycolysis.

The major source of energy for the body is the glucose produced when we digest the carbohydrates in our food or from glycogen, a polysaccharide stored in the liver and skeletal muscle. Glucose in the bloodstream enters our cells for further degradation in a pathway called *glycolysis*. Early organisms used glycolysis to produce energy from simple nutrients long before there was any oxygen in Earth's atmosphere. Glycolysis is an **anaerobic** process; no oxygen is required.

In **glycolysis**, a six-carbon glucose molecule is broken down to yield two molecules of three-carbon pyruvate. (See Figure 22.9.) All the reactions in glycolysis take place in the cytoplasm of the cell where the enzymes for glycolysis are located. In the first five reactions (1–5), the energy of two ATPs is used to add phosphoryl groups to form sugar phosphates. (See Figure 22.10.) In reactions 4 and 5, the six-carbon sugar phosphate is split to yield two molecules of three-carbon sugar phosphate. In the last five reactions (6–10), energy to synthesize four ATP is produced as the phosphoryl groups are hydrolyzed in these

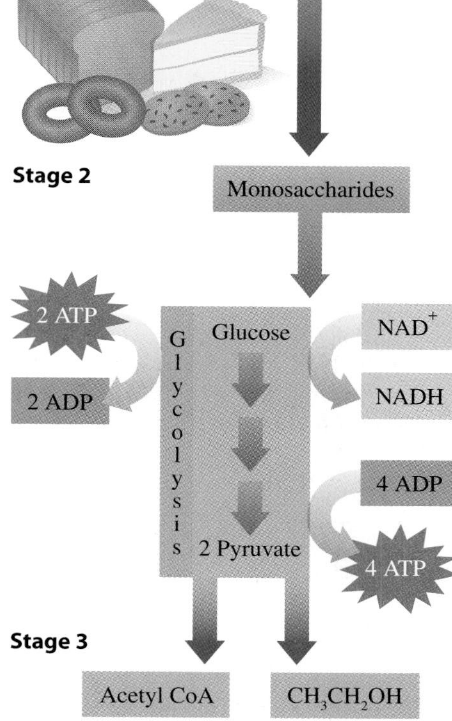


**FIGURE 22.9** Glucose obtained from the digestion (stage 1) of polysaccharides is degraded in a metabolic pathway called glycolysis to give pyruvate.

Q What is the end product of glycolysis?

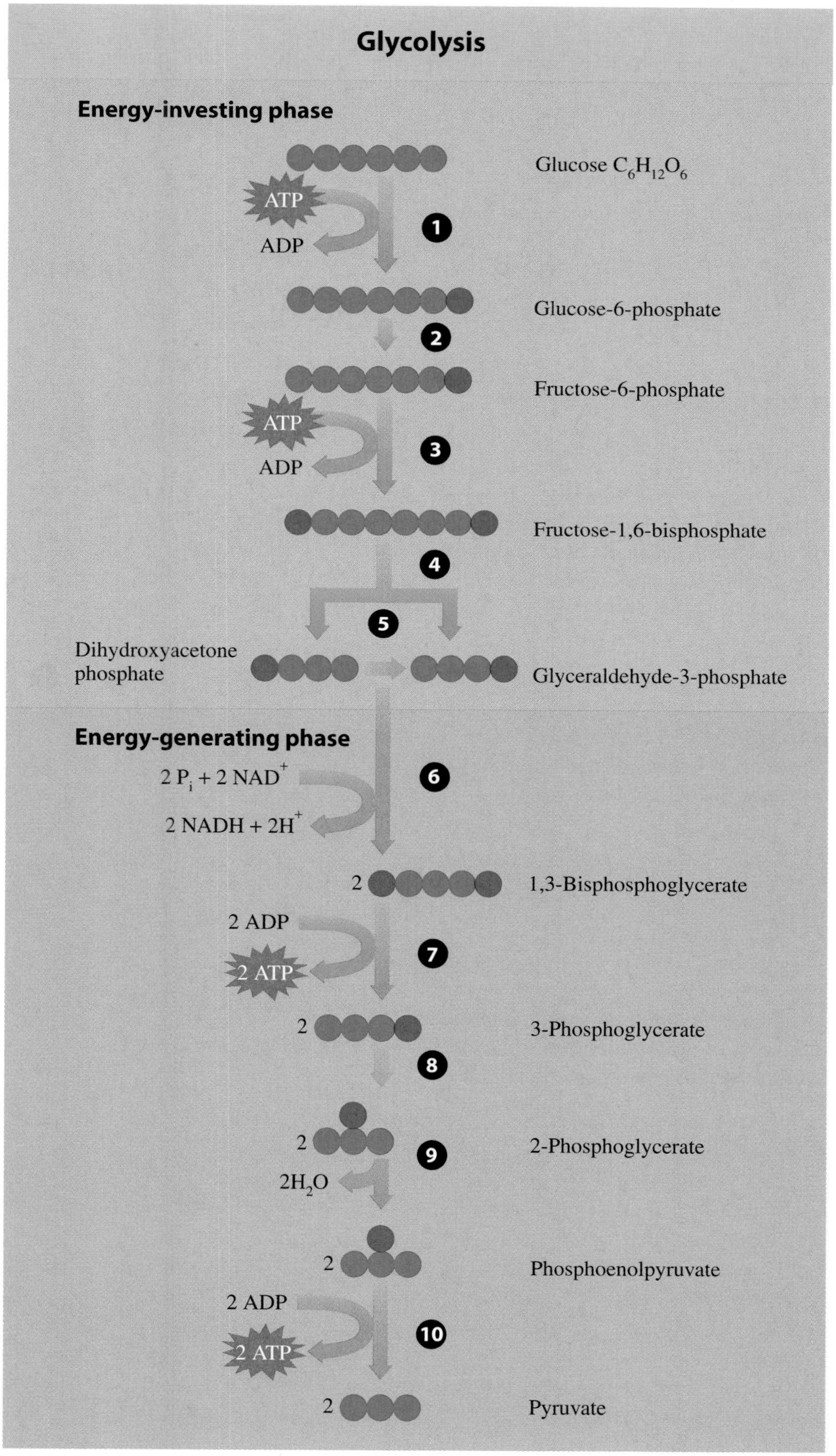

## Glycolysis

### Energy-investing phase

Glucose $C_6H_{12}O_6$

ATP → ADP (1)

Glucose-6-phosphate

(2)

Fructose-6-phosphate

ATP → ADP (3)

Fructose-1,6-bisphosphate

(4)

(5)

Dihydroxyacetone phosphate → Glyceraldehyde-3-phosphate

### Energy-generating phase

$2\ P_i + 2\ NAD^+$ → $2\ NADH + 2H^+$ (6)

2 1,3-Bisphosphoglycerate

2 ADP → 2 ATP (7)

2 3-Phosphoglycerate

(8)

2 2-Phosphoglycerate

$2H_2O$ (9)

2 Phosphoenolpyruvate

2 ADP → 2 ATP (10)

2 Pyruvate

MC™ SELF STUDY ACTIVITY Glycolysis

**FIGURE 22.10** In glycolysis, the six-carbon glucose molecule is degraded to yield two three-carbon pyruvate molecules. A net of two ATPs are produced along with two NADH.

Q Where in the glycolysis pathway is glucose cleaved to yield two three-carbon compounds?

energy-rich compounds of 1,3-bisphosphoglycerate and phosphoenolpyruvate. The final products are two pyruvate and two reduced NADH.

MC™ TUTORIAL
The Glycolysis Pathway

## Energy-Investing Reactions: 1–5

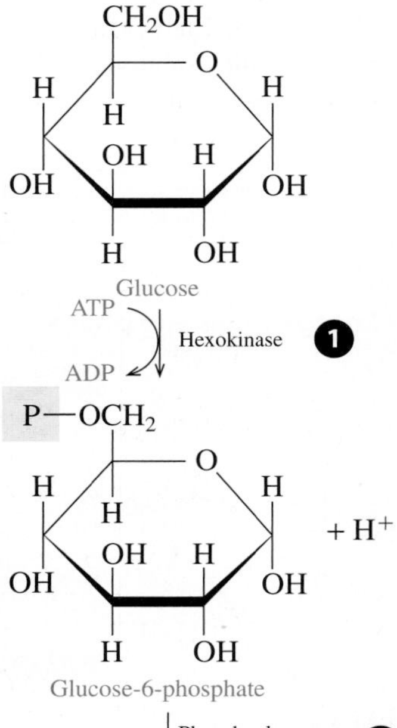


### Reaction 1 Phosphorylation: first ATP invested

Glucose is converted to glucose-6-phosphate by a reaction with ATP catalyzed by the enzyme *hexokinase*.

$$\text{P} = -\overset{\overset{\displaystyle \text{O}}{\|}}{\underset{\underset{\displaystyle \text{O}^-}{|}}{\text{P}}}-\text{O}^- = -\text{PO}_3^{2-}$$

### Reaction 2 Isomerization

The enzyme *phosphoglucose isomerase* converts glucose-6-phosphate, an aldose, to fructose-6-phosphate, a ketose.

Phosphoglucose isomerase **2**

### Reaction 3 Phosphorylation: second ATP invested

The enzyme *phosphofructokinase* catalyzes the addition of a second ATP to fructose-6-phosphate to give fructose-1,6-bisphosphate. The word *bisphosphate* is used to show that the phosphates are on different carbons in fructose and not connected to each other.

Fructose-6-phosphate

ATP → ADP, Phosphofructokinase **3**

Fructose-1,6-bisphosphate + $H^+$

### Reaction 4 Cleavage: formation of two three-carbon intermediates

Fructose-1,6-bisphosphate is "split" into two three-carbon intermediates (dihydroxyacetone phosphate and glyceraldehyde-3-phosphate) catalyzed by *aldolase*.

**4** Aldolase

Dihydroxyacetone phosphate

Glyceraldehyde-3-phosphate

### Reaction 5 Isomerization

In this reaction, *triose phosphate isomerase* converts one of the three-carbon intermediates, dihydroxyacetone phosphate, to a second molecule of glyceraldehyde-3-phosphate. Now all six carbon atoms from glucose are in two identical three-carbon compounds.

Triose phosphate isomerase **5**

Glyceraldehyde-3-phosphate

## Energy-Generating Reactions: 6–10

### Reaction 6 First energy-rich compound

Now we look at reactions 6–10 that involve the two three-carbon compounds from the initial glucose. In reaction 6, the aldehyde group of glyceraldehyde-3-phosphate is oxidized and phosphorylated by *glyceraldehyde-3-phosphate dehydrogenase*. The product is a high-energy three-carbon compound called *1,3-bisphosphoglycerate*. The coenzyme $NAD^+$ is reduced to NADH and $H^+$.

### Reaction 7 Formation of first ATP

Now, a *phosphoglycerate kinase* transfers a phosphoryl group from 1,3-bisphosphoglycerate to ADP to form ATP. This process is called a *substrate-level phosphorylation*. At this point in glycolysis, the reactions of two 1,3-bisphosphoglycerate molecules pays back the two ATP invested in reactions 1 and 3.

### Reaction 8 Formation of 2-phosphoglycerate

A *phosphoglycerate mutase* transfers the phosphoryl group from carbon 3 of 3-phosphoglycerate to carbon 2 to yield 2-phosphoglycerate.

### Reaction 9 Second energy-rich compound

An *enolase* catalyzes the removal of water from phosphoglycerate to yield a high-energy compound called *phosphoenolpyruvate*.

### Reaction 10 Formation of second ATP

In a second direct substrate phosphorylation, catalyzed by *pyruvate kinase*, a phosphoryl group is transferred from phosphoenolpyruvate to ADP to yield pyruvate and ATP. From the reaction of two three-carbon compounds, two more ATP are produced.

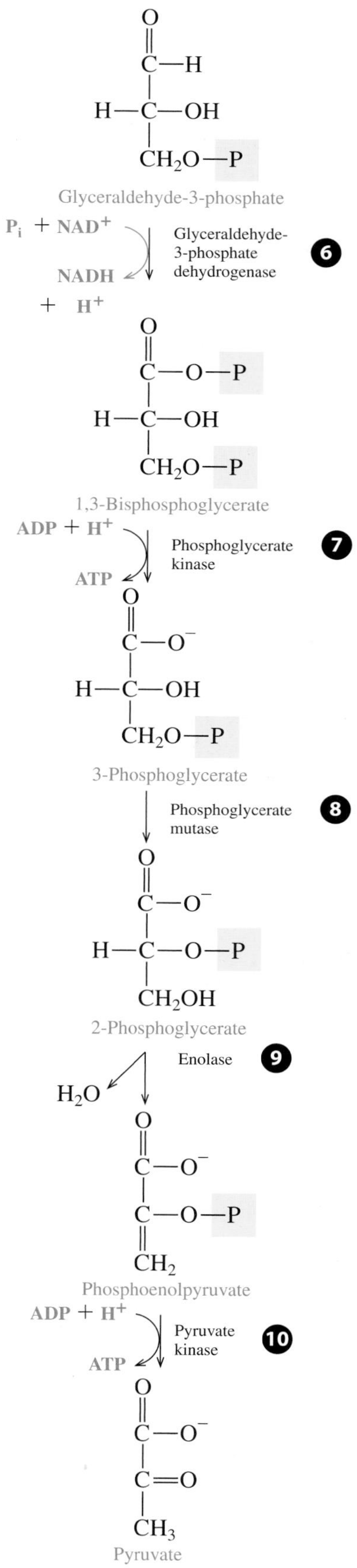

Glyceraldehyde-3-phosphate

$P_i + NAD^+$ → NADH + $H^+$ — Glyceraldehyde-3-phosphate dehydrogenase (6)

1,3-Bisphosphoglycerate

$ADP + H^+$ → ATP — Phosphoglycerate kinase (7)

3-Phosphoglycerate

Phosphoglycerate mutase (8)

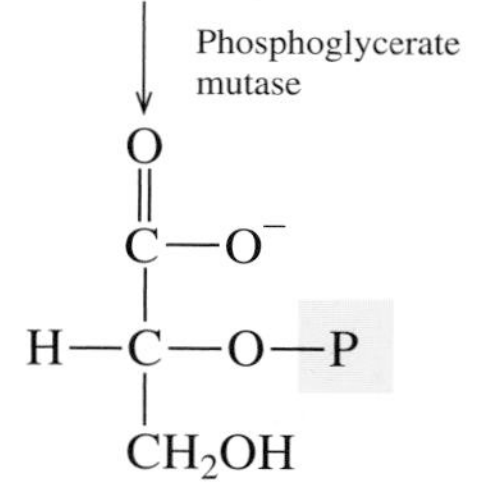


2-Phosphoglycerate

Enolase (9) → $H_2O$

Phosphoenolpyruvate

$ADP + H^+$ → ATP — Pyruvate kinase (10)

Pyruvate

## Summary of Glycolysis

In the glycolysis pathway, a glucose molecule is converted to two molecules of pyruvate. Initially, two ATP are required to form a sugar diphosphate. Later, from reactions 7 and 10, a total of four ATP are generated, which gives a net gain of two ATP. Overall, glycolysis yields two ATP and two NADH for each glucose that is converted to pyruvate:

$$\underset{\text{Glucose}}{C_6H_{12}O_6} + 2NAD^+ \xrightarrow{2ADP + 2P_i \;\rightarrow\; 2ATP} \underset{\text{Pyruvate}}{2CH_3{-}\overset{\displaystyle O}{\overset{\|}{C}}{-}COO^-} + 2NADH + 4H^+ + 2H_2O$$

**CONCEPT CHECK 22.4**

### Glycolysis

What reaction in glycolysis is catalyzed by each of the following?

**a.** phosphoglucose isomerase
**b.** aldolase
**c.** phosphoglycerate mutase

ANSWER

**a.** Phosphoglucose isomerase catalyzes the isomerization of glucose-6-phosphate to fructose-6-phosphate (reaction 2).
**b.** Aldolase catalyzes the splitting of the six-carbon fructose-1,6-bisphosphate into two three-carbon compounds: glyceraldehyde-3-phosphate and dihydroxyacetone phosphate (reaction 4).
**c.** Phosphoglycerate mutase catalyzes the transfer of a phosphoryl group from carbon 3 of 3-phosphoglycerate to carbon 2 to form 2-phosphoglycerate (reaction 8).

**SAMPLE PROBLEM 22.4**

### Glycolysis

What are the reactions in glycolysis that generate ATP?

SOLUTION

ATP is produced when phosphoryl groups are transferred directly to ADP from 1,3-bisphosphoglycerate (reaction 7) and from phosphoenolpyruvate (reaction 10).

STUDY CHECK

If four ATP molecules are produced in glycolysis, why is there a net yield of only two ATP?

It appears right now that glycolysis does a lot of work to produce only two ATP, two NADH, and two pyruvate. However, under aerobic conditions, stage 3 operates to reoxidize NADH to produce more ATP, and pyruvate enters the citric acid cycle where it generates considerably more energy. We will look at the oxidative pathways of stage 3 in Chapter 23.

## Other Hexoses Enter Glycolysis

Other monosaccharides enter glycolysis after they are converted to intermediates of the pathway. Digestion of carbohydrates produces galactose from lactose in milk products and fructose from fruits and sucrose. Galactose reacts with ATP to yield galactose-1-phosphate, which is converted to glucose-6-phosphate, an intermediate of glycolysis. In the liver, fructose is converted to fructose-1-phosphate, which is cleaved in a reaction similar to reaction 4 to give dihydroxyacetone phosphate and glyceraldehyde. Dihydroxyacetone phosphate isomerizes to glyceraldehyde-3-phosphate, and glyceraldehyde is phosphorylated to glyceraldehyde-3-phosphate, a reactant in reaction 6. In the muscles and kidneys, fructose is phosphorylated to fructose-6-phosphate, which enters glycolysis in reaction 3.

Galactose —(ATP → ADP + $P_i$)→ galactose-1-phosphate ⟶ glucose-6-phosphate —2→ Glycolysis

Glyceraldehyde-3-phosphate —6→ Glycolysis

Fructose —(ATP → ADP + $P_i$)→ fructose-1-phosphate ⟶ glyceraldehyde + dihydroxyacetone phosphate

glyceraldehyde —(ATP → ADP + $P_i$)→ Glyceraldehyde-3-phosphate

dihydroxyacetone phosphate —5→ Glycolysis

## Regulation of Glycolysis

Metabolic pathways such as glycolysis do not run at the same rates all the time. The amount of glucose that is broken down is controlled by the requirements in the cells for pyruvate, ATP, and other intermediates of glycolysis. Within the glycolysis sequence, three enzymes respond to the levels of ATP and other products.

### Reaction 1 Hexokinase

The amount of glucose entering the glycolysis pathway decreases when high levels of glucose-6-phosphate are present in the cell. This phosphorylation product inhibits hexokinase, which prevents glucose from reacting with ATP. This is a feedback control, which is a type of enzyme regulation we discussed in Chapter 20.

### Reaction 3 Phosphofructokinase

The reaction catalyzed by phosphofructokinase is a very important control point for glycolysis. Once fructose-1,6-bisphosphate is formed, it must continue through the remaining reactions to pyruvate. As an allosteric enzyme, phosphofructokinase is inhibited by high levels of ATP and activated by high levels of ADP and AMP. High levels of ADP and AMP indicate that the cell has used up much of its ATP. As a regulator, phosphofructokinase increases the rate of pyruvate production for ATP synthesis when the cell needs to replenish ATP and slows or stops the reaction when ATP is plentiful.

### Reaction 10 Pyruvate Kinase

In the last reaction of glycolysis, high levels of ATP as well as acetyl CoA inhibit pyruvate kinase, which is another allosteric enzyme.

## Summary of Regulation

Reactions 1, 3, and 10 are examples of how metabolic pathways shut off enzymes to stop the production of molecules that are not needed. Since pyruvate can be used to synthesize ATP, several enzymes in glycolysis respond to ATP levels in the cell. When ATP levels are high, enzymes in glycolysis slow or stop the synthesis of pyruvate. With phosphofructokinase and pyruvate kinase inhibited by ATP, glucose-6-phosphate accumulates and inhibits the first reaction, and glucose does not enter the glycolysis pathway. The glycolysis pathway is shut down until ATP is once again needed in the cell. When ATP levels are low or AMP/ADP levels are high, these enzymes are activated and pyruvate production starts again.

CONCEPT CHECK 22.5

**Regulation of Glycolysis**

How is glycolysis regulated by each of the following enzymes?

**a.** hexokinase **b.** phosphofructokinase **c.** pyruvate kinase

ANSWER

**a.** High levels of glucose-6-phosphate inhibit hexokinase, which stops the addition of a phosphoryl group to glucose in reaction 1.

**b.** Phosphofructokinase, which catalyzes the formation of fructose-1,6-bisphosphate, is inhibited by high levels of ATP, and activated by high levels of ADP and AMP.

**c.** High levels of ATP or acetyl CoA inhibit pyruvate kinase, which stops the formation of pyruvate in reaction 10.

## QUESTIONS AND PROBLEMS

### Glycolysis: Oxidation of Glucose

22.21 What is the starting compound of glycolysis?

**22.22** What is the three-carbon product of glycolysis?

22.23 How is ATP used in the initial steps of glycolysis?

**22.24** How many ATP molecules are used in the initial steps of glycolysis?

22.25 What three-carbon intermediates are obtained when fructose-1,6-bisphosphate splits?

**22.26** Why does one of the three-carbon intermediates undergo isomerization?

22.27 How does substrate phosphorylation account for the production of ATP in glycolysis?

**22.28** Why are there two ATP molecules formed for one molecule of glucose?

22.29 Indicate the enzyme(s) that catalyze each of the following reactions in glycolysis:
**a.** phosphorylation **b.** direct transfer of a phosphoryl group

**22.30** Indicate the enzyme(s) that catalyze each of the following reactions in glycolysis:
**a.** isomerization
**b.** formation of a three-carbon ketone and a three-carbon aldehyde

22.31 How many ATP or NADH are produced (or required) in each of the following steps in glycolysis?
**a.** glucose to glucose-6-phosphate
**b.** glyceraldehyde-3-phosphate to 1,3-bisphosphoglycerate
**c.** glucose to pyruvate

**22.32** How many ATP or NADH are produced (or required) in each of the following steps in glycolysis?
**a.** 1,3-bisphosphoglycerate to 3-phosphoglycerate
**b.** fructose-6-phosphate to fructose-1,6-bisphosphate
**c.** phosphoenolpyruvate to pyruvate

22.33 Which step(s) in glycolysis involve the following?
**a.** The first ATP molecule is hydrolyzed.
**b.** Direct substrate phosphorylation occurs.
**c.** Six-carbon sugar splits into two three-carbon molecules.

**22.34** Which step(s) in glycolysis involve the following?
**a.** Isomerization takes place.
**b.** $NAD^+$ is reduced.
**c.** A second ATP molecule is synthesized.

22.35 How do galactose and fructose, obtained from the digestion of carbohydrates, enter glycolysis?

**22.36** What are three enzymes that regulate glycolysis?

22.37 Indicate whether each of the following would activate or inhibit phosphofructokinase:
**a.** low levels of ATP **b.** high levels of ATP

**22.38** Indicate whether each of the following would activate or inhibit pyruvate kinase:
**a.** low levels of ATP **b.** high levels of ATP

# 22.6 Pathways for Pyruvate

LEARNING GOAL

Give the conditions for the conversion of pyruvate to lactate, ethanol, and acetyl coenzyme A.

The pyruvate produced from glucose can now enter pathways that continue to extract energy. The available pathway depends on whether there is sufficient oxygen in the cell. During **aerobic** conditions, oxygen is available to convert pyruvate to acetyl coenzyme A (acetyl CoA). When oxygen levels are low, pyruvate is reduced to lactate. In yeast cells, which are anaerobic, pyruvate is converted to ethanol.

## Aerobic Conditions

MC™ TUTORIAL
Pathways for Pyruvate

In glycolysis, two ATP molecules were generated when one glucose molecule was converted to two pyruvate. However, much more energy is still available. The greatest amount of energy is obtained from glucose when oxygen levels are high in the cells. Under aerobic conditions, pyruvate moves from the cytoplasm (where glycolysis took place) into the matrix of the mitochondria to be oxidized further. In a complex reaction, pyruvate is oxidized, and a carbon atom is removed from pyruvate as $CO_2$. The coenzyme $NAD^+$ is required for the

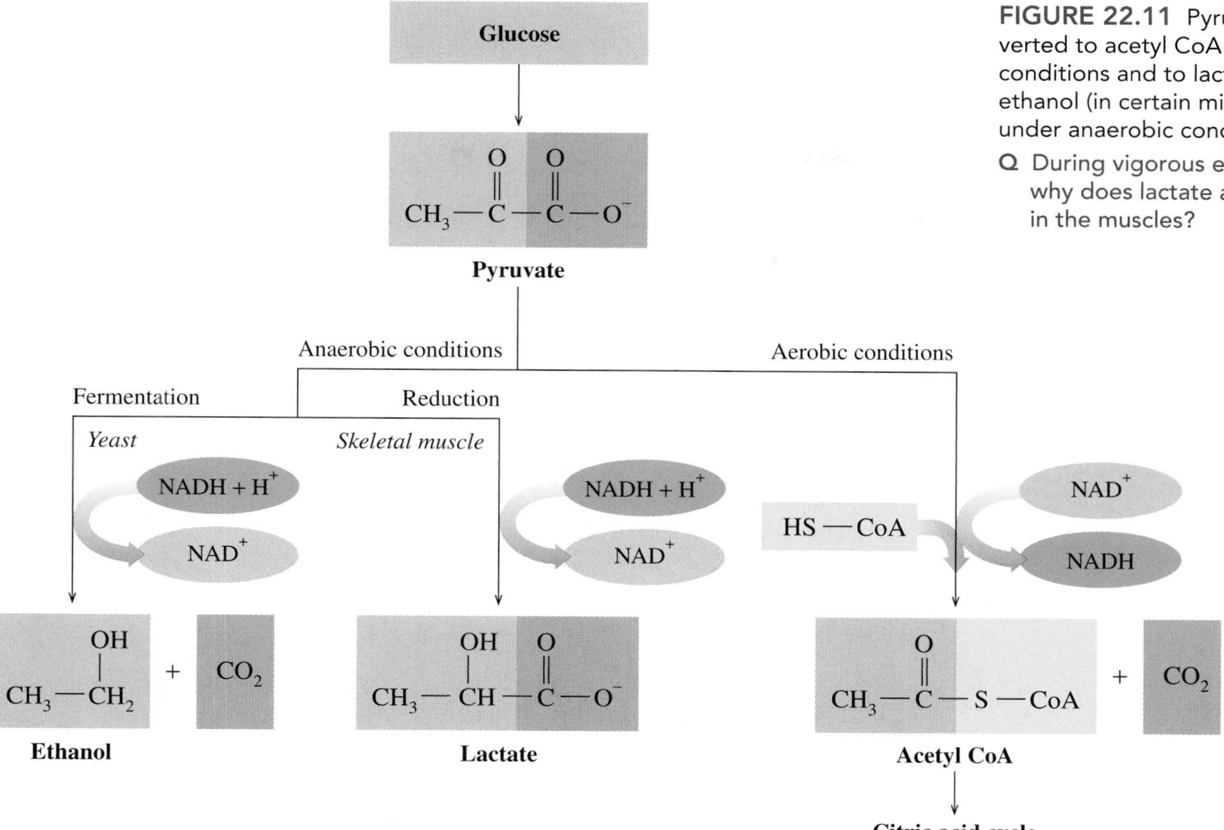


**FIGURE 22.11** Pyruvate is converted to acetyl CoA under aerobic conditions and to lactate or ethanol (in certain microorganisms) under anaerobic conditions.

**Q** During vigorous exercise, why does lactate accumulate in the muscles?

oxidation. The resulting two-carbon acetyl compound is attached to CoA, producing acetyl CoA, an important intermediate in many metabolic pathways. (See Figure 22.11.)

$$\underset{\text{Pyruvate}}{CH_3-\overset{O}{\overset{\|}{C}}-\overset{O}{\overset{\|}{C}}-O^-} + HS-CoA + NAD^+ \xrightarrow{\text{Pyruvate dehydrogenase}} \underset{\text{Acetyl CoA}}{CH_3-\overset{O}{\overset{\|}{C}}-S-CoA} + CO_2 + NADH$$

## Anaerobic Conditions

When we engage in strenuous exercise, the oxygen stored in our muscle cells is quickly depleted. Under anaerobic conditions, pyruvate remains in the cytoplasm where it is reduced to lactate. $NAD^+$ is produced and used to oxidize more glyceraldehyde-3-phosphate in the glycolysis pathway, which produces a small but needed amount of ATP:

$$\underset{\text{Pyruvate (oxidized)}}{CH_3-\overset{O}{\overset{\|}{C}}-\overset{O}{\overset{\|}{C}}-O^-} \underset{\text{Lactate dehydrogenase}}{\overset{NADH + H^+ \quad NAD^+}{\rightleftharpoons}} \underset{\text{Lactate (reduced)}}{CH_3-\overset{OH}{\overset{|}{\underset{H}{\underset{|}{C}}}}-\overset{O}{\overset{\|}{C}}-O^-}$$

The accumulation of lactate causes the muscles to tire rapidly and become sore. After exercise, a person continues to breathe rapidly to repay the oxygen debt incurred during exercise. Most of the lactate is transported to the liver, where it is converted back into pyruvate. Under anaerobic conditions, the only ATP production in glycolysis occurs during the steps that phosphorylate ADP directly, giving a net gain of only two ATP molecules:

$$\underset{\text{Glucose}}{C_6H_{12}O_6} + 2ADP + 2P_i \longrightarrow \underset{\text{Lactate}}{2CH_3-\overset{OH}{\overset{|}{CH}}-COO^-} + 2ATP + 2H_2O$$

Bacteria also convert pyruvate to lactate under anaerobic conditions. In the preparation of kimchee and sauerkraut, cabbage is covered with salt brine. The glucose obtained from the starches in the cabbage is converted to lactate. This acidic environment acts as a preservative that prevents the growth of other bacteria. The pickling of olives and cucumbers gives similar products. When cultures of bacteria that produce lactate are added to milk, the acid denatures the milk proteins to give sour cream and yogurt.

CONCEPT CHECK 22.6

■ **Pathways for Pyruvate**

When is pyruvate converted to each of the following?

**a.** acetyl CoA **b.** lactate

ANSWER

**a.** Pyruvate is converted to acetyl CoA and NADH under aerobic conditions. The NADH must be oxidized back to $NAD^+$ to allow glycolysis to continue.

**b.** Pyruvate is converted to lactate and $NAD^+$ under anaerobic conditions, which provides $NAD^+$ for glycolysis.

## Fermentation

SELF STUDY ACTIVITY
Fermentation

Some microorganisms, particularly yeast, convert sugars to ethanol under anaerobic conditions by a process called **fermentation**. After pyruvate is formed in glycolysis, a carbon atom is removed in the form of $CO_2$ (**decarboxylation**). The $NAD^+$ for continued glycolysis is regenerated when the acetaldehyde is reduced to ethanol:

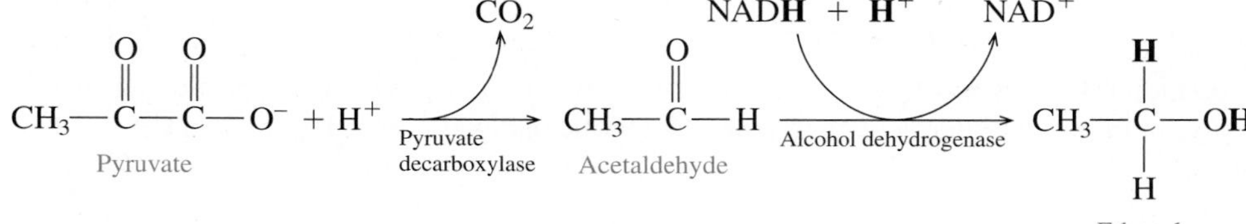

The process of fermentation by yeast is one of the oldest known chemical reactions. Enzymes in the yeast convert the sugars in a variety of carbohydrate sources to glucose and then to ethanol. The evolution of $CO_2$ gas produces bubbles in beer, sparkling wines, and champagne. The type of carbohydrate used determines the taste associated with a particular alcoholic beverage. Beer is made from the fermentation of barley malt, wine and champagne from the sugars in grapes, vodka from potatoes or grain, sake from rice, and whiskeys from corn or rye. Fermentation produces solutions up to about 15% alcohol by volume. At this concentration, the alcohol kills the yeast, and fermentation stops.

SAMPLE PROBLEM 22.5

■ **Fermentation of Pyruvate**

In the production of wine, the fermentation process converts pyruvate to acetaldehyde, which is converted to ethanol using NADH and $H^+$. Using pyruvate ($C_3H_3O_3^-$) + $H^+$ as the starting reactants, write the balanced chemical equations. How does fermentation supply $NAD^+$?

SOLUTION

Fermentation takes places under anaerobic conditions. Pyruvate ($C_3H_3O_3^-$) undergoes decarboxylation to acetaldehyde ($C_2H_4O$), which is reduced by NADH and $H^+$ to ethanol ($C_2H_6O$) and $NAD^+$.

$$C_3H_3O_3^- + H^+ \longrightarrow C_2H_4O + CO_2$$

$$C_2H_4O + NADH + H^+ \longrightarrow C_2H_6O + NAD^+$$

In fermentation, $NAD^+$ is supplied when NADH and $H^+$ reduce the C=O in acetaldehyde.

STUDY CHECK

After strenuous exercise, some lactate is oxidized back to pyruvate by lactate dehydrogenase using $NAD^+$. Write an equation to show this reaction.

## QUESTIONS AND PROBLEMS

### Pathways for Pyruvate

22.39 What condition is needed in the cell to convert pyruvate to acetyl CoA?

**22.40** What coenzymes are needed for the oxidation of pyruvate to acetyl CoA?

22.41 Write the overall equation for the conversion of pyruvate to acetyl CoA.

**22.42** What are the possible products of pyruvate under anaerobic conditions?

22.43 How does the formation of lactate permit glycolysis to continue under anaerobic conditions?

**22.44** After running a marathon, a runner has muscle pain and cramping. What might have occurred in the muscle cells to cause this?

22.45 In fermentation, a carbon atom is removed from pyruvate. What is the compound formed by that carbon atom?

**22.46** Some students decided to make some wine by placing yeast and grape juice in a container with a tight lid. A few weeks later, the container exploded. What reaction could account for the explosion?

# 22.7 Glycogen Metabolism

LEARNING GOAL

Describe the breakdown and synthesis of glycogen.

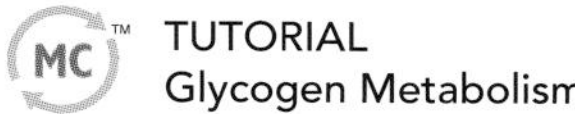

TUTORIAL
Glycogen Metabolism

We have just eaten a large meal that has supplied us with all the glucose we need to produce pyruvate and ATP by glycolysis. Then we use excess glucose to replenish our energy reserves by synthesizing glycogen that is stored in limited amounts in our skeletal muscle and liver. When glycogen stores are full, any remaining glucose is converted to triacylglycerols and stored as body fat, as we will see in Chapter 24. When our diet does not supply sufficient glucose or we have utilized our blood glucose, we degrade the stored glycogen and release glucose.

## Glycogenesis

Glycogen is a polymer of glucose with $\alpha$-1,4 glycosidic bonds and multiple branches attached by $\alpha$-1,6 glycosidic bonds, as seen in Chapter 15. **Glycogenesis** is the synthesis of glycogen from glucose molecules, which occurs when the digestion of polysaccharides produces high levels of glucose. The synthesis of glycogen starts with the glucose-6-phosphate obtained from the first reaction in glycolysis. (See Figure 22.12.) It is converted to an isomer glucose-1-phosphate, which is activated using high-energy UTP (uridine triphosphate) to yield UDP (uridine diphosphate)-glucose. The reaction is driven by the energy released from the hydrolysis of pyrophosphate ($PP_i$).

$$\text{Glucose-6-phosphate} \xrightleftharpoons{\text{Phosphoglucomutase}} \text{glucose-1-phosphate}$$

$$\text{Glucose-1-phosphate} + \text{UTP} \xrightarrow{\text{UDP-glucose pyrophosphorylase}} \text{UDP-glucose} + PP_i$$

$$PP_i + H_2O \xrightarrow{\text{Inorganic pyrophosphatase}} 2P_i$$

UDP-glucose (uridine diphosphate glucose)

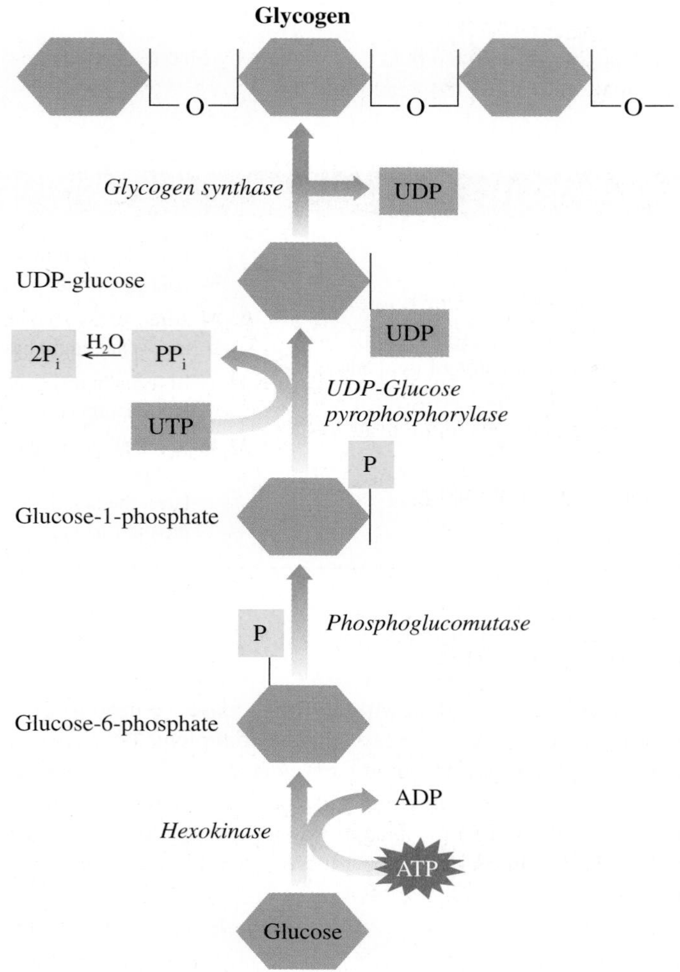


**FIGURE 22.12** In glycogenesis, glucose is used to synthesize glycogen.

**Q** What is the function of UTP in glycogen synthesis?

The UDP-glucose attaches to the end of a glycogen chain releasing UDP, which reacts with ATP to regenerate UTP:

$$\text{UDP-glucose} + \text{glycogen} \xrightarrow{\text{Glycogen synthase}} \text{glucose—glycogen} + \text{UDP}$$

$$\text{UDP} + \text{ATP} \longrightarrow \text{UTP} + \text{ADP}$$

## Glycogenolysis

Glucose is the primary energy source for muscle contractions, red blood cells, and the brain. When blood glucose is depleted, glycogen breaks down to glucose in a process called **glycogenolysis**. Glucose molecules are removed one by one from the end of the glycogen chain and phosphorylated to yield glucose-1-phosphate:

$$\text{Glucose—glycogen} + P_i \xrightarrow{\text{Glycogen phosphorylase}} \text{glucose-1-phosphate} + \text{glycogen}$$

Glucose-1-phosphate is converted to glucose-6-phosphate, which enters the glycolysis pathway to replenish ATP:

$$\text{Glucose-1-phosphate} \xrightleftharpoons{\text{Phosphoglucomutase}} \text{glucose-6-phosphate}$$

Free glucose is needed for energy by the brain and muscle. While glucose can diffuse across cell membranes, glucose phosphates cannot. Only cells in the liver and kidneys have a glucose-6-phosphatase that hydrolyzes the glucose-6-phosphate to yield free glucose.

$$\text{Glucose-6-phosphate} \xrightarrow{\text{Glucose-6-phosphatase}} \text{glucose} + P_i$$

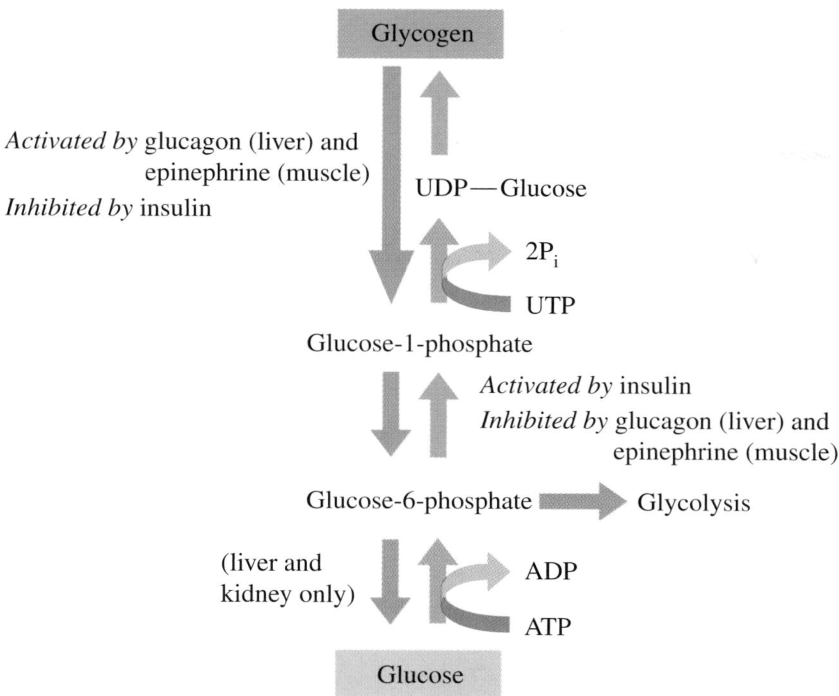


## Regulation of Glycogen Metabolism

The brain, skeletal muscles, and red blood cells require large amounts of glucose every day to function properly. To protect the brain, hormones with opposing actions control blood glucose levels. When glucose is low, *glucagon*, a hormone produced in the pancreas, is secreted into the bloodstream. In the liver, glucagon accelerates the rate of glycogenolysis, which raises blood glucose levels. At the same time, glucagon inhibits the synthesis of glycogen.

Glycogen in skeletal muscle is broken down quickly when the body requires a "burst of energy," often referred to as "fight or flight." *Epinephrine* released from the adrenal glands converts *glycogen phosphorylase* from an inactive to an active form. The secretion of only a few molecules of epinephrine can break down a huge number of glycogen molecules.

Soon after we have eaten and digested a meal, our blood glucose level rises, which stimulates the pancreas to secrete the hormone insulin into our bloodstream. Insulin promotes the use of glucose in the cells by accelerating glycogen synthesis as well as degradation reactions such as glycolysis. At the same time, insulin inhibits the synthesis of glucose, which we will discuss in the next section.

CONCEPT CHECK 22.7

### Glycogen Metabolism

What are the conditions and hormones that promote each of the following?

**a.** glycogenesis **b.** glycogenolysis

ANSWER

**a.** Glycogenesis occurs when glucose levels are high, particularly after digestion of carbohydrates. High glucose levels stimulate the pancreas to secrete insulin, which accelerates the synthesis of glycogen.

**b.** Glycogenolysis occurs when blood glucose levels are depleted and glucose is needed for energy by muscle and the brain. The secretion of the hormone glucagon by the pancreas accelerates the breakdown of glycogen in the liver to glucose. In "fight or flight" situations, epinephrine from the adrenal glands accelerates glycogenolysis in muscle to raise the blood glucose level quickly.

SAMPLE PROBLEM 22.6

**Glycogen Metabolism**

Identify each of the following as part of the reaction pathways of (1) glycolysis, (2) glycogenolysis, or (3) glycogenesis:

**a.** Glucose-1-phosphate is converted to glucose-6-phosphate.
**b.** Glucose-1-phosphate forms UDP-glucose.
**c.** An isomerase converts glucose-6-phosphate to fructose-6-phosphate.

SOLUTION

**a.** (2) glycogenolysis **b.** (3) glycogenesis **c.** (1) glycolysis

STUDY CHECK

Why do cells in the liver and kidneys provide glucose to raise blood glucose levels, but cells in skeletal muscle do not?

## QUESTIONS AND PROBLEMS

### Glycogen Metabolism

22.47 What is meant by the term *glycogenesis*?

**22.48** What is meant by the term *glycogenolysis*?

22.49 How do muscle cells use glycogen to provide energy?

**22.50** How does the liver raise blood glucose levels?

22.51 What is the function of *glycogen phosphorylase*?

**22.52** Why is the enzyme *phosphoglucomutase* used in both glycogenolysis and glycogenesis?

## 22.8 Gluconeogenesis: Glucose Synthesis

LEARNING GOAL

Describe how glucose is synthesized from noncarbohydrate molecules.

Glycogen stored in our liver and muscles can supply us with about one day's requirement of glucose. However, glycogen stores are quickly depleted if we fast for more than one day or participate in heavy exercise. Then glucose is synthesized from carbon atoms obtained from noncarbohydrate compounds in a process called **gluconeogenesis**. Most glucose is synthesized in the cytosol of liver cells. (See Figure 22.13.)

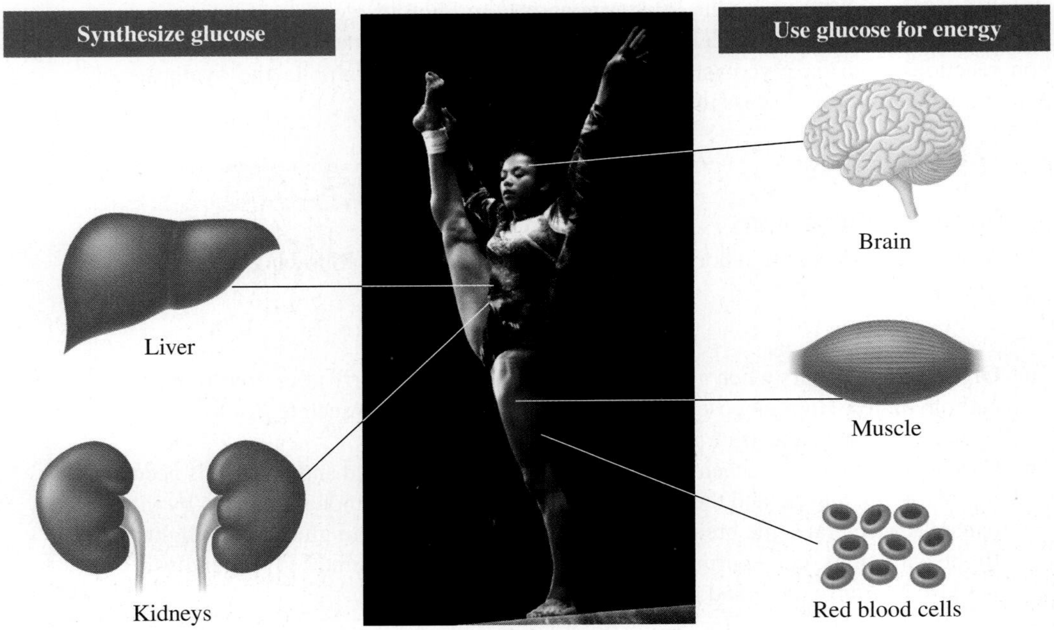

**FIGURE 22.13** Glucose is synthesized in the tissues of the liver and kidneys. Tissues that use glucose as their main energy source are the brain, skeletal muscles, and red blood cells.

Q Why does the body need a pathway for the synthesis of glucose from noncarbohydrate sources?

Carbon atoms for glucose can be obtained from lactate and food sources, such as amino acids, and glycerol from fats. Each is converted to pyruvate or an intermediate for the synthesis of glucose. Most of the reactions in gluconeogenesis are the reverse of glycolysis and are catalyzed by the same enzymes. However, three of the glycolysis reactions are not reversible: the ones catalyzed by hexokinase, phosphofructokinase, and pyruvate kinase—glycolysis reactions 1, 3, and 10, respectively. Different enzymes are used to replace them, but all the other reactions simply reverse glycolysis and use the same enzymes. We will now look at these three reactions in gluconeogenesis that differ from the reactions of glycolysis.

## Converting Pyruvate to Phosphoenolpyruvate

To start the synthesis of glucose, two steps are needed. The first step converts pyruvate to oxaloacetate, and the second step converts oxaloacetate to phosphoenolpyruvate. The hydrolysis of ATP and GTP are used to drive the reactions. (See Figure 22.14.)

$$\underset{\text{Pyruvate}}{CH_3{-}\overset{\overset{\displaystyle O}{\|}}{C}{-}COO^-} + CO_2 + ATP + H_2O \xrightarrow{\text{Pyruvate carboxylase}} \underset{\text{Oxaloacetate}}{{}^-OOC{-}CH_2{-}\overset{\overset{\displaystyle O}{\|}}{C}{-}COO^-} + ADP + P_i$$

$$\underset{\text{Oxaloacetate}}{{}^-OOC{-}CH_2{-}\overset{\overset{\displaystyle O}{\|}}{C}{-}COO^-} + GTP \xrightarrow{\text{Phosphoenolpyruvate carboxykinase}} \underset{\text{Phosphoenolpyruvate}}{CH_2{=}\overset{\overset{\displaystyle O{-}P}{|}}{C}{-}COO^-} + CO_2 + GDP$$

Molecules of phosphoenolpyruvate now enter the next five reverse reactions in glycolysis using the same enzymes to form fructose-1,6-bisphosphate.

## Converting Fructose-1,6-bisphosphate to Fructose-6-phosphate

The second irreversible reaction in glycolysis is bypassed using *fructose-1,6-bisphosphatase* to cleave a phosphoryl group from fructose-1,6-bisphosphate by hydrolysis with water and releasing the energy that drives the reaction:

$$\text{Fructose-1,6-bisphosphate} + H_2O \xrightarrow{\text{Fructose-1,6-bisphosphatase}} \text{fructose-6-phosphate} + P_i$$

Then fructose-6-phosphate undergoes a reversible reaction to yield glucose-6-phosphate.

## Converting Glucose-6-phosphate to Glucose

In the final reaction, glucose-6-phosphate is converted to glucose by a different enzyme than used in glycolysis. *Glucose-6-phosphatase* catalyzes the hydrolysis of glucose-6-phosphate with water:

$$\text{Glucose-6-phosphate} + H_2O \xrightarrow{\text{Glucose-6-phosphatase}} \text{glucose} + P_i$$

## Energy Cost of Gluconeogenesis

The pathway of gluconeogenesis consists of seven reversible reactions of glycolysis and four new reactions that replace the three irreversible reactions. Overall, this synthesis of glucose requires four ATPs, two GTPs, and two NADHs. If all the reactions were simply the reverse of glycolysis, the synthesis of glucose would not be energetically favorable.

**FIGURE 22.14** In gluconeogenesis, three irreversible reactions of glycolysis are bypassed using four different enzymes.

**Q** Why are 11 enzymes required for gluconeogenesis and only 10 for glycolysis?

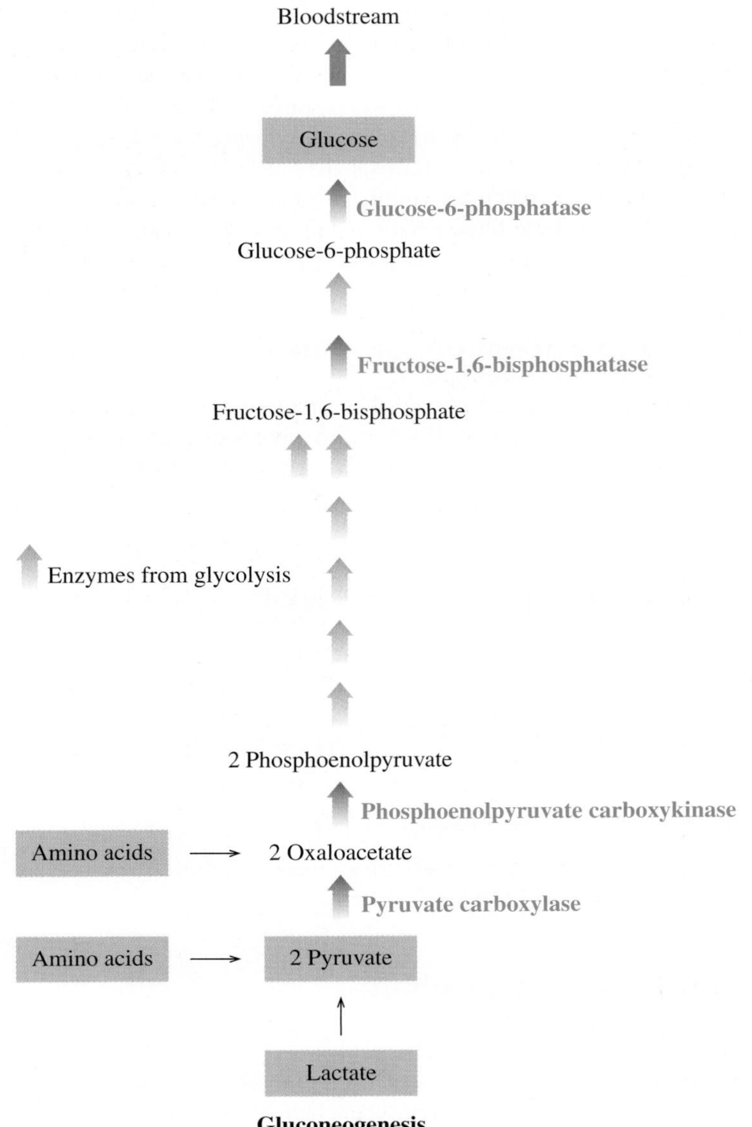


By using the energy resources and bypassing the three irreversible and energy-requiring reactions, gluconeogenesis becomes favorable in terms of energy. The overall equation for gluconeogenesis is written as follows:

$$2\,\text{Pyruvate} + 4\,\text{ATP} + 2\,\text{GTP} + 2\,\text{NADH} + 2\text{H}^+ + 6\text{H}_2\text{O} \longrightarrow$$
$$\text{glucose} + 4\,\text{ADP} + 2\,\text{GDP} + 6\text{P}_\text{i} + 2\,\text{NAD}^+$$

## Lactate and the Cori Cycle

When a person exercises vigorously, anaerobic conditions cause the reduction of pyruvate to lactate, which accumulates in the muscle. This reaction is necessary to oxidize NADH to $NAD^+$, which allows glycolysis to continue to produce a small amount of ATP. Lactate is an important source of carbon for gluconeogenesis. Lactate is transported to the liver where it is oxidized to pyruvate, which is used to synthesize glucose. Glucose enters the bloodstream and returns to the muscle to rebuild glycogen stores. This flow of lactate and glucose between the muscle and liver, known as the **Cori cycle**, is very active when a person has just completed a period of vigorous exercise. (See Figure 22.15.)

The relationship between the metabolic reactions of glucose for stage 1 and stage 2 are summarized in Figure 22.16.

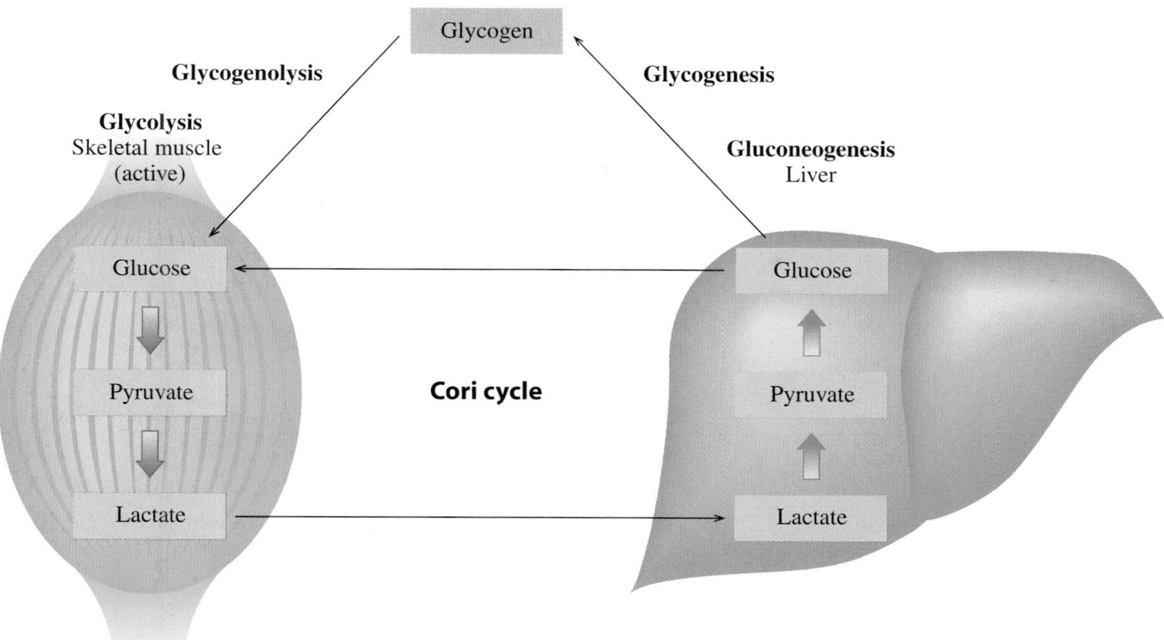


**FIGURE 22.15** Different pathways connect the utilization and synthesis of glucose.
**Q** Why is lactate formed in the muscle converted to glucose in the liver?

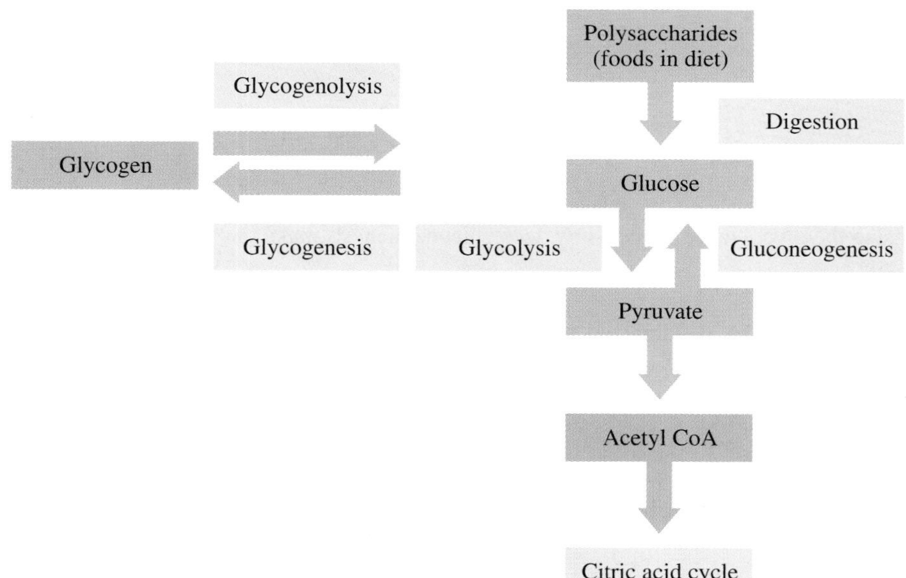


**FIGURE 22.16** Glycogenolysis and glycogenesis involve the breakdown and synthesis of glycogen. Glycolysis involves the breakdown of glucose, and gluconeogenesis involves the synthesis of glucose.
**Q** Why does glycogenesis operate after the digestion of a meal high in carbohydrates?

## Regulation of Gluconeogenesis

Gluconeogenesis is a pathway that protects the brain and nervous system from experiencing a loss of glucose, which causes impairment of function. It is also a pathway that is utilized when vigorous activity depletes blood glucose and glycogen stores. Thus, the level of carbohydrate available from the diet controls gluconeogenesis. When a diet is high in carbohydrate, the gluconeogenesis pathway is not utilized. However, when a diet is low in carbohydrate, the pathway is very active.

As long as conditions in a cell favor glycolysis, there is no synthesis of glucose. But when the cell requires the synthesis of glucose, glycolysis is turned off. The same three reactions that control glycolysis also control gluconeogenesis, but with different enzymes. Let's look at how high levels of certain compounds activate or inhibit the two processes (see Table 22.2).

**TABLE 22.2** Regulation of Glycolysis and Gluconeogenesis

| | Glycolysis | Gluconeogenesis |
|---|---|---|
| **Enzyme** | **Hexokinase** | **Glucose-6-phosphatase** |
| Activated by | High glucose levels, insulin, epinephrine | Low glucose levels, glucose-6-phosphate |
| Inhibited by | Glucose-6-phosphate | |
| **Enzyme** | **Phosphofructokinase** | **Fructose-1,6-bisphosphatase** |
| Activated by | AMP | Low glucose levels, glucagon |
| Inhibited by | ATP | AMP, insulin |
| **Enzyme** | **Pyruvate kinase** | **Pyruvate carboxylase** |
| Activated by | Fructose-1,6-bisphosphate | Low glucose level, glucagon |
| Inhibited by | ATP, acetyl CoA | Insulin |

CONCEPT CHECK 22.8

### Gluconeogenesis

Under what conditions does gluconeogenesis operate in a cell?

ANSWER

Gluconeogenesis operates when glycogen in the liver is depleted and the blood glucose level is extremely low. If the diet is not providing sufficient glucose for energy, glucose is produced from carbon atoms in noncarbohydrate sources, including amino acids, fatty acids, glycerol, and lactate.

SAMPLE PROBLEM 22.7

### Gluconeogenesis

The conversion of fructose-1,6-bisphosphate to fructose-6-phosphate is an irreversible reaction using the glycolytic enzyme. How does gluconeogenesis make this reaction happen?

SOLUTION

This reverse reaction is catalyzed by a different enzyme, *fructose-1,6-bisphosphatase*, which cleaves a phosphoryl group using a hydrolysis reaction, a reaction that is energetically favorable.

STUDY CHECK

Why is hexokinase in glycolysis replaced by glucose-6-phosphatase in gluconeogenesis?

## QUESTIONS AND PROBLEMS

### Gluconeogenesis: Glucose Synthesis

22.53 What is the function of gluconeogenesis in the body?

**22.54** What enzymes in glycolysis are not used in gluconeogenesis?

22.55 What enzymes in glycolysis are used in gluconeogenesis?

**22.56** How is the lactate produced in skeletal muscle used for glucose synthesis?

22.57 Indicate whether each of the following activates or inhibits gluconeogenesis:
**a.** low glucose levels **b.** glucagon **c.** insulin

**22.58** Indicate whether each of the following activates or inhibits glycolysis:
**a.** low glucose levels **b.** insulin **c.** glucagon

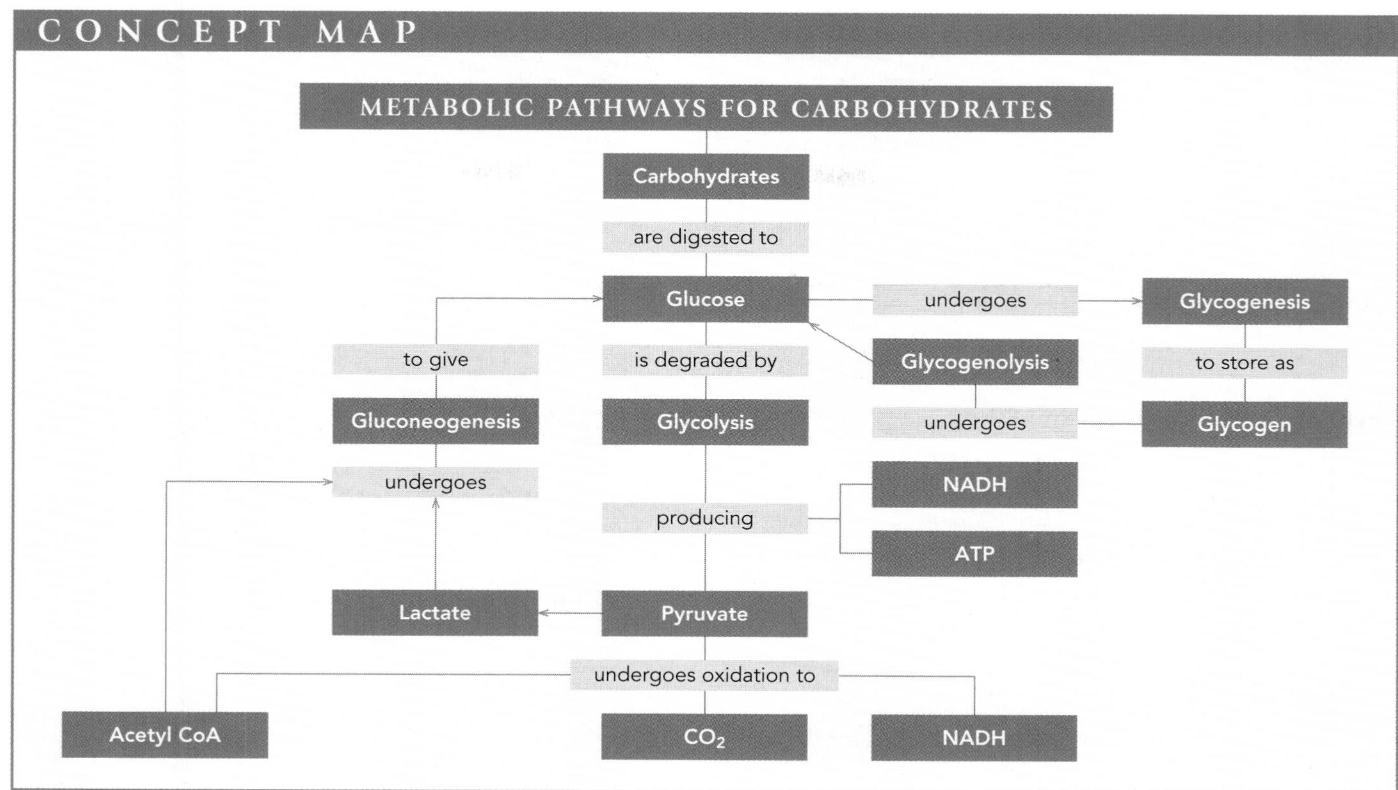


## CHAPTER REVIEW

### 22.1 Metabolism and Cell Structure

**LEARNING GOAL:** *Describe three stages of metabolism.*

Metabolism includes all the catabolic and anabolic reactions that occur in the cells. Catabolic reactions degrade large molecules into smaller ones with an accompanying release of energy. Anabolic reactions require energy to synthesize larger molecules from smaller ones. The three stages of metabolism are digestion of food, degradation of monomers such as glucose to pyruvate, and the extraction of energy from the two- and three-carbon compounds from stage 2. Many of the metabolic enzymes are present in the cytosol of the cell where metabolic reactions take place.

### 22.2 ATP and Energy

**LEARNING GOAL:** *Describe the role of ATP in catabolic and anabolic reactions.*

Energy obtained from catabolic reactions is stored primarily in adenosine triphosphate (ATP), a high-energy compound that is hydrolyzed when energy is required by anabolic reactions.

### 22.3 Important Coenzymes in Metabolic Pathways

**LEARNING GOAL:** *Describe the components and functions of the coenzymes FAD, NAD$^+$, and coenzyme A.*

FAD and NAD$^+$ are the oxidized forms of coenzymes that participate in oxidation–reduction reactions. When FAD and NAD$^+$ pick up hydrogen ions and electrons, they are reduced to $FADH_2$ and NADH + $H^+$. Coenzyme A contains a thiol group that usually bonds with a two-carbon acetyl group (acetyl CoA).

### 22.4 Digestion of Carbohydrates

**LEARNING GOAL:** *Give the sites and products of the digestion of carbohydrates.*

The digestion of carbohydrates is a series of reactions that breaks down polysaccharides into hexose monomers such as glucose, galactose, and fructose. These monomers can be absorbed through the intestinal wall into the bloodstream to be carried to cells where they provide energy and carbon atoms for synthesis of new molecules.

### 22.5 Glycolysis: Oxidation of Glucose

**LEARNING GOAL:** *Describe the conversion of glucose to pyruvate in glycolysis.*

Glycolysis, which occurs in the cytosol, consists of ten reactions that degrade glucose (six carbons) to two pyruvate molecules (three carbons each). The overall series of reactions yields two molecules of the reduced coenzyme NADH and two ATP.

### 22.6 Pathways for Pyruvate

**LEARNING GOAL:** *Give the conditions for the conversion of pyruvate to lactate, ethanol, and acetyl coenzyme A.*

Under aerobic conditions, pyruvate is oxidized in the mitochondria to acetyl CoA. In the absence of oxygen, pyruvate is reduced to lactate and NAD$^+$ is regenerated for the continuation of glycolysis, while microorganisms such as yeast reduce pyruvate to ethanol, a process known as fermentation.

### 22.7 Glycogen Metabolism

**LEARNING GOAL:** *Describe the breakdown and synthesis of glycogen.*

Glycogenolysis breaks down glycogen to glucose when glucose and ATP levels are low. When blood glucose levels are high, glycogenesis converts glucose to glycogen, which is stored in the liver.

### 22.8 Gluconeogenesis: Glucose Synthesis

**LEARNING GOAL:** *Describe how glucose is synthesized from noncarbohydrate molecules.*

When blood glucose levels are low and glycogen stores in the liver are depleted, glucose is synthesized from compounds such as pyruvate and lactate.

# SUMMARY OF KEY REACTIONS

## HYDROLYSIS OF ATP

$$\text{ATP} \longrightarrow \text{ADP} + \text{P}_i + 7.3\ \text{kcal/mole}\ (31\ \text{kJ/mole})$$

## HYDROLYSIS OF ADP

$$\text{ATP} \longrightarrow \text{AMP} + \text{P}_i + 7.3\ \text{kcal/mole}\ (31\ \text{kJ/mole})$$

## FORMATION OF ATP

$$\text{ADP} + \text{P}_i + 7.3\ \text{kcal/mole}\ (31\ \text{kJ/mole}) \longrightarrow \text{ATP}$$

## REDUCTION OF FAD AND NAD+

$$\text{FAD} + 2\text{H}^+ + 2e^- \longrightarrow \text{FADH}_2$$

$$\text{NAD}^+ + 2\text{H}^+ + 2e^- \longrightarrow \text{NADH} + \text{H}^+$$

## HYDROLYSIS OF DISACCHARIDES

$$\text{Lactose} + \text{H}_2\text{O} \xrightarrow{\text{Lactase}} \text{galactose} + \text{glucose}$$

$$\text{Sucrose} + \text{H}_2\text{O} \xrightarrow{\text{Sucrase}} \text{fructose} + \text{glucose}$$

$$\text{Maltose} + \text{H}_2\text{O} \xrightarrow{\text{Maltase}} \text{glucose} + \text{glucose}$$

## GLYCOLYSIS

$$\underset{\text{Glucose}}{\text{C}_6\text{H}_{12}\text{O}_6} + 2\text{ADP} + 2\text{P}_i + 2\text{NAD}^+ \longrightarrow \underset{\text{Pyruvate}}{2\text{CH}_3\text{—}\overset{\text{O}}{\overset{\|}{\text{C}}}\text{—COO}^-} + 2\text{ATP} + 2\text{NADH} + 4\text{H}^+ + 2\text{H}_2\text{O}$$

## OXIDATION OF PYRUVATE TO ACETYL CoA

$$\underset{\text{Pyruvate}}{\text{CH}_3\text{—}\overset{\text{O}}{\overset{\|}{\text{C}}}\text{—COO}^-} + \text{NAD}^+ + \text{HS—CoA} \xrightarrow{\text{Pyruvate dehydrogenase}} \underset{\text{Acetyl CoA}}{\text{CH}_3\text{—}\overset{\text{O}}{\overset{\|}{\text{C}}}\text{—S—CoA}} + \text{NADH} + \text{CO}_2$$

## REDUCTION OF PYRUVATE TO LACTATE

$$\underset{\text{Pyruvate}}{\text{CH}_3\text{—}\overset{\text{O}}{\overset{\|}{\text{C}}}\text{—COO}^-} + \text{NADH} + \text{H}^+ \longrightarrow \underset{\text{Lactate}}{\text{CH}_3\text{—}\overset{\text{OH}}{\overset{|}{\text{C}}\text{H}}\text{—COO}^-} + \text{NAD}^+$$

## OXIDATION OF GLUCOSE TO LACTATE

$$\text{Glucose} + 2\text{ADP} + 2\text{P}_i \longrightarrow 2\text{lactate} + 2\text{ATP}$$

## REDUCTION OF PYRUVATE TO ETHANOL

$$\underset{\text{Pyruvate}}{\text{CH}_3\text{—}\overset{\text{O}}{\overset{\|}{\text{C}}}\text{—COO}^-} + \text{NADH} + 2\text{H}^+ \longrightarrow \underset{\text{Ethanol}}{\text{CH}_3\text{—CH}_2\text{—OH}} + \text{NAD}^+ + \text{CO}_2$$

## GLYCOGENESIS

$$\text{Glucose} \longrightarrow \text{glycogen}$$

## GLYCOGENOLYSIS

$$\text{Glycogen} \longrightarrow \text{glucose}$$

## GLUCONEOGENESIS

$$\text{Pyruvate (or lactate)} \longrightarrow \text{glucose}$$

$$2\text{Pyruvate} + 4\text{ATP} + 2\text{GTP} + 2\text{NADH} + 2\text{H}^+ + 6\text{H}_2\text{O} \longrightarrow \text{Glucose} + 4\text{ADP} + 2\text{GDP} + 6\text{P}_i + 2\text{NAD}^+$$

# KEY TERMS

**acetyl CoA** The compound that forms when a two-carbon acetyl unit bonds to coenzyme A.

**ADP** Adenosine diphosphate, formed by the hydrolysis of ATP; consists of adenine, a ribose sugar, and two phosphoryl groups.

**aerobic** An oxygen-containing environment in the cells.

**anabolic reaction** A metabolic reaction that requires energy to build large molecules from small molecules.

**anaerobic** A condition in cells when there is no oxygen.

**ATP** Adenosine triphosphate, a high-energy compound that stores energy in the cells; consists of adenine, a ribose sugar, and three phosphoryl groups.

**catabolic reaction** A metabolic reaction that produces energy for the cell by the degradation and oxidation of glucose and other molecules.

**coenzyme A (CoA)** A coenzyme that transports acyl and acetyl groups.

**Cori cycle** A cyclic process in which lactate produced in muscle is transferred to the liver to be synthesized to glucose, which can be used again by muscle.

**cytoplasm** The material in eukaryotic cells between the nucleus and the cell membrane.

**cytosol** The fluid of the cytoplasm, which is an aqueous solution of electrolytes and enzymes.

**decarboxylation** The loss of a carbon atom in the form of $CO_2$.

**digestion** The processes in the gastrointestinal tract that break down large food molecules to smaller ones that pass through the intestinal membrane into the bloodstream.

**FAD** A coenzyme (flavin adenine dinucleotide) for dehydrogenase enzymes that form carbon–carbon double bonds.

**fermentation** The anaerobic conversion of glucose by enzymes in yeast to yield alcohol and $CO_2$.
**gluconeogenesis** The synthesis of glucose from noncarbohydrate compounds.
**glycogenesis** The synthesis of glycogen from glucose molecules.
**glycogenolysis** The breakdown of glycogen into glucose molecules.
**glycolysis** The ten oxidation reactions of glucose that yield two pyruvate molecules.
**metabolism** All the chemical reactions in living cells that carry out molecular and energy transformations.
**mitochondria** The components of cells where energy-producing reactions take place.
**$NAD^+$** The hydrogen acceptor used in oxidation reactions that form carbon–oxygen double bonds.

## UNDERSTANDING THE CONCEPTS

22.59 On a hike, you expend 350 kcal per hour. How many moles of ATP will you use if you hike for 2.5 h?

**22.60** Identify each of the following as a 6-carbon or a 3-carbon compound and arrange them in the order in which they occur in glycolysis:
**a.** 3-phosphoglycerate
**b.** pyruvate
**c.** glucose-6-phosphate
**d.** glucose
**e.** fructose-1,6-bisphosphate

## ADDITIONAL QUESTIONS AND PROBLEMS

*For instructor-assigned homework, go to* ***www.masteringchemistry.com***.

22.61 What is meant by the term metabolism?

**22.62** How do catabolic reactions differ from anabolic reactions?

22.63 What stage of metabolism involves the digestion of large food polymers?

**22.64** What stage of metabolism degrades monomers such as glucose into smaller molecules?

22.65 What type of cell has a nucleus?

**22.66** What is the function of each of the following cell components:
**a.** cell membrane **b.** mitochondria **c.** cytoplasm

22.67 What is the full name of ATP?

**22.68** What is the full name of ADP?

22.69 Write an abbreviated equation for the hydrolysis of ATP to ADP.

**22.70** Write the abbreviated equation for the hydrolysis of ADP to AMP.

22.71 What is the full name of FAD?

**22.72** What type of reaction uses FAD as the coenzyme?

22.73 What is the full name of $NAD^+$?

**22.74** What type of reaction uses $NAD^+$ as the coenzyme?

22.75 Write the abbreviations for the reduced forms of each of the following:
**a.** FAD **b.** $NAD^+$

**22.76** What is the name of the vitamin in the structure of each of the following?
**a.** FAD **b.** $NAD^+$ **c.** coenzyme A

22.77 How and where does lactose undergo digestion in the body? What are the products?

**22.78** How and where does sucrose undergo digestion in the body? What are the products?

22.79 How do galactose and fructose enter glycolysis?

**22.80** What is the general type of reaction that takes place in the digestion of carbohydrates?

22.81 What are the reactant and product of glycolysis?

**22.82** What is the coenzyme used in glycolysis?

22.83 In glycolysis, which reactions involve phosphorylation? Which reactions involve a direct substrate phosphorylation to generate ATP?

**22.84** How do ADP and ATP regulate the glycolysis pathway?

22.85 What reaction and enzyme in glycolysis convert a hexose bisphosphate into two three-carbon intermediates?

**22.86** How does the investment and generation of ATP give a net gain of ATP for glycolysis?

22.87 What compound is converted to fructose-6-phosphate by phosphoglucose isomerase?

**22.88** What product forms when glyceraldehyde-3-phosphate adds a phosphoryl group?

22.89 When is pyruvate converted to lactate in the body?

**22.90** When pyruvate is used to form acetyl CoA or ethanol in fermentation, the product has only two carbon atoms. What happened to the third carbon?

**22.91** How does phosphofructokinase regulate the rate of glycolysis?

**22.92** How does pyruvate kinase regulate the rate of glycolysis?

**22.93** When does the rate of glycogenolysis increase in the cells?

**22.94** If glucose-1-phosphate is the product from glycogen, how does it enter glycolysis?

**22.95** What is the end product of glycogenolysis in the liver?

**22.96** What is the end product of glycogenolysis in skeletal muscle?

**22.97** Indicate whether each of the following conditions would increase or decrease the rate of glycogenolysis in the liver:
**a.** low blood glucose level **b.** secretion of insulin
**c.** secretion of glucagon **d.** high levels of ATP

**22.98** Indicate whether each of the following conditions would increase or decrease the rate of glycogenesis in the liver:
**a.** low blood glucose level **b.** secretion of insulin
**c.** secretion of glucagon **d.** high levels of ATP

**22.99** Indicate whether each of the following conditions would increase or decrease the rate of gluconeogenesis:
**a.** high blood glucose level **b.** secretion of insulin
**c.** secretion of glucagon **d.** high levels of ATP

**22.100** Indicate whether each of the following conditions would increase or decrease the rate of glycolysis:
**a.** high blood glucose level **b.** secretion of insulin
**c.** secretion of glucagon **d.** high levels of ATP

## CHALLENGE QUESTIONS

**22.101** Why is glucose provided by glycogenolysis in the liver but not in skeletal muscle?

**22.102** When does the rate of glycogenesis increase in the cells?

**22.103** How do the hormones insulin and glucagon affect the rates of glycogenesis, glycogenolysis, and glycolysis?

**22.104** What is the function of gluconeogenesis?

**22.105** Where does the Cori cycle operate?

**22.106** Identify each of the following as part of glycolysis, glycogenolysis, glycogenesis, or gluconeogenesis:
**a.** Glycogen is broken down to glucose in the liver.
**b.** Glucose is synthesized from noncarbohydrate sources.
**c.** Glucose is degraded to pyruvate.
**d.** Glycogen is synthesized from glucose.

**22.107** One cell at work may break down 2 million (2 000 000) ATP molecules in 1 second. Researchers estimate that the human body has about $10^{13}$ cells.
**a.** How much energy, in kcal, could be produced by the cells in the body in 24 hours?
**b.** If ATP has a molar mass of 507 g/mole, how many grams of ATP are hydrolyzed in 24 hours?

## ANSWERS

### ANSWERS TO STUDY CHECKS

**22.1** 7.3 kcal/mole or 31 kJ/mole

**22.2** $FADH_2$

**22.3** The digestion of amylose begins in the mouth when salivary amylase hydrolyzes some of the glycosidic bonds. In the small intestine, pancreatic amylase hydrolyzes more glycosidic bonds, and finally maltose is hydrolyzed by maltase to yield glucose.

**22.4** In the initial reactions of glycolysis, energy in the form of two ATP is invested to activate glucose and convert it to fructose-1,6-bisphosphate.

**22.5**
$$CH_3-\overset{\underset{|}{OH}}{CH}-\overset{\underset{\|}{O}}{C}-O^- + NAD^+ \xrightarrow{\text{Lactate dehydrogenase}} CH_3-\overset{\underset{\|}{O}}{C}-\overset{\underset{\|}{O}}{C}-O^- + NADH + H^+$$

**22.6** Only liver and kidney cells contain the phosphatase enzyme that converts glucose-6-phosphate to free glucose.

**22.7** The reaction catalyzed by hexokinase in glycolysis is irreversible.

### ANSWERS TO SELECTED QUESTIONS AND PROBLEMS

**22.1** The digestion of polysaccharides takes place in stage 1.

**22.3** In metabolism, a catabolic reaction breaks apart large molecules, releasing energy.

**22.5** **a.** (3) smooth endoplasmic reticulum
**b.** (1) lysosome
**c.** (2) Golgi complex

**22.7** When a phosphoryl group is cleaved from ATP, sufficient energy is released for energy-requiring processes in the cell.

**22.9** **a.** PEP $\longrightarrow$ pyruvate + $P_i$ + 14.8 kcal/mole
**b.** ADP + $P_i$ + 7.3 kcal/mole $\longrightarrow$ ATP
**c.** PEP + ADP $\longrightarrow$ ATP + pyruvate + 7.5 kcal/mole

**22.11** **a.** coenzyme A **b.** $NAD^+$ **c.** FAD

**22.13** **a.** NADH **b.** FAD

**22.15** FAD

**22.17** Hydrolysis is the main reaction involved in the digestion of carbohydrates.

**22.19** **a.** lactose
**b.** glucose and fructose
**c.** glucose

**22.21** glucose

**22.23** ATP is required in phosphorylation reactions.

**22.25** glyceraldehyde-3-phosphate and dihydroxyacetone phosphate

**22.27** ATP is produced in glycolysis by transferring a phosphoryl group from 1,3-bisphosphoglycerate and from phosphoenolpyruvate directly to ADP.

**22.29** **a.** hexokinase; phosphofructokinase
**b.** phosphoglycerate kinase; pyruvate kinase

**22.31** **a.** 1 ATP required
**b.** 1 NADH is produced
**c.** 2 ATP and 2 NADH

**22.33** **a.** In reaction 1, a hexokinase uses ATP to phosphorylate glucose.
**b.** In reactions 7 and 10, phosphoryl groups are transferred from 1,3-bisphosphoglycerate and phosphoenolpyruvate directly to ADP to produce ATP.
**c.** In reaction 4, the six-carbon molecule fructose-1,6-bisphosphate is split into two three-carbon molecules, glyceraldehyde-3-phosphate and dihydroxyacetone phosphate.

**22.35** Galactose reacts with ATP to yield galactose-1-phosphate, which is converted to glucose-6-phosphate, an intermediate in glycolysis. Fructose reacts with ATP to yield fructose-1-phosphate, which is cleaved to give dihydroxyacetone phosphate and glyceraldehyde. Dihydroxyacetone phosphate isomerizes to glyceraldehyde-3-phosphate, and glyceraldehyde is phosphorylated to glyceraldehyde-3-phosphate, which is an intermediate in glycolysis.

**22.37** **a.** activate **b.** inhibit

**22.39** Aerobic (oxygen) conditions are needed.

**22.41** The oxidation of pyruvate converts $NAD^+$ to NADH and produces acetyl CoA and $CO_2$.

$$\text{Pyruvate} + NAD^+ + \text{CoA} \longrightarrow \text{Acetyl CoA} + CO_2 + NADH + H^+$$

**22.43** When pyruvate is reduced to lactate, the $NAD^+$ is used to oxidize glyceraldehyde-3-phosphate, which recycles NADH.

**22.45** carbon dioxide, $CO_2$

**22.47** Glycogenesis is the synthesis of glycogen from glucose molecules.

**22.49** Muscle cells break down glycogen to glucose-6-phosphate, which enters glycolysis.

**22.51** Glycogen phosphorylase cleaves the glycosidic bonds at the ends of glycogen chains to remove glucose as glucose-1-phosphate.

**22.53** When there are no glycogen stores remaining in the liver, gluconeogenesis synthesizes glucose from noncarbohydrate compounds such as pyruvate and lactate.

**22.55** phosphoglucose isomerase, aldolase, triose phosphate isomerase, glyceraldehyde-3-phosphate dehydrogenase, phosphoglycerate kinase, phosphoglycerate mutase, and enolase

**22.57** **a.** activates **b.** activates **c.** inhibits

**22.59** 120 moles of ATP

**22.61** Metabolism includes all the reactions in cells that provide energy and material for cell growth.

**22.63** stage 1

**22.65** eukaryotic cell

**22.67** adenosine triphosphate

**22.69** $ATP \longrightarrow ADP + P_i + 7.3$ kcal/mole (31 kJ/mole)

**22.71** flavin adenine dinucleotide

**22.73** nicotinamide adenine dinucleotide

**22.75** **a.** $FADH_2$ **b.** $NADH + H^+$

**22.77** Lactose undergoes digestion in the small intestine to yield galactose and glucose.

**22.79** Galactose and fructose are converted in the liver to glucose phosphate compounds that can enter the glycolysis pathway.

**22.81** Glucose is the reactant and pyruvate is the product of glycolysis.

**22.83** Reactions 1 and 3 involve phosphorylation of hexoses with ATP, and reactions 7 and 10 involve direct substrate phosphorylation that generates ATP.

**22.85** Reaction 4, which converts fructose-1,6-bisphosphate into two three-carbon intermediates, is catalyzed by aldolase.

**22.87** glucose-6-phosphate

**22.89** Pyruvate is converted to lactate when oxygen is not present in the cell (anaerobic) to regenerate $NAD^+$ for glycolysis.

**22.91** Phosphofructokinase is an allosteric enzyme that is activated by high levels of AMP and ADP because the cell needs to produce more ATP. When ATP levels are high due to a decrease in energy needs, ATP inhibits phosphofructokinase, which reduces its catalysis of fructose-6-phosphate.

**22.93** The rate of glycogenolysis increases when blood glucose levels are low and glucagon has been secreted, which accelerates the breakdown of glycogen.

**22.95** glucose

**22.97** **a.** increase **b.** decrease
**c.** increase **d.** decrease

**22.99** **a.** decrease **b.** decrease
**c.** increase **d.** decrease

**22.101** The cells in the liver, but not skeletal muscle, contain a phosphatase enzyme needed to convert glucose-6-phosphate to free glucose that can diffuse through cell membranes into the bloodstream. Glucose-6-phosphate, which is the end product of glycogenolysis in muscle cells, cannot diffuse easily across cell membranes.

**22.103** Insulin increases the rate of glycogenesis and glycolysis and decreases the rate of glycogenolysis. Glucagon decreases the rate of glycogenesis and glycolysis and increases the rate of glycogenolysis.

**22.105** The Cori cycle is a cyclic process that involves the transfer of lactate from muscle to the liver where glucose is synthesized, which can be used again by the muscle.

**22.107** **a.** 21 kcal **b.** 1500 g of ATP

# 23 Metabolism and Energy Production

LOOKING AHEAD


**23.1** The Citric Acid Cycle

**23.2** Electron Carriers

**23.3** Electron Transport

**23.4** Oxidative Phosphorylation and ATP

**23.5** ATP Energy from Glucose


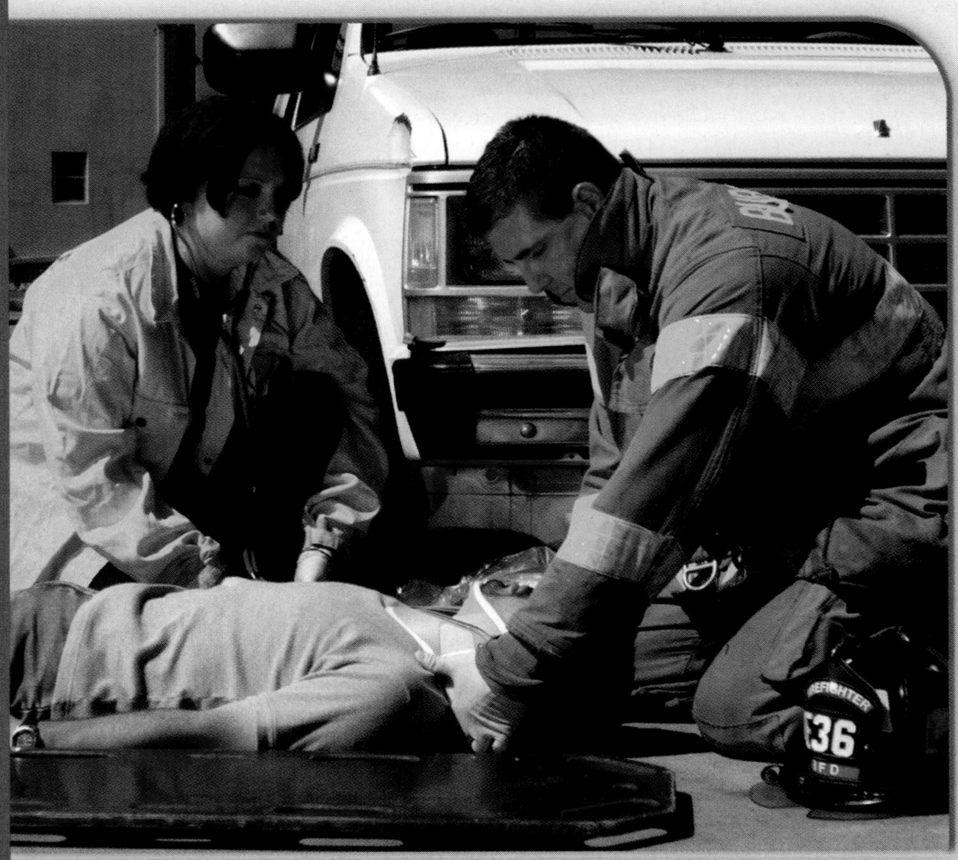

*"I am trained in basic life support. I work with the ER staff to assist in patient care," says Mandy Dornell, emergency medical technician at Seaton Medical Center. "In the ER, I take vital signs, do patient assessment, and perform CPR. If someone has a motor vehicle accident, I may suspect a neck or back injury. Then I may use a backboard or a cervical collar, which prevents the patient from moving and causing further damage. When people have difficulty breathing, I insert an airway—nasal or oral—to assist ventilation. I also set up and monitor IVs, and I am trained in childbirth."*

*When someone is critically ill or injured, the quick reactions of emergency medical technicians (EMTs) and paramedics provide immediate medical care and transport to an ER or trauma center.*

Visit **www.masteringchemistry.com** for self-study materials and instructor-assigned homework.

In Chapter 22, we described the digestion of carbohydrates to glucose and the degradation of glucose to pyruvate during glycolysis. We saw that pyruvate is converted to acetyl CoA when oxygen is plentiful in the cell and to lactate when oxygen levels are low. Although glycolysis produces a small amount of ATP, most of the ATP in the cells is produced in stage 3 of metabolism during the conversion of pyruvate, when oxygen is available in the cell. In a process known as *respiration*, oxygen is required to complete the oxidation of glucose to $CO_2$ and $H_2O$.

In the *citric acid cycle*, a series of metabolic reactions in the mitochondria oxidizes the two carbon atoms in the acetyl component of acetyl CoA to two molecules of carbon dioxide. The reduced coenzymes NADH and $FADH_2$ enter *electron transport*, or the *respiratory chain*, where they provide hydrogen ions and electrons that combine with oxygen ($O_2$) to form $H_2O$. The energy released during electron transport is used to synthesize ATP from ADP.

# 23.1 The Citric Acid Cycle

The **citric acid cycle** is a series of reactions that uses the two-carbon acetyl group in acetyl CoA to produce $CO_2$, NADH + $H^+$, and $FADH_2$. (See Figure 23.1.) The citric acid cycle connects the intermediate acetyl CoA from stages 1 and 2 with electron transport and the synthesis of ATP in stage 3. As a central pathway in metabolism, the citric acid cycle uses acetyl CoA from the degradation of carbohydrates as well as lipids and proteins.

The citric acid cycle is named for the citrate ion from citric acid ($C_6H_8O_7$), a tricarboxylic acid, that forms in the first reaction. The citric acid cycle is also known as the tricarboxylic acid (TCA) cycle or the Krebs cycle, named for H. A. Krebs, who recognized it as the major pathway for the production of energy.

**LEARNING GOAL**

Describe the oxidation of acetyl CoA in the citric acid cycle.

SELF STUDY ACTIVITY
Krebs Cycle

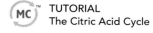

MC TUTORIAL
The Citric Acid Cycle

## Overview of the Citric Acid Cycle

The citric acid cycle has a total of eight reactions and eight enzymes, which we can separate into two parts. In part 1, an acetyl group (2C) in acetyl CoA bonds with oxaloacetate (4C) to yield citrate (6C). Then, two decarboxylation reactions remove two carbon atoms as $CO_2$ molecules to give a succinyl CoA (4C). In part 2, succinyl CoA is converted to other four-carbon compounds and eventually to oxaloacetate, which combines with another acetyl CoA and goes through the cycle again. (See Figure 23.2.) In one turn of the citric acid cycle, four oxidation reactions provide hydrogen ions and electrons, which are used to reduce FAD and $NAD^+$ coenzymes.

## Part 1 Decarboxylation Removes Two Carbon Atoms

### Reaction 1 Formation of citrate

In the first reaction, *citrate synthase* catalyzes the combination of an acetyl group (2C) from acetyl CoA with oxaloacetate (4C) to yield citrate (6C) and coenzyme A. (See Figure 23.3.)

$$CH_3-\overset{\overset{\displaystyle O}{\|}}{C}-S-CoA + \underset{\underset{\displaystyle COO^-}{|}}{\underset{\displaystyle CH_2}{\underset{|}{\overset{\overset{\displaystyle COO^-}{|}}{C}}}}{=}O + H_2O \xrightarrow[]{\text{Citrate synthase}} HO-\underset{\underset{\underset{\displaystyle COO^-}{|}}{\displaystyle CH_2}}{\underset{|}{\overset{\overset{\overset{\displaystyle COO^-}{|}}{\displaystyle CH_2}}{\overset{|}{C}}}}-COO^- + HS-CoA + H^+$$

Acetyl CoA — Oxaloacetate — Citrate

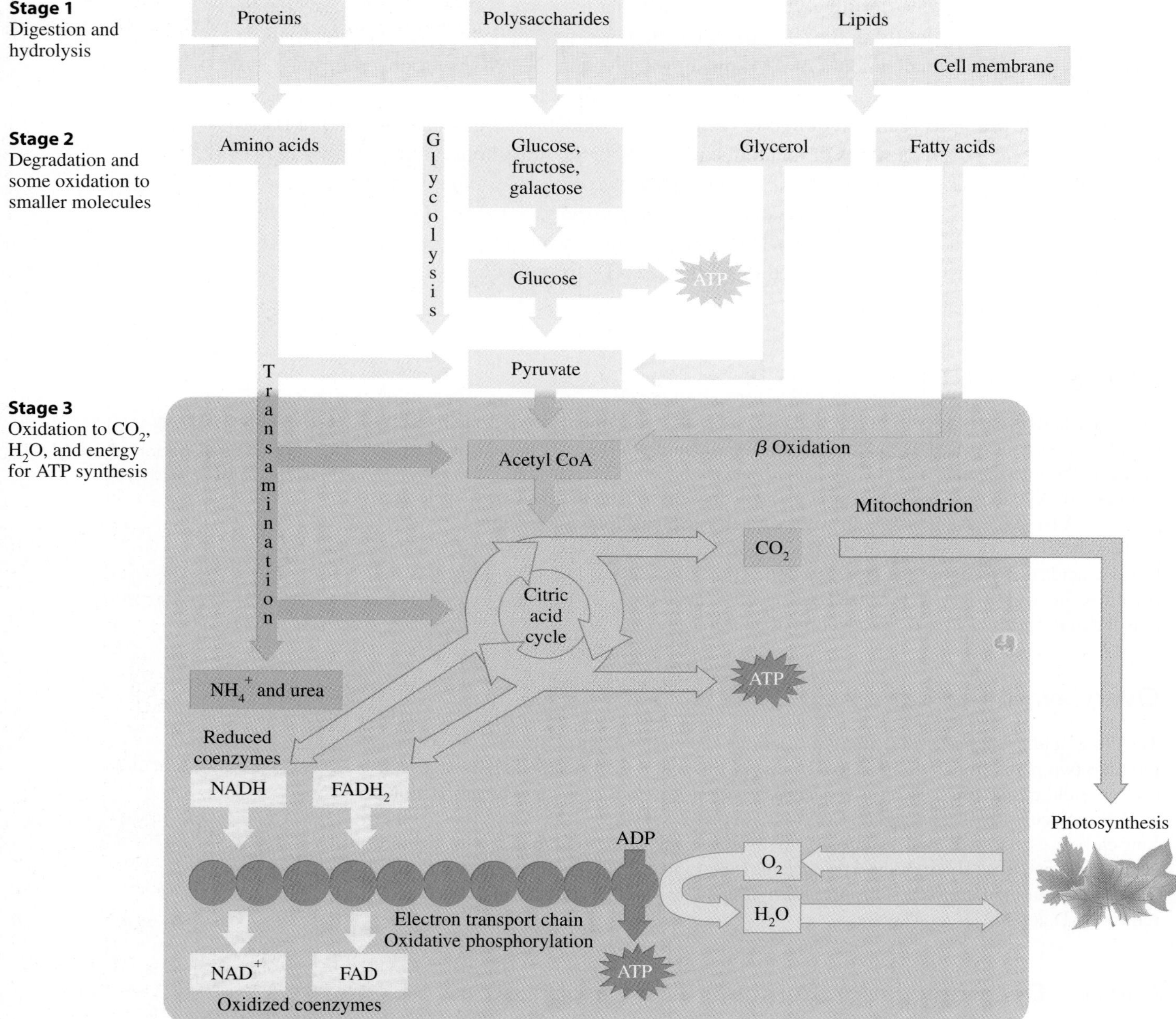


**FIGURE 23.1** The citric acid cycle connects the catabolic pathways that begin with the digestion and degradation of foods in stages 1 and 2 with the oxidation of substrates in stage 3 that generates most of the energy for ATP synthesis.

**Q** Why is the citric acid cycle called a central metabolic pathway?

### Reaction 2 Isomerization to isocitrate

The steps in this reaction produce an isomer that is more easily oxidized than citrate. Initially, *aconitase* catalyzes the dehydration of citrate to yield *cis*-aconitate. Then, *aconitase* catalyzes a hydration that forms isocitrate. The combination of these two steps converts the tertiary hydroxyl (—OH) group in citrate to a secondary hydroxyl group in isocitrate that is oxidized in the next reaction.

$$\underset{\text{Citrate}}{\begin{array}{c} COO^- \\ | \\ CH_2 \\ | \\ HO-C-COO^- \\ | \\ H-C-H \\ | \\ COO^- \end{array}} \xrightarrow[\;H_2O\;]{\text{aconitase}} \underset{\text{Aconitate}}{\begin{array}{c} COO^- \\ | \\ CH_2 \\ | \\ C-COO^- \\ \| \\ C-H \\ | \\ COO^- \end{array}} \xrightarrow[\;H_2O\;]{\text{aconitase}} \underset{\text{Isocitrate}}{\begin{array}{c} COO^- \\ | \\ CH_2 \\ | \\ H-C-COO^- \\ | \\ HO-C-H \\ | \\ COO^- \end{array}}$$

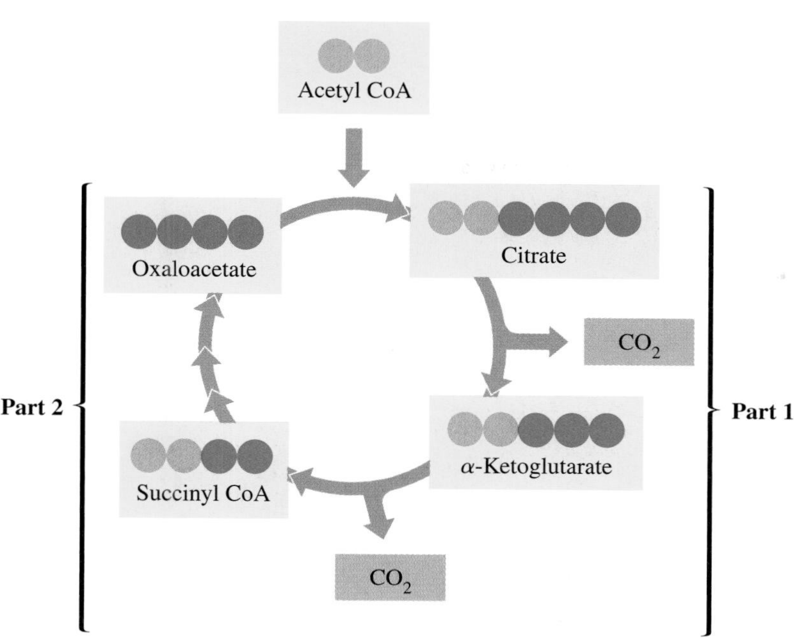


**FIGURE 23.2** In part 1 of the citric acid cycle, two carbon atoms are removed as $CO_2$ from six-carbon citrate to give four-carbon succinyl CoA, which is converted in part 2 to four-carbon oxaloacetate.

**Q** What is the difference in part 1 and part 2 of the citric acid cycle?

### Reaction 3 First oxidation and decarboxylation

Here, an oxidation and a decarboxylation take place for the first time in the citric acid cycle. The enzyme *isocitrate dehydrogenase* catalyzes the oxidation of the hydroxyl group to form a ketone and a **decarboxylation** that converts a carboxylate group ($COO^-$) to a $CO_2$ molecule. The ketone produced, α-ketoglutarate, is a compound with five carbon atoms. The oxidation of isocitrate provides hydrogen that reduces $NAD^+$ to NADH and $H^+$. (The production of ATP from reduced coenzymes is discussed in Section 23.4.)

$$\begin{array}{c} COO^- \\ | \\ CH_2 \\ | \\ H-C-COO^- \\ | \\ HO-C-H \\ | \\ COO^- \\ \text{Isocitrate} \end{array} + \mathbf{NAD^+} \xrightarrow[\text{dehydrogenase}]{\text{Isocitrate}} \begin{array}{c} COO^- \\ | \\ CH_2 \\ | \\ H-C-H \\ | \\ C=O \\ | \\ COO^- \\ \alpha\text{-Ketoglutarate} \end{array} + CO_2 + \mathbf{NADH}$$

### Reaction 4 Second oxidation and decarboxylation

In this reaction, a second $CO_2$ is removed when *α-ketoglutarate dehydrogenase* catalyzes the decarboxylation of α-ketoglutarate (5C) and combines the product with coenzyme A to form succinyl CoA. Again, an oxidation provides hydrogen for the reduction of $NAD^+$ to NADH:

$$\begin{array}{c} COO^- \\ | \\ CH_2 \\ | \\ CH_2 \\ | \\ C=O \\ | \\ COO^- \\ \alpha\text{-Ketoglutarate} \end{array} + NAD^+ + CoA-SH \xrightarrow[\text{dehydrogenase}]{\alpha\text{-Ketoglutarate}} \begin{array}{c} COO^- \\ | \\ CH_2 \\ | \\ CH_2 \\ | \\ C=O \\ | \\ S-CoA \\ \text{Succinyl CoA} \end{array} + CO_2 + NADH$$

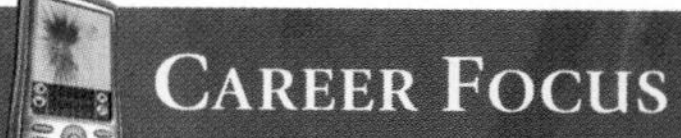


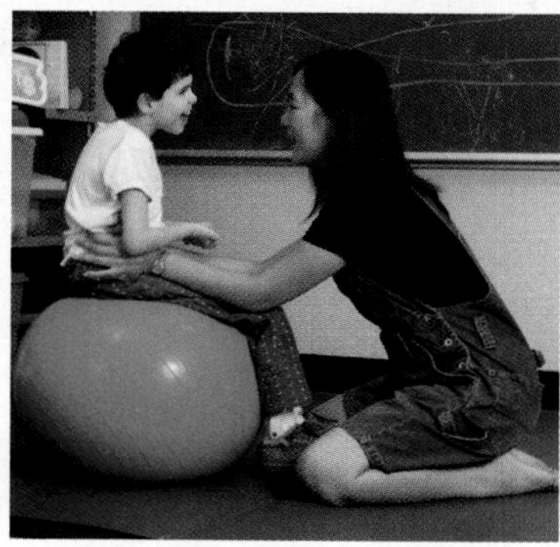

### Physical Therapist

"We do all kinds of activities that are typical of the things kids would do," says Helen Tong, physical therapist. "For example, we play with toys to help improve motor control. When a child can't do something, we use adaptive equipment to help him or her do that activity in a different way, which still allows participation. In school, we learn how the body works, and why it does not work. Then we can figure out what to do to help a child learn new skills. For example, this child with Rett syndrome has motor difficulties. Although she has difficulty talking, she does amazing work at a computer. There has been a real growth in assisted technology for children, and it has changed our work tremendously."

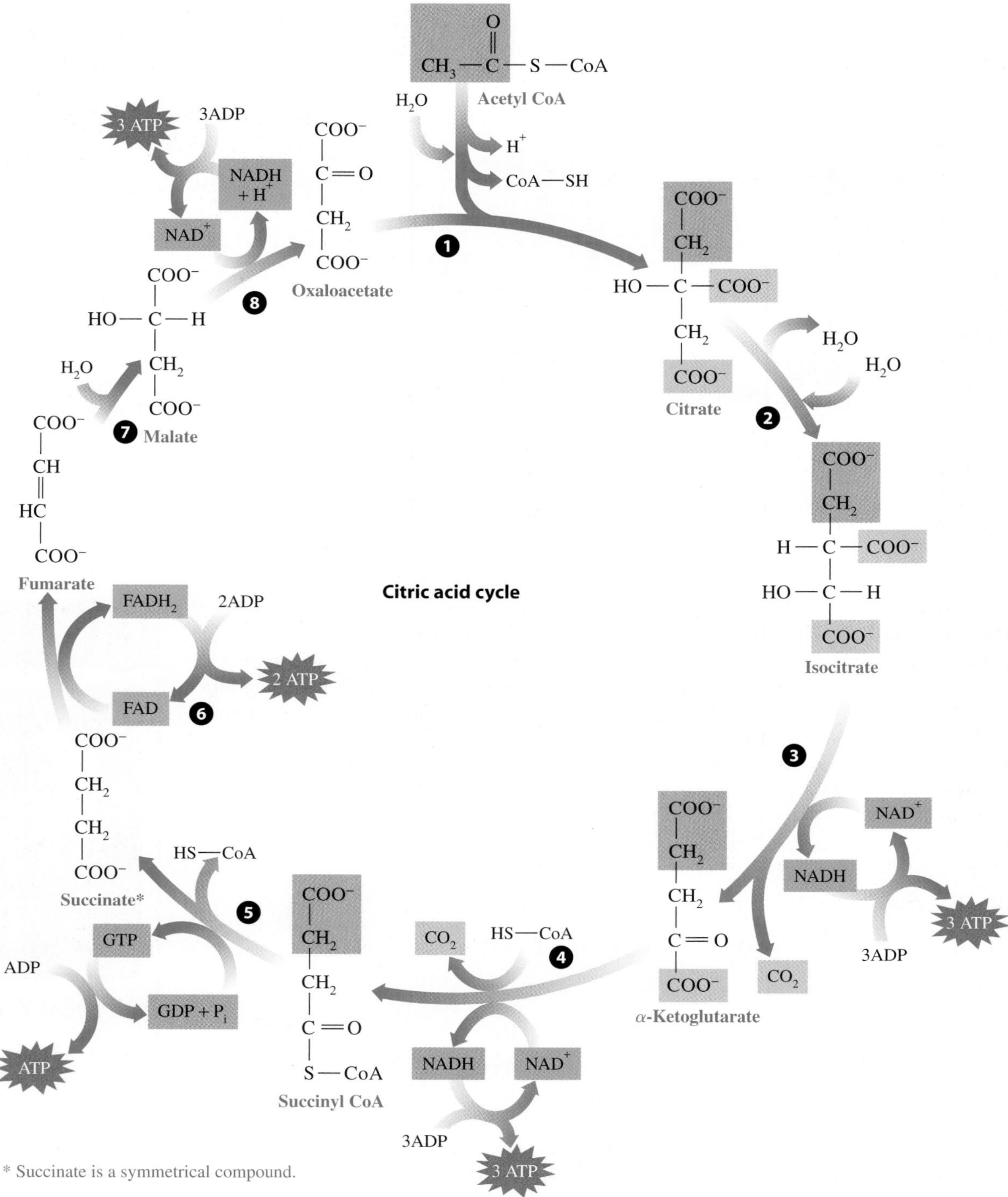


**FIGURE 23.3** In the citric acid cycle, oxidation reactions produce two $CO_2$, create reduced coenzymes NADH and $FADH_2$, and regenerate oxaloacetate.

**Q** How many reactions in the citric acid cycle produce a reduced coenzyme?

**CONCEPT CHECK 23.1**

### Reactions of the Citric Acid Cycle

**a.** What is the function of reaction 1 in the citric acid cycle?

**b.** Why is water removed and added in reaction 2?

ANSWER

**a.** Reaction 1 in the citric acid cycle combines acetyl (2C) with oxaloacetate (4C) to prepare citrate (6C) for the citric acid cycle.

**b.** In reaction 2, the —OH on the tertiary carbon of citrate is removed forming a double bond. Then water is added, but this time —OH forms on the secondary carbon, which can be oxidized in reaction 3.

## Part 2 Converting Four Carbon Compounds to Oxaloacetate

### Reaction 5 Hydrolysis of succinyl CoA

Here, *succinyl CoA synthetase* catalyses the hydrolysis of the thioester bond in succinyl CoA to yield succinate and CoA. The energy released when the thioester bond is broken is used to add a phosphoryl group to GDP (guanosine diphosphate) to form GTP, a high-energy compound similar to ATP. (See Chapter 21 to compare the structures of guanine and adenine.)

$$\underset{\text{Succinyl CoA}}{\begin{array}{l}COO^-\\ |\\ CH_2\\ |\\ CH_2\\ |\\ C{=}O\\ |\\ S{-}CoA\end{array}} + GDP + P_i + H^+ \xrightarrow[\text{synthetase}]{\text{Succinyl CoA}} \underset{\text{Succinate}}{\begin{array}{l}COO^-\\ |\\ CH_2\\ |\\ CH_2\\ |\\ COO^-\end{array}} + GTP + HS{-}CoA$$

Eventually, the GTP undergoes hydrolysis with a release of energy that is used to phosphorylate ADP to form ATP. At the same time, the reaction regenerates GDP to use again in the citric acid cycle. This reaction is the only time in the citric acid cycle that ATP is produced by a direct phosphorylation of ADP:

$$GTP + ADP \longrightarrow GDP + ATP$$

### Reaction 6 Dehydrogenation of succinate

In reaction 6 and the next two reactions, four-carbon compounds are converted eventually to oxaloacetate to start the citric acid cycle again. In this reaction, *succinate dehydrogenase* catalyzes the oxidation of succinate to produce fumarate, a compound with a trans double bond. The formation of a carbon–carbon (C═C) double bond requires the coenzyme FAD, which accepts 2H when it is reduced to $FADH_2$. This reaction is the only one in the citric acid cycle that involves the reduction of FAD to $FADH_2$:

$$\underset{\text{Succinate}}{\begin{array}{l}COO^-\\ |\\ CH_2\\ |\\ CH_2\\ |\\ COO^-\end{array}} + FAD \xrightarrow[\text{dehydrogenase}]{\text{Succinate}} \underset{\text{Fumarate}}{\begin{array}{c}{}^-OOC\diagdown\quad\diagup H\\ C\\ \|\\ C\\ H\diagup\quad\diagdown COO^-\end{array}} + FADH_2$$

### Reaction 7 Hydration

A hydration, catalyzed by *fumarase*, adds water to the double bond of fumarate to yield malate:

$$\underset{\text{Fumarate}}{\begin{array}{c}{}^-OOC\diagdown\quad\diagup H\\ C\\ \|\\ C\\ H\diagup\quad\diagdown COO^-\end{array}} + H_2O \xrightarrow{\text{Fumarase}} \underset{\text{Malate}}{\begin{array}{c}COO^-\\ |\\ HO{-}C{-}H\\ |\\ H{-}C{-}H\\ |\\ COO^-\end{array}}$$

### Reaction 8 Dehydrogenation forms oxaloacetate

In the last step of the citric acid cycle, *malate dehydrogenase* catalyzes the oxidation of the hydroxyl (—OH) group in malate to yield oxaloacetate. For the third time in the citric acid cycle, an oxidation provides hydrogen for the reduction of $NAD^+$ to NADH and $H^+$:

$$\underset{\text{Malate}}{\begin{array}{c}COO^-\\ |\\ HO{-}C{-}H\\ |\\ CH_2\\ |\\ COO^-\end{array}} + NAD^+ \xrightarrow[\text{dehydrogenase}]{\text{Malate}} \underset{\text{Oxaloacetate}}{\begin{array}{l}COO^-\\ |\\ C{=}O\\ |\\ CH_2\\ |\\ COO^-\end{array}} + NADH + H^+$$

CONCEPT CHECK 23.2

**Enzymes of the Citric Acid Cycle**

Four dehydrogenase enzymes catalyze oxidation reactions in the citric acid cycle.

**a.** What are the names of the four types of dehydrogenase enzymes?
**b.** Why does only one use the coenzyme FAD?

ANSWER

**a.** The four dehydrogenase enzymes are isocitrate dehydrogenase, $\alpha$-ketoglutarate dehydrogenase, succinate dehydrogenase, and malate dehydrogenase.
**b.** Succinate dehydrogenase uses FAD because the reaction it catalyzes involves the removal of 2H from a carbon–carbon single bond in succinate to form a carbon–carbon double bond in fumarate.

## Summary of Products from the Citric Acid Cycle

We have seen that the citric acid cycle begins when a two-carbon acetyl group from acetyl CoA combines with oxaloacetate to form citrate. In part 1 of the cycle, two carbon atoms are removed from citrate to yield two $CO_2$ and a four-carbon compound that undergoes reaction in part 2 to regenerate oxaloacetate. In the four oxidation reactions of one turn of the citric acid cycle, three $NAD^+$ and one FAD are reduced to three NADH and one $FADH_2$. In reaction 5, one GDP is converted to one GTP by a direct phosphorylation of GDP, which is used to convert one ADP to ATP. We can write an overall chemical equation for one complete turn of the citric acid cycle as follows:

$$3NAD^+ + FAD + GDP + P_i + \text{acetyl CoA} + 2H_2O \longrightarrow 3NADH + 3H^+ + FADH_2 + GTP + CoA + 2CO_2$$

## Regulation of Citric Acid Cycle

The primary function of the citric acid cycle is to produce high-energy compounds for ATP synthesis. When the cell needs energy, low levels of ATP stimulate the conversion of pyruvate to acetyl CoA, the fuel for the citric acid cycle. When ATP and NADH levels are high, there is a decrease in the production of acetyl CoA from pyruvate.

In the citric acid cycle, the enzymes that catalyze reactions 3 and 4 respond to allosteric activation and inhibition (Chapter 20). In reaction 3, isocitrate dehydrogenase is activated by high levels of ADP and inhibited by high levels of ATP and NADH. In reaction 4, $\alpha$-ketoglutarate dehydrogenase is activated by high levels of ADP and inhibited by high levels of NADH and succinyl CoA. (See Figure 23.4.)

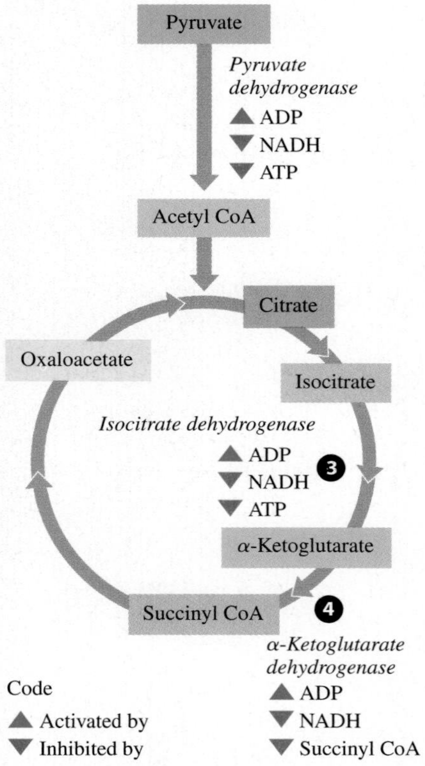

**FIGURE 23.4** High levels of ADP activate enzymes for the production of acetyl CoA and the citric acid cycle, whereas high levels of ATP, NADH, and succinyl CoA inhibit enzymes in the citric acid cycle.

**Q** How do high levels of ATP affect the rate of the citric acid cycle?

SAMPLE PROBLEM 23.1

**Citric Acid Cycle**

When one acetyl CoA completes the citric acid cycle, how many of each of the following is produced?

**a.** NADH **b.** ketone group **c.** $CO_2$

SOLUTION

**a.** One turn of the citric acid cycle produces three molecules of NADH.
**b.** Two ketone groups form when the secondary alcohol groups in isocitrate and malate are oxidized by $NAD^+$.
**c.** Two molecules of $CO_2$ are produced by the decarboxylation of isocitrate and $\alpha$-ketoglutarate.

STUDY CHECK

What compound is a substrate in the first reaction of the citric acid cycle and a product in the last reaction?

## QUESTIONS AND PROBLEMS

### The Citric Acid Cycle

23.1 What other names are used for the citric acid cycle?

**23.2** What compounds are needed to start the citric acid cycle?

23.3 What are the products from one turn of the citric acid cycle?

**23.4** What compound is regenerated in each turn of the citric acid cycle?

23.5 Which reaction(s) of the citric acid cycle involve oxidative decarboxylation?

**23.6** Which reaction(s) of the citric acid cycle involve a dehydration reaction?

23.7 Which reaction(s) of the citric acid cycle reduce $NAD^+$?

**23.8** Which reaction(s) of the citric acid cycle reduce FAD?

23.9 Which reaction(s) in the citric acid cycle involve a direct substrate phosphorylation?

**23.10** What is the total NADH and total $FADH_2$ produced in one turn of the citric acid cycle?

23.11 Refer to the diagram of the citric acid cycle to answer each of the following:
**a.** What are the six-carbon compounds?
**b.** How is the number of carbon atoms decreased?
**c.** What is the five-carbon compound?
**d.** Which reactions are oxidation reactions?
**e.** In which reactions are secondary alcohols oxidized?

**23.12** Refer to the diagram of the citric acid cycle to answer each of the following:
**a.** What is the yield of $CO_2$ molecules?
**b.** What are the four-carbon compounds?
**c.** What is the yield of GTP molecules?
**d.** What are the decarboxylation reactions?
**e.** Where does a hydration occur?

23.13 Indicate the name of the enzyme for each of the following reactions in the citric acid cycle:
**a.** joins acetyl CoA to oxaloacetate
**b.** forms a carbon–carbon double bond
**c.** adds water to fumarate

**23.14** Indicate the name of the enzyme for each of the following reactions in the citric acid cycle:
**a.** isomerizes citrate
**b.** oxidizes and decarboxylates $\alpha$-ketoglutarate
**c.** hydrolyzes succinyl CoA and adds $P_i$ to GDP

23.15 Indicate the reactant that accepts a hydrogen or a phosphoryl group in each of the following:
**a.** isocitrate $\longrightarrow$ $\alpha$-ketoglutarate
**b.** succinyl CoA $\longrightarrow$ succinate

**23.16** Indicate the reactant that accepts a hydrogen or a phosphoryl group in each of the following:
**a.** malate $\longrightarrow$ oxaloacetate
**b.** $\alpha$-ketoglutarate $\longrightarrow$ succinyl CoA

23.17 What enzymes in the citric acid cycle are allosteric enzymes?

**23.18** How does NADH affect the rate of the citric acid cycle?

23.19 How do high levels of ADP affect the rate of the citric acid cycle?

**23.20** Why does the rate of the oxidation of pyruvate affect the rate of the citric acid cycle?

## 23.2 Electron Carriers

**LEARNING GOAL**

Describe the electron carriers involved in electron transport.

MC TUTORIAL Electron Carriers

At this point, the metabolic cycles of glycolysis, the oxidation of two pyruvates, and the citric acid cycle for two acetyl CoA would produce four ATP along with ten NADH and two $FADH_2$ from the degradation of one glucose:

| From Glucose | ATP | Reduced Coenzymes | |
|---|---|---|---|
| Glycolysis: | 2 | 2 NADH | |
| Oxidation (2 pyruvate): | | 2 NADH | |
| Citric acid cycle (2 acetyl CoA): | 2 | 6 NADH | 2 $FADH_2$ |

Now we will see how the oxidation of these reduced coenzymes provides the energy for the synthesis of considerably more ATP. In **electron transport**, or the *respiratory chain*, hydrogen ions and electrons from NADH and $FADH_2$ are passed from one electron acceptor to the next until they combine with oxygen to form $H_2O$. The electron acceptors in this transport system are known as **electron carriers**. The energy released during electron transport is used to synthesize ATP from ADP and $P_i$, a process called *oxidative phosphorylation.* (See Section 23.4.) As long as oxygen is available for the mitochondria in the cell, electron transport and oxidative phosphorylation function to produce most of the ATP energy manufactured in the cell.

Glucose
2 NADH
2 ATP
2 Pyruvate
2 NADH
2 Acetyl CoA
Citric acid cycle
6 NADH
2 $FADH_2$
2 ATP
Electron carriers
Flavins
Iron–sulfur clusters
Coenzyme Q
Cytochromes
$NAD^+$
FAD
$4H^+ + O_2$
$4e^-$
$2H_2O$
ADP + $P_i$
ATP

## Oxidation and Reduction of Electron Carriers

The electron carriers in electron transport include flavins, iron–sulfur proteins, coenyzme Q, and cytochromes. Each type of electron carrier contains a group or ion that is reduced when electrons are accepted and oxidized when electrons are removed. That is, the transfer of hydrogen ions and electrons from reduced $AH_2$ to the carrier B forms reduced $BH_2$ and oxidized carrier A:

Oxidized carrier **A** ← → Reduced carrier **B**$H_2$

Reduced carrier **A**$H_2$ → Oxidized carrier **B**

Four types of electron carriers make up the electron transport system:

1. **FMN (flavin mononucleotide)** is a coenzyme derived from riboflavin (vitamin $B_2$). In riboflavin, the flavin ring system is attached to ribitol (a sugar alcohol of ribose). (See Figure 23.5.) The reduced product is $FMNH_2$.
2. **Fe–S (iron–sulfur) clusters** are groups of proteins that contain iron–sulfur clusters embedded in the proteins involved in electron transport. The clusters contain iron ions, inorganic sulfides, and several cysteine groups. The iron in the Fe–S clusters is oxidized to $Fe^{3+}$ and reduced to $Fe^{2+}$ as electrons are lost and gained. (See Figure 23.6.)
3. **Coenzyme Q (Q** or **CoQ)** is derived from quinone, which is a six-carbon cyclic compound with two double bonds and two keto groups attached to a long carbon chain. (See Figure 23.7.) Coenzyme Q is reduced when the keto groups accept hydrogen ions and electrons.
4. **Cytochromes (cyt)** are proteins that contain a heme group with an iron ion. The different cytochromes are indicated by letters following the abbreviation for cytochrome (cyt): cyt *b*, cyt $c_1$, cyt *c*, cyt *a*, and cyt $a_3$. In each cytochrome, the $Fe^{3+}$ accepts a single electron to form $Fe^{2+}$, which is oxidized back to $Fe^{3+}$ when the electron is passed to the next cytochrome:

$$Fe^{3+} + e^- \rightleftharpoons Fe^{2+}$$

The structures of the nitrogen-containing rings and iron ion of the heme groups are similar in all of the cytochromes. (See Figure 23.8.) The differences in the cytochromes are due to side groups attached to the rings and the attachment of cytochromes *c* and $c_1$ to protein.

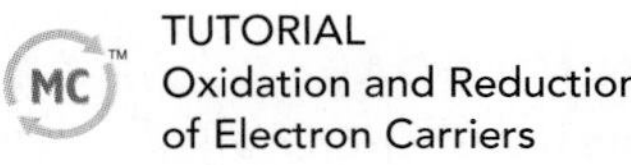

TUTORIAL
Oxidation and Reduction of Electron Carriers

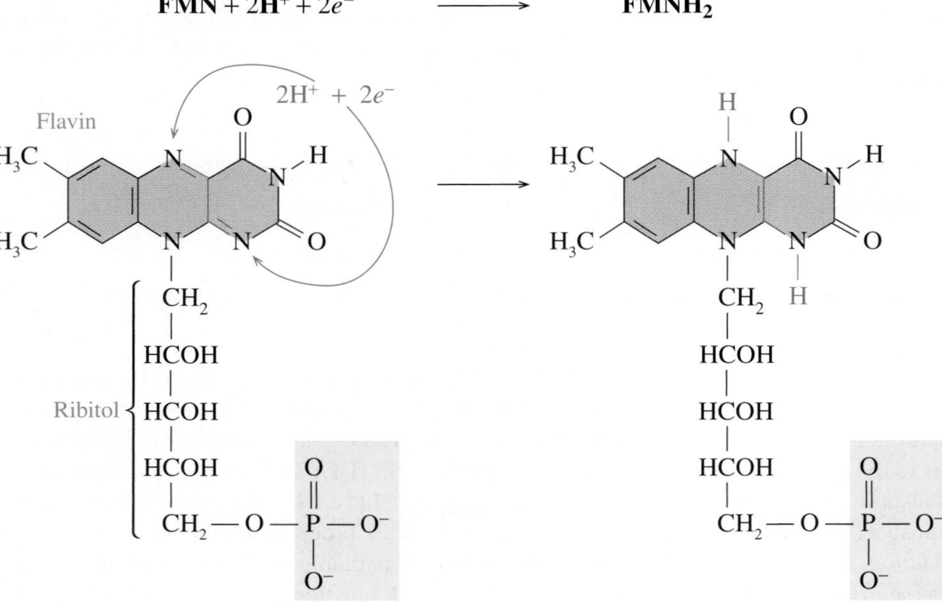


**FIGURE 23.5** The electron carrier FMN consists of a flavin ring system containing the reactive center, ribitol, and a phosphoryl group.

**Q** What part of the FMN molecule is reduced when hydrogen ions and electrons are accepted?

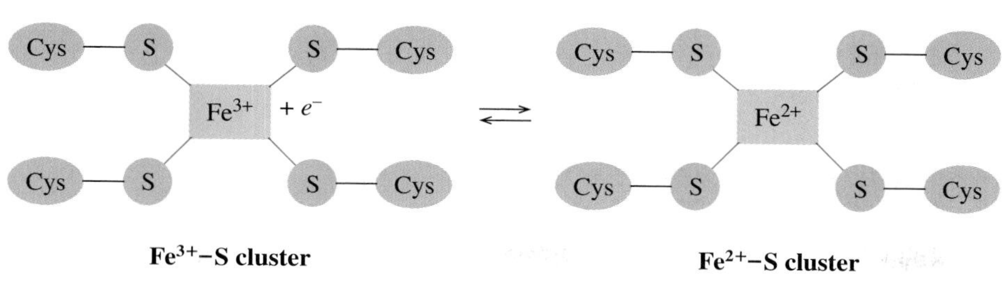

**FIGURE 23.6** In typical iron–sulfur clusters, iron ions bond to sulfur atoms in the thiol (—SH) groups of four cysteine groups in proteins.

**Q** In an iron–sulfur cluster, what are the ionic charges of the oxidized and reduced iron ions?

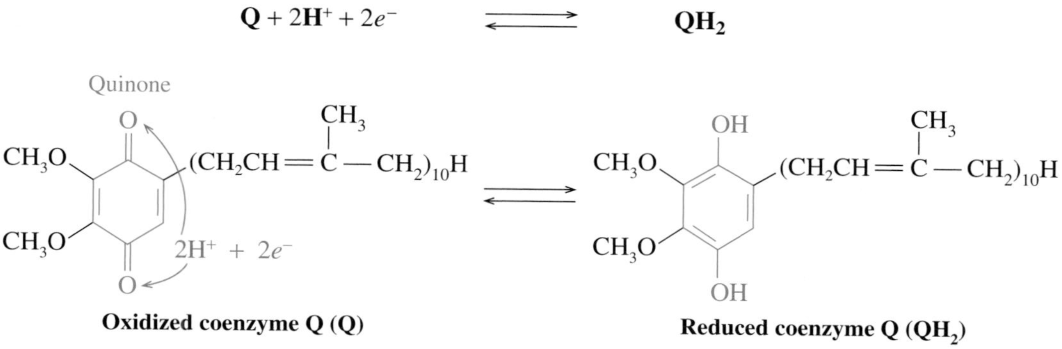

**FIGURE 23.7** The electron carrier coenzyme Q accepts $2H^+$ and $2e^-$ from $FADH_2$ and $FMNH_2$ and passes them to the cytochromes.

**Q** How does reduced coenzyme Q compare to the oxidized form?

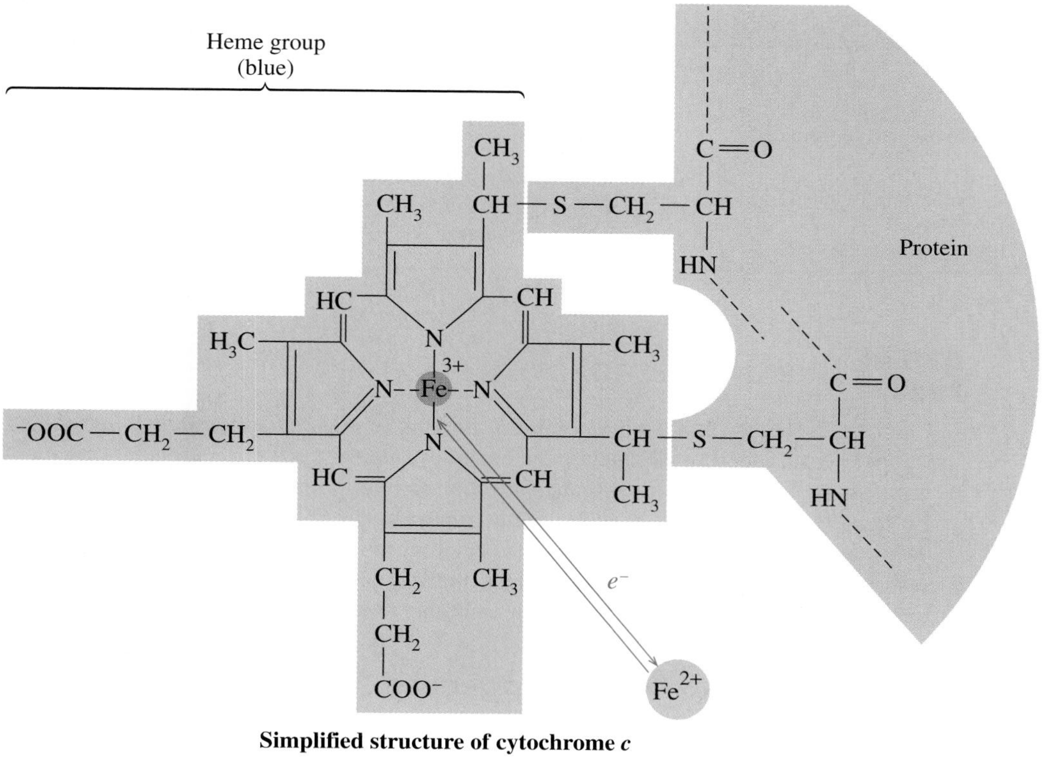

**FIGURE 23.8** The iron-containing proteins known as cytochromes are identified as *b*, *c*, $c_1$, *a*, and $a_3$.

**Q** What are the reduced and oxidized forms of the cytochromes?

CONCEPT CHECK 23.3

**Electron Carriers**

1. Give the abbreviation for each of the following carriers:
   a. the oxidized form of flavin mononucleotide
   b. the reduced form of coenzyme Q
2. What is the oxidized form of iron in cyt $a_3$?

ANSWER

1. a. In the oxidized form, flavin mononucleotide has the formula FMN.
   b. When coenzyme Q is reduced, it gains two hydrogen ions and two electrons, which gives the formula $QH_2$.
2. When $Fe^{2+}$ in cyt $a_3$ is oxidized, an electron is lost to give $Fe^{3+}$.

SAMPLE PROBLEM 23.2

**Oxidation and Reduction**

Identify the following steps in electron transport as oxidation or reduction:

**a.** $FMN + 2H^+ + 2e^- \longrightarrow FMNH_2$ **b.** $\text{cyt } c(Fe^{2+}) \longrightarrow \text{cyt } c(Fe^{3+}) + e^-$

SOLUTION

**a.** The gain of two electrons is reduction. **b.** The loss of an electron is oxidation.

STUDY CHECK

Identify each of the following as oxidation or reduction:

**a.** $QH_2 \longrightarrow Q + 2H^+ + 2e^-$ **b.** $\text{cyt } b(Fe^{3+}) + e^- \longrightarrow \text{cyt } b(Fe^{2+})$

## QUESTIONS AND PROBLEMS

### Electron Carriers

23.21 Is cyt $b$ ($Fe^{3+}$) the abbreviation for the oxidized or reduced form of cytochrome $b$?

**23.22** Is $FMNH_2$ the abbreviation for the oxidized or reduced form of flavin mononucleotide?

23.23 Identify each of the following as oxidation or reduction:
   a. $FMNH_2 \longrightarrow FMN + 2H^+ + 2e^-$
   b. $Q + 2H^+ + 2e^- \longrightarrow QH_2$

**23.24** Identify each of the following as oxidation or reduction:
   a. $\text{cyt } c(Fe^{3+}) + e^- \longrightarrow \text{cyt } c(Fe^{2+})$
   b. $Fe^{2+}\text{—S cluster} \longrightarrow Fe^{3+}\text{—S cluster} + e^-$

## 23.3 Electron Transport

LEARNING GOAL

Describe the role of the electron carriers in electron transport.

SELF STUDY ACTIVITY Electron Transport

In Chapter 22, we saw that a mitochondrion contains an inner and outer membrane. Along the highly folded inner membrane are the enzymes and electron carriers required for electron transport. Within these membranes are four distinct protein complexes. Within each complex are electron carriers needed for electron transport.

Two electron carriers, coenzyme Q and cytochrome $c$, are not firmly attached to the membrane. They function as mobile carriers shuttling electrons between the protein complexes that are tightly bound to the inner membrane. (See Figure 23.9.)

### Complex I NADH Dehydrogenase

At complex I, NADH transfers hydrogen ions and electrons to FMN to yield reduced $FMNH_2$. NADH is oxidized back to $NAD^+$, which makes it available to oxidize more substrates in oxidative pathways such as the citric acid cycle:

$$NADH + H^+ + FMN \longrightarrow NAD^+ + FMNH_2$$

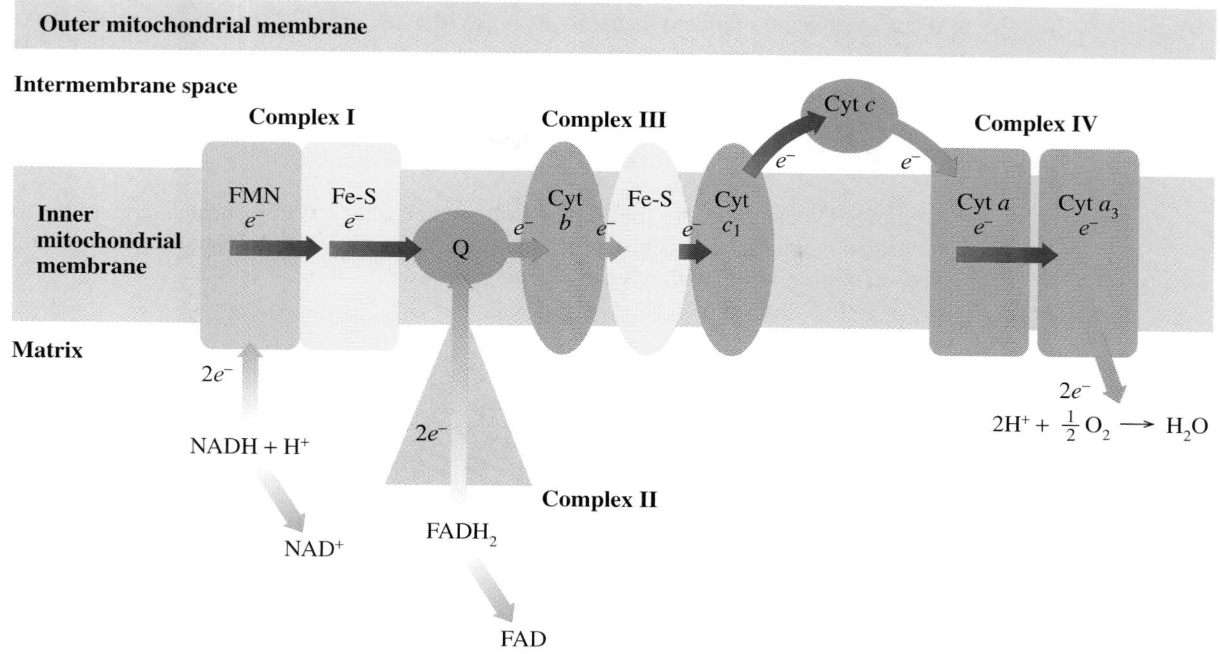


FIGURE 23.9 Most of the electron carriers in electron transport are found in protein complexes bound to the inner membrane of the mitochondria. Two are mobile carriers that carry electrons between the protein complexes.
Q What is the function of the electron carriers coenzyme Q and cytochrome c?

Within complex I, electrons are transferred from $FMNH_2$ to Fe–S clusters and from Fe–S to coenzyme Q:

$$FMNH_2 + Q \longrightarrow QH_2 + FMN$$

NADH + $H^+$ → $NAD^+$; FMN → $FMNH_2$; $FMNH_2$ → FMN; $Fe^{2+}S$ → $Fe^{3+}S$; $Fe^{3+}S$ → $Fe^{2+}S$; Q → $QH_2$

The overall reaction sequence in complex I can be written as follows:

$$NADH + H^+ + Q \longrightarrow QH_2 + NAD^+$$

## Complex II Succinate Dehydrogenase

Complex II is used when $FADH_2$ is generated by the conversion of succinate to fumarate in the citric acid cycle. The electrons from $FADH_2$ are transferred to coenzyme Q to yield $QH_2$. Because complex II is at a lower energy level than complex I, the electrons from $FADH_2$ enter electron transport at a lower energy level than those from NADH.

$$FADH_2 + Q \longrightarrow FAD + QH_2$$

## Complex III Coenzyme Q–Cytochrome *c* Reductase

The mobile carrier $QH_2$ transfers electrons from NADH and $FADH_2$ to an iron–sulfur (Fe–S) cluster, and then to cytochrome *b*, the first cytochrome in complex III:

$$QH_2 + 2\text{cyt } b(Fe^{3+}) \longrightarrow Q + 2\text{cyt } b(Fe^{2+}) + 2H^+$$

From cyt *b*, the electrons are transferred to an Fe–S cluster, then to cytochrome $c_1$, and then to cytochrome *c*. Each time an $Fe^{3+}$ ion accepts an electron, it is reduced to $Fe^{2+}$ and then oxidized back to $Fe^{3+}$ as the electron is passed on to the next cytochrome. Cytochrome *c*, another mobile carrier moves the electron from complex III to complex IV.

## Complex IV Cytochrome *c* Oxidase

At complex IV, electrons are transferred from cytochrome *c* to cytochrome *a*, and then to cytochrome $a_3$, the last cytochrome. In the final step of electron transport, electrons and hydrogen ions combine with oxygen ($O_2$) to form water:

$$2H^+ + 2e^- + \frac{1}{2}O_2 \longrightarrow H_2O$$

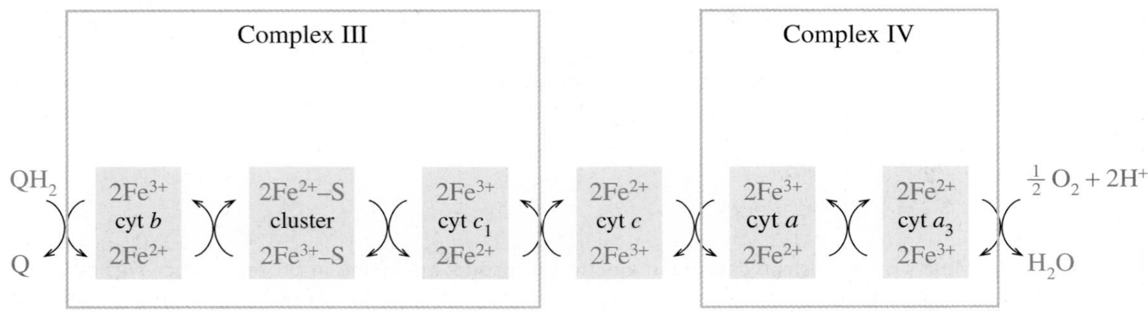


**CONCEPT CHECK 23.4**

### Electron Transport

Identify each of the following as an oxidation or reduction:

**a.** cyt *a*($Fe^{2+}$) $\longrightarrow$ cyt *a*($Fe^{3+}$)
**b.** Q $\longrightarrow$ $QH_2$
**c.** $2H^+ + \frac{1}{2}O_2 \longrightarrow H_2O$

ANSWER

**a.** Oxidation occurs when the iron ion in cyt *a* loses an electron and changes from $Fe^{2+}$ to $Fe^{3+}$.
**b.** Reduction occurs when coenzyme Q combines with two hydrogen atoms.
**c.** Reduction occurs when hydrogen ions and oxygen combine with two electrons to form water:

$$2H^+ + \frac{1}{2}O_2 + 2e^- \longrightarrow H_2O$$

**SAMPLE PROBLEM 23.3**

### Electron Transport

Identify which of the following are mobile carriers:

**a.** cyt *c* **b.** FMN **c.** Fe–S clusters **d.** Q

SOLUTION

**a** and **d,** cyt *c* and Q, are mobile carriers.

STUDY CHECK

What is the final substance that accepts electrons in electron transport?

## HEALTH NOTE

### Toxins: Inhibitors of Electron Transport

Several substances can inhibit the electron carriers in electron transport. Rotenone, a product from a plant root used as an insecticide, blocks electron transport between FMN (complex I) and coenzyme Q. The barbiturates Amytal and Demerol also inhibit FMN. Another inhibitor is the antibiotic antimycin A, which blocks the flow of electrons between cytochrome *b* and cytochrome $c_1$ (complex III). Another group of compounds, including cyanide ($CN^-$) and carbon monoxide, inhibit cytochrome *c* oxidase (complex IV). The toxic nature of these compounds makes it clear that an organism relies heavily on the process of electron transport.

Rotenone

Amytal

Antimycin A

When an inhibitor blocks a step in electron transport, the carriers preceding that step are unable to transfer electrons, remaining in their reduced forms. All the carriers after the blocked step remain oxidized without a source of electrons. Thus, any of these inhibitors can shut down the flow of electrons through electron transport. Consequently, respiration stops, and the cells die.

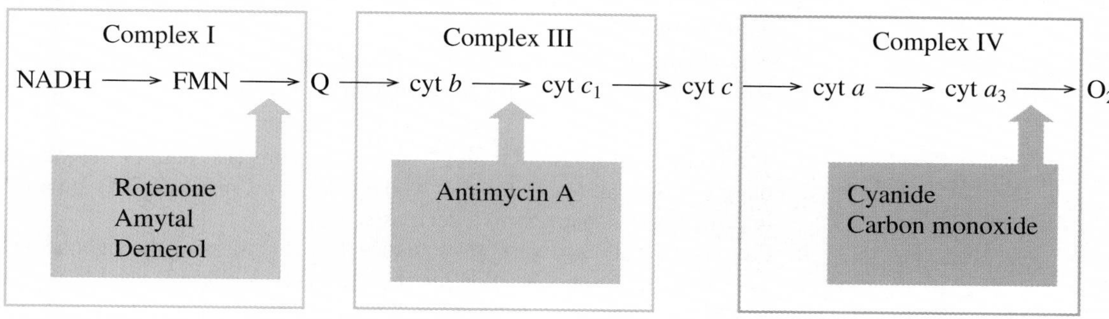


## QUESTIONS AND PROBLEMS

### Electron Transport

**23.25** What reduced coenzymes provide the electrons for electron transport?

**23.26** What happens to the energy level as electrons move through electron transport?

**23.27** Arrange the following in the order in which they appear in electron transport: cytochrome *c*, cytochrome *b*, FAD, and coenzyme Q.

**23.28** Arrange the following in the order in which they appear in electron transport: $O_2$, $NAD^+$, cytochrome $a_3$, and FMN.

**23.29** How are electrons carried from complex I to complex III?

**23.30** How are electrons carried from complex III to complex IV?

**23.31** How is NADH oxidized in electron transport?

**23.32** How is $FADH_2$ oxidized in electron transport?

**23.33** Complete each of the following reactions in electron transport:

**a.** $NADH + H^+ +$ ______ $\longrightarrow$ ______ $+ FMNH_2$

**b.** $QH_2 + 2$ cyt *b* $(Fe^{3+}) \longrightarrow$ ______ $+$ ______ $+ 2H^+$

**23.34** Complete each of the following reactions in electron transport:

**a.** $Q +$ ______ $\longrightarrow$ ______ $+ FAD$

**b.** 2 cyt *a* $(Fe^{3+})$ + 2 cyt $a_3$ $(Fe^{2+}) \longrightarrow$ ______ $+$ ______

## 23.4 Oxidative Phosphorylation and ATP

**LEARNING GOAL**

Describe the process of oxidative phosphorylation in ATP synthesis.

We have seen that energy is generated when electrons from the oxidation of substrates flow through electron transport. Now we will look at how that energy is coupled with the production of ATP in the process called **oxidative phosphorylation**.

### Chemiosmotic Model

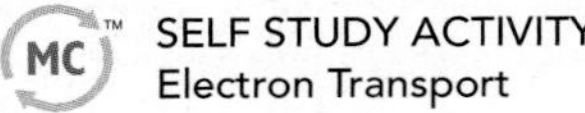


SELF STUDY ACTIVITY
Electron Transport

In 1978, Peter Mitchell received the Nobel Prize in Chemistry for his theory called the **chemiosmotic model**, which links the energy from electron transport to a proton gradient that drives the synthesis of ATP. Three of the complexes (I, III, and IV) extend through the inner mitochondrial membrane, with one end of each complex in the matrix and the other end in the intermembrane space. In the chemiosmotic model, each of these complexes act as a **proton pump** by pushing protons ($H^+$) out of the matrix and into the intermembrane space. This increase in protons in the intermembrane space lowers the pH and creates a proton gradient. Because protons are positively charged, both the lower pH and the electrical charge of the proton gradient produce an electrochemical gradient. (See Figure 23.10.)

To equalize the pH between the intermembrane space and the matrix within a mitochondrion, there is a tendency by the protons to return to the matrix. However, protons cannot diffuse through the inner membrane. The only way protons can return to the matrix is to pass through a protein complex called **ATP synthase**. As the protons flow through ATP synthase, energy generated from the proton gradient is used to drive the ATP synthesis. Thus, the process of oxidative phosphorylation couples the energy from electron transport to the synthesis of ATP from ADP and $P_i$:

$$\text{ADP} + \text{P}_i + \text{energy} \xrightarrow{\text{ATP synthase}} \text{ATP}$$

MC TUTORIAL
The Chemiosmotic Model

**CONCEPT CHECK 23.5**

**Chemiosmotic Model**

Consider the process of proton pumping in the chemiosmotic model.

**a.** What changes in pH take place in the mitochondrial matrix and in the intermembrane space?
**b.** How do the protons return to the matrix to rebalance the pH?
**c.** How is energy obtained for the synthesis of ATP?

ANSWER

**a.** The process of proton pumping "pushes" protons ($H^+$) out of the mitochondrial matrix, which increases the pH. At the same time, protons ($H^+$) are added to the intermembrane space, which decreases its pH.
**b.** Protons return to the matrix to rebalance the pH by passing through the ATP synthase.
**c.** The energy from protons flowing through ATP synthase is used to synthesize ATP.

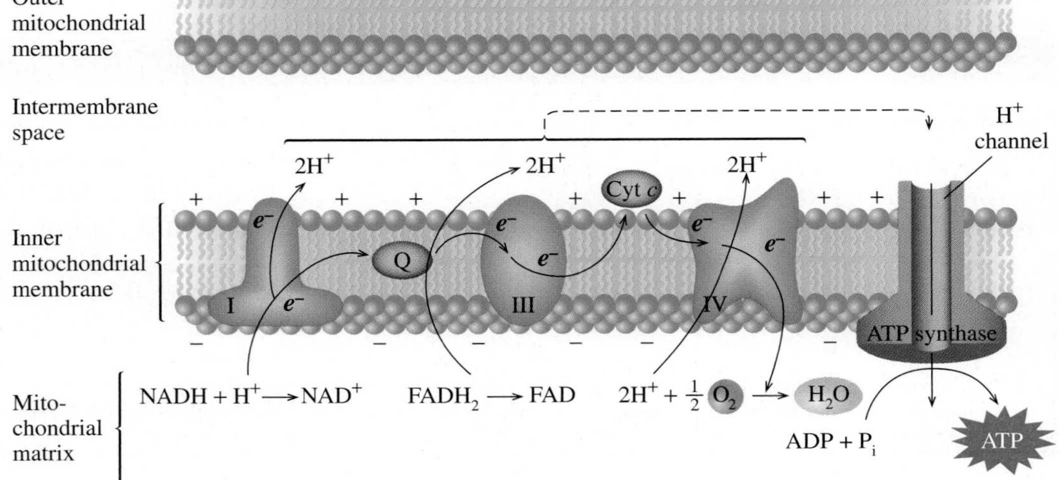


**FIGURE 23.10** In electron transport, protein complexes oxidize and reduce coenzymes to provide electrons and protons that move into the intermembrane space where they create a proton gradient that drives ATP synthesis.

**Q** What is the major source of NADH for electron transport?

## Details of ATP Synthase

ATP synthase consists of two enzyme complexes. (See Figure 23.11.) The $F_0$ complex contains the channel for the return of protons to the matrix. The $F_1$ section consists of a center subunit ($\gamma$) and three surrounding protein subunits, which have three active sites with different shapes or conformations known as loose (L), tight (T), and open (O). As the protons flow through the $F_0$ channel, the energy released turns the center subunit ($\gamma$). We might think of the flow of protons as a stream or river that turns a water wheel. As the center unit supplies energy to the three active sites, their shapes change.

ATP synthesis begins when the substrates ADP and $P_i$ enter a loose (L) active site. As the shape of a loose (L) site converts to a tight (T) shape, ATP is formed. However, the ATP is bound to the active site (T). When energy turns the $\gamma$ unit, the tight site (T) converts to an open (O) site, which has little affinity for ATP, and releases the ATP. The open site converts to an L site and accepts new substrates ADP and $P_i$. According to Paul Boyer, who earned the 1997 Nobel Prize in Chemistry for his work on ATP synthase, the formation of ATP is spontaneous, whereas its release from the synthase requires the energy supplied by the proton gradient. (See Figure 23.12.)

In summary, the energy from protons flowing through $F_0$ turns the center $\gamma$ unit in $F_1$. The shapes of the active sites change from loose (L), where ADP and $P_i$ bind, to tight (T), where ATP forms, and then to open (O), which releases ATP. This process of oxidative phosphorylation continues as long as energy from the electron transport system is generated, which pumps the protons into the intermembrane space and produces the proton gradient to fuel ATP synthase.

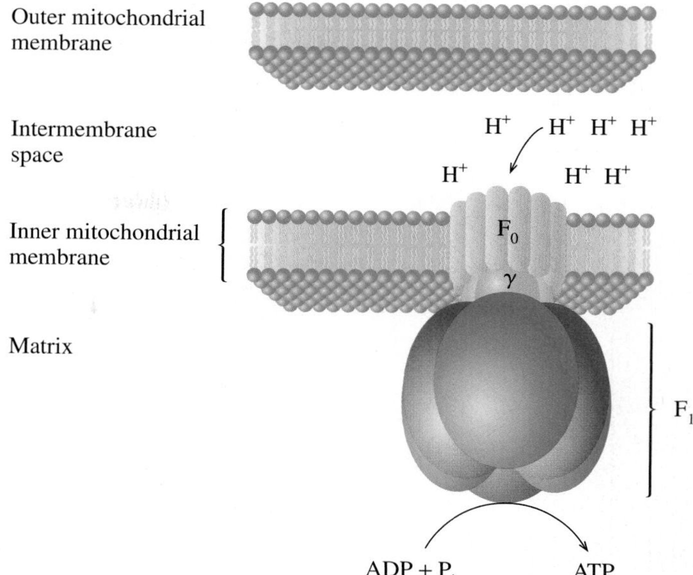


**FIGURE 23.11** ATP synthase consists of two protein complexes. An $F_0$ section contains the channel for proton flow, and an $F_1$ section uses the energy from the proton gradient to drive the synthesis of ATP.

**Q** What are the functions of the $F_0$ and $F_1$ sections of ATP synthase?

## Electron Transport and ATP Synthesis

We have seen that oxidative phosphorylation couples the energy from electron transport with the synthesis of ATP. Because NADH enters electron transport at complex I, energy is released from the oxidation of NADH to synthesize three ATP. However, $FADH_2$ enters at complex II, which is at a lower energy level, where it provides energy for the synthesis of only two ATP. The overall equation for the oxidation of NADH and $FADH_2$ can be written as follows:

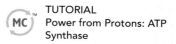

TUTORIAL
Power from Protons: ATP Synthase

$$\boxed{\textbf{NADH + H}^+} + \tfrac{1}{2}O_2 + 3\text{ ADP} + 3P_i \longrightarrow NAD^+ + H_2O + \boxed{\textbf{3 ATP}}$$

$$\boxed{\textbf{FADH}_2} + \tfrac{1}{2}O_2 + 2\text{ ADP} + 2P_i \longrightarrow FAD + H_2O + \boxed{\textbf{2 ATP}}$$

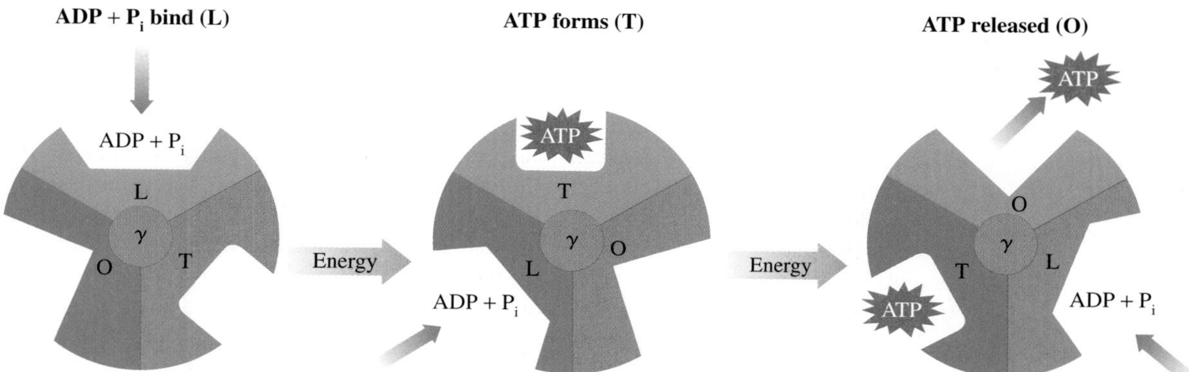


**FIGURE 23.12** In the $F_1$ ATP synthase, ATP is formed when loose (L) active site containing ADP and $P_i$ converts to a tight (T) site. When energy from the proton flow in $F_0$ changes the site to an open (O) site, ATP is released.

**Q** What shape of an active site in $F_1$ ATP synthase accepts the substrates, and which shape releases the ATP?

## Regulation of Electron Transport and Oxidative Phosphorylation

Electron transport is regulated by the availability of ADP, $P_i$, oxygen ($O_2$), and NADH. Low levels of any of these compounds will decrease the activity of electron transport and the formation of ATP. When a cell is active and ATP is consumed rapidly, the elevated levels of ADP will activate the synthesis of ATP. Therefore, the activity of electron transport is strongly dependent on the levels of ADP for ATP synthesis.

SAMPLE PROBLEM 23.4

**ATP Synthesis**

How much ATP is formed by the oxidation of NADH and $FADH_2$ in electron transport?

SOLUTION

Electrons from the oxidation of NADH enter electron transport at a higher energy level than $FADH_2$. The oxidation of NADH provides energy to form three ATP, whereas the oxidation $FADH_2$ provides energy for two ATP.

STUDY CHECK

What complexes on the inner mitochondrial membrane act as proton pumps?

## QUESTIONS AND PROBLEMS

### Oxidative Phosphorylation and ATP

23.35 What is meant by oxidative phosphorylation?

**23.36** How is the proton gradient established?

23.37 According to the chemiosmotic theory, how does the proton gradient provide energy to synthesize ATP?

**23.38** How does the phosphorylation of ADP occur?

23.39 How are glycolysis and the citric acid cycle linked to the production of ATP by electron transport?

**23.40** Why does $FADH_2$ have a yield of two ATP via electron transport, whereas NADH yields three ATP?

23.41 What are the parts of ATP synthase?

**23.42** What is the role of each part of ATP synthase in ATP synthesis?

23.43 What type of active site in ATP synthase binds ADP and $P_i$?

**23.44** How is the ATP released from ATP synthase?

# 23.5 ATP Energy from Glucose

LEARNING GOAL

Account for the ATP produced by the complete oxidation of glucose.

MC™ TUTORIAL
ATP Energy from Glucose

Under aerobic conditions, glycolysis, the citric acid cycle, and electron transport produce ATP from NADH and $FADH_2$. Let's see how much ATP is associated with each of these metabolic cycles.

## ATP from Glycolysis

In glycolysis, the oxidation of glucose stores energy in two NADH molecules as well as two ATP molecules from direct substrate phosphorylation. However, glycolysis occurs in the cytoplasm, and the NADH produced cannot pass through the mitochondrial membrane.

Therefore, the hydrogen ions and electrons from NADH in the cytoplasm are transferred to compounds that can enter the mitochondria. In this shuttle system, dihydroxyacetone phosphate, a compound in glycolysis, is reduced to glycerol-3-phosphate, and $NAD^+$ is regenerated. After glycerol-3-phosphate crosses the mitochondrial membrane, the hydrogen ions and electrons are transferred to FAD. $FADH_2$ is produced along with glycerol-3-phosphate, which returns to the cytoplasm. The overall reaction for the glycerol-3-phosphate shuttle is

$$\underset{\text{In cytoplasm}}{NADH + H^+} + FAD \longrightarrow NAD^+ + \underset{\text{In mitochondria}}{FADH_2}$$

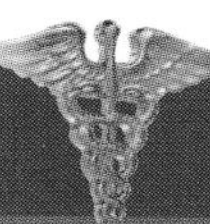

## HEALTH NOTE

### ATP Synthase and Heating the Body

Some types of compounds called *uncouplers* separate the electron transport system from the ATP synthase. They do this by disrupting the proton gradient needed for the synthesis of ATP. The electrons are transported to $O_2$ in electron transport, but ATP is not formed by ATP synthase.

Some uncouplers transport the protons through the inner mitochondrial membrane, which is normally impermeable to protons; others block the channel in the $F_0$ portion of ATP synthase. Compounds such as dicumarol and 2,4-dinitrophenol (DNP) are hydrophobic and bind with protons that carry them across the inner membrane. An antibiotic, oligomycin, binds to the $F_0$ complex and blocks the channel, which does not allow any protons to return to the matrix. By removing protons or blocking the $F_0$ channel, there is no proton flow through the $F_0$ channel to generate energy for ATP synthesis.

Dicumarol

2,4-Dinitrophenol (DNP)

When there is no mechanism for ATP synthesis, the energy of electron transport is released as heat. Certain animals that are adapted to cold climates have developed their own uncoupling system, which allows them to use electron transport energy for heat production. These animals have large amounts of a tissue called *brown fat*, which contains a high concentration of mitochondria. This tissue is brown because of the color of iron in the cytochromes of the mitochondria. The proton pumps still operate in brown tissue, but a protein embedded in the inner membrane allows the protons to bypass ATP synthase. The energy that would be used to synthesize ATP is released as heat. In newborn babies, brown fat is used to generate heat, because newborns have not stored much fat. The brown fat deposits are located near major blood vessels, which carry the warmed blood throughout the body. Infants have a small mass but a large surface area, and they need to produce more heat than do adults. Most adults have little or no brown fat, although someone who works outdoors in a cold climate will develop some brown fat deposits.

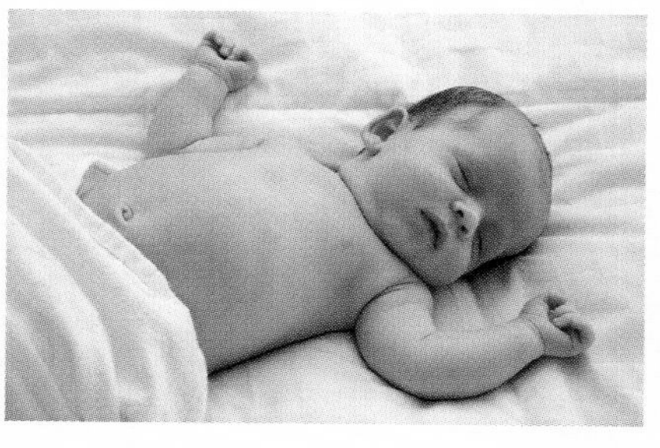

Plants also use uncouplers. Some plants use uncoupling agents to volatize fragrant compounds that attract insects to pollinate the plants. Skunk cabbage uses this system. In other plants, heat is used to warm early shoots of plants under the snow, which helps them melt the snow around the plants.

Therefore, the transfer of electrons from NADH in the cytoplasm to $FADH_2$ produces only two ATP, rather than three. In glycolysis, glucose yields six ATP: four ATP from two NADH, and two ATP from direct phosphorylation:

$$\text{Glucose} \longrightarrow 2\text{ pyruvate} + 2\text{ ATP} + 2\text{ NADH} (\longrightarrow 2\text{ FADH}_2)$$

$$\text{Glucose} \longrightarrow 2\text{ pyruvate} + 6\text{ ATP}$$

## ATP from the Oxidation of Two Pyruvate

Under aerobic conditions, pyruvate enters the mitochondria, where it is oxidized to give acetyl CoA, $CO_2$, and NADH. Because glucose yields two pyruvate, two NADH enter electron transport. The oxidation of two pyruvate leads to the production of six ATP molecules:

$$2\text{ Pyruvate} \longrightarrow 2\text{ acetyl CoA} + 6\text{ ATP}$$

## ATP from the Citric Acid Cycle

One turn of the citric acid cycle produces two $CO_2$, three NADH, one $FADH_2$, and one ATP by direct substrate phosphorylation. When the NADH and $FADH_2$ enter electron transport, three NADH produce nine ATP molecules, and one $FADH_2$ produces two more ATP. Thus, one turn of the citric acid cycle generates energy for the synthesis of a total of 12 ATP molecules:

$$\begin{aligned} 3\text{ NADH} \times 3\text{ ATP} &= 9\text{ ATP} \\ 1\text{ FADH}_2 \times 2\text{ ATP} &= 2\text{ ATP} \\ 1\text{ GTP} \times 1\text{ ATP} &= 1\text{ ATP} \\ \hline \text{Total (one turn)} &= 12\text{ ATP} \end{aligned}$$

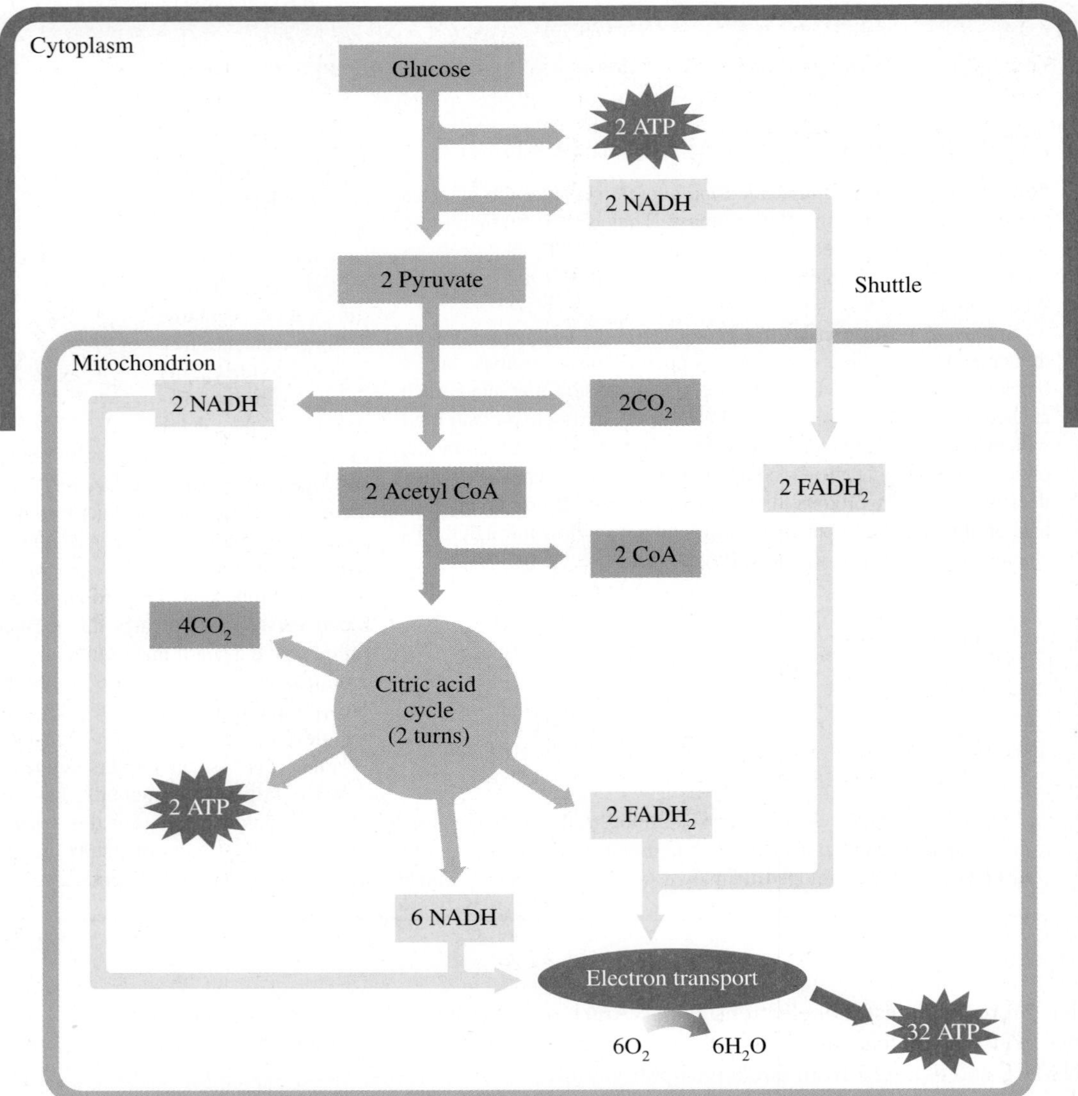


**FIGURE 23.13** The complete oxidation of glucose to $CO_2$ and $H_2O$ yields 36 ATP.

**Q** What metabolic pathway produces most of the ATP from the oxidation of glucose?

Because one glucose produces two acetyl CoA molecules, two turns of the citric acid cycle produces 24 ATP.

$$\text{Acetyl CoA} \longrightarrow 2CO_2 + 12\ \text{ATP (one turn of citric acid cycle)}$$

$$2\ \text{Acetyl CoA} \longrightarrow 4CO_2 + 24\ \text{ATP (two turns of citric acid cycle)}$$

## ATP from the Complete Oxidation of Glucose

The total ATP production for the complete oxidation of glucose is calculated by combining the ATP produced from glycolysis plus the oxidation of pyruvate plus the citric acid cycle. (See Figure 23.13.) The ATP produced for these reactions is given in Table 23.1.

**CONCEPT CHECK 23.6**

### ATP Production from Glucose

How many turns of the citric acid cycle are needed by the intermediate products formed by glucose in glycolysis under aerobic conditions?

ANSWER

When glucose with six carbons is degraded in glycolysis, two pyruvate (3C) are produced. The decarboxylation of two pyruvate gives two acetyl CoA (2C) that enter the citric acid cycle under aerobic conditions. In one turn of the citric acid cycle, two carbon atoms from the acetyl group are oxidized to two $CO_2$. For two acetyl groups from two acetyl CoA molecules, two turns of the citric acid cycle are needed.

**TABLE 23.1** ATP Produced by the Complete Oxidation of Glucose

| Reaction | ATP for 1 Glucose |
|---|---|
| **ATP from Glycolysis** | |
| Activation of glucose | −2 ATP |
| Oxidation of glyceraldehyde-3-phosphate (2 NADH) | 6 ATP |
| Conversion of 2 NADH $\longrightarrow$ 2 $FADH_2$ | −2 ATP |
| Direct ADP phosphorylation (two triose phosphate) | 4 ATP |
| Summary: $\underset{\text{Glucose}}{C_6H_{12}O_6} \longrightarrow 2\,\text{pyruvate} + 2H_2O$ | 6 ATP |
| **ATP from Pyruvate** | |
| 2 Pyruvate $\longrightarrow$ 2 acetyl CoA (2 NADH) | 6 ATP |
| **ATP from Citric Acid Cycle** | |
| Oxidation of 2 isocitrate (2 NADH) | 6 ATP |
| Oxidation of 2 $\alpha$-ketoglutarate (2 NADH) | 6 ATP |
| 2 Direct substrate phosphorylations (2 GTP) | 2 ATP |
| Oxidation of 2 succinate (2 $FADH_2$) | 4 ATP |
| Oxidation of 2 malate (2 NADH) | 6 ATP |
| Summary: 2 acetyl CoA $\longrightarrow 4CO_2 + 2H_2O$ | 24 ATP |
| **Overall ATP Production for 1 Glucose** | |
| $\underset{\text{Glucose}}{C_6H_{12}O_6} + 6O_2 + 36\,\text{ADP} + 36\,P_i \longrightarrow 6CO_2 + 6H_2O + 36\,\text{ATP}$ | |

SAMPLE PROBLEM 23.5

### ATP Production

Indicate the amount of ATP produced by each of the following oxidation reactions:

**a.** pyruvate to acetyl CoA **b.** glucose to acetyl CoA

SOLUTION

**a.** The oxidation of pyruvate to acetyl CoA produces one NADH, which yields three ATP.
**b.** Six ATP are produced from the oxidation of glucose to two pyruvate molecules. Six more ATP result from the oxidation of two pyruvate molecules to two acetyl CoA molecules. Thus, a total of twelve ATP are produced when glucose is oxidized to yield two acetyl CoA.

STUDY CHECK

What are the sources of ATP in the citric acid cycle?

When the cells do not immediately use glucose for energy, it is stored as glycogen in the liver and muscles. When the levels of glucose in the brain or blood become low, the glycogen reserves are hydrolyzed, and glucose is released into the blood. If glycogen stores are depleted, some glucose can be synthesized from noncarbohydrate sources. The balance of all these reactions maintains the necessary blood glucose level available to our cells and provides the necessary amount of ATP for our energy needs. (See Figure 23.14.)

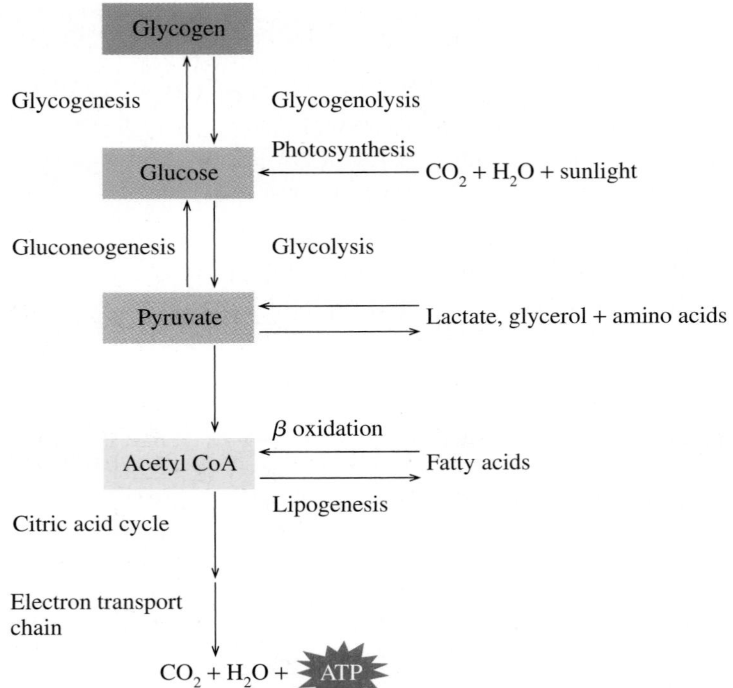


**FIGURE 23.14** The ATP level is maintained by metabolic pathways that increase or decrease the glucose according to the energy requirements in the cell.

**Q** What metabolic pathways do low ATP levels stimulate?

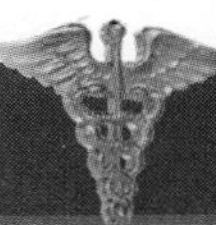

## HEALTH NOTE

### Efficiency of ATP Production

In a laboratory, a calorimeter is used to measure the heat energy from the combustion of glucose. In a calorimeter, 1 mole of glucose produces 680 kcal:

$$C_6H_{12}O_6 + 6O_2 \longrightarrow 6CO_2 + 6H_2O + 680 \text{ kcal/mole}$$

Let's compare the amount of energy produced from 1 mole of glucose in a calorimeter with the ATP energy produced in the mitochondria. We can use the energy of the hydrolysis of ATP, which is 7.3 kcal/mole of ATP. Because 1 mole of glucose generates energy for 36 moles of ATP, the total energy from the oxidation of 1 mole of glucose in the cells would be 260 kcal/mole:

$$\frac{36 \text{ } \cancel{\text{moles ATP}}}{1 \text{ mole glucose}} \times \frac{7.3 \text{ kcal (31 kJ)}}{1 \text{ } \cancel{\text{mole ATP}}} = 260 \text{ kcal per 1 mole of glucose}$$

Compared to the energy produced by burning glucose in a calorimeter, our cells are about 38% efficient in converting the total available chemical energy in glucose to ATP:

$$\frac{260 \text{ kcal (cells)}}{680 \text{ kcal (calorimeter)}} \times 100\% = 38\%$$

The rest of the energy from glucose produced during the oxidation of glucose in our cells is lost as heat.

| Calorimeter | Cells |
|---|---|
| Energy produced by 1 mole of glucose (680 kcal) | Stored as ATP (260 kcal) |
| | Lost as heat (420 kcal) |

## QUESTIONS AND PROBLEMS

### ATP Energy from Glucose

23.45 Why does the NADH produced in glycolysis yield only two ATP?

**23.46** Under aerobic conditions, what is the maximum number of ATP molecules that can be produced from one glucose molecule?

23.47 What is the energy yield in ATP molecules associated with each of the following?

**a.** NADH $\longrightarrow$ $NAD^+$

**b.** glucose $\longrightarrow$ 2 pyruvate

**c.** 2 pyruvate $\longrightarrow$ 2 acetyl CoA + $2CO_2$

**23.48** What is the energy yield in ATP molecules associated with each of the following?

**a.** $FADH_2 \longrightarrow FAD$

**b.** glucose + $6O_2 \longrightarrow 6CO_2 + 6H_2O$

**c.** acetyl CoA $\longrightarrow$ $2CO_2$

## CONCEPT MAP

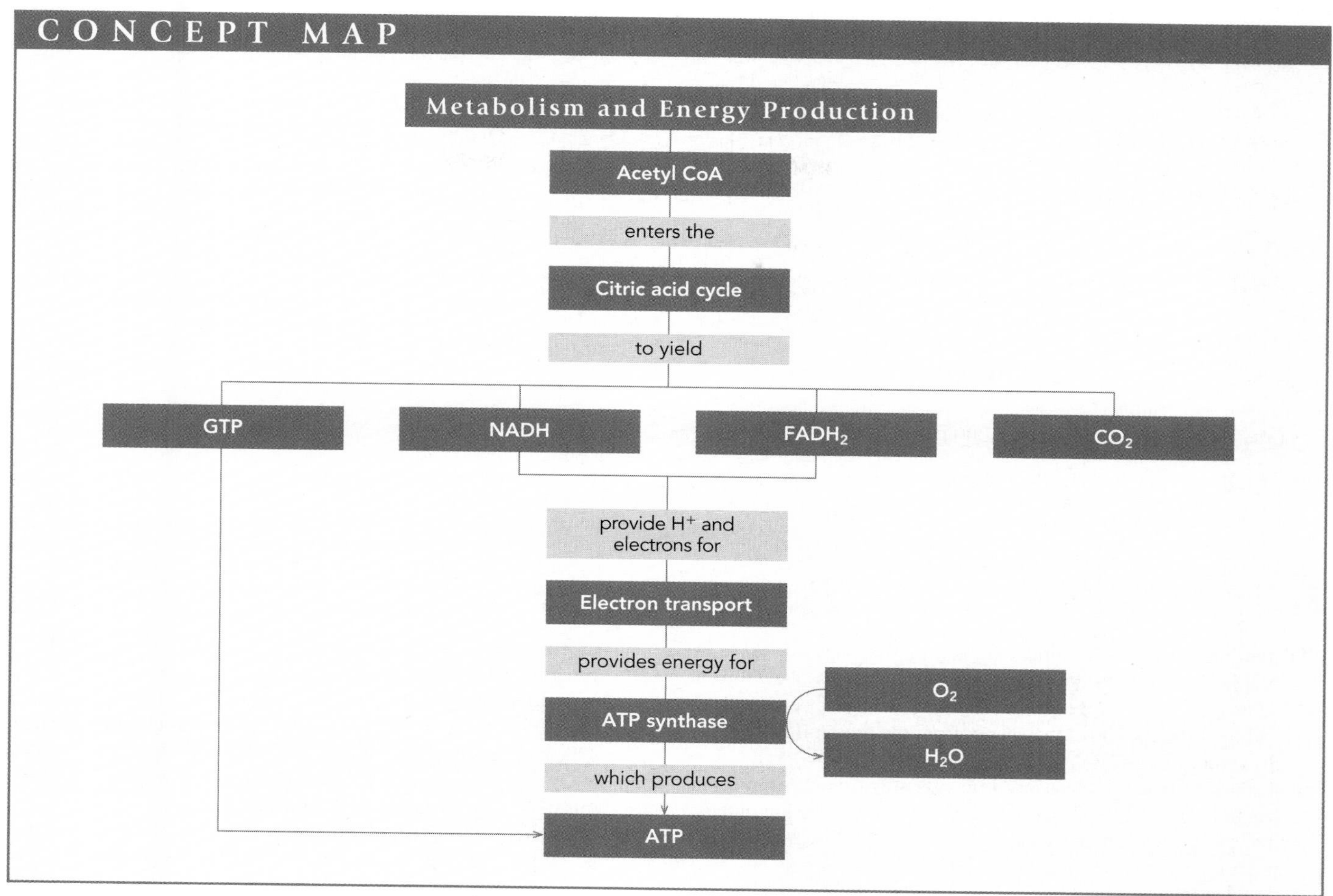


## CHAPTER REVIEW

### 23.1 The Citric Acid Cycle

**LEARNING GOAL:** *Describe the oxidation of acetyl CoA in the citric acid cycle.*

In a sequence of reactions called the citric acid cycle, an acetyl group is combined with oxaloacetate to yield citrate. Citrate undergoes oxidation and decarboxylation to yield two $CO_2$, GTP, three NADH, and $FADH_2$ with the regeneration of oxaloacetate. The direct phosphorylation of ADP by GTP yields ATP.

### 23.2 Electron Carriers

**LEARNING GOAL:** *Describe the electron carriers involved in electron transport.*

Electron carriers that transfer hydrogen ions and electrons include FMN, iron–sulfur clusters, coenzyme Q, and several cytochromes. Both iron–sulfur clusters and cytochromes contain iron ions that are reduced to $Fe^{2+}$ and reoxidized to $Fe^{3+}$ as electrons are accepted and then passed to the next electron carrier.

### 23.3 Electron Transport

**LEARNING GOAL:** *Describe the role of the electron carriers in electron transport.*

The reduced coenzymes NADH and $FADH_2$ from various metabolic pathways are oxidized to $NAD^+$ and FAD when their protons and electrons are transferred to the electron transport system. The final acceptor, $O_2$, combines with protons and electrons to yield $H_2O$. The energy decrease provides the necessary energy for ATP synthesis.

### 23.4 Oxidative Phosphorylation and ATP

**LEARNING GOAL:** *Describe the process of oxidative phosphorylation in ATP synthesis.*

The protein complexes in electron transport act as proton pumps to move protons into the intermembrane space, which produces a proton gradient. As the protons return to the matrix by way of ATP synthase, energy is generated. This energy is used to drive the synthesis of ATP in a process known as oxidative phosphorylation. The available ADP and ATP levels in the cells control the activity of electron transport.

### 23.5 ATP Energy from Glucose

**LEARNING GOAL:** *Account for the ATP produced by the complete oxidation of glucose.*

With the exception of the NADH produced from glycolysis, the oxidation of NADH yields three ATP molecules, and $FADH_2$ yields two ATP. The energy from the NADH produced in the cytoplasm is used to form $FADH_2$. Under aerobic conditions, the complete oxidation of glucose yields a total of 36 ATP from the oxidation of the reduced coenzymes NADH and $FADH_2$ by electron transport, oxidative phosphorylation, and from some direct substrate phosphorylation.

## SUMMARY OF KEY REACTIONS

### CITRIC ACID CYCLE

$$\text{Acetyl CoA} + 3\text{NAD}^+ + \text{FAD} + \text{GDP} + \text{P}_i + 2\text{H}_2\text{O} \longrightarrow 2\text{CO}_2 + 3\ \text{NADH} + 3\text{H}^+ + \text{FADH}_2 + \text{HS—CoA} + \text{GTP}$$

### ELECTRON TRANSPORT

$$\text{NADH} + \text{H}^+ + 3\text{ADP} + 3\ \text{P}_i + \tfrac{1}{2}\text{O}_2 \longrightarrow \text{NAD}^+ + 3\ \text{ATP} + \text{H}_2\text{O}$$

$$\text{FADH}_2 + 2\ \text{ADP} + 2\ \text{P}_i + \tfrac{1}{2}\text{O}_2 \longrightarrow \text{FAD} + 2\ \text{ATP} + \text{H}_2\text{O}$$

### PHOSPHORYLATION OF ADP

$$\text{ADP} + \text{P}_i \longrightarrow \text{ATP} + \text{H}_2\text{O}$$

### COMPLETE OXIDATION OF GLUCOSE

$$\text{C}_6\text{H}_{12}\text{O}_6 + 6\text{O}_2 + 36\ \text{ADP} + 36\text{P}_i \longrightarrow 6\text{CO}_2 + 6\text{H}_2\text{O} + 36\ \text{ATP}$$

## KEY TERMS

**ATP synthase** An enzyme complex that links the energy released by protons returning to the matrix with the synthesis of ATP from ADP and $P_i$. The $F_0$ section contains the channel for proton flow, and the $F_1$ section uses the energy from the proton flow to drive the synthesis of ATP.

**chemiosmotic model** The conservation of energy from the transfer of electrons in electron transport that results from pumping protons into the intermembrane space to produce a proton gradient that provides the energy to synthesize ATP.

**citric acid cycle** A series of oxidation reactions in the mitochondria that converts acetyl CoA to $CO_2$ and yields NADH and $FADH_2$. It is also called the tricarboxylic acid cycle or the Krebs cycle.

**coenzyme Q (CoQ, Q)** A mobile carrier that transfers electrons from NADH and $FADH_2$ to cytochrome *b* in complex III.

**cytochromes (cyt)** Iron-containing proteins that transfer electrons from $QH_2$ to oxygen.

**decarboxylation** A reaction in which a $CO_2$ molecule is produced.

**electron carriers** A group of proteins that accept and pass on electrons as they are reduced and oxidized. Most of the carriers are tightly attached to the inner mitochondrial membrane, but two are mobile carriers, which move electrons between the complexes containing the other carriers.

**electron transport** A series of reactions in the mitochondria that transfer electrons from NADH and $FADH_2$ to electron carriers, which are arranged from higher to lower energy levels, and finally to $O_2$, which produces $H_2O$. Energy changes during three of these transfers provide energy for ATP synthesis.

**Fe–S (iron–sulfur) clusters** Proteins containing iron and sulfur in which the iron ions accept electrons from $FMNH_2$ and cytochrome *b*.

**FMN (flavin mononucleotide)** An electron carrier derived from riboflavin (vitamin $B_2$) that transfers hydrogen ions and electrons from NADH entering electron transport.

**oxidative phosphorylation** The synthesis of ATP from ADP and $P_i$ using energy generated by the oxidation reactions in electron transport.

**proton pumps** The enzyme complexes I, III, and IV that move protons from the matrix into the intermembrane space, creating a proton gradient.

## UNDERSTANDING THE CONCEPTS

**23.49** Identify each of the following as a substance that is part of the citric acid cycle, electron transport, or both:

**a.** succinate **b.** $QH_2$
**c.** FAD **d.** cyt *c* ($Fe^{2+}$)
**e.** cytochrome *c* oxidase **f.** $H_2O$
**g.** malate **h.** $NAD^+$

**23.50** Complete the names of the missing compounds in the citric acid cycle:

citrate ⟶ ________ ⟶ ________ ⟶
succinyl CoA ⟶ ________ ⟶ ________ ⟶
malate ⟶ ________

**23.51** Arrange the following components of electron transport in order of appearance:

**a.** cyt $a_3$ **b.** $O_2$ **c.** cyt *a*
**d.** cyt *c* **e.** $QH_2$ **f.** $FMNH_2$
**g.** cyt $c_1$ **h.** cyt *b*

**23.52** Identify the reactant and product for each of the following enzymes in the citric acid cycle:

**a.** aconitase **b.** succinate dehydrogenase
**c.** fumarase **d.** isocitrate dehydrogenase
**e.** succinyl CoA synthetase **f.** malate dehydrogenase

**23.53** For each of the given enzymes (**a** to **f**), indicate which of the following are needed: $NAD^+$, $H_2O$, FAD, GDP.

**a.** aconitase **b.** succinate dehydrogenase
**c.** fumarase **d.** isocitrate dehydrogenase
**e.** succinyl CoA synthetase **f.** malate dehydrogenase

**23.54** Identify the type of reaction(s)—(1) oxidation, (2) decarboxylation, (3) hydrolysis, (4) hydration—catalyzed by each of the following enzymes (**a** to **f**):

**a.** aconitase **b.** succinate dehydrogenase
**c.** fumarase **d.** isocitrate dehydrogenase
**e.** $\alpha$-ketoglutarate dehydrogenase **f.** malate dehydrogenase

# ADDITIONAL QUESTIONS AND PROBLEMS

*For instructor-assigned homework, go to* **www.masteringchemistry.com**.

23.55 What is the main function of the citric acid cycle in energy production?

**23.56** Most metabolic pathways are not considered cycles. Why is the citric acid cycle considered a metabolic cycle?

23.57 If there are no reactions in the citric acid cycle that use oxygen, $O_2$, why does the cycle operate only in aerobic conditions?

**23.58** What products of the citric acid cycle are needed for electron transport?

23.59 Identify the compounds in the citric acid cycle that have the following:
**a.** six carbon atoms
**b.** five carbon atoms
**c.** a keto group

**23.60** Identify the compounds in the citric acid cycle that have the following:
**a.** four carbon atoms
**b.** a hydroxyl group
**c.** a double bond

23.61 In which reaction of the citric acid cycle does each of the following occur?
**a.** A five-carbon keto acid is decarboxylated.
**b.** A double bond is hydrated.
**c.** $NAD^+$ is reduced.
**d.** A secondary hydroxyl group is oxidized.

**23.62** In which reaction of the citric acid cycle does each of the following occur?
**a.** FAD is reduced.
**b.** A six-carbon keto acid is decarboxylated.
**c.** A carbon–carbon double bond is formed.
**d.** GDP undergoes direct phosphorylation.

23.63 Indicate the coenzyme(s) for each of the following reactions:
**a.** isocitrate $\longrightarrow$ $\alpha$-ketoglutarate
**b.** $\alpha$-ketoglutarate $\longrightarrow$ succinyl CoA

**23.64** Indicate the coenzyme(s) for each of the following reactions:
**a.** succinate $\longrightarrow$ fumarate
**b.** malate $\longrightarrow$ oxaloacetate

23.65 How does each of the following regulate the citric acid cycle?
**a.** high levels of NADH **b.** high levels of ATP

**23.66** How does each of the following regulate the citric acid cycle?
**a.** high levels of ADP **b.** low levels of NADH

23.67 Identify each of the following as part of the structure of one of the components in electron transport as (1) FMN, (2) Fe–S cluster, (3) CoQ, or (4) cytochrome:
**a.** a heme group **b.** a ribitol group

**23.68** Identify each of the following as part of the structure of one of the components in electron transport as (1) FMN, (2) Fe–S cluster, (3) CoQ, or (4) cytochrome:
**a.** contains the three-ring system of flavins
**b.** a six-atom ring attached to a long-carbon chain

23.69 Identify each of the following electron carriers as part of a complex or as a mobile carrier. If part of a complex, indicate which one.
**a.** CoQ **b.** Fe–S clusters **c.** cyt $a_3$

**23.70** Identify each of the following electron carriers as part of a complex or as a mobile carrier. If part of a complex, indicate which one.
**a.** cyt *b* **b.** cyt *c* **c.** FMN

23.71 Identify the complex where each of the following reactions take place. Complete the equations.
**a.** $FADH_2 + Q \longrightarrow$
**b.** cyt *a* $(Fe^{2+})$ + cyt $a_3$ $(Fe^{3+}) \longrightarrow$

**23.72** Identify the complex where each of the following are oxidized or reduced. Complete the equations.
**a.** cyt *c* $(Fe^{2+})$ + cyt *a* $(Fe^{3+}) \longrightarrow$
**b.** $NADH + H^+ \longrightarrow$

23.73 Complete the following by adding the substances that are missing:

**a.**
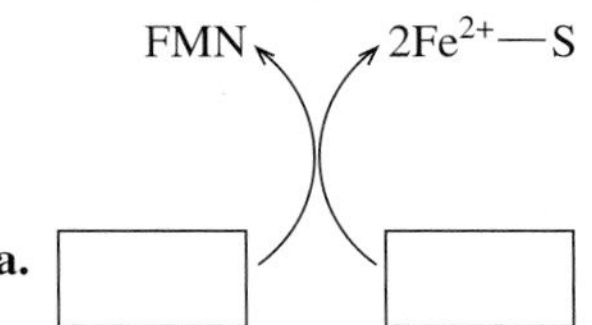


**b.**
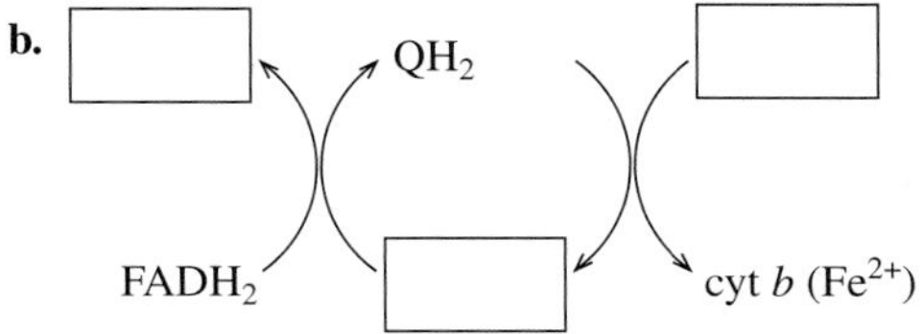


**23.74** Complete the following by adding the substances that are missing:

**a.**
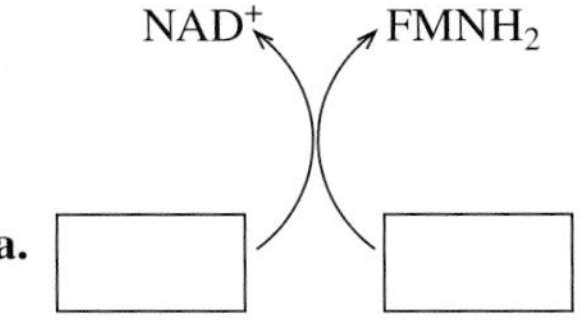


**b.**
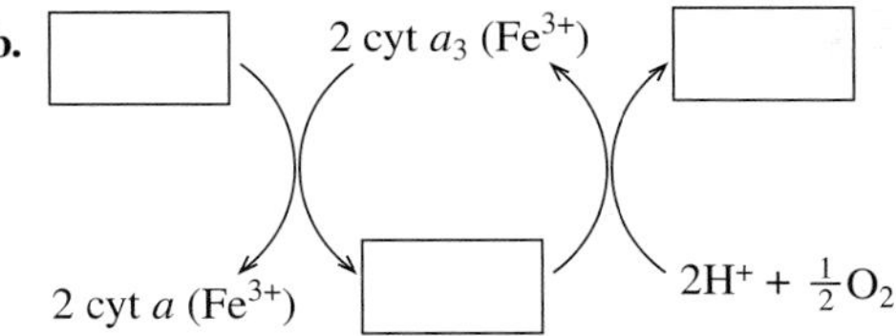


23.75 At which parts of the electron transport system are protons pumped into the intermembrane space?

**23.76** What is the effect of proton accumulation in the intermembrane space?

23.77 In the chemiosmotic model, how is energy provided to synthesize ATP?

**23.78** In what part of electron transport does the synthesis of ATP take place?

23.79 Why do protons tend to leave the intermembrane space and return to the matrix within a mitochondrion?

**23.80** Why do the enzyme complexes that pump protons extend across the mitochondrial membrane from the matrix to the intermembrane space?

23.81 How many ATP molecules are produced by energy generated when electrons flow from $FADH_2$ to oxygen $(O_2)$?

**23.82** How many ATP molecules are produced by energy generated when electrons flow from NADH to oxygen $(O_2)$?

23.83 What part of electron transport is inhibited by each of the following?
**a.** Amytal and rotenone
**b.** antimycin A
**c.** cyanide and carbon monoxide

**23.84** **a.** When an inhibitor blocks electron transport, how are the coenzymes that precede the blocked site affected?
**b.** When an inhibitor blocks electron transport, how are the coenzymes that follow the blocked site affected?

23.85 How many ATP are produced when glucose is oxidized to pyruvate compared to when glucose is oxidized to $CO_2$ and $H_2O$?

**23.86** Why do the two NADH produced in glycolysis provide a net of two ATP and not three?

23.87 Where is ATP synthase for oxidative phosphorylation located in the cell?

**23.88** Considering the efficiency of ATP synthesis, how many kcal of energy would be conserved from the complete oxidation of 4.0 moles of glucose?

23.89 How is the energy from the proton gradient utilized by ATP synthase?

**23.90** In electron transport, would the solution in the space between the outer and inner mitochondrial membrane be more or less acidic than the solution in the matrix?

23.91 Why would a bear that is hibernating have more brown fat than one that is active?

**23.92** How do the active sites on $F_1$ ATP synthase change during ATP production?

# CHALLENGE QUESTIONS

23.93 Using the value 7.3 kcal/mole for ATP, how many kcal are conserved as ATP from 1 mole of glucose in each of the following?
**a.** glycolysis
**b.** oxidation of pyruvate to acetyl CoA
**c.** citric acid cycle
**d.** complete oxidation of glucose to $CO_2$ and $H_2O$

**23.94** What percentage of ATP energy is conserved from 1 mole of glucose in problem 23.93 **a.–d.**

23.95 What does it mean to say that the cell is 38% efficient in storing the energy from the complete combustion of glucose?

**23.96** A student is considering using 2,4-dinitrophenol, which is an uncoupler, to lose weight. Explain how the uncoupler will affect the body temperature of the student. How would you advise the student if the dosage of DNP needed to lose weight is close to toxic levels?

23.97 If acetyl CoA has a molar mass of 809 g/mole, how many moles of ATP are produced when 1.0 $\mu$g of acetyl CoA completes the citric acid cycle?

# ANSWERS

## ANSWERS TO STUDY CHECKS

**23.1** oxaloacetate

**23.2** a. oxidation b. reduction

**23.3** Oxygen ($O_2$) is the last substance that accepts electrons.

**23.4** The protein complexes I, III, and IV pump protons from the matrix to the intermembrane space.

**23.5** Three NADH provide nine ATP, one $FADH_2$ provides two ATP, and one direct phosphorylation provides one ATP.

## ANSWERS TO SELECTED QUESTIONS AND PROBLEMS

**23.1** Krebs cycle and tricarboxylic acid cycle

**23.3** $2CO_2$, 3 NADH + $3H^+$, $FADH_2$, GTP (ATP), and HS—CoA.

**23.5** Two reactions, reactions 3 and 4, involve oxidative decarboxylation.

**23.7** $NAD^+$ is reduced in reactions 3, 4, and 8 of the citric acid cycle.

**23.9** In reaction 5, GDP undergoes a direct substrate phosphorylation.

**23.11** **a.** citrate and isocitrate
**b.** A carbon atom is lost as $CO_2$ in decarboxylation.
**c.** $\alpha$-ketoglutarate
**d.** isocitrate $\longrightarrow$ $\alpha$-ketoglutarate; $\alpha$-ketoglutarate $\longrightarrow$ succinyl CoA; succinate $\longrightarrow$ fumarate; malate $\longrightarrow$ oxaloacetate
**e.** reactions 3, 8

**23.13** **a.** citrate synthase
**b.** succinate dehydrogenase and aconitase
**c.** fumarase

**23.15** **a.** $NAD^+$ **b.** GDP

**23.17** Isocitrate dehydrogenase and $\alpha$-ketoglutarate dehydrogenase are allosteric enzymes.

**23.19** High levels of ADP increase the rate of the citric acid cycle.

**23.21** oxidized

**23.23** **a.** oxidation **b.** reduction

**23.25** NADH and $FADH_2$

**23.27** FAD, coenzyme Q, cytochrome *b*, cytochrome *c*

**23.29** The mobile carrier Q transfers electrons from complex I to complex III.

**23.31** NADH transfers electrons to FMN in complex I to give $NAD^+$.

**23.33** **a.** $NADH + H^+ + FMN \longrightarrow NAD^+ + FMNH_2$
**b.** $QH_2 + 2\ \text{cyt}\ b\ (Fe^{3+}) \longrightarrow Q + 2\ \text{cyt}\ b\ (Fe^{2+}) + 2H^+$

**23.35** In oxidative phosphorylation, the energy from the oxidation reactions in electron transport is used to drive ATP synthesis.

**23.37** As protons return to the lower energy environment in the matrix, they pass through ATP synthase where they release energy to drive the synthesis of ATP.

**23.39** The oxidation of the reduced coenzymes NADH and $FADH_2$ by electron transport generates energy to drive the synthesis of ATP.

**23.41** ATP synthase consists of two protein complexes, $F_0$ and $F_1$.

**23.43** The loose (L) site in ATP synthase binds ADP and $P_i$.

**23.45** Glycolysis takes place in the cytoplasm, not in the mitochondria. Because NADH cannot cross the mitochondrial membrane, the hydrogen ions and electrons from NADH are used to form glycerol-3-phosphate, which crosses the mitochondrial membrane. Then the hydrogen ions and electrons are transferred to FAD to form $FADH_2$. The resulting $FADH_2$ produces only two ATP for each NADH produced in glycolysis.

**23.47** **a.** 3 ATP **b.** 6 ATP **c.** 6 ATP

**23.49** **a.** citric acid cycle **b.** electron transport
**c.** both **d.** electron transport
**e.** electron transport **f.** both
**g.** citric acid cycle **h.** both

**23.51** $FMNH_2$ (**f**) $\longrightarrow$ $QH_2$ (**e**) $\longrightarrow$ cyt$b$ (**h**) $\longrightarrow$ cyt $c_1$ (**g**)
cyt$c$ (**d**) $\longrightarrow$ cyt$a$ (**c**) $\longrightarrow$ cyt$a_3$ (**a**) $\longrightarrow$ $O_2$ (**b**)

**23.53** **a.** Aconitase uses $H_2O$.
**b.** Succinate dehydrogenase uses FAD.
**c.** Fumarase uses $H_2O$.
**d.** Isocitrate dehydrogenase uses $NAD^+$.
**e.** Succinyl CoA synthetase uses GDP.
**f.** Malate dehydrogenase uses $NAD^+$.

**23.55** The oxidation reactions of the citric acid cycle produce a source of reduced coenzymes for electron transport and ATP synthesis.

**23.57** The oxidized coenzymes $NAD^+$ and FAD needed for the citric acid cycle are regenerated by electron transport which requires oxygen.

**23.59** **a.** citrate, isocitrate
**b.** $\alpha$-ketoglutarate
**c.** $\alpha$-ketoglutarate, succinyl CoA, oxaloacetate

**23.61** **a.** In reaction 4, $\alpha$-ketoglutarate, a five-carbon keto acid, is decarboxylated.
**b.** In reaction 2 and reaction 7, double bonds in aconitate and fumarate are hydrated.
**c.** $NAD^+$ is reduced in reactions 3, 4, and 8.
**d.** In reactions 3 and 8, a secondary hydroxyl group in isocitrate and malate is oxidized.

**23.63** **a.** $NAD^+$ **b.** $NAD^+$ and CoA

**23.65** **a.** High levels of NADH inhibit isocitrate dehydrogenase and $\alpha$-ketoglutarate dehydrogenase to slow the rate of the citric acid cycle.
**b.** High levels of ATP inhibit isocitrate dehydrogenase to slow the rate of the citric acid cycle.

**23.67** **a.** (4) cytochrome **b.** (1) FMN

**23.69** **a.** CoQ is a mobile carrier.
**b.** Fe-S clusters are found in complex I, III, and IV.
**c.** cyt $a_3$ is part of complex IV.

**23.71** **a.** complex II, $FADH_2 + Q \longrightarrow FAD + QH_2$
**b.** complex IV, cyt $a$ ($Fe^{2+}$) + cyt $a_3$ ($Fe^{3+}$) $\longrightarrow$ cyt $a$ ($Fe^{3+}$) + cyt $a_3$ ($Fe^{2+}$)

**23.73**

**a.**

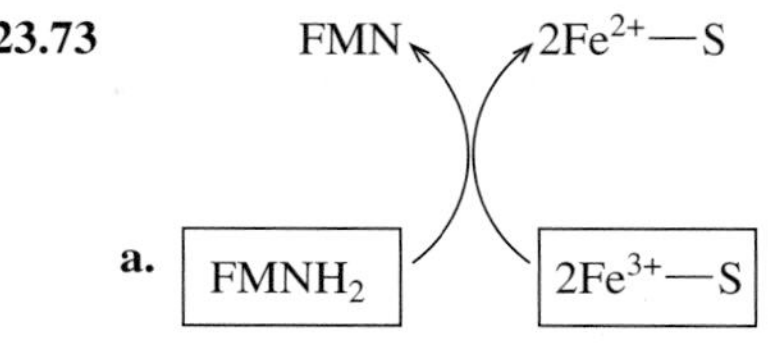


**b.**

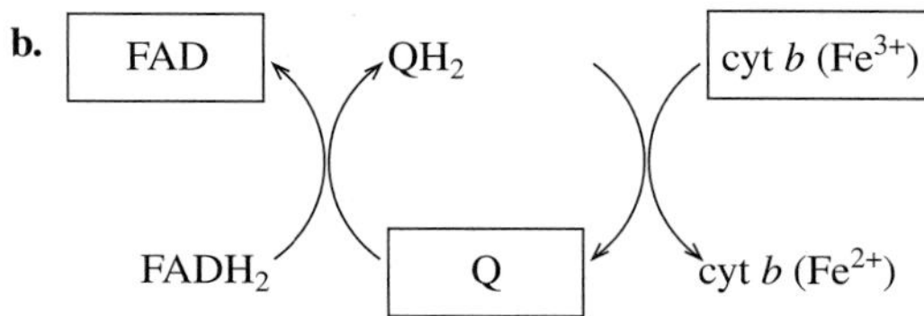


**23.75** complex I, III, and IV

**23.77** Energy released as protons flow through ATP synthase back to the matrix is utilized for the synthesis of ATP.

**23.79** Protons flow into the matrix where $H^+$ concentration is lower.

**23.81** Two ATP molecules are produced from $FADH_2$.

**23.83** **a.** NADH dehydrogenase (complex I)
**b.** electron flow from cyt $b$ to cyt $c_1$ (complex III)
**c.** cytochrome $c$ oxidase (complex IV)

**23.85** The oxidation of glucose to pyruvate produces 6 ATP, whereas the oxidation of glucose to $CO_2$ and $H_2O$ produces 36 ATP.

**23.87** The ATP synthase extends through the inner mitochondrial membrane with the $F_0$ part in contact with the proton gradient in the intermembrane space, while the $F_1$ complex is in the matrix.

**23.89** As protons from the proton gradient move through the ATP synthase to return to the matrix, energy is released and used to drive ATP synthesis at $F_1$ ATP synthase.

**23.91** A hibernating bear has more brown fat because it can be used during the winter for heat rather than ATP energy.

**23.93** **a.** 44 kcal **b.** 44 kcal
**c.** 180 kcal **d.** 260 kcal

**23.95** If the combustion of glucose produces 680 kcal, but only 260 kcal (from 36 ATP) in cells, the efficiency of glucose use in the cells is 260 kcal/680 kcal or 38%.

**23.97** $1.5 \times 10^{-8}$ mole of ATP

# 24 Metabolic Pathways for Lipids and Amino Acids

LOOKING AHEAD


24.1 Digestion of Triacylglycerols
24.2 Oxidation of Fatty Acids
24.3 ATP and Fatty Acid Oxidation
24.4 Ketogenesis and Ketone Bodies
24.5 Fatty Acid Synthesis
24.6 Digestion of Proteins
24.7 Degradation of Amino Acids
24.8 Urea Cycle
24.9 Fates of the Carbon Atoms from Amino Acids
24.10 Synthesis of Amino Acids


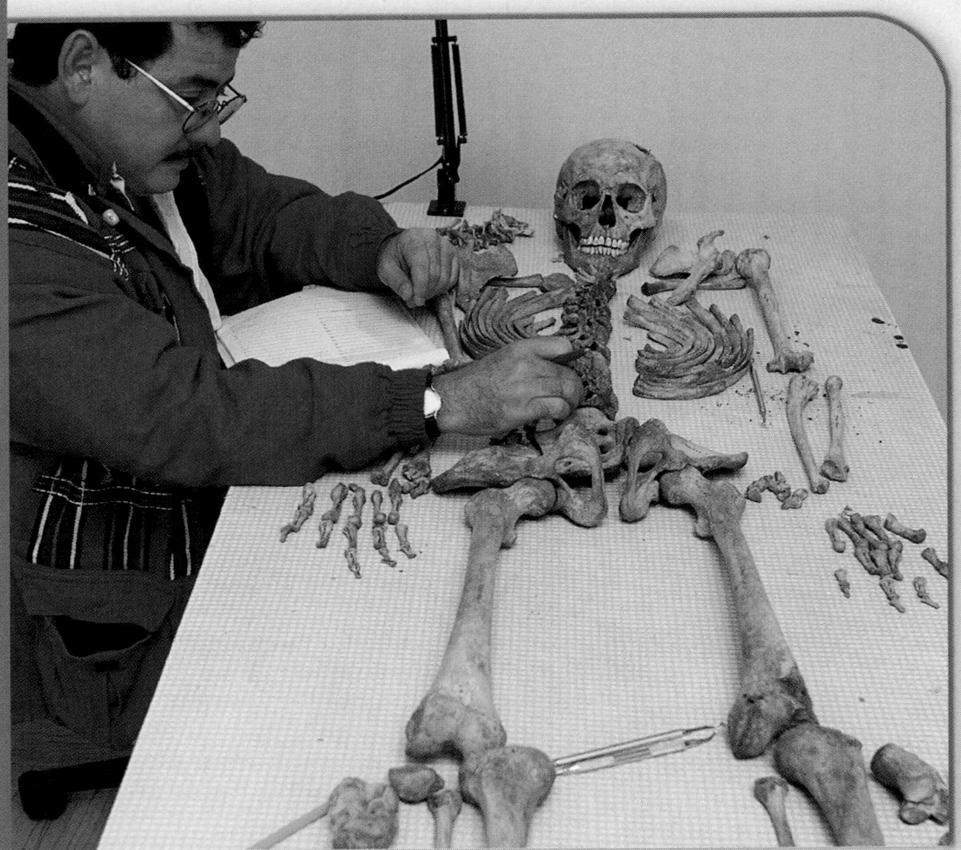

*"Chemistry plays an integral part in all aspects of medical legal death investigation," says Charles L. Cecil, forensic anthropologist and medical legal death investigator, San Francisco Medical Examiner's Office. "Crime-scene analysis of blood droplets determines whether they are human or nonhuman, the analyses of toxicological samples of blood and/or other fluids help determine the cause and time of death. Specialists in forensic anthropology can analyze trace-element ratios in bones to identify the number of individuals in mixed human bone situations. These conditions are quite often found during investigations of massive human-rights violations, such as the site of El Mozote in El Salvador."*

*Forensic anthropologists help police identify skeletal remains by determining the gender, approximate age, height, and cause of death. Analysis of bone can also provide information about illnesses or trauma a person may have experienced.*

Visit **www.masteringchemistry.com** for self-study materials and instructor-assigned homework.

In previous chapters, we focused on carbohydrates because glucose is the primary fuel for the synthesis of ATP. However, lipids and proteins also play an important role in metabolism and energy production. In this chapter, we will look at how the digestion of lipids produces fatty acids and glycerol and how the digestion of proteins gives amino acids. Almost all of our energy is stored in the form of triacylglycerols in fat cells of adipose tissue. Many people go on diets after they discover that adipose tissue can store unlimited quantities of fat. This fact has become quite apparent in the large number of people in the U.S. that are considered obese. When our caloric intake exceeds the nutritional and metabolic needs of our bodies, excess carbohydrates and fatty acids are converted to triacylglycerols and added to our fat cells.

The digestion and degradation of dietary proteins as well as body proteins provide amino acids, which are needed to synthesize nitrogen-containing compounds in our cells, such as new proteins and nucleic acids. Although amino acids are not considered a primary source of fuel, energy can be extracted from amino acids if glycogen and fat reserves have been depleted. However, when a person who is fasting or starving utilizes amino acids as the only source of energy, the breakdown of the body's own proteins eventually destroys essential body tissues, particularly muscles.

## 24.1 Digestion of Triacylglycerols

**LEARNING GOAL**

Describe the sites and products obtained from the digestion of triacylglycerols.

Our adipose tissue is made of fat cells called *adipocytes*, which store triacylglycerols. (See Figure 24.1.) Let's compare the amount of energy stored in the fat cells to the energy from glucose, glycogen, and protein. A typical 70-kg (150-lb) person has about 135 000 kcal of energy stored as fat, 24 000 kcal as protein, 720 kcal as glycogen reserves, and 80 kcal as blood glucose. Therefore, the energy available from stored fats is about 85% of the total energy available in the body. Thus, body fat is our major source of stored energy.

### Digestion of Dietary Fats

MC TUTORIAL Digestion of Triacylglycerols

The digestion of dietary fats begins in the small intestine, where the hydrophobic fat globules mix with bile salts released from the gallbladder. (See Chapter 17 to review lipids and bile salts.) In a process called *emulsification*, the bile salts break the fat globules into smaller droplets called *micelles*. Then, *pancreatic lipases* released from the pancreas hydrolyze the triacylglycerols in the micelles to yield monoacylglycerols and free fatty acids. These digestion products are absorbed into the intestinal lining, where they recombine to form triacylglycerols, which are coated with proteins to form lipoproteins called **chylomicrons**. The chylomicrons transport the triacylglycerols through the lymphatic system and into the bloodstream to be carried to cells of the heart, muscle, and adipose tissues.

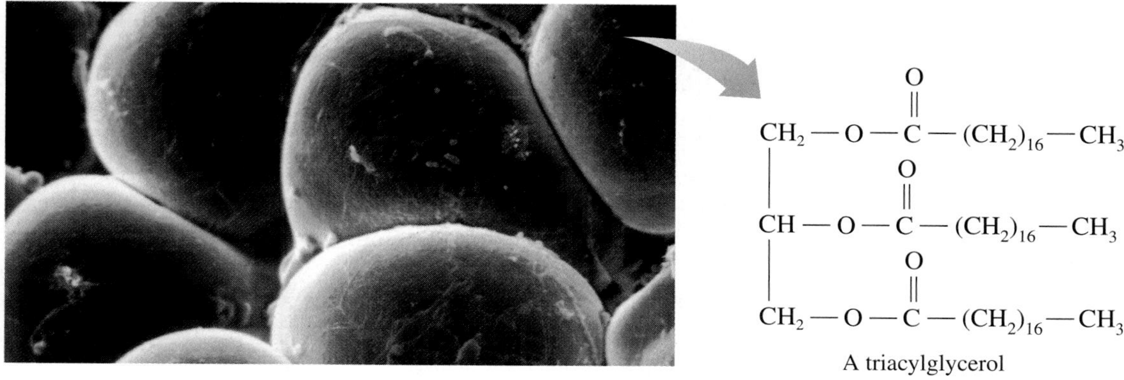


**FIGURE 24.1** The fat cells (adipocytes) that make up adipose tissue are capable of storing unlimited quantities of triacylglycerols.

Q What are some sources of fats in our diet?

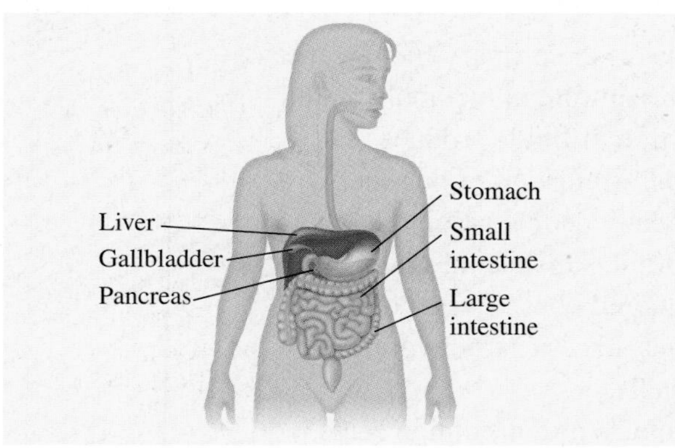


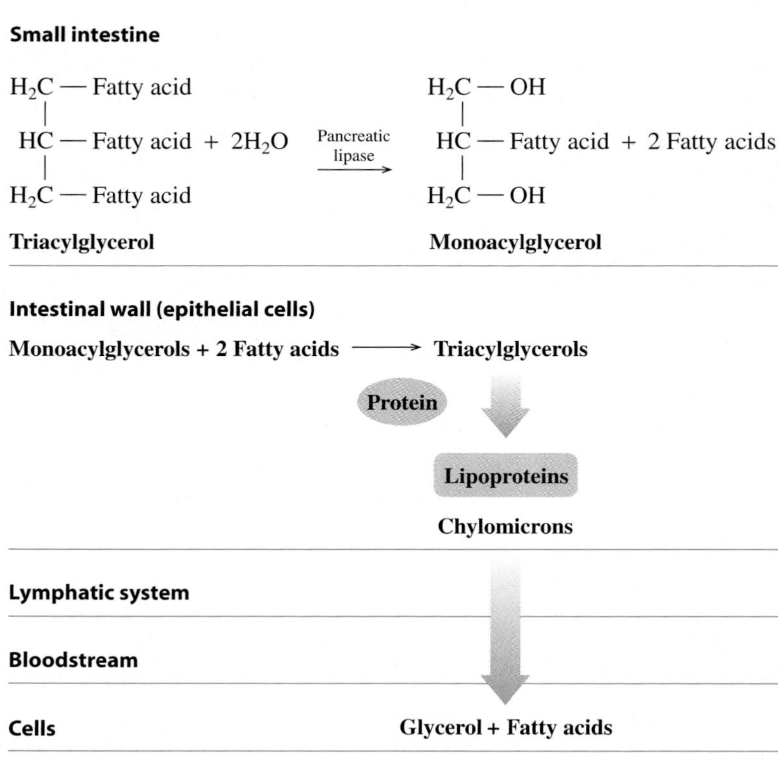


**FIGURE 24.2** The triacylglycerols that reform in the intestinal wall from the digestion products monoacylglycerols and fatty acids bind to proteins for transport through the lymphatic system and bloodstream to the cells.

**Q** What kinds of enzymes are secreted from the pancreas into the small intestine to hydrolyze triacylglycerols?

(See Figure 24.2.) We can write the overall equation for the digestion of triacylglycerols as follows:

$$\text{Triacylglycerols} + 2H_2O \xrightarrow{\text{Pancreatic lipase}} \text{monoacylglycerols} + 2 \text{ fatty acids}$$

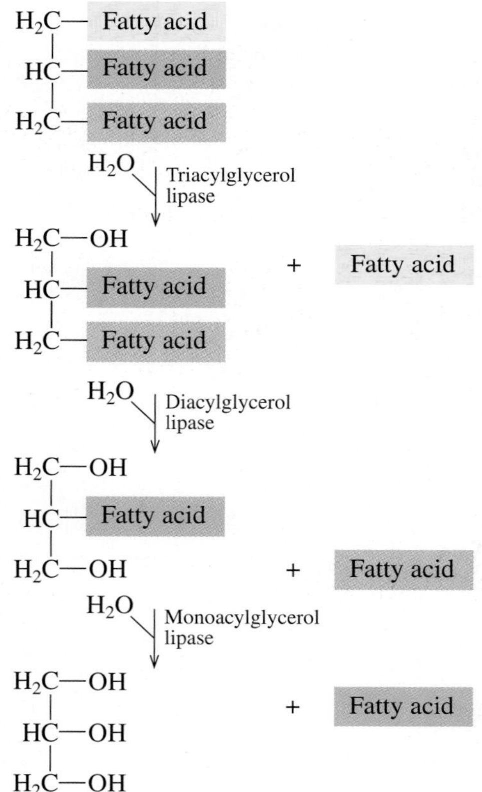


In the cells, enzymes hydrolyze the triacylglycerols to yield glycerol and free fatty acids, which can be used for energy production. Fatty acids, which are the preferred fuel of the heart, are oxidized to acetyl CoA molecules for ATP synthesis. However, the brain and red blood cells cannot utilize fatty acids. Fatty acids cannot diffuse across the blood-brain barrier, and red blood cells have no mitochondria, which are where fatty acids are oxidized. Therefore, glucose and glycogen are the only sources of energy for the brain and red blood cells.

## Mobilization of Fat Stores

When blood glucose is depleted and glycogen stores are low, the process of **fat mobilization** breaks down triacylglycerols in adipose tissue to fatty acids and glycerol. The mobilization occurs when the hormones *glucagon* or *epinephrine* are secreted into the bloodstream, where they bind to receptors on the membrane of adipose cells. This process activates enzymes within the fat cells that begin the hydrolysis of a triacylglycerol. A fatty acid is hydrolyzed from carbon 1 or carbon 3, followed by the hydrolysis of the second and third fatty acids.

We can write the overall reaction for the mobilization of fats in fat cells as follows:

$$\text{Triacylglycerols} + 3H_2O \xrightarrow{\text{Lipases}} \text{glycerol} + 3 \text{ fatty acids}$$

The products of fat mobilization, glycerol and fatty acids, diffuse into the bloodstream and bind with plasma proteins (albumin) to be transported to the tissues. Most of the glycerol goes into the liver, where it is converted to glucose.

## Metabolism of Glycerol

Enzymes in the liver convert glycerol to dihydroxyacetone phosphate in two steps. In the first step, glycerol is phosphorylated using ATP to yield glycerol-3-phosphate. In the second step, the hydroxyl group is oxidized to yield dihydroxyacetone phosphate, which is an intermediate in several metabolic pathways including glycolysis and gluconeogenesis. (See Chapter 22.)

$$\underset{\text{Glycerol}}{\begin{array}{c} H_2C-OH \\ | \\ H-C-OH \\ | \\ H_2C-OH \end{array}} \xrightarrow[\text{ATP} \;\; \text{ADP}]{\text{Glycerol kinase}} \underset{\text{Glycerol-3-phosphate}}{\begin{array}{c} H_2C-OH \\ | \\ H-C-OH \\ | \\ H_2C-O-\mathbf{P} \end{array}} \xrightarrow[\text{NAD}^+ \;\; \text{NADH} + \text{H}^+]{\text{Glycerol-3-phosphate dehydrogenase}} \underset{\text{Dihydroxyacetone phosphate}}{\begin{array}{c} H_2C-OH \\ | \\ C=O \\ | \\ H_2C-O-\mathbf{P} \end{array}}$$

Dihydroxyacetone phosphate → Glycolysis, Gluconeogenesis

**P** = phosphoryl

The overall reaction for the metabolism of glycerol is written as follows:

$$\text{Glycerol} + \text{ATP} + \text{NAD}^+ \longrightarrow \text{dihydroxyacetone phosphate} + \text{ADP} + \text{NADH} + \text{H}^+$$

**CONCEPT CHECK 24.1**

### Fats and Digestion

Answer each of the following for the digestion of triacylglycerols:

**a.** What are the sites, enzymes, and products of the digestion of triacylglycerols?

**b.** What happens to the products from the digestion of triacylglycerols in the membrane of the small intestine?

ANSWER

**a.** The digestion of triacylglycerols takes place in the small intestine where pancreatic lipase catalyzes their hydrolysis to monoacylglycerols and fatty acids.

**b.** Monoacylglycerols and fatty acids recombine in the membrane of the small intestine to form triacylglycerols. The triacylglycerols combine with proteins to form chylomicrons for transport to the lymphatic system and the bloodstream.

### Digestion of Fats

Place some water and several drops of vegetable oil in a container with a top. Cap the container and shake. Observe. Add a few drops of liquid soap to the oil and water, cap the container again, and shake. Observe.

QUESTIONS

1. Why does the oil separate from the water?
2. How does the appearance of the oil change after soap is added?
3. How is soap like the bile salts in the digestion of fats?
4. Where does fat digestion occur in the body?
5. Many people with gallbladder problems take lipase medication. Why is this necessary?

## QUESTIONS AND PROBLEMS

### Digestion of Triacylglycerols

24.1 What is the role of bile salts in lipid digestion?

**24.2** How are insoluble triacylglycerols transported to the tissues?

24.3 When are fats released from fat stores?

**24.4** What happens to the glycerol produced from the hydrolysis of triacylglycerols in adipose tissues?

24.5 How is glycerol converted to an intermediate of glycolysis?

**24.6** How can glycerol be used to synthesize glucose?

## 24.2 Oxidation of Fatty Acids

LEARNING GOAL

Describe the metabolic pathway of $\beta$ oxidation.

A large amount of energy is obtained when fatty acids undergo oxidation in the mitochondria to yield acetyl CoA. In stage 2 of fat metabolism, fatty acids undergo **beta oxidation ($\beta$ oxidation)**, which removes two-carbon segments, one at a time, from a fatty acid. The remaining carbon chain is given the symbol R.

$\beta$ oxidation occurs here

$$CH_3-(CH_2)_{14}-\underset{\beta}{CH_2}-\underset{\alpha}{CH_2}-\overset{O}{\overset{\|}{C}}-OH$$

Stearic acid

Each cycle in $\beta$ oxidation produces acetyl CoA and a fatty acid that is shorter by two carbons. The cycle repeats until the original fatty acid is completely degraded to two-carbon acetyl CoA molecules. Each acetyl CoA can then enter the citric acid cycle in the same way as the acetyl CoA molecules derived from glucose.

## Fatty Acid Activation

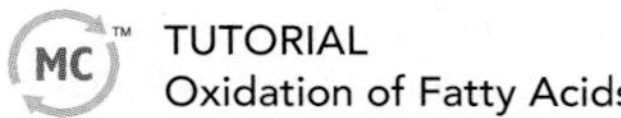
TUTORIAL
Oxidation of Fatty Acids

Before a fatty acid can enter the mitochondrion, it undergoes activation in the cytosol. The activation process combines a fatty acid with coenzyme A to yield fatty acyl CoA. The energy released by the hydrolysis of two phosphate groups from ATP is used to drive the reaction. The products are AMP and pyrophosphate ($PP_i$), which hydrolyzes to yield two inorganic phosphates ($2P_i$). Then, fatty acyl CoA moves from the cytosol into the intermembrane space:

$$\underset{\text{Fatty acid}}{R{-}CH_2{-}CH_2{-}\overset{\overset{\large O}{\|}}{C}{-}OH} + ATP + HS{-}CoA \xrightarrow[\text{synthetase}]{\text{Acyl CoA}} \underset{\text{Fatty acyl CoA}}{R{-}CH_2{-}CH_2{-}\overset{\overset{\large O}{\|}}{C}{-}S{-}CoA} + AMP + 2P_i + H_2O$$

## Transport of Fatty Acyl CoA

The long hydrocarbon chain prevents the fatty acyl CoA molecule from crossing the inner mitochondrial membrane into the matrix. Then, the fatty acyl group binds to a charged carrier called *carnitine* to form fatty acyl carnitine, which transports the fatty acyl group across the inner mitochondrial membrane into the matrix. (See Figure 24.3.)

$$\underset{\text{Fatty acyl CoA}}{R{-}CH_2{-}CH_2{-}\overset{\overset{\large O}{\|}}{C}{-}S{-}CoA} + \underset{\text{Carnitine}}{H{-}\underset{\underset{COO^-}{|}}{\underset{CH_2}{|}}{\overset{\overset{\overset{+}{N}(CH_3)_3}{|}}{\overset{CH_2}{|}}{C}}{-}OH} \rightleftharpoons \underset{\text{Fatty acyl carnitine}}{H{-}\underset{\underset{COO^-}{|}}{\underset{CH_2}{|}}{\overset{\overset{\overset{+}{N}(CH_3)_3}{|}}{\overset{CH_2}{|}}{C}}{-}O{-}\overset{\overset{\large O}{\|}}{C}{-}CH_2{-}CH_2{-}R} + HS{-}CoA$$

In the matrix, the fatty acyl group is transferred back to coenzyme A to form fatty acyl CoA. The released carnitine returns to the inner mitochondrial membrane. While it may seem like a complicated way to move fatty acyl CoA into the matrix, this transport system provides a way to regulate degradation (oxidation) and synthesis of fatty acids. When fatty acids are being synthesized in the cytosol, the transport of fatty acyl CoA into the matrix is blocked, which prevents fatty acid degradation.

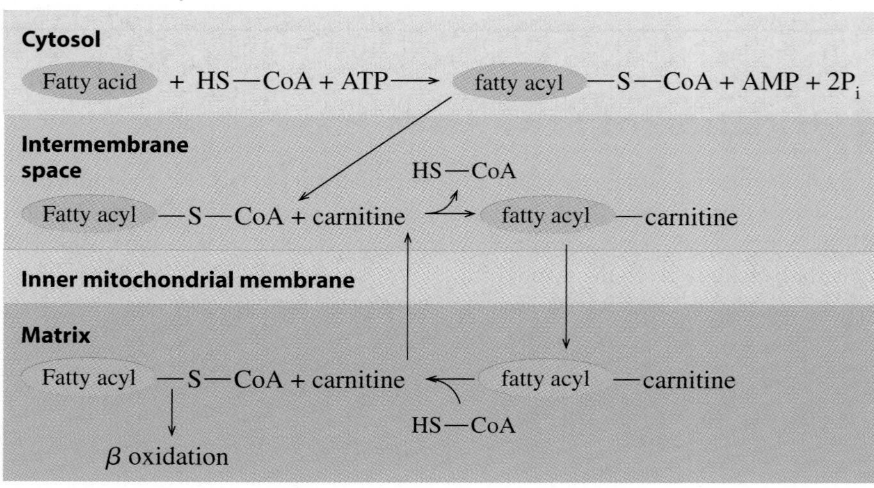


**FIGURE 24.3** Fatty acids are activated and transported by carnitine through the inner mitochondrial membrane into the matrix.

Q Why is carnitine used to transport a fatty acid into the matrix?

## Reactions of β-Oxidation Cycle

In the mitochondrial matrix, fatty acyl CoA molecules undergo $\beta$ oxidation, which is a cycle of four reactions that convert the $-CH_2-$ of the $\beta$ carbon to a $\beta$-keto group. Once the $\beta$-keto group is formed, a two-carbon acetyl group can be split from the chain, which shortens the fatty acyl group.

## β-Oxidation Pathway

**Reaction 1 Oxidation (Dehydrogenation)**
In the first reaction of $\beta$ oxidation, the FAD coenzyme removes hydrogen atoms from the $\alpha$ and $\beta$ carbons of the activated fatty acid to form a trans carbon-carbon double bond and $FADH_2$.

**Reaction 2 Hydration**
A water molecule now adds to the trans double bond, which places a hydroxyl group (—OH) on the $\beta$ carbon.

**Reaction 3 Oxidation (Dehydrogenation)**
The hydroxyl group on the $\beta$ carbon is oxidized to yield a ketone. The hydrogen atoms removed in the dehydrogenation reduce coenzyme $NAD^+$ to $NADH + H^+$. At this point, the $\beta$ carbon has been oxidized to a keto group.

**Reaction 4 Cleavage of Acetyl CoA**
In the final step of $\beta$ oxidation, the $C_\alpha$—$C_\beta$ bond splits to yield free acetyl CoA and a fatty acyl CoA molecule that is shorter by two carbon atoms. This shorter fatty acyl CoA is ready to go through the $\beta$-oxidation cycle again.

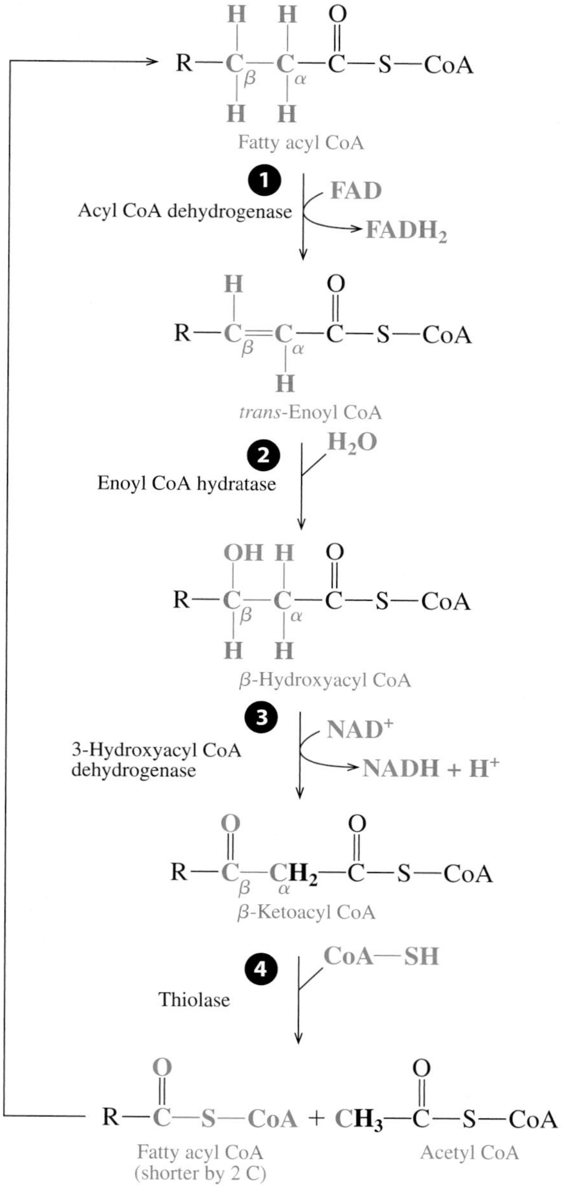

$$R-CH_2(\beta)-CH_2(\alpha)-C(=O)-S-CoA$$
Fatty acyl CoA

1 Acyl CoA dehydrogenase: FAD → $FADH_2$

$$R-CH(\beta)=CH(\alpha)-C(=O)-S-CoA$$
*trans*-Enoyl CoA

2 Enoyl CoA hydratase: $H_2O$

$$R-CH(OH)(\beta)-CH_2(\alpha)-C(=O)-S-CoA$$
$\beta$-Hydroxyacyl CoA

3 3-Hydroxyacyl CoA dehydrogenase: $NAD^+$ → $NADH + H^+$

$$R-C(=O)(\beta)-CH_2(\alpha)-C(=O)-S-CoA$$
$\beta$-Ketoacyl CoA

4 Thiolase: CoA—SH

$$R-C(=O)-S-CoA + CH_3-C(=O)-S-CoA$$
Fatty acyl CoA (shorter by 2 C) + Acetyl CoA

The reaction for one cycle of $\beta$ oxidation is written as follows:

$$\underset{\text{Fatty acyl CoA}}{R-CH_2-CH_2-\overset{O}{\overset{\|}{C}}-S-CoA} + FAD + H_2O + NAD^+ + HS-CoA \longrightarrow$$

$$\underset{\text{New fatty acyl }(-2\text{ C})\text{ CoA}}{R-\overset{O}{\overset{\|}{C}}-S-CoA} + \underset{\text{Acetyl CoA}}{CH_3-\overset{O}{\overset{\|}{C}}-S-CoA} + FADH_2 + NADH + H^+$$

## Fatty Acid Length Determines Cycle Repeats

The number of carbon atoms in a fatty acid determines the number of times the cycle repeats and the number of acetyl CoA units it produces. For example, the complete $\beta$ oxidation of myristic acid ($C_{14}$) produces seven acetyl CoA groups, which is equal to one-half the number of carbon atoms in the chain. Because the final turn of the cycle produces two acetyl CoA groups, the total number of times the cycle repeats is one less than the total number of acetyl groups it produces. Therefore, the $C_{14}$ fatty acid goes through the cycle six times. (See Figure 24.4.)

| Fatty acid | Number of Acetyl CoA | $\beta$-Oxidation Cycles |
|---|---|---|
| Myristic acid $C_{14}$ | 7 | 6 |
| Palmitic acid $C_{16}$ | 8 | 7 |
| Stearic acid $C_{18}$ | 9 | 8 |

We can write an overall equation for the complete oxidation of myristyl CoA as follows:

$$\text{Myristyl CoA} + 6\text{HS—CoA} + 6\text{FAD} + 6\text{NAD}^+ + 6\text{H}_2\text{O} \longrightarrow 7\text{ acetyl CoA} + 6\text{FADH}_2 + 6\text{NADH} + 6\text{H}^+$$

## Oxidation of Unsaturated Fatty Acids

The $\beta$-oxidation sequence we have described applies to saturated fatty acids with an even number of carbon atoms. However, the fats in our diets, particularly the oils, contain unsaturated fatty acids, which have one or more cis double bonds. The hydration reaction adds water to trans double bonds, not cis. When the double bond in an unsaturated fatty acid is ready for hydration, an isomerase forms a trans double bond between the $\alpha$ and $\beta$ carbon atoms, which is the arrangement needed for the hydration reaction.

$$\text{R—CH=CH—CH}_2\text{—C(=O)—S—CoA} \xrightarrow{\text{Enoyl CoA isomerase}} \text{R—CH}_2\text{—CH=CH—C(=O)—S—CoA}$$

*cis*-Fatty acyl CoA (β and α carbons: the double-bond carbons are β, and CH₂ is α) → *trans*-Fatty acyl CoA

2 $H_2O$, Enoyl CoA hydratase

$$\text{R—CH}_2\text{—CH(OH)—CH}_2\text{—C(=O)—S—CoA}$$

$\beta$-Hydroxyacyl CoA

Because the isomerization provides the trans double bond for the hydration in reaction 2, it bypasses the first reaction. Therefore, the energy released by the $\beta$ oxidation of an unsaturated fatty acid is slightly less because no $FADH_2$ is produced in that cycle.

SAMPLE PROBLEM 24.1

### $\beta$ Oxidation

Match each of the following with reactions in the $\beta$-oxidation cycle:

(1) first oxidation (2) hydration (3) second oxidation (4) cleavage

**a.** Water is added to a trans double bond.
**b.** An acetyl CoA is removed.
**c.** FAD is reduced to $FADH_2$.
**d.** Reaction which is bypassed during the oxidation of unsaturated fatty acids.

SOLUTION

**a.** (2) hydration **b.** (4) cleavage **c.** (1) first oxidation **d.** (1) first oxidation

STUDY CHECK

Which coenzyme is needed in reaction 3 when a $\beta$-hydroxyl group is converted to a $\beta$-keto group?

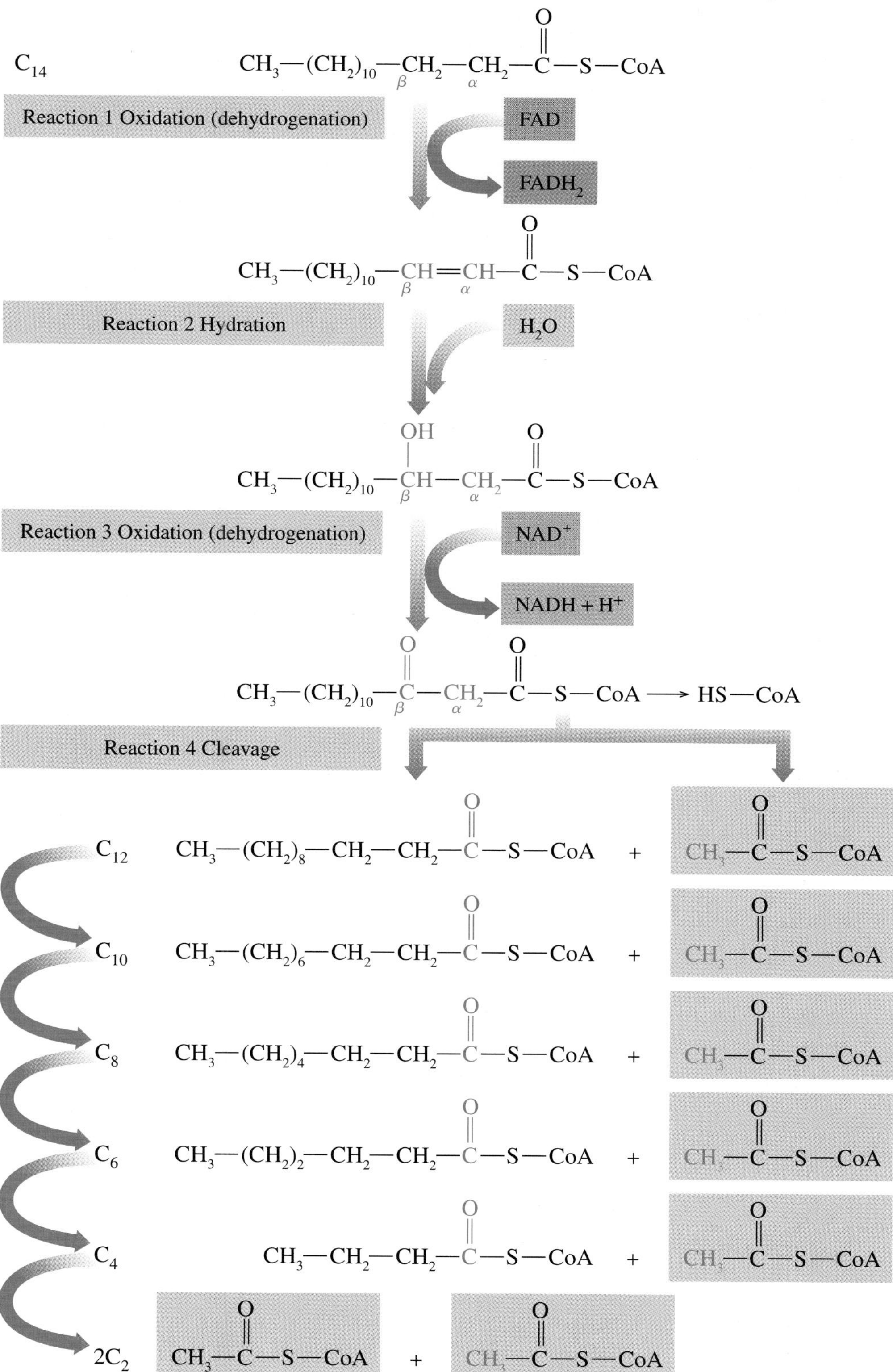


**FIGURE 24.4** Myristic acid ($C_{14}$) undergoes six oxidation cycles that repeat reactions 1–4 to yield seven acetyl CoA molecules.

**Q** How many NADH and $FADH_2$ are produced in one turn of the fatty acid cycle of $\beta$ oxidation?

## QUESTIONS AND PROBLEMS

### Oxidation of Fatty Acids

**24.7** Where in the cell are fatty acids activated?

**24.8** What is the function of carnitine in the degradation of fatty acids?

**24.9** What coenzymes are required for $\beta$ oxidation?

**24.10** When does an isomerization occur during the $\beta$ oxidation of a fatty acid?

**24.11** In each of the following acyl CoA molecules, identify the $\beta$ carbon:

**a.** $CH_3—CH_2—CH_2—CH_2—CH_2—CH_2—CH_2—\overset{O}{\overset{\|}{C}}—S—CoA$

**b.** $CH_3—(CH_2)_{14}—CH_2—CH_2—\overset{O}{\overset{\|}{C}}—S—CoA$

**c.** $CH_3—CH_2—CH{=}CH—CH_2—CH_2—CH_2—CH_2—CH_2—\overset{O}{\overset{\|}{C}}—S—CoA$

**24.12** Write the product when each of the following undergoes the indicated reaction in $\beta$ oxidation:

**a.** $CH_3—(CH_2)_{12}—CH{=}CH—\overset{O}{\overset{\|}{C}}—S—CoA + H_2O \xrightarrow{\text{Enoyl CoA hydratase}}$

**b.** $CH_3—(CH_2)_6—CH_2—CH_2—\overset{O}{\overset{\|}{C}}—S—CoA \xrightarrow{\text{Acyl CoA dehydrogenase}}$

**c.** $CH_3—(CH_2)_4—\overset{O}{\overset{\|}{C}}—CH_2—\overset{O}{\overset{\|}{C}}—S—CoA + HS—CoA \xrightarrow{\text{Thiolase}}$

**24.13** Capric acid, $CH_3—(CH_2)_8—COOH$, is a $C_{10}$ fatty acid.

**a.** Write the formula of the activated form of capric acid.
**b.** Indicate the $\alpha$ and $\beta$ carbon atoms in the fatty acid.
**c.** Write the overall equation for the first cycle of $\beta$ oxidation for capric acid.
**d.** Write the overall equation for the complete $\beta$ oxidation of capric acid.

**24.14** Arachidic acid, $CH_3—(CH_2)_{18}—COOH$, is a $C_{20}$ fatty acid.

**a.** Write the formula of the activated form of arachidic acid.
**b.** Indicate the $\alpha$ and $\beta$ carbon atoms in the fatty acid.
**c.** Write the overall equation for the first cycle of $\beta$ oxidation for arachidic acid.
**d.** Write the overall equation for the complete $\beta$ oxidation of arachidic acid.

## 24.3 ATP and Fatty Acid Oxidation

**LEARNING GOAL**

Calculate the total ATP produced by the complete oxidation of a fatty acid.

We can now determine the total energy yield from the oxidation of a particular fatty acid. In each $\beta$-oxidation cycle, one NADH, one $FADH_2$, and one acetyl CoA are produced. From Chapter 23, we know that hydrogen ions and electrons transferred from NADH to coenzyme Q in the electron transport chain generate sufficient energy to synthesize three ATP, whereas $FADH_2$ leads to the synthesis of two ATP. However, the greatest amount of energy produced from a fatty acid is generated by the production of the acetyl CoA units that enter the citric acid cycle. We saw in Chapter 23 that one acetyl CoA leads to the synthesis of 12 ATP.

So far, we know that the $C_{14}$ acid produces seven acetyl CoA units and goes through six turns of the cycle. We also need to remember that activation of the myristic acid requires two ATP. We can set up the calculation as follows:

**ATP Production for Myristic Acid**

| | |
|---|---|
| **Activation** | −2 ATP |
| **7 Acetyl CoA** | |
| $7\ \cancel{\text{acetyl CoA}} \times \dfrac{12\text{ ATP}}{\cancel{\text{acetyl CoA}}}$ | 84 ATP |
| **6 $\beta$-oxidation cycles** | |
| $6\ \cancel{FADH_2} \times \dfrac{2\text{ ATP}}{\cancel{FADH_2}}$ | 12 ATP |
| $6\ \cancel{NADH} \times \dfrac{3\text{ ATP}}{\cancel{NADH}}$ | 18 ATP |
| Total | 112 ATP |

## The Energy Yield from Fats

Myristic acid, $C_{14}H_{28}O_2$, has a molar mass of 228 g/mole. We can calculate the ATP produced per gram of the fatty acid as follows:

$$\frac{112 \text{ moles ATP}}{\cancel{1 \text{ mole myristic acid}}} \times \frac{\cancel{1 \text{ mole myristic acid}}}{228 \text{ g myristic acid}} = 0.491 \text{ mole of ATP/g of myristic acid (fat)}$$

In Chapter 23, we saw that the complete oxidation of glucose generated 36 ATP. Glucose, $C_6H_{12}O_6$, has a molar mass of 180. g. We can calculate the ATP produced per gram of glucose as follows:

$$\frac{36 \text{ moles ATP}}{\cancel{1 \text{ mole glucose}}} \times \frac{\cancel{1 \text{ mole glucose}}}{180. \text{ g glucose}} = 0.200 \text{ mole of ATP/g of glucose}$$

From these calculations, we see that 1 g of fat produces more than twice the ATP energy as 1 g of glucose. This also means that we obtain more than double the number of nutritional calories from 1 g of fat (9 kcal/g of fat) than we do from 1 g of carbohydrate (4 kcal/g). This is one reason a low-fat diet is recommended when we are trying to lose weight.

## Health Note

### Stored Fat and Obesity

The storage of fat is an important survival feature in the lives of many animals. In hibernating animals, large amounts of stored fat provide the energy for the entire hibernation period, which can be several months. In camels, large amounts of food are stored in the camel's hump, which is actually a huge fat deposit. When food resources are low, the camel can survive months without food or water by utilizing the fat reserves in the hump. Migratory birds preparing to fly long distances also store large amounts of fat. Whales are kept warm by a layer of body fat called "blubber" (which can be as thick as 2 feet) under their skin. Blubber also provides energy when whales must survive long periods of starvation. Penguins also have blubber, which protects them from the cold and provides energy when they are incubating their eggs.

Humans also have the capability to store large amounts of fat, although they do not hibernate or usually have to survive for long periods without food. When humans survived on sparse diets that were mostly vegetarian, about 20% of the dietary calories were from fat. Today, a typical diet includes more dairy products and foods with high fat levels, and as much as 60% of the calories are from fat. The U.S. Public Health Service now estimates that in the United States, more than one-third of adults are obese. Obesity is defined as a body weight that is more than 20% over an ideal weight. Obesity is a major factor in health problems such as diabetes, heart disease, high blood pressure, stroke, and gallstones, as well as some cancers and forms of arthritis.

At one time, we thought that obesity was simply a problem of eating too much. However, research now indicates that certain pathways in lipid and carbohydrate metabolism may cause excessive weight gain in some people. In 1995, scientists discovered that a hormone called *leptin* is produced in fat cells. When fat cells are full, high levels of leptin signal the brain to limit the intake of food. When fat stores are low, leptin production decreases, which signals the brain to increase food intake. Some obese persons have high levels of leptin, which means that leptin does not cause them to decrease how much they eat.

The causes of obesity have become a major research field. Scientists are studying differences in the rate of leptin production, degrees of resistance to leptin, and possible combinations of these factors. After a person has dieted and lost weight, the leptin level drops. This decrease in leptin may cause an increase in hunger, slow metabolism, and increased food intake, which starts the weight-gain cycle all over again. Currently, studies are being made to assess the safety of leptin therapy following a weight loss.

EXPLORE YOUR WORLD

## Fat Storage and Blubber

Obtain four plastic freezer bags, masking tape, and some solid vegetable fat used for cooking. Fill a bucket or container with enough water to cover both of your hands. Add ice until the water feels very cold.

Place 3 or 4 tablespoons of the vegetable fat in one of the plastic bags. Place another plastic bag inside the first bag containing the fat. Tape the outside edges of the two bags together leaving the inside bag open. Using the remaining two plastic bags, place one inside the other, and tape the outside edges together leaving the inside bag open. Now place one hand inside the bag with the vegetable fat and distribute the fat around until a layer of about 2/3 in. (2 cm) of the fat covers your hand. Place your other hand inside the other double bags and submerge both your hands in the ice water. Measure the time it takes for one hand to feel uncomfortably cold. Remove your hands before they get too cold.

### QUESTIONS

1. How effective is the double bag with "blubber" in protecting your hand from the cold?
2. How would increasing the amount of vegetable fat affect your results?
3. How does "blubber" help an animal survive starvation?
4. Why would animals in warm climates, such as camels and migratory birds, need to store fat?
5. If you placed 300. g of vegetable fat in the double bag, how many moles of ATP could it provide if the fat were used for energy production (assume the fat produces the same amount of ATP as myristic acid)?

CONCEPT CHECK 24.2

### Number of $\beta$-Oxidation Cycles

For each of the following saturated fatty acids, give the number of $\beta$-oxidation cycles and number of acetyl CoA produced:

**a.** caprylic acid ($C_8$) **b.** lauric acid ($C_{12}$) **c.** behenic acid ($C_{22}$)

ANSWER

**a.** Caprylic acid ($C_8$) requires three $\beta$-oxidation cycles, and four acetyl CoA are produced.
**b.** Lauric acid ($C_{12}$) requires five $\beta$-oxidation cycles, and six acetyl CoA are produced.
**c.** Behenic acid ($C_{22}$) requires 10 $\beta$-oxidation cycles, and 11 acetyl CoA are produced.

SAMPLE PROBLEM 24.2

### ATP Production from $\beta$ Oxidation

How much ATP will be produced from the $\beta$ oxidation of palmitic acid, a $C_{16}$ saturated fatty acid?

SOLUTION

A 16-carbon fatty acid will produce 8 acetyl CoA units and go through 7 $\beta$-oxidation cycles, which produces 7 $FADH_2$ and 7 NADH. Each acetyl CoA can produce 12 ATP by way of the citric acid cycle. During electron transport, each $FADH_2$ produces 2 ATP, and each NADH produces 3 ATP.

**ATP Production from Palmitic Acid ($C_{16}H_{32}O_2$)**

| | |
|---|---|
| Activation of palmitic acid to palmityl CoA | −2 ATP |
| $8\ \cancel{\text{acetyl CoA}} \times \dfrac{12\text{ ATP}}{\cancel{\text{acetyl CoA}}}$ (citric acid cycle) | 96 ATP |
| $7\ \cancel{FADH_2} \times \dfrac{2\text{ ATP}}{\cancel{FADH_2}}$ (electron transport) | 14 ATP |
| $7\ \cancel{\text{NADH}} \times \dfrac{3\text{ ATP}}{\cancel{\text{NADH}}}$ (electron transport) | 21 ATP |
| Total | 129 ATP |

STUDY CHECK

Compare the total ATP from reduced coenzymes and from acetyl CoA in the $\beta$ oxidation of palmitic acid.

## QUESTIONS AND PROBLEMS

### ATP and Fatty Acid Oxidation

**24.15** Why is the energy of fatty acid activation from ATP to AMP considered the same as the hydrolysis of 2 ATP $\longrightarrow$ 2 ADP?

**24.16** What is the number of ATP molecules obtained from one molecule of acetyl CoA in the citric acid cycle?

**24.17** Consider the complete oxidation of one molecule of capric acid, $CH_3—(CH_2)_8—COOH$, a $C_{10}$ fatty acid.
**a.** How many acetyl CoA molecules are produced?
**b.** How many cycles of $\beta$ oxidation are needed?
**c.** How many molecules of ATP are generated from the oxidation of one molecule of capric acid?

**24.18** Consider the complete oxidation of one molecule of arachidic acid, $CH_3—(CH_2)_{18}—COOH$, a $C_{20}$ fatty acid.
**a.** How many molecules of acetyl CoA are produced?
**b.** How many cycles of $\beta$ oxidation are needed?
**c.** How many molecules of ATP are generated from the oxidation of one molecule of arachidic acid?

# 24.4 Ketogenesis and Ketone Bodies

**LEARNING GOAL**

Describe the pathway of ketogenesis.

When carbohydrates are not available to meet energy needs, the body breaks down body fat. However, the oxidation of large amounts of fatty acids can cause acetyl CoA molecules to accumulate in the liver. Then acetyl CoA molecules combine to form compounds called **ketone bodies** in a pathway known as **ketogenesis**. (See Figure 24.5.)

1. In ketogenesis, two molecules of acetyl CoA combine to form acetoacetyl CoA, which reverses the last reaction in $\beta$ oxidation.
2. The hydrolysis of acetoacetyl CoA forms acetoacetate, a ketone body, which reacts further to produce two other ketone bodies.
3. Acetoacetate can be reduced to yield $\beta$-hydroxybutyrate, which is considered a ketone body even though it does not contain a keto group.
4. Acetone forms when acetoacetate undergoes decarboxylation.

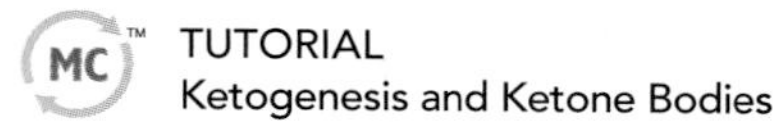

TUTORIAL
Ketogenesis and Ketone Bodies

Ketone bodies are produced mostly in the liver and transported to cells in the heart, brain, and skeletal muscle, where small amounts of energy can be obtained by converting acetoacetate or $\beta$-hydroxybutyrate to acetyl CoA:

$$\beta\text{-Hydroxybutyrate} \longrightarrow \text{acetoacetate} \longrightarrow \text{acetoacetyl CoA} \longrightarrow 2\ \text{acetyl CoA}$$

## Ketosis

When ketone bodies accumulate, they may not be completely metabolized by the body, which may lead to a condition called **ketosis**. Ketosis is found in severe diabetes, diets high in fat and low in carbohydrates, and starvation. Two of the ketone bodies are acids that dissociate to acetoacetate and $\beta$-hydroxybutyrate. The production of ketone bodies can cause **acidosis** (a blood pH below 7.4), a condition that often accompanies ketosis. A decrease in blood pH may interfere with the ability of the blood to carry oxygen and cause breathing difficulties.

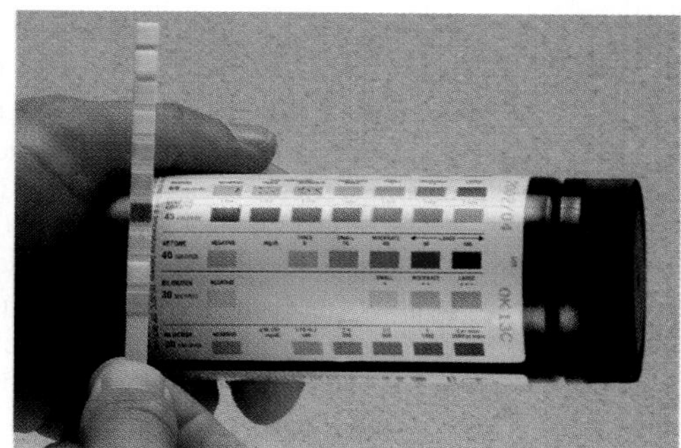

A test strip determines the level of ketone bodies in a urine sample.

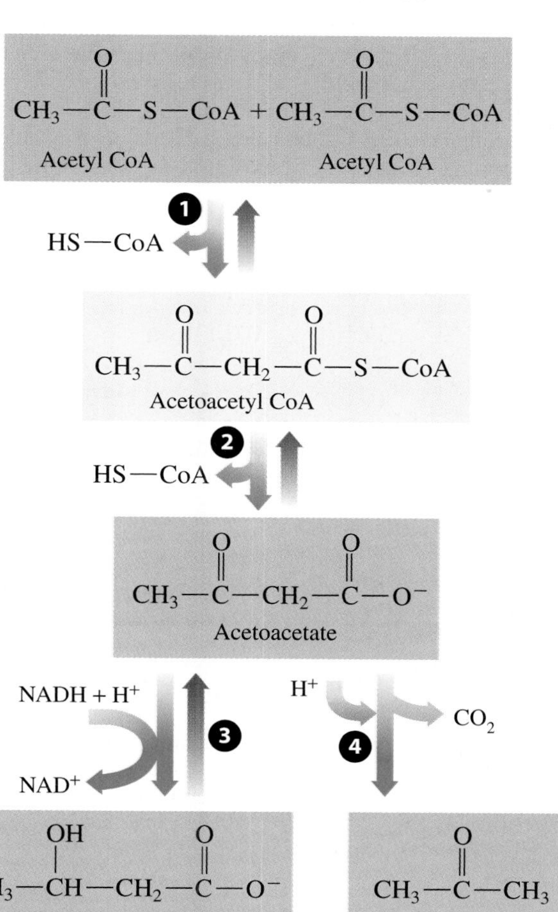


**FIGURE 24.5** In ketogenesis, acetyl CoA molecules combine to produce ketone bodies: acetoacetate, $\beta$-hydroxybutyrate, and acetone.

**Q** What condition in the body leads to the formation of ketone bodies?

CONCEPT CHECK 24.3

## Ketogenesis

The process called ketogenesis takes place in the liver.

**a.** What are the conditions that promote ketogenesis?
**b.** What are the names of the three compounds that are called ketone bodies?
**c.** What ketone bodies are responsible for the acidosis that occurs in ketogenesis?

ANSWER

**a.** When excess acetyl CoA cannot be processed by the citric acid cycle, acetyl CoA enters the ketogenesis pathway, where it forms ketone bodies.
**b.** The ketone bodies in ketogenesis are acetoacetate, β-hydroxybutyrate, and acetone.
**c.** The ketone bodies acetoacetate and β-hydroxybutyrate are formed by the dissociation of acids, which decrease the pH of the blood (acidosis).

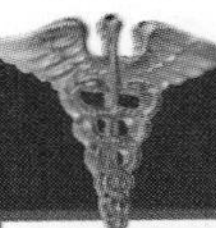

# HEALTH NOTE

## Ketone Bodies and Diabetes

The blood glucose is elevated within 30 minutes following a meal containing carbohydrates. The elevated level of glucose stimulates the secretion of the hormone *insulin* from the pancreas, which increases the flow of glucose into muscle and adipose tissue for the synthesis of glycogen. As blood glucose levels drop, the secretion of insulin decreases. When blood glucose is low, another hormone, *glucagon*, is secreted by the pancreas, which stimulates the breakdown of glycogen in the liver to yield glucose.

In *diabetes mellitus*, glucose cannot be utilized or stored as glycogen, because *insulin* is not secreted or does not function properly. In Type I, *insulin-dependent diabetes*, which often begins in childhood, the pancreas produces inadequate levels of insulin. This type of diabetes can result from damage to the pancreas by viral infections or from genetic mutations. In Type II, *insulin-resistant diabetes*, which usually occurs in adults, insulin is produced, but insulin receptors are not responsive. Thus, a person with Type II diabetes does not respond to insulin therapy. *Gestational diabetes* can occur during pregnancy, but blood glucose levels usually return to normal after the baby is born. Pregnant women with diabetes tend to gain weight and have large babies.

In all types of diabetes, insufficient amounts of glucose are available in the muscle, liver, and adipose tissue. As a result, liver cells synthesize glucose from noncarbohydrate sources (gluconeogenesis) and break down fat, which elevates the level of acetyl CoA. Excess acetyl CoA undergoes ketogenesis, and ketone bodies accumulate in the blood. The odor of acetone can be detected on the breath of a person with uncontrolled diabetes who is in ketosis.

In uncontrolled diabetes, the concentration of blood glucose exceeds the ability of the kidney to reabsorb glucose, and glucose appears in the urine. High levels of glucose increase the osmotic pressure in the blood, which leads to an increase in urine output. Symptoms of diabetes include frequent urination and excessive thirst. Treatment for diabetes includes diet changes to limit carbohydrate intake and may require medication such as a daily injection of insulin.

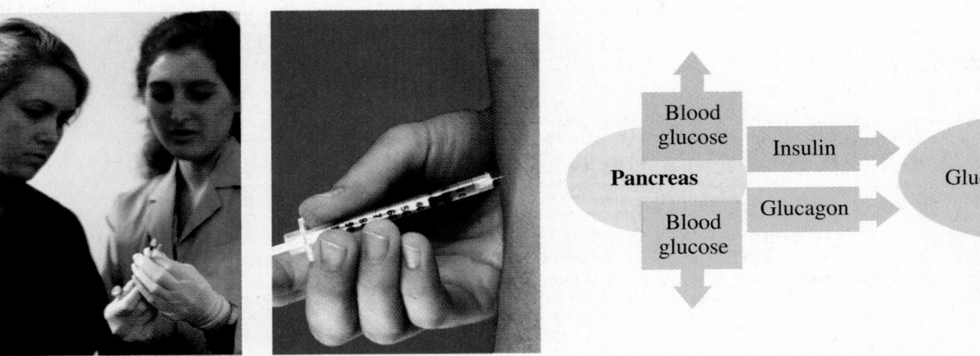

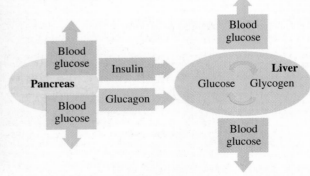

# QUESTIONS AND PROBLEMS

## Ketogenesis and Ketone Bodies

24.19 What is ketogenesis?

**24.20** If a person were fasting, why would they have high levels of acetyl CoA?

24.21 What type of reaction converts acetoacetate to β-hydroxybutyrate?

**24.22** How is acetone formed from acetoacetate?

24.23 What is ketosis?

**24.24** Why do diabetics produce high levels of ketone bodies?

## 24.5 Fatty Acid Synthesis

**LEARNING GOAL**

Describe the biosynthesis of fatty acids from acetyl CoA.

When the body has met all its energy needs and the glycogen stores are full, acetyl CoA from the breakdown of carbohydrates and fatty acids is used to form new fatty acids. In the pathway called **lipogenesis**, 2-carbon acetyl units are linked together to give a 16-carbon fatty acid, palmitic acid. Although the reactions appear much like the reverse of the reactions we discussed in fatty acid oxidation, the synthesis of fatty acids proceeds in a separate pathway with different enzymes. Fatty acid oxidation occurs in the mitochondria and uses FAD and $NAD^+$, whereas fatty acid synthesis occurs in the cytosol and uses the reduced coenzyme NADPH. NADPH is similar to NADH, except it has a phosphoryl group.

### Acyl Carrier Protein (ACP)

In $\beta$ oxidation, acetyl and acyl groups are activated using coenzyme A (CoA). In fatty acid synthesis, an acyl carrier protein (ACP—SH) activates the acyl compounds. In the ACP—SH molecule, the thiol and pantothenic acid found in CoA are attached to a protein:

MC TUTORIAL Fatty Acid Synthesis

$$\underbrace{HS-CH_2-CH_2-NH}_{\text{2-Aminoethanethiol}}-\underbrace{\overset{O}{\overset{\|}{C}}-CH_2-CH_2-NH-\overset{O}{\overset{\|}{C}}-\overset{OH}{\overset{|}{C}H}-\underset{H}{\underset{|}{\overset{CH_3}{\overset{|}{C}}}}-CH_2}_{\text{Pantothenic acid}}-O-\underset{O^-}{\underset{|}{\overset{O}{\overset{\|}{P}}}}-O-CH_2-\text{Protein}$$

Acyl carrier protein (ACP)

For fatty acid synthesis, transferring an acetyl or acyl group to ACP—SH produces the activated forms of malonyl-ACP and acetyl-ACP:

$$\underset{\text{Acetyl CoA}}{CH_3-\overset{O}{\overset{\|}{C}}-S-CoA} + HS-ACP \xrightarrow[\text{transacylase}]{\text{Acetyl CoA}} \underset{\text{Acetyl-ACP}}{CH_3-\overset{O}{\overset{\|}{C}}-S-ACP} + HS-CoA$$

$$\underset{\text{Malonyl CoA}}{^-O-\overset{O}{\overset{\|}{C}}-CH_2-\overset{O}{\overset{\|}{C}}-S-CoA} + HS-ACP \xrightarrow[\text{transacylase}]{\text{Malonyl CoA}} \underset{\text{Malonyl-ACP}}{^-O-\overset{O}{\overset{\|}{C}}-CH_2-\overset{O}{\overset{\|}{C}}-S-ACP} + HS-CoA$$

### Synthesis of Malonyl CoA

Fatty acid synthesis begins when acetyl CoA combines with bicarbonate to form a three-carbon compound, malonyl CoA. The hydrolysis of ATP provides the energy for the reaction.

$$\underset{\text{Acetyl CoA}}{CH_3-\overset{O}{\overset{\|}{C}}-S-CoA} + HCO_3^- + ATP \xrightarrow[\text{carboxylase}]{\text{Acetyl CoA}} \underset{\text{Malonyl CoA}}{^-O-\overset{O}{\overset{\|}{C}}-CH_2-\overset{O}{\overset{\|}{C}}-S-CoA} + ADP + P_i + H^+$$

### Synthesis of Palmitate

The next four reactions occur in a cycle that adds two-carbon acetyl groups to a carbon chain. (See Figure 24.6.)

#### Reaction 1 Condensation

Acetyl-ACP and malonyl-ACP condense to yield acetoacetyl-ACP and $CO_2$.

#### Reaction 2 Reduction

The keto group on the $\beta$ carbon is reduced to a hydroxyl group using hydrogen from the reduced coenzyme NADPH.

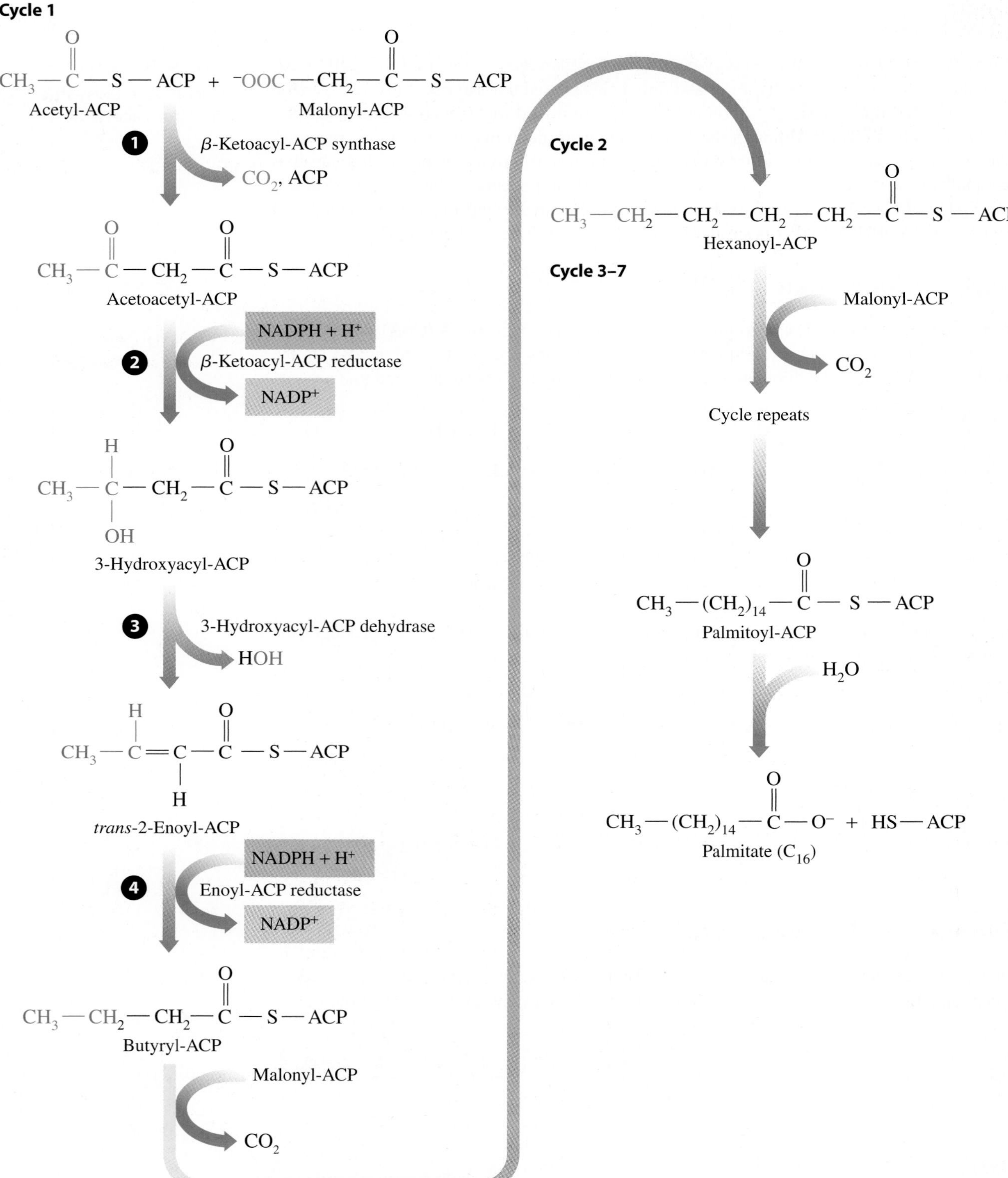


**FIGURE 24.6** In fatty acid synthesis (lipogenesis), two-carbon units from acetyl CoA are added together to form palmitate.
**Q** Identify each of the reactions 1–4 as reduction, dehydration, or condensation.

**Reaction 3 Dehydration**
The alcohol is dehydrated to form a trans double bond in *trans*-enoyl-ACP.

**Reaction 4 Reduction**
NADPH reduces the double bond to a single bond, which forms butyryl-ACP, a saturated four-carbon compound.

## Cycle Repeats

The cycle repeats as the longer four-carbon butyryl-ACP reacts with another malonyl-ACP to produce hexanoyl-ACP. After seven cycles, the product, $C_{16}$ palmitoyl-ACP, is hydrolyzed to yield palmitate and HS-ACP. We can write this synthesis of palmitate ($C_{16}$) from acetyl CoA and 7 malonyl CoA as follows:

$$\text{(1) Acetyl CoA} + 7 \text{ malonyl CoA} + 14 \text{ NADPH} + 7\text{H}^+ \longrightarrow \text{palmitate} + 7\text{CO}_2 + 14 \text{ NADP}^+ + 8 \text{ CoA—SH} + 6\text{H}_2\text{O}$$

Initially, malonyl CoA was prepared from acetyl CoA in a reaction that requires ATP and NADPH. To simplify this reaction, the $HCO_3^-$ in the cell is shown as $CO_2$:

$$\text{(2) } 7 \text{ Acetyl CoA} + 7\text{CO}_2 + 7 \text{ ATP} \longrightarrow 7 \text{ malonyl CoA} + 7 \text{ ADP} + 7\text{P}_\text{i} + 7\text{H}^+$$

When reactions (1) and (2) are added together, the overall reaction for the synthesis of palmitate from acetyl CoA is

$$8 \text{ Acetyl CoA} + 14 \text{ NADPH} + 7 \text{ ATP} \longrightarrow \text{palmitate} + 8 \text{ CoA—SH} + 14 \text{ NADP}^+ + 6\text{H}_2\text{O} + 7 \text{ ADP} + 7\text{P}_\text{i}$$

## Longer and Shorter Fatty Acids

Although we have looked at the synthesis of the fatty acid palmitate, shorter and longer fatty acids are also produced in cells. Shorter fatty acids are released before there are 16 carbon atoms in the chain. Longer fatty acids are produced with special enzymes that add two-carbon units to the carboxyl end of the fatty acid chain. An unsaturated cis bond can also be incorporated into a 10-carbon fatty acid followed by the same elongation reactions we have seen.

## Regulation of Fatty Acid Synthesis

Fatty acid synthesis takes place primarily in the adipose tissue, where triacylglycerols are formed and stored. The hormone *insulin* stimulates the formation of fatty acids. When blood glucose is high, insulin moves glucose into the cells. In the cell, insulin stimulates glycolysis and the oxidation of pyruvate, thereby producing acetyl CoA for fatty acid synthesis. During lipogenesis, the production of malonyl CoA blocks the transport of fatty acyl groups into the matrix of the mitochondria, which prevents their oxidation.

## Comparison of $\beta$ Oxidation and Fatty Acid Synthesis

We have seen that many of the steps in the synthesis of palmitate are similar to those that occur in the $\beta$ oxidation of palmitate. Synthesis combines two-carbon units, whereas $\beta$ oxidation removes two-carbon units. Synthesis involves reduction and dehydration, whereas $\beta$ oxidation involves oxidation and hydration. We can distinguish between the two pathways by comparing some of their features in Table 24.1.

**TABLE 24.1** A Comparison of $\beta$ Oxidation and Fatty Acid Synthesis

| | $\beta$ Oxidation | Fatty Acid Synthesis (lipogenesis) |
|---|---|---|
| **Site** | Mitochondrial matrix | Cytosol |
| **Activated by** | Glucagon<br>Low blood glucose | Insulin<br>High blood glucose |
| **Activator** | Coenzyme A (CoA) | Acyl carrier protein (ACP) |
| **Initial substrate** | Fatty acid | Acetyl CoA |
| **Initial coenzymes** | FAD, $NAD^+$ | NADPH |
| **Types of reaction** | Oxidation<br>Hydration<br>Cleavage | Reduction<br>Dehydration<br>Condensation |
| **Function** | Cleaves two-carbon acyl group | Adds two-carbon acyl group |
| **Final product** | Acetyl CoA | Palmitate ($C_{16}$) or other fatty acids |
| **Final coenzymes** | $FADH_2$, NADH | $NADP^+$ |

CONCEPT CHECK 24.4

**Fatty Acid Synthesis**

Malonyl-ACP is required for the elongation of fatty acid chains.

**a.** Complete the following equation for the formation of malonyl-ACP from the starting material acetyl CoA:

$$\text{Acetyl CoA} + HCO_3^- + \text{ATP} \longrightarrow$$

**b.** What enzyme catalyzes this reaction?

**c.** If malonyl-ACP is a three-carbon acyl group, why are only two carbon atoms added each time malonyl-ACP is combined with a fatty acid chain?

ANSWER

**a.** Acetyl CoA combines with bicarbonate to form malonyl CoA, which reacts with ACP to form malonyl-ACP.

$$\text{Acetyl CoA} + HCO_3^- + \text{ATP} \longrightarrow \text{malonyl CoA} + \text{ADP} + P_i + H^+$$

$$\text{Malonyl CoA} + \text{HS-ACP} \longrightarrow \text{malonyl-ACP} + \text{HC-CoA}$$

**b.** The enzyme for this reaction is acetyl CoA carboxylase.

**c.** In each cycle of fatty acid synthesis, a two-carbon acetyl group from the three-carbon group in malonyl-ACP adds to the growing fatty acid chain and one carbon forms $CO_2$.

## QUESTIONS AND PROBLEMS

### Fatty Acid Synthesis

24.25 Where does fatty acid synthesis occur in the cell?

**24.26** What compound is involved in the activation of acyl compounds in fatty acid synthesis?

24.27 What is the starting material for fatty acid synthesis?

**24.28** What is the function of malonyl-ACP in fatty acid synthesis?

24.29 Identify the reaction catalyzed by each of the following enzymes:
(1) acetyl CoA carboxylase (2) acetyl CoA transacylase
(3) malonyl CoA transacylase

**a.** converts malonyl CoA to malonyl-ACP
**b.** combines acetyl CoA with bicarbonate to give malonyl CoA
**c.** converts acetyl CoA to acetyl-ACP

**24.30** Identify the reaction catalyzed by each of the following enzymes: (1) $\beta$-ketoacyl-ACP synthase, (2) $\beta$-ketoacyl-ACP reductase, (3) 3-hydroxyacyl-ACP dehydrase, (4) enoyl-ACP reductase

**a.** catalyzes the dehydration of an alcohol
**b.** converts a carbon–carbon double bond to a carbon–carbon single bond
**c.** combines a two-carbon acetyl group with a three-carbon acyl group accompanied by the loss of $CO_2$
**d.** reduces a keto group to a hydroxyl group

24.31 Determine the number of each of the following components involved in the synthesis of one molecule of capric acid, a fatty acid with 10 carbon atoms, $C_{10}H_{20}O_2$:

**a.** $HCO_3^-$ **b.** ATP
**c.** acetyl CoA **d.** malonyl-ACP
**e.** NADPH **f.** $CO_2$ removed

**24.32** Determine the number of each of the following components in the synthesis of one molecule of myristic acid, a fatty acid with 14 carbon atoms, $C_{14}H_{28}O_2$:

**a.** $HCO_3^-$ **b.** ATP
**c.** acetyl CoA **d.** malonyl-ACP
**e.** NADPH **f.** $CO_2$ removed

## 24.6 Digestion of Proteins

LEARNING GOAL

Describe the hydrolysis of dietary protein and absorption of amino acids.

The major role of proteins is to provide amino acids for the synthesis of new proteins for the body and nitrogen atoms for the synthesis of compounds such as nucleotides. We have seen that carbohydrates and lipids are the major sources of energy, but when they are not available, amino acids are degraded to substrates that enter energy-producing pathways.

In stage 1, the digestion of proteins begins in the stomach, where hydrochloric acid (HCl) at pH 2 denatures proteins and activates enzymes such as *pepsin* that begin to hydrolyze peptide bonds. Polypeptides move from the stomach into the small intestine where *trypsin* and *chymotrypsin* complete the hydrolysis of the peptides to amino acids. The amino acids are absorbed through the intestinal walls into the bloodstream for transport to the cells. (See Figure 24.7.)

SAMPLE PROBLEM 24.3

## Digestion of Proteins

What are the sites and end products for the digestion of proteins?

SOLUTION

Proteins begin digestion in the stomach and complete digestion in the small intestine to yield amino acids.

STUDY CHECK

What is the function of HCl in the stomach?

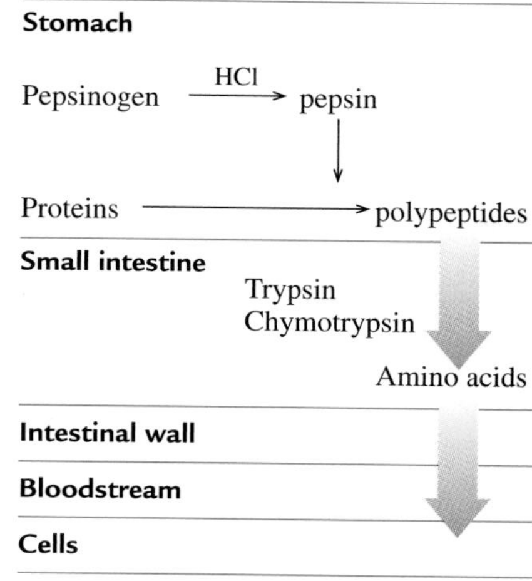


**FIGURE 24.7** Proteins are hydrolyzed to polypeptides in the stomach and to amino acids in the small intestine.

Q What enzyme, secreted into the small intestine, hydrolyzes peptides?

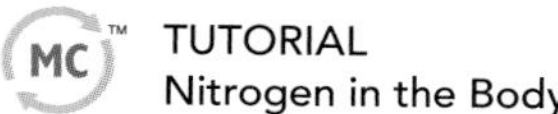


## Protein Turnover

Our bodies are constantly replacing old proteins with new ones. The process of synthesizing proteins and breaking them down is called **protein turnover**. Many types of proteins, including enzymes, hormones, and hemoglobin, are synthesized in the cells and then degraded. For example, the hormone *insulin* has a half-life of 10 minutes, whereas the half-lives of *lactate dehydrogenase* is about 2 days, and hemoglobin is 120 days. Damaged and ineffective proteins are also degraded and replaced. While most amino acids are used to build proteins, other compounds also require nitrogen for their synthesis, as seen in Table 24.2. (See Figure 24.8.)

**TABLE 24.2** Nitrogen-Containing Compounds

| Type of Compound | Example |
|---|---|
| Nonessential amino acids | Alanine, aspartate, cysteine, glycine |
| Proteins | Muscle protein, enzymes |
| Neurotransmitters | Acetylcholine, dopamine, serotonin |
| Amino alcohols | Choline, ethanolamine |
| Heme | Hemoglobin |
| Hormones | Thyroxine, epinephrine, insulin |
| Nucleotides (nucleic acids) | Purines, pyrimidines |

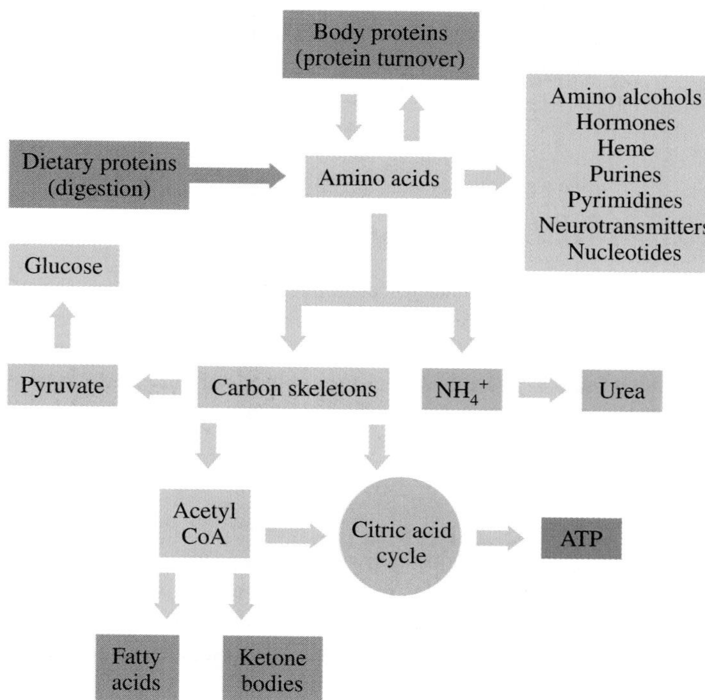


**FIGURE 24.8** Proteins are used in the synthesis of nitrogen-containing compounds or degraded to urea and carbon skeletons that enter other metabolic pathways.

Q What are some compounds that require nitrogen for their synthesis?

Usually, we maintain a nitrogen balance in the cells so that the amount of protein we break down is equal to the amount that is reused. A diet that is high in protein, however, has a positive nitrogen balance because it supplies more nitrogen than we need. Because the body cannot store nitrogen, the excess is excreted as urea. A diet that does not provide sufficient nitrogen has a negative nitrogen balance, which is a condition that occurs during starvation and fasting.

### Energy from Amino Acids

Normally, only a small amount (about 10%) of our energy needs is supplied by amino acids. However, more energy is extracted from amino acids in conditions such as fasting or starvation, when carbohydrate and fat stores are exhausted. If amino acids remain the only source of energy for a long period, the breakdown of body proteins eventually leads to a destruction of essential body tissues. In anorexia, the loss of protein decreases muscle mass and may severely weaken heart muscle and impair heart function.

**SAMPLE PROBLEM 24.4**

**Nitrogen Balance**

In positive nitrogen balance, why are excess amino acids excreted?

SOLUTION

Because the body cannot store nitrogen, amino acids that are not needed for the synthesis of proteins are excreted.

STUDY CHECK

Under what condition does the body have a negative nitrogen balance?

## QUESTIONS AND PROBLEMS

**Digestion of Proteins**

24.33 Where do dietary proteins undergo digestion in the body?

**24.34** What is meant by protein turnover?

24.35 What are some nitrogen-containing compounds that need amino acids for their synthesis?

**24.36** What is the fate of the amino acids obtained from a high protein diet?

## 24.7 Degradation of Amino Acids

**LEARNING GOAL**

Describe the reactions of transamination and oxidative deamination in the degradation of amino acids.

When dietary protein exceeds the nitrogen needed for protein synthesis, all excess amino acids are degraded in a similar way. The $\alpha$-amino group is removed to yield a keto acid, which can be converted to an intermediate of other metabolic pathways. The carbon atoms from amino acids are used in the citric acid cycle as well as the synthesis of fatty acids, ketone bodies, and glucose.

MC TUTORIAL Transamination and Deamination

### Transamination

The degradation of amino acids occurs primarily in the liver. In a **transamination** reaction, an $\alpha$-amino group is transferred from an amino acid to an $\alpha$-keto acid, usually $\alpha$-ketoglutarate. A new amino acid and a new $\alpha$-keto acid are produced. The enzymes for the transfer of amino groups are known as *transaminases* or *aminotransferases*. We can write an equation to show the transfer of the amino group from alanine to $\alpha$-ketoglutarate to yield glutamate, the new amino acid, and the α-keto acid pyruvate. The α-keto acid often used in transamination reactions is α-ketoglutarate, which is converted to glutamate.

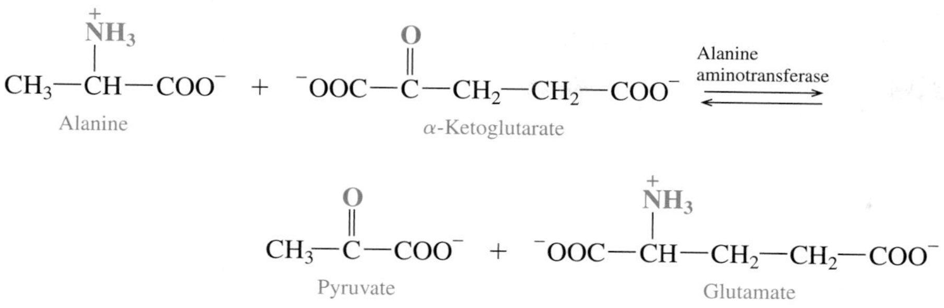

$$\underset{\text{Alanine}}{CH_3-\overset{\overset{+}{N}H_3}{\overset{|}{C}H}-COO^-} + \underset{\alpha\text{-Ketoglutarate}}{^-OOC-\overset{O}{\overset{\|}{C}}-CH_2-CH_2-COO^-} \xrightleftharpoons{\text{Alanine aminotransferase}}$$

$$\underset{\text{Pyruvate}}{CH_3-\overset{O}{\overset{\|}{C}}-COO^-} + \underset{\text{Glutamate}}{^-OOC-\overset{\overset{+}{N}H_3}{\overset{|}{C}H}-CH_2-CH_2-COO^-}$$

## SAMPLE PROBLEM 24.5

### Transamination

Write the products that form from the transamination of alanine and oxaloacetate.

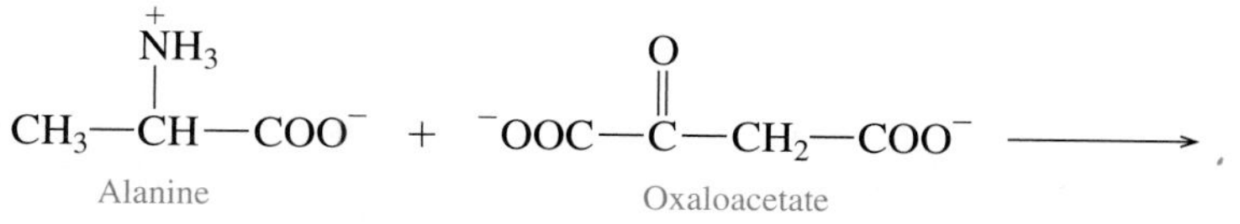

$$\underset{\text{Alanine}}{CH_3-\overset{\overset{+}{N}H_3}{\overset{|}{C}H}-COO^-} + \underset{\text{Oxaloacetate}}{^-OOC-\overset{O}{\overset{\|}{C}}-CH_2-COO^-} \longrightarrow$$

SOLUTION

The transamination product of alanine is pyruvate, and the transamination product of oxaloacetate is aspartate:

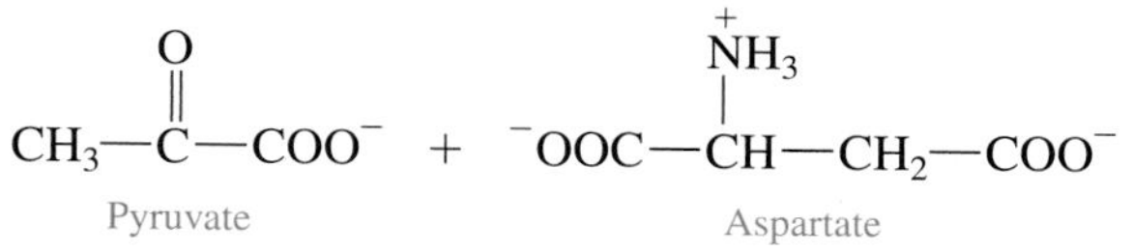

$$\underset{\text{Pyruvate}}{CH_3-\overset{O}{\overset{\|}{C}}-COO^-} + \underset{\text{Aspartate}}{^-OOC-\overset{\overset{+}{N}H_3}{\overset{|}{C}H}-CH_2-COO^-}$$

STUDY CHECK

What is a possible name for the enzyme that catalyzes the reaction above?

## Oxidative Deamination

In a process called **oxidative deamination**, the amino group in glutamate is removed as an ammonium ion, $NH_4^+$. The reaction is catalyzed by *glutamate dehydrogenase*, which uses either $NAD^+$ or $NADP^+$ as a coenzyme:

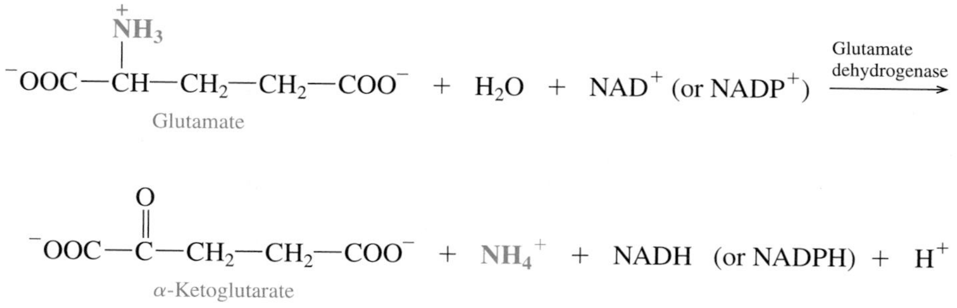

$$\underset{\text{Glutamate}}{^-OOC-\overset{\overset{+}{N}H_3}{\overset{|}{C}H}-CH_2-CH_2-COO^-} + H_2O + NAD^+ \text{ (or } NADP^+\text{)} \xrightarrow{\text{Glutamate dehydrogenase}}$$

$$\underset{\alpha\text{-Ketoglutarate}}{^-OOC-\overset{O}{\overset{\|}{C}}-CH_2-CH_2-COO^-} + NH_4^+ + NADH \text{ (or NADPH)} + H^+$$

Therefore, the amino group from any amino acid can be used to form glutamate, which undergoes oxidative deamination converting the amino group to an ammonium ion. Then, the ammonium ion is converted to urea, which we will discuss in the next section.

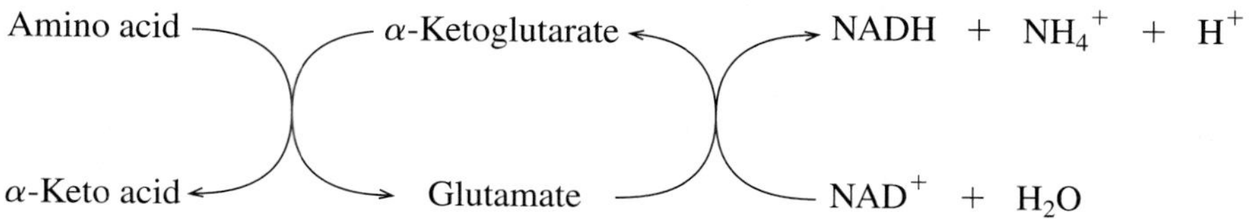

Amino acid → α-Ketoglutarate ⇄ Glutamate coupled reactions:

Amino acid — α-Ketoglutarate ← — → NADH + $NH_4^+$ + $H^+$

α-Keto acid ← — → Glutamate — — NAD$^+$ + $H_2O$

CONCEPT CHECK 24.5

**Transamination and Oxidative Deamination**

Indicate whether each of the following represents a transamination or an oxidative deamination:

**a.** Glutamate is converted to $\alpha$-ketoglutarate and $NH_4^+$.
**b.** Alanine and $\alpha$-ketoglutarate react to form pyruvate and glutamate.
**c.** A reaction is catalyzed by glutamate dehydrogenase, which requires $NAD^+$.

ANSWER

**a.** Oxidative deamination occurs when the amino group in glutamate is removed as an ammonium ion.
**b.** Transamination occurs when an amino group is transferred from an amino acid to an $\alpha$-ketoacid such as $\alpha$-ketoglutarate.
**c.** Oxidative deamination is catalyzed by glutamate dehydrogenase, which requires $NAD^+$ or $NADP^+$.

## QUESTIONS AND PROBLEMS

### Degradation of Amino Acids

24.37 What are the reactants and products in transamination reactions?

**24.38** What types of enzymes catalyze transamination reactions?

24.39 Draw the structure of the $\alpha$-keto acid produced from each of the following in transamination:

a. 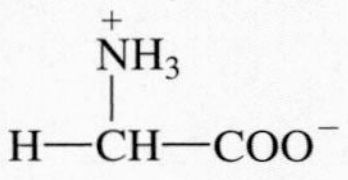 $H-CH(NH_3^+)-COO^-$ Glycine

b. 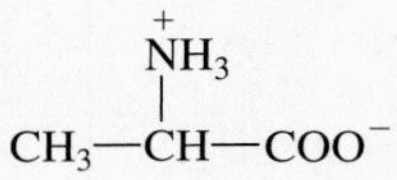 $CH_3-CH(NH_3^+)-COO^-$ Alanine

c. 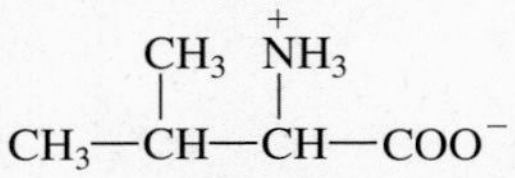 $CH_3-CH(CH_3)-CH(NH_3^+)-COO^-$ Valine

**24.40** Draw the structure of the $\alpha$-keto acid produced from each of the following in transamination:

a. 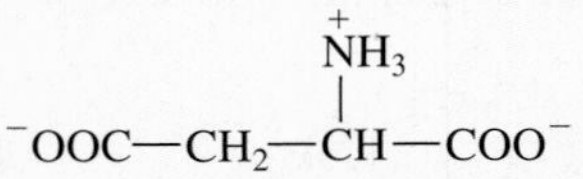 $^-OOC-CH_2-CH(NH_3^+)-COO^-$ Aspartate

b. 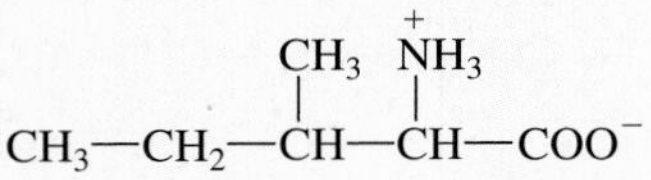 $CH_3-CH_2-CH(CH_3)-CH(NH_3^+)-COO^-$ Isoleucine

c. 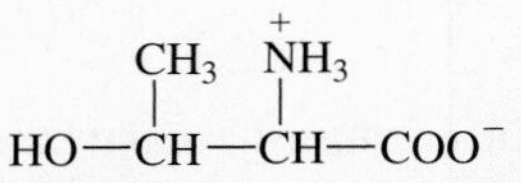 $HO-CH(CH_3)-CH(NH_3^+)-COO^-$ Serine

24.41 Write the reaction for the oxidative deamination of glutamate.

**24.42** How do the amino groups from all 20 amino acids produce ammonium ions when glutamate undergoes oxidative deamination?

## 24.8 Urea Cycle

LEARNING GOAL

Describe the formation of urea from ammonium ion.

The ammonium ion, which is the end product of amino acid degradation, is toxic if it is allowed to accumulate. In the liver, the **urea cycle** converts ammonium ions to urea, which is transported to the kidneys to form urine.

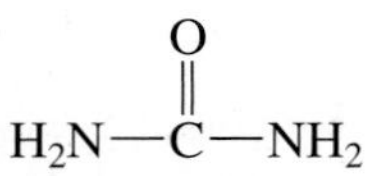

$$H_2N-\overset{\displaystyle O}{\overset{\|}{C}}-NH_2$$

Urea

In one day, a typical adult may excrete about 25–30 g of urea in the urine. This amount increases when a diet is high in protein. If urea is not properly excreted, it builds up quickly to a toxic level. To detect renal disease, the blood urea nitrogen (BUN) level is measured. If the BUN is high, protein intake must be reduced, and hemodialysis may be needed to remove toxic nitrogen waste from the blood.

MC™ TUTORIAL Detoxifying Ammonia In the Body

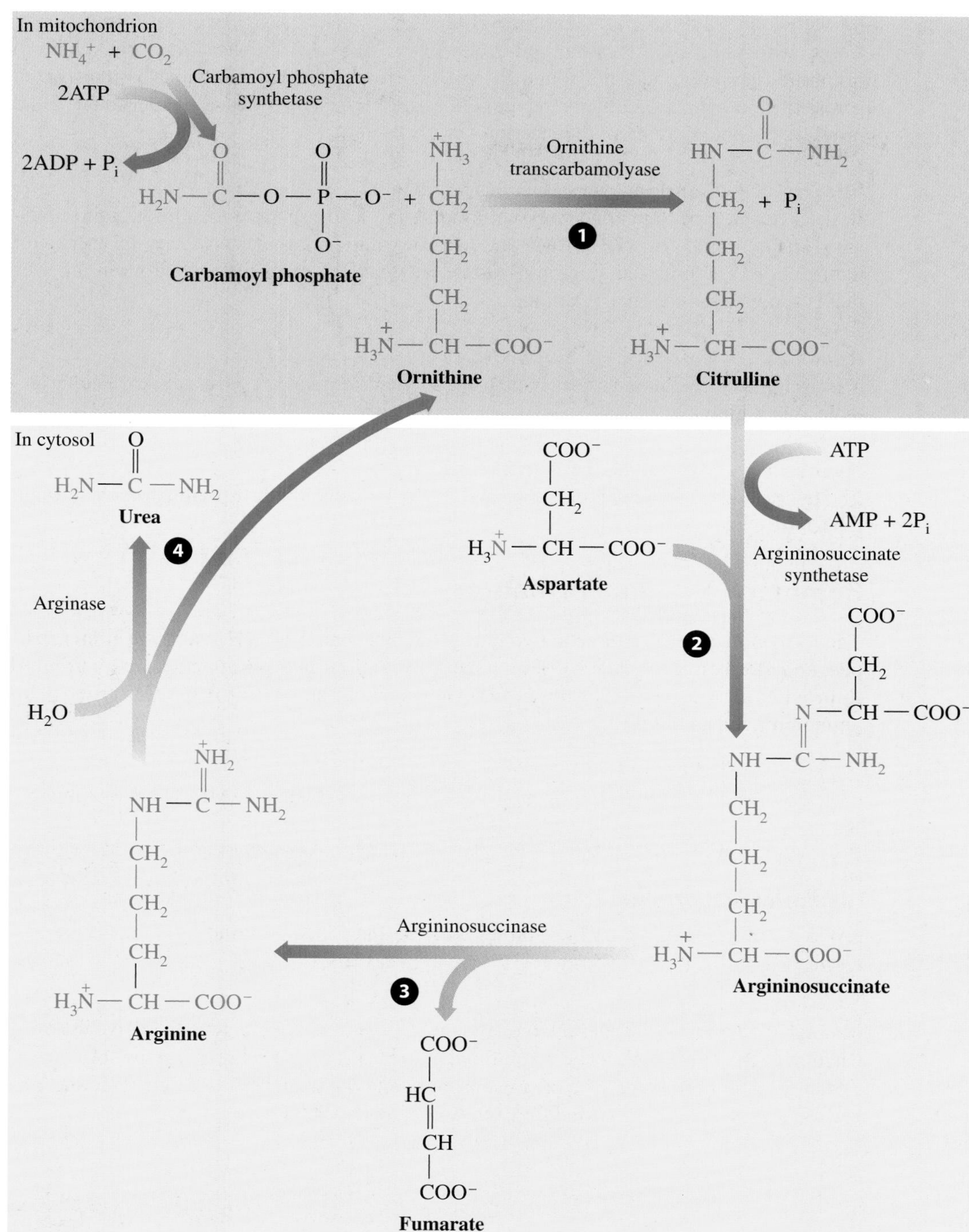


FIGURE 24.9 In the urea cycle, urea is formed from a carbon and nitrogen (blue) from carbamoyl phosphate (initially an ammonium ion from oxidative deamination) and a nitrogen atom from aspartate (pink).

Q Where in the cell is urea formed?

## Urea Cycle

The urea cycle in the liver cells consists of reactions that take place in both the mitochondria and cytosol. (See Figure 24.9.) In preparation for the urea cycle, the ammonium ions react with carbon dioxide from the citric acid cycle and two ATP to yield carbamoyl phosphate.

$$NH_4^+ + CO_2 + 2\,ATP + H_2O \xrightarrow{\text{Carbamoyl phosphate synthetase}} H_2N-\overset{\overset{\displaystyle O}{\|}}{C}-O-\overset{\overset{\displaystyle O}{\|}}{\underset{\underset{\displaystyle O^-}{|}}{P}}-O^- + 2\,ADP + P_i$$

Carbamoyl phosphate

**Reaction 1 Transfer of Carbamoyl Group**

In the mitochondria, the carbamoyl group is transferred from carbamoyl phosphate to ornithine (an amino acid not found in proteins) to yield citrulline, which is transported across the mitochondrial membrane into the cytosol. The hydrolysis of the phosphate bond provides the energy to drive the reaction.

**Reaction 2 Condensation with Aspartate**

In the cytosol, citrulline condenses with the amino acid aspartate to form argininosuccinate. The hydrolysis of ATP to AMP and two inorganic phosphates provides the energy for the reaction. The nitrogen atom in aspartate becomes the other nitrogen atom in the urea that is produced in the final reaction.

**Reaction 3 Cleavage of Fumarate**

The argininosuccinate undergoes a cleavage to yield fumarate, a citric acid cycle intermediate, and arginine.

**Reaction 4 Hydrolysis to Form Urea**

The hydrolysis of arginine yields urea and ornithine, which returns to the mitochondria to repeat the cycle.

## Summary of Urea Formation

The formation of urea starts with two nitrogen atoms, one from $NH_4^+$ and one from aspartate, and a carbon atom from $CO_2$. In the urea cycle, four phosphate bonds are hydrolyzed to provide the energy for the reactions. We can write an overall reaction starting with ammonium ion as follows:

$$NH_4^+ + CO_2 + 3\text{ ATP} + \text{aspartate} + 2H_2O \longrightarrow \text{urea} + 2\text{ ADP} + \text{AMP} + 4P_i + \text{fumarate}$$

CONCEPT CHECK 24.6

### Formation of Urea

Why would a person on a high-protein diet be instructed to drink large quantities of water?

ANSWER

A high-protein diet provides a large amount of protein that undergoes oxidative deamination in the liver. High levels of ammonium ion, $NH_4^+$, would result in the formation of large amounts of urea. The urea is transported to the kidneys where large amounts of water are needed to form urine for excretion. High levels of urea can be toxic.

SAMPLE PROBLEM 24.6

### Urea Cycle

Indicate the reaction in the urea cycle where each of the following compounds is a reactant:

**a.** aspartate **b.** ornithine **c.** arginine

SOLUTION

**a.** Aspartate condenses with citrulline in reaction 2.
**b.** Ornithine accepts the carbamoyl group in reaction 1.
**c.** Arginine is cleaved in reaction 4.

STUDY CHECK

Name the products of each reaction in Sample Problem 24.6.

## QUESTIONS AND PROBLEMS

### Urea Cycle

**24.43** Why does the body convert $NH_4^+$ to urea?

**24.44** Where is the energy source for the formation of urea?

**24.45** What is the structure of urea?

**24.46** What is the structure of carbamoyl phosphate?

**24.47** What is the source of carbon in urea?

**24.48** How much ATP energy is required to drive one turn of the urea cycle?

# 24.9 Fates of the Carbon Atoms from Amino Acids

**LEARNING GOAL**

Describe where carbon atoms from amino acids enter the citric acid cycle or other pathways.

The carbon skeletons from the transamination of amino acids are used as intermediates of the citric acid cycle or other metabolic pathways. We can classify the amino acids according to the number of carbon atoms in those intermediates. (See Figure 24.10.) The amino acids that provide three-carbon compounds are converted to pyruvate. The amino acids with four carbon atoms are converted to oxaloacetate, and the five-carbon amino acids provide α-ketoglutarate. Some amino acids are listed twice because they can enter different pathways to form citric acid cycle intermediates.

A **glucogenic amino acid** generates pyruvate or oxaloacetate, which can be converted to glucose by gluconeogenesis. A **ketogenic amino acid** produces acetoacetyl CoA or acetyl

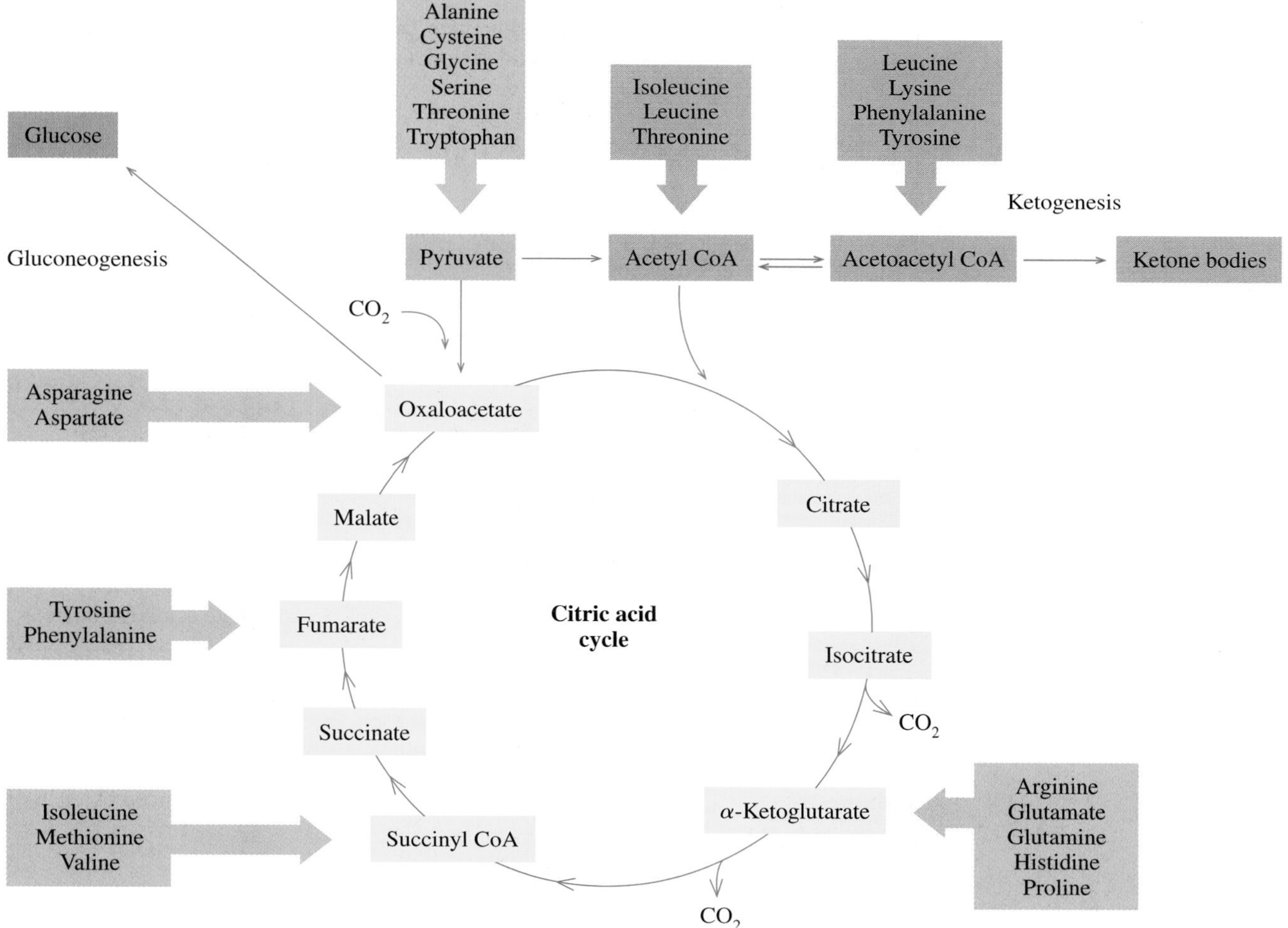


**FIGURE 24.10** Carbon atoms from degraded amino acids are converted to the intermediates of the citric acid cycle or other pathways. Glucogenic amino acids (orange boxes) produce carbon skeletons that can form glucose, and ketogenic amino acids (green boxes) can produce ketone bodies.

**Q** Why is aspartate glucogenic, but leucine ketogenic?

CoA, which can enter the ketogenesis pathway to form ketone bodies or the lipogenesis pathway to form fatty acids.

## Amino Acids that Form Three-Carbon Compounds

The carbon atoms from alanine, serine, and cysteine are converted to pyruvate in transamination reactions:

$$\text{Alanine} + \alpha\text{-ketoglutarate} \longrightarrow \text{pyruvate} + \text{glutamate}$$

Glycine is converted to serine and then to pyruvate. Tryptophan is degraded by using only the three carbon atoms that are not part of the ring system to form alanine. Threonine with four carbon atoms is degraded to glycine and acetaldehyde. The oxidation of acetaldehyde gives acetyl CoA.

## Amino Acids That Form Four-Carbon Compounds

Aspartate, a four-carbon amino acid, undergoes transamination to form oxaloacetate, a four-carbon $\alpha$-keto acid:

$$\text{Aspartate} + \alpha\text{-ketoglutarate} \longrightarrow \text{oxaloacetate} + \text{glutamate}$$

Asparagine hydrolyzes to give $NH_4^+$ and aspartate, which goes to oxaloacetate. The degradation pathways of other four-carbon amino acids—isoleucine, methionine, and valine—produce succinyl CoA, another intermediate of the citric acid cycle.

## Amino Acids that Form Five-Carbon Compounds

The five-carbon amino acids glutamine, glutamate, proline, arginine, and histidine are converted to glutamate, which undergoes oxidative deamination to yield $\alpha$-ketoglutarate and ammonium ion.

## Degradation of Ketogenic Amino Acids

Two ketogenic amino acids—leucine and lysine—are degraded to acetoacetyl CoA, which is an intermediate in the production of ketone bodies. Leucine also produces acetyl CoA. Some of the carbon atoms of the aromatic amino acids phenylalanine and tyrosine are converted to acetoacetate as well as fumarate.

**CONCEPT CHECK 24.7**

### Degradation of Amino Acids

What is the citric acid intermediate formed by each of the following amino acids?

**a.** methionine **b.** serine **c.** glutamate

ANSWER

**a.** Carbon atoms from methionine form the citric acid cycle intermediate succinyl CoA.
**b.** Carbon atoms from serine form the citric acid cycle intermediate oxaloacetate.
**c.** Carbon atoms from glutamate form the citric acid cycle intermediate $\alpha$-ketoglutarate.

**SAMPLE PROBLEM 24.7**

### Degradation of Amino Acids

Determine the citric acid cycle intermediate and the number of ATP produced by each of the following amino acids:

**a.** proline **b.** tyrosine **c.** tryptophan

SOLUTION

**a.** Proline is converted to the citric acid cycle intermediate $\alpha$-ketoglutarate. The reactions in the remaining part of the citric acid cycle from $\alpha$-ketoglutarate to oxaloacetate produce two NADH, one GTP, and one $FADH_2$. The two NADH provide six ATP, one GTP provides one ATP, and one $FADH_2$ provides two ATP, for a total of nine ATP from proline.

**b.** Tyrosine is converted to the citric acid cycle intermediate fumarate. The reactions in the remaining part of the citric acid cycle from fumarate to oxaloacetate produce one NADH, which provides three ATP.

**c.** Tryptophan is converted to the citric acid cycle intermediate oxaloacetate. The reactions in the citric acid cycle starting with oxaloacetate produce 3 NADH, 1 GTP, and 1 $FADH_2$. The 3 NADH provide 9 ATP, 1 GTP provides 1 ATP, and 1 $FADH_2$ provides 2 ATP, for a total of 12 ATP from tryptophan.

STUDY CHECK

Why does the citric acid cycle intermediate from leucine supply more ATP than the intermediate from phenylalanine?

## QUESTIONS AND PROBLEMS

### Fates of the Carbon Atoms from Amino Acids

24.49 What is the function of a glucogenic amino acid?

**24.50** What is the function of a ketogenic amino acid?

24.51 What metabolic substrate(s) can be produced from the carbon atoms of each of the following amino acids?
**a.** alanine **b.** aspartate
**c.** valine **d.** glutamine

**24.52** What metabolic substrate(s) can be produced from the carbon atoms of each of the following amino acids?
**a.** leucine **b.** asparagine
**c.** cysteine **d.** arginine

# 24.10 Synthesis of Amino Acids

LEARNING GOAL

Illustrate how some nonessential amino acids are synthesized from intermediates in the citric acid cycle and other metabolic pathways.

Plants and bacteria such as *E. coli* produce all of their amino acids using $NH_4^+$ and $NO_3^-$. However, humans can synthesize only 10 of the 20 amino acids found in their proteins. The nonessential amino acids are synthesized in the body (discussed in Chapter 19), whereas the essential amino acids must be obtained from the diet. (See Table 24.3.) Two amino acids, arginine and histidine, are essential in diets for children due to their rapid growth requirements, but not for adults.

TABLE 24.3 Essential and Nonessential Amino Acids in Humans

| Essential | |
|---|---|
| Arginine* | Methionine |
| Histidine* | Phenylalanine |
| Isoleucine | Threonine |
| Leucine | Tryptophan |
| Lysine | Valine |
| **Nonessential** | |
| Alanine | Glutamine |
| Asparagine | Glycine |
| Aspartate | Proline |
| Cysteine | Serine |
| Glutamate | Tyrosine |

*Essential for children only

## Some Pathways for Amino Acid Synthesis

A variety of pathways are involved in the synthesis of nonessential amino acids. When the body synthesizes nonessential amino acids, the $\alpha$-keto acid skeletons are obtained from the citric acid cycle or glycolysis and converted to amino acids by transamination. (See Figure 24.11.)

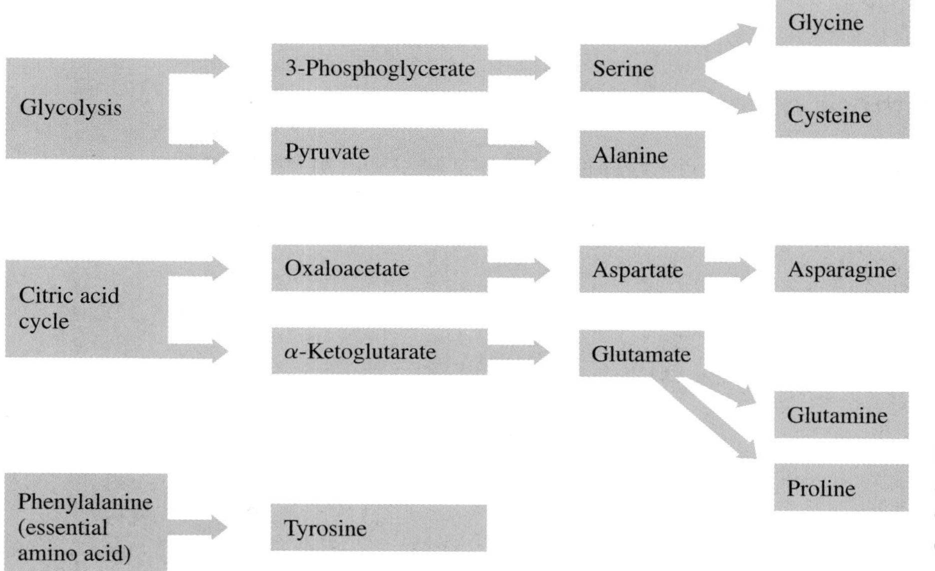


FIGURE 24.11 Nonessential amino acids are synthesized from intermediates of glycolysis and the citric acid cycle.

Q How is alanine formed from pyruvate?

Some of the amino acids are formed from a simple transamination. For example, the transfer of the amino group from glutamate to pyruvate, a three-carbon $\alpha$-keto acid, produces alanine, an amino acid with three carbons:

$$\underset{\text{Pyruvate}}{CH_3-\overset{\overset{\displaystyle O}{\|}}{C}-COO^-} + \underset{\text{Glutamate}}{^-OOC-\overset{\overset{\displaystyle \overset{+}{N}H_3}{|}}{C}H-CH_2-CH_2-COO^-} \xrightarrow[\text{transaminase}]{\text{Glutamate pyruvate}}$$

$$\underset{\text{Alanine}}{CH_3-\overset{\overset{\displaystyle \overset{+}{N}H_3}{|}}{C}H-COO^-} + \underset{\alpha\text{-Ketoglutarate}}{^-OOC-\overset{\overset{\displaystyle O}{\|}}{C}-CH_2-CH_2-COO^-}$$

In another transamination using glutamate, the four-carbon oxaloacetate from the citric acid cycle is converted to aspartate:

$$\underset{\text{Oxaloacetate}}{^-OOC-CH_2-\overset{\overset{\displaystyle O}{\|}}{C}-COO^-} + \underset{\text{Glutamate}}{^-OOC-\overset{\overset{\displaystyle \overset{+}{N}H_3}{|}}{C}H-CH_2-CH_2-COO^-} \xrightarrow[\text{transaminase}]{\text{Glutamate oxaloacetate}}$$

$$\underset{\text{Aspartate}}{^-OOC-CH_2-\overset{\overset{\displaystyle \overset{+}{N}H_3}{|}}{C}H-COO^-} + \underset{\alpha\text{-Ketoglutarate}}{^-OOC-\overset{\overset{\displaystyle O}{\|}}{C}-CH_2-CH_2-COO^-}$$

These two *transaminases* are abundant in the cells of the liver and heart, but they are present only in low levels in the bloodstream. When an injury or disease occurs, they are released from the damaged cells into the bloodstream. Elevated levels of *serum glutamate pyruvate transaminase* (SGPT) and *serum glutamate oxaloacetate transaminase* (SGOT) provide a means to diagnose the extent of damage to the liver or the heart.

## Synthesis of Glutamine

The synthesis of the other nonessential amino acids requires several reactions in addition to transamination. For example, glutamine is synthesized when a second amino group is added to glutamate using the energy from the hydrolysis of ATP:

$$\underset{\text{Glutamate}}{^-OOC-\overset{\overset{\displaystyle \overset{+}{N}H_3}{|}}{C}H-CH_2-CH_2-COO^-} + NH_3 \xrightarrow[\text{ATP} \;\; \text{ADP} + P_i]{\text{Glutamine synthetase}} \underset{\text{Glutamine}}{^-OOC-\overset{\overset{\displaystyle \overset{+}{N}H_3}{|}}{C}H-CH_2-CH_2-\overset{\overset{\displaystyle O}{\|}}{C}-NH_2}$$

## Synthesis of Serine and Cysteine

In the synthesis of serine, three steps are required starting with 3-phosphoglycerate from glycolysis. In this pathway, the —OH group of glycerate is oxidized to give an $\alpha$-keto acid, which undergoes transamination by glutamate accompanied by the loss of the phosphate group:

$$\underset{\text{3-Phosphoglycerate}}{^-OOC-\overset{\overset{\displaystyle OH}{|}}{C}H-CH_2-O-\underset{\underset{\displaystyle O^-}{|}}{\overset{\overset{\displaystyle O}{\|}}{P}}-O^-} + NAD^+ + \text{glutamate} + H_2O \longrightarrow$$

$$\underset{\text{Serine}}{^-OOC-\overset{\overset{\displaystyle \overset{+}{N}H_3}{|}}{C}H-CH_2-OH} + NADH + H^+ + \alpha\text{-ketoglutarate} + P_i$$

Once serine is formed, its —OH group is replaced by —SH from a reaction with homocysteine:

$$^{-}OOC{-}\overset{\overset{+}{N}H_3}{\overset{|}{C}H}{-}CH_2{-}OH \;+\; ^{-}OOC{-}\overset{\overset{+}{N}H_3}{\overset{|}{C}H}{-}CH_2{-}CH_2{-}\mathbf{SH} \xrightarrow{\text{Cysteine synthase}}$$

Serine — Homocysteine

$$^{-}OOC{-}\overset{\overset{+}{N}H_3}{\overset{|}{C}H}{-}CH_2{-}\mathbf{SH} \;+\; ^{-}OOC{-}\overset{O}{\overset{\|}{C}}{-}CH_2{-}CH_3 \;+\; NH_4^{+}$$

Cysteine — $\alpha$-Ketobutyrate

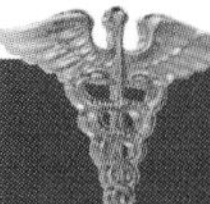

## HEALTH NOTE

### Phenylketonuria (PKU)

In the genetic disease *phenylketonuria* (PKU), a person cannot convert phenylalanine to tyrosine, because the gene for an enzyme in the conversion is defective. As a result, large amounts of phenylalanine accumulate. In a different pathway, phenylalanine undergoes transamination to form phenylpyruvate, which is decarboxylated to phenylacetate. Large amounts of these compounds are excreted in the urine.

In infants, high levels of phenylpyruvate and phenylacetate cause severe mental retardation. However, the defect can be identified at birth, and all newborns are now tested for PKU. By detecting PKU early, retardation is avoided by using a diet with proteins that are low in phenylalanine and high in tyrosine. It is also important to avoid the use of sweeteners and soft drinks containing aspartame, which contains phenylalanine as one of two amino acids in its structure. In adulthood, some persons with PKU can eat a nearly normal diet as long as they are checked for phenylpyruvate periodically.

$$C_6H_5{-}CH_2{-}\overset{\overset{+}{N}H_3}{\overset{|}{C}H}{-}COO^{-} \xrightarrow{\text{Transamination}} C_6H_5{-}CH_2{-}\overset{O}{\overset{\|}{C}}{-}COO^{-}$$

Phenylalanine — Phenylpyruvate

Phenylalanine ⟶ (Phenylalanine hydroxylase, blocked ✕) ⟶ Tyrosine

$$HO{-}C_6H_4{-}CH_2{-}\overset{\overset{+}{N}H_3}{\overset{|}{C}H}{-}COO^{-}$$

Tyrosine

Phenylpyruvate ⟶ ($CO_2$ released) ⟶ Phenylacetate

$$C_6H_5{-}CH_2{-}COO^{-}$$

Phenylacetate

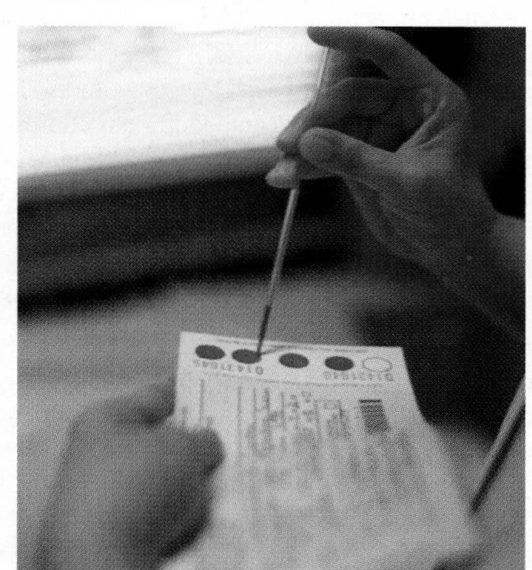

## Synthesis of Tyrosine

Tyrosine, an aromatic amino acid with a hydroxyl group, is formed from phenylalanine, an essential amino acid:

$$C_6H_5{-}CH_2{-}\overset{\overset{+}{N}H_3}{\overset{|}{C}H}{-}COO^{-} + \mathbf{O_2} \xrightarrow{\text{Phenylalanine hydroxylase}} \mathbf{HO}{-}C_6H_4{-}CH_2{-}\overset{\overset{+}{N}H_3}{\overset{|}{C}H}{-}COO^{-} + H_2\mathbf{O}$$

Phenylalanine — Tyrosine

SAMPLE PROBLEM 24.8

**Synthesis of Amino Acids**

What compound is typically the source of amino groups when transamination is used to synthesize nonessential amino acids?

SOLUTION

Glutamate is the usual source of amino groups in the synthesis of nonessential amino acids.

STUDY CHECK

What are the sources of the reactants for the synthesis of nonessential amino acids?

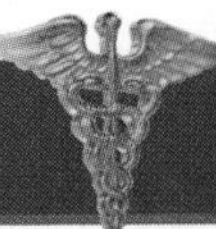

# HEALTH NOTE

## Homocysteine and Coronary Heart Disease

We obtain most of our methionine, an essential amino acid, from the proteins in meat. In the body, methionine is degraded to homocysteine. In turn, homocysteine can be used to synthesize methionine in a process that requires folic acid and vitamin $B_{12}$ (cobalamin). In a study at Harvard during the 1960s, children suffering from *homocystinuria*, a genetic disorder, were found to have high homocysteine levels. They were also found to have advanced *atherosclerosis*, which led to strokes and heart attacks early in life. This relationship was one of the first indications of a link between elevated homocysteine levels and heart disease. In the past few years, additional clinical research has indicated that elevated blood levels of homocysteine are associated with increased risk of coronary heart disease, which can also lead to stroke and myocardial infarction (heart attack). Researchers also found that low levels of folic acid accompanied the elevated levels of homocysteine. This finding suggests that inadequate levels of folic acid limit the synthesis of methionine from homocysteine causing an accumulation of homocysteine.

When the body has adequate amounts of vitamin $B_6$, $B_{12}$, and folic acid, the synthesis of methionine maintains proper levels of homocysteine, which we need for healthy tissues. However, a deficiency of any one of these vitamins can lead to increased homocysteine levels, which may be damaging to the heart. Folic acid is recommended as a supplement for pregnant women to avoid folic acid deficiencies during the growth of a fetus.

$$HS-CH_2-CH_2-CH(\overset{+}{N}H_3)-COO^- \xrightarrow[\text{Methionine synthase}]{CH_3-B_{12} \;\rightarrow\; B_{12}} CH_3-S-CH_2-CH_2-CH(\overset{+}{N}H_3)-COO^-$$

Homocysteine → Methionine

## Overview of Metabolism

In these chapters, we have seen that catabolic pathways degrade large molecules to small molecules that are used for energy production via the citric acid cycle and electron transport. We have also looked at the anabolic pathways that lead to the synthesis of larger molecules in the cell. In the overall view of metabolism, compounds may be degraded for energy or used to synthesize larger molecules from several branch points. For example, glucose can be degraded to acetyl CoA for the citric acid cycle to produce energy or converted to glycogen for storage. When glycogen stores are depleted, fatty acids are degraded for energy. Amino acids normally used to synthesize nitrogen-containing compounds in the cells can also be used for energy after they are degraded to intermediates of the citric acid cycle. In the synthesis of nonessential amino acids, $\alpha$-keto acids of the citric acid cycle enter a variety of reactions that convert them to amino acids through transamination by glutamate. (See Figure 24.12.)

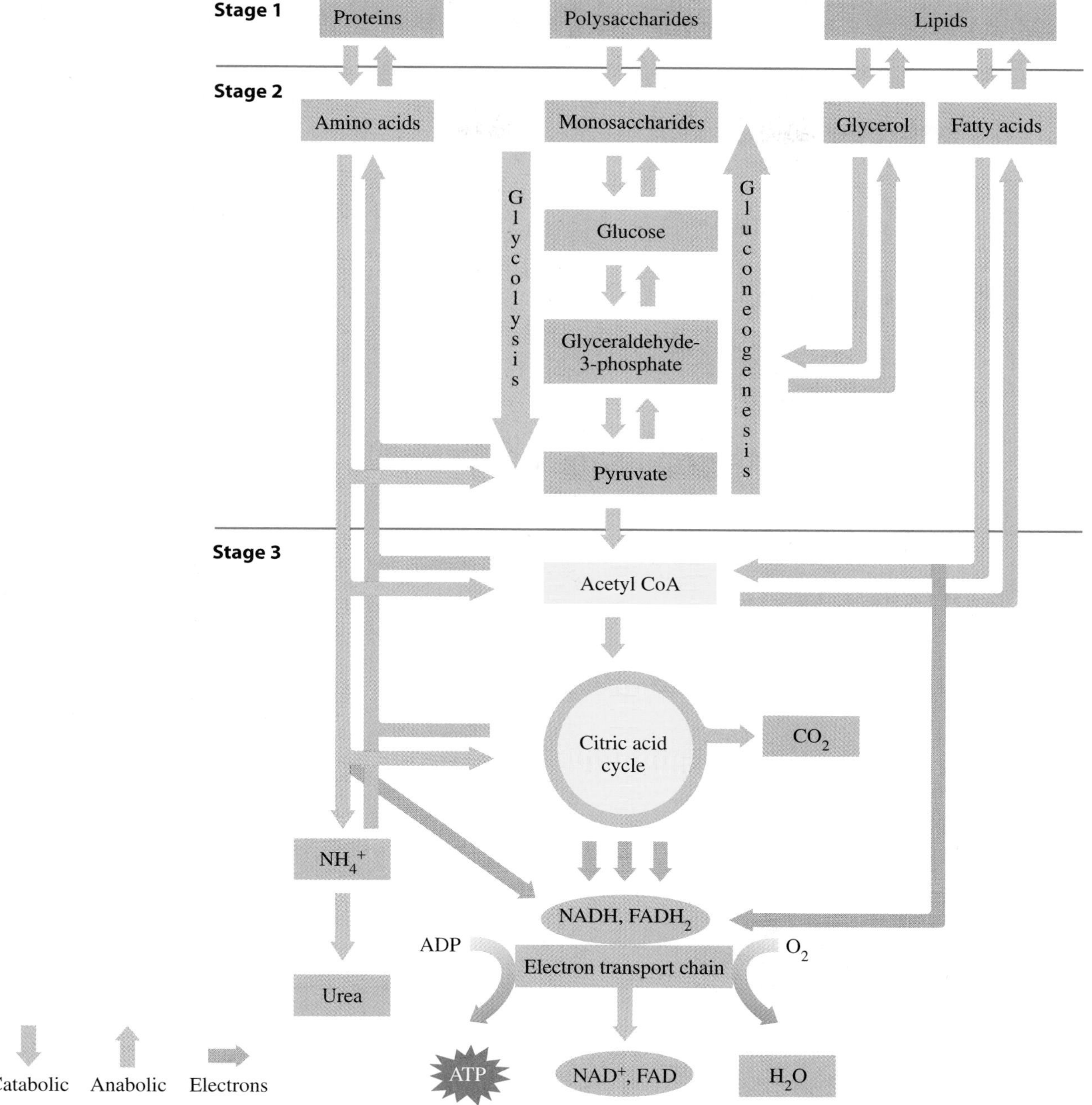


**FIGURE 24.12** Catabolic and anabolic pathways in the cells provide the energy and necessary compounds for the cells.

**Q** Under what conditions in the cell are amino acids degraded for energy?

## QUESTIONS AND PROBLEMS

### Synthesis of Amino Acids

**24.53** What do we call the amino acids that humans can synthesize?

**24.54** How do humans obtain the amino acids that cannot be synthesized in the body?

**24.55** How is glutamate converted to glutamine?

**24.56** What amino acid is needed for the synthesis of tyrosine?

**24.57** What do the letters PKU mean?

**24.58** How is PKU treated?

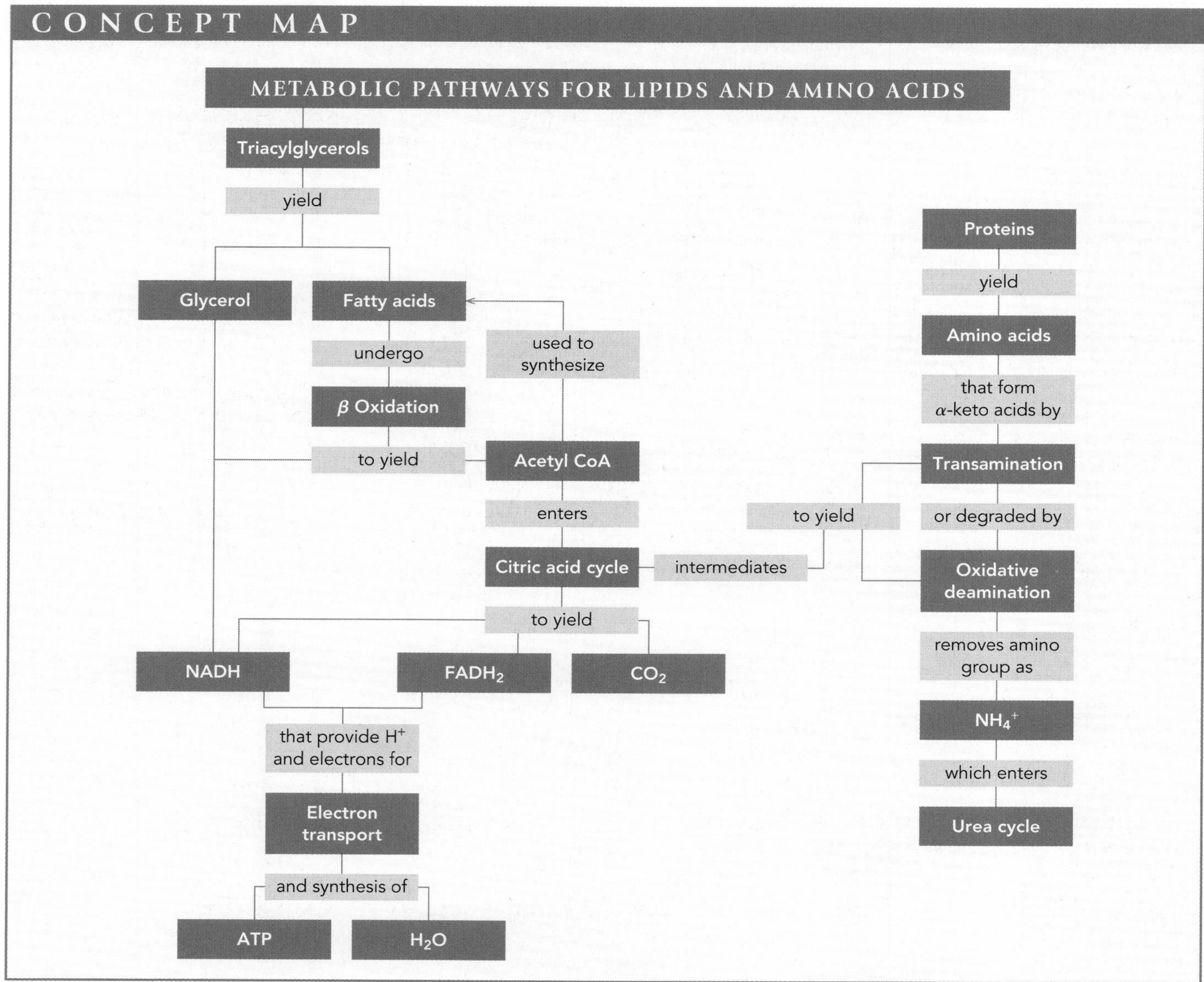


## CHAPTER REVIEW

### 24.1 Digestion of Triacylglycerols

***LEARNING GOAL:*** *Describe the sites and products obtained from the digestion of triacylglycerols.*

Triacylglycerols are hydrolyzed in the small intestine to yield monoacylglycerols and fatty acids, which enter the intestinal wall and form new triacylglycerols. They bind with proteins to form chylomicrons, which transport them through the lymphatic system and bloodstream to the tissues.

### 24.2 Oxidation of Fatty Acids

***LEARNING GOAL:*** *Describe the metabolic pathway of β oxidation.*

When needed as an energy source, fatty acids are linked to coenzyme A and transported into the mitochondria, where they undergo β oxidation. The fatty acyl chain is oxidized to yield a shorter fatty acid, acetyl CoA, and the reduced coenzymes NADH and $FADH_2$.

### 24.3 ATP and Fatty Acid Oxidation

***LEARNING GOAL:*** *Calculate the total ATP produced by the complete oxidation of a fatty acid.*

The activation of a fatty acid for β oxidation requires an input of 2 ATP. The energy obtained from a particular fatty acid depends on its length, with each oxidation cycle yielding 5 ATP and an additional 12 ATP from each acetyl CoA that enters the citric acid cycle.

### 24.4 Ketogenesis and Ketone Bodies

***LEARNING GOAL:*** *Describe the pathway of ketogenesis.*

When high levels of acetyl CoA are present in the cell, they enter the ketogenesis pathway, forming ketone bodies such as acetoacetate, which can cause ketosis and acidosis.

### 24.5 Fatty Acid Synthesis

***LEARNING GOAL:*** *Describe the biosynthesis of fatty acids from acetyl CoA.*

When there is an excess of acetyl CoA in the cell, the two-carbon acetyl CoA units link together to synthesize palmitate, which is converted to triacylglycerols and stored in the adipose tissue.

### 24.6 Digestion of Proteins

**LEARNING GOAL:** *Describe the hydrolysis of dietary protein and absorption of amino acids.*

The digestion of proteins, which begins in the stomach and continues in the small intestine, involves the hydrolysis of peptide bonds by proteases to yield amino acids that are absorbed through the intestinal wall and transported to the cells.

### 24.7 Degradation of Amino Acids

**LEARNING GOAL:** *Describe the reactions of transamination and oxidative deamination in the degradation of amino acids.*

When the amount of amino acids in the cells exceeds that needed for synthesis of nitrogen compounds, the process of transamination converts them to $\alpha$-keto acids and glutamate. Oxidative deamination of glutamate produces ammonium ions and $\alpha$-ketoglutarate.

### 24.8 Urea Cycle

**LEARNING GOAL:** *Describe the formation of urea from ammonium ion.*

Ammonium ions from oxidative deamination combine with bicarbonate and ATP to form carbamoyl phosphate, which is converted to urea.

### 24.9 Fates of the Carbon Atoms from Amino Acids

**LEARNING GOAL:** *Describe where carbon atoms from amino acids enter the citric acid cycle or other pathways.*

The carbon atoms from the degradation of glucogenic amino acids enter the citric acid cycle or gluconeogenesis whereas ketogenic amino acids provide acetyl CoA or acetoacetate for ketogenesis.

### 24.10 Synthesis of Amino Acids

**LEARNING GOAL:** *Illustrate how some nonessential amino acids are synthesized from intermediates in the citric acid cycle and other metabolic pathways.*

Nonessential amino acids are synthesized when amino groups from glutamate are transferred to an $\alpha$-keto acid obtained from glycolysis or the citric acid cycle.

## SUMMARY OF KEY REACTIONS

### DIGESTION OF TRIACYLGLYCEROLS

$$\text{Triacylglycerols} + 2H_2O \xrightarrow{\text{Pancreatic lipase}} \text{monoacylglycerols} + 2\text{ fatty acids}$$

### MOBILIZATION OF FATS

$$\text{Triacylglycerols} + 3H_2O \xrightarrow{\text{Lipases}} \text{glycerol} + 3\text{ fatty acids}$$

### METABOLISM OF GLYCEROL

$$\text{Glycerol} + \text{ATP} + \text{NAD}^+ \longrightarrow \text{dihydroxyacetone phosphate} + \text{ADP} + \text{NADH} + H^+$$

### $\beta$ OXIDATION OF FATTY ACID

$$\text{Myristyl CoA} + 6\text{ HS—CoA} + 6\text{ FAD} + 6\text{ NAD}^+ + 6H_2O \longrightarrow 7\text{ acetyl CoA} + 6\text{ FADH}_2 + 6\text{ NADH} + 6H^+$$

### FATTY ACID SYNTHESIS

$$8\text{ Acetyl CoA} + 14\text{ NADPH} + 14H^+ + 7\text{ ATP} \longrightarrow \text{palmitate } (C_{16}) + 8\text{ HS—CoA} + 14\text{ NADP}^+ + 6H_2O + 7\text{ ADP} + 7P_i$$

### TRANSAMINATION

$$\underset{\text{Alanine}}{CH_3\text{—}CH(\overset{+}{N}H_3)\text{—}COO^-} + \underset{\alpha\text{-Ketoglutarate}}{^-OOC\text{—}C(=O)\text{—}CH_2\text{—}CH_2\text{—}COO^-} \xrightleftharpoons{\text{Alanine aminotransferase}} \underset{\text{Pyruvate}}{CH_3\text{—}C(=O)\text{—}COO^-} + \underset{\text{Glutamate}}{^-OOC\text{—}CH(\overset{+}{N}H_3)\text{—}CH_2\text{—}CH_2\text{—}COO^-}$$

### OXIDATIVE DEAMINATION

$$\underset{\text{Glutamate}}{^-OOC\text{—}CH(\overset{+}{N}H_3)\text{—}CH_2\text{—}CH_2\text{—}COO^-} + H_2O + NAD^+\ (NADP^+) \xrightleftharpoons{\text{Glutamate dehydrogenase}} \underset{\alpha\text{-Ketoglutarate}}{^-OOC\text{—}C(=O)\text{—}CH_2\text{—}CH_2\text{—}COO^-} + NH_4^+ + NADH\ (NADPH) + H^+$$

## UREA CYCLE

$$NH_4^+ + CO_2 + 3\ ATP + \text{aspartate} + 2H_2O \longrightarrow \text{urea} + 2\ ADP + AMP + 4P_i + \text{fumarate}$$

# KEY TERMS

**acidosis** Low blood pH resulting from the formation of acidic ketone bodies.

**beta ($\beta$) oxidation** The degradation of fatty acids that removes two-carbon segments from a fatty acid chain.

**chylomicrons** Lipoproteins formed by coating triacylglycerols with proteins for transport in the lymphatic system and bloodstream.

**fat mobilization** The hydrolysis of triacylglycerols in the adipose tissue to yield fatty acids and glycerol for energy production.

**glucogenic amino acid** An amino acid that provides carbon atoms for the synthesis of glucose.

**ketogenesis** The pathway that converts acetyl CoA to four-carbon acetoacetate and other ketone bodies.

**ketogenic amino acid** An amino acid that provides carbon atoms for the synthesis of fatty acids or ketone bodies.

**ketone bodies** The products of ketogenesis: acetoacetate, $\beta$-hydroxybutyrate, and acetone.

**ketosis** A condition in which high levels of ketone bodies cannot be metabolized, leading to lower blood pH.

**lipogenesis** The synthesis of fatty acid in which two-carbon acetyl units link together to yield fatty acids, primarily palmitic acid.

**oxidative deamination** The loss of ammonium ion when glutamate is degraded to $\alpha$-ketoglutarate.

**protein turnover** The amount of protein that we break down from our diet and utilize for synthesis of proteins and nitrogen-containing compounds.

**transamination** The transfer of an amino group from an amino acid to an $\alpha$-keto acid.

**urea cycle** The process in which ammonium ions from the degradation of amino acids and $CO_2$ form carbamoyl phosphate, which is converted to urea.

# UNDERSTANDING THE CONCEPTS

**24.59** Lauric acid, $CH_3—(CH_2)_{10}—COOH$, found in coconut oil, is a saturated fatty acid.

a. Write the formula of the activated form of lauric acid.
b. Indicate the $\alpha$ and $\beta$ carbon atoms in the fatty acyl molecule.
c. Write the overall equation for the complete $\beta$ oxidation of lauric acid.
d. How many acetyl CoA units are produced?
e. How many cycles of $\beta$ oxidation are needed?
f. Account for the total ATP yield from $\beta$ oxidation of lauric acid ($C_{12}$ fatty acid) by completing the following calculations:

| | |
|---|---|
| ___Activation | −2 ATP |
| ___Acetyl CoA | ___ATP |
| ___$FADH_2$ | ___ATP |
| ___NADH | ___ATP |
| **Total** | ___ATP |

**24.60** Arachidic acid is a saturated 20-carbon fatty acid found in peanut and fish oils.

a. Write the formula of the activated form of arachidic acid.
b. Indicate the $\alpha$ and $\beta$ carbon atoms in the fatty acyl molecule.
c. Write the overall equation for the complete $\beta$ oxidation of arachidic acid.
d. How many acetyl CoA units are produced?
e. How many cycles of $\beta$ oxidation are needed?
f. Account for the total ATP yield from $\beta$ oxidation of arachidic acid by completing the following calculations:

| | |
|---|---|
| ___Activation | −2 ATP |
| ___Acetyl CoA | ___ATP |
| ___$FADH_2$ | ___ATP |
| ___NADH | ___ATP |
| **Total** | ___ATP |

## ADDITIONAL QUESTIONS AND PROBLEMS

*For instructor-assigned homework, go to* ***www.masteringchemistry.com***.

24.61 How are dietary triacylglycerols digested?

**24.62** What is a chylomicron?

24.63 Why are the fats in the adipose tissues of the body considered the major form of stored energy?

**24.64** How are fatty acids obtained from stored fats?

24.65 Why doesn't the brain utilize fatty acids for energy?

**24.66** Why don't red blood cells utilize fatty acids for energy?

24.67 A triacylglycerol is hydrolyzed in fat cells of adipose tissues and the fatty acid is transported to the liver.
  **a.** What happens to the glycerol?
  **b.** Where in the liver cells is the fatty acid activated for $\beta$ oxidation?
  **c.** What is the energy cost for activation of the fatty acid?
  **d.** What is the purpose of activating fatty acids?

**24.68** Consider the $\beta$ oxidation of a saturated fatty acid.
  **a.** What is the activated form of the fatty acid?
  **b.** Why is the oxidation called $\beta$ oxidation?
  **c.** What reactions in the fatty acid cycle require coenzymes?
  **d.** What is the yield in ATP for one cycle of $\beta$ oxidation?

24.69 Identify each of the following as involved in $\beta$ oxidation or in fatty acid synthesis:
  **a.** $NAD^+$
  **b.** occurs in the mitochondrial matrix
  **c.** malonyl-ACP
  **d.** cleavage of two-carbon acetyl group
  **e.** acyl carrier protein
  **f.** acetyl CoA carboxylase

**24.70** Identify each of the following as involved in $\beta$ oxidation or fatty acid synthesis:
  **a.** NADPH
  **b.** takes place in the cytosol
  **c.** FAD
  **d.** oxidation of a hydroxyl group
  **e.** coenzyme A
  **f.** hydration of a double bond

24.71 The metabolism of triacylglycerols and carbohydrates is influenced by the hormones insulin and glucagon. Indicate the results of each of the following as stimulating (1) fatty acid oxidation or (2) the synthesis of fatty acids:
  **a.** low blood glucose
  **b.** glucagon secreted

**24.72** The metabolism of triacylglycerols and carbohydrates is influenced by the hormones insulin and glucagon. Indicate the results of each of the following as stimulating (1) fatty acid oxidation or (2) the synthesis of fatty acids:
  **a.** high blood glucose
  **b.** insulin secreted

24.73 Why is ammonium ion produced in the liver converted immediately to urea?

**24.74** Calculate the total ATP produced in the complete oxidation of caproic acid, $C_6H_{12}O_2$, and compare with the total ATP produced from the oxidation of glucose, $C_6H_{12}O_6$.

24.75 Indicate the reactant in the urea cycle that reacts with each of the following compounds:
  **a.** aspartate
  **b.** ornithine

**24.76** Indicate the products in the urea cycle from the step that uses each of the following compounds:
  **a.** arginine
  **b.** argininosuccinate

24.77 What metabolic substrate(s) can be produced from the carbon atoms of each of the following amino acids?
  **a.** serine
  **b.** lysine
  **c.** methionine
  **d.** glutamate

**24.78** What metabolic substrate(s) can be produced from the carbon atoms of each of the following amino acids?
  **a.** leucine
  **b.** isoleucine
  **c.** cysteine
  **d.** phenylalanine

24.79 How much ATP can be produced by the degradation of serine?

**24.80** What compound is regenerated to repeat the urea cycle?

## CHALLENGE QUESTIONS

23.81 A camel hump contains 14 kg of triacylglycerols.
  **a.** Using the value of 0.491 mole of ATP per gram of fat, how many moles of ATP could be produced by the fat in the camel's hump?
  **b.** If the hydrolysis of ATP releases 7.3 kcal/mole, how many kcal are produced by the utilization of the fat?

**24.82** Identify each of the following reactions in the $\beta$ oxidation of palmitic acid ($C_{16}$), a fatty acid, as (1) activation, (2) first dehydrogenation (oxidation), (3) hydration, (4) second dehydrogenation, or (5) cleavage of acetyl CoA.
  **a.** Palmityl CoA and FAD form $\alpha,\beta$-unsaturated palmityl CoA and $FADH_2$.
  **b.** $\beta$-Ketopalmityl CoA forms myristyl CoA and acetyl CoA.
  **c.** Palmitic acid, acetyl CoA, and ATP form palmityl CoA.
  **d.** $\alpha,\beta$-Unsaturated palmityl CoA and $H_2O$ form $\beta$-hydroxypalmityl CoA.
  **e.** $\beta$-Hydroxypalmityl CoA and $NAD^+$ form $\beta$-ketopalmityl CoA and NADH + $H^+$.

24.83 Write the structure and name of the amino acid formed when the following $\alpha$-keto acids undergo transamination with glutamate:

**a.** $CH_3-CH(CH_3)-C(=O)-C(=O)-O^-$

**b.** $CH_3-CH_2-CH(CH_3)-C(=O)-C(=O)-O^-$

**c.** $^-O-C(=O)-CH_2-C(=O)-C(=O)-O^-$

# ANSWERS

## ANSWERS TO STUDY CHECKS

**24.1** $NAD^+$

**24.2** 8 acetyl CoA give 96 ATP; NADH and $FADH_2$ give 35 ATP.

**24.3** HCl denatures proteins and activates enzymes such as pepsin.

**24.4** In conditions such as fasting or starvation, a diet insufficient in protein leads to a negative nitrogen balance.

**24.5** alanine transaminase or alanine aminotransferase

**24.6** **a.** argininosuccinate **b.** citrulline
**c.** urea and ornithine

**24.7** Leucine forms the citric acid cycle intermediate acetyl CoA that enters the beginning of the citric acid cycle to provide 12 ATP. Phenylalanine forms the citric acid cycle intermediate fumarate that enters later in the citric acid cycle to provide 3 ATP.

**24.8** Substrates for the synthesis of most of the nonessential amino acids are 3-phosophoglycerate, pyruvate, oxaloacetate, and $\alpha$-ketoglutarate, which are obtained from glycolysis and the citric acid cycle. The essential amino acid phenylalanine is the resource for synthesis of tyrosine.

## ANSWERS TO SELECTED QUESTIONS AND PROBLEMS

**24.1** The bile salts emulsify fat to give small fat globules for lipase hydrolysis.

**24.3** Fats are released from fat stores when blood glucose and glycogen stores are depleted.

**24.5** Glycerol is converted to glycerol-3-phosphate, then to dihydroxyacetone phosphate, an intermediate of glycolysis.

**24.7** in the cytosol at the outer mitochondrial membrane

**24.9** FAD, $NAD^+$, and HS—CoA

**24.11** **a.** $CH_3{-}CH_2{-}CH_2{-}CH_2{-}CH_2{-}\underset{\beta}{CH_2}{-}CH_2{-}\overset{O}{\overset{\|}{C}}{-}S{-}CoA$

**b.** $CH_3{-}(CH_2)_{14}{-}\underset{\beta}{CH_2}{-}CH_2{-}\overset{O}{\overset{\|}{C}}{-}S{-}CoA$

**c.** $CH_3{-}CH_2{-}CH{=}CH{-}CH_2{-}CH_2{-}CH_2{-}\underset{\beta}{CH_2}{-}CH_2{-}\overset{O}{\overset{\|}{C}}{-}S{-}CoA$

**24.13** **a and b,** $CH_3{-}(CH_2)_6{-}\underset{\beta}{CH_2}{-}\underset{\alpha}{CH_2}{-}\overset{O}{\overset{\|}{C}}{-}S{-}CoA$

**c.** $CH_3{-}(CH_2)_8{-}\overset{O}{\overset{\|}{C}}{-}S{-}CoA + NAD^+ + FAD + H_2O + HS{-}CoA \longrightarrow$

$CH_3{-}(CH_2)_6{-}\overset{O}{\overset{\|}{C}}{-}S{-}CoA + CH_3{-}\overset{O}{\overset{\|}{C}}{-}S{-}CoA + NADH + H^+ + FADH_2$

**d.** $CH_3{-}(CH_2)_8{-}COOH + 4\ HS{-}CoA + 4\ FAD + 4\ NAD^+ + 4H_2O \longrightarrow$
$5\text{ acetyl CoA} + 4\ FADH_2 + 4\ NADH + 4H^+$

**24.15** The hydrolysis of ATP to AMP hydrolyzes ATP to ADP, and ADP to AMP, which provides the same amount of energy as the hydrolysis of two ATP to two ADP.

**24.17** **a.** 5 acetyl CoA molecules
**b.** 4 cycles of $\beta$ oxidation
**c.** 60 ATP from 5 acetyl CoA (citric acid cycle) + 12 ATP from 4 NADH + 8 ATP from 4 $FADH_2$ − 2 ATP (activation) = 80 − 2 = 78 ATP

**24.19** Ketogenesis is the synthesis of ketone bodies from excess acetyl CoA from fatty acid oxidation, which occurs when glucose is not available for energy, particularly in starvation, low-carbohydrate diets, fasting, and diabetes.

**24.21** Acetoacetate undergoes reduction using NADH + $H^+$ to yield $\beta$-hydroxybutyrate.

**24.23** High levels of ketone bodies lead to ketosis, a condition characterized by acidosis (a drop in blood pH values), excessive urination, and strong thirst.

**24.25** in the cytosol of cells in liver and adipose tissue

**24.27** acetyl CoA, $HCO_3^-$, and ATP

**24.29** **a.** (3) malonyl CoA transacylase
**b.** (1) acetyl CoA carboxylase
**c.** (2) acetyl CoA transacylase

**24.31** **a.** 4 $HCO_3^-$
**b.** 4 ATP
**c.** 5 acetyl CoA
**d.** 4 malonyl-ACP
**e.** 8 NADPH
**f.** 4 $CO_2$ removed

**24.33** The digestion of proteins begins in the stomach and is completed in the small intestine.

**24.35** Hormones, heme, purines and pyrimidines for nucleotides, proteins, nonessential amino acids, amino alcohols, and neurotransmitters require nitrogen obtained from amino acids.

**24.37** The reactants are an amino acid and an $\alpha$-keto acid, and the products are a new amino acid and a new $\alpha$-keto acid.

**24.39** **a.** $H-\overset{\overset{O}{\|}}{C}-COO^-$ **b.** $CH_3-\overset{\overset{O}{\|}}{C}-COO^-$

**c.** $CH_3-\overset{\overset{CH_3}{|}}{CH}-\overset{\overset{O}{\|}}{C}-COO^-$

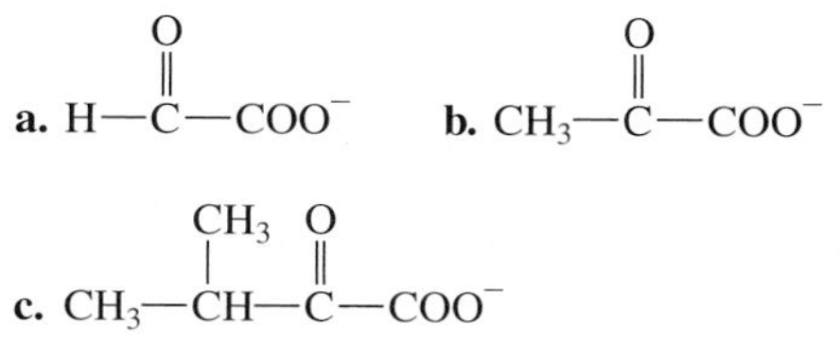

**24.41**

$$^-OOC-\overset{\overset{\overset{+}{N}H_3}{|}}{CH}-CH_2-CH_2-COO^- + H_2O + NAD^+ (NADP^+) \xrightarrow{\text{Glutamate dehydrogenase}}$$

Glutamate

$$^-OOC-\overset{\overset{O}{\|}}{C}-CH_2-CH_2-COO^- + NH_4^+ + NADH\ (NADPH) + H^+$$

α-Ketoglutarate

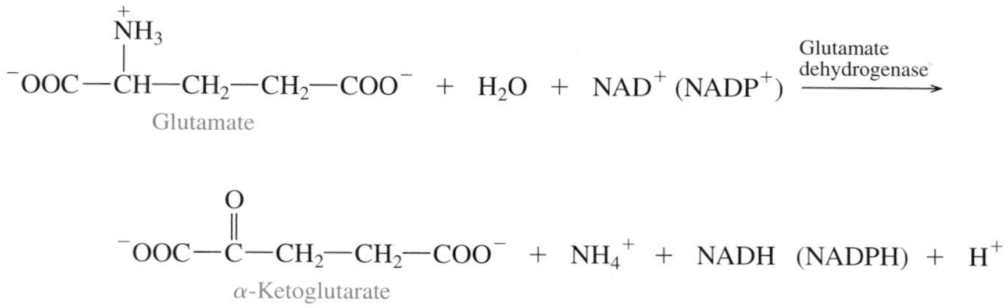

**24.43** $NH_4^+$ is toxic if allowed to accumulate in the liver.

**24.45**

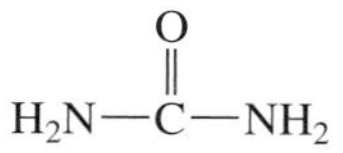

$$H_2N-\overset{\overset{O}{\|}}{C}-NH_2$$

**24.47** $CO_2$ from the citric acid cycle

**24.49** Glucogenic amino acids produce compounds used to synthesis glucose.

**24.51** **a.** pyruvate
**b.** oxaloacetate
**c.** succinyl CoA
**d.** α-ketoglutarate

**24.53** nonessential amino acids

**24.55** Glutamine synthetase catalyzes the addition of an amino group to glutamate using energy from the hydrolysis of ATP.

**24.57** **p**henyl**k**eton**u**ria

**24.59** **a** and **b**

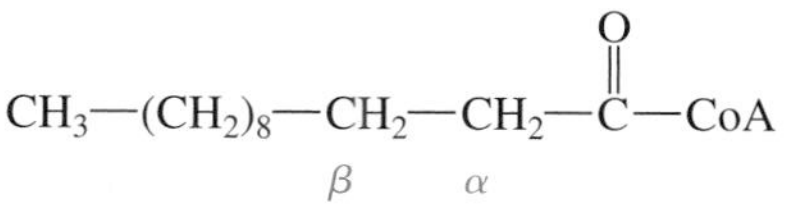

$$CH_3-(CH_2)_8-\underset{\beta}{CH_2}-\underset{\alpha}{CH_2}-\overset{\overset{O}{\|}}{C}-CoA$$

**c.** Lauryl CoA + 5 HS — CoA + 5 FAD + 5 NAD$^+$ + $5H_2O \longrightarrow$ 6 acetyl CoA + 5 $FADH_2$ + 5 NADH + 5H$^+$
**d.** Six acetyl CoA units are produced.
**e.** Five cycles of β oxidation are needed.
**f.**

| | | |
|---|---|---|
| Activation | ⟶ | −2 ATP |
| 6 Acetyl CoA × 12 | ⟶ | 72 ATP |
| 5 $FADH_2$ × 2 | ⟶ | 10 ATP |
| 5 NADH × 3 | ⟶ | 15 ATP |
| **Total** | | 95 ATP |

**24.61** Triacylglycerols are hydrolyzed to monoacylglycerols and fatty acids in the small intestine, which reform triacylglycerols in the intestinal lining for transport as lipoproteins to the tissues.

**24.63** Fats can be stored in unlimited amounts in adipose tissue compared to the limited storage of carbohydrates as glycogen.

**24.65** The fatty acids cannot diffuse across the blood-brain barrier.

**24.67** **a.** Glycerol is converted to glycerol-3-phosphate and to dihydroxyacetone phosphate, which enters glycolysis or gluconeogenesis.
**b.** Activation of fatty acids occurs in the cytosol at the outer mitochondrial membrane.
**c.** The energy cost is equal to two ATP.
**d.** Only fatty acyl CoA can move into the intermembrane space for transport by carnitine into the matrix.

**24.69** **a.** β oxidation
**b.** β oxidation
**c.** fatty acid synthesis
**d.** β oxidation
**e.** fatty acid synthesis
**f.** fatty acid synthesis

**24.71** **a.** (1) fatty acid oxidation
**b.** (1) fatty acid oxidation

**24.73** Ammonium ion is toxic if allowed to accumulate in the liver.

**24.75** **a.** citrulline
**b.** carbamoyl phosphate

**24.77** **a.** pyruvate
**b.** acetoacetyl CoA
**c.** succinyl CoA
**d.** α-ketoglutarate

**24.79** Serine is degraded to pyruvate, which is oxidized to acetyl CoA. The oxidation produces NADH + H$^+$, which provides 3 ATP. In one turn of the citric acid cycle, the acetyl CoA provides 12 ATP. Thus, serine can provide 15 ATP.

**24.81** **a.** 6900 moles of ATP
**b.** 50 000 kcal

**24.83** **a.** $CH_3-\overset{\overset{CH_3}{|}}{CH}-\overset{\overset{\overset{+}{N}H_3}{|}}{CH}-\overset{\overset{O}{\|}}{C}-O^-$ Valine

**b.** $CH_3-CH_2-\overset{\overset{CH_3}{|}}{CH}-\overset{\overset{\overset{+}{N}H_3}{|}}{CH}-\overset{\overset{O}{\|}}{C}-O^-$ Isoleucine

**c.** $^-O-\overset{\overset{O}{\|}}{C}-CH_2-\overset{\overset{\overset{+}{N}H_3}{|}}{CH}-\overset{\overset{O}{\|}}{C}-O^-$ Aspartic acid

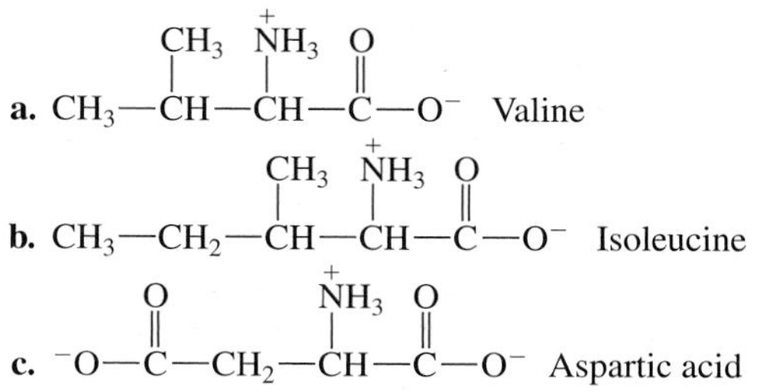

# COMBINING IDEAS FROM CHAPTERS 21 TO 24

**CI.37** Identify each of the following as a substance that is part of the citric acid cycle, electron transport, or both:

**a.** GTP
**b.** FMN
**c.** $FADH_2$
**d.** cyt *a* ($Fe^{3+}$)
**e.** succinate dehydrogenase
**f.** complex I
**g.** isocitrate
**h.** $NAD^+$

**CI.38** Use the value of 7.3 kcal per mole of ATP to determine the total kcal stored as ATP from each of the following:

**a.** the reactions of 1 mole of glucose in glycolysis
**b.** the oxidation of 2 moles of pyruvate to 2 moles of acetyl CoA
**c.** the complete oxidation of 1 mole of glucose to $CO_2$ and $H_2O$
**d.** the $\beta$ oxidation of 1 mole of lauric acid, a $C_{12}$ fatty acid
**e.** the reaction of 1 mole of glutamate (from protein) in the citric acid cycle

**CI.39** Acetyl coenzyme A is the fuel for the citric acid cycle. It has the formula $C_{23}H_{38}N_7O_{17}P_3S$.

**a.** What are the components of acetyl coenzyme A?
**b.** What is the function of HS—CoA
**c.** Where does the acetyl group attach in HS-CoA?
**d.** What is the molar mass to three significant figures for acetyl CoA?
**e.** How many moles of ATP are produced when 1.0 $\mu$g of acetyl CoA completes one turn of the citric acid cycle?

**CI.40** State if each of the following produces or consumes ATP:

**a.** citric acid cycle
**b.** glucose forms two pyruvate
**c.** pyruvate yields acetyl CoA
**d.** glucose forms glucose-6-phosphate
**e.** oxidation of $\alpha$-ketoglutarate
**f.** transport of NADH across the mitochondrial membrane
**g.** activation of a fatty acid

**CI.41** Butter is a fat that contains 80.% by mass triacylglycerols. Assume the triacylglycerol in butter is glyceryl tripalmitate.

**a.** Write an equation for the hydrolysis of glyceryl tripalmitate.
**b.** What is the molar mass of glyceryl tripalmitate, $C_{51}H_{98}O_6$?
**c.** Calculate the ATP yield from 1 mole of palmitic acid.
**d.** How many kcal are released from the palmitic acid in a 0.50-oz pat of butter?
**e.** If running for exactly 1 h uses 750 kcal, how many pats of butter would provide the energy (kcal) for a 45-min run?

**CI.42** Match these ATP yields with the given reactions: 2 ATP, 3 ATP, 6 ATP, 12 ATP, 18 ATP, 36 ATP, and 44 ATP.

**a.** Glucose yields two pyruvate.
**b.** Pyruvate yields acetyl CoA.
**c.** Glucose yields two acetyl CoA.
**d.** Acetyl CoA goes through one turn of the citric acid cycle.
**e.** Caproic acid ($C_6$) is completely oxidized.
**f.** $NADH + H^+$ is oxidized to $NAD^+$.
**g.** $FADH_2$ is oxidized to FAD.

**CI.43** Which of the following molecules will produce more ATP per mole when each is completely oxidized?

**a.** glucose or maltose
**b.** myristic acid, $CH_3—(CH_2)_{12}—COOH$ or stearic acid, $CH_3—(CH_2)_{16}—COOH$
**c.** glucose or two acetyl CoA
**d.** glucose or caprylic acid ($C_8$)
**e.** citrate or succinate in one turn of the citric acid cycle

**CI.44**

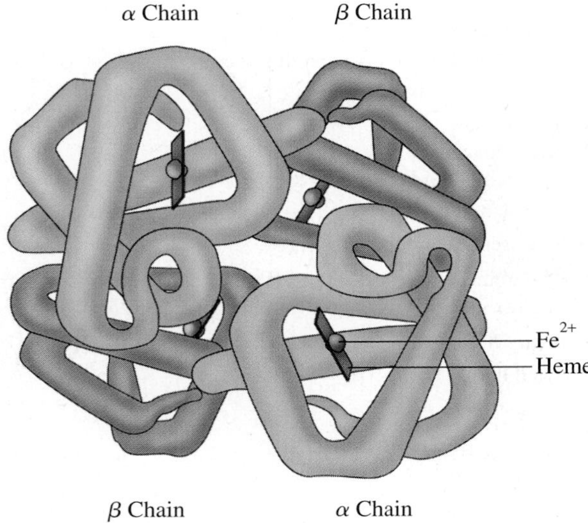


Thalassemia is an inherited genetic mutation that limits the production of the beta chain needed for the formation of hemoglobin. If low levels of the beta chain are produced, there is a shortage of red blood cells (anemia). As a result, the body does not have sufficient amounts of oxygen. In one form of thalassemia, a single nucleotide is deleted in the DNA that codes for the beta chain. This mutation involves the deletion of thymine (T) from section 91 in the following segment of normal DNA:

| 89 | 90 | 91 | 92 | 93 | 94 |
|---|---|---|---|---|---|
| —AGT— | GAG— | CTG— | CAC— | TGT— | GAC—A. . . . |

**a.** Write the complementary strand for this normal DNA segment.
**b.** Write the mRNA sequence from normal DNA using the complementary strand in part **a**.
**c.** What amino acids are placed in the beta chain by this portion of mRNA?
**d.** What is the order of nucleotides in the mutation?

**e.** Write the complementary strand for the mutated DNA segment.

**f.** Write the mRNA sequence from the mutated DNA segment using the complementary strand in part **e**.

**g.** What amino acids are placed in the beta chain by the mutated DNA segment?

**h.** What type of mutation occurs in this form of thalassemia?

**i.** How might the properties of this segment of the beta chain be different from the properties of the normal protein?

**j.** How might the level of structure in hemoglobin be affected if beta chains are not produced?

## ANSWERS

**CI.37** **a.** citric acid cycle **b.** electron transport
**c.** both **d.** electron transport
**e.** citric acid cycle **f.** electron transport
**g.** citric acid cycle **h.** both

**CI.39** **a.** aminoethanethiol, pantothenic acid (vitamin $B_5$), diphosphate of adenosine 3′-phosphate (phosphorylated ADP)
**b.** Coenzyme A carries an acetyl group to the citric acid cycle for oxidation.
**c.** The acetyl group links to the sulfur atom (—S—) in the aminoethanethiol part of CoA.
**d.** 809 g/mole
**e.** $1.5 \times 10^{-8}$ mole of ATP

**CI.41** **a.**

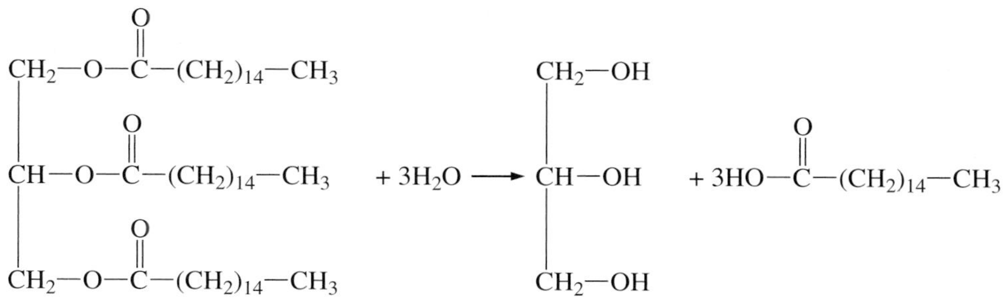

$$\begin{array}{l} CH_2-O-\overset{O}{\overset{\|}{C}}-(CH_2)_{14}-CH_3 \\ | \\ CH-O-\overset{O}{\overset{\|}{C}}-(CH_2)_{14}-CH_3 \\ | \\ CH_2-O-\overset{O}{\overset{\|}{C}}-(CH_2)_{14}-CH_3 \end{array} + 3H_2O \longrightarrow \begin{array}{l} CH_2-OH \\ | \\ CH-OH \\ | \\ CH_2-OH \end{array} + 3HO-\overset{O}{\overset{\|}{C}}-(CH_2)_{14}-CH_3$$

**b.** 806 g/mole
**c.** 129 moles of ATP
**d.** 36 kcal
**e.** 16 pats of butter

**CI.43** **a.** maltose
**b.** stearic acid
**c.** glucose
**d.** caprylic acid
**e.** citrate

# CREDITS

p. ii Foodcollection\Getty Images, Inc - Foodcollection Royalty Free

**Prologue**

p. 1 San Francisco Museum of Art
p. 2 *top:* Pearson Education/Pearson Science
p. 2 *bottom:* Pearson Education/Pearson Science
p. 3 *top:* Robert Mathena\Fundamental Photographs, NYC
p. 3 *bottom:* Photodisc/Getty Images
p. 4 Thomas Hollyman\Photo Researchers, Inc.
p. 5 Bill Bachmann\Photo Researchers, Inc.
p. 6 *left:* The Alchimist's Workshop, 1570, Jan van der Straet (Jannes Stradanus), Palazzo Vecchio, Florence, Italy/Bridgeman Art Library
p. 6 *right:* Erich Lessing\Art Resource, N.Y.
p. 8 [Photographer]/Stone/Getty Images
p. 12 H. Armstrong Roberts\Corbis -

**Chapter 1**

p. 14 Pearson Education/Pearson Science
p. 16 *top:* Pearson Education/Pearson Science
p. 16 *bottom:* Pearson Education/Pearson Science
p. 17 *top:* Pearson Education/Pearson Science
p. 17 *bottom:* Pearson Education/Pearson Science
p. 18 *left:* Photolibrary.com
p. 18 *right:* Anatomy/University "la Sapienza". Rome/Science Photo Library
p. 20 Texas Instruments Incorporated
p. 24 Pearson Education/Pearson Science
p. 29 Shutterstock
p. 30 *top:* Pearson Education/Pearson Science
p. 30 *center:* istockphoto.com
p. 30 *bottom:* Pearson Education/Pearson Science
p. 32 Pearson Education/Pearson Science
p. 33 *top:* Pearson Education/Pearson Science
p. 33 *bottom:* Pearson Education/Pearson Science
p. 35 *top:* Pearson Education/Pearson Science
p. 35 *bottom:* Pearson Science
p. 36 istockphoto.com
p. 39 Getty Images/Digital Vision
p. 41 Christopher Cormack\Corbis
p. 43 Pearson Education/Pearson Science
p. 45 *top, left:* Pearson Education/Pearson Science
p. 45 *top, right:* Pearson Education/ Pearson Science
p. 45 *bottom:* istockphoto.com
p. 46 *top, left:* Prof. P. La Motta, Dept. Anatomy, University La Sapienza, Rome\Photo Researchers, Inc.
p. 46 *top, right:* Phanie\Photo Researchers, Inc.
p. 46 *bottom:* Pearson Education/Pearson Science
p. 47 Michael R. Wrigth
p. 48 Joav Levy\Alamy Images

**Chapter 2**

p. 55 Pearson Education/Pearson Science
p. 56 istockphoto.com
p. 57 *top:* istockphoto.com
p. 57 *center:* Pearson Education/Pearson Science
p. 57 *bottom:* Pearson Education/Pearson Science
p. 58 Jack Star\Getty Images/Digital Vision
p. 65 istockphoto.com
p. 71 Getty Images - Photodisc
p. 72 *top:* Pearson Education/Pearson Science
p. 72 *bottom, left:* Richard Megna\ Fundamental Photographs, NYC
p. 72 *bottom, right:* Pearson Education/Pearson Science
p. 73 *left, middle:* Pearson Education/ Pearson Science
p. 73 *right:* Pearson Education/Pearson Science
p. 73 *left:* istockphoto.com
p. 73 *right, middle:* Shutterstock
p. 73 *bottom, left:* Dave King © Dorling Kindersley
p. 73 *bottom, right:* David Murray and Jules Selmes © Dorling Kindersley
p. 74 Pearson Education/Pearson Science
p. 75 *top:* Siede Preis\Getty Images, Inc.- Photodisc.
p. 75 *center, left:* Pearson Education/ Pearson Science
p. 75 *bottom, right:* Pearson Education/Pearson Science
p. 76 *top, right:* Pearson Education/ Pearson Science
p. 76 *top, left:* Pearson Education/Pearson Science
p. 76 *bottom:* Shutterstock
p. 77 Pearson Education/Pearson Science
p. 79 Pearson Education/Pearson Science
p. 81 Pearson Education/Pearson Science
p. 82 *right:* istockphoto.com
p. 82 *middle:* Helene Canada\ istockphoto.com
p. 82 *left:* Pearson Education/Pearson Science
p. 83 Comstock Complete
p. 89 *top:* istockphoto.com
p. 89 *bottom:* istockphoto.com
p. 90 *top, left:* Pearson Education/Pearson Science
p. 90 *top, middle:* Masterfile Royalty Free Division
p. 90 *top, right:* Spencer Jones\Getty Images, Inc.- Photodisc.
p. 90 *center:* Jonathan Wood\Getty Images - BC
p. 90 *bottom:* Mark Dahners\AP Wide World Photos

**Chapter 3**

p. 93 *top, left:* Photolibrary\ Photolibrary.com - Royalty Free
p. 93 *bottom, left:* Plush Studios\Getty Images/Royalty Free
p. 93 *bottom, right:* Pearson Education/Pearson Science
p. 94 *left:* Photolibrary\Photolibrary.com - Royalty Free
p. 94 *right:* Masterfile Royalty Free Division;
p. 95 Getty Images/Digital Vision
p. 97(A) Pearson Education/Pearson Science
p. 97(B) Pearson Education/Pearson Science
p. 97(C) Pearson Education/Pearson Science
p. 97(D) Pearson Education/Pearson Science
p. 97(E) Pearson Education/Pearson Science
p. 98 Mary Ann Sullivan
p. 101 *left:* Pearson Education/Pearson Science
p. 101 *middle:* Pearson Education/Pearson Science
p. 101 *right:* Pearson Education/Pearson Science
p. 102 Pearson Education/Pearson Science
p. 103 Pearson Education/Pearson Science
p. 105 Lawrence Berkeley National Laboratory
p. 106 Pearson Education/Pearson Science
p. 108 *left:* Pearson Education/Pearson Science
p. 108 *right:* Pearson Education/Pearson Science
p. 109 Pearson Education/Pearson Science
p. 111 Pearson Education/Pearson Science
p. 114 istockphoto.com
p. 115 *top:* Pearson Education/Pearson Science
p. 115 *bottom:* Pearson Education/Pearson Science
p. 116 Shutterstock
p. 117 David Young Wolff\PhotoEdit Inc.
p. 126 Pearson Education/Pearson Science

## Chapter 4

p. 138 Pearson Education/Pearson Science
p. 141 istockphoto.com
p. 142 Health Protection Agengy\Photo Researchers, Inc.
p. 146 Pearson Education/Pearson Science
p. 148 David Parker/SPL\Photo Researchers, Inc.
p. 150 *top:* Rich Frishman\Getty Images Inc. - Stone Allstock
p. 150 *center, left:* Don Farrall\Getty Images, Inc.- Photodisc.
p. 150 *bottom:* Stanford Dosimetry, LLC
p. 151 Pearson Education/Pearson Science
p. 152 *left:* Courtesy of Cytyc/Hologic
p. 152 *right:* Courtesy of Cytyc/Hologic
p. 156 Corbis
p. 157 *left:* Phannie.com\Photo Researchers, Inc.
p. 157 *right:* Pasieka/Science Photo Library\Photo Researchers, Inc.
p. 158 Getty Images, Inc.- Photodisc.
p. 159 *left:* Getty Images, Inc.- Photodisc.
p. 159 *right:* GJLLP/CNRI\Phototake NYC
p. 162 istockphoto.com
p. 164 SuperStock, Inc.
p. 166 Augustin Ochsenreite\AP Wide World Photos

## Chapter 5

p. 168 Pearson Education/Pearson Science
p. 169 Colin Keates © Dorling Kindersley, Courtesy of the Natural History Museum, London
p. 172 Shutterstock
p. 173 Pearson Education/Pearson Science
p. 174 *left:* Pearson Education/Pearson Science
p. 174 *middle:* Pearson Education/Pearson Science
p. 175 Pearson Education/Pearson Science
p. 180 *top:* Pearson Education/Pearson Science
p. 180 *bottom:* Pearson Education/Pearson Science

## Chapter 6

p. 210 Pearson Education/Pearson Science
p. 211 Pearson Education/Pearson Science
p. 212 *top:* Pearson Education/Pearson Science
p. 212 *bottom:* Pearson Education/Pearson Science
p. 213 Pearson Education/Pearson Science
p. 215 Richard Megna\Fundamental Photographs, NYC
p. 217 *left:* Pearson Education/Pearson Science
p. 217 *middle:* Pearson Education/Pearson Science
p. 217 *right:* Pearson Education/Pearson Science
p. 218 *top:* Tom Bochsler\Pearson Education/PH College
p. 218 *bottom, left:* Pearson Education/ Pearson Science
p. 218 *bottom, right:* Pearson Education/Pearson Science
p. 219 Pearson Education/Pearson Science
p. 220 Patrick Clark\Getty Images, Inc.- Photodisc.
p. 221 Mitch Hrdlicka\Getty Images/Digital Vision
p. 222 *left:* Pearson Education/Pearson Science
p. 222 *middle:* Pearson Education/Pearson Science
p. 222 *bottom:* Pearson Education/Pearson Science
p. 223 Renn Sminkey, Pearson Science
p. 225 Photos.com\www.indexopen.com
p. 226 Pearson Education/Pearson Science
p. 227 © Ken Karp/Omni-Photo Communications, Inc
p. 228 Pearson Education/Pearson Science
p. 230 Pearson Education/Pearson Science
p. 231(A) Pearson Education/Pearson Science
p. 231(B) Pearson Education/Pearson Science
p. 231(C) Pearson Education/Pearson Science
p. 231(D) Pearson Education/Pearson Science
p. 231(E) Pearson Education/Pearson Science
p. 233 Pearson Education/Pearson Science
p. 235 *left:* Pearson Education/Pearson Science
p. 235 *middle:* Pearson Education/Pearson Science
p. 235 *right:* Pearson Education/Pearson Science
p. 236 *left:* Pearson Education/Pearson Science
p. 236 *middle:* Pearson Education/Pearson Science
p. 236 *right:* Pearson Education/Pearson Science
p. 242 Pearson Education/Pearson Science
p. 249 Pearson Education/Pearson Science
p. 252 Pearson Education/Pearson Science
p. 253 *top:* istockphoto.com
p. 253 *bottom:* CDV LLC, Creative Digital Visions
p. 254 Pearson Education/Pearson Science
p. 258 Getty Images, Inc.- Photodisc.
p. 258 *left:* AlsoSalt
p. 258 *top,:* Family Safety Products, Inc.
p. 259 *top:* Pearson Education/Pearson Science
p. 259 *center:* istockphoto.com
p. 260 *bottom:* Wikipedia, The Free Encyclopedia
p. 260 *top:* Photolibrary.com - Royalty Free
p. 260 *bottom:* Marianna Day Massey/ZUMA\Corbis

## Chapter 7

p. 261 Pearson Education/Pearson Science
p. 265 Yva Momatiuk & John Eastcott\ Minden Pictures
p. 266 Pearson Education/Pearson Science
p. 268 Pearson Education/Pearson Science
p. 270 Larry Brownstein\Getty Images, Inc.- Photodisc.
p. 275 *left:* Pearson Education/Pearson Science
p. 275 *right:* Pearson Education/Pearson Science
p. 277 T. O'Keefe\Getty Images, Inc.- Photodisc.
p. 279 istockphoto.com
p. 281 Gary Rhijnsburger\Masterfile Corporation
p. 288 Phanie.com\Photo Researchers, Inc.
p. 291 The Image Works

## Chapter 8

p. 295 Pearson Education/Pearson Science
p. 296 *left:* Pearson Education/Pearson Science
p. 296 *right:* Pearson Education/Pearson Science
p. 297 Pearson Education/Pearson Science
p. 298 Comstock Images
p. 299 Pearson Education/Pearson Science
p. 301 *right, top:* Pearson Education/ Pearson Science
p. 301 *right, center:* Pearson Education/Pearson Science
p. 301 *right, bottom:* Pearson Education/Pearson Science
p. 301 *top, left:* Pearson Education/Pearson Science
p. 301 *top, right:* Pearson Education/ Pearson Science
p. 304 Pearson Education/Pearson Science
p. 305 *left:* Pearson Education/Pearson Science
p. 305 *right:* Pearson Education/Pearson Science
p. 306 *left:* ISM\Phototake NYC
p. 306 *right:* NMSB\Custom Medical Stock Photo, Inc.
p. 309 *top, left:* Pearson Education/Pearson Science
p. 309 *top, right:* Pearson Education/ Pearson Science
p. 309 *bottom, left:* Pearson Education/ Pearson Science
p. 309 *bottom, right:* Pearson Education/Pearson Science
p. 310 CNRI/Science Photo Library\Photo Researchers, Inc.
p. 311 Pearson Education/Pearson Science
p. 313 *top:* Pearson Education/Pearson Science
p. 313 *bottom:* Pearson Education/Pearson Science
p. 314 Pearson Education/Pearson Science
p. 318 *left:* Pearson Education/Pearson Science
p. 318 *middle:* Pearson Education/Pearson Science
p. 318 *right:* Pearson Education/Pearson Science
p. 318 *bottom, left:* Pearson Education/ Pearson Science
p. 318 *bottom, right:* Pearson Education/Pearson Science
p. 320 Pearson Education/Pearson Science
p. 324 *top:* Florida Images\Alamy Images
p. 324 *bottom:* istockphoto.com
p. 326 *left:* Dennis Kunkel\Dennis Kunkel Microscopy, Inc.
p. 326 *middle:* Dennis Kunkel\Dennis Kunkel Microscopy, Inc.
p. 326 *right:* Dennis Kunkel\Dennis Kunkel Microscopy, Inc.
p. 328 Hans Eick/DocStock\ Photolibrary.com
p. 331 *left:* istockphoto.com
p. 331 *right:* Corbis RF
p. 332 *bottom, left:* Dennis Kunkel\ Phototake NYC
p. 332 *bottom, middle:* Dennis Kunkel\ Phototake NYC
p. 332 *bottom, right:* Dennis Kunkel\ Phototake NYC

## Chapter 9

p. 336 Claudia Benitez-Nelson
p. 337 *top, left:* Pearson Education/Pearson Science
p. 337 *center, left:* Pearson Education/ Pearson Science
p. 337 *top, right:* Pearson Education/ Pearson Science
p. 337 *bottom, left:* Pearson Education/ Pearson Science
p. 337 *right, bottom:* Pearson Education/Pearson Science
p. 337 *center, right:* Pearson Education/Pearson Science
p. 339 Pearson Education/Pearson Science
p. 344 Steve Mason\Getty Images, Inc.- Photodisc.
p. 357 Robert Holmes\Corbis
p. 362 *top:* Photodisc/Getty Images
p. 362 *bottom:* Photodisc/Getty Images

## Chapter 10

p. 371 Pearson Education/Pearson Science
p. 372 istockphoto.com
p. 378 Pearson Education/Pearson Science
p. 379 Pearson Education/Pearson Science
p. 380 Pearson Education/Pearson Science
p. 387 *top, left:* Pearson Education/Pearson Science
p. 387 *top, middle:* Pearson Education/ Pearson Science
p. 387 *top, right:* Pearson Education/ Pearson Science
p. 387 *center, left:* Pearson Education/ Pearson Science
p. 387 *center, middle:* Pearson Education/Pearson Science
p. 387 *center, right:* Pearson Education/Pearson Science
p. 387 *bottom, left:* Pearson Education/ Pearson Science
p. 387 *bottom, middle:* Pearson Education/Pearson Science
p. 387 *bottom, right:* Pearson Education/Pearson Science
p. 388 *left:* Pearson Education/Pearson Science
p. 388 *center:* Pearson Education/Pearson Science
p. 388 *right:* Pearson Education/Pearson Science
p. 394 *top:* Kristen Brochmann\Fundamental Photographs, NYC
p. 394 *bottom:* Will & Deni McIntyre\Corbis
p. 396 Pearson Education, Pearson Science
p. 397 Renn Sminkey, Pearson Science
p. 407 *left:* Pearson Education/Pearson Science
p. 407 *middle:* Pearson Education/Pearson Science
p. 407 *right:* Pearson Education/Pearson Science
p. 408 istockphoto.com
p. 412 *top, left:* Center for Liquefied Natural Gas
p. 409 MARK EDWARDS\Peter Arnold, Inc.
p. 412 *bottom, left:* Shutterstock
p. 412 *top, right:* istockphoto.com
p. 412 *bottom, right:* Richard Megna\ Fundamental Photographs, NYC
p. 413 *top, left:* istockphoto.com
p. 413 *bottom, left:* Isifa Image Service\Alamy Images
p. 413 *top, right:* Charles D. Winters\Photo Researchers, Inc.
p. 413 *bottom, right:* Renn Sminkey/ Pearson Science

## Chapter 11

p. 415 Pearson Education/Pearson Science
p. 416 Pearson Education/Pearson Science
p. 417 *right:* Pearson Education/ Pearson Science
p. 417 *left:* istockphoto.com
p. 428 *top:* istockphoto.com
p. 428 *bottom:* Mark Dahners\AP Wide World Photos
p. 430 *top:* Natalie Fobes\Corbis
p. 430 *bottom:* Pearson Education/ Pearson Science
p. 431 Pearson Education/Pearson Science
p. 433 Photodisc/Getty Images
p. 427 Caroline R. Abadie\Pearson Education/Pearson Science
p. 441 *top, right:* Photolibrary.com
p. 441 *bottom:* istockphoto.com
p. 434 NASA
p. 438 Pearson Education/Pearson Science
p. 441 *top, left:* Getty Images/Digital Vision
p. 442 *top:* Andy Crawford © Dorling Kindersley
p. 442 *bottom, left:* Courtesy of www.istockphoto.com
p. 442 *bottom, right:* Pearson Education/Pearson Science

## Chapter 12

p. 446 Pearson Education/Pearson Science
p. 447 Don Tremain\Getty Images, Inc.- Photodisc.
p. 448 Tim Hall\Getty Images, Inc.- Photodisc.
p. 450 Shutterstock
p. 453 *bottom:* Alastair Shay/Papilio\Corbis
p. 453 *top, left:* Pearson Education/ Pearson Science
p. 453 *center:* Pearson Education/ Pearson Science
p. 458 Pearson Education/Pearson Science
p. 457 *top, left:* Pearson Education/ Pearson Science
p. 457 *top, right:* Pearson Education/ Pearson Science
p. 457 *bottom, left:* Pearson Education/ Pearson Science
p. 457 *bottom, right:* Pearson Education/ Pearson Science
p. 460 Pearson Education/Pearson Science
p. 463 SIU\Visuals Unlimited
p. 464 *top, left:* Pearson Education/ Pearson Science
p. 464 *top, center:* Pearson Education/ Pearson Science
p. 464 *top, right:* Pearson Education/ Pearson Science
p. 464 *bottom, left:* Pearson Education/ Pearson Science
p. 464 *bottom, center:* Pearson Education/Pearson Science
p. 464 *bottom, right:* Pearson Education/Pearson Science
p. 464 *center:* Pearson Education/Pearson Science
p. 464 *bottom:* istockphoto.com
p. 467 Martin Rotker\Phototake NYC
p. 473 *top, left:* istockphoto.com
p. 473 *bottom, left:* Getty Images, Inc.- Photodisc.
p. 473 *top, right:* Jupiter Images - PictureArts Corporation/Brand X Pictures Royalty Free
p. 473 *bottom, right:* Shutterstock
p. 475 Comstock Images

## Chapter 13

p. 479 Pearson Education/Pearson Science
p. 483 Pearson Education/Pearson Science
p. 484 Pearson Education/Pearson Science
p. 485 Pearson Education/Pearson Science
p. 489 ©2006, 2007 Koi Health. All rights reserved. Contents may be freely reproduced in their entirety for educational purposes with appropriate credit.
Koihealth.org is sponsored by a small private foundation for educational purposes.
p. 494 © Al Assid/CORBIS All Rights Reserved
p. 498 istockphoto.com
p. 499 dbimages\Alamy Images
p. 502 *top, left:* istockphoto.com
p. 502 *top, right:* Nancy R. Cohen\Getty Images, Inc.- Photodisc.
p. 502 *bottom, left:* Ian O'Leary © Dorling Kindersley.
p. 502 *bottom, right:* Pearson Education/Pearson Science
p. 505 Shutterstock

## Chapter 14

p. 508 Pearson Education/Pearson Science
p. 512 *top:* Pearson Education/Pearson Science
p. 512 *bottom:* Pearson Education/Pearson Science
p. 513 *top:* Pearson Education/Pearson Science
p. 513 *bottom:* Pearson Education/Pearson Science
p. 518 *top, left:* Pearson Education/Pearson Science
p. 518 *top, right:* Pearson Education/ Pearson Science
p. 518 *bottom:* Pearson Education/Pearson Science
p. 525 *left:* Pearson Education/Pearson Science
p. 525 *center:* Pearson Education/Pearson Science
p. 525 *right:* Pearson Education/Pearson Science
p. 526 *top, left:* Pearson Education/Pearson Science
p. 526 *top, center:* Pearson Education/ Pearson Science
p. 526 *top, right:* Pearson Education/ Pearson Science
p. 526 *bottom, left:* Pearson Education/ Pearson Science
p. 526 *bottom, center:* Pearson Education/Pearson Science

p. 526 *bottom, right:* Pearson Education/Pearson Science
p. 534 Pearson Education/Pearson Science
p. 535 *center, left:* istockphoto.com
p. 535 *top, right:* Pearson Education/Pearson Science
p. 535 *center, right:* Anne Hyde © Dorling Kindersley
p. 535 *top, right:* C Squared Studios\Getty Images, Inc.- Photodisc.
p. 535 *bottom, left:* Pearson Education/Pearson Science
p. 535 *bottom, right:* © Dorling Kindersley
p. 536 *left:* Frank Greenaway © Dorling Kindersley
p. 536 *right:* Frank Greenaway © Dorling Kindersley

## Chapter 15

p. 542 Pearson Education/Pearson Science
p. 543 Pearson Education/Pearson Science
p. 548 Pearson Education/Pearson Science
p. 549 Addison Wesley Longman, Inc./San Francisco
p. 555 *top:* Pearson Education/Pearson Science
p. 555 *bottom:* Pearson Education/Pearson Science
p. 556 Custom Medical Stock Photo, Inc.
p. 559 *top:* Pearson Education/Pearson Science
p. 559 *bottom:* Pearson Education/Pearson Science
p. 560 Pearson Education/Pearson Science
p. 562 Pearson Education/Pearson Science
p. 561 Getty Images, Inc. - PhotoDisc
p. 564 Pearson Education/Pearson Science
p. 565 Richard Hamilton Smith/CORBIS\Corbis
p. 569 *top, left:* Pearson Education/Pearson Science
p. 569 *top, right:* Richard Hamilton Smith/CORBIS\Corbis
p. 569 *bottom, left:* Pearson Education/Pearson Science
p. 569 *bottom, right:* Pearson Education/Pearson Science
p. 573 *top, left:* istockphoto.com
p. 573 *top, right:* istockphoto.com
p. 573 *bottom, left:* Shutterstock

## Chapter 16

p. 575 Pearson Education/Pearson Science
p. 577 istockphoto.com
p. 578 Pearson Education/Pearson Science
p. 579 Pearson Education/Pearson Science
p. 583 Pearson Education/Pearson Science
p. 584 *top:* Shutterstock
p. 584 *right:* istockphoto.com
p. 584 *bottom:* Pearson Education/Pearson Science
p. 586 Pearson Education/Pearson Science
p. 587 Pearson Education/Pearson Science
p. 589 Pearson Education/Pearson Science
p. 593 Pearson Education/Pearson Science
p. 596 *left:* Anthony Johnson © Dorling Kindersley

## Chapter 17

p. 602 Pearson Education/Pearson Science
p. 607 *left:* Pearson Education/Pearson Science
p. 607 *right:* Pearson Education/Pearson Science
p. 610 Lawson Wood\Corbis
p. 612 *top:* Shutterstock
p. 612 *bottom:* George D. Lepp\Corbis
p. 614 Pearson Education/Pearson Science
p. 616 *top:* Pearson Education/Pearson Science
p. 616 *bottom:* Pearson Education/Pearson Science
p. 618 Pearson Education/Pearson Science
p. 619 L.G. Patterson\AP Wide World Photos
p. 626 Steve Gschmeissner\Photo Researchers, Inc.
p. 628 *top:* National Heart, Lung, and Blood Institute
p. 628 *bottom:* National Heart, Lung, and Blood Institute
p. 629 Martin \Custom Medical Stock Photo, Inc.
p. 632 SFP\Getty Images - Iconica
p. 638 *top, left:* istockphoto.com
p. 638 *bottom, left:* istockphoto.com
p. 638 *top, right:* istockphoto.com
p. 638 *top, left:* Pearson Education/Pearson Science
p. 639 Pearson Education/Pearson Science
p. 640 Photolibrary.com

## Chapter 18

p. 644 Pearson Education/Pearson Science
p. 652 *top:* Pearson Education/Pearson Science
p. 652 *bottom:* Pearson Education/Pearson Science
p. 653 istockphoto.com
p. 655 Pearson Education/Pearson Science
p. 656 *top, right:* Pearson Education/Pearson Science
p. 656 *top, left:* Ed Drews\Photo Researchers, Inc.
p. 656 *bottom:* Pearson Education/Pearson Science
p. 657 Michael S. Yamashita\Corbis
p. 662 Pearson Education/Pearson Science
p. 667 *left:* Pearson Science
p. 667 *right:* Ariel Skelley\Corbis/Stock Market
p. 668 *top:* Pearson Education/Pearson Science
p. 668 *bottom:* © Judith Miller / Dorling Kindersley / Wallis and Wallis
p. 669 Shutterstock

## Chapter 19

p. 672 Pearson Education/Pearson Science
p. 673 Pearson Education/Pearson Science
p. 682 Pearson Education/Pearson Science
p. 684 istockphoto.com
p. 686 Jilly Wendell\Getty Images, Inc. / Riser
p. 687 Pearson Education/Pearson Science
p. 690 *left:* Richard Hamilton Smith/CORBIS/CORBIS-NY
p. 690 *Middle:* Eric and David Hosking/CORBIS/CORBIS-NY
p. 690 *Right:* Bruice Wilson/Getty Images, Inc./Stone Alstock
p. 692 Lewin/Royal Free Hospital\Photo Researchers, Inc.
p. 694 Pearson Education/Pearson Science
p. 698 *left:* Pearson Education/Pearson Science
p. 698 *right:* Miep van Damm\Pearson Education/Pearson Science

## Chapter 20

p. 702 Pearson Education/Pearson Science
p. 725 Pearson Education/Pearson Science
p. 727 Pearson Education/Pearson Science
p. 731 *top, left:* Pearson Education/Pearson Science
p. 731 *bottom, left:* Pearson Education/Pearson Science
p. 731 *top, middle:* Andy Crawford © Dorling Kindersley
p. 731 *top, right:* Dave Rudkin © Dorling Kindersley
p. 731 *bottom, right:* Courtesy of GlaxoSmithKline
p. 735 Shutterstock
p. 736 Shutterstock

## Chapter 21

p. 738 Pearson Education/Pearson Science
p. 746 M. Freeman\Getty Images, Inc. - PhotoDisc
p. 747 Pearson Education/Pearson Science
p. 749 Pearson Education/Pearson Science
p. 764 istockphoto.com
p. 767 Courtesy of the Library of Congress

## Chapter 22

p. 778 Pearson Education/Pearson Science
p. 784 istockphoto.com
p. 790 Pearson Education/Pearson Science
p. 797 Joel W. Rogert/CORBIS\Corbis
p. 798 Pearson Education/Pearson Science
p. 802 Neal Preston\Corbis
p. 809 Karen Timberlake

## Chapter 23

p. 812 Pearson Education/Pearson Science
p. 815 Pearson Education/Pearson Science
p. 829 Shutterstock

## Chapter 24

p. 838 Thomas Hoepker\Magnum Photos, Inc.
p. 839 Custom Medical Stock Photo, Inc.
p. 847 *left:* istockphoto.com
p. 847 *right:* istockphoto.com
p. 849 Pearson Education/Pearson Science
p. 850 *left:* Custom Medical Stock Photo, Inc.
p. 850 *right:* SIU\Custom Medical Stock Photo, Inc.
p. 865 Custom Medical Stock Photo, Inc.
p. 870 *left:* istockphoto.com
p. 870 *right:* Pearson Education/Pearson Science
p. 874 Pearson Education/Pearson Science

## Design features

Tree in a lightbulb, Courtesy of www.istockphoto.com; Collection of Gerberas, Courtesy of www.istockphoto.com; Golden caduceus, Tom Grill\Getty Images Inc. RF; Close-up of a personal data assistant, Photodisc/Getty Images; Internet concept, Courtesy of www.istockphoto.com

# GLOSSARY/INDEX

*t* = table;
*Italic number* = figure

## A


Abbreviated configuration, 120
Absolute zero, 62, 62*t*
Acceptor stem, 752, *752*, *759*
**Acetal** The product of the addition of two alcohols to an aldehyde or ketone. 522, 534
Acetaldehyde
  from alcohol oxidation, 496, 498
  ball-and-stick model, *511*
  oxidization of, 502, 862
  produced in liver, 498
  from threonine degradation, 862
Acetaminophen (Tylenol), 645, 662
Acetic acid, 438, 577, 577*t*
  buffers, 402–403, *402*
Acetoacetate, 849, *849*
  from amino acid degradation, 862
Acetoacetyl CoA, 861–862, *861*
Acetone, 438, 513
  ketosis and, 849, *849*, 850
Acetyl-ACP, *852*
Acetylcholinesterase, inhibitors, 715
**Acetyl CoA** The compound that is formed when a two-carbon acetyl unit bonds to coenzyme A. 779, *780*, 787–788
  accumulation in liver, ketone bodies and, 849
  from acetaldehyde, 862
  from amino acid degradation, 862
  beta oxidation and, 842, 843–844
  citric acid cycle and, 818, *818*, *867*
  cleavage of, 843
  ketogenesis and, 849, *849*, 850
  ketogenic amino acid and, 861–862, *861*
  lipogenesis and, 851
  from pyruvate, 9, 796, *797*, *805*
Acetylene (ethyne), 447–448, *447*
Acetylsalicylic acid (aspirin), 2, 36*t*, 438, 586, 610
**Achiral** Molecules with mirror images that are superimposable. 526–527, *526*
Achiral compound, *528*
**Acid** A substance that dissolves in water and produces hydrogen ions ($H^+$), according to the Arrhenius theory. All acids are proton donors, according to the Brønsted-Lowry theory. 371–414
  amphoteric, 383–384
  bases and (neutralization), 394–396
  Brønsted-Lowry, 374, 375*t*
  characteristics of, 375*t*, 382*t*
  conjugate acid-base pair, 375–377, 387*t*
  denaturing protein, 694, *694*
  naming, 372, 373*t*
  reactions of, 393–398
  salts forming acidic solutions, 399–401, 400*t*
  stomach, 388
  strength of, 377–383
  strong, 378–379, 378*t*, *379*, 382*t*
  titration, 396–398, *396*
  weak, 378–382, 378*t*, *379*
Acid-base properties of salt solutions, 399–401, 400*t*
Acid-base titration, 396–398, *396*
**Acid dissociation constant ($K_a$)** The product of the concentrations of the ions from the dissociation of a weak acid divided by the concentration of the weak acid. 381–382, 382*t*
**Acidic amino acid** An amino acid that has an R group with a carboxylate ($—COO^-$). 674
Acidic solution, 374, 384, *384*
  cation and anion of salt, 400*t*
  examples of, 384*t*
  forming from salt, 399
  pH of, 386
  stomach acid, 388
**Acidosis** Low blood pH resulting from the formation of acidic ketone bodies. 405, 405*t*, 849
Acid rain, 394
Aconitase, 814
ACP (acyl carrier protein), 851, *852*, 853
Acquired immune deficiency syndrome (AIDS), 770–771
Actin, 784
Actinides, *99*, 100
**Activation energy** The energy needed to break the bonds of reacting molecules. 338–339, *338*
Active learning, 9, 10*t*
**Active site** A pocket in a part of the tertiary enzyme structure that binds substrate and catalyzes a reaction. 706–707, *706*
Active transport, 635, *635*
**Activity** The rate at which an enzyme catalyzes the reaction that converts substrate to product. 710–713
Actron, 609
**Actual yield** The actual amount of product produced by a reaction. 240–241
Acyl carrier protein (ACP), 851, *852*, 853
Acyl CoA synthetase, 842
**Addition** A reaction in which atoms or groups of atoms bond to a double bond. Addition reactions include the addition of hydrogen (hydrogenation), halogens (halogenation), hydrogen halides (hydrohalogenation), or water (hydration). 455–462, 456*t*
Addition (mathematical), significant figures and, 25–27
Adenine (A), 739–740, *740*, 742*t*
Adenosine 5'-diphosphate (ADP), 742, 742t, 742*t*
Adenosine 5'-monophosphate (AMP), *741*, 742, *742*, 742*t*
Adenosine 5'-triphosphate (ATP), 742, *742*
Adenosine diphosphate. *See* ADP
Adenosine triphosphate. *See* ATP
Adipocytes, 839, *839*
Adipose tissue, 48
**ADP** Adenosine diphosphate, formed by the hydrolysis of ATP; consists of adenine, a ribose sugar, and two phosphate groups. 782–783, *783*
  activating enzymes in citric acid cycle, 818, *818*
  metabolism and, *867*
  as nucleotide, 742, *742*
Adrenal corticosteroid, 632
Adrenal gland, 632
Adrenaline (epinephrine), 530, 647
**Aerobic** An oxygen-containing environment in the cells. 796
Agent Orange, 490
Agitation, 695
Agricultural technologist, 672
AIDS (acquired immune deficiency syndrome), 770–771
Air
  as gas mixture, 286, 296
  typical composition, 286*t*
Alanine, 675*t*
  from conversion of tryptophan, 862
  converting to pyruvate, 862
  as nonessential amino acid, 863*t*
  synthesis, *863*, 864
Albinism, 764, *764*
Alchemists, 4
**Alcohol** An organic compound that contains the hydroxyl (—OH) functional group attached to a carbon chain. 435, 437*t*, 480–486
  abuse of, 498
  ball-and-stick model, 480, *480*
  blood alcohol content, 498
  boiling point, 491–492, 492*t*
  breathalyzer test, 498
  classifying, 437*t*, 480–481
  combustion, *494*
  dehydrating to form alkene, 494–495
  disinfectant, 695
  fermentation, *787*, 798
  functional group, 437*t*
  heats of fusion and vaporization, 82*t*
  household products, 482
  hydroxyl groups in, 436, 480, 481
  important, 483
  isomers, 488–489
  naming, 481–482, 501
  oxidation, 496–498
  oxidation in body, 488*t*, 498
  oxidation to acetaldehyde, 496
  reactions of, 494–500
  solubility in water, 492–493, 492*t*
  sugar, 556, 560*t*

**Aldehyde** An organic compound with a carbonyl functional group and at least one hydrogen attached to the carbon in the carbonyl group. 435, 437*t*, 438, 507–515
addition reactions, 521–525, 534
boiling point, 515, *516*
important, 513
naming, 510–511, 533
oxidation and reduction, 517–521, *518*, 533–534
physical properties, 515–517, *516*
solubility in water, 516, *516*
structure, 509–510, *509*
Alditol, 555
Aldohexose, 545
Aldolase, 792
**Aldose** A monosaccharide that contains an aldehyde group. 544
Alginate, 508
**Alkali metal** An element in Group 1A (1), except hydrogen, that is a soft, shiny metal with one electron in its outermost energy level. 101–102, *101*
**Alkaline earth metal** An element in Group 2A (2) that has 2 electrons in its outermost energy level. *101*, 102
**Alkaloid** Amines having physiological activity that are produced in plants. 438, 645, 655–657
medicinal use, 438
Alkalosis, 405, 405*t*
**Alkanes** Hydrocarbons containing only single bonds between carbon atoms. 419–422
ball-and-stick model, 423, 423*t*
boiling point, 430, 431*t*
branch, substituents in, 423–429, 424*t*
combustion, 430–432, *431*
comparing name, 448*t*
cycloalkanes, 421, 422*t*
haloalkanes, 427, 428
melting point, 430
naming, 419, 419*t*, 424–426
naming with substituents, 424–425
properties of, 429–434
solubility and density, 430, *430*, 492*t*
structural formulas, 419–421, *420*
structural formulas, drawing, 426–427
uses of, 430, *430*
waxy coating on fruit, *430*
**Alkene** A hydrocarbon containing a carbon-carbon double bond. 435, 437*t*, 447–451
addition reactions, 455–462, 456*t*
cis-trans isomer, 451–455, *452*
from dehydration of alcohol, 494–495
fragrance, 450
identifying, 447
naming, 448–450, 448*t*, 471
polymers, 462–465, *463*, 463*t*, *464*
structure, 447–448, *447*
**Alkoxy group** A group that contains oxygen bonded to an alkyl group. 487
**Alkyl group** An alkane minus one hydrogen atom. Alkyl groups are named like the alkanes except a *yl* ending replaces *ane*. 423–424
Alkyl halide, 427
**Alkyne** A hydrocarbon containing a carbon-carbon triple bond. 435, 437*t*, 447–451
identifying, 447
naming, 448–450, 448*t*, 471
structure, 447–448, *447*
**Allosteric enzyme** An enzyme that regulates the rate of a reaction when a regulator molecule attaches to a site other than the active site. 719
$\alpha$-amylase, 789
Alpha emission, 143*t*, 144–145, *147*
**$\alpha$ (alpha) helix** A secondary level of protein structure, in which hydrogen bonds connect the N—H of one peptide bond with the C=O of a peptide bond farther down the chain to form a coiled or corkscrew structure. 684, *685*
Alpha hydroxy acid (AHA), 579
**$\alpha$-keratin** Fibrous proteins that contain mostly $\alpha$-helixes found in hair, nails, and skin. 689, *690*
**Alpha particle** A nuclear particle identical to a helium nucleus with symbol $\alpha$ or ${}^{4}_{2}He$. 140, 141*t*
alpha decay, 143*t*, 144–145
protecting from, 141–142, 142*t*
Altitude
atmospheric pressure and, 265*t*
boiling point and, 274–275, 274*t*
high, 357
oxygen-hemoglobin equilibrium and, 357
Amethyst, 75, *75*
**Amidation** The formation of an amide from a carboxylic acid and ammonia or an amine. 658–659
**Amide** Organic compounds containing the carbonyl group attached to an amino group or a substituted nitrogen atom. 437, 437*t*, 645, 658–663
cyclic, 662
in health and medicine, 662
hydrolysis, 663–665, 667
melting point, 661
naming, 659–661, 666
physical properties, 661
preparation (amidation), 658–659, 666
primary, secondary, and tertiary, 661
**Amine** Organic compounds containing a nitrogen atom attached to one, two, or three hydrocarbon groups. 437, 437*t*, 645–650
aromatic, 649
basicity/equilibrium constant, 651
biogenic, 647
boiling point, 650
classification, 645–646
in health and medicine, 647
heterocyclic, 654–655
ionization in water, 651
IUPAC names, 647–648
line-bond formula, 645
naming, 646–649, 666
neutralization, 652
properties of, 650–654
solubility in water, 650, *651*
**Amine salt** An ionic compound produced from an amine and an acid. 652–653, 666
properties of, 652–653
**Amino acid** The building block of proteins, consisting of an ammonium group, a carboxylate group, and a unique R group attached to the $\alpha$ carbon. 673–677
20 amino acids, 675*t*
amidation reaction, 658–659
carbon atoms from, fates of, 861–863
classification of, 674, 861
codons for, 757, *757*
deficiency, 687*t*
degradation, 856–858
electrophoresis of, 679, *679*
energy from, 856
essential, 687, 687*t*, 863, 863*t*
forming five-carbon compounds, 862
forming four-carbon compounds, 862
forming three-carbon compounds, 862
genetic code and, 757, *757*
glucogenic, 861–862, *861*
ketogenic, 861–862, *861*
metabolism, 854–866, *867*
N and C terminal, 681
nonessential, 855*t*, *863*, 863*t*
oxidative deamination, 857–858
polar and nonpolar, 674, 675*t*
protein synthesis (translation), 758–761, *759–760*
stereoisomers, 676
structure, 673–674, 675*t*
synthesis, 863–866
transamination, 856–857, 858
urea cycle and, 858–861, *859*
as zwitterions, 677–680
Aminoacyl-tRNA synthetase, 759
Amino group, protein, 857
Aminotransferase, 856–857
Ammonia, 645
Ammonium ion, 180, 180*t*, 652
amino acid degradation and, 862
oxidative deamination and, 857
urea cycle and, 858–860, *859*
Amoxicillin, 716*t*
AMP (adenosine 5'-monophosphate), *741*, 742, *742*, 742*t*, 783
Amphetamines, 647
**Amphoteric** Substances that can act as either an acid or a base in water. 383–384
Ampicillin, 716*t*
Amylase, 565, 711*t*, 788–789
**Amylopectin** A branched-chain polymer of starch composed of glucose units joined by $\alpha$-1,4- and $\alpha$-1,6-glycosidic bonds. 563, *564*, 567
**Amylose** An unbranched polymer of starch composed of glucose units joined by $\alpha$-1,4-glycosidic bonds. 563, *564*, 567
Amyotrophic lateral sclerosis, 767
Amytal, 825
**Anabolic reaction** A metabolic reaction that requires energy to build large molecules from small molecules. 779, 866, *867*
Anabolic steroid, 632
**Anaerobic** A condition in cells when there is no oxygen. glycolysis, 790–796
Androgen, 631
Androsterone, 631
Anesthesia, 428, 446, 489
Aniline, 466
Animal
brown fat, 829
fat, 447
hibernating, 612

**Anion** A negatively charged ion such as $Cl^-$, $O^{2-}$, or $SO_4^{2-}$. 170
Anode, 679
**Anomer** The isomers of cyclic hemiacetals of monosaccharides that have a hydroxyl group on carbon 1 (or carbon 2). In the $\alpha$ anomer, the —OH is drawn downward; in the $\beta$ isomer the —OH is up. 552
Antabuse (disulfiram), 498
Antacids, 397, 397*t*
**Antibiotic** Substances usually produced by bacteria, mold, or yeast that inhibit the growth of bacteria. 715–716, 716*t*
  inhibiting electron transport, 825
  protein synthesis inhibition by, 759, 759*t*
Antibodies, monoclonal, 766*t*
**Anticodon** The triplet of bases in the center loop of tRNA that is complementary to a codon on mRNA. 752, *752*, 758–759, *759–760*
Antidiuretic hormone, 684
Antihistamine, 405*t*, 647, 655
Antimatter, 140
Antimycin A, 825
Antioxidants, 3
Antiretroviral treatment, 770
Aqueous solution, 300–301
Arachidonic acid, 606*t*, 610
  converting to prostaglandin, 609
Area, 24
Arginase, in urea cycle, *859*
Arginine, 675*t*
  degradation, 862
  essential for children but not adults, 863
  in urea cycle, *859*, 860
Arginosuccinate, *859*, 860
Argon (Ar), 121
**Aromatic** Compounds that usually have fragrant odors and often contain the ring structure of benzene. 435, 437*t*, 465–472
  naming, 466–467, 471
  properties of, 467–469
Aromatic amine, 649
Aromatic group, 480
Aromatic ring, 480
Arrhenius theory, 372–373, 375*t*
Artery, 266
Arthritis, 632
Artificial kidney, 328
Artificial sweeteners, 560, 560*t*
Ascorbic acid (vitamin C), 724*t*, 725–726, *726*
Asparagine, 675*t*
  degradation, 862
  as nonessential amino acid, 863*t*
  synthesis, *863*
Aspartame, 560, 560*t*, 662
Aspartate, *859*, 860
  degradation, 862
  synthesis, *863*, 864
Aspartic acid, 675*t*
Aspirin, 2, 36*t*, 438, 586, 610
  substitutes, 662
Asthma, 632
Atherosclerosis, 603, 610, 866
**Atmosphere (atm)** The pressure exerted by a column of mercury 760 mm high, 262, 263, 265, 265*t*
**Atmospheric pressure** The pressure exerted by the atmosphere. 263, *263*, 286
  altitude and, 265*t*
**Atom** The smallest particle of an element that retains the characteristics of the element. 105–107
  composition of, representative, 109*t*
  electrical charges in, 105, *105*, 107
  isotopes, 110–113
  mass of, 106–107, 110–113
  particles in (subatomic), 105, 107*t*
  sizes of, 172
  structure of, 105–106, *106*
Atomic clock, 17
Atomic energy, 160
**Atomic mass** The weighted average mass of all the naturally occurring isotopes of an element. 106–107, 110–113
  calculating, 111–113
  of common elements, 112*t*
  isotopes and, 110–113
**Atomic mass unit (amu)** A small mass unit used to describe the mass of extremely small particles such as atoms and subatomic particles; 1 amu is equal to one-twelfth the mass of a ${}^{12}_{6}C$ atom. 107, 107*t*
**Atomic number** A number that is equal to the number of protons in an atom, 107–110, 109*t*
  changing due to radiation, 143*t*
Atomic radius, 127–128, *128*
Atomic size, 127–128, *128*
**Atomic spectrum** A series of lines specific for each element produced by photons emitted by electrons dropping to lower energy levels. 114, *115*
**Atomic symbol** An abbreviation used to indicate the mass number and atomic number of an isotope. 110, 111*t*
Atomic theory, 105
**ATP** Adenosine triphosphate; a high-energy compound that stores energy in the cells, consists of adenine, a ribose sugar, and three phosphate groups. 828–832
  citric acid cycle and, 818, 829–830, *830*, 831*t*
  energy and, 782–785, *783*
  energy from glucose, 828–832, *830*
  fatty acid oxidation and, 846–848
  formation in glycolysis, 793, 828–829, 831*t*
  hydrolysis of, 782–783, *783*
  muscle contraction and, 784
  as nucleotide, 742, *742*
  number produced by complete oxidation of glucose, 803, *830*, 831*t*
  oxidative phosphorylation and, 826–828, *826*
  production, efficiency of, 832
  proton gradient and, 826–827, *827*
  pyruvate and, 829, 831*t*
  synthesis, electron transport and, 827
**ATP synthase** An enzyme complex that links the energy released by protons returning to the matrix with the synthesis of ATP from ADP and $P_i$. The $F_0$ section contains the channel for proton flow, and the $F_1$ section uses the energy from the proton flow to drive the synthesis of ATP. 826–827, *827*
  electron transport and, 827, *827*
  heating the body, 829
  uncouplers, 829
Atropine, 656
Attractive force, 79
  in compounds, 200–202, 201*t*
  types of, 200–202, 201*t*
Autoclave, 275
Avogadro, Amedeo, 226
**Avogadro's law** A gas law that states that the volume of gas is directly related to the number of moles of gas in the sample when pressure and temperature do not change. 277–281, *278*
**Avogadro's number** The number of items in a mole, equal to $6.02 \times 10^{23}$. 226–227, 226*t*
AZT (azidothymine), 770

## B

Background radiation, 151–152, 152*t*
Bacteria
  antibiotics and, 715–716, 716*t*
  disinfectant and, 695
  lipid composition, 633*t*
Balance, 230
**Balanced equation** The final form of a chemical equation that shows the same number of atoms of each element in the reactants and products. 213–216
Ball-and-stick model
  alcohols, 480, *480*
  branched alkanes, 423, 423*t*
  butene, *452*
  cycloalkane, 421, 422*t*
  ethane, 418, *418*
  ethene (ethylene), *447*
  ethyne (acetylene), *447*
  hexane, *419*
  methane, 418, *418*
Barbiturates, 662
  electron transport inhibition by, 825
Barium sulfate, 309–310, *310*
Barometer, 265, *265*
**Base (chemical)** A substance that dissolves in water and produces hydroxide ions ($OH^-$) according to the Arrhenius theory. All bases are proton acceptors, according to the Brønsted-Lowry theory. 371–414
  acids and (neutralization), 394–396
  amphoteric, 383–384
  Brønsted-Lowry, 374, 375*t*
  characteristics of, 375*t*
  conjugate acid-base pair, 375–377, 387*t*
  denaturing protein, 694, *694*
  naming, 373
  reactions of, 393–398
  salts forming basic solutions, 399–401, 400*t*
  strength of, 377–383
  strong, 380
  weak, 380
**Base (nucleic acid)** Nitrogen-containing compounds found in DNA and RNA: adenosine (A), thymine (T), cytosine (C), guanine (G), and uracil (U). 739–740, *740*
  complementary base pairs, 746, *747*
**Basic amino acid** An amino acid that contains an R group with an ammonium ($—NH_3^+$) ion. 674

Basic solution, 374, 384, *384*
cation and anion of salt, 400*t*
examples of, 384*t*
forming from salt, 399
pH of, 386
Beano, 731
**Becquerel (Bq)** A unit of activity of a radioactive sample equal to one disintegration per second. 150, 150*t*
Beer fermentation, 798
Beeswax, 611, 611*t*
Belladonna, 656
Benadryl, 652
"Bends", scuba diving and, 288
Benedict's reagent, 555
**Benedict's test** A test for aldehydes with adjacent hydroxyl groups in which $Cu^{2+}$ ($CuSO_4$) ions in Benedict's reagent are reduced to a brick-red solid of $Cu_2O$. 518, *518*, 556
**Bent** The shape of a molecule with two bonded atoms and two lone pairs. 196, 197, 198*t*
Benzaldehyde, 513
Benzedrine, 647
**Benzene** A ring of six carbon atoms each of which is attached to a hydrogen atom $C_6H_6$. 465
in aromatics, 435, 465–472
Beryllium (Be), 99
Beta emitters in medicine, 147
Beta-galactosidase, 754–755, *756*
Beta hydroxybutyrate, 849, *849*
$\beta$-keratins, 689
**Beta oxidation ($\beta$ oxidation)** The degradation of fatty acids that removes two-carbon segments from a fatty acid chain. 841–846, 869
compared to fatty acid synthesis, 853, 853*t*
number of cycles, 844
pathway, 843
**Beta particle** A particle identical to an electron with symbol $\beta$ or ${}^{0}_{-1}e$ that forms in the nucleus when a neutron changes to a proton and an electron. 140, 141*t*
beta decay, 143*t*, 145–146, *147*
protecting from, 142, 142*t*
**$\beta$ (beta)-pleated sheet** A secondary level of protein structure that consists of hydrogen bonds between peptide links in parallel polypeptide chains. 684, *685*
Bicarbonate, 180
Bile salt, 628–629, *629*
cholesterol and, 627, 628, 630
excreting, 630
structure, *604*, 628
synthesizing, 628
Bilirubin, 629
**Biodiesel** A nonpetroleum fuel that can be used in place of diesel fuel; produced from renewable biological resources. 619
Biogenic amine, 647
Biotin, 724*t*, 726
Birth-control pill, 631
Bisphenol A (BPA), 483
Bisphosphate, 792
Blimp, helium, 172
Block elements, 122–124, *123*
Blood
buffers in, 405, 405*t*
crime scene analysis, 1
partial pressures of gases in, 287*t*
plasma, 298, 304, 304*t*
Blood alcohol content, 498
Blood-brain barrier, 840
Blood clotting, 104*t*, 610, 718, 727
Blood clotting factor, 766*t*
Blood gas, 287, 287*t*
Blood glucose, 549, 850
Blood group compatibility, 561*t*
Blood pressure, measuring, 266
Blood sugar. *See* Glucose
Blood types, 561, 561*t*
Blood urea nitrogen (BUN), 858
Blood vessels, plaque in, 603, 628, *628*
Blubber, 847, 848
Body fat, 35, *35*, 48
Body, human. *See* Human body
Body temperature, 362
**Boiling** The formation of bubbles of gas throughout a liquid. 80–81, *81*
**Boiling point** The temperature at which a liquid changes to gas (boils) and gas changes to liquid (condenses). 80
alcohols/ethers, 491–492, 492*t*
aldehyde and ketone, 515, *516*
alkane, 430, 431*t*
amine, 650
carboxylic acid, 580–581, 581*t*
Celsius (°C) scale, 59, *60*
effect of solutes on, 324, 324*t*
Fahrenheit (°F) scale, 59, *60*
inorganic compound, 417*t*
Kelvin (K) scale, *60*, 62*t*
organic compound, 417*t*
of water, 59, *60*
of water, altitude and, 274–275, 274*t*
Bombykol, 453
Bonding, 72, 168–209
attractive forces in, 200–202, 201*t*
comparison of, 201*t*
covalent, 183–189
electronegativity and polarity, 192–195, 194*t*
ionic bond, 169
molecule shape and, 195–198
octet rule, 169–174
polarity and, 192–200
types of, 193–194, *193*, 194*t*
variation, 194, 194*t*
Bonding pair, 184
Bone
density, 46
disease, diagnosing, 710*t*
hydroxyapatite, 182, 362
polyatomic ions, 182
Bovine spongiform encephalopathy (BSE), 690
**Boyle's law** A gas law stating that the pressure of a gas is inversely related to the volume when temperature (K) and amount (moles) of the gas do not change. 267–270, *267*, 276*t*
Brachytherapy, 152
Bradykinin, 684
Brain
body temperature and, 62
computed tomography (CT), 159, *159*
function, PET and, 158
mercury and, 98
PET of, 158
radioisotopes and, 148, 157*t*
scans, 148, 157*t*
**Branch** A carbon group bonded to the main carbon chain. 423
**Branched alkane** A single-bonded hydrocarbon containing a substituent bonded to the main chain. 423
Breast cancer, 152, 617
Breathalyzer test, 498
Breathing
partial pressure of gas, 287*t*
pressure-volume relationship, 269
Bromine, 102, *102*
Bronchodilator, 642
**Brønsted-Lowry acids and bases** An acid is a proton donor; a base is a proton acceptor. 374, 375*t*
Brown fat, 829
Buffer, 401–405, *402*
in blood, 405, 405*t*
calculating pH, 403–404
**Buffer solution** A solution of a weak acid and its conjugate base or a weak base and its conjugate acid maintains the pH by neutralizing added acid or base. 401–405, *402*
BUN (blood urea nitrogen), 858
Buoyant force, 48
Butanal, *511*
Butane, 420, *420*
Butyraldehyde, 438, *511*
Butyric acid, 577, 577*t*
Butyryl-ACP, *852*, 853


## C


Cadaverine, 438
Caffeine, 36*t*, 655, *656*
Calcium
ion, 173*t*
muscle contraction and, 784
Calculator, scientific notation and, 19–20
**Caloric value** The kilocalories obtained per gram of the food types: carbohydrate, fat and protein. *68*, 69–70, 69*t*, 70*t*
**Calorie (cal)** The amount of heat energy that raises the temperature of exactly 1 g of water exactly 1 °C. 58
ATP and, 832
calculating value, 69–70
counting, 70
**Calorie (Cal)** A nutritional unit of energy equal to 1000 cal, or 1 kcal. 68
Calorimeter, 832
Cancellation of units, 38
Cancer, 771
breast, 152, 617
carcinogens and, 490, 771*t*
dietary recommendation, 603
mutagens and, 761
prostate, 710*t*
radiation therapy, 152, 158
retinoblastoma, 771
skin (melanoma), 771
viruses and, 771, 771*t*
Carbamoyl group, 859–860, *859*
Carbamoyl phosphate, 859–860, *859*
**Carbocation** A carbon cation that has only three bonds and a positive charge and is formed during the addition reactions of hydration and hydrohalogenation. 459

**Carbohydrate** A simple or complex sugar composed of carbon, hydrogen, and oxygen. 542–574
digestion of, 788–790, *789*
energy content, 70*t*
as energy source, 782–785, *783*
metabolic pathways, 778–811, *780*
oxidization, 780–786, *791*, *867*
reactions, 567–568
types, 543–544, 567
Carbolic acid (phenol), 493
Carbon
five-carbon compounds, 862
four-carbon compounds, 862
polyatomic ions, 180*t*
three-carbon compounds, 862
Carbon-14 dating, 155*t*, 156
Carbonate, acids and, 393
Carbonated drinks, 296, 297, 307–308
Carbon atom
amino acid degradation and, 856–858
fates from amino acid degradation, 861–863, *861*
in organic compounds, 416, 418, *418*
Carbon cycle, 543
**Carbon dating** A technique used to date ancient specimens that contain carbon. The age is determined by the amount of active carbon-14 that remains in the samples. 156
Carbon dioxide
in carbonated drinks, 296, 297, 307–308
global warming and, 66
partial pressure in blood and tissue, 287, 287*t*
producing and returning to atmosphere, 263
Carbon monoxide, 432, 825
Carbon skeleton
amino acid, 861–863, *861*
citric acid cycle and, 861, *861*
Carbon tetrachloride, 428
**Carbonyl group** A functional group that contains a double bond between a carbon atom and an oxygen atom (C=O). 435, 509
aldehyde and ketone, 509–510, *509*
**Carboxylate group** The anion produced when a carboxylic acid donates a proton to water. 576, 673, 676
**Carboxylate ion** The anion produced when a carboxylic acid donates a proton to water. 582
**Carboxyl group** A functional group found in carboxylic acids composed of carbonyl and hydroxyl groups. 437*t*, 576–577
**Carboxylic acid** An organic compound containing the carboxyl group. 436, 576–580
acidity, 582
alpha hydroxy acids (AHAs), 579
boiling point, 580–581, 581*t*
in metabolism, 584
naming, 576–578, 577*t*, 595
natural sources, 577*t*, 579
neutralization, 582–583, 595
preparing, 578–579
properties, 580–585
solubility in water, 581, *581*, 581*t*, 595
**Carboxylic acid salt** The product of neutralization of a carboxylic acid; a carboxylate ion and the metal ion from the base. 582–583, 595
Carcinogens, 490, 771*t*
Career Focus
geologist, 427
histologist, 76
laboratory technologist, 460
occupational therapist, 749
optician, 109
phlebotomist, 562
physical therapist, 815
rehabilitation specialist, 682
surgical technologist, 55
veterinary technician (VT), 33
Carnauba wax, 611, 611*t*
Carnitine, 842, *842*
Carvone enantiomer, 530
Casein, 673*t*
**Catabolic reaction** A metabolic reaction that produces energy for the cell by the degradation and oxidation of glucose and other molecules. 779, *780*, *789*, 866, *867*
**Catalyst** A substance that increases the rate of reaction by lowering the activation energy. 340, 703
effect on equilibrium constant, 355–356, 361*t*
reaction rate and, 340, 340*t*
Catalytic converters, 341
Cataract, 548
Cathode rays, 105
**Cation** A positively charged ion such as $Na^+$, $Mg^{2+}$, $Al^{3+}$, and $NH_4^+$, 128, 170
Cell
cholesterol as a component, 633*t*, 634, *634*
eukaryotic vs. prokaryotic, 781
structures in, 779–781, *781*, 781*t*
Cell division
DNA replication in, *753*
uncontrolled (in cancer), 771
Cell membrane, 633–636, 779, *781*
diffusion, 634–635, *635*
facilitated transport, 635, *635*
fluid mosaic model, 634, *634*
functions of, 781*t*
hydrophilic and hydrophobic layers, 634, *634*
lipid bilayer, 634, *634*
lipid composition, 622, *622*, 633*t*
transport through, 634–635, *635*
Cellophane, 327
**Cellulose** An unbranched polysaccharide composed of glucose units linked by β-1,4-glycosidic bonds that cannot be hydrolyzed by the human digestive system. 543, 564–565, *565*, 567
**Celsius (°C) temperature scale** A temperature scale on which water has a freezing point of 0 °C and a boiling point of 100 °C. 17, 59–62
boiling and freezing point of water, 59, *60*, 62*t*
comparison of temperature scales, *60*, 62*t*
converting to Fahrenheit temperature, 59
*Centi* (c), 27, 28*t*
**Centimeter (cm)** A unit of length in the metric system; there are 2.54 cm in 1 inch. 15, *15*
**Cephalin** A glycerophospholipid found in brain and nerve tissues that incorporates the amino alcohol serine or ethanolamine. 622
**Ceramide** A lipid in which sphingosine is attached to a fatty acid by an *amide* link. 624
**Cerebroside** A glycolipid consisting of sphingosine, a fatty acid, and a monosaccharide (usually galactose). 624–625
Cesium-141, 157*t*
**Chain reaction** A fission reaction that will continue once it has been initiated by a high-energy neutron bombarding a heavy nucleus such as U-235. 160, *161*
**Change of state** The transformation of one state of matter to another; for example solid to liquid, liquid to solid, liquid to gas. 79–87, *79*
Changes of energy levels, 115–116, *115*
Chargaff's rules, 745
**Charles' law** A gas law stating that the volume of a gas changes directly with a change in Kelvin temperature when pressure and amount (moles) of the gas do not change. 270–273, *271*, 276*t*
**Chemical** A substance that has the same composition and properties wherever it is found. 2–4
chemicals in the kitchen, *3*
chemicals in toothpaste, 3*t*
Chemical bond, 183–189
**Chemical change** A change during which the original substance is converted into a new substance with a different composition and new chemical and physical properties. 2, 77, 77*t*, 211
Chemical compound. *See* Compound
**Chemical equation** A shorthand way to represent a chemical reaction using chemical formulas to indicate the reactants and products and coefficients to show reacting ratios. 311
balanced, identifying, 213
balanced, information from, 235*t*
balancing, 213–216
mole relationship, 235–237, 235*t*
symbols used in, 213*t*
**Chemical equilibrium** The point at which the forward and reverse reactions take place at the same rate so that there is no further change in concentrations of reactants and products. 342–344, *343*
*See also* Equilibrium
**Chemical properties** The properties that indicate the ability of a substance to change to a new substance. 77, 77*t*
**Chemical reaction** The process by which a chemical change takes place. 210–260
activation energy, 338–339, *338*
collision theory, 337–338, *338*
energy changes in, 246–249
ideal gas law and, 283–284
mass calculations, 237–240
moles and molar mass, 226–237
oxidation-reduction, 221–225, *222*
percent yield and limiting reactants, 240–246
rate, 337–342, *337*, *339*, 340*t*
solutions and, 319–320, *320*
types of, 216–221, *217–219*
*See also* Equilibrium
**Chemical symbol** An abbreviation that represents the name of an element. 96
**Chemiosmotic model** The conservation of energy from transfer of electrons in the electron that results from pumping protons into the intermembrane space to produce a proton gradient that provides the energy to synthesize ATP. 826

**Chemistry** A science that studies the composition of substances and they way they interact with other substances. 1–13
study plan for, 9–11, 10*t*
Chernobyl nuclear power plant, 152
**Chiral carbon** A carbon atom that is bonded to four different atoms or groups of atoms. 527–528, *527–528*, 546
**Chiral molecule** Objects or molecules that have nonsuperimposable mirror images. 525–532, *526*
Chloral hydrate, 522
Chloramphenicol, 759*t*
Chloride ion, 173*t*
Chlorine, polyatomic ions, 180*t*
Chloroethane (ethyl chloride), 428
Chlorofluorocarbons (CFCs), 2, 262, 272–273
ozone depletion and, 434
Chloroform, 428, 603
Cholecaliferol, 727, 727*t*
**Cholesterol** The most prevalent of the steroid compounds; needed for cellular membranes and the synthesis of vitamin D, hormones, and bile acids. 627, 629–631
"bad" and "good," 630–631
bile salts and, 627, 628, 630
in blood (value), 30*t*, 628
in blood, elevated, 628
in body, 627–628
cell membrane, 633*t*, 634, *634*
dietary recommendations, 628
excess, *628*, 764
food content, 628*t*
gallstones and, 628–629
HDL and LDL, 617, 630
high-cholesterol diet, 628, 628*t*
hypercholesterolemia, familial, 764*t*
laboratory values/testing, 30*t*, 460
plaque and, 628, *628*
serum, 628
structure, *604*, 627
trans fatty acids and hydrogenation and, 617
transporting, 629–630, *630*
vitamin D and, 727
Cholesteryl ester, 629, *629*
Choline, 622
Chromium-51, 155*t*
**Chylomicrons** Lipoproteins formed by coating triacylglycerols with proteins for transport in the lymphatic system and bloodstream. 630, *630*, 839
Chymotrypsin, 854, *855*
Chymotrypsinogen, 718–719, 718*t*
Cinchona tree, 656
Cirrhosis, 548, 710*t*
**Cis isomer** An isomer of an alkene in which large groups are attached to the same side of the double bond. 451–455, *452*
modeling, 453
night vision, 454
Citrate, 365, 813
Citrate synthetase, 813
Citric acid, 579
**Citric acid cycle** A series of oxidation reactions in the mitochondria that convert acetyl CoA to $CO_2$ and yield NADH and $FADH_2$. It is also called the tricarboxylic acid cycle or the Krebs cycle. 584, 813–819, *816*
ATP from, 829–830, *830*, 831*t*
carbon skeletons and, 861, *861*
dehydrogenases in, 815, 817
eight reaction(s), 813–817
metabolism and, 779, *780*, *867*
nonessential amino acid synthesis and, *863*
overview and summary of, 813, *816*, 818
oxidation reactions in, *816*
primary function of, 818
product summary for, 818, *818*
regulation of, 818, *818*
Citrulline, *859*, 860
Cleavage
acetyl CoA, 843
in glycolysis, 792
urea cycle reaction, 860
Clinical calculations, 40–41
Cloning, gene, 765–766, *766*
Clotting, 104*t*, 718, 727
Clotting factor, 766*t*
Cobalamin (vitamin $B_{12}$), 724*t*, 725, 866
Cocaine, 653, 657
Codeine, 656, *657*
**Codon** A sequence of three bases in mRNA that specifies a certain amino acid to be placed in a protein. A few codons signal the start or stop of protein synthesis. 757, *757*, *759*, *760*
for amino acids, *757*
messenger RNA (mRNA), 757, *757*, 769
start, 759
**Coefficient** Whole numbers placed in front of the formulas to balance the number of atoms or moles of atoms of each element on both sides of an equation. 213
**Coenzyme** An organic molecule, usually a vitamin, required as a cofactor in enzyme action. 721–729, 723*t*, *724*
metabolic cycle and, *780*, 785–788, *786–787*
reduced, citric acid cycle and, *816*, 819
**Coenzyme A (CoA)** A coenzyme that transports acyl and acetyl groups. 787–788, *787*
**Coenzyme Q (CoQ, Q)** A mobile carrier that transfers electrons from NADH and $FADH_2$ to cytochrome *b* in complex III. 820, *821*, 823–824
**Cofactor** A metal ion or an organic molecule that is necessary for a biologically functional enzyme. 721–729, 721*t*, 723*t*
Coffee, 655, *656*
Cold pack, 249
**Collagen** The most abundant form of protein in the body, which is composed of fibrils of triple helices with hydrogen bonding between —OH groups of hydroxyproline and hydroxylysine. 673*t*, 684–686, *686*
vitamin C and, 725
Colligative properties, 324
**Collision theory** A model for a chemical reaction that states that molecules must collide with sufficient energy in order to form products. 337–338, *338*
**Colloid** A mixture having particles that are moderately large. Colloids pass through filters but cannot pass through semipermeable membranes. 322, 322*t*
comparison to solution and suspension, 323*t*
in human body, 322
properties of, *323*
**Combination reaction** A reaction in which reactants combine to form a single product. 216–217, *217*
**Combined gas law** A relationship that combines several gas laws relating pressure, volume, and temperature. 276–277, 276*t*
**Combustion** A chemical reaction in which an alkane reacts with oxygen to produce $CO_2$, $H_2O$, and energy. 430–432, *431*
alcohol, *494*
incomplete, 432
Compact fluorescent light (CFL), 116
**Competitive inhibitor** A molecule with a structure similar to the substrate that inhibits enzyme action by competing for the active site. 713–714, *714*
**Complementary base pairs** In DNA, adenine is always paired with thymine (A—T or T—A), and guanine is always paired with cytosine (G—C or C—G). In forming RNA, adenine is paired with uracil (A—U). 746, *747*
Complete protein, 687
**Compound** A pure substance consisting of two or more elements, with a definite composition, that can be broken down into simpler substances only by chemical methods. 72, *73*, 74*t*, 168–209
attractive forces in, 200–202
containing polyatomic ion, 180–183, 182*t*
covalent, 183–192
ionic, 174–176
molar mass, 230–232, *234*
naming and writing formulas, 176–179, 189–192, *191*
polarity of, 192–200
Computed tomography (CT), 159, *159*
**Concentration** A measure of the amount of solute that is dissolved in a specified amount of solution. 312–316
calculating at equilibrium, 352–353
effect of change on equilibrium, 339, *339*, 340*t*, 354–356, *354*, 356*t*
**Condensation** The change of state of a gas to a liquid. 80–81
heat of, 82
**Condensed structural formula** A structural formula that shows the arrangement of the carbon atoms in a molecule but groups each carbon atom with its bonded hydrogen atoms. 420, *420*
Conductor, 101
Coniine, 655
**Conjugate acid-base pair** An acid and base that differ by one $H^+$. When an acid donates a proton, the product is its conjugate base, which is capable of accepting a proton in the reverse reaction. 375–377, 387*t*
Conservation of mass, 235
**Continuous alkane** An alkane in which the carbon atoms are connected in a row, one after the other. 419
naming, 419, 419*t*

**Control site** A section of DNA that regulates protein synthesis. 755, *756*
**Conversion factor** A ratio in which the numerator and denominator are quantities from an equality or given relationship. For example, the conversion factors for the relationship 1 kg = 2.20 lb are written as the following

$$\frac{2.20\ \text{lb}}{1\ \text{kg}} \text{ and } \frac{1\ \text{kg}}{2.20\ \text{lb}}, 32\text{–}37$$

clinical calculations, 40–41
Guide to Problem Solving (GPS) using, 37–39
metric-U.S. system, 33–34
molarity, 317, 317*t*
molar volume, 279
percentage, ppm, and ppb, 35–36, *35*, 41–42
percent concentration, 314, 315*t*
problem solving with, 37–43
stated within a problem, 34
**Cooling curve** A diagram that illustrates temperature changes and changes of states for a substance as heat is removed. 84–85, *84*
Copper (Cu), 104*t*
**Cori cycle** A cyclic process in which lactate produced in muscle is transferred to the liver to be synthesized to glucose, which can be used again by muscle. 804, *805*
Coronary heart disease, 603, 610, 628, 866
Corticosteroid, 632
Cortisone, 632
Cosmic ray, *114*
**Covalent bond** A bond created by the sharing of valence electrons by atoms. 183–189
electron-dot formula, 184, 185*t*
forming, 184
multiple, 186–187
nonpolar, 193, *193*
organic compound, 435*t*
polar, 193, *193*
resonance structures, 187–189
**Covalent compound** A combination of atoms in which noble gas configurations are attained by sharing electrons. 183–189
bonding pattern of nonmetal, 185, *185*t
naming and writing formulas, 189–192, *191*
prefix used in naming, 189*t*
Covalent formula, 189–192
Covalent molecule, 184, 184*t*
CPR, 812
"Crack cocaine," 653
"Crank," 647
Creatinine kinase, 709*t*, 710, 710*t*
**Crenation** The shriveling of a cell due to water leaving the cell when the cell is placed in a hypertonic solution. *326*, 327
Cresol, 482
Creutzfeldt-Jakob disease (CJD), 690
Crick, Francis, 746
Crime scene analysis of blood, 1
Cross-links, in protein structure, 687–689, *688*, 688*t*
Crude oil, 430
distilling, 433, 433*t*
Cryostat, 76
Crystal, 75, *75*
**C terminal** The end amino acid in a peptide chain with a free carboxylate ($—COO^-$) group. 681
CT scan. *See* Computed tomography
**Cubic centimeter ($cm^3$, cc)** The volume of a cube that has 1-cm sides, equal to 1 mL. 30, *31*
Cubic meter ($m^3$), 16
Curie, Marie and Pierre, 150
**Curie (Ci)** A unit of radiation equal to $3.7 \times 10^{10}$ disintegrations/s. 150, 150*t*
Cyanide, 716*t*, 825
Cyclic acetal, 524
Cyclic amide, 662
**Cyclic ether** Compounds that contain an oxygen atom in a carbon ring. 489–490, 501
Cyclic hemiacetal, 524, 551
Cyclic organic compound, 654–655
**Cycloalkane** An alkane that is a ring or cyclic structure. 421
boiling point, 431*t*
formula, 422*t*
naming, 425
Cycloalkanol, 481
**Cycloalkene** A cyclic hydrocarbon that contains a double bond in the ring, 448, 449, 471
Cyclohexane ring, 627
Cysteine
converting to pyruvate, 862
as nonessential amino acid, 863*t*
synthesis, *863*, 864–865
Cystic fibrosis, 764*t*
**Cytochrome (cyt)** Iron-containing proteins that transfer electrons from $QH_2$ to oxygen. 820, *821*, 823–824, *823*
Cytochrome c, 821, *821*
**Cytoplasm** The material in eukaryotic cells between the nucleus and the cell membrane. 779, *781*, 781*t*
Cytosine (C), 739–740, *740*, 742*t*
**Cytosol** The fluid of the cytoplasm, which is an aqueous solution of electrolytes and enzymes. 779, *781*, 781*t*

## D

Dacron, 483
Daily value (DV), 28*t*
Dalton, John, 105, 107
**Dalton's law** A gas law stating that the total pressure exerted by a mixture of gases in a container is the sum of the partial pressures that each gas would exert alone. 285–288
Dating, with half-lives, 155, 156
***d* block element** The block of ten elements from Groups 3B (3) to 2B (12) in which electrons fill the five *d* orbitals in *d* sublevels. 123–124, *123*
DDT (dichlorodiphenyltricholorethane), 8
Dead Sea Scroll, 156
**Decarboxylation** A reaction in which a $CO_2$ molecule is produced. 798
in citric acid cycle, 813, 815
**Decay curve** A diagram of the decay of a radioactive element. 154, *154*
*Deci* (d), 27, 28*t*
Deciliter (dL), 30
Decimal point, 18–19
power of ten, 18–19, 19*t*
**Decomposition reaction** A reaction in which a single reactant splits into two or more simpler substances. 217, *218*
Decompression, 288
Decongestants, 652, *652*
Deforestation, 66
Dehydrogenases, 703, 704*t*
in citric acid cycle, 815, 817
Dehydrogenation. *See* Oxidation
Demerol, 657, 825
**Denaturation** The loss of secondary and tertiary protein structure caused by heat, acids, bases, organic compounds, heavy metals, and/or agitation. 693–696
enzyme, 710–711, *711*
milk protein, 694
protein, 693–696, *694*, 854
**Density** The relationship of the mass of an object to its volume expressed as grams per cubic centimeter ($g/cm^3$), grams per milliliter (g/mL), or grams per liter (g/L). 43–49, *43*
bone density, 46
of common substances, 43*t*
guide to calculating, 44
problem solving using, 46–47
sink or float?, 46
of solids, 43*t*, 45, *45*
Denture, 508
Deoxyribonucleic acid. *See* DNA
Deoxyribose, 740
Deposition, 81
Desalinization, 325
Dextrose. *See* Glucose
Diabetes
gestational, 850
insulin and, 850
ketone bodies and, 850
obesity and, 847
Type I vs. Type II, 850
**Dialysis** A process in which water and small solute particles pass through a semipermeable membrane. 296, 327–328
Dialyzing membrane, 327
Diaphragm, 269
Diastolic blood pressure, 266
Diatomic molecule, 184*t*, 185
Diazepam, 662
Dichloromethane, 428
Dicumarol, 829
Diet
high-cholesterol, 628, 628*t*
high-fat, 603, 610, 847
high-protein, 858
obesity and, 847
recommendations, 603
Diffusion, 634–635, *635*
**Digestion** The processes in the gastrointestinal tract that break down large food molecules to smaller ones that pass through the intestinal membrane into the bloodstream.
carbohydrate, 788–790, *789*
dietary fats, 839–841, *840*
lipids, 839–854
protein and amino acids, 854–866
**Dilution** A process by which water (solvent) is added to a solution to increase the volume and decrease (dilute) the concentration of the solute. 318–320, *318*
Dimethylamine, 645
Dinitrogen oxide ($N_2O$), 272
2,4-Dinitrophenol (DNP), 829
Dioxane, 490

Dioxin, 490
Diphenhydramine, 652
Diphenylhydramine, 647
**Dipole** The separation of positive and negative charge in a polar bond indicated by an arrow that is drawn from the more positive atom to the more negative atom. 194, 199
**Dipole-dipole attractions** Attractive forces between oppositely charged ends of polar molecules. 201, 201*t*
**Direct relationship** A relationship in which two properties increase or decrease together. 270
**Disaccharide** Carbohydrates composed of two monosaccharides joined by a glycosidic bond. 543, 557–563, 567
  digestion of, 789
  reactions, 567, 568
  sweetness of, 560*t*
Disease
  genetic, 763–764, 764*t*
  lipid, 626, 626*t*
  vaccine against, 768
  viral infection and, 768*t*
Disinfectant, 695
**Dispersion forces** Weak dipole bonding that results from a momentary polarization of nonpolar molecules in a substance. 201, 201*t*
**Dissociation** The separation of an acid or base into ions in water. 300, 377
  constant for weak acid, 381–382, 382*t*
**Disulfide** A compound formed from thiols; disulfides contain the —S—S— functional group. 498–499, 501
**Disulfide bond** Covalent —S—S— bonds that form between the —SH group of two cysteines in a protein to stabilize the tertiary structure. 499, 688, 688*t*
Disulfiram (antabuse), 498
Diver. *See* Scuba diver
Division, 25
**DNA (deoxyribonucleic acid)** The genetic material of all cells, containing nucleotides with deoxyribose sugar, phosphate, and the four bases adenine, thymine, guanine, and cytosine. 739–750
  base pairs in, 746, *747*
  bases in, 739–740, *740*, 746*t*
  components of, 739–743
  daughter DNAs, 749
  deoxyribose in, 740
  double helix, 745–747, *746*
  genetic code and, 757
  introns and exons in, 754, *755*
  model, construction of, 763
  mutations, 761–765, *762*
  nucleotides and nucleosides in, 739–743, *739*, *741*, 742*t*
  primary structure, 743–744
  recombinant, 765–768
  replication, 747–750, *748*
  synthesis, 747–749, *748*
  transcription of, 753–754, *753*, *754*
DNA fingerprinting, 766–767, *767*
DNA fragment, 749, *750*
DNA polymerase, 749, *750*
DNA viruses, 771, 771*t*
Docosahexaenoic acid (DHA), 610
Dopamine, 647
Dosage, 36, 40–41
**Double bond** A sharing of two pairs of electrons by two atoms. 186–187
**Double helix** The helical shape of the double chain of DNA that is like a spiral staircase with a sugar-phosphate backbone on the outside and base pairs like stair steps on the inside. 745–747, *746*
**Double replacement reaction** A reaction in which parts of two different reactants exchange places. 219, *219*
Down syndrome, 764*t*
Drug
  detecting in urine, 479
  synthesizing, 657
Dry cleaner, 428


## E


*E. coli* (*Escherichia coli*)
  gene cloning, 765–766, *766*
  recombinant DNA and, 765–766
Eggs (ova), 141
Egg whites, 695
Eicosanoids, 608–609
Eicosapentaenoic acid (EPA), 610
Electrical charge
  in atom, 105
  static electricity, 105
**Electrolyte** A substance that produces ions when dissolved in water; its solution conducts electricity. 300–304, *301*
  in blood plasma, 304, 304*t*
  in body fluids, 304, 304*t*, 306
  equivalents, 302–303, 302*t*
  in intravenous fluid, 304*t*
Electromagnetic radiation, 114
Electromagnetic spectrum, 114, *115*
**Electron** A negatively charged subatomic particle having a minute mass that is usually ignored in mass calculations; its symbol is $e^-$. 105, *106*, 107*t*
  energy level changes, 115–116, *115*
  energy levels, 114–119, *115*
  energy sublevels, 116–117, *116*, 117*t*
  ground vs. excited state, 115
  high-energy (beta particle), 140
  orbitals, 118, *118*
  sharing, 183–186
  valence, 126–127, 126*t*
**Electron carrier** A group of proteins that accept and pass on electrons as they are reduced and oxidized. Most of the carriers are tightly attached to the inner mitochondrial membrane, but two are mobile carriers, which move electrons between the complexes containing the other carriers. 819–822, *820–821*
**Electron configuration** A list of the number of electrons in each sublevel within an atom, arranged by increasing energy. 119–126, *120*
  abbreviated, 120
  Period 1, 119–120
  Period 2, 120–121
  Period 3, 121–122
  Period 4, 123–124
  periodic table and, 122–123, *123*
  writing using sublevel blocks, 123
Electron-dot formula
  covalent compound, 184, 185*t*
  writing, 186
**Electron-dot symbol** The representation of an atom that shows valence electrons as dots around the symbol of the element. 126–127, 127*t*
**Electronegativity** The relative ability of an element to attract electrons in a bond. 192–195, *193*, 194*t*
**Electron transport** A series of reactions in the mitochondria that transfer electrons from NADH and $FADH_2$ to electron carriers, which are arranged from higher to lower energy levels, and finally to $O_2$, which produces $H_2O$. Energy changes during three of these transfers provide energy for ATP synthesis. *780*, 822–825, *823*
  ATP synthase and, 827, *827*
  driving ATP synthesis (chemiosmotic model), 826, *826*
  electron carriers, 819–822
  energy from, 819
  metabolism and, 819–828, *823*, *826*, *867*
  regulation of, 828
  toxins inhibiting, 825
**Electrophoresis** The use of electrical current to separate proteins or other charged molecules with different isoelectric points. 679, *679*
**Element** A pure substance containing only one type of matter, which cannot be broken down by chemical methods. 72, *72*, *73*, 74*t*, 96–98
  atom, 105–107
  atomic mass, 106–107
  covalent bond, 183–189
  as diatomic molecule, 184*t*, 185
  essential to health, 100, 100*t*
  ionic charge, 170, 171, 171*t*
  Latin names in clinical usage, 96, 97
  molar mass, 230–234, *234*
  names and symbols of, 96*t*, 97*t*
  periodic table of, 98–104, *99*
  representative, 99–100
  trace, 104, 104*t*
  transition, 100, *101*
  *See also* Periodic table
Emergency medical technician (EMT), 812
EMT (emergency medical technician), 812
Emulsification, 839
**Enantiomer** Stereoisomers that are mirror images that cannot be superimposed. 527–528, *527–528*
  in biological systems, 530, *530*
Endoplasmic reticulum, 779, *781*, 781*t*
Endorphins, 684
**Endothermic reaction** A reaction in which the energy of the products is greater than that of the reactants. 247
  in cold pack, 249
  equilibrium shifting from temperature change, 360, 360*t*, 361*t*
**Energy** The ability to do work. 55–94
  activation, 338–339, *338*
  amino acid as a source, 856
  atomic, 160
  ATP and, 782–785, *783*
  for brain and red blood cells, 840
  caloric value of foods, *68*, 69–70, 69*t*, 70*t*

carbohydrate metabolism and, 782–785, *783*
catabolic and anabolic pathways, 779, *780*, *867*
changes in chemical reactions, 246–249
citric acid cycle and, 813–819
collision theory, 337–338, *338*
combining calculations, 85–86
DNA replication and, 747–749, *749*
electron transport and, 819–828, *823*, *826*
energy-rich compounds, 793
fat as a source of, 70*t*, 846–848
fatty acid oxidation and, 846–848
fusion reaction and, 160–162
gluconeogenesis and, 803–804
glycolysis and, 790–796, *791*, *867*
heat and units of, 57–59
heat of fusion, 79–80, 82*t*
ionization, 128, *129*
levels, atomic, 114–119, *115*
nuclear fission, 160, *161*
nuclear power plant, 162
nutrition and, 68–71, *68*, 70*t*
oxidative phosphorylation and, 826–828, *826*
potential and kinetic, 56, *56*
production, metabolism and, 812–837
radiant, 771
specific heat, 63–67, 64*t*
storage as glycogen, 831, *832*
summary of metabolic pathways for, *867*
sun, 57
temperature, 59–63
typical requirements for adults, 71*t*
units of, 57–59

Enkephalins, 684
Enolase, 793
Enteropeptidase, 718
Environmental Notes
catalytic converters, 341
CFCs and ozone depletion, 434
dating ancient objects, 156
DDT, 8
fragrant alkenes, 450
functional groups in familiar compounds, 438
pheromones in insect communication, 453
plastics, 587
soaps, cleaning action, 593
toxic ethers, 490
toxicity of mercury, 98
vanilla, 512

Environmental Protection Agency (EPA)
DDT and, 8
mercury in fish, 98
radioactive hazardous waste and, 662
recommended radon level, 146

**Enzyme** Globular proteins, sometimes with cofactors, that catalyze biological reactions. 673*t*, 702–737
action, 706–710
active site, 706–707, *706*
activity, factors affecting, 710–713
activity, regulation of, 717–721
allosteric, 719
as catalyst, 703, *703*
catalyzed reactions, 707–708, *707*
classification, 703–705, 704*t*
cofactors and vitamins, 721–729, 721*t*, 723*t*
denaturation, 710–711, *711*
feedback control, 719–720, *719*
increasing concentration, 711–712, *712*
induced-fit model, 707–708, *708*
inhibition/inhibitors, 713–717, *714–715*, 716*t*
isoenzymes, diagnosis and, 709–710, 709*t*–710*t*
lock-and-key model, 707, *708*
naming, 703
pH and, 711, 711*t*
simple, 721
specificities of, 707–708, 707*t*
substrate concentration and, 711–712, *712*
synthesizing as zymogen, 717–719, 718*t*
temperature and, 710–711, *711*
types of, 704*t*, 707*t*
zymogens and, 717–719, 718*t*

Enzyme-catalyzed reaction, 707–708, *707*

**Enzyme induction** A model of cellular regulation in which protein synthesis is induced by a substrate. 755, *756*

**Enzyme-substrate (ES) complex** An intermediate consisting of an enzyme that binds to a substrate in an enzyme-catalyzed reaction. *706*

Epinephrine (adrenaline), 647, 801
fat mobilization and, 840

Epstein-Barr virus, 771*t*

**Equality** A relationship between two units that measure the same quantity
common, 33*t*
conversion factors for, 32–37
length, 29, *30*
mass, 31
prefixes and, 28*t*
volume, 30

Equanil (meprobamate), 662

Equation
balanced, 213–216
chemical, 311

Equilibrium, 336–370
calculating concentration at, 352–353
catalysts and, 340, 340*t*, 355–356, 361*t*
changing conditions/Le Châtelier's principle, 353–362, 356*t*, 361*t*
chemical, 342–344, *343*
concentration change and, 339, *339*, 340*t*, 354–356, *354*, 356*t*, 361*t*
forward, reserve, and reversible reactions, 342–343, *343*
heterogenous and homogenous, 346, *346*
oxygen-hemoglobin equilibrium, 357
rate of reaction, 337–342, *338*, *339*, 340*t*
saturated solutions, 362–365
shifting, 354–356, *354*, 356*t*
state of reactants and products at, 342–344, *343*
temperature change and, 339, 340*t*, 359–361, 360*t*, 361*t*
volume (pressure) change and, 356–359, *357*, 361*t*

**Equilibrium constant ($K_c$)** The numerical value obtained by substituting the equilibrium concentrations of the components into the equilibrium constant expression. 344–348
calculating, 347–348, 347*t*
large, 349–350, *349*, *350*, 351*t*
predicting reaction, 349
small, 350–352, *351*, 351*t*
using, 348–353

**Equilibrium constant expression** The ratio of the concentrations of products to the concentrations of reactants with each component raised to an exponent equal to the coefficient of that compound in the chemical equation. 344–346

**Equivalent (Eq)** The amount of a positive or negative ion that supplies 1 mole of electrical charge. 302–303, 302*t*

**Equivalent dose** The measure of biological damage from an absorbed dose that has been adjusted for the type of radiation. 150

Erythromycin, 759*t*
*Escherichia coli. See E. coli*
Eskimos, 610

**Essential amino acid** Amino acids that must be supplied by the diet because they are not synthesized by the body. 687, 687*t*, 863, 863*t*
for children but not adults, 863

Essential fatty acid, 605

**Ester** An organic compound in which an alkyl group replaces the hydrogen atom in a carboxylic acid. 436, 437*t*, 585–588
acid hydrolysis, 591–592, 595
base hydrolysis (saponification), 592–593, 595
fruit and flavoring, 438, 589*t*
naming, 588–590, 595
properties, 591–594
solubility in water, 591

Ester bond, 587, *611*

**Esterification** The formation of an ester from a carboxylic acid and an alcohol with the elimination of a molecule of water in the presence of an acid catalyst. 585–587, 595, 637

Estradiol, 631
Estrogen, 631
Ethanal, 496, 498
Ethane, 418, *418*
Ethanediol (ethylene glycol), 483, 731
Ethanoic acid, 496, 517
Ethanol (ethyl alcohol), 483
as abused drug, 498
combustion, *494*
disinfectant, 695
lactate fermentation and, *797*, 798
$LD_{50}$ value, 36*t*
oxidation of, 496
*See also* Alcohol

Ethanolamine, 621
Ethene (ethylene), 447–448, *447*, 463*t*

**Ether** An organic compound in which an oxygen atom is bonded to two alkyl or two aromatic groups or a mix of the two. 435, 437*t*, 486–491
anesthesia, 489
boiling point, 491–492, 492*t*
cyclic, 489–490
forming, 496
isomers, 488–489
naming, 487–488, 501
solubility in water, 492–493, 492*t*
toxic, 490

Ethrane, 489
Ethyl alcohol, 438
Ethylbenzene, 466
Ethyl chloride (chloroethane), 428
Ethylene (Ethene), 447–448, *447*, 463*t*
Ethylene glycol, 483, 731
Ethyne (acetylene), 447–448, *447*
Eukaryotic cell, 779
  major component(s), 779–781, *781*, 781*t*
**Evaporation** The formation of a gas (vapor) by the escape of high-energy molecules from the surface of a liquid. 80, *81*
**Exact number** A number obtained by counting or definition. 22–23, 23*t*
**Excess reactant** The reactant that remains when the limiting reactant is used up in a reaction. 242
Excited state, 115
Exercise, lactic acid and, 584
Exhalation, 269
**Exons** The sections in a DNA template that code for proteins. 754, *755*
**Exothermic reaction** A reaction in which the energy of the reactants is greater than that of the products. 247
  equilibrium shifting from temperature change, 360, 360*t*, 361*t*
  in hot pack, 249
**Expanded structural formula** A type of structural formula that shows the arrangement of the atoms by showing each bond in the hydrocarbon as C—H, C—C, C=C, or C≡C. 418, *420*
  butane, *420*
  hexane, *420*
**Experiment** A procedure that tests the validity of a hypothesis. 4, 5
EXP function key, 19
Expiration, 269
*Exxon Valdez* oil spill, 430

## F

Fabry's disease, 626, 626*t*
Facilitated transport, 635, *635*
**FAD** A coenzyme (flavin adenine dinucleotide) for dehydrogenase enzymes that form carbon-carbon double bonds. 786–787, *787*, *867*
Fahrenheit (°F) temperature scale, 59–62
  boiling and freezing point of water, 59, *60*, 62*t*
  comparison of temperature scales, *60*, 62*t*
  converting to Celsius temperature, 61
Faraday, Michael, 465
**Fat** A triacylglycerol that is solid at room temperature and usually comes from animal sources. 612–613
  adipose tissue, 48
  blubber, 847, 848
  brown, 829
  cells, 839, *839*
  in diet, 847
  digestion of, 839–841, *840*
  energy content, 70*t*, 846–848
  hibernation and, 612
  high-fat diet, 603, 610, 847
  hydrogenation, 615–617, *616*, 637
  hydrolysis, 618, 637
  leptin and, 847
  melting point, 613–615, *614*
  metabolism of, 839–854, *867*
  obesity and, 847
  oxidation, 618, 841–848
  saponification, 618, 637
  saturated, 603, 617, 628
  solubility, 609
  source of energy, 839–841
  source of energy during hibernation, 612
  stored/storage of, 847, 848
  substitute (Olestra), 616
  types of, 620
  unsaturation, 456
**Fat mobilization** The hydrolysis of triacylglycerols in the adipose tissue to yield fatty acids and glycerol for energy production. 840, 869
**Fat-soluble vitamin** Vitamins that are not soluble in water and can be stored in the liver and body fat. 727–728, 727*t*
**Fatty acid** A long-chain carboxylic acids found in many lipids. 604–611
  activation, 842, *842*
  blood-brain barrier and, 840
  degradation, 866, *867*
  essential, 605
  length, beta oxidation cycles and, 844
  length, synthesis cycles and, 853
  melting points, 606*t*
  in metabolism summary, *867*
  monounsaturated, 605, 606*t*
  omega-3, 610
  oxidation, 841–846, 869
  oxidation, ATP and, 846–848
  polyunsaturated, 605, 606*t*
  properties of, 606–607, *607*
  saturated, 605, 606*t*, 617
  structures, 606*t*
  synthesis (lipogenesis), 851–854, *852*, 853*t*, 869
  synthesis, regulation of, 853
  trans, 617
  transporting, 842
Fatty acid synthesis, 851–854, *852*, 853*t*, 869
  comparing to beta-oxidation, 853, 853*t*
***f* block element** The block of 14 elements in the rows at the bottom of the periodic table in which electrons fill the seven *f* orbitals in 4*f* and 5*f* sublevels. 123, *123*
FDA. *See* Food and Drug Administration (FDA)
**Feedback control** A type of inhibition in which an end product inhibits the first enzyme in a sequence of enzyme-catalyzed reactions. 719–720, *719*
*Femto* (f), 28*t*
**Fermentation** The anaerobic conversion of glucose by enzymes in yeast to yield alcohol and $CO_2$. *797*, 798
Ferritin, 673*t*
Fertilizer, 180
**Fe-S (iron-sulfur) clusters** Proteins containing iron and sulfur in which the iron ions accept electrons from $FMNH_2$ and cytochrome *b*. 820, *821*
Fever, 711
Fibril
  collagen, 686
  fibrous protein, 689, *690*
  hair, 689
Fibrinogen, 718*t*
**Fibrous protein** Proteins that are insoluble in water; consisting of polypeptide chains with $\alpha$-helixes or $\beta$-pleated sheets, that make up the fibers of hair, wool, skin nails, and silk. 689, *690*
Fibrous proteins, 689, *689*
"Fight or flight," 647
Filament
  light bulb
  muscle protein, 784
Fingerprinting, DNA, 766–767, *767*
Fischer, Emil, 528
**Fischer projection** A system for drawing stereoisomers; carbon atoms are shown at the intersections of horizontal lines for bonds projecting forward and vertical lines for bonds projecting backward. The most highly oxidized carbon is at the top. 528–531, *529*
  monosaccharides, 546–550
Fish
  mercury level in, 98
  odor of, 438
  oil, 610
**Fission** A process in which large nuclei are split into smaller pieces, releasing large amounts of energy. 160, *161*
Five-carbon compounds, 862
Flammability, 415
  inorganic compound, 417*t*
  organic compound, 417*t*
**Flavin adenine dinucleotide (FAD)** A coenzyme for dehydrogenase enzymes that form carbon-carbon double bonds. 786–787, *787*
**FMN (flavin mononucleotide)** An electron carrier derived from riboflavin (vitamin $B_2$) that transfers hydrogen ions and electrons from NADH entering electron transport. 820, *820*
Flavin ring system, *820*
Flavor, esters and, 585, 589*t*
**Fluid mosaic model** The concept that cell membranes are lipid bilayer structures that contain an assortment of polar lipids and proteins in a dynamic fluid arrangement. 634, *634*
Fluoride, 168
Fluorine, 104*t*
Fluothane, 428

**FMN (flavin mononucleotide)** An electron carrier derived from riboflavin (vitamin $B_2$) that transfers hydrogen ions and electrons from NADH entering electron transport. 820, *820*

Folate, 724*t*, 726, 866
Folic acid (folate), 724*t*, 726, 866
Food
  digestion of, *780*, 788–790, *789*
  irradiating, 151, *151*
  mercury content, 98
  nutrition labeling, 70
  water percentage, 298*t*
Food technologist, 210
Forane, 489
Force
  attractive, 75, 200–202, 201*t*
  buoyant, 48
  dispersion, 201, 201*t*
  *See also* Pressure
Forensic anthropologist, 1

Formaldehyde, *511*, 513
Formalin, 521
Formic acid, 577, 577*t*
**Formula** The group of symbols and subscripts that represent the atoms or ions in a compound. 175–179
 *See also* Condensed Structural formula; Expanded structural formula
**Formula unit** The group of ions represented by the formula of an ionic compound. 226
Forward reaction, 342–343, *343*
Fossil fuel, 272
Four-carbon compounds, 862, 864
**Frameshift mutation** A mutation that inserts or deletes a base in a DNA sequence. *762*, 763
Freeze-dried foods, 81–82
Freezer burn, 81
**Freezing** A change of state from liquid to solid. 79, *79*
**Freezing point (fp)** The temperature at which a liquid changes to a solid (freezes) and a solid changes to a liquid (melts). 79
 Celsius (°C) scale, 59, *60*, 62*t*
 Fahrenheit (°F) scale, 59, *60*, 62*t*
 Kelvin (K) scale, *60*, 62*t*
 lowering with solutes, 324, 324*t*
**Fructose** A monosaccharide, also called levulose and fruit sugar, that is found in honey and fruit juices; it is combined with glucose in sucrose. 547, 548–549, *548*, 567
 digestion (glycolysis) and, 794–795
 Haworth structure, 553
 reducing sugar, 555
Fructose-1,6-bisphosphate, 803, *804*, 806*t*
Fructose-6-phosphate, 803, *804*
Fruits
 enzymes and, 711
 flavor and aroma, 585, 589*t*
 oxidation of, 223
 ripening, 448
 waxy coating on, *430*
Fuel cells, 225
Fumarase, 817
Fumarate, *816*
 from amino acid degradation, 862
 in urea cycle, *859*, 860
Fumaric acid, 584
**Functional group** A group of atoms that determine the physical and chemical properties and naming of a class of organic compounds. 434–439, 435*t*
Furan, 489
**Fusion** A reaction in which large amounts of energy are released when small nuclei combine to form larger nuclei. 160–162


## G


**Galactose** A monosaccharide that occurs combined with glucose in lactose. 547, 548, 567
 digestion (glycolysis) and, 794–795
 Haworth structure, 552
Galactosemia, 548, 764*t*
Gallstones, 628–629, *629*
Gamma emission, 143*t*, 147, *147*
**Gamma ray** High-energy radiation with symbol ${}^{0}_{0}\gamma$ that is emitted by an unstable nucleus. 114, *114*, 141, 141*t*
 killing bacteria in food with, 151, *151*
 protecting from, 142, 142*t*
**Ganglioside** A glycolipid consisting of sphingosine, a fatty acid, and two or more monosaccharides. 625
**Gas** A state of matter characterized by no definite shape or volume. Particles in a gas move rapidly. 75, *75*, 76*t*, 261–294
 blood gases, 287, 287*t*
 density of common gases, 43*t*
 forming, 264
 kinetic molecular theory of, 262–263
 laws, 267–285, 276*t*
 noble gases, *101*, 102, 169
 partial pressures (Dalton's Law), 285–288
 pressure, 263, *263*, 264–266, 264*t*, 307–308
 problem solving reactions involving, 280
 properties of, 76*t*, 262–264, *263*, 264*t*, 281
 as solution, 297*t*
 STP, 278–280, *279*
 volume and moles (Avogadro's Law), 277–281, *278*
 *See also* Gas laws
Gas chromatograph, 602
Gas laws
 combined gas law, 276–277
 ideal gas law, 281–285
 partial pressures (Dalton's Law), 285–288
 pressure and volume (Boyle's Law), 267–270, *267*
 summary of, 276*t*
 temperature (Kelvin) in calculations of, 270, 273
 temperature and pressure (Gay-Lussac's Law), 273–276, *273*
 temperature and volume (Charles's Law), 270–273, *271*
 volume and moles (Avogadro's Law), 277–281, *278*
Gaucher's disease, 626, 626*t*
**Gay-Lussac's law** A gas law stating that the pressure of a gas changes directly with a change in temperature when the number of moles of a gas and its volume do not change. 273–276, *273*, 276*t*
Geiger counter, 150
Gene cloning, 765–766, *766*
Genes, 739
 regulatory, 755
 structural, 755, *756*
**Genetic code** The sequence of codons in mRNA that specifies the amino acid order for the synthesis of protein. 757–758, *757*
 mRNA codons for amino acids, 757, *757*
**Genetic disease** A physical malformation or metabolic dysfunction caused by a mutation in the base sequence of DNA. 763–764, 764*t*
Genetic information. *See* DNA; RNA
Genetic mutations, 761–765, *762*
Genetic screening, 767
Genome, 739, 767
Geologist, 427
Gestational diabetes, 850
*Giga* (G), 28*t*
Global warming, 66, 272–273
**Globular protein** Proteins that acquire a compact shape from attractions between the R group of the amino acids in the protein. 687, 689, *689*
 denaturation, 694
Glomerulus, 328
Glucagon, 801, 840
 diabetes and, 850
**Glucogenic amino acid** An amino acid that provides carbon atoms for the synthesis of glucose. 861–862, *861*
**Gluconeogenesis** The synthesis of glucose from noncarbohydrate compounds. 802–806, *802*, *804*
 carbon skeletons and, *861*
 energy cost of, 803–804
 irreversible reactions in, 803, *804*
 regulation of, 805–806, 806*t*
 summary of, *805*
**Glucose** The most prevalent monosaccharide in the diet. An aldohexose that is found in fruits, vegetables, corn syrup and honey. Also known as blood sugar and dextrose. Most polysaccharides are polymers of glucose. 547–548
 ATP energy from, 830, *830*
 blood, 549, 850
 energy for brain and red blood cells, 840
 as energy source, 782–785, *783*
 mutarotation, 552
 oxidation of (glycolysis), 780–786, *791*, *867*
 oxidation of, ATP from, 830, *830*
 synthesis (gluconeogenesis), 802–806, *802*, *867*
 in urine, testing, 556, 556*t*
Glucose-6-phosphate, converting to glucose, 803, *804*, 806*t*
Glutamate, 857–858
 from amino acid degradation, 862
 degradation, 862
 as nonessential amino acid, 863*t*
 synthesis, *863*
Glutamate dehydrogenase, 857
Glutamine, 675*t*
 degradation, 862
 as nonessential amino acid, 863*t*
 synthesis, *863*, 864
Glyceraldehyde 3-phosphate, 793, *867*
Glycerol, 483
 metabolism of, 841, 869
**Glycerophospholipid** A polar lipid of glycerol attached to two fatty acids and a phosphate group connected to an amino alcohol such as choline, serine, or ethanolamine. 621–623
 cell membrane and, 622, *622*
 phosphate esters, 621–623, *622*
Glycine, 675*t*
 converting to pyruvate, 862
 as nonessential amino acid, 863*t*
 synthesis, *863*
 from threonine degradation, 862
**Glycogen** A polysaccharide formed in the liver and muscles for the storage of glucose as an energy reserve. It is composed of glucose in a highly branched polymer joined by $\alpha$-1,4- and $\alpha$-1,6-glycosidic bonds. 563, 567
 energy for brain and red blood cells, 840
 energy storage, 831, *832*
 metabolism, 799–802
 metabolism, regulating, 801
 synthesis (glycogenesis), 799–800, *800*, *805*

**Glycogenesis** The synthesis of glycogen from glucose molecules. 799–800, *800*, *805*
**Glycogenolysis** The breakdown of glycogen into glucose molecules. 800, *805*, *867*
Glycogen phosphorylase, 801
Glycolic acid, 579
**Glycolysis** The ten oxidation reactions of glucose that yield two pyruvate molecules. 790–796, *791*
  as anaerobic process, 790
  ATP from, 828–832, *830*, 831*t*
  nonessential amino acid synthesis and, *863*
  other hexoses, 794–795
  regulation of, 795, 806*t*
  summary of, 794, *867*
**Glycosidic bond** The bond that forms when the hydroxyl group of one monosaccharide reacts with the hydroxyl group of another monosaccharide; it is the type of bond that links monosaccharide units in di- or polysaccharides. 558
**Glycosphingolipid** The phospholipid that combines sphingosine with a fatty acid bonded to the nitrogen group and one or more monosaccharides bonded by a glycosidic link which replaces the —OH group of sphingosine. 624–625
Gold-foil experiment, 105–106, *106*
Golgi complex, 779–780, *781*, 781*t*
Gonorrhea, 695
Gore, Al, 273
Gout, 306
Grain (gr), 40
**Gram (g)** The metric unit used in measurements of mass. 16, *16*
Graphite, *105*
**Gray (Gy)** A unit of absorbed dose equal to 100 rads. 150, 150*t*
Green Chemistry Notes
  acid rain, 394
  biodiesel, 619
  carbon dioxide and global warming, 66
  crude oil, 433, 433*t*
  energy-saving lightbulbs, 116
  fuel cells: clean energy for the future, 225
  nuclear power plants, 162
  radon in our homes, 146
  toxicology and risk-benefit assessment, 36
Greenhouse gases, 272–273
Ground state, 115
**Group** A vertical column in the periodic table that contains elements having similar physical and chemical properties. 99–103, *100*
  classification of, 101–102, *101–102*, 101*t*, 103*t*
Group number, 126
  ionic charge and, 171, 171*t*
Growth hormone, 766*t*
Guanine (G), 739–740, *740*, 742*t*
Guide to Problem Solving (GPS), 37–39
Gypsum, 508

## H

Hair
  disulfide bonds in, 499
  fibril, 689
  mercury testing and, 98
  number and width of, 18, *18*
  "permanent" and, 499
  sprays, CFCs and, 434
**Half-life** The length of time it takes for one-half of a radioactive sample to decay. 153–156, 154*t*, 157*t*
  carbon-14, 156
  decay curve, 154, *154*
  modeling, 155
  proteins, 855
  radioisotopes, examples, 155*t*
Hallucinogens, 438
**Haloalkane** A type of alkane that contains one or more halogen atoms. 427, 437*t*
  common use, 428
**Halogen** An element in Group 7A (17)—fluorine, chlorine, bromine, iodine and astatine—that has seven electrons in its outermost energy level. 102, *102*
**Halogenation** The addition of $Cl_2$ or $Br_2$ to an alkene or benzene to form halogen-containing compounds. 456*t*, 457–458, *457*, 469
Halothane, 427
Handedness, 525–528, *525*
**Haworth structure** The cyclic structure that represents the closed chain of a monosaccharide. 551–554
  alpha and beta glucose, 552
  drawing for cyclic form, 551–552, 553–554
  fructose, 553
  galactose, 552
Hazardous wastes, 162
HDL (high-density lipoprotein), 630–631, *630*
HDL-cholesterol, 617
Health Notes
  alcohol, oxidation in the body, 498, 498*t*
  alpha hydroxy acids (AHA), 579
  amides in health and medicine, 662
  amines in health and medicine, 647
  antacids, 397
  aromatic compounds, 466
  beta emitters in medicine, 147
  blood gases, 287, 287*t*
  blood types and carbohydrates, 561, 561*t*
  bone density, 46
  brachytherapy, 152
  buffers in the blood, 405, 405*t*
  carboxylic acids in metabolism, 584
  colloids and solutions in the body, 322
  determination of percentage body fat, 48
  dialysis by kidneys and artifical kidney, 328
  drugs, synthesizing, 657
  early chemists: the alchemists, 6
  electrolytes in body fluids, 304, 304*t*
  elements essential to health, 100, 100*t*
  enantiomers in biological systems, 530, *530*
  essential amino acids, 687, 687*t*
  ethers as anesthetics, 389
  glucose in urine, testing for, 556, 556*t*
  gout and kidney stones, 306
  haloalkanes, common uses of, 428
  homeostasis: regulation of body temperature, 362
  homocysteine and coronary heart disease, 866
  hot and cold packs, 249
  hydrogenation of unsaturated fats, 458
  hyper- and hypoglycemia, 549
  hyperbaric chambers, 288
  important alcohols and phenols, 483
  important aldehydes and ketones, 513
  important ions in the body, 173, 173*t*
  isoenzymes as diagnostic tools, 709–710, 709*t*, 710*t*
  ketone bodies and diabetes, 850
  lactose intolerance, 790
  Latin names for elements in clinical usage, 97
  lipid diseases, 626, 626*t*
  losing and gaining weight, 71, 71*t*
  measuring blood pressure, 266
  methanol poisoning, 496
  muscle contraction, $Ca^{2+}$ and ATP and, 784
  night vision, cis-trans isomers for, 454
  Olestra: a fat substitute, 616
  omega-3 fatty acids in fish oils, 610
  oxygen-hemoglobin equilibrium and hypoxia, 357
  phenylketonuria (PKU), 865
  polycyclic aromatic hydrocarbons (PAHs), 467
  polypeptides in the body, 684
  pressure-volume relationship in breathing, 269
  radiation and food, 151, *151*
  radiation doses in medical procedures, 158, 158*t*
  salicylic acid and pain relievers, 586
  sickle-cell anemia, 692
  smog and health concerns, 220
  steam burns, 84
  stomach acid, HCl, 388
  sweeteners, sweetness of, 560, 560*t*
  toxicity of carbon monoxide, 432
  trace elements in the body, 104, 104*t*
  trans fatty acids and hydrogenation, 617
  uses for noble gases, 172
  variation in body temperature, 62
  water in the body, 298
Heart attack, *628*, 630 diagnosis, 710*t*
Heart damage, diagnosing, 864
Heart disease, 603, 610, 866
**Heat** The energy associated with the motion of particles in a substance. 57–59
  body, heating, 829
  brown fat and, 829
  calculating in reaction, 248
  calculating to melt or freeze water, 80
  calculations using specific heat, 65–67
  denaturing protein, 694, *694*
  specific, 63–67, 64*t*
  units of, 57–59
Heat extractor, 76
**Heating curve** A diagram that shows the temperature changes and changes of state of a substance as it is heated. 84–85, *84*
Heat of condensation, 82
**Heat of fusion** The energy required to melt exactly 1 g of a substance at its melting point. For water, 80. cal are needed to melt 1 g of ice; 80. cal are released when 1 g of water freezes. 79–80, 82*t*
**Heat of reaction** The heat (symbol $\Delta H$) absorbed or released when a reaction takes place at constant pressure. 246–249

**Heat of vaporization** The energy required to vaporize 1 g of a substance at its boiling point. For water, 540 calories are needed to vaporize exactly 1 g of liquid; 1 g of steam gives off 540 cal when it condenses. 82–84, *82*, 82*t*
Height, measuring, 15
Helicase, 747, 749, *750*
Helium (He), 119–120
  uses of, 172
Helium balloon, 172
Helix
  double, 745–747, *746*
  triple, 686, *686*
Hemotoxin, 76
**Hemiacetal** The product of the addition of one alcohol to the double bond of the carbonyl group in aldehydes and ketones.
  cyclic, 524
  intermediate, forming, 522–523, 534
Hemlock, 655
**Hemodialysis** A mechanical cleansing of the blood by an artificial kidney using the principle of dialysis. 328
Hemoglobin, 673*t*
  carrying oxygen, 673, 673*t*
  half-life, 855
  quaternary structure, 689, *691*
**Hemolysis** A swelling and bursting of red blood cells in a hypotonic solution due to an increase in fluid volume. 326, *326*
Hemophilia, 764*t*
**Henry's law** The solubility of a gas in a liquid is directly related to the pressure of that gas above the liquid. 307–308
Hepatitis, diagnosis, 710*t*
Hepatitis B virus (HBV), 771*t*
Heroin, 656
Herpes simplex virus, 771*t*
**Heterocyclic amine** A cyclic organic compound that contains one or more nitrogen atoms in the ring. 654–655
Heterocyclic compound, 489
**Heterogeneous equilibrium** An equilibrium system in which the components are in different states. 346, *346*
Heterogeneous mixture, 74, 74*t*
Hexane, *420*
Hexokinase, 792, 795, 803, 806*t*
Hexose, 544
Hibernation, 612
High-density lipoprotein (HDL), 630, *630*
Hip replacement, *463*
Histamine, 647
Histidine, 675*t*
  degradation, 862
  essential for children but not adults, 863
Histologist, 76
HIV (human immunodeficiency virus), 770, *770*
  AIDS and, 770–771
Homeostasis, 362
Homocysteine, 866
Homocystinuria, 866
**Homogenous equilibrium** An equilibrium system in which all components are in the same state. 346, *346*
Homogenous mixture, 73, 74*t*
Honey, *548*
Hormone, 673*t*
  antidiuretic, 684
  half-life, 855
  human growth, 766*t*
  prostaglandins, 2, 608–610
  sex, 631
  steroid, 631
Hot pack, 249
Human body
  body fat, 35, *35*, 48
  body temperature, 362
  electrolytes in plasma, 304, 304*t*
  essential and nonessential amino acids, 863–866, *863*, 863*t*
  hair on scalp, 18, *18*
  homeostasis and, 362
  nonessential amino acid, synthesizing, 863–864, *863*
  trace elements in, 104, 104*t*
Human Genome Project, 767
Human growth hormone, 766*t*
Human immunodeficiency virus. *See* HIV
Huntington's disease, 764*t*, 767
**Hydration** An addition reaction in which the components of water, H— and —OH, bond to the carbon-carbon double bond to form an alcohol. 299, *299*, 456*t*, 460–461
  beta-oxidation cycle, 843
**Hydrocarbon** Organic compounds consisting of only carbon and hydrogen. 418
  saturated and unsaturated, 419
Hydrochloric acid (HCl), 388
Hydrofluorocarbon (HFC), 273
Hydrogen (H), 119–120
  molecule, 184
  in periodic table, 102
**Hydrogenation** The addition of hydrogen ($H_2$) to the double bond of alkenes to yield alkanes. 456–457, 456*t*
**Hydrogenation** The addition of hydrogen to unsaturated fats. 458, 615–617, *616*, 637
**Hydrogen bond** The interactions between water and the polar R groups such as —OH, —$NH_3^+$, and —COOH on the outside surface of a polypeptide chain. 201, 201*t*, 688, 688*t*
  acetaldehyde and acetone with water, *516*
  in DNA double helix, 746, *747*
  in triple helix, 686
  in water, 297
**Hydrohalogenation** The addition of a hydrogen halide such as HCl or HBr to a double bond. 456*t*, 458–459
**Hydrolysis** The splitting of a molecule by the addition of water.
  amide, 663–665
  ATP, 782–783, *783*
  enzymes (hydrolases), 704*t*
  esters, 591–592, 637
  protein, 693–696
  urea cycle reaction, 860
Hydrometer, 47, *47*
**Hydronium ion ($H_3O^+$)** The ion formed by the attraction of a proton ($H^+$) to an $H_2O$ molecule. 374
  calculating from pH, 390–392, 392*t*
Hydrophilic, 593
  cell membrane layer, 634, *634*
  polar amino acid, 674
**Hydrophilic interaction** The attraction between polar R groups on the protein surface and water. 688, 688*t*
Hydrophobic, 593
  cell membrane layer, 634, *634*
  nonpolar amino acid, 674
**Hydrophobic interaction** The attraction between nonpolar R groups on the inside of a globular protein. 688, 688*t*
Hydroxide ion, 180*t*
Hydroxyapatite, 182, 362
**Hydroxyl group** The —OH functional group. 436, 437*t*, 480
  in alcohols, 436, 480, 481
  Benedict's test and, 518, *518*
  cyclic hemiacetal, 524
  phenol, 480, 482
Hydroxylysine, 686
Hydroxyproline, 686
Hyperbaric chambers, 288
Hyperglycemia, 549
Hypertension, 632
Hyperthermia, 62
Hyperthyroidism, 139
**Hypertonic solution** A solution that has a higher osmotic pressure than the red blood cells of the body. 326–327, *326*
Hypo (prefix), 180
Hypoglycemia, 549
Hypothermia, 62
**Hypothesis** An unverified explanation of a natural phenomenon. 4, 5
**Hypotonic solution** A solution that has a lower osmotic pressure than the red blood cells of the body. 326, *326*
Hypoxia, 357

**I**

Ibuprofen, 530, 609–610
**Ideal gas constant (*R*)** A numerical value that relates the quantities *P*, *V*, *n*, and *T* in the ideal gas law. 281
**Ideal gas law** A law that combines the four measured properties of a gas in the equation $PV = nRT$. 281–285
Imaging
  CT scans, 159, *159*
  PET and, 158
  radioisotopes and, 148, 157*t*
Imidazole, 654
Inch, 15
Incomplete protein, 687
Indicator (pH), 393, 396
Indinavir, 771
**Induced-fit model** A model of enzyme action in which the shape of a substrate and the active site of the enzyme adjust to give an optimal fit. 707–708, *708*
Inducer, 755, *756*
Industrial smog, 220
Inflammation
  aspirin and, 2
  cold pack and, 249
  NSAIDs and, 609
  reducing, 2, 249, 609
  in sickle-cell anemia, 692
Infrared, 114, *114*
Inhalation, 269
**Inhibitor** Substances that make an enzyme inactive by interfering with its ability to react with a substrate. 713–717
  reversible inhibition, 713–714, *714*
Inorganic compound, 417, 417*t*

Insecticide, 715, 716*t*
  electron transport inhibition by, 825
**Insoluble salts** Ionic compounds that do not dissolve in water. 308–310, *309*, 309*t*
Inspiration, 269
Insulator, 102
Insulin, 673*t*, 766*t*
  diabetes and, 850
  half-life, 855
  proinsulin, 718, 718*t*
Interferon, 766*t*
*International System of Units*. *See* SI unit
International Union of Pure and Applied Chemistry. *See* IUPAC system
Intestine
  disaccharide digestion and, 789
  protein/amino acid digestion and, *855*
  triacylglycerol (lipid) digestion and, 840, *840*
Intravenous fluid, electrolyte concentration, 304*t*
**Introns** The sections in DNA that do not code for protein. 754, *755*
Inuit people, 610
**Inverse relationship** A relationship in which two properties change in opposite directions. 267
Invirase (Saquinavir), 771
Iodine, 102, *102*, 104*t*
  radioactive, 139–140, *154*, 155*t*
  stable and radioactive isotope, 140*t*
Iodine-125, 152, 157*t*
Iodine-131, *154*, 155*t*, 157*t*
**Iodine test** A test for amylose that forms a blue-black color after iodine is added to the sample. 565
**Ion** An atom or group of atoms having an electrical charge because of a loss or gain of electrons.
  in body, 173, 173*t*
  name and formula, 171*t*
  negative, 170
  oxidation-reduction involving, 221–223, *222*
  polyatomic, 180–183, 180*t*
  positive, 169–170, 177–178, 177*t*, 178*t*
  sizes of, 172
**Ionic bond** The attraction between oppositely charged ions. 169, 174, 193, 201*t*
**Ionic charge** The difference between the number of protons (positive) and the number of electrons (negative) written in the upper right corner of the symbol for the element or polyatomic ion. 170
  group number and, 171, 171*t*
  writing ionic formula, 175–176
**Ionic compound** A compound of positive and negative ions held together by ionic bonds. 169, 174–176, *174*
  attractive force, 200–202
  charge balance, 175
  formula, 175, 176–179
  metals forming positive ion, 177*t*
  naming, 176–179, 176*t*
  properties, 174
  solubility, 308–310, 309*t*
**Ionic equation** An equation for a reaction in solution that gives all the individual ions, both reacting ions and spectator ions. 310–311
Ionic formula, 175, 176–179
Ionization
  gamma ray, 151, *151*
  water, 383–386, *384*, 384*t*
**Ionization energy** The energy needed to remove the least tightly bound electron from the outermost energy level of an atom. 128, *129*
  increasing and decreasing, *129*
Ionizing radiation
  protecting from, 141–142
  treating food with, 151, *151*
**Ion-product constant of water, $K_w$** The product of $[H_3O^+]$ and $[OH^-]$ in solution; $K_w = [H_3O^+][OH^-]$. 384, 384*t*
Iridium-192, 155*t*
Iron (Fe)
  in the body, 104, 104*t*
  rust and, 2, 77, 77*t*
Iron-59, 155*t*
**Iron-sulfur cluster (Fe-S)** Proteins containing iron and sulfur in which the iron ions accept electrons from $FMNH_2$ and cytochrome *b*. 820, *821*
Irradiated foods, 151, *151*
**Irreversible inhibition** The loss of enzymatic activity that cannot be reversed. 715–716, 716*t*
Isocitrate, 814, *816*
Isocitrate dehydrogenase, 815
**Isoelectric point (pI)** The pH at which an amino acid exists as a zwitterion with a net charge of zero. 677
Isoenzymes, 709–710, 709*t*, 710*t*
Isoleucine, 675*t*
  degradation, 862
  as essential amino acid, 863*t*
**Isomer** Organic compounds in which identical molecular formulas have different arrangements of atoms. 423, *423*
  alcohol, 488–489
  ether, 488–489
Isomerase, 704*t*
Isomerization
  beta-oxidation cycle, 844
  in citric acid cycle, 814
  in glycolysis, 792
Isopropyl alcohol, 695
**Isotonic solution** A solution that has the same osmotic pressure as that of the red blood cells of the body. 326, *326*
**Isotope** An atom that differs only in mass number from another atom of the same element. Isotopes have the same atomic number (number of protons) but different numbers of neutrons. 110–113
  half-life, 153–156, 157*t*
  radioactive, 139–143, 140*t*, 155*t*, 156–159, 157*t*
  stable and radioactive, 140*t*
**IUPAC system**The system for naming organic compounds devised by the International Union of Pure and Applied Chemistry. 419
  alkanes, 419*t*, 425

## J

Jojoba wax, 611, 611*t*
**Joule (J)** The SI unit of heat energy; 4.184 J = 1 cal. 57

## K

Kaposi's sarcoma, 770
Kekulé, August, 465
Kelvin (K), 17, 62
**Kelvin (K) temperature scale** A temperature scale on which the lowest possible temperature is 0 K. 17, 62–63
  comparison of temperature scales, *60*, 62*t*
Keratin, 673*t*, 689, *690*
Keto acid, 856
**Ketogenesis** The pathway that converts acetyl CoA to four-carbon acetoacetate and other ketone bodies. 849–850, *849*
**Ketogenic amino acid** An amino acid that provides carbon atoms for the synthesis of fatty acids or ketone bodies. 861–862, *861*
  degradation, 862
Ketohexose, 555
**Ketone** An organic compound in which the carbonyl functional group is bonded to two alkyl or aromatic groups. 435, 437*t*, 438
  boiling point, 515, *516*
  important, 513
  naming, 512–514, 533
  oxidation and reduction, 517–521, *518*, 533–534
  physical properties, 515–517, *516*
  solubility in water, 516, *516*
  structure, 509–510, *509*
**Ketone bodies** The products of ketogenesis: acetoacetate, β-hydroxybutyrate, and acetone. 849–850, *849*
  diabetes and, 850
Ketoprofen, 609–610
**Ketose** A monosaccharide that contains a ketone group. 544
**Ketosis** A condition in which high levels of ketone bodies cannot be metabolized leading to lower blood pH. 849
Kidney
  adrenal gland and, 632
  damage from NSAID, 609–610
  dialysis, 327–328
  glomerulus, 328
  malfunction of, 662
  sodium reabsorption, 632
Kidney stones, 306
*Kilo* (k), 28, 28*t*
**Kilocalorie (kcal)** An amount of heat energy equal to 1000 calories. 57
**Kilogram (kg)** A metric mass of 1000 g equal to 2.20 lb. The kilogram is the SI standard unit of mass. 16
Kilojoule (kJ), 57, 58
**Kinetic energy** The energy of motion. 56
**Kinetic molecular theory of gases** A model used to explain the behavior of gases. 262–263
Krebs cycle, 584
  *See also* Citric acid cycle
Kuru disease, 690

## L

Labeling, food nutrition, 70
Laboratory technician/technologist, 371, 460, 479
Laboratory test values, 30*t*
Lactase, 558
Lactate
  accumulating in muscle, 797

Cori cycle and, 804, *805*
pyruvate conversion to, 797–798, *797*
Lactate dehydrogenase
half-life, 855
isoenzyme, 709, 709*t*, 710*t*
Lactic acid, 497–498, 579, 584
**Lactose** A disaccharide consisting of glucose and galactose found in milk and milk products. 558, *559*
intolerance, 790
operon, 755, *756*
Lamb Lac, 672
Lanolin, 611
Lanthanides, *99*, 100
Lard, 603
Laughing gas, 168
Lauric acid, 606*t*
Law of conservation of mass, 235
Laws, scientific, 7, 7*t*
$LD_{50}$ (lethal dose), 36
LDL (low-density lipoprotein), 630–631, *630*
LDL-cholesterol, 617
L-dopa, 530
**Le Châtelier's Principle** When a stress is placed on a system at equilibrium, the equilibrium shifts to relieve that stress. 353–355, 356*t*, 361*t*
**Lecithin** Glycerophospholipids containing choline as the amino alcohol. 622
Length
equalities, 29, *30*, 33*t*
measuring, 29, *30*
units of measurement, 15, *15*
Leptin, 847
Lethal dose ($LD_{50}$), 36
Leucine, 862, 863*t*
Leukemia, 771*t*
Levulose, 549
Lidocaine, 654, 657
Light, 114, *114*
Lightbulbs, energy-saving, 116
"Like dissolves like," 299, *299*, 300
Limestone, 284, 394
**Limiting reactant** The reactant used up during a chemical reaction; it limits the amount of product that can form. 241–246
calculating mass of product, 244–245
calculating mole of product, 242–244
percent yield, 240–241
**Linear** The shape of a molecule that has two bonded atoms and no lone pair. 196, 198*t*
**Line-bond formula** A type of structural formula that shows only the bonds from carbon to carbon. 420
butane, *420*
hexane, *420*
Linoleic acid, 606*t*, 610
Lipase, 618, 704, 711*t*
pancreatic, 839, 840
**Lipid** A family of compounds that is nonpolar in nature and not soluble in water; includes fats, waxes, phospholipids, and steroids. 447, 602–643
composition in cell membrane, 622, *622*, 633*t*
digestion of, 839–841
diseases, 626, 626*t*
emulsification of, 839
metabolism of, 839–854, *867*
nonpolar, *622*
polar, *622*
structures, *604*
types of, 603–604, *604*
*See also* Fat; Fatty acid
**Lipid bilayer** A model of a cell membrane in which glycerophospholipids are arranged in two rows. 634, *634*
**Lipogenesis** The synthesis of fatty acid in which two-carbon acetyl units link together to yield fatty acids, primarily palmitic acid. 851–854, *852*
**Lipoprotein** A combination of nonpolar lipids with glycerophospholipids and proteins to form a polar complex that can be transported through body fluids. 629–631, 673*t*
composition and properties, 630, 630*t*
HDL and LDL, 617
transporting nonpolar lipids, 629–631, *629*, *630*
types of, 630, 630*t*
*See also* Cholesterol
**Liquid** A state of matter that takes the shape of its container but has a definite volume. 75, *75*, 76*t*
density of common liquids, 43*t*
properties of, 76*t*
solutions, 297*t*
**Liter (L)** The metric unit for volume that is slightly larger than a quart. 16
measuring volume, 30, *31*
unit of measurement, 16, *16*
Lithium (Li)
alkali metal, 101, *101*
electron configuration, 120–121
Liver
damage, diagnosing, 710*t*, 864
damage from NSAIDs, 609–610
synthesizing cholesterol, 627, *630*
synthesizing glucose, *802*
urea cycle and, 859
**Lock-and-key model** A model of enzyme action in which the substrate is like a key that fits the specific shape of the active site (the lock). 707, *708*
London smog, 220
Lone pair, 184
Lou Gehrig's disease, 767
Low-density lipoprotein (LDL), 630, *630*
Low-pressure system, 265
LSD, 438, 658
Luminal (phenobarbital), 662
Lysergic acid (LSD), 658
Lysine, 675*t*
degradation, 862
as essential amino acid, 863*t*
Lysosome, 780, *781*, 781*t*

## M

Mad cow disease, 690
Magnesium
electron-dot symbols, 127
ion, 173*t*
isotope, 110, 111*t*
Magnetic resonance imaging (MRI), 159, *159*
Malaria, 656
Malate, *816*, 817
Malate dehydrogenase, 817
Malic acid, 579, 584
Malonate, 714
Malonyl CoA, 851, *852*, 853
**Maltose** A disaccharide consisting of two glucose units; it is obtained from the hydrolysis of starch and in germinating grains. 558, 560*t*
Manganese, 104*t*
Mannitol, 556
Mannose, 556
Margarine, 458, 616, *616*
**Markovnikov's rule** When adding HX or HOH to alkenes with different numbers of groups attached to the double bonds the H-adds to the carbon that has the greater number of hydrogen atoms. 459–460
**Mass** A measure of the quantity of material in an object. 16
calculations for reactions, 237–240
conservation of, 235
equalities, 31, 33*t*
measuring, 31
relation to moles and particles, *234*, 235–237
units of measurement, 16, *16*
**Mass number** The total number of neutrons and protons in the nucleus of an atom. 107–110, 109*t*
alpha and beta particle, 141*t*
changing due to radiation, 143*t*
**Mass percent (m/m)** The grams of solute in exactly 100 grams of solution. 312–313
Mass spectrometer, 479
**Mass/volume percent (m/v)** The grams of solute in exactly 100 mL of solution. 314
Materials science, 95
Matrix, cellular, 780, 842
**Matter** Anything that has mass and occupies space. 2, 56, 72–74
changes of state, 79–87
classifying, 72–74, *73*, 74*t*
organizing, *73*
states and properties of, 75–79, *75*, 76*t*, 77*t*
**Measured number** A number obtained when a quantity is determined by using a measuring device. 21–22, *21*
Measurement, 14–54
body fat, 35, *35*, 48
density, 43–49
length, 15, *15*, 29, *30*
mass, 16, *16*, 31
measured numbers, 21–22
prefixes and equalities, 27–32
pressure, 263, 265, 265*t*
problem solving, 37–43
radiation, 150–153, 150*t*
scientific notation, 18–21, 19*t*
significant figures, 21–27
specific gravity (sp gr), 47–48, *47*
temperature, 17, *17*
time, 17
units of, 15–18, 17*t*
volume, 16, *16*, 30, *30*, *31*
volume displacement, 45, *45*
weight, 16
writing conversion factors, 32–37
writing in scientific notation, 18–19, 19*t*
*Mega* (M), 28*t*
Melanin, 764
Melanoma, 771
**Melting** A change of state that involves the conversion of a solid to a liquid. 79, *79*

**Melting point (mp)** The temperature at which a solid becomes a liquid (melts). It is the same temperature as the freezing point. 79
alkane, 430
amide, 661
bond type and, 201*t*
fat and oil, 613–615, *614*
fatty acid, 606*t*
inorganic compound, 417*t*
ionic compound, 174
organic compound, 417*t*
Membrane, cell. *See* Cell membrane
Menaquinone (vitamin K), 727*t*, 728
Mendeleev, Dmitri, 98
Menstruation, 631
Mental retardation, 548
Menthol, 480
Meperidine, 657
Meprobamate, 662
Mercury
in fish, 98
millimeters of (mmHg), 263
toxicity of, 98
**Messenger RNA**. *See* **MRNA**
**Meta (m)** A method of naming that indicates two substituents at carbons 1 and 3 of a benzene ring. 466, 482, 577
Metabolic acidosis/alkalosis, 405, 405*t*
**Metabolism** All the chemical reactions in living cells that carry out molecular and energy transformations. 778–875
amino acid and protein, 854–866
ATP, energy from glucose, 828–832, *830*
ATP, oxidative phosphorylation and, 826–828
carbohydrate pathways for, 778–811, *780*
catabolism and anabolism, 779, *780*, 866, *867*
cell structure for, 779–781, *781*, 781*t*
chemiosmotic model, 826, *826*
citric acid cycle and, 779, *780*, 813–819
coenzymes and, 785–788, *786–787*
defined, 779
digesting carbohydrate, 788–790, *789*
digesting protein, 839, 854–856, *855*
electron transport and, 819–828, *823*, *826*
energy production and, 812–837
glycogen, 799–802
lipid, 839–854
obesity, 847
overview of, 866, *867*
oxidative phosphorylation and ATP and, 826–828, *826*
pyruvate, 796–799
stages of, *780*, *814*, *867*
**Metal** An element that is shiny, malleable, ductile, and a good conductor of heat and electricity. The metals are located to the left of the heavy zigzag line in the periodic table. 102
acids and, 393
alkali metals, 101–102, *101*
alkaline earth metals, *101*, 102
characteristics of, 103*t*
forming positive ion, 177–178, 177*t*, 178*t*
ionic charge, 177–178
ions, as cofactors, 721–722, 721*t*
ions, common, 171*t*
in periodic table, *99*
variable charge, 177–178
**Metalloid** Elements with properties of both metals and nonmetals located along the heavy zigzag line on the periodic table. 102, *102*, 103*t*
Metastable, 147
**Meter (m)** The metric unit for length that is slightly longer than a yard The meter is the SI standard unit of length. 15
Methamphetamine, 647
Methandienone, 632
Methane ($CH_4$), 272
Methanethiol, 484
Methanol, 483
poisoning, 496
producing blindness, 483
Methedrine, 647
Methionine, 675*t*
degradation, 862
as essential amino acid, 863*t*
synthesis, 866
Methotrexate, 726
Methoxyflurane, 489
Methylamine, 438, 645
Methylene chloride, 602
Methyl group, 424*t*, 452, 468
ester, 487
Methyl salicylate, 584
**Metric system** A system of measurement used by scientists and in most countries of the world. 15, 17*t*, *33*
conversion factors, 33–34
exact number, 23*t*
measuring length, 15, *15*
measuring mass, 16, *16*
measuring volume, 16, *16*
prefixes, 27–28, 28*t*
unit of time, 17
*See also* Measurement
Micelles, 839
*Micro* (μ), 28*t*
Microscope, 105, *105*
Microwaves, 114, *114*
Milk, lactose intolerance and, 790
Milk protein, denaturation, 694
Milk sugar (lactose), 558
*Milli* (m), 27, 28*t*
Millicurie (mCi), 151
**Milliliter (mL)** A metric unit of volume equal to one-thousandth of a L (0.001 L). 16, *16*
Millimeter (mm), 29, *30*
Millirem (Mrem), 150
Mirror image, 525–528, *525*
archiral compound, *528*
Mirrors, making, 517–518, *518*
Mitchell, Peter, 826
**Mitochondria** The components of the cells where energy-producing reactions take place. 780, *781*, 781*t*
Mitosis (cell division)
DNA replication in, *753*
uncontrolled (in cancer), 771
**Mixture** The physical combination of two or more substances that does not change the identities of the substances. 73–74, *73*
types of (classifying), 73–74, *73*, 74*t*
MmHg, 263
**Molarity** The number of moles of solute in exactly 1 L of solution. 316–318, 317*t*
**Molar mass** The mass in grams of 1 mole of an element equal numerically to its atomic mass. The molar mass of a compound is equal to the sum of the masses of the elements in the formula. 230–234, *234*
**Molar volume** A volume of 22.4 L occupied by 1 mole of a gas at STP conditions of 0°C (273 K) and 1 atm. 278–280, *279*
**Mole** A group of atoms, molecules, or formula units that contains $6.02 \times 10^{23}$ of these items. 226–230, 226*t*
calculating from limiting reactant, 242–244
calculating in the kitchen, 232
in chemical equations, 235–237, 235*t*
of elements in formula, 228–229
molar mass calculations, 230–234
relation to mass and particles, *234*
**Molecule** The smallest unit of two or more atoms held together by covalent bonds. 183–186
collision theory, 337–338, *338*
number in one-mole sample, 226–228, 226*t*
polarity, 199–200
shape, 195–198, 198*t*
**Mole-mole factor** A conversion factor that relates the number of moles of two compounds derived from the coefficients in an equation. 236–237
Monoacylglycerols, 839–840, *840*
**Monomer** The small organic molecule that is repeated many times in a polymer. 462–463, 463*t*
**Monosaccharide** A polyhydroxy compound that contains an aldehyde or ketone group. 543, 544–545
chemical properties, 555–557
Fischer projections, 546–550
Haworth structures, 551–554
important, 547–548
metabolism and, *867*
oxidation, 555, 568
reduction, 555–556, 568
sweetness of, 560*t*
types, 544, 567
Monosodium glutamate (MSG), 583
**Monounsaturated fatty acid** A fatty acid with one double bond. 605
melting point and structure, 606*t*
Morphine, 656, *657*
MRI (magnetic resonance imaging), 159, *159*
**mRNA** Messenger RNA; produced in the nucleus from DNA to carry the genetic information to the ribosomes for the construction of a protein. 751, 751*t*
codons, 757, *757*, *759*
pre-mRNA, 754, *755*
processing, 754–755, *755*
producing (transcription), 753–755, *753*, *754*
protein synthesis (translation) and, 753, *753*, 758
Multiple sclerosis, 626
Multiplication, 25
Muscle
anabolic steroid and, 632
contraction, ATP and, 784

filaments, 784
lactate accumulation in, 797
Muscular dystrophy (MD), 764*t*
Mutagens, 761
**Mutarotation** The conversion between $\alpha$ and $\beta$ anomers. 552
**Mutation** A change in the DNA base sequence that alters the formation of a protein in the cell. 761–765
effects of, 763
types of, 761–763, *762*
Myelin sheath, 622
Mylar, 587
Myocardial infarction, 603, 630
Myoglobin, *689*
carrying oxygen, 673, 673*t*
Myosin, 673*t*, 784
Myristic acid, 606*t*
ATP production from, 846–847
beta oxidation and, *845*

## N

Nabumetone, 609–610
**NAD$^+$** The hydrogen acceptor used in oxidation reactions that form carbon-oxygen double bonds. 785–786, *786, 867*
NADH dehydrogenase, 822–823, *823*
Nandrolone, 632
*Nano* (n), 28*t*
Naproxen, 609–610
Negative ion, 170, 177*t*
Nembutal (pentobarbital), 662
Neon (Ne), 102, 120–121
in lighting tubes, 172
Neoplasm. *See* Cancer
Neo-Synephrine (phenylephrine), 647
Neotame, 560, 560*t*
Nerve gas, 715, 716*t*
Nervous system stimulants, 655
**Net ionic equation** An equation for a reaction that gives only the reactants and products involved in a chemical change. 310–311
**Neutralization** A reaction between an acid and a base to form a salt and water. 394–396
endpoint, 397
**Neutral solution** The term that describes a solution with equal concentrations of $H_3O^+$ and $OH^-$. 384, 384*t*
cation and anion of salt, 400*t*
salts that form, 399, 400*t*
**Neutron** A neutral subatomic particle having a mass of 1 amu and found in the nucleus of an atom; its symbol is $n$ or $n^0$. 106, *106*, 107*t*
mass number, 141*t*
Niacin (vitamin $B_3$), 723*t*, 724
**Nicotinamide adenine dinucleotide (NAD$^+$)** The hydrogen acceptor used in oxidation reactions that form carbon-oxygen double bonds. 785–786, *786, 867*
Nicotine, 530, 655
Niemann-Pick disease, 626*t*
Night vision, 454, 727*t*
Nitrate, 180*t*
Nitration, 469
Nitrogen (N), 96, 97*t*, 99
atomic number and composition, 109
balance, in cells, 856
blood urea nitrogen (BUN), 858
in carbohydrates, 100
compounds containing, 855, 855*t*
dietary, 856
excreting (urea cycle), 858–861, *859*
freezing, 79
polyatomic ions, 180*t*
smog and, 2, 220
Nitrogen-13, 147
Nitrogen-14, 145, 156
**Nitrogen-containing base** Nitrogen-containing compounds found in DNA and RNA: adenine (A) thymine (T), cytosine (C), guanine (G), and uracil (U). 739–740, *740*
Nitrogen-containing compounds, 855, 855*t*
Nitrogen dioxide, 168
smog and, 220, 394
**Noble gas** An element in Group 8A (18) of the periodic table, generally unreactive and seldom found in combination with other elements, that has eight electrons in its outermost energy level. *101*, 102, 169
uses of, 172
**Noncompetitive inhibitor** A type of inhibitor that alters the shape of an enzyme as well as the active site so that the substrate cannot bind properly. 714, *715*
**Nonelectrolyte** A substance that dissolves in water as molecules; its solution will not conduct an electrical current. 301, *301*
**Nonessential amino acid** An amino acid that can be synthesized by reactions including transamination of $\alpha$-keto acids in the body. 855*t*
in human body, 863*t*
synthesizing in body, 863–864, *863*
**Nonmetal** An element with little or no luster that is a poor conductor of heat and electricity. The nonmetals are located to the right of the heavy zigzag line in the periodic table. 102, 103*t*
bonding pattern, 185, 185*t*
polyatomic ion, 180–183
**Nonpolar amino acid** Amino acids with nonpolar R groups containing only C and H atoms. 674, 675*t*, 677–678
**Nonpolar covalent bond** A covalent bond in which the electrons are shared equally between atoms. 193, *193*
Nonpolar lipid, *622*
transport of, *630*
**Nonpolar molecule** A molecule that has only nonpolar bonds or in which the bond dipoles cancel. 199
Nonpolar tail, *622*, 633–634, *634*
Nonsteroidal anti-inflammatory drugs (NSAIDs), 609–610
Noradrenaline (norepinephrine), 647
Norepinephrine (noradrenaline), 647
Norethindrone, 631
Novocaine, 168
NSAIDs, 609–610
**N terminal** The end amino acid in a peptide with a free $—NH_3^+$ group. 681
Nuclear chemistry, 138–167
half-life of radioisotopes, 153–156
medical applications, 156–159
natural radioactivity, 139–143, 140*t*
nuclear fission and fusion, 160–162, *161*
nuclear reactions, 143–149
radiation measurement, 150–153
*See also* Radiation
Nuclear equation, completing, 144–145
Nuclear fission, 160–162, *161*
Nuclear fusion, 160–162
Nuclear medicine, 156–159
Nuclear power plant, 162
Chernobyl, 152
Nuclear reactions, 143–149
**Nucleic acids** Large molecules composed of nucleotides; found as a double helix in DNA and as the single strands of RNA. 738–758
bases in, 739–740, *740*
components of, 739–743
nucleotide structure, 739–743, *739, 741, 742*
primary structure, 743–745
**Nucleoside** The combination of a pentose sugar and a base. 741–743, *741*, 742*t*
forming of di- and triphosphates, 742, *742*
name in DNA and RNA, 741–742, 742*t*
producing, 740
Nucleoside triphosphate, 742, *742*
**Nucleotide** Building blocks of a nucleic acid consisting of a base, a pentose sugar (ribose or deoxyribose), and a phosphate group. 739–743
in DNA, 741–742, *741*, 742*t*
forming, 741
name in DNA and RNA, 741–742, *741*, 742*t*
in RNA, 741–742, *741*, 742*t*
structure, *739, 741, 742*
Nucleotide sequence, 744, 752, 761, *767*
**Nucleus** (of atom) The compact, extremely dense center of an atom, containing the protons and neutrons of the atom. 106, *106*
changing due to radiation, 143*t*, *147*
fusion, 160
splitting, *161*
**Nucleus** (of cell), *781*, 781*t*
Numerator, 32
Nurse, 14
NutraSweet, 560, 560*t*
Nutrient
food labeling, 70
recommended daily amounts, 28*t*
Nutrition, 68–71, *68*
caloric value of foods, *68*, 69–70, 69*t*, 70*t*
Nutrition Facts label, 70

## O

Obesity, 847
**Observation** Information determined by noting and recording a natural phenomenon. 4, 5
Occupational therapist, 749
Oceanographer, 336
**Octet rule** Elements in Groups 1-7A (1, 2, 13-17) react with other elements by forming ionic or covalent bonds to produce a noble gas configuration, usually 8 electrons in the outer shell. 169–174
exceptions, 185
Odor
alkenes and, 450
fish, 438
fruit, 585, 589*t*

**Oil** A triacylglycerol that is usually a liquid at room temperature and is obtained from a plant source. 447, 613
- fish, 610
- hydrogenation, 615–617, *616*, 637
- melting point, 613–615, *614*
- palm, 603
- polyunsaturated, 613
- solubility, 608
- unsaturated fat, 458
- unsaturation, 456
- vegetable, 458, 617
- *See also* Crude oil

Oil spill, 430, *430*

**Okazaki fragments** The short segments formed by DNA polymerase in the daughter DNA strand that runs in the 3' to 5' direction. 749, *750*

Oleic acid, 458, 606*t*

Olestra, 616

Omega-3 fatty acid, 610

Oncogenic viruses, 771, 771*t*

**Operon** A group of genes, including a control site and structural genes, whose transcription is controlled by the same regulatory gene. 755, *756*

Opium, 656, *657*

Optician, 109

**Optimum pH** The pH at which an enzyme is most active. 711, 711*t*

**Optimum temperature** The temperature at which an enzyme is most active. 710–711, *711*

**Orbital** The region around the nucleus where electrons of a certain energy are more likely to be found. The *s* orbitals are spherical; the *p* orbitals have two lobes. 118, *118*
- shape of, 118, *118*

**Orbital diagram** A diagram that shows the distribution of electrons in the orbitals of the energy levels. 119, *120*
- Period 1, 119–120
- Period 2, 120–121
- Period 3, 121–122

Organelle, cellular, 779–781, *781*, 781*t*

Organic chemistry, 416

**Organic compound** Compounds made of carbon that typically have covalent bonds, are nonpolar molecules, have low melting and boiling points, are insoluble in water, and are flammable. 416–419
- alkanes, 419–422
- bonding, 417*t*, 418
- classification of, 437*t*
- covalent bonds, 435*t*
- cyclic, 654–655
- functional groups, 434–439, 435*t*
- naming, 419, 419*t*
- properties of, 416–419, 417*t*
- tetrahedral structure of carbon, 418, *418*

Organic solvent, 438, 602
- lipids and, 603

Ornithine, *859*, 860

**Ortho** A method of naming that indicates two substituents at carbons 1 and 2 of a benzene ring. 466, 482, 577

**Osmosis** The flow of a solvent, usually water, through a semipermeable membrane into a solution of higher solute concentration. 296, 324–325

**Osmotic pressure** The pressure that prevents the flow of water into the more concentrated solution. 324–325

Osteoporosis, 46

Oxaloacetate, 803, *804*
- from aspartate or asparagine degradation, 862
- in citric acid cycle, *815*, *816*, 817
- glucogenic amino acid and, 861–862, *861*

Oxaloacetic acid, 584

Oxandrolone, 632

**Oxidation** The loss of two hydrogen atoms from a reactant to give a more oxidized compound. 221, 224*t*, 785
- alcohol, 496–498
- alcohol in body, 498, 498*t*
- aldehyde, 517–519, *518*, 533
- beta-oxidation cycle, 841–846
- in biological systems, 223–224
- carbohydrate, 780–786, *791*, *867*
- characteristics of, *816*
- citric acid cycle, *816*
- coenzymes, 820, *820–821*
- electron carriers, 820, *820–821*
- enzymes (oxidases), 703, 704*t*
- fatty acid, 841–846
- fruits and vegetables, 223
- glucose, 780–786, *791*
- monosaccharide, 555, 568
- thiol, 498–499

**Oxidation-reduction reaction** A reaction in which the oxidation of one reactant is always accompanied by the reduction of another reactant. 221–223, *222*

**Oxidative deamination** The loss of ammonium ion when glutamate is degraded to $\alpha$-ketoglutarate. 857–858, 869

**Oxidative phosphorylation** The synthesis of ATP from ADP and $P_i$ using energy generated by the oxidation reactions in electron transport. 826–828, *826*
- electron carriers, 819–822

Oxygen (O)
- aerobic condition, 796
- anaerobic condition, 790–796
- in carbohydrates, 100
- density of, 43*t*
- discovery of, 7*t*
- hydroxyl group, 436, 437*t*, 480
- partial pressure in blood and tissue, 287, 287*t*
- smog and, 2

Oxygenation, 62

Oxygen-hemoglobin equilibrium, 357

Oxytocin, 684

Ozone, 2
- depletion, CFCs and, 434

## P

PABA (*p*-aminobenzoic acid), 714, 726

Pain
- prostaglandins and, 609
- relievers, 586, 609–610, 656–657

Palmitate, synthesis, 851–853, *852*

Palmitic acid, 606*t*

Palm oil, 603

Pancreatic lipase, 839, 840

Pancreatitis, 718

Pantothenic acid (vitamin $B_5$), 723*t*, 724–725

Papain, 704

Papilloma virus, 771*t*

**Para** A method of naming that indicates two substituents at carbons 1 and 4 of a benzene ring. 466, 482, 577

Paracelsus, 6, 36

Paramedic, 812

Parathion, 716*t*

Parkinson's disease, 647

**Partial pressure** The pressure exerted by a single gas in a gas mixture. 285–288, 286*t*

Particle, *234*

Pascal (Pa), 265*t*

Passive transport, 634–635, *635*

Pauling, Linus, 4

***p* block element** The elements in Groups 3A (13) to 8A (18) in which electrons fill the *p* orbitals in the *p* sublevels. 122, *123*

PCR (polymerase chain reaction), 767, *768*

Peanut butter, 458

Penicillin, 645, 715–716, 716*t*

Penthrane, 489

Pentobarbital (Nembutal), 662

Pentose, 544

Pepper, 654

Pepsin, 704, 711, 711*t*, 854, *855*

Pepsinogen, 718, 718*t*, *855*

**Peptide** The combination of two or more amino acids joined by peptide bonds; dipeptide, tripeptide, and so on. 680–682
- forming, 680–682
- naming, 681

**Peptide bond** The amide bond in peptides that joins the carboxylate group of one amino acid with the ammonium group in the next amino acid. 680–681, *681*
- hydrolyzing, 693–696

Peptide chain, 683

Percentage, 35–36, *35*
- as a conversion factor, 41–42

Percent concentration, 312–316, 315*t*

**Percent yield** The ratio of the actual yield of a reaction to the theoretical yield possible for the reaction that is multiplied by 100%. 240–241

**Period** A horizontal row of elements in the periodic table. 99–100, *100*

Periodic properties, 126–130

**Periodic table** An arrangement of elements by increasing atomic number such that elements having similar chemical behavior are grouped in vertical columns. 98–104, *99*
- electron configurations and, 122–123, *123*
- period and groups in, 99–103, *100*
- trends in, 126–130

Permanent (hair treatment), 499

Pesticides, $LD_{50}$ values, 36*t*

*Peta* (P), 28*t*

PETE (polyethyleneterphthalate), 464, 587

**pH** A measure of the $[H_3O^+]$ in a solution; $pH = -\log[H_3O^+]$. 386–393, *387*
- acidosis and, 849
- calculating, 388–390
- calculating of buffer, 403–404
- determining, methods of, *388*
- enzyme activity and, 711, 711*t*
- $[H_3O^+]$ and $[OH^-]$ values, 392*t*
- indicators, 393, 396
- scale, *387*, 392*t*
- stomach, 711
- vegetables and fruit as indicators of, 393

Phenobarbital (Luminal), 662
**Phenol** An organic compound that has an —OH group attached to a benzene ring. 466, 480
important, 483
naming, 482–484, 501
structure, 466
Phenolphthalein, 396
Phenylalanine, 862
as essential amino acid, 863*t*
phenylketonuria and, 865
synthesis, *863*
Phenyl group, 466
Phenylketonuria (PKU), 560, 764–765, 865
Phenylpyruvate, 764
Pheromones, 453
Phlebotomist, 562
Phosphate ester, 621–623, *622*
**Phosphodiester bond** The phosphate link that joins the 3' hydroxyl group in one nucleotide to the phosphate group on the 5'-carbon atom in the next nucleotide. 743–744
Phosphoenolpyruvate, 803, *804*
Phosphofructokinase, 792, 795, 803, 806*t*
Phosphoglucose isomerase, 792
Phospholipid bilayer, 634, *634*
Phosphorus
polyatomic ions, 180*t*
Phosphorus-32, 147, 157*t*
Phosphorylation, 792, 793
Phosphoryl group, 739, *739*
Photochemical smog, 220
Photon, 114
Photosynthesis, 543, *543*
Phylloquinone (vitamin K), 727*t*, 728
**Physical change** A change in which the physical appearance of a substance changes, but the chemical composition stays the same. 77, 77*t*
**Physical properties** The properties that can be observed or measured without affecting the identity of a substance, 75–76, 76*t*, 77*t*
Physical therapist, 175, 815
**Physiological solution** A solution that exerts the same osmotic pressure as normal body fluids. 326
*Pico* (p), 28*t*
Piperidine, 655
PKU (phenylketonuria), 560, 764–765, 865
Plaque, 603, 628, *628*
Plasma, 298
electrolytes in, 304, 304*t*
Plasmids, recombinant DNA and, 765–766, *766*
Plaster, 180
Plastics, 416, 462–463
recycling, 463, 464
Platelet clotting, 610
*Pneumocystis carinii,* 770
**Polar amino acid** Amino acids with polar R groups. 674, 675*t*, 677–678
**Polar covalent bond** A covalent bond in which the electrons are shared unequally between atoms. 193, *193*
Polar head, *622*, 633–634, *634*
Polar lipid, *622*
**Polar molecule** A molecule containing bond dipoles that do not cancel. 199–200
Polar solute, 29, *299*
Polar solvent, 297
**Polyatomic ion** A group of covalently bonded nonmetal atoms that has an overall electrical charge. 180–183
bones and teeth, 182
compounds containing, 182–183, 182*t*
naming, 180, 180*t*, 183
products containing, *180*
writing formula, 181–182
Polycyclic aromatic hydrocarbons (PAHs), 467
Polydichloroethylene (Saran™), 463*t*, *464*
Polyester, 416
Polyethylene, 463*t*, 464, *464*
Polyethyleneterphthalate (PETE), 464, 587
**Polymer** A very large molecule that is composed of many small, repeating structural units that are identical. 462
alkene, 462–465, *463*, 463*t*, *464*
recycling, 463, 464
synthetic, *463*, *464*
**Polymerase chain reaction (PCR)** A procedure in which a strand of DNA is copied many times by mixing it with DNA polymerase and a mixture of deoxyribonucleotides. 767, *768*
Polypeptides, 683, 684
Polypropylene, 463*t*, 464, *464*
**Polysaccharide** Polymers of many monosaccharide units, usually glucose. Polysaccharides differ in the types of glycosidic bonds and the amount of branching in the polymer. 544, 563–566, 567
cellulose, 564–565, *565*
digesting, 565, *867*
Polysome, 759
Polystyrene, 463*t*, 464, *464*
Polytetrafluoroethylene (Teflon®), 463*t*, *464*
Polyunsaturated fat
dietary consumption, 610
oil, 613
**Polyunsaturated fatty acid** A fatty acid that contain two or more double bonds. 605
melting point and structure, 606*t*
Polyvinyl chloride (PVC), 463*t*, 464, *464*
Positive ion, 169–170, 177–178, 177*t*, 178*t*
**Positron** A particle with minute mass and a positive charge produced when a proton is transformed into a neutron and a positron. 140, 141*t*
Positron emission, 147
Positron emission tomography (PET), 158, *158*
Potassium (K)
alkali metal, 101, *101*
ion in the body, 173*t*
Potassium-40, 155*t*
**Potential energy** An inactive type of energy that is stored for future use. 56, *56*
Pound, 16
conversion factor, 33
Power of ten, 18–19, 19*t*
Power plant, nuclear, 162
Chernobyl, 152
Precipitate, 310
Prednisone, 632
**Prefix** The part of the name of a metric unit that precedes the base unit and specifies the size of the measurement. All prefixes are related on a decimal scale. 27–29, 28*t*, 466
Pregnancy
folic acid and, 866
gestational diabetes, 850
Pre-mRNA, 754, *755*
Preservative, 583, *583*
**Pressure** The force exerted by gas particles that hit the walls of a container. 263, *263*, 264
altitude and, 265*t*
atmospheric, 263, *263*, 265, *265*
blood, measuring, 266
in breathing, 269
change, equilibrium and, 356–359, *357*
gas, 263, *263*, 264–266, 264*t*
gradient, 269
measuring, 263, 265, 265*t*
osmotic, 324–325
partial, 285–288, 286*t*
solubility and (Henry's law), 307–308
standard (STP), 278–280, *279*
temperature and (Gay-Lussac's Law), 273–276, *273*
vapor, 274–275, 274*t*
volume and (Boyle's Law), 267–270, *267*
**Primary (1°) alcohol** An alcohol that has one alkyl group bonded to the alcohol carbon atom. 480, 496–498
Primary (1°) amine, 645
Primary amide, 661
**Primary structure (nucleic acid)** The specific sequence of the nucleotides in nucleic acids. 743–745, *744*
**Primary structure (protein)** The specific sequence of the amino acids in a protein. 683, *683*
Principal quantum number (*n*), 114, 115
Prions, 690
Problem solving, 37–43
cancellation of units, 38
clinical calculations using conversion factors, 40–41
Guide to Problem Solving (GPS), 37–39
with specific gravity, 47–48
using density, 46–47
using metric factors, 39
using two or more conversion factors, 39–40
Procaine, 654, 657
Procarboxypeptidase, 718–719
**Products** The substances formed as a result of a chemical reaction. 213
Proenzyme, 717–719, 718*t*
Progesterone, 631
Progestin, 631
Proinsulin, 718, 718*t*
Prokaryotic cell, 781
Proline, 862, 863*t*
Propanal, *511*
Propane, 416, *417*, 417*t*
combustion of, 431, *431*
Propanetriol (glycerol, glycerin), 483
Propionaldehyde, *511*
Propionic acid, 577, 577*t*
**Prostaglandins (PGs)** A number of compounds derived from arachidonic acid that regulate several physiological processes. 2, 608–610
physiological effect, 2
Prostate cancer, diagnosing, 710*t*
Prostate specific antigen (PSA), 710*t*

Protease inhibitors, 771
**Protein** Polypeptides containing many amino acids linked together by peptide bonds that are biologically active. 672–701
20 amino acids in, 675*t*
classification of, 673*t*
complete and incomplete, 687
cross-links and, 687–689, *688*, 688*t*
denaturation, 693–696, *694*, 854
digestion of, 839, 854–856, *855*
disulfide bonds, 499
energy content, 70*t*
half-life, 855
hydrolysis, 693–696
metabolism, 854–866, *855*, *867*
nitrogen-containing compounds, 855*t*
peptides and, 680–682
primary structure, 683, *683*
secondary structure, 683–686, *685*
structure, summary of, 691, *691*, 691*t*
synthesis, 758–761, *760*
tertiary and quaternary structure, 687–693, *688–691*, 688*t*, 691*t*
urea cycle and, 858–861, *859*
Protein synthesis, 758–761, *760*
antibiotics and, 759, 759*t*
**Protein turnover** The amount of protein that we break down from our diet and utilize for synthesis of proteins and nitrogen-containing compounds. 855–856, *855*
Prothrombin, 718*t*
**Proton** A positively charged subatomic particle having a mass of 1 amu and found in the nucleus of an atom; its symbol is $p$ or $p^+$. 105, *106*, 107*t*
**Proton pump** The enzyme complexes I, III, and IV that move protons from the matrix into the intermembrane space creating a proton gradient. 826, *826*
Provirus, *769*, 770
PSA (prostate specific antigen), 710*t*
psi (pound per square inch), 265, 265*t*
**Pure substance** Matter composed of elements or compounds that has a definite composition. 72, *73*, 74*t*
Purine, 739–740, *740*, 746
Puromycin, 759*t*
Putrescine, 438
Pyran, 490
Pyrex glass, 431
Pyridine, 655
Pyridoxine (vitamin $B_6$), 724*t*, 725
Pyrimidine, 739–740, *740*, 746
Pyrophosphate, *749*, 842
Pyrrole, 654
Pyrrolidine, 654
Pyruvate
aerobic conditions (converting to acetyl CoA), 796–797, *797*
anaerobic conditions (converting to lactate, ethanol), 797–798, *797*
ATP from oxidizing, 829, 831*t*
digestion/metabolism and, 779, *780*, 793
glucogenic amino acid and, 861–862, *861*
in metabolism summary, *867*
pathways for, 796–799, *797*, 803, *804*
Pyruvate carboxylase, 803, 806*t*
Pyruvate kinase, 793, 795, 803, 806*t*
Pyruvic acid, 497–498, 584


## Q


Quantum number ($n$), 114, 115
Quart, 16
Quartz, 75, *75*
**Quaternary ammonium ion** An amine ion in which the nitrogen atom is bonded to four carbon groups. 652
**Quaternary structure** A protein structure in which two or more protein subunits form an active protein. 689–691, *691*
Quinine, 656


## R


**Rad (radiation absorbed dose)** A measure of an amount of radiation absorbed by the body. 150, 150*t*
Radar, 114, *114*
Radiant energy, 771
**Radiation** Energy or particles released by radioactive atoms. 139
average annual per person, 152*t*
background, 151–152, 152*t*
biological effects of, 141
common forms, 152, 152*t*
doses in medical procedures, 158, 158*t*
exposure, 151–152, 152*t*
food and, 151, *151*
lethal dosage, 153, 153*t*
measuring, 150–153, 150*t*
medical applications, 156–159
protecting from, 141–142
sickness, 152–153
treating food, 151, *151*
types of, 140–141
**Radiation therapy** The use of high doses of radiation to destroy harmful tissues in the body. 152, 158
**Radioactive** The process by which an unstable nucleus breaks down with the release of high-energy radiation. 139–140
**Radioactive decay** The process by which an unstable nucleus breaks down and releases high-energy radiation. 143–149, 143*t*, *147*
Radioactive iodine, 139–140
Radioactive iodine uptake (RAIU), 157
Radioactive isotope, 139–143, 140*t*
producing, 147–149
Radioactive waste, 160, 162
Radioactivity, 156–159
**Radioisotope** A radioactive atom of an element. 139–143, 140*t*
emitting positron, 147
half-life, 153–156, 157*t*
medical applications, 155*t*, 156–159, *157*, 157*t*
scans with, 157–159, *157*, *158*, *159*
Radio waves, 114, *114*
Radium-226, 155*t*
Radon (Rn), 102, 146
**Rate of reaction** The speed at which reactants are used to form product(s). 337–342, *337*
factors affecting, 339–340, *339*, 340*t*
formula, 339
substrate concentration and, 711–712, *712*
**Reactant** The initial substances that undergo change in a chemical reaction. 211, *211*, 213
excess, 242
increasing concentration, 339, 340*t*
limiting, 241–246
mole-mole factor calculation, 236–237
Reaction
catalysts and, 340, 340*t*, 703, 707
direction of, 380–381
heat of, 246–249
*See also* Chemical reaction; Rate of reaction
Reactive center, *820*
**Recombinant DNA** DNA combined from different organisms to form new, synthetic DNA. 765–768
forming, 765–766, *766*
therapeutic products of, 766*t*
Recommended Daily Amounts (RDA), 28*t*
Recycling
plastics, 463, 464
plastics, symbols for, 464
Red blood cell
lipid composition, 633*t*
radiation and, 141
**Reducing sugar** A carbohydrate with a free aldehyde group capable of reducing the $Cu^{2+}$ in Benedict's reagent. 555
**Reduction** A decrease in the number of carbon-oxygen bonds by the addition of hydrogen to a carbonyl bond. Biological reduction may involve the loss of oxygen or the gain of hydrogen. 221, 223–224, 224*t*, 785
aldehyde and ketone, 519–520
coenzymes, 820, *820–821*
electron carriers, 820
enzymes (reductases), 704*t*
fatty acid synthesis, 851–852
monosaccharide, 555–556, 568
**Regulatory gene** A gene in front of the control site that produces a repressor. 755
Rehabilitation specialist, 682
Relafen, 609
Release factors, 759
**Rem (radiation equivalent in humans)** A measure of the biological damage caused by the various kinds of radiation (rad × radiation biological factor). 150, 150*t*
Renal disease, 858
Rennin, 704
**Replication** The process of duplicating DNA by pairing the bases on each parent strand with their complementary base. 747–750, *748*
direction of, 749, *750*
semi-conservative, 749
**Replication forks** The open sections in unwound DNA strands where DNA polymerase begins the replication process. 749, *750*
**Representative element** An element in the first two columns on the left of the periodic table and the last six columns on the right that has a group number of 1A through 8A or 1, 2 and 13 through 18. 99–100
**Repressor** A protein that interacts with the control site in an operon to prevent the transcription of mRNA. 755, *756*
Repulsion and attraction, 107
**Resonance structure** Two or more electron-dot formulas that can be written for a

molecule by placing a multiple bond between different atoms. 187–189
Respiration, 543, 813
Respiratory acidosis/alkalosis, 405, 405*t*
Respiratory chain, 819
Restriction enzyme, 765, *766*
Restriction fragment length polymorphism (RFLP), 766
Retardation, 548
Retina, 454
Retinal (aldehyde), 454, 727
Retinoblastoma, 771
Retinoic acid (carboxylic acid), 727
Retinol (vitamin A), 727, *727*, 727*t*
**Retrovirus** A virus that contains RNA as its genetic material and that synthesizes a complementary DNA strand inside a cell. *769*, 770
Reverse osmosis, 325
Reverse reaction, 342–343, *343*
Reverse transcriptase, *769*, 770
Reverse transcription, 770
**Reversible inhibition** The loss of enzymatic activity by an inhibitor whose effect can be reversed. 713
**Reversible reaction** A reaction in which a forward reaction occurs from reactants to products, and a reverse reaction occurs from products back to reactants. 342–343, *343*
RFLP (restriction fragment length polymorphism), 766
Rheumatoid arthritis, 632
Rhodopsin, 454
Ribitol, 724
Riboflavin (vitamin $B_2$), 723*t*, 724
Ribonucleic acid. *See* RNA
Ribose, 740
**Ribosomal RNA (rRNA)** The most prevalent type of RNA and a major component of the ribosomes. 751, 751*t*
Ribosome, 751, *751*, 779, *781*, 781*t*
  polysome, 759
  protein synthesis and, 759, *760*
Rickets, 722, 727*t*
Rigor mortis, 784
Risk-benefit assessment, 36
Ritonavir, 771
**RNA** Ribonucleic acid; a type of nucleic acid that is a single strand of nucleotides containing adenine, cytosine, guanine, and uracil. 739–745, 751–756
  base pairs in, 746, *747*
  bases in, 739–740, *740*
  genetic code and, 757–758, 757*t*
  nucleotides and nucleosides in, 739–743, *739*, *741*, 742*t*
  primary structure, 743–745, *744*
  protein synthesis and (translation), 753, *753*, 758–761
  ribose in, 740
  types of, 751–753, 751*t*
  *See also* MRNA; RRNA; TRNA
RNA polymerase, *754*, 763
RNA viruses, 771, 771*t*
Rotenone, 825
Rounding off, 24–27
**rRNA** Ribosomal RNA; the most prevalent type of RNA and a major component of the ribosomes. 751, 751*t*
Rust, 2, 77, 77*t*
Rutherford, Ernest, 105, *106*

## S

Saccharin, 560, 560*t*, 662
Salicylic acid, 586
Saliva, 565
Salt (NaCl), *174*
  decomposition of, 72, *72*
  $LD_{50}$ value, 36*t*
**Salt bridge** The attraction between the ionized R groups of basic and acidic amino acids in the tertiary structure of a protein. 688, 688*t*
Salts
  forming acidic solutions, 399–400, 400*t*
  forming neutral and basic solutions, 399, 400*t*
  soluble and insoluble, 308–310, 309*t*
**Saponification** The hydrolysis of an ester with a strong base to produce a salt of the carboxylic acid and an alcohol. 592–593, 595, 618, 637
Saquinavir (Invirase), 771
Saran™, 463*t*, *464*
Sarin, 716*t*
Saturated fat, 603, 617
  health concerns, 603
  stimulating synthesis of cholesterol, 628
**Saturated fatty acid** Fatty acids that have no double bonds; they have higher melting points than unsaturated fatty acids and are usually solid at room temperatures. 605, 617
  melting point and structure, 606*t*
Saturated hydrocarbon, 418, 447
**Saturated solution** A solution containing the maximum amount of solute that can dissolve at a given temperature. Any additional solute will remain undissolved in the container. 305
  equilibrium in, 362–365
  supersaturated, 307
  temperature and, 307
**Saytzeff's rule** In the dehydration of an alcohol, hydrogen is removed from the carbon that already has the smallest number of hydrogen atoms, to form an alkene. 494
***s* block element** The elements in Groups 1A (1) and 2A (2) in which electrons fill the *s* orbitals. 122, *123*
**Scan** The image of a site in the body created by the detection of radiation from radioactive isotopes that have accumulated in that site. 157–159, *157*, *158*, *159*
Scanning electron micrograph (SEM), 46
Scanning tunneling microscope (STM), 105, *105*
Scientific discoveries, laws, theories, and technological innovations, 7, 7*t*
**Scientific method** The process of making observations, proposing a hypothesis, testing the hypothesis, and developing a theory that explains a natural event. 4–8
  in everyday life, 5–6
**Scientific notation** A form of writing large and small numbers using a coefficient from 1 to 9, followed by a power of 10. 18–21
  calculators and, 19–20
  converting to standard number, 20
  measurements in, 19*t*
  powers of ten, 18–19, 19*t*
  significant figure, 22–27
  writing a number in, 18–19, *18*
Scuba diver
  decompression and, 288
  gases breathed by, 172
  helium used by, 172
  pressure and, 265
Scurvy, 722
Sealant, 168
Secobarbital (Seconal), 662
Seconal (secobarbital), 662
**Second** The standard unit of time in the SI and metric system. 17
**Secondary (2°) alcohol** An alcohol that has two alkyl groups bonded to the carbon atom with the —OH group. 480
  dehydrating, 496–498
Secondary amide, 661
Secondary amine, 645, 648
**Secondary structure** The formation of an $\alpha$ helix, $\beta$-pleated sheet, or triple helix. 683–686, *685*
SEM. *See* Scanning electron micrograph
Semiconductors, 95, 102
Semi-conservative replication, 749
**Semipermeable membrane** A membrane that permits the passage of certain substances while blocking or retaining others. 322
Serine, 675*t*
  converting to pyruvate, 862
  as nonessential amino acid, 863*t*
  synthesis, *863*, 864–866
Serotonin, 658
Serum cholesterol, 628
Serum glutamate oxaloacetate transaminase (SGOT), 864
Serum glutamate pyruvate transaminase (SGPT), 864
Sex hormones, 631
SGOT (serum glutamate oxaloacetate transaminase), 864
SGPT (serum glutamate pyruvate transaminase), 864
Shapes, of molecules, 195–198, 198*t*
**Shielding** Materials used to provide protection from radioactive sources. 141–142
Sickle-cell anemia, 692, 764*t*
**Sievert (Sv)** A unit of biological damage (equivalent dose) equal to 100 rems. 150, 150*t*
**Significant figure** The number recorded in a measurement. 22–27
  addition and subtraction, 26–27
  in calculation, 24–27
  in measured numbers, 22*t*
  multiplication and division, 25
  rounding off, 24–25
  significant zeros, 22, 22*t*
  significant zeros, adding, 25–26
Silver (Ag), 103*t*
Silver mirror, 517–518
**Simple enzyme** An enzyme that is active as a polypeptide only. 721
**Single replacement reaction** A reaction in which an element replaces a different element in a compound. 217, *218*

**SI unit** The international system of units that modifies the metric system. 15–18
conversion factors, 33–34
joule, 57
Skin cancer, 771
Smog, 2, 220, 394
Soap
cleaning action, 593
saponification, 592–593
Sodium (Na)
alkali metal, 101, *101*
electron configuration, 121
ion, 173*t*
Sodium chloride, *174*
*See also* Salt
Sodium propionate, 583
**Solid** A state of matter that has its own shape and volume. 75, *75*, 76*t*
calculating density, 43*t*, 45, *45*
crystal, 75, *75*
formation of, 310–311
properties of, 76*t*
as solution, 297
**Solubility** The maximum amount of solute that can dissolve in exactly 100 g of solvent, usually water, at a given temperature. 305–312
alcohols and ethers, 492–493, 492*t*
aldehyde and ketone, 516, *516*
alkanes, 430, *430*, 492*t*
amine, 650, *651*
formation of a solid, 310–311
organic compound in water, 417*t*
pressure and (Henry's law), 307–308
rules, 309*t*
salts, 308–310, 309*t*
solubility product constant and, 364–365
temperature and, 307, *307*
**Solubility product constant, $K_{sp}$** The product of the concentrations of the ions in a saturated solution of a slightly soluble salt with each concentration raised to a power equal to its coefficient in the equilibrium equation. 363–365, 364*t*
**Soluble salts** An ionic compounds that dissolves in water. 308–310, 309*t*
**Solute** The component in a solution that changes state upon dissolving; if no change in state occurs, it is the component present in the smaller quantity. 296–297, 297*t*
freezing and boiling points and, 324, 324*t*
ionic and polar, 299, *299*
**Solution** A homogeneous mixture in which the solute is made up of small particles (ions or molecules) that can pass through filters and semipermeable membranes. 295–335
acidic, 374, 384, *384*
acidic, forming from salt, 399
basic, 374, 384, *384*
basic, forming from salt, 399
basic properties of, 296–299, *296*
buffer, 401–405, *402*
calculating concentration of, 312–316
calculating pH, 388–390
chemical reactions and, 319–320, *320*
comparison to colloid and suspension, 323*t*
electrolytes and nonelectrolytes, 300–304, *301*
formation, 298–299, 298*t*
homogenous mixture, 73
in human body, 322
isotonic, hypotonic, and hypertonic, 326–327, *326*
molarity and dilution, 316–321
neutral, 384, 384*t*
neutral, forming from salt, 399, 400*t*
percent concentration, 312–316
physical properties of, 322–329, *323*
preparing, 307
salts, soluble and insoluble, 308–310, 309*t*
saturation, 305
supersaturated, 307
**Solvent** The substance in which the solute dissolves; usually the component present in greater amount. 296–297, 297*t*
Sorbitol, 555–556, 560*t*
**Specific gravity (sp gr)** A relationship between the density of a substance and the density of water:

$$\text{sp gr} = \frac{\text{density of sample}}{\text{density of water}}.\ 47\text{–}48,\ \mathit{47}$$

**Specific heat (SH)** A quantity of heat that changes the temperature of exactly 1 g of a substance by exactly 1 °C. 63–67, 64*t*
calculations using, 65–67
Spectrum
atomic, 114, *115*
electromagnetic, 114, *114*
"Speed," 647
Sperm, 141, 631, 761
**Sphingolipid** Types of lipids in which glycerol is replaced by sphingosine. 624–627
**Sphingomyelin** Sphingolipid that consists of ceramide attached to a phosphate ester of choline, an amino alcohol. 624
Sphingosine, 624
Sphygmomanometer, 266
Standard number, 20
Standard temperature and pressure (STP), 278–280, *279*
Stanozolol, 632
Starch, 471, 543, 558
animal (glycogen), 563
composition of, 563
cornstarch, 558
digesting, 221
hydrolysis, 563
in insoluble granules, 563
iodine test for, 565
plant, 563
Start codon, 759
States of matter, 75–79, *75*, 76*t*
changes in, 79–87
Static electricity, 105
Steam, 84, *84*
burns, 84
nuclear power plants and, 162
sterilization with, 55
Stearic acid
melting point and structure, 606*t*
$\beta$ oxidation and, 841–842
saturated fatty acid, 458
**Stereoisomer** Isomers that have atoms bonded in the same order, but with different arrangements in space. 525
amino acid, 676
Fischer projections, 528–531, *529*
**Steroid** Types of lipid composed of a multicyclic ring system. 627–633
anabolic, 632
Steroid hormone, 631
Stimulant
caffeine, 36*t*, 655, *656*
central nervous system, 655
nicotine, 530, 655
Stomach acid, 388
Stomach pH, 711
Stomach ulcer, 610
**STP (standard temperature and pressure)** Standard conditions of 0 °C (273 K) temperature and 1 atm pressure used for the comparison of gases. 278–280, *279*
Streptomycin, 759*t*
Stress, on equilibrium, 354–356, *354*, 356*t*
**Strong acid** An acid that completely ionizes in water. 378–379, 378*t*, *379*, 382*t*
**Strong base** A base that completely ionizes in water. 380
**Strong electrolyte** A polar or ionic compound that ionizes completely when it dissolves in water. Its solution is a good conductor of electricity. 300–301, *301*
Strontium-85, 157*t*
**Structural genes** The sections of DNA that code for the synthesis of proteins. 755, *756*
Study plan, 9–11, 10*t*
**Subatomic particle** A particle within an atom; protons, neutrons, and electrons are subatomic particles. 105, 107*t*
**Sublevel** A group of orbitals of equal energy within principal energy levels. The number of sublevels in each energy level is the same as the principal quantum number (*n*). 116–117, *116*, 117*t*
block order, exceptions in, 124
electron configurations using, 119–126
**Sublimation** The change of state in which a solid is transformed directly to a gas without forming a liquid first. 81–82
**Substituent** Groups of atoms such as an alkyl group or a halogen bonded to the main chain or ring of carbon atoms. 423
in alkanes, 423–429, 424*t*
**Substitution** The reactions of benzene and other aromatic compounds in which an atom or group of atoms replaces a hydrogen on a benzene ring. 468–469
**Substitution mutation** A mutation that replaces one base in a DNA with a different base. 762, *762*
**Substrate** The molecule that reacts in the active site in an enzyme-catalyzed reaction. 706–707, *706*
concentration, 711–712, *712*
Subtraction, 26–27
Succinate, 817
Succinate dehydrogenase, 817, 822, *823*
Succinic acid, 584
Succinyl CoA, *815*, *816*, 817
from amino acid degradation, 862
Succinyl CoA synthetase, 817
Sucralose, 560, 560*t*

**Sucrose** A disaccharide composed of glucose and fructose; a nonreducing sugar, commonly called table sugar or "sugar". 558–559, *559*, 567
Sudafed, 652
Sugar(s)
in DNA and RNA, 740
milk (lactose), 558
reducing, 555
*See also* Sucrose
Sugar alcohols, 556, 560*t*
Sugar beet, 559
Sugar cane, 559
Sugar-phosphate bond, 770
Sulfanilamide, 714
Sulfonation, 469
Sulfur, 103*t*
Sun, energy from, 57, 771
Superimposing, mirror image and, 525–528
Supersaturated solution, 307
Surgical technologist, 55
**Suspension** A mixture in which the solute particles are large enough and heavy enough to settle out and be retained by both filters and semipermeable membranes. 322, *323*
comparison to solution and colloid, 323*t*
Sweeteners, 556, 558
artificial, 560, 560*t*
sweetness of, 548, 558, 560, 560*t*
Symbol
electron-dot, 126–127, 127*t*
element names and, 96, 96*t*, 97*t*
plastic recycling symbol, 464
writing chemical equation, 213*t*
Synthetic polymer, *463*, 464
Systeme International (SI). *See* SI unit
Systolic blood pressure, 266

## T

Tannic acid, 694
Tartaric acid, 579
Tay-Sachs disease, 625, 764*t*
Technetium (Tc), 147, 148
Technetium-99m, 155*t*, 157*t*
Technology, 7, 7*t*
Teeth
polyatomic ions, 182
sealant, 168
toothpaste, 168
Teflon®, 463*t*, *464*, 473
**Temperature** An indicator of the hotness or coldness of an object. 17, 59–63
body, homeostasis in, 362
body, variation in, 62
change, equilibrium and, 339, 340*t*, 359–361, 360*t*, 361*t*
comparing on three scales, 59–62, *60*
enzyme activity and, 710–711, *711*
equilibrium, effect on, 339, 340*t*, 359–361, 360*t*, 361*t*
gas, 263–264, 264*t*
in gas law calculations (Kelvin), 270, 273
measuring, 17, *17*
pressure and (Gay-Lussac's Law), 273–276, *273*
reaction rate and, 339, 340*t*
solubility and, 307, *307*
solubility, effect on, 307, *307*
standard (STP), 278–280, *279*
units of measurement, 17, *17*
volume and (Charles's Law), 270–273, *271*
Temperature scale. *See* Celsius scale; Fahrenheit scale; Kelvin scale
Ten, powers of, 18–19, 19*t*
*Tera* (T), 28*t*
**Tertiary (3°) alcohol** An alcohol that has three alkyl groups bonded to the carbon atom with the —OH. 480
Tertiary (3°) amine, 645, 648
Tertiary amide, 661
**Tertiary structure** The folding of the secondary structure of a protein into a compact structure that is stabilized by the interactions of R groups such as ionic and disulfide bonds. 687–689, *688*, 688*t*
Testosterone, 631
Tetracycline, 759*t*
**Tetrahedral** The shape of a molecule with four bonded atoms. 196–197, 198*t*
structure of carbon, 418, *418*
Tetrahydrofolate (THF), 726
Tetrose, 544
**Theoretical yield** The maximum amount of product that a reaction can produce from a given amount of reactant. 240–241
**Theory** An explanation of an observation that has been validated by experiments that support a hypothesis. 4–5, 7*t*
Arrhenius, 372–373, 375*t*
Brønsted-Lowry, 374, 375*t*
Valence shell electron-pair repulsion, 195, 198, 418
Thermometer, 17, 264
Thiamin (vitamin $B_1$), 723–724, 723*t*
Thioester, 787, *788*
**Thiol** An organic compound that contains a thiol (—SH) group. 435, 437*t*, 480, *485*
naming, 484–485, 501
oxidation, 498–499
Three-carbon compounds, 862, 864
Threonine, 675*t*
degrading, 862
as essential amino acid, 863*t*
Thymine (T), 739–740, *740*, 742*t*
Thyroid gland, hyperactive, 139
Thyroid scan, 157–158, *157*
Time
equalities, 33*t*
unit of measurement (second), 17
Tissue, 142, 147
frozen sections, 76
**Titration** The addition of base to an acid sample to determine the concentration of the acid. 396–398, *396*
TNT (trinitrotoluene), 466
Tocopherol, 727*t*, 728
Tollens' reagent, 517
**Tollens' test** A test for aldehydes in which $Ag^+$ in Tollens' reagent is reduced to metallic silver, which forms a "silver mirror" on the walls of the container. 517–518, *518*
Toluene, 466
Toothpaste, 3*t*, 168
*Torr*, 263, 265, 265*t*
Torricelli, Evangelista, 265
Toxicity of mercury, 98
Toxicology, 36
Toxins, inhibiting electron transport, 825
Trace elements in body, 104, 104*t*
Transacylase, 851
Transaminase, 856–857, 864
serum glutamate oxaloacetate transaminase (SGOT), 864
serum glutamate pyruvate transaminase (SGPT), 864
**Transamination** The transfer of an amino group from an amino acid to an α-keto acid. *814*, 856–857, 862
amino acid synthesis and, 863, 864
summary of reactions, 869
**Transcription** The transfer of genetic information from DNA by the formation of mRNA. 753–755, *753*, *754*
regulation of, 754–755, *756*
transcription bubble, 753
Trans fatty acid, 617
Transferase, 704*t*
**Transfer RNA**. *See* **tRNA**
**Trans isomer** An isomer of an alkene in which large groups are attached to different sides of the double bond. 451–455, *452*
modeling, 453
night vision, 454
**Transition element** An element in the center of the periodic table that is designated with the letter "B" or the group number of 3 through 12. 100, *101*
**Translation** The interpretation of the codons in mRNA as amino acids in a peptide. 758–761, *760*
mRNA and, 753, *753*, 758
**Translocation** The shift of a ribosome along mRNA from one codon (three bases) to the next codon during translation. 759
Transmutation, 147
Transport, through cell membrane, 634–635, *635*
**Triacylglycerol** A family of lipids composed of three fatty acids bonded through ester bonds to glycerol, a trihydroxy alcohol. 612–613
chemical properties, 615–621
digestion of, 839–841, *840*, 869
fat mobilization, 840, 869
fatty acid synthesis, 851–854, *852*, 853*t*, 869
hydrogenation, 615–617, *616*, 637
transporting to tissue, 842
*See also* Fat
Tricarboxylic acid, 584
*See also* Citric acid cycle
Trichloromethane, 428
Triglyceride. *See* Triacylglycerol
**Trigonal planar** The shape of a molecule with three bonded atoms and no lone pair. 196, 198*t*
**Trigonal pyramidal** The shape of a molecule that has three bonded atoms and one lone pair. 197, 198*t*
Trimethylamine, 645
Trinitrotoluene, 466
Triose, 544
Triose phosphate isomerase, 792
**Triple bond** A sharing of three pairs of electrons by two atoms. 186

**Triple helix** The protein structure found in collagen consisting of three polypeptide chains woven together like a braid. 686, *686*
Tristearin, 612
**tRNA** Transfer RNA; an RNA that places a specific amino acid into a peptide chain at the ribosome. There is one or more tRNA for each of the 20 different amino acids. 751–752, 751*t*
  activation of, 758–759
  anticodons on, 758–759, *759*
  protein synthesis and, 758–761, *760*
  structure of, 751–752, 751*t*
Trypsin, 704, 711*t*, 718–719, 854, *855*
Trypsinogen, 718–719, 718*t*
Tryptophan, 675*t*
  converting to alanine, 862
  as essential amino acid, 863*t*
Tungsten filament, 116
Tylenol (acetaminophen), 645, 662
Tyrosine, 675*t*
  degradation, 862
  melanin formation and, 764
  as nonessential amino acid, 863*t*
  synthesis, 865

## U

Ulcers, 610
Ultraviolet, 114, *114*
Uncouplers, 829
Unit of measurement, 15–18, 17*t*
  *See also* SI unit
**Universal gas constant R** A numerical value that relates the quantities *P*, *V*, *n*, and *T* in the ideal gas law, $PV = nRT$. 281–285
Unsaturated fat, 456, 458
  hydrogenation, 458, 615–617, *616*
  oxidation, 618, 637
  vegetable oil, 458, 617
Unsaturated fatty acid, 605
  cis and trans isomers, 605
  oxidation, 637
**Unsaturated hydrocarbon** A compound of carbon and hydrogen in which the carbon chain contains at least one double (alkene) or triple carbon-carbon bond (alkyne). An unsaturated compound is capable of an addition reaction with hydrogen, which converts the double or triple bonds to single carbon-carbon bonds. 447, *447*
**Unsaturated solution** A solution that contains less solute than can be dissolved. 305
Uracil (U), 739–740, *740*, 742*t*
Uranium
  nuclear power plant and, 662
Uranium-235, *161*, 662
Uranium-238, 155*t*
Urea, 662, *867*
  ammonium ion and, 858, *859*
  amount excreted per day, 858
  formation of, *859*, 860
  toxicity, 858
**Urea cycle** The process in which ammonium ions from the degradation of amino acids and $CO_2$ form carbamoyl phosphate, which is converted to urea. 858–861, *859*
  reactions, 859–860
Uremia, 662
Uric acid, 306
Uridine diphosphate (UDP), 799
Uridine monophosphate (UMP), *741*, 742*t*
Uridine triphosphate (UTP), 799
Urine, 365
  glucose in, 518
  measuring drugs in, 479
  pH of, 386, *387*
  water loss from, 298
U.S. Food and Drug Administration. *See* Food and Drug Administration (FDA)
U.S. System, *33*
  conversion factors (to metric), 33–34

## V

Vaccines, 768
Valence, variable, 177–178
**Valence electron** Electron in the outermost energy level of an atom. 126–127, 126*t*
  bonding and, 169
  sharing, 183–186
**Valence shell electron-pair repulsion (VSEPR) theory** A theory that predicts the shape of a molecule by placing the electron pairs on a central atom as far apart as possible to minimize the mutual repulsion of the electrons, 195, 198, 418
Valine, 675*t*
  degradation, 862
  as essential amino acid, 863*t*
  sickle-cell anemia and, 692
Valium, 662
Vanilla, 512
Vanillin, 466
Vaporization, *79*, 80
  heat of, 82–84, *82*, 82*t*
**Vapor pressure** The pressure exerted by the particles of vapor above a liquid. 274–275, 274*t*
Variable charge, 177–178
Vaseline, 430
Vasopressin, 684
Vegetable oil, 617
  unsaturated fat, 458
Very-low-density lipoprotein (VLDL), 630, *630*
Veterinary technician (VT), 33
Vinegar, 578, *578*
**Virus** Small particles containing DNA or RNA in a protein coat that require a host cell for replication. 768–772
  attaching to host cell, *769*
  diseases caused by, 768*t*
  oncogenic (cancer-causing), 771, 771*t*
  provirus, *769*, 770
  retrovirus, *769*, 770
  vaccines, 768
Visible light, 114, *114*
Vision, 727*t*
  night vision, 454, 727*t*
**Vitamin(s)** Organic molecules that are essential for normal health and growth and are obtained in small amounts from the diet. 722–729
  fat-soluble, 727–728, 727*t*
  water-soluble, 723–726, 723*t*
Vitamin A, 727, 727*t*
  night vision and, 454
Vitamin B, 723–725, 723*t*, 866
Vitamin C, 724*t*, 725–726, *726*
Vitamin D, 46, 727, 727*t*
Vitamin E (tocopherol), 727*t*, 728
Vitamin K (phylloquinone), 727*t*, 728
VLDL (very-low-density lipoprotein), 630, *630*
**Volume** The amount of space occupied by a substance.
  change, equilibrium and, 356–359, *357*, 361*t*
  displacement, in calculating solid density, 45, *45*
  equalities, 30, 33*t*
  gas, 263, 264*t*, 277–281, *278*
  gas, moles and (Avogadro's Law), 277–281, *278*
  measuring, 30, *30*, *31*
  pressure and (Boyle's Law), 267–270, *267*
  temperature and (Charles's Law), 270–273, *271*
  units of measurement, 16, *16*
**Volume percent (v/v)** A percent concentration that relates the volume of the solute to the volume of the solution. 314
VSEPR. *See* Valence shell electron-pair repulsion theory

## W

Water
  adding to aldehyde and ketone, 521–522, 534
  boiling and freezing points, 59, *60*, 62*t*, 79, 274–275, 274*t*
  in foods, 298*t*
  heat of fusion, 79–80, 82*t*
  heat of sublimation, 81
  heat of vaporization, 82, *82*, 82*t*
  in human body, 298
  ionization of, 383–386, *384*, 384*t*
  retention, kidney and, 632
  as solvent, 297
  specific heat, 63, 64*t*
  vapor pressure, 274–275, 274*t*
**Water-soluble vitamin** Vitamins that are soluble in water; they cannot be stored in the body, are easily destroyed by heat, ultraviolet light, and oxygen, and function as coenzymes. 723–726, 723*t*
Watson, James, 746
Wavelength, 114, *115*
**Wax** The ester of a long-chain alcohol and a long-chain saturated fatty acid. 611, 611*t*
**Weak acid** An acid that is a poor donor of $H^+$ and dissociates only slightly in water. 378–379, 378*t*, *379*, 382*t*
  dissociation constants for, 381–382, 382*t*
**Weak base** A base that is a poor acceptor of $H^+$ and produced only a small number of ions in water. 380
**Weak electrolyte** A substance that produces only a few ions along with many molecules when it dissolves in water. Its solution is a weak conductor of electricity. 300–301, *301*
Weather, 263–265
Weight
  losing and gaining, 71, 71*t*
  measuring, 16

Wine making, 798
Wintergreen oil, 584
Wood alcohol (methanol), 496
**Work** An activity that requires energy. 56

## X

X-ray, 114, *114*
  radiation from, 152*t*
Xylitol, 556, 560*t*
Xylocaine, 654
Xylose, 556

## Y

Yard (length measurement), 15
Yeast fermentation, 798
Yield, 240–241
Yogurt, 694

## Z

Zeros, significant, 22, 22*t*
  adding, 25–26
Zinc ion (cofactor), 721–722, *722*
**Zwitterion** The dipolar form of an amino acid consisting of two oppositely charged ionic regions, $—NH_3^+$ and $—COO^-$. 677–680
**Zymogen** An inactive form of an enzyme that is activated by removing a peptide portion from one end of the protein. 717–719, 718*t*

## METRIC AND SI UNITS AND SOME USEFUL CONVERSION FACTORS

| Length SI unit meter (m) | Volume SI unit cubic meter ($m^3$) | Mass SI unit kilogram (kg) |
|---|---|---|
| 1 meter (m) = 100 centimeters (cm) | 1 liter (L) = 1000 milliliters (mL) | 1 kilogram (kg) = 1000 grams (g) |
| 1 meter (m) = 1000 millimeters (mm) | 1 mL = 1 $cm^3$ | 1 g = 1000 milligrams (mg) |
| 1 cm = 10 mm | 1 L = 1.06 quart (qt) | 1 kg = 2.20 lb |
| 1 kilometer (km) = 0.6214 mile (mi) | 1 qt = 946 mL | 1 lb = 454 g |
| 1 inch (in.) = 2.54 cm (exact) | | 1 mole = $6.02 \times 10^{23}$ particles |
| | | **Water** |
| | | density = 1.00 g/mL |

| Temperature SI unit kelvin (K) | Pressure SI unit pascal (Pa) | Energy SI unit joule (J) |
|---|---|---|
| °F = 1.8(°C) + 32 | 1 atm = 760 mmHg | 1 calorie (cal) = 4.184 J |
| $°C = \frac{(°F - 32)}{1.8}$ | 1 atm = 760 torr | 1 kcal = 1000 cal |
| K = °C + 273 | 1 mole (STP) = 22.4 L | **Water** |
| | R = 0.0821 L · atm/mole · K | Heat of fusion = 80. cal/g; 334 J/g |
| | R = 62.4 L · mmHg/mole · K | Heat of vaporization = 540 cal/g; 2260 J/g |
| | | Specific heat = 4.184 J/g°C; 1 cal/g°C |

## PREFIXES FOR METRIC (SI) UNITS

| Prefix | Symbol | Power of Ten |
|---|---|---|
| **Values greater than 1** | | |
| peta | P | $10^{15}$ |
| tera | T | $10^{12}$ |
| giga | G | $10^{9}$ |
| mega | M | $10^{6}$ |
| kilo | k | $10^{3}$ |
| **Values less than 1** | | |
| deci | d | $10^{-1}$ |
| centi | c | $10^{-2}$ |
| milli | m | $10^{-3}$ |
| micro | $\mu$ | $10^{-6}$ |
| nano | n | $10^{-9}$ |
| pico | p | $10^{-12}$ |
| femto | f | $10^{-15}$ |

## FORMULAS AND MOLAR MASSES OF SOME TYPICAL COMPOUNDS

| Name | Formula | Molar Mass (g/mole) | Name | Formula | Molar Mass (g/mole) |
|---|---|---|---|---|---|
| Ammonia | $NH_3$ | 17.0 | Hydrogen chloride | HCl | 36.5 |
| Ammonium chloride | $NH_4Cl$ | 53.5 | Iron(III) oxide | $Fe_2O_3$ | 159.8 |
| Ammonium sulfate | $(NH_4)_2SO_4$ | 132.1 | Magnesium oxide | MgO | 40.3 |
| Bromine | $Br_2$ | 159.8 | Methane | $CH_4$ | 16.0 |
| Butane | $C_4H_{10}$ | 58.0 | Nitrogen | $N_2$ | 28.0 |
| Calcium carbonate | $CaCO_3$ | 100.1 | Oxygen | $O_2$ | 32.0 |
| Calcium chloride | $CaCl_2$ | 111.1 | Potassium carbonate | $K_2CO_3$ | 138.2 |
| Calcium oxide | CaO | 56.1 | Propane | $C_3H_8$ | 44.0 |
| Carbon dioxide | $CO_2$ | 44.0 | Sodium chloride | NaCl | 58.5 |
| Chlorine | $Cl_2$ | 71.0 | Sodium hydroxide | NaOH | 40.0 |
| Copper(II) sulfide | CuS | 95.7 | Sulfur dioxide | $SO_2$ | 64.1 |
| Hydrogen | $H_2$ | 2.0 | Water | $H_2O$ | 18.0 |